RSMeans
Quarterly Updates
700 Longwater Drive
Norwell, MA 02061
USA

Tips for Customizing Your RSMeans Cost Data By Location

The cost data found throughout the book reflects national averages.

Customize your cost data for over 930 locations throughout the U.S. and Canada.

☑ To adjust costs to your region, use the *Location Factors* found in the back of the book.

☑ To compare costs from region-to-region, use the *City Cost Indexes* found in the back of the book.

☑ For additional guidance, refer to the *How RSMeans Data Works* section towards the front of the book.

Metric Conversion Formulas

Length

cm = 0.3937 in.
meter = 3.2808 ft.
meter = 1.0936 yd.
km = 0.6214 mile

in. = 2.5400 cm
ft. = 0.3048 m
yd. = 0.9144 m
mile = 1.6093 km

Weight

gram = 15.4324 grains
gram = 0.0353 oz.
kg = 2.2046 lbs.

grain = 0.0648 g
oz. = 28.3495 g
lb. = 0.4536 kg

Area

sq. cm = 0.1550 sq. in.
sq. m = 10.7639 sq. ft.
sq. m = 1.1960 sq. yd.
hectare = 2.4710 acres
sq. km = 0.3861 sq. mile

sq.in. = 6.4516 sq. cm
sq. ft. = 0.0929 sq. m
sq. yd. = 0.8361 sq. m
acre = 0.4047 hectare
sq. mile = 2.5900 sq. km

Weight, cont.

kg = 0.0011 ton (short)
ton (met.) = 1.1023 ton (short)
ton (met.) = 0.9842 ton (large)

ton (short) = 907.1848 kg
ton (short) = 0.9072 ton (met.)
ton (long) = 1.0160 ton (met.)

Common Units of Measure

Abbreviation	Measurement	Formula
SF	Square feet	Length (in feet) x Width (in feet)
SY	Square yards	Square feet / 9
CF	Cubic feet	Length (in feet) x Width (in feet) x Depth (in feet)
CY	Cubic yards	Cubic feet / 27
BF	Board foot	Length (in inches) x width (in inches) x thickness (in inches)/144
MBF	Thousand board foot	Board foot / 1,000
LF	Linear feet	12 inches of the item
SFCA	Square foot of contact area	A square foot of concrete formwork
SQ	Square	100 square feet
Ton	Ton	2,000 pounds

$174.95 per copy (in United States)
Price is subject to change without prior notice.

0022

2012

RSMeans Mechanical Cost Data

35TH ANNUAL EDITION

RSMeans
A division of Reed Construction Data
Construction Publishers & Consultants
700 Longwater Drive
Norwell, MA 02061
USA
1-800-334-3509
www.rsmeans.com

Copyright 2011 by RSMeans
A division of Reed Construction Data
All rights reserved.

Printed in the United States of America
ISSN 0748-2698
ISBN 978-1-936335-41-1

Senior Editor
Melville J. Mossman, PE

Contributing Editors
Christopher Babbitt
Ted Baker
Barbara Balboni
Adrian C. Charest, PE
Gary W. Christensen
David G. Drain, PE
Cheryl Elsmore
Robert J. Kuchta
Robert C. McNichols
Jeannene D. Murphy
Marilyn Phelan, AIA
Stephen C. Plotner
Eugene R. Spencer
Phillip R. Waier, PE

Cover Design
Wendy McBay
Paul Robertson
Wayne Engebretson

President & CEO
Iain Melville

Vice President, Product & Development
Richard Remington

Vice President, Finance & Operations
David C. Walsh

Vice President, Data Aquisition & Fulfillment
Marco Piovesan

Chief Customer Officer
Lisa Fiondella

Senior Director, Product Management
Daimon Bridge

Vice President, Marketing & Business
Steven Ritchie

Engineering Director
Bob Mewis, CCC

Product Manager
Andrea Sillah

Product Marketing Manager
Ryan Cummings

Manager, Product Management
Jennifer Johnson

Production Manager
Michael Kokernak

Production Coordinator
Jill Goodman

Production Supervisor
Paula Reale-Camelio

Production
Jonathan Forgit
Mary Lou Geary
Debbie Panarelli
Sheryl A. Rose
Caroline Sullivan

Technical Support
Christopher Anderson
Tom Dion
Gary L. Hoitt
Genevieve Medeiros
Sharon Proulx
Kathryn S. Rodriguez

This book is printed using soy-based printing ink.
This book is recyclable.

Related RSMeans Products and Services

The engineers at RSMeans suggest the following products and services as companion information resources to *RSMeans Mechanical Cost Data:*

Construction Cost Data Books
Assemblies Cost Data 2012
Square Foot Costs 2012

Reference Books
Estimating Building Costs
RSMeans Estimating Handbook
Green Building: Project Planning & Estimating
How to Estimate with RSMeans Data
Plan Reading & Material Takeoff
Project Scheduling & Management for Construction
Repair & Remodeling Estimating Methods
Universal Design

Seminars and In-House Training
Unit Price Estimating
Means CostWorks® Training
RSMeans Data for Job Order Contracting (JOC)
Practical Project Management for Construction Professionals
Scheduling with MSProject for Construction Professionals
Mechanical & Electrical Estimating

RSMeans on the Internet
Visit RSMeans at **www.rsmeans.com** for a one-stop portal for the most reliable and current resources available on the market. Here you can learn about our more than 20 annual cost data books, also available on CD and online versions, as well as about RSMeans seminars.

RSMeans Electronic Data
Get the information found in RSMeans cost books electronically on CD or on the Web at **MeansCostWorks.com.**

RSMeans Business Solutions
Cost engineers and analysts conduct facility life cycle and benchmark research studies and predictive cost modeling, as well as offer consultation services for conceptual estimating, real property management, and job order contracting. Research studies are designed with the application of proprietary cost and project data from Reed Construction Data and RSMeans' extensive North American databases. Analysts offer building product manufacturers qualitative and quantitative market research, as well as time/motion studies for new products, and Web-based dashboards for market opportunity analysis. Clients are from both the public and private sectors, including federal, state, and municipal agencies; corporations; institutions; construction management firms; hospitals; and associations.

RSMeans for Job Order Contracting (JOC)
Best practice job order contracting (JOC) services support the owner in the development of their program. RSMeans develops all required contracting documents, works with stakeholders, and develops qualified and experienced contractor lists. RSMeans JOCWorks™ software is the best of class in the functional tools that meet JOC specific requirements. RSMeans data is organized to meet JOC cost estimating requirements.

Construction Costs for Software Applications
Over 25 unit price and assemblies cost databases are available through a number of leading estimating and facilities management software providers (listed below). For more information see the "Other RSMeans Products" pages at the back of this publication.
RSMeansData™ is also available to federal, state, and local government agencies as multi-year, multi-seat licenses.

- 4Clicks-Solutions, LLC
- ArenaSoft Estimating
- Assetworks
- Beck Technology
- BSD – Building Systems Design, Inc.
- CMS – Construction Management Software
- Corecon Technologies, Inc.
- CorVet Systems
- Hard Dollar Corporation
- Maxwell Systems
- MC^2
- Parsons Corporation
- ProEst
- Sage Timberline Office
- UDA Technologies, Inc.
- US Cost, Inc.
- VFA – Vanderweil Facility Advisers
- WinEstimator, Inc.
- R & K Solutions
- Tririga

Table of Contents

Foreword

Our Mission

Since 1942, RSMeans has been actively engaged in construction cost publishing and consulting throughout North America.

Today, more than 65 years after RSMeans began, our primary objective remains the same: to provide you, the construction and facilities professional, with the most current and comprehensive construction cost data possible.

Whether you are a contractor, owner, architect, engineer, facilities manager, or anyone else who needs a reliable construction cost estimate, you'll find this publication to be a highly useful and necessary tool.

With the constant flow of new construction methods and materials today, it's difficult to find the time to look at and evaluate all the different construction cost possibilities. In addition, because labor and material costs keep changing, last year's cost information is not a reliable basis for today's estimate or budget.

That's why so many construction professionals turn to RSMeans. We keep track of the costs for you, along with a wide range of other key information, from city cost indexes . . . to productivity rates . . . to crew composition . . . to contractor's overhead and profit rates.

RSMeans performs these functions by collecting data from all facets of the industry and organizing it in a format that is instantly accessible to you. From the preliminary budget to the detailed unit price estimate, you'll find the data in this book useful for all phases of construction cost determination.

The Staff, the Organization, and Our Services

When you purchase one of RSMeans' publications, you are, in effect, hiring the services of a full-time staff of construction and engineering professionals.

Our thoroughly experienced and highly qualified staff works daily at collecting, analyzing, and disseminating comprehensive cost information for your needs. These staff members have years of practical construction experience and engineering training prior to joining the firm. As a result, you can count on them not only for accurate cost figures, but also for additional background reference information that will help you create a realistic estimate.

The RSMeans organization is always prepared to help you solve construction problems through its variety of data solutions, including online, CD, and print book formats, as well as cost estimating expertise available via our business solutions, training, and seminars.

Besides a full array of construction cost estimating books, RSMeans also publishes a number of other reference works for the construction industry. Subjects include construction estimating and project and business management, special topics such as green building and job order contracting, and a library of facility management references.

In addition, you can access all of our construction cost data electronically in convenient CD format or on the Web. Visit **MeansCostWorks.com** for more information on our 24/7 online cost data.

What's more, you can increase your knowledge and improve your construction estimating and management performance with an RSMeans construction seminar or in-house training program. These two-day seminar programs offer unparalleled opportunities for everyone in your organization to become updated on a wide variety of construction-related issues.

RSMeans is also a worldwide provider of construction cost management and analysis services for commercial and government owners.

In short, RSMeans can provide you with the tools and expertise for constructing accurate and dependable construction estimates and budgets in a variety of ways.

Robert Snow Means Established a Tradition of Quality That Continues Today

Robert Snow Means spent years building RSMeans, making certain he always delivered a quality product.

Today, at RSMeans, we do more than talk about the quality of our data and the usefulness of our books. We stand behind all of our data, from historical cost indexes to construction materials and techniques to current costs.

If you have any questions about our products or services, please call us toll-free at 1-800-334-3509. Our customer service representatives will be happy to assist you. You can also visit our Web site at **www.rsmeans.com**

How the Book Is Built: An Overview

The Construction Specifications Institute (CSI) and Construction Specifications Canada (CSC) have produced the 2010 edition of MasterFormat™, a system of titles and numbers used extensively to organize construction information.

All unit price data in the RSMeans cost data books is now arranged in the 50-division MasterFormat™ 2010 system.

A Powerful Construction Tool

You have in your hands one of the most powerful construction tools available today. A successful project is built on the foundation of an accurate and dependable estimate. This book will enable you to construct just such an estimate.

For the casual user the book is designed to be:

• quickly and easily understood so you can get right to your estimate.

• filled with valuable information so you can understand the necessary factors that go into the cost estimate.

For the regular user, the book is designed to be:

• a handy desk reference that can be quickly referred to for key costs.

• a comprehensive, fully reliable source of current construction costs and productivity rates so you'll be prepared to estimate any project.

• a source book for preliminary project cost, product selections, and alternate materials and methods.

To meet all of these requirements, we have organized the book into the following clearly defined sections.

New: Quick Start

See our new "Quick Start" instructions on the following page to get started right away.

Estimating with RSMeans Unit Price Cost Data

Please refer to these steps for guidance on completing an estimate using RSMeans unit price cost data.

How to Use the Book:
The Details

This section contains an in-depth explanation of how the book is arranged . . . and how you can use it to determine a reliable construction cost estimate. It includes information about how we develop our cost figures and how to completely prepare your estimate.

Unit Price Section

All cost data has been divided into the 50 divisions according to the MasterFormat system of classification and numbering. For a listing of these divisions and an outline of their subdivisions, see the Unit Price Section Table of Contents.

Estimating tips are included at the beginning of each division.

Assemblies Section

The cost data in this section has been organized in an "Assemblies" format. These assemblies are the functional elements of a building and are arranged according to the 7 elements of the UNIFORMAT II classification system. For a complete explanation of a typical "Assemblies" page, see "How to Use the Assemblies Cost Tables."

Reference Section

This section includes information on Equipment Rental Costs, Crew Listings, Historical Cost Indexes, City Cost Indexes, Location Factors, Reference Tables, Change Orders, Square Foot Costs, and a listing of Abbreviations.

Equipment Rental Costs: This section contains the average costs to rent and operate hundreds of pieces of construction equipment.

Crew Listings: This section lists all of the crews referenced in the book. For the purposes of this book, a crew is composed of more than one trade classification and/or the addition of power equipment to any trade classification. Power equipment is included in the cost of the crew. Costs are shown both with bare labor rates and with the installing contractor's overhead and profit added. For each, the total crew cost per eight-hour day and the composite cost per labor-hour are listed.

Historical Cost Indexes: These indexes provide you with data to adjust construction costs over time.

City Cost Indexes: All costs in this book are U.S. national averages. Costs vary because of the regional economy. You can adjust costs by CSI Division to over 700 locations throughout the U.S. and Canada by using the data in this section.

Location Factors: You can adjust total project costs to over 900 locations throughout the U.S. and Canada by using the data in this section.

Reference Tables: At the beginning of selected major classifications in the Unit Price section are reference numbers shown in a shaded box. These numbers refer you to related information in the Reference Section. In this section, you'll find reference tables, explanations, estimating information that support how we develop the unit price data, technical data, and estimating procedures.

Change Orders: This section includes information on the factors that influence the pricing of change orders.

Square Foot Costs: This section contains costs for 59 different building types that allow you to make a rough estimate for the overall cost of a project or its major components.

Abbreviations: A listing of abbreviations used throughout this book, along with the terms they represent, is included in this section.

Index

A comprehensive listing of all terms and subjects in this book will help you quickly find what you need when you are not sure where it occurs in MasterFormat.

The Scope of This Book

This book is designed to be as comprehensive and as easy to use as possible. To that end we have made certain assumptions and limited its scope in two key ways:

1. We have established material prices based on a national average.

2. We have computed labor costs based on a 30-city national average of union wage rates.

For a more detailed explanation of how the cost data is developed, see "How to Use the Book: The Details."

Project Size/Type

The material prices in Means data cost books are "contractor's prices." They are the prices that contractors can expect to pay at the lumberyards, suppliers/distributers warehouses, etc. Small orders of speciality items would be higher than the costs shown, while very large orders, such as truckload lots, would be less. The variation would depend on the size, timing, and negotiating power of the contractor. The labor costs are primarily for new construction or major renovation rather than repairs or minor alterations.

With reasonable exercise of judgment, the figures can be used for any building work.

Absolute Essentials for a Quick Start

If you feel you are ready to use this book and don't think you will need the detailed instructions that begin on the following page, this Absolute Essentials for a Quick Start page is for you. These steps will allow you to get started estimating in a matter of minutes.

1 Scope

Think through the project that you will be estimating, and identify the many individual work tasks that will need to be covered in your estimate.

2 Quantify

Determine the number of units that will be required for each work task that you identified.

3 Pricing

Locate individual Unit Price line items that match the work tasks you identified. The Unit Price Section Table of Contents that begins on page 1 and the Index in the back of the book will help you find these line items.

4 Multiply

Multiply the Total Incl O&P cost for a Unit Price line item in the book by your quantity for that item. The price you calculate will be an estimate for a completed item of work performed by a subcontractor. Keep adding line items in this manner to build your estimate.

5 Project Overhead

Include project overhead items in your estimate. These items are needed to make the job run and are typically, but not always, provided by the General Contractor. They can be found in Division 1. An alternate method of estimating project overhead costs is to apply a percentage of the total project cost.

Include rented tools not included in crews, waste, rubbish handling, and cleanup.

6 Estimate Summary

Include General Contractor's markup on subcontractors, General Contractor's office overhead and profit, and sales tax on materials and equipment.

Adjust your estimate to the project's location by using the City Cost Indexes or Location Factors found in the Reference Section.

Editors' Note: We urge you to spend time reading and understanding the supporting material in the front of this book. An accurate estimate requires experience, knowledge, and careful calculation. The more you know about how we at RSMeans developed the data, the more accurate your estimate will be. In addition, it is important to take into consideration the reference material in the back of the book such as Equipment Listings, Crew Listings, City Cost Indexes, Location Factors, and Reference Numbers.

Estimating with RSMeans Unit Price Cost Data

Following these steps will allow you to complete an accurate estimate using RSMeans Unit Price cost data.

1 Scope Out the Project

- Identify the individual work tasks that will need to be covered in your estimate.
- The Unit Price data in this book has been divided into 50 Divisions according to the CSI MasterFormat 2010—their titles are listed on the back cover of your book.
- Think through the project and identify those CSI Divisions needed in your estimate.
- The Unit Price Section Table of Contents on page 1 may also be helpful when scoping out your project.
- Experienced estimators find it helpful to begin with Division 2 and continue through completion. Division 1 can be estimated after the full project scope is known.

2 Quantify

- Determine the number of units required for each work task that you identified.
- Experienced estimators include an allowance for waste in their quantities. (Waste is not included in RSMeans Unit Price line items unless so stated.)

3 Price the Quantities

- Use the Unit Price Table of Contents, and the Index, to locate individual Unit Price line items for your estimate.
- Reference Numbers indicated within a Unit Price section refer to additional information that you may find useful.
- The crew indicates who is performing the work for that task. Crew codes are expanded in the Crew Listings in the Reference Section to include all trades and equipment that comprise the crew.
- The Daily Output is the amount of work the crew is expected to do in one day.
- The Labor-Hours value is the amount of time it will take for the crew to install one unit of work.

- The abbreviated Unit designation indicates the unit of measure upon which the crew, productivity, and prices are based.
- Bare Costs are shown for materials, labor, and equipment needed to complete the Unit Price line item. Bare costs do not include waste, project overhead, payroll insurance, payroll taxes, main office overhead, or profit.
- The Total Incl O&P cost is the billing rate or invoice amount of the installing contractor or subcontractor who performs the work for the Unit Price line item.

4 Multiply

- Multiply the total number of units needed for your project by the Total Incl O&P cost for each Unit Price line item.
- Be careful that your take off unit of measure matches the unit of measure in the Unit column.
- The price you calculate is an estimate for a completed item of work.
- Keep scoping individual tasks, determining the number of units required for those tasks, matching each task with individual Unit Price line items in the book, and multiply quantities by Total Incl O&P costs.
- An estimate completed in this manner is priced as if a subcontractor, or set of subcontractors, is performing the work. The estimate does not yet include Project Overhead or Estimate Summary components such as General Contractor markups on subcontracted work, General Contractor office overhead and profit, contingency, and location factor.

5 Project Overhead

- Include project overhead items from Division 1 – General Requirements.
- These items are needed to make the job run. They are typically, but not always, provided by the General Contractor. Items include, but are not limited to, field personnel, insurance, performance bond, permits, testing, temporary utilities, field office and storage facilities, temporary scaffolding and platforms, equipment mobilization and demobilization, temporary roads and sidewalks, winter protection, temporary barricades and fencing, temporary security, temporary signs, field engineering and layout, final cleaning and commissioning.
- Each item should be quantified, and matched to individual Unit Price line items in Division 1, and then priced and added to your estimate.
- An alternate method of estimating project overhead costs is to apply a percentage of the total project cost, usually 5% to 15% with an average of 10% (see General Conditions, page ix).
- Include other project related expenses in your estimate such as:
  - Rented equipment not itemized in the Crew Listings
  - Rubbish handling throughout the project (see 02 41 19.19)

6 Estimate Summary

- Include sales tax as required by laws of your state or country.
- Include the General Contractor's markup on self-performed work, usually 5% to 15% with an average of 10%.
- Include the General Contractor's markup on subcontracted work, usually 5% to 15% with an average of 10%.
- Include General Contractor's main office overhead and profit.
- RSMeans gives general guidelines on the General Contractor's main office overhead (see section 01 31 13.50 and Reference Number R013113-50).
- RSMeans gives no guidance on the General Contractor's profit.
- Markups will depend on the size of the General Contractor's operations, his projected annual revenue, the level of risk he is taking on, and on the level of competition in the local area and for this project in particular.
- Include a contingency, usually 3% to 5%, if appropriate.

- Adjust your estimate to the project's location by using the City Cost Indexes or the Location Factors in the Reference Section.
- Look at the rules on the pages for How to Use the City Cost Indexes to see how to apply the Indexes for your location.
- When the proper Index or Factor has been identified for the project's location, convert it to a multiplier by dividing it by 100, and then multiply that multiplier by your estimated total cost. The original estimated total cost will now be adjusted up or down from the national average to a total that is appropriate for your location.

Editors' Notes:

1) *We urge you to spend time reading and understanding the supporting material in the front of this book. An accurate estimate requires experience, knowledge, and careful calculation. The more you know about how we at RSMeans developed the data, the more accurate your estimate will be. In addition, it is important to take into consideration the reference material in the back of the book such as Equipment Listings, Crew Listings, City Cost Indexes, Location Factors, and Reference Numbers.*

2) *Contractors who are bidding or are involved in JOC, DOC, SABER, or IDIQ type contracts are cautioned that workers' compensation insurance, federal and state payroll taxes, waste, project supervision, project overhead, main office overhead, and profit are not included in bare costs. The coefficient or multiplier must cover these costs.*

How to Use the Book: The Details

What's Behind the Numbers? The Development of Cost Data

The staff at RSMeans continually monitors developments in the construction industry in order to ensure reliable, thorough, and up-to-date cost information. While overall construction costs may vary relative to general economic conditions, price fluctuations within the industry are dependent upon many factors. Individual price variations may, in fact, be opposite to overall economic trends. Therefore, costs are constantly tracked and complete updates are published yearly. Also, new items are frequently added in response to changes in materials and methods.

Costs—$ (U.S.)

All costs represent U.S. national averages and are given in U.S. dollars. The RSMeans City Cost Indexes can be used to adjust costs to a particular location. The City Cost Indexes for Canada can be used to adjust U.S. national averages to local costs in Canadian dollars. No exchange rate conversion is necessary.

G   The processes or products identified by the green symbol in our publications have been determined to be environmentally responsible and/or resource-efficient solely by the RSMeans engineering staff. The inclusion of the green symbol does not represent compliance with any specific industry association or standard.

Material Costs

The RSMeans staff contacts manufacturers, dealers, distributors, and contractors all across the U.S. and Canada to determine national average material costs. If you have access to current material costs for your specific location, you may wish to make adjustments to reflect differences from the national average. Included within material costs are fasteners for a normal installation. RSMeans engineers use manufacturers' recommendations, written specifications, and/or standard construction practice for size and spacing of fasteners. Adjustments to material costs may be required for your specific application or location. Material costs do not include sales tax.

Labor Costs

Labor costs are based on the average of wage rates from 30 major U.S. cities. Rates are determined from labor union agreements or prevailing wages for construction trades for the current year. Rates, along with overhead and profit markups, are listed on the inside back cover of this book.

- If wage rates in your area vary from those used in this book, or if rate increases are expected within a given year, labor costs should be adjusted accordingly.

Labor costs reflect productivity based on actual working conditions. In addition to actual installation, these figures include time spent during a normal weekday on tasks such as, material receiving and handling, mobilization at site, site movement, breaks, and cleanup. Productivity data is developed over an extended period so as not to be influenced by abnormal variations and reflects a typical average.

Equipment Costs

Equipment costs include not only rental, but also operating costs for equipment under normal use. The operating costs include parts and labor for routine servicing such as repair and replacement of pumps, filters, and worn lines. Normal operating expendables, such as fuel, lubricants, tires, and electricity (where applicable), are also included. Extraordinary operating expendables with highly variable wear patterns, such as diamond bits and blades, are excluded. These costs are included under materials. Equipment rental rates are obtained from industry sources throughout North America—contractors, suppliers, dealers, manufacturers, and distributors.

Rental rates can also be treated as reimbursement costs for contractor-owned equipment. Owned equipment costs include depreciation, loan payments, interest, taxes, insurance, storage and major repairs.

Equipment costs do not include operators' wages; nor do they include the cost to move equipment to a job site (mobilization) or from a job site (demobilization).

Equipment Cost/Day——The cost of power equipment required for each crew is included in the Crew Listings in the Reference Section (small tools that are considered as essential everyday tools are not listed out separately). The Crew Listings itemize specialized tools and heavy equipment along with labor trades. The daily cost of itemized equipment included in a crew is based on dividing the weekly bare rental rate by 5 (number of working days per week) and then adding the hourly operating cost times 8 (the number of hours per day). This Equipment Cost/Day is shown in the last column of the Equipment Rental Cost pages in the Reference Section.

Mobilization/Demobilization——The cost to move construction equipment from an equipment yard or rental company to the job site and back again is not included in equipment costs. Mobilization (to the site) and demobilization (from the site) costs can be found in the Unit Price Section. If a piece of equipment is already at the job site, it is not appropriate to utilize mob./demob. costs again in an estimate.

Overhead and Profit

Total Cost including O&P for the *Installing Contractor* is shown in the last column on the Unit Price and/or the Assemblies pages of this book. This figure is the sum of the bare material cost plus 10% for profit, the bare labor cost plus total overhead and profit, and the bare equipment cost plus 10% for profit. Details for the calculation of Overhead and Profit on labor are shown on the inside back cover and in the Reference Section of this book. (See the "How to Use the Unit Price Pages" for an example of this calculation.)

General Conditions

Cost data in this book is presented in two ways: Bare Costs and Total Cost including O&P (Overhead and Profit). General Conditions, or General Requirements, of the contract should also be added to the Total Cost including O&P when applicable. Costs for General Conditions are listed in Division 1 of the Unit Price Section and the Reference

Section of this book. General Conditions for the *Installing Contractor* may range from 0% to 10% of the Total Cost including O&P. For the *General* or *Prime Contractor*, costs for General Conditions may range from 5% to 15% of the Total Cost including O&P, with a figure of 10% as the most typical allowance. If applicable, the Assemblies and Models sections of this book use costs that include the installing contractor's overhead and profit (O&P).

Factors Affecting Costs

Costs can vary depending upon a number of variables. Here's how we have handled the main factors affecting costs.

Quality——The prices for materials and the workmanship upon which productivity is based represent sound construction work. They are also in line with U.S. government specifications.

Overtime——We have made no allowance for overtime. If you anticipate premium time or work beyond normal working hours, be sure to make an appropriate adjustment to your labor costs.

Productivity——The productivity, daily output, and labor-hour figures for each line item are based on working an eight-hour day in daylight hours in moderate temperatures. For work that extends beyond normal work hours or is performed under adverse conditions, productivity may decrease. (See the section in "How To Use the Unit Price Pages" for more on productivity.)

Size of Project——The size, scope of work, and type of construction project will have a significant impact on cost. Economies of scale can reduce costs for large projects. Unit costs can often run higher for small projects.

Location——Material prices in this book are for metropolitan areas. However, in dense urban areas, traffic and site storage limitations may increase costs. Beyond a 20-mile radius of large cities, extra trucking or transportation charges may also increase the material costs slightly. On the other hand, lower wage rates may be in effect. Be sure to consider both of these factors when preparing an estimate, particularly if the job site is located in a central city or remote rural location. In addition, highly specialized subcontract items may require travel and per-diem expenses for mechanics.

Other Factors—

- season of year
- contractor management
- weather conditions
- local union restrictions
- building code requirements
- availability of:
  - adequate energy
  - skilled labor
  - building materials
- owner's special requirements/restrictions
- safety requirements
- environmental considerations

Unpredictable Factors——General business conditions influence "in-place" costs of all items. Substitute materials and construction methods may have to be employed. These may affect the installed cost and/or life cycle costs. Such factors may be difficult to evaluate and cannot necessarily be predicted on the basis of the job's location in a particular section of the country. Thus, where these factors apply, you may find significant but unavoidable cost variations for which you will have to apply a measure of judgment to your estimate.

Rounding of Costs

In general, all unit prices in excess of $5.00 have been rounded to make them easier to use and still maintain adequate precision of the results. The rounding rules we have chosen are in the following table.

Prices from . . .	Rounded to the nearest . . .
$.01 to $5.00	$.01
$5.01 to $20.00	$.05
$20.01 to $100.00	$.50
$100.01 to $300.00	$1.00
$300.01 to $1,000.00	$5.00
$1,000.01 to $10,000.00	$25.00
$10,000.01 to $50,000.00	$100.00
$50,000.01 and above	$500.00

How Subcontracted Items Affect Costs

A considerable portion of all large construction jobs is usually subcontracted. In fact, the percentage done by subcontractors is constantly increasing and may run over 90%. Since the workers employed by these companies do nothing else but install their particular product, they soon become expert in that line. The result is, installation by these firms is accomplished so efficiently that the total in-place cost, even adding the general contractor's overhead and profit, is no more, and often less, than if the principal contractor had handled the installation himself/herself. Companies that deal with construction specialties are anxious to have their product perform well and, consequently, the installation will be the best possible.

Contingencies

The allowance for contingencies generally provides for unforeseen construction difficulties. On alterations or repair jobs, 20% is not too much. If drawings are final and only field contingencies are being considered, 2% or 3% is probably sufficient, and often nothing need be added. Contractually, changes in plans will be covered by extras. The contractor should consider inflationary price trends and possible material shortages during the course of the job. These escalation factors are dependent upon both economic conditions and the anticipated time between the estimate and actual construction. If drawings are not complete or approved, or a budget cost is wanted, it is wise to add 5% to 10%. Contingencies, then, are a matter of judgment. Additional allowances for contingencies are shown in Division 1.

Important Estimating Considerations

The "productivity," or daily output, of each craftsman includes mobilization and cleanup time, break time and plan layout time, as well as an allowance to carry stock from the storage trailer or location on the job site up to 200' into the building and to the first or second floor. If material has to be transported over greater distances or to higher floors, an additional allowance should be considered by the estimator. An allowance has also been included in the piping and fittings installation time for leak checking and minor tightening. Equipment installation time includes the following applicable items: positioning, leveling and securing the unit in place, connecting all associated piping, ducts, vents, etc., which shall have been estimated separately, connecting to an adjacent power source, filling/bleeding, startup, adjusting the controls up and down to ensure proper response, setting the integral controls/valves/regulators/thermostats for proper operation (does not include external building type control systems, DDC systems, etc.), explaining/training owner's operator, and warranty. A reasonable breakdown of the labor costs is as follows:

1. Movement into building, installation/ setting of equipment 35%
2. Connection to piping/duct/power, etc. 25%
3. Filling/flushing/cleaning/touchup, etc. 15%
4. Startup/running adjustments 5%
5. Training owner's representative 5%
6. Warranty/call back/service 15%

Note that cranes or other lifting equipment are not included on any lines in the Mechanical divisions. For example, if a crane is required to lift a heavy piece of pipe into place high above a gym floor, or to put a rooftop unit on the roof of a four-story building, etc., it must be added. Due to the potential for extreme variation—from nothing additional required to a major crane or helicopter—we feel that including a nominal amount for "lifting contingency" would be useless and detract from the accuracy of the estimate. When using equipment rental from RSMeans, remember to include the cost of the operator(s).

Estimating Labor-Hours

The labor-hours expressed in this publication are based on Average Installation time, using an efficiency level of approximately 60%–65% (see item 7), which has been found reasonable and acceptable by many contractors. The book uses this national efficiency average to establish a consistent benchmark. For bid situations, adjustments to this efficiency level should be the responsibility of the contractor bidding the project. The unit labor-hour is divided in the following manner. A typical day for a journeyman might be:

1.	Study Plans	3%	14.4 min.
2.	Material Procurement	3%	14.4 min.
3.	Receiving and Storing	3%	14.4 min
4.	Mobilization	5%	24.0 min.
5.	Site Movement	5%	24.0 min.
6.	Layout and Marking	8%	38.4 min.
7.	Actual Installation	64%	307.2 min.
8.	Cleanup	3%	14.4 min.
9.	Breaks, Nonproductive	6%	28.8 min.
		100%	480.0 min.

If any of the percentages expressed in this breakdown do not apply to the particular work or project situation, then that percentage or a portion of it may be deducted from or added to labor-hours.

Final Checklist

Estimating can be a straightforward process provided you remember the basics. Here's a checklist of some of the steps you should remember to complete before finalizing your estimate. Did you remember to . . .

- factor in the City Cost Index for your locale?
- take into consideration which items have been marked up and by how much?
- mark up the entire estimate sufficiently for your purposes?
- read the background information on techniques and technical matters that could impact your project time span and cost?
- include all components of your project in the final estimate?
- double check your figures for accuracy?
- call RSMeans if you have any questions about your estimate or the data you've found in our publications? Remember, RSMeans stands behind its publications. If you have any questions about your estimate . . . about the costs you've used from our books . . . or even about the technical aspects of the job that may affect your estimate, feel free to call the RSMeans editors at 1-800-334-3509.

Unit Price Section

Table of Contents

Table of Contents (cont.)

How RSMeans Data Works

All RSMeans unit price data is organized in the same way.

It is important to understand the structure, so that you can find information easily and use it correctly.

RSMeans **Line Numbers** consist of 12 characters, which identify a unique location in the database for each task. The first 6 or 8 digits conform to the Construction Specifications Institute MasterFormat 2010. The remainder of the digits are a further breakdown by RSMeans in order to arrange items in understandable groups of similar tasks. Line numbers are consistent across all RSMeans publications, so a line number in any RSMeans product will always refer to the same unit of work.

RSMeans engineers have created **reference** information to assist you in your estimate. If there is information that applies to a section, it will be indicated at the start of the section. In this case, R033105-10 provides information on the proportionate quantities of formwork, reinforcing, and concrete used in cast-in-place concrete items such as footings, slabs, beams, and columns. The reference section is located in the back of the book on the pages with a gray edge.

RSMeans **Descriptions** are shown in a hierarchical structure to make them readable. In order to read a complete description, read up through the indents to the top of the section. Include everything that is above and to the left that is not contradicted by information below. For instance, the complete description for line 03 30 53.40 3550 is "Concrete in place, including forms (4 uses), reinforcing steel, concrete, placement, and finishing unless otherwise indicated; Equipment pad (3000 psi), 4' x 4' x 6" thick."

When using **RSMeans data**, it is important to read through an entire section to ensure that you use the data that most closely matches your work. Note that sometimes there is additional information shown in the section that may improve your price. There are frequently lines that further describe, add to, or adjust data for specific situations.

03 30 Cast-In-Place Concrete

03 30 53 – Miscellaneous Cast-In-Place Concrete

03 30 53.40 Concrete In Place

0010	**CONCRETE IN PLACE**	R033105-10
0020	Including forms (4 uses), reinforcing steel, concrete, placement,	R033105-20
0050	and finishing unless otherwise indicated	R033105-50
0300	Beams (3500 psi), 5 kip per L.F., 10' span	R033105-65
0350	25' span	R033105-70
0500	Chimney foundations (5000 psi), industrial, minimum	R033105-85
0510	Maximum	
0700	Columns, square (4000 psi), 12" x 12", minimum reinforcing	
3500	Add per floor for 3 to 6 stories high	
3520	For 7 to 20 stories high	
3540	Equipment pad (3000 psi), 3' x 3' x 6" thick	
3550	4' x 4' x 6" thick	
3560	5' x 5' x 8" thick	
3570	6' x 6' x 8" thick	

The data published in RSMeans print books represents a "national average" cost. This data should be modified to the project location using the **City Cost Indexes** or **Location Factors** tables found in the reference section (see pages 647–695). Use the location factors to adjust estimate totals if the project covers multiple trades. Use the city cost indexes (CCI) for single trade projects or projects where a more detailed analysis is required. All figures in the two tables are derived from the same research. The last row of data in the CCI, the weighted average, is the same as the numbers reported for each location in the location factor table.

Crews include labor or labor and equipment necessary to accomplish each task. In this case, Crew C-14H is used. RSMeans selects a crew to represent the workers and equipment that are typically used for that task. In this case, Crew C-14H consists of one carpenter foreman (outside), two carpenters, one rodman, one laborer, one cement finisher, and one gas engine vibrator. Details of all crews can be found in the reference section.

Crews

Crew No.	Bare Costs		Incl. Subs O&P		Cost Per Labor-Hour	
Crew C-14H	Hr.	Daily	Hr.	Daily	Bare Costs	Incl. O&P
1 Carpenter Foreman (outside)	$46.10	$368.80	$70.95	$567.60	$43.48	$66.89
2 Carpenters	44.10	705.60	67.85	1085.60		
1 Rodman (reinf.)	49.10	392.80	78.40	627.20		
1 Laborer	35.10	280.80	54.00	432.00		
1 Cement Finisher	42.35	338.80	62.30	498.40		
1 Gas Engine Vibrator		27.40		30.14	.57	.63
48 L.H., Daily Totals		$2114.20		$3240.94	$44.05	$67.52

The **Daily Output** is the amount of work that the crew can do in a normal 8-hour workday, including mobilization, layout, movement of materials, and cleanup. In this case, crew C-14H can install thirty 4' x 4' x 6" thick concrete pads in a day. Daily output is variable, based on many factors, including the size of the job, location, and environmental conditions. RSMeans data represents work done in daylight (or adequate lighting) and temperate conditions.

Bare Costs are the costs of materials, labor, and equipment that the installing contractor pays. They represent the cost, in U.S. dollars, for one unit of work. They do not include any markups for profit or labor burden.

Crew	Daily Output	Labor-Hours	Unit	Material	2012 Bare Costs Labor	Equipment	Total	Total Incl O&P
C-14A	15.62	12.804	C.Y.	305	565	47.50	917.50	1,275
"	18.55	10.782		320	480	40	840	1,125
C-14C	32.22	3.476		144	147	.83	291.83	385
"	23.71	4.724		168	200	1.13	369.13	495
C-14A	11.96	16.722		350	740	62	1,152	1,600
	31800	.002			.07	.02	.09	.12
	21200	.003			.10	.03	.13	.20
C-14H	45	1.067	Ea.	44	46.50	.61	91.11	121
	30	1.600		66	69.50	.91	136.41	181
	18	2.667		118	116	1.52	235.52	310
	14	3.429		159	149	1.95	309.95	405

The **Total Incl O&P column** is the total cost, including overhead and profit, that the installing contractor will charge the customer. This represents the cost of materials plus 10% profit, the cost of labor plus labor burden and 10% profit, and the cost of equipment plus 10% profit. It does not include the general contractor's overhead and profit. Note: See the inside back cover for details of how RSMeans calculates labor burden.

The **Total column** represents the total bare cost for the installing contractor, in U.S. dollars. In this case, the sum of $66 for material + $69.50 for labor + $.91 for equipment is $136.41.

The figure in the **Labor Hours** column is the amount of labor required to perform one unit of work—in this case the amount of labor required to construct one 4' x 4' equipment pad. This figure is calculated by dividing the number of hours of labor in the crew by the daily output (48 labor hours divided by 30 pads = 1.6 hours of labor per pad). Multiply 1.600 times 60 to see the value in minutes: 60 x 1.6 = 96 minutes. Note: the labor hour figure is not dependent on the crew size. A change in crew size will result in a corresponding change in daily output, but the labor hours per unit of work will not change.

All RSMeans unit cost data includes the typical **Unit of Measure** used for estimating that item. For concrete-in-place the typical unit is cubic yards (C.Y.) or each (Ea.). For installing broadloom carpet it is square yard, and for gypsum board it is square foot. The estimator needs to take special care that the unit in the data matches the unit in the take-off. Unit conversions may be found in the Reference Section.

Sample Estimate

This sample demonstrates the elements of an estimate, including a tally of the RSMeans data lines, and a summary of the markups on a contractor's work to arrive at a total cost to the owner. The RSMeans Location Factor is added at the bottom of the estimate to adjust the cost of the work to a specific location.

Work Performed: The body of the estimate shows the RSMeans data selected, including line number, a brief description of each item, its take-off unit and quantity, and the bare costs of materials, labor, and equipment. This estimate also includes a column titled "SubContract." This data is taken from the RSMeans column "Total Incl O&P," and represents the total that a subcontractor would charge a general contractor for the work, including the sub's markup for overhead and profit.

General Requirements: This item covers project-wide needs provided by the general contractor. These items vary by project, but may include temporary facilities and utilities, security, testing, project cleanup, etc. For small projects a percentage can be used, typically between 5% and 15% of project cost. For large projects the costs may be itemized and priced individually.

Bonds: Bond costs should be added to the estimate. The figures here represent a typical performance bond, ensuring the owner that if the general contractor does not complete the obligations in the construction contract the bonding company will pay the cost for completion of the work.

Location Adjustment: RSMeans published data is based on national average costs. If necessary, adjust the total cost of the project using a location factor from the "Location Factor" table or the "City Cost Index" table. Use location factors if the work is general, covering multiple trades. If the work is by a single trade (e.g., masonry) use the more specific data found in the "City Cost Indexes."

This estimate is based on an interactive spreadsheet.
A copy of this spreadsheet is located on the RSMeans website at
http://www.reedconstructiondata.com/rsmeans/extras/546011.
You are free to download it and adjust it to your methodology.

Project Name:	Pre-Engineered Steel Building	Architect: As Shown			
Location:	**Anywhere, USA**				
Line Number	**Description**	**Qty**	**Unit**	**Material**	
03 30 53.40 3950	Strip footing, 12" x 36"	33.33	C.Y.	$4,699.53	
03 30 53.40 3940	Strip footing, 12" x24"	14.8	C.Y.	$2,175.60	
03 31 05.35 0300	Concrete ready mix, 4000 psi, for slab	185.2	C.Y.	$19,631.20	
03 31 05.70 4300	Placing concrete, slab on grade	185.2	C.Y.	$0.00	
03 11 13.65 3000	Concrete forms	500	L.F.	$190.00	
03 22 05.50 0200	WWF	150	C.S.F.	$3,975.00	
03 39 23.13 0300	Curing	150	C.S.F.	$787.50	
03 35 29.30 0250	Concrete finishing	15000	S.F.	$0.00	
03 35 29.35 0160	Control joints	650	L.F.	$84.50	
Division 03	**Subtotal**			**$31,543.33**	
08 33 23.10 0100	10' x 10' OH Door	8	Ea.	$14,000.00	
08 33 23.10 3300	Add for enamel finish	800	S.F.	$1,216.00	
Division 8	**Subtotal**			**$15,216.00**	
13 34 19.50 1000	Pre-Engineered Steel Building	15,000	SF Flr.		
13 34 19.50 6050	Framing for doors, 3' x 7'	4	Opng.	$0.00	
13 34 19.50 6100	Framing for doors, 10' x 10'	8	Opng.	$0.00	
13 34 19.50 6200	Framing for windows, 3' x 4'	6	Opng.	$0.00	
13 34 19.50 5750	PESB doors	4	Opng.	$1,740.00	
13 34 19.50 7750	PESB windows	6	Opng.	$2,100.00	
13 34 19.50 6550	Gutters	380	L.F.	$2,679.00	
13 34 19.50 8650	Roof vent	15	Ea.	$382.50	
13 34 19.50 6900	Insulation	25,000	S.F.	$12,750.00	
Division 13	**Subtotal**			**$19,651.50**	
Estimate Subtotal				**$66,410.83**	
			Gen. Requirements	4,648.76	
			Sales Tax	3,320.54	
			Subtotal	74,380.13	
			GC O & P	7,438.01	
			Subtotal	81,818.14	
			Contingency	@5%	
			Subtotal		
			Bond	$12/1000 +10% O&P	
			Subtotal		
			Location Adjustment	Factor	
			Grand Total		

This example shows the cost to construct a pre-engineered steel building. The foundation, doors, windows, and insulation will be installed by the general contractor. A subcontractor will install the structural steel, roofing, and siding.

	01/01/12			
Labor	Equipment	SubContract	EstimateTotal	
$2,383.10	$14.33	$0.00		
$1,324.60	$7.99	$0.00		
$0.00	$0.00	$0.00		
$2,666.88	$87.04	$0.00		
$1,010.00	$0.00	$0.00		
$3,450.00	$0.00	$0.00		
$795.00	$0.00	$0.00		
$7,500.00	$300.00	$0.00		
$247.00	$58.50	$0.00		
$19,376.58	**$467.86**	**$0.00**	**$51,387.77**	**Division 03**
$4,080.00	$0.00	$0.00		
$0.00	$0.00	$0.00		
$4,080.00	**$0.00**	**$0.00**	**$19,296.00**	**Division 0**
		$287,250.00		
$0.00	$0.00	$1,900.00		
$0.00	$0.00	$8,400.00		
$0.00	$0.00	$3,450.00		
$572.00	$0.00	$0.00		
$483.00	$61.80	$0.00		
$851.20	$0.00	$0.00		
$2,685.00	$0.00	$0.00		
$7,000.00	$0.00	$0.00		
$11,591.20	**$61.80**	**$301,000.00**	**$3?2,304.50**	**Division 13**
$35,047.78	**$529.66**	**$301,000.00**	**$402,988.27**	
2,453.34	37.08	21,070.00		Gen. Requirements
	26.48	7,525.00		Sales Tax
37,501.12	593.22	329,595.00		Subtotal
3,750.11	59.32	32,959.50		GC O & P
41,251.24	652.54	362,554.50	$486,276.42	Subtotal
			24,313.82	Contingency
			$510,590.24	Subtotal
			6,739.79	Bond
			$517,330.03	Subtotal
102.30			11,898.59	Location Adjustment
			$529,228.62	**Grand Total**

Sales Tax: If the work is subject to state or local sales taxes, the amount must be added to the estimate. Sales tax may be added to material costs, equipment costs, and subcontracted work. In this case, sales tax was added in all three categories. It was assumed that approximately half the subcontracted work would be material cost, so the tax was applied to 50% of the subcontract total.

GC O&P: This entry represents the general contractor's markup on material, labor, equipment, and subcontractor costs. RSMeans' standard markup on materials, equipment, and subcontracted work is 10%. In this estimate, the markup on the labor performed by the GC's workers uses "Skilled Workers Average" shown in Column F on the table "Installing Contractor's Overhead & Profit," which can be found on the inside-back cover of the book.

Contingency: A factor for contingency may be added to any estimate to represent the cost of unknowns that may occur between the time that the estimate is performed and the time the project is constructed. The amount of the allowance will depend on the stage of design at which the estimate is done, and the contractor's assessment of the risk involved. Refer to section 01 21 16.50 for contigency allowances.

Estimating Tips

01 20 00 Price and Payment Procedures

- Allowances that should be added to estimates to cover contingencies and job conditions that are not included in the national average material and labor costs are shown in section 01 21.

- When estimating historic preservation projects (depending on the condition of the existing structure and the owner's requirements), a 15%–20% contingency or allowance is recommended, regardless of the stage of the drawings.

01 30 00 Administrative Requirements

- Before determining a final cost estimate, it is a good practice to review all the items listed in Subdivisions 01 31 and 01 32 to make final adjustments for items that may need customizing to specific job conditions.

- Requirements for initial and periodic submittals can represent a significant cost to the General Requirements of a job. Thoroughly check the submittal specifications when estimating a project to determine any costs that should be included.

01 40 00 Quality Requirements

- All projects will require some degree of Quality Control. This cost is not included in the unit cost of construction listed in each division. Depending upon the terms of the contract, the various costs of inspection and testing can be the responsibility of either the owner or the contractor. Be sure to include the required costs in your estimate.

01 50 00 Temporary Facilities and Controls

- Barricades, access roads, safety nets, scaffolding, security, and many more requirements for the execution of a safe project are elements of direct cost. These costs can easily be overlooked when preparing an estimate. When looking through the major classifications of this subdivision, determine which items apply to each division in your estimate.

- Construction Equipment Rental Costs can be found in the Reference Section in section 01 54 33. Operators' wages are not included in equipment rental costs.

- Equipment mobilization and demobilization costs are not included in equipment rental costs and must be considered separately in section 01 54 36.50.

- The cost of small tools provided by the installing contractor for his workers is covered in the "Overhead" column on the "Installing Contractor's Overhead and Profit" table that lists labor trades, base rates and markups and, therefore, is included in the "Total Incl. O&P" cost of any Unit Price line item. For those users who are constrained by contract terms to use only bare costs, there are two line items in section 01 54 39.70 for small tools as a percentage of bare labor cost. If some of those users are further constrained by contract terms to refrain from using line items from Division 1, you are advised to cover the cost of small tools within your coefficient or multiplier.

01 70 00 Execution and Closeout Requirements

- When preparing an estimate, thoroughly read the specifications to determine the requirements for Contract Closeout. Final cleaning, record documentation, operation and maintenance data, warranties and bonds, and spare parts and maintenance materials can all be elements of cost for the completion of a contract. Do not overlook these in your estimate.

Reference Numbers

Reference numbers are shown in shaded boxes at the beginning of some major classifications. These numbers refer to related items in the Reference Section. The reference information may be an estimating procedure, an alternate pricing method, or technical information.

Note: Not all subdivisions listed here necessarily appear in this publication.

01 11 Summary of Work
01 11 31 – Professional Consultants

01 11 31.10 Architectural Fees		Crew	Daily Output	Labor-Hours	Unit	Material	2012 Bare Costs Labor	Equipment	Total	Total Incl O&P
0010	**ARCHITECTURAL FEES** R011110-10									
2000	For "Greening" of building ⒼG				Project					3%

01 11 31.30 Engineering Fees

01 11 31.30 Engineering Fees		Crew	Daily Output	Labor-Hours	Unit	Material	2012 Bare Costs Labor	Equipment	Total	Total Incl O&P
0010	**ENGINEERING FEES** R011110-30									
0020	Educational planning consultant, minimum				Project					.50%
0100	Maximum				"					2.50%
0200	Electrical, minimum				Contrct					4.10%
0300	Maximum									10.10%
0400	Elevator & conveying systems, minimum									2.50%
0500	Maximum									5%
0600	Food service & kitchen equipment, minimum									8%
0700	Maximum									12%
1000	Mechanical (plumbing & HVAC), minimum									4.10%
1100	Maximum									10.10%

01 21 Allowances
01 21 16 – Contingency Allowances

01 21 16.50 Contingencies

01 21 16.50 Contingencies		Crew	Daily Output	Labor-Hours	Unit	Material	2012 Bare Costs Labor	Equipment	Total	Total Incl O&P
0010	**CONTINGENCIES**, Add to estimate									
0020	Conceptual stage				Project					20%
0050	Schematic stage									15%
0100	Preliminary working drawing stage (Design Dev.)									10%
0150	Final working drawing stage									3%

01 21 53 – Factors Allowance

01 21 53.50 Factors

01 21 53.50 Factors		Crew	Daily Output	Labor-Hours	Unit	Material	2012 Bare Costs Labor	Equipment	Total	Total Incl O&P
0010	**FACTORS** Cost adjustments R012153-10									
0100	Add to construction costs for particular job requirements									
0500	Cut & patch to match existing construction, add, minimum				Costs	2%	3%			
0550	Maximum					5%	9%			
0800	Dust protection, add, minimum					1%	2%			
0850	Maximum					4%	11%			
1100	Equipment usage curtailment, add, minimum					1%	1%			
1150	Maximum					3%	10%			
1400	Material handling & storage limitation, add, minimum					1%	1%			
1450	Maximum					6%	7%			
1700	Protection of existing work, add, minimum					2%	2%			
1750	Maximum					5%	7%			
2000	Shift work requirements, add, minimum						5%			
2050	Maximum						30%			
2300	Temporary shoring and bracing, add, minimum					2%	5%			
2350	Maximum					5%	12%			
2400	Work inside prisons and high security areas, add, minimum						30%			
2450	Maximum						50%			

01 21 55 – Job Conditions Allowance

01 21 55.50 Job Conditions

01 21 55.50 Job Conditions		Crew	Daily Output	Labor-Hours	Unit	Material	2012 Bare Costs Labor	Equipment	Total	Total Incl O&P
0010	**JOB CONDITIONS** Modifications to applicable									
0020	cost summaries									
0100	Economic conditions, favorable, deduct				Project				2%	2%
0200	Unfavorable, add								5%	5%
0300	Hoisting conditions, favorable, deduct								2%	2%

01 21 Allowances

01 21 55 – Job Conditions Allowance

01 21 55.50 Job Conditions		Crew	Daily Output	Labor-Hours	Unit	Material	2012 Bare Costs Labor	Equipment	Total	Total Incl O&P
0400	Unfavorable, add				Project				5%	5%
0700	Labor availability, surplus, deduct								1%	1%
0800	Shortage, add								10%	10%
0900	Material storage area, available, deduct								1%	1%
1000	Not available, add								2%	2%
1100	Subcontractor availability, surplus, deduct								5%	5%
1200	Shortage, add								12%	12%
1300	Work space, available, deduct								2%	2%
1400	Not available, add								5%	5%

01 21 57 – Overtime Allowance

01 21 57.50 Overtime

0010	**OVERTIME** for early completion of projects or where	R012909-90								
0020	labor shortages exist, add to usual labor, up to					Costs		100%		

01 21 61 – Cost Indexes

01 21 61.10 Construction Cost Index

0010	**CONSTRUCTION COST INDEX** (Reference) over 930 zip code locations in									
0020	the U.S. and Canada, total bldg. cost, min. (Guymon, OK)					%				67.50%
0050	Average									100%
0100	Maximum (New York, NY)									132.20%

01 21 61.20 Historical Cost Indexes

0010	**HISTORICAL COST INDEXES** (See Reference Section)									

01 21 61.30 Labor Index

0010	**LABOR INDEX** (Reference) For over 930 zip code locations in									
0020	the U.S. and Canada, minimum (Guymon, OK)					%	31%			
0050	Average						100%			
0100	Maximum (New York, NY)						166.90%			

01 21 61.50 Material Index

0011	**MATERIAL INDEX** For over 930 zip code locations in									
0020	the U.S. and Canada, minimum (Elizabethtown, KY)					%	91.40%			
0040	Average						100%			
0060	Maximum (Ketchikan, AK)						141.30%			

01 21 63 – Taxes

01 21 63.10 Taxes

0010	**TAXES**	R012909-80								
0020	Sales tax, State, average					%	5.07%			
0050	Maximum	R012909-85					9.25%			
0200	Social Security, on first $110,100 of wages							7.65%		
0300	Unemployment, combined Federal and State, minimum							.80%		
0350	Average							7.80%		
0400	Maximum							14.36%		

01 31 Project Management and Coordination

01 31 13 – Project Coordination

01 31 13.20 Field Personnel

	01 31 13.20 Field Personnel	Crew	Daily Output	Labor-Hours	Unit	Material	2012 Bare Costs Labor	Equipment	Total	Total Incl O&P
0010	**FIELD PERSONNEL**									
0020	Clerk, average				Week		420		420	650
0100	Field engineer, minimum						995		995	1,550
0120	Average						1,300		1,300	2,000
0140	Maximum						1,475		1,475	2,275
0160	General purpose laborer, average						1,375		1,375	2,125
0180	Project manager, minimum						1,850		1,850	2,850
0200	Average						2,125		2,125	3,275
0220	Maximum						2,425		2,425	3,750
0240	Superintendent, minimum						1,800		1,800	2,775
0260	Average						1,975		1,975	3,050
0280	Maximum						2,250		2,250	3,475
0290	Timekeeper, average						1,150		1,150	1,775

01 31 13.30 Insurance

	01 31 13.30 Insurance		Crew	Daily Output	Labor-Hours	Unit	Material	2012 Bare Costs Labor	Equipment	Total	Total Incl O&P
0010	**INSURANCE**	R013113-40									
0020	Builders risk, standard, minimum					Job					.24%
0050	Maximum	R013113-50									.64%
0200	All-risk type, minimum										.25%
0250	Maximum	R013113-60									.62%
0400	Contractor's equipment floater, minimum					Value					.50%
0450	Maximum					"					1.50%
0600	Public liability, average					Job					2.02%
0800	Workers' compensation & employer's liability, average										
0850	by trade, carpentry, general					Payroll		14.96%			
1000	Electrical							5.58%			
1150	Insulation							11.85%			
1450	Plumbing							6.91%			
1550	Sheet metal work (HVAC)							8.47%			

01 31 13.50 General Contractor's Mark-Up

	01 31 13.50 General Contractor's Mark-Up	Crew	Daily Output	Labor-Hours	Unit	Material	2012 Bare Costs Labor	Equipment	Total	Total Incl O&P
0010	**GENERAL CONTRACTOR'S MARK-UP** on Change Orders									
0200	Extra work, by subcontractors, add				%					10%
0250	By General Contractor, add									15%
0400	Omitted work, by subcontractors, deduct all but									5%
0450	By General Contractor, deduct all but									7.50%
0600	Overtime work, by subcontractors, add									15%
0650	By General Contractor, add									10%

01 31 13.60 Installing Contractor's Main Office Overhead

	01 31 13.60 Installing Contractor's Main Office Overhead	Crew	Daily Output	Labor-Hours	Unit	Material	2012 Bare Costs Labor	Equipment	Total	Total Incl O&P
0010	**INSTALLING CONTRACTOR'S MAIN OFFICE OVERHEAD**									
0020	As percent of direct costs, minimum				%					5%
0050	Average									13%
0100	Maximum									30%

01 31 13.80 Overhead and Profit

	01 31 13.80 Overhead and Profit	Crew	Daily Output	Labor-Hours	Unit	Material	2012 Bare Costs Labor	Equipment	Total	Total Incl O&P
0010	**OVERHEAD & PROFIT** Allowance to add to items in this									
0020	book that do not include Subs O&P, average				%					25%
0100	Allowance to add to items in this book that									
0110	do include Subs O&P, minimum				%					5%
0150	Average									10%
0200	Maximum									15%
0300	Typical, by size of project, under $100,000									30%
0350	$500,000 project									25%
0400	$2,000,000 project									20%
0450	Over $10,000,000 project									15%

01 31 Project Management and Coordination

01 31 13 – Project Coordination

01 31 13.90 Performance Bond		Crew	Daily Output	Labor-Hours	Unit	Material	2012 Bare Costs Labor	Equipment	Total	Total Incl O&P
0010	**PERFORMANCE BOND**	R013113-80								
0020	For buildings, minimum				Job					.60%
0100	Maximum				"					2.50%

01 32 Construction Progress Documentation

01 32 33 – Photographic Documentation

01 32 33.50 Photographs

		Crew	Daily Output	Labor-Hours	Unit	Material	Labor	Equipment	Total	Total Incl O&P
0010	**PHOTOGRAPHS**									
0020	8" x 10", 4 shots, 2 prints ea., std. mounting				Set	475			475	520
0100	Hinged linen mounts					530			530	580
0200	8" x 10", 4 shots, 2 prints each, in color					415			415	460
0300	For I.D. slugs, add to all above					5.30			5.30	5.85
1500	Time lapse equipment, camera and projector, buy					845			845	930
1550	Rent per month					305			305	335
1700	Cameraman and film, including processing, B.&W.				Day	1,375			1,375	1,525
1720	Color				"	1,375			1,375	1,525

01 41 Regulatory Requirements

01 41 26 – Permit Requirements

01 41 26.50 Permits

		Crew	Daily Output	Labor-Hours	Unit	Material	Labor	Equipment	Total	Total Incl O&P
0010	**PERMITS**									
0020	Rule of thumb, most cities, minimum				Job					.50%
0100	Maximum				"					2%

01 45 Quality Control

01 45 23 – Testing and Inspecting Services

01 45 23.50 Testing

		Crew	Daily Output	Labor-Hours	Unit	Material	Labor	Equipment	Total	Total Incl O&P
0010	**TESTING** and Inspecting Services									
5820	Non-destructive metal testing, dye penetrant				Day				310	340
5840	Magnetic particle								310	340
5860	Radiography								450	495
5880	Ultrasonic								310	340
9000	Thermographic testing, for bldg envelope heat loss, average 2,000 S.F. [G]				Ea.					500

01 51 Temporary Utilities

01 51 13 – Temporary Electricity

01 51 13.80 Temporary Utilities

		Crew	Daily Output	Labor-Hours	Unit	Material	Labor	Equipment	Total	Total Incl O&P
0010	**TEMPORARY UTILITIES**									
0100	Heat, incl. fuel and operation, per week, 12 hrs. per day	1 Skwk	100	.080	CSF Flr	36.50	3.63		40.13	45.50
0200	24 hrs. per day	"	60	.133		69.50	6.05		75.55	86
0350	Lighting, incl. service lamps, wiring & outlets, minimum	1 Elec	34	.235		2.80	12.15		14.95	21
0360	Maximum	"	17	.471		5.85	24.50		30.35	43
0400	Power for temp lighting only, 6.6 KWH, per month								.92	1.01
0430	11.8 KWH, per month								1.65	1.82
0450	23.6 KWH, per month								3.30	3.63

01 51 Temporary Utilities

01 51 13 – Temporary Electricity

01 51 13.80 Temporary Utilities	Crew	Daily Output	Labor-Hours	Unit	Material	2012 Bare Costs Labor	Equipment	Total	Total Incl O&P
0600	Power for job duration incl. elevator, etc., minimum				CSF Flr				47	51.50
0650	Maximum				↓				110	121
1000	Toilet, portable, see Equip. Rental 01 54 33 in Reference Section									

01 52 Construction Facilities

01 52 13 – Field Offices and Sheds

01 52 13.20 Office and Storage Space

		Crew	Daily Output	Labor-Hours	Unit	Material	Labor	Equipment	Total	Total Incl O&P
0010	**OFFICE AND STORAGE SPACE**									
0020	Office trailer, furnished, no hookups, 20' x 8', buy	2 Skwk	1	16	Ea.	8,550	725		9,275	10,500
0250	Rent per month					144			144	158
0300	32' x 8', buy	2 Skwk	.70	22.857		13,600	1,050		14,650	16,600
0350	Rent per month					185			185	203
0400	50' x 10', buy	2 Skwk	.60	26.667		22,300	1,200		23,500	26,500
0450	Rent per month					279			279	305
0500	50' x 12', buy	2 Skwk	.50	32		27,000	1,450		28,450	32,000
0550	Rent per month					365			365	400
0700	For air conditioning, rent per month, add				↓	41.50			41.50	45.50
0800	For delivery, add per mile				Mile	4.60			4.60	5.05
0890	Delivery each way				Ea.	200			200	220
0900	Bunk house trailer, 8' x 40' duplex dorm with kitchen, no hookups, buy	2 Carp	1	16		37,300	705		38,005	42,100
0910	9 man with kitchen and bath, no hookups, buy		1	16		38,000	705		38,705	42,900
0920	18 man sleeper with bath, no hookups, buy		1	16	↓	49,000	705		49,705	55,000
1000	Portable buildings, prefab, on skids, economy, 8' x 8'		265	.060	S.F.	86	2.66		88.66	98.50
1100	Deluxe, 8' x 12'	↓	150	.107	"	96	4.70		100.70	113
1200	Storage boxes, 20' x 8', buy	2 Skwk	1.80	8.889	Ea.	2,625	405		3,030	3,500
1250	Rent per month					72			72	79
1300	40' x 8', buy	2 Skwk	1.40	11.429		3,325	520		3,845	4,450
1350	Rent per month				↓	94			94	103

01 52 13.40 Field Office Expense

					Unit	Material			Total	Total Incl O&P
0010	**FIELD OFFICE EXPENSE**									
0100	Office equipment rental average				Month	200			200	220
0120	Office supplies, average				"	75			75	82.50
0125	Office trailer rental, see Section 01 52 13.20									
0140	Telephone bill; avg. bill/month incl. long dist.				Month	81			81	89
0160	Lights & HVAC				"	152			152	167

01 54 Construction Aids

01 54 16 – Temporary Hoists

01 54 16.50 Weekly Forklift Crew

		Crew	Daily Output	Labor-Hours	Unit	Material	Labor	Equipment	Total	Total Incl O&P
0010	**WEEKLY FORKLIFT CREW**									
0100	All-terrain forklift, 45' lift, 35' reach, 9000 lb. capacity	A-3P	.20	40	Week		1,800	2,400	4,200	5,350

01 54 19 – Temporary Cranes

01 54 19.50 Daily Crane Crews

		Crew	Daily Output	Labor-Hours	Unit	Material	Labor	Equipment	Total	Total Incl O&P
0010	**DAILY CRANE CREWS** for small jobs, portal to portal									
0100	12-ton truck-mounted hydraulic crane	A-3H	1	8	Day		380	825	1,205	1,475
0200	25-ton	A-3I	1	8			380	955	1,335	1,625
0300	40-ton	A-3J	1	8			380	1,175	1,555	1,875
0400	55-ton	A-3K	1	16	↓		710	1,625	2,335	2,850

01 54 Construction Aids

01 54 19 – Temporary Cranes

01 54 19.50 Daily Crane Crews

		Crew	Daily Output	Labor-Hours	Unit	Material	2012 Bare Costs Labor	Equipment	Total	Total Incl O&P
0500	80-ton	A-3L	1	16	Day		710	2,275	2,985	3,575
0600	100-ton	A-3M	1	16	↓		710	2,275	2,985	3,575

01 54 19.60 Monthly Tower Crane Crew

		Crew	Daily Output	Labor-Hours	Unit	Material	Labor	Equipment	Total	Total Incl O&P
0010	**MONTHLY TOWER CRANE CREW**, excludes concrete footing									
0100	Static tower crane, 130' high, 106' jib, 6200 lb. capacity	A-3N	.05	176	Month		8,425	22,100	30,525	37,000

01 54 23 – Temporary Scaffolding and Platforms

01 54 23.70 Scaffolding

			Crew	Daily Output	Labor-Hours	Unit	Material	Labor	Equipment	Total	Total Incl O&P
0010	**SCAFFOLDING**	R015423-10									
0015	Steel tube, regular, no plank, labor only to erect & dismantle										
0090	Building exterior, wall face, 1 to 5 stories, 6'-4" x 5' frames		3 Carp	8	3	C.S.F.		132		132	204
0200	6 to 12 stories		4 Carp	8	4			176		176	271
0301	13 to 20 stories		5 Clab	8	5			176		176	270
0460	Building interior, wall face area, up to 16' high		3 Carp	12	2			88		88	136
0560	16' to 40' high			10	2.400	↓		106		106	163
0800	Building interior floor area, up to 30' high		↓	150	.160	C.C.F.		7.05		7.05	10.85
0900	Over 30' high		4 Carp	160	.200	"		8.80		8.80	13.55
0906	Complete system for face of walls, no plank, material only rent/mo					C.S.F.	36			36	39.50
0908	Interior spaces, no plank, material only rent/mo					C.C.F.	3.42			3.42	3.76
0910	Steel tubular, heavy duty shoring, buy										
0920	Frames 5' high 2' wide					Ea.	81.50			81.50	90
0925	5' high 4' wide						93			93	102
0930	6' high 2' wide						93.50			93.50	103
0935	6' high 4' wide					↓	109			109	120
0940	Accessories										
0945	Cross braces					Ea.	15.85			15.85	17.40
0950	U-head, 8" x 8"						19.10			19.10	21
0955	J-head, 4" x 8"						13.90			13.90	15.30
0960	Base plate, 8" x 8"						15.50			15.50	17.05
0965	Leveling jack					↓	33.50			33.50	36.50
1000	Steel tubular, regular, buy										
1100	Frames 3' high 5' wide					Ea.	75			75	82.50
1150	5' high 5' wide						88			88	96.50
1200	6'-4" high 5' wide						118			118	129
1350	7'-6" high 6' wide						158			158	173
1500	Accessories cross braces						15.50			15.50	17.05
1550	Guardrail post						16.40			16.40	18.05
1600	Guardrail 7' section						6.30			6.30	6.95
1650	Screw jacks & plates						21.50			21.50	24
1700	Sidearm brackets						25.50			25.50	28.50
1750	8" casters						31			31	34
1800	Plank 2" x 10" x 16'-0"						24.50			24.50	27
1900	Stairway section						275			275	305
1910	Stairway starter bar						32			32	35
1920	Stairway inside handrail						53			53	58
1930	Stairway outside handrail						81.50			81.50	90
1940	Walk-thru frame guardrail					↓	41.50			41.50	46
2000	Steel tubular, regular, rent/mo.										
2100	Frames 3' high 5' wide					Ea.	5			5	5.50
2150	5' high 5' wide						5			5	5.50
2200	6'-4" high 5' wide						5.15			5.15	5.65
2250	7'-6" high 6' wide						7			7	7.70
2500	Accessories, cross braces					↓	1			1	1.10

01 54 23 – Temporary Scaffolding and Platforms

01 54 23.70 Scaffolding	Crew	Daily Output	Labor-Hours	Unit	Material	2012 Bare Costs Labor	Equipment	Total	Total Incl O&P
2550 Guardrail post				Ea.	1			1	1.10
2600 Guardrail 7' section					1			1	1.10
2650 Screw jacks & plates					2			2	2.20
2700 Sidearm brackets					2			2	2.20
2750 8" casters					8			8	8.80
2800 Outrigger for rolling tower					3			3	3.30
2850 Plank 2" x 10" x 16'-0"					6			6	6.60
2900 Stairway section					40			40	44
2940 Walk-thru frame guardrail				↓	2.50			2.50	2.75
3000 Steel tubular, heavy duty shoring, rent/mo.									
3250 5' high 2' & 4' wide				Ea.	5			5	5.50
3300 6' high 2' & 4' wide					5			5	5.50
3500 Accessories, cross braces					1			1	1.10
3600 U - head, 8" x 8"					1			1	1.10
3650 J - head, 4" x 8"					1			1	1.10
3700 Base plate, 8" x 8"					1			1	1.10
3750 Leveling jack				↓	2			2	2.20
5700 Planks, 2" x 10" x 16'-0", labor only to erect & remove to 50' H	3 Carp	72	.333			14.70		14.70	22.50
5800 Over 50' high	4 Carp	80	.400	↓		17.65		17.65	27
6000 Heavy duty shoring for elevated slab forms to 8'-2" high, floor area									
6100 Labor only to erect & dismantle	4 Carp	16	2	C.S.F.		88		88	136
6110 Materials only, rent.mo				"	29.50			29.50	32.50
6500 To 14'-8" high									
6600 Labor only to erect & dismantle	4 Carp	10	3.200	C.S.F.		141		141	217
6610 Materials only, rent/mo				"	43			43	47.50

01 54 23.75 Scaffolding Specialties

	Crew	Daily Output	Labor-Hours	Unit	Material	2012 Bare Costs Labor	Equipment	Total	Total Incl O&P
0010 **SCAFFOLDING SPECIALTIES**									
1200 Sidewalk bridge, heavy duty steel posts & beams, including									
1210 parapet protection & waterproofing									
1220 8' to 10' wide, 2 posts	3 Carp	15	1.600	L.F.	32	70.50		102.50	144
1230 3 posts	"	10	2.400	"	48.50	106		154.50	217
1500 Sidewalk bridge using tubular steel									
1510 scaffold frames, including planking	3 Carp	45	.533	L.F.	5.60	23.50		29.10	42
1600 For 2 uses per month, deduct from all above					50%				
1700 For 1 use every 2 months, add to all above					100%				
1900 Catwalks, 20" wide, no guardrails, 7' span, buy				Ea.	133			133	146
2000 10' span, buy					186			186	205
3720 Putlog, standard, 8' span, with hangers, buy					66.50			66.50	73
3730 Rent per month					10			10	11
3750 12' span, buy					99			99	109
3755 Rent per month					15			15	16.50
3760 Trussed type, 16' span, buy					228			228	251
3770 Rent per month					20			20	22
3790 22' span, buy					274			274	300
3795 Rent per month					30			30	33
3800 Rolling ladders with handrails, 30" wide, buy, 2 step					229			229	252
4000 7 step					710			710	780
4050 10 step					985			985	1,075
4100 Rolling towers, buy, 5' wide, 7' long, 10' high					1,200			1,200	1,325
4200 For 5' high added sections, to buy, add				↓	207			207	228
4300 Complete incl. wheels, railings, outriggers,									
4350 21' high, to buy				Ea.	2,025			2,025	2,225

01 54 Construction Aids

01 54 23 – Temporary Scaffolding and Platforms

01 54 23.75 Scaffolding Specialties		Crew	Daily Output	Labor-Hours	Unit	Material	2012 Bare Costs Labor	Equipment	Total	Total Incl O&P
4400	Rent/month = 5% of purchase cost				Ea.	113			113	124

01 54 36 – Equipment Mobilization

01 54 36.50 Mobilization

			Crew	Daily Output	Labor-Hours	Unit	Material	Labor	Equipment	Total	Total Incl O&P
0010	**MOBILIZATION** (Use line item again for demobilization)	R015433-10									
0015	Up to 25 mi haul dist (50 mi RT for mob/demob crew)										
0020	Dozer, loader, backhoe, excav., grader, paver, roller, 70 to 150 H.P.		B-34N	4	2	Ea.		70.50	126	196.50	246
0100	Above 150 HP		B-34K	3	2.667			94	283	377	455
0900	Shovel or dragline, 3/4 C.Y.		"	3.60	2.222			78.50	236	314.50	380
1100	Small equipment, placed in rear of, or towed by pickup truck		A-3A	8	1			34.50	17.40	51.90	71
1150	Equip up to 70 HP, on flatbed trailer behind pickup truck		A-3D	4	2			68.50	62	130.50	172
2000	Crane, truck-mounted, up to 75 ton, (driver only, one-way)		1 Eqhv	7.20	1.111			53		53	80
2100	Crane, truck-mounted, over 75 ton		A-3E	2.50	6.400			266	55.50	321.50	460
2200	Crawler-mounted, up to 75 ton		A-3F	2	8			330	435	765	985
2300	Over 75 ton		A-3G	1.50	10.667			445	660	1,105	1,400
2500	For each additional 5 miles haul distance, add							10%	10%		
3000	For large pieces of equipment, allow for assembly/knockdown										
3100	For mob/demob of micro-tunneling equip, see Section 33 05 23.19										

01 54 39 – Construction Equipment

01 54 39.70 Small Tools

			Crew	Daily Output	Labor-Hours	Unit	Material	Labor	Equipment	Total	Total Incl O&P
0010	**SMALL TOOLS**	R013113-50									
0020	As % of contractor's bare labor cost for project, minimum					Total		.50%			
0100	Maximum					"		2%			

01 55 Vehicular Access and Parking

01 55 23 – Temporary Roads

01 55 23.50 Roads and Sidewalks

			Crew	Daily Output	Labor-Hours	Unit	Material	Labor	Equipment	Total	Total Incl O&P
0010	**ROADS AND SIDEWALKS** Temporary										
0050	Roads, gravel fill, no surfacing, 4" gravel depth		B-14	715	.067	S.Y.	4.15	2.49	.47	7.11	8.90
0100	8" gravel depth		"	615	.078	"	8.30	2.89	.54	11.73	14.20
1000	Ramp, 3/4" plywood on 2" x 6" joists, 16" O.C.		2 Carp	300	.053	S.F.	1.23	2.35		3.58	4.98
1100	On 2" x 10" joists, 16" O.C.		"	275	.058	"	1.70	2.57		4.27	5.80

01 56 Temporary Barriers and Enclosures

01 56 13 – Temporary Air Barriers

01 56 13.60 Tarpaulins

			Crew	Daily Output	Labor-Hours	Unit	Material	Labor	Equipment	Total	Total Incl O&P
0010	**TARPAULINS**										
0020	Cotton duck, 10 oz. to 13.13 oz. per S.Y., minimum					S.F.	.78			.78	.86
0050	Maximum						.80			.80	.88
0100	Polyvinyl coated nylon, 14 oz. to 18 oz., minimum						.48			.48	.53
0150	Maximum						.68			.68	.75
0200	Reinforced polyethylene 3 mils thick, white						.15			.15	.17
0300	4 mils thick, white, clear or black						.20			.20	.22
0400	5.5 mils thick, clear						.23			.23	.25
0500	White, fire retardant						.35			.35	.39
0600	12 mils, oil resistant, fire retardant						.28			.28	.31
0700	8.5 mils, black						.57			.57	.63
0710	Woven polyethylene, 6 mils thick						.35			.35	.39
0730	Polyester reinforced w/integral fastening system 11 mils thick						1.07			1.07	1.18

01 56 Temporary Barriers and Enclosures

01 56 13 – Temporary Air Barriers

01 56 13.60 Tarpaulins

		Crew	Daily Output	Labor-Hours	Unit	Material	2012 Bare Costs Labor	Equipment	Total	Total Incl O&P
0740	Mylar polyester, non-reinforced, 7 mils thick				S.F.	1.17			1.17	1.29

01 56 13.90 Winter Protection

		Crew	Daily Output	Labor-Hours	Unit	Material	2012 Bare Costs Labor	Equipment	Total	Total Incl O&P
0010	**WINTER PROTECTION**									
0100	Framing to close openings	2 Clab	750	.021	S.F.	.39	.75		1.14	1.58
0200	Tarpaulins hung over scaffolding, 8 uses, not incl. scaffolding		1500	.011		.25	.37		.62	.86
0250	Tarpaulin polyester reinf. w/integral fastening system 11 mils thick		1600	.010		.80	.35		1.15	1.42
0300	Prefab fiberglass panels, steel frame, 8 uses		1200	.013		.85	.47		1.32	1.66

01 56 16 – Temporary Dust Barriers

01 56 16.10 Dust Barriers, Temporary

		Crew	Daily Output	Labor-Hours	Unit	Material	2012 Bare Costs Labor	Equipment	Total	Total Incl O&P
0010	**DUST BARRIERS, TEMPORARY**									
0020	Spring loaded telescoping pole & head, to 12', erect and dismantle	1 Clab	240	.033	Ea.		1.17		1.17	1.80
0025	Cost per day (based upon 250 days)				Day	.24			.24	.26
0030	To 21', erect and dismantle	1 Clab	240	.033	Ea.		1.17		1.17	1.80
0035	Cost per day (based upon 250 days)				Day	.39			.39	.42
0040	Accessories, caution tape reel, erect and dismantle	1 Clab	480	.017	Ea.		.59		.59	.90
0045	Cost per day (based upon 250 days)				Day	.05			.05	.05
0060	Foam rail and connector, erect and dismantle	1 Clab	240	.033	Ea.		1.17		1.17	1.80
0065	Cost per day (based upon 250 days)				Day	.10			.10	.11
0070	Caution tape	1 Clab	384	.021	C.L.F.	2.65	.73		3.38	4.03
0080	Zipper, standard duty		60	.133	Ea.	8	4.68		12.68	16
0090	Heavy duty		48	.167	"	9.50	5.85		15.35	19.45
0100	Polyethylene sheet, 4 mil		37	.216	Sq.	3.23	7.60		10.83	15.25
0110	6 mil		37	.216	"	4.54	7.60		12.14	16.70
1000	Dust partition, 6 mil polyethylene, 1" x 3" frame	2 Carp	2000	.008	S.F.	.27	.35		.62	.84
1080	2" x 4" frame	"	2000	.008	"	.29	.35		.64	.86

01 56 23 – Temporary Barricades

01 56 23.10 Barricades

		Crew	Daily Output	Labor-Hours	Unit	Material	2012 Bare Costs Labor	Equipment	Total	Total Incl O&P
0010	**BARRICADES**									
0020	5' high, 3 rail @ 2" x 8", fixed	2 Carp	20	.800	L.F.	5.30	35.50		40.80	60.50
0150	Movable		30	.533		4.35	23.50		27.85	41
1000	Guardrail, wooden, 3' high, 1" x 6", on 2" x 4" posts		200	.080		1.15	3.53		4.68	6.70
1100	2" x 6", on 4" x 4" posts		165	.097		2.26	4.28		6.54	9.10
1200	Portable metal with base pads, buy					15.25			15.25	16.75
1250	Typical installation, assume 10 reuses	2 Carp	600	.027		2.50	1.18		3.68	4.56
1300	Barricade tape, polyethylene, 7 mil, 3" wide x 500' long roll				Ea.	25			25	27.50

01 56 26 – Temporary Fencing

01 56 26.50 Temporary Fencing

		Crew	Daily Output	Labor-Hours	Unit	Material	2012 Bare Costs Labor	Equipment	Total	Total Incl O&P
0010	**TEMPORARY FENCING**									
0020	Chain link, 11 ga, 5' high	2 Clab	400	.040	L.F.	4.50	1.40		5.90	7.10
0100	6' high		300	.053		5.30	1.87		7.17	8.75
0200	Rented chain link, 6' high, to 1000' (up to 12 mo.)		400	.040		6.30	1.40		7.70	9.10
0250	Over 1000' (up to 12 mo.)		300	.053		3.29	1.87		5.16	6.50
0350	Plywood, painted, 2" x 4" frame, 4' high	A-4	135	.178		5.45	7.50		12.95	17.45
0400	4" x 4" frame, 8' high	"	110	.218		10.20	9.20		19.40	25.50
0500	Wire mesh on 4" x 4" posts, 4' high	2 Carp	100	.160		9.25	7.05		16.30	21
0550	8' high	"	80	.200		13.90	8.80		22.70	29

01 56 29 – Temporary Protective Walkways

01 56 29.50 Protection

		Crew	Daily Output	Labor-Hours	Unit	Material	2012 Bare Costs Labor	Equipment	Total	Total Incl O&P
0010	**PROTECTION**									
0020	Stair tread, 2" x 12" planks, 1 use	1 Carp	75	.107	Tread	3.83	4.70		8.53	11.45

01 56 Temporary Barriers and Enclosures

01 56 29 – Temporary Protective Walkways

01 56 29.50 Protection	Crew	Daily Output	Labor-Hours	Unit	Material	2012 Bare Costs Labor	Equipment	Total	Total Incl O&P
0100	Exterior plywood, 1/2" thick, 1 use	1 Carp	65	.123	Tread	1.41	5.45		6.86	9.90
0200	3/4" thick, 1 use		60	.133	↓	2.10	5.90		8	11.35
2200	Sidewalks, 2" x 12" planks, 2 uses		350	.023	S.F.	.64	1.01		1.65	2.25
2300	Exterior plywood, 2 uses, 1/2" thick		750	.011		.24	.47		.71	.98
2400	5/8" thick		650	.012		.31	.54		.85	1.18
2500	3/4" thick	↓	600	.013	↓	.35	.59		.94	1.29

01 58 Project Identification

01 58 13 – Temporary Project Signage

01 58 13.50 Signs

		Crew	Daily Output	Labor-Hours	Unit	Material	2012 Bare Costs Labor	Equipment	Total	Total Incl O&P
0010	**SIGNS**									
0020	High intensity reflectorized, no posts, buy				S.F.	34			34	37.50

01 74 Cleaning and Waste Management

01 74 13 – Progress Cleaning

01 74 13.20 Cleaning Up

		Crew	Daily Output	Labor-Hours	Unit	Material	2012 Bare Costs Labor	Equipment	Total	Total Incl O&P
0010	**CLEANING UP**									
0020	After job completion, allow, minimum				Job					.30%
0040	Maximum				"					1%
0050	Cleanup of floor area, continuous, per day, during const.	A-5	24	.750	M.S.F.	1.75	26.50	2.20	30.45	45
0100	Final by GC at end of job	"	11.50	1.565	"	2.78	55	4.59	62.37	92
1000	Mechanical demolition, see Section 02 41 19									

01 91 Commissioning

01 91 13 – General Commissioning Requirements

01 91 13.50 Building Commissioning

		Crew	Daily Output	Labor-Hours	Unit	Material	2012 Bare Costs Labor	Equipment	Total	Total Incl O&P
0010	**BUILDING COMMISSIONING**									
0100	Basic building commissioning, minimum				%					.25%
0150	Maximum									.50%
0200	Enhanced building commissioning, minimum									.50%
0250	Maximum				↓					1%

01 93 Facility Maintenance

01 93 13 – Facility Maintenance Procedures

01 93 13.15 Mechanical Facilities Maintenance

		Crew	Daily Output	Labor-Hours	Unit	Material	2012 Bare Costs Labor	Equipment	Total	Total Incl O&P
0010	**MECHANICAL FACILITIES MAINTENANCE**									
0100	Air conditioning system maintenance									
0130	Belt, replace	1 Stpi	15	.533	Ea.		29.50		29.50	45
0170	Fan, clean		16	.500			28		28	42
0180	Filter, remove, clean, replace		12	.667			37		37	56
0190	Flexible coupling alignment, inspect		40	.200			11.15		11.15	16.80
0200	Gas leak locate and repair		4	2			111		111	168
0250	Pump packing gland, remove and replace		11	.727			40.50		40.50	61
0270	Tighten		32	.250			13.95		13.95	21
0290	Pump disassemble and assemble	↓	4	2			111		111	168
0300	Air pressure regulator, disassemble, clean, assemble	1 Skwk	4	2	↓		91		91	140

01 93 13 – Facility Maintenance Procedures

01 93 13.15 Mechanical Facilities Maintenance		Crew	Daily Output	Labor-Hours	Unit	Material	2012 Bare Costs Labor	Equipment	Total	Total Incl O&P
0310	Repair or replace part	1 Skwk	6	1.333	Ea.		60.50		60.50	93.50
0320	Purging system	1 Stpi	16	.500			28		28	42
0400	Compressor, air, remove or install fan wheel	1 Skwk	20	.400			18.15		18.15	28
0410	Disassemble or assemble 2 cylinder, 2 stage		4	2			91		91	140
0420	4 cylinder, 4 stage		1	8			365		365	560
0430	Repair or replace part	↓	2	4	↓		182		182	281
0700	Demolition, for mech. demolition see Section 23 05 05.10 or 22 05 05.10									
0800	Ductwork, clean									
0810	Rectangular									
0820	6" [G]	1 Shee	187.50	.043	L.F.		2.23		2.23	3.39
0830	8" [G]		140.63	.057			2.97		2.97	4.52
0840	10" [G]		112.50	.071			3.71		3.71	5.65
0850	12" [G]		93.75	.085			4.45		4.45	6.80
0860	14" [G]		80.36	.100			5.20		5.20	7.90
0870	16" [G]	↓	70.31	.114	↓		5.95		5.95	9.05
0900	Round									
0910	4" [G]	1 Shee	358.10	.022	L.F.		1.17		1.17	1.78
0920	6" [G]		238.73	.034			1.75		1.75	2.66
0930	8" [G]		179.05	.045			2.33		2.33	3.55
0940	10" [G]		143.24	.056			2.91		2.91	4.44
0950	12" [G]		119.37	.067			3.50		3.50	5.35
0960	16" [G]	↓	89.52	.089	↓		4.66		4.66	7.10
1000	Expansion joint, not screwed, install or remove	1 Stpi	3	2.667	Ea.		149		149	224
1010	Repack	"	6	1.333	"		74.50		74.50	112
1200	Fire protection equipment									
1220	Fire hydrant, replace	Q-1	3	5.333	Ea.		262		262	395
1230	Service, lubricate, inspect, flush, clean	1 Plum	7	1.143			62.50		62.50	94
1240	Test	"	11	.727	↓		39.50		39.50	60
1310	Inspect valves, pressure, nozzle,	1 Spri	4	2	System		108		108	163
1500	Instrumentation preventive maintenance, rule of thumb									
1510	Annual cost per instrument for calibration & trouble shooting									
1520	Includes flow meters, analytical transmitters, flow control									
1530	chemical feed systems, recorders and distrib. control sys.				Ea.					325
1800	Plumbing fixtures, for installation see Section 22 41 00									
1801	Plumbing fixtures									
1840	Open drain with snake	1 Plum	13	.615	Ea.		33.50		33.50	50.50
1850	Open drain with toilet auger		16	.500			27.50		27.50	41
1860	Grease trap, clean		2	4			218		218	330
1870	Plaster trap, clean	↓	6	1.333			73		73	110
1881	Clean commode	1 Clab	20	.400		.43	14.05		14.48	22
1882	Clean commode seat		48	.167		.22	5.85		6.07	9.25
1883	Clean single sink		28	.286		.28	10.05		10.33	15.75
1884	Clean double sink		20	.400		.43	14.05		14.48	22
1885	Clean lavatory		28	.286		.28	10.05		10.33	15.75
1886	Clean bathtub		12	.667		.87	23.50		24.37	37
1887	Clean fiberglass shower		12	.667		.87	23.50		24.37	37
1888	Clean fiberglass tub/shower		8	1		1.09	35		36.09	55
1889	Clean faucet set		32	.250		.17	8.80		8.97	13.70
1891	Clean shower head		80	.100		.02	3.51		3.53	5.40
1893	Clean water heater	↓	16	.500		1.52	17.55		19.07	28.50
1900	Relief valve, test and adjust	1 Stpi	20	.400			22.50		22.50	33.50
1910	Clean pump, heater, or motor for whirlpool	1 Clab	16	.500		.22	17.55		17.77	27
1920	Clean thermal cover for whirlpool	"	16	.500	↓	2.17	17.55		19.72	29.50

01 93 Facility Maintenance

01 93 13 – Facility Maintenance Procedures

01 93 13.15 Mechanical Facilities Maintenance	Crew	Daily Output	Labor-Hours	Unit	Material	2012 Bare Costs Labor	2012 Bare Costs Equipment	Total	Total Incl O&P
2000	Repair or replace-steam trap	1 Stpi	8	1	Ea.		55.50		55.50	84
2020	Y-type or bell strainer		6	1.333			74.50		74.50	112
2040	Water trap or vacuum breaker, screwed joints	↓	13	.615	↓		34.50		34.50	51.50
2100	Steam specialties, clean									
2120	Air separator with automatic trap, 1" fittings	1 Stpi	12	.667	Ea.		37		37	56
2130	Bucket trap, 2" pipe		7	1.143			63.50		63.50	96
2150	Drip leg, 2" fitting		45	.178			9.90		9.90	14.95
2200	Thermodynamic trap, 1" fittings		50	.160			8.90		8.90	13.45
2210	Thermostatic		65	.123			6.85		6.85	10.35
2240	Screen and seat in y-type strainer, plug type.		25	.320			17.80		17.80	27
2242	Screen and seat in y-type strainer, flange type.		12	.667			37		37	56
2500	Valve, replace broken handwheel	↓	24	.333	↓		18.55		18.55	28
3000	Valve, overhaul, regulator, relief, flushometer, mixing									
3040	Cold water, gas	1 Stpi	5	1.600	Ea.		89		89	134
3050	Hot water, steam		3	2.667			149		149	224
3080	Globe, gate, check up to 4" cold water, gas		10	.800			44.50		44.50	67
3090	Hot water, steam		5	1.600			89		89	134
3100	Over 4" ID hot or cold line	↓	1.40	5.714			320		320	480
3120	Remove and replace, gate, globe or check up to 4"	Q-5	6	2.667			134		134	202
3130	Over 4"	"	2	8			400		400	605
3150	Repack up to 4"	1 Stpi	13	.615			34.50		34.50	51.50
3160	Over 4"	"	4	2	↓		111		111	168

Division Notes

	CREW	DAILY OUTPUT	LABOR-HOURS	UNIT	2012 BARE COSTS				TOTAL INCL O&P
					MAT.	LABOR	EQUIP.	TOTAL	

Estimating Tips

02 30 00 Subsurface Investigation

In preparing estimates on structures involving earthwork or foundations, all information concerning soil characteristics should be obtained. Look particularly for hazardous waste, evidence of prior dumping of debris, and previous stream beds.

02 41 00 Demolition and Structure Moving

The costs shown for selective demolition do not include rubbish handling or disposal. These items should be estimated separately using RSMeans data or other sources.

- Historic preservation often requires that the contractor remove materials from the existing structure, rehab them, and replace them. The estimator must be aware of any related measures and precautions that must be taken when doing selective demolition and cutting and patching. Requirements may include special handling and storage, as well as security.

- In addition to Subdivision 02 41 00, you can find selective demolition items in each division. Example: Roofing demolition is in Division 7.

02 42 10 Building Deconstruction

This section provides costs for the careful dismantling and recycling of most of low-rise building materials.

02 56 13 Containment of Hazardous Waste

This section addresses on-site hazardous waste disposal costs.

02 80 00 Hazardous Material Disposal/ Remediation

This subdivision includes information on hazardous waste handling, asbestos remediation, lead remediation, and mold remediation. See reference R028213-20 and R028319-60 for further guidance in using these unit price lines.

02 91 10 Monitoring Chemical Sampling, Testing Analysis

This section provides costs for on-site sampling and testing hazardous waste.

Reference Numbers

Reference numbers are shown in shaded boxes at the beginning of some major classifications. These numbers refer to related items in the Reference Section. The reference information may be an estimating procedure, an alternate pricing method, or technical information.

Note: Not all subdivisions listed here necessarily appear in this publication.

02 41 Demolition

02 41 13 – Selective Site Demolition

02 41 13.17 Demolish, Remove Pavement and Curb

02 41 13.17 Demolish, Remove Pavement and Curb		Crew	Daily Output	Labor-Hours	Unit	Material	2012 Bare Costs Labor	2012 Bare Costs Equipment	Total	Total Incl O&P
0010	DEMOLISH, REMOVE PAVEMENT AND CURB	R024119-10								
5010	Pavement removal, bituminous roads, 3" thick	B-38	690	.058	S.Y.		2.30	1.71	4.01	5.40
5050	4" to 6" thick		420	.095			3.78	2.82	6.60	8.85
5100	Bituminous driveways		640	.063			2.48	1.85	4.33	5.80
5200	Concrete to 6" thick, hydraulic hammer, mesh reinforced		255	.157			6.25	4.64	10.89	14.60
5300	Rod reinforced		200	.200			7.95	5.90	13.85	18.60
5400	Concrete, 7" to 24" thick, plain		33	1.212	C.Y.		48	36	84	113
5500	Reinforced		24	1.667	"		66	49.50	115.50	155
5600	With hand held air equipment, bituminous, to 6" thick	B-39	1900	.025	S.F.		.94	.11	1.05	1.55
5700	Concrete to 6" thick, no reinforcing		1600	.030			1.11	.13	1.24	1.84
5800	Mesh reinforced		1400	.034			1.27	.15	1.42	2.11
5900	Rod reinforced		765	.063			2.32	.27	2.59	3.86

02 41 13.33 Minor Site Demolition

02 41 13.33 Minor Site Demolition		Crew	Daily Output	Labor-Hours	Unit	Material	Labor	Equipment	Total	Total Incl O&P
0010	MINOR SITE DEMOLITION	R024119-10								
0015	No hauling, abandon catch basin or manhole	B-6	7	3.429	Ea.		131	47.50	178.50	254
0020	Remove existing catch basin or manhole, masonry		4	6			230	83.50	313.50	440
0030	Catch basin or manhole frames and covers, stored		13	1.846			70.50	25.50	96	137
0040	Remove and reset		7	3.429			131	47.50	178.50	254
0900	Hydrants, fire, remove only	B-21A	5	8			350	89.50	439.50	630
0950	Remove and reset	"	2	20			875	224	1,099	1,575
4000	Sidewalk removal, bituminous, 2-1/2" thick	B-6	325	.074	S.Y.		2.83	1.03	3.86	5.45
4050	Brick, set in mortar		185	.130			4.97	1.81	6.78	9.60
4100	Concrete, plain, 4"		160	.150			5.75	2.09	7.84	11.10
4200	Mesh reinforced		150	.160			6.15	2.23	8.38	11.80

02 41 19 – Selective Demolition

02 41 19.13 Selective Building Demolition

02 41 19.13 Selective Building Demolition		Crew	Daily Output	Labor-Hours	Unit	Material	Labor	Equipment	Total	Total Incl O&P
0010	SELECTIVE BUILDING DEMOLITION									
0020	Costs related to selective demolition of specific building components									
0025	are included under Common Work Results (XX 05)									
0030	in the component's appropriate division.									

02 41 19.19 Selective Facility Services Demolition

02 41 19.19 Selective Facility Services Demolition		Crew	Daily Output	Labor-Hours	Unit	Material	Labor	Equipment	Total	Total Incl O&P
0010	SELECTIVE FACILITY SERVICES DEMOLITION, Rubbish Handling R024119-10									
0020	The following are to be added to the demolition prices									
0400	Chute, circular, prefabricated steel, 18" diameter	B-1	40	.600	L.F.	52	21.50		73.50	90.50
0440	30" diameter	"	30	.800	"	46.50	28.50		75	95
0600	Dumpster, weekly rental, 1 dump/week, 6 C.Y. capacity (2 Tons)				Week	460			460	505
0700	10 C.Y. capacity (3 Tons)					535			535	590
0725	20 C.Y. capacity (8 Tons) R024119-20					630			630	695
0800	30 C.Y. capacity (7 Tons)					810			810	890
0840	40 C.Y. capacity (10 Tons)					860			860	945
2000	Load, haul, dump and return, 50' haul, hand carried	2 Clab	24	.667	C.Y.		23.50		23.50	36
2005	Wheeled		37	.432			15.20		15.20	23.50
2040	51' to 100' haul, hand carried		16.50	.970			34		34	52.50
2045	Wheeled		25	.640			22.50		22.50	34.50
2080	Over 100' haul, add per 100 L.F., hand carried		35.50	.451			15.80		15.80	24.50
2085	Wheeled		54	.296			10.40		10.40	16
2120	In elevators, per 10 floors, add		140	.114			4.01		4.01	6.15
2130	Load, haul, dump and return, up to 50' haul, incl. up to 5 rsr stair, hand		23	.696			24.50		24.50	37.50
2135	Wheeled		35	.457			16.05		16.05	24.50
2140	6 – 10 riser stairs, hand carried		22	.727			25.50		25.50	39.50
2145	Wheeled		34	.471			16.50		16.50	25.50
2150	11 – 20 riser stairs, hand carried		20	.800			28		28	43

02 41 Demolition

02 41 19 – Selective Demolition

02 41 19.19 Selective Facility Services Demolition

		Crew	Daily Output	Labor-Hours	Unit	Material	2012 Bare Costs		Total	Total Incl O&P
							Labor	Equipment		
2155	Wheeled	2 Clab	31	.516	C.Y.		18.10		18.10	28
2160	21 – 40 riser stairs, hand carried		16	1			35		35	54
2165	Wheeled		24	.667			23.50		23.50	36
2170	100' haul, incl. 5 riser stair, hand carried		15	1.067			37.50		37.50	57.50
2175	Wheeled		23	.696			24.50		24.50	37.50
2180	6 – 10 riser stair, hand carried		14	1.143			40		40	61.50
2185	Wheeled		21	.762			26.50		26.50	41
2190	11 – 20 riser stair, hand carried		12	1.333			47		47	72
2195	Wheeled		18	.889			31		31	48
2200	21 – 40 riser stair, hand carried		8	2			70		70	108
2205	Wheeled		12	1.333			47		47	72
2210	Over 100' haul, add per 100 L.F., hand carried		35.50	.451			15.80		15.80	24.50
2215	Wheeled		54	.296			10.40		10.40	16
2220	For each additional flight of stairs, up to 5 risers, add		550	.029	Flight		1.02		1.02	1.57
2225	6 – 10 risers, add		275	.058			2.04		2.04	3.14
2230	11 – 20 risers, add		138	.116			4.07		4.07	6.25
2235	21 – 40 risers, add		69	.232			8.15		8.15	12.50
3000	Loading & trucking, including 2 mile haul, chute loaded	B-16	45	.711	C.Y.		25.50	13	38.50	53.50
3040	Hand loading truck, 50' haul	"	48	.667			24	12.20	36.20	50
3080	Machine loading truck	B-17	120	.267			10	5.75	15.75	21.50
5000	Haul, per mile, up to 8 C.Y. truck	B-34B	1165	.007			.24	.50	.74	.92
5100	Over 8 C.Y. truck	"	1550	.005			.18	.38	.56	.69

02 41 19.20 Selective Demolition, Dump Charges

		Crew	Daily Output	Labor-Hours	Unit	Material	2012 Bare Costs		Total	Total Incl O&P
							Labor	Equipment		
0010	**SELECTIVE DEMOLITION, DUMP CHARGES**	R024119-10								
0020	Dump charges, typical urban city, tipping fees only									
0100	Building construction materials				Ton	82			82	90
0200	Trees, brush, lumber					70			70	77
0300	Rubbish only					70			70	77
0500	Reclamation station, usual charge					82			82	90

02 41 19.27 Selective Demolition, Torch Cutting

		Crew	Daily Output	Labor-Hours	Unit	Material	2012 Bare Costs		Total	Total Incl O&P
							Labor	Equipment		
0010	**SELECTIVE DEMOLITION, TORCH CUTTING**	R024119-10								
0020	Steel, 1" thick plate	1 Clab	360	.022	L.F.	.37	.78		1.15	1.61
0040	1" diameter bar	"	210	.038	Ea.		1.34		1.34	2.06
1000	Oxygen lance cutting, reinforced concrete walls									
1040	12" to 16" thick walls	1 Clab	10	.800	L.F.		28		28	43
1080	24" thick walls	"	6	1.333	"		47		47	72

02 65 Underground Storage Tank Removal

02 65 10 – Underground Tank and Contaminated Soil Removal

02 65 10.30 Removal of Underground Storage Tanks

			Crew	Daily Output	Labor-Hours	Unit	Material	2012 Bare Costs		Total	Total Incl O&P
								Labor	Equipment		
0010	**REMOVAL OF UNDERGROUND STORAGE TANKS**		R026510-20								
0011	Petroleum storage tanks, non-leaking										
0100	Excavate & load onto trailer										
0110	3000 gal. to 5000 gal. tank	G	B-14	4	12	Ea.		445	83.50	528.50	770
0120	6000 gal. to 8000 gal. tank	G	B-3A	3	13.333			500	320	820	1,125
0130	9000 gal. to 12000 gal. tank	G	"	2	20			750	480	1,230	1,675
0190	Known leaking tank, add					%				100%	100%
0200	Remove sludge, water and remaining product from tank bottom										
0201	of tank with vacuum truck										
0300	3000 gal. to 5000 gal. tank	G	A-13	5	1.600	Ea.		71.50	147	218.50	270

02 65 10 – Underground Tank and Contaminated Soil Removal

02 65 10.30 Removal of Underground Storage Tanks		Crew	Daily Output	Labor-Hours	Unit	Material	2012 Bare Costs Labor	Equipment	Total	Total Incl O&P
0310	6000 gal. to 8000 gal. tank [G]	A-13	4	2	Ea.		89.50	184	273.50	335
0320	9000 gal. to 12000 gal. tank [G]	↓	3	2.667	↓		119	245	364	450
0390	Dispose of sludge off-site, average				Gal.				6	6.60
0400	Insert inert solid CO$_2$ "dry ice" into tank									
0401	For cleaning/transporting tanks (1.5 lb./100 gal. cap) [G]	1 Clab	500	.016	Lb.	.94	.56		1.50	1.89
1020	Haul tank to certified salvage dump, 100 miles round trip									
1023	3000 gal. to 5000 gal. tank				Ea.				745	820
1026	6000 gal. to 8000 gal. tank								850	9,350
1029	9,000 gal. to 12,000 gal. tank				↓				1,000	1,100
1100	Disposal of contaminated soil to landfill									
1110	Minimum				C.Y.				125	140
1111	Maximum				"				400	440
1120	Disposal of contaminated soil to									
1121	bituminous concrete batch plant									
1130	Minimum				C.Y.				70	77
1131	Maximum				"				110	120
2010	Decontamination of soil on site incl poly tarp on top/bottom									
2011	Soil containment berm, and chemical treatment									
2020	Minimum [G]	B-11C	100	.160	C.Y.	7.10	6.55	3.34	16.99	21.50
2021	Maximum [G]	"	100	.160	↓	9.20	6.55	3.34	19.09	23.50
2050	Disposal of decontaminated soil, minimum								125	140
2055	Maximum				↓				400	440

02 82 Asbestos Remediation

02 82 13 – Asbestos Abatement

02 82 13.39 Asbestos Remediation Plans and Methods

0010	**ASBESTOS REMEDIATION PLANS AND METHODS**									
0100	Building Survey-Commercial Building				Ea.				2,000	2,200
0200	Asbestos Abatement Remediation Plan				"				1,200	1,325

02 82 13.41 Asbestos Abatement Equip.

0010	**ASBESTOS ABATEMENT EQUIP.** R028213-20									
0011	Equipment and supplies, buy									
0200	Air filtration device, 2000 CFM				Ea.	885			885	975
0250	Large volume air sampling pump, minimum					365			365	400
0260	Maximum					530			530	585
0300	Airless sprayer unit, 2 gun					4,900			4,900	5,400
0350	Light stand, 500 watt				↓	46.50			46.50	51.50
0400	Personal respirators									
0410	Negative pressure, 1/2 face, dual operation, min.				Ea.	26			26	28.50
0420	Maximum					32.50			32.50	35.50
0450	P.A.P.R., full face, minimum					109			109	120
0460	Maximum					199			199	219
0470	Supplied air, full face, incl. air line, minimum					191			191	210
0480	Maximum					395			395	435
0500	Personnel sampling pump					226			226	248
1500	Power panel, 20 unit, incl. G.F.I.					565			565	620
1600	Shower unit, including pump and filters					1,200			1,200	1,300
1700	Supplied air system (type C)					5,425			5,425	5,975
1750	Vacuum cleaner, HEPA, 16 gal., stainless steel, wet/dry					1,200			1,200	1,325
1760	55 gallon					1,950			1,950	2,150
1800	Vacuum loader, 9 – 18 ton/hr.				↓	92,000			92,000	101,000

02 82 13 – Asbestos Abatement

02 82 13.41 Asbestos Abatement Equip.

		Crew	Daily Output	Labor-Hours	Unit	Material	2012 Bare Costs Labor	Equipment	Total	Total Incl O&P
1900	Water atomizer unit, including 55 gal. drum				Ea.	235			235	258
2000	Worker protection, whole body, foot, head cover & gloves, plastic					8.90			8.90	9.80
2500	Respirator, single use					29.50			29.50	32.50
2550	Cartridge for respirator					7			7	7.70
2570	Glove bag, 7 mil, 50" x 64"					17.60			17.60	19.35
2580	10 mil, 44" x 60"					5.50			5.50	6.05
2590	6 mil, 44" x 60"					5.50			5.50	6.05
3000	HEPA vacuum for work area, minimum					1,400			1,400	1,525
3050	Maximum					1,475			1,475	1,600
6000	Disposable polyethylene bags, 6 mil, 3 C.F.					2.35			2.35	2.59
6300	Disposable fiber drums, 3 C.F.					17.25			17.25	19
6400	Pressure sensitive caution labels, 3" x 5"					3.22			3.22	3.54
6450	11" x 17"					7.15			7.15	7.90
6500	Negative air machine, 1800 CFM					820			820	905

02 82 13.42 Preparation of Asbestos Containment Area

		Crew	Daily Output	Labor-Hours	Unit	Material	2012 Bare Costs Labor	Equipment	Total	Total Incl O&P
0010	**PREPARATION OF ASBESTOS CONTAINMENT AREA** R028213-20									
0100	Pre-cleaning, HEPA vacuum and wet wipe, flat surfaces	A-9	12000	.005	S.F.	.02	.26		.28	.43
0200	Protect carpeted area, 2 layers 6 mil poly on 3/4" plywood	"	1000	.064		2	3.13		5.13	7.10
0300	Separation barrier, 2" x 4" @ 16", 1/2" plywood ea. side, 8' high	2 Carp	400	.040		3	1.76		4.76	6
0310	12' high		320	.050		3	2.21		5.21	6.70
0320	16' high		200	.080		2	3.53		5.53	7.65
0400	Personnel decontam. chamber, 2" x 4" @ 16", 3/4" ply ea. side		280	.057		4	2.52		6.52	8.30
0450	Waste decontam. chamber, 2" x 4" studs @ 16", 3/4" ply ea. side		360	.044		4	1.96		5.96	7.40
0500	Cover surfaces with polyethylene sheeting									
0501	Including glue and tape									
0550	Floors, each layer, 6 mil	A-9	8000	.008	S.F.	.05	.39		.44	.66
0551	4 mil		9000	.007		.03	.35		.38	.58
0560	Walls, each layer, 6 mil		6000	.011		.05	.52		.57	.86
0561	4 mil		7000	.009		.03	.45		.48	.74
0570	For heights above 12', add						20%			
0575	For heights above 20', add						30%			
0580	For fire retardant poly, add					100%				
0590	For large open areas, deduct					10%	20%			
0600	Seal floor penetrations with foam firestop to 36 sq. in.	2 Carp	200	.080	Ea.	7.60	3.53		11.13	13.85
0610	36 sq. in. to 72 sq. in.		125	.128		15.25	5.65		20.90	25.50
0615	72 sq. in. to 144 sq. in.		80	.200		30.50	8.80		39.30	47
0620	Wall penetrations, to 36 square inches		180	.089		7.60	3.92		11.52	14.45
0630	36 sq. in. to 72 sq. in.		100	.160		15.25	7.05		22.30	27.50
0640	72 sq. in. to 144 sq. in.		60	.267		30.50	11.75		42.25	51.50
0800	Caulk seams with latex	1 Carp	230	.035	L.F.	.15	1.53		1.68	2.53
0900	Set up neg. air machine, 1-2k CFM/25 M.C.F. volume	1 Asbe	4.30	1.860	Ea.		91		91	142

02 82 13.43 Bulk Asbestos Removal

		Crew	Daily Output	Labor-Hours	Unit	Material	2012 Bare Costs Labor	Equipment	Total	Total Incl O&P
0010	**BULK ASBESTOS REMOVAL**									
0020	Includes disposable tools and 2 suits and 1 respirator filter/day/worker									
0200	Boiler insulation	A-9	480	.133	S.F.	.48	6.50		6.98	10.70
0210	With metal lath, add				%		50%			
0300	Boiler breeching or flue insulation	A-9	520	.123	S.F.	.38	6		6.38	9.80
0310	For active boiler, add				%		100%			
0400	Duct or AHU insulation	A-10B	440	.073	S.F.	.23	3.56		3.79	5.80
0500	Duct vibration isolation joints, up to 24 sq. in. duct	A-9	56	1.143	Ea.	3.54	56		59.54	91
0520	25 sq. in. to 48 sq. in. duct		48	1.333		4.13	65		69.13	107
0530	49 sq. in. to 76 sq. in. duct		40	1.600		4.96	78.50		83.46	127

02 82 13 – Asbestos Abatement

02 82 13.43 Bulk Asbestos Removal

		Crew	Daily Output	Labor-Hours	Unit	Material	2012 Bare Costs Labor	2012 Bare Costs Equipment	Total	Total Incl O&P
0600	Pipe insulation, air cell type, up to 4" diameter pipe	A-9	900	.071	L.F.	.22	3.48		3.70	5.65
0610	4" to 8" diameter pipe		800	.080		.25	3.91		4.16	6.35
0620	10" to 12" diameter pipe		700	.091		.28	4.47		4.75	7.25
0630	14" to 16" diameter pipe		550	.116		.36	5.70		6.06	9.25
0650	Over 16" diameter pipe		650	.098	S.F.	.31	4.82		5.13	7.85
0700	With glove bag up to 3" diameter pipe		200	.320	L.F.	6.05	15.65		21.70	31
1000	Pipe fitting insulation up to 4" diameter pipe		320	.200	Ea.	.62	9.80		10.42	15.95
1100	6" to 8" diameter pipe		304	.211		.65	10.30		10.95	16.75
1110	10" to 12" diameter pipe		192	.333		1.03	16.30		17.33	26.50
1120	14" to 16" diameter pipe		128	.500		1.55	24.50		26.05	39.50
1130	Over 16" diameter pipe		176	.364	S.F.	1.13	17.80		18.93	28.50
1200	With glove bag, up to 8" diameter pipe		75	.853	L.F.	6.55	41.50		48.05	72
2000	Scrape foam fireproofing from flat surface		2400	.027	S.F.	.08	1.30		1.38	2.12
2100	Irregular surfaces		1200	.053		.17	2.61		2.78	4.24
3000	Remove cementitious material from flat surface		1800	.036		.11	1.74		1.85	2.83
3100	Irregular surface		1000	.064		.14	3.13		3.27	5.05
6000	Remove contaminated soil from crawl space by hand		400	.160	C.F.	.50	7.85		8.35	12.75
6100	With large production vacuum loader	A-12	700	.091	"	.28	4.47	1.05	5.80	8.40
7000	Radiator backing, not including radiator removal	A-9	1200	.053	S.F.	.17	2.61		2.78	4.24
9000	For type B (supplied air) respirator equipment, add				%					10%

02 82 13.44 Demolition In Asbestos Contaminated Area

		Crew	Daily Output	Labor-Hours	Unit	Material	2012 Bare Costs Labor	2012 Bare Costs Equipment	Total	Total Incl O&P
0010	**DEMOLITION IN ASBESTOS CONTAMINATED AREA**									
0200	Ceiling, including suspension system, plaster and lath	A-9	2100	.030	S.F.	.09	1.49		1.58	2.42
0210	Finished plaster, leaving wire lath		585	.109		.34	5.35		5.69	8.70
0220	Suspended acoustical tile		3500	.018		.06	.89		.95	1.45
0230	Concealed tile grid system		3000	.021		.07	1.04		1.11	1.70
0240	Metal pan grid system		1500	.043		.13	2.09		2.22	3.40
0250	Gypsum board		2500	.026		.08	1.25		1.33	2.04
0260	Lighting fixtures up to 2' x 4'		72	.889	Ea.	2.75	43.50		46.25	70.50
0400	Partitions, non load bearing									
0410	Plaster, lath, and studs	A-9	690	.093	S.F.	.86	4.54		5.40	8
0450	Gypsum board and studs	"	1390	.046	"	.14	2.25		2.39	3.67
9000	For type B (supplied air) respirator equipment, add				%					10%

02 82 13.45 OSHA Testing

		Crew	Daily Output	Labor-Hours	Unit	Material	2012 Bare Costs Labor	2012 Bare Costs Equipment	Total	Total Incl O&P
0010	**OSHA TESTING**									
0100	Certified technician, minimum				Day				200	220
0110	Maximum								300	330
0120	Industrial hygienist, minimum								300	330
0130	Maximum								400	440
0200	Asbestos sampling and PCM analysis, NIOSH 7400, minimum	1 Asbe	8	1	Ea.	2.75	49		51.75	79
0210	Maximum		4	2		3	97.50		100.50	155
1000	Cleaned area samples		8	1		2.63	49		51.63	79
1100	PCM air sample analysis, NIOSH 7400, minimum		8	1		30.50	49		79.50	110
1110	Maximum		4	2		3.20	97.50		100.70	156
1200	TEM air sample analysis, NIOSH 7402, minimum								90	120
1210	Maximum								360	450

02 82 13.46 Decontamination of Asbestos Containment Area

		Crew	Daily Output	Labor-Hours	Unit	Material	2012 Bare Costs Labor	2012 Bare Costs Equipment	Total	Total Incl O&P
0010	**DECONTAMINATION OF ASBESTOS CONTAINMENT AREA**									
0100	Spray exposed substrate with surfactant (bridging)									
0200	Flat surfaces	A-9	6000	.011	S.F.	.36	.52		.88	1.21
0250	Irregular surfaces		4000	.016	"	.31	.78		1.09	1.56
0300	Pipes, beams, and columns		2000	.032	L.F.	.56	1.57		2.13	3.06

02 82 Asbestos Remediation

02 82 13 – Asbestos Abatement

02 82 13.46 Decontamination of Asbestos Containment Area

		Crew	Daily Output	Labor-Hours	Unit	Material	2012 Bare Costs Labor	Equipment	Total	Total Incl O&P
1000	Spray encapsulate polyethylene sheeting	A-9	8000	.008	S.F.	.31	.39		.70	.95
1100	Roll down polyethylene sheeting		8000	.008	"		.39		.39	.61
1500	Bag polyethylene sheeting		400	.160	Ea.	.77	7.85		8.62	13.05
2000	Fine clean exposed substrate, with nylon brush		2400	.027	S.F.		1.30		1.30	2.03
2500	Wet wipe substrate		4800	.013			.65		.65	1.02
2600	Vacuum surfaces, fine brush		6400	.010			.49		.49	.76
3000	Structural demolition									
3100	Wood stud walls	A-9	2800	.023	S.F.		1.12		1.12	1.74
3500	Window manifolds, not incl. window replacement		4200	.015			.75		.75	1.16
3600	Plywood carpet protection		2000	.032			1.57		1.57	2.44
4000	Remove custom decontamination facility	A-10A	8	3	Ea.	15	147		162	246
4100	Remove portable decontamination facility	3 Asbe	12	2	"	12.75	97.50		110.25	166
5000	HEPA vacuum, shampoo carpeting	A-9	4800	.013	S.F.	.05	.65		.70	1.08
9000	Final cleaning of protected surfaces	A-10A	8000	.003	"		.15		.15	.23

02 82 13.47 Asbestos Waste Pkg., Handling, and Disp.

		Crew	Daily Output	Labor-Hours	Unit	Material	2012 Bare Costs Labor	Equipment	Total	Total Incl O&P
0010	**ASBESTOS WASTE PACKAGING, HANDLING, AND DISPOSAL**									
0100	Collect and bag bulk material, 3 C.F. bags, by hand	A-9	400	.160	Ea.	2.35	7.85		10.20	14.80
0200	Large production vacuum loader	A-12	880	.073		.80	3.56	.83	5.19	7.35
1000	Double bag and decontaminate	A-9	960	.067		2.35	3.26		5.61	7.70
2000	Containerize bagged material in drums, per 3 C.F. drum	"	800	.080		17.25	3.91		21.16	25
3000	Cart bags 50' to dumpster	2 Asbe	400	.040			1.95		1.95	3.04
5000	Disposal charges, not including haul, minimum				C.Y.				60	66
5020	Maximum				"				350	385
5100	Remove refrigerant from system	1 Stpi	40	.200	Lb.		11.15		11.15	16.80
9000	For type B (supplied air) respirator equipment, add				%					10%

02 82 13.48 Asbestos Encapsulation With Sealants

		Crew	Daily Output	Labor-Hours	Unit	Material	2012 Bare Costs Labor	Equipment	Total	Total Incl O&P
0010	**ASBESTOS ENCAPSULATION WITH SEALANTS**									
0100	Ceilings and walls, minimum	A-9	21000	.003	S.F.	.27	.15		.42	.53
0110	Maximum		10600	.006	"	.42	.30		.72	.92
0300	Pipes to 12" diameter including minor repairs, minimum		800	.080	L.F.	.37	3.91		4.28	6.50
0310	Maximum		400	.160	"	1.04	7.85		8.89	13.35

02 85 Mold Remediation

02 85 16 – Mold Remediation Preparation and Containment

02 85 16.50 Preparation of Mold Containment Area

		Crew	Daily Output	Labor-Hours	Unit	Material	2012 Bare Costs Labor	Equipment	Total	Total Incl O&P
0010	**PREPARATION OF MOLD CONTAINMENT AREA** R028213-20									
0100	Pre-cleaning, HEPA vacuum and wet wipe, flat surfaces	A-9	12000	.005	S.F.	.02	.26		.28	.43
0300	Separation barrier, 2" x 4" @ 16", 1/2" plywood ea. side, 8' high	2 Carp	400	.040		3	1.76		4.76	6
0310	12' high		320	.050		3	2.21		5.21	6.70
0320	16' high		200	.080		2	3.53		5.53	7.65
0400	Personnel decontam. chamber, 2" x 4" @ 16", 3/4" ply ea. side		280	.057		4	2.52		6.52	8.30
0450	Waste decontam. chamber, 2" x 4" studs @ 16", 3/4" ply each side		360	.044		4	1.96		5.96	7.40
0500	Cover surfaces with polyethylene sheeting									
0501	Including glue and tape									
0550	Floors, each layer, 6 mil	A-9	8000	.008	S.F.	.06	.39		.45	.68
0551	4 mil		9000	.007		.04	.35		.39	.59
0560	Walls, each layer, 6 mil		6000	.011		.09	.52		.61	.91
0561	4 mil		7000	.009		.07	.45		.52	.78
0570	For heights above 12', add						20%			
0575	For heights above 20', add						30%			

02 85 Mold Remediation

02 85 16 – Mold Remediation Preparation and Containment

	02 85 16.50 Preparation of Mold Containment Area	Crew	Daily Output	Labor-Hours	Unit	Material	2012 Bare Costs Labor	Equipment	Total	Total Incl O&P
0580	For fire retardant poly, add					100%				
0590	For large open areas, deduct					10%	20%			
0600	Seal floor penetrations with foam firestop to 36 sq. in.	2 Carp	200	.080	Ea.	7.60	3.53		11.13	13.85
0610	36 sq. in. to 72 sq. in.		125	.128		15.25	5.65		20.90	25.50
0615	72 sq. in. to 144 sq. in.		80	.200		30.50	8.80		39.30	47
0620	Wall penetrations, to 36 square inches		180	.089		7.60	3.92		11.52	14.45
0630	36 sq. in. to 72 sq. in.		100	.160		15.25	7.05		22.30	27.50
0640	72 sq. in. to 144 sq. in.	↓	60	.267	↓	30.50	11.75		42.25	51.50
0800	Caulk seams with latex caulk	1 Carp	230	.035	L.F.	.15	1.53		1.68	2.53
0900	Set up neg. air machine, 1-2k CFM/25 M.C.F. volume	1 Asbe	4.30	1.860	Ea.		91		91	142

02 85 33 – Removal and Disposal of Materials with Mold

02 85 33.50 Demolition in Mold Contaminated Area

		Crew	Daily Output	Labor-Hours	Unit	Material	2012 Bare Costs Labor	Equipment	Total	Total Incl O&P
0010	**DEMOLITION IN MOLD CONTAMINATED AREA**									
0200	Ceiling, including suspension system, plaster and lath	A-9	2100	.030	S.F.	.09	1.49		1.58	2.42
0210	Finished plaster, leaving wire lath		585	.109		.34	5.35		5.69	8.70
0220	Suspended acoustical tile		3500	.018		.06	.89		.95	1.45
0230	Concealed tile grid system		3000	.021		.07	1.04		1.11	1.70
0240	Metal pan grid system		1500	.043		.13	2.09		2.22	3.40
0250	Gypsum board		2500	.026		.08	1.25		1.33	2.04
0255	Plywood		2500	.026	↓	.08	1.25		1.33	2.04
0260	Lighting fixtures up to 2' x 4'	↓	72	.889	Ea.	2.75	43.50		46.25	70.50
0400	Partitions, non load bearing									
0410	Plaster, lath, and studs	A-9	690	.093	S.F.	.86	4.54		5.40	8
0450	Gypsum board and studs		1390	.046		.14	2.25		2.39	3.67
0465	Carpet & pad		1390	.046	↓	.14	2.25		2.39	3.67
0600	Pipe insulation, air cell type, up to 4" diameter pipe		900	.071	L.F.	.22	3.48		3.70	5.65
0610	4" to 8" diameter pipe		800	.080		.25	3.91		4.16	6.35
0620	10" to 12" diameter pipe		700	.091	↓	.28	4.47		4.75	7.25
0630	14" to 16" diameter pipe	↓	550	.116	↓	.36	5.70		6.06	9.25
0650	Over 16" diameter pipe		650	.098	S.F.	.31	4.82		5.13	7.85
9000	For type B (supplied air) respirator equipment, add				%					10%

Estimating Tips

General

- Carefully check all the plans and specifications. Concrete often appears on drawings other than structural drawings, including mechanical and electrical drawings for equipment pads. The cost of cutting and patching is often difficult to estimate. See Subdivision 03 81 for Concrete Cutting, Subdivision 02 41 19.16 for Cutout Demolition, Subdivision 03 05 05.10 for Concrete Demolition, and Subdivision 02 41 19.23 for Rubbish Handling (handling, loading and hauling of debris).
- Always obtain concrete prices from suppliers near the job site. A volume discount can often be negotiated, depending upon competition in the area. Remember to add for waste, particularly for slabs and footings on grade.

03 10 00 Concrete Forming and Accessories

- A primary cost for concrete construction is forming. Most jobs today are constructed with prefabricated forms. The selection of the forms best suited for the job and the total square feet of forms required for efficient concrete forming and placing are key elements in estimating concrete construction. Enough forms must be available for erection to make efficient use of the concrete placing equipment and crew.

- Concrete accessories for forming and placing depend upon the systems used. Study the plans and specifications to ensure that all special accessory requirements have been included in the cost estimate, such as anchor bolts, inserts, and hangers.
- Included within costs for forms-in-place are all necessary bracing and shoring.

03 20 00 Concrete Reinforcing

- Ascertain that the reinforcing steel supplier has included all accessories, cutting, bending, and an allowance for lapping, splicing, and waste. A good rule of thumb is 10% for lapping, splicing, and waste. Also, 10% waste should be allowed for welded wire fabric.
- The unit price items in the subdivisions for Reinforcing In Place, Glass Fiber Reinforcing, and Welded Wire Fabric include the labor to install accessories such as beam and slab bolsters, high chairs, and bar ties and tie wire. The material cost for these accessories is not included; they may be obtained from the Accessories Division.

03 30 00 Cast-In-Place Concrete

- When estimating structural concrete, pay particular attention to requirements for concrete additives, curing methods, and surface treatments. Special consideration for climate, hot or cold, must be included in your estimate. Be sure to include requirements for concrete placing equipment, and concrete finishing.

- For accurate concrete estimating, the estimator must consider each of the following major components individually: forms, reinforcing steel, ready-mix concrete, placement of the concrete, and finishing of the top surface. For faster estimating, Subdivision 03 30 53.40 for Concrete-In-Place can be used; here, various items of concrete work are presented that include the costs of all five major components (unless specifically stated otherwise).

03 40 00 Precast Concrete
03 50 00 Cast Decks and Underlayment

- The cost of hauling precast concrete structural members is often an important factor. For this reason, it is important to get a quote from the nearest supplier. It may become economically feasible to set up precasting beds on the site if the hauling costs are prohibitive.

Reference Numbers

Reference numbers are shown in shaded boxes at the beginning of some major classifications. These numbers refer to related items in the Reference Section. The reference information may be an estimating procedure, an alternate pricing method, or technical information.
Note: Not all subdivisions listed here necessarily appear in this publication.

03 01 Maintenance of Concrete

03 01 30 – Maintenance of Cast-In-Place Concrete

03 01 30.62 Concrete Patching

		Crew	Daily Output	Labor-Hours	Unit	Material	2012 Bare Costs Labor	Equipment	Total	Total Incl O&P
0010	**CONCRETE PATCHING**									
0100	Floors, 1/4" thick, small areas, regular grout	1 Cefi	170	.047	S.F.	1.23	1.99		3.22	4.28
0150	Epoxy grout	"	100	.080	"	7.30	3.39		10.69	13
2000	Walls, including chipping, cleaning and epoxy grout									
2100	1/4" deep	1 Cefi	65	.123	S.F.	7.30	5.20		12.50	15.65
2150	1/2" deep		50	.160		14.55	6.80		21.35	26
2200	3/4" deep		40	.200		22	8.45		30.45	36.50

03 11 Concrete Forming

03 11 13 – Structural Cast-In-Place Concrete Forming

03 11 13.40 Forms In Place, Equipment Foundations

		Crew	Daily Output	Labor-Hours	Unit	Material	2012 Bare Costs Labor	Equipment	Total	Total Incl O&P
0010	**FORMS IN PLACE, EQUIPMENT FOUNDATIONS**									
0020	1 use	C-2	160	.300	SFCA	2.93	12.90		15.83	23
0050	2 use		190	.253		1.61	10.85		12.46	18.45
0100	3 use		200	.240		1.17	10.30		11.47	17.15
0150	4 use		205	.234		.96	10.05		11.01	16.50

03 11 13.45 Forms In Place, Footings

		Crew	Daily Output	Labor-Hours	Unit	Material	2012 Bare Costs Labor	Equipment	Total	Total Incl O&P
0010	**FORMS IN PLACE, FOOTINGS**									
0020	Continuous wall, plywood, 1 use	C-1	375	.085	SFCA	5.95	3.57		9.52	12
0050	2 use		440	.073		3.26	3.04		6.30	8.25
0100	3 use		470	.068		2.37	2.85		5.22	7
0150	4 use		485	.066		1.93	2.76		4.69	6.35
5000	Spread footings, job-built lumber, 1 use		305	.105		1.90	4.39		6.29	8.85
5050	2 use		371	.086		1.06	3.61		4.67	6.70
5100	3 use		401	.080		.76	3.34		4.10	6
5150	4 use		414	.077		.62	3.23		3.85	5.65

03 11 13.65 Forms In Place, Slab On Grade

		Crew	Daily Output	Labor-Hours	Unit	Material	2012 Bare Costs Labor	Equipment	Total	Total Incl O&P
0010	**FORMS IN PLACE, SLAB ON GRADE**									
3000	Edge forms, wood, 4 use, on grade, to 6" high	C-1	600	.053	L.F.	.29	2.23		2.52	3.75
6000	Trench forms in floor, wood, 1 use		160	.200	SFCA	1.56	8.35		9.91	14.60
6050	2 use		175	.183		.86	7.65		8.51	12.70
6100	3 use		180	.178		.62	7.45		8.07	12.15
6150	4 use		185	.173		.51	7.25		7.76	11.70
8760	Void form, corrugated fiberboard, 4" x 12", 4' long	G	3000	.011	S.F.	2.64	.45		3.09	3.59
8770	6" x 12", 4' long		3000	.011		3.10	.45		3.55	4.10
8780	1/4" thick hardboard protective cover for void form	2 Carp	1500	.011		.57	.47		1.04	1.35

03 15 Concrete Accessories

03 15 05 – Concrete Forming Accessories

03 15 05.75 Sleeves and Chases

		Crew	Daily Output	Labor-Hours	Unit	Material	2012 Bare Costs Labor	Equipment	Total	Total Incl O&P
0010	**SLEEVES AND CHASES**									
0100	Plastic, 1 use, 12" long, 2" diameter	1 Carp	100	.080	Ea.	2.19	3.53		5.72	7.85
0150	4" diameter		90	.089		6.45	3.92		10.37	13.15
0200	6" diameter		75	.107		11.35	4.70		16.05	19.70
0250	12" diameter		60	.133		32	5.90		37.90	44
5000	Sheet metal, 2" diameter	G	100	.080		1.57	3.53		5.10	7.15
5100	4" diameter	G	90	.089		1.96	3.92		5.88	8.20
5150	6" diameter	G	75	.107		1.96	4.70		6.66	9.40
5200	12" diameter	G	60	.133		3.90	5.90		9.80	13.35

03 15 Concrete Accessories

03 15 05 – Concrete Forming Accessories

03 15 05.75 Sleeves and Chases

		Crew	Daily Output	Labor-Hours	Unit	Material	2012 Bare Costs Labor	Equipment	Total	Total Incl O&P
6000	Steel pipe, 2" diameter	G 1 Carp	100	.080	Ea.	9.10	3.53		12.63	15.45
6100	4" diameter	G	90	.089		29.50	3.92		33.42	38.50
6150	6" diameter	G	75	.107		44	4.70		48.70	56
6200	12" diameter	G	60	.133		60.50	5.90		66.40	75.50

03 21 Reinforcement Bars

03 21 10 – Uncoated Reinforcing Steel

03 21 10.60 Reinforcing In Place

		Crew	Daily Output	Labor-Hours	Unit	Material	2012 Bare Costs Labor	Equipment	Total	Total Incl O&P
0015	**REINFORCING IN PLACE**, 50-60 ton lots, A615 Grade 60									
0020	Includes labor, but not material cost, to install accessories									
0030	Made from recycled materials	G								
0502	Footings, #4 to #7	G 4 Rodm	4200	.008	Lb.	.51	.37		.88	1.16
0552	#8 to #18	G	7200	.004		.51	.22		.73	.91
0602	Slab on grade, #3 to #7	G	4200	.008		.49	.37		.86	1.14
0900	For other than 50 – 60 ton lots									
1000	Under 10 ton job, #3 to #7, add					25%	10%			
1010	#8 to #18, add					20%	10%			
1050	10 – 50 ton job, #3 to #7, add					10%				
1060	#8 to #18, add					5%				
1100	60 – 100 ton job, #3 to #7, deduct					5%				
1110	#8 to #18, deduct					10%				
1150	Over 100 ton job, #3 to #7, deduct					10%				
1160	#8 to #18, deduct					15%				

03 22 Fabric and Grid Reinforcing

03 22 05 – Uncoated Welded Wire Fabric

03 22 05.50 Welded Wire Fabric

		Crew	Daily Output	Labor-Hours	Unit	Material	2012 Bare Costs Labor	Equipment	Total	Total Incl O&P
0010	**WELDED WIRE FABRIC** ASTM A185									
0020	Includes labor, but not material cost, to install accessories									
0030	Made from recycled materials	G								
0050	Sheets									
0100	6 x 6 - W1.4 x W1.4 (10 x 10) 21 lb. per C.S.F.	G 2 Rodm	35	.457	C.S.F.	13.80	22.50		36.30	51

03 30 Cast-In-Place Concrete

03 30 53 – Miscellaneous Cast-In-Place Concrete

03 30 53.40 Concrete In Place

		Crew	Daily Output	Labor-Hours	Unit	Material	2012 Bare Costs Labor	Equipment	Total	Total Incl O&P
0010	**CONCRETE IN PLACE**									
0020	Including forms (4 uses), reinforcing steel, concrete, placement,									
0050	and finishing unless otherwise indicated									
0500	Chimney foundations (5000 psi), industrial, minimum	C-14C	32.22	3.476	C.Y.	144	147	.83	291.83	385
0510	Maximum	"	23.71	4.724	"	168	200	1.13	369.13	495
3540	Equipment pad (3000 psi), 3' x 3' x 6" thick	C-14H	45	1.067	Ea.	44	46.50	.61	91.11	121
3550	4' x 4' x 6" thick		30	1.600		66	69.50	.91	136.41	181
3560	5' x 5' x 8" thick		18	2.667		118	116	1.52	235.52	310
3570	6' x 6' x 8" thick		14	3.429		159	149	1.95	309.95	405
3580	8' x 8' x 10" thick		8	6		335	261	3.42	599.42	775
3590	10' x 10' x 12" thick		5	9.600		575	415	5.45	995.45	1,275

03 30 Cast-In-Place Concrete

03 30 53 – Miscellaneous Cast-In-Place Concrete

03 30 53.40 Concrete In Place

03 30 53.40 Concrete In Place	Crew	Daily Output	Labor-Hours	Unit	Material	2012 Bare Costs Labor	Equipment	Total	Total Incl O&P
3800	Footings (3000 psi), spread under 1 C.Y.	C-14C	28	4	C.Y.	166	169	.96	335.96	445
3825	1 C.Y. to 5 C.Y.		43	2.605		192	110	.63	302.63	380
3850	Over 5 C.Y.		75	1.493		177	63	.36	240.36	293
3900	Footings, strip (3000 psi), 18" x 9", unreinforced	C-14L	40	2.400		121	98.50	.70	220.20	285
3920	18" x 9", reinforced	C-14C	35	3.200		145	135	.77	280.77	370
3925	20" x 10", unreinforced	C-14L	45	2.133		118	87.50	.62	206.12	265
3930	20" x 10", reinforced	C-14C	40	2.800		137	118	.67	255.67	335
3935	24" x 12", unreinforced	C-14L	55	1.745		117	72	.51	189.51	240
3940	24" x 12", reinforced	C-14C	48	2.333		136	98.50	.56	235.06	305
3945	36" x 12", unreinforced	C-14L	70	1.371		114	56.50	.40	170.90	212
3950	36" x 12", reinforced	C-14C	60	1.867		131	79	.45	210.45	267
4000	Foundation mat (3000 psi), under 10 C.Y.		38.67	2.896		202	122	.70	324.70	415
4050	Over 20 C.Y.		56.40	1.986		178	84	.48	262.48	325
4650	Slab on grade (3500 psi), not including finish, 4" thick	C-14E	60.75	1.449		118	63	.45	181.45	228
4700	6" thick	"	92	.957		114	41.50	.30	155.80	190
4701	Thickened slab edge (3500 psi), for slab on grade poured									
4702	monolithically with slab; depth is in addition to slab thickness;									
4703	formed vertical outside edge, earthen bottom and inside slope									
4705	8" deep x 8" wide bottom, unreinforced	C-14L	2190	.044	L.F.	3.18	1.80	.01	4.99	6.25
4710	8" x 8", reinforced	C-14C	1670	.067		5.50	2.83	.02	8.35	10.45
4715	12" deep x 12" wide bottom, unreinforced	C-14L	1800	.053		6.55	2.19	.02	8.76	10.60
4720	12" x 12", reinforced	C-14C	1310	.086		10.75	3.61	.02	14.38	17.40
4725	16" deep x 16" wide bottom, unreinforced	C-14L	1440	.067		11.05	2.74	.02	13.81	16.40
4730	16" x 16", reinforced	C-14C	1120	.100		16.10	4.23	.02	20.35	24
4735	20" deep x 20" wide bottom, unreinforced	C-14L	1150	.083		16.85	3.43	.02	20.30	24
4740	20" x 20", reinforced	C-14C	920	.122		23	5.15	.03	28.18	33.50
4745	24" deep x 24" wide bottom, unreinforced	C-14L	930	.103		24	4.24	.03	28.27	32.50
4750	24" x 24", reinforced	C-14C	740	.151		32	6.40	.04	38.44	45.50
4751	Slab on grade (3500 psi), incl. troweled finish, not incl. forms									
4760	or reinforcing, over 10,000 S.F., 4" thick	C-14F	3425	.021	S.F.	1.29	.84	.01	2.14	2.69
4820	6" thick		3350	.021		1.89	.86	.01	2.76	3.38
4840	8" thick		3184	.023		2.59	.91	.01	3.51	4.21
4900	12" thick		2734	.026		3.88	1.06	.01	4.95	5.85
4950	15" thick		2505	.029		4.88	1.15	.01	6.04	7.10

03 31 Structural Concrete

03 31 05 – Normal Weight Structural Concrete

03 31 05.35 Normal Weight Concrete, Ready Mix

03 31 05.35 Normal Weight Concrete, Ready Mix	Crew	Daily Output	Labor-Hours	Unit	Material	2012 Bare Costs Labor	Equipment	Total	Total Incl O&P
0010	**NORMAL WEIGHT CONCRETE, READY MIX**, delivered									
0012	Includes local aggregate, sand, Portland cement, and water									
0015	Excludes all additives and treatments									
0020	2000 psi				C.Y.	91.50			91.50	101
0100	2500 psi					94			94	103
0150	3000 psi					102			102	112
0200	3500 psi					99.50			99.50	110
0300	4000 psi					103			103	113
0350	4500 psi					106			106	116
0400	5000 psi					109			109	120
0411	6000 psi					124			124	136
0412	8000 psi					202			202	223
0413	10,000 psi					287			287	315

03 31 Structural Concrete

03 31 05 – Normal Weight Structural Concrete

03 31 05.35 Normal Weight Concrete, Ready Mix	Crew	Daily Output	Labor-Hours	Unit	Material	2012 Bare Costs Labor	2012 Bare Costs Equipment	Total	Total Incl O&P
0414 12,000 psi				C.Y.	345			345	380
1000 For high early strength cement, add					10%				
1300 For winter concrete (hot water), add					4.25			4.25	4.68
1400 For hot weather concrete (ice), add					9.35			9.35	10.25
1410 For mid-range water reducer, add					4.13			4.13	4.54
1420 For high-range water reducer/superplasticizer, add					6.35			6.35	6.95
1430 For retarder, add					2.71			2.71	2.98
1440 For non-Chloride accelerator, add					4.83			4.83	5.30
1450 For Chloride accelerator, per 1%, add					3.28			3.28	3.61
1460 For fiber reinforcing, synthetic (1 lb./C.Y.), add					6.65			6.65	7.30
1500 For Saturday delivery, add					8.85			8.85	9.70
1510 For truck holding/waiting time past 1st hour per load, add				Hr.	87.50			87.50	96.50
1520 For short load (less than 4 C.Y.), add per load				Ea.	112			112	124
2000 For all lightweight aggregate, add				C.Y.	45%				

03 31 05.70 Placing Concrete	Crew	Daily Output	Labor-Hours	Unit	Material	Labor	Equipment	Total	Total Incl O&P
0010 **PLACING CONCRETE**									
0020 Includes labor and equipment to place, strike off and consolidate									
1900 Footings, continuous, shallow, direct chute	C-6	120	.400	C.Y.		14.65	.46	15.11	23
1950 Pumped	C-20	150	.427			16.10	5.15	21.25	30
2000 With crane and bucket	C-7	90	.800			30.50	13.10	43.60	61
2100 Footings, continuous, deep, direct chute	C-6	140	.343			12.55	.39	12.94	19.60
2150 Pumped	C-20	160	.400			15.10	4.82	19.92	28.50
2200 With crane and bucket	C-7	110	.655			25	10.70	35.70	50
2400 Footings, spread, under 1 C.Y., direct chute	C-6	55	.873			32	.99	32.99	50
2450 Pumped	C-20	65	.985			37	11.85	48.85	69.50
2500 With crane and bucket	C-7	45	1.600			61	26	87	122
2600 Over 5 C.Y., direct chute	C-6	120	.400			14.65	.46	15.11	23
2650 Pumped	C-20	150	.427			16.10	5.15	21.25	30
2700 With crane and bucket	C-7	100	.720			27.50	11.75	39.25	55
2900 Foundation mats, over 20 C.Y., direct chute	C-6	350	.137			5	.16	5.16	7.80
2950 Pumped	C-20	400	.160			6.05	1.93	7.98	11.30
3000 With crane and bucket	C-7	300	.240			9.15	3.92	13.07	18.20

03 35 Concrete Finishing

03 35 29 – Tooled Concrete Finishing

03 35 29.30 Finishing Floors	Crew	Daily Output	Labor-Hours	Unit	Material	Labor	Equipment	Total	Total Incl O&P
0010 **FINISHING FLOORS**									
0012 Finishing requires that concrete first be placed, struck off & consolidated									
0015 Basic finishing for various unspecified flatwork									
0100 Bull float only	C-10	4000	.006	S.F.		.24		.24	.36
0125 Bull float & manual float		2000	.012			.48		.48	.71
0150 Bull float, manual float, & broom finish, w/edging & joints		1850	.013			.52		.52	.77
0200 Bull float, manual float & manual steel trowel		1265	.019			.76		.76	1.13
0210 For specified Random Access Floors in ACI Classes 1, 2, 3 and 4 to achieve									
0215 Composite Overall Floor Flatness and Levelness values up to F35/F25									
0250 Bull float, machine float & machine trowel (walk-behind)	C-10C	1715	.014	S.F.		.56	.03	.59	.86
0300 Power screed, bull float, machine float & trowel (walk-behind)	C-10D	2400	.010			.40	.05	.45	.65
0350 Power screed, bull float, machine float & trowel (ride-on)	C-10E	4000	.006			.24	.06	.30	.43
0352 For specified Random Access Floors in ACI Classes 5, 6, 7 and 8 to achieve									
0354 Composite Overall Floor Flatness and Levelness values up to F50/F50									
0356 Add for two-dimensional restraightening after power float	C-10	6000	.004	S.F.		.16		.16	.24

03 35 Concrete Finishing

03 35 29 – Tooled Concrete Finishing

03 35 29.30 Finishing Floors

		Crew	Daily Output	Labor-Hours	Unit	Material	2012 Bare Costs Labor	Equipment	Total	Total Incl O&P
0358	For specified Random or Defined Access Floors in ACI Class 9 to achieve									
0360	Composite Overall Floor Flatness and Levelness values up to F100/F100									
0362	Add for two-dimensional restraightening after bull float & power float	C-10	3000	.008	S.F.		.32		.32	.48
0364	For specified Superflat Defined Access Floors in ACI Class 9 to achieve									
0366	Minimum Floor Flatness and Levelness values of F100/F100									
0368	Add for 2-dim'l restraightening after bull float, power float, power trowel	C-10	2000	.012	S.F.		.48		.48	.71

03 35 29.35 Control Joints, Saw Cut

		Crew	Daily Output	Labor-Hours	Unit	Material	2012 Bare Costs Labor	Equipment	Total	Total Incl O&P
0010	**CONTROL JOINTS, SAW CUT**									
0100	Sawcut control joints in green concrete									
0120	1" depth	C-27	2000	.008	L.F.	.03	.34	.07	.44	.62
0140	1-1/2" depth		1800	.009		.05	.38	.08	.51	.70
0160	2" depth	↓	1600	.010	↓	.07	.42	.09	.58	.79
0180	Sawcut joint reservoir in cured concrete									
0182	3/8" wide x 3/4" deep, with single saw blade	C-27	1000	.016	L.F.	.05	.68	.15	.88	1.22
0184	1/2" wide x 1" deep, with double saw blades		900	.018		.10	.75	.16	1.01	1.40
0186	3/4" wide x 1-1/2" deep, with double saw blades	↓	800	.020		.20	.85	.19	1.24	1.67
0190	Water blast joint to wash away laitance, 2 passes	C-29	2500	.003			.11	.03	.14	.20
0200	Air blast joint to blow out debris and air dry, 2 passes	C-28	2000	.004	↓		.17	.01	.18	.26
0300	For backer rod, see Section 07 91 23.10									
0342	For joint sealant, see Section 07 92 13.20									

03 54 Cast Underlayment

03 54 16 – Hydraulic Cement Underlayment

03 54 16.50 Cement Underlayment

		Crew	Daily Output	Labor-Hours	Unit	Material	2012 Bare Costs Labor	Equipment	Total	Total Incl O&P
0010	**CEMENT UNDERLAYMENT**									
2510	Underlayment, P.C based self-leveling, 4100 psi, pumped, 1/4"	C-8	20000	.003	S.F.	1.43	.11	.04	1.58	1.78
2520	1/2"		19000	.003		2.85	.12	.04	3.01	3.35
2530	3/4"		18000	.003		4.28	.12	.04	4.44	4.92
2540	1"		17000	.003		5.70	.13	.04	5.87	6.50
2550	1-1/2"	↓	15000	.004		8.55	.15	.05	8.75	9.65
2560	Hand placed, 1/2"	C-18	450	.020		2.85	.71	.13	3.69	4.37
2610	Topping, P.C. based self-level/dry 6100 psi, pumped, 1/4"	C-8	20000	.003		2.16	.11	.04	2.31	2.58
2620	1/2"		19000	.003		4.32	.12	.04	4.48	4.96
2630	3/4"		18000	.003		6.45	.12	.04	6.61	7.30
2660	1"		17000	.003		8.65	.13	.04	8.82	9.75
2670	1-1/2"	↓	15000	.004		12.95	.15	.05	13.15	14.50
2680	Hand placed, 1/2"	C-18	450	.020	↓	4.32	.71	.13	5.16	6

03 63 Epoxy Grouting

03 63 05 – Grouting of Dowels and Fasteners

03 63 05.10 Epoxy Only

		Crew	Daily Output	Labor-Hours	Unit	Material	2012 Bare Costs Labor	Equipment	Total	Total Incl O&P
0010	**EPOXY ONLY**									
1500	Chemical anchoring, epoxy cartridge, excludes layout, drilling, fastener									
1530	For fastener 3/4" diam. x 6" embedment	2 Skwk	72	.222	Ea.	5.10	10.10		15.20	21
1535	1" diam. x 8" embedment		66	.242		7.65	11		18.65	25.50
1540	1-1/4" diam. x 10" embedment		60	.267		15.30	12.10		27.40	35.50
1545	1-3/4" diam. x 12" embedment		54	.296		25.50	13.45		38.95	49
1550	14" embedment		48	.333		30.50	15.15		45.65	57
1555	2" diam. x 12" embedment	↓	42	.381	↓	41	17.30		58.30	71.50

03 63 Epoxy Grouting

03 63 05 – Grouting of Dowels and Fasteners

03 63 05.10 Epoxy Only	Crew	Daily Output	Labor-Hours	Unit	Material	2012 Bare Costs Labor	Equipment	Total	Total Incl O&P
1560	18" embedment	2 Skwk	32	.500	Ea.	51	22.50		73.50	91

03 82 Concrete Boring

03 82 13 – Concrete Core Drilling

03 82 13.10 Core Drilling

		Crew	Daily Output	Labor-Hours	Unit	Material	2012 Bare Costs Labor	Equipment	Total	Total Incl O&P
0010	**CORE DRILLING**									
0020	Reinf. conc slab, up to 6" thick, incl. bit, layout & set up									
0100	1" diameter core	B-89A	17	.941	Ea.	.18	38	6.50	44.68	66
0150	Each added inch thick in same hole, add		1440	.011		.03	.45	.08	.56	.80
0200	2" diameter core		16.50	.970		.29	39	6.70	45.99	67.50
0250	Each added inch thick in same hole, add		1080	.015		.05	.60	.10	.75	1.08
0300	3" diameter core		16	1		.41	40.50	6.90	47.81	70
0350	Each added inch thick in same hole, add		720	.022		.07	.89	.15	1.11	1.62
0500	4" diameter core		15	1.067		.49	43	7.35	50.84	74.50
0550	Each added inch thick in same hole, add		480	.033		.49	1.34	.23	2.06	2.86
0700	6" diameter core		14	1.143		.81	46	7.85	54.66	80.50
0750	Each added inch thick in same hole, add		360	.044		.13	1.79	.31	2.23	3.25
0900	8" diameter core		13	1.231		1.03	49.50	8.50	59.03	87
0950	Each added inch thick in same hole, add		288	.056		.17	2.24	.38	2.79	4.06
1100	10" diameter core		12	1.333		1.50	53.50	9.20	64.20	95
1150	Each added inch thick in same hole, add		240	.067		.25	2.68	.46	3.39	4.92
1300	12" diameter core		11	1.455		1.65	58.50	10	70.15	103
1350	Each added inch thick in same hole, add		206	.078		.27	3.13	.54	3.94	5.70
1500	14" diameter core		10	1.600		2.07	64.50	11	77.57	114
1550	Each added inch thick in same hole, add		180	.089		.34	3.58	.61	4.53	6.55
1700	18" diameter core		9	1.778		2.75	71.50	12.25	86.50	127
1750	Each added inch thick in same hole, add		144	.111		.46	4.47	.77	5.70	8.25
1754	24" diameter core		8	2		3.89	80.50	13.80	98.19	143
1756	Each added inch thick in same hole, add		120	.133		.65	5.35	.92	6.92	10
1760	For horizontal holes, add to above						20%	20%		
1770	Prestressed hollow core plank, 8" thick									
1780	1" diameter core	B-89A	17.50	.914	Ea.	.25	37	6.30	43.55	64
1790	Each added inch thick in same hole, add		3840	.004		.03	.17	.03	.23	.32
1794	2" diameter core		17.25	.928		.39	37.50	6.40	44.29	65
1796	Each added inch thick in same hole, add		2880	.006		.05	.22	.04	.31	.44
1800	3" diameter core		17	.941		.54	38	6.50	45.04	66.50
1810	Each added inch thick in same hole, add		1920	.008		.07	.34	.06	.47	.65
1820	4" diameter core		16.50	.970		.65	39	6.70	46.35	68
1830	Each added inch thick in same hole, add		1280	.013		.08	.50	.09	.67	.96
1840	6" diameter core		15.50	1.032		1.08	41.50	7.10	49.68	73
1850	Each added inch thick in same hole, add		960	.017		.13	.67	.11	.91	1.32
1860	8" diameter core		15	1.067		1.37	43	7.35	51.72	75.50
1870	Each added inch thick in same hole, add		768	.021		.17	.84	.14	1.15	1.64
1880	10" diameter core		14	1.143		2	46	7.85	55.85	82
1890	Each added inch thick in same hole, add		640	.025		.25	1.01	.17	1.43	2.01
1900	12" diameter core		13.50	1.185		2.20	47.50	8.15	57.85	85
1910	Each added inch thick in same hole, add		548	.029		.27	1.18	.20	1.65	2.33

03 82 Concrete Boring

03 82 16 – Concrete Drilling

03 82 16.10 Concrete Impact Drilling	Crew	Daily Output	Labor- Hours	Unit	Material	2012 Bare Costs Labor	Equipment	Total	Total Incl O&P
0010 **CONCRETE IMPACT DRILLING**									
0050 Up to 4" deep in conc/brick floor/wall, incl. bit & layout, no anchor									
0100 Holes, 1/4" diameter	1 Carp	75	.107	Ea.	.05	4.70		4.75	7.30
0150 For each additional inch of depth, add		430	.019		.01	.82		.83	1.27
0200 3/8" diameter		63	.127		.05	5.60		5.65	8.65
0250 For each additional inch of depth, add		340	.024		.01	1.04		1.05	1.61
0300 1/2" diameter		50	.160		.05	7.05		7.10	10.90
0350 For each additional inch of depth, add		250	.032		.01	1.41		1.42	2.18
0400 5/8" diameter		48	.167		.08	7.35		7.43	11.40
0450 For each additional inch of depth, add		240	.033		.02	1.47		1.49	2.28
0500 3/4" diameter		45	.178		.10	7.85		7.95	12.15
0550 For each additional inch of depth, add		220	.036		.03	1.60		1.63	2.50
0600 7/8" diameter		43	.186		.13	8.20		8.33	12.75
0650 For each additional inch of depth, add		210	.038		.03	1.68		1.71	2.63
0700 1" diameter		40	.200		.15	8.80		8.95	13.70
0750 For each additional inch of depth, add		190	.042		.04	1.86		1.90	2.90
0800 1-1/4" diameter		38	.211		.23	9.30		9.53	14.55
0850 For each additional inch of depth, add		180	.044		.06	1.96		2.02	3.08
0900 1-1/2" diameter		35	.229		.35	10.10		10.45	15.90
0950 For each additional inch of depth, add		165	.048		.09	2.14		2.23	3.39
1000 For ceiling installations, add						40%			

Estimating Tips

04 05 00 Common Work Results for Masonry

- The terms *mortar* and *grout* are often used interchangeably, and incorrectly. Mortar is used to bed masonry units, seal the entry of air and moisture, provide architectural appearance, and allow for size variations in the units. Grout is used primarily in reinforced masonry construction and is used to bond the masonry to the reinforcing steel. Common mortar types are M(2500 psi), S(1800 psi), N(750 psi), and O(350 psi), and conform to ASTM C270. Grout is either fine or coarse and conforms to ASTM C476, and in-place strengths generally exceed 2500 psi. Mortar and grout are different components of masonry construction and are placed by entirely different methods. An estimator should be aware of their unique uses and costs.

- Mortar is included in all assembled masonry line items. The mortar cost, part of the assembled masonry material cost, includes all ingredients, all labor, and all equipment required. Please see reference number R040513-10.

- Waste, specifically the loss/droppings of mortar and the breakage of brick and block, is included in all masonry assemblies in this division. A factor of 25% is added for mortar and 3% for brick and concrete masonry units.

- Scaffolding or staging is not included in any of the Division 4 costs. Refer to Subdivision 01 54 23 for scaffolding and staging costs.

04 20 00 Unit Masonry

- The most common types of unit masonry are brick and concrete masonry. The major classifications of brick are building brick (ASTM C62), facing brick (ASTM C216), glazed brick, fire brick, and pavers. Many varieties of texture and appearance can exist within these classifications, and the estimator would be wise to check local custom and availability within the project area. For repair and remodeling jobs, matching the existing brick may be the most important criteria.

- Brick and concrete block are priced by the piece and then converted into a price per square foot of wall. Openings less than two square feet are generally ignored by the estimator because any savings in units used is offset by the cutting and trimming required.

- It is often difficult and expensive to find and purchase small lots of historic brick. Costs can vary widely. Many design issues affect costs, selection of mortar mix, and repairs or replacement of masonry materials. Cleaning techniques must be reflected in the estimate.

- All masonry walls, whether interior or exterior, require bracing. The cost of bracing walls during construction should be included by the estimator, and this bracing must remain in place until permanent bracing is complete. Permanent bracing of masonry walls is accomplished by masonry itself, in the form of pilasters or abutting wall corners, or by anchoring the walls to the structural frame. Accessories in the form of anchors, anchor slots, and ties are used, but their supply and installation can be by different trades. For instance, anchor slots on spandrel beams and columns are supplied and welded in place by the steel fabricator, but the ties from the slots into the masonry are installed by the bricklayer. Regardless of the installation method, the estimator must be certain that these accessories are accounted for in pricing.

Reference Numbers

Reference numbers are shown in shaded boxes at the beginning of some major classifications. These numbers refer to related items in the Reference Section. The reference information may be an estimating procedure, an alternate pricing method, or technical information.

Note: Not all subdivisions listed here necessarily appear in this publication.

04 05 Common Work Results for Masonry

04 05 23 – Masonry Accessories

04 05 23.19 Masonry Cavity Drainage, Weepholes, and Vents	Crew	Daily Output	Labor-Hours	Unit	Material	2012 Bare Costs Labor	Equipment	Total	Total Incl O&P
0010 **MASONRY CAVITY DRAINAGE, WEEPHOLES, AND VENTS**									
0020 Extruded aluminum, 4" deep, 2-3/8" x 8-1/8"	1 Bric	30	.267	Ea.	31.50	11.75		43.25	52.50
0050 5" x 8-1/8"		25	.320		41	14.10		55.10	67
0100 2-1/4" x 25"		25	.320		71.50	14.10		85.60	101
0150 5" x 16-1/2"		22	.364		62.50	16.05		78.55	92.50
0200 6" x 16-1/2"		22	.364		83.50	16.05		99.55	116
0250 7-3/4" x 16-1/2"		20	.400		71	17.65		88.65	105
0400 For baked enamel finish, add					35%				
0500 For cast aluminum, painted, add					60%				
1000 Stainless steel ventilators, 6" x 6"	1 Bric	25	.320		126	14.10		140.10	160
1050 8" x 8"		24	.333		132	14.70		146.70	168
1100 12" x 12"		23	.348		153	15.35		168.35	191
1150 12" x 6"		24	.333		134	14.70		148.70	169
1200 Foundation block vent, galv., 1-1/4" thk, 8" high, 16" long, no damper		30	.267		24.50	11.75		36.25	45
1250 For damper, add					8.20			8.20	9

04 21 Clay Unit Masonry

04 21 13 – Brick Masonry

04 21 13.15 Chimney

	Crew	Daily Output	Labor-Hours	Unit	Material	2012 Bare Costs Labor	Equipment	Total	Total Incl O&P
0010 **CHIMNEY**, excludes foundation, scaffolding, grout and reinforcing									
0100 Brick, 16" x 16", 8" flue	D-1	18.20	.879	V.L.F.	21.50	35		56.50	76.50
0150 16" x 20" with one 8" x 12" flue		16	1		34	40		74	97.50
0200 16" x 24" with two 8" x 8" flues		14	1.143		50.50	45.50		96	125
0250 20" x 20" with one 12" x 12" flue		13.70	1.168		38.50	46.50		85	113
0300 20" x 24" with two 8" x 12" flues		12	1.333		57	53		110	143
0350 20" x 32" with two 12" x 12" flues		10	1.600		68	64		132	172
1800 Metal, high temp. steel jacket, factory lining, 24" diam.	E-2	65	.862		210	41.50	23	274.50	330
1900 60" diameter	"	30	1.867		765	90	50	905	1,050
2100 Poured concrete, brick lining, 200' high x 10' diam.					7,275			7,275	8,000
2800 500' x 20' diameter					12,700			12,700	14,000

Estimating Tips

05 05 00 Common Work Results for Metals

- Nuts, bolts, washers, connection angles, and plates can add a significant amount to both the tonnage of a structural steel job and the estimated cost. As a rule of thumb, add 10% to the total weight to account for these accessories.

- Type 2 steel construction, commonly referred to as "simple construction," consists generally of field-bolted connections with lateral bracing supplied by other elements of the building, such as masonry walls or x-bracing. The estimator should be aware, however, that shop connections may be accomplished by welding or bolting. The method may be particular to the fabrication shop and may have an impact on the estimated cost.

05 12 23 Structural Steel

- Steel items can be obtained from two sources: a fabrication shop or a metals service center. Fabrication shops can fabricate items under more controlled conditions than can crews in the field. They are also more efficient and can produce items more economically. Metal service centers serve as a source of long mill shapes to both fabrication shops and contractors.

- Most line items in this structural steel subdivision, and most items in 05 50 00 Metal Fabrications, are indicated as being shop fabricated. The bare material cost for these shop fabricated items is the "Invoice Cost" from the shop and includes the mill base price of steel plus mill extras, transportation to the shop, shop drawings and detailing where warranted, shop fabrication and handling, sandblasting and a shop coat of primer paint, all necessary structural bolts, and delivery to the job site. The bare labor cost and bare equipment cost for these shop fabricated items is for field installation or erection.

- Line items in Subdivision 05 12 23.40 Lightweight Framing, and other items scattered in Division 5, are indicated as being field fabricated. The bare material cost for these field fabricated items is the "Invoice Cost" from the metals service center and includes the mill base price of steel plus mill extras, transportation to the metals service center, material handling, and delivery of long lengths of mill shapes to the job site. Material costs for structural bolts and welding rods should be added to the estimate. The bare labor cost and bare equipment cost for these items is for both field fabrication and field installation or erection, and include time for cutting, welding and drilling in the fabricated metal items. Drilling into concrete and fasteners to fasten field fabricated items to other work are not included and should be added to the estimate.

05 20 00 Steel Joist Framing

- In any given project the total weight of open web steel joists is determined by the loads to be supported and the design. However, economies can be realized in minimizing the amount of labor used to place the joists. This is done by maximizing the joist spacing, and therefore minimizing the number of joists required to be installed on the job. Certain spacings and locations may be required by the design, but in other cases maximizing the spacing and keeping it as uniform as possible will keep the costs down.

05 30 00 Steel Decking

- The takeoff and estimating of metal deck involves more than simply the area of the floor or roof and the type of deck specified or shown on the drawings. Many different sizes and types of openings may exist. Small openings for individual pipes or conduits may be drilled after the floor/roof is installed, but larger openings may require special deck lengths as well as reinforcing or structural support. The estimator should determine who will be supplying this reinforcing. Additionally, some deck terminations are part of the deck package, such as screed angles and pour stops, and others will be part of the steel contract, such as angles attached to structural members and cast-in-place angles and plates. The estimator must ensure that all pieces are accounted for in the complete estimate.

05 50 00 Metal Fabrications

- The most economical steel stairs are those that use common materials, standard details, and most importantly, a uniform and relatively simple method of field assembly. Commonly available A36 channels and plates are very good choices for the main stringers of the stairs, as are angles and tees for the carrier members. Risers and treads are usually made by specialty shops, and it is most economical to use a typical detail in as many places as possible. The stairs should be pre-assembled and shipped directly to the site. The field connections should be simple and straightforward to be accomplished efficiently, and with minimum equipment and labor.

Reference Numbers

Reference numbers are shown in shaded boxes at the beginning of some major classifications. These numbers refer to related items in the Reference Section. The reference information may be an estimating procedure, an alternate pricing method, or technical information. *Note:* Not all subdivisions listed here necessarily appear in this publication.

05 05 21 – Fastening Methods for Metal

05 05 21.15 Drilling Steel		Crew	Daily Output	Labor-Hours	Unit	Material	2012 Bare Costs Labor	Equipment	Total	Total Incl O&P
0010	**DRILLING STEEL**									
1910	Drilling & layout for steel, up to 1/4" deep, no anchor									
1920	Holes, 1/4" diameter	1 Sswk	112	.071	Ea.	.07	3.53		3.60	6.40
1925	For each additional 1/4" depth, add		336	.024		.07	1.18		1.25	2.18
1930	3/8" diameter		104	.077		.08	3.80		3.88	6.90
1935	For each additional 1/4" depth, add		312	.026		.08	1.27		1.35	2.35
1940	1/2" diameter		96	.083		.09	4.11		4.20	7.45
1945	For each additional 1/4" depth, add		288	.028		.09	1.37		1.46	2.54
1950	5/8" diameter		88	.091		.12	4.49		4.61	8.15
1955	For each additional 1/4" depth, add		264	.030		.12	1.50		1.62	2.80
1960	3/4" diameter		80	.100		.15	4.94		5.09	9
1965	For each additional 1/4" depth, add		240	.033		.15	1.64		1.79	3.11
1970	7/8" diameter		72	.111		.20	5.50		5.70	10
1975	For each additional 1/4" depth, add		216	.037		.20	1.83		2.03	3.49
1980	1" diameter		64	.125		.21	6.15		6.36	11.30
1985	For each additional 1/4" depth, add		192	.042		.21	2.06		2.27	3.91
1990	For drilling up, add						40%			

05 05 23 – Metal Fastenings

05 05 23.05 Anchor Bolts			Crew	Daily Output	Labor-Hours	Unit	Material	2012 Bare Costs Labor	Equipment	Total	Total Incl O&P
0010	**ANCHOR BOLTS**										
0015	Made from recycled materials	G									
0025	Single bolts installed in fresh concrete, no templates										
0030	Hooked w/nut and washer, 1/2" diameter, 8" long	G	1 Carp	132	.061	Ea.	1.39	2.67		4.06	5.65
0040	12" long	G		131	.061		1.54	2.69		4.23	5.85
0050	5/8" diameter, 8" long	G		129	.062		3	2.74		5.74	7.50
0060	12" long	G		127	.063		3.70	2.78		6.48	8.35
0070	3/4" diameter, 8" long	G		127	.063		3.70	2.78		6.48	8.35
0080	12" long	G		125	.064		4.62	2.82		7.44	9.45
0090	2-bolt pattern, including job-built 2-hole template, per set										
0100	J-type, incl. hex nut & washer, 1/2" diameter x 6" long	G	1 Carp	21	.381	Set	4.55	16.80		21.35	31
0110	12" long	G		21	.381		5.15	16.80		21.95	31.50
0120	18" long	G		21	.381		6.10	16.80		22.90	32.50
0130	3/4" diameter x 8" long	G		20	.400		9.50	17.65		27.15	37.50
0140	12" long	G		20	.400		11.35	17.65		29	39.50
0150	18" long	G		20	.400		14.10	17.65		31.75	42.50
0160	1" diameter x 12" long	G		19	.421		19.90	18.55		38.45	50.50
0170	18" long	G		19	.421		23.50	18.55		42.05	54.50
0180	24" long	G		19	.421		28.50	18.55		47.05	59.50
0190	36" long	G		18	.444		38	19.60		57.60	72
0200	1-1/2" diameter x 18" long	G		17	.471		60	21		81	98
0210	24" long	G		16	.500		71.50	22		93.50	113
0300	L-type, incl. hex nut & washer, 3/4" diameter x 12" long	G		20	.400		10.75	17.65		28.40	39
0310	18" long	G		20	.400		13.15	17.65		30.80	41.50
0320	24" long	G		20	.400		15.60	17.65		33.25	44
0330	30" long	G		20	.400		19.25	17.65		36.90	48
0340	36" long	G		20	.400		21.50	17.65		39.15	51
0350	1" diameter x 12" long	G		19	.421		16.95	18.55		35.50	47
0360	18" long	G		19	.421		20.50	18.55		39.05	51
0370	24" long	G		19	.421		25	18.55		43.55	56
0380	30" long	G		19	.421		29	18.55		47.55	60.50
0390	36" long	G		18	.444		33	19.60		52.60	66.50
0400	42" long	G		18	.444		39.50	19.60		59.10	73.50

05 05 23 – Metal Fastenings

05 05 23.05 Anchor Bolts			Crew	Daily Output	Labor-Hours	Unit	Material	2012 Bare Costs Labor	Equipment	Total	Total Incl O&P
0410	48" long	G	1 Carp	18	.444	Set	44	19.60		63.60	78.50
0420	1-1/4" diameter x 18" long	G		18	.444		30	19.60		49.60	63
0430	24" long	G		18	.444		35	19.60		54.60	69
0440	30" long	G		17	.471		40.50	21		61.50	76.50
0450	36" long	G		17	.471		45.50	21		66.50	82.50
0460	42" long	G	2 Carp	32	.500		51.50	22		73.50	90.50
0470	48" long	G		32	.500		58.50	22		80.50	98
0480	54" long	G		31	.516		68.50	23		91.50	110
0490	60" long	G		31	.516		75	23		98	118
0500	1-1/2" diameter x 18" long	G		33	.485		43.50	21.50		65	81
0510	24" long	G		32	.500		50.50	22		72.50	89.50
0520	30" long	G		31	.516		57	23		80	97.50
0540	42" long	G		30	.533		74	23.50		97.50	117
0550	48" long	G		29	.552		82.50	24.50		107	129
0560	54" long	G		28	.571		100	25		125	149
0570	60" long	G		28	.571		110	25		135	160
0580	1-3/4" diameter x 18" long	G		31	.516		61.50	23		84.50	103
0590	24" long	G		30	.533		72	23.50		95.50	115
0600	30" long	G		29	.552		83.50	24.50		108	129
0610	36" long	G		28	.571		95	25		120	143
0620	42" long	G		27	.593		106	26		132	157
0630	48" long	G		26	.615		116	27		143	170
0640	54" long	G		26	.615		144	27		171	200
0650	60" long	G		25	.640		155	28		183	215
0660	2" diameter x 24" long	G		27	.593		96.50	26		122.50	146
0670	30" long	G		27	.593		108	26		134	159
0680	36" long	G		26	.615		119	27		146	173
0690	42" long	G		25	.640		132	28		160	190
0700	48" long	G		24	.667		152	29.50		181.50	212
0710	54" long	G		23	.696		180	30.50		210.50	245
0720	60" long	G		23	.696		194	30.50		224.50	260
0730	66" long	G		22	.727		207	32		239	278
0740	72" long	G		21	.762		227	33.50		260.50	300
1000	4-bolt pattern, including job-built 4-hole template, per set										
1100	J-type, incl. hex nut & washer, 1/2" diameter x 6" long	G	1 Carp	19	.421	Set	7	18.55		25.55	36
1110	12" long	G		19	.421		8.25	18.55		26.80	37.50
1120	18" long	G		18	.444		10.10	19.60		29.70	41
1130	3/4" diameter x 8" long	G		17	.471		16.85	21		37.85	50.50
1140	12" long	G		17	.471		20.50	21		41.50	54.50
1150	18" long	G		17	.471		26	21		47	60.50
1160	1" diameter x 12" long	G		16	.500		38	22		60	75.50
1170	18" long	G		15	.533		45	23.50		68.50	85.50
1180	24" long	G		15	.533		54.50	23.50		78	96
1190	36" long	G		15	.533		74	23.50		97.50	118
1200	1-1/2" diameter x 18" long	G		13	.615		118	27		145	172
1210	24" long	G		12	.667		140	29.50		169.50	200
1300	L-type, incl. hex nut & washer, 3/4" diameter x 12" long	G		17	.471		19.35	21		40.35	53.50
1310	18" long	G		17	.471		24	21		45	58.50
1320	24" long	G		17	.471		29	21		50	64
1330	30" long	G		16	.500		36.50	22		58.50	74
1340	36" long	G		16	.500		41	22		63	79.50
1350	1" diameter x 12" long	G		16	.500		32	22		54	69
1360	18" long	G		15	.533		39	23.50		62.50	79

05 05 Common Work Results for Metals

05 05 23 – Metal Fastenings

05 05 23.05 Anchor Bolts

			Crew	Daily Output	Labor-Hours	Unit	Material	2012 Bare Costs Labor	Equipment	Total	Total Incl O&P
1370	24" long	G	1 Carp	15	.533	Set	48	23.50		71.50	88.50
1380	30" long	G		15	.533		56	23.50		79.50	97.50
1390	36" long	G		15	.533		64	23.50		87.50	107
1400	42" long	G		14	.571		77	25		102	124
1410	48" long	G		14	.571		86.50	25		111.50	134
1420	1-1/4" diameter x 18" long	G		14	.571		58	25		83	103
1430	24" long	G		14	.571		68.50	25		93.50	114
1440	30" long	G		13	.615		79	27		106	129
1450	36" long	G		13	.615		89.50	27		116.50	140
1460	42" long	G	2 Carp	25	.640		101	28		129	155
1470	48" long	G		24	.667		115	29.50		144.50	171
1480	54" long	G		23	.696		135	30.50		165.50	195
1490	60" long	G		23	.696		148	30.50		178.50	209
1500	1-1/2" diameter x 18" long	G		25	.640		85	28		113	137
1510	24" long	G		24	.667		99	29.50		128.50	154
1520	30" long	G		23	.696		112	30.50		142.50	170
1540	42" long	G		22	.727		146	32		178	210
1550	48" long	G		21	.762		163	33.50		196.50	231
1560	54" long	G		20	.800		198	35.50		233.50	273
1570	60" long	G		20	.800		217	35.50		252.50	294
1580	1-3/4" diameter x 18" long	G		22	.727		121	32		153	183
1590	24" long	G		21	.762		142	33.50		175.50	208
1600	30" long	G		21	.762		165	33.50		198.50	233
1610	36" long	G		20	.800		187	35.50		222.50	261
1620	42" long	G		19	.842		210	37		247	288
1630	48" long	G		18	.889		231	39		270	315
1640	54" long	G		18	.889		286	39		325	375
1650	60" long	G		17	.941		310	41.50		351.50	405
1660	2" diameter x 24" long	G		19	.842		191	37		228	267
1670	30" long	G		18	.889		215	39		254	297
1680	36" long	G		18	.889		236	39		275	320
1690	42" long	G		17	.941		263	41.50		304.50	355
1700	48" long	G		16	1		300	44		344	400
1710	54" long	G		15	1.067		360	47		407	470
1720	60" long	G		15	1.067		385	47		432	500
1730	66" long	G		14	1.143		410	50.50		460.50	535
1740	72" long	G		14	1.143		450	50.50		500.50	575
1990	For galvanized, add					Ea.	75%				

05 05 23.15 Chemical Anchors

0010	**CHEMICAL ANCHORS**										
0020	Includes layout & drilling										
1430	Chemical anchor, w/rod & epoxy cartridge, 3/4" diam. x 9-1/2" long		B-89A	27	.593	Ea.	8.55	24	4.08	36.63	51
1435	1" diameter x 11-3/4" long			24	.667		15.50	27	4.59	47.09	63.50
1440	1-1/4" diameter x 14" long			21	.762		32	30.50	5.25	67.75	88.50
1445	1-3/4" diameter x 15" long			20	.800		60	32	5.50	97.50	122
1450	18" long			17	.941		72	38	6.50	116.50	145
1455	2" diameter x 18" long			16	1		87	40.50	6.90	134.40	166
1460	24" long			15	1.067		113	43	7.35	163.35	198

05 05 23.20 Expansion Anchors

0010	**EXPANSION ANCHORS**										
0100	Anchors for concrete, brick or stone, no layout and drilling										
0200	Expansion shields, zinc, 1/4" diameter, 1-5/16" long, single	G	1 Carp	90	.089	Ea.	.42	3.92		4.34	6.50

44

05 05 23 – Metal Fastenings

05 05 23.20 Expansion Anchors		Crew	Daily Output	Labor-Hours	Unit	Material	2012 Bare Costs Labor	Equipment	Total	Total Incl O&P
0300	1-3/8" long, double	G 1 Carp	85	.094	Ea.	.54	4.15		4.69	7
0400	3/8" diameter, 1-1/2" long, single	G	85	.094		.73	4.15		4.88	7.20
0500	2" long, double	G	80	.100		1.17	4.41		5.58	8.10
0600	1/2" diameter, 2-1/16" long, single	G	80	.100		1.40	4.41		5.81	8.35
0700	2-1/2" long, double	G	75	.107		1.82	4.70		6.52	9.25
0800	5/8" diameter, 2-5/8" long, single	G	75	.107		2.54	4.70		7.24	10.05
0900	2-3/4" long, double	G	70	.114		2.59	5.05		7.64	10.60
1000	3/4" diameter, 2-3/4" long, single	G	70	.114		2.79	5.05		7.84	10.80
1100	3-15/16" long, double	G	65	.123		5	5.45		10.45	13.85
2100	Hollow wall anchors for gypsum wall board, plaster or tile									
2300	1/8" diameter, short	G 1 Carp	160	.050	Ea.	.20	2.21		2.41	3.61
2400	Long	G	150	.053		.23	2.35		2.58	3.87
2500	3/16" diameter, short	G	150	.053		.36	2.35		2.71	4.02
2600	Long	G	140	.057		.49	2.52		3.01	4.42
2700	1/4" diameter, short	G	140	.057		.53	2.52		3.05	4.46
2800	Long	G	130	.062		.53	2.71		3.24	4.76
3000	Toggle bolts, bright steel, 1/8" diameter, 2" long	G	85	.094		.18	4.15		4.33	6.60
3100	4" long	G	80	.100		.22	4.41		4.63	7.05
3200	3/16" diameter, 3" long	G	80	.100		.22	4.41		4.63	7.05
3300	6" long	G	75	.107		.32	4.70		5.02	7.60
3400	1/4" diameter, 3" long	G	75	.107		.28	4.70		4.98	7.55
3500	6" long	G	70	.114		.45	5.05		5.50	8.25
3600	3/8" diameter, 3" long	G	70	.114		.67	5.05		5.72	8.50
3700	6" long	G	60	.133		1.18	5.90		7.08	10.35
3800	1/2" diameter, 4" long	G	60	.133		1.69	5.90		7.59	10.90
3900	6" long	G	50	.160		2.08	7.05		9.13	13.15
5000	Screw anchors for concrete, masonry,									
5100	stone & tile, no layout or drilling included									
5700	Lag screw shields, 1/4" diameter, short	G 1 Carp	90	.089	Ea.	.32	3.92		4.24	6.40
5800	Long	G	85	.094		.39	4.15		4.54	6.85
5900	3/8" diameter, short	G	85	.094		.62	4.15		4.77	7.10
6000	Long	G	80	.100		.76	4.41		5.17	7.65
6100	1/2" diameter, short	G	80	.100		1.02	4.41		5.43	7.90
6200	Long	G	75	.107		1.24	4.70		5.94	8.60
6300	5/8" diameter, short	G	70	.114		1.63	5.05		6.68	9.55
6400	Long	G	65	.123		2.13	5.45		7.58	10.70
6600	Lead, #6 & #8, 3/4" long	G	260	.031		.16	1.36		1.52	2.27
6700	#10 - #14, 1-1/2" long	G	200	.040		.27	1.76		2.03	3.01
6800	#16 & #18, 1-1/2" long	G	160	.050		.32	2.21		2.53	3.74
6900	Plastic, #6 & #8, 3/4" long	G	260	.031		.04	1.36		1.40	2.13
7000	#8 & #10, 7/8" long	G	240	.033		.04	1.47		1.51	2.30
7100	#10 & #12, 1" long	G	220	.036		.05	1.60		1.65	2.53
7200	#14 & #16, 1-1/2" long	G	160	.050		.07	2.21		2.28	3.47
8000	Wedge anchors, not including layout or drilling									
8050	Carbon steel, 1/4" diameter, 1-3/4" long	G 1 Carp	150	.053	Ea.	.36	2.35		2.71	4.02
8100	3-1/4" long	G	140	.057		.48	2.52		3	4.41
8150	3/8" diameter, 2-1/4" long	G	145	.055		.44	2.43		2.87	4.22
8200	5" long	G	140	.057		.77	2.52		3.29	4.73
8250	1/2" diameter, 2-3/4" long	G	140	.057		.89	2.52		3.41	4.86
8300	7" long	G	125	.064		1.53	2.82		4.35	6
8350	5/8" diameter, 3-1/2" long	G	130	.062		1.60	2.71		4.31	5.95
8400	8-1/2" long	G	115	.070		3.40	3.07		6.47	8.45
8450	3/4" diameter, 4-1/4" long	G	115	.070		2.38	3.07		5.45	7.35

05 05 Common Work Results for Metals

05 05 23 – Metal Fastenings

05 05 23.20 Expansion Anchors		Crew	Daily Output	Labor-Hours	Unit	Material	2012 Bare Costs Labor	Equipment	Total	Total Incl O&P
8500	10" long	G 1 Carp	95	.084	Ea.	5.40	3.71		9.11	11.65
8550	1" diameter, 6" long	G	100	.080		8.60	3.53		12.13	14.90
8575	9" long	G	85	.094		11.20	4.15		15.35	18.70
8600	12" long	G	75	.107		12.05	4.70		16.75	20.50
8650	1-1/4" diameter, 9" long	G	70	.114		24	5.05		29.05	34
8700	12" long	G	60	.133		30.50	5.90		36.40	42.50
8750	For type 303 stainless steel, add					350%				
8800	For type 316 stainless steel, add					450%				
8950	Self-drilling concrete screw, hex washer head, 3/16" diam. x 1-3/4" long	G	1 Carp	300	.027	Ea.	.19	1.18		1.37	2.02
8960	2-1/4" long	G	250	.032		.20	1.41		1.61	2.39
8970	Phillips flat head, 3/16" diam. x 1-3/4" long	G	300	.027		.18	1.18		1.36	2.01
8980	2-1/4" long	G	250	.032		.20	1.41		1.61	2.39

05 05 23.30 Lag Screws										
0010	**LAG SCREWS**									
0020	Steel, 1/4" diameter, 2" long	G 1 Carp	200	.040	Ea.	.07	1.76		1.83	2.79
0100	3/8" diameter, 3" long	G	150	.053		.25	2.35		2.60	3.90
0200	1/2" diameter, 3" long	G	130	.062		.49	2.71		3.20	4.72
0300	5/8" diameter, 3" long	G	120	.067		1.01	2.94		3.95	5.65

05 05 23.35 Machine Screws										
0010	**MACHINE SCREWS**									
0020	Steel, round head, #8 x 1" long	G 1 Carp	4.80	1.667	C	3.76	73.50		77.26	117
0110	#8 x 2" long	G	2.40	3.333		5.85	147		152.85	232
0200	#10 x 1" long	G	4	2		5.85	88		93.85	142
0300	#10 x 2" long	G	2	4		7.95	176		183.95	280

05 05 23.40 Machinery Anchors										
0010	**MACHINERY ANCHORS**, heavy duty, incl. sleeve, floating base nut,									
0020	lower stud & coupling nut, fiber plug, connecting stud, washer & nut.									
0030	For flush mounted embedment in poured concrete heavy equip. pads.									
0200	Stud & bolt, 1/2" diameter	G E-16	40	.400	Ea.	68.50	20	3.04	91.54	115
0300	5/8" diameter	G	35	.457		76	23	3.47	102.47	128
0500	3/4" diameter	G	30	.533		87.50	27	4.05	118.55	149
0600	7/8" diameter	G	25	.640		95.50	32	4.86	132.36	168
0800	1" diameter	G	20	.800		100	40.50	6.10	146.60	189
0900	1-1/4" diameter	G	15	1.067		133	53.50	8.10	194.60	252

05 05 23.50 Powder Actuated Tools and Fasteners										
0010	**POWDER ACTUATED TOOLS & FASTENERS**									
0020	Stud driver, .22 caliber, buy, minimum				Ea.	95			95	105
0100	Maximum				"	370			370	405
0300	Powder charges for above, low velocity				C	5.10			5.10	5.65
0400	Standard velocity					7			7	7.70
0600	Drive pins & studs, 1/4" & 3/8" diam., to 3" long, minimum	G 1 Carp	4.80	1.667		4.75	73.50		78.25	118
0700	Maximum	G "	4	2		11.40	88		99.40	149

05 05 23.55 Rivets										
0010	**RIVETS**									
0100	Aluminum rivet & mandrel, 1/2" grip length x 1/8" diameter	G 1 Carp	4.80	1.667	C	6.65	73.50		80.15	120
0200	3/16" diameter	G	4	2		11.75	88		99.75	149
0300	Aluminum rivet, steel mandrel, 1/8" diameter	G	4.80	1.667		9.10	73.50		82.60	123
0400	3/16" diameter	G	4	2		14.60	88		102.60	152
0500	Copper rivet, steel mandrel, 1/8" diameter	G	4.80	1.667		8.35	73.50		81.85	122
1200	Steel rivet and mandrel, 1/8" diameter	G	4.80	1.667		8.05	73.50		81.55	122
1300	3/16" diameter	G	4	2		11.20	88		99.20	148

05 05 Common Work Results for Metals

05 05 23 – Metal Fastenings

05 05 23.55 Rivets

		Crew	Daily Output	Labor-Hours	Unit	Material	2012 Bare Costs Labor	Equipment	Total	Total Incl O&P
1400	Hand riveting tool, minimum				Ea.	65.50			65.50	72
1500	Maximum					271			271	298
1600	Power riveting tool, minimum					475			475	525
1700	Maximum					2,650			2,650	2,925

05 05 23.70 Structural Blind Bolts

			Crew	Daily Output	Labor-Hours	Unit	Material	Labor	Equipment	Total	Total Incl O&P
0010	**STRUCTURAL BLIND BOLTS**										
0100	1/4" diameter x 1/4" grip	G	1 Sswk	240	.033	Ea.	1.24	1.64		2.88	4.30
0150	1/2" grip	G		216	.037		1.33	1.83		3.16	4.73
0200	3/8" diameter x 1/2" grip	G		232	.034		1.75	1.70		3.45	4.97
0250	3/4" grip	G		208	.038		1.83	1.90		3.73	5.40
0300	1/2" diameter x 1/2" grip	G		224	.036		5.15	1.76		6.91	8.80
0350	3/4" grip	G		200	.040		5.60	1.97		7.57	9.70
0400	5/8" diameter x 3/4" grip	G		216	.037		8.25	1.83		10.08	12.35
0450	1" grip	G		192	.042		9.50	2.06		11.56	14.15

05 12 Structural Steel Framing

05 12 23 – Structural Steel for Buildings

05 12 23.40 Lightweight Framing

			Crew	Daily Output	Labor-Hours	Unit	Material	Labor	Equipment	Total	Total Incl O&P
0010	**LIGHTWEIGHT FRAMING**										
0015	Made from recycled materials	G									
0400	Angle framing, field fabricated, 4" and larger	G	E-3	440	.055	Lb.	.73	2.73	.28	3.74	6
0450	Less than 4" angles	G		265	.091		.75	4.53	.46	5.74	9.45
0600	Channel framing, field fabricated, 8" and larger	G		500	.048		.75	2.40	.24	3.39	5.40
0650	Less than 8" channels	G		335	.072		.75	3.58	.36	4.69	7.65
1000	Continuous slotted channel framing system, shop fab, minimum	G	2 Sswk	2400	.007		3.88	.33		4.21	4.85
1200	Maximum	G	"	1600	.010		4.38	.49		4.87	5.70
1250	Plate & bar stock for reinforcing beams and trusses	G					1.38			1.38	1.51
1300	Cross bracing, rods, shop fabricated, 3/4" diameter	G	E-3	700	.034		1.50	1.72	.17	3.39	4.91
1310	7/8" diameter	G		850	.028		1.50	1.41	.14	3.05	4.34
1320	1" diameter	G		1000	.024		1.50	1.20	.12	2.82	3.93
1330	Angle, 5" x 5" x 3/8"	G		2800	.009		1.50	.43	.04	1.97	2.47
1350	Hanging lintels, shop fabricated, average	G		850	.028		1.50	1.41	.14	3.05	4.34
1380	Roof frames, shop fabricated, 3'-0" square, 5' span	G	E-2	4200	.013		1.50	.64	.36	2.50	3.14
1400	Tie rod, not upset, 1-1/2" to 4" diameter, with turnbuckle	G	2 Sswk	800	.020		1.63	.99		2.62	3.56
1420	No turnbuckle	G		700	.023		1.56	1.13		2.69	3.74
1500	Upset, 1-3/4" to 4" diameter, with turnbuckle	G		800	.020		1.63	.99		2.62	3.56
1520	No turnbuckle	G		700	.023		1.56	1.13		2.69	3.74

05 12 23.60 Pipe Support Framing

			Crew	Daily Output	Labor-Hours	Unit	Material	Labor	Equipment	Total	Total Incl O&P
0010	**PIPE SUPPORT FRAMING**										
0020	Under 10#/L.F., shop fabricated	G	E-4	3900	.008	Lb.	1.68	.41	.03	2.12	2.60
0200	10.1 to 15#/L.F.	G		4300	.007		1.65	.37	.03	2.05	2.51
0400	15.1 to 20#/L.F.	G		4800	.007		1.63	.33	.03	1.99	2.41
0600	Over 20#/L.F.	G		5400	.006		1.60	.30	.02	1.92	2.31

Division Notes

	CREW	DAILY OUTPUT	LABOR-HOURS	UNIT	2012 BARE COSTS				TOTAL INCL O&P
					MAT.	LABOR	EQUIP.	TOTAL	

Estimating Tips

06 05 00 Common Work Results for Wood, Plastics, and Composites

- Common to any wood-framed structure are the accessory connector items such as screws, nails, adhesives, hangers, connector plates, straps, angles, and hold-downs. For typical wood-framed buildings, such as residential projects, the aggregate total for these items can be significant, especially in areas where seismic loading is a concern. For floor and wall framing, the material cost is based on 10 to 25 lbs. per MBF. Hold-downs, hangers, and other connectors should be taken off by the piece.

  Included with material costs are fasteners for a normal installation. RSMeans engineers use manufacturer's recommendations, written specifications, and/or standard construction practice for size and spacing of fasteners. Prices for various fasteners are shown for informational purposes only. Adjustments should be made if unusual fastening conditions exist.

06 10 00 Carpentry

- Lumber is a traded commodity and therefore sensitive to supply and demand in the marketplace. Even in "budgetary" estimating of wood-framed projects, it is advisable to call local suppliers for the latest market pricing.

- Common quantity units for wood-framed projects are "thousand board feet" (MBF). A board foot is a volume of wood, 1" x 1' x 1', or 144 cubic inches. Board-foot quantities are generally calculated using nominal material dimensions—dressed sizes are ignored. Board foot per lineal foot of any stick of lumber can be calculated by dividing the nominal cross-sectional area by 12. As an example, 2,000 lineal feet of 2 x 12 equates to 4 MBF by dividing the nominal area, 2 x 12, by 12, which equals 2, and multiplying by 2,000 to give 4,000 board feet. This simple rule applies to all nominal dimensioned lumber.

- Waste is an issue of concern at the quantity takeoff for any area of construction. Framing lumber is sold in even foot lengths, i.e., 10', 12', 14', 16', and depending on spans, wall heights, and the grade of lumber, waste is inevitable. A rule of thumb for lumber waste is 5%–10% depending on material quality and the complexity of the framing.

- Wood in various forms and shapes is used in many projects, even where the main structural framing is steel, concrete, or masonry. Plywood as a back-up partition material and 2x boards used as blocking and cant strips around roof edges are two common examples. The estimator should ensure that the costs of all wood materials are included in the final estimate.

06 20 00 Finish Carpentry

- It is necessary to consider the grade of workmanship when estimating labor costs for erecting millwork and interior finish. In practice, there are three grades: premium, custom, and economy. The RSMeans daily output for base and case moldings is in the range of 200 to 250 L.F. per carpenter per day. This is appropriate for most average custom-grade projects. For premium projects, an adjustment to productivity of 25%–50% should be made, depending on the complexity of the job.

Reference Numbers

Reference numbers are shown in shaded boxes at the beginning of some major classifications. These numbers refer to related items in the Reference Section. The reference information may be an estimating procedure, an alternate pricing method, or technical information.

Note: Not all subdivisions listed here necessarily appear in this publication.

Division 6 - Wood, Plastics, and Composites

06 05 23 – Wood, Plastic, and Composite Fastenings

06 05 23.10 Nails

		Crew	Daily Output	Labor-Hours	Unit	Material	2012 Bare Costs Labor	Equipment	Total	Total Incl O&P
0010	**NAILS**, material only, based upon 50# box purchase									
0020	Copper nails, plain				Lb.	10			10	11
0400	Stainless steel, plain					7.80			7.80	8.60
0500	Box, 3d to 20d, bright					1.25			1.25	1.38
0520	Galvanized					1.77			1.77	1.95
0600	Common, 3d to 60d, plain					1.30			1.30	1.43
0700	Galvanized					1.56			1.56	1.72
0800	Aluminum					5.80			5.80	6.40
1000	Annular or spiral thread, 4d to 60d, plain					1.80			1.80	1.98
1200	Galvanized					3			3	3.30
1400	Drywall nails, plain					3.59			3.59	3.95
1600	Galvanized					2.19			2.19	2.41
1800	Finish nails, 4d to 10d, plain					1.36			1.36	1.50
2000	Galvanized					1.79			1.79	1.97
2100	Aluminum					5.80			5.80	6.40
2300	Flooring nails, hardened steel, 2d to 10d, plain					3.10			3.10	3.41
2400	Galvanized					4			4	4.40
2500	Gypsum lath nails, 1-1/8", 13 ga. flathead, blued					3.59			3.59	3.95
2600	Masonry nails, hardened steel, 3/4" to 3" long, plain					2.20			2.20	2.42
2700	Galvanized					3.75			3.75	4.13
5000	Add to prices above for cement coating					.11			.11	.12
5200	Zinc or tin plating					.14			.14	.15
5500	Vinyl coated sinkers, 8d to 16d					.65			.65	.72

06 05 23.40 Sheet Metal Screws

		Crew	Daily Output	Labor-Hours	Unit	Material	2012 Bare Costs Labor	Equipment	Total	Total Incl O&P
0010	**SHEET METAL SCREWS**									
0020	Steel, standard, #8 x 3/4", plain				C	2.92			2.92	3.21
0100	Galvanized					2.92			2.92	3.21
0300	#10 x 1", plain					4.03			4.03	4.43
0400	Galvanized					4.03			4.03	4.43
0600	With washers, #14 x 1", plain					12.35			12.35	13.60
0700	Galvanized					12.35			12.35	13.60
0900	#14 x 2", plain					16.90			16.90	18.60
1000	Galvanized					16.90			16.90	18.60
1500	Self-drilling, with washers, (pinch point) #8 x 3/4", plain					7.80			7.80	8.55
1600	Galvanized					7.80			7.80	8.55
1800	#10 x 3/4", plain					8.90			8.90	9.80
1900	Galvanized					8.90			8.90	9.80
3000	Stainless steel w/aluminum or neoprene washers, #14 x 1", plain					30			30	33
3100	#14 x 2", plain					40			40	44

06 05 23.50 Wood Screws

		Crew	Daily Output	Labor-Hours	Unit	Material	2012 Bare Costs Labor	Equipment	Total	Total Incl O&P
0010	**WOOD SCREWS**									
0020	#8 x 1" long, steel				C	3.41			3.41	3.75
0100	Brass					10.50			10.50	11.55
0200	#8, 2" long, steel					5.25			5.25	5.80
0300	Brass					19.95			19.95	22
0400	#10, 1" long, steel					3.65			3.65	4.02
0500	Brass					14.15			14.15	15.60
0600	#10, 2" long, steel					5.85			5.85	6.45
0700	Brass					24.50			24.50	27
0800	#10, 3" long, steel					9.80			9.80	10.75
1000	#12, 2" long, steel					8.05			8.05	8.85
1100	Brass					29.50			29.50	32

06 05 Common Work Results for Wood, Plastics, and Composites

06 05 23 – Wood, Plastic, and Composite Fastenings

06 05 23.50 Wood Screws		Crew	Daily Output	Labor-Hours	Unit	Material	2012 Bare Costs			Total	Total Incl O&P
							Labor	Equipment			
1500	#12, 3" long, steel				C	11.65				11.65	12.80
2000	#12, 4" long, steel				↓	21.50				21.50	23.50

06 16 Sheathing

06 16 36 – Wood Panel Product Sheathing

06 16 36.10 Sheathing

		Crew	Daily Output	Labor-Hours	Unit	Material	2012 Bare Costs			Total	Total Incl O&P
							Labor	Equipment			
0010	**SHEATHING**										
0012	Plywood on roofs, CDX										
0030	5/16" thick	2 Carp	1600	.010	S.F.	.55	.44			.99	1.28
0035	Pneumatic nailed		1952	.008		.55	.36			.91	1.16
0050	3/8" thick		1525	.010		.47	.46			.93	1.23
0055	Pneumatic nailed		1860	.009		.47	.38			.85	1.10
0100	1/2" thick		1400	.011		.47	.50			.97	1.30
0105	Pneumatic nailed		1708	.009		.47	.41			.88	1.16
0200	5/8" thick		1300	.012		.62	.54			1.16	1.52
0205	Pneumatic nailed		1586	.010		.62	.45			1.07	1.36
0300	3/4" thick		1200	.013		.70	.59			1.29	1.67
0305	Pneumatic nailed		1464	.011		.70	.48			1.18	1.51
0500	Plywood on walls with exterior CDX, 3/8" thick		1200	.013		.47	.59			1.06	1.42
0505	Pneumatic nailed		1488	.011		.47	.47			.94	1.25
0600	1/2" thick		1125	.014		.47	.63			1.10	1.48
0605	Pneumatic nailed		1395	.011		.47	.51			.98	1.30
0700	5/8" thick		1050	.015		.62	.67			1.29	1.71
0705	Pneumatic nailed		1302	.012		.62	.54			1.16	1.51
0800	3/4" thick		975	.016		.70	.72			1.42	1.88
0805	Pneumatic nailed	↓	1209	.013	↓	.70	.58			1.28	1.67

Division Notes

		CREW	DAILY OUTPUT	LABOR-HOURS	UNIT	2012 BARE COSTS				TOTAL INCL O&P
						MAT.	LABOR	EQUIP.	TOTAL	

Estimating Tips

07 10 00 Dampproofing and Waterproofing

- Be sure of the job specifications before pricing this subdivision. The difference in cost between waterproofing and dampproofing can be great. Waterproofing will hold back standing water. Dampproofing prevents the transmission of water vapor. Also included in this section are vapor retarding membranes.

07 20 00 Thermal Protection

- Insulation and fireproofing products are measured by area, thickness, volume or R-value. Specifications may give only what the specific R-value should be in a certain situation. The estimator may need to choose the type of insulation to meet that R-value.

07 30 00 Steep Slope Roofing
07 40 00 Roofing and Siding Panels

- Many roofing and siding products are bought and sold by the square. One square is equal to an area that measures 100 square feet.

This simple change in unit of measure could create a large error if the estimator is not observant. Accessories necessary for a complete installation must be figured into any calculations for both material and labor.

07 50 00 Membrane Roofing
07 60 00 Flashing and Sheet Metal
07 70 00 Roofing and Wall Specialties and Accessories

- The items in these subdivisions compose a roofing system. No one component completes the installation, and all must be estimated. Built-up or single-ply membrane roofing systems are made up of many products and installation trades. Wood blocking at roof perimeters or penetrations, parapet coverings, reglets, roof drains, gutters, downspouts, sheet metal flashing, skylights, smoke vents, and roof hatches all need to be considered along with the roofing material. Several different installation trades will need to work together on the roofing system. Inherent difficulties in the scheduling and coordination of various trades must be accounted for when estimating labor costs.

07 90 00 Joint Protection

- To complete the weather-tight shell, the sealants and caulkings must be estimated. Where different materials meet—at expansion joints, at flashing penetrations, and at hundreds of other locations throughout a construction project—they provide another line of defense against water penetration. Often, an entire system is based on the proper location and placement of caulking or sealants. The detailed drawings that are included as part of a set of architectural plans show typical locations for these materials. When caulking or sealants are shown at typical locations, this means the estimator must include them for all the locations where this detail is applicable. Be careful to keep different types of sealants separate, and remember to consider backer rods and primers if necessary.

Reference Numbers

Reference numbers are shown in shaded boxes at the beginning of some major classifications. These numbers refer to related items in the Reference Section. The reference information may be an estimating procedure, an alternate pricing method, or technical information.

Note: Not all subdivisions listed here necessarily appear in this publication.

07 65 Flexible Flashing

07 65 10 – Sheet Metal Flashing

07 65 10.10 Sheet Metal Flashing and Counter Flashing	Crew	Daily Output	Labor-Hours	Unit	Material	2012 Bare Costs Labor	Equipment	Total	Total Incl O&P
0010 **SHEET METAL FLASHING AND COUNTER FLASHING**									
0011 Including up to 4 bends									
0020 Aluminum, mill finish, .013" thick	1 Rofc	145	.055	S.F.	.73	2.06		2.79	4.26
0030 .016" thick		145	.055		.84	2.06		2.90	4.38
0060 .019" thick		145	.055		1.07	2.06		3.13	4.64
0100 .032" thick		145	.055		1.25	2.06		3.31	4.84
0200 .040" thick		145	.055		2.14	2.06		4.20	5.80
0300 .050" thick		145	.055		2.25	2.06		4.31	5.95
0400 Painted finish, add					.34			.34	.37
1600 Copper, 16 oz., sheets, under 1000 lb.	1 Rofc	115	.070		7.85	2.60		10.45	13
1700 Over 4000 lb.		155	.052		7.85	1.93		9.78	11.90
1900 20 oz. sheets, under 1000 lb.		110	.073		9.85	2.72		12.57	15.40
2000 Over 4000 lb.		145	.055		9.35	2.06		11.41	13.75
2200 24 oz. sheets, under 1000 lb.		105	.076		12.10	2.85		14.95	18.15
2300 Over 4000 lb.		135	.059		11.50	2.22		13.72	16.35
2500 32 oz. sheets, under 1000 lb.		100	.080		16.15	2.99		19.14	23
2600 Over 4000 lb.		130	.062		15.35	2.30		17.65	21
5800 Lead, 2.5 lb. per S.F., up to 12" wide		135	.059		5.40	2.22		7.62	9.65
5900 Over 12" wide		135	.059		4.43	2.22		6.65	8.60
8900 Stainless steel sheets, 32 ga, .010" thick		155	.052		4	1.93		5.93	7.65
9000 28 ga, .015" thick		155	.052		5.65	1.93		7.58	9.45
9100 26 ga, .018" thick		155	.052		7.25	1.93		9.18	11.25
9200 24 ga, .025" thick		155	.052		8.90	1.93		10.83	13.05
9400 Terne coated stainless steel, .015" thick, 28 ga		155	.052		7.35	1.93		9.28	11.35
9500 .018" thick, 26 ga		155	.052		8.30	1.93		10.23	12.35
9600 Zinc and copper alloy (brass), .020" thick		155	.052		11.10	1.93		13.03	15.45
9700 .027" thick		155	.052		15.60	1.93		17.53	20.50
9800 .032" thick		155	.052		18.80	1.93		20.73	23.50
9900 .040" thick		155	.052		21	1.93		22.93	26

07 65 13 – Laminated Sheet Flashing

07 65 13.10 Laminated Sheet Flashing

	Crew	Daily Output	Labor-Hours	Unit	Material	2012 Bare Costs Labor	Equipment	Total	Total Incl O&P
0010 **LAMINATED SHEET FLASHING**, Including up to 4 bends									
4300 Copper-clad stainless steel, .015" thick, under 500 lb.	1 Rofc	115	.070	S.F.	5.80	2.60		8.40	10.75
4400 Over 2000 lb.		155	.052		5.55	1.93		7.48	9.35
4600 .018" thick, under 500 lb.		100	.080		6.55	2.99		9.54	12.20
4700 Over 2000 lb.		145	.055		6.20	2.06		8.26	10.30
8550 3 ply copper and fabric, 3 oz.		155	.052		2.19	1.93		4.12	5.65
8600 7 oz.		155	.052		3.25	1.93		5.18	6.80
8700 Lead on copper and fabric, 5 oz.		155	.052		3.04	1.93		4.97	6.60
8800 7 oz.		155	.052		5.25	1.93		7.18	9.05

07 65 19 – Plastic Sheet Flashing

07 65 19.10 Plastic Sheet Flashing and Counter Flashing

	Crew	Daily Output	Labor-Hours	Unit	Material	2012 Bare Costs Labor	Equipment	Total	Total Incl O&P
0010 **PLASTIC SHEET FLASHING AND COUNTER FLASHING**									
7300 Polyvinyl chloride, black, .010" thick	1 Rofc	285	.028	S.F.	.21	1.05		1.26	1.99
7400 .020" thick		285	.028		.30	1.05		1.35	2.09
7600 .030" thick		285	.028		.39	1.05		1.44	2.19
7700 .056" thick		285	.028		.94	1.05		1.99	2.79
7900 Black or white for exposed roofs, .060" thick		285	.028		2	1.05		3.05	3.96
8060 PVC tape, 5" x 45 mils, for joint covers, 100 L.F./roll				Ea.	136			136	150
8850 Polyvinyl chloride, .030" thick	1 Rofc	160	.050	S.F.	.44	1.87		2.31	3.62

07 71 Roof Specialties

07 71 23 – Manufactured Gutters and Downspouts

07 71 23.10 Downspouts		Crew	Daily Output	Labor-Hours	Unit	Material	2012 Bare Costs Labor	Equipment	Total	Total Incl O&P
0010	**DOWNSPOUTS**									
0020	Aluminum 2" x 3", .020" thick, embossed	1 Shee	190	.042	L.F.	.97	2.20		3.17	4.42
0100	Enameled		190	.042		1.26	2.20		3.46	4.74
4800	Steel, galvanized, round, corrugated, 2" or 3" diameter, 28 gauge		190	.042		1.84	2.20		4.04	5.35
4900	4" diameter, 28 gauge		145	.055		2.54	2.88		5.42	7.20
5100	5" diameter, 28 gauge		130	.062		3.61	3.21		6.82	8.85
5200	26 gauge		130	.062		4	3.21		7.21	9.30
5400	6" diameter, 28 gauge		105	.076		4	3.97		7.97	10.45
5500	26 gauge		105	.076		5.80	3.97		9.77	12.45

07 72 Roof Accessories

07 72 26 – Ridge Vents

07 72 26.10 Ridge Vents and Accessories		Crew	Daily Output	Labor-Hours	Unit	Material	2012 Bare Costs Labor	Equipment	Total	Total Incl O&P
0010	**RIDGE VENTS AND ACCESSORIES**									
2300	Ridge vent strip, mill finish	1 Shee	155	.052	L.F.	2.95	2.69		5.64	7.35

07 72 53 – Snow Guards

07 72 53.10 Snow Guard Options		Crew	Daily Output	Labor-Hours	Unit	Material	2012 Bare Costs Labor	Equipment	Total	Total Incl O&P
0010	**SNOW GUARD OPTIONS**									
0100	Slate & asphalt shingle roofs, fastened with nails	1 Rofc	160	.050	Ea.	9.40	1.87		11.27	13.50
0200	Standing seam metal roofs, fastened with set screws		48	.167		15.60	6.25		21.85	27.50
0300	Surface mount for metal roofs, fastened with solder		48	.167		6.05	6.25		12.30	17.10
0400	Double rail pipe type, including pipe		130	.062	L.F.	22.50	2.30		24.80	29

07 72 73 – Pitch Pockets

07 72 73.10 Pitch Pockets, Variable Sizes		Crew	Daily Output	Labor-Hours	Unit	Material	2012 Bare Costs Labor	Equipment	Total	Total Incl O&P
0010	**PITCH POCKETS, VARIABLE SIZES**									
0100	Adjustable, 4" to 7", welded corners, 4" deep	1 Rofc	48	.167	Ea.	15	6.25		21.25	27
0200	Side extenders, 6"	"	240	.033	"	2	1.25		3.25	4.29

07 84 Firestopping

07 84 13 – Penetration Firestopping

07 84 13.10 Firestopping			Crew	Daily Output	Labor-Hours	Unit	Material	2012 Bare Costs Labor	Equipment	Total	Total Incl O&P
0010	**FIRESTOPPING**	R078413-30									
0100	Metallic piping, non insulated										
0110	Through walls, 2" diameter		1 Carp	16	.500	Ea.	14.65	22		36.65	50
0120	4" diameter			14	.571		22.50	25		47.50	63.50
0130	6" diameter			12	.667		30	29.50		59.50	78
0140	12" diameter			10	.800		53	35.50		88.50	113
0150	Through floors, 2" diameter			32	.250		8.85	11.05		19.90	26.50
0160	4" diameter			28	.286		12.75	12.60		25.35	33.50
0170	6" diameter			24	.333		16.75	14.70		31.45	41
0180	12" diameter			20	.400		28.50	17.65		46.15	58
0190	Metallic piping, insulated										
0200	Through walls, 2" diameter		1 Carp	16	.500	Ea.	20.50	22		42.50	57
0210	4" diameter			14	.571		28.50	25		53.50	70
0220	6" diameter			12	.667		36	29.50		65.50	84.50
0230	12" diameter			10	.800		59	35.50		94.50	120
0240	Through floors, 2" diameter			32	.250		15	11.05		26.05	33.50
0250	4" diameter			28	.286		18.85	12.60		31.45	40

07 84 13.10 Firestopping		Crew	Daily Output	Labor-Hours	Unit	Material	2012 Bare Costs Labor	Equipment	Total	Total Incl O&P
0260	6" diameter	1 Carp	24	.333	Ea.	23	14.70		37.70	47.50
0270	12" diameter		20	.400		28.50	17.65		46.15	58
0280	Non metallic piping, non insulated									
0290	Through walls, 2" diameter	1 Carp	12	.667	Ea.	60	29.50		89.50	112
0300	4" diameter		10	.800		75.50	35.50		111	138
0310	6" diameter		8	1		105	44		149	184
0330	Through floors, 2" diameter		16	.500		47	22		69	86
0340	4" diameter		6	1.333		58.50	59		117.50	155
0350	6" diameter		6	1.333		70.50	59		129.50	168
0370	Ductwork, insulated & non insulated, round									
0380	Through walls, 6" diameter	1 Carp	12	.667	Ea.	30.50	29.50		60	79
0390	12" diameter		10	.800		61	35.50		96.50	122
0400	18" diameter		8	1		99	44		143	177
0410	Through floors, 6" diameter		16	.500		16.75	22		38.75	52.50
0420	12" diameter		14	.571		30.50	25		55.50	73
0430	18" diameter		12	.667		53	29.50		82.50	104
0440	Ductwork, insulated & non insulated, rectangular									
0450	With stiffener/closure angle, through walls, 6" x 12"	1 Carp	8	1	Ea.	25.50	44		69.50	96
0460	12" x 24"		6	1.333		33.50	59		92.50	128
0470	24" x 48"		4	2		96.50	88		184.50	242
0480	With stiffener/closure angle, through floors, 6" x 12"		10	.800		13.75	35.50		49.25	69.50
0490	12" x 24"		8	1		25	44		69	95.50
0500	24" x 48"		6	1.333		48.50	59		107.50	144
0510	Multi trade openings									
0520	Through walls, 6" x 12"	1 Carp	2	4	Ea.	53	176		229	330
0530	12" x 24"	"	1	8		215	355		570	780
0540	24" x 48"	2 Carp	1	16		860	705		1,565	2,025
0550	48" x 96"	"	.75	21.333		3,450	940		4,390	5,250
0560	Through floors, 6" x 12"	1 Carp	2	4		53	176		229	330
0570	12" x 24"	"	1	8		215	355		570	780
0580	24" x 48"	2 Carp	.75	21.333		860	940		1,800	2,400
0590	48" x 96"	"	.50	32		3,450	1,400		4,850	5,975
0600	Structural penetrations, through walls									
0610	Steel beams, W8 x 10	1 Carp	8	1	Ea.	33.50	44		77.50	105
0620	W12 x 14		6	1.333		53	59		112	149
0630	W21 x 44		5	1.600		107	70.50		177.50	227
0640	W36 x 135		3	2.667		260	118		378	465
0650	Bar joists, 18" deep		6	1.333		49	59		108	145
0660	24" deep		6	1.333		61	59		120	158
0670	36" deep		5	1.600		91.50	70.50		162	210
0680	48" deep		4	2		107	88		195	254
0690	Construction joints, floor slab at exterior wall									
0700	Precast, brick, block or drywall exterior									
0710	2" wide joint	1 Carp	125	.064	L.F.	7.60	2.82		10.42	12.75
0720	4" wide joint	"	75	.107	"	15.25	4.70		19.95	24
0730	Metal panel, glass or curtain wall exterior									
0740	2" wide joint	1 Carp	40	.200	L.F.	18.05	8.80		26.85	33.50
0750	4" wide joint	"	25	.320	"	25	14.10		39.10	49
0760	Floor slab to drywall partition									
0770	Flat joint	1 Carp	100	.080	L.F.	7.50	3.53		11.03	13.70
0780	Fluted joint		50	.160		15.25	7.05		22.30	27.50
0790	Etched fluted joint		75	.107		9.90	4.70		14.60	18.15
0800	Floor slab to concrete/masonry partition									

07 84 Firestopping

07 84 13 – Penetration Firestopping

07 84 13.10 Firestopping		Crew	Daily Output	Labor-Hours	Unit	Material	2012 Bare Costs Labor	2012 Bare Costs Equipment	Total	Total Incl O&P
0810	Flat joint	1 Carp	75	.107	L.F.	16.75	4.70		21.45	25.50
0820	Fluted joint	"	50	.160	"	19.85	7.05		26.90	33
0830	Concrete/CMU wall joints									
0840	1" wide	1 Carp	100	.080	L.F.	9.15	3.53		12.68	15.50
0850	2" wide		75	.107		16.75	4.70		21.45	25.50
0860	4" wide	↓	50	.160	↓	32	7.05		39.05	46
0870	Concrete/CMU floor joints									
0880	1" wide	1 Carp	200	.040	L.F.	4.59	1.76		6.35	7.75
0890	2" wide	↓	150	.053		8.40	2.35		10.75	12.80
0900	4" wide	↓	100	.080	↓	16	3.53		19.53	23

07 91 Preformed Joint Seals

07 91 13 – Compression Seals

07 91 13.10 Compression Seals

		Crew	Daily Output	Labor-Hours	Unit	Material	2012 Bare Costs Labor	2012 Bare Costs Equipment	Total	Total Incl O&P
0010	**COMPRESSION SEALS**									
4900	O-ring type cord, 1/4"	1 Bric	472	.017	L.F.	.48	.75		1.23	1.66
4910	1/2"		440	.018		1.79	.80		2.59	3.18
4920	3/4"		424	.019		3.62	.83		4.45	5.25
4930	1"		408	.020		6.95	.86		7.81	8.95
4940	1-1/4"		384	.021		13.75	.92		14.67	16.50
4950	1-1/2"		368	.022		17.40	.96		18.36	20.50
4960	1-3/4"		352	.023		36.50	1		37.50	41.50
4970	2"	↓	344	.023	↓	64.50	1.03		65.53	72

07 91 16 – Joint Gaskets

07 91 16.10 Joint Gaskets

		Crew	Daily Output	Labor-Hours	Unit	Material	2012 Bare Costs Labor	2012 Bare Costs Equipment	Total	Total Incl O&P
0010	**JOINT GASKETS**									
4400	Joint gaskets, neoprene, closed cell w/adh, 1/8" x 3/8"	1 Bric	240	.033	L.F.	.27	1.47		1.74	2.52
4500	1/4" x 3/4"		215	.037		.59	1.64		2.23	3.13
4700	1/2" x 1"		200	.040		1.31	1.76		3.07	4.10
4800	3/4" x 1-1/2"	↓	165	.048	↓	1.45	2.14		3.59	4.83

07 91 23 – Backer Rods

07 91 23.10 Backer Rods

		Crew	Daily Output	Labor-Hours	Unit	Material	2012 Bare Costs Labor	2012 Bare Costs Equipment	Total	Total Incl O&P
0010	**BACKER RODS**									
0030	Backer rod, polyethylene, 1/4" diameter	1 Bric	4.60	1.739	C.L.F.	2.75	76.50		79.25	119
0050	1/2" diameter		4.60	1.739		5.65	76.50		82.15	122
0070	3/4" diameter		4.60	1.739		7.30	76.50		83.80	124
0090	1" diameter	↓	4.60	1.739	↓	13.65	76.50		90.15	131

07 91 26 – Joint Fillers

07 91 26.10 Joint Fillers

		Crew	Daily Output	Labor-Hours	Unit	Material	2012 Bare Costs Labor	2012 Bare Costs Equipment	Total	Total Incl O&P
0010	**JOINT FILLERS**									
4360	Butyl rubber filler, 1/4" x 1/4"	1 Bric	290	.028	L.F.	.14	1.22		1.36	2
4365	1/2" x 1/2"		250	.032		.57	1.41		1.98	2.76
4370	1/2" x 3/4"		210	.038		.86	1.68		2.54	3.48
4375	3/4" x 3/4"		230	.035		1.28	1.53		2.81	3.73
4380	1" x 1"	↓	180	.044	↓	1.71	1.96		3.67	4.84
4390	For coloring, add					12%				
4980	Polyethylene joint backing, 1/4" x 2"	1 Bric	2.08	3.846	C.L.F.	12	170		182	269
4990	1/4" x 6"		1.28	6.250	"	28	276		304	445
5600	Silicone, room temp vulcanizing foam seal, 1/4" x 1/2"	↓	1312	.006	L.F.	.31	.27		.58	.76

07 91 Preformed Joint Seals

07 91 26 – Joint Fillers

07 91 26.10 Joint Fillers

		Crew	Daily Output	Labor-Hours	Unit	Material	2012 Bare Costs Labor	Equipment	Total	Total Incl O&P
5610	1/2" x 1/2"	1 Bric	656	.012	L.F.	.63	.54		1.17	1.50
5620	1/2" x 3/4"		442	.018		.94	.80		1.74	2.25
5630	3/4" x 3/4"		328	.024		1.41	1.08		2.49	3.17
5640	1/8" x 1"		1312	.006		.31	.27		.58	.76
5650	1/8" x 3"		442	.018		.94	.80		1.74	2.25
5670	1/4" x 3"		295	.027		1.88	1.20		3.08	3.88
5680	1/4" x 6"		148	.054		3.77	2.38		6.15	7.75
5690	1/2" x 6"		82	.098		7.55	4.30		11.85	14.80
5700	1/2" x 9"		52.50	.152		11.30	6.70		18	22.50
5710	1/2" x 12"		33	.242		15.05	10.70		25.75	33

07 92 Joint Sealants

07 92 13 – Elastomeric Joint Sealants

07 92 13.20 Caulking and Sealant Options

		Crew	Daily Output	Labor-Hours	Unit	Material	2012 Bare Costs Labor	Equipment	Total	Total Incl O&P
0010	**CAULKING AND SEALANT OPTIONS**									
0050	Latex acrylic based, bulk				Gal.	29.50			29.50	32.50
0055	Bulk in place 1/4" x 1/4" bead	1 Bric	300	.027	L.F.	.09	1.18		1.27	1.88
0060	1/4" x 3/8"		294	.027		.16	1.20		1.36	1.98
0065	1/4" x 1/2"		288	.028		.21	1.23		1.44	2.08
0075	3/8" x 3/8"		284	.028		.23	1.24		1.47	2.13
0080	3/8" x 1/2"		280	.029		.31	1.26		1.57	2.24
0085	3/8" x 5/8"		276	.029		.39	1.28		1.67	2.36
0095	3/8" x 3/4"		272	.029		.46	1.30		1.76	2.47
0100	1/2" x 1/2"		275	.029		.41	1.28		1.69	2.40
0105	1/2" x 5/8"		269	.030		.52	1.31		1.83	2.55
0110	1/2" x 3/4"		263	.030		.62	1.34		1.96	2.71
0115	1/2" x 7/8"		256	.031		.72	1.38		2.10	2.88
0120	1/2" x 1"		250	.032		.83	1.41		2.24	3.04
0125	3/4" x 3/4"		244	.033		.93	1.45		2.38	3.21
0130	3/4" x 1"		225	.036		1.24	1.57		2.81	3.74
0135	1" x 1"		200	.040		1.66	1.76		3.42	4.48
0190	Cartridges				Gal.	25.50			25.50	28
0200	11 fl. oz. cartridge				Ea.	2.20			2.20	2.42
0500	1/4" x 1/2"	1 Bric	288	.028	L.F.	.18	1.23		1.41	2.05
0600	1/2" x 1/2"		275	.029		.36	1.28		1.64	2.34
0800	3/4" x 3/4"		244	.033		.81	1.45		2.26	3.07
0900	3/4" x 1"		225	.036		1.08	1.57		2.65	3.56
1000	1" x 1"		200	.040		1.35	1.76		3.11	4.14
1400	Butyl based, bulk				Gal.	28.50			28.50	31.50
1500	Cartridges				"	32			32	35
1700	1/4" x 1/2", 154 L.F./gal.	1 Bric	288	.028	L.F.	.19	1.23		1.42	2.05
1800	1/2" x 1/2", 77 L.F./gal.	"	275	.029	"	.37	1.28		1.65	2.35
2300	Polysulfide compounds, 1 component, bulk				Gal.	56			56	61.50
2600	1 or 2 component, in place, 1/4" x 1/4", 308 L.F./gal.	1 Bric	300	.027	L.F.	.18	1.18		1.36	1.98
2700	1/2" x 1/4", 154 L.F./gal.		288	.028		.36	1.23		1.59	2.25
2900	3/4" x 3/8", 68 L.F./gal.		272	.029		.82	1.30		2.12	2.87
3000	1" x 1/2", 38 L.F./gal.		250	.032		1.47	1.41		2.88	3.75
3200	Polyurethane, 1 or 2 component				Gal.	51			51	56
3300	Cartridges				"	70			70	77
3500	Bulk, in place, 1/4" x 1/4"	1 Bric	300	.027	L.F.	.17	1.18		1.35	1.96
3655	1/2" x 1/4"		288	.028		.33	1.23		1.56	2.21

07 92 Joint Sealants

07 92 13 – Elastomeric Joint Sealants

07 92 13.20 Caulking and Sealant Options

		Crew	Daily Output	Labor-Hours	Unit	Material	2012 Bare Costs Labor	Equipment	Total	Total Incl O&P
3800	3/4" x 3/8"	1 Bric	272	.029	L.F.	.75	1.30		2.05	2.79
3900	1" x 1/2"	↓	250	.032	↓	1.33	1.41		2.74	3.59
4100	Silicone rubber, bulk				Gal.	42			42	46
4200	Cartridges				"	41			41	45

07 92 16 – Rigid Joint Sealants

07 92 16.10 Rigid Joint Sealants

		Crew	Daily Output	Labor-Hours	Unit	Material	2012 Bare Costs Labor	Equipment	Total	Total Incl O&P
0010	**RIGID JOINT SEALANTS**									
5800	Tapes, sealant, P.V.C. foam adhesive, 1/16" x 1/4"				C.L.F.	6			6	6.60
5900	1/16" x 1/2"					8			8	8.80
5950	1/16" x 1"					15			15	16.50
6000	1/8" x 1/2"				↓	9			9	9.90

07 92 19 – Acoustical Joint Sealants

07 92 19.10 Acoustical Sealant

		Crew	Daily Output	Labor-Hours	Unit	Material	2012 Bare Costs Labor	Equipment	Total	Total Incl O&P
0010	**ACOUSTICAL SEALANT**									
0020	Acoustical sealant, elastomeric, cartridges				Ea.	6.25			6.25	6.90
0025	In place, 1/4" x 1/4"	1 Bric	300	.027	L.F.	.26	1.18		1.44	2.06
0030	1/4" x 1/2"		288	.028		.51	1.23		1.74	2.41
0035	1/2" x 1/2"		275	.029		1.02	1.28		2.30	3.06
0040	1/2" x 3/4"		263	.030		1.53	1.34		2.87	3.72
0045	3/4" x 3/4"		244	.033		2.30	1.45		3.75	4.71
0050	1" x 1"	↓	200	.040	↓	4.09	1.76		5.85	7.15

Division Notes

	CREW	DAILY OUTPUT	LABOR-HOURS	UNIT	2012 BARE COSTS				TOTAL INCL O&P
					MAT.	LABOR	EQUIP.	TOTAL	

Estimating Tips

08 10 00 Doors and Frames

All exterior doors should be addressed for their energy conservation (insulation and seals).

- Most metal doors and frames look alike, but there may be significant differences among them. When estimating these items, be sure to choose the line item that most closely compares to the specification or door schedule requirements regarding:
  - type of metal
  - metal gauge
  - door core material
  - fire rating
  - finish
- Wood and plastic doors vary considerably in price. The primary determinant is the veneer material. Lauan, birch, and oak are the most common veneers. Other variables include the following:
  - hollow or solid core
  - fire rating
  - flush or raised panel
  - finish

08 30 00 Specialty Doors and Frames

- There are many varieties of special doors, and they are usually priced per each. Add frames, hardware, or operators required for a complete installation.

08 40 00 Entrances, Storefronts, and Curtain Walls

- Glazed curtain walls consist of the metal tube framing and the glazing material. The cost data in this subdivision is presented for the metal tube framing alone or the composite wall. If your estimate requires a detailed takeoff of the framing, be sure to add the glazing cost.

08 50 00 Windows

- Most metal windows are delivered preglazed. However, some metal windows are priced without glass. Refer to 08 80 00 Glazing for glass pricing. The grade C indicates commercial grade windows, usually ASTM C-35.
- All wood windows and vinyl are priced preglazed. The glazing is insulating glass. Some wood windows may have single pane float glass. Add the cost of screens and grills if required, and not already included.

08 70 00 Hardware

- Hardware costs add considerably to the cost of a door. The most efficient method to determine the hardware requirements for a project is to review the door schedule.

- Door hinges are priced by the pair, with most doors requiring 1-1/2 pairs per door. The hinge prices do not include installation labor because it is included in door installation. Hinges are classified according to the frequency of use.

08 80 00 Glazing

- Different openings require different types of glass. The most common types are:
  - float
  - tempered
  - insulating
  - impact-resistant
  - ballistic-resistant
- Most exterior windows are glazed with insulating glass. Entrance doors and window walls, where the glass is less than 18" from the floor, are generally glazed with tempered glass. Interior windows and some residential windows are glazed with float glass.
- Coastal communities require the use of impact-resistant glass.
- The insulation or 'u' value is a strong consideration, along with solar heat gain, to determine total energy efficiency.

Reference Numbers

Reference numbers are shown in shaded boxes at the beginning of some major classifications. These numbers refer to related items in the Reference Section. The reference information may be an estimating procedure, an alternate pricing method, or technical information.

Note: Not all subdivisions listed here necessarily appear in this publication.

08 34 Special Function Doors

08 34 13 - Cold Storage Doors

08 34 13.10 Doors for Cold Area Storage

		Crew	Daily Output	Labor-Hours	Unit	Material	2012 Bare Costs Labor	Equipment	Total	Total Incl O&P
0010	**DOORS FOR COLD AREA STORAGE**									
0020	Single, 20 ga. galvanized steel									
0300	Horizontal sliding, 5' x 7', manual operation, 3.5" thick	2 Carp	2	8	Ea.	3,200	355		3,555	4,075
0400	4" thick		2	8		3,225	355		3,580	4,100
0500	6" thick		2	8		3,400	355		3,755	4,300
0800	5' x 7', power operation, 2" thick		1.90	8.421		5,525	370		5,895	6,650
0900	4" thick		1.90	8.421		5,650	370		6,020	6,800
1000	6" thick		1.90	8.421		6,450	370		6,820	7,675
1300	9' x 10', manual operation, 2" insulation		1.70	9.412		4,500	415		4,915	5,600
1400	4" insulation		1.70	9.412		4,600	415		5,015	5,725
1500	6" insulation		1.70	9.412		5,550	415		5,965	6,750
1800	Power operation, 2" insulation		1.60	10		7,625	440		8,065	9,050
1900	4" insulation		1.60	10		7,850	440		8,290	9,325
2000	6" insulation		1.70	9.412		8,850	415		9,265	10,400
2300	For stainless steel face, add					25%				
3000	Hinged, lightweight, 3' x 7'-0", 2" thick	2 Carp	2	8	Ea.	1,400	355		1,755	2,100
3050	4" thick		1.90	8.421		1,750	370		2,120	2,500
3300	Aluminum doors, 3' x 7'-0", 4" thick		1.90	8.421		1,325	370		1,695	2,050
3350	6" thick		1.40	11.429		2,325	505		2,830	3,350
3600	Stainless steel, 3' x 7'-0", 4" thick		1.90	8.421		1,725	370		2,095	2,475
3650	6" thick		1.40	11.429		2,925	505		3,430	4,000
3900	Painted, 3' x 7'-0", 4" thick		1.90	8.421		1,250	370		1,620	1,950
3950	6" thick		1.40	11.429		2,325	505		2,830	3,350
5000	Bi-parting, electric operated									
5010	6' x 8' opening, galv. faces, 4" thick for cooler	2 Carp	.80	20	Opng.	7,200	880		8,080	9,275
5050	For freezer, 4" thick		.80	20		7,950	880		8,830	10,100
5300	For door buck framing and door protection, add		2.50	6.400		635	282		917	1,125
6000	Galvanized batten door, galvanized hinges, 4' x 7'		2	8		1,800	355		2,155	2,525
6050	6' x 8'		1.80	8.889		2,450	390		2,840	3,300
6500	Fire door, 3 hr., 6' x 8', single slide		.80	20		8,275	880		9,155	10,500
6550	Double, bi-parting		.70	22.857		12,200	1,000		13,200	15,000

08 91 Louvers

08 91 19 - Fixed Louvers

08 91 19.10 Aluminum Louvers

		Crew	Daily Output	Labor-Hours	Unit	Material	2012 Bare Costs Labor	Equipment	Total	Total Incl O&P
0010	**ALUMINUM LOUVERS**									
0020	Aluminum with screen, residential, 8" x 8"	1 Carp	38	.211	Ea.	13.50	9.30		22.80	29
0100	12" x 12"		38	.211		15	9.30		24.30	31
0200	12" x 18"		35	.229		19	10.10		29.10	36.50
0250	14" x 24"		30	.267		26	11.75		37.75	46.50
0300	18" x 24"		27	.296		29	13.05		42.05	52
0500	24" x 30"		24	.333		40	14.70		54.70	66.50
0700	Triangle, adjustable, small		20	.400		37.50	17.65		55.15	68.50
0800	Large		15	.533		46.50	23.50		70	87
1200	Extruded aluminum, see Section 23 37 15.40									
2100	Midget, aluminum, 3/4" deep, 1" diameter	1 Carp	85	.094	Ea.	.72	4.15		4.87	7.20
2150	3" diameter		60	.133		2	5.90		7.90	11.25
2200	4" diameter		50	.160		3.64	7.05		10.69	14.85
2250	6" diameter		30	.267		3.85	11.75		15.60	22.50

08 95 Vents

08 95 13 − Soffit Vents

08 95 13.10 Wall Louvers

		Crew	Daily Output	Labor-Hours	Unit	Material	2012 Bare Costs Labor	Equipment	Total	Total Incl O&P
0010	**WALL LOUVERS**									
2330	Soffit vent, continuous, 3" wide, aluminum, mill finish	1 Carp	200	.040	L.F.	.52	1.76		2.28	3.28
2340	Baked enamel finish		200	.040	"	.57	1.76		2.33	3.34
2400	Under eaves vent, aluminum, mill finish, 16" x 4"		48	.167	Ea.	1.84	7.35		9.19	13.30
2500	16" x 8"		48	.167	"	2.14	7.35		9.49	13.65

08 95 16 − Wall Vents

08 95 16.10 Louvers

		Crew	Daily Output	Labor-Hours	Unit	Material	2012 Bare Costs Labor	Equipment	Total	Total Incl O&P
0010	**LOUVERS**									
0020	Redwood, 2'-0" diameter, full circle	1 Carp	16	.500	Ea.	174	22		196	225
0100	Half circle		16	.500		192	22		214	245
0200	Octagonal		16	.500		132	22		154	179
0300	Triangular, 5/12 pitch, 5'-0" at base		16	.500		194	22		216	247
1100	Rectangular, 1'-4" x 1'-8"		16	.500		26	22		48	62.50
1200	1'-4" x 2'-2"		15	.533		30	23.50		53.50	69
1300	1'-9" x 2'-2"		15	.533		36.50	23.50		60	76
1400	2'-3" x 2'-2"		14	.571		48	25		73	92
1700	2'-4" x 2'-11"		13	.615		48	27		75	95
2000	Aluminum, 12" x 16"		25	.320		15.90	14.10		30	39
2010	16" x 20"		25	.320		24	14.10		38.10	48
2020	24" x 30"		25	.320		53	14.10		67.10	80
2100	6' triangle		12	.667		166	29.50		195.50	228
7000	Vinyl gable vent, 8" x 8"		38	.211		12.60	9.30		21.90	28
7020	12" x 12"		38	.211		24	9.30		33.30	41
7080	12" x 18"		35	.229		31	10.10		41.10	49.50
7200	18" x 24"		30	.267		38	11.75		49.75	60

Division Notes

		CREW	DAILY OUTPUT	LABOR-HOURS	UNIT	2012 BARE COSTS				TOTAL INCL O&P
						MAT.	LABOR	EQUIP.	TOTAL	

Estimating Tips

General

- Room Finish Schedule: A complete set of plans should contain a room finish schedule. If one is not available, it would be well worth the time and effort to obtain one.

09 20 00 Plaster and Gypsum Board

- Lath is estimated by the square yard plus a 5% allowance for waste. Furring, channels, and accessories are measured by the linear foot. An extra foot should be allowed for each accessory miter or stop.

- Plaster is also estimated by the square yard. Deductions for openings vary by preference, from zero deduction to 50% of all openings over 2 feet in width. The estimator should allow one extra square foot for each linear foot of horizontal interior or exterior angle located below the ceiling level. Also, double the areas of small radius work.

- Drywall accessories, studs, track, and acoustical caulking are all measured by the linear foot. Drywall taping is figured by the square foot. Gypsum wallboard is estimated by the square foot. No material deductions should be made for door or window openings under 32 S.F.

09 60 00 Flooring

- Tile and terrazzo areas are taken off on a square foot basis. Trim and base materials are measured by the linear foot. Accent tiles are listed per each. Two basic methods of installation are used. Mud set is approximately 30% more expensive than thin set. In terrazzo work, be sure to include the linear footage of embedded decorative strips, grounds, machine rubbing, and power cleanup.

- Wood flooring is available in strip, parquet, or block configuration. The latter two types are set in adhesives with quantities estimated by the square foot. The laying pattern will influence labor costs and material waste. In addition to the material and labor for laying wood floors, the estimator must make allowances for sanding and finishing these areas unless the flooring is prefinished.

- Sheet flooring is measured by the square yard. Roll widths vary, so consideration should be given to use the most economical width, as waste must be figured into the total quantity. Consider also the installation methods available, direct glue down or stretched.

09 70 00 Wall Finishes

- Wall coverings are estimated by the square foot. The area to be covered is measured, length by height of wall above baseboards, to calculate the square footage of each wall. This figure is divided by the number of square feet in the single roll which is being used. Deduct, in full, the areas of openings such as doors and windows. Where a pattern match is required allow 25%-30% waste.

09 80 00 Acoustic Treatment

- Acoustical systems fall into several categories. The takeoff of these materials should be by the square foot of area with a 5% allowance for waste. Do not forget about scaffolding, if applicable, when estimating these systems.

09 90 00 Painting and Coating

- A major portion of the work in painting involves surface preparation. Be sure to include cleaning, sanding, filling, and masking costs in the estimate.

- Protection of adjacent surfaces is not included in painting costs. When considering the method of paint application, an important factor is the amount of protection and masking required. These must be estimated separately and may be the determining factor in choosing the method of application.

Reference Numbers

Reference numbers are shown in shaded boxes at the beginning of some major classifications. These numbers refer to related items in the Reference Section. The reference information may be an estimating procedure, an alternate pricing method, or technical information.

Note: Not all subdivisions listed here necessarily appear in this publication.

09 22 Supports for Plaster and Gypsum Board

09 22 03 – Fastening Methods for Finishes

09 22 03.20 Drilling Plaster/Drywall		Crew	Daily Output	Labor-Hours	Unit	Material	2012 Bare Costs Labor	Equipment	Total	Total Incl O&P
0010	**DRILLING PLASTER/DRYWALL**									
1100	Drilling & layout for drywall/plaster walls, up to 1" deep, no anchor									
1200	Holes, 1/4" diameter	1 Carp	150	.053	Ea.	.01	2.35		2.36	3.63
1300	3/8" diameter		140	.057		.01	2.52		2.53	3.89
1400	1/2" diameter		130	.062		.01	2.71		2.72	4.19
1500	3/4" diameter		120	.067		.01	2.94		2.95	4.53
1600	1" diameter		110	.073		.02	3.21		3.23	4.95
1700	1-1/4" diameter		100	.080		.03	3.53		3.56	5.50
1800	1-1/2" diameter		90	.089		.04	3.92		3.96	6.10
1900	For ceiling installations, add						40%			

09 69 Access Flooring

09 69 13 – Rigid-Grid Access Flooring

09 69 13.10 Access Floors

		Crew	Daily Output	Labor-Hours	Unit	Material	2012 Bare Costs Labor	Equipment	Total	Total Incl O&P
0010	**ACCESS FLOORS**									
0015	Access floor package including panel, pedestal, stringers & laminate cover									
0100	Computer room, greater than 6,000 S.F.	4 Carp	750	.043	S.F.	7.50	1.88		9.38	11.15
0110	Less than 6,000 S.F.	2 Carp	375	.043		8.15	1.88		10.03	11.90
0120	Office, greater than 6,000 S.F.	4 Carp	1050	.030		5.35	1.34		6.69	7.95
0250	Panels, particle board or steel, 1250# load, no covering, under 6,000 S.F.	2 Carp	600	.027		3.75	1.18		4.93	5.95
0300	Over 6,000 S.F.		640	.025		3.21	1.10		4.31	5.25
0400	Aluminum, 24" panels		500	.032		33	1.41		34.41	38.50
0600	For carpet covering, add					8.75			8.75	9.65
0700	For vinyl floor covering, add					7			7	7.70
0900	For high pressure laminate covering, add					5.45			5.45	6
0910	For snap on stringer system, add	2 Carp	1000	.016		1.44	.71		2.15	2.67
0950	Office applications, steel or concrete panels,									
0960	no covering, over 6,000 S.F.	2 Carp	960	.017	S.F.	10.65	.74		11.39	12.85
1000	Machine cutouts after initial installation	1 Carp	50	.160	Ea.	5.05	7.05		12.10	16.40
1050	Pedestals, 6" to 12"	2 Carp	85	.188		8.35	8.30		16.65	22
1100	Air conditioning grilles, 4" x 12"	1 Carp	17	.471		66	21		87	105
1150	4" x 18"	"	14	.571		90.50	25		115.50	139
1200	Approach ramps, minimum	2 Carp	60	.267	S.F.	25.50	11.75		37.25	46
1300	Maximum	"	40	.400	"	33.50	17.65		51.15	63.50
1500	Handrail, 2 rail, aluminum	1 Carp	15	.533	L.F.	97.50	23.50		121	143

09 91 Painting

09 91 23 – Interior Painting

09 91 23.52 Miscellaneous, Interior

		Crew	Daily Output	Labor-Hours	Unit	Material	2012 Bare Costs Labor	Equipment	Total	Total Incl O&P
0010	**MISCELLANEOUS, INTERIOR** R099100-10									
3800	Grilles, per side, oil base, primer coat, brushwork	1 Pord	520	.015	S.F.	.12	.59		.71	1.01
3850	Spray		1140	.007		.13	.27		.40	.54
3880	Paint 1 coat, brushwork		520	.015		.22	.59		.81	1.12
3900	Spray		1140	.007		.24	.27		.51	.66
3920	Paint 2 coats, brushwork		325	.025		.42	.94		1.36	1.87
3940	Spray		650	.012		.48	.47		.95	1.23
3950	Prime & paint 1 coat		325	.025		.34	.94		1.28	1.78
3960	Prime & paint 2 coats		270	.030		.33	1.13		1.46	2.05
4500	Louvers, one side, primer, brushwork		524	.015		.07	.58		.65	.95

09 91 Painting

09 91 23 – Interior Painting

09 91 23.52 Miscellaneous, Interior	Crew	Daily Output	Labor-Hours	Unit	Material	2012 Bare Costs Labor	Equipment	Total	Total Incl O&P
4520	Paint one coat, brushwork	1 Pord	520	.015	S.F.	.10	.59		.69	.99
4530	Spray		1140	.007		.11	.27		.38	.52
4540	Paint two coats, brushwork		325	.025		.19	.94		1.13	1.62
4550	Spray		650	.012		.22	.47		.69	.94
4560	Paint three coats, brushwork		270	.030		.29	1.13		1.42	2.01
4570	Spray		500	.016		.32	.61		.93	1.27
5000	Pipe, 1" - 4" diameter, primer or sealer coat, oil base, brushwork	2 Pord	1250	.013	L.F.	.08	.49		.57	.81
5100	Spray		2165	.007		.07	.28		.35	.50
5200	Paint 1 coat, brushwork		1250	.013		.12	.49		.61	.86
5300	Spray		2165	.007		.10	.28		.38	.53
5350	Paint 2 coats, brushwork		775	.021		.20	.79		.99	1.40
5400	Spray		1240	.013		.23	.49		.72	.99
5420	Paint 3 coats, brushwork		775	.021		.30	.79		1.09	1.51
5450	5" - 8" diameter, primer or sealer coat, brushwork		620	.026		.15	.99		1.14	1.65
5500	Spray		1085	.015		.25	.56		.81	1.12
5550	Paint 1 coat, brushwork		620	.026		.31	.99		1.30	1.82
5600	Spray		1085	.015		.34	.56		.90	1.22
5650	Paint 2 coats, brushwork		385	.042		.41	1.59		2	2.83
5700	Spray		620	.026		.45	.99		1.44	1.98
5720	Paint 3 coats, brushwork		385	.042		.61	1.59		2.20	3.05
5750	9" - 12" diameter, primer or sealer coat, brushwork		415	.039		.23	1.47		1.70	2.46
5800	Spray		725	.022		.37	.84		1.21	1.67
5850	Paint 1 coat, brushwork		415	.039		.31	1.47		1.78	2.56
6000	Spray		725	.022		.35	.84		1.19	1.64
6200	Paint 2 coats, brushwork		260	.062		.61	2.35		2.96	4.19
6250	Spray		415	.039		.68	1.47		2.15	2.95
6270	Paint 3 coats, brushwork		260	.062		.91	2.35		3.26	4.52
6300	13" - 16" diameter, primer or sealer coat, brushwork		310	.052		.31	1.97		2.28	3.29
6350	Spray		540	.030		.34	1.13		1.47	2.06
6400	Paint 1 coat, brushwork		310	.052		.42	1.97		2.39	3.41
6450	Spray		540	.030		.47	1.13		1.60	2.20
6500	Paint 2 coats, brushwork		195	.082		.82	3.14		3.96	5.60
6550	Spray		310	.052		.91	1.97		2.88	3.95
6600	Radiators, per side, primer, brushwork	1 Pord	520	.015	S.F.	.07	.59		.66	.96
6620	Paint, one coat		520	.015		.07	.59		.66	.96
6640	Two coats		340	.024		.19	.90		1.09	1.56
6660	Three coats		283	.028		.29	1.08		1.37	1.94

Division Notes

	CREW	DAILY OUTPUT	LABOR-HOURS	UNIT	2012 BARE COSTS				TOTAL INCL O&P
					MAT.	LABOR	EQUIP.	TOTAL	

Estimating Tips

General

- The items in this division are usually priced per square foot or each.

- Many items in Division 10 require some type of support system or special anchors that are not usually furnished with the item. The required anchors must be added to the estimate in the appropriate division.

- Some items in Division 10, such as lockers, may require assembly before installation. Verify the amount of assembly required. Assembly can often exceed installation time.

10 20 00 Interior Specialties

- Support angles and blocking are not included in the installation of toilet compartments, shower/dressing compartments, or cubicles. Appropriate line items from Divisions 5 or 6 may need to be added to support the installations.

- Toilet partitions are priced by the stall. A stall consists of a side wall, pilaster, and door with hardware. Toilet tissue holders and grab bars are extra.

- The required acoustical rating of a folding partition can have a significant impact on costs. Verify the sound transmission coefficient rating of the panel priced to the specification requirements.

- Grab bar installation does not include supplemental blocking or backing to support the required load. When grab bars are installed at an existing facility, provisions must be made to attach the grab bars to solid structure.

Reference Numbers

Reference numbers are shown in shaded boxes at the beginning of some major classifications. These numbers refer to related items in the Reference Section. The reference information may be an estimating procedure, an alternate pricing method, or technical information.

Note: Not all subdivisions listed here necessarily appear in this publication.

Division 10 - Specialties

10 31 Manufactured Fireplaces

10 31 13 – Manufactured Fireplace Chimneys

10 31 13.10 Fireplace Chimneys	Crew	Daily Output	Labor-Hours	Unit	Material	2012 Bare Costs Labor	Equipment	Total	Total Incl O&P
0010 **FIREPLACE CHIMNEYS**									
0500 Chimney dbl. wall, all stainless, over 8'-6", 7" diam., add to fireplace	1 Carp	33	.242	V.L.F.	81	10.70		91.70	105
0600 10" diameter, add to fireplace		32	.250		119	11.05		130.05	147
0700 12" diameter, add to fireplace		31	.258		210	11.40		221.40	249
0800 14" diameter, add to fireplace		30	.267		233	11.75		244.75	274
1000 Simulated brick chimney top, 4' high, 16" x 16"		10	.800	Ea.	425	35.50		460.50	525
1100 24" x 24"		7	1.143	"	520	50.50		570.50	650

10 31 23 – Prefabricated Fireplaces

10 31 23.10 Fireplace, Prefabricated

	Crew	Daily Output	Labor-Hours	Unit	Material	2012 Bare Costs Labor	Equipment	Total	Total Incl O&P
0010 **FIREPLACE, PREFABRICATED**, free standing or wall hung									
0100 With hood & screen, minimum	1 Carp	1.30	6.154	Ea.	1,200	271		1,471	1,750
0150 Average		1	8		1,425	355		1,780	2,100
0200 Maximum		.90	8.889		2,725	390		3,115	3,600
1500 Simulated logs, gas fired, 40,000 BTU, 2' long, minimum		7	1.143	Set	500	50.50		550.50	630
1600 Maximum		6	1.333		1,100	59		1,159	1,325
1700 Electric, 1,500 BTU, 1'-6" long, minimum		7	1.143		200	50.50		250.50	298
1800 11,500 BTU, maximum		6	1.333		450	59		509	585

10 35 Stoves

10 35 13 – Heating Stoves

10 35 13.10 Woodburning Stoves

	Crew	Daily Output	Labor-Hours	Unit	Material	2012 Bare Costs Labor	Equipment	Total	Total Incl O&P
0010 **WOODBURNING STOVES**									
0015 Cast iron, minimum	2 Carp	1.30	12.308	Ea.	905	545		1,450	1,825
0020 Average		1	16		1,675	705		2,380	2,925
0030 Maximum		.80	20		2,450	880		3,330	4,050
0050 For gas log lighter, add					42.50			42.50	46.50

Estimating Tips

General

- The items in this division are usually priced per square foot or each. Many of these items are purchased by the owner for installation by the contractor. Check the specifications for responsibilities and include time for receiving, storage, installation, and mechanical and electrical hookups in the appropriate divisions.

- Many items in Division 11 require some type of support system that is not usually furnished with the item. Examples of these systems include blocking for the attachment of casework and support angles for ceiling-hung projection screens. The required blocking or supports must be added to the estimate in the appropriate division.

- Some items in Division 11 may require assembly or electrical hookups. Verify the amount of assembly required or the need for a hard electrical connection and add the appropriate costs.

Reference Numbers

Reference numbers are shown in shaded boxes at the beginning of some major classifications. These numbers refer to related items in the Reference Section. The reference information may be an estimating procedure, an alternate pricing method, or technical information.

Note: Not all subdivisions listed here necessarily appear in this publication.

11 11 Vehicle Service Equipment

11 11 13 – Compressed-Air Vehicle Service Equipment

11 11 13.10 Compressed Air Equipment		Crew	Daily Output	Labor-Hours	Unit	Material	2012 Bare Costs Labor	Equipment	Total	Total Incl O&P
0010	**COMPRESSED AIR EQUIPMENT**									
0030	Compressors, electric, 1-1/2 H.P., standard controls	L-4	1.50	16	Ea.	420	660		1,080	1,475
0550	Dual controls		1.50	16		765	660		1,425	1,875
0600	5 H.P., 115/230 volt, standard controls		1	24		2,025	995		3,020	3,750
0650	Dual controls		1	24		2,575	995		3,570	4,350

11 11 19 – Vehicle Lubrication Equipment

11 11 19.10 Lubrication Equipment		Crew	Daily Output	Labor-Hours	Unit	Material	2012 Bare Costs Labor	Equipment	Total	Total Incl O&P
0010	**LUBRICATION EQUIPMENT**									
3000	Lube equipment, 3 reel type, with pumps, not including piping	L-4	.50	48	Set	8,700	1,975		10,675	12,600
3700	Pump lubrication, pneumatic, not incl. air compressor									
3710	Oil/gear lube	Q-1	9.60	1.667	Ea.	780	82		862	980
3720	Grease	"	9.60	1.667	"	1,075	82		1,157	1,300

11 11 33 – Vehicle Spray Painting Equipment

11 11 33.10 Spray Painting Equipment		Crew	Daily Output	Labor-Hours	Unit	Material	2012 Bare Costs Labor	Equipment	Total	Total Incl O&P
0010	**SPRAY PAINTING EQUIPMENT**									
4000	Spray painting booth, 26' long, complete	L-4	.40	60	Ea.	17,600	2,475		20,075	23,200

11 23 Commercial Laundry and Dry Cleaning Equipment

11 23 16 – Drying and Conditioning Equipment

11 23 16.13 Dryers		Crew	Daily Output	Labor-Hours	Unit	Material	2012 Bare Costs Labor	Equipment	Total	Total Incl O&P
0010	**DRYERS**, Not including rough-in									
1500	Industrial, 30 lb. capacity	1 Plum	2	4	Ea.	3,025	218		3,243	3,650
1600	50 lb. capacity	"	1.70	4.706	"	3,250	257		3,507	3,975

11 23 26 – Commercial Washers and Extractors

11 23 26.13 Washers and Extractors		Crew	Daily Output	Labor-Hours	Unit	Material	2012 Bare Costs Labor	Equipment	Total	Total Incl O&P
0010	**WASHERS AND EXTRACTORS**, not including rough-in									
6000	Combination washer/extractor, 20 lb. capacity	L-6	1.50	8	Ea.	5,700	430		6,130	6,925
6100	30 lb. capacity		.80	15		8,975	805		9,780	11,100
6200	50 lb. capacity		.68	17.647		10,500	945		11,445	13,000
6300	75 lb. capacity		.30	40		19,900	2,150		22,050	25,100
6350	125 lb. capacity		.16	75		27,300	4,025		31,325	36,200

11 23 33 – Coin-Operated Laundry Equipment

11 23 33.13 Coin Operated Washers and Dryers		Crew	Daily Output	Labor-Hours	Unit	Material	2012 Bare Costs Labor	Equipment	Total	Total Incl O&P
0010	**COIN OPERATED WASHERS AND DRYERS**									
0990	Dryer, gas fired									
1000	Commercial, 30 lb. capacity, coin operated, single	1 Plum	3	2.667	Ea.	3,150	146		3,296	3,700
1100	Double stacked	"	2	4	"	6,825	218		7,043	7,825
5290	Clothes washer									
5300	Commercial, coin operated, average	1 Plum	3	2.667	Ea.	1,250	146		1,396	1,600

11 24 Maintenance Equipment

11 24 19 – Vacuum Cleaning Systems

11 24 19.10 Vacuum Cleaning	Crew	Daily Output	Labor-Hours	Unit	Material	2012 Bare Costs Labor	Equipment	Total	Total Incl O&P
0010 **VACUUM CLEANING**									
0020 Central, 3 inlet, residential	1 Skwk	.90	8.889	Total	1,025	405		1,430	1,775
0200 Commercial		.70	11.429		1,225	520		1,745	2,150
0400 5 inlet system, residential		.50	16		1,450	725		2,175	2,725
0600 7 inlet system, commercial		.40	20		1,675	910		2,585	3,250
0800 9 inlet system, residential		.30	26.667		3,600	1,200		4,800	5,825
4010 Rule of thumb: First 1200 S.F., installed								1,425	1,575
4020 For each additional S.F., add				S.F.					.26

11 26 Unit Kitchens

11 26 13 – Metal Unit Kitchens

11 26 13.10 Commercial Unit Kitchens

	Crew	Daily Output	Labor-Hours	Unit	Material	2012 Bare Costs Labor	Equipment	Total	Total Incl O&P
0010 **COMMERCIAL UNIT KITCHENS**									
1500 Combination range, refrigerator and sink, 30" wide, minimum	L-1	2	8	Ea.	1,125	425		1,550	1,875
1550 Maximum		1	16		3,875	850		4,725	5,525
1570 60" wide, average		1.40	11.429		3,375	605		3,980	4,625
1590 72" wide, average		1.20	13.333		4,400	710		5,110	5,925
1600 Office model, 48" wide		2	8		2,725	425		3,150	3,650
1620 Refrigerator and sink only		2.40	6.667		2,850	355		3,205	3,650
1640 Combination range, refrigerator, sink, microwave									
1660 Oven and ice maker	L-1	.80	20	Ea.	4,675	1,050		5,725	6,725

11 27 Photographic Processing Equipment

11 27 13 – Darkroom Processing Equipment

11 27 13.10 Darkroom Equipment

	Crew	Daily Output	Labor-Hours	Unit	Material	2012 Bare Costs Labor	Equipment	Total	Total Incl O&P
0010 **DARKROOM EQUIPMENT**									
0020 Developing sink, 5" deep, 24" x 48"	Q-1	2	8	Ea.	5,625	395		6,020	6,775
0050 48" x 52"		1.70	9.412		5,675	465		6,140	6,925
0200 10" deep, 24" x 48"		1.70	9.412		7,775	465		8,240	9,250
0250 24" x 108"		1.50	10.667		10,200	525		10,725	12,100
3500 Washers, round, minimum sheet 11" x 14"		2	8		3,400	395		3,795	4,350
3550 Maximum sheet 20" x 24"		1	16		3,475	785		4,260	5,000
3800 Square, minimum sheet 20" x 24"		1	16		3,125	785		3,910	4,600
3900 Maximum sheet 50" x 56"		.80	20		4,850	985		5,835	6,800
4500 Combination tank sink, tray sink, washers, with									
4510 Dry side tables, average	Q-1	.45	35.556	Ea.	10,600	1,750		12,350	14,300

11 31 Residential Appliances

11 31 13 – Residential Kitchen Appliances

11 31 13.13 Cooking Equipment

	Crew	Daily Output	Labor-Hours	Unit	Material	2012 Bare Costs Labor	Equipment	Total	Total Incl O&P
0010 **COOKING EQUIPMENT**									
0020 Cooking range, 30" free standing, 1 oven, minimum	2 Clab	10	1.600	Ea.	405	56		461	530
0050 Maximum		4	4		1,775	140		1,915	2,175
0150 2 oven, minimum		10	1.600		1,100	56		1,156	1,275
0200 Maximum		10	1.600		1,175	56		1,231	1,350

11 31 13.23 Refrigeration Equipment

0010 **REFRIGERATION EQUIPMENT**									

11 31 Residential Appliances

11 31 13 – Residential Kitchen Appliances

11 31 13.23 Refrigeration Equipment	Crew	Daily Output	Labor-Hours	Unit	Material	2012 Bare Costs Labor	2012 Bare Costs Equipment	Total	Total Incl O&P
5200 Icemaker, automatic, 20 lb. per day	1 Plum	7	1.143	Ea.	920	62.50		982.50	1,125
5350 51 lb. per day	"	2	4	"	1,350	218		1,568	1,800

11 31 13.33 Kitchen Cleaning Equipment

	Crew	Daily Output	Labor-Hours	Unit	Material	Labor	Equipment	Total	Total Incl O&P
0010 **KITCHEN CLEANING EQUIPMENT**									
2750 Dishwasher, built-in, 2 cycles, minimum	L-1	4	4	Ea.	212	212		424	555
2800 Maximum		2	8		400	425		825	1,075
2950 4 or more cycles, minimum		4	4		325	212		537	680
2960 Average		4	4		435	212		647	795
3000 Maximum		2	8		1,100	425		1,525	1,875

11 31 13.43 Waste Disposal Equipment

	Crew	Daily Output	Labor-Hours	Unit	Material	Labor	Equipment	Total	Total Incl O&P
0010 **WASTE DISPOSAL EQUIPMENT**									
3300 Garbage disposal, sink type, minimum	L-1	10	1.600	Ea.	83	85		168	219
3350 Maximum	"	10	1.600	"	197	85		282	345

11 31 13.53 Kitchen Ventilation Equipment

	Crew	Daily Output	Labor-Hours	Unit	Material	Labor	Equipment	Total	Total Incl O&P
0010 **KITCHEN VENTILATION EQUIPMENT**									
4150 Hood for range, 2 speed, vented, 30" wide, minimum	L-3	5	3.200	Ea.	57.50	154		211.50	297
4200 Maximum		3	5.333		750	256		1,006	1,225
4300 42" wide, minimum		5	3.200		181	154		335	435
4330 Custom		5	3.200		1,650	154		1,804	2,025
4350 Maximum		3	5.333		2,000	256		2,256	2,600
4500 For ventless hood, 2 speed, add					17.90			17.90	19.70
4650 For vented 1 speed, deduct from maximum					47.50			47.50	52.50

11 31 23 – Residential Laundry Appliances

11 31 23.13 Washers

	Crew	Daily Output	Labor-Hours	Unit	Material	Labor	Equipment	Total	Total Incl O&P
0010 **WASHERS**									
5000 Residential, 4 cycle, average	1 Plum	3	2.667	Ea.	850	146		996	1,150
6650 Washing machine, automatic, minimum		3	2.667		415	146		561	675
6700 Maximum		1	8		1,500	435		1,935	2,300

11 31 23.23 Dryers

	Crew	Daily Output	Labor-Hours	Unit	Material	Labor	Equipment	Total	Total Incl O&P
0010 **DRYERS**									
0500 Gas fired residential, 16 lb. capacity, average	1 Plum	3	2.667	Ea.	645	146		791	930
7450 Vent kits for dryers	1 Carp	10	.800	"	41	35.50		76.50	99.50

11 31 33 – Miscellaneous Residential Appliances

11 31 33.13 Sump Pumps

	Crew	Daily Output	Labor-Hours	Unit	Material	Labor	Equipment	Total	Total Incl O&P
0010 **SUMP PUMPS**									
6400 Cellar drainer, pedestal, 1/3 H.P., molded PVC base	1 Plum	3	2.667	Ea.	128	146		274	360
6450 Solid brass	"	2	4	"	272	218		490	630
6460 Sump pump, see also Section 22 14 29.16									

11 31 33.23 Water Heaters

	Crew	Daily Output	Labor-Hours	Unit	Material	Labor	Equipment	Total	Total Incl O&P
0010 **WATER HEATERS**									
6900 Electric, glass lined, 30 gallon, minimum	L-1	5	3.200	Ea.	520	170		690	825
6950 Maximum		3	5.333		720	283		1,003	1,225
7100 80 gallon, minimum		2	8		935	425		1,360	1,675
7150 Maximum		1	16		1,300	850		2,150	2,700
7180 Gas, glass lined, 30 gallon, minimum	2 Plum	5	3.200		805	175		980	1,150
7220 Maximum		3	5.333		1,125	291		1,416	1,675
7260 50 gallon, minimum		2.50	6.400		845	350		1,195	1,450
7300 Maximum		1.50	10.667		1,175	580		1,755	2,150

11 31 Residential Appliances

11 31 33 – Miscellaneous Residential Appliances

11 31 33.43 Air Quality

		Crew	Daily Output	Labor-Hours	Unit	Material	2012 Bare Costs Labor	Equipment	Total	Total Incl O&P
0010	**AIR QUALITY**									
2450	Dehumidifier, portable, automatic, 15 pint				Ea.	162			162	178
2550	40 pint					212			212	233
3550	Heater, electric, built-in, 1250 watt, ceiling type, minimum	1 Elec	4	2		102	103		205	266
3600	Maximum		3	2.667		166	137		303	385
3700	Wall type, minimum		4	2		164	103		267	335
3750	Maximum		3	2.667		176	137		313	400
3900	1500 watt wall type, with blower		4	2		164	103		267	335
3950	3000 watt		3	2.667		335	137		472	575
4850	Humidifier, portable, 8 gallons per day					173			173	191
5000	15 gallons per day					208			208	229

11 41 Foodservice Storage Equipment

11 41 13 – Refrigerated Food Storage Cases

11 41 13.10 Refrigerated Food Cases

		Crew	Daily Output	Labor-Hours	Unit	Material	2012 Bare Costs Labor	Equipment	Total	Total Incl O&P
0010	**REFRIGERATED FOOD CASES**									
0030	Dairy, multi-deck, 12' long	Q-5	3	5.333	Ea.	11,200	267		11,467	12,700
0100	For rear sliding doors, add					1,725			1,725	1,900
0200	Delicatessen case, service deli, 12' long, single deck	Q-5	3.90	4.103		6,575	206		6,781	7,550
0300	Multi-deck, 18 S.F. shelf display		3	5.333		6,225	267		6,492	7,250
0400	Freezer, self-contained, chest-type, 30 C.F.		3.90	4.103		7,425	206		7,631	8,475
0500	Glass door, upright, 78 C.F.		3.30	4.848		11,900	243		12,143	13,500
0600	Frozen food, chest type, 12' long		3.30	4.848		7,975	243		8,218	9,150
0700	Glass door, reach-in, 5 door		3	5.333		13,900	267		14,167	15,700
0800	Island case, 12' long, single deck		3.30	4.848		7,200	243		7,443	8,300
0900	Multi-deck		3	5.333		8,400	267		8,667	9,650
1000	Meat case, 12' long, single deck		3.30	4.848		6,000	243		6,243	6,975
1050	Multi-deck		3.10	5.161		10,300	259		10,559	11,700
1100	Produce, 12' long, single deck		3.30	4.848		6,775	243		7,018	7,825
1200	Multi-deck		3.10	5.161		8,625	259		8,884	9,875

11 41 13.20 Refrigerated Food Storage Equipment

		Crew	Daily Output	Labor-Hours	Unit	Material	2012 Bare Costs Labor	Equipment	Total	Total Incl O&P
0010	**REFRIGERATED FOOD STORAGE EQUIPMENT**									
2350	Cooler, reach-in, beverage, 6' long	Q-1	6	2.667	Ea.	3,625	131		3,756	4,175
4300	Freezers, reach-in, 44 C.F.		4	4		2,625	197		2,822	3,200
4500	68 C.F.		3	5.333		4,550	262		4,812	5,425

11 44 Food Cooking Equipment

11 44 13 – Commercial Ranges

11 44 13.10 Cooking Equipment

		Crew	Daily Output	Labor-Hours	Unit	Material	2012 Bare Costs Labor	Equipment	Total	Total Incl O&P
0010	**COOKING EQUIPMENT**									
0020	Bake oven, gas, one section	Q-1	8	2	Ea.	4,800	98.50		4,898.50	5,425
0300	Two sections		7	2.286		9,175	112		9,287	10,300
0600	Three sections		6	2.667		14,900	131		15,031	16,600
0900	Electric convection, single deck	L-7	4	7		6,425	298		6,723	7,525
6350	Kettle, w/steam jacket, tilting, w/positive lock, SS, 20 gallons		7	4		7,375	170		7,545	8,350
6600	60 gallons		6	4.667		10,400	199		10,599	11,700

11 47 Ice Machines

11 47 10 – Commercial Ice Machines

11 47 10.10 Commercial Ice Equipment	Crew	Daily Output	Labor-Hours	Unit	Material	2012 Bare Costs Labor	Equipment	Total	Total Incl O&P
0010 **COMMERCIAL ICE EQUIPMENT**									
5800 Ice cube maker, 50 pounds per day	Q-1	6	2.667	Ea.	1,475	131		1,606	1,825
6050 500 pounds per day	"	4	4	"	2,750	197		2,947	3,325

11 48 Cleaning and Disposal Equipment

11 48 13 – Commercial Dishwashers

11 48 13.10 Dishwashers

11 48 13.10 Dishwashers	Crew	Daily Output	Labor-Hours	Unit	Material	2012 Bare Costs Labor	Equipment	Total	Total Incl O&P
0010 **DISHWASHERS**									
2700 Dishwasher, commercial, rack type									
2720 10 to 12 racks per hour	Q-1	3.20	5	Ea.	4,300	246		4,546	5,100
2730 Energy star rated, 35 to 40 racks/hour ⒢		1.30	12.308		4,725	605		5,330	6,100
2740 50 to 60 racks/hour ⒢		1.30	12.308		10,200	605		10,805	12,100
2800 Automatic, 190 to 230 racks per hour	L-6	.35	34.286		13,500	1,825		15,325	17,600
2820 235 to 275 racks per hour		.25	48		31,900	2,575		34,475	39,000
2840 8,750 to 12,500 dishes per hour		.10	120		49,500	6,425		55,925	64,000

11 53 Laboratory Equipment

11 53 13 – Laboratory Fume Hoods

11 53 13.13 Recirculating Laboratory Fume Hoods

11 53 13.13 Recirculating Laboratory Fume Hoods	Crew	Daily Output	Labor-Hours	Unit	Material	2012 Bare Costs Labor	Equipment	Total	Total Incl O&P
0010 **RECIRCULATING LABORATORY FUME HOODS**									
0600 Fume hood, with countertop & base, not including HVAC									
0610 Simple, minimum	2 Carp	5.40	2.963	L.F.	620	131		751	880
0620 Complex, including fixtures		2.40	6.667		1,850	294		2,144	2,475
0630 Special, maximum		1.70	9.412		825	415		1,240	1,550
0670 Service fixtures, average				Ea.	295			295	325
0680 For sink assembly with hot and cold water, add	1 Plum	1.40	5.714	"	725	310		1,035	1,275

11 53 13.23 Exhaust Hoods

11 53 13.23 Exhaust Hoods	Crew	Daily Output	Labor-Hours	Unit	Material	2012 Bare Costs Labor	Equipment	Total	Total Incl O&P
0010 **EXHAUST HOODS**									
0650 Ductwork, minimum	2 Shee	1	16	Hood	3,725	835		4,560	5,375
0660 Maximum	"	.50	32	"	5,750	1,675		7,425	8,875

11 53 19 – Laboratory Sterilizers

11 53 19.13 Sterilizers

11 53 19.13 Sterilizers	Crew	Daily Output	Labor-Hours	Unit	Material	2012 Bare Costs Labor	Equipment	Total	Total Incl O&P
0010 **STERILIZERS**									
0700 Glassware washer, undercounter, minimum	L-1	1.80	8.889	Ea.	6,000	470		6,470	7,300
0710 Maximum	"	1	16		12,200	850		13,050	14,700
1850 Utensil washer-sanitizer	1 Plum	2	4		11,100	218		11,318	12,500

11 53 33 – Emergency Safety Appliances

11 53 33.13 Emergency Equipment

11 53 33.13 Emergency Equipment	Crew	Daily Output	Labor-Hours	Unit	Material	2012 Bare Costs Labor	Equipment	Total	Total Incl O&P
0010 **EMERGENCY EQUIPMENT**									
1400 Safety equipment, eye wash, hand held				Ea.	405			405	445
1450 Deluge shower				"	740			740	815

11 53 43 – Service Fittings and Accessories

11 53 43.13 Fittings

11 53 43.13 Fittings	Crew	Daily Output	Labor-Hours	Unit	Material	2012 Bare Costs Labor	Equipment	Total	Total Incl O&P
0010 **FITTINGS**									
1600 Sink, one piece plastic, flask wash, hose, free standing	1 Plum	1.60	5	Ea.	1,850	273		2,123	2,425
1610 Epoxy resin sink, 25" x 16" x 10"	"	2	4	"	204	218		422	555
8000 Alternate pricing method: as percent of lab furniture									

11 53 Laboratory Equipment

11 53 43 – Service Fittings and Accessories

11 53 43.13 Fittings

	11 53 43.13 Fittings	Crew	Daily Output	Labor-Hours	Unit	Material	2012 Bare Costs Labor	Equipment	Total	Total Incl O&P
8050	Installation, not incl. plumbing & duct work				% Furn.				20%	22%
8100	Plumbing, final connections, simple system								9.09%	10%
8110	Moderately complex system								13.64%	15%
8120	Complex system								18.18%	20%
8150	Electrical, simple system								9.09%	10%
8160	Moderately complex system								18.18%	20%
8170	Complex system								31.80%	35%

11 71 Medical Sterilizing Equipment

11 71 10 – Medical Sterilizers & Distillers

11 71 10.10 Sterilizers and Distillers

	11 71 10.10 Sterilizers and Distillers	Crew	Daily Output	Labor-Hours	Unit	Material	2012 Bare Costs Labor	Equipment	Total	Total Incl O&P
0010	**STERILIZERS AND DISTILLERS**									
0700	Distiller, water, steam heated, 50 gal. capacity	1 Plum	1.40	5.714	Ea.	19,000	310		19,310	21,400
5600	Sterilizers, floor loading, 26" x 62" x 42", single door, steam					115,000			115,000	126,500
5650	Double door, steam					204,000			204,000	224,000
5800	General purpose, 20" x 20" x 38", single door					13,000			13,000	14,300
6000	Portable, counter top, steam, minimum					3,300			3,300	3,625
6020	Maximum					5,475			5,475	6,025
6050	Portable, counter top, gas, 17" x 15" x 32-1/2"					39,300			39,300	43,200
6150	Manual washer/sterilizer, 16" x 16" x 26"	1 Plum	2	4		54,000	218		54,218	59,500
6200	Steam generators, electric 10 kW to 180 kW, freestanding									
6250	Minimum	1 Elec	3	2.667	Ea.	7,750	137		7,887	8,725
6300	Maximum	"	.70	11.429		28,800	590		29,390	32,600
8200	Bed pan washer-sanitizer	1 Plum	2	4		7,275	218		7,493	8,325

11 73 Patient Care Equipment

11 73 10 – Patient Treatment Equipment

11 73 10.10 Treatment Equipment

	11 73 10.10 Treatment Equipment	Crew	Daily Output	Labor-Hours	Unit	Material	2012 Bare Costs Labor	Equipment	Total	Total Incl O&P
0010	**TREATMENT EQUIPMENT**									
1800	Heat therapy unit, humidified, 26" x 78" x 28"				Ea.	3,500			3,500	3,850
8400	Whirlpool bath, mobile, sst, 18" x 24" x 60"					4,600			4,600	5,050
8450	Fixed, incl. mixing valves	1 Plum	2	4		9,400	218		9,618	10,600

11 74 Dental Equipment

11 74 10 – Dental Office Equipment

11 74 10.10 Diagnostic and Treatment Equipment

	11 74 10.10 Diagnostic and Treatment Equipment	Crew	Daily Output	Labor-Hours	Unit	Material	2012 Bare Costs Labor	Equipment	Total	Total Incl O&P
0010	**DIAGNOSTIC AND TREATMENT EQUIPMENT**									
0020	Central suction system, minimum	1 Plum	1.20	6.667	Ea.	1,550	365		1,915	2,250
0100	Maximum	"	.90	8.889		4,250	485		4,735	5,400
0600	Chair, electric or hydraulic, minimum	1 Skwk	.50	16		2,300	725		3,025	3,650
0700	Maximum		.25	32		8,125	1,450		9,575	11,200
2000	Light, ceiling mounted, minimum		8	1		1,125	45.50		1,170.50	1,325
2100	Maximum		8	1		1,700	45.50		1,745.50	1,950
2200	Unit light, minimum	2 Skwk	5.33	3.002		620	136		756	890
2210	Maximum		5.33	3.002		1,375	136		1,511	1,700
2220	Track light, minimum		3.20	5		1,500	227		1,727	2,000
2230	Maximum		3.20	5		2,700	227		2,927	3,325

11 74 Dental Equipment

11 74 10 – Dental Office Equipment

11 74 10.10 Diagnostic and Treatment Equipment	Crew	Daily Output	Labor-Hours	Unit	Material	2012 Bare Costs Labor	Equipment	Total	Total Incl O&P
2300	Sterilizers, steam portable, minimum				Ea.	1,350			1,350	1,500
2350	Maximum					10,400			10,400	11,400
2600	Steam, institutional					3,250			3,250	3,550
2650	Dry heat, electric, portable, 3 trays					1,225			1,225	1,325

11 78 Mortuary Equipment

11 78 13 – Mortuary Refrigerators

11 78 13.10 Mortuary and Autopsy Equipment

		Crew	Daily Output	Labor-Hours	Unit	Material	2012 Bare Costs Labor	Equipment	Total	Total Incl O&P
0010	**MORTUARY AND AUTOPSY EQUIPMENT**									
0015	Autopsy table, standard	1 Plum	1	8	Ea.	9,175	435		9,610	10,800
0020	Deluxe	"	.60	13.333		15,600	730		16,330	18,200
3200	Mortuary refrigerator, end operated, 2 capacity					13,100			13,100	14,400
3300	6 capacity					21,000			21,000	23,100

11 78 16 – Crematorium Equipment

11 78 16.10 Crematory

		Crew	Daily Output	Labor-Hours	Unit	Material	2012 Bare Costs Labor	Equipment	Total	Total Incl O&P
0010	**CREMATORY**									
1500	Crematory, not including building, 1 place	Q-3	.20	160	Ea.	65,000	8,325		73,325	84,000
1750	2 place	"	.10	320	"	93,000	16,600		109,600	127,000

11 82 Solid Waste Handling Equipment

11 82 19 – Packaged Incinerators

11 82 19.10 Packaged Gas Fired Incinerators

		Crew	Daily Output	Labor-Hours	Unit	Material	2012 Bare Costs Labor	Equipment	Total	Total Incl O&P
0010	**PACKAGED GAS FIRED INCINERATORS**									
4400	Incinerator, gas, not incl. chimney, elec. or pipe, 50#/hr., minimum	Q-3	.80	40	Ea.	11,900	2,075		13,975	16,100
4420	Maximum		.70	45.714		38,200	2,375		40,575	45,700
4440	200 lb. per hr., minimum (batch type)		.60	53.333		65,500	2,775		68,275	76,000
4460	Maximum (with feeder)		.50	64		93,000	3,325		96,325	107,000
4480	400 lb. per hr., minimum (batch type)		.30	106		72,500	5,550		78,050	88,500
4500	Maximum (with feeder)		.25	128		98,500	6,650		105,150	118,000
4520	800 lb. per hr., with feeder, minimum		.20	160		118,500	8,325		126,825	143,000
4540	Maximum		.17	188		164,000	9,800		173,800	195,500
4560	1,200 lb. per hr., with feeder, minimum		.15	213		159,500	11,100		170,600	192,000
4580	Maximum		.11	290		190,500	15,100		205,600	232,500
4600	2,000 lb. per hr., with feeder, minimum		.10	320		390,500	16,600		407,100	454,500
4620	Maximum		.05	640		534,500	33,300		567,800	638,000
4700	For heat recovery system, add, minimum		.25	128		75,500	6,650		82,150	93,000
4710	Add, maximum		.11	290		241,000	15,100		256,100	288,000
4720	For automatic ash conveyer, add		.50	64		31,600	3,325		34,925	39,800
4750	Large municipal incinerators, incl. stack, minimum		.25	128	Ton/day	19,200	6,650		25,850	31,200
4850	Maximum		.10	320	"	51,000	16,600		67,600	81,500

11 82 26 – Facility Waste Compactors

11 82 26.10 Compactors

		Crew	Daily Output	Labor-Hours	Unit	Material	2012 Bare Costs Labor	Equipment	Total	Total Incl O&P
0010	**COMPACTORS**									
0020	Compactors, 115 volt, 250#/hr., chute fed	L-4	1	24	Ea.	11,900	995		12,895	14,600
0100	Hand fed		2.40	10		8,725	415		9,140	10,200
0300	Multi-bag, 230 volt, 600#/hr., chute fed		1	24		10,800	995		11,795	13,400
0400	Hand fed		1	24		9,275	995		10,270	11,700
0500	Containerized, hand fed, 2 to 6 C.Y. containers, 250#/hr.		1	24		11,500	995		12,495	14,100

11 82 Solid Waste Handling Equipment

11 82 26 – Facility Waste Compactors

11 82 26.10 Compactors	Crew	Daily Output	Labor-Hours	Unit	Material	2012 Bare Costs Labor	Equipment	Total	Total Incl O&P
0550 For chute fed, add per floor	L-4	1	24	Ea.	1,325	995		2,320	2,975
1000 Heavy duty industrial compactor, 0.5 C.Y. capacity		1	24		7,750	995		8,745	10,100
1050 1.0 C.Y. capacity		1	24		11,800	995		12,795	14,500
1100 3.0 C.Y. capacity		.50	48		16,100	1,975		18,075	20,800
1150 5.0 C.Y. capacity		.50	48		19,900	1,975		21,875	25,000
1200 Combination shredder/compactor (5,000 lb./hr.)		.50	48		39,500	1,975		41,475	46,500
1400 For handling hazardous waste materials, 55 gallon drum packer, std.					18,300			18,300	20,200
1410 55 gallon drum packer w/HEPA filter					22,900			22,900	25,200
1420 55 gallon drum packer w/charcoal & HEPA filter					30,600			30,600	33,600
1430 All of the above made explosion proof, add					13,900			13,900	15,300
5800 Shredder, industrial, minimum					22,500			22,500	24,800
5850 Maximum					121,000			121,000	133,000
5900 Baler, industrial, minimum					9,025			9,025	9,925
5950 Maximum					527,500			527,500	580,000

Division Notes

	CREW	DAILY OUTPUT	LABOR-HOURS	UNIT	2012 BARE COSTS				TOTAL INCL O&P
					MAT.	LABOR	EQUIP.	TOTAL	

Estimating Tips

General

- The items and systems in this division are usually estimated, purchased, supplied, and installed as a unit by one or more subcontractors. The estimator must ensure that all parties are operating from the same set of specifications and assumptions, and that all necessary items are estimated and will be provided. Many times the complex items and systems are covered, but the more common ones, such as excavation or a crane, are overlooked for the very reason that everyone assumes nobody could miss them. The estimator should be the central focus and be able to ensure that all systems are complete.

- Another area where problems can develop in this division is at the interface between systems. The estimator must ensure, for instance, that anchor bolts, nuts, and washers are estimated and included for the air-supported structures and pre-engineered buildings to be bolted to their foundations. Utility supply is a common area where essential items or pieces of equipment can be missed or overlooked due to the fact that each subcontractor may feel it is another's responsibility. The estimator should also be aware of certain items which may be supplied as part of a package but installed by others, and ensure that the installing contractor's estimate includes the cost of installation. Conversely, the estimator must also ensure that items are not costed by two different subcontractors, resulting in an inflated overall estimate.

13 30 00 Special Structures

- The foundations and floor slab, as well as rough mechanical and electrical, should be estimated, as this work is required for the assembly and erection of the structure. Generally, as noted in the book, the pre-engineered building comes as a shell. Pricing is based on the size and structural design parameters stated in the reference section. Additional features, such as windows and doors with their related structural framing, must also be included by the estimator. Here again, the estimator must have a clear understanding of the scope of each portion of the work and all the necessary interfaces.

Reference Numbers

Reference numbers are shown in shaded boxes at the beginning of some major classifications. These numbers refer to related items in the Reference Section. The reference information may be an estimating procedure, an alternate pricing method, or technical information.

Note: Not all subdivisions listed here necessarily appear in this publication.

13 11 Swimming Pools

13 11 13 – Below-Grade Swimming Pools

13 11 13.50 Swimming Pools

		Crew	Daily Output	Labor-Hours	Unit	Material	2012 Bare Costs Labor	Equipment	Total	Total Incl O&P
0010	**SWIMMING POOLS** Residential in-ground, vinyl lined, concrete									
0020	Sides including equipment, sand bottom	B-52	300	.187	SF Surf	17.55	7.60	1.84	26.99	33
0100	Metal or polystyrene sides	B-14	410	.117		14.70	4.34	.81	19.85	23.50
0200	Add for vermiculite bottom					1.12			1.12	1.23
0500	Gunite bottom and sides, white plaster finish									
0600	12' x 30' pool	B-52	145	.386	SF Surf	32.50	15.75	3.82	52.07	64
0720	16' x 32' pool		155	.361		29.50	14.75	3.57	47.82	59
0750	20' x 40' pool		250	.224		26.50	9.15	2.21	37.86	45.50
0810	Concrete bottom and sides, tile finish									
0820	12' x 30' pool	B-52	80	.700	SF Surf	33	28.50	6.90	68.40	87.50
0830	16' x 32' pool		95	.589		27.50	24	5.80	57.30	73.50
0840	20' x 40' pool		130	.431		21.50	17.60	4.26	43.36	55.50
1100	Motel, gunite with plaster finish, incl. medium									
1150	capacity filtration & chlorination	B-52	115	.487	SF Surf	40	19.85	4.81	64.66	80.50
1200	Municipal, gunite with plaster finish, incl. high									
1250	capacity filtration & chlorination	B-52	100	.560	SF Surf	52	23	5.55	80.55	98
1350	Add for formed gutters				L.F.	76.50			76.50	84
1360	Add for stainless steel gutters				"	226			226	249
1700	Filtration and deck equipment only, as % of total				Total				20%	20%
1800	Deck equipment, rule of thumb, 20' x 40' pool				SF Pool				1.18	1.30
1900	5000 S.F. pool				"				1.73	1.90
3000	Painting pools, preparation + 3 coats, 20' x 40' pool, epoxy	2 Pord	.33	48.485	Total	1,700	1,850		3,550	4,625
3100	Rubber base paint, 18 gallons	"	.33	48.485		1,100	1,850		2,950	3,975
3500	42' x 82' pool, 75 gallons, epoxy paint	3 Pord	.14	171		7,150	6,550		13,700	17,700
3600	Rubber base paint	"	.14	171		4,500	6,550		11,050	14,800

13 11 46 – Swimming Pool Accessories

13 11 46.50 Swimming Pool Equipment

		Crew	Daily Output	Labor-Hours	Unit	Material	2012 Bare Costs Labor	Equipment	Total	Total Incl O&P
0010	**SWIMMING POOL EQUIPMENT**									
0020	Diving stand, stainless steel, 3 meter	2 Carp	.40	40	Ea.	11,100	1,775		12,875	14,900
0300	1 meter	"	2.70	5.926		6,450	261		6,711	7,475
2100	Lights, underwater, 12 volt, with transformer, 300 watt	1 Elec	1	8		274	410		684	915
2200	110 volt, 500 watt, standard		1	8		208	410		618	845
2400	Low water cutoff type		1	8		257	410		667	900
2800	Heaters, see Section 23 52 28.10									

13 18 Ice Rinks

13 18 13 – Ice Rink Floor Systems

13 18 13.50 Ice Skating

		Crew	Daily Output	Labor-Hours	Unit	Material	2012 Bare Costs Labor	Equipment	Total	Total Incl O&P
0010	**ICE SKATING** Equipment incl. refrigeration, plumbing & cooling									
0020	coils & concrete slab, 85' x 200' rink									
0300	55° system, 5 mos., 100 ton				Total	575,000			575,000	632,500
0700	90° system, 12 mos., 135 ton				"	650,000			650,000	715,000
1200	Subsoil heating system (recycled from compressor), 85' x 200'	Q-7	.27	118	Ea.	40,000	6,275		46,275	53,500
1300	Subsoil insulation, 2 lb. polystyrene with vapor barrier, 85' x 200'	2 Carp	.14	114	"	30,000	5,050		35,050	40,800

13 18 16 – Ice Rink Dasher Boards

13 18 16.50 Ice Rink Dasher Boards

		Crew	Daily Output	Labor-Hours	Unit	Material	2012 Bare Costs Labor	Equipment	Total	Total Incl O&P
0010	**ICE RINK DASHER BOARDS**									
1000	Dasher boards, 1/2" H.D. polyethylene faced steel frame, 3' acrylic									
1020	screen at sides, 5' acrylic ends, 85' x 200'	F-5	.06	533	Ea.	135,000	23,800		158,800	185,000
1100	Fiberglass & aluminum construction, same sides and ends	"	.06	533	"	155,000	23,800		178,800	207,000

13 21 13 – Clean Rooms

13 21 13.50 Clean Room Components

		Crew	Daily Output	Labor-Hours	Unit	Material	2012 Bare Costs Labor	Equipment	Total	Total Incl O&P
0010	**CLEAN ROOM COMPONENTS**									
1100	Clean room, soft wall, 12' x 12', Class 100	1 Carp	.18	44.444	Ea.	16,400	1,950		18,350	21,000
1110	Class 1,000		.18	44.444		13,200	1,950		15,150	17,600
1120	Class 10,000		.21	38.095		11,600	1,675		13,275	15,400
1130	Class 100,000	↓	.21	38.095	↓	10,900	1,675		12,575	14,600
2800	Ceiling grid support, slotted channel struts 4'-0" O.C., ea. way				S.F.				5.90	6.50
3000	Ceiling panel, vinyl coated foil on mineral substrate									
3020	Sealed, non-perforated				S.F.				1.27	1.40
4000	Ceiling panel seal, silicone sealant, 150 L.F./gal.	1 Carp	150	.053	L.F.	.30	2.35		2.65	3.95
4100	Two sided adhesive tape	"	240	.033	"	.13	1.47		1.60	2.40
4200	Clips, one per panel				Ea.	1.04			1.04	1.14
6000	HEPA filter, 2' x 4', 99.97% eff., 3" dp beveled frame (silicone seal)					455			455	500
6040	6" deep skirted frame (channel seal)					390			390	430
6100	99.99% efficient, 3" deep beveled frame (silicone seal)					530			530	585
6140	6" deep skirted frame (channel seal)					405			405	445
6200	99.999% efficient, 3" deep beveled frame (silicone seal)					600			600	660
6240	6" deep skirted frame (channel seal)				↓	420			420	465
7000	Wall panel systems, including channel strut framing									
7020	Polyester coated aluminum, particle board				S.F.				18.20	20
7100	Porcelain coated aluminum, particle board								32	35
7400	Wall panel support, slotted channel struts, to 12' high				↓				16.35	18

13 21 26 – Cold Storage Rooms

13 21 26.50 Refrigeration

		Crew	Daily Output	Labor-Hours	Unit	Material	2012 Bare Costs Labor	Equipment	Total	Total Incl O&P
0010	**REFRIGERATION**									
0020	Curbs, 12" high, 4" thick, concrete	2 Carp	58	.276	L.F.	4.61	12.15		16.76	24
1000	Doors, see Section 08 34 13.10									
2400	Finishes, 2 coat portland cement plaster, 1/2" thick	1 Plas	48	.167	S.F.	1.27	6.75		8.02	11.45
2500	For galvanized reinforcing mesh, add	1 Lath	335	.024		.84	.94		1.78	2.30
2700	3/16" thick latex cement	1 Plas	88	.091		2.16	3.67		5.83	7.90
2900	For glass cloth reinforced ceilings, add	"	450	.018		.52	.72		1.24	1.64
3100	Fiberglass panels, 1/8" thick	1 Carp	149.45	.054		2.86	2.36		5.22	6.80
3200	Polystyrene, plastic finish ceiling, 1" thick		274	.029		2.64	1.29		3.93	4.88
3400	2" thick		274	.029		3.01	1.29		4.30	5.30
3500	4" thick	↓	219	.037		3.34	1.61		4.95	6.15
3800	Floors, concrete, 4" thick	1 Cefi	93	.086		1.32	3.64		4.96	6.80
3900	6" thick	"	85	.094	↓	2.07	3.99		6.06	8.15
4000	Insulation, 1" to 6" thick, cork				B.F.	1.22			1.22	1.34
4100	Urethane					.51			.51	.56
4300	Polystyrene, regular					.50			.50	.55
4400	Bead board				↓	.28			.28	.31
4600	Installation of above, add per layer	2 Carp	657.60	.024	S.F.	.40	1.07		1.47	2.09
4700	Wall and ceiling juncture		298.90	.054	L.F.	1.97	2.36		4.33	5.80
4900	Partitions, galvanized sandwich panels, 4" thick, stock		219.20	.073	S.F.	8.25	3.22		11.47	14.05
5000	Aluminum or fiberglass	↓	219.20	.073	"	9.05	3.22		12.27	14.90
5200	Prefab walk-in, 7'-6" high, aluminum, incl. door & floors,									
5210	not incl. partitions or refrigeration, 6' x 6' O.D. nominal	2 Carp	54.80	.292	SF Flr.	148	12.90		160.90	183
5500	10' x 10' O.D. nominal		82.20	.195		119	8.60		127.60	144
5700	12' x 14' O.D. nominal		109.60	.146		107	6.45		113.45	127
5800	12' x 20' O.D. nominal	↓	109.60	.146		93	6.45		99.45	112
6100	For 8'-6" high, add					5%				
6300	Rule of thumb for complete units, w/o doors & refrigeration, cooler	2 Carp	146	.110		134	4.83		138.83	154
6400	Freezer	↓	109.60	.146	↓	158	6.45		164.45	184

13 21 Controlled Environment Rooms

13 21 26 – Cold Storage Rooms

13 21 26.50 Refrigeration

		Crew	Daily Output	Labor-Hours	Unit	Material	2012 Bare Costs Labor	Equipment	Total	Total Incl O&P
6600	Shelving, plated or galvanized, steel wire type	2 Carp	360	.044	SF Hor.	11.75	1.96		13.71	15.90
6700	Slat shelf type	↓	375	.043		14.45	1.88		16.33	18.80
6900	For stainless steel shelving, add					300%				
7000	Vapor barrier, on wood walls	2 Carp	1644	.010	S.F.	.17	.43		.60	.85
7200	On masonry walls	"	1315	.012	"	.44	.54		.98	1.31
7500	For air curtain doors, see Section 23 34 33.10									

13 24 Special Activity Rooms

13 24 16 – Saunas

13 24 16.50 Saunas and Heaters

		Crew	Daily Output	Labor-Hours	Unit	Material	2012 Bare Costs Labor	Equipment	Total	Total Incl O&P
0010	**SAUNAS AND HEATERS**									
0020	Prefabricated, incl. heater & controls, 7' high, 6' x 4', C/C	L-7	2.20	12.727	Ea.	5,125	540		5,665	6,475
0050	6' x 4', C/P		2	14		4,300	595		4,895	5,650
0400	6' x 5', C/C		2	14		5,225	595		5,820	6,675
0450	6' x 5', C/P		2	14		4,450	595		5,045	5,825
0600	6' x 6', C/C		1.80	15.556		5,550	665		6,215	7,125
0650	6' x 6', C/P		1.80	15.556		4,750	665		5,415	6,250
0800	6' x 9', C/C		1.60	17.500		6,875	745		7,620	8,700
0850	6' x 9', C/P		1.60	17.500		6,425	745		7,170	8,225
1000	8' x 12', C/C		1.10	25.455		11,200	1,075		12,275	14,000
1050	8' x 12', C/P		1.10	25.455		9,900	1,075		10,975	12,600
1200	8' x 8', C/C		1.40	20		8,525	850		9,375	10,700
1250	8' x 8', C/P		1.40	20		7,750	850		8,600	9,825
1400	8' x 10', C/C		1.20	23.333		9,450	995		10,445	11,900
1450	8' x 10', C/P		1.20	23.333		8,500	995		9,495	10,900
1600	10' x 12', C/C		1	28		11,800	1,200		13,000	14,800
1650	10' x 12', C/P	↓	1	28		10,300	1,200		11,500	13,200
2500	Heaters only (incl. above), wall mounted, to 200 C.F.					615			615	675
2750	To 300 C.F.					795			795	875
3000	Floor standing, to 720 C.F., 10,000 watts, w/controls	1 Elec	3	2.667		2,100	137		2,237	2,500
3250	To 1,000 C.F., 16,000 watts	"	3	2.667	↓	2,700	137		2,837	3,150

13 24 26 – Steam Baths

13 24 26.50 Steam Baths and Components

		Crew	Daily Output	Labor-Hours	Unit	Material	2012 Bare Costs Labor	Equipment	Total	Total Incl O&P
0010	**STEAM BATHS AND COMPONENTS**									
0020	Heater, timer & head, single, to 140 C.F.	1 Plum	1.20	6.667	Ea.	2,100	365		2,465	2,850
0500	To 300 C.F.		1.10	7.273		2,425	395		2,820	3,275
1000	Commercial size, with blow-down assembly, to 800 C.F.		.90	8.889		7,800	485		8,285	9,300
1500	To 2500 C.F.	↓	.80	10		8,775	545		9,320	10,500
2000	Multiple, motels, apts., 2 baths, w/blow-down assm., 500 C.F.	Q-1	1.30	12.308		5,900	605		6,505	7,400
2500	4 baths	"	.70	22.857		7,450	1,125		8,575	9,900
2700	Conversion unit for residential tub, including door				↓	4,100			4,100	4,500

13 34 Fabricated Engineered Structures

13 34 23 – Fabricated Structures

13 34 23.10 Comfort Stations	Crew	Daily Output	Labor-Hours	Unit	Material	2012 Bare Costs Labor	2012 Bare Costs Equipment	Total	Total Incl O&P
0010 **COMFORT STATIONS** Prefab., stock, w/doors, windows & fixt.									
0100 Not incl. interior finish or electrical									
0300 Mobile, on steel frame, minimum				S.F.	48			48	52.50
0350 Maximum					81			81	89
0400 Permanent, including concrete slab, minimum	B-12J	50	.320		199	13.25	16.90	229.15	258
0500 Maximum	"	43	.372	↓	288	15.40	19.65	323.05	360
0600 Alternate pricing method, mobile, minimum				Fixture	2,150			2,150	2,375
0650 Maximum					3,175			3,175	3,500
0700 Permanent, minimum	B-12J	.70	22.857		12,200	945	1,200	14,345	16,300
0750 Maximum	"	.50	32	↓	20,400	1,325	1,700	23,425	26,300

13 34 23.16 Fabricated Control Booths

	Crew	Daily Output	Labor-Hours	Unit	Material	2012 Bare Costs Labor	2012 Bare Costs Equipment	Total	Total Incl O&P
0010 **FABRICATED CONTROL BOOTHS**									
0100 Guard House, prefab conc w/bullet resistant doors & windows, roof & wiring									
0110 8' x 8', Level III	L-10	1	24	Ea.	24,200	1,200	610	26,010	29,300
0120 8' x 8', Level IV	"	1	24	"	30,300	1,200	610	32,110	36,000

Division Notes

	CREW	DAILY OUTPUT	LABOR-HOURS	UNIT	2012 BARE COSTS				TOTAL INCL O&P
					MAT.	LABOR	EQUIP.	TOTAL	

Estimating Tips

General

- Many products in Division 14 will require some type of support or blocking for installation not included with the item itself. Examples are supports for conveyors or tube systems, attachment points for lifts, and footings for hoists or cranes. Add these supports in the appropriate division.

14 10 00 Dumbwaiters
14 20 00 Elevators

- Dumbwaiters and elevators are estimated and purchased in a method similar to buying a car. The manufacturer has a base unit with standard features. Added to this base unit price will be whatever options the owner or specifications require. Increased load capacity, additional vertical travel, additional stops, higher speed, and cab finish options are items to be considered. When developing an estimate for dumbwaiters and elevators, remember that some items needed by the installers may have to be included as part of the general contract.

Examples are:
— shaftway
— rail support brackets
— machine room
— electrical supply
— sill angles
— electrical connections
— pits
— roof penthouses
— pit ladders

Check the job specifications and drawings before pricing.

- Installation of elevators and handicapped lifts in historic structures can require significant additional costs. The associated structural requirements may involve cutting into and repairing finishes, mouldings, flooring, etc. The estimator must account for these special conditions.

14 30 00 Escalators and Moving Walks

- Escalators and moving walks are specialty items installed by specialty contractors. There are numerous options associated with these items. For specific options, contact a manufacturer or contractor. In a method similar to estimating dumbwaiters and elevators, you should verify the extent of general contract work and add items as necessary.

14 40 00 Lifts
14 90 00 Other Conveying Equipment

- Products such as correspondence lifts, chutes, and pneumatic tube systems, as well as other items specified in this subdivision, may require trained installers. The general contractor might not have any choice as to who will perform the installation or when it will be performed. Long lead times are often required for these products, making early decisions in scheduling necessary.

Reference Numbers

Reference numbers are shown in shaded boxes at the beginning of some major classifications. These numbers refer to related items in the Reference Section. The reference information may be an estimating procedure, an alternate pricing method, or technical information.

Note: Not all subdivisions listed here necessarily appear in this publication.

14 91 Facility Chutes

14 91 33 – Laundry and Linen Chutes

14 91 33.10 Chutes	Crew	Daily Output	Labor-Hours	Unit	Material	2012 Bare Costs Labor	Equipment	Total	Total Incl O&P
0011	**CHUTES**, linen, trash or refuse									
0050	Aluminized steel, 16 ga., 18" diameter	2 Shee	3.50	4.571	Floor	1,700	238		1,938	2,250
0100	24" diameter		3.20	5		1,775	261		2,036	2,350
0200	30" diameter		3	5.333		2,125	278		2,403	2,750
0300	36" diameter		2.80	5.714		2,625	298		2,923	3,350
0400	Galvanized steel, 16 ga., 18" diameter		3.50	4.571		1,000	238		1,238	1,475
0500	24" diameter		3.20	5		1,125	261		1,386	1,650
0600	30" diameter		3	5.333		1,275	278		1,553	1,825
0700	36" diameter		2.80	5.714		1,500	298		1,798	2,100
0800	Stainless steel, 18" diameter		3.50	4.571		3,000	238		3,238	3,675
0900	24" diameter		3.20	5		3,150	261		3,411	3,850
1000	30" diameter		3	5.333		3,750	278		4,028	4,550
1005	36" diameter		2.80	5.714		3,950	298		4,248	4,775
1200	Linen chute bottom collector, aluminized steel		4	4	Ea.	1,400	209		1,609	1,875
1300	Stainless steel		4	4		1,800	209		2,009	2,300
1500	Refuse, bottom hopper, aluminized steel, 18" diameter		3	5.333		1,025	278		1,303	1,550
1600	24" diameter		3	5.333		1,250	278		1,528	1,800
1800	36" diameter		3	5.333		2,500	278		2,778	3,175

14 91 82 – Trash Chutes

14 91 82.10 Trash Chutes and Accessories

		Crew	Daily Output	Labor-Hours	Unit	Material	2012 Bare Costs Labor	Equipment	Total	Total Incl O&P
0010	**TRASH CHUTES AND ACCESSORIES**									
2900	Package chutes, spiral type, minimum	2 Shee	4.50	3.556	Floor	2,425	185		2,610	2,950
3000	Maximum	"	1.50	10.667	"	6,325	555		6,880	7,825

14 92 Pneumatic Tube Systems

14 92 10 – Conventional, Automatic and Computer Controlled Pneumatic Tube Systems

14 92 10.10 Pneumatic Tube Systems

		Crew	Daily Output	Labor-Hours	Unit	Material	2012 Bare Costs Labor	Equipment	Total	Total Incl O&P
0010	**PNEUMATIC TUBE SYSTEMS**									
0020	100' long, single tube, 2 stations, stock									
0100	3" diameter	2 Stpi	.12	133	Total	6,600	7,425		14,025	18,500
0300	4" diameter	"	.09	177	"	7,450	9,900		17,350	23,100
0400	Twin tube, two stations or more, conventional system									
0600	2-1/2" round	2 Stpi	62.50	.256	L.F.	13.30	14.25		27.55	36
0700	3" round		46	.348		15.25	19.35		34.60	46
0900	4" round		49.60	.323		16.90	17.95		34.85	45.50
1000	4" x 7" oval		37.60	.426		24.50	23.50		48	62.50
1050	Add for blower		2	8	System	5,200	445		5,645	6,400
1110	Plus for each round station, add		7.50	2.133	Ea.	585	119		704	825
1150	Plus for each oval station, add		7.50	2.133	"	585	119		704	825
1200	Alternate pricing method: base cost, minimum		.75	21.333	Total	6,375	1,200		7,575	8,825
1300	Maximum		.25	64	"	12,700	3,575		16,275	19,300
1500	Plus total system length, add, minimum		93.40	.171	L.F.	8.20	9.55		17.75	23.50
1600	Maximum		37.60	.426	"	24.50	23.50		48	62
1800	Completely automatic system, 4" round, 15 to 50 stations		.29	55.172	Station	20,100	3,075		23,175	26,700
2200	51 to 144 stations		.32	50		15,600	2,775		18,375	21,400
2400	6" round or 4" x 7" oval, 15 to 50 stations		.24	66.667		25,200	3,725		28,925	33,300
2800	51 to 144 stations		.23	69.565		21,100	3,875		24,975	29,100

88

Estimating Tips

22 10 00 Plumbing Piping and Pumps

This subdivision is primarily basic pipe and related materials. The pipe may be used by any of the mechanical disciplines, i.e., plumbing, fire protection, heating, and air conditioning.

Note: CPVC plastic piping approved for tire protection is located in 21 11 13.

- The labor adjustment factors listed in Subdivision 22 01 02.20 apply throughout Divisions 21, 22, and 23. CAUTION: the correct percentage may vary for the same items. For example, the percentage add for the basic pipe installation should be based on the maximum height that the craftsman must install for that particular section. If the pipe is to be located 14' above the floor but it is suspended on threaded rod from beams, the bottom flange of which is 18' high (4' rods), then the height is actually 18' and the add is 20%. The pipe coverer, however, does not have to go above the 14', and so his or her add should be 10%.

- Most pipe is priced first as straight pipe with a joint (coupling, weld, etc.) every 10' and a hanger usually every 10'.

There are exceptions with hanger spacing such as for cast iron pipe (5') and plastic pipe (3 per 10'). Following each type of pipe there are several lines listing sizes and the amount to be subtracted to delete couplings and hangers. This is for pipe that is to be buried or supported together on trapeze hangers. The reason that the couplings are deleted is that these runs are usually long, and frequently longer lengths of pipe are used. By deleting the couplings, the estimator is expected to look up and add back the correct reduced number of couplings.

- When preparing an estimate, it may be necessary to approximate the fittings. Fittings usually run between 25% and 50% of the cost of the pipe. The lower percentage is for simpler runs, and the higher number is for complex areas, such as mechanical rooms.

- For historic restoration projects, the systems must be as invisible as possible, and pathways must be sought for pipes, conduit, and ductwork. While installations in accessible spaces (such as basements and attics) are relatively straightforward to estimate, labor costs may be more difficult to determine when delivery systems must be concealed.

22 40 00 Plumbing Fixtures

- Plumbing fixture costs usually require two lines: the fixture itself and its "rough-in, supply, and waste."

- In the Assemblies Section (Plumbing D2010) for the desired fixture, the System Components Group at the center of the page shows the fixture on the first line. The rest of the list (fittings, pipe, tubing, etc.) will total up to what we refer to in the Unit Price section as "Rough-in, supply, waste, and vent." Note that for most fixtures we allow a nominal 5' of tubing to reach from the fixture to a main or riser.

- Remember that gas- and oil-fired units need venting.

Reference Numbers

Reference numbers are shown in shaded boxes at the beginning of some major classifications. These numbers refer to related items in the Reference Section. The reference information may be an estimating procedure, an alternate pricing method, or technical information.

Note: Not all subdivisions listed here necessarily appear in this publication.

Note: **Trade Service,** *in part, has been used as a reference source for some of the material prices used in Division 22.*

22 01 Operation and Maintenance of Plumbing

22 01 02 – Labor Adjustments

22 01 02.10 Boilers, General

		Crew	Daily Output	Labor-Hours	Unit	Material	2012 Bare Costs Labor	Equipment	Total	Total Incl O&P
0010	**BOILERS, GENERAL**, Prices do not include flue piping, elec. wiring,									
0020	gas or oil piping, boiler base, pad, or tankless unless noted									
0100	Boiler H.P.: 10 KW = 34 lb./steam/hr. = 33,475 BTU/hr. R235000-50									
0150	To convert SFR to BTU rating: Hot water, 150 x SFR;									
0160	Forced hot water, 180 x SFR; steam, 240 x SFR									

22 01 02.20 Labor Adjustment Factors

		Crew	Daily Output	Labor-Hours	Unit	Material	2012 Bare Costs Labor	Equipment	Total	Total Incl O&P
0010	**LABOR ADJUSTMENT FACTORS**, (For Div. 21, 22 and 23) R220102-20									
1000	Add to labor for elevated installation (Above floor level)									
1080	10' to 14.5' high R221113-70						10%			
1100	15' to 19.5' high						20%			
1120	20' to 24.5' high						25%			
1140	25' to 29.5' high						35%			
1160	30' to 34.5' high						40%			
1180	35' to 39.5' high						50%			
1200	40' and higher						55%			
2000	Add to labor for crawl space									
2100	3' high						40%			
2140	4' high						30%			
3000	Add to labor for multi-story building									
3100	Add per floor for floors 3 thru 19						2%			
3140	Add per floor for floors 20 and up						4%			
4000	Add to labor for working in existing occupied buildings									
4100	Hospital						35%			
4140	Office building						25%			
4180	School						20%			
4220	Factory or warehouse						15%			
4260	Multi dwelling						15%			
5000	Add to labor, miscellaneous									
5100	Cramped shaft						35%			
5140	Congested area						15%			
5180	Excessive heat or cold						30%			
9000	Labor factors, The above are reasonable suggestions, however									
9010	each project should be evaluated for its own peculiarities.									
9100	Other factors to be considered are:									
9140	Movement of material and equipment through finished areas									
9180	Equipment room									
9220	Attic space									
9260	No service road									
9300	Poor unloading/storage area									
9340	Congested site area/heavy traffic									

22 05 Common Work Results for Plumbing

22 05 05 – Selective Plumbing Demolition

22 05 05.10 Plumbing Demolition

		Crew	Daily Output	Labor-Hours	Unit	Material	2012 Bare Costs Labor	2012 Bare Costs Equipment	Total	Total Incl O&P
0010	**PLUMBING DEMOLITION** R220105-10									
0400	Air compressor, up thru 2 H.P.	Q-1	10	1.600	Ea.		78.50		78.50	119
0410	3 H.P. thru 7-1/2 H.P.		5.60	2.857			140		140	212
0420	10 H.P. thru 15 H.P.		1.40	11.429			560		560	845
0430	20 H.P. thru 30 H.P.	Q-2	1.30	18.462			940		940	1,425
0500	Backflow preventer, up thru 2" diameter	1 Plum	17	.471			25.50		25.50	39
0510	2-1/2" thru 3" diameter	Q-1	10	1.600			78.50		78.50	119
0520	4" thru 6" diameter	"	5	3.200			157		157	237
0530	8" thru 10" diameter	Q-2	3	8			410		410	615
0700	Carriers and supports									
0710	Fountains, sinks, lavatories and urinals	1 Plum	14	.571	Ea.		31		31	47
0720	Water closets	"	12	.667	"		36.50		36.50	55
0730	Grinder pump or sewage ejector system									
0732	Simplex	Q-1	7	2.286	Ea.		112		112	169
0734	Duplex	"	2.80	5.714			281		281	425
0738	Hot water dispenser	1 Plum	36	.222			12.15		12.15	18.30
0740	Hydrant, wall		26	.308			16.80		16.80	25.50
0744	Ground		12	.667			36.50		36.50	55
0760	Cleanouts and drains, up thru 4" pipe diameter		10	.800			43.50		43.50	66
0764	5" thru 8" pipe diameter	Q-1	10	1.600			78.50		78.50	119
0780	Industrial safety fixtures	1 Plum	8	1			54.50		54.50	82.50
1020	Fixtures, including 10' piping									
1100	Bathtubs, cast iron	1 Plum	4	2	Ea.		109		109	165
1120	Fiberglass		6	1.333			73		73	110
1140	Steel		5	1.600			87.50		87.50	132
1150	Bidet	Q-1	7	2.286			112		112	169
1200	Lavatory, wall hung	1 Plum	10	.800			43.50		43.50	66
1220	Counter top		8	1			54.50		54.50	82.50
1300	Sink, single compartment		8	1			54.50		54.50	82.50
1320	Double compartment		7	1.143			62.50		62.50	94
1340	Shower, stall and receptor	Q-1	6	2.667			131		131	198
1350	Group	"	7	2.286			112		112	169
1400	Water closet, floor mounted	1 Plum	8	1			54.50		54.50	82.50
1420	Wall mounted	"	7	1.143			62.50		62.50	94
1440	Wash fountain, 36" diameter	Q-2	8	3			153		153	231
1442	54" diameter	"	7	3.429			175		175	264
1500	Urinal, floor mounted	1 Plum	4	2			109		109	165
1520	Wall mounted	"	7	1.143			62.50		62.50	94
1590	Whirl pool or hot tub	Q-1	2.60	6.154			300		300	455
1600	Water fountains, free standing	1 Plum	8	1			54.50		54.50	82.50
1620	Wall or deck mounted		6	1.333			73		73	110
1800	Medical gas specialties		8	1			54.50		54.50	82.50
1810	Plumbing demo, Floor drain, Remove		12	.667			36.50		36.50	55
1900	Piping fittings, single connection, up thru 1-1/2" diameter		30	.267			14.55		14.55	22
1910	2" thru 4" diameter		14	.571			31		31	47
1980	Pipe hanger/support removal		80	.100			5.45		5.45	8.25
1990	Glass pipe with fittings, 1" thru 3" diameter		200	.040	L.F.		2.18		2.18	3.29
1992	4" thru 6" diameter		150	.053			2.91		2.91	4.39
2000	Piping, metal, up thru 1-1/2" diameter		200	.040			2.18		2.18	3.29
2050	2" thru 3-1/2" diameter		150	.053			2.91		2.91	4.39
2100	4" thru 6" diameter	2 Plum	100	.160			8.75		8.75	13.20
2150	8" thru 14" diameter	"	60	.267			14.55		14.55	22
2153	16" thru 20" diameter	Q-18	70	.343			17.80	.53	18.33	27.50

22 05 05.10 Plumbing Demolition		Crew	Daily Output	Labor-Hours	Unit	Material	2012 Bare Costs Labor	2012 Bare Costs Equipment	Total	Total Incl O&P
2155	24" thru 26" diameter	Q-18	55	.436	L.F.		22.50	.67	23.17	34.50
2156	30" thru 36" diameter	↓	40	.600			31	.92	31.92	48
2160	Plastic pipe with fittings, up thru 1-1/2" diameter	1 Plum	250	.032			1.75		1.75	2.64
2162	2" thru 3" diameter	"	200	.040			2.18		2.18	3.29
2164	4" thru 6" diameter	Q-1	200	.080			3.93		3.93	5.95
2166	8" thru 14" diameter		150	.107			5.25		5.25	7.90
2168	16" diameter		100	.160	↓		7.85		7.85	11.85
2170	Prison fixtures, lavatory or sink		18	.889	Ea.		43.50		43.50	66
2172	Shower		5.60	2.857			140		140	212
2174	Urinal or water closet		13	1.231			60.50		60.50	91
2180	Pumps, all fractional horse-power		12	1.333			65.50		65.50	99
2184	1 H.P. thru 5 H.P.		6	2.667			131		131	198
2186	7-1/2 H.P. thru 15 H.P.	↓	2.50	6.400			315		315	475
2188	20 H.P. thru 25 H.P.	Q-2	4	6			305		305	460
2190	30 H.P. thru 60 H.P.		.80	30			1,525		1,525	2,300
2192	75 H.P. thru 100 H.P.		.60	40			2,050		2,050	3,075
2194	150 H.P.	↓	.50	48			2,450		2,450	3,700
2198	Pump, sump or submersible	1 Plum	12	.667			36.50		36.50	55
2200	Receptors and interceptors, up thru 20 GPM	"	8	1			54.50		54.50	82.50
2204	25 thru 100 GPM	Q-1	6	2.667			131		131	198
2208	125 thru 300 GPM	"	2.40	6.667			330		330	495
2211	325 thru 500 GPM	Q-2	2.60	9.231	↓		470		470	710
2212	Deduct for salvage, aluminum scrap				Ton				700	770
2214	Brass scrap								2,450	2,675
2216	Copper scrap								3,200	3,525
2218	Lead scrap								520	570
2220	Steel scrap				↓				180	200
2230	Temperature maintenance cable	1 Plum	1200	.007	L.F.		.36		.36	.55
2250	Water heater, 40 gal.	"	6	1.333	Ea.		73		73	110
3100	Tanks, water heaters and liquid containers									
3110	Up thru 45 gallons	Q-1	22	.727	Ea.		36		36	54
3120	50 thru 120 gallons		14	1.143			56		56	84.50
3130	130 thru 240 gallons		7.60	2.105			103		103	156
3140	250 thru 500 gallons	↓	5.40	2.963			146		146	220
3150	600 thru 1000 gallons	Q-2	1.60	15			765		765	1,150
3160	1100 thru 2000 gallons		.70	34.286			1,750		1,750	2,625
3170	2100 thru 4000 gallons	↓	.50	48			2,450		2,450	3,700
6000	Remove and reset fixtures, minimum	1 Plum	6	1.333			73		73	110
6100	Maximum	"	4	2			109		109	165
9100	Valve, metal valves, strainers and similar, up thru 1-1/2" diameter	1 Stpi	28	.286			15.90		15.90	24
9110	2" thru 3" diameter	Q-1	11	1.455			71.50		71.50	108
9120	4" thru 6" diameter	"	8	2			98.50		98.50	148
9130	8" thru 14" diameter	Q-2	8	3			153		153	231
9140	16" thru 20" diameter		2	12			610		610	920
9150	24" diameter	↓	1.20	20			1,025		1,025	1,525
9200	Valve, plastic, up thru 1-1/2" diameter	1 Plum	42	.190			10.40		10.40	15.70
9210	2" thru 3" diameter		15	.533			29		29	44
9220	4" thru 6" diameter		12	.667			36.50		36.50	55
9300	Vent flashing and caps	↓	55	.145			7.95		7.95	12
9350	Water filter, commercial, 1" thru 1-1/2"	Q-1	2	8			395		395	595
9360	2" thru 2-1/2"	"	1.60	10	↓		490		490	740
9400	Water heaters									
9410	Up thru 245 GPH	Q-1	2.40	6.667	Ea.		330		330	495

22 05 Common Work Results for Plumbing

22 05 05 – Selective Plumbing Demolition

22 05 05.10 Plumbing Demolition

		Crew	Daily Output	Labor-Hours	Unit	Material	2012 Bare Costs Labor	Equipment	Total	Total Incl O&P
9420	250 thru 756 GPH	Q-1	1.60	10	Ea.		490		490	740
9430	775 thru 1640 GPH	↓	.80	20			985		985	1,475
9440	1650 thru 4000 GPH	Q-2	.50	48			2,450		2,450	3,700
9470	Water softener	Q-1	2	8	↓		395		395	595

22 05 23 – General-Duty Valves for Plumbing Piping

22 05 23.10 Valves, Brass

		Crew	Daily Output	Labor-Hours	Unit	Material	2012 Bare Costs Labor	Equipment	Total	Total Incl O&P
0010	**VALVES, BRASS**									
0032	For motorized valves, see Section 23 09 53.10									
0500	Gas cocks, threaded									
0510	1/4"	1 Plum	26	.308	Ea.	14.70	16.80		31.50	41.50
0520	3/8"		24	.333		14.70	18.20		32.90	43.50
0530	1/2"		24	.333		13.15	18.20		31.35	42
0540	3/4"		22	.364		15.50	19.85		35.35	47
0550	1"		19	.421		31	23		54	68.50
0560	1-1/4"		15	.533		44.50	29		73.50	93
0570	1-1/2"		13	.615		61	33.50		94.50	118
0580	2"	↓	11	.727	↓	103	39.50		142.50	174
0672	For larger sizes use lubricated plug valve, Section 23 05 23.70									

22 05 23.20 Valves, Bronze

		Crew	Daily Output	Labor-Hours	Unit	Material	2012 Bare Costs Labor	Equipment	Total	Total Incl O&P
0010	**VALVES, BRONZE** R220523-90									
1020	Angle, 150 lb., rising stem, threaded									
1030	1/8"	1 Plum	24	.333	Ea.	119	18.20		137.20	159
1040	1/4"		24	.333		119	18.20		137.20	159
1050	3/8"		24	.333		119	18.20		137.20	159
1060	1/2"		22	.364		119	19.85		138.85	161
1070	3/4"		20	.400		162	22		184	211
1080	1"		19	.421		234	23		257	292
1090	1-1/4"		15	.533		300	29		329	375
1100	1-1/2"		13	.615		360	33.50		393.50	445
1110	2"	↓	11	.727	↓	630	39.50		669.50	755
1300	Ball									
1304	Soldered									
1312	3/8"	1 Plum	21	.381	Ea.	12.60	21		33.60	45.50
1316	1/2"		18	.444		12.60	24.50		37.10	50.50
1320	3/4"		17	.471		21	25.50		46.50	62
1324	1"		15	.533		26	29		55	73
1328	1-1/4"		13	.615		44	33.50		77.50	99
1332	1-1/2"		11	.727		56	39.50		95.50	122
1336	2"		9	.889		70	48.50		118.50	151
1340	2-1/2"		7	1.143		380	62.50		442.50	515
1344	3"	↓	5	1.600	↓	505	87.50		592.50	685
1350	Single union end									
1358	3/8"	1 Plum	21	.381	Ea.	17.90	21		38.90	51
1362	1/2"		18	.444		17.90	24.50		42.40	56
1366	3/4"		17	.471		32.50	25.50		58	74.50
1370	1"		15	.533		43.50	29		72.50	92
1374	1-1/4"		13	.615		74	33.50		107.50	132
1378	1-1/2"		11	.727		93	39.50		132.50	162
1382	2"	↓	9	.889	↓	145	48.50		193.50	233
1398	150 psi, threaded									
1400	1/4"	1 Plum	24	.333	Ea.	12.70	18.20		30.90	41.50
1430	3/8"	↓	24	.333		12.70	18.20		30.90	41.50

22 05 23.20 Valves, Bronze		Crew	Daily Output	Labor-Hours	Unit	Material	2012 Bare Costs Labor	Equipment	Total	Total Incl O&P
1450	1/2"	1 Plum	22	.364	Ea.	12.70	19.85		32.55	44
1460	3/4"		20	.400		21	22		43	56
1470	1"		19	.421		28.50	23		51.50	66
1480	1-1/4"		15	.533		50	29		79	99
1490	1-1/2"		13	.615		65	33.50		98.50	122
1500	2"		11	.727		78.50	39.50		118	147
1510	2-1/2"		9	.889		263	48.50		311.50	365
1520	3"	▼	8	1	▼	400	54.50		454.50	525
1600	Butterfly, 175 psi, full port, solder or threaded ends									
1610	Stainless steel disc and stem									
1620	1/4"	1 Plum	24	.333	Ea.	14.75	18.20		32.95	43.50
1630	3/8"		24	.333		14.75	18.20		32.95	43.50
1640	1/2"		22	.364		14.75	19.85		34.60	46
1650	3/4"		20	.400		22.50	22		44.50	57.50
1660	1"		19	.421		28.50	23		51.50	65.50
1670	1-1/4"		15	.533		45.50	29		74.50	94
1680	1-1/2"		13	.615		56.50	33.50		90	113
1690	2"	▼	11	.727	▼	68.50	39.50		108	136
1750	Check, swing, class 150, regrinding disc, threaded									
1800	1/8"	1 Plum	24	.333	Ea.	91	18.20		109.20	128
1830	1/4"		24	.333		91	18.20		109.20	128
1840	3/8"		24	.333		88.50	18.20		106.70	125
1850	1/2"		24	.333		107	18.20		125.20	146
1860	3/4"		20	.400		142	22		164	189
1870	1"		19	.421		145	23		168	194
1880	1-1/4"		15	.533		198	29		227	262
1890	1-1/2"		13	.615		292	33.50		325.50	370
1900	2"	▼	11	.727		400	39.50		439.50	495
1910	2-1/2"	Q-1	15	1.067		615	52.50		667.50	755
1920	3"	"	13	1.231	▼	910	60.50		970.50	1,100
2000	For 200 lb., add					5%	10%			
2040	For 300 lb., add					15%	15%			
2060	Check swing, 300#, sweat, 3/8" size	1 Plum	24	.333	Ea.	37	18.20		55.20	68
2070	1/2"		24	.333		37	18.20		55.20	68
2080	3/4"		20	.400		63	22		85	102
2090	1"		19	.421		65	23		88	107
2100	1-1/4"		15	.533		84.50	29		113.50	137
2110	1-1/2"		13	.615		112	33.50		145.50	174
2120	2"	▼	11	.727		169	39.50		208.50	246
2130	2-1/2"	Q-1	15	1.067		400	52.50		452.50	520
2140	3"	"	13	1.231	▼	535	60.50		595.50	680
2350	Check, lift, class 150, horizontal composition disc, threaded									
2430	1/4"	1 Plum	24	.333	Ea.	128	18.20		146.20	169
2440	3/8"		24	.333		163	18.20		181.20	207
2450	1/2"		24	.333		142	18.20		160.20	184
2460	3/4"		20	.400		173	22		195	223
2470	1"		19	.421		246	23		269	305
2480	1-1/4"		15	.533		330	29		359	410
2490	1-1/2"		13	.615		395	33.50		428.50	485
2500	2"	▼	11	.727	▼	655	39.50		694.50	785
2850	Gate, N.R.S., soldered, 125 psi									
2900	3/8"	1 Plum	24	.333	Ea.	48	18.20		66.20	80.50
2920	1/2"	▼	24	.333	▼	41	18.20		59.20	72.50

22 05 23.20 Valves, Bronze		Crew	Daily Output	Labor-Hours	Unit	Material	2012 Bare Costs Labor	Equipment	Total	Total Incl O&P
2940	3/4"	1 Plum	20	.400	Ea.	47	22		69	84.50
2950	1"		19	.421		66.50	23		89.50	108
2960	1-1/4"		15	.533		102	29		131	156
2970	1-1/2"		13	.615		114	33.50		147.50	176
2980	2"		11	.727		161	39.50		200.50	237
2990	2-1/2"	Q-1	15	1.067		405	52.50		457.50	525
3000	3"	"	13	1.231		525	60.50		585.50	670
3350	Threaded, class 150									
3410	1/4"	1 Plum	24	.333	Ea.	63.50	18.20		81.70	97
3420	3/8"		24	.333		63.50	18.20		81.70	97
3430	1/2"		24	.333		60	18.20		78.20	93
3440	3/4"		20	.400		68.50	22		90.50	108
3450	1"		19	.421		86.50	23		109.50	130
3460	1-1/4" size		15	.533		117	29		146	172
3470	1-1/2"		13	.615		167	33.50		200.50	235
3480	2"		11	.727		199	39.50		238.50	279
3490	2-1/2"	Q-1	15	1.067		465	52.50		517.50	590
3500	3" size	"	13	1.231		660	60.50		720.50	815
3600	Gate, flanged, 150 lb.									
3610	1"	1 Plum	7	1.143	Ea.	1,050	62.50		1,112.50	1,250
3620	1-1/2"		6	1.333		1,325	73		1,398	1,550
3630	2"		5	1.600		1,925	87.50		2,012.50	2,250
3634	2-1/2"	Q-1	5	3.200		3,000	157		3,157	3,500
3640	3"	"	4.50	3.556		3,475	175		3,650	4,100
3850	Rising stem, soldered, 300 psi									
3900	3/8"	1 Plum	24	.333	Ea.	86	18.20		104.20	122
3920	1/2"		24	.333		86	18.20		104.20	122
3940	3/4"		20	.400		93.50	22		115.50	136
3950	1"		19	.421		136	23		159	185
3960	1-1/4"		15	.533		189	29		218	251
3970	1-1/2"		13	.615		222	33.50		255.50	295
3980	2"		11	.727		360	39.50		399.50	455
3990	2-1/2"	Q-1	15	1.067		805	52.50		857.50	965
4000	3"	"	13	1.231		1,150	60.50		1,210.50	1,350
4250	Threaded, class 150									
4310	1/4"	1 Plum	24	.333	Ea.	62.50	18.20		80.70	96.50
4320	3/8"		24	.333		62.50	18.20		80.70	96.50
4330	1/2"		24	.333		57.50	18.20		75.70	91
4340	3/4"		20	.400		67	22		89	107
4350	1"		19	.421		90	23		113	134
4360	1-1/4"		15	.533		122	29		151	179
4370	1-1/2"		13	.615		154	33.50		187.50	220
4380	2"		11	.727		208	39.50		247.50	289
4390	2-1/2"	Q-1	15	1.067		485	52.50		537.50	615
4400	3"	"	13	1.231		675	60.50		735.50	835
4500	For 300 psi, threaded, add					100%	15%			
4540	For chain operated type, add					15%				
4850	Globe, class 150, rising stem, threaded									
4920	1/4"	1 Plum	24	.333	Ea.	88.50	18.20		106.70	125
4940	3/8" size		24	.333		88.50	18.20		106.70	125
4950	1/2"		24	.333		88.50	18.20		106.70	125
4960	3/4"		20	.400		119	22		141	164
4970	1"		19	.421		187	23		210	240

22 05 23.20 Valves, Bronze	Crew	Daily Output	Labor-Hours	Unit	Material	2012 Bare Costs Labor	Equipment	Total	Total Incl O&P
4980	1-1/4"	1 Plum	15	.533	Ea.	298	29		327	375
4990	1-1/2"		13	.615		360	33.50		393.50	450
5000	2"		11	.727		540	39.50		579.50	655
5010	2-1/2"	Q-1	15	1.067		1,100	52.50		1,152.50	1,275
5020	3"	"	13	1.231		1,425	60.50		1,485.50	1,675
5120	For 300 lb. threaded, add					50%	15%			
5130	Globe, 300 lb., sweat, 3/8" size	1 Plum	24	.333	Ea.	111	18.20		129.20	150
5140	1/2"		24	.333		114	18.20		132.20	153
5150	3/4"		20	.400		158	22		180	206
5160	1"		19	.421		214	23		237	270
5170	1-1/4"		15	.533		340	29		369	415
5180	1-1/2"		13	.615		335	33.50		368.50	420
5190	2"		11	.727		590	39.50		629.50	710
5200	2-1/2"	Q-1	15	1.067		1,175	52.50		1,227.50	1,375
5210	3"	"	13	1.231		1,525	60.50		1,585.50	1,775
5600	Relief, pressure & temperature, self-closing, ASME, threaded									
5640	3/4"	1 Plum	28	.286	Ea.	142	15.60		157.60	180
5650	1"		24	.333		217	18.20		235.20	266
5660	1-1/4"		20	.400		420	22		442	495
5670	1-1/2"		18	.444		800	24.50		824.50	915
5680	2"		16	.500		870	27.50		897.50	1,000
5950	Pressure, poppet type, threaded									
6000	1/2"	1 Plum	30	.267	Ea.	37.50	14.55		52.05	63.50
6040	3/4"	"	28	.286	"	40	15.60		55.60	67.50
6400	Pressure, water, ASME, threaded									
6440	3/4"	1 Plum	28	.286	Ea.	80	15.60		95.60	112
6450	1"		24	.333		170	18.20		188.20	215
6460	1-1/4"		20	.400		270	22		292	330
6470	1-1/2"		18	.444		375	24.50		399.50	445
6480	2"		16	.500		540	27.50		567.50	635
6490	2-1/2"		15	.533		2,650	29		2,679	2,975
6900	Reducing, water pressure									
6920	300 psi to 25-75 psi, threaded or sweat									
6940	1/2"	1 Plum	24	.333	Ea.	257	18.20		275.20	310
6950	3/4"		20	.400		257	22		279	315
6960	1"		19	.421		400	23		423	475
6970	1-1/4"		15	.533		715	29		744	830
6980	1-1/2"		13	.615		1,075	33.50		1,108.50	1,225
6990	2"		11	.727		1,550	39.50		1,589.50	1,750
7100	For built-in by-pass or 10-35 psi, add					26.50			26.50	29
7700	High capacity, 250 psi to 25-75 psi, threaded									
7740	1/2"	1 Plum	24	.333	Ea.	350	18.20		368.20	415
7780	3/4"		20	.400		350	22		372	420
7790	1"		19	.421		505	23		528	590
7800	1-1/4"		15	.533		870	29		899	1,000
7810	1-1/2"		13	.615		1,275	33.50		1,308.50	1,450
7820	2"		11	.727		1,850	39.50		1,889.50	2,100
7830	2-1/2"		9	.889		2,650	48.50		2,698.50	3,000
7840	3"		8	1		3,175	54.50		3,229.50	3,575
7850	3" flanged (iron body)	Q-1	10	1.600		3,150	78.50		3,228.50	3,575
7860	4" flanged (iron body)	"	8	2		4,150	98.50		4,248.50	4,725
7920	For higher pressure, add					25%				
8000	Silent check, bronze trim									

22 05 23 – General-Duty Valves for Plumbing Piping

22 05 23.20 Valves, Bronze	Crew	Daily Output	Labor-Hours	Unit	Material	2012 Bare Costs Labor	Equipment	Total	Total Incl O&P
8010	Compact wafer type, for 125 or 150 lb. flanges								
8020	1-1/2"	1 Plum	11	.727	Ea.	305	39.50		344.50	400
8021	2"	"	9	.889		325	48.50		373.50	430
8022	2-1/2"	Q-1	9	1.778		340	87.50		427.50	505
8023	3"		8	2		380	98.50		478.50	570
8024	4"		5	3.200		650	157		807	950
8025	5"	Q-2	6	4		860	204		1,064	1,250
8026	6"		5	4.800		1,025	245		1,270	1,500
8027	8"		4.50	5.333		2,175	272		2,447	2,800
8028	10"		4	6		3,975	305		4,280	4,825
8029	12"		3	8		9,000	410		9,410	10,500
8050	For 250 or 300 lb. flanges, thru 6" no change								
8051	For 8" and 10", add				Ea.	40%	10%			
8060	Full flange wafer type, 150 lb.								
8061	1"	1 Plum	14	.571	Ea.	320	31		351	400
8062	1-1/4"		12	.667		335	36.50		371.50	425
8063	1-1/2"		11	.727		405	39.50		444.50	505
8064	2"		9	.889		545	48.50		593.50	675
8065	2-1/2"	Q-1	9	1.778		615	87.50		702.50	805
8066	3"		8	2		680	98.50		778.50	900
8067	4"		5	3.200		1,000	157		1,157	1,325
8068	5"	Q-2	6	4		1,300	204		1,504	1,725
8069	6"	"	5	4.800		1,700	245		1,945	2,250
8080	For 300 lb., add					40%	10%			
8100	Globe type, 150 lb.								
8110	2"	1 Plum	9	.889	Ea.	635	48.50		683.50	775
8111	2-1/2"	Q-1	9	1.778		785	87.50		872.50	995
8112	3"		8	2		940	98.50		1,038.50	1,175
8113	4"		5	3.200		1,300	157		1,457	1,650
8114	5"	Q-2	6	4		1,600	204		1,804	2,050
8115	6"	"	5	4.800		2,225	245		2,470	2,825
8130	For 300 lb., add					20%	10%			
8140	Screwed end type, 250 lb.								
8141	1/2"	1 Plum	24	.333	Ea.	57	18.20		75.20	90.50
8142	3/4"		20	.400		57	22		79	96
8143	1"		19	.421		65	23		88	106
8144	1-1/4"		15	.533		90	29		119	143
8145	1-1/2"		13	.615		101	33.50		134.50	162
8146	2"		11	.727		136	39.50		175.50	210
8350	Tempering, water, sweat connections								
8400	1/2"	1 Plum	24	.333	Ea.	85	18.20		103.20	121
8440	3/4"	"	20	.400	"	104	22		126	148
8650	Threaded connections								
8700	1/2"	1 Plum	24	.333	Ea.	128	18.20		146.20	169
8740	3/4"		20	.400		475	22		497	560
8750	1"		19	.421		535	23		558	625
8760	1-1/4"		15	.533		830	29		859	955
8770	1-1/2"		13	.615		905	33.50		938.50	1,050
8780	2"		11	.727		1,350	39.50		1,389.50	1,550

22 05 23.60 Valves, Plastic	Crew	Daily Output	Labor-Hours	Unit	Material	2012 Bare Costs Labor	2012 Bare Costs Equipment	Total	Total Incl O&P
0010 **VALVES, PLASTIC** R220523-90									
1100 Angle, PVC, threaded									
1110 1/4"	1 Plum	26	.308	Ea.	74	16.80		90.80	107
1120 1/2"		26	.308		74	16.80		90.80	107
1130 3/4"		25	.320		87.50	17.45		104.95	123
1140 1"		23	.348		106	19		125	146
1150 Ball, PVC, socket or threaded, single union									
1230 1/2"	1 Plum	26	.308	Ea.	26.50	16.80		43.30	55
1240 3/4"		25	.320		30.50	17.45		47.95	60
1250 1"		23	.348		38.50	19		57.50	70.50
1260 1-1/4"		21	.381		51.50	21		72.50	88.50
1270 1-1/2"		20	.400		61.50	22		83.50	101
1280 2"		17	.471		89	25.50		114.50	137
1290 2-1/2"	Q-1	26	.615		375	30.50		405.50	460
1300 3"		24	.667		455	33		488	550
1310 4"		20	.800		770	39.50		809.50	910
1360 For PVC, flanged, add					100%	15%			
1450 Double union 1/2"	1 Plum	26	.308		34	16.80		50.80	63
1460 3/4"		25	.320		40	17.45		57.45	70.50
1470 1"		23	.348		48	19		67	81
1480 1-1/4"		21	.381		66.50	21		87.50	105
1490 1-1/2"		20	.400		80	22		102	121
1500 2"		17	.471		105	25.50		130.50	155
1650 CPVC, socket or threaded, single union									
1700 1/2"	1 Plum	26	.308	Ea.	53	16.80		69.80	84
1720 3/4"		25	.320		66.50	17.45		83.95	100
1730 1"		23	.348		80	19		99	117
1750 1-1/4"		21	.381		127	21		148	172
1760 1-1/2"		20	.400		127	22		149	173
1770 2"		17	.471		176	25.50		201.50	232
1780 3"	Q-1	24	.667		725	33		758	845
1840 For CPVC, flanged, add					65%	15%			
1880 For true union, socket or threaded, add					50%	5%			
2050 Polypropylene, threaded									
2100 1/4"	1 Plum	26	.308	Ea.	40	16.80		56.80	69.50
2120 3/8"		26	.308		40	16.80		56.80	69.50
2130 1/2"		26	.308		40	16.80		56.80	69.50
2140 3/4"		25	.320		49	17.45		66.45	80
2150 1"		23	.348		56	19		75	90
2160 1-1/4"		21	.381		75	21		96	114
2170 1-1/2"		20	.400		93	22		115	135
2180 2"		17	.471		125	25.50		150.50	176
2190 3"	Q-1	24	.667		282	33		315	360
2200 4"	"	20	.800		500	39.50		539.50	610
2550 PVC, three way, socket or threaded									
2600 1/2"	1 Plum	26	.308	Ea.	62.50	16.80		79.30	94
2640 3/4"		25	.320		71	17.45		88.45	105
2650 1"		23	.348		76.50	19		95.50	113
2660 1-1/2"		20	.400		181	22		203	232
2670 2"		17	.471		206	25.50		231.50	266
2680 3"	Q-1	24	.667		430	33		463	525
2740 For flanged, add					60%	15%			

22 05 23 – General-Duty Valves for Plumbing Piping

22 05 23.60 Valves, Plastic		Crew	Daily Output	Labor-Hours	Unit	Material	2012 Bare Costs Labor	Equipment	Total	Total Incl O&P
3150	Ball check, PVC, socket or threaded									
3200	1/4"	1 Plum	26	.308	Ea.	41.50	16.80		58.30	71.50
3220	3/8"		26	.308		41.50	16.80		58.30	71.50
3240	1/2"		26	.308		41.50	16.80		58.30	71.50
3250	3/4"		25	.320		46.50	17.45		63.95	78
3260	1"		23	.348		58.50	19		77.50	92.50
3270	1-1/4"		21	.381		98	21		119	140
3280	1-1/2"		20	.400		98	22		120	141
3290	2"		17	.471		133	25.50		158.50	186
3310	3"	Q-1	24	.667		370	33		403	455
3320	4"	"	20	.800		525	39.50		564.50	635
3360	For PVC, flanged, add					50%	15%			
3750	CPVC, socket or threaded									
3800	1/2"	1 Plum	26	.308	Ea.	64	16.80		80.80	96
3840	3/4"		25	.320		75.50	17.45		92.95	110
3850	1"		23	.348		90.50	19		109.50	129
3860	1-1/2"		20	.400		156	22		178	204
3870	2"		17	.471		156	25.50		181.50	210
3880	3"	Q-1	24	.667		565	33		598	670
3920	4"	"	20	.800		765	39.50		804.50	900
3930	For CPVC, flanged, add					40%	15%			
4340	Polypropylene, threaded									
4360	1/2"	1 Plum	26	.308	Ea.	38.50	16.80		55.30	67.50
4400	3/4"		25	.320		45	17.45		62.45	76
4440	1"		23	.348		57	19		76	91
4450	1-1/2"		20	.400		110	22		132	154
4460	2"		17	.471		138	25.50		163.50	191
4500	For polypropylene flanged, add					200%	15%			
4850	Foot valve, PVC, socket or threaded									
4900	1/2"	1 Plum	34	.235	Ea.	66.50	12.85		79.35	92.50
4930	3/4"		32	.250		75	13.65		88.65	103
4940	1"		28	.286		97.50	15.60		113.10	131
4950	1-1/4"		27	.296		187	16.20		203.20	231
4960	1-1/2"		26	.308		187	16.80		203.80	232
4970	2"		24	.333		218	18.20		236.20	267
4980	3"		20	.400		520	22		542	605
4990	4"		18	.444		915	24.50		939.50	1,025
5000	For flanged, add					25%	10%			
5050	CPVC, socket or threaded									
5060	1/2"	1 Plum	34	.235	Ea.	72	12.85		84.85	99
5070	3/4"		32	.250		83	13.65		96.65	112
5080	1"		28	.286		102	15.60		117.60	137
5090	1-1/4"		27	.296		164	16.20		180.20	205
5100	1-1/2"		26	.308		164	16.80		180.80	206
5110	2"		24	.333		211	18.20		229.20	260
5120	3"		20	.400		430	22		452	505
5130	4"		18	.444		780	24.50		804.50	890
5140	For flanged, add					25%	10%			
5280	Needle valve, PVC, threaded									
5300	1/4"	1 Plum	26	.308	Ea.	47	16.80		63.80	77.50
5340	3/8"		26	.308		54.50	16.80		71.30	85.50
5360	1/2"		26	.308		54.50	16.80		71.30	85.50
5380	For polypropylene, add					10%				

22 05 23 – General-Duty Valves for Plumbing Piping

22 05 23.60 Valves, Plastic		Crew	Daily Output	Labor-Hours	Unit	Material	2012 Bare Costs Labor	Equipment	Total	Total Incl O&P
5800	Y check, PVC, socket or threaded									
5820	1/2"	1 Plum	26	.308	Ea.	55	16.80		71.80	86
5840	3/4"		25	.320		89	17.45		106.45	124
5850	1"		23	.348		96.50	19		115.50	135
5860	1-1/4"		21	.381		151	21		172	199
5870	1-1/2"		20	.400		165	22		187	215
5880	2"		17	.471		205	25.50		230.50	265
5890	2-1/2"		15	.533		435	29		464	520
5900	3"	Q-1	24	.667		435	33		468	525
5910	4"	"	20	.800		710	39.50		749.50	840
5960	For PVC flanged, add					45%	15%			
6350	Y sediment strainer, PVC, socket or threaded									
6400	1/2"	1 Plum	26	.308	Ea.	49	16.80		65.80	79
6440	3/4"		24	.333		52	18.20		70.20	84.50
6450	1"		23	.348		62.50	19		81.50	97
6460	1-1/4"		21	.381		104	21		125	146
6470	1-1/2"		20	.400		104	22		126	147
6480	2"		17	.471		128	25.50		153.50	180
6490	2-1/2"		15	.533		270	29		299	340
6500	3"	Q-1	24	.667		270	33		303	345
6510	4"	"	20	.800		520	39.50		559.50	630
6560	For PVC, flanged, add					55%	15%			

22 05 29 – Hangers and Supports for Plumbing Piping and Equipment

22 05 29.10 Hangers & Supp. for Plumb'g/HVAC Pipe/Equip.		Crew	Daily Output	Labor-Hours	Unit	Material	2012 Bare Costs Labor	Equipment	Total	Total Incl O&P
0010	**HANGERS AND SUPPORTS FOR PLUMB'G/HVAC PIPE/EQUIP.**									
0011	TYPE numbers per MSS-SP58									
0050	Brackets									
0060	Beam side or wall, malleable iron, TYPE 34									
0070	3/8" threaded rod size	1 Plum	48	.167	Ea.	3.42	9.10		12.52	17.50
0080	1/2" threaded rod size		48	.167		6.05	9.10		15.15	20.50
0090	5/8" threaded rod size		48	.167		9.25	9.10		18.35	24
0100	3/4" threaded rod size		48	.167		11.20	9.10		20.30	26
0110	7/8" threaded rod size		48	.167		13.15	9.10		22.25	28.50
0120	For concrete installation, add						30%			
0150	Wall, welded steel, medium, TYPE 32									
0160	0 size, 12" wide, 18" deep	1 Plum	34	.235	Ea.	227	12.85		239.85	269
0170	1 size, 18" wide, 24" deep		34	.235		270	12.85		282.85	315
0180	2 size, 24" wide, 30" deep		34	.235		355	12.85		367.85	415
0200	Beam attachment, welded, TYPE 22									
0202	3/8"	Q-15	80	.200	Ea.	8.35	9.85	.46	18.66	24.50
0203	1/2"		76	.211		8.35	10.35	.49	19.19	25.50
0204	5/8"		72	.222		8.80	10.90	.51	20.21	26.50
0205	3/4"		68	.235		9.60	11.55	.54	21.69	28.50
0206	7/8"		64	.250		13.90	12.30	.58	26.78	34.50
0207	1"		56	.286		18.90	14.05	.66	33.61	42.50
0300	Clamps									
0310	C-clamp, for mounting on steel beam flange, w/locknut, TYPE 23									
0320	3/8" threaded rod size	1 Plum	160	.050	Ea.	3.31	2.73		6.04	7.75
0330	1/2" threaded rod size		160	.050		4.12	2.73		6.85	8.65
0340	5/8" threaded rod size		160	.050		6.30	2.73		9.03	11.05
0350	3/4" threaded rod size		160	.050		8.50	2.73		11.23	13.45
0352	7/8" threaded-rod size		140	.057		27	3.12		30.12	34

22 05 29.10 Hangers & Supp. for Plumb'g/HVAC Pipe/Equip.	Crew	Daily Output	Labor-Hours	Unit	Material	2012 Bare Costs Labor	Equipment	Total	Total Incl O&P
0400	High temperature to 1050°F, alloy steel								
0410	4" pipe size	Q-1	106	.151	Ea.	27	7.40		34.40	40.50
0420	6" pipe size		106	.151		45.50	7.40		52.90	61
0430	8" pipe size		97	.165		51.50	8.10		59.60	69
0440	10" pipe size		84	.190		81.50	9.35		90.85	104
0450	12" pipe size		72	.222		94.50	10.90		105.40	120
0460	14" pipe size		64	.250		248	12.30		260.30	292
0470	16" pipe size		56	.286		259	14.05		273.05	305
0480	Beam clamp, flange type, TYPE 25									
0482	For 3/8" bolt	1 Plum	48	.167	Ea.	12.50	9.10		21.60	27.50
0483	For 1/2" bolt		44	.182		17.35	9.95		27.30	34
0484	For 5/8" bolt		40	.200		17.90	10.90		28.80	36
0485	For 3/4" bolt		36	.222		17.90	12.15		30.05	38
0486	For 1" bolt		32	.250		17.90	13.65		31.55	40
0500	I-beam, for mounting on bottom flange, strap iron, TYPE 21									
0510	2" flange size	1 Plum	96	.083	Ea.	15.10	4.55		19.65	23.50
0520	3" flange size		95	.084		17.95	4.60		22.55	26.50
0530	4" flange size		93	.086		7.85	4.70		12.55	15.70
0540	5" flange size		92	.087		8.65	4.75		13.40	16.65
0550	6" flange size		90	.089		9.90	4.85		14.75	18.15
0560	7" flange size		88	.091		10.85	4.96		15.81	19.45
0570	8" flange size		86	.093		11.60	5.10		16.70	20.50
0600	One hole, vertical mounting, malleable iron									
0610	1/2" pipe size	1 Plum	160	.050	Ea.	1.17	2.73		3.90	5.40
0620	3/4" pipe size		145	.055		1.42	3.01		4.43	6.10
0630	1" pipe size		136	.059		1.97	3.21		5.18	7
0640	1-1/4" pipe size		128	.063		2.35	3.41		5.76	7.75
0650	1-1/2" pipe size		120	.067		2.61	3.64		6.25	8.35
0660	2" pipe size		112	.071		3.81	3.90		7.71	10.10
0670	2-1/2" pipe size		104	.077		7.45	4.20		11.65	14.55
0680	3" pipe size		96	.083		10.60	4.55		15.15	18.50
0690	3-1/2" pipe size		90	.089		12.95	4.85		17.80	21.50
0700	4" pipe size		84	.095		14.30	5.20		19.50	23.50
0750	Riser or extension pipe, carbon steel, TYPE 8									
0756	1/2" pipe size	1 Plum	52	.154	Ea.	4.77	8.40		13.17	17.90
0760	3/4" pipe size		48	.167		4.77	9.10		13.87	19
0770	1" pipe size		47	.170		4.95	9.30		14.25	19.45
0780	1-1/4" pipe size		46	.174		6.10	9.50		15.60	21
0790	1-1/2" pipe size		45	.178		6.55	9.70		16.25	22
0800	2" pipe size		43	.186		6.80	10.15		16.95	23
0810	2-1/2" pipe size		41	.195		7.40	10.65		18.05	24
0820	3" pipe size		40	.200		8.20	10.90		19.10	25.50
0830	3-1/2" pipe size		39	.205		10	11.20		21.20	28
0840	4" pipe size		38	.211		10.25	11.50		21.75	28.50
0850	5" pipe size		37	.216		13.90	11.80		25.70	33
0860	6" pipe size		36	.222		17.15	12.15		29.30	37
0870	8" pipe size		34	.235		29.50	12.85		42.35	52
0880	10" pipe size		32	.250		40	13.65		53.65	64.50
0890	12" pipe size		28	.286		57	15.60		72.60	86
0900	For plastic coating 3/4" to 4", add					190%				
0910	For copper plating 3/4" to 4", add					58%				
0950	Two piece, complete, carbon steel, medium weight, TYPE 4									
0960	1/2" pipe size	Q-1	137	.117	Ea.	3.46	5.75		9.21	12.45

22 05 29 – Hangers and Supports for Plumbing Piping and Equipment

22 05 29.10 Hangers & Supp. for Plumb'g/HVAC Pipe/Equip.		Crew	Daily Output	Labor-Hours	Unit	Material	2012 Bare Costs		Total	Total Incl O&P
							Labor	Equipment		
0970	3/4" pipe size	Q-1	134	.119	Ea.	3.46	5.85		9.31	12.65
0980	1" pipe size		132	.121		3.49	5.95		9.44	12.85
0990	1-1/4" pipe size		130	.123		4.58	6.05		10.63	14.15
1000	1-1/2" pipe size		126	.127		4.58	6.25		10.83	14.45
1010	2" pipe size		124	.129		5.35	6.35		11.70	15.40
1020	2-1/2" pipe size		120	.133		5.70	6.55		12.25	16.15
1030	3" pipe size		117	.137		6.30	6.70		13	17.10
1040	3-1/2" pipe size		114	.140		8.95	6.90		15.85	20.50
1050	4" pipe size		110	.145		8.95	7.15		16.10	20.50
1060	5" pipe size		106	.151		17.20	7.40		24.60	30
1070	6" pipe size		104	.154		22	7.55		29.55	35.50
1080	8" pipe size		100	.160		26	7.85		33.85	40.50
1090	10" pipe size		96	.167		47	8.20		55.20	64
1100	12" pipe size		89	.180		60	8.85		68.85	79.50
1110	14" pipe size		82	.195		116	9.60		125.60	141
1120	16" pipe size	▼	68	.235		125	11.55		136.55	155
1130	For galvanized, add				▼	45%				
1150	Insert, concrete									
1160	Wedge type, carbon steel body, malleable iron nut, galvanized									
1170	1/4" threaded rod size	1 Plum	96	.083	Ea.	2.25	4.55		6.80	9.35
1180	3/8" threaded rod size		96	.083		2.26	4.55		6.81	9.35
1190	1/2" threaded rod size		96	.083		2.54	4.55		7.09	9.65
1200	5/8" threaded rod size		96	.083		3.02	4.55		7.57	10.15
1210	3/4" threaded rod size		96	.083		3.58	4.55		8.13	10.80
1220	7/8" threaded rod size	▼	96	.083	▼	7.85	4.55		12.40	15.50
1250	Pipe guide sized for insulation									
1260	No. 1, 1" pipe size, 1" thick insulation	1 Stpi	26	.308	Ea.	148	17.15		165.15	189
1270	No. 2, 1-1/4"-2" pipe size, 1" thick insulation		23	.348		173	19.35		192.35	219
1280	No. 3, 1-1/4"-2" pipe size, 1-1/2" thick insulation		21	.381		173	21		194	222
1290	No. 4, 2-1/2"-3-1/2" pipe size, 1-1/2" thick insulation		18	.444		173	25		198	228
1300	No. 5, 4"-5" pipe size, 1-1/2" thick insulation	▼	16	.500		194	28		222	255
1310	No. 6, 5"-6" pipe size, 2" thick insulation	Q-5	21	.762		215	38		253	295
1320	No. 7, 8" pipe size, 2" thick insulation		16	1		296	50		346	400
1330	No. 8, 10" pipe size, 2" thick insulation	▼	12	1.333		490	67		557	640
1340	No. 9, 12" pipe size, 2" thick insulation	Q-6	17	1.412		490	73.50		563.50	650
1350	No. 10, 12"-14" pipe size, 2-1/2" thick insulation		16	1.500		545	78		623	720
1360	No. 11, 16" pipe size, 2-1/2" thick insulation		10.50	2.286		545	119		664	780
1370	No. 12, 16"-18" pipe size, 3" thick insulation		9	2.667		770	139		909	1,050
1380	No. 13, 20" pipe size, 3" thick insulation		7.50	3.200		770	166		936	1,100
1390	No. 14, 24" pipe size, 3" thick insulation	▼	7	3.429	▼	1,050	178		1,228	1,425
1400	Bands									
1410	Adjustable band, carbon steel, for non-insulated pipe, TYPE 7									
1420	1/2" pipe size	Q-1	142	.113	Ea.	.74	5.55		6.29	9.15
1430	3/4" pipe size		140	.114		.74	5.60		6.34	9.25
1440	1" pipe size		137	.117		.74	5.75		6.49	9.45
1450	1-1/4" pipe size		134	.119		.80	5.85		6.65	9.75
1460	1-1/2" pipe size		131	.122		.80	6		6.80	9.95
1470	2" pipe size		129	.124		.80	6.10		6.90	10.10
1480	2-1/2" pipe size		125	.128		1.45	6.30		7.75	11.10
1490	3" pipe size		122	.131		1.56	6.45		8.01	11.40
1500	3-1/2" pipe size		119	.134		2.53	6.60		9.13	12.75
1510	4" pipe size		114	.140		2.53	6.90		9.43	13.20
1520	5" pipe size	▼	110	.145	▼	4.25	7.15		11.40	15.50

22 05 Common Work Results for Plumbing

22 05 29 - Hangers and Supports for Plumbing Piping and Equipment

22 05 29.10 Hangers & Supp. for Plumb'g/HVAC Pipe/Equip.	Crew	Daily Output	Labor-Hours	Unit	Material	2012 Bare Costs Labor	Equipment	Total	Total Incl O&P
1530	6" pipe size	Q-1	108	.148	Ea.	4.73	7.30		12.03	16.20
1540	8" pipe size	↓	104	.154	↓	6.40	7.55		13.95	18.40
1550	For copper plated, add					50%				
1560	For galvanized, add					30%				
1570	For plastic coating, add					30%				
1600	Adjusting nut malleable iron, steel band, TYPE 9									
1610	1/2" pipe size, galvanized band	Q-1	137	.117	Ea.	1.35	5.75		7.10	10.15
1620	3/4" pipe size, galvanized band		135	.119		1.49	5.85		7.34	10.45
1630	1" pipe size, galvanized band		132	.121		1.49	5.95		7.44	10.65
1640	1-1/4" pipe size, galvanized band		129	.124		1.62	6.10		7.72	11
1650	1-1/2" pipe size, galvanized band		126	.127		1.62	6.25		7.87	11.20
1660	2" pipe size, galvanized band		124	.129		1.71	6.35		8.06	11.45
1670	2-1/2" pipe size, galvanized band		120	.133		2.79	6.55		9.34	12.95
1680	3" pipe size, galvanized band		117	.137		2.93	6.70		9.63	13.35
1690	3-1/2" pipe size, galvanized band		114	.140		3.92	6.90		10.82	14.70
1700	4" pipe size, cadmium plated band	↓	110	.145		3.92	7.15		11.07	15.10
1740	For plastic coated band, add					35%				
1750	For completely copper coated, add				↓	45%				
1800	Clevis, adjustable, carbon steel, for non-insulated pipe, TYPE 1									
1810	1/2" pipe size	Q-1	137	.117	Ea.	1.77	5.75		7.52	10.60
1820	3/4" pipe size		135	.119		1.77	5.85		7.62	10.75
1830	1" pipe size		132	.121		1.80	5.95		7.75	11
1840	1-1/4" pipe size		129	.124		1.94	6.10		8.04	11.35
1850	1-1/2" pipe size		126	.127		2	6.25		8.25	11.60
1860	2" pipe size		124	.129		2.45	6.35		8.80	12.25
1870	2-1/2" pipe size		120	.133		3.85	6.55		10.40	14.15
1880	3" pipe size		117	.137		4.61	6.70		11.31	15.20
1890	3-1/2" pipe size		114	.140		5.05	6.90		11.95	15.95
1900	4" pipe size		110	.145		5.75	7.15		12.90	17.15
1910	5" pipe size		106	.151		7.65	7.40		15.05	19.60
1920	6" pipe size		104	.154		10.20	7.55		17.75	22.50
1930	8" pipe size		100	.160		15.85	7.85		23.70	29.50
1940	10" pipe size		96	.167		29	8.20		37.20	44.50
1950	12" pipe size		89	.180		38	8.85		46.85	55.50
1960	14" pipe size		82	.195		49.50	9.60		59.10	69
1970	16" pipe size		68	.235		74.50	11.55		86.05	99.50
1971	18" pipe size		54	.296		90	14.55		104.55	121
1972	20" pipe size	↓	38	.421	↓	170	20.50		190.50	218
1980	For galvanized, add					66%				
1990	For copper plated 1/2" to 4", add					77%				
2000	For light weight 1/2" to 4", deduct					13%				
2010	Insulated pipe type, 3/4" to 12" pipe, add					180%				
2020	Insulated pipe type, chrome-moly U-strap, add					530%				
2250	Split ring, malleable iron, for non-insulated pipe, TYPE 11									
2260	1/2" pipe size	Q-1	137	.117	Ea.	6.05	5.75		11.80	15.30
2270	3/4" pipe size		135	.119		6.10	5.85		11.95	15.55
2280	1" pipe size		132	.121		6.50	5.95		12.45	16.15
2290	1-1/4" pipe size		129	.124		8.05	6.10		14.15	18.05
2300	1-1/2" pipe size		126	.127		9.75	6.25		16	20
2310	2" pipe size		124	.129		11.05	6.35		17.40	21.50
2320	2-1/2" pipe size		120	.133		15.95	6.55		22.50	27.50
2330	3" pipe size		117	.137		19.95	6.70		26.65	32
2340	3-1/2" pipe size		114	.140		21	6.90		27.90	33.50

22 05 29.10 Hangers & Supp. for Plumb'g/HVAC Pipe/Equip.		Crew	Daily Output	Labor-Hours	Unit	Material	2012 Bare Costs Labor	2012 Bare Costs Equipment	Total	Total Incl O&P
2350	4" pipe size	Q-1	110	.145	Ea.	21	7.15		28.15	34
2360	5" pipe size		106	.151		27.50	7.40		34.90	41.50
2370	6" pipe size		104	.154		61.50	7.55		69.05	79.50
2380	8" pipe size		100	.160		101	7.85		108.85	124
2390	For copper plated, add					8%				
2500	Washer, flat steel									
2502	3/8"	1 Plum	240	.033	Ea.	.04	1.82		1.86	2.78
2503	1/2"		220	.036		.13	1.99		2.12	3.13
2504	5/8"		200	.040		.24	2.18		2.42	3.55
2505	3/4"		180	.044		.35	2.43		2.78	4.05
2506	7/8"		160	.050		.49	2.73		3.22	4.66
2507	1"		140	.057		.58	3.12		3.70	5.35
2508	1-1/4"		120	.067		.84	3.64		4.48	6.40
2520	Nut, steel, hex									
2522	3/8"	1 Plum	200	.040	Ea.	.92	2.18		3.10	4.30
2523	1/2"		180	.044		1.77	2.43		4.20	5.60
2524	5/8"		160	.050		2.99	2.73		5.72	7.40
2525	3/4"		140	.057		4.52	3.12		7.64	9.70
2526	7/8"		120	.067		7.20	3.64		10.84	13.45
2527	1"		100	.080		10.40	4.37		14.77	18.05
2528	1-1/4"		80	.100		19.85	5.45		25.30	30.50
2532	Turnbuckle, TYPE 13									
2534	3/8"	1 Plum	80	.100	Ea.	3.46	5.45		8.91	12.05
2535	1/2"		72	.111		5.45	6.05		11.50	15.15
2536	5/8"		64	.125		9.65	6.85		16.50	21
2537	3/4"		56	.143		12.55	7.80		20.35	25.50
2538	7/8"		48	.167		29.50	9.10		38.60	46.50
2539	1"		40	.200		38.50	10.90		49.40	59
2540	1-1/4"		32	.250		69.50	13.65		83.15	96.50
2650	Rods, carbon steel									
2660	Continuous thread									
2670	1/4" thread size	1 Plum	144	.056	L.F.	1.45	3.03		4.48	6.20
2680	3/8" thread size		144	.056		1.55	3.03		4.58	6.30
2690	1/2" thread size		144	.056		2.44	3.03		5.47	7.25
2700	5/8" thread size		144	.056		3.47	3.03		6.50	8.40
2710	3/4" thread size		144	.056		6.10	3.03		9.13	11.35
2720	7/8" thread size		144	.056		7.65	3.03		10.68	13.05
2721	1" thread size	Q-1	160	.100		13.05	4.92		17.97	22
2722	1-1/8" thread size	"	120	.133		21.50	6.55		28.05	34
2725	1/4" thread size, bright finish	1 Plum	144	.056		1.90	3.03		4.93	6.65
2726	1/2" thread size, bright finish	"	144	.056		3.42	3.03		6.45	8.35
2730	For galvanized, add					40%				
2750	Both ends machine threaded 18" length									
2760	3/8" thread size	1 Plum	240	.033	Ea.	5.90	1.82		7.72	9.25
2770	1/2" thread size		240	.033		9.50	1.82		11.32	13.20
2780	5/8" thread size		240	.033		13.60	1.82		15.42	17.70
2790	3/4" thread size		240	.033		21.50	1.82		23.32	26
2800	7/8" thread size		240	.033		29.50	1.82		31.32	35
2810	1" thread size		240	.033		35	1.82		36.82	40.50
2820	Rod couplings									
2821	3/8"	1 Plum	60	.133	Ea.	1.87	7.30		9.17	13.05
2822	1/2"		54	.148		2.48	8.10		10.58	14.95
2823	5/8"		48	.167		2.80	9.10		11.90	16.85

22 05 29.10 Hangers & Supp. for Plumb'g/HVAC Pipe/Equip.		Crew	Daily Output	Labor-Hours	Unit	Material	2012 Bare Costs Labor	Equipment	Total	Total Incl O&P
2824	3/4"	1 Plum	44	.182	Ea.	3.93	9.95		13.88	19.25
2825	7/8"		40	.200		6.55	10.90		17.45	23.50
2826	1"		34	.235		8.85	12.85		21.70	29
2827	1-1/8"		30	.267		40.50	14.55		55.05	66.50
2860	Pipe hanger assy, adj. clevis, saddle, rod, clamp, insul. allowance									
2864	1/2" pipe size	Q-5	35	.457	Ea.	41.50	23		64.50	80
2866	3/4" pipe size		34.80	.460		42.50	23		65.50	82
2868	1" pipe size		34.60	.462		45.50	23		68.50	85
2869	1-1/4" pipe size		34.30	.466		46	23.50		69.50	86
2870	1-1/2" pipe size		33.90	.472		47	23.50		70.50	87.50
2872	2" pipe size		33.30	.480		52.50	24		76.50	94
2874	2-1/2" pipe size		32.30	.495		58	25		83	101
2876	3" pipe size		31.20	.513		66	25.50		91.50	112
2880	4" pipe size		30.70	.521		72	26		98	119
2884	6" pipe size		29.80	.537		88.50	27		115.50	138
2888	8" pipe size		28	.571		122	28.50		150.50	177
2892	10" pipe size		25.20	.635		137	32		169	199
2896	12" pipe size		23.20	.690		197	34.50		231.50	268
2900	Rolls									
2910	Adjustable yoke, carbon steel with CI roll, TYPE 43									
2918	2" pipe size	Q-1	140	.114	Ea.	16.60	5.60		22.20	26.50
2920	2-1/2" pipe size		137	.117		16.60	5.75		22.35	27
2930	3" pipe size		131	.122		18.45	6		24.45	29.50
2940	3-1/2" pipe size		124	.129		24.50	6.35		30.85	36.50
2950	4" pipe size		117	.137		24.50	6.70		31.20	37
2960	5" pipe size		110	.145		28.50	7.15		35.65	42.50
2970	6" pipe size		104	.154		38	7.55		45.55	53
2980	8" pipe size		96	.167		53.50	8.20		61.70	71
2990	10" pipe size		80	.200		67.50	9.85		77.35	89.50
3000	12" pipe size		68	.235		99.50	11.55		111.05	126
3010	14" pipe size		56	.286		248	14.05		262.05	294
3020	16" pipe size		48	.333		305	16.40		321.40	360
3050	Chair, carbon steel with CI roll									
3060	2" pipe size	1 Plum	68	.118	Ea.	22	6.40		28.40	33.50
3070	2-1/2" pipe size		65	.123		23.50	6.70		30.20	36
3080	3" pipe size		62	.129		24	7.05		31.05	37
3090	3-1/2" pipe size		60	.133		31	7.30		38.30	45
3100	4" pipe size		58	.138		33	7.55		40.55	48
3110	5" pipe size		56	.143		36	7.80		43.80	51.50
3120	6" pipe size		53	.151		50	8.25		58.25	67.50
3130	8" pipe size		50	.160		67.50	8.75		76.25	87.50
3140	10" pipe size		48	.167		85	9.10		94.10	107
3150	12" pipe size		46	.174		124	9.50		133.50	150
3170	Single pipe roll, (see line 2650 for rods), TYPE 41, 1" pipe size	Q-1	137	.117		14.95	5.75		20.70	25
3180	1-1/4" pipe size		131	.122		15.50	6		21.50	26
3190	1-1/2" pipe size		129	.124		16	6.10		22.10	27
3200	2" pipe size		124	.129		16.55	6.35		22.90	28
3210	2-1/2" pipe size		118	.136		17.75	6.65		24.40	29.50
3220	3" pipe size		115	.139		18.80	6.85		25.65	31
3230	3-1/2" pipe size		113	.142		21	6.95		27.95	33.50
3240	4" pipe size		112	.143		22	7		29	35
3250	5" pipe size		110	.145		26.50	7.15		33.65	40
3260	6" pipe size		101	.158		38	7.80		45.80	54

22 05 Common Work Results for Plumbing

22 05 29 – Hangers and Supports for Plumbing Piping and Equipment

22 05 29.10 Hangers & Supp. for Plumb'g/HVAC Pipe/Equip.	Crew	Daily Output	Labor-Hours	Unit	Material	2012 Bare Costs Labor	Equipment	Total	Total Incl O&P
3270	8" pipe size	Q-1	90	.178	Ea.	53	8.75		61.75	71.50
3280	10" pipe size		80	.200		63	9.85		72.85	84
3290	12" pipe size		68	.235		97	11.55		108.55	124
3291	14" pipe size		56	.286		151	14.05		165.05	187
3292	16" pipe size		48	.333		205	16.40		221.40	250
3293	18" pipe size		40	.400		220	19.65		239.65	272
3294	20" pipe size		35	.457		300	22.50		322.50	365
3296	24" pipe size		30	.533		475	26		501	565
3297	30" pipe size		25	.640		940	31.50		971.50	1,075
3298	36" pipe size	▼	20	.800	▼	1,150	39.50		1,189.50	1,325
3300	Saddles (add vertical pipe riser, usually 3" diameter)									
3310	Pipe support, complete, adjust., CI saddle, TYPE 36									
3320	2-1/2" pipe size	1 Plum	96	.083	Ea.	122	4.55		126.55	141
3330	3" pipe size		88	.091		123	4.96		127.96	144
3340	3-1/2" pipe size		79	.101		127	5.55		132.55	147
3350	4" pipe size		68	.118		179	6.40		185.40	206
3360	5" pipe size		64	.125		181	6.85		187.85	209
3370	6" pipe size		59	.136		190	7.40		197.40	220
3380	8" pipe size		53	.151		207	8.25		215.25	240
3390	10" pipe size		50	.160		229	8.75		237.75	265
3400	12" pipe size	▼	48	.167	▼	237	9.10		246.10	275
3450	For standard pipe support, one piece, CI deduct					34%				
3460	For stanchion support, CI with steel yoke, deduct					60%				
3550	Insulation shield 1" thick, 1/2" pipe size, TYPE 40	1 Asbe	100	.080	Ea.	6.20	3.91		10.11	12.95
3560	3/4" pipe size		100	.080		7.15	3.91		11.06	13.95
3570	1" pipe size		98	.082		7.70	3.99		11.69	14.70
3580	1-1/4" pipe size		98	.082		8.25	3.99		12.24	15.25
3590	1-1/2" pipe size		96	.083		8.25	4.07		12.32	15.40
3600	2" pipe size		96	.083		8.55	4.07		12.62	15.75
3610	2-1/2" pipe size		94	.085		8.80	4.16		12.96	16.20
3620	3" pipe size		94	.085		9.45	4.16		13.61	16.85
3630	2" thick, 3-1/2" pipe size		92	.087		10.55	4.25		14.80	18.25
3640	4" pipe size		92	.087		15.05	4.25		19.30	23
3650	5" pipe size		90	.089		18.70	4.34		23.04	27.50
3660	6" pipe size		90	.089		22	4.34		26.34	31.50
3670	8" pipe size		88	.091		33.50	4.44		37.94	44
3680	10" pipe size		88	.091		45.50	4.44		49.94	57
3690	12" pipe size		86	.093		52	4.54		56.54	64
3700	14" pipe size		86	.093		100	4.54		104.54	117
3710	16" pipe size		84	.095		106	4.65		110.65	124
3720	18" pipe size		84	.095		118	4.65		122.65	137
3730	20" pipe size		82	.098		130	4.77		134.77	150
3732	24" pipe size		80	.100		157	4.89		161.89	181
3733	30" pipe size		78	.103		505	5		510	565
3735	36" pipe size	▼	75	.107	▼	730	5.20		735.20	810
3750	Covering protection saddle, TYPE 39									
3760	1" covering size									
3770	3/4" pipe size	1 Plum	68	.118	Ea.	11.25	6.40		17.65	22
3780	1" pipe size		68	.118		11.25	6.40		17.65	22
3790	1-1/4" pipe size		68	.118		11.25	6.40		17.65	22
3800	1-1/2" pipe size		66	.121		12.20	6.60		18.80	23.50
3810	2" pipe size		66	.121		12.20	6.60		18.80	23.50
3820	2-1/2" pipe size	▼	64	.125		12.20	6.85		19.05	24

22 05 29.10 Hangers & Supp. for Plumb'g/HVAC Pipe/Equip.	Crew	Daily Output	Labor-Hours	Unit	Material	2012 Bare Costs Labor	Equipment	Total	Total Incl O&P
3830	3" pipe size	1 Plum	64	.125	Ea.	17.10	6.85		23.95	29
3840	3-1/2" pipe size		62	.129		18.15	7.05		25.20	30.50
3850	4" pipe size		62	.129		18.15	7.05		25.20	30.50
3860	5" pipe size		60	.133		18.15	7.30		25.45	31
3870	6" pipe size		60	.133		22	7.30		29.30	35
3900	1-1/2" covering size									
3910	3/4" pipe size	1 Plum	68	.118	Ea.	13.70	6.40		20.10	25
3920	1" pipe size		68	.118		13.40	6.40		19.80	24.50
3930	1-1/4" pipe size		68	.118		13.70	6.40		20.10	25
3940	1-1/2" pipe size		66	.121		13.70	6.60		20.30	25
3950	2" pipe size		66	.121		14.85	6.60		21.45	26.50
3960	2-1/2" pipe size		64	.125		17.55	6.85		24.40	29.50
3970	3" pipe size		64	.125		17.55	6.85		24.40	29.50
3980	3-1/2" pipe size		62	.129		17.75	7.05		24.80	30
3990	4" pipe size		62	.129		17.75	7.05		24.80	30
4000	5" pipe size		60	.133		17.75	7.30		25.05	30.50
4010	6" pipe size		60	.133		25.50	7.30		32.80	39
4020	8" pipe size		58	.138		32	7.55		39.55	46.50
4022	10" pipe size		56	.143		32	7.80		39.80	47
4024	12" pipe size		54	.148		57	8.10		65.10	75
4028	2" covering size									
4029	2-1/2" pipe size	1 Plum	62	.129	Ea.	19.70	7.05		26.75	32
4032	3" pipe size		60	.133		19.75	7.30		27.05	33
4033	4" pipe size		58	.138		19.75	7.55		27.30	33.50
4034	6" pipe size		56	.143		28.50	7.80		36.30	43
4035	8" pipe size		54	.148		33.50	8.10		41.60	48.50
4080	10" pipe size		58	.138		35.50	7.55		43.05	50.50
4090	12" pipe size		56	.143		64	7.80		71.80	82.50
4100	14" pipe size		56	.143		64	7.80		71.80	82.50
4110	16" pipe size		54	.148		92.50	8.10		100.60	114
4120	18" pipe size		54	.148		92.50	8.10		100.60	114
4130	20" pipe size		52	.154		103	8.40		111.40	126
4150	24" pipe size		50	.160		120	8.75		128.75	145
4160	30" pipe size		48	.167		132	9.10		141.10	159
4180	36" pipe size		45	.178		145	9.70		154.70	175
4186	2-1/2" covering size									
4187	3" pipe size	1 Plum	58	.138	Ea.	19.05	7.55		26.60	32.50
4188	4" pipe size		56	.143		20.50	7.80		28.30	35
4189	6" pipe size		52	.154		31.50	8.40		39.90	47.50
4190	8" pipe size		48	.167		38.50	9.10		47.60	56.50
4191	10" pipe size		44	.182		42	9.95		51.95	61.50
4192	12" pipe size		40	.200		70	10.90		80.90	93.50
4193	14" pipe size		36	.222		70	12.15		82.15	95.50
4194	16" pipe size		32	.250		97	13.65		110.65	128
4195	18" pipe size		28	.286		108	15.60		123.60	143
4200	Sockets									
4210	Rod end, malleable iron, TYPE 16									
4220	1/4" thread size	1 Plum	240	.033	Ea.	2.07	1.82		3.89	5
4230	3/8" thread size		240	.033		2.07	1.82		3.89	5
4240	1/2" thread size		230	.035		2.45	1.90		4.35	5.55
4250	5/8" thread size		225	.036		4.83	1.94		6.77	8.25
4260	3/4" thread size		220	.036		7.90	1.99		9.89	11.70
4270	7/8" thread size		210	.038		14.35	2.08		16.43	18.95

22 05 29.10 Hangers & Supp. for Plumb'g/HVAC Pipe/Equip.	Crew	Daily Output	Labor-Hours	Unit	Material	2012 Bare Costs Labor	Equipment	Total	Total Incl O&P
4290	Strap, 1/2" pipe size, TYPE 26	Q-1	142	.113	Ea.	4.32	5.55		9.87	13.10
4300	3/4" pipe size		140	.114		4.42	5.60		10.02	13.30
4310	1" pipe size		137	.117		4.61	5.75		10.36	13.70
4320	1-1/4" pipe size		134	.119		5.10	5.85		10.95	14.45
4330	1-1/2" pipe size		131	.122		6.40	6		12.40	16.10
4340	2" pipe size		129	.124		6.60	6.10		12.70	16.45
4350	2-1/2" pipe size		125	.128		11.90	6.30		18.20	22.50
4360	3" pipe size		122	.131		12.50	6.45		18.95	23.50
4370	3-1/2" pipe size		119	.134		14.90	6.60		21.50	26.50
4380	4" pipe size	▼	114	.140	▼	15.80	6.90		22.70	28
4400	U-bolt, carbon steel									
4410	Standard, with nuts, TYPE 42									
4420	1/2" pipe size	1 Plum	160	.050	Ea.	1.97	2.73		4.70	6.30
4430	3/4" pipe size		158	.051		1.97	2.76		4.73	6.35
4450	1" pipe size		152	.053		2.03	2.87		4.90	6.55
4460	1-1/4" pipe size		148	.054		2.48	2.95		5.43	7.20
4470	1-1/2" pipe size		143	.056		2.60	3.05		5.65	7.45
4480	2" pipe size		139	.058		2.83	3.14		5.97	7.85
4490	2-1/2" pipe size		134	.060		4.69	3.26		7.95	10.05
4500	3" pipe size		128	.063		4.91	3.41		8.32	10.55
4510	3-1/2" pipe size		122	.066		5.15	3.58		8.73	11.10
4520	4" pipe size		117	.068		5.30	3.73		9.03	11.45
4530	5" pipe size		114	.070		5.30	3.83		9.13	11.65
4540	6" pipe size		111	.072		10.90	3.94		14.84	17.95
4550	8" pipe size		109	.073		12.95	4.01		16.96	20.50
4560	10" pipe size		107	.075		23	4.08		27.08	31.50
4570	12" pipe size	▼	104	.077	▼	31.50	4.20		35.70	41.50
4580	For plastic coating on 1/2" thru 6" size, add					150%				
4700	U-hook, carbon steel, requires mounting screws or bolts									
4710	3/4" thru 2" pipe size									
4720	6" long	1 Plum	96	.083	Ea.	.76	4.55		5.31	7.70
4730	8" long		96	.083		.94	4.55		5.49	7.90
4740	10" long		96	.083		1.05	4.55		5.60	8
4750	12" long	▼	96	.083		1.40	4.55		5.95	8.40
4760	For copper plated, add					50%				
8000	Pipe clamp, plastic, 1/2" CTS	1 Plum	80	.100		.22	5.45		5.67	8.50
8010	3/4" CTS		73	.110		.23	6		6.23	9.25
8020	1" CTS		68	.118		.52	6.40		6.92	10.25
8080	Economy clamp, 1/4" CTS		175	.046		.05	2.50		2.55	3.82
8090	3/8" CTS		168	.048		.07	2.60		2.67	4
8100	1/2" CTS		160	.050		.07	2.73		2.80	4.20
8110	3/4" CTS		145	.055		.14	3.01		3.15	4.69
8200	Half clamp, 1/2" CTS		80	.100		.08	5.45		5.53	8.35
8210	3/4" CTS		73	.110		.12	6		6.12	9.15
8300	Suspension clamp, 1/2" CTS		80	.100		.22	5.45		5.67	8.50
8310	3/4" CTS		73	.110		.23	6		6.23	9.25
8320	1" CTS		68	.118		.52	6.40		6.92	10.25
8400	Insulator, 1/2" CTS		80	.100		.36	5.45		5.81	8.65
8410	3/4" CTS		73	.110		.37	6		6.37	9.40
8420	1" CTS		68	.118		.38	6.40		6.78	10.10
8500	J hook clamp with nail 1/2" CTS		240	.033	▼	.13	1.82		1.95	2.88
8501	3/4" CTS	▼	240	.033	▼	.13	1.82		1.95	2.88
8800	Wire cable support system									

22 05 29 – Hangers and Supports for Plumbing Piping and Equipment

22 05 29.10 Hangers & Supp. for Plumb'g/HVAC Pipe/Equip.	Crew	Daily Output	Labor-Hours	Unit	Material	2012 Bare Costs Labor	Equipment	Total	Total Incl O&P
8810	Cable with hook terminal and locking device									
8830	2 mm, (.079") dia cable, (100 lb. cap.)									
8840	1 m, (3.3') length, with hook	1 Shee	96	.083	Ea.	3.03	4.35		7.38	9.95
8850	2 m, (6.6') length, with hook		84	.095		3.50	4.97		8.47	11.40
8860	3 m, (9.9') length, with hook		72	.111		3.97	5.80		9.77	13.20
8870	5 m, (16.4') length, with hook	Q-9	60	.267		4.97	12.50		17.47	24.50
8880	10 m, (32.8') length, with hook	"	30	.533		7.20	25		32.20	46
8900	3mm, (.118") dia cable, (200 lb. cap.)									
8910	1 m, (3.3') length, with hook	1 Shee	96	.083	Ea.	3.88	4.35		8.23	10.85
8920	2 m, (6.6') length, with hook		84	.095		4.36	4.97		9.33	12.35
8930	3 m, (9.9') length, with hook		72	.111		4.81	5.80		10.61	14.15
8940	5 m, (16.4') length, with hook	Q-9	60	.267		5.95	12.50		18.45	25.50
8950	10 m, (32.8') length, with hook	"	30	.533		8.55	25		33.55	47.50
9000	Cable system accessories									
9010	Anchor bolt, 3/8", with nut	1 Shee	140	.057	Ea.	1.16	2.98		4.14	5.80
9020	Air duct corner protector		160	.050		.52	2.61		3.13	4.55
9030	Air duct support attachment		140	.057		.99	2.98		3.97	5.65
9040	Flange clip, hammer-on style									
9044	For flange thickness 3/32" - 9/64", 160 lb. cap.	1 Shee	180	.044	Ea.	.29	2.32		2.61	3.85
9048	For flange thickness 1/8" - 1/4", 200 lb. cap.		160	.050		.29	2.61		2.90	4.30
9052	For flange thickness 5/16" - 1/2", 200 lb. cap.		150	.053		.56	2.78		3.34	4.86
9056	For flange thickness 9/16" - 3/4", 200 lb. cap.		140	.057		.75	2.98		3.73	5.35
9060	Wire insulation protection tube		180	.044	L.F.	.34	2.32		2.66	3.90
9070	Wire cutter				Ea.	41.50			41.50	45.50

22 05 48 – Vibration and Seismic Controls for Plumbing Piping and Equipment

22 05 48.40 Vibration Absorbers

		Crew	Daily Output	Labor-Hours	Unit	Material	2012 Bare Costs Labor	Equipment	Total	Total Incl O&P
0010	**VIBRATION ABSORBERS**									
0100	Hangers, neoprene flex									
0200	10 – 120 lb. capacity				Ea.	23.50			23.50	26
0220	75 – 550 lb. capacity					32			32	35
0240	250 – 1100 lb. capacity					57.50			57.50	63.50
0260	1000 – 4000 lb. capacity					104			104	115
0500	Spring flex, 60 lb. capacity					33			33	36.50
0520	450 lb. capacity					43.50			43.50	48
0540	900 lb. capacity					57.50			57.50	63.50
0560	1100 – 1300 lb. capacity					57.50			57.50	63.50
0600	Rubber in shear									
0610	45 – 340 lb., up to 1/2" rod size	1 Stpi	22	.364	Ea.	14.30	20.50		34.80	46.50
0620	130 – 700 lb., up to 3/4" rod size		20	.400		31	22.50		53.50	67.50
0630	50 – 1000 lb., up to 3/4" rod size		18	.444		36.50	25		61.50	77.50
1000	Mounts, neoprene, 45 – 380 lb. capacity					16.15			16.15	17.80
1020	250 – 1100 lb. capacity					42.50			42.50	47
1040	1000 – 4000 lb. capacity					95.50			95.50	105
1100	Spring flex, 60 lb. capacity					66			66	72.50
1120	165 lb. capacity					66			66	72.50
1140	260 lb. capacity					66			66	72.50
1160	450 lb. capacity					88			88	97
1180	600 lb. capacity					88			88	97
1200	750 lb. capacity					88			88	97
1220	900 lb. capacity					91			91	100
1240	1100 lb. capacity					97			97	107
1260	1300 lb. capacity					97			97	107

22 05 Common Work Results for Plumbing

22 05 48 – Vibration and Seismic Controls for Plumbing Piping and Equipment

22 05 48.40 Vibration Absorbers

		Crew	Daily Output	Labor-Hours	Unit	Material	2012 Bare Costs Labor	Equipment	Total	Total Incl O&P
1280	1500 lb. capacity				Ea.	144			144	158
1300	1800 lb. capacity					155			155	170
1320	2200 lb. capacity					155			155	170
1340	2600 lb. capacity					155			155	170
1399	Spring type									
1400	2 Piece									
1410	50 – 1000 lb.	1 Stpi	12	.667	Ea.	130	37		167	199
1420	1100 – 1600 lb.	"	12	.667	"	141	37		178	211
1500	Double spring open									
1510	150 – 450 lb.	1 Stpi	24	.333	Ea.	89	18.55		107.55	126
1520	500 – 1000 lb.		24	.333		89	18.55		107.55	126
1530	1100 – 1600 lb.		24	.333		89	18.55		107.55	126
1540	1700 – 2400 lb.		24	.333		97	18.55		115.55	134
1550	2500 – 3400 lb.		24	.333		165	18.55		183.55	210
2000	Pads, cork rib, 18" x 18" x 1", 10-50 psi					153			153	169
2020	18" x 36" x 1", 10-50 psi					305			305	335
2100	Shear flexible pads, 18" x 18" x 3/8", 20-70 psi					72			72	79.50
2120	18" x 36" x 3/8", 20-70 psi					153			153	169
2150	Laminated neoprene and cork									
2160	1" thick	1 Stpi	16	.500	S.F.	76	28		104	126
2200	Neoprene elastomer isolation bearing pad									
3000	Note overlap in capacities due to deflections									

22 05 53 – Identification for Plumbing Piping and Equipment

22 05 53.10 Piping System Identification Labels

		Crew	Daily Output	Labor-Hours	Unit	Material	2012 Bare Costs Labor	Equipment	Total	Total Incl O&P
0010	**PIPING SYSTEM IDENTIFICATION LABELS**									
0100	Indicate contents and flow direction									
0106	Pipe markers									
0110	Plastic snap around									
0114	1/2" pipe	1 Plum	80	.100	Ea.	6.50	5.45		11.95	15.40
0116	3/4" pipe		80	.100		6.50	5.45		11.95	15.40
0118	1" pipe		80	.100		6.50	5.45		11.95	15.40
0120	2" pipe		75	.107		7.70	5.80		13.50	17.25
0122	3" pipe		70	.114		12.60	6.25		18.85	23.50
0124	4" pipe		60	.133		12.60	7.30		19.90	25
0126	6" pipe		60	.133		12.60	7.30		19.90	25
0128	8" pipe		56	.143		16.70	7.80		24.50	30
0130	10" pipe		56	.143		16.70	7.80		24.50	30
0200	Over 10" pipe size		50	.160		20.50	8.75		29.25	35.50
1110	Self adhesive									
1114	1" pipe	1 Plum	80	.100	Ea.	3.20	5.45		8.65	11.75
1116	2" pipe		75	.107		3.20	5.80		9	12.30
1118	3" pipe		70	.114		4.90	6.25		11.15	14.80
1120	4" pipe		60	.133		4.90	7.30		12.20	16.40
1122	6" pipe		60	.133		4.90	7.30		12.20	16.40
1124	8" pipe		56	.143		4.90	7.80		12.70	17.15
1126	10" pipe		56	.143		9.90	7.80		17.70	22.50
1200	Over 10" pipe size		50	.160		9.90	8.75		18.65	24
2000	Valve tags									
2010	Numbered plus identifying legend									
2100	Brass, 2" diameter	1 Plum	40	.200	Ea.	2.95	10.90		13.85	19.70
2200	Plastic, 1-1/2" Dia.	"	40	.200	"	2.70	10.90		13.60	19.40

22 07 Plumbing Insulation

22 07 16 – Plumbing Equipment Insulation

22 07 16.10 Insulation for Plumbing Equipment

		Crew	Daily Output	Labor-Hours	Unit	Material	2012 Bare Costs Labor	Equipment	Total	Total Incl O&P
0010	**INSULATION FOR PLUMBING EQUIPMENT**									
2900	Domestic water heater wrap kit									
2920	1-1/2" with vinyl jacket, 20-60 gal. [G]	1 Plum	8	1	Ea.	17.60	54.50		72.10	102

22 07 19 – Plumbing Piping Insulation

22 07 19.10 Piping Insulation

		Crew	Daily Output	Labor-Hours	Unit	Material	2012 Bare Costs Labor	Equipment	Total	Total Incl O&P
0010	**PIPING INSULATION**									
0100	Rule of thumb, as a percentage of total mechanical costs				Job				10%	
0110	Insulation req'd is based on the surface size/area to be covered									
0230	Insulated protectors, (ADA)									
0235	For exposed piping under sinks or lavatories									
0240	Vinyl coated foam, velcro tabs									
0245	P Trap, 1-1/4" or 1-1/2"	1 Plum	32	.250	Ea.	20.50	13.65		34.15	43
0260	Valve and supply cover									
0265	1/2", 3/8", and 7/16" pipe size	1 Plum	32	.250	Ea.	19.35	13.65		33	42
0280	Tailpiece offset (wheelchair)									
0285	1-1/4" pipe size	1 Plum	32	.250	Ea.	16.55	13.65		30.20	38.50
0600	Pipe covering (price copper tube one size less than IPS)									
1000	Mineral wool [G]									
1010	Preformed, 1200°F, plain [G]									
1014	1" wall [G]									
1016	1/2" iron pipe size [G]	Q-14	230	.070	L.F.	1.65	3.06		4.71	6.60
1018	3/4" iron pipe size [G]		220	.073		1.72	3.20		4.92	6.85
1022	1" iron pipe size [G]		210	.076		1.77	3.35		5.12	7.15
1024	1-1/4" iron pipe size [G]		205	.078		1.82	3.43		5.25	7.35
1026	1-1/2" iron pipe size [G]		205	.078		1.90	3.43		5.33	7.45
1028	2" iron pipe size [G]		200	.080		2.32	3.52		5.84	8.05
1030	2-1/2" iron pipe size [G]		190	.084		2.46	3.70		6.16	8.45
1032	3" iron pipe size [G]		180	.089		2.55	3.91		6.46	8.90
1034	4" iron pipe size [G]		150	.107		3.14	4.69		7.83	10.75
1036	5" iron pipe size [G]		140	.114		3.55	5.05		8.60	11.75
1038	6" iron pipe size [G]		120	.133		3.79	5.85		9.64	13.30
1040	7" iron pipe size [G]		110	.145		4.43	6.40		10.83	14.80
1042	8" iron pipe size [G]		100	.160		6.10	7.05		13.15	17.65
1044	9" iron pipe size [G]		90	.178		6.65	7.80		14.45	19.50
1046	10" iron pipe size [G]		90	.178		7.50	7.80		15.30	20.50
1050	1-1/2" wall [G]									
1052	1/2" iron pipe size [G]	Q-14	225	.071	L.F.	2.82	3.13		5.95	7.95
1054	3/4" iron pipe size [G]		215	.074		2.89	3.27		6.16	8.30
1056	1" iron pipe size		205	.078		2.93	3.43		6.36	8.55
1058	1-1/4" iron pipe size [G]		200	.080		2.99	3.52		6.51	8.80
1060	1-1/2" iron pipe size [G]		200	.080		3.14	3.52		6.66	8.95
1062	2" iron pipe size		190	.084		3.32	3.70		7.02	9.40
1064	2-1/2" iron pipe size		180	.089		3.62	3.91		7.53	10.10
1066	3" iron pipe size		165	.097		3.77	4.26		8.03	10.80
1068	4" iron pipe size		140	.114		4.53	5.05		9.58	12.85
1070	5" iron pipe size		130	.123		4.84	5.40		10.24	13.75
1072	6" iron pipe size		110	.145		4.99	6.40		11.39	15.45
1074	7" iron pipe size		100	.160		5.90	7.05		12.95	17.45
1076	8" iron pipe size		90	.178		6.55	7.80		14.35	19.40
1078	9" iron pipe size		85	.188		7.55	8.30		15.85	21
1080	10" iron pipe size		80	.200		8.30	8.80		17.10	23
1082	12" iron pipe size		75	.213		9.45	9.40		18.85	25

22 07 19.10 Piping Insulation		Crew	Daily Output	Labor-Hours	Unit	Material	2012 Bare Costs Labor	Equipment	Total	Total Incl O&P
1084	14" iron pipe size	G Q-14	70	.229	L.F.	10.80	10.05		20.85	27.50
1086	16" iron pipe size	G	65	.246		12.30	10.85		23.15	30.50
1088	18" iron pipe size	G	60	.267		13.85	11.75		25.60	33.50
1090	20" iron pipe size	G	55	.291		15.25	12.80		28.05	37
1092	22" iron pipe size	G	50	.320		17.45	14.05		31.50	41
1094	24" iron pipe size		45	.356		18.65	15.65		34.30	45
1100	2" wall	G								
1102	1/2" iron pipe size	G Q-14	220	.073	L.F.	3.65	3.20		6.85	9
1104	3/4" iron pipe size	G	210	.076		3.78	3.35		7.13	9.35
1106	1" iron pipe size	G	200	.080		4.01	3.52		7.53	9.90
1108	1-1/4" iron pipe size	G	190	.084		4.30	3.70		8	10.50
1110	1-1/2" iron pipe size	G	190	.084		4.48	3.70		8.18	10.70
1112	2" iron pipe size	G	180	.089		4.70	3.91		8.61	11.25
1114	2-1/2" iron pipe size	G	170	.094		5.30	4.14		9.44	12.30
1116	3" iron pipe size	G	160	.100		5.70	4.40		10.10	13.10
1118	4" iron pipe size	G	130	.123		6.60	5.40		12	15.75
1120	5" iron pipe size	G	120	.133		7.35	5.85		13.20	17.25
1122	6" iron pipe size	G	100	.160		7.65	7.05		14.70	19.35
1124	8" iron pipe size	G	80	.200		9.25	8.80		18.05	24
1126	10" iron pipe size	G	70	.229		11.35	10.05		21.40	28
1128	12" iron pipe size	G	65	.246		12.55	10.85		23.40	30.50
1130	14" iron pipe size	G	60	.267		14.05	11.75		25.80	33.50
1132	16" iron pipe size	G	55	.291		15.90	12.80		28.70	37.50
1134	18" iron pipe size	G	50	.320		17.20	14.05		31.25	41
1136	20" iron pipe size	G	45	.356		19.80	15.65		35.45	46.50
1138	22" iron pipe size	G	45	.356		21.50	15.65		37.15	48
1140	24" iron pipe size	G	40	.400		22.50	17.60		40.10	52.50
1150	4" wall	G								
1152	1-1/4" iron pipe size	G Q-14	170	.094	L.F.	11.65	4.14		15.79	19.25
1154	1-1/2" iron pipe size	G	165	.097		12.10	4.26		16.36	20
1156	2" iron pipe size	G	155	.103		12.35	4.54		16.89	20.50
1158	4" iron pipe size	G	105	.152		15.60	6.70		22.30	27.50
1160	6" iron pipe size	G	75	.213		18.40	9.40		27.80	34.50
1162	8" iron pipe size	G	60	.267		21	11.75		32.75	41.50
1164	10" iron pipe size	G	50	.320		25	14.05		39.05	49.50
1166	12" iron pipe size	G	45	.356		27.50	15.65		43.15	55
1168	14" iron pipe size	G	40	.400		29.50	17.60		47.10	60
1170	16" iron pipe size	G	35	.457		33.50	20		53.50	68
1172	18" iron pipe size	G	32	.500		36	22		58	74
1174	20" iron pipe size	G	30	.533		38.50	23.50		62	79
1176	22" iron pipe size	G	28	.571		43.50	25		68.50	86.50
1178	24" iron pipe size	G	26	.615		46	27		73	92.50
4280	Cellular glass, closed cell foam, all service jacket, sealant,									
4281	working temp. (-450°F to +900°F), 0 water vapor transmission									
4284	1" wall									
4286	1/2" iron pipe size	G Q-14	120	.133	L.F.	5	5.85		10.85	14.65
4300	1-1/2" wall,									
4301	1" iron pipe size	G Q-14	105	.152	L.F.	8.70	6.70		15.40	20
4304	2-1/2" iron pipe size	G	90	.178		15.40	7.80		23.20	29
4306	3" iron pipe size	G	85	.188		15.40	8.30		23.70	30
4308	4" iron pipe size	G	70	.229		16.30	10.05		26.35	33.50
4310	5" iron pipe size	G	65	.246		19	10.85		29.85	38
4320	2" wall,									

22 07 Plumbing Insulation

22 07 19 - Plumbing Piping Insulation

22 07 19.10 Piping Insulation		Crew	Daily Output	Labor-Hours	Unit	Material	2012 Bare Costs Labor	Equipment	Total	Total Incl O&P
4322	1" iron pipe size [G]	Q-14	100	.160	L.F.	11.60	7.05		18.65	23.50
4324	2-1/2" iron pipe size [G]		85	.188		18.70	8.30		27	33.50
4326	3" iron pipe size [G]		80	.200		18.70	8.80		27.50	34
4328	4" iron pipe size [G]		65	.246		20.50	10.85		31.35	39.50
4330	5" iron pipe size [G]		60	.267		23.50	11.75		35.25	44
4332	6" iron pipe size [G]		50	.320		27.50	14.05		41.55	52.50
4336	8" iron pipe size [G]		40	.400		32	17.60		49.60	62.50
4338	10" iron pipe size [G]		35	.457		39	20		59	74.50
4350	2-1/2" wall,									
4360	12" iron pipe size [G]	Q-14	32	.500	L.F.	53	22		75	93
4362	14" iron pipe size [G]	"	28	.571	"	57	25		82	102
4370	3" wall,									
4378	6" iron pipe size [G]	Q-14	48	.333	L.F.	36.50	14.65		51.15	63
4380	8" iron pipe size [G]		38	.421		45.50	18.50		64	79
4382	10" iron pipe size [G]		33	.485		54	21.50		75.50	92
4384	16" iron pipe size [G]		25	.640		72.50	28		100.50	124
4386	18" iron pipe size [G]		22	.727		82.50	32		114.50	141
4388	20" iron pipe size [G]		20	.800		89.50	35		124.50	154
4400	3-1/2" wall,									
4412	12" iron pipe size [G]	Q-14	27	.593	L.F.	69	26		95	116
4414	14" iron pipe size [G]	"	25	.640	"	71	28		99	122
4430	4" wall,									
4446	16" iron pipe size [G]	Q-14	22	.727	L.F.	92.50	32		124.50	152
4448	18" iron pipe size [G]		20	.800		101	35		136	166
4450	20" iron pipe size [G]		18	.889		114	39		153	186
4480	Fittings, average with fabric and mastic									
4484	1" wall,									
4486	1/2" iron pipe size [G]	1 Asbe	40	.200	Ea.	5.65	9.75		15.40	21.50
4500	1-1/2" wall,									
4502	1" iron pipe size [G]	1 Asbe	38	.211	Ea.	7.50	10.30		17.80	24.50
4504	2-1/2" iron pipe size [G]		32	.250		13.60	12.20		25.80	34
4506	3" iron pipe size [G]		30	.267		13.60	13.05		26.65	35.50
4508	4" iron pipe size [G]		28	.286		17.15	13.95		31.10	40.50
4510	5" iron pipe size [G]		24	.333		21	16.30		37.30	48.50
4520	2" wall,									
4522	1" iron pipe size [G]	1 Asbe	36	.222	Ea.	10.90	10.85		21.75	29
4524	2-1/2" iron pipe size [G]		30	.267		17.15	13.05		30.20	39.50
4526	3" iron pipe size [G]		28	.286		17.15	13.95		31.10	40.50
4528	4" iron pipe size [G]		24	.333		21	16.30		37.30	48.50
4530	5" iron pipe size [G]		22	.364		31	17.75		48.75	61.50
4532	6" iron pipe size [G]		20	.400		44	19.55		63.55	78.50
4536	8" iron pipe size [G]		12	.667		73.50	32.50		106	131
4538	10" iron pipe size [G]		8	1		85	49		134	170
4550	2-1/2" wall,									
4560	12" iron pipe size [G]	1 Asbe	6	1.333	Ea.	156	65		221	273
4562	14" iron pipe size [G]	"	4	2	"	206	97.50		303.50	380
4570	3" wall,									
4578	6" iron pipe size [G]	1 Asbe	16	.500	Ea.	63	24.50		87.50	108
4580	8" iron pipe size [G]		10	.800		94.50	39		133.50	165
4582	10" iron pipe size [G]		6	1.333		128	65		193	241
4900	Calcium silicate, with 8 oz. canvas cover									
5100	1" wall, 1/2" iron pipe size [G]	Q-14	170	.094	L.F.	3.07	4.14		7.21	9.85
5130	3/4" iron pipe size [G]		170	.094		3.10	4.14		7.24	9.85

113

22 07 19.10 Piping Insulation		Crew	Daily Output	Labor-Hours	Unit	Material	2012 Bare Costs Labor	Equipment	Total	Total Incl O&P
5140	1" iron pipe size	G	Q-14	170	.094	L.F.	3	4.14		7.14	9.75
5150	1-1/4" iron pipe size	G		165	.097		3.07	4.26		7.33	10.05
5160	1-1/2" iron pipe size	G		165	.097		3.12	4.26		7.38	10.10
5170	2" iron pipe size	G		160	.100		3.58	4.40		7.98	10.80
5180	2-1/2" iron pipe size	G		160	.100		3.80	4.40		8.20	11.05
5190	3" iron pipe size	G		150	.107		4.12	4.69		8.81	11.85
5200	4" iron pipe size	G		140	.114		5.10	5.05		10.15	13.45
5210	5" iron pipe size	G		135	.119		5.40	5.20		10.60	14
5220	6" iron pipe size	G		130	.123		5.70	5.40		11.10	14.75
5280	1-1/2" wall, 1/2" iron pipe size	G		150	.107		3.32	4.69		8.01	10.95
5310	3/4" iron pipe size	G		150	.107		3.38	4.69		8.07	11
5320	1" iron pipe size	G		150	.107		3.68	4.69		8.37	11.35
5330	1-1/4" iron pipe size	G		145	.110		3.96	4.85		8.81	11.90
5340	1-1/2" iron pipe size	G		145	.110		4.25	4.85		9.10	12.25
5350	2" iron pipe size	G		140	.114		4.68	5.05		9.73	13
5360	2-1/2" iron pipe size	G		140	.114		5.10	5.05		10.15	13.45
5370	3" iron pipe size	G		135	.119		5.35	5.20		10.55	14
5380	4" iron pipe size	G		125	.128		6.20	5.65		11.85	15.55
5390	5" iron pipe size	G		120	.133		7	5.85		12.85	16.85
5400	6" iron pipe size	G		110	.145		7.20	6.40		13.60	17.90
5402	8" iron pipe size	G		95	.168		9.45	7.40		16.85	22
5404	10" iron pipe size	G		85	.188		12.35	8.30		20.65	26.50
5406	12" iron pipe size	G		80	.200		14.65	8.80		23.45	30
5408	14" iron pipe size	G		75	.213		16.45	9.40		25.85	32.50
5410	16" iron pipe size	G		70	.229		18.40	10.05		28.45	36
5412	18" iron pipe size	G		65	.246		20.50	10.85		31.35	39.50
5460	2" wall, 1/2" iron pipe size	G		135	.119		5.10	5.20		10.30	13.75
5490	3/4" iron pipe size	G		135	.119		5.40	5.20		10.60	14.05
5500	1" iron pipe size	G		135	.119		5.70	5.20		10.90	14.35
5510	1-1/4" iron pipe size	G		130	.123		6.10	5.40		11.50	15.15
5520	1-1/2" iron pipe size	G		130	.123		6.35	5.40		11.75	15.45
5530	2" iron pipe size	G		125	.128		6.70	5.65		12.35	16.15
5540	2-1/2" iron pipe size	G		125	.128		7.95	5.65		13.60	17.50
5550	3" iron pipe size	G		120	.133		8.05	5.85		13.90	18
5560	4" iron pipe size	G		115	.139		9.30	6.10		15.40	19.75
5570	5" iron pipe size	G		110	.145		10.55	6.40		16.95	21.50
5580	6" iron pipe size	G		105	.152		11.55	6.70		18.25	23
5581	8" iron pipe size	G		95	.168		13.75	7.40		21.15	26.50
5582	10" iron pipe size	G		85	.188		17.15	8.30		25.45	32
5583	12" iron pipe size	G		80	.200		19.10	8.80		27.90	34.50
5584	14" iron pipe size	G		75	.213		21	9.40		30.40	37.50
5585	16" iron pipe size	G		70	.229		23	10.05		33.05	41
5586	18" iron pipe size	G		65	.246		25.50	10.85		36.35	45
5587	3" wall, 1-1/4" iron pipe size	G		100	.160		9.40	7.05		16.45	21.50
5588	1-1/2" iron pipe size	G		100	.160		9.50	7.05		16.55	21.50
5589	2" iron pipe size	G		95	.168		9.80	7.40		17.20	22.50
5590	2-1/2" iron pipe size	G		95	.168		11.45	7.40		18.85	24
5591	3" iron pipe size	G		90	.178		11.60	7.80		19.40	25
5592	4" iron pipe size	G		85	.188		14.65	8.30		22.95	29
5593	6" iron pipe size	G		80	.200		17.85	8.80		26.65	33.50
5594	8" iron pipe size	G		75	.213		21	9.40		30.40	38
5595	10" iron pipe size	G		65	.246		25.50	10.85		36.35	45
5596	12" iron pipe size	G		60	.267		28.50	11.75		40.25	49.50

22 07 19 – Plumbing Piping Insulation

22 07 19.10 Piping Insulation		Crew	Daily Output	Labor-Hours	Unit	Material	2012 Bare Costs Labor	Equipment	Total	Total Incl O&P
5597	14" iron pipe size	G	Q-14	55	.291	L.F.	31.50	12.80		44.30	55
5598	16" iron pipe size	G		50	.320		35	14.05		49.05	60.50
5599	18" iron pipe size	G		45	.356		38.50	15.65		54.15	66.50
5600	Calcium silicate, no cover										
5720	1" wall, 1/2" iron pipe size	G	Q-14	180	.089	L.F.	2.80	3.91		6.71	9.20
5740	3/4" iron pipe size	G		180	.089		2.80	3.91		6.71	9.20
5750	1" iron pipe size	G		180	.089		2.68	3.91		6.59	9.05
5760	1-1/4" iron pipe size	G		175	.091		2.72	4.02		6.74	9.25
5770	1-1/2" iron pipe size	G		175	.091		2.75	4.02		6.77	9.30
5780	2" iron pipe size	G		170	.094		3.17	4.14		7.31	9.95
5790	2-1/2" iron pipe size	G		170	.094		3.35	4.14		7.49	10.15
5800	3" iron pipe size	G		160	.100		3.60	4.40		8	10.80
5810	4" iron pipe size	G		150	.107		4.50	4.69		9.19	12.25
5820	5" iron pipe size	G		145	.110		4.68	4.85		9.53	12.70
5830	6" iron pipe size	G		140	.114		4.92	5.05		9.97	13.25
5900	1-1/2" wall, 1/2" iron pipe size	G		160	.100		2.95	4.40		7.35	10.10
5920	3/4" iron pipe size	G		160	.100		3	4.40		7.40	10.15
5930	1" iron pipe size	G		160	.100		3.28	4.40		7.68	10.45
5940	1-1/4" iron pipe size	G		155	.103		3.53	4.54		8.07	10.95
5950	1-1/2" iron pipe size	G		155	.103		3.79	4.54		8.33	11.20
5960	2" iron pipe size	G		150	.107		4.18	4.69		8.87	11.90
5970	2-1/2" iron pipe size	G		150	.107		4.56	4.69		9.25	12.30
5980	3" iron pipe size	G		145	.110		4.76	4.85		9.61	12.80
5990	4" iron pipe size	G		135	.119		5.50	5.20		10.70	14.15
6000	5" iron pipe size	G		130	.123		6.20	5.40		11.60	15.30
6010	6" iron pipe size	G		120	.133		6.35	5.85		12.20	16.15
6020	7" iron pipe size	G		115	.139		7.45	6.10		13.55	17.75
6030	8" iron pipe size	G		105	.152		8.40	6.70		15.10	19.70
6040	9" iron pipe size	G		100	.160		10.10	7.05		17.15	22
6050	10" iron pipe size	G		95	.168		11.15	7.40		18.55	24
6060	12" iron pipe size	G		90	.178		13.20	7.80		21	27
6070	14" iron pipe size	G		85	.188		14.95	8.30		23.25	29.50
6080	16" iron pipe size	G		80	.200		16.70	8.80		25.50	32
6090	18" iron pipe size	G		75	.213		18.50	9.40		27.90	35
6120	2" wall, 1/2" iron pipe size	G		145	.110		4.67	4.85		9.52	12.70
6140	3/4" iron pipe size	G		145	.110		4.92	4.85		9.77	12.95
6150	1" iron pipe size	G		145	.110		5.20	4.85		10.05	13.25
6160	1-1/4" iron pipe size	G		140	.114		5.55	5.05		10.60	13.95
6170	1-1/2" iron pipe size	G		140	.114		5.80	5.05		10.85	14.25
6180	2" iron pipe size	G		135	.119		6.10	5.20		11.30	14.80
6190	2-1/2" iron pipe size	G		135	.119		7.30	5.20		12.50	16.15
6200	3" iron pipe size	G		130	.123		7.35	5.40		12.75	16.50
6210	4" iron pipe size	G		125	.128		8.50	5.65		14.15	18.10
6220	5" iron pipe size	G		120	.133		9.70	5.85		15.55	19.80
6230	6" iron pipe size	G		115	.139		10.60	6.10		16.70	21
6240	7" iron pipe size	G		110	.145		11.50	6.40		17.90	22.50
6250	8" iron pipe size	G		105	.152		12.60	6.70		19.30	24.50
6260	9" iron pipe size	G		100	.160		14.30	7.05		21.35	26.50
6270	10" iron pipe size	G		95	.168		15.85	7.40		23.25	29
6280	12" iron pipe size	G		90	.178		17.60	7.80		25.40	31.50
6290	14" iron pipe size	G		85	.188		19.35	8.30		27.65	34.50
6300	16" iron pipe size	G		80	.200		21.50	8.80		30.30	37
6310	18" iron pipe size	G		75	.213		23.50	9.40		32.90	40

22 07 Plumbing Insulation

22 07 19 – Plumbing Piping Insulation

22 07 19.10 Piping Insulation		Crew	Daily Output	Labor-Hours	Unit	Material	Labor	Equipment	Total	Total Incl O&P
6320	20" iron pipe size	G Q-14	65	.246	L.F.	28.50	10.85		39.35	48.50
6330	22" iron pipe size	G	60	.267		32	11.75		43.75	53.50
6340	24" iron pipe size	G	55	.291		32.50	12.80		45.30	55.50
6360	3" wall, 1/2" iron pipe size	G	115	.139		8.45	6.10		14.55	18.85
6380	3/4" iron pipe size	G	115	.139		8.50	6.10		14.60	18.90
6390	1" iron pipe size	G	115	.139		8.60	6.10		14.70	19
6400	1-1/4" iron pipe size	G	110	.145		8.70	6.40		15.10	19.50
6410	1-1/2" iron pipe size	G	110	.145		8.75	6.40		15.15	19.60
6420	2" iron pipe size	G	105	.152		9.05	6.70		15.75	20.50
6430	2-1/2" iron pipe size	G	105	.152		10.65	6.70		17.35	22
6440	3" iron pipe size	G	100	.160		10.75	7.05		17.80	23
6450	4" iron pipe size	G	95	.168		13.70	7.40		21.10	26.50
6460	5" iron pipe size	G	90	.178		14.85	7.80		22.65	28.50
6470	6" iron pipe size	G	90	.178		16.70	7.80		24.50	30.50
6480	7" iron pipe size	G	85	.188		18.60	8.30		26.90	33.50
6490	8" iron pipe size	G	85	.188		19.90	8.30		28.20	35
6500	9" iron pipe size	G	80	.200		22.50	8.80		31.30	38.50
6510	10" iron pipe size	G	75	.213		24	9.40		33.40	41
6520	12" iron pipe size	G	70	.229		26.50	10.05		36.55	45
6530	14" iron pipe size	G	65	.246		30	10.85		40.85	50
6540	16" iron pipe size	G	60	.267		33	11.75		44.75	55
6550	18" iron pipe size	G	55	.291		36	12.80		48.80	60
6560	20" iron pipe size	G	50	.320		43	14.05		57.05	69.50
6570	22" iron pipe size	G	45	.356		46.50	15.65		62.15	76
6580	24" iron pipe size	G	40	.400		50	17.60		67.60	82.50
6600	Fiberglass, with all service jacket									
6640	1/2" wall, 1/2" iron pipe size	G Q-14	250	.064	L.F.	.74	2.81		3.55	5.20
6660	3/4" iron pipe size	G	240	.067		.83	2.93		3.76	5.50
6670	1" iron pipe size	G	230	.070		.86	3.06		3.92	5.70
6680	1-1/4" iron pipe size	G	220	.073		.92	3.20		4.12	6
6690	1-1/2" iron pipe size	G	220	.073		1.06	3.20		4.26	6.15
6700	2" iron pipe size	G	210	.076		1.13	3.35		4.48	6.45
6710	2-1/2" iron pipe size	G	200	.080		1.18	3.52		4.70	6.80
6840	1" wall, 1/2" iron pipe size	G	240	.067		.89	2.93		3.82	5.55
6860	3/4" iron pipe size	G	230	.070		.97	3.06		4.03	5.85
6870	1" iron pipe size	G	220	.073		1.04	3.20		4.24	6.10
6880	1-1/4" iron pipe size	G	210	.076		1.13	3.35		4.48	6.45
6890	1-1/2" iron pipe size	G	210	.076		1.22	3.35		4.57	6.55
6900	2" iron pipe size	G	200	.080		1.32	3.52		4.84	6.95
6910	2-1/2" iron pipe size	G	190	.084		1.50	3.70		5.20	7.40
6920	3" iron pipe size	G	180	.089		1.60	3.91		5.51	7.85
6930	3-1/2" iron pipe size	G	170	.094		1.74	4.14		5.88	8.35
6940	4" iron pipe size	G	150	.107		2.12	4.69		6.81	9.65
6950	5" iron pipe size	G	140	.114		2.39	5.05		7.44	10.50
6960	6" iron pipe size	G	120	.133		2.54	5.85		8.39	11.95
6970	7" iron pipe size	G	110	.145		3.02	6.40		9.42	13.25
6980	8" iron pipe size	G	100	.160		4.15	7.05		11.20	15.50
6990	9" iron pipe size	G	90	.178		4.38	7.80		12.18	17
7000	10" iron pipe size	G	90	.178		4.40	7.80		12.20	17.05
7010	12" iron pipe size	G	80	.200		4.80	8.80		13.60	19
7020	14" iron pipe size	G	80	.200		5.75	8.80		14.55	20
7030	16" iron pipe size	G	70	.229		7.30	10.05		17.35	23.50
7040	18" iron pipe size	G	70	.229		8.10	10.05		18.15	24.50

116

22 07 19.10 Piping Insulation		Crew	Daily Output	Labor-Hours	Unit	Material	2012 Bare Costs Labor	Equipment	Total	Total Incl O&P
7050	20" iron pipe size	G	Q-14	60	.267	L.F.	9.05	11.75		20.80	28
7060	24" iron pipe size	G		60	.267		11.05	11.75		22.80	30.50
7080	1-1/2" wall, 1/2" iron pipe size	G		230	.070		1.69	3.06		4.75	6.65
7100	3/4" iron pipe size	G		220	.073		1.69	3.20		4.89	6.85
7110	1" iron pipe size	G		210	.076		1.81	3.35		5.16	7.20
7120	1-1/4" iron pipe size	G		200	.080		1.97	3.52		5.49	7.65
7130	1-1/2" iron pipe size	G		200	.080		2.07	3.52		5.59	7.80
7140	2" iron pipe size	G		190	.084		2.28	3.70		5.98	8.25
7150	2-1/2" iron pipe size	G		180	.089		2.44	3.91		6.35	8.80
7160	3" iron pipe size	G		170	.094		2.56	4.14		6.70	9.25
7170	3-1/2" iron pipe size	G		160	.100		2.80	4.40		7.20	9.95
7180	4" iron pipe size	G		140	.114		2.91	5.05		7.96	11.05
7190	5" iron pipe size	G		130	.123		3.26	5.40		8.66	12.05
7200	6" iron pipe size	G		110	.145		3.44	6.40		9.84	13.75
7210	7" iron pipe size	G		100	.160		3.82	7.05		10.87	15.15
7220	8" iron pipe size	G		90	.178		4.82	7.80		12.62	17.50
7230	9" iron pipe size	G		85	.188		5	8.30		13.30	18.40
7240	10" iron pipe size	G		80	.200		5.20	8.80		14	19.40
7250	12" iron pipe size	G		75	.213		5.90	9.40		15.30	21
7260	14" iron pipe size	G		70	.229		7.05	10.05		17.10	23.50
7270	16" iron pipe size	G		65	.246		9.15	10.85		20	27
7280	18" iron pipe size	G		60	.267		10.30	11.75		22.05	29.50
7290	20" iron pipe size	G		55	.291		10.50	12.80		23.30	31.50
7300	24" iron pipe size	G		50	.320		12.85	14.05		26.90	36
7320	2" wall, 1/2" iron pipe size	G		220	.073		2.62	3.20		5.82	7.85
7340	3/4" iron pipe size	G		210	.076		2.70	3.35		6.05	8.15
7350	1" iron pipe size	G		200	.080		2.88	3.52		6.40	8.65
7360	1-1/4" iron pipe size	G		190	.084		3.04	3.70		6.74	9.10
7370	1-1/2" iron pipe size	G		190	.084		3.17	3.70		6.87	9.25
7380	2" iron pipe size	G		180	.089		3.34	3.91		7.25	9.75
7390	2-1/2" iron pipe size	G		170	.094		3.60	4.14		7.74	10.40
7400	3" iron pipe size	G		160	.100		3.82	4.40		8.22	11.05
7410	3-1/2" iron pipe size	G		150	.107		4.14	4.69		8.83	11.85
7420	4" iron pipe size	G		130	.123		4.45	5.40		9.85	13.35
7430	5" iron pipe size	G		120	.133		5.10	5.85		10.95	14.75
7440	6" iron pipe size	G		100	.160		5.25	7.05		12.30	16.75
7450	7" iron pipe size	G		90	.178		6	7.80		13.80	18.80
7460	8" iron pipe size	G		80	.200		6.40	8.80		15.20	20.50
7470	9" iron pipe size	G		75	.213		7	9.40		16.40	22.50
7480	10" iron pipe size	G		70	.229		7.65	10.05		17.70	24
7490	12" iron pipe size	G		65	.246		8.55	10.85		19.40	26.50
7500	14" iron pipe size	G		60	.267		11.05	11.75		22.80	30.50
7510	16" iron pipe size	G		55	.291		12.10	12.80		24.90	33.50
7520	18" iron pipe size	G		50	.320		13.50	14.05		27.55	37
7530	20" iron pipe size	G		45	.356		15.35	15.65		31	41.50
7540	24" iron pipe size	G		40	.400		16.45	17.60		34.05	45.50
7560	2-1/2" wall, 1/2" iron pipe size	G		210	.076		3.10	3.35		6.45	8.60
7562	3/4" iron pipe size	G		200	.080		3.24	3.52		6.76	9.05
7564	1" iron pipe size	G		190	.084		3.38	3.70		7.08	9.45
7566	1-1/4" iron pipe size	G		185	.086		3.50	3.80		7.30	9.75
7568	1-1/2" iron pipe size	G		180	.089		3.68	3.91		7.59	10.15
7570	2" iron pipe size	G		170	.094		3.86	4.14		8	10.70
7572	2-1/2" iron pipe size	G		160	.100		4.45	4.40		8.85	11.75

22 07 19 – Plumbing Piping Insulation

22 07 19.10 Piping Insulation		Crew	Daily Output	Labor-Hours	Unit	Material	2012 Bare Costs Labor	Equipment	Total	Total Incl O&P
7574	3" iron pipe size	G	Q-14	150	.107	L.F.	4.68	4.69		9.37	12.45
7576	3-1/2" iron pipe size	G		140	.114		5.10	5.05		10.15	13.45
7578	4" iron pipe size	G		120	.133		5.35	5.85		11.20	15.05
7580	5" iron pipe size	G		110	.145		6.40	6.40		12.80	17
7582	6" iron pipe size	G		90	.178		7.70	7.80		15.50	20.50
7584	7" iron pipe size	G		80	.200		7.75	8.80		16.55	22.50
7586	8" iron pipe size	G		70	.229		8.25	10.05		18.30	24.50
7588	9" iron pipe size	G		65	.246		9	10.85		19.85	27
7590	10" iron pipe size	G		60	.267		9.80	11.75		21.55	29
7592	12" iron pipe size	G		55	.291		11.90	12.80		24.70	33
7594	14" iron pipe size	G		50	.320		13.90	14.05		27.95	37.50
7596	16" iron pipe size	G		45	.356		15.95	15.65		31.60	42
7598	18" iron pipe size	G		40	.400		17.30	17.60		34.90	46.50
7602	24" iron pipe size	G		30	.533		23	23.50		46.50	61.50
7620	3" wall, 1/2" iron pipe size	G		200	.080		3.97	3.52		7.49	9.85
7622	3/4" iron pipe size	G		190	.084		4.20	3.70		7.90	10.35
7624	1" iron pipe size	G		180	.089		4.45	3.91		8.36	11
7626	1-1/4" iron pipe size	G		175	.091		4.54	4.02		8.56	11.25
7628	1-1/2" iron pipe size	G		170	.094		4.74	4.14		8.88	11.65
7630	2" iron pipe size	G		160	.100		5.10	4.40		9.50	12.50
7632	2-1/2" iron pipe size	G		150	.107		5.35	4.69		10.04	13.15
7634	3" iron pipe size	G		140	.114		5.65	5.05		10.70	14.10
7636	3-1/2" iron pipe size	G		130	.123		6.25	5.40		11.65	15.35
7638	4" iron pipe size	G		110	.145		6.75	6.40		13.15	17.35
7640	5" iron pipe size	G		100	.160		7.60	7.05		14.65	19.35
7642	6" iron pipe size	G		80	.200		8.15	8.80		16.95	22.50
7644	7" iron pipe size	G		70	.229		9.30	10.05		19.35	26
7646	8" iron pipe size	G		60	.267		10.15	11.75		21.90	29.50
7648	9" iron pipe size	G		55	.291		10.95	12.80		23.75	32
7650	10" iron pipe size	G		50	.320		11.75	14.05		25.80	35
7652	12" iron pipe size	G		45	.356		14.60	15.65		30.25	40.50
7654	14" iron pipe size	G		40	.400		16.85	17.60		34.45	46
7656	16" iron pipe size	G		35	.457		19.10	20		39.10	52.50
7658	18" iron pipe size	G		32	.500		20.50	22		42.50	57
7660	20" iron pipe size	G		30	.533		22	23.50		45.50	61
7662	24" iron pipe size	G		28	.571		28	25		53	70
7664	26" iron pipe size	G		26	.615		31	27		58	76
7666	30" iron pipe size	G		24	.667		37	29.50		66.50	86
7800	For fiberglass with standard canvas jacket, deduct						5%			
7802	For fittings, add 3 L.F. for each fitting									
7804	plus 4 L.F. for each flange of the fitting									
7810	Finishes									
7814	For single layer of felt, add						10%	10%		
7816	For roofing paper, 45 lb. to 55 lb., add						25%	10%		
7820	Polyethylene tubing flexible closed cell foam, UV resistant									
7828	Standard temperature (-90°F to +212°F)									
7830	3/8" wall, 1/8" iron pipe size	G	1 Asbe	130	.062	L.F.	.22	3.01		3.23	4.92
7831	1/4" iron pipe size	G		130	.062		.23	3.01		3.24	4.93
7832	3/8" iron pipe size	G		130	.062		.26	3.01		3.27	4.97
7833	1/2" iron pipe size	G		126	.063		.29	3.10		3.39	5.15
7834	3/4" iron pipe size	G		122	.066		.34	3.20		3.54	5.35
7835	1" iron pipe size	G		120	.067		.39	3.26		3.65	5.50
7836	1-1/4" iron pipe size	G		118	.068		.47	3.31		3.78	5.65

22 07 19 – Plumbing Piping Insulation

22 07 19.10 Piping Insulation		Crew	Daily Output	Labor-Hours	Unit	Material	2012 Bare Costs Labor	Equipment	Total	Total Incl O&P
7837	1-1/2" iron pipe size	G 1 Asbe	118	.068	L.F.	.60	3.31		3.91	5.80
7838	2" iron pipe size	G	116	.069		.79	3.37		4.16	6.10
7839	2-1/2" iron pipe size	G	114	.070		1.01	3.43		4.44	6.45
7840	3" iron pipe size	G	112	.071		1.56	3.49		5.05	7.15
7842	1/2" wall, 1/8" iron pipe size	G	120	.067		.33	3.26		3.59	5.40
7843	1/4" iron pipe size	G	120	.067		.35	3.26		3.61	5.45
7844	3/8" iron pipe size	G	120	.067		.39	3.26		3.65	5.50
7845	1/2" iron pipe size	G	118	.068		.43	3.31		3.74	5.60
7846	3/4" iron pipe size	G	116	.069		.49	3.37		3.86	5.80
7847	1" iron pipe size	G	114	.070		.55	3.43		3.98	5.95
7848	1-1/4" iron pipe size	G	112	.071		.65	3.49		4.14	6.15
7849	1-1/2" iron pipe size	G	110	.073		.77	3.55		4.32	6.40
7850	2" iron pipe size	G	108	.074		1.11	3.62		4.73	6.85
7851	2-1/2" iron pipe size	G	106	.075		1.37	3.69		5.06	7.25
7852	3" iron pipe size	G	104	.077		1.89	3.76		5.65	7.95
7853	3-1/2" iron pipe size	G	102	.078		2.14	3.83		5.97	8.30
7854	4" iron pipe size	G	100	.080		2.44	3.91		6.35	8.80
7855	3/4" wall, 1/8" iron pipe size	G	110	.073		.50	3.55		4.05	6.10
7856	1/4" iron pipe size	G	110	.073		.53	3.55		4.08	6.15
7857	3/8" iron pipe size	G	108	.074		.61	3.62		4.23	6.30
7858	1/2" iron pipe size	G	106	.075		.73	3.69		4.42	6.55
7859	3/4" iron pipe size	G	104	.077		.88	3.76		4.64	6.80
7860	1" iron pipe size	G	102	.078		1.01	3.83		4.84	7.05
7861	1-1/4" iron pipe size	G	100	.080		1.38	3.91		5.29	7.60
7862	1-1/2" iron pipe size	G	100	.080		1.56	3.91		5.47	7.80
7863	2" iron pipe size	G	98	.082		1.98	3.99		5.97	8.40
7864	2-1/2" iron pipe size	G	96	.083		2.39	4.07		6.46	9
7865	3" iron pipe size	G	94	.085		3.15	4.16		7.31	9.95
7866	3-1/2" iron pipe size	G	92	.087		3.51	4.25		7.76	10.45
7867	4" iron pipe size	G	90	.089		3.92	4.34		8.26	11.05
7868	1" wall, 1/4" iron pipe size	G	100	.080		1.06	3.91		4.97	7.25
7869	3/8" iron pipe size	G	98	.082		1.08	3.99		5.07	7.40
7870	1/2" iron pipe size	G	96	.083		1.35	4.07		5.42	7.85
7871	3/4" iron pipe size	G	94	.085		1.57	4.16		5.73	8.25
7872	1" iron pipe size	G	92	.087		1.91	4.25		6.16	8.70
7873	1-1/4" iron pipe size	G	90	.089		2.17	4.34		6.51	9.15
7874	1-1/2" iron pipe size	G	90	.089		2.48	4.34		6.82	9.50
7875	2" iron pipe size	G	88	.091		3.23	4.44		7.67	10.45
7876	2-1/2" iron pipe size	G	86	.093		4.22	4.54		8.76	11.75
7877	3" iron pipe size	G	84	.095		4.74	4.65		9.39	12.45
7878	Contact cement, quart can	G			Ea.	10.50			10.50	11.55
7879	Rubber tubing, flexible closed cell foam									
7880	3/8" wall, 1/4" iron pipe size	G 1 Asbe	120	.067	L.F.	.38	3.26		3.64	5.45
7900	3/8" iron pipe size	G	120	.067		.43	3.26		3.69	5.50
7910	1/2" iron pipe size	G	115	.070		.48	3.40		3.88	5.85
7920	3/4" iron pipe size	G	115	.070		.55	3.40		3.95	5.90
7930	1" iron pipe size	G	110	.073		.63	3.55		4.18	6.25
7940	1-1/4" iron pipe size	G	110	.073		.77	3.55		4.32	6.40
7950	1-1/2" iron pipe size	G	110	.073		.85	3.55		4.40	6.50
8100	1/2" wall, 1/4" iron pipe size	G	90	.089		.57	4.34		4.91	7.40
8120	3/8" iron pipe size	G	90	.089		.64	4.34		4.98	7.45
8130	1/2" iron pipe size	G	89	.090		.71	4.39		5.10	7.65
8140	3/4" iron pipe size	G	89	.090		.79	4.39		5.18	7.70

22 07 19 – Plumbing Piping Insulation

22 07 19.10 Piping Insulation		Crew	Daily Output	Labor-Hours	Unit	Material	2012 Bare Costs Labor	Equipment	Total	Total Incl O&P
8150	1" iron pipe size	G	1 Asbe	88	.091	L.F.	.87	4.44		5.31	7.85
8160	1-1/4" iron pipe size	G		87	.092		1	4.49		5.49	8.10
8170	1-1/2" iron pipe size	G		87	.092		1.21	4.49		5.70	8.35
8180	2" iron pipe size	G		86	.093		1.55	4.54		6.09	8.80
8190	2-1/2" iron pipe size	G		86	.093		1.96	4.54		6.50	9.25
8200	3" iron pipe size	G		85	.094		2.18	4.60		6.78	9.55
8210	3-1/2" iron pipe size	G		85	.094		3.03	4.60		7.63	10.50
8220	4" iron pipe size	G		80	.100		3.24	4.89		8.13	11.15
8230	5" iron pipe size	G		80	.100		4.41	4.89		9.30	12.45
8240	6" iron pipe size	G		75	.107		4.41	5.20		9.61	12.95
8300	3/4" wall, 1/4" iron pipe size	G		90	.089		.90	4.34		5.24	7.75
8320	3/8" iron pipe size	G		90	.089		.98	4.34		5.32	7.85
8330	1/2" iron pipe size	G		89	.090		1.17	4.39		5.56	8.15
8340	3/4" iron pipe size	G		89	.090		1.43	4.39		5.82	8.40
8350	1" iron pipe size	G		88	.091		1.63	4.44		6.07	8.70
8360	1-1/4" iron pipe size	G		87	.092		2.17	4.49		6.66	9.40
8370	1-1/2" iron pipe size	G		87	.092		2.46	4.49		6.95	9.70
8380	2" iron pipe size	G		86	.093		2.84	4.54		7.38	10.20
8390	2-1/2" iron pipe size	G		86	.093		3.79	4.54		8.33	11.25
8400	3" iron pipe size	G		85	.094		4.32	4.60		8.92	11.90
8410	3-1/2" iron pipe size	G		85	.094		5.10	4.60		9.70	12.75
8420	4" iron pipe size	G		80	.100		5.45	4.89		10.34	13.55
8430	5" iron pipe size	G		80	.100		6.55	4.89		11.44	14.80
8440	6" iron pipe size	G		80	.100		7.90	4.89		12.79	16.30
8444	1" wall, 1/2" iron pipe size	G		86	.093		2.17	4.54		6.71	9.50
8445	3/4" iron pipe size	G		84	.095		2.63	4.65		7.28	10.15
8446	1" iron pipe size	G		84	.095		3.06	4.65		7.71	10.60
8447	1-1/4" iron pipe size	G		82	.098		3.42	4.77		8.19	11.15
8448	1-1/2" iron pipe size	G		82	.098		3.98	4.77		8.75	11.80
8449	2" iron pipe size	G		80	.100		5.25	4.89		10.14	13.35
8450	2-1/2" iron pipe size	G		80	.100		6.85	4.89		11.74	15.10
8456	Rubber insulation tape, 1/8" x 2" x 30'	G				Ea.	12.05			12.05	13.25
8460	Polyolefin tubing, flexible closed cell foam, UV stabilized, work										
8462	temp.-165°F to +210°F, 0 water vapor transmission										
8464	3/8" wall, 1/8" iron pipe size	G	1 Asbe	140	.057	L.F.	.39	2.79		3.18	4.78
8466	1/4" iron pipe size	G		140	.057		.41	2.79		3.20	4.80
8468	3/8" iron pipe size	G		140	.057		.45	2.79		3.24	4.85
8470	1/2" iron pipe size	G		136	.059		.50	2.87		3.37	5.05
8472	3/4" iron pipe size	G		132	.061		.50	2.96		3.46	5.15
8474	1" iron pipe size	G		130	.062		.58	3.01		3.59	5.30
8476	1-1/4" iron pipe size	G		128	.063		.63	3.05		3.68	5.45
8478	1-1/2" iron pipe size	G		128	.063		.83	3.05		3.88	5.65
8480	2" iron pipe size	G		126	.063		1.06	3.10		4.16	6
8482	2-1/2" iron pipe size	G		123	.065		1.49	3.18		4.67	6.60
8484	3" iron pipe size	G		121	.066		1.83	3.23		5.06	7.05
8486	4" iron pipe size	G		118	.068		3.29	3.31		6.60	8.75
8500	1/2" wall, 1/8" iron pipe size	G		130	.062		.58	3.01		3.59	5.30
8502	1/4" iron pipe size	G		130	.062		.62	3.01		3.63	5.35
8504	3/8" iron pipe size	G		130	.062		.66	3.01		3.67	5.40
8506	1/2" iron pipe size	G		128	.063		.73	3.05		3.78	5.55
8508	3/4" iron pipe size	G		126	.063		.75	3.10		3.85	5.65
8510	1" iron pipe size	G		123	.065		.84	3.18		4.02	5.85
8512	1-1/4" iron pipe size	G		121	.066		.91	3.23		4.14	6.05

22 07 Plumbing Insulation

22 07 19 – Plumbing Piping Insulation

22 07 19.10 Piping Insulation

		Crew	Daily Output	Labor-Hours	Unit	Material	2012 Bare Costs Labor	Equipment	Total	Total Incl O&P
8514	1-1/2" iron pipe size G	1 Asbe	119	.067	L.F.	.96	3.28		4.24	6.15
8516	2" iron pipe size G		117	.068		1.36	3.34		4.70	6.70
8518	2-1/2" iron pipe size G		114	.070		1.85	3.43		5.28	7.40
8520	3" iron pipe size G		112	.071		2.38	3.49		5.87	8.05
8522	4" iron pipe size G		110	.073		3.46	3.55		7.01	9.35
8534	3/4" wall, 1/8" iron pipe size G		120	.067		.88	3.26		4.14	6
8536	1/4" iron pipe size G		120	.067		.94	3.26		4.20	6.10
8538	3/8" iron pipe size G		117	.068		1.07	3.34		4.41	6.40
8540	1/2" iron pipe size G		114	.070		1.18	3.43		4.61	6.65
8542	3/4" iron pipe size G		112	.071		1.28	3.49		4.77	6.85
8544	1" iron pipe size G		110	.073		1.53	3.55		5.08	7.25
8546	1-1/4" iron pipe size G		108	.074		1.77	3.62		5.39	7.60
8548	1-1/2" iron pipe size G		108	.074		2.40	3.62		6.02	8.30
8550	2" iron pipe size G		106	.075		2.80	3.69		6.49	8.85
8552	2-1/2" iron pipe size G		104	.077		3.75	3.76		7.51	10
8554	3" iron pipe size G		102	.078		4.80	3.83		8.63	11.25
8556	4" iron pipe size G		100	.080		6.15	3.91		10.06	12.90
8570	1" wall, 1/8" iron pipe size G		110	.073		1.59	3.55		5.14	7.30
8572	1/4" iron pipe size G		108	.074		1.92	3.62		5.54	7.75
8574	3/8" iron pipe size G		106	.075		1.66	3.69		5.35	7.60
8576	1/2" iron pipe size G		104	.077		1.79	3.76		5.55	7.80
8578	3/4" iron pipe size G		102	.078		2.07	3.83		5.90	8.25
8580	1" iron pipe size G		100	.080		2.31	3.91		6.22	8.65
8582	1-1/4" iron pipe size G		97	.082		2.67	4.03		6.70	9.25
8584	1-1/2" iron pipe size G		97	.082		3.04	4.03		7.07	9.65
8586	2" iron pipe size G		95	.084		3.47	4.11		7.58	10.20
8588	2-1/2" iron pipe size G		93	.086		5.15	4.20		9.35	12.20
8590	3" iron pipe size G		91	.088		6.75	4.29		11.04	14.10
8606	Contact adhesive (R-320) G				Qt.	24			24	26.50
8608	Contact adhesive (R-320) G				Gal.	85.50			85.50	94
8610	NOTE: Preslit/preglued vs unslit, same price									

22 07 19.30 Piping Insulation Protective Jacketing, PVC

		Crew	Daily Output	Labor-Hours	Unit	Material	2012 Bare Costs Labor	Equipment	Total	Total Incl O&P
0010	**PIPING INSULATION PROTECTIVE JACKETING, PVC**									
0100	PVC, white, 48" lengths cut from roll goods									
0120	20 mil thick									
0140	Size based on OD of insulation									
0150	1-1/2" ID	Q-14	270	.059	L.F.	.20	2.61		2.81	4.28
0152	2" ID		260	.062		.27	2.71		2.98	4.52
0154	2-1/2" ID		250	.064		.32	2.81		3.13	4.73
0156	3" ID		240	.067		.39	2.93		3.32	5
0158	3-1/2" ID		230	.070		.44	3.06		3.50	5.25
0160	4" ID		220	.073		.50	3.20		3.70	5.55
0162	4-1/2" ID		210	.076		.56	3.35		3.91	5.80
0164	5" ID		200	.080		.61	3.52		4.13	6.15
0166	5-1/2" ID		190	.084		.67	3.70		4.37	6.50
0168	6" ID		180	.089		.73	3.91		4.64	6.90
0170	6-1/2" ID		175	.091		.79	4.02		4.81	7.10
0172	7" ID		170	.094		.84	4.14		4.98	7.35
0174	7-1/2" ID		164	.098		.91	4.29		5.20	7.70
0176	8" ID		161	.099		.96	4.37		5.33	7.85
0178	8-1/2" ID		158	.101		1.02	4.45		5.47	8.05
0180	9" ID		155	.103		1.08	4.54		5.62	8.25

22 07 19.30 Piping Insulation Protective Jacketing, PVC		Crew	Daily Output	Labor-Hours	Unit	Material	2012 Bare Costs Labor	Equipment	Total	Total Incl O&P
0182	9-1/2" ID	Q-14	152	.105	L.F.	1.14	4.63		5.77	8.45
0184	10" ID		149	.107		1.19	4.72		5.91	8.65
0186	10-1/2" ID		146	.110		1.25	4.82		6.07	8.90
0188	11" ID		143	.112		1.31	4.92		6.23	9.10
0190	11-1/2" ID		140	.114		1.37	5.05		6.42	9.35
0192	12" ID		137	.117		1.42	5.15		6.57	9.55
0194	12-1/2" ID		134	.119		1.49	5.25		6.74	9.85
0195	13" ID		132	.121		1.54	5.35		6.89	10
0196	13-1/2" ID		132	.121		1.60	5.35		6.95	10.05
0198	14" ID		130	.123		1.66	5.40		7.06	10.30
0200	15" ID		128	.125		1.78	5.50		7.28	10.50
0202	16" ID		126	.127		1.89	5.60		7.49	10.80
0204	17" ID		124	.129		2.01	5.65		7.66	11.05
0206	18" ID		122	.131		2.13	5.75		7.88	11.35
0208	19" ID		120	.133		2.24	5.85		8.09	11.60
0210	20" ID		118	.136		2.35	5.95		8.30	11.90
0212	21" ID		116	.138		2.47	6.05		8.52	12.15
0214	22" ID		114	.140		2.58	6.15		8.73	12.45
0216	23" ID		112	.143		2.69	6.30		8.99	12.75
0218	24" ID		110	.145		2.81	6.40		9.21	13.05
0220	25" ID		108	.148		2.93	6.50		9.43	13.35
0222	26" ID		106	.151		3.04	6.65		9.69	13.70
0224	27" ID		104	.154		3.16	6.75		9.91	14.05
0226	28" ID		102	.157		3.27	6.90		10.17	14.35
0228	29" ID		100	.160		3.39	7.05		10.44	14.70
0230	30" ID	▼	98	.163	▼	3.51	7.20		10.71	15.05
0300	For colors, add				Ea.	10%				
1000	30 mil thick									
1010	Size based on OD of insulation									
1020	2" ID	Q-14	260	.062	L.F.	.40	2.71		3.11	4.66
1022	2-1/2" ID		250	.064		.48	2.81		3.29	4.91
1024	3" ID		240	.067		.58	2.93		3.51	5.20
1026	3-1/2" ID		230	.070		.65	3.06		3.71	5.50
1028	4" ID		220	.073		.74	3.20		3.94	5.80
1030	4-1/2" ID		210	.076		.82	3.35		4.17	6.10
1032	5" ID		200	.080		.91	3.52		4.43	6.50
1034	5-1/2" ID		190	.084		.99	3.70		4.69	6.85
1036	6" ID		180	.089		1.08	3.91		4.99	7.30
1038	6-1/2" ID		175	.091		1.16	4.02		5.18	7.55
1040	7" ID		170	.094		1.25	4.14		5.39	7.85
1042	7-1/2" ID		164	.098		1.34	4.29		5.63	8.15
1044	8" ID		161	.099		1.43	4.37		5.80	8.35
1046	8-1/2" ID		158	.101		1.51	4.45		5.96	8.60
1048	9" ID		155	.103		1.60	4.54		6.14	8.80
1050	9-1/2" ID		152	.105		1.68	4.63		6.31	9.05
1052	10" ID		149	.107		1.77	4.72		6.49	9.30
1054	10-1/2" ID		146	.110		1.85	4.82		6.67	9.55
1056	11" ID		143	.112		1.94	4.92		6.86	9.80
1058	11-1/2" ID		140	.114		2.02	5.05		7.07	10.05
1060	12" ID		137	.117		2.11	5.15		7.26	10.30
1062	12-1/2" ID		134	.119		2.20	5.25		7.45	10.60
1063	13" ID		132	.121		2.29	5.35		7.64	10.80
1064	13-1/2" ID	▼	132	.121	▼	2.37	5.35		7.72	10.90

22 07 19.30 Piping Insulation Protective Jacketing, PVC	Crew	Daily Output	Labor-Hours	Unit	Material	2012 Bare Costs Labor	Equipment	Total	Total Incl O&P
1066	14" ID	Q-14	130	.123	L.F.	2.46	5.40		7.86	11.15
1068	15" ID		128	.125		2.63	5.50		8.13	11.45
1070	16" ID		126	.127		2.80	5.60		8.40	11.80
1072	17" ID		124	.129		2.97	5.65		8.62	12.10
1074	18" ID		122	.131		3.15	5.75		8.90	12.45
1076	19" ID		120	.133		3.32	5.85		9.17	12.80
1078	20" ID		118	.136		3.49	5.95		9.44	13.15
1080	21" ID		116	.138		3.66	6.05		9.71	13.50
1082	22" ID		114	.140		3.83	6.15		9.98	13.80
1084	23" ID		112	.143		4	6.30		10.30	14.20
1086	24" ID		110	.145		4.17	6.40		10.57	14.55
1088	25" ID		108	.148		4.34	6.50		10.84	14.90
1090	26" ID		106	.151		4.51	6.65		11.16	15.30
1092	27" ID		104	.154		4.68	6.75		11.43	15.70
1094	28" ID		102	.157		4.85	6.90		11.75	16.10
1096	29" ID		100	.160		5	7.05		12.05	16.45
1098	30" ID		98	.163		5.20	7.20		12.40	16.90
1300	For colors, add				Ea.	10%				
2000	PVC, white, fitting covers									
2020	Fiberglass insulation inserts included with sizes 1-3/4" thru 9-3/4"									
2030	Size is based on OD of insulation									
2040	90° Elbow fitting									
2060	1-3/4"	Q-14	135	.119	Ea.	.47	5.20		5.67	8.60
2062	2"		130	.123		.58	5.40		5.98	9.10
2064	2-1/4"		128	.125		.65	5.50		6.15	9.25
2068	2-1/2"		126	.127		.71	5.60		6.31	9.50
2070	2-3/4"		123	.130		.77	5.70		6.47	9.75
2072	3"		120	.133		.82	5.85		6.67	10.05
2074	3-3/8"		116	.138		.93	6.05		6.98	10.45
2076	3-3/4"		113	.142		1.04	6.25		7.29	10.85
2078	4-1/8"		110	.145		1.31	6.40		7.71	11.40
2080	4-3/4"		105	.152		1.58	6.70		8.28	12.20
2082	5-1/4"		100	.160		1.84	7.05		8.89	12.95
2084	5-3/4"		95	.168		2.43	7.40		9.83	14.20
2086	6-1/4"		90	.178		4.05	7.80		11.85	16.65
2088	6-3/4"		87	.184		4.27	8.10		12.37	17.30
2090	7-1/4"		85	.188		5.35	8.30		13.65	18.80
2092	7-3/4"		83	.193		5.60	8.50		14.10	19.35
2094	8-3/4"		80	.200		7.20	8.80		16	21.50
2096	9-3/4"		77	.208		9.65	9.15		18.80	25
2098	10-7/8"		74	.216		10.75	9.50		20.25	26.50
2100	11-7/8"		71	.225		12.35	9.90		22.25	29
2102	12-7/8"		68	.235		15.55	10.35		25.90	33.50
2104	14-1/8"		66	.242		17.80	10.65		28.45	36
2106	15-1/8"		64	.250		19.15	11		30.15	38
2108	16-1/8"		63	.254		21	11.15		32.15	40.50
2110	17-1/8"		62	.258		23	11.35		34.35	43
2112	18-1/8"		61	.262		30	11.55		41.55	51
2114	19-1/8"		60	.267		40.50	11.75		52.25	63
2116	20-1/8"		59	.271		52	11.95		63.95	76
2200	45° Elbow fitting									
2220	1-3/4" thru 9-3/4" same price as 90° Elbow fitting									
2320	10-7/8"	Q-14	74	.216	Ea.	10.75	9.50		20.25	26.50

22 07 19.30 Piping Insulation Protective Jacketing, PVC		Crew	Daily Output	Labor-Hours	Unit	Material	2012 Bare Costs Labor	Equipment	Total	Total Incl O&P
2322	11-7/8"	Q-14	71	.225	Ea.	11.85	9.90		21.75	28.50
2324	12-7/8"		68	.235		13.25	10.35		23.60	30.50
2326	14-1/8"		66	.242		15.10	10.65		25.75	33.50
2328	15-1/8"		64	.250		16.25	11		27.25	35
2330	16-1/8"		63	.254		18.55	11.15		29.70	38
2332	17-1/8"		62	.258		21	11.35		32.35	40.50
2334	18-1/8"		61	.262		25.50	11.55		37.05	46
2336	19-1/8"		60	.267		35	11.75		46.75	57
2338	20-1/8"		59	.271		39.50	11.95		51.45	62
2400	Tee fitting									
2410	1-3/4"	Q-14	96	.167	Ea.	.88	7.35		8.23	12.35
2412	2"		94	.170		1	7.50		8.50	12.75
2414	2-1/4"		91	.176		1.09	7.75		8.84	13.25
2416	2-1/2"		88	.182		1.19	8		9.19	13.75
2418	2-3/4"		85	.188		1.31	8.30		9.61	14.35
2420	3"		82	.195		1.42	8.60		10.02	14.90
2422	3-3/8"		79	.203		1.63	8.90		10.53	15.65
2424	3-3/4"		76	.211		1.85	9.25		11.10	16.45
2426	4-1/8"		73	.219		2.19	9.65		11.84	17.40
2428	4-3/4"		70	.229		2.73	10.05		12.78	18.65
2430	5-1/4"		67	.239		3.28	10.50		13.78	19.95
2432	5-3/4"		63	.254		4.36	11.15		15.51	22
2434	6-1/4"		60	.267		5.75	11.75		17.50	24.50
2436	6-3/4"		59	.271		7.10	11.95		19.05	26.50
2438	7-1/4"		57	.281		11.45	12.35		23.80	32
2440	7-3/4"		54	.296		12.55	13.05		25.60	34.50
2442	8-3/4"		52	.308		15.30	13.55		28.85	38
2444	9-3/4"		50	.320		18	14.05		32.05	42
2446	10-7/8"		48	.333		18.25	14.65		32.90	43
2448	11-7/8"		47	.340		20.50	14.95		35.45	46
2450	12-7/8"		46	.348		22.50	15.30		37.80	48.50
2452	14-1/8"		45	.356		24.50	15.65		40.15	51.50
2454	15-1/8"		44	.364		26.50	16		42.50	54
2456	16-1/8"		43	.372		28.50	16.35		44.85	56.50
2458	17-1/8"		42	.381		30.50	16.75		47.25	59.50
2460	18-1/8"		41	.390		33.50	17.15		50.65	63.50
2462	19-1/8"		40	.400		36.50	17.60		54.10	67.50
2464	20-1/8"		39	.410		40	18.05		58.05	72
4000	Mechanical grooved fitting cover, including insert									
4020	90° Elbow fitting									
4030	3/4" & 1"	Q-14	140	.114	Ea.	3.70	5.05		8.75	11.90
4040	1-1/4" & 1-1/2"		135	.119		4.68	5.20		9.88	13.25
4042	2"		130	.123		7.40	5.40		12.80	16.60
4044	2-1/2"		125	.128		8.20	5.65		13.85	17.75
4046	3"		120	.133		9.20	5.85		15.05	19.25
4048	3-1/2"		115	.139		10.65	6.10		16.75	21.50
4050	4"		110	.145		11.85	6.40		18.25	23
4052	5"		100	.160		14.75	7.05		21.80	27
4054	6"		90	.178		22	7.80		29.80	36
4056	8"		80	.200		23.50	8.80		32.30	39.50
4058	10"		75	.213		30.50	9.40		39.90	48
4060	12"		68	.235		43.50	10.35		53.85	64
4062	14"		65	.246		43.50	10.85		54.35	65

22 07 Plumbing Insulation

22 07 19 – Plumbing Piping Insulation

22 07 19.30 Piping Insulation Protective Jacketing, PVC

		Crew	Daily Output	Labor-Hours	Unit	Material	2012 Bare Costs Labor	Equipment	Total	Total Incl O&P
4064	16"	Q-14	63	.254	Ea.	59.50	11.15		70.65	83
4066	18"	↓	61	.262	↓	81.50	11.55		93.05	108
4100	45° Elbow fitting									
4120	3/4" & 1"	Q-14	140	.114	Ea.	3.29	5.05		8.34	11.45
4130	1-1/4" & 1-1/2"		135	.119		4.19	5.20		9.39	12.70
4140	2"		130	.123		6.60	5.40		12	15.70
4142	2-1/2"		125	.128		7.30	5.65		12.95	16.80
4144	3"		120	.133		8.20	5.85		14.05	18.15
4146	3-1/2"		115	.139		8.65	6.10		14.75	19.05
4148	4"		110	.145		10.55	6.40		16.95	21.50
4150	5"		100	.160		13.10	7.05		20.15	25.50
4152	6"		90	.178		19.35	7.80		27.15	33.50
4154	8"		80	.200		21	8.80		29.80	36.50
4156	10"		75	.213		27	9.40		36.40	44
4158	12"		68	.235		39	10.35		49.35	58.50
4160	14"		65	.246		50.50	10.85		61.35	72.50
4162	16"		63	.254		61	11.15		72.15	85
4164	18"	↓	61	.262	↓	72	11.55		83.55	97.50
4200	Tee fitting									
4220	3/4" & 1"	Q-14	93	.172	Ea.	4.82	7.55		12.37	17.10
4230	1-1/4" & 1-1/2"		90	.178		6.10	7.80		13.90	18.90
4240	2"		87	.184		9.60	8.10		17.70	23
4242	2-1/2"		84	.190		10.70	8.40		19.10	25
4244	3"		80	.200		11.95	8.80		20.75	27
4246	3-1/2"		77	.208		12.65	9.15		21.80	28
4248	4"		73	.219		15.45	9.65		25.10	32
4250	5"		67	.239		17.05	10.50		27.55	35
4252	6"		60	.267		25	11.75		36.75	46
4254	8"		54	.296		27.50	13.05		40.55	50.50
4256	10"		50	.320		39.50	14.05		53.55	65.50
4258	12"		46	.348		56.50	15.30		71.80	86.50
4260	14"		43	.372		68.50	16.35		84.85	101
4262	16"		42	.381		82	16.75		98.75	117
4264	18"	↓	41	.390	↓	90.50	17.15		107.65	126

22 07 19.40 Pipe Insulation Protective Jacketing, Aluminum

		Crew	Daily Output	Labor-Hours	Unit	Material	2012 Bare Costs Labor	Equipment	Total	Total Incl O&P
0010	**PIPE INSULATION PROTECTIVE JACKETING, ALUMINUM**									
0100	Metal roll jacketing									
0120	Aluminum with polykraft moisture barrier									
0140	Smooth, based on OD of insulation, .016" thick									
0180	1/2" ID	Q-14	220	.073	L.F.	.20	3.20		3.40	5.20
0190	3/4" ID		215	.074		.26	3.27		3.53	5.40
0200	1" ID		210	.076		.32	3.35		3.67	5.55
0210	1-1/4" ID		205	.078		.38	3.43		3.81	5.75
0220	1-1/2" ID		202	.079		.44	3.48		3.92	5.95
0230	1-3/4" ID		199	.080		.51	3.54		4.05	6.05
0240	2" ID		195	.082		.57	3.61		4.18	6.25
0250	2-1/4" ID		191	.084		.63	3.68		4.31	6.45
0260	2-1/2" ID		187	.086		.69	3.76		4.45	6.60
0270	2-3/4" ID		184	.087		.75	3.82		4.57	6.80
0280	3" ID		180	.089		.82	3.91		4.73	7
0290	3-1/4" ID		176	.091		.88	4		4.88	7.20
0300	3-1/2" ID	↓	172	.093		.94	4.09		5.03	7.40

22 07 19.40 Pipe Insulation Protective Jacketing, Aluminum		Crew	Daily Output	Labor-Hours	Unit	Material	2012 Bare Costs Labor	Equipment	Total	Total Incl O&P
0310	3-3/4" ID	Q-14	169	.095	L.F.	1	4.16		5.16	7.60
0320	4" ID		165	.097		1.06	4.26		5.32	7.80
0330	4-1/4" ID		161	.099		1.12	4.37		5.49	8.05
0340	4-1/2" ID		157	.102		1.19	4.48		5.67	8.30
0350	4-3/4" ID		154	.104		1.25	4.57		5.82	8.50
0360	5" ID		150	.107		1.31	4.69		6	8.75
0370	5-1/4" ID		146	.110		1.37	4.82		6.19	9
0380	5-1/2" ID		143	.112		1.43	4.92		6.35	9.20
0390	5-3/4" ID		139	.115		1.49	5.05		6.54	9.55
0400	6" ID		135	.119		1.55	5.20		6.75	9.80
0410	6-1/4" ID		133	.120		1.61	5.30		6.91	10
0420	6-1/2" ID		131	.122		1.67	5.35		7.02	10.20
0430	7" ID		128	.125		1.79	5.50		7.29	10.50
0440	7-1/4" ID		125	.128		1.86	5.65		7.51	10.80
0450	7-1/2" ID		123	.130		1.92	5.70		7.62	11
0460	8" ID		121	.132		2.04	5.80		7.84	11.30
0470	8-1/2" ID		119	.134		2.17	5.90		8.07	11.60
0480	9" ID		116	.138		2.29	6.05		8.34	11.95
0490	9-1/2" ID		114	.140		2.41	6.15		8.56	12.25
0500	10" ID		112	.143		2.54	6.30		8.84	12.60
0510	10-1/2" ID		110	.145		2.66	6.40		9.06	12.90
0520	11" ID		107	.150		2.78	6.60		9.38	13.30
0530	11-1/2" ID		105	.152		2.90	6.70		9.60	13.65
0540	12" ID		103	.155		3.02	6.85		9.87	13.95
0550	12-1/2" ID		100	.160		3.14	7.05		10.19	14.40
0560	13" ID		99	.162		3.27	7.10		10.37	14.65
0570	14" ID		98	.163		3.52	7.20		10.72	15.05
0580	15" ID		96	.167		3.76	7.35		11.11	15.55
0590	16" ID		95	.168		4.01	7.40		11.41	15.95
0600	17" ID		93	.172		4.25	7.55		11.80	16.50
0610	18" ID		92	.174		4.42	7.65		12.07	16.75
0620	19" ID		90	.178		4.74	7.80		12.54	17.40
0630	20" ID		89	.180		4.99	7.90		12.89	17.80
0640	21" ID		87	.184		5.25	8.10		13.35	18.35
0650	22" ID		86	.186		5.50	8.20		13.70	18.80
0660	23" ID		84	.190		5.70	8.40		14.10	19.35
0670	24" ID		83	.193		5.95	8.50		14.45	19.75
0710	For smooth .020" thick, add					27%	10%			
0720	For smooth .024" thick, add					52%	20%			
0730	For smooth .032" thick, add					104%	33%			
0800	For stucco embossed, add					1%				
0820	For corrugated, add					2.50%				
0900	White aluminum with polysurlyn moisture barrier									
0910	Smooth, % is an add to polykraft lines of same thickness									
0940	For smooth .016" thick, add				L.F.	35%				
0960	For smooth .024" thick, add				"	22%				
1000	Aluminum fitting covers									
1010	Size is based on OD of insulation									
1020	90° LR elbow, 2 piece									
1100	1-1/2"	Q-14	140	.114	Ea.	3.45	5.05		8.50	11.65
1110	1-3/4"		135	.119		3.45	5.20		8.65	11.90
1120	2"		130	.123		4.34	5.40		9.74	13.20
1130	2-1/4"		128	.125		4.34	5.50		9.84	13.30

22 07 19 – Plumbing Piping Insulation

22 07 19.40 Pipe Insulation Protective Jacketing, Aluminum		Crew	Daily Output	Labor-Hours	Unit	Material	2012 Bare Costs Labor	Equipment	Total	Total Incl O&P
1140	2-1/2"	Q-14	126	.127	Ea.	4.34	5.60		9.94	13.45
1150	2-3/4"		123	.130		4.34	5.70		10.04	13.65
1160	3"		120	.133		4.71	5.85		10.56	14.35
1170	3-1/4"		117	.137		4.71	6		10.71	14.55
1180	3-1/2"		115	.139		5.55	6.10		11.65	15.70
1190	3-3/4"		113	.142		5.70	6.25		11.95	16
1200	4"		110	.145		6	6.40		12.40	16.55
1210	4-1/4"		108	.148		6.15	6.50		12.65	16.90
1220	4-1/2"		106	.151		6.15	6.65		12.80	17.10
1230	4-3/4"		104	.154		6.15	6.75		12.90	17.30
1240	5"		102	.157		6.95	6.90		13.85	18.35
1250	5-1/4"		100	.160		8	7.05		15.05	19.75
1260	5-1/2"		97	.165		9.95	7.25		17.20	22.50
1270	5-3/4"		95	.168		9.95	7.40		17.35	22.50
1280	6"		92	.174		8.50	7.65		16.15	21.50
1290	6-1/4"		90	.178		8.50	7.80		16.30	21.50
1300	6-1/2"		87	.184		10.25	8.10		18.35	24
1310	7"		85	.188		12.40	8.30		20.70	26.50
1320	7-1/4"		84	.190		12.40	8.40		20.80	26.50
1330	7-1/2"		83	.193		18.25	8.50		26.75	33
1340	8"		82	.195		13.60	8.60		22.20	28.50
1350	8-1/2"		80	.200		25	8.80		33.80	41
1360	9"		78	.205		25	9		34	41.50
1370	9-1/2"		77	.208		18.50	9.15		27.65	35
1380	10"		76	.211		18.50	9.25		27.75	35
1390	10-1/2"		75	.213		18.90	9.40		28.30	35.50
1400	11"		74	.216		18.90	9.50		28.40	36
1410	11-1/2"		72	.222		21.50	9.75		31.25	38.50
1420	12"		71	.225		21.50	9.90		31.40	39
1430	12-1/2"		69	.232		38	10.20		48.20	58
1440	13"		68	.235		38	10.35		48.35	58
1450	14"		66	.242		51.50	10.65		62.15	73
1460	15"		64	.250		53.50	11		64.50	76
1470	16"		63	.254		58.50	11.15		69.65	82
2000	45° Elbow, 2 piece									
2010	2-1/2"	Q-14	126	.127	Ea.	3.59	5.60		9.19	12.65
2020	2-3/4"		123	.130		3.59	5.70		9.29	12.85
2030	3"		120	.133		4.05	5.85		9.90	13.60
2040	3-1/4"		117	.137		4.05	6		10.05	13.80
2050	3-1/2"		115	.139		4.62	6.10		10.72	14.65
2060	3-3/4"		113	.142		4.62	6.25		10.87	14.80
2070	4"		110	.145		4.70	6.40		11.10	15.10
2080	4-1/4"		108	.148		5.35	6.50		11.85	16.05
2090	4-1/2"		106	.151		5.35	6.65		12	16.25
2100	4-3/4"		104	.154		5.35	6.75		12.10	16.45
2110	5"		102	.157		6.30	6.90		13.20	17.70
2120	5-1/4"		100	.160		6.30	7.05		13.35	17.90
2130	5-1/2"		97	.165		6.60	7.25		13.85	18.55
2140	6"		92	.174		6.60	7.65		14.25	19.15
2150	6-1/2"		87	.184		9.10	8.10		17.20	22.50
2160	7"		85	.188		9.10	8.30		17.40	23
2170	7-1/2"		83	.193		9.20	8.50		17.70	23.50
2180	8"		82	.195		9.20	8.60		17.80	23.50

22 07 19.40 Pipe Insulation Protective Jacketing, Aluminum	Crew	Daily Output	Labor-Hours	Unit	Material	2012 Bare Costs Labor	2012 Bare Costs Equipment	Total	Total Incl O&P
2190	8-1/2"	Q-14	80	.200	Ea.	11.45	8.80		20.25	26.50
2200	9"		78	.205		11.45	9		20.45	26.50
2210	9-1/2"		77	.208		15.90	9.15		25.05	32
2220	10"		76	.211		15.90	9.25		25.15	32
2230	10-1/2"		75	.213		14.85	9.40		24.25	31
2240	11"		74	.216		14.85	9.50		24.35	31
2250	11-1/2"		72	.222		17.85	9.75		27.60	35
2260	12"		71	.225		17.85	9.90		27.75	35
2270	13"		68	.235		21	10.35		31.35	39
2280	14"		66	.242		25.50	10.65		36.15	45
2290	15"		64	.250		39.50	11		50.50	60.50
2300	16"		63	.254		43	11.15		54.15	65
2310	17"		62	.258		42	11.35		53.35	63.50
2320	18"		61	.262		48	11.55		59.55	70.50
2330	19"		60	.267		58.50	11.75		70.25	83
2340	20"		59	.271		56.50	11.95		68.45	80.50
2350	21"		58	.276		61	12.15		73.15	86
3000	Tee, 4 piece									
3010	2-1/2"	Q-14	88	.182	Ea.	29	8		37	44.50
3020	2-3/4"		86	.186		29	8.20		37.20	45
3030	3"		84	.190		32.50	8.40		40.90	49
3040	3-1/4"		82	.195		32.50	8.60		41.10	49.50
3050	3-1/2"		80	.200		34.50	8.80		43.30	51
3060	4"		78	.205		34.50	9		43.50	52
3070	4-1/4"		76	.211		36.50	9.25		45.75	54.50
3080	4-1/2"		74	.216		36.50	9.50		46	55
3090	4-3/4"		72	.222		36.50	9.75		46.25	55
3100	5"		70	.229		37.50	10.05		47.55	57
3110	5-1/4"		68	.235		37.50	10.35		47.85	57.50
3120	5-1/2"		66	.242		39.50	10.65		50.15	60
3130	6"		64	.250		39.50	11		50.50	60.50
3140	6-1/2"		60	.267		43.50	11.75		55.25	66
3150	7"		58	.276		43.50	12.15		55.65	66.50
3160	7-1/2"		56	.286		48	12.55		60.55	72.50
3170	8"		54	.296		48	13.05		61.05	73.50
3180	8-1/2"		52	.308		49.50	13.55		63.05	75.50
3190	9"		50	.320		49.50	14.05		63.55	76.50
3200	9-1/2"		49	.327		36.50	14.35		50.85	63
3210	10"		48	.333		36.50	14.65		51.15	63.50
3220	10-1/2"		47	.340		39	14.95		53.95	66.50
3230	11"		46	.348		39	15.30		54.30	67
3240	11-1/2"		45	.356		41	15.65		56.65	70
3250	12"		44	.364		41	16		57	70.50
3260	13"		43	.372		43	16.35		59.35	73
3270	14"		42	.381		45.50	16.75		62.25	76
3280	15"		41	.390		49	17.15		66.15	80.50
3290	16"		40	.400		50.50	17.60		68.10	83
3300	17"		39	.410		58	18.05		76.05	91.50
3310	18"		38	.421		60	18.50		78.50	95
3320	19"		37	.432		66.50	19		85.50	103
3330	20"		36	.444		68	19.55		87.55	105
3340	22"		35	.457		86.50	20		106.50	127
3350	23"		34	.471		89	20.50		109.50	130

22 07 Plumbing Insulation

22 07 19 – Plumbing Piping Insulation

22 07 19.40 Pipe Insulation Protective Jacketing, Aluminum	Crew	Daily Output	Labor-Hours	Unit	Material	2012 Bare Costs Labor	Equipment	Total	Total Incl O&P
3360	24"	Q-14	31	.516	Ea.	91	22.50		113.50	136

22 07 19.50 Pipe Insulation Protective Jacketing, St. Stl.

		Crew	Daily Output	Labor-Hours	Unit	Material	2012 Bare Costs Labor	Equipment	Total	Total Incl O&P
0010	**PIPE INSULATION PROTECTIVE JACKETING, STAINLESS STEEL**									
0100	Metal roll jacketing									
0120	Type 304 with moisture barrier									
0140	Smooth, based on OD of insulation, .010" thick									
0260	2-1/2" ID	Q-14	250	.064	L.F.	2.06	2.81		4.87	6.65
0270	2-3/4" ID		245	.065		2.24	2.87		5.11	6.95
0280	3" ID		240	.067		2.42	2.93		5.35	7.25
0290	3-1/4" ID		235	.068		2.60	2.99		5.59	7.50
0300	3-1/2" ID		230	.070		2.79	3.06		5.85	7.85
0310	3-3/4" ID		225	.071		2.97	3.13		6.10	8.15
0320	4" ID		220	.073		3.16	3.20		6.36	8.45
0330	4-1/4" ID		215	.074		3.34	3.27		6.61	8.75
0340	4-1/2" ID		210	.076		3.52	3.35		6.87	9.05
0350	5" ID		200	.080		3.89	3.52		7.41	9.80
0360	5-1/2" ID		190	.084		4.25	3.70		7.95	10.45
0370	6" ID		180	.089		4.61	3.91		8.52	11.15
0380	6-1/2" ID		175	.091		4.98	4.02		9	11.75
0390	7" ID		170	.094		5.35	4.14		9.49	12.35
0400	7-1/2" ID		164	.098		5.70	4.29		9.99	13
0410	8" ID		161	.099		6.10	4.37		10.47	13.50
0420	8-1/2" ID		158	.101		6.45	4.45		10.90	14.05
0430	9" ID		155	.103		6.80	4.54		11.34	14.55
0440	9-1/2" ID		152	.105		7.15	4.63		11.78	15.10
0450	10" ID		149	.107		7.55	4.72		12.27	15.65
0460	10-1/2" ID		146	.110		7.90	4.82		12.72	16.20
0470	11" ID		143	.112		8.25	4.92		13.17	16.75
0480	12" ID		137	.117		9	5.15		14.15	17.90
0490	13" ID		132	.121		9.75	5.35		15.10	19
0500	14" ID		130	.123		10.45	5.40		15.85	19.95
0700	For smooth .016" thick, add					45%	33%			
1000	Stainless steel, Type 316, fitting covers									
1010	Size is based on OD of insulation									
1020	90° LR Elbow, 2 piece									
1100	1-1/2"	Q-14	126	.127	Ea.	12.50	5.60		18.10	22.50
1110	2-3/4"		123	.130		12.50	5.70		18.20	22.50
1120	3"		120	.133		13.05	5.85		18.90	23.50
1130	3-1/4"		117	.137		13.05	6		19.05	24
1140	3-1/2"		115	.139		13.75	6.10		19.85	24.50
1150	3-3/4"		113	.142		14.50	6.25		20.75	25.50
1160	4"		110	.145		15.95	6.40		22.35	27.50
1170	4-1/4"		108	.148		21	6.50		27.50	33.50
1180	4-1/2"		106	.151		21	6.65		27.65	34
1190	5"		102	.157		21.50	6.90		28.40	35
1200	5-1/2"		97	.165		32.50	7.25		39.75	47
1210	6"		92	.174		35.50	7.65		43.15	51
1220	6-1/2"		87	.184		49	8.10		57.10	66
1230	7"		85	.188		49	8.30		57.30	66.50
1240	7-1/2"		83	.193		57	8.50		65.50	75.50
1250	8"		80	.200		57	8.80		65.80	76
1260	8-1/2"		80	.200		59	8.80		67.80	78.50

22 07 Plumbing Insulation

22 07 19 – Plumbing Piping Insulation

22 07 19.50 Pipe Insulation Protective Jacketing, St. Stl.	Crew	Daily Output	Labor-Hours	Unit	Material	2012 Bare Costs Labor	Equipment	Total	Total Incl O&P
1270	9"	Q-14	78	.205	Ea.	89.50	9		98.50	113
1280	9-1/2"		77	.208		88	9.15		97.15	111
1290	10"		76	.211		88	9.25		97.25	111
1300	10-1/2"		75	.213		105	9.40		114.40	131
1310	11"		74	.216		101	9.50		110.50	126
1320	12"		71	.225		114	9.90		123.90	141
1330	13"		68	.235		158	10.35		168.35	190
1340	14"		66	.242		159	10.65		169.65	192
2000	45° Elbow, 2 piece									
2010	2-1/2"	Q-14	126	.127	Ea.	10.40	5.60		16	20
2020	2-3/4"		123	.130		10.40	5.70		16.10	20.50
2030	3"		120	.133		11.20	5.85		17.05	21.50
2040	3-1/4"		117	.137		11.20	6		17.20	21.50
2050	3-1/2"		115	.139		11.35	6.10		17.45	22
2060	3-3/4"		113	.142		11.35	6.25		17.60	22
2070	4"		110	.145		14.60	6.40		21	26
2080	4-1/4"		108	.148		20.50	6.50		27	32.50
2090	4-1/2"		106	.151		20.50	6.65		27.15	33
2100	4-3/4"		104	.154		20.50	6.75		27.25	33
2110	5"		102	.157		21	6.90		27.90	34
2120	5-1/2"		97	.165		21	7.25		28.25	34.50
2130	6"		92	.174		24.50	7.65		32.15	39
2140	6-1/2"		87	.184		24.50	8.10		32.60	39.50
2150	7"		85	.188		42	8.30		50.30	59
2160	7-1/2"		83	.193		42.50	8.50		51	60
2170	8"		82	.195		42.50	8.60		51.10	60.50
2180	8-1/2"		80	.200		50	8.80		58.80	68.50
2190	9"		78	.205		50	9		59	69
2200	9-1/2"		77	.208		58.50	9.15		67.65	79
2210	10"		76	.211		58.50	9.25		67.75	79
2220	10-1/2"		75	.213		70.50	9.40		79.90	92
2230	11"		74	.216		70.50	9.50		80	92.50
2240	12"		71	.225		76.50	9.90		86.40	99.50
2250	13"		68	.235		90	10.35		100.35	115

22 11 Facility Water Distribution

22 11 13 – Facility Water Distribution Piping

22 11 13.14 Pipe, Brass

		Crew	Daily Output	Labor-Hours	Unit	Material	2012 Bare Costs Labor	Equipment	Total	Total Incl O&P
0010	**PIPE, BRASS**, Plain end									
0900	Field threaded, coupling & clevis hanger assembly 10' O.C.									
0920	Regular weight									
1120	1/2" diameter	1 Plum	48	.167	L.F.	6.35	9.10		15.45	20.50
1140	3/4" diameter		46	.174		8.45	9.50		17.95	23.50
1160	1" diameter		43	.186		12.25	10.15		22.40	29
1180	1-1/4" diameter	Q-1	72	.222		18.65	10.90		29.55	37
1200	1-1/2" diameter		65	.246		22.50	12.10		34.60	43
1220	2" diameter		53	.302		31	14.85		45.85	57
1240	2-1/2" diameter		41	.390		48.50	19.20		67.70	82.50
1260	3" diameter		31	.516		68.50	25.50		94	114
1300	4" diameter	Q-2	37	.649		120	33		153	182
1930	To delete coupling & hanger, subtract									

22 11 Facility Water Distribution

22 11 13 – Facility Water Distribution Piping

22 11 13.14 Pipe, Brass

		Crew	Daily Output	Labor-Hours	Unit	Material	2012 Bare Costs Labor	Equipment	Total	Total Incl O&P
1940	1/2" diam.					14%	46%			
1950	3/4" diam. to 1-1/2" diam.					8%	47%			
1960	2" diam. to 4" diam.					10%	37%			

22 11 13.16 Pipe Fittings, Brass

		Crew	Daily Output	Labor-Hours	Unit	Material	2012 Bare Costs Labor	Equipment	Total	Total Incl O&P
0010	**PIPE FITTINGS, BRASS**, Rough bronze, threaded.									
1000	Standard wt., 90° Elbow									
1040	1/8"	1 Plum	13	.615	Ea.	16.60	33.50		50.10	69
1060	1/4"		13	.615		16.60	33.50		50.10	69
1080	3/8"		13	.615		16.60	33.50		50.10	69
1100	1/2"		12	.667		16.60	36.50		53.10	73.50
1120	3/4"		11	.727		22	39.50		61.50	84.50
1140	1"		10	.800		36	43.50		79.50	106
1160	1-1/4"	Q-1	17	.941		58	46.50		104.50	134
1180	1-1/2"		16	1		72	49		121	154
1200	2"		14	1.143		116	56		172	213
1220	2-1/2"		11	1.455		281	71.50		352.50	420
1240	3"		8	2		430	98.50		528.50	625
1260	4"	Q-2	11	2.182		870	111		981	1,125
1280	5"		8	3		2,400	153		2,553	2,875
1300	6"		7	3.429		3,550	175		3,725	4,175
1500	45° Elbow, 1/8"	1 Plum	13	.615		20.50	33.50		54	73
1540	1/4"		13	.615		20.50	33.50		54	73
1560	3/8"		13	.615		20.50	33.50		54	73
1580	1/2"		12	.667		20.50	36.50		57	77.50
1600	3/4"		11	.727		29	39.50		68.50	92
1620	1"		10	.800		49.50	43.50		93	121
1640	1-1/4"	Q-1	17	.941		78.50	46.50		125	156
1660	1-1/2"		16	1		98.50	49		147.50	182
1680	2"		14	1.143		160	56		216	260
1700	2-1/2"		11	1.455		305	71.50		376.50	445
1720	3"		8	2		470	98.50		568.50	665
1740	4"	Q-2	11	2.182		1,050	111		1,161	1,325
1760	5"		8	3		1,950	153		2,103	2,375
1780	6"		7	3.429		2,700	175		2,875	3,250
2000	Tee, 1/8"	1 Plum	9	.889		22	48.50		70.50	97
2040	1/4"		9	.889		22	48.50		70.50	97
2060	3/8"		9	.889		22	48.50		70.50	97
2080	1/2"		8	1		22	54.50		76.50	107
2100	3/4"		7	1.143		27.50	62.50		90	125
2120	1"		6	1.333		50	73		123	165
2140	1-1/4"	Q-1	10	1.600		86	78.50		164.50	214
2160	1-1/2"		9	1.778		97	87.50		184.50	239
2180	2"		8	2		161	98.50		259.50	325
2200	2-1/2"		7	2.286		385	112		497	590
2220	3"		5	3.200		585	157		742	880
2240	4"	Q-2	7	3.429		1,450	175		1,625	1,875
2260	5"		5	4.800		3,025	245		3,270	3,700
2280	6"		4	6		4,725	305		5,030	5,650
2500	Coupling, 1/8"	1 Plum	26	.308		13.85	16.80		30.65	41
2540	1/4"		22	.364		13.85	19.85		33.70	45.50
2560	3/8"		18	.444		13.85	24.50		38.35	52
2580	1/2"		15	.533		13.85	29		42.85	59.50

22 11 Facility Water Distribution

22 11 13 – Facility Water Distribution Piping

22 11 13.16 Pipe Fittings, Brass

		Crew	Daily Output	Labor-Hours	Unit	Material	2012 Bare Costs Labor	Equipment	Total	Total Incl O&P
2600	3/4"	1 Plum	14	.571	Ea.	19.45	31		50.45	68.50
2620	1"	↓	13	.615		33	33.50		66.50	87
2640	1-1/4"	Q-1	22	.727		55.50	36		91.50	115
2660	1-1/2"		20	.800		72	39.50		111.50	139
2680	2"		18	.889		119	43.50		162.50	197
2700	2-1/2"		14	1.143		203	56		259	310
2720	3"	↓	10	1.600		281	78.50		359.50	430
2740	4"	Q-2	12	2		580	102		682	795
2760	5"		10	2.400		1,075	122		1,197	1,375
2780	6"	↓	9	2.667	↓	1,550	136		1,686	1,900
3000	Union, 125 lb.									
3020	1/8"	1 Plum	12	.667	Ea.	47	36.50		83.50	107
3040	1/4"		12	.667		47	36.50		83.50	107
3060	3/8"		12	.667		47	36.50		83.50	107
3080	1/2"		11	.727		47	39.50		86.50	112
3100	3/4"		10	.800		65	43.50		108.50	138
3120	1"	↓	9	.889		98	48.50		146.50	181
3140	1-1/4"	Q-1	16	1		141	49		190	230
3160	1-1/2"		15	1.067		168	52.50		220.50	264
3180	2"		13	1.231		227	60.50		287.50	340
3200	2-1/2"		10	1.600		620	78.50		698.50	800
3220	3"	↓	7	2.286		965	112		1,077	1,225
3240	4"	Q-2	10	2.400	↓	3,000	122		3,122	3,475
3320	For 250 lb. (navy pattern), add					100%				

22 11 13.23 Pipe/Tube, Copper

		Crew	Daily Output	Labor-Hours	Unit	Material	2012 Bare Costs Labor	Equipment	Total	Total Incl O&P
0010	**PIPE/TUBE, COPPER**, Solder joints R221113-50									
0100	Solder									
0120	Solder, lead free, roll				Lb.	15.35			15.35	16.85
1000	Type K tubing, couplings & clevis hanger assemblies 10' O.C.									
1100	1/4" diameter	1 Plum	84	.095	L.F.	4.94	5.20		10.14	13.30
1120	3/8" diameter		82	.098		4.72	5.35		10.07	13.25
1140	1/2" diameter		78	.103		5.40	5.60		11	14.40
1160	5/8" diameter		77	.104		7	5.65		12.65	16.25
1180	3/4" diameter		74	.108		9.55	5.90		15.45	19.45
1200	1" diameter		66	.121		12.85	6.60		19.45	24
1220	1-1/4" diameter		56	.143		16	7.80		23.80	29.50
1240	1-1/2" diameter		50	.160		21	8.75		29.75	36
1260	2" diameter	↓	40	.200		32	10.90		42.90	51.50
1280	2-1/2" diameter	Q-1	60	.267		49	13.10		62.10	74
1300	3" diameter		54	.296		69	14.55		83.55	97.50
1320	3-1/2" diameter		42	.381		95.50	18.70		114.20	133
1330	4" diameter		38	.421		118	20.50		138.50	161
1340	5" diameter	↓	32	.500		261	24.50		285.50	325
1360	6" diameter	Q-2	38	.632		385	32		417	475
1380	8" diameter	"	34	.706		645	36		681	760
1390	For other than full hard temper, add				↓	13%				
1440	For silver solder, add						15%			
1800	For medical clean, (oxygen class), add					12%				
1950	To delete cplgs. & hngrs., 1/4"-1" pipe, subtract					27%	60%			
1960	1-1/4"-3" pipe, subtract					14%	52%			
1970	3-1/2"-5" pipe, subtract					10%	60%			
1980	6"-8" pipe, subtract					19%	53%			

22 11 Facility Water Distribution

22 11 13 – Facility Water Distribution Piping

22 11 13.23 Pipe/Tube, Copper

		Crew	Daily Output	Labor-Hours	Unit	Material	2012 Bare Costs Labor	Equipment	Total	Total Incl O&P
2000	Type L tubing, couplings & clevis hanger assemblies 10' O.C.									
2100	1/4" diameter	1 Plum	88	.091	L.F.	2.69	4.96		7.65	10.45
2120	3/8" diameter		84	.095		3.73	5.20		8.93	11.95
2140	1/2" diameter		81	.099		4.30	5.40		9.70	12.90
2160	5/8" diameter		79	.101		6.25	5.55		11.80	15.25
2180	3/4" diameter		76	.105		6.60	5.75		12.35	15.90
2200	1" diameter		68	.118		9.85	6.40		16.25	20.50
2220	1-1/4" diameter		58	.138		13.45	7.55		21	26
2240	1-1/2" diameter		52	.154		17.25	8.40		25.65	31.50
2260	2" diameter		42	.190		27	10.40		37.40	45.50
2280	2-1/2" diameter	Q-1	62	.258		42	12.70		54.70	65
2300	3" diameter		56	.286		57	14.05		71.05	84
2320	3-1/2" diameter		43	.372		81	18.30		99.30	117
2340	4" diameter		39	.410		99	20		119	140
2360	5" diameter		34	.471		211	23		234	267
2380	6" diameter	Q-2	40	.600		300	30.50		330.50	375
2400	8" diameter	"	36	.667		485	34		519	585
2410	For other than full hard temper, add					21%				
2590	For silver solder, add						15%			
2900	For medical clean, (oxygen class), add					12%				
2940	To delete cplgs. & hngrs., 1/4"-1" pipe, subtract					37%	63%			
2960	1-1/4"-3" pipe, subtract					12%	53%			
2970	3-1/2"-5" pipe, subtract					12%	63%			
2980	6"-8" pipe, subtract					24%	55%			
3000	Type M tubing, couplings & clevis hanger assemblies 10' O.C.									
3100	1/4" diameter	1 Plum	90	.089	L.F.	3.02	4.85		7.87	10.60
3120	3/8" diameter		87	.092		3.08	5		8.08	10.95
3140	1/2" diameter		84	.095		3.31	5.20		8.51	11.50
3160	5/8" diameter		81	.099		4.94	5.40		10.34	13.60
3180	3/4" diameter		78	.103		5.05	5.60		10.65	14
3200	1" diameter		70	.114		7.65	6.25		13.90	17.85
3220	1-1/4" diameter		60	.133		11.25	7.30		18.55	23.50
3240	1-1/2" diameter		54	.148		15.20	8.10		23.30	29
3260	2" diameter		44	.182		24	9.95		33.95	41
3280	2-1/2" diameter	Q-1	64	.250		37	12.30		49.30	59
3300	3" diameter		58	.276		50	13.55		63.55	75.50
3320	3-1/2" diameter		45	.356		73.50	17.50		91	107
3340	4" diameter		40	.400		91	19.65		110.65	130
3360	5" diameter		36	.444		211	22		233	265
3370	6" diameter	Q-2	42	.571		300	29		329	375
3380	8" diameter	"	38	.632		485	32		517	585
3440	For silver solder, add						15%			
3960	To delete cplgs. & hngrs., 1/4"-1" pipe, subtract					35%	65%			
3970	1-1/4"-3" pipe, subtract					19%	56%			
3980	3-1/2"-5" pipe, subtract					13%	65%			
3990	6"-8" pipe, subtract					28%	58%			
4000	Type DWV tubing, couplings & clevis hanger assemblies 10' O.C.									
4100	1-1/4" diameter	1 Plum	60	.133	L.F.	11.95	7.30		19.25	24
4120	1-1/2" diameter		54	.148		14.95	8.10		23.05	28.50
4140	2" diameter		44	.182		21	9.95		30.95	38
4160	3" diameter	Q-1	58	.276		39	13.55		52.55	63
4180	4" diameter		40	.400		70	19.65		89.65	107
4200	5" diameter		36	.444		191	22		213	243

22 11 13.23 Pipe/Tube, Copper		Crew	Daily Output	Labor-Hours	Unit	Material	2012 Bare Costs Labor	Equipment	Total	Total Incl O&P
4220	6" diameter	Q-2	42	.571	L.F.	280	29		309	355
4240	8" diameter	"	38	.632	↓	610	32		642	720
4730	To delete cplgs. & hngrs., 1-1/4"-2" pipe, subtract					16%	53%			
4740	3"-4" pipe, subtract					13%	60%			
4750	5"-8" pipe, subtract					23%	58%			
5200	ACR tubing, type L, hard temper, cleaned and									
5220	capped, no couplings or hangers									
5240	3/8" OD				L.F.	2.05			2.05	2.26
5250	1/2" OD					3.12			3.12	3.43
5260	5/8" OD					3.80			3.80	4.18
5270	3/4" OD					5.35			5.35	5.90
5280	7/8" OD					5.95			5.95	6.55
5290	1-1/8" OD					8.65			8.65	9.50
5300	1-3/8" OD					11.60			11.60	12.75
5310	1-5/8" OD					14.85			14.85	16.35
5320	2-1/8" OD					23.50			23.50	25.50
5330	2-5/8" OD					35			35	38.50
5340	3-1/8" OD					46.50			46.50	51.50
5350	3-5/8" OD					61			61	67
5360	4-1/8" OD				↓	77.50			77.50	85
5380	ACR tubing, type L, hard, cleaned and capped									
5381	No couplings or hangers									
5384	3/8"	1 Stpi	160	.050	L.F.	2.05	2.79		4.84	6.45
5385	1/2"		160	.050		3.12	2.79		5.91	7.65
5386	5/8"		160	.050		3.80	2.79		6.59	8.40
5387	3/4"		130	.062		5.35	3.43		8.78	11.05
5388	7/8"		130	.062		5.95	3.43		9.38	11.70
5389	1-1/8"		115	.070		8.65	3.88		12.53	15.35
5390	1-3/8"		100	.080		11.60	4.46		16.06	19.45
5391	1-5/8"		90	.089		14.85	4.95		19.80	24
5392	2-1/8"	↓	80	.100		23.50	5.55		29.05	34
5393	2-5/8"	Q-5	125	.128		35	6.40		41.40	48
5394	3-1/8"		105	.152		46.50	7.65		54.15	63
5395	4-1/8"	↓	95	.168	↓	77.50	8.45		85.95	98
5800	Refrigeration tubing, dryseal, 50' coils									
5840	1/8" OD				Coil	46			46	50.50
5850	3/16" OD					53.50			53.50	59
5860	1/4" OD					61.50			61.50	67.50
5870	5/16" OD					82.50			82.50	91
5880	3/8" OD					91.50			91.50	101
5890	1/2" OD					124			124	136
5900	5/8" OD					168			168	185
5910	3/4" OD					202			202	222
5920	7/8" OD					300			300	330
5930	1-1/8" OD					435			435	475
5940	1-3/8" OD					680			680	750
5950	1-5/8" OD				↓	865			865	950
9400	Sub assemblies used in assembly systems									
9410	Chilled water unit, coil connections per unit under 10 ton	Q-5	.80	20	System	1,375	1,000		2,375	3,025
9420	Chilled water unit, coil connections per unit 10 ton and up		1	16		2,000	800		2,800	3,375
9430	Chilled water dist. piping per ton, less than 61 ton systems	↓	26	.615		34.50	31		65.50	84.50
9440	Chilled water dist. piping per ton, 61 through 120 ton systems	Q-6	31	.774		53	40		93	119
9450	Chilled water dist. piping/ton, 135 ton systems and up	Q-8	25.40	1.260	↓	75	67	1.45	143.45	185

22 11 Facility Water Distribution

22 11 13 – Facility Water Distribution Piping

22 11 13.23 Pipe/Tube, Copper

		Crew	Daily Output	Labor-Hours	Unit	Material	2012 Bare Costs Labor	Equipment	Total	Total Incl O&P
9510	Refrigerant piping/ton of cooling for remote condensers	Q-5	2	8	System	540	400		940	1,200
9520	Refrigerant piping per ton up to 10 ton w/remote condensing unit		2.40	6.667		221	335		556	750
9530	Refrigerant piping per ton, 20 ton w/remote condensing unit		2	8		335	400		735	975
9540	Refrigerant piping per ton, 40 ton w/remote condensing unit		1.90	8.421		455	420		875	1,125
9550	Refrigerant piping per ton, 75-80 ton w/remote condensing unit	Q-6	2.40	10		675	520		1,195	1,525
9560	Refrigerant piping per ton, 100 ton w/remote condensing unit	"	2.20	10.909		905	565		1,470	1,850

22 11 13.25 Pipe/Tube Fittings, Copper

		Crew	Daily Output	Labor-Hours	Unit	Material	2012 Bare Costs Labor	Equipment	Total	Total Incl O&P
0010	**PIPE/TUBE FITTINGS, COPPER**, Wrought unless otherwise noted									
0040	Solder joints, copper x copper									
0070	90° elbow, 1/4"	1 Plum	22	.364	Ea.	8.95	19.85		28.80	40
0090	3/8"		22	.364		8.50	19.85		28.35	39.50
0100	1/2"		20	.400		2.84	22		24.84	36
0110	5/8"		19	.421		9.55	23		32.55	45
0120	3/4"		19	.421		6.40	23		29.40	41.50
0130	1"		16	.500		15.70	27.50		43.20	58.50
0140	1-1/4"		15	.533		23.50	29		52.50	70
0150	1-1/2"		13	.615		37	33.50		70.50	91
0160	2"		11	.727		67.50	39.50		107	134
0170	2-1/2"	Q-1	13	1.231		135	60.50		195.50	239
0180	3"		11	1.455		180	71.50		251.50	305
0190	3-1/2"		10	1.600		630	78.50		708.50	810
0200	4"		9	1.778		460	87.50		547.50	635
0210	5"		6	2.667		1,925	131		2,056	2,325
0220	6"	Q-2	9	2.667		2,575	136		2,711	3,025
0230	8"	"	8	3		9,525	153		9,678	10,700
0250	45° elbow, 1/4"	1 Plum	22	.364		15.95	19.85		35.80	47.50
0270	3/8"		22	.364		13.70	19.85		33.55	45
0280	1/2"		20	.400		5.25	22		27.25	39
0290	5/8"		19	.421		26	23		49	63
0300	3/4"		19	.421		9.15	23		32.15	44.50
0310	1"		16	.500		23	27.50		50.50	66.50
0320	1-1/4"		15	.533		31	29		60	78
0330	1-1/2"		13	.615		37.50	33.50		71	91.50
0340	2"		11	.727		62.50	39.50		102	129
0350	2-1/2"	Q-1	13	1.231		134	60.50		194.50	238
0360	3"		13	1.231		197	60.50		257.50	310
0370	3-1/2"		10	1.600		320	78.50		398.50	470
0380	4"		9	1.778		420	87.50		507.50	595
0390	5"		6	2.667		1,625	131		1,756	2,000
0400	6"	Q-2	9	2.667		2,575	136		2,711	3,025
0410	8"	"	8	3		8,725	153		8,878	9,825
0450	Tee, 1/4"	1 Plum	14	.571		17.90	31		48.90	66.50
0470	3/8"		14	.571		14.40	31		45.40	63
0480	1/2"		13	.615		4.88	33.50		38.38	56
0490	5/8"		12	.667		31.50	36.50		68	89.50
0500	3/4"		12	.667		11.70	36.50		48.20	68
0510	1"		10	.800		36	43.50		79.50	106
0520	1-1/4"		9	.889		49.50	48.50		98	128
0530	1-1/2"		8	1		76.50	54.50		131	167
0540	2"		7	1.143		119	62.50		181.50	225
0550	2-1/2"	Q-1	8	2		240	98.50		338.50	410
0560	3"		7	2.286		365	112		477	575

22 11 Facility Water Distribution

22 11 13 – Facility Water Distribution Piping

22 11 13.25 Pipe/Tube Fittings, Copper		Crew	Daily Output	Labor-Hours	Unit	Material	2012 Bare Costs Labor	Equipment	Total	Total Incl O&P
0570	3-1/2"	Q-1	6	2.667	Ea.	1,050	131		1,181	1,375
0580	4"		5	3.200		885	157		1,042	1,200
0590	5"		4	4		2,900	197		3,097	3,500
0600	6"	Q-2	6	4		3,975	204		4,179	4,650
0610	8"	"	5	4.800		15,300	245		15,545	17,200
0612	Tee, reducing on the outlet, 1/4"	1 Plum	15	.533		30.50	29		59.50	77.50
0613	3/8"		15	.533		28.50	29		57.50	75.50
0614	1/2"		14	.571		25	31		56	74.50
0615	5/8"		13	.615		48	33.50		81.50	104
0616	3/4"		12	.667		13.20	36.50		49.70	69.50
0617	1"		11	.727		44.50	39.50		84	109
0618	1-1/4"		10	.800		53.50	43.50		97	125
0619	1-1/2"		9	.889		57	48.50		105.50	136
0620	2"		8	1		92.50	54.50		147	185
0621	2-1/2"	Q-1	9	1.778		280	87.50		367.50	440
0622	3"		8	2		310	98.50		408.50	490
0623	4"		6	2.667		590	131		721	850
0624	5"		5	3.200		2,900	157		3,057	3,425
0625	6"	Q-2	7	3.429		3,775	175		3,950	4,425
0626	8"	"	6	4		15,300	204		15,504	17,100
0630	Tee, reducing on the run, 1/4"	1 Plum	15	.533		38	29		67	86
0631	3/8"		15	.533		51	29		80	100
0632	1/2"		14	.571		34.50	31		65.50	85
0633	5/8"		13	.615		51	33.50		84.50	107
0634	3/4"		12	.667		13.80	36.50		50.30	70
0635	1"		11	.727		43	39.50		82.50	108
0636	1-1/4"		10	.800		68.50	43.50		112	142
0637	1-1/2"		9	.889		114	48.50		162.50	198
0638	2"		8	1		161	54.50		215.50	260
0639	2-1/2"	Q-1	9	1.778		360	87.50		447.50	530
0640	3"		8	2		535	98.50		633.50	735
0641	4"		6	2.667		1,175	131		1,306	1,500
0642	5"		5	3.200		2,750	157		2,907	3,250
0643	6"	Q-2	7	3.429		4,175	175		4,350	4,875
0644	8"	"	6	4		15,300	204		15,504	17,100
0650	Coupling, 1/4"	1 Plum	24	.333		2.07	18.20		20.27	30
0670	3/8"		24	.333		2.75	18.20		20.95	30.50
0680	1/2"		22	.364		2.15	19.85		22	32.50
0690	5/8"		21	.381		6.50	21		27.50	38.50
0700	3/4"		21	.381		4.33	21		25.33	36.50
0710	1"		18	.444		8.65	24.50		33.15	46
0715	1-1/4"		17	.471		15.30	25.50		40.80	56
0716	1-1/2"		15	.533		20.50	29		49.50	66.50
0718	2"		13	.615		34	33.50		67.50	87.50
0721	2-1/2"	Q-1	15	1.067		72	52.50		124.50	158
0722	3"		13	1.231		108	60.50		168.50	210
0724	3-1/2"		8	2		207	98.50		305.50	375
0726	4"		7	2.286		227	112		339	420
0728	5"		6	2.667		560	131		691	815
0731	6"	Q-2	8	3		925	153		1,078	1,250
0732	8"	"	7	3.429		3,000	175		3,175	3,575
0741	Coupling, reducing, concentric									
0743	1/2"	1 Plum	23	.348	Ea.	5.60	19		24.60	34.50

22 11 13.25 Pipe/Tube Fittings, Copper		Crew	Daily Output	Labor-Hours	Unit	Material	2012 Bare Costs Labor	Equipment	Total	Total Incl O&P
0745	3/4"	1 Plum	21.50	.372	Ea.	10.05	20.50		30.55	41.50
0747	1"		19.50	.410		15.40	22.50		37.90	51
0748	1-1/4"		18	.444		22	24.50		46.50	60.50
0749	1-1/2"		16	.500		28.50	27.50		56	72
0751	2"		14	.571		60	31		91	113
0752	2-1/2"		13	.615		124	33.50		157.50	187
0753	3"	Q-1	14	1.143		149	56		205	249
0755	4"	"	8	2		315	98.50		413.50	495
0757	5"	Q-2	7.50	3.200		1,675	163		1,838	2,075
0759	6"		7	3.429		2,650	175		2,825	3,200
0761	8"		6.50	3.692		5,500	188		5,688	6,325
0771	Cap, sweat									
0773	1/2"	1 Plum	40	.200	Ea.	2.07	10.90		12.97	18.75
0775	3/4"		38	.211		3.86	11.50		15.36	21.50
0777	1"		32	.250		9.15	13.65		22.80	30.50
0778	1-1/4"		29	.276		12.25	15.05		27.30	36
0779	1-1/2"		26	.308		17.90	16.80		34.70	45
0781	2"		22	.364		33	19.85		52.85	66.50
0791	Flange, sweat									
0793	3"	Q-1	22	.727	Ea.	440	36		476	540
0795	4"		18	.889		610	43.50		653.50	740
0797	5"		12	1.333		1,150	65.50		1,215.50	1,350
0799	6"	Q-2	18	1.333		1,200	68		1,268	1,425
0801	8"	"	16	1.500		3,000	76.50		3,076.50	3,425
0850	Unions, 1/4"	1 Plum	21	.381		62.50	21		83.50	101
0870	3/8"		21	.381		63	21		84	101
0880	1/2"		19	.421		33.50	23		56.50	71.50
0890	5/8"		18	.444		143	24.50		167.50	194
0900	3/4"		18	.444		42	24.50		66.50	83
0910	1"		15	.533		72.50	29		101.50	124
0920	1-1/4"		14	.571		126	31		157	185
0930	1-1/2"		12	.667		165	36.50		201.50	237
0940	2"		10	.800		282	43.50		325.50	375
0950	2-1/2"	Q-1	12	1.333		615	65.50		680.50	780
0960	3"	"	10	1.600		1,600	78.50		1,678.50	1,875
0980	Adapter, copper x male IPS, 1/4"	1 Plum	20	.400		29.50	22		51.50	65.50
0990	3/8"		20	.400		14.70	22		36.70	49
1000	1/2"		18	.444		5.95	24.50		30.45	43
1010	3/4"		17	.471		10	25.50		35.50	50
1020	1"		15	.533		26	29		55	72.50
1030	1-1/4"		13	.615		38	33.50		71.50	92.50
1040	1-1/2"		12	.667		44	36.50		80.50	104
1050	2"		11	.727		74.50	39.50		114	142
1060	2-1/2"	Q-1	10.50	1.524		285	75		360	430
1070	3"		10	1.600		375	78.50		453.50	535
1080	3-1/2"		9	1.778		465	87.50		552.50	640
1090	4"		8	2		510	98.50		608.50	710
1200	5"		6	2.667		2,400	131		2,531	2,850
1210	6"	Q-2	8.50	2.824		2,700	144		2,844	3,175
1214	Adapter, copper x female IPS									
1216	1/2"	1 Plum	18	.444	Ea.	9.45	24.50		33.95	47
1218	3/4"		17	.471		12.95	25.50		38.45	53.50
1220	1"		15	.533		30	29		59	77

22 11 13.25 Pipe/Tube Fittings, Copper		Crew	Daily Output	Labor-Hours	Unit	Material	2012 Bare Costs Labor	Equipment	Total	Total Incl O&P
1221	1-1/4"	1 Plum	13	.615	Ea.	44	33.50		77.50	99
1222	1-1/2"		12	.667		68.50	36.50		105	131
1224	2"		11	.727		93	39.50		132.50	163
1250	Cross, 1/2"		10	.800		45.50	43.50		89	116
1260	3/4"		9.50	.842		88.50	46		134.50	167
1270	1"		8	1		150	54.50		204.50	248
1280	1-1/4"		7.50	1.067		216	58		274	325
1290	1-1/2"		6.50	1.231		305	67		372	440
1300	2"		5.50	1.455		580	79.50		659.50	760
1310	2-1/2"	Q-1	6.50	2.462		1,350	121		1,471	1,650
1320	3"	"	5.50	2.909		1,675	143		1,818	2,075
1500	Tee fitting, mechanically formed, (Type 1, 'branch sizes up to 2 in.')									
1520	1/2" run size, 3/8" to 1/2" branch size	1 Plum	80	.100	Ea.		5.45		5.45	8.25
1530	3/4" run size, 3/8" to 3/4" branch size		60	.133			7.30		7.30	11
1540	1" run size, 3/8" to 1" branch size		54	.148			8.10		8.10	12.20
1550	1-1/4" run size, 3/8" to 1-1/4" branch size		48	.167			9.10		9.10	13.75
1560	1-1/2" run size, 3/8" to 1-1/2" branch size		40	.200			10.90		10.90	16.45
1570	2" run size, 3/8" to 2" branch size		35	.229			12.50		12.50	18.80
1580	2-1/2" run size, 1/2" to 2" branch size		32	.250			13.65		13.65	20.50
1590	3" run size, 1" to 2" branch size		26	.308			16.80		16.80	25.50
1600	4" run size, 1" to 2" branch size		24	.333			18.20		18.20	27.50
1640	Tee fitting, mechanically formed, (Type 2, branches 2-1/2" thru 4")									
1650	2-1/2" run size, 2-1/2" branch size	1 Plum	12.50	.640	Ea.		35		35	52.50
1660	3" run size, 2-1/2" to 3" branch size		12	.667			36.50		36.50	55
1670	3-1/2" run size, 2-1/2" to 3-1/2" branch size		11	.727			39.50		39.50	60
1680	4" run size, 2-1/2" to 4" branch size		10.50	.762			41.50		41.50	62.50
1698	5" run size, 2" to 4" branch size		9.50	.842			46		46	69.50
1700	6" run size, 2" to 4" branch size		8.50	.941			51.50		51.50	77.50
1710	8" run size, 2" to 4" branch size		7	1.143			62.50		62.50	94
1800	ACR fittings, OD size									
1802	Tee, straight									
1808	5/8"	1 Stpi	12	.667	Ea.	4.86	37		41.86	61.50
1810	3/4"		12	.667		31.50	37		68.50	90.50
1812	7/8"		10	.800		11.70	44.50		56.20	80
1813	1"		10	.800		85	44.50		129.50	161
1814	1-1/8"		10	.800		36	44.50		80.50	107
1816	1-3/8"		9	.889		49.50	49.50		99	129
1818	1-5/8"		8	1		76.50	55.50		132	168
1820	2-1/8"		7	1.143		119	63.50		182.50	227
1822	2-5/8"	Q-5	8	2		240	100		340	415
1824	3-1/8"		7	2.286		365	115		480	580
1826	4-1/8"		5	3.200		885	160		1,045	1,225
1830	90° elbow									
1836	5/8"	1 Stpi	19	.421	Ea.	9.55	23.50		33.05	46
1838	3/4"		19	.421		17.30	23.50		40.80	54.50
1840	7/8"		16	.500		17.30	28		45.30	61
1842	1-1/8"		16	.500		23	28		51	67.50
1844	1-3/8"		15	.533		23.50	29.50		53	71
1846	1-5/8"		13	.615		37	34.50		71.50	92
1848	2-1/8"		11	.727		67.50	40.50		108	135
1850	2-5/8"	Q-5	13	1.231		135	61.50		196.50	241
1852	3-1/8"		11	1.455		180	73		253	310
1854	4-1/8"		9	1.778		460	89		549	640

22 11 Facility Water Distribution

22 11 13 – Facility Water Distribution Piping

22 11 13.25 Pipe/Tube Fittings, Copper		Crew	Daily Output	Labor-Hours	Unit	Material	2012 Bare Costs Labor	Equipment	Total	Total Incl O&P
1860	Coupling									
1866	5/8"	1 Stpi	21	.381	Ea.	2.15	21		23.15	34.50
1868	3/4"		21	.381		6.20	21		27.20	39
1870	7/8"		18	.444		4.33	25		29.33	42.50
1871	1"		18	.444		14.70	25		39.70	53.50
1872	1-1/8"		18	.444		8.70	25		33.70	47
1874	1-3/8"		17	.471		15.30	26		41.30	56.50
1876	1-5/8"		15	.533		20.50	29.50		50	67.50
1878	2-1/8"		13	.615		34	34.50		68.50	88.50
1880	2-5/8"	Q-5	15	1.067		76	53.50		129.50	165
1882	3-1/8"		13	1.231		110	61.50		171.50	214
1884	4-1/8"		7	2.286		251	115		366	450
2000	DWV, solder joints, copper x copper									
2030	90° Elbow, 1-1/4"	1 Plum	13	.615	Ea.	27.50	33.50		61	81
2050	1-1/2"		12	.667		41	36.50		77.50	101
2070	2"		10	.800		54	43.50		97.50	125
2090	3"	Q-1	10	1.600		133	78.50		211.50	265
2100	4"	"	9	1.778		715	87.50		802.50	915
2150	45° Elbow, 1-1/4"	1 Plum	13	.615		25.50	33.50		59	78.50
2170	1-1/2"		12	.667		21	36.50		57.50	78
2180	2"		10	.800		48	43.50		91.50	119
2190	3"	Q-1	10	1.600		102	78.50		180.50	232
2200	4"	"	9	1.778		490	87.50		577.50	670
2250	Tee, Sanitary, 1-1/4"	1 Plum	9	.889		54.50	48.50		103	133
2270	1-1/2"		8	1		67.50	54.50		122	157
2290	2"		7	1.143		78.50	62.50		141	180
2310	3"	Q-1	7	2.286		320	112		432	525
2330	4"	"	6	2.667		815	131		946	1,100
2400	Coupling, 1-1/4"	1 Plum	14	.571		12.90	31		43.90	61
2420	1-1/2"		13	.615		16	33.50		49.50	68
2440	2"		11	.727		22	39.50		61.50	84.50
2460	3"	Q-1	11	1.455		43	71.50		114.50	156
2480	4"	"	10	1.600		137	78.50		215.50	270
2602	Traps, see Section 22 13 16.60									
3500	Compression joint fittings									
3510	As used for plumbing and oil burner work									
3520	Fitting price includes nuts and sleeves									
3540	Sleeve, 1/8"				Ea.	.20			.20	.22
3550	3/16"					.20			.20	.22
3560	1/4"					.08			.08	.09
3570	5/16"					.21			.21	.23
3580	3/8"					.43			.43	.47
3600	1/2"					.56			.56	.62
3620	Nut, 1/8"					.30			.30	.33
3630	3/16"					.31			.31	.34
3640	1/4"					.31			.31	.34
3650	5/16"					.45			.45	.50
3660	3/8"					.49			.49	.54
3670	1/2"					.88			.88	.97
3710	Union, 1/8"	1 Plum	26	.308		1.84	16.80		18.64	27.50
3720	3/16"		24	.333		1.76	18.20		19.96	29.50
3730	1/4"		24	.333		1.84	18.20		20.04	29.50
3740	5/16"		23	.348		2.37	19		21.37	31

22 11 13.25 Pipe/Tube Fittings, Copper		Crew	Daily Output	Labor-Hours	Unit	Material	2012 Bare Costs Labor	Equipment	Total	Total Incl O&P
3750	3/8"	1 Plum	22	.364	Ea.	2.44	19.85		22.29	32.50
3760	1/2"		22	.364		3.67	19.85		23.52	34
3780	5/8"		21	.381		4.06	21		25.06	36
3820	Union tee, 1/8"		17	.471		7	25.50		32.50	46.50
3830	3/16"		16	.500		4.05	27.50		31.55	45.50
3840	1/4"		15	.533		3.67	29		32.67	48
3850	5/16"		15	.533		5.15	29		34.15	49.50
3860	3/8"		15	.533		5.25	29		34.25	50
3870	1/2"		15	.533		8.85	29		37.85	54
3910	Union elbow, 1/4"		24	.333		2.26	18.20		20.46	30
3920	5/16"		23	.348		3.99	19		22.99	33
3930	3/8"		22	.364		3.85	19.85		23.70	34
3940	1/2"		22	.364		6.30	19.85		26.15	37
3980	Female connector, 1/8"		26	.308		1.42	16.80		18.22	27
4000	3/16" x 1/8"		24	.333		1.82	18.20		20.02	29.50
4010	1/4" x 1/8"		24	.333		1.61	18.20		19.81	29.50
4020	1/4"		24	.333		2.16	18.20		20.36	30
4030	3/8" x 1/4"		22	.364		2.16	19.85		22.01	32.50
4040	1/2" x 3/8"		22	.364		3.44	19.85		23.29	34
4050	5/8" x 1/2"		21	.381		3.93	21		24.93	36
4090	Male connector, 1/8"		26	.308		1.15	16.80		17.95	27
4100	3/16" x 1/8"		24	.333		1.18	18.20		19.38	29
4110	1/4" x 1/8"		24	.333		1.23	18.20		19.43	29
4120	1/4"		24	.333		1.23	18.20		19.43	29
4130	5/16" x 1/8"		23	.348		1.45	19		20.45	30
4140	5/16" x 1/4"		23	.348		1.63	19		20.63	30.50
4150	3/8" x 1/8"		22	.364		1.72	19.85		21.57	32
4160	3/8" x 1/4"		22	.364		1.97	19.85		21.82	32
4170	3/8"		22	.364		1.97	19.85		21.82	32
4180	3/8" x 1/2"		22	.364		2.71	19.85		22.56	33
4190	1/2" x 3/8"		22	.364		2.63	19.85		22.48	33
4200	1/2"		22	.364		2.95	19.85		22.80	33.50
4210	5/8" x 1/2"		21	.381		3.40	21		24.40	35
4240	Male elbow, 1/8"		26	.308		2.37	16.80		19.17	28
4250	3/16" x 1/8"		24	.333		2.61	18.20		20.81	30.50
4260	1/4" x 1/8"		24	.333		1.97	18.20		20.17	29.50
4270	1/4"		24	.333		2.25	18.20		20.45	30
4280	3/8" x 1/4"		22	.364		2.86	19.85		22.71	33
4290	3/8"		22	.364		4.90	19.85		24.75	35.50
4300	1/2" x 1/4"		22	.364		4.72	19.85		24.57	35
4310	1/2" x 3/8"		22	.364		7.45	19.85		27.30	38
4340	Female elbow, 1/8"		26	.308		5.05	16.80		21.85	31
4350	1/4" x 1/8"		24	.333		2.88	18.20		21.08	30.50
4360	1/4"		24	.333		3.79	18.20		21.99	31.50
4370	3/8" x 1/4"		22	.364		3.74	19.85		23.59	34
4380	1/2" x 3/8"		22	.364		6.40	19.85		26.25	37
4390	1/2"		22	.364		8.60	19.85		28.45	39.50
4420	Male run tee, 1/4" x 1/8"		15	.533		3.54	29		32.54	48
4430	5/16" x 1/8"		15	.533		6.10	29		35.10	51
4440	3/8" x 1/4"		15	.533		5.45	29		34.45	50
4480	Male branch tee, 1/4" x 1/8"		15	.533		4.11	29		33.11	48.50
4490	1/4"		15	.533		4.41	29		33.41	49
4500	3/8" x 1/4"		15	.533		5.15	29		34.15	49.50

22 11 Facility Water Distribution

22 11 13 – Facility Water Distribution Piping

22 11 13.25 Pipe/Tube Fittings, Copper	Crew	Daily Output	Labor-Hours	Unit	Material	2012 Bare Costs Labor	Equipment	Total	Total Incl O&P
4510　　　　1/2" x 3/8"	1 Plum	15	.533	Ea.	8	29		37	53
4520　　　　1/2"	↓	15	.533	↓	12.80	29		41.80	58
4800　Flare joint fittings									
4810　　Refrigeration fittings									
4820　　Flare joint nuts and labor not incl. in price. Add 1 nut per jnt.									
4830　　　90° Elbow, 1/4"				Ea.	2.79			2.79	3.07
4840　　　　3/8"					3.93			3.93	4.32
4850　　　　1/2"					5.70			5.70	6.25
4860　　　　5/8"					8.35			8.35	9.20
4870　　　　3/4"					12.65			12.65	13.90
5030　　　Tee, 1/4"					2.82			2.82	3.10
5040　　　　5/16"					3.29			3.29	3.62
5050　　　　3/8"					3.57			3.57	3.93
5060　　　　1/2"					5.40			5.40	5.95
5070　　　　5/8"					6.85			6.85	7.50
5080　　　　3/4"					7.80			7.80	8.55
5140　　　Union, 3/16"					1.26			1.26	1.39
5150　　　　1/4"					.87			.87	.96
5160　　　　5/16"					1.56			1.56	1.72
5170　　　　3/8"					1.45			1.45	1.60
5180　　　　1/2"					2.16			2.16	2.38
5190　　　　5/8"					3.47			3.47	3.82
5200　　　　3/4"					9.65			9.65	10.65
5260　　　Long flare nut, 3/16"	1 Stpi	42	.190		2.22	10.60		12.82	18.45
5270　　　　1/4"		41	.195		.88	10.85		11.73	17.35
5280　　　　5/16"		40	.200		1.60	11.15		12.75	18.55
5290　　　　3/8"		39	.205		1.92	11.45		13.37	19.35
5300　　　　1/2"		38	.211		3.07	11.75		14.82	21
5310　　　　5/8"		37	.216		2.02	12.05		14.07	20.50
5320　　　　3/4"		34	.235		6.70	13.10		19.80	27
5380　　　Short flare nut, 3/16"		42	.190		3.72	10.60		14.32	20
5390　　　　1/4"		41	.195		.62	10.85		11.47	17.10
5400　　　　5/16"		40	.200		.74	11.15		11.89	17.60
5410　　　　3/8"		39	.205		1.22	11.45		12.67	18.60
5420　　　　1/2"		38	.211		1.45	11.75		13.20	19.30
5430　　　　5/8"		36	.222		2.02	12.40		14.42	21
5440　　　　3/4"	↓	34	.235		6.75	13.10		19.85	27
5500　　　90° Elbow flare by MIPS, 1/4"					2.59			2.59	2.85
5510　　　　3/8"					2.86			2.86	3.15
5520　　　　1/2"					4.56			4.56	5
5530　　　　5/8"					7.55			7.55	8.30
5540　　　　3/4"					12.25			12.25	13.50
5600　　　Flare by FIPS, 1/4"					4.34			4.34	4.77
5610　　　　3/8"					4.70			4.70	5.15
5620　　　　1/2"					6.75			6.75	7.45
5670　　　Flare by sweat, 1/4"					2.42			2.42	2.66
5680　　　　3/8"					3.15			3.15	3.47
5690　　　　1/2"					6.45			6.45	7.10
5700　　　　5/8"					21			21	23
5760　　　Tee flare by IPS, 1/4"					4.34			4.34	4.77
5770　　　　3/8"					6.10			6.10	6.70
5780　　　　1/2"					10.20			10.20	11.20
5790　　　　5/8"	↓			↓	6.95			6.95	7.60

22 11 13.25 Pipe/Tube Fittings, Copper		Crew	Daily Output	Labor-Hours	Unit	Material	2012 Bare Costs Labor	Equipment	Total	Total Incl O&P
5850	Connector, 1/4"				Ea.	.94			.94	1.03
5860	3/8"					1.40			1.40	1.54
5870	1/2"					2.29			2.29	2.52
5880	5/8"					2.15			2.15	2.37
5890	3/4"					6.45			6.45	7.10
5950	Seal cap, 1/4"					.77			.77	.85
5960	3/8"					.93			.93	1.02
5970	1/2"					1.16			1.16	1.28
5980	5/8"					2.41			2.41	2.65
5990	3/4"					7.05			7.05	7.75
6000	Water service fittings									
6010	Flare joints nut and labor are included in the fitting price.									
6020	90° Elbow, C x C, 3/8"	1 Plum	19	.421	Ea.	113	23		136	159
6030	1/2"		18	.444		113	24.50		137.50	161
6040	3/4"		16	.500		143	27.50		170.50	199
6050	1"		15	.533		272	29		301	345
6080	2"		10	.800		935	43.50		978.50	1,100
6090	90° Elbow, C x MPT, 3/8"		19	.421		81	23		104	124
6100	1/2"		18	.444		81	24.50		105.50	126
6110	3/4"		16	.500		94	27.50		121.50	144
6120	1"		15	.533		256	29		285	325
6130	1-1/4"		13	.615		410	33.50		443.50	500
6140	1-1/2"		12	.667		410	36.50		446.50	505
6150	2"		10	.800		690	43.50		733.50	820
6160	90° Elbow, C x FPT, 3/8"		19	.421		87	23		110	130
6170	1/2"		18	.444		87	24.50		111.50	132
6180	3/4"		16	.500		108	27.50		135.50	160
6190	1"		15	.533		248	29		277	315
6200	1-1/4"		13	.615		277	33.50		310.50	355
6210	1-1/2"		12	.667		1,075	36.50		1,111.50	1,225
6220	2"		10	.800		1,525	43.50		1,568.50	1,775
6230	Tee, C x C x C, 3/8"		13	.615		164	33.50		197.50	232
6240	1/2"		12	.667		164	36.50		200.50	236
6250	3/4"		11	.727		193	39.50		232.50	272
6260	1"		10	.800		340	43.50		383.50	440
6330	Tube nut, C x nut seat, 3/8"		40	.200		33.50	10.90		44.40	53
6340	1/2"		38	.211		33.50	11.50		45	54
6350	3/4"		34	.235		33.50	12.85		46.35	56
6360	1"		32	.250		60.50	13.65		74.15	87
6380	Coupling, C x C, 3/8"		19	.421		101	23		124	146
6390	1/2"		18	.444		101	24.50		125.50	148
6400	3/4"		16	.500		128	27.50		155.50	182
6410	1"		15	.533		236	29		265	305
6420	1-1/4"		12	.667		380	36.50		416.50	475
6430	1-1/2"		12	.667		580	36.50		616.50	690
6440	2"		10	.800		870	43.50		913.50	1,025
6450	Adapter, C x FPT, 3/8"		19	.421		76.50	23		99.50	119
6460	1/2"		18	.444		76.50	24.50		101	121
6470	3/4"		16	.500		92	27.50		119.50	142
6480	1"		15	.533		197	29		226	260
6490	1-1/4"		13	.615		420	33.50		453.50	510
6500	1-1/2"		12	.667		420	36.50		456.50	515
6510	2"		10	.800		545	43.50		588.50	665

22 11 13.25 Pipe/Tube Fittings, Copper

		Crew	Daily Output	Labor-Hours	Unit	Material	2012 Bare Costs Labor	Equipment	Total	Total Incl O&P
6520	Adapter, C x MPT, 3/8"	1 Plum	19	.421	Ea.	68	23		91	110
6530	1/2"		18	.444		68	24.50		92.50	112
6540	3/4"		16	.500		94	27.50		121.50	144
6550	1"		15	.533		166	29		195	227
6560	1-1/4"		13	.615		415	33.50		448.50	505
6570	1-1/2"		12	.667		415	36.50		451.50	510
6580	2"		10	.800		560	43.50		603.50	685
6992	Tube connector fittings, See Section 22 11 13.76 for plastic ftng.									
7000	Insert type Brass/copper, 100 psi @ 180°F, CTS									
7010	Adapter MPT 3/8" x 3/8" CTS	1 Plum	29	.276	Ea.	2.22	15.05		17.27	25
7020	1/2" x 1/2"		26	.308		2.22	16.80		19.02	28
7030	3/4" x 1/2"		26	.308		3.77	16.80		20.57	29.50
7040	3/4" x 3/4"		25	.320		3.28	17.45		20.73	30
7050	Adapter CTS 1/2" x 1/2" sweat		24	.333		1.38	18.20		19.58	29
7060	3/4" x 3/4" sweat		22	.364		1.05	19.85		20.90	31
7070	Coupler center set 3/8" CTS		25	.320		1.09	17.45		18.54	27.50
7080	1/2" CTS		23	.348		.83	19		19.83	29.50
7090	3/4" CTS		22	.364		1.05	19.85		20.90	31
7100	Elbow 90°, copper 3/8"		25	.320		2.38	17.45		19.83	29
7110	1/2" CTS		23	.348		1.51	19		20.51	30
7120	3/4" CTS		22	.364		1.85	19.85		21.70	32
7130	Tee copper 3/8" CTS		17	.471		2.82	25.50		28.32	42
7140	1/2" CTS		15	.533		1.94	29		30.94	46
7150	3/4" CTS		14	.571		2.98	31		33.98	50.50
7160	3/8" x 3/8" x 1/2"		16	.500		2.98	27.50		30.48	44.50
7170	1/2" x 3/8" x 1/2"		15	.533		1.93	29		30.93	46
7180	3/4" x 1/2" x 3/4"		14	.571		2.98	31		33.98	50.50

22 11 13.27 Pipe/Tube, Grooved Joint for Copper

		Crew	Daily Output	Labor-Hours	Unit	Material	2012 Bare Costs Labor	Equipment	Total	Total Incl O&P
0010	**PIPE/TUBE, GROOVED JOINT FOR COPPER**									
4000	Fittings: coupling material required at joints not incl. in fitting price.									
4001	Add 1 selected coupling, material only, per joint for installed price.									
4010	Coupling, rigid style									
4018	2" diameter	1 Plum	50	.160	Ea.	16	8.75		24.75	31
4020	2-1/2" diameter	Q-1	80	.200		18.20	9.85		28.05	35
4022	3" diameter		67	.239		20	11.75		31.75	39.50
4024	4" diameter		50	.320		30.50	15.75		46.25	57
4026	5" diameter		40	.400		52	19.65		71.65	86.50
4028	6" diameter	Q-2	50	.480		68.50	24.50		93	113
4100	Elbow, 90° or 45°									
4108	2" diameter	1 Plum	25	.320	Ea.	28.50	17.45		45.95	57.50
4110	2-1/2" diameter	Q-1	40	.400		31	19.65		50.65	63.50
4112	3" diameter		33	.485		43.50	24		67.50	83.50
4114	4" diameter		25	.640		100	31.50		131.50	158
4116	5" diameter		20	.800		285	39.50		324.50	375
4118	6" diameter	Q-2	25	.960		455	49		504	575
4200	Tee									
4208	2" diameter	1 Plum	17	.471	Ea.	47	25.50		72.50	90.50
4210	2-1/2" diameter	Q-1	27	.593		50	29		79	99
4212	3" diameter		22	.727		74.50	36		110.50	136
4214	4" diameter		17	.941		164	46.50		210.50	250
4216	5" diameter		13	1.231		460	60.50		520.50	595
4218	6" diameter	Q-2	17	1.412		565	72		637	735

22 11 Facility Water Distribution

22 11 13 – Facility Water Distribution Piping

22 11 13.27 Pipe/Tube, Grooved Joint for Copper

		Crew	Daily Output	Labor-Hours	Unit	Material	2012 Bare Costs Labor	Equipment	Total	Total Incl O&P
4300	Reducer, concentric									
4310	3" x 2-1/2" diameter	Q-1	35	.457	Ea.	41	22.50		63.50	79
4312	4" x 2-1/2" diameter		32	.500		84.50	24.50		109	130
4314	4" x 3" diameter		29	.552		84.50	27		111.50	134
4316	5" x 3" diameter		25	.640		238	31.50		269.50	310
4318	5" x 4" diameter		22	.727		238	36		274	315
4320	6" x 3" diameter	Q-2	28	.857		258	43.50		301.50	350
4322	6" x 4" diameter		26	.923		258	47		305	355
4324	6" x 5" diameter		24	1		258	51		309	360
4350	Flange, w/groove gasket									
4351	ANSI class 125 and 150									
4355	2" diameter	1 Plum	23	.348	Ea.	124	19		143	166
4356	2-1/2" diameter	Q-1	37	.432		129	21.50		150.50	174
4358	3" diameter		31	.516		136	25.50		161.50	188
4360	4" diameter		23	.696		149	34		183	216
4362	5" diameter		19	.842		200	41.50		241.50	283
4364	6" diameter	Q-2	23	1.043		218	53		271	320

22 11 13.44 Pipe, Steel

		Crew	Daily Output	Labor-Hours	Unit	Material	2012 Bare Costs Labor	Equipment	Total	Total Incl O&P
0010	**PIPE, STEEL**	R221113-50								
0020	All pipe sizes are to Spec. A-53 unless noted otherwise	R221113-70								
0032	Schedule 10, see Line 22 11 13.48 0500									
0050	Schedule 40, threaded, with couplings, and clevis hanger									
0060	assemblies sized for covering, 10' O.C.									
0540	Black, 1/4" diameter	1 Plum	66	.121	L.F.	6	6.60		12.60	16.60
0550	3/8" diameter		65	.123		6.75	6.70		13.45	17.60
0560	1/2" diameter		63	.127		4.38	6.95		11.33	15.25
0570	3/4" diameter		61	.131		5.15	7.15		12.30	16.45
0580	1" diameter		53	.151		7.55	8.25		15.80	21
0590	1-1/4" diameter	Q-1	89	.180		9.50	8.85		18.35	24
0600	1-1/2" diameter		80	.200		11.15	9.85		21	27
0610	2" diameter		64	.250		14.90	12.30		27.20	35
0620	2-1/2" diameter		50	.320		23	15.75		38.75	48.50
0630	3" diameter		43	.372		29.50	18.30		47.80	60
0640	3-1/2" diameter		40	.400		40	19.65		59.65	73.50
0650	4" diameter		36	.444		43.50	22		65.50	80.50
0809	A-106, gr. A/B, seamless w/cplgs. & clevis hanger assemblies									
0811	1/4" diameter	1 Plum	66	.121	L.F.	7.75	6.60		14.35	18.55
0812	3/8" diameter		65	.123		7.75	6.70		14.45	18.65
0813	1/2" diameter		63	.127		8.95	6.95		15.90	20.50
0814	3/4" diameter		61	.131		10.95	7.15		18.10	23
0815	1" diameter		53	.151		12	8.25		20.25	25.50
0816	1-1/4" diameter	Q-1	89	.180		14.55	8.85		23.40	29.50
0817	1-1/2" diameter		80	.200		22	9.85		31.85	39.50
0819	2" diameter		64	.250		24	12.30		36.30	45
0821	2-1/2" diameter		50	.320		29	15.75		44.75	55.50
0822	3" diameter		43	.372		31.50	18.30		49.80	62.50
0823	4" diameter		36	.444		49	22		71	86.50
1220	To delete coupling & hanger, subtract									
1230	1/4" diam. to 3/4" diam.					31%	56%			
1240	1" diam. to 1-1/2" diam.					23%	51%			
1250	2" diam. to 4" diam.					23%	41%			
1280	All pipe sizes are to Spec. A-53 unless noted otherwise									

22 11 13.44 Pipe, Steel	Crew	Daily Output	Labor-Hours	Unit	Material	2012 Bare Costs Labor	Equipment	Total	Total Incl O&P
1281 Schedule 40, threaded, with couplings and clevis hanger									
1282 assemblies sized for covering, 10' O. C.									
1290 Galvanized, 1/4" diameter	1 Plum	66	.121	L.F.	8.10	6.60		14.70	18.90
1300 3/8" diameter		65	.123		8.95	6.70		15.65	20
1310 1/2" diameter		63	.127		6.35	6.95		13.30	17.45
1320 3/4" diameter		61	.131		7.60	7.15		14.75	19.15
1330 1" diameter		53	.151		10.40	8.25		18.65	24
1340 1-1/4" diameter	Q-1	89	.180		13.30	8.85		22.15	28
1350 1-1/2" diameter		80	.200		15.65	9.85		25.50	32
1360 2" diameter		64	.250		21	12.30		33.30	41.50
1370 2-1/2" diameter		50	.320		34.50	15.75		50.25	61.50
1380 3" diameter		43	.372		44	18.30		62.30	76
1390 3-1/2" diameter		40	.400		55.50	19.65		75.15	90.50
1400 4" diameter		36	.444		63.50	22		85.50	103
1750 To delete coupling & hanger, subtract									
1760 1/4" diam. to 3/4" diam.					31%	56%			
1770 1" diam. to 1-1/2" diam.					23%	51%			
1780 2" diam. to 4" diam.					23%	41%			
2000 Welded, sch. 40, on yoke & roll hanger assy's, sized for covering, 10' O.C.									
2040 Black, 1" diameter	Q-15	93	.172	L.F.	6.80	8.45	.40	15.65	20.50
2050 1-1/4" diameter		84	.190		8.70	9.35	.44	18.49	24
2060 1-1/2" diameter		76	.211		9.75	10.35	.49	20.59	27
2070 2" diameter		61	.262		12.35	12.90	.61	25.86	33.50
2080 2-1/2" diameter		47	.340		21	16.75	.79	38.54	49
2090 3" diameter		43	.372		25.50	18.30	.86	44.66	57
2100 3-1/2" diameter		39	.410		33	20	.95	53.95	67.50
2110 4" diameter		37	.432		35	21.50	1	57.50	71.50
2120 5" diameter		32	.500		38	24.50	1.16	63.66	80
2130 6" diameter	Q-16	36	.667		50.50	34	1.03	85.53	108
2140 8" diameter		29	.828		55	42	1.27	98.27	125
2150 10" diameter		24	1		64	51	1.54	116.54	149
2160 12" diameter		19	1.263		87.50	64.50	1.95	153.95	195
2170 14" diameter, (two rod roll type hanger for 14" dia. and up)		15	1.600		106	81.50	2.46	189.96	243
2180 16" diameter, (two rod roll type hanger)		13	1.846		123	94	2.84	219.84	280
2190 18" diameter, (two rod roll type hanger)		11	2.182		144	111	3.36	258.36	330
2200 20" diameter, (two rod roll type hanger)		9	2.667		169	136	4.11	309.11	395
2220 24" diameter, (two rod roll type hanger)		8	3		235	153	4.62	392.62	495
2345 Sch. 40, A-53, gr. A/B, ERW, welded w/hngrs.									
2346 2" diameter	Q-15	61	.262	L.F.	8.40	12.90	.61	21.91	29.50
2347 2-1/2" diameter		47	.340		10.45	16.75	.79	27.99	37.50
2348 3" diameter		43	.372		13.05	18.30	.86	32.21	43
2349 4" diameter		38	.421		17.55	20.50	.97	39.02	51.50
2350 6" diameter	Q-16	37	.649		36.50	33	1	70.50	91
2351 8" diameter		29	.828		53.50	42	1.27	96.77	124
2352 10" diameter		24	1		63	51	1.54	115.54	148
2560 To delete hanger, subtract									
2570 1" diam. to 1-1/2" diam.					15%	34%			
2580 2" diam. to 3-1/2" diam.					9%	21%			
2590 4" diam. to 12" diam.					5%	12%			
2596 14" diam. to 36" diam.					3%	10%			
2640 Galvanized, 1" diameter	Q-15	93	.172	L.F.	8.75	8.45	.40	17.60	23
2650 1-1/4" diameter		84	.190		11.20	9.35	.44	20.99	27
2660 1-1/2" diameter		76	.211		12.75	10.35	.49	23.59	30

22 11 Facility Water Distribution

22 11 13 – Facility Water Distribution Piping

22 11 13.44 Pipe, Steel		Crew	Daily Output	Labor-Hours	Unit	Material	2012 Bare Costs Labor	Equipment	Total	Total Incl O&P
2670	2" diameter	Q-15	61	.262	L.F.	16.30	12.90	.61	29.81	38
2680	2-1/2" diameter		47	.340		29.50	16.75	.79	47.04	58.50
2690	3" diameter		43	.372		38.50	18.30	.86	57.66	70.50
2700	3-1/2" diameter		39	.410		44	20	.95	64.95	80
2710	4" diameter		37	.432		53.50	21.50	1	76	91.50
2720	5" diameter	▼	32	.500		57	24.50	1.16	82.66	101
2730	6" diameter	Q-16	36	.667		63	34	1.03	98.03	122
2740	8" diameter		29	.828		71.50	42	1.27	114.77	143
2750	10" diameter		24	1		112	51	1.54	164.54	202
2760	12" diameter	▼	19	1.263	▼	151	64.50	1.95	217.45	265
3160	To delete hanger, subtract									
3170	1" diam. to 1-1/2" diam.					30%	34%			
3180	2" diam. to 3-1/2" diam.					19%	21%			
3190	4" diam. to 12" diam.					10%	12%			
3250	Flanged, 150 lb. weld neck, on yoke & roll hangers									
3260	sized for covering, 10' O.C.									
3290	Black, 1" diameter	Q-15	70	.229	L.F.	12	11.25	.53	23.78	30.50
3300	1-1/4" diameter		64	.250		13.90	12.30	.58	26.78	34.50
3310	1-1/2" diameter		58	.276		14.95	13.55	.64	29.14	37.50
3320	2" diameter		45	.356		18.35	17.50	.82	36.67	47.50
3330	2-1/2" diameter		36	.444		27.50	22	1.03	50.53	64.50
3340	3" diameter		32	.500		33	24.50	1.16	58.66	75
3350	3-1/2" diameter		29	.552		42	27	1.27	70.27	89
3360	4" diameter		26	.615		44	30.50	1.42	75.92	95
3370	5" diameter	▼	21	.762		52.50	37.50	1.76	91.76	116
3380	6" diameter	Q-16	25	.960		66.50	49	1.48	116.98	149
3390	8" diameter		19	1.263		82	64.50	1.95	148.45	189
3400	10" diameter		16	1.500		119	76.50	2.31	197.81	249
3410	12" diameter	▼	14	1.714		149	87.50	2.64	239.14	299
3470	For 300 lb. flanges, add					63%				
3480	For 600 lb. flanges, add				▼	310%				
3960	To delete flanges & hanger, subtract									
3970	1" diam. to 2" diam.					76%	65%			
3980	2-1/2" diam. to 4" diam.					62%	59%			
3990	5" diam. to 12" diam.					60%	46%			
4040	Galvanized, 1" diameter	Q-15	70	.229	L.F.	13.95	11.25	.53	25.73	33
4050	1-1/4" diameter		64	.250		16.45	12.30	.58	29.33	37
4060	1-1/2" diameter		58	.276		18	13.55	.64	32.19	41
4070	2" diameter		45	.356		21.50	17.50	.82	39.82	51
4080	2-1/2" diameter		36	.444		36.50	22	1.03	59.53	74
4090	3" diameter		32	.500		45	24.50	1.16	70.66	88
4100	3-1/2" diameter		29	.552		52	27	1.27	80.27	99.50
4110	4" diameter		26	.615		62.50	30.50	1.42	94.42	116
4120	5" diameter	▼	21	.762		72	37.50	1.76	111.26	137
4130	6" diameter	Q-16	25	.960		79.50	49	1.48	129.98	163
4140	8" diameter		19	1.263		88.50	64.50	1.95	154.95	197
4150	10" diameter		16	1.500		153	76.50	2.31	231.81	286
4160	12" diameter	▼	14	1.714		183	87.50	2.64	273.14	335
4220	For 300 lb. flanges, add					65%				
4240	For 600 lb. flanges, add				▼	350%				
4660	To delete flanges & hanger, subtract									
4670	1" diam. to 2" diam.					73%	65%			
4680	2-1/2" diam. to 4" diam.					58%	59%			

22 11 13 – Facility Water Distribution Piping

22 11 13.44 Pipe, Steel	Crew	Daily Output	Labor-Hours	Unit	2012 Bare Costs				Total Incl O&P
					Material	Labor	Equipment	Total	
4690 5" diam. to 12" diam.					43%	46%			
4750 Schedule 80, threaded, with couplings, and clevis hanger assemblies									
4760 sized for covering, 10' O.C.									
4790 Black, 1/4" diameter	1 Plum	54	.148	L.F.	7.95	8.10		16.05	21
4800 3/8" diameter		53	.151		10.20	8.25		18.45	23.50
4810 1/2" diameter		52	.154		6.50	8.40		14.90	19.80
4820 3/4" diameter		50	.160		7.95	8.75		16.70	22
4830 1" diameter	▼	45	.178		10.80	9.70		20.50	26.50
4840 1-1/4" diameter	Q-1	75	.213		14.20	10.50		24.70	31.50
4850 1-1/2" diameter		69	.232		16.70	11.40		28.10	35.50
4860 2" diameter		56	.286		22.50	14.05		36.55	46
4870 2-1/2" diameter		44	.364		35	17.85		52.85	65.50
4880 3" diameter		38	.421		46.50	20.50		67	82
4890 3-1/2" diameter		35	.457		56.50	22.50		79	96.50
4900 4" diameter	▼	32	.500		67.50	24.50		92	112
5061 A-106, gr. A/B seamless with cplgs. & clevis hanger assemblies, 1/4" dia.	1 Plum	63	.127		9.85	6.95		16.80	21.50
5062 3/8" diameter		62	.129		11.50	7.05		18.55	23.50
5063 1/2" diameter		61	.131		9.95	7.15		17.10	22
5064 3/4" diameter		57	.140		11.50	7.65		19.15	24
5065 1" diameter	▼	51	.157		13.65	8.55		22.20	28
5066 1-1/4" diameter	Q-1	85	.188		18.05	9.25		27.30	34
5067 1-1/2" diameter		77	.208		28	10.20		38.20	46
5071 2" diameter		61	.262		33.50	12.90		46.40	56.50
5072 2-1/2" diameter		48	.333		36	16.40		52.40	64
5073 3" diameter		41	.390		44.50	19.20		63.70	78
5074 4" diameter	▼	35	.457	▼	63.50	22.50		86	104
5430 To delete coupling & hanger, subtract									
5440 1/4" diam. to 1/2" diam.					31%	54%			
5450 3/4" diam. to 1-1/2" diam.					28%	49%			
5460 2" diam. to 4" diam.					21%	40%			
5510 Galvanized, 1/4" diameter	1 Plum	54	.148	L.F.	7.45	8.10		15.55	20.50
5520 3/8" diameter		53	.151		8.20	8.25		16.45	21.50
5530 1/2" diameter		52	.154		8.70	8.40		17.10	22.50
5540 3/4" diameter		50	.160		10.55	8.75		19.30	25
5550 1" diameter	▼	45	.178		14.70	9.70		24.40	31
5560 1-1/4" diameter	Q-1	75	.213		19.60	10.50		30.10	37.50
5570 1-1/2" diameter		69	.232		23	11.40		34.40	42.50
5580 2" diameter		56	.286		32	14.05		46.05	56
5590 2-1/2" diameter		44	.364		49.50	17.85		67.35	81.50
5600 3" diameter		38	.421		65.50	20.50		86	103
5610 3-1/2" diameter		35	.457		78	22.50		100.50	120
5620 4" diameter	▼	32	.500	▼	93	24.50		117.50	139
5930 To delete coupling & hanger, subtract									
5940 1/4" diam. to 1/2" diam.					31%	54%			
5950 3/4" diam. to 1-1/2" diam.					28%	49%			
5960 2" diam. to 4" diam.					21%	40%			
6000 Welded, on yoke & roller hangers									
6010 sized for covering, 10' O.C.									
6040 Black, 1" diameter	Q-15	85	.188	L.F.	11.50	9.25	.43	21.18	27
6050 1-1/4" diameter		79	.203		15.10	9.95	.47	25.52	32
6060 1-1/2" diameter		72	.222		17.55	10.90	.51	28.96	36.50
6070 2" diameter		57	.281		23	13.80	.65	37.45	46.50
6080 2-1/2" diameter	▼	44	.364	▼	34.50	17.85	.84	53.19	66

22 11 13.44 Pipe, Steel	Crew	Daily Output	Labor-Hours	Unit	Material	2012 Bare Costs Labor	Equipment	Total	Total Incl O&P
6090	3" diameter	Q-15	40	.400	L.F.	45.50	19.65	.92	66.07	80.50
6100	3-1/2" diameter		34	.471		55.50	23	1.09	79.59	97
6110	4" diameter		33	.485		66	24	1.12	91.12	110
6120	5" diameter		26	.615		71	30.50	1.42	102.92	125
6130	6" diameter	Q-16	30	.800		90.50	41	1.23	132.73	163
6140	8" diameter		25	.960		108	49	1.48	158.48	195
6150	10" diameter		20	1.200		202	61	1.85	264.85	315
6160	12" diameter		15	1.600		360	81.50	2.46	443.96	520
6540	To delete hanger, subtract									
6550	1" diam. to 1-1/2" diam.					30%	14%			
6560	2" diam. to 3" diam.					23%	9%			
6570	3-1/2" diam. to 5" diam.					12%	6%			
6580	6" diam. to 12" diam.					10%	4%			
6610	Galvanized, 1" diameter	Q-15	85	.188	L.F.	15.45	9.25	.43	25.13	31.50
6650	1-1/4" diameter		79	.203		20.50	9.95	.47	30.92	38
6660	1-1/2" diameter		72	.222		24	10.90	.51	35.41	43.50
6670	2" diameter		57	.281		32	13.80	.65	46.45	57
6680	2-1/2" diameter		44	.364		49.50	17.85	.84	68.19	82
6690	3" diameter		40	.400		64.50	19.65	.92	85.07	102
6700	3-1/2" diameter		34	.471		77	23	1.09	101.09	121
6710	4" diameter		33	.485		91	24	1.12	116.12	137
6720	5" diameter		26	.615		93.50	30.50	1.42	125.42	150
6730	6" diameter	Q-16	30	.800		119	41	1.23	161.23	194
6740	8" diameter		25	.960		141	49	1.48	191.48	232
6750	10" diameter		20	1.200		264	61	1.85	326.85	385
6760	12" diameter		15	1.600		475	81.50	2.46	558.96	650
7150	To delete hanger, subtract									
7160	1" diam. to 1-1/2" diam.					26%	14%			
7170	2" diam. to 3" diam.					16%	9%			
7180	3-1/2" diam. to 5" diam.					10%	6%			
7190	6" diam. to 12" diam.					7%	4%			
7250	Flanged, 300 lb. weld neck, on yoke & roll hangers									
7260	sized for covering, 10' O.C.									
7290	Black, 1" diameter	Q-15	66	.242	L.F.	17.90	11.90	.56	30.36	38.50
7300	1-1/4" diameter		61	.262		21.50	12.90	.61	35.01	43.50
7310	1-1/2" diameter		54	.296		24	14.55	.68	39.23	49.50
7320	2" diameter		42	.381		31	18.70	.88	50.58	63
7330	2-1/2" diameter		33	.485		44	24	1.12	69.12	85.50
7340	3" diameter		29	.552		55	27	1.27	83.27	103
7350	3-1/2" diameter		24	.667		71	33	1.54	105.54	129
7360	4" diameter		23	.696		81.50	34	1.61	117.11	143
7370	5" diameter		19	.842		94.50	41.50	1.95	137.95	169
7380	6" diameter	Q-16	23	1.043		113	53	1.61	167.61	206
7390	8" diameter		17	1.412		147	72	2.17	221.17	273
7400	10" diameter		14	1.714		277	87.50	2.64	367.14	440
7410	12" diameter		12	2		455	102	3.08	560.08	655
7470	For 600 lb. flanges, add					100%				
7940	To delete flanges & hanger, subtract									
7950	1" diam. to 1-1/2" diam.					75%	66%			
7960	2" diam. to 3" diam.					62%	60%			
7970	3-1/2" diam. to 5" diam.					54%	66%			
7980	6" diam. to 12" diam.					55%	62%			
8040	Galvanized, 1" diameter water	Q-15	66	.242	L.F.	22	11.90	.56	34.46	42.50

22 11 Facility Water Distribution

22 11 13 – Facility Water Distribution Piping

22 11 13.44 Pipe, Steel	Crew	Daily Output	Labor-Hours	Unit	Material	2012 Bare Costs		Total	Total Incl O&P
						Labor	Equipment		
8050 1-1/4" diameter	Q-15	61	.262	L.F.	27	12.90	.61	40.51	49.50
8060 1-1/2" diameter		54	.296		30.50	14.55	.68	45.73	56.50
8070 2" diameter		42	.381		40.50	18.70	.88	60.08	73.50
8080 2-1/2" diameter		33	.485		58.50	24	1.12	83.62	102
8090 3" diameter		29	.552		74	27	1.27	102.27	124
8100 3-1/2" diameter		24	.667		92.50	33	1.54	127.04	153
8110 4" diameter		23	.696		107	34	1.61	142.61	170
8120 5" diameter		19	.842		117	41.50	1.95	160.45	194
8130 6" diameter	Q-16	23	1.043		141	53	1.61	195.61	237
8140 8" diameter		17	1.412		180	72	2.17	254.17	310
8150 10" diameter		14	1.714		340	87.50	2.64	430.14	505
8160 12" diameter		12	2		570	102	3.08	675.08	780
8240 For 600 lb. flanges, add					100%				
8900 To delete flanges & hangers, subtract									
8910 1" diam. to 1-1/2" diam.					72%	66%			
8920 2" diam. to 3" diam.					59%	60%			
8930 3-1/2" diam. to 5" diam.					51%	66%			
8940 6" diam. to 12" diam.					49%	62%			
9000 Threading pipe labor, one end, all schedules through 80									
9010 1/4" through 3/4" pipe size	1 Plum	80	.100	Ea.		5.45		5.45	8.25
9020 1" through 2" pipe size		73	.110			6		6	9
9030 2-1/2" pipe size		53	.151			8.25		8.25	12.45
9040 3" pipe size		50	.160			8.75		8.75	13.20
9050 3-1/2" pipe size	Q-1	89	.180			8.85		8.85	13.35
9060 4" pipe size		73	.219			10.75		10.75	16.25
9070 5" pipe size		53	.302			14.85		14.85	22.50
9080 6" pipe size		46	.348			17.10		17.10	26
9090 8" pipe size		29	.552			27		27	41
9100 10" pipe size		21	.762			37.50		37.50	56.50
9110 12" pipe size		13	1.231			60.50		60.50	91
9200 Welding labor per joint									
9210 Schedule 40,									
9230 1/2" pipe size	Q-15	32	.500	Ea.		24.50	1.16	25.66	38.50
9240 3/4" pipe size		27	.593			29	1.37	30.37	45.50
9250 1" pipe size		23	.696			34	1.61	35.61	53.50
9260 1-1/4" pipe size		20	.800			39.50	1.85	41.35	61.50
9270 1-1/2" pipe size		19	.842			41.50	1.95	43.45	64.50
9280 2" pipe size		16	1			49	2.31	51.31	76.50
9290 2-1/2" pipe size		13	1.231			60.50	2.84	63.34	94
9300 3" pipe size		12	1.333			65.50	3.08	68.58	102
9310 4" pipe size		10	1.600			78.50	3.70	82.20	123
9320 5" pipe size		9	1.778			87.50	4.11	91.61	137
9330 6" pipe size		8	2			98.50	4.62	103.12	153
9340 8" pipe size		5	3.200			157	7.40	164.40	245
9350 10" pipe size		4	4			197	9.25	206.25	305
9360 12" pipe size		3	5.333			262	12.30	274.30	410
9370 14" pipe size		2.60	6.154			300	14.20	314.20	470
9380 16" pipe size		2.20	7.273			355	16.80	371.80	560
9390 18" pipe size		2	8			395	18.50	413.50	615
9400 20" pipe size		1.80	8.889			435	20.50	455.50	685
9410 22" pipe size		1.70	9.412			465	21.50	486.50	725
9420 24" pipe size		1.50	10.667			525	24.50	549.50	815
9450 Schedule 80,									

22 11 13 – Facility Water Distribution Piping

22 11 13.44 Pipe, Steel

		Crew	Daily Output	Labor-Hours	Unit	Material	Labor	Equipment	Total	Total Incl O&P
9460	1/2" pipe size	Q-15	27	.593	Ea.		29	1.37	30.37	45.50
9470	3/4" pipe size		23	.696			34	1.61	35.61	53.50
9480	1" pipe size		20	.800			39.50	1.85	41.35	61.50
9490	1-1/4" pipe size		19	.842			41.50	1.95	43.45	64.50
9500	1-1/2" pipe size		18	.889			43.50	2.05	45.55	68.50
9510	2" pipe size		15	1.067			52.50	2.46	54.96	81.50
9520	2-1/2" pipe size		12	1.333			65.50	3.08	68.58	102
9530	3" pipe size		11	1.455			71.50	3.36	74.86	112
9540	4" pipe size		8	2			98.50	4.62	103.12	153
9550	5" pipe size		6	2.667			131	6.15	137.15	205
9560	6" pipe size		5	3.200			157	7.40	164.40	245
9570	8" pipe size		4	4			197	9.25	206.25	305
9580	10" pipe size		3	5.333			262	12.30	274.30	410
9590	12" pipe size	▼	2	8			395	18.50	413.50	615
9600	14" pipe size	Q-16	2.60	9.231			470	14.20	484.20	725
9610	16" pipe size		2.30	10.435			530	16.05	546.05	820
9620	18" pipe size		2	12			610	18.50	628.50	940
9630	20" pipe size		1.80	13.333			680	20.50	700.50	1,050
9640	22" pipe size		1.60	15			765	23	788	1,175
9650	24" pipe size	▼	1.50	16	▼		815	24.50	839.50	1,250

22 11 13.45 Pipe Fittings, Steel, Threaded

		Crew	Daily Output	Labor-Hours	Unit	Material	Labor	Equipment	Total	Total Incl O&P
0010	**PIPE FITTINGS, STEEL, THREADED**									
0020	Cast Iron									
0040	Standard weight, black									
0060	90° Elbow, straight									
0070	1/4"	1 Plum	16	.500	Ea.	8.50	27.50		36	50.50
0080	3/8"		16	.500		12.25	27.50		39.75	54.50
0090	1/2"		15	.533		5.40	29		34.40	50
0100	3/4"		14	.571		5.60	31		36.60	53
0110	1"	▼	13	.615		6.65	33.50		40.15	58
0120	1-1/4"	Q-1	22	.727		9.40	36		45.40	64.50
0130	1-1/2"		20	.800		13	39.50		52.50	74
0140	2"		18	.889		20.50	43.50		64	88.50
0150	2-1/2"		14	1.143		48.50	56		104.50	138
0160	3"		10	1.600		80	78.50		158.50	207
0170	3-1/2"		8	2		217	98.50		315.50	385
0180	4"	▼	6	2.667	▼	148	131		279	360
0250	45° Elbow, straight									
0260	1/4"	1 Plum	16	.500	Ea.	10.45	27.50		37.95	52.50
0270	3/8"		16	.500		11.25	27.50		38.75	53.50
0280	1/2"		15	.533		8.20	29		37.20	53
0300	3/4"		14	.571		8.25	31		39.25	56
0320	1"	▼	13	.615		9.70	33.50		43.20	61
0330	1-1/4"	Q-1	22	.727		13.05	36		49.05	68.50
0340	1-1/2"		20	.800		21.50	39.50		61	83.50
0350	2"		18	.889		25	43.50		68.50	93.50
0360	2-1/2"		14	1.143		65	56		121	156
0370	3"		10	1.600		103	78.50		181.50	232
0380	3-1/2"		8	2		234	98.50		332.50	405
0400	4"	▼	6	2.667	▼	214	131		345	435
0500	Tee, straight									
0510	1/4"	1 Plum	10	.800	Ea.	13.25	43.50		56.75	80.50

22 11 13 – Facility Water Distribution Piping

22 11 13.45 Pipe Fittings, Steel, Threaded	Crew	Daily Output	Labor-Hours	Unit	Material	2012 Bare Costs Labor	Equipment	Total	Total Incl O&P
0520	3/8"	1 Plum	10	.800	Ea.	12.90	43.50		56.40	80
0530	1/2"		9	.889		8.35	48.50		56.85	82
0540	3/4"		9	.889		9.80	48.50		58.30	84
0550	1"		8	1		8.70	54.50		63.20	92
0560	1-1/4"	Q-1	14	1.143		15.85	56		71.85	102
0570	1-1/2"		13	1.231		20.50	60.50		81	114
0580	2"		11	1.455		28.50	71.50		100	140
0590	2-1/2"		9	1.778		74.50	87.50		162	214
0600	3"		6	2.667		114	131		245	325
0610	3-1/2"		5	3.200		231	157		388	490
0620	4"		4	4		223	197		420	545
0660	Tee, reducing, run or outlet									
0661	1/2"	1 Plum	9	.889	Ea.	20.50	48.50		69	95.50
0662	3/4"		9	.889		17.95	48.50		66.45	93
0663	1"		8	1		20	54.50		74.50	105
0664	1-1/4"	Q-1	14	1.143		28.50	56		84.50	116
0665	1-1/2"		13	1.231		33.50	60.50		94	128
0666	2"		11	1.455		52.50	71.50		124	166
0667	2-1/2"		9	1.778		98	87.50		185.50	240
0668	3"		6	2.667		200	131		331	420
0669	3-1/2"		5	3.200		360	157		517	635
0670	4"		4	4		390	197		587	720
0674	Reducer, concentric									
0675	3/4"	1 Plum	18	.444	Ea.	15	24.50		39.50	53
0676	1"	"	15	.533		10.15	29		39.15	55
0677	1-1/4"	Q-1	26	.615		30.50	30.50		61	79
0678	1-1/2"		24	.667		47.50	33		80.50	102
0679	2"		21	.762		54	37.50		91.50	116
0680	2-1/2"		18	.889		77	43.50		120.50	151
0681	3"		14	1.143		120	56		176	217
0682	3-1/2"		12	1.333		207	65.50		272.50	325
0683	4"		10	1.600		226	78.50		304.50	365
0687	Reducer, eccentric									
0688	3/4"	1 Plum	16	.500	Ea.	31.50	27.50		59	76
0689	1"	"	14	.571		34	31		65	84.50
0690	1-1/4"	Q-1	25	.640		54.50	31.50		86	108
0691	1-1/2"		22	.727		72	36		108	134
0692	2"		20	.800		104	39.50		143.50	174
0693	2-1/2"		16	1		143	49		192	231
0694	3"		12	1.333		226	65.50		291.50	345
0695	3-1/2"		10	1.600		315	78.50		393.50	465
0696	4"		9	1.778		405	87.50		492.50	575
0700	Standard weight, galvanized cast iron									
0720	90° Elbow, straight									
0730	1/4"	1 Plum	16	.500	Ea.	13.15	27.50		40.65	55.50
0740	3/8"		16	.500		13.15	27.50		40.65	55.50
0750	1/2"		15	.533		15	29		44	60.50
0760	3/4"		14	.571		14.70	31		45.70	63
0770	1"		13	.615		17	33.50		50.50	69
0780	1-1/4"	Q-1	22	.727		26.50	36		62.50	83
0790	1-1/2"		20	.800		36.50	39.50		76	99.50
0800	2"		18	.889		53.50	43.50		97	125
0810	2-1/2"		14	1.143		110	56		166	206

22 11 13.45 Pipe Fittings, Steel, Threaded		Crew	Daily Output	Labor-Hours	Unit	Material	2012 Bare Costs Labor	Equipment	Total	Total Incl O&P
0820	3"	Q-1	10	1.600	Ea.	167	78.50		245.50	305
0830	3-1/2"		8	2		267	98.50		365.50	440
0840	4"		6	2.667		305	131		436	540
0900	45° Elbow, straight									
0910	1/4"	1 Plum	16	.500	Ea.	15	27.50		42.50	57.50
0920	3/8"		16	.500		15	27.50		42.50	57.50
0930	1/2"		15	.533		15	29		44	60.50
0940	3/4"		14	.571		17.15	31		48.15	66
0950	1"		13	.615		21	33.50		54.50	73.50
0960	1-1/4"	Q-1	22	.727		31.50	36		67.50	88.50
0970	1-1/2"		20	.800		44.50	39.50		84	109
0980	2"		18	.889		62.50	43.50		106	135
0990	2-1/2"		14	1.143		123	56		179	221
1000	3"		10	1.600		197	78.50		275.50	335
1010	3-1/2"		8	2		315	98.50		413.50	495
1020	4"		6	2.667		360	131		491	595
1100	Tee, straight									
1110	1/4"	1 Plum	10	.800	Ea.	15.85	43.50		59.35	83.50
1120	3/8"		10	.800		15.85	43.50		59.35	83.50
1130	1/2"		9	.889		15.85	48.50		64.35	90.50
1140	3/4"		9	.889		21	48.50		69.50	96.50
1150	1"		8	1		23	54.50		77.50	108
1160	1-1/4"	Q-1	14	1.143		40	56		96	129
1170	1-1/2"		13	1.231		53	60.50		113.50	150
1180	2"		11	1.455		66.50	71.50		138	181
1190	2-1/2"		9	1.778		135	87.50		222.50	280
1200	3"		6	2.667		350	131		481	585
1210	3-1/2"		5	3.200		380	157		537	650
1220	4"		4	4		425	197		622	765
1300	Extra heavy weight, black									
1310	Couplings, steel straight									
1320	1/4"	1 Plum	19	.421	Ea.	3.30	23		26.30	38
1330	3/8"		19	.421		3.62	23		26.62	38.50
1340	1/2"		19	.421		4.90	23		27.90	40
1350	3/4"		18	.444		5.25	24.50		29.75	42.50
1360	1"		15	.533		6.65	29		35.65	51.50
1370	1-1/4"	Q-1	26	.615		10.70	30.50		41.20	57.50
1380	1-1/2"		24	.667		10.70	33		43.70	61.50
1390	2"		21	.762		16.25	37.50		53.75	74.50
1400	2-1/2"		18	.889		24	43.50		67.50	92.50
1410	3"		14	1.143		28.50	56		84.50	116
1420	3-1/2"		12	1.333		38.50	65.50		104	142
1430	4"		10	1.600		45.50	78.50		124	169
1510	90° Elbow, straight									
1520	1/2"	1 Plum	15	.533	Ea.	27.50	29		56.50	74
1530	3/4"		14	.571		28	31		59	78
1540	1"		13	.615		34	33.50		67.50	88
1550	1-1/4"	Q-1	22	.727		50.50	36		86.50	110
1560	1-1/2"		20	.800		63	39.50		102.50	129
1580	2"		18	.889		77.50	43.50		121	152
1590	2-1/2"		14	1.143		187	56		243	290
1600	3"		10	1.600		247	78.50		325.50	390
1610	4"		6	2.667		515	131		646	765

22 11 13 – Facility Water Distribution Piping

22 11 13.45 Pipe Fittings, Steel, Threaded	Crew	Daily Output	Labor-Hours	Unit	Material	2012 Bare Costs Labor	Equipment	Total	Total Incl O&P
1650	45° Elbow, straight								
1660	1/2"	1 Plum	15	.533	Ea.	39	29		68	87
1670	3/4"		14	.571		37.50	31		68.50	88.50
1680	1"		13	.615		45.50	33.50		79	101
1690	1-1/4"	Q-1	22	.727		74.50	36		110.50	136
1700	1-1/2"		20	.800		82	39.50		121.50	150
1710	2"		18	.889		117	43.50		160.50	194
1720	2-1/2"		14	1.143		202	56		258	305
1800	Tee, straight								
1810	1/2"	1 Plum	9	.889	Ea.	43	48.50		91.50	121
1820	3/4"		9	.889		43	48.50		91.50	121
1830	1"		8	1		52	54.50		106.50	140
1840	1-1/4"	Q-1	14	1.143		78	56		134	170
1850	1-1/2"		13	1.231		100	60.50		160.50	201
1860	2"		11	1.455		124	71.50		195.50	245
1870	2-1/2"		9	1.778		265	87.50		352.50	425
1880	3"		6	2.667		360	131		491	595
1890	4"		4	4		705	197		902	1,075
4000	Standard weight, black								
4010	Couplings, steel straight, merchants								
4030	1/4"	1 Plum	19	.421	Ea.	.89	23		23.89	35.50
4040	3/8"		19	.421		1.07	23		24.07	35.50
4050	1/2"		19	.421		1.14	23		24.14	36
4060	3/4"		18	.444		1.46	24.50		25.96	38
4070	1"		15	.533		2.04	29		31.04	46
4080	1-1/4"	Q-1	26	.615		2.60	30.50		33.10	48.50
4090	1-1/2"		24	.667		3.29	33		36.29	53
4100	2"		21	.762		4.71	37.50		42.21	61.50
4110	2-1/2"		18	.889		13.40	43.50		56.90	81
4120	3"		14	1.143		18.85	56		74.85	105
4130	3-1/2"		12	1.333		33.50	65.50		99	136
4140	4"		10	1.600		33.50	78.50		112	156
4166	Plug, 1/4"	1 Plum	38	.211		2.39	11.50		13.89	20
4167	3/8"		38	.211		2.39	11.50		13.89	20
4168	1/2"		38	.211		2.39	11.50		13.89	20
4169	3/4"		32	.250		7.20	13.65		20.85	28.50
4170	1"		30	.267		7.70	14.55		22.25	30.50
4171	1-1/4"	Q-1	52	.308		8.85	15.10		23.95	32.50
4172	1-1/2"		48	.333		12.55	16.40		28.95	38.50
4173	2"		42	.381		16.20	18.70		34.90	46
4176	2-1/2"		36	.444		24	22		46	59.50
4180	4"		20	.800		41.50	39.50		81	105
4200	Standard weight, galvanized								
4210	Couplings, steel straight, merchants								
4230	1/4"	1 Plum	19	.421	Ea.	1.03	23		24.03	35.50
4240	3/8"		19	.421		1.32	23		24.32	36
4250	1/2"		19	.421		1.40	23		24.40	36
4260	3/4"		18	.444		1.75	24.50		26.25	38.50
4270	1"		15	.533		2.45	29		31.45	46.50
4280	1-1/4"	Q-1	26	.615		3.13	30.50		33.63	49
4290	1-1/2"		24	.667		3.89	33		36.89	54
4300	2"		21	.762		5.80	37.50		43.30	63
4310	2-1/2"		18	.889		16.50	43.50		60	84

22 11 13.45 Pipe Fittings, Steel, Threaded		Crew	Daily Output	Labor-Hours	Unit	Material	2012 Bare Costs Labor	Equipment	Total	Total Incl O&P
4320	3"	Q-1	14	1.143	Ea.	22	56		78	109
4330	3-1/2"		12	1.333		38.50	65.50		104	142
4340	4"	▼	10	1.600	▼	38.50	78.50		117	162
4370	Plug, galvanized, square head									
4374	1/2"	1 Plum	38	.211	Ea.	5.75	11.50		17.25	23.50
4375	3/4"		32	.250		5.75	13.65		19.40	27
4376	1"	▼	30	.267		5.75	14.55		20.30	28.50
4377	1-1/4"	Q-1	52	.308		9.65	15.10		24.75	33.50
4378	1-1/2"		48	.333		13	16.40		29.40	39
4379	2"		42	.381		16.15	18.70		34.85	46
4380	2-1/2"		36	.444		34	22		56	70.50
4381	3"		28	.571		43.50	28		71.50	90.50
4382	4"	▼	20	.800	▼	120	39.50		159.50	192
4700	Nipple, black									
4710	1/2" x 4" long	1 Plum	19	.421	Ea.	1.92	23		24.92	36.50
4712	3/4" x 4" long		18	.444		2.33	24.50		26.83	39
4714	1" x 4" long	▼	15	.533		3.24	29		32.24	47.50
4716	1-1/4" x 4" long	Q-1	26	.615		4.06	30.50		34.56	50
4718	1-1/2" x 4" long		24	.667		4.80	33		37.80	55
4720	2" x 4" long		21	.762		6.70	37.50		44.20	64
4722	2-1/2" x 4" long		18	.889		18.25	43.50		61.75	86
4724	3" x 4" long		14	1.143		23	56		79	110
4726	4" x 4" long	▼	10	1.600	▼	34	78.50		112.50	157
4800	Nipple, galvanized									
4810	1/2" x 4" long	1 Plum	19	.421	Ea.	2.37	23		25.37	37
4812	3/4" x 4" long		18	.444		2.93	24.50		27.43	39.50
4814	1" x 4" long	▼	15	.533		3.95	29		32.95	48.50
4816	1-1/4" x 4" long	Q-1	26	.615		4.85	30.50		35.35	51
4818	1-1/2" x 4" long		24	.667		6.15	33		39.15	56.50
4820	2" x 4" long		21	.762		7.80	37.50		45.30	65
4822	2-1/2" x 4" long		18	.889		20.50	43.50		64	88.50
4824	3" x 4" long		14	1.143		27.50	56		83.50	115
4826	4" x 4" long	▼	10	1.600	▼	36.50	78.50		115	159
5000	Malleable iron, 150 lb.									
5020	Black									
5040	90° elbow, straight									
5060	1/4"	1 Plum	16	.500	Ea.	4.17	27.50		31.67	45.50
5070	3/8"		16	.500		4.17	27.50		31.67	45.50
5080	1/2"		15	.533		2.89	29		31.89	47
5090	3/4"		14	.571		3.49	31		34.49	51
5100	1"	▼	13	.615		6.05	33.50		39.55	57
5110	1-1/4"	Q-1	22	.727		10	36		46	65
5120	1-1/2"		20	.800		13.15	39.50		52.65	74
5130	2"		18	.889		22.50	43.50		66	91
5140	2-1/2"		14	1.143		50.50	56		106.50	140
5150	3"		10	1.600		74	78.50		152.50	200
5160	3-1/2"		8	2		203	98.50		301.50	370
5170	4"	▼	6	2.667	▼	159	131		290	370
5250	45° elbow, straight									
5270	1/4"	1 Plum	16	.500	Ea.	6.30	27.50		33.80	48
5280	3/8"		16	.500		6.30	27.50		33.80	48
5290	1/2"		15	.533		4.77	29		33.77	49.50
5300	3/4"	▼	14	.571		5.90	31		36.90	53.50

22 11 Facility Water Distribution

22 11 13 – Facility Water Distribution Piping

22 11 13.45 Pipe Fittings, Steel, Threaded	Crew	Daily Output	Labor-Hours	Unit	Material	2012 Bare Costs Labor	Equipment	Total	Total Incl O&P
5310	1"	1 Plum	13	.615	Ea.	7.45	33.50		40.95	58.50
5320	1-1/4"	Q-1	22	.727		13.35	36		49.35	68.50
5330	1-1/2"		20	.800		16.25	39.50		55.75	77.50
5340	2"		18	.889		24.50	43.50		68	93
5350	2-1/2"		14	1.143		71	56		127	163
5360	3"		10	1.600		92.50	78.50		171	221
5370	3-1/2"		8	2		181	98.50		279.50	345
5380	4"		6	2.667		181	131		312	395
5450	Tee, straight									
5470	1/4"	1 Plum	10	.800	Ea.	6.05	43.50		49.55	72.50
5480	3/8"		10	.800		6.05	43.50		49.55	72.50
5490	1/2"		9	.889		3.86	48.50		52.36	77.50
5500	3/4"		9	.889		5.55	48.50		54.05	79
5510	1"		8	1		9.50	54.50		64	93
5520	1-1/4"	Q-1	14	1.143		15.40	56		71.40	101
5530	1-1/2"		13	1.231		19.10	60.50		79.60	112
5540	2"		11	1.455		32.50	71.50		104	144
5550	2-1/2"		9	1.778		70.50	87.50		158	210
5560	3"		6	2.667		104	131		235	310
5570	3-1/2"		5	3.200		240	157		397	500
5580	4"		4	4		250	197		447	570
5601	Tee, reducing, on outlet									
5602	1/2"	1 Plum	9	.889	Ea.	9.50	48.50		58	83.50
5603	3/4"		9	.889		9.15	48.50		57.65	83
5604	1"		8	1		15.20	54.50		69.70	99.50
5605	1-1/4"	Q-1	14	1.143		27	56		83	114
5606	1-1/2"		13	1.231		27	60.50		87.50	121
5607	2"		11	1.455		37	71.50		108.50	149
5608	2-1/2"		9	1.778		107	87.50		194.50	249
5609	3"		6	2.667		145	131		276	360
5610	3-1/2"		5	3.200		345	157		502	615
5611	4"		4	4		296	197		493	620
5650	Coupling									
5670	1/4"	1 Plum	19	.421	Ea.	5.20	23		28.20	40
5680	3/8"		19	.421		5.20	23		28.20	40
5690	1/2"		19	.421		3.99	23		26.99	39
5700	3/4"		18	.444		4.68	24.50		29.18	41.50
5710	1"		15	.533		7	29		36	51.50
5720	1-1/4"	Q-1	26	.615		9.10	30.50		39.60	55.50
5730	1-1/2"		24	.667		12.25	33		45.25	63
5740	2"		21	.762		18.15	37.50		55.65	76.50
5750	2-1/2"		18	.889		50	43.50		93.50	121
5760	3"		14	1.143		68	56		124	159
5770	3-1/2"		12	1.333		137	65.50		202.50	249
5780	4"		10	1.600		137	78.50		215.50	269
5840	Reducer, concentric, 1/4"	1 Plum	19	.421		5.45	23		28.45	40.50
5850	3/8"		19	.421		7	23		30	42
5860	1/2"		19	.421		5.50	23		28.50	40.50
5870	3/4"		16	.500		6.55	27.50		34.05	48
5880	1"		15	.533		11	29		40	56
5890	1-1/4"	Q-1	26	.615		12.35	30.50		42.85	59
5900	1-1/2"		24	.667		17.70	33		50.70	69
5910	2"		21	.762		25.50	37.50		63	84.50

22 11 13.45 Pipe Fittings, Steel, Threaded		Crew	Daily Output	Labor-Hours	Unit	Material	2012 Bare Costs Labor	Equipment	Total	Total Incl O&P
5911	2-1/2"	Q-1	18	.889	Ea.	57	43.50		100.50	129
5912	3"		14	1.143		70.50	56		126.50	162
5913	3-1/2"		12	1.333		219	65.50		284.50	340
5914	4"		10	1.600		166	78.50		244.50	300
5981	Bushing, 1/4"	1 Plum	19	.421		1.16	23		24.16	36
5982	3/8"		19	.421		5	23		28	40
5983	1/2"		19	.421		5	23		28	40
5984	3/4"		16	.500		5.20	27.50		32.70	47
5985	1"		15	.533		7.60	29		36.60	52.50
5986	1-1/4"	Q-1	26	.615		9.45	30.50		39.95	56
5987	1-1/2"		24	.667		8.15	33		41.15	58.50
5988	2"		21	.762		10.30	37.50		47.80	68
5989	Cap, 1/4"	1 Plum	38	.211		5.20	11.50		16.70	23
5991	3/8"		38	.211		3.37	11.50		14.87	21
5992	1/2"		38	.211		2.92	11.50		14.42	20.50
5993	3/4"		32	.250		3.96	13.65		17.61	25
5994	1"		30	.267		4.78	14.55		19.33	27.50
5995	1-1/4"	Q-1	52	.308		6.20	15.10		21.30	30
5996	1-1/2"		48	.333		8.65	16.40		25.05	34
5997	2"		42	.381		12.65	18.70		31.35	42
6000	For galvanized elbows, tees, and couplings add					20%				
6058	For galvanized reducers, caps and bushings add					20%				
6100	90° Elbow, galvanized, 150 lb., reducing									
6110	3/4" x 1/2"	1 Plum	15.40	.519	Ea.	8.30	28.50		36.80	52
6112	1" x 3/4"		14	.571		10.65	31		41.65	59
6114	1" x 1/2"		14.50	.552		11.30	30		41.30	58
6116	1-1/4" x 1"	Q-1	24.20	.661		17.85	32.50		50.35	68.50
6118	1-1/4" x 3/4"		25.40	.630		21.50	31		52.50	70
6120	1-1/4" x 1/2"		26.20	.611		23	30		53	70.50
6122	1-1/2" x 1-1/4"		21.60	.741		28.50	36.50		65	86.50
6124	1-1/2" x 1"		23.50	.681		28.50	33.50		62	82
6126	1-1/2" x 3/4"		24.60	.650		28.50	32		60.50	79.50
6128	2" x 1-1/2"		20.50	.780		33.50	38.50		72	94.50
6130	2" x 1-1/4"		21	.762		38.50	37.50		76	98.50
6132	2" x 1"		22.80	.702		39.50	34.50		74	95.50
6134	2" x 3/4"		23.90	.669		40.50	33		73.50	94
6136	2-1/2" x 2"		12.30	1.301		113	64		177	221
6138	2-1/2" x 1-1/2"		12.50	1.280		126	63		189	234
6140	3" x 2-1/2"		8.60	1.860		206	91.50		297.50	365
6142	3" x 2"		11.80	1.356		179	66.50		245.50	297
6144	4" x 3"		8.20	1.951		465	96		561	655
6160	90° Elbow, black, 150 lb., reducing									
6170	1" x 3/4"	1 Plum	14	.571	Ea.	7.30	31		38.30	55
6174	1-1/2" x 1"	Q-1	23.50	.681		17.25	33.50		50.75	69.50
6178	1-1/2" x 3/4"		24.60	.650		19.75	32		51.75	69.50
6182	2" x 1-1/2"		20.50	.780		25	38.50		63.50	85.50
6186	2" x 1"		22.80	.702		28.50	34.50		63	83.50
6190	2" x 3/4"		23.90	.669		30	33		63	82.50
6194	2-1/2" x 2"		12.30	1.301		68.50	64		132.50	172
7000	Union, with brass seat									
7010	1/4"	1 Plum	15	.533	Ea.	20.50	29		49.50	66.50
7020	3/8"		15	.533		14.10	29		43.10	59.50
7030	1/2"		14	.571		12.75	31		43.75	61

22 11 13 – Facility Water Distribution Piping

22 11 13.45 Pipe Fittings, Steel, Threaded		Crew	Daily Output	Labor-Hours	Unit	Material	2012 Bare Costs Labor	Equipment	Total	Total Incl O&P
7040	3/4"	1 Plum	13	.615	Ea.	14.70	33.50		48.20	66.50
7050	1"		12	.667		19.15	36.50		55.65	76
7060	1-1/4"	Q-1	21	.762		27.50	37.50		65	86.50
7070	1-1/2"		19	.842		34	41.50		75.50	100
7080	2"		17	.941		40	46.50		86.50	114
7090	2-1/2"		13	1.231		119	60.50		179.50	221
7100	3"		9	1.778		143	87.50		230.50	289
7120	Union, galvanized									
7124	1/2"	1 Plum	14	.571	Ea.	16.95	31		47.95	65.50
7125	3/4"		13	.615		19.50	33.50		53	72
7126	1"		12	.667		25.50	36.50		62	83
7127	1-1/4"	Q-1	21	.762		37	37.50		74.50	97
7128	1-1/2"		19	.842		44.50	41.50		86	112
7129	2"		17	.941		51.50	46.50		98	127
7130	2-1/2"		13	1.231		178	60.50		238.50	287
7131	3"		9	1.778		250	87.50		337.50	405
7500	Malleable iron, 300 lb.									
7520	Black									
7540	90° Elbow, straight, 1/4"	1 Plum	16	.500	Ea.	14.70	27.50		42.20	57
7560	3/8"		16	.500		13	27.50		40.50	55.50
7570	1/2"		15	.533		16.85	29		45.85	62.50
7580	3/4"		14	.571		19.05	31		50.05	68
7590	1"		13	.615		24.50	33.50		58	77.50
7600	1-1/4"	Q-1	22	.727		35.50	36		71.50	93
7610	1-1/2"		20	.800		42	39.50		81.50	106
7620	2"		18	.889		60	43.50		103.50	133
7630	2-1/2"		14	1.143		156	56		212	257
7640	3"		10	1.600		179	78.50		257.50	315
7650	4"		6	2.667		420	131		551	665
7700	45° Elbow, straight, 1/4"	1 Plum	16	.500		22	27.50		49.50	65
7720	3/8"		16	.500		22	27.50		49.50	65
7730	1/2"		15	.533		24	29		53	70.50
7740	3/4"		14	.571		27	31		58	76.50
7750	1"		13	.615		30	33.50		63.50	83.50
7760	1-1/4"	Q-1	22	.727		48	36		84	107
7770	1-1/2"		20	.800		62.50	39.50		102	128
7780	2"		18	.889		94	43.50		137.50	170
7790	2-1/2"		14	1.143		210	56		266	315
7800	3"		10	1.600		277	78.50		355.50	425
7810	4"		6	2.667		630	131		761	890
7850	Tee, straight, 1/4"	1 Plum	10	.800		18.45	43.50		61.95	86.50
7870	3/8"		10	.800		19.50	43.50		63	87.50
7880	1/2"		9	.889		25	48.50		73.50	101
7890	3/4"		9	.889		27	48.50		75.50	103
7900	1"		8	1		32.50	54.50		87	118
7910	1-1/4"	Q-1	14	1.143		35.50	56		91.50	124
7920	1-1/2"		13	1.231		54	60.50		114.50	151
7930	2"		11	1.455		79.50	71.50		151	196
7940	2-1/2"		9	1.778		194	87.50		281.50	345
7950	3"		6	2.667		276	131		407	505
7960	4"		4	4		785	197		982	1,150
8050	Couplings, straight, 1/4"	1 Plum	19	.421		13.20	23		36.20	49
8070	3/8"		19	.421		13.20	23		36.20	49

22 11 13 – Facility Water Distribution Piping

22 11 13.45 Pipe Fittings, Steel, Threaded		Crew	Daily Output	Labor-Hours	Unit	Material	2012 Bare Costs Labor	Equipment	Total	Total Incl O&P
8080	1/2"	1 Plum	19	.421	Ea.	14.75	23		37.75	50.50
8090	3/4"		18	.444		16.95	24.50		41.45	55
8100	1"	▼	15	.533		19.40	29		48.40	65.50
8110	1-1/4"	Q-1	26	.615		23	30.50		53.50	71
8120	1-1/2"		24	.667		34.50	33		67.50	87.50
8130	2"		21	.762		49.50	37.50		87	111
8140	2-1/2"		18	.889		91.50	43.50		135	167
8150	3"		14	1.143		132	56		188	230
8160	4"	▼	10	1.600	▼	240	78.50		318.50	385
8200	Galvanized									
8220	90° Elbow, straight, 1/4"	1 Plum	16	.500	Ea.	26	27.50		53.50	70
8222	3/8"		16	.500		13	27.50		40.50	55.50
8224	1/2"		15	.533		16.85	29		45.85	62.50
8226	3/4"		14	.571		19.05	31		50.05	68
8228	1"	▼	13	.615		24.50	33.50		58	77.50
8230	1-1/4"	Q-1	22	.727		35.50	36		71.50	93
8232	1-1/2"		20	.800		42	39.50		81.50	106
8234	2"		18	.889		60	43.50		103.50	133
8236	2-1/2"		14	1.143		289	56		345	405
8238	3"		10	1.600		345	78.50		423.50	500
8240	4"	▼	6	2.667	▼	1,025	131		1,156	1,325
8280	45° Elbow, straight									
8282	1/2"	1 Plum	15	.533	Ea.	47.50	29		76.50	96
8284	3/4"		14	.571		54.50	31		85.50	107
8286	1"	▼	13	.615		59.50	33.50		93	116
8288	1-1/4"	Q-1	22	.727		92.50	36		128.50	156
8290	1-1/2"		20	.800		120	39.50		159.50	192
8292	2"	▼	18	.889		166	43.50		209.50	249
8310	Tee, straight, 1/4"	1 Plum	10	.800		41	43.50		84.50	111
8312	3/8"		10	.800		38	43.50		81.50	108
8314	1/2"		9	.889		47.50	48.50		96	126
8316	3/4"		9	.889		52.50	48.50		101	131
8318	1"	▼	8	1		64.50	54.50		119	154
8320	1-1/4"	Q-1	14	1.143		92	56		148	186
8322	1-1/2"		13	1.231		96	60.50		156.50	196
8324	2"		11	1.455		153	71.50		224.50	277
8326	2-1/2"		9	1.778		485	87.50		572.50	665
8328	3"		6	2.667		550	131		681	805
8330	4"	▼	4	4		1,400	197		1,597	1,850
8380	Couplings, straight, 1/4"	1 Plum	19	.421		17.20	23		40.20	53.50
8382	3/8"		19	.421		24.50	23		47.50	61.50
8384	1/2"		19	.421		25.50	23		48.50	62.50
8386	3/4"		18	.444		28.50	24.50		53	68
8388	1"	▼	15	.533		38	29		67	85.50
8390	1-1/4"	Q-1	26	.615		49.50	30.50		80	100
8392	1-1/2"		24	.667		70	33		103	126
8394	2"		21	.762		84.50	37.50		122	149
8396	2-1/2"		18	.889		222	43.50		265.50	310
8398	3"		14	1.143		264	56		320	375
8399	4"	▼	10	1.600	▼	425	78.50		503.50	585
8529	Black									
8530	Reducer, concentric, 1/4"	1 Plum	19	.421	Ea.	17.45	23		40.45	53.50
8531	3/8"	↓	19	.421	↓	17.45	23		40.45	53.50

22 11 13.45 Pipe Fittings, Steel, Threaded

		Crew	Daily Output	Labor-Hours	Unit	Material	2012 Bare Costs Labor	2012 Bare Costs Equipment	Total	Total Incl O&P
8532	1/2"	1 Plum	17	.471	Ea.	21	25.50		46.50	62
8533	3/4"		16	.500		30	27.50		57.50	74
8534	1"		15	.533		31.50	29		60.50	78.50
8535	1-1/4"	Q-1	26	.615		53.50	30.50		84	105
8536	1-1/2"		24	.667		55.50	33		88.50	111
8537	2"		21	.762		80.50	37.50		118	145
8550	Cap, 1/4"	1 Plum	38	.211		13.55	11.50		25.05	32.50
8551	3/8"		38	.211		13.55	11.50		25.05	32.50
8552	1/2"		34	.235		13.45	12.85		26.30	34
8553	3/4"		32	.250		16.95	13.65		30.60	39
8554	1"		30	.267		22	14.55		36.55	46.50
8555	1-1/4"	Q-1	52	.308		24.50	15.10		39.60	50
8556	1-1/2"		48	.333		36	16.40		52.40	64
8557	2"		42	.381		50	18.70		68.70	83
8570	Plug, 1/4"	1 Plum	38	.211		3.28	11.50		14.78	21
8571	3/8"		38	.211		3.44	11.50		14.94	21
8572	1/2"		34	.235		3.60	12.85		16.45	23.50
8573	3/4"		32	.250		4.49	13.65		18.14	25.50
8574	1"		30	.267		6.85	14.55		21.40	29.50
8575	1-1/4"	Q-1	52	.308		14.15	15.10		29.25	38.50
8576	1-1/2"		48	.333		16.20	16.40		32.60	42.50
8577	2"		42	.381		25.50	18.70		44.20	56
9500	Union with brass seat, 1/4"	1 Plum	15	.533		30	29		59	77
9530	3/8"		15	.533		30.50	29		59.50	77.50
9540	1/2"		14	.571		24.50	31		55.50	74
9550	3/4"		13	.615		27	33.50		60.50	80.50
9560	1"		12	.667		35.50	36.50		72	94
9570	1-1/4"	Q-1	21	.762		57.50	37.50		95	120
9580	1-1/2"		19	.842		60.50	41.50		102	129
9590	2"		17	.941		75	46.50		121.50	153
9600	2-1/2"		13	1.231		241	60.50		301.50	355
9610	3"		9	1.778		310	87.50		397.50	475
9620	4"		5	3.200		990	157		1,147	1,325
9630	Union, all iron, 1/4"	1 Plum	15	.533		46.50	29		75.50	95
9650	3/8"		15	.533		46.50	29		75.50	95
9660	1/2"		14	.571		49	31		80	101
9670	3/4"		13	.615		52.50	33.50		86	108
9680	1"		12	.667		64	36.50		100.50	126
9690	1-1/4"	Q-1	21	.762		98.50	37.50		136	165
9700	1-1/2"		19	.842		120	41.50		161.50	195
9710	2"		17	.941		152	46.50		198.50	238
9720	2-1/2"		13	1.231		270	60.50		330.50	390
9730	3"		9	1.778		515	87.50		602.50	695
9750	For galvanized unions, add					15%				
9757	Forged steel, 3000 lb.									
9758	Black									
9760	90° Elbow, 1/4"	1 Plum	16	.500	Ea.	19.35	27.50		46.85	62.50
9761	3/8"		16	.500		19.35	27.50		46.85	62.50
9762	1/2"		15	.533		14.80	29		43.80	60.50
9763	3/4"		14	.571		18.60	31		49.60	67.50
9764	1"		13	.615		27.50	33.50		61	81
9765	1-1/4"	Q-1	22	.727		52.50	36		88.50	112
9766	1-1/2"		20	.800		67.50	39.50		107	134

22 11 13 – Facility Water Distribution Piping

22 11 13.45 Pipe Fittings, Steel, Threaded	Crew	Daily Output	Labor-Hours	Unit	Material	2012 Bare Costs Labor	2012 Bare Costs Equipment	Total	Total Incl O&P
9767	2"	Q-1	18	.889	Ea.	82	43.50		125.50	157
9780	45° Elbow 1/4"	1 Plum	16	.500		24.50	27.50		52	68
9781	3/8"		16	.500		24.50	27.50		52	68
9782	1/2"		15	.533		24	29		53	70.50
9783	3/4"		14	.571		28	31		59	78
9784	1"		13	.615		38	33.50		71.50	92.50
9785	1-1/4"	Q-1	22	.727		52.50	36		88.50	112
9786	1-1/2"		20	.800		75.50	39.50		115	143
9787	2"		18	.889		104	43.50		147.50	181
9800	Tee, 1/4"	1 Plum	10	.800		23.50	43.50		67	92
9801	3/8"		10	.800		23.50	43.50		67	92
9802	1/2"		9	.889		21	48.50		69.50	96.50
9803	3/4"		9	.889		28.50	48.50		77	105
9804	1"		8	1		37.50	54.50		92	124
9805	1-1/4"	Q-1	14	1.143		73	56		129	165
9806	1-1/2"		13	1.231		85	60.50		145.50	185
9807	2"		11	1.455		110	71.50		181.50	228
9820	Reducer, concentric, 1/4"	1 Plum	19	.421		11.80	23		34.80	47.50
9821	3/8"		19	.421		12.30	23		35.30	48
9822	1/2"		17	.471		12.30	25.50		37.80	52.50
9823	3/4"		16	.500		14.60	27.50		42.10	57
9824	1"		15	.533		19.05	29		48.05	65
9825	1-1/4"	Q-1	26	.615		33.50	30.50		64	82
9826	1-1/2"		24	.667		36	33		69	89.50
9827	2"		21	.762		52.50	37.50		90	115
9840	Cap, 1/4"	1 Plum	38	.211		6.90	11.50		18.40	25
9841	3/8"		38	.211		7.25	11.50		18.75	25.50
9842	1/2"		34	.235		7.05	12.85		19.90	27
9843	3/4"		32	.250		9.85	13.65		23.50	31.50
9844	1"		30	.267		15.10	14.55		29.65	38.50
9845	1-1/4"	Q-1	52	.308		24.50	15.10		39.60	50
9846	1-1/2"		48	.333		29	16.40		45.40	56.50
9847	2"		42	.381		42	18.70		60.70	74
9860	Plug, 1/4"	1 Plum	38	.211		3.28	11.50		14.78	21
9861	3/8"		38	.211		3.44	11.50		14.94	21
9862	1/2"		34	.235		3.60	12.85		16.45	23.50
9863	3/4"		32	.250		4.49	13.65		18.14	25.50
9864	1"		30	.267		6.85	14.55		21.40	29.50
9865	1-1/4"	Q-1	52	.308		14.15	15.10		29.25	38.50
9866	1-1/2"		48	.333		16.20	16.40		32.60	42.50
9867	2"		42	.381		25.50	18.70		44.20	56
9880	Union, bronze seat, 1/4"	1 Plum	15	.533		53.50	29		82.50	103
9881	3/8"		15	.533		53.50	29		82.50	103
9882	1/2"		14	.571		51.50	31		82.50	104
9883	3/4"		13	.615		69	33.50		102.50	126
9884	1"		12	.667		77.50	36.50		114	141
9885	1-1/4"	Q-1	21	.762		151	37.50		188.50	223
9886	1-1/2"		19	.842		155	41.50		196.50	234
9887	2"		17	.941		184	46.50		230.50	273
9900	Coupling, 1/4"	1 Plum	19	.421		7.55	23		30.55	43
9901	3/8"		19	.421		7.55	23		30.55	43
9902	1/2"		17	.471		6.20	25.50		31.70	46
9903	3/4"		16	.500		8.05	27.50		35.55	50

22 11 13 – Facility Water Distribution Piping

22 11 13.45 Pipe Fittings, Steel, Threaded

		Crew	Daily Output	Labor-Hours	Unit	Material	2012 Bare Costs Labor	Equipment	Total	Total Incl O&P
9904	1"	1 Plum	15	.533	Ea.	14	29		43	59.50
9905	1-1/4"	Q-1	26	.615		23.50	30.50		54	71
9906	1-1/2"		24	.667		30	33		63	82.50
9907	2"	▼	21	.762	▼	37.50	37.50		75	98

22 11 13.47 Pipe Fittings, Steel

		Crew	Daily Output	Labor-Hours	Unit	Material	2012 Bare Costs Labor	Equipment	Total	Total Incl O&P
0010	**PIPE FITTINGS, STEEL**, Flanged, Welded & Special									
0020	Flanged joints, C.I., standard weight, black. One gasket & bolt									
0040	set, mat'l only, required at each joint, not included (see line 0620)									
0060	90° Elbow, straight, 1-1/2" pipe size	Q-1	14	1.143	Ea.	475	56		531	610
0080	2" pipe size		13	1.231		283	60.50		343.50	400
0090	2-1/2" pipe size		12	1.333		305	65.50		370.50	435
0100	3" pipe size		11	1.455		255	71.50		326.50	390
0110	4" pipe size		8	2		315	98.50		413.50	495
0120	5" pipe size	▼	7	2.286		745	112		857	990
0130	6" pipe size	Q-2	9	2.667		495	136		631	750
0140	8" pipe size		8	3		855	153		1,008	1,175
0150	10" pipe size		7	3.429		1,875	175		2,050	2,325
0160	12" pipe size	▼	6	4	▼	3,775	204		3,979	4,450
0171	90° Elbow, reducing									
0172	2-1/2" by 2" pipe size	Q-1	12	1.333	Ea.	925	65.50		990.50	1,125
0173	3" by 2-1/2" pipe size		11	1.455		945	71.50		1,016.50	1,150
0174	4" by 3" pipe size		8	2		700	98.50		798.50	920
0175	5" by 3" pipe size	▼	7	2.286		1,500	112		1,612	1,800
0176	6" by 4" pipe size	Q-2	9	2.667		870	136		1,006	1,150
0177	8" by 6" pipe size		8	3		1,275	153		1,428	1,625
0178	10" by 8" pipe size		7	3.429		2,400	175		2,575	2,925
0179	12" by 10" pipe size	▼	6	4		4,625	204		4,829	5,375
0200	45° Elbow, straight, 1-1/2" pipe size	Q-1	14	1.143		575	56		631	720
0220	2" pipe size		13	1.231		410	60.50		470.50	540
0230	2-1/2" pipe size		12	1.333		435	65.50		500.50	580
0240	3" pipe size		11	1.455		425	71.50		496.50	575
0250	4" pipe size		8	2		480	98.50		578.50	675
0260	5" pipe size	▼	7	2.286		1,150	112		1,262	1,425
0270	6" pipe size	Q-2	9	2.667		780	136		916	1,075
0280	8" pipe size		8	3		1,150	153		1,303	1,475
0290	10" pipe size		7	3.429		2,425	175		2,600	2,925
0300	12" pipe size	▼	6	4	▼	3,700	204		3,904	4,350
0310	Cross, straight									
0311	2-1/2" pipe size	Q-1	6	2.667	Ea.	900	131		1,031	1,200
0312	3" pipe size		5	3.200		945	157		1,102	1,250
0313	4" pipe size		4	4		1,225	197		1,422	1,650
0314	5" pipe size	▼	3	5.333		2,575	262		2,837	3,225
0315	6" pipe size	Q-2	5	4.800		2,575	245		2,820	3,200
0316	8" pipe size		4	6		4,150	305		4,455	5,025
0317	10" pipe size		3	8		4,925	410		5,335	6,050
0318	12" pipe size	▼	2	12		7,525	610		8,135	9,200
0350	Tee, straight, 1-1/2" pipe size	Q-1	10	1.600		550	78.50		628.50	725
0370	2" pipe size		9	1.778		310	87.50		397.50	470
0380	2-1/2" pipe size		8	2		450	98.50		548.50	645
0390	3" pipe size		7	2.286		315	112		427	515
0400	4" pipe size		5	3.200		480	157		637	765
0410	5" pipe size	▼	4	4	▼	1,275	197		1,472	1,725

22 11 13.47 Pipe Fittings, Steel		Crew	Daily Output	Labor-Hours	Unit	Material	2012 Bare Costs Labor	2012 Bare Costs Equipment	Total	Total Incl O&P
0420	6" pipe size	Q-2	6	4	Ea.	695	204		899	1,075
0430	8" pipe size		5	4.800		1,200	245		1,445	1,675
0440	10" pipe size		4	6		3,200	305		3,505	3,975
0450	12" pipe size		3	8		5,025	410		5,435	6,175
0459	Tee, reducing on outlet									
0460	2-1/2" by 2" pipe size	Q-1	8	2	Ea.	940	98.50		1,038.50	1,175
0461	3" by 2-1/2" pipe size		7	2.286		940	112		1,052	1,200
0462	4" by 3" pipe size		5	3.200		990	157		1,147	1,325
0463	5" by 4" pipe size		4	4		2,150	197		2,347	2,650
0464	6" by 4" pipe size	Q-2	6	4		950	204		1,154	1,350
0465	8" by 6" pipe size		5	4.800		1,475	245		1,720	2,000
0466	10" by 8" pipe size		4	6		3,400	305		3,705	4,200
0467	12" by 10" pipe size		3	8		5,875	410		6,285	7,100
0476	Reducer, concentric									
0477	3" by 2-1/2"	Q-1	12	1.333	Ea.	565	65.50		630.50	725
0478	4" by 3"		9	1.778		635	87.50		722.50	830
0479	5" by 4"		8	2		985	98.50		1,083.50	1,225
0480	6" by 4"	Q-2	10	2.400		850	122		972	1,125
0481	8" by 6"		9	2.667		1,075	136		1,211	1,375
0482	10" by 8"		8	3		2,200	153		2,353	2,650
0483	12" by 10"		7	3.429		3,825	175		4,000	4,475
0492	Reducer, eccentric									
0493	4" by 3"	Q-1	8	2	Ea.	1,025	98.50		1,123.50	1,275
0494	5" by 4"	"	7	2.286		1,575	112		1,687	1,900
0495	6" by 4"	Q-2	9	2.667		975	136		1,111	1,275
0496	8" by 6"		8	3		1,225	153		1,378	1,575
0497	10" by 8"		7	3.429		3,150	175		3,325	3,725
0498	12" by 10"		6	4		4,275	204		4,479	5,000
0500	For galvanized elbows and tees, add					100%				
0520	For extra heavy weight elbows and tees, add					140%				
0620	Gasket and bolt set, 150#, 1/2" pipe size	1 Plum	20	.400		2.50	22		24.50	36
0622	3/4" pipe size		19	.421		2.64	23		25.64	37.50
0624	1" pipe size		18	.444		2.67	24.50		27.17	39.50
0626	1-1/4" pipe size		17	.471		2.80	25.50		28.30	42
0628	1-1/2" pipe size		15	.533		2.98	29		31.98	47.50
0630	2" pipe size		13	.615		4.85	33.50		38.35	56
0640	2-1/2" pipe size		12	.667		5.60	36.50		42.10	61
0650	3" pipe size		11	.727		5.80	39.50		45.30	66.50
0660	3-1/2" pipe size		9	.889		9.40	48.50		57.90	83.50
0670	4" pipe size		8	1		10.40	54.50		64.90	94
0680	5" pipe size		7	1.143		17.10	62.50		79.60	113
0690	6" pipe size		6	1.333		18.10	73		91.10	130
0700	8" pipe size		5	1.600		19.55	87.50		107.05	154
0710	10" pipe size		4.50	1.778		35.50	97		132.50	185
0720	12" pipe size		4.20	1.905		37.50	104		141.50	199
0730	14" pipe size		4	2		39.50	109		148.50	209
0740	16" pipe size		3	2.667		41.50	146		187.50	266
0750	18" pipe size		2.70	2.963		80.50	162		242.50	335
0760	20" pipe size		2.30	3.478		131	190		321	430
0780	24" pipe size		1.90	4.211		164	230		394	525
0790	26" pipe size		1.60	5		222	273		495	655
0810	30" pipe size		1.40	5.714		430	310		740	945
0830	36" pipe size		1.10	7.273		810	395		1,205	1,500

22 11 Facility Water Distribution

22 11 13 – Facility Water Distribution Piping

22 11 13.47 Pipe Fittings, Steel

		Crew	Daily Output	Labor-Hours	Unit	Material	2012 Bare Costs Labor	2012 Bare Costs Equipment	Total	Total Incl O&P
0850	For 300 lb. gasket set, add					40%				
2000	Flanged unions, 125 lb., black, 1/2" pipe size	1 Plum	17	.471	Ea.	72	25.50		97.50	119
2040	3/4" pipe size		17	.471		95	25.50		120.50	144
2050	1" pipe size		16	.500		92	27.50		119.50	142
2060	1-1/4" pipe size	Q-1	28	.571		109	28		137	163
2070	1-1/2" pipe size		27	.593		101	29		130	155
2080	2" pipe size		26	.615		118	30.50		148.50	176
2090	2-1/2" pipe size		24	.667		160	33		193	226
2100	3" pipe size		22	.727		181	36		217	253
2110	3-1/2" pipe size		18	.889		305	43.50		348.50	405
2120	4" pipe size		16	1		246	49		295	345
2130	5" pipe size		14	1.143		575	56		631	715
2140	6" pipe size	Q-2	19	1.263		540	64.50		604.50	690
2150	8" pipe size	"	16	1.500		1,225	76.50		1,301.50	1,475
2200	For galvanized unions, add					150%				
2290	Threaded flange									
2300	Cast iron									
2310	Black, 125 lb., per flange									
2320	1" pipe size	1 Plum	27	.296	Ea.	41	16.20		57.20	70
2330	1-1/4" pipe size	Q-1	44	.364		49.50	17.85		67.35	81.50
2340	1-1/2" pipe size		40	.400		45.50	19.65		65.15	79.50
2350	2" pipe size		36	.444		45.50	22		67.50	83
2360	2-1/2" pipe size		28	.571		53	28		81	101
2370	3" pipe size		20	.800		68.50	39.50		108	135
2380	3-1/2" pipe size		16	1		96	49		145	180
2390	4" pipe size		12	1.333		92.50	65.50		158	201
2400	5" pipe size		10	1.600		131	78.50		209.50	263
2410	6" pipe size	Q-2	14	1.714		148	87.50		235.50	294
2420	8" pipe size		12	2		233	102		335	410
2430	10" pipe size		10	2.400		415	122		537	640
2440	12" pipe size		8	3		910	153		1,063	1,225
2460	For galvanized flanges, add					95%				
2490	Blind flange									
2492	Cast iron									
2494	Black, 125 lb., per flange									
2496	1" pipe size	1 Plum	27	.296	Ea.	65.50	16.20		81.70	96.50
2500	1-1/2" pipe size	Q-1	40	.400		73.50	19.65		93.15	111
2502	2" pipe size		36	.444		83	22		105	125
2504	2-1/2" pipe size		28	.571		91.50	28		119.50	144
2506	3" pipe size		20	.800		110	39.50		149.50	180
2508	4" pipe size		12	1.333		140	65.50		205.50	253
2510	5" pipe size		10	1.600		228	78.50		306.50	370
2512	6" pipe size	Q-2	14	1.714		248	87.50		335.50	405
2514	8" pipe size		12	2		390	102		492	585
2516	10" pipe size		10	2.400		575	122		697	820
2518	12" pipe size		8	3		1,075	153		1,228	1,425
2520	For galvanized flanges, add					80%				
2570	Threaded flange									
2580	Forged steel,									
2590	Black 150 lb., per flange									
2600	1/2" pipe size	1 Plum	30	.267	Ea.	26.50	14.55		41.05	51
2610	3/4" pipe size		28	.286		26.50	15.60		42.10	52.50
2620	1" pipe size		27	.296		26.50	16.20		42.70	53.50

22 11 13.47 Pipe Fittings, Steel		Crew	Daily Output	Labor-Hours	Unit	Material	2012 Bare Costs Labor	Equipment	Total	Total Incl O&P
2630	1-1/4" pipe size	Q-1	44	.364	Ea.	26.50	17.85		44.35	56
2640	1-1/2" pipe size		40	.400		26.50	19.65		46.15	58.50
2650	2" pipe size		36	.444		29.50	22		51.50	65.50
2660	2-1/2" pipe size		28	.571		36	28		64	82.50
2670	3" pipe size		20	.800		36.50	39.50		76	99.50
2690	4" pipe size		12	1.333		42.50	65.50		108	146
2700	5" pipe size		10	1.600		66.50	78.50		145	193
2710	6" pipe size	Q-2	14	1.714		73	87.50		160.50	213
2720	8" pipe size		12	2		126	102		228	292
2730	10" pipe size		10	2.400		228	122		350	435
2860	Black 300 lb., per flange									
2870	1/2" pipe size	1 Plum	30	.267	Ea.	29	14.55		43.55	54
2880	3/4" pipe size		28	.286		29	15.60		44.60	55.50
2890	1" pipe size		27	.296		29	16.20		45.20	56.50
2900	1-1/4" pipe size	Q-1	44	.364		29	17.85		46.85	59
2910	1-1/2" pipe size		40	.400		29	19.65		48.65	61.50
2920	2" pipe size		36	.444		34	22		56	70.50
2930	2-1/2" pipe size		28	.571		47.50	28		75.50	94.50
2940	3" pipe size		20	.800		50.50	39.50		90	115
2960	4" pipe size		12	1.333		73	65.50		138.50	179
2970	6" pipe size	Q-2	14	1.714		136	87.50		223.50	282
3000	Weld joint, butt, carbon steel, standard weight									
3040	90° elbow, long radius									
3050	1/2" pipe size	Q-15	16	1	Ea.	45	49	2.31	96.31	126
3060	3/4" pipe size		16	1		45	49	2.31	96.31	126
3070	1" pipe size		16	1		21	49	2.31	72.31	99.50
3080	1-1/4" pipe size		14	1.143		21	56	2.64	79.64	110
3090	1-1/2" pipe size		13	1.231		21	60.50	2.84	84.34	117
3100	2" pipe size		10	1.600		22.50	78.50	3.70	104.70	148
3110	2-1/2" pipe size		8	2		27.50	98.50	4.62	130.62	184
3120	3" pipe size		7	2.286		29	112	5.30	146.30	207
3130	4" pipe size		5	3.200		48	157	7.40	212.40	298
3136	5" pipe size		4	4		103	197	9.25	309.25	420
3140	6" pipe size	Q-16	5	4.800		106	245	7.40	358.40	495
3150	8" pipe size		3.75	6.400		200	325	9.85	534.85	720
3160	10" pipe size		3	8		400	410	12.30	822.30	1,075
3170	12" pipe size		2.50	9.600		590	490	14.80	1,094.80	1,400
3180	14" pipe size		2	12		970	610	18.50	1,598.50	2,025
3190	16" pipe size		1.50	16		1,325	815	24.50	2,164.50	2,725
3191	18" pipe size		1.25	19.200		1,525	980	29.50	2,534.50	3,175
3192	20" pipe size		1.15	20.870		2,450	1,075	32	3,557	4,325
3194	24" pipe size		1.02	23.529		3,450	1,200	36	4,686	5,650
3200	45° Elbow, long									
3210	1/2" pipe size	Q-15	16	1	Ea.	62.50	49	2.31	113.81	145
3220	3/4" pipe size		16	1		62.50	49	2.31	113.81	145
3230	1" pipe size		16	1		22	49	2.31	73.31	101
3240	1-1/4" pipe size		14	1.143		22	56	2.64	80.64	112
3250	1-1/2" pipe size		13	1.231		22	60.50	2.84	85.34	119
3260	2" pipe size		10	1.600		22	78.50	3.70	104.20	148
3270	2-1/2" pipe size		8	2		26.50	98.50	4.62	129.62	182
3280	3" pipe size		7	2.286		27.50	112	5.30	144.80	205
3290	4" pipe size		5	3.200		49.50	157	7.40	213.90	300
3296	5" pipe size		4	4		75	197	9.25	281.25	390

22 11 13 – Facility Water Distribution Piping

22 11 13.47 Pipe Fittings, Steel		Crew	Daily Output	Labor-Hours	Unit	Material	2012 Bare Costs Labor	Equipment	Total	Total Incl O&P
3300	6" pipe size	Q-16	5	4.800	Ea.	97.50	245	7.40	349.90	485
3310	8" pipe size		3.75	6.400		163	325	9.85	497.85	680
3320	10" pipe size		3	8		325	410	12.30	747.30	985
3330	12" pipe size		2.50	9.600		460	490	14.80	964.80	1,250
3340	14" pipe size		2	12		615	610	18.50	1,243.50	1,625
3341	16" pipe size		1.50	16		1,100	815	24.50	1,939.50	2,475
3342	18" pipe size		1.25	19.200		1,550	980	29.50	2,559.50	3,225
3343	20" pipe size		1.15	20.870		1,625	1,075	32	2,732	3,400
3345	24" pipe size		1.05	22.857		2,300	1,175	35	3,510	4,325
3346	26" pipe size		.85	28.235		2,700	1,450	43.50	4,193.50	5,200
3347	30" pipe size		.45	53.333		2,975	2,725	82	5,782	7,475
3349	36" pipe size		.38	63.158		3,275	3,225	97.50	6,597.50	8,575
3350	Tee, straight									
3352	For reducing tees and concentrics see starting line 4600									
3360	1/2" pipe size	Q-15	10	1.600	Ea.	110	78.50	3.70	192.20	244
3370	3/4" pipe size		10	1.600		110	78.50	3.70	192.20	244
3380	1" pipe size		10	1.600		54.50	78.50	3.70	136.70	183
3390	1-1/4" pipe size		9	1.778		68.50	87.50	4.11	160.11	212
3400	1-1/2" pipe size		8	2		68.50	98.50	4.62	171.62	229
3410	2" pipe size		6	2.667		54.50	131	6.15	191.65	265
3420	2-1/2" pipe size		5	3.200		75.50	157	7.40	239.90	330
3430	3" pipe size		4	4		84	197	9.25	290.25	400
3440	4" pipe size		3	5.333		118	262	12.30	392.30	540
3446	5" pipe size		2.50	6.400		195	315	14.80	524.80	705
3450	6" pipe size	Q-16	3	8		203	410	12.30	625.30	850
3460	8" pipe size		2.50	9.600		355	490	14.80	859.80	1,150
3470	10" pipe size		2	12		695	610	18.50	1,323.50	1,700
3480	12" pipe size		1.60	15		975	765	23	1,763	2,250
3481	14" pipe size		1.30	18.462		1,700	940	28.50	2,668.50	3,325
3482	16" pipe size		1	24		1,900	1,225	37	3,162	4,000
3483	18" pipe size		.80	30		3,025	1,525	46	4,596	5,675
3484	20" pipe size		.75	32		4,750	1,625	49.50	6,424.50	7,725
3486	24" pipe size		.70	34.286		6,150	1,750	53	7,953	9,425
3487	26" pipe size		.55	43.636		6,775	2,225	67	9,067	10,900
3488	30" pipe size		.30	80		7,425	4,075	123	11,623	14,400
3490	36" pipe size		.25	96		8,200	4,900	148	13,248	16,500
3491	Eccentric reducer, 1-1/2" pipe size	Q-15	14	1.143		30.50	56	2.64	89.14	121
3492	2" pipe size		11	1.455		43	71.50	3.36	117.86	159
3493	2-1/2" pipe size		9	1.778		50	87.50	4.11	141.61	192
3494	3" pipe size		8	2		59	98.50	4.62	162.12	218
3495	4" pipe size		6	2.667		75.50	131	6.15	212.65	288
3496	6" pipe size	Q-16	5	4.800		232	245	7.40	484.40	635
3497	8" pipe size		4	6		345	305	9.25	659.25	850
3498	10" pipe size		3	8		435	410	12.30	857.30	1,100
3499	12" pipe size		2.50	9.600		385	490	14.80	889.80	1,175
3501	Cap, 1-1/2" pipe size	Q-15	28	.571		25.50	28	1.32	54.82	72
3502	2" pipe size		22	.727		25.50	36	1.68	63.18	84
3503	2-1/2" pipe size		18	.889		26.50	43.50	2.05	72.05	97.50
3504	3" pipe size		16	1		26.50	49	2.31	77.81	106
3505	4" pipe size		12	1.333		38.50	65.50	3.08	107.08	144
3506	6" pipe size	Q-16	10	2.400		65.50	122	3.70	191.20	260
3507	8" pipe size		8	3		99	153	4.62	256.62	345
3508	10" pipe size		6	4		180	204	6.15	390.15	510

22 11 13 – Facility Water Distribution Piping

	22 11 13.47 Pipe Fittings, Steel	Crew	Daily Output	Labor-Hours	Unit	Material	2012 Bare Costs Labor	Equipment	Total	Total Incl O&P
3509	12" pipe size	Q-16	5	4.800	Ea.	272	245	7.40	524.40	675
3511	14" pipe size		4	6		293	305	9.25	607.25	795
3512	16" pipe size		4	6		455	305	9.25	769.25	970
3513	18" pipe size		3	8		575	410	12.30	997.30	1,275
3517	Weld joint, butt, carbon steel, extra strong									
3519	90° elbow, long									
3520	1/2" pipe size	Q-15	13	1.231	Ea.	55.50	60.50	2.84	118.84	156
3530	3/4" pipe size		12	1.333		55.50	65.50	3.08	124.08	164
3540	1" pipe size		11	1.455		27	71.50	3.36	101.86	142
3550	1-1/4" pipe size		10	1.600		27	78.50	3.70	109.20	153
3560	1-1/2" pipe size		9	1.778		27	87.50	4.11	118.61	167
3570	2" pipe size		8	2		27.50	98.50	4.62	130.62	184
3580	2-1/2" pipe size		7	2.286		38.50	112	5.30	155.80	217
3590	3" pipe size		6	2.667		49.50	131	6.15	186.65	259
3600	4" pipe size		4	4		81.50	197	9.25	287.75	395
3606	5" pipe size		3.50	4.571		195	225	10.55	430.55	565
3610	6" pipe size	Q-16	4.50	5.333		206	272	8.20	486.20	645
3620	8" pipe size		3.50	6.857		395	350	10.55	755.55	965
3630	10" pipe size		2.50	9.600		830	490	14.80	1,334.80	1,675
3640	12" pipe size		2.25	10.667		1,025	545	16.45	1,586.45	1,975
3650	45° Elbow, long									
3660	1/2" pipe size	Q-15	13	1.231	Ea.	62	60.50	2.84	125.34	162
3670	3/4" pipe size		12	1.333		62	65.50	3.08	130.58	170
3680	1" pipe size		11	1.455		29	71.50	3.36	103.86	143
3690	1-1/4" pipe size		10	1.600		29	78.50	3.70	111.20	155
3700	1-1/2" pipe size		9	1.778		29	87.50	4.11	120.61	168
3710	2" pipe size		8	2		29	98.50	4.62	132.12	185
3720	2-1/2" pipe size		7	2.286		64	112	5.30	181.30	245
3730	3" pipe size		6	2.667		37	131	6.15	174.15	246
3740	4" pipe size		4	4		58.50	197	9.25	264.75	370
3746	5" pipe size		3.50	4.571		139	225	10.55	374.55	505
3750	6" pipe size	Q-16	4.50	5.333		160	272	8.20	440.20	595
3760	8" pipe size		3.50	6.857		277	350	10.55	637.55	840
3770	10" pipe size		2.50	9.600		535	490	14.80	1,039.80	1,350
3780	12" pipe size		2.25	10.667		790	545	16.45	1,351.45	1,700
3800	Tee, straight									
3810	1/2" pipe size	Q-15	9	1.778	Ea.	136	87.50	4.11	227.61	286
3820	3/4" pipe size		8.50	1.882		131	92.50	4.35	227.85	289
3830	1" pipe size		8	2		72.50	98.50	4.62	175.62	233
3840	1-1/4" pipe size		7	2.286		67	112	5.30	184.30	249
3850	1-1/2" pipe size		6	2.667		81.50	131	6.15	218.65	295
3860	2" pipe size		5	3.200		68.50	157	7.40	232.90	320
3870	2-1/2" pipe size		4	4		114	197	9.25	320.25	430
3880	3" pipe size		3.50	4.571		106	225	10.55	341.55	470
3890	4" pipe size		2.50	6.400		171	315	14.80	500.80	680
3896	5" pipe size		2.25	7.111		375	350	16.45	741.45	955
3900	6" pipe size	Q-16	2.25	10.667		288	545	16.45	849.45	1,150
3910	8" pipe size		2	12		545	610	18.50	1,173.50	1,550
3920	10" pipe size		1.75	13.714		965	700	21	1,686	2,150
3930	12" pipe size		1.50	16		1,400	815	24.50	2,239.50	2,800
4000	Eccentric reducer, 1-1/2" pipe size	Q-15	10	1.600		17.30	78.50	3.70	99.50	142
4010	2" pipe size		9	1.778		47.50	87.50	4.11	139.11	189
4020	2-1/2" pipe size		8	2		71.50	98.50	4.62	174.62	232

22 11 Facility Water Distribution

22 11 13 – Facility Water Distribution Piping

22 11 13.47 Pipe Fittings, Steel

		Crew	Daily Output	Labor-Hours	Unit	Material	2012 Bare Costs Labor	2012 Bare Costs Equipment	Total	Total Incl O&P
4030	3" pipe size	Q-15	7	2.286	Ea.	59	112	5.30	176.30	240
4040	4" pipe size		5	3.200		95.50	157	7.40	259.90	350
4046	5" pipe size		4.70	3.404		245	167	7.85	419.85	530
4050	6" pipe size	Q-16	4.50	5.333		259	272	8.20	539.20	705
4060	8" pipe size		3.50	6.857		390	350	10.55	750.55	965
4070	10" pipe size		2.50	9.600		665	490	14.80	1,169.80	1,475
4080	12" pipe size		2.25	10.667		855	545	16.45	1,416.45	1,775
4090	14" pipe size		2.10	11.429		1,575	585	17.60	2,177.60	2,625
4100	16" pipe size		1.90	12.632		2,025	645	19.45	2,689.45	3,225
4151	Cap, 1-1/2" pipe size	Q-15	24	.667		31.50	33	1.54	66.04	86
4152	2" pipe size		18	.889		25.50	43.50	2.05	71.05	96.50
4153	2-1/2" pipe size		16	1		34.50	49	2.31	85.81	115
4154	3" pipe size		14	1.143		38.50	56	2.64	97.14	129
4155	4" pipe size		10	1.600		89	78.50	3.70	171.20	221
4156	6" pipe size	Q-16	9	2.667		107	136	4.11	247.11	325
4157	8" pipe size		7	3.429		160	175	5.30	340.30	445
4158	10" pipe size		5	4.800		245	245	7.40	497.40	645
4159	12" pipe size		4	6		330	305	9.25	644.25	830
4190	Weld fittings, reducing, standard weight									
4200	Welding ring w/spacer pins, 2" pipe size				Ea.	3.57			3.57	3.93
4210	2-1/2" pipe size					4.32			4.32	4.75
4220	3" pipe size					4.47			4.47	4.92
4230	4" pipe size					4.65			4.65	5.10
4236	5" pipe size					5.45			5.45	6
4240	6" pipe size					5.45			5.45	6
4250	8" pipe size					6.45			6.45	7.10
4260	10" pipe size					7.90			7.90	8.70
4270	12" pipe size					9.10			9.10	10
4280	14" pipe size					10.55			10.55	11.60
4290	16" pipe size					11.90			11.90	13.10
4300	18" pipe size					13.75			13.75	15.10
4310	20" pipe size					14.55			14.55	16.05
4330	24" pipe size					16.95			16.95	18.65
4340	26" pipe size					22.50			22.50	25
4350	30" pipe size					22.50			22.50	25
4370	36" pipe size					25.50			25.50	28
4600	Tee, reducing on outlet									
4601	2-1/2" x 2" pipe size	Q-15	5	3.200	Ea.	98	157	7.40	262.40	355
4602	3" x 2-1/2" pipe size		4	4		118	197	9.25	324.25	435
4604	4" x 3" pipe size		3	5.333		124	262	12.30	398.30	545
4605	5" x 4" pipe size		2.50	6.400		268	315	14.80	597.80	785
4606	6" x 5" pipe size	Q-16	3	8		370	410	12.30	792.30	1,050
4607	8" x 6" pipe size		2.50	9.600		460	490	14.80	964.80	1,250
4608	10" x 8" pipe size		2	12		850	610	18.50	1,478.50	1,875
4609	12" x 10" pipe size		1.60	15		1,250	765	23	2,038	2,550
4610	16" x 12" pipe size		1.50	16		2,000	815	24.50	2,839.50	3,450
4611	14" x 12" pipe size		1.52	15.789		1,900	805	24.50	2,729.50	3,325
4618	Reducer, concentric									
4619	2-1/2" by 2" pipe size	Q-15	10	1.600	Ea.	42.50	78.50	3.70	124.70	170
4620	3" by 2-1/2" pipe size		9	1.778		35	87.50	4.11	126.61	175
4621	3-1/2" by 3" pipe size		8	2		89.50	98.50	4.62	192.62	251
4622	4" by 2-1/2" pipe size		7	2.286		54.50	112	5.30	171.80	235
4623	5" by 3" pipe size		7	2.286		114	112	5.30	231.30	300

22 11 13.47 Pipe Fittings, Steel

		Crew	Daily Output	Labor-Hours	Unit	Material	2012 Bare Costs Labor	Equipment	Total	Total Incl O&P
4624	6" by 4" pipe size	Q-16	6	4	Ea.	94	204	6.15	304.15	415
4625	8" by 6" pipe size		5	4.800		124	245	7.40	376.40	515
4626	10" by 8" pipe size		4	6		256	305	9.25	570.25	750
4627	12" by 10" pipe size	▼	3	8	▼	296	410	12.30	718.30	955
4660	Reducer, eccentric									
4662	3" x 2" pipe size	Q-15	8	2	Ea.	59	98.50	4.62	162.12	218
4664	4" x 3" pipe size		6	2.667		71.50	131	6.15	208.65	284
4666	4" x 2" pipe size	▼	6	2.667		87.50	131	6.15	224.65	300
4670	6" x 4" pipe size	Q-16	5	4.800		148	245	7.40	400.40	540
4672	6" x 3" pipe size		5	4.800		232	245	7.40	484.40	635
4676	8" x 6" pipe size		4	6		188	305	9.25	502.25	675
4678	8" x 4" pipe size		4	6		345	305	9.25	659.25	850
4682	10" x 8" pipe size		3	8		247	410	12.30	669.30	900
4684	10" x 6" pipe size		3	8		435	410	12.30	857.30	1,100
4688	12" x 10" pipe size		2.50	9.600		385	490	14.80	889.80	1,175
4690	12" x 8" pipe size		2.50	9.600		605	490	14.80	1,109.80	1,425
4691	14" x 12" pipe size		2.20	10.909		675	555	16.80	1,246.80	1,600
4693	16" x 14" pipe size		1.80	13.333		1,025	680	20.50	1,725.50	2,175
4694	16" x 12" pipe size		2	12		1,375	610	18.50	2,003.50	2,450
4696	18" x 16" pipe size	▼	1.60	15	▼	1,875	765	23	2,663	3,250
5000	Weld joint, socket, forged steel, 3000 lb., schedule 40 pipe									
5010	90° elbow, straight									
5020	1/4" pipe size	Q-15	22	.727	Ea.	23.50	36	1.68	61.18	82
5030	3/8" pipe size		22	.727		23.50	36	1.68	61.18	82
5040	1/2" pipe size		20	.800		13.20	39.50	1.85	54.55	76
5050	3/4" pipe size		20	.800		13.70	39.50	1.85	55.05	76.50
5060	1" pipe size		20	.800		17.60	39.50	1.85	58.95	81
5070	1-1/4" pipe size		18	.889		34	43.50	2.05	79.55	106
5080	1-1/2" pipe size		16	1		39.50	49	2.31	90.81	120
5090	2" pipe size		12	1.333		58	65.50	3.08	126.58	166
5100	2-1/2" pipe size		10	1.600		165	78.50	3.70	247.20	305
5110	3" pipe size		8	2		284	98.50	4.62	387.12	470
5120	4" pipe size	▼	6	2.667	▼	750	131	6.15	887.15	1,025
5130	45° Elbow, straight									
5134	1/4" pipe size	Q-15	22	.727	Ea.	24	36	1.68	61.68	82
5135	3/8" pipe size		22	.727		24	36	1.68	61.68	82
5136	1/2" pipe size		20	.800		17.55	39.50	1.85	58.90	81
5137	3/4" pipe size		20	.800		20.50	39.50	1.85	61.85	84
5140	1" pipe size		20	.800		26.50	39.50	1.85	67.85	91
5150	1-1/4" pipe size		18	.889		36.50	43.50	2.05	82.05	109
5160	1-1/2" pipe size		16	1		45	49	2.31	96.31	126
5170	2" pipe size		12	1.333		72	65.50	3.08	140.58	182
5180	2-1/2" pipe size		10	1.600		190	78.50	3.70	272.20	330
5190	3" pipe size		8	2		315	98.50	4.62	418.12	500
5200	4" pipe size	▼	6	2.667	▼	620	131	6.15	757.15	890
5250	Tee, straight									
5254	1/4" pipe size	Q-15	15	1.067	Ea.	26	52.50	2.46	80.96	110
5255	3/8" pipe size		15	1.067		26	52.50	2.46	80.96	110
5256	1/2" pipe size		13	1.231		16.35	60.50	2.84	79.69	112
5257	3/4" pipe size		13	1.231		19.95	60.50	2.84	83.29	116
5260	1" pipe size		13	1.231		27	60.50	2.84	90.34	124
5270	1-1/4" pipe size		12	1.333		41.50	65.50	3.08	110.08	148
5280	1-1/2" pipe size	▼	11	1.455	▼	55	71.50	3.36	129.86	173

22 11 Facility Water Distribution

22 11 13 – Facility Water Distribution Piping

22 11 13.47 Pipe Fittings, Steel		Crew	Daily Output	Labor-Hours	Unit	Material	2012 Bare Costs Labor	Equipment	Total	Total Incl O&P
5290	2" pipe size	Q-15	8	2	Ea.	80	98.50	4.62	183.12	241
5300	2-1/2" pipe size		6	2.667		229	131	6.15	366.15	455
5310	3" pipe size		5	3.200		550	157	7.40	714.40	845
5320	4" pipe size		4	4		880	197	9.25	1,086.25	1,275
5350	For reducing sizes, add					60%				
5450	Couplings									
5451	1/4" pipe size	Q-15	23	.696	Ea.	15	34	1.61	50.61	70
5452	3/8" pipe size		23	.696		15	34	1.61	50.61	70
5453	1/2" pipe size		21	.762		6.95	37.50	1.76	46.21	66
5454	3/4" pipe size		21	.762		8.95	37.50	1.76	48.21	68.50
5460	1" pipe size		20	.800		9.90	39.50	1.85	51.25	72.50
5470	1-1/4" pipe size		20	.800		17.55	39.50	1.85	58.90	81
5480	1-1/2" pipe size		18	.889		19.40	43.50	2.05	64.95	90
5490	2" pipe size		14	1.143		31	56	2.64	89.64	121
5500	2-1/2" pipe size		12	1.333		69.50	65.50	3.08	138.08	179
5510	3" pipe size		9	1.778		156	87.50	4.11	247.61	310
5520	4" pipe size		7	2.286		234	112	5.30	351.30	435
5570	Union, 1/4" pipe size		21	.762		32	37.50	1.76	71.26	94
5571	3/8" pipe size		21	.762		32	37.50	1.76	71.26	94
5572	1/2" pipe size		19	.842		27	41.50	1.95	70.45	94
5573	3/4" pipe size		19	.842		31.50	41.50	1.95	74.95	99
5574	1" pipe size		19	.842		40.50	41.50	1.95	83.95	109
5575	1-1/4" pipe size		17	.941		65.50	46.50	2.17	114.17	144
5576	1-1/2" pipe size		15	1.067		71	52.50	2.46	125.96	160
5577	2" pipe size		11	1.455		102	71.50	3.36	176.86	224
5600	Reducer, 1/4" pipe size		23	.696		38.50	34	1.61	74.11	95.50
5601	3/8" pipe size		23	.696		40.50	34	1.61	76.11	98
5602	1/2" pipe size		21	.762		24.50	37.50	1.76	63.76	85.50
5603	3/4" pipe size		21	.762		24.50	37.50	1.76	63.76	85.50
5604	1" pipe size		21	.762		34.50	37.50	1.76	73.76	96.50
5605	1-1/4" pipe size		19	.842		44	41.50	1.95	87.45	113
5607	1-1/2" pipe size		17	.941		47	46.50	2.17	95.67	124
5608	2" pipe size		13	1.231		52	60.50	2.84	115.34	152
5612	Cap, 1/4" pipe size		46	.348		14.30	17.10	.80	32.20	42.50
5613	3/8" pipe size		46	.348		14.30	17.10	.80	32.20	42.50
5614	1/2" pipe size		42	.381		8.75	18.70	.88	28.33	38.50
5615	3/4" pipe size		42	.381		10.20	18.70	.88	29.78	40
5616	1" pipe size		42	.381		15.45	18.70	.88	35.03	46
5617	1-1/4" pipe size		38	.421		18.20	20.50	.97	39.67	52
5618	1-1/2" pipe size		34	.471		25.50	23	1.09	49.59	64
5619	2" pipe size		26	.615		39	30.50	1.42	70.92	90
5630	T-O-L, 1/4" pipe size, nozzle		23	.696		7.10	34	1.61	42.71	61
5631	3/8" pipe size, nozzle		23	.696		7.20	34	1.61	42.81	61
5632	1/2" pipe size, nozzle		22	.727		7.10	36	1.68	44.78	63.50
5633	3/4" pipe size, nozzle		21	.762		8.20	37.50	1.76	47.46	67.50
5634	1" pipe size, nozzle		20	.800		9.55	39.50	1.85	50.90	72
5635	1-1/4" pipe size, nozzle		18	.889		15.10	43.50	2.05	60.65	85
5636	1-1/2" pipe size, nozzle		16	1		15.10	49	2.31	66.41	93
5637	2" pipe size, nozzle		12	1.333		17.20	65.50	3.08	85.78	121
5638	2-1/2" pipe size, nozzle		10	1.600		57.50	78.50	3.70	139.70	187
5639	4" pipe size, nozzle		6	2.667		131	131	6.15	268.15	350
5640	W-O-L, 1/4" pipe size, nozzle		23	.696		16.80	34	1.61	52.41	71.50
5641	3/8" pipe size, nozzle		23	.696		15.85	34	1.61	51.46	70.50

22 11 Facility Water Distribution

22 11 13 – Facility Water Distribution Piping

22 11 13.47 Pipe Fittings, Steel		Crew	Daily Output	Labor-Hours	Unit	Material	2012 Bare Costs Labor	Equipment	Total	Total Incl O&P
5642	1/2" pipe size, nozzle	Q-15	22	.727	Ea.	14.70	36	1.68	52.38	72
5643	3/4" pipe size, nozzle		21	.762		15.50	37.50	1.76	54.76	75.50
5644	1" pipe size, nozzle		20	.800		16.20	39.50	1.85	57.55	79.50
5645	1-1/4" pipe size, nozzle		18	.889		19.25	43.50	2.05	64.80	89.50
5646	1-1/2" pipe size, nozzle		16	1		19.25	49	2.31	70.56	97.50
5647	2" pipe size, nozzle		12	1.333		19.45	65.50	3.08	88.03	124
5648	2-1/2" pipe size, nozzle		10	1.600		44.50	78.50	3.70	126.70	172
5649	3" pipe size, nozzle		8	2		48.50	98.50	4.62	151.62	207
5650	4" pipe size, nozzle		6	2.667		61.50	131	6.15	198.65	272
5651	5" pipe size, nozzle		5	3.200		152	157	7.40	316.40	410
5652	6" pipe size, nozzle		4	4		177	197	9.25	383.25	500
5653	8" pipe size, nozzle		3	5.333		340	262	12.30	614.30	785
5654	10" pipe size, nozzle		2.60	6.154		490	300	14.20	804.20	1,000
5655	12" pipe size, nozzle		2.20	7.273		930	355	16.80	1,301.80	1,575
5674	S-O-L, 1/4" pipe size, outlet		23	.696		9.45	34	1.61	45.06	63.50
5675	3/8" pipe size, outlet		23	.696		9.45	34	1.61	45.06	63.50
5676	1/2" pipe size, outlet		22	.727		8.80	36	1.68	46.48	65.50
5677	3/4" pipe size, outlet		21	.762		8.95	37.50	1.76	48.21	68.50
5678	1" pipe size, outlet		20	.800		9.90	39.50	1.85	51.25	72.50
5679	1-1/4" pipe size, outlet		18	.889		16.55	43.50	2.05	62.10	86.50
5680	1-1/2" pipe size, outlet		16	1		16.55	49	2.31	67.86	94.50
5681	2" pipe size, outlet	↓	12	1.333	↓	18.80	65.50	3.08	87.38	123
6000	Weld-on flange, forged steel									
6020	Slip-on, 150 lb. flange (welded front and back)									
6050	1/2" pipe size	Q-15	18	.889	Ea.	23.50	43.50	2.05	69.05	94.50
6060	3/4" pipe size		18	.889		23.50	43.50	2.05	69.05	94.50
6070	1" pipe size		17	.941		23.50	46.50	2.17	72.17	98.50
6080	1-1/4" pipe size		16	1		23.50	49	2.31	74.81	103
6090	1-1/2" pipe size		15	1.067		23.50	52.50	2.46	78.46	108
6100	2" pipe size		12	1.333		23.50	65.50	3.08	92.08	128
6110	2-1/2" pipe size		10	1.600		23.50	78.50	3.70	105.70	149
6120	3" pipe size		9	1.778		23.50	87.50	4.11	115.11	163
6130	3-1/2" pipe size		7	2.286		23.50	112	5.30	140.80	201
6140	4" pipe size		6	2.667		33	131	6.15	170.15	241
6150	5" pipe size	↓	5	3.200		57.50	157	7.40	221.90	310
6160	6" pipe size	Q-16	6	4		54.50	204	6.15	264.65	370
6170	8" pipe size		5	4.800		82.50	245	7.40	334.90	470
6180	10" pipe size		4	6		143	305	9.25	457.25	625
6190	12" pipe size		3	8		212	410	12.30	634.30	865
6191	14" pipe size		2.50	9.600		281	490	14.80	785.80	1,075
6192	16" pipe size	↓	1.80	13.333	↓	440	680	20.50	1,140.50	1,525
6200	300 lb. flange									
6210	1/2" pipe size	Q-15	17	.941	Ea.	23.50	46.50	2.17	72.17	98
6220	3/4" pipe size		17	.941		23.50	46.50	2.17	72.17	98
6230	1" pipe size		16	1		23.50	49	2.31	74.81	102
6240	1-1/4" pipe size		13	1.231		23.50	60.50	2.84	86.84	120
6250	1-1/2" pipe size		12	1.333		23.50	65.50	3.08	92.08	128
6260	2" pipe size		11	1.455		31	71.50	3.36	105.86	146
6270	2-1/2" pipe size		9	1.778		35	87.50	4.11	126.61	175
6280	3" pipe size		7	2.286		38	112	5.30	155.30	217
6290	4" pipe size		6	2.667		55.50	131	6.15	192.65	266
6300	5" pipe size	↓	4	4		95	197	9.25	301.25	410
6310	6" pipe size	Q-16	5	4.800	↓	95.50	245	7.40	347.90	485

22 11 13.47 Pipe Fittings, Steel		Crew	Daily Output	Labor-Hours	Unit	Material	2012 Bare Costs Labor	Equipment	Total	Total Incl O&P
6320	8" pipe size	Q-16	4	6	Ea.	163	305	9.25	477.25	650
6330	10" pipe size		3.40	7.059		278	360	10.85	648.85	860
6340	12" pipe size		2.80	8.571		340	435	13.20	788.20	1,050
6400	Welding neck, 150 lb. flange									
6410	1/2" pipe size	Q-15	40	.400	Ea.	25.50	19.65	.92	46.07	58.50
6420	3/4" pipe size		36	.444		25.50	22	1.03	48.53	62
6430	1" pipe size		32	.500		25.50	24.50	1.16	51.16	66.50
6440	1-1/4" pipe size		29	.552		25.50	27	1.27	53.77	70.50
6450	1-1/2" pipe size		26	.615		25.50	30.50	1.42	57.42	75
6460	2" pipe size		20	.800		29.50	39.50	1.85	70.85	93.50
6470	2-1/2" pipe size		16	1		32	49	2.31	83.31	112
6480	3" pipe size		14	1.143		35	56	2.64	93.64	126
6500	4" pipe size		10	1.600		42.50	78.50	3.70	124.70	170
6510	5" pipe size		8	2		66.50	98.50	4.62	169.62	227
6520	6" pipe size	Q-16	10	2.400		64	122	3.70	189.70	258
6530	8" pipe size		7	3.429		113	175	5.30	293.30	395
6540	10" pipe size		6	4		180	204	6.15	390.15	510
6550	12" pipe size		5	4.800		262	245	7.40	514.40	665
6551	14" pipe size		4.50	5.333		380	272	8.20	660.20	835
6552	16" pipe size		3	8		570	410	12.30	992.30	1,250
6553	18" pipe size		2.50	9.600		800	490	14.80	1,304.80	1,625
6554	20" pipe size		2.30	10.435		975	530	16.05	1,521.05	1,900
6556	24" pipe size		2	12		1,300	610	18.50	1,928.50	2,400
6557	26" pipe size		1.70	14.118		1,425	720	21.50	2,166.50	2,675
6558	30" pipe size		.90	26.667		1,650	1,350	41	3,041	3,900
6559	36" pipe size		.75	32		1,900	1,625	49.50	3,574.50	4,575
6560	300 lb. flange									
6570	1/2" pipe size	Q-15	36	.444	Ea.	31	22	1.03	54.03	68
6580	3/4" pipe size		34	.471		31	23	1.09	55.09	70
6590	1" pipe size		30	.533		31	26	1.23	58.23	75
6600	1-1/4" pipe size		28	.571		31	28	1.32	60.32	78
6610	1-1/2" pipe size		24	.667		31	33	1.54	65.54	85
6620	2" pipe size		18	.889		38.50	43.50	2.05	84.05	110
6630	2-1/2" pipe size		14	1.143		44	56	2.64	102.64	136
6640	3" pipe size		12	1.333		44.50	65.50	3.08	113.08	151
6650	4" pipe size		8	2		73	98.50	4.62	176.12	233
6660	5" pipe size		7	2.286		111	112	5.30	228.30	297
6670	6" pipe size	Q-16	9	2.667		113	136	4.11	253.11	335
6680	8" pipe size		6	4		195	204	6.15	405.15	525
6690	10" pipe size		5	4.800		355	245	7.40	607.40	770
6700	12" pipe size		4	6		455	305	9.25	769.25	970
6710	14" pipe size		3.50	6.857		980	350	10.55	1,340.55	1,600
6720	16" pipe size		2	12		1,150	610	18.50	1,778.50	2,225
7740	Plain ends for plain end pipe, mechanically coupled									
7750	Cplg. & labor required at joints not included, add 1 per									
7760	joint for installed price, see line 9180									
7770	Malleable iron, painted, unless noted otherwise									
7800	90° Elbow 1"				Ea.	86			86	95
7810	1-1/2"					102			102	112
7820	2"					152			152	167
7830	2-1/2"					178			178	196
7840	3"					185			185	203
7860	4"					209			209	230

22 11 13.47 Pipe Fittings, Steel	Crew	Daily Output	Labor-Hours	Unit	Material	2012 Bare Costs Labor	Equipment	Total	Total Incl O&P
7870	5" welded steel				Ea.	241			241	265
7880	6"					305			305	335
7890	8" welded steel					570			570	630
7900	10" welded steel					755			755	830
7910	12" welded steel					840			840	925
7970	45° Elbow 1"					51.50			51.50	56.50
7980	1-1/2"					77			77	84.50
7990	2"					161			161	177
8000	2-1/2"					161			161	177
8010	3"					185			185	203
8030	4"					193			193	212
8040	5" welded steel					241			241	265
8050	6"					276			276	305
8060	8"					325			325	355
8070	10" welded steel					345			345	380
8080	12" welded steel					625			625	690
8140	Tee, straight 1"					96.50			96.50	106
8150	1-1/2"					124			124	136
8160	2"					124			124	136
8170	2-1/2"					162			162	178
8180	3"					249			249	274
8200	4"					355			355	390
8210	5" welded steel					490			490	535
8220	6"					425			425	465
8230	8" welded steel					610			610	675
8240	10" welded steel					960			960	1,050
8250	12" welded steel					1,175			1,175	1,275
8340	Segmentally welded steel, painted									
8390	Wye 2"				Ea.	155			155	170
8400	2-1/2"					155			155	170
8410	3"					173			173	191
8430	4"					259			259	285
8440	5"					315			315	345
8450	6"					435			435	475
8460	8"					560			560	615
8470	10"					825			825	910
8480	12"					1,275			1,275	1,400
8540	Wye, lateral 2"					168			168	185
8550	2-1/2"					193			193	212
8560	3"					229			229	252
8580	4"					315			315	345
8590	5"					535			535	590
8600	6"					555			555	610
8610	8"					930			930	1,025
8620	10"					965			965	1,050
8630	12"					1,775			1,775	1,950
8690	Cross, 2"					164			164	180
8700	2-1/2"					164			164	180
8710	3"					195			195	215
8730	4"					267			267	294
8740	5"					380			380	415
8750	6"					500			500	550
8760	8"					640			640	705

22 11 13.47 Pipe Fittings, Steel		Crew	Daily Output	Labor-Hours	Unit	Material	2012 Bare Costs Labor	Equipment	Total	Total Incl O&P
8770	10"				Ea.	935			935	1,025
8780	12"					1,350			1,350	1,475
8800	Tees, reducing 2" x 1"					106			106	117
8810	2" x 1-1/2"					106			106	117
8820	3" x 1"					106			106	117
8830	3" x 1-1/2"					106			106	117
8840	3" x 2"					107			107	118
8850	4" x 1"					156			156	172
8860	4" x 1-1/2"					156			156	172
8870	4" x 2"					154			154	169
8880	4" x 2-1/2"					158			158	174
8890	4" x 3"					158			158	174
8900	6" x 2"					231			231	254
8910	6" x 3"					249			249	274
8920	6" x 4"					300			300	330
8930	8" x 2"					315			315	345
8940	8" x 3"					310			310	340
8950	8" x 4"					310			310	340
8960	8" x 5"					330			330	365
8970	8" x 6"					365			365	400
8980	10" x 4"					475			475	525
8990	10" x 6"					475			475	525
9000	10" x 8"					505			505	555
9010	12" x 6"					735			735	805
9020	12" x 8"					735			735	810
9030	12" x 10"					765			765	840
9080	Adapter nipples 3" long									
9090	1"				Ea.	14.60			14.60	16.05
9100	1-1/2"					14.60			14.60	16.05
9110	2"					14.60			14.60	16.05
9120	2-1/2"					17			17	18.70
9130	3"					20.50			20.50	22.50
9140	4"					34			34	37.50
9150	6"					90			90	99
9180	Coupling, mechanical, plain end pipe to plain end pipe or fitting									
9190	1"	Q-1	29	.552	Ea.	52	27		79	98
9200	1-1/2"		28	.571		52	28		80	99.50
9210	2"		27	.593		52	29		81	101
9220	2-1/2"		26	.615		52	30.50		82.50	103
9230	3"		25	.640		76	31.50		107.50	131
9240	3-1/2"		24	.667		88	33		121	147
9250	4"		22	.727		88	36		124	151
9260	5"	Q-2	28	.857		125	43.50		168.50	204
9270	6"		24	1		153	51		204	245
9280	8"		19	1.263		270	64.50		334.50	395
9290	10"		16	1.500		350	76.50		426.50	500
9300	12"		12	2		440	102		542	640
9310	Outlets for precut holes through pipe wall									
9331	Strapless type, with gasket									
9332	4" to 8" pipe x 1/2"	1 Plum	13	.615	Ea.	56.50	33.50		90	113
9333	4" to 8" pipe x 3/4"		13	.615		60.50	33.50		94	117
9334	10" pipe and larger x 1/2"		11	.727		56.50	39.50		96	123
9335	10" pipe and larger x 3/4"		11	.727		60.50	39.50		100	127

22 11 Facility Water Distribution

22 11 13 – Facility Water Distribution Piping

22 11 13.47 Pipe Fittings, Steel

		Crew	Daily Output	Labor-Hours	Unit	Material	2012 Bare Costs Labor	Equipment	Total	Total Incl O&P
9341	Thermometer wells with gasket									
9342	4" to 8" pipe, 6" stem	1 Plum	14	.571	Ea.	85.50	31		116.50	141
9343	8" pipe and larger, 6" stem	"	13	.615	"	85.50	33.50		119	145
9940	For galvanized fittings for plain end pipe, add					20%				

22 11 13.48 Pipe, Fittings and Valves, Steel, Grooved-Joint

		Crew	Daily Output	Labor-Hours	Unit	Material	2012 Bare Costs Labor	Equipment	Total	Total Incl O&P
0010	**PIPE, FITTINGS AND VALVES, STEEL, GROOVED-JOINT**									
0012	Fittings are ductile iron. Steel fittings noted.									
0020	Pipe includes coupling & clevis type hanger assemblies, 10' O.C.									
0500	Schedule 10, black									
0550	2" diameter	1 Plum	43	.186	L.F.	5.70	10.15		15.85	21.50
0560	2-1/2" diameter	Q-1	61	.262		7.35	12.90		20.25	27.50
0570	3" diameter		55	.291		8.60	14.30		22.90	31
0580	3-1/2" diameter		53	.302		10.05	14.85		24.90	33.50
0590	4" diameter		49	.327		11.55	16.05		27.60	36.50
0600	5" diameter		40	.400		13.75	19.65		33.40	44.50
0610	6" diameter	Q-2	46	.522		17.95	26.50		44.45	60
0620	8" diameter	"	41	.585		24.50	30		54.50	72
0700	To delete couplings & hangers, subtract									
0710	2" diam. to 5" diam.					25%	20%			
0720	6" diam. to 8" diam.					27%	15%			
1000	Schedule 40, black									
1040	3/4" diameter	1 Plum	71	.113	L.F.	6.30	6.15		12.45	16.20
1050	1" diameter		63	.127		6.30	6.95		13.25	17.40
1060	1-1/4" diameter		58	.138		8	7.55		15.55	20
1070	1-1/2" diameter		51	.157		9.25	8.55		17.80	23
1080	2" diameter		40	.200		11.85	10.90		22.75	29.50
1090	2-1/2" diameter	Q-1	57	.281		20.50	13.80		34.30	43.50
1100	3" diameter		50	.320		26	15.75		41.75	52
1110	4" diameter		45	.356		35	17.50		52.50	65
1120	5" diameter		37	.432		38.50	21.50		60	74.50
1130	6" diameter	Q-2	42	.571		53	29		82	103
1140	8" diameter		37	.649		60.50	33		93.50	117
1150	10" diameter		31	.774		75.50	39.50		115	143
1160	12" diameter		27	.889		87	45.50		132.50	165
1170	14" diameter		20	1.200		104	61		165	206
1180	16" diameter		17	1.412		125	72		197	247
1190	18" diameter		14	1.714		144	87.50		231.50	291
1200	20" diameter		12	2		169	102		271	340
1210	24" diameter		10	2.400		200	122		322	405
1740	To delete coupling & hanger, subtract									
1750	3/4" diam. to 2" diam.					65%	27%			
1760	2-1/2" diam. to 5" diam.					41%	18%			
1770	6" diam. to 12" diam.					31%	13%			
1780	14" diam. to 24" diam.					35%	10%			
1800	Galvanized									
1840	3/4" diameter	1 Plum	71	.113	L.F.	8.70	6.15		14.85	18.85
1850	1" diameter		63	.127		8.25	6.95		15.20	19.55
1860	1-1/4" diameter		58	.138		10.55	7.55		18.10	23
1870	1-1/2" diameter		51	.157		12.25	8.55		20.80	26.50
1880	2" diameter		40	.200		15.80	10.90		26.70	34
1890	2-1/2" diameter	Q-1	57	.281		30	13.80		43.80	54
1900	3" diameter		50	.320		38.50	15.75		54.25	65.50

22 11 13.48 Pipe, Fittings and Valves, Steel, Grooved-Joint	Crew	Daily Output	Labor-Hours	Unit	Material	2012 Bare Costs Labor	Equipment	Total	Total Incl O&P
1910	4" diameter	Q-1	45	.356	L.F.	53.50	17.50		71	85.50
1920	5" diameter		37	.432		58	21.50		79.50	96
1930	6" diameter	Q-2	42	.571		65.50	29		94.50	116
1940	8" diameter		37	.649		77	33		110	135
1950	10" diameter		31	.774		123	39.50		162.50	195
1960	12" diameter		27	.889		151	45.50		196.50	235
2540	To delete coupling & hanger, subtract									
2550	3/4" diam. to 2" diam.					36%	27%			
2560	2-1/2" diam. to 5" diam.					19%	18%			
2570	6" diam. to 12" diam.					14%	13%			
2600	Schedule 80, black									
2610	3/4" diameter	1 Plum	65	.123	L.F.	8.70	6.70		15.40	19.70
2650	1" diameter		61	.131		11.15	7.15		18.30	23
2660	1-1/4" diameter		55	.145		14.60	7.95		22.55	28
2670	1-1/2" diameter		49	.163		17.25	8.90		26.15	32.50
2680	2" diameter		38	.211		22.50	11.50		34	42.50
2690	2-1/2" diameter	Q-1	54	.296		34.50	14.55		49.05	60
2700	3" diameter		48	.333		46	16.40		62.40	75
2710	4" diameter		44	.364		66.50	17.85		84.35	100
2720	5" diameter		35	.457		72	22.50		94.50	114
2730	6" diameter	Q-2	40	.600		89.50	30.50		120	145
2740	8" diameter		35	.686		109	35		144	173
2750	10" diameter		29	.828		199	42		241	283
2760	12" diameter		24	1		355	51		406	465
3240	To delete coupling & hanger, subtract									
3250	3/4" diam. to 2" diam.					30%	25%			
3260	2-1/2" diam. to 5" diam.					14%	17%			
3270	6" diam. to 12" diam.					12%	12%			
3300	Galvanized									
3310	3/4" diameter	1 Plum	65	.123	L.F.	11.30	6.70		18	22.50
3350	1" diameter		61	.131		15.10	7.15		22.25	27.50
3360	1-1/4" diameter		55	.145		20	7.95		27.95	34
3370	1-1/2" diameter		46	.174		23.50	9.50		33	40.50
3380	2" diameter		38	.211		32	11.50		43.50	52.50
3390	2-1/2" diameter	Q-1	54	.296		49	14.55		63.55	76
3400	3" diameter		48	.333		65	16.40		81.40	96
3410	4" diameter		44	.364		91.50	17.85		109.35	128
3420	5" diameter		35	.457		93.50	22.50		116	137
3430	6" diameter	Q-2	40	.600		117	30.50		147.50	175
3440	8" diameter		35	.686		141	35		176	208
3450	10" diameter		29	.828		259	42		301	350
3460	12" diameter		24	1		465	51		516	590
3920	To delete coupling & hanger, subtract									
3930	3/4" diam. to 2" diam.					30%	25%			
3940	2-1/2" diam. to 5" diam.					15%	17%			
3950	6" diam. to 12" diam.					11%	12%			
3990	Fittings: coupling material required at joints not incl. in fitting price.									
3994	Add 1 selected coupling, material only, per joint for installed price.									
4000	Elbow, 90° or 45°, painted									
4030	3/4" diameter	1 Plum	50	.160	Ea.	46	8.75		54.75	63.50
4040	1" diameter		50	.160		24.50	8.75		33.25	40
4050	1-1/4" diameter		40	.200		24.50	10.90		35.40	43.50
4060	1-1/2" diameter		33	.242		24.50	13.25		37.75	47

22 11 13 – Facility Water Distribution Piping

22 11 13.48 Pipe, Fittings and Valves, Steel, Grooved-Joint	Crew	Daily Output	Labor-Hours	Unit	Material	2012 Bare Costs Labor	Equipment	Total	Total Incl O&P
4070	2" diameter	1 Plum	25	.320	Ea.	24.50	17.45		41.95	53.50
4080	2-1/2" diameter	Q-1	40	.400		24.50	19.65		44.15	56.50
4090	3" diameter		33	.485		43	24		67	83.50
4100	4" diameter		25	.640		47	31.50		78.50	99
4110	5" diameter		20	.800		112	39.50		151.50	184
4120	6" diameter	Q-2	25	.960		132	49		181	219
4130	8" diameter		21	1.143		275	58.50		333.50	395
4140	10" diameter		18	1.333		500	68		568	650
4150	12" diameter		15	1.600		800	81.50		881.50	1,000
4170	14" diameter		12	2		860	102		962	1,100
4180	16" diameter		11	2.182		1,125	111		1,236	1,400
4190	18" diameter	Q-3	15	2.133		1,425	111		1,536	1,725
4200	20" diameter		13	2.462		1,875	128		2,003	2,250
4210	24" diameter		11	2.909		2,700	151		2,851	3,200
4250	For galvanized elbows, add					26%				
4690	Tee, painted									
4700	3/4" diameter	1 Plum	38	.211	Ea.	49	11.50		60.50	71.50
4740	1" diameter		33	.242		38	13.25		51.25	61.50
4750	1-1/4" diameter		27	.296		38	16.20		54.20	66
4760	1-1/2" diameter		22	.364		38	19.85		57.85	71.50
4770	2" diameter		17	.471		38	25.50		63.50	80.50
4780	2-1/2" diameter	Q-1	27	.593		38	29		67	85.50
4790	3" diameter		22	.727		52	36		88	111
4800	4" diameter		17	.941		79.50	46.50		126	158
4810	5" diameter		13	1.231		185	60.50		245.50	295
4820	6" diameter	Q-2	17	1.412		214	72		286	345
4830	8" diameter		14	1.714		470	87.50		557.50	645
4840	10" diameter		12	2		975	102		1,077	1,225
4850	12" diameter		10	2.400		1,150	122		1,272	1,450
4851	14" diameter		9	2.667		1,400	136		1,536	1,725
4852	16" diameter		8	3		1,550	153		1,703	1,925
4853	18" diameter	Q-3	11	2.909		1,625	151		1,776	2,025
4854	20" diameter		10	3.200		2,325	166		2,491	2,825
4855	24" diameter		8	4		3,550	208		3,758	4,225
4900	For galvanized tees, add					24%				
4906	Couplings, rigid style, painted									
4908	1" diameter	1 Plum	100	.080	Ea.	18.40	4.37		22.77	26.50
4909	1-1/4" diameter		100	.080		18.40	4.37		22.77	26.50
4910	1-1/2" diameter		67	.119		18.40	6.50		24.90	30
4912	2" diameter		50	.160		20.50	8.75		29.25	35.50
4914	2-1/2" diameter	Q-1	80	.200		23.50	9.85		33.35	40.50
4916	3" diameter		67	.239		27	11.75		38.75	47.50
4918	4" diameter		50	.320		38	15.75		53.75	65.50
4920	5" diameter		40	.400		49	19.65		68.65	83.50
4922	6" diameter	Q-2	50	.480		65	24.50		89.50	109
4924	8" diameter		42	.571		103	29		132	157
4926	10" diameter		35	.686		169	35		204	239
4928	12" diameter		32	.750		189	38		227	266
4930	14" diameter		24	1		211	51		262	310
4931	16" diameter		20	1.200		274	61		335	390
4932	18" diameter		18	1.333		315	68		383	450
4933	20" diameter		16	1.500		435	76.50		511.50	590
4934	24" diameter		13	1.846		555	94		649	750

22 11 13 – Facility Water Distribution Piping

22 11 13.48 Pipe, Fittings and Valves, Steel, Grooved-Joint	Crew	Daily Output	Labor-Hours	Unit	Material	2012 Bare Costs Labor	Equipment	Total	Total Incl O&P
4940	Flexible, standard, painted									
4950	3/4" diameter	1 Plum	100	.080	Ea.	13.40	4.37		17.77	21.50
4960	1" diameter		100	.080		13.40	4.37		17.77	21.50
4970	1-1/4" diameter		80	.100		17.60	5.45		23.05	27.50
4980	1-1/2" diameter		67	.119		19.20	6.50		25.70	31
4990	2" diameter		50	.160		20.50	8.75		29.25	35.50
5000	2-1/2" diameter	Q-1	80	.200		24	9.85		33.85	41.50
5010	3" diameter		67	.239		27	11.75		38.75	47
5020	3-1/2" diameter		57	.281		38	13.80		51.80	63
5030	4" diameter		50	.320		38.50	15.75		54.25	66
5040	5" diameter		40	.400		58.50	19.65		78.15	94
5050	6" diameter	Q-2	50	.480		69.50	24.50		94	114
5070	8" diameter		42	.571		113	29		142	168
5090	10" diameter		35	.686		184	35		219	256
5110	12" diameter		32	.750		209	38		247	288
5120	14" diameter		24	1		217	51		268	315
5130	16" diameter		20	1.200		285	61		346	405
5140	18" diameter		18	1.333		335	68		403	465
5150	20" diameter		16	1.500		445	76.50		521.50	605
5160	24" diameter		13	1.846		575	94		669	770
5176	Lightweight style, painted									
5178	1-1/2" diameter	1 Plum	67	.119	Ea.	17	6.50		23.50	28.50
5180	2" diameter	"	50	.160		20.50	8.75		29.25	35.50
5182	2-1/2" diameter	Q-1	80	.200		24	9.85		33.85	41.50
5184	3" diameter		67	.239		27	11.75		38.75	47
5186	3-1/2" diameter		57	.281		33	13.80		46.80	57
5188	4" diameter		50	.320		38.50	15.75		54.25	66
5190	5" diameter		40	.400		58.50	19.65		78.15	94
5192	6" diameter	Q-2	50	.480		69.50	24.50		94	114
5194	8" diameter		42	.571		113	29		142	168
5196	10" diameter		35	.686		229	35		264	305
5198	12" diameter		32	.750		255	38		293	340
5200	For galvanized couplings, add					33%				
5220	Tee, reducing, painted									
5225	2" x 1-1/2" diameter	Q-1	38	.421	Ea.	80	20.50		100.50	119
5226	2-1/2" x 2" diameter		28	.571		80	28		108	131
5227	3" x 2-1/2" diameter		23	.696		71	34		105	130
5228	4" x 3" diameter		18	.889		95.50	43.50		139	171
5229	5" x 4" diameter		15	1.067		204	52.50		256.50	305
5230	6" x 4" diameter	Q-2	18	1.333		225	68		293	350
5231	8" x 6" diameter		15	1.600		470	81.50		551.50	640
5232	10" x 8" diameter		13	1.846		615	94		709	815
5233	12" x 10" diameter		11	2.182		940	111		1,051	1,200
5234	14" x 12" diameter		10	2.400		840	122		962	1,100
5235	16" x 12" diameter		9	2.667		1,225	136		1,361	1,550
5236	18" x 12" diameter	Q-3	12	2.667		1,250	139		1,389	1,575
5237	18" x 16" diameter		11	2.909		1,575	151		1,726	1,950
5238	20" x 16" diameter		10	3.200		2,050	166		2,216	2,525
5239	24" x 20" diameter		9	3.556		3,250	185		3,435	3,850
5240	Reducer, concentric, painted									
5241	2-1/2" x 2" diameter	Q-1	43	.372	Ea.	28.50	18.30		46.80	59
5242	3" x 2-1/2" diameter		35	.457		34.50	22.50		57	72
5243	4" x 3" diameter		29	.552		41.50	27		68.50	87

22 11 13 – Facility Water Distribution Piping

22 11 13.48 Pipe, Fittings and Valves, Steel, Grooved-Joint	Crew	Daily Output	Labor-Hours	Unit	Material	2012 Bare Costs Labor	Equipment	Total	Total Incl O&P
5244 5" x 4" diameter	Q-1	22	.727	Ea.	57.50	36		93.50	117
5245 6" x 4" diameter	Q-2	26	.923		66.50	47		113.50	145
5246 8" x 6" diameter		23	1.043		173	53		226	270
5247 10" x 8" diameter		20	1.200		350	61		411	475
5248 12" x 10" diameter		16	1.500		630	76.50		706.50	810
5255 Eccentric, painted									
5256 2-1/2" x 2" diameter	Q-1	42	.381	Ea.	60	18.70		78.70	94
5257 3" x 2-1/2" diameter		34	.471		68	23		91	110
5258 4" x 3" diameter		28	.571		83	28		111	134
5259 5" x 4" diameter		21	.762		113	37.50		150.50	182
5260 6" x 4" diameter	Q-2	25	.960		132	49		181	219
5261 8" x 6" diameter		22	1.091		266	55.50		321.50	375
5262 10" x 8" diameter		19	1.263		730	64.50		794.50	895
5263 12" x 10" diameter		15	1.600		1,000	81.50		1,081.50	1,225
5270 Coupling, reducing, painted									
5272 2" x 1-1/2" diameter	1 Plum	52	.154	Ea.	28	8.40		36.40	43.50
5274 2-1/2" x 2" diameter	Q-1	82	.195		36.50	9.60		46.10	54.50
5276 3" x 2" diameter		69	.232		41.50	11.40		52.90	63
5278 4" x 2" diameter		52	.308		66	15.10		81.10	95.50
5280 5" x 4" diameter		42	.381		74	18.70		92.70	110
5282 6" x 4" diameter	Q-2	52	.462		112	23.50		135.50	159
5284 8" x 6" diameter	"	44	.545		168	28		196	226
5290 Outlet coupling, painted									
5294 1-1/2" x 1" pipe size	1 Plum	65	.123	Ea.	36.50	6.70		43.20	50
5296 2" x 1" pipe size	"	48	.167		37	9.10		46.10	55
5298 2-1/2" x 1" pipe size	Q-1	78	.205		57	10.10		67.10	78
5300 2-1/2" x 1-1/4" pipe size	1 Plum	70	.114		64.50	6.25		70.75	80.50
5302 3" x 1" pipe size	Q-1	65	.246		73	12.10		85.10	99
5304 4" x 3/4" pipe size		48	.333		81	16.40		97.40	114
5306 4" x 1-1/2" pipe size		46	.348		115	17.10		132.10	153
5308 6" x 1-1/2" pipe size	Q-2	44	.545		163	28		191	221
5750 Flange, w/groove gasket, black steel									
5754 See Line 22 11 13.47 0620 for gasket & bolt set									
5760 ANSI class 125 and 150, painted									
5780 2" pipe size	1 Plum	23	.348	Ea.	81.50	19		100.50	118
5790 2-1/2" pipe size	Q-1	37	.432		101	21.50		122.50	143
5800 3" pipe size		31	.516		109	25.50		134.50	159
5820 4" pipe size		23	.696		146	34		180	212
5830 5" pipe size		19	.842		169	41.50		210.50	249
5840 6" pipe size	Q-2	23	1.043		184	53		237	283
5850 8" pipe size		17	1.412		208	72		280	340
5860 10" pipe size		14	1.714		330	87.50		417.50	490
5870 12" pipe size		12	2		430	102		532	630
5880 14" pipe size		10	2.400		845	122		967	1,100
5890 16" pipe size		9	2.667		980	136		1,116	1,275
5900 18" pipe size		6	4		1,200	204		1,404	1,625
5910 20" pipe size		5	4.800		1,450	245		1,695	1,975
5920 24" pipe size		4.50	5.333		1,850	272		2,122	2,450
5940 ANSI class 350, painted									
5946 2" pipe size	1 Plum	23	.348	Ea.	102	19		121	141
5948 2-1/2" pipe size	Q-1	37	.432		118	21.50		139.50	161
5950 3" pipe size		31	.516		161	25.50		186.50	216
5952 4" pipe size		23	.696		214	34		248	288

22 11 Facility Water Distribution

22 11 13 – Facility Water Distribution Piping

22 11 13.48 Pipe, Fittings and Valves, Steel, Grooved-Joint	Crew	Daily Output	Labor-Hours	Unit	Material	2012 Bare Costs Labor	Equipment	Total	Total Incl O&P
5954	5" pipe size	Q-1	19	.842	Ea.	244	41.50		285.50	330
5956	6" pipe size	Q-2	23	1.043		283	53		336	390
5958	8" pipe size		17	1.412		325	72		397	470
5960	10" pipe size	↓	14	1.714		515	87.50		602.50	700
5962	12" pipe size	1 Plum	12	.667	↓	550	36.50		586.50	665
6100	Cross, painted									
6110	2" diameter	1 Plum	12.50	.640	Ea.	68	35		103	127
6112	2-1/2" diameter	Q-1	20	.800		68	39.50		107.50	134
6114	3" diameter		15.50	1.032		121	50.50		171.50	210
6116	4" diameter	↓	12.50	1.280		201	63		264	315
6118	6" diameter	Q-2	12.50	1.920		525	98		623	730
6120	8" diameter		10.50	2.286		690	117		807	935
6122	10" diameter		9	2.667		1,175	136		1,311	1,500
6124	12" diameter	↓	7.50	3.200	↓	1,700	163		1,863	2,125
7400	Suction diffuser									
7402	Grooved end inlet x flanged outlet									
7410	3" x 3"	Q-1	50	.320	Ea.	660	15.75		675.75	750
7412	4" x 4"		38	.421		895	20.50		915.50	1,025
7414	5" x 5"	↓	30	.533		1,050	26		1,076	1,200
7416	6" x 6"	Q-2	38	.632		1,325	32		1,357	1,500
7418	8" x 8"		27	.889		2,450	45.50		2,495.50	2,775
7420	10" x 10"		20	1.200		3,300	61		3,361	3,725
7422	12" x 12"		16	1.500		5,500	76.50		5,576.50	6,175
7424	14" x 14"		15	1.600		6,025	81.50		6,106.50	6,775
7426	16" x 14"	↓	14	1.714	↓	6,225	87.50		6,312.50	6,950
7500	Strainer, tee type, painted									
7506	2" pipe size	1 Plum	38	.211	Ea.	440	11.50		451.50	500
7508	2-1/2" pipe size	Q-1	62	.258		465	12.70		477.70	530
7510	3" pipe size		50	.320		520	15.75		535.75	595
7512	4" pipe size		38	.421		590	20.50		610.50	675
7514	5" pipe size	↓	30	.533		850	26		876	975
7516	6" pipe size	Q-2	38	.632		925	32		957	1,075
7518	8" pipe size		27	.889		1,425	45.50		1,470.50	1,625
7520	10" pipe size		20	1.200		2,075	61		2,136	2,400
7522	12" pipe size		16	1.500		2,675	76.50		2,751.50	3,075
7524	14" pipe size		15	1.600		8,400	81.50		8,481.50	9,350
7526	16" pipe size	↓	14	1.714		10,400	87.50		10,487.50	11,600
7570	Expansion joint, max. 3" travel									
7572	2" diameter	1 Plum	38	.211	Ea.	555	11.50		566.50	625
7574	3" diameter	Q-1	50	.320		640	15.75		655.75	725
7576	4" diameter	"	38	.421		840	20.50		860.50	955
7578	6" diameter	Q-2	38	.632	↓	1,300	32		1,332	1,500
7800	Ball valve w/handle, carbon steel trim									
7810	1-1/2" pipe size	1 Plum	50	.160	Ea.	126	8.75		134.75	151
7812	2" pipe size	"	38	.211		140	11.50		151.50	170
7814	2-1/2" pipe size	Q-1	62	.258		305	12.70		317.70	355
7816	3" pipe size		50	.320		490	15.75		505.75	565
7818	4" pipe size	↓	38	.421		760	20.50		780.50	865
7820	6" pipe size	Q-2	30	.800	↓	2,325	41		2,366	2,625
7830	With gear operator									
7834	2-1/2" pipe size	Q-1	62	.258	Ea.	615	12.70		627.70	695
7836	3" pipe size		50	.320		870	15.75		885.75	985
7838	4" pipe size	↓	38	.421		1,100	20.50		1,120.50	1,250

179

22 11 13.48 Pipe, Fittings and Valves, Steel, Grooved-Joint	Crew	Daily Output	Labor-Hours	Unit	Material	2012 Bare Costs Labor	Equipment	Total	Total Incl O&P
7840	6" pipe size	Q-2	30	.800	Ea.	2,625	41		2,666	2,925
7870	Check valve									
7874	2-1/2" pipe size	Q-1	62	.258	Ea.	210	12.70		222.70	250
7876	3" pipe size		50	.320		249	15.75		264.75	297
7878	4" pipe size		38	.421		263	20.50		283.50	320
7880	5" pipe size		30	.533		435	26		461	520
7882	6" pipe size	Q-2	38	.632		520	32		552	620
7884	8" pipe size		27	.889		710	45.50		755.50	850
7886	10" pipe size		20	1.200		2,050	61		2,111	2,350
7888	12" pipe size		16	1.500		2,425	76.50		2,501.50	2,800
7900	Plug valve, balancing, w/lever operator									
7906	3" pipe size	Q-1	50	.320	Ea.	520	15.75		535.75	600
7908	4" pipe size	"	38	.421		640	20.50		660.50	735
7909	6" pipe size	Q-2	30	.800		985	41		1,026	1,125
7916	With gear operator									
7920	3" pipe size	Q-1	50	.320	Ea.	990	15.75		1,005.75	1,125
7922	4" pipe size	"	38	.421		1,025	20.50		1,045.50	1,150
7924	6" pipe size	Q-2	38	.632		1,375	32		1,407	1,575
7926	8" pipe size		27	.889		2,125	45.50		2,170.50	2,425
7928	10" pipe size		20	1.200		2,900	61		2,961	3,300
7930	12" pipe size		16	1.500		4,425	76.50		4,501.50	5,000
8000	Butterfly valve, 2 position handle, with standard trim									
8010	1-1/2" pipe size	1 Plum	50	.160	Ea.	198	8.75		206.75	231
8020	2" pipe size	"	38	.211		198	11.50		209.50	235
8030	3" pipe size	Q-1	50	.320		284	15.75		299.75	340
8050	4" pipe size	"	38	.421		315	20.50		335.50	375
8070	6" pipe size	Q-2	38	.632		630	32		662	745
8080	8" pipe size		27	.889		850	45.50		895.50	1,000
8090	10" pipe size		20	1.200		1,500	61		1,561	1,750
8200	With stainless steel trim									
8240	1-1/2" pipe size	1 Plum	50	.160	Ea.	251	8.75		259.75	289
8250	2" pipe size	"	38	.211		251	11.50		262.50	293
8270	3" pipe size	Q-1	50	.320		340	15.75		355.75	395
8280	4" pipe size	"	38	.421		365	20.50		385.50	435
8300	6" pipe size	Q-2	38	.632		685	32		717	800
8310	8" pipe size		27	.889		1,700	45.50		1,745.50	1,925
8320	10" pipe size		20	1.200		3,050	61		3,111	3,450
8322	12" pipe size		16	1.500		3,500	76.50		3,576.50	3,975
8324	14" pipe size		15	1.600		4,150	81.50		4,231.50	4,700
8326	16" pipe size		14	1.714		6,000	87.50		6,087.50	6,725
8328	18" pipe size	Q-3	12	2.667		7,400	139		7,539	8,325
8330	20" pipe size		11	2.909		9,100	151		9,251	10,200
8332	24" pipe size		10	3.200		12,200	166		12,366	13,700
8336	Note: sizes 8" up w/manual gear operator									
9000	Cut one groove, labor									
9010	3/4" pipe size	Q-1	152	.105	Ea.		5.15		5.15	7.80
9020	1" pipe size		140	.114			5.60		5.60	8.45
9030	1-1/4" pipe size		124	.129			6.35		6.35	9.55
9040	1-1/2" pipe size		114	.140			6.90		6.90	10.40
9050	2" pipe size		104	.154			7.55		7.55	11.40
9060	2-1/2" pipe size		96	.167			8.20		8.20	12.35
9070	3" pipe size		88	.182			8.95		8.95	13.50
9080	3-1/2" pipe size		83	.193			9.45		9.45	14.30

22 11 Facility Water Distribution

22 11 13 – Facility Water Distribution Piping

22 11 13.48 Pipe, Fittings and Valves, Steel, Grooved-Joint		Crew	Daily Output	Labor-Hours	Unit	Material	2012 Bare Costs Labor	2012 Bare Costs Equipment	Total	Total Incl O&P
9090	4" pipe size	Q-1	78	.205	Ea.		10.10		10.10	15.20
9100	5" pipe size		72	.222			10.90		10.90	16.45
9110	6" pipe size		70	.229			11.25		11.25	16.95
9120	8" pipe size		54	.296			14.55		14.55	22
9130	10" pipe size		38	.421			20.50		20.50	31
9140	12" pipe size		30	.533			26		26	39.50
9150	14" pipe size		20	.800			39.50		39.50	59.50
9160	16" pipe size		19	.842			41.50		41.50	62.50
9170	18" pipe size		18	.889			43.50		43.50	66
9180	20" pipe size		17	.941			46.50		46.50	70
9190	24" pipe size		15	1.067			52.50		52.50	79
9210	Roll one groove									
9220	3/4" pipe size	Q-1	266	.060	Ea.		2.96		2.96	4.46
9230	1" pipe size		228	.070			3.45		3.45	5.20
9240	1-1/4" pipe size		200	.080			3.93		3.93	5.95
9250	1-1/2" pipe size		178	.090			4.42		4.42	6.65
9260	2" pipe size		116	.138			6.80		6.80	10.20
9270	2-1/2" pipe size		110	.145			7.15		7.15	10.80
9280	3" pipe size		100	.160			7.85		7.85	11.85
9290	3-1/2" pipe size		94	.170			8.35		8.35	12.60
9300	4" pipe size		86	.186			9.15		9.15	13.80
9310	5" pipe size		84	.190			9.35		9.35	14.10
9320	6" pipe size		80	.200			9.85		9.85	14.85
9330	8" pipe size		66	.242			11.90		11.90	17.95
9340	10" pipe size		58	.276			13.55		13.55	20.50
9350	12" pipe size		46	.348			17.10		17.10	26
9360	14" pipe size		30	.533			26		26	39.50
9370	16" pipe size		28	.571			28		28	42.50
9380	18" pipe size		27	.593			29		29	44
9390	20" pipe size		25	.640			31.50		31.50	47.50
9400	24" pipe size		23	.696			34		34	51.50

22 11 13.60 Tubing, Stainless Steel

		Crew	Daily Output	Labor-Hours	Unit	Material	2012 Bare Costs Labor	2012 Bare Costs Equipment	Total	Total Incl O&P
0010	**TUBING, STAINLESS STEEL**									
5010	Type 304, no joints, no hangers									
5020	.035 wall									
5021	1/4"	1 Plum	160	.050	L.F.	2.46	2.73		5.19	6.85
5022	3/8"		160	.050		3.10	2.73		5.83	7.55
5023	1/2"		160	.050		3.99	2.73		6.72	8.50
5024	5/8"		160	.050		4.89	2.73		7.62	9.50
5025	3/4"		133	.060		5.90	3.28		9.18	11.45
5026	7/8"		133	.060		7	3.28		10.28	12.65
5027	1"		114	.070		6.85	3.83		10.68	13.30
5040	.049 wall									
5041	1/4"	1 Plum	160	.050	L.F.	2.88	2.73		5.61	7.30
5042	3/8"		160	.050		3.99	2.73		6.72	8.50
5043	1/2"		160	.050		4.42	2.73		7.15	9
5044	5/8"		160	.050		6	2.73		8.73	10.70
5045	3/4"		133	.060		6.35	3.28		9.63	11.95
5046	7/8"		133	.060		7.45	3.28		10.73	13.15
5047	1"		114	.070		7.95	3.83		11.78	14.50
5060	.065 wall									
5061	1/4"	1 Plum	160	.050	L.F.	3.23	2.73		5.96	7.65

22 11 13 – Facility Water Distribution Piping

22 11 13.60 Tubing, Stainless Steel		Crew	Daily Output	Labor-Hours	Unit	Material	2012 Bare Costs Labor	Equipment	Total	Total Incl O&P
5062	3/8"	1 Plum	160	.050	L.F.	4.46	2.73		7.19	9.05
5063	1/2"		160	.050		5.40	2.73		8.13	10.05
5064	5/8"		160	.050		6.55	2.73		9.28	11.30
5065	3/4"		133	.060		6.95	3.28		10.23	12.60
5066	7/8"		133	.060		9	3.28		12.28	14.85
5067	1"		114	.070		8.80	3.83		12.63	15.45
5210	Type 316									
5220	.035 wall									
5221	1/4"	1 Plum	160	.050	L.F.	3.71	2.73		6.44	8.20
5222	3/8"		160	.050		4.74	2.73		7.47	9.30
5223	1/2"		160	.050		6.45	2.73		9.18	11.20
5224	5/8"		160	.050		10.20	2.73		12.93	15.30
5225	3/4"		133	.060		8.95	3.28		12.23	14.80
5226	7/8"		133	.060		14.30	3.28		17.58	20.50
5227	1"		114	.070		9.35	3.83		13.18	16.10
5240	.049 wall									
5241	1/4"	1 Plum	160	.050	L.F.	5.55	2.73		8.28	10.25
5242	3/8"		160	.050		5.95	2.73		8.68	10.65
5243	1/2"		160	.050		6.95	2.73		9.68	11.75
5244	5/8"		160	.050		9.95	2.73		12.68	15
5245	3/4"		133	.060		7.70	3.28		10.98	13.45
5246	7/8"		133	.060		11.95	3.28		15.23	18.10
5247	1"		114	.070		12	3.83		15.83	19
5260	.065 wall									
5261	1/4"	1 Plum	160	.050	L.F.	4.59	2.73		7.32	9.15
5262	3/8"		160	.050		9.70	2.73		12.43	14.80
5263	1/2"		160	.050		9.75	2.73		12.48	14.80
5264	5/8"		160	.050		12.80	2.73		15.53	18.20
5265	3/4"		133	.060		12.90	3.28		16.18	19.15
5266	7/8"		133	.060		14	3.28		17.28	20.50
5267	1"		114	.070		13.30	3.83		17.13	20.50

22 11 13.61 Tubing Fittings, Stainless Steel

		Crew	Daily Output	Labor-Hours	Unit	Material	2012 Bare Costs Labor	Equipment	Total	Total Incl O&P
0010	**TUBING FITTINGS, STAINLESS STEEL**									
8200	Tube fittings, compression type									
8202	Type 316									
8204	90° elbow									
8206	1/4"	1 Plum	24	.333	Ea.	14.40	18.20		32.60	43.50
8207	3/8"		22	.364		17.60	19.85		37.45	49.50
8208	1/2"		22	.364		29	19.85		48.85	62
8209	5/8"		21	.381		32.50	21		53.50	67.50
8210	3/4"		21	.381		51.50	21		72.50	88
8211	7/8"		20	.400		78.50	22		100.50	120
8212	1"		20	.400		98	22		120	141
8220	Union tee									
8222	1/4"	1 Plum	15	.533	Ea.	20.50	29		49.50	66.50
8224	3/8"		15	.533		26	29		55	72.50
8225	1/2"		15	.533		40.50	29		69.50	88.50
8226	5/8"		14	.571		45	31		76	96.50
8227	3/4"		14	.571		60.50	31		91.50	114
8228	7/8"		13	.615		113	33.50		146.50	176
8229	1"		13	.615		129	33.50		162.50	193
8234	Union									

22 11 Facility Water Distribution

22 11 13 – Facility Water Distribution Piping

22 11 13.61 Tubing Fittings, Stainless Steel

		Crew	Daily Output	Labor-Hours	Unit	Material	2012 Bare Costs Labor	Equipment	Total	Total Incl O&P
8236	1/4"	1 Plum	24	.333	Ea.	9.95	18.20		28.15	38.50
8237	3/8"		22	.364		14.15	19.85		34	45.50
8238	1/2"		22	.364		21	19.85		40.85	53
8239	5/8"		21	.381		27.50	21		48.50	61.50
8240	3/4"		21	.381		34	21		55	69
8241	7/8"		20	.400		56	22		78	94.50
8242	1"	▼	20	.400	▼	59	22		81	98
8250	Male connector									
8252	1/4" x 1/4"	1 Plum	24	.333	Ea.	6.40	18.20		24.60	34.50
8253	3/8" x 3/8"		22	.364		9.95	19.85		29.80	41
8254	1/2" x 1/2"		22	.364		14.70	19.85		34.55	46
8256	3/4" x 3/4"		21	.381		22.50	21		43.50	56.50
8258	1" x 1"	▼	20	.400	▼	39.50	22		61.50	76.50

22 11 13.64 Pipe, Stainless Steel

		Crew	Daily Output	Labor-Hours	Unit	Material	2012 Bare Costs Labor	Equipment	Total	Total Incl O&P
0010	**PIPE, STAINLESS STEEL**									
0020	Welded, with clevis type hanger assemblies, 10' O.C.									
0500	Schedule 5, type 304									
0540	1/2" diameter	Q-15	128	.125	L.F.	6.05	6.15	.29	12.49	16.20
0550	3/4" diameter		116	.138		7.75	6.80	.32	14.87	19.10
0560	1" diameter		103	.155		9.40	7.65	.36	17.41	22
0570	1-1/4" diameter		93	.172		13.05	8.45	.40	21.90	27.50
0580	1-1/2" diameter		85	.188		17.55	9.25	.43	27.23	33.50
0590	2" diameter		69	.232		29.50	11.40	.54	41.44	50.50
0600	2-1/2" diameter		53	.302		32	14.85	.70	47.55	59
0610	3" diameter		48	.333		39	16.40	.77	56.17	68
0620	4" diameter		44	.364		49.50	17.85	.84	68.19	82.50
0630	5" diameter	▼	36	.444		101	22	1.03	124.03	145
0640	6" diameter	Q-16	42	.571		93	29	.88	122.88	147
0650	8" diameter		34	.706		143	36	1.09	180.09	213
0660	10" diameter		26	.923		199	47	1.42	247.42	292
0670	12" diameter	▼	21	1.143	▼	262	58.50	1.76	322.26	380
0700	To delete hangers, subtract									
0710	1/2" diam. to 1-1/2" diam.					8%	19%			
0720	2" diam. to 5" diam.					4%	9%			
0730	6" diam. to 12" diam.					3%	4%			
0750	For small quantities, add				L.F.	10%				
1250	Schedule 5, type 316									
1290	1/2" diameter	Q-15	128	.125	L.F.	10.40	6.15	.29	16.84	21
1300	3/4" diameter		116	.138		13.55	6.80	.32	20.67	25.50
1310	1" diameter		103	.155		13.95	7.65	.36	21.96	27
1320	1-1/4" diameter		93	.172		16.80	8.45	.40	25.65	31.50
1330	1-1/2" diameter		85	.188		24	9.25	.43	33.68	40.50
1340	2" diameter		69	.232		41	11.40	.54	52.94	63
1350	2-1/2" diameter		53	.302		53	14.85	.70	68.55	81.50
1360	3" diameter		48	.333		67	16.40	.77	84.17	99.50
1370	4" diameter		44	.364		83.50	17.85	.84	102.19	119
1380	5" diameter	▼	36	.444		159	22	1.03	182.03	209
1390	6" diameter	Q-16	42	.571		155	29	.88	184.88	216
1400	8" diameter		34	.706		234	36	1.09	271.09	315
1410	10" diameter		26	.923		335	47	1.42	383.42	445
1420	12" diameter	▼	21	1.143	▼	430	58.50	1.76	490.26	565
1490	For small quantities, add					10%				

22 11 13.64 Pipe, Stainless Steel

		Crew	Daily Output	Labor-Hours	Unit	Material	2012 Bare Costs Labor	Equipment	Total	Total Incl O&P
1940	To delete hanger, subtract									
1950	1/2" diam. to 1-1/2" diam.					5%	19%			
1960	2" diam. to 5" diam.					3%	9%			
1970	6" diam. to 12" diam.					2%	4%			
2000	Schedule 10, type 304									
2040	1/4" diameter	Q-15	131	.122	L.F.	3.85	6	.28	10.13	13.60
2050	3/8" diameter		128	.125		5.10	6.15	.29	11.54	15.15
2060	1/2" diameter		125	.128		10	6.30	.30	16.60	21
2070	3/4" diameter		113	.142		10.20	6.95	.33	17.48	22
2080	1" diameter		100	.160		10.25	7.85	.37	18.47	23.50
2090	1-1/4" diameter		91	.176		11.75	8.65	.41	20.81	26.50
2100	1-1/2" diameter		83	.193		13.15	9.45	.45	23.05	29
2110	2" diameter		67	.239		16.10	11.75	.55	28.40	36
2120	2-1/2" diameter		51	.314		21	15.40	.72	37.12	47.50
2130	3" diameter		46	.348		25.50	17.10	.80	43.40	55
2140	4" diameter		42	.381		31	18.70	.88	50.58	63.50
2150	5" diameter	↓	35	.457		40.50	22.50	1.06	64.06	79.50
2160	6" diameter	Q-16	40	.600		49.50	30.50	.92	80.92	102
2170	8" diameter		33	.727		86.50	37	1.12	124.62	153
2180	10" diameter		25	.960		121	49	1.48	171.48	209
2190	12" diameter	↓	21	1.143		151	58.50	1.76	211.26	256
2250	For small quantities, add				↓	10%				
2650	To delete hanger, subtract									
2660	1/4" diam. to 3/4" diam.					9%	22%			
2670	1" diam. to 2" diam.					4%	15%			
2680	2-1/2" diam. to 5" diam.					3%	8%			
2690	6" diam. to 12" diam.					3%	4%			
2750	Schedule 10, type 316									
2790	1/4" diameter	Q-15	131	.122	L.F.	5.20	6	.28	11.48	15.10
2800	3/8" diameter		128	.125		7	6.15	.29	13.44	17.25
2810	1/2" diameter		125	.128		7.60	6.30	.30	14.20	18.20
2820	3/4" diameter		113	.142		9.05	6.95	.33	16.33	21
2830	1" diameter		100	.160		12	7.85	.37	20.22	25.50
2840	1-1/4" diameter		91	.176		16.85	8.65	.41	25.91	32
2850	1-1/2" diameter		83	.193		18.70	9.45	.45	28.60	35.50
2860	2" diameter		67	.239		21.50	11.75	.55	33.80	42
2870	2-1/2" diameter		51	.314		29.50	15.40	.72	45.62	57
2880	3" diameter		46	.348		35.50	17.10	.80	53.40	66
2890	4" diameter		42	.381		45	18.70	.88	64.58	78.50
2900	5" diameter	↓	35	.457		55	22.50	1.06	78.56	95.50
2910	6" diameter	Q-16	40	.600		71.50	30.50	.92	102.92	126
2920	8" diameter		33	.727		127	37	1.12	165.12	197
2930	10" diameter		25	.960		169	49	1.48	219.48	262
2940	12" diameter	↓	21	1.143		211	58.50	1.76	271.26	320
2990	For small quantities, add				↓	10%				
3430	To delete hanger, subtract									
3440	1/4" diam. to 3/4" diam.					6%	22%			
3450	1" diam. to 2" diam.					3%	15%			
3460	2-1/2" diam. to 5" diam.					2%	8%			
3470	6" diam. to 12" diam.					2%	4%			
3500	Threaded, couplings and clevis hanger assemblies, 10' O.C.									
3520	Schedule 40, type 304									
3540	1/4" diameter	1 Plum	54	.148	L.F.	6.65	8.10		14.75	19.50

22 11 13.64 Pipe, Stainless Steel		Crew	Daily Output	Labor-Hours	Unit	Material	2012 Bare Costs Labor	Equipment	Total	Total Incl O&P
3550	3/8" diameter	1 Plum	53	.151	L.F.	8.45	8.25		16.70	22
3560	1/2" diameter		52	.154		7.55	8.40		15.95	21
3570	3/4" diameter		51	.157		11.65	8.55		20.20	25.50
3580	1" diameter		45	.178		16.15	9.70		25.85	32.50
3590	1-1/4" diameter	Q-1	76	.211		22	10.35		32.35	39.50
3600	1-1/2" diameter		69	.232		25.50	11.40		36.90	45
3610	2" diameter		57	.281		35.50	13.80		49.30	60
3620	2-1/2" diameter		44	.364		61	17.85		78.85	94
3630	3" diameter		38	.421		84	20.50		104.50	124
3640	4" diameter	Q-2	51	.471		101	24		125	147
3740	For small quantities, add					10%				
4200	To delete couplings & hangers, subtract									
4210	1/4" diam. to 3/4" diam.					15%	56%			
4220	1" diam. to 2" diam.					18%	49%			
4230	2-1/2" diam. to 4" diam.					34%	40%			
4250	Schedule 40, type 316									
4290	1/4" diameter	1 Plum	54	.148	L.F.	8	8.10		16.10	21
4300	3/8" diameter		53	.151		9.10	8.25		17.35	22.50
4310	1/2" diameter		52	.154		11.95	8.40		20.35	26
4320	3/4" diameter		51	.157		14.65	8.55		23.20	29
4330	1" diameter		45	.178		21	9.70		30.70	37.50
4340	1-1/4" diameter	Q-1	76	.211		29	10.35		39.35	47.50
4350	1-1/2" diameter		69	.232		33	11.40		44.40	53
4360	2" diameter		57	.281		46.50	13.80		60.30	72.50
4370	2-1/2" diameter		44	.364		81	17.85		98.85	116
4380	3" diameter		38	.421		106	20.50		126.50	147
4390	4" diameter	Q-2	51	.471		150	24		174	201
4490	For small quantities, add					10%				
4900	To delete couplings & hangers, subtract									
4910	1/4" diam. to 3/4" diam.					12%	56%			
4920	1" diam. to 2" diam.					14%	49%			
4930	2-1/2" diam. to 4" diam.					27%	40%			
5000	Schedule 80, type 304									
5040	1/4" diameter	1 Plum	53	.151	L.F.	17.20	8.25		25.45	31.50
5050	3/8" diameter		52	.154		19.70	8.40		28.10	34
5060	1/2" diameter		51	.157		24	8.55		32.55	39
5070	3/4" diameter		48	.167		25.50	9.10		34.60	42
5080	1" diameter		43	.186		32	10.15		42.15	50.50
5090	1-1/4" diameter	Q-1	73	.219		41.50	10.75		52.25	62.50
5100	1-1/2" diameter		67	.239		54.50	11.75		66.25	77.50
5110	2" diameter		54	.296		68	14.55		82.55	97
5190	For small quantities, add					10%				
5700	To delete couplings & hangers, subtract									
5710	1/4" diam. to 3/4" diam.					10%	53%			
5720	1" diam. to 2" diam.					14%	47%			
5750	Schedule 80, type 316									
5790	1/4" diameter	1 Plum	53	.151	L.F.	20.50	8.25		28.75	35
5800	3/8" diameter		52	.154		23	8.40		31.40	38
5810	1/2" diameter		51	.157		30	8.55		38.55	46
5820	3/4" diameter		48	.167		33	9.10		42.10	50.50
5830	1" diameter		43	.186		43.50	10.15		53.65	63
5840	1-1/4" diameter	Q-1	73	.219		62	10.75		72.75	85
5850	1-1/2" diameter		67	.239		67	11.75		78.75	91

22 11 13 – Facility Water Distribution Piping

22 11 13.64 Pipe, Stainless Steel

		Crew	Daily Output	Labor-Hours	Unit	Material	2012 Bare Costs Labor	Equipment	Total	Total Incl O&P
5860	2" diameter	Q-1	54	.296	L.F.	84.50	14.55		99.05	115
5950	For small quantities, add				▼	10%				
7000	To delete couplings & hangers, subtract									
7010	1/4" diam. to 3/4" diam.					9%	53%			
7020	1" diam. to 2" diam.					14%	47%			
8000	Weld joints with clevis type hanger assemblies, 10' O.C.									
8010	Schedule 40, type 304									
8050	1/8" pipe size	Q-15	126	.127	L.F.	5.20	6.25	.29	11.74	15.45
8060	1/4" pipe size		125	.128		5.40	6.30	.30	12	15.80
8070	3/8" pipe size		122	.131		7	6.45	.30	13.75	17.75
8080	1/2" pipe size		118	.136		5.60	6.65	.31	12.56	16.60
8090	3/4" pipe size		109	.147		9.10	7.20	.34	16.64	21.50
8100	1" pipe size		95	.168		12	8.30	.39	20.69	26
8110	1-1/4" pipe size		86	.186		15.30	9.15	.43	24.88	31
8120	1-1/2" pipe size		78	.205		18	10.10	.47	28.57	35.50
8130	2" pipe size		62	.258		23	12.70	.60	36.30	45.50
8140	2-1/2" pipe size		49	.327		32.50	16.05	.75	49.30	60.50
8150	3" pipe size		44	.364		45	17.85	.84	63.69	77.50
8160	3-1/2" pipe size		44	.364		46	17.85	.84	64.69	78.50
8170	4" pipe size		39	.410		46	20	.95	66.95	82.50
8180	5" pipe size	▼	32	.500		65.50	24.50	1.16	91.16	110
8190	6" pipe size	Q-16	37	.649		76.50	33	1	110.50	135
8200	8" pipe size		29	.828		153	42	1.27	196.27	233
8210	10" pipe size		24	1		260	51	1.54	312.54	365
8220	12" pipe size	▼	20	1.200	▼	293	61	1.85	355.85	420
8300	Schedule 40, type 316									
8310	1/8" pipe size	Q-15	126	.127	L.F.	7.10	6.25	.29	13.64	17.50
8320	1/4" pipe size		125	.128		6.55	6.30	.30	13.15	17.05
8330	3/8" pipe size		122	.131		7.35	6.45	.30	14.10	18.10
8340	1/2" pipe size		118	.136		9.65	6.65	.31	16.61	21
8350	3/4" pipe size		109	.147		11.60	7.20	.34	19.14	24
8360	1" pipe size		95	.168		16	8.30	.39	24.69	30.50
8370	1-1/4" pipe size		86	.186		21	9.15	.43	30.58	38
8380	1-1/2" pipe size		78	.205		24	10.10	.47	34.57	42
8390	2" pipe size		62	.258		32	12.70	.60	45.30	55
8400	2-1/2" pipe size		49	.327		46.50	16.05	.75	63.30	76
8410	3" pipe size		44	.364		59	17.85	.84	77.69	93
8420	3-1/2" pipe size		44	.364		73.50	17.85	.84	92.19	109
8430	4" pipe size		39	.410		84	20	.95	104.95	124
8440	5" pipe size	▼	32	.500		128	24.50	1.16	153.66	179
8450	6" pipe size	Q-16	37	.649		145	33	1	179	210
8460	8" pipe size		29	.828		280	42	1.27	323.27	375
8470	10" pipe size		24	1		375	51	1.54	427.54	490
8480	12" pipe size	▼	20	1.200	▼	510	61	1.85	572.85	655
8500	Schedule 80, type 304									
8510	1/4" pipe size	Q-15	110	.145	L.F.	15.80	7.15	.34	23.29	28.50
8520	3/8" pipe size		109	.147		18.10	7.20	.34	25.64	31
8530	1/2" pipe size		106	.151		22	7.40	.35	29.75	35.50
8540	3/4" pipe size		96	.167		23	8.20	.39	31.59	38
8550	1" pipe size		87	.184		27.50	9.05	.42	36.97	44
8560	1-1/4" pipe size		81	.198		31	9.70	.46	41.16	49
8570	1-1/2" pipe size		74	.216		42	10.65	.50	53.15	62.50
8580	2" pipe size	▼	58	.276	▼	51.50	13.55	.64	65.69	78

22 11 Facility Water Distribution

22 11 13 – Facility Water Distribution Piping

22 11 13.64 Pipe, Stainless Steel	Crew	Daily Output	Labor-Hours	Unit	Material	2012 Bare Costs Labor	Equipment	Total	Total Incl O&P
8590	2-1/2" pipe size	Q-15	46	.348	L.F.	106	17.10	.80	123.90	144
8600	3" pipe size		41	.390		143	19.20	.90	163.10	187
8610	4" pipe size	↓	33	.485		224	24	1.12	249.12	283
8630	6" pipe size	Q-16	30	.800	↓	490	41	1.23	532.23	605
8640	Schedule 80, type 316									
8650	1/4" pipe size	Q-15	110	.145	L.F.	18.95	7.15	.34	26.44	32
8660	3/8" pipe size		109	.147		21.50	7.20	.34	29.04	35
8670	1/2" pipe size		106	.151		27.50	7.40	.35	35.25	42
8680	3/4" pipe size		96	.167		29.50	8.20	.39	38.09	45.50
8690	1" pipe size		87	.184		37.50	9.05	.42	46.97	55
8700	1-1/4" pipe size		81	.198		48.50	9.70	.46	58.66	68.50
8710	1-1/2" pipe size		74	.216		51	10.65	.50	62.15	73
8720	2" pipe size		58	.276		62.50	13.55	.64	76.69	89.50
8730	2-1/2" pipe size		46	.348		168	17.10	.80	185.90	212
8740	3" pipe size		41	.390		196	19.20	.90	216.10	245
8760	4" pipe size	↓	33	.485		272	24	1.12	297.12	335
8770	6" pipe size	Q-16	30	.800	↓	735	41	1.23	777.23	870
9100	Threading pipe labor, sst, one end, schedules 40 & 80									
9110	1/4" through 3/4" pipe size	1 Plum	61.50	.130	Ea.		7.10		7.10	10.70
9120	1" through 2" pipe size		55.90	.143			7.80		7.80	11.80
9130	2-1/2" pipe size		41.50	.193			10.55		10.55	15.85
9140	3" pipe size	↓	38.50	.208			11.35		11.35	17.10
9150	3-1/2" pipe size	Q-1	68.40	.234			11.50		11.50	17.35
9160	4" pipe size		73	.219			10.75		10.75	16.25
9170	5" pipe size		40.70	.393			19.30		19.30	29
9180	6" pipe size		35.40	.452			22		22	33.50
9190	8" pipe size		22.30	.717			35.50		35.50	53
9200	10" pipe size		16.10	.994			49		49	73.50
9210	12" pipe size	↓	12.30	1.301	↓		64		64	96.50
9250	Welding labor per joint for stainless steel									
9260	Schedule 5 and 10									
9270	1/4" pipe size	Q-15	36	.444	Ea.		22	1.03	23.03	34
9280	3/8" pipe size		35	.457			22.50	1.06	23.56	35
9290	1/2" pipe size		35	.457			22.50	1.06	23.56	35
9300	3/4" pipe size		28	.571			28	1.32	29.32	44
9310	1" pipe size		25	.640			31.50	1.48	32.98	49
9320	1-1/4" pipe size		22	.727			36	1.68	37.68	56
9330	1-1/2" pipe size		21	.762			37.50	1.76	39.26	58.50
9340	2" pipe size		18	.889			43.50	2.05	45.55	68.50
9350	2-1/2" pipe size		12	1.333			65.50	3.08	68.58	102
9360	3" pipe size		9.73	1.644			81	3.80	84.80	126
9370	4" pipe size		7.37	2.171			107	5	112	167
9380	5" pipe size		6.15	2.602			128	6	134	200
9390	6" pipe size		5.71	2.802			138	6.45	144.45	215
9400	8" pipe size		3.69	4.336			213	10	223	330
9410	10" pipe size		2.91	5.498			270	12.70	282.70	425
9420	12" pipe size	↓	2.31	6.926	↓		340	16	356	535
9500	Schedule 40									
9510	1/4" pipe size	Q-15	28	.571	Ea.		28	1.32	29.32	44
9520	3/8" pipe size		27	.593			29	1.37	30.37	45.50
9530	1/2" pipe size		25.40	.630			31	1.46	32.46	48
9540	3/4" pipe size		22.22	.720			35.50	1.66	37.16	55.50
9550	1" pipe size	↓	20.25	.790			39	1.83	40.83	60.50

187

22 11 13.64 Pipe, Stainless Steel

		Crew	Daily Output	Labor-Hours	Unit	Material	Labor	Equipment	Total	Total Incl O&P
							2012 Bare Costs			
9560	1-1/4" pipe size	Q-15	18.82	.850	Ea.		42	1.96	43.96	65
9570	1-1/2" pipe size		17.78	.900			44	2.08	46.08	69
9580	2" pipe size		15.09	1.060			52	2.45	54.45	81
9590	2-1/2" pipe size		7.96	2.010			99	4.64	103.64	154
9600	3" pipe size		6.43	2.488			122	5.75	127.75	190
9610	4" pipe size		4.88	3.279			161	7.55	168.55	251
9620	5" pipe size		4.26	3.756			185	8.70	193.70	288
9630	6" pipe size		3.77	4.244			209	9.80	218.80	325
9640	8" pipe size		2.44	6.557			320	15.15	335.15	500
9650	10" pipe size		1.92	8.333			410	19.25	429.25	640
9660	12" pipe size	↓	1.52	10.526	↓		515	24.50	539.50	805
9750	Schedule 80									
9760	1/4" pipe size	Q-15	21.55	.742	Ea.	36.50	1.72		38.22	57
9770	3/8" pipe size		20.75	.771		38	1.78		39.78	59
9780	1/2" pipe size		19.54	.819		40.50	1.89		42.39	62.50
9790	3/4" pipe size		17.09	.936		46	2.16		48.16	72
9800	1" pipe size		15.58	1.027		50.50	2.37		52.87	78.50
9810	1-1/4" pipe size		14.48	1.105		54.50	2.55		57.05	85
9820	1-1/2" pipe size		13.68	1.170		57.50	2.70		60.20	89.50
9830	2" pipe size		11.61	1.378		67.50	3.18		70.68	106
9840	2-1/2" pipe size		6.12	2.614		129	6.05		135.05	201
9850	3" pipe size		4.94	3.239		159	7.50		166.50	248
9860	4" pipe size		3.75	4.267		210	9.85		219.85	325
9870	5" pipe size		3.27	4.893		240	11.30		251.30	375
9880	6" pipe size		2.90	5.517		271	12.75		283.75	425
9890	8" pipe size		1.87	8.556		420	19.75		439.75	655
9900	10" pipe size		1.48	10.811		530	25		555	830
9910	12" pipe size		1.17	13.675		670	31.50		701.50	1,050
9920	Schedule 160, 1/2" pipe size		17	.941		46.50	2.17		48.67	72.50
9930	3/4" pipe size		14.81	1.080		53	2.50		55.50	82.50
9940	1" pipe size		13.50	1.185		58.50	2.74		61.24	91
9950	1-1/4" pipe size		12.55	1.275		62.50	2.95		65.45	97.50
9960	1-1/2" pipe size		11.85	1.350		66.50	3.12		69.62	103
9970	2" pipe size		10	1.600		78.50	3.70		82.20	123
9980	3" pipe size		4.28	3.738		184	8.65		192.65	287
9990	4" pipe size	↓	3.25	4.923	↓	242	11.35		253.35	380

22 11 13.66 Pipe Fittings, Stainless Steel

		Crew	Daily Output	Labor-Hours	Unit	Material	Labor	Equipment	Total	Total Incl O&P
0010	**PIPE FITTINGS, STAINLESS STEEL**									
0100	Butt weld joint, schedule 5, type 304									
0120	90° Elbow, long									
0140	1/2"	Q-15	17.50	.914	Ea.	19.80	45	2.11	66.91	92.50
0150	3/4"		14	1.143		19.80	56	2.64	78.44	109
0160	1"		12.50	1.280		21	63	2.96	86.96	121
0170	1-1/4"		11	1.455		28.50	71.50	3.36	103.36	143
0180	1-1/2"		10.50	1.524		24	75	3.52	102.52	143
0190	2"		9	1.778		28.50	87.50	4.11	120.11	168
0200	2-1/2"		6	2.667		66	131	6.15	203.15	277
0210	3"		4.86	3.292		72.50	162	7.60	242.10	330
0220	3-1/2"		4.27	3.747		182	184	8.65	374.65	490
0230	4"		3.69	4.336		99	213	10	322	440
0240	5"	↓	3.08	5.195		385	255	12	652	825
0250	6"	Q-16	4.29	5.594	↓	297	285	8.60	590.60	765

22 11 13.66 Pipe Fittings, Stainless Steel		Crew	Daily Output	Labor-Hours	Unit	Material	2012 Bare Costs Labor	Equipment	Total	Total Incl O&P
0260	8″	Q-16	2.76	8.696	Ea.	625	445	13.40	1,083.40	1,375
0270	10″		2.18	11.009		970	560	16.95	1,546.95	1,950
0280	12″		1.73	13.873		1,375	705	21.50	2,101.50	2,625
0320	For schedule 5, type 316, add					30%				
0600	45° Elbow, long									
0620	1/2″	Q-15	17.50	.914	Ea.	19.80	45	2.11	66.91	92.50
0630	3/4″		14	1.143		19.80	56	2.64	78.44	109
0640	1″		12.50	1.280		21	63	2.96	86.96	121
0650	1-1/4″		11	1.455		28.50	71.50	3.36	103.36	143
0660	1-1/2″		10.50	1.524		24	75	3.52	102.52	143
0670	2″		9	1.778		28.50	87.50	4.11	120.11	168
0680	2-1/2″		6	2.667		66	131	6.15	203.15	277
0690	3″		4.86	3.292		72.50	162	7.60	242.10	330
0700	3-1/2″		4.27	3.747		182	184	8.65	374.65	490
0710	4″		3.69	4.336		83.50	213	10	306.50	425
0720	5″		3.08	5.195		310	255	12	577	740
0730	6″	Q-16	4.29	5.594		209	285	8.60	502.60	670
0740	8″		2.76	8.696		440	445	13.40	898.40	1,175
0750	10″		2.18	11.009		770	560	16.95	1,346.95	1,700
0760	12″		1.73	13.873		965	705	21.50	1,691.50	2,150
0800	For schedule 5, type 316, add					25%				
1100	Tee, straight									
1130	1/2″	Q-15	11.66	1.372	Ea.	59.50	67.50	3.17	130.17	171
1140	3/4″		9.33	1.715		59.50	84.50	3.96	147.96	197
1150	1″		8.33	1.921		62.50	94.50	4.44	161.44	216
1160	1-1/4″		7.33	2.183		50.50	107	5.05	162.55	223
1170	1-1/2″		7	2.286		49.50	112	5.30	166.80	229
1180	2″		6	2.667		51.50	131	6.15	188.65	262
1190	2-1/2″		4	4		124	197	9.25	330.25	445
1200	3″		3.24	4.938		198	243	11.40	452.40	595
1210	3-1/2″		2.85	5.614		260	276	12.95	548.95	715
1220	4″		2.46	6.504		141	320	15	476	650
1230	5″		2	8		445	395	18.50	858.50	1,100
1240	6″	Q-16	2.85	8.421		350	430	12.95	792.95	1,050
1250	8″		1.84	13.043		750	665	20	1,435	1,850
1260	10″		1.45	16.552		1,200	845	25.50	2,070.50	2,625
1270	12″		1.15	20.870		1,675	1,075	32	2,782	3,475
1320	For schedule 5, type 316, add					25%				
2000	Butt weld joint, schedule 10, type 304									
2020	90° elbow, long									
2040	1/2″	Q-15	17	.941	Ea.	14.85	46.50	2.17	63.52	88.50
2050	3/4″		14	1.143		16.35	56	2.64	74.99	105
2060	1″		12.50	1.280		14.25	63	2.96	80.21	114
2070	1-1/4″		11	1.455		21.50	71.50	3.36	96.36	135
2080	1-1/2″		10.50	1.524		16.50	75	3.52	95.02	135
2090	2″		9	1.778		19.50	87.50	4.11	111.11	158
2100	2-1/2″		6	2.667		49.50	131	6.15	186.65	259
2110	3″		4.86	3.292		46	162	7.60	215.60	305
2120	3-1/2″		4.27	3.747		136	184	8.65	328.65	440
2130	4″		3.69	4.336		70.50	213	10	293.50	410
2140	5″		3.08	5.195		289	255	12	556	720
2150	6″	Q-16	4.29	5.594		203	285	8.60	496.60	660
2160	8″		2.76	8.696		430	445	13.40	888.40	1,150

22 11 13.66 Pipe Fittings, Stainless Steel		Crew	Daily Output	Labor-Hours	Unit	Material	2012 Bare Costs		Total	Total Incl O&P
							Labor	Equipment		
2170	10"	Q-16	2.18	11.009	Ea.	665	560	16.95	1,241.95	1,600
2180	12"	↓	1.73	13.873	↓	940	705	21.50	1,666.50	2,125
2500	45° elbow, long									
2520	1/2"	Q-15	17.50	.914	Ea.	14.85	45	2.11	61.96	86.50
2530	3/4"		14	1.143		14.85	56	2.64	73.49	104
2540	1"		12.50	1.280		14.25	63	2.96	80.21	114
2550	1-1/4"		11	1.455		21.50	71.50	3.36	96.36	135
2560	1-1/2"		10.50	1.524		16.50	75	3.52	95.02	135
2570	2"		9	1.778		19.50	87.50	4.11	111.11	158
2580	2-1/2"		6	2.667		49.50	131	6.15	186.65	259
2590	3"		4.86	3.292		37	162	7.60	206.60	293
2600	3-1/2"		4.27	3.747		136	184	8.65	328.65	440
2610	4"		3.69	4.336		57	213	10	280	395
2620	5"	↓	3.08	5.195		231	255	12	498	650
2630	6"	Q-16	4.29	5.594		143	285	8.60	436.60	595
2640	8"		2.76	8.696		300	445	13.40	758.40	1,025
2650	10"		2.18	11.009		525	560	16.95	1,101.95	1,450
2660	12"	↓	1.73	13.873	↓	655	705	21.50	1,381.50	1,825
2670	Reducer, concentric									
2674	1" x 3/4"	Q-15	13.25	1.208	Ea.	29.50	59.50	2.79	91.79	125
2676	2" x 1-1/2"	"	9.75	1.641		24	80.50	3.79	108.29	153
2678	6" x 4"	Q-16	4.91	4.888	↓	72	249	7.55	328.55	460
2680	Caps									
2682	1"	Q-15	25	.640	Ea.	30	31.50	1.48	62.98	82
2684	1-1/2"		21	.762		36	37.50	1.76	75.26	98
2685	2"		18	.889		34	43.50	2.05	79.55	105
2686	4"	↓	7.38	2.168		54	107	5	166	226
2687	6"	Q-16	8.58	2.797	↓	86.50	143	4.31	233.81	315
3000	Tee, straight									
3030	1/2"	Q-15	11.66	1.372	Ea.	44.50	67.50	3.17	115.17	154
3040	3/4"		9.33	1.715		44.50	84.50	3.96	132.96	180
3050	1"		8.33	1.921		43	94.50	4.44	141.94	194
3060	1-1/4"		7.33	2.183		57.50	107	5.05	169.55	231
3070	1-1/2"		7	2.286		34	112	5.30	151.30	212
3080	2"		6	2.667		35.50	131	6.15	172.65	244
3090	2-1/2"		4	4		93	197	9.25	299.25	410
3100	3"		3.24	4.938		73.50	243	11.40	327.90	460
3110	3-1/2"		2.85	5.614		108	276	12.95	396.95	550
3120	4"		2.46	6.504		96	320	15	431	605
3130	5"	↓	2	8		335	395	18.50	748.50	985
3140	6"	Q-16	2.85	8.421		240	430	12.95	682.95	925
3150	8"		1.84	13.043		510	665	20	1,195	1,575
3151	10"		1.45	16.552		825	845	25.50	1,695.50	2,225
3152	12"	↓	1.15	20.870		1,150	1,075	32	2,257	2,875
3154	For schedule 10, type 316, add				↓	25%				
3281	Butt weld joint, schedule 40, type 304									
3284	90° Elbow, long, 1/2"	Q-15	12.70	1.260	Ea.	17.35	62	2.91	82.26	116
3288	3/4"		11.10	1.441		17.35	71	3.33	91.68	130
3289	1"		10.13	1.579		18.15	77.50	3.65	99.30	141
3290	1-1/4"		9.40	1.702		24	83.50	3.93	111.43	157
3300	1-1/2"		8.89	1.800		19	88.50	4.16	111.66	159
3310	2"		7.55	2.119		27	104	4.90	135.90	192
3320	2-1/2"	↓	3.98	4.020	↓	52	198	9.30	259.30	365

22 11 Facility Water Distribution

22 11 13 – Facility Water Distribution Piping

22 11 13.66 Pipe Fittings, Stainless Steel		Crew	Daily Output	Labor-Hours	Unit	Material	2012 Bare Costs Labor	Equipment	Total	Total Incl O&P
3330	3"	Q-15	3.21	4.984	Ea.	67	245	11.50	323.50	455
3340	3-1/2"		2.83	5.654		248	278	13.05	539.05	705
3350	4"		2.44	6.557		116	320	15.15	451.15	630
3360	5"	↓	2.13	7.512		390	370	17.35	777.35	1,000
3370	6"	Q-16	2.83	8.481		340	430	13.05	783.05	1,025
3380	8"		1.83	13.115		615	670	20	1,305	1,700
3390	10"		1.44	16.667		1,300	850	25.50	2,175.50	2,725
3400	12"	↓	1.14	21.053	↓	1,650	1,075	32.50	2,757.50	3,475
3410	For schedule 40, type 316, add					25%				
3460	45° Elbow, long, 1/2"	Q-15	12.70	1.260	Ea.	17.35	62	2.91	82.26	116
3470	3/4"		11.10	1.441		17.35	71	3.33	91.68	130
3480	1"		10.13	1.579		18.15	77.50	3.65	99.30	141
3490	1-1/4"		9.40	1.702		24	83.50	3.93	111.43	157
3500	1-1/2"		8.89	1.800		19	88.50	4.16	111.66	159
3510	2"		7.55	2.119		27	104	4.90	135.90	192
3520	2-1/2"		3.98	4.020		52	198	9.30	259.30	365
3530	3"		3.21	4.984		53	245	11.50	309.50	440
3540	3-1/2"		2.83	5.654		248	278	13.05	539.05	705
3550	4"		2.44	6.557		82.50	320	15.15	417.65	595
3560	5"	↓	2.13	7.512		272	370	17.35	659.35	875
3570	6"	Q-16	2.83	8.481		239	430	13.05	682.05	925
3580	8"		1.83	13.115		430	670	20	1,120	1,500
3590	10"		1.44	16.667		910	850	25.50	1,785.50	2,300
3600	12"	↓	1.14	21.053	↓	1,150	1,075	32.50	2,257.50	2,925
3610	For schedule 40, type 316, add					25%				
3660	Tee, straight 1/2"	Q-15	8.46	1.891	Ea.	44.50	93	4.37	141.87	194
3670	3/4"		7.40	2.162		44.50	106	4.99	155.49	215
3680	1"		6.74	2.374		47	117	5.50	169.50	234
3690	1-1/4"		6.27	2.552		110	125	5.90	240.90	315
3700	1-1/2"		5.92	2.703		50.50	133	6.25	189.75	262
3710	2"		5.03	3.181		75	156	7.35	238.35	325
3720	2-1/2"		2.65	6.038		95	297	13.95	405.95	570
3730	3"		2.14	7.477		95.50	365	17.25	477.75	680
3740	3-1/2"		1.88	8.511		181	420	19.65	620.65	850
3750	4"		1.62	9.877		181	485	23	689	955
3760	5"	↓	1.42	11.268		415	555	26	996	1,325
3770	6"	Q-16	1.88	12.766		370	650	19.65	1,039.65	1,400
3780	8"		1.22	19.672		735	1,000	30.50	1,765.50	2,350
3790	10"		.96	25		1,425	1,275	38.50	2,738.50	3,550
3800	12"	↓	.76	31.579	↓	1,900	1,600	48.50	3,548.50	4,575
3810	For schedule 40, type 316, add					25%				
3820	Tee, reducing on outlet, 3/4" x 1/2"	Q-15	7.73	2.070	Ea.	59.50	102	4.78	166.28	224
3822	1" x 1/2"		7.24	2.210		64.50	109	5.10	178.60	241
3824	1" x 3/4"		6.96	2.299		59.50	113	5.30	177.80	241
3826	1-1/4" x 1"		6.43	2.488		145	122	5.75	272.75	350
3828	1-1/2" x 1/2"		6.58	2.432		87.50	120	5.60	213.10	282
3830	1-1/2" x 3/4"		6.35	2.520		81.50	124	5.80	211.30	283
3832	1-1/2" x 1"		6.18	2.589		62.50	127	6	195.50	268
3834	2" x 1"		5.50	2.909		112	143	6.70	261.70	345
3836	2" x 1-1/2"		5.30	3.019		94	148	6.95	248.95	335
3838	2-1/2" x 2"		3.15	5.079		142	250	11.75	403.75	545
3840	3" x 1-1/2"		2.72	5.882		144	289	13.60	446.60	610
3842	3" x 2"	↓	2.65	6.038	↓	120	297	13.95	430.95	595

22 11 13 – Facility Water Distribution Piping

22 11 13.66 Pipe Fittings, Stainless Steel	Crew	Daily Output	Labor-Hours	Unit	Material	2012 Bare Costs Labor	Equipment	Total	Total Incl O&P
3844	4" x 2"	Q-15	2.10	7.619	Ea.	299	375	17.60	691.60	915
3846	4" x 3"		1.77	9.040		217	445	21	683	930
3848	5" x 4"	↓	1.48	10.811		500	530	25	1,055	1,375
3850	6" x 3"	Q-16	2.19	10.959		555	560	16.90	1,131.90	1,475
3852	6" x 4"		2.04	11.765		480	600	18.10	1,098.10	1,450
3854	8" x 4"		1.46	16.438		1,125	840	25.50	1,990.50	2,525
3856	10" x 8"		.69	34.783		1,875	1,775	53.50	3,703.50	4,800
3858	12" x 10"	↓	.55	43.636		2,525	2,225	67	4,817	6,200
3950	Reducer, concentric, 3/4" x 1/2"	Q-15	11.85	1.350		33	66.50	3.12	102.62	140
3952	1" x 3/4"		10.60	1.509		34.50	74	3.49	111.99	154
3954	1-1/4" x 3/4"		10.19	1.570		85	77	3.63	165.63	213
3956	1-1/4" x 1"		9.76	1.639		43	80.50	3.79	127.29	173
3958	1-1/2" x 3/4"		9.88	1.619		72	79.50	3.74	155.24	203
3960	1-1/2" x 1"		9.47	1.690		58	83	3.90	144.90	193
3962	2" x 1"		8.65	1.850		25	91	4.27	120.27	169
3964	2" x 1-1/2"		8.16	1.961		29	96.50	4.53	130.03	182
3966	2-1/2" x 1"		5.71	2.802		125	138	6.45	269.45	350
3968	2-1/2" x 2"		5.21	3.071		63.50	151	7.10	221.60	305
3970	3" x 1"		4.88	3.279		86	161	7.55	254.55	345
3972	3" x 1-1/2"		4.72	3.390		43.50	167	7.85	218.35	310
3974	3" x 2"		4.51	3.548		41.50	174	8.20	223.70	320
3976	4" x 2"		3.69	4.336		58.50	213	10	281.50	395
3978	4" x 3"		2.77	5.776		43.50	284	13.35	340.85	495
3980	5" x 3"		2.56	6.250		261	305	14.45	580.45	770
3982	5" x 4"	↓	2.27	7.048		210	345	16.30	571.30	775
3984	6" x 3"	Q-16	3.57	6.723		134	345	10.35	489.35	675
3986	6" x 4"		3.19	7.524		111	385	11.60	507.60	715
3988	8" x 4"		2.44	9.836		315	500	15.15	830.15	1,125
3990	8" x 6"		2.22	10.811		236	550	16.65	802.65	1,100
3992	10" x 6"		1.91	12.565		440	640	19.35	1,099.35	1,475
3994	10" x 8"		1.61	14.907		365	760	23	1,148	1,575
3995	12" x 6"		1.63	14.724		745	750	22.50	1,517.50	1,975
3996	12" x 8"		1.41	17.021		675	870	26	1,571	2,075
3997	12" x 10"	↓	1.27	18.898	↓	435	965	29	1,429	1,950
4000	Socket weld joint, 3000 lb., type 304									
4100	90° Elbow									
4140	1/4"	Q-15	13.47	1.188	Ea.	44	58.50	2.74	105.24	140
4150	3/8"		12.97	1.234		57	60.50	2.85	120.35	158
4160	1/2"		12.21	1.310		62.50	64.50	3.03	130.03	169
4170	3/4"		10.68	1.498		72	73.50	3.46	148.96	194
4180	1"		9.74	1.643		108	80.50	3.79	192.29	245
4190	1-1/4"		9.05	1.768		189	87	4.08	280.08	345
4200	1-1/2"		8.55	1.871		229	92	4.32	325.32	395
4210	2"	↓	7.26	2.204	↓	370	108	5.10	483.10	575
4300	45° Elbow									
4340	1/4"	Q-15	13.47	1.188	Ea.	83	58.50	2.74	144.24	182
4350	3/8"		12.97	1.234		83	60.50	2.85	146.35	186
4360	1/2"		12.21	1.310		83	64.50	3.03	150.53	191
4370	3/4"		10.68	1.498		94	73.50	3.46	170.96	218
4380	1"		9.74	1.643		136	80.50	3.79	220.29	276
4390	1-1/4"		9.05	1.768		224	87	4.08	315.08	380
4400	1-1/2"		8.55	1.871		225	92	4.32	321.32	390
4410	2"	↓	7.26	2.204		410	108	5.10	523.10	620

22 11 13.66 Pipe Fittings, Stainless Steel	Crew	Daily Output	Labor-Hours	Unit	Material	2012 Bare Costs Labor	Equipment	Total	Total Incl O&P
4500 Tee									
4540 1/4"	Q-15	8.97	1.784	Ea.	58	87.50	4.12	149.62	200
4550 3/8"		8.64	1.852		69	91	4.28	164.28	218
4560 1/2"		8.13	1.968		85	96.50	4.55	186.05	245
4570 3/4"		7.12	2.247		98	110	5.20	213.20	281
4580 1"		6.48	2.469		132	121	5.70	258.70	335
4590 1-1/4"		6.03	2.653		234	130	6.15	370.15	460
4600 1-1/2"		5.69	2.812		335	138	6.50	479.50	585
4610 2"		4.83	3.313		510	163	7.65	680.65	815
5000 Socket weld joint, 3000 lb., type 316									
5100 90° Elbow									
5140 1/4"	Q-15	13.47	1.188	Ea.	54	58.50	2.74	115.24	150
5150 3/8"		12.97	1.234		63	60.50	2.85	126.35	164
5160 1/2"		12.21	1.310		76	64.50	3.03	143.53	184
5170 3/4"		10.68	1.498		100	73.50	3.46	176.96	225
5180 1"		9.74	1.643		142	80.50	3.79	226.29	282
5190 1-1/4"		9.05	1.768		253	87	4.08	344.08	415
5200 1-1/2"		8.55	1.871		286	92	4.32	382.32	460
5210 2"		7.26	2.204		485	108	5.10	598.10	705
5300 45° Elbow									
5340 1/4"	Q-15	13.47	1.188	Ea.	104	58.50	2.74	165.24	205
5350 3/8"		12.97	1.234		104	60.50	2.85	167.35	209
5360 1/2"		12.21	1.310		104	64.50	3.03	171.53	214
5370 3/4"		10.68	1.498		121	73.50	3.46	197.96	248
5380 1"		9.74	1.643		182	80.50	3.79	266.29	325
5390 1-1/4"		9.05	1.768		258	87	4.08	349.08	420
5400 1-1/2"		8.55	1.871		292	92	4.32	388.32	465
5410 2"		7.26	2.204		435	108	5.10	548.10	650
5500 Tee									
5540 1/4"	Q-15	8.97	1.784	Ea.	73	87.50	4.12	164.62	217
5550 3/8"		8.64	1.852		89.50	91	4.28	184.78	240
5560 1/2"		8.13	1.968		99.50	96.50	4.55	200.55	260
5570 3/4"		7.12	2.247		123	110	5.20	238.20	310
5580 1"		6.48	2.469		188	121	5.70	314.70	395
5590 1-1/4"		6.03	2.653		299	130	6.15	435.15	535
5600 1-1/2"		5.69	2.812		420	138	6.50	564.50	680
5610 2"		4.83	3.313		670	163	7.65	840.65	995
5700 For socket weld joint, 6000 lb., type 304 and 316, add					100%				
6000 Threaded companion flange									
6010 Stainless steel, 150 lb., type 304									
6020 1/2" diam.	1 Plum	30	.267	Ea.	45	14.55		59.55	71.50
6030 3/4" diam.		28	.286		50	15.60		65.60	78.50
6040 1" diam.		27	.296		55	16.20		71.20	85
6050 1-1/4" diam.	Q-1	44	.364		71	17.85		88.85	105
6060 1-1/2" diam.		40	.400		71	19.65		90.65	108
6070 2" diam.		36	.444		93	22		115	135
6080 2-1/2" diam.		28	.571		130	28		158	186
6090 3" diam.		20	.800		136	39.50		175.50	210
6110 4" diam.		12	1.333		186	65.50		251.50	305
6130 6" diam.	Q-2	14	1.714		335	87.50		422.50	495
6140 8" diam.	"	12	2		645	102		747	865
6150 For type 316 add					40%				
6260 Weld flanges, stainless steel, type 304									

22 11 13.66 Pipe Fittings, Stainless Steel		Crew	Daily Output	Labor-Hours	Unit	Material	2012 Bare Costs Labor	Equipment	Total	Total Incl O&P
6270	Slip on, 150 lb. (welded, front and back)									
6280	1/2" diam.	Q-15	12.70	1.260	Ea.	40	62	2.91	104.91	141
6290	3/4" diam.		11.11	1.440		41	71	3.33	115.33	156
6300	1" diam.		10.13	1.579		45	77.50	3.65	126.15	171
6310	1-1/4" diam.		9.41	1.700		61	83.50	3.93	148.43	197
6320	1-1/2" diam.		8.89	1.800		61	88.50	4.16	153.66	205
6330	2" diam.		7.55	2.119		79	104	4.90	187.90	249
6340	2-1/2" diam.		3.98	4.020		111	198	9.30	318.30	430
6350	3" diam.		3.21	4.984		119	245	11.50	375.50	515
6370	4" diam.	▼	2.44	6.557		162	320	15.15	497.15	680
6390	6" diam.	Q-16	1.89	12.698		247	645	19.55	911.55	1,275
6400	8" diam.	"	1.22	19.672	▼	465	1,000	30.50	1,495.50	2,050
6410	For type 316, add					40%				
6530	Weld neck 150 lb.									
6540	1/2" diam.	Q-15	25.40	.630	Ea.	16.15	31	1.46	48.61	66
6550	3/4" diam.		22.22	.720		20	35.50	1.66	57.16	77.50
6560	1" diam.		20.25	.790		24.50	39	1.83	65.33	87
6570	1-1/4" diam.		18.82	.850		38	42	1.96	81.96	107
6580	1-1/2" diam.		17.78	.900		31.50	44	2.08	77.58	103
6590	2" diam.		15.09	1.060		30	52	2.45	84.45	114
6600	2-1/2" diam.		7.96	2.010		51.50	99	4.64	155.14	211
6610	3" diam.		6.43	2.488		50.50	122	5.75	178.25	246
6630	4" diam.		4.88	3.279		84	161	7.55	252.55	345
6640	5" diam.	▼	4.26	3.756		104	185	8.70	297.70	400
6650	6" diam.	Q-16	5.66	4.240		105	216	6.55	327.55	450
6652	8" diam.		3.65	6.575		210	335	10.15	555.15	745
6654	10" diam.		2.88	8.333		296	425	12.85	733.85	980
6656	12" diam.	▼	2.28	10.526	▼	460	535	16.20	1,011.20	1,325
6670	For type 316 add					23%				
7000	Threaded joint, 150 lb., type 304									
7030	90° elbow									
7040	1/8"	1 Plum	13	.615	Ea.	25.50	33.50		59	78.50
7050	1/4"		13	.615		25.50	33.50		59	78.50
7070	3/8"		13	.615		28	33.50		61.50	81
7080	1/2"		12	.667		25	36.50		61.50	82.50
7090	3/4"		11	.727		29.50	39.50		69	92.50
7100	1"	▼	10	.800		39.50	43.50		83	110
7110	1-1/4"	Q-1	17	.941		61	46.50		107.50	137
7120	1-1/2"		16	1		70.50	49		119.50	152
7130	2"		14	1.143		102	56		158	197
7140	2-1/2"		11	1.455		255	71.50		326.50	390
7150	3"	▼	8	2		370	98.50		468.50	560
7160	4"	Q-2	11	2.182	▼	630	111		741	865
7180	45° elbow									
7190	1/8"	1 Plum	13	.615	Ea.	37	33.50		70.50	91.50
7200	1/4"		13	.615		37	33.50		70.50	91.50
7210	3/8"		13	.615		35	33.50		68.50	89
7220	1/2"		12	.667		35.50	36.50		72	94
7230	3/4"		11	.727		38.50	39.50		78	103
7240	1"	▼	10	.800		44.50	43.50		88	115
7250	1-1/4"	Q-1	17	.941		60.50	46.50		107	137
7260	1-1/2"		16	1		78	49		127	160
7270	2"	▼	14	1.143	▼	111	56		167	207

22 11 Facility Water Distribution

22 11 13 – Facility Water Distribution Piping

22 11 13.66 Pipe Fittings, Stainless Steel		Crew	Daily Output	Labor-Hours	Unit	Material	2012 Bare Costs Labor	Equipment	Total	Total Incl O&P
7280	2-1/2"	Q-1	11	1.455	Ea.	360	71.50		431.50	505
7290	3"		8	2		530	98.50		628.50	730
7300	4"	Q-2	11	2.182		955	111		1,066	1,225
7320	Tee, straight									
7330	1/8"	1 Plum	9	.889	Ea.	39	48.50		87.50	116
7340	1/4"		9	.889		39	48.50		87.50	116
7350	3/8"		9	.889		39.50	48.50		88	116
7360	1/2"		8	1		37.50	54.50		92	124
7370	3/4"		7	1.143		40	62.50		102.50	138
7380	1"		6.50	1.231		49.50	67		116.50	156
7390	1-1/4"	Q-1	11	1.455		83	71.50		154.50	200
7400	1-1/2"		10	1.600		106	78.50		184.50	236
7410	2"		9	1.778		132	87.50		219.50	277
7420	2-1/2"		7	2.286		365	112		477	575
7430	3"		5	3.200		560	157		717	850
7440	4"	Q-2	7	3.429		1,375	175		1,550	1,800
7460	Coupling, straight									
7470	1/8"	1 Plum	19	.421	Ea.	10.25	23		33.25	46
7480	1/4"		19	.421		12.10	23		35.10	48
7490	3/8"		19	.421		14.50	23		37.50	50.50
7500	1/2"		19	.421		19.30	23		42.30	55.50
7510	3/4"		18	.444		25.50	24.50		50	65
7520	1"		15	.533		41.50	29		70.50	89.50
7530	1-1/4"	Q-1	26	.615		66.50	30.50		97	119
7540	1-1/2"		24	.667		74.50	33		107.50	132
7550	2"		21	.762		123	37.50		160.50	193
7560	2-1/2"		18	.889		287	43.50		330.50	380
7570	3"		14	1.143		390	56		446	515
7580	4"	Q-2	16	1.500		550	76.50		626.50	720
7600	Reducer, concentric, 1/2"	1 Plum	12	.667		20.50	36.50		57	78
7610	3/4"		11	.727		26.50	39.50		66	89.50
7612	1"		10	.800		44.50	43.50		88	115
7614	1-1/4"	Q-1	17	.941		94.50	46.50		141	174
7616	1-1/2"		16	1		103	49		152	187
7618	2"		14	1.143		161	56		217	262
7620	2-1/2"		11	1.455		400	71.50		471.50	550
7622	3"		8	2		445	98.50		543.50	640
7624	4"	Q-2	11	2.182		735	111		846	980
7710	Union									
7720	1/8"	1 Plum	12	.667	Ea.	47.50	36.50		84	108
7730	1/4"		12	.667		47.50	36.50		84	108
7740	3/8"		12	.667		55.50	36.50		92	116
7750	1/2"		11	.727		69.50	39.50		109	137
7760	3/4"		10	.800		96	43.50		139.50	171
7770	1"		9	.889		138	48.50		186.50	225
7780	1-1/4"	Q-1	16	1		320	49		369	430
7790	1-1/2"		15	1.067		350	52.50		402.50	465
7800	2"		13	1.231		440	60.50		500.50	575
7810	2-1/2"		10	1.600		830	78.50		908.50	1,025
7820	3"		7	2.286		1,100	112		1,212	1,400
7830	4"	Q-2	10	2.400		1,525	122		1,647	1,850
7838	Caps									
7840	1/2"	1 Plum	24	.333	Ea.	12.95	18.20		31.15	42

22 11 13.66 Pipe Fittings, Stainless Steel		Crew	Daily Output	Labor-Hours	Unit	Material	2012 Bare Costs Labor	Equipment	Total	Total Incl O&P
7841	3/4"	1 Plum	22	.364	Ea.	18.80	19.85		38.65	50.50
7842	1"	↓	20	.400		30	22		52	66
7843	1-1/2"	Q-1	32	.500		71.50	24.50		96	116
7844	2"	"	28	.571		90.50	28		118.50	142
7845	4"	Q-2	22	1.091		355	55.50		410.50	475
7850	For 150 lb., type 316, add				↓	25%				
8750	Threaded joint, 2000 lb., type 304									
8770	90° Elbow									
8780	1/8"	1 Plum	13	.615	Ea.	32.50	33.50		66	86
8790	1/4"		13	.615		32.50	33.50		66	86
8800	3/8"		13	.615		40	33.50		73.50	94.50
8810	1/2"		12	.667		54.50	36.50		91	115
8820	3/4"		11	.727		63	39.50		102.50	130
8830	1"	↓	10	.800		83.50	43.50		127	158
8840	1-1/4"	Q-1	17	.941		136	46.50		182.50	220
8850	1-1/2"		16	1		218	49		267	315
8860	2"	↓	14	1.143	↓	305	56		361	420
8880	45° Elbow									
8890	1/8"	1 Plum	13	.615	Ea.	67.50	33.50		101	125
8900	1/4"		13	.615		67.50	33.50		101	125
8910	3/8"		13	.615		84.50	33.50		118	144
8920	1/2"		12	.667		84.50	36.50		121	148
8930	3/4"		11	.727		93	39.50		132.50	162
8940	1"	↓	10	.800		111	43.50		154.50	188
8950	1-1/4"	Q-1	17	.941		194	46.50		240.50	283
8960	1-1/2"		16	1		260	49		309	360
8970	2"	↓	14	1.143	↓	299	56		355	415
8990	Tee, straight									
9000	1/8"	1 Plum	9	.889	Ea.	42	48.50		90.50	119
9010	1/4"		9	.889		42	48.50		90.50	119
9020	3/8"		9	.889		54	48.50		102.50	132
9030	1/2"		8	1		69	54.50		123.50	159
9040	3/4"		7	1.143		78.50	62.50		141	180
9050	1"	↓	6.50	1.231		108	67		175	220
9060	1-1/4"	Q-1	11	1.455		182	71.50		253.50	310
9070	1-1/2"		10	1.600		305	78.50		383.50	455
9080	2"	↓	9	1.778	↓	420	87.50		507.50	595
9100	For couplings and unions use 3000 lb., type 304									
9120	2000 lb., type 316									
9130	90° Elbow									
9140	1/8"	1 Plum	13	.615	Ea.	40.50	33.50		74	95
9150	1/4"		13	.615		40.50	33.50		74	95
9160	3/8"		13	.615		47	33.50		80.50	103
9170	1/2"		12	.667		61	36.50		97.50	123
9180	3/4"		11	.727		75	39.50		114.50	143
9190	1"	↓	10	.800		111	43.50		154.50	189
9200	1-1/4"	Q-1	17	.941		202	46.50		248.50	292
9210	1-1/2"		16	1		233	49		282	330
9220	2"	↓	14	1.143	↓	395	56		451	520
9240	45° Elbow									
9250	1/8"	1 Plum	13	.615	Ea.	85.50	33.50		119	145
9260	1/4"	↓	13	.615		85.50	33.50		119	145
9270	3/8"	↓	13	.615	↓	85.50	33.50		119	145

22 11 13.66 Pipe Fittings, Stainless Steel		Crew	Daily Output	Labor-Hours	Unit	Material	2012 Bare Costs Labor	Equipment	Total	Total Incl O&P
9280	1/2"	1 Plum	12	.667	Ea.	85.50	36.50		122	149
9300	3/4"		11	.727		96.50	39.50		136	166
9310	1"	↓	10	.800		146	43.50		189.50	226
9320	1-1/4"	Q-1	17	.941		208	46.50		254.50	299
9330	1-1/2"		16	1		285	49		334	390
9340	2"	↓	14	1.143	↓	350	56		406	470
9360	Tee, straight									
9370	1/8"	1 Plum	9	.889	Ea.	51.50	48.50		100	130
9380	1/4"		9	.889		51.50	48.50		100	130
9390	3/8"		9	.889		63	48.50		111.50	142
9400	1/2"		8	1		78	54.50		132.50	169
9410	3/4"		7	1.143		96.50	62.50		159	200
9420	1"	↓	6.50	1.231		147	67		214	263
9430	1-1/4"	Q-1	11	1.455		239	71.50		310.50	370
9440	1-1/2"		10	1.600		345	78.50		423.50	495
9450	2"	↓	9	1.778	↓	545	87.50		632.50	730
9470	For couplings and unions use 3000 lb., type 316									
9490	3000 lb., type 304									
9510	Coupling									
9520	1/8"	1 Plum	19	.421	Ea.	12.80	23		35.80	48.50
9530	1/4"		19	.421		13.90	23		36.90	50
9540	3/8"		19	.421		16.20	23		39.20	52.50
9550	1/2"		19	.421		19.50	23		42.50	56
9560	3/4"		18	.444		26	24.50		50.50	65
9570	1"	↓	15	.533		44	29		73	92.50
9580	1-1/4"	Q-1	26	.615		107	30.50		137.50	163
9590	1-1/2"		24	.667		125	33		158	188
9600	2"	↓	21	.762	↓	165	37.50		202.50	238
9620	Union									
9630	1/8"	1 Plum	12	.667	Ea.	98	36.50		134.50	163
9640	1/4"		12	.667		98	36.50		134.50	163
9650	3/8"		12	.667		105	36.50		141.50	170
9660	1/2"		11	.727		105	39.50		144.50	175
9670	3/4"		10	.800		128	43.50		171.50	207
9680	1"	↓	9	.889		198	48.50		246.50	290
9690	1-1/4"	Q-1	16	1		350	49		399	460
9700	1-1/2"		15	1.067		410	52.50		462.50	535
9710	2"	↓	13	1.231	↓	550	60.50		610.50	695
9730	3000 lb., type 316									
9750	Coupling									
9770	1/8"	1 Plum	19	.421	Ea.	14.40	23		37.40	50.50
9780	1/4"		19	.421		16.25	23		39.25	52.50
9790	3/8"		19	.421		17.40	23		40.40	53.50
9800	1/2"		19	.421		24.50	23		47.50	61.50
9810	3/4"		18	.444		36.50	24.50		61	76.50
9820	1"	↓	15	.533		60.50	29		89.50	111
9830	1-1/4"	Q-1	26	.615		136	30.50		166.50	196
9840	1-1/2"		24	.667		159	33		192	225
9850	2"	↓	21	.762	↓	219	37.50		256.50	298
9870	Union									
9880	1/8"	1 Plum	12	.667	Ea.	108	36.50		144.50	173
9890	1/4"		12	.667		108	36.50		144.50	173
9900	3/8"	↓	12	.667	↓	125	36.50		161.50	192

22 11 Facility Water Distribution

22 11 13 – Facility Water Distribution Piping

22 11 13.66 Pipe Fittings, Stainless Steel

		Crew	Daily Output	Labor-Hours	Unit	Material	2012 Bare Costs Labor	Equipment	Total	Total Incl O&P
9910	1/2"	1 Plum	11	.727	Ea.	125	39.50		164.50	197
9920	3/4"		10	.800		163	43.50		206.50	245
9930	1"	↓	9	.889		257	48.50		305.50	355
9940	1-1/4"	Q-1	16	1		450	49		499	570
9950	1-1/2"	↓	15	1.067		555	52.50		607.50	690
9960	2"	↓	13	1.231	↓	705	60.50		765.50	865

22 11 13.74 Pipe, Plastic

		Crew	Daily Output	Labor-Hours	Unit	Material	2012 Bare Costs Labor	Equipment	Total	Total Incl O&P
0010	**PIPE, PLASTIC**									
0020	Fiberglass reinforced, couplings 10' O.C., clevis hanger assy's, 3 per 10'									
0080	General service									
0120	2" diameter	Q-1	59	.271	L.F.	7.80	13.35		21.15	28.50
0140	3" diameter		52	.308		11.25	15.10		26.35	35.50
0150	4" diameter		48	.333		15.25	16.40		31.65	41.50
0160	6" diameter	↓	39	.410		27.50	20		47.50	61
0170	8" diameter	Q-2	49	.490		44.50	25		69.50	86.50
0180	10" diameter		41	.585		66	30		96	118
0190	12" diameter	↓	36	.667	↓	85.50	34		119.50	146
0600	PVC, high impact/pressure, cplgs. 10' O.C., clevis hanger assy's, 3 per 10'									
1020	Schedule 80									
1070	1/2" diameter	1 Plum	50	.160	L.F.	4.58	8.75		13.33	18.25
1080	3/4" diameter		47	.170		5.55	9.30		14.85	20
1090	1" diameter		43	.186		7.10	10.15		17.25	23
1100	1-1/4" diameter		39	.205		9.20	11.20		20.40	27
1110	1-1/2" diameter	↓	34	.235		10.65	12.85		23.50	31
1120	2" diameter	Q-1	55	.291		13.80	14.30		28.10	36.50
1140	3" diameter		50	.320		28	15.75		43.75	54
1150	4" diameter		46	.348		39.50	17.10		56.60	69.50
1170	6" diameter	↓	38	.421	↓	88.50	20.50		109	129
1730	To delete coupling & hangers, subtract									
1740	1/4" diam. to 1/2" diam.					62%	80%			
1750	3/4" diam. to 1-1/4" diam.					58%	73%			
1760	1-1/2" diam. to 6" diam.					40%	57%			
1770	8" diam. to 12" diam.					34%	50%			
1800	PVC, couplings 10' O.C., clevis hanger assemblies, 3 per 10'									
1820	Schedule 40									
1860	1/2" diameter	1 Plum	54	.148	L.F.	2.83	8.10		10.93	15.30
1870	3/4" diameter		51	.157		3.17	8.55		11.72	16.40
1880	1" diameter		46	.174		3.59	9.50		13.09	18.25
1890	1-1/4" diameter		42	.190		4.33	10.40		14.73	20.50
1900	1-1/2" diameter	↓	36	.222		4.59	12.15		16.74	23.50
1910	2" diameter	Q-1	59	.271		5.75	13.35		19.10	26.50
1920	2-1/2" diameter		56	.286		8.40	14.05		22.45	30.50
1930	3" diameter		53	.302		10.70	14.85		25.55	34.50
1940	4" diameter		48	.333		14.35	16.40		30.75	40.50
1950	5" diameter		43	.372		20	18.30		38.30	49.50
1960	6" diameter	↓	39	.410		26	20		46	59.50
1970	8" diameter	Q-2	48	.500		38.50	25.50		64	81
1980	10" diameter		43	.558		76	28.50		104.50	127
1990	12" diameter		42	.571		92	29		121	145
2000	14" diameter		31	.774		146	39.50		185.50	220
2010	16" diameter	↓	23	1.043	↓	208	53		261	310
2340	To delete coupling & hangers, subtract									

22 11 13 – Facility Water Distribution Piping

22 11 13.74 Pipe, Plastic		Crew	Daily Output	Labor-Hours	Unit	Material	2012 Bare Costs Labor	Equipment	Total	Total Incl O&P
2360	1/2" diam. to 1-1/4" diam.					65%	74%			
2370	1-1/2" diam. to 6" diam.					44%	57%			
2380	8" diam. to 12" diam.					41%	53%			
2390	14" diam. to 16" diam.					48%	45%			
2420	Schedule 80									
2440	1/4" diameter	1 Plum	58	.138	L.F.	2.28	7.55		9.83	13.85
2450	3/8" diameter		55	.145		2.28	7.95		10.23	14.50
2460	1/2" diameter		50	.160		2.97	8.75		11.72	16.45
2470	3/4" diameter		47	.170		3.36	9.30		12.66	17.70
2480	1" diameter		43	.186		3.89	10.15		14.04	19.60
2490	1-1/4" diameter		39	.205		4.78	11.20		15.98	22
2500	1-1/2" diameter		34	.235		5.10	12.85		17.95	25
2510	2" diameter	Q-1	55	.291		6.15	14.30		20.45	28.50
2520	2-1/2" diameter		52	.308		8.40	15.10		23.50	32.50
2530	3" diameter		50	.320		12.40	15.75		28.15	37
2540	4" diameter		46	.348		16.80	17.10		33.90	44.50
2550	5" diameter		42	.381		24.50	18.70		43.20	55
2560	6" diameter		38	.421		37	20.50		57.50	72
2570	8" diameter	Q-2	47	.511		47	26		73	91.50
2580	10" diameter		42	.571		90	29		119	143
2590	12" diameter		38	.632		112	32		144	173
2830	To delete coupling & hangers, subtract									
2840	1/4" diam. to 1/2" diam.					66%	80%			
2850	3/4" diam. to 1-1/4" diam.					61%	73%			
2860	1-1/2" diam. to 6" diam.					41%	57%			
2870	8" diam. to 12" diam.					31%	50%			
2900	Schedule 120									
2910	1/2" diameter	1 Plum	50	.160	L.F.	3.14	8.75		11.89	16.65
2950	3/4" diameter		47	.170		3.57	9.30		12.87	17.90
2960	1" diameter		43	.186		4.17	10.15		14.32	19.90
2970	1-1/4" diameter		39	.205		5.20	11.20		16.40	22.50
2980	1-1/2" diameter		33	.242		5.75	13.25		19	26.50
2990	2" diameter	Q-1	54	.296		7.10	14.55		21.65	30
3000	2-1/2" diameter		52	.308		11.60	15.10		26.70	36
3010	3" diameter		49	.327		14.25	16.05		30.30	39.50
3020	4" diameter		45	.356		21	17.50		38.50	49.50
3030	6" diameter		37	.432		39.50	21.50		61	75.50
3240	To delete coupling & hangers, subtract									
3250	1/2" diam. to 1-1/4" diam.					52%	74%			
3260	1-1/2" diam. to 4" diam.					30%	57%			
3270	6" diam.					17%	50%			
3300	PVC, pressure, couplings 10' O.C., clevis hanger assy's, 3 per 10'									
3310	SDR 26, 160 psi									
3350	1-1/4" diameter	1 Plum	42	.190	L.F.	3.47	10.40		13.87	19.50
3360	1-1/2" diameter	"	36	.222		3.67	12.15		15.82	22.50
3370	2" diameter	Q-1	59	.271		4.26	13.35		17.61	24.50
3380	2-1/2" diameter		56	.286		6.35	14.05		20.40	28
3390	3" diameter		53	.302		8.55	14.85		23.40	32
3400	4" diameter		48	.333		11.70	16.40		28.10	37.50
3420	6" diameter		39	.410		23	20		43	56
3430	8" diameter	Q-2	48	.500		35.50	25.50		61	77.50
3660	To delete coupling & clevis hanger assy's, subtract									
3670	1-1/4" diam.					63%	68%			

22 11 13.74 Pipe, Plastic		Crew	Daily Output	Labor-Hours	Unit	Material	2012 Bare Costs Labor	Equipment	Total	Total Incl O&P
3680	1-1/2" diam. to 4" diam.					48%	57%			
3690	6" diam. to 8" diam.					60%	54%			
3720	SDR 21, 200 psi, 1/2" diameter	1 Plum	54	.148	L.F.	2.53	8.10		10.63	15
3740	3/4" diameter		51	.157		2.79	8.55		11.34	15.95
3750	1" diameter		46	.174		2.97	9.50		12.47	17.55
3760	1-1/4" diameter		42	.190		3.58	10.40		13.98	19.65
3770	1-1/2" diameter		36	.222		3.81	12.15		15.96	22.50
3780	2" diameter	Q-1	59	.271		4.49	13.35		17.84	25
3790	2-1/2" diameter		56	.286		8.10	14.05		22.15	30
3800	3" diameter		53	.302		9	14.85		23.85	32.50
3810	4" diameter		48	.333		13.95	16.40		30.35	40
3830	6" diameter		39	.410		25	20		45	58
3840	8" diameter	Q-2	48	.500		38.50	25.50		64	80.50
4000	To delete coupling & hangers, subtract									
4010	1/2" diam. to 3/4" diam.					71%	77%			
4020	1" diam. to 1-1/4" diam.					63%	70%			
4030	1-1/2" diam. to 6" diam.					44%	57%			
4040	8" diam.					46%	54%			
4100	DWV type, schedule 40, couplings 10' O.C., clevis hanger assy's, 3 per 10'									
4210	ABS, schedule 40, foam core type									
4212	Plain end black									
4214	1-1/2" diameter	1 Plum	39	.205	L.F.	2.97	11.20		14.17	20
4216	2" diameter	Q-1	62	.258		3.44	12.70		16.14	23
4218	3" diameter		56	.286		6.15	14.05		20.20	28
4220	4" diameter		51	.314		8.55	15.40		23.95	33
4222	6" diameter		42	.381		17.90	18.70		36.60	47.50
4240	To delete coupling & hangers, subtract									
4244	1-1/2" diam. to 6" diam.					43%	48%			
4400	PVC									
4410	1-1/4" diameter	1 Plum	42	.190	L.F.	3.21	10.40		13.61	19.25
4420	1-1/2" diameter	"	36	.222		3.01	12.15		15.16	21.50
4460	2" diameter	Q-1	59	.271		3.46	13.35		16.81	24
4470	3" diameter		53	.302		6.15	14.85		21	29.50
4480	4" diameter		48	.333		8.30	16.40		24.70	33.50
4490	6" diameter		39	.410		15.65	20		35.65	47.50
4500	8" diameter	Q-2	48	.500		24.50	25.50		50	65.50
4510	To delete coupling & hangers, subtract									
4520	1-1/4" diam. to 1-1/2" diam.					48%	60%			
4530	2" diam. to 8" diam.					42%	54%			
4550	PVC, schedule 40, foam core type									
4552	Plain end, white									
4554	1-1/2" diameter	1 Plum	39	.205	L.F.	2.75	11.20		13.95	19.90
4556	2" diameter	Q-1	62	.258		3.14	12.70		15.84	22.50
4558	3" diameter		56	.286		5.55	14.05		19.60	27
4560	4" diameter		51	.314		7.40	15.40		22.80	31.50
4562	6" diameter		42	.381		13.80	18.70		32.50	43
4564	8" diameter	Q-2	51	.471		21.50	24		45.50	59.50
4568	10" diameter		48	.500		26	25.50		51.50	67
4570	12" diameter		46	.522		31	26.50		57.50	74
4580	To delete coupling & hangers, subtract									
4582	1-1/2" dia to 2" dia					58%	54%			
4584	3" dia to 12" dia					46%	42%			
4800	PVC, clear pipe, cplgs. 10' O.C., clevis hanger assy's 3 per 10', Sched. 40									

22 11 13.74 Pipe, Plastic	Crew	Daily Output	Labor-Hours	Unit	Material	2012 Bare Costs Labor	Equipment	Total	Total Incl O&P
4840	1/4" diameter	1 Plum	59	.136	L.F.	2.81	7.40		10.21	14.25
4850	3/8" diameter		56	.143		3.13	7.80		10.93	15.20
4860	1/2" diameter		54	.148		3.75	8.10		11.85	16.30
4870	3/4" diameter		51	.157		4.40	8.55		12.95	17.75
4880	1" diameter		46	.174		5.70	9.50		15.20	20.50
4890	1-1/4" diameter		42	.190		7.05	10.40		17.45	23.50
4900	1-1/2" diameter		36	.222		8.10	12.15		20.25	27
4910	2" diameter	Q-1	59	.271		10.35	13.35		23.70	31.50
4920	2-1/2" diameter		56	.286		16.15	14.05		30.20	39
4930	3" diameter		53	.302		20.50	14.85		35.35	45
4940	3-1/2" diameter		50	.320		29	15.75		44.75	55.50
4950	4" diameter		48	.333		30	16.40		46.40	57.50
5250	To delete coupling & hangers, subtract									
5260	1/4" diam. to 3/8" diam.					60%	81%			
5270	1/2" diam. to 3/4" diam.					41%	77%			
5280	1" diam. to 1-1/2" diam.					26%	67%			
5290	2" diam. to 4" diam.					16%	58%			
5300	CPVC, socket joint, couplings 10' O.C., clevis hanger assemblies, 3 per 10'									
5302	Schedule 40									
5304	1/2" diameter	1 Plum	54	.148	L.F.	3.58	8.10		11.68	16.15
5305	3/4" diameter		51	.157		4.17	8.55		12.72	17.50
5306	1" diameter		46	.174		5.25	9.50		14.75	20
5307	1-1/4" diameter		42	.190		6.60	10.40		17	23
5308	1-1/2" diameter		36	.222		7.60	12.15		19.75	26.50
5309	2" diameter	Q-1	59	.271		9.35	13.35		22.70	30.50
5310	2-1/2" diameter		56	.286		15.65	14.05		29.70	38
5311	3" diameter		53	.302		18.85	14.85		33.70	43
5312	4" diameter		48	.333		26	16.40		42.40	53
5314	6" diameter		43	.372		49	18.30		67.30	81.50
5318	To delete coupling & hangers, subtract									
5319	1/2" diam. to 3/4" diam.					37%	77%			
5320	1" diam. to 1-1/4" diam.					27%	70%			
5321	1-1/2" diam. to 3" diam.					21%	57%			
5322	4" diam. to 6" diam.					16%	57%			
5324	Schedule 80									
5325	1/2" diameter	1 Plum	50	.160	L.F.	3.79	8.75		12.54	17.35
5326	3/4" diameter		47	.170		4.50	9.30		13.80	18.95
5327	1" diameter		43	.186		5.75	10.15		15.90	21.50
5328	1-1/4" diameter		39	.205		7.35	11.20		18.55	25
5329	1-1/2" diameter		34	.235		8.55	12.85		21.40	29
5330	2" diameter	Q-1	55	.291		10.90	14.30		25.20	33.50
5331	2-1/2" diameter		52	.308		17.65	15.10		32.75	42.50
5332	3" diameter		50	.320		20.50	15.75		36.25	46
5333	4" diameter		46	.348		28.50	17.10		45.60	57.50
5334	6" diameter		38	.421		56.50	20.50		77	93
5335	8" diameter	Q-2	47	.511		110	26		136	161
5339	To delete couplings & hangers, subtract									
5340	1/2" diam. to 3/4" diam.					44%	77%			
5341	1" diam. to 1-1/4" diam.					32%	71%			
5342	1-1/2" diam. to 4" diam.					25%	58%			
5343	6" diam. to 8" diam.					20%	53%			
5360	CPVC, threaded, couplings 10' O.C., clevis hanger assemblies, 3 per 10'									
5380	Schedule 40									

22 11 13.74 Pipe, Plastic	Crew	Daily Output	Labor-Hours	Unit	Material	2012 Bare Costs Labor	Equipment	Total	Total Incl O&P
5460 1/2" diameter	1 Plum	54	.148	L.F.	4.34	8.10		12.44	16.95
5470 3/4" diameter		51	.157		5.50	8.55		14.05	18.95
5480 1" diameter		46	.174		6.60	9.50		16.10	21.50
5490 1-1/4" diameter		42	.190		7.65	10.40		18.05	24
5500 1-1/2" diameter	▼	36	.222		8.50	12.15		20.65	27.50
5510 2" diameter	Q-1	59	.271		10.45	13.35		23.80	31.50
5520 2-1/2" diameter		56	.286		16.80	14.05		30.85	39.50
5530 3" diameter		53	.302		20.50	14.85		35.35	45
5540 4" diameter		48	.333		32.50	16.40		48.90	60.50
5550 6" diameter	▼	43	.372	▼	52	18.30		70.30	85
5730 To delete coupling & hangers, subtract									
5740 1/2" diam. to 3/4" diam.					37%	77%			
5750 1" diam. to 1-1/4" diam.					27%	70%			
5760 1-1/2" diam. to 3" diam.					21%	57%			
5770 4" diam. to 6" diam.					16%	57%			
5800 Schedule 80									
5860 1/2" diameter	1 Plum	50	.160	L.F.	4.55	8.75		13.30	18.20
5870 3/4" diameter		47	.170		5.80	9.30		15.10	20.50
5880 1" diameter		43	.186		7.10	10.15		17.25	23
5890 1-1/4" diameter		39	.205		8.40	11.20		19.60	26
5900 1-1/2" diameter	▼	34	.235		9.45	12.85		22.30	30
5910 2" diameter	Q-1	55	.291		12	14.30		26.30	34.50
5920 2-1/2" diameter		52	.308		18.80	15.10		33.90	43.50
5930 3" diameter		50	.320		22	15.75		37.75	48
5940 4" diameter		46	.348		35.50	17.10		52.60	65
5950 6" diameter	▼	38	.421		60	20.50		80.50	96.50
5960 8" diameter	Q-2	47	.511	▼	110	26		136	160
6060 To delete couplings & hangers, subtract									
6070 1/2" diam. to 3/4" diam.					44%	77%			
6080 1" diam. to 1-1/4" diam.					32%	71%			
6090 1-1/2" diam. to 4" diam.					25%	58%			
6100 6" diam. to 8" diam.					20%	53%			
6240 CTS, 1/2" diameter	1 Plum	54	.148	L.F.	2.32	8.10		10.42	14.75
6250 3/4" diameter		51	.157		2.90	8.55		11.45	16.10
6260 1" diameter		46	.174		4.25	9.50		13.75	18.95
6270 1 1/4"		42	.190		5.50	10.40		15.90	22
6280 1 1/2" diameter	▼	36	.222		6.75	12.15		18.90	26
6290 2" diameter	Q-1	59	.271	▼	10.45	13.35		23.80	31.50
6370 To delete coupling & hangers, subtract									
6380 1/2" diam.					51%	79%			
6390 3/4" diam.					40%	76%			
6392 1" thru 2" diam.					72%	68%			
7280 PEX, flexible, no couplings or hangers									
7282 Note: For labor costs add 25% to the couplings and fittings labor total.									
7285 For fittings see section 23 83 16.10 7000									
7300 Non-barrier type, hot/cold tubing rolls									
7310 1/4" diameter x 100'				L.F.	.46			.46	.51
7350 3/8" diameter x 100'					.51			.51	.56
7360 1/2" diameter x 100'					.57			.57	.63
7370 1/2" diameter x 500'					.57			.57	.63
7380 1/2" diameter x 1000'					.57			.57	.63
7400 3/4" diameter x 100'					1.05			1.05	1.16
7410 3/4" diameter x 500'				▼	1.05			1.05	1.16

22 11 13 – Facility Water Distribution Piping

22 11 13.74 Pipe, Plastic	Crew	Daily Output	Labor-Hours	Unit	Material	2012 Bare Costs Labor	Equipment	Total	Total Incl O&P
7420	3/4" diameter x 1000'				L.F.	1.05			1.05	1.16
7460	1" diameter x 100'					1.80			1.80	1.98
7470	1" diameter x 300'					1.80			1.80	1.98
7480	1" diameter x 500'					1.78			1.78	1.96
7500	1-1/4" diameter x 100'					3.04			3.04	3.34
7510	1-1/4" diameter x 300'					3.04			3.04	3.34
7540	1-1/2" diameter x 100'					4.15			4.15	4.57
7550	1-1/2" diameter x 300'				↓	4.15			4.15	4.57
7596	Most sizes available in red or blue									
7700	Non-barrier type, hot/cold tubing straight lengths									
7710	1/2" diameter x 20'				L.F.	.57			.57	.63
7750	3/4" diameter x 20'					1.05			1.05	1.16
7760	1" diameter x 20'					1.80			1.80	1.98
7770	1-1/4" diameter x 20'					3.04			3.04	3.34
7780	1-1/2" diameter x 20'				↓	4.15			4.15	4.57
7796	Most sizes available in red or blue									
9000	Polypropylene pipe									
9002	For fusion weld fittings and accessories see line 22 11 13.76 9400									
9004	Note: sizes 1/2" thru 4" use socket fusion									
9005	Sizes 6" thru 10" use butt fusion									
9010	SDR 7.4, (domestic hot water piping)									
9011	Enhanced to minimize thermal expansion and high temperature life									
9016	13' lengths, size is ID, includes joints 13' O.C. and hangers 3 per 10'									
9020	3/8" diameter	1 Plum	53	.151	L.F.	2.86	8.25		11.11	15.60
9022	1/2" diameter		52	.154		3.25	8.40		11.65	16.20
9024	3/4" diameter		50	.160		3.74	8.75		12.49	17.30
9026	1" diameter		45	.178		4.70	9.70		14.40	19.80
9028	1-1/4" diameter		40	.200		6.60	10.90		17.50	23.50
9030	1-1/2" diameter	↓	35	.229		9.05	12.50		21.55	29
9032	2" diameter	Q-1	58	.276		12.55	13.55		26.10	34.50
9034	2-1/2" diameter		55	.291		17.05	14.30		31.35	40.50
9036	3" diameter		52	.308		23	15.10		38.10	48.50
9038	3-1/2" diameter		49	.327		33	16.05		49.05	60
9040	4" diameter		46	.348		37	17.10		54.10	67
9042	6" diameter	↓	39	.410		44	20		64	79
9044	8" diameter	Q-2	48	.500		67.50	25.50		93	113
9046	10" diameter	"	43	.558	↓	108	28.50		136.50	162
9050	To delete joint & hangers, subtract									
9052	3/8" diam. to 1" diam.					45%	65%			
9054	1-1/4" diam. to 4" diam.					15%	45%			
9056	6" diam. to 10" diam.					5%	24%			
9060	SDR 11, (domestic cold water piping)									
9062	13' lengths, size is ID, includes joints 13' O.C. and hangers 3 per 10'									
9064	1/2" diameter	1 Plum	57	.140	L.F.	2.95	7.65		10.60	14.80
9066	3/4" diameter		54	.148		3.25	8.10		11.35	15.75
9068	1" diameter		49	.163		3.82	8.90		12.72	17.65
9070	1-1/4" diameter		45	.178		5.30	9.70		15	20.50
9072	1-1/2" diameter	↓	40	.200		6.80	10.90		17.70	24
9074	2" diameter	Q-1	62	.258		9.35	12.70		22.05	29.50
9076	2-1/2" diameter		59	.271		12.15	13.35		25.50	33.50
9078	3" diameter		56	.286		16.75	14.05		30.80	39.50
9080	3-1/2" diameter		53	.302		24	14.85		38.85	48.50
9082	4" diameter	↓	50	.320		26.50	15.75		42.25	53

22 11 Facility Water Distribution

22 11 13 - Facility Water Distribution Piping

22 11 13.74 Pipe, Plastic

		Crew	Daily Output	Labor-Hours	Unit	Material	2012 Bare Costs Labor	Equipment	Total	Total Incl O&P
9084	6" diameter	Q-1	47	.340	L.F.	30.50	16.75		47.25	58.50
9086	8" diameter	Q-2	51	.471		50	24		74	91
9088	10" diameter	"	46	.522	↓	76.50	26.50		103	124
9090	To delete joint & hangers, subtract									
9092	3/8" diam. to 1" diam.					45%	65%			
9094	1-1/4" diam. to 4" diam.					15%	45%			
9096	6" diam. to 10" diam.					5%	24%			

22 11 13.76 Pipe Fittings, Plastic

		Crew	Daily Output	Labor-Hours	Unit	Material	2012 Bare Costs Labor	Equipment	Total	Total Incl O&P
0010	**PIPE FITTINGS, PLASTIC**									
0030	Epoxy resin, fiberglass reinforced, general service									
0090	Elbow, 90°, 2"	Q-1	33.10	.483	Ea.	102	24		126	148
0100	3"		20.80	.769		113	38		151	181
0110	4"		16.50	.970		115	47.50		162.50	198
0120	6"	↓	10.10	1.584		225	78		303	365
0130	8"	Q-2	9.30	2.581		415	132		547	655
0140	10"		8.50	2.824		520	144		664	790
0150	12"	↓	7.60	3.158	↓	750	161		911	1,075
0160	45° Elbow, same as 90°									
0170	Elbow, 90°, flanged									
0172	2"	Q-1	23	.696	Ea.	146	34		180	213
0173	3"		16	1		167	49		216	258
0174	4"		13	1.231		218	60.50		278.50	330
0176	6"	↓	8	2		395	98.50		493.50	585
0177	8"	Q-2	9	2.667		715	136		851	995
0178	10"		7	3.429		980	175		1,155	1,350
0179	12"	↓	5	4.800	↓	1,325	245		1,570	1,825
0186	Elbow, 45°, flanged									
0188	2"	Q-1	23	.696	Ea.	146	34		180	213
0189	3"		16	1		167	49		216	258
0190	4"		13	1.231		218	60.50		278.50	330
0192	6"	↓	8	2		395	98.50		493.50	585
0193	8"	Q-2	9	2.667		680	136		816	950
0194	10"		7	3.429		865	175		1,040	1,225
0195	12"	↓	5	4.800		1,100	245		1,345	1,600
0290	Tee, 2"	Q-1	20	.800		54	39.50		93.50	119
0300	3"		13.90	1.151		64.50	56.50		121	157
0310	4"		11	1.455		89.50	71.50		161	206
0320	6"	↓	6.70	2.388		225	117		342	425
0330	8"	Q-2	6.20	3.871		1,600	197		1,797	2,050
0340	10"		5.70	4.211		1,800	215		2,015	2,325
0350	12"	↓	5.10	4.706	↓	2,200	240		2,440	2,775
0352	Tee, flanged									
0354	2"	Q-1	17	.941	Ea.	198	46.50		244.50	288
0355	3"		10	1.600		262	78.50		340.50	405
0356	4"		8	2		293	98.50		391.50	475
0358	6"	↓	5	3.200		505	157		662	790
0359	8"	Q-2	6	4		955	204		1,159	1,350
0360	10"		5	4.800		1,400	245		1,645	1,900
0361	12"	↓	4	6	↓	1,925	305		2,230	2,550
0365	Wye, flanged									
0367	2"	Q-1	17	.941	Ea.	390	46.50		436.50	500
0368	3"		10	1.600	↓	540	78.50		618.50	715

22 11 13.76 Pipe Fittings, Plastic		Crew	Daily Output	Labor-Hours	Unit	Material	2012 Bare Costs Labor	Equipment	Total	Total Incl O&P
0369	4"	Q-1	8	2	Ea.	720	98.50		818.50	940
0371	6"		5	3.200		1,000	157		1,157	1,325
0372	8"	Q-2	6	4		1,650	204		1,854	2,125
0373	10"		5	4.800		2,575	245		2,820	3,225
0374	12"		4	6		3,750	305		4,055	4,575
0380	Couplings									
0410	2"	Q-1	33.10	.483	Ea.	17	24		41	54.50
0420	3"		20.80	.769		18.20	38		56.20	77
0430	4"		16.50	.970		24.50	47.50		72	98.50
0440	6"		10.10	1.584		58	78		136	181
0450	8"	Q-2	9.30	2.581		99	132		231	305
0460	10"		8.50	2.824		146	144		290	375
0470	12"		7.60	3.158		194	161		355	455
0473	High corrosion resistant couplings, add					30%				
0474	Reducer, concentric, flanged									
0475	2" x 1-1/2"	Q-1	30	.533	Ea.	380	26		406	460
0476	3" x 2"		24	.667		415	33		448	505
0477	4" x 3"		19	.842		465	41.50		506.50	575
0479	6" x 4"		15	1.067		465	52.50		517.50	590
0480	8" x 6"	Q-2	16	1.500		765	76.50		841.50	955
0481	10" x 8"		13	1.846		710	94		804	920
0482	12" x 10"		11	2.182		1,100	111		1,211	1,375
0486	Adapter, bell x male or female									
0488	2"	Q-1	28	.571	Ea.	18.90	28		46.90	63.50
0489	3"		20	.800		28	39.50		67.50	90
0491	4"		17	.941		37.50	46.50		84	112
0492	6"		12	1.333		79	65.50		144.50	186
0493	8"	Q-2	15	1.600		114	81.50		195.50	249
0494	10"	"	11	2.182		165	111		276	350
0528	Flange									
0532	2"	Q-1	46	.348	Ea.	28	17.10		45.10	56.50
0533	3"		32	.500		34	24.50		58.50	74.50
0534	4"		26	.615		45	30.50		75.50	95
0536	6"		16	1		85	49		134	168
0537	8"	Q-2	18	1.333		130	68		198	245
0538	10"		14	1.714		184	87.50		271.50	335
0539	12"		10	2.400		232	122		354	440
2100	PVC schedule 80, socket joint									
2110	90° elbow, 1/2"	1 Plum	30.30	.264	Ea.	2.36	14.40		16.76	24
2130	3/4"		26	.308		3.01	16.80		19.81	29
2140	1"		22.70	.352		4.84	19.25		24.09	34.50
2150	1-1/4"		20.20	.396		6.50	21.50		28	39.50
2160	1-1/2"		18.20	.440		6.95	24		30.95	43.50
2170	2"	Q-1	33.10	.483		8.40	24		32.40	45.50
2180	3"		20.80	.769		22	38		60	81.50
2190	4"		16.50	.970		33.50	47.50		81	109
2200	6"		10.10	1.584		95.50	78		173.50	222
2210	8"	Q-2	9.30	2.581		264	132		396	490
2250	45° elbow, 1/2"	1 Plum	30.30	.264		4.43	14.40		18.83	26.50
2270	3/4"		26	.308		6.75	16.80		23.55	33
2280	1"		22.70	.352		10.15	19.25		29.40	40
2290	1-1/4"		20.20	.396		12.95	21.50		34.45	46.50
2300	1-1/2"		18.20	.440		15.30	24		39.30	53

22 11 13.76 Pipe Fittings, Plastic		Crew	Daily Output	Labor-Hours	Unit	Material	2012 Bare Costs Labor	Equipment	Total	Total Incl O&P
2310	2"	Q-1	33.10	.483	Ea.	19.85	24		43.85	58
2320	3"		20.80	.769		50.50	38		88.50	113
2330	4"		16.50	.970		91	47.50		138.50	172
2340	6"		10.10	1.584		115	78		193	243
2350	8"	Q-2	9.30	2.581		249	132		381	470
2400	Tee, 1/2"	1 Plum	20.20	.396		6.65	21.50		28.15	40
2420	3/4"		17.30	.462		6.95	25.50		32.45	45.50
2430	1"		15.20	.526		8.70	28.50		37.20	53
2440	1-1/4"		13.50	.593		24	32.50		56.50	75.50
2450	1-1/2"		12.10	.661		24	36		60	81
2460	2"	Q-1	20	.800		30	39.50		69.50	92.50
2470	3"		13.90	1.151		40.50	56.50		97	130
2480	4"		11	1.455		47	71.50		118.50	160
2490	6"		6.70	2.388		161	117		278	355
2500	8"	Q-2	6.20	3.871		375	197		572	710
2510	Flange, socket, 150 lb., 1/2"	1 Plum	55.60	.144		12.90	7.85		20.75	26
2514	3/4"		47.60	.168		13.80	9.20		23	29
2518	1"		41.70	.192		15.35	10.50		25.85	32.50
2522	1-1/2"		33.30	.240		16.15	13.10		29.25	37.50
2526	2"	Q-1	60.60	.264		21.50	13		34.50	43
2530	4"		30.30	.528		46.50	26		72.50	90
2534	6"		18.50	.865		73	42.50		115.50	145
2538	8"	Q-2	17.10	1.404		131	71.50		202.50	252
2550	Coupling, 1/2"	1 Plum	30.30	.264		4.26	14.40		18.66	26
2570	3/4"		26	.308		5.75	16.80		22.55	32
2580	1"		22.70	.352		5.95	19.25		25.20	35.50
2590	1-1/4"		20.20	.396		9.05	21.50		30.55	42.50
2600	1-1/2"		18.20	.440		9.75	24		33.75	46.50
2610	2"	Q-1	33.10	.483		10.45	24		34.45	47.50
2620	3"		20.80	.769		29.50	38		67.50	89.50
2630	4"		16.50	.970		37	47.50		84.50	113
2640	6"		10.10	1.584		79.50	78		157.50	205
2650	8"	Q-2	9.30	2.581		108	132		240	315
2660	10"		8.50	2.824		370	144		514	625
2670	12"		7.60	3.158		430	161		591	715
2700	PVC (white), schedule 40, socket joints									
2760	90° elbow, 1/2"	1 Plum	33.30	.240	Ea.	.46	13.10		13.56	20.50
2770	3/4"		28.60	.280		.51	15.25		15.76	23.50
2780	1"		25	.320		.92	17.45		18.37	27.50
2790	1-1/4"		22.20	.360		1.63	19.70		21.33	31.50
2800	1-1/2"		20	.400		1.76	22		23.76	35
2810	2"	Q-1	36.40	.440		2.75	21.50		24.25	35.50
2820	2-1/2"		26.70	.599		8.60	29.50		38.10	54
2830	3"		22.90	.699		10	34.50		44.50	63
2840	4"		18.20	.879		17.90	43		60.90	84.50
2850	5"		12.10	1.322		46	65		111	149
2860	6"		11.10	1.441		57	71		128	170
2870	8"	Q-2	10.30	2.330		146	119		265	340
2980	45° elbow, 1/2"	1 Plum	33.30	.240		.76	13.10		13.86	20.50
2990	3/4"		28.60	.280		1.17	15.25		16.42	24.50
3000	1"		25	.320		1.41	17.45		18.86	28
3010	1-1/4"		22.20	.360		1.97	19.70		21.67	31.50
3020	1-1/2"		20	.400		2.47	22		24.47	35.50

22 11 13 – Facility Water Distribution Piping

22 11 13.76 Pipe Fittings, Plastic		Crew	Daily Output	Labor-Hours	Unit	Material	2012 Bare Costs Labor	Equipment	Total	Total Incl O&P
3030	2"	Q-1	36.40	.440	Ea.	3.21	21.50		24.71	36
3040	2-1/2"		26.70	.599		8.35	29.50		37.85	53.50
3050	3"		22.90	.699		13	34.50		47.50	66.50
3060	4"		18.20	.879		23.50	43		66.50	90.50
3070	5"		12.10	1.322		46	65		111	149
3080	6"		11.10	1.441		57.50	71		128.50	171
3090	8"	Q-2	10.30	2.330		138	119		257	330
3180	Tee, 1/2"	1 Plum	22.20	.360		.57	19.70		20.27	30
3190	3/4"		19	.421		.65	23		23.65	35
3200	1"		16.70	.479		1.22	26		27.22	41
3210	1-1/4"		14.80	.541		1.91	29.50		31.41	46.50
3220	1-1/2"		13.30	.602		2.33	33		35.33	52
3230	2"	Q-1	24.20	.661		3.38	32.50		35.88	52.50
3240	2-1/2"		17.80	.899		11.15	44		55.15	79
3250	3"		15.20	1.053		14.65	51.50		66.15	94
3260	4"		12.10	1.322		26.50	65		91.50	127
3270	5"		8.10	1.975		64	97		161	217
3280	6"		7.40	2.162		89.50	106		195.50	259
3290	8"	Q-2	6.80	3.529		207	180		387	500
3380	Coupling, 1/2"	1 Plum	33.30	.240		.30	13.10		13.40	20
3390	3/4"		28.60	.280		.41	15.25		15.66	23.50
3400	1"		25	.320		.73	17.45		18.18	27.50
3410	1-1/4"		22.20	.360		1.01	19.70		20.71	30.50
3420	1-1/2"		20	.400		1.07	22		23.07	34
3430	2"	Q-1	36.40	.440		1.64	21.50		23.14	34.50
3440	2-1/2"		26.70	.599		3.62	29.50		33.12	48.50
3450	3"		22.90	.699		5.65	34.50		40.15	58.50
3460	4"		18.20	.879		8.20	43		51.20	74
3470	5"		12.10	1.322		15	65		80	115
3480	6"		11.10	1.441		26	71		97	136
3490	8"	Q-2	10.30	2.330		48.50	119		167.50	233
3600	Cap, schedule 40, PVC socket 1/2"	1 Plum	60.60	.132		.41	7.20		7.61	11.30
3610	3/4"		51.90	.154		.48	8.40		8.88	13.25
3620	1"		45.50	.176		.76	9.60		10.36	15.35
3630	1-1/4"		40.40	.198		1.07	10.80		11.87	17.50
3640	1-1/2"		36.40	.220		1.17	12		13.17	19.40
3650	2"	Q-1	66.10	.242		1.41	11.90		13.31	19.50
3660	2-1/2"		48.50	.330		4.49	16.20		20.69	29.50
3670	3"		41.60	.385		4.91	18.90		23.81	34
3680	4"		33.10	.483		11.15	24		35.15	48.50
3690	6"		20.20	.792		27	39		66	88
3700	8"	Q-2	18.60	1.290		67.50	66		133.50	173
3710	Reducing insert, schedule 40, socket weld									
3712	3/4"	1 Plum	31.50	.254	Ea.	.48	13.85		14.33	21.50
3713	1"		27.50	.291		.87	15.90		16.77	25
3715	1-1/2"		22	.364		1.24	19.85		21.09	31.50
3716	2"	Q-1	40	.400		2.05	19.65		21.70	32
3717	4"		20	.800		10.85	39.50		50.35	71.50
3718	6"		12.20	1.311		27	64.50		91.50	127
3719	8"	Q-2	11.30	2.124		106	108		214	280
3730	Reducing insert, socket weld x female/male thread									
3732	1/2"	1 Plum	38.30	.209	Ea.	2.17	11.40		13.57	19.60
3733	3/4"		32.90	.243		1.34	13.30		14.64	21.50

22 11 13.76 Pipe Fittings, Plastic		Crew	Daily Output	Labor-Hours	Unit	Material	2012 Bare Costs Labor	Equipment	Total	Total Incl O&P
3734	1"	1 Plum	28.80	.278	Ea.	1.88	15.15		17.03	25
3736	1-1/2"	↓	23	.348		3.38	19		22.38	32
3737	2"	Q-1	41.90	.382		3.62	18.75		22.37	32.50
3738	4"	"	20.90	.766	↓	34.50	37.50		72	95
3742	Male adapter, socket weld x male thread									
3744	1/2"	1 Plum	38.30	.209	Ea.	.73	11.40		12.13	18
3745	3/4"		32.90	.243		.83	13.30		14.13	21
3746	1"		28.80	.278		1.43	15.15		16.58	24.50
3748	1-1/2"	↓	23	.348		2.36	19		21.36	31
3749	2"	Q-1	41.90	.382		2.90	18.75		21.65	31.50
3750	4"	"	20.90	.766	↓	9.70	37.50		47.20	67.50
3754	Female adapter, socket weld x female thread									
3756	1/2"	1 Plum	38.30	.209	Ea.	.51	11.40		11.91	17.75
3757	3/4"		32.90	.243		.65	13.30		13.95	20.50
3758	1"		28.80	.278		.76	15.15		15.91	24
3760	1-1/2"	↓	23	.348		1.34	19		20.34	30
3761	2"	Q-1	41.90	.382		1.80	18.75		20.55	30.50
3762	4"	"	20.90	.766	↓	10.15	37.50		47.65	68
3800	PVC, schedule 80, socket joints									
3810	Reducing insert									
3812	3/4"	1 Plum	28.60	.280	Ea.	1.37	15.25		16.62	24.50
3813	1"		25	.320		3.93	17.45		21.38	31
3815	1-1/2"	↓	20	.400		8.40	22		30.40	42.50
3816	2"	Q-1	36.40	.440		12	21.50		33.50	45.50
3817	4"		18.20	.879		45.50	43		88.50	116
3818	6"	↓	11.10	1.441		63.50	71		134.50	177
3819	8"	Q-2	10.20	2.353	↓	365	120		485	580
3830	Reducing insert, socket weld x female/male thread									
3832	1/2"	1 Plum	34.80	.230	Ea.	8.60	12.55		21.15	28.50
3833	3/4"		29.90	.268		5.25	14.60		19.85	28
3834	1"		26.10	.307		8.25	16.75		25	34
3836	1-1/2"	↓	20.90	.383		10.40	21		31.40	43
3837	2"	Q-1	38	.421		15.20	20.50		35.70	48
3838	4"	"	19	.842	↓	73.50	41.50		115	144
3844	Adapter, male socket x male thread									
3846	1/2"	1 Plum	34.80	.230	Ea.	3.32	12.55		15.87	22.50
3847	3/4"		29.90	.268		3.66	14.60		18.26	26
3848	1"		26.10	.307		6.35	16.75		23.10	32
3850	1-1/2"	↓	20.90	.383		10.65	21		31.65	43
3851	2"	Q-1	38	.421		15.40	20.50		35.90	48
3852	4"	"	19	.842	↓	34.50	41.50		76	101
3860	Adapter, female socket x female thread									
3862	1/2"	1 Plum	34.80	.230	Ea.	3.99	12.55		16.54	23.50
3863	3/4"		29.90	.268		5.95	14.60		20.55	28.50
3864	1"		26.10	.307		8.75	16.75		25.50	34.50
3866	1-1/2"	↓	20.90	.383		17.35	21		38.35	50.50
3867	2"	Q-1	38	.421		30.50	20.50		51	64.50
3868	4"	"	19	.842	↓	92.50	41.50		134	165
3872	Union, socket joints									
3874	1/2"	1 Plum	25.80	.310	Ea.	8.75	16.95		25.70	35
3875	3/4"		22.10	.362		11.10	19.75		30.85	42
3876	1"		19.30	.415		12.65	22.50		35.15	48
3878	1-1/2"	↓	15.50	.516	↓	28.50	28		56.50	74

22 11 Facility Water Distribution

22 11 13 – Facility Water Distribution Piping

22 11 13.76 Pipe Fittings, Plastic	Crew	Daily Output	Labor-Hours	Unit	Material	2012 Bare Costs Labor	Equipment	Total	Total Incl O&P
3879 2"	Q-1	28.10	.569	Ea.	38.50	28		66.50	84.50
3888 Cap									
3890 1/2"	1 Plum	54.50	.147	Ea.	4.17	8		12.17	16.70
3891 3/4"		46.70	.171		4.40	9.35		13.75	18.95
3892 1"		41	.195		7.80	10.65		18.45	24.50
3894 1-1/2"		32.80	.244		9.40	13.30		22.70	30.50
3895 2"	Q-1	59.50	.269		25	13.20		38.20	47.50
3896 4"		30	.533		75	26		101	122
3897 6"		18.20	.879		186	43		229	270
3898 8"	Q-2	16.70	1.437		239	73.50		312.50	375
4500 DWV, ABS, non pressure, socket joints									
4540 1/4 Bend, 1-1/4"	1 Plum	20.20	.396	Ea.	3.73	21.50		25.23	36.50
4560 1-1/2"	"	18.20	.440		2.84	24		26.84	39
4570 2"	Q-1	33.10	.483		4.10	24		28.10	40.50
4580 3"		20.80	.769		11.40	38		49.40	69.50
4590 4"		16.50	.970		23	47.50		70.50	97
4600 6"		10.10	1.584		97.50	78		175.50	224
4650 1/8 Bend, same as 1/4 Bend									
4800 Tee, sanitary									
4820 1-1/4"	1 Plum	13.50	.593	Ea.	4.95	32.50		37.45	54.50
4830 1-1/2"	"	12.10	.661		4.33	36		40.33	59.50
4840 2"	Q-1	20	.800		6.70	39.50		46.20	67
4850 3"		13.90	1.151		18.40	56.50		74.90	106
4860 4"		11	1.455		32.50	71.50		104	144
4862 Tee, sanitary, reducing, 2" x 1-1/2"		22	.727		6.75	36		42.75	61.50
4864 3" x 2"		15.30	1.046		13.40	51.50		64.90	92.50
4868 4" x 3"		12.10	1.322		32	65		97	133
4870 Combination Y and 1/8 bend									
4872 1-1/2"	1 Plum	12.10	.661	Ea.	10.35	36		46.35	66
4874 2"	Q-1	20	.800		11.60	39.50		51.10	72.50
4876 3"		13.90	1.151		26.50	56.50		83	115
4878 4"		11	1.455		52.50	71.50		124	166
4880 3" x 1-1/2"		15.50	1.032		27	50.50		77.50	106
4882 4" x 3"		12.10	1.322		52.50	65		117.50	156
4900 Wye, 1-1/4"	1 Plum	13.50	.593		5.70	32.50		38.20	55.50
4902 1-1/2"	"	12.10	.661		6.90	36		42.90	62
4904 2"	Q-1	20	.800		8.65	39.50		48.15	69
4906 3"		13.90	1.151		20.50	56.50		77	108
4908 4"		11	1.455		41.50	71.50		113	154
4910 6"		6.70	2.388		124	117		241	315
4918 3" x 1-1/2"		15.50	1.032		16.35	50.50		66.85	94.50
4920 4" x 3"		12.10	1.322		33	65		98	134
4922 6" x 4"		6.90	2.319		102	114		216	285
4930 Double Wye, 1-1/2"	1 Plum	9.10	.879		20	48		68	94.50
4932 2"	Q-1	16.60	.964		24	47.50		71.50	97.50
4934 3"		10.40	1.538		54.50	75.50		130	174
4936 4"		8.25	1.939		106	95.50		201.50	261
4940 2" x 1-1/2"		16.80	.952		21	47		68	93.50
4942 3" x 2"		10.60	1.509		40	74		114	156
4944 4" x 3"		8.45	1.893		84	93		177	233
4946 6" x 4"		7.25	2.207		130	108		238	305
4950 Reducer bushing, 2" x 1-1/2"		36.40	.440		2.33	21.50		23.83	35
4952 3" x 1-1/2"		27.30	.586		9.85	29		38.85	54.50

22 11 Facility Water Distribution

22 11 13 – Facility Water Distribution Piping

22 11 13.76 Pipe Fittings, Plastic		Crew	Daily Output	Labor-Hours	Unit	Material	2012 Bare Costs Labor	Equipment	Total	Total Incl O&P
4954	4" x 2"	Q-1	18.20	.879	Ea.	18.85	43		61.85	86
4956	6" x 4"	↓	11.10	1.441		50.50	71		121.50	163
4960	Couplings, 1-1/2"	1 Plum	18.20	.440		1.42	24		25.42	37.50
4962	2"	Q-1	33.10	.483		1.90	24		25.90	38
4963	3"		20.80	.769		5.50	38		43.50	63
4964	4"		16.50	.970		9.90	47.50		57.40	83
4966	6"		10.10	1.584		41.50	78		119.50	163
4970	2" x 1-1/2"		33.30	.480		4.07	23.50		27.57	40
4972	3" x 1-1/2"		21	.762		11.35	37.50		48.85	69
4974	4" x 3"	↓	16.70	.958		18	47		65	91
4978	Closet flange, 4"	1 Plum	32	.250		8.55	13.65		22.20	30
4980	4" x 3"	"	34	.235	↓	10.75	12.85		23.60	31
5000	DWV, PVC, schedule 40, socket joints									
5040	1/4 bend, 1-1/4"	1 Plum	20.20	.396	Ea.	7.45	21.50		28.95	40.50
5060	1-1/2"	"	18.20	.440		2.05	24		26.05	38.50
5070	2"	Q-1	33.10	.483		3.23	24		27.23	39.50
5080	3"		20.80	.769		9.55	38		47.55	67.50
5090	4"		16.50	.970		18.80	47.50		66.30	92.50
5100	6"	↓	10.10	1.584		66	78		144	190
5105	8"	Q-2	9.30	2.581		133	132		265	345
5106	10"	"	8.50	2.824		234	144		378	475
5110	1/4 bend, long sweep, 1-1/2"	1 Plum	18.20	.440		4.92	24		28.92	41.50
5112	2"	Q-1	33.10	.483		5.30	24		29.30	42
5114	3"		20.80	.769		12.55	38		50.55	71
5116	4"	↓	16.50	.970		24	47.50		71.50	98.50
5150	1/8 bend, 1-1/4"	1 Plum	20.20	.396		4.88	21.50		26.38	38
5170	1-1/2"	"	18.20	.440		2.01	24		26.01	38
5180	2"	Q-1	33.10	.483		2.90	24		26.90	39
5190	3"		20.80	.769		8.55	38		46.55	66.50
5200	4"		16.50	.970		14.95	47.50		62.45	88.50
5210	6"	↓	10.10	1.584		60.50	78		138.50	184
5215	8"	Q-2	9.30	2.581		78.50	132		210.50	285
5216	10"		8.50	2.824		196	144		340	435
5217	12"	↓	7.60	3.158		270	161		431	540
5250	Tee, sanitary 1-1/4"	1 Plum	13.50	.593		7.50	32.50		40	57.50
5254	1-1/2"	"	12.10	.661		3.72	36		39.72	58.50
5255	2"	Q-1	20	.800		5.45	39.50		44.95	65.50
5256	3"		13.90	1.151		14	56.50		70.50	101
5257	4"		11	1.455		24.50	71.50		96	135
5259	6"	↓	6.70	2.388		106	117		223	294
5261	8"	Q-2	6.20	3.871	↓	320	197		517	650
5276	Tee, sanitary, reducing									
5281	2" x 1-1/2" x 1-1/2"	Q-1	23	.696	Ea.	4.80	34		38.80	57
5282	2" x 1-1/2" x 2"		22	.727		5.85	36		41.85	60.50
5283	2" x 2" x 1-1/2"		22	.727		4.83	36		40.83	59.50
5284	3" x 3" x 1-1/2"		15.50	1.032		10.15	50.50		60.65	87.50
5285	3" x 3" x 2"		15.30	1.046		10.70	51.50		62.20	89.50
5286	4" x 4" x 1-1/2"		12.30	1.301		27.50	64		91.50	127
5287	4" x 4" x 2"		12.20	1.311		23	64.50		87.50	122
5288	4" x 4" x 3"		12.10	1.322		31	65		96	132
5291	6" x 6" x 4"	↓	6.90	2.319	↓	103	114		217	285
5294	Tee, double sanitary									
5295	1-1/2"	1 Plum	9.10	.879	Ea.	8.25	48		56.25	81.50

210

22 11 13 – Facility Water Distribution Piping

22 11 13.76 Pipe Fittings, Plastic		Crew	Daily Output	Labor-Hours	Unit	Material	2012 Bare Costs Labor	Equipment	Total	Total Incl O&P
5296	2"	Q-1	16.60	.964	Ea.	11.15	47.50		58.65	84
5297	3"		10.40	1.538		31	75.50		106.50	149
5298	4"	↓	8.25	1.939	↓	50	95.50		145.50	199
5303	Wye, reducing									
5304	2" x 1-1/2" x 1-1/2"	Q-1	23	.696	Ea.	9.40	34		43.40	62
5305	2" x 2" x 1-1/2"		22	.727		8.15	36		44.15	63
5306	3" x 3" x 2"		15.30	1.046		26.50	51.50		78	107
5307	4" x 4" x 2"		12.20	1.311		19.60	64.50		84.10	119
5309	4" x 4" x 3"	↓	12.10	1.322		26.50	65		91.50	127
5314	Combination Y & 1/8 bend, 1-1/2"	1 Plum	12.10	.661		8.95	36		44.95	64.50
5315	2"	Q-1	20	.800		9.60	39.50		49.10	70
5317	3"		13.90	1.151		24	56.50		80.50	112
5318	4"		11	1.455		47.50	71.50		119	160
5319	6"	↓	6.70	2.388		170	117		287	365
5320	8"	Q-2	6.20	3.871		310	197		507	640
5321	10"		5.70	4.211		680	215		895	1,075
5322	12"	↓	5.10	4.706	↓	790	240		1,030	1,225
5324	Combination Y & 1/8 bend, reducing									
5325	2" x 2" x 1-1/2"	Q-1	22	.727	Ea.	12.60	36		48.60	68
5327	3" x 3" x 1-1/2"		15.50	1.032		22	50.50		72.50	101
5328	3" x 3" x 2"		15.30	1.046		15.80	51.50		67.30	95
5329	4" x 4" x 2"	↓	12.20	1.311		25.50	64.50		90	126
5331	Wye, 1-1/4"	1 Plum	13.50	.593		9.50	32.50		42	59.50
5332	1-1/2"	"	12.10	.661		7	36		43	62
5333	2"	Q-1	20	.800		6.65	39.50		46.15	67
5334	3"		13.90	1.151		17.90	56.50		74.40	105
5335	4"		11	1.455		32.50	71.50		104	144
5336	6"	↓	6.70	2.388		98.50	117		215.50	285
5337	8"	Q-2	6.20	3.871		229	197		426	550
5338	10"		5.70	4.211		495	215		710	870
5339	12"	↓	5.10	4.706		810	240		1,050	1,250
5341	2" x 1-1/2"	Q-1	22	.727		8.15	36		44.15	63
5342	3" x 1-1/2"		15.50	1.032		11.75	50.50		62.25	89.50
5343	4" x 3"		12.10	1.322		26.50	65		91.50	127
5344	6" x 4"	↓	6.90	2.319		72.50	114		186.50	252
5345	8" x 6"	Q-2	6.40	3.750		173	191		364	480
5347	Double wye, 1-1/2"	1 Plum	9.10	.879		15.15	48		63.15	89
5348	2"	Q-1	16.60	.964		17.05	47.50		64.55	90.50
5349	3"		10.40	1.538		35.50	75.50		111	153
5350	4"	↓	8.25	1.939	↓	72.50	95.50		168	224
5353	Double wye, reducing									
5354	2" x 2" x 1-1/2" x 1-1/2"	Q-1	16.80	.952	Ea.	15.45	47		62.45	87.50
5355	3" x 3" x 2" x 2"		10.60	1.509		26.50	74		100.50	141
5356	4" x 4" x 3" x 3"		8.45	1.893		57	93		150	203
5357	6" x 6" x 4" x 4"	↓	7.25	2.207		187	108		295	370
5374	Coupling, 1-1/4"	1 Plum	20.20	.396		4.52	21.50		26.02	37.50
5376	1-1/2"	"	18.20	.440		1.03	24		25.03	37
5378	2"	Q-1	33.10	.483		1.32	24		25.32	37.50
5380	3"		20.80	.769		4.58	38		42.58	62
5390	4"		16.50	.970		8.10	47.50		55.60	81
5400	6"	↓	10.10	1.584		26.50	78		104.50	146
5402	8"	Q-2	9.30	2.581		64.50	132		196.50	269
5404	2" x 1-1/2"	Q-1	33.30	.480	↓	2.95	23.50		26.45	39

22 11 Facility Water Distribution

22 11 13 – Facility Water Distribution Piping

22 11 13.76 Pipe Fittings, Plastic	Crew	Daily Output	Labor-Hours	Unit	Material	2012 Bare Costs Labor	Equipment	Total	Total Incl O&P
5406	3" x 1-1/2"	Q-1	21	.762	Ea.	9	37.50		46.50	66.50
5408	4" x 3"		16.70	.958		14.65	47		61.65	87
5410	Reducer bushing, 2" x 1-1/4"		36.50	.438		4.20	21.50		25.70	37
5411	2" x 1-1/2"		36.40	.440		1.76	21.50		23.26	34.50
5412	3" x 1-1/2"		27.30	.586		8.40	29		37.40	53
5413	3" x 2"		27.10	.590		4.40	29		33.40	49
5414	4" x 2"		18.20	.879		14.65	43		57.65	81
5415	4" x 3"		16.70	.958		7.50	47		54.50	79.50
5416	6" x 4"		11.10	1.441		39	71		110	150
5418	8" x 6"	Q-2	10.20	2.353		84.50	120		204.50	274
5425	Closet flange 4"	Q-1	32	.500		10.35	24.50		34.85	48.50
5426	4" x 3"	"	34	.471		10.30	23		33.30	46.50
5450	Solvent cement for PVC, industrial grade, per quart				Qt.	19.90			19.90	22
5500	CPVC, Schedule 80, threaded joints									
5540	90° Elbow, 1/4"	1 Plum	32	.250	Ea.	11.55	13.65		25.20	33
5560	1/2"		30.30	.264		6.70	14.40		21.10	29
5570	3/4"		26	.308		10	16.80		26.80	36.50
5580	1"		22.70	.352		14.05	19.25		33.30	44.50
5590	1-1/4"		20.20	.396		27	21.50		48.50	62.50
5600	1-1/2"		18.20	.440		29	24		53	68
5610	2"	Q-1	33.10	.483		39	24		63	79
5620	2-1/2"		24.20	.661		121	32.50		153.50	182
5630	3"		20.80	.769		130	38		168	200
5640	4"		16.50	.970		203	47.50		250.50	296
5650	6"		10.10	1.584		240	78		318	380
5660	45° Elbow same as 90° Elbow									
5700	Tee, 1/4"	1 Plum	22	.364	Ea.	22.50	19.85		42.35	54.50
5702	1/2"		20.20	.396		22.50	21.50		44	57
5704	3/4"		17.30	.462		32.50	25.50		58	73.50
5706	1"		15.20	.526		35	28.50		63.50	82
5708	1-1/4"		13.50	.593		35	32.50		67.50	87.50
5710	1-1/2"		12.10	.661		36.50	36		72.50	95
5712	2"	Q-1	20	.800		41	39.50		80.50	105
5714	2-1/2"		16.20	.988		156	48.50		204.50	244
5716	3"		13.90	1.151		233	56.50		289.50	340
5718	4"		11	1.455		550	71.50		621.50	715
5720	6"		6.70	2.388		635	117		752	875
5730	Coupling, 1/4"	1 Plum	32	.250		14.70	13.65		28.35	36.50
5732	1/2"		30.30	.264		12.10	14.40		26.50	35
5734	3/4"		26	.308		19.55	16.80		36.35	47
5736	1"		22.70	.352		22	19.25		41.25	53.50
5738	1-1/4"		20.20	.396		23.50	21.50		45	58.50
5740	1-1/2"		18.20	.440		25.50	24		49.50	64
5742	2"	Q-1	33.10	.483		30	24		54	69
5744	2-1/2"		24.20	.661		53.50	32.50		86	108
5746	3"		20.80	.769		62	38		100	126
5748	4"		16.50	.970		127	47.50		174.50	212
5750	6"		10.10	1.584		173	78		251	305
5752	8"	Q-2	9.30	2.581		370	132		502	605
5900	CPVC, Schedule 80, socket joints									
5904	90° Elbow, 1/4"	1 Plum	32	.250	Ea.	11	13.65		24.65	32.50
5906	1/2"		30.30	.264		4.31	14.40		18.71	26
5908	3/4"		26	.308		5.50	16.80		22.30	31.50

22 11 13 – Facility Water Distribution Piping

22 11 13.76 Pipe Fittings, Plastic		Crew	Daily Output	Labor-Hours	Unit	Material	2012 Bare Costs Labor	Equipment	Total	Total Incl O&P
5910	1"	1 Plum	22.70	.352	Ea.	8.70	19.25		27.95	38.50
5912	1-1/4"		20.20	.396		18.85	21.50		40.35	53.50
5914	1-1/2"	↓	18.20	.440		21	24		45	59
5916	2"	Q-1	33.10	.483		25.50	24		49.50	64
5918	2-1/2"		24.20	.661		58.50	32.50		91	114
5920	3"		20.80	.769		66	38		104	130
5922	4"		16.50	.970		119	47.50		166.50	203
5924	6"		10.10	1.584		240	78		318	380
5926	8"	↓	9.30	1.720		585	84.50		669.50	775
5930	45° Elbow, 1/4"	1 Plum	32	.250		16.35	13.65		30	38.50
5932	1/2"		30.30	.264		5.25	14.40		19.65	27.50
5934	3/4"		26	.308		7.60	16.80		24.40	34
5936	1"		22.70	.352		12.10	19.25		31.35	42.50
5938	1-1/4"		20.20	.396		24	21.50		45.50	58.50
5940	1-1/2"	↓	18.20	.440		24.50	24		48.50	63
5942	2"	Q-1	33.10	.483		27.50	24		51.50	66
5944	2-1/2"		24.20	.661		56	32.50		88.50	111
5946	3"		20.80	.769		72	38		110	136
5948	4"		16.50	.970		98.50	47.50		146	180
5950	6"		10.10	1.584		305	78		383	450
5952	8"	↓	9.30	1.720		630	84.50		714.50	825
5960	Tee, 1/4"	1 Plum	22	.364		10.10	19.85		29.95	41
5962	1/2"		20.20	.396		10.10	21.50		31.60	43.50
5964	3/4"		17.30	.462		10.25	25.50		35.75	49.50
5966	1"		15.20	.526		12.60	28.50		41.10	57.50
5968	1-1/4"		13.50	.593		26.50	32.50		59	78
5970	1-1/2"	↓	12.10	.661		30.50	36		66.50	88
5972	2"	Q-1	20	.800		34	39.50		73.50	96.50
5974	2-1/2"		16.20	.988		86	48.50		134.50	168
5976	3"		13.90	1.151		86	56.50		142.50	181
5978	4"		11	1.455		115	71.50		186.50	234
5980	6"	↓	6.70	2.388		298	117		415	505
5982	8"	Q-2	6.20	3.871		835	197		1,032	1,225
5990	Coupling, 1/4"	1 Plum	32	.250		11.70	13.65		25.35	33.50
5992	1/2"		30.30	.264		4.55	14.40		18.95	26.50
5994	3/4"		26	.308		6.35	16.80		23.15	32.50
5996	1"		22.70	.352		8.55	19.25		27.80	38.50
5998	1-1/4"		20.20	.396		12.80	21.50		34.30	46.50
6000	1-1/2"	↓	18.20	.440		16.15	24		40.15	54
6002	2"	Q-1	33.10	.483		18.75	24		42.75	56.50
6004	2-1/2"		24.20	.661		41.50	32.50		74	95
6006	3"		20.80	.769		45.50	38		83.50	107
6008	4"		16.50	.970		59.50	47.50		107	138
6010	6"	↓	10.10	1.584		140	78		218	271
6012	8"	Q-2	9.30	2.581	↓	380	132		512	615
6200	CTS, 100 psi at 180°F, hot and cold water									
6230	90° Elbow, 1/2"	1 Plum	20	.400	Ea.	.34	22		22.34	33.50
6250	3/4"		19	.421		.60	23		23.60	35
6251	1"		16	.500		1.75	27.50		29.25	43
6252	1-1/4"		15	.533		2.86	29		31.86	47
6253	1-1/2"	↓	14	.571		5.15	31		36.15	52.50
6254	2"	Q-1	23	.696		9.65	34		43.65	62
6260	45° Elbow, 1/2"	1 Plum	20	.400	↓	.46	22		22.46	33.50

22 11 13.76 Pipe Fittings, Plastic		Crew	Daily Output	Labor-Hours	Unit	Material	2012 Bare Costs Labor	Equipment	Total	Total Incl O&P
6280	3/4"	1 Plum	19	.421	Ea.	.80	23		23.80	35.50
6281	1"		16	.500		1.66	27.50		29.16	43
6282	1-1/4"		15	.533		3.30	29		32.30	47.50
6283	1-1/2"	▼	14	.571		4.78	31		35.78	52.50
6284	2"	Q-1	23	.696		10	34		44	62.50
6290	Tee, 1/2"	1 Plum	13	.615		.47	33.50		33.97	51
6310	3/4"		12	.667		.87	36.50		37.37	56
6311	1"		11	.727		3.76	39.50		43.26	64
6312	1-1/4"		10	.800		5.75	43.50		49.25	72.50
6313	1-1/2"	▼	10	.800		7.50	43.50		51	74.50
6314	2"	Q-1	17	.941		12.15	46.50		58.65	83.50
6320	Coupling, 1/2"	1 Plum	22	.364		.30	19.85		20.15	30.50
6340	3/4"		21	.381		.40	21		21.40	32
6341	1"		18	.444		1.46	24.50		25.96	38
6342	1-1/4"		17	.471		1.76	25.50		27.26	41
6343	1-1/2"	▼	16	.500		2.49	27.50		29.99	43.50
6344	2"	Q-1	28	.571	▼	5.05	28		33.05	48
6360	Solvent cement for CPVC, commercial grade, per quart				Qt.	34			34	37.50
7340	PVC flange, slip-on, Sch 80 std., 1/2"	1 Plum	22	.364	Ea.	12.90	19.85		32.75	44
7350	3/4"		21	.381		13.75	21		34.75	46.50
7360	1"		18	.444		15.35	24.50		39.85	53.50
7370	1-1/4"		17	.471		15.80	25.50		41.30	56.50
7380	1-1/2"	▼	16	.500		16.15	27.50		43.65	59
7390	2"	Q-1	26	.615		21.50	30.50		52	69
7400	2-1/2"		24	.667		33	33		66	86
7410	3"		18	.889		36.50	43.50		80	107
7420	4"		15	1.067		46.50	52.50		99	130
7430	6"	▼	10	1.600		73	78.50		151.50	200
7440	8"	Q-2	11	2.182		131	111		242	310
7550	Union, schedule 40, socket joints, 1/2"	1 Plum	19	.421		4.49	23		27.49	39.50
7560	3/4"		18	.444		5.10	24.50		29.60	42
7570	1"		15	.533		5.25	29		34.25	50
7580	1-1/4"		14	.571		15.85	31		46.85	64.50
7590	1-1/2"	▼	13	.615		17.65	33.50		51.15	70
7600	2"	Q-1	20	.800	▼	24	39.50		63.50	85.50
7992	Polybutyl/polyethyl pipe, for copper fittings see Line 22 11 13.25 7000									
8000	Compression type, PVC, 160 psi cold water									
8010	Coupling, 3/4" CTS	1 Plum	21	.381	Ea.	3.48	21		24.48	35.50
8020	1" CTS		18	.444		4.32	24.50		28.82	41.50
8030	1-1/4" CTS		17	.471		6.10	25.50		31.60	45.50
8040	1-1/2" CTS		16	.500		8.30	27.50		35.80	50
8050	2" CTS		15	.533		11.65	29		40.65	57
8060	Female adapter, 3/4" FPT x 3/4" CTS		23	.348		5.70	19		24.70	35
8070	3/4" FPT x 1" CTS		21	.381		6.60	21		27.60	39
8080	1" FPT x 1" CTS		20	.400		6.60	22		28.60	40.50
8090	1-1/4" FPT x 1-1/4" CTS		18	.444		8.65	24.50		33.15	46
8100	1-1/2" FPT x 1-1/2" CTS		16	.500		9.90	27.50		37.40	52
8110	2" FPT x 2" CTS		13	.615		14.35	33.50		47.85	66.50
8130	Male adapter, 3/4" MPT x 3/4" CTS		23	.348		4.74	19		23.74	33.50
8140	3/4" MPT x 1" CTS		21	.381		5.65	21		26.65	37.50
8150	1" MPT x 1" CTS		20	.400		5.65	22		27.65	39
8160	1-1/4" MPT x 1-1/4" CTS		18	.444		7.60	24.50		32.10	45
8170	1-1/2" MPT x 1-1/2" CTS		16	.500	▼	9.15	27.50		36.65	51

22 11 13 – Facility Water Distribution Piping

22 11 13.76 Pipe Fittings, Plastic	Crew	Daily Output	Labor-Hours	Unit	Material	2012 Bare Costs Labor	Equipment	Total	Total Incl O&P
8180	2" MPT x 2" CTS	1 Plum	13	.615	Ea.	11.85	33.50		45.35	63.50
8200	Spigot adapter, 3/4" IPS x 3/4" CTS		23	.348		2.70	19		21.70	31.50
8210	3/4" IPS x 1" CTS		21	.381		3.30	21		24.30	35
8220	1" IPS x 1" CTS		20	.400		3.30	22		25.30	36.50
8230	1-1/4" IPS x 1-1/4" CTS		18	.444		4.99	24.50		29.49	42
8240	1-1/2" IPS x 1-1/2" CTS		16	.500		5.25	27.50		32.75	47
8250	2" IPS x 2" CTS	▼	13	.615	▼	6.45	33.50		39.95	57.50
8270	Price includes insert stiffeners									
8280	250 psi is same price as 160 psi									
8300	Insert type, nylon, 160 & 250 psi, cold water									
8310	Clamp ring stainless steel, 3/4" IPS	1 Plum	115	.070	Ea.	2.38	3.80		6.18	8.35
8320	1" IPS		107	.075		2.43	4.08		6.51	8.80
8330	1-1/4" IPS		101	.079		2.45	4.32		6.77	9.20
8340	1-1/2" IPS		95	.084		3.28	4.60		7.88	10.55
8350	2" IPS		85	.094		3.77	5.15		8.92	11.90
8370	Coupling, 3/4" IPS		22	.364		.84	19.85		20.69	31
8390	1-1/4" IPS		18	.444		1.30	24.50		25.80	38
8400	1-1/2" IPS		17	.471		1.54	25.50		27.04	40.50
8410	2" IPS		16	.500		2.91	27.50		30.41	44
8430	Elbow, 90°, 3/4" IPS		22	.364		1.68	19.85		21.53	32
8440	1" IPS		19	.421		1.86	23		24.86	36.50
8450	1-1/4" IPS		18	.444		2.08	24.50		26.58	39
8460	1-1/2" IPS		17	.471		2.45	25.50		27.95	41.50
8470	2" IPS		16	.500		3.42	27.50		30.92	45
8490	Male adapter, 3/4" IPS x 3/4" MPT		25	.320		.84	17.45		18.29	27.50
8500	1" IPS x 1" MPT		21	.381		.87	21		21.87	32.50
8510	1-1/4" IPS x 1-1/4" MPT		20	.400		1.37	22		23.37	34.50
8520	1-1/2" IPS x 1-1/2" MPT		18	.444		1.54	24.50		26.04	38
8530	2" IPS x 2" MPT		15	.533		2.95	29		31.95	47.50
8550	Tee, 3/4" IPS		14	.571		1.63	31		32.63	49
8560	1" IPS		13	.615		2.12	33.50		35.62	53
8570	1-1/4" IPS		12	.667		3.31	36.50		39.81	58.50
8580	1-1/2" IPS		11	.727		3.75	39.50		43.25	64
8590	2" IPS	▼	10	.800	▼	7.40	43.50		50.90	74
8610	Insert type, PVC, 100 psi @ 180°F, hot & cold water									
8620	Coupler, male, 3/8" CTS x 3/8" MPT	1 Plum	29	.276	Ea.	.68	15.05		15.73	23.50
8630	3/8" CTS x 1/2" MPT		28	.286		.68	15.60		16.28	24.50
8640	1/2" CTS x 1/2" MPT		27	.296		.68	16.20		16.88	25.50
8650	1/2" CTS x 3/4" MPT		26	.308		2.18	16.80		18.98	28
8660	3/4" CTS x 1/2" MPT		25	.320		1.98	17.45		19.43	28.50
8670	3/4" CTS x 3/4" MPT		25	.320		2.34	17.45		19.79	29
8700	Coupling, 3/8" CTS x 1/2" CTS		25	.320		3.37	17.45		20.82	30
8710	1/2" CTS		23	.348		3.94	19		22.94	33
8730	3/4" CTS		22	.364		6.20	19.85		26.05	37
8750	Elbow 90°, 3/8" CTS		25	.320		4	17.45		21.45	31
8760	1/2" CTS		23	.348		4.73	19		23.73	33.50
8770	3/4" CTS		22	.364		7.25	19.85		27.10	38
8800	Rings, crimp, copper, 3/8" CTS		120	.067		.22	3.64		3.86	5.75
8810	1/2" CTS		117	.068		.22	3.73		3.95	5.90
8820	3/4" CTS		115	.070		.29	3.80		4.09	6.05
8850	Reducer tee, 3/8" x 3/8" x 1/2" CTS		17	.471		1.64	25.50		27.14	41
8860	1/2" x 3/8" x 1/2" CTS		15	.533		1.64	29		30.64	46
8870	3/4" x 1/2" x 1/2" CTS	▼	14	.571		2.54	31		33.54	50

22 11 13.76 Pipe Fittings, Plastic	Crew	Daily Output	Labor-Hours	Unit	Material	2012 Bare Costs Labor	Equipment	Total	Total Incl O&P
8890	3/4" x 3/4" x 1/2" CTS	1 Plum	14	.571	Ea.	2.54	31		33.54	50
8900	3/4" x 1/2" x 3/8" CTS		14	.571		2.54	31		33.54	50
8930	Tee, 3/8" CTS		17	.471		2.70	25.50		28.20	42
8940	1/2" CTS		15	.533		2.86	29		31.86	47
8950	3/4" CTS		14	.571		3.05	31		34.05	50.50
8960	Copper rings included in fitting price									
9000	Flare type, assembled, acetal, hot & cold water									
9010	Coupling, 1/4" & 3/8" CTS	1 Plum	24	.333	Ea.	3.36	18.20		21.56	31
9020	1/2" CTS		22	.364		3.84	19.85		23.69	34
9030	3/4" CTS		21	.381		5.70	21		26.70	38
9040	1" CTS		18	.444		7.25	24.50		31.75	44.50
9050	Elbow 90°, 1/4" CTS		26	.308		3.73	16.80		20.53	29.50
9060	3/8" CTS		24	.333		4	18.20		22.20	32
9070	1/2" CTS		22	.364		4.73	19.85		24.58	35
9080	3/4" CTS		21	.381		7.25	21		28.25	39.50
9090	1" CTS		18	.444		9.15	24.50		33.65	46.50
9110	Tee, 1/4" CTS		16	.500		4.09	27.50		31.59	45.50
9114	3/8" CTS		15	.533		4.13	29		33.13	48.50
9120	1/2" CTS		14	.571		5.25	31		36.25	53
9130	3/4" CTS		13	.615		8.25	33.50		41.75	59.50
9140	1" CTS		12	.667		11.05	36.50		47.55	67
9400	Polypropylene, fittings and accessories									
9404	Fittings fusion welded, sizes are I.D.									
9408	Note: sizes 1/2" thru 4" use socket fusion									
9410	Sizes 6" thru 10" use butt fusion									
9416	Coupling									
9420	3/8"	1 Plum	39	.205	Ea.	.84	11.20		12.04	17.80
9422	1/2"		37.40	.214		1.09	11.70		12.79	18.80
9424	3/4"		35.40	.226		1.22	12.35		13.57	19.95
9426	1"		29.70	.269		1.61	14.70		16.31	24
9428	1-1/4"		27.60	.290		1.93	15.85		17.78	26
9430	1-1/2"		24.80	.323		4.05	17.60		21.65	31
9432	2"	Q-1	43	.372		8.10	18.30		26.40	36.50
9434	2-1/2"		35.60	.449		9.05	22		31.05	43.50
9436	3"		30.90	.518		19.90	25.50		45.40	60.50
9438	3-1/2"		27.80	.576		32.50	28.50		61	78
9440	4"		25	.640		42.50	31.50		74	94.50
9442	Reducing coupling, female to female									
9446	2" to 1-1/2"	Q-1	49	.327	Ea.	11.65	16.05		27.70	37
9448	2-1/2" to 2"		41.20	.388		12.80	19.10		31.90	43
9450	3" to 2-1/2"		33.10	.483		17.25	24		41.25	55
9470	Reducing bushing, female to female									
9472	1/2" to 3/8"	1 Plum	38.20	.209	Ea.	1.09	11.45		12.54	18.45
9474	3/4" to 3/8" or 1/2"		36.50	.219		1.22	11.95		13.17	19.40
9476	1" to 3/4" or 1/2"		33.10	.242		1.63	13.20		14.83	21.50
9478	1-1/4" to 3/4" or 1"		28.70	.279		2.51	15.20		17.71	26
9480	1-1/2" to 1/2" thru 1-1/4"		26.20	.305		4.15	16.65		20.80	29.50
9482	2" to 1/2" thru 1-1/2"	Q-1	43	.372		8.30	18.30		26.60	36.50
9484	2-1/2" to 1/2" thru 2"		41.20	.388		9.30	19.10		28.40	39
9486	3" to 1-1/2" thru 2-1/2"		33.10	.483		20.50	24		44.50	58.50
9488	3-1/2" to 2" thru 3"		29.20	.548		33	27		60	77
9490	4" to 2-1/2" thru 3-1/2"		26.20	.611		40.50	30		70.50	90
9491	6" to 4" SDR 7.4		16.50	.970		62	47.50		109.50	140

22 11 13 – Facility Water Distribution Piping

22 11 13.76 Pipe Fittings, Plastic	Crew	Daily Output	Labor-Hours	Unit	Material	2012 Bare Costs Labor	Equipment	Total	Total Incl O&P
9492	6" to 4" SDR 11	Q-1	16.50	.970	Ea.	62	47.50		109.50	140
9493	8" to 6" SDR 7.4		10.10	1.584		91	78		169	217
9494	8" to 6" SDR 11		10.10	1.584		83.50	78		161.50	209
9495	10" to 8" SDR 7.4		7.80	2.051		125	101		226	289
9496	10" to 8" SDR 11	▼	7.80	2.051	▼	109	101		210	272
9500	90° Elbow									
9504	3/8"	1 Plum	39	.205	Ea.	.92	11.20		12.12	17.90
9506	1/2"		37.40	.214		1.17	11.70		12.87	18.90
9508	3/4"		35.40	.226		1.50	12.35		13.85	20.50
9510	1"		29.70	.269		2.17	14.70		16.87	24.50
9512	1-1/4"		27.60	.290		3.34	15.85		19.19	27.50
9514	1-1/2"	▼	24.80	.323		7.20	17.60		24.80	34.50
9516	2"	Q-1	43	.372		11.05	18.30		29.35	39.50
9518	2-1/2"		35.60	.449		24.50	22		46.50	60.50
9520	3"		30.90	.518		45.50	25.50		71	88.50
9522	3-1/2"		27.80	.576		64.50	28.50		93	114
9524	4"		25	.640		99.50	31.50		131	157
9526	6" SDR 7.4		5.55	2.883		114	142		256	340
9528	6" SDR 11	▼	5.55	2.883		94.50	142		236.50	320
9530	8" SDR 7.4	Q-2	8.10	2.963		395	151		546	665
9532	8" SDR 11		8.10	2.963		305	151		456	565
9534	10" SDR 7.4		7.50	3.200		555	163		718	855
9536	10" SDR 11	▼	7.50	3.200	▼	510	163		673	810
9551	45° Elbow									
9554	3/8"	1 Plum	39	.205	Ea.	.90	11.20		12.10	17.90
9556	1/2"		37.40	.214		1.17	11.70		12.87	18.90
9558	3/4"		35.40	.226		1.50	12.35		13.85	20.50
9564	1"		29.70	.269		2.17	14.70		16.87	24.50
9566	1-1/4"		27.60	.290		3.34	15.85		19.19	27.50
9568	1-1/2"	▼	24.80	.323		7.20	17.60		24.80	34.50
9570	2"	Q-1	43	.372		10.95	18.30		29.25	39.50
9572	2-1/2"		35.60	.449		24	22		46	60
9574	3"		30.90	.518		44.50	25.50		70	87.50
9576	3-1/2"		27.80	.576		63.50	28.50		92	113
9578	4"		25	.640		98	31.50		129.50	156
9580	6" SDR 7.4		5.55	2.883		113	142		255	340
9582	6" SDR 11	▼	5.55	2.883		93.50	142		235.50	315
9584	8" SDR 7.4	Q-2	8.10	2.963		310	151		461	570
9586	8" SDR 11		8.10	2.963		271	151		422	525
9588	10" SDR 7.4		7.50	3.200		500	163		663	795
9590	10" SDR 11	▼	7.50	3.200	▼	410	163		573	695
9600	Tee									
9604	3/8"	1 Plum	26	.308	Ea.	1.16	16.80		17.96	27
9606	1/2"		24.90	.321		1.58	17.55		19.13	28
9608	3/4"		23.70	.338		2.17	18.45		20.62	30.50
9610	1"		19.90	.402		2.76	22		24.76	36
9612	1-1/4"		18.50	.432		4.21	23.50		27.71	40
9614	1-1/2"	▼	16.60	.482		12.05	26.50		38.55	53
9616	2"	Q-1	26.80	.597		17.25	29.50		46.75	63.50
9618	2-1/2"		23.80	.672		29	33		62	82
9620	3"		20.60	.777		53	38		91	116
9622	3-1/2"		18.40	.870		82.50	42.50		125	156
9624	4"	▼	16.70	.958		105	47		152	186

22 11 13 – Facility Water Distribution Piping

22 11 13.76 **Pipe Fittings, Plastic**	Crew	Daily Output	Labor-Hours	Unit	Material	2012 Bare Costs Labor	Equipment	Total	Total Incl O&P
9626	6" SDR 7.4	Q-1	3.70	4.324	Ea.	123	213		336	455
9628	6" SDR 11	↓	3.70	4.324		93.50	213		306.50	425
9630	8" SDR 7.4	Q-2	5.40	4.444		335	227		562	710
9632	8" SDR 11		5.40	4.444		291	227		518	660
9634	10" SDR 7.4		5	4.800		580	245		825	1,000
9636	10" SDR 11	↓	5	4.800	↓	470	245		715	885
9638	For reducing tee use same tee price									
9660	End cap									
9662	3/8"	1 Plum	78	.103	Ea.	1.16	5.60		6.76	9.75
9664	1/2"		74.60	.107		1.72	5.85		7.57	10.75
9666	3/4"		71.40	.112		2.17	6.10		8.27	11.65
9668	1"		59.50	.134		2.63	7.35		9.98	13.95
9670	1-1/4"		55.60	.144		4.15	7.85		12	16.40
9672	1-1/2"	↓	49.50	.162		5.70	8.80		14.50	19.60
9674	2"	Q-1	80	.200		9.55	9.85		19.40	25.50
9676	2-1/2"		71.40	.224		13.90	11		24.90	32
9678	3"		61.70	.259		31.50	12.75		44.25	53.50
9680	3-1/2"		55.20	.290		37.50	14.25		51.75	63
9682	4"		50	.320		57.50	15.75		73.25	86.50
9684	6" SDR 7.4		26.50	.604		79	29.50		108.50	132
9686	6" SDR 11	↓	26.50	.604		79	29.50		108.50	132
9688	8" SDR 7.4	Q-2	16.30	1.472		79	75		154	200
9690	8" SDR 11		16.30	1.472		68.50	75		143.50	189
9692	10" SDR 7.4		14.90	1.611		118	82		200	254
9694	10" SDR 11	↓	14.90	1.611	↓	101	82		183	235
9800	Accessories and tools									
9802	Pipe clamps for suspension, not including rod or beam clamp									
9804	3/8"	1 Plum	74	.108	Ea.	2.03	5.90		7.93	11.15
9805	1/2"		70	.114		2.54	6.25		8.79	12.20
9806	3/4"		68	.118		2.93	6.40		9.33	12.90
9807	1"		66	.121		3.19	6.60		9.79	13.50
9808	1-1/4"		64	.125		3.28	6.85		10.13	13.90
9809	1-1/2"	↓	62	.129		3.58	7.05		10.63	14.60
9810	2"	Q-1	110	.145		4.44	7.15		11.59	15.70
9811	2-1/2"		104	.154		5.70	7.55		13.25	17.65
9812	3"		98	.163		6.10	8		14.10	18.85
9813	3-1/2"		92	.174		6.70	8.55		15.25	20.50
9814	4"		86	.186		7.55	9.15		16.70	22
9815	6"	↓	70	.229		9.20	11.25		20.45	27
9816	8"	Q-2	100	.240		33	12.25		45.25	54.50
9817	10"	"	94	.255	↓	37.50	13		50.50	61
9820	Pipe cutter									
9822	For 3/8" thru 1-1/4"				Ea.	112			112	123
9824	For 1-1/2" thru 4"				"	296			296	325
9826	Note: Pipes may be cut with standard									
9827	iron saw with blades for plastic.									
9830	Manual welding device, 800 W, 110 V									
9831	For 3/8" thru 2"				Ea.	355			355	390
9834	Manual welding device, 1400 W, 110 V									
9835	For 1-1/2" thru 4"				Ea.	695			695	765
9838	Butt welding machine									
9839	For 6" thru 10"				Ea.	24,200			24,200	26,600
9982	For plastic hangers see Line 22 05 29.10 8000									

22 11 Facility Water Distribution

22 11 13 - Facility Water Distribution Piping

22 11 13.76 Pipe Fittings, Plastic	Crew	Daily Output	Labor-Hours	Unit	Material	2012 Bare Costs Labor	Equipment	Total	Total Incl O&P
9986	For copper/brass fittings see Line 22 11 13.25 7000									

22 11 13.78 Pipe, High Density Polyethylene Plastic (HDPE)

	22 11 13.78 Pipe, High Density Polyethylene Plastic (HDPE)	Crew	Daily Output	Labor-Hours	Unit	Material	2012 Bare Costs Labor	Equipment	Total	Total Incl O&P
0010	**PIPE, HIGH DENSITY POLYETHYLENE PLASTIC (HDPE)**									
0020	Not incl. hangers, trenching, backfill, hoisting or digging equipment.									
0030	Standard length is 40', add a weld for each joint									
0040	Single wall									
0050	Straight									
0054	1" diameter DR 11				L.F.	.72			.72	.79
0058	1-1/2" diameter DR 11					.91			.91	1
0062	2" diameter DR 11					1.52			1.52	1.67
0066	3" diameter DR 11					1.83			1.83	2.01
0070	3" diameter DR 17					1.46			1.46	1.61
0074	4" diameter DR 11					3.05			3.05	3.36
0078	4" diameter DR 17					3.05			3.05	3.36
0082	6" diameter DR 11					7.60			7.60	8.35
0086	6" diameter DR 17					5.05			5.05	5.55
0090	8" diameter DR 11					12.65			12.65	13.90
0094	8" diameter DR 26					5.95			5.95	6.50
0098	10" diameter DR 11					19.80			19.80	22
0102	10" diameter DR 26					9.15			9.15	10.05
0106	12" diameter DR 11					29			29	32
0110	12" diameter DR 26					13.70			13.70	15.05
0114	16" diameter DR 11					44			44	48.50
0118	16" diameter DR 26					19.80			19.80	22
0122	18" diameter DR 11					56.50			56.50	62
0126	18" diameter DR 26					26			26	28.50
0130	20" diameter DR 11					68.50			68.50	75.50
0134	20" diameter DR 26					30.50			30.50	33.50
0138	22" diameter DR 11					83.50			83.50	92
0142	22" diameter DR 26					38			38	42
0146	24" diameter DR 11					99			99	109
0150	24" diameter DR 26					44			44	48.50
0154	28" diameter DR 17					91.50			91.50	100
0158	28" diameter DR 26					61			61	67
0162	30" diameter DR 21					85.50			85.50	94
0166	30" diameter DR 26					70			70	77
0170	36" diameter DR 26					70			70	77
0174	42" diameter DR 26					135			135	149
0178	48" diameter DR 26					178			178	196
0182	54" diameter DR 26					224			224	246
0300	90° Elbow									
0304	1" diameter DR 11				Ea.	5.35			5.35	5.85
0308	1-1/2" diameter DR 11					6.70			6.70	7.35
0312	2" diameter DR 11					6.70			6.70	7.35
0316	3" diameter DR 11					13.35			13.35	14.65
0320	3" diameter DR 17					13.35			13.35	14.65
0324	4" diameter DR 11					18.70			18.70	20.50
0328	4" diameter DR 17					18.70			18.70	20.50
0332	6" diameter DR 11					42.50			42.50	47
0336	6" diameter DR 17					42.50			42.50	47
0340	8" diameter DR 11					105			105	116
0344	8" diameter DR 26					93.50			93.50	103

22 11 13 – Facility Water Distribution Piping

22 11 13.78 Pipe, High Density Polyethylene Plastic (HDPE)	Crew	Daily Output	Labor-Hours	Unit	Material	2012 Bare Costs Labor	Equipment	Total	Total Incl O&P
0348	10" diameter DR 11				Ea.	395			395	435
0352	10" diameter DR 26					365			365	400
0356	12" diameter DR 11					415			415	460
0360	12" diameter DR 26					375			375	415
0364	16" diameter DR 11					490			490	540
0368	16" diameter DR 26					485			485	535
0372	18" diameter DR 11					615			615	680
0376	18" diameter DR 26					580			580	640
0380	20" diameter DR 11					730			730	800
0384	20" diameter DR 26					705			705	775
0388	22" diameter DR 11					750			750	825
0392	22" diameter DR 26					730			730	800
0396	24" diameter DR 11					850			850	935
0400	24" diameter DR 26					825			825	905
0404	28" diameter DR 17					1,025			1,025	1,125
0408	28" diameter DR 26					970			970	1,075
0412	30" diameter DR 17					1,450			1,450	1,600
0416	30" diameter DR 26					1,325			1,325	1,475
0420	36" diameter DR 26					1,700			1,700	1,875
0424	42" diameter DR 26					2,175			2,175	2,400
0428	48" diameter DR 26					2,550			2,550	2,800
0432	54" diameter DR 26					6,075			6,075	6,675
0500	45° Elbow									
0512	2" diameter DR 11				Ea.	5.35			5.35	5.85
0516	3" diameter DR 11					13.35			13.35	14.65
0520	3" diameter DR 17					13.35			13.35	14.65
0524	4" diameter DR 11					18.70			18.70	20.50
0528	4" diameter DR 17					18.70			18.70	20.50
0532	6" diameter DR 11					42.50			42.50	47
0536	6" diameter DR 17					42.50			42.50	47
0540	8" diameter DR 11					105			105	116
0544	8" diameter DR 26					61.50			61.50	67.50
0548	10" diameter DR 11					395			395	435
0552	10" diameter DR 26					365			365	400
0556	12" diameter DR 11					415			415	460
0560	12" diameter DR 26					375			375	415
0564	16" diameter DR 11					218			218	240
0568	16" diameter DR 26					206			206	227
0572	18" diameter DR 11					232			232	255
0576	18" diameter DR 26					212			212	233
0580	20" diameter DR 11					350			350	385
0584	20" diameter DR 26					335			335	365
0588	22" diameter DR 11					485			485	535
0592	22" diameter DR 26					460			460	505
0596	24" diameter DR 11					595			595	655
0600	24" diameter DR 26					570			570	625
0604	28" diameter DR 17					675			675	740
0608	28" diameter DR 26					655			655	720
0612	30" diameter DR 17					835			835	920
0616	30" diameter DR 26					815			815	895
0620	36" diameter DR 26					1,025			1,025	1,125
0624	42" diameter DR 26					1,325			1,325	1,450
0628	48" diameter DR 26					1,450			1,450	1,600

22 11 13 – Facility Water Distribution Piping

22 11 13.78 Pipe, High Density Polyethylene Plastic (HDPE)	Crew	Daily Output	Labor-Hours	Unit	Material	2012 Bare Costs Labor	Equipment	Total	Total Incl O&P
0632	54" diameter DR 26				Ea.	1,925			1,925	2,125
0700	Tee									
0704	1" diameter DR 11				Ea.	6.95			6.95	7.65
0708	1-1/2" diameter DR 11					9.75			9.75	10.75
0712	2" diameter DR 11					8.35			8.35	9.20
0716	3" diameter DR 11					15.35			15.35	16.85
0720	3" diameter DR 17					15.35			15.35	16.85
0724	4" diameter DR 11					22.50			22.50	24.50
0728	4" diameter DR 17					22.50			22.50	24.50
0732	6" diameter DR 11					56			56	61.50
0736	6" diameter DR 17					56			56	61.50
0740	8" diameter DR 11					138			138	152
0744	8" diameter DR 17					138			138	152
0748	10" diameter DR 11					410			410	450
0752	10" diameter DR 17					410			410	450
0756	12" diameter DR 11					550			550	605
0760	12" diameter DR 17					550			550	605
0764	16" diameter DR 11					290			290	320
0768	16" diameter DR 17					239			239	263
0772	18" diameter DR 11					410			410	450
0776	18" diameter DR 17					335			335	370
0780	20" diameter DR 11					500			500	550
0784	20" diameter DR 17					410			410	450
0788	22" diameter DR 11					640			640	705
0792	22" diameter DR 17					505			505	555
0796	24" diameter DR 11					795			795	870
0800	24" diameter DR 17					670			670	735
0804	28" diameter DR 17					1,300			1,300	1,425
0812	30" diameter DR 17					1,475			1,475	1,625
0820	36" diameter DR 17					2,450			2,450	2,700
0824	42" diameter DR 26					2,725			2,725	3,000
0828	48" diameter DR 26				▽	2,925			2,925	3,225
1000	Flange adptr, w/back-up ring and 1/2 cost of plated bolt set									
1004	1" diameter DR 11				Ea.	26.50			26.50	29
1008	1-1/2" diameter DR 11					26.50			26.50	29
1012	2" diameter DR 11					16.75			16.75	18.40
1016	3" diameter DR 11					19.55			19.55	21.50
1020	3" diameter DR 17					19.55			19.55	21.50
1024	4" diameter DR 11					26.50			26.50	29
1028	4" diameter DR 17					26.50			26.50	29
1032	6" diameter DR 11					37.50			37.50	41.50
1036	6" diameter DR 17					37.50			37.50	41.50
1040	8" diameter DR 11					54.50			54.50	60
1044	8" diameter DR 26					54.50			54.50	60
1048	10" diameter DR 11					86.50			86.50	95
1052	10" diameter DR 26					86.50			86.50	95
1056	12" diameter DR 11					127			127	140
1060	12" diameter DR 26					127			127	140
1064	16" diameter DR 11					272			272	299
1068	16" diameter DR 26					272			272	299
1072	18" diameter DR 11					355			355	390
1076	18" diameter DR 26					355			355	390
1080	20" diameter DR 11					490			490	540

22 11 13.78 Pipe, High Density Polyethylene Plastic (HDPE)	Crew	Daily Output	Labor-Hours	Unit	Material	2012 Bare Costs Labor	Equipment	Total	Total Incl O&P
1084	20" diameter DR 26				Ea.	490			490	540
1088	22" diameter DR 11					530			530	585
1092	22" diameter DR 26					530			530	585
1096	24" diameter DR 17					575			575	635
1100	24" diameter DR 32.5					575			575	635
1104	28" diameter DR 15.5					780			780	860
1108	28" diameter DR 32.5					780			780	860
1112	30" diameter DR 11					905			905	995
1116	30" diameter DR 21					905			905	995
1120	36" diameter DR 26					990			990	1,100
1124	42" diameter DR 26					1,125			1,125	1,250
1128	48" diameter DR 26					1,375			1,375	1,525
1132	54" diameter DR 26					1,675			1,675	1,850
1200	Reducer									
1208	2" x 1-1/2" diameter DR 11				Ea.	8			8	8.80
1212	3" x 2" diameter DR 11					8			8	8.80
1216	4" x 2" diameter DR 11					9.35			9.35	10.25
1220	4" x 3" diameter DR 11					12			12	13.20
1224	6" x 4" diameter DR 11					28			28	31
1228	8" x 6" diameter DR 11					42.50			42.50	47
1232	10" x 8" diameter DR 11					73.50			73.50	80.50
1236	12" x 8" diameter DR 11					120			120	132
1240	12" x 10" diameter DR 11					96			96	106
1244	14" x 12" diameter DR 11					107			107	117
1248	16" x 14" diameter DR 11					136			136	150
1252	18" x 16" diameter DR 11					165			165	182
1256	20" x 18" diameter DR 11					330			330	360
1260	22" x 20" diameter DR 11					405			405	445
1264	24" x 22" diameter DR 11					455			455	500
1268	26" x 24" diameter DR 11					535			535	585
1272	28" x 24" diameter DR 11					680			680	750
1276	32" x 28" diameter DR 17					880			880	970
1280	36" x 32" diameter DR 17					1,200			1,200	1,325
4000	Welding labor per joint, not including welding machine									
4010	Pipe joint size (cost based on thickest wall for each dia.)									
4030	1" pipe size	4 Skwk	273	.117	Ea.		5.30		5.30	8.25
4040	1-1/2" pipe size		175	.183			8.30		8.30	12.85
4050	2" pipe size		128	.250			11.35		11.35	17.55
4060	3" pipe size		100	.320			14.55		14.55	22.50
4070	4" pipe size		77	.416			18.85		18.85	29
4080	6" pipe size	5 Skwk	63	.635			29		29	44.50
4090	8" pipe size		48	.833			38		38	58.50
4100	10" pipe size		40	1			45.50		45.50	70
4110	12" pipe size	6 Skwk	41	1.171			53		53	82
4120	16" pipe size		34	1.412			64		64	99
4130	18" pipe size		32	1.500			68		68	105
4140	20" pipe size	8 Skwk	37	1.730			78.50		78.50	121
4150	22" pipe size		35	1.829			83		83	128
4160	24" pipe size		34	1.882			85.50		85.50	132
4170	28" pipe size		33	1.939			88		88	136
4180	30" pipe size		32	2			91		91	140
4190	36" pipe size		31	2.065			93.50		93.50	145
4200	42" pipe size		30	2.133			97		97	150

22 11 Facility Water Distribution

22 11 13 – Facility Water Distribution Piping

22 11 13.78 Pipe, High Density Polyethylene Plastic (HDPE)	Crew	Daily Output	Labor-Hours	Unit	Material	2012 Bare Costs Labor	Equipment	Total	Total Incl O&P
4210	48" pipe size	9 Skwk	33	2.182	Ea.		99		99	153
4220	54" pipe size	"	31	2.323	↓		105		105	163
4300	Note: Cost for set up each time welder is moved.									
4301	Add 50% of a weld cost									
4310	Welder usually remains stationary with pipe moved through it.									
4340	Weld machine, rental per day based on dia. capacity									
4350	1" thru 2" diameter				Ea.			40.50	40.50	44.50
4360	3" thru 4" diameter							46	46	50.50
4370	6" thru 8" diameter							103	103	113
4380	10" thru 12" diameter							178	178	196
4390	16" thru 18" diameter							259	259	285
4400	20" thru 24" diameter							500	500	550
4410	28" thru 32" diameter							545	545	600
4420	36" diameter							570	570	625
4430	42" thru 54" diameter				↓			890	890	980
5000	Dual wall contained pipe									
5040	Straight									
5054	1" DR 11 x 3" DR 11				L.F.	6.75			6.75	7.40
5058	1" DR 11 x 4" DR 11					7.20			7.20	7.90
5062	1-1/2" DR 11 x 4" DR 17					7.40			7.40	8.15
5066	2" DR 11 x 4" DR 17					7.95			7.95	8.75
5070	2" DR 11 x 6" DR 17					11.90			11.90	13.10
5074	3" DR 11 x 6" DR 17					13.30			13.30	14.60
5078	3" DR 11 x 6" DR 26					11.40			11.40	12.55
5086	3" DR 17 x 8" DR 17					16.85			16.85	18.55
5090	4" DR 11 x 8" DR 17					19.75			19.75	21.50
5094	4" DR 17 x 8" DR 26					15.60			15.60	17.15
5098	6" DR 11 x 10" DR 17					30.50			30.50	33.50
5102	6" DR 17 x 10" DR 26					23			23	25
5106	6" DR 26 x 10" DR 26					21.50			21.50	24
5110	8" DR 17 x 12" DR 26					32.50			32.50	36
5114	8" DR 26 x 12" DR 32.5					27.50			27.50	30.50
5118	10" DR 17 x 14" DR 26					45			45	50
5122	10" DR 17 x 16" DR 26					49.50			49.50	54.50
5126	10" DR 26 x 16" DR 26					45			45	49.50
5130	12" DR 26 x 16" DR 26					51			51	56.50
5134	12" DR 17 x 18" DR 26					65.50			65.50	72
5138	12" DR 26 x 18" DR 26					58.50			58.50	64.50
5142	14" DR 26 x 20" DR 32.5					64			64	70.50
5146	16" DR 26 x 22" DR 32.5					97			97	107
5150	18" DR 26 x 24" DR 32.5					89			89	98
5154	20" DR 32.5 x 28" DR 32.5					115			115	127
5158	22" DR 32.5 x 30" DR 32.5					115			115	127
5162	24" DR 32.5 x 32" DR 32.5				↓	147			147	162
5166	36" DR 32.5 x 42" DR 32.5					249			249	274
5300	Force transfer coupling									
5354	1" DR 11 x 3" DR 11				Ea.	243			243	267
5358	1" DR 11 x 4" DR 17					255			255	280
5362	1-1/2" DR 11 x 4" DR 17					267			267	293
5366	2" DR 11 x 4" DR 17					279			279	305
5370	2" DR 11 x 6" DR 17					405			405	445
5374	3" DR 11 x 6" DR 17					405			405	445
5378	3" DR 11 x 6" DR 26				↓	405			405	445

223

22 11 13 – Facility Water Distribution Piping

22 11 13.78 Pipe, High Density Polyethylene Plastic (HDPE)	Crew	Daily Output	Labor-Hours	Unit	Material	2012 Bare Costs Labor	Equipment	Total	Total Incl O&P
5382	3" DR 11 x 8" DR 11				Ea.	430			430	470
5386	3" DR 11 x 8" DR 17					430			430	470
5390	4" DR 11 x 8" DR 17					430			430	470
5394	4" DR 17 x 8" DR 26					375			375	415
5398	6" DR 11 x 10" DR 17					545			545	595
5402	6" DR 17 x 10" DR 26					445			445	490
5406	6" DR 26 x 10" DR 26					445			445	490
5410	8" DR 17 x 12" DR 26					595			595	655
5414	8" DR 26 x 12" DR 32.5					480			480	530
5418	10" DR 17 x 14" DR 26					780			780	855
5422	10" DR 17 x 16" DR 26					780			780	855
5426	10" DR 26 x 16" DR 26					780			780	855
5430	12" DR 26 x 16" DR 26					975			975	1,075
5434	12" DR 17 x 18" DR 26					1,000			1,000	1,100
5438	12" DR 26 x 18" DR 26					1,000			1,000	1,100
5442	14" DR 26 x 20" DR 32.5					1,050			1,050	1,150
5446	16" DR 26 x 22" DR 32.5					1,100			1,100	1,200
5450	18" DR 26 x 24" DR 32.5					1,175			1,175	1,300
5454	20" DR 32.5 x 28" DR 32.5					1,425			1,425	1,575
5458	22" DR 32.5 x 30" DR 32.5					1,575			1,575	1,750
5462	24" DR 32.5 x 32" DR 32.5					1,725			1,725	1,900
5466	36" DR 32.5 x 42" DR 32.5					2,850			2,850	3,125
5600	90° Elbow									
5654	1" DR 11 x 3" DR 11				Ea.	200			200	220
5658	1" DR 11 x 4" DR 17					192			192	211
5662	1-1/2" DR 11 x 4" DR 17					210			210	231
5666	2" DR 11 x 4" DR 17					222			222	244
5670	2" DR 11 x 6" DR 17					283			283	310
5674	3" DR 11 x 6" DR 17					325			325	355
5678	3" DR 17 x 6" DR 26					258			258	284
5682	3" DR 17 x 8" DR 11					520			520	575
5686	3" DR 17 x 8" DR 17					405			405	445
5690	4" DR 11 x 8" DR 17					480			480	525
5694	4" DR 17 x 8" DR 26					380			380	415
5698	6" DR 11 x 10" DR 17					635			635	700
5702	6" DR 17 x 10" DR 26					485			485	535
5706	6" DR 26 x 10" DR 26					455			455	500
5710	8" DR 17 x 12" DR 26					725			725	795
5714	8" DR 26 x 12" DR 32.5					670			670	735
5718	10" DR 17 x 14" DR 26					1,150			1,150	1,250
5722	10" DR 17 x 16" DR 26					1,100			1,100	1,200
5726	10" DR 26 x 16" DR 26					1,000			1,000	1,100
5730	12" DR 26 x 16" DR 26					1,125			1,125	1,225
5734	12" DR 17 x 18" DR 26					1,325			1,325	1,475
5738	12" DR 26 x 18" DR 26					1,225			1,225	1,350
5742	14" DR 26 x 20" DR 32.5					1,625			1,625	1,775
5746	16" DR 26 x 22" DR 32.5					1,625			1,625	1,800
5750	18" DR 26 x 24" DR 32.5					2,000			2,000	2,200
5754	20" DR 32.5 x 28" DR 32.5					2,300			2,300	2,525
5758	22" DR 32.5 x 30" DR 32.5					3,150			3,150	3,450
5762	24" DR 32.5 x 32" DR 32.5					3,050			3,050	3,350
5766	36" DR 32.5 x 42" DR 32.5					4,950			4,950	5,450
5800	45° Elbow									

22 11 Facility Water Distribution

22 11 13 – Facility Water Distribution Piping

22 11 13.78 Pipe, High Density Polyethylene Plastic (HDPE)	Crew	Daily Output	Labor-Hours	Unit	Material	2012 Bare Costs Labor	Equipment	Total	Total Incl O&P
5804	1" DR 11 x 3" DR 11				Ea.	120			120	132
5808	1" DR 11 x 4" DR 17					119			119	131
5812	1-1/2" DR 11 x 4" DR 17					128			128	141
5816	2" DR 11 x 4" DR 17					140			140	154
5820	2" DR 11 x 6" DR 17					175			175	193
5824	3" DR 11 x 6" DR 17					195			195	214
5828	3" DR 17 x 6" DR 26					161			161	177
5832	3" DR 17 x 8" DR 11					298			298	330
5836	3" DR 17 x 8" DR 17					238			238	262
5840	4" DR 11 x 8" DR 17					278			278	305
5844	4" DR 17 x 8" DR 26					227			227	250
5848	6" DR 11 x 10" DR 17					365			365	405
5852	6" DR 17 x 10" DR 26					288			288	315
5856	6" DR 26 x 10" DR 26					271			271	299
5860	8" DR 17 x 12" DR 26					440			440	480
5864	8" DR 26 x 12" DR 32.5					410			410	450
5868	10" DR 17 x 14" DR 26					685			685	755
5872	10" DR 17 x 16" DR 26					670			670	740
5876	10" DR 26 x 16" DR 26					630			630	690
5880	12" DR 26 x 16" DR 26					710			710	780
5884	12" DR 17 x 18" DR 26					835			835	920
5888	12" DR 26 x 18" DR 26					780			780	855
5892	14" DR 26 x 20" DR 32.5					1,000			1,000	1,100
5896	16" DR 26 x 22" DR 32.5					1,050			1,050	1,150
5900	18" DR 26 x 24" DR 32.5					1,250			1,250	1,375
5904	20" DR 32.5 x 28" DR 32.5					1,525			1,525	1,675
5908	22" DR 32.5 x 30" DR 32.5					1,925			1,925	2,125
5912	24" DR 32.5 x 32" DR 32.5					1,925			1,925	2,125
5916	36" DR 32.5 x 42" DR 32.5					3,000			3,000	3,275
6000	Access port with 4" riser									
6050	1" DR 11 x 4" DR 17				Ea.	262			262	288
6054	1-1/2" DR 11 x 4" DR 17					267			267	294
6058	2" DR 11 x 6" DR 17					325			325	360
6062	3" DR 11 x 6" DR 17					330			330	360
6066	3" DR 17 x 6" DR 26					320			320	355
6070	3" DR 17 x 8" DR 11					370			370	405
6074	3" DR 17 x 8" DR 17					350			350	385
6078	4" DR 11 x 8" DR 17					365			365	400
6082	4" DR 17 x 8" DR 26					350			350	385
6086	6" DR 11 x 10" DR 17					455			455	500
6090	6" DR 17 x 10" DR 26					420			420	460
6094	6" DR 26 x 10" DR 26					410			410	450
6098	8" DR 17 x 12" DR 26					440			440	485
6102	8" DR 26 x 12" DR 32.5					420			420	460
6200	End termination with vent plug									
6204	1" DR 11 x 3" DR 11				Ea.	217			217	238
6208	1" DR 11 x 4" DR 17					232			232	255
6212	1-1/2" DR 11 x 4" DR 17					232			232	255
6216	2" DR 11 x 4" DR 17					252			252	277
6220	2" DR 11 x 6" DR 17					287			287	315
6224	3" DR 11 x 6" DR 17					287			287	315
6228	3" DR 17 x 6" DR 26					287			287	315
6232	3" DR 17 x 8" DR 11					400			400	435

22 11 13.78 Pipe, High Density Polyethylene Plastic (HDPE)	Crew	Daily Output	Labor-Hours	Unit	Material	2012 Bare Costs Labor	Equipment	Total	Total Incl O&P
6236	3" DR 17 x 8" DR 17				Ea.	400			400	435
6240	4" DR 11 x 8" DR 17					400			400	435
6244	4" DR 17 x 8" DR 26					345			345	380
6248	6" DR 11 x 10" DR 17					470			470	520
6252	6" DR 17 x 10" DR 26					390			390	425
6256	6" DR 26 x 10" DR 26					390			390	425
6260	8" DR 17 x 12" DR 26					575			575	630
6264	8" DR 26 x 12" DR 32.5					460			460	505
6268	10" DR 17 x 14" DR 26					595			595	655
6272	10" DR 17 x 16" DR 26					595			595	655
6276	10" DR 26 x 16" DR 26					595			595	655
6280	12" DR 26 x 16" DR 26					595			595	655
6284	12" DR 17 x 18" DR 26					785			785	865
6288	12" DR 26 x 18" DR 26					785			785	865
6292	14" DR 26 x 20" DR 32.5					800			800	880
6296	16" DR 26 x 22" DR 32.5					930			930	1,025
6300	18" DR 26 x 24" DR 32.5					960			960	1,050
6304	20" DR 32.5 x 28" DR 32.5					1,225			1,225	1,350
6308	22" DR 32.5 x 30" DR 32.5					1,350			1,350	1,475
6312	24" DR 32.5 x 32" DR 32.5					1,500			1,500	1,650
6316	36" DR 32.5 x 42" DR 32.5				▼	2,175			2,175	2,400
6600	Tee									
6604	1" DR 11 x 3" DR 11				Ea.	221			221	243
6608	1" DR 11 x 4" DR 17					274			274	300
6612	1-1/2" DR 11 x 4" DR 17					305			305	335
6616	2" DR 11 x 4" DR 17					335			335	365
6620	2" DR 11 x 6" DR 17					405			405	445
6624	3" DR 11 x 6" DR 17					465			465	510
6628	3" DR 17 x 6" DR 26					455			455	500
6632	3" DR 17 x 8" DR 11					550			550	605
6636	3" DR 17 x 8" DR 17					520			520	575
6640	4" DR 11 x 8" DR 17					570			570	625
6644	4" DR 17 x 8" DR 26					545			545	600
6648	6" DR 11 x 10" DR 17					710			710	780
6652	6" DR 17 x 10" DR 26					675			675	740
6656	6" DR 26 x 10" DR 26					665			665	735
6660	8" DR 17 x 12" DR 26					665			665	735
6664	8" DR 26 x 12" DR 32.5					870			870	955
6668	10" DR 17 x 14" DR 26					1,000			1,000	1,100
6672	10" DR 17 x 16" DR 26					1,050			1,050	1,150
6676	10" DR 26 x 16" DR 26					1,050			1,050	1,150
6680	12" DR 26 x 16" DR 26					1,150			1,150	1,250
6684	12" DR 17 x 18" DR 26					1,150			1,150	1,250
6688	12" DR 26 x 18" DR 26					1,250			1,250	1,400
6692	14" DR 26 x 20" DR 32.5					1,675			1,675	1,825
6696	16" DR 26 x 22" DR 32.5					2,050			2,050	2,250
6700	18" DR 26 x 24" DR 32.5					2,225			2,225	2,450
6704	20" DR 32.5 x 28" DR 32.5					2,800			2,800	3,100
6708	22" DR 32.5 x 30" DR 32.5					3,325			3,325	3,675
6712	24" DR 32.5 x 32" DR 32.5					4,000			4,000	4,375
6716	36" DR 32.5 x 42" DR 32.5				▼	8,125			8,125	8,950
6800	Wye									
6816	2" DR 11 x 4" DR 17				Ea.	420			420	460

22 11 13 – Facility Water Distribution Piping

22 11 13.78 Pipe, High Density Polyethylene Plastic (HDPE)	Crew	Daily Output	Labor-Hours	Unit	Material	2012 Bare Costs Labor		Equipment	Total	Total Incl O&P
6820	2" DR 11 x 6" DR 17				Ea.	475				475	525
6824	3" DR 11 x 6" DR 17					480				480	530
6828	3" DR 17 x 6" DR 26					465				465	515
6832	3" DR 17 x 8" DR 11					585				585	645
6836	3" DR 17 x 8" DR 17					545				545	600
6840	4" DR 11 x 8" DR 17					595				595	655
6844	4" DR 17 x 8" DR 26					565				565	625
6848	6" DR 11 x 10" DR 17					740				740	815
6852	6" DR 17 x 10" DR 26					685				685	755
6856	6" DR 26 x 10" DR 26					685				685	750
6860	8" DR 17 x 12" DR 26					980				980	1,075
6864	8" DR 26 x 12" DR 32.5					945				945	1,050
6868	10" DR 17 x 14" DR 26					1,175				1,175	1,300
6872	10" DR 17 x 16" DR 26					1,250				1,250	1,375
6876	10" DR 26 x 16" DR 26					1,225				1,225	1,350
6880	12" DR 26 x 16" DR 26					1,375				1,375	1,525
6884	12" DR 17 x 18" DR 26					1,550				1,550	1,725
6888	12" DR 26 x 18" DR 26					1,575				1,575	1,750
6892	14" DR 26 x 20" DR 32.5					1,925				1,925	2,125
6896	16" DR 26 x 22" DR 32.5					2,775				2,775	3,050
6900	18" DR 26 x 24" DR 32.5					3,250				3,250	3,575
6904	20" DR 32.5 x 28" DR 32.5					4,075				4,075	4,500
6908	22" DR 32.5 x 30" DR 32.5					4,650				4,650	5,125
6912	24" DR 32.5 x 32" DR 32.5				▼	5,300				5,300	5,825
9000	Welding labor per joint, not including welding machine										
9010	Pipe joint size, outer pipe (cost based on the thickest walls)										
9020	Straight pipe										
9050	3" pipe size	4 Skwk	96	.333	Ea.		15.15			15.15	23.50
9060	4" pipe size	"	77	.416			18.85			18.85	29
9070	6" pipe size	5 Skwk	60	.667			30.50			30.50	47
9080	8" pipe size	"	40	1			45.50			45.50	70
9090	10" pipe size	6 Skwk	41	1.171			53			53	82
9100	12" pipe size		39	1.231			56			56	86.50
9110	14" pipe size		38	1.263			57.50			57.50	88.50
9120	16" pipe size	▼	35	1.371			62.50			62.50	96.50
9130	18" pipe size	8 Skwk	45	1.422			64.50			64.50	100
9140	20" pipe size		42	1.524			69			69	107
9150	22" pipe size		40	1.600			72.50			72.50	112
9160	24" pipe size		38	1.684			76.50			76.50	118
9170	28" pipe size		37	1.730			78.50			78.50	121
9180	30" pipe size		36	1.778			80.50			80.50	125
9190	32" pipe size		35	1.829			83			83	128
9200	42" pipe size	▼	32	2	▼		91			91	140
9300	Note: Cost for set up each time welder is moved.										
9301	Add 100% of weld labor cost										
9310	For handling between fitting welds add 50% of weld labor cost										
9320	Welder usually remains stationary with pipe moved through it										
9360	Weld machine, rental per day based on dia. capacity										
9380	3" thru 4" diameter				Ea.				63.50	63.50	70
9390	6" thru 8" diameter								207	207	228
9400	10" thru 12" diameter								310	310	340
9410	14" thru 18" diameter								420	420	460
9420	20" thru 24" diameter				▼				750	750	825

22 11 Facility Water Distribution

22 11 13 – Facility Water Distribution Piping

22 11 13.78 Pipe, High Density Polyethylene Plastic (HDPE)	Crew	Daily Output	Labor-Hours	Unit	Material	2012 Bare Costs Labor	Equipment	Total	Total Incl O&P
9430	28" thru 32" diameter				Ea.			880	880	970
9440	42" thru 58" diameter				↓			910	910	1,000

22 11 19 – Domestic Water Piping Specialties

22 11 19.10 Flexible Connectors

		Crew	Daily Output	Labor-Hours	Unit	Material	Labor	Equipment	Total	Total Incl O&P
0010	**FLEXIBLE CONNECTORS**, Corrugated, 7/8" O.D., 1/2" I.D.									
0050	Gas, seamless brass, steel fittings									
0200	12" long	1 Plum	36	.222	Ea.	16.30	12.15		28.45	36
0220	18" long		36	.222		20	12.15		32.15	40.50
0240	24" long		34	.235		24	12.85		36.85	46
0260	30" long		34	.235		25.50	12.85		38.35	47.50
0280	36" long		32	.250		28.50	13.65		42.15	52
0320	48" long		30	.267		36	14.55		50.55	62
0340	60" long		30	.267		43	14.55		57.55	69.50
0360	72" long	↓	30	.267	↓	50	14.55		64.55	76.50
2000	Water, copper tubing, dielectric separators									
2100	12" long	1 Plum	36	.222	Ea.	15.95	12.15		28.10	36
2220	15" long		36	.222		17.70	12.15		29.85	38
2240	18" long		36	.222		19.25	12.15		31.40	39.50
2260	24" long	↓	34	.235	↓	23.50	12.85		36.35	45.50

22 11 19.14 Flexible Metal Hose

		Crew	Daily Output	Labor-Hours	Unit	Material	Labor	Equipment	Total	Total Incl O&P
0010	**FLEXIBLE METAL HOSE**, Connectors, standard lengths									
0100	Bronze braided, bronze ends									
0120	3/8" diameter x 12"	1 Stpi	26	.308	Ea.	18.85	17.15		36	47
0140	1/2" diameter x 12"		24	.333		17.95	18.55		36.50	48
0160	3/4" diameter x 12"		20	.400		26.50	22.50		49	62.50
0180	1" diameter x 18"		19	.421		34	23.50		57.50	73
0200	1-1/2" diameter x 18"		13	.615		53.50	34.50		88	111
0220	2" diameter x 18"	↓	11	.727	↓	64.50	40.50		105	132
1000	Carbon steel ends									
1020	1/4" diameter x 12"	1 Stpi	28	.286	Ea.	13.60	15.90		29.50	39
1040	3/8" diameter x 12"		26	.308		13.95	17.15		31.10	41.50
1060	1/2" diameter x 12"		24	.333		15.40	18.55		33.95	45
1080	1/2" diameter x 24"		24	.333		42	18.55		60.55	74
1120	3/4" diameter x 12"		20	.400		25	22.50		47.50	61
1140	3/4" diameter x 24"		20	.400		52	22.50		74.50	90.50
1160	3/4" diameter x 36"		20	.400		61.50	22.50		84	101
1180	1" diameter x 18"		19	.421		31.50	23.50		55	70
1200	1" diameter x 30"		19	.421		96	23.50		119.50	141
1220	1" diameter x 36"		19	.421		72.50	23.50		96	115
1240	1-1/4" diameter x 18"		15	.533		43	29.50		72.50	92.50
1260	1-1/4" diameter x 36"		15	.533		97	29.50		126.50	151
1280	1-1/2" diameter x 18"		13	.615		61	34.50		95.50	119
1300	1-1/2" diameter x 36"		13	.615		105	34.50		139.50	168
1320	2" diameter x 24"		11	.727		88.50	40.50		129	159
1340	2" diameter x 36"		11	.727		129	40.50		169.50	203
1360	2-1/2" diameter x 24"		9	.889		202	49.50		251.50	298
1380	2-1/2" diameter x 36"		9	.889		253	49.50		302.50	355
1400	3" diameter x 24"		7	1.143		279	63.50		342.50	400
1420	3" diameter x 36"	↓	7	1.143	↓	96	63.50		159.50	202
2000	Carbon steel braid, carbon steel solid ends									
2100	1/2" diameter x 12"	1 Stpi	24	.333	Ea.	38.50	18.55		57.05	70
2120	3/4" diameter x 12"	↓	20	.400	↓	58	22.50		80.50	97.50

22 11 19.14 Flexible Metal Hose		Crew	Daily Output	Labor-Hours	Unit	Material	2012 Bare Costs Labor	Equipment	Total	Total Incl O&P
2140	1" diameter x 12"	1 Stpi	19	.421	Ea.	82	23.50		105.50	126
2160	1-1/4" diameter x 12"		15	.533		27	29.50		56.50	74.50
2180	1-1/2" diameter x 12"		13	.615		29	34.50		63.50	83.50
3000	Stainless steel braid, welded on carbon steel ends									
3100	1/2" diameter x 12"	1 Stpi	24	.333	Ea.	50.50	18.55		69.05	83.50
3120	3/4" diameter x 12"		20	.400		62.50	22.50		85	103
3140	3/4" diameter x 24"		20	.400		49	22.50		71.50	87.50
3160	3/4" diameter x 36"		20	.400		52.50	22.50		75	91.50
3180	1" diameter x 12"		19	.421		59.50	23.50		83	101
3200	1" diameter x 24"		19	.421		55	23.50		78.50	96
3220	1" diameter x 36"		19	.421		102	23.50		125.50	148
3240	1-1/4" diameter x 12"		15	.533		111	29.50		140.50	167
3260	1-1/4" diameter x 24"		15	.533		121	29.50		150.50	178
3280	1-1/4" diameter x 36"		15	.533		137	29.50		166.50	195
3300	1-1/2" diameter x 12"		13	.615		43	34.50		77.50	99
3320	1-1/2" diameter x 24"		13	.615		132	34.50		166.50	197
3340	1-1/2" diameter x 36"		13	.615		154	34.50		188.50	222
3400	Metal stainless steel braid, over corrugated stainless steel, flanged ends									
3410	150 PSI									
3420	1/2" diameter x 12"	1 Stpi	24	.333	Ea.	144	18.55		162.55	186
3430	1" diameter x 12"		20	.400		180	22.50		202.50	232
3440	1-1/2" diameter x 12"		15	.533		204	29.50		233.50	269
3450	2-1/2" diameter x 9"		12	.667		108	37		145	175
3460	3" diameter x 9"		9	.889		93	49.50		142.50	177
3470	4" diameter x 9"		7	1.143		113	63.50		176.50	220
3480	4" diameter x 30"		5	1.600		560	89		649	750
3490	4" diameter x 36"		4.80	1.667		580	93		673	780
3500	6" diameter x 11"		5	1.600		188	89		277	340
3510	6" diameter x 36"		3.80	2.105		685	117		802	925
3520	8" diameter x 12"		4	2		410	111		521	620
3530	10" diameter x 13"		3	2.667		625	149		774	915
3540	12" diameter x 14"	Q-5	4	4		950	201		1,151	1,350
6000	Molded rubber with helical wire reinforcement									
6010	150 PSI									
6020	1-1/2" diameter x 12"	1 Stpi	15	.533	Ea.	88	29.50		117.50	142
6030	2" diameter x 12"		12	.667		240	37		277	320
6040	3" diameter x 12"		8	1		251	55.50		306.50	360
6050	4" diameter x 12"		6	1.333		320	74.50		394.50	460
6060	6" diameter x 18"		4	2		475	111		586	695
6070	8" diameter x 24"		3	2.667		665	149		814	960
6080	10" diameter x 24"		2	4		810	223		1,033	1,225
6090	12" diameter x 24"	Q-5	3	5.333		925	267		1,192	1,425
7000	Molded teflon with stainless steel flanges									
7010	150 PSI									
7020	2-1/2" diameter x 3-3/16"	Q-1	7.80	2.051	Ea.	2,325	101		2,426	2,700
7030	3" diameter x 3-5/8"		6.50	2.462		1,625	121		1,746	1,950
7040	4" diameter x 3-5/8"		5	3.200		2,100	157		2,257	2,550
7050	6" diameter x 4"		4.30	3.721		2,950	183		3,133	3,525
7060	8" diameter x 6"		3.80	4.211		4,700	207		4,907	5,475

22 11 Facility Water Distribution

22 11 19 – Domestic Water Piping Specialties

22 11 19.18 Mixing Valve	Crew	Daily Output	Labor-Hours	Unit	Material	2012 Bare Costs Labor	Equipment	Total	Total Incl O&P
0010 **MIXING VALVE**, Automatic, water tempering.									
0040 1/2" size	1 Stpi	19	.421	Ea.	505	23.50		528.50	590
0050 3/4" size		18	.444		505	25		530	595
0100 1" size		16	.500		745	28		773	860
0120 1-1/4" size		13	.615		1,025	34.50		1,059.50	1,175
0140 1-1/2" size		10	.800		1,225	44.50		1,269.50	1,425
0160 2" size		8	1		1,525	55.50		1,580.50	1,750
0170 2-1/2" size		6	1.333		1,525	74.50		1,599.50	1,775
0180 3" size		4	2		3,600	111		3,711	4,125
0190 4" size	▼	3	2.667	▼	3,600	149		3,749	4,175

22 11 19.22 Pressure Reducing Valve

22 11 19.22 Pressure Reducing Valve	Crew	Daily Output	Labor-Hours	Unit	Material	2012 Bare Costs Labor	Equipment	Total	Total Incl O&P
0010 **PRESSURE REDUCING VALVE**, Steam, pilot operated.									
0100 Threaded, iron body									
0200 1-1/2" size	1 Stpi	8	1	Ea.	1,700	55.50		1,755.50	1,950
0220 2" size	"	5	1.600	"	1,950	89		2,039	2,275
1000 Flanged, iron body, 125 lb. flanges									
1020 2" size	1 Stpi	8	1	Ea.	1,975	55.50		2,030.50	2,250
1040 2-1/2" size	"	4	2		2,375	111		2,486	2,800
1060 3" size	Q-5	4.50	3.556		2,875	178		3,053	3,450
1080 4" size	"	3	5.333		4,150	267		4,417	4,975
1500 For 250 lb. flanges, add				▼	5%				

22 11 19.26 Pressure Regulators

22 11 19.26 Pressure Regulators	Crew	Daily Output	Labor-Hours	Unit	Material	2012 Bare Costs Labor	Equipment	Total	Total Incl O&P
0010 **PRESSURE REGULATORS**									
0100 Gas appliance regulators									
0106 Main burner and pilot applications									
0108 Rubber seat poppet type									
0109 1/8" pipe size	1 Stpi	24	.333	Ea.	14.80	18.55		33.35	44.50
0110 1/4" pipe size		24	.333		17.05	18.55		35.60	47
0112 3/8" pipe size		24	.333		18.15	18.55		36.70	48
0113 1/2" pipe size		24	.333		20	18.55		38.55	50
0114 3/4" pipe size	▼	20	.400	▼	23.50	22.50		46	59.50
0122 Lever action type									
0123 3/8" pipe size	1 Stpi	24	.333	Ea.	22.50	18.55		41.05	53
0124 1/2" pipe size		24	.333		22.50	18.55		41.05	53
0125 3/4" pipe size		20	.400		44.50	22.50		67	82.50
0126 1" pipe size	▼	19	.421	▼	44.50	23.50		68	84.50
0132 Double diaphragm type									
0133 3/8" pipe size	1 Stpi	24	.333	Ea.	33	18.55		51.55	64.50
0134 1/2" pipe size		24	.333		46	18.55		64.55	78.50
0135 3/4" pipe size		20	.400		76.50	22.50		99	118
0136 1" pipe size		19	.421		96	23.50		119.50	141
0137 1-1/4" pipe size		15	.533		325	29.50		354.50	400
0138 1-1/2" pipe size		13	.615		600	34.50		634.50	710
0139 2" pipe size	▼	11	.727		600	40.50		640.50	720
0140 2-1/2" pipe size	Q-5	15	1.067		1,150	53.50		1,203.50	1,350
0141 3" pipe size		13	1.231		1,150	61.50		1,211.50	1,375
0142 4" pipe size (flanged)	▼	8	2	▼	2,075	100		2,175	2,425
0160 Main burner only									
0162 Straight-thru-flow design									
0163 1/2" pipe size	1 Stpi	24	.333	Ea.	37.50	18.55		56.05	69
0164 3/4" pipe size		20	.400		51	22.50		73.50	89.50
0165 1" pipe size	▼	19	.421	▼	72.50	23.50		96	115

22 11 Facility Water Distribution

22 11 19 – Domestic Water Piping Specialties

22 11 19.26 Pressure Regulators	Crew	Daily Output	Labor-Hours	Unit	Material	2012 Bare Costs Labor	Equipment	Total	Total Incl O&P
0166 1-1/4" pipe size	1 Stpi	15	.533	Ea.	72.50	29.50		102	125
0200 Oil, light, hot water, ordinary steam, threaded									
0220 Bronze body, 1/4" size	1 Stpi	24	.333	Ea.	143	18.55		161.55	186
0230 3/8" size		24	.333		155	18.55		173.55	198
0240 1/2" size		24	.333		192	18.55		210.55	240
0250 3/4" size		20	.400		229	22.50		251.50	286
0260 1" size		19	.421		350	23.50		373.50	420
0270 1-1/4" size		15	.533		470	29.50		499.50	560
0280 1-1/2" size		13	.615		505	34.50		539.50	605
0290 2" size		11	.727		920	40.50		960.50	1,050
0320 Iron body, 1/4" size		24	.333		112	18.55		130.55	151
0330 3/8" size		24	.333		132	18.55		150.55	173
0340 1/2" size		24	.333		140	18.55		158.55	182
0350 3/4" size		20	.400		170	22.50		192.50	221
0360 1" size		19	.421		221	23.50		244.50	280
0370 1-1/4" size		15	.533		305	29.50		334.50	385
0380 1-1/2" size		13	.615		340	34.50		374.50	425
0390 2" size	▼	11	.727	▼	495	40.50		535.50	605
0500 Oil, heavy, viscous fluids, threaded									
0520 Bronze body, 3/8" size	1 Stpi	24	.333	Ea.	246	18.55		264.55	299
0530 1/2" size		24	.333		315	18.55		333.55	380
0540 3/4" size		20	.400		355	22.50		377.50	425
0550 1" size		19	.421		440	23.50		463.50	520
0560 1-1/4" size		15	.533		620	29.50		649.50	730
0570 1-1/2" size		13	.615		710	34.50		744.50	835
0600 Iron body, 3/8" size		24	.333		196	18.55		214.55	244
0620 1/2" size		24	.333		238	18.55		256.55	290
0630 3/4" size		20	.400		270	22.50		292.50	330
0640 1" size		19	.421		320	23.50		343.50	385
0650 1-1/4" size		15	.533		460	29.50		489.50	550
0660 1-1/2" size	▼	13	.615	▼	495	34.50		529.50	595
0800 Process steam, wet or super heated, monel trim, threaded									
0820 Bronze body, 1/4" size	1 Stpi	24	.333	Ea.	560	18.55		578.55	645
0830 3/8" size		24	.333		560	18.55		578.55	645
0840 1/2" size		24	.333		645	18.55		663.55	740
0850 3/4" size		20	.400		760	22.50		782.50	870
0860 1" size		19	.421		955	23.50		978.50	1,075
0870 1-1/4" size		15	.533		1,175	29.50		1,204.50	1,350
0880 1-1/2" size		13	.615		1,425	34.50		1,459.50	1,625
0920 Iron body, max 125 PSIG press out, 1/4" size		24	.333		745	18.55		763.55	850
0930 3/8" size		24	.333		745	18.55		763.55	850
0940 1/2" size		24	.333		925	18.55		943.55	1,050
0950 3/4" size		20	.400		1,125	22.50		1,147.50	1,275
0960 1" size		19	.421		1,425	23.50		1,448.50	1,600
0970 1-1/4" size		15	.533		1,725	29.50		1,754.50	1,950
0980 1-1/2" size	▼	13	.615	▼	2,125	34.50		2,159.50	2,400
3000 Steam, high capacity, bronze body, stainless steel trim									
3020 Threaded, 1/2" diameter	1 Stpi	24	.333	Ea.	1,550	18.55		1,568.55	1,750
3030 3/4" diameter		24	.333		1,550	18.55		1,568.55	1,750
3040 1" diameter		19	.421		1,750	23.50		1,773.50	1,950
3060 1-1/4" diameter		15	.533		1,925	29.50		1,954.50	2,175
3080 1-1/2" diameter		13	.615		2,200	34.50		2,234.50	2,475
3100 2" diameter	▼	11	.727	▼	2,700	40.50		2,740.50	3,025

22 11 19.26 Pressure Regulators

		Crew	Daily Output	Labor-Hours	Unit	Material	2012 Bare Costs Labor	Equipment	Total	Total Incl O&P
3120	2-1/2" diameter	Q-5	12	1.333	Ea.	3,375	67		3,442	3,825
3140	3" diameter	"	11	1.455	↓	3,850	73		3,923	4,350
3500	Flanged connection, iron body, 125 lb. W.S.P.									
3520	3" diameter	Q-5	11	1.455	Ea.	4,225	73		4,298	4,750
3540	4" diameter	"	5	3.200	"	5,325	160		5,485	6,100
9002	For water pressure regulators, see Section 22 05 23.20									

22 11 19.30 Pressure and Temperature Safety Plug

		Crew	Daily Output	Labor-Hours	Unit	Material	2012 Bare Costs Labor	Equipment	Total	Total Incl O&P
0010	**PRESSURE & TEMPERATURE SAFETY PLUG**									
1000	3/4" external thread, 3/8" diam. element									
1020	Carbon steel									
1050	7-1/2" insertion	1 Stpi	32	.250	Ea.	87	13.95		100.95	117
1120	304 stainless steel									
1150	7-1/2" insertion	1 Stpi	32	.250	Ea.	81.50	13.95		95.45	111
1220	316 Stainless steel									
1250	7-1/2" insertion	1 Stpi	32	.250	Ea.	85.50	13.95		99.45	115

22 11 19.34 Sleeves and Escutcheons

		Crew	Daily Output	Labor-Hours	Unit	Material	2012 Bare Costs Labor	Equipment	Total	Total Incl O&P
0010	**SLEEVES & ESCUTCHEONS**									
0100	Pipe sleeve									
0110	Steel, w/water stop, 12" long, with link seal									
0120	2" diam. for 1/2" carrier pipe	1 Plum	8.40	.952	Ea.	50	52		102	134
0130	2-1/2" diam. for 3/4" carrier pipe		8	1		57	54.50		111.50	145
0140	2-1/2" diam. for 1" carrier pipe		8	1		53.50	54.50		108	142
0150	3" diam. for 1-1/4" carrier pipe		7.20	1.111		69.50	60.50		130	168
0160	3-1/2" diam. for 1-1/2" carrier pipe		6.80	1.176		69	64		133	173
0170	4" diam. for 2" carrier pipe		6	1.333		75	73		148	193
0180	4" diam. for 2-1/2" carrier pipe		6	1.333		76.50	73		149.50	194
0190	5" diam. for 3" carrier pipe		5.40	1.481		89.50	81		170.50	221
0200	6" diam. for 4" carrier pipe	↓	4.80	1.667		101	91		192	248
0210	10" diam. for 6" carrier pipe	Q-1	8	2		174	98.50		272.50	340
0220	12" diam. for 8" carrier pipe		7.20	2.222		244	109		353	435
0230	14" diam. for 10" carrier pipe		6.40	2.500		281	123		404	495
0240	16" diam. for 12" carrier pipe		5.80	2.759		320	136		456	560
0250	18" diam. for 14" carrier pipe		5.20	3.077		470	151		621	750
0260	24" diam. for 18" carrier pipe		4	4		735	197		932	1,100
0270	24" diam. for 20" carrier pipe		4	4		640	197		837	1,000
0280	30" diam. for 24" carrier pipe	↓	3.20	5	↓	975	246		1,221	1,450
0500	Wall sleeve									
0510	Ductile iron with rubber gasket seal									
0520	3"	1 Plum	8.40	.952	Ea.	700	52		752	850
0530	4"		7.20	1.111		750	60.50		810.50	915
0540	6"		6	1.333		920	73		993	1,125
0550	8"		4	2		1,125	109		1,234	1,425
0560	10"		3	2.667		1,375	146		1,521	1,750
0570	12"	↓	2.40	3.333	↓	1,625	182		1,807	2,075
5000	Escutcheon									
5100	Split ring, pipe									
5110	Chrome plated									
5120	1/2"	1 Plum	160	.050	Ea.	1.05	2.73		3.78	5.30
5130	3/4"		160	.050		1.16	2.73		3.89	5.40
5140	1"		135	.059		1.25	3.24		4.49	6.25
5150	1-1/2"		115	.070		1.76	3.80		5.56	7.70
5160	2"	↓	100	.080	↓	1.96	4.37		6.33	8.75

22 11 Facility Water Distribution

22 11 19 – Domestic Water Piping Specialties

22 11 19.34 Sleeves and Escutcheons		Crew	Daily Output	Labor-Hours	Unit	Material	2012 Bare Costs Labor	Equipment	Total	Total Incl O&P
5170	4"	1 Plum	80	.100	Ea.	4.35	5.45		9.80	13.05
5180	6"	↓	68	.118	↓	7.25	6.40		13.65	17.70
5400	Shallow flange type									
5410	Chrome plated steel									
5420	1/2" CTS	1 Plum	180	.044	Ea.	.32	2.43		2.75	4.01
5430	3/4" CTS		180	.044		.25	2.43		2.68	3.94
5440	1/2" IPS		180	.044		.34	2.43		2.77	4.03
5450	3/4" IPS		180	.044		.38	2.43		2.81	4.08
5460	1" IPS		175	.046		.44	2.50		2.94	4.24
5470	1-1/2" IPS		170	.047		.72	2.57		3.29	4.67
5480	2" IPS	↓	160	.050	↓	.86	2.73		3.59	5.05

22 11 19.38 Water Supply Meters

		Crew	Daily Output	Labor-Hours	Unit	Material	2012 Bare Costs Labor	Equipment	Total	Total Incl O&P
0010	**WATER SUPPLY METERS**									
1000	Detector, serves dual systems such as fire and domestic or									
1020	process water, wide range cap., UL and FM approved									
1100	3" mainline x 2" by-pass, 400 GPM	Q-1	3.60	4.444	Ea.	6,825	218		7,043	7,825
1140	4" mainline x 2" by-pass, 700 GPM	"	2.50	6.400		6,825	315		7,140	7,975
1180	6" mainline x 3" by-pass, 1600 GPM	Q-2	2.60	9.231		10,400	470		10,870	12,200
1220	8" mainline x 4" by-pass, 2800 GPM		2.10	11.429		15,500	585		16,085	17,900
1260	10" mainline x 6" by-pass, 4400 GPM		2	12		22,100	610		22,710	25,200
1300	10" x 12" mainlines x 6" by-pass, 5400 GPM	↓	1.70	14.118	↓	30,000	720		30,720	34,100
2000	Domestic/commercial, bronze									
2020	Threaded									
2060	5/8" diameter, to 20 GPM	1 Plum	16	.500	Ea.	46	27.50		73.50	91.50
2080	3/4" diameter, to 30 GPM		14	.571		83.50	31		114.50	139
2100	1" diameter, to 50 GPM	↓	12	.667	↓	127	36.50		163.50	195
2300	Threaded/flanged									
2340	1-1/2" diameter, to 100 GPM	1 Plum	8	1	Ea.	310	54.50		364.50	425
2360	2" diameter, to 160 GPM	"	6	1.333	"	420	73		493	570
2600	Flanged, compound									
2640	3" diameter, 320 GPM	Q-1	3	5.333	Ea.	2,850	262		3,112	3,550
2660	4" diameter, to 500 GPM		1.50	10.667		4,575	525		5,100	5,825
2680	6" diameter, to 1,000 GPM		1	16		7,300	785		8,085	9,200
2700	8" diameter, to 1,800 GPM	↓	.80	20	↓	11,500	985		12,485	14,100
7000	Turbine									
7260	Flanged									
7300	2" diameter, to 160 GPM	1 Plum	7	1.143	Ea.	560	62.50		622.50	710
7320	3" diameter, to 450 GPM	Q-1	3.60	4.444		1,175	218		1,393	1,600
7340	4" diameter, to 650 GPM	"	2.50	6.400		1,925	315		2,240	2,600
7360	6" diameter, to 1800 GPM	Q-2	2.60	9.231		3,450	470		3,920	4,500
7380	8" diameter, to 2500 GPM		2.10	11.429		5,475	585		6,060	6,900
7400	10" diameter, to 5500 GPM	↓	1.70	14.118	↓	7,400	720		8,120	9,200

22 11 19.42 Backflow Preventers

		Crew	Daily Output	Labor-Hours	Unit	Material	2012 Bare Costs Labor	Equipment	Total	Total Incl O&P
0010	**BACKFLOW PREVENTERS**, Includes valves									
0020	and four test cocks, corrosion resistant, automatic operation									
1000	Double check principle									
1010	Threaded, with ball valves									
1020	3/4" pipe size	1 Plum	16	.500	Ea.	220	27.50		247.50	283
1030	1" pipe size		14	.571		252	31		283	325
1040	1-1/2" pipe size		10	.800		535	43.50		578.50	655
1050	2" pipe size	↓	7	1.143	↓	615	62.50		677.50	775
1080	Threaded, with gate valves									

22 11 19.42 Backflow Preventers	Crew	Daily Output	Labor-Hours	Unit	Material	2012 Bare Costs Labor	Equipment	Total	Total Incl O&P
1100	3/4" pipe size	1 Plum	16	.500	Ea.	1,025	27.50		1,052.50	1,175
1120	1" pipe size		14	.571		1,050	31		1,081	1,200
1140	1-1/2" pipe size		10	.800		1,350	43.50		1,393.50	1,550
1160	2" pipe size		7	1.143		1,650	62.50		1,712.50	1,900
1200	Flanged, valves are gate									
1210	3" pipe size	Q-1	4.50	3.556	Ea.	2,650	175		2,825	3,200
1220	4" pipe size	"	3	5.333		2,750	262		3,012	3,450
1230	6" pipe size	Q-2	3	8		4,075	410		4,485	5,100
1240	8" pipe size		2	12		7,400	610		8,010	9,075
1250	10" pipe size		1	24		11,000	1,225		12,225	14,000
1300	Flanged, valves are OS&Y									
1370	1" pipe size	1 Plum	5	1.600	Ea.	1,125	87.50		1,212.50	1,375
1374	1-1/2" pipe size		5	1.600		1,450	87.50		1,537.50	1,725
1378	2" pipe size		4.80	1.667		1,750	91		1,841	2,050
1380	3" pipe size	Q-1	4.50	3.556		3,550	175		3,725	4,200
1400	4" pipe size	"	3	5.333		5,250	262		5,512	6,175
1420	6" pipe size	Q-2	3	8		8,200	410		8,610	9,650
1430	8" pipe size	"	2	12		16,200	610		16,810	18,700
4000	Reduced pressure principle									
4100	Threaded, bronze, valves are ball									
4120	3/4" pipe size	1 Plum	16	.500	Ea.	420	27.50		447.50	505
4140	1" pipe size		14	.571		455	31		486	545
4150	1-1/4" pipe size		12	.667		835	36.50		871.50	975
4160	1-1/2" pipe size		10	.800		915	43.50		958.50	1,075
4180	2" pipe size		7	1.143		1,025	62.50		1,087.50	1,225
5000	Flanged, bronze, valves are OS&Y									
5060	2-1/2" pipe size	Q-1	5	3.200	Ea.	6,100	157		6,257	6,950
5080	3" pipe size		4.50	3.556		7,100	175		7,275	8,100
5100	4" pipe size		3	5.333		8,325	262		8,587	9,575
5120	6" pipe size	Q-2	3	8		13,300	410		13,710	15,200
5200	Flanged, iron, valves are gate									
5210	2-1/2" pipe size	Q-1	5	3.200	Ea.	2,525	157		2,682	3,000
5220	3" pipe size		4.50	3.556		2,650	175		2,825	3,175
5230	4" pipe size		3	5.333		3,575	262		3,837	4,325
5240	6" pipe size	Q-2	3	8		5,025	410		5,435	6,150
5250	8" pipe size		2	12		9,025	610		9,635	10,800
5260	10" pipe size		1	24		12,700	1,225		13,925	15,900
5600	Flanged, iron, valves are OS&Y									
5660	2-1/2" pipe size	Q-1	5	3.200	Ea.	3,150	157		3,307	3,700
5680	3" pipe size		4.50	3.556		3,425	175		3,600	4,050
5700	4" pipe size		3	5.333		3,800	262		4,062	4,575
5720	6" pipe size	Q-2	3	8		5,500	410		5,910	6,675
5740	8" pipe size		2	12		9,675	610		10,285	11,500
5760	10" pipe size		1	24		12,900	1,225		14,125	16,100

22 11 19.50 Vacuum Breakers

		Crew	Daily Output	Labor-Hours	Unit	Material	2012 Bare Costs Labor	Equipment	Total	Total Incl O&P
0010	**VACUUM BREAKERS**									
0013	See also backflow preventers Section 22 11 19.42									
1000	Anti-siphon continuous pressure type									
1010	Max. 150 PSI - 210°F									
1020	Bronze body									
1030	1/2" size	1 Stpi	24	.333	Ea.	171	18.55		189.55	216
1040	3/4" size		20	.400		171	22.50		193.50	222

22 11 Facility Water Distribution

22 11 19 – Domestic Water Piping Specialties

22 11 19.50 Vacuum Breakers

		Crew	Daily Output	Labor-Hours	Unit	Material	2012 Bare Costs Labor	2012 Bare Costs Equipment	Total	Total Incl O&P
1050	1" size	1 Stpi	19	.421	Ea.	177	23.50		200.50	230
1060	1-1/4" size		15	.533		350	29.50		379.50	430
1070	1-1/2" size		13	.615		430	34.50		464.50	520
1080	2" size		11	.727		445	40.50		485.50	545
1200	Max. 125 PSI with atmospheric vent									
1210	Brass, in-line construction									
1220	1/4" size	1 Stpi	24	.333	Ea.	68	18.55		86.55	103
1230	3/8" size	"	24	.333		68	18.55		86.55	103
1260	For polished chrome finish, add					13%				
2000	Anti-siphon, non-continuous pressure type									
2010	Hot or cold water 125 PSI - 210°F									
2020	Bronze body									
2030	1/4" size	1 Stpi	24	.333	Ea.	43.50	18.55		62.05	75.50
2040	3/8" size		24	.333		43.50	18.55		62.05	75.50
2050	1/2" size		24	.333		49	18.55		67.55	82
2060	3/4" size		20	.400		58	22.50		80.50	97.50
2070	1" size		19	.421		91	23.50		114.50	136
2080	1-1/4" size		15	.533		159	29.50		188.50	220
2090	1-1/2" size		13	.615		187	34.50		221.50	258
2100	2" size		11	.727		291	40.50		331.50	380
2110	2-1/2" size		8	1		840	55.50		895.50	1,000
2120	3" size		6	1.333		1,125	74.50		1,199.50	1,325
2150	For polished chrome finish, add					50%				

22 11 19.54 Water Hammer Arresters/Shock Absorbers

		Crew	Daily Output	Labor-Hours	Unit	Material	2012 Bare Costs Labor	2012 Bare Costs Equipment	Total	Total Incl O&P
0010	**WATER HAMMER ARRESTERS/SHOCK ABSORBERS**									
0490	Copper									
0500	3/4" male I.P.S. For 1 to 11 fixtures	1 Plum	12	.667	Ea.	21.50	36.50		58	79
0600	1" male I.P.S. For 12 to 32 fixtures		8	1		34	54.50		88.50	120
0700	1-1/4" male I.P.S. For 33 to 60 fixtures		8	1		44	54.50		98.50	131
0800	1-1/2" male I.P.S. For 61 to 113 fixtures		8	1		63	54.50		117.50	152
0900	2" male I.P.S. For 114 to 154 fixtures		8	1		92	54.50		146.50	184
1000	2-1/2" male I.P.S. For 155 to 330 fixtures		4	2		285	109		394	480
4000	Bellows type									
4010	3/4" FNPT, to 11 fixture units	1 Plum	10	.800	Ea.	221	43.50		264.50	310
4020	1" FNPT, to 32 fixture units		8.80	.909		445	49.50		494.50	565
4030	1" FNPT, to 60 fixture units		8.80	.909		670	49.50		719.50	815
4040	1" FNPT, to 113 fixture units		8.80	.909		1,675	49.50		1,724.50	1,925
4050	1" FNPT, to 154 fixture units		6.60	1.212		1,900	66		1,966	2,200
4060	1-1/2" FNPT, to 300 fixture units		5	1.600		2,325	87.50		2,412.50	2,700

22 11 19.64 Hydrants

		Crew	Daily Output	Labor-Hours	Unit	Material	2012 Bare Costs Labor	2012 Bare Costs Equipment	Total	Total Incl O&P
0010	**HYDRANTS**									
0050	Wall type, moderate climate, bronze, encased									
0200	3/4" IPS connection	1 Plum	16	.500	Ea.	650	27.50		677.50	755
0300	1" IPS connection	"	14	.571		745	31		776	865
0500	Anti-siphon type, 3/4" connection					560			560	615
1000	Non-freeze, bronze, exposed									
1100	3/4" IPS connection, 4" to 9" thick wall	1 Plum	14	.571	Ea.	440	31		471	530
1120	10" to 14" thick wall		12	.667		475	36.50		511.50	575
1140	15" to 19" thick wall		12	.667		530	36.50		566.50	640
1160	20" to 24" thick wall		10	.800		575	43.50		618.50	695
1200	For 1" IPS connection, add					15%	10%			
1240	For 3/4" adapter type vacuum breaker, add				Ea.	55.50			55.50	61

22 11 19.64 Hydrants		Crew	Daily Output	Labor-Hours	Unit	Material	2012 Bare Costs Labor	Equipment	Total	Total Incl O&P
1280	For anti-siphon type, add				Ea.	115			115	126
2000	Non-freeze bronze, encased, anti-siphon type									
2100	3/4" IPS connection, 5" to 9" thick wall	1 Plum	14	.571	Ea.	1,125	31		1,156	1,275
2120	10" to 14" thick wall		12	.667		1,150	36.50		1,186.50	1,300
2140	15" to 19" thick wall		12	.667		1,200	36.50		1,236.50	1,375
2160	20" to 24" thick wall		10	.800		1,250	43.50		1,293.50	1,450
2200	For 1" IPS connection, add					10%	10%			
3000	Ground box type, bronze frame, 3/4" IPS connection									
3080	Non-freeze, all bronze, polished face, set flush									
3100	2 feet depth of bury	1 Plum	8	1	Ea.	830	54.50		884.50	995
3120	3 feet depth of bury		8	1		890	54.50		944.50	1,075
3140	4 feet depth of bury		8	1		955	54.50		1,009.50	1,125
3160	5 feet depth of bury		7	1.143		1,025	62.50		1,087.50	1,225
3180	6 feet depth of bury		7	1.143		1,075	62.50		1,137.50	1,300
3200	7 feet depth of bury		6	1.333		1,150	73		1,223	1,350
3220	8 feet depth of bury		5	1.600		1,200	87.50		1,287.50	1,450
3240	9 feet depth of bury		4	2		1,275	109		1,384	1,575
3260	10 feet depth of bury		4	2		1,325	109		1,434	1,650
3400	For 1" IPS connection, add					15%	10%			
3450	For 1-1/4" IPS connection, add					325%	14%			
3500	For 1-1/2" connection, add					370%	18%			
3550	For 2" connection, add					445%	24%			
3600	For tapped drain port in box, add					75			75	82.50
4000	Non-freeze, CI body, bronze frame & scoriated cover									
4010	with hose storage									
4100	2 feet depth of bury	1 Plum	7	1.143	Ea.	1,525	62.50		1,587.50	1,775
4120	3 feet depth of bury		7	1.143		1,600	62.50		1,662.50	1,850
4140	4 feet depth of bury		7	1.143		1,650	62.50		1,712.50	1,900
4160	5 feet depth of bury		6.50	1.231		1,675	67		1,742	1,950
4180	6 feet depth of bury		6	1.333		1,700	73		1,773	1,975
4200	7 feet depth of bury		5.50	1.455		1,775	79.50		1,854.50	2,075
4220	8 feet depth of bury		5	1.600		1,825	87.50		1,912.50	2,125
4240	9 feet depth of bury		4.50	1.778		1,875	97		1,972	2,225
4260	10 feet depth of bury		4	2		1,950	109		2,059	2,325
4280	For 1" IPS connection, add					335			335	370
4300	For tapped drain port in box, add					75			75	82.50
5000	Moderate climate, all bronze, polished face									
5020	and scoriated cover, set flush									
5100	3/4" IPS connection	1 Plum	16	.500	Ea.	575	27.50		602.50	670
5120	1" IPS connection	"	14	.571		705	31		736	820
5200	For tapped drain port in box, add					75			75	82.50
6000	Ground post type, all non-freeze, all bronze, aluminum casing									
6010	guard, exposed head, 3/4" IPS connection									
6100	2 feet depth of bury	1 Plum	8	1	Ea.	810	54.50		864.50	975
6120	3 feet depth of bury		8	1		875	54.50		929.50	1,050
6140	4 feet depth of bury		8	1		945	54.50		999.50	1,100
6160	5 feet depth of bury		7	1.143		1,000	62.50		1,062.50	1,200
6180	6 feet depth of bury		7	1.143		1,075	62.50		1,137.50	1,300
6200	7 feet depth of bury		6	1.333		1,150	73		1,223	1,375
6220	8 feet depth of bury		5	1.600		1,225	87.50		1,312.50	1,475
6240	9 feet depth of bury		4	2		1,300	109		1,409	1,600
6260	10 feet depth of bury		4	2		1,375	109		1,484	1,700
6300	For 1" IPS connection, add					40%	10%			

22 11 Facility Water Distribution

22 11 19 – Domestic Water Piping Specialties

22 11 19.64 Hydrants		Crew	Daily Output	Labor-Hours	Unit	Material	2012 Bare Costs Labor	Equipment	Total	Total Incl O&P
6350	For 1-1/4" IPS connection, add					140%	14%			
6400	For 1-1/2" IPS connection, add					225%	18%			
6450	For 2" IPS connection, add					315%	24%			

22 11 23 – Domestic Water Pumps

22 11 23.10 General Utility Pumps

		Crew	Daily Output	Labor-Hours	Unit	Material	2012 Bare Costs Labor	Equipment	Total	Total Incl O&P
0010	**GENERAL UTILITY PUMPS**									
2000	Single stage									
3000	Double suction,									
3190	75 HP, to 2500 GPM	Q-3	.28	114	Ea.	19,800	5,950		25,750	30,800
3220	100 HP, to 3000 GPM		.26	123		25,200	6,400		31,600	37,400
3240	150 HP, to 4000 GPM	↓	.24	133	↓	35,300	6,925		42,225	49,400
4000	Centrifugal, end suction, mounted on base									
4010	Horizontal mounted, with drip proof motor, rated @ 100' head									
4020	Vertical split case, single stage									
4040	100 GPM, 5 HP, 1-1/2" discharge	Q-1	1.70	9.412	Ea.	3,650	465		4,115	4,700
4050	200 GPM, 10 HP, 2" discharge		1.30	12.308		3,950	605		4,555	5,225
4060	250 GPM, 10 HP, 3" discharge	↓	1.28	12.500		4,400	615		5,015	5,775
4070	300 GPM, 15 HP, 2" discharge	Q-2	1.56	15.385		5,150	785		5,935	6,850
4080	500 GPM, 20 HP, 4" discharge		1.44	16.667		5,425	850		6,275	7,225
4090	750 GPM, 30 HP, 4" discharge		1.20	20		6,200	1,025		7,225	8,350
4100	1050 GPM, 40 HP, 5" discharge		1	24		9,000	1,225		10,225	11,700
4110	1500 GPM, 60 HP, 6" discharge		.60	40		13,100	2,050		15,150	17,500
4120	2000 GPM, 75 HP, 6" discharge		.50	48		14,300	2,450		16,750	19,400
4130	3000 GPM, 100 HP, 8" discharge	↓	.40	60	↓	32,500	3,050		35,550	40,400
4200	Horizontal split case, single stage									
4210	100 GPM, 7.5 HP, 1-1/2" discharge	Q-1	1.70	9.412	Ea.	7,600	465		8,065	9,050
4220	250 GPM, 15 HP, 2-1/2" discharge	"	1.30	12.308		7,825	605		8,430	9,500
4230	500 GPM, 20 HP, 4" discharge	Q-2	1.60	15		9,550	765		10,315	11,700
4240	750 GPM, 25 HP, 5" discharge		1.54	15.584		9,950	795		10,745	12,100
4250	1000 GPM, 40 HP, 5" discharge	↓	1.20	20		13,800	1,025		14,825	16,600
4260	1500 GPM, 50 HP, 6" discharge	Q-3	1.42	22.535		19,800	1,175		20,975	23,600
4270	2000 GPM, 75 HP, 8" discharge		1.14	28.070		22,000	1,450		23,450	26,400
4280	3000 GPM, 100 HP, 10" discharge		.96	33.333		24,600	1,725		26,325	29,700
4290	3500 GPM, 150 HP, 10" discharge		.86	37.209		32,200	1,925		34,125	38,400
4300	4000 GPM, 200 HP, 10" discharge	↓	.66	48.485	↓	35,300	2,525		37,825	42,700
4330	Horizontal split case, two stage, 500' head									
4340	100 GPM, 40 HP, 1-1/2" discharge	Q-2	1.70	14.118	Ea.	15,500	720		16,220	18,200
4350	200 GPM, 50 HP, 1-1/2" discharge	"	1.44	16.667		16,300	850		17,150	19,200
4360	300 GPM, 75 HP, 2" discharge	Q-3	1.57	20.382		22,300	1,050		23,350	26,200
4370	400 GPM, 100 HP, 3" discharge		1.14	28.070		26,400	1,450		27,850	31,300
4380	800 GPM, 200 HP, 4" discharge	↓	.86	37.209	↓	35,000	1,925		36,925	41,400
5000	Centrifugal, in-line									
5006	Vertical mount, iron body, 125 lb. flgd, 3550 RPM TEFC mtr									
5010	Single stage									
5020	50 GPM, 3 HP, 1-1/2" discharge	Q-1	2.30	6.957	Ea.	1,125	340		1,465	1,750
5030	75 GPM, 5 HP, 1-1/2" discharge		1.60	10		1,200	490		1,690	2,075
5040	100 GPM, 7.5 HP, 1-1/2" discharge	↓	1.30	12.308		1,500	605		2,105	2,550
5050	125 GPM, 10 HP, 1-1/2" discharge	Q-2	1.70	14.118		1,725	720		2,445	2,975
5060	150 GPM, 15 HP, 1-1/2" discharge		1.60	15		2,900	765		3,665	4,350
5080	250 GPM, 40 HP, 2" discharge		1.40	17.143		4,350	875		5,225	6,100
5090	300 GPM, 50 HP, 3" discharge	↓	1.30	18.462		4,650	940		5,590	6,550
5100	400 GPM, 75 HP, 3" discharge	Q-3	.60	53.333	↓	5,900	2,775		8,675	10,700

22 11 Facility Water Distribution

22 11 23 – Domestic Water Pumps

22 11 23.10 General Utility Pumps	Crew	Daily Output	Labor-Hours	Unit	Material	2012 Bare Costs Labor	Equipment	Total	Total Incl O&P
5110 600 GPM, 100 HP, 3" discharge	Q-3	.50	64	Ea.	6,200	3,325		9,525	11,900

22 11 23.11 Miscellaneous Pumps

		Crew	Daily Output	Labor-Hours	Unit	Material	2012 Bare Costs Labor	Equipment	Total	Total Incl O&P
0010	**MISCELLANEOUS PUMPS**									
0020	Water pump, portable, gasoline powered									
0100	170 GPH, 2" discharge	Q-1	11	1.455	Ea.	570	71.50		641.50	735
0110	343 GPH, 3" discharge		10.50	1.524		735	75		810	920
0120	608 GPH, 4" discharge	↓	10	1.600	↓	1,675	78.50		1,753.50	1,975
0500	Pump, propylene body, housing and impeller									
0510	22 GPM, 1/3 HP, 40' HD	1 Plum	5	1.600	Ea.	520	87.50		607.50	705
0520	33 GPM, 1/2 HP, 40' HD	Q-1	5	3.200		565	157		722	855
0530	53 GPM, 3/4 HP, 40' HD	"	4	4	↓	925	197		1,122	1,325
0600	Rotary pump, CI									
0614	202 GPH, 3/4 HP, 1" discharge	Q-1	4.50	3.556	Ea.	1,200	175		1,375	1,600
0618	277 GPH, 1 HP, 1" discharge		4	4		1,200	197		1,397	1,625
0624	1100 GPH, 1.5 HP, 1-1/4" discharge		3.60	4.444		3,025	218		3,243	3,650
0628	1900 GPH, 2 HP, 1-1/4" discharge	↓	3.20	5	↓	4,175	246		4,421	4,975
1000	Turbine pump, CI									
1010	50 GPM, 2 HP, 3" discharge	Q-1	.80	20	Ea.	3,325	985		4,310	5,125
1020	100 GPM, 3 HP, 4" discharge	Q-2	.96	25		5,475	1,275		6,750	7,950
1030	250 GPM, 15 HP, 6" discharge	"	.94	25.532		6,800	1,300		8,100	9,450
1040	500 GPM, 25 HP, 6" discharge	Q-3	1.22	26.230		6,850	1,375		8,225	9,600
1050	1000 GPM, 50 HP, 8" discharge		1.14	28.070		9,450	1,450		10,900	12,600
1060	2000 GPM, 100 HP, 10" discharge		1	32		11,200	1,675		12,875	14,800
1070	3000 GPM, 150 HP, 10" discharge		.80	40		18,000	2,075		20,075	22,900
1080	4000 GPM, 200 HP, 12" discharge		.70	45.714		19,700	2,375		22,075	25,300
1090	6000 GPM, 300 HP, 14" discharge		.60	53.333		30,100	2,775		32,875	37,300
1100	10,000 GPM, 300 HP, 18" discharge	↓	.58	55.172	↓	34,800	2,875		37,675	42,500
2000	Centrifugal stainless steel pumps									
2100	100 GPM, 100' TDH, 3 HP	Q-1	1.80	8.889	Ea.	9,925	435		10,360	11,600
2130	250 GPM, 100' TDH, 10 HP	"	1.28	12.500		13,900	615		14,515	16,200
2160	500 GPM, 100' TDH, 20 HP	Q-2	1.44	16.667	↓	15,900	850		16,750	18,800
2200	Vertical turbine stainless steel pumps									
2220	100 GPM, 100' TDH, 7.5 HP	Q-2	.95	25.263	Ea.	55,500	1,300		56,800	63,000
2240	250 GPM, 100' TDH, 15 HP		.94	25.532		61,500	1,300		62,800	69,500
2260	500 GPM, 100' TDH, 20 HP	↓	.93	25.806		67,500	1,325		68,825	76,000
2280	750 GPM, 100' TDH, 30 HP	Q-3	1.19	26.891		73,500	1,400		74,900	82,500
2300	1000 GPM, 100' TDH, 40 HP	"	1.16	27.586		79,500	1,425		80,925	89,500
2320	100 GPM, 200' TDH, 15 HP	Q-2	.94	25.532		85,500	1,300		86,800	96,000
2340	250 GPM, 200' TDH, 25 HP	Q-3	1.22	26.230		91,000	1,375		92,375	102,500
2360	500 GPM, 200' TDH, 40 HP		1.16	27.586		97,000	1,425		98,425	109,000
2380	750 GPM, 200' TDH, 60 HP		1.13	28.319		98,000	1,475		99,475	109,500
2400	1000 GPM, 200' TDH, 75 HP	↓	1.12	28.571	↓	101,000	1,475		102,475	113,500

22 11 23.13 Domestic-Water Packaged Booster Pumps

		Crew	Daily Output	Labor-Hours	Unit	Material	2012 Bare Costs Labor	Equipment	Total	Total Incl O&P
0010	**DOMESTIC-WATER PACKAGED BOOSTER PUMPS**									
0200	Pump system, with diaphragm tank, control, press. switch									
0300	1 HP pump	Q-1	1.30	12.308	Ea.	6,000	605		6,605	7,500
0400	1-1/2 HP pump		1.25	12.800		6,075	630		6,705	7,625
0420	2 HP pump		1.20	13.333		6,225	655		6,880	7,825
0440	3 HP pump	↓	1.10	14.545		6,300	715		7,015	8,025
0460	5 HP pump	Q-2	1.50	16		6,975	815		7,790	8,900
0480	7-1/2 HP pump		1.42	16.901		7,775	860		8,635	9,850
0500	10 HP pump	↓	1.34	17.910	↓	8,125	915		9,040	10,300

22 11 Facility Water Distribution

22 11 23 – Domestic Water Pumps

22 11 23.13 Domestic-Water Packaged Booster Pumps	Crew	Daily Output	Labor-Hours	Unit	Material	2012 Bare Costs Labor	Equipment	Total	Total Incl O&P
2000 Pump system, variable speed, base, controls, starter									
2010 Duplex, 100' head									
2020 400 GPM, 7-1/2HP, 4" discharge	Q-2	.70	34.286	Ea.	35,000	1,750		36,750	41,100
2025 Triplex, 100' head									
2030 1000 GPM, 15HP, 6" discharge	Q-2	.50	48	Ea.	52,000	2,450		54,450	60,500
2040 1700 GPM, 30HP, 6" discharge	"	.30	80	"	63,000	4,075		67,075	75,500

22 12 Facility Potable-Water Storage Tanks

22 12 21 – Facility Underground Potable-Water Storage Tanks

22 12 21.13 Fiberglass, Underground Potable-Water Storage Tanks

		Crew	Daily Output	Labor-Hours	Unit	Material	2012 Bare Costs Labor	Equipment	Total	Total Incl O&P
0010	**FIBERGLASS, UNDERGROUND POTABLE-WATER STORAGE TANKS**									
0020	Excludes excavation, backfill, & piping									
2000	600 gallon capacity	B-21B	3.75	10.667	Ea.	6,800	405	163	7,368	8,300
2010	1,000 gallon capacity		3.50	11.429		7,700	435	175	8,310	9,325
2020	2,000 gallon capacity		3.25	12.308		9,825	470	188	10,483	11,700
2030	4,000 gallon capacity		3	13.333		11,200	505	204	11,909	13,300
2040	6,000 gallon capacity		2.65	15.094		13,700	575	231	14,506	16,200
2050	8,000 gallon capacity		2.30	17.391		16,100	660	266	17,026	19,000
2060	10,000 gallon capacity		2	20		17,800	760	305	18,865	21,100
2070	12,000 gallon capacity		1.50	26.667		19,600	1,025	410	21,035	23,600
2080	15,000 gallon capacity		1	40		24,700	1,525	610	26,835	30,200
2090	20,000 gallon capacity		.75	53.333		30,800	2,025	815	33,640	37,900
2100	25,000 gallon capacity		.50	80		44,400	3,050	1,225	48,675	55,000
2110	30,000 gallon capacity		.35	114		53,500	4,350	1,750	59,600	67,000
2120	40,000 gallon capacity		.30	133		75,000	5,075	2,050	82,125	92,500

22 12 23 – Facility Indoor Potable-Water Storage Tanks

22 12 23.13 Facility Steel, Indoor Pot.-Water Storage Tanks

		Crew	Daily Output	Labor-Hours	Unit	Material	2012 Bare Costs Labor	Equipment	Total	Total Incl O&P
0010	**FACILITY STEEL, INDOOR POT.-WATER STORAGE TANKS**									
2000	Galvanized steel, 15 gal., 14" diam., 26" LOA	1 Plum	12	.667	Ea.	1,325	36.50		1,361.50	1,525
2060	30 gal., 14" diam. x 49" LOA		11	.727		1,575	39.50		1,614.50	1,775
2080	80 gal., 20" diam. x 64" LOA		9	.889		2,450	48.50		2,498.50	2,775
2100	135 gal., 24" diam. x 75" LOA		6	1.333		3,575	73		3,648	4,025
2120	240 gal., 30" diam. x 86" LOA		4	2		7,000	109		7,109	7,875
2140	300 gal., 36" diam. x 76" LOA		3	2.667		9,950	146		10,096	11,100
2160	400 gal., 36" diam. x 100" LOA	Q-1	4	4		12,200	197		12,397	13,800
2180	500 gal., 36" diam., x 126" LOA	"	3	5.333		15,100	262		15,362	17,000
3000	Glass lined, P.E., 80 gal., 20" diam. x 60" LOA	1 Plum	9	.889		2,475	48.50		2,523.50	2,800
3060	140 gal., 24" diam. x 80" LOA		6	1.333		3,425	73		3,498	3,875
3080	225 gal., 30" diam. x 78" LOA		4	2		5,050	109		5,159	5,725
3100	325 gal., 36" diam. x 81" LOA		3	2.667		6,450	146		6,596	7,325
3120	460 gal., 42" diam. x 84" LOA	Q-1	4	4		6,800	197		6,997	7,775
3140	605 gal., 48" diam. x 87" LOA		3	5.333		13,000	262		13,262	14,700
3160	740 gal., 54" diam. x 91" LOA		3	5.333		14,600	262		14,862	16,500
3180	940 gal., 60" diam. x 93" LOA		2.50	6.400		16,900	315		17,215	19,100
3200	1330 gal., 66" diam. x 107" LOA		2	8		23,100	395		23,495	26,000
3220	1615 gal., 72" diam. x 110" LOA		1.50	10.667		26,300	525		26,825	29,700
3240	2285 gal., 84" diam. x 128" LOA		1	16		32,500	785		33,285	37,000
3260	3440 gal., 96" diam. x 157" LOA	Q-2	1.50	16		48,100	815		48,915	54,000

22 13 16.40 Pipe Fittings, Cast Iron for Drainage	Crew	Daily Output	Labor-Hours	Unit	Material	2012 Bare Costs Labor	Equipment	Total	Total Incl O&P
0010 **PIPE FITTINGS, CAST IRON FOR DRAINAGE**, Special									
1000 Drip pan elbow, (safety valve discharge elbow)									
1010 Cast iron, threaded inlet									
1014 2-1/2"	Q-1	8	2	Ea.	1,125	98.50		1,223.50	1,400
1015 3"	↓	6.40	2.500	↓	1,200	123		1,323	1,500
1017 4"	↓	4.80	3.333	↓	1,625	164		1,789	2,050
1018 Cast iron, flanged inlet									
1019 6"	Q-2	3.60	6.667	Ea.	1,700	340		2,040	2,375
1020 8"	"	2.60	9.231	"	1,800	470		2,270	2,675
22 13 16.60 Traps									
0010 **TRAPS**									
4700 Copper, drainage, drum trap									
4800 3" x 5" solid, 1-1/2" pipe size	1 Plum	16	.500	Ea.	256	27.50		283.50	325
4840 3" x 6" swivel, 1-1/2" pipe size	"	16	.500	"	405	27.50		432.50	485
5100 P trap, standard pattern									
5200 1-1/4" pipe size	1 Plum	18	.444	Ea.	189	24.50		213.50	245
5240 1-1/2" pipe size		17	.471		183	25.50		208.50	240
5260 2" pipe size		15	.533		282	29		311	355
5280 3" pipe size	↓	11	.727	↓	675	39.50		714.50	805
5340 With cleanout, swivel joint and slip joint									
5360 1-1/4" pipe size	1 Plum	18	.444	Ea.	134	24.50		158.50	184
5400 1-1/2" pipe size		17	.471		278	25.50		303.50	345
5420 2" pipe size	↓	15	.533	↓	450	29		479	540
6710 ABS DWV P trap, solvent weld joint									
6720 1-1/2" pipe size	1 Plum	18	.444	Ea.	9.35	24.50		33.85	47
6722 2" pipe size		17	.471		12.30	25.50		37.80	52.50
6724 3" pipe size		15	.533		48.50	29		77.50	97.50
6726 4" pipe size	↓	14	.571	↓	96.50	31		127.50	153
6732 PVC DWV P trap, solvent weld joint									
6733 1-1/2" pipe size	1 Plum	18	.444	Ea.	7.10	24.50		31.60	44.50
6734 2" pipe size		17	.471		9.60	25.50		35.10	49.50
6735 3" pipe size		15	.533		32.50	29		61.50	80
6736 4" pipe size		14	.571		74	31		105	129
6760 PP DWV, dilution trap, 1-1/2" pipe size		16	.500		202	27.50		229.50	263
6770 P trap, 1-1/2" pipe size		17	.471		50	25.50		75.50	94
6780 2" pipe size		16	.500		74	27.50		101.50	123
6790 3" pipe size		14	.571		136	31		167	196
6800 4" pipe size		13	.615		229	33.50		262.50	305
6830 S trap, 1-1/2" pipe size		16	.500		41.50	27.50		69	86.50
6840 2" pipe size		15	.533		62	29		91	112
6850 Universal trap, 1-1/2" pipe size		14	.571		81.50	31		112.50	137
6860 PVC DWV hub x hub, basin trap, 1-1/4" pipe size		18	.444		10.90	24.50		35.40	48.50
6870 Sink P trap, 1-1/2" pipe size		18	.444		10.90	24.50		35.40	48.50
6880 Tubular S trap, 1-1/2" pipe size	↓	17	.471	↓	20	25.50		45.50	61
6890 PVC sch. 40 DWV, drum trap									
6900 1-1/2" pipe size	1 Plum	16	.500	Ea.	30	27.50		57.50	74
6910 P trap, 1-1/2" pipe size		18	.444		7.45	24.50		31.95	44.50
6920 2" pipe size		17	.471		10.05	25.50		35.55	50
6930 3" pipe size		15	.533		34	29		63	81.50
6940 4" pipe size		14	.571		77.50	31		108.50	133
6950 P trap w/clean out, 1-1/2" pipe size		18	.444		12.30	24.50		36.80	50
6960 2" pipe size	↓	17	.471	↓	20.50	25.50		46	61.50

22 13 Facility Sanitary Sewerage

22 13 16 – Sanitary Waste and Vent Piping

22 13 16.60 Traps

		Crew	Daily Output	Labor-Hours	Unit	Material	2012 Bare Costs Labor	2012 Bare Costs Equipment	Total	Total Incl O&P
6970	P trap adjustable, 1-1/2" pipe size	1 Plum	17	.471	Ea.	9.50	25.50		35	49.50
6980	P trap adj. w/union & cleanout, 1-1/2" pipe size	↓	16	.500	↓	36.50	27.50		64	81

22 13 16.80 Vent Flashing and Caps

		Crew	Daily Output	Labor-Hours	Unit	Material	2012 Bare Costs Labor	2012 Bare Costs Equipment	Total	Total Incl O&P
0010	**VENT FLASHING AND CAPS**									
0120	Vent caps									
0140	Cast iron									
0180	2-1/2" - 3-5/8" pipe	1 Plum	21	.381	Ea.	40	21		61	75.50
0190	4" - 4-1/8" pipe	"	19	.421	"	48	23		71	87.50
0900	Vent flashing									
1000	Aluminum with lead ring									
1020	1-1/4" pipe	1 Plum	20	.400	Ea.	11.20	22		33.20	45.50
1030	1-1/2" pipe		20	.400		13.40	22		35.40	47.50
1040	2" pipe		18	.444		12.05	24.50		36.55	50
1050	3" pipe		17	.471		13.30	25.50		38.80	53.50
1060	4" pipe	↓	16	.500	↓	16.05	27.50		43.55	58.50
1350	Copper with neoprene ring									
1400	1-1/4" pipe	1 Plum	20	.400	Ea.	19.95	22		41.95	55
1430	1-1/2" pipe		20	.400		19.95	22		41.95	55
1440	2" pipe		18	.444		21	24.50		45.50	59.50
1450	3" pipe		17	.471		24.50	25.50		50	66
1460	4" pipe	↓	16	.500	↓	27	27.50		54.50	71
2000	Galvanized with neoprene ring									
2020	1-1/4" pipe	1 Plum	20	.400	Ea.	15.60	22		37.60	50
2030	1-1/2" pipe		20	.400		15.60	22		37.60	50
2040	2" pipe		18	.444		16.15	24.50		40.65	54.50
2050	3" pipe		17	.471		17.05	25.50		42.55	58
2060	4" pipe	↓	16	.500		19.80	27.50		47.30	63
2980	Neoprene, one piece									
3000	1-1/4" pipe	1 Plum	24	.333	Ea.	7.25	18.20		25.45	35.50
3030	1-1/2" pipe		24	.333		7.95	18.20		26.15	36.50
3040	2" pipe		23	.348		7.30	19		26.30	36.50
3050	3" pipe		21	.381		8.40	21		29.40	40.50
3060	4" pipe	↓	20	.400	↓	12.45	22		34.45	46.50
4000	Lead, 4#, 8" skirt, VTR									
4100	2" pipe	1 Plum	18	.444	Ea.	38	24.50		62.50	78
4110	3" pipe		17	.471		45	25.50		70.50	88.50
4120	4" pipe		16	.500		51.50	27.50		79	97.50
4130	6" pipe	↓	14	.571		73.50	31		104.50	128

22 13 26 – Sanitary Waste Separators

22 13 26.10 Separators

		Crew	Daily Output	Labor-Hours	Unit	Material	2012 Bare Costs Labor	2012 Bare Costs Equipment	Total	Total Incl O&P
0010	**SEPARATORS**, Entrainment eliminator, steel body, 150 PSIG.									
0100	1/4" size	1 Stpi	24	.333	Ea.	246	18.55		264.55	299
0120	1/2" size		24	.333		254	18.55		272.55	305
0140	3/4" size		20	.400		266	22.50		288.50	325
0160	1" size		19	.421		274	23.50		297.50	335
0180	1-1/4" size		15	.533		291	29.50		320.50	365
0200	1-1/2" size		13	.615		320	34.50		354.50	405
0220	2" size	↓	11	.727		355	40.50		395.50	455
0240	2-1/2" size	Q-5	15	1.067		1,525	53.50		1,578.50	1,750
0260	3" size		13	1.231		1,725	61.50		1,786.50	2,000
0280	4" size		10	1.600		1,950	80		2,030	2,250
0300	5" size	↓	6	2.667		2,300	134		2,434	2,750

22 13 Facility Sanitary Sewerage

22 13 26 – Sanitary Waste Separators

22 13 26.10 Separators

		Crew	Daily Output	Labor-Hours	Unit	Material	2012 Bare Costs Labor	Equipment	Total	Total Incl O&P
0320	6" size	Q-5	3	5.333	Ea.	2,500	267		2,767	3,150
0340	8" size	Q-6	4.40	5.455		3,200	284		3,484	3,925
0360	10" size	"	4	6		4,525	310		4,835	5,450
1000	For 300 PSIG, add					15%				

22 13 29 – Sanitary Sewerage Pumps

22 13 29.13 Wet-Pit-Mounted, Vertical Sewerage Pumps

		Crew	Daily Output	Labor-Hours	Unit	Material	2012 Bare Costs Labor	Equipment	Total	Total Incl O&P
0010	**WET-PIT-MOUNTED, VERTICAL SEWERAGE PUMPS**									
0020	Controls incl. alarm/disconnect panel w/wire. Excavation not included									
0260	Simplex, 9 GPM at 60 PSIG, 91 gal. tank				Ea.	3,150			3,150	3,450
0300	Unit with manway, 26" I.D., 18" high					3,575			3,575	3,950
0340	26" I.D., 36" high					3,625			3,625	4,000
0380	43" I.D., 4' high					3,750			3,750	4,125
0600	Simplex, 9 GPM at 60 PSIG, 150 gal. tank, indoor					3,425			3,425	3,775
0700	Unit with manway, 26" I.D., 36" high					4,100			4,100	4,500
0740	26" I.D., 4' high					4,200			4,200	4,625
2000	Duplex, 18 GPM at 60 PSIG, 150 gal. tank, indoor					6,825			6,825	7,525
2060	Unit with manway, 43" I.D., 4' high					7,625			7,625	8,400
2400	For core only					1,775			1,775	1,950
3000	Indoor residential type installation									
3020	Simplex, 9 GPM at 60 PSIG, 91 gal. HDPE tank				Ea.	3,125			3,125	3,450

22 13 29.14 Sewage Ejector Pumps

		Crew	Daily Output	Labor-Hours	Unit	Material	2012 Bare Costs Labor	Equipment	Total	Total Incl O&P
0010	**SEWAGE EJECTOR PUMPS,** With operating and level controls									
0100	Simplex system incl. tank, cover, pump 15' head									
0500	37 gal. PE tank, 12 GPM, 1/2 HP, 2" discharge	Q-1	3.20	5	Ea.	455	246		701	870
0510	3" discharge		3.10	5.161		495	254		749	930
0530	87 GPM, .7 HP, 2" discharge		3.20	5		690	246		936	1,125
0540	3" discharge		3.10	5.161		750	254		1,004	1,200
0600	45 gal. coated stl tank, 12 GPM, 1/2 HP, 2" discharge		3	5.333		805	262		1,067	1,275
0610	3" discharge		2.90	5.517		840	271		1,111	1,325
0630	87 GPM, .7 HP, 2" discharge		3	5.333		1,025	262		1,287	1,525
0640	3" discharge		2.90	5.517		1,100	271		1,371	1,600
0660	134 GPM, 1 HP, 2" discharge		2.80	5.714		1,125	281		1,406	1,650
0680	3" discharge		2.70	5.926		1,175	291		1,466	1,750
0700	70 gal. PE tank, 12 GPM, 1/2 HP, 2" discharge		2.60	6.154		880	300		1,180	1,425
0710	3" discharge		2.40	6.667		935	330		1,265	1,525
0730	87 GPM, 0.7 HP, 2" discharge		2.50	6.400		1,125	315		1,440	1,700
0740	3" discharge		2.30	6.957		1,200	340		1,540	1,850
0760	134 GPM, 1 HP, 2" discharge		2.20	7.273		1,225	355		1,580	1,900
0770	3" discharge		2	8		1,300	395		1,695	2,025
0800	75 gal. coated stl. tank, 12 GPM, 1/2 HP, 2" discharge		2.40	6.667		965	330		1,295	1,575
0810	3" discharge		2.20	7.273		1,000	355		1,355	1,650
0830	87 GPM, .7 HP, 2" discharge		2.30	6.957		1,225	340		1,565	1,850
0840	3" discharge		2.10	7.619		1,275	375		1,650	1,975
0860	134 GPM, 1 HP, 2" discharge		2	8		1,300	395		1,695	2,025
0880	3" discharge		1.80	8.889		1,375	435		1,810	2,150
1040	Duplex system incl. tank, covers, pumps									
1060	110 gal. fiberglass tank, 24 GPM, 1/2 HP, 2" discharge	Q-1	1.60	10	Ea.	1,750	490		2,240	2,700
1080	3" discharge		1.40	11.429		1,850	560		2,410	2,875
1100	174 GPM, .7 HP, 2" discharge		1.50	10.667		2,250	525		2,775	3,275
1120	3" discharge		1.30	12.308		2,350	605		2,955	3,475
1140	268 GPM, 1 HP, 2" discharge		1.20	13.333		2,450	655		3,105	3,700
1160	3" discharge		1	16		2,525	785		3,310	3,975

22 13 Facility Sanitary Sewerage

22 13 29 – Sanitary Sewerage Pumps

22 13 29.14 Sewage Ejector Pumps		Crew	Daily Output	Labor-Hours	Unit	Material	2012 Bare Costs Labor	Equipment	Total	Total Incl O&P
1260	135 gal. coated stl. tank, 24 GPM, 1/2 HP, 2" discharge	Q-2	1.70	14.118	Ea.	1,800	720		2,520	3,050
2000	3" discharge		1.60	15		1,900	765		2,665	3,250
2640	174 GPM, .7 HP, 2" discharge		1.60	15		2,350	765		3,115	3,750
2660	3" discharge		1.50	16		2,475	815		3,290	3,950
2700	268 GPM, 1 HP, 2" discharge		1.30	18.462		2,550	940		3,490	4,250
3040	3" discharge		1.10	21.818		2,725	1,100		3,825	4,675
3060	275 gal. coated stl. tank, 24 GPM, 1/2 HP, 2" discharge		1.50	16		2,250	815		3,065	3,700
3080	3" discharge		1.40	17.143		2,275	875		3,150	3,825
3100	174 GPM, .7 HP, 2" discharge		1.40	17.143		2,900	875		3,775	4,525
3120	3" discharge		1.30	18.462		3,075	940		4,015	4,800
3140	268 GPM, 1 HP, 2" discharge		1.10	21.818		3,175	1,100		4,275	5,175
3160	3" discharge		.90	26.667		3,350	1,350		4,700	5,750
3260	Pump system accessories, add									
3300	Alarm horn and lights, 115 V mercury switch	Q-1	8	2	Ea.	94	98.50		192.50	251
3340	Switch, mag. contactor, alarm bell, light, 3 level control		5	3.200		460	157		617	740
3380	Alternator, mercury switch activated		4	4		830	197		1,027	1,200

22 14 Facility Storm Drainage

22 14 29 – Sump Pumps

22 14 29.13 Wet-Pit-Mounted, Vertical Sump Pumps

0010	WET-PIT-MOUNTED, VERTICAL SUMP PUMPS									
0400	Molded PVC base, 21 GPM at 15' head, 1/3 HP	1 Plum	5	1.600	Ea.	128	87.50		215.50	272
0800	Iron base, 21 GPM at 15' head, 1/3 HP		5	1.600		156	87.50		243.50	305
1200	Solid brass, 21 GPM at 15' head, 1/3 HP		5	1.600		272	87.50		359.50	430

22 14 29.16 Submersible Sump Pumps

0010	SUBMERSIBLE SUMP PUMPS									
7000	Sump pump, automatic									
7100	Plastic, 1-1/4" discharge, 1/4 HP	1 Plum	6	1.333	Ea.	126	73		199	249
7140	1/3 HP		5	1.600		189	87.50		276.50	340
7160	1/2 HP		5	1.600		207	87.50		294.50	360
7180	1-1/2" discharge, 1/2 HP		4	2		256	109		365	445
7500	Cast iron, 1-1/4" discharge, 1/4 HP		6	1.333		177	73		250	305
7540	1/3 HP		6	1.333		209	73		282	340
7560	1/2 HP		5	1.600		252	87.50		339.50	410

22 14 53 – Rainwater Storage Tanks

22 14 53.13 Fiberglass, Rainwater Storage Tank

0010	FIBERGLASS, RAINWATER STORAGE TANK									
2000	600 gallon	B-21B	3.75	10.667	Ea.	5,150	405	163	5,718	6,475
2010	1,000 gallon		3.50	11.429		6,025	435	175	6,635	7,500
2020	2,000 gallon		3.25	12.308		8,150	470	188	8,808	9,900
2030	4,000 gallon		3	13.333		9,525	505	204	10,234	11,500
2040	6,000 gallon		2.65	15.094		11,700	575	231	12,506	14,000
2050	8,000 gallon		2.30	17.391		13,700	660	266	14,626	16,400
2060	10,000 gallon		2	20		15,100	760	305	16,165	18,100
2070	12,000 gallon		1.50	26.667		16,500	1,025	410	17,935	20,200
2080	15,000 gallon		1	40		21,900	1,525	610	24,035	27,100
2090	20,000 gallon		.75	53.333		27,400	2,025	815	30,240	34,200
2100	25,000 gallon		.50	80		39,000	3,050	1,225	43,275	48,900
2110	30,000 gallon		.35	114		46,600	4,350	1,750	52,700	59,500
2120	40,000 gallon		.30	133		65,500	5,075	2,050	72,625	82,000

22 15 General Service Compressed-Air Systems

22 15 13 – General Service Compressed-Air Piping

22 15 13.10 Compressor Accessories		Crew	Daily Output	Labor-Hours	Unit	Material	2012 Bare Costs Labor	Equipment	Total	Total Incl O&P
0010	**COMPRESSOR ACCESSORIES**									
1700	Refrigerated air dryers with ambient air filters									
1710	10 CFM	Q-5	8	2	Ea.	675	100		775	895
1720	25 CFM		6.60	2.424		920	122		1,042	1,200
1730	50 CFM		6.20	2.581		1,300	129		1,429	1,625
1740	75 CFM		5.80	2.759		2,375	138		2,513	2,825
1750	100 CFM	↓	5.60	2.857	↓	2,700	143		2,843	3,200
4000	Couplers, air line, sleeve type									
4010	Female, connection size NPT									
4020	1/4"	1 Stpi	38	.211	Ea.	8.55	11.75		20.30	27
4030	3/8"		36	.222		14.25	12.40		26.65	34.50
4040	1/2"		35	.229		20.50	12.75		33.25	42
4050	3/4"	↓	34	.235	↓	20.50	13.10		33.60	43
4100	Male									
4110	1/4"	1 Stpi	38	.211	Ea.	8.90	11.75		20.65	27.50
4120	3/8"		36	.222		9.75	12.40		22.15	29.50
4130	1/2"		35	.229		21	12.75		33.75	42
4140	3/4"	↓	34	.235	↓	22	13.10		35.10	44
4150	Coupler, combined male and female halves									
4160	1/2"	1 Stpi	17	.471	Ea.	41.50	26		67.50	85
4170	3/4"	"	15	.533	"	42.50	29.50		72	92

22 15 19 – General Service Packaged Air Compressors and Receivers

22 15 19.10 Air Compressors

		Crew	Daily Output	Labor-Hours	Unit	Material	2012 Bare Costs Labor	Equipment	Total	Total Incl O&P
0010	**AIR COMPRESSORS**									
5250	Air, reciprocating air cooled, splash lubricated, tank mounted									
5300	Single stage, 1 phase, 140 psi									
5303	1/2 HP, 30 gal. tank	1 Stpi	3	2.667	Ea.	1,750	149		1,899	2,150
5305	3/4 HP, 30 gal. tank		2.60	3.077		1,775	171		1,946	2,200
5307	1 HP, 30 gal. tank	↓	2.20	3.636		2,175	203		2,378	2,700
5309	2 HP, 30 gal. tank	Q-5	4	4		2,650	201		2,851	3,225
5310	3 HP, 30 gal. tank		3.60	4.444		2,800	223		3,023	3,400
5314	3 HP, 60 gal. tank		3.50	4.571		3,375	229		3,604	4,075
5320	5 HP, 60 gal. tank		3.20	5		3,550	251		3,801	4,275
5330	5 HP, 80 gal. tank		3	5.333		3,900	267		4,167	4,700
5340	7.5 HP, 80 gal. tank	↓	2.60	6.154	↓	5,050	310		5,360	6,025
5600	2 stage pkg., 3 phase									
5650	6 CFM at 125 psi 1-1/2 HP, 60 gal. tank	Q-5	3	5.333	Ea.	3,200	267		3,467	3,925
5670	10.9 CFM at 125 psi, 3 HP, 80 gal. tank		1.50	10.667		3,600	535		4,135	4,775
5680	38.7 CFM at 125 psi, 10 HP, 120 gal. tank	↓	.60	26.667		6,500	1,325		7,825	9,175
5690	105 CFM at 125 psi, 25 HP, 250 gal. tank	Q-6	.60	40	↓	14,700	2,075		16,775	19,200
5800	With single stage pump									
5850	8.3 CFM at 125 psi, 2 HP, 80 gal. tank	Q-6	3.50	6.857	Ea.	3,575	355		3,930	4,500
5860	38.7 CFM at 125 psi, 10 HP, 120 gal. tank	"	.90	26.667	"	7,150	1,375		8,525	9,975
6000	Reciprocating, 2 stage, tank mtd, 3 Ph., Cap. rated @175 PSIG									
6050	Pressure lubricated, hvy duty, 9.7 CFM, 3 HP, 120 gal. tank	Q-5	1.30	12.308	Ea.	5,500	615		6,115	6,975
6054	5 CFM, 1-1/2 HP, 80 gal. tank		2.80	5.714		3,425	286		3,711	4,175
6056	6.4 CFM, 2 HP, 80 gal. tank		2	8		3,575	400		3,975	4,550
6058	8.1 CFM, 3 HP, 80 gal. tank		1.70	9.412		3,600	470		4,070	4,675
6059	14.8 CFM, 5 HP, 80 gal. tank		1	16		3,900	800		4,700	5,500
6060	16.5 CFM, 5 HP, 120 gal. tank		1	16		5,600	800		6,400	7,375
6063	13 CFM, 6 HP, 80 gal. tank		.90	17.778		5,600	890		6,490	7,525
6066	19.8 CFM, 7.5 HP, 80 gal. tank	↓	.80	20	↓	5,600	1,000		6,600	7,675

22 15 General Service Compressed-Air Systems

22 15 19 – General Service Packaged Air Compressors and Receivers

22 15 19.10 Air Compressors		Crew	Daily Output	Labor-Hours	Unit	Material	2012 Bare Costs Labor	Equipment	Total	Total Incl O&P
6070	25.8 CFM, 7-1/2 HP, 120 gal. tank	Q-5	.80	20	Ea.	8,450	1,000		9,450	10,800
6078	34.8 CFM, 10 HP, 80 gal. tank		.70	22.857		8,100	1,150		9,250	10,600
6080	34.8 CFM, 10 HP, 120 gal. tank	↓	.60	26.667		9,325	1,325		10,650	12,300
6090	53.7 CFM, 15 HP, 120 gal. tank	Q-6	.80	30		9,775	1,550		11,325	13,100
6100	76.7 CFM, 20 HP, 120 gal. tank		.70	34.286		12,800	1,775		14,575	16,800
6104	76.7 CFM, 20 HP, 240 gal. tank		.68	35.294		14,100	1,825		15,925	18,300
6110	90.1 CFM, 25 HP, 120 gal. tank		.63	38.095		13,400	1,975		15,375	17,800
6120	101 CFM, 30 HP, 120 gal. tank		.57	42.105		14,400	2,200		16,600	19,200
6130	101 CFM, 30 HP, 250 gal. tank	↓	.52	46.154		15,600	2,400		18,000	20,800
6200	Oil-less, 13.6 CFM, 5 HP, 120 gal. tank	Q-5	.88	18.182		16,100	910		17,010	19,100
6210	13.6 CFM, 5 HP, 250 gal. tank		.80	20		17,300	1,000		18,300	20,500
6220	18.2 CFM, 7.5 HP, 120 gal. tank		.73	21.918		16,100	1,100		17,200	19,400
6230	18.2 CFM, 7.5 HP, 250 gal. tank		.67	23.881		17,300	1,200		18,500	20,800
6250	30.5 CFM, 10 HP, 120 gal. tank		.57	28.070		19,000	1,400		20,400	23,000
6260	30.5 CFM, 10 HP, 250 gal. tank	↓	.53	30.189		20,200	1,525		21,725	24,500
6270	41.3 CFM, 15 HP, 120 gal. tank	Q-6	.70	34.286		20,600	1,775		22,375	25,400
6280	41.3 CFM, 15 HP, 250 gal. tank	"	.67	35.821		21,800	1,850		23,650	26,800

22 31 Domestic Water Softeners

22 31 13 – Residential Domestic Water Softeners

22 31 13.10 Residential Water Softeners

0010	**RESIDENTIAL WATER SOFTENERS**									
7350	Water softener, automatic, to 30 grains per gallon	2 Plum	5	3.200	Ea.	340	175		515	640
7400	To 100 grains per gallon	"	4	4	"	680	218		898	1,075

22 35 Domestic Water Heat Exchangers

22 35 30 – Water Heating by Steam

22 35 30.10 Water Heating Transfer Package

0010	**WATER HEATING TRANSFER PACKAGE**, Complete controls,									
0020	expansion tank, converter, air separator									
1000	Hot water, 180°F enter, 200°F leaving, 15# steam									
1010	One pump system, 28 GPM	Q-6	.75	32	Ea.	18,700	1,675		20,375	23,100
1020	35 GPM		.70	34.286		20,300	1,775		22,075	25,100
1040	55 GPM		.65	36.923		23,900	1,925		25,825	29,200
1060	130 GPM		.55	43.636		30,100	2,275		32,375	36,600
1080	255 GPM		.40	60		39,400	3,125		42,525	48,100
1100	550 GPM		.30	80		50,000	4,150		54,150	61,500
1120	800 GPM		.25	96		63,500	5,000		68,500	77,500
1220	Two pump system, 28 GPM		.70	34.286		25,300	1,775		27,075	30,500
1240	35 GPM		.65	36.923		29,500	1,925		31,425	35,300
1260	55 GPM		.60	40		31,700	2,075		33,775	38,000
1280	130 GPM		.50	48		41,600	2,500		44,100	49,600
1300	255 GPM		.35	68.571		53,000	3,575		56,575	64,000
1320	550 GPM		.25	96		67,000	5,000		72,000	81,000
1340	800 GPM	↓	.20	120	↓	86,000	6,250		92,250	104,000

22 41 Residential Plumbing Fixtures

22 41 39 – Residential Faucets, Supplies and Trim

22 41 39.10 Faucets and Fittings	Crew	Daily Output	Labor-Hours	Unit	Material	2012 Bare Costs Labor	Equipment	Total	Total Incl O&P
0010 **FAUCETS AND FITTINGS**									
5000 Sillcock, compact, brass, IPS or copper to hose	1 Plum	24	.333	Ea.	13.30	18.20		31.50	42
6000 Stop and waste valves, bronze									
6100 Angle, solder end 1/2"	1 Plum	24	.333	Ea.	11.35	18.20		29.55	40
6110 3/4"		20	.400		13.30	22		35.30	47.50
6300 Straightway, solder end 3/8"		24	.333		11.35	18.20		29.55	40
6310 1/2"		24	.333		11.60	18.20		29.80	40.50
6320 3/4"		20	.400		17.20	22		39.20	52
6410 Straightway, threaded 1/2"		24	.333		15	18.20		33.20	44
6420 3/4"		20	.400		21	22		43	56
6430 1"		19	.421		12.60	23		35.60	48.50

22 51 Swimming Pool Plumbing Systems

22 51 19 – Swimming Pool Water Treatment Equipment

22 51 19.50 Swimming Pool Filtration Equipment	Crew	Daily Output	Labor-Hours	Unit	Material	2012 Bare Costs Labor	Equipment	Total	Total Incl O&P
0010 **SWIMMING POOL FILTRATION EQUIPMENT**									
0900 Filter system, sand or diatomite type, incl. pump, 6,000 gal./hr.	2 Plum	1.80	8.889	Total	1,775	485		2,260	2,675
1020 Add for chlorination system, 800 S.F. pool		3	5.333	Ea.	105	291		396	555
1040 5,000 S.F. pool		3	5.333	"	1,875	291		2,166	2,525

22 52 Fountain Plumbing Systems

22 52 16 – Fountain Pumps

22 52 16.10 Fountain Water Pumps	Crew	Daily Output	Labor-Hours	Unit	Material	2012 Bare Costs Labor	Equipment	Total	Total Incl O&P
0010 **FOUNTAIN WATER PUMPS**									
0100 Pump w/controls									
0200 Single phase, 100' cord, 1/2 H.P. pump	2 Skwk	4.40	3.636	Ea.	1,225	165		1,390	1,600
0300 3/4 H.P. pump		4.30	3.721		2,125	169		2,294	2,575
0400 1 H.P. pump		4.20	3.810		2,300	173		2,473	2,800
0500 1-1/2 H.P. pump		4.10	3.902		2,700	177		2,877	3,250
0600 2 H.P. pump		4	4		3,675	182		3,857	4,325
0700 Three phase, 200' cord, 5 H.P. pump		3.90	4.103		5,025	186		5,211	5,825
0800 7-1/2 H.P. pump		3.80	4.211		8,725	191		8,916	9,900
0900 10 H.P. pump		3.70	4.324		9,550	196		9,746	10,800
1000 15 H.P. pump		3.60	4.444		11,500	202		11,702	13,000
2000 DESIGN NOTE: Use two horsepower per surface acre.									

22 52 33 – Fountain Ancillary

22 52 33.10 Fountain Miscellaneous	Crew	Daily Output	Labor-Hours	Unit	Material	2012 Bare Costs Labor	Equipment	Total	Total Incl O&P
0010 **FOUNTAIN MISCELLANEOUS**									
1100 Nozzles, minimum	2 Skwk	8	2	Ea.	149	91		240	305
1200 Maximum		8	2		320	91		411	490
1300 Lights w/mounting kits, 200 watt		18	.889		1,050	40.50		1,090.50	1,225
1400 300 watt		18	.889		1,275	40.50		1,315.50	1,475
1500 500 watt		18	.889		1,425	40.50		1,465.50	1,650
1600 Color blender		12	1.333		555	60.50		615.50	705

22 62 Vacuum Systems for Laboratory and Healthcare Facilities

22 62 19 – Vacuum Equipment for Laboratory and Healthcare Facilities

22 62 19.70 Healthcare Vacuum Equipment	Crew	Daily Output	Labor-Hours	Unit	Material	2012 Bare Costs Labor	Equipment	Total	Total Incl O&P
0010 **HEALTHCARE VACUUM EQUIPMENT**									
0100 Medical, with receiver									
0110 Duplex									
0120 20 SCFM	Q-1	1.14	14.035	Ea.	16,800	690		17,490	19,600
0130 60 SCFM, 10 HP	Q-2	1.20	20	"	30,500	1,025		31,525	35,000
0200 Triplex									
0220 180 SCFM	Q-2	.86	27.907	Ea.	47,300	1,425		48,725	54,000
0300 Dental oral									
0310 Duplex									
0330 165 SCFM with 77 gal. separator	Q-2	1.30	18.462	Ea.	49,400	940		50,340	56,000
1100 Vacuum system									
1110 Vacuum outlet alarm panel	1 Plum	3.20	2.500	Ea.	1,050	137		1,187	1,350

22 63 Gas Systems for Laboratory and Healthcare Facilities

22 63 13 – Gas Piping for Laboratory and Healthcare Facilities

22 63 13.70 Healthcare Gas Piping

	Crew	Daily Output	Labor-Hours	Unit	Material	2012 Bare Costs Labor	Equipment	Total	Total Incl O&P
0010 **HEALTHCARE GAS PIPING**									
1000 Nitrogen or oxygen system									
1010 Cylinder manifold									
1020 5 cylinder	1 Plum	.80	10	Ea.	5,675	545		6,220	7,050
1026 10 cylinder	"	.40	20	"	6,825	1,100		7,925	9,150
3000 Outlets and valves									
3010 Recessed, wall mounted									
3012 Single outlet	1 Plum	3.20	2.500	Ea.	68.50	137		205.50	281
3100 Ceiling outlet									
3190 Zone valve with box									
3210 2" valve size	1 Plum	3.20	2.500	Ea.	420	137		557	665
4000 Alarm panel, medical gases and vacuum									
4010 Alarm panel	1 Plum	3.20	2.500	Ea.	1,050	137		1,187	1,350

Division Notes

	CREW	DAILY OUTPUT	LABOR-HOURS	UNIT	2012 BARE COSTS				TOTAL INCL O&P
					MAT.	LABOR	EQUIP.	TOTAL	

Estimating Tips

The labor adjustment factors listed in Subdivision 22 01 02.20 also apply to Division 23.

23 10 00 Facility Fuel Systems

- The prices in this subdivision for above- and below-ground storage tanks do not include foundations or hold-down slabs, unless noted. The estimator should refer to Divisions 3 and 31 for foundation system pricing. In addition to the foundations, required tank accessories, such as tank gauges, leak detection devices, and additional manholes and piping, must be added to the tank prices.

23 50 00 Central Heating Equipment

- When estimating the cost of an HVAC system, check to see who is responsible for providing and installing the temperature control system. It is possible to overlook controls, assuming that they would be included in the electrical estimate.
- When looking up a boiler, be careful on specified capacity. Some manufacturers rate their products on output while others use input.
- Include HVAC insulation for pipe, boiler, and duct (wrap and liner).
- Be careful when looking up mechanical items to get the correct pressure rating and connection type (thread, weld, flange).

23 70 00 Central HVAC Equipment

- Combination heating and cooling units are sized by the air conditioning requirements. (See Reference No. R236000-20 for preliminary sizing guide.)
- A ton of air conditioning is nominally 400 CFM.
- Rectangular duct is taken off by the linear foot for each size, but its cost is usually estimated by the pound. Remember that SMACNA standards now base duct on internal pressure.
- Prefabricated duct is estimated and purchased like pipe: straight sections and fittings.
- Note that cranes or other lifting equipment are not included on any lines in Division 23. For example, if a crane is required to lift a heavy piece of pipe into place high above a gym floor, or to put a rooftop unit on the roof of a four-story building, etc., it must be added. Due to the potential for extreme variation—from nothing additional required to a major crane or helicopter—we feel that including a nominal amount for "lifting contingency" would be useless and detract from the accuracy of the estimate. When using equipment rental cost data from RSMeans, do not forget to include the cost of the operator(s).

Reference Numbers

Reference numbers are shown in shaded boxes at the beginning of some major classifications. These numbers refer to related items in the Reference Section. The reference information may be an estimating procedure, an alternate pricing method, or technical information.

Note: Not all subdivisions listed here necessarily appear in this publication.

Note: **Trade Service,** *in part, has been used as a reference source for some of the material prices used in Division 23.*

23 05 Common Work Results for HVAC

23 05 02 – HVAC General

23 05 02.10 Air Conditioning, General	Crew	Daily Output	Labor-Hours	Unit	Material	2012 Bare Costs Labor	Equipment	Total	Total Incl O&P
0010 **AIR CONDITIONING, GENERAL** Prices are for standard efficiencies (SEER 13)									
0020 for upgrade to SEER 14 add					20%				

23 05 05 – Selective HVAC Demolition

23 05 05.10 HVAC Demolition

		Crew	Daily Output	Labor-Hours	Unit	Material	Labor	Equipment	Total	Total Incl O&P
0010	**HVAC DEMOLITION** R220105-10									
0100	Air conditioner, split unit, 3 ton	Q-5	2	8	Ea.		400		400	605
0150	Package unit, 3 ton	Q-6	3	8			415		415	625
0190	Rooftop, self contained, up to 5 ton	1 Plum	1.20	6.667			365		365	550
0250	Air curtain	Q-9	20	.800	L.F.		37.50		37.50	57
0254	Air filters, up thru 16,000 CFM		20	.800	Ea.		37.50		37.50	57
0256	20,000 thru 60,000 CFM		16	1			47		47	71.50
0297	Boiler blowdown	Q-5	8	2			100		100	151
0298	Boilers									
0300	Electric, up thru 148 kW	Q-19	2	12	Ea.		605		605	915
0310	150 thru 518 kW	"	1	24			1,225		1,225	1,825
0320	550 thru 2000 kW	Q-21	.40	80			4,150		4,150	6,250
0330	2070 kW and up	"	.30	106			5,525		5,525	8,325
0340	Gas and/or oil, up thru 150 MBH	Q-7	2.20	14.545			770		770	1,175
0350	160 thru 2000 MBH		.80	40			2,125		2,125	3,200
0360	2100 thru 4500 MBH		.50	64			3,400		3,400	5,125
0370	4600 thru 7000 MBH		.30	106			5,650		5,650	8,525
0380	7100 thru 12,000 MBH		.16	200			10,600		10,600	16,000
0390	12,200 thru 25,000 MBH		.12	266			14,100		14,100	21,300
0400	Central station air handler unit, up thru 15 ton	Q-5	1.60	10			500		500	755
0410	17.5 thru 30 ton	"	.80	20			1,000		1,000	1,500
0430	Computer room unit									
0434	Air cooled split, up thru 10 ton	Q-5	.67	23.881	Ea.		1,200		1,200	1,800
0436	12 thru 23 ton		.53	30.189			1,525		1,525	2,275
0440	Chilled water, up thru 10 ton		1.30	12.308			615		615	930
0444	12 thru 23 ton		1	16			800		800	1,200
0450	Glycol system, up thru 10 ton		.53	30.189			1,525		1,525	2,275
0454	12 thru 23 ton		.40	40			2,000		2,000	3,025
0460	Water cooled, not including condenser, up thru 10 ton		.80	20			1,000		1,000	1,500
0464	12 thru 23 ton		.60	26.667			1,325		1,325	2,025
0600	Condenser, up thru 50 ton		1	16			800		800	1,200
0610	51 thru 100 ton	Q-6	.80	30			1,550		1,550	2,350
0620	101 thru 1000 ton	"	.16	150			7,800		7,800	11,800
0660	Condensing unit, up thru 10 ton	Q-5	1.25	12.800			640		640	970
0670	11 thru 50 ton	"	.40	40			2,000		2,000	3,025
0680	60 thru 100 ton	Q-6	.30	80			4,150		4,150	6,275
0700	Cooling tower, up thru 400 ton		.80	30			1,550		1,550	2,350
0710	450 thru 600 ton		.53	45.283			2,350		2,350	3,550
0720	700 thru 1300 ton		.40	60			3,125		3,125	4,700
0780	Dehumidifier, up thru 155 lb./hr.	Q-1	8	2			98.50		98.50	148
0790	240 lb./hr. and up	"	2	8			395		395	595
1560	Ductwork									
1570	Metal, steel, sst, fabricated	Q-9	1000	.016	Lb.		.75		.75	1.14
1580	Aluminum, fabricated		485	.033	"		1.55		1.55	2.36
1590	Spiral, prefabricated		400	.040	L.F.		1.88		1.88	2.86
1600	Fiberglass, prefabricated		400	.040			1.88		1.88	2.86
1610	Flex, prefabricated		500	.032			1.50		1.50	2.29
1620	Glass fiber reinforced plastic, prefabricated		280	.057			2.68		2.68	4.09

23 05 Common Work Results for HVAC

23 05 05 – Selective HVAC Demolition

	23 05 05.10 HVAC Demolition	Crew	Daily Output	Labor-Hours	Unit	Material	Labor	Equipment	Total	Total Incl O&P
1630	Diffusers, registers or grills, up thru 20" max dimension	1 Shee	50	.160	Ea.		8.35		8.35	12.70
1640	21 thru 36" max dimension		36	.222			11.60		11.60	17.65
1650	Above 36" max dimension	↓	30	.267			13.90		13.90	21
1700	Evaporator, up thru 12,000 BTUH	Q-5	5.30	3.019			151		151	228
1710	12,500 thru 30,000 BTUH	"	2.70	5.926			297		297	450
1720	31,000 BTUH and up	Q-6	1.50	16			830		830	1,250
1730	Evaporative cooler, up thru 5 H.P.	Q-9	2.70	5.926			278		278	425
1740	10 thru 30 H.P.	"	.67	23.881	↓		1,125		1,125	1,700
1750	Exhaust systems									
1760	Exhaust components	1 Shee	8	1	System		52		52	79.50
1770	Weld fume hoods	"	20	.400	Ea.		21		21	32
2120	Fans, up thru 1 H.P. or 2000 CFM	Q-9	8	2			94		94	143
2124	1-1/2 thru 10 H.P. or 20,000 CFM	↓	5.30	3.019			142		142	216
2128	15 thru 30 H.P. or above 20,000 CFM	↓	4	4			188		188	286
2150	Fan coil air conditioner, chilled water, up thru 7.5 ton	Q-5	14	1.143			57.50		57.50	86.50
2154	Direct expansion, up thru 10 ton		8	2			100		100	151
2158	11 thru 30 ton	↓	2	8			400		400	605
2170	Flue shutter damper	Q-9	8	2			94		94	143
2200	Furnace, electric	Q-20	2	10			480		480	725
2300	Gas or oil, under 120 MBH	Q-9	4	4			188		188	286
2340	Over 120 MBH	"	3	5.333			250		250	380
2730	Heating and ventilating unit	Q-5	2.70	5.926			297		297	450
2740	Heater, electric, wall, baseboard and quartz	1 Elec	10	.800			41		41	61.50
2750	Heater, electric, unit, cabinet, fan and convector	"	8	1			51.50		51.50	77
2760	Heat exchanger, shell and tube type	Q-5	1.60	10			500		500	755
2770	Plate type	Q-6	.60	40	↓		2,075		2,075	3,125
2810	Heat pump									
2820	Air source, split, up thru 10 ton	Q-5	.90	17.778	Ea.		890		890	1,350
2830	15 thru 25 ton	Q-6	.80	30			1,550		1,550	2,350
2850	Single package, up thru 12 ton	Q-5	1	16			800		800	1,200
2860	Water source, up thru 15 ton	"	.90	17.778			890		890	1,350
2870	20 thru 50 ton	Q-6	.80	30			1,550		1,550	2,350
2910	Heat recovery package, up thru 20,000 CFM	Q-5	2	8			400		400	605
2920	25,000 CFM and up		1.20	13.333			670		670	1,000
2930	Heat transfer package, up thru 130 GPM		.80	20			1,000		1,000	1,500
2934	255 thru 800 GPM		.42	38.095			1,900		1,900	2,875
2940	Humidifier		10.60	1.509			75.50		75.50	114
2961	Hydronic unit heaters, up thru 200 MBH		14	1.143			57.50		57.50	86.50
2962	Above 200 MBH		8	2			100		100	151
2964	Valance units	↓	32	.500	↓		25		25	38
2966	Radiant floor heating									
2967	System valves, controls, manifolds	Q-5	16	1	Ea.		50		50	75.50
2968	Per room distribution		8	2			100		100	151
2970	Hydronic heating, baseboard radiation		16	1			50		50	75.50
2976	Convectors and free standing radiators	↓	18	.889			44.50		44.50	67
2980	Induced draft fan, up thru 1 H.P.	Q-9	4.60	3.478			163		163	249
2984	1-1/2 H.P. thru 7-1/2 H.P.	"	2.20	7.273			340		340	520
2988	Infrared unit	Q-5	16	1	↓		50		50	75.50
2992	Louvers	1 Shee	46	.174	S.F.		9.05		9.05	13.85
3000	Mechanical equipment, light items. Unit is weight, not cooling.	Q-5	.90	17.778	Ton		890		890	1,350
3600	Heavy items	"	1.10	14.545	"		730		730	1,100
3700	Deduct for salvage (when applicable), minimum				Job				73	80
3710	Maximum				"				455	500

23 05 05 – Selective HVAC Demolition

	23 05 05.10 HVAC Demolition	Crew	Daily Output	Labor-Hours	Unit	Material	2012 Bare Costs Labor	2012 Bare Costs Equipment	Total	Total Incl O&P
3720	Make up air unit, up thru 6000 CFM	Q-5	3	5.333	Ea.		267		267	405
3730	6500 thru 30,000 CFM	"	1.60	10			500		500	755
3740	35,000 thru 75,000 CFM	Q-6	1	24			1,250		1,250	1,875
3800	Mixing boxes, constant and VAV	Q-9	18	.889			41.50		41.50	63.50
4000	Packaged terminal air conditioner, up thru 18,000 BTUH	Q-5	8	2			100		100	151
4010	24,000 thru 48,000 BTUH	"	2.80	5.714			286		286	430
5000	Refrigerant compressor, reciprocating or scroll									
5010	Up thru 5 ton	1 Stpi	6	1.333	Ea.		74.50		74.50	112
5020	5.08 thru 10 ton	Q-5	6	2.667			134		134	202
5030	15 thru 50 ton	"	.40	40			2,000		2,000	3,025
5040	60 thru 130 ton	Q-6	.48	50			2,600		2,600	3,925
5100	Roof top air conditioner, up thru 10 ton	Q-5	1.40	11.429			575		575	865
5110	12 thru 40 ton	Q-6	1	24			1,250		1,250	1,875
5120	50 thru 140 ton		.50	48			2,500		2,500	3,775
5130	150 thru 300 ton		.30	80			4,150		4,150	6,275
6000	Self contained single package air conditioner, up thru 10 ton	Q-5	1.60	10			500		500	755
6010	15 thru 60 ton	Q-6	1.20	20			1,050		1,050	1,575
6100	Space heaters, up thru 200 MBH	Q-5	10	1.600			80		80	121
6110	Over 200 MBH		5	3.200			160		160	242
6200	Split ductless, both sections		8	2			100		100	151
6300	Steam condensate meter	1 Stpi	11	.727			40.50		40.50	61
6600	Thru-the-wall air conditioner	L-2	8	2			77.50		77.50	119
7000	Vent chimney, prefabricated, up thru 12" diameter	Q-9	94	.170	V.L.F.		8		8	12.20
7010	14" thru 36" diameter		40	.400			18.75		18.75	28.50
7020	38" thru 48" diameter		32	.500			23.50		23.50	36
7030	54" thru 60" diameter	Q-10	14	1.714			83.50		83.50	127
7400	Ventilators, up thru 14" neck diameter	Q-9	58	.276	Ea.		12.95		12.95	19.75
7410	16" thru 50" neck diameter		40	.400			18.75		18.75	28.50
7450	Relief vent, up thru 24" x 96"		22	.727			34		34	52
7460	48" x 60" thru 96" x 144"		10	1.600			75		75	114
8000	Water chiller up thru 10 ton	Q-5	2.50	6.400			320		320	485
8010	15 thru 100 ton	Q-6	.48	50			2,600		2,600	3,925
8020	110 thru 500 ton	Q-7	.29	110			5,850		5,850	8,825
8030	600 thru 1000 ton		.23	139			7,375		7,375	11,100
8040	1100 ton and up		.20	160			8,475		8,475	12,800
8400	Window air conditioner	1 Carp	16	.500			22		22	34

23 05 23 – General-Duty Valves for HVAC Piping

23 05 23.30 Valves, Iron Body

		Crew	Daily Output	Labor-Hours	Unit	Material	2012 Bare Costs Labor	2012 Bare Costs Equipment	Total	Total Incl O&P
0010	**VALVES, IRON BODY** R220523-90									
0022	For grooved joint, see Section 22 11 13.48									
0100	Angle, 125 lb.									
0110	Flanged									
0116	2"	1 Plum	5	1.600	Ea.	1,500	87.50		1,587.50	1,775
0118	4"	Q-1	3	5.333		1,850	262		2,112	2,450
0120	6"	Q-2	3	8		3,625	410		4,035	4,600
0122	8"	"	2.50	9.600		6,475	490		6,965	7,875
0560	Butterfly, lug type, pneumatic operator, 2" size	1 Stpi	14	.571		865	32		897	1,000
0570	3"	Q-1	8	2		875	98.50		973.50	1,125
0580	4"	"	5	3.200		925	157		1,082	1,250
0590	6"	Q-2	5	4.800		1,025	245		1,270	1,525
0600	8"		4.50	5.333		1,025	272		1,297	1,525
0610	10"		4	6		1,350	305		1,655	1,950

23 05 Common Work Results for HVAC

23 05 23 – General-Duty Valves for HVAC Piping

23 05 23.30 Valves, Iron Body

		Crew	Daily Output	Labor-Hours	Unit	Material	2012 Bare Costs Labor	Equipment	Total	Total Incl O&P
0620	12"	Q-2	3	8	Ea.	1,650	410		2,060	2,425
0630	14"		2.30	10.435		2,125	530		2,655	3,125
0640	18"		1.50	16		3,350	815		4,165	4,900
0650	20"		1	24		4,075	1,225		5,300	6,350
0790	Butterfly, lug type, gear operated, 2" size, 200 lb. except noted	1 Plum	14	.571		320	31		351	400
0800	2-1/2"	Q-1	9	1.778		325	87.50		412.50	490
0810	3"		8	2		340	98.50		438.50	525
0820	4"		5	3.200		385	157		542	655
0830	5"	Q-2	5	4.800		480	245		725	895
0840	6"		5	4.800		530	245		775	950
0850	8"		4.50	5.333		685	272		957	1,175
0860	10"		4	6		960	305		1,265	1,500
0870	12"		3	8		1,325	410		1,735	2,075
0880	14", 150 lb.		2.30	10.435		2,650	530		3,180	3,725
0890	16", 150 lb.		1.75	13.714		3,850	700		4,550	5,300
0900	18", 150 lb.		1.50	16		4,250	815		5,065	5,900
0910	20", 150 lb.		1	24		5,500	1,225		6,725	7,900
0930	24", 150 lb.		.75	32		9,500	1,625		11,125	12,900
1020	Butterfly, wafer type, gear actuator, 200 lb.									
1030	2"	1 Plum	14	.571	Ea.	172	31		203	237
1040	2-1/2"	Q-1	9	1.778		178	87.50		265.50	325
1050	3"		8	2		184	98.50		282.50	350
1060	4"		5	3.200		209	157		366	465
1070	5"	Q-2	5	4.800		278	245		523	675
1080	6"		5	4.800		315	245		560	715
1090	8"		4.50	5.333		420	272		692	870
1100	10"		4	6		525	305		830	1,025
1110	12"		3	8		730	410		1,140	1,425
1200	Wafer type, lever actuator, 200 lb.									
1220	2"	1 Plum	14	.571	Ea.	143	31		174	204
1230	2-1/2"	Q-1	9	1.778		147	87.50		234.50	294
1240	3"		8	2		156	98.50		254.50	320
1250	4"		5	3.200		189	157		346	445
1260	5"	Q-2	5	4.800		263	245		508	660
1270	6"		5	4.800		320	245		565	720
1280	8"		4.50	5.333		495	272		767	950
1290	10"		4	6		690	305		995	1,225
1300	12"		3	8		1,250	410		1,660	2,000
1600	Gate, threaded, 125 lb.									
1603	1-1/2"	1 Plum	13	.615	Ea.	247	33.50		280.50	325
1604	2"		11	.727		980	39.50		1,019.50	1,125
1605	2-1/2"		10	.800		1,075	43.50		1,118.50	1,250
1606	3"		8	1		1,275	54.50		1,329.50	1,475
1607	4"		5	1.600		1,800	87.50		1,887.50	2,100
1650	Gate, 125 lb., N.R.S.									
2150	Flanged									
2200	2"	1 Plum	5	1.600	Ea.	610	87.50		697.50	800
2240	2-1/2"	Q-1	5	3.200		625	157		782	920
2260	3"		4.50	3.556		700	175		875	1,025
2280	4"		3	5.333		1,000	262		1,262	1,500
2290	5"	Q-2	3.40	7.059		1,700	360		2,060	2,425
2300	6"		3	8		1,700	410		2,110	2,500
2320	8"		2.50	9.600		2,925	490		3,415	3,975

23 05 23.30 Valves, Iron Body		Crew	Daily Output	Labor-Hours	Unit	Material	2012 Bare Costs Labor	Equipment	Total	Total Incl O&P
2340	10"	Q-2	2.20	10.909	Ea.	5,150	555		5,705	6,525
2360	12"		1.70	14.118		7,075	720		7,795	8,850
2370	14"		1.30	18.462		10,100	940		11,040	12,500
2380	16"	↓	1	24	↓	14,000	1,225		15,225	17,300
2420	For 250 lb. flanged, add					200%	10%			
3500	OS&Y, 125 lb., (225# noted), threaded									
3504	3/4" (225 lb.)	1 Plum	18	.444	Ea.	440	24.50		464.50	520
3505	1" (225 lb.)		16	.500		500	27.50		527.50	590
3506	1-1/2" (225 lb.)		13	.615		730	33.50		763.50	850
3507	2"	↓	11	.727	↓	940	39.50		979.50	1,075
3550	OS&Y, 125 lb., flanged									
3600	2"	1 Plum	5	1.600	Ea.	315	87.50		402.50	475
3640	2-1/2"	Q-1	5	3.200		405	157		562	680
3660	3"		4.50	3.556		445	175		620	750
3670	3-1/2"		3	5.333		520	262		782	965
3680	4"	↓	3	5.333		635	262		897	1,100
3690	5"	Q-2	3.40	7.059		1,050	360		1,410	1,700
3700	6"		3	8		1,050	410		1,460	1,775
3720	8"		2.50	9.600		1,850	490		2,340	2,800
3740	10"		2.20	10.909		3,400	555		3,955	4,575
3760	12"		1.70	14.118		4,525	720		5,245	6,050
3770	14"		1.30	18.462		9,125	940		10,065	11,400
3780	16"		1	24		13,000	1,225		14,225	16,200
3790	18"		.80	30		17,400	1,525		18,925	21,400
3800	20"		.60	40		24,200	2,050		26,250	29,800
3830	24"	↓	.50	48	↓	36,000	2,450		38,450	43,300
3900	For 175 lb., flanged, add					200%	10%			
4350	Globe, OS&Y									
4540	Class 125, flanged									
4550	2"	1 Plum	5	1.600	Ea.	785	87.50		872.50	995
4560	2-1/2"	Q-1	5	3.200		790	157		947	1,100
4570	3"		4.50	3.556		960	175		1,135	1,325
4580	4"	↓	3	5.333		1,375	262		1,637	1,900
4590	5"	Q-2	3.40	7.059		2,500	360		2,860	3,300
4600	6"		3	8		2,500	410		2,910	3,375
4610	8"		2.50	9.600		4,900	490		5,390	6,150
4612	10"		2.20	10.909		7,650	555		8,205	9,275
4614	12"	↓	1.70	14.118	↓	7,950	720		8,670	9,825
5040	Class 250, flanged									
5050	2"	1 Plum	4.50	1.778	Ea.	1,250	97		1,347	1,525
5060	2-1/2"	Q-1	4.50	3.556		1,625	175		1,800	2,075
5070	3"		4	4		1,700	197		1,897	2,150
5080	4"	↓	2.70	5.926		2,475	291		2,766	3,175
5090	5"	Q-2	3	8		4,425	410		4,835	5,500
5100	6"		2.70	8.889		4,275	455		4,730	5,400
5110	8"		2.20	10.909		7,525	555		8,080	9,125
5120	10"		2	12		13,100	610		13,710	15,300
5130	12"	↓	1.60	15		20,400	765		21,165	23,600
5240	Valve sprocket rim w/chain, for 2" valve	1 Stpi	30	.267		117	14.85		131.85	152
5250	2-1/2" valve		27	.296		117	16.50		133.50	154
5260	3-1/2" valve		25	.320		117	17.80		134.80	156
5270	6" valve		20	.400		117	22.50		139.50	163
5280	8" valve	↓	18	.444	↓	143	25		168	195

23 05 23.30 Valves, Iron Body		Crew	Daily Output	Labor-Hours	Unit	Material	2012 Bare Costs Labor	Equipment	Total	Total Incl O&P
5290	12" valve	1 Stpi	16	.500	Ea.	143	28		171	199
5300	16" valve		12	.667		197	37		234	273
5310	20" valve		10	.800		197	44.50		241.50	284
5320	36" valve		8	1		350	55.50		405.50	470
5450	Swing check, 125 lb., threaded									
5470	1"	1 Plum	13	.615	Ea.	575	33.50		608.50	685
5500	2"	"	11	.727		780	39.50		819.50	915
5540	2-1/2"	Q-1	15	1.067		675	52.50		727.50	825
5550	3"		13	1.231		750	60.50		810.50	915
5560	4"		10	1.600		1,300	78.50		1,378.50	1,550
5950	Flanged									
5994	1"	1 Plum	7	1.143	Ea.	172	62.50		234.50	284
5998	1-1/2"		6	1.333		240	73		313	375
6000	2"		5	1.600		335	87.50		422.50	500
6040	2-1/2"	Q-1	5	3.200		340	157		497	605
6050	3"		4.50	3.556		345	175		520	640
6060	4"		3	5.333		540	262		802	985
6070	6"	Q-2	3	8		920	410		1,330	1,625
6080	8"		2.50	9.600		1,725	490		2,215	2,650
6090	10"		2.20	10.909		3,025	555		3,580	4,175
6100	12"		1.70	14.118		4,800	720		5,520	6,350
6110	18"		1.30	18.462		12,400	940		13,340	15,000
6114	24"		.75	32		23,400	1,625		25,025	28,200
6160	For 250 lb. flanged, add					200%	20%			
6600	Silent check, bronze trim									
6610	Compact wafer type, for 125 or 150 lb. flanges									
6630	1-1/2"	1 Plum	11	.727	Ea.	124	39.50		163.50	197
6640	2"	"	9	.889		149	48.50		197.50	237
6650	2-1/2"	Q-1	9	1.778		163	87.50		250.50	310
6660	3"		8	2		175	98.50		273.50	340
6670	4"		5	3.200		223	157		380	480
6680	5"	Q-2	6	4		291	204		495	625
6690	6"		6	4		390	204		594	735
6700	8"		4.50	5.333		695	272		967	1,175
6710	10"		4	6		1,200	305		1,505	1,775
6720	12"		3	8		2,300	410		2,710	3,150
6740	For 250 or 300 lb. flanges, thru 6" no change									
6741	For 8" and 10", add				Ea.	11%	10%			
6750	Twin disc									
6752	2"	1 Plum	9	.889	Ea.	272	48.50		320.50	370
6754	4"	Q-1	5	3.200		445	157		602	725
6756	6"	Q-2	5	4.800		675	245		920	1,100
6758	8"		4.50	5.333		1,025	272		1,297	1,525
6760	10"		4	6		1,625	305		1,930	2,225
6762	12"		3	8		2,100	410		2,510	2,925
6764	18"		1.50	16		9,075	815		9,890	11,200
6766	24"		.75	32		12,800	1,625		14,425	16,600
6800	Full flange type, 150 lb.									
6810	1"	1 Plum	14	.571	Ea.	146	31		177	207
6811	1-1/4"		12	.667		153	36.50		189.50	224
6812	1-1/2"		11	.727		178	39.50		217.50	256
6813	2"		9	.889		204	48.50		252.50	298
6814	2-1/2"	Q-1	9	1.778		247	87.50		334.50	405

23 05 23 – General-Duty Valves for HVAC Piping

23 05 23.30 Valves, Iron Body

		Crew	Daily Output	Labor-Hours	Unit	Material	2012 Bare Costs Labor	Equipment	Total	Total Incl O&P
6815	3"	Q-1	8	2	Ea.	256	98.50		354.50	430
6816	4"	↓	5	3.200		315	157		472	585
6817	5"	Q-2	6	4		500	204		704	855
6818	6"		5	4.800		655	245		900	1,100
6819	8"		4.50	5.333		1,100	272		1,372	1,625
6820	10"	↓	4	6		1,400	305		1,705	2,000
6840	For 250 lb., add				↓	30%	10%			
6900	Globe type, 125 lb.									
6910	2"	1 Plum	9	.889	Ea.	335	48.50		383.50	445
6911	2-1/2"	Q-1	9	1.778		370	87.50		457.50	535
6912	3"		8	2		395	98.50		493.50	585
6913	4"	↓	5	3.200		535	157		692	820
6914	5"	Q-2	6	4		685	204		889	1,050
6915	6"		5	4.800		860	245		1,105	1,325
6916	8"		4.50	5.333		1,575	272		1,847	2,125
6917	10"		4	6		1,975	305		2,280	2,625
6918	12"		3	8		3,300	410		3,710	4,250
6919	14"		2.30	10.435		4,475	530		5,005	5,725
6920	16"		1.75	13.714		6,475	700		7,175	8,150
6921	18"		1.50	16		9,350	815		10,165	11,500
6922	20"		1	24		11,300	1,225		12,525	14,400
6923	24"	↓	.75	32		14,000	1,625		15,625	17,900
6940	For 250 lb., add				↓	40%	10%			
6980	Screwed end type, 125 lb.									
6981	1"	1 Plum	19	.421	Ea.	51.50	23		74.50	91
6982	1-1/4"		15	.533		66.50	29		95.50	118
6983	1-1/2"		13	.615		81.50	33.50		115	140
6984	2"	↓	11	.727	↓	112	39.50		151.50	183

23 05 23.50 Valves, Multipurpose

		Crew	Daily Output	Labor-Hours	Unit	Material	2012 Bare Costs Labor	Equipment	Total	Total Incl O&P
0010	**VALVES, MULTIPURPOSE**									
0100	Functions as a shut off, balancing, check & metering valve									
1000	Cast iron body									
1010	Threaded									
1020	1-1/2" size	1 Stpi	11	.727	Ea.	360	40.50		400.50	455
1030	2" size	"	8	1		435	55.50		490.50	565
1040	2-1/2" size	Q-5	5	3.200	↓	470	160		630	755
1200	Flanged									
1210	3" size	Q-5	4.20	3.810	Ea.	540	191		731	885
1220	4" size	"	3	5.333		1,100	267		1,367	1,600
1230	5" size	Q-6	3.80	6.316		1,300	330		1,630	1,925
1240	6" size		3	8		1,625	415		2,040	2,400
1250	8" size		2.50	9.600		2,800	500		3,300	3,825
1260	10" size		2.20	10.909		4,000	565		4,565	5,250
1270	12" size		2.10	11.429		7,225	595		7,820	8,850
1280	14" size	↓	2	12	↓	10,500	625		11,125	12,400

23 05 23.70 Valves, Semi-Steel

		Crew	Daily Output	Labor-Hours	Unit	Material	2012 Bare Costs Labor	Equipment	Total	Total Incl O&P
0010	**VALVES, SEMI-STEEL** R220523-90									
1020	Lubricated plug valve, threaded, 200 psi									
1030	1/2"	1 Plum	18	.444	Ea.	82	24.50		106.50	127
1040	3/4"		16	.500		82	27.50		109.50	131
1050	1"		14	.571		104	31		135	162
1060	1-1/4"	↓	12	.667	↓	124	36.50		160.50	191

23 05 23.70 Valves, Semi-Steel

		Crew	Daily Output	Labor-Hours	Unit	Material	2012 Bare Costs Labor	2012 Bare Costs Equipment	Total	Total Incl O&P
1070	1-1/2"	1 Plum	11	.727	Ea.	134	39.50		173.50	207
1080	2"	↓	8	1		159	54.50		213.50	258
1090	2-1/2"	Q-1	5	3.200		246	157		403	510
1100	3"	"	4.50	3.556	↓	300	175		475	595
6990	Flanged, 200 psi									
7000	2"	1 Plum	8	1	Ea.	197	54.50		251.50	300
7010	2-1/2"	Q-1	5	3.200		283	157		440	545
7020	3"		4.50	3.556		340	175		515	640
7030	4"		3	5.333		430	262		692	865
7036	5"	↓	2.50	6.400		840	315		1,155	1,400
7040	6"	Q-2	3	8		705	410		1,115	1,400
7050	8"		2.50	9.600		1,375	490		1,865	2,250
7060	10"		2.20	10.909		2,175	555		2,730	3,250
7070	12"	↓	1.70	14.118	↓	4,700	720		5,420	6,250

23 05 23.80 Valves, Steel

		Crew	Daily Output	Labor-Hours	Unit	Material	2012 Bare Costs Labor	2012 Bare Costs Equipment	Total	Total Incl O&P
0010	**VALVES, STEEL** R220523-90									
0800	Cast									
1350	Check valve, swing type, 150 lb., flanged									
1370	1"	1 Plum	10	.800	Ea.	390	43.50		433.50	495
1400	2"	"	8	1		660	54.50		714.50	810
1440	2-1/2"	Q-1	5	3.200		765	157		922	1,075
1450	3"		4.50	3.556		780	175		955	1,125
1460	4"	↓	3	5.333		1,125	262		1,387	1,625
1470	6"	Q-2	3	8		1,750	410		2,160	2,550
1480	8"		2.50	9.600		2,850	490		3,340	3,900
1490	10"		2.20	10.909		4,225	555		4,780	5,500
1500	12"		1.70	14.118		6,025	720		6,745	7,725
1510	14"		1.30	18.462		8,725	940		9,665	11,000
1520	16"	↓	1	24		9,875	1,225		11,100	12,800
1548	For 600 lb., flanged, add					110%	20%			
1571	300 lb., 2"	1 Plum	7.40	1.081		700	59		759	860
1572	2-1/2"	Q-1	4.20	3.810		1,050	187		1,237	1,425
1573	3"		4	4		1,050	197		1,247	1,450
1574	4"	↓	2.80	5.714		1,375	281		1,656	1,925
1575	6"	Q-2	2.90	8.276		2,650	420		3,070	3,550
1576	8"		2.40	10		3,825	510		4,335	5,000
1577	10"		2.10	11.429		5,675	585		6,260	7,125
1578	12"		1.60	15		7,950	765		8,715	9,875
1579	14"		1.20	20		12,000	1,025		13,025	14,700
1581	16"	↓	.90	26.667	↓	15,500	1,350		16,850	19,200
1950	Gate valve, 150 lb., flanged									
2000	2"	1 Plum	8	1	Ea.	710	54.50		764.50	865
2040	2-1/2"	Q-1	5	3.200		1,000	157		1,157	1,325
2050	3"		4.50	3.556		1,000	175		1,175	1,375
2060	4"	↓	3	5.333		1,250	262		1,512	1,775
2070	6"	Q-2	3	8		1,850	410		2,260	2,650
2080	8"		2.50	9.600		1,925	490		2,415	2,875
2090	10"		2.20	10.909		4,400	555		4,955	5,675
2100	12"		1.70	14.118		5,975	720		6,695	7,650
2110	14"		1.30	18.462		9,500	940		10,440	11,900
2120	16"		1	24		12,300	1,225		13,525	15,400
2130	18"	↓	.80	30	↓	14,900	1,525		16,425	18,700

23 05 23.80 Valves, Steel		Crew	Daily Output	Labor-Hours	Unit	Material	2012 Bare Costs Labor	Equipment	Total	Total Incl O&P
2140	20"	Q-2	.60	40	Ea.	17,900	2,050		19,950	22,800
2650	300 lb., flanged									
2700	2"	1 Plum	7.40	1.081	Ea.	965	59		1,024	1,150
2740	2-1/2"	Q-1	4.20	3.810		1,300	187		1,487	1,700
2750	3"		4	4		1,300	197		1,497	1,725
2760	4"		2.80	5.714		1,825	281		2,106	2,425
2770	6"	Q-2	2.90	8.276		3,075	420		3,495	4,000
2780	8"		2.40	10		4,800	510		5,310	6,050
2790	10"		2.10	11.429		6,450	585		7,035	7,975
2800	12"		1.60	15		9,300	765		10,065	11,400
2810	14"		1.20	20		17,600	1,025		18,625	20,900
2820	16"		.90	26.667		22,100	1,350		23,450	26,400
2830	18"		.70	34.286		31,500	1,750		33,250	37,300
2840	20"		.50	48		35,100	2,450		37,550	42,300
3650	Globe valve, 150 lb., flanged									
3700	2"	1 Plum	8	1	Ea.	890	54.50		944.50	1,075
3740	2-1/2"	Q-1	5	3.200		1,125	157		1,282	1,475
3750	3"		4.50	3.556		1,125	175		1,300	1,525
3760	4"		3	5.333		1,650	262		1,912	2,225
3770	6"	Q-2	3	8		2,600	410		3,010	3,475
3780	8"		2.50	9.600		4,750	490		5,240	6,000
3790	10"		2.20	10.909		8,425	555		8,980	10,100
3800	12"		1.70	14.118		11,400	720		12,120	13,600
4080	300 lb., flanged									
4100	2"	1 Plum	7.40	1.081	Ea.	1,200	59		1,259	1,400
4140	2-1/2"	Q-1	4.20	3.810		1,625	187		1,812	2,050
4150	3"		4	4		1,625	197		1,822	2,075
4160	4"		2.80	5.714		2,250	281		2,531	2,900
4170	6"	Q-2	2.90	8.276		4,050	420		4,470	5,075
4180	8"		2.40	10		6,625	510		7,135	8,050
4190	10"		2.10	11.429		12,500	585		13,085	14,600
4200	12"		1.60	15		14,500	765		15,265	17,100
4680	600 lb., flanged									
4700	2"	1 Plum	7	1.143	Ea.	1,650	62.50		1,712.50	1,925
4740	2-1/2"	Q-1	4	4		2,475	197		2,672	3,025
4750	3"		3.60	4.444		2,475	218		2,693	3,050
4760	4"		2.50	6.400		4,000	315		4,315	4,875
4770	6"	Q-2	2.60	9.231		8,325	470		8,795	9,850
4780	8"	"	2.10	11.429		13,500	585		14,085	15,800
4800	Silent check, 316 S.S. trim									
4810	Full flange type, 150 lb.									
4811	1"	1 Plum	14	.571	Ea.	515	31		546	615
4812	1-1/4"		12	.667		515	36.50		551.50	625
4813	1-1/2"		11	.727		565	39.50		604.50	680
4814	2"		9	.889		680	48.50		728.50	825
4815	2-1/2"	Q-1	9	1.778		820	87.50		907.50	1,025
4816	3"		8	2		955	98.50		1,053.50	1,200
4817	4"		5	3.200		1,300	157		1,457	1,650
4818	5"	Q-2	6	4		1,625	204		1,829	2,100
4819	6"		5	4.800		2,100	245		2,345	2,700
4820	8"		4.50	5.333		3,050	272		3,322	3,775
4821	10"		4	6		4,300	305		4,605	5,200
4840	For 300 lb., add					20%	10%			

23 05 23.80 Valves, Steel		Crew	Daily Output	Labor-Hours	Unit	Material	2012 Bare Costs Labor	Equipment	Total	Total Incl O&P
4860	For 600 lb., add				Ea.	50%	15%			
4900	Globe type, 150 lb.									
4910	2"	1 Plum	9	.889	Ea.	810	48.50		858.50	965
4911	2-1/2"	Q-1	9	1.778		975	87.50		1,062.50	1,200
4912	3"		8	2		1,075	98.50		1,173.50	1,350
4913	4"		5	3.200		1,450	157		1,607	1,800
4914	5"	Q-2	6	4		1,800	204		2,004	2,300
4915	6"		5	4.800		2,250	245		2,495	2,850
4916	8"		4.50	5.333		3,125	272		3,397	3,825
4917	10"		4	6		5,350	305		5,655	6,325
4918	12"		3	8		6,650	410		7,060	7,925
4919	14"		2.30	10.435		10,100	530		10,630	11,900
4920	16"		1.75	13.714		14,000	700		14,700	16,500
4921	18"		1.50	16		14,800	815		15,615	17,400
4940	For 300 lb., add					30%	10%			
4960	For 600 lb., add					60%	15%			
5150	Forged									
5340	Ball valve, 1500 psi, threaded, 1/4" size	1 Plum	24	.333	Ea.	71.50	18.20		89.70	107
5350	3/8"		24	.333		71.50	18.20		89.70	107
5360	1/2"		24	.333		88.50	18.20		106.70	125
5370	3/4"		20	.400		118	22		140	163
5380	1"		19	.421		147	23		170	197
5390	1-1/4"		15	.533		196	29		225	259
5400	1-1/2"		13	.615		255	33.50		288.50	330
5410	2"		11	.727		340	39.50		379.50	430
5460	Ball valve, 800 lb., socket weld, 1/4" size	Q-15	19	.842		71.50	41.50	1.95	114.95	144
5470	3/8"		19	.842		71.50	41.50	1.95	114.95	144
5480	1/2"		19	.842		88.50	41.50	1.95	131.95	162
5490	3/4"		19	.842		118	41.50	1.95	161.45	195
5500	1"		15	1.067		147	52.50	2.46	201.96	244
5510	1-1/4"		13	1.231		196	60.50	2.84	259.34	310
5520	1-1/2"		11	1.455		305	71.50	3.36	379.86	445
5530	2"		8.50	1.882		340	92.50	4.35	436.85	515
5550	Ball valve, 150 lb., flanged									
5560	4"	Q-1	3	5.333	Ea.	780	262		1,042	1,250
5570	6"	Q-2	3	8		1,875	410		2,285	2,675
5580	8"	"	2.50	9.600		4,775	490		5,265	6,000
5650	Check valve, class 800, horizontal, socket									
5652	1/4"	Q-15	19	.842	Ea.	94.50	41.50	1.95	137.95	169
5654	3/8"		19	.842		94.50	41.50	1.95	137.95	169
5656	1/2"		19	.842		94.50	41.50	1.95	137.95	169
5658	3/4"		19	.842		101	41.50	1.95	144.45	176
5660	1"		15	1.067		119	52.50	2.46	173.96	213
5662	1-1/4"		13	1.231		233	60.50	2.84	296.34	350
5664	1-1/2"		11	1.455		233	71.50	3.36	307.86	370
5666	2"		8.50	1.882		325	92.50	4.35	421.85	505
5698	Threaded									
5700	1/4"	1 Plum	24	.333	Ea.	94.50	18.20		112.70	132
5720	3/8"		24	.333		94.50	18.20		112.70	132
5730	1/2"		24	.333		94.50	18.20		112.70	132
5740	3/4"		20	.400		101	22		123	144
5750	1"		19	.421		119	23		142	166
5760	1-1/4"		15	.533		233	29		262	300

23 05 23.80 Valves, Steel

		Crew	Daily Output	Labor-Hours	Unit	Material	2012 Bare Costs Labor	Equipment	Total	Total Incl O&P
5770	1-1/2"	1 Plum	13	.615	Ea.	233	33.50		266.50	305
5780	2"	↓	11	.727		325	39.50		364.50	420
5840	For class 150, flanged, add					100%	15%			
5860	For class 300, flanged, add				↓	120%	20%			
6100	Gate, class 800, OS&Y, socket									
6102	3/8"	Q-15	19	.842	Ea.	65.50	41.50	1.95	108.95	137
6103	1/2"		19	.842		65.50	41.50	1.95	108.95	137
6104	3/4"		19	.842		72	41.50	1.95	115.45	144
6105	1"		15	1.067		87	52.50	2.46	141.96	178
6106	1-1/4"		13	1.231		165	60.50	2.84	228.34	275
6107	1-1/2"		11	1.455		165	71.50	3.36	239.86	293
6108	2"	↓	8.50	1.882	↓	185	92.50	4.35	281.85	350
6118	Threaded									
6120	3/8"	1 Plum	24	.333	Ea.	65.50	18.20		83.70	99.50
6130	1/2"		24	.333		65.50	18.20		83.70	99.50
6140	3/4"		20	.400		72	22		94	112
6150	1"		19	.421		87	23		110	131
6160	1-1/4"		15	.533		165	29		194	225
6170	1-1/2"		13	.615		165	33.50		198.50	232
6180	2"	↓	11	.727	↓	185	39.50		224.50	264
6260	For OS&Y, flanged, add					100%	20%			
6700	Globe, OS&Y, class 800, socket									
6710	1/4"	Q-15	19	.842	Ea.	101	41.50	1.95	144.45	176
6720	3/8"		19	.842		101	41.50	1.95	144.45	176
6730	1/2"		19	.842		101	41.50	1.95	144.45	176
6740	3/4"		19	.842		116	41.50	1.95	159.45	193
6750	1"		15	1.067		151	52.50	2.46	205.96	248
6760	1-1/4"		13	1.231		295	60.50	2.84	358.34	420
6770	1-1/2"		11	1.455		295	71.50	3.36	369.86	435
6780	2"	↓	8.50	1.882		380	92.50	4.35	476.85	560
6860	For OS&Y, flanged, add				↓	300%	20%			
6880	Threaded									
6882	1/4"	1 Plum	24	.333	Ea.	101	18.20		119.20	139
6884	3/8"		24	.333		101	18.20		119.20	139
6886	1/2"		24	.333		101	18.20		119.20	139
6888	3/4"		20	.400		116	22		138	161
6890	1"		19	.421		151	23		174	201
6892	1-1/4"		15	.533		295	29		324	370
6894	1-1/2"		13	.615		295	33.50		328.50	375
6896	2"	↓	11	.727	↓	380	39.50		419.50	475

23 05 23.90 Valves, Stainless Steel

		Crew	Daily Output	Labor-Hours	Unit	Material	2012 Bare Costs Labor	Equipment	Total	Total Incl O&P
0010	**VALVES, STAINLESS STEEL** R220523-90									
1610	Ball, threaded 1/4"	1 Stpi	24	.333	Ea.	47	18.55		65.55	80
1620	3/8"		24	.333		47	18.55		65.55	80
1630	1/2"		22	.364		47	20.50		67.50	82.50
1640	3/4"		20	.400		78	22.50		100.50	120
1650	1"		19	.421		95	23.50		118.50	141
1660	1-1/4		15	.533		181	29.50		210.50	244
1670	1-1/2"		13	.615		189	34.50		223.50	260
1680	2"	↓	11	.727	↓	245	40.50		285.50	330
1700	Check, 200 lb., threaded									
1710	1/4"	1 Plum	24	.333	Ea.	130	18.20		148.20	171

23 05 23.90 Valves, Stainless Steel		Crew	Daily Output	Labor-Hours	Unit	Material	2012 Bare Costs Labor	Equipment	Total	Total Incl O&P
1720	1/2"	1 Plum	22	.364	Ea.	130	19.85		149.85	173
1730	3/4"		20	.400		142	22		164	189
1750	1"		19	.421		182	23		205	235
1760	1-1/2"		13	.615		350	33.50		383.50	435
1770	2"		11	.727		585	39.50		624.50	705
1800	150 lb., flanged									
1810	2-1/2"	Q-1	5	3.200	Ea.	1,400	157		1,557	1,775
1820	3"		4.50	3.556		1,400	175		1,575	1,825
1830	4"		3	5.333		2,100	262		2,362	2,700
1840	6"	Q-2	3	8		3,725	410		4,135	4,725
1850	8"	"	2.50	9.600		6,250	490		6,740	7,625
2100	Gate, OS&Y, 150 lb., flanged									
2120	1/2"	1 Plum	18	.444	Ea.	415	24.50		439.50	490
2140	3/4"		16	.500		440	27.50		467.50	525
2150	1"		14	.571		540	31		571	640
2160	1-1/2"		11	.727		750	39.50		789.50	890
2170	2"		8	1		845	54.50		899.50	1,000
2180	2-1/2"	Q-1	5	3.200		1,400	157		1,557	1,750
2190	3"		4.50	3.556		2,050	175		2,225	2,525
2200	4"		3	5.333		2,050	262		2,312	2,650
2205	5"		2.80	5.714		3,550	281		3,831	4,350
2210	6"	Q-2	3	8		3,550	410		3,960	4,550
2220	8"		2.50	9.600		5,725	490		6,215	7,050
2230	10"		2.30	10.435		9,375	530		9,905	11,100
2240	12"		1.90	12.632		12,000	645		12,645	14,200
2260	For 300 lb., flanged, add					120%	15%			
2600	600 lb., flanged									
2620	1/2"	1 Plum	16	.500	Ea.	213	27.50		240.50	275
2640	3/4"		14	.571		230	31		261	300
2650	1"		12	.667		277	36.50		313.50	360
2660	1-1/2"		10	.800		445	43.50		488.50	550
2670	2"		7	1.143		610	62.50		672.50	765
2680	2-1/2"	Q-1	4	4		4,950	197		5,147	5,750
2690	3"	"	3.60	4.444		4,950	218		5,168	5,775
3100	Globe, OS&Y, 150 lb., flanged									
3120	1/2"	1 Plum	18	.444	Ea.	415	24.50		439.50	490
3140	3/4"		16	.500		460	27.50		487.50	545
3150	1"		14	.571		570	31		601	670
3160	1-1/2"		11	.727		845	39.50		884.50	990
3170	2"		8	1		1,025	54.50		1,079.50	1,200
3180	2-1/2"	Q-1	5	3.200		2,225	157		2,382	2,675
3190	3"		4.50	3.556		2,225	175		2,400	2,725
3200	4"		3	5.333		2,600	262		2,862	3,275
3210	6"	Q-2	3	8		4,575	410		4,985	5,675
5000	Silent check, 316 S.S. body and trim									
5010	Compact wafer type, 300 lb.									
5020	1"	1 Plum	14	.571	Ea.	850	31		881	980
5021	1-1/4"		12	.667		925	36.50		961.50	1,075
5022	1-1/2"		11	.727		955	39.50		994.50	1,100
5023	2"		9	.889		1,100	48.50		1,148.50	1,275
5024	2-1/2"	Q-1	9	1.778		1,500	87.50		1,587.50	1,775
5025	3"	"	8	2		1,725	98.50		1,823.50	2,050
5100	Full flange wafer type, 150 lb.									

23 05 23 – General-Duty Valves for HVAC Piping

23 05 23.90 Valves, Stainless Steel

		Crew	Daily Output	Labor-Hours	Unit	Material	2012 Bare Costs Labor	Equipment	Total	Total Incl O&P
5110	1"	1 Plum	14	.571	Ea.	600	31		631	705
5111	1-1/4"		12	.667		645	36.50		681.50	765
5112	1-1/2"		11	.727		735	39.50		774.50	870
5113	2"		9	.889		965	48.50		1,013.50	1,125
5114	2-1/2"	Q-1	9	1.778		1,125	87.50		1,212.50	1,375
5115	3"		8	2		1,300	98.50		1,398.50	1,575
5116	4"		5	3.200		1,925	157		2,082	2,350
5117	5"	Q-2	6	4		2,225	204		2,429	2,750
5118	6"		5	4.800		2,800	245		3,045	3,450
5119	8"		4.50	5.333		4,675	272		4,947	5,550
5120	10"		4	6		6,475	305		6,780	7,575
5200	Globe type, 300 lb.									
5210	2"	1 Plum	9	.889	Ea.	1,100	48.50		1,148.50	1,275
5211	2-1/2"	Q-1	9	1.778		1,350	87.50		1,437.50	1,600
5212	3"		8	2		1,675	98.50		1,773.50	1,975
5213	4"		5	3.200		2,325	157		2,482	2,775
5214	5"	Q-2	6	4		3,250	204		3,454	3,875
5215	6"		5	4.800		3,675	245		3,920	4,400
5216	8"		4.50	5.333		5,175	272		5,447	6,100
5217	10"		4	6		7,325	305		7,630	8,525
5300	Screwed end type, 300 lb.									
5310	1/2"	1 Plum	24	.333	Ea.	75.50	18.20		93.70	111
5311	3/4"		20	.400		89.50	22		111.50	132
5312	1"		19	.421		104	23		127	149
5313	1-1/4"		15	.533		139	29		168	197
5314	1-1/2"		13	.615		149	33.50		182.50	215
5315	2"		11	.727		185	39.50		224.50	263

23 05 93 – Testing, Adjusting, and Balancing for HVAC

23 05 93.10 Balancing, Air

		Crew	Daily Output	Labor-Hours	Unit	Material	2012 Bare Costs Labor	Equipment	Total	Total Incl O&P
0010	**BALANCING, AIR** (Subcontractor's quote incl. material and labor) R230500-10									
0900	Heating and ventilating equipment									
1000	Centrifugal fans, utility sets				Ea.				340	375
1100	Heating and ventilating unit								515	565
1200	In-line fan								515	565
1300	Propeller and wall fan								97	107
1400	Roof exhaust fan								230	251
2000	Air conditioning equipment, central station								745	815
2100	Built-up low pressure unit								685	755
2200	Built-up high pressure unit								800	880
2300	Built-up high pressure dual duct								1,250	1,375
2400	Built-up variable volume								1,475	1,625
2500	Multi-zone A.C. and heating unit								515	565
2600	For each zone over one, add								114	126
2700	Package A.C. unit								286	315
2800	Rooftop heating and cooling unit								400	440
3000	Supply, return, exhaust, registers & diffusers, avg. height ceiling								68	75
3100	High ceiling								103	113
3200	Floor height								57	63
3300	Off mixing box								45.50	50
3500	Induction unit								74.50	81.50
3600	Lab fume hood								345	375
3700	Linear supply								172	189

23 05 93.10 Balancing, Air

		Crew	Daily Output	Labor-Hours	Unit	Material	2012 Bare Costs Labor	Equipment	Total	Total Incl O&P
3800	Linear supply high				Ea.				200	220
4000	Linear return								57	63
4100	Light troffers								68.50	75.50
4200	Moduline - master								68.50	75.50
4300	Moduline - slaves								34.50	37.50
4400	Regenerators								455	500
4500	Taps into ceiling plenums								85.50	94
4600	Variable volume boxes								68.50	75.50

23 05 93.20 Balancing, Water

		Crew	Daily Output	Labor-Hours	Unit	Material	2012 Bare Costs Labor	Equipment	Total	Total Incl O&P
0010	**BALANCING, WATER** (Subcontractor's quote incl. material and labor) R230500-10									
0050	Air cooled condenser				Ea.				215	235
0080	Boiler								430	475
0100	Cabinet unit heater								73.50	80.50
0200	Chiller								520	570
0300	Convector								61	67
0400	Converter								305	335
0500	Cooling tower								400	435
0600	Fan coil unit, unit ventilator								110	121
0700	Fin tube and radiant panels								122	134
0800	Main and duct re-heat coils								113	124
0810	Heat exchanger								113	124
0900	Main balancing cocks								91.50	101
1000	Pumps								269	296
1100	Unit heater								85.50	94

23 05 93.50 Piping, Testing

		Crew	Daily Output	Labor-Hours	Unit	Material	2012 Bare Costs Labor	Equipment	Total	Total Incl O&P
0010	**PIPING, TESTING**									
0100	Nondestructive testing									
0110	Nondestructive hydraulic pressure test, isolate & 1 hr. hold									
0120	1" - 4" pipe									
0140	0 – 250 L.F.	1 Stpi	1.33	6.015	Ea.		335		335	505
0160	250 – 500 L.F.	"	.80	10			555		555	840
0180	500 – 1000 L.F.	Q-5	1.14	14.035			705		705	1,050
0200	1000 – 2000 L.F.	"	.80	20			1,000		1,000	1,500
0300	6" - 10" pipe									
0320	0 – 250 L.F.	Q-5	1	16	Ea.		800		800	1,200
0340	250 – 500 L.F.		.73	21.918			1,100		1,100	1,650
0360	500 – 1000 L.F.		.53	30.189			1,525		1,525	2,275
0380	1000 – 2000 L.F.		.38	42.105			2,100		2,100	3,175
1000	Pneumatic pressure test, includes soaping joints									
1120	1" - 4" pipe									
1140	0 – 250 L.F.	Q-5	2.67	5.993	Ea.	14.25	300		314.25	470
1160	250 – 500 L.F.		1.33	12.030		28.50	605		633.50	940
1180	500 – 1000 L.F.		.80	20		42.50	1,000		1,042.50	1,550
1200	1000 – 2000 L.F.		.50	32		57	1,600		1,657	2,500
1300	6" - 10" pipe									
1320	0 – 250 L.F.	Q-5	1.33	12.030	Ea.	14.25	605		619.25	925
1340	250 – 500 L.F.		.67	23.881		28.50	1,200		1,228.50	1,825
1360	500 – 1000 L.F.		.40	40		57	2,000		2,057	3,100
1380	1000 – 2000 L.F.		.25	64		71	3,200		3,271	4,925
2000	X-Ray of welds									
2110	2" diam.	1 Stpi	8	1	Ea.	11.60	55.50		67.10	97
2120	3" diam.		8	1		11.60	55.50		67.10	97

23 05 Common Work Results for HVAC

23 05 93 – Testing, Adjusting, and Balancing for HVAC

23 05 93.50 Piping, Testing		Crew	Daily Output	Labor-Hours	Unit	Material	2012 Bare Costs Labor	Equipment	Total	Total Incl O&P
2130	4" diam.	1 Stpi	8	1	Ea.	17.40	55.50		72.90	103
2140	6" diam.		8	1		17.40	55.50		72.90	103
2150	8" diam.		6.60	1.212		17.40	67.50		84.90	121
2160	10" diam.		6	1.333		23	74.50		97.50	138
3000	Liquid penetration of welds									
3110	2" diam.	1 Stpi	14	.571	Ea.	3.55	32		35.55	52
3120	3" diam.		13.60	.588		3.55	33		36.55	53.50
3130	4" diam.		13.40	.597		3.55	33.50		37.05	54
3140	6" diam.		13.20	.606		3.55	34		37.55	55
3150	8" diam.		13	.615		5.35	34.50		39.85	57.50
3160	10" diam.		12.80	.625		5.35	35		40.35	58.50

23 07 HVAC Insulation

23 07 13 – Duct Insulation

23 07 13.10 Duct Thermal Insulation

23 07 13.10 Duct Thermal Insulation			Crew	Daily Output	Labor-Hours	Unit	Material	2012 Bare Costs Labor	Equipment	Total	Total Incl O&P
0010	**DUCT THERMAL INSULATION**										
0100	Rule of thumb, as a percentage of total mechanical costs					Job				10%	
0110	Insulation req'd is based on the surface size/area to be covered										
3000	Ductwork										
3020	Blanket type, fiberglass, flexible										
3140	FSK vapor barrier wrap, .75 lb. density										
3160	1" thick	G	Q-14	350	.046	S.F.	.18	2.01		2.19	3.33
3170	1-1/2" thick	G		320	.050		.21	2.20		2.41	3.66
3180	2" thick	G		300	.053		.26	2.35		2.61	3.94
3190	3" thick	G		260	.062		.37	2.71		3.08	4.63
3200	4" thick	G		242	.066		.60	2.91		3.51	5.20
3210	Vinyl jacket, same as FSK										
3280	Unfaced, 1 lb. density										
3310	1" thick	G	Q-14	360	.044	S.F.	.19	1.95		2.14	3.25
3320	1-1/2" thick	G		330	.048		.23	2.13		2.36	3.57
3330	2" thick	G		310	.052		.31	2.27		2.58	3.88
3400	FSK facing, 1 lb. density										
3420	1-1/2" thick	G	Q-14	310	.052	S.F.	.28	2.27		2.55	3.85
3430	2" thick	G	"	300	.053	"	.33	2.35		2.68	4.01
3450	FSK facing, 1.5 lb. density										
3470	1-1/2" thick	G	Q-14	300	.053	S.F.	.37	2.35		2.72	4.06
3480	2" thick	G	"	290	.055	"	.48	2.43		2.91	4.31
3730	Sheet insulation										
3760	Polyethylene foam, closed cell, UV resistant										
3770	Standard temperature (-90°F to +212°F)										
3771	1/4" thick	G	Q-14	450	.036	S.F.	1.51	1.56		3.07	4.10
3772	3/8" thick	G		440	.036		2.15	1.60		3.75	4.86
3773	1/2" thick	G		420	.038		2.65	1.68		4.33	5.55
3774	3/4" thick	G		400	.040		3.78	1.76		5.54	6.90
3775	1" thick	G		380	.042		5.10	1.85		6.95	8.50
3776	1-1/2" thick	G		360	.044		8.10	1.95		10.05	11.95
3777	2" thick	G		340	.047		10.85	2.07		12.92	15.10
3778	2-1/2" thick	G		320	.050		13.70	2.20		15.90	18.55
3779	Adhesive (see line 7878)										
3780	Foam, rubber										
3782	1" thick	G	1 Stpi	50	.160	S.F.	3.06	8.90		11.96	16.80

23 07 HVAC Insulation

23 07 13 – Duct Insulation

23 07 13.10 Duct Thermal Insulation

	23 07 13.10 Duct Thermal Insulation		Crew	Daily Output	Labor-Hours	Unit	Material	2012 Bare Costs Labor	Equipment	Total	Total Incl O&P
3795	Finishes										
3800	Stainless steel woven mesh		Q-14	100	.160	S.F.	.70	7.05		7.75	11.70
3810	For .010" stainless steel, add			160	.100		2.79	4.40		7.19	9.90
3820	18 oz. fiberglass cloth, pasted on			170	.094		.67	4.14		4.81	7.20
3900	8 oz. canvas, pasted on			180	.089		.19	3.91		4.10	6.30
3940	For .016" aluminum jacket, add			200	.080		.94	3.52		4.46	6.55
7000	Board insulation	G									
7020	Mineral wool, 1200° F	G									
7022	6 lb. density, plain	G									
7024	1" thick	G	Q-14	370	.043	S.F.	.29	1.90		2.19	3.28
7026	1-1/2" thick	G		350	.046		.44	2.01		2.45	3.61
7028	2" thick	G		330	.048		.58	2.13		2.71	3.96
7030	3" thick	G		300	.053		.87	2.35		3.22	4.61
7032	4" thick	G		280	.057		1.16	2.51		3.67	5.20
7038	8 lb. density, plain	G									
7040	1" thick	G	Q-14	360	.044	S.F.	.34	1.95		2.29	3.41
7042	1-1/2" thick	G		340	.047		.51	2.07		2.58	3.78
7044	2" thick	G		320	.050		.68	2.20		2.88	4.18
7046	3" thick	G		290	.055		1.02	2.43		3.45	4.90
7048	4" thick	G		270	.059		1.36	2.61		3.97	5.55
7060	10 lb. density, plain	G									
7062	1" thick	G	Q-14	350	.046	S.F.	.41	2.01		2.42	3.58
7064	1-1/2" thick	G		330	.048		.62	2.13		2.75	4
7066	2" thick	G		310	.052		.82	2.27		3.09	4.44
7068	3" thick	G		280	.057		1.24	2.51		3.75	5.25
7070	4" thick	G		260	.062		1.65	2.71		4.36	6.05
7878	Contact cement, quart can					Ea.	10.50			10.50	11.55

23 07 16 – HVAC Equipment Insulation

23 07 16.10 HVAC Equipment Thermal Insulation

	23 07 16.10 HVAC Equipment Thermal Insulation		Crew	Daily Output	Labor-Hours	Unit	Material	2012 Bare Costs Labor	Equipment	Total	Total Incl O&P
0010	**HVAC EQUIPMENT THERMAL INSULATION**										
0100	Rule of thumb, as a percentage of total mechanical costs					Job				10%	
0110	Insulation req'd is based on the surface size/area to be covered										
1000	Boiler, 1-1/2" calcium silicate only	G	Q-14	110	.145	S.F.	3.50	6.40		9.90	13.80
1020	Plus 2" fiberglass	G	"	80	.200	"	4.47	8.80		13.27	18.60
2000	Breeching, 2" calcium silicate										
2020	Rectangular	G	Q-14	42	.381	S.F.	6.85	16.75		23.60	33.50
2040	Round	G	"	38.70	.413	"	7.15	18.20		25.35	36.50
2300	Calcium silicate block, + 200°F to + 1200°F										
2310	On irregular surfaces, valves and fittings										
2340	1" thick	G	Q-14	30	.533	S.F.	3.11	23.50		26.61	40
2360	1-1/2" thick	G		25	.640		3.50	28		31.50	48
2380	2" thick	G		22	.727		4.60	32		36.60	55
2400	3" thick	G		18	.889		7.05	39		46.05	69
2410	On plane surfaces										
2420	1" thick	G	Q-14	126	.127	S.F.	3.11	5.60		8.71	12.10
2430	1-1/2" thick	G		120	.133		3.50	5.85		9.35	13
2440	2" thick	G		100	.160		4.60	7.05		11.65	16
2450	3" thick	G		70	.229		7.05	10.05		17.10	23.50

23 09 Instrumentation and Control for HVAC

23 09 13 – Instrumentation and Control Devices for HVAC

23 09 13.60 Water Level Controls	Crew	Daily Output	Labor-Hours	Unit	Material	2012 Bare Costs Labor	Equipment	Total	Total Incl O&P
0010 **WATER LEVEL CONTROLS**									
1000 Electric water feeder	1 Stpi	12	.667	Ea.	188	37		225	262
2000 Feeder cut-off combination									
2100 Steam system up to 5000 sq. ft.	1 Stpi	12	.667	Ea.	565	37		602	675
2200 Steam system above 5000 sq. ft.		12	.667		695	37		732	820
2300 Steam and hot water, high pressure	↓	10	.800	↓	815	44.50		859.50	960
3000 Low water cut-off for hot water boiler, 50 psi maximum									
3100 1" top & bottom equalizing pipes, manual reset	1 Stpi	14	.571	Ea.	315	32		347	395
3200 1" top & bottom equalizing pipes		14	.571		315	32		347	395
3300 2-1/2" side connection for nipple-to-boiler	↓	14	.571	↓	285	32		317	365
4000 Low water cut-off for low pressure steam with quick hook-up ftgs.									
4100 For installation in gauge glass tappings	1 Stpi	16	.500	Ea.	229	28		257	294
4200 Built-in type, 2-1/2" tap - 3-1/8" insertion		16	.500		188	28		216	248
4300 Built-in type, 2-1/2" tap - 1-3/4" insertion		16	.500		203	28		231	265
4400 Side connection to 2-1/2" tapping		16	.500		218	28		246	281
5000 Pump control, low water cut-off and alarm switch	↓	14	.571	↓	605	32		637	715
9000 Water gauges, complete									
9010 Rough brass, wheel type									
9020 125 PSI at 350°F									
9030 3/8" pipe size	1 Stpi	11	.727	Ea.	58.50	40.50		99	125
9040 1/2" pipe size	"	10	.800	"	64	44.50		108.50	137
9060 200 PSI at 400°F									
9070 3/8" pipe size	1 Stpi	11	.727	Ea.	73	40.50		113.50	142
9080 1/2" pipe size		10	.800		73	44.50		117.50	148
9090 3/4" pipe size	↓	9	.889	↓	92.50	49.50		142	177
9130 Rough brass, chain lever type									
9140 250 PSI at 400°F									
9200 Polished brass, wheel type									
9210 200 PSI at 400°F									
9220 3/8" pipe size	1 Stpi	11	.727	Ea.	137	40.50		177.50	211
9230 1/2" pipe size		10	.800		139	44.50		183.50	219
9240 3/4" pipe size	↓	9	.889	↓	147	49.50		196.50	236
9260 Polished brass, chain lever type									
9270 250 PSI at 400°F									
9280 1/2" pipe size	1 Stpi	10	.800	Ea.	200	44.50		244.50	288
9290 3/4" pipe size	"	9	.889	"	218	49.50		267.50	315
9400 Bronze, high pressure, ASME									
9410 1/2" pipe size	1 Stpi	10	.800	Ea.	252	44.50		296.50	345
9420 3/4" pipe size	"	9	.889	"	267	49.50		316.50	370
9460 Chain lever type									
9470 1/2" pipe size	1 Stpi	10	.800	Ea.	320	44.50		364.50	415
9480 3/4" pipe size	"	9	.889	"	355	49.50		404.50	465
9500 316 stainless steel, high pressure, ASME									
9510 500 PSI at 450°F									
9520 1/2" pipe size	1 Stpi	10	.800	Ea.	755	44.50		799.50	900
9530 3/4" pipe size	"	9	.889	"	735	49.50		784.50	885

23 09 23 – Direct-Digital Control System for HVAC

23 09 23.10 Control Components/DDC Systems

	Crew	Daily Output	Labor-Hours	Unit	Material	Labor	Equipment	Total	Total Incl O&P
0010 **CONTROL COMPONENTS/DDC SYSTEMS** (Sub's quote incl. M & L)									
0100 Analog inputs									
0110 Sensors (avg. 50' run in 1/2" EMT)									
0120 Duct temperature				Ea.				360	395

23 09 23.10 Control Components/DDC Systems	Crew	Daily Output	Labor-Hours	Unit	Material	2012 Bare Costs Labor	Equipment	Total	Total Incl O&P
0130 Space temperature				Ea.				575	635
0140 Duct humidity, +/- 3%								605	665
0150 Space humidity, +/- 2%								925	1,025
0160 Duct static pressure								490	540
0170 CFM/Transducer								660	730
0172 Water temp. (see Section 23 21 20 for well tap add)								570	625
0174 Water flow (see Section 23 21 20 for circuit sensor add)								2,075	2,300
0176 Water pressure differential (see Section 23 21 20 for tap add)								850	935
0177 Steam flow (see Section 23 21 20 for circuit sensor add)								2,075	2,300
0178 Steam pressure (see Section 23 21 20 for tap add)								890	980
0180 K.W./Transducer								1,175	1,300
0182 K.W.H. totalization (not incl. elec. meter pulse xmtr.)								545	600
0190 Space static pressure				↓				925	1,025
1000 Analog outputs (avg. 50' run in 1/2" EMT)									
1010 P/I Transducer				Ea.				550	605
1020 Analog output, matl. in MUX								265	291
1030 Pneumatic (not incl. control device)								560	615
1040 Electric (not incl control device)				↓				330	365
2000 Status (Alarms)									
2100 Digital inputs (avg. 50' run in 1/2" EMT)									
2110 Freeze				Ea.				380	415
2120 Fire								340	375
2130 Differential pressure, (air)								520	570
2140 Differential pressure, (water)								850	935
2150 Current sensor								380	415
2160 Duct high temperature thermostat								495	545
2170 Duct smoke detector				↓				615	675
2200 Digital output (avg. 50' run in 1/2" EMT)									
2210 Start/stop				Ea.				297	325
2220 On/off (maintained contact)				"				510	560
3000 Controller M.U.X. panel, incl. function boards									
3100 48 point				Ea.				4,575	5,050
3110 128 point				"				6,300	6,925
3200 D.D.C. controller (avg. 50' run in conduit)									
3210 Mechanical room									
3214 16 point controller (incl. 120 volt/1 phase power supply)				Ea.				1,925	3,125
3229 32 point controller (incl. 120 volt/1 phase power supply)				"				4,725	5,200
3230 Includes software programming and checkout									
3260 Space									
3266 V.A.V. terminal box (incl. space temp. sensor)				Ea.				735	805
3280 Host computer (avg. 50' run in conduit)									
3281 Package complete with PC, keyboard,									
3282 printer, color CRT, modem, basic software				Ea.				8,500	9,375
4000 Front end costs									
4100 Computer (P.C.)/software program				Ea.				5,675	6,250
4200 Color graphics software								3,400	3,750
4300 Color graphics slides								425	470
4350 Additional dot matrix printer				↓				850	935
4400 Communications trunk cable				L.F.				3.31	3.64
4500 Engineering labor, (not incl. dftg.)				Point				82	90
4600 Calibration labor								105	115
4700 Start-up, checkout labor				↓				105	115
4800 Programming labor, as req'd									

23 09 Instrumentation and Control for HVAC

23 09 23 – Direct-Digital Control System for HVAC

23 09 23.10 Control Components/DDC Systems

	23 09 23.10 Control Components/DDC Systems	Crew	Daily Output	Labor-Hours	Unit	Material	2012 Bare Costs Labor	Equipment	Total	Total Incl O&P
5000	Communications bus (data transmission cable)									
5010	#18 twisted shielded pair in 1/2" EMT conduit				C.L.F.				330	365
8000	Applications software									
8050	Basic maintenance manager software (not incl. data base entry)				Ea.				1,700	1,875
8100	Time program				Point				5.95	6.55
8120	Duty cycle								11.85	13.05
8140	Optimum start/stop								36	39.50
8160	Demand limiting								17.80	19.55
8180	Enthalpy program								36	39.50
8200	Boiler optimization				Ea.				1,075	1,175
8220	Chiller optimization				"				1,425	1,550
8240	Custom applications									
8260	Cost varies with complexity									

23 09 33 – Electric and Electronic Control System for HVAC

23 09 33.10 Electronic Control Systems

	23 09 33.10 Electronic Control Systems	Crew	Daily Output	Labor-Hours	Unit	Material	2012 Bare Costs Labor	Equipment	Total	Total Incl O&P
0010	**ELECTRONIC CONTROL SYSTEMS** R230500-10									
0020	For electronic costs, add to Section 23 09 43.10				Ea.					15%

23 09 43 – Pneumatic Control System for HVAC

23 09 43.10 Pneumatic Control Systems

	23 09 43.10 Pneumatic Control Systems	Crew	Daily Output	Labor-Hours	Unit	Material	2012 Bare Costs Labor	Equipment	Total	Total Incl O&P
0010	**PNEUMATIC CONTROL SYSTEMS** R230500-10									
0011	Including a nominal 50 ft. of tubing. Add control panelboard if req'd.									
0100	Heating and ventilating, split system									
0200	Mixed air control, economizer cycle, panel readout, tubing									
0220	Up to 10 tons	Q-19	.68	35.294	Ea.	3,800	1,775		5,575	6,875
0240	For 10 to 20 tons		.63	37.915		4,075	1,925		6,000	7,350
0260	For over 20 tons		.58	41.096		4,425	2,075		6,500	7,975
0270	Enthalpy cycle, up to 10 tons		.50	48.387		4,200	2,450		6,650	8,300
0280	For 10 to 20 tons		.46	52.174		4,550	2,650		7,200	8,975
0290	For over 20 tons		.42	56.604		4,925	2,875		7,800	9,725
0300	Heating coil, hot water, 3 way valve,									
0320	Freezestat, limit control on discharge, readout	Q-5	.69	23.088	Ea.	2,825	1,150		3,975	4,850
0500	Cooling coil, chilled water, room									
0520	Thermostat, 3 way valve	Q-5	2	8	Ea.	1,250	400		1,650	1,975
0600	Cooling tower, fan cycle, damper control,									
0620	Control system including water readout in/out at panel	Q-19	.67	35.821	Ea.	5,000	1,825		6,825	8,225
1000	Unit ventilator, day/night operation,									
1100	freezestat, ASHRAE, cycle 2	Q-19	.91	26.374	Ea.	2,775	1,325		4,100	5,050
2000	Compensated hot water from boiler, valve control,									
2100	readout and reset at panel, up to 60 GPM	Q-19	.55	43.956	Ea.	5,175	2,225		7,400	9,050
2120	For 120 GPM		.51	47.059		5,550	2,375		7,925	9,675
2140	For 240 GPM		.49	49.180		5,800	2,500		8,300	10,200
3000	Boiler room combustion air, damper to 5 S.F., controls		1.37	17.582		2,500	890		3,390	4,100
3500	Fan coil, heating and cooling valves, 4 pipe control system		3	8		1,125	405		1,530	1,850
3600	Heat exchanger system controls		.86	27.907		2,425	1,400		3,825	4,800
3900	Multizone control (one per zone), includes thermostat, damper									
3910	motor and reset of discharge temperature	Q-5	.51	31.373	Ea.	2,500	1,575		4,075	5,125
4000	Pneumatic thermostat, including controlling room radiator valve	"	2.43	6.593		755	330		1,085	1,325
4040	Program energy saving optimizer	Q-19	1.21	19.786		6,250	1,000		7,250	8,375
4060	Pump control system	"	3	8		1,150	405		1,555	1,875
4080	Reheat coil control system, not incl coil	Q-5	2.43	6.593		980	330		1,310	1,575
4500	Air supply for pneumatic control system									
4600	Tank mounted duplex compressor, starter, alternator,									

23 09 Instrumentation and Control for HVAC

23 09 43 – Pneumatic Control System for HVAC

23 09 43.10 Pneumatic Control Systems

		Crew	Daily Output	Labor-Hours	Unit	Material	2012 Bare Costs Labor	2012 Bare Costs Equipment	Total	Total Incl O&P
4620	piping, dryer, PRV station and filter									
4630	1/2 HP	Q-19	.68	35.139	Ea.	9,300	1,775		11,075	12,900
4640	3/4 HP		.64	37.383		9,750	1,900		11,650	13,600
4650	1 HP		.61	39.539		10,700	2,000		12,700	14,700
4660	1-1/2 HP		.58	41.739		11,400	2,100		13,500	15,700
4680	3 HP		.55	43.956		15,500	2,225		17,725	20,400
4690	5 HP		.42	57.143		27,000	2,900		29,900	34,100
4800	Main air supply, includes 3/8" copper main and labor	Q-5	1.82	8.791	C.L.F.	315	440		755	1,000
4810	If poly tubing used, deduct									30%
7000	Static pressure control for air handling unit, includes pressure									
7010	sensor, receiver controller, readout and damper motors	Q-19	.64	37.383	Ea.	7,400	1,900		9,300	11,000
7020	If return air fan requires control, add									70%
8600	VAV boxes, incl. thermostat, damper motor, reheat coil & tubing	Q-5	1.46	10.989		1,150	550		1,700	2,100
8610	If no reheat coil, deduct									204
9400	Sub assemblies for assembly systems									

23 09 53 – Pneumatic and Electric Control System for HVAC

23 09 53.10 Control Components

		Crew	Daily Output	Labor-Hours	Unit	Material	2012 Bare Costs Labor	2012 Bare Costs Equipment	Total	Total Incl O&P
0010	**CONTROL COMPONENTS**									
0500	Aquastats									
0508	Immersion type									
0510	High/low limit, breaks contact w/temp rise	1 Stpi	4	2	Ea.	385	111		496	595
0514	Sequencing, break 2 switches w/temp rise		4	2		271	111		382	465
0518	Circulating, makes contact w/temp rise		4	2		246	111		357	440
0600	Carbon monoxide detector system									
0606	Panel	1 Stpi	4	2	Ea.	1,350	111		1,461	1,675
0610	Sensor	"	7.30	1.096	"	785	61		846	955
0700	Controller, receiver									
0730	Pneumatic, panel mount, single input	1 Plum	8	1	Ea.	410	54.50		464.50	535
0740	With conversion mounting bracket		8	1		410	54.50		464.50	535
0750	Dual input, with control point adjustment		7	1.143		565	62.50		627.50	715
0850	Electric, single snap switch	1 Elec	4	2		450	103		553	650
0860	Dual snap switches		3	2.667		605	137		742	870
0870	Humidity controller		8	1		217	51.50		268.50	315
0880	Load limiting controller		8	1		800	51.50		851.50	955
0890	Temperature controller		8	1		450	51.50		501.50	570
0900	Control panel readout									
0910	Panel up to 12 indicators	1 Stpi	1.20	6.667	Ea.	287	370		657	875
0914	Panel up to 24 indicators		.86	9.302		355	520		875	1,175
0918	Panel up to 48 indicators		.50	16		860	890		1,750	2,300
1000	Enthalpy control, boiler water temperature control									
1010	governed by outdoor temperature, with timer	1 Elec	3	2.667	Ea.	330	137		467	570
1300	Energy control/monitor									
1320	BTU computer meter and controller	1 Stpi	1	8	Ea.	1,425	445		1,870	2,225
1600	Flow meters									
1610	Gas	1 Stpi	4	2	Ea.	123	111		234	305
1620	Liquid	"	4	2	"	123	111		234	305
1640	Freezestat									
1644	20' sensing element, adjustable	1 Stpi	3.50	2.286	Ea.	72.50	127		199.50	272
2000	Gauges, pressure or vacuum									
2100	2" diameter dial	1 Stpi	32	.250	Ea.	14.30	13.95		28.25	36.50
2200	2-1/2" diameter dial		32	.250		15.65	13.95		29.60	38.50
2300	3-1/2" diameter dial		32	.250		35.50	13.95		49.45	60.50

23 09 53.10 Control Components		Crew	Daily Output	Labor-Hours	Unit	Material	2012 Bare Costs Labor	2012 Bare Costs Equipment	Total	Total Incl O&P
2400	4-1/2" diameter dial	1 Stpi	32	.250	Ea.	52.50	13.95		66.45	79
2700	Flanged iron case, black ring									
2800	3-1/2" diameter dial	1 Stpi	32	.250	Ea.	102	13.95		115.95	133
2900	4-1/2" diameter dial		32	.250		105	13.95		118.95	137
3000	6" diameter dial		32	.250		167	13.95		180.95	204
3010	Steel case, 0 – 300 psi									
3012	2" diam. dial	1 Stpi	16	.500	Ea.	7.70	28		35.70	50.50
3014	4" diam. dial	"	16	.500	"	39.50	28		67.50	85.50
3020	Aluminum case, 0 – 300 psi									
3022	3-1/2" diam. dial	1 Stpi	16	.500	Ea.	33.50	28		61.50	79
3024	4-1/2" diam. dial		16	.500		101	28		129	153
3026	6" diam. dial		16	.500		173	28		201	233
3028	8-1/2" diam. dial		16	.500		295	28		323	365
3030	Brass case, 0 – 300 psi									
3032	2" diam. dial	1 Stpi	16	.500	Ea.	42	28		70	88
3034	4-1/2" diam. dial	"	16	.500	"	107	28		135	160
3040	Steel case, high pressure, 0 -10,000 psi									
3042	4-1/2" diam. dial	1 Stpi	16	.500	Ea.	274	28		302	340
3044	6-1/2" diam. dial		16	.500		298	28		326	370
3046	8-1/2" diam. dial		16	.500		330	28		358	405
3080	Pressure gauge, differential, magnehelic									
3084	0 – 2" W.C., with air filter kit	1 Stpi	6	1.333	Ea.	98.50	74.50		173	220
3300	For compound pressure-vacuum, add					18%				
3350	Humidistat									
3360	Pneumatic operation									
3361	Room humidistat, direct acting	1 Stpi	12	.667	Ea.	299	37		336	385
3362	Room humidistat, reverse acting		12	.667		299	37		336	385
3363	Room humidity transmitter		17	.471		320	26		346	390
3364	Duct mounted controller		12	.667		350	37		387	440
3365	Duct mounted transmitter		12	.667		320	37		357	405
3366	Humidity indicator, 3-1/2"		28	.286		123	15.90		138.90	159
3390	Electric operated	1 Shee	8	1		82	52		134	170
3400	Relays									
3430	Pneumatic/electric	1 Plum	16	.500	Ea.	310	27.50		337.50	385
3440	Pneumatic proportioning		8	1		216	54.50		270.50	320
3450	Pneumatic switching		12	.667		142	36.50		178.50	211
3460	Selector, 3 point		6	1.333		101	73		174	221
3470	Pneumatic time delay		8	1		273	54.50		327.50	385
3500	Sensor, air operated									
3520	Humidity	1 Plum	16	.500	Ea.	350	27.50		377.50	425
3540	Pressure		16	.500		60	27.50		87.50	107
3560	Temperature		12	.667		152	36.50		188.50	222
3600	Electric operated									
3620	Humidity	1 Elec	8	1	Ea.	91.50	51.50		143	178
3650	Pressure		8	1		1,550	51.50		1,601.50	1,775
3680	Temperature		10	.800		97	41		138	169
3700	Switches									
3710	Minimum position									
3720	Electrical	1 Stpi	4	2	Ea.	20.50	111		131.50	191
3730	Pneumatic	"	4	2	"	93.50	111		204.50	271
4000	Thermometers									
4100	Dial type, 3-1/2" diameter, vapor type, union connection	1 Stpi	32	.250	Ea.	227	13.95		240.95	271
4120	Liquid type, union connection		32	.250		440	13.95		453.95	505

23 09 53.10 Control Components	Crew	Daily Output	Labor-Hours	Unit	Material	2012 Bare Costs Labor	2012 Bare Costs Equipment	Total	Total Incl O&P
4130 Remote reading, 15' capillary	1 Stpi	32	.250	Ea.	172	13.95		185.95	210
4500 Stem type, 6-1/2" case, 2" stem, 1/2" NPT		32	.250		60.50	13.95		74.45	87.50
4520 4" stem, 1/2" NPT		32	.250		74	13.95		87.95	103
4600 9" case, 3-1/2" stem, 3/4" NPT		28	.286		115	15.90		130.90	150
4620 6" stem, 3/4" NPT		28	.286		133	15.90		148.90	170
4640 8" stem, 3/4" NPT		28	.286		169	15.90		184.90	210
4660 12" stem, 1" NPT		26	.308		184	17.15		201.15	228
4670 Bi-metal, dial type, steel case brass stem									
4672 2" dial, 4" - 9" stem	1 Stpi	16	.500	Ea.	34	28		62	79
4673 2-1/2" dial, 4" - 9" stem		16	.500		34	28		62	79
4674 3-1/2" dial, 4" - 9" stem		16	.500		41.50	28		69.50	87.50
4680 Mercury filled, industrial, union connection type									
4682 Angle stem, 7" scale	1 Stpi	16	.500	Ea.	63	28		91	112
4683 9" scale		16	.500		169	28		197	228
4684 12" scale		16	.500		218	28		246	282
4686 Straight stem, 7" scale		16	.500		149	28		177	206
4687 9" scale		16	.500		151	28		179	208
4688 12" scale		16	.500		183	28		211	243
4690 Mercury filled, industrial, separable socket type, with well									
4692 Angle stem, with socket, 7" scale	1 Stpi	16	.500	Ea.	69	28		97	118
4693 9" scale		16	.500		71.50	28		99.50	121
4694 12" scale		16	.500		224	28		252	289
4696 Straight stem, with socket, 7" scale		16	.500		37.50	28		65.50	83.50
4697 9" scale		16	.500		90.50	28		118.50	142
4698 12" scale		16	.500		98	28		126	150
5000 Thermostats									
5030 Manual	1 Stpi	8	1	Ea.	45	55.50		100.50	133
5040 1 set back, electric, timed G		8	1		35	55.50		90.50	123
5050 2 set back, electric, timed G		8	1		161	55.50		216.50	261
5100 Locking cover		20	.400		18.80	22.50		41.30	54
5200 24 hour, automatic, clock G	1 Shee	8	1		142	52		194	236
5220 Electric, low voltage, 2 wire	1 Elec	13	.615		32.50	31.50		64	83
5230 3 wire		10	.800		31.50	41		72.50	96
5236 Heating/cooling, low voltage, with clock		8	1		238	51.50		289.50	340
5240 Pneumatic									
5250 Single temp., single pressure	1 Stpi	8	1	Ea.	200	55.50		255.50	305
5251 Dual pressure		8	1		280	55.50		335.50	395
5252 Dual temp., dual pressure		8	1		257	55.50		312.50	365
5253 Reverse acting w/averaging element		8	1		205	55.50		260.50	310
5254 Heating-cooling w/deadband		8	1		445	55.50		500.50	575
5255 Integral w/piston top valve actuator		8	1		183	55.50		238.50	285
5256 Dual temp., dual pressure		8	1		187	55.50		242.50	289
5257 Low limit, 8' averaging element		8	1		171	55.50		226.50	272
5258 Room single temp. proportional		8	1		71.50	55.50		127	163
5260 Dual temp, direct acting for VAV fan		8	1		287	55.50		342.50	400
5262 Capillary tube type, 20', 30°F to 100°F		8	1		475	55.50		530.50	605
5300 Transmitter, pneumatic									
5320 Temperature averaging element	Q-1	8	2	Ea.	119	98.50		217.50	279
5350 Pressure differential	1 Plum	7	1.143		1,000	62.50		1,062.50	1,200
5370 Humidity, duct		8	1		320	54.50		374.50	435
5380 Room		12	.667		320	36.50		356.50	405
5390 Temperature, with averaging element		6	1.333		164	73		237	290
5500 Timer/time clocks									

23 09 53 – Pneumatic and Electric Control System for HVAC

23 09 53.10 Control Components	Crew	Daily Output	Labor-Hours	Unit	Material	2012 Bare Costs Labor	Equipment	Total	Total Incl O&P
5510 7 day, 12 hr. battery	1 Stpi	2.60	3.077	Ea.	192	171		363	470
5600 Recorders									
5610 Hydrograph humidity, wall mtd., aluminum case, grad. chart									
5612 8"	1 Stpi	1.60	5	Ea.	745	279		1,024	1,225
5614 10"	"	1.60	5	"	715	279		994	1,200
5620 Thermo-hydrograph, wall mtd., grad. chart, 5' SS probe									
5622 8"	1 Stpi	1.60	5	Ea.	655	279		934	1,150
5624 10"	"	1.60	5	"	1,125	279		1,404	1,675
5630 Time of operation, wall mtd., 1 pen cap, 24 hr. clock									
5632 6"	1 Stpi	1.60	5	Ea.	420	279		699	880
5634 8"	"	1.60	5	"	650	279		929	1,125
5640 Pressure & vacuum, bourdon tube type									
5642 Flush mount, 1 pen									
5644 4"	1 Stpi	1.60	5	Ea.	450	279		729	915
5645 6"		1.60	5		450	279		729	915
5646 8"		1.60	5		700	279		979	1,200
5648 10"		1.60	5		875	279		1,154	1,375
6000 Valves, motorized zone									
6100 Sweat connections, 1/2" C x C	1 Stpi	20	.400	Ea.	159	22.50		181.50	209
6110 3/4" C x C		20	.400		163	22.50		185.50	214
6120 1" C x C		19	.421		212	23.50		235.50	270
6140 1/2" C x C, with end switch, 2 wire		20	.400		161	22.50		183.50	211
6150 3/4" C x C, with end switch, 2 wire		20	.400		172	22.50		194.50	223
6160 1" C x C, with end switch, 2 wire		19	.421		196	23.50		219.50	251
7090 Valves, motor controlled, including actuator									
7100 Electric motor actuated									
7200 Brass, two way, screwed									
7210 1/2" pipe size	L-6	36	.333	Ea.	261	17.85		278.85	315
7220 3/4" pipe size		30	.400		475	21.50		496.50	550
7230 1" pipe size		28	.429		550	23		573	640
7240 1-1/2" pipe size		19	.632		600	34		634	710
7250 2" pipe size		16	.750		870	40		910	1,025
7350 Brass, three way, screwed									
7360 1/2" pipe size	L-6	33	.364	Ea.	254	19.50		273.50	310
7370 3/4" pipe size		27	.444		296	24		320	360
7380 1" pipe size		25.50	.471		385	25		410	465
7384 1-1/4" pipe size		21	.571		490	30.50		520.50	585
7390 1-1/2" pipe size		17	.706		560	38		598	670
7400 2" pipe size		14	.857		745	46		791	890
7550 Iron body, two way, flanged									
7560 2-1/2" pipe size	L-6	4	3	Ea.	1,125	161		1,286	1,475
7570 3" pipe size		3	4		1,175	214		1,389	1,600
7580 4" pipe size		2	6		2,025	320		2,345	2,700
7850 Iron body, three way, flanged									
7860 2-1/2" pipe size	L-6	3	4	Ea.	1,125	214		1,339	1,550
7870 3" pipe size		2.50	4.800		1,300	257		1,557	1,800
7880 4" pipe size		2	6		1,625	320		1,945	2,250
8000 Pneumatic, air operated									
8050 Brass, two way, screwed									
8060 1/2" pipe size, class 250	1 Plum	24	.333	Ea.	164	18.20		182.20	208
8070 3/4" pipe size, class 250		20	.400		196	22		218	249
8080 1" pipe size, class 250		19	.421		229	23		252	287
8090 1-1/4" pipe size, class 125		15	.533		285	29		314	360

23 09 53 – Pneumatic and Electric Control System for HVAC

23 09 53.10 Control Components	Crew	Daily Output	Labor-Hours	Unit	Material	2012 Bare Costs Labor	Equipment	Total	Total Incl O&P
8100	1-1/2" pipe size, class 125	1 Plum	13	.615	Ea.	365	33.50		398.50	450
8110	2" pipe size, class 125	↓	11	.727	↓	420	39.50		459.50	525
8180	Brass, three way, screwed									
8190	1/2" pipe size, class 250	1 Plum	22	.364	Ea.	180	19.85		199.85	228
8200	3/4" pipe size, class 250		18	.444		223	24.50		247.50	282
8210	1" pipe size, class 250		17	.471		262	25.50		287.50	325
8214	1-1/4" pipe size, class 250		14	.571		365	31		396	450
8220	1-1/2" pipe size, class 125		11	.727		435	39.50		474.50	540
8230	2" pipe size, class 125	↓	9	.889	↓	525	48.50		573.50	650
8450	Iron body, two way, flanged									
8460	2-1/2" pipe size, 250 lb. flanges	Q-1	5	3.200	Ea.	2,125	157		2,282	2,550
8470	3" pipe size, 250 lb. flanges		4.50	3.556		2,200	175		2,375	2,675
8480	4" pipe size, 250 lb. flanges		3	5.333		2,525	262		2,787	3,200
8510	2-1/2" pipe size, class 125		5	3.200		890	157		1,047	1,225
8520	3" pipe size, class 125		4.50	3.556		975	175		1,150	1,350
8530	4" pipe size, class 125	↓	3	5.333		1,250	262		1,512	1,775
8540	5" pipe size, class 125	Q-2	3.40	7.059		2,675	360		3,035	3,500
8550	6" pipe size, class 125	"	3	8	↓	3,100	410		3,510	4,050
8560	Iron body, three way, flanged									
8570	2-1/2" pipe size, class 125	Q-1	4.50	3.556	Ea.	960	175		1,135	1,325
8580	3" pipe size, class 125		4	4		1,100	197		1,297	1,525
8590	4" pipe size, class 125	↓	2.50	6.400		2,225	315		2,540	2,925
8600	6" pipe size, class 125	Q-2	3	8	↓	3,400	410		3,810	4,350
9005	Pneumatic system misc. components									
9010	Adding/subtracting repeater	1 Stpi	20	.400	Ea.	156	22.50		178.50	206
9020	Adjustable ratio network		16	.500		147	28		175	204
9030	Comparator	↓	20	.400	↓	310	22.50		332.50	375
9040	Cumulator									
9041	Air switching	1 Stpi	20	.400	Ea.	142	22.50		164.50	190
9042	Averaging		20	.400		132	22.50		154.50	179
9043	2:1 ratio		20	.400		297	22.50		319.50	360
9044	Sequencing		20	.400		90.50	22.50		113	133
9045	Two-position		16	.500		177	28		205	236
9046	Two-position pilot	↓	16	.500	↓	340	28		368	410
9050	Damper actuator									
9051	For smoke control	1 Stpi	8	1	Ea.	270	55.50		325.50	380
9052	For ventilation	"	8	1	"	199	55.50		254.50	305
9053	Series duplex pedestal mounted									
9054	For inlet vanes on fans, compressors	1 Stpi	6	1.333	Ea.	1,525	74.50		1,599.50	1,775
9060	Enthalpy logic center		16	.500		296	28		324	365
9070	High/low pressure selector		22	.364		57	20.50		77.50	93.50
9080	Signal limiter		20	.400		90.50	22.50		113	133
9081	Transmitter	↓	28	.286	↓	34.50	15.90		50.40	62
9090	Optimal start									
9092	Mass temperature transmitter	1 Stpi	18	.444	Ea.	135	25		160	187
9100	Step controller with positioner, time delay restrictor									
9110	recycler air valve, switches and cam settings									
9112	With cabinet									
9113	6 points	1 Stpi	4	2	Ea.	910	111		1,021	1,175
9114	6 points, 6 manual sequences		2	4		800	223		1,023	1,225
9115	8 points	↓	3	2.667	↓	1,000	149		1,149	1,325
9200	Pressure controller and switches									
9210	High static pressure limit	1 Stpi	8	1	Ea.	250	55.50		305.50	360

23 09 53.10 Control Components	Crew	Daily Output	Labor-Hours	Unit	Material	2012 Bare Costs Labor	Equipment	Total	Total Incl O&P
9220	Pressure transmitter	1 Stpi	8	1	Ea.	213	55.50		268.50	320
9230	Differential pressure transmitter		8	1		835	55.50		890.50	1,000
9240	Static pressure transmitter		8	1		865	55.50		920.50	1,025
9250	Proportional-only control, single input		6	1.333		410	74.50		484.50	560
9260	Proportional plus integral, single input		6	1.333		610	74.50		684.50	780
9270	Proportional-only, dual input		6	1.333		565	74.50		639.50	730
9280	Proportional plus integral, dual input		6	1.333		745	74.50		819.50	930
9281	Time delay for above proportional units		16	.500		148	28		176	205
9290	Proportional/2 position controller units		6	1.333		430	74.50		504.50	585
9300	Differential pressure control direct/reverse	▼	6	1.333	▼	380	74.50		454.50	525
9310	Air pressure reducing valve									
9311	1/8" size	1 Stpi	18	.444	Ea.	31.50	25		56.50	72
9315	Precision valve, 1/4" size		17	.471		176	26		202	233
9320	Air flow controller		12	.667		164	37		201	236
9330	Booster relay volume amplifier		18	.444		97	25		122	145
9340	Series restrictor, straight		60	.133		4.99	7.45		12.44	16.70
9341	T-fitting		40	.200		7.25	11.15		18.40	25
9342	In-line adjustable		48	.167		32	9.30		41.30	49.50
9350	Diode tee		40	.200		16.70	11.15		27.85	35
9351	Restrictor tee		40	.200		16.70	11.15		27.85	35
9360	Pneumatic gradual switch		8	1		279	55.50		334.50	390
9361	Selector switch		8	1		101	55.50		156.50	195
9370	Electro-pneumatic motor driven servo		10	.800		910	44.50		954.50	1,075
9390	Fan control switch and mounting base		16	.500		101	28		129	153
9400	Circulating pump sequencer	▼	14	.571	▼	1,150	32		1,182	1,325
9410	Pneumatic tubing, fittings and accessories									
9414	Tubing, urethane									
9415	1/8" OD x 1/16" ID	1 Stpi	120	.067	L.F.	.66	3.71		4.37	6.35
9416	1/4" OD x 1/8" ID		115	.070		1.30	3.88		5.18	7.30
9417	5/32" OD x 3/32" ID	▼	110	.073	▼	.74	4.05		4.79	6.90
9420	Coupling, straight									
9422	Barb x barb									
9423	1/4" x 5/32"	1 Stpi	160	.050	Ea.	.74	2.79		3.53	5
9424	1/4" x 1/4"		158	.051		.57	2.82		3.39	4.88
9425	3/8" x 3/8"		154	.052		.54	2.89		3.43	4.95
9426	3/8" x 1/4"		150	.053		.51	2.97		3.48	5.05
9427	1/2" x 1/4"		148	.054		4.73	3.01		7.74	9.75
9428	1/2" x 3/8"		144	.056		.99	3.09		4.08	5.75
9429	1/2" x 1/2"	▼	140	.057	▼	.65	3.18		3.83	5.50
9440	Tube x tube									
9441	1/4" x 1/4"	1 Stpi	100	.080	Ea.	2.03	4.46		6.49	8.95
9442	3/8" x 1/4"		96	.083		3.77	4.64		8.41	11.15
9443	3/8" x 3/8"		92	.087		2.52	4.84		7.36	10.05
9444	1/2" x 3/8"		88	.091		4.17	5.05		9.22	12.25
9445	1/2" x 1/2"	▼	84	.095	▼	4.62	5.30		9.92	13.10
9450	Elbow coupling									
9452	Barb x barb									
9454	1/4" x 1/4"	1 Stpi	158	.051	Ea.	1.15	2.82		3.97	5.50
9455	3/8" x 3/8"		154	.052		3.09	2.89		5.98	7.75
9456	1/2" x 1/2"	▼	140	.057	▼	1.37	3.18		4.55	6.30
9460	Tube x tube									
9462	1/2" x 1/2"	1 Stpi	84	.095	Ea.	6.65	5.30		11.95	15.30
9470	Tee coupling									

23 09 Instrumentation and Control for HVAC

23 09 53 – Pneumatic and Electric Control System for HVAC

23 09 53.10 Control Components

		Crew	Daily Output	Labor-Hours	Unit	Material	2012 Bare Costs Labor	2012 Bare Costs Equipment	Total	Total Incl O&P
9472	Barb x barb x barb									
9474	1/4" x 1/4" x 5/32"	1 Stpi	108	.074	Ea.	1.35	4.13		5.48	7.70
9475	1/4" x 1/4" x 1/4"		104	.077		.91	4.28		5.19	7.45
9476	3/8" x 3/8" x 5/32"		102	.078		2.84	4.37		7.21	9.70
9477	3/8" x 3/8" x 1/4"		99	.081		1.35	4.50		5.85	8.30
9478	3/8" x 3/8" x 3/8"		98	.082		3.09	4.55		7.64	10.25
9479	1/2" x 1/2" x 1/4"		96	.083		3.68	4.64		8.32	11.05
9480	1/2" x 1/2" x 3/8"		95	.084		3.07	4.69		7.76	10.45
9481	1/2" x 1/2" x 1/2"	↓	92	.087	↓	4.12	4.84		8.96	11.85
9484	Tube x tube x tube									
9485	1/4" x 1/4" x 1/4"	1 Stpi	66	.121	Ea.	4.16	6.75		10.91	14.80
9486	3/8" x 1/4" x 1/4"		64	.125		12.30	6.95		19.25	24
9487	3/8" x 3/8" x 1/4"		61	.131		5.85	7.30		13.15	17.40
9488	3/8" x 3/8" x 3/8"		60	.133		6.10	7.45		13.55	17.95
9489	1/2" x 1/2" x 3/8"		58	.138		13.20	7.70		20.90	26
9490	1/2" x 1/2" x 1/2"	↓	56	.143	↓	8.90	7.95		16.85	22
9492	Needle valve									
9494	Tube x tube									
9495	1/4" x 1/4"	1 Stpi	86	.093	Ea.	7.15	5.20		12.35	15.70
9496	3/8" x 3/8"	"	82	.098	"	10.60	5.45		16.05	19.90
9600	Electronic system misc. components									
9610	Electric motor damper actuator	1 Elec	8	1	Ea.	475	51.50		526.50	595
9620	Damper position indicator		10	.800		118	41		159	192
9630	Pneumatic-electronic transducer	↓	12	.667	↓	61.50	34.50		96	119
9700	Modulating step controller									
9701	2-5 steps	1 Elec	5.30	1.509	Ea.	900	78		978	1,100
9702	6-10 steps		3.20	2.500		1,150	129		1,279	1,475
9703	11-15 steps		2.70	2.963		1,625	153		1,778	2,025
9704	16-20 steps	↓	1.60	5	↓	2,400	258		2,658	3,025
9710	Staging network									
9740	Accessory unit regulator									
9750	Accessory power supply	1 Elec	18	.444	Ea.	181	23		204	233
9760	Step down transformer	"	16	.500	"	181	26		207	238

23 11 Facility Fuel Piping

23 11 13 – Facility Fuel-Oil Piping

23 11 13.10 Fuel Oil Specialties

		Crew	Daily Output	Labor-Hours	Unit	Material	2012 Bare Costs Labor	2012 Bare Costs Equipment	Total	Total Incl O&P
0010	**FUEL OIL SPECIALTIES**									
0020	Foot valve, single poppet, metal to metal construction									
0040	Bevel seat, 1/2" diameter	1 Stpi	20	.400	Ea.	61.50	22.50		84	102
0060	3/4" diameter		18	.444		71	25		96	116
0080	1" diameter		16	.500		91	28		119	142
0100	1-1/4" diameter		15	.533		118	29.50		147.50	175
0120	1-1/2" diameter		13	.615		163	34.50		197.50	232
0140	2" diameter	↓	11	.727	↓	169	40.50		209.50	247
0160	Foot valve, double poppet, metal to metal construction									
0164	1" diameter	1 Stpi	15	.533	Ea.	137	29.50		166.50	196
0166	1-1/2" diameter	"	12	.667	"	185	37		222	260
0400	Fuel fill box, flush type									
0408	Nonlocking, watertight									
0410	1-1/2" diameter	1 Stpi	12	.667	Ea.	19.40	37		56.40	77.50

23 11 13 – Facility Fuel-Oil Piping

23 11 13.10 Fuel Oil Specialties		Crew	Daily Output	Labor-Hours	Unit	Material	2012 Bare Costs Labor	Equipment	Total	Total Incl O&P
0440	2" diameter	1 Stpi	10	.800	Ea.	16.75	44.50		61.25	85.50
0450	2-1/2" diameter		9	.889		56	49.50		105.50	137
0460	3" diameter		7	1.143		54	63.50		117.50	156
0470	4" diameter		5	1.600		75	89		164	217
0500	Locking inner cover									
0510	2" diameter	1 Stpi	8	1	Ea.	82.50	55.50		138	175
0520	2-1/2" diameter		7	1.143		110	63.50		173.50	217
0530	3" diameter		5	1.600		118	89		207	264
0540	4" diameter		4	2		152	111		263	335
0600	Fuel system components									
0620	Spill container	1 Stpi	4	2	Ea.	670	111		781	905
0640	Fill adapter, 4", straight drop		8	1		54.50	55.50		110	144
0680	Fill cap, 4"		30	.267		32	14.85		46.85	57.50
0700	Extractor fitting, 4" x 1-1/2"		8	1		355	55.50		410.50	475
0740	Vapor hose adapter, 4"		8	1		90.50	55.50		146	184
0760	Wood gage stick, 10'					11.40			11.40	12.55
1000	Oil filters, 3/8" IPT., 20 gal. per hour	1 Stpi	20	.400		19.25	22.50		41.75	54.50
1020	32 gal. per hour		18	.444		34.50	25		59.50	75.50
1040	40 gal. per hour		16	.500		37	28		65	83
1060	50 gal. per hour		14	.571		38.50	32		70.50	90
2000	Remote tank gauging system, self contained									
2100	Single tank kit/8 sensors inputs w/printer	1 Stpi	2.50	3.200	Ea.	3,875	178		4,053	4,525
2120	Two tank kit/8 sensors inputs w/printer		2	4		5,200	223		5,423	6,050
3000	Valve, ball check, globe type, 3/8" diameter		24	.333		12.80	18.55		31.35	42
3500	Fusible, 3/8" diameter		24	.333		13.10	18.55		31.65	42.50
3600	1/2" diameter		24	.333		32	18.55		50.55	63
3610	3/4" diameter		20	.400		70	22.50		92.50	111
3620	1" diameter		19	.421		205	23.50		228.50	262
4000	Nonfusible, 3/8" diameter		24	.333		22.50	18.55		41.05	52.50
4500	Shutoff, gate type, lever handle, spring-fusible kit									
4520	1/4" diameter	1 Stpi	14	.571	Ea.	34.50	32		66.50	86
4540	3/8" diameter		12	.667		33.50	37		70.50	93
4560	1/2" diameter		10	.800		49.50	44.50		94	122
4570	3/4" diameter		8	1		86	55.50		141.50	179
4580	Lever handle, requires weight and fusible kit									
4600	1" diameter	1 Stpi	9	.889	Ea.	261	49.50		310.50	360
4620	1-1/4" diameter		8	1		275	55.50		330.50	390
4640	1-1/2" diameter		7	1.143		300	63.50		363.50	430
4660	2" diameter		6	1.333		395	74.50		469.50	545
4680	For fusible link, weight and braided wire, add					5%				
5000	Vent alarm, whistling signal					26			26	28.50
5500	Vent protector/breather, 1-1/4" diameter	1 Stpi	32	.250		12.80	13.95		26.75	35
5520	1-1/2" diameter		32	.250		14.40	13.95		28.35	37
5540	2" diameter		32	.250		29	13.95		42.95	52.50
5560	3" diameter		28	.286		45	15.90		60.90	73.50
5580	4" diameter		24	.333		53.50	18.55		72.05	87
5600	Dust cap, breather, 2"		40	.200		11.70	11.15		22.85	29.50
8000	Fuel oil and tank heaters									
8020	Electric, capacity rated at 230 volts									
8040	Immersion element in steel manifold									
8060	96 GPH at 50°F rise	Q-5	6.40	2.500	Ea.	1,150	125		1,275	1,450
8070	128 GPH at 50°F rise		6.20	2.581		1,175	129		1,304	1,500
8080	160 GPH at 50°F rise		5.90	2.712		1,300	136		1,436	1,650

23 11 Facility Fuel Piping

23 11 13 – Facility Fuel-Oil Piping

23 11 13.10 Fuel Oil Specialties		Crew	Daily Output	Labor-Hours	Unit	Material	2012 Bare Costs Labor	Equipment	Total	Total Incl O&P
8090	192 GPH at 50°F rise	Q-5	5.50	2.909	Ea.	1,425	146		1,571	1,800
8100	240 GPH at 50°F rise		5.10	3.137		1,650	157		1,807	2,050
8110	288 GPH at 50°F rise		4.60	3.478		1,850	174		2,024	2,325
8120	384 GPH at 50°F rise		3.10	5.161		2,175	259		2,434	2,775
8130	480 GPH at 50°F rise		2.30	6.957		2,725	350		3,075	3,525
8140	576 GPH at 50°F rise		2.10	7.619		2,725	380		3,105	3,575
8300	Suction stub, immersion type									
8320	75" long, 750 watts	1 Stpi	14	.571	Ea.	775	32		807	905
8330	99" long, 2000 watts		12	.667		1,100	37		1,137	1,250
8340	123" long, 3000 watts		10	.800		1,175	44.50		1,219.50	1,375
8660	Steam, cross flow, rated at 5 PSIG									
8680	42 GPH	Q-5	7	2.286	Ea.	1,800	115		1,915	2,150
8690	73 GPH		6.70	2.388		2,100	120		2,220	2,475
8700	112 GPH		6.20	2.581		2,175	129		2,304	2,575
8710	158 GPH		5.80	2.759		2,375	138		2,513	2,800
8720	187 GPH		4	4		3,250	201		3,451	3,875
8730	270 GPH		3.60	4.444		3,500	223		3,723	4,175
8740	365 GPH	Q-6	4.90	4.898		4,100	255		4,355	4,875
8750	635 GPH		3.70	6.486		5,175	335		5,510	6,200
8760	845 GPH		2.50	9.600		7,600	500		8,100	9,100
8770	1420 GPH		1.60	15		12,400	780		13,180	14,800
8780	2100 GPH		1.10	21.818		17,000	1,125		18,125	20,400

23 11 23 – Facility Natural-Gas Piping

23 11 23.10 Gas Meters

		Crew	Daily Output	Labor-Hours	Unit	Material	Labor	Equipment	Total	Total Incl O&P
0010	**GAS METERS**									
4000	Residential									
4010	Gas meter, residential, 3/4" pipe size	1 Plum	14	.571	Ea.	178	31		209	243
4020	Gas meter, residential, 1" pipe size		12	.667		179	36.50		215.50	252
4030	Gas meter, residential, 1-1/4" pipe size		10	.800		181	43.50		224.50	265

23 12 Facility Fuel Pumps

23 12 13 – Facility Fuel-Oil Pumps

23 12 13.10 Pump and Motor Sets

		Crew	Daily Output	Labor-Hours	Unit	Material	Labor	Equipment	Total	Total Incl O&P
0010	**PUMP AND MOTOR SETS**									
1810	Light fuel and diesel oils									
1820	20 GPH 1/3 HP	Q-5	6	2.667	Ea.	1,025	134		1,159	1,325
1830	27 GPH, 1/3 HP		6	2.667		1,025	134		1,159	1,325
1840	80 GPH, 1/3 HP		5	3.200		1,025	160		1,185	1,375
1850	145 GPH, 1/2 HP		4	4		1,075	201		1,276	1,500
1860	277 GPH, 1 HP		4	4		1,200	201		1,401	1,625
1870	700 GPH, 1-1/2 HP		3	5.333		2,575	267		2,842	3,225
1880	1000 GPH, 2 HP		3	5.333		3,025	267		3,292	3,725
1890	1800 GPH, 5 HP		1.80	8.889		4,175	445		4,620	5,275

23 13 Facility Fuel-Storage Tanks

23 13 13 – Facility Underground Fuel-Oil, Storage Tanks

23 13 13.09 Single-Wall Steel Fuel-Oil Tanks

		Crew	Daily Output	Labor-Hours	Unit	Material	2012 Bare Costs Labor	Equipment	Total	Total Incl O&P
0010	**SINGLE-WALL STEEL FUEL-OIL TANKS**									
5000	Tanks, steel ugnd, sti-p3, not incl hold-down bars									
5500	Excavation, pad, pumps and piping not included									
5510	Single wall, 500 gallon capacity, 7 gauge shell	Q-5	2.70	5.926	Ea.	2,050	297		2,347	2,700
5520	1,000 gallon capacity, 7 gauge shell	"	2.50	6.400		3,475	320		3,795	4,300
5530	2,000 gallon capacity, 1/4" thick shell	Q-7	4.60	6.957		5,625	370		5,995	6,750
5535	2,500 gallon capacity, 7 gauge shell	Q-5	3	5.333		6,225	267		6,492	7,250
5540	5,000 gallon capacity, 1/4" thick shell	Q-7	3.20	10		10,500	530		11,030	12,300
5560	10,000 gallon capacity, 1/4" thick shell		2	16		11,200	850		12,050	13,600
5580	15,000 gallon capacity, 5/16" thick shell		1.70	18.824		18,100	1,000		19,100	21,400
5600	20,000 gallon capacity, 5/16" thick shell		1.50	21.333		33,000	1,125		34,125	38,000
5610	25,000 gallon capacity, 3/8" thick shell		1.30	24.615		32,300	1,300		33,600	37,500
5620	30,000 gallon capacity, 3/8" thick shell		1.10	29.091		34,900	1,550		36,450	40,700
5630	40,000 gallon capacity, 3/8" thick shell		.90	35.556		35,600	1,875		37,475	42,100
5640	50,000 gallon capacity, 3/8" thick shell		.80	40		39,500	2,125		41,625	46,700

23 13 13.13 Dbl-Wall Steel, Undrgrnd Fuel-Oil, Stor. Tanks

		Crew	Daily Output	Labor-Hours	Unit	Material	2012 Bare Costs Labor	Equipment	Total	Total Incl O&P
0010	**DOUBLE-WALL STEEL, UNDERGROUND FUEL-OIL, STORAGE TANKS**									
6200	Steel, underground, 360°, double wall, U.L. listed,									
6210	with sti-P3 corrosion protection,									
6220	(dielectric coating, cathodic protection, electrical									
6230	isolation) 30 year warranty,									
6240	not incl. manholes or hold-downs.									
6250	500 gallon capacity	Q-5	2.40	6.667	Ea.	4,300	335		4,635	5,225
6260	1,000 gallon capactiy	"	2.25	7.111		6,275	355		6,630	7,450
6270	2,000 gallon capacity	Q-7	4.16	7.692		8,225	410		8,635	9,675
6280	3,000 gallon capacity		3.90	8.205		10,900	435		11,335	12,700
6290	4,000 gallon capacity		3.64	8.791		13,300	465		13,765	15,300
6300	5,000 gallon capacity		2.91	10.997		18,100	585		18,685	20,800
6310	6,000 gallon capacity		2.42	13.223		21,400	700		22,100	24,700
6320	8,000 gallon capacity		2.08	15.385		22,300	815		23,115	25,800
6330	10,000 gallon capacity		1.82	17.582		25,200	935		26,135	29,100
6340	12,000 gallon capacity		1.70	18.824		27,900	1,000		28,900	32,100
6350	15,000 gallon capacity		1.33	24.060		29,000	1,275		30,275	33,800
6360	20,000 gallon capacity		1.33	24.060		32,700	1,275		33,975	37,800
6370	25,000 gallon capacity		1.16	27.586		66,000	1,475		67,475	74,500
6380	30,000 gallon capacity		1.03	31.068		79,500	1,650		81,150	90,000
6390	40,000 gallon capacity		.80	40		102,000	2,125		104,125	115,500
6395	50,000 gallon capacity		.73	43.836		124,000	2,325		126,325	140,000
6400	For hold-downs 500-2000 gal., add		16	2	Set	166	106		272	345
6410	For hold-downs 3000-6000 gal., add		12	2.667		335	141		476	585
6420	For hold-downs 8000-12,000 gal., add		11	2.909		405	154		559	680
6430	For hold-downs 15,000 gal., add		9	3.556		580	189		769	925
6440	For hold-downs 20,000 gal., add		8	4		670	212		882	1,050
6450	For hold-downs 20,000 gal. plus, add		6	5.333		870	283		1,153	1,375
6500	For manways, add				Ea.	1,650			1,650	1,800
6600	In place with hold-downs									
6652	550 gallon capacity	Q-5	1.84	8.696	Ea.	4,475	435		4,910	5,575

23 13 13.23 Glass-Fiber-Reinfcd-Plastic, Fuel-Oil, Storage

		Crew	Daily Output	Labor-Hours	Unit	Material	2012 Bare Costs Labor	Equipment	Total	Total Incl O&P
0010	**GLASS-FIBER-REINFCD-PLASTIC, UNDERGRND FUEL-OIL, STORAGE**									
0210	Fiberglass, underground, single wall, U.L. listed, not including									
0220	manway or hold-down strap									
0225	550 gallon capacity	Q-5	2.67	5.993	Ea.	3,950	300		4,250	4,775

23 13 13 – Facility Underground Fuel-Oil, Storage Tanks

23 13 13.23 Glass-Fiber-Reinfcd-Plastic, Fuel-Oil, Storage	Crew	Daily Output	Labor-Hours	Unit	Material	2012 Bare Costs Labor	Equipment	Total	Total Incl O&P
0230	1,000 gallon capacity	Q-5	2.46	6.504	Ea.	4,800	325		5,125	5,775
0240	2,000 gallon capacity	Q-7	4.57	7.002		6,700	370		7,070	7,925
0250	4,000 gallon capacity		3.55	9.014		9,525	480		10,005	11,200
0260	6,000 gallon capacity		2.67	11.985		10,600	635		11,235	12,600
0270	8,000 gallon capacity		2.29	13.974		12,500	740		13,240	14,900
0280	10,000 gallon capacity		2	16		14,200	850		15,050	16,900
0282	12,000 gallon capacity		1.88	17.021		23,900	905		24,805	27,700
0284	15,000 gallon capacity		1.68	19.048		26,300	1,000		27,300	30,500
0290	20,000 gallon capacity		1.45	22.069		28,900	1,175		30,075	33,600
0300	25,000 gallon capacity		1.28	25		42,800	1,325		44,125	49,100
0320	30,000 gallon capacity		1.14	28.070		51,500	1,500		53,000	59,500
0340	40,000 gallon capacity		.89	35.955		73,500	1,900		75,400	84,000
0360	48,000 gallon capacity	▼	.81	39.506		86,500	2,100		88,600	98,500
0500	For manway, fittings and hold-downs, add					20%	15%			
0600	For manways, add					2,125			2,125	2,350
1000	For helical heating coil, add	Q-5	2.50	6.400	▼	4,200	320		4,520	5,075
1020	Fiberglass, underground, double wall, U.L. listed									
1030	includes manways, not incl. hold-down straps									
1040	600 gallon capacity	Q-5	2.42	6.612	Ea.	7,875	330		8,205	9,150
1050	1,000 gallon capacity	"	2.25	7.111		10,600	355		10,955	12,100
1060	2,500 gallon capacity	Q-7	4.16	7.692		15,100	410		15,510	17,200
1070	3,000 gallon capacity		3.90	8.205		16,400	435		16,835	18,700
1080	4,000 gallon capacity		3.64	8.791		16,500	465		16,965	18,900
1090	6,000 gallon capacity		2.42	13.223		21,800	700		22,500	25,100
1100	8,000 gallon capacity		2.08	15.385		24,700	815		25,515	28,400
1110	10,000 gallon capacity		1.82	17.582		27,000	935		27,935	31,100
1120	12,000 gallon capacity		1.70	18.824		33,100	1,000		34,100	37,900
1122	15,000 gallon capacity		1.52	21.053		43,300	1,125		44,425	49,300
1124	20,000 gallon capacity		1.33	24.060		53,000	1,275		54,275	60,000
1126	25,000 gallon capacity		1.16	27.586		69,500	1,475		70,975	78,500
1128	30,000 gallon capacity	▼	1.03	31.068		83,500	1,650		85,150	94,500
1140	For hold-down straps, add				▼	2%	10%			
1150	For hold-downs 500-4000 gal., add	Q-7	16	2	Set	405	106		511	605
1160	For hold-downs 5000-15000 gal., add		8	4		810	212		1,022	1,200
1170	For hold-downs 20,000 gal., add		5.33	6.004		1,225	320		1,545	1,800
1180	For hold-downs 25,000 gal., add		4	8		1,625	425		2,050	2,425
1190	For hold-downs 30,000 gal., add	▼	2.60	12.308	▼	2,425	655		3,080	3,650
2210	Fiberglass, underground, single wall, U.L. listed, including									
2220	hold-down straps, no manways									
2225	550 gallon capacity	Q-5	2	8	Ea.	4,350	400		4,750	5,375
2230	1,000 gallon capacity	"	1.88	8.511		5,200	425		5,625	6,375
2240	2,000 gallon capacity	Q-7	3.55	9.014		7,100	480		7,580	8,525
2250	4,000 gallon capacity		2.90	11.034		9,925	585		10,510	11,800
2260	6,000 gallon capacity		2	16		11,400	850		12,250	13,800
2270	8,000 gallon capacity		1.78	17.978		13,400	955		14,355	16,200
2280	10,000 gallon capacity		1.60	20		15,000	1,050		16,050	18,100
2282	12,000 gallon capacity		1.52	21.053		24,800	1,125		25,925	28,900
2284	15,000 gallon capacity		1.39	23.022		27,100	1,225		28,325	31,800
2290	20,000 gallon capacity		1.14	28.070		30,100	1,500		31,600	35,400
2300	25,000 gallon capacity		.96	33.333		44,400	1,775		46,175	51,500
2320	30,000 gallon capacity	▼	.80	40	▼	54,000	2,125		56,125	62,500
3020	Fiberglass, underground, double wall, U.L. listed									
3030	includes manways and hold-down straps									

23 13 Facility Fuel-Storage Tanks

23 13 13 – Facility Underground Fuel-Oil, Storage Tanks

23 13 13.23 Glass-Fiber-Reinfcd-Plastic, Fuel-Oil, Storage

		Crew	Daily Output	Labor-Hours	Unit	Material	2012 Bare Costs Labor	Equipment	Total	Total Incl O&P
3040	600 gallon capacity	Q-5	1.86	8.602	Ea.	8,275	430		8,705	9,750
3050	1,000 gallon capacity	"	1.70	9.412		11,000	470		11,470	12,800
3060	2,500 gallon capacity	Q-7	3.29	9.726		15,500	515		16,015	17,900
3070	3,000 gallon capacity		3.13	10.224		16,800	540		17,340	19,300
3080	4,000 gallon capacity		2.93	10.922		16,900	580		17,480	19,500
3090	6,000 gallon capacity		1.86	17.204		22,600	915		23,515	26,200
3100	8,000 gallon capacity		1.65	19.394		25,500	1,025		26,525	29,700
3110	10,000 gallon capacity		1.48	21.622		27,800	1,150		28,950	32,300
3120	12,000 gallon capacity		1.40	22.857		33,900	1,200		35,100	39,100
3122	15,000 gallon capacity		1.28	25		44,100	1,325		45,425	50,500
3124	20,000 gallon capacity		1.06	30.189		54,000	1,600		55,600	62,000
3126	25,000 gallon capacity		.90	35.556		71,000	1,875		72,875	81,000
3128	30,000 gallon capacity		.74	43.243		86,000	2,300		88,300	98,000

23 13 23 – Facility Aboveground Fuel-Oil, Storage Tanks

23 13 23.13 Vertical, Steel, Abvground Fuel-Oil, Stor. Tanks

		Crew	Daily Output	Labor-Hours	Unit	Material	2012 Bare Costs Labor	Equipment	Total	Total Incl O&P
0010	**VERTICAL, STEEL, ABOVEGROUND FUEL-OIL, STORAGE TANKS**									
4000	Fixed roof oil storage tanks, steel, (1 BBL=42 gal. w/foundation 3'D x 1'W)									
4200	5,000 barrels				Ea.				194,000	213,500
4300	24,000 barrels								333,500	367,000
4500	56,000 barrels								729,000	802,000
4600	110,000 barrels								1,060,000	1,166,000
4800	143,000 barrels								1,250,000	1,375,000
4900	225,000 barrels								1,360,000	1,496,000
5100	Floating roof gasoline tanks, steel, 5,000 barrels (w/foundation 3'D x 1'W)								204,000	225,000
5200	25,000 barrels								381,000	419,000
5400	55,000 barrels								839,000	923,000
5500	100,000 barrels								1,253,000	1,379,000
5700	150,000 barrels								1,532,000	1,685,000
5800	225,000 barrels								2,300,000	2,783,000

23 13 23.16 Horizontal, Stl, Abvgrd Fuel-Oil, Storage Tanks

		Crew	Daily Output	Labor-Hours	Unit	Material	2012 Bare Costs Labor	Equipment	Total	Total Incl O&P
0010	**HORIZONTAL, STEEL, ABOVEGROUND FUEL-OIL, STORAGE TANKS**									
3000	Steel, storage, above ground, including cradles, coating,									
3020	fittings, not including foundation, pumps or piping									
3040	Single wall, 275 gallon	Q-5	5	3.200	Ea.	445	160		605	730
3060	550 gallon	"	2.70	5.926		3,100	297		3,397	3,850
3080	1,000 gallon	Q-7	5	6.400		5,075	340		5,415	6,100
3100	1,500 gallon		4.75	6.737		7,250	355		7,605	8,525
3120	2,000 gallon		4.60	6.957		8,800	370		9,170	10,200
3140	5,000 gallon		3.20	10		19,100	530		19,630	21,800
3150	10,000 gallon		2	16		29,000	850		29,850	33,200
3160	15,000 gallon		1.70	18.824		37,300	1,000		38,300	42,500
3170	20,000 gallon		1.45	22.069		48,200	1,175		49,375	55,000
3180	25,000 gallon		1.30	24.615		56,500	1,300		57,800	64,000
3190	30,000 gallon		1.10	29.091		67,500	1,550		69,050	76,500
3320	Double wall, 500 gallon capacity	Q-5	2.40	6.667		2,375	335		2,710	3,125
3330	2000 gallon capacity	Q-7	4.15	7.711		9,075	410		9,485	10,600
3340	4000 gallon capacity		3.60	8.889		16,200	470		16,670	18,500
3350	6000 gallon capacity		2.40	13.333		19,100	705		19,805	22,100
3360	8000 gallon capacity		2	16		24,500	850		25,350	28,300
3370	10000 gallon capacity		1.80	17.778		27,500	945		28,445	31,600
3380	15000 gallon capacity		1.50	21.333		41,700	1,125		42,825	47,600
3390	20000 gallon capacity		1.30	24.615		47,500	1,300		48,800	54,500

23 13 Facility Fuel-Storage Tanks

23 13 23 – Facility Aboveground Fuel-Oil, Storage Tanks

23 13 23.16 Horizontal, Stl, Abvgrd Fuel-Oil, Storage Tanks	Crew	Daily Output	Labor-Hours	Unit	Material	2012 Bare Costs Labor	Equipment	Total	Total Incl O&P
3400	25000 gallon capacity	Q-7	1.15	27.826	Ea.	57,500	1,475		58,975	65,500
3410	30000 gallon capacity	↓	1	32	↓	63,500	1,700		65,200	72,000

23 21 Hydronic Piping and Pumps

23 21 20 – Hydronic HVAC Piping Specialties

23 21 20.10 Air Control

		Crew	Daily Output	Labor-Hours	Unit	Material	2012 Bare Costs Labor	Equipment	Total	Total Incl O&P
0010	**AIR CONTROL**									
0030	Air separator, with strainer									
0040	2" diameter	Q-5	6	2.667	Ea.	905	134		1,039	1,200
0080	2-1/2" diameter		5	3.200		1,025	160		1,185	1,375
0100	3" diameter		4	4		1,550	201		1,751	2,025
0120	4" diameter	↓	3	5.333		2,250	267		2,517	2,875
0130	5" diameter	Q-6	3.60	6.667		2,875	345		3,220	3,700
0140	6" diameter		3.40	7.059		3,450	365		3,815	4,350
0160	8" diameter		3	8		5,150	415		5,565	6,300
0180	10" diameter		2.20	10.909		8,025	565		8,590	9,675
0200	12" diameter		1.70	14.118		13,400	735		14,135	15,900
0210	14" diameter		1.30	18.462		16,000	960		16,960	19,100
0220	16" diameter		1	24		24,100	1,250		25,350	28,400
0230	18" diameter		.80	30		31,600	1,550		33,150	37,200
0240	20" diameter	↓	.60	40	↓	35,400	2,075		37,475	42,100
0300	Without strainer									
0310	2" diameter	Q-5	6	2.667	Ea.	705	134		839	975
0320	2-1/2" diameter		5	3.200		840	160		1,000	1,175
0330	3" diameter		4	4		1,175	201		1,376	1,600
0340	4" diameter		3	5.333		1,850	267		2,117	2,450
0350	5" diameter	↓	2.40	6.667		2,525	335		2,860	3,275
0360	6" diameter	Q-6	3.40	7.059		2,875	365		3,240	3,725
0370	8" diameter		3	8		3,950	415		4,365	4,975
0380	10" diameter		2.20	10.909		5,825	565		6,390	7,275
0390	12" diameter		1.70	14.118		8,975	735		9,710	11,000
0400	14" diameter		1.30	18.462		13,400	960		14,360	16,300
0410	16" diameter		1	24		18,800	1,250		20,050	22,600
0420	18" diameter		.80	30		24,500	1,550		26,050	29,300
0430	20" diameter	↓	.60	40	↓	29,300	2,075		31,375	35,400
1000	Micro-bubble separator for total air removal, closed loop system									
1010	Requires bladder type tank in system.									
1020	Water (hot or chilled) or glycol system									
1030	Threaded									
1040	3/4" diameter	1 Stpi	20	.400	Ea.	88.50	22.50		111	131
1050	1" diameter		19	.421		99.50	23.50		123	145
1060	1-1/4" diameter		16	.500		138	28		166	193
1070	1-1/2" diameter		13	.615		179	34.50		213.50	249
1080	2" diameter	↓	11	.727		865	40.50		905.50	1,025
1090	2-1/2" diameter	Q-5	15	1.067		965	53.50		1,018.50	1,125
1100	3" diameter		13	1.231		1,375	61.50		1,436.50	1,625
1110	4" diameter	↓	10	1.600	↓	1,500	80		1,580	1,775
1230	Flanged									
1250	2" diameter	1 Stpi	8	1	Ea.	1,100	55.50		1,155.50	1,300
1260	2-1/2" diameter	Q-5	5	3.200		1,200	160		1,360	1,575
1270	3" diameter	↓	4.50	3.556	↓	1,625	178		1,803	2,050

23 21 Hydronic Piping and Pumps

23 21 20 – Hydronic HVAC Piping Specialties

23 21 20.10 Air Control

		Crew	Daily Output	Labor-Hours	Unit	Material	2012 Bare Costs Labor	Equipment	Total	Total Incl O&P
1280	4" diameter	Q-5	3	5.333	Ea.	1,775	267		2,042	2,375
1290	5" diameter	Q-6	3.40	7.059		2,850	365		3,215	3,700
1300	6" diameter	"	3	8		3,475	415		3,890	4,450
1400	Larger sizes available									
1590	With extended tank dirt catcher									
1600	Flanged									
1620	2" diameter	1 Stpi	7.40	1.081	Ea.	1,450	60		1,510	1,700
1630	2-1/2" diameter	Q-5	4.20	3.810		1,525	191		1,716	2,000
1640	3" diameter		4	4		2,000	201		2,201	2,500
1650	4" diameter		2.80	5.714		2,175	286		2,461	2,825
1660	5" diameter	Q-6	3.10	7.742		3,200	400		3,600	4,125
1670	6" diameter	"	2.90	8.276		3,925	430		4,355	4,975
1800	With drain/dismantle/cleaning access flange									
1810	Flanged									
1820	2" diameter	1 Stpi	7	1.143	Ea.	2,275	63.50		2,338.50	2,600
1830	2-1/2" diameter	Q-5	4	4		2,450	201		2,651	3,000
1840	3" diameter		3.60	4.444		3,325	223		3,548	3,975
1850	4" diameter		2.50	6.400		3,675	320		3,995	4,500
1860	5" diameter	Q-6	2.80	8.571		5,475	445		5,920	6,700
1870	6" diameter	"	2.60	9.231		7,125	480		7,605	8,575
2000	Boiler air fitting, separator									
2010	1-1/4"	Q-5	22	.727	Ea.	203	36.50		239.50	278
2020	1-1/2"		20	.800		390	40		430	485
2021	2"		18	.889		670	44.50		714.50	805
2400	Compression tank air fitting									
2410	For tanks 9" to 24" diameter	1 Stpi	15	.533	Ea.	69	29.50		98.50	121
2420	For tanks 100 gallon or larger	"	12	.667	"	259	37		296	340

23 21 20.14 Air Purging Scoop

		Crew	Daily Output	Labor-Hours	Unit	Material	2012 Bare Costs Labor	Equipment	Total	Total Incl O&P
0010	**AIR PURGING SCOOP**, With tappings.									
0020	For air vent and expansion tank connection									
0100	1" pipe size, threaded	1 Stpi	19	.421	Ea.	23	23.50		46.50	60.50
0110	1-1/4" pipe size, threaded		15	.533		23	29.50		52.50	70
0120	1-1/2" pipe size, threaded		13	.615		50.50	34.50		85	107
0130	2" pipe size, threaded		11	.727		57.50	40.50		98	125
0140	2-1/2" pipe size, threaded	Q-5	15	1.067		123	53.50		176.50	216
0150	3" pipe size, threaded		13	1.231		160	61.50		221.50	269
0160	4" 150 lb. flanges		3	5.333		360	267		627	800

23 21 20.18 Automatic Air Vent

		Crew	Daily Output	Labor-Hours	Unit	Material	2012 Bare Costs Labor	Equipment	Total	Total Incl O&P
0010	**AUTOMATIC AIR VENT**									
0020	Cast iron body, stainless steel internals, float type									
0060	1/2" NPT inlet, 300 psi	1 Stpi	12	.667	Ea.	93.50	37		130.50	159
0140	3/4" NPT inlet, 300 psi		12	.667		93.50	37		130.50	159
0180	1/2" NPT inlet, 250 psi		10	.800		299	44.50		343.50	395
0220	3/4" NPT inlet, 250 psi		10	.800		299	44.50		343.50	395
0260	1" NPT inlet, 250 psi		10	.800		435	44.50		479.50	545
0340	1-1/2" NPT inlet, 250 psi	Q-5	12	1.333		925	67		992	1,125
0380	2" NPT inlet, 250 psi	"	12	1.333		925	67		992	1,125
0600	Forged steel body, stainless steel internals, float type									
0640	1/2" NPT inlet, 750 psi	1 Stpi	12	.667	Ea.	980	37		1,017	1,125
0680	3/4" NPT inlet, 750 psi		12	.667		980	37		1,017	1,125
0760	3/4" NPT inlet, 1000 psi		10	.800		1,475	44.50		1,519.50	1,675
0800	1" NPT inlet, 1000 psi	Q-5	12	1.333		1,475	67		1,542	1,700

23 21 Hydronic Piping and Pumps

23 21 20 – Hydronic HVAC Piping Specialties

23 21 20.18 Automatic Air Vent

		Crew	Daily Output	Labor-Hours	Unit	Material	2012 Bare Costs Labor	Equipment	Total	Total Incl O&P
0880	1-1/2" NPT inlet, 1000 psi	Q-5	10	1.600	Ea.	4,125	80		4,205	4,650
0920	2" NPT inlet, 1000 psi	↓	10	1.600	↓	4,125	80		4,205	4,650
1100	Formed steel body, noncorrosive									
1110	1/8" NPT inlet 150 psi	1 Stpi	32	.250	Ea.	11.75	13.95		25.70	34
1120	1/4" NPT inlet 150 psi		32	.250		39.50	13.95		53.45	64.50
1130	3/4" NPT inlet 150 psi	↓	32	.250	↓	39.50	13.95		53.45	64.50
1300	Chrome plated brass, automatic/manual, for radiators									
1310	1/8" NPT inlet, nickel plated brass	1 Stpi	32	.250	Ea.	6.85	13.95		20.80	28.50

23 21 20.22 Circuit Sensor

		Crew	Daily Output	Labor-Hours	Unit	Material	2012 Bare Costs Labor	Equipment	Total	Total Incl O&P
0010	**CIRCUIT SENSOR**, Flow meter									
0020	Metering stations									
0040	Wafer orifice insert type									
0060	2-1/2" pipe size	Q-5	12	1.333	Ea.	193	67		260	315
0100	3" pipe size		11	1.455		214	73		287	345
0140	4" pipe size		8	2		245	100		345	420
0180	5" pipe size		7.30	2.192		310	110		420	510
0220	6" pipe size	↓	6.40	2.500		375	125		500	600
0260	8" pipe size	Q-6	5.30	4.528		520	235		755	925
0280	10" pipe size		4.60	5.217		590	271		861	1,050
0360	12" pipe size	↓	4.20	5.714	↓	985	297		1,282	1,525
2000	In-line probe type									
2200	Copper, soldered									
2210	1/2" size	1 Stpi	24	.333	Ea.	173	18.55		191.55	218
2220	3/4" size		20	.400		180	22.50		202.50	232
2230	1" size		19	.421		204	23.50		227.50	260
2240	1-1/4" size		15	.533		214	29.50		243.50	281
2250	1-1/2" size		13	.615		255	34.50		289.50	330
2260	2" size	↓	11	.727		284	40.50		324.50	370
2270	2-1/2" size	Q-5	15	1.067		299	53.50		352.50	410
2280	3" size	"	13	1.231	↓	325	61.50		386.50	450
2500	Brass, threaded									
2510	1" size	1 Stpi	19	.421	Ea.	214	23.50		237.50	272
2520	1-1/4" size		15	.533		236	29.50		265.50	305
2530	1-1/2" size		13	.615		284	34.50		318.50	360
2540	2" size	↓	11	.727		299	40.50		339.50	390
2550	2-1/2" size	Q-5	15	1.067		325	53.50		378.50	435
2560	3" size	"	13	1.231	↓	335	61.50		396.50	460
2700	Steel, threaded									
2710	1" size	1 Stpi	19	.421	Ea.	205	23.50		228.50	262
2720	1-1/4" size		15	.533		222	29.50		251.50	290
2730	1-1/2" size		13	.615		253	34.50		287.50	330
2740	2" size	↓	11	.727		282	40.50		322.50	370
2750	2-1/2" size	Q-5	15	1.067		299	53.50		352.50	410
2760	3" size	"	13	1.231	↓	325	61.50		386.50	455
3000	Pitot tube probe type									
3100	Weld-on mounting with probe									
3110	2" size	Q-17	18	.889	Ea.	232	44.50	2.05	278.55	325
3120	2-1/2" size		18	.889		236	44.50	2.05	282.55	330
3130	3" size		18	.889		251	44.50	2.05	297.55	345
3140	4" size		18	.889		335	44.50	2.05	381.55	435
3150	5" size		17	.941		375	47	2.17	424.17	485
3160	6" size	↓	17	.941	↓	485	47	2.17	534.17	605

23 21 20.22 Circuit Sensor		Crew	Daily Output	Labor-Hours	Unit	Material	2012 Bare Costs Labor	2012 Bare Costs Equipment	Total	Total Incl O&P
3170	8" size	Q-17	16	1	Ea.	690	50	2.31	742.31	840
3180	10" size		15	1.067		745	53.50	2.46	800.96	905
3190	12" size		15	1.067		800	53.50	2.46	855.96	965
3200	14" size		14	1.143		915	57.50	2.64	975.14	1,100
3210	16" size		14	1.143		1,075	57.50	2.64	1,135.14	1,300
3220	18" size		13	1.231		1,150	61.50	2.84	1,214.34	1,375
3230	20" size		13	1.231		1,250	61.50	2.84	1,314.34	1,475
3240	24" size	▼	12	1.333	▼	1,325	67	3.08	1,395.08	1,550
3400	Weld-on wet tap with probe									
3410	2" size, 5/16" probe dia.	Q-17	14	1.143	Ea.	560	57.50	2.64	620.14	710
3420	2-1/2" size, 5/16" probe dia.		14	1.143		570	57.50	2.64	630.14	715
3430	3" size, 5/16" probe dia.		14	1.143		605	57.50	2.64	665.14	760
3440	4" size, 5/16" probe dia.		14	1.143		705	57.50	2.64	765.14	865
3450	5" size, 3/8" probe dia.		13	1.231		725	61.50	2.84	789.34	890
3460	6" size, 3/8" probe dia.		13	1.231		695	61.50	2.84	759.34	860
3470	8" size, 1/2" probe dia.		12	1.333		720	67	3.08	790.08	895
3480	10" size, 3/4" probe dia.		11	1.455		790	73	3.36	866.36	985
3490	12" size, 3/4" probe dia.		11	1.455		835	73	3.36	911.36	1,025
3500	14" size, 1" probe dia.		10	1.600		945	80	3.70	1,028.70	1,175
3510	16" size, 1" probe dia.		10	1.600		1,125	80	3.70	1,208.70	1,375
3520	18" size, 1" probe dia.		9	1.778		1,225	89	4.11	1,318.11	1,475
3530	20" size, 1" probe dia.		8	2		1,300	100	4.62	1,404.62	1,575
3540	24" size, 1" probe dia.	▼	8	2	▼	1,450	100	4.62	1,554.62	1,750
3700	Clamp-on wet tap with probe									
3710	2" size, 5/16" probe dia.	Q-5	16	1	Ea.	810	50		860	965
3720	2-1/2" size, 5/16" probe dia.		16	1		705	50		755	850
3730	3" size, 5/16" probe dia.		15	1.067		705	53.50		758.50	855
3740	4" size, 5/16" probe dia.		15	1.067		815	53.50		868.50	975
3750	5" size, 3/8" probe dia.		14	1.143		860	57.50		917.50	1,025
3760	6" size, 3/8" probe dia.		14	1.143		910	57.50		967.50	1,075
3770	8" size, 1/2" probe dia.		13	1.231		1,000	61.50		1,061.50	1,200
3780	10" size, 3/4" probe dia.		12	1.333		1,050	67		1,117	1,250
3790	12" size, 3/4" probe dia.		12	1.333		1,225	67		1,292	1,425
3800	14" size, 1" probe dia.		11	1.455		1,575	73		1,648	1,825
3810	16" size, 1" probe dia.		11	1.455		1,825	73		1,898	2,125
3820	18" size, 1" probe dia.		10	1.600		1,975	80		2,055	2,300
3830	20" size, 1" probe dia		9	1.778		2,250	89		2,339	2,600
3840	24" size, 1" probe dia.	▼	9	1.778	▼	2,325	89		2,414	2,675
4000	Wet tap drills									
4010	3/8" dia. for 5/16" probe				Ea.	135			135	149
4020	1/2" dia. for 3/8" probe					140			140	154
4030	5/8" dia for 1/2" probe					166			166	183
4040	7/8" dia for 3/4" probe					217			217	238
4050	1-3/16" dia for 1" probe				▼	231			231	254
4100	Wet tap punch									
4110	5/16" dia for 5/16" probe				Ea.	139			139	153
4120	3/8" dia for 3/8" probe					150			150	165
4130	1/2" dia for 1/2" probe				▼	180			180	198
4150	Note: labor for wet tap drill or punch									
4160	is included with the mounting and probe assembly									
9000	Readout instruments									
9200	Gauges									
9220	GPM gauge				Ea.	2,275			2,275	2,500

23 21 Hydronic Piping and Pumps

23 21 20 – Hydronic HVAC Piping Specialties

23 21 20.22 Circuit Sensor

		Crew	Daily Output	Labor-Hours	Unit	Material	2012 Bare Costs Labor	Equipment	Total	Total Incl O&P
9230	Dual gauge kit				Ea.	2,375			2,375	2,600

23 21 20.26 Circuit Setter

		Crew	Daily Output	Labor-Hours	Unit	Material	2012 Bare Costs Labor	Equipment	Total	Total Incl O&P
0010	**CIRCUIT SETTER**, Balance valve									
0012	Bronze body, soldered									
0013	1/2" size	1 Stpi	24	.333	Ea.	68	18.55		86.55	103
0014	3/4" size	"	20	.400	"	71.50	22.50		94	112
0018	Threaded									
0019	1/2" pipe size	1 Stpi	22	.364	Ea.	70.50	20.50		91	108
0020	3/4" pipe size		20	.400		75	22.50		97.50	117
0040	1" pipe size		18	.444		97.50	25		122.50	145
0050	1-1/4" pipe size		15	.533		143	29.50		172.50	202
0060	1-1/2" pipe size		12	.667		169	37		206	241
0080	2" pipe size		10	.800		241	44.50		285.50	330
0100	2-1/2" pipe size	Q-5	15	1.067		545	53.50		598.50	680
0120	3" pipe size	"	10	1.600		770	80		850	965
0130	Cast iron body, flanged									
0136	3" pipe size, flanged	Q-5	4	4	Ea.	770	201		971	1,150
0140	4" pipe size	"	3	5.333		1,150	267		1,417	1,675
0200	For differential meter, accurate to 1%, add					885			885	975
0300	For differential meter 400 psi/200°F continuous, add					2,200			2,200	2,400

23 21 20.30 Cocks, Drains and Specialties

		Crew	Daily Output	Labor-Hours	Unit	Material	2012 Bare Costs Labor	Equipment	Total	Total Incl O&P
0010	**COCKS, DRAINS AND SPECIALTIES**									
1000	Boiler drain									
1010	Pipe thread to hose									
1020	Bronze									
1030	1/2" size	1 Stpi	36	.222	Ea.	11.15	12.40		23.55	31
1040	3/4" size	"	34	.235	"	12.15	13.10		25.25	33
1100	Solder to hose									
1110	Bronze									
1120	1/2" size	1 Stpi	46	.174	Ea.	11.15	9.70		20.85	27
1130	3/4" size	"	44	.182	"	12.15	10.15		22.30	28.50
1600	With built-in vacuum breaker									
1610	1/2" IP or solder	1 Stpi	36	.222	Ea.	32	12.40		44.40	53.50
1630	With tamper proof vacuum breaker									
1640	1/2" IP or solder	1 Stpi	36	.222	Ea.	36	12.40		48.40	58.50
1650	3/4" IP or solder	"	34	.235	"	37	13.10		50.10	60.50
3000	Cocks									
3010	Air, lever or tee handle									
3020	Bronze, single thread									
3030	1/8" size	1 Stpi	52	.154	Ea.	9.75	8.55		18.30	23.50
3040	1/4" size		46	.174		10.30	9.70		20	26
3050	3/8" size		40	.200		10.40	11.15		21.55	28.50
3060	1/2" size		36	.222		12.30	12.40		24.70	32
3100	Bronze, double thread									
3110	1/8" size	1 Stpi	26	.308	Ea.	12.20	17.15		29.35	39.50
3120	1/4" size		22	.364		12.80	20.50		33.30	44.50
3130	3/8" size		18	.444		13.30	25		38.30	52
3140	1/2" size		15	.533		16.30	29.50		45.80	63
4000	Steam									
4010	Bronze									
4020	1/8" size	1 Stpi	26	.308	Ea.	37.50	17.15		54.65	67
4030	1/4" size		22	.364		32.50	20.50		53	66

23 21 20.30 Cocks, Drains and Specialties		Crew	Daily Output	Labor-Hours	Unit	Material	2012 Bare Costs Labor	2012 Bare Costs Equipment	Total	Total Incl O&P
4040	3/8" size	1 Stpi	18	.444	Ea.	47	25		72	89
4050	1/2" size		15	.533		49.50	29.50		79	99.50
4060	3/4" size		14	.571		58.50	32		90.50	113
4070	1" size		13	.615		76.50	34.50		111	136
4080	1-1/4" size		11	.727		117	40.50		157.50	190
4090	1-1/2" size		10	.800		151	44.50		195.50	234
4100	2" size		9	.889		250	49.50		299.50	350
4300	Bronze, 3 way									
4320	1/4" size	1 Stpi	15	.533	Ea.	55.50	29.50		85	106
4330	3/8" size		12	.667		55.50	37		92.50	117
4340	1/2" size		10	.800		55.50	44.50		100	128
4350	3/4" size		9.50	.842		95.50	47		142.50	176
4360	1" size		8.50	.941		115	52.50		167.50	206
4370	1-1/4" size		7.50	1.067		173	59.50		232.50	280
4380	1-1/2" size		6.50	1.231		200	68.50		268.50	325
4390	2" size		6	1.333		250	74.50		324.50	385
4500	Gauge cock, brass									
4510	1/4" FPT	1 Stpi	24	.333	Ea.	10.30	18.55		28.85	39.50
4512	1/4" MPT	"	24	.333	"	12.95	18.55		31.50	42.50
4600	Pigtail, steam syphon									
4604	1/4"	1 Stpi	24	.333	Ea.	18.80	18.55		37.35	48.50
4650	Snubber valve									
4654	1/4"	1 Stpi	22	.364	Ea.	12.15	20.50		32.65	44
4660	Nipple, black steel									
4664	1/4" x 3"	1 Stpi	37	.216	Ea.	2.14	12.05		14.19	20.50

23 21 20.34 Dielectric Unions

		Crew	Daily Output	Labor-Hours	Unit	Material	2012 Bare Costs Labor	2012 Bare Costs Equipment	Total	Total Incl O&P
0010	**DIELECTRIC UNIONS**, Standard gaskets for water and air									
0020	250 psi maximum pressure									
0280	Female IPT to sweat, straight									
0300	1/2" pipe size	1 Plum	24	.333	Ea.	5.45	18.20		23.65	33.50
0340	3/4" pipe size		20	.400		6.10	22		28.10	39.50
0360	1" pipe size		19	.421		8.30	23		31.30	43.50
0380	1-1/4" pipe size		15	.533		12.85	29		41.85	58
0400	1-1/2" pipe size		13	.615		19.30	33.50		52.80	71.50
0420	2" pipe size		11	.727		26	39.50		65.50	88.50
0580	Female IPT to brass pipe thread, straight									
0600	1/2" pipe size	1 Plum	24	.333	Ea.	11.80	18.20		30	40.50
0640	3/4" pipe size		20	.400		13.05	22		35.05	47.50
0660	1" pipe size		19	.421		24	23		47	61
0680	1-1/4" pipe size		15	.533		29.50	29		58.50	76.50
0700	1-1/2" pipe size		13	.615		43	33.50		76.50	97.50
0720	2" pipe size		11	.727		84	39.50		123.50	153
0780	Female IPT to female IPT, straight									
0800	1/2" pipe size	1 Plum	24	.333	Ea.	10.35	18.20		28.55	39
0840	3/4" pipe size		20	.400		11.70	22		33.70	46
0860	1" pipe size		19	.421		15.65	23		38.65	51.50
0880	1-1/4" pipe size		15	.533		21	29		50	67.50
0900	1-1/2" pipe size		13	.615		32.50	33.50		66	86
0920	2" pipe size		11	.727		47.50	39.50		87	112
2000	175 psi maximum pressure									
2180	Female IPT to sweat									
2240	2" pipe size	1 Plum	9	.889	Ea.	140	48.50		188.50	227

23 21 Hydronic Piping and Pumps

23 21 20 – Hydronic HVAC Piping Specialties

23 21 20.34 Dielectric Unions

		Crew	Daily Output	Labor-Hours	Unit	Material	2012 Bare Costs Labor	2012 Bare Costs Equipment	Total	Total Incl O&P
2260	2-1/2" pipe size	Q-1	15	1.067	Ea.	150	52.50		202.50	244
2280	3" pipe size		14	1.143		208	56		264	315
2300	4" pipe size	↓	11	1.455	↓	550	71.50		621.50	715
2480	Female IPT to brass pipe									
2500	1-1/2" pipe size	1 Plum	11	.727	Ea.	162	39.50		201.50	238
2540	2" pipe size	"	9	.889		190	48.50		238.50	282
2560	2-1/2" pipe size	Q-1	15	1.067		279	52.50		331.50	385
2580	3" pipe size		14	1.143		325	56		381	440
2600	4" pipe size	↓	11	1.455		585	71.50		656.50	750

23 21 20.38 Expansion Couplings

		Crew	Daily Output	Labor-Hours	Unit	Material	2012 Bare Costs Labor	2012 Bare Costs Equipment	Total	Total Incl O&P
0010	**EXPANSION COUPLINGS**, Hydronic									
0100	Copper to copper, sweat									
1000	Baseboard riser fitting, 5" stub by coupling 12" long									
1020	1/2" diameter	1 Stpi	24	.333	Ea.	17.20	18.55		35.75	47
1040	3/4" diameter		20	.400		24.50	22.50		47	60
1060	1" diameter		19	.421		34	23.50		57.50	73
1080	1-1/4" diameter	↓	15	.533	↓	44.50	29.50		74	94
1180	9" Stub by tubing 8" long									
1200	1/2" diameter	1 Stpi	24	.333	Ea.	15.40	18.55		33.95	45
1220	3/4" diameter		20	.400		20.50	22.50		43	56
1240	1" diameter		19	.421		28.50	23.50		52	66.50
1260	1-1/4" diameter	↓	15	.533	↓	38	29.50		67.50	86.50

23 21 20.42 Expansion Joints

		Crew	Daily Output	Labor-Hours	Unit	Material	2012 Bare Costs Labor	2012 Bare Costs Equipment	Total	Total Incl O&P
0010	**EXPANSION JOINTS**									
0100	Bellows type, neoprene cover, flanged spool									
0140	6" face to face, 1-1/4" diameter	1 Stpi	11	.727	Ea.	255	40.50		295.50	340
0160	1-1/2" diameter	"	10.60	.755		255	42		297	345
0180	2" diameter	Q-5	13.30	1.203		258	60.50		318.50	375
0190	2-1/2" diameter		12.40	1.290		267	64.50		331.50	390
0200	3" diameter		11.40	1.404		299	70.50		369.50	435
0210	4" diameter		8.40	1.905		325	95.50		420.50	500
0220	5" diameter		7.60	2.105		395	106		501	595
0230	6" diameter		6.80	2.353		405	118		523	630
0240	8" diameter		5.40	2.963		475	149		624	745
0250	10" diameter		5	3.200		650	160		810	955
0260	12" diameter		4.60	3.478		745	174		919	1,075
0480	10" face to face, 2" diameter		13	1.231		370	61.50		431.50	505
0500	2-1/2" diameter		12	1.333		390	67		457	530
0520	3" diameter		11	1.455		400	73		473	550
0540	4" diameter		8	2		455	100		555	650
0560	5" diameter		7	2.286		540	115		655	770
0580	6" diameter		6	2.667		560	134		694	815
0600	8" diameter		5	3.200		670	160		830	975
0620	10" diameter		4.60	3.478		735	174		909	1,075
0640	12" diameter		4	4		910	201		1,111	1,300
0660	14" diameter		3.80	4.211		1,125	211		1,336	1,575
0680	16" diameter		2.90	5.517		1,300	277		1,577	1,850
0700	18" diameter		2.50	6.400		1,475	320		1,795	2,100
0720	20" diameter		2.10	7.619		1,550	380		1,930	2,275
0740	24" diameter		1.80	8.889		1,800	445		2,245	2,650
0760	26" diameter		1.40	11.429		2,025	575		2,600	3,100
0780	30" diameter	↓	1.20	13.333	↓	2,250	670		2,920	3,475

23 21 Hydronic Piping and Pumps

23 21 20 – Hydronic HVAC Piping Specialties

23 21 20.42 Expansion Joints

		Crew	Daily Output	Labor-Hours	Unit	Material	2012 Bare Costs Labor	Equipment	Total	Total Incl O&P
0800	36" diameter	Q-5	1	16	Ea.	2,800	800		3,600	4,275
1000	Bellows with internal sleeves and external covers									
1010	Stainless steel, 150 lb.									
1020	With male threads									
1040	3/4" diameter	1 Stpi	20	.400	Ea.	142	22.50		164.50	190
1050	1" diameter		19	.421		150	23.50		173.50	200
1060	1-1/4" diameter		16	.500		156	28		184	214
1070	1-1/2" diameter		13	.615		191	34.50		225.50	262
1080	2" diameter		11	.727		243	40.50		283.50	330
1110	With flanged ends									
1120	1-1/4" diameter	1 Stpi	12	.667	Ea.	195	37		232	270
1130	1-1/2" diameter		11	.727		238	40.50		278.50	325
1140	2" diameter		9	.889		305	49.50		354.50	410
1150	3" diameter	Q-5	8	2		530	100		630	730
1160	4" diameter	"	5	3.200		895	160		1,055	1,225
1170	5" diameter	Q-6	6	4		1,075	208		1,283	1,500
1180	6" diameter		5	4.800		1,275	250		1,525	1,775
1190	8" diameter		4.50	5.333		1,800	277		2,077	2,400
1200	10" diameter		4	6		2,175	310		2,485	2,850
1210	12" diameter		3.60	6.667		3,375	345		3,720	4,250

23 21 20.46 Expansion Tanks

		Crew	Daily Output	Labor-Hours	Unit	Material	2012 Bare Costs Labor	Equipment	Total	Total Incl O&P
0010	**EXPANSION TANKS**									
1400	Plastic, corrosion resistant, see Plumbing Cost Data									
1507	Underground fuel-oil storage tanks, see Section 23 13 13									
1512	Tank leak detection systems, see Section 28 33 33.50									
2000	Steel, liquid expansion, ASME, painted, 15 gallon capacity	Q-5	17	.941	Ea.	595	47		642	725
2020	24 gallon capacity		14	1.143		635	57.50		692.50	785
2040	30 gallon capacity		12	1.333		665	67		732	835
2060	40 gallon capacity		10	1.600		780	80		860	980
2080	60 gallon capacity		8	2		935	100		1,035	1,175
2100	80 gallon capacity		7	2.286		1,000	115		1,115	1,275
2120	100 gallon capacity		6	2.667		1,350	134		1,484	1,700
2130	120 gallon capacity		5	3.200		1,450	160		1,610	1,850
2140	135 gallon capacity		4.50	3.556		1,500	178		1,678	1,925
2150	175 gallon capacity		4	4		2,375	201		2,576	2,900
2160	220 gallon capacity		3.60	4.444		2,700	223		2,923	3,300
2170	240 gallon capacity		3.30	4.848		2,800	243		3,043	3,475
2180	305 gallon capacity		3	5.333		3,975	267		4,242	4,750
2190	400 gallon capacity		2.80	5.714		4,850	286		5,136	5,750
2360	Galvanized									
2370	15 gallon capacity	Q-5	17	.941	Ea.	1,050	47		1,097	1,225
2380	24 gallon capacity		14	1.143		1,075	57.50		1,132.50	1,250
2390	30 gallon capacity		12	1.333		1,250	67		1,317	1,475
2400	40 gallon capacity		10	1.600		1,475	80		1,555	1,750
2410	60 gallon capacity		8	2		1,700	100		1,800	2,000
2420	80 gallon capacity		7	2.286		1,950	115		2,065	2,300
2430	100 gallon capacity		6	2.667		2,525	134		2,659	2,975
2440	120 gallon capacity		5	3.200		2,700	160		2,860	3,225
2450	135 gallon capacity		4.50	3.556		2,850	178		3,028	3,425
2460	175 gallon capacity		4	4		4,650	201		4,851	5,400
2470	220 gallon capacity		3.60	4.444		5,300	223		5,523	6,150
2480	240 gallon capacity		3.30	4.848		5,550	243		5,793	6,475

23 21 Hydronic Piping and Pumps

23 21 20 – Hydronic HVAC Piping Specialties

23 21 20.46 Expansion Tanks

		Crew	Daily Output	Labor-Hours	Unit	Material	2012 Bare Costs Labor	2012 Bare Costs Equipment	Total	Total Incl O&P
2490	305 gallon capacity	Q-5	3	5.333	Ea.	8,050	267		8,317	9,250
2500	400 gallon capacity		2.80	5.714		9,900	286		10,186	11,300
3000	Steel ASME expansion, rubber diaphragm, 19 gal. cap. accept.		12	1.333		2,450	67		2,517	2,800
3020	31 gallon capacity		8	2		2,600	100		2,700	3,000
3040	61 gallon capacity		6	2.667		3,650	134		3,784	4,225
3060	79 gallon capacity		5	3.200		3,700	160		3,860	4,325
3080	119 gallon capacity		4	4		3,925	201		4,126	4,625
3100	158 gallon capacity		3.80	4.211		5,475	211		5,686	6,350
3120	211 gallon capacity		3.30	4.848		6,325	243		6,568	7,325
3140	317 gallon capacity		2.80	5.714		8,250	286		8,536	9,500
3160	422 gallon capacity		2.60	6.154		12,200	310		12,510	13,900
3180	528 gallon capacity		2.40	6.667		13,400	335		13,735	15,200

23 21 20.50 Float Valves

		Crew	Daily Output	Labor-Hours	Unit	Material	Labor	Equipment	Total	Total Incl O&P
0010	**FLOAT VALVES**									
0020	With ball and bracket									
0030	Single seat, threaded									
0040	Brass body									
0050	1/2"	1 Stpi	11	.727	Ea.	72.50	40.50		113	141
0060	3/4"		9	.889		84	49.50		133.50	167
0070	1"		7	1.143		124	63.50		187.50	232
0080	1-1/2"		4.50	1.778		182	99		281	350
0090	2"		3.60	2.222		185	124		309	390
0300	For condensate receivers, CI, in-line mount									
0320	1" inlet	1 Stpi	7	1.143	Ea.	124	63.50		187.50	232
0360	For condensate receiver, CI, external float, flanged tank mount									
0370	3/4" inlet	1 Stpi	5	1.600	Ea.	93	89		182	236

23 21 20.54 Flow Check Control

		Crew	Daily Output	Labor-Hours	Unit	Material	Labor	Equipment	Total	Total Incl O&P
0010	**FLOW CHECK CONTROL**									
0100	Bronze body, soldered									
0110	3/4" size	1 Stpi	20	.400	Ea.	60.50	22.50		83	100
0120	1" size	"	19	.421	"	72.50	23.50		96	115
0200	Cast iron body, threaded									
0210	3/4" size	1 Stpi	20	.400	Ea.	46.50	22.50		69	84.50
0220	1" size		19	.421		52.50	23.50		76	93
0230	1-1/4" size		15	.533		63.50	29.50		93	115
0240	1-1/2" size		13	.615		97	34.50		131.50	159
0250	2" size		11	.727		140	40.50		180.50	215
0300	Flanged inlet, threaded outlet									
0310	2-1/2" size	1 Stpi	8	1	Ea.	291	55.50		346.50	405
0320	3" size	Q-5	9	1.778		345	89		434	515
0330	4" size	"	7	2.286		675	115		790	920

23 21 20.58 Hydronic Heating Control Valves

		Crew	Daily Output	Labor-Hours	Unit	Material	Labor	Equipment	Total	Total Incl O&P
0010	**HYDRONIC HEATING CONTROL VALVES**									
0050	Hot water, nonelectric, thermostatic									
0100	Radiator supply, 1/2" diameter	1 Stpi	24	.333	Ea.	59.50	18.55		78.05	93
0120	3/4" diameter		20	.400		62.50	22.50		85	102
0140	1" diameter		19	.421		77.50	23.50		101	121
0160	1-1/4" diameter		15	.533		111	29.50		140.50	167
0500	For low pressure steam, add					25%				
1000	Manual, radiator supply									
1010	1/2" pipe size, angle union	1 Stpi	24	.333	Ea.	44.50	18.55		63.05	77
1020	3/4" pipe size, angle union		20	.400		56	22.50		78.50	95.50

23 21 Hydronic Piping and Pumps

23 21 20 - Hydronic HVAC Piping Specialties

23 21 20.58 Hydronic Heating Control Valves

		Crew	Daily Output	Labor-Hours	Unit	Material	2012 Bare Costs Labor	Equipment	Total	Total Incl O&P
1030	1" pipe size, angle union	1 Stpi	19	.421	Ea.	72.50	23.50		96	116
1100	Radiator, balancing, straight, sweat connections									
1110	1/2" pipe size	1 Stpi	24	.333	Ea.	17	18.55		35.55	46.50
1120	3/4" pipe size		20	.400		24	22.50		46.50	59.50
1130	1" pipe size		19	.421		38.50	23.50		62	78
1200	Steam, radiator, supply									
1210	1/2" pipe size, angle union	1 Stpi	24	.333	Ea.	43.50	18.55		62.05	76
1220	3/4" pipe size, angle union		20	.400		47.50	22.50		70	85.50
1230	1" pipe size, angle union		19	.421		54.50	23.50		78	95.50
1240	1-1/4" pipe size, angle union		15	.533		70	29.50		99.50	122
8000	System balancing and shut-off									
8020	Butterfly, quarter turn, calibrated, threaded or solder									
8040	Bronze, -30°F to +350°F, pressure to 175 psi									
8060	1/2" size	1 Stpi	22	.364	Ea.	14.75	20.50		35.25	46.50
8070	3/4" size		20	.400		22.50	22.50		45	58
8080	1" size		19	.421		28.50	23.50		52	66.50
8090	1-1/4" size		15	.533		45.50	29.50		75	95
8100	1-1/2" size		13	.615		56.50	34.50		91	114
8110	2" size		11	.727		68.50	40.50		109	137

23 21 20.62 Liquid Drainers

		Crew	Daily Output	Labor-Hours	Unit	Material	2012 Bare Costs Labor	Equipment	Total	Total Incl O&P
0010	**LIQUID DRAINERS**									
0100	Guided lever type									
0110	Cast iron body, threaded									
0120	1/2" pipe size	1 Stpi	22	.364	Ea.	93.50	20.50		114	134
0130	3/4" pipe size		20	.400		249	22.50		271.50	310
0140	1" pipe size		19	.421		395	23.50		418.50	470
0150	1-1/2" pipe size		11	.727		865	40.50		905.50	1,000
0160	2" pipe size		8	1		865	55.50		920.50	1,025
0200	Forged steel body, threaded									
0210	1/2" pipe size	1 Stpi	18	.444	Ea.	925	25		950	1,075
0220	3/4" pipe size		16	.500		925	28		953	1,075
0230	1" pipe size		14	.571		1,375	32		1,407	1,575
0240	1-1/2" pipe size	Q-5	10	1.600		4,025	80		4,105	4,550
0250	2" pipe size	"	8	2		4,025	100		4,125	4,575
0300	Socket weld									
0310	1/2" pipe size	Q-17	16	1	Ea.	1,075	50	2.31	1,127.31	1,250
0320	3/4" pipe size		14	1.143		1,075	57.50	2.64	1,135.14	1,275
0330	1" pipe size		12	1.333		1,075	67	3.08	1,145.08	1,275
0340	1-1/2" pipe size		9	1.778		4,200	89	4.11	4,293.11	4,750
0350	2" pipe size		7	2.286		4,200	115	5.30	4,320.30	4,775
0400	Flanged									
0410	1/2" pipe size	1 Stpi	12	.667	Ea.	2,200	37		2,237	2,475
0420	3/4" pipe size		10	.800		2,200	44.50		2,244.50	2,500
0430	1" pipe size		7	1.143		2,775	63.50		2,838.50	3,150
0440	1-1/2" pipe size	Q-5	9	1.778		5,625	89		5,714	6,300
0450	2" pipe size	"	7	2.286		5,625	115		5,740	6,350
1000	Fixed lever and snap action type									
1100	Cast iron body, threaded									
1110	1/2" pipe size	1 Stpi	22	.364	Ea.	146	20.50		166.50	192
1120	3/4" pipe size		20	.400		385	22.50		407.50	460
1130	1" pipe size		19	.421		385	23.50		408.50	460
1200	Forged steel body, threaded									

23 21 Hydronic Piping and Pumps

23 21 20 – Hydronic HVAC Piping Specialties

23 21 20.62 Liquid Drainers	Crew	Daily Output	Labor-Hours	Unit	Material	2012 Bare Costs Labor	Equipment	Total	Total Incl O&P
1210	1/2" pipe size	1 Stpi	18	.444	Ea.	1,000	25		1,025	1,150
1220	3/4" pipe size		16	.500		1,000	28		1,028	1,150
1230	1" pipe size		14	.571		2,475	32		2,507	2,775
1240	1-1/4" pipe size		12	.667		2,475	37		2,512	2,775
2000	High pressure high leverage type									
2100	Forged steel body, threaded									
2110	1/2" pipe size	1 Stpi	18	.444	Ea.	1,950	25		1,975	2,200
2120	3/4" pipe size		16	.500		1,950	28		1,978	2,200
2130	1" pipe size		14	.571		3,275	32		3,307	3,675
2140	1-1/4" pipe size		12	.667		3,275	37		3,312	3,675
2150	1-1/2" pipe size	Q-5	10	1.600		4,950	80		5,030	5,575
2160	2" pipe size	"	8	2		4,950	100		5,050	5,600
2200	Socket weld									
2210	1/2" pipe size	Q-17	16	1	Ea.	2,125	50	2.31	2,177.31	2,400
2220	3/4" pipe size		14	1.143		2,125	57.50	2.64	2,185.14	2,425
2230	1" pipe size		12	1.333		3,450	67	3.08	3,520.08	3,900
2240	1-1/4" pipe size		11	1.455		3,450	73	3.36	3,526.36	3,925
2250	1-1/2" pipe size		9	1.778		6,125	89	4.11	6,218.11	6,900
2260	2" pipe size		7	2.286		6,125	115	5.30	6,245.30	6,925
2300	Flanged									
2310	1/2" pipe size	1 Stpi	12	.667	Ea.	2,850	37		2,887	3,175
2320	3/4" pipe size		10	.800		2,850	44.50		2,894.50	3,200
2330	1" pipe size		7	1.143		4,500	63.50		4,563.50	5,050
2340	1-1/4" pipe size		6	1.333		4,500	74.50		4,574.50	5,050
2350	1-1/2" pipe size	Q-5	9	1.778		6,150	89		6,239	6,875
2360	2" pipe size	"	7	2.286		6,150	115		6,265	6,925
3000	Guided lever dual gravity type									
3100	Cast iron body, threaded									
3110	1/2" pipe size	1 Stpi	22	.364	Ea.	360	20.50		380.50	425
3120	3/4" pipe size		20	.400		360	22.50		382.50	430
3130	1" pipe size		19	.421		525	23.50		548.50	610
3140	1-1/2" pipe size		11	.727		1,000	40.50		1,040.50	1,150
3150	2" pipe size		8	1		1,000	55.50		1,055.50	1,175
3200	Forged steel body, threaded									
3210	1/2" pipe size	1 Stpi	18	.444	Ea.	1,075	25		1,100	1,225
3220	3/4" pipe size		16	.500		1,075	28		1,103	1,225
3230	1" pipe size		14	.571		1,600	32		1,632	1,800
3240	1-1/2" pipe size	Q-5	10	1.600		4,225	80		4,305	4,775
3250	2" pipe size	"	8	2		4,225	100		4,325	4,800
3300	Socket weld									
3310	1/2" pipe size	Q-17	16	1	Ea.	1,200	50	2.31	1,252.31	1,400
3320	3/4" pipe size		14	1.143		1,200	57.50	2.64	1,260.14	1,425
3330	1" pipe size		12	1.333		1,750	67	3.08	1,820.08	2,025
3340	1-1/2" pipe size		9	1.778		4,400	89	4.11	4,493.11	4,975
3350	2" pipe size		7	2.286		4,400	115	5.30	4,520.30	5,000
3400	Flanged									
3410	1/2" pipe size	1 Stpi	12	.667	Ea.	1,950	37		1,987	2,200
3420	3/4" pipe size		10	.800		1,950	44.50		1,994.50	2,225
3430	1" pipe size		7	1.143		2,550	63.50		2,613.50	2,900
3440	1-1/2" pipe size	Q-5	9	1.778		5,425	89		5,514	6,075
3450	2" pipe size	"	7	2.286		5,425	115		5,540	6,125

23 21 Hydronic Piping and Pumps

23 21 20 – Hydronic HVAC Piping Specialties

23 21 20.66 Monoflow Tee Fitting

		Crew	Daily Output	Labor-Hours	Unit	Material	2012 Bare Costs Labor	Equipment	Total	Total Incl O&P
0010	**MONOFLOW TEE FITTING**									
1100	For one pipe hydronic, supply and return									
1110	Copper, soldered									
1120	3/4" x 1/2" size	1 Stpi	13	.615	Ea.	18.75	34.50		53.25	72
1130	1" x 1/2" size		12	.667		18.75	37		55.75	76.50
1140	1" x 3/4" size		11	.727		18.75	40.50		59.25	81.50
1150	1-1/4" x 1/2" size		11	.727		19.50	40.50		60	82.50
1160	1-1/4" x 3/4" size		10	.800		19.50	44.50		64	88.50
1170	1-1/2" x 3/4" size		10	.800		27.50	44.50		72	97
1180	1-1/2" x 1" size		9	.889		27.50	49.50		77	105
1190	2" x 3/4" size		9	.889		42.50	49.50		92	121
1200	2" x 1" size	▼	8	1	▼	42.50	55.50		98	131

23 21 20.70 Steam Traps

		Crew	Daily Output	Labor-Hours	Unit	Material	2012 Bare Costs Labor	Equipment	Total	Total Incl O&P
0010	**STEAM TRAPS**									
0030	Cast iron body, threaded									
0040	Inverted bucket									
0050	1/2" pipe size	1 Stpi	12	.667	Ea.	136	37		173	205
0070	3/4" pipe size		10	.800		236	44.50		280.50	325
0100	1" pipe size		9	.889		365	49.50		414.50	475
0120	1-1/4" pipe size		8	1		550	55.50		605.50	690
0130	1-1/2" pipe size		7	1.143		690	63.50		753.50	855
0140	2" pipe size	▼	6	1.333	▼	1,075	74.50		1,149.50	1,300
0200	With thermic vent & check valve									
0202	1/2" pipe size	1 Stpi	12	.667	Ea.	160	37		197	232
0204	3/4" pipe size		10	.800		271	44.50		315.50	365
0206	1" pipe size		9	.889		395	49.50		444.50	510
0208	1-1/4" pipe size		8	1		595	55.50		650.50	740
0210	1-1/2" pipe size		7	1.143		660	63.50		723.50	820
0212	2" pipe size	▼	6	1.333	▼	1,000	74.50		1,074.50	1,200
1000	Float & thermostatic, 15 psi									
1010	3/4" pipe size	1 Stpi	16	.500	Ea.	109	28		137	162
1020	1" pipe size		15	.533		131	29.50		160.50	189
1030	1-1/4" pipe size		13	.615		159	34.50		193.50	227
1040	1-1/2" pipe size		9	.889		231	49.50		280.50	330
1060	2" pipe size	▼	6	1.333		425	74.50		499.50	580
1100	For vacuum breaker, add				▼	58			58	63.50
1110	Differential condensate controller									
1120	With union and manual metering valve									
1130	1/2" pipe size	1 Stpi	24	.333	Ea.	510	18.55		528.55	590
1140	3/4" pipe size		20	.400		595	22.50		617.50	690
1150	1" pipe size		19	.421		800	23.50		823.50	915
1160	1-1/4" pipe size		15	.533		1,075	29.50		1,104.50	1,225
1170	1-1/2" pipe size		13	.615		1,300	34.50		1,334.50	1,475
1180	2" pipe size	▼	11	.727	▼	1,700	40.50		1,740.50	1,900
1290	Brass body, threaded									
1300	Thermostatic, angle union, 25 psi									
1310	1/2" pipe size	1 Stpi	24	.333	Ea.	57	18.55		75.55	90.50
1320	3/4" pipe size		20	.400		86.50	22.50		109	129
1330	1" pipe size	▼	19	.421		128	23.50		151.50	176
1990	Carbon steel body, threaded									
2000	Controlled disc, integral strainer & blow down									
2010	Threaded									

23 21 20.70 Steam Traps		Crew	Daily Output	Labor-Hours	Unit	Material	2012 Bare Costs Labor	Equipment	Total	Total Incl O&P
2020	3/8" pipe size	1 Stpi	24	.333	Ea.	229	18.55		247.55	280
2030	1/2" pipe size		24	.333		229	18.55		247.55	280
2040	3/4" pipe size		20	.400		305	22.50		327.50	375
2050	1" pipe size		19	.421		395	23.50		418.50	470
2100	Socket weld									
2110	3/8" pipe size	Q-17	17	.941	Ea.	274	47	2.17	323.17	375
2120	1/2" pipe size		16	1		274	50	2.31	326.31	380
2130	3/4" pipe size		14	1.143		355	57.50	2.64	415.14	480
2140	1" pipe size		12	1.333		445	67	3.08	515.08	595
2170	Flanged, 600 lb. ASA									
2180	3/8" pipe size	1 Stpi	12	.667	Ea.	615	37		652	735
2190	1/2" pipe size		12	.667		615	37		652	735
2200	3/4" pipe size		10	.800		740	44.50		784.50	875
2210	1" pipe size		7	1.143		875	63.50		938.50	1,050
5000	Forged steel body									
5010	Inverted bucket									
5020	Threaded									
5030	1/2" pipe size	1 Stpi	12	.667	Ea.	410	37		447	505
5040	3/4" pipe size		10	.800		705	44.50		749.50	845
5050	1" pipe size		9	.889		1,050	49.50		1,099.50	1,250
5060	1-1/4" pipe size		8	1		1,550	55.50		1,605.50	1,775
5070	1-1/2" pipe size		7	1.143		2,175	63.50		2,238.50	2,500
5080	2" pipe size		6	1.333		3,825	74.50		3,899.50	4,325
5100	Socket weld									
5110	1/2" pipe size	Q-17	16	1	Ea.	490	50	2.31	542.31	620
5120	3/4" pipe size		14	1.143		790	57.50	2.64	850.14	960
5130	1" pipe size		12	1.333		1,150	67	3.08	1,220.08	1,350
5140	1-1/4" pipe size		10	1.600		1,625	80	3.70	1,708.70	1,900
5150	1-1/2" pipe size		9	1.778		2,275	89	4.11	2,368.11	2,650
5160	2" pipe size		7	2.286		3,925	115	5.30	4,045.30	4,500
5200	Flanged									
5210	1/2" pipe size	1 Stpi	12	.667	Ea.	755	37		792	885
5220	3/4" pipe size		10	.800		1,250	44.50		1,294.50	1,450
5230	1" pipe size		7	1.143		1,675	63.50		1,738.50	1,950
5240	1-1/4" pipe size		6	1.333		2,275	74.50		2,349.50	2,600
5250	1-1/2" pipe size	Q-5	9	1.778		2,925	89		3,014	3,350
5260	2" pipe size	"	7	2.286		4,600	115		4,715	5,225
6000	Stainless steel body									
6010	Inverted bucket									
6020	Threaded									
6030	1/2" pipe size	1 Stpi	12	.667	Ea.	136	37		173	205
6040	3/4" pipe size		10	.800		178	44.50		222.50	263
6050	1" pipe size		9	.889		635	49.50		684.50	770
6100	Threaded with thermic vent									
6110	1/2" pipe size	1 Stpi	12	.667	Ea.	155	37		192	226
6120	3/4" pipe size		10	.800		199	44.50		243.50	286
6130	1" pipe size		9	.889		660	49.50		709.50	800
6200	Threaded with check valve									
6210	1/2" pipe size	1 Stpi	12	.667	Ea.	129	37		166	198
6220	3/4" pipe size	"	10	.800	"	264	44.50		308.50	355
6300	Socket weld									
6310	1/2" pipe size	Q-17	16	1	Ea.	157	50	2.31	209.31	251
6320	3/4" pipe size	"	14	1.143	"	203	57.50	2.64	263.14	315

23 21 Hydronic Piping and Pumps

23 21 20 – Hydronic HVAC Piping Specialties

23 21 20.74 Strainers, Basket Type	Crew	Daily Output	Labor-Hours	Unit	Material	2012 Bare Costs Labor	Equipment	Total	Total Incl O&P
0010 **STRAINERS, BASKET TYPE**, Perforated stainless steel basket									
0100 Brass or monel available									
2000 Simplex style									
2300 Bronze body									
2320 Screwed, 3/8" pipe size	1 Stpi	22	.364	Ea.	157	20.50		177.50	204
2340 1/2" pipe size		20	.400		252	22.50		274.50	310
2360 3/4" pipe size		17	.471		335	26		361	410
2380 1" pipe size		15	.533		335	29.50		364.50	415
2400 1-1/4" pipe size		13	.615		480	34.50		514.50	580
2420 1-1/2" pipe size		12	.667		480	37		517	585
2440 2" pipe size		10	.800		715	44.50		759.50	850
2460 2-1/2" pipe size	Q-5	15	1.067		705	53.50		758.50	860
2480 3" pipe size	"	14	1.143		1,025	57.50		1,082.50	1,200
2600 Flanged, 2" pipe size	1 Stpi	6	1.333		750	74.50		824.50	935
2620 2-1/2" pipe size	Q-5	4.50	3.556		1,175	178		1,353	1,575
2640 3" pipe size		3.50	4.571		1,325	229		1,554	1,800
2660 4" pipe size		3	5.333		2,250	267		2,517	2,875
2680 5" pipe size	Q-6	3.40	7.059		3,450	365		3,815	4,325
2700 6" pipe size		3	8		4,375	415		4,790	5,425
2710 8" pipe size		2.50	9.600		7,100	500		7,600	8,575
3600 Iron body									
3700 Screwed, 3/8" pipe size	1 Stpi	22	.364	Ea.	98.50	20.50		119	140
3720 1/2" pipe size		20	.400		102	22.50		124.50	146
3740 3/4" pipe size		17	.471		130	26		156	183
3760 1" pipe size		15	.533		133	29.50		162.50	191
3780 1-1/4" pipe size		13	.615		173	34.50		207.50	242
3800 1-1/2" pipe size		12	.667		191	37		228	266
3820 2" pipe size		10	.800		228	44.50		272.50	320
3840 2-1/2" pipe size	Q-5	15	1.067		305	53.50		358.50	415
3860 3" pipe size	"	14	1.143		370	57.50		427.50	490
4000 Flanged, 2" pipe size	1 Stpi	6	1.333		355	74.50		429.50	500
4020 2-1/2" pipe size	Q-5	4.50	3.556		475	178		653	795
4040 3" pipe size		3.50	4.571		500	229		729	895
4060 4" pipe size		3	5.333		760	267		1,027	1,250
4080 5" pipe size	Q-6	3.40	7.059		1,150	365		1,515	1,825
4100 6" pipe size		3	8		1,475	415		1,890	2,250
4120 8" pipe size		2.50	9.600		2,675	500		3,175	3,700
4140 10" pipe size		2.20	10.909		5,875	565		6,440	7,325
6000 Cast steel body									
6400 Screwed, 1" pipe size	1 Stpi	15	.533	Ea.	195	29.50		224.50	260
6410 1-1/4" pipe size		13	.615		295	34.50		329.50	375
6420 1-1/2" pipe size		12	.667		320	37		357	405
6440 2" pipe size		10	.800		405	44.50		449.50	510
6460 2-1/2" pipe size	Q-5	15	1.067		570	53.50		623.50	710
6480 3" pipe size	"	14	1.143		750	57.50		807.50	910
6560 Flanged, 2" pipe size	1 Stpi	6	1.333		655	74.50		729.50	830
6580 2-1/2" pipe size	Q-5	4.50	3.556		980	178		1,158	1,350
6600 3" pipe size		3.50	4.571		1,050	229		1,279	1,500
6620 4" pipe size		3	5.333		1,500	267		1,767	2,025
6640 6" pipe size	Q-6	3	8		2,725	415		3,140	3,625
6660 8" pipe size	"	2.50	9.600		4,400	500		4,900	5,600
7000 Stainless steel body									

23 21 Hydronic Piping and Pumps

23 21 20 – Hydronic HVAC Piping Specialties

23 21 20.74 Strainers, Basket Type		Crew	Daily Output	Labor-Hours	Unit	Material	2012 Bare Costs Labor	Equipment	Total	Total Incl O&P
7200	Screwed, 1" pipe size	1 Stpi	15	.533	Ea.	283	29.50		312.50	355
7210	1-1/4" pipe size		13	.615		440	34.50		474.50	535
7220	1-1/2" pipe size		12	.667		440	37		477	540
7240	2" pipe size		10	.800		655	44.50		699.50	785
7260	2-1/2" pipe size	Q-5	15	1.067		925	53.50		978.50	1,100
7280	3" pipe size	"	14	1.143		1,275	57.50		1,332.50	1,475
7400	Flanged, 2" pipe size	1 Stpi	6	1.333		1,075	74.50		1,149.50	1,275
7420	2-1/2" pipe size	Q-5	4.50	3.556		1,950	178		2,128	2,400
7440	3" pipe size		3.50	4.571		1,975	229		2,204	2,525
7460	4" pipe size		3	5.333		3,125	267		3,392	3,825
7480	6" pipe size	Q-6	3	8		5,425	415		5,840	6,600
7500	8" pipe size	"	2.50	9.600		15,000	500		15,500	17,300
8100	Duplex style									
8200	Bronze body									
8240	Screwed, 3/4" pipe size	1 Stpi	16	.500	Ea.	1,100	28		1,128	1,275
8260	1" pipe size		14	.571		1,100	32		1,132	1,275
8280	1-1/4" pipe size		12	.667		2,175	37		2,212	2,450
8300	1-1/2" pipe size		11	.727		2,175	40.50		2,215.50	2,450
8320	2" pipe size		9	.889		3,525	49.50		3,574.50	3,950
8340	2-1/2" pipe size	Q-5	14	1.143		4,550	57.50		4,607.50	5,075
8420	Flanged, 2" pipe size	1 Stpi	6	1.333		3,775	74.50		3,849.50	4,250
8440	2-1/2" pipe size	Q-5	4.50	3.556		5,225	178		5,403	6,025
8460	3" pipe size		3.50	4.571		5,700	229		5,929	6,600
8480	4" pipe size		3	5.333		8,175	267		8,442	9,375
8500	5" pipe size	Q-6	3.40	7.059		18,200	365		18,565	20,600
8520	6" pipe size	"	3	8		18,200	415		18,615	20,600
8700	Iron body									
8740	Screwed, 3/4" pipe size	1 Stpi	16	.500	Ea.	665	28		693	770
8760	1" pipe size		14	.571		665	32		697	780
8780	1-1/4" pipe size		12	.667		1,175	37		1,212	1,325
8800	1-1/2" pipe size		11	.727		1,175	40.50		1,215.50	1,325
8820	2" pipe size		9	.889		1,975	49.50		2,024.50	2,250
8840	2-1/2" pipe size	Q-5	14	1.143		2,175	57.50		2,232.50	2,475
9000	Flanged, 2" pipe size	1 Stpi	6	1.333		2,100	74.50		2,174.50	2,425
9020	2-1/2" pipe size	Q-5	4.50	3.556		2,250	178		2,428	2,750
9040	3" pipe size		3.50	4.571		2,450	229		2,679	3,050
9060	4" pipe size		3	5.333		4,150	267		4,417	4,950
9080	5" pipe size	Q-6	3.40	7.059		8,200	365		8,565	9,575
9100	6" pipe size		3	8		8,200	415		8,615	9,650
9120	8" pipe size		2.50	9.600		15,000	500		15,500	17,300
9140	10" pipe size		2.20	10.909		20,800	565		21,365	23,800
9160	12" pipe size		1.70	14.118		23,100	735		23,835	26,500
9170	14" pipe size		1.40	17.143		28,000	890		28,890	32,200
9180	16" pipe size		1	24		35,100	1,250		36,350	40,500
9300	Cast steel body									
9340	Screwed, 1" pipe size	1 Stpi	14	.571	Ea.	1,350	32		1,382	1,525
9360	1-1/2" pipe size		11	.727		2,175	40.50		2,215.50	2,450
9380	2" pipe size		9	.889		2,875	49.50		2,924.50	3,250
9460	Flanged, 2" pipe size		6	1.333		3,225	74.50		3,299.50	3,650
9480	2-1/2" pipe size	Q-5	4.50	3.556		5,200	178		5,378	5,975
9500	3" pipe size		3.50	4.571		5,650	229		5,879	6,575
9520	4" pipe size		3	5.333		6,975	267		7,242	8,075
9540	6" pipe size	Q-6	3	8		13,100	415		13,515	15,000

295

23 21 Hydronic Piping and Pumps

23 21 20 – Hydronic HVAC Piping Specialties

23 21 20.74 Strainers, Basket Type

		Crew	Daily Output	Labor-Hours	Unit	Material	2012 Bare Costs Labor	Equipment	Total	Total Incl O&P
9560	8" pipe size	Q-6	2.50	9.600	Ea.	31,500	500		32,000	35,400
9700	Stainless steel body									
9740	Screwed, 1" pipe size	1 Stpi	14	.571	Ea.	1,900	32		1,932	2,125
9760	1-1/2" pipe size		11	.727		2,850	40.50		2,890.50	3,200
9780	2" pipe size		9	.889		4,000	49.50		4,049.50	4,475
9860	Flanged, 2" pipe size		6	1.333		4,350	74.50		4,424.50	4,900
9880	2-1/2" pipe size	Q-5	4.50	3.556		7,300	178		7,478	8,300
9900	3" pipe size		3.50	4.571		7,950	229		8,179	9,100
9920	4" pipe size		3	5.333		10,400	267		10,667	11,800
9940	6" pipe size	Q-6	3	8		15,800	415		16,215	18,000
9960	8" pipe size	"	2.50	9.600		44,200	500		44,700	49,400

23 21 20.76 Strainers, Y Type, Bronze Body

		Crew	Daily Output	Labor-Hours	Unit	Material	2012 Bare Costs Labor	Equipment	Total	Total Incl O&P
0010	**STRAINERS, Y TYPE, BRONZE BODY**									
0050	Screwed, 125 lb., 1/4" pipe size	1 Stpi	24	.333	Ea.	22	18.55		40.55	52
0070	3/8" pipe size		24	.333		29	18.55		47.55	59.50
0100	1/2" pipe size		20	.400		29	22.50		51.50	65
0120	3/4" pipe size		19	.421		32.50	23.50		56	71.50
0140	1" pipe size		17	.471		38.50	26		64.50	81.50
0150	1-1/4" pipe size		15	.533		77.50	29.50		107	130
0160	1-1/2" pipe size		14	.571		83	32		115	140
0180	2" pipe size		13	.615		110	34.50		144.50	173
0182	3" pipe size		12	.667		835	37		872	975
0200	300 lb., 2-1/2" pipe size	Q-5	17	.941		485	47		532	605
0220	3" pipe size		16	1		960	50		1,010	1,125
0240	4" pipe size		15	1.067		2,200	53.50		2,253.50	2,475
0500	For 300 lb. rating 1/4" thru 2", add					15%				
1000	Flanged, 150 lb., 1-1/2" pipe size	1 Stpi	11	.727	Ea.	450	40.50		490.50	555
1020	2" pipe size	"	8	1		610	55.50		665.50	755
1030	2-1/2" pipe size	Q-5	5	3.200		905	160		1,065	1,225
1040	3" pipe size		4.50	3.556		1,125	178		1,303	1,500
1060	4" pipe size		3	5.333		1,700	267		1,967	2,250
1080	5" pipe size	Q-6	3.40	7.059		1,700	365		2,065	2,400
1100	6" pipe size		3	8		3,225	415		3,640	4,175
1106	8" pipe size		2.60	9.231		3,550	480		4,030	4,625
1500	For 300 lb. rating, add					40%				

23 21 20.78 Strainers, Y Type, Iron Body

		Crew	Daily Output	Labor-Hours	Unit	Material	2012 Bare Costs Labor	Equipment	Total	Total Incl O&P
0010	**STRAINERS, Y TYPE, IRON BODY**									
0050	Screwed, 250 lb., 1/4" pipe size	1 Stpi	20	.400	Ea.	10.55	22.50		33.05	45
0070	3/8" pipe size		20	.400		10.55	22.50		33.05	45
0100	1/2" pipe size		20	.400		10.55	22.50		33.05	45
0120	3/4" pipe size		18	.444		12.50	25		37.50	51.50
0140	1" pipe size		16	.500		17.30	28		45.30	61
0150	1-1/4" pipe size		15	.533		23	29.50		52.50	70.50
0160	1-1/2" pipe size		12	.667		28.50	37		65.50	87
0180	2" pipe size		8	1		42.50	55.50		98	131
0200	2-1/2" pipe size	Q-5	12	1.333		255	67		322	380
0220	3" pipe size		11	1.455		275	73		348	415
0240	4" pipe size		5	3.200		465	160		625	755
0500	For galvanized body, add					50%				
1000	Flanged, 125 lb., 1-1/2" pipe size	1 Stpi	11	.727	Ea.	147	40.50		187.50	223
1020	2" pipe size	"	8	1		108	55.50		163.50	203
1030	2-1/2" pipe size	Q-5	5	3.200		110	160		270	365

23 21 Hydronic Piping and Pumps

23 21 20 – Hydronic HVAC Piping Specialties

23 21 20.78 Strainers, Y Type, Iron Body

		Crew	Daily Output	Labor-Hours	Unit	Material	2012 Bare Costs Labor	Equipment	Total	Total Incl O&P
1040	3" pipe size	Q-5	4.50	3.556	Ea.	143	178		321	425
1060	4" pipe size		3	5.333		260	267		527	690
1080	5" pipe size	Q-6	3.40	7.059		405	365		770	1,000
1100	6" pipe size		3	8		495	415		910	1,175
1120	8" pipe size		2.50	9.600		830	500		1,330	1,675
1140	10" pipe size		2	12		1,600	625		2,225	2,700
1160	12" pipe size		1.70	14.118		2,375	735		3,110	3,725
1170	14" pipe size		1.30	18.462		4,400	960		5,360	6,300
1180	16" pipe size		1	24		6,225	1,250		7,475	8,725
1500	For 250 lb. rating, add					20%				
2000	For galvanized body, add					50%				
2500	For steel body, add					40%				

23 21 20.80 Suction Diffusers

		Crew	Daily Output	Labor-Hours	Unit	Material	2012 Bare Costs Labor	Equipment	Total	Total Incl O&P
0010	**SUCTION DIFFUSERS**									
0100	Cast iron body with integral straightening vanes, strainer									
1000	Flanged									
1010	2" inlet, 1-1/2" pump side	1 Stpi	6	1.333	Ea.	335	74.50		409.50	475
1020	2" pump side	"	5	1.600		345	89		434	515
1030	3" inlet, 2" pump side	Q-5	6.50	2.462		370	123		493	595
1040	2-1/2" pump side		5.30	3.019		620	151		771	910
1050	3" pump side		4.50	3.556		625	178		803	955
1060	4" inlet, 3" pump side		3.50	4.571		730	229		959	1,150
1070	4" pump side		3	5.333		825	267		1,092	1,300
1080	5" inlet, 4" pump side	Q-6	3.80	6.316		965	330		1,295	1,575
1090	5" pump side		3.40	7.059		1,150	365		1,515	1,825
1100	6" inlet, 4" pump side		3.30	7.273		1,000	380		1,380	1,675
1110	5" pump side		3.10	7.742		1,200	400		1,600	1,925
1120	6" pump side		3	8		1,275	415		1,690	2,025
1130	8" inlet, 6" pump side		2.70	8.889		1,375	460		1,835	2,200
1140	8" pump side		2.50	9.600		2,375	500		2,875	3,350
1150	10" inlet, 6" pump side		2.40	10		3,275	520		3,795	4,400
1160	8" pump side		2.30	10.435		3,700	540		4,240	4,875
1170	10" pump side		2.20	10.909		3,975	565		4,540	5,225
1180	12" inlet, 8" pump side		2	12		4,200	625		4,825	5,575
1190	10" pump side		1.80	13.333		4,650	695		5,345	6,175
1200	12" pump side		1.70	14.118		5,225	735		5,960	6,850
1210	14" inlet, 12" pump side		1.50	16		6,775	830		7,605	8,700
1220	14" pump side		1.30	18.462		6,925	960		7,885	9,050

23 21 20.84 Thermoflo Indicator

		Crew	Daily Output	Labor-Hours	Unit	Material	2012 Bare Costs Labor	Equipment	Total	Total Incl O&P
0010	**THERMOFLO INDICATOR**, For balancing									
1000	Sweat connections, 1-1/4" pipe size	1 Stpi	12	.667	Ea.	585	37		622	700
1020	1-1/2" pipe size		10	.800		595	44.50		639.50	720
1040	2" pipe size		8	1		625	55.50		680.50	775
1060	2-1/2" pipe size		7	1.143		955	63.50		1,018.50	1,150
2000	Flange connections, 3" pipe size	Q-5	5	3.200		1,150	160		1,310	1,500
2020	4" pipe size		4	4		1,375	201		1,576	1,800
2030	5" pipe size		3.50	4.571		1,725	229		1,954	2,225
2040	6" pipe size		3	5.333		1,850	267		2,117	2,425
2060	8" pipe size		2	8		2,225	400		2,625	3,050

23 21 20.88 Venturi Flow

		Crew	Daily Output	Labor-Hours	Unit	Material	2012 Bare Costs Labor	Equipment	Total	Total Incl O&P
0010	**VENTURI FLOW**, Measuring device									
0050	1/2" diameter	1 Stpi	24	.333	Ea.	281	18.55		299.55	340

23 21 Hydronic Piping and Pumps

23 21 20 – Hydronic HVAC Piping Specialties

23 21 20.88 Venturi Flow

		Crew	Daily Output	Labor-Hours	Unit	Material	2012 Bare Costs Labor	Equipment	Total	Total Incl O&P
0100	3/4" diameter	1 Stpi	20	.400	Ea.	257	22.50		279.50	315
0120	1" diameter		19	.421		276	23.50		299.50	340
0140	1-1/4" diameter		15	.533		340	29.50		369.50	420
0160	1-1/2" diameter		13	.615		355	34.50		389.50	440
0180	2" diameter		11	.727		365	40.50		405.50	465
0200	2-1/2" diameter	Q-5	16	1		500	50		550	625
0220	3" diameter		14	1.143		515	57.50		572.50	655
0240	4" diameter		11	1.455		775	73		848	960
0260	5" diameter	Q-6	4	6		1,025	310		1,335	1,600
0280	6" diameter		3.50	6.857		1,125	355		1,480	1,800
0300	8" diameter		3	8		1,450	415		1,865	2,225
0320	10" diameter		2	12		3,425	625		4,050	4,725
0330	12" diameter		1.80	13.333		4,950	695		5,645	6,500
0340	14" diameter		1.60	15		5,600	780		6,380	7,350
0350	16" diameter		1.40	17.143		6,250	890		7,140	8,225
0500	For meter, add					2,125			2,125	2,350

23 21 20.94 Weld End Ball Joints

		Crew	Daily Output	Labor-Hours	Unit	Material	2012 Bare Costs Labor	Equipment	Total	Total Incl O&P
0010	**WELD END BALL JOINTS**, Steel									
0050	2-1/2" diameter	Q-17	13	1.231	Ea.	615	61.50	2.84	679.34	775
0100	3" diameter		12	1.333		720	67	3.08	790.08	895
0120	4" diameter		11	1.455		1,175	73	3.36	1,251.36	1,400
0140	5" diameter	Q-18	14	1.714		1,350	89	2.64	1,441.64	1,600
0160	6" diameter		12	2		2,000	104	3.08	2,107.08	2,350
0180	8" diameter		9	2.667		3,025	139	4.11	3,168.11	3,550
0200	10" diameter		8	3		4,075	156	4.62	4,235.62	4,725
0220	12" diameter		6	4		6,500	208	6.15	6,714.15	7,475

23 21 20.98 Zone Valves

		Crew	Daily Output	Labor-Hours	Unit	Material	2012 Bare Costs Labor	Equipment	Total	Total Incl O&P
0010	**ZONE VALVES**									
1000	Bronze body									
1010	2 way, 125 psi									
1020	Standard, 65' pump head									
1030	1/2" soldered	1 Stpi	24	.333	Ea.	120	18.55		138.55	160
1040	3/4" soldered		20	.400		120	22.50		142.50	166
1050	1" soldered		19	.421		129	23.50		152.50	178
1060	1-1/4" soldered		15	.533		151	29.50		180.50	211
1200	High head, 125' pump head									
1210	1/2" soldered	1 Stpi	24	.333	Ea.	164	18.55		182.55	208
1220	3/4" soldered		20	.400		169	22.50		191.50	220
1230	1" soldered		19	.421		185	23.50		208.50	239
1300	Geothermal, 150' pump head									
1310	3/4" soldered	1 Stpi	20	.400	Ea.	195	22.50		217.50	248
1320	1" soldered		19	.421		206	23.50		229.50	263
1330	3/4" threaded		20	.400		171	22.50		193.50	222
3000	3 way, 125 psi									
3200	Bypass, 65' pump head									
3210	1/2" soldered	1 Stpi	24	.333	Ea.	195	18.55		213.55	242
3220	3/4" soldered		20	.400		176	22.50		198.50	228
3230	1" soldered		19	.421		201	23.50		224.50	257
9000	Transformer, for up to 3 zone valves		20	.400		24.50	22.50		47	60.50

23 21 23.13 In-Line Centrifugal Hydronic Pumps	Crew	Daily Output	Labor-Hours	Unit	Material	2012 Bare Costs Labor	Equipment	Total	Total Incl O&P
0010 **IN-LINE CENTRIFUGAL HYDRONIC PUMPS**									
0600 Bronze, sweat connections, 1/40 HP, in line									
0640 3/4" size	Q-1	16	1	Ea.	206	49		255	300
1000 Flange connection, 3/4" to 1-1/2" size									
1040 1/12 HP	Q-1	6	2.667	Ea.	530	131		661	785
1060 1/8 HP		6	2.667		915	131		1,046	1,200
1100 1/3 HP		6	2.667		1,025	131		1,156	1,325
1140 2" size, 1/6 HP		5	3.200		1,325	157		1,482	1,675
1180 2-1/2" size, 1/4 HP		5	3.200		1,675	157		1,832	2,075
1220 3" size, 1/4 HP		4	4		1,750	197		1,947	2,225
1260 1/3 HP		4	4		2,150	197		2,347	2,675
1300 1/2 HP		4	4		2,200	197		2,397	2,700
1340 3/4 HP		4	4		2,400	197		2,597	2,925
1380 1 HP		4	4		3,875	197		4,072	4,550
2000 Cast iron, flange connection									
2040 3/4" to 1-1/2" size, in line, 1/12 HP	Q-1	6	2.667	Ea.	345	131		476	580
2060 1/8 HP		6	2.667		575	131		706	830
2100 1/3 HP		6	2.667		640	131		771	905
2140 2" size, 1/6 HP		5	3.200		700	157		857	1,000
2180 2-1/2" size, 1/4 HP		5	3.200		905	157		1,062	1,225
2220 3" size, 1/4 HP		4	4		920	197		1,117	1,300
2260 1/3 HP		4	4		1,250	197		1,447	1,675
2300 1/2 HP		4	4		1,300	197		1,497	1,725
2340 3/4 HP		4	4		1,500	197		1,697	1,950
2380 1 HP		4	4		2,150	197		2,347	2,675
2600 For non-ferrous impeller, add					3%				
3000 High head, bronze impeller									
3030 1-1/2" size 1/2 HP	Q-1	5	3.200	Ea.	1,100	157		1,257	1,425
3040 1-1/2" size 3/4 HP		5	3.200		1,175	157		1,332	1,525
3050 2" size 1 HP		4	4		1,450	197		1,647	1,900
3090 2" size 1-1/2 HP		4	4		1,775	197		1,972	2,275
4000 Close coupled, end suction, bronze impeller									
4040 1-1/2" size, 1-1/2 HP, to 40 GPM	Q-1	3	5.333	Ea.	2,075	262		2,337	2,675
4090 2" size, 2 HP, to 50 GPM		3	5.333		2,450	262		2,712	3,100
4100 2" size, 3 HP, to 90 GPM		2.30	6.957		2,550	340		2,890	3,325
4190 2-1/2" size, 3 HP, to 150 GPM		2	8		2,750	395		3,145	3,625
4300 3" size, 5 HP, to 225 GPM		1.80	8.889		2,900	435		3,335	3,850
4410 3" size, 10 HP, to 350 GPM		1.60	10		4,250	490		4,740	5,425
4420 4" size, 7-1/2 HP, to 350 GPM		1.60	10		4,125	490		4,615	5,275
4520 4" size, 10 HP, to 600 GPM	Q-2	1.70	14.118		4,700	720		5,420	6,250
4530 5" size, 15 HP, to 1000 GPM		1.70	14.118		4,725	720		5,445	6,275
4610 5" size, 20 HP, to 1350 GPM		1.50	16		5,025	815		5,840	6,750
4620 5" size, 25 HP, to 1550 GPM		1.50	16		6,850	815		7,665	8,750
5000 Base mounted, bronze impeller, coupling guard									
5040 1-1/2" size, 1-1/2 HP, to 40 GPM	Q-1	2.30	6.957	Ea.	5,600	340		5,940	6,675
5090 2" size, 2 HP, to 50 GPM		2.30	6.957		6,200	340		6,540	7,350
5100 2" size, 3 HP, to 90 GPM		2	8		6,575	395		6,970	7,825
5190 2-1/2" size, 3 HP, to 150 GPM		1.80	8.889		7,150	435		7,585	8,500
5300 3" size, 5 HP, to 225 GPM		1.60	10		7,475	490		7,965	8,975
5410 4" size, 5 HP, to 350 GPM		1.50	10.667		8,150	525		8,675	9,775
5420 4" size, 7-1/2 HP, to 350 GPM		1.50	10.667		8,400	525		8,925	10,000
5520 5" size, 10 HP, to 600 GPM	Q-2	1.60	15		10,400	765		11,165	12,700

23 21 23 – Hydronic Pumps

23 21 23.13 In-Line Centrifugal Hydronic Pumps		Crew	Daily Output	Labor-Hours	Unit	Material	2012 Bare Costs Labor	Equipment	Total	Total Incl O&P
5530	5" size, 15 HP, to 1000 GPM	Q-2	1.60	15	Ea.	11,700	765		12,465	14,100
5610	6" size, 20 HP, to 1350 GPM	↓	1.40	17.143		12,100	875		12,975	14,600
5620	6" size, 25 HP, to 1550 GPM	↓	1.40	17.143	↓	13,400	875		14,275	16,000
5800	The above pump capacities are based on 1800 RPM,									
5810	at a 60 foot head. Increasing the RPM									
5820	or decreasing the head will increase the GPM.									

23 21 29 – Automatic Condensate Pump Units

23 21 29.10 Condensate Removal Pump System

0010	**CONDENSATE REMOVAL PUMP SYSTEM**									
0020	Pump with 1 gal. ABS tank	G								
0100	115 V	G								
0120	1/50 HP, 200 GPH	G	1 Stpi	12	.667	Ea.	185	37		222	260
0140	1/18 HP, 270 GPH	G		10	.800		205	44.50		249.50	293
0160	1/5 HP, 450 GPH	G	↓	8	1	↓	445	55.50		500.50	570
0200	230 V	G								
0240	1/18 HP, 270 GPH	G	1 Stpi	10	.800	Ea.	192	44.50		236.50	278
0260	1/5 HP, 450 GPH	G	"	8	1	"	485	55.50		540.50	620

23 22 13 – Steam and Condensate Heating Piping

23 22 13.23 Aboveground Steam and Condensate Piping

		Crew	Daily Output	Labor-Hours	Unit	Material	Labor	Equipment	Total	Total Incl O&P
0010	**ABOVEGROUND STEAM AND CONDENSATE HEATING PIPING**									
0020	Condensate meter									
0100	500 lb. per hour	1 Stpi	14	.571	Ea.	2,350	32		2,382	2,650
0140	1500 lb. per hour		7	1.143		2,550	63.50		2,613.50	2,900
0160	3000 lb. per hour	↓	5	1.600		3,425	89		3,514	3,875
0200	12,000 lb. per hour	Q-5	3.50	4.571	↓	4,575	229		4,804	5,375

23 22 23 – Steam Condensate Pumps

23 22 23.10 Condensate Return System

		Crew	Daily Output	Labor-Hours	Unit	Material	Labor	Equipment	Total	Total Incl O&P
0010	**CONDENSATE RETURN SYSTEM**									
2000	Simplex									
2010	With pump, motor, CI receiver, float switch									
2020	3/4 HP, 15 GPM	Q-1	1.80	8.889	Ea.	5,825	435		6,260	7,050
2100	Duplex									
2110	With 2 pumps and motors, CI receiver, float switch, alternator									
2120	3/4 HP, 15 GPM, 15 gal. CI rcvr	Q-1	1.40	11.429	Ea.	6,350	560		6,910	7,825
2130	1 HP, 25 GPM		1.20	13.333		7,625	655		8,280	9,375
2140	1-1/2 HP, 45 GPM		1	16		8,850	785		9,635	10,900
2150	1-1/2 HP, 60 GPM	↓	1	16	↓	9,925	785		10,710	12,100

23 22 23.23 Pumps, Pneumatic Ejector

		Crew	Daily Output	Labor-Hours	Unit	Material	Labor	Equipment	Total	Total Incl O&P
0010	**PUMPS, PNEUMATIC EJECTOR**									
0020	With steel receiver, level controls, inlet/outlet gate/check valves									
0030	Cross connect. not incl. compressor, fittings or piping									
0040	Duplex									
0050	30 GPM	Q-2	1.70	14.118	Ea.	29,500	720		30,220	33,600
0060	50 GPM		1.56	15.385		30,500	785		31,285	34,800
0070	100 GPM		1.30	18.462		60,000	940		60,940	67,500
0080	150 GPM		1.10	21.818		70,000	1,100		71,100	78,500
0090	200 GPM	↓	.85	28.235		75,000	1,450		76,450	84,500
0100	250 GPM	Q-3	.91	35.165	↓	80,000	1,825		81,825	91,000

23 22 Steam and Condensate Piping and Pumps

23 22 23 – Steam Condensate Pumps

23 22 23.23 Pumps, Pneumatic Ejector	Crew	Daily Output	Labor-Hours	Unit	Material	2012 Bare Costs Labor	Equipment	Total	Total Incl O&P
0110 300 GPM	Q-3	.57	56.140	Ea.	130,000	2,925		132,925	147,500

23 23 Refrigerant Piping

23 23 13 – Refrigerant Piping Valves

23 23 13.10 Valves

		Crew	Daily Output	Labor-Hours	Unit	Material	2012 Bare Costs Labor	Equipment	Total	Total Incl O&P
0010	**VALVES**									
8100	Check valve, soldered									
8110	5/8"	1 Stpi	36	.222	Ea.	115	12.40		127.40	145
8114	7/8"		26	.308		132	17.15		149.15	172
8118	1-1/8"		18	.444		158	25		183	211
8122	1-3/8"		14	.571		217	32		249	287
8126	1-5/8"		13	.615		279	34.50		313.50	355
8130	2-1/8"		12	.667		310	37		347	395
8134	2-5/8"	Q-5	22	.727		465	36.50		501.50	565
8138	3-1/8"	"	20	.800		615	40		655	735
8500	Refrigeration valve, packless, soldered									
8510	1/2"	1 Stpi	38	.211	Ea.	37.50	11.75		49.25	58.50
8514	5/8"		36	.222		39	12.40		51.40	61
8518	7/8"		26	.308		132	17.15		149.15	171
8520	Packed, soldered									
8522	1-1/8"	1 Stpi	18	.444	Ea.	161	25		186	215
8526	1-3/8"		14	.571		284	32		316	360
8530	1-5/8"		13	.615		315	34.50		349.50	395
8534	2-1/8"		12	.667		500	37		537	605
8538	2-5/8"	Q-5	22	.727		680	36.50		716.50	800
8542	3-1/8"		20	.800		785	40		825	925
8546	4-1/8"		18	.889		1,375	44.50		1,419.50	1,600
8600	Solenoid valve, flange/solder									
8610	1/2"	1 Stpi	38	.211	Ea.	163	11.75		174.75	198
8614	5/8"		36	.222		205	12.40		217.40	244
8618	3/4"		30	.267		256	14.85		270.85	305
8622	7/8"		26	.308		320	17.15		337.15	380
8626	1-1/8"		18	.444		420	25		445	500
8630	1-3/8"		14	.571		510	32		542	610
8634	1-5/8"		13	.615		715	34.50		749.50	835
8638	2-1/8"		12	.667		785	37		822	920
8800	Thermostatic valve, flange/solder									
8810	1/2 – 3 ton, 3/8" x 5/8"	1 Stpi	9	.889	Ea.	182	49.50		231.50	275
8814	4 – 5 ton, 1/2" x 7/8"		7	1.143		213	63.50		276.50	330
8818	6 – 8 ton, 5/8" x 7/8"		5	1.600		213	89		302	370
8822	7 – 12 ton, 7/8" x 1-1/8"		4	2		249	111		360	440
8826	15 – 20 ton, 7/8" x 1-3/8"		3.20	2.500		249	139		388	485

23 23 16 – Refrigerant Piping Specialties

23 23 16.10 Refrigerant Piping Component Specialties

		Crew	Daily Output	Labor-Hours	Unit	Material	2012 Bare Costs Labor	Equipment	Total	Total Incl O&P
0010	**REFRIGERANT PIPING COMPONENT SPECIALTIES**									
0600	Accumulator									
0610	3/4"	1 Stpi	8.80	.909	Ea.	70.50	50.50		121	154
0614	7/8"		6.40	1.250		80.50	69.50		150	194
0618	1-1/8"		4.80	1.667		111	93		204	262
0622	1-3/8"		4	2		145	111		256	330

23 23 16 – Refrigerant Piping Specialties

23 23 16.10 Refrigerant Piping Component Specialties		Crew	Daily Output	Labor-Hours	Unit	Material	2012 Bare Costs		Total	Total Incl O&P
							Labor	Equipment		
0626	1-5/8"	1 Stpi	3.20	2.500	Ea.	157	139		296	380
0630	2-1/8"		2.40	3.333		375	186		561	695
0700	Condensate drip/drain pan, 10" x 9" x 2-3/4"		24	.333		132	18.55		150.55	173
1000	Filter dryer									
1010	Replaceable core type, solder									
1020	1/2"	1 Stpi	20	.400	Ea.	153	22.50		175.50	202
1030	5/8"		19	.421		154	23.50		177.50	206
1040	7/8"		18	.444		154	25		179	208
1050	1-1/8"		15	.533		168	29.50		197.50	230
1060	1-3/8"		14	.571		168	32		200	233
1070	1-5/8"		12	.667		172	37		209	245
1080	2-1/8"		10	.800		181	44.50		225.50	266
1090	2-5/8"		9	.889		188	49.50		237.50	282
1100	3-1/8"		8	1		195	55.50		250.50	298
1200	Sealed in-line, solder									
1210	1/4", 3 cubic inches	1 Stpi	22	.364	Ea.	8.10	20.50		28.60	39.50
1220	3/8", 5 cubic inches		21	.381		7.40	21		28.40	40
1230	1/2", 9 cubic inches		20	.400		12	22.50		34.50	46.50
1240	1/2", 16 cubic inches		20	.400		15.45	22.50		37.95	50.50
1250	5/8", 16 cubic inches		19	.421		16.35	23.50		39.85	53.50
1260	5/8", 30 cubic inches		19	.421		26.50	23.50		50	64.50
1270	7/8", 30 cubic inches		18	.444		28	25		53	68.50
1280	7/8", 41 cubic inches		17	.471		37.50	26		63.50	81
1290	1-1/8", 60 cubic inches		15	.533		52	29.50		81.50	103
4000	P-Trap, suction line, solder									
4010	5/8"	1 Stpi	19	.421	Ea.	86.50	23.50		110	131
4020	3/4"		19	.421		129	23.50		152.50	178
4030	7/8"		18	.444		96.50	25		121.50	144
4040	1-1/8"		15	.533		147	29.50		176.50	206
4050	1-3/8"		14	.571		266	32		298	340
4060	1-5/8"		12	.667		370	37		407	465
4070	2-1/8"		10	.800		760	44.50		804.50	900
5000	Sightglass									
5010	Moisture and liquid indicator, solder									
5020	1/4"	1 Stpi	22	.364	Ea.	19.65	20.50		40.15	52
5030	3/8"		21	.381		20	21		41	54
5040	1/2"		20	.400		24	22.50		46.50	60
5050	5/8"		19	.421		25	23.50		48.50	63
5060	7/8"		18	.444		36.50	25		61.50	78
5070	1-1/8"		15	.533		39.50	29.50		69	88.50
5080	1-3/8"		14	.571		63	32		95	117
5090	1-5/8"		12	.667		71	37		108	134
5100	2-1/8"		10	.800		89	44.50		133.50	165
7400	Vacuum pump set									
7410	Two stage, high vacuum continuous duty	1 Stpi	8	1	Ea.	3,500	55.50		3,555.50	3,925

23 23 23 – Refrigerants

23 23 23.10 Anti-Freeze

		Crew	Daily Output	Labor-Hours	Unit	Material	2012 Bare Costs		Total	Total Incl O&P
							Labor	Equipment		
0010	**ANTI-FREEZE**, Inhibited									
0900	Ethylene glycol concentrated									
1000	55 gallon drums, small quantities				Gal.	9.80			9.80	10.80
1200	Large quantities					8.80			8.80	9.70
2000	Propylene glycol, for solar heat, small quantities					14.50			14.50	15.95

23 23 Refrigerant Piping

23 23 23 – Refrigerants

23 23 23.10 Anti-Freeze		Crew	Daily Output	Labor-Hours	Unit	Material	2012 Bare Costs Labor	Equipment	Total	Total Incl O&P
2100	Large quantities				Gal.	12.70			12.70	13.95

23 23 23.20 Refrigerant

		Crew	Daily Output	Labor-Hours	Unit	Material	Labor	Equipment	Total	Total Incl O&P
0010	**REFRIGERANT**									
4420	R-22, 30 lb. disposable cylinder				Lb.	12.15			12.15	13.40
4428	R-134A, 30 lb. disposable cylinder					11.10			11.10	12.20
4434	R-407C, 30 lb. disposable cylinder					16.60			16.60	18.25
4440	R-408A, 25 lb. disposable cylinder					22			22	24
4450	R-410A, 25 lb. disposable cylinder					14.55			14.55	16
4470	R-507, 25 lb. disposable cylinder					17.75			17.75	19.55

23 31 HVAC Ducts and Casings

23 31 13 – Metal Ducts

23 31 13.13 Rectangular Metal Ducts

			Crew	Daily Output	Labor-Hours	Unit	Material	Labor	Equipment	Total	Total Incl O&P
0010	**RECTANGULAR METAL DUCTS**	R233100-20									
0020	Fabricated rectangular, includes fittings, joints, supports,										
0030	allowance for flexible connections, no insulation	R233100-30									
0031	NOTE: Fabrication and installation are combined										
0040	as LABOR cost. Approx. 25% fittings assumed.	R233100-40									
0042	Fabrication/Inst. is to commercial quality standards										
0043	(SMACNA or equiv.) for structure, sealing, leak testing, etc.	R233100-50									
0050	Add to labor for elevated installation										
0051	of fabricated ductwork										
0052	10' to 15' high							6%			
0053	15' to 20' high							12%			
0054	20' to 25' high							15%			
0055	25' to 30' high							21%			
0056	30' to 35' high							24%			
0057	35' to 40' high							30%			
0058	Over 40' high							33%			
0072	For duct insulation see Line 23 07 13.10 3000										
0100	Aluminum, alloy 3003-H14, under 100 lb.		Q-10	75	.320	Lb.	3.58	15.55		19.13	27.50
0110	100 to 500 lb.			80	.300		2.34	14.60		16.94	25
0120	500 to 1,000 lb.			95	.253		2.21	12.30		14.51	21
0140	1,000 to 2,000 lb.			120	.200		2.13	9.75		11.88	17.20
0150	2,000 to 5,000 lb.			130	.185		2.13	9		11.13	16.05
0160	Over 5,000 lb.			145	.166		2.13	8.05		10.18	14.65
0500	Galvanized steel, under 200 lb.			235	.102		.70	4.97		5.67	8.35
0520	200 to 500 lb.			245	.098		.69	4.77		5.46	8
0540	500 to 1,000 lb.			255	.094		.68	4.58		5.26	7.75
0560	1,000 to 2,000 lb.			265	.091		.67	4.41		5.08	7.45
0570	2,000 to 5,000 lb.			275	.087		.66	4.25		4.91	7.20
0580	Over 5,000 lb.			285	.084		.66	4.10		4.76	7
0600	For large quantities special prices available from supplier										
1000	Stainless steel, type 304, under 100 lb.		Q-10	165	.145	Lb.	6.35	7.10		13.45	17.75
1020	100 to 500 lb.			175	.137		4.05	6.65		10.70	14.60
1030	500 to 1,000 lb.			190	.126		2.95	6.15		9.10	12.60
1040	1,000 to 2,000 lb.			200	.120		2.89	5.85		8.74	12.10
1050	2,000 to 5,000 lb.			225	.107		2.39	5.20		7.59	10.55
1060	Over 5,000 lb.			235	.102		2.35	4.97		7.32	10.20
1080	Note: Minimum order cost exceeds per lb. cost for min. wt.										
1100	For medium pressure ductwork, add					Lb.		15%			

23 31 HVAC Ducts and Casings

23 31 13 – Metal Ducts

23 31 13.13 Rectangular Metal Ducts

		Crew	Daily Output	Labor-Hours	Unit	Material	2012 Bare Costs Labor	Equipment	Total	Total Incl O&P
1200	For high pressure ductwork, add				Lb.		40%			
1210	For welded ductwork, add						85%			
1220	For 30% fittings, add						11%			
1224	For 40% fittings, add						34%			
1228	For 50% fittings, add						56%			
1232	For 60% fittings, add						79%			
1236	For 70% fittings, add						101%			
1240	For 80% fittings, add						124%			
1244	For 90% fittings, add						147%			
1248	For 100% fittings, add						169%			
1252	Note: Fittings add includes time for detailing and installation.									
1276	Duct tape, 2" x 60 yd roll				Ea.	5.20			5.20	5.70

23 31 13.16 Round and Flat-Oval Spiral Ducts

		Crew	Daily Output	Labor-Hours	Unit	Material	2012 Bare Costs Labor	Equipment	Total	Total Incl O&P
0010	**ROUND AND FLAT-OVAL SPIRAL DUCTS**									
1280	Add to labor for elevated installation									
1282	of prefabricated (purchased) ductwork									
1283	10' to 15' high						10%			
1284	15' to 20' high						20%			
1285	20' to 25' high						25%			
1286	25' to 30' high						35%			
1287	30' to 35' high						40%			
1288	35' to 40' high						50%			
1289	Over 40' high						55%			
5400	Spiral preformed, steel, galv., straight lengths, Max 10" spwg.									
5410	4" diameter, 26 ga.	Q-9	360	.044	L.F.	1.96	2.09		4.05	5.35
5416	5" diameter, 26 ga.		320	.050		1.96	2.35		4.31	5.75
5420	6" diameter, 26 ga.		280	.057		1.96	2.68		4.64	6.25
5425	7" diameter, 26 ga.		240	.067		2.28	3.13		5.41	7.30
5430	8" diameter, 26 ga.		200	.080		2.61	3.75		6.36	8.55
5440	10" diameter, 26 ga.		160	.100		3.26	4.69		7.95	10.75
5450	12" diameter, 26 ga.		120	.133		3.90	6.25		10.15	13.85
5460	14" diameter, 26 ga.		80	.200		4.55	9.40		13.95	19.30
5480	16" diameter, 24 ga.		60	.267		6.05	12.50		18.55	26
5490	18" diameter, 24 ga.		50	.320		6.80	15		21.80	30.50
5500	20" diameter, 24 ga.	Q-10	65	.369		7.60	17.95		25.55	36
5510	22" diameter, 24 ga.		60	.400		8.35	19.45		27.80	38.50
5520	24" diameter, 24 ga.		55	.436		9.10	21		30.10	42.50
5540	30" diameter, 22 ga.		45	.533		13.45	26		39.45	54.50
5600	36" diameter, 22 ga.		40	.600		16.15	29		45.15	62.50
5800	Connector, 4" diameter	Q-9	100	.160	Ea.	2.84	7.50		10.34	14.55
5810	5" diameter		94	.170		3.01	8		11.01	15.50
5820	6" diameter		88	.182		3.20	8.55		11.75	16.50
5840	8" diameter		78	.205		3.60	9.65		13.25	18.60
5860	10" diameter		70	.229		4.20	10.75		14.95	21
5880	12" diameter		50	.320		4.70	15		19.70	28
5900	14" diameter		44	.364		5.05	17.05		22.10	31.50
5920	16" diameter		40	.400		5.50	18.75		24.25	34.50
5930	18" diameter		37	.432		5.85	20.50		26.35	37.50
5940	20" diameter		34	.471		6.65	22		28.65	41
5950	22" diameter		31	.516		7.80	24		31.80	45.50
5960	24" diameter		28	.571		8.25	27		35.25	50
5980	30" diameter		22	.727		11.05	34		45.05	64

23 31 13.16 Round and Flat-Oval Spiral Ducts	Crew	Daily Output	Labor-Hours	Unit	Material	2012 Bare Costs Labor	Equipment	Total	Total Incl O&P
6000	36" diameter	Q-9	18	.889	Ea.	32	41.50		73.50	99
6300	Elbow, 45°, 4" diameter		60	.267		6.05	12.50		18.55	25.50
6310	5" diameter		52	.308		6.70	14.45		21.15	29.50
6320	6" diameter		44	.364		6.70	17.05		23.75	33.50
6340	8" diameter		28	.571		8.10	27		35.10	50
6360	10" diameter		18	.889		8.50	41.50		50	73
6380	12" diameter		13	1.231		9.20	58		67.20	98
6400	14" diameter		11	1.455		12.75	68.50		81.25	118
6420	16" diameter		10	1.600		18.30	75		93.30	134
6430	18" diameter		9.60	1.667		24	78		102	146
6440	20" diameter	Q-10	14	1.714		30.50	83.50		114	161
6450	22" diameter		13	1.846		51.50	90		141.50	194
6460	24" diameter		12	2		63.50	97.50		161	218
6480	30" diameter		9	2.667		91.50	130		221.50	299
6500	36" diameter		7	3.429		111	167		278	375
6600	Elbow, 90°, 4" diameter	Q-9	60	.267		4.60	12.50		17.10	24
6610	5" diameter		52	.308		4.60	14.45		19.05	27
6620	6" diameter		44	.364		4.60	17.05		21.65	31
6625	7" diameter		36	.444		5.15	21		26.15	37.50
6630	8" diameter		28	.571		5.65	27		32.65	47
6640	10" diameter		18	.889		7.40	41.50		48.90	71.50
6650	12" diameter		13	1.231		9.25	58		67.25	98
6660	14" diameter		11	1.455		15.85	68.50		84.35	121
6670	16" diameter		10	1.600		23	75		98	139
6676	18" diameter		9.60	1.667		30	78		108	152
6680	20" diameter	Q-10	14	1.714		38	83.50		121.50	169
6684	22" diameter		13	1.846		62	90		152	205
6690	24" diameter		12	2		76	97.50		173.50	232
6700	30" diameter		9	2.667		145	130		275	355
6710	36" diameter		7	3.429		223	167		390	500
6720	End cap									
6722	4"	Q-9	110	.145	Ea.	4.38	6.85		11.23	15.20
6724	6"		94	.170		4.38	8		12.38	17
6725	8"		88	.182		5.50	8.55		14.05	19.05
6726	10"		78	.205		6.85	9.65		16.50	22
6727	12"		70	.229		7.45	10.75		18.20	24.50
6728	14"		50	.320		10.45	15		25.45	34.50
6729	16"		44	.364		11.65	17.05		28.70	39
6730	18"		40	.400		16	18.75		34.75	46
6731	20"		37	.432		32.50	20.50		53	67
6732	22"		34	.471		36.50	22		58.50	74
6733	24"		30	.533		41	25		66	83
6800	Reducing coupling, 6" x 4"		46	.348		13.40	16.30		29.70	40
6820	8" x 6"		40	.400		13.40	18.75		32.15	43.50
6840	10" x 8"		32	.500		14.70	23.50		38.20	52
6860	12" x 10"		24	.667		16.80	31.50		48.30	66
6880	14" x 12"		20	.800		18	37.50		55.50	77
6900	16" x 14"		18	.889		23	41.50		64.50	88.50
6920	18" x 16"		16	1		30	47		77	105
6940	20" x 18"	Q-10	24	1		48	48.50		96.50	127
6950	22" x 20"		23	1.043		51	51		102	134
6960	24" x 22"		22	1.091		61.50	53		114.50	149
6980	30" x 28"		18	1.333		154	65		219	268

23 31 HVAC Ducts and Casings

23 31 13 - Metal Ducts

23 31 13.16 Round and Flat-Oval Spiral Ducts	Crew	Daily Output	Labor-Hours	Unit	Material	2012 Bare Costs Labor	Equipment	Total	Total Incl O&P
7000	36" x 34"	Q-10	16	1.500	Ea.	192	73		265	320
7100	Tee, 90°, 4" diameter	Q-9	40	.400		21	18.75		39.75	51.50
7110	5" diameter		34.60	.462		31.50	21.50		53	68
7120	6" diameter		30	.533		31.50	25		56.50	73
7130	8" diameter		19	.842		41	39.50		80.50	105
7140	10" diameter		12	1.333		56.50	62.50		119	158
7150	12" diameter		9	1.778		68.50	83.50		152	203
7160	14" diameter		7	2.286		104	107		211	278
7170	16" diameter		6.70	2.388		120	112		232	305
7176	18" diameter		6	2.667		175	125		300	385
7180	20" diameter	Q-10	8.70	2.759		208	134		342	435
7190	24" diameter		7	3.429		325	167		492	615
7200	30" diameter		6	4		400	195		595	735
7210	36" diameter		5	4.800		510	234		744	915
7400	Steel, PVC coated both sides, straight lengths									
7410	4" diameter, 26 ga.	Q-9	360	.044	L.F.	3.60	2.09		5.69	7.15
7416	5" diameter, 26 ga.		240	.067		3.60	3.13		6.73	8.75
7420	6" diameter, 26 ga.		280	.057		3.60	2.68		6.28	8.05
7440	8" diameter, 26 ga.		200	.080		4.90	3.75		8.65	11.10
7460	10" diameter, 26 ga.		160	.100		6.10	4.69		10.79	13.85
7480	12" diameter, 26 ga.		120	.133		7.30	6.25		13.55	17.60
7500	14" diameter, 26 ga.		80	.200		8.50	9.40		17.90	23.50
7520	16" diameter, 24 ga.		60	.267		9.70	12.50		22.20	29.50
7540	18" diameter, 24 ga.		45	.356		10.90	16.70		27.60	37.50
7560	20" diameter, 24 ga.	Q-10	65	.369		12.10	17.95		30.05	41
7580	24" diameter, 24 ga.		55	.436		14.50	21		35.50	48.50
7600	30" diameter, 22 ga.		45	.533		22	26		48	63.50
7620	36" diameter, 22 ga.		40	.600		26	29		55	73.50
7890	Connector, 4" diameter	Q-9	100	.160	Ea.	2.60	7.50		10.10	14.30
7896	5" diameter		83	.193		2.90	9.05		11.95	17
7900	6" diameter		88	.182		3.30	8.55		11.85	16.65
7920	8" diameter		78	.205		3.90	9.65		13.55	18.95
7940	10" diameter		70	.229		4.50	10.75		15.25	21.50
7960	12" diameter		50	.320		5.30	15		20.30	29
7980	14" diameter		44	.364		5.60	17.05		22.65	32
8000	16" diameter		40	.400		6.10	18.75		24.85	35
8020	18" diameter		37	.432		6.80	20.50		27.30	38.50
8040	20" diameter		34	.471		8.90	22		30.90	43.50
8060	24" diameter		28	.571		11	27		38	53
8080	30" diameter		22	.727		14.70	34		48.70	68
8100	36" diameter		18	.889		17.90	41.50		59.40	83
8390	Elbow, 45°, 4" diameter		60	.267		9.45	12.50		21.95	29.50
8396	5" diameter		36	.444		9.70	21		30.70	42.50
8400	6" diameter		44	.364		10.05	17.05		27.10	37
8420	8" diameter		28	.571		10.90	27		37.90	53
8440	10" diameter		18	.889		11.50	41.50		53	76
8460	12" diameter		13	1.231		12.75	58		70.75	102
8480	14" diameter		11	1.455		13.70	68.50		82.20	119
8500	16" diameter		10	1.600		19.75	75		94.75	136
8520	18" diameter		9	1.778		25	83.50		108.50	155
8540	20" diameter	Q-10	13	1.846		57	90		147	200
8560	24" diameter		11	2.182		81.50	106		187.50	252
8580	30" diameter		9	2.667		129	130		259	340

23 31 HVAC Ducts and Casings

23 31 13 – Metal Ducts

23 31 13.16 Round and Flat-Oval Spiral Ducts

		Crew	Daily Output	Labor-Hours	Unit	Material	2012 Bare Costs Labor	Equipment	Total	Total Incl O&P
8600	36" diameter	Q-10	7	3.429	Ea.	157	167		324	425
8800	Elbow, 90°, 4" diameter	Q-9	60	.267		13.35	12.50		25.85	34
8804	5" diameter		52	.308		13.65	14.45		28.10	37
8806	6" diameter		44	.364		13.95	17.05		31	41.50
8808	8" diameter		28	.571		14.55	27		41.55	57
8810	10" diameter		18	.889		15.15	41.50		56.65	80
8812	12" diameter		13	1.231		15.75	58		73.75	105
8814	14" diameter		11	1.455		22	68.50		90.50	128
8816	16" diameter		10	1.600		29	75		104	146
8818	18" diameter		9.60	1.667		35.50	78		113.50	158
8820	20" diameter	Q-10	14	1.714		45	83.50		128.50	177
8822	24" diameter		12	2		98	97.50		195.50	256
8824	30" diameter		9	2.667		175	130		305	390
8826	36" diameter		7	3.429		285	167		452	570
9000	Reducing coupling									
9040	6" x 4"	Q-9	46	.348	Ea.	19.50	16.30		35.80	46.50
9060	8" x 6"		40	.400		19.50	18.75		38.25	50
9080	10" x 8"		32	.500		20.50	23.50		44	58.50
9100	12" x 10"		24	.667		23.50	31.50		55	73.50
9120	14" x 12"		20	.800		25	37.50		62.50	84.50
9140	16" x 14"		18	.889		32	41.50		73.50	99
9160	18" x 16"		16	1		39	47		86	115
9180	20" x 18"	Q-10	24	1		45.50	48.50		94	124
9200	24" x 22"		22	1.091		58.50	53		111.50	146
9220	30" x 28"		18	1.333		104	65		169	213
9240	36" x 34"		16	1.500		143	73		216	268
9800	Steel, stainless, straight lengths									
9810	3" diameter, 26 Ga.	Q-9	400	.040	L.F.	14.20	1.88		16.08	18.45
9820	4" diameter, 26 Ga.		360	.044		16.45	2.09		18.54	21.50
9830	5" diameter, 26 Ga.		320	.050		17.75	2.35		20.10	23
9840	6" diameter, 26 Ga.		280	.057		17.75	2.68		20.43	23.50
9850	7" diameter, 26 Ga.		240	.067		19.55	3.13		22.68	26.50
9860	8" diameter, 26 Ga.		200	.080		23	3.75		26.75	31
9870	9" diameter, 26 Ga.		180	.089		33.50	4.17		37.67	43.50
9880	10" diameter, 26 Ga.		160	.100		43.50	4.69		48.19	55
9890	12" diameter, 26 Ga.		120	.133		61.50	6.25		67.75	77
9900	14" diameter, 26 Ga.		80	.200		65	9.40		74.40	86

23 31 13.17 Round Grease Duct

		Crew	Daily Output	Labor-Hours	Unit	Material	2012 Bare Costs Labor	Equipment	Total	Total Incl O&P
0010	**ROUND GREASE DUCT**									
1280	Add to labor for elevated installation									
1282	of prefabricated (purchased) ductwork									
1283	10' to 15' high						10%			
1284	15' to 20' high						20%			
1285	20' to 25' high						25%			
1286	25' to 30' high						35%			
1287	30' to 35' high						40%			
1288	35' to 40' high						50%			
1289	Over 40' high						55%			
4020	Zero clearance, 2 hr. fire rated, UL listed, 3" double wall									
4030	304 interior, aluminized exterior, all sizes are ID									
4032	For 316 interior and aluminized exterior, add						6%			
4034	For 304 interior and 304 exterior, add						21%			

23 31 13.17 Round Grease Duct		Crew	Daily Output	Labor-Hours	Unit	Material	2012 Bare Costs Labor	Equipment	Total	Total Incl O&P
4036	For 316 interior and 316 exterior, add					40%				
4040	Straight									
4052	6"	Q-9	34.20	.468	L.F.	73.50	22		95.50	114
4054	8"		29.64	.540		84	25.50		109.50	131
4056	10"		27.36	.585		94	27.50		121.50	145
4058	12"		25.10	.637		108	30		138	164
4060	14"		23.94	.668		121	31.50		152.50	181
4062	16"		22.80	.702		136	33		169	200
4064	18"		21.66	.739		154	34.50		188.50	222
4066	20"	Q-10	20.52	1.170		175	57		232	279
4068	22"		19.38	1.238		197	60.50		257.50	310
4070	24"		18.24	1.316		223	64		287	345
4072	26"		17.67	1.358		240	66		306	365
4074	28"		17.10	1.404		257	68.50		325.50	385
4076	30"		15.96	1.504		269	73		342	410
4078	32"		15.39	1.559		290	76		366	435
4080	36"		14.25	1.684		325	82		407	480
4100	Adjustable section, 30" long									
4104	6"	Q-9	17.10	.936	Ea.	221	44		265	310
4106	8"		14.82	1.080		276	50.50		326.50	380
4108	10"		13.68	1.170		315	55		370	430
4110	12"		12.54	1.276		350	60		410	475
4112	14"		11.97	1.337		395	62.50		457.50	530
4114	16"		11.40	1.404		445	66		511	590
4116	18"		10.83	1.477		505	69.50		574.50	660
4118	20"	Q-10	10.26	2.339		575	114		689	805
4120	22"		9.69	2.477		650	121		771	900
4122	24"		9.12	2.632		735	128		863	1,000
4124	26"		8.83	2.718		790	132		922	1,075
4126	28"		8.55	2.807		845	137		982	1,150
4128	30"		8.26	2.906		900	141		1,041	1,200
4130	32"		7.98	3.008		955	146		1,101	1,275
4132	36"		6.84	3.509		1,050	171		1,221	1,425
4140	Tee, 90°, grease									
4144	6"	Q-9	13.68	1.170	Ea.	390	55		445	515
4146	8"		12.54	1.276		425	60		485	560
4148	10"		11.97	1.337		480	62.50		542.50	625
4150	12"		11.40	1.404		555	66		621	715
4152	14"		10.26	1.559		635	73		708	810
4154	16"		9.12	1.754		700	82.50		782.50	895
4156	18"		7.98	2.005		825	94		919	1,050
4158	20"		9.69	1.651		955	77.50		1,032.50	1,175
4160	22"		8.26	1.937		1,050	91		1,141	1,325
4162	24"		6.84	2.339		1,175	110		1,285	1,475
4164	26"		6.55	2.443		1,300	115		1,415	1,600
4166	28"	Q-10	6.27	3.828		1,425	186		1,611	1,825
4168	30"		5.98	4.013		1,700	195		1,895	2,175
4170	32"		5.70	4.211		2,000	205		2,205	2,500
4172	36"		5.13	4.678		2,200	228		2,428	2,775
4180	Cleanout Tee Cap									
4184	6"	Q-9	21.09	.759	Ea.	80	35.50		115.50	143
4186	8"		19.38	.826		84	38.50		122.50	152
4188	10"		18.24	.877		90.50	41		131.50	163

23 31 13.17 Round Grease Duct		Crew	Daily Output	Labor-Hours	Unit	Material	2012 Bare Costs Labor	Equipment	Total	Total Incl O&P
4190	12"	Q-9	17.10	.936	Ea.	97	44		141	174
4192	14"		15.96	1.003		103	47		150	185
4194	16"		14.25	1.123		113	52.50		165.50	206
4196	18"		13.68	1.170		120	55		175	216
4198	20"	Q-10	15.39	1.559		133	76		209	262
4200	22"		12.54	1.914		144	93		237	300
4202	24"		11.97	2.005		157	97.50		254.50	320
4204	26"		11.40	2.105		171	102		273	345
4206	28"		10.83	2.216		186	108		294	370
4208	30"		10.26	2.339		202	114		316	395
4210	32"		9.69	2.477		220	121		341	425
4212	36"		8.55	2.807		258	137		395	490
4220	Elbow, 45°									
4224	6"	Q-9	17.10	.936	Ea.	276	44		320	370
4226	8"		14.82	1.080		310	50.50		360.50	415
4228	10"		13.68	1.170		355	55		410	475
4230	12"		12.54	1.276		405	60		465	535
4232	14"		11.97	1.337		455	62.50		517.50	595
4234	16"		11.40	1.404		510	66		576	665
4236	18"		10.83	1.477		580	69.50		649.50	740
4238	20"	Q-10	10.26	2.339		655	114		769	895
4240	22"		9.69	2.477		735	121		856	990
4242	24"		9.12	2.632		840	128		968	1,125
4244	26"		8.83	2.718		890	132		1,022	1,175
4246	28"		8.55	2.807		1,050	137		1,187	1,350
4248	30"		8.26	2.906		1,050	141		1,191	1,375
4250	32"		7.98	3.008		1,275	146		1,421	1,625
4252	36"		6.84	3.509		1,700	171		1,871	2,125
4260	Elbow, 90°									
4264	6"	Q-9	17.10	.936	Ea.	555	44		599	675
4266	8"		14.82	1.080		625	50.50		675.50	760
4268	10"		13.68	1.170		710	55		765	865
4270	12"		12.54	1.276		800	60		860	975
4272	14"		11.97	1.337		905	62.50		967.50	1,100
4274	16"		11.40	1.404		1,025	66		1,091	1,225
4276	18"		10.83	1.477		1,250	69.50		1,319.50	1,475
4278	20"	Q-10	10.26	2.339		1,300	114		1,414	1,600
4280	22"		9.69	2.477		1,475	121		1,596	1,775
4282	24"		9.12	2.632		1,675	128		1,803	2,050
4284	26"		8.83	2.718		1,775	132		1,907	2,150
4286	28"		8.55	2.807		1,875	137		2,012	2,275
4288	30"		8.26	2.906		2,100	141		2,241	2,550
4290	32"		7.98	3.008		2,550	146		2,696	3,025
4292	36"		6.84	3.509		3,400	171		3,571	4,000
4300	Support strap									
4304	6"	Q-9	25.50	.627	Ea.	97	29.50		126.50	152
4306	8"		22	.727		113	34		147	177
4308	10"		20.50	.780		117	36.50		153.50	184
4310	12"		18.80	.851		125	40		165	199
4312	14"		17.90	.894		135	42		177	213
4314	16"		17	.941		136	44		180	218
4316	18"		16.20	.988		138	46.50		184.50	223
4318	20"	Q-10	15.40	1.558		153	76		229	285

23 31 13.17 Round Grease Duct		Crew	Daily Output	Labor-Hours	Unit	Material	2012 Bare Costs Labor	Equipment	Total	Total Incl O&P
4320	22"	Q-10	14.50	1.655	Ea.	170	80.50		250.50	310
4340	Plate Support Assembly									
4344	6"	Q-9	14.82	1.080	Ea.	136	50.50		186.50	227
4346	8"		12.54	1.276		159	60		219	267
4348	10"		11.40	1.404		173	66		239	290
4350	12"		10.26	1.559		181	73		254	310
4352	14"		9.69	1.651		215	77.50		292.50	355
4354	16"		9.12	1.754		227	82.50		309.50	375
4356	18"		8.55	1.871		239	88		327	395
4358	20"	Q-10	9.12	2.632		251	128		379	470
4360	22"		8.55	2.807		256	137		393	490
4362	24"		7.98	3.008		260	146		406	510
4364	26"		7.69	3.121		293	152		445	550
4366	28"		7.41	3.239		320	158		478	590
4368	30"		7.12	3.371		355	164		519	645
4370	32"		6.84	3.509		390	171		561	690
4372	36"		5.70	4.211		470	205		675	830
4380	Wall Guide Assembly									
4384	6"	Q-9	19.10	.838	Ea.	180	39.50		219.50	258
4386	8"		16.50	.970		204	45.50		249.50	295
4388	10"		15.30	1.046		216	49		265	315
4390	12"		14.10	1.135		226	53.50		279.50	330
4392	14"		13.40	1.194		244	56		300	355
4394	16"		12.75	1.255		247	59		306	360
4396	18"		12.10	1.322		251	62		313	370
4398	20"	Q-10	11.50	2.087		280	102		382	465
4400	22"		10.90	2.202		300	107		407	495
4402	24"		10.20	2.353		340	115		455	550
4404	26"		9.90	2.424		375	118		493	590
4406	28"		9.60	2.500		385	122		507	610
4408	30"		9.30	2.581		440	126		566	675
4410	32"		9	2.667		470	130		600	715
4412	36"		7.60	3.158		515	154		669	800
4420	Hood Transition, Flanged or Unflanged									
4424	6"	Q-9	15.60	1.026	Ea.	76.50	48		124.50	158
4426	8"		13.50	1.185		87.50	55.50		143	181
4428	10"		12.50	1.280		97	60		157	199
4430	12"		11.40	1.404		117	66		183	228
4432	14"		10.90	1.468		125	69		194	243
4434	16"		10.40	1.538		135	72		207	259
4436	18"		9.80	1.633		154	76.50		230.50	287
4438	20"	Q-10	9.40	2.553		164	124		288	370
4440	22"		8.80	2.727		173	133		306	390
4442	24"		8.30	2.892		193	141		334	430
4444	26"		8.10	2.963		202	144		346	440
4446	28"		7.80	3.077		213	150		363	460
4448	30"		7.50	3.200		231	156		387	490
4450	32"		7.30	3.288		242	160		402	510
4452	36"		6.20	3.871		269	188		457	585
4460	Fan Adapter									
4464	6"	Q-9	15	1.067	Ea.	215	50		265	315
4466	8"		13	1.231		244	58		302	355
4468	10"		12	1.333		267	62.50		329.50	390

23 31 HVAC Ducts and Casings

23 31 13 – Metal Ducts

23 31 13.17 Round Grease Duct		Crew	Daily Output	Labor-Hours	Unit	Material	2012 Bare Costs Labor	Equipment	Total	Total Incl O&P
4470	12"	Q-9	11	1.455	Ea.	298	68.50		366.50	435
4472	14"		10.50	1.524		325	71.50		396.50	465
4474	16"		10	1.600		350	75		425	500
4476	18"		9.50	1.684		380	79		459	535
4478	20"	Q-10	9	2.667		410	130		540	650
4480	22"		8.50	2.824		435	137		572	690
4482	24"		8	3		460	146		606	730
4484	26"		7.70	3.117		490	152		642	765
4486	28"		7.50	3.200		515	156		671	805
4488	30"		7.20	3.333		545	162		707	845
4490	32"		7	3.429		570	167		737	885
4492	36"		6	4		625	195		820	985
4500	Tapered Increaser/Reducer									
4530	6" x 10" dia	Q-9	13.40	1.194	Ea.	276	56		332	390
4540	6" x 20" dia		10.10	1.584		276	74.50		350.50	420
4550	8" x 10" dia		13.20	1.212		335	57		392	450
4560	8" x 20" dia		9.90	1.616		335	76		411	480
4570	10" x 20" dia		10.60	1.509		385	71		456	535
4580	10" x 28" dia	Q-10	8.60	2.791		385	136		521	630
4590	12" x 20" dia		8.80	2.727		445	133		578	690
4600	14" x 28" dia		8.40	2.857		505	139		644	765
4610	16" x 20" dia		8.60	2.791		555	136		691	820
4620	16" x 30" dia		8.30	2.892		555	141		696	830
4630	18" x 24" dia		8.80	2.727		615	133		748	875
4640	18" x 30" dia		8.10	2.963		615	144		759	895
4650	20" x 24" dia		8.30	2.892		670	141		811	950
4660	20" x 32" dia		8	3		670	146		816	960
4670	24" x 26" dia		8	3		785	146		931	1,075
4680	24" x 36" dia		7.30	3.288		785	160		945	1,100
4690	28" x 30" dia		7.90	3.038		895	148		1,043	1,200
4700	28" x 36" dia		7.10	3.380		895	165		1,060	1,225
4710	30" x 36" dia		6.90	3.478		950	169		1,119	1,300
4730	Many intermediate standard sizes of tapered fittings are available									

23 31 13.19 Metal Duct Fittings

		Crew	Daily Output	Labor-Hours	Unit	Material	2012 Bare Costs Labor	Equipment	Total	Total Incl O&P
0010	**METAL DUCT FITTINGS**									
0350	Duct collar, spin-in type									
0352	Without damper									
0354	Round									
0356	4"	1 Shee	32	.250	Ea.	2.61	13.05		15.66	23
0357	5"		30	.267		3.16	13.90		17.06	24.50
0358	6"		28	.286		3.49	14.90		18.39	26.50
0359	7"		26	.308		3.80	16.05		19.85	28.50
0360	8"		24	.333		3.80	17.40		21.20	30.50
0361	9"		22	.364		3.80	18.95		22.75	33
0362	10"		20	.400		4.18	21		25.18	36.50
0363	12"		17	.471		5.25	24.50		29.75	43.50
2000	Fabrics for flexible connections, with metal edge		100	.080	L.F.	2.17	4.17		6.34	8.75
2100	Without metal edge		160	.050	"	1.64	2.61		4.25	5.80

23 31 16.13 Fibrous-Glass Ducts

	23 31 16.13 Fibrous-Glass Ducts	Crew	Daily Output	Labor-Hours	Unit	Material	2012 Bare Costs Labor	Equipment	Total	Total Incl O&P
0010	**FIBROUS-GLASS DUCTS** R233100-20									
1280	Add to labor for elevated installation									
1282	of prefabricated (purchased) ductwork									
1283	10' to 15' high						10%			
1284	15' to 20' high						20%			
1285	20' to 25' high						25%			
1286	25' to 30' high						35%			
1287	30' to 35' high						40%			
1288	35' to 40' high						50%			
1289	Over 40' high						55%			
3490	Rigid fiberglass duct board, foil reinf. kraft facing									
3500	Rectangular, 1" thick, alum. faced, (FRK), std. weight	Q-10	350	.069	SF Surf	.77	3.34		4.11	5.95

23 31 16.16 Thermoset Fiberglass-Reinforced Plastic Ducts

	23 31 16.16 Thermoset Fiberglass-Reinforced Plastic Ducts	Crew	Daily Output	Labor-Hours	Unit	Material	2012 Bare Costs Labor	Equipment	Total	Total Incl O&P
0010	**THERMOSET FIBERGLASS-REINFORCED PLASTIC DUCTS** R233100-20									
1280	Add to labor for elevated installation									
1282	of prefabricated (purchased) ductwork									
1283	10' to 15' high						10%			
1284	15' to 20' high						20%			
1285	20' to 25' high						25%			
1286	25' to 30' high						35%			
1287	30' to 35' high						40%			
1288	35' to 40' high						50%			
1289	Over 40' high						55%			
3550	Rigid fiberglass reinforced plastic, FM approved									
3552	for acid fume and smoke exhaust system, nonflammable									
3554	Straight, 4" diameter	Q-9	200	.080	L.F.	11.15	3.75		14.90	17.95
3555	6" diameter		146	.110		14.60	5.15		19.75	24
3556	8" diameter		106	.151		17.70	7.10		24.80	30.50
3557	10" diameter		85	.188		21	8.85		29.85	37
3558	12" diameter		68	.235		25	11.05		36.05	44.50
3559	14" diameter		50	.320		36.50	15		51.50	63.50
3560	16" diameter		40	.400		41	18.75		59.75	73.50
3561	18" diameter		31	.516		45.50	24		69.50	87
3562	20" diameter	Q-10	44	.545		50	26.50		76.50	95.50
3563	22" diameter		40	.600		54.50	29		83.50	104
3564	24" diameter		37	.649		58.50	31.50		90	113
3565	26" diameter		34	.706		63	34.50		97.50	122
3566	28" diameter		28	.857		67.50	41.50		109	138
3567	30" diameter		24	1		72	48.50		120.50	153
3568	32" diameter		22.60	1.062		76.50	51.50		128	163
3569	34" diameter		21.60	1.111		80.50	54		134.50	171
3570	36" diameter		20.60	1.165		85.50	56.50		142	181
3571	38" diameter		19.80	1.212		131	59		190	234
3572	42" diameter		18.30	1.311		147	64		211	260
3573	46" diameter		17	1.412		162	68.50		230.50	284
3574	50" diameter		15.90	1.509		177	73.50		250.50	305
3575	54" diameter		14.90	1.611		194	78.50		272.50	335
3576	60" diameter		13.60	1.765		222	86		308	375
3577	64" diameter		12.80	1.875		325	91.50		416.50	500
3578	68" diameter		12.20	1.967		345	95.50		440.50	525
3579	72" diameter		11.90	2.017		370	98		468	560

23 31 HVAC Ducts and Casings

23 31 16 – Nonmetal Ducts

23 31 16.16 Thermoset Fiberglass-Reinforced Plastic Ducts	Crew	Daily Output	Labor-Hours	Unit	Material	2012 Bare Costs Labor	Equipment	Total	Total Incl O&P
3584	Note: joints are cemented with									
3586	fiberglass resin, included in material cost.									
3590	Elbow, 90°, 4" diameter	Q-9	20.30	.788	Ea.	54	37		91	116
3591	6" diameter		13.80	1.159		75	54.50		129.50	166
3592	8" diameter		10	1.600		82.50	75		157.50	205
3593	10" diameter		7.80	2.051		109	96.50		205.50	266
3594	12" diameter		6.50	2.462		138	116		254	325
3595	14" diameter		5.50	2.909		169	137		306	395
3596	16" diameter		4.80	3.333		201	156		357	460
3597	18" diameter		4.40	3.636		287	171		458	575
3598	20" diameter	Q-10	5.90	4.068		305	198		503	635
3599	22" diameter		5.40	4.444		370	216		586	740
3600	24" diameter		4.90	4.898		430	238		668	835
3601	26" diameter		4.60	5.217		435	254		689	865
3602	28" diameter		4.20	5.714		545	278		823	1,025
3603	30" diameter		3.90	6.154		605	300		905	1,125
3604	32" diameter		3.70	6.486		670	315		985	1,225
3605	34" diameter		3.45	6.957		790	340		1,130	1,375
3606	36" diameter		3.20	7.500		910	365		1,275	1,550
3607	38" diameter		3.07	7.818		1,300	380		1,680	2,000
3608	42" diameter		2.70	8.889		1,550	435		1,985	2,350
3609	46" diameter		2.54	9.449		1,800	460		2,260	2,700
3610	50" diameter		2.33	10.300		2,100	500		2,600	3,075
3611	54" diameter		2.14	11.215		2,400	545		2,945	3,475
3612	60" diameter		1.94	12.371		3,200	600		3,800	4,450
3613	64" diameter		1.82	13.187		4,650	640		5,290	6,100
3614	68" diameter		1.71	14.035		5,175	685		5,860	6,725
3615	72" diameter		1.62	14.815		5,725	720		6,445	7,375
3626	Elbow, 45°, 4" diameter	Q-9	22.30	.717		51.50	33.50		85	109
3627	6" diameter		15.20	1.053		71.50	49.50		121	154
3628	8" diameter		11	1.455		76	68.50		144.50	188
3629	10" diameter		8.60	1.860		80	87.50		167.50	221
3630	12" diameter		7.20	2.222		88	104		192	256
3631	14" diameter		6.10	2.623		108	123		231	305
3632	16" diameter		5.28	3.030		128	142		270	360
3633	18" diameter		4.84	3.306		150	155		305	400
3634	20" diameter	Q-10	6.50	3.692		174	180		354	465
3635	22" diameter		5.94	4.040		237	197		434	560
3636	24" diameter		5.40	4.444		270	216		486	625
3637	26" diameter		5.06	4.743		305	231		536	685
3638	28" diameter		4.62	5.195		330	253		583	750
3639	30" diameter		4.30	5.581		385	272		657	835
3640	32" diameter		4.07	5.897		425	287		712	900
3641	34" diameter		3.80	6.316		500	305		805	1,025
3642	36" diameter		3.52	6.818		580	330		910	1,150
3643	38" diameter		3.38	7.101		810	345		1,155	1,425
3644	42" diameter		2.97	8.081		970	395		1,365	1,675
3645	46" diameter		2.80	8.571		1,125	415		1,540	1,875
3646	50" diameter		2.56	9.375		1,325	455		1,780	2,150
3647	54" diameter		2.35	10.213		1,500	495		1,995	2,400
3648	60" diameter		2.13	11.268		2,025	550		2,575	3,050
3649	64" diameter		2	12		2,925	585		3,510	4,125
3650	68" diameter		1.88	12.766		3,225	620		3,845	4,500

23 31 16.16 Thermoset Fiberglass-Reinforced Plastic Ducts	Crew	Daily Output	Labor-Hours	Unit	Material	2012 Bare Costs Labor	Equipment	Total	Total Incl O&P
3651	72" diameter	Q-10	1.78	13.483	Ea.	3,575	655		4,230	4,925
3660	Tee, 90°, 4" diameter	Q-9	14.06	1.138		29.50	53.50		83	114
3661	6" diameter		9.52	1.681		45	79		124	170
3662	8" diameter		6.98	2.292		61.50	108		169.50	232
3663	10" diameter		5.45	2.936		80	138		218	298
3664	12" diameter		4.60	3.478		100	163		263	360
3665	14" diameter		3.86	4.145		146	195		341	455
3666	16" diameter		3.40	4.706		174	221		395	525
3667	18" diameter		3.05	5.246		206	246		452	600
3668	20" diameter	Q-10	4.12	5.825		241	284		525	695
3669	22" diameter		3.78	6.349		275	310		585	775
3670	24" diameter		3.46	6.936		310	340		650	855
3671	26" diameter		3.20	7.500		350	365		715	940
3672	28" diameter		2.96	8.108		395	395		790	1,025
3673	30" diameter		2.75	8.727		440	425		865	1,125
3674	32" diameter		2.54	9.449		485	460		945	1,225
3675	34" diameter		2.40	10		535	485		1,020	1,325
3676	36" diameter		2.27	10.573		585	515		1,100	1,425
3677	38" diameter		2.15	11.163		880	545		1,425	1,800
3678	42" diameter		1.91	12.565		1,050	610		1,660	2,100
3679	46" diameter		1.78	13.483		1,250	655		1,905	2,375
3680	50" diameter		1.63	14.724		1,450	715		2,165	2,700
3681	54" diameter		1.50	16		1,675	780		2,455	3,025
3682	60" diameter		1.35	17.778		2,100	865		2,965	3,625
3683	64" diameter		1.27	18.898		3,150	920		4,070	4,875
3684	68" diameter		1.20	20		3,525	975		4,500	5,350
3685	72" diameter		1.13	21.239		3,925	1,025		4,950	5,900
3690	For Y @ 45°, add					22%				
3700	Blast gate, 4" diameter	Q-9	22.30	.717		143	33.50		176.50	209
3701	6" diameter		15.20	1.053		161	49.50		210.50	253
3702	8" diameter		11	1.455		217	68.50		285.50	345
3703	10" diameter		8.60	1.860		248	87.50		335.50	405
3704	12" diameter		7.20	2.222		305	104		409	495
3705	14" diameter		6.10	2.623		335	123		458	560
3706	16" diameter		5.28	3.030		370	142		512	625
3707	18" diameter		4.84	3.306		395	155		550	670
3708	20" diameter	Q-10	6.50	3.692		440	180		620	760
3709	22" diameter		5.94	4.040		475	197		672	825
3710	24" diameter		5.40	4.444		510	216		726	895
3711	26" diameter		5.06	4.743		550	231		781	955
3712	28" diameter		4.62	5.195		590	253		843	1,025
3713	30" diameter		4.30	5.581		625	272		897	1,100
3714	32" diameter		4.07	5.897		680	287		967	1,175
3715	34" diameter		3.80	6.316		745	305		1,050	1,300
3716	36" diameter		3.52	6.818		800	330		1,130	1,375
3717	38" diameter		3.38	7.101		1,075	345		1,420	1,725
3718	42" diameter		2.97	8.081		1,250	395		1,645	1,975
3719	46" diameter		2.80	8.571		1,425	415		1,840	2,200
3720	50" diameter		2.56	9.375		1,625	455		2,080	2,500
3721	54" diameter		2.35	10.213		1,825	495		2,320	2,775
3722	60" diameter		2.13	11.268		2,150	550		2,700	3,175
3723	64" diameter		2	12		2,375	585		2,960	3,525
3724	68" diameter		1.88	12.766		2,625	620		3,245	3,850

23 31 16.16 Thermoset Fiberglass-Reinforced Plastic Ducts	Crew	Daily Output	Labor-Hours	Unit	Material	2012 Bare Costs Labor	Equipment	Total	Total Incl O&P
3725	72" diameter	Q-10	1.78	13.483	Ea.	2,900	655		3,555	4,175
3740	Reducers, 4" diameter	Q-9	24.50	.653		35.50	30.50		66	86
3741	6" diameter		16.70	.958		53.50	45		98.50	127
3742	8" diameter		12	1.333		72	62.50		134.50	175
3743	10" diameter		9.50	1.684		89	79		168	218
3744	12" diameter		7.90	2.025		107	95		202	262
3745	14" diameter		6.70	2.388		124	112		236	305
3746	16" diameter		5.80	2.759		142	129		271	355
3747	18" diameter	▼	5.30	3.019		160	142		302	390
3748	20" diameter	Q-10	7.20	3.333		178	162		340	445
3749	22" diameter		6.50	3.692		286	180		466	590
3750	24" diameter		5.90	4.068		310	198		508	640
3751	26" diameter		5.60	4.286		335	209		544	690
3752	28" diameter		5.10	4.706		365	229		594	755
3753	30" diameter		4.70	5.106		395	249		644	810
3754	32" diameter		4.50	5.333		420	260		680	855
3755	34" diameter		4.20	5.714		445	278		723	915
3756	36" diameter		3.90	6.154		470	300		770	975
3757	38" diameter		3.70	6.486		715	315		1,030	1,275
3758	42" diameter		3.30	7.273		785	355		1,140	1,400
3759	46" diameter		3.10	7.742		865	375		1,240	1,525
3760	50" diameter		2.80	8.571		935	415		1,350	1,650
3761	54" diameter		2.60	9.231		1,025	450		1,475	1,800
3762	60" diameter		2.34	10.256		1,125	500		1,625	2,000
3763	64" diameter		2.20	10.909		1,750	530		2,280	2,725
3764	68" diameter		2.06	11.650		1,850	565		2,415	2,925
3765	72" diameter	▼	1.96	12.245		2,000	595		2,595	3,100
3780	Flange, per each, 4" diameter	Q-9	40.60	.394		86.50	18.50		105	123
3781	6" diameter		27.70	.578		101	27		128	153
3782	8" diameter		20.50	.780		126	36.50		162.50	195
3783	10" diameter		16.30	.982		151	46		197	236
3784	12" diameter		13.90	1.151		174	54		228	274
3785	14" diameter		11.30	1.416		201	66.50		267.50	320
3786	16" diameter		9.70	1.649		225	77.50		302.50	365
3787	18" diameter	▼	8.30	1.928		250	90.50		340.50	415
3788	20" diameter	Q-10	11.30	2.124		275	103		378	465
3789	22" diameter		10.40	2.308		300	112		412	500
3790	24" diameter		9.50	2.526		325	123		448	545
3791	26" diameter		8.80	2.727		350	133		483	585
3792	28" diameter		8.20	2.927		375	142		517	630
3793	30" diameter		7.60	3.158		400	154		554	675
3794	32" diameter		7.20	3.333		425	162		587	710
3795	34" diameter		6.80	3.529		450	172		622	755
3796	36" diameter		6.40	3.750		475	183		658	805
3797	38" diameter		6.10	3.934		500	191		691	840
3798	42" diameter		5.50	4.364		550	212		762	930
3799	46" diameter		5	4.800		600	234		834	1,025
3800	50" diameter		4.60	5.217		650	254		904	1,100
3801	54" diameter		4.20	5.714		700	278		978	1,200
3802	60" diameter		3.80	6.316		775	305		1,080	1,325
3803	64" diameter		3.60	6.667		820	325		1,145	1,400
3804	68" diameter		3.40	7.059		875	345		1,220	1,475
3805	72" diameter	▼	3.20	7.500	▼	925	365		1,290	1,575

23 31 HVAC Ducts and Casings

23 31 16 – Nonmetal Ducts

23 31 16.19 PVC Ducts

		Crew	Daily Output	Labor-Hours	Unit	Material	2012 Bare Costs Labor	Equipment	Total	Total Incl O&P
0010	**PVC DUCTS**									
4000	Rigid plastic, corrosive fume resistant PVC									
4020	Straight, 6" diameter	Q-9	220	.073	L.F.	10.05	3.41		13.46	16.25
4040	8" diameter		160	.100		15.35	4.69		20.04	24
4060	10" diameter		120	.133		19.40	6.25		25.65	31
4070	12" diameter		100	.160		22.50	7.50		30	36.50
4080	14" diameter		70	.229		28	10.75		38.75	47.50
4090	16" diameter		62	.258		32.50	12.10		44.60	54.50
4100	18" diameter		58	.276		44.50	12.95		57.45	69
4110	20" diameter	Q-10	75	.320		54.50	15.55		70.05	83.50
4130	24" diameter	"	55	.436		57.50	21		78.50	95.50
4250	Coupling, 6" diameter	Q-9	88	.182	Ea.	22	8.55		30.55	37
4270	8" diameter		78	.205		28.50	9.65		38.15	45.50
4290	10" diameter		70	.229		32.50	10.75		43.25	52.50
4300	12" diameter		55	.291		35.50	13.65		49.15	60
4310	14" diameter		44	.364		46	17.05		63.05	76.50
4320	16" diameter		40	.400		48.50	18.75		67.25	82
4330	18" diameter		38	.421		63	19.75		82.75	99
4340	20" diameter	Q-10	55	.436		75.50	21		96.50	116
4360	24" diameter	"	45	.533		94.50	26		120.50	144
4470	Elbow, 90°, 6" diameter	Q-9	44	.364		99	17.05		116.05	135
4490	8" diameter		28	.571		111	27		138	164
4510	10" diameter		18	.889		135	41.50		176.50	213
4520	12" diameter		15	1.067		154	50		204	246
4530	14" diameter		11	1.455		178	68.50		246.50	299
4540	16" diameter		10	1.600		231	75		306	370
4550	18" diameter	Q-10	15	1.600		320	78		398	470
4560	20" diameter		14	1.714		480	83.50		563.50	650
4580	24" diameter		12	2		590	97.50		687.50	795
4750	Elbow 45°, use 90° and deduct					25%				

23 31 16.21 Polypropylene Ducts

		Crew	Daily Output	Labor-Hours	Unit	Material	2012 Bare Costs Labor	Equipment	Total	Total Incl O&P
0010	**POLYPROPYLENE DUCTS**									
0020	Rigid plastic, corrosive fume resistant, flame retardant, PP									
0110	Straight, 4" diameter	Q-9	200	.080	L.F.	7.55	3.75		11.30	14
0120	6" diameter		146	.110		10.75	5.15		15.90	19.65
0140	8" diameter		106	.151		13.75	7.10		20.85	26
0160	10" diameter		85	.188		20.50	8.85		29.35	36
0170	12" diameter		68	.235		39	11.05		50.05	60
0180	14" diameter		50	.320		44	15		59	71.50
0190	16" diameter		40	.400		59.50	18.75		78.25	94
0200	18" diameter		31	.516		97	24		121	143
0210	20" diameter	Q-10	44	.545		123	26.50		149.50	176
0220	22" diameter		40	.600		137	29		166	196
0230	24" diameter		37	.649		186	31.50		217.50	253
0250	28" diameter		28	.857		221	41.50		262.50	305
0270	30" diameter		24	1		249	48.50		297.50	350
0400	Coupling									
0410	4" diameter	Q-9	23	.696	Ea.	21	32.50		53.50	73
0420	6" diameter		16	1		21.50	47		68.50	95.50
0430	8" diameter		11.40	1.404		31	66		97	135
0440	10" diameter		9	1.778		41	83.50		124.50	172
0450	12" diameter		8	2		48	94		142	196

23 31 16 – Nonmetal Ducts

23 31 16.21 Polypropylene Ducts		Crew	Daily Output	Labor-Hours	Unit	Material	2012 Bare Costs Labor	Equipment	Total	Total Incl O&P
0460	14" diameter	Q-9	6.60	2.424	Ea.	93.50	114		207.50	276
0470	16" diameter		5.70	2.807		103	132		235	315
0480	18" diameter		5.20	3.077		123	144		267	355
0490	20" diameter	Q-10	6.80	3.529		134	172		306	410
0500	22" diameter		6.20	3.871		340	188		528	660
0510	24" diameter		5.80	4.138		435	201		636	785
0800	Elbow, 90°									
0810	4" diameter	Q-9	22	.727	Ea.	35	34		69	90.50
0820	6" diameter		15.40	1.039		49.50	49		98.50	129
0830	8" diameter		11	1.455		60	68.50		128.50	170
0840	10" diameter		8.60	1.860		86.50	87.50		174	228
0850	12" diameter		7.70	2.078		225	97.50		322.50	395
0860	14" diameter		6.40	2.500		260	117		377	465
0870	16" diameter		5.40	2.963		273	139		412	510
0880	18" diameter	Q-10	7.50	3.200		705	156		861	1,025
0890	20" diameter		6.60	3.636		775	177		952	1,125
0900	24" diameter		5.60	4.286		1,100	209		1,309	1,550
1000	Elbow, 45°									
1020	4" diameter	Q-9	22	.727	Ea.	23	34		57	77.50
1030	6" diameter		15.40	1.039		41.50	49		90.50	121
1040	8" diameter		11	1.455		48	68.50		116.50	157
1050	10" diameter		8.60	1.860		65	87.50		152.50	205
1060	12" diameter		7.70	2.078		174	97.50		271.50	340
1070	14" diameter		6.40	2.500		194	117		311	395
1080	16" diameter		5.40	2.963		226	139		365	460
1090	18" diameter	Q-10	7.50	3.200		445	156		601	725
1100	20" diameter		6.60	3.636		575	177		752	905
1110	24" diameter		5.60	4.286		760	209		969	1,150
1200	Tee									
1210	4" diameter	Q-9	16.50	.970	Ea.	150	45.50		195.50	235
1220	6" diameter		11.60	1.379		183	64.50		247.50	300
1230	8" diameter		8.30	1.928		228	90.50		318.50	390
1240	10" diameter		6.50	2.462		315	116		431	520
1250	12" diameter		5.80	2.759		415	129		544	650
1260	14" diameter		4.80	3.333		540	156		696	835
1270	16" diameter		4.05	3.951		600	185		785	940
1280	18" diameter	Q-10	5.60	4.286		790	209		999	1,200
1290	20" diameter		4.90	4.898		855	238		1,093	1,300
1300	22" diameter		4.40	5.455		1,025	265		1,290	1,525
1310	24" diameter		4.20	5.714		1,300	278		1,578	1,850

23 33 13.13 Volume-Control Dampers	Crew	Daily Output	Labor-Hours	Unit	Material	2012 Bare Costs Labor	Equipment	Total	Total Incl O&P
0010	**VOLUME-CONTROL DAMPERS**								
5990	Multi-blade dampers, opposed blade, 8" x 6"	1 Shee	24	.333	Ea.	21	17.40		38.40	50
5994	8" x 8"		22	.364		22	18.95		40.95	53
5996	10" x 10"		21	.381		25.50	19.85		45.35	59
6000	12" x 12"		21	.381		28.50	19.85		48.35	62
6020	12" x 18"		18	.444		38.50	23		61.50	78
6030	14" x 10"		20	.400		28	21		49	63
6031	14" x 14"		17	.471		34	24.50		58.50	75
6032	16" x 10"		18	.444		30	23		53	69
6033	16" x 12"		17	.471		34	24.50		58.50	75
6035	16" x 16"		16	.500		42.50	26		68.50	86.50
6036	18" x 14"		16	.500		42.50	26		68.50	86.50
6037	18" x 16"		15	.533		47	28		75	94
6038	18" x 18"		15	.533		50.50	28		78.50	98
6040	18" x 24"		12	.667		65	35		100	125
6060	18" x 28"		10	.800		75.50	41.50		117	147
6068	20" x 6"		18	.444		27	23		50	65.50
6069	20" x 8"		16	.500		32	26		58	75
6070	20" x 16"		14	.571		50.50	30		80.50	101
6071	20" x 18"		13	.615		54.50	32		86.50	109
6072	20" x 20"		13	.615		60.50	32		92.50	116
6073	22" x 6"		20	.400		28	21		49	63
6074	22" x 18"		14	.571		60.50	30		90.50	112
6075	22" x 20"		12	.667		66	35		101	126
6076	24" x 16"		11	.727		59.50	38		97.50	124
6077	22" x 22"		10	.800		70.50	41.50		112	141
6078	24" x 20"		8	1		70.50	52		122.50	157
6080	24" x 24"		8	1		82.50	52		134.50	170
6100	24" x 28"		6	1.333		97	69.50		166.50	212
6110	26" x 26"		6	1.333		90.50	69.50		160	206
6120	28" x 28"	Q-9	11	1.455		103	68.50		171.50	217
6130	30" x 18"		10	1.600		87.50	75		162.50	211
6132	30" x 24"		7	2.286		110	107		217	285
6133	30" x 30"		6.60	2.424		130	114		244	315
6135	32" x 32"		6.40	2.500		151	117		268	345
6150	34" x 34"		6	2.667		169	125		294	375
6151	36" x 12"		10	1.600		69	75		144	190
6152	36" x 16"		8	2		93.50	94		187.50	246
6156	36" x 32"		6.30	2.540		169	119		288	365
6157	36" x 34"		6.20	2.581		177	121		298	380
6158	36" x 36"		6	2.667		185	125		310	395
6160	44" x 28"		5.80	2.759		191	129		320	405
6180	48" x 36"		5.60	2.857		249	134		383	480
6200	56" x 36"		5.40	2.963		300	139		439	540
6220	60" x 36"		5.20	3.077		320	144		464	575
6240	60" x 44"		5	3.200		380	150		530	645
7500	Variable volume modulating motorized damper, incl. elect. mtr.									
7504	8" x 6"	1 Shee	15	.533	Ea.	115	28		143	169
7506	10" x 6"		14	.571		115	30		145	172
7510	10" x 10"		13	.615		118	32		150	179
7520	12" x 12"		12	.667		123	35		158	189
7522	12" x 16"		11	.727		124	38		162	194
7524	16" x 10"		12	.667		121	35		156	186

23 33 Air Duct Accessories

23 33 13 – Dampers

23 33 13.13 Volume-Control Dampers

		Crew	Daily Output	Labor-Hours	Unit	Material	2012 Bare Costs Labor	Equipment	Total	Total Incl O&P
7526	16" x 14"	1 Shee	10	.800	Ea.	126	41.50		167.50	202
7528	16" x 18"		9	.889		131	46.50		177.50	215
7540	18" x 12"		10	.800		126	41.50		167.50	203
7542	18" x 18"		8	1		134	52		186	227
7544	20" x 14"		8	1		137	52		189	231
7546	20" x 18"		7	1.143		143	59.50		202.50	248
7560	24" x 12"		8	1		138	52		190	232
7562	24" x 18"		7	1.143		150	59.50		209.50	256
7568	28" x 10"		7	1.143		138	59.50		197.50	243
7580	28" x 16"		6	1.333		156	69.50		225.50	278
7590	30" x 14"		5	1.600		147	83.50		230.50	288
7600	30" x 18"		4	2		189	104		293	365
7610	30" x 24"	↓	3.80	2.105		251	110		361	445
7690	48" x 48"	Q-9	6	2.667		895	125		1,020	1,175
7694	6' x 14' w/2 motors	"	3	5.333		3,225	250		3,475	3,925
7700	For thermostat, add	1 Shee	8	1		42.50	52		94.50	126
7800	For transformer 40 VA capacity, add	"	16	.500	↓	18.90	26		44.90	61
8000	Multi-blade dampers, parallel blade									
8100	8" x 8"	1 Shee	24	.333	Ea.	82	17.40		99.40	117
8120	12" x 8"		22	.364		82	18.95		100.95	119
8140	16" x 10"		20	.400		103	21		124	146
8160	18" x 12"		18	.444		113	23		136	160
8180	22" x 12"		15	.533		122	28		150	177
8200	24" x 16"		11	.727		134	38		172	206
8220	28" x 16"		10	.800		150	41.50		191.50	229
8240	30" x 16"		8	1		152	52		204	248
8260	30" x 18"	↓	7	1.143	↓	186	59.50		245.50	295
8400	Round damper, butterfly, vol. control w/lever lock reg.									
8410	6" diam.	1 Shee	22	.364	Ea.	24	18.95		42.95	55.50
8412	7" diam.		21	.381		25	19.85		44.85	58
8414	8" diam.		20	.400		25.50	21		46.50	60.50
8416	9" diam.		19	.421		27	22		49	63
8418	10" diam.		18	.444		29.50	23		52.50	68
8420	12" diam.		16	.500		30	26		56	73.50
8422	14" diam.		14	.571		39.50	30		69.50	88.50
8424	16" diam.		13	.615		42.50	32		74.50	95.50
8426	18" diam.		12	.667		52	35		87	111
8428	20" diam.		11	.727		63.50	38		101.50	128
8430	24" diam.		10	.800		79	41.50		120.50	151
8432	30" diam.		9	.889		111	46.50		157.50	193
8434	36" diam.	↓	8	1	↓	148	52		200	243
8500	Round motor operated damper									
8510	6" dia.	1 Shee	22	.364	Ea.	59.50	18.95		78.45	94.50
8512	7" dia.		21	.381		63	19.85		82.85	99.50
8514	8" dia.		20	.400		65	21		86	104
8516	10" dia.		18	.444		72	23		95	115
8518	12" dia.		16	.500		77	26		103	125
8520	14" dia.	↓	14	.571	↓	87.50	30		117.50	142

23 33 13.16 Fire Dampers

		Crew	Daily Output	Labor-Hours	Unit	Material	2012 Bare Costs Labor	Equipment	Total	Total Incl O&P
0010	**FIRE DAMPERS**									
3000	Fire damper, curtain type, 1-1/2 hr. rated, vertical, 6" x 6"	1 Shee	24	.333	Ea.	24	17.40		41.40	53
3020	8" x 6"	↓	22	.364	↓	24	18.95		42.95	55.50

23 33 Air Duct Accessories

23 33 13 – Dampers

23 33 13.16 Fire Dampers		Crew	Daily Output	Labor-Hours	Unit	Material	2012 Bare Costs Labor	Equipment	Total	Total Incl O&P
3021	8" x 8"	1 Shee	22	.364	Ea.	24	18.95		42.95	55.50
3030	10" x 10"		22	.364		24	18.95		42.95	55.50
3040	12" x 6"		22	.364		24	18.95		42.95	55.50
3044	12" x 12"		20	.400		28.50	21		49.50	63.50
3060	20" x 6"		18	.444		32	23		55	70.50
3080	12" x 8"		22	.364		24	18.95		42.95	55.50
3100	24" x 8"		16	.500		36.50	26		62.50	80
3120	12" x 10"		21	.381		24	19.85		43.85	57
3140	24" x 10"		15	.533		39	28		67	85.50
3160	36" x 10"		12	.667		50.50	35		85.50	109
3180	16" x 12"		20	.400		33	21		54	68.50
3200	24" x 12"		13	.615		41.50	32		73.50	94.50
3220	48" x 12"		10	.800		64	41.50		105.50	134
3238	14" x 14"		19	.421		36	22		58	73
3240	16" x 14"		18	.444		44	23		67	84
3260	24" x 14"		12	.667		53	35		88	111
3280	30" x 14"		11	.727		50.50	38		88.50	114
3298	16" x 16"		18	.444		40	23		63	79.50
3300	18" x 16"		17	.471		43	24.50		67.50	84.50
3320	24" x 16"		11	.727		46	38		84	109
3340	36" x 16"		10	.800		58.50	41.50		100	128
3356	18" x 18"		16	.500		44	26		70	88.50
3360	24" x 18"		10	.800		54	41.50		95.50	123
3380	48" x 18"		8	1		77.50	52		129.50	165
3398	20" x 20"		10	.800		47.50	41.50		89	116
3400	24" x 20"		8	1		54	52		106	139
3420	36" x 20"		7	1.143		65	59.50		124.50	163
3440	24" x 22"		7	1.143		55.50	59.50		115	152
3460	30" x 22"		6	1.333		60.50	69.50		130	173
3478	24" x 24"		8	1		56.50	52		108.50	142
3480	26" x 24"		7	1.143		56.50	59.50		116	153
3484	32" x 24"	Q-9	13	1.231		67	58		125	162
3500	48" x 24"		12	1.333		87	62.50		149.50	191
3520	28" x 26"		13	1.231		63.50	58		121.50	158
3540	30" x 28"		12	1.333		70	62.50		132.50	173
3560	48" x 30"		11	1.455		102	68.50		170.50	216
3580	48" x 36"		10	1.600		136	75		211	263
3590	32" x 40"		10	1.600		105	75		180	230
3600	44" x 44"		10	1.600		144	75		219	273
3620	48" x 48"		8	2		161	94		255	320
3700	U.L. label included in above									
3800	For horizontal operation, add				Ea.	20%				
3900	For cap for blades out of air stream, add					20%				
4000	For 10" 22 ga., U.L. approved sleeve, add					35%				
4100	For 10" 22 ga., U.L. sleeve, 100% free area, add					65%				
4200	For oversize openings group dampers									
4210	Fire damper, round, Type A									
4214	4" diam.	1 Shee	20	.400	Ea.	59	21		80	96.50
4216	5" diam.		16	.500		50	26		76	95
4218	6" diam.		14.30	.559		50	29		79	99.50
4220	7" diam.		13.30	.602		50	31.50		81.50	103
4222	8" diam.		11.40	.702		50	36.50		86.50	111
4224	9" diam.		10.80	.741		55.50	38.50		94	120

23 33 Air Duct Accessories

23 33 13 — Dampers

23 33 13.16 Fire Dampers

		Crew	Daily Output	Labor-Hours	Unit	Material	2012 Bare Costs Labor	Equipment	Total	Total Incl O&P
4226	10" diam.	1 Shee	10	.800	Ea.	55.50	41.50		97	125
4228	12" diam.		9.50	.842		62.50	44		106.50	136
4230	14" diam.		8.20	.976		77.50	51		128.50	163
4232	16" diam.		7.60	1.053		77.50	55		132.50	169
4234	18" diam.		7.20	1.111		94	58		152	192
4236	20" diam.		6.40	1.250		97	65		162	206
4238	22" diam.		6.10	1.311		106	68.50		174.50	221
4240	24" diam.		5.70	1.404		111	73		184	234
4242	26" diam.		5.50	1.455		125	76		201	254
4244	28" diam.		5.40	1.481		131	77.50		208.50	262
4246	30" diam.	▼	5.30	1.509	▼	138	78.50		216.50	271
4500	Fire/smoke combination damper, louver type, UL									
4506	6" x 6"	1 Shee	24	.333	Ea.	38	17.40		55.40	68.50
4510	8" x 8"		22	.364		134	18.95		152.95	176
4520	16" x 8"		20	.400		146	21		167	193
4540	18" x 8"		18	.444		146	23		169	197
4560	20" x 8"		16	.500		157	26		183	212
4580	10" x 10"		21	.381		151	19.85		170.85	198
4600	24" x 10"		15	.533		178	28		206	239
4620	30" x 10"		12	.667		184	35		219	255
4640	12" x 12"		20	.400		158	21		179	206
4660	18" x 12"		18	.444		161	23		184	213
4680	24" x 12"		13	.615		170	32		202	235
4700	30" x 12"		11	.727		176	38		214	252
4720	14" x 14"		17	.471		170	24.50		194.50	225
4740	16" x 14"		18	.444		175	23		198	228
4760	20" x 14"		14	.571		178	30		208	242
4780	24" x 14"		12	.667		183	35		218	254
4800	30" x 14"		10	.800		193	41.50		234.50	277
4820	16" x 16"		16	.500		188	26		214	247
4840	20" x 16"		14	.571		193	30		223	259
4860	24" x 16"		11	.727		199	38		237	277
4880	30" x 16"		8	1		208	52		260	310
4900	18" x 18"		15	.533		186	28		214	248
5000	24" x 18"		10	.800		199	41.50		240.50	283
5020	36" x 18"		7	1.143		218	59.50		277.50	330
5040	20" x 20"		13	.615		208	32		240	278
5060	24" x 20"		8	1		213	52		265	315
5080	30" x 20"		8	1		224	52		276	325
5100	36" x 20"		7	1.143		236	59.50		295.50	350
5120	24" x 24"		8	1		230	52		282	335
5130	30" x 24"	▼	7.60	1.053		218	55		273	325
5140	36" x 24"	Q-9	12	1.333		252	62.50		314.50	375
5141	36" x 30"		10	1.600		266	75		341	405
5142	40" x 36"		8	2		470	94		564	665
5143	48" x 48"	▼	4	4		920	188		1,108	1,300
5150	Damper operator motor, 24 or 120 volt	1 Shee	16	.500	▼	252	26		278	315

23 33 13.25 Exhaust Vent Damper

		Crew	Daily Output	Labor-Hours	Unit	Material	2012 Bare Costs Labor	Equipment	Total	Total Incl O&P
0010	**EXHAUST VENT DAMPER**, Auto, OB with elect. actuator.									
1110	6" x 6"	1 Shee	24	.333	Ea.	62	17.40		79.40	94.50
1114	8" x 6"		23	.348		63.50	18.15		81.65	97.50
1116	8" x 8"	▼	22	.364	▼	66	18.95		84.95	102

23 33 13 – Dampers

23 33 13.25 Exhaust Vent Damper

		Crew	Daily Output	Labor-Hours	Unit	Material	2012 Bare Costs Labor	2012 Bare Costs Equipment	Total	Total Incl O&P
1118	10" x 6"	1 Shee	23	.348	Ea.	66	18.15		84.15	100
1120	10" x 10"		22	.364		70.50	18.95		89.45	107
1122	12" x 6"		22	.364		66.50	18.95		85.45	102
1124	12" x 10"		21	.381		74	19.85		93.85	112
1126	12" x 12"		20	.400		78	21		99	118
1128	14" x 6"		21	.381		69	19.85		88.85	106
1130	14" x 10"		19	.421		78	22		100	119
1132	16" x 6"		21	.381		69.50	19.85		89.35	107
1134	16" x 8"		20	.400		77	21		98	117
1136	18" x 6"		20	.400		73.50	21		94.50	113
1138	18" x 8"		19	.421		78	22		100	119

23 33 13.28 Splitter Damper Assembly

		Crew	Daily Output	Labor-Hours	Unit	Material	2012 Bare Costs Labor	2012 Bare Costs Equipment	Total	Total Incl O&P
0009	**SPLITTER DAMPER ASSEMBLY**									
0010	Self locking, 1' rod	1 Shee	24	.333	Ea.	23.50	17.40		40.90	52
7020	3' rod		22	.364		30	18.95		48.95	62
7040	4' rod		20	.400		33.50	21		54.50	69
7060	6' rod		18	.444		41	23		64	80.50

23 33 13.32 Relief Damper

		Crew	Daily Output	Labor-Hours	Unit	Material	2012 Bare Costs Labor	2012 Bare Costs Equipment	Total	Total Incl O&P
0010	**RELIEF DAMPER**, Electronic bypass with tight seal									
8310	8" x 6"	1 Shee	22	.364	Ea.	171	18.95		189.95	218
8314	10" x 6"		22	.364		171	18.95		189.95	218
8318	10" x 10"		21	.381		178	19.85		197.85	227
8322	12" x 12"		20	.400		181	21		202	232
8326	12" x 16"		19	.421		189	22		211	242
8330	16" x 10"		20	.400		199	21		220	251
8334	16" x 14"		18	.444		204	23		227	260
8338	16" x 18"		17	.471		221	24.50		245.50	281
8342	18" x 12"		18	.444		221	23		244	279
8346	18" x 18"		15	.533		209	28		237	273
8350	20" x 14"		14	.571		206	30		236	273
8354	20" x 18"		13	.615		215	32		247	286
8358	24" x 12"		13	.615		210	32		242	280
8362	24" x 18"		10	.800		164	41.50		205.50	244
8363	24" x 24"		10	.800		229	41.50		270.50	315
8364	24" x 36"		9	.889		272	46.50		318.50	370
8365	24" x 48"		6	1.333		305	69.50		374.50	440
8366	28" x 10"		13	.615		151	32		183	215
8370	28" x 16"		10	.800		232	41.50		273.50	320
8374	30" x 14"		11	.727		159	38		197	233
8378	30" x 18"		8	1		240	52		292	345
8382	30" x 24"		6	1.333		254	69.50		323.50	385
8390	46" x 36"		4	2		335	104		439	530
8394	48" x 48"		3	2.667		365	139		504	615
8396	54" x 36"		2	4		390	209		599	750

23 33 19 – Duct Silencers

23 33 19.10 Duct Silencers

		Crew	Daily Output	Labor-Hours	Unit	Material	2012 Bare Costs Labor	2012 Bare Costs Equipment	Total	Total Incl O&P
0009	**DUCT SILENCERS**									
0010	Silencers, noise control for air flow, duct				MCFM	57			57	63
9004	Duct sound trap, packaged									
9010	12" x 18" x 36", 2000 CFM	1 Shee	12	.667	Ea.	445	35		480	545
9011	24" x 18" x 36", 9000 CFM	Q-9	80	.200		510	9.40		519.40	580
9012	24" x 24" x 36", 9000 CFM		60	.267		770	12.50		782.50	865

23 33 Air Duct Accessories

23 33 19 – Duct Silencers

23 33 19.10 Duct Silencers

23 33 19.10 Duct Silencers	Crew	Daily Output	Labor-Hours	Unit	Material	2012 Bare Costs Labor	Equipment	Total	Total Incl O&P
9013	24" x 30" x 36", 9000 CFM	Q-9	50	.320	Ea.	820	15		835	925
9014	24" x 36" x 36", 9000 CFM		40	.400		1,025	18.75		1,043.75	1,150
9015	24" x 48" x 36", 9000 CFM		28	.571		1,325	27		1,352	1,525
9018	36" x 18" x 36", 6300 CFM		42	.381		1,025	17.90		1,042.90	1,150
9019	36" x 36" x 36", 6300 CFM		21	.762		2,050	36		2,086	2,300
9020	36" x 48" x 36", 6300 CFM		14	1.143		2,675	53.50		2,728.50	3,000
9021	36" x 60" x 36", 6300 CFM		13	1.231		3,375	58		3,433	3,825
9022	48" x 48" x 36", 6300 CFM		12	1.333		3,575	62.50		3,637.50	4,050
9023	24" x 24" x 60", 6000 CFM		3.60	4.444		1,175	209		1,384	1,625
9026	24" x 30" x 60", 7000 CFM		3.50	4.571		1,325	215		1,540	1,775
9030	24" x 36" x 60", 8000 CFM		3.40	4.706		1,450	221		1,671	1,925
9034	24" x 48" x 60", 11,000 CFM		3.30	4.848		1,250	228		1,478	1,725
9038	36" x 18" x 60", 6300 CFM		3.50	4.571		980	215		1,195	1,400
9042	36" x 36" x 60", 12,000 CFM		3.30	4.848		1,575	228		1,803	2,075
9046	36" x 48" x 60", 17,000 CFM		3.10	5.161		2,075	242		2,317	2,650
9050	36" x 60" x 60", 20,000 CFM		2.80	5.714		2,525	268		2,793	3,175
9054	48" x 48" x 60", 23,000 CFM		2.60	6.154		2,900	289		3,189	3,650
9056	48" x 60" x 60", 23,000 CFM		2.10	7.619		3,650	360		4,010	4,550

23 33 23 – Turning Vanes

23 33 23.13 Air Turning Vanes

		Crew	Daily Output	Labor-Hours	Unit	Material	Labor	Equipment	Total	Total Incl O&P
0010	**AIR TURNING VANES**									
9400	Turning vane components									
9410	Turning vane rail	1 Shee	160	.050	L.F.	.75	2.61		3.36	4.81
9420	Double thick, factory fab. vane		300	.027		1.17	1.39		2.56	3.41
9428	12" high set		170	.047		1.68	2.45		4.13	5.60
9432	14" high set		160	.050		1.96	2.61		4.57	6.15
9434	16" high set		150	.053		2.24	2.78		5.02	6.70
9436	18" high set		144	.056		2.52	2.90		5.42	7.20
9438	20" high set		138	.058		2.80	3.02		5.82	7.70
9440	22" high set		130	.062		3.08	3.21		6.29	8.30
9442	24" high set		124	.065		3.36	3.36		6.72	8.85
9444	26" high set		116	.069		3.64	3.60		7.24	9.50
9446	30" high set		112	.071		4.20	3.73		7.93	10.30

23 33 33 – Duct-Mounting Access Doors

23 33 33.13 Duct Access Doors

		Crew	Daily Output	Labor-Hours	Unit	Material	Labor	Equipment	Total	Total Incl O&P
0010	**DUCT ACCESS DOORS**									
1000	Duct access door, insulated, 6" x 6"	1 Shee	14	.571	Ea.	16.05	30		46.05	63
1020	10" x 10"		11	.727		18.45	38		56.45	78.50
1040	12" x 12"		10	.800		20	41.50		61.50	85.50
1050	12" x 18"		9	.889		37	46.50		83.50	111
1060	16" x 12"		9	.889		29.50	46.50		76	103
1070	18" x 18"		8	1		32.50	52		84.50	115
1074	24" x 18"		8	1		44	52		96	128
1080	24" x 24"		8	1		48	52		100	133

23 33 46 – Flexible Ducts

23 33 46.10 Flexible Air Ducts

		Crew	Daily Output	Labor-Hours	Unit	Material	Labor	Equipment	Total	Total Incl O&P
0010	**FLEXIBLE AIR DUCTS**	R233100-20								
1280	Add to labor for elevated installation									
1282	of prefabricated (purchased) ductwork									
1283	10' to 15' high						10%			
1284	15' to 20' high						20%			

23 33 46.10 Flexible Air Ducts		Crew	Daily Output	Labor-Hours	Unit	Material	2012 Bare Costs Labor	Equipment	Total	Total Incl O&P
1285	20' to 25' high						25%			
1286	25' to 30' high						35%			
1287	30' to 35' high						40%			
1288	35' to 40' high						50%			
1289	Over 40' high						55%			
1300	Flexible, coated fiberglass fabric on corr. resist. metal helix									
1400	pressure to 12" (WG) UL-181									
1500	Non-insulated, 3" diameter		Q-9	400	.040	L.F.	1.12	1.88		3	4.09
1520	4" diameter			360	.044		1.12	2.09		3.21	4.41
1540	5" diameter			320	.050		1.12	2.35		3.47	4.81
1560	6" diameter			280	.057		1.40	2.68		4.08	5.65
1580	7" diameter			240	.067		1.46	3.13		4.59	6.40
1600	8" diameter			200	.080		1.76	3.75		5.51	7.65
1620	9" diameter			180	.089		1.82	4.17		5.99	8.35
1640	10" diameter			160	.100		2.28	4.69		6.97	9.65
1660	12" diameter			120	.133		2.73	6.25		8.98	12.55
1680	14" diameter			80	.200		3.23	9.40		12.63	17.85
1700	16" diameter			60	.267		5.05	12.50		17.55	24.50
1800	For adjustable clamps, add					Ea.	.77			.77	.85
1900	Insulated, 1" thick, PE jacket, 3" diameter	G	Q-9	380	.042	L.F.	2.22	1.98		4.20	5.45
1910	4" diameter	G		340	.047		2.22	2.21		4.43	5.80
1920	5" diameter	G		300	.053		2.23	2.50		4.73	6.25
1940	6" diameter	G		260	.062		2.50	2.89		5.39	7.15
1960	7" diameter	G		220	.073		2.73	3.41		6.14	8.20
1980	8" diameter	G		180	.089		3.01	4.17		7.18	9.65
2000	9" diameter	G		160	.100		3.17	4.69		7.86	10.65
2020	10" diameter	G		140	.114		3.66	5.35		9.01	12.25
2040	12" diameter	G		100	.160		4.20	7.50		11.70	16.05
2060	14" diameter	G		80	.200		5.10	9.40		14.50	19.95
2080	16" diameter	G		60	.267		7.25	12.50		19.75	27
2100	18" diameter	G		45	.356		8.35	16.70		25.05	34.50
2120	20" diameter	G	Q-10	65	.369		9.45	17.95		27.40	38
2500	Insulated, heavy duty, coated fiberglass fabric									
2520	4" diameter	G	Q-9	340	.047	L.F.	3.20	2.21		5.41	6.90
2540	5" diameter	G		300	.053		3.32	2.50		5.82	7.45
2560	6" diameter	G		260	.062		3.71	2.89		6.60	8.50
2580	7" diameter	G		220	.073		4.13	3.41		7.54	9.75
2600	8" diameter	G		180	.089		4.53	4.17		8.70	11.35
2620	9" diameter	G		160	.100		5.05	4.69		9.74	12.75
2640	10" diameter	G		140	.114		5.70	5.35		11.05	14.50
2660	12" diameter	G		100	.160		6.65	7.50		14.15	18.75
2680	14" diameter	G		80	.200		8.05	9.40		17.45	23
2700	16" diameter	G		60	.267		11.35	12.50		23.85	31.50
2720	18" diameter	G		45	.356		13.25	16.70		29.95	40
2800	Flexible, aluminum, pressure to 12" (WG) UL-181									
2820	Non-insulated									
2830	3" diameter		Q-9	400	.040	L.F.	1.14	1.88		3.02	4.11
2831	4" diameter			360	.044		1.23	2.09		3.32	4.53
2832	5" diameter			320	.050		1.57	2.35		3.92	5.30
2833	6" diameter			280	.057		2.01	2.68		4.69	6.30
2834	7" diameter			240	.067		2.44	3.13		5.57	7.45
2835	8" diameter			200	.080		2.75	3.75		6.50	8.75
2836	9" diameter			180	.089		3.25	4.17		7.42	9.95

23 33 46 – Flexible Ducts

23 33 46.10 Flexible Air Ducts		Crew	Daily Output	Labor-Hours	Unit	Material	2012 Bare Costs Labor	Equipment	Total	Total Incl O&P
2837	10" diameter	Q-9	160	.100	L.F.	3.86	4.69		8.55	11.40
2838	12" diameter		120	.133		5.05	6.25		11.30	15.10
2839	14" diameter		80	.200		5.70	9.40		15.10	20.50
2840	15" diameter		70	.229		7.70	10.75		18.45	25
2841	16" diameter		60	.267		8.90	12.50		21.40	29
2842	18" diameter		45	.356		10.10	16.70		26.80	36.50
2843	20" diameter	Q-10	65	.369		11.65	17.95		29.60	40.50
2880	Insulated, 1" thick with 3/4 lb., PE jacket									
2890	3" diameter G	Q-9	380	.042	L.F.	2.84	1.98		4.82	6.15
2891	4" diameter G		340	.047		2.84	2.21		5.05	6.50
2892	5" diameter G		300	.053		3.25	2.50		5.75	7.40
2893	6" diameter G		260	.062		3.87	2.89		6.76	8.65
2894	7" diameter G		220	.073		4.68	3.41		8.09	10.35
2895	8" diameter G		180	.089		4.79	4.17		8.96	11.60
2896	9" diameter G		160	.100		5.55	4.69		10.24	13.25
2897	10" diameter G		140	.114		6.60	5.35		11.95	15.45
2898	12" diameter G		100	.160		7.70	7.50		15.20	19.90
2899	14" diameter G		80	.200		8.75	9.40		18.15	24
2900	15" diameter G		70	.229		10.75	10.75		21.50	28
2901	16" diameter G		60	.267		12.40	12.50		24.90	32.50
2902	18" diameter G		45	.356		14.60	16.70		31.30	41.50
3000	Transitions, 3" deep, square to round									
3010	6" x 6" to round	Q-9	44	.364	Ea.	9.90	17.05		26.95	37
3014	6" x 12" to round		42	.381		17.60	17.90		35.50	47
3018	8" x 8" to round		40	.400		11.55	18.75		30.30	41
3022	9" x 9" to round		38	.421		11.55	19.75		31.30	42.50
3026	9" x 12" to round		37	.432		22.50	20.50		43	56
3030	9" x 15" to round		36	.444		26.50	21		47.50	61
3034	10" x 10" to round		34	.471		13.75	22		35.75	48.50
3038	10" x 22" to round		32	.500		32.50	23.50		56	71.50
3042	12" x 12" to round		30	.533		13.75	25		38.75	53
3046	12" x 18" to round		28	.571		32.50	27		59.50	76.50
3050	12" x 24" to round		26	.615		32.50	29		61.50	79.50
3054	15" x 15" to round		25	.640		18.70	30		48.70	66.50
3058	15" x 18" to round		24	.667		35	31.50		66.50	86
3062	18" x 18" to round		22	.727		26.50	34		60.50	81
3066	21" x 21" to round		21	.762		29	36		65	86.50
3070	22" x 22" to round		20	.800		29	37.50		66.50	89
3074	24" x 24" to round		18	.889		33	41.50		74.50	100
5000	Flexible, aluminum, acoustical, pressure to 2" (wg), NFPA-90A									
5010	Fiberglass insulation 1-1/2" thick, 1/2 lb. density									
5020	Polyethylene jacket, UL approved									
5026	5" diameter	Q-9	300	.053	L.F.	3.89	2.50		6.39	8.10
5030	6" diameter		260	.062		4.65	2.89		7.54	9.50
5034	7" diameter		220	.073		5.60	3.41		9.01	11.35
5038	8" diameter		180	.089		5.75	4.17		9.92	12.65
5042	9" diameter		160	.100		6.65	4.69		11.34	14.50
5046	10" diameter		140	.114		8.85	5.35		14.20	17.95
5050	12" diameter		100	.160		9.75	7.50		17.25	22
5054	14" diameter		80	.200		10.45	9.40		19.85	26
5058	16" diameter		60	.267		14.85	12.50		27.35	35.50
5072	Hospital grade, PE jacket, UL approved									
5076	5" diameter	Q-9	300	.053	L.F.	4.28	2.50		6.78	8.50

23 33 46 – Flexible Ducts

23 33 46.10 Flexible Air Ducts		Crew	Daily Output	Labor-Hours	Unit	Material	2012 Bare Costs Labor	Equipment	Total	Total Incl O&P
5080	6" diameter	Q-9	260	.062	L.F.	4.57	2.89		7.46	9.45
5084	7" diameter		220	.073		6.15	3.41		9.56	12
5088	8" diameter		180	.089		6.30	4.17		10.47	13.30
5092	9" diameter		160	.100		7.30	4.69		11.99	15.20
5096	10" diameter		140	.114		9.75	5.35		15.10	18.95
5100	12" diameter		100	.160		10.70	7.50		18.20	23.50
5104	14" diameter		80	.200		11.50	9.40		20.90	27
5108	16" diameter	▼	60	.267	▼	16.05	12.50		28.55	36.50
5140	Flexible, aluminum, silencer, pressure to 12" (wg), NFPA-90A									
5144	Fiberglass insulation 1-1/2" thick, 1/2 lb. density									
5148	Aluminum outer shell, UL approved									
5152	5" diameter	Q-9	290	.055	L.F.	16.70	2.59		19.29	22.50
5156	6" diameter		250	.064		17.70	3		20.70	24
5160	7" diameter		210	.076		19.45	3.58		23.03	27
5164	8" diameter		170	.094		21	4.42		25.42	30
5168	9" diameter		150	.107		23	5		28	32.50
5172	10" diameter		130	.123		24	5.80		29.80	35.50
5176	12" diameter		90	.178		28	8.35		36.35	43
5180	14" diameter		70	.229		32	10.75		42.75	52
5184	16" diameter	▼	50	.320	▼	41.50	15		56.50	68.50
5200	Hospital grade, aluminum shell, UL approved									
5204	5" diameter	Q-9	280	.057	L.F.	17.15	2.68		19.83	23
5208	6" diameter		240	.067		18.25	3.13		21.38	25
5212	7" diameter		200	.080		20	3.75		23.75	27.50
5216	8" diameter		160	.100		21.50	4.69		26.19	30.50
5220	9" diameter		140	.114		23.50	5.35		28.85	34
5224	10" diameter		130	.123		25	5.80		30.80	36.50
5228	12" diameter		80	.200		29	9.40		38.40	46
5232	14" diameter		60	.267		33	12.50		45.50	55.50
5236	16" diameter	▼	40	.400	▼	43	18.75		61.75	76

23 33 53 – Duct Liners

23 33 53.10 Duct Liner Board

			Crew	Daily Output	Labor-Hours	Unit	Material	Labor	Equipment	Total	Total Incl O&P
0010	**DUCT LINER BOARD**										
3340	Board type fiberglass liner, FSK, 1-1/2 lb. density										
3344	1" thick	G	Q-14	150	.107	S.F.	.60	4.69		5.29	7.95
3345	1-1/2" thick	G		130	.123		.66	5.40		6.06	9.20
3346	2" thick	G		120	.133		.77	5.85		6.62	10
3348	3" thick	G		110	.145		.99	6.40		7.39	11.05
3350	4" thick	G		100	.160		1.22	7.05		8.27	12.30
3356	3 lb. density, 1" thick	G		150	.107		.77	4.69		5.46	8.15
3358	1-1/2" thick	G		130	.123		.97	5.40		6.37	9.50
3360	2" thick	G		120	.133		1.18	5.85		7.03	10.45
3362	2-1/2" thick	G		110	.145		1.38	6.40		7.78	11.45
3364	3" thick	G		100	.160		1.59	7.05		8.64	12.70
3366	4" thick			90	.178		2	7.80		9.80	14.40
3370	6 lb. density, 1" thick			140	.114		1.09	5.05		6.14	9.05
3374	1-1/2" thick			120	.133		1.46	5.85		7.31	10.75
3378	2" thick		▼	100	.160	▼	1.82	7.05		8.87	12.95
3490	Board type, fiberglass liner, 3 lb. density										
3680	No finish										
3700	1" thick	G	Q-14	170	.094	S.F.	.43	4.14		4.57	6.90
3710	1-1/2" thick	G	↓	140	.114	↓	.64	5.05		5.69	8.55

23 33 Air Duct Accessories

23 33 53 – Duct Liners

23 33 53.10 Duct Liner Board		Crew	Daily Output	Labor-Hours	Unit	Material	2012 Bare Costs Labor	Equipment	Total	Total Incl O&P
3720	2" thick	G	Q-14	130	.123	S.F.	.86	5.40		6.26	9.40
3940	Board type, non-fibrous foam										
3950	Temperature, bacteria and fungi resistant										
3960	1" thick	G	Q-14	150	.107	S.F.	2.25	4.69		6.94	9.80
3970	1-1/2" thick	G		130	.123		2.95	5.40		8.35	11.70
3980	2" thick	G	↓	120	.133	↓	3.60	5.85		9.45	13.10

23 34 HVAC Fans

23 34 13 – Axial HVAC Fans

23 34 13.10 Axial Flow HVAC Fans

			Crew	Daily Output	Labor-Hours	Unit	Material	2012 Bare Costs Labor	Equipment	Total	Total Incl O&P
0010	**AXIAL FLOW HVAC FANS**	R233100-10									
0020	Air conditioning and process air handling										
0030	Axial flow, compact, low sound, 2.5" S.P.	R233400-10									
0050	3,800 CFM, 5 HP		Q-20	3.40	5.882	Ea.	4,800	281		5,081	5,700
0080	6,400 CFM, 5 HP			2.80	7.143		5,350	340		5,690	6,425
0100	10,500 CFM, 7-1/2 HP			2.40	8.333		6,675	400		7,075	7,925
0120	15,600 CFM, 10 HP			1.60	12.500		8,400	600		9,000	10,200
0140	23,000 CFM, 15 HP			.70	28.571		12,900	1,375		14,275	16,300
0160	28,000 CFM, 20 HP		↓	.40	50	↓	14,400	2,400		16,800	19,400
0500	Axial flow, constant speed										
0505	Direct drive, 1/8" S.P.										
0510	12", 1060 CFM, 1/6 HP		Q-20	3	6.667	Ea.	560	320		880	1,100
0514	12", 2095 CFM, 1/2 HP			3	6.667		660	320		980	1,200
0518	16", 2490 CFM, 1/3 HP			2.80	7.143		660	340		1,000	1,250
0522	20", 4130 CFM, 3/4 HP			2.60	7.692		785	370		1,155	1,425
0526	22", 4700 CFM, 3/4 HP			2.60	7.692		1,175	370		1,545	1,825
0530	24", 5850 CFM, 1 HP			2.50	8		1,200	385		1,585	1,900
0534	24", 7925 CFM, 1-1/2 HP			2.40	8.333		1,475	400		1,875	2,225
0538	30", 10640 CFM, 2 HP			2.20	9.091		1,900	435		2,335	2,750
0542	30", 14765 CFM, 2-1/2 HP			2.10	9.524		2,225	455		2,680	3,150
0546	36", 16780 CFM, 2 HP			2.10	9.524		2,275	455		2,730	3,225
0550	36", 22920 CFM, 5 HP		↓	1.80	11.111	↓	2,500	530		3,030	3,575
0560	Belt drive, 1/8" S.P.										
0562	15", 2800 CFM, 1/3 HP		Q-20	3.20	6.250	Ea.	940	299		1,239	1,475
0564	15", 3400 CFM, 1/2 HP			3	6.667		965	320		1,285	1,550
0568	18", 3280 CFM, 1/3 HP			2.80	7.143		1,025	340		1,365	1,650
0572	18", 3900 CFM, 1/2 HP			2.80	7.143		1,050	340		1,390	1,675
0576	18", 5250 CFM, 1 HP			2.70	7.407		1,175	355		1,530	1,825
0584	24", 6430 CFM, 1 HP			2.50	8		1,525	385		1,910	2,250
0588	24", 8860 CFM, 2 HP			2.40	8.333		1,875	400		2,275	2,650
0592	30", 9250 CFM, 1 HP			2.20	9.091		1,950	435		2,385	2,800
0596	30", 16900 CFM, 5 HP			2	10		2,075	480		2,555	3,000
0604	36", 14475 CFM, 2 HP			2.30	8.696		2,175	415		2,590	3,025
0608	36", 20080 CFM, 5 HP			1.80	11.111		2,350	530		2,880	3,400
0612	36", 14475 CFM, 7-1/2 HP			1.60	12.500		2,550	600		3,150	3,700
0616	42", 29000 CFM, 7-1/2 HP		↓	1.40	14.286	↓	3,050	685		3,735	4,425
1000	Return air fan										
1010	9200 CFM		Q-20	1.40	14.286	Ea.	3,925	685		4,610	5,350
1020	13,200 CFM			1.30	15.385		5,625	735		6,360	7,300
1030	16,500 CFM			1.20	16.667		7,025	800		7,825	8,925
1040	19,500 CFM		↓	1	20		8,300	955		9,255	10,600

23 34 HVAC Fans

23 34 13 – Axial HVAC Fans

23 34 13.10 Axial Flow HVAC Fans

		Crew	Daily Output	Labor-Hours	Unit	Material	2012 Bare Costs Labor	Equipment	Total	Total Incl O&P
1500	Vaneaxial, low pressure, 2000 CFM, 1/2 HP	Q-20	3.60	5.556	Ea.	2,025	266		2,291	2,625
1520	4,000 CFM, 1 HP		3.20	6.250		2,375	299		2,674	3,050
1540	8,000 CFM, 2 HP		2.80	7.143		3,000	340		3,340	3,825
1560	16,000 CFM, 5 HP	↓	2.40	8.333	↓	4,225	400		4,625	5,250

23 34 14 – Blower HVAC Fans

23 34 14.10 Blower Type HVAC Fans

		Crew	Daily Output	Labor-Hours	Unit	Material	2012 Bare Costs Labor	Equipment	Total	Total Incl O&P
0010	**BLOWER TYPE HVAC FANS**									
2000	Blowers, direct drive with motor, complete									
2020	1045 CFM @ .5" S.P., 1/5 HP	Q-20	18	1.111	Ea.	254	53		307	360
2040	1385 CFM @ .5" S.P., 1/4 HP		18	1.111		256	53		309	360
2060	1640 CFM @ .5" S.P., 1/3 HP		18	1.111		232	53		285	335
2080	1760 CFM @ .5" S.P., 1/2 HP	↓	18	1.111	↓	242	53		295	345
2090	4 speed									
2100	1164 to 1739 CFM @ .5" S.P., 1/3 HP	Q-20	16	1.250	Ea.	249	60		309	365
2120	1467 to 2218 CFM @ 1.0" S.P., 3/4 HP	"	14	1.429	"	288	68.50		356.50	420
2500	Ceiling fan, right angle, extra quiet, 0.10" S.P.									
2520	95 CFM	Q-20	20	1	Ea.	264	48		312	365
2540	210 CFM		19	1.053		310	50.50		360.50	420
2560	385 CFM		18	1.111		395	53		448	515
2580	885 CFM		16	1.250		780	60		840	950
2600	1,650 CFM		13	1.538		1,075	73.50		1,148.50	1,300
2620	2,960 CFM	↓	11	1.818		1,450	87		1,537	1,700
2640	For wall or roof cap, add	1 Shee	16	.500		264	26		290	330
2660	For straight thru fan, add					10%				
2680	For speed control switch, add	1 Elec	16	.500	↓	144	26		170	198
7500	Utility set, steel construction, pedestal, 1/4" S.P.									
7520	Direct drive, 150 CFM, 1/8 HP	Q-20	6.40	3.125	Ea.	805	150		955	1,100
7540	485 CFM, 1/6 HP		5.80	3.448		1,025	165		1,190	1,375
7560	1950 CFM, 1/2 HP		4.80	4.167		1,200	199		1,399	1,600
7580	2410 CFM, 3/4 HP		4.40	4.545		2,200	218		2,418	2,725
7600	3328 CFM, 1-1/2 HP	↓	3	6.667	↓	2,450	320		2,770	3,150
7680	V-belt drive, drive cover, 3 phase									
7700	800 CFM, 1/4 HP	Q-20	6	3.333	Ea.	900	160		1,060	1,225
7720	1,300 CFM, 1/3 HP		5	4		940	191		1,131	1,325
7740	2,000 CFM, 1 HP		4.60	4.348		1,125	208		1,333	1,550
7760	2,900 CFM, 3/4 HP		4.20	4.762		1,500	228		1,728	2,000
7780	3,600 CFM, 3/4 HP		4	5		1,850	239		2,089	2,400
7800	4,800 CFM, 1 HP		3.50	5.714		2,175	273		2,448	2,825
7820	6,700 CFM, 1-1/2 HP		3	6.667		2,700	320		3,020	3,450
7830	7,500 CFM, 2 HP		2.50	8		3,650	385		4,035	4,600
7840	11,000 CFM, 3 HP		2	10		4,900	480		5,380	6,100
7860	13,000 CFM, 3 HP		1.60	12.500		4,975	600		5,575	6,350
7880	15,000 CFM, 5 HP		1	20		5,150	955		6,105	7,100
7900	17,000 CFM, 7-1/2 HP		.80	25		5,500	1,200		6,700	7,875
7920	20,000 CFM, 7-1/2 HP	↓	.80	25	↓	6,550	1,200		7,750	9,050

23 34 16 – Centrifugal HVAC Fans

23 34 16.10 Centrifugal Type HVAC Fans

		Crew	Daily Output	Labor-Hours	Unit	Material	2012 Bare Costs Labor	Equipment	Total	Total Incl O&P
0010	**CENTRIFUGAL TYPE HVAC FANS**									
0200	In-line centrifugal, supply/exhaust booster									
0220	aluminum wheel/hub, disconnect switch, 1/4" S.P.									
0240	500 CFM, 10" diameter connection	Q-20	3	6.667	Ea.	1,150	320		1,470	1,750
0260	1,380 CFM, 12" diameter connection	↓	2	10	↓	1,225	480		1,705	2,075

23 34 16.10 Centrifugal Type HVAC Fans	Crew	Daily Output	Labor-Hours	Unit	Material	2012 Bare Costs Labor	2012 Bare Costs Equipment	Total	Total Incl O&P
0280	1,520 CFM, 16" diameter connection	Q-20	2	10	Ea.	1,325	480		1,805	2,175
0300	2,560 CFM, 18" diameter connection		1	20		1,450	955		2,405	3,050
0320	3,480 CFM, 20" diameter connection		.80	25		1,725	1,200		2,925	3,700
0326	5,080 CFM, 20" diameter connection		.75	26.667		1,875	1,275		3,150	3,975
0340	7,500 CFM, 22" diameter connection		.70	28.571		2,225	1,375		3,600	4,525
0350	10,000 CFM, 27" diameter connection		.65	30.769		2,700	1,475		4,175	5,200
3500	Centrifugal, airfoil, motor and drive, complete									
3520	1000 CFM, 1/2 HP	Q-20	2.50	8	Ea.	1,725	385		2,110	2,475
3540	2,000 CFM, 1 HP		2	10		1,950	480		2,430	2,875
3560	4,000 CFM, 3 HP		1.80	11.111		2,500	530		3,030	3,550
3580	8,000 CFM, 7-1/2 HP		1.40	14.286		3,750	685		4,435	5,175
3600	12,000 CFM, 10 HP		1	20		5,000	955		5,955	6,950
4000	Single width, belt drive, not incl. motor, capacities									
4020	at 2000 fpm, 2.5" S.P. for indicated motor									
4040	6900 CFM, 5 HP	Q-9	2.40	6.667	Ea.	3,500	315		3,815	4,325
4060	10,340 CFM, 7-1/2 HP		2.20	7.273		4,875	340		5,215	5,875
4080	15,320 CFM, 10 HP		2	8		5,750	375		6,125	6,900
4100	22,780 CFM, 15 HP		1.80	8.889		8,550	415		8,965	10,000
4120	33,840 CFM, 20 HP		1.60	10		11,300	470		11,770	13,200
4140	41,400 CFM, 25 HP		1.40	11.429		15,000	535		15,535	17,300
4160	50,100 CFM, 30 HP		.80	20		19,100	940		20,040	22,400
4200	Double width wheel, 12,420 CFM, 7.5 HP		2.20	7.273		5,000	340		5,340	6,025
4220	18,620 CFM, 15 HP		2	8		7,175	375		7,550	8,450
4240	27,580 CFM, 20 HP		1.80	8.889		8,750	415		9,165	10,300
4260	40,980 CFM, 25 HP		1.50	10.667		13,700	500		14,200	15,900
4280	60,920 CFM, 40 HP		1	16		18,500	750		19,250	21,500
4300	74,520 CFM, 50 HP		.80	20		21,900	940		22,840	25,500
4320	90,160 CFM, 50 HP		.70	22.857		30,000	1,075		31,075	34,600
4340	110,300 CFM, 60 HP		.50	32		40,600	1,500		42,100	46,900
4360	134,960 CFM, 75 HP		.40	40		54,000	1,875		55,875	62,500
4500	Corrosive fume resistant, plastic									
4600	roof ventilators, centrifugal, V belt drive, motor									
4620	1/4" S.P., 250 CFM, 1/4 HP	Q-20	6	3.333	Ea.	4,150	160		4,310	4,825
4640	895 CFM, 1/3 HP		5	4		4,525	191		4,716	5,275
4660	1630 CFM, 1/2 HP		4	5		5,350	239		5,589	6,250
4680	2240 CFM, 1 HP		3	6.667		5,575	320		5,895	6,600
4700	3810 CFM, 2 HP		2	10		6,200	480		6,680	7,550
4710	5000 CFM, 2 HP		1.80	11.111		13,000	530		13,530	15,100
4715	8000 CFM, 5 HP		1.40	14.286		14,500	685		15,185	17,000
4720	11760 CFM, 5 HP		1	20		14,700	955		15,655	17,700
4740	18810 CFM, 10 HP		.70	28.571		15,200	1,375		16,575	18,900
4800	For intermediate capacity, motors may be varied									
4810	For explosion proof motor, add				Ea.	15%				
5000	Utility set, centrifugal, V belt drive, motor									
5020	1/4" S.P., 1200 CFM, 1/4 HP	Q-20	6	3.333	Ea.	1,450	160		1,610	1,825
5040	1520 CFM, 1/3 HP		5	4		1,775	191		1,966	2,275
5060	1850 CFM, 1/2 HP		4	5		1,775	239		2,014	2,350
5080	2180 CFM, 3/4 HP		3	6.667		2,125	320		2,445	2,800
5100	1/2" S.P., 3600 CFM, 1 HP		2	10		2,450	480		2,930	3,400
5120	4250 CFM, 1-1/2 HP		1.60	12.500		2,675	600		3,275	3,850
5140	4800 CFM, 2 HP		1.40	14.286		3,000	685		3,685	4,350
5160	6920 CFM, 5 HP		1.30	15.385		3,700	735		4,435	5,200
5180	7700 CFM, 7-1/2 HP		1.20	16.667		4,125	800		4,925	5,750

23 34 16 – Centrifugal HVAC Fans

23 34 16.10 Centrifugal Type HVAC Fans		Crew	Daily Output	Labor- Hours	Unit	Material	2012 Bare Costs Labor	Equipment	Total	Total Incl O&P
5200	For explosion proof motor, add					15%				
5300	Fume exhauster without hose and intake nozzle									
5310	630 CFM, 1-1/2 HP	Q-20	2	10	Ea.	750	480		1,230	1,550
5320	Hose extension kit 5'	"	20	1	"	59	48		107	138
5500	Fans, industrial exhauster, for air which may contain granular matl.									
5520	1000 CFM, 1-1/2 HP	Q-20	2.50	8	Ea.	2,625	385		3,010	3,475
5540	2000 CFM, 3 HP		2	10		3,200	480		3,680	4,250
5560	4000 CFM, 7-1/2 HP		1.80	11.111		4,450	530		4,980	5,700
5580	8000 CFM, 15 HP		1.40	14.286		5,750	685		6,435	7,375
5600	12,000 CFM, 30 HP	↓	1	20	↓	9,350	955		10,305	11,800
7000	Roof exhauster, centrifugal, aluminum housing, 12" galvanized									
7020	curb, bird screen, back draft damper, 1/4" S.P.									
7100	Direct drive, 320 CFM, 11" sq. damper	Q-20	7	2.857	Ea.	625	137		762	900
7120	600 CFM, 11" sq. damper		6	3.333		785	160		945	1,100
7140	815 CFM, 13" sq. damper		5	4		785	191		976	1,150
7160	1450 CFM, 13" sq. damper		4.20	4.762		1,275	228		1,503	1,750
7180	2050 CFM, 16" sq. damper		4	5		1,525	239		1,764	2,050
7200	V-belt drive, 1650 CFM, 12" sq. damper		6	3.333		1,125	160		1,285	1,500
7220	2750 CFM, 21" sq. damper		5	4		1,350	191		1,541	1,775
7230	3500 CFM, 21" sq. damper		4.50	4.444		1,525	213		1,738	2,000
7240	4910 CFM, 23" sq. damper		4	5		1,850	239		2,089	2,400
7260	8525 CFM, 28" sq. damper		3	6.667		2,475	320		2,795	3,200
7280	13,760 CFM, 35" sq. damper		2	10		3,325	480		3,805	4,375
7300	20,558 CFM, 43" sq. damper	↓	1	20		6,925	955		7,880	9,075
7320	For 2 speed winding, add					15%				
7340	For explosionproof motor, add					495			495	545
7360	For belt driven, top discharge, add				↓	15%				
7400	Roof mounted kitchen exhaust, aluminum, centrifugal									
7410	Direct drive, 2 speed, temp to 200°F									
7412	1/12 HP, 9-3/4"	Q-20	8	2.500	Ea.	595	120		715	835
7414	1/3 HP, 12-5/8"		7	2.857		735	137		872	1,025
7416	1/2 HP, 13-1/2"		6	3.333		810	160		970	1,125
7418	3/4 HP, 15"	↓	5	4	↓	1,150	191		1,341	1,575
7424	Belt drive, temp to 250°F									
7426	3/4 HP, 20"	Q-20	5	4	Ea.	2,550	191		2,741	3,100
7428	1-1/2 HP, 24-1/2"		4	5		2,825	239		3,064	3,475
7430	1-1/2 HP, 30"	↓	4	5	↓	3,725	239		3,964	4,475
7450	Upblast, propeller, w/BDD, BS, + C									
7454	30,300 CFM @ 3/8" S.P., 5 HP	Q-20	1.60	12.500	Ea.	4,100	600		4,700	5,425
7458	36,000 CFM @ 1/2" S.P., 15 HP	"	1.60	12.500	"	5,825	600		6,425	7,325
8500	Wall exhausters, centrifugal, auto damper, 1/8" S.P.									
8520	Direct drive, 610 CFM, 1/20 HP	Q-20	14	1.429	Ea.	385	68.50		453.50	525
8540	796 CFM, 1/12 HP		13	1.538		755	73.50		828.50	940
8560	822 CFM, 1/6 HP		12	1.667		975	80		1,055	1,200
8580	1,320 CFM, 1/4 HP		12	1.667		1,100	80		1,180	1,325
8600	1756 CFM, 1/4 HP		11	1.818		1,150	87		1,237	1,375
8620	1983 CFM, 1/4 HP		10	2		1,175	95.50		1,270.50	1,450
8640	2900 CFM, 1/2 HP		9	2.222		1,250	106		1,356	1,525
8660	3307 CFM, 3/4 HP		8	2.500		1,350	120		1,470	1,650
8670	5940 CFM, 1 HP		7	2.857	↓	1,400	137		1,537	1,750
9500	V-belt drive, 3 phase									
9520	2,800 CFM, 1/4 HP	Q-20	9	2.222	Ea.	1,750	106		1,856	2,075
9540	3,740 CFM, 1/2 HP	↓	8	2.500	↓	1,800	120		1,920	2,175

23 34 HVAC Fans

23 34 16 – Centrifugal HVAC Fans

23 34 16.10 Centrifugal Type HVAC Fans		Crew	Daily Output	Labor-Hours	Unit	Material	2012 Bare Costs Labor	Equipment	Total	Total Incl O&P
9560	4400 CFM, 3/4 HP	Q-20	7	2.857	Ea.	1,825	137		1,962	2,225
9580	5700 CFM, 1-1/2 HP	↓	6	3.333	↓	1,900	160		2,060	2,350

23 34 23 – HVAC Power Ventilators

23 34 23.10 HVAC Power Circulators and Ventilators

			Crew	Daily Output	Labor-Hours	Unit	Material	Labor	Equipment	Total	Total Incl O&P
0010	**HVAC POWER CIRCULATORS AND VENTILATORS**										
3000	Paddle blade air circulator, 3 speed switch										
3020	42", 5,000 CFM high, 3000 CFM low	G	1 Elec	2.40	3.333	Ea.	154	172		326	425
3040	52", 6,500 CFM high, 4000 CFM low	G	"	2.20	3.636	"	161	187		348	455
3100	For antique white motor, same cost										
3200	For brass plated motor, same cost										
3300	For light adaptor kit, add	G				Ea.	38.50			38.50	42.50
3310	Industrial grade, reversible, 4 blade										
3312	5500 CFM		Q-20	5	4	Ea.	170	191		361	480
3314	7600 CFM			5	4		185	191		376	495
3316	21,015 CFM		↓	4	5	↓	240	239		479	630
6000	Propeller exhaust, wall shutter, 1/4" S.P.										
6020	Direct drive, two speed										
6100	375 CFM, 1/10 HP		Q-20	10	2	Ea.	450	95.50		545.50	640
6120	730 CFM, 1/7 HP			9	2.222		505	106		611	715
6140	1000 CFM, 1/8 HP			8	2.500		700	120		820	950
6160	1890 CFM, 1/4 HP			7	2.857		715	137		852	995
6180	3275 CFM, 1/2 HP			6	3.333		725	160		885	1,050
6200	4720 CFM, 1 HP		↓	5	4	↓	1,125	191		1,316	1,525
6300	V-belt drive, 3 phase										
6320	6175 CFM, 3/4 HP		Q-20	5	4	Ea.	945	191		1,136	1,350
6340	7500 CFM, 3/4 HP			5	4		1,000	191		1,191	1,400
6360	10,100 CFM, 1 HP			4.50	4.444		1,100	213		1,313	1,525
6380	14,300 CFM, 1-1/2 HP			4	5		1,375	239		1,614	1,875
6400	19,800 CFM, 2 HP			3	6.667		1,575	320		1,895	2,200
6420	26,250 CFM, 3 HP			2.60	7.692		1,950	370		2,320	2,700
6440	38,500 CFM, 5 HP			2.20	9.091		2,300	435		2,735	3,200
6460	46,000 CFM, 7-1/2 HP			2	10		2,475	480		2,955	3,450
6480	51,500 CFM, 10 HP		↓	1.80	11.111	↓	2,575	530		3,105	3,625
6490	V-belt drive, 115 V, residential, whole house										
6500	Ceiling-wall, 5200 CFM, 1/4 HP, 30" x 30"		1 Shee	6	1.333	Ea.	490	69.50		559.50	645
6510	7500 CFM, 1/3 HP, 36" x 36"			5	1.600		515	83.50		598.50	690
6520	10,500 CFM, 1/3 HP, 42" x 42"			5	1.600		540	83.50		623.50	715
6530	13,200 CFM, 1/3 HP, 48" x 48"			4	2		595	104		699	815
6540	15,445 CFM, 1/2 HP, 48" x 48"			4	2		620	104		724	840
6550	17,025 CFM, 1/2 HP, 54" x 54"		↓	4	2	↓	1,200	104		1,304	1,450
6560	For two speed motor, add						20%				
6570	Shutter, automatic, ceiling/wall										
6580	30" x 30"		1 Shee	8	1	Ea.	160	52		212	256
6590	36" x 36"			8	1		183	52		235	281
6600	42" x 42"			8	1		229	52		281	330
6610	48" x 48"			7	1.143		248	59.50		307.50	365
6620	54" x 54"			6	1.333		325	69.50		394.50	465
6630	Timer, shut off, to 12 hour		↓	20	.400	↓	52.50	21		73.50	90
6650	Residential, bath exhaust, grille, back draft damper										
6660	50 CFM		Q-20	24	.833	Ea.	49	40		89	115
6670	110 CFM			22	.909		82	43.50		125.50	156
6672	180 CFM		↓	22	.909		159	43.50		202.50	241

23 34 HVAC Fans

23 34 23 – HVAC Power Ventilators

23 34 23.10 HVAC Power Circulators and Ventilators		Crew	Daily Output	Labor-Hours	Unit	Material	2012 Bare Costs Labor	Equipment	Total	Total Incl O&P
6673	210 CFM	Q-20	22	.909	Ea.	214	43.50		257.50	300
6674	260 CFM		22	.909		240	43.50		283.50	330
6675	300 CFM		22	.909		325	43.50		368.50	425
6680	Light combination, squirrel cage, 100 watt, 70 CFM		24	.833		92.50	40		132.50	163
6700	Light/heater combination, ceiling mounted									
6710	70 CFM, 1450 watt	Q-20	24	.833	Ea.	174	40		214	252
6800	Heater combination, recessed, 70 CFM		24	.833		55	40		95	121
6820	With 2 infrared bulbs		23	.870		86	41.50		127.50	158
6840	Wall mount, 170 CFM		22	.909		246	43.50		289.50	335
6846	Ceiling mount, 180 CFM		22	.909		248	43.50		291.50	340
6900	Kitchen exhaust, grille, complete, 160 CFM		22	.909		92	43.50		135.50	167
6910	180 CFM		20	1		78	48		126	159
6920	270 CFM		18	1.111		141	53		194	236
6930	350 CFM		16	1.250		110	60		170	212
6940	Residential roof jacks and wall caps									
6944	Wall cap with back draft damper									
6946	3" & 4" dia. round duct	1 Shee	11	.727	Ea.	22.50	38		60.50	82.50
6948	6" dia. round duct	"	11	.727	"	55.50	38		93.50	119
6958	Roof jack with bird screen and back draft damper									
6960	3" & 4" dia. round duct	1 Shee	11	.727	Ea.	22.50	38		60.50	82.50
6962	3-1/4" x 10" rectangular duct	"	10	.800	"	42	41.50		83.50	110
6980	Transition									
6982	3-1/4" x 10" to 6" dia. round	1 Shee	20	.400	Ea.	25.50	21		46.50	60
8020	Attic, roof type									
8030	Aluminum dome, damper & curb									
8040	6" diameter, 300 CFM	1 Elec	16	.500	Ea.	460	26		486	550
8050	7" diameter, 450 CFM		15	.533		505	27.50		532.50	595
8060	9" diameter, 900 CFM		14	.571		555	29.50		584.50	655
8080	12" diameter, 1000 CFM (gravity)		10	.800		520	41		561	630
8090	16" diameter, 1500 CFM (gravity)		9	.889		625	46		671	760
8100	20" diameter, 2500 CFM (gravity)		8	1		770	51.50		821.50	920
8110	26" diameter, 4000 CFM (gravity)		7	1.143		930	59		989	1,125
8120	32" diameter, 6500 CFM (gravity)		6	1.333		1,275	68.50		1,343.50	1,500
8130	38" diameter, 8000 CFM (gravity)		5	1.600		1,900	82.50		1,982.50	2,200
8140	50" diameter, 13,000 CFM (gravity)		4	2		2,750	103		2,853	3,175
8160	Plastic, ABS dome									
8180	1050 CFM	1 Elec	14	.571	Ea.	153	29.50		182.50	212
8200	1600 CFM	"	12	.667	"	229	34.50		263.50	305
8240	Attic, wall type, with shutter, one speed									
8250	12" diameter, 1000 CFM	1 Elec	14	.571	Ea.	365	29.50		394.50	445
8260	14" diameter, 1500 CFM		12	.667		395	34.50		429.50	485
8270	16" diameter, 2000 CFM		9	.889		445	46		491	560
8290	Whole house, wall type, with shutter, one speed									
8300	30" diameter, 4800 CFM	1 Elec	7	1.143	Ea.	955	59		1,014	1,150
8310	36" diameter, 7000 CFM		6	1.333		1,050	68.50		1,118.50	1,250
8320	42" diameter, 10,000 CFM		5	1.600		1,175	82.50		1,257.50	1,400
8330	48" diameter, 16,000 CFM		4	2		1,450	103		1,553	1,750
8340	For two speed, add					87			87	96
8350	Whole house, lay-down type, with shutter, one speed									
8360	30" diameter, 4500 CFM	1 Elec	8	1	Ea.	1,025	51.50		1,076.50	1,200
8370	36" diameter, 6500 CFM		7	1.143		1,100	59		1,159	1,300
8380	42" diameter, 9000 CFM		6	1.333		1,200	68.50		1,268.50	1,425
8390	48" diameter, 12,000 CFM		5	1.600		1,375	82.50		1,457.50	1,625

23 34 HVAC Fans

23 34 23 – HVAC Power Ventilators

23 34 23.10 HVAC Power Circulators and Ventilators	Crew	Daily Output	Labor-Hours	Unit	Material	2012 Bare Costs Labor	2012 Bare Costs Equipment	Total	Total Incl O&P
8440 For two speed, add				Ea.	65.50			65.50	72
8450 For 12 hour timer switch, add	1 Elec	32	.250	↓	65.50	12.90		78.40	91.50

23 34 33 – Air Curtains

23 34 33.10 Air Barrier Curtains

	Crew	Daily Output	Labor-Hours	Unit	Material	Labor	Equipment	Total	Total Incl O&P
0010 **AIR BARRIER CURTAINS**, Incl. motor starters, transformers,									
0050 and door switches									
2450 Conveyor openings or service windows									
3000 Service window, 5' high x 25" wide	2 Shee	5	3.200	Ea.	350	167		517	640
3100 Environmental separation									
3110 Door heights up to 8', low profile, super quiet									
3120 Unheated, variable speed									
3130 36" wide	2 Shee	4	4	Ea.	620	209		829	1,000
3134 42" wide		3.80	4.211		650	220		870	1,050
3138 48" wide		3.60	4.444		675	232		907	1,100
3142 60" wide	↓	3.40	4.706		705	245		950	1,150
3146 72" wide	Q-3	4.60	6.957		895	360		1,255	1,525
3150 96" wide		4.40	7.273		1,350	380		1,730	2,075
3154 120" wide		4.20	7.619		1,450	395		1,845	2,200
3158 144" wide	↓	4	8	↓	1,800	415		2,215	2,600
3200 Door heights up to 10'									
3210 Unheated									
3230 36" wide	2 Shee	3.80	4.211	Ea.	620	220		840	1,025
3234 42" wide	↓	3.60	4.444		640	232		872	1,050
3238 48" wide		3.40	4.706		660	245		905	1,100
3242 60" wide	↓	3.20	5		1,000	261		1,261	1,500
3246 72" wide	Q-3	4.40	7.273		1,075	380		1,455	1,750
3250 96" wide		4.20	7.619		1,275	395		1,670	2,000
3254 120" wide		4	8		1,775	415		2,190	2,575
3258 144" wide	↓	3.80	8.421	↓	1,925	440		2,365	2,775
3300 Door heights up to 12'									
3310 Unheated									
3334 42" wide	2 Shee	3.40	4.706	Ea.	875	245		1,120	1,350
3338 48" wide		3.20	5		885	261		1,146	1,375
3342 60" wide	↓	3	5.333		905	278		1,183	1,425
3346 72" wide	Q-3	4.20	7.619		1,650	395		2,045	2,400
3350 96" wide		4	8		1,800	415		2,215	2,600
3354 120" wide		3.80	8.421		2,225	440		2,665	3,100
3358 144" wide	↓	3.60	8.889	↓	2,375	460		2,835	3,300
3400 Door heights up to 16'									
3410 Unheated									
3438 48" wide	2 Shee	3	5.333	Ea.	985	278		1,263	1,500
3442 60" wide	"	2.80	5.714		1,025	298		1,323	1,575
3446 72" wide	Q-3	3.80	8.421		1,925	440		2,365	2,775
3450 96" wide		3.60	8.889		2,025	460		2,485	2,925
3454 120" wide		3.40	9.412		2,575	490		3,065	3,575
3458 144" wide	↓	3.20	10	↓	2,650	520		3,170	3,700
3470 Heated, electric									
3474 48" wide	2 Shee	2.90	5.517	Ea.	1,925	288		2,213	2,575
3478 60" wide	"	2.70	5.926		1,950	310		2,260	2,625
3482 72" wide	Q-3	3.70	8.649		3,325	450		3,775	4,350
3486 96" wide		3.50	9.143		3,450	475		3,925	4,525
3490 120" wide	↓	3.30	9.697		4,625	505		5,130	5,850

23 34 HVAC Fans

23 34 33 – Air Curtains

23 34 33.10 Air Barrier Curtains	Crew	Daily Output	Labor-Hours	Unit	Material	2012 Bare Costs Labor	Equipment	Total	Total Incl O&P
3494	144" wide	Q-3	3.10	10.323	Ea.	4,725	535		5,260	6,000

23 35 Special Exhaust Systems

23 35 16 – Engine Exhaust Systems

23 35 16.10 Engine Exhaust Removal Systems

	23 35 16.10 Engine Exhaust Removal Systems	Crew	Daily Output	Labor-Hours	Unit	Material	2012 Bare Costs Labor	Equipment	Total	Total Incl O&P
0010	**ENGINE EXHAUST REMOVAL SYSTEMS** D3090-320									
0500	Engine exhaust, garage, in-floor system									
0510	Single tube outlet assemblies									
0520	For transite pipe ducting, self-storing tube									
0530	3" tubing adapter plate	1 Shee	16	.500	Ea.	300	26		326	370
0540	4" tubing adapter plate		16	.500		305	26		331	375
0550	5" tubing adapter plate		16	.500		305	26		331	375
0600	For vitrified tile ducting									
0610	3" tubing adapter plate, self-storing tube	1 Shee	16	.500	Ea.	300	26		326	370
0620	4" tubing adapter plate, self-storing tube		16	.500		300	26		326	370
0660	5" tubing adapter plate, self-storing tube		16	.500		300	26		326	370
0800	Two tube outlet assemblies									
0810	For transite pipe ducting, self-storing tube									
0820	3" tubing, dual exhaust adapter plate	1 Shee	16	.500	Ea.	315	26		341	390
0850	For vitrified tile ducting									
0860	3" tubing, dual exhaust, self-storing tube	1 Shee	16	.500	Ea.	315	26		341	390
0870	3" tubing, double outlet, non-storing tubes	"	16	.500	"	315	26		341	390
0900	Accessories for metal tubing, (overhead systems also)									
0910	Adapters, for metal tubing end									
0920	3" tail pipe type				Ea.	62			62	68.50
0930	4" tail pipe type					66.50			66.50	73.50
0940	5" tail pipe type					68			68	74.50
0990	5" diesel stack type					400			400	440
1000	6" diesel stack type					415			415	455
1100	Bullnose (guide) required for in-floor assemblies									
1110	3" tubing size				Ea.	34.50			34.50	38
1120	4" tubing size					37			37	40.50
1130	5" tubing size					39			39	43
1150	Plain rings, for tubing end									
1160	3" tubing size				Ea.	30			30	33
1170	4" tubing size				"	33.50			33.50	36.50
1200	Tubing, galvanized, flexible, (for overhead systems also)									
1210	3" ID				L.F.	14.60			14.60	16.05
1220	4" ID					17.95			17.95	19.75
1230	5" ID					21			21	23.50
1240	6" ID					24.50			24.50	27
1250	Stainless steel, flexible, (for overhead system, also)									
1260	3" ID				L.F.	3.25			3.25	3.58
1270	4" ID					4.45			4.45	4.90
1280	5" ID					5.05			5.05	5.55
1290	6" ID					5.90			5.90	6.45
1500	Engine exhaust, garage, overhead components, for neoprene tubing									
1510	Alternate metal tubing & accessories see above									
1550	Adapters, for neoprene tubing end									
1560	3" tail pipe, adjustable, neoprene				Ea.	60			60	66
1570	3" tail pipe, heavy wall neoprene					66.50			66.50	73.50

23 35 16.10 Engine Exhaust Removal Systems	Crew	Daily Output	Labor-Hours	Unit	Material	2012 Bare Costs Labor	Equipment	Total	Total Incl O&P
1580	4" tail pipe, heavy wall neoprene				Ea.	128			128	140
1590	5" tail pipe, heavy wall neoprene				↓	135			135	148
1650	Connectors, tubing									
1660	3" interior, aluminum				Ea.	26			26	28.50
1670	4" interior, aluminum					33.50			33.50	36.50
1710	5" interior, neoprene					64.50			64.50	71
1750	3" spiralock, neoprene					30			30	33
1760	4" spiralock, neoprene					33.50			33.50	36.50
1780	Y for 3" ID tubing, neoprene, dual exhaust					251			251	276
1790	Y for 4" ID tubing, aluminum, dual exhaust				↓	251			251	276
1850	Elbows, aluminum, splice into tubing for strap									
1860	3" neoprene tubing size				Ea.	62			62	68.50
1870	4" neoprene tubing size				↓	52			52	57
1900	Flange assemblies, connect tubing to overhead duct				↓	47.50			47.50	52.50
2000	Hardware and accessories									
2020	Cable, galvanized, 1/8" diameter				L.F.	.51			.51	.56
2040	Cleat, tie down cable or rope				Ea.	5.75			5.75	6.35
2060	Pulley					7.95			7.95	8.75
2080	Pulley hook, universal				↓	5.75			5.75	6.35
2100	Rope, nylon, 1/4" diameter				L.F.	.43			.43	.47
2120	Winch, 1" diameter				Ea.	123			123	135
2150	Lifting strap, mounts on neoprene									
2160	3" tubing size				Ea.	29			29	32
2170	4" tubing size					29			29	32
2180	5" tubing size					29			29	32
2190	6" tubing size				↓	29			29	32
2200	Tubing, neoprene, 11' lengths									
2210	3" ID				L.F.	12.35			12.35	13.55
2220	4" ID					20			20	22
2230	5" ID				↓	28			28	31
2500	Engine exhaust, thru-door outlet									
2510	3" tube size	1 Carp	16	.500	Ea.	68	22		90	109
2530	4" tube size	"	16	.500	"	68	22		90	109
3000	Tubing, exhaust, flex hose, with									
3010	coupler, damper and tail pipe adapter									
3020	Neoprene									
3040	3" x 20'	1 Shee	6	1.333	Ea.	375	69.50		444.50	515
3050	4" x 15'		5.40	1.481		495	77.50		572.50	660
3060	4" x 20'		5	1.600		595	83.50		678.50	780
3070	5" x 15'	↓	4.40	1.818	↓	660	95		755	870
3100	Galvanized									
3110	3" x 20'	1 Shee	6	1.333	Ea.	415	69.50		484.50	560
3120	4" x 17'		5.60	1.429		435	74.50		509.50	595
3130	4" x 20'		5	1.600		490	83.50		573.50	665
3140	5" x 17'	↓	4.60	1.739	↓	530	90.50		620.50	720
8000	Blower, for tailpipe exhaust system									
8010	Direct drive									
8012	495 CFM, 1/3 HP	Q-9	5	3.200	Ea.	1,900	150		2,050	2,300
8014	1445 CFM, 3/4 HP		4	4		2,350	188		2,538	2,850
8016	1840 CFM, 1-1/2 HP	↓	3	5.333	↓	2,775	250		3,025	3,450
8030	Beltdrive									
8032	1400 CFM, 1 HP	Q-9	4	4	Ea.	2,350	188		2,538	2,850
8034	2023 CFM, 1-1/2 HP	↓	3	5.333	↓	3,175	250		3,425	3,875

23 35 Special Exhaust Systems

23 35 16 – Engine Exhaust Systems

23 35 16.10 Engine Exhaust Removal Systems

		Crew	Daily Output	Labor-Hours	Unit	Material	2012 Bare Costs Labor	2012 Bare Costs Equipment	Total	Total Incl O&P
8036	2750 CFM, 2 HP	Q-9	2	8	Ea.	3,775	375		4,150	4,750
8038	4400 CFM, 3 HP		1.80	8.889		5,575	415		5,990	6,750
8040	7060 CFM, 5 HP		1.40	11.429		8,050	535		8,585	9,675

23 35 43 – Welding Fume Elimination Systems

23 35 43.10 Welding Fume Elimination System Components

		Crew	Daily Output	Labor-Hours	Unit	Material	2012 Bare Costs Labor	2012 Bare Costs Equipment	Total	Total Incl O&P
0010	**WELDING FUME ELIMINATION SYSTEM COMPONENTS**									
7500	Welding fume elimination accessories for garage exhaust systems									
7600	Cut off (blast gate)									
7610	3" tubing size, 3" x 6" opening	1 Shee	24	.333	Ea.	30	17.40		47.40	59.50
7620	4" tubing size, 4" x 8" opening		24	.333		31	17.40		48.40	60.50
7630	5" tubing size, 5" x 10" opening		24	.333		37	17.40		54.40	67
7640	6" tubing size		24	.333		39	17.40		56.40	69.50
7650	8" tubing size		24	.333		54	17.40		71.40	86
7700	Hoods, magnetic, with handle & screen									
7710	3" tubing size, 3" x 6" opening	1 Shee	24	.333	Ea.	108	17.40		125.40	146
7720	4" tubing size, 4" x 8" opening		24	.333		108	17.40		125.40	146
7730	5" tubing size, 5" x 10" opening		24	.333		108	17.40		125.40	146

23 36 Air Terminal Units

23 36 13 – Constant-Air-Volume Units

23 36 13.10 Constant Volume Mixing Boxes

		Crew	Daily Output	Labor-Hours	Unit	Material	2012 Bare Costs Labor	2012 Bare Costs Equipment	Total	Total Incl O&P
0010	**CONSTANT VOLUME MIXING BOXES**									
5180	Mixing box, includes electric or pneumatic motor									
5192	Recommend use with silencer, see Line 23 33 19.10 0010									
5200	Constant volume, 150 to 270 CFM	Q-9	12	1.333	Ea.	670	62.50		732.50	830
5210	270 to 600 CFM		11	1.455		685	68.50		753.50	860
5230	550 to 1000 CFM		9	1.778		685	83.50		768.50	880
5240	1000 to 1600 CFM		8	2		705	94		799	920
5250	1300 to 1900 CFM		6	2.667		720	125		845	980
5260	550 to 2640 CFM		5.60	2.857		795	134		929	1,075
5270	650 to 3120 CFM		5.20	3.077		845	144		989	1,150

23 36 16 – Variable-Air-Volume Units

23 36 16.10 Variable Volume Mixing Boxes

		Crew	Daily Output	Labor-Hours	Unit	Material	2012 Bare Costs Labor	2012 Bare Costs Equipment	Total	Total Incl O&P
0010	**VARIABLE VOLUME MIXING BOXES**									
5180	Mixing box, includes electric or pneumatic motor									
5192	Recommend use with attenuator, see Line 23 33 19.10 0010									
5500	VAV Cool only, pneumatic, pressure independent 300 to 600 CFM	Q-9	11	1.455	Ea.	385	68.50		453.50	525
5510	500 to 1000 CFM		9	1.778		395	83.50		478.50	555
5520	800 to 1600 CFM		9	1.778		405	83.50		488.50	570
5530	1100 to 2000 CFM		8	2		415	94		509	600
5540	1500 to 3000 CFM		7	2.286		440	107		547	650
5550	2000 to 4000 CFM		6	2.667		445	125		570	680
5560	For electric, w/thermostat, pressure dependent, add					23			23	25.50
5600	VAV Cool & HW coils, damper, actuator and t'stat									
5610	200 CFM	Q-9	11	1.455	Ea.	750	68.50		818.50	930
5620	400 CFM		10	1.600		760	75		835	950
5630	600 CFM		10	1.600		760	75		835	950
5640	800 CFM		8	2		780	94		874	1,000
5650	1000 CFM		8	2		780	94		874	1,000
5660	1250 CFM		6	2.667		855	125		980	1,125

23 36 Air Terminal Units

23 36 16 – Variable-Air-Volume Units

23 36 16.10 Variable Volume Mixing Boxes

		Crew	Daily Output	Labor-Hours	Unit	Material	2012 Bare Costs Labor	Equipment	Total	Total Incl O&P
5670	1500 CFM	Q-9	6	2.667	Ea.	855	125		980	1,125
5680	2000 CFM		4	4		930	188		1,118	1,300
5684	3000 CFM	↓	3.80	4.211	↓	1,000	198		1,198	1,425
5700	VAV Cool only, fan powered, damper, actuator, thermostat									
5710	200 CFM	Q-9	10	1.600	Ea.	1,025	75		1,100	1,250
5720	400 CFM		9	1.778		1,075	83.50		1,158.50	1,300
5730	600 CFM		9	1.778		1,075	83.50		1,158.50	1,300
5740	800 CFM		7	2.286		1,150	107		1,257	1,425
5750	1000 CFM		7	2.286		1,150	107		1,257	1,425
5760	1250 CFM		5	3.200		1,225	150		1,375	1,575
5770	1500 CFM		5	3.200		1,225	150		1,375	1,575
5780	2000 CFM	↓	4	4	↓	1,350	188		1,538	1,775
5800	VAV Fan powr'd, cooling, with HW coils, dampers, actuators, t'stat									
5810	200 CFM	Q-9	10	1.600	Ea.	1,250	75		1,325	1,500
5820	400 CFM		9	1.778		1,275	83.50		1,358.50	1,525
5830	600 CFM		9	1.778		1,275	83.50		1,358.50	1,525
5840	800 CFM		7	2.286		1,350	107		1,457	1,675
5850	1000 CFM		7	2.286		1,350	107		1,457	1,675
5860	1250 CFM		5	3.200		1,550	150		1,700	1,925
5870	1500 CFM		5	3.200		1,550	150		1,700	1,925
5880	2000 CFM	↓	3.50	4.571	↓	1,650	215		1,865	2,150

23 37 Air Outlets and Inlets

23 37 13 – Diffusers, Registers, and Grilles

23 37 13.10 Diffusers

			Crew	Daily Output	Labor-Hours	Unit	Material	2012 Bare Costs Labor	Equipment	Total	Total Incl O&P
0010	**DIFFUSERS**, Aluminum, opposed blade damper unless noted	R233100-10									
0100	Ceiling, linear, also for sidewall										
0120	2" wide	R233100-30	1 Shee	32	.250	L.F.	44.50	13.05		57.55	69
0140	3" wide			30	.267		51.50	13.90		65.40	77.50
0160	4" wide	R233700-60		26	.308		60	16.05		76.05	90.50
0180	6" wide			24	.333		74	17.40		91.40	108
0200	8" wide			22	.364		86.50	18.95		105.45	125
0220	10" wide			20	.400		99	21		120	141
0240	12" wide		↓	18	.444	↓	117	23		140	164
0260	For floor or sill application, add						15%				
0500	Perforated, 24" x 24" lay-in panel size, 6" x 6"		1 Shee	16	.500	Ea.	151	26		177	206
0520	8" x 8"			15	.533		159	28		187	218
0530	9" x 9"			14	.571		161	30		191	223
0540	10" x 10"			14	.571		162	30		192	224
0560	12" x 12"			12	.667		168	35		203	238
0580	15" x 15"			11	.727		188	38		226	265
0590	16" x 16"			11	.727		189	38		227	265
0600	18" x 18"			10	.800		202	41.50		243.50	286
0610	20" x 20"			10	.800		218	41.50		259.50	305
0620	24" x 24"			9	.889		239	46.50		285.50	335
1000	Rectangular, 1 to 4 way blow, 6" x 6"			16	.500		50	26		76	95
1010	8" x 8"			15	.533		58	28		86	106
1014	9" x 9"			15	.533		64.50	28		92.50	114
1016	10" x 10"			15	.533		80	28		108	130
1020	12" x 6"			15	.533		71.50	28		99.50	121
1040	12" x 9"		↓	14	.571	↓	75.50	30		105.50	129

23 37 13.10 Diffusers		Crew	Daily Output	Labor-Hours	Unit	Material	2012 Bare Costs Labor	Equipment	Total	Total Incl O&P
1060	12" x 12"	1 Shee	12	.667	Ea.	84	35		119	146
1070	14" x 6"		13	.615		77.50	32		109.50	135
1074	14" x 14"		12	.667		128	35		163	193
1080	18" x 12"		11	.727		137	38		175	209
1120	15" x 15"		10	.800		108	41.50		149.50	183
1140	18" x 15"		9	.889		155	46.50		201.50	242
1150	18" x 18"		9	.889		136	46.50		182.50	220
1160	21" x 21"		8	1		215	52		267	315
1170	24" x 12"		10	.800		163	41.50		204.50	244
1180	24" x 24"		7	1.143		270	59.50		329.50	385
1500	Round, butterfly damper, steel, diffuser size, 6" diameter		18	.444		24.50	23		47.50	62.50
1520	8" diameter		16	.500		26	26		52	68.50
1540	10" diameter		14	.571		32	30		62	81
1560	12" diameter		12	.667		42	35		77	99.50
1580	14" diameter		10	.800		52	41.50		93.50	121
1600	18" diameter		9	.889		134	46.50		180.50	219
1610	20" diameter		9	.889		144	46.50		190.50	230
1620	22" diameter		8	1		158	52		210	254
1630	24" diameter		8	1		173	52		225	271
1640	28" diameter		7	1.143		213	59.50		272.50	325
1650	32" diameter		6	1.333		238	69.50		307.50	370
1700	Round, steel, adjustable core, annular segmented damper, diffuser size									
1704	6" diameter	1 Shee	18	.444	Ea.	82	23		105	126
1708	8" diameter		16	.500		88	26		114	137
1712	10" diameter		14	.571		99	30		129	155
1716	12" diameter		12	.667		110	35		145	174
1720	14" diameter		10	.800		122	41.50		163.50	198
1724	18" diameter		9	.889		187	46.50		233.50	277
1728	20" diameter		9	.889		216	46.50		262.50	310
1732	24" diameter		8	1		335	52		387	450
1736	30" diameter		7	1.143		585	59.50		644.50	735
1740	36" diameter		6	1.333		715	69.50		784.50	890
2000	T bar mounting, 24" x 24" lay-in frame, 6" x 6"		16	.500		45.50	26		71.50	90
2020	8" x 8"		14	.571		47	30		77	97.50
2040	12" x 12"		12	.667		55.50	35		90.50	114
2060	16" x 16"		11	.727		75	38		113	141
2080	18" x 18"		10	.800		83	41.50		124.50	155
2500	Combination supply and return									
2520	21" x 21" supply, 15" x 15" return	Q-9	10	1.600	Ea.	330	75		405	480
2540	24" x 24" supply, 18" x 18" return		9.50	1.684		420	79		499	580
2560	27" x 27" supply, 18" x 18" return		9	1.778		510	83.50		593.50	685
2580	30" x 30" supply, 21" x 21" return		8.50	1.882		645	88.50		733.50	845
2600	33" x 33" supply, 24" x 24" return		8	2		695	94		789	910
2620	36" x 36" supply, 24" x 24" return		7.50	2.133		890	100		990	1,125
3000	Baseboard, white enameled steel									
3100	18" long	1 Shee	20	.400	Ea.	13.55	21		34.55	47
3120	24" long		18	.444		26.50	23		49.50	64.50
3140	48" long		16	.500		48.50	26		74.50	93
3400	For matching return, deduct					10%				
4000	Floor, steel, adjustable pattern									
4100	2" x 10"	1 Shee	34	.235	Ea.	18.15	12.25		30.40	38.50
4120	2" x 12"		32	.250		19.95	13.05		33	42
4140	2" x 14"		30	.267		22.50	13.90		36.40	46

23 37 13 – Diffusers, Registers, and Grilles

23 37 13.10 Diffusers

		Crew	Daily Output	Labor-Hours	Unit	Material	Labor	2012 Bare Costs Equipment	Total	Total Incl O&P
4200	4" x 10"	1 Shee	28	.286	Ea.	21	14.90		35.90	45.50
4220	4" x 12"		26	.308		23	16.05		39.05	50
4240	4" x 14"		25	.320		26	16.70		42.70	54.50
4260	6" x 10"		26	.308		31.50	16.05		47.55	59.50
4280	6" x 12"		24	.333		33	17.40		50.40	63
4300	6" x 14"		22	.364		34.50	18.95		53.45	67
4500	Linear bar diffuser in wall, sill or ceiling									
4510	2" wide	1 Shee	32	.250	L.F.	37	13.05		50.05	61
4512	3" wide		30	.267		40	13.90		53.90	65
4514	4" wide		26	.308		49.50	16.05		65.55	79
4516	6" wide		24	.333		61.50	17.40		78.90	94
4520	10" wide		20	.400		81.50	21		102.50	122
4522	12" wide		18	.444		91.50	23		114.50	137
5000	Sidewall, aluminum, 3 way dispersion									
5100	8" x 4"	1 Shee	24	.333	Ea.	9.95	17.40		27.35	37.50
5110	8" x 6"		24	.333		10.65	17.40		28.05	38
5120	10" x 4"		22	.364		10.45	18.95		29.40	40.50
5130	10" x 6"		22	.364		11.20	18.95		30.15	41.50
5140	10" x 8"		20	.400		15.25	21		36.25	49
5160	12" x 4"		18	.444		11.25	23		34.25	48
5170	12" x 6"		17	.471		12.45	24.50		36.95	51
5180	12" x 8"		16	.500		16.15	26		42.15	58
5200	14" x 4"		15	.533		12.55	28		40.55	56.50
5220	14" x 6"		14	.571		13.85	30		43.85	60.50
5240	14" x 8"		13	.615		18	32		50	69
5260	16" x 6"		12.50	.640		19.75	33.50		53.25	72.50
6000	For steel diffusers instead of aluminum, deduct					10%				

23 37 13.30 Grilles

		Crew	Daily Output	Labor-Hours	Unit	Material	Labor	2012 Bare Costs Equipment	Total	Total Incl O&P
0010	**GRILLES**									
0020	Aluminum									
0100	Air supply, single deflection, adjustable									
0120	8" x 4"	1 Shee	30	.267	Ea.	20	13.90		33.90	43
0140	8" x 8"		28	.286		24.50	14.90		39.40	49.50
0160	10" x 4"		24	.333		22	17.40		39.40	51
0180	10" x 10"		23	.348		29.50	18.15		47.65	59.50
0200	12" x 6"		23	.348		26.50	18.15		44.65	56.50
0220	12" x 12"		22	.364		34.50	18.95		53.45	67
0230	14" x 6"		23	.348		29.50	18.15		47.65	59.50
0240	14" x 8"		23	.348		31.50	18.15		49.65	62
0260	14" x 14"		22	.364		42.50	18.95		61.45	75.50
0270	18" x 8"		23	.348		36	18.15		54.15	67
0280	18" x 10"		23	.348		41.50	18.15		59.65	73
0300	18" x 18"		21	.381		64.50	19.85		84.35	102
0320	20" x 12"		22	.364		47	18.95		65.95	80.50
0340	20" x 20"		21	.381		78	19.85		97.85	117
0350	24" x 8"		20	.400		45	21		66	81.50
0360	24" x 14"		18	.444		63.50	23		86.50	106
0380	24" x 24"		15	.533		110	28		138	164
0400	30" x 8"		20	.400		58	21		79	96
0420	30" x 10"		19	.421		64	22		86	104
0440	30" x 12"		18	.444		70.50	23		93.50	113
0460	30" x 16"		17	.471		91.50	24.50		116	139

23 37 13 - Diffusers, Registers, and Grilles

23 37 13.30 Grilles		Crew	Daily Output	Labor-Hours	Unit	Material	2012 Bare Costs Labor	Equipment	Total	Total Incl O&P
0480	30" x 18"	1 Shee	17	.471	Ea.	102	24.50		126.50	151
0500	30" x 30"		14	.571		182	30		212	247
0520	36" x 12"		17	.471		87.50	24.50		112	134
0540	36" x 16"		16	.500		111	26		137	163
0560	36" x 18"		15	.533		124	28		152	179
0570	36" x 20"		15	.533		135	28		163	192
0580	36" x 24"		14	.571		172	30		202	235
0600	36" x 28"		13	.615		195	32		227	264
0620	36" x 30"		12	.667		237	35		272	315
0640	36" x 32"		12	.667		254	35		289	335
0660	36" x 34"		11	.727		283	38		321	370
0680	36" x 36"		11	.727		305	38		343	395
0700	For double deflecting, add					70%				
1000	Air return, steel, 6" x 6"	1 Shee	26	.308		18.15	16.05		34.20	44.50
1020	10" x 6"		24	.333		18.15	17.40		35.55	46.50
1040	14" x 6"		23	.348		21	18.15		39.15	50.50
1060	10" x 8"		23	.348		21	18.15		39.15	50.50
1080	16" x 8"		22	.364		26.50	18.95		45.45	58
1100	12" x 12"		22	.364		26.50	18.95		45.45	58
1120	24" x 12"		18	.444		34.50	23		57.50	73.50
1140	30" x 12"		16	.500		44	26		70	88.50
1160	14" x 14"		22	.364		30.50	18.95		49.45	62.50
1180	16" x 16"		22	.364		32.50	18.95		51.45	64.50
1200	18" x 18"		21	.381		37.50	19.85		57.35	71.50
1220	24" x 18"		16	.500		42.50	26		68.50	86.50
1240	36" x 18"		15	.533		65.50	28		93.50	115
1260	24" x 24"		15	.533		50.50	28		78.50	98
1280	36" x 24"		14	.571		73	30		103	126
1300	48" x 24"		12	.667		125	35		160	191
1320	48" x 30"		11	.727		162	38		200	236
1340	36" x 36"		13	.615		97.50	32		129.50	156
1360	48" x 36"		11	.727		201	38		239	279
1380	48" x 48"		8	1		248	52		300	350
2000	Door grilles, 12" x 12"		22	.364		65	18.95		83.95	101
2020	18" x 12"		22	.364		75	18.95		93.95	112
2040	24" x 12"		18	.444		84	23		107	128
2060	18" x 18"		18	.444		104	23		127	150
2080	24" x 18"		16	.500		118	26		144	169
2100	24" x 24"		15	.533		167	28		195	227
3000	Filter grille with filter, 12" x 12"		24	.333		51	17.40		68.40	83
3020	18" x 12"		20	.400		68	21		89	107
3040	24" x 18"		18	.444		80.50	23		103.50	124
3060	24" x 24"		16	.500		94	26		120	143
3080	30" x 24"		14	.571		115	30		145	172
3100	30" x 30"		13	.615		136	32		168	198
3950	Eggcrate, framed, 6" x 6" opening		26	.308		14.85	16.05		30.90	41
3954	8" x 8" opening		24	.333		18.15	17.40		35.55	46.50
3960	10" x 10" opening		23	.348		22	18.15		40.15	51.50
3970	12" x 12" opening		22	.364		25.50	18.95		44.45	57
3980	14" x 14" opening		22	.364		32.50	18.95		51.45	64.50
3984	16" x 16" opening		21	.381		36.50	19.85		56.35	70.50
3990	18" x 18" opening		21	.381		43.50	19.85		63.35	78.50
4020	22" x 22" opening		17	.471		50.50	24.50		75	93

23 37 Air Outlets and Inlets

23 37 13 – Diffusers, Registers, and Grilles

23 37 13.30 Grilles

		Crew	Daily Output	Labor-Hours	Unit	Material	2012 Bare Costs Labor	Equipment	Total	Total Incl O&P
4040	24" x 24" opening	1 Shee	15	.533	Ea.	65	28		93	114
4044	28" x 28" opening		14	.571		100	30		130	156
4048	36" x 36" opening		12	.667		114	35		149	179
4050	48" x 24" opening		12	.667		145	35		180	213
4060	Eggcrate, lay-in, T-bar system									
4070	48" x 24" sheet	1 Shee	40	.200	Ea.	64.50	10.45		74.95	87
5000	Transfer grille, vision proof, 8" x 4"		30	.267		37	13.90		50.90	62
5020	8" x 6"		28	.286		37	14.90		51.90	63.50
5040	8" x 8"		26	.308		41.50	16.05		57.55	70
5060	10" x 6"		24	.333		38.50	17.40		55.90	69
5080	10" x 10"		23	.348		49	18.15		67.15	81
5090	12" x 6"		23	.348		40	18.15		58.15	71.50
5100	12" x 10"		22	.364		53.50	18.95		72.45	87.50
5110	12" x 12"		22	.364		58	18.95		76.95	92.50
5120	14" x 10"		22	.364		58	18.95		76.95	92.50
5140	16" x 8"		21	.381		58	19.85		77.85	94
5160	18" x 12"		20	.400		75.50	21		96.50	115
5170	18" x 18"		21	.381		107	19.85		126.85	148
5180	20" x 12"		20	.400		81.50	21		102.50	122
5200	20" x 20"		19	.421		129	22		151	176
5220	24" x 12"		17	.471		91.50	24.50		116	139
5240	24" x 24"		16	.500		176	26		202	234
5260	30" x 6"		15	.533		81.50	28		109.50	132
5280	30" x 8"		15	.533		95	28		123	147
5300	30" x 12"		14	.571		118	30		148	176
5320	30" x 16"		13	.615		141	32		173	204
5340	30" x 20"		12	.667		178	35		213	248
5360	30" x 24"		11	.727		219	38		257	299
5380	30" x 30"		10	.800		288	41.50		329.50	380
6000	For steel grilles instead of aluminum in above, deduct					10%				
6200	Plastic, eggcrate, lay-in, T-bar system									
6210	48" x 24" sheet	1 Shee	50	.160	Ea.	19.25	8.35		27.60	33.50
6250	Steel door louver									
6270	With fire link, steel only									
6350	12" x 18"	1 Shee	22	.364	Ea.	208	18.95		226.95	258
6410	12" x 24"		21	.381		238	19.85		257.85	293
6470	18" x 18"		20	.400		232	21		253	287
6530	18" x 24"		19	.421		267	22		289	330
6600	18" x 36"		17	.471		310	24.50		334.50	380
6660	24" x 24"		15	.533		269	28		297	340
6720	24" x 30"		15	.533		310	28		338	385
6780	30" x 30"		13	.615		365	32		397	450
6840	30" x 36"		12	.667		420	35		455	520
6900	36" x 36"		10	.800		505	41.50		546.50	625

23 37 13.60 Registers

		Crew	Daily Output	Labor-Hours	Unit	Material	2012 Bare Costs Labor	Equipment	Total	Total Incl O&P
0010	**REGISTERS**									
0980	Air supply									
1000	Ceiling/wall, O.B. damper, anodized aluminum									
1010	One or two way deflection, adj. curved face bars									
1014	6" x 6"	1 Shee	24	.333	Ea.	34.50	17.40		51.90	64.50
1020	8" x 4"		26	.308		34.50	16.05		50.55	62.50
1040	8" x 8"		24	.333		43.50	17.40		60.90	74

23 37 13.60 **Registers**		Crew	Daily Output	Labor-Hours	Unit	Material	2012 Bare Costs Labor	Equipment	Total	Total Incl O&P
1060	10" x 6"	1 Shee	20	.400	Ea.	40	21		61	76
1080	10" x 10"		19	.421		53.50	22		75.50	92.50
1100	12" x 6"		19	.421		40	22		62	77.50
1120	12" x 12"		18	.444		63.50	23		86.50	106
1140	14" x 8"		17	.471		55.50	24.50		80	98.50
1160	14" x 14"		18	.444		74	23		97	117
1170	16" x 16"		17	.471		82	24.50		106.50	128
1180	18" x 8"		18	.444		61.50	23		84.50	104
1200	18" x 18"		17	.471		113	24.50		137.50	162
1220	20" x 4"		19	.421		56.50	22		78.50	96
1240	20" x 6"		18	.444		56.50	23		79.50	98
1260	20" x 8"		18	.444		62	23		85	104
1280	20" x 20"		17	.471		137	24.50		161.50	189
1290	22" x 22"		15	.533		157	28		185	216
1300	24" x 4"		17	.471		70	24.50		94.50	115
1320	24" x 6"		16	.500		70	26		96	117
1340	24" x 8"		13	.615		76.50	32		108.50	133
1350	24" x 18"		12	.667		142	35		177	209
1360	24" x 24"		11	.727		193	38		231	271
1380	30" x 4"		16	.500		87.50	26		113.50	137
1400	30" x 6"		15	.533		87.50	28		115.50	139
1420	30" x 8"		14	.571		100	30		130	156
1440	30" x 24"		12	.667		249	35		284	325
1460	30" x 30"	▼	10	.800	▼	320	41.50		361.50	415
1504	4 way deflection, adjustable curved face bars									
1510	6" x 6"	1 Shee	26	.308	Ea.	41.50	16.05		57.55	70.50
1514	8" x 8"		24	.333		52	17.40		69.40	83.50
1518	10" x 10"		19	.421		64.50	22		86.50	105
1522	12" x 6"		19	.421		48	22		70	86.50
1526	12" x 12"		18	.444		76	23		99	119
1530	14" x 14"		18	.444		89	23		112	134
1534	16" x 16"		17	.471		98.50	24.50		123	146
1538	18" x 18"		17	.471		135	24.50		159.50	187
1542	22" x 22"	▼	16	.500	▼	189	26		215	248
1980	One way deflection, adj. vert. or horiz. face bars									
1990	6" x 6"	1 Shee	26	.308	Ea.	36.50	16.05		52.55	64.50
2000	8" x 4"		26	.308		35.50	16.05		51.55	63.50
2020	8" x 8"		24	.333		42.50	17.40		59.90	73
2040	10" x 6"		20	.400		42.50	21		63.50	79
2060	10" x 10"		19	.421		50	22		72	88
2080	12" x 6"		19	.421		46	22		68	84
2100	12" x 12"		18	.444		60	23		83	102
2120	14" x 8"		17	.471		55	24.50		79.50	98
2140	14" x 12"		18	.444		66	23		89	108
2160	14" x 14"		18	.444		74.50	23		97.50	117
2180	16" x 6"		18	.444		55	23		78	96
2200	16" x 12"		18	.444		72.50	23		95.50	116
2220	16" x 16"		17	.471		92	24.50		116.50	139
2240	18" x 8"		18	.444		64	23		87	106
2260	18" x 12"		17	.471		78	24.50		102.50	123
2280	18" x 18"		16	.500		113	26		139	164
2300	20" x 10"		18	.444		76	23		99	119
2320	20" x 16"	▼	16	.500	▼	110	26		136	161

23 37 13.60 Registers		Crew	Daily Output	Labor-Hours	Unit	Material	2012 Bare Costs Labor	Equipment	Total	Total Incl O&P
2340	20" x 20"	1 Shee	16	.500	Ea.	138	26		164	192
2360	24" x 12"		15	.533		95.50	28		123.50	148
2380	24" x 16"		14	.571		128	30		158	186
2400	24" x 20"		12	.667		159	35		194	228
2420	24" x 24"		10	.800		195	41.50		236.50	278
2440	30" x 12"		13	.615		124	32		156	185
2460	30" x 16"		13	.615		161	32		193	226
2480	30" x 24"		11	.727		251	38		289	335
2500	30" x 30"		9	.889		325	46.50		371.50	425
2520	36" x 12"		11	.727		154	38		192	228
2540	36" x 24"		10	.800		310	41.50		351.50	405
2560	36" x 36"		8	1		520	52		572	650
2600	For 2 way deflect., adj. vert. or horiz. face bars, add					40%				
2700	Above registers in steel instead of aluminum, deduct					10%				
3000	Baseboard, hand adj. damper, enameled steel									
3012	8" x 6"	1 Shee	26	.308	Ea.	14.85	16.05		30.90	41
3020	10" x 6"		24	.333		16.15	17.40		33.55	44.50
3040	12" x 5"		23	.348		17.50	18.15		35.65	47
3060	12" x 6"		23	.348		17.50	18.15		35.65	47
3080	12" x 8"		22	.364		25.50	18.95		44.45	57
3100	14" x 6"		20	.400		19	21		40	53
4000	Floor, toe operated damper, enameled steel									
4020	4" x 8"	1 Shee	32	.250	Ea.	27.50	13.05		40.55	50
4040	4" x 12"		26	.308		32	16.05		48.05	60
4060	6" x 8"		28	.286		29.50	14.90		44.40	55
4080	6" x 14"		22	.364		37.50	18.95		56.45	70
4100	8" x 10"		22	.364		33.50	18.95		52.45	66
4120	8" x 16"		20	.400		56	21		77	93.50
4140	10" x 10"		20	.400		40	21		61	76
4160	10" x 16"		18	.444		61	23		84	103
4180	12" x 12"		18	.444		49.50	23		72.50	90
4200	12" x 24"		16	.500		171	26		197	228
4220	14" x 14"		16	.500		141	26		167	195
4240	14" x 20"		15	.533		188	28		216	250
4300	Spiral pipe supply register									
4310	Aluminum, double deflection, w/damper extractor									
4320	4" x 12", for 6" thru 10" diameter duct	1 Shee	25	.320	Ea.	62	16.70		78.70	93.50
4330	4" x 18", for 6" thru 10" diameter duct		18	.444		77	23		100	120
4340	6" x 12", for 8" thru 12" diameter duct		19	.421		67.50	22		89.50	108
4350	6" x 18", for 8" thru 12" diameter duct		18	.444		88	23		111	132
4360	6" x 24", for 8" thru 12" diameter duct		16	.500		109	26		135	160
4370	6" x 30", for 8" thru 12" diameter duct		15	.533		138	28		166	195
4380	8" x 18", for 10" thru 14" diameter duct		18	.444		94	23		117	139
4390	8" x 24", for 10" thru 14" diameter duct		15	.533		117	28		145	172
4400	8" x 30", for 10" thru 14" diameter duct		14	.571		156	30		186	217
4410	10" x 24", for 12" thru 18" diameter duct		13	.615		129	32		161	191
4420	10" x 30", for 12" thru 18" diameter duct		12	.667		170	35		205	240
4430	10" x 36", for 12" thru 18" diameter duct		11	.727		211	38		249	290
4980	Air return									
5000	Ceiling or wall, fixed 45° face blades									
5010	Adjustable O.B. damper, anodized aluminum									
5020	4" x 8"	1 Shee	26	.308	Ea.	28.50	16.05		44.55	56
5040	6" x 8"		24	.333		28.50	17.40		45.90	58

23 37 13.60 Registers		Crew	Daily Output	Labor-Hours	Unit	Material	2012 Bare Costs Labor	Equipment	Total	Total Incl O&P
5060	6" x 10"	1 Shee	19	.421	Ea.	28.50	22		50.50	65
5070	6" x 12"		19	.421		32.50	22		54.50	69
5080	6" x 16"		18	.444		38.50	23		61.50	78
5100	8" x 10"		19	.421		32.50	22		54.50	69
5120	8" x 12"		16	.500		34.50	26		60.50	78
5140	10" x 10"		18	.444		36.50	23		59.50	75.50
5160	10" x 16"		17	.471		43	24.50		67.50	84.50
5170	12" x 12"		18	.444		37.50	23		60.50	76.50
5180	12" x 18"		18	.444		49	23		72	89.50
5184	12" x 24"		14	.571		56	30		86	107
5200	12" x 30"		12	.667		75.50	35		110.50	136
5210	12" x 36"		10	.800		103	41.50		144.50	178
5220	16" x 16"		17	.471		51.50	24.50		76	94.50
5240	18" x 18"		16	.500		61.50	26		87.50	108
5250	18" x 24"		13	.615		74.50	32		106.50	131
5254	18" x 30"		11	.727		114	38		152	184
5260	18" x 36"		10	.800		135	41.50		176.50	213
5270	20" x 20"		10	.800		72	41.50		113.50	143
5274	20" x 24"		12	.667		85.50	35		120.50	147
5280	24" x 24"		11	.727		94.50	38		132.50	162
5290	24" x 30"		10	.800		106	41.50		147.50	181
5300	24" x 36"		8	1		151	52		203	246
5320	24" x 48"		6	1.333		225	69.50		294.50	355
5340	30" x 30"	▼	6.50	1.231		176	64		240	292
5344	30" x 120"	Q-9	6	2.667		760	125		885	1,025
5360	36" x 36"	1 Shee	6	1.333		385	69.50		454.50	530
5370	40" x 32"	"	6	1.333	▼	480	69.50		549.50	630
5400	Ceiling or wall, removable-reversible core, single deflection									
5402	Adjustable O.B. damper, radiused frame with border, aluminum									
5410	8" x 4"	1 Shee	26	.308	Ea.	31.50	16.05		47.55	59
5414	8" x 6"		24	.333		31.50	17.40		48.90	61
5418	10" x 6"		19	.421		40	22		62	77.50
5422	10" x 10"		18	.444		45.50	23		68.50	85.50
5426	12" x 6"		19	.421		40	22		62	77.50
5430	12" x 12"		18	.444		51	23		74	92
5434	16" x 16"		16	.500		77	26		103	125
5438	18" x 18"		17	.471		97	24.50		121.50	144
5442	20" x 20"		16	.500		117	26		143	168
5446	24" x 12"		15	.533		77	28		105	127
5450	24" x 18"		13	.615		117	32		149	177
5454	24" x 24"		11	.727		162	38		200	236
5458	30" x 12"		13	.615		102	32		134	162
5462	30" x 18"		12.50	.640		148	33.50		181.50	214
5466	30" x 24"		11	.727		208	38		246	286
5470	30" x 30"		9	.889		259	46.50		305.50	355
5474	36" x 12"		11	.727		128	38		166	199
5478	36" x 18"		10.50	.762		179	39.50		218.50	258
5482	36" x 24"		10	.800		250	41.50		291.50	340
5486	36" x 30"		9	.889		335	46.50		381.50	440
5490	36" x 36"	▼	8	1	▼	430	52		482	555
6000	For steel construction instead of aluminum, deduct					10%				

23 37 Air Outlets and Inlets

23 37 15 – Louvers

23 37 15.40 HVAC Louvers	Crew	Daily Output	Labor-Hours	Unit	Material	2012 Bare Costs Labor	Equipment	Total	Total Incl O&P
0010 **HVAC LOUVERS**									
0100 Aluminum, extruded, with screen, mill finish									
1002 Brick vent, see also Section 04 05 23.19									
1100 Standard, 4" deep, 8" wide, 5" high	1 Shee	24	.333	Ea.	34.50	17.40		51.90	64
1200 Modular, 4" deep, 7-3/4" wide, 5" high		24	.333		36	17.40		53.40	66
1300 Speed brick, 4" deep, 11-5/8" wide, 3-7/8" high		24	.333		36	17.40		53.40	66
1400 Fuel oil brick, 4" deep, 8" wide, 5" high		24	.333		61.50	17.40		78.90	94.50
2000 Cooling tower and mechanical equip., screens, light weight		40	.200	S.F.	15.40	10.45		25.85	33
2020 Standard weight		35	.229		41	11.90		52.90	63
2500 Dual combination, automatic, intake or exhaust		20	.400		56	21		77	93.50
2520 Manual operation		20	.400		41.50	21		62.50	78
2540 Electric or pneumatic operation		20	.400		41.50	21		62.50	78
2560 Motor, for electric or pneumatic		14	.571	Ea.	480	30		510	575
3000 Fixed blade, continuous line									
3100 Mullion type, stormproof	1 Shee	28	.286	S.F.	41.50	14.90		56.40	68.50
3200 Stormproof		28	.286		41.50	14.90		56.40	68.50
3300 Vertical line		28	.286		49.50	14.90		64.40	76.50
3500 For damper to use with above, add					50%	30%			
3520 Motor, for damper, electric or pneumatic	1 Shee	14	.571	Ea.	480	30		510	575
4000 Operating, 45°, manual, electric or pneumatic		24	.333	S.F.	50	17.40		67.40	81.50
4100 Motor, for electric or pneumatic		14	.571	Ea.	480	30		510	575
4200 Penthouse, roof		56	.143	S.F.	24.50	7.45		31.95	38.50
4300 Walls		40	.200		58	10.45		68.45	80
5000 Thinline, under 4" thick, fixed blade		40	.200		24	10.45		34.45	42.50
5010 Finishes, applied by mfr. at additional cost, available in colors									
5020 Prime coat only, add				S.F.	3.30			3.30	3.63
5040 Baked enamel finish coating, add					6.10			6.10	6.70
5060 Anodized finish, add					6.60			6.60	7.25
5080 Duranodic finish, add					12			12	13.20
5100 Fluoropolymer finish coating, add					18.90			18.90	21
9980 For small orders (under 10 pieces), add					25%				

23 37 23 – HVAC Gravity Ventilators

23 37 23.10 HVAC Gravity Air Ventilators

	Crew	Daily Output	Labor-Hours	Unit	Material	2012 Bare Costs Labor	Equipment	Total	Total Incl O&P
0010 **HVAC GRAVITY AIR VENTILATORS**, Incl. base and damper									
1280 Rotary ventilators, wind driven, galvanized									
1300 4" neck diameter	Q-9	20	.800	Ea.	50	37.50		87.50	112
1320 5" neck diameter		18	.889		56	41.50		97.50	125
1340 6" neck diameter		16	1		56	47		103	133
1360 8" neck diameter		14	1.143		58	53.50		111.50	146
1380 10" neck diameter		12	1.333		75	62.50		137.50	178
1400 12" neck diameter		10	1.600		81	75		156	204
1420 14" neck diameter		10	1.600		113	75		188	238
1440 16" neck diameter		9	1.778		136	83.50		219.50	277
1460 18" neck diameter, 1700 CFM		9	1.778		158	83.50		241.50	300
1480 20" neck diameter, 2100 CFM		8	2		176	94		270	335
1500 24" neck diameter, 3,100 CFM		8	2		236	94		330	405
1520 30" neck diameter, 4500 CFM		7	2.286		490	107		597	705
1540 36" neck diameter, 5,500 CFM		6	2.667		695	125		820	955
1600 For aluminum, add					300%				
1620 For stainless steel, add					600%				
1630 For copper, add					600%				
2000 Stationary, gravity, syphon, galvanized									

23 37 23 – HVAC Gravity Ventilators

23 37 23.10 HVAC Gravity Air Ventilators		Crew	Daily Output	Labor-Hours	Unit	Material	2012 Bare Costs Labor	Equipment	Total	Total Incl O&P
2100	3" neck diameter, 40 CFM	Q-9	24	.667	Ea.	45.50	31.50		77	97.50
2120	4" neck diameter, 50 CFM		20	.800		49.50	37.50		87	112
2140	5" neck diameter, 58 CFM		18	.889		50	41.50		91.50	119
2160	6" neck diameter, 66 CFM		16	1		53	47		100	130
2180	7" neck diameter, 86 CFM		15	1.067		54.50	50		104.50	137
2200	8" neck diameter, 110 CFM		14	1.143		55	53.50		108.50	142
2220	10" neck diameter, 140 CFM		12	1.333		71	62.50		133.50	174
2240	12" neck diameter, 160 CFM		10	1.600		91	75		166	214
2260	14" neck diameter, 250 CFM		10	1.600		114	75		189	240
2280	16" neck diameter, 380 CFM		9	1.778		153	83.50		236.50	295
2300	18" neck diameter, 500 CFM		9	1.778		203	83.50		286.50	350
2320	20" neck diameter, 625 CFM		8	2		215	94		309	380
2340	24" neck diameter, 900 CFM		8	2		248	94		342	415
2360	30" neck diameter, 1375 CFM		7	2.286		565	107		672	785
2380	36" neck diameter, 2,000 CFM		6	2.667		775	125		900	1,050
2400	42" neck diameter, 3000 CFM		4	4		1,100	188		1,288	1,475
2410	48" neck diameter, 4000 CFM		3	5.333		1,475	250		1,725	2,000
2500	For aluminum, add					300%				
2520	For stainless steel, add					600%				
2530	For copper, add					600%				
3000	Rotating chimney cap, galvanized, 4" neck diameter	Q-9	20	.800		39	37.50		76.50	99.50
3020	5" neck diameter		18	.889		40	41.50		81.50	107
3040	6" neck diameter		16	1		40.50	47		87.50	116
3060	7" neck diameter		15	1.067		44	50		94	125
3080	8" neck diameter		14	1.143		45.50	53.50		99	132
3100	10" neck diameter		12	1.333		58.50	62.50		121	160
3600	Stationary chimney rain cap, galvanized, 3" neck diameter		24	.667		34	31.50		65.50	85
3620	4" neck diameter		20	.800		35	37.50		72.50	95.50
3640	6" neck diameter		16	1		36.50	47		83.50	112
3680	8" neck diameter		14	1.143		39	53.50		92.50	125
3700	10" neck diameter		12	1.333		49.50	62.50		112	150
3720	12" neck diameter		10	1.600		82.50	75		157.50	205
3740	14" neck diameter		10	1.600		88	75		163	211
3760	16" neck diameter		9	1.778		108	83.50		191.50	246
3770	18" neck diameter		9	1.778		156	83.50		239.50	298
3780	20" neck diameter		8	2		208	94		302	370
3790	24" neck diameter		8	2		243	94		337	410
4200	Stationary mushroom, aluminum, 16" orifice diameter		10	1.600		565	75		640	735
4220	26" orifice diameter		6.15	2.602		830	122		952	1,100
4230	30" orifice diameter		5.71	2.802		1,225	132		1,357	1,550
4240	38" orifice diameter		5	3.200		1,750	150		1,900	2,150
4250	42" orifice diameter		4.70	3.404		2,300	160		2,460	2,800
4260	50" orifice diameter		4.44	3.604		2,750	169		2,919	3,275
5000	Relief vent									
5500	Rectangular, aluminum, galvanized curb									
5510	intake/exhaust, 0.033" SP									
5580	500 CFM, 12" x 12"	Q-9	8.60	1.860	Ea.	645	87.50		732.50	845
5600	600 CFM, 12" x 16"		8	2		730	94		824	945
5620	750 CFM, 12" x 20"		7.20	2.222		780	104		884	1,025
5640	1000 CFM, 12" x 24"		6.60	2.424		820	114		934	1,075
5660	1500 CFM, 12" x 36"		5.80	2.759		1,100	129		1,229	1,400
5680	3000 CFM, 20" x 42"		4	4		1,450	188		1,638	1,850
5700	5000 CFM, 20" x 72"		3	5.333		2,075	250		2,325	2,650

23 37 Air Outlets and Inlets

23 37 23 – HVAC Gravity Ventilators

23 37 23.10 HVAC Gravity Air Ventilators

		Crew	Daily Output	Labor-Hours	Unit	Material	2012 Bare Costs Labor	Equipment	Total	Total Incl O&P
5720	6000 CFM, 24" x 72"	Q-9	2.30	6.957	Ea.	2,225	325		2,550	2,950
5740	10,000 CFM, 48" x 60"		1.80	8.889		2,850	415		3,265	3,750
5760	12,000 CFM, 48" x 72"		1.60	10		3,375	470		3,845	4,425
5780	13,750 CFM, 60" x 66"		1.40	11.429		3,725	535		4,260	4,925
5800	15,000 CFM, 60" x 72"		1.30	12.308		3,975	580		4,555	5,250
5820	18,000 CFM, 72" x 72"	↓	1.20	13.333	↓	4,525	625		5,150	5,925
5880	Size is throat area, volume is at 500 fpm									
7000	Note: sizes based on exhaust. Intake, with 0.125" SP									
7100	loss, approximately twice listed capacity.									

23 38 Ventilation Hoods

23 38 13 – Commercial-Kitchen Hoods

23 38 13.10 Hood and Ventilation Equipment

		Crew	Daily Output	Labor-Hours	Unit	Material	2012 Bare Costs Labor	Equipment	Total	Total Incl O&P
0010	**HOOD AND VENTILATION EQUIPMENT**									
2970	Exhaust hood, sst, gutter on all sides, 4' x 4' x 2'	1 Carp	1.80	4.444	Ea.	4,675	196		4,871	5,425
2980	4' x 4' x 7'	"	1.60	5	"	7,425	221		7,646	8,525
7800	Vent hood, wall canopy with fire protection	L-3A	9	1.333	L.F.	385	64		449	520
7810	Without fire protection		10	1.200		268	57.50		325.50	385
7820	Island canopy with fire protection		7	1.714		405	82.50		487.50	570
7830	Without fire protection		8	1.500		292	72		364	430
7840	Back shelf with fire protection		11	1.091		385	52.50		437.50	500
7850	Without fire protection	↓	12	1	↓	268	48		316	370
7860	Range hood & CO_2 system, minimum	1 Carp	2.50	3.200	Ea.	2,825	141		2,966	3,325
7870	Maximum	"	1	8		33,800	355		34,155	37,600
7950	Hood fire protection system, minimum	Q-1	3	5.333		4,400	262		4,662	5,250
8050	Maximum	"	1	16	↓	35,300	785		36,085	40,100

23 38 13.20 Kitchen Ventilation

		Crew	Daily Output	Labor-Hours	Unit	Material	2012 Bare Costs Labor	Equipment	Total	Total Incl O&P
0010	**KITCHEN VENTILATION**, Commercial									
1010	Heat reclaim unit, air to air									
1100	Heat pipe exchanger									
1110	Combined supply/exhaust air volume									
1120	2.5 to 6.0 MCFM	Q-10	2.80	8.571	MCFM	7,225	415		7,640	8,575
1130	6 to 16 MCFM		5	4.800		4,425	234		4,659	5,225
1140	16 to 22 MCFM	↓	6	4	↓	3,450	195		3,645	4,100
2010	Packaged ventilation									
2100	Combined supply/exhaust air volume									
2110	With ambient supply									
2120	3 to 7 MCFM	Q-10	5	4.800	MCFM	1,300	234		1,534	1,775
2130	7 to 12 MCFM		7.10	3.380		870	165		1,035	1,200
2140	12 to 22 MCFM	↓	10.70	2.243	↓	615	109		724	840
2400	With tempered supply									
2410	3 to 7 MCFM	Q-10	5	4.800	MCFM	2,275	234		2,509	2,850
2420	7 to 12 MCFM		7.10	3.380		1,450	165		1,615	1,850
2430	12 to 22 MCFM	↓	10.70	2.243	↓	1,075	109		1,184	1,350
6000	Exhaust hoods									
6100	Centrifugal grease extraction									
6110	Water wash type									
6120	Per foot of length, minimum	Q-10	7.10	3.380	L.F.	1,675	165		1,840	2,100
6130	Maximum	"	7.10	3.380	"	2,875	165		3,040	3,400
6200	Non water wash type									
6210	Per foot of length	Q-10	13.40	1.791	L.F.	1,225	87		1,312	1,475

23 38 Ventilation Hoods

23 38 13 – Commercial-Kitchen Hoods

23 38 13.20 Kitchen Ventilation		Crew	Daily Output	Labor-Hours	Unit	Material	2012 Bare Costs Labor	Equipment	Total	Total Incl O&P
6400	Island style ventilator									
6410	Water wash type									
6420	Per foot of length, minimum	Q-10	7.10	3.380	L.F.	2,225	165		2,390	2,700
6430	Maximum	"	7.10	3.380	"	3,725	165		3,890	4,350
6460	Non water wash type									
6470	Per foot of length, minimum	Q-10	13.40	1.791	L.F.	965	87		1,052	1,200
6480	Maximum	"	13.40	1.791	"	1,975	87		2,062	2,300

23 41 Particulate Air Filtration

23 41 13 – Panel Air Filters

23 41 13.10 Panel Type Air Filters

	23 41 13.10 Panel Type Air Filters	Crew	Daily Output	Labor-Hours	Unit	Material	2012 Bare Costs Labor	Equipment	Total	Total Incl O&P
0010	**PANEL TYPE AIR FILTERS**									
2950	Mechanical media filtration units									
3000	High efficiency type, with frame, non-supported [G]				MCFM	45			45	49.50
3100	Supported type [G]				"	60			60	66
5500	Throwaway glass or paper media type				Ea.	3.35			3.35	3.69

23 41 16 – Renewable-Media Air Filters

23 41 16.10 Disposable Media Air Filters

	23 41 16.10 Disposable Media Air Filters	Crew	Daily Output	Labor-Hours	Unit	Material	2012 Bare Costs Labor	Equipment	Total	Total Incl O&P
0010	**DISPOSABLE MEDIA AIR FILTERS**									
5000	Renewable disposable roll				MCFM	11.50			11.50	12.65
5800	Filter, bag type									
5810	90-95% efficiency									
5820	24" x 12" x 29", .75-1.25 MCFM	1 Shee	1.90	4.211	Ea.	61.50	220		281.50	405
5830	24" x 24" x 29", 1.5-2.5 MCFM	"	1.90	4.211	"	109	220		329	455
5850	80-85% efficiency									
5860	24" x 12" x 29", .75-1.25 MCFM	1 Shee	1.90	4.211	Ea.	53	220		273	395
5870	24" x 24" x 29", 1.5-2.5 MCFM	"	1.90	4.211	"	87	220		307	430

23 41 19 – Washable Air Filters

23 41 19.10 Permanent Air Filters

	23 41 19.10 Permanent Air Filters	Crew	Daily Output	Labor-Hours	Unit	Material	2012 Bare Costs Labor	Equipment	Total	Total Incl O&P
0010	**PERMANENT AIR FILTERS**									
4500	Permanent washable [G]				MCFM	20			20	22

23 41 23 – Extended Surface Filters

23 41 23.10 Expanded Surface Filters

	23 41 23.10 Expanded Surface Filters	Crew	Daily Output	Labor-Hours	Unit	Material	2012 Bare Costs Labor	Equipment	Total	Total Incl O&P
0010	**EXPANDED SURFACE FILTERS**									
4000	Medium efficiency, extended surface [G]				MCFM	5.50			5.50	6.05

23 41 33 – High-Efficiency Particulate Filtration

23 41 33.10 HEPA Filters

	23 41 33.10 HEPA Filters	Crew	Daily Output	Labor-Hours	Unit	Material	2012 Bare Costs Labor	Equipment	Total	Total Incl O&P
0010	**HEPA FILTERS**									
6000	HEPA filter complete w/particle board,									
6010	kraft paper frame, separator material									
6020	95% DOP efficiency									
6030	12" x 12" x 6", 150 CFM	1 Shee	3.70	2.162	Ea.	44	113		157	221
6034	24" x 12" x 6", 375 CFM		1.90	4.211		73.50	220		293.50	415
6038	24" x 18" x 6", 450 CFM		1.90	4.211		90	220		310	435
6042	24" x 24" x 6", 700 CFM		1.90	4.211		101	220		321	445
6046	12" x 12" x 12", 250 CFM		3.70	2.162		74.50	113		187.50	254
6050	24" x 12" x 12", 500 CFM		1.90	4.211		105	220		325	450
6054	24" x 18" x 12", 875 CFM		1.90	4.211		146	220		366	495
6058	24" x 24" x 12", 1000 CFM		1.90	4.211		158	220		378	510

23 41 Particulate Air Filtration

23 41 33 – High-Efficiency Particulate Filtration

23 41 33.10 HEPA Filters

		Crew	Daily Output	Labor-Hours	Unit	Material	2012 Bare Costs Labor	Equipment	Total	Total Incl O&P
6100	99% DOP efficiency									
6110	12" x 12" x 6", 150 CFM	1 Shee	3.70	2.162	Ea.	46	113		159	223
6114	24" x 12" x 6", 325 CFM		1.90	4.211		76	220		296	420
6118	24" x 18" x 6", 550 CFM		1.90	4.211		93	220		313	435
6122	24" x 24" x 6", 775 CFM		1.90	4.211		105	220		325	450
6124	24" x 48" x 6", 775 CFM		1.30	6.154		201	320		521	710
6126	12" x 12" x 12", 250 CFM		3.60	2.222		77	116		193	262
6130	24" x 12" x 12", 500 CFM		1.90	4.211		109	220		329	455
6134	24" x 18" x 12", 775 CFM		1.90	4.211		152	220		372	500
6138	24" x 24" x 12", 1100 CFM	↓	1.90	4.211	↓	164	220		384	515
6500	HEPA filter housing, 14 ga. galv. sheet metal									
6510	12" x 12" x 6"	1 Shee	2.50	3.200	Ea.	660	167		827	980
6514	24" x 12" x 6"		2	4		740	209		949	1,125
6518	12" x 12" x 12"		2.40	3.333		660	174		834	990
6522	14" x 12" x 12"		2.30	3.478		660	181		841	1,000
6526	24" x 18" x 6"		1.90	4.211		940	220		1,160	1,350
6530	24" x 24" x 6"		1.80	4.444		855	232		1,087	1,300
6534	24" x 48" x 6"		1.70	4.706		1,150	245		1,395	1,625
6538	24" x 72" x 6"		1.60	5		1,475	261		1,736	2,025
6542	24" x 18" x 12"		1.80	4.444		940	232		1,172	1,375
6546	24" x 24" x 12"		1.70	4.706		1,050	245		1,295	1,525
6550	24" x 48" x 12"		1.60	5		1,225	261		1,486	1,750
6554	24" x 72" x 12"	↓	1.50	5.333		1,525	278		1,803	2,125
6558	48" x 48" x 6"	Q-9	2.80	5.714		1,700	268		1,968	2,250
6562	48" x 72" x 6"		2.60	6.154		2,025	289		2,314	2,675
6566	48" x 96" x 6"		2.40	6.667		2,575	315		2,890	3,300
6570	48" x 48" x 12"		2.70	5.926		1,700	278		1,978	2,275
6574	48" x 72" x 12"		2.50	6.400		2,025	300		2,325	2,675
6578	48" x 96" x 12"		2.30	6.957		2,575	325		2,900	3,325
6582	114" x 72" x 12"	↓	2	8	↓	3,550	375		3,925	4,475

23 42 Gas-Phase Air Filtration

23 42 13 – Activated-Carbon Air Filtration

23 42 13.10 Charcoal Type Air Filtration

		Crew	Daily Output	Labor-Hours	Unit	Material	2012 Bare Costs Labor	Equipment	Total	Total Incl O&P
0010	**CHARCOAL TYPE AIR FILTRATION**									
0050	Activated charcoal type, full flow				MCFM	600			600	660
0060	Full flow, impregnated media 12" deep					225			225	248
0070	HEPA filter & frame for field erection					300			300	330
0080	HEPA filter-diffuser, ceiling install.				↓	300			300	330

23 42 16 – Chemically-Impregnated Adsorption Air Filtration

23 42 16.10 Chemical Adsorption Air Filtration

		Crew	Daily Output	Labor-Hours	Unit	Material	2012 Bare Costs Labor	Equipment	Total	Total Incl O&P
0010	**CHEMICAL ADSORPTION AIR FILTRATION**									
0500	Chemical media filtration type									
1100	Industrial air fume & odor scrubber unit w/pump & motor									
1110	corrosion resistant PVC construction									
1120	Single pack filter, horizontal type									
1130	500 CFM	Q-9	14	1.143	Ea.	6,500	53.50		6,553.50	7,225
1140	1000 CFM		11	1.455		7,625	68.50		7,693.50	8,500
1150	2000 CFM		8	2		9,250	94		9,344	10,300
1160	3000 CFM	↓	7	2.286	↓	10,700	107		10,807	12,000

23 42 Gas-Phase Air Filtration

23 42 16 – Chemically-Impregnated Adsorption Air Filtration

23 42 16.10 Chemical Adsorption Air Filtration		Crew	Daily Output	Labor-Hours	Unit	Material	2012 Bare Costs Labor	Equipment	Total	Total Incl O&P
1170	5000 CFM	Q-9	5	3.200	Ea.	14,000	150		14,150	15,500
1180	8000 CFM		4	4		19,500	188		19,688	21,800
1190	12,000 CFM		3	5.333		25,900	250		26,150	28,900
1200	16,000 CFM		2.50	6.400		32,000	300		32,300	35,700
1210	20,000 CFM		2	8		40,100	375		40,475	44,700
1220	26,000 CFM		1.50	10.667		46,100	500		46,600	51,500
1230	30,000 CFM	Q-10	2	12		52,500	585		53,085	58,500
1240	40,000 CFM	"	1.50	16		68,500	780		69,280	76,500
1250	50,000 CFM	Q-11	2	16		83,500	795		84,295	93,000
1260	55,000 CFM		1.80	17.778		91,000	885		91,885	102,000
1270	60,000 CFM		1.50	21.333		98,000	1,050		99,050	109,500
1300	Double pack filter, horizontal type									
1310	500 CFM	Q-9	10	1.600	Ea.	8,450	75		8,525	9,425
1320	1000 CFM		8	2		10,100	94		10,194	11,300
1330	2000 CFM		6	2.667		12,200	125		12,325	13,600
1340	3000 CFM		5	3.200		14,600	150		14,750	16,300
1350	5000 CFM		4	4		18,600	188		18,788	20,700
1360	8000 CFM		3	5.333		24,500	250		24,750	27,400
1370	12,000 CFM		2.50	6.400		33,300	300		33,600	37,100
1380	16,000 CFM		2	8		43,400	375		43,775	48,400
1390	20,000 CFM		1.50	10.667		52,500	500		53,000	59,000
1400	26,000 CFM		1	16		61,000	750		61,750	68,000
1410	30,000 CFM	Q-10	1.50	16		71,500	780		72,280	79,500
1420	40,000 CFM	"	1.30	18.462		91,500	900		92,400	102,000
1430	50,000 CFM	Q-11	1.50	21.333		114,500	1,050		115,550	127,500
1440	55,000 CFM		1.30	24.615		125,000	1,225		126,225	140,000
1450	60,000 CFM		1	32		135,500	1,600		137,100	151,500
1500	Single pack filter, vertical type									
1510	500 CFM	Q-9	24	.667	Ea.	6,200	31.50		6,231.50	6,875
1520	1000 CFM		18	.889		7,325	41.50		7,366.50	8,150
1530	2000 CFM		12	1.333		8,800	62.50		8,862.50	9,775
1540	3000 CFM		9	1.778		10,300	83.50		10,383.50	11,400
1550	5000 CFM		6	2.667		13,700	125		13,825	15,300
1560	8000 CFM		4	4		19,500	188		19,688	21,800
1570	12,000 CFM		3	5.333		26,600	250		26,850	29,600
1580	16,000 CFM		2	8		31,100	375		31,475	34,800
1590	20,000 CFM		1.80	8.889		39,200	415		39,615	43,700
1600	24,000 CFM		1.60	10		43,800	470		44,270	48,800
1650	Double pack filter, vertical type									
1660	500 CFM	Q-9	22	.727	Ea.	8,050	34		8,084	8,900
1670	1000 CFM		16	1		9,600	47		9,647	10,700
1680	2000 CFM		10	1.600		11,500	75		11,575	12,800
1690	3000 CFM		7	2.286		13,600	107		13,707	15,100
1700	5000 CFM		5	3.200		17,800	150		17,950	19,800
1710	8000 CFM		3	5.333		24,300	250		24,550	27,100
1720	12,000 CFM		2.50	6.400		32,900	300		33,200	36,600
1730	16,000 CFM		2	8		41,300	375		41,675	46,000
1740	20,000 CFM		1.50	10.667		51,500	500		52,000	57,500
1750	24,000 CFM		1	16		57,500	750		58,250	64,000
1800	Inlet or outlet transition, horizontal									
1810	Single pack to 12,000 CFM, add					4%				
1820	Single pack to 30,000 CFM, add					6%				
1830	Single pack to 60,000 CFM, add					8%				

23 42 Gas-Phase Air Filtration

23 42 16 – Chemically-Impregnated Adsorption Air Filtration

23 42 16.10 Chemical Adsorption Air Filtration		Crew	Daily Output	Labor-Hours	Unit	Material	2012 Bare Costs Labor	Equipment	Total	Total Incl O&P
1840	Double pack to 12,000 CFM, add					3%				
1850	Double pack to 30,000 CFM, add					5%				
1860	Double pack to 60,000 CFM, add					6%				
1870	Inlet or outlet transition, vertical									
1880	Single pack to 5000 CFM, add					2%				
1890	Single pack to 24,000 CFM, add					3%				
1900	Double pack to 24,000 CFM, add					2%				

23 43 Electronic Air Cleaners

23 43 13 – Washable Electronic Air Cleaners

23 43 13.10 Electronic Air Cleaners

		Crew	Daily Output	Labor-Hours	Unit	Material	Labor	Equipment	Total	Total Incl O&P
0010	**ELECTRONIC AIR CLEANERS**									
2000	Electronic air cleaner, duct mounted									
2150	1000 CFM	1 Shee	4	2	Ea.	380	104		484	580
2200	1200 CFM		3.80	2.105		430	110		540	640
2250	1400 CFM		3.60	2.222		435	116		551	655
2260	2000 CFM		3.20	2.500		480	130		610	730

23 51 Breechings, Chimneys, and Stacks

23 51 13 – Draft Control Devices

23 51 13.13 Draft-Induction Fans

		Crew	Daily Output	Labor-Hours	Unit	Material	Labor	Equipment	Total	Total Incl O&P
0010	**DRAFT-INDUCTION FANS**									
1000	Breeching installation									
1800	Hot gas, 600°F, variable pitch pulley and motor									
1840	6" diam. inlet, 1/4 H.P., 1 phase, 400 CFM	Q-9	6	2.667	Ea.	1,875	125		2,000	2,250
1860	8" diam. inlet, 1/4 H.P., 1phase, 1120 CFM		4	4		2,675	188		2,863	3,225
1870	9" diam. inlet, 3/4 H.P., 1 phase, 1440 CFM		3.60	4.444		3,300	209		3,509	3,950
1880	10" diam. inlet, 3/4 H.P., 1 phase, 2000 CFM		3.30	4.848		3,300	228		3,528	3,975
1900	12" diam. inlet, 3/4 H.P., 3 phase, 2960 CFM		3	5.333		3,650	250		3,900	4,400
1910	14" diam. inlet, 1 H.P., 3 phase, 4160 CFM		2.60	6.154		3,675	289		3,964	4,500
1920	16" diam. inlet, 2 H.P., 3 phase, 5500 CFM		2.30	6.957		4,075	325		4,400	4,975
1950	20" diam. inlet, 3 H.P., 3 phase, 9760 CFM		1.50	10.667		5,850	500		6,350	7,225
1960	22" diam. inlet, 5 H.P., 3 phase, 13,360 CFM		1	16		9,525	750		10,275	11,700
1980	24" diam. inlet, 7-1/2 H.P., 3 phase, 17,760 CFM		.80	20		10,500	940		11,440	12,900
2300	For multi-blade damper at fan inlet, add					20%				
3600	Chimney-top installation									
3700	6" size	1 Shee	8	1	Ea.	835	52		887	995
3740	8" size		7	1.143		840	59.50		899.50	1,000
3750	10" size		6.50	1.231		1,100	64		1,164	1,300
3780	13" size		6	1.333		1,125	69.50		1,194.50	1,350
3880	For speed control switch, add					63.50			63.50	70
3920	For thermal fan control, add					63.50			63.50	70
5500	Flue blade style damper for draft control,									
5510	locking quadrant blade									
5550	8" size	Q-9	8	2	Ea.	405	94		499	590
5560	9" size		7.50	2.133		405	100		505	600
5570	10" size		7	2.286		415	107		522	620
5580	12" size		6.50	2.462		420	116		536	640
5590	14" size		6	2.667		430	125		555	665

23 51 Breechings, Chimneys, and Stacks

23 51 13 – Draft Control Devices

23 51 13.13 Draft-Induction Fans

		Crew	Daily Output	Labor-Hours	Unit	Material	2012 Bare Costs Labor	Equipment	Total	Total Incl O&P
5600	16" size	Q-9	5.50	2.909	Ea.	445	137		582	700
5610	18" size		5	3.200		465	150		615	740
5620	20" size		4.50	3.556		490	167		657	795
5630	22" size		4	4		515	188		703	850
5640	24" size		3.50	4.571		545	215		760	920
5650	27" size		3	5.333		570	250		820	1,000
5660	30" size		2.50	6.400		625	300		925	1,150
5670	32" size		2	8		655	375		1,030	1,300
5680	36" size	↓	1.50	10.667	↓	725	500		1,225	1,550

23 51 13.16 Vent Dampers

		Crew	Daily Output	Labor-Hours	Unit	Material	2012 Bare Costs Labor	Equipment	Total	Total Incl O&P
0010	**VENT DAMPERS**									
5000	Vent damper, bi-metal, gas, 3" diameter	Q-9	24	.667	Ea.	44	31.50		75.50	96
5010	4" diameter		24	.667		44	31.50		75.50	96
5020	5" diameter		23	.696		44	32.50		76.50	98.50
5030	6" diameter		22	.727		44	34		78	101
5040	7" diameter		21	.762		45.50	36		81.50	105
5050	8" diameter	↓	20	.800	↓	49	37.50		86.50	111

23 51 13.19 Barometric Dampers

		Crew	Daily Output	Labor-Hours	Unit	Material	2012 Bare Costs Labor	Equipment	Total	Total Incl O&P
0010	**BAROMETRIC DAMPERS**									
1000	Barometric, gas fired system only, 6" size for 5" and 6" pipes	1 Shee	20	.400	Ea.	63	21		84	102
1020	7" size, for 6" and 7" pipes		19	.421		67.50	22		89.50	108
1040	8" size, for 7" and 8" pipes		18	.444		87	23		110	132
1060	9" size, for 8" and 9" pipes	↓	16	.500	↓	98	26		124	148
2000	All fuel, oil, oil/gas, coal									
2020	10" for 9" and 10" pipes	1 Shee	15	.533	Ea.	146	28		174	204
2040	12" for 11" and 12" pipes		15	.533		191	28		219	253
2060	14" for 13" and 14" pipes		14	.571		248	30		278	320
2080	16" for 15" and 16" pipes		13	.615		345	32		377	430
2100	18" for 17" and 18" pipes		12	.667		460	35		495	560
2120	20" for 19" and 21" pipes	↓	10	.800		550	41.50		591.50	670
2140	24" for 22" and 25" pipes	Q-9	12	1.333		675	62.50		737.50	835
2160	28" for 26" and 30" pipes		10	1.600		835	75		910	1,025
2180	32" for 31" and 34" pipes	↓	8	2		1,075	94		1,169	1,325
3260	For thermal switch for above, add	1 Shee	24	.333	↓	60	17.40		77.40	93

23 51 23 – Gas Vents

23 51 23.10 Gas Chimney Vents

		Crew	Daily Output	Labor-Hours	Unit	Material	2012 Bare Costs Labor	Equipment	Total	Total Incl O&P
0010	**GAS CHIMNEY VENTS**, Prefab metal, U.L. listed									
0020	Gas, double wall, galvanized steel									
0080	3" diameter	Q-9	72	.222	V.L.F.	4.65	10.45		15.10	21
0100	4" diameter		68	.235		6.35	11.05		17.40	24
0120	5" diameter		64	.250		7.20	11.75		18.95	26
0140	6" diameter		60	.267		9.05	12.50		21.55	29
0160	7" diameter		56	.286		10.40	13.40		23.80	32
0180	8" diameter		52	.308		15.80	14.45		30.25	39.50
0200	10" diameter		48	.333		30	15.65		45.65	57
0220	12" diameter		44	.364		36	17.05		53.05	65.50
0240	14" diameter		42	.381		60	17.90		77.90	93.50
0260	16" diameter		40	.400		86	18.75		104.75	124
0280	18" diameter	↓	38	.421		106	19.75		125.75	147
0300	20" diameter	Q-10	36	.667		125	32.50		157.50	188
0320	22" diameter		34	.706		159	34.50		193.50	228
0340	24" diameter	↓	32	.750	↓	197	36.50		233.50	272

23 51 23.10 Gas Chimney Vents		Crew	Daily Output	Labor-Hours	Unit	Material	2012 Bare Costs Labor	Equipment	Total	Total Incl O&P
0600	For 4", 5" and 6" oval, add					50%				
0650	Gas, double wall, galvanized steel, fittings									
0660	Elbow 45°, 3" diameter	Q-9	36	.444	Ea.	11.90	21		32.90	45
0670	4" diameter		34	.471		13.95	22		35.95	49
0680	5" diameter		32	.500		16.80	23.50		40.30	54.50
0690	6" diameter		30	.533		20.50	25		45.50	61
0700	7" diameter		28	.571		31.50	27		58.50	75.50
0710	8" diameter		26	.615		42	29		71	90
0720	10" diameter		24	.667		89	31.50		120.50	146
0730	12" diameter		22	.727		95	34		129	157
0740	14" diameter		21	.762		149	36		185	219
0750	16" diameter		20	.800		193	37.50		230.50	270
0760	18" diameter	▼	19	.842		254	39.50		293.50	340
0770	20" diameter	Q-10	18	1.333		284	65		349	410
0780	22" diameter		17	1.412		455	68.50		523.50	605
0790	24" diameter	▼	16	1.500	▼	580	73		653	745
0916	Adjustable length									
0918	3" diameter, to 12"	Q-9	36	.444	Ea.	10.95	21		31.95	44
0920	4" diameter, to 12"		34	.471		12.75	22		34.75	47.50
0924	6" diameter, to 12"		30	.533		16.45	25		41.45	56
0928	8" diameter, to 12"		26	.615		29.50	29		58.50	76
0930	10" diameter, to 18"		24	.667		90	31.50		121.50	147
0932	12" diameter, to 18"		22	.727		91.50	34		125.50	153
0936	16" diameter, to 18"		20	.800		185	37.50		222.50	260
0938	18" diameter, to 18"	▼	19	.842		287	39.50		326.50	375
0944	24" diameter, to 18"	Q-10	16	1.500		405	73		478	555
0950	Elbow 90°, adjustable, 3" diameter	Q-9	36	.444		20.50	21		41.50	54.50
0960	4" diameter		34	.471		24	22		46	59.50
0970	5" diameter		32	.500		29.50	23.50		53	68.50
0980	6" diameter		30	.533		34.50	25		59.50	76
0990	7" diameter		28	.571		49.50	27		76.50	95.50
1010	8" diameter		26	.615		57	29		86	107
1020	Wall thimble, 4 to 7" adjustable, 3" diameter		36	.444		12.70	21		33.70	46
1022	4" diameter		34	.471		14.30	22		36.30	49.50
1024	5" diameter		32	.500		21	23.50		44.50	59
1026	6" diameter		30	.533		23.50	25		48.50	64
1028	7" diameter		28	.571		27.50	27		54.50	71.50
1030	8" diameter		26	.615		43	29		72	91.50
1040	Roof flashing, 3" diameter		36	.444		7.50	21		28.50	40.50
1050	4" diameter		34	.471		8.70	22		30.70	43
1060	5" diameter		32	.500		16.05	23.50		39.55	53.50
1070	6" diameter		30	.533		21	25		46	61
1080	7" diameter		28	.571		26	27		53	69.50
1090	8" diameter		26	.615		31.50	29		60.50	79
1100	10" diameter		24	.667		37.50	31.50		69	88.50
1110	12" diameter		22	.727		52.50	34		86.50	110
1120	14" diameter		20	.800		149	37.50		186.50	221
1130	16" diameter		18	.889		185	41.50		226.50	267
1140	18" diameter	▼	16	1		196	47		243	288
1150	20" diameter	Q-10	18	1.333		325	65		390	455
1160	22" diameter		14	1.714		410	83.50		493.50	575
1170	24" diameter	▼	12	2		450	97.50		547.50	645
1200	Tee, 3" diameter	Q-9	27	.593	▼	31	28		59	76.50

23 51 23.10 Gas Chimney Vents		Crew	Daily Output	Labor-Hours	Unit	Material	2012 Bare Costs Labor	Equipment	Total	Total Incl O&P
1210	4" diameter	Q-9	26	.615	Ea.	33.50	29		62.50	81
1220	5" diameter		25	.640		37	30		67	86.50
1230	6" diameter		24	.667		40	31.50		71.50	91.50
1240	7" diameter		23	.696		52.50	32.50		85	108
1250	8" diameter		22	.727		59.50	34		93.50	118
1260	10" diameter		21	.762		159	36		195	230
1270	12" diameter		20	.800		163	37.50		200.50	237
1280	14" diameter		18	.889		415	41.50		456.50	520
1290	16" diameter		16	1		430	47		477	545
1300	18" diameter		14	1.143		520	53.50		573.50	650
1310	20" diameter	Q-10	17	1.412		1,000	68.50		1,068.50	1,200
1320	22" diameter		13	1.846		1,025	90		1,115	1,250
1330	24" diameter		12	2		1,050	97.50		1,147.50	1,300
1460	Tee cap, 3" diameter	Q-9	45	.356		3.11	16.70		19.81	29
1470	4" diameter		42	.381		3.50	17.90		21.40	31.50
1480	5" diameter		40	.400		4.63	18.75		23.38	33.50
1490	6" diameter		37	.432		5.40	20.50		25.90	37
1500	7" diameter		35	.457		8.75	21.50		30.25	42
1510	8" diameter		34	.471		10.30	22		32.30	45
1520	10" diameter		32	.500		21.50	23.50		45	59.50
1530	12" diameter		30	.533		28.50	25		53.50	69
1540	14" diameter		28	.571		58.50	27		85.50	105
1550	16" diameter		25	.640		67.50	30		97.50	121
1560	18" diameter		24	.667		76.50	31.50		108	132
1570	20" diameter	Q-10	27	.889		82	43.50		125.50	156
1580	22" diameter		22	1.091		94	53		147	184
1590	24" diameter		21	1.143		106	55.50		161.50	201
1750	Top, 3" diameter	Q-9	46	.348		16.35	16.30		32.65	43
1760	4" diameter		44	.364		21.50	17.05		38.55	49.50
1770	5" diameter		42	.381		24	17.90		41.90	54
1780	6" diameter		40	.400		30	18.75		48.75	61.50
1790	7" diameter		38	.421		44	19.75		63.75	78.50
1800	8" diameter		36	.444		57.50	21		78.50	95.50
1810	10" diameter		34	.471		104	22		126	149
1820	12" diameter		32	.500		118	23.50		141.50	166
1830	14" diameter		30	.533		151	25		176	204
1840	16" diameter		28	.571		219	27		246	282
1850	18" diameter		26	.615		300	29		329	375
1860	20" diameter	Q-10	28	.857		800	41.50		841.50	945
1870	22" diameter		22	1.091		860	53		913	1,025
1880	24" diameter		20	1.200		875	58.50		933.50	1,050
1900	Gas, double wall, galvanized steel, oval									
1904	4" x 1'	Q-9	68	.235	V.L.F.	15.60	11.05		26.65	34
1906	5"		64	.250		37	11.75		48.75	58.50
1908	5"/6" x 1'		60	.267		34	12.50		46.50	56.50
1910	Oval fittings									
1912	Adjustable length									
1914	4" diameter to 12" lg	Q-9	34	.471	Ea.	15.05	22		37.05	50
1916	5" diameter to 12" lg		32	.500		42	23.50		65.50	82
1918	5"/6" diameter to 12"		30	.533		38	25		63	80
1920	Elbow 45°									
1922	4"	Q-9	34	.471	Ea.	27.50	22		49.50	64
1924	5"		32	.500		52	23.50		75.50	93.50

23 51 Breechings, Chimneys, and Stacks

23 51 23 – Gas Vents

23 51 23.10 Gas Chimney Vents

		Crew	Daily Output	Labor-Hours	Unit	Material	2012 Bare Costs Labor	Equipment	Total	Total Incl O&P
1926	5"/6"	Q-9	30	.533	Ea.	49.50	25		74.50	92.50
1930	Elbow 45°, flat									
1932	4"	Q-9	34	.471	Ea.	27.50	22		49.50	64
1934	5"		32	.500		52	23.50		75.50	93.50
1936	5"/6"		30	.533		49.50	25		74.50	92.50
1940	Top									
1942	4"	Q-9	44	.364	Ea.	33	17.05		50.05	62
1944	5"		42	.381		23	17.90		40.90	52.50
1946	5"/6"		40	.400		55.50	18.75		74.25	89.50
1950	Adjustable flashing									
1952	4"	Q-9	34	.471	Ea.	8.55	22		30.55	43
1954	5"		32	.500		27	23.50		50.50	66
1956	5"/6"		30	.533		28.50	25		53.50	69.50
1960	Tee									
1962	4"	Q-9	26	.615	Ea.	41	29		70	89
1964	5"		25	.640		85.50	30		115.50	141
1966	5"/6"		24	.667		79	31.50		110.50	135
1970	Tee with short snout									
1972	4"	Q-9	26	.615	Ea.	41	29		70	89

23 51 26 – All-Fuel Vent Chimneys

23 51 26.10 All-Fuel Vent Chimneys, Press. Tight, Dbl. Wall

		Crew	Daily Output	Labor-Hours	Unit	Material	2012 Bare Costs Labor	Equipment	Total	Total Incl O&P
0010	**ALL-FUEL VENT CHIMNEYS, PRESSURE TIGHT, DOUBLE WALL**									
3200	All fuel, pressure tight, double wall, 1" insulation, U.L. listed, 1400°F.									
3210	304 stainless steel liner, aluminized steel outer jacket									
3220	6" diameter	Q-9	60	.267	L.F.	53.50	12.50		66	78
3221	8" diameter		52	.308		59	14.45		73.45	87
3222	10" diameter		48	.333		66	15.65		81.65	96.50
3223	12" diameter		44	.364		75.50	17.05		92.55	110
3224	14" diameter		42	.381		85	17.90		102.90	121
3225	16" diameter		40	.400		95.50	18.75		114.25	134
3226	18" diameter		38	.421		109	19.75		128.75	150
3227	20" diameter	Q-10	36	.667		123	32.50		155.50	185
3228	24" diameter		32	.750		158	36.50		194.50	229
3229	28" diameter		30	.800		181	39		220	259
3230	32" diameter		27	.889		205	43.50		248.50	291
3231	36" diameter		25	.960		228	46.50		274.50	320
3232	42" diameter		22	1.091		267	53		320	375
3233	48" diameter		19	1.263		305	61.50		366.50	430
3260	For 316 stainless steel liner add					30%				
3280	All fuel, pressure tight, double wall fittings									
3284	304 stainless steel inner, aluminized steel jacket									
3288	Adjustable 20"/29" section									
3292	6" diameter	Q-9	30	.533	Ea.	187	25		212	244
3293	8" diameter		26	.615		195	29		224	258
3294	10" diameter		24	.667		220	31.50		251.50	290
3295	12" diameter		22	.727		248	34		282	325
3296	14" diameter		21	.762		280	36		316	365
3297	16" diameter		20	.800		315	37.50		352.50	400
3298	18" diameter		19	.842		355	39.50		394.50	450
3299	20" diameter	Q-10	18	1.333		405	65		470	545
3300	24" diameter		16	1.500		520	73		593	680
3301	28" diameter		15	1.600		555	78		633	735

23 51 26.10 All-Fuel Vent Chimneys, Press. Tight, Dbl. Wall		Crew	Daily Output	Labor-Hours	Unit	Material	2012 Bare Costs Labor	Equipment	Total	Total Incl O&P
3302	32" diameter	Q-10	14	1.714	Ea.	675	83.50		758.50	865
3303	36" diameter		12	2		750	97.50		847.50	975
3304	42" diameter		11	2.182		880	106		986	1,125
3305	48" diameter		10	2.400		1,000	117		1,117	1,275
3350	Elbow 90° fixed									
3354	6" diameter	Q-9	30	.533	Ea.	390	25		415	470
3355	8" diameter		26	.615		440	29		469	530
3356	10" diameter		24	.667		500	31.50		531.50	600
3357	12" diameter		22	.727		565	34		599	675
3358	14" diameter		21	.762		640	36		676	760
3359	16" diameter		20	.800		720	37.50		757.50	850
3360	18" diameter		19	.842		815	39.50		854.50	955
3361	20" diameter	Q-10	18	1.333		925	65		990	1,125
3362	24" diameter		16	1.500		1,175	73		1,248	1,400
3363	28" diameter		15	1.600		1,325	78		1,403	1,575
3364	32" diameter		14	1.714		1,800	83.50		1,883.50	2,100
3365	36" diameter		12	2		2,400	97.50		2,497.50	2,800
3366	42" diameter		11	2.182		2,850	106		2,956	3,300
3367	48" diameter		10	2.400		3,200	117		3,317	3,700
3380	For 316 stainless steel liner, add					30%				
3400	Elbow 45°									
3404	6" diameter	Q-9	30	.533	Ea.	195	25		220	252
3405	8" diameter		26	.615		219	29		248	285
3406	10" diameter		24	.667		249	31.50		280.50	320
3407	12" diameter		22	.727		285	34		319	365
3408	14" diameter		21	.762		320	36		356	405
3409	16" diameter		20	.800		360	37.50		397.50	450
3410	18" diameter		19	.842		410	39.50		449.50	510
3411	20" diameter	Q-10	18	1.333		460	65		525	610
3412	24" diameter		16	1.500		590	73		663	760
3413	28" diameter		15	1.600		665	78		743	850
3414	32" diameter		14	1.714		895	83.50		978.50	1,100
3415	36" diameter		12	2		1,200	97.50		1,297.50	1,475
3416	42" diameter		11	2.182		1,400	106		1,506	1,700
3417	48" diameter		10	2.400		1,600	117		1,717	1,925
3430	For 316 stainless steel liner, add					30%				
3450	Tee 90°									
3454	6" diameter	Q-9	24	.667	Ea.	229	31.50		260.50	300
3455	8" diameter		22	.727		251	34		285	330
3456	10" diameter		21	.762		283	36		319	365
3457	12" diameter		20	.800		330	37.50		367.50	415
3458	14" diameter		18	.889		375	41.50		416.50	475
3459	16" diameter		16	1		410	47		457	520
3460	18" diameter		14	1.143		485	53.50		538.50	610
3461	20" diameter	Q-10	17	1.412		560	68.50		628.50	720
3462	24" diameter		12	2		700	97.50		797.50	920
3463	28" diameter		11	2.182		830	106		936	1,075
3464	32" diameter		10	2.400		1,150	117		1,267	1,450
3465	36" diameter		9	2.667		1,300	130		1,430	1,625
3466	42" diameter		6	4		1,525	195		1,720	1,975
3467	48" diameter		5	4.800		1,750	234		1,984	2,275
3480	For Tee Cap, add					35%	20%			
3500	For 316 stainless steel liner, add					30%				

23 51 Breechings, Chimneys, and Stacks

23 51 26 – All-Fuel Vent Chimneys

23 51 26.10 All-Fuel Vent Chimneys, Press. Tight, Dbl. Wall		Crew	Daily Output	Labor-Hours	Unit	Material	2012 Bare Costs Labor	Equipment	Total	Total Incl O&P
3520	Plate support, galvanized									
3524	6" diameter	Q-9	26	.615	Ea.	115	29		144	170
3525	8" diameter		22	.727		134	34		168	199
3526	10" diameter		20	.800		146	37.50		183.50	217
3527	12" diameter		18	.889		153	41.50		194.50	232
3528	14" diameter		17	.941		181	44		225	267
3529	16" diameter		16	1		191	47		238	282
3530	18" diameter		15	1.067		201	50		251	298
3531	20" diameter	Q-10	16	1.500		211	73		284	345
3532	24" diameter		14	1.714		219	83.50		302.50	370
3533	28" diameter		13	1.846		269	90		359	435
3534	32" diameter		12	2		330	97.50		427.50	515
3535	36" diameter		10	2.400		400	117		517	615
3536	42" diameter		9	2.667		465	130		595	710
3537	48" diameter		8	3		530	146		676	810
3570	Bellows, lined									
3574	6" diameter	Q-9	30	.533	Ea.	1,250	25		1,275	1,425
3575	8" diameter		26	.615		1,300	29		1,329	1,500
3576	10" diameter		24	.667		1,325	31.50		1,356.50	1,525
3577	12" diameter		22	.727		1,375	34		1,409	1,550
3578	14" diameter		21	.762		1,425	36		1,461	1,600
3579	16" diameter		20	.800		1,475	37.50		1,512.50	1,675
3580	18" diameter		19	.842		1,525	39.50		1,564.50	1,725
3581	20" diameter	Q-10	18	1.333		1,575	65		1,640	1,825
3582	24" diameter		16	1.500		1,825	73		1,898	2,100
3583	28" diameter		15	1.600		1,950	78		2,028	2,250
3584	32" diameter		14	1.714		2,175	83.50		2,258.50	2,500
3585	36" diameter		12	2		2,375	97.50		2,472.50	2,775
3586	42" diameter		11	2.182		2,675	106		2,781	3,100
3587	48" diameter		10	2.400		3,075	117		3,192	3,550
3600	Ventilated roof thimble, 304 stainless steel									
3620	6" diameter	Q-9	26	.615	Ea.	239	29		268	305
3624	8" diameter		22	.727		248	34		282	325
3625	10" diameter		20	.800		256	37.50		293.50	340
3626	12" diameter		18	.889		263	41.50		304.50	355
3627	14" diameter		17	.941		273	44		317	370
3628	16" diameter		16	1		294	47		341	395
3629	18" diameter		15	1.067		320	50		370	425
3630	20" diameter	Q-10	16	1.500		335	73		408	475
3631	24" diameter		14	1.714		365	83.50		448.50	525
3632	28" diameter		13	1.846		400	90		490	570
3633	32" diameter		12	2		430	97.50		527.50	620
3634	36" diameter		10	2.400		460	117		577	685
3635	42" diameter		9	2.667		510	130		640	760
3636	48" diameter		8	3		555	146		701	840
3650	For 316 stainless steel, add					30%				
3670	Exit cone, 316 stainless steel only									
3674	6" diameter	Q-9	46	.348	Ea.	181	16.30		197.30	224
3675	8" diameter		42	.381		187	17.90		204.90	233
3676	10" diameter		40	.400		197	18.75		215.75	246
3677	12" diameter		38	.421		210	19.75		229.75	261
3678	14" diameter		37	.432		225	20.50		245.50	278
3679	16" diameter		36	.444		282	21		303	340

23 51 26 – All-Fuel Vent Chimneys

23 51 26.10 All-Fuel Vent Chimneys, Press. Tight, Dbl. Wall		Crew	Daily Output	Labor-Hours	Unit	Material	2012 Bare Costs Labor	Equipment	Total	Total Incl O&P
3680	18" diameter	Q-9	35	.457	Ea.	305	21.50		326.50	370
3681	20" diameter	Q-10	28	.857		365	41.50		406.50	465
3682	24" diameter		26	.923		480	45		525	595
3683	28" diameter		25	.960		545	46.50		591.50	670
3684	32" diameter		24	1		670	48.50		718.50	815
3685	36" diameter		22	1.091		815	53		868	980
3686	42" diameter		21	1.143		955	55.50		1,010.50	1,125
3687	48" diameter	▼	20	1.200	▼	1,075	58.50		1,133.50	1,300
3720	Roof guide, 304 stainless steel									
3724	6" diameter	Q-9	25	.640	Ea.	83	30		113	137
3725	8" diameter		21	.762		96.50	36		132.50	161
3726	10" diameter		19	.842		106	39.50		145.50	176
3727	12" diameter		17	.941		109	44		153	188
3728	14" diameter		16	1		127	47		174	212
3729	16" diameter		15	1.067		135	50		185	225
3730	18" diameter	▼	14	1.143		143	53.50		196.50	239
3731	20" diameter	Q-10	15	1.600		150	78		228	284
3732	24" diameter		13	1.846		157	90		247	310
3733	28" diameter		12	2		191	97.50		288.50	360
3734	32" diameter		11	2.182		235	106		341	420
3735	36" diameter		9	2.667		280	130		410	510
3736	42" diameter		8	3		325	146		471	585
3737	48" diameter	▼	7	3.429		370	167		537	665
3750	For 316 stainless steel, add				▼	30%				
3770	Rain cap with bird screen									
3774	6" diameter	Q-9	46	.348	Ea.	280	16.30		296.30	335
3775	8" diameter		42	.381		325	17.90		342.90	385
3776	10" diameter		40	.400		380	18.75		398.75	445
3777	12" diameter		38	.421		440	19.75		459.75	510
3778	14" diameter		37	.432		495	20.50		515.50	575
3779	16" diameter		36	.444		565	21		586	650
3780	18" diameter	▼	35	.457		655	21.50		676.50	755
3781	20" diameter	Q-10	28	.857		740	41.50		781.50	880
3782	24" diameter		26	.923		890	45		935	1,050
3783	28" diameter		25	.960		1,050	46.50		1,096.50	1,250
3784	32" diameter		24	1		1,200	48.50		1,248.50	1,400
3785	36" diameter		22	1.091		1,425	53		1,478	1,650
3786	42" diameter		21	1.143		1,675	55.50		1,730.50	1,900
3787	48" diameter	▼	20	1.200	▼	1,875	58.50		1,933.50	2,175

23 51 26.30 All-Fuel Vent Chimneys, Double Wall, St. Stl.

		Crew	Daily Output	Labor-Hours	Unit	Material	2012 Bare Costs Labor	Equipment	Total	Total Incl O&P
0010	**ALL-FUEL VENT CHIMNEYS, DOUBLE WALL, STAINLESS STEEL**									
7780	All fuel, pressure tight, double wall, 4" insulation, U.L. listed, 1400°F.									
7790	304 stainless steel liner, aluminized steel outer jacket									
7800	6" diameter	Q-9	60	.267	V.L.F.	62	12.50		74.50	87
7804	8" diameter		52	.308		71	14.45		85.45	100
7806	10" diameter		48	.333		79	15.65		94.65	111
7808	12" diameter		44	.364		90.50	17.05		107.55	126
7810	14" diameter	▼	42	.381	▼	102	17.90		119.90	140
7880	For 316 stainless steel liner add				L.F.	30%				
8000	All fuel, double wall, stainless steel fittings									
8010	Roof support 6" diameter	Q-9	30	.533	Ea.	109	25		134	158
8030	8" diameter	↓	26	.615	↓	127	29		156	184

23 51 Breechings, Chimneys, and Stacks

23 51 26 – All-Fuel Vent Chimneys

23 51 26.30 All-Fuel Vent Chimneys, Double Wall, St. Stl.		Crew	Daily Output	Labor-Hours	Unit	Material	2012 Bare Costs Labor	Equipment	Total	Total Incl O&P
8040	10" diameter	Q-9	24	.667	Ea.	135	31.50		166.50	196
8050	12" diameter		22	.727		143	34		177	209
8060	14" diameter		21	.762		150	36		186	220
8100	Elbow 45°, 6" diameter		30	.533		233	25		258	294
8140	8" diameter		26	.615		262	29		291	330
8160	10" diameter		24	.667		298	31.50		329.50	380
8180	12" diameter		22	.727		340	34		374	425
8200	14" diameter		21	.762		380	36		416	475
8300	Insulated tee, 6" diameter		30	.533		274	25		299	340
8360	8" diameter		26	.615		300	29		329	375
8380	10" diameter		24	.667		335	31.50		366.50	420
8400	12" diameter		22	.727		380	34		414	470
8420	14" diameter		20	.800		445	37.50		482.50	545
8500	Boot tee, 6" diameter		28	.571		525	27		552	615
8520	8" diameter		24	.667		570	31.50		601.50	675
8530	10" diameter		22	.727		665	34		699	780
8540	12" diameter		20	.800		785	37.50		822.50	920
8550	14" diameter		18	.889		895	41.50		936.50	1,050
8600	Rain cap with bird screen, 6" diameter		30	.533		280	25		305	350
8640	8" diameter		26	.615		325	29		354	400
8660	10" diameter		24	.667		380	31.50		411.50	465
8680	12" diameter		22	.727		440	34		474	530
8700	14" diameter		21	.762		495	36		531	600
8800	Flat roof flashing, 6" diameter		30	.533		103	25		128	151
8840	8" diameter		26	.615		112	29		141	167
8860	10" diameter		24	.667		120	31.50		151.50	180
8880	12" diameter		22	.727		132	34		166	197
8900	14" diameter		21	.762		135	36		171	203

23 51 33 – Insulated Sectional Chimneys

23 51 33.10 Prefabricated Insulated Sectional Chimneys		Crew	Daily Output	Labor-Hours	Unit	Material	2012 Bare Costs Labor	Equipment	Total	Total Incl O&P
0010	**PREFABRICATED INSULATED SECTIONAL CHIMNEYS**									
9000	High temp. (2000°F), steel jacket, acid resistant refractory lining									
9010	11 ga. galvanized jacket, U.L. listed									
9020	Straight section, 48" long, 10" diameter	Q-10	13.30	1.805	Ea.	400	88		488	575
9030	12" diameter		11.20	2.143		440	104		544	640
9040	18" diameter		7.40	3.243		615	158		773	915
9050	24" diameter		4.60	5.217		840	254		1,094	1,300
9060	30" diameter		3.70	6.486		1,075	315		1,390	1,650
9070	36" diameter		2.70	8.889		1,325	435		1,760	2,100
9080	42" diameter	Q-11	3.10	10.323		1,625	515		2,140	2,575
9090	48" diameter		2.70	11.852		1,925	590		2,515	3,000
9100	54" diameter		2.20	14.545		2,325	720		3,045	3,650
9110	60" diameter		2	16		3,050	795		3,845	4,550
9120	Tee section, 10" diameter	Q-10	4.40	5.455		855	265		1,120	1,350
9130	12" diameter		3.70	6.486		900	315		1,215	1,475
9140	18" diameter		2.40	10		1,225	485		1,710	2,100
9150	24" diameter		1.50	16		1,675	780		2,455	3,025
9160	30" diameter		1.20	20		2,350	975		3,325	4,075
9170	36" diameter		.80	30		3,975	1,450		5,425	6,600
9180	42" diameter	Q-11	1	32		5,225	1,600		6,825	8,175
9190	48" diameter		.90	35.556		6,775	1,775		8,550	10,200
9200	54" diameter		.70	45.714		9,900	2,275		12,175	14,400

359

23 51 33 – Insulated Sectional Chimneys

23 51 33.10 Prefabricated Insulated Sectional Chimneys	Crew	Daily Output	Labor-Hours	Unit	Material	2012 Bare Costs Labor	Equipment	Total	Total Incl O&P
9210	60" diameter	Q-11	.60	53.333	Ea.	12,500	2,650		15,150	17,800
9220	Cleanout pier section, 10" diameter	Q-10	3.50	6.857		655	335		990	1,225
9230	12" diameter		2.50	9.600		690	465		1,155	1,475
9240	18" diameter		1.90	12.632		885	615		1,500	1,900
9250	24" diameter		1.30	18.462		1,125	900		2,025	2,600
9260	30" diameter		1	24		1,375	1,175		2,550	3,275
9270	36" diameter	↓	.75	32		1,625	1,550		3,175	4,150
9280	42" diameter	Q-11	.90	35.556		2,050	1,775		3,825	4,975
9290	48" diameter		.75	42.667		2,475	2,125		4,600	5,950
9300	54" diameter		.60	53.333		2,950	2,650		5,600	7,275
9310	60" diameter	↓	.50	64		3,775	3,175		6,950	9,000
9320	For drain, add					53%				
9330	Elbow, 30° and 45°, 10" diameter	Q-10	6.60	3.636		555	177		732	880
9340	12" diameter		5.60	4.286		600	209		809	975
9350	18" diameter		3.70	6.486		900	315		1,215	1,475
9360	24" diameter		2.30	10.435		1,350	510		1,860	2,250
9370	30" diameter		1.85	12.973		1,850	630		2,480	2,975
9380	36" diameter	↓	1.30	18.462		2,225	900		3,125	3,825
9390	42" diameter	Q-11	1.60	20		3,050	995		4,045	4,900
9400	48" diameter		1.35	23.704		3,900	1,175		5,075	6,075
9410	54" diameter		1.10	29.091		5,050	1,450		6,500	7,750
9420	60" diameter	↓	1	32		6,150	1,600		7,750	9,200
9430	For 60° and 90° elbow, add					112%				
9440	End cap, 10" diameter	Q-10	26	.923		955	45		1,000	1,125
9450	12" diameter		22	1.091		1,100	53		1,153	1,275
9460	18" diameter		15	1.600		1,350	78		1,428	1,600
9470	24" diameter		9	2.667		1,650	130		1,780	2,025
9480	30" diameter		7.30	3.288		2,050	160		2,210	2,500
9490	36" diameter	↓	5	4.800		2,350	234		2,584	2,950
9500	42" diameter	Q-11	6.30	5.079		2,950	252		3,202	3,600
9510	48" diameter		5.30	6.038		3,475	300		3,775	4,250
9520	54" diameter		4.40	7.273		3,975	360		4,335	4,900
9530	60" diameter	↓	3.90	8.205		4,675	405		5,080	5,775
9540	Increaser (1 diameter), 10" diameter	Q-10	6.60	3.636		475	177		652	790
9550	12" diameter		5.60	4.286		505	209		714	875
9560	18" diameter		3.70	6.486		740	315		1,055	1,300
9570	24" diameter		2.30	10.435		1,050	510		1,560	1,950
9580	30" diameter		1.85	12.973		1,325	630		1,955	2,400
9590	36" diameter	↓	1.30	18.462		1,450	900		2,350	2,975
9592	42" diameter	Q-11	1.60	20		1,600	995		2,595	3,275
9594	48" diameter		1.35	23.704		1,925	1,175		3,100	3,900
9596	54" diameter	↓	1.10	29.091		2,325	1,450		3,775	4,750
9600	For expansion joints, add to straight section					7%				
9610	For 1/4" hot rolled steel jacket, add					157%				
9620	For 2950°F very high temperature, add				↓	89%				
9630	26 ga. aluminized jacket, straight section, 48" long									
9640	10" diameter	Q-10	15.30	1.569	V.L.F.	237	76.50		313.50	375
9650	12" diameter		12.90	1.860		252	90.50		342.50	415
9660	18" diameter		8.50	2.824		365	137		502	615
9670	24" diameter		5.30	4.528		520	220		740	905
9680	30" diameter		4.30	5.581		665	272		937	1,150
9690	36" diameter	↓	3.10	7.742	↓	845	375		1,220	1,500
9700	Accessories (all models)									

23 51 Breechings, Chimneys, and Stacks

23 51 33 - Insulated Sectional Chimneys

	23 51 33.10 Prefabricated Insulated Sectional Chimneys	Crew	Daily Output	Labor-Hours	Unit	Material	2012 Bare Costs Labor	Equipment	Total	Total Incl O&P
9710	Guy band, 10" diameter	Q-10	32	.750	Ea.	74	36.50		110.50	137
9720	12" diameter		30	.800		78	39		117	145
9730	18" diameter		26	.923		102	45		147	181
9740	24" diameter		24	1		149	48.50		197.50	237
9750	30" diameter		20	1.200		173	58.50		231.50	279
9760	36" diameter		18	1.333		191	65		256	310
9770	42" diameter	Q-11	22	1.455		345	72		417	490
9780	48" diameter		20	1.600		380	79.50		459.50	535
9790	54" diameter		16	2		420	99.50		519.50	610
9800	60" diameter		12	2.667		455	132		587	700
9810	Draw band, galv. stl., 11 gauge, 10" diameter	Q-10	32	.750		65	36.50		101.50	127
9820	12" diameter		30	.800		69	39		108	135
9830	18" diameter		26	.923		86	45		131	163
9840	24" diameter		24	1		110	48.50		158.50	195
9850	30" diameter		20	1.200		127	58.50		185.50	228
9860	36" diameter		18	1.333		146	65		211	259
9870	42" diameter	Q-11	22	1.455		196	72		268	325
9880	48" diameter		20	1.600		251	79.50		330.50	400
9890	54" diameter		16	2		291	99.50		390.50	470
9900	60" diameter		12	2.667		370	132		502	605
9910	Draw band, aluminized stl., 26 gauge, 10" diameter	Q-10	32	.750		18.95	36.50		55.45	76.50
9920	12" diameter		30	.800		18.95	39		57.95	80.50
9930	18" diameter		26	.923		24	45		69	95
9940	24" diameter		24	1		28	48.50		76.50	105
9950	30" diameter		20	1.200		32	58.50		90.50	124
9960	36" diameter		18	1.333		43	65		108	146
9962	42" diameter	Q-11	22	1.455		43	72		115	157
9964	48" diameter		20	1.600		51	79.50		130.50	177
9966	54" diameter		16	2		51	99.50		150.50	207
9968	60" diameter		12	2.667		56	132		188	264

23 52 Heating Boilers

23 52 13 - Electric Boilers

23 52 13.10 Electric Boilers, ASME

			Crew	Daily Output	Labor-Hours	Unit	Material	2012 Bare Costs Labor	Equipment	Total	Total Incl O&P
0010	**ELECTRIC BOILERS, ASME**, Standard controls and trim	R235000-30									
1000	Steam, 6 KW, 20.5 MBH		Q-19	1.20	20	Ea.	3,625	1,000		4,625	5,525
1040	9 KW, 30.7 MBH	D3020-102		1.20	20		3,775	1,000		4,775	5,675
1060	18 KW, 61.4 MBH			1.20	20		3,875	1,000		4,875	5,800
1080	24 KW, 81.8 MBH	D3020-104		1.10	21.818		4,525	1,100		5,625	6,625
1120	36 KW, 123 MBH			1.10	21.818		5,000	1,100		6,100	7,150
1160	60 KW, 205 MBH			1	24		6,250	1,225		7,475	8,700
1220	112 KW, 382 MBH			.75	32		8,550	1,625		10,175	11,800
1240	148 KW, 505 MBH			.65	36.923		9,000	1,875		10,875	12,700
1260	168 KW, 573 MBH			.60	40		11,800	2,025		13,825	16,100
1280	222 KW, 758 MBH			.55	43.636		13,500	2,200		15,700	18,200
1300	296 KW, 1010 MBH			.45	53.333		13,600	2,700		16,300	19,100
1320	300 KW, 1023 MBH			.40	60		17,500	3,025		20,525	23,900
1340	370 KW, 1263 MBH			.35	68.571		18,800	3,475		22,275	25,900
1360	444 KW, 1515 MBH			.30	80		20,200	4,050		24,250	28,300
1380	518 KW, 1768 MBH		Q-21	.36	88.889		22,800	4,600		27,400	32,100
1400	592 KW, 2020 MBH			.34	94.118		25,800	4,875		30,675	35,800

23 52 13 – Electric Boilers

23 52 13.10 Electric Boilers, ASME	Crew	Daily Output	Labor-Hours	Unit	Material	2012 Bare Costs Labor	Equipment	Total	Total Incl O&P
1420	666 KW, 2273 MBH	Q-21	.32	100	Ea.	27,200	5,200		32,400	37,700
1460	740 KW, 2526 MBH		.28	114		28,500	5,925		34,425	40,200
1480	814 KW, 2778 MBH		.25	128		31,900	6,650		38,550	45,100
1500	962 KW, 3283 MBH		.22	145		32,800	7,550		40,350	47,400
1520	1036 KW, 3536 MBH		.20	160		34,400	8,300		42,700	50,500
1540	1110 KW, 3788 MBH		.19	168		36,100	8,750		44,850	53,000
1560	2070 KW, 7063 MBH		.18	177		50,500	9,225		59,725	69,500
1580	2250 KW, 7677 MBH		.17	188		59,000	9,775		68,775	79,500
1600	2,340 KW, 7984 MBH		.16	200		65,500	10,400		75,900	87,500
2000	Hot water, 7.5 KW, 25.6 MBH	Q-19	1.30	18.462		3,825	935		4,760	5,600
2020	15 KW, 51.2 MBH		1.30	18.462		3,925	935		4,860	5,725
2040	30 KW, 102 MBH		1.20	20		4,075	1,000		5,075	6,000
2060	45 KW, 164 MBH		1.20	20		4,550	1,000		5,550	6,525
2070	60 KW, 205 MBH		1.20	20		4,800	1,000		5,800	6,825
2080	75 KW, 256 MBH		1.10	21.818		5,175	1,100		6,275	7,350
2100	90 KW, 307 MBH		1.10	21.818		5,575	1,100		6,675	7,775
2120	105 KW, 358 MBH		1	24		5,950	1,225		7,175	8,375
2140	120 KW, 410 MBH		.90	26.667		6,250	1,350		7,600	8,900
2160	135 KW, 461 MBH		.75	32		6,775	1,625		8,400	9,875
2180	150 KW, 512 MBH		.65	36.923		7,050	1,875		8,925	10,600
2200	165 KW, 563 MBH		.60	40		7,300	2,025		9,325	11,100
2220	296 KW, 1010 MBH		.55	43.636		11,900	2,200		14,100	16,400
2280	370 KW, 1263 MBH		.40	60		13,200	3,025		16,225	19,100
2300	444 KW, 1515 MBH		.35	68.571		16,000	3,475		19,475	22,800
2340	518 KW, 1768 MBH	Q-21	.44	72.727		17,700	3,775		21,475	25,200
2360	592 KW, 2020 MBH		.43	74.419		19,600	3,850		23,450	27,300
2400	666 KW, 2273 MBH		.40	80		20,900	4,150		25,050	29,300
2420	740 KW, 2526 MBH		.39	82.051		21,400	4,250		25,650	30,000
2440	814 KW, 2778 MBH		.38	84.211		22,100	4,375		26,475	30,900
2460	888 KW, 3031 MBH		.37	86.486		23,300	4,475		27,775	32,400
2480	962 KW, 3283 MBH		.36	88.889		26,100	4,600		30,700	35,700
2500	1036 KW, 3536 MBH		.34	94.118		27,700	4,875		32,575	37,900
2520	1110 KW, 3788 MBH		.33	96.970		30,700	5,025		35,725	41,300
2540	1440 KW, 4915 MBH		.32	100		35,200	5,200		40,400	46,500
2560	1560 KW, 5323 MBH		.31	103		39,600	5,350		44,950	51,500
2580	1680 KW, 5733 MBH		.30	106		42,200	5,525		47,725	55,000
2600	1800 KW, 6143 MBH		.29	110		44,500	5,725		50,225	57,500
2620	1980 KW, 6757 MBH		.28	114		47,500	5,925		53,425	61,500
2640	2100 KW, 7167 MBH		.27	118		53,000	6,150		59,150	68,000
2660	2220 KW, 7576 MBH		.26	123		55,000	6,375		61,375	69,500
2680	2400 KW, 8191 MBH		.25	128		58,000	6,650		64,650	73,500
2700	2610 KW, 8905 MBH		.24	133		62,000	6,925		68,925	79,000
2720	2790 KW, 9519 MBH		.23	139		65,000	7,225		72,225	82,500
2740	2970 KW, 10133 MBH		.21	152		66,500	7,900		74,400	85,000
2760	3150 KW, 10748 MBH		.19	168		73,000	8,750		81,750	93,000
2780	3240 KW, 11055 MBH		.18	177		74,000	9,225		83,225	95,500
2800	3420 KW, 11669 MBH		.17	188		78,500	9,775		88,275	101,000
2820	3600 KW, 12,283 MBH		.16	200		81,500	10,400		91,900	105,000

23 52 Heating Boilers

23 52 16 – Condensing Boilers

23 52 16.24 Condensing Boilers

		Crew	Daily Output	Labor-Hours	Unit	Material	2012 Bare Costs Labor	Equipment	Total	Total Incl O&P
0010	**CONDENSING BOILERS**, Cast iron									
0020	Packaged with standard controls, circulator and trim									
0030	Intermittent (spark) pilot, natural or LP gas									
0040	Hot water, DOE MBH output, (AFUE)									
0100	42 MBH, (84.0%) [G]	Q-5	1.80	8.889	Ea.	1,400	445		1,845	2,225
0120	57 MBH, (84.3%) [G]		1.60	10		1,575	500		2,075	2,475
0140	85 MBH, (84.0%) [G]		1.40	11.429		1,725	575		2,300	2,750
0160	112 MBH, (83.7%) [G]		1.20	13.333		1,925	670		2,595	3,125
0180	140 MBH, (83.3%) [G]	Q-6	1.60	15		2,175	780		2,955	3,575
0200	167 MBH, (83.0%) [G]		1.40	17.143		2,450	890		3,340	4,050
0220	194 MBH, (82.7%) [G]		1.20	20		2,675	1,050		3,725	4,525

23 52 19 – Pulse Combustion Boilers

23 52 19.20 Pulse Type Combustion Boilers

		Crew	Daily Output	Labor-Hours	Unit	Material	2012 Bare Costs Labor	Equipment	Total	Total Incl O&P
0010	**PULSE TYPE COMBUSTION BOILERS**									
7990	Special feature gas fired boilers									
8000	Pulse combustion, standard controls/trim									
8050	88,000 BTU [G]	Q-5	1.40	11.429	Ea.	4,625	575		5,200	5,975
8080	134,000 BTU [G]	"	1.20	13.333	"	5,200	670		5,870	6,725

23 52 23 – Cast-Iron Boilers

23 52 23.20 Gas-Fired Boilers

		Crew	Daily Output	Labor-Hours	Unit	Material	2012 Bare Costs Labor	Equipment	Total	Total Incl O&P
0010	**GAS-FIRED BOILERS**, Natural or propane, standard controls, packaged R235000-10									
1000	Cast iron, with insulated jacket									
2000	Steam, gross output, 81 MBH R235000-20	Q-7	1.40	22.857	Ea.	1,950	1,200		3,150	3,975
2020	102 MBH		1.30	24.615		2,200	1,300		3,500	4,400
2040	122 MBH R235000-30		1	32		2,375	1,700		4,075	5,150
2060	163 MBH		.90	35.556		2,375	1,875		4,250	5,475
2080	203 MBH R235000-50		.90	35.556		3,100	1,875		4,975	6,275
2100	240 MBH		.85	37.647		3,100	2,000		5,100	6,425
2120	280 MBH R235000-70		.80	40		4,150	2,125		6,275	7,750
2140	320 MBH		.70	45.714		4,400	2,425		6,825	8,475
2160	360 MBH R235000-80		.63	51.200		5,000	2,725		7,725	9,575
2180	400 MBH		.56	56.838		5,200	3,025		8,225	10,300
2200	440 MBH		.51	62.500		5,525	3,325		8,850	11,100
2220	544 MBH		.45	71.588		8,575	3,800		12,375	15,200
2240	765 MBH		.43	74.419		10,300	3,950		14,250	17,400
2260	892 MBH		.38	84.211		12,000	4,475		16,475	19,900
2280	1275 MBH		.34	94.118		14,600	5,000		19,600	23,600
2300	1530 MBH		.32	100		15,700	5,300		21,000	25,200
2320	1,875 MBH		.30	106		16,400	5,650		22,050	26,500
2340	2170 MBH		.26	122		17,800	6,475		24,275	29,400
2360	2675 MBH		.20	163		20,500	8,650		29,150	35,600
2380	3060 MBH		.19	172		22,100	9,125		31,225	38,100
2400	3570 MBH		.18	181		24,600	9,650		34,250	41,600
2420	4207 MBH		.16	205		27,200	10,900		38,100	46,300
2440	4,720 MBH		.15	207		73,500	11,000		84,500	97,000
2460	5660 MBH		.15	220		78,500	11,700		90,200	104,000
2480	6,100 MBH		.13	246		81,000	13,100		94,100	109,000
2500	6390 MBH		.12	266		83,500	14,100		97,600	113,000
2520	6680 MBH		.11	290		85,500	15,400		100,900	117,500
2540	6,970 MBH		.10	320		88,500	17,000		105,500	123,000
3000	Hot water, gross output, 80 MBH		1.46	21.918		1,775	1,175		2,950	3,725

23 52 Heating Boilers

23 52 23 – Cast-Iron Boilers

23 52 23.20 Gas-Fired Boilers

		Crew	Daily Output	Labor-Hours	Unit	Material	2012 Bare Costs Labor	Equipment	Total	Total Incl O&P
3020	100 MBH	Q-7	1.35	23.704	Ea.	2,050	1,250		3,300	4,150
3040	122 MBH		1.10	29.091		2,200	1,550		3,750	4,750
3060	163 MBH		1	32		2,675	1,700		4,375	5,500
3080	203 MBH		1	32		2,950	1,700		4,650	5,800
3100	240 MBH		.95	33.684		3,100	1,775		4,875	6,125
3120	280 MBH		.90	35.556		3,875	1,875		5,750	7,125
3140	320 MBH		.80	40		4,200	2,125		6,325	7,825
3160	360 MBH		.71	45.070		4,700	2,400		7,100	8,750
3180	400 MBH		.64	50		4,975	2,650		7,625	9,475
3200	440 MBH		.58	54.983		5,300	2,925		8,225	10,300
3220	544 MBH		.51	62.992		8,300	3,350		11,650	14,200
3240	765 MBH		.46	70.022		10,000	3,725		13,725	16,600
3260	1,088 MBH		.40	80		12,500	4,250		16,750	20,100
3280	1,275 MBH		.36	89.888		14,300	4,775		19,075	22,900
3300	1,530 MBH		.31	104		15,400	5,575		20,975	25,400
3320	2,000 MBH		.26	125		18,100	6,625		24,725	29,900
3340	2,312 MBH		.22	148		20,700	7,850		28,550	34,700
3360	2,856 MBH		.20	160		22,100	8,475		30,575	37,100
3380	3,264 MBH		.18	179		23,500	9,525		33,025	40,300
3400	3,996 MBH		.16	195		25,800	10,300		36,100	44,000
3420	4,488 MBH		.15	210		28,600	11,200		39,800	48,300
3440	4,720 MBH		.15	220		73,500	11,700		85,200	98,000
3460	5,520 MBH		.14	228		78,500	12,100		90,600	105,000
3480	6,100 MBH		.13	250		81,000	13,300		94,300	109,500
3500	6,390 MBH		.11	285		83,500	15,200		98,700	114,500
3520	6,680 MBH		.10	310		85,500	16,500		102,000	119,000
3540	6,970 MBH		.09	359		88,500	19,100		107,600	126,500
7000	For tankless water heater, add					10%				
7050	For additional zone valves up to 312 MBH add					157			157	173

23 52 23.30 Gas/Oil Fired Boilers

		Crew	Daily Output	Labor-Hours	Unit	Material	2012 Bare Costs Labor	Equipment	Total	Total Incl O&P
0010	**GAS/OIL FIRED BOILERS**, Combination with burners and controls, packaged									
1000	Cast iron with insulated jacket									
2000	Steam, gross output, 720 MBH	Q-7	.43	74.074	Ea.	13,300	3,925		17,225	20,600
2020	810 MBH		.38	83.990		13,300	4,450		17,750	21,400
2040	1,084 MBH		.34	93.023		15,400	4,925		20,325	24,400
2060	1,360 MBH		.33	98.160		17,600	5,200		22,800	27,300
2080	1,600 MBH		.30	107		18,900	5,675		24,575	29,400
2100	2,040 MBH		.25	130		22,500	6,900		29,400	35,100
2120	2,450 MBH		.21	156		24,000	8,275		32,275	39,000
2140	2,700 MBH		.19	165		25,400	8,800		34,200	41,300
2160	3,000 MBH		.18	175		27,200	9,325		36,525	44,000
2180	3,270 MBH		.17	183		29,800	9,750		39,550	47,400
2200	3,770 MBH		.17	191		61,000	10,200		71,200	83,000
2220	4,070 MBH		.16	200		64,500	10,600		75,100	87,000
2240	4,650 MBH		.15	210		68,000	11,200		79,200	91,500
2260	5,230 MBH		.14	223		75,000	11,900		86,900	100,500
2280	5,520 MBH		.14	235		82,000	12,500		94,500	109,000
2300	5,810 MBH		.13	248		82,500	13,200		95,700	111,000
2320	6,100 MBH		.12	260		83,500	13,800		97,300	113,000
2340	6,390 MBH		.11	296		88,000	15,700		103,700	120,000
2360	6,680 MBH		.10	320		90,500	17,000		107,500	125,500
2380	6,970 MBH		.09	372		93,000	19,700		112,700	132,500

23 52 Heating Boilers

23 52 23 – Cast-Iron Boilers

23 52 23.30 Gas/Oil Fired Boilers

		Crew	Daily Output	Labor-Hours	Unit	Material	2012 Bare Costs Labor	Equipment	Total	Total Incl O&P
2900	Hot water, gross output									
2910	200 MBH	Q-6	.62	39.024	Ea.	8,925	2,025		10,950	12,900
2920	300 MBH		.49	49.080		8,925	2,550		11,475	13,700
2930	400 MBH		.41	57.971		10,400	3,025		13,425	16,100
2940	500 MBH		.36	67.039		11,300	3,475		14,775	17,700
3000	584 MBH	Q-7	.44	72.072		12,400	3,825		16,225	19,500
3020	876 MBH		.41	79.012		16,400	4,200		20,600	24,400
3040	1,168 MBH		.31	103		19,900	5,500		25,400	30,200
3060	1,460 MBH		.28	113		24,800	6,000		30,800	36,300
3080	2,044 MBH		.26	122		27,400	6,475		33,875	39,900
3100	2,628 MBH		.21	150		33,300	7,975		41,275	48,600
3120	3,210 MBH		.18	174		41,000	9,275		50,275	59,000
3140	3,796 MBH		.17	186		45,900	9,875		55,775	65,500
3160	4,088 MBH		.16	195		52,000	10,300		62,300	73,000
3180	4,672 MBH		.16	203		57,000	10,800		67,800	79,000
3200	5,256 MBH		.15	217		58,500	11,500		70,000	82,000
3220	6,000 MBH, 179 BHP		.13	256		91,500	13,600		105,100	121,000
3240	7,130 MBH, 213 BHP		.08	385		96,000	20,400		116,400	136,500
3260	9,800 MBH, 286 BHP		.06	533		110,000	28,300		138,300	163,500
3280	10,900 MBH, 325.6 BHP		.05	592		133,500	31,400		164,900	194,500
3290	12,200 MBH, 364.5 BHP		.05	666		146,000	35,400		181,400	214,000
3300	13,500 MBH, 403.3 BHP		.04	727		161,500	38,600		200,100	235,500

23 52 23.40 Oil-Fired Boilers

		Crew	Daily Output	Labor-Hours	Unit	Material	2012 Bare Costs Labor	Equipment	Total	Total Incl O&P
0010	**OIL-FIRED BOILERS**, Standard controls, flame retention burner, packaged									
1000	Cast iron, with insulated flush jacket									
2000	Steam, gross output, 109 MBH	Q-7	1.20	26.667	Ea.	2,025	1,425		3,450	4,350
2020	144 MBH		1.10	29.091		2,275	1,550		3,825	4,825
2040	173 MBH		1	32		2,550	1,700		4,250	5,350
2060	207 MBH		.90	35.556		2,775	1,875		4,650	5,900
2080	236 MBH		.85	37.647		3,250	2,000		5,250	6,575
2100	300 MBH		.70	45.714		3,825	2,425		6,250	7,875
2120	480 MBH		.50	64		4,925	3,400		8,325	10,500
2140	665 MBH		.45	71.111		6,700	3,775		10,475	13,100
2160	794 MBH		.41	78.049		7,925	4,150		12,075	15,000
2180	1,084 MBH		.38	85.106		9,400	4,525		13,925	17,100
2200	1,360 MBH		.33	98.160		10,800	5,200		16,000	19,800
2220	1,600 MBH		.26	122		12,100	6,475		18,575	23,100
2240	2,175 MBH		.24	133		17,300	7,100		24,400	29,800
2260	2,480 MBH		.21	156		18,600	8,275		26,875	32,900
2280	3,000 MBH		.19	170		21,600	9,025		30,625	37,300
2300	3,550 MBH		.17	187		23,900	9,925		33,825	41,300
2320	3,820 MBH		.16	200		34,000	10,600		44,600	53,500
2340	4,360 MBH		.15	214		37,300	11,400		48,700	58,000
2360	4,940 MBH		.14	225		58,500	12,000		70,500	82,000
2380	5,520 MBH		.14	235		68,500	12,500		81,000	94,500
2400	6,100 MBH		.13	256		78,500	13,600		92,100	107,000
2420	6,390 MBH		.11	290		83,000	15,400		98,400	114,500
2440	6,680 MBH		.10	313		85,000	16,600		101,600	118,500
2460	6,970 MBH		.09	363		88,000	19,300		107,300	126,000
3000	Hot water, same price as steam									
4000	For tankless coil in smaller sizes, add				Ea.	15%				

23 52 Heating Boilers

23 52 23 – Cast-Iron Boilers

23 52 23.60 Solid-Fuel Boilers

		Crew	Daily Output	Labor-Hours	Unit	Material	2012 Bare Costs Labor	Equipment	Total	Total Incl O&P
0010	**SOLID-FUEL BOILERS**									
3000	Stoker fired (coal) cast iron with flush jacket and									
3400	insulation, steam or water, gross output, 1280 MBH	Q-6	.36	66.667	Ea.	38,400	3,475		41,875	47,400
3420	1460 MBH		.30	80		42,100	4,150		46,250	52,500
3440	1640 MBH		.28	85.714		44,900	4,450		49,350	56,000
3460	1820 MBH		.26	92.308		48,100	4,800		52,900	60,000
3480	2000 MBH		.25	96		51,000	5,000		56,000	64,000
3500	2360 MBH		.23	104		58,000	5,425		63,425	71,500
3540	2725 MBH	▼	.20	120		64,500	6,250		70,750	80,500
3800	2950 MBH	Q-7	.16	200		107,500	10,600		118,100	134,500
3820	3210 MBH		.15	213		113,000	11,300		124,300	141,500
3840	3480 MBH		.14	228		118,000	12,100		130,100	148,500
3860	3745 MBH		.14	228		124,000	12,100		136,100	154,500
3880	4000 MBH		.13	246		129,000	13,100		142,100	161,000
3900	4200 MBH		.13	246		134,500	13,100		147,600	167,500
3920	4400 MBH		.12	266		139,500	14,100		153,600	175,000
3940	4600 MBH	▼	.12	266	▼	145,000	14,100		159,100	181,000

23 52 26 – Steel Boilers

23 52 26.40 Oil-Fired Boilers

		Crew	Daily Output	Labor-Hours	Unit	Material	2012 Bare Costs Labor	Equipment	Total	Total Incl O&P
0010	**OIL-FIRED BOILERS**, Standard controls, flame retention burner									
5000	Steel, with insulated flush jacket									
7000	Hot water, gross output, 103 MBH	Q-6	1.60	15	Ea.	1,800	780		2,580	3,150
7020	122 MBH		1.45	16.506		1,900	860		2,760	3,400
7040	137 MBH		1.36	17.595		2,025	915		2,940	3,600
7060	168 MBH		1.30	18.405		2,125	955		3,080	3,800
7080	225 MBH		1.22	19.704		2,700	1,025		3,725	4,500
7100	315 MBH		.96	25.105		5,225	1,300		6,525	7,725
7120	420 MBH		.70	34.483		5,500	1,800		7,300	8,750
7140	525 MBH		.57	42.403		6,525	2,200		8,725	10,500
7180	735 MBH		.48	50.104		7,650	2,600		10,250	12,400
7220	1,050 MBH		.37	65.753		14,400	3,425		17,825	21,000
7280	2,310 MBH		.21	114		25,000	5,975		30,975	36,500
7320	3,150 MBH	▼	.13	184		37,100	9,600		46,700	55,500
7340	For tankless coil in steam or hot water, add				▼	7%				

23 52 26.70 Packaged Water Tube Boilers

		Crew	Daily Output	Labor-Hours	Unit	Material	2012 Bare Costs Labor	Equipment	Total	Total Incl O&P
0010	**PACKAGED WATER TUBE BOILERS**									
2000	Packaged water tube, #2 oil, steam or hot water, gross output									
2010	200 MBH	Q-6	1.50	16	Ea.	4,625	830		5,455	6,325
2014	275 MBH		1.40	17.143		4,875	890		5,765	6,725
2018	360 MBH		1.10	21.818		5,225	1,125		6,350	7,450
2022	520 MBH		.65	36.923		6,300	1,925		8,225	9,825
2026	600 MBH		.60	40		6,425	2,075		8,500	10,200
2030	720 MBH		.55	43.636		7,650	2,275		9,925	11,900
2034	960 MBH	▼	.48	50		9,475	2,600		12,075	14,300
2040	1200 MBH	Q-7	.50	64		16,800	3,400		20,200	23,600
2044	1440 MBH		.45	71.111		22,500	3,775		26,275	30,500
2060	1600 MBH		.40	80		26,500	4,250		30,750	35,600
2068	1920 MBH		.35	91.429		28,700	4,850		33,550	38,900
2072	2160 MBH		.33	96.970		31,900	5,150		37,050	42,800
2080	2400 MBH		.30	106		35,700	5,650		41,350	47,700
2100	3200 MBH	▼	.25	128	▼	40,800	6,800		47,600	55,000

23 52 Heating Boilers

23 52 26 – Steel Boilers

23 52 26.70 Packaged Water Tube Boilers

		Crew	Daily Output	Labor-Hours	Unit	Material	2012 Bare Costs Labor	Equipment	Total	Total Incl O&P
2120	4800 MBH	Q-7	.20	160	Ea.	53,000	8,475		61,475	71,500
2200	Gas fired									
2204	200 MBH	Q-6	1.50	16	Ea.	4,625	830		5,455	6,325
2208	275 MBH		1.40	17.143		4,875	890		5,765	6,725
2212	360 MBH		1.10	21.818		5,225	1,125		6,350	7,450
2216	520 MBH		.65	36.923		6,300	1,925		8,225	9,825
2220	600 MBH		.60	40		6,425	2,075		8,500	10,200
2224	720 MBH		.55	43.636		7,650	2,275		9,925	11,900
2228	960 MBH		.48	50		9,475	2,600		12,075	14,300
2232	1220 MBH	Q-7	.50	64		14,200	3,400		17,600	20,700
2236	1440 MBH		.45	71.111		14,600	3,775		18,375	21,700
2240	1680 MBH		.40	80		22,500	4,250		26,750	31,100
2244	1920 MBH		.35	91.429		22,600	4,850		27,450	32,100
2248	2160 MBH		.33	96.970		22,900	5,150		28,050	33,000
2252	2400 MBH		.30	106		25,800	5,650		31,450	36,800

23 52 28 – Swimming Pool Boilers

23 52 28.10 Swimming Pool Heaters

		Crew	Daily Output	Labor-Hours	Unit	Material	2012 Bare Costs Labor	Equipment	Total	Total Incl O&P
0010	**SWIMMING POOL HEATERS**, Not including wiring, external									
0020	piping, base or pad,									
0160	Gas fired, input, 155 MBH	Q-6	1.50	16	Ea.	1,700	830		2,530	3,100
0200	199 MBH		1	24		1,800	1,250		3,050	3,850
0220	250 MBH		.70	34.286		1,950	1,775		3,725	4,850
0240	300 MBH		.60	40		2,050	2,075		4,125	5,375
0260	399 MBH		.50	48		2,300	2,500		4,800	6,300
0280	500 MBH		.40	60		7,650	3,125		10,775	13,100
0300	650 MBH		.35	68.571		8,125	3,575		11,700	14,300
0320	750 MBH		.33	72.727		8,875	3,775		12,650	15,500
0360	990 MBH		.22	109		11,900	5,675		17,575	21,700
0370	1,260 MBH		.21	114		14,000	5,950		19,950	24,400
0380	1,440 MBH		.19	126		14,900	6,575		21,475	26,300
0400	1,800 MBH		.14	171		16,600	8,900		25,500	31,700
0410	2,070 MBH		.13	184		19,600	9,600		29,200	36,000
2000	Electric, 12 KW, 4,800 gallon pool	Q-19	3	8		2,050	405		2,455	2,850
2020	15 KW, 7,200 gallon pool		2.80	8.571		2,075	435		2,510	2,950
2040	24 KW, 9,600 gallon pool		2.40	10		2,400	505		2,905	3,400
2060	30 KW, 12,000 gallon pool		2	12		2,450	605		3,055	3,625
2080	36 KW, 14,400 gallon pool		1.60	15		2,825	760		3,585	4,250
2100	57 KW, 24,000 gallon pool		1.20	20		3,525	1,000		4,525	5,400
9000	To select pool heater: 12 BTUH x S.F. pool area									
9010	X temperature differential = required output									
9050	For electric, KW = gallons x 2.5 divided by 1000									
9100	For family home type pool, double the									
9110	Rated gallon capacity = 1/2°F rise per hour									

23 52 39 – Fire-Tube Boilers

23 52 39.13 Scotch Marine Boilers

		Crew	Daily Output	Labor-Hours	Unit	Material	2012 Bare Costs Labor	Equipment	Total	Total Incl O&P
0010	**SCOTCH MARINE BOILERS**									
1000	Packaged fire tube, #2 oil, gross output									
1006	15 PSI steam									
1010	1005 MBH, 30 HP	Q-6	.33	72.072	Ea.	37,300	3,750		41,050	46,700
1014	1675 MBH, 50 HP	"	.26	93.023		46,800	4,825		51,625	59,000
1020	3348 MBH, 100 HP	Q-7	.21	152		63,000	8,075		71,075	81,000
1030	5025 MBH, 150 HP		.17	192		79,000	10,200		89,200	102,500

23 52 Heating Boilers

23 52 39 – Fire-Tube Boilers

23 52 39.13 Scotch Marine Boilers	Crew	Daily Output	Labor-Hours	Unit	Material	2012 Bare Costs Labor	Equipment	Total	Total Incl O&P
1040	6696 MBH, 200 HP	Q-7	.14	223	Ea.	94,000	11,900		105,900	121,500
1050	8375 MBH, 250 HP		.14	231		111,000	12,300		123,300	141,000
1060	10,044 MBH, 300 HP		.13	251		120,000	13,400		133,400	152,000
1080	16,740 MBH, 500 HP		.08	380		163,000	20,200		183,200	209,500
1100	23,435 MBH, 700 HP		.07	484		199,500	25,700		225,200	258,500
1140	To fire #6, and gas, add	↓	.42	76.190	↓	17,800	4,050		21,850	25,600
1180	For duplex package feed system									
1200	To 3348 MBH boiler, add	Q-7	.54	59.259	Ea.	9,550	3,150		12,700	15,300
1220	To 6696 MBH boiler, add		.41	78.049		11,300	4,150		15,450	18,800
1240	To 10,044 MBH boiler, add		.38	84.211		13,000	4,475		17,475	21,000
1260	To 16,740 MBH boiler, add		.28	114		14,800	6,050		20,850	25,500
1280	To 23,435 MBH boiler, add	↓	.25	128	↓	17,500	6,800		24,300	29,400
1300	150 PSI steam									
1310	1005 MBH, 30 HP	Q-6	.33	72.072	Ea.	43,700	3,750		47,450	53,500
1320	1675 MBH, 50 HP	"	.26	93.023		52,500	4,825		57,325	65,500
1330	3350 MBH, 100 HP	Q-7	.21	152		75,500	8,075		83,575	95,000
1340	5025 MBH, 150 HP		.17	192		96,000	10,200		106,200	121,500
1350	6700 MBH, 200 HP		.14	223		107,000	11,900		118,900	135,500
1360	10,050 MBH, 300 HP	↓	.13	251	↓	150,000	13,400		163,400	185,000
1400	Packaged scotch marine, #6 oil									
1410	15 PSI steam									
1420	1675 MBH, 50 HP	Q-6	.25	97.166	Ea.	57,500	5,050		62,550	70,500
1430	3350 MBH, 100 HP	Q-7	.20	159		75,000	8,450		83,450	95,000
1440	5025 MBH, 150 HP		.16	202		91,500	10,700		102,200	116,500
1450	6700 MBH, 200 HP		.14	233		104,500	12,400		116,900	133,500
1460	8375 MBH, 250 HP		.13	244		119,500	13,000		132,500	151,000
1470	10,050 MBH, 300 HP		.12	262		134,500	13,900		148,400	169,000
1480	13,400 MBH, 400 HP	↓	.09	351	↓	165,500	18,700		184,200	210,000
1500	150 PSI steam									
1510	1675 MBH, 50 HP	Q-6	.25	97.166	Ea.	68,000	5,050		73,050	82,500
1520	3350 MBH, 100 HP	Q-7	.20	159		86,000	8,450		94,450	107,000
1530	5025 MBH, 150 HP		.16	202		106,500	10,700		117,200	133,000
1540	6700 MBH, 200 HP		.14	233		117,000	12,400		129,400	147,000
1550	8375 MBH, 250 HP		.13	244		142,000	13,000		155,000	175,500
1560	10,050 MBH, 300 HP		.12	262		158,000	13,900		171,900	194,500
1570	13,400 MBH, 400 HP	↓	.09	351		183,000	18,700		201,700	229,500

23 52 84 – Boiler Blowdown

23 52 84.10 Boiler Blowdown Systems

0010	**BOILER BLOWDOWN SYSTEMS**									
1010	Boiler blowdown, auto/manual to 2000 MBH	Q-5	3.75	4.267	Ea.	3,550	214		3,764	4,250
1020	7300 MBH	"	3	5.333	"	5,025	267		5,292	5,950

23 52 88 – Burners

23 52 88.10 Replacement Type Burners

0010	**REPLACEMENT TYPE BURNERS**									
0990	Residential, conversion, gas fired, LP or natural									
1000	Gun type, atmospheric input 50 to 225 MBH	Q-1	2.50	6.400	Ea.	720	315		1,035	1,275
1020	100 to 400 MBH		2	8		1,200	395		1,595	1,925
1040	300 to 1000 MBH	↓	1.70	9.412	↓	3,625	465		4,090	4,675
2000	Commercial and industrial, gas/oil, input									
2050	400 MBH	Q-1	1.50	10.667	Ea.	3,500	525		4,025	4,650
2090	670 MBH		1.40	11.429		3,500	560		4,060	4,700
2140	1155 MBH	↓	1.30	12.308	↓	3,900	605		4,505	5,200

23 52 Heating Boilers

23 52 88 – Burners

23 52 88.10 Replacement Type Burners

		Crew	Daily Output	Labor-Hours	Unit	Material	2012 Bare Costs Labor	Equipment	Total	Total Incl O&P
2200	1800 MBH	Q-1	1.20	13.333	Ea.	3,925	655		4,580	5,300
2260	3000 MBH		1.10	14.545		4,700	715		5,415	6,250
2320	4100 MBH		1	16		4,825	785		5,610	6,475
2500	Impinged jet, rectangular, burner only, 3-1/2" WC,									
2520	Gas fired, input, 420 to 640 MBH	Q-1	2	8	Ea.	975	395		1,370	1,675
2540	560 to 860 MBH		2	8		1,500	395		1,895	2,250
2560	630 to 950 MBH		1.90	8.421		1,700	415		2,115	2,500
2580	950 to 1200 MBH		1.80	8.889		2,275	435		2,710	3,150
2600	1120 to 1700 MBH		1.80	8.889		3,025	435		3,460	3,975
2620	1700 to 1900 MBH		1.70	9.412		3,400	465		3,865	4,450
2640	1400 to 2100 MBH		1.60	10		3,775	490		4,265	4,900
2660	1600 to 2400 MBH		1.60	10		3,900	490		4,390	5,050
2680	1700 to 2500 MBH		1.50	10.667		4,525	525		5,050	5,775
2700	1880 to 2880 MBH		1.40	11.429		4,650	560		5,210	5,950
2720	2260 to 3680 MBH		1.40	11.429		5,125	560		5,685	6,500
2740	2590 to 4320 MBH		1.30	12.308		6,800	605		7,405	8,375
2760	3020 to 5040 MBH		1.20	13.333		7,925	655		8,580	9,725
2780	3450 to 5760 MBH		1.20	13.333		9,075	655		9,730	11,000
2850	Burner pilot		50	.320		25	15.75		40.75	51
2860	Thermocouple		50	.320		26	15.75		41.75	52
2870	Thermocouple & pilot bracket		45	.356		94.50	17.50		112	131
2900	For 7" W.C. pressure, increase MBH 40%									
3000	Flame retention oil fired assembly, input									
3020	.50 to 2.25 GPH	Q-1	2.40	6.667	Ea.	289	330		619	815
3040	2.0 to 5.0 GPH		2	8		345	395		740	975
3060	3.0 to 7.0 GPH		1.80	8.889		620	435		1,055	1,350
3080	6.0 to 12.0 GPH		1.60	10		990	490		1,480	1,825
4600	Gas safety, shut off valve, 3/4" threaded	1 Stpi	20	.400		178	22.50		200.50	230
4610	1" threaded		19	.421		172	23.50		195.50	226
4620	1-1/4" threaded		15	.533		194	29.50		223.50	258
4630	1-1/2" threaded		13	.615		210	34.50		244.50	283
4640	2" threaded		11	.727		235	40.50		275.50	320
4650	2-1/2" threaded	Q-1	15	1.067		269	52.50		321.50	375
4660	3" threaded		13	1.231		370	60.50		430.50	495
4670	4" flanged		3	5.333		2,625	262		2,887	3,300
4680	6" flanged	Q-2	3	8		5,875	410		6,285	7,100

23 53 Heating Boiler Feedwater Equipment

23 53 24 – Shot Chemical Feeder

23 53 24.10 Chemical Feeder

		Crew	Daily Output	Labor-Hours	Unit	Material	2012 Bare Costs Labor	Equipment	Total	Total Incl O&P
0010	**CHEMICAL FEEDER**									
0200	Shot chem feeder, by pass, in line mount, 125 PSIG, 1.7 gallon	2 Stpi	1.80	8.889	Ea.	298	495		793	1,075
0220	Floor mount, 175 PSIG, 5 gallon		1.24	12.903		350	720		1,070	1,450
0230	12 gallon		.93	17.204		545	960		1,505	2,050
0300	150 lb., ASME, 5 gallon		1.24	12.903		350	720		1,070	1,450
0320	10 gallon		.93	17.204		500	960		1,460	2,000
0400	300 lb., ASME, 5 gallon		1.24	12.903		350	720		1,070	1,450
0420	10 gallon		.93	17.204		500	960		1,460	2,000

23 54 Furnaces

23 54 13 – Electric-Resistance Furnaces

23 54 13.10 Electric Furnaces

23 54 13.10 Electric Furnaces	Crew	Daily Output	Labor-Hours	Unit	Material	2012 Bare Costs Labor	Equipment	Total	Total Incl O&P
0010 **ELECTRIC FURNACES**, Hot air, blowers, std. controls									
0011 not including gas, oil or flue piping									
1000 Electric, UL listed									
1020 10.2 MBH	Q-20	5	4	Ea.	475	191		666	810
1040 17.1 MBH		4.80	4.167		495	199		694	850
1060 27.3 MBH		4.60	4.348		600	208		808	975
1100 34.1 MBH		4.40	4.545		635	218		853	1,025
1120 51.6 MBH		4.20	4.762		685	228		913	1,100
1140 68.3 MBH		4	5		735	239		974	1,175
1160 85.3 MBH	▼	3.80	5.263	▼	745	252		997	1,200

23 54 16 – Fuel-Fired Furnaces

23 54 16.13 Gas-Fired Furnaces

23 54 16.13 Gas-Fired Furnaces	Crew	Daily Output	Labor-Hours	Unit	Material	2012 Bare Costs Labor	Equipment	Total	Total Incl O&P
0010 **GAS-FIRED FURNACES**									
3000 Gas, AGA certified, upflow, direct drive models									
3020 45 MBH input	Q-9	4	4	Ea.	620	188		808	965
3040 60 MBH input		3.80	4.211		645	198		843	1,000
3060 75 MBH input		3.60	4.444		665	209		874	1,050
3100 100 MBH input		3.20	5		720	235		955	1,150
3120 125 MBH input		3	5.333		750	250		1,000	1,200
3130 150 MBH input		2.80	5.714		770	268		1,038	1,250
3140 200 MBH input		2.60	6.154		2,800	289		3,089	3,525
3160 300 MBH input		2.30	6.957		3,100	325		3,425	3,925
3180 400 MBH input	▼	2	8	▼	3,450	375		3,825	4,375
3200 Gas fired wall furnace									
3204 Horizontal flow									
3208 7.7 MBH	Q-9	7	2.286	Ea.	470	107		577	685
3212 14 MBH		6.50	2.462		470	116		586	695
3216 24 MBH		5	3.200		495	150		645	775
3220 49 MBH		4	4		705	188		893	1,050
3224 65 MBH	▼	3.60	4.444	▼	895	209		1,104	1,300
3240 Up-flow									
3244 7.7 MBH	Q-9	7	2.286	Ea.	470	107		577	685
3248 14 MBH		6.50	2.462		470	116		586	695
3252 24 MBH		5	3.200		610	150		760	900
3254 35 MBH		4.50	3.556		745	167		912	1,075
3256 49 MBH		4	4		920	188		1,108	1,275
3260 65 MBH	▼	3.60	4.444	▼	1,025	209		1,234	1,450
3500 Gas furnace									
3510 Up-flow									
3514 1200 CFM, 45 MBH	Q-9	4	4	Ea.	865	188		1,053	1,225
3518 75 MBH		3.60	4.444		865	209		1,074	1,275
3522 100 MBH		3.20	5		1,000	235		1,235	1,450
3526 125 MBH		3	5.333		1,050	250		1,300	1,550
3530 150 MBH		2.80	5.714		1,200	268		1,468	1,700
3540 2000 CFM, 75 MBH		3.60	4.444		1,050	209		1,259	1,475
3544 100 MBH		3.20	5		1,175	235		1,410	1,650
3548 120 MBH	▼	3	5.333	▼	1,250	250		1,500	1,750
3560 Horizontal flow									
3564 1200 CFM, 45 MBH	Q-9	4	4	Ea.	1,000	188		1,188	1,375
3568 60 MBH		3.80	4.211		1,050	198		1,248	1,450
3572 70 MBH		3.60	4.444		1,075	209		1,284	1,500
3576 2000 CFM, 90 MBH	▼	3.30	4.848	▼	1,150	228		1,378	1,625

23 54 Furnaces

23 54 16 – Fuel-Fired Furnaces

23 54 16.13 Gas-Fired Furnaces	Crew	Daily Output	Labor-Hours	Unit	Material	2012 Bare Costs Labor	Equipment	Total	Total Incl O&P
3580	110 MBH	Q-9	3.10	5.161	Ea.	1,200	242		1,442	1,675

23 54 16.16 Oil-Fired Furnaces

		Crew	Daily Output	Labor-Hours	Unit	Material	2012 Bare Costs Labor	Equipment	Total	Total Incl O&P
0010	**OIL-FIRED FURNACES**									
6000	Oil, UL listed, atomizing gun type burner									
6020	56 MBH output	Q-9	3.60	4.444	Ea.	1,475	209		1,684	1,950
6030	84 MBH output		3.50	4.571		1,850	215		2,065	2,375
6040	95 MBH output		3.40	4.706		1,875	221		2,096	2,400
6060	134 MBH output		3.20	5		2,175	235		2,410	2,750
6080	151 MBH output		3	5.333		2,250	250		2,500	2,850
6100	200 MBH input		2.60	6.154		2,450	289		2,739	3,150
6120	300 MBH input		2.30	6.957		3,600	325		3,925	4,475
6140	400 MBH input		2	8		3,900	375		4,275	4,875
6200	Up flow									
6210	105 MBH	Q-9	3.40	4.706	Ea.	1,575	221		1,796	2,075
6220	140 MBH		3.30	4.848		1,725	228		1,953	2,225
6230	168 MBH		2.90	5.517		2,425	259		2,684	3,075
6260	Lo-boy style									
6270	105 MBH	Q-9	3.40	4.706	Ea.	1,575	221		1,796	2,075
6280	140 MBH		3.30	4.848		1,725	228		1,953	2,225
6290	189 MBH		2.80	5.714		2,425	268		2,693	3,075
6320	Down flow									
6330	105 MBH	Q-9	3.40	4.706	Ea.	1,525	221		1,746	2,000
6340	140 MBH		3.30	4.848		1,725	228		1,953	2,225
6350	168 MBH		2.90	5.517		2,425	259		2,684	3,075
6380	Horizontal									
6390	105 MBH	Q-9	3.40	4.706	Ea.	1,575	221		1,796	2,075
6400	140 MBH		3.30	4.848		1,725	228		1,953	2,225
6410	189 MBH		2.80	5.714		2,225	268		2,493	2,850

23 54 16.21 Solid Fuel-Fired Furnaces

			Crew	Daily Output	Labor-Hours	Unit	Material	2012 Bare Costs Labor	Equipment	Total	Total Incl O&P
0010	**SOLID FUEL-FIRED FURNACES**										
6020	Wood fired furnaces										
6030	Includes hot water coil, thermostat, and auto draft control										
6040	24" long firebox	G	Q-9	4	4	Ea.	4,075	188		4,263	4,775
6050	30" long firebox	G		3.60	4.444		4,800	209		5,009	5,600
6060	With fireplace glass doors	G		3.20	5		6,175	235		6,410	7,150
6200	Wood/oil fired furnaces, includes two thermostats										
6210	Includes hot water coil and auto draft control										
6240	24" long firebox	G	Q-9	3.40	4.706	Ea.	4,975	221		5,196	5,800
6250	30" long firebox	G		3	5.333		5,575	250		5,825	6,500
6260	With fireplace glass doors	G		2.80	5.714		6,900	268		7,168	7,975
6400	Wood/gas fired furnaces, includes two thermostats										
6410	Includes hot water coil and auto draft control										
6440	24" long firebox	G	Q-9	2.80	5.714	Ea.	5,625	268		5,893	6,575
6450	30" long firebox	G		2.40	6.667		6,325	315		6,640	7,450
6460	With fireplace glass doors	G		2	8		7,625	375		8,000	8,975
6600	Wood/oil/gas fired furnaces, optional accessories										
6610	Hot air plenum		Q-9	16	1	Ea.	96	47		143	177
6620	Safety heat dump			24	.667		84.50	31.50		116	141
6630	Auto air intake			18	.889		136	41.50		177.50	214
6640	Cold air return package			14	1.143		146	53.50		199.50	243
6650	Wood fork						45.50			45.50	50
6700	Wood fired outdoor furnace										

23 54 Furnaces

23 54 16 – Fuel-Fired Furnaces

23 54 16.21 Solid Fuel-Fired Furnaces

		Crew	Daily Output	Labor-Hours	Unit	Material	2012 Bare Costs Labor	2012 Bare Costs Equipment	Total	Total Incl O&P
6740	24" long firebox Ⓖ	Q-9	3.80	4.211	Ea.	4,325	198		4,523	5,050
6760	Wood fired outdoor furnace, optional accessories									
6770	Chimney section, stainless steel, 6" ID x 3' lg. Ⓖ	Q-9	36	.444	Ea.	125	21		146	169
6780	Chimney cap, stainless steel Ⓖ	"	40	.400	"	68	18.75		86.75	104
6800	Wood fired hot water furnace									
6820	Includes 200 gal. hot water storage, thermostat, and auto draft control									
6840	30" long firebox Ⓖ	Q-9	2.10	7.619	Ea.	8,525	360		8,885	9,925
6850	Water to air heat exchanger									
6870	Includes mounting kit and blower relay									
6880	140 MBH, 18.75" W x 18.75" L	Q-9	7.50	2.133	Ea.	380	100		480	575
6890	200 MBH, 24" W x 24" L	"	7	2.286	"	540	107		647	760
6900	Water to water heat exchanger									
6940	100 MBH	Q-9	6.50	2.462	Ea.	385	116		501	595
6960	290 MBH	"	6	2.667	"	550	125		675	795
7000	Optional accessories									
7010	Large volume circulation pump, (2 Included)	Q-9	14	1.143	Ea.	249	53.50		302.50	355
7020	Air bleed fittings, (package)		24	.667		50.50	31.50		82	103
7030	Domestic water preheater		6	2.667		226	125		351	440
7040	Smoke pipe kit		4	4		76.50	188		264.50	370

23 54 24 – Furnace Components for Cooling

23 54 24.10 Furnace Components and Combinations

		Crew	Daily Output	Labor-Hours	Unit	Material	2012 Bare Costs Labor	2012 Bare Costs Equipment	Total	Total Incl O&P
0010	**FURNACE COMPONENTS AND COMBINATIONS**									
0080	Coils, A/C evaporator, for gas or oil furnaces									
0090	Add-on, with holding charge									
0100	Upflow									
0120	1-1/2 ton cooling	Q-5	4	4	Ea.	261	201		462	585
0130	2 ton cooling		3.70	4.324		292	217		509	645
0140	3 ton cooling		3.30	4.848		455	243		698	865
0150	4 ton cooling		3	5.333		565	267		832	1,025
0160	5 ton cooling		2.70	5.926		575	297		872	1,075
0300	Downflow									
0330	2-1/2 ton cooling	Q-5	3	5.333	Ea.	345	267		612	785
0340	3-1/2 ton cooling		2.60	6.154		535	310		845	1,050
0350	5 ton cooling		2.20	7.273		575	365		940	1,175
0600	Horizontal									
0630	2 ton cooling	Q-5	3.90	4.103	Ea.	390	206		596	735
0640	3 ton cooling		3.50	4.571		430	229		659	820
0650	4 ton cooling		3.20	5		550	251		801	985
0660	5 ton cooling		2.90	5.517		550	277		827	1,025
2000	Cased evaporator coils for air handlers									
2100	1-1/2 ton cooling	Q-5	4.40	3.636	Ea.	320	182		502	625
2110	2 ton cooling		4.10	3.902		365	196		561	700
2120	2-1/2 ton cooling		3.90	4.103		385	206		591	735
2130	3 ton cooling		3.70	4.324		430	217		647	800
2140	3-1/2 ton cooling		3.50	4.571		550	229		779	950
2150	4 ton cooling		3.20	5		625	251		876	1,075
2160	5 ton cooling		2.90	5.517		705	277		982	1,200
3010	Air handler, modular									
3100	With cased evaporator cooling coil									
3120	1-1/2 ton cooling	Q-5	3.80	4.211	Ea.	1,275	211		1,486	1,725
3130	2 ton cooling		3.50	4.571		1,325	229		1,554	1,800
3140	2-1/2 ton cooling		3.30	4.848		1,425	243		1,668	1,950

23 54 Furnaces

23 54 24 – Furnace Components for Cooling

23 54 24.10 Furnace Components and Combinations

		Crew	Daily Output	Labor-Hours	Unit	Material	2012 Bare Costs Labor	Equipment	Total	Total Incl O&P
3150	3 ton cooling	Q-5	3.10	5.161	Ea.	1,525	259		1,784	2,100
3160	3-1/2 ton cooling		2.90	5.517		1,575	277		1,852	2,175
3170	4 ton cooling		2.50	6.400		1,775	320		2,095	2,425
3180	5 ton cooling		2.10	7.619		2,025	380		2,405	2,800
3500	With no cooling coil									
3520	1-1/2 ton coil size	Q-5	12	1.333	Ea.	685	67		752	850
3530	2 ton coil size		10	1.600		685	80		765	870
3540	2-1/2 ton coil size		10	1.600		815	80		895	1,025
3554	3 ton coil size		9	1.778		925	89		1,014	1,150
3560	3-1/2 ton coil size		9	1.778		935	89		1,024	1,150
3570	4 ton coil size		8.50	1.882		1,125	94.50		1,219.50	1,400
3580	5 ton coil size		8	2		1,425	100		1,525	1,725
4000	With heater									
4120	5 kW, 17.1 MBH	Q-5	16	1	Ea.	670	50		720	810
4130	7.5 kW, 25.6 MBH		15.60	1.026		825	51.50		876.50	985
4140	10 kW, 34.2 MBH		15.20	1.053		875	53		928	1,050
4150	12.5 KW, 42.7 MBH		14.80	1.081		940	54		994	1,100
4160	15 KW, 51.2 MBH		14.40	1.111		1,000	55.50		1,055.50	1,175
4170	25 KW, 85.4 MBH		14.40	1.111		1,350	55.50		1,405.50	1,575
4180	30 KW, 102 MBH		14.40	1.111		1,575	55.50		1,630.50	1,800

23 55 Fuel-Fired Heaters

23 55 13 – Fuel-Fired Duct Heaters

23 55 13.16 Gas-Fired Duct Heaters

		Crew	Daily Output	Labor-Hours	Unit	Material	2012 Bare Costs Labor	Equipment	Total	Total Incl O&P
0010	**GAS-FIRED DUCT HEATERS**, Includes burner, controls, stainless steel									
0020	heat exchanger. Gas fired, electric ignition									
0030	Indoor installation									
0080	100 MBH output	Q-5	5	3.200	Ea.	1,875	160		2,035	2,325
0100	120 MBH output		4	4		2,125	201		2,326	2,650
0130	200 MBH output		2.70	5.926		2,850	297		3,147	3,575
0140	240 MBH output		2.30	6.957		2,975	350		3,325	3,775
0160	280 MBH output		2	8		3,350	400		3,750	4,300
0180	320 MBH output		1.60	10		3,550	500		4,050	4,675
0300	For powered venter and adapter, add					460			460	510
0502	For required flue pipe, see Section 23 51 23.10									
1000	Outdoor installation, with power venter									
1020	75 MBH output	Q-5	4	4	Ea.	2,775	201		2,976	3,350
1040	94 MBH output		4	4		3,125	201		3,326	3,750
1060	120 MBH output		4	4		3,525	201		3,726	4,200
1080	157 MBH output		3.50	4.571		4,100	229		4,329	4,850
1100	187 MBH output		3	5.333		5,050	267		5,317	5,950
1120	225 MBH output		2.50	6.400		5,225	320		5,545	6,225
1140	300 MBH output		1.80	8.889		6,100	445		6,545	7,375
1160	375 MBH output		1.60	10		6,425	500		6,925	7,825
1180	450 MBH output		1.40	11.429		7,450	575		8,025	9,075
1200	600 MBH output		1	16		8,400	800		9,200	10,400
1300	Aluminized exchanger, subtract					15%				
1500	For two stage gas valve, add					190			190	208

23 55 Fuel-Fired Heaters

23 55 33 – Fuel-Fired Unit Heaters

23 55 33.13 Oil-Fired Unit Heaters

		Crew	Daily Output	Labor-Hours	Unit	Material	2012 Bare Costs Labor	2012 Bare Costs Equipment	Total	Total Incl O&P
0010	**OIL-FIRED UNIT HEATERS**, Cabinet, grilles, fan, ctrl, burner, no piping									
6000	Oil fired, suspension mounted, 94 MBH output	Q-5	4	4	Ea.	3,400	201		3,601	4,025
6040	140 MBH output		3	5.333		3,625	267		3,892	4,375
6060	184 MBH output		3	5.333		3,900	267		4,167	4,700

23 55 33.16 Gas-Fired Unit Heaters

		Crew	Daily Output	Labor-Hours	Unit	Material	2012 Bare Costs Labor	2012 Bare Costs Equipment	Total	Total Incl O&P
0010	**GAS-FIRED UNIT HEATERS**, Cabinet, grilles, fan, ctrls., burner, no piping									
0022	thermostat, no piping. For flue see Section 23 51 23.10									
1000	Gas fired, floor mounted									
1100	60 MBH output	Q-5	10	1.600	Ea.	830	80		910	1,025
1120	80 MBH output		9	1.778		840	89		929	1,050
1140	100 MBH output		8	2		915	100		1,015	1,150
1160	120 MBH output		7	2.286		1,075	115		1,190	1,375
1180	180 MBH output		6	2.667		1,300	134		1,434	1,650
1500	Rooftop mounted, power vent, stainless steel exchanger									
1520	75 MBH input	Q-6	4	6	Ea.	4,200	310		4,510	5,100
1540	100 MBH input		3.60	6.667		4,425	345		4,770	5,400
1560	125 MBH input		3.30	7.273		4,625	380		5,005	5,675
1580	150 MBH input		3	8		5,050	415		5,465	6,175
1600	175 MBH input		2.60	9.231		5,200	480		5,680	6,425
1620	225 MBH input		2.30	10.435		6,050	540		6,590	7,475
1640	300 MBH input		1.90	12.632		7,125	655		7,780	8,825
1660	350 MBH input		1.40	17.143		7,825	890		8,715	9,950
1680	450 MBH input		1.20	20		8,250	1,050		9,300	10,700
1720	700 MBH input		.80	30		10,300	1,550		11,850	13,700
1760	1200 MBH input		.30	80		10,700	4,150		14,850	18,000
1900	For aluminized steel exchanger, subtract					10%				
2000	Suspension mounted, propeller fan, 20 MBH output	Q-5	8.50	1.882		985	94.50		1,079.50	1,225
2020	40 MBH output		7.50	2.133		1,075	107		1,182	1,350
2040	60 MBH output		7	2.286		1,200	115		1,315	1,500
2060	80 MBH output		6	2.667		1,225	134		1,359	1,550
2080	100 MBH output		5.50	2.909		1,375	146		1,521	1,725
2100	130 MBH output		5	3.200		1,500	160		1,660	1,900
2120	140 MBH output		4.50	3.556		1,550	178		1,728	1,975
2140	160 MBH output		4	4		1,600	201		1,801	2,050
2160	180 MBH output		3.50	4.571		1,700	229		1,929	2,225
2180	200 MBH output		3	5.333		1,800	267		2,067	2,375
2200	240 MBH output		2.70	5.926		2,075	297		2,372	2,725
2220	280 MBH output		2.30	6.957		2,425	350		2,775	3,200
2240	320 MBH output		2	8		2,650	400		3,050	3,500
2500	For powered venter and adapter, add					355			355	390
3000	Suspension mounted, blower type, 40 MBH output	Q-5	6.80	2.353		915	118		1,033	1,175
3020	60 MBH output		6.60	2.424		930	122		1,052	1,200
3040	84 MBH output		5.80	2.759		945	138		1,083	1,250
3060	104 MBH output		5.20	3.077		975	154		1,129	1,300
3080	140 MBH output		4.30	3.721		985	187		1,172	1,350
3100	180 MBH output		3.30	4.848		1,050	243		1,293	1,525
3120	240 MBH output		2.50	6.400		1,450	320		1,770	2,075
3140	280 MBH output		2	8		1,600	400		2,000	2,375
4000	Suspension mounted, sealed combustion system,									
4020	Aluminized steel exchanger, powered vent									
4040	100 MBH output	Q-5	5	3.200	Ea.	1,800	160		1,960	2,250
4060	120 MBH output		4.70	3.404		2,025	171		2,196	2,475

23 55 Fuel-Fired Heaters

23 55 33 – Fuel-Fired Unit Heaters

23 55 33.16 Gas-Fired Unit Heaters

		Crew	Daily Output	Labor-Hours	Unit	Material	2012 Bare Costs Labor	Equipment	Total	Total Incl O&P
4080	160 MBH output	Q-5	3.70	4.324	Ea.	2,225	217		2,442	2,750
4100	200 MBH output		2.90	5.517		2,650	277		2,927	3,350
4120	240 MBH output		2.50	6.400		2,850	320		3,170	3,600
4140	320 MBH output		1.70	9.412		3,400	470		3,870	4,425
5000	Wall furnace, 17.5 MBH output		6	2.667		715	134		849	985
5020	24 MBH output		5	3.200		835	160		995	1,150
5040	35 MBH output	↓	4	4	↓	960	201		1,161	1,350

23 56 Solar Energy Heating Equipment

23 56 16 – Packaged Solar Heating Equipment

23 56 16.40 Solar Heating Systems

			Crew	Daily Output	Labor-Hours	Unit	Material	2012 Bare Costs Labor	Equipment	Total	Total Incl O&P
0010	**SOLAR HEATING SYSTEMS**	R235616-60									
0020	System/Package prices, not including connecting										
0030	pipe, insulation, or special heating/plumbing fixtures										
0152	For solar ultraviolet pipe insulation see Section 22 07 19.10										
0500	Hot water, standard package, low temperature										
0540	1 collector, circulator, fittings, 65 gal. tank	G	Q-1	.50	32	Ea.	1,625	1,575		3,200	4,150
0580	2 collectors, circulator, fittings, 120 gal. tank	G		.40	40		2,375	1,975		4,350	5,575
0620	3 collectors, circulator, fittings, 120 gal. tank	G	↓	.34	47.059	↓	3,225	2,325		5,550	7,050
0700	Medium temperature package										
0720	1 collector, circulator, fittings, 80 gal. tank	G	Q-1	.50	32	Ea.	2,375	1,575		3,950	4,975
0740	2 collectors, circulator, fittings, 120 gal. tank	G		.40	40		3,425	1,975		5,400	6,750
0780	3 collectors, circulator, fittings, 120 gal. tank	G	↓	.30	53.333		4,450	2,625		7,075	8,850
0980	For each additional 120 gal. tank, add	G					1,550			1,550	1,700

23 56 19 – Solar Heating Components

23 56 19.50 Solar Heating Ancillary

			Crew	Daily Output	Labor-Hours	Unit	Material	2012 Bare Costs Labor	Equipment	Total	Total Incl O&P
0010	**SOLAR HEATING ANCILLARY**										
2300	Circulators, air										
2310	Blowers										
2330	100-300 S.F. system, 1/10 HP	G	Q-9	16	1	Ea.	229	47		276	325
2340	300-500 S.F. system, 1/5 HP	G		15	1.067		299	50		349	405
2350	Two speed, 100-300 S.F., 1/10 HP	G		14	1.143		142	53.50		195.50	239
2400	Reversible fan, 20" diameter, 2 speed	G		18	.889		113	41.50		154.50	188
2550	Booster fan 6" diameter, 120 CFM	G		16	1		36.50	47		83.50	112
2570	6" diameter, 225 CFM	G		16	1		45	47		92	121
2580	8" diameter, 150 CFM	G		16	1		41	47		88	117
2590	8" diameter, 310 CFM	G		14	1.143		63.50	53.50		117	152
2600	8" diameter, 425 CFM	G		14	1.143		71	53.50		124.50	160
2650	Rheostat	G		32	.500		15.45	23.50		38.95	53
2660	Shutter/damper	G		12	1.333		52	62.50		114.50	153
2670	Shutter motor	G	↓	16	1		129	47		176	214
2800	Circulators, liquid, 1/25 HP, 5.3 GPM	G	Q-1	14	1.143		268	56		324	380
2820	1/20 HP, 17 GPM	G		12	1.333		161	65.50		226.50	276
2850	1/20 HP, 17 GPM, stainless steel	G		12	1.333		254	65.50		319.50	380
2870	1/12 HP, 30 GPM	G	↓	10	1.600	↓	345	78.50		423.50	500
3000	Collector panels, air with aluminum absorber plate										
3010	Wall or roof mount										
3040	Flat black, plastic glazing										
3080	4' x 8'	G	Q-9	6	2.667	Ea.	660	125		785	920
3100	4' x 10'	G	↓	5	3.200	"	815	150		965	1,125

23 56 19 – Solar Heating Components

23 56 19.50 Solar Heating Ancillary		Crew	Daily Output	Labor-Hours	Unit	Material	2012 Bare Costs Labor	2012 Bare Costs Equipment	Total	Total Incl O&P
3200	Flush roof mount, 10' to 16' x 22" wide	G	Q-9	96	.167	L.F.	470	7.80		477.80	525
3210	Manifold, by L.F. width of collectors	▼	↓	160	.100	"	127	4.69		131.69	147
3300	Collector panels, liquid with copper absorber plate										
3320	Black chrome, tempered glass glazing										
3330	Alum. frame, 4' x 8', 5/32" single glazing	G	Q-1	9.50	1.684	Ea.	995	83		1,078	1,225
3390	Alum. frame, 4' x 10', 5/32" single glazing	G		6	2.667		1,150	131		1,281	1,450
3450	Flat black, alum. frame, 3.5' x 7.5'	G		9	1.778		690	87.50		777.50	890
3500	4' x 8'	G		5.50	2.909		865	143		1,008	1,175
3520	4' x 10'	G		10	1.600		970	78.50		1,048.50	1,200
3540	4' x 12.5'	G	▼	5	3.200	▼	1,175	157		1,332	1,500
3550	Liquid with fin tube absorber plate										
3560	Alum. frame 4' x 8' tempered glass	G	Q-1	10	1.600	Ea.	515	78.50		593.50	685
3580	Liquid with vacuum tubes, 4' x 6'-10"	G		9	1.778		850	87.50		937.50	1,075
3600	Liquid, full wetted, plastic, alum. frame, 4' x 10'	G		5	3.200		234	157		391	495
3650	Collector panel mounting, flat roof or ground rack	G		7	2.286	▼	228	112		340	420
3670	Roof clamps	G	▼	70	.229	Set	2.46	11.25		13.71	19.65
3700	Roof strap, teflon	G	1 Plum	205	.039	L.F.	19.95	2.13		22.08	25
3900	Differential controller with two sensors										
3930	Thermostat, hard wired	G	1 Plum	8	1	Ea.	83	54.50		137.50	174
3950	Line cord and receptacle	G		12	.667		550	36.50		586.50	660
4050	Pool valve system	G		2.50	3.200		278	175		453	570
4070	With 12 VAC actuator	G		2	4		290	218		508	650
4080	Pool pump system, 2" pipe size	G		6	1.333		181	73		254	310
4100	Five station with digital read-out	G	▼	3	2.667	▼	229	146		375	470
4150	Sensors										
4200	Brass plug, 1/2" MPT	G	1 Plum	32	.250	Ea.	18.85	13.65		32.50	41
4210	Brass plug, reversed	G		32	.250		25.50	13.65		39.15	48.50
4220	Freeze prevention	G		32	.250		23	13.65		36.65	45.50
4240	Screw attached	G		32	.250		8.75	13.65		22.40	30
4250	Brass, immersion	G	▼	32	.250		27.50	13.65		41.15	51
4300	Heat exchanger										
4330	Fluid to air coil, up flow, 45 MBH	G	Q-1	4	4	Ea.	310	197		507	635
4380	70 MBH	G		3.50	4.571		350	225		575	720
4400	80 MBH	G	▼	3	5.333	▼	465	262		727	905
4580	Fluid to fluid package includes two circulating pumps										
4590	expansion tank, check valve, relief valve										
4600	controller, high temperature cutoff and sensors	G	Q-1	2.50	6.400	Ea.	725	315		1,040	1,275
4650	Heat transfer fluid										
4700	Propylene glycol, inhibited anti-freeze	G	1 Plum	28	.286	Gal.	14.50	15.60		30.10	39.50
4800	Solar storage tanks, knocked down										
4810	Air, galvanized steel clad, double wall, 4" fiberglass										
4820	insulation, 20 Mil PVC lining										
4870	4' high, 4' x 4', = 64 C.F./450 gallons	G	Q-9	2	8	Ea.	2,400	375		2,775	3,200
4880	4' x 8' = 128 C.F./900 gallons	G		1.50	10.667		3,375	500		3,875	4,500
4890	4' x 12' = 190 C.F./1300 gallons	G		1.30	12.308		4,500	580		5,080	5,850
4900	8' x 8' = 250 C.F./1700 gallons	G	▼	1	16		5,050	750		5,800	6,700
5010	6'-3" high, 7' x 7' = 306 C.F./2000 gallons	G	Q-10	1.20	20		12,300	975		13,275	15,000
5020	7' x 10'-6" = 459 C.F./3000 gallons	G		.80	30		15,500	1,450		16,950	19,200
5030	7' x 14' = 613 C.F./4000 gallons	G		.60	40		18,100	1,950		20,050	22,900
5040	10'-6" x 10'-6" = 689 C.F./4500 gallons	G		.50	48		18,700	2,325		21,025	24,100
5050	10'-6" x 14' = 919 C.F./6000 gallons	G	▼	.40	60		22,000	2,925		24,925	28,700
5060	14' x 14' = 1225 C.F./8000 gallons	G	Q-11	.40	80		25,700	3,975		29,675	34,400
5070	14' x 17'-6" = 1531 C.F./10,000 gallons	G	▼	.30	106	▼	29,000	5,300		34,300	40,000

23 56 Solar Energy Heating Equipment

23 56 19 – Solar Heating Components

23 56 19.50 Solar Heating Ancillary		Crew	Daily Output	Labor-Hours	Unit	Material	2012 Bare Costs Labor	Equipment	Total	Total Incl O&P
5080	17'-6" x 17'-6" = 1914 C.F./12,500 gallons	G	Q-11	.25	128	Ea.	34,100	6,350		40,450	47,200
5090	17'-6" x 21' = 2297 C.F./15,000 gallons	G		.20	160		38,000	7,950		45,950	54,000
5100	21' x 21' = 2756 C.F./18,000 gallons	G	↓	.18	177	↓	43,500	8,825		52,325	61,500
5120	30 Mil reinforced Chemflex lining,										
5140	4' high, 4' x 4' = 64 C.F./450 gallons	G	Q-9	2	8	Ea.	2,650	375		3,025	3,500
5150	4' x 8' = 128 C.F./900 gallons	G		1.50	10.667		4,000	500		4,500	5,175
5160	4' x 12' = 190 C.F./1300 gallons	G		1.30	12.308		5,300	580		5,880	6,725
5170	8' x 8' = 250 C.F./1700 gallons	G		1	16		5,925	750		6,675	7,675
5190	6'-3" high, 7' x 7' = 306 C.F./2000 gallons	G	Q-10	1.20	20		13,100	975		14,075	15,900
5200	7' x 10'-6" = 459 C.F./3000 gallons	G		.80	30		16,000	1,450		17,450	19,800
5210	7' x 14' = 613 C.F./4000 gallons	G		.60	40		18,600	1,950		20,550	23,500
5220	10'-6" x 10'-6" = 689 C.F./4500 gallons	G		.50	48		19,200	2,325		21,525	24,700
5230	10'-6" x 14' = 919 C.F./6000 gallons	G	↓	.40	60		22,500	2,925		25,425	29,300
5240	14' x 14' = 1225 C.F./8000 gallons	G	Q-11	.40	80		26,400	3,975		30,375	35,100
5250	14' x 17'-6" = 1531 C.F./10,000 gallons	G		.30	106		29,500	5,300		34,800	40,600
5260	17'-6" x 17'-6" = 1914 C.F./12,500 gallons	G		.25	128		34,800	6,350		41,150	47,900
5270	17'-6" x 21' = 2297 C.F./15,000 gallons	G		.20	160		39,100	7,950		47,050	55,000
5280	21' x 21' = 2756 C.F./18,000 gallons	G	↓	.18	177	↓	44,900	8,825		53,725	63,000
5290	30 Mil reinforced Hypalon lining, add						.02%				
7000	Solar control valves and vents										
7050	Air purger, 1" pipe size	G	1 Plum	12	.667	Ea.	45	36.50		81.50	105
7070	Air eliminator, automatic 3/4" size	G		32	.250		30	13.65		43.65	53.50
7090	Air vent, automatic, 1/8" fitting	G		32	.250		17.25	13.65		30.90	39.50
7100	Manual, 1/8" NPT	G		32	.250		2.73	13.65		16.38	23.50
7120	Backflow preventer, 1/2" pipe size	G		16	.500		120	27.50		147.50	173
7130	3/4" pipe size	G		16	.500		121	27.50		148.50	175
7150	Balancing valve, 3/4" pipe size	G		20	.400		49.50	22		71.50	87.50
7180	Draindown valve, 1/2" copper tube	G		9	.889		212	48.50		260.50	305
7200	Flow control valve, 1/2" pipe size	G		22	.364		151	19.85		170.85	197
7220	Expansion tank, up to 5 gal.	G		32	.250		64	13.65		77.65	91
7250	Hydronic controller (aquastat)	G		8	1		179	54.50		233.50	280
7400	Pressure gauge, 2" dial	G		32	.250		23	13.65		36.65	46
7450	Relief valve, temp. and pressure 3/4" pipe size	G	↓	30	.267	↓	18.65	14.55		33.20	42.50
7500	Solenoid valve, normally closed										
7520	Brass, 3/4" NPT, 24V	G	1 Plum	9	.889	Ea.	112	48.50		160.50	196
7530	1" NPT, 24V	G		9	.889		1,050	48.50		1,098.50	1,225
7750	Vacuum relief valve, 3/4" pipe size	G	↓	32	.250		27.50	13.65		41.15	51
7800	Thermometers										
7820	Digital temperature monitoring, 4 locations	G	1 Plum	2.50	3.200	Ea.	135	175		310	410
7900	Upright, 1/2" NPT	G		8	1		25.50	54.50		80	111
7970	Remote probe, 2" dial	G		8	1		32	54.50		86.50	118
7990	Stem, 2" dial, 9" stem	G	↓	16	.500	↓	21	27.50		48.50	64
8250	Water storage tank with heat exchanger and electric element										
8270	66 gal. with 2" x 2 lb. density insulation	G	1 Plum	1.60	5	Ea.	1,100	273		1,373	1,600
8300	80 gal. with 2" x 2 lb. density insulation	G		1.60	5		1,100	273		1,373	1,600
8380	120 gal. with 2" x 2 lb. density insulation	G		1.40	5.714		1,250	310		1,560	1,850
8400	120 gal. with 2" x 2 lb. density insul., 40 S.F. heat coil	G	↓	1.40	5.714	↓	1,575	310		1,885	2,200
8500	Water storage module, plastic										
8600	Tubular, 12" diameter, 4' high	G	1 Carp	48	.167	Ea.	103	7.35		110.35	124
8610	12" diameter, 8' high	G		40	.200		159	8.80		167.80	189
8620	18" diameter, 5' high	G		38	.211		174	9.30		183.30	205
8630	18" diameter, 10' high	G	↓	32	.250		229	11.05		240.05	269
8640	58" diameter, 5' high	G	2 Carp	32	.500	↓	490	22		512	570

23 56 Solar Energy Heating Equipment

23 56 19 - Solar Heating Components

23 56 19.50 Solar Heating Ancillary	Crew	Daily Output	Labor-Hours	Unit	Material	2012 Bare Costs Labor	Equipment	Total	Total Incl O&P
8650	Cap, 12" diameter	G			Ea.	19			19	21
8660	18" diameter	G			▼	24			24	26.50

23 57 Heat Exchangers for HVAC

23 57 16 - Steam-to-Water Heat Exchangers

23 57 16.10 Shell/Tube Type Steam-to-Water Heat Exch.

		Crew	Daily Output	Labor-Hours	Unit	Material	2012 Bare Costs Labor	Equipment	Total	Total Incl O&P
0010	**SHELL AND TUBE TYPE STEAM-TO-WATER HEAT EXCHANGERS**									
0016	Shell & tube type, 2 or 4 pass, 3/4" O.D. copper tubes,									
0020	C.I. heads, C.I. tube sheet, steel shell									
0100	Hot water 40°F to 180°F, by steam at 10 PSI									
0120	8 GPM	Q-5	6	2.667	Ea.	1,925	134		2,059	2,325
0140	10 GPM		5	3.200		2,900	160		3,060	3,450
0160	40 GPM		4	4		4,500	201		4,701	5,250
0180	64 GPM		2	8		6,900	400		7,300	8,200
0200	96 GPM	▼	1	16		9,250	800		10,050	11,400
0220	120 GPM	Q-6	1.50	16		12,100	830		12,930	14,600
0240	168 GPM		1	24		14,900	1,250		16,150	18,300
0260	240 GPM		.80	30		23,300	1,550		24,850	28,000
0300	600 GPM	▼	.70	34.286	▼	49,900	1,775		51,675	57,500
0500	For bronze head and tube sheet, add					50%				

23 57 19 - Liquid-to-Liquid Heat Exchangers

23 57 19.13 Plate-Type, Liquid-to-Liquid Heat Exchangers

		Crew	Daily Output	Labor-Hours	Unit	Material	2012 Bare Costs Labor	Equipment	Total	Total Incl O&P
0010	**PLATE-TYPE, LIQUID-TO-LIQUID HEAT EXCHANGERS**									
3000	Plate type,									
3100	400 GPM	Q-6	.80	30	Ea.	33,600	1,550		35,150	39,300
3120	800 GPM	"	.50	48		58,000	2,500		60,500	67,500
3140	1200 GPM	Q-7	.34	94.118		86,000	5,000		91,000	102,000
3160	1800 GPM	"	.24	133	▼	114,000	7,075		121,075	136,000

23 57 19.16 Shell-Type, Liquid-to-Liquid Heat Exchangers

		Crew	Daily Output	Labor-Hours	Unit	Material	2012 Bare Costs Labor	Equipment	Total	Total Incl O&P
0010	**SHELL-TYPE, LIQUID-TO-LIQUID HEAT EXCHANGERS**									
1000	Hot water 40°F to 140°F, by water at 200°F									
1020	7 GPM	Q-5	6	2.667	Ea.	2,375	134		2,509	2,800
1040	16 GPM		5	3.200		3,350	160		3,510	3,950
1060	34 GPM		4	4		5,100	201		5,301	5,900
1080	55 GPM		3	5.333		7,400	267		7,667	8,525
1100	74 GPM		1.50	10.667		9,225	535		9,760	10,900
1120	86 GPM	▼	1.40	11.429		12,300	575		12,875	14,500
1140	112 GPM	Q-6	2	12		15,400	625		16,025	17,800
1160	126 GPM		1.80	13.333		19,200	695		19,895	22,200
1180	152 GPM	▼	1	24	▼	24,500	1,250		25,750	28,800

23 61 Refrigerant Compressors

23 61 15 – Rotary Refrigerant Compressors

23 61 15.10 Rotary Compressors

23 61 15.10 Rotary Compressors	Crew	Daily Output	Labor-Hours	Unit	Material	2012 Bare Costs Labor	Equipment	Total	Total Incl O&P
0010 **ROTARY COMPRESSORS**									
0100 Refrigeration, hermetic, switches and protective devices									
0210 1.25 ton	1 Stpi	3	2.667	Ea.	221	149		370	465
0220 1.42 ton		3	2.667		223	149		372	470
0230 1.68 ton		2.80	2.857		243	159		402	505
0240 2.00 ton		2.60	3.077		250	171		421	535
0250 2.37 ton		2.50	3.200		282	178		460	580
0260 2.67 ton		2.40	3.333		296	186		482	605
0270 3.53 ton		2.30	3.478		325	194		519	645
0280 4.43 ton		2.20	3.636		415	203		618	760
0290 5.08 ton		2.10	3.810		455	212		667	820
0300 5.22 ton		2	4		640	223		863	1,050
0310 7.31 ton	Q-5	3	5.333		1,025	267		1,292	1,525
0320 9.95 ton		2.60	6.154		1,200	310		1,510	1,800
0330 11.6 ton		2.50	6.400		1,550	320		1,870	2,175
0340 15.25 ton		2.30	6.957		2,125	350		2,475	2,850
0350 17.7 ton		2.10	7.619		2,275	380		2,655	3,075

23 61 16 – Reciprocating Refrigerant Compressors

23 61 16.10 Reciprocating Compressors

23 61 16.10 Reciprocating Compressors	Crew	Daily Output	Labor-Hours	Unit	Material	2012 Bare Costs Labor	Equipment	Total	Total Incl O&P
0010 **RECIPROCATING COMPRESSORS**									
0990 Refrigeration, recip. hermetic, switches & protective devices									
1000 10 ton	Q-5	1	16	Ea.	8,850	800		9,650	10,900
1100 20 ton	Q-6	.72	33.333		13,400	1,725		15,125	17,300
1200 30 ton		.64	37.500		15,100	1,950		17,050	19,600
1300 40 ton		.44	54.545		16,600	2,825		19,425	22,600
1400 50 ton		.20	120		17,500	6,250		23,750	28,600
1500 75 ton	Q-7	.27	118		19,300	6,275		25,575	30,800
1600 130 ton	"	.21	152		22,100	8,075		30,175	36,500

23 61 19 – Scroll Refrigerant Compressors

23 61 19.10 Scroll Compressors

23 61 19.10 Scroll Compressors	Crew	Daily Output	Labor-Hours	Unit	Material	2012 Bare Costs Labor	Equipment	Total	Total Incl O&P
0010 **SCROLL COMPRESSORS**									
1800 Refrigeration, scroll type									
1810 1.5 ton	1 Stpi	2.70	2.963	Ea.	885	165		1,050	1,225
1820 2.5 ton		2.50	3.200		885	178		1,063	1,250
1830 2.75 ton		2.35	3.404		935	190		1,125	1,300
1840 3 ton		2.30	3.478		940	194		1,134	1,325
1850 3.5 ton		2.25	3.556		965	198		1,163	1,350
1860 4 ton		2.20	3.636		1,075	203		1,278	1,475
1870 5 ton		2.10	3.810		1,175	212		1,387	1,600
1880 6 ton	Q-5	3.70	4.324		1,550	217		1,767	2,025
1900 7.5 ton		3.20	5		2,600	251		2,851	3,225
1910 10 ton		3.10	5.161		2,750	259		3,009	3,425
1920 13 ton		2.90	5.517		2,975	277		3,252	3,700
1960 25 ton		2.20	7.273		5,075	365		5,440	6,150

23 62 Packaged Compressor and Condenser Units

23 62 13 – Packaged Air-Cooled Refrigerant Compressor and Condenser Units

23 62 13.10 Packaged Air-Cooled Refrig. Condensing Units

23 62 13.10 Packaged Air-Cooled Refrig. Condensing Units	Crew	Daily Output	Labor-Hours	Unit	Material	2012 Bare Costs Labor	Equipment	Total	Total Incl O&P
0010 **PACKAGED AIR-COOLED REFRIGERANT CONDENSING UNITS**									
0020 Condensing unit									
0030 Air cooled, compressor, standard controls									
0050 1.5 ton	Q-5	2.50	6.400	Ea.	1,125	320		1,445	1,700
0100 2 ton		2.10	7.619		1,350	380		1,730	2,050
0200 2.5 ton		1.70	9.412		1,400	470		1,870	2,225
0300 3 ton		1.30	12.308		1,425	615		2,040	2,500
0350 3.5 ton		1.10	14.545		1,650	730		2,380	2,925
0400 4 ton		.90	17.778		1,875	890		2,765	3,400
0500 5 ton		.60	26.667		2,250	1,325		3,575	4,525
0550 7.5 ton		.55	29.091		3,700	1,450		5,150	6,250
0560 8.5 ton		.53	30.189		4,550	1,525		6,075	7,300
0600 10 ton		.50	32		4,950	1,600		6,550	7,875
0620 12.5 ton		.48	33.333		7,475	1,675		9,150	10,700
0650 15 ton	↓	.40	40		8,275	2,000		10,275	12,100
0700 20 ton	Q-6	.40	60		11,200	3,125		14,325	17,000
0720 25 ton		.35	68.571		15,500	3,575		19,075	22,400
0750 30 ton		.30	80		17,800	4,150		21,950	25,900
0800 40 ton		.20	120		22,500	6,250		28,750	34,200
0840 50 ton		.18	133		26,800	6,925		33,725	40,000
0860 60 ton		.16	150		30,900	7,800		38,700	45,800
0900 70 ton		.14	171		35,300	8,900		44,200	52,000
1000 80 ton		.12	200		39,200	10,400		49,600	59,000
1100 100 ton	↓	.09	266	↓	48,100	13,900		62,000	74,000

23 62 23 – Packaged Water-Cooled Refrigerant Compressor and Condenser Units

23 62 23.10 Packaged Water-Cooled Refrigerant Condensing Units

	Crew	Daily Output	Labor-Hours	Unit	Material	2012 Bare Costs Labor	Equipment	Total	Total Incl O&P
0010 **PACKAGED WATER-COOLED REFRIGERANT CONDENSING UNITS**									
2000 Water cooled, compressor, heat exchanger, controls									
2100 5 ton	Q-5	.70	22.857	Ea.	12,600	1,150		13,750	15,600
2110 10 ton		.60	26.667		14,700	1,325		16,025	18,200
2200 15 ton	↓	.50	32		19,900	1,600		21,500	24,300
2300 20 ton	Q-6	.40	60		23,000	3,125		26,125	30,000
2310 30 ton		.30	80		26,400	4,150		30,550	35,300
2400 40 ton		.20	120		28,700	6,250		34,950	41,000
2410 60 ton		.18	133		42,000	6,925		48,925	56,500
2420 80 ton		.14	171		48,500	8,900		57,400	67,000
2500 100 ton		.11	218		59,500	11,300		70,800	82,500
2510 120 ton	↓	.10	240	↓	95,500	12,500		108,000	124,500

23 63 Refrigerant Condensers

23 63 13 – Air-Cooled Refrigerant Condensers

23 63 13.10 Air-Cooled Refrig. Condensers

	Crew	Daily Output	Labor-Hours	Unit	Material	2012 Bare Costs Labor	Equipment	Total	Total Incl O&P
0010 **AIR-COOLED REFRIG. CONDENSERS**, Ratings for 30°F TD, R-22.									
0080 Air cooled, belt drive, propeller fan									
0220 45 ton	Q-6	.70	34.286	Ea.	9,625	1,775		11,400	13,300
0240 50 ton		.69	34.985		10,400	1,825		12,225	14,200
0260 54 ton		.64	37.795		11,300	1,975		13,275	15,500
0280 59 ton		.58	41.308		12,400	2,150		14,550	17,000
0300 65 ton		.53	45.541		14,800	2,375		17,175	19,900
0320 73 ton	↓	.47	51.173	↓	16,300	2,650		18,950	21,900

23 63 13 – Air-Cooled Refrigerant Condensers

23 63 13.10 Air-Cooled Refrig. Condensers

		Crew	Daily Output	Labor-Hours	Unit	Material	2012 Bare Costs Labor	Equipment	Total	Total Incl O&P
0340	81 ton	Q-6	.42	56.738	Ea.	17,900	2,950		20,850	24,200
0360	86 ton		.40	60.302		18,800	3,125		21,925	25,400
0380	88 ton		.39	61.697		20,200	3,200		23,400	27,000
0400	101 ton	Q-7	.45	70.640		25,800	3,750		29,550	34,000
0500	159 ton		.31	102		35,500	5,450		40,950	47,200
0600	228 ton		.22	148		50,000	7,850		57,850	67,000
1500	May be specified single or multi-circuit									
1550	Air cooled, direct drive, propeller fan									
1590	1 ton	Q-5	3.80	4.211	Ea.	685	211		896	1,075
1600	1-1/2 ton		3.60	4.444		840	223		1,063	1,250
1620	2 ton		3.20	5		900	251		1,151	1,375
1630	3 ton		2.40	6.667		1,000	335		1,335	1,600
1640	5 ton		2	8		1,825	400		2,225	2,625
1650	8 ton		1.80	8.889		2,300	445		2,745	3,225
1660	10 ton		1.40	11.429		2,825	575		3,400	3,975
1670	12 ton		1.30	12.308		3,175	615		3,790	4,425
1680	14 ton		1.20	13.333		3,625	670		4,295	5,000
1690	16 ton		1.10	14.545		3,975	730		4,705	5,475
1700	21 ton		1	16		4,575	800		5,375	6,250
1720	26 ton		.84	19.002		5,150	955		6,105	7,100
1740	30 ton		.70	22.792		8,825	1,150		9,975	11,400
1760	41 ton	Q-6	.77	31.008		9,700	1,600		11,300	13,100
1780	52 ton		.66	36.419		13,800	1,900		15,700	18,100
1800	63 ton		.55	44.037		15,300	2,300		17,600	20,300
1820	76 ton		.45	52.980		17,300	2,750		20,050	23,300
1840	86 ton		.40	60		21,400	3,125		24,525	28,300
1860	97 ton		.35	67.989		24,400	3,525		27,925	32,100
1880	105 ton	Q-7	.44	73.563		28,100	3,900		32,000	36,800
1890	118 ton		.39	82.687		30,300	4,375		34,675	39,900
1900	126 ton		.36	88.154		35,200	4,675		39,875	45,800
1910	136 ton		.34	95.238		39,400	5,050		44,450	51,000
1920	142 ton		.32	99.379		40,400	5,275		45,675	52,500

23 63 30 – Lubricants

23 63 30.10 Lubricant Oils

		Crew	Daily Output	Labor-Hours	Unit	Material	2012 Bare Costs Labor	Equipment	Total	Total Incl O&P
0010	**LUBRICANT OILS**									
8000	Oils									
8100	Lubricating									
8120	Oil, lubricating				Oz.	.32			.32	.35
8500	Refrigeration									
8520	Oil, refrigeration				Gal.	41.50			41.50	45.50
8525	Oil, refrigeration				Qt.	10.40			10.40	11.40

23 63 33 – Evaporative Refrigerant Condensers

23 63 33.10 Evaporative Condensers

		Crew	Daily Output	Labor-Hours	Unit	Material	2012 Bare Costs Labor	Equipment	Total	Total Incl O&P
0010	**EVAPORATIVE CONDENSERS**									
3400	Evaporative, copper coil, pump, fan motor									
3440	10 ton	Q-5	.54	29.630	Ea.	8,725	1,475		10,200	11,900
3460	15 ton		.50	32		8,925	1,600		10,525	12,300
3480	20 ton		.47	34.043		9,200	1,700		10,900	12,700
3500	25 ton		.45	35.556		9,400	1,775		11,175	13,000
3520	30 ton		.42	38.095		9,875	1,900		11,775	13,800
3540	40 ton	Q-6	.49	48.980		10,800	2,550		13,350	15,700
3560	50 ton		.39	61.538		12,200	3,200		15,400	18,200

23 63 Refrigerant Condensers

23 63 33 – Evaporative Refrigerant Condensers

23 63 33.10 Evaporative Condensers	Crew	Daily Output	Labor-Hours	Unit	Material	2012 Bare Costs Labor	Equipment	Total	Total Incl O&P
3580	65 ton	Q-6	.35	68.571	Ea.	13,000	3,575		16,575	19,700
3600	80 ton		.33	72.727		14,400	3,775		18,175	21,500
3620	90 ton		.29	82.759		15,800	4,300		20,100	23,800
3640	100 ton	Q-7	.36	88.889		17,400	4,725		22,125	26,200
3660	110 ton		.33	96.970		18,200	5,150		23,350	27,900
3680	125 ton		.30	106		19,700	5,650		25,350	30,200
3700	135 ton		.28	114		20,800	6,050		26,850	32,000
3720	150 ton		.25	128		22,600	6,800		29,400	35,000
3740	165 ton		.23	139		23,900	7,375		31,275	37,400
3760	185 ton		.22	145		27,000	7,725		34,725	41,300
3860	For fan damper control, add	Q-5	2	8		820	400		1,220	1,500

23 64 Packaged Water Chillers

23 64 13 – Absorption Water Chillers

23 64 13.13 Direct-Fired Absorption Water Chillers

		Crew	Daily Output	Labor-Hours	Unit	Material	2012 Bare Costs Labor	Equipment	Total	Total Incl O&P
0010	**DIRECT-FIRED ABSORPTION WATER CHILLERS**									
3000	Gas fired, air cooled									
3220	5 ton	Q-5	.60	26.667	Ea.	9,325	1,325		10,650	12,200
3270	10 ton	"	.40	40	"	25,500	2,000		27,500	31,000
4000	Water cooled, duplex									
4130	100 ton	Q-7	.13	246	Ea.	136,000	13,100		149,100	169,000
4140	200 ton		.11	283		183,000	15,000		198,000	224,000
4150	300 ton		.11	299		219,500	15,900		235,400	265,500
4160	400 ton		.10	316		285,500	16,800		302,300	339,500
4170	500 ton		.10	329		359,500	17,500		377,000	421,500
4180	600 ton		.09	340		424,500	18,100		442,600	493,500
4190	700 ton		.09	359		470,500	19,100		489,600	546,500
4200	800 ton		.08	380		568,000	20,200		588,200	655,500
4210	900 ton		.08	400		658,000	21,200		679,200	756,000
4220	1000 ton		.08	421		731,500	22,300		753,800	838,000

23 64 13.16 Indirect-Fired Absorption Water Chillers

		Crew	Daily Output	Labor-Hours	Unit	Material	2012 Bare Costs Labor	Equipment	Total	Total Incl O&P
0010	**INDIRECT-FIRED ABSORPTION WATER CHILLERS**									
0020	Steam or hot water, water cooled									
0050	100 ton	Q-7	.13	240	Ea.	125,000	12,700		137,700	156,500
0100	148 ton		.12	258		207,500	13,700		221,200	248,500
0200	200 ton		.12	275		231,000	14,600		245,600	276,000
0240	250 ton		.11	290		254,000	15,400		269,400	303,000
0300	354 ton		.11	304		317,500	16,200		333,700	373,500
0400	420 ton		.10	323		347,000	17,100		364,100	407,500
0500	665 ton		.09	340		487,000	18,100		505,100	563,000
0600	750 ton		.09	363		569,000	19,300		588,300	655,000
0700	850 ton		.08	385		607,500	20,400		627,900	699,500
0800	955 ton		.08	410		649,500	21,800		671,300	747,500
0900	1125 ton		.08	421		750,000	22,300		772,300	858,500
1000	1250 ton		.07	444		806,500	23,600		830,100	922,500
1100	1465 ton		.07	463		956,000	24,600		980,600	1,089,000
1200	1660 ton		.07	477		1,125,000	25,300		1,150,300	1,275,500
2000	For two stage unit, add					80%	25%			

23 64 Packaged Water Chillers

23 64 16 – Centrifugal Water Chillers

23 64 16.10 Centrifugal Type Water Chillers	Crew	Daily Output	Labor-Hours	Unit	Material	Labor	Equipment	Total	Total Incl O&P
0010 **CENTRIFUGAL TYPE WATER CHILLERS**, With standard controls									
0020 Centrifugal liquid chiller, water cooled									
0030 not including water tower									
0100 2000 ton (twin 1000 ton units)	Q-7	.07	477	Ea.	865,500	25,300		890,800	990,000
0274 Centrifugal, packaged unit, water cooled, not incl. tower									
0280 400 ton	Q-7	.11	283	Ea.	129,500	15,000		144,500	165,000
0282 450 ton		.11	290		194,500	15,400		209,900	237,500
0290 500 ton		.11	296		216,500	15,700		232,200	261,500
0292 550 ton		.11	304		238,000	16,200		254,200	286,500
0300 600 ton		.10	310		259,500	16,500		276,000	310,500
0302 650 ton		.10	320		281,500	17,000		298,500	335,000
0304 700 ton		.10	326		303,000	17,300		320,300	359,000
0306 750 ton		.10	333		324,500	17,700		342,200	383,500
0310 800 ton		.09	340		346,000	18,100		364,100	408,000
0312 850 ton		.09	351		368,000	18,700		386,700	432,500
0316 900 ton		.09	359		389,500	19,100		408,600	457,500
0318 950 ton		.09	363		411,000	19,300		430,300	481,000
0320 1000 ton		.09	372		433,000	19,700		452,700	506,000
0324 1100 ton		.08	385		463,000	20,400		483,400	540,500
0330 1200 ton		.08	395		505,000	21,000		526,000	587,000
0340 1300 ton		.08	410		547,000	21,800		568,800	635,000
0350 1400 ton		.08	421		589,500	22,300		611,800	681,000
0360 1500 ton		.08	426		631,500	22,600		654,100	728,500
0370 1600 ton		.07	438		673,500	23,300		696,800	776,000
0380 1700 ton		.07	450		715,500	23,900		739,400	823,000
0390 1800 ton		.07	457		757,500	24,200		781,700	870,000
0400 1900 ton		.07	470		799,500	25,000		824,500	917,000
0430 2000 ton		.07	492		842,000	26,100		868,100	965,500
0440 2500 ton	▼	.06	524	▼	1,052,000	27,800		1,079,800	1,199,500

23 64 19 – Reciprocating Water Chillers

23 64 19.10 Reciprocating Type Water Chillers

	Crew	Daily Output	Labor-Hours	Unit	Material	Labor	Equipment	Total	Total Incl O&P
0010 **RECIPROCATING TYPE WATER CHILLERS**, With standard controls									
0494 Water chillers, integral air cooled condenser									
0538 60 ton cooling	Q-7	.28	115	Ea.	47,700	6,100		53,800	61,500
0546 70 ton cooling		.27	119		54,500	6,350		60,850	69,500
0552 80 ton cooling		.26	123		59,000	6,525		65,525	75,000
0554 90 ton cooling		.25	125		63,500	6,675		70,175	79,500
0600 100 ton cooling		.25	129		71,500	6,850		78,350	89,000
0620 110 ton cooling		.24	132		76,500	7,025		83,525	94,500
0630 130 ton cooling		.24	135		91,000	7,150		98,150	111,000
0640 150 ton cooling		.23	137		101,000	7,325		108,325	122,000
0650 175 ton cooling		.23	140		113,000	7,475		120,475	136,000
0654 190 ton cooling		.22	144		124,500	7,650		132,150	148,500
0660 210 ton cooling		.22	148		128,000	7,850		135,850	153,000
0662 250 ton cooling		.21	151		148,500	8,050		156,550	175,500
0664 275 ton cooling		.21	156		154,000	8,275		162,275	181,500
0666 300 ton cooling		.20	160		172,000	8,475		180,475	202,500
0668 330 ton cooling		.20	164		201,000	8,700		209,700	234,000
0670 360 ton cooling		.19	168		221,000	8,925		229,925	256,500
0672 390 ton cooling		.19	172		234,000	9,175		243,175	271,500
0674 420 ton cooling	▼	.18	177	▼	244,500	9,425		253,925	283,000
0980 Water cooled, multiple compressor, semi-hermetic, tower not incl.									

23 64 Packaged Water Chillers

23 64 19 – Reciprocating Water Chillers

23 64 19.10 Reciprocating Type Water Chillers		Crew	Daily Output	Labor-Hours	Unit	Material	2012 Bare Costs Labor	Equipment	Total	Total Incl O&P
1000	15 ton cooling	Q-6	.36	65.934	Ea.	17,500	3,425		20,925	24,500
1020	25 ton cooling	Q-7	.41	78.049		18,900	4,150		23,050	27,100
1040	28 ton cooling		.36	89.888		20,200	4,775		24,975	29,400
1060	35 ton cooling		.31	101		22,600	5,400		28,000	33,000
1080	40 ton cooling		.30	108		30,200	5,725		35,925	41,900
1100	50 ton cooling		.28	113		32,300	6,050		38,350	44,600
1120	60 ton cooling		.25	125		35,400	6,675		42,075	49,000
1130	75 ton cooling		.23	139		48,900	7,375		56,275	65,000
1140	85 ton cooling		.21	151		51,000	8,050		59,050	68,000
1150	95 ton cooling		.19	164		54,500	8,750		63,250	73,000
1160	100 ton cooling		.18	179		58,500	9,525		68,025	79,000
1170	115 ton cooling		.17	190		61,500	10,100		71,600	82,500
1180	125 ton cooling		.16	196		66,500	10,400		76,900	88,500
1200	145 ton cooling		.16	202		77,500	10,700		88,200	101,500
1210	155 ton cooling		.15	210		82,000	11,200		93,200	107,000
1300	Water cooled, single compressor, semi-hermetic, tower not incl.									
1320	40 ton cooling,	Q-7	.30	108	Ea.	16,800	5,725		22,525	27,200
1340	50 ton cooling		.28	113		20,800	6,050		26,850	32,000
1360	60 ton cooling		.25	125		23,100	6,675		29,775	35,600
1451	Water cooled, dual compressors, semi-hermetic, tower not incl.									
1500	80 ton cooling	Q-7	.14	222	Ea.	28,800	11,800		40,600	49,400
1520	100 ton cooling		.14	228		38,800	12,100		50,900	61,000
1540	120 ton cooling		.14	231		47,100	12,300		59,400	70,500
4000	Packaged chiller, remote air cooled condensers not incl.									
4020	15 ton cooling	Q-7	.30	108	Ea.	14,600	5,725		20,325	24,800
4030	20 ton cooling		.28	115		15,900	6,150		22,050	26,800
4040	25 ton cooling		.25	125		18,000	6,675		24,675	29,900
4050	35 ton cooling		.24	133		19,400	7,100		26,500	32,000
4060	40 ton cooling		.22	144		22,700	7,650		30,350	36,400
4070	50 ton cooling		.21	153		26,300	8,150		34,450	41,300
4080	60 ton cooling		.20	164		30,700	8,700		39,400	46,800
4090	75 ton cooling		.18	173		39,300	9,225		48,525	57,000
4100	85 ton cooling		.17	183		41,300	9,750		51,050	60,000
4110	95 ton cooling		.17	193		44,500	10,300		54,800	64,500
4120	105 ton cooling		.16	203		48,000	10,800		58,800	69,500
4130	115 ton cooling		.15	213		52,000	11,300		63,300	74,000
4140	125 ton cooling		.14	223		55,500	11,900		67,400	79,000
4150	145 ton cooling		.14	233		77,500	12,400		89,900	104,000

23 64 23 – Scroll Water Chillers

23 64 23.10 Scroll Water Chillers

		Crew	Daily Output	Labor-Hours	Unit	Material	2012 Bare Costs Labor	Equipment	Total	Total Incl O&P
0010	**SCROLL WATER CHILLERS**, With standard controls									
0490	Packaged w/integral air cooled condenser, 15 ton cool	Q-7	.37	86.486	Ea.	20,400	4,575		24,975	29,400
0500	20 ton cooling		.34	94.118		26,400	5,000		31,400	36,500
0510	25 ton cooling		.34	94.118		27,600	5,000		32,600	37,900
0515	30 ton cooling		.31	101		28,300	5,400		33,700	39,300
0517	35 ton cooling		.31	104		31,800	5,575		37,375	43,400
0520	40 ton cooling		.30	108		34,100	5,725		39,825	46,200
0528	45 ton cooling		.29	109		35,300	5,825		41,125	47,700
0536	50 ton cooling		.28	113		39,000	6,000		45,000	52,000
0680	Scroll water cooled, single compressor, hermetic, tower not incl.									
0700	2 ton cooling	Q-5	.57	28.070	Ea.	3,400	1,400		4,800	5,850
0710	5 ton cooling		.57	28.070		4,050	1,400		5,450	6,575

23 64 Packaged Water Chillers

23 64 23 – Scroll Water Chillers

23 64 23.10 Scroll Water Chillers

23 64 23.10 Scroll Water Chillers		Crew	Daily Output	Labor-Hours	Unit	Material	2012 Bare Costs Labor	Equipment	Total	Total Incl O&P
0720	6 ton cooling	Q-5	.42	38.005	Ea.	5,100	1,900		7,000	8,475
0740	8 ton cooling	↓	.31	52.117		5,575	2,625		8,200	10,100
0760	10 ton cooling	Q-6	.36	67.039		6,425	3,475		9,900	12,300
0780	15 ton cooling	"	.33	72.727		10,100	3,775		13,875	16,800
0800	20 ton cooling	Q-7	.38	83.990		11,500	4,450		15,950	19,300
0820	30 ton cooling	"	.33	96.096	↓	12,900	5,100		18,000	21,800

23 64 26 – Rotary-Screw Water Chillers

23 64 26.10 Rotary-Screw Type Water Chillers

23 64 26.10 Rotary-Screw Type Water Chillers		Crew	Daily Output	Labor-Hours	Unit	Material	2012 Bare Costs Labor	Equipment	Total	Total Incl O&P
0010	**ROTARY-SCREW TYPE WATER CHILLERS**, With standard controls									
0110	Screw, liquid chiller, air cooled, insulated evaporator									
0120	130 ton	Q-7	.14	228	Ea.	86,500	12,100		98,600	113,500
0124	160 ton		.13	246		106,500	13,100		119,600	136,500
0128	180 ton		.13	250		119,500	13,300		132,800	151,500
0132	210 ton		.12	258		132,000	13,700		145,700	165,500
0136	270 ton		.12	266		150,500	14,100		164,600	187,500
0140	320 ton	↓	.12	275	↓	189,000	14,600		203,600	230,000
0200	Packaged unit, water cooled, not incl. tower									
0210	80 ton	Q-7	.14	223	Ea.	43,400	11,900		55,300	65,500
0220	100 ton		.14	230		54,000	12,200		66,200	78,000
0230	150 ton		.13	240		72,000	12,800		84,800	98,000
0240	200 ton		.13	251		82,000	13,400		95,400	110,000
0250	250 ton		.12	260		98,000	13,800		111,800	129,000
0260	300 ton		.12	266		113,000	14,100		127,100	145,500
0270	350 ton	↓	.12	275	↓	162,000	14,600		176,600	200,000
1450	Water cooled, tower not included									
1560	135 ton cooling, screw compressors	Q-7	.14	235	Ea.	57,500	12,500		70,000	82,500
1580	150 ton cooling, screw compressors		.13	240		67,000	12,800		79,800	92,500
1620	200 ton cooling, screw compressors		.13	250		92,000	13,300		105,300	121,500
1660	291 ton cooling, screw compressors	↓	.12	260	↓	96,000	13,800		109,800	127,000

23 64 33 – Direct Expansion Water Chillers

23 64 33.10 Direct Expansion Type Water Chillers

23 64 33.10 Direct Expansion Type Water Chillers		Crew	Daily Output	Labor-Hours	Unit	Material	2012 Bare Costs Labor	Equipment	Total	Total Incl O&P
0010	**DIRECT EXPANSION TYPE WATER CHILLERS**, With standard controls									
8000	Direct expansion, shell and tube type, for built up systems									
8020	1 ton	Q-5	2	8	Ea.	6,900	400		7,300	8,200
8030	5 ton		1.90	8.421		11,500	420		11,920	13,200
8040	10 ton		1.70	9.412		14,200	470		14,670	16,300
8050	20 ton		1.50	10.667		16,300	535		16,835	18,700
8060	30 ton		1	16		20,700	800		21,500	24,000
8070	50 ton	↓	.90	17.778		33,200	890		34,090	38,000
8080	100 ton	Q-6	.90	26.667	↓	59,000	1,375		60,375	67,000

385

23 65 Cooling Towers

23 65 13 – Forced-Draft Cooling Towers

23 65 13.10 Forced-Draft Type Cooling Towers	Crew	Daily Output	Labor-Hours	Unit	Material	2012 Bare Costs Labor	Equipment	Total	Total Incl O&P
0010 **FORCED-DRAFT TYPE COOLING TOWERS**, Packaged units D3030-310									
0070 Galvanized steel									
0080 Induced draft, crossflow									
0100 Vertical, belt drive, 61 tons	Q-6	90	.267	TonAC	197	13.85		210.85	237
0150 100 ton		100	.240		190	12.50		202.50	228
0200 115 ton		109	.220		165	11.45		176.45	199
0250 131 ton		120	.200		198	10.40		208.40	234
0260 162 ton		132	.182		160	9.45		169.45	191
1000 For higher capacities, use multiples									
1500 Induced air, double flow									
1900 Vertical, gear drive, 167 ton	Q-6	126	.190	TonAC	156	9.90		165.90	186
2000 297 ton		129	.186		96	9.65		105.65	121
2100 582 ton		132	.182		53.50	9.45		62.95	73
2150 849 ton		142	.169		72	8.80		80.80	92.50
2200 1016 ton		150	.160		72.50	8.30		80.80	92.50
2500 Blow through, centrifugal type									
2510 50 ton	Q-6	2.28	10.526	Ea.	11,200	545		11,745	13,100
2520 75 ton		1.52	15.789		14,400	820		15,220	17,200
2524 100 ton		1.22	19.672		17,100	1,025		18,125	20,400
2528 125 ton	Q-7	1.31	24.427		19,900	1,300		21,200	23,900
2532 200 ton		.82	39.216		26,800	2,075		28,875	32,600
2536 250 ton		.65	49.231		31,100	2,600		33,700	38,200
2540 300 ton		.54	59.259		35,800	3,150		38,950	44,100
2544 350 ton		.47	68.085		40,400	3,600		44,000	50,000
2548 400 ton		.41	78.049		42,100	4,150		46,250	52,500
2552 450 ton		.36	88.154		50,500	4,675		55,175	62,500
2556 500 ton		.32	100		54,000	5,300		59,300	67,500
2560 550 ton		.30	107		58,000	5,725		63,725	72,500
2564 600 ton		.27	117		61,000	6,250		67,250	76,500
2568 650 ton		.25	127		68,000	6,750		74,750	84,500
2572 700 ton		.23	137		79,500	7,275		86,775	98,500
2576 750 ton		.22	146		85,500	7,775		93,275	105,500
2580 800 ton		.21	152		92,500	8,075		100,575	113,500
2584 850 ton		.20	156		98,000	8,325		106,325	120,500
2588 900 ton		.20	161		104,000	8,575		112,575	127,500
2592 950 ton		.19	170		109,500	9,025		118,525	134,000
2596 1000 ton		.18	180		113,000	9,600		122,600	139,000
2700 Axial fan, induced draft									
2710 50 ton	Q-6	2.28	10.526	Ea.	9,725	545		10,270	11,500
2720 75 ton		1.52	15.789		11,400	820		12,220	13,900
2724 100 ton		1.22	19.672		12,100	1,025		13,125	14,900
2728 125 ton	Q-7	1.31	24.427		14,900	1,300		16,200	18,400
2732 200 ton		.82	39.216		25,300	2,075		27,375	30,900
2736 250 ton		.65	49.231		28,500	2,600		31,100	35,400
2740 300 ton		.54	59.259		33,300	3,150		36,450	41,500
2744 350 ton		.47	68.085		35,700	3,600		39,300	44,800
2748 400 ton		.41	78.049		40,900	4,150		45,050	51,500
2752 450 ton		.36	88.154		45,400	4,675		50,075	57,000
2756 500 ton		.32	100		48,200	5,300		53,500	61,000
2760 550 ton		.30	107		54,000	5,725		59,725	68,000
2764 600 ton		.27	117		57,000	6,250		63,250	72,000
2768 650 ton		.25	127		62,000	6,750		68,750	78,500
2772 700 ton		.23	137		70,500	7,275		77,775	88,500

23 65 Cooling Towers

23 65 13 – Forced-Draft Cooling Towers

23 65 13.10 Forced-Draft Type Cooling Towers

		Crew	Daily Output	Labor-Hours	Unit	Material	2012 Bare Costs Labor	Equipment	Total	Total Incl O&P
2776	750 ton	Q-7	.22	146	Ea.	73,500	7,775		81,275	92,000
2780	800 ton		.21	152		76,500	8,075		84,575	96,000
2784	850 ton		.20	156		77,000	8,325		85,325	97,500
2788	900 ton		.20	161		80,000	8,575		88,575	101,000
2792	950 ton		.19	170		84,500	9,025		93,525	106,000
2796	1000 ton		.18	180		89,000	9,600		98,600	112,500
3000	For higher capacities, use multiples									
3500	For pumps and piping, add	Q-6	38	.632	TonAC	98.50	33		131.50	158
4000	For absorption systems, add				"	75%	75%			
4100	Cooling water chemical feeder	Q-5	3	5.333	Ea.	345	267		612	785
5000	Fiberglass tower on galvanized steel support structure									
5010	Draw thru									
5100	100 ton	Q-6	1.40	17.143	Ea.	10,100	890		10,990	12,500
5120	120 ton		1.20	20		11,700	1,050		12,750	14,500
5140	140 ton		1	24		12,700	1,250		13,950	15,900
5160	160 ton		.80	30		14,100	1,550		15,650	17,900
5180	180 ton		.65	36.923		16,000	1,925		17,925	20,500
5200	200 ton		.48	50		18,100	2,600		20,700	23,800
5300	For stainless steel support structure, add					30%				
5360	For higher capacities, use multiples of each size									
6000	Stainless steel									
6010	Induced draft, crossflow, horizontal, belt drive									
6100	57 ton	Q-6	1.50	16	Ea.	25,300	830		26,130	29,100
6120	91 ton		.99	24.242		30,600	1,250		31,850	35,500
6140	111 ton		.43	55.814		38,900	2,900		41,800	47,100
6160	126 ton		.22	109		38,900	5,675		44,575	51,500
6170	Induced draft, crossflow, vertical, gear drive									
6172	167 ton	Q-6	.75	32	Ea.	49,600	1,675		51,275	57,000
6174	297 ton		.43	55.814		55,000	2,900		57,900	65,000
6176	582 ton		.23	104		87,500	5,425		92,925	104,000
6178	849 ton		.17	141		123,500	7,350		130,850	146,500
6180	1016 ton		.15	160		148,000	8,325		156,325	175,500

23 72 Air-to-Air Energy Recovery Equipment

23 72 13 – Heat-Wheel Air-to-Air Energy-Recovery Equipment

23 72 13.10 Heat-Wheel Air-to-Air Energy Recovery Equip.

			Crew	Daily Output	Labor-Hours	Unit	Material	2012 Bare Costs Labor	Equipment	Total	Total Incl O&P
0010	**HEAT-WHEEL AIR-TO-AIR ENERGY RECOVERY EQUIPMENT**										
0100	Air to air										
4000	Enthalpy recovery wheel										
4010	1000 max CFM	G	Q-9	1.20	13.333	Ea.	6,225	625		6,850	7,800
4020	2000 max CFM	G		1	16		7,300	750		8,050	9,175
4030	4000 max CFM	G		.80	20		8,450	940		9,390	10,700
4040	6000 max CFM	G		.70	22.857		9,850	1,075		10,925	12,400
4050	8000 max CFM	G	Q-10	1	24		10,900	1,175		12,075	13,800
4060	10,000 max CFM	G		.90	26.667		13,000	1,300		14,300	16,300
4070	20,000 max CFM	G		.80	30		23,600	1,450		25,050	28,200
4080	25,000 max CFM	G		.70	34.286		28,900	1,675		30,575	34,400
4090	30,000 max CFM	G		.50	48		32,000	2,325		34,325	38,900
4100	40,000 max CFM	G		.45	53.333		44,200	2,600		46,800	52,500
4110	50,000 max CFM	G		.40	60		51,500	2,925		54,425	61,000

23 72 Air-to-Air Energy Recovery Equipment

23 72 16 – Heat-Pipe Air-To-Air Energy-Recovery Equipment

23 72 16.10 Heat Pipes	Crew	Daily Output	Labor-Hours	Unit	Material	2012 Bare Costs Labor	Equipment	Total	Total Incl O&P
0010 **HEAT PIPES**									
8000 Heat pipe type, glycol, 50% efficient									
8010 100 MBH, 1700 CFM	1 Stpi	.80	10	Ea.	3,925	555		4,480	5,150
8020 160 MBH, 2700 CFM		.60	13.333		5,250	745		5,995	6,900
8030 620 MBH, 4000 CFM	↓	.40	20	↓	7,950	1,125		9,075	10,400

23 73 Indoor Central-Station Air-Handling Units

23 73 13 – Modular Indoor Central-Station Air-Handling Units

23 73 13.10 Air Handling Units

	Crew	Daily Output	Labor-Hours	Unit	Material	2012 Bare Costs Labor	Equipment	Total	Total Incl O&P
0010 **AIR HANDLING UNITS**, Built-Up									
0100 With cooling/heating coil section, filters, mixing box									
0880 Single zone, horizontal/vertical									
0890 Constant volume									
0900 1600 CFM	Q-5	1.20	13.333	Ea.	3,425	670		4,095	4,775
0906 2000 CFM		1.10	14.545		4,300	730		5,030	5,825
0910 3000 CFM		1	16		5,350	800		6,150	7,100
0916 4000 CFM	↓	.95	16.842		7,150	845		7,995	9,125
0920 5000 CFM	Q-6	1.40	17.143		8,925	890		9,815	11,200
0926 6500 CFM		1.30	18.462		11,600	960		12,560	14,300
0930 7500 CFM		1.20	20		13,400	1,050		14,450	16,300
0936 9200 CFM		1.10	21.818		16,400	1,125		17,525	19,800
0940 11,500 CFM		1	24		18,100	1,250		19,350	21,800
0946 13,200 CFM		.90	26.667		20,800	1,375		22,175	24,900
0950 16,500 CFM		.80	30		25,900	1,550		27,450	30,900
0960 19,500 CFM		.70	34.286		30,700	1,775		32,475	36,400
0970 22,000 CFM		.60	40		34,600	2,075		36,675	41,200
0980 27,000 CFM		.50	48		38,600	2,500		41,100	46,300
0990 34,000 CFM		.40	60		48,600	3,125		51,725	58,000
1000 40,000 CFM		.30	80		53,000	4,150		57,150	65,000
1010 47,000 CFM	↓	.20	120		67,000	6,250		73,250	83,500
1140 60,000 CFM	Q-7	.18	177		75,000	9,425		84,425	96,000
1160 75,000 CFM	"	.16	200	↓	93,500	10,600		104,100	119,000
2000 Variable air volume									
2100 75,000 CFM	Q-7	.12	266	Ea.	94,500	14,100		108,600	125,500
2140 100,000 CFM		.11	290		129,000	15,400		144,400	165,500
2160 150,000 CFM	↓	.10	320	↓	197,000	17,000		214,000	242,500
2300 Multi-zone, horizontal or vertical, blow-thru fan									
2310 3000 CFM	Q-5	1	16	Ea.	6,250	800		7,050	8,075
2314 4000 CFM	"	.95	16.842		8,250	845		9,095	10,400
2318 5000 CFM	Q-6	1.40	17.143		10,300	890		11,190	12,700
2322 6500 CFM		1.30	18.462		13,300	960		14,260	16,200
2326 7500 CFM		1.20	20		15,400	1,050		16,450	18,500
2330 9200 CFM		1.10	21.818		19,000	1,125		20,125	22,600
2334 11,500 CFM		1	24		20,900	1,250		22,150	24,900
2336 13,200 CFM		.90	26.667		23,900	1,375		25,275	28,400
2340 16,500 CFM		.80	30		29,800	1,550		31,350	35,200
2344 19,500 CFM		.70	34.286		35,200	1,775		36,975	41,400
2348 22,000 CFM		.60	40		39,700	2,075		41,775	46,800
2352 27,000 CFM		.50	48		44,400	2,500		46,900	52,500
2356 34,000 CFM	↓	.40	60	↓	56,000	3,125		59,125	66,000

23 73 Indoor Central-Station Air-Handling Units

23 73 13 – Modular Indoor Central-Station Air-Handling Units

23 73 13.10 Air Handling Units

		Crew	Daily Output	Labor-Hours	Unit	Material	2012 Bare Costs Labor	Equipment	Total	Total Incl O&P
2360	40,000 CFM	Q-6	.30	80	Ea.	60,500	4,150		64,650	73,500
2364	47,000 CFM	↓	.20	120	↓	77,000	6,250		83,250	94,500

23 73 13.20 Air Handling Units, Packaged Indoor Type

		Crew	Daily Output	Labor-Hours	Unit	Material	2012 Bare Costs Labor	Equipment	Total	Total Incl O&P
0010	**AIR HANDLING UNITS, PACKAGED INDOOR TYPE**									
0040	Cooling coils may be chilled water or DX									
0050	Heating coils may be hot water, steam or electric									
1090	Constant volume									
1200	2000 CFM	Q-5	1.10	14.545	Ea.	9,950	730		10,680	12,000
1400	5000 CFM	Q-6	.80	30		14,600	1,550		16,150	18,400
1550	10,000 CFM		.54	44.444		32,400	2,300		34,700	39,100
1670	15,000 CFM		.38	63.158		46,700	3,275		49,975	56,500
1700	20,000 CFM		.31	77.419		58,500	4,025		62,525	70,000
1710	30,000 CFM	↓	.27	88.889	↓	78,500	4,625		83,125	93,500
2300	Variable air volume									
2330	2000 CFM	Q-5	1	16	Ea.	12,100	800		12,900	14,500
2340	5000 CFM	Q-6	.70	34.286		18,000	1,775		19,775	22,500
2350	10,000 CFM		.50	48		34,600	2,500		37,100	41,900
2360	15,000 CFM		.40	60		49,500	3,125		52,625	59,000
2370	20,000 CFM		.29	82.759		64,500	4,300		68,800	77,500
2380	30,000 CFM	↓	.20	120		88,500	6,250		94,750	107,000

23 73 39 – Indoor, Direct Gas-Fired Heating and Ventilating Units

23 73 39.10 Make-Up Air Unit

		Crew	Daily Output	Labor-Hours	Unit	Material	2012 Bare Costs Labor	Equipment	Total	Total Incl O&P
0010	**MAKE-UP AIR UNIT**									
0020	Indoor suspension, natural/LP gas, direct fired,									
0032	standard control. For flue see Section 23 51 23.10									
0040	70°F temperature rise, MBH is input									
0100	75 MBH input	Q-6	3.60	6.667	Ea.	2,400	345		2,745	3,175
0120	100 MBH input		3.40	7.059		2,425	365		2,790	3,225
0140	125 MBH input		3.20	7.500		2,550	390		2,940	3,400
0160	150 MBH input		3	8		2,850	415		3,265	3,750
0180	175 MBH input		2.80	8.571		2,950	445		3,395	3,900
0200	200 MBH input		2.60	9.231		3,050	480		3,530	4,075
0220	225 MBH input		2.40	10		3,300	520		3,820	4,400
0240	250 MBH input		2	12		3,925	625		4,550	5,250
0260	300 MBH input		1.90	12.632		4,025	655		4,680	5,450
0280	350 MBH input		1.75	13.714		4,825	715		5,540	6,375
0300	400 MBH input		1.60	15		7,450	780		8,230	9,350
0320	840 MBH input		1.20	20		10,400	1,050		11,450	13,100
0340	1200 MBH input	↓	.88	27.273		14,900	1,425		16,325	18,600
0600	For discharge louver assembly, add					5%				
0700	For filters, add					10%				
0800	For air shut-off damper section, add				↓	30%				

23 74 Packaged Outdoor HVAC Equipment

23 74 13 – Packaged, Outdoor, Central-Station Air-Handling Units

23 74 13.10 Packaged, Outdoor Type, Central-Station AHU		Crew	Daily Output	Labor-Hours	Unit	Material	2012 Bare Costs Labor	Equipment	Total	Total Incl O&P
0010	**PACKAGED, OUTDOOR TYPE, CENTRAL-STATION AIR-HANDLING UNITS**									
2900	Cooling coils may be chilled water or DX									
2910	Heating coils may be hot water, steam or electric									
3000	Weathertight, ground or rooftop									
3010	Constant volume									
3100	2000 CFM	Q-6	1	24	Ea.	10,100	1,250		11,350	13,000
3140	5000 CFM		.79	30.380		24,500	1,575		26,075	29,400
3150	10,000 CFM		.52	46.154		52,000	2,400		54,400	60,500
3160	15,000 CFM		.41	58.537		76,500	3,050		79,550	88,500
3170	20,000 CFM		.30	80		106,000	4,150		110,150	123,000
3180	30,000 CFM		.24	100		158,000	5,200		163,200	182,000
3200	Variable air volume									
3210	2000 CFM	Q-6	.96	25	Ea.	12,200	1,300		13,500	15,400
3240	5000 CFM		.73	32.877		27,600	1,700		29,300	33,000
3250	10,000 CFM		.50	48		58,500	2,500		61,000	68,000
3260	15,000 CFM		.40	60		87,500	3,125		90,625	100,500
3270	20,000 CFM		.29	82.759		112,000	4,300		116,300	129,500
3280	30,000 CFM		.20	120		158,000	6,250		164,250	183,500

23 74 23 – Packaged, Outdoor, Heating-Only Makeup-Air Units

23 74 23.16 Packaged, Ind.-Fired, In/Outdoor

		Crew	Daily Output	Labor-Hours	Unit	Material	Labor	Equipment	Total	Total Incl O&P
0010	**PACKAGED, IND.-FIRED, IN/OUTDOOR,** Heat-Only Makeup-Air Units									
1000	Rooftop unit, natural gas, gravity vent, S.S. exchanger									
1010	70°F temperature rise, MBH is input									
1020	250 MBH	Q-6	4	6	Ea.	11,400	310		11,710	13,000
1040	400 MBH		3.60	6.667		11,400	345		11,745	13,100
1060	550 MBH		3.30	7.273		12,500	380		12,880	14,300
1080	750 MBH		3	8		13,800	415		14,215	15,800
1100	1000 MBH		2.60	9.231		16,400	480		16,880	18,700
1120	1750 MBH		2.30	10.435		20,600	540		21,140	23,500
1140	2500 MBH		1.90	12.632		26,900	655		27,555	30,600
1160	3250 MBH		1.40	17.143		32,500	890		33,390	37,200
1180	4000 MBH		1.20	20		39,700	1,050		40,750	45,300
1200	6000 MBH		1	24		49,400	1,250		50,650	56,500
1600	For cleanable filters, add					5%				
1700	For electric modulating gas control, add					10%				
8000	Rooftop unit, electric, with curb, controls									
8010	33 kW	Q-5	4	4	Ea.	3,750	201		3,951	4,425
8020	100 kW		3.60	4.444		6,300	223		6,523	7,250
8030	150 kW		3.20	5		7,225	251		7,476	8,325
8040	250 kW		2.80	5.714		9,475	286		9,761	10,800
8050	400 kW		2.20	7.273		14,000	365		14,365	16,000

23 74 33 – Dedicated Outdoor-Air Units

23 74 33.10 Roof Top Air Conditioners

			Crew	Daily Output	Labor-Hours	Unit	Material	Labor	Equipment	Total	Total Incl O&P
0010	**ROOF TOP AIR CONDITIONERS,** Standard controls, curb, economizer										
1000	Single zone, electric cool, gas heat										
1100	3 ton cooling, 60 MBH heating	D3050-150	Q-5	.70	22.857	Ea.	3,600	1,150		4,750	5,675
1120	4 ton cooling, 95 MBH heating	D3050-155		.61	26.403		4,250	1,325		5,575	6,675
1140	5 ton cooling, 112 MBH heating	R236000-10		.56	28.521		4,975	1,425		6,400	7,625
1145	6 ton cooling, 140 MBH heating	R236000-20		.52	30.769		5,825	1,550		7,375	8,750
1150	7.5 ton cooling, 170 MBH heating			.50	32.258		7,650	1,625		9,275	10,900
1160	10 ton cooling, 200 MBH heating		Q-6	.67	35.982		10,600	1,875		12,475	14,400
1170	12.5 ton cooling, 230 MBH heating			.63	37.975		13,400	1,975		15,375	17,700

23 74 33.10 Roof Top Air Conditioners		Crew	Daily Output	Labor-Hours	Unit	Material	2012 Bare Costs Labor	Equipment	Total	Total Incl O&P
1180	15 ton cooling, 270 MBH heating	Q-6	.57	42.032	Ea.	15,900	2,175		18,075	20,800
1190	17.5 ton cooling, 330 MBH heating	↓	.52	45.889		18,800	2,375		21,175	24,300
1200	20 ton cooling, 360 MBH heating	Q-7	.67	47.976		21,900	2,550		24,450	28,000
1210	25 ton cooling, 450 MBH heating		.56	57.554		25,000	3,050		28,050	32,100
1220	30 ton cooling, 540 MBH heating		.47	68.376		25,500	3,625		29,125	33,600
1240	40 ton cooling, 675 MBH heating		.35	91.168		33,400	4,825		38,225	44,000
1260	50 ton cooling, 810 MBH heating		.28	113		39,500	6,050		45,550	52,500
1265	60 ton cooling, 900 MBH heating		.23	136		47,800	7,250		55,050	63,500
1270	80 ton cooling, 1000 MBH heating		.20	160		79,000	8,475		87,475	100,000
1275	90 ton cooling, 1200 MBH heating		.17	188		82,000	9,975		91,975	105,000
1280	100 ton cooling, 1350 MBH heating	↓	.14	228	↓	100,000	12,100		112,100	128,500
1300	Electric cool, electric heat									
1310	5 ton	Q-5	.63	25.600	Ea.	3,900	1,275		5,175	6,200
1314	10 ton	Q-6	.74	32.432		7,075	1,675		8,750	10,300
1318	15 ton	"	.64	37.795		10,600	1,975		12,575	14,700
1322	20 ton	Q-7	.74	43.185		14,200	2,300		16,500	19,100
1326	25 ton		.62	51.696		17,700	2,750		20,450	23,600
1330	30 ton		.52	61.657		21,200	3,275		24,475	28,300
1334	40 ton		.39	82.051		28,300	4,350		32,650	37,700
1338	50 ton		.31	102		33,600	5,450		39,050	45,200
1342	60 ton		.26	123		40,300	6,525		46,825	54,500
1346	75 ton	↓	.21	153	↓	50,500	8,150		58,650	68,000
2000	Multizone, electric cool, gas heat, economizer									
2100	15 ton cooling, 360 MBH heating	Q-7	.61	52.545	Ea.	59,500	2,775		62,275	69,500
2120	20 ton cooling, 360 MBH heating		.53	60.038		64,000	3,175		67,175	75,500
2140	25 ton cooling, 450 MBH heating		.45	71.910		77,000	3,825		80,825	90,500
2160	28 ton cooling, 450 MBH heating		.41	79.012		87,500	4,200		91,700	103,000
2180	30 ton cooling, 540 MBH heating		.37	85.562		98,500	4,550		103,050	115,500
2200	40 ton cooling, 540 MBH heating		.28	113		112,500	6,050		118,550	133,000
2210	50 ton cooling, 540 MBH heating		.23	142		140,000	7,550		147,550	165,500
2220	70 ton cooling, 1500 MBH heating		.16	198		151,500	10,500		162,000	182,500
2240	80 ton cooling, 1500 MBH heating		.14	228		173,000	12,100		185,100	209,000
2260	90 ton cooling, 1500 MBH heating		.13	256		181,500	13,600		195,100	220,000
2280	105 ton cooling, 1500 MBH heating	↓	.11	290		200,000	15,400		215,400	243,500
2400	For hot water heat coil, deduct					5%				
2500	For steam heat coil, deduct					2%				
2600	For electric heat, deduct				↓	3%	5%			
4000	Single zone, electric cool, gas heat, variable air volume									
4100	12.5 ton cooling, 230 MBH heating	Q-6	.55	43.716	Ea.	15,200	2,275		17,475	20,100
4120	18 ton cooling, 330 MBH heating	"	.46	52.747		20,900	2,750		23,650	27,100
4140	25 ton cooling, 450 MBH heating	Q-7	.48	66.116		27,600	3,500		31,100	35,600
4160	40 ton cooling, 675 MBH heating		.31	104		38,000	5,575		43,575	50,000
4180	60 ton cooling, 900 MBH heating		.20	157		55,500	8,350		63,850	74,000
4200	80 ton cooling, 1000 MBH heating	↓	.15	209	↓	88,000	11,100		99,100	113,500
5000	Single zone, electric cool only									
5050	3 ton cooling	Q-5	.88	18.203	Ea.	2,475	910		3,385	4,100
5060	4 ton cooling		.76	21.108		2,875	1,050		3,925	4,750
5070	5 ton cooling		.70	22.792		3,525	1,150		4,675	5,600
5080	6 ton cooling		.65	24.502		3,975	1,225		5,200	6,225
5090	7.5 ton cooling		.62	25.806		5,550	1,300		6,850	8,050
5100	8.5 ton cooling	↓	.59	26.981		6,200	1,350		7,550	8,875
5110	10 ton cooling	Q-6	.83	28.812		7,325	1,500		8,825	10,300
5120	12.5 ton cooling	↓	.80	30	↓	9,350	1,550		10,900	12,700

23 74 33.10 Roof Top Air Conditioners	Crew	Daily Output	Labor-Hours	Unit	Material	2012 Bare Costs Labor	Equipment	Total	Total Incl O&P
5130	15 ton cooling	Q-6	.71	33.613	Ea.	15,100	1,750		16,850	19,300
5140	17.5 ton cooling	↓	.65	36.697		18,600	1,900		20,500	23,400
5150	20 ton cooling	Q-7	.83	38.415		20,700	2,050		22,750	25,900
5160	25 ton cooling		.70	45.977		22,700	2,450		25,150	28,700
5170	30 ton cooling		.59	54.701		24,200	2,900		27,100	31,000
5180	40 ton cooling	↓	.44	73.059		32,500	3,875		36,375	41,700
5400	For low heat, add					7%				
5410	For high heat, add				↓	10%				
6000	Single zone electric cooling with variable volume distribution									
6020	20 ton cooling	Q-7	.72	44.199	Ea.	24,600	2,350		26,950	30,500
6030	25 ton cooling		.61	52.893		28,900	2,800		31,700	36,000
6040	30 ton cooling		.51	62.868		29,700	3,325		33,025	37,700
6050	40 ton cooling		.38	83.990		39,900	4,450		44,350	50,500
6060	50 ton cooling		.31	104		44,200	5,575		49,775	57,000
6070	60 ton cooling	↓	.25	125		52,000	6,675		58,675	67,500
6200	For low heat, add					7%				
6210	For high heat, add				↓	10%				
7000	Multizone, cool/heat, variable volume distribution									
7100	50 ton cooling	Q-7	.20	164	Ea.	104,000	8,700		112,700	127,500
7110	70 ton cooling		.14	228		145,500	12,100		157,600	178,500
7120	90 ton cooling		.11	296		167,000	15,700		182,700	207,500
7130	105 ton cooling		.10	333		187,000	17,700		204,700	232,000
7140	120 ton cooling		.08	380		213,500	20,200		233,700	265,500
7150	140 ton cooling	↓	.07	444	↓	229,000	23,600		252,600	287,500
7300	Penthouse unit, cool/heat, variable volume distribution									
7400	150 ton cooling	Q-7	.10	310	Ea.	374,000	16,500		390,500	436,500
7410	170 ton cooling		.10	320		399,500	17,000		416,500	465,000
7420	200 ton cooling		.10	326		470,500	17,300		487,800	543,500
7430	225 ton cooling		.09	340		514,500	18,100		532,600	593,000
7440	250 ton cooling		.09	359		531,000	19,100		550,100	613,000
7450	270 ton cooling		.09	363		573,500	19,300		592,800	659,500
7460	300 ton cooling	↓	.09	372	↓	637,000	19,700		656,700	731,000
9400	Sub assemblies for assembly systems									
9410	Ductwork, per ton, rooftop 1 zone units	Q-9	.96	16.667	Ton	259	780		1,039	1,475
9420	Ductwork, per ton, rooftop multizone units		.50	32		355	1,500		1,855	2,700
9430	Ductwork, VAV cooling/ton, rooftop multizone, 1 zone/ton		.32	50		480	2,350		2,830	4,100
9440	Ductwork per ton, packaged water & air cooled units		1.26	12.698		74.50	595		669.50	990
9450	Ductwork per ton, split system remote condensing units		1.32	12.121	↓	70	570		640	940
9500	Ductwork package for residential units, 1 ton		.80	20	Ea.	350	940		1,290	1,800
9520	2 ton		.40	40		695	1,875		2,570	3,625
9530	3 ton	↓	.27	59.259		1,050	2,775		3,825	5,400
9540	4 ton	Q-10	.30	80		1,400	3,900		5,300	7,450
9550	5 ton		.23	104		1,750	5,075		6,825	9,675
9560	6 ton		.20	120		2,100	5,850		7,950	11,200
9570	7 ton		.17	141		2,450	6,875		9,325	13,200
9580	8 ton	↓	.15	160	↓	2,800	7,775		10,575	15,000

23 76 Evaporative Air-Cooling Equipment

23 76 13 – Direct Evaporative Air Coolers

23 76 13.10 Evaporative Coolers

		Crew	Daily Output	Labor-Hours	Unit	Material	2012 Bare Costs Labor	Equipment	Total	Total Incl O&P
0010	**EVAPORATIVE COOLERS**, (Swamp Coolers) ducted, not incl. duct.									
0100	Side discharge style, capacities at .25" S.P.									
0120	1785 CFM, 1/3 HP, 115 V [G]	Q-9	5	3.200	Ea.	445	150		595	720
0140	2740 CFM, 1/3 HP, 115 V [G]		4.50	3.556		540	167		707	850
0160	3235 CFM, 1/2 HP, 115 V [G]		4	4		555	188		743	895
0180	3615 CFM, 1/2 HP, 230 V [G]		3.60	4.444		685	209		894	1,075
0200	4215 CFM, 3/4 HP, 230 V [G]		3.20	5		710	235		945	1,150
0220	5255 CFM, 1 HP, 115/230 V [G]		3	5.333		1,400	250		1,650	1,925
0240	6090 CFM, 1 HP, 230/460 V [G]		2.80	5.714		1,475	268		1,743	2,025
0260	8300 CFM, 1-1/2 HP, 230/460 V [G]		2.60	6.154		2,150	289		2,439	2,825
0280	8360 CFM, 1-1/2 HP, 230/460 V [G]		2.20	7.273		2,150	340		2,490	2,900
0300	9725 CFM, 2 HP, 230/460 V [G]		1.80	8.889		2,275	415		2,690	3,125
0320	11,715 CFM, 3 HP, 230/460 V [G]		1.40	11.429		2,800	535		3,335	3,900
0340	14,410 CFM, 5 HP, 230/460 V [G]	↓	1	16	↓	2,875	750		3,625	4,300
0400	For two-speed motor, add					5%				
0500	For down discharge style, add					10%				

23 76 26 – Fan Coil Evaporators for Coolers/Freezers

23 76 26.10 Evaporators

		Crew	Daily Output	Labor-Hours	Unit	Material	2012 Bare Costs Labor	Equipment	Total	Total Incl O&P
0010	**EVAPORATORS**, DX coils, remote compressors not included.									
1000	Coolers, reach-in type, above freezing temperatures									
1300	Shallow depth, wall mount, 7 fins per inch, air defrost									
1310	600 BTUH, 8" fan, rust-proof core	Q-5	3.80	4.211	Ea.	665	211		876	1,050
1320	900 BTUH, 8" fan, rust-proof core		3.30	4.848		770	243		1,013	1,225
1330	1200 BTUH, 8" fan, rust-proof core		3	5.333		870	267		1,137	1,350
1340	1800 BTUH, 8" fan, rust-proof core		2.40	6.667		1,000	335		1,335	1,600
1350	2500 BTUH, 10" fan, rust-proof core		2.20	7.273		1,025	365		1,390	1,700
1360	3500 BTUH, 10" fan		2	8		1,175	400		1,575	1,900
1370	4500 BTUH, 10" fan	↓	1.90	8.421		1,225	420		1,645	1,975
1390	For pan drain, add				↓	57.50			57.50	63
1600	Undercounter refrigerators, ceiling or wall mount,									
1610	8 fins per inch, air defrost, rust-proof core									
1630	800 BTUH, one 6" fan	Q-5	5	3.200	Ea.	300	160		460	570
1640	1300 BTUH, two 6" fans		4	4		365	201		566	700
1650	1700 BTUH, two 6" fans	↓	3.60	4.444	↓	405	223		628	780
2000	Coolers, reach-in and walk-in types, above freezing temperatures									
2600	Two-way discharge, ceiling mount, 150-4100 CFM,									
2610	above 34°F applications, air defrost									
2630	900 BTUH, 7 fins per inch, 8" fan	Q-5	4	4	Ea.	540	201		741	895
2660	2500 BTUH, 7 fins per inch, 10" fan		2.60	6.154		845	310		1,155	1,400
2690	5500 BTUH, 7 fins per inch, 12" fan		1.70	9.412		1,450	470		1,920	2,300
2720	8500 BTUH, 8 fins per inch, 16" fan		1.20	13.333		1,750	670		2,420	2,925
2750	15,000 BTUH, 7 fins per inch, 18" fan		1.10	14.545		2,450	730		3,180	3,775
2770	24,000 BTUH, 7 fins per inch, two 16" fans		1	16		3,675	800		4,475	5,225
2790	30,000 BTUH, 7 fins per inch, two 18" fans	↓	.90	17.778	↓	4,550	890		5,440	6,350
2850	Two-way discharge, low profile, ceiling mount,									
2860	8 fins per inch, 200-570 CFM, air defrost									
2880	800 BTUH, one 6" fan	Q-5	4	4	Ea.	360	201		561	695
2890	1300 BTUH, two 6" fans		3.50	4.571		430	229		659	815
2900	1800 BTUH, two 6" fans		3.30	4.848		450	243		693	860
2910	2700 BTUH, three 6" fans	↓	2.70	5.926	↓	530	297		827	1,025
3000	Coolers, walk-in type, above freezing temperatures									
3300	General use, ceiling mount, 108-2080 CFM									

23 76 26.10 Evaporators	Crew	Daily Output	Labor-Hours	Unit	Material	2012 Bare Costs Labor	Equipment	Total	Total Incl O&P
3320	600 BTUH, 7 fins per inch, 6" fan	Q-5	5.20	3.077	Ea.	320	154		474	585
3340	1200 BTUH, 7 fins per inch, 8" fan		3.70	4.324		440	217		657	810
3360	1800 BTUH, 7 fins per inch, 10" fan		2.70	5.926		620	297		917	1,125
3380	3500 BTUH, 7 fins per inch, 12" fan		2.40	6.667		910	335		1,245	1,500
3400	5500 BTUH, 8 fins per inch, 12" fan		2	8		1,025	400		1,425	1,725
3430	8500 BTUH, 8 fins per inch, 16" fan		1.40	11.429		1,500	575		2,075	2,525
3460	15,000 BTUH, 7 fins per inch, two 16" fans		1.10	14.545		2,425	730		3,155	3,775
3640	Low velocity, high latent load, ceiling mount,									
3650	1050-2420 CFM, air defrost, 6 fins per inch									
3670	6700 BTUH, two 10" fans	Q-5	1.30	12.308	Ea.	2,000	615		2,615	3,125
3680	10,000 BTUH, three 10" fans		1	16		2,525	800		3,325	3,975
3690	13,500 BTUH, three 10" fans		1	16		2,875	800		3,675	4,375
3700	18,000 BTUH, four 10" fans		1	16		3,900	800		4,700	5,500
3710	26,500 BTUH, four 10" fans		.80	20		4,550	1,000		5,550	6,525
3730	For electric defrost, add					17%				
5000	Freezers and coolers, reach-in type, above 34°F									
5030	to sub-freezing temperature range, low latent load,									
5050	air defrost, 7 fins per inch									
5070	1200 BTUH, 8" fan, rustproof core	Q-5	4.40	3.636	Ea.	590	182		772	925
5080	1500 BTUH, 8" fan, rustproof core		4.20	3.810		605	191		796	955
5090	1800 BTUH, 8" fan, rustproof core		3.70	4.324		625	217		842	1,000
5100	2500 BTUH, 10" fan, rustproof core		2.90	5.517		675	277		952	1,150
5110	3500 BTUH, 10" fan, rustproof core		2.50	6.400		845	320		1,165	1,425
5120	4500 BTUH, 12" fan, rustproof core		2.10	7.619		1,050	380		1,430	1,725
6000	Freezers and coolers, walk-in type									
6050	1960-18,000 CFM, medium profile									
6060	Standard motor, 6 fins per inch, to -30°F, all aluminum									
6080	10,500 BTUH, air defrost, one 18" fan	Q-5	1.40	11.429	Ea.	1,600	575		2,175	2,650
6090	12,500 BTUH, air defrost, one 18" fan		1.40	11.429		1,725	575		2,300	2,775
6100	16,400 BTUH, air defrost, one 18" fan		1.30	12.308		1,750	615		2,365	2,850
6110	20,900 BTUH, air defrost, one 18" fans		1	16		2,050	800		2,850	3,450
6120	27,000 BTUH, air defrost, two 18" fans		1	16		3,025	800		3,825	4,525
6130	32,900 BTUH, air defrost, two 20" fans	Q-6	1.30	18.462		3,375	960		4,335	5,175
6140	39,000 BTUH, air defrost, two 20" fans		1.25	19.200		3,925	1,000		4,925	5,825
6150	44,100 BTUH, air defrost, three 20" fans		1	24		4,475	1,250		5,725	6,800
6155	53,000 BTUH, air defrost, three 20" fans		1	24		4,475	1,250		5,725	6,800
6160	66,200 BTUH, air defrost, four 20" fans		1	24		5,075	1,250		6,325	7,475
6170	78,000 BTUH, air defrost, four 20" fans		.80	30		6,325	1,550		7,875	9,300
6180	88,200 BTUH, air defrost, four 24" fans		.60	40		6,725	2,075		8,800	10,500
6190	110,000 BTUH, air defrost, four 24" fans		.50	48		7,625	2,500		10,125	12,200
6330	Hot gas defrost, standard motor units, add					35%				
6370	Electric defrost, 230V, standard motor, add					16%				
6410	460V, standard or high capacity motor, add					25%				
6800	Eight fins per inch, increases BTUH 75%									
6810	Standard capacity, add				Ea.	5%				
6830	Hot gas & electric defrost not recommended									
7000	800-4150 CFM, 12" fans									
7010	Four fins per inch									
7030	3400 BTUH, 1 fan	Q-5	2.80	5.714	Ea.	540	286		826	1,025
7040	4200 BTUH, 1 fan		2.40	6.667		740	335		1,075	1,325
7050	5300 BTUH, 1 fan		1.90	8.421		820	420		1,240	1,525
7060	6800 BTUH, 1 fan		1.70	9.412		970	470		1,440	1,775
7070	8400 BTUH, 2 fans		1.60	10		1,250	500		1,750	2,125

23 76 Evaporative Air-Cooling Equipment

23 76 26 – Fan Coil Evaporators for Coolers/Freezers

23 76 26.10 Evaporators

23 76 26.10 Evaporators		Crew	Daily Output	Labor-Hours	Unit	Material	2012 Bare Costs Labor	2012 Bare Costs Equipment	Total	Total Incl O&P
7080	10,500 BTUH, 2 fans	Q-5	1.40	11.429	Ea.	1,400	575		1,975	2,425
7090	13,000 BTUH, 3 fans		1.30	12.308		1,925	615		2,540	3,050
7100	17,000 BTUH, 4 fans		1.20	13.333		2,475	670		3,145	3,725
7110	21,500 BTUH, 5 fans		1	16		3,050	800		3,850	4,550
7160	Six fins per inch increases BTUH 35%, add					5%				
7180	Eight fins per inch increases BTUH 53%,									
7190	not recommended for below 35°F, add				Ea.	8%				
7210	For 12°F temperature differential, add					20%				
7230	For adjustable thermostat control, add					137			137	151
7240	For hot gas defrost, except 8 fin models									
7250	on applications below 35°F, add				Ea.	58%				
7260	For electric defrost, except 8 fin models									
7270	on applications below 35°F, add				Ea.	36%				
8000	Freezers, pass-thru door uprights, walk-in storage									
8300	Low temperature, thin profile, electric defrost									
8310	138-1800 CFM, 5 fins per inch									
8320	900 BTUH, one 6" fan	Q-5	3.30	4.848	Ea.	495	243		738	910
8340	1500 BTUH, two 6" fans		2.20	7.273		775	365		1,140	1,400
8360	2600 BTUH, three 6" fans		1.90	8.421		1,050	420		1,470	1,775
8370	3300 BTUH, four 6" fans		1.70	9.412		1,225	470		1,695	2,050
8380	4400 BTUH, five 6" fans		1.40	11.429		1,700	575		2,275	2,750
8400	7000 BTUH, three 10" fans		1.30	12.308		1,925	615		2,540	3,050
8410	8700 BTUH, four 10" fans		1.10	14.545		2,325	730		3,055	3,675
8450	For air defrost, deduct					250			250	275

23 81 Decentralized Unitary HVAC Equipment

23 81 13 – Packaged Terminal Air-Conditioners

23 81 13.10 Packaged Cabinet Type Air-Conditioners

23 81 13.10		Crew	Daily Output	Labor-Hours	Unit	Material	Labor	Equipment	Total	Total Incl O&P
0010	**PACKAGED CABINET TYPE AIR-CONDITIONERS**, Cabinet, wall sleeve,									
0100	louver, electric heat, thermostat, manual changeover, 208 V									
0200	6,000 BTUH cooling, 8800 BTU heat	Q-5	6	2.667	Ea.	720	134		854	990
0220	9,000 BTUH cooling, 13,900 BTU heat		5	3.200		785	160		945	1,100
0240	12,000 BTUH cooling, 13,900 BTU heat		4	4		850	201		1,051	1,225
0260	15,000 BTUH cooling, 13,900 BTU heat		3	5.333		1,050	267		1,317	1,550
0280	18,000 BTUH cooling, 10 KW heat		2.40	6.667		1,775	335		2,110	2,450
0300	24,000 BTUH cooling, 10 KW heat		1.90	8.421		1,800	420		2,220	2,600
0320	30,000 BTUH cooling, 10 KW heat		1.40	11.429		2,025	575		2,600	3,100
0340	36,000 BTUH cooling, 10 KW heat		1.25	12.800		2,150	640		2,790	3,325
0360	42,000 BTUH cooling, 10 KW heat		1	16		2,625	800		3,425	4,075
0380	48,000 BTUH cooling, 10 KW heat		.90	17.778		2,775	890		3,665	4,400
0500	For hot water coil, increase heat by 10%, add					5%	10%			
1000	For steam, increase heat output by 30%, add					8%	10%			

23 81 19 – Self-Contained Air-Conditioners

23 81 19.10 Window Unit Air Conditioners

23 81 19.10		Crew	Daily Output	Labor-Hours	Unit	Material	Labor	Equipment	Total	Total Incl O&P
0010	**WINDOW UNIT AIR CONDITIONERS**									
4000	Portable/window, 15 amp 125 V grounded receptacle required									
4060	5000 BTUH	1 Carp	8	1	Ea.	263	44		307	355
4340	6000 BTUH		8	1		300	44		344	400
4480	8000 BTUH		6	1.333		410	59		469	540
4500	10,000 BTUH		6	1.333		525	59		584	670

23 81 Decentralized Unitary HVAC Equipment

23 81 19 – Self-Contained Air-Conditioners

23 81 19.10 Window Unit Air Conditioners

		Crew	Daily Output	Labor-Hours	Unit	Material	2012 Bare Costs Labor	Equipment	Total	Total Incl O&P
4520	12,000 BTUH	L-2	8	2	Ea.	645	77.50		722.50	825
4600	Window/thru-the-wall, 15 amp 230 V grounded receptacle required									
4780	18,000 BTUH	L-2	6	2.667	Ea.	865	103		968	1,100
4940	25,000 BTUH		4	4		1,100	155		1,255	1,450
4960	29,000 BTUH		4	4		1,200	155		1,355	1,575

23 81 19.20 Self-Contained Single Package

		Crew	Daily Output	Labor-Hours	Unit	Material	2012 Bare Costs Labor	Equipment	Total	Total Incl O&P
0010	**SELF-CONTAINED SINGLE PACKAGE**									
0100	Air cooled, for free blow or duct, not incl. remote condenser									
0110	Constant volume									
0200	3 ton cooling	Q-5	1	16	Ea.	3,475	800		4,275	5,025
0210	4 ton cooling	"	.80	20		3,800	1,000		4,800	5,675
0220	5 ton cooling	Q-6	1.20	20		4,150	1,050		5,200	6,150
0230	7.5 ton cooling	"	.90	26.667		5,300	1,375		6,675	7,925
0240	10 ton cooling	Q-7	1	32		7,000	1,700		8,700	10,300
0250	15 ton cooling		.95	33.684		9,725	1,775		11,500	13,400
0260	20 ton cooling		.90	35.556		15,600	1,875		17,475	20,100
0270	25 ton cooling		.85	37.647		17,200	2,000		19,200	21,900
0280	30 ton cooling		.80	40		23,600	2,125		25,725	29,200
0300	40 ton cooling		.60	53.333		34,200	2,825		37,025	41,900
0320	50 ton cooling		.50	64		44,500	3,400		47,900	54,000
0340	60 ton cooling	Q-8	.40	80		53,500	4,250	92	57,842	65,500
0380	With hot water heat, variable air volume									
0390	10 ton cooling	Q-7	.96	33.333	Ea.	9,175	1,775		10,950	12,800
0400	20 ton cooling		.86	37.209		19,700	1,975		21,675	24,700
0410	30 ton cooling		.76	42.105		29,900	2,225		32,125	36,300
0420	40 ton cooling		.58	55.172		42,200	2,925		45,125	51,000
0430	50 ton cooling		.48	66.667		54,500	3,525		58,025	65,500
0440	60 ton cooling	Q-8	.38	84.211		67,000	4,475	97	71,572	80,500
0490	For duct mounting no price change									
0500	For steam heating coils, add				Ea.	10%	10%			
0550	Packaged, with electric heat									
0552	Constant volume									
0560	5 ton cooling	Q-6	1.20	20	Ea.	7,525	1,050		8,575	9,875
0570	10 ton cooling	Q-7	1	32		12,200	1,700		13,900	16,000
0580	20 ton cooling		.90	35.556		23,000	1,875		24,875	28,200
0590	30 ton cooling		.80	40		36,100	2,125		38,225	42,900
0600	40 ton cooling		.60	53.333		47,600	2,825		50,425	57,000
0610	50 ton cooling		.50	64		63,000	3,400		66,400	74,500
0700	Variable air volume									
0710	10 ton cooling	Q-7	1	32	Ea.	13,700	1,700		15,400	17,600
0720	20 ton cooling		.90	35.556		25,500	1,875		27,375	31,000
0730	30 ton cooling		.80	40		39,900	2,125		42,025	47,100
0740	40 ton cooling		.60	53.333		52,000	2,825		54,825	62,000
0750	50 ton cooling		.50	64		69,000	3,400		72,400	80,500
0760	60 ton cooling	Q-8	.40	80		78,500	4,250	92	82,842	93,000
1000	Water cooled for free blow or duct, not including tower									
1010	Constant volume									
1100	3 ton cooling	Q-6	1	24	Ea.	3,475	1,250		4,725	5,700
1120	5 ton cooling		1	24		4,550	1,250		5,800	6,900
1130	7.5 ton cooling		.80	30		6,400	1,550		7,950	9,400
1140	10 ton cooling	Q-7	.90	35.556		8,550	1,875		10,425	12,300
1150	15 ton cooling		.85	37.647		14,100	2,000		16,100	18,500

23 81 19 – Self-Contained Air-Conditioners

23 81 19.20 Self-Contained Single Package

		Crew	Daily Output	Labor-Hours	Unit	Material	2012 Bare Costs Labor	Equipment	Total	Total Incl O&P
1160	20 ton cooling	Q-7	.80	40	Ea.	26,800	2,125		28,925	32,700
1170	25 ton cooling		.75	42.667		31,600	2,275		33,875	38,200
1180	30 ton cooling		.70	45.714		35,500	2,425		37,925	42,800
1200	40 ton cooling		.40	80		45,000	4,250		49,250	56,000
1220	50 ton cooling		.30	106		56,000	5,650		61,650	70,000
1240	60 ton cooling	Q-8	.30	106		65,500	5,650	123	71,273	80,500
1300	For hot water or steam heat coils, add					12%	10%			
2000	Water cooled with electric heat, not including tower									
2010	Constant volume									
2100	5 ton cooling	Q-6	1.20	20	Ea.	7,950	1,050		9,000	10,300
2120	10 ton cooling	Q-7	1	32		13,700	1,700		15,400	17,700
2130	15 ton cooling	"	.90	35.556		21,500	1,875		23,375	26,600
2400	Variable air volume									
2440	10 ton cooling	Q-7	1	32	Ea.	15,200	1,700		16,900	19,400
2450	15 ton cooling	"	.90	35.556	"	24,100	1,875		25,975	29,400
2600	Water cooled, hot water coils, not including tower									
2610	Variable air volume									
2640	10 ton cooling	Q-7	1	32	Ea.	10,900	1,700		12,600	14,600
2650	15 ton cooling	"	.80	40	"	18,100	2,125		20,225	23,100

23 81 23 – Computer-Room Air-Conditioners

23 81 23.10 Computer Room Units

			Crew	Daily Output	Labor-Hours	Unit	Material	2012 Bare Costs Labor	Equipment	Total	Total Incl O&P
0010	**COMPUTER ROOM UNITS**	D3050-185									
1000	Air cooled, includes remote condenser but not										
1020	interconnecting tubing or refrigerant										
1080	3 ton		Q-5	.50	32	Ea.	17,800	1,600		19,400	22,000
1120	5 ton			.45	35.556		19,100	1,775		20,875	23,700
1160	6 ton			.30	53.333		33,600	2,675		36,275	40,900
1200	8 ton			.27	59.259		35,600	2,975		38,575	43,700
1240	10 ton			.25	64		37,200	3,200		40,400	45,800
1260	12 ton			.24	66.667		38,600	3,350		41,950	47,500
1280	15 ton			.22	72.727		40,900	3,650		44,550	50,500
1290	18 ton			.20	80		46,600	4,000		50,600	57,000
1300	20 ton		Q-6	.26	92.308		49,000	4,800		53,800	61,000
1320	22 ton			.24	100		49,700	5,200		54,900	62,500
1360	30 ton			.21	114		61,000	5,950		66,950	76,000
2200	Chilled water, for connection to										
2220	existing chiller system of adequate capacity										
2260	5 ton		Q-5	.74	21.622	Ea.	13,600	1,075		14,675	16,600
2280	6 ton			.52	30.769		13,800	1,550		15,350	17,400
2300	8 ton			.50	32		13,800	1,600		15,400	17,600
2320	10 ton			.49	32.653		13,900	1,625		15,525	17,800
2330	12 ton			.49	32.990		14,300	1,650		15,950	18,300
2360	15 ton			.48	33.333		14,600	1,675		16,275	18,600
2400	20 ton			.46	34.783		15,500	1,750		17,250	19,700
2440	25 ton		Q-6	.63	38.095		16,600	1,975		18,575	21,200
2460	30 ton			.57	42.105		17,900	2,200		20,100	23,000
2480	35 ton			.52	46.154		18,100	2,400		20,500	23,600
2500	45 ton			.46	52.174		19,200	2,700		21,900	25,200
2520	50 ton			.42	57.143		22,000	2,975		24,975	28,700
2540	60 ton			.38	63.158		23,400	3,275		26,675	30,700
2560	77 ton			.35	68.571		39,500	3,575		43,075	48,800
2580	95 ton			.32	75		46,100	3,900		50,000	56,500

23 81 Decentralized Unitary HVAC Equipment

23 81 23 – Computer-Room Air-Conditioners

23 81 23.10 Computer Room Units		Crew	Daily Output	Labor-Hours	Unit	Material	2012 Bare Costs Labor	Equipment	Total	Total Incl O&P
4000	Glycol system, complete except for interconnecting tubing									
4060	3 ton	Q-5	.40	40	Ea.	22,300	2,000		24,300	27,600
4100	5 ton		.38	42.105		24,500	2,100		26,600	30,100
4120	6 ton		.25	64		35,900	3,200		39,100	44,300
4140	8 ton		.23	69.565		39,300	3,475		42,775	48,600
4160	10 ton		.21	76.190		41,800	3,825		45,625	52,000
4180	12 ton		.19	84.211		45,400	4,225		49,625	56,500
4200	15 ton	Q-6	.26	92.308		52,000	4,800		56,800	64,000
4240	20 ton		.24	100		57,000	5,200		62,200	70,500
4280	22 ton		.23	104		60,000	5,425		65,425	74,000
4430	30 ton		.22	109		74,500	5,675		80,175	90,000
8000	Water cooled system, not including condenser,									
8020	water supply or cooling tower									
8060	3 ton	Q-5	.62	25.806	Ea.	18,100	1,300		19,400	22,000
8100	5 ton		.54	29.630		19,700	1,475		21,175	24,000
8120	6 ton		.35	45.714		30,700	2,300		33,000	37,300
8140	8 ton		.33	48.485		32,300	2,425		34,725	39,300
8160	10 ton		.31	51.613		33,500	2,575		36,075	40,700
8180	12 ton		.29	55.172		36,300	2,775		39,075	44,100
8200	15 ton		.27	59.259		39,200	2,975		42,175	47,700
8240	20 ton	Q-6	.38	63.158		42,200	3,275		45,475	51,500
8280	22 ton		.35	68.571		44,200	3,575		47,775	54,000
8300	30 ton		.30	80		55,000	4,150		59,150	67,000

23 81 26 – Split-System Air-Conditioners

23 81 26.10 Split Ductless Systems		Crew	Daily Output	Labor-Hours	Unit	Material	2012 Bare Costs Labor	Equipment	Total	Total Incl O&P
0010	**SPLIT DUCTLESS SYSTEMS**									
0100	Cooling only, single zone									
0110	Wall mount									
0120	3/4 ton cooling	Q-5	2	8	Ea.	690	400		1,090	1,375
0130	1 ton cooling		1.80	8.889		765	445		1,210	1,525
0140	1-1/2 ton cooling		1.60	10		1,225	500		1,725	2,100
0150	2 ton cooling		1.40	11.429		1,400	575		1,975	2,425
1000	Ceiling mount									
1020	2 ton cooling	Q-5	1.40	11.429	Ea.	1,250	575		1,825	2,250
1030	3 ton cooling	"	1.20	13.333	"	1,600	670		2,270	2,750
3000	Multizone									
3010	Wall mount									
3020	2 @ 3/4 ton cooling	Q-5	1.80	8.889	Ea.	2,100	445		2,545	3,000
5000	Cooling/Heating									
5010	Wall mount									
5110	1 ton cooling	Q-5	1.70	9.412	Ea.	765	470		1,235	1,550
5120	1-1/2 ton cooling	"	1.50	10.667	"	1,225	535		1,760	2,150
7000	Accessories for all split ductless systems									
7010	Add for ambient frost control	Q-5	8	2	Ea.	79	100		179	238
7020	Add for tube/wiring kit, (Line sets)									
7030	15' kit	Q-5	32	.500	Ea.	96	25		121	144
7036	25' kit		28	.571		116	28.50		144.50	171
7040	35' kit		24	.667		169	33.50		202.50	237
7050	50' kit		20	.800		207	40		247	289

23 81 Decentralized Unitary HVAC Equipment

23 81 43 – Air-Source Unitary Heat Pumps

23 81 43.10 Air-Source Heat Pumps

		Crew	Daily Output	Labor-Hours	Unit	Material	2012 Bare Costs Labor	2012 Bare Costs Equipment	Total	Total Incl O&P
0010	**AIR-SOURCE HEAT PUMPS**, Not including interconnecting tubing									
1000	Air to air, split system, not including curbs, pads, fan coil and ductwork									
1010	For curbs/pads see Section 23 91 00									
1012	Outside condensing unit only, for fan coil see Section 23 82 19.10									
1015	1.5 ton cooling, 7 MBH heat @ 0°F	Q-5	2.40	6.667	Ea.	2,075	335		2,410	2,775
1020	2 ton cooling, 8.5 MBH heat @ 0°F		2	8		2,125	400		2,525	2,925
1030	2.5 ton cooling, 10 MBH heat @ 0°F		1.60	10		2,350	500		2,850	3,325
1040	3 ton cooling, 13 MBH heat @ 0°F		1.20	13.333		2,650	670		3,320	3,925
1050	3.5 ton cooling, 18 MBH heat @ 0°F		1	16		2,850	800		3,650	4,325
1054	4 ton cooling, 24 MBH heat @ 0°F		.80	20		3,150	1,000		4,150	4,950
1060	5 ton cooling, 27 MBH heat @ 0°F		.50	32		3,425	1,600		5,025	6,200
1080	7.5 ton cooling, 33 MBH heat @ 0°F		.45	35.556		5,925	1,775		7,700	9,200
1100	10 ton cooling, 50 MBH heat @ 0°F	Q-6	.64	37.500		8,250	1,950		10,200	12,000
1120	15 ton cooling, 64 MBH heat @ 0°F		.50	48		12,200	2,500		14,700	17,200
1130	20 ton cooling, 85 MBH heat @ 0°F		.35	68.571		16,000	3,575		19,575	23,000
1140	25 ton cooling, 119 MBH heat @ 0°F		.25	96		19,300	5,000		24,300	28,700
1500	Single package, not including curbs, pads, or plenums									
1502	1/2 ton cooling, supplementary heat not incl.	Q-5	8	2	Ea.	2,200	100		2,300	2,575
1504	3/4 ton cooling, supplementary heat not incl.		6	2.667		2,400	134		2,534	2,850
1506	1 ton cooling, supplementary heat not incl.		4	4		2,475	201		2,676	3,025
1510	1.5 ton cooling, 5 MBH heat @ 0°F		1.55	10.323		2,550	515		3,065	3,575
1520	2 ton cooling, 6.5 MBH heat @ 0°F		1.50	10.667		2,750	535		3,285	3,825
1540	2.5 ton cooling, 8 MBH heat @ 0°F		1.40	11.429		3,000	575		3,575	4,175
1560	3 ton cooling, 10 MBH heat @ 0°F		1.20	13.333		3,275	670		3,945	4,600
1570	3.5 ton cooling, 11 MBH heat @ 0°F		1	16		3,575	800		4,375	5,150
1580	4 ton cooling, 13 MBH heat @ 0°F		.96	16.667		3,850	835		4,685	5,500
1620	5 ton cooling, 27 MBH heat @ 0°F		.65	24.615		4,150	1,225		5,375	6,425
1640	7.5 ton cooling, 35 MBH heat @ 0°F		.40	40		6,850	2,000		8,850	10,600
1648	10 ton cooling, 45 MBH heat @ 0°F	Q-6	.40	60		9,000	3,125		12,125	14,600
1652	12 ton cooling, 50 MBH heat @ 0°F	"	.36	66.667		10,400	3,475		13,875	16,600
1696	Supplementary electric heat coil incl., except as noted									

23 81 46 – Water-Source Unitary Heat Pumps

23 81 46.10 Water Source Heat Pumps

		Crew	Daily Output	Labor-Hours	Unit	Material	2012 Bare Costs Labor	2012 Bare Costs Equipment	Total	Total Incl O&P
0010	**WATER SOURCE HEAT PUMPS**, Not incl. connecting tubing or water source									
2000	Water source to air, single package									
2100	1 ton cooling, 13 MBH heat @ 75°F	Q-5	2	8	Ea.	1,700	400		2,100	2,450
2120	1.5 ton cooling, 17 MBH heat @ 75°F		1.80	8.889		1,775	445		2,220	2,650
2140	2 ton cooling, 19 MBH heat @ 75°F		1.70	9.412		1,875	470		2,345	2,775
2160	2.5 ton cooling, 25 MBH heat @ 75°F		1.60	10		1,975	500		2,475	2,925
2180	3 ton cooling, 27 MBH heat @ 75°F		1.40	11.429		2,025	575		2,600	3,125
2190	3.5 ton cooling, 29 MBH heat @ 75°F		1.30	12.308		2,300	615		2,915	3,475
2200	4 ton cooling, 31 MBH heat @ 75°F		1.20	13.333		2,475	670		3,145	3,725
2220	5 ton cooling, 29 MBH heat @ 75°F		.90	17.778		2,825	890		3,715	4,450
2240	7.5 ton cooling, 35 MBH heat @ 75°F		.60	26.667		6,600	1,325		7,925	9,275
2250	8.5 ton cooling, 40 MBH heat @ 75°F		.58	27.586		8,025	1,375		9,400	10,900
2260	10 ton cooling, 50 MBH heat @ 75°F		.53	30.189		8,575	1,525		10,100	11,700
2280	15 ton cooling, 64 MBH heat @ 75°F	Q-6	.47	51.064		14,000	2,650		16,650	19,400
2300	20 ton cooling, 100 MBH heat @ 75°F		.41	58.537		15,300	3,050		18,350	21,400
2310	25 ton cooling, 100 MBH heat @ 75°F		.32	75		20,800	3,900		24,700	28,800
2320	30 ton cooling, 128 MBH heat @ 75°F		.24	102		22,800	5,300		28,100	33,100
2340	40 ton cooling, 200 MBH heat @ 75°F		.21	117		32,200	6,075		38,275	44,600
2360	50 ton cooling, 200 MBH heat @ 75°F		.15	160		36,400	8,325		44,725	52,500

23 81 Decentralized Unitary HVAC Equipment

23 81 46 – Water-Source Unitary Heat Pumps

23 81 46.10 Water Source Heat Pumps	Crew	Daily Output	Labor-Hours	Unit	Material	2012 Bare Costs Labor	Equipment	Total	Total Incl O&P
3960	For supplementary heat coil, add				Ea.	10%				
4000	For increase in capacity thru use									
4020	of solar collector, size boiler at 60%									

23 82 Convection Heating and Cooling Units

23 82 13 – Valance Heating and Cooling Units

23 82 13.16 Valance Units

		Crew	Daily Output	Labor-Hours	Unit	Material	2012 Bare Costs Labor	Equipment	Total	Total Incl O&P
0010	**VALANCE UNITS**									
6000	Valance units, complete with 1/2" cooling coil, enclosure									
6020	2 tube	Q-5	18	.889	L.F.	30.50	44.50		75	101
6040	3 tube		16	1		36.50	50		86.50	116
6060	4 tube		16	1		41.50	50		91.50	121
6080	5 tube		15	1.067		47	53.50		100.50	133
6100	6 tube		15	1.067		52	53.50		105.50	138
6120	8 tube		14	1.143		75.50	57.50		133	170
6200	For 3/4" cooling coil, add					10%				

23 82 16 – Air Coils

23 82 16.10 Flanged Coils

		Crew	Daily Output	Labor-Hours	Unit	Material	2012 Bare Costs Labor	Equipment	Total	Total Incl O&P
0010	**FLANGED COILS**									
0100	Basic water, DX, or condenser coils									
0110	Copper tubes, alum. fins, galv. end sheets									
0112	H is finned height, L is finned length									
0120	3/8" x .016 tube, .0065 aluminum fins									
0130	2 row, 8 fins per inch									
0140	4" H x 12" L	Q-5	48	.333	Ea.	655	16.70		671.70	745
0150	4" H x 24" L		38.38	.417		680	21		701	775
0160	4" H x 48" L		19.25	.831		720	41.50		761.50	860
0170	4" H x 72" L		12.80	1.250		930	62.50		992.50	1,125
0180	6" H x 12" L		48	.333		635	16.70		651.70	720
0190	6" H x 24" L		25.60	.625		660	31.50		691.50	775
0200	6" H x 48" L		12.80	1.250		715	62.50		777.50	880
0210	6" H x 72" L		8.53	1.876		940	94		1,034	1,175
0220	10" H x 12" L		30.73	.521		675	26		701	780
0230	10" H x 24" L		15.33	1.044		715	52.50		767.50	865
0240	10" H x 48" L		7.69	2.081		795	104		899	1,025
0250	10" H x 72" L		5.12	3.125		1,050	157		1,207	1,400
0260	12" H x 12" L		25.60	.625		690	31.50		721.50	810
0270	12" H x 24" L		12.80	1.250		740	62.50		802.50	905
0280	12" H x 48" L		6.40	2.500		835	125		960	1,100
0290	12" H x 72" L		4.27	3.747		1,125	188		1,313	1,500
0300	16" H x 16" L		14.38	1.113		750	56		806	910
0310	16" H x 24" L		9.59	1.668		795	83.50		878.50	995
0320	16" H x 48" L		4.80	3.333		1,000	167		1,167	1,350
0330	16" H x 72" L		3.20	5		1,225	251		1,476	1,725
0340	20" H x 24" L		7.69	2.081		880	104		984	1,125
0350	20" H x 48" L		3.84	4.167		1,125	209		1,334	1,550
0360	20" H x 72" L		2.56	6.250		1,375	315		1,690	2,000
0370	24" H x 24" L		6.40	2.500		950	125		1,075	1,250
0380	24" H x 48" L		3.20	5		1,225	251		1,476	1,725
0390	24" H x 72" L		2.13	7.512		1,525	375		1,900	2,250

23 82 16 – Air Coils

23 82 16.10 Flanged Coils		Crew	Daily Output	Labor-Hours	Unit	Material	2012 Bare Costs Labor	Equipment	Total	Total Incl O&P
0400	30" H x 28" L	Q-5	4.39	3.645	Ea.	1,200	183		1,383	1,575
0410	30" H x 48" L		2.56	6.250		1,400	315		1,715	2,025
0420	30" H x 72" L		1.71	9.357		1,750	470		2,220	2,625
0430	30" H x 84" L		1.46	10.959		1,900	550		2,450	2,925
0440	34" H x 32" L		3.39	4.720		1,325	237		1,562	1,800
0450	34" H x 48" L		2.26	7.080		1,500	355		1,855	2,175
0460	34" H x 72" L		1.51	10.596		1,875	530		2,405	2,850
0470	34" H x 84" L	▼	1.29	12.403	▼	2,050	620		2,670	3,200
0600	For 10 fins per inch, add					1%				
0610	For 12 fins per inch, add					3%				
0620	For 4 row, add				Ea.	30%	50%			
0630	For 6 row, add					60%	100%			
0640	For 8 row, add				▼	80%	150%			
1100	1/2" x .017 tube, .0065 aluminum fins									
1110	2 row, 8 fins per inch									
1120	5" H x 5" L	Q-5	40	.400	Ea.	650	20		670	745
1130	5" H x 20" L		37.10	.431		685	21.50		706.50	790
1140	5" H x 45" L		16.41	.975		745	49		794	895
1150	5" H x 90" L		8.21	1.949		1,100	97.50		1,197.50	1,350
1160	7.5" H x 5" L		38.50	.416		625	21		646	720
1170	7.5" H x 20" L		24.62	.650		675	32.50		707.50	795
1180	7.5" H x 45" L		10.94	1.463		760	73.50		833.50	945
1190	7.5" H x 90" L		5.46	2.930		1,150	147		1,297	1,500
1200	12.5" H x 10" L		29.49	.543		715	27		742	825
1210	12.5" H x 20" L		14.75	1.085		765	54.50		819.50	920
1220	12.5" H x 45" L		6.55	2.443		890	122		1,012	1,175
1230	12.5" H x 90" L		3.28	4.878		1,375	245		1,620	1,900
1240	15" H x 15" L		16.41	.975		765	49		814	920
1250	15" H x 30" L		8.21	1.949		855	97.50		952.50	1,075
1260	15" H x 45" L		5.46	2.930		945	147		1,092	1,275
1270	15" H x 90" L		2.73	5.861		1,475	294		1,769	2,075
1280	20" H x 20" L		9.22	1.735		875	87		962	1,100
1290	20" H x 45" L		4.10	3.902		1,150	196		1,346	1,575
1300	20" H x 90" L		2.05	7.805		1,700	390		2,090	2,475
1310	25" H x 25" L		5.90	2.712		1,050	136		1,186	1,350
1320	25" H x 45" L		3.28	4.878		1,325	245		1,570	1,825
1330	25" H x 90" L		1.64	9.756		1,950	490		2,440	2,900
1340	30" H x 30" L		4.10	3.902		1,275	196		1,471	1,700
1350	30" H x 45" L		2.73	5.861		1,475	294		1,769	2,075
1360	30" H x 90" L		1.37	11.679		2,175	585		2,760	3,275
1370	35" H x 35" L		3.01	5.316		1,450	266		1,716	2,000
1380	35" H x 45" L		2.34	6.838		1,600	345		1,945	2,300
1390	35" H x 90" L		1.17	13.675		2,400	685		3,085	3,675
1400	42.5" H x 45" L		1.93	8.290		1,850	415		2,265	2,675
1410	42.5" H x 75" L		1.16	13.793		2,475	690		3,165	3,775
1420	42.5" H x 105" L	▼	.83	19.277		3,050	965		4,015	4,825
1600	For 10 fins per inch, add					2%				
1610	For 12 fins per inch, add					5%				
1620	For 4 row, add					35%	50%			
1630	For 6 row, add					65%	100%			
1640	For 8 row, add				▼	90%	150%			
2010	5/8" x .020" tube, .0065 aluminum fins									
2020	2 row, 8 fins per inch									

23 82 Convection Heating and Cooling Units

23 82 16 – Air Coils

23 82 16.10 Flanged Coils		Crew	Daily Output	Labor-Hours	Unit	Material	2012 Bare Costs Labor	Equipment	Total	Total Incl O&P
2030	6" H x 6" L	Q-5	38	.421	Ea.	670	21		691	765
2040	6" H x 24" L		24.96	.641		720	32		752	845
2050	6" H x 48" L		12.48	1.282		795	64.50		859.50	965
2060	6" H x 96" L		6.24	2.564		1,175	129		1,304	1,500
2070	12" H x 12" L		24.96	.641		695	32		727	815
2080	12" H x 24" L		12.48	1.282		760	64.50		824.50	930
2090	12" H x 48" L		6.24	2.564		885	129		1,014	1,175
2100	12" H x 96" L		3.12	5.128		1,400	257		1,657	1,950
2110	18" H x 24" L		8.32	1.923		895	96.50		991.50	1,125
2120	18" H x 48" L		4.16	3.846		1,175	193		1,368	1,575
2130	18" H x 96" L		2.08	7.692		1,725	385		2,110	2,475
2140	24" H x 24" L		6.24	2.564		995	129		1,124	1,300
2150	24" H x 48" L		3.12	5.128		1,325	257		1,582	1,875
2160	24" H x 96" L		1.56	10.256		2,025	515		2,540	3,000
2170	30" H x 30" L		3.99	4.010		1,300	201		1,501	1,725
2180	30" H x 48" L		2.50	6.400		1,550	320		1,870	2,175
2190	30" H x 96" L		1.25	12.800		2,350	640		2,990	3,550
2200	30" H x 120" L		1	16		2,750	800		3,550	4,225
2210	36" H x 36" L		2.77	5.776		1,550	290		1,840	2,125
2220	36" H x 48" L		2.08	7.692		1,725	385		2,110	2,475
2230	36" H x 90" L		1.11	14.414		2,550	725		3,275	3,925
2240	36" H x 120" L		.83	19.277		3,125	965		4,090	4,875
2250	42" H x 48" L		1.78	8.989		1,925	450		2,375	2,775
2260	42" H x 90" L		.95	16.842		2,850	845		3,695	4,400
2270	42" H x 120" L		.71	22.535		3,475	1,125		4,600	5,525
2280	51" H x 48" L		1.47	10.884		2,250	545		2,795	3,300
2290	51" H x 96" L		.73	21.918		3,475	1,100		4,575	5,475
2300	51" H x 120" L		.59	27.119		4,075	1,350		5,425	6,550
2500	For 10 fins per inch, add					3%				
2510	For 12 fins per inch, add					6%				
2520	For 4 row, add				Ea.	40%	50%			
2530	For 6 row, add					80%	100%			
2540	For 8 row, add					110%	150%			
3000	Hot water booster coils									
3010	Copper tubes, alum. fins, galv. end sheets									
3012	H is finned height, L is finned length									
3020	1/2" x .017" tube, .0065 Al fins									
3030	1 row, 10 fins per inch									
3040	5"H x 10"L	Q-5	40	.400	Ea.	305	20		325	365
3050	5"H x 25"L		33.18	.482		335	24		359	400
3060	10"H x 10"L		39	.410		335	20.50		355.50	400
3070	10"H x 20"L		20.73	.772		360	38.50		398.50	460
3080	10"H x 30"L		13.83	1.157		390	58		448	520
3090	15"H x 15"L		18.44	.868		380	43.50		423.50	480
3110	15"H x 20"L		13.83	1.157		400	58		458	530
3120	15"H x 30"L		9.22	1.735		435	87		522	610
3130	20"H x 20"L		10.37	1.543		435	77.50		512.50	595
3140	20"H x 30"L		6.91	2.315		485	116		601	710
3150	20"H x 40"L		5.18	3.089		535	155		690	820
3160	25"H x 25"L		6.64	2.410		500	121		621	730
3170	25"H x 35"L		4.74	3.376		640	169		809	960
3180	25"H x 45"L		3.69	4.336		720	217		937	1,125
3190	30"H x 30"L		4.61	3.471		655	174		829	985

23 82 16 – Air Coils

23 82 16.10 Flanged Coils		Crew	Daily Output	Labor-Hours	Unit	Material	2012 Bare Costs Labor	Equipment	Total	Total Incl O&P
3200	30"H x 40"L	Q-5	3.46	4.624	Ea.	750	232		982	1,175
3210	30"H x 50"L	↓	2.76	5.797		835	291		1,126	1,350
3300	For 2 row, add				↓	20%	50%			
3400	1/2" x .020" tube, .008 Al fins									
3410	2 row, 10 fins per inch									
3420	20" H x 27" L	Q-5	7.27	2.201	Ea.	645	110		755	870
3430	20" H x 36" L		5.44	2.941		730	147		877	1,025
3440	20" H x 45" L		4.35	3.678		905	184		1,089	1,275
3450	25" H x 45" L		3.49	4.585		1,050	230		1,280	1,500
3460	25" H x 54" L		2.90	5.517		1,250	277		1,527	1,800
3470	30" H x 54" L		2.42	6.612		1,425	330		1,755	2,050
3480	35" H x 54" L		2.07	7.729		1,575	385		1,960	2,300
3490	35" H x 63" L		1.78	8.989		1,725	450		2,175	2,575
3500	40" H x 72" L		1.36	11.765		2,125	590		2,715	3,225
3510	55" H x 63" L		1.13	14.159		2,500	710		3,210	3,825
3520	55" H x 72" L		.99	16.162		2,750	810		3,560	4,250
3530	55" H x 81" L		.88	18.182		3,050	910		3,960	4,750
3540	75" H x 81" L		.64	25		3,975	1,250		5,225	6,275
3550	75" H x 90" L		.58	27.586		4,350	1,375		5,725	6,850
3560	75" H x 108" L	↓	.48	33.333	↓	5,100	1,675		6,775	8,125
3800	5/8" x .020" tubing, .0065 aluminum fins									
3810	1 row, 10 fins per inch									
3820	6" H x 12" L	Q-5	38	.421	Ea.	340	21		361	405
3830	6" H x 24" L		28.80	.556		345	28		373	420
3840	6" H x 30" L		23.04	.694		350	35		385	440
3850	12" H x 12" L		28.80	.556		350	28		378	425
3860	12" H x 24" L		14.40	1.111		380	55.50		435.50	505
3870	12" H x 30" L		11.52	1.389		400	69.50		469.50	545
3880	18" H x 18" L		12.80	1.250		400	62.50		462.50	535
3890	18" H x 24" L		9.60	1.667		425	83.50		508.50	590
3900	18" H x 36" L		6.40	2.500		475	125		600	710
3910	24" H x 24" L		7.20	2.222		470	111		581	685
3920	24" H x 30" L		4.80	3.333		615	167		782	925
3930	24" H x 36" L		5.05	3.168		665	159		824	975
3940	30" H x 30" L		4.61	3.471		690	174		864	1,025
3950	30" H x 36" L		3.85	4.159		745	209		954	1,125
3960	30" H x 42" L		3.29	4.863		810	244		1,054	1,250
3970	36" H x 36" L		3.20	5		825	251		1,076	1,300
3980	36" H x 42" L	↓	2.74	5.839		900	293		1,193	1,425
4100	For 2 row, add				↓	30%	50%			
4400	Steam and hot water heating coils									
4410	Copper tubes, alum. fins. galv. end sheets									
4412	H is finned height, L is finned length									
4420	5/8" tubing, to 175 psig working pressure									
4430	1 row, 8 fins per inch									
4440	6"H x 6"L	Q-5	38	.421	Ea.	635	21		656	730
4450	6"H x 12"L		37	.432		650	21.50		671.50	750
4460	6"H x 24"L		24.48	.654		675	33		708	795
4470	6"H x 36"L		16.32	.980		700	49		749	845
4480	6"H x 48"L		12.24	1.307		730	65.50		795.50	905
4490	6"H x 84"L		6.99	2.289		1,400	115		1,515	1,725
4500	6" H x 108" L		5.44	2.941		1,575	147		1,722	1,950
4510	12" H x 12" L	↓	24.48	.654	↓	765	33		798	890

23 82 16.10 Flanged Coils		Crew	Daily Output	Labor-Hours	Unit	Material	2012 Bare Costs Labor	Equipment	Total	Total Incl O&P
4520	12" H x 24" L	Q-5	12.24	1.307	Ea.	810	65.50		875.50	995
4530	12" H x 36" L		8.16	1.961		860	98.50		958.50	1,100
4540	12" H x 48" L		6.12	2.614		995	131		1,126	1,300
4550	12" H x 84" L		3.50	4.571		1,750	229		1,979	2,275
4560	12" H x 108" L		2.72	5.882		2,025	295		2,320	2,675
4570	18" H x 18" L		10.88	1.471		910	73.50		983.50	1,100
4580	18" H x 24" L		8.16	1.961		950	98.50		1,048.50	1,200
4590	18" H x 48" L		4.08	3.922		1,175	197		1,372	1,600
4600	18" H x 84" L		2.33	6.867		2,100	345		2,445	2,850
4610	18" H x 108" L		1.81	8.840		2,425	445		2,870	3,350
4620	24" H x 24" L		6.12	2.614		1,150	131		1,281	1,475
4630	24" H x 48" L		3.06	5.229		1,375	262		1,637	1,925
4640	24" H x 84" L		1.75	9.143		2,475	460		2,935	3,425
4650	24" H x 108" L		1.36	11.765		2,875	590		3,465	4,050
4660	36" H x 36" L		2.72	5.882		1,600	295		1,895	2,225
4670	36" H x 48" L		2.04	7.843		1,750	395		2,145	2,525
4680	36" H x 84" L		1.17	13.675		3,175	685		3,860	4,500
4690	36" H x 108" L		.91	17.582		3,725	880		4,605	5,425
4700	48"H x 48"L		1.53	10.458		2,150	525		2,675	3,150
4710	48"H x 84"L		.87	18.391		3,900	920		4,820	5,700
4720	48"H x 108"L		.68	23.529		4,625	1,175		5,800	6,850
4730	48"H x 126"L	↓	.58	27.586	↓	4,950	1,375		6,325	7,500
4910	For 10 fins per inch, add					2%				
4920	For 12 fins per inch, add					5%				
4930	For 2 row, add					30%	50%			
4940	For 3 row, add					50%	100%			
4950	For 4 row, add					80%	123%			
4960	For 230 PSIG heavy duty, add					20%	30%			
6000	Steam, heavy duty, 200 PSIG									
6010	Copper tubes, alum. fins, galv. end sheets									
6012	H is finned height, L is finned length									
6020	1" x .035" tubing, .010 aluminum fins									
6030	1 row, 8 fins per inch									
6040	12"H x 12"L	Q-5	24.48	.654	Ea.	915	33		948	1,050
6050	12"H x 24"L		12.24	1.307		1,025	65.50		1,090.50	1,250
6060	12"H x 36"L		8.16	1.961		1,150	98.50		1,248.50	1,425
6070	12"H x 48"L		6.12	2.614		1,375	131		1,506	1,700
6080	12"H x 84"L		3.50	4.571		1,925	229		2,154	2,450
6090	12"H x 108"L		2.72	5.882		2,275	295		2,570	2,950
6100	18"H x 24"L		8.16	1.961		1,275	98.50		1,373.50	1,550
6110	18"H x 36"L		5.44	2.941		1,550	147		1,697	1,925
6120	18"H x 48"L		4.08	3.922		1,750	197		1,947	2,225
6130	18"H x 84"L		2.33	6.867		2,475	345		2,820	3,225
6140	18"H x 108"L		1.81	8.840		2,975	445		3,420	3,950
6150	24"H x 24"L		6.12	2.614		1,650	131		1,781	2,025
6160	24"H x 36"L		4.08	3.922		1,850	197		2,047	2,350
6170	24"H x 48"L		3.06	5.229		2,100	262		2,362	2,725
6180	24"H x 84"L		1.75	9.143		3,025	460		3,485	4,025
6190	24"H x 108"L		1.36	11.765		3,650	590		4,240	4,925
6200	30"H x 36"L		3.26	4.908		2,175	246		2,421	2,750
6210	30"H x 48"L		2.45	6.531		2,475	325		2,800	3,225
6220	30"H x 84"L		1.40	11.429		3,575	575		4,150	4,800
6230	30"H x 108"L	↓	1.09	14.679	↓	4,350	735		5,085	5,875

23 82 16 – Air Coils

23 82 16.10 Flanged Coils

		Crew	Daily Output	Labor-Hours	Unit	Material	2012 Bare Costs Labor	Equipment	Total	Total Incl O&P
6240	36"H x 36"L	Q-5	2.72	5.882	Ea.	2,475	295		2,770	3,175
6250	36"H x 48"L		2.04	7.843		2,850	395		3,245	3,725
6260	36"H x 84"L		1.17	13.675		4,125	685		4,810	5,575
6270	36"H x 108"L		.91	17.582		5,050	880		5,930	6,875
6280	36"H x 120"L		.82	19.512		5,425	980		6,405	7,425
6290	48"H x 48"L		1.53	10.458		5,200	525		5,725	6,500
6300	48"H x 84"L		.87	18.391		5,250	920		6,170	7,175
6310	48"H x 108"L		.68	23.529		6,450	1,175		7,625	8,850
6320	48"H x 120"L		.61	26.230		6,925	1,325		8,250	9,600
6400	For 10 fins per inch, add					4%				
6410	For 12 fins per inch, add					10%				

23 82 16.20 Duct Heaters

		Crew	Daily Output	Labor-Hours	Unit	Material	2012 Bare Costs Labor	Equipment	Total	Total Incl O&P
0010	**DUCT HEATERS**, Electric, 480 V, 3 Ph.									
0020	Finned tubular insert, 500°F									
0100	8" wide x 6" high, 4.0 kW	Q-20	16	1.250	Ea.	740	60		800	905
0120	12" high, 8.0 kW		15	1.333		1,225	64		1,289	1,450
0140	18" high, 12.0 kW		14	1.429		1,725	68.50		1,793.50	2,000
0160	24" high, 16.0 kW		13	1.538		2,225	73.50		2,298.50	2,525
0180	30" high, 20.0 kW		12	1.667		2,700	80		2,780	3,100
0300	12" wide x 6" high, 6.7 kW		15	1.333		785	64		849	960
0320	12" high, 13.3 kW		14	1.429		1,275	68.50		1,343.50	1,500
0340	18" high, 20.0 kW		13	1.538		1,775	73.50		1,848.50	2,050
0360	24" high, 26.7 kW		12	1.667		2,275	80		2,355	2,650
0380	30" high, 33.3 kW		11	1.818		2,800	87		2,887	3,200
0500	18" wide x 6" high, 13.3 kW		14	1.429		845	68.50		913.50	1,025
0520	12" high, 26.7 kW		13	1.538		1,450	73.50		1,523.50	1,700
0540	18" high, 40.0 kW		12	1.667		1,925	80		2,005	2,250
0560	24" high, 53.3 kW		11	1.818		2,575	87		2,662	2,950
0580	30" high, 66.7 kW		10	2		3,225	95.50		3,320.50	3,675
0700	24" wide x 6" high, 17.8 kW		13	1.538		935	73.50		1,008.50	1,125
0720	12" high, 35.6 kW		12	1.667		1,575	80		1,655	1,850
0740	18" high, 53.3 kW		11	1.818		2,200	87		2,287	2,550
0760	24" high, 71.1 kW		10	2		2,850	95.50		2,945.50	3,300
0780	30" high, 88.9 kW		9	2.222		3,500	106		3,606	4,000
0900	30" wide x 6" high, 22.2 kW		12	1.667		990	80		1,070	1,200
0920	12" high, 44.4 kW		11	1.818		1,675	87		1,762	1,950
0940	18" high, 66.7 kW		10	2		2,350	95.50		2,445.50	2,725
0960	24" high, 88.9 kW		9	2.222		2,875	106		2,981	3,325
0980	30" high, 111.0 kW		8	2.500		3,700	120		3,820	4,250
1400	Note decreased kW available for									
1410	each duct size at same cost									
1420	See line 5000 for modifications and accessories									
2000	Finned tubular flange with insulated									
2020	terminal box, 500°F									
2100	12" wide x 36" high, 54 kW	Q-20	10	2	Ea.	3,650	95.50		3,745.50	4,150
2120	40" high, 60 kW		9	2.222		4,200	106		4,306	4,750
2200	24" wide x 36" high, 118.8 kW		9	2.222		4,450	106		4,556	5,050
2220	40" high, 132 kW		8	2.500		4,900	120		5,020	5,575
2400	36" wide x 8" high, 40 kW		11	1.818		1,850	87		1,937	2,175
2420	16" high, 80 kW		10	2		2,475	95.50		2,570.50	2,875
2440	24" high, 120 kW		9	2.222		3,250	106		3,356	3,725
2460	32" high, 160 kW		8	2.500		4,150	120		4,270	4,750

23 82 16 – Air Coils

23 82 16.20 Duct Heaters	Crew	Daily Output	Labor-Hours	Unit	Material	2012 Bare Costs Labor	Equipment	Total	Total Incl O&P
2480	36" high, 180 kW	Q-20	7	2.857	Ea.	5,125	137		5,262	5,825
2500	40" high, 200 kW		6	3.333		5,675	160		5,835	6,475
2600	40" wide x 8" high, 45 kW		11	1.818		1,925	87		2,012	2,250
2620	16" high, 90 kW		10	2		2,675	95.50		2,770.50	3,075
2640	24" high, 135 kW		9	2.222		3,375	106		3,481	3,875
2660	32" high, 180 kW		8	2.500		4,500	120		4,620	5,125
2680	36" high, 202.5 kW		7	2.857		5,200	137		5,337	5,900
2700	40" high, 225 kW		6	3.333		5,925	160		6,085	6,750
2800	48" wide x 8" high, 54.8 kW		10	2		2,025	95.50		2,120.50	2,375
2820	16" high, 109.8 kW		9	2.222		2,825	106		2,931	3,250
2840	24" high, 164.4 kW		8	2.500		3,575	120		3,695	4,125
2860	32" high, 219.2 kW		7	2.857		4,775	137		4,912	5,450
2880	36" high, 246.6 kW		6	3.333		5,500	160		5,660	6,300
2900	40" high, 274 kW		5	4		6,225	191		6,416	7,125
3000	56" wide x 8" high, 64 kW		9	2.222		2,300	106		2,406	2,700
3020	16" high, 128 kW		8	2.500		3,200	120		3,320	3,700
3040	24" high, 192 kW		7	2.857		3,875	137		4,012	4,475
3060	32" high, 256 kW		6	3.333		5,425	160		5,585	6,225
3080	36" high, 288kW		5	4		6,225	191		6,416	7,150
3100	40" high, 320kW		4	5		6,875	239		7,114	7,950
3200	64" wide x 8" high, 74kW		8	2.500		2,375	120		2,495	2,800
3220	16" high, 148kW		7	2.857		3,300	137		3,437	3,825
3240	24" high, 222kW		6	3.333		4,200	160		4,360	4,875
3260	32" high, 296kW		5	4		5,625	191		5,816	6,475
3280	36" high, 333kW		4	5		6,700	239		6,939	7,750
3300	40" high, 370kW		3	6.667		7,400	320		7,720	8,600
3800	Note decreased kW available for									
3820	each duct size at same cost									
5000	Duct heater modifications and accessories									
5120	T.C.O. limit auto or manual reset	Q-20	42	.476	Ea.	121	23		144	168
5140	Thermostat		28	.714		520	34		554	620
5160	Overheat thermocouple (removable)		7	2.857		735	137		872	1,025
5180	Fan interlock relay		18	1.111		177	53		230	276
5200	Air flow switch		20	1		153	48		201	241
5220	Split terminal box cover		100	.200		50.50	9.55		60.05	70
8000	To obtain BTU multiply kW by 3413									

23 82 19 – Fan Coil Units

23 82 19.10 Fan Coil Air Conditioning

		Crew	Daily Output	Labor-Hours	Unit	Material	2012 Bare Costs Labor	Equipment	Total	Total Incl O&P
0010	**FAN COIL AIR CONDITIONING** Cabinet mounted, filters, controls									
0100	Chilled water, 1/2 ton cooling	Q-5	8	2	Ea.	710	100		810	930
0110	3/4 ton cooling		7	2.286		735	115		850	985
0120	1 ton cooling		6	2.667		815	134		949	1,100
0140	1.5 ton cooling		5.50	2.909		920	146		1,066	1,225
0150	2 ton cooling		5.25	3.048		1,150	153		1,303	1,500
0160	2.5 ton cooling		5	3.200		1,525	160		1,685	1,925
0180	3 ton cooling		4	4		1,725	201		1,926	2,200
0262	For hot water coil, add					40%	10%			
0300	Console, 2 pipe with electric heat									
0310	1/2 ton cooling	Q-5	8	2	Ea.	1,225	100		1,325	1,500
0315	3/4 ton cooling		7	2.286		1,350	115		1,465	1,650
0320	1 ton cooling		6	2.667		1,450	134		1,584	1,800
0330	1.5 ton cooling		5.50	2.909		1,775	146		1,921	2,175

23 82 19.10 Fan Coil Air Conditioning		Crew	Daily Output	Labor-Hours	Unit	Material	2012 Bare Costs Labor	Equipment	Total	Total Incl O&P
0340	2 ton cooling	Q-5	4.70	3.404	Ea.	2,350	171		2,521	2,850
0345	2-1/2 ton cooling		4.70	3.404		3,425	171		3,596	4,000
0350	3 ton cooling		4	4		4,725	201		4,926	5,475
0360	4 ton cooling		4	4		4,900	201		5,101	5,700
0940	Direct expansion, for use w/air cooled condensing unit, 1.5 ton cooling		5	3.200		690	160		850	1,000
0950	2 ton cooling		4.80	3.333		750	167		917	1,075
0960	2.5 ton cooling		4.40	3.636		790	182		972	1,150
0970	3 ton cooling		3.80	4.211		985	211		1,196	1,400
0980	3.5 ton cooling		3.60	4.444		1,025	223		1,248	1,475
0990	4 ton cooling		3.40	4.706		1,150	236		1,386	1,625
1000	5 ton cooling		3	5.333		1,325	267		1,592	1,850
1020	7.5 ton cooling		3	5.333		2,475	267		2,742	3,125
1040	10 ton cooling	Q-6	2.60	9.231		2,975	480		3,455	4,000
1042	12.5 ton cooling		2.30	10.435		3,875	540		4,415	5,075
1050	15 ton cooling		1.60	15		4,100	780		4,880	5,675
1060	20 ton cooling		.70	34.286		5,575	1,775		7,350	8,850
1070	25 ton cooling		.65	36.923		7,000	1,925		8,925	10,600
1080	30 ton cooling		.60	40		7,350	2,075		9,425	11,200
1500	For hot water coil, add					40%	10%			
1512	For condensing unit add see Section 23 62									
3000	Chilled water, horizontal unit, housing, 2 pipe, fan control, no valves									
3100	1/2 ton cooling	Q-5	8	2	Ea.	1,150	100		1,250	1,400
3110	1 ton cooling		6	2.667		1,375	134		1,509	1,725
3120	1.5 ton cooling		5.50	2.909		1,650	146		1,796	2,050
3130	2 ton cooling		5.25	3.048		1,975	153		2,128	2,400
3140	3 ton cooling		4	4		2,300	201		2,501	2,825
3150	3.5 ton cooling		3.80	4.211		2,525	211		2,736	3,100
3160	4 ton cooling		3.80	4.211		2,525	211		2,736	3,100
3170	5 ton cooling		3.40	4.706		2,925	236		3,161	3,575
3180	6 ton cooling		3.40	4.706		2,925	236		3,161	3,575
3190	7 ton cooling		2.90	5.517		3,200	277		3,477	3,950
3200	8 ton cooling		2.90	5.517		3,200	277		3,477	3,950
3210	10 ton cooling	Q-6	2.80	8.571		3,750	445		4,195	4,800
3240	For hot water coil, add					40%	10%			
4000	With electric heat, 2 pipe									
4100	1/2 ton cooling	Q-5	8	2	Ea.	1,400	100		1,500	1,675
4105	3/4 ton cooling		7	2.286		1,550	115		1,665	1,875
4110	1 ton cooling		6	2.667		1,700	134		1,834	2,050
4120	1.5 ton cooling		5.50	2.909		1,875	146		2,021	2,300
4130	2 ton cooling		5.25	3.048		2,375	153		2,528	2,825
4135	2.5 ton cooling		4.80	3.333		3,275	167		3,442	3,850
4140	3 ton cooling		4	4		4,500	201		4,701	5,250
4150	3.5 ton cooling		3.80	4.211		5,375	211		5,586	6,250
4160	4 ton cooling		3.60	4.444		6,225	223		6,448	7,175
4170	5 ton cooling		3.40	4.706		7,400	236		7,636	8,475
4180	6 ton cooling		3.20	5		7,400	251		7,651	8,500
4190	7 ton cooling		2.90	5.517		7,350	277		7,627	8,500
4200	8 ton cooling		2.20	7.273		8,300	365		8,665	9,700
4210	10 ton cooling	Q-6	2.80	8.571		8,825	445		9,270	10,400

23 82 Convection Heating and Cooling Units

23 82 19 – Fan Coil Units

23 82 19.20 Heating and Ventilating Units	Crew	Daily Output	Labor-Hours	Unit	Material	2012 Bare Costs Labor	Equipment	Total	Total Incl O&P
0010 **HEATING AND VENTILATING UNITS**, Classroom units									
0020 Includes filter, heating/cooling coils, standard controls									
0080 750 CFM, 2 tons cooling	Q-6	2	12	Ea.	3,900	625		4,525	5,250
0100 1000 CFM, 2-1/2 tons cooling		1.60	15		4,600	780		5,380	6,250
0120 1250 CFM, 3 tons cooling		1.40	17.143		4,750	890		5,640	6,575
0140 1500 CFM, 4 tons cooling		.80	30		5,100	1,550		6,650	7,950
0160 2000 CFM 5 tons cooling	↓	.50	48		5,975	2,500		8,475	10,400
0500 For electric heat, add					35%				
1000 For no cooling, deduct				↓	25%	10%			

23 82 27 – Infrared Units

23 82 27.10 Infrared Type Heating Units

	Crew	Daily Output	Labor-Hours	Unit	Material	2012 Bare Costs Labor	Equipment	Total	Total Incl O&P
0010 **INFRARED TYPE HEATING UNITS**									
0020 Gas fired, unvented, electric ignition, 100% shutoff.									
0030 Piping and wiring not included									
0060 Input, 15 MBH	Q-5	7	2.286	Ea.	520	115		635	745
0100 30 MBH		6	2.667		1,075	134		1,209	1,400
0120 45 MBH		5	3.200		1,500	160		1,660	1,900
0140 50 MBH		4.50	3.556		1,575	178		1,753	2,000
0160 60 MBH		4	4		1,600	201		1,801	2,075
0180 75 MBH		3	5.333		1,625	267		1,892	2,175
0200 90 MBH		2.50	6.400		1,725	320		2,045	2,375
0220 105 MBH		2	8		1,850	400		2,250	2,625
0240 120 MBH	↓	2	8	↓	1,975	400		2,375	2,750
2000 Electric, single or three phase									
2050 6 kW, 20,478 BTU	1 Elec	2.30	3.478	Ea.	550	179		729	875
2100 13.5 KW, 40,956 BTU		2.20	3.636		795	187		982	1,150
2150 24 KW, 81,912 BTU	↓	2	4	↓	1,600	206		1,806	2,075
3000 Oil fired, pump, controls, fusible valve, oil supply tank									
3050 91,000 BTU	Q-5	2.50	6.400	Ea.	6,425	320		6,745	7,550
3080 105,000 BTU		2.25	7.111		6,800	355		7,155	8,050
3110 119,000 BTU	↓	2	8	↓	7,450	400		7,850	8,800

23 82 29 – Radiators

23 82 29.10 Hydronic Heating

	Crew	Daily Output	Labor-Hours	Unit	Material	2012 Bare Costs Labor	Equipment	Total	Total Incl O&P
0010 **HYDRONIC HEATING**, Terminal units, not incl. main supply pipe									
1000 Radiation									
1100 Panel, baseboard, C.I., including supports, no covers	Q-5	46	.348	L.F.	35.50	17.45		52.95	65.50
3000 Radiators, cast iron									
3100 Free standing or wall hung, 6 tube, 25" high	Q-5	96	.167	Section	37.50	8.35		45.85	54
3150 4 tube 25" high		96	.167		28	8.35		36.35	43.50
3200 4 tube, 19" high	↓	96	.167	↓	26	8.35		34.35	41.50
3250 Adj. brackets, 2 per wall radiator up to 30 sections	1 Stpi	32	.250	Ea.	36.50	13.95		50.45	61
3500 Recessed, 20" high x 5" deep, without grille	Q-5	60	.267	Section	32	13.35		45.35	55
3600 For inlet grille, add				"	2.21			2.21	2.43
9500 To convert SFR to BTU rating: Hot water, 150 x SFR									
9510 Forced hot water, 180 x SFR; steam, 240 x SFR									

23 82 33 – Convectors

23 82 33.10 Convector Units

	Crew	Daily Output	Labor-Hours	Unit	Material	2012 Bare Costs Labor	Equipment	Total	Total Incl O&P
0010 **CONVECTOR UNITS**, Terminal units, not incl. main supply pipe									
2204 Convector, multifin, 2 pipe w/cabinet									
2210 17" H x 24" L	Q-5	10	1.600	Ea.	99.50	80		179.50	231

23 82 Convection Heating and Cooling Units

23 82 33 – Convectors

23 82 33.10 Convector Units		Crew	Daily Output	Labor-Hours	Unit	Material	2012 Bare Costs Labor	Equipment	Total	Total Incl O&P
2214	17" H x 36" L	Q-5	8.60	1.860	Ea.	149	93.50		242.50	305
2218	17" H x 48" L		7.40	2.162		199	108		307	380
2222	21" H x 24" L		9	1.778		99.50	89		188.50	244
2226	21" H x 36" L		8.20	1.951		149	98		247	310
2228	21" H x 48" L		6.80	2.353		199	118		317	395
2240	For knob operated damper, add					140%				
2241	For metal trim strips, add	Q-5	64	.250	Ea.	19.25	12.55		31.80	40
2243	For snap-on inlet grille, add					10%	10%			
2245	For hinged access door, add	Q-5	64	.250	Ea.	35.50	12.55		48.05	58
2246	For air chamber, auto-venting, add	"	58	.276	"	6.85	13.85		20.70	28.50

23 82 36 – Finned-Tube Radiation Heaters

23 82 36.10 Finned Tube Radiation

		Crew	Daily Output	Labor-Hours	Unit	Material	Labor	Equipment	Total	Total Incl O&P
0010	**FINNED TUBE RADIATION**, Terminal units, not incl. main supply pipe									
1150	Fin tube, wall hung, 14" slope top cover, with damper									
1200	1-1/4" copper tube, 4-1/4" alum. fin	Q-5	38	.421	L.F.	42.50	21		63.50	78.50
1250	1-1/4" steel tube, 4-1/4" steel fin		36	.444		39	22.50		61.50	76.50
1255	2" steel tube, 4-1/4" steel fin		32	.500		42	25		67	84.50
1260	21", two tier, slope top, w/damper									
1262	1-1/4" copper tube, 4-1/4" alum. fin	Q-5	30	.533	L.F.	50	26.50		76.50	95.50
1264	1-1/4" steel tube, 4-1/4" steel fin		28	.571		46.50	28.50		75	94
1266	2" steel tube, 4-1/4" steel fin		25	.640		49.50	32		81.50	103
1270	10", flat top, with damper									
1272	1-1/4" copper tube, 4-1/4" alum. fin	Q-5	38	.421	L.F.	21	21		42	55
1274	1-1/4" steel tube, 4-1/4" steel fin		36	.444		39	22.50		61.50	76.50
1276	2" steel tube, 4-1/4" steel fin		32	.500		42	25		67	84.50
1280	17", two tier, flat top, w/damper									
1282	1-1/4" copper tube, 4-1/4" alum. fin	Q-5	30	.533	L.F.	50	26.50		76.50	95.50
1284	1-1/4" steel tube, 4-1/4" steel fin		28	.571		46.50	28.50		75	94
1286	2" steel tube, 4-1/4" steel fin		25	.640		49.50	32		81.50	103
1301	Rough in wall hung, steel fin w/supply & balance valves	1 Stpi	.91	8.791	Ea.	294	490		784	1,075
1310	Baseboard, pkgd, 1/2" copper tube, alum. fin, 7" high	Q-5	60	.267	L.F.	7.65	13.35		21	28.50
1320	3/4" copper tube, alum. fin, 7" high		58	.276		8.40	13.85		22.25	30.50
1340	1" copper tube, alum. fin, 8-7/8" high		56	.286		18.30	14.30		32.60	41.50
1360	1-1/4" copper tube, alum. fin, 8-7/8" high		54	.296		30	14.85		44.85	55.50
1380	1-1/4" IPS steel tube with steel fins		52	.308		27	15.40		42.40	53
1381	Rough in baseboard panel & fin tube, supply & balance valves	1 Stpi	1.06	7.547	Ea.	315	420		735	980
1500	Note: fin tube may also require corners, caps, etc.									

23 82 39 – Unit Heaters

23 82 39.13 Cabinet Unit Heaters

		Crew	Daily Output	Labor-Hours	Unit	Material	Labor	Equipment	Total	Total Incl O&P
0010	**CABINET UNIT HEATERS**									
5400	Cabinet, horizontal, hot water, blower type									
5420	20 MBH	Q-5	10	1.600	Ea.	815	80		895	1,025
5430	60 MBH		7	2.286		1,425	115		1,540	1,750
5440	100 MBH		5	3.200		1,475	160		1,635	1,875
5450	120 MBH		4	4		1,550	201		1,751	2,000

23 82 39.16 Propeller Unit Heaters

		Crew	Daily Output	Labor-Hours	Unit	Material	Labor	Equipment	Total	Total Incl O&P
0010	**PROPELLER UNIT HEATERS**									
3950	Unit heaters, propeller, 115 V 2 psi steam, 60°F entering air									
4000	Horizontal, 12 MBH	Q-5	12	1.333	Ea.	345	67		412	480
4020	28.2 MBH		10	1.600		445	80		525	610
4040	36.5 MBH		8	2		520	100		620	725

23 82 Convection Heating and Cooling Units

23 82 39 – Unit Heaters

23 82 39.16 Propeller Unit Heaters	Crew	Daily Output	Labor-Hours	Unit	Material	2012 Bare Costs Labor	Equipment	Total	Total Incl O&P
4060	43.9 MBH	Q-5	8	2	Ea.	520	100		620	725
4080	56.5 MBH		7.50	2.133		555	107		662	770
4100	65.6 MBH		7	2.286		570	115		685	800
4120	87.6 MBH		6.50	2.462		620	123		743	865
4140	96.8 MBH		6	2.667		760	134		894	1,025
4160	133.3 MBH		5	3.200		820	160		980	1,150
4180	157.6 MBH		4	4		1,000	201		1,201	1,400
4200	197.7 MBH		3	5.333		1,150	267		1,417	1,650
4220	257.2 MBH		2.50	6.400		1,425	320		1,745	2,025
4240	286.9 MBH		2	8		1,575	400		1,975	2,325
4250	326.0 MBH		1.90	8.421		1,825	420		2,245	2,625
4260	364 MBH		1.80	8.889		1,975	445		2,420	2,850
4270	404 MBH	▼	1.60	10		2,500	500		3,000	3,500
4300	For vertical diffuser, add					174			174	191
4310	Vertical flow, 40 MBH	Q-5	11	1.455		735	73		808	920
4314	58.5 MBH		8	2		765	100		865	990
4318	92 MBH		7	2.286		975	115		1,090	1,250
4322	109.7 MBH		6	2.667		1,150	134		1,284	1,475
4326	131.0 MBH		4	4		1,150	201		1,351	1,575
4330	160.0 MBH		3	5.333		1,225	267		1,492	1,750
4334	194.0 MBH		2.20	7.273		1,400	365		1,765	2,100
4338	212.0 MBH		2.10	7.619		1,750	380		2,130	2,500
4342	247.0 MBH		1.96	8.163		2,075	410		2,485	2,900
4346	297.0 MBH	▼	1.80	8.889		2,200	445		2,645	3,100
4350	333.0 MBH	Q-6	1.90	12.632		2,400	655		3,055	3,625
4354	420 MBH, (460 V)		1.80	13.333		3,375	695		4,070	4,775
4358	500 MBH, (460 V)		1.71	14.035		4,700	730		5,430	6,275
4362	570 MBH, (460 V)		1.40	17.143		5,975	890		6,865	7,925
4366	620 MBH, (460 V)		1.30	18.462		6,525	960		7,485	8,625
4370	960 MBH, (460 V)	▼	1.10	21.818	▼	7,200	1,125		8,325	9,600
4400	Unit heaters, propeller, hot water, 115 V, 60 Deg. F entering air									
4404	Horizontal									
4408	6 MBH	Q-5	11	1.455	Ea.	345	73		418	490
4412	12 MBH		11	1.455		345	73		418	490
4416	16 MBH		10	1.600		385	80		465	545
4420	24 MBH		9	1.778		445	89		534	625
4424	29 MBH		8	2		520	100		620	725
4428	47 MBH		7	2.286		570	115		685	800
4432	63 MBH		6	2.667		620	134		754	880
4436	81 MBH		5.50	2.909		760	146		906	1,050
4440	90 MBH		5	3.200		820	160		980	1,150
4460	133 MBH		4	4		1,000	201		1,201	1,400
4464	139 MBH		3.50	4.571		1,150	229		1,379	1,600
4468	198 MBH		2.50	6.400		1,425	320		1,745	2,025
4472	224 MBH		2	8		1,575	400		1,975	2,325
4476	273 MBH	▼	1.50	10.667	▼	2,150	535		2,685	3,175
4500	Vertical									
4504	8 MBH	Q-5	13	1.231	Ea.	735	61.50		796.50	905
4508	12 MBH		13	1.231		735	61.50		796.50	905
4512	16 MBH		13	1.231		735	61.50		796.50	905
4516	30 MBH		12	1.333		735	67		802	910
4520	43 MBH		11	1.455		765	73		838	950
4524	57 MBH	▼	8	2	▼	935	100		1,035	1,175

410

23 82 Convection Heating and Cooling Units

23 82 39 – Unit Heaters

23 82 39.16 Propeller Unit Heaters		Crew	Daily Output	Labor-Hours	Unit	Material	2012 Bare Costs Labor	2012 Bare Costs Equipment	Total	Total Incl O&P
4528	68 MBH	Q-5	7	2.286	Ea.	975	115		1,090	1,250
4540	105 MBH		6	2.667		1,150	134		1,284	1,475
4544	123 MBH		5	3.200		1,225	160		1,385	1,600
4550	140 MBH		5	3.200		1,400	160		1,560	1,800
4554	156 MBH		4	4		1,750	201		1,951	2,225
4560	210 MBH		4	4		2,200	201		2,401	2,725
4564	223 MBH		3	5.333		2,400	267		2,667	3,025
4568	257 MBH		2	8		2,400	400		2,800	3,225

23 83 Radiant Heating Units

23 83 16 – Radiant-Heating Hydronic Piping

23 83 16.10 Radiant Floor Heating

		Crew	Daily Output	Labor-Hours	Unit	Material	2012 Bare Costs Labor	2012 Bare Costs Equipment	Total	Total Incl O&P
0010	**RADIANT FLOOR HEATING**									
0100	Tubing, PEX (cross-linked polyethylene)									
0110	Oxygen barrier type for systems with ferrous materials									
0120	1/2"	Q-5	800	.020	L.F.	.99	1		1.99	2.60
0130	3/4"		535	.030		1.40	1.50		2.90	3.80
0140	1"		400	.040		2.19	2.01		4.20	5.45
0200	Non barrier type for ferrous free systems									
0210	1/2"	Q-5	800	.020	L.F.	.57	1		1.57	2.14
0220	3/4"		535	.030		1.05	1.50		2.55	3.42
0230	1"		400	.040		1.80	2.01		3.81	5
1000	Manifolds									
1110	Brass									
1120	With supply and return valves, flow meter, thermometer,									
1122	auto air vent and drain/fill valve.									
1130	1", 2 circuit	Q-5	14	1.143	Ea.	245	57.50		302.50	355
1140	1", 3 circuit		13.50	1.185		280	59.50		339.50	400
1150	1", 4 circuit		13	1.231		305	61.50		366.50	430
1154	1", 5 circuit		12.50	1.280		365	64		429	495
1158	1", 6 circuit		12	1.333		395	67		462	535
1162	1", 7 circuit		11.50	1.391		430	70		500	580
1166	1", 8 circuit		11	1.455		480	73		553	635
1172	1", 9 circuit		10.50	1.524		515	76.50		591.50	680
1174	1", 10 circuit		10	1.600		555	80		635	730
1178	1", 11 circuit		9.50	1.684		575	84.50		659.50	760
1182	1", 12 circuit		9	1.778		635	89		724	835
1610	Copper manifold header, (cut to size)									
1620	1" header, 12 – 1/2" sweat outlets	Q-5	3.33	4.805	Ea.	91	241		332	465
1630	1-1/4" header, 12 – 1/2" sweat outlets		3.20	5		106	251		357	495
1640	1-1/4" header, 12 – 3/4" sweat outlets		3	5.333		114	267		381	530
1650	1-1/2" header, 12 – 3/4" sweat outlets		3.10	5.161		139	259		398	545
1660	2" header, 12 – 3/4" sweat outlets		2.90	5.517		201	277		478	635
3000	Valves									
3110	Thermostatic zone valve actuator with end switch	Q-5	40	.400	Ea.	36.50	20		56.50	70
3114	Thermostatic zone valve actuator	"	36	.444	"	81	22.50		103.50	123
3120	Motorized straight zone valve with operator complete									
3130	3/4"	Q-5	35	.457	Ea.	125	23		148	173
3140	1"		32	.500		137	25		162	189
3150	1-1/4"		29.60	.541		165	27		192	223
3500	4 Way mixing valve, manual, brass									

23 83 Radiant Heating Units

23 83 16 – Radiant-Heating Hydronic Piping

23 83 16.10 Radiant Floor Heating		Crew	Daily Output	Labor-Hours	Unit	Material	2012 Bare Costs Labor	Equipment	Total	Total Incl O&P
3530	1"	Q-5	13.30	1.203	Ea.	126	60.50		186.50	230
3540	1-1/4"		11.40	1.404		137	70.50		207.50	257
3550	1-1/2"		11	1.455		203	73		276	335
3560	2"		10.60	1.509		288	75.50		363.50	430
3800	Mixing valve motor, 4 way for valves, 1" and 1-1/4"		34	.471		310	23.50		333.50	375
3810	Mixing valve motor, 4 way for valves, 1-1/2" and 2"	▼	30	.533	▼	355	26.50		381.50	430
5000	Radiant floor heating, zone control panel									
5120	4 Zone actuator valve control, expandable	Q-5	20	.800	Ea.	163	40		203	240
5130	6 Zone actuator valve control, expandable		18	.889		199	44.50		243.50	286
6070	Thermal track, straight panel for long continuous runs, 5.333 S.F.		40	.400		20	20		40	52
6080	Thermal track, utility panel, for direction reverse at run end, 5.333 S.F.		40	.400		20	20		40	52
6090	Combination panel, for direction reverse plus straight run, 5.333 S.F.	▼	40	.400	▼	20	20		40	52
7000	PEX tubing fittings									
7100	Compression type									
7116	Coupling									
7120	1/2" x 1/2"	1 Stpi	27	.296	Ea.	6.40	16.50		22.90	32
7124	3/4" x 3/4"	"	23	.348	"	10.60	19.35		29.95	40.50
7130	Adapter									
7132	1/2" x female sweat 1/2"	1 Stpi	27	.296	Ea.	4.33	16.50		20.83	30
7134	1/2" x female sweat 3/4"		26	.308		4.88	17.15		22.03	31.50
7136	5/8" x female sweat 3/4"	▼	24	.333	▼	7	18.55		25.55	35.50
7140	Elbow									
7142	1/2" x female sweat 1/2"	1 Stpi	27	.296	Ea.	6.65	16.50		23.15	32.50
7144	1/2" x female sweat 3/4"		26	.308		7.80	17.15		24.95	34.50
7146	5/8" x female sweat 3/4"	▼	24	.333	▼	8.75	18.55		27.30	37.50
7200	Insert type									
7206	PEX x male NPT									
7210	1/2" x 1/2"	1 Stpi	29	.276	Ea.	2.48	15.35		17.83	25.50
7220	3/4" x 3/4"		27	.296		3.67	16.50		20.17	29
7230	1" x 1"	▼	26	.308	▼	6.05	17.15		23.20	32.50
7300	PEX coupling									
7310	1/2" x 1/2"	1 Stpi	30	.267	Ea.	.94	14.85		15.79	23.50
7320	3/4" x 3/4"		29	.276		1.17	15.35		16.52	24.50
7330	1" x 1"	▼	28	.286	▼	2.20	15.90		18.10	26.50
7400	PEX stainless crimp ring									
7410	1/2" x 1/2"	1 Stpi	86	.093	Ea.	.34	5.20		5.54	8.15
7420	3/4" x 3/4"		84	.095		.47	5.30		5.77	8.50
7430	1" x 1"	▼	82	.098	▼	.68	5.45		6.13	8.95

23 83 33 – Electric Radiant Heaters

23 83 33.10 Electric Heating

		Crew	Daily Output	Labor-Hours	Unit	Material	2012 Bare Costs Labor	Equipment	Total	Total Incl O&P
0010	**ELECTRIC HEATING**, not incl. conduit or feed wiring									
1100	Rule of thumb: Baseboard units, including control	1 Elec	4.40	1.818	kW	98	93.50		191.50	248
1300	Baseboard heaters, 2' long, 375 watt		8	1	Ea.	40	51.50		91.50	121
1400	3' long, 500 watt		8	1		46	51.50		97.50	128
1600	4' long, 750 watt		6.70	1.194		64	61.50		125.50	163
1800	5' long, 935 watt		5.70	1.404		68	72.50		140.50	183
2000	6' long, 1125 watt		5	1.600		74	82.50		156.50	205
2200	7' long, 1310 watt		4.40	1.818		84	93.50		177.50	233
2400	8' long, 1500 watt		4	2		92	103		195	255
2600	9' long, 1680 watt		3.60	2.222		104	115		219	285
2800	10' long, 1875 watt	▼	3.30	2.424	▼	193	125		318	400
2950	Wall heaters with fan, 120 to 277 volt									

23 83 33 – Electric Radiant Heaters

23 83 33.10 Electric Heating		Crew	Daily Output	Labor-Hours	Unit	Material	2012 Bare Costs Labor	Equipment	Total	Total Incl O&P
3160	Recessed, residential, 750 watt	1 Elec	6	1.333	Ea.	134	68.50		202.50	250
3170	1000 watt		6	1.333		134	68.50		202.50	250
3180	1250 watt		5	1.600		134	82.50		216.50	270
3190	1500 watt		4	2		134	103		237	300
3210	2000 watt		4	2		134	103		237	300
3230	2500 watt		3.50	2.286		335	118		453	545
3240	3000 watt		3	2.667		495	137		632	745
3250	4000 watt		2.70	2.963		495	153		648	775
3260	Commercial, 750 watt		6	1.333		181	68.50		249.50	300
3270	1000 watt		6	1.333		181	68.50		249.50	300
3280	1250 watt		5	1.600		181	82.50		263.50	320
3290	1500 watt		4	2		181	103		284	355
3300	2000 watt		4	2		181	103		284	355
3310	2500 watt		3.50	2.286		181	118		299	375
3320	3000 watt		3	2.667		330	137		467	565
3330	4000 watt		2.70	2.963		330	153		483	590
3600	Thermostats, integral		16	.500		30	26		56	71.50
3800	Line voltage, 1 pole		8	1		31	51.50		82.50	111
3810	2 pole		8	1		29.50	51.50		81	110
3820	Low voltage, 1 pole		8	1		34.50	51.50		86	115
4000	Heat trace system, 400 degree									
4020	115 V, 2.5 watts per L.F.	1 Elec	530	.015	L.F.	7.35	.78		8.13	9.25
4030	5 watts per L.F.		530	.015		7.35	.78		8.13	9.25
4050	10 watts per L.F.		530	.015		7.35	.78		8.13	9.25
4060	208 V, 5 watts per L.F.		530	.015		7.35	.78		8.13	9.25
4080	480 V, 8 watts per L.F.		530	.015		7.35	.78		8.13	9.25
4200	Heater raceway									
4260	Heat transfer cement									
4280	1 gallon				Ea.	57			57	62.50
4300	5 gallon				"	220			220	242
4320	Snap band, clamp									
4340	3/4" pipe size	1 Elec	470	.017	Ea.		.88		.88	1.31
4360	1" pipe size		444	.018			.93		.93	1.39
4380	1-1/4" pipe size		400	.020			1.03		1.03	1.54
4400	1-1/2" pipe size		355	.023			1.16		1.16	1.74
4420	2" pipe size		320	.025			1.29		1.29	1.93
4440	3" pipe size		160	.050			2.58		2.58	3.85
4460	4" pipe size		100	.080			4.12		4.12	6.15
4480	Thermostat NEMA 3R, 22 amp, 0-150 Deg, 10' cap.		8	1		236	51.50		287.50	335
4500	Thermostat NEMA 4X, 25 amp, 40 Deg, 5-1/2' cap.		7	1.143		236	59		295	350
4520	Thermostat NEMA 4X, 22 amp, 25-325 Deg, 10' cap.		7	1.143		635	59		694	790
4540	Thermostat NEMA 4X, 22 amp, 15-140 Deg,		6	1.333		535	68.50		603.50	695
4580	Thermostat NEMA 4,7,9, 22 amp, 25-325 Deg, 10' cap.		3.60	2.222		785	115		900	1,025
4600	Thermostat NEMA 4,7,9, 22 amp, 15-140 Deg,		3	2.667		775	137		912	1,050
4720	Fiberglass application tape, 36 yard roll		11	.727		74	37.50		111.50	138
5000	Radiant heating ceiling panels, 2' x 4', 500 watt		16	.500		252	26		278	315
5050	750 watt		16	.500		288	26		314	355
5200	For recessed plaster frame, add		32	.250		102	12.90		114.90	131
5300	Infrared quartz heaters, 120 volts, 1000 watts		6.70	1.194		255	61.50		316.50	375
5350	1500 watt		5	1.600		255	82.50		337.50	405
5400	240 volts, 1500 watt		5	1.600		255	82.50		337.50	405
5450	2000 watt		4	2		255	103		358	435
5500	3000 watt		3	2.667		283	137		420	515

23 83 Radiant Heating Units

23 83 33 – Electric Radiant Heaters

23 83 33.10 Electric Heating		Crew	Daily Output	Labor-Hours	Unit	Material	2012 Bare Costs Labor	Equipment	Total	Total Incl O&P
5550	4000 watt	1 Elec	2.60	3.077	Ea.	283	159		442	545
5570	Modulating control	↓	.80	10	↓	305	515		820	1,100
5600	Unit heaters, heavy duty, with fan & mounting bracket									
5650	Single phase, 208-240-277 volt, 3 kW	1 Elec	3.20	2.500	Ea.	420	129		549	655
5750	5 kW		2.40	3.333		430	172		602	730
5800	7 kW		1.90	4.211		665	217		882	1,050
5850	10 kW		1.30	6.154		760	315		1,075	1,325
5950	15 kW		.90	8.889		1,225	460		1,685	2,025
6000	480 volt, 3 kW		3.30	2.424		455	125		580	685
6020	4 kW		3	2.667		465	137		602	715
6040	5 kW		2.60	3.077		480	159		639	760
6060	7 kW		2	4		715	206		921	1,100
6080	10 kW		1.40	5.714		780	295		1,075	1,300
6100	13 kW		1.10	7.273		1,225	375		1,600	1,900
6120	15 kW		1	8		1,225	410		1,635	1,975
6140	20 kW		.90	8.889		1,600	460		2,060	2,425
6300	3 phase, 208-240 volt, 5 kW		2.40	3.333		410	172		582	705
6320	7 kW		1.90	4.211		630	217		847	1,025
6340	10 kW		1.30	6.154		680	315		995	1,225
6360	15 kW		.90	8.889		1,150	460		1,610	1,925
6380	20 kW		.70	11.429		1,625	590		2,215	2,650
6400	25 kW		.50	16		1,875	825		2,700	3,300
6500	480 volt, 5 kW		2.60	3.077		570	159		729	865
6520	7 kW		2	4		720	206		926	1,100
6540	10 kW		1.40	5.714		760	295		1,055	1,275
6560	13 kW		1.10	7.273		1,250	375		1,625	1,925
6580	15 kW		1	8		1,250	410		1,660	2,000
6600	20 kW		.90	8.889		1,600	460		2,060	2,425
6620	25 kW		.60	13.333		1,925	685		2,610	3,125
6630	30 kW		.70	11.429		2,225	590		2,815	3,325
6640	40 kW		.60	13.333		2,825	685		3,510	4,150
6650	50 kW	↓	.50	16	↓	3,425	825		4,250	4,975
6800	Vertical discharge heaters, with fan									
6820	Single phase, 208-240-277 volt, 10 kW	1 Elec	1.30	6.154	Ea.	705	315		1,020	1,250
6840	15 kW		.90	8.889		1,175	460		1,635	1,975
6900	3 phase, 208-240 volt, 10 kW		1.30	6.154		680	315		995	1,225
6920	15 kW		.90	8.889		1,150	460		1,610	1,925
6940	20 kW		.70	11.429		1,625	590		2,215	2,650
6960	25 kW		.50	16		1,925	825		2,750	3,325
6980	30 kW		.40	20		2,225	1,025		3,250	4,000
7000	40 kW		.36	22.222		2,825	1,150		3,975	4,825
7020	50 kW		.32	25		3,425	1,300		4,725	5,675
7100	480 volt, 10 kW		1.40	5.714		760	295		1,055	1,275
7120	15 kW		1	8		1,225	410		1,635	1,975
7140	20 kW		.90	8.889		1,600	460		2,060	2,425
7160	25 kW		.60	13.333		1,925	685		2,610	3,125
7180	30 kW		.50	16		2,225	825		3,050	3,675
7200	40 kW		.40	20		2,825	1,025		3,850	4,675
7220	50 kW	↓	.35	22.857	↓	3,425	1,175		4,600	5,500
7900	Cabinet convector heaters, 240 volt									
7920	3' long, 2000 watt	1 Elec	5.30	1.509	Ea.	1,900	78		1,978	2,225
7940	3000 watt		5.30	1.509		2,000	78		2,078	2,300
7960	4000 watt	↓	5.30	1.509	↓	2,050	78		2,128	2,375

23 83 33.10 Electric Heating	Crew	Daily Output	Labor-Hours	Unit	Material	2012 Bare Costs Labor	Equipment	Total	Total Incl O&P
7980	6000 watt	1 Elec	4.60	1.739	Ea.	2,125	89.50		2,214.50	2,450
8000	8000 watt		4.60	1.739		2,200	89.50		2,289.50	2,550
8020	4' long, 4000 watt		4.60	1.739		2,075	89.50		2,164.50	2,400
8040	6000 watt		4	2		2,150	103		2,253	2,525
8060	8000 watt		4	2		2,225	103		2,328	2,600
8080	10,000 watt		4	2		2,250	103		2,353	2,625
8100	Available also in 208 or 277 volt									
8200	Cabinet unit heaters, 120 to 277 volt, 1 pole,									
8220	wall mounted, 2 kW	1 Elec	4.60	1.739	Ea.	2,000	89.50		2,089.50	2,325
8230	3 kW		4.60	1.739		2,075	89.50		2,164.50	2,425
8240	4 kW		4.40	1.818		2,150	93.50		2,243.50	2,500
8250	5 kW		4.40	1.818		2,200	93.50		2,293.50	2,575
8260	6 kW		4.20	1.905		2,225	98		2,323	2,600
8270	8 kW		4	2		2,300	103		2,403	2,675
8280	10 kW		3.80	2.105		2,325	109		2,434	2,725
8290	12 kW		3.50	2.286		2,375	118		2,493	2,800
8300	13.5 kW		2.90	2.759		2,475	142		2,617	2,950
8310	16 kW		2.70	2.963		3,000	153		3,153	3,525
8320	20 kW		2.30	3.478		3,550	179		3,729	4,175
8330	24 kW		1.90	4.211		3,600	217		3,817	4,300
8350	Recessed, 2 kW		4.40	1.818		2,075	93.50		2,168.50	2,425
8370	3 kW		4.40	1.818		2,150	93.50		2,243.50	2,525
8380	4 kW		4.20	1.905		2,200	98		2,298	2,575
8390	5 kW		4.20	1.905		2,275	98		2,373	2,650
8400	6 kW		4	2		2,300	103		2,403	2,675
8410	8 kW		3.80	2.105		2,375	109		2,484	2,750
8420	10 kW		3.50	2.286		2,900	118		3,018	3,350
8430	12 kW		2.90	2.759		2,900	142		3,042	3,425
8440	13.5 kW		2.70	2.963		2,950	153		3,103	3,475
8450	16 kW		2.30	3.478		2,950	179		3,129	3,525
8460	20 kW		1.90	4.211		3,475	217		3,692	4,150
8470	24 kW		1.60	5		3,525	258		3,783	4,250
8490	Ceiling mounted, 2 kW		3.20	2.500		2,000	129		2,129	2,400
8510	3 kW		3.20	2.500		2,075	129		2,204	2,500
8520	4 kW		3	2.667		2,125	137		2,262	2,550
8530	5 kW		3	2.667		2,200	137		2,337	2,625
8540	6 kW		2.80	2.857		2,275	147		2,422	2,750
8550	8 kW		2.40	3.333		2,300	172		2,472	2,775
8560	10 kW		2.20	3.636		2,325	187		2,512	2,850
8570	12 kW		2	4		2,375	206		2,581	2,925
8580	13.5 kW		1.50	5.333		2,475	275		2,750	3,125
8590	16 kW		1.30	6.154		2,475	315		2,790	3,200
8600	20 kW		.90	8.889		3,550	460		4,010	4,575
8610	24 kW		.60	13.333		3,600	685		4,285	5,000
8630	208 to 480 V, 3 pole									
8650	Wall mounted, 2 kW	1 Elec	4.60	1.739	Ea.	2,000	89.50		2,089.50	2,325
8670	3 kW		4.60	1.739		2,075	89.50		2,164.50	2,425
8680	4 kW		4.40	1.818		2,125	93.50		2,218.50	2,500
8690	5 kW		4.40	1.818		2,200	93.50		2,293.50	2,575
8700	6 kW		4.20	1.905		2,225	98		2,323	2,600
8710	8 kW		4	2		2,300	103		2,403	2,675
8720	10 kW		3.80	2.105		2,325	109		2,434	2,725
8730	12 kW		3.50	2.286		2,375	118		2,493	2,800

23 83 Radiant Heating Units

23 83 33 – Electric Radiant Heaters

23 83 33.10 Electric Heating

		Crew	Daily Output	Labor-Hours	Unit	Material	2012 Bare Costs Labor	Equipment	Total	Total Incl O&P
8740	13.5 kW	1 Elec	2.90	2.759	Ea.	2,475	142		2,617	2,950
8750	16 kW		2.70	2.963		2,475	153		2,628	2,950
8760	20 kW		2.30	3.478		3,550	179		3,729	4,175
8770	24 kW		1.90	4.211		3,600	217		3,817	4,300
8790	Recessed, 2 kW		4.40	1.818		2,000	93.50		2,093.50	2,350
8810	3 kW		4.40	1.818		2,075	93.50		2,168.50	2,450
8820	4 kW		4.20	1.905		2,200	98		2,298	2,575
8830	5 kW		4.20	1.905		2,225	98		2,323	2,600
8840	6 kW		4	2		2,300	103		2,403	2,675
8850	8 kW		3.80	2.105		2,325	109		2,434	2,725
8860	10 kW		3.50	2.286		2,375	118		2,493	2,800
8870	12 kW		2.90	2.759		2,475	142		2,617	2,950
8880	13.5 kW		2.70	2.963		2,475	153		2,628	2,950
8890	16 kW		2.30	3.478		3,550	179		3,729	4,175
8900	20 kW		1.90	4.211		3,600	217		3,817	4,300
8920	24 kW		1.60	5		3,650	258		3,908	4,400
8940	Ceiling mount, 2 kW		3.20	2.500		2,075	129		2,204	2,500
8950	3 kW		3.20	2.500		2,125	129		2,254	2,550
8960	4 kW		3	2.667		2,200	137		2,337	2,625
8970	5 kW		3	2.667		2,225	137		2,362	2,650
8980	6 kW		2.80	2.857		2,225	147		2,372	2,675
8990	8 kW		2.40	3.333		2,300	172		2,472	2,775
9000	10 kW		2.20	3.636		2,325	187		2,512	2,825
9020	13.5 kW		1.50	5.333		2,475	275		2,750	3,125
9030	16 kW		1.30	6.154		3,500	315		3,815	4,325
9040	20 kW		.90	8.889		3,550	460		4,010	4,575
9060	24 kW		.60	13.333		3,600	685		4,285	5,000

23 84 Humidity Control Equipment

23 84 13 – Humidifiers

23 84 13.10 Humidifier Units

		Crew	Daily Output	Labor-Hours	Unit	Material	2012 Bare Costs Labor	Equipment	Total	Total Incl O&P
0010	**HUMIDIFIER UNITS**									
0520	Steam, room or duct, filter, regulators, auto. controls, 220 V									
0540	11 lb. per hour	Q-5	6	2.667	Ea.	2,450	134		2,584	2,900
0560	22 lb. per hour		5	3.200		2,700	160		2,860	3,225
0580	33 lb. per hour		4	4		2,775	201		2,976	3,350
0600	50 lb. per hour		4	4		3,400	201		3,601	4,050
0620	100 lb. per hour		3	5.333		4,075	267		4,342	4,875
0640	150 lb. per hour		2.50	6.400		5,400	320		5,720	6,400
0660	200 lb. per hour		2	8		6,675	400		7,075	7,950
0700	With blower									
0720	11 lb. per hour	Q-5	5.50	2.909	Ea.	3,625	146		3,771	4,225
0740	22 lb. per hour		4.75	3.368		3,875	169		4,044	4,500
0760	33 lb. per hour		3.75	4.267		3,925	214		4,139	4,650
0780	50 lb. per hour		3.50	4.571		4,525	229		4,754	5,325
0800	100 lb. per hour		2.75	5.818		5,025	292		5,317	5,975
0820	150 lb. per hour		2	8		7,525	400		7,925	8,875
0840	200 lb. per hour		1.50	10.667		8,750	535		9,285	10,400
1000	Steam for duct installation, manifold with pneum. controls									
1010	3 – 191 lb./hr., 24" x 24"	Q-5	5	3.200	Ea.	1,900	160		2,060	2,325
1020	3 – 191 lb./hr., 48" x 48"		4.60	3.478		3,675	174		3,849	4,325

23 84 Humidity Control Equipment

23 84 13 – Humidifiers

23 84 13.10 Humidifier Units

		Crew	Daily Output	Labor-Hours	Unit	Material	2012 Bare Costs Labor	Equipment	Total	Total Incl O&P
1030	65 – 334 lb./hr., 36" x 36"	Q-5	4.80	3.333	Ea.	3,600	167		3,767	4,200
1040	65 – 334 lb./hr., 72" x 72"		4	4		3,875	201		4,076	4,575
1050	100 – 690 lb./hr., 48" x 48"		4	4		5,050	201		5,251	5,850
1060	100 – 690 lb./hr., 84" x 84"		3.60	4.444		5,200	223		5,423	6,050
1070	220 – 2000 lb./hr., 72" x 72"		3.80	4.211		5,275	211		5,486	6,125
1080	220 – 2000 lb./hr., 144" x 144"		3.40	4.706		6,175	236		6,411	7,125
1090	For electrically controlled unit, add					805			805	885
1092	For additional manifold, add					25%	15%			
1200	Electric steam, self generating, with manifold									
1210	1 – 96 lb./hr., 12" x 72"	Q-5	3.60	4.444	Ea.	8,225	223		8,448	9,375
1220	20 – 168 lb./hr., 12" x 72"		3.60	4.444		14,400	223		14,623	16,200
1290	For room mounting, add		16	1		236	50		286	335
5000	Furnace type, wheel bypass									
5020	10 GPD	1 Stpi	4	2	Ea.	267	111		378	460
5040	14 GPD		3.80	2.105		285	117		402	490
5060	19 GPD		3.60	2.222		300	124		424	515

23 84 16 – Mechanical Dehumidification Units

23 84 16.10 Dehumidifier Units

		Crew	Daily Output	Labor-Hours	Unit	Material	2012 Bare Costs Labor	Equipment	Total	Total Incl O&P
0010	**DEHUMIDIFIER UNITS**									
6000	Self contained with filters and standard controls									
6040	1.5 lb./hr., 50 CFM	1 Plum	8	1	Ea.	5,300	54.50		5,354.50	5,900
6060	3 lb./hr., 150 CFM	Q-1	12	1.333		5,525	65.50		5,590.50	6,175
6065	6 lb./hr., 150 CFM		9	1.778		9,000	87.50		9,087.50	10,100
6070	16 to 20 lb./hr., 600 CFM		5	3.200		18,300	157		18,457	20,400
6080	30 to 40 lb./hr., 1125 CFM		4	4		28,600	197		28,797	31,700
6090	60 to 75 lb./hr., 2250 CFM		3	5.333		37,300	262		37,562	41,400
6100	120 to 155 lb./hr., 4500 CFM		2	8		66,000	395		66,395	73,000
6110	240 to 310 lb./hr., 9000 CFM		1.50	10.667		94,500	525		95,025	105,000
6120	400 to 515 lb./hr., 15,000 CFM	Q-2	1.60	15		128,000	765		128,765	142,000
6130	530 to 690 lb./hr., 20,000 CFM		1.40	17.143		139,000	875		139,875	154,000
6140	800 to 1030 lb./hr., 30,000 CFM		1.20	20		158,000	1,025		159,025	175,500
6150	1060 to 1375 lb./hr., 40,000 CFM		1	24		220,000	1,225		221,225	244,000

23 91 Prefabricated Equipment Supports

23 91 10 – Prefabricated Curbs, Pads and Stands

23 91 10.10 Prefabricated Pads and Stands

		Crew	Daily Output	Labor-Hours	Unit	Material	2012 Bare Costs Labor	Equipment	Total	Total Incl O&P
0010	**PREFABRICATED PADS AND STANDS**									
6000	Pad, fiberglass reinforced concrete with polystyrene foam core									
6050	Condenser, 2" thick, 20" x 38"	1 Shee	8	1	Ea.	25.50	52		77.50	108
6070	24" x 24"		16	.500		20	26		46	62
6090	24" x 36"		12	.667		32.50	35		67.50	88.50
6110	24" x 42"		8	1		42.50	52		94.50	127
6150	26" x 36"	Q-9	8	2		35.50	94		129.50	182
6170	28" x 38"	1 Shee	8	1		40	52		92	124
6190	30" x 30"		12	.667		34	35		69	90
6220	30" x 36"		8	1		40	52		92	124
6240	30" x 40"	Q-9	8	2		43.50	94		137.50	191
6260	32" x 32"		7	2.286		38	107		145	206
6280	36" x 36"		8	2		46.50	94		140.50	194
6300	36" x 40"		7	2.286		53	107		160	222

23 91 Prefabricated Equipment Supports

23 91 10 - Prefabricated Curbs, Pads and Stands

23 91 10.10 Prefabricated Pads and Stands	Crew	Daily Output	Labor-Hours	Unit	Material	2012 Bare Costs Labor	Equipment	Total	Total Incl O&P
6320	36" x 48"	Q-9	7	2.286	Ea.	62	107		169	232
6340	36" x 54"		6	2.667		75	125		200	274
6360	36" x 60" x 3"		7	2.286		89	107		196	262
6400	41" x 47" x 3"		6	2.667		83	125		208	282
6490	26" round		10	1.600		19.95	75		94.95	136
6550	30" round		9	1.778		26	83.50		109.50	156
6600	36" round	↓	8	2		36	94		130	183
6700	For 3" thick pad, add				↓	20%	5%			
8800	Stand, corrosion-resistant plastic									
8850	Heat pump, 6" high	1 Shee	32	.250	Ea.	4.60	13.05		17.65	25
8870	12" high	"	32	.250	"	11.35	13.05		24.40	32.50

Estimating Tips

26 05 00 Common Work Results for Electrical

- Conduit should be taken off in three main categories—power distribution, branch power, and branch lighting—so the estimator can concentrate on systems and components, therefore making it easier to ensure all items have been accounted for.

- For cost modifications for elevated conduit installation, add the percentages to labor according to the height of installation, and only to the quantities exceeding the different height levels, not to the total conduit quantities.

- Remember that aluminum wiring of equal ampacity is larger in diameter than copper and may require larger conduit.

- If more than three wires at a time are being pulled, deduct percentages from the labor hours of that grouping of wires.

- When taking off grounding systems, identify separately the type and size of wire, and list each unique type of ground connection.

- The estimator should take the weights of materials into consideration when completing a takeoff. Topics to consider include: How will the materials be supported? What methods of support are available? How high will the support structure have to reach? Will the final support structure be able to withstand the total burden? Is the support material included or separate from the fixture, equipment, and material specified?

- Do not overlook the costs for equipment used in the installation. If scaffolding or highlifts are available in the field, contractors may use them in lieu of the proposed ladders and rolling staging.

26 20 00 Low-Voltage Electrical Transmission

- Supports and concrete pads may be shown on drawings for the larger equipment, or the support system may be only a piece of plywood for the back of a panelboard. In either case, it must be included in the costs.

26 40 00 Electrical and Cathodic Protection

- When taking off cathodic protections systems, identify the type and size of cable, and list each unique type of anode connection.

26 50 00 Lighting

- Fixtures should be taken off room by room, using the fixture schedule, specifications, and the ceiling plan. For large concentrations of lighting fixtures in the same area, deduct the percentages from labor hours.

Reference Numbers

Reference numbers are shown in shaded boxes at the beginning of some major classifications. These numbers refer to related items in the Reference Section. The reference information may be an estimating procedure, an alternate pricing method, or technical information.

Note: Not all subdivisions listed here necessarily appear in this publication.

Note: **Trade Service,** *in part, has been used as a reference source for some of the material prices used in Division 26.*

26 05 33.95 Cutting and Drilling	Crew	Daily Output	Labor-Hours	Unit	Material	2012 Bare Costs Labor	Equipment	Total	Total Incl O&P
0010 CUTTING AND DRILLING									
0100 Hole drilling to 10' high, concrete wall									
0110 8" thick, 1/2" pipe size	R-31	12	.667	Ea.	.25	34.50	3.92	38.67	56
0120 3/4" pipe size		12	.667		.25	34.50	3.92	38.67	56
0130 1" pipe size		9.50	.842		.39	43.50	4.95	48.84	71
0140 1-1/4" pipe size		9.50	.842		.39	43.50	4.95	48.84	71
0150 1-1/2" pipe size		9.50	.842		.39	43.50	4.95	48.84	71
0160 2" pipe size		4.40	1.818		.54	93.50	10.70	104.74	152
0170 2-1/2" pipe size		4.40	1.818		.54	93.50	10.70	104.74	152
0180 3" pipe size		4.40	1.818		.54	93.50	10.70	104.74	152
0190 3-1/2" pipe size		3.30	2.424		.65	125	14.25	139.90	203
0200 4" pipe size		3.30	2.424		.65	125	14.25	139.90	203
0500 12" thick, 1/2" pipe size		9.40	.851		.37	44	5	49.37	71.50
0520 3/4" pipe size		9.40	.851		.37	44	5	49.37	71.50
0540 1" pipe size		7.30	1.096		.58	56.50	6.45	63.53	92
0560 1-1/4" pipe size		7.30	1.096		.58	56.50	6.45	63.53	92
0570 1-1/2" pipe size		7.30	1.096		.58	56.50	6.45	63.53	92
0580 2" pipe size		3.60	2.222		.81	115	13.05	128.86	186
0590 2-1/2" pipe size		3.60	2.222		.81	115	13.05	128.86	186
0600 3" pipe size		3.60	2.222		.81	115	13.05	128.86	186
0610 3-1/2" pipe size		2.80	2.857		.98	147	16.80	164.78	240
0630 4" pipe size		2.50	3.200		.98	165	18.80	184.78	269
0650 16" thick, 1/2" pipe size		7.60	1.053		.49	54.50	6.20	61.19	88.50
0670 3/4" pipe size		7	1.143		.49	59	6.70	66.19	96
0690 1" pipe size		6	1.333		.78	68.50	7.85	77.13	112
0710 1-1/4" pipe size		5.50	1.455		.78	75	8.55	84.33	122
0730 1-1/2" pipe size		5.50	1.455		.78	75	8.55	84.33	122
0750 2" pipe size		3	2.667		1.08	137	15.70	153.78	223
0770 2-1/2" pipe size		2.70	2.963		1.08	153	17.40	171.48	248
0790 3" pipe size		2.50	3.200		1.08	165	18.80	184.88	269
0810 3-1/2" pipe size		2.30	3.478		1.30	179	20.50	200.80	292
0830 4" pipe size		2	4		1.30	206	23.50	230.80	335
0850 20" thick, 1/2" pipe size		6.40	1.250		.61	64.50	7.35	72.46	105
0870 3/4" pipe size		6	1.333		.61	68.50	7.85	76.96	112
0890 1" pipe size		5	1.600		.97	82.50	9.40	92.87	134
0910 1-1/4" pipe size		4.80	1.667		.97	86	9.80	96.77	140
0930 1-1/2" pipe size		4.60	1.739		.97	89.50	10.25	100.72	146
0950 2" pipe size		2.70	2.963		1.35	153	17.40	171.75	249
0970 2-1/2" pipe size		2.40	3.333		1.35	172	19.60	192.95	280
0990 3" pipe size		2.20	3.636		1.35	187	21.50	209.85	305
1010 3-1/2" pipe size		2	4		1.63	206	23.50	231.13	340
1030 4" pipe size		1.70	4.706		1.63	243	27.50	272.13	395
1050 24" thick, 1/2" pipe size		5.50	1.455		.74	75	8.55	84.29	122
1070 3/4" pipe size		5.10	1.569		.74	81	9.20	90.94	132
1090 1" pipe size		4.30	1.860		1.16	96	10.95	108.11	156
1110 1-1/4" pipe size		4	2		1.16	103	11.75	115.91	168
1130 1-1/2" pipe size		4	2		1.16	103	11.75	115.91	168
1150 2" pipe size		2.40	3.333		1.63	172	19.60	193.23	280
1170 2-1/2" pipe size		2.20	3.636		1.63	187	21.50	210.13	305
1190 3" pipe size		2	4		1.63	206	23.50	231.13	340
1210 3-1/2" pipe size		1.80	4.444		1.95	229	26	256.95	370
1230 4" pipe size		1.50	5.333		1.95	275	31.50	308.45	445
1500 Brick wall, 8" thick, 1/2" pipe size		18	.444		.25	23	2.61	25.86	37

26 05 33 – Raceway and Boxes for Electrical Systems

26 05 33.95 Cutting and Drilling		Crew	Daily Output	Labor-Hours	Unit	Material	2012 Bare Costs			Total Incl O&P
							Labor	Equipment	Total	
1520	3/4" pipe size	R-31	18	.444	Ea.	.25	23	2.61	25.86	37
1540	1" pipe size		13.30	.602		.39	31	3.54	34.93	51
1560	1-1/4" pipe size		13.30	.602		.39	31	3.54	34.93	51
1580	1-1/2" pipe size		13.30	.602		.39	31	3.54	34.93	51
1600	2" pipe size		5.70	1.404		.54	72.50	8.25	81.29	118
1620	2-1/2" pipe size		5.70	1.404		.54	72.50	8.25	81.29	118
1640	3" pipe size		5.70	1.404		.54	72.50	8.25	81.29	118
1660	3-1/2" pipe size		4.40	1.818		.65	93.50	10.70	104.85	152
1680	4" pipe size		4	2		.65	103	11.75	115.40	168
1700	12" thick, 1/2" pipe size		14.50	.552		.37	28.50	3.24	32.11	46.50
1720	3/4" pipe size		14.50	.552		.37	28.50	3.24	32.11	46.50
1740	1" pipe size		11	.727		.58	37.50	4.28	42.36	61.50
1760	1-1/4" pipe size		11	.727		.58	37.50	4.28	42.36	61.50
1780	1-1/2" pipe size		11	.727		.58	37.50	4.28	42.36	61.50
1800	2" pipe size		5	1.600		.81	82.50	9.40	92.71	134
1820	2-1/2" pipe size		5	1.600		.81	82.50	9.40	92.71	134
1840	3" pipe size		5	1.600		.81	82.50	9.40	92.71	134
1860	3-1/2" pipe size		3.80	2.105		.98	109	12.40	122.38	177
1880	4" pipe size		3.30	2.424		.98	125	14.25	140.23	204
1900	16" thick, 1/2" pipe size		12.30	.650		.49	33.50	3.82	37.81	54.50
1920	3/4" pipe size		12.30	.650		.49	33.50	3.82	37.81	54.50
1940	1" pipe size		9.30	.860		.78	44.50	5.05	50.33	73
1960	1-1/4" pipe size		9.30	.860		.78	44.50	5.05	50.33	73
1980	1-1/2" pipe size		9.30	.860		.78	44.50	5.05	50.33	73
2000	2" pipe size		4.40	1.818		1.08	93.50	10.70	105.28	153
2010	2-1/2" pipe size		4.40	1.818		1.08	93.50	10.70	105.28	153
2030	3" pipe size		4.40	1.818		1.08	93.50	10.70	105.28	153
2050	3-1/2" pipe size		3.30	2.424		1.30	125	14.25	140.55	204
2070	4" pipe size		3	2.667		1.30	137	15.70	154	224
2090	20" thick, 1/2" pipe size		10.70	.748		.61	38.50	4.40	43.51	63
2110	3/4" pipe size		10.70	.748		.61	38.50	4.40	43.51	63
2130	1" pipe size		8	1		.97	51.50	5.90	58.37	84.50
2150	1-1/4" pipe size		8	1		.97	51.50	5.90	58.37	84.50
2170	1-1/2" pipe size		8	1		.97	51.50	5.90	58.37	84.50
2190	2" pipe size		4	2		1.35	103	11.75	116.10	168
2210	2-1/2" pipe size		4	2		1.35	103	11.75	116.10	168
2230	3" pipe size		4	2		1.35	103	11.75	116.10	168
2250	3-1/2" pipe size		3	2.667		1.63	137	15.70	154.33	224
2270	4" pipe size		2.70	2.963		1.63	153	17.40	172.03	249
2290	24" thick, 1/2" pipe size		9.40	.851		.74	44	5	49.74	72
2310	3/4" pipe size		9.40	.851		.74	44	5	49.74	72
2330	1" pipe size		7.10	1.127		1.16	58	6.65	65.81	95.50
2350	1-1/4" pipe size		7.10	1.127		1.16	58	6.65	65.81	95.50
2370	1-1/2" pipe size		7.10	1.127		1.16	58	6.65	65.81	95.50
2390	2" pipe size		3.60	2.222		1.63	115	13.05	129.68	187
2410	2-1/2" pipe size		3.60	2.222		1.63	115	13.05	129.68	187
2430	3" pipe size		3.60	2.222		1.63	115	13.05	129.68	187
2450	3-1/2" pipe size		2.80	2.857		1.95	147	16.80	165.75	241
2470	4" pipe size		2.50	3.200		1.95	165	18.80	185.75	270
3000	Knockouts to 8' high, metal boxes & enclosures									
3020	With hole saw, 1/2" pipe size	1 Elec	53	.151	Ea.		7.80		7.80	11.65
3040	3/4" pipe size		47	.170			8.75		8.75	13.10
3050	1" pipe size		40	.200			10.30		10.30	15.40

26 05 33 – Raceway and Boxes for Electrical Systems

26 05 33.95 Cutting and Drilling		Crew	Daily Output	Labor-Hours	Unit	Material	2012 Bare Costs Labor	Equipment	Total	Total Incl O&P
3060	1-1/4" pipe size	1 Elec	36	.222	Ea.		11.45		11.45	17.10
3070	1-1/2" pipe size		32	.250			12.90		12.90	19.25
3080	2" pipe size		27	.296			15.25		15.25	23
3090	2-1/2" pipe size		20	.400			20.50		20.50	31
4010	3" pipe size		16	.500			26		26	38.50
4030	3-1/2" pipe size		13	.615			31.50		31.50	47.50
4050	4" pipe size		11	.727			37.50		37.50	56
4070	With hand punch set, 1/2" pipe size		40	.200			10.30		10.30	15.40
4090	3/4" pipe size		32	.250			12.90		12.90	19.25
4110	1" pipe size		30	.267			13.75		13.75	20.50
4130	1-1/4" pipe size		28	.286			14.75		14.75	22
4150	1-1/2" pipe size		26	.308			15.85		15.85	23.50
4170	2" pipe size		20	.400			20.50		20.50	31
4190	2-1/2" pipe size		17	.471			24.50		24.50	36.50
4200	3" pipe size		15	.533			27.50		27.50	41
4220	3-1/2" pipe size		12	.667			34.50		34.50	51.50
4240	4" pipe size		10	.800			41		41	61.50
4260	With hydraulic punch, 1/2" pipe size		44	.182			9.35		9.35	14
4280	3/4" pipe size		38	.211			10.85		10.85	16.20
4300	1" pipe size		38	.211			10.85		10.85	16.20
4320	1-1/4" pipe size		38	.211			10.85		10.85	16.20
4340	1-1/2" pipe size		38	.211			10.85		10.85	16.20
4360	2" pipe size		32	.250			12.90		12.90	19.25
4380	2-1/2" pipe size		27	.296			15.25		15.25	23
4400	3" pipe size		23	.348			17.95		17.95	27
4420	3-1/2" pipe size		20	.400			20.50		20.50	31
4440	4" pipe size		18	.444			23		23	34

26 05 80 – Wiring Connections

26 05 80.10 Motor Connections		Crew	Daily Output	Labor-Hours	Unit	Material	2012 Bare Costs Labor	Equipment	Total	Total Incl O&P
0010	**MOTOR CONNECTIONS**									
0020	Flexible conduit and fittings, 115 volt, 1 phase, up to 1 HP motor	1 Elec	8	1	Ea.	10.30	51.50		61.80	88.50
0050	2 HP motor		6.50	1.231		10.55	63.50		74.05	107
0100	3 HP motor		5.50	1.455		16.50	75		91.50	130
0120	230 volt, 10 HP motor, 3 phase		4.20	1.905		17.55	98		115.55	166
0150	15 HP motor		3.30	2.424		30.50	125		155.50	221
0200	25 HP motor		2.70	2.963		36	153		189	268
0400	50 HP motor		2.20	3.636		89	187		276	380
0600	100 HP motor		1.50	5.333		217	275		492	650
1500	460 volt, 5 HP motor, 3 phase		8	1		11.15	51.50		62.65	89.50
1520	10 HP motor		8	1		11.15	51.50		62.65	89.50
1530	25 HP motor		6	1.333		19.65	68.50		88.15	125
1540	30 HP motor		6	1.333		19.65	68.50		88.15	125
1550	40 HP motor		5	1.600		30.50	82.50		113	157
1560	50 HP motor		5	1.600		34	82.50		116.50	161
1570	60 HP motor		3.80	2.105		38.50	109		147.50	204
1580	75 HP motor		3.50	2.286		51.50	118		169.50	233
1590	100 HP motor		2.50	3.200		76.50	165		241.50	330
1600	125 HP motor		2	4		101	206		307	420
1610	150 HP motor		1.80	4.444		106	229		335	455
1620	200 HP motor		1.50	5.333		166	275		441	595
2005	460 Volt, 5 HP motor, 3 Phase, w/sealtite		8	1		17.60	51.50		69.10	96.50
2010	10 HP motor		8	1		17.60	51.50		69.10	96.50

26 05 Common Work Results for Electrical

26 05 80 – Wiring Connections

26 05 80.10 Motor Connections

		Crew	Daily Output	Labor-Hours	Unit	Material	2012 Bare Costs Labor	Equipment	Total	Total Incl O&P
2015	25 HP motor	1 Elec	6	1.333	Ea.	31.50	68.50		100	138
2020	30 HP motor		6	1.333		31.50	68.50		100	138
2025	40 HP motor		5	1.600		59	82.50		141.50	188
2030	50 HP motor		5	1.600		59	82.50		141.50	188
2035	60 HP motor		3.80	2.105		92.50	109		201.50	264
2040	75 HP motor		3.50	2.286		96.50	118		214.50	282
2045	100 HP motor		2.50	3.200		129	165		294	390
2055	150 HP motor		1.80	4.444		135	229		364	490
2060	200 HP motor		1.50	5.333		965	275		1,240	1,450

26 05 90 – Residential Applications

26 05 90.10 Residential Wiring

		Crew	Daily Output	Labor-Hours	Unit	Material	2012 Bare Costs Labor	Equipment	Total	Total Incl O&P
0010	**RESIDENTIAL WIRING**									
0020	20' avg. runs and #14/2 wiring incl. unless otherwise noted									
1000	Service & panel, includes 24' SE-AL cable, service eye, meter,									
1010	Socket, panel board, main bkr., ground rod, 15 or 20 amp									
1020	1-pole circuit breakers, and misc. hardware									
1100	100 amp, with 10 branch breakers	1 Elec	1.19	6.723	Ea.	590	345		935	1,175
1110	With PVC conduit and wire		.92	8.696		670	450		1,120	1,400
1120	With RGS conduit and wire		.73	10.959		845	565		1,410	1,775
1150	150 amp, with 14 branch breakers		1.03	7.767		915	400		1,315	1,600
1170	With PVC conduit and wire		.82	9.756		1,075	505		1,580	1,925
1180	With RGS conduit and wire		.67	11.940		1,400	615		2,015	2,475
1200	200 amp, with 18 branch breakers	2 Elec	1.80	8.889		1,200	460		1,660	2,000
1220	With PVC conduit and wire		1.46	10.959		1,375	565		1,940	2,350
1230	With RGS conduit and wire		1.24	12.903		1,825	665		2,490	3,025
1800	Lightning surge suppressor for above services, add	1 Elec	32	.250		59.50	12.90		72.40	84.50
2000	Switch devices									
2100	Single pole, 15 amp, Ivory, with a 1-gang box, cover plate,									
2110	Type NM (Romex) cable	1 Elec	17.10	.468	Ea.	13.95	24		37.95	51.50
2120	Type MC (BX) cable		14.30	.559		30	29		59	76
2130	EMT & wire		5.71	1.401		38	72		110	150
2150	3-way, #14/3, type NM cable		14.55	.550		18.60	28.50		47.10	63
2170	Type MC cable		12.31	.650		40.50	33.50		74	94.50
2180	EMT & wire		5	1.600		42	82.50		124.50	170
2200	4-way, #14/3, type NM cable		14.55	.550		28	28.50		56.50	73.50
2220	Type MC cable		12.31	.650		50	33.50		83.50	105
2230	EMT & wire		5	1.600		51.50	82.50		134	180
2250	S.P., 20 amp, #12/2, type NM cable		13.33	.600		21.50	31		52.50	70
2270	Type MC cable		11.43	.700		35	36		71	92.50
2280	EMT & wire		4.85	1.649		47	85		132	179
2290	S.P. rotary dimmer, 600W, no wiring		17	.471		24	24.50		48.50	63
2300	S.P. rotary dimmer, 600W, type NM cable		14.55	.550		30	28.50		58.50	75.50
2320	Type MC cable		12.31	.650		46	33.50		79.50	101
2330	EMT & wire		5	1.600		55.50	82.50		138	185
2350	3-way rotary dimmer, type NM cable		13.33	.600		37.50	31		68.50	87
2370	Type MC cable		11.43	.700		53.50	36		89.50	113
2380	EMT & wire		4.85	1.649		63	85		148	197
2400	Interval timer wall switch, 20 amp, 1-30 min., #12/2									
2410	Type NM cable	1 Elec	14.55	.550	Ea.	59	28.50		87.50	107
2420	Type MC cable		12.31	.650		65.50	33.50		99	122
2430	EMT & wire		5	1.600		84	82.50		166.50	216
2500	Decorator style									

26 05 90.10 Residential Wiring	Crew	Daily Output	Labor-Hours	Unit	Material	2012 Bare Costs Labor	Equipment	Total	Total Incl O&P
2510	S.P., 15 amp, type NM cable	1 Elec	17.10	.468	Ea.	18.85	24		42.85	56.50
2520	Type MC cable		14.30	.559		35	29		64	81.50
2530	EMT & wire		5.71	1.401		43	72		115	156
2550	3-way, #14/3, type NM cable		14.55	.550		23.50	28.50		52	68.50
2570	Type MC cable		12.31	.650		45	33.50		78.50	99.50
2580	EMT & wire		5	1.600		47	82.50		129.50	175
2600	4-way, #14/3, type NM cable		14.55	.550		33	28.50		61.50	79
2620	Type MC cable		12.31	.650		54.50	33.50		88	110
2630	EMT & wire		5	1.600		56.50	82.50		139	185
2650	S.P., 20 amp, #12/2, type NM cable		13.33	.600		26.50	31		57.50	75
2670	Type MC cable		11.43	.700		40	36		76	98
2680	EMT & wire		4.85	1.649		52	85		137	184
2700	S.P., slide dimmer, type NM cable		17.10	.468		37.50	24		61.50	77.50
2720	Type MC cable		14.30	.559		54	29		83	103
2730	EMT & wire		5.71	1.401		63.50	72		135.50	178
2750	S.P., touch dimmer, type NM cable		17.10	.468		32.50	24		56.50	71.50
2770	Type MC cable		14.30	.559		48.50	29		77.50	96.50
2780	EMT & wire		5.71	1.401		58.50	72		130.50	172
2800	3-way touch dimmer, type NM cable		13.33	.600		52.50	31		83.50	104
2820	Type MC cable		11.43	.700		68.50	36		104.50	130
2830	EMT & wire	▼	4.85	1.649	▼	78	85		163	213
3000	Combination devices									
3100	S.P. switch/15 amp recpt., Ivory, 1-gang box, plate									
3110	Type NM cable	1 Elec	11.43	.700	Ea.	26.50	36		62.50	83.50
3120	Type MC cable		10	.800		43	41		84	109
3130	EMT & wire		4.40	1.818		52.50	93.50		146	198
3150	S.P. switch/pilot light, type NM cable		11.43	.700		27.50	36		63.50	84.50
3170	Type MC cable		10	.800		44	41		85	110
3180	EMT & wire		4.43	1.806		53.50	93		146.50	198
3190	2-S.P. switches, 2-#14/2, no wiring		14	.571		8.90	29.50		38.40	54
3200	2-S.P. switches, 2-#14/2, type NM cables		10	.800		31.50	41		72.50	96
3220	Type MC cable		8.89	.900		56	46.50		102.50	132
3230	EMT & wire		4.10	1.951		56.50	101		157.50	212
3250	3-way switch/15 amp recpt., #14/3, type NM cable		10	.800		35.50	41		76.50	101
3270	Type MC cable		8.89	.900		57	46.50		103.50	133
3280	EMT & wire		4.10	1.951		59	101		160	215
3300	2-3 way switches, 2-#14/3, type NM cables		8.89	.900		46.50	46.50		93	121
3320	Type MC cable		8	1		82.50	51.50		134	168
3330	EMT & wire		4	2		67	103		170	228
3350	S.P. switch/20 amp recpt., #12/2, type NM cable		10	.800		39.50	41		80.50	105
3370	Type MC cable		8.89	.900		46.50	46.50		93	121
3380	EMT & wire	▼	4.10	1.951	▼	65	101		166	222
3400	Decorator style									
3410	S.P. switch/15 amp recpt., type NM cable	1 Elec	11.43	.700	Ea.	31.50	36		67.50	89
3420	Type MC cable		10	.800		48	41		89	114
3430	EMT & wire		4.40	1.818		57.50	93.50		151	203
3450	S.P. switch/pilot light, type NM cable		11.43	.700		32.50	36		68.50	90
3470	Type MC cable		10	.800		48.50	41		89.50	115
3480	EMT & wire		4.40	1.818		58.50	93.50		152	204
3500	2-S.P. switches, 2-#14/2, type NM cables		10	.800		36.50	41		77.50	102
3520	Type MC cable		8.89	.900		61	46.50		107.50	137
3530	EMT & wire		4.10	1.951		61.50	101		162.50	218
3550	3-way/15 amp recpt., #14/3, type NM cable	▼	10	.800	▼	40.50	41		81.50	106

26 05 90 − Residential Applications

26 05 90.10 Residential Wiring	Crew	Daily Output	Labor-Hours	Unit	Material	2012 Bare Costs Labor	Equipment	Total	Total Incl O&P
3570 Type MC cable	1 Elec	8.89	.900	Ea.	62	46.50		108.50	138
3580 EMT & wire		4.10	1.951		64	101		165	221
3650 2-3 way switches, 2-#14/3, type NM cables		8.89	.900		51.50	46.50		98	127
3670 Type MC cable		8	1		87	51.50		138.50	173
3680 EMT & wire		4	2		72	103		175	233
3700 S.P. switch/20 amp recpt., #12/2, type NM cable		10	.800		44.50	41		85.50	111
3720 Type MC cable		8.89	.900		51.50	46.50		98	126
3730 EMT & wire	▼	4.10	1.951	▼	70	101		171	227
4000 Receptacle devices									
4010 Duplex outlet, 15 amp recpt., Ivory, 1-gang box, plate									
4015 Type NM cable	1 Elec	14.55	.550	Ea.	12.45	28.50		40.95	56
4020 Type MC cable		12.31	.650		28.50	33.50		62	81.50
4030 EMT & wire		5.33	1.501		36.50	77.50		114	157
4050 With #12/2, type NM cable		12.31	.650		15.55	33.50		49.05	67
4070 Type MC cable		10.67	.750		29	38.50		67.50	89.50
4080 EMT & wire		4.71	1.699		41	87.50		128.50	176
4100 20 amp recpt., #12/2, type NM cable		12.31	.650		25	33.50		58.50	77.50
4120 Type MC cable		10.67	.750		38.50	38.50		77	100
4130 EMT & wire	▼	4.71	1.699	▼	50.50	87.50		138	187
4140 For GFI see Section 26 05 90.10 line 4300 below									
4150 Decorator style, 15 amp recpt., type NM cable	1 Elec	14.55	.550	Ea.	17.30	28.50		45.80	61.50
4170 Type MC cable		12.31	.650		33.50	33.50		67	87
4180 EMT & wire		5.33	1.501		41.50	77.50		119	162
4200 With #12/2, type NM cable		12.31	.650		20.50	33.50		54	72.50
4220 Type MC cable		10.67	.750		33.50	38.50		72	95
4230 EMT & wire		4.71	1.699		45.50	87.50		133	181
4250 20 amp recpt. #12/2, type NM cable		12.31	.650		30	33.50		63.50	83
4270 Type MC cable		10.67	.750		43	38.50		81.50	106
4280 EMT & wire		4.71	1.699		55	87.50		142.50	192
4300 GFI, 15 amp recpt., type NM cable		12.31	.650		48	33.50		81.50	103
4320 Type MC cable		10.67	.750		64.50	38.50		103	129
4330 EMT & wire		4.71	1.699		72.50	87.50		160	211
4350 GFI with #12/2, type NM cable		10.67	.750		51.50	38.50		90	115
4370 Type MC cable		9.20	.870		64.50	45		109.50	138
4380 EMT & wire		4.21	1.900		76.50	98		174.50	230
4400 20 amp recpt., #12/2 type NM cable		10.67	.750		53.50	38.50		92	117
4420 Type MC cable		9.20	.870		66.50	45		111.50	141
4430 EMT & wire		4.21	1.900		78.50	98		176.50	233
4500 Weather-proof cover for above receptacles, add	▼	32	.250	▼	5.65	12.90		18.55	25.50
4550 Air conditioner outlet, 20 amp-240 volt recpt.									
4560 30' of #12/2, 2 pole circuit breaker									
4570 Type NM cable	1 Elec	10	.800	Ea.	65.50	41		106.50	134
4580 Type MC cable		9	.889		82	46		128	159
4590 EMT & wire		4	2		90	103		193	253
4600 Decorator style, type NM cable		10	.800		70.50	41		111.50	139
4620 Type MC cable		9	.889		86.50	46		132.50	164
4630 EMT & wire	▼	4	2	▼	95	103		198	258
4650 Dryer outlet, 30 amp-240 volt recpt., 20' of #10/3									
4660 2 pole circuit breaker									
4670 Type NM cable	1 Elec	6.41	1.248	Ea.	73	64.50		137.50	177
4680 Type MC cable		5.71	1.401		81.50	72		153.50	198
4690 EMT & wire	▼	3.48	2.299	▼	86.50	119		205.50	272
4700 Range outlet, 50 amp-240 volt recpt., 30' of #8/3									

26 05 90.10 Residential Wiring	Crew	Daily Output	Labor-Hours	Unit	Material	2012 Bare Costs Labor	2012 Bare Costs Equipment	Total	Total Incl O&P
4710	Type NM cable	1 Elec	4.21	1.900	Ea.	105	98		203	262
4720	Type MC cable		4	2		167	103		270	340
4730	EMT & wire		2.96	2.703		119	139		258	340
4750	Central vacuum outlet, Type NM cable		6.40	1.250		71	64.50		135.50	175
4770	Type MC cable		5.71	1.401		94	72		166	211
4780	EMT & wire	▼	3.48	2.299	▼	98	119		217	285
4800	30 amp-110 volt locking recpt., #10/2 circ. bkr.									
4810	Type NM cable	1 Elec	6.20	1.290	Ea.	82.50	66.50		149	190
4830	EMT & wire	"	3.20	2.500	"	109	129		238	310
4900	Low voltage outlets									
4910	Telephone recpt., 20' of 4/C phone wire	1 Elec	26	.308	Ea.	12.15	15.85		28	37
4920	TV recpt., 20' of RG59U coax wire, F type connector	"	16	.500	"	20.50	26		46.50	61
4950	Door bell chime, transformer, 2 buttons, 60' of bellwire									
4970	Economy model	1 Elec	11.50	.696	Ea.	76.50	36		112.50	138
4980	Custom model		11.50	.696		119	36		155	185
4990	Luxury model, 3 buttons	▼	9.50	.842	▼	320	43.50		363.50	420
6000	Lighting outlets									
6050	Wire only (for fixture), type NM cable	1 Elec	32	.250	Ea.	8.05	12.90		20.95	28
6070	Type MC cable		24	.333		17.30	17.20		34.50	44.50
6080	EMT & wire		10	.800		24	41		65	88
6100	Box (4"), and wire (for fixture), type NM cable		25	.320		20.50	16.50		37	47
6120	Type MC cable		20	.400		29.50	20.50		50	63.50
6130	EMT & wire	▼	11	.727	▼	36	37.50		73.50	96
6200	Fixtures (use with lines 6050 or 6100 above)									
6210	Canopy style, economy grade	1 Elec	40	.200	Ea.	37	10.30		47.30	56.50
6220	Custom grade		40	.200		57	10.30		67.30	78
6250	Dining room chandelier, economy grade		19	.421		92.50	21.50		114	135
6260	Custom grade		19	.421		272	21.50		293.50	330
6270	Luxury grade		15	.533		610	27.50		637.50	715
6310	Kitchen fixture (fluorescent), economy grade		30	.267		68.50	13.75		82.25	96
6320	Custom grade		25	.320		188	16.50		204.50	232
6350	Outdoor, wall mounted, economy grade		30	.267		35	13.75		48.75	59
6360	Custom grade		30	.267		120	13.75		133.75	153
6370	Luxury grade		25	.320		272	16.50		288.50	325
6410	Outdoor PAR floodlights, 1 lamp, 150 watt		20	.400		37.50	20.50		58	72.50
6420	2 lamp, 150 watt each		20	.400		62.50	20.50		83	99.50
6430	For infrared security sensor, add		32	.250		126	12.90		138.90	157
6450	Outdoor, quartz-halogen, 300 watt flood		20	.400		45.50	20.50		66	81
6600	Recessed downlight, round, pre-wired, 50 or 75 watt trim		30	.267		46.50	13.75		60.25	71.50
6610	With shower light trim		30	.267		57.50	13.75		71.25	83.50
6620	With wall washer trim		28	.286		69.50	14.75		84.25	98
6630	With eye-ball trim	▼	28	.286		69.50	14.75		84.25	98
6640	For direct contact with insulation, add					2.47			2.47	2.72
6700	Porcelain lamp holder	1 Elec	40	.200		4.83	10.30		15.13	20.50
6710	With pull switch		40	.200		5.65	10.30		15.95	21.50
6750	Fluorescent strip, 1-20 watt tube, wrap around diffuser, 24"		24	.333		58	17.20		75.20	89.50
6770	2-34 watt tubes, 48"		20	.400		88.50	20.50		109	129
6780	With residential ballast		20	.400		99.50	20.50		120	140
6800	Bathroom heat lamp, 1-250 watt		28	.286		51	14.75		65.75	78
6810	2-250 watt lamps	▼	28	.286	▼	81.50	14.75		96.25	112
6820	For timer switch, see Section 26 05 90.10 line 2400									
6900	Outdoor post lamp, incl. post, fixture, 35' of #14/2									
6910	Type NMC cable	1 Elec	3.50	2.286	Ea.	207	118		325	405

26 05 90 – Residential Applications

26 05 90.10 Residential Wiring	Crew	Daily Output	Labor-Hours	Unit	Material	2012 Bare Costs Labor	Equipment	Total	Total Incl O&P
6920	Photo-eye, add	1 Elec	27	.296	Ea.	37.50	15.25		52.75	64.50
6950	Clock dial time switch, 24 hr., w/enclosure, type NM cable		11.43	.700		72	36		108	133
6970	Type MC cable		11	.727		88	37.50		125.50	153
6980	EMT & wire		4.85	1.649		96	85		181	233
7000	Alarm systems									
7050	Smoke detectors, box, #14/3, type NM cable	1 Elec	14.55	.550	Ea.	37	28.50		65.50	83
7070	Type MC cable		12.31	.650		52.50	33.50		86	108
7080	EMT & wire		5	1.600		54	82.50		136.50	183
7090	For relay output to security system, add					14			14	15.40
8000	Residential equipment									
8050	Disposal hook-up, incl. switch, outlet box, 3' of flex									
8060	20 amp-1 pole circ. bkr., and 25' of #12/2									
8070	Type NM cable	1 Elec	10	.800	Ea.	36.50	41		77.50	102
8080	Type MC cable		8	1		51	51.50		102.50	133
8090	EMT & wire		5	1.600		64	82.50		146.50	193
8100	Trash compactor or dishwasher hook-up, incl. outlet box,									
8110	3' of flex, 15 amp-1 pole circ. bkr., and 25' of #14/2									
8120	Type NM cable	1 Elec	10	.800	Ea.	27	41		68	91
8130	Type MC cable		8	1		45.50	51.50		97	127
8140	EMT & wire		5	1.600		55	82.50		137.50	184
8150	Hot water sink dispensor hook-up, use line 8100									
8200	Vent/exhaust fan hook-up, type NM cable	1 Elec	32	.250	Ea.	8.05	12.90		20.95	28
8220	Type MC cable		24	.333		17.30	17.20		34.50	44.50
8230	EMT & wire		10	.800		24	41		65	88
8250	Bathroom vent fan, 50 CFM (use with above hook-up)									
8260	Economy model	1 Elec	15	.533	Ea.	27	27.50		54.50	70.50
8270	Low noise model		15	.533		36.50	27.50		64	81
8280	Custom model		12	.667		126	34.50		160.50	190
8300	Bathroom or kitchen vent fan, 110 CFM									
8310	Economy model	1 Elec	15	.533	Ea.	74.50	27.50		102	123
8320	Low noise model	"	15	.533	"	92.50	27.50		120	143
8350	Paddle fan, variable speed (w/o lights)									
8360	Economy model (AC motor)	1 Elec	10	.800	Ea.	124	41		165	198
8362	With light kit		10	.800		162	41		203	240
8370	Custom model (AC motor)		10	.800		195	41		236	277
8372	With light kit		10	.800		234	41		275	320
8380	Luxury model (DC motor)		8	1		385	51.50		436.50	500
8382	With light kit		8	1		425	51.50		476.50	545
8390	Remote speed switch for above, add		12	.667		32	34.50		66.50	87
8500	Whole house exhaust fan, ceiling mount, 36", variable speed									
8510	Remote switch, incl. shutters, 20 amp-1 pole circ. bkr.									
8520	30' of #12/2, type NM cable	1 Elec	4	2	Ea.	1,200	103		1,303	1,450
8530	Type MC cable		3.50	2.286		1,200	118		1,318	1,500
8540	EMT & wire		3	2.667		1,225	137		1,362	1,550
8600	Whirlpool tub hook-up, incl. timer switch, outlet box									
8610	3' of flex, 20 amp-1 pole GFI circ. bkr.									
8620	30' of #12/2, type NM cable	1 Elec	5	1.600	Ea.	133	82.50		215.50	269
8630	Type MC cable		4.20	1.905		142	98		240	305
8640	EMT & wire		3.40	2.353		154	121		275	350
8650	Hot water heater hook-up, incl. 1-2 pole circ. bkr., box;									
8660	3' of flex, 20' of #10/2, type NM cable	1 Elec	5	1.600	Ea.	37.50	82.50		120	165
8670	Type MC cable		4.20	1.905		58	98		156	211
8680	EMT & wire		3.40	2.353		58	121		179	245

26 05 Common Work Results for Electrical

26 05 90 – Residential Applications

26 05 90.10 Residential Wiring

		Crew	Daily Output	Labor-Hours	Unit	Material	2012 Bare Costs Labor	Equipment	Total	Total Incl O&P
9000	Heating/air conditioning									
9050	Furnace/boiler hook-up, incl. firestat, local on-off switch									
9060	Emergency switch, and 40' of type NM cable	1 Elec	4	2	Ea.	62	103		165	223
9070	Type MC cable		3.50	2.286		87	118		205	272
9080	EMT & wire		1.50	5.333		101	275		376	520
9100	Air conditioner hook-up, incl. local 60 amp disc. switch									
9110	3' sealtite, 40 amp, 2 pole circuit breaker									
9130	40' of #8/2, type NM cable	1 Elec	3.50	2.286	Ea.	234	118		352	435
9140	Type MC cable		3	2.667		330	137		467	565
9150	EMT & wire		1.30	6.154		273	315		588	775
9200	Heat pump hook-up, 1-40 & 1-100 amp 2 pole circ. bkr.									
9210	Local disconnect switch, 3' sealtite									
9220	40' of #8/2 & 30' of #3/2									
9230	Type NM cable	1 Elec	1.30	6.154	Ea.	615	315		930	1,150
9240	Type MC cable		1.08	7.407		760	380		1,140	1,400
9250	EMT & wire		.94	8.511		670	440		1,110	1,400
9500	Thermostat hook-up, using low voltage wire									
9520	Heating only, 25' of #18-3	1 Elec	24	.333	Ea.	10.95	17.20		28.15	37.50
9530	Heating/cooling, 25' of #18-4	"	20	.400	"	13.20	20.50		33.70	45.50

26 24 Switchboards and Panelboards

26 24 19 – Motor-Control Centers

26 24 19.40 Motor Starters and Controls

		Crew	Daily Output	Labor-Hours	Unit	Material	2012 Bare Costs Labor	Equipment	Total	Total Incl O&P
0010	**MOTOR STARTERS AND CONTROLS**									
0050	Magnetic, FVNR, with enclosure and heaters, 480 volt									
0080	2 HP, size 00	1 Elec	3.50	2.286	Ea.	207	118		325	405
0100	5 HP, size 0		2.30	3.478		259	179		438	555
0200	10 HP, size 1		1.60	5		291	258		549	705
0300	25 HP, size 2	2 Elec	2.20	7.273		545	375		920	1,150
0400	50 HP, size 3		1.80	8.889		890	460		1,350	1,675
0500	100 HP, size 4		1.20	13.333		1,975	685		2,660	3,200
0600	200 HP, size 5		.90	17.778		4,625	915		5,540	6,475
0610	400 HP, size 6		.80	20		19,300	1,025		20,325	22,800
0620	NEMA 7, 5 HP, size 0	1 Elec	1.60	5		1,425	258		1,683	1,950
0630	10 HP, size 1	"	1.10	7.273		1,500	375		1,875	2,200
0640	25 HP, size 2	2 Elec	1.80	8.889		2,425	460		2,885	3,325
0650	50 HP, size 3		1.20	13.333		3,625	685		4,310	5,025
0660	100 HP, size 4		.90	17.778		5,850	915		6,765	7,825
0670	200 HP, size 5		.50	32		14,000	1,650		15,650	17,900
0700	Combination, with motor circuit protectors, 5 HP, size 0	1 Elec	1.80	4.444		815	229		1,044	1,225
0800	10 HP, size 1	"	1.30	6.154		845	315		1,160	1,400
0900	25 HP, size 2	2 Elec	2	8		1,175	410		1,585	1,925
1000	50 HP, size 3		1.32	12.121		1,700	625		2,325	2,800
1200	100 HP, size 4		.80	20		3,725	1,025		4,750	5,650
1220	NEMA 7, 5 HP, size 0	1 Elec	1.30	6.154		2,725	315		3,040	3,450
1230	10 HP, size 1	"	1	8		2,775	410		3,185	3,675
1240	25 HP, size 2	2 Elec	1.32	12.121		3,725	625		4,350	5,000
1250	50 HP, size 3		.80	20		6,125	1,025		7,150	8,300
1260	100 HP, size 4		.60	26.667		9,550	1,375		10,925	12,600
1270	200 HP, size 5		.40	40		20,800	2,050		22,850	25,900
1400	Combination, with fused switch, 5 HP, size 0	1 Elec	1.80	4.444		620	229		849	1,025

26 24 Switchboards and Panelboards

26 24 19 – Motor-Control Centers

26 24 19.40 Motor Starters and Controls

		Crew	Daily Output	Labor-Hours	Unit	Material	2012 Bare Costs Labor	Equipment	Total	Total Incl O&P
1600	10 HP, size 1	1 Elec	1.30	6.154	Ea.	665	315		980	1,200
1800	25 HP, size 2	2 Elec	2	8		1,075	410		1,485	1,800
2000	50 HP, size 3		1.32	12.121		1,825	625		2,450	2,925
2200	100 HP, size 4		.80	20		3,175	1,025		4,200	5,050
3500	Magnetic FVNR with NEMA 12, enclosure & heaters, 480 volt									
3600	5 HP, size 0	1 Elec	2.20	3.636	Ea.	236	187		423	540
3700	10 HP, size 1	"	1.50	5.333		355	275		630	800
3800	25 HP, size 2	2 Elec	2	8		665	410		1,075	1,350
3900	50 HP, size 3		1.60	10		1,025	515		1,540	1,900
4000	100 HP, size 4		1	16		2,450	825		3,275	3,925
4100	200 HP, size 5		.80	20		5,875	1,025		6,900	8,000
4200	Combination, with motor circuit protectors, 5 HP, size 0	1 Elec	1.70	4.706		780	243		1,023	1,225
4300	10 HP, size 1	"	1.20	6.667		815	345		1,160	1,400
4400	25 HP, size 2	2 Elec	1.80	8.889		1,225	460		1,685	2,000
4500	50 HP, size 3		1.20	13.333		1,975	685		2,660	3,200
4600	100 HP, size 4		.74	21.622		4,475	1,125		5,600	6,600
4700	Combination, with fused switch, 5 HP, size 0	1 Elec	1.70	4.706		755	243		998	1,200
4800	10 HP, size 1	"	1.20	6.667		790	345		1,135	1,375
4900	25 HP, size 2	2 Elec	1.80	8.889		1,200	460		1,660	2,000
5000	50 HP, size 3		1.20	13.333		1,925	685		2,610	3,150
5100	100 HP, size 4		.74	21.622		3,900	1,125		5,025	5,975
5200	Factory installed controls, adders to size 0 thru 5									
5300	Start-stop push button	1 Elec	32	.250	Ea.	49.50	12.90		62.40	74
5400	Hand-off-auto-selector switch		32	.250		49.50	12.90		62.40	74
5500	Pilot light		32	.250		92.50	12.90		105.40	121
5600	Start-stop-pilot		32	.250		142	12.90		154.90	175
5700	Auxiliary contact, NO or NC		32	.250		68	12.90		80.90	94.50
5800	NO-NC		32	.250		136	12.90		148.90	169

26 29 Low-Voltage Controllers

26 29 13 – Enclosed Controllers

26 29 13.20 Control Stations

		Crew	Daily Output	Labor-Hours	Unit	Material	2012 Bare Costs Labor	Equipment	Total	Total Incl O&P
0010	**CONTROL STATIONS**									
0050	NEMA 1, heavy duty, stop/start	1 Elec	8	1	Ea.	135	51.50		186.50	226
0100	Stop/start, pilot light		6.20	1.290		184	66.50		250.50	305
0200	Hand/off/automatic		6.20	1.290		100	66.50		166.50	210
0400	Stop/start/reverse		5.30	1.509		182	78		260	315
0500	NEMA 7, heavy duty, stop/start		6	1.333		400	68.50		468.50	545
0600	Stop/start, pilot light		4	2		490	103		593	695

26 29 23 – Variable-Frequency Motor Controllers

26 29 23.10 Variable Frequency Drives/Adj. Frequency Drives

			Crew	Daily Output	Labor-Hours	Unit	Material	2012 Bare Costs Labor	Equipment	Total	Total Incl O&P
0010	**VARIABLE FREQUENCY DRIVES/ADJ. FREQUENCY DRIVES**										
0100	Enclosed (NEMA 1), 460 volt, for 3 HP motor size	G	1 Elec	.80	10	Ea.	1,100	515		1,615	2,000
0110	5 HP motor size	G		.80	10		1,250	515		1,765	2,150
0120	7.5 HP motor size	G		.67	11.940		1,500	615		2,115	2,575
0130	10 HP motor size	G		.67	11.940		1,775	615		2,390	2,875
0140	15 HP motor size	G	2 Elec	.89	17.978		2,125	925		3,050	3,700
0150	20 HP motor size	G		.89	17.978		2,525	925		3,450	4,150
0160	25 HP motor size	G		.67	23.881		3,125	1,225		4,350	5,300
0170	30 HP motor size	G		.67	23.881		3,850	1,225		5,075	6,100

26 29 Low-Voltage Controllers

26 29 23 – Variable-Frequency Motor Controllers

26 29 23.10 Variable Frequency Drives/Adj. Frequency Drives		Crew	Daily Output	Labor-Hours	Unit	Material	2012 Bare Costs Labor	Equipment	Total	Total Incl O&P
0180	40 HP motor size	G 2 Elec	.67	23.881	Ea.	4,625	1,225		5,850	6,925
0190	50 HP motor size	G	.53	30.189		5,775	1,550		7,325	8,675
0200	60 HP motor size	G R-3	.56	35.714		6,875	1,825	236	8,936	10,600
0210	75 HP motor size	G	.56	35.714		7,950	1,825	236	10,011	11,700
0220	100 HP motor size	G	.50	40		9,275	2,050	265	11,590	13,500
0230	125 HP motor size	G	.50	40		10,300	2,050	265	12,615	14,700
0240	150 HP motor size	G	.50	40		11,900	2,050	265	14,215	16,300
0250	200 HP motor size	G	.42	47.619		15,400	2,425	315	18,140	20,900
1100	Custom-engineered, 460 volt, for 3 HP motor size	G 1 Elec	.56	14.286		2,575	735		3,310	3,925
1110	5 HP motor size	G	.56	14.286		2,575	735		3,310	3,925
1120	7.5 HP motor size	G	.47	17.021		2,700	875		3,575	4,275
1130	10 HP motor size	G	.47	17.021		2,825	875		3,700	4,400
1140	15 HP motor size	G 2 Elec	.62	25.806		3,525	1,325		4,850	5,900
1150	20 HP motor size	G	.62	25.806		3,975	1,325		5,300	6,375
1160	25 HP motor size	G	.47	34.043		4,650	1,750		6,400	7,750
1170	30 HP motor size	G	.47	34.043		5,825	1,750		7,575	9,025
1180	40 HP motor size	G	.47	34.043		6,875	1,750		8,625	10,200
1190	50 HP motor size	G	.37	43.243		7,900	2,225		10,125	12,000
1200	60 HP motor size	G R-3	.39	51.282		11,900	2,625	340	14,865	17,400
1210	75 HP motor size	G	.39	51.282		12,700	2,625	340	15,665	18,200
1220	100 HP motor size	G	.35	57.143		13,900	2,925	380	17,205	20,100
1230	125 HP motor size	G	.35	57.143		14,800	2,925	380	18,105	21,100
1240	150 HP motor size	G	.35	57.143		17,000	2,925	380	20,305	23,500
1250	200 HP motor size	G	.29	68.966		22,200	3,525	455	26,180	30,200
2000	For complex & special design systems to meet specific									
2010	requirements, obtain quote from vendor.									

26 42 Cathodic Protection

26 42 16 – Passive Cathodic Protection for Underground Storage Tank

26 42 16.50 Cathodic Protection Wiring Methods

		Crew	Daily Output	Labor-Hours	Unit	Material	2012 Bare Costs Labor	Equipment	Total	Total Incl O&P
0010	**CATHODIC PROTECTION WIRING METHODS**									
1000	Anodes, magnesium type, 9 #	R-15	18.50	2.595	Ea.	38.50	131	17.50	187	258
1010	17 #		13	3.692		70	186	25	281	385
1020	32 #		10	4.800		122	242	32.50	396.50	535
1030	48 #		7.20	6.667		160	335	45	540	730
1100	Graphite type w/epoxy cap, 3" x 60" (32 #)	R-22	8.40	4.438		125	194		319	430
1110	4" x 80" (68 #)		6	6.213		237	272		509	670
1120	6" x 72" (80 #)		5.20	7.169		1,475	315		1,790	2,100
1130	6" x 36" (45 #)		9.60	3.883		745	170		915	1,075
2000	Rectifiers, silicon type, air cooled, 28 V/10 A	R-19	3.50	5.714		2,275	295		2,570	2,950
2010	20 V/20 A		3.50	5.714		2,325	295		2,620	3,000
2100	Oil immersed, 28 V/10 A		3	6.667		3,100	345		3,445	3,925
2110	20 V/20 A		3	6.667		3,125	345		3,470	3,950
3000	Anode backfill, coke breeze	R-22	3850	.010	Lb.	.22	.42		.64	.88
4000	Cable, HMWPE, No. 8		2.40	15.533	M.L.F.	490	680		1,170	1,575
4010	No. 6		2.40	15.533		730	680		1,410	1,825
4020	No. 4		2.40	15.533		1,100	680		1,780	2,250
4030	No. 2		2.40	15.533		1,725	680		2,405	2,925
4040	No. 1		2.20	16.945		2,350	740		3,090	3,725
4050	No. 1/0		2.20	16.945		2,925	740		3,665	4,325
4060	No. 2/0		2.20	16.945		4,525	740		5,265	6,125

26 42 16.50 Cathodic Protection Wiring Methods	Crew	Daily Output	Labor-Hours	Unit	Material	2012 Bare Costs Labor	Equipment	Total	Total Incl O&P
4070	No. 4/0	R-22	2	18.640	M.L.F.	5,875	815		6,690	7,700
5000	Test station, 7 terminal box, flush curb type w/lockable cover	R-19	12	1.667	Ea.	70.50	86		156.50	207
5010	Reference cell, 2" dia PVC conduit, cplg., plug, set flush	"	4.80	4.167	"	148	215		363	485

Division Notes

		CREW	DAILY OUTPUT	LABOR-HOURS	UNIT	2012 BARE COSTS				TOTAL INCL O&P
						MAT.	LABOR	EQUIP.	TOTAL	

Estimating Tips

- When estimating material costs for electronic safety and security systems, it is always prudent to obtain manufacturers' quotations for equipment prices and special installation requirements that affect the total cost.
- Fire alarm systems consist of control panels, annunciator panels, battery with rack, charger, and fire alarm actuating and indicating devices. Some fire alarm systems include speakers, telephone lines, door closer controls, and other components. Be careful not to overlook the costs related to installation for these items.

Also be aware of costs for integrated automation instrumentation and terminal devices, control equipment, control wiring, and programming.

- Security equipment includes items such as CCTV, access control, and other detection and identification systems to perform alert and alarm functions. Be sure to consider the costs related to installation for this security equipment, such as for integrated automation instrumentation and terminal devices, control equipment, control wiring, and programming.

Reference Numbers

Reference numbers are shown in shaded boxes at the beginning of some major classifications. These numbers refer to related items in the Reference Section. The reference information may be an estimating procedure, an alternate pricing method, or technical information.

Note: Not all subdivisions listed here necessarily appear in this publication.

28 13 Access Control

28 13 53 – Security Access Detection

28 13 53.13 Security Access Metal Detectors

28 13 53.13 Security Access Metal Detectors	Crew	Daily Output	Labor-Hours	Unit	Material	2012 Bare Costs Labor	Equipment	Total	Total Incl O&P
0010 **SECURITY ACCESS METAL DETECTORS**									
0240 Metal detector, hand-held, wand type, unit only				Ea.	89			89	98
0250 Metal detector, walk through portal type, single zone	1 Elec	2	4		3,150	206		3,356	3,750
0260 Multi-zone	"	2	4		4,000	206		4,206	4,700

28 13 53.16 Security Access X-Ray Equipment

28 13 53.16 Security Access X-Ray Equipment	Crew	Daily Output	Labor-Hours	Unit	Material	2012 Bare Costs Labor	Equipment	Total	Total Incl O&P
0010 **SECURITY ACCESS X-RAY EQUIPMENT**									
0290 X-ray machine, desk top, for mail/small packages/letters	1 Elec	4	2	Ea.	3,350	103		3,453	3,850
0300 Conveyor type, incl monitor, minimum		2	4		15,700	206		15,906	17,500
0310 Maximum		2	4		28,000	206		28,206	31,100
0320 X-ray machine, large unit, for airports, incl monitor, min	2 Elec	1	16		39,200	825		40,025	44,300
0330 Maximum	"	.50	32		67,000	1,650		68,650	76,500

28 13 53.23 Security Access Explosive Detection Equipment

28 13 53.23 Security Access Explosive Detection Equipment	Crew	Daily Output	Labor-Hours	Unit	Material	2012 Bare Costs Labor	Equipment	Total	Total Incl O&P
0010 **SECURITY ACCESS EXPLOSIVE DETECTION EQUIPMENT**									
0270 Explosives detector, walk through portal type	1 Elec	2	4	Ea.	43,300	206		43,506	47,900
0280 Hand-held, battery operated				"				25,500	28,100

28 16 Intrusion Detection

28 16 16 – Intrusion Detection Systems Infrastructure

28 16 16.50 Intrusion Detection

28 16 16.50 Intrusion Detection	Crew	Daily Output	Labor-Hours	Unit	Material	2012 Bare Costs Labor	Equipment	Total	Total Incl O&P
0010 **INTRUSION DETECTION**, not including wires & conduits									
0100 Burglar alarm, battery operated, mechanical trigger	1 Elec	4	2	Ea.	272	103		375	455
0200 Electrical trigger		4	2		325	103		428	510
0400 For outside key control, add		8	1		82	51.50		133.50	168
0600 For remote signaling circuitry, add		8	1		122	51.50		173.50	212
0800 Card reader, flush type, standard		2.70	2.963		910	153		1,063	1,225
1000 Multi-code		2.70	2.963		1,175	153		1,328	1,525

28 23 Video Surveillance

28 23 23 – Video Surveillance Systems Infrastructure

28 23 23.50 Video Surveillance Equipments

28 23 23.50 Video Surveillance Equipments	Crew	Daily Output	Labor-Hours	Unit	Material	2012 Bare Costs Labor	Equipment	Total	Total Incl O&P
0010 **VIDEO SURVEILLANCE EQUIPMENTS**									
0200 Video cameras, wireless, hidden in exit signs, clocks, etc, incl receiver	1 Elec	3	2.667	Ea.	106	137		243	320
0210 Accessories for video recorder, single camera		3	2.667		179	137		316	400
0220 For multiple cameras		3	2.667		1,725	137		1,862	2,100
0230 Video cameras, wireless, for under vehicle searching, complete		2	4		9,975	206		10,181	11,300

28 31 Fire Detection and Alarm

28 31 23 – Fire Detection and Alarm Annunciation Panels and Fire Stations

28 31 23.50 Alarm Panels and Devices

28 31 23.50 Alarm Panels and Devices	Crew	Daily Output	Labor-Hours	Unit	Material	2012 Bare Costs Labor	Equipment	Total	Total Incl O&P
0010 **ALARM PANELS AND DEVICES**, not including wires & conduits									
3594 Fire, alarm control panel									
3600 4 zone	2 Elec	2	8	Ea.	390	410		800	1,050
3800 8 zone		1	16		760	825		1,585	2,050
4000 12 zone		.67	23.988		2,325	1,225		3,550	4,400
4020 Alarm device	1 Elec	8	1		231	51.50		282.50	330
4050 Actuating device		8	1		325	51.50		376.50	435
4200 Battery and rack		4	2		400	103		503	595

28 31 Fire Detection and Alarm

28 31 23 – Fire Detection and Alarm Annunciation Panels and Fire Stations

28 31 23.50 Alarm Panels and Devices

		Crew	Daily Output	Labor-Hours	Unit	Material	2012 Bare Costs Labor	Equipment	Total	Total Incl O&P
4400	Automatic charger	1 Elec	8	1	Ea.	565	51.50		616.50	700
4600	Signal bell		8	1		71	51.50		122.50	155
4800	Trouble buzzer or manual station		8	1		81	51.50		132.50	166
5600	Strobe and horn		5.30	1.509		148	78		226	278
5800	Fire alarm horn		6.70	1.194		59	61.50		120.50	157
6000	Door holder, electro-magnetic		4	2		99.50	103		202.50	264
6200	Combination holder and closer		3.20	2.500		120	129		249	325
6600	Drill switch		8	1		360	51.50		411.50	470
6800	Master box		2.70	2.963		6,225	153		6,378	7,075
7000	Break glass station		8	1		65.50	51.50		117	149
7800	Remote annunciator, 8 zone lamp	↓	1.80	4.444		203	229		432	565
8000	12 zone lamp	2 Elec	2.60	6.154		325	315		640	835
8200	16 zone lamp	"	2.20	7.273	↓	405	375		780	1,000

28 31 43 – Fire Detection Sensors

28 31 43.50 Fire and Heat Detectors

		Crew	Daily Output	Labor-Hours	Unit	Material	2012 Bare Costs Labor	Equipment	Total	Total Incl O&P
0010	**FIRE & HEAT DETECTORS**									
5000	Detector, rate of rise	1 Elec	8	1	Ea.	49.50	51.50		101	132
5100	Fixed temperature	"	8	1	"	49.50	51.50		101	132

28 31 46 – Smoke Detection Sensors

28 31 46.50 Smoke Detectors

		Crew	Daily Output	Labor-Hours	Unit	Material	2012 Bare Costs Labor	Equipment	Total	Total Incl O&P
0010	**SMOKE DETECTORS**									
5200	Smoke detector, ceiling type	1 Elec	6.20	1.290	Ea.	127	66.50		193.50	240
5400	Duct type	"	3.20	2.500	"	320	129		449	545

28 33 Gas Detection and Alarm

28 33 33 – Gas Detection Sensors

28 33 33.50 Tank Leak Detection Systems

		Crew	Daily Output	Labor-Hours	Unit	Material	2012 Bare Costs Labor	Equipment	Total	Total Incl O&P
0010	**TANK LEAK DETECTION SYSTEMS** Liquid and vapor									
0100	For hydrocarbons and hazardous liquids/vapors									
0120	Controller, data acquisition, incl. printer, modem, RS232 port									
0140	24 channel, for use with all probes				Ea.	4,050			4,050	4,450
0160	9 channel, for external monitoring				"	890			890	980
0200	Probes									
0210	Well monitoring									
0220	Liquid phase detection				Ea.	460			460	505
0230	Hydrocarbon vapor, fixed position					460			460	505
0240	Hydrocarbon vapor, float mounted					460			460	505
0250	Both liquid and vapor hydrocarbon				↓	460			460	505
0300	Secondary containment, liquid phase									
0310	Pipe trench/manway sump				Ea.	800			800	880
0320	Double wall pipe and manual sump					800			800	880
0330	Double wall fiberglass annular space					315			315	345
0340	Double wall steel tank annular space				↓	325			325	360
0500	Accessories									
0510	Modem, non-dedicated phone line				Ea.	294			294	325
0600	Monitoring, internal									
0610	Automatic tank gauge, incl. overfill				Ea.	1,125			1,125	1,225
0620	Product line				"	1,125			1,125	1,225
0700	Monitoring, special									
0710	Cathodic protection				Ea.	700			700	770
0720	Annular space chemical monitor				"	955			955	1,050

Division Notes

		CREW	DAILY OUTPUT	LABOR-HOURS	UNIT	2012 BARE COSTS				TOTAL INCL O&P
						MAT.	LABOR	EQUIP.	TOTAL	

Estimating Tips

31 05 00 Common Work Results for Earthwork

- Estimating the actual cost of performing earthwork requires careful consideration of the variables involved. This includes items such as type of soil, whether water will be encountered, dewatering, whether banks need bracing, disposal of excavated earth, and length of haul to fill or spoil sites, etc. If the project has large quantities of cut or fill, consider raising or lowering the site to reduce costs, while paying close attention to the effect on site drainage and utilities.
- If the project has large quantities of fill, creating a borrow pit on the site can significantly lower the costs.
- It is very important to consider what time of year the project is scheduled for completion. Bad weather can create large cost overruns from dewatering, site repair, and lost productivity from cold weather.
- New lines have been added for marine piling.

Reference Numbers

Reference numbers are shown in shaded boxes at the beginning of some major classifications. These numbers refer to related items in the Reference Section. The reference information may be an estimating procedure, an alternate pricing method, or technical information.

Note: Not all subdivisions listed here necessarily appear in this publication.

Division 31 - Earthwork

31 05 Common Work Results for Earthwork

31 05 23 – Cement and Concrete for Earthwork

31 05 23.30 Plant Mixed Bituminous Concrete	Crew	Daily Output	Labor-Hours	Unit	Material	2012 Bare Costs Labor	Equipment	Total	Total Incl O&P
0010	**PLANT MIXED BITUMINOUS CONCRETE**									
0020	Asphaltic concrete plant mix (145 lb. per C.F.)				Ton	62			62	68
0040	Asphaltic concrete less than 300 tons add trucking costs									
0050	See Section 31 23 23.20 for hauling costs									
0200	All weather patching mix, hot				Ton	68			68	75
0250	Cold patch					68			68	75
0300	Berm mix					68			68	75

31 23 Excavation and Fill

31 23 16 – Excavation

31 23 16.13 Excavating, Trench

		Crew	Daily Output	Labor-Hours	Unit	Material	2012 Bare Costs Labor	Equipment	Total	Total Incl O&P
0010	**EXCAVATING, TRENCH** G1030–805									
0011	Or continuous footing									
0020	Common earth with no sheeting or dewatering included									
0050	1' to 4' deep, 3/8 C.Y. excavator	B-11C	150	.107	B.C.Y.		4.36	2.23	6.59	9.10
0060	1/2 C.Y. excavator	B-11M	200	.080			3.27	1.82	5.09	6.95
0090	4' to 6' deep, 1/2 C.Y. excavator	"	200	.080			3.27	1.82	5.09	6.95
0100	5/8 C.Y. excavator	B-12Q	250	.064			2.65	2.21	4.86	6.45
0110	3/4 C.Y. excavator	B-12F	300	.053			2.21	2.16	4.37	5.75
0300	1/2 C.Y. excavator, truck mounted	B-12J	200	.080			3.32	4.22	7.54	9.70
0500	6' to 10' deep, 3/4 C.Y. excavator	B-12F	225	.071			2.95	2.88	5.83	7.65
0600	1 C.Y. excavator, truck mounted	B-12K	400	.040			1.66	2.40	4.06	5.15
0900	10' to 14' deep, 3/4 C.Y. excavator	B-12F	200	.080			3.32	3.24	6.56	8.60
1000	1-1/2 C.Y. excavator	B-12B	540	.030			1.23	1.78	3.01	3.83
1300	14' to 20' deep, 1 C.Y. excavator	B-12A	320	.050			2.07	2.34	4.41	5.70
1340	20' to 24' deep, 1 C.Y. excavator	"	288	.056			2.30	2.60	4.90	6.35
1352	4' to 6' deep, 1/2 C.Y. excavator w/trench box	B-13H	188	.085			3.53	5.10	8.63	10.95
1354	5/8 C.Y. excavator	"	235	.068			2.82	4.07	6.89	8.80
1356	3/4 C.Y. excavator	B-13G	282	.057			2.35	2.70	5.05	6.55
1362	6' to 10' deep, 3/4 C.Y. excavator w/trench box		212	.075			3.13	3.59	6.72	8.70
1374	10' to 14' deep, 3/4 C.Y. excavator w/trench box		188	.085			3.53	4.05	7.58	9.80
1376	1-1/2 C.Y. excavator	B-13E	508	.032			1.31	2.11	3.42	4.32
1381	14' to 20' deep, 1 C.Y. excavator w/trench box	B-13D	301	.053			2.20	2.86	5.06	6.50
1386	20' to 24' deep, 1 C.Y. excavator w/trench box	"	271	.059			2.45	3.18	5.63	7.20
1400	By hand with pick and shovel 2' to 6' deep, light soil	1 Clab	8	1			35		35	54
1500	Heavy soil	"	4	2			70		70	108
1700	For tamping backfilled trenches, air tamp, add	A-1G	100	.080	E.C.Y.		2.81	.50	3.31	4.87
1900	Vibrating plate, add	B-18	180	.133	"		4.77	.23	5	7.60
2100	Trim sides and bottom for concrete pours, common earth		1500	.016	S.F.		.57	.03	.60	.91
2300	Hardpan		600	.040	"		1.43	.07	1.50	2.27
5020	Loam & Sandy clay with no sheeting or dewatering included									
5050	1' to 4' deep, 3/8 C.Y. tractor loader/backhoe	B-11C	162	.099	B.C.Y.		4.03	2.06	6.09	8.40
5060	1/2 C.Y. excavator	B-11M	216	.074			3.02	1.68	4.70	6.45
5080	4' to 6' deep, 1/2 C.Y. excavator	"	216	.074			3.02	1.68	4.70	6.45
5090	5/8 C.Y. excavator	B-12Q	276	.058			2.40	2	4.40	5.85
5100	3/4 C.Y. excavator	B-12F	324	.049			2.05	2	4.05	5.30
5130	1/2 C.Y. excavator, truck mounted	B-12J	216	.074			3.07	3.91	6.98	8.95
5140	6' to 10' deep, 3/4 C.Y. excavator	B-12F	243	.066			2.73	2.66	5.39	7.10
5160	1 C.Y. excavator, truck mounted	B-12K	432	.037			1.54	2.23	3.77	4.79
5190	10' to 14' deep, 3/4 C.Y. excavator	B-12F	216	.074			3.07	3	6.07	7.95
5210	1-1/2 C.Y. excavator	B-12B	583	.027			1.14	1.65	2.79	3.54

31 23 16 – Excavation

31 23 16.13 Excavating, Trench

		Crew	Daily Output	Labor-Hours	Unit	Material	2012 Bare Costs Labor	Equipment	Total	Total Incl O&P
5250	14' to 20' deep, 1 C.Y. excavator	B-12A	346	.046	B.C.Y.		1.92	2.16	4.08	5.30
5300	20' to 24' deep, 1 C.Y. excavator	"	311	.051			2.13	2.41	4.54	5.90
5352	4' to 6' deep, 1/2 C.Y. excavator w/trench box	B-13H	205	.078			3.24	4.67	7.91	10.05
5354	5/8 C.Y. excavator	"	257	.062			2.58	3.73	6.31	8.05
5356	3/4 C.Y. excavator	B-13G	308	.052			2.15	2.47	4.62	6
5362	6' to 10' deep, 3/4 C.Y. excavator w/trench box		231	.069			2.87	3.29	6.16	8
5370	10' to 14' deep, 3/4 C.Y. excavator w/trench box		205	.078			3.24	3.71	6.95	9
5374	1-1/2 C.Y. excavator	B-13E	554	.029			1.20	1.94	3.14	3.95
5382	14' to 20' deep, 1 C.Y. excavator w/trench box	B-13D	329	.049			2.02	2.62	4.64	5.95
5392	20' to 24' deep, 1 C.Y. excavator w/trench box	"	295	.054			2.25	2.92	5.17	6.65
6020	Sand & gravel with no sheeting or dewatering included									
6050	1' to 4' deep, 3/8 C.Y. excavator	B-11C	165	.097	B.C.Y.		3.96	2.02	5.98	8.25
6060	1/2 C.Y. excavator	B-11M	220	.073			2.97	1.65	4.62	6.35
6080	4' to 6' deep, 1/2 C.Y. excavator	"	220	.073			2.97	1.65	4.62	6.35
6090	5/8 C.Y. excavator	B-12Q	275	.058			2.41	2.01	4.42	5.90
6100	3/4 C.Y. excavator	B-12F	330	.048			2.01	1.96	3.97	5.20
6130	1/2 C.Y. excavator, truck mounted	B-12J	220	.073			3.01	3.84	6.85	8.80
6140	6' to 10' deep, 3/4 C.Y. excavator	B-12F	248	.065			2.67	2.61	5.28	6.95
6160	1 C.Y. excavator, truck mounted	B-12K	440	.036			1.51	2.18	3.69	4.69
6190	10' to 14' deep, 3/4 C.Y. excavator	B-12F	220	.073			3.01	2.94	5.95	7.85
6210	1-1/2 C.Y. excavator	B-12B	594	.027			1.12	1.62	2.74	3.48
6250	14' to 20' deep, 1 C.Y. excavator	B-12A	352	.045			1.88	2.13	4.01	5.20
6300	20' to 24' deep, 1 C.Y. excavator	"	317	.050			2.09	2.36	4.45	5.80
6352	4' to 6' deep, 1/2 C.Y. excavator w/trench box	B-13H	209	.077			3.17	4.58	7.75	9.90
6354	5/8 C.Y. excavator	"	261	.061			2.54	3.67	6.21	7.90
6356	3/4 C.Y. excavator	B-13G	314	.051			2.11	2.42	4.53	5.85
6362	6' to 10' deep, 3/4 C.Y. excavator w/trench box		236	.068			2.81	3.22	6.03	7.85
6370	10' to 14' deep, 3/4 C.Y. excavator w/trench box		209	.077			3.17	3.64	6.81	8.85
6374	1-1/2 C.Y. excavator	B-13E	564	.028			1.18	1.90	3.08	3.88
6382	14' to 20' deep, 1 C.Y. excavator w/trench box	B-13D	334	.048			1.99	2.58	4.57	5.85
6392	20' to 24' deep, 1 C.Y. excavator w/trench box	"	301	.053			2.20	2.86	5.06	6.50
7020	Dense hard clay with no sheeting or dewatering included									
7050	1' to 4' deep, 3/8 C.Y. excavator	B-11C	132	.121	B.C.Y.		4.95	2.53	7.48	10.35
7060	1/2 C.Y. excavator	B-11M	176	.091			3.71	2.07	5.78	7.90
7080	4' to 6' deep, 1/2 C.Y. excavator	"	176	.091			3.71	2.07	5.78	7.90
7090	5/8 C.Y. excavator	B-12Q	220	.073			3.01	2.51	5.52	7.35
7100	3/4 C.Y. excavator	B-12F	264	.061			2.51	2.45	4.96	6.50
7130	1/2 C.Y. excavator, truck mounted	B-12J	176	.091			3.77	4.80	8.57	11.05
7140	6' to 10' deep, 3/4 C.Y. excavator	B-12F	198	.081			3.35	3.27	6.62	8.70
7160	1 C.Y. excavator, truck mounted	B-12K	352	.045			1.88	2.73	4.61	5.85
7190	10' to 14' deep, 3/4 C.Y. excavator	B-12F	176	.091			3.77	3.68	7.45	9.80
7210	1-1/2 C.Y. excavator	B-12B	475	.034			1.40	2.02	3.42	4.34
7250	14' to 20' deep, 1 C.Y. excavator	B-12A	282	.057			2.35	2.65	5	6.50
7300	20' to 24' deep, 1 C.Y. excavator	"	254	.063			2.61	2.95	5.56	7.20

31 23 16.14 Excavating, Utility Trench

		Crew	Daily Output	Labor-Hours	Unit	Material	2012 Bare Costs Labor	Equipment	Total	Total Incl O&P
0010	**EXCAVATING, UTILITY TRENCH**									
0011	Common earth									
0050	Trenching with chain trencher, 12 H.P., operator walking									
0100	4" wide trench, 12" deep	B-53	800	.010	L.F.		.45	.08	.53	.77
0150	18" deep		750	.011			.48	.08	.56	.81
0200	24" deep		700	.011			.51	.09	.60	.87
0300	6" wide trench, 12" deep		650	.012			.55	.10	.65	.94

31 23 16.14 Excavating, Utility Trench

		Crew	Daily Output	Labor-Hours	Unit	Material	2012 Bare Costs Labor	Equipment	Total	Total Incl O&P
0350	18" deep	B-53	600	.013	L.F.		.60	.10	.70	1.02
0400	24" deep		550	.015			.65	.11	.76	1.11
0450	36" deep		450	.018			.80	.14	.94	1.35
0600	8" wide trench, 12" deep		475	.017			.75	.13	.88	1.29
0650	18" deep		400	.020			.90	.16	1.06	1.52
0700	24" deep		350	.023			1.02	.18	1.20	1.74
0750	36" deep	▼	300	.027	▼		1.19	.21	1.40	2.03
1000	Backfill by hand including compaction, add									
1050	4" wide trench, 12" deep	A-1G	800	.010	L.F.		.35	.06	.41	.61
1100	18" deep		530	.015			.53	.09	.62	.91
1150	24" deep		400	.020			.70	.12	.82	1.22
1300	6" wide trench, 12" deep		540	.015			.52	.09	.61	.90
1350	18" deep		405	.020			.69	.12	.81	1.21
1400	24" deep		270	.030			1.04	.18	1.22	1.80
1450	36" deep		180	.044			1.56	.28	1.84	2.70
1600	8" wide trench, 12" deep		400	.020			.70	.12	.82	1.22
1650	18" deep		265	.030			1.06	.19	1.25	1.84
1700	24" deep		200	.040			1.40	.25	1.65	2.43
1750	36" deep	▼	135	.059	▼		2.08	.37	2.45	3.61
2000	Chain trencher, 40 H.P. operator riding									
2050	6" wide trench and backfill, 12" deep	B-54	1200	.007	L.F.		.30	.26	.56	.74
2100	18" deep		1000	.008			.36	.31	.67	.88
2150	24" deep		975	.008			.37	.32	.69	.90
2200	36" deep		900	.009			.40	.35	.75	.98
2250	48" deep		750	.011			.48	.42	.90	1.18
2300	60" deep		650	.012			.55	.48	1.03	1.36
2400	8" wide trench and backfill, 12" deep		1000	.008			.36	.31	.67	.88
2450	18" deep		950	.008			.38	.33	.71	.93
2500	24" deep		900	.009			.40	.35	.75	.98
2550	36" deep		800	.010			.45	.39	.84	1.11
2600	48" deep		650	.012			.55	.48	1.03	1.36
2700	12" wide trench and backfill, 12" deep		975	.008			.37	.32	.69	.90
2750	18" deep		860	.009			.42	.36	.78	1.03
2800	24" deep		800	.010			.45	.39	.84	1.11
2850	36" deep		725	.011			.49	.43	.92	1.22
3000	16" wide trench and backfill, 12" deep		835	.010			.43	.37	.80	1.06
3050	18" deep		750	.011			.48	.42	.90	1.18
3100	24" deep	▼	700	.011	▼		.51	.45	.96	1.26
3200	Compaction with vibratory plate, add								35%	35%
5100	Hand excavate and trim for pipe bells after trench excavation									
5200	8" pipe	1 Clab	155	.052	L.F.		1.81		1.81	2.79
5300	18" pipe	"	130	.062	"		2.16		2.16	3.32

31 23 16.16 Structural Excavation for Minor Structures

		Crew	Daily Output	Labor-Hours	Unit	Material	2012 Bare Costs Labor	Equipment	Total	Total Incl O&P
0010	**STRUCTURAL EXCAVATION FOR MINOR STRUCTURES**									
0015	Hand, pits to 6' deep, sandy soil	1 Clab	8	1	B.C.Y.		35		35	54
0100	Heavy soil or clay		4	2			70		70	108
0300	Pits 6' to 12' deep, sandy soil		5	1.600			56		56	86.50
0500	Heavy soil or clay		3	2.667			93.50		93.50	144
0700	Pits 12' to 18' deep, sandy soil		4	2			70		70	108
0900	Heavy soil or clay	▼	2	4	▼		140		140	216
1500	For wet or muck hand excavation, add to above								50%	50%

31 23 Excavation and Fill

31 23 16 – Excavation

31 23 16.30 Drilling and Blasting Rock	Crew	Daily Output	Labor-Hours	Unit	Material	2012 Bare Costs Labor	Equipment	Total	Total Incl O&P
0010 **DRILLING AND BLASTING ROCK**									
0020 Rock, open face, under 1500 C.Y.	B-47	225	.107	B.C.Y.	3.05	4.16	6.40	13.61	16.70
0100 Over 1500 C.Y.		300	.080		3.05	3.12	4.78	10.95	13.35
0200 Areas where blasting mats are required, under 1500 C.Y.		175	.137		3.05	5.35	8.20	16.60	20.50
0250 Over 1500 C.Y.		250	.096		3.05	3.74	5.75	12.54	15.35
2200 Trenches, up to 1500 C.Y.		22	1.091		8.85	42.50	65	116.35	146
2300 Over 1500 C.Y.		26	.923		8.85	36	55	99.85	125

31 23 19 – Dewatering

31 23 19.20 Dewatering Systems

31 23 19.20 Dewatering Systems	Crew	Daily Output	Labor-Hours	Unit	Material	2012 Bare Costs Labor	Equipment	Total	Total Incl O&P
0010 **DEWATERING SYSTEMS**									
0020 Excavate drainage trench, 2' wide, 2' deep	B-11C	90	.178	C.Y.		7.25	3.71	10.96	15.15
0100 2' wide, 3' deep, with backhoe loader	"	135	.119			4.84	2.47	7.31	10.05
0200 Excavate sump pits by hand, light soil	1 Clab	7.10	1.127			39.50		39.50	61
0300 Heavy soil	"	3.50	2.286			80		80	123
0500 Pumping 8 hr., attended 2 hrs. per day, including 20 L.F.									
0550 of suction hose & 100 L.F. discharge hose									
0600 2" diaphragm pump used for 8 hours	B-10H	4	3	Day		128	18.50	146.50	215
0650 4" diaphragm pump used for 8 hours	B-10I	4	3			128	31	159	228
0800 8 hrs. attended, 2" diaphragm pump	B-10H	1	12			515	74	589	860
0900 3" centrifugal pump	B-10J	1	12			515	83	598	870
1000 4" diaphragm pump	B-10I	1	12			515	124	639	915
1100 6" centrifugal pump	B-10K	1	12			515	345	860	1,150
1300 CMP, incl. excavation 3' deep, 12" diameter	B-6	115	.209	L.F.	10.50	8	2.91	21.41	27
1400 18" diameter		100	.240	"	15.75	9.20	3.34	28.29	35
1600 Sump hole construction, incl. excavation and gravel, pit		1250	.019	C.F.	1	.74	.27	2.01	2.51
1700 With 12" gravel collar, 12" pipe, corrugated, 16 ga.		70	.343	L.F.	24	13.15	4.77	41.92	52
1800 15" pipe, corrugated, 16 ga.		55	.436		31	16.70	6.05	53.75	66
1900 18" pipe, corrugated, 16 ga.		50	.480		36	18.40	6.70	61.10	75
2000 24" pipe, corrugated, 14 ga.		40	.600		43.50	23	8.35	74.85	91.50
2200 Wood lining, up to 4' x 4', add		300	.080	SFCA	16.65	3.07	1.11	20.83	24.50
9950 See Section 31 23 19.40 for wellpoints									
9960 See Section 31 23 19.30 for deep well systems									

31 23 19.30 Wells

31 23 19.30 Wells	Crew	Daily Output	Labor-Hours	Unit	Material	2012 Bare Costs Labor	Equipment	Total	Total Incl O&P
0010 **WELLS**									
0011 For dewatering 10' to 20' deep, 2' diameter									
0020 with steel casing, minimum	B-6	165	.145	V.L.F.	37	5.55	2.02	44.57	51
0050 Average		98	.245		42	9.40	3.41	54.81	64
0100 Maximum		49	.490		47.50	18.75	6.80	73.05	88
0300 For dewatering pumps see 01 54 33 in Reference Section									
0500 For domestic water wells, see Section 33 21 13.10									

31 23 19.40 Wellpoints

31 23 19.40 Wellpoints	Crew	Daily Output	Labor-Hours	Unit	Material	2012 Bare Costs Labor	Equipment	Total	Total Incl O&P
0010 **WELLPOINTS** R312319-90									
0011 For equipment rental, see 01 54 33 in Reference Section									
0100 Installation and removal of single stage system									
0110 Labor only, .75 labor-hours per L.F.	1 Clab	10.70	.748	LF Hdr		26		26	40.50
0200 2.0 labor-hours per L.F.	"	4	2	"		70		70	108
0400 Pump operation, 4 @ 6 hr. shifts									
0410 Per 24 hour day	4 Eqlt	1.27	25.197	Day		1,125		1,125	1,700
0500 Per 168 hour week, 160 hr. straight, 8 hr. double time		.18	177	Week		7,950		7,950	12,000
0550 Per 4.3 week month		.04	800	Month		35,800		35,800	54,000
0600 Complete installation, operation, equipment rental, fuel &									

31 23 Excavation and Fill

31 23 19 – Dewatering

31 23 19.40 Wellpoints

		Crew	Daily Output	Labor-Hours	Unit	Material	2012 Bare Costs Labor	Equipment	Total	Total Incl O&P
0610	removal of system with 2" wellpoints 5' O.C.									
0700	100' long header, 6" diameter, first month	4 Eqlt	3.23	9.907	LF Hdr	155	445		600	840
0800	Thereafter, per month		4.13	7.748		124	345		469	660
1000	200' long header, 8" diameter, first month		6	5.333		140	239		379	515
1100	Thereafter, per month		8.39	3.814		69.50	171		240.50	335
1300	500' long header, 8" diameter, first month		10.63	3.010		54	135		189	263
1400	Thereafter, per month		20.91	1.530		38.50	68.50		107	146
1600	1,000' long header, 10" diameter, first month		11.62	2.754		46.50	123		169.50	237
1700	Thereafter, per month		41.81	.765		23	34.50		57.50	77
1900	Note: above figures include pumping 168 hrs. per week									
1910	and include the pump operator and one stand-by pump.									

31 23 23 – Fill

31 23 23.13 Backfill

		Crew	Daily Output	Labor-Hours	Unit	Material	2012 Bare Costs Labor	Equipment	Total	Total Incl O&P
0010	**BACKFILL** G1030–805									
0015	By hand, no compaction, light soil	1 Clab	14	.571	L.C.Y.		20		20	31
0100	Heavy soil		11	.727	"		25.50		25.50	39.50
0300	Compaction in 6" layers, hand tamp, add to above		20.60	.388	E.C.Y.		13.65		13.65	21
0400	Roller compaction operator walking, add	B-10A	100	.120			5.15	1.72	6.87	9.70
0500	Air tamp, add	B-9D	190	.211			7.45	1.27	8.72	12.90
0600	Vibrating plate, add	A-1D	60	.133			4.68	.54	5.22	7.80
0800	Compaction in 12" layers, hand tamp, add to above	1 Clab	34	.235			8.25		8.25	12.70
0900	Roller compaction operator walking, add	B-10A	150	.080			3.42	1.14	4.56	6.45
1000	Air tamp, add	B-9	285	.140			4.98	.73	5.71	8.45
1100	Vibrating plate, add	A-1E	90	.089			3.12	.45	3.57	5.30
1300	Dozer backfilling, bulk, up to 300' haul, no compaction	B-10B	1200	.010	L.C.Y.		.43	1.04	1.47	1.79
1400	Air tamped, add	B-11B	80	.200	E.C.Y.		8	3.35	11.35	15.85
1600	Compacting backfill, 6" to 12" lifts, vibrating roller	B-10C	800	.015			.64	2.04	2.68	3.21
1700	Sheepsfoot roller	B-10D	750	.016			.68	2.22	2.90	3.48
1900	Dozer backfilling, trench, up to 300' haul, no compaction	B-10B	900	.013	L.C.Y.		.57	1.38	1.95	2.38
2000	Air tamped, add	B-11B	80	.200	E.C.Y.		8	3.35	11.35	15.85
2200	Compacting backfill, 6" to 12" lifts, vibrating roller	B-10C	700	.017			.73	2.33	3.06	3.67
2300	Sheepsfoot roller	B-10D	650	.018			.79	2.56	3.35	4.01

31 23 23.16 Fill By Borrow and Utility Bedding

		Crew	Daily Output	Labor-Hours	Unit	Material	2012 Bare Costs Labor	Equipment	Total	Total Incl O&P
0010	**FILL BY BORROW AND UTILITY BEDDING**									
0049	Utility bedding, for pipe & conduit, not incl. compaction									
0050	Crushed or screened bank run gravel	B-6	150	.160	L.C.Y.	26	6.15	2.23	34.38	40.50
0100	Crushed stone 3/4" to 1/2"		150	.160		31.50	6.15	2.23	39.88	46.50
0200	Sand, dead or bank		150	.160		17	6.15	2.23	25.38	30.50
0500	Compacting bedding in trench	A-1D	90	.089	E.C.Y.		3.12	.36	3.48	5.20
0600	If material source exceeds 2 miles, add for extra mileage.									
0610	See Section 31 23 23.20 for hauling mileage add.									

31 23 23.17 General Fill

		Crew	Daily Output	Labor-Hours	Unit	Material	2012 Bare Costs Labor	Equipment	Total	Total Incl O&P
0010	**GENERAL FILL**									
0011	Spread dumped material, no compaction									
0020	By dozer, no compaction	B-10B	1000	.012	L.C.Y.		.51	1.24	1.75	2.15
0100	By hand	1 Clab	12	.667	"		23.50		23.50	36
0500	Gravel fill, compacted, under floor slabs, 4" deep	B-37	10000	.005	S.F.	.43	.18	.01	.62	.76
0600	6" deep		8600	.006		.64	.21	.02	.87	1.04
0700	9" deep		7200	.007		1.06	.25	.02	1.33	1.57
0800	12" deep		6000	.008		1.49	.30	.02	1.81	2.12
1000	Alternate pricing method, 4" deep		120	.400	E.C.Y.	32	14.80	1.24	48.04	59
1100	6" deep		160	.300		32	11.10	.93	44.03	53

31 23 Excavation and Fill

31 23 23 – Fill

31 23 23.17 General Fill	Crew	Daily Output	Labor-Hours	Unit	Material	2012 Bare Costs Labor	2012 Bare Costs Equipment	Total	Total Incl O&P
1200 9" deep	B-37	200	.240	E.C.Y.	32	8.90	.75	41.65	49.50
1300 12" deep	↓	220	.218	↓	32	8.10	.68	40.78	48
1400 Granular fill				L.C.Y.	21.50			21.50	23.50

31 23 23.20 Hauling

	Crew	Daily Output	Labor-Hours	Unit	Material	2012 Bare Costs Labor	2012 Bare Costs Equipment	Total	Total Incl O&P
0010 **HAULING**									
0011 Excavated or borrow, loose cubic yards									
0012 no loading equipment, including hauling, waiting, loading/dumping									
0013 time per cycle (wait, load, travel, unload or dump & return)									
0014 8 C.Y. truck, 15 MPH ave, cycle 0.5 miles, 10 min. wait/Ld./Uld.	B-34A	320	.025	L.C.Y.		.88	1.12	2	2.57
0016 cycle 1 mile		272	.029			1.04	1.31	2.35	3.02
0018 cycle 2 miles		208	.038			1.36	1.72	3.08	3.95
0020 cycle 4 miles		144	.056			1.96	2.48	4.44	5.70
0022 cycle 6 miles		112	.071			2.52	3.19	5.71	7.35
0024 cycle 8 miles		88	.091			3.21	4.06	7.27	9.35
0026 20 MPH ave, cycle 0.5 mile		336	.024			.84	1.06	1.90	2.45
0028 cycle 1 mile		296	.027			.95	1.21	2.16	2.78
0030 cycle 2 miles		240	.033			1.18	1.49	2.67	3.42
0032 cycle 4 miles		176	.045			1.60	2.03	3.63	4.66
0034 cycle 6 miles		136	.059			2.08	2.63	4.71	6.05
0036 cycle 8 miles		112	.071			2.52	3.19	5.71	7.35
0044 25 MPH ave, cycle 4 miles		192	.042			1.47	1.86	3.33	4.28
0046 cycle 6 miles		160	.050			1.77	2.23	4	5.15
0048 cycle 8 miles		128	.063			2.21	2.79	5	6.40
0050 30 MPH ave, cycle 4 miles		216	.037			1.31	1.65	2.96	3.80
0052 cycle 6 miles		176	.045			1.60	2.03	3.63	4.66
0054 cycle 8 miles		144	.056			1.96	2.48	4.44	5.70
0114 15 MPH ave, cycle 0.5 mile, 15 min. wait/Ld./Uld.		224	.036			1.26	1.60	2.86	3.66
0116 cycle 1 mile		200	.040			1.41	1.79	3.20	4.11
0118 cycle 2 miles		168	.048			1.68	2.13	3.81	4.89
0120 cycle 4 miles		120	.067			2.35	2.98	5.33	6.85
0122 cycle 6 miles		96	.083			2.94	3.72	6.66	8.55
0124 cycle 8 miles		80	.100			3.53	4.47	8	10.25
0126 20 MPH ave, cycle 0.5 mile		232	.034			1.22	1.54	2.76	3.54
0128 cycle 1 mile		208	.038			1.36	1.72	3.08	3.95
0130 cycle 2 miles		184	.043			1.53	1.94	3.47	4.47
0132 cycle 4 miles		144	.056			1.96	2.48	4.44	5.70
0134 cycle 6 miles		112	.071			2.52	3.19	5.71	7.35
0136 cycle 8 miles		96	.083			2.94	3.72	6.66	8.55
0144 25 MPH ave, cycle 4 miles		152	.053			1.86	2.35	4.21	5.40
0146 cycle 6 miles		128	.063			2.21	2.79	5	6.40
0148 cycle 8 miles		112	.071			2.52	3.19	5.71	7.35
0150 30 MPH ave, cycle 4 miles		168	.048			1.68	2.13	3.81	4.89
0152 cycle 6 miles		144	.056			1.96	2.48	4.44	5.70
0154 cycle 8 miles		120	.067			2.35	2.98	5.33	6.85
0214 15 MPH ave, cycle 0.5 mile, 20 min wait/Ld./Uld.		176	.045			1.60	2.03	3.63	4.66
0216 cycle 1 mile		160	.050			1.77	2.23	4	5.15
0218 cycle 2 miles		136	.059			2.08	2.63	4.71	6.05
0220 cycle 4 miles		104	.077			2.72	3.44	6.16	7.90
0222 cycle 6 miles		88	.091			3.21	4.06	7.27	9.35
0224 cycle 8 miles		72	.111			3.92	4.96	8.88	11.40
0226 20 MPH ave, cycle 0.5 mile		176	.045			1.60	2.03	3.63	4.66
0228 cycle 1 mile	↓	168	.048	↓		1.68	2.13	3.81	4.89

31 23 23 - Fill

31 23 23.20 Hauling		Crew	Daily Output	Labor-Hours	Unit	Material	2012 Bare Costs Labor	Equipment	Total	Total Incl O&P
0230	cycle 2 miles	B-34A	144	.056	L.C.Y.		1.96	2.48	4.44	5.70
0232	cycle 4 miles		120	.067			2.35	2.98	5.33	6.85
0234	cycle 6 miles		96	.083			2.94	3.72	6.66	8.55
0236	cycle 8 miles		88	.091			3.21	4.06	7.27	9.35
0244	25 MPH ave, cycle 4 miles		128	.063			2.21	2.79	5	6.40
0246	cycle 6 miles		112	.071			2.52	3.19	5.71	7.35
0248	cycle 8 miles		96	.083			2.94	3.72	6.66	8.55
0250	30 MPH ave, cycle 4 miles		136	.059			2.08	2.63	4.71	6.05
0252	cycle 6 miles		120	.067			2.35	2.98	5.33	6.85
0254	cycle 8 miles		104	.077			2.72	3.44	6.16	7.90
0314	15 MPH ave, cycle 0.5 mile, 25 min wait/Ld./Uld.		144	.056			1.96	2.48	4.44	5.70
0316	cycle 1 mile		128	.063			2.21	2.79	5	6.40
0318	cycle 2 miles		112	.071			2.52	3.19	5.71	7.35
0320	cycle 4 miles		96	.083			2.94	3.72	6.66	8.55
0322	cycle 6 miles		80	.100			3.53	4.47	8	10.25
0324	cycle 8 miles		64	.125			4.41	5.60	10.01	12.85
0326	20 MPH ave, cycle 0.5 mile		144	.056			1.96	2.48	4.44	5.70
0328	cycle 1 mile		136	.059			2.08	2.63	4.71	6.05
0330	cycle 2 miles		120	.067			2.35	2.98	5.33	6.85
0332	cycle 4 miles		104	.077			2.72	3.44	6.16	7.90
0334	cycle 6 miles		88	.091			3.21	4.06	7.27	9.35
0336	cycle 8 miles		80	.100			3.53	4.47	8	10.25
0344	25 MPH ave, cycle 4 miles		112	.071			2.52	3.19	5.71	7.35
0346	cycle 6 miles		96	.083			2.94	3.72	6.66	8.55
0348	cycle 8 miles		88	.091			3.21	4.06	7.27	9.35
0350	30 MPH ave, cycle 4 miles		112	.071			2.52	3.19	5.71	7.35
0352	cycle 6 miles		104	.077			2.72	3.44	6.16	7.90
0354	cycle 8 miles		96	.083			2.94	3.72	6.66	8.55
0414	15 MPH ave, cycle 0.5 mile, 30 min wait/Ld./Uld.		120	.067			2.35	2.98	5.33	6.85
0416	cycle 1 mile		112	.071			2.52	3.19	5.71	7.35
0418	cycle 2 miles		96	.083			2.94	3.72	6.66	8.55
0420	cycle 4 miles		80	.100			3.53	4.47	8	10.25
0422	cycle 6 miles		72	.111			3.92	4.96	8.88	11.40
0424	cycle 8 miles		64	.125			4.41	5.60	10.01	12.85
0426	20 MPH ave, cycle 0.5 mile		120	.067			2.35	2.98	5.33	6.85
0428	cycle 1 mile		112	.071			2.52	3.19	5.71	7.35
0430	cycle 2 miles		104	.077			2.72	3.44	6.16	7.90
0432	cycle 4 miles		88	.091			3.21	4.06	7.27	9.35
0434	cycle 6 miles		80	.100			3.53	4.47	8	10.25
0436	cycle 8 miles		72	.111			3.92	4.96	8.88	11.40
0444	25 MPH ave, cycle 4 miles		96	.083			2.94	3.72	6.66	8.55
0446	cycle 6 miles		88	.091			3.21	4.06	7.27	9.35
0448	cycle 8 miles		80	.100			3.53	4.47	8	10.25
0450	30 MPH ave, cycle 4 miles		96	.083			2.94	3.72	6.66	8.55
0452	cycle 6 miles		88	.091			3.21	4.06	7.27	9.35
0454	cycle 8 miles		80	.100			3.53	4.47	8	10.25
0514	15 MPH ave, cycle 0.5 mile, 35 min wait/Ld./Uld.		104	.077			2.72	3.44	6.16	7.90
0516	cycle 1 mile		96	.083			2.94	3.72	6.66	8.55
0518	cycle 2 miles		88	.091			3.21	4.06	7.27	9.35
0520	cycle 4 miles		72	.111			3.92	4.96	8.88	11.40
0522	cycle 6 miles		64	.125			4.41	5.60	10.01	12.85
0524	cycle 8 miles		56	.143			5.05	6.40	11.45	14.65
0526	20 MPH ave, cycle 0.5 mile		104	.077			2.72	3.44	6.16	7.90

31 23 Excavation and Fill

31 23 23 – Fill

31 23 23.20 Hauling		Crew	Daily Output	Labor-Hours	Unit	Material	2012 Bare Costs Labor	2012 Bare Costs Equipment	Total	Total Incl O&P
0528	cycle 1 mile	B-34A	96	.083	L.C.Y.		2.94	3.72	6.66	8.55
0530	cycle 2 miles		96	.083			2.94	3.72	6.66	8.55
0532	cycle 4 miles		80	.100			3.53	4.47	8	10.25
0534	cycle 6 miles		72	.111			3.92	4.96	8.88	11.40
0536	cycle 8 miles		64	.125			4.41	5.60	10.01	12.85
0544	25 MPH ave, cycle 4 miles		88	.091			3.21	4.06	7.27	9.35
0546	cycle 6 miles		80	.100			3.53	4.47	8	10.25
0548	cycle 8 miles		72	.111			3.92	4.96	8.88	11.40
0550	30 MPH ave, cycle 4 miles		88	.091			3.21	4.06	7.27	9.35
0552	cycle 6 miles		80	.100			3.53	4.47	8	10.25
0554	cycle 8 miles		72	.111			3.92	4.96	8.88	11.40
1014	12 C.Y. truck, cycle 0.5 mile, 15 MPH ave, 15 min. wait/Ld./Uld.	B-34B	336	.024			.84	1.74	2.58	3.19
1016	cycle 1 mile		300	.027			.94	1.95	2.89	3.57
1018	cycle 2 miles		252	.032			1.12	2.32	3.44	4.25
1020	cycle 4 miles		180	.044			1.57	3.25	4.82	5.95
1022	cycle 6 miles		144	.056			1.96	4.06	6.02	7.45
1024	cycle 8 miles		120	.067			2.35	4.87	7.22	8.90
1025	cycle 10 miles		96	.083			2.94	6.10	9.04	11.15
1026	20 MPH ave, cycle 0.5 mile		348	.023			.81	1.68	2.49	3.08
1028	cycle 1 mile		312	.026			.91	1.87	2.78	3.43
1030	cycle 2 miles		276	.029			1.02	2.12	3.14	3.88
1032	cycle 4 miles		216	.037			1.31	2.71	4.02	4.96
1034	cycle 6 miles		168	.048			1.68	3.48	5.16	6.40
1036	cycle 8 miles		144	.056			1.96	4.06	6.02	7.45
1038	cycle 10 miles		120	.067			2.35	4.87	7.22	8.90
1040	25 MPH ave, cycle 4 miles		228	.035			1.24	2.56	3.80	4.70
1042	cycle 6 miles		192	.042			1.47	3.05	4.52	5.60
1044	cycle 8 miles		168	.048			1.68	3.48	5.16	6.40
1046	cycle 10 miles		144	.056			1.96	4.06	6.02	7.45
1050	30 MPH ave, cycle 4 miles		252	.032			1.12	2.32	3.44	4.25
1052	cycle 6 miles		216	.037			1.31	2.71	4.02	4.96
1054	cycle 8 miles		180	.044			1.57	3.25	4.82	5.95
1056	cycle 10 miles		156	.051			1.81	3.75	5.56	6.85
1060	35 MPH ave, cycle 4 miles		264	.030			1.07	2.21	3.28	4.06
1062	cycle 6 miles		228	.035			1.24	2.56	3.80	4.70
1064	cycle 8 miles		204	.039			1.38	2.87	4.25	5.25
1066	cycle 10 miles		180	.044			1.57	3.25	4.82	5.95
1068	cycle 20 miles		120	.067			2.35	4.87	7.22	8.90
1069	cycle 30 miles		84	.095			3.36	6.95	10.31	12.75
1070	cycle 40 miles		72	.111			3.92	8.10	12.02	14.90
1072	40 MPH ave, cycle 6 miles		240	.033			1.18	2.44	3.62	4.46
1074	cycle 8 miles		216	.037			1.31	2.71	4.02	4.96
1076	cycle 10 miles		192	.042			1.47	3.05	4.52	5.60
1078	cycle 20 miles		120	.067			2.35	4.87	7.22	8.90
1080	cycle 30 miles		96	.083			2.94	6.10	9.04	11.15
1082	cycle 40 miles		72	.111			3.92	8.10	12.02	14.90
1084	cycle 50 miles		60	.133			4.71	9.75	14.46	17.85
1094	45 MPH ave, cycle 8 miles		216	.037			1.31	2.71	4.02	4.96
1096	cycle 10 miles		204	.039			1.38	2.87	4.25	5.25
1098	cycle 20 miles		132	.061			2.14	4.43	6.57	8.10
1100	cycle 30 miles		108	.074			2.61	5.40	8.01	9.90
1102	cycle 40 miles		84	.095			3.36	6.95	10.31	12.75
1104	cycle 50 miles		72	.111			3.92	8.10	12.02	14.90

31 23 Excavation and Fill

31 23 23 – Fill

31 23 23.20 Hauling		Crew	Daily Output	Labor-Hours	Unit	Material	2012 Bare Costs Labor	Equipment	Total	Total Incl O&P
1106	50 MPH ave, cycle 10 miles	B-34B	216	.037	L.C.Y.		1.31	2.71	4.02	4.96
1108	cycle 20 miles		144	.056			1.96	4.06	6.02	7.45
1110	cycle 30 miles		108	.074			2.61	5.40	8.01	9.90
1112	cycle 40 miles		84	.095			3.36	6.95	10.31	12.75
1114	cycle 50 miles		72	.111			3.92	8.10	12.02	14.90
1214	15 MPH ave, cycle 0.5 mile, 20 min. wait/Ld./Uld.		264	.030			1.07	2.21	3.28	4.06
1216	cycle 1 mile		240	.033			1.18	2.44	3.62	4.46
1218	cycle 2 miles		204	.039			1.38	2.87	4.25	5.25
1220	cycle 4 miles		156	.051			1.81	3.75	5.56	6.85
1222	cycle 6 miles		132	.061			2.14	4.43	6.57	8.10
1224	cycle 8 miles		108	.074			2.61	5.40	8.01	9.90
1225	cycle 10 miles		96	.083			2.94	6.10	9.04	11.15
1226	20 MPH ave, cycle 0.5 mile		264	.030			1.07	2.21	3.28	4.06
1228	cycle 1 mile		252	.032			1.12	2.32	3.44	4.25
1230	cycle 2 miles		216	.037			1.31	2.71	4.02	4.96
1232	cycle 4 miles		180	.044			1.57	3.25	4.82	5.95
1234	cycle 6 miles		144	.056			1.96	4.06	6.02	7.45
1236	cycle 8 miles		132	.061			2.14	4.43	6.57	8.10
1238	cycle 10 miles		108	.074			2.61	5.40	8.01	9.90
1240	25 MPH ave, cycle 4 miles		192	.042			1.47	3.05	4.52	5.60
1242	cycle 6 miles		168	.048			1.68	3.48	5.16	6.40
1244	cycle 8 miles		144	.056			1.96	4.06	6.02	7.45
1246	cycle 10 miles		132	.061			2.14	4.43	6.57	8.10
1250	30 MPH ave, cycle 4 miles		204	.039			1.38	2.87	4.25	5.25
1252	cycle 6 miles		180	.044			1.57	3.25	4.82	5.95
1254	cycle 8 miles		156	.051			1.81	3.75	5.56	6.85
1256	cycle 10 miles		144	.056			1.96	4.06	6.02	7.45
1260	35 MPH ave, cycle 4 miles		216	.037			1.31	2.71	4.02	4.96
1262	cycle 6 miles		192	.042			1.47	3.05	4.52	5.60
1264	cycle 8 miles		168	.048			1.68	3.48	5.16	6.40
1266	cycle 10 miles		156	.051			1.81	3.75	5.56	6.85
1268	cycle 20 miles		108	.074			2.61	5.40	8.01	9.90
1269	cycle 30 miles		72	.111			3.92	8.10	12.02	14.90
1270	cycle 40 miles		60	.133			4.71	9.75	14.46	17.85
1272	40 MPH ave, cycle 6 miles		192	.042			1.47	3.05	4.52	5.60
1274	cycle 8 miles		180	.044			1.57	3.25	4.82	5.95
1276	cycle 10 miles		156	.051			1.81	3.75	5.56	6.85
1278	cycle 20 miles		108	.074			2.61	5.40	8.01	9.90
1280	cycle 30 miles		84	.095			3.36	6.95	10.31	12.75
1282	cycle 40 miles		72	.111			3.92	8.10	12.02	14.90
1284	cycle 50 miles		60	.133			4.71	9.75	14.46	17.85
1294	45 MPH ave, cycle 8 miles		180	.044			1.57	3.25	4.82	5.95
1296	cycle 10 miles		168	.048			1.68	3.48	5.16	6.40
1298	cycle 20 miles		120	.067			2.35	4.87	7.22	8.90
1300	cycle 30 miles		96	.083			2.94	6.10	9.04	11.15
1302	cycle 40 miles		72	.111			3.92	8.10	12.02	14.90
1304	cycle 50 miles		60	.133			4.71	9.75	14.46	17.85
1306	50 MPH ave, cycle 10 miles		180	.044			1.57	3.25	4.82	5.95
1308	cycle 20 miles		132	.061			2.14	4.43	6.57	8.10
1310	cycle 30 miles		96	.083			2.94	6.10	9.04	11.15
1312	cycle 40 miles		84	.095			3.36	6.95	10.31	12.75
1314	cycle 50 miles		72	.111			3.92	8.10	12.02	14.90
1414	15 MPH ave, cycle 0.5 mile, 25 min. wait/Ld./Uld.		204	.039			1.38	2.87	4.25	5.25

31 23 Excavation and Fill

31 23 23 – Fill

31 23 23.20 Hauling		Crew	Daily Output	Labor-Hours	Unit	Material	2012 Bare Costs Labor	Equipment	Total	Total Incl O&P
1416	cycle 1 mile	B-34B	192	.042	L.C.Y.		1.47	3.05	4.52	5.60
1418	cycle 2 miles		168	.048			1.68	3.48	5.16	6.40
1420	cycle 4 miles		132	.061			2.14	4.43	6.57	8.10
1422	cycle 6 miles		120	.067			2.35	4.87	7.22	8.90
1424	cycle 8 miles		96	.083			2.94	6.10	9.04	11.15
1425	cycle 10 miles		84	.095			3.36	6.95	10.31	12.75
1426	20 MPH ave, cycle 0.5 mile		216	.037			1.31	2.71	4.02	4.96
1428	cycle 1 mile		204	.039			1.38	2.87	4.25	5.25
1430	cycle 2 miles		180	.044			1.57	3.25	4.82	5.95
1432	cycle 4 miles		156	.051			1.81	3.75	5.56	6.85
1434	cycle 6 miles		132	.061			2.14	4.43	6.57	8.10
1436	cycle 8 miles		120	.067			2.35	4.87	7.22	8.90
1438	cycle 10 miles		96	.083			2.94	6.10	9.04	11.15
1440	25 MPH ave, cycle 4 miles		168	.048			1.68	3.48	5.16	6.40
1442	cycle 6 miles		144	.056			1.96	4.06	6.02	7.45
1444	cycle 8 miles		132	.061			2.14	4.43	6.57	8.10
1446	cycle 10 miles		108	.074			2.61	5.40	8.01	9.90
1450	30 MPH ave, cycle 4 miles		168	.048			1.68	3.48	5.16	6.40
1452	cycle 6 miles		156	.051			1.81	3.75	5.56	6.85
1454	cycle 8 miles		132	.061			2.14	4.43	6.57	8.10
1456	cycle 10 miles		120	.067			2.35	4.87	7.22	8.90
1460	35 MPH ave, cycle 4 miles		180	.044			1.57	3.25	4.82	5.95
1462	cycle 6 miles		156	.051			1.81	3.75	5.56	6.85
1464	cycle 8 miles		144	.056			1.96	4.06	6.02	7.45
1466	cycle 10 miles		132	.061			2.14	4.43	6.57	8.10
1468	cycle 20 miles		96	.083			2.94	6.10	9.04	11.15
1469	cycle 30 miles		72	.111			3.92	8.10	12.02	14.90
1470	cycle 40 miles		60	.133			4.71	9.75	14.46	17.85
1472	40 MPH ave, cycle 6 miles		168	.048			1.68	3.48	5.16	6.40
1474	cycle 8 miles		156	.051			1.81	3.75	5.56	6.85
1476	cycle 10 miles		144	.056			1.96	4.06	6.02	7.45
1478	cycle 20 miles		96	.083			2.94	6.10	9.04	11.15
1480	cycle 30 miles		84	.095			3.36	6.95	10.31	12.75
1482	cycle 40 miles		60	.133			4.71	9.75	14.46	17.85
1484	cycle 50 miles		60	.133			4.71	9.75	14.46	17.85
1494	45 MPH ave, cycle 8 miles		156	.051			1.81	3.75	5.56	6.85
1496	cycle 10 miles		144	.056			1.96	4.06	6.02	7.45
1498	cycle 20 miles		108	.074			2.61	5.40	8.01	9.90
1500	cycle 30 miles		84	.095			3.36	6.95	10.31	12.75
1502	cycle 40 miles		72	.111			3.92	8.10	12.02	14.90
1504	cycle 50 miles		60	.133			4.71	9.75	14.46	17.85
1506	50 MPH ave, cycle 10 miles		156	.051			1.81	3.75	5.56	6.85
1508	cycle 20 miles		120	.067			2.35	4.87	7.22	8.90
1510	cycle 30 miles		96	.083			2.94	6.10	9.04	11.15
1512	cycle 40 miles		72	.111			3.92	8.10	12.02	14.90
1514	cycle 50 miles		60	.133			4.71	9.75	14.46	17.85
1614	15 MPH, cycle 0.5 mile, 30 min. wait/Ld./Uld.		180	.044			1.57	3.25	4.82	5.95
1616	cycle 1 mile		168	.048			1.68	3.48	5.16	6.40
1618	cycle 2 miles		144	.056			1.96	4.06	6.02	7.45
1620	cycle 4 miles		120	.067			2.35	4.87	7.22	8.90
1622	cycle 6 miles		108	.074			2.61	5.40	8.01	9.90
1624	cycle 8 miles		84	.095			3.36	6.95	10.31	12.75
1625	cycle 10 miles		84	.095			3.36	6.95	10.31	12.75

31 23 23 – Fill

31 23 23.20 Hauling		Crew	Daily Output	Labor-Hours	Unit	Material	2012 Bare Costs		Total	Total Incl O&P
							Labor	Equipment		
1626	20 MPH ave, cycle 0.5 mile	B-34B	180	.044	L.C.Y.		1.57	3.25	4.82	5.95
1628	cycle 1 mile		168	.048			1.68	3.48	5.16	6.40
1630	cycle 2 miles		156	.051			1.81	3.75	5.56	6.85
1632	cycle 4 miles		132	.061			2.14	4.43	6.57	8.10
1634	cycle 6 miles		120	.067			2.35	4.87	7.22	8.90
1636	cycle 8 miles		108	.074			2.61	5.40	8.01	9.90
1638	cycle 10 miles		96	.083			2.94	6.10	9.04	11.15
1640	25 MPH ave, cycle 4 miles		144	.056			1.96	4.06	6.02	7.45
1642	cycle 6 miles		132	.061			2.14	4.43	6.57	8.10
1644	cycle 8 miles		108	.074			2.61	5.40	8.01	9.90
1646	cycle 10 miles		108	.074			2.61	5.40	8.01	9.90
1650	30 MPH ave, cycle 4 miles		144	.056			1.96	4.06	6.02	7.45
1652	cycle 6 miles		132	.061			2.14	4.43	6.57	8.10
1654	cycle 8 miles		120	.067			2.35	4.87	7.22	8.90
1656	cycle 10 miles		108	.074			2.61	5.40	8.01	9.90
1660	35 MPH ave, cycle 4 miles		156	.051			1.81	3.75	5.56	6.85
1662	cycle 6 miles		144	.056			1.96	4.06	6.02	7.45
1664	cycle 8 miles		132	.061			2.14	4.43	6.57	8.10
1666	cycle 10 miles		120	.067			2.35	4.87	7.22	8.90
1668	cycle 20 miles		84	.095			3.36	6.95	10.31	12.75
1669	cycle 30 miles		72	.111			3.92	8.10	12.02	14.90
1670	cycle 40 miles		60	.133			4.71	9.75	14.46	17.85
1672	40 MPH, cycle 6 miles		144	.056			1.96	4.06	6.02	7.45
1674	cycle 8 miles		132	.061			2.14	4.43	6.57	8.10
1676	cycle 10 miles		120	.067			2.35	4.87	7.22	8.90
1678	cycle 20 miles		96	.083			2.94	6.10	9.04	11.15
1680	cycle 30 miles		72	.111			3.92	8.10	12.02	14.90
1682	cycle 40 miles		60	.133			4.71	9.75	14.46	17.85
1684	cycle 50 miles		48	.167			5.90	12.20	18.10	22.50
1694	45 MPH ave, cycle 8 miles		144	.056			1.96	4.06	6.02	7.45
1696	cycle 10 miles		132	.061			2.14	4.43	6.57	8.10
1698	cycle 20 miles		96	.083			2.94	6.10	9.04	11.15
1700	cycle 30 miles		84	.095			3.36	6.95	10.31	12.75
1702	cycle 40 miles		60	.133			4.71	9.75	14.46	17.85
1704	cycle 50 miles		60	.133			4.71	9.75	14.46	17.85
1706	50 MPH ave, cycle 10 miles		132	.061			2.14	4.43	6.57	8.10
1708	cycle 20 miles		108	.074			2.61	5.40	8.01	9.90
1710	cycle 30 miles		84	.095			3.36	6.95	10.31	12.75
1712	cycle 40 miles		72	.111			3.92	8.10	12.02	14.90
1714	cycle 50 miles		60	.133			4.71	9.75	14.46	17.85
2000	Hauling, 8 C.Y. truck, small project cost per hour	B-34A	8	1	Hr.		35.50	44.50	80	103
2100	12 C.Y. Truck	B-34B	8	1			35.50	73	108.50	134
2150	16.5 C.Y. Truck	B-34C	8	1			35.50	80.50	116	142
2175	18 C.Y. 8 wheel Truck	B-34I	8	1			35.50	93	128.50	156
2200	20 C.Y. Truck	B-34D	8	1			35.50	82.50	118	145
2300	Grading at dump, or embankment if required, by dozer	B-10B	1000	.012	L.C.Y.		.51	1.24	1.75	2.15
2310	Spotter at fill or cut, if required	1 Clab	8	1	Hr.		35		35	54
9014	18 C.Y. truck, 8 wheels,15 min. wait/Ld./Uld.,15 MPH, cycle 0.5 mi.	B-34I	504	.016	L.C.Y.		.56	1.48	2.04	2.48
9016	cycle 1 mile		450	.018			.63	1.66	2.29	2.77
9018	cycle 2 miles		378	.021			.75	1.97	2.72	3.30
9020	cycle 4 miles		270	.030			1.05	2.76	3.81	4.63
9022	cycle 6 miles		216	.037			1.31	3.45	4.76	5.75
9024	cycle 8 miles		180	.044			1.57	4.14	5.71	6.95

31 23 23.20 Hauling		Crew	Daily Output	Labor-Hours	Unit	Material	2012 Bare Costs Labor	Equipment	Total	Total Incl O&P
9025	cycle 10 miles	B-34I	144	.056	L.C.Y.		1.96	5.15	7.11	8.70
9026	20 MPH ave, cycle 0.5 mile		522	.015			.54	1.43	1.97	2.39
9028	cycle 1 mile		468	.017			.60	1.59	2.19	2.67
9030	cycle 2 miles		414	.019			.68	1.80	2.48	3.01
9032	cycle 4 miles		324	.025			.87	2.30	3.17	3.85
9034	cycle 6 miles		252	.032			1.12	2.96	4.08	4.95
9036	cycle 8 miles		216	.037			1.31	3.45	4.76	5.75
9038	cycle 10 miles		180	.044			1.57	4.14	5.71	6.95
9040	25 MPH ave, cycle 4 miles		342	.023			.83	2.18	3.01	3.65
9042	cycle 6 miles		288	.028			.98	2.59	3.57	4.34
9044	cycle 8 miles		252	.032			1.12	2.96	4.08	4.95
9046	cycle 10 miles		216	.037			1.31	3.45	4.76	5.75
9050	30 MPH ave, cycle 4 miles		378	.021			.75	1.97	2.72	3.30
9052	cycle 6 miles		324	.025			.87	2.30	3.17	3.85
9054	cycle 8 miles		270	.030			1.05	2.76	3.81	4.63
9056	cycle 10 miles		234	.034			1.21	3.18	4.39	5.35
9060	35 MPH ave, cycle 4 miles		396	.020			.71	1.88	2.59	3.15
9062	cycle 6 miles		342	.023			.83	2.18	3.01	3.65
9064	cycle 8 miles		288	.028			.98	2.59	3.57	4.34
9066	cycle 10 miles		270	.030			1.05	2.76	3.81	4.63
9068	cycle 20 miles		162	.049			1.74	4.60	6.34	7.70
9070	cycle 30 miles		126	.063			2.24	5.90	8.14	9.90
9072	cycle 40 miles		90	.089			3.14	8.30	11.44	13.85
9074	40 MPH ave, cycle 6 miles		360	.022			.78	2.07	2.85	3.47
9076	cycle 8 miles		324	.025			.87	2.30	3.17	3.85
9078	cycle 10 miles		288	.028			.98	2.59	3.57	4.34
9080	cycle 20 miles		180	.044			1.57	4.14	5.71	6.95
9082	cycle 30 miles		144	.056			1.96	5.15	7.11	8.70
9084	cycle 40 miles		108	.074			2.61	6.90	9.51	11.55
9086	cycle 50 miles		90	.089			3.14	8.30	11.44	13.85
9094	45 MPH ave, cycle 8 miles		324	.025			.87	2.30	3.17	3.85
9096	cycle 10 miles		306	.026			.92	2.43	3.35	4.08
9098	cycle 20 miles		198	.040			1.43	3.76	5.19	6.30
9100	cycle 30 miles		144	.056			1.96	5.15	7.11	8.70
9102	cycle 40 miles		126	.063			2.24	5.90	8.14	9.90
9104	cycle 50 miles		108	.074			2.61	6.90	9.51	11.55
9106	50 MPH ave, cycle 10 miles		324	.025			.87	2.30	3.17	3.85
9108	cycle 20 miles		216	.037			1.31	3.45	4.76	5.75
9110	cycle 30 miles		162	.049			1.74	4.60	6.34	7.70
9112	cycle 40 miles		126	.063			2.24	5.90	8.14	9.90
9114	cycle 50 miles		108	.074			2.61	6.90	9.51	11.55
9214	20 min. wait/Ld./Uld.,15 MPH, cycle 0.5 mi.		396	.020			.71	1.88	2.59	3.15
9216	cycle 1 mile		360	.022			.78	2.07	2.85	3.47
9218	cycle 2 miles		306	.026			.92	2.43	3.35	4.08
9220	cycle 4 miles		234	.034			1.21	3.18	4.39	5.35
9222	cycle 6 miles		198	.040			1.43	3.76	5.19	6.30
9224	cycle 8 miles		162	.049			1.74	4.60	6.34	7.70
9225	cycle 10 miles		144	.056			1.96	5.15	7.11	8.70
9226	20 MPH ave, cycle 0.5 mile		396	.020			.71	1.88	2.59	3.15
9228	cycle 1 mile		378	.021			.75	1.97	2.72	3.30
9230	cycle 2 miles		324	.025			.87	2.30	3.17	3.85
9232	cycle 4 miles		270	.030			1.05	2.76	3.81	4.63
9234	cycle 6 miles		216	.037			1.31	3.45	4.76	5.75

31 23 23.20 Hauling		Crew	Daily Output	Labor-Hours	Unit	Material	2012 Bare Costs Labor	Equipment	Total	Total Incl O&P
9236	cycle 8 miles	B-34I	198	.040	L.C.Y.		1.43	3.76	5.19	6.30
9238	cycle 10 miles		162	.049			1.74	4.60	6.34	7.70
9240	25 MPH ave, cycle 4 miles		288	.028			.98	2.59	3.57	4.34
9242	cycle 6 miles		252	.032			1.12	2.96	4.08	4.95
9244	cycle 8 miles		216	.037			1.31	3.45	4.76	5.75
9246	cycle 10 miles		198	.040			1.43	3.76	5.19	6.30
9250	30 MPH ave, cycle 4 miles		306	.026			.92	2.43	3.35	4.08
9252	cycle 6 miles		270	.030			1.05	2.76	3.81	4.63
9254	cycle 8 miles		234	.034			1.21	3.18	4.39	5.35
9256	cycle 10 miles		216	.037			1.31	3.45	4.76	5.75
9260	35 MPH ave, cycle 4 miles		324	.025			.87	2.30	3.17	3.85
9262	cycle 6 miles		288	.028			.98	2.59	3.57	4.34
9264	cycle 8 miles		252	.032			1.12	2.96	4.08	4.95
9266	cycle 10 miles		234	.034			1.21	3.18	4.39	5.35
9268	cycle 20 miles		162	.049			1.74	4.60	6.34	7.70
9270	cycle 30 miles		108	.074			2.61	6.90	9.51	11.55
9272	cycle 40 miles		90	.089			3.14	8.30	11.44	13.85
9274	40 MPH ave, cycle 6 miles		288	.028			.98	2.59	3.57	4.34
9276	cycle 8 miles		270	.030			1.05	2.76	3.81	4.63
9278	cycle 10 miles		234	.034			1.21	3.18	4.39	5.35
9280	cycle 20 miles		162	.049			1.74	4.60	6.34	7.70
9282	cycle 30 miles		126	.063			2.24	5.90	8.14	9.90
9284	cycle 40 miles		108	.074			2.61	6.90	9.51	11.55
9286	cycle 50 miles		90	.089			3.14	8.30	11.44	13.85
9294	45 MPH ave, cycle 8 miles		270	.030			1.05	2.76	3.81	4.63
9296	cycle 10 miles		252	.032			1.12	2.96	4.08	4.95
9298	cycle 20 miles		180	.044			1.57	4.14	5.71	6.95
9300	cycle 30 miles		144	.056			1.96	5.15	7.11	8.70
9302	cycle 40 miles		108	.074			2.61	6.90	9.51	11.55
9304	cycle 50 miles		90	.089			3.14	8.30	11.44	13.85
9306	50 MPH ave, cycle 10 miles		270	.030			1.05	2.76	3.81	4.63
9308	cycle 20 miles		198	.040			1.43	3.76	5.19	6.30
9310	cycle 30 miles		144	.056			1.96	5.15	7.11	8.70
9312	cycle 40 miles		126	.063			2.24	5.90	8.14	9.90
9314	cycle 50 miles		108	.074			2.61	6.90	9.51	11.55
9414	25 min. wait/Ld./Uld.,15 MPH, cycle 0.5 mi.		306	.026			.92	2.43	3.35	4.08
9416	cycle 1 mile		288	.028			.98	2.59	3.57	4.34
9418	cycle 2 miles		252	.032			1.12	2.96	4.08	4.95
9420	cycle 4 miles		198	.040			1.43	3.76	5.19	6.30
9422	cycle 6 miles		180	.044			1.57	4.14	5.71	6.95
9424	cycle 8 miles		144	.056			1.96	5.15	7.11	8.70
9425	cycle 10 miles		126	.063			2.24	5.90	8.14	9.90
9426	20 MPH ave, cycle 0.5 mile		324	.025			.87	2.30	3.17	3.85
9428	cycle 1 mile		306	.026			.92	2.43	3.35	4.08
9430	cycle 2 miles		270	.030			1.05	2.76	3.81	4.63
9432	cycle 4 miles		234	.034			1.21	3.18	4.39	5.35
9434	cycle 6 miles		198	.040			1.43	3.76	5.19	6.30
9436	cycle 8 miles		180	.044			1.57	4.14	5.71	6.95
9438	cycle 10 miles		144	.056			1.96	5.15	7.11	8.70
9440	25 MPH ave, cycle 4 miles		252	.032			1.12	2.96	4.08	4.95
9442	cycle 6 miles		216	.037			1.31	3.45	4.76	5.75
9444	cycle 8 miles		198	.040			1.43	3.76	5.19	6.30
9446	cycle 10 miles		180	.044			1.57	4.14	5.71	6.95

31 23 Excavation and Fill

31 23 23 – Fill

31 23 23.20 Hauling		Crew	Daily Output	Labor-Hours	Unit	Material	2012 Bare Costs		Total	Total Incl O&P
							Labor	Equipment		
9450	30 MPH ave, cycle 4 miles	B-34I	252	.032	L.C.Y.		1.12	2.96	4.08	4.95
9452	cycle 6 miles		234	.034			1.21	3.18	4.39	5.35
9454	cycle 8 miles		198	.040			1.43	3.76	5.19	6.30
9456	cycle 10 miles		180	.044			1.57	4.14	5.71	6.95
9460	35 MPH ave, cycle 4 miles		270	.030			1.05	2.76	3.81	4.63
9462	cycle 6 miles		234	.034			1.21	3.18	4.39	5.35
9464	cycle 8 miles		216	.037			1.31	3.45	4.76	5.75
9466	cycle 10 miles		198	.040			1.43	3.76	5.19	6.30
9468	cycle 20 miles		144	.056			1.96	5.15	7.11	8.70
9470	cycle 30 miles		108	.074			2.61	6.90	9.51	11.55
9472	cycle 40 miles		90	.089			3.14	8.30	11.44	13.85
9474	40 MPH ave, cycle 6 miles		252	.032			1.12	2.96	4.08	4.95
9476	cycle 8 miles		234	.034			1.21	3.18	4.39	5.35
9478	cycle 10 miles		216	.037			1.31	3.45	4.76	5.75
9480	cycle 20 miles		144	.056			1.96	5.15	7.11	8.70
9482	cycle 30 miles		126	.063			2.24	5.90	8.14	9.90
9484	cycle 40 miles		90	.089			3.14	8.30	11.44	13.85
9486	cycle 50 miles		90	.089			3.14	8.30	11.44	13.85
9494	45 MPH ave, cycle 8 miles		234	.034			1.21	3.18	4.39	5.35
9496	cycle 10 miles		216	.037			1.31	3.45	4.76	5.75
9498	cycle 20 miles		162	.049			1.74	4.60	6.34	7.70
9500	cycle 30 miles		126	.063			2.24	5.90	8.14	9.90
9502	cycle 40 miles		108	.074			2.61	6.90	9.51	11.55
9504	cycle 50 miles		90	.089			3.14	8.30	11.44	13.85
9506	50 MPH ave, cycle 10 miles		234	.034			1.21	3.18	4.39	5.35
9508	cycle 20 miles		180	.044			1.57	4.14	5.71	6.95
9510	cycle 30 miles		144	.056			1.96	5.15	7.11	8.70
9512	cycle 40 miles		108	.074			2.61	6.90	9.51	11.55
9514	cycle 50 miles		90	.089			3.14	8.30	11.44	13.85
9614	30 min. wait/Ld./Uld.,15 MPH, cycle 0.5 mi.		270	.030			1.05	2.76	3.81	4.63
9616	cycle 1 mile		252	.032			1.12	2.96	4.08	4.95
9618	cycle 2 miles		216	.037			1.31	3.45	4.76	5.75
9620	cycle 4 miles		180	.044			1.57	4.14	5.71	6.95
9622	cycle 6 miles		162	.049			1.74	4.60	6.34	7.70
9624	cycle 8 miles		126	.063			2.24	5.90	8.14	9.90
9625	cycle 10 miles		126	.063			2.24	5.90	8.14	9.90
9626	20 MPH ave, cycle 0.5 mile		270	.030			1.05	2.76	3.81	4.63
9628	cycle 1 mile		252	.032			1.12	2.96	4.08	4.95
9630	cycle 2 miles		234	.034			1.21	3.18	4.39	5.35
9632	cycle 4 miles		198	.040			1.43	3.76	5.19	6.30
9634	cycle 6 miles		180	.044			1.57	4.14	5.71	6.95
9636	cycle 8 miles		162	.049			1.74	4.60	6.34	7.70
9638	cycle 10 miles		144	.056			1.96	5.15	7.11	8.70
9640	25 MPH ave, cycle 4 miles		216	.037			1.31	3.45	4.76	5.75
9642	cycle 6 miles		198	.040			1.43	3.76	5.19	6.30
9644	cycle 8 miles		180	.044			1.57	4.14	5.71	6.95
9646	cycle 10 miles		162	.049			1.74	4.60	6.34	7.70
9650	30 MPH ave, cycle 4 miles		216	.037			1.31	3.45	4.76	5.75
9652	cycle 6 miles		198	.040			1.43	3.76	5.19	6.30
9654	cycle 8 miles		180	.044			1.57	4.14	5.71	6.95
9656	cycle 10 miles		162	.049			1.74	4.60	6.34	7.70
9660	35 MPH ave, cycle 4 miles		234	.034			1.21	3.18	4.39	5.35
9662	cycle 6 miles		216	.037			1.31	3.45	4.76	5.75

31 23 23 – Fill

31 23 23.20 Hauling		Crew	Daily Output	Labor-Hours	Unit	Material	2012 Bare Costs		Total	Total Incl O&P
							Labor	Equipment		
9664	cycle 8 miles	B-34I	198	.040	L.C.Y.		1.43	3.76	5.19	6.30
9666	cycle 10 miles		180	.044			1.57	4.14	5.71	6.95
9668	cycle 20 miles		126	.063			2.24	5.90	8.14	9.90
9670	cycle 30 miles		108	.074			2.61	6.90	9.51	11.55
9672	cycle 40 miles		90	.089			3.14	8.30	11.44	13.85
9674	40 MPH ave, cycle 6 miles		216	.037			1.31	3.45	4.76	5.75
9676	cycle 8 miles		198	.040			1.43	3.76	5.19	6.30
9678	cycle 10 miles		180	.044			1.57	4.14	5.71	6.95
9680	cycle 20 miles		144	.056			1.96	5.15	7.11	8.70
9682	cycle 30 miles		108	.074			2.61	6.90	9.51	11.55
9684	cycle 40 miles		90	.089			3.14	8.30	11.44	13.85
9686	cycle 50 miles		72	.111			3.92	10.35	14.27	17.35
9694	45 MPH ave, cycle 8 miles		216	.037			1.31	3.45	4.76	5.75
9696	cycle 10 miles		198	.040			1.43	3.76	5.19	6.30
9698	cycle 20 miles		144	.056			1.96	5.15	7.11	8.70
9700	cycle 30 miles		126	.063			2.24	5.90	8.14	9.90
9702	cycle 40 miles		108	.074			2.61	6.90	9.51	11.55
9704	cycle 50 miles		90	.089			3.14	8.30	11.44	13.85
9706	50 MPH ave, cycle 10 miles		198	.040			1.43	3.76	5.19	6.30
9708	cycle 20 miles		162	.049			1.74	4.60	6.34	7.70
9710	cycle 30 miles		126	.063			2.24	5.90	8.14	9.90
9712	cycle 40 miles		108	.074			2.61	6.90	9.51	11.55
9714	cycle 50 miles		90	.089			3.14	8.30	11.44	13.85

31 41 Shoring

31 41 16 – Sheet Piling

31 41 16.10 Sheet Piling Systems

	31 41 16.10 Sheet Piling Systems		Crew	Daily Output	Labor-Hours	Unit	Material	2012 Bare Costs		Total	Total Incl O&P
								Labor	Equipment		
0010	**SHEET PILING SYSTEMS**										
0020	Sheet piling steel, not incl. wales, 22 psf, 15' excav., left in place		B-40	10.81	5.920	Ton	1,525	261	320	2,106	2,425
0100	Drive, extract & salvage	R314116-45		6	10.667		530	470	575	1,575	1,950
0300	20' deep excavation, 27 psf, left in place			12.95	4.942		1,525	218	266	2,009	2,300
0400	Drive, extract & salvage			6.55	9.771		530	430	525	1,485	1,850
1200	15' deep excavation, 22 psf, left in place			983	.065	S.F.	17.65	2.87	3.51	24.03	28
1300	Drive, extract & salvage			545	.117		5.95	5.20	6.35	17.50	21.50
1500	20' deep excavation, 27 psf, left in place			960	.067		22	2.94	3.59	28.53	33
1600	Drive, extract & salvage			485	.132		7.75	5.80	7.10	20.65	25.50
2100	Rent steel sheet piling and wales, first month					Ton	305			305	335
2200	Per added month						30.50			30.50	33.50
2300	Rental piling left in place, add to rental						1,225			1,225	1,325
2500	Wales, connections & struts, 2/3 salvage						485			485	535
3900	Wood, solid sheeting, incl. wales, braces and spacers,	R314116-40									
3910	drive, extract & salvage, 8' deep excavation		B-31	330	.121	S.F.	1.56	4.52	.59	6.67	9.30
4000	10' deep, 50 S.F./hr. in & 150 S.F./hr. out			300	.133		1.61	4.97	.65	7.23	10.15
4100	12' deep, 45 S.F./hr. in & 135 S.F./hr. out			270	.148		1.66	5.55	.72	7.93	11.10
4200	14' deep, 42 S.F./hr. in & 126 S.F./hr. out			250	.160		1.71	5.95	.78	8.44	11.95
4300	16' deep, 40 S.F./hr. in & 120 S.F./hr. out			240	.167		1.76	6.20	.81	8.77	12.40
4400	18' deep, 38 S.F./hr. in & 114 S.F./hr. out			230	.174		1.82	6.50	.85	9.17	12.95
4520	Left in place, 8' deep, 55 S.F./hr.			440	.091		2.82	3.39	.44	6.65	8.80
4540	10' deep, 50 S.F./hr.			400	.100		2.96	3.73	.49	7.18	9.55
4560	12' deep, 45 S.F./hr.			360	.111		3.13	4.14	.54	7.81	10.45
4565	14' deep, 42 S.F./hr.			335	.119		3.31	4.45	.58	8.34	11.15

31 41 Shoring

31 41 16 – Sheet Piling

31 41 16.10 Sheet Piling Systems	Crew	Daily Output	Labor-Hours	Unit	Material	2012 Bare Costs Labor	Equipment	Total	Total Incl O&P
4570	16' deep, 40 S.F./hr.	B-31	320	.125	S.F.	3.52	4.66	.61	8.79	11.70
4700	Alternate pricing, left in place, 8' deep		1.76	22.727	M.B.F.	635	850	111	1,596	2,125
4800	Drive, extract and salvage, 8' deep		1.32	30.303	"	565	1,125	148	1,838	2,525

31 52 Cofferdams

31 52 16 – Timber Cofferdams

31 52 16.10 Cofferdams

		Crew	Daily Output	Labor-Hours	Unit	Material	2012 Bare Costs Labor	Equipment	Total	Total Incl O&P
0010	**COFFERDAMS**									
0011	Incl. mobilization and temporary sheeting									
0080	Soldier beams & lagging H piles with 3" wood sheeting									
0090	horizontal between piles, including removal of wales & braces									
0100	No hydrostatic head, 15' deep, 1 line of braces, minimum	B-50	545	.206	S.F.	6.40	8.65	4.26	19.31	25.50
0200	Maximum		495	.226		7.10	9.50	4.69	21.29	28
1300	No hydrostatic head, left in place, 15' dp., 1 line of braces, min.		635	.176		8.50	7.40	3.65	19.55	25
1400	Maximum		575	.195		9.10	8.20	4.04	21.34	27.50
2350	Lagging only, 3" thick wood between piles 8' O.C., minimum	B-46	400	.120		1.42	4.71	.11	6.24	9.15
2370	Maximum		250	.192		2.13	7.55	.17	9.85	14.45
2400	Open sheeting no bracing, for trenches to 10' deep, min.		1736	.028		.64	1.09	.03	1.76	2.44
2450	Maximum		1510	.032		.71	1.25	.03	1.99	2.78
2500	Tie-back method, add to open sheeting, add, minimum								20%	20%
2550	Maximum								60%	60%
2700	Tie-backs only, based on tie-backs total length, minimum	B-46	86.80	.553	L.F.	14	21.50	.50	36	50.50
2750	Maximum		38.50	1.247	"	24.50	49	1.13	74.63	105
3500	Tie-backs only, typical average, 25' long		2	24	Ea.	615	945	22	1,582	2,175
3600	35' long		1.58	30.380	"	820	1,200	27.50	2,047.50	2,800

Division Notes

	CREW	DAILY OUTPUT	LABOR-HOURS	UNIT	2012 BARE COSTS				TOTAL INCL O&P
					MAT.	LABOR	EQUIP.	TOTAL	

Estimating Tips

32 01 00 Operations and Maintenance of Exterior Improvements

- Recycling of asphalt pavement is becoming very popular and is an alternative to removal and replacement. It can be a good value engineering proposal if removed pavement can be recycled, either at the project site or at another site that is reasonably close to the project site. Two new sections on repair of flexible and rigid pavement have been added.

32 10 00 Bases, Ballasts, and Paving

- When estimating paving, keep in mind the project schedule. If an asphaltic paving project is in a colder climate and runs through to the spring, consider placing the base course in the autumn and then topping it in the spring, just prior to completion. This could save considerable costs in spring repair. Keep in mind that prices for asphalt and concrete are generally higher in the cold seasons. New lines have been added for pavement markings including tactile warning systems and new fence lines.

32 90 00 Planting

- The timing of planting and guarantee specifications often dictate the costs for establishing tree and shrub growth and a stand of grass or ground cover. Establish the work performance schedule to coincide with the local planting season. Maintenance and growth guarantees can add from 20%–100% to the total landscaping cost. The cost to replace trees and shrubs can be as high as 5% of the total cost, depending on the planting zone, soil conditions, and time of year.

Reference Numbers

Reference numbers are shown in shaded boxes at the beginning of some major classifications. These numbers refer to related items in the Reference Section. The reference information may be an estimating procedure, an alternate pricing method, or technical information.

Note: Not all subdivisions listed here necessarily appear in this publication.

32 12 Flexible Paving

32 12 16 – Asphalt Paving

32 12 16.13 Plant-Mix Asphalt Paving

		Crew	Daily Output	Labor-Hours	Unit	Material	2012 Bare Costs Labor	Equipment	Total	Total Incl O&P
0010	**PLANT-MIX ASPHALT PAVING**									
0020	And large paved areas with no hauling included									
0025	See Section 31 23 23.20 for hauling costs									
0080	Binder course, 1-1/2" thick	B-25	7725	.011	S.Y.	5.05	.44	.33	5.82	6.65
0120	2" thick		6345	.014		6.75	.53	.40	7.68	8.65
0130	2-1/2" thick		5620	.016		8.45	.60	.45	9.50	10.65
0160	3" thick		4905	.018		10.10	.69	.52	11.31	12.75
0170	3-1/2" thick		4520	.019		11.80	.75	.56	13.11	14.75
0200	4" thick		4140	.021		13.50	.82	.61	14.93	16.75
0300	Wearing course, 1" thick	B-25B	10575	.009		3.34	.35	.26	3.95	4.51
0340	1-1/2" thick		7725	.012		5.60	.49	.36	6.45	7.35
0380	2" thick		6345	.015		7.55	.59	.44	8.58	9.70
0420	2-1/2" thick		5480	.018		9.30	.68	.50	10.48	11.85
0460	3" thick		4900	.020		11.10	.77	.56	12.43	14
0470	3-1/2" thick		4520	.021		13.05	.83	.61	14.49	16.30
0480	4" thick		4140	.023		14.90	.91	.67	16.48	18.45
0500	Open graded friction course	B-25C	5000	.010		2.70	.38	.44	3.52	4.04
0800	Alternate method of figuring paving costs									
0810	Binder course, 1-1/2" thick	B-25	630	.140	Ton	62	5.35	4.03	71.38	80.50
0811	2" thick		690	.128		62	4.90	3.68	70.58	79.50
0812	3" thick		800	.110		62	4.22	3.17	69.39	78
0813	4" thick		900	.098		62	3.75	2.82	68.57	77
0850	Wearing course, 1" thick	B-25B	575	.167		68	6.50	4.81	79.31	90.50
0851	1-1/2" thick		630	.152		68	5.95	4.39	78.34	89
0852	2" thick		690	.139		68	5.45	4.01	77.46	87.50
0853	2-1/2" thick		765	.125		68	4.90	3.61	76.51	86.50
0854	3" thick		800	.120		68	4.69	3.46	76.15	86
1000	Pavement replacement over trench, 2" thick	B-37	90	.533	S.Y.	6.95	19.75	1.66	28.36	40
1050	4" thick		70	.686		13.80	25.50	2.13	41.43	56.50
1080	6" thick		55	.873		22	32.50	2.71	57.21	76.50

32 12 16.14 Asphaltic Concrete Paving

		Crew	Daily Output	Labor-Hours	Unit	Material	2012 Bare Costs Labor	Equipment	Total	Total Incl O&P
0011	**ASPHALTIC CONCRETE PAVING**, parking lots & driveways									
0015	No asphalt hauling included									
0018	Use 6.05 C. Y. per inch per M.S.F. for hauling									
0020	6" stone base, 2" binder course, 1" topping	B-25C	9000	.005	S.F.	1.70	.21	.25	2.16	2.46
0025	2" binder course, 2" topping		9000	.005		2.11	.21	.25	2.57	2.91
0030	3" binder course, 2" topping		9000	.005		2.49	.21	.25	2.95	3.32
0035	4" binder course, 2" topping		9000	.005		2.86	.21	.25	3.32	3.73
0040	1.5" binder course, 1" topping		9000	.005		1.51	.21	.25	1.97	2.25
0042	3" binder course, 1" topping		9000	.005		2.07	.21	.25	2.53	2.87
0045	3" binder course, 3" topping		9000	.005		2.90	.21	.25	3.36	3.78
0050	4" binder course, 3" topping		9000	.005		3.27	.21	.25	3.73	4.19
0055	4" binder course, 4" topping		9000	.005		3.68	.21	.25	4.14	4.64
0300	Binder course, 1-1/2" thick		35000	.001		.56	.05	.06	.67	.77
0400	2" thick		25000	.002		.73	.08	.09	.90	1.02
0500	3" thick		15000	.003		1.13	.13	.15	1.41	1.59
0600	4" thick		10800	.004		1.48	.17	.21	1.86	2.12
0800	Sand finish course, 3/4" thick		41000	.001		.32	.05	.05	.42	.48
0900	1" thick		34000	.001		.39	.06	.07	.52	.58
1000	Fill pot holes, hot mix, 2" thick	B-16	4200	.008		.84	.27	.14	1.25	1.49
1100	4" thick		3500	.009		1.23	.33	.17	1.73	2.03
1120	6" thick		3100	.010		1.65	.37	.19	2.21	2.59

456

32 12 Flexible Paving

32 12 16 – Asphalt Paving

32 12 16.14 Asphaltic Concrete Paving	Crew	Daily Output	Labor-Hours	Unit	Material	2012 Bare Costs Labor	Equipment	Total	Total Incl O&P
1140	Cold patch, 2" thick	B-51	3000	.016	S.F.	.85	.57	.07	1.49	1.89
1160	4" thick		2700	.018		1.62	.63	.08	2.33	2.83
1180	6" thick		1900	.025		2.52	.89	.11	3.52	4.26

32 84 Planting Irrigation

32 84 23 – Underground Sprinklers

32 84 23.10 Sprinkler Irrigation System

		Crew	Daily Output	Labor-Hours	Unit	Material	2012 Bare Costs Labor	Equipment	Total	Total Incl O&P
0010	**SPRINKLER IRRIGATION SYSTEM**									
0011	For lawns									
0100	Golf course with fully automatic system	C-17	.05	1600	9 holes	98,000	73,500		171,500	221,500
0200	24' diam. head at 15' O.C incl. piping, auto oper., minimum	B-20	70	.343	Head	22	13.45		35.45	45
0300	Maximum		40	.600		54.50	23.50		78	96.50
0500	60' diam. head at 40' O.C. incl. piping, auto oper., minimum		28	.857		69.50	33.50		103	128
0600	Maximum		23	1.043		192	41		233	274
0800	Residential system, custom, 1" supply		2000	.012	S.F.	.34	.47		.81	1.10
0900	1-1/2" supply		1800	.013	"	.39	.52		.91	1.24

Division Notes

	CREW	DAILY OUTPUT	LABOR-HOURS	UNIT	2012 BARE COSTS				TOTAL INCL O&P
					MAT.	LABOR	EQUIP.	TOTAL	

Estimating Tips

33 10 00 Water Utilities
33 30 00 Sanitary Sewerage Utilities
33 40 00 Storm Drainage Utilities

- Never assume that the water, sewer, and drainage lines will go in at the early stages of the project. Consider the site access needs before dividing the site in half with open trenches, loose pipe, and machinery obstructions. Always inspect the site to establish that the site drawings are complete. Check off all existing utilities on your drawings as you locate them. Be especially careful with underground utilities because appurtenances are sometimes buried during regrading or repaving operations. If you find any discrepancies, mark up the site plan for further research. Differing site conditions can be very costly if discovered later in the project.

- See also Section 33 01 00 for restoration of pipe where removal/replacement may be undesirable. Use of new types of piping materials can reduce the overall project cost. Owners/design engineers should consider the installing contractor as a valuable source of current information on utility products and local conditions that could lead to significant cost savings.

Reference Numbers

Reference numbers are shown in shaded boxes at the beginning of some major classifications. These numbers refer to related items in the Reference Section. The reference information may be an estimating procedure, an alternate pricing method, or technical information.

Note: Not all subdivisions listed here necessarily appear in this publication.

33 01 10.10 Corrosion Resistance	Crew	Daily Output	Labor-Hours	Unit	Material	2012 Bare Costs Labor	Equipment	Total	Total Incl O&P
0010	**CORROSION RESISTANCE**									
0012	Wrap & coat, add to pipe, 4" diameter				L.F.	2.24			2.24	2.46
0020	5" diameter					2.81			2.81	3.09
0040	6" diameter					3.36			3.36	3.70
0060	8" diameter					4.36			4.36	4.80
0080	10" diameter					5.50			5.50	6.05
0100	12" diameter					6.60			6.60	7.25
0120	14" diameter					7.60			7.60	8.35
0140	16" diameter					8.60			8.60	9.45
0160	18" diameter					9.45			9.45	10.40
0180	20" diameter					10.45			10.45	11.50
0200	24" diameter					12.70			12.70	13.95
0220	Small diameter pipe, 1" diameter, add					1.46			1.46	1.61
0240	2" diameter					1.60			1.60	1.76
0260	2-1/2" diameter					1.76			1.76	1.94
0280	3" diameter					2.11			2.11	2.32
0300	Fittings, field covered, add				S.F.	9.20			9.20	10.10
0500	Coating, bituminous, per diameter inch, 1 coat, add				L.F.	.55			.55	.61
0540	3 coat					1.65			1.65	1.82
0560	Coal tar epoxy, per diameter inch, 1 coat, add					.28			.28	.31
0600	3 coat					.84			.84	.92
1000	Polyethylene H.D. extruded, .025" thk., 1/2" diameter add					.35			.35	.39
1020	3/4" diameter					.37			.37	.41
1040	1" diameter					.42			.42	.46
1060	1-1/4" diameter					.52			.52	.57
1080	1-1/2" diameter					.54			.54	.59
1100	.030" thk., 2" diameter					.58			.58	.64
1120	2-1/2" diameter					.67			.67	.74
1140	.035" thk., 3" diameter					.84			.84	.92
1160	3-1/2" diameter					.95			.95	1.05
1180	4" diameter					1.02			1.02	1.12
1200	.040" thk, 5" diameter					1.39			1.39	1.53
1220	6" diameter					1.47			1.47	1.62
1240	8" diameter					1.90			1.90	2.09
1260	10" diameter					2.35			2.35	2.59
1280	12" diameter					2.80			2.80	3.08
1300	.060" thk., 14" diameter					3.84			3.84	4.22
1320	16" diameter					4.55			4.55	5
1340	18" diameter					5.25			5.25	5.80
1360	20" diameter					5.95			5.95	6.55
1380	Fittings, field wrapped, add				S.F.	6.10			6.10	6.70

33 01 10.20 Pipe Repair

33 01 10.20 Pipe Repair	Crew	Daily Output	Labor-Hours	Unit	Material	2012 Bare Costs Labor	Equipment	Total	Total Incl O&P
0010	**PIPE REPAIR**									
0020	Not including excavation or backfill									
0100	Clamp, stainless steel, lightweight, for steel pipe									
0110	3" long, 1/2" diameter pipe	1 Plum	34	.235	Ea.	13.15	12.85		26	34
0120	3/4" diameter pipe		32	.250		13.60	13.65		27.25	35.50
0130	1" diameter pipe		30	.267		14.40	14.55		28.95	38
0140	1-1/4" diameter pipe		28	.286		15.20	15.60		30.80	40
0150	1-1/2" diameter pipe		26	.308		15.95	16.80		32.75	43
0160	2" diameter pipe		24	.333		17.50	18.20		35.70	47
0170	2-1/2" diameter pipe		23	.348		18.70	19		37.70	49

33 01 10 – Operation and Maintenance of Water Utilities

33 01 10.20 Pipe Repair	Crew	Daily Output	Labor-Hours	Unit	Material	2012 Bare Costs Labor	Equipment	Total	Total Incl O&P
0180	3" diameter pipe	1 Plum	22	.364	Ea.	20.50	19.85		40.35	52.50
0190	3-1/2" diameter pipe		21	.381		21.50	21		42.50	55.50
0200	4" diameter pipe	B-20	44	.545		21.50	21.50		43	57
0210	5" diameter pipe		42	.571		28.50	22.50		51	65.50
0220	6" diameter pipe		38	.632		29.50	25		54.50	70.50
0230	8" diameter pipe		30	.800		35	31.50		66.50	87
0240	10" diameter pipe		28	.857		95	33.50		128.50	157
0250	12" diameter pipe		24	1		105	39		144	177
0260	14" diameter pipe		22	1.091		218	43		261	305
0270	16" diameter pipe		20	1.200		235	47		282	330
0280	18" diameter pipe		18	1.333		247	52.50		299.50	355
0290	20" diameter pipe		16	1.500		262	59		321	380
0300	24" diameter pipe		14	1.714		291	67		358	425
0360	For 6" long, add					100%	40%			
0370	For 9" long, add					200%	100%			
0380	For 12" long, add					300%	150%			
0390	For 18" long, add					500%	200%			
0400	Pipe Freezing for live repairs of systems 3/8 inch to 6 inch									
0410	Note: Pipe Freezing can also be used to install a valve into a live system									
0420	Pipe Freezing each side 3/8 inch	2 Skwk	8	2	Ea.	510	91		601	700
0425	Pipe Freezing each side 3/8 inch, second location same kit		8	2		21	91		112	163
0430	Pipe Freezing each side 3/4 inch		8	2		510	91		601	700
0435	Pipe Freezing each side 3/4 inch, second location same kit		8	2		21	91		112	163
0440	Pipe Freezing each side 1-1/2 inch		6	2.667		510	121		631	745
0445	Pipe Freezing each side 1-1/2 inch , second location same kit		6	2.667		21	121		142	210
0450	Pipe Freezing each side 2 inch		6	2.667		680	121		801	935
0455	Pipe Freezing each side 2 inch, second location same kit		6	2.667		21	121		142	210
0460	Pipe Freezing each side 2-1/2 inch-3 inch		6	2.667		900	121		1,021	1,175
0465	Pipe Freeze each side 2-1/2 -3 inch, second location same kit		6	2.667		42	121		163	233
0470	Pipe Freezing each side 4 inch		4	4		1,500	182		1,682	1,925
0475	Pipe Freezing each side 4 inch, second location same kit		4	4		68.50	182		250.50	355
0480	Pipe Freezing each side 5-6 inch		4	4		3,950	182		4,132	4,625
0485	Pipe Freezing each side 5-6 inch, second location same kit		4	4		206	182		388	505
0490	Pipe Frz extra 20 lb. CO_2 cylinders (3/8" to 2" - 1 ea, 3" -2 ea)					205			205	226
0500	Pipe Freezing extra 50 lb. CO_2 cylinders (4" - 2 ea, 5"-6" -6 ea)					495			495	545
1000	Clamp, stainless steel, with threaded service tap									
1040	Full seal for iron, steel, PVC pipe									
1100	6" long, 2" diameter pipe	1 Plum	17	.471	Ea.	130	25.50		155.50	182
1110	2-1/2" diameter pipe		16	.500		133	27.50		160.50	187
1120	3" diameter pipe		15.60	.513		145	28		173	202
1130	3-1/2" diameter pipe		15	.533		150	29		179	209
1140	4" diameter pipe	B-20	32	.750		156	29.50		185.50	218
1150	6" diameter pipe		28	.857		181	33.50		214.50	251
1160	8" diameter pipe		21	1.143		214	45		259	305
1170	10" diameter pipe		20	1.200		250	47		297	345
1180	12" diameter pipe		17	1.412		282	55.50		337.50	395
1205	For 9" long, add					20%	45%			
1210	For 12" long, add					40%	80%			
1220	For 18" long, add					70%	110%			
1600	Clamp, stainless steel, single section									
1640	Full seal for iron, steel, PVC pipe									
1700	6" long, 2" diameter pipe	1 Plum	17	.471	Ea.	75.50	25.50		101	122
1710	2-1/2" diameter pipe		16	.500		78.50	27.50		106	128

33 01 Operation and Maintenance of Utilities

33 01 10 – Operation and Maintenance of Water Utilities

33 01 10.20 Pipe Repair		Crew	Daily Output	Labor-Hours	Unit	Material	2012 Bare Costs Labor	Equipment	Total	Total Incl O&P
1720	3" diameter pipe	1 Plum	15.60	.513	Ea.	91.50	28		119.50	142
1730	3-1/2" diameter pipe	↓	15	.533		95.50	29		124.50	149
1740	4" diameter pipe	B-20	32	.750		102	29.50		131.50	158
1750	6" diameter pipe		27	.889		127	35		162	193
1760	8" diameter pipe		21	1.143		161	45		206	246
1770	10" diameter pipe		20	1.200		196	47		243	289
1780	12" diameter pipe	↓	17	1.412		229	55.50		284.50	340
1800	For 9" long, add					40%	45%			
1810	For 12" long, add					60%	80%			
1820	For 18" long, add				↓	120%	110%			
2000	Clamp, stainless steel, two section									
2040	Full seal, for iron, steel, PVC pipe									
2100	6" long, 4" diameter pipe	B-20	24	1	Ea.	155	39		194	232
2110	6" diameter pipe		20	1.200		180	47		227	270
2120	8" diameter pipe		13	1.846		203	72.50		275.50	335
2130	10" diameter pipe		12	2		215	78.50		293.50	360
2140	12" diameter pipe		10	2.400		275	94		369	450
2200	9" long, 4" diameter pipe		16	1.500		206	59		265	320
2210	6" diameter pipe		13	1.846		232	72.50		304.50	365
2220	8" diameter pipe		9	2.667		258	105		363	445
2230	10" diameter pipe		8	3		345	118		463	560
2240	12" diameter pipe		7	3.429		380	134		514	625
2250	14" diameter pipe		6.40	3.750		640	147		787	930
2260	16" diameter pipe		6	4		715	157		872	1,025
2270	18" diameter pipe		5	4.800		725	188		913	1,100
2280	20" diameter pipe		4.60	5.217		785	205		990	1,175
2290	24" diameter pipe	↓	4	6		1,025	235		1,260	1,500
2320	For 12" long, add to 9"					15%	25%			
2330	For 18" long, add to 9"				↓	70%	55%			
8000	For internal cleaning and inspection, see Section 33 01 30.16									
8100	For pipe testing, see Section 23 05 93.50									

33 01 30 – Operation and Maintenance of Sewer Utilities

33 01 30.16 TV Inspection of Sewer Pipelines

		Crew	Daily Output	Labor-Hours	Unit	Material	2012 Bare Costs Labor	Equipment	Total	Total Incl O&P
0010	**TV INSPECTION OF SEWER PIPELINES**									
0100	Pipe internal cleaning & inspection, cleaning, pressure pipe systems									
0120	Pig method, lengths 1000' to 10,000'									
0140	4" diameter thru 24" diameter, minimum				L.F.				4	4.60
0160	Maximum				"				17.50	20.50
6000	Sewage/sanitary systems									
6100	Power rodder with header & cutters									
6110	Mobilization charge, minimum				Total				695	800
6120	Mobilization charge, maximum				"				8,950	10,300
6140	Cleaning 4"-12" diameter				L.F.				3.70	4.25
6190	14"-24" diameter								4.33	4.98
6240	30" diameter								6.30	7.25
6250	36" diameter								7.35	8.45
6260	48" diameter								8.40	9.65
6270	60" diameter								9.45	10.85
6280	72" diameter				↓				10.50	12.10
9000	Inspection, television camera with video									
9060	up to 500 linear feet				Total				765	880

33 01 Operation and Maintenance of Utilities

33 01 30 – Operation and Maintenance of Sewer Utilities

33 01 30.71 Pipebursting

		Crew	Daily Output	Labor-Hours	Unit	Material	2012 Bare Costs Labor	Equipment	Total	Total Incl O&P
0010	**PIPEBURSTING**									
0011	300' runs, replace with HDPE pipe									
0020	Not including excavation, backfill, shoring, or dewatering									
0100	6" to 15" diameter, minimum				L.F.				100	110
0200	Maximum								200	220
0300	18" to 36" diameter, minimum								200	220
0400	Maximum								410	450
0500	Mobilize and demobilize, minimum				Job				3,000	3,300
0600	Maximum				"				30,000	33,000

33 01 30.74 HDPE Pipe Lining

		Crew	Daily Output	Labor-Hours	Unit	Material	2012 Bare Costs Labor	Equipment	Total	Total Incl O&P
0010	**HDPE PIPE LINING**, excludes cleaning and video inspection									
0020	Pipe relined with one pipe size smaller than original (4" for 6")									
0100	6" diameter, original size	B-6B	600	.080	L.F.	4.03	2.86	1.42	8.31	10.40
0150	8" diameter, original size		600	.080		9.15	2.86	1.42	13.43	16
0200	10" diameter, original size		600	.080		12.50	2.86	1.42	16.78	19.70
0250	12" diameter, original size		400	.120		19.75	4.29	2.13	26.17	30.50
0300	14" diameter, original size		400	.120		31	4.29	2.13	37.42	43
0350	16" diameter, original size	B-6C	300	.160		36	5.70	5.05	46.75	54.50
0400	18" diameter, original size	"	300	.160		41.50	5.70	5.05	52.25	60
1000	Pipe HDPE lining, make service line taps	B-6	4	6	Ea.	105	230	83.50	418.50	555

33 05 Common Work Results for Utilities

33 05 23 – Trenchless Utility Installation

33 05 23.19 Microtunneling

		Crew	Daily Output	Labor-Hours	Unit	Material	2012 Bare Costs Labor	Equipment	Total	Total Incl O&P
0010	**MICROTUNNELING**									
0011	Not including excavation, backfill, shoring,									
0020	or dewatering, average 50'/day, slurry method									
0100	24" to 48" outside diameter, minimum				L.F.				830	915
0110	Adverse conditions, add				%				50%	50%
1000	Rent microtunneling machine, average monthly lease				Month				92,000	101,000
1010	Operating technician				Day				610	680
1100	Mobilization and demobilization, minimum				Job				40,000	45,000
1110	Maximum				"				420,000	462,000

33 05 23.20 Horizontal Boring

		Crew	Daily Output	Labor-Hours	Unit	Material	2012 Bare Costs Labor	Equipment	Total	Total Incl O&P
0010	**HORIZONTAL BORING**									
0011	Casing only, 100' minimum,									
0020	not incl. jacking pits or dewatering									
0100	Roadwork, 1/2" thick wall, 24" diameter casing	B-42	20	3.200	L.F.	146	126	63.50	335.50	430
0200	36" diameter		16	4		220	158	79	457	575
0300	48" diameter		15	4.267		294	168	84.50	546.50	680
0500	Railroad work, 24" diameter		15	4.267		146	168	84.50	398.50	520
0600	36" diameter		14	4.571		220	181	90.50	491.50	625
0700	48" diameter		12	5.333		294	211	106	611	770
0900	For ledge, add									20%
1000	Small diameter boring, 3", sandy soil	B-82	900	.018		23	.71	.09	23.80	26
1040	Rocky soil	"	500	.032		23	1.28	.15	24.43	27
1100	Prepare jacking pits, incl. mobilization & demobilization, minimum				Ea.				3,150	3,625
1101	Maximum				"				21,000	24,200

33 05 Common Work Results for Utilities

33 05 26 – Utility Identification

33 05 26.10 Utility Accessories		Crew	Daily Output	Labor-Hours	Unit	Material	2012 Bare Costs Labor	Equipment	Total	Total Incl O&P
0010	**UTILITY ACCESSORIES**	G1030–805									
0400	Underground tape, detectable, reinforced, alum. foil core, 2"	1 Clab	150	.053	C.L.F.	2.05	1.87		3.92	5.15
0500	6"	"	140	.057	"	5.60	2.01		7.61	9.25

33 11 Water Utility Distribution Piping

33 11 13 – Public Water Utility Distribution Piping

33 11 13.15 Water Supply, Ductile Iron Pipe

		Crew	Daily Output	Labor-Hours	Unit	Material	Labor	Equipment	Total	Total Incl O&P
0010	**WATER SUPPLY, DUCTILE IRON PIPE** R331113-80									
0020	Not including excavation or backfill									
2000	Pipe, class 50 water piping, 18' lengths									
2020	Mechanical joint, 4" diameter	B-21A	200	.200	L.F.	12.60	8.75	2.24	23.59	29.50
2040	6" diameter		160	.250		14.75	10.90	2.80	28.45	36
2060	8" diameter		133.33	.300		21.50	13.10	3.36	37.96	47
2080	10" diameter		114.29	.350		26	15.30	3.92	45.22	56
2100	12" diameter		105.26	.380		31.50	16.60	4.26	52.36	64
2120	14" diameter		100	.400		49	17.45	4.48	70.93	85
2140	16" diameter		72.73	.550		50.50	24	6.15	80.65	99
2160	18" diameter		68.97	.580		53.50	25.50	6.50	85.50	105
2170	20" diameter		57.14	.700		56.50	30.50	7.85	94.85	117
2180	24" diameter		47.06	.850		61.50	37	9.55	108.05	135
3000	Tyton, push-on joint, 4" diameter		400	.100		11.40	4.37	1.12	16.89	20.50
3020	6" diameter		333.33	.120		15.80	5.25	1.35	22.40	27
3040	8" diameter		200	.200		22	8.75	2.24	32.99	40
3060	10" diameter		181.82	.220		31.50	9.60	2.47	43.57	52
3080	12" diameter		160	.250		33	10.90	2.80	46.70	56
3100	14" diameter		133.33	.300		36.50	13.10	3.36	52.96	63.50
3120	16" diameter		114.29	.350		49.50	15.30	3.92	68.72	82
3140	18" diameter		100	.400		55	17.45	4.48	76.93	92
3160	20" diameter		88.89	.450		57.50	19.65	5.05	82.20	98.50
3180	24" diameter		76.92	.520		72	22.50	5.85	100.35	120
8000	Fittings, mechanical joint									
8006	90° bend, 4" diameter	B-20A	16	2	Ea.	251	85.50		336.50	405
8020	6" diameter		12.80	2.500		375	107		482	570
8040	8" diameter		10.67	2.999		665	128		793	925
8060	10" diameter	B-21A	11.43	3.500		890	153	39	1,082	1,250
8080	12" diameter		10.53	3.799		1,250	166	42.50	1,458.50	1,675
8100	14" diameter		10	4		1,675	175	45	1,895	2,175
8120	16" diameter		7.27	5.502		2,175	240	61.50	2,476.50	2,825
8140	18" diameter		6.90	5.797		2,925	253	65	3,243	3,675
8160	20" diameter		5.71	7.005		3,675	305	78.50	4,058.50	4,600
8180	24" diameter		4.70	8.511		5,675	370	95.50	6,140.50	6,925
8200	Wye or tee, 4" diameter	B-20A	10.67	2.999		405	128		533	640
8220	6" diameter		8.53	3.751		615	160		775	920
8240	8" diameter		7.11	4.501		975	192		1,167	1,375
8260	10" diameter	B-21A	7.62	5.249		1,400	229	59	1,688	1,975
8280	12" diameter		7.02	5.698		1,850	249	64	2,163	2,475
8300	14" diameter		6.67	5.997		2,750	262	67	3,079	3,500
8320	16" diameter		4.85	8.247		3,550	360	92.50	4,002.50	4,550
8340	18" diameter		4.60	8.696		4,400	380	97.50	4,877.50	5,500
8360	20" diameter		3.81	10.499		6,200	460	118	6,778	7,650

33 11 13.15 Water Supply, Ductile Iron Pipe

		Crew	Daily Output	Labor-Hours	Unit	Material	2012 Bare Costs Labor	Equipment	Total	Total Incl O&P
8380	24" diameter	B-21A	3.14	12.739	Ea.	10,500	555	143	11,198	12,500
8398	45° bends, 4" diameter	B-20A	16	2		234	85.50		319.50	385
8400	6" diameter	"	12.80	2.500		340	107		447	530
8410	12" diameter	B-21A	10.53	3.799		1,075	166	42.50	1,283.50	1,475
8420	16" diameter		7.27	5.502		1,925	240	61.50	2,226.50	2,525
8430	20" diameter		5.71	7.005		3,000	305	78.50	3,383.50	3,850
8440	24" diameter		4.70	8.511		4,175	370	95.50	4,640.50	5,275
8450	Decreaser, 6" x 4" diameter	B-20A	14.22	2.250		330	96		426	510
8460	8" x 6" diameter	"	11.64	2.749		485	117		602	710
8470	10" x 6" diameter	B-21A	13.33	3.001		590	131	33.50	754.50	885
8480	12" x 6" diameter		12.70	3.150		730	138	35.50	903.50	1,050
8490	16" x 6" diameter		10	4		1,300	175	45	1,520	1,750
8500	20" x 6" diameter		8.42	4.751		2,750	207	53.50	3,010.50	3,400
8552	For water utility valves see Section 33 12 16									
8700	Joint restraint, ductile iron mechanical joints									
8710	4" diameter	B-20A	32	1	Ea.	36	42.50		78.50	105
8720	6" diameter		25.60	1.250		43	53.50		96.50	128
8730	8" diameter		21.33	1.500		63.50	64		127.50	167
8740	10" diameter		18.28	1.751		92.50	74.50		167	216
8750	12" diameter		16.84	1.900		132	81		213	269
8760	14" diameter		16	2		180	85.50		265.50	330
8770	16" diameter		11.64	2.749		239	117		356	440
8780	18" diameter		11.03	2.901		335	124		459	555
8785	20" diameter		9.14	3.501		410	149		559	675
8790	24" diameter		7.53	4.250		485	181		666	810
9600	Steel sleeve with tap, 4" diameter	B-20	3	8		410	315		725	935
9620	6" diameter		2	12		465	470		935	1,225
9630	8" diameter		2	12		520	470		990	1,300

33 11 13.25 Water Supply, Polyvinyl Chloride Pipe

		Crew	Daily Output	Labor-Hours	Unit	Material	2012 Bare Costs Labor	Equipment	Total	Total Incl O&P
0010	**WATER SUPPLY, POLYVINYL CHLORIDE PIPE** R331113-80									
0020	Not including excavation or backfill, unless specified									
2100	PVC pipe, Class 150, 1-1/2" diameter	Q-1A	750	.013	L.F.	.33	.73		1.06	1.47
2120	2" diameter		686	.015		.45	.80		1.25	1.71
2140	2-1/2" diameter		500	.020		.65	1.10		1.75	2.38
2160	3" diameter	B-20	430	.056		.93	2.19		3.12	4.39
3010	AWWA C905, PR 100, DR 25									
3030	14" diameter	B-20A	213	.150	L.F.	14	6.40		20.40	25
3040	16" diameter		200	.160		14.20	6.80		21	26
3050	18" diameter		160	.200		24	8.55		32.55	39.50
3060	20" diameter		133	.241		30	10.25		40.25	48.50
3070	24" diameter		107	.299		43	12.75		55.75	66.50
3080	30" diameter		80	.400		80	17.05		97.05	114
3090	36" diameter		80	.400		124	17.05		141.05	162
3100	42" diameter		60	.533		166	22.50		188.50	218
3200	48" diameter		60	.533		217	22.50		239.50	273
4520	Pressure pipe Class 150, SDR 18, AWWA C900, 4" diameter		380	.084		2.34	3.59		5.93	8
4530	6" diameter		316	.101		5.70	4.32		10.02	12.85
4540	8" diameter		264	.121		9.50	5.15		14.65	18.30
4550	10" diameter		220	.145		12.45	6.20		18.65	23
4560	12" diameter		186	.172		17.60	7.35		24.95	30.50
8000	Fittings with rubber gasket									
8003	Class 150, D.R. 18									

33 11 13.25 Water Supply, Polyvinyl Chloride Pipe	Crew	Daily Output	Labor-Hours	Unit	Material	2012 Bare Costs Labor	Equipment	Total	Total Incl O&P
8006	90° Bend , 4" diameter	B-20	100	.240	Ea.	49.50	9.40		58.90	69
8020	6" diameter		90	.267		88	10.45		98.45	113
8040	8" diameter		80	.300		158	11.75		169.75	191
8060	10" diameter		50	.480		330	18.80		348.80	390
8080	12" diameter		30	.800		425	31.50		456.50	515
8100	Tee, 4" diameter		90	.267		58	10.45		68.45	79.50
8120	6" diameter		80	.300		145	11.75		156.75	178
8140	8" diameter		70	.343		190	13.45		203.45	230
8160	10" diameter		40	.600		565	23.50		588.50	655
8180	12" diameter		20	1.200		710	47		757	855
8200	45° Bend, 4" diameter		100	.240		47	9.40		56.40	66
8220	6" diameter		90	.267		85.50	10.45		95.95	110
8240	8" diameter		50	.480		167	18.80		185.80	212
8260	10" diameter		50	.480		330	18.80		348.80	390
8280	12" diameter		30	.800		420	31.50		451.50	510
8300	Reducing tee 6" x 4"		100	.240		129	9.40		138.40	157
8320	8" x 6"		90	.267		248	10.45		258.45	288
8330	10" x 6"		90	.267		350	10.45		360.45	400
8340	10" x 8"		90	.267		365	10.45		375.45	415
8350	12" x 6"		90	.267		430	10.45		440.45	485
8360	12" x 8"		90	.267		470	10.45		480.45	530
8400	Tapped service tee (threaded type) 6" x 6" x 3/4"		100	.240		95	9.40		104.40	120
8430	6" x 6" x 1"		90	.267		95	10.45		105.45	121
8440	6" x 6" x 1-1/2"		90	.267		95	10.45		105.45	121
8450	6" x 6" x 2"		90	.267		95	10.45		105.45	121
8460	8" x 8" x 3/4"		90	.267		140	10.45		150.45	170
8470	8" x 8" x 1"		90	.267		140	10.45		150.45	170
8480	8" x 8" x 1-1/2"		90	.267		140	10.45		150.45	170
8490	8" x 8" x 2"		90	.267		140	10.45		150.45	170
8500	Repair coupling 4"		100	.240		25.50	9.40		34.90	42.50
8520	6" diameter		90	.267		40	10.45		50.45	60
8540	8" diameter		50	.480		96	18.80		114.80	135
8560	10" diameter		50	.480		202	18.80		220.80	251
8580	12" diameter		50	.480		295	18.80		313.80	355
8600	Plug end 4"		100	.240		22.50	9.40		31.90	39.50
8620	6" diameter		90	.267		40.50	10.45		50.95	60.50
8640	8" diameter		50	.480		69.50	18.80		88.30	105
8660	10" diameter		50	.480		96.50	18.80		115.30	135
8680	12" diameter	↓	50	.480	↓	118	18.80		136.80	159
8700	PVC pipe, joint restraint									
8710	4" diameter	B-20A	32	1	Ea.	41	42.50		83.50	110
8720	6" diameter		25.60	1.250		50.50	53.50		104	137
8730	8" diameter		21.33	1.500		72	64		136	177
8740	10" diameter		18.28	1.751		132	74.50		206.50	259
8750	12" diameter		16.84	1.900		138	81		219	275
8760	14" diameter		16	2		216	85.50		301.50	370
8770	16" diameter		11.64	2.749		268	117		385	475
8780	18" diameter		11.03	2.901		325	124		449	545
8785	20" diameter		9.14	3.501		395	149		544	660
8790	24" diameter	↓	7.53	4.250	↓	455	181		636	775

33 11 Water Utility Distribution Piping

33 11 13 — Public Water Utility Distribution Piping

33 11 13.35 Water Supply, HDPE	Crew	Daily Output	Labor-Hours	Unit	Material	2012 Bare Costs Labor	Equipment	Total	Total Incl O&P
0010 **WATER SUPPLY, HDPE**									
0011 Butt fusion joints, SDR 21 40' lengths not including excavation or backfill									
0100 4" diameter	B-22A	400	.100	L.F.	4.03	4.01	1.60	9.64	12.35
0200 6" diameter		380	.105		9.15	4.22	1.69	15.06	18.35
0300 8" diameter		320	.125		12.50	5	2	19.50	23.50
0400 10" diameter		300	.133		19.75	5.35	2.14	27.24	32
0500 12" diameter		260	.154		31	6.15	2.47	39.62	46
0600 14" diameter	B-22B	220	.182		36	7.30	4.87	48.17	56.50
0700 16" diameter		180	.222		41.50	8.90	5.95	56.35	65.50
0800 18" diameter		140	.286		46.50	11.45	7.65	65.60	77
0900 24" diameter		100	.400		67	16.05	10.70	93.75	110
1000 Fittings									
1100 Elbows, 90 degrees									
1200 4" diameter	B-22A	32	1.250	Ea.	32.50	50	20	102.50	135
1300 6" diameter		28	1.429		70	57.50	23	150.50	190
1400 8" diameter		24	1.667		165	67	26.50	258.50	315
1500 10" diameter		18	2.222		670	89	35.50	794.50	910
1600 12" diameter		12	3.333		640	134	53.50	827.50	970
1700 14" diameter	B-22B	9	4.444		755	178	119	1,052	1,225
1800 16" diameter		6	6.667		865	267	178	1,310	1,550
1900 18" diameter		4	10		980	400	268	1,648	1,975
2000 24" diameter		3	13.333		1,325	535	355	2,215	2,675
2100 Tees									
2200 4" diameter	B-22A	30	1.333	Ea.	35.50	53.50	21.50	110.50	145
2300 6" diameter		26	1.538		88.50	61.50	24.50	174.50	219
2400 8" diameter		22	1.818		222	73	29	324	390
2500 10" diameter		15	2.667		293	107	43	443	530
2600 12" diameter		10	4		920	160	64	1,144	1,325
2700 14" diameter	B-22B	8	5		1,075	201	134	1,410	1,650
2800 16" diameter		6	6.667		1,275	267	178	1,720	2,000
2900 18" diameter		4	10		1,400	400	268	2,068	2,425
3000 24" diameter		2	20		1,850	800	535	3,185	3,875

33 12 Water Utility Distribution Equipment

33 12 13 — Water Service Connections

33 12 13.15 Tapping, Crosses and Sleeves

	Crew	Daily Output	Labor-Hours	Unit	Material	2012 Bare Costs Labor	Equipment	Total	Total Incl O&P
0010 **TAPPING, CROSSES AND SLEEVES**									
4000 Drill and tap pressurized main (labor only)									
4100 6" main, 1" to 2" service	Q-1	3	5.333	Ea.		262		262	395
4150 8" main, 1" to 2" service	"	2.75	5.818	"		286		286	430
4500 Tap and insert gate valve									
4600 8" main, 4" branch	B-21	3.20	8.750	Ea.		355	41.50	396.50	590
4650 6" branch		2.70	10.370			420	49	469	700
4700 10" Main, 4" branch		2.70	10.370			420	49	469	700
4750 6" branch		2.35	11.915			480	56.50	536.50	800
4800 12" main, 6" branch		2.35	11.915			480	56.50	536.50	800
4850 8" branch		2.35	11.915			480	56.50	536.50	800
7020 Crosses, 4" x 4"		37	.757		1,325	30.50	3.58	1,359.08	1,500
7030 6" x 4"		25	1.120		1,125	45.50	5.30	1,175.80	1,300
7040 6" x 6"		25	1.120		1,125	45.50	5.30	1,175.80	1,300

33 12 Water Utility Distribution Equipment

33 12 13 – Water Service Connections

33 12 13.15 Tapping, Crosses and Sleeves	Crew	Daily Output	Labor-Hours	Unit	Material	2012 Bare Costs Labor	Equipment	Total	Total Incl O&P
7060	8" x 6"	B-21	21	1.333	Ea.	1,375	54	6.30	1,435.30	1,600
7080	8" x 8"		21	1.333		1,450	54	6.30	1,510.30	1,675
7100	10" x 6"		21	1.333		2,250	54	6.30	2,310.30	2,575
7120	10" x 10"		21	1.333		2,400	54	6.30	2,460.30	2,750
7140	12" x 6"		18	1.556		2,250	63	7.35	2,320.35	2,575
7160	12" x 12"		18	1.556		3,125	63	7.35	3,195.35	3,550
7180	14" x 6"		16	1.750		6,100	71	8.30	6,179.30	6,850
7200	14" x 14"		16	1.750		6,450	71	8.30	6,529.30	7,225
7220	16" x 6"		14	2		6,450	81	9.45	6,540.45	7,225
7240	16" x 10"		14	2		6,625	81	9.45	6,715.45	7,425
7260	16" x 16"		14	2		6,975	81	9.45	7,065.45	7,800
7280	18" x 6"		10	2.800		9,775	113	13.25	9,901.25	11,000
7300	18" x 12"		10	2.800		9,850	113	13.25	9,976.25	11,000
7320	18" x 18"		10	2.800		9,000	113	13.25	9,126.25	10,100
7340	20" x 6"		8	3.500		7,900	142	16.55	8,058.55	8,925
7360	20" x 12"		8	3.500		8,475	142	16.55	8,633.55	9,550
7380	20" x 20"		8	3.500		12,400	142	16.55	12,558.55	13,800
7400	24" x 6"		6	4.667		10,200	189	22	10,411	11,500
7420	24" x 12"		6	4.667		10,400	189	22	10,611	11,700
7440	24" x 18"		6	4.667		15,500	189	22	15,711	17,300
7460	24" x 24"		6	4.667		16,100	189	22	16,311	18,000
7600	Cut-in sleeves with rubber gaskets, 4"		18	1.556		241	63	7.35	311.35	370
7620	6"		12	2.333		289	94.50	11.05	394.55	475
7640	8"		10	2.800		380	113	13.25	506.25	610
7660	10"		10	2.800		485	113	13.25	611.25	725
7680	12"		9	3.111		645	126	14.70	785.70	920
7800	Cut-in valves with rubber gaskets, 4"		18	1.556		350	63	7.35	420.35	490
7820	6"		12	2.333		470	94.50	11.05	575.55	670
7840	8"		10	2.800		730	113	13.25	856.25	995
7860	10"		10	2.800		760	113	13.25	886.25	1,025
7880	12"		9	3.111		905	126	14.70	1,045.70	1,200
7900	Tapping Valve 4 inch, MJ, ductile iron		18	1.556		640	63	7.35	710.35	810
7920	6 inch, MJ, ductile iron		12	2.333		870	94.50	11.05	975.55	1,100
8000	Sleeves with rubber gaskets, 4" x 4"		37	.757		720	30.50	3.58	754.08	840
8010	6" x 4"		25	1.120		755	45.50	5.30	805.80	905
8020	6" x 6"		25	1.120		815	45.50	5.30	865.80	970
8030	8" x 4"		21	1.333		765	54	6.30	825.30	930
8040	8" x 6"		21	1.333		835	54	6.30	895.30	1,000
8060	8" x 8"		21	1.333		1,100	54	6.30	1,160.30	1,325
8070	10" x 4"		21	1.333		840	54	6.30	900.30	1,025
8080	10" x 6"		21	1.333		1,300	54	6.30	1,360.30	1,525
8090	10" x 8"		21	1.333		1,650	54	6.30	1,710.30	1,900
8100	10" x 10"		21	1.333		2,050	54	6.30	2,110.30	2,350
8110	12" x 4"		18	1.556		1,500	63	7.35	1,570.35	1,750
8120	12" x 6"		18	1.556		1,525	63	7.35	1,595.35	1,775
8130	12" x 8"		18	1.556		1,700	63	7.35	1,770.35	1,950
8135	12" x 10"		18	1.556		2,250	63	7.35	2,320.35	2,575
8140	12" x 12"		18	1.556		2,375	63	7.35	2,445.35	2,700
8160	14" x 6"		16	1.750		1,525	71	8.30	1,604.30	1,825
8180	14" x 14"		16	1.750		2,950	71	8.30	3,029.30	3,375
8200	16" x 6"		14	2		1,800	81	9.45	1,890.45	2,100
8220	16" x 10"		14	2		2,900	81	9.45	2,990.45	3,325
8240	16" x 16"		14	2		3,075	81	9.45	3,165.45	3,500

33 12 Water Utility Distribution Equipment

33 12 13 – Water Service Connections

33 12 13.15 Tapping, Crosses and Sleeves

		Crew	Daily Output	Labor-Hours	Unit	Material	2012 Bare Costs Labor	Equipment	Total	Total Incl O&P
8260	18" x 6"	B-21	10	2.800	Ea.	1,850	113	13.25	1,976.25	2,225
8280	18" x 12"		10	2.800		3,150	113	13.25	3,276.25	3,675
8300	18" x 18"		10	2.800		8,675	113	13.25	8,801.25	9,750
8320	20" x 6"		8	3.500		2,150	142	16.55	2,308.55	2,575
8340	20" x 12"		8	3.500		3,625	142	16.55	3,783.55	4,225
8360	20" x 20"		8	3.500		10,400	142	16.55	10,558.55	11,700
8380	24" x 6"		6	4.667		2,250	189	22	2,461	2,800
8400	24" x 12"		6	4.667		3,775	189	22	3,986	4,475
8420	24" x 18"		6	4.667		9,325	189	22	9,536	10,600
8440	24" x 24"		6	4.667		13,600	189	22	13,811	15,300
8800	Hydrant valve box, 6' long	B-20	20	1.200		220	47		267	315
8820	8' long		18	1.333		270	52.50		322.50	380
8830	Valve box w/lid 4' deep		14	1.714		157	67		224	277
8840	Valve box and large base w/lid		14	1.714		298	67		365	435

33 12 16 – Water Utility Distribution Valves

33 12 16.10 Valves

		Crew	Daily Output	Labor-Hours	Unit	Material	2012 Bare Costs Labor	Equipment	Total	Total Incl O&P
0010	**VALVES**, water distribution									
0011	See Sections 22 05 23.20 and 22 05 23.60									
3000	Butterfly valves with boxes, cast iron, mech. jt.									
3100	4" diameter	B-6	6	4	Ea.	960	153	55.50	1,168.50	1,350
3140	6" diameter		6	4		1,000	153	55.50	1,208.50	1,400
3180	8" diameter		6	4		1,275	153	55.50	1,483.50	1,725
3300	10" diameter		6	4		1,850	153	55.50	2,058.50	2,350
3340	12" diameter		6	4		2,600	153	55.50	2,808.50	3,150
3400	14" diameter		4	6		4,400	230	83.50	4,713.50	5,300
3440	16" diameter		4	6		5,125	230	83.50	5,438.50	6,075
3460	18" diameter		4	6		6,850	230	83.50	7,163.50	7,975
3480	20" diameter		4	6		7,875	230	83.50	8,188.50	9,100
3500	24" diameter		4	6		10,400	230	83.50	10,713.50	11,900
3600	With lever operator									
3610	4" diameter	B-6	6	4	Ea.	800	153	55.50	1,008.50	1,175
3614	6" diameter		6	4		850	153	55.50	1,058.50	1,225
3616	8" diameter		6	4		1,125	153	55.50	1,333.50	1,550
3618	10" diameter		6	4		1,700	153	55.50	1,908.50	2,175
3620	12" diameter		6	4		2,425	153	55.50	2,633.50	2,975
3622	14" diameter		4	6		4,100	230	83.50	4,413.50	4,975
3624	16" diameter		4	6		4,825	230	83.50	5,138.50	5,750
3626	18" diameter		4	6		6,550	230	83.50	6,863.50	7,650
3628	20" diameter		4	6		7,575	230	83.50	7,888.50	8,775
3630	24" diameter		4	6		10,200	230	83.50	10,513.50	11,600
3700	Check valves, flanged									
3710	4" diameter	B-6	6	4	Ea.	850	153	55.50	1,058.50	1,225
3714	6" diameter		6	4		1,150	153	55.50	1,358.50	1,575
3716	8" diameter		6	4		1,625	153	55.50	1,833.50	2,100
3718	10" diameter		6	4		2,975	153	55.50	3,183.50	3,575
3720	12" diameter		6	4		4,375	153	55.50	4,583.50	5,125
3722	14" diameter		4	6		6,125	230	83.50	6,438.50	7,200
3724	16" diameter		4	6		2,950	230	83.50	3,263.50	3,675
3726	18" diameter		4	6		4,900	230	83.50	5,213.50	5,850
3728	20" diameter		4	6		7,000	230	83.50	7,313.50	8,150
3730	24" diameter		4	6		12,600	230	83.50	12,913.50	14,300
3800	Gate valves, C.I., 250 PSI, mechanical joint, w/boxes									

33 12 16.10 Valves		Crew	Daily Output	Labor-Hours	Unit	Material	2012 Bare Costs Labor	Equipment	Total	Total Incl O&P
3810	4" diameter	B-6	6	4	Ea.	455	153	55.50	663.50	800
3814	6" diameter		6	4		655	153	55.50	863.50	1,025
3816	8" diameter		6	4		855	153	55.50	1,063.50	1,250
3818	10" diameter		6	4		1,250	153	55.50	1,458.50	1,675
3820	12" diameter		6	4		1,550	153	55.50	1,758.50	2,025
3822	14" diameter		4	6		4,150	230	83.50	4,463.50	5,025
3824	16" diameter		4	6		4,500	230	83.50	4,813.50	5,400
3826	18" diameter		4	6		7,300	230	83.50	7,613.50	8,475
3828	20" diameter		4	6		10,300	230	83.50	10,613.50	11,700
3830	24" diameter		4	6		12,900	230	83.50	13,213.50	14,600
3831	30" diameter		4	6		33,900	230	83.50	34,213.50	37,700
3832	36" diameter		4	6		49,300	230	83.50	49,613.50	54,500

33 12 16.20 Valves										
0010	**VALVES**									
0011	Special trim or use									
9000	Valves, gate valve, N.R.S. PIV with post, 4" diameter	B-6	6	4	Ea.	1,375	153	55.50	1,583.50	1,825
9020	6" diameter		6	4		1,575	153	55.50	1,783.50	2,050
9040	8" diameter		6	4		1,775	153	55.50	1,983.50	2,250
9060	10" diameter		6	4		2,175	153	55.50	2,383.50	2,700
9080	12" diameter		6	4		2,475	153	55.50	2,683.50	3,025
9100	14" diameter		6	4		4,925	153	55.50	5,133.50	5,725
9120	O.S.&Y., 4" diameter		6	4		585	153	55.50	793.50	940
9140	6" diameter		6	4		835	153	55.50	1,043.50	1,225
9160	8" diameter		6	4		1,375	153	55.50	1,583.50	1,800
9180	10" diameter		6	4		2,225	153	55.50	2,433.50	2,750
9200	12" diameter		6	4		2,900	153	55.50	3,108.50	3,500
9220	14" diameter		4	6		4,250	230	83.50	4,563.50	5,125
9400	Check valves, rubber disc, 2-1/2" diameter		6	4		700	153	55.50	908.50	1,075
9420	3" diameter		6	4		700	153	55.50	908.50	1,075
9440	4" diameter		6	4		850	153	55.50	1,058.50	1,225
9480	6" diameter		6	4		1,150	153	55.50	1,358.50	1,575
9500	8" diameter		6	4		1,625	153	55.50	1,833.50	2,100
9520	10" diameter		6	4		2,975	153	55.50	3,183.50	3,575
9540	12" diameter		6	4		4,375	153	55.50	4,583.50	5,125
9542	14" diameter		4	6		6,125	230	83.50	6,438.50	7,200
9700	Detector check valves, reducing, 4" diameter		6	4		1,450	153	55.50	1,658.50	1,875
9720	6" diameter		6	4		1,925	153	55.50	2,133.50	2,400
9740	8" diameter		6	4		2,800	153	55.50	3,008.50	3,375
9760	10" diameter		6	4		4,950	153	55.50	5,158.50	5,750
9800	Galvanized, 4" diameter		6	4		2,025	153	55.50	2,233.50	2,525
9820	6" diameter		6	4		2,750	153	55.50	2,958.50	3,325
9840	8" diameter		6	4		4,325	153	55.50	4,533.50	5,050
9860	10" diameter		6	4		4,700	153	55.50	4,908.50	5,475

33 16 Water Utility Storage Tanks

33 16 13 – Aboveground Water Utility Storage Tanks

33 16 13.13 Steel Water Storage Tanks

		Crew	Daily Output	Labor-Hours	Unit	Material	2012 Bare Costs Labor	Equipment	Total	Total Incl O&P
0010	**STEEL WATER STORAGE TANKS**									
0910	Steel, ground level, ht./diam. less than 1, not incl. fdn., 100,000 gallons				Ea.				180,000	217,500
1000	250,000 gallons								263,000	288,500
1200	500,000 gallons								372,000	408,500
1250	750,000 gallons								479,500	527,500
1300	1,000,000 gallons								588,000	647,000
1500	2,000,000 gallons								1,022,500	1,023,000
1600	4,000,000 gallons								1,890,500	2,079,000
1800	6,000,000 gallons								2,758,500	3,034,500
1850	8,000,000 gallons								3,625,500	3,988,000
1910	10,000,000 gallons								4,501,000	4,950,500
2100	Steel standpipes, ht./diam. more than 1, 100' to overflow, no fdn									
2200	500,000 gallons				Ea.				487,500	535,000
2400	750,000 gallons								644,000	708,000
2500	1,000,000 gallons								945,000	1,040,000
2700	1,500,000 gallons								1,558,500	1,714,000
2800	2,000,000 gallons								2,074,000	2,281,000

33 16 13.16 Prestressed Conc. Aboveground Water Utility Storage Tanks

		Crew	Daily Output	Labor-Hours	Unit	Material	2012 Bare Costs Labor	Equipment	Total	Total Incl O&P
0010	**PRESTRESSED CONC. ABOVEGROUND WATER UTILITY STORAGE TANKS**									
0020	Not including fdn., pipe or pumps, 250,000 gallons				Ea.				267,500	295,000
0100	500,000 gallons								436,500	480,000
0300	1,000,000 gallons								633,000	696,000
0400	2,000,000 gallons								960,000	1,056,000
0600	4,000,000 gallons								1,528,000	1,680,000
0700	6,000,000 gallons								2,030,000	2,232,000
0750	8,000,000 gallons								2,619,000	2,880,000
0800	10,000,000 gallons								3,164,000	3,848,000

33 16 13.23 Plastic-Coated Fabric Pillow Water Tanks

		Crew	Daily Output	Labor-Hours	Unit	Material	2012 Bare Costs Labor	Equipment	Total	Total Incl O&P
0010	**PLASTIC-COATED FABRIC PILLOW WATER TANKS**									
7000	Water tanks, vinyl coated fabric pillow tanks, freestanding, 5,000 gallons	4 Clab	4	8	Ea.	4,600	281		4,881	5,475
7100	Supporting embankment not included, 25,000 gallons	6 Clab	2	24		10,500	840		11,340	12,900
7200	50,000 gallons	8 Clab	1.50	42.667		18,500	1,500		20,000	22,700
7300	100,000 gallons	9 Clab	.90	80		40,000	2,800		42,800	48,300
7400	150,000 gallons		.50	144		57,500	5,050		62,550	71,500
7500	200,000 gallons		.40	180		70,000	6,325		76,325	86,500
7600	250,000 gallons		.30	240		100,000	8,425		108,425	123,000

33 16 19 – Elevated Water Utility Storage Tanks

33 16 19.50 Elevated Water Storage Tanks

		Crew	Daily Output	Labor-Hours	Unit	Material	2012 Bare Costs Labor	Equipment	Total	Total Incl O&P
0010	**ELEVATED WATER STORAGE TANKS**									
0011	Not incl. pipe, pumps or foundation									
3000	Elevated water tanks, 100' to bottom capacity line, incl. painting									
3010	50,000 gallons				Ea.				167,000	184,000
3300	100,000 gallons								255,000	280,000
3400	250,000 gallons								706,000	776,000
3600	500,000 gallons								1,255,000	1,380,000
3700	750,000 gallons								1,523,000	1,675,000
3900	1,000,000 gallons								2,180,000	2,400,000

33 21 13.10 Wells and Accessories	Crew	Daily Output	Labor-Hours	Unit	Material	2012 Bare Costs			Total	Total Incl O&P
						Labor	Equipment		Total	
0010 **WELLS & ACCESSORIES**										
0011 Domestic										
0100 Drilled, 4" to 6" diameter	B-23	120	.333	L.F.		11.85	22.50		34.35	43
0200 8" diameter	"	95.20	.420	"		14.90	28.50		43.40	54.50
0400 Gravel pack well, 40' deep, incl. gravel & casing, complete										
0500 24" diameter casing x 18" diameter screen	B-23	.13	307	Total	36,200	10,900	20,800		67,900	79,500
0600 36" diameter casing x 18" diameter screen		.12	333	"	37,400	11,800	22,500		71,700	84,000
0800 Observation wells, 1-1/4" riser pipe	↓	163	.245	V.L.F.	18.20	8.70	16.60		43.50	51.50
0900 For flush Buffalo roadway box, add	1 Skwk	16.60	.482	Ea.	49.50	22			71.50	88.50
1200 Test well, 2-1/2" diameter, up to 50' deep (15 to 50 GPM)	B-23	1.51	26.490	"	745	940	1,800		3,485	4,250
1300 Over 50' deep, add	"	121.80	.328	L.F.	19.85	11.65	22		53.50	64.50
1500 Pumps, installed in wells to 100' deep, 4" submersible										
1510 1/2 H.P.	Q-1	3.22	4.969	Ea.	420	244			664	830
1520 3/4 H.P.	↓	2.66	6.015		625	296			921	1,125
1600 1 H.P.	↓	2.29	6.987		680	345			1,025	1,275
1700 1-1/2 H.P.	Q-22	1.60	10		780	490	385		1,655	2,025
1800 2 H.P.		1.33	12.030		850	590	460		1,900	2,325
1900 3 H.P.		1.14	14.035		1,325	690	535		2,550	3,125
2000 5 H.P.		1.14	14.035		2,225	690	535		3,450	4,100
2050 Remove and install motor only, 4 H.P.		1.14	14.035		1,200	690	535		2,425	2,975
3000 Pump, 6" submersible, 25' to 150' deep, 25 H.P., 249 to 297 GPM		.89	17.978		7,350	885	690		8,925	10,200
3100 25' to 500' deep, 30 H.P., 100 to 300 GPM	↓	.73	21.918	↓	8,650	1,075	840		10,565	12,000
8110 Well screen assembly, stainless steel, 2" diameter	B-23A	273	.088	L.F.	87.50	3.48	9.40		100.38	112
8120 3" diameter		253	.095		123	3.75	10.15		136.90	152
8130 4" diameter		200	.120		150	4.75	12.85		167.60	186
8140 5" diameter		168	.143		180	5.65	15.30		200.95	223
8150 6" diameter		126	.190		211	7.55	20.50		239.05	266
8160 8" diameter		98.50	.244		281	9.65	26		316.65	355
8170 10" diameter		73	.329		350	13	35		398	445
8180 12" diameter		62.50	.384		400	15.20	41		456.20	510
8190 14" diameter		54.30	.442		455	17.50	47.50		520	580
8200 16" diameter		48.30	.497		505	19.65	53		577.65	645
8210 18" diameter		39.20	.612		630	24	65.50		719.50	800
8220 20" diameter		31.20	.769		700	30.50	82.50		813	905
8230 24" diameter		23.80	1.008		845	40	108		993	1,100
8240 26" diameter		21	1.143		915	45	122		1,082	1,200
8300 Slotted PVC, 1-1/4" diameter		521	.046		3.23	1.82	4.93		9.98	11.75
8310 1-1/2" diameter		488	.049		3.43	1.95	5.25		10.63	12.55
8320 2" diameter		273	.088		3.91	3.48	9.40		16.79	19.95
8330 3" diameter		253	.095		5.30	3.75	10.15		19.20	23
8340 4" diameter		200	.120		6.65	4.75	12.85		24.25	28.50
8350 5" diameter		168	.143		8.85	5.65	15.30		29.80	35
8360 6" diameter		126	.190		11.80	7.55	20.50		39.85	47
8370 8" diameter	↓	98.50	.244		17.50	9.65	26		53.15	62.50
8400 Artificial gravel pack, 2" screen, 6" casing	B-23B	174	.138		3.34	5.45	16.55		25.34	30
8405 8" casing		111	.216		4.28	8.55	26		38.83	46.50
8410 10" casing		74.50	.322		6.10	12.75	38.50		57.35	68.50
8415 12" casing		60	.400		8.55	15.85	48		72.40	86
8420 14" casing		50.20	.478		9.95	18.90	57.50		86.35	103
8425 16" casing		40.70	.590		12.60	23.50	70.50		106.60	127
8430 18" casing		36	.667		15.15	26.50	80		121.65	145
8435 20" casing		29.50	.814		17.80	32	97.50		147.30	176
8440 24" casing	↓	25.70	.934	↓	20.50	37	112		169.50	202

33 21 Water Supply Wells

33 21 13 – Public Water Supply Wells

33 21 13.10 Wells and Accessories

		Crew	Daily Output	Labor-Hours	Unit	Material	2012 Bare Costs Labor	Equipment	Total	Total Incl O&P
8445	26" casing	B-23B	24.60	.976	L.F.	22.50	38.50	117	178	213
8450	30" casing		20	1.200		26	47.50	144	217.50	259
8455	36" casing		16.40	1.463	↓	29	58	175	262	315
8500	Develop well		8	3	Hr.	305	119	360	784	910
8550	Pump test well		8	3		80.50	119	360	559.50	665
8560	Standby well	B-23A	8	3		79	119	320	518	625
8570	Standby, drill rig		8	3	↓		119	320	439	535
8580	Surface seal well, concrete filled	↓	1	24	Ea.	810	950	2,575	4,335	5,175
8590	Well test pump, install & remove	B-23	1	40			1,425	2,700	4,125	5,150
8600	Well sterilization, chlorine	2 Clab	1	16		130	560		690	1,000
8610	Well water pressure switch	1 Clab	12	.667		58.50	23.50		82	101
8630	Well, water pressure switch with manual reset	"	12	.667	↓	27	23.50		50.50	65.50
9950	See Section 31 23 19.40 for wellpoints									
9960	See Section 31 23 19.30 for drainage wells									

33 21 13.20 Water Supply Wells, Pumps

		Crew	Daily Output	Labor-Hours	Unit	Material	2012 Bare Costs Labor	Equipment	Total	Total Incl O&P
0010	**WATER SUPPLY WELLS, PUMPS**									
0011	With pressure control									
1000	Deep well, jet, 42 gal. galvanized tank									
1040	3/4 HP	1 Plum	.80	10	Ea.	1,350	545		1,895	2,300
3000	Shallow well, jet, 30 gal. galvanized tank									
3040	1/2 HP	1 Plum	2	4	Ea.	1,050	218		1,268	1,500

33 31 Sanitary Utility Sewerage Piping

33 31 13 – Public Sanitary Utility Sewerage Piping

33 31 13.15 Sewage Collection, Concrete Pipe

		Crew	Daily Output	Labor-Hours	Unit	Material	2012 Bare Costs Labor	Equipment	Total	Total Incl O&P
0010	**SEWAGE COLLECTION, CONCRETE PIPE**									
0020	See Section 33 41 13.60 for sewage/drainage collection, concrete pipe									

33 31 13.25 Sewage Collection, Polyvinyl Chloride Pipe

		Crew	Daily Output	Labor-Hours	Unit	Material	2012 Bare Costs Labor	Equipment	Total	Total Incl O&P
0010	**SEWAGE COLLECTION, POLYVINYL CHLORIDE PIPE**									
0020	Not including excavation or backfill									
2000	20' lengths, S.D.R. 35, B&S, 4" diameter	B-20	375	.064	L.F.	1.64	2.51		4.15	5.65
2040	6" diameter		350	.069		3.45	2.69		6.14	7.95
2080	13' lengths , S.D.R. 35, B&S, 8" diameter	↓	335	.072		7.85	2.81		10.66	12.95
2120	10" diameter	B-21	330	.085		12.70	3.43	.40	16.53	19.65
2160	12" diameter		320	.088		14.70	3.54	.41	18.65	22
2200	15" diameter	↓	240	.117		15.15	4.72	.55	20.42	24.50
4000	Piping, DWV PVC, no exc./bkfill., 10' L, Sch 40, 4" diameter	B-20	375	.064		4.09	2.51		6.60	8.35
4010	6" diameter		350	.069		8.45	2.69		11.14	13.45
4020	8" diameter	↓	335	.072	↓	15.30	2.81		18.11	21

33 41 Storm Utility Drainage Piping

33 41 13 – Public Storm Utility Drainage Piping

33 41 13.40 Piping, Storm Drainage, Corrugated Metal

	33 41 13.40 Piping, Storm Drainage, Corrugated Metal	Crew	Daily Output	Labor-Hours	Unit	Material	2012 Bare Costs Labor	Equipment	Total	Total Incl O&P
0010	**PIPING, STORM DRAINAGE, CORRUGATED METAL**									
0020	Not including excavation or backfill									
2000	Corrugated metal pipe, galvanized									
2020	Bituminous coated with paved invert, 20' lengths									
2040	8" diameter, 16 ga.	B-14	330	.145	L.F.	11.10	5.40	1.01	17.51	21.50
2060	10" diameter, 16 ga.		260	.185		11.55	6.85	1.29	19.69	24.50
2080	12" diameter, 16 ga.		210	.229		14	8.45	1.59	24.04	30
2100	15" diameter, 16 ga.		200	.240		19.45	8.90	1.67	30.02	37
2120	18" diameter, 16 ga.		190	.253		21	9.35	1.76	32.11	39.50
2140	24" diameter, 14 ga.	▼	160	.300		25	11.10	2.09	38.19	47
2160	30" diameter, 14 ga.	B-13	120	.467		28	17.75	5.80	51.55	64.50
2180	36" diameter, 12 ga.		120	.467		35	17.75	5.80	58.55	72
2200	48" diameter, 12 ga.	▼	100	.560		55	21.50	6.95	83.45	101
2220	60" diameter, 10 ga.	B-13B	75	.747		85	28.50	14.65	128.15	153
2240	72" diameter, 8 ga.	"	45	1.244	▼	95	47.50	24.50	167	205
2500	Galvanized, uncoated, 20' lengths									
2520	8" diameter, 16 ga.	B-14	355	.135	L.F.	8.30	5	.94	14.24	17.90
2540	10" diameter, 16 ga.		280	.171		8.80	6.35	1.19	16.34	21
2560	12" diameter, 16 ga.		220	.218		9.80	8.10	1.52	19.42	25
2580	15" diameter, 16 ga.		220	.218		12.90	8.10	1.52	22.52	28.50
2600	18" diameter, 16 ga.		205	.234		15	8.65	1.63	25.28	31.50
2620	24" diameter, 14 ga.	▼	175	.274		19.20	10.15	1.91	31.26	38.50
2640	30" diameter, 14 ga.	B-13	130	.431		24.50	16.40	5.35	46.25	58
2660	36" diameter, 12 ga.		130	.431		31.50	16.40	5.35	53.25	65.50
2680	48" diameter, 12 ga.	▼	110	.509		46.50	19.40	6.35	72.25	87.50
2690	60" diameter, 10 ga.	B-13B	78	.718	▼	69	27.50	14.10	110.60	134
2780	End sections, 8" diameter	B-14	35	1.371	Ea.	65.50	51	9.55	126.05	161
2785	10" diameter		35	1.371		69.50	51	9.55	130.05	165
2790	12" diameter		35	1.371		103	51	9.55	163.55	202
2800	18" diameter	▼	30	1.600		125	59.50	11.15	195.65	241
2810	24" diameter	B-13	25	2.240		188	85.50	28	301.50	370
2820	30" diameter		25	2.240		297	85.50	28	410.50	485
2825	36" diameter		20	2.800		455	107	35	597	700
2830	48" diameter	▼	10	5.600		900	213	69.50	1,182.50	1,400
2835	60" diameter	B-13B	5	11.200		1,550	425	220	2,195	2,600
2840	72" diameter	"	4	14	▼	1,850	535	275	2,660	3,175

33 41 13.60 Sewage/Drainage Collection, Concrete Pipe

	33 41 13.60 Sewage/Drainage Collection, Concrete Pipe	Crew	Daily Output	Labor-Hours	Unit	Material	2012 Bare Costs Labor	Equipment	Total	Total Incl O&P
0010	**SEWAGE/DRAINAGE COLLECTION, CONCRETE PIPE**									
0020	Not including excavation or backfill									
1000	Non-reinforced pipe, extra strength, B&S or T&G joints									
1010	6" diameter	B-14	265.04	.181	L.F.	6.40	6.70	1.26	14.36	18.75
1020	8" diameter		224	.214		7.05	7.95	1.49	16.49	21.50
1030	10" diameter		216	.222		7.80	8.25	1.55	17.60	23
1040	12" diameter		200	.240		9.55	8.90	1.67	20.12	26
1050	15" diameter		180	.267		13.05	9.90	1.86	24.81	31.50
1060	18" diameter		144	.333		15.40	12.35	2.32	30.07	38.50
1070	21" diameter		112	.429		18.95	15.85	2.98	37.78	49
1080	24" diameter	▼	100	.480	▼	25.50	17.80	3.34	46.64	59
2000	Reinforced culvert, class 3, no gaskets									
2010	12" diameter	B-14	150	.320	L.F.	11.75	11.85	2.23	25.83	33.50
2020	15" diameter		150	.320		16	11.85	2.23	30.08	38
2030	18" diameter	▼	132	.364	▼	20	13.45	2.53	35.98	45.50

33 41 Storm Utility Drainage Piping

33 41 13 – Public Storm Utility Drainage Piping

33 41 13.60 Sewage/Drainage Collection, Concrete Pipe

		Crew	Daily Output	Labor-Hours	Unit	Material	2012 Bare Costs Labor	Equipment	Total	Total Incl O&P
2035	21" diameter	B-14	120	.400	L.F.	24	14.80	2.78	41.58	52
2040	24" diameter	↓	100	.480		28	17.80	3.34	49.14	62
2045	27" diameter	B-13	92	.609		41	23	7.60	71.60	89
2050	30" diameter	↓	88	.636		49	24	7.90	80.90	99.50
2060	36" diameter	↓	72	.778		59	29.50	9.70	98.20	121
2070	42" diameter	B-13B	72	.778		78	29.50	15.30	122.80	148
2080	48" diameter		64	.875		97.50	33.50	17.20	148.20	177
2090	60" diameter		48	1.167		125	44.50	23	192.50	231
2100	72" diameter		40	1.400		204	53.50	27.50	285	335
2120	84" diameter		32	1.750		293	66.50	34.50	394	465
2140	96" diameter	↓	24	2.333		350	89	46	485	570
2200	With gaskets, class 3, 12" diameter	B-21	168	.167		12.90	6.75	.79	20.44	25.50
2220	15" diameter		160	.175		17.60	7.10	.83	25.53	31
2230	18" diameter		152	.184		22	7.45	.87	30.32	37
2240	24" diameter	↓	136	.206		34.50	8.30	.97	43.77	52
2260	30" diameter	B-13	88	.636		56	24	7.90	87.90	107
2270	36" diameter	"	72	.778		67.50	29.50	9.70	106.70	131
2290	48" diameter	B-13B	64	.875		109	33.50	17.20	159.70	190
2310	72" diameter	"	40	1.400		222	53.50	27.50	303	355
2330	Flared ends, 6'-1" long, 12" diameter	B-21	190	.147		37.50	5.95	.70	44.15	51
2340	15" diameter		155	.181		40.50	7.30	.85	48.65	56.50
2400	6'-2" long, 18" diameter		122	.230		52	9.30	1.09	62.39	73
2420	24" diameter	↓	88	.318		56	12.85	1.51	70.36	83
2440	36" diameter	B-13	60	.933		129	35.50	11.60	176.10	209
3080	Radius pipe, add to pipe prices, 12" to 60" diameter					50%				
3090	Over 60" diameter, add				↓	20%				
3500	Reinforced elliptical, 8' lengths, C507 class 3									
3520	14" x 23" inside, round equivalent 18" diameter	B-21	82	.341	L.F.	55.50	13.80	1.62	70.92	84.50
3530	24" x 38" inside, round equivalent 30" diameter	B-13	58	.966		82.50	37	12	131.50	160
3540	29" x 45" inside, round equivalent 36" diameter		52	1.077		99	41	13.40	153.40	186
3550	38" x 60" inside, round equivalent 48" diameter		38	1.474		164	56	18.35	238.35	287
3560	48" x 76" inside, round equivalent 60" diameter		26	2.154		208	82	27	317	385
3570	58" x 91" inside, round equivalent 72" diameter	↓	22	2.545	↓	315	97	31.50	443.50	530
3780	Concrete slotted pipe, class 4 mortar joint									
3800	12" diameter	B-21	168	.167	L.F.	35.50	6.75	.79	43.04	50.50
3840	18" diameter	"	152	.184	"	41	7.45	.87	49.32	57.50
3900	Concrete slotted pipe, Class 4 O-ring joint									
3940	12" diameter	B-21	168	.167	L.F.	35.50	6.75	.79	43.04	50.50
3960	18" diameter	"	152	.184	"	41	7.45	.87	49.32	57.50

33 42 Culverts

33 42 16 – Concrete Culverts

33 42 16.15 Oval Arch Culverts

		Crew	Daily Output	Labor-Hours	Unit	Material	2012 Bare Costs Labor	Equipment	Total	Total Incl O&P
0010	**OVAL ARCH CULVERTS**									
3000	Corrugated galvanized or aluminum, coated & paved									
3020	17" x 13", 16 ga., 15" equivalent	B-14	200	.240	L.F.	17	8.90	1.67	27.57	34
3040	21" x 15", 16 ga., 18" equivalent		150	.320		20.50	11.85	2.23	34.58	43
3060	28" x 20", 14 ga., 24" equivalent		125	.384		28	14.20	2.67	44.87	56
3080	35" x 24", 14 ga., 30" equivalent	↓	100	.480		34	17.80	3.34	55.14	68.50
3100	42" x 29", 12 ga., 36" equivalent	B-13	100	.560		39	21.50	6.95	67.45	83
3120	49" x 33", 12 ga., 42" equivalent	↓	90	.622	↓	49	23.50	7.75	80.25	98.50

33 42 Culverts

33 42 16 – Concrete Culverts

33 42 16.15 Oval Arch Culverts		Crew	Daily Output	Labor-Hours	Unit	Material	2012 Bare Costs Labor	Equipment	Total	Total Incl O&P
3140	57" x 38", 12 ga., 48" equivalent	B-13	75	.747	L.F.	58	28.50	9.30	95.80	118
3160	Steel, plain oval arch culverts, plain									
3180	17" x 13", 16 ga., 15" equivalent	B-14	225	.213	L.F.	12	7.90	1.48	21.38	27
3200	21" x 15", 16 ga., 18" equivalent		175	.274		15.25	10.15	1.91	27.31	34.50
3220	28" x 20", 14 ga., 24" equivalent		150	.320		22	11.85	2.23	36.08	45
3240	35" x 24", 14 ga., 30" equivalent	B-13	108	.519		27	19.75	6.45	53.20	67
3260	42" x 29", 12 ga., 36" equivalent		108	.519		34.50	19.75	6.45	60.70	75
3280	49" x 33", 12 ga., 42" equivalent		92	.609		44	23	7.60	74.60	92.50
3300	57" x 38", 12 ga., 48" equivalent		75	.747		53	28.50	9.30	90.80	112
3320	End sections, 17" x 13"		22	2.545	Ea.	130	97	31.50	258.50	325
3340	42" x 29"		17	3.294	"	360	125	41	526	630
3360	Multi-plate arch, steel	B-20	1690	.014	Lb.	1.25	.56		1.81	2.24

33 44 Storm Utility Water Drains

33 44 13 – Utility Area Drains

33 44 13.13 Catchbasins

		Crew	Daily Output	Labor-Hours	Unit	Material	2012 Bare Costs Labor	Equipment	Total	Total Incl O&P
0010	**CATCHBASINS**									
0011	Not including footing & excavation									
1600	Frames & covers, C.I., 24" square, 500 lb.	B-6	7.80	3.077	Ea.	320	118	43	481	575
1700	26" D shape, 600 lb.		7	3.429		480	131	47.50	658.50	785
1800	Light traffic, 18" diameter, 100 lb.		10	2.400		115	92	33.50	240.50	305
1900	24" diameter, 300 lb.		8.70	2.759		192	106	38.50	336.50	415
2000	36" diameter, 900 lb.		5.80	4.138		560	159	57.50	776.50	920
2100	Heavy traffic, 24" diameter, 400 lb.		7.80	3.077		250	118	43	411	500
2200	36" diameter, 1150 lb.		3	8		800	305	111	1,216	1,475
2300	Mass. State standard, 26" diameter, 475 lb.		7	3.429		270	131	47.50	448.50	550
2400	30" diameter, 620 lb.		7	3.429		350	131	47.50	528.50	640
2500	Watertight, 24" diameter, 350 lb.		7.80	3.077		237	118	43	398	485
2600	26" diameter, 500 lb.		7	3.429		390	131	47.50	568.50	685
2700	32" diameter, 575 lb.		6	4		750	153	55.50	958.50	1,125
2800	3 piece cover & frame, 10" deep,									
2900	1200 lb., for heavy equipment	B-6	3	8	Ea.	1,000	305	111	1,416	1,700
3000	Raised for paving 1-1/4" to 2" high									
3100	4 piece expansion ring									
3200	20" to 26" diameter	1 Clab	3	2.667	Ea.	147	93.50		240.50	305
3300	30" to 36" diameter	"	3	2.667	"	205	93.50		298.50	370
3320	Frames and covers, existing, raised for paving, 2", including									
3340	row of brick, concrete collar, up to 12" wide frame	B-6	18	1.333	Ea.	46.50	51	18.55	116.05	150
3360	20" to 26" wide frame		11	2.182		69.50	83.50	30.50	183.50	238
3380	30" to 36" wide frame		9	2.667		86	102	37	225	292
3400	Inverts, single channel brick	D-1	3	5.333		100	213		313	430
3500	Concrete		5	3.200		78	128		206	279
3600	Triple channel, brick		2	8		153	320		473	650
3700	Concrete		3	5.333		132	213		345	465

33 46 Subdrainage

33 46 16 – Subdrainage Piping

33 46 16.25 Piping, Subdrainage, Corrugated Metal

		Crew	Daily Output	Labor-Hours	Unit	Material	2012 Bare Costs Labor	Equipment	Total	Total Incl O&P
0010	**PIPING, SUBDRAINAGE, CORRUGATED METAL**									
0021	Not including excavation and backfill									
2010	Aluminum, perforated									
2020	6" diameter, 18 ga.	B-14	380	.126	L.F.	6	4.68	.88	11.56	14.70
2200	8" diameter, 16 ga.		370	.130		11.10	4.81	.90	16.81	20.50
2220	10" diameter, 16 ga.		360	.133		13.90	4.94	.93	19.77	24
2240	12" diameter, 16 ga.		285	.168		15.55	6.25	1.17	22.97	28
2260	18" diameter, 16 ga.		205	.234		23.50	8.65	1.63	33.78	40.50
3000	Uncoated galvanized, perforated									
3020	6" diameter, 18 ga.	B-20	380	.063	L.F.	5.50	2.48		7.98	9.85
3200	8" diameter, 16 ga.	"	370	.065		8.30	2.54		10.84	13.05
3220	10" diameter, 16 ga.	B-21	360	.078		8.80	3.14	.37	12.31	14.95
3240	12" diameter, 16 ga.		285	.098		9.80	3.97	.46	14.23	17.35
3260	18" diameter, 16 ga.		205	.137		15	5.50	.65	21.15	25.50
4000	Steel, perforated, asphalt coated									
4020	6" diameter 18 ga.	B-20	380	.063	L.F.	5.50	2.48		7.98	9.85
4030	8" diameter 18 ga.	"	370	.065		8.30	2.54		10.84	13.05
4040	10" diameter 16 ga.	B-21	360	.078		8.80	3.14	.37	12.31	14.95
4050	12" diameter 16 ga.		285	.098		9.80	3.97	.46	14.23	17.40
4060	18" diameter 16 ga.		205	.137		15	5.50	.65	21.15	25.50

33 46 16.30 Piping, Subdrainage, Plastic

		Crew	Daily Output	Labor-Hours	Unit	Material	2012 Bare Costs Labor	Equipment	Total	Total Incl O&P
0010	**PIPING, SUBDRAINAGE, PLASTIC**									
0020	Not including excavation and backfill									
2100	Perforated PVC, 4" diameter	B-14	314	.153	L.F.	1.64	5.65	1.06	8.35	11.65
2110	6" diameter		300	.160		3.45	5.95	1.11	10.51	14.10
2120	8" diameter		290	.166		7.15	6.15	1.15	14.45	18.50
2130	10" diameter		280	.171		10.15	6.35	1.19	17.69	22
2140	12" diameter		270	.178		14.70	6.60	1.24	22.54	27.50

33 49 Storm Drainage Structures

33 49 13 – Storm Drainage Manholes, Frames, and Covers

33 49 13.10 Storm Drainage Manholes, Frames and Covers

		Crew	Daily Output	Labor-Hours	Unit	Material	2012 Bare Costs Labor	Equipment	Total	Total Incl O&P
0010	**STORM DRAINAGE MANHOLES, FRAMES & COVERS**									
0020	Excludes footing, excavation, backfill (See line items for frame & cover)									
0050	Brick, 4' inside diameter, 4' deep	D-1	1	16	Ea.	410	640		1,050	1,425
0100	6' deep		.70	22.857		570	910		1,480	2,000
0150	8' deep		.50	32		730	1,275		2,005	2,725
0200	For depths over 8', add		4	4	V.L.F.	85	159		244	335
0400	Concrete blocks (radial), 4' I.D., 4' deep		1.50	10.667	Ea.	375	425		800	1,050
0500	6' deep		1	16		500	640		1,140	1,525
0600	8' deep		.70	22.857		630	910		1,540	2,075
0700	For depths over 8', add		5.50	2.909	V.L.F.	66	116		182	248
0800	Concrete, cast in place, 4' x 4', 8" thick, 4' deep	C-14H	2	24	Ea.	445	1,050	13.70	1,508.70	2,100
0900	6' deep		1.50	32		635	1,400	18.25	2,053.25	2,875
1000	8' deep		1	48		925	2,075	27.50	3,027.50	4,250
1100	For depths over 8', add		8	6	V.L.F.	101	261	3.42	365.42	515
1110	Precast, 4' I.D., 4' deep	B-22	4.10	7.317	Ea.	775	299	48.50	1,122.50	1,375
1120	6' deep		3	10		900	410	66	1,376	1,700
1130	8' deep		2	15		1,025	615	99.50	1,739.50	2,175
1140	For depths over 8', add		16	1.875	V.L.F.	121	76.50	12.40	209.90	265
1150	5' I.D., 4' deep	B-6	3	8	Ea.	1,625	305	111	2,041	2,400

33 49 Storm Drainage Structures

33 49 13 – Storm Drainage Manholes, Frames, and Covers

33 49 13.10 Storm Drainage Manholes, Frames and Covers		Crew	Daily Output	Labor-Hours	Unit	Material	2012 Bare Costs Labor	Equipment	Total	Total Incl O&P
1160	6' deep	B-6	2	12	Ea.	2,025	460	167	2,652	3,100
1170	8' deep		1.50	16	↓	2,475	615	223	3,313	3,900
1180	For depths over 8', add		12	2	V.L.F.	305	76.50	28	409.50	485
1190	6' I.D., 4' deep		2	12	Ea.	2,100	460	167	2,727	3,200
1200	6' deep		1.50	16		2,525	615	223	3,363	3,950
1210	8' deep		1	24	↓	3,100	920	335	4,355	5,200
1220	For depths over 8', add	↓	8	3	V.L.F.	360	115	42	517	620
1250	Slab tops, precast, 8" thick									
1300	4' diameter manhole	B-6	8	3	Ea.	272	115	42	429	520
1400	5' diameter manhole		7.50	3.200		425	123	44.50	592.50	705
1500	6' diameter manhole	↓	7	3.429		635	131	47.50	813.50	955
3800	Steps, heavyweight cast iron, 7" x 9"	1 Bric	40	.200		18.05	8.80		26.85	33
3900	8" x 9"		40	.200		21.50	8.80		30.30	37.50
3928	12" x 10-1/2"		40	.200		25.50	8.80		34.30	41.50
4000	Standard sizes, galvanized steel		40	.200		24	8.80		32.80	40
4100	Aluminum	↓	40	.200	↓	24	8.80		32.80	40

33 51 Natural-Gas Distribution

33 51 13 – Natural-Gas Piping

33 51 13.10 Piping, Gas Service and Distribution, P.E.

0010	**PIPING, GAS SERVICE AND DISTRIBUTION, POLYETHYLENE**									
0020	Not including excavation or backfill									
1000	60 psi coils, compression coupling @ 100', 1/2" diameter, SDR 11	B-20A	608	.053	L.F.	.91	2.24		3.15	4.41
1010	1" diameter, SDR 11		544	.059		2.03	2.51		4.54	6.05
1040	1-1/4" diameter, SDR 11		544	.059		2.04	2.51		4.55	6.05
1100	2" diameter, SDR 11		488	.066		3.36	2.80		6.16	7.95
1160	3" diameter, SDR 11	↓	408	.078		4.37	3.34		7.71	9.90
1500	60 PSI 40' joints with coupling, 3" diameter, SDR 11	B-21A	408	.098		4.37	4.28	1.10	9.75	12.50
1540	4" diameter, SDR 11		352	.114		9.15	4.96	1.27	15.38	19
1600	6" diameter, SDR 11		328	.122		26.50	5.30	1.37	33.17	38.50
1640	8" diameter, SDR 11	↓	272	.147	↓	32.50	6.40	1.65	40.55	47

33 52 Liquid Fuel Distribution

33 52 16 – Gasoline Distribution

33 52 16.13 Gasoline Piping

0010	**GASOLINE PIPING**									
0020	Primary containment pipe, fiberglass-reinforced									
0030	Plastic pipe 15' & 30' lengths									
0040	2" diameter	Q-6	425	.056	L.F.	5.60	2.94		8.54	10.65
0050	3" diameter		400	.060		8.60	3.12		11.72	14.15
0060	4" diameter	↓	375	.064	↓	11.25	3.33		14.58	17.40
0100	Fittings									
0110	Elbows, 90° & 45°, bell-ends, 2"	Q-6	24	1	Ea.	41	52		93	124
0120	3" diameter		22	1.091		51.50	56.50		108	143
0130	4" diameter		20	1.200		66	62.50		128.50	167
0200	Tees, bell ends, 2"		21	1.143		57	59.50		116.50	152
0210	3" diameter		18	1.333		60.50	69.50		130	172
0220	4" diameter		15	1.600		79.50	83		162.50	212
0230	Flanges bell ends, 2"	↓	24	1	↓	31.50	52		83.50	113

33 52 Liquid Fuel Distribution

33 52 16 – Gasoline Distribution

33 52 16.13 Gasoline Piping

		Crew	Daily Output	Labor-Hours	Unit	Material	2012 Bare Costs Labor	2012 Bare Costs Equipment	Total	Total Incl O&P
0240	3" diameter	Q-6	22	1.091	Ea.	37	56.50		93.50	126
0250	4" diameter		20	1.200		42.50	62.50		105	141
0260	Sleeve couplings, 2"		21	1.143		13.50	59.50		73	104
0270	3" diameter		18	1.333		17.10	69.50		86.60	124
0280	4" diameter		15	1.600		24.50	83		107.50	152
0290	Threaded adapters 2"		21	1.143		17.10	59.50		76.60	108
0300	3" diameter		18	1.333		32.50	69.50		102	141
0310	4" diameter		15	1.600		36	83		119	165
0320	Reducers, 2"		27	.889		26	46		72	98
0330	3" diameter		22	1.091		26	56.50		82.50	114
0340	4" diameter		20	1.200		35	62.50		97.50	133
1010	Gas station product line for secondary containment (double wall)									
1100	Fiberglass reinforced plastic pipe 25' lengths									
1120	Pipe, plain end, 3" diameter	Q-6	375	.064	L.F.	6.75	3.33		10.08	12.45
1130	4" diameter		350	.069		7.90	3.56		11.46	14.10
1140	5" diameter		325	.074		13.80	3.84		17.64	21
1150	6" diameter		300	.080		14.20	4.16		18.36	22
1200	Fittings									
1230	Elbows, 90° & 45°, 3" diameter	Q-6	18	1.333	Ea.	56.50	69.50		126	167
1240	4" diameter		16	1.500		105	78		183	234
1250	5" diameter		14	1.714		280	89		369	445
1260	6" diameter		12	2		320	104		424	505
1270	Tees, 3" diameter		15	1.600		86	83		169	220
1280	4" diameter		12	2		131	104		235	300
1290	5" diameter		9	2.667		300	139		439	540
1300	6" diameter		6	4		365	208		573	720
1310	Couplings, 3" diameter		18	1.333		55	69.50		124.50	166
1320	4" diameter		16	1.500		115	78		193	245
1330	5" diameter		14	1.714		250	89		339	410
1340	6" diameter		12	2		310	104		414	495
1350	Cross-over nipples, 3" diameter		18	1.333		10	69.50		79.50	116
1360	4" diameter		16	1.500		12	78		90	131
1370	5" diameter		14	1.714		15	89		104	151
1380	6" diameter		12	2		18	104		122	177
1400	Telescoping, reducers, concentric 4" x 3"		18	1.333		45	69.50		114.50	155
1410	5" x 4"		17	1.412		90	73.50		163.50	210
1420	6" x 5"		16	1.500		220	78		298	360

33 61 Hydronic Energy Distribution

33 61 13 – Underground Hydronic Energy Distribution

33 61 13.20 Pipe Conduit, Prefabricated/Preinsulated

		Crew	Daily Output	Labor-Hours	Unit	Material	2012 Bare Costs Labor	2012 Bare Costs Equipment	Total	Total Incl O&P
0010	**PIPE CONDUIT, PREFABRICATED/PREINSULATED**									
0020	Does not include trenching, fittings or crane.									
0300	For cathodic protection, add 12 to 14%									
0310	of total built-up price (casing plus service pipe)									
0580	Polyurethane insulated system, 250°F. max. temp.									
0620	Black steel service pipe, standard wt., 1/2" insulation									
0660	3/4" diam. pipe size	Q-17	54	.296	L.F.	61.50	14.85	.68	77.03	91
0670	1" diam. pipe size		50	.320		67.50	16.05	.74	84.29	99.50
0680	1-1/4" diam. pipe size		47	.340		75.50	17.05	.79	93.34	109
0690	1-1/2" diam. pipe size		45	.356		82	17.80	.82	100.62	118

33 61 Hydronic Energy Distribution

33 61 13 – Underground Hydronic Energy Distribution

33 61 13.20 Pipe Conduit, Prefabricated/Preinsulated	Crew	Daily Output	Labor-Hours	Unit	Material	2012 Bare Costs Labor	Equipment	Total	Total Incl O&P
0700	2" diam. pipe size	Q-17	42	.381	L.F.	85	19.10	.88	104.98	123
0710	2-1/2" diam. pipe size		34	.471		86	23.50	1.09	110.59	132
0720	3" diam. pipe size		28	.571		100	28.50	1.32	129.82	154
0730	4" diam. pipe size		22	.727		126	36.50	1.68	164.18	196
0740	5" diam. pipe size		18	.889		161	44.50	2.05	207.55	246
0750	6" diam. pipe size	Q-18	23	1.043		187	54	1.61	242.61	289
0760	8" diam. pipe size		19	1.263		274	65.50	1.95	341.45	400
0770	10" diam. pipe size		16	1.500		345	78	2.31	425.31	500
0780	12" diam. pipe size		13	1.846		430	96	2.84	528.84	625
0790	14" diam. pipe size		11	2.182		480	113	3.36	596.36	705
0800	16" diam. pipe size		10	2.400		550	125	3.70	678.70	795
0810	18" diam. pipe size		8	3		635	156	4.62	795.62	940
0820	20" diam. pipe size		7	3.429		705	178	5.30	888.30	1,050
0830	24" diam. pipe size		6	4		865	208	6.15	1,079.15	1,275
0900	For 1" thick insulation, add					10%				
0940	For 1-1/2" thick insulation, add					13%				
0980	For 2" thick insulation, add					20%				
1500	Gland seal for system, 3/4" diam. pipe size	Q-17	32	.500	Ea.	830	25	1.16	856.16	955
1510	1" diam. pipe size		32	.500		830	25	1.16	856.16	955
1540	1-1/4" diam. pipe size		30	.533		890	26.50	1.23	917.73	1,025
1550	1-1/2" diam. pipe size		30	.533		890	26.50	1.23	917.73	1,025
1560	2" diam. pipe size		28	.571		1,050	28.50	1.32	1,079.82	1,200
1570	2-1/2" diam. pipe size		26	.615		1,150	31	1.42	1,182.42	1,300
1580	3" diam. pipe size		24	.667		1,225	33.50	1.54	1,260.04	1,400
1590	4" diam. pipe size		22	.727		1,450	36.50	1.68	1,488.18	1,650
1600	5" diam. pipe size		19	.842		1,775	42	1.95	1,818.95	2,025
1610	6" diam. pipe size	Q-18	26	.923		1,900	48	1.42	1,949.42	2,150
1620	8" diam. pipe size		25	.960		2,200	50	1.48	2,251.48	2,500
1630	10" diam. pipe size		23	1.043		2,575	54	1.61	2,630.61	2,900
1640	12" diam. pipe size		21	1.143		2,825	59.50	1.76	2,886.26	3,225
1650	14" diam. pipe size		19	1.263		3,175	65.50	1.95	3,242.45	3,600
1660	16" diam. pipe size		18	1.333		3,725	69.50	2.05	3,796.55	4,200
1670	18" diam. pipe size		16	1.500		3,975	78	2.31	4,055.31	4,500
1680	20" diam. pipe size		14	1.714		4,525	89	2.64	4,616.64	5,100
1690	24" diam. pipe size		12	2		5,025	104	3.08	5,132.08	5,675
2000	Elbow, 45° for system									
2020	3/4" diam. pipe size	Q-17	14	1.143	Ea.	525	57.50	2.64	585.14	665
2040	1" diam. pipe size		13	1.231		540	61.50	2.84	604.34	690
2050	1-1/4" diam. pipe size		11	1.455		610	73	3.36	686.36	790
2060	1-1/2" diam. pipe size		9	1.778		640	89	4.11	733.11	845
2070	2" diam. pipe size		6	2.667		670	134	6.15	810.15	945
2080	2-1/2" diam. pipe size		4	4		725	201	9.25	935.25	1,100
2090	3" diam. pipe size		3.50	4.571		835	229	10.55	1,074.55	1,275
2100	4" diam. pipe size		3	5.333		975	267	12.30	1,254.30	1,500
2110	5" diam. pipe size		2.80	5.714		1,250	286	13.20	1,549.20	1,825
2120	6" diam. pipe size	Q-18	4	6		1,425	310	9.25	1,744.25	2,025
2130	8" diam. pipe size		3	8		2,050	415	12.30	2,477.30	2,925
2140	10" diam. pipe size		2.40	10		2,525	520	15.40	3,060.40	3,575
2150	12" diam. pipe size		2	12		3,325	625	18.50	3,968.50	4,600
2160	14" diam. pipe size		1.80	13.333		4,125	695	20.50	4,840.50	5,600
2170	16" diam. pipe size		1.60	15		4,900	780	23	5,703	6,600
2180	18" diam. pipe size		1.30	18.462		6,150	960	28.50	7,138.50	8,250
2190	20" diam. pipe size		1	24		7,750	1,250	37	9,037	10,400

33 61 Hydronic Energy Distribution

33 61 13 – Underground Hydronic Energy Distribution

33 61 13.20 Pipe Conduit, Prefabricated/Preinsulated

	33 61 13.20 Pipe Conduit, Prefabricated/Preinsulated	Crew	Daily Output	Labor-Hours	Unit	Material	2012 Bare Costs Labor	Equipment	Total	Total Incl O&P
2200	24" diam. pipe size	Q-18	.70	34.286	Ea.	9,750	1,775	53	11,578	13,500
2260	For elbow, 90°, add					25%				
2300	For tee, straight, add					85%	30%			
2340	For tee, reducing, add					170%	30%			
2380	For weldolet, straight, add					50%				
2400	Polyurethane insulation, 1"									
2410	FRP carrier and casing									
2420	4"	Q-5	18	.889	L.F.	53	44.50		97.50	125
2422	6"	Q-6	23	1.043		91.50	54		145.50	183
2424	8"		19	1.263		149	65.50		214.50	263
2426	10"		16	1.500		201	78		279	340
2428	12"		13	1.846		262	96		358	435
2430	FRP carrier and PVC casing									
2440	4"	Q-5	18	.889	L.F.	21	44.50		65.50	90
2444	8"	Q-6	19	1.263		43.50	65.50		109	147
2446	10"		16	1.500		62.50	78		140.50	187
2448	12"		13	1.846		80	96		176	233
2450	PVC carrier and casing									
2460	4"	Q-1	36	.444	L.F.	10.30	22		32.30	44.50
2462	6"	"	29	.552		14.40	27		41.40	57
2464	8"	Q-2	36	.667		20	34		54	73.50
2466	10"		32	.750		27.50	38		65.50	87.50
2468	12"		31	.774		32	39.50		71.50	94.50

33 63 Steam Energy Distribution

33 63 13 – Underground Steam and Condensate Distribution Piping

33 63 13.10 Calcium Silicate Insulated System

	33 63 13.10 Calcium Silicate Insulated System	Crew	Daily Output	Labor-Hours	Unit	Material	2012 Bare Costs Labor	Equipment	Total	Total Incl O&P
0010	**CALCIUM SILICATE INSULATED SYSTEM**									
0011	High temp. (1200 degrees F)									
2840	Steel casing with protective exterior coating									
2850	6-5/8" diameter	Q-18	52	.462	L.F.	114	24	.71	138.71	162
2860	8-5/8" diameter		50	.480		124	25	.74	149.74	175
2870	10-3/4" diameter		47	.511		145	26.50	.79	172.29	201
2880	12-3/4" diameter		44	.545		158	28.50	.84	187.34	218
2890	14" diameter		41	.585		178	30.50	.90	209.40	243
2900	16" diameter		39	.615		191	32	.95	223.95	261
2910	18" diameter		36	.667		211	34.50	1.03	246.53	286
2920	20" diameter		34	.706		238	36.50	1.09	275.59	320
2930	22" diameter		32	.750		330	39	1.16	370.16	425
2940	24" diameter		29	.828		375	43	1.27	419.27	480
2950	26" diameter		26	.923		430	48	1.42	479.42	545
2960	28" diameter		23	1.043		535	54	1.61	590.61	675
2970	30" diameter		21	1.143		570	59.50	1.76	631.26	715
2980	32" diameter		19	1.263		640	65.50	1.95	707.45	805
2990	34" diameter		18	1.333		645	69.50	2.05	716.55	815
3000	36" diameter		16	1.500		695	78	2.31	775.31	880
3040	For multi-pipe casings, add					10%				
3060	For oversize casings, add					2%				
3400	Steel casing gland seal, single pipe									
3420	6-5/8" diameter	Q-18	25	.960	Ea.	1,575	50	1.48	1,626.48	1,825
3440	8-5/8" diameter		23	1.043		1,850	54	1.61	1,905.61	2,100

33 63 13 – Underground Steam and Condensate Distribution Piping

33 63 13.10 Calcium Silicate Insulated System		Crew	Daily Output	Labor-Hours	Unit	Material	2012 Bare Costs Labor	Equipment	Total	Total Incl O&P
3450	10-3/4" diameter	Q-18	21	1.143	Ea.	2,075	59.50	1.76	2,136.26	2,375
3460	12-3/4" diameter		19	1.263		2,475	65.50	1.95	2,542.45	2,825
3470	14" diameter		17	1.412		2,700	73.50	2.17	2,775.67	3,100
3480	16" diameter		16	1.500		3,175	78	2.31	3,255.31	3,600
3490	18" diameter		15	1.600		3,525	83	2.46	3,610.46	4,000
3500	20" diameter		13	1.846		3,900	96	2.84	3,998.84	4,425
3510	22" diameter		12	2		4,400	104	3.08	4,507.08	4,975
3520	24" diameter		11	2.182		4,925	113	3.36	5,041.36	5,575
3530	26" diameter		10	2.400		5,600	125	3.70	5,728.70	6,375
3540	28" diameter		9.50	2.526		6,325	131	3.89	6,459.89	7,175
3550	30" diameter		9	2.667		6,475	139	4.11	6,618.11	7,350
3560	32" diameter		8.50	2.824		7,250	147	4.35	7,401.35	8,200
3570	34" diameter		8	3		7,925	156	4.62	8,085.62	8,975
3580	36" diameter	▼	7	3.429	▼	8,425	178	5.30	8,608.30	9,525
3620	For multi-pipe casings, add					5%				
4000	Steel casing anchors, single pipe									
4020	6-5/8" diameter	Q-18	8	3	Ea.	1,425	156	4.62	1,585.62	1,800
4040	8-5/8" diameter		7.50	3.200		1,475	166	4.93	1,645.93	1,875
4050	10-3/4" diameter		7	3.429		1,950	178	5.30	2,133.30	2,425
4060	12-3/4" diameter		6.50	3.692		2,075	192	5.70	2,272.70	2,575
4070	14" diameter		6	4		2,450	208	6.15	2,664.15	3,000
4080	16" diameter		5.50	4.364		2,850	227	6.70	3,083.70	3,475
4090	18" diameter		5	4.800		3,200	250	7.40	3,457.40	3,900
4100	20" diameter		4.50	5.333		3,525	277	8.20	3,810.20	4,300
4110	22" diameter		4	6		3,925	310	9.25	4,244.25	4,800
4120	24" diameter		3.50	6.857		4,300	355	10.55	4,665.55	5,275
4130	26" diameter		3	8		4,850	415	12.30	5,277.30	5,975
4140	28" diameter		2.50	9.600		5,325	500	14.80	5,839.80	6,625
4150	30" diameter		2	12		5,650	625	18.50	6,293.50	7,150
4160	32" diameter		1.50	16		6,775	830	24.50	7,629.50	8,725
4170	34" diameter		1	24		7,600	1,250	37	8,887	10,300
4180	36" diameter	▼	1	24		8,250	1,250	37	9,537	11,000
4220	For multi-pipe, add				▼	5%	20%			
4800	Steel casing elbow									
4820	6-5/8" diameter	Q-18	15	1.600	Ea.	1,950	83	2.46	2,035.46	2,275
4830	8-5/8" diameter		15	1.600		2,075	83	2.46	2,160.46	2,400
4850	10-3/4" diameter		14	1.714		2,500	89	2.64	2,591.64	2,875
4860	12-3/4" diameter		13	1.846		2,975	96	2.84	3,073.84	3,425
4870	14" diameter		12	2		3,175	104	3.08	3,282.08	3,625
4880	16" diameter		11	2.182		3,475	113	3.36	3,591.36	3,975
4890	18" diameter		10	2.400		3,950	125	3.70	4,078.70	4,550
4900	20" diameter		9	2.667		4,225	139	4.11	4,368.11	4,875
4910	22" diameter		8	3		4,550	156	4.62	4,710.62	5,250
4920	24" diameter		7	3.429		5,025	178	5.30	5,208.30	5,800
4930	26" diameter		6	4		5,475	208	6.15	5,689.15	6,350
4940	28" diameter		5	4.800		5,900	250	7.40	6,157.40	6,875
4950	30" diameter		4	6		5,950	310	9.25	6,269.25	7,000
4960	32" diameter		3	8		6,775	415	12.30	7,202.30	8,100
4970	34" diameter		2	12		7,425	625	18.50	8,068.50	9,125
4980	36" diameter	▼	2	12	▼	7,925	625	18.50	8,568.50	9,675
5500	Black steel service pipe, std. wt., 1" thick insulation									
5510	3/4" diameter pipe size	Q-17	54	.296	L.F.	51.50	14.85	.68	67.03	80
5540	1" diameter pipe size	▼	50	.320	▼	53.50	16.05	.74	70.29	84

33 63 Steam Energy Distribution

33 63 13 – Underground Steam and Condensate Distribution Piping

33 63 13.10 Calcium Silicate Insulated System	Crew	Daily Output	Labor-Hours	Unit	Material	2012 Bare Costs Labor	Equipment	Total	Total Incl O&P
5550	1-1/4" diameter pipe size	Q-17	47	.340	L.F.	60	17.05	.79	77.84	92.50
5560	1-1/2" diameter pipe size		45	.356		65.50	17.80	.82	84.12	100
5570	2" diameter pipe size		42	.381		72.50	19.10	.88	92.48	110
5580	2-1/2" diameter pipe size		34	.471		76.50	23.50	1.09	101.09	121
5590	3" diameter pipe size		28	.571		87	28.50	1.32	116.82	140
5600	4" diameter pipe size		22	.727		112	36.50	1.68	150.18	180
5610	5" diameter pipe size	▼	18	.889		151	44.50	2.05	197.55	235
5620	6" diameter pipe size	Q-18	23	1.043	▼	165	54	1.61	220.61	265
6000	Black steel service pipe, std. wt., 1-1/2" thick insul.									
6010	3/4" diameter pipe size	Q-17	54	.296	L.F.	52.50	14.85	.68	68.03	81
6040	1" diameter pipe size		50	.320		58.50	16.05	.74	75.29	89
6050	1-1/4" diameter pipe size		47	.340		65.50	17.05	.79	83.34	98.50
6060	1-1/2" diameter pipe size		45	.356		71.50	17.80	.82	90.12	106
6070	2" diameter pipe size		42	.381		77.50	19.10	.88	97.48	115
6080	2-1/2" diameter pipe size		34	.471		83	23.50	1.09	107.59	128
6090	3" diameter pipe size		28	.571		92.50	28.50	1.32	122.32	146
6100	4" diameter pipe size		22	.727		118	36.50	1.68	156.18	187
6110	5" diameter pipe size	▼	18	.889		151	44.50	2.05	197.55	235
6120	6" diameter pipe size	Q-18	23	1.043		172	54	1.61	227.61	273
6130	8" diameter pipe size		19	1.263		247	65.50	1.95	314.45	375
6140	10" diameter pipe size		16	1.500		310	78	2.31	390.31	460
6150	12" diameter pipe size	▼	13	1.846		370	96	2.84	468.84	555
6190	For 2" thick insulation, add					15%				
6220	For 2-1/2" thick insulation, add					25%				
6260	For 3" thick insulation, add				▼	30%				
6800	Black steel service pipe, ex. hvy. wt., 1" thick insul.									
6820	3/4" diameter pipe size	Q-17	50	.320	L.F.	54	16.05	.74	70.79	84.50
6840	1" diameter pipe size		47	.340		57.50	17.05	.79	75.34	90
6850	1-1/4" diameter pipe size		44	.364		66.50	18.25	.84	85.59	102
6860	1-1/2" diameter pipe size		42	.381		70.50	19.10	.88	90.48	108
6870	2" diameter pipe size		40	.400		75	20	.92	95.92	114
6880	2-1/2" diameter pipe size		31	.516		92.50	26	1.19	119.69	142
6890	3" diameter pipe size		27	.593		104	29.50	1.37	134.87	162
6900	4" diameter pipe size		21	.762		137	38	1.76	176.76	210
6910	5" diameter pipe size	▼	17	.941		192	47	2.17	241.17	284
6920	6" diameter pipe size	Q-18	22	1.091	▼	177	56.50	1.68	235.18	282
7400	Black steel service pipe, ex. hvy. wt., 1-1/2" thick insul.									
7420	3/4" diameter pipe size	Q-17	50	.320	L.F.	45	16.05	.74	61.79	74.50
7440	1" diameter pipe size		47	.340		51.50	17.05	.79	69.34	83
7450	1-1/4" diameter pipe size		44	.364		60	18.25	.84	79.09	94.50
7460	1-1/2" diameter pipe size		42	.381		65.50	19.10	.88	85.48	102
7470	2" diameter pipe size		40	.400		66	20	.92	86.92	104
7480	2-1/2" diameter pipe size		31	.516		78.50	26	1.19	105.69	126
7490	3" diameter pipe size		27	.593		92	29.50	1.37	122.87	148
7500	4" diameter pipe size		21	.762		120	38	1.76	159.76	191
7510	5" diameter pipe size	▼	17	.941		166	47	2.17	215.17	256
7520	6" diameter pipe size	Q-18	22	1.091		183	56.50	1.68	241.18	288
7530	8" diameter pipe size		18	1.333		275	69.50	2.05	346.55	405
7540	10" diameter pipe size		15	1.600		325	83	2.46	410.46	490
7550	12" diameter pipe size	▼	13	1.846		400	96	2.84	498.84	590
7590	For 2" thick insulation, add					13%				
7640	For 2-1/2" thick insulation, add					18%				
7680	For 3" thick insulation, add				▼	24%				

33 63 Steam Energy Distribution

33 63 13 – Underground Steam and Condensate Distribution Piping

33 63 13.20 Combined Steam Pipe With Condensate Return	Crew	Daily Output	Labor-Hours	Unit	Material	2012 Bare Costs Labor	Equipment	Total	Total Incl O&P
9000	**COMBINED STEAM PIPE WITH CONDENSATE RETURN**								
9010	8" and 4" in 24" case	Q-18	100	.240	L.F.	580	12.50	.37	592.87	655
9020	6" and 3" in 20" case		104	.231		395	12	.36	407.36	455
9030	3" and 1-1/2" in 16" case		110	.218		296	11.35	.34	307.69	340
9040	2" and 1-1/4" in 12-3/4" case		114	.211		257	10.95	.32	268.27	300
9050	1-1/2" and 1-1/4" in 10-3/4" case	↓	116	.207	↓	225	10.75	.32	236.07	265
9100	Steam pipe only (no return)									
9110	6" in 18" case	Q-18	108	.222	L.F.	325	11.55	.34	336.89	375
9120	4" in 14" case		112	.214		257	11.15	.33	268.48	300
9130	3" in 14" case		114	.211		238	10.95	.32	249.27	279
9140	2-1/2" in 12-3/4" case		118	.203		222	10.55	.31	232.86	260
9150	2" in 12-3/4" case	↓	122	.197	↓	212	10.25	.30	222.55	249

Estimating Tips

This section involves equipment and construction costs for air noise and odor pollution control systems.

These systems may be interrelated and care must be taken that the complete systems are estimated. For example, air pollution equipment may include dust and air-entrained particles that have to be collected. The vacuum systems could be noisy, requiring silencers to reduce noise pollution, and the collected solids have to be disposed of to prevent solid pollution.

Reference Numbers

Reference numbers are shown in shaded boxes at the beginning of some major classifications. These numbers refer to related items in the Reference Section. The reference information may be an estimating procedure, an alternate pricing method, or technical information.

Note: Not all subdivisions listed here necessarily appear in this publication.

Division 44 - Pollution Control Equipment

44 11 16.10 Dust Collection Systems	Crew	Daily Output	Labor-Hours	Unit	Material	2012 Bare Costs Labor	Equipment	Total	Total Incl O&P
0010 **DUST COLLECTION SYSTEMS** Commercial/Industrial									
0120 Central vacuum units									
0130 Includes stand, filters and motorized shaker									
0200 500 CFM, 10" inlet, 2 HP	Q-20	2.40	8.333	Ea.	3,900	400		4,300	4,900
0220 1000 CFM, 10" inlet, 3 HP		2.20	9.091		4,100	435		4,535	5,175
0240 1500 CFM, 10" inlet, 5 HP		2	10		4,325	480		4,805	5,475
0260 3000 CFM, 13" inlet, 10 HP		1.50	13.333		12,200	640		12,840	14,400
0280 5000 CFM, 16" inlet, 2 @ 10 HP		1	20		12,900	955		13,855	15,700
1000 Vacuum tubing, galvanized									
1100 2-1/8" OD, 16 ga.	Q-9	440	.036	L.F.	2.80	1.71		4.51	5.70
1110 2-1/2" OD, 16 ga.		420	.038		3.23	1.79		5.02	6.30
1120 3" OD, 16 ga.		400	.040		3.69	1.88		5.57	6.90
1130 3-1/2" OD, 16 ga.		380	.042		5.35	1.98		7.33	8.85
1140 4" OD, 16 ga.		360	.044		6	2.09		8.09	9.80
1150 5" OD, 14 ga.		320	.050		10.75	2.35		13.10	15.45
1160 6" OD, 14 ga.		280	.057		12.45	2.68		15.13	17.80
1170 8" OD, 14 ga.		200	.080		18.75	3.75		22.50	26
1180 10" OD, 12 ga.		160	.100		29.50	4.69		34.19	39.50
1190 12" OD, 12 ga.		120	.133		32.50	6.25		38.75	45.50
1200 14" OD, 12 ga.		80	.200		39.50	9.40		48.90	58
1940 Hose, flexible wire reinforced rubber									
1956 3" dia.	Q-9	400	.040	L.F.	8.20	1.88		10.08	11.85
1960 4" dia.		360	.044		9.50	2.09		11.59	13.65
1970 5" dia.		320	.050		11.90	2.35		14.25	16.70
1980 6" dia.		280	.057		12.90	2.68		15.58	18.25
2000 90° Elbow, slip fit									
2110 2-1/8" dia.	Q-9	70	.229	Ea.	11.70	10.75		22.45	29
2120 2-1/2" dia.		65	.246		16.35	11.55		27.90	35.50
2130 3" dia.		60	.267		22	12.50		34.50	43.50
2140 3-1/2" dia.		55	.291		27.50	13.65		41.15	51
2150 4" dia.		50	.320		34	15		49	60.50
2160 5" dia.		45	.356		64.50	16.70		81.20	96.50
2170 6" dia.		40	.400		89	18.75		107.75	127
2180 8" dia.		30	.533		169	25		194	224
2400 45° Elbow, slip fit									
2410 2-1/8" dia.	Q-9	70	.229	Ea.	10.25	10.75		21	27.50
2420 2-1/2" dia.		65	.246		15.10	11.55		26.65	34
2430 3" dia.		60	.267		18.20	12.50		30.70	39
2440 3-1/2" dia.		55	.291		23	13.65		36.65	46
2450 4" dia.		50	.320		29.50	15		44.50	55.50
2460 5" dia.		45	.356		50	16.70		66.70	80.50
2470 6" dia.		40	.400		68	18.75		86.75	103
2480 8" dia.		35	.457		133	21.50		154.50	179
2800 90° TY, slip fit thru 6" dia.									
2810 2-1/8" dia.	Q-9	42	.381	Ea.	23	17.90		40.90	52.50
2820 2-1/2" dia.		39	.410		30	19.25		49.25	62.50
2830 3" dia.		36	.444		39.50	21		60.50	75.50
2840 3-1/2" dia.		33	.485		50	23		73	89.50
2850 4" dia.		30	.533		72	25		97	117
2860 5" dia.		27	.593		137	28		165	194
2870 6" dia.		24	.667		186	31.50		217.50	253
2880 8" dia., butt end					395			395	435
2890 10" dia., butt end					715			715	785

44 11 Particulate Control Equipment

44 11 16 – Fugitive Dust Barrier Systems

44 11 16.10 Dust Collection Systems		Crew	Daily Output	Labor-Hours	Unit	Material	2012 Bare Costs Labor	Equipment	Total	Total Incl O&P
2900	12" dia., butt end				Ea.	715			715	785
2910	14" dia., butt end					1,300			1,300	1,425
2920	6" x 4" dia., butt end					114			114	125
2930	8" x 4" dia., butt end					215			215	237
2940	10" x 4" dia., butt end					282			282	310
2950	12" x 4" dia., butt end				▼	325			325	355
3100	90° Elbow, butt end segmented									
3110	8" dia., butt end, segmented				Ea.	169			169	186
3120	10" dia., butt end, segmented					420			420	460
3130	12" dia., butt end, segmented					530			530	585
3140	14" dia., butt end, segmented				▼	665			665	735
3200	45° Elbow, butt end segmented									
3210	8" dia., butt end, segmented				Ea.	133			133	146
3220	10" dia., butt end, segmented					305			305	335
3230	12" dia., butt end, segmented					310			310	340
3240	14" dia., butt end, segmented				▼	380			380	420
3400	All butt end fittings require one coupling per joint.									
3410	Labor for fitting included with couplings.									
3460	Compression coupling, galvanized, neoprene gasket									
3470	2-1/8" dia.	Q-9	44	.364	Ea.	13.55	17.05		30.60	41
3480	2-1/2" dia.		44	.364		13.55	17.05		30.60	41
3490	3" dia.		38	.421		19.55	19.75		39.30	51.50
3500	3-1/2" dia.		35	.457		22	21.50		43.50	57
3510	4" dia.		33	.485		24	23		47	61
3520	5" dia.		29	.552		27.50	26		53.50	69.50
3530	6" dia.		26	.615		27.50	29		56.50	74.50
3540	8" dia.		22	.727		57.50	34		91.50	115
3550	10" dia.		20	.800		77.50	37.50		115	142
3560	12" dia.		18	.889		96	41.50		137.50	169
3570	14" dia.	▼	16	1	▼	122	47		169	207
3800	Air gate valves, galvanized									
3810	2-1/8" dia.	Q-9	30	.533	Ea.	198	25		223	256
3820	2-1/2" dia.		28	.571		219	27		246	282
3830	3" dia.		26	.615		239	29		268	305
3840	4" dia.		23	.696		300	32.50		332.50	380
3850	6" dia.	▼	18	.889	▼	405	41.50		446.50	510

44 11 96 – Dry Plate Electrostatic Precipitator Equipment

44 11 96.10 Electrostatic Precipitators		Crew	Daily Output	Labor-Hours	Unit	Material	2012 Bare Costs Labor	Equipment	Total	Total Incl O&P
0010	**ELECTROSTATIC PRECIPITATORS**									
4100	Smoke pollution control									
4110	Exhaust air volume									
4120	1 to 2.4 MCFM	Q-10	2.15	11.163	MCFM	8,225	545		8,770	9,875
4130	2.4 to 4.8 MCFM		2.70	8.889		9,350	435		9,785	11,000
4140	4.8 to 7.2 MCFM		3.60	6.667		9,525	325		9,850	11,000
4150	7.2 to 12 MCFM	▼	5.40	4.444	▼	9,950	216		10,166	11,300
4400	Electrostatic precipitators with built-in exhaust fans									
4410	Smoke pollution control									
4420	Exhaust air volume									
4440	1 to 2.4 MCFM	Q-10	2.15	11.163	MCFM	9,900	545		10,445	11,700
4450	2.4 to 4.8 MCFM		2.70	8.889		7,850	435		8,285	9,275
4460	4.8 to 7.2 MCFM		3.60	6.667		6,725	325		7,050	7,900
4470	7.2 to 12 MCFM	▼	5.40	4.444		5,775	216		5,991	6,700

Division Notes

	CREW	DAILY OUTPUT	LABOR-HOURS	UNIT	2012 BARE COSTS				TOTAL INCL O&P
					MAT.	LABOR	EQUIP.	TOTAL	

Estimating Tips

This new division contains information about water and wastewater equipment and systems, which was formerly located in Division 44.

The main areas of focus are total wastewater treatment plants and components of wastewater treatment plants. In addition, there are assemblies such as sewage treatment lagoons that can be found in some publications under G30 Site Mechanical Utilities.

Also included in this section are oil/water separators for wastewater treatment.

New sections added for this year are for activated sludge cells and air diffuser systems for wastewater treatment.

Reference Numbers

Reference numbers are shown in shaded boxes at the beginning of some major classifications. These numbers refer to related items in the Reference Section. The reference information may be an estimating procedure, an alternate pricing method, or technical information.

Note: Not all subdivisions listed here necessarily appear in this publication.

46 23 Grit Removal And Handling Equipment

46 23 23 – Vortex Grit Removal Equipment

46 23 23.10 Rainwater Filters	Crew	Daily Output	Labor-Hours	Unit	Material	2012 Bare Costs Labor	Equipment	Total	Total Incl O&P
0010 **RAINWATER FILTERS**									
0100 42 gal./min	B-21	3.50	8	Ea.	22,400	325	38	22,763	25,200
0200 65 gal./min		3.50	8		22,300	325	38	22,663	25,000
0300 208 gal./min		3.50	8		22,300	325	38	22,663	25,000

46 25 Oil and Grease Separation and Removal Equipment

46 25 13 – Coalescing Oil-Water Separators

46 25 13.20 Oil/Water Separators

	Crew	Daily Output	Labor-Hours	Unit	Material	2012 Bare Costs Labor	Equipment	Total	Total Incl O&P
0010 **OIL/WATER SEPARATORS**									
0020 Underground, tank only									
0030 Excludes excavation, backfill, & piping									
0100 200 GPM	B-21	3.50	8	Ea.	22,300	325	38	22,663	25,000
0110 400 GPM		3.25	8.615		35,800	350	41	36,191	40,000
0120 600 GPM		2.75	10.182		41,400	410	48	41,858	46,300
0130 800 GPM		2.50	11.200		48,700	455	53	49,208	54,500
0140 1000 GPM		2	14		57,000	565	66	57,631	63,500
0150 1200 GPM		1.50	18.667		63,000	755	88.50	63,843.50	70,500
0160 1500 GPM		1	28		71,000	1,125	132	72,257	80,000

46 25 16 – API Oil-Water Separators

46 25 16.10 Oil/Water Separators

	Crew	Daily Output	Labor-Hours	Unit	Material	2012 Bare Costs Labor	Equipment	Total	Total Incl O&P
0010 **OIL/WATER SEPARATORS**									
0020 Complete system, not including excavation and backfill									
0100 Treated capacity 0.2 cubic feet per second	B-22	1	30	Ea.	10,400	1,225	199	11,824	13,500
0200 0.5 cubic foot per second	B-13	.75	74.667		15,800	2,850	930	19,580	22,800
0300 1.0 cubic foot per second		.60	93.333		22,600	3,550	1,150	27,300	31,500
0400 2.4 – 3 cubic feet per second		.30	186		44,600	7,100	2,325	54,025	62,500
0500 11 cubic feet per second		.17	329	Ea.	50,000	12,500	4,100	66,600	78,500
0600 22 cubic feet per second	B-13	.10	560	Ea.	74,500	21,300	6,975	102,775	122,500

Assemblies Section

Table of Contents

How to Use the Assemblies Cost Tables

The following is a detailed explanation of a sample Assemblies Cost Table. Most Assembly Tables are separated into three parts: (1) an illustration of the system to be estimated, (2) the components and related costs of a typical system, and (3) the costs for similar systems with dimensional and/or size variations. For costs of the components that comprise these systems, or assemblies, refer to the Unit Price Section. Next to each bold number below is the described item with the appropriate component of the sample entry following in parentheses. In most cases, if the work is to be subcontracted, the general contractor will need to add an additional markup (RSMeans suggests using 10%) to the "Total" figures.

1 System/Line Numbers (D3010 510 1760)

Each Assemblies Cost Line has been assigned a unique identification number based on the UniFormat classification sytem.

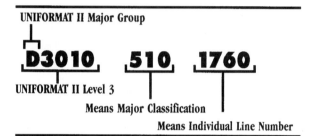

UNIFORMAT II Major Group

D3010   510   1760

UNIFORMAT II Level 3

Means Major Classification

Means Individual Line Number

D30 HVAC

D3010 Energy Supply 1

2

Basis for Heat Loss Estimate, Apartment Type Structures:

1. Masonry walls and flat roof are insulated. U factor is assumed at .08.
2. Window glass area taken as BOCA minimum, 1/10th of floor area. Double insulating glass with 1/4" air space, U = .65.
3. Infiltration = 0.3 C.F. per hour per S.F. of net wall.
4. Concrete floor loss is 2 BTUH per S.F.
5. Temperature difference taken as 70°F.
6. Ventilating or makeup air has not been included and must be added if desired. Air shafts are not used.

System Components	QUANTITY 4	UNIT 5	MAT. 7	INST. 8	TOTAL 9
SYSTEM D3010 510 1760					
HEATING SYSTEM, FIN TUBE RADIATION, FORCED HOT WATER					
1,000 S.F. AREA, 10,000 C.F. VOLUME					
3 Boiler, oil fired, CI, burner, ctrls/insul/breech/pipe/fttng/valves, 109 MBH	1.000	Ea.	3,893.75	3,718.75	7,612.50
Circulating pump, CI flange connection, 1/12 HP	1.000	Ea.	380	198	578
Expansion tank, painted steel, ASME 18 Gal capacity	1.000	Ea.	700	86.50	786.50
Storage tank, steel, above ground, 275 Gal capacity w/supports	1.000	Ea.	490	242	732
Copper tubing type L, solder joint, hanger 10' OC, 3/4" diam	100.000	L.F.	725	865	1,590
Radiation, 3/4" copper tube w/alum fin baseboard pkg, 7" high	30.000	L.F.	277.50	630	907.50
Pipe covering, calcium silicate w/cover, 1' wall, 3/4' diam	100.000	L.F.	338	645	983
TOTAL			6,804.25	6,385.25	13,189.50
COST PER S.F.			6.80	6.39	13.19

D3010 510	Apartment Building Heating - Fin Tube Radiation		COST PER S.F.		
			MAT.	INST.	TOTAL
1740	Heating systems, fin tube radiation, forced hot water				
1760	1,000 S.F. area, 10,000 C.F. volume		6.80	6.38	13.18
1800	10,000 S.F. area, 100,000 C.F. volume	R235000 -10	3.42	3.86	7.28
1840	20,000 S.F. area, 200,000 C.F. volume		3.89	4.32	8.21
1880	30,000 S.F. area, 300,000 C.F. volume	R235000 -20	3.77	4.18	7.95
1890					

Illustration

2 At the top of most assembly pages are an illustration, a brief description, and the design criteria used to develop the cost.

System Components

3 The components of a typical system are listed separately to show what has been included in the development of the total system price. The table below contains prices for other similar systems with dimensional and/or size variations.

Quantity

4 This is the number of line item units required for one system unit. For example, we assume that it will take 30 linear feet of radiation for the 1,000 S.F. area shown.

Unit of Measure for Each Item

5 The abbreviated designation indicates the unit of measure, as defined by industry standards, upon which the price of the component is based. For example, baseboard radiation is priced by the linear foot. For a complete listing of abbreviations, see the Reference Section.

Unit of Measure for Each System (Each)

6 Costs shown in the three right-hand columns have been adjusted by the component quantity and unit of measure for the entire system. In this example, "Cost Each" is the unit of measure for this system, or assembly.

Materials (6,804.25)

7 This column contains the Materials Cost of each component. These cost figures are bare costs plus 10% for profit.

Installation (6,385.25)

8 Installation includes labor and equipment plus the installing contractor's overhead and profit. Equipment costs are the bare rental costs plus 10% for profit. The labor overhead and profit is defined on the inside back cover of this book.

Total (13,189.50)

9 The figure in this column is the sum of the material and installation costs.

Material Cost	+	Installation Cost	=	Total
$6,804.25	+	$6,385.25	=	$13,189.50

A Substructure

A20 Basement Construction

A2020 Basement Walls

A2020 220	Subdrainage Piping	COST PER L.F.		
		MAT.	INST.	TOTAL
2000	Piping, excavation & backfill excluded, PVC, perforated			
2110	3" diameter	1.80	3.87	5.67
2130	4" diameter	1.80	3.87	5.67
2140	5" diameter	3.80	4.14	7.94
2150	6" diameter	3.80	4.14	7.94
3000	Metal alum. or steel, perforated asphalt coated			
3150	6" diameter	6.60	8.10	14.70
3160	8" diameter	12.20	8.35	20.55
3170	10" diameter	15.25	8.55	23.80
3180	12" diameter	17.10	10.85	27.95
3220	18" diameter	25.50	15.10	40.60
4000	Corrugated HDPE tubing			
4130	4" diameter	.69	.72	1.41
4150	6" diameter	2.20	.96	3.16
4160	8" diameter	3.08	1.23	4.31
4180	12" diameter	7.35	4.27	11.62
4200	15" diameter	8.75	4.83	13.58
4220	18" diameter	13.90	6.85	20.75

In this closed-loop indirect collection system, fluid with a low freezing temperature, such as propylene glycol, transports heat from the collectors to water storage. The transfer fluid is contained in a closed-loop consisting of collectors, supply and return piping, and a remote heat exchanger. The heat exchanger transfers heat energy from the

fluid in the collector loop to potable water circulated in a storage loop. A typical two-or-three panel system contains 5 to 6 gallons of heat transfer fluid.

When the collectors become approximately 20°F warmer than the storage temperature, a controller activates the circulator on the collector and storage

loops. The circulators will move the fluid and potable water through the heat exchanger until heat collection no longer occurs. At that point, the system shuts down. Since the heat transfer medium is a fluid with a very low freezing temperature, there is no need for it to be drained from the system between periods of collection.

D2020 Domestic Water Distribution

System Components	QUANTITY	UNIT	COST EACH		
			MAT.	INST.	TOTAL
SYSTEM D2020 265 2760					
SOLAR, CLOSED LOOP, ADD-ON HOT WATER SYS., EXTERNAL HEAT EXCHANGER					
3/4" TUBING, TWO 3'X7' BLACK CHROME COLLECTORS					
A,B,G,L,K,M Heat exchanger fluid-fluid pkg incl 2 circulators, expansion tank,					
Check valve, relief valve, controller, hi temp cutoff, & 2 sensors	1.000	Ea.	795	475	1,270
C Thermometer, 2" dial	3.000	Ea.	69	123	192
D, T Fill & drain valve, brass, 3/4" connection	1.000	Ea.	14.65	27.50	42.15
E Air vent, manual, 1/8" fitting	2.000	Ea.	6	41	47
F Air purger	1.000	Ea.	50	55	105
H Strainer, Y type, bronze body, 3/4" IPS	1.000	Ea.	36	35.50	71.50
I Valve, gate, bronze, NRS, soldered 3/4" diam	6.000	Ea.	309	198	507
J Neoprene vent flashing	2.000	Ea.	27.40	66	93.40
N-1, N Relief valve temp & press, 150 psi 210°F self-closing 3/4" IPS	1.000	Ea.	20.50	22	42.50
O Pipe covering, urethane, ultraviolet cover, 1" wall 3/4" diam	20.000	L.F.	45.60	119	164.60
P Pipe covering, fiberglass, all service jacket, 1" wall, 3/4" diam	50.000	L.F.	53.50	238.50	292
Q Collector panel solar energy blk chrome on copper, 1/8" temp glass 3'x7'	2.000	Ea.	2,200	250	2,450
Roof clamps for solar energy collector panels	2.000	Set	5.42	33.90	39.32
R Valve, swing check, bronze, regrinding disc, 3/4" diam	2.000	Ea.	312	66	378
S Pressure gauge, 60 psi, 2" dial	1.000	Ea.	25.50	20.50	46
U Valve, water tempering, bronze, sweat connections, 3/4" diam	1.000	Ea.	115	33	148
W-2, V Tank water storage w/heating element, drain, relief valve, existing	1.000	Ea.			
Copper tubing type L, solder joint, hanger 10' OC 3/4" diam	20.000	L.F.	145	173	318
Copper tubing, type M, solder joint, hanger 10' OC 3/4" diam	70.000	L.F.	388.50	591.50	980
Sensor wire, #22-2 conductor multistranded	.500	C.L.F.	8.05	30.75	38.80
Solar energy heat transfer fluid, propylene glycol anti-freeze	6.000	Gal.	95.70	141	236.70
Wrought copper fittings & solder, 3/4" diam	76.000	Ea.	535.80	2,622	3,157.80
TOTAL			5,257.62	5,362.15	10,619.77

D2020 265	Solar, Closed Loop, Add-On Hot Water Systems	COST EACH		
		MAT.	INST.	TOTAL
2550	Solar, closed loop, add-on hot water system, external heat exchanger			
2570	3/8" tubing, 3 ea. 4' x 4'-4" vacuum tube collectors	5,675	5,025	10,700
2580	1/2" tubing, 4 ea. 4 x 4'-4" vacuum tube collectors	6,175	5,450	11,625
2600	2 ea. 3'x7' black chrome collectors [R235616 -60]	4,625	5,125	9,750
2620	3 ea. 3'x7' black chrome collectors	5,725	5,275	11,000
2640	2 ea. 3'x7' flat black collectors	3,950	5,150	9,100
2660	3 ea. 3'x7' flat black collectors	4,700	5,300	10,000
2700	3/4" tubing, 3 ea. 3'x7' black chrome collectors	6,350	5,500	11,850
2720	3 ea. 3'x7' flat black absorber plate collectors	5,350	5,525	10,875
2740	2 ea. 4'x9' flat black w/plastic glazing collectors	4,950	5,550	10,500
2760	2 ea. 3'x7' black chrome collectors	5,250	5,350	10,600
2780	1" tubing, 4 ea 2'x9' plastic absorber & glazing collectors	6,525	6,225	12,750
2800	4 ea. 3'x7' black chrome absorber collectors	8,650	6,250	14,900
2820	4 ea. 3'x7' flat black absorber collectors	7,300	6,275	13,575

In the drainback indirect-collection system, the heat transfer fluid is distilled water contained in a loop consisting of collectors, supply and return piping, and an unpressurized holding tank. A large heat exchanger containing incoming potable water is immersed in the holding tank. When a controller activates solar collection, the distilled water is pumped through the collectors and heated and pumped back down to the holding tank. When the temperature differential between the water in the collectors and water in storage is such that collection no longer occurs, the pump turns off and gravity causes the distilled water in the collector loop to drain back to the holding tank. All the loop piping is pitched so that the water can drain out of the collectors and piping and not freeze there. As hot water is needed in the home, incoming water first flows through the holding tank with the immersed heat exchanger and is warmed and then flows through a conventional heater for any supplemental heating that is necessary.

D2020 Domestic Water Distribution

System Components	QUANTITY	UNIT	COST EACH		
			MAT.	INST.	TOTAL
SYSTEM D2020 270 2760					
SOLAR, DRAINBACK, ADD ON, HOT WATER, IMMERSED HEAT EXCHANGER					
3/4″ TUBING, THREE EA 3′X7′ BLACK CHROME COLLECTOR					
A, B Differential controller 2 sensors, thermostat, solar energy system	1.000	Ea.	605	55	660
C Thermometer 2″ dial	3.000	Ea.	69	123	192
D, T Fill & drain valve, brass, 3/4″ connection	1.000	Ea.	14.65	27.50	42.15
E-1 Automatic air vent 1/8″ fitting	1.000	Ea.	18.95	20.50	39.45
H Strainer, Y type, bronze body, 3/4″ IPS	1.000	Ea.	36	35.50	71.50
I Valve, gate, bronze, NRS, soldered 3/4″ diam	2.000	Ea.	103	66	169
J Neoprene vent flashing	2.000	Ea.	27.40	66	93.40
L Circulator, solar heated liquid, 1/20 HP	1.000	Ea.	177	99	276
N Relief valve temp. & press. 150 psi 210°F self-closing 3/4″ IPS	1.000	Ea.	20.50	22	42.50
O Pipe covering, urethane, ultraviolet cover, 1″ wall, 3/4″ diam	20.000	L.F.	45.60	119	164.60
P Pipe covering, fiberglass, all service jacket, 1″ wall, 3/4″ diam	50.000	L.F.	53.50	238.50	292
Q Collector panel solar energy blk chrome on copper, 1/8″ temp glas 3′x7′	3.000	Ea.	3,300	375	3,675
Roof clamps for solar energy collector panels	3.000	Set	8.13	50.85	58.98
R Valve, swing check, bronze, regrinding disc, 3/4″ diam	1.000	Ea.	156	33	189
U Valve, water tempering, bronze sweat connections, 3/4″ diam	1.000	Ea.	115	33	148
V Tank, water storage w/heating element, drain, relief valve, existing	1.000	Ea.			
W Tank, water storage immersed heat exchr elec 2″x1/2# insul 120 gal	1.000	Ea.	1,375	470	1,845
X Valve, globe, bronze, rising stem, 3/4″ diam, soldered	3.000	Ea.	393	99	492
Y Flow control valve	1.000	Ea.	167	30	197
Z Valve, ball, bronze, solder 3/4″ diam, solar loop flow control	1.000	Ea.	23	33	56
Copper tubing, type L, solder joint, hanger 10′ OC 3/4″ diam	20.000	L.F.	145	173	318
Copper tubing, type M, solder joint, hanger 10′ OC 3/4″ diam	70.000	L.F.	388.50	591.50	980
Sensor wire, #22-2 conductor, multistranded	.500	C.L.F.	8.05	30.75	38.80
Wrought copper fittings & solder, 3/4″ diam	76.000	Ea.	535.80	2,622	3,157.80
TOTAL			7,785.08	5,413.10	13,198.18

D2020 270	Solar, Drainback, Hot Water Systems		COST EACH		
			MAT.	INST.	TOTAL
2550	Solar, drainback, hot water, immersed heat exchanger	R235616 -60			
2560	3/8″ tubing, 3 ea. 4′ x 4′-4″ vacuum tube collectors		6,875	4,900	11,775
2580	1/2″ tubing, 4 ea 4′ x 4′-4″ vacuum tube collectors, 80 gal tank		7,375	5,300	12,675
2600	120 gal tank		7,550	5,350	12,900
2640	2 ea. 3′x7′ blk chrome collectors, 80 gal tank		5,825	5,000	10,825
2660	3 ea. 3′x7′ blk chrome collectors, 120 gal tank		7,100	5,200	12,300
2700	2 ea. 3′x7′ flat blk collectors, 120 gal tank		5,325	5,075	10,400
2720	3 ea. 3′x7′ flat blk collectors, 120 gal tank		6,075	5,225	11,300
2760	3/4″ tubing, 3 ea 3′x7′ black chrome collectors, 120 gal tank		7,775	5,425	13,200
2780	3 ea. 3′x7′ flat black absorber collectors, 120 gal tank		6,775	5,425	12,200
2800	2 ea. 4′x9′ flat blk w/plastic glazing collectors 120 gal tank		6,375	5,450	11,825
2840	1″ tubing, 4 ea. 2′x9′ plastic absorber & glazing collectors, 120 gal tank		8,100	6,150	14,250
2860	4 ea. 3′x7′ black chrome absorber collectors, 120 gal tank		10,200	6,175	16,375
2880	4 ea. 3′x7′ flat black absorber collectors, 120 gal tank		8,875	6,200	15,075

In the draindown direct-collection system, incoming domestic water is heated in the collectors. When the controller activates solar collection, domestic water is first heated as it flows through the collectors and is then pumped to storage. When conditions are no longer suitable for heat collection, the pump shuts off and the water in the loop drains down and out of the system by means of solenoid valves and properly pitched piping.

D2020 Domestic Water Distribution

System Components	QUANTITY	UNIT	COST EACH		
			MAT.	INST.	TOTAL
SYSTEM D2020 275 2760					
SOLAR, DRAINDOWN, HOT WATER, DIRECT COLLECTION					
3/4″ TUBING, THREE 3′X7′ BLACK CHROME COLLECTORS					
A, B Differential controller, 2 sensors, thermostat, solar energy system	1.000	Ea.	605	55	660
A-1 Solenoid valve, solar heating loop, brass, 3/4″ diam, 24 volts	3.000	Ea.	369	219	588
B-1 Solar energy sensor, freeze prevention	1.000	Ea.	25	20.50	45.50
C Thermometer, 2″ dial	3.000	Ea.	69	123	192
E-1 Vacuum relief valve, 3/4″ diam	1.000	Ea.	30.50	20.50	51
F-1 Air vent, automatic, 1/8″ fitting	1.000	Ea.	18.95	20.50	39.45
H Strainer, Y type, bronze body, 3/4″ IPS	1.000	Ea.	36	35.50	71.50
I Valve, gate, bronze, NRS, soldered, 3/4″ diam	2.000	Ea.	103	66	169
J Vent flashing neoprene	2.000	Ea.	27.40	66	93.40
K Circulator, solar heated liquid, 1/25 HP	1.000	Ea.	295	84.50	379.50
N Relief valve temp & press 150 psi 210°F self-closing 3/4″ IPS	1.000	Ea.	20.50	22	42.50
O Pipe covering, urethane, ultraviolet cover, 1″ wall, 3/4″ diam	20.000	L.F.	45.60	119	164.60
P Pipe covering, fiberglass, all service jacket, 1″ wall, 3/4″ diam	50.000	L.F.	53.50	238.50	292
Roof clamps for solar energy collector panels	3.000	Set	8.13	50.85	58.98
Q Collector panel solar energy blk chrome on copper, 1/8″ temp glass 3′x7′	3.000	Ea.	3,300	375	3,675
R Valve, swing check, bronze, regrinding disc, 3/4″ diam, soldered	2.000	Ea.	312	66	378
T Drain valve, brass, 3/4″ connection	2.000	Ea.	29.30	55	84.30
U Valve, water tempering, bronze, sweat connections, 3/4″ diam	1.000	Ea.	115	33	148
W-2, W Tank, water storage elec elem 2″x1/2# insul 120 gal	1.000	Ea.	1,375	470	1,845
X Valve, globe, bronze, rising stem, 3/4″ diam, soldered	1.000	Ea.	131	33	164
Copper tubing, type L, solder joints, hangers 10′ OC 3/4″ diam	20.000	L.F.	145	173	318
Copper tubing, type M, solder joints, hangers 10′ OC 3/4″ diam	70.000	L.F.	388.50	591.50	980
Sensor wire, #22-2 conductor, multistranded	.500	C.L.F.	8.05	30.75	38.80
Wrought copper fittings & solder, 3/4″ diam	76.000	Ea.	535.80	2,622	3,157.80
TOTAL			8,046.23	5,590.10	13,636.33

D2020 275	Solar, Draindown, Hot Water Systems		COST EACH		
			MAT.	INST.	TOTAL
2550	Solar, draindown, hot water				
2560	3/8″ tubing, 3 ea. 4′ x 4′-4″ vacuum tube collectors, 80 gal tank		6,725	5,350	12,075
2580	1/2″ tubing, 4 ea. 4′ x 4′-4″ vacuum tube collectors, 80 gal tank	R235616 -60	7,675	5,475	13,150
2600	120 gal tank		7,850	5,550	13,400
2640	2 ea. 3′x7′ black chrome collectors, 80 gal tank		6,125	5,175	11,300
2660	3 ea. 3′x7′ black chrome collectors, 120 gal tank		7,400	5,375	12,775
2700	2 ea. 3′x7′ flat black collectors, 120 gal tank		5,625	5,250	10,875
2720	3 ea. 3′x7′ flat black collectors, 120 gal tank		6,275	5,375	11,650
2760	3/4″ tubing, 3 ea. 3′x7′ black chrome collectors, 120 gal tank		8,050	5,600	13,650
2780	3 ea. 3′x7′ flat collectors, 120 gal tank		7,025	5,600	12,625
2800	2 ea. 4′x9′ flat black & plastic glazing collectors, 120 gal tank		6,650	5,625	12,275
2840	1″ tubing, 4 ea. 2′x9′ plastic absorber & glazing collectors, 120 gal tank		11,300	6,325	17,625
2860	4 ea. 3′x7′ black chrome absorber collectors, 120 gal tank		13,400	6,350	19,750
2880	4 ea. 3′x7′ flat black absorber collectors, 120 gal tank		12,100	6,375	18,475

In the recirculation system, (a direct-collection system), incoming domestic water is heated in the collectors. When the controller activates solar collection, domestic water is heated as it flows through the collectors and then it flows back to storage. When conditions are not suitable for heat collection, the pump shuts off and the flow of the water stops. In this type of system, water remains in the collector loop at all times. A "frost sensor" at the collector activates the circulation of warm water from storage through the collectors when protection from freezing is required.

D20 Plumbing

D2020 Domestic Water Distribution

System Components	QUANTITY	UNIT	COST EACH MAT.	COST EACH INST.	COST EACH TOTAL
SYSTEM D2020 280 2820					
SOLAR, RECIRCULATION, HOT WATER					
3/4″ TUBING, TWO 3′X7′ BLACK CHROME COLLECTORS					
A, B Differential controller 2 sensors, thermostat, for solar energy system	1.000	Ea.	605	55	660
A-1 Solenoid valve, solar heating loop, brass, 3/4″ IPS, 24 volts	2.000	Ea.	246	146	392
B-1 Solar energy sensor freeze prevention	1.000	Ea.	25	20.50	45.50
C Thermometer, 2″ dial	3.000	Ea.	69	123	192
D Drain valve, brass, 3/4″ connection	1.000	Ea.	14.65	27.50	42.15
F-1 Air vent, automatic, 1/8″ fitting	1.000	Ea.	18.95	20.50	39.45
H Strainer, Y type, bronze body, 3/4″ IPS	1.000	Ea.	36	35.50	71.50
I Valve, gate, bronze, 125 lb, soldered 3/4″ diam	3.000	Ea.	154.50	99	253.50
J Vent flashing, neoprene	2.000	Ea.	27.40	66	93.40
L Circulator, solar heated liquid, 1/20 HP	1.000	Ea.	177	99	276
N Relief valve, temp & press 150 psi 210° F self-closing 3/4″ IPS	2.000	Ea.	41	44	85
O Pipe covering, urethane, ultraviolet cover, 1″ wall, 3/4″ diam	20.000	L.F.	45.60	119	164.60
P Pipe covering, fiberglass, all service jacket, 1″ wall 3/4″ diam	50.000	L.F.	53.50	238.50	292
Q Collector panel solar energy blk chrome on copper, 1/8″ temp glass 3′x7′	2.000	Ea.	2,200	250	2,450
Roof clamps for solar energy collector panels	2.000	Set	5.42	33.90	39.32
R Valve, swing check, bronze, 125 lb, regrinding disc, soldered 3/4″ diam	2.000	Ea.	312	66	378
U Valve, water tempering, bronze, sweat connections, 3/4″ diam	1.000	Ea.	115	33	148
V Tank, water storage, w/heating element, drain, relief valve, existing	1.000	Ea.			
X Valve, globe, bronze, 125 lb, 3/4″ diam	2.000	Ea.	262	66	328
Copper tubing, type L, solder joints, hangers 10′ OC 3/4″ diam	20.000	L.F.	145	173	318
Copper tubing, type M, solder joints, hangers 10′ OC 3/4″ diam	70.000	L.F.	388.50	591.50	980
Wrought copper fittings & solder, 3/4″ diam	76.000	Ea.	535.80	2,622	3,157.80
Sensor wire, #22-2 conductor, multistranded	.500	C.L.F.	8.05	30.75	38.80
TOTAL			5,485.37	4,959.65	10,445.02

D2020 280	Solar Recirculation, Domestic Hot Water Systems		COST EACH MAT.	COST EACH INST.	COST EACH TOTAL
2550	Solar recirculation, hot water				
2560	3/8″ tubing, 3 ea. 4′ x 4′-4″ vacuum tube collectors		5,850	4,650	10,500
2580	1/2″ tubing, 4 ea. 4′ x 4′-4″ vacuum tube collectors		6,350	5,050	11,400
2640	2 ea. 3′x7′ black chrome collectors	R235616 -60	4,800	4,725	9,525
2660	3 ea. 3′x7′ black chrome collectors		5,900	4,875	10,775
2700	2 ea. 3′x7′ flat black collectors		4,125	4,750	8,875
2720	3 ea. 3′x7′ flat black collectors		4,875	4,900	9,775
2760	3/4″ tubing, 3 ea. 3′x7′ black chrome collectors		6,600	5,100	11,700
2780	3 ea. 3′x7′ flat black absorber plate collectors		5,575	5,125	10,700
2800	2 ea. 4′x9′ flat black w/plastic glazing collectors		5,175	5,150	10,325
2820	2 ea. 3′x7′ black chrome collectors		5,475	4,950	10,425
2840	1″ tubing, 4 ea. 2′x9′ black plastic absorber & glazing collectors		8,875	5,825	14,700
2860	4 ea. 3′x7′ black chrome absorber collectors		11,000	5,850	16,850
2880	4 ea. 3′x7′ flat black absorber collectors		9,675	5,875	15,550

The thermosyphon domestic hot water system, a direct collection system, operates under city water pressure and does not require pumps for system operation. An insulated water storage tank is located above the collectors. As the sun heats the collectors, warm water in them rises by means of natural convection; the colder water in the storage tank flows into the collectors by means of gravity. As long as the sun is shining the water continues to flow through the collectors and to become warmer.

To prevent freezing, the system must be drained or the collectors covered with an insulated lid when the temperature drops below 32°F.

D20 Plumbing

D2020 Domestic Water Distribution

System Components	QUANTITY	UNIT	COST EACH MAT.	COST EACH INST.	COST EACH TOTAL
SYSTEM D2020 285 0960					
SOLAR, THERMOSYPHON, WATER HEATER					
3/4″ TUBING, TWO 3′X7′ BLACK CHROME COLLECTORS					
D-1 Framing lumber, fir, 2″ x 6″ x 8′, tank cradle	.008	M.B.F.	4.68	6.96	11.64
F-1 Framing lumber, fir, 2″ x 4″ x 24′, sleepers	.016	M.B.F.	8.64	20.80	29.44
I Valve, gate, bronze, 125 lb, soldered 1/2″ diam	2.000	Ea.	90	55	145
J Vent flashing, neoprene	4.000	Ea.	54.80	132	186.80
O Pipe covering, urethane, ultraviolet cover, 1″ wall, 1/2″diam	40.000	L.F.	78.80	234	312.80
P Pipe covering fiberglass all service jacket 1″ wall 1/2″ diam	160.000	L.F.	156.80	731.20	888
Q Collector panel solar, blk chrome on copper, 3/16″ temp glass 3′-6″ x 7.5′	2.000	Ea.	1,520	264	1,784
Y Flow control valve, globe, bronze, 125#, soldered, 1/2″ diam	1.000	Ea.	97.50	27.50	125
U Valve, water tempering, bronze,sweat connections, 1/2″ diam	1.000	Ea.	93.50	27.50	121
W Tank, water storage, solar energy system, 80 Gal, 2″ x 1/2 lb insul	1.000	Ea.	1,200	410	1,610
Copper tubing type L, solder joints, hangers 10′ OC 1/2″ diam	150.000	L.F.	709.50	1,222.50	1,932
Copper tubing type M, solder joints, hangers 10′ OC 1/2″ diam	50.000	L.F.	182.50	392.50	575
Sensor wire, #22-2 gauge multistranded	.500	C.L.F.	8.05	30.75	38.80
Wrought copper fittings & solder, 1/2″ diam	75.000	Ea.	234	2,475	2,709
TOTAL			4,438.77	6,029.71	10,468.48

D2020 285	Thermosyphon, Hot Water		COST EACH MAT.	COST EACH INST.	COST EACH TOTAL
0960	Solar, thermosyphon, hot water, two collector system	R235616 -60	4,450	6,025	10,475
0970					

ATTIC FLOOR

CWS

HWS

This domestic hot water pre-heat system
includes heat exchanger with a
circulating pump, blower, air-to-water,
coil and controls, mounted in the upper
collector manifold. Heat from the hot air
coming out of the collectors is transferred
through the heat exchanger. For each
degree of DHW preheating gained, one
degree less heating is needed from the
fuel fired water heater. The system is
simple, inexpensive to operate and can
provide a substantial portion of DHW
requirements for modest additional cost.

D2020 Domestic Water Distribution

System Components	QUANTITY	UNIT	COST EACH		
			MAT.	INST.	TOTAL
SYSTEM D2020 290 2560					
SOLAR, HOT WATER, AIR TO WATER HEAT EXCHANGE					
THREE COLLECTORS, OPTICAL BLACK ON ALUMINUM, 10'X2', 80 GAL TANK					
A, B — Differential controller, 2 sensors, thermostat, solar energy system	1.000	Ea.	605	55	660
C — Thermometer, 2" dial	2.000	Ea.	46	82	128
C-1 — Heat exchanger, air to fluid, up flow 70 MBH	1.000	Ea.	380	340	720
E — Air vent, manual, for solar energy system 1/8" fitting	1.000	Ea.	3	20.50	23.50
F — Air purger	1.000	Ea.	50	55	105
G — Expansion tank	1.000	Ea.	70.50	20.50	91
H — Strainer, Y type, bronze body, 1/2" IPS	1.000	Ea.	31.50	33.50	65
I — Valve, gate, bronze, 125 lb, NRS, soldered 1/2" diam	5.000	Ea.	225	137.50	362.50
N — Relief valve, temp & pressure solar 150 psi 210°F self-closing	1.000	Ea.	20.50	22	42.50
P — Pipe covering, fiberglass, all service jacket, 1" wall, 1/2" diam	60.000	L.F.	58.80	274.20	333
Q — Collector panel solar energy, air, black on alum plate, flush mount, 10'x2'	30.000	L.F.	15,450	357	15,807
B-1, R-1 — Shutter damper for solar heater circulator	1.000	Ea.	57	95.50	152.50
B-1, R-1 — Shutter motor for solar heater circulator	1.000	Ea.	142	71.50	213.50
R — Backflow preventer, 1/2" pipe size	2.000	Ea.	264	82	346
T — Drain valve, brass, 3/4" connection	1.000	Ea.	14.65	27.50	42.15
U — Valve, water tempering, bronze, sweat connections, 1/2" diam	1.000	Ea.	93.50	27.50	121
W — Tank, water storage, solar energy system, 80 Gal, 2" x 2 lb insul	1.000	Ea.	1,200	410	1,610
V — Tank, water storage, w/heating element, drain, relief valve, existing	1.000	System			
X — Valve, globe, bronze, 125 lb, rising stem, 1/2" diam	1.000	Ea.	97.50	27.50	125
Copper tubing type M, solder joints, hangers 10' OC, 1/2" diam	50.000	L.F.	182.50	392.50	575
Copper tubing type L, solder joints, hangers 10' OC 1/2" diam	10.000	L.F.	47.30	81.50	128.80
Wrought copper fittings & solder, 1/2" diam	10.000	Ea.	31.20	330	361.20
Sensor wire, #22-2 conductor multistranded	.500	C.L.F.	8.05	30.75	38.80
Q-1, Q-2 — Ductwork, fiberglass, aluminized jacket, 1-1/2" thick, 8" diam	32.000	S.F.	159.36	203.20	362.56
Q-3 — Manifold for flush mount solar energy collector panels, air	6.000	L.F.	840	42.90	882.90
TOTAL			20,077.36	3,219.55	23,296.91

D2020 290	Solar Hot Water, Air To Water Heat Exchange		COST EACH		
			MAT.	INST.	TOTAL
2550	Solar hot water, air to water heat exchange				
2560	Three collectors, optical black on aluminum, 10' x 2', 80 Gal tank		20,100	3,225	23,325
2580	Four collectors, optical black on aluminum, 10' x 2', 80 Gal tank	R235616	25,600	3,400	29,000
2600	Four collectors, optical black on aluminum, 10' x 2', 120 Gal tank	-60	25,700	3,450	29,150

In this closed-loop indirect collection system, fluid with a low freezing temperature, such as propylene glycol, transports heat from the collectors to water storage. The transfer fluid is contained in a closed-loop consisting of collectors, supply and return piping, and a heat exchanger immersed in the storage tank. A typical two-or-three panel system contains 5 to 6 gallons of heat transfer fluid.

When the collectors become approximately 20°F warmer than the storage temperature, a controller activates the circulator. The circulator moves the fluid continuously through the collectors until the temperature difference between the collectors and storage is such that heat collection no longer occurs; at that point, the circulator shuts off. Since the heat transfer fluid has a very low freezing temperature, there is no need for it to be drained from the collectors between periods of collection.

D20 Plumbing

D2020 Domestic Water Distribution

System Components	QUANTITY	UNIT	COST EACH		
			MAT.	INST.	TOTAL
SYSTEM D2020 295 2760					
SOLAR, CLOSED LOOP, HOT WATER SYSTEM, IMMERSED HEAT EXCHANGER					
3/4" TUBING, THREE 3' X 7' BLACK CHROME COLLECTORS					
A, B Differential controller, 2 sensors, thermostat, solar energy system	1.000	Ea.	605	55	660
C Thermometer 2" dial	3.000	Ea.	69	123	192
D, T Fill & drain valves, brass, 3/4" connection	3.000	Ea.	43.95	82.50	126.45
E Air vent, manual, 1/8" fitting	1.000	Ea.	3	20.50	23.50
F Air purger	1.000	Ea.	50	55	105
G Expansion tank	1.000	Ea.	70.50	20.50	91
I Valve, gate, bronze, NRS, soldered 3/4" diam	3.000	Ea.	154.50	99	253.50
J Neoprene vent flashing	2.000	Ea.	27.40	66	93.40
K Circulator, solar heated liquid, 1/25 HP	1.000	Ea.	295	84.50	379.50
N-1, N Relief valve, temp & press 150 psi 210°F self-closing 3/4" IPS	2.000	Ea.	41	44	85
O Pipe covering, urethane ultraviolet cover, 1" wall, 3/4" diam	20.000	L.F.	45.60	119	164.60
P Pipe covering, fiberglass, all service jacket, 1" wall, 3/4" diam	50.000	L.F.	53.50	238.50	292
Roof clamps for solar energy collector panel	3.000	Set	8.13	50.85	58.98
Q Collector panel solar blk chrome on copper, 1/8" temp glass, 3'x7'	3.000	Ea.	3,300	375	3,675
R-1 Valve, swing check, bronze, regrinding disc, 3/4" diam, soldered	1.000	Ea.	156	33	189
S Pressure gauge, 60 psi, 2-1/2" dial	1.000	Ea.	25.50	20.50	46
U Valve, water tempering, bronze, sweat connections, 3/4" diam	1.000	Ea.	115	33	148
W-2, W Tank, water storage immersed heat exchr elec elem 2"x2# insul 120 Gal	1.000	Ea.	1,375	470	1,845
X Valve, globe, bronze, rising stem, 3/4" diam, soldered	1.000	Ea.	131	33	164
Copper tubing type L, solder joint, hanger 10' OC 3/4" diam	20.000	L.F.	145	173	318
Copper tubing, type M, solder joint, hanger 10' OC 3/4" diam	70.000	L.F.	388.50	591.50	980
Sensor wire, #22-2 conductor multistranded	.500	C.L.F.	8.05	30.75	38.80
Solar energy heat transfer fluid, propylene glycol, anti-freeze	6.000	Gal.	95.70	141	236.70
Wrought copper fittings & solder, 3/4" diam	76.000	Ea.	535.80	2,622	3,157.80
TOTAL			7,742.13	5,581.10	13,323.23

D2020 295	Solar, Closed Loop, Hot Water Systems		COST EACH		
			MAT.	INST.	TOTAL
2550	Solar, closed loop, hot water system, immersed heat exchanger				
2560	3/8" tubing, 3 ea. 4' x 4'-4" vacuum tube collectors, 80 gal. tank		6,925	5,075	12,000
2580	1/2" tubing, 4 ea. 4' x 4'-4" vacuum tube collectors, 80 gal. tank		7,400	5,475	12,875
2600	120 gal. tank		7,575	5,550	13,125
2640	2 ea. 3'x7' black chrome collectors, 80 gal. tank	R235616 -60	5,900	5,225	11,125
2660	120 gal. tank		6,025	5,225	11,250
2700	2 ea. 3'x7' flat black collectors, 120 gal. tank		5,350	5,250	10,600
2720	3 ea. 3'x7' flat black collectors, 120 gal. tank		6,125	5,400	11,525
2760	3/4" tubing, 3 ea. 3'x7' black chrome collectors, 120 gal. tank		7,750	5,575	13,325
2780	3 ea. 3'x7' flat black collectors, 120 gal. tank		6,725	5,600	12,325
2800	2 ea. 4'x9' flat black w/plastic glazing collectors 120 gal. tank		6,350	5,625	11,975
2840	1" tubing, 4 ea. 2'x9' plastic absorber & glazing collectors 120 gal. tank		7,825	6,275	14,100
2860	4 ea. 3'x7' black chrome collectors, 120 gal. tank		9,975	6,300	16,275
2880	4 ea. 3'x7' flat black absorber collectors, 120 gal. tank		8,625	6,325	14,950

D3010 Energy Supply

Basis for Heat Loss Estimate, Apartment Type Structures:

1. Masonry walls and flat roof are insulated. U factor is assumed at .08.
2. Window glass area taken as BOCA minimum, 1/10th of floor area. Double insulating glass with 1/4″ air space, U = .65.
3. Infiltration = 0.3 C.F. per hour per S.F. of net wall.
4. Concrete floor loss is 2 BTUH per S.F.
5. Temperature difference taken as 70°F.
6. Ventilating or makeup air has not been included and must be added if desired. Air shafts are not used.

System Components	QUANTITY	UNIT	COST EACH		
			MAT.	INST.	TOTAL
SYSTEM D3010 510 1760					
HEATING SYSTEM, FIN TUBE RADIATION, FORCED HOT WATER					
1,000 S.F. AREA, 10,000 C.F. VOLUME					
Boiler, oil fired, CI, burner, ctrls/insul/breech/pipe/fttng/valves, 109 MBH	1.000	Ea.	3,893.75	3,718.75	7,612.50
Circulating pump, CI flange connection, 1/12 HP	1.000	Ea.	380	198	578
Expansion tank, painted steel, ASME 18 Gal capacity	1.000	Ea.	700	86.50	786.50
Storage tank, steel, above ground, 275 Gal capacity w/supports	1.000	Ea.	490	242	732
Copper tubing type L, solder joint, hanger 10′ OC, 3/4″ diam	100.000	L.F.	725	865	1,590
Radiation, 3/4″ copper tube w/alum fin baseboard pkg, 7″ high	30.000	L.F.	277.50	630	907.50
Pipe covering, calcium silicate w/cover, 1′ wall, 3/4′ diam	100.000	L.F.	338	645	983
TOTAL			6,804.25	6,385.25	13,189.50
COST PER S.F.			6.80	6.39	13.19

D3010 510	Apartment Building Heating - Fin Tube Radiation	COST PER S.F.		
		MAT.	INST.	TOTAL
1740	Heating systems, fin tube radiation, forced hot water			
1760	1,000 S.F. area, 10,000 C.F. volume	6.80	6.38	13.18
1800	10,000 S.F. area, 100,000 C.F. volume	3.42	3.86	7.28
1840	20,000 S.F. area, 200,000 C.F. volume [R235000 -10]	3.89	4.32	8.21
1880	30,000 S.F. area, 300,000 C.F. volume	3.77	4.18	7.95
1890	[R235000 -20]			

D3010 Energy Supply

Fin Tube Radiator

Basis for Heat Loss Estimate, Factory or Commercial Type Structures:

1. Walls and flat roof are of lightly insulated concrete block or metal. U factor is assumed at .17.
2. Windows and doors are figured at 1-1/2 S.F. per linear foot of building perimeter. The U factor for flat single glass is 1.13.
3. Infiltration is approximately 5 C.F. per hour per S.F. of wall.
4. Concrete floor loss is 2 BTUH per S.F. of floor.
5. Temperature difference is assumed at 70°F.
6. Ventilation or makeup air has not been included and must be added if desired.

System Components	QUANTITY	UNIT	COST EACH MAT.	COST EACH INST.	COST EACH TOTAL
SYSTEM D3010 520 1960					
HEATING SYSTEM, FIN TUBE RADIATION, FORCED HOT WATER					
1,000 S.F. BLDG., ONE FLOOR					
Boiler, oil fired, CI, burner/ctrls/insul/breech/pipe/ftngs/valves, 109 MBH	1.000	Ea.	3,893.75	3,718.75	7,612.50
Expansion tank, painted steel, ASME 18 Gal capacity	1.000	Ea.	2,700	101	2,801
Storage tank, steel, above ground, 550 Gal capacity w/supports	1.000	Ea.	3,400	450	3,850
Circulating pump, CI flanged, 1/8 HP	1.000	Ea.	630	198	828
Pipe, steel, black, sch. 40, threaded, cplg & hngr 10'OC, 1-1/2" diam.	260.000	L.F.	3,185	3,861	7,046
Pipe covering, calcium silicate w/cover , 1" wall, 1-1/2" diam	260.000	L.F.	891.80	1,729	2,620.80
Radiation, steel 1-1/4" tube & 4-1/4" fin w/cover & damper, wall hung	42.000	L.F.	1,806	1,407	3,213
Rough in, steel fin tube radiation w/supply & balance valves	4.000	Set	1,300	2,960	4,260
TOTAL			17,806.55	14,424.75	32,231.30
COST PER S.F.			17.81	14.42	32.23

D3010 520	Commercial Building Heating - Fin Tube Radiation		COST PER S.F. MAT.	COST PER S.F. INST.	COST PER S.F. TOTAL
1940	Heating systems, fin tube radiation, forced hot water				
1960	1,000 S.F. bldg, one floor		17.80	14.40	32.20
2000	10,000 S.F., 100,000 C.F., total two floors		5.20	5.45	10.65
2040	100,000 S.F., 1,000,000 C.F., total three floors	R235000 -10	2.10	2.41	4.51
2080	1,000,000 S.F., 10,000,000 C.F., total five floors	R235000 -20	1.22	1.26	2.48
2090					

Unit Heater

Basis for Heat Loss Estimate, Factory or Commercial Type Structures:

1. Walls and flat roof are of lightly insulated concrete block or metal. U factor is assumed at .17.
2. Windows and doors are figured at 1-1/2 S.F. per linear foot of building perimeter. The U factor for flat single glass is 1.13.
3. Infiltration is approximately 5 C.F. per hour per S.F. of wall.
4. Concrete floor loss is 2 BTUH per S.F. of floor.
5. Temperature difference is assumed at 70°F.
6. Ventilation or makeup air has not been included and must be added if desired.

System Components	QUANTITY	UNIT	COST EACH		
			MAT.	INST.	TOTAL
SYSTEM D3010 530 1880					
HEATING SYSTEM, TERMINAL UNIT HEATERS, FORCED HOT WATER					
1,000 S.F. BLDG., ONE FLOOR					
Boiler oil fired, CI, burner/ctrls/insul/breech/pipe/ftngs/valves, 109 MBH	1.000	Ea.	3,893.75	3,718.75	7,612.50
Expansion tank, painted steel, ASME 18 Gal capacity	1.000	Ea.	2,700	101	2,801
Storage tank, steel, above ground, 550 Gal capacity w/supports	1.000	Ea.	3,400	450	3,850
Circulating pump, CI, flanged, 1/8 HP	1.000	Ea.	630	198	828
Pipe, steel, black, schedule 40, threaded, cplg & hngr 10' OC 1-1/2" diam	260.000	L.F.	3,185	3,861	7,046
Pipe covering, calcium silicate w/cover, 1" wall, 1-1/2" diam	260.000	L.F.	891.80	1,729	2,620.80
Unit heater, 1 speed propeller, horizontal, 200° EWT, 26.9 MBH	2.000	Ea.	1,150	302	1,452
Unit heater piping hookup with controls	2.000	Set	1,550	2,850	4,400
TOTAL			17,400.55	13,209.75	30,610.30
COST PER S.F.			17.40	13.21	30.61

D3010 530	Commercial Bldg. Heating - Terminal Unit Heaters		COST PER S.F.		
			MAT.	INST.	TOTAL
1860	Heating systems, terminal unit heaters, forced hot water				
1880	1,000 S.F. bldg., one floor		17.40	13.20	30.60
1920	10,000 S.F. bldg., 100,000 C.F. total two floors	R235000 -10	4.69	4.52	9.21
1960	100,000 S.F. bldg., 1,000,000 C.F. total three floors		2.11	2.21	4.32
2000	1,000,000 S.F. bldg., 10,000,000 C.F. total five floors	R235000 -20	1.48	1.42	2.90
2010					

Many styles of active solar energy systems exist. Those shown on the following page represent the majority of systems now being installed in different regions of the country.

The five active domestic hot water (DHW) systems which follow are typically specified as two or three panel systems with additional variations being the type of glazing and size of the storage tanks. Various combinations have been costed for the user's evaluation and comparison. The basic specifications from which the following systems were developed satisfy the construction detail requirements specified in the HUD Intermediate Minimum Property Standards (IMPS). If these standards are not complied with, the renewable energy system's costs could be significantly lower than shown.

To develop the system's specifications and costs it was necessary to make a number of assumptions about the systems. Certain systems are more appropriate to one climatic region than another or the systems may require modifications to be usable in particular locations. Specific instances in which the systems are not appropriate throughout the country as specified, or in which modification will be needed include the following:

- The freeze protection mechanisms provided in the DHW systems vary greatly. In harsh climates, where freeze is a major concern, a closed-loop indirect collection system may be more appropriate than a direct collection system.

- The thermosyphon water heater system described cannot be used when temperatures drop below 32°F.

- In warm climates it may be necessary to modify the systems installed to prevent overheating.

For each renewable resource (solar) system a schematic diagram and descriptive summary of the system is provided along with a list of all the components priced as part of the system. The costs were developed based on these specifications.

Considerations affecting costs which may increase or decrease beyond the estimates presented here include the following:

- Special structural qualities (allowance for earthquake, future expansion, high winds, and unusual spans or shapes);

- Isolated building site or rough terrain that would affect the transportation of personnel, material, or equipment;

- Unusual climatic conditions during the construction process;

- Substitution of other materials or system components for those used in the system specifications.

In this closed-loop indirect collection system, fluid with a low freezing temperature, propylene glycol, transports heat from the collectors to water storage. The transfer fluid is contained in a closed loop consisting of collectors, supply and return piping, and a heat exchanger immersed in the storage tank.

When the collectors become approximately 20°F warmer than the storage temperature, the controller activates the circulator. The circulator moves the fluid continuously until the temperature difference between fluid in the collectors and storage is such that the collection will no longer occur and then the circulator turns off. Since the heat transfer fluid has a very low freezing temperature, there is no need for it to be drained from the collectors between periods of collection.

D3010 Energy Supply

System Components	QUANTITY	UNIT	COST EACH		
			MAT.	INST.	TOTAL
SYSTEM D3010 650 2750					
SOLAR, CLOSED LOOP, SPACE/HOT WATER					
1" TUBING, TEN 3'X7' BLK CHROME ON COPPER ABSORBER COLLECTORS					
A, B Differential controller 2 sensors, thermostat, solar energy system	2.000	Ea.	1,210	110	1,320
C Thermometer, 2" dial	10.000	Ea.	230	410	640
C-1 Heat exchanger, solar energy system, fluid to air, up flow, 80 MBH	1.000	Ea.	510	395	905
D, T Fill & drain valves, brass, 3/4" connection	5.000	Ea.	73.25	137.50	210.75
D-1 Fan center	1.000	Ea.	129	137	266
E Air vent, manual, 1/8" fitting	1.000	Ea.	3	20.50	23.50
E-2 Thermostat, 2 stage for sensing room temperature	1.000	Ea.	177	84	261
F Air purger	2.000	Ea.	100	110	210
F-1 Controller, liquid temperature, solar energy system	1.000	Ea.	111	132	243
G Expansion tank	2.000	Ea.	141	41	182
I Valve, gate, bronze, 125 lb, soldered, 1" diam	5.000	Ea.	365	172.50	537.50
J Vent flashing, neoprene	2.000	Ea.	27.40	66	93.40
K Circulator, solar heated liquid, 1/25 HP	2.000	Ea.	590	169	759
L Circulator, solar heated liquid, 1/20 HP	1.000	Ea.	177	99	276
N Relief valve, temp & pressure 150 psi 210°F self-closing	4.000	Ea.	82	88	170
N-1 Relief valve, pressure poppet, bronze, 30 psi, 3/4" IPS	3.000	Ea.	132	70.50	202.50
O Pipe covering, urethane, ultraviolet cover, 1" wall, 1" diam	50.000	L.F.	114	297.50	411.50
P Pipe covering, fiberglass, all service jacket, 1" wall, 1" diam	60.000	L.F.	64.20	286.20	350.40
Q Collector panel solar energy blk chrome on copper 1/8" temp glass 3'x7'	10.000	Ea.	11,000	1,250	12,250
Roof clamps for solar energy collector panel	10.000	Set	27.10	169.50	196.60
R Valve, swing check, bronze, 125 lb, regrinding disc, 3/4" & 1" diam	4.000	Ea.	636	138	774
S Pressure gage, 0-60 psi, for solar energy system	2.000	Ea.	51	41	92
U Valve, water tempering, bronze, sweat connections, 3/4" diam	1.000	Ea.	115	33	148
W-2, W-1, W Tank, water storage immersed heat xchr elec elem 2"x1/2# ins 120 gal	4.000	Ea.	5,500	1,880	7,380
X Valve, globe, bronze, 125 lb, rising stem, 1" diam	3.000	Ea.	615	103.50	718.50
Y Valve, flow control	1.000	Ea.	167	30	197
Copper tubing, type M, solder joint, hanger 10' OC 1" diam	110.000	L.F.	929.50	1,034	1,963.50
Copper tubing, type L, solder joint, hanger 10' OC 3/4" diam	20.000	L.F.	145	173	318
Wrought copper fittings & solder, 3/4" & 1" diam	121.000	Ea.	2,087.25	4,961	7,048.25
Sensor, wire, #22-2 conductor, multistranded	.700	C.L.F.	11.27	43.05	54.32
Ductwork, galvanized steel, for heat exchanger	8.000	Lb.	6.16	60.80	66.96
Solar energy heat transfer fluid propylene glycol, anti-freeze	25.000	Gal.	398.75	587.50	986.25
TOTAL			25,924.88	13,330.05	39,254.93

D3010 650	Solar, Closed Loop, Space/Hot Water Systems		COST EACH		
			MAT.	INST.	TOTAL
2540	Solar, closed loop, space/hot water				
2550	1/2" tubing, 12 ea. 4'x4'4" vacuum tube collectors		23,300	12,500	35,800
2600	3/4" tubing, 12 ea. 4'x4'4" vacuum tube collectors	R235616 -60	24,700	12,800	37,500
2650	10 ea. 3' x 7' black chrome absorber collectors		24,500	12,400	36,900
2700	10 ea. 3' x 7' flat black absorber collectors		21,100	12,500	33,600
2750	1" tubing, 10 ea. 3' x 7' black chrome absorber collectors		25,900	13,300	39,200
2800	10 ea. 3' x 7' flat black absorber collectors		22,700	13,400	36,100
2850	6 ea. 4' x 9' flat black w/plastic glazing collectors		20,700	13,300	34,000
2900	12 ea. 2' x 9' plastic absorber and glazing collectors		21,800	13,600	35,400

This draindown pool system uses a differential thermostat similar to those used in solar domestic hot water and space heating applications. To heat the pool, the pool water passes through the conventional pump-filter loop and then flows through the collectors. When collection is not possible, or when the pool temperature is reached, all water drains from the solar loop back to the pool through the existing piping. The modes are controlled by solenoid valves or other automatic valves in conjunction with a vacuum breaker relief valve, which facilitates draindown.

D3010 Energy Supply

System Components	QUANTITY	UNIT	COST EACH		
			MAT.	INST.	TOTAL
SYSTEM D3010 660 2640					
SOLAR SWIMMING POOL HEATER, ROOF MOUNTED COLLECTORS					
TEN 4′ X 10′ FULLY WETTED UNGLAZED PLASTIC ABSORBERS					
A Differential thermostat/controller, 110V, adj pool pump system	1.000	Ea.	320	330	650
A-1 Solenoid valve, PVC, normally 1 open 1 closed (included)	2.000	Ea.			
B Sensor, thermistor type (included)	2.000	Ea.			
E-1 Valve, vacuum relief	1.000	Ea.	30.50	20.50	51
Q Collector panel, solar energy, plastic, liquid full wetted, 4′ x 10′	10.000	Ea.	2,570	2,370	4,940
R Valve, ball check, PVC, socket, 1-1/2″ diam	1.000	Ea.	108	33	141
Z Valve, ball, PVC, socket, 1-1/2″ diam	3.000	Ea.	202.50	99	301.50
Pipe, PVC, sch 40, 1-1/2″ diam	80.000	L.F.	404	1,464	1,868
Pipe fittings, PVC sch 40, socket joint, 1-1/2″ diam	10.000	Ea.	19.40	330	349.40
Sensor wire, #22-2 conductor, multistranded	.500	C.L.F.	8.05	30.75	38.80
Roof clamps for solar energy collector panels	10.000	Set	27.10	169.50	196.60
Roof strap, teflon for solar energy collector panels	26.000	L.F.	572	83.46	655.46
TOTAL			4,261.55	4,930.21	9,191.76

D3010 660	Solar Swimming Pool Heater Systems		COST EACH		
			MAT.	INST.	TOTAL
2530	Solar swimming pool heater systems, roof mounted collectors				
2540	10 ea. 3′x7′ black chrome absorber, 1/8″ temp. glass		12,700	3,800	16,500
2560	10 ea. 4′x8′ black chrome absorber, 3/16″ temp. glass	R235616 -60	14,200	4,550	18,750
2580	10 ea. 3′8″x6′ flat black absorber, 3/16″ temp. glass		9,300	3,875	13,175
2600	10 ea. 4′x9′ flat black absorber, plastic glazing		11,200	4,725	15,925
2620	10 ea. 2′x9′ rubber absorber, plastic glazing		13,000	5,100	18,100
2640	10 ea. 4′x10′ fully wetted unglazed plastic absorber		4,250	4,925	9,175
2660	Ground mounted collectors				
2680	10 ea. 3′x7′ black chrome absorber, 1/8″ temp. glass		12,800	4,275	17,075
2700	10 ea. 4′x8′ black chrome absorber, 3/16″ temp. glass		14,300	5,000	19,300
2720	10 ea. 3′8″x6′ flat blk absorber, 3/16″ temp. glass		9,425	4,325	13,750
2740	10 ea. 4′x9′ flat blk absorber, plastic glazing		11,300	5,175	16,475
2760	10 ea. 2′x9′ rubber absorber, plastic glazing		13,100	5,400	18,500
2780	10 ea. 4′x10′ fully wetted unglazed plastic absorber		4,400	5,375	9,775

The complete Solar Air Heating System provides maximum savings of conventional fuel with both space heating and year-round domestic hot water heating. It allows for the home air conditioning to operate simultaneously and independently from the solar domestic water heating in summer. The system's modes of operation are:

Mode 1: The building is heated directly from the collectors with air circulated by the Solar Air Mover.

Mode 2: When heat is not needed in the building, the dampers change within the air mover to circulate the air from the collectors to the rock storage bin.

Mode 3: When heat is not available from the collector array and is available in rock storage, the air mover draws heated air from rock storage and directs it into the building. When heat is not available from the collectors or the rock storage bin, the auxiliary heating unit will provide heat for the building. The size of the collector array is typically 25% the size of the main floor area.

D3010 Energy Supply

System Components	QUANTITY	UNIT	COST EACH		
			MAT.	INST.	TOTAL
SYSTEM D3010 675 1210					
SOLAR, SPACE/HOT WATER, AIR TO WATER HEAT EXCHANGE					
A, B Differential controller 2 sensors thermos., solar energy sys liquid loop	1.000	Ea.	605	55	660
A-1, B Differential controller 2 sensors 6 station solar energy sys air loop	1.000	Ea.	251	220	471
B-1 Solar energy sensor, freeze prevention	1.000	Ea.	25	20.50	45.50
C Thermometer for solar energy system, 2" dial	2.000	Ea.	46	82	128
C-1 Heat exchanger, solar energy system, air to fluid, up flow, 70 MBH	1.000	Ea.	380	340	720
D Drain valve, brass, 3/4" connection	2.000	Ea.	29.30	55	84.30
E Air vent, manual, for solar energy system 1/8" fitting	1.000	Ea.	3	20.50	23.50
E-1 Thermostat, 2 stage for sensing room temperature	1.000	Ea.	177	84	261
F Air purger	1.000	Ea.	50	55	105
G Expansion tank, for solar energy system	1.000	Ea.	70.50	20.50	91
I Valve, gate, bronze, 125 lb, NRS, soldered 3/4" diam	2.000	Ea.	103	66	169
K Circulator, solar heated liquid, 1/25 HP	1.000	Ea.	295	84.50	379.50
N Relief valve temp & press 150 psi 210°F self-closing, 3/4" IPS	1.000	Ea.	20.50	22	42.50
N-1 Relief valve, pressure, poppet, bronze, 30 psi, 3/4" IPS	1.000	Ea.	44	23.50	67.50
P Pipe covering, fiberglass, all service jacket, 1" wall, 3/4" diam	60.000	L.F.	64.20	286.20	350.40
Q-3 Manifold for flush mount solar energy collector panels	20.000	L.F.	2,800	143	2,943
Q Collector panel solar energy, air, black on alum. plate, flush mount 10'x2'	100.000	L.F.	51,500	1,190	52,690
R Valve, swing check, bronze, 125 lb, regrinding disc, 3/4" diam	2.000	Ea.	312	66	378
S Pressure gage, 2" dial, for solar energy system	1.000	Ea.	25.50	20.50	46
U Valve, water tempering, bronze, sweat connections, 3/4" diam	1.000	Ea.	115	33	148
W-2, W Tank, water storage, solar, elec element 2"x1/2# insul, 80 Gal	1.000	Ea.	1,200	410	1,610
X Valve, globe, bronze, 125 lb, soldered, 3/4" diam	1.000	Ea.	131	33	164
Copper tubing type L, solder joints, hangers 10' OC 3/4" diam	10.000	L.F.	72.50	86.50	159
Copper tubing type M, solder joints, hangers 10' OC 3/4" diam	60.000	L.F.	333	507	840
Wrought copper fittings & solder, 3/4" diam	26.000	Ea.	183.30	897	1,080.30
Sensor wire, #22-2 conductor multistranded	1.200	C.L.F.	19.32	73.80	93.12
Q-1 Duct work, rigid fiberglass, rectangular	400.000	S.F.	340	2,040	2,380
12" x 10"	8.000	Ea.	208	380	588
R-2 Shutter/damper for solar heater circulator	9.000	Ea.	513	859.50	1,372.50
K-1 Shutter motor for solar heater circulator blower	9.000	Ea.	1,278	643.50	1,921.50
K-1 Fan, solar energy heated air circulator, space & DHW system	1.000	Ea.	1,700	2,300	4,000
Z-1 Tank, solar energy air storage, 6'-3"H 7'x7' = 306 CF/2000 Gal	1.000	Ea.	13,500	1,475	14,975
Z-2 Crushed stone 1-1/2"	11.000	C.Y.	379.50	78.65	458.15
C-2 Thermometer, remote probe, 2" dial	1.000	Ea.	35	82.50	117.50
R-1 Solenoid valve	1.000	Ea.	123	73	196
V, R-4, R-3 Furnace, supply diffusers, return grilles, existing	1.000	Ea.	13,500	1,475	14,975
TOTAL			90,431.62	14,301.65	104,733.27

D3010 675	Air To Water Heat Exchange		COST EACH		
			MAT.	INST.	TOTAL
1210	Solar, air to water heat exchange, for space/hot water heating	R235616	90,500	14,300	104,800
1220		-60			

D3020 Heat Generating Systems

Boiler

Baseboard Radiation

**Small Electric Boiler
System Considerations:**
1. Terminal units are fin tube baseboard radiation rated at 720 BTU/hr with 200° water temperature or 820 BTU/hr steam.
2. Primary use being for residential or smaller supplementary areas, the floor levels are based on 7-1/2' ceiling heights.
3. All distribution piping is copper for boilers through 205 MBH. All piping for larger systems is steel pipe.

System Components	QUANTITY	UNIT	COST EACH		
			MAT.	INST.	TOTAL
SYSTEM D3020 102 1120					
SMALL HEATING SYSTEM, HYDRONIC, ELECTRIC BOILER					
1,480 S.F., 61 MBH, STEAM, 1 FLOOR					
Boiler, electric steam, std cntrls, trim, ftngs and valves, 18 KW, 61.4 MBH	1.000	Ea.	4,702.50	1,677.50	6,380
Copper tubing type L, solder joint, hanger 10'OC, 1-1/4" diam	160.000	L.F.	2,368	1,816	4,184
Radiation, 3/4" copper tube w/alum fin baseboard pkg 7" high	60.000	L.F.	555	1,260	1,815
Rough in baseboard panel or fin tube with valves & traps	10.000	Set	3,450	6,350	9,800
Pipe covering, calcium silicate w/cover, 2" wall 1-1/4" diam	160.000	L.F.	540.80	1,064	1,604.80
Low water cut-off, quick hookup, in gage glass tappings	1.000	Ea.	252	42	294
TOTAL			11,868.30	12,209.50	24,077.80
COST PER S.F.			8.02	8.25	16.27

D3020 102	Small Heating Systems, Hydronic, Electric Boilers		COST PER S.F.		
			MAT.	INST.	TOTAL
1100	Small heating systems, hydronic, electric boilers				
1120	Steam, 1 floor, 1480 S.F., 61 M.B.H.		8.04	8.24	16.28
1160	3,000 S.F., 123 M.B.H.	R235000 -10	6.35	7.25	13.60
1200	5,000 S.F., 205 M.B.H.		5.65	6.70	12.35
1240	2 floors, 12,400 S.F., 512 M.B.H.	R235000 -20	4.64	6.65	11.29
1280	3 floors, 24,800 S.F., 1023 M.B.H.		4.82	6.55	11.37
1320	34,750 S.F., 1,433 M.B.H.	R235000 -30	4.45	6.40	10.85
1360	Hot water, 1 floor, 1,000 S.F., 41 M.B.H.		10.90	4.58	15.48
1400	2,500 S.F., 103 M.B.H.		9.20	8.25	17.45
1440	2 floors, 4,850 S.F., 205 M.B.H.		9.70	9.90	19.60
1480	3 floors, 9,700 S.F., 410 M.B.H.		10.90	10.20	21.10

D3020 Heat Generating Systems

Boiler

Unit Heater

Large Electric Boiler System Considerations:

1. Terminal units are all unit heaters of the same size. Quantities are varied to accommodate total requirements.
2. All air is circulated through the heaters a minimum of three times per hour.
3. As the capacities are adequate for commercial use, floor levels are based on 10′ ceiling heights.
4. All distribution piping is black steel pipe.

System Components	QUANTITY	UNIT	COST EACH MAT.	COST EACH INST.	COST EACH TOTAL
SYSTEM D3020 104 1240					
LARGE HEATING SYSTEM, HYDRONIC, ELECTRIC BOILER					
9,280 S.F., 135 KW, 461 MBH, 1 FLOOR					
Boiler, electric hot water, std ctrls, trim, ftngs, valves, 135 KW, 461 MBH	1.000	Ea.	11,175	3,637.50	14,812.50
Expansion tank, painted steel, 60 Gal capacity ASME	1.000	Ea.	4,025	202	4,227
Circulating pump, CI, close cpld, 50 GPM, 2 HP, 2″ pipe conn	1.000	Ea.	2,700	395	3,095
Unit heater, 1 speed propeller, horizontal, 200° EWT, 72.7 MBH	7.000	Ea.	5,845	1,540	7,385
Unit heater piping hookup with controls	7.000	Set	5,425	9,975	15,400
Pipe, steel, black, schedule 40, welded, 2-1/2″ diam	380.000	L.F.	8,740	9,826.80	18,566.80
Pipe covering, calcium silicate w/cover, 1″ wall, 2-1/2″ diam	380.000	L.F.	1,588.40	2,603	4,191.40
TOTAL			39,498.40	28,179.30	67,677.70
COST PER S.F.			4.26	3.04	7.30

D3020 104	Large Heating Systems, Hydronic, Electric Boilers		COST PER S.F. MAT.	COST PER S.F. INST.	COST PER S.F. TOTAL
1230	Large heating systems, hydronic, electric boilers				
1240	9,280 S.F., 135 K.W., 461 M.B.H., 1 floor		4.26	3.04	7.30
1280	14,900 S.F., 240 K.W., 820 M.B.H., 2 floors	R235000 -10	5.75	4.89	10.64
1320	18,600 S.F., 296 K.W., 1,010 M.B.H., 3 floors		5.90	5.35	11.25
1360	26,100 S.F., 420 K.W., 1,432 M.B.H., 4 floors	R235000 -20	5.80	5.20	11
1400	39,100 S.F., 666 K.W., 2,273 M.B.H., 4 floors		4.90	4.37	9.27
1440	57,700 S.F., 900 K.W., 3,071 M.B.H., 5 floors	R235000 -30	4.89	4.29	9.18
1480	111,700 S.F., 1,800 K.W., 6,148 M.B.H., 6 floors		4.35	3.72	8.07
1520	149,000 S.F., 2,400 K.W., 8,191 M.B.H., 8 floors		4.34	3.70	8.04
1560	223,300 S.F., 3,600 K.W., 12,283 M.B.H., 14 floors		4.73	4.19	8.92

D30 HVAC

D3020 Heat Generating Systems

Unit Heater

Fossil Fuel Boiler System Considerations:

1. Terminal units are horizontal unit heaters. Quantities are varied to accommodate total heat loss per building.
2. Unit heater selection was determined by their capacity to circulate the building volume a minimum of three times per hour in addition to the BTU output.
3. Systems shown are forced hot water. Steam boilers cost slightly more than hot water boilers. However, this is compensated for by the smaller size or fewer terminal units required with steam.
4. Floor levels are based on 10' story heights.
5. MBH requirements are gross boiler output.

System Components	QUANTITY	UNIT	COST EACH		
			MAT.	INST.	TOTAL
SYSTEM D3020 108 1280					
HEATING SYSTEM, HYDRONIC, FOSSIL FUEL, TERMINAL UNIT HEATERS					
CAST IRON BOILER, GAS, 80 MBH, 1,070 S.F. BUILDING					
Boiler, gas, hot water, CI, burner, controls, insulation, breeching, 80 MBH	1.000	Ea.	2,073.75	1,837.50	3,911.25
Pipe, steel, black, schedule 40, threaded, cplg & hngr 10'OC, 2" diam	200.000	L.F.	3,280	3,710	6,990
Unit heater, 1 speed propeller, horizontal, 200° EWT, 72.7 MBH	2.000	Ea.	1,670	440	2,110
Unit heater piping hookup with controls	2.000	Set	1,550	2,850	4,400
Expansion tank, painted steel, ASME, 18 Gal capacity	1.000	Ea.	2,700	101	2,801
Circulating pump, CI, flange connection, 1/12 HP	1.000	Ea.	380	198	578
Pipe covering, calcium silicate w/cover, 1" wall, 2" diam	200.000	L.F.	788	1,370	2,158
TOTAL			12,441.75	10,506.50	22,948.25
COST PER S.F.			11.63	9.82	21.45

D3020 108	Heating Systems, Unit Heaters		COST PER S.F.		
			MAT.	INST.	TOTAL
1260	Heating systems, hydronic, fossil fuel, terminal unit heaters,				
1280	Cast iron boiler, gas, 80 M.B.H., 1,070 S.F. bldg.		11.59	9.81	21.40
1320	163 M.B.H., 2,140 S.F. bldg.	R235000 -10	7.65	6.65	14.30
1360	544 M.B.H., 7,250 S.F. bldg.		5.70	4.65	10.35
1400	1,088 M.B.H., 14,500 S.F. bldg.	R235000 -20	4.97	4.39	9.36
1440	3,264 M.B.H., 43,500 S.F. bldg.		3.87	3.35	7.22
1480	5,032 M.B.H., 67,100 S.F. bldg.	R235000 -30	4.80	3.44	8.24
1520	Oil, 109 M.B.H., 1,420 S.F. bldg.		12	8.75	20.75
1560	235 M.B.H., 3,150 S.F. bldg.		7.90	6.15	14.05
1600	940 M.B.H., 12,500 S.F. bldg.		5.60	4.05	9.65
1640	1,600 M.B.H., 21,300 S.F. bldg.		5.25	3.89	9.14
1680	2,480 M.B.H., 33,100 S.F. bldg.		5.25	3.49	8.74
1720	3,350 M.B.H., 44,500 S.F. bldg.		4.90	3.57	8.47
1760	Coal, 148 M.B.H., 1,975 S.F. bldg.		10.40	5.70	16.10
1800	300 M.B.H., 4,000 S.F. bldg.		7.95	4.47	12.42
1840	2,360 M.B.H., 31,500 S.F. bldg.		5.70	3.56	9.26

D3020   Heat Generating Systems

Fin Tube Radiator

Fossil Fuel Boiler System Considerations:

1. Terminal units are commercial steel fin tube radiation. Quantities are varied to accommodate total heat loss per building.
2. Systems shown are forced hot water. Steam boilers cost slightly more than hot water boilers. However, this is compensated for by the smaller size or fewer terminal units required with steam.
3. Floor levels are based on 10' story heights.
4. MBH requirements are gross boiler output.

System Components	QUANTITY	UNIT	COST EACH		
			MAT.	INST.	TOTAL
SYSTEM D3020 110 3240					
HEATING SYSTEM, HYDRONIC, FOSSIL FUEL, FIN TUBE RADIATION					
CAST IRON BOILER, GAS, 80 MBH, 1,070 S.F. BLDG.					
Boiler, gas, hot water, CI, burner, controls, insulation, breeching, 80 MBH	1.000	Ea.	2,073.75	1,837.50	3,911.25
Pipe, steel, black, schedule 40, threaded, 2" diam	200.000	L.F.	3,280	3,710	6,990
Radiation, steel 1-1/4" tube & 4-1/4" fin w/cover & damper, wall hung	80.000	L.F.	3,440	2,680	6,120
Rough-in, wall hung steel fin radiation with supply & balance valves	8.000	Set	2,600	5,920	8,520
Expansion tank, painted steel, ASME, 18 Gal capacity	1.000	Ea.	2,700	101	2,801
Circulating pump, CI flanged, 1/12 HP	1.000	Ea.	380	198	578
Pipe covering, calcium silicate w/cover, 1" wall, 2" diam	200.000	L.F.	788	1,370	2,158
TOTAL			15,261.75	15,816.50	31,078.25
COST PER S.F.			14.26	14.78	29.04

D3020 110	Heating System, Fin Tube Radiation		COST PER S.F.		
			MAT.	INST.	TOTAL
3230	Heating systems, hydronic, fossil fuel, fin tube radiation				
3240	Cast iron boiler, gas, 80 MBH, 1,070 S.F. bldg.		14.30	14.77	29.07
3280	169 M.B.H., 2,140 S.F. bldg.	R235000 -10	8.90	9.35	18.25
3320	544 M.B.H., 7,250 S.F. bldg.		7.55	7.95	15.50
3360	1,088 M.B.H., 14,500 S.F. bldg.	R235000 -20	6.95	7.80	14.75
3400	3,264 M.B.H., 43,500 S.F. bldg.		6	6.90	12.90
3440	5,032 M.B.H., 67,100 S.F. bldg.	R235000 -30	6.95	7	13.95
3480	Oil, 109 M.B.H., 1,420 S.F. bldg.		16.50	16.15	32.65
3520	235 M.B.H., 3,150 S.F. bldg.		9.75	9.40	19.15
3560	940 M.B.H., 12,500 S.F. bldg.		7.65	7.50	15.15
3600	1,600 M.B.H., 21,300 S.F. bldg.		7.40	7.45	14.85
3640	2,480 M.B.H., 33,100 S.F. bldg.		7.40	7.10	14.50
3680	3,350 M.B.H., 44,500 S.F. bldg.		7.05	7.15	14.20
3720	Coal, 148 M.B.H., 1,975 S.F. bldg.		12.25	8.95	21.20
3760	300 M.B.H., 4,000 S.F. bldg.		9.75	7.65	17.40
3800	2,360 M.B.H., 31,500 S.F. bldg.		7.80	7.10	14.90
4080	Steel boiler, oil, 97 M.B.H., 1,300 S.F. bldg.		13.70	13.30	27
4120	315 M.B.H., 4,550 S.F. bldg.		6.70	6.75	13.45
4160	525 M.B.H., 7,000 S.F. bldg.		9	7.70	16.70
4200	1,050 M.B.H., 14,000 S.F. bldg.		8.05	7.70	15.75
4240	2,310 M.B.H., 30,800 S.F. bldg.		7.75	7.15	14.90
4280	3,150 M.B.H., 42,000 S.F. bldg.		7.55	7.25	14.80

D3020 Heat Generating Systems

Electric Boiler, Hot Water

System Components	QUANTITY	UNIT	COST EACH		
			MAT.	INST.	TOTAL
SYSTEM D3020 126 1010					
BOILER, ELECTRIC, HOT WATER, 15 kW, 52 MBH					
Boilers, electric, ASME, hot water, 15 KW, 52 MBH	1.000	Ea.	4,325	1,400	5,725
Pipe, black steel, Sch 40, threaded, W/coupling & hangers, 10' OC, 3/4" dia	10.000	L.F.	64.98	124.20	189.18
Pipe, black steel, Sch 40, threaded, W/coupling & hangers, 10' OC, 1" dia	20.000	L.F.	178.45	267.68	446.13
Elbow, 90°, black, straight, 3/4" dia.	6.000	Ea.	23.04	282	305.04
Elbow, 90°, black, straight, 1" dia.	6.000	Ea.	39.90	303	342.90
Tee, black, straight, 3/4" dia.	1.000	Ea.	6.10	73	79.10
Tee, black, straight, 1" dia.	2.000	Ea.	20.90	165	185.90
Tee, black, reducing, 1" dia.	2.000	Ea.	33.50	165	198.50
Union, black with brass seat, 3/4" dia.	1.000	Ea.	16.15	50.50	66.65
Union, black with brass seat, 1" dia.	2.000	Ea.	42	110	152
Pipe nipples, 3/4" diam.	3.000	Ea.	8.48	16.20	24.68
Pipe nipples, 1" diam.	3.000	Ea.	12.45	18.68	31.13
Valves, bronze, gate, N.R.S., threaded, class 150, 3/4" size	2.000	Ea.	150	66	216
Valves, bronze, gate, N.R.S., threaded, class 150, 1" size	2.000	Ea.	190	69	259
Thermometer, stem type, 9" case, 8" stem, 3/4" NPT	1.000	Ea.	372	48	420
Tank, steel, liquid expansion, ASME, painted, 15 gallon capacity	1.000	Ea.	655	71	726
Pump, circulating, bronze, flange connection, 3/4" to 1-1/2" size, 1/8 HP	1.000	Ea.	1,000	198	1,198
Insulation, fiberglass pipe covering, 1" wall, 1" IPS	20.000	L.F.	22.80	99.60	122.40
TOTAL			7,160.75	3,526.86	10,687.61

D3020 126	Electric Boiler, Hot Water	COST EACH		
		MAT.	INST.	TOTAL
1010	Boiler, electric, hot water, 15 kW, 52 MBH	7,150	3,525	10,675
1020	30 kW, 103 MBH	8,025	3,725	11,750
1030	60 kW, 205 MBH	8,225	3,850	12,075
1040	120 kW, 410 MBH	10,900	4,625	15,525
1050	150 kW, 510 MBH	16,800	8,775	25,575
1060	210 kW, 716 MBH	19,400	9,675	29,075
1070	296 kW, 1010 MBH	24,700	9,975	34,675
1080	444 kW, 1515 MBH	29,800	13,500	43,300
1090	666 kW, 2273 MBH	35,500	14,600	50,100
1100	900 kW, 3071 MBH	44,200	17,000	61,200
1110	1320 kW, 4505 MBH	52,500	17,800	70,300
1120	2100 kW, 7167 MBH	78,500	21,700	100,200
1130	2610 kW, 8905 MBH	97,000	26,000	123,000
1140	3600 kW, 12,283 MBH	118,000	31,200	149,200

D30 HVAC

D3020 Heat Generating Systems

D3020 128	Electric Boiler, Steam	COST EACH		
		MAT.	INST.	TOTAL
1010	Boiler, electric, steam, 18 kW, 61.4 MBH	5,500	3,400	8,900
1020	36 kW, 123 MBH	6,900	3,575	10,475
1030	60 kW, 205 MBH	14,300	7,300	21,600
1040	120 kW, 409 MBH	16,900	8,025	24,925
1050	150 kW, 512 MBH	20,500	12,000	32,500
1060	210 kW, 716 MBH	26,300	12,900	39,200
1070	300 kW, 1023 MBH	30,700	14,100	44,800
1080	510 kW, 1740 MBH	38,400	18,500	56,900
1090	720 kW, 2456 MBH	43,200	19,300	62,500
1100	1080 kW, 3685 MBH	50,500	23,000	73,500
1110	1260 kW, 4300 MBH	53,500	24,600	78,100
1120	1620 kW, 5527 MBH	56,000	27,700	83,700
1130	2070 kW, 7063 MBH	74,000	29,100	103,100
1140	2340 kW, 7984 MBH	96,500	33,000	129,500

Cast Iron Boiler, Hot Water, Gas Fired

System Components	QUANTITY	UNIT	COST EACH		
			MAT.	INST.	TOTAL
SYSTEM D3020 130 1010					
BOILER, CAST IRON, GAS, HOT WATER, 100 MBH					
Boilers, gas fired, std controls, CI, insulated, HW, gross output 100 MBH	1.000	Ea.	2,250	1,900	4,150
Pipe, black steel, Sch 40, threaded, W/coupling & hangers, 10' OC, 3/4" dia	20.000	L.F.	127.13	243	370.13
Pipe, black steel, Sch 40, threaded, W/coupling & hangers, 10' OC, 1" dia.	20.000	L.F.	178.45	267.68	446.13
Elbow, 90°, black, straight, 3/4" dia.	9.000	Ea.	34.56	423	457.56
Elbow, 90°, black, straight, 1" dia.	6.000	Ea.	39.90	303	342.90
Tee, black, straight, 3/4" dia.	2.000	Ea.	12.20	146	158.20
Tee, black, straight, 1" dia.	2.000	Ea.	20.90	165	185.90
Tee, black, reducing, 1" dia.	2.000	Ea.	33.50	165	198.50
Pipe cap, black, 3/4" dia.	1.000	Ea.	4.36	20.50	24.86
Union, black with brass seat, 3/4" dia.	2.000	Ea.	32.30	101	133.30
Union, black with brass seat, 1" dia.	2.000	Ea.	42	110	152
Pipe nipples, black, 3/4" dia.	5.000	Ea.	14.13	27	41.13
Pipe nipples, black, 1" dia.	3.000	Ea.	12.45	18.68	31.13
Valves, bronze, gate, N.R.S., threaded, class 150, 3/4" size	2.000	Ea.	150	66	216
Valves, bronze, gate, N.R.S., threaded, class 150, 1" size	2.000	Ea.	190	69	259
Gas cock, brass, 3/4" size	1.000	Ea.	17.05	30	47.05
Thermometer, stem type, 9" case, 8" stem, 3/4" NPT	2.000	Ea.	372	48	420
Tank, steel, liquid expansion, ASME, painted, 15 gallon capacity	1.000	Ea.	655	71	726
Pump, circulating, bronze, flange connection, 3/4" to 1-1/2" size, 1/8 HP	1.000	Ea.	1,000	198	1,198
Vent chimney, all fuel, pressure tight, double wall, SS, 6" dia.	20.000	L.F.	1,180	381	1,561
Vent chimney, elbow, 90° fixed, 6" dia.	2.000	Ea.	860	76	936
Vent chimney, Tee, 6" dia.	2.000	Ea.	504	95	599
Vent chimney, ventilated roof thimble, 6" dia.	1.000	Ea.	263	44	307
Vent chimney, flat roof flashing, 6" dia.	1.000	Ea.	113	38	151
Vent chimney, stack cap, 6" diameter	1.000	Ea.	310	25	335
Insulation, fiberglass pipe covering, 1" wall, 1" IPS	20.000	L.F.	22.80	99.60	122.40
TOTAL			8,438.73	5,130.46	13,569.19

D3020 130	Boiler, Cast Iron, Hot Water, Gas	COST EACH		
		MAT.	INST.	TOTAL
1010	Boiler, cast iron, gas, hot water, 100 MBH	8,450	5,125	13,575
1020	200 MBH	9,650	5,850	15,500
1030	320 MBH	10,100	6,400	16,500
1040	440 MBH	13,600	8,250	21,850
1050	544 MBH	22,400	12,800	35,200
1060	765 MBH	27,000	13,800	40,800

D3020 Heat Generating Systems

D3020 130	Boiler, Cast Iron, Hot Water, Gas	COST EACH		
		MAT.	INST.	TOTAL
1070	1088 MBH	29,900	14,700	44,600
1080	1530 MBH	35,000	19,500	54,500
1090	2312 MBH	40,800	23,000	63,800
1100	2856 MBH	48,100	24,800	72,900
1110	3808 MBH	53,500	29,000	82,500
1120	4720 MBH	107,000	32,600	139,600
1130	6100 MBH	116,500	36,200	152,700
1140	6970 MBH	124,500	44,800	169,300

D3020 134	Boiler, Cast Iron, Steam, Gas	COST EACH		
		MAT.	INST.	TOTAL
1010	Boiler, cast iron, gas, steam, 100 MBH	7,075	4,975	12,050
1020	200 MBH	14,100	9,350	23,450
1030	320 MBH	16,000	10,500	26,500
1040	544 MBH	23,800	16,300	40,100
1050	765 MBH	27,100	17,000	44,100
1060	1275 MBH	32,000	18,700	50,700
1070	2675 MBH	41,300	27,300	68,600
1080	3570 MBH	49,000	30,600	79,600
1090	4720 MBH	102,500	32,700	135,200
1100	6100 MBH	114,500	38,100	152,600
1110	6970 MBH	122,500	44,600	167,100

D3020 136	Boiler, Cast Iron, Hot Water, Gas/Oil	COST EACH		
		MAT.	INST.	TOTAL
1010	Boiler, cast iron, gas & oil, hot water, 584 MBH	27,300	14,200	41,500
1020	876 MBH	34,700	15,300	50,000
1030	1168 MBH	38,500	17,200	55,700
1040	1460 MBH	45,500	20,800	66,300
1050	2044 MBH	48,400	21,500	69,900
1060	2628 MBH	62,000	26,000	88,000
1070	3210 MBH	70,500	28,000	98,500
1080	3796 MBH	76,000	28,900	104,900
1090	4672 MBH	88,000	30,300	118,300
1100	5256 MBH	101,000	36,700	137,700
1110	6000 MBH	128,000	37,400	165,400
1120	9800 MBH	159,500	64,000	223,500
1130	12,200 MBH	199,000	75,000	274,000
1140	13,500 MBH	216,000	79,500	295,500

D3020 138	Boiler, Cast Iron, Steam, Gas/Oil	COST EACH		
		MAT.	INST.	TOTAL
1010	Boiler, cast iron, gas & oil, steam, 810 MBH	30,800	18,500	49,300
1020	1360 MBH	35,700	19,700	55,400
1030	2040 MBH	44,000	25,300	69,300
1040	2700 MBH	47,300	28,200	75,500
1050	3270 MBH	55,000	31,500	86,500
1060	3770 MBH	90,000	32,100	122,100
1070	4650 MBH	100,000	36,500	136,500
1080	5520 MBH	115,500	38,500	154,000
1090	6100 MBH	117,500	40,500	158,000
1100	6970 MBH	128,000	49,500	177,500

D3020 Heat Generating Systems

Flow ↓   ↑ Flow

Gate Valve →

Y Strainer →

← Combination Valve

Pressure Gauge →

← Pressure Gauge

Expansion Joint →

← Expansion Joint

Base Mounted End—Suction Pump

System Components	QUANTITY	UNIT	COST EACH		
			MAT.	INST.	TOTAL
SYSTEM D3020 330 1010					
PUMP, BASE MTD. WITH MOTOR, END-SUCTION, 2-1/2″ SIZE, 3 HP, TO 150 GPM					
Pump, circulating, CI, base mounted, 2-1/2″ size, 3 HP, to 150 GPM	1.000	Ea.	7,850	660	8,510
Pipe, black steel, Sch. 40, on yoke & roll hangers, 10′ O.C., 2-1/2″ dia	12.000	L.F.	276	310.32	586.32
Elbow, 90°, weld joint, steel, 2-1/2″ pipe size	1.000	Ea.	30.50	153.10	183.60
Flange, weld neck, 150 LB, 2-1/2″ pipe size	8.000	Ea.	280	612.32	892.32
Valve, iron body, gate, 125 lb., N.R.S., flanged, 2-1/2″ size	1.000	Ea.	685	237	922
Strainer, Y type, iron body, flanged, 125 lb., 2-1/2″ pipe size	1.000	Ea.	121	242	363
Multipurpose valve, CI body, 2″ size	1.000	Ea.	480	84	564
Expansion joint, flanged spool, 6″ F to F, 2-1/2″ dia	2.000	Ea.	588	195	783
T-O-L, weld joint, socket, 1/4″ pipe size, nozzle	2.000	Ea.	15.60	106.54	122.14
T-O-L, weld joint, socket, 1/2″ pipe size, nozzle	2.000	Ea.	15.60	111.70	127.30
Control gauges, pressure or vacuum, 3-1/2″ diameter dial	2.000	Ea.	79	42	121
Pressure/temperature relief plug, 316 SS, 3/4″ OD, 7-1/2″ insertion	2.000	Ea.	188	42	230
Insulation, fiberglass pipe covering, 1-1/2″ wall, 2-1/2″ IPS	12.000	L.F.	32.16	73.20	105.36
Pump control system	1.000	Ea.	1,275	610	1,885
Pump balancing	1.000	Ea.		296	296
TOTAL			11,915.86	3,775.18	15,691.04

D3020 330	Circulating Pump Systems, End Suction	COST EACH		
		MAT.	INST.	TOTAL
1010	Pump, base mtd with motor, end-suction, 2-1/2″ size, 3 HP, to 150 GPM	11,900	3,775	15,675
1020	3″ size, 5 HP, to 225 GPM	13,400	4,325	17,725
1030	4″ size, 7-1/2 HP, to 350 GPM	15,000	5,200	20,200
1040	5″ size, 15 HP, to 1000 GPM	21,500	7,900	29,400
1050	6″ size, 25 HP, to 1550 GPM	27,200	9,600	36,800

D3020 340	Circulating Pump Systems, Double Suction	COST EACH		
		MAT.	INST.	TOTAL
1010	Pump, base mtd w/motor, double suction, 6″ size, 50 HP, to 1200 GPM	22,400	13,900	36,300
1020	8″ size, 75 HP, to 2500 GPM	40,400	18,700	59,100
1030	8″ size, 100 HP, to 3000 GPM	54,000	20,900	74,900
1040	10″ size, 150 HP, to 4000 GPM	79,500	23,800	103,300

D3030 Cooling Generating Systems

Chilled Water Supply & Return Piping

Air Cooled Water Chiller Unit

Roof

Insulate
Return → Fan Coil Unit → Supply — Finish Ceiling

Design Assumptions: The chilled water, air cooled systems priced, utilize reciprocating hermetic compressors and propeller-type condenser fans. Piping with pumps and expansion tanks is included based on a two pipe system. No ducting is included and the fan-coil units are cooling only. Water treatment and balancing are not included. Chilled water piping is insulated. Area distribution is through the use of multiple fan coil units. Fewer but larger fan coil units with duct distribution would be approximately the same S.F. cost.

System Components	QUANTITY	UNIT	COST EACH		
			MAT.	INST.	TOTAL
SYSTEM D3030 110 1200					
PACKAGED CHILLER, AIR COOLED, WITH FAN COIL UNIT					
APARTMENT CORRIDORS, 3,000 S.F., 5.50 TON					
Fan coil air conditioning unit, cabinet mounted & filters chilled water	1.000	Ea.	3,482.70	549.90	4,032.60
Water chiller, air conditioning unit, air cooled	1.000	Ea.	7,975	2,069.38	10,044.38
Chilled water unit coil connections	1.000	Ea.	1,525	1,500	3,025
Chilled water distribution piping	440.000	L.F.	16,720	20,460	37,180
TOTAL			29,702.70	24,579.28	54,281.98
COST PER S.F.			9.90	8.19	18.09

*Cooling requirements would lead to choosing a water cooled unit.

D3030 110	Chilled Water, Air Cooled Condenser Systems	COST PER S.F.		
		MAT.	INST.	TOTAL
1180	Packaged chiller, air cooled, with fan coil unit			
1200	Apartment corridors, 3,000 S.F., 5.50 ton	9.90	8.20	18.10
1240	6,000 S.F., 11.00 ton	8.20	6.55	14.75
1280	10,000 S.F., 18.33 ton	6.85	4.98	11.83
1320	20,000 S.F., 36.66 ton	4.97	3.61	8.58
1360	40,000 S.F., 73.33 ton	5.40	3.62	9.02
1440	Banks and libraries, 3,000 S.F., 12.50 ton	14.20	9.65	23.85
1480	6,000 S.F., 25.00 ton	12.70	7.85	20.55
1520	10,000 S.F., 41.66 ton	9.10	5.50	14.60
1560	20,000 S.F., 83.33 ton	9	4.93	13.93
1600	40,000 S.F., 167 ton*			
1680	Bars and taverns, 3,000 S.F., 33.25 ton	21.50	11.45	32.95
1720	6,000 S.F., 66.50 ton	19.10	8.75	27.85
1760	10,000 S.F., 110.83 ton	13.60	2.83	16.43
1800	20,000 S.F., 220 ton*			
1840	40,000 S.F., 440 ton*			
1920	Bowling alleys, 3,000 S.F., 17.00 ton	17.40	10.80	28.20
1960	6,000 S.F., 34.00 ton	12.45	7.60	20.05
2000	10,000 S.F., 56.66 ton	10.55	5.50	16.05
2040	20,000 S.F., 113.33 ton	10	5	15
2080	40,000 S.F., 227 ton*			
2160	Department stores, 3,000 S.F., 8.75 ton	12.90	9.10	22
2200	6,000 S.F., 17.50 ton	10.10	7.05	17.15
2240	10,000 S.F., 29.17 ton	7.50	5.10	12.60
2280	20,000 S.F., 58.33 ton	6.25	3.75	10
2320	40,000 S.F., 116.66 ton	6.65	3.75	10.40

D3030 Cooling Generating Systems

D3030 110	Chilled Water, Air Cooled Condenser Systems	COST PER S.F.		
		MAT.	INST.	TOTAL
2400	Drug stores, 3,000 S.F., 20.00 ton	19.35	11.20	30.55
2440	6,000 S.F., 40.00 ton	14.45	8.30	22.75
2480	10,000 S.F., 66.66 ton	13.75	7.05	20.80
2520	20,000 S.F., 133.33 ton	12.05	5.30	17.35
2560	40,000 S.F., 267 ton*			
2640	Factories, 2,000 S.F., 10.00 ton	12.70	9.25	21.95
2680	6,000 S.F., 20.00 ton	11.20	7.45	18.65
2720	10,000 S.F., 33.33 ton	8.05	5.25	13.30
2760	20,000 S.F., 66.66 ton	7.95	4.69	12.64
2800	40,000 S.F., 133.33 ton	7.20	3.86	11.06
2880	Food supermarkets, 3,000 S.F., 8.50 ton	12.70	9.05	21.75
2920	6,000 S.F., 17.00 ton	9.95	7.05	17
2960	10,000 S.F., 28.33 ton	7.20	4.96	12.16
3000	20,000 S.F., 56.66 ton	6.05	3.68	9.73
3040	40,000 S.F., 113.33 ton	6.35	3.76	10.11
3120	Medical centers, 3,000 S.F., 7.00 ton	11.65	8.85	20.50
3160	6,000 S.F., 14.00 ton	9.05	6.80	15.85
3200	10,000 S.F., 23.33 ton	7.75	5.20	12.95
3240	20,000 S.F., 46.66 ton	5.75	3.80	9.55
3280	40,000 S.F., 93.33 ton	5.85	3.68	9.53
3360	Offices, 3,000 S.F., 9.50 ton	12	9	21
3400	6,000 S.F., 19.00 ton	10.90	7.35	18.25
3440	10,000 S.F., 31.66 ton	7.85	5.20	13.05
3480	20,000 S.F., 63.33 ton	7.95	4.76	12.71
3520	40,000 S.F., 126.66 ton	7.10	3.88	10.98
3600	Restaurants, 3,000 S.F., 15.00 ton	15.70	10	25.70
3640	6,000 S.F., 30.00 ton	11.95	7.60	19.55
3680	10,000 S.F., 50.00 ton	10.20	5.55	15.75
3720	20,000 S.F., 100.00 ton	10.20	5.25	15.45
3760	40,000 S.F., 200 ton*			
3840	Schools and colleges, 3,000 S.F., 11.50 ton	13.60	9.50	23.10
3880	6,000 S.F., 23.00 ton	12.10	7.70	19.80
3920	10,000 S.F., 38.33 ton	8.70	5.40	14.10
3960	20,000 S.F., 76.66 ton	8.85	4.97	13.82
4000	40,000 S.F., 153 ton*			

D30 HVAC

D3030 Cooling Generating Systems

Reciprocating Package Chiller
Condenser Water
Cooling Tower
Cooling Tower Water Makeup
Chilled Water Supply & Return Piping
Roof Structure
Finish Ceiling
Insulate
Return
Supply
Fan Coil Unit

General: Water cooled chillers are available in the same sizes as air cooled units. They are also available in larger capacities.

Design Assumptions: The chilled water systems with water cooled condenser include reciprocating hermetic compressors, water cooling tower, pumps, piping and expansion tanks and are based on a two pipe system. Chilled water piping is insulated. No ducts are included and fan-coil units are cooling only. Area distribution is through use of multiple fan coil units. Fewer but larger fan coil units with duct distribution would be approximately the same S.F. cost. Water treatment and balancing are not included.

System Components	QUANTITY	UNIT	COST EACH		
			MAT.	INST.	TOTAL
SYSTEM D3030 115 1320					
PACKAGED CHILLER, WATER COOLED, WITH FAN COIL UNIT					
APARTMENT CORRIDORS, 4,000 S.F., 7.33 TON					
Fan coil air conditioner unit, cabinet mounted & filters, chilled water	2.000	Ea.	4,641.70	732.90	5,374.60
Water chiller, water cooled, 1 compressor, hermetic scroll,	1.000	Ea.	5,633.40	3,618.20	9,251.60
Cooling tower, draw thru single flow, belt drive	1.000	Ea.	1,583.28	153.93	1,737.21
Cooling tower pumps & piping	1.000	System	791.64	362.84	1,154.48
Chilled water unit coil connections	2.000	Ea.	3,050	3,000	6,050
Chilled water distribution piping	520.000	L.F.	19,760	24,180	43,940
TOTAL			35,460.02	32,047.87	67,507.89
COST PER S.F.			8.87	8.01	16.88

*Cooling requirements would lead to choosing a water cooled unit.

D3030 115	Chilled Water, Cooling Tower Systems		COST PER S.F.		
			MAT.	INST.	TOTAL
1300	Packaged chiller, water cooled, with fan coil unit				
1320	Apartment corridors, 4,000 S.F., 7.33 ton		8.88	8	16.88
1360	6,000 S.F., 11.00 ton	R236000	7.55	6.90	14.45
1400	10,000 S.F., 18.33 ton	-20	6.90	5.10	12
1440	20,000 S.F., 26.66 ton		5.40	3.83	9.23
1480	40,000 S.F., 73.33 ton		5.15	3.91	9.06
1520	60,000 S.F., 110.00 ton		5.40	4.01	9.41
1600	Banks and libraries, 4,000 S.F., 16.66 ton		13.90	8.80	22.70
1640	6,000 S.F., 25.00 ton		11.70	7.75	19.45
1680	10,000 S.F., 41.66 ton		10	5.80	15.80
1720	20,000 S.F., 83.33 ton		8.35	5.55	13.90
1760	40,000 S.F., 166.66 ton		9.45	6.65	16.10
1800	60,000 S.F., 250.00 ton		9.75	7.05	16.80
1880	Bars and taverns, 4,000 S.F., 44.33 ton		23	11.15	34.15
1920	6,000 S.F., 66.50 ton		22.50	11.50	34
1960	10,000 S.F., 110.83 ton		18.15	9.10	27.25
2000	20,000 S.F., 221.66 ton		21.50	9.20	30.70
2040	40,000 S.F., 440 ton*				
2080	60,000 S.F., 660 ton*				
2160	Bowling alleys, 4,000 S.F., 22.66 ton		15.95	9.65	25.60
2200	6,000 S.F., 34.00 ton		14	8.55	22.55
2240	10,000 S.F., 56.66 ton		11.75	6.25	18
2280	20,000 S.F., 113.33 ton		10.35	5.80	16.15
2320	40,000 S.F., 226.66 ton		12.50	6.65	19.15

D3030 Cooling Generating Systems

D3030 115	Chilled Water, Cooling Tower Systems	COST PER S.F.		
		MAT.	INST.	TOTAL
2360	60,000 S.F., 340 ton			
2440	Department stores, 4,000 S.F., 11.66 ton	9.80	8.70	18.50
2480	6,000 S.F., 17.50 ton	10.55	7.15	17.70
2520	10,000 S.F., 29.17 ton	7.95	5.35	13.30
2560	20,000 S.F., 58.33 ton	6.45	3.98	10.43
2600	40,000 S.F., 116.66 ton	6.35	4.11	10.46
2640	60,000 S.F., 175.00 ton	8.75	6.40	15.15
2720	Drug stores, 4,000 S.F., 26.66 ton	16.65	10	26.65
2760	6,000 S.F., 40.00 ton	15.60	8.55	24.15
2800	10,000 S.F., 66.66 ton	14.55	7.75	22.30
2840	20,000 S.F., 133.33 ton	11.80	6.10	17.90
2880	40,000 S.F., 266.67 ton	12.75	7.55	20.30
2920	60,000 S.F., 400 ton*			
3000	Factories, 4,000 S.F., 13.33 ton	12.30	8.40	20.70
3040	6,000 S.F., 20.00 ton	10.65	7.25	17.90
3080	10,000 S.F., 33.33 ton	8.55	5.55	14.10
3120	20,000 S.F., 66.66 ton	8.20	4.97	13.17
3160	40,000 S.F., 133.33 ton	7.05	4.25	11.30
3200	60,000 S.F., 200.00 ton	8.85	6.75	15.60
3280	Food supermarkets, 4,000 S.F., 11.33 ton	9.70	8.65	18.35
3320	6,000 S.F., 17.00 ton	9.70	7.05	16.75
3360	10,000 S.F., 28.33 ton	7.80	5.30	13.10
3400	20,000 S.F., 56.66 ton	6.55	4.01	10.56
3440	40,000 S.F., 113.33 ton	6.35	4.13	10.48
3480	60,000 S.F., 170.00 ton	8.70	6.40	15.10
3560	Medical centers, 4.000 S.F., 9.33 ton	8.65	7.95	16.60
3600	6,000 S.F., 14.00 ton	9.45	6.90	16.35
3640	10,000 S.F., 23.33 ton	7.20	5.15	12.35
3680	20,000 S.F., 46.66 ton	5.95	3.89	9.84
3720	40,000 S.F., 93.33 ton	5.80	4.04	9.84
3760	60,000 S.F., 140.00 ton	7.45	6.50	13.95
3840	Offices, 4,000 S.F., 12.66 ton	12	8.30	20.30
3880	6,000 S.F., 19.00 ton	10.65	7.40	18.05
3920	10,000 S.F., 31.66 ton	8.50	5.60	14.10
3960	20,000 S.F., 63.33 ton	8.10	4.97	13.07
4000	40,000 S.F., 126.66 ton	7.95	6.40	14.35
4040	60,000 S.F., 190.00 ton	8.60	6.65	15.25
4120	Restaurants, 4,000 S.F., 20.00 ton	14.45	9	23.45
4160	6,000 S.F., 30.00 ton	12.80	8	20.80
4200	10,000 S.F., 50.00 ton	10.90	6	16.90
4240	20,000 S.F., 100.00 ton	9.75	5.80	15.55
4280	40,000 S.F., 200.00 ton	9.95	6.45	16.40
4320	60,000 S.F., 300.00 ton	10.75	7.30	18.05
4400	Schools and colleges, 4,000 S.F., 15.33 ton	13.30	8.65	21.95
4440	6,000 S.F., 23.00 ton	11.20	7.60	18.80
4480	10,000 S.F., 38.33 ton	9.50	5.65	15.15
4520	20,000 S.F., 76.66 ton	8.10	5.45	13.55
4560	40,000 S.F., 153.33 ton	9	6.50	15.50
4600	60,000 S.F., 230.00 ton	9.05	6.75	15.80

D30 HVAC

D3030 Cooling Generating Systems

Chilled Water Piping

Reciprocating Chiller, Water Cooled

Condenser Water Piping

System Components	QUANTITY	UNIT	COST EACH		
			MAT.	INST.	TOTAL
SYSTEM D3030 130 1010					
CHILLER, RECIPROCATING, WATER COOLED, STD. CONTROLS, 60 TON					
Water chiller, reciprocating, water cooled, 60 ton cooling	1.000	Ea.	38,900	10,100	49,000
Pipe, black steel, welded, Sch. 40, on yoke & roll hgrs, 10' O.C., 4" dia	40.000	L.F.	1,540	1,324	2,864
Elbow, 90°, weld joint, butt, 4" pipe size	8.000	Ea.	424	1,961.20	2,385.20
Flange, welding neck, 150 lb., 4" pipe size	16.000	Ea.	744	1,968.96	2,712.96
Valves, iron body, butterfly, lug type, lever actuator, 4" size	4.000	Ea.	832	948	1,780
Expansion joints, bellows type, flange spool, 6" F to F, 4" dia	4.000	Ea.	1,420	576	1,996
T-O-L socket, weld joint, 1/4" pipe size, nozzle	4.000	Ea.	31.20	213.08	244.28
T-O-L socket, weld joint, 3/4" pipe size, nozzle	4.000	Ea.	36	233.76	269.76
Thermometers, stem type, 9" case, 8" stem, 3/4" NPT	4.000	Ea.	744	96	840
Gauges, pressure or vacuum, 3-1/2" diameter dial	4.000	Ea.	158	84	242
Insulation, fiberglass pipe covering, 1-1/2" wall, 4" IPS	20.000	L.F.	64	157	221
Chiller balancing	1.000	Ea.		570	570
TOTAL			44,893.20	18,232	63,125.20

D3030 130	Reciprocating Chiller, Water Cooled	COST EACH		
		MAT.	INST.	TOTAL
1010	Chiller, reciprocating, water cooled, std. controls, 60 Ton	44,900	18,200	63,100
1020	100 Ton	49,600	27,500	77,100
1030	150 Ton	81,500	30,200	111,700
1040	200 Ton	110,000	31,900	141,900

D3030 135	Reciprocating Chiller, Air Cooled	COST EACH		
		MAT.	INST.	TOTAL
1010	Chiller, reciprocating, air cooled, std. controls, 20 Ton	31,300	10,800	42,100
1020	30 Ton	33,400	11,400	44,800
1030	40 Ton	40,100	12,200	52,300
1040	60 Ton	55,500	13,600	69,100
1050	70 Ton	63,000	14,000	77,000
1060	80 Ton	68,000	14,300	82,300
1070	90 Ton	72,500	14,500	87,000
1080	100 Ton	81,500	14,700	96,200
1090	110 Ton	88,000	15,900	103,900
1100	130 Ton	104,000	16,100	120,100

D30 HVAC

D3030 Cooling Generating Systems

D3030 135	Reciprocating Chiller, Air Cooled	COST EACH		
		MAT.	INST.	TOTAL
1110	150 Ton	115,000	16,300	131,300
1120	175 Ton	128,500	16,600	145,100
1130	210 Ton	145,500	18,200	163,700

D3030 Cooling Generating Systems

Chilled Water Piping

Centrifugal Chiller, Water Cooled, Hermetic

Condenser Water Piping

System Components	QUANTITY	UNIT	COST EACH		
			MAT.	INST.	TOTAL
SYSTEM D3030 140 1010					
CHILLER, CENTRIF., WATER COOLED, PKGD. HERMETIC, STD. CONTROLS, 200 TON					
Water chiller, screw, water cooled, not incl tower, 200 ton	1.000	Ea.	90,000	20,200	110,200
Pipe, black steel, welded, Sch. 40, on yoke & roll hgrs, 10' o.c., 6" dia	40.000	L.F.	2,220	2,105.20	4,325.20
Elbow, 90°, weld joint, 6" pipe size	8.000	Ea.	928	3,024.80	3,952.80
Flange, welding neck, 150 lb., 6" pipe size	16.000	Ea.	1,120	3,008.96	4,128.96
Valves, iron body, butterfly, lug type, lever actuator, 6" size	4.000	Ea.	1,400	1,480	2,880
Expansion joints, bellows type, flange spool, 6" F to F, 6" dia	4.000	Ea.	1,800	712	2,512
T-O-L socket, weld jiont, 1/4" pipe size, nozzle	4.000	Ea.	31.20	213.08	244.28
T-O-L socket, weld joint, 3/4" pipe size, nozzle	4.000	Ea.	36	233.76	269.76
Thermometers, stem type, 9" case, 8" stem, 3/4" NPT	4.000	Ea.	744	96	840
Gauges, pressure or vacuum, 3-1/2" diameter dial	4.000	Ea.	158	84	242
Insulation, fiberglass pipe covering, 1-1/2" wall, 6" IPS	40.000	L.F.	151.20	398	549.20
Chiller balancing	1.000	Ea.		570	570
TOTAL			98,588.40	32,125.80	130,714.20

D3030 140	Centrifugal Chiller, Water Cooled	COST EACH		
		MAT.	INST.	TOTAL
1010	Chiller, centrif., water cooled, pkgd. hermetic, std controls, 200 Ton	98,500	32,100	130,600
1020	400 Ton	157,500	44,000	201,500
1030	1,000 Ton	514,000	66,500	580,500
1040	1,500 Ton	753,500	80,500	834,000

D3030 Cooling Generating Systems

Chilled Water Piping
(Condenser Water Piping Similar)

Gas Absorption Chiller, Water Cooled

Gas Piping

System Components	QUANTITY	UNIT	COST EACH		
			MAT.	INST.	TOTAL
SYSTEM D3030 145 1010					
CHILLER, GAS FIRED ABSORPTION, WATER COOLED, STD. CONTROLS, 800 TON					
Absorption water chiller, gas fired, water cooled, 800 ton	1.000	Ea.	625,000	30,500	655,500
Pipe, black steel, weld, Sch. 40, on yoke & roll hangers, 10' O.C., 10" dia	20.000	L.F.	1,410	1,573.80	2,983.80
Pipe, black steel, welded, Sch. 40, 14" dia., (two rod roll type hanger)	44.000	L.F.	5,148	5,530.80	10,678.80
Pipe, black steel, welded, Sch. 40, on yoke & roll hangers, 10' O.C., 4" di	20.000	L.F.	770	662	1,432
Elbow, 90°, weld joint, 10" pipe size	4.000	Ea.	1,740	2,514	4,254
Elbow, 90°, weld joint, 14" pipe size	6.000	Ea.	6,450	5,643	12,093
Elbow, 90°, weld joint, 4" pipe size	3.000	Ea.	159	735.45	894.45
Flange, welding neck, 150 lb., 10" pipe size	8.000	Ea.	1,592	2,494	4,086
Flange, welding neck, 150 lb., 14" pipe size	14.000	Ea.	5,810	5,866	11,676
Flange, welding neck, 150 lb., 4" pipe size	3.000	Ea.	139.50	369.18	508.68
Valves, iron body, butterfly, lug type, gear operated, 10" size	2.000	Ea.	2,100	920	3,020
Valves, iron body, butterfly, lug type, gear operated, 14" size	5.000	Ea.	14,625	4,000	18,625
Valves, semi-steel, lubricated plug valve, flanged, 4" pipe size	1.000	Ea.	470	395	865
Expansion joints, bellows type, flange spool, 6" F to F, 10" dia	2.000	Ea.	1,430	484	1,914
Expansion joints, bellows type, flange spool, 10" F to F, 14" dia	2.000	Ea.	2,500	640	3,140
T-O-L socket, weld joint, 1/4" pipe size, nozzle	4.000	Ea.	31.20	213.08	244.28
T-O-L socket, weld joint, 3/4" pipe size, nozzle	4.000	Ea.	36	233.76	269.76
Thermometers, stem type, 9" case, 8" stem, 3/4" NPT	4.000	Ea.	744	96	840
Gauges, pressure or vacuum, 3-1/2" diameter dial	4.000	Ea.	158	84	242
Insulation, fiberglass pipe covering, 2" wall, 10" IPS	20.000	L.F.	168	313	481
Vent chimney, all fuel, pressure tight, double wall, SS, 12" dia	20.000	L.F.	1,670	520	2,190
Chiller balancing	1.000	Ea.		570	570
TOTAL			672,150.70	64,357.07	736,507.77

D3030 145	Gas Absorption Chiller, Water Cooled	COST EACH		
		MAT.	INST.	TOTAL
1010	Chiller, gas fired absorption, water cooled, std. ctrls, 800 Ton	672,000	64,500	736,500
1020	1000 Ton	877,500	82,500	960,000

D3030 150	Steam Absorption Chiller, Water Cooled	COST EACH		
		MAT.	INST.	TOTAL
1010	Chiller, steam absorption, water cooled, std. ctrls, 750 Ton	689,500	76,500	766,000
1020	955 Ton	800,500	91,000	891,500
1030	1465 Ton	1,162,500	104,000	1,266,500
1040	1660 Ton	1,399,000	118,500	1,517,500

D30 HVAC

D3030 Cooling Generating Systems

Cold Water Fill

Drain To Waste Piping

Cooling Tower

Condenser Water Piping

System Components	QUANTITY	UNIT	COST EACH MAT.	COST EACH INST.	COST EACH TOTAL
SYSTEM D3030 310 1010					
COOLING TOWER, GALVANIZED STEEL, PACKAGED UNIT, DRAW THRU, 60 TON					
Cooling towers, draw thru, single flow, belt drive, 60 tons	1.000	Ea.	12,960	1,260	14,220
Pipe, black steel, welded, Sch. 40, on yoke & roll hangers, 10' OC, 4" dia.	40.000	L.F.	1,540	1,324	2,864
Tubing, copper, Type L, couplings & hangers 10' OC, 1-1/2" dia.	20.000	L.F.	379	253	632
Elbow, 90°, copper, cu x cu, 1-1/2" dia.	3.000	Ea.	121.50	151.50	273
Elbow, 90°, weld joint, 4" pipe size	6.000	Ea.	318	1,470.90	1,788.90
Flange, welding neck, 150 lb., 4" pipe size	6.000	Ea.	279	738.36	1,017.36
Valves, bronze, gate, N.R.S., soldered, 125 psi, 1-1/2" size	1.000	Ea.	125	50.50	175.50
Valves, iron body, butterfly, lug type, lever actuator, 4" size	2.000	Ea.	416	474	890
Electric heat trace system, 400 degree, 115v, 5 watts per L.F.	160.000	L.F.	1,296	185.60	1,481.60
Insulation, fiberglass pipe covering, , 1-1/2" wall, 4" IPS	40.000	L.F.	128	314	442
Insulation, fiberglass pipe covering, 1" wall, 1-1/2" IPS	20.000	L.F.	26.80	104	130.80
Cooling tower condenser control system	1.000	Ea.	5,500	2,725	8,225
Cooling tower balancing	1.000	Ea.		435	435
TOTAL			23,089.30	9,485.86	32,575.16

D3030 310	Galvanized Draw Through Cooling Tower	COST EACH MAT.	COST EACH INST.	COST EACH TOTAL
1010	Cooling tower, galvanized steel, packaged unit, draw thru, 60 Ton	23,100	9,500	32,600
1020	110 Ton	31,000	11,100	42,100
1030	300 Ton	45,100	16,900	62,000
1040	600 Ton	55,500	25,200	80,700
1050	1000 Ton	115,500	37,100	152,600

D3030 320	Fiberglass Draw Through Cooling Tower	COST EACH MAT.	COST EACH INST.	COST EACH TOTAL
1010	Cooling tower, fiberglass, packaged unit, draw thru, 100 Ton	21,200	9,575	30,775
1020	120 Ton	23,900	10,800	34,700
1030	140 Ton	27,300	14,400	41,700
1040	160 Ton	36,100	19,000	55,100
1050	180 Ton	53,000	27,500	80,500

D3030 330	Stainless Steel Draw Through Cooling Tower	COST EACH MAT.	COST EACH INST.	COST EACH TOTAL
1010	Cooling tower, stainless steel, packaged unit, draw thru, 60 Ton	37,900	9,475	47,375
1020	110 Ton	44,600	11,100	55,700
1030	300 Ton	74,000	16,900	90,900
1040	600 Ton	116,500	24,800	141,300
1050	1000 Ton	198,500	37,100	235,600

D3040 Distribution Systems

Two-Way Valve Piping

Three-Way Valve Piping

Built-Up Air Handling Unit

System Components	QUANTITY	UNIT	COST EACH		
			MAT.	INST.	TOTAL
SYSTEM D3040 106 1010					
AHU, FIELD FAB., BLT. UP, COOL/HEAT COILS, FLTRS., CONST. VOL., 40,000 CFM					
AHU, Built-up, cool/heat coils, filters, mix box, constant volume	1.000	Ea.	58,500	6,275	64,775
Pipe, black steel, welded, Sch. 40, on yoke & roll hgrs, 10' OC, 3" dia.	26.000	L.F.	741	739.70	1,480.70
Pipe, black steel, welded, Sch. 40, on yoke & roll hgrs, 10' OC, 4" dia	20.000	L.F.	770	662	1,432
Elbow, 90°, weld joint, 3" pipe size	5.000	Ea.	160	874	1,034
Elbow, 90°, weld joint, 4" pipe size	4.000	Ea.	212	980.60	1,192.60
Tee, welded, reducing on outlet, 3" by 2-1/2" pipe	3.000	Ea.	390	921.45	1,311.45
Tee, welded, reducing on outlet, 4" by 3" pipe	2.000	Ea.	274	817.10	1,091.10
Reducer, eccentric, weld joint, 3" pipe size	4.000	Ea.	260	612.40	872.40
Reducer, eccentric, weld joint, 4" pipe size	4.000	Ea.	332	819	1,151
Flange, weld neck, 150 LB, 2-1/2" pipe size	3.000	Ea.	105	229.62	334.62
Flange, weld neck, 150 lb., 3" pipe size	14.000	Ea.	539	1,223.60	1,762.60
Flange, weld neck, 150 lb., 4" pipe size	10.000	Ea.	465	1,230.60	1,695.60
Valves, iron body, butterfly, lug type, lever actuator, 3" size	2.000	Ea.	344	296	640
Valves, iron body, butterfly, lug type, lever actuator, 4" size	2.000	Ea.	416	474	890
Strainer, Y type, iron body, flanged, 125 lb., 3" pipe size	1.000	Ea.	157	269	426
Strainer, Y type, iron body, flanged, 125 lb., 4" pipe size	1.000	Ea.	286	405	691
Valve, electric motor actuated, iron body, 3 way, flanged, 2-1/2" pipe	1.000	Ea.	1,225	320	1,545
Valve, electric motor actuated, iron body, two way, flanged, 3" pipe size	1.000	Ea.	1,275	320	1,595
Expansion joints, bellows type, flange spool, 6" F to F, 3" dia	2.000	Ea.	660	212	872
Expansion joints, bellows type, flange spool, 6" F to F, 4" dia	2.000	Ea.	710	288	998
T-O-L socket, weld joint, 1/4" pipe size, nozzle	4.000	Ea.	31.20	213.08	244.28
T-O-L socket, weld joint, 1/2" pipe size, nozzle	12.000	Ea.	93.60	670.20	763.80
Thermometers, stem type, 9" case, 8" stem, 3/4" NPT	4.000	Ea.	744	96	840
Pressure/temperature relief plug, 316 SS, 3/4"OD, 7-1/2" insertion	4.000	Ea.	376	84	460
Insulation, fiberglass pipe covering, 1-1/2" wall, 3" IPS	26.000	L.F.	73.32	167.70	241.02
Insulation, fiberglass pipe covering, 1-1/2" wall, 4" IPS	20.000	L.F.	64	157	221
Fan coil control system	1.000	Ea.	1,250	610	1,860
Re-heat coil balancing	2.000	Ea.		248	248
Air conditioner balancing	1.000	Ea.		765	765
TOTAL			70,453.12	20,980.05	91,433.17

D3040 106	Field Fabricated Air Handling Unit	COST EACH		
		MAT.	INST.	TOTAL
1010	AHU, Field fab, blt up, cool/heat coils, fltrs, const vol, 40,000 CFM	70,500	20,900	91,400
1020	60,000 CFM	98,000	32,600	130,600
1030	75,000 CFM	119,000	34,400	153,400

D3040 Distribution Systems

D3040 108	Field Fabricated VAV Air Handling Unit	COST EACH		
		MAT.	INST.	TOTAL
1010	AHU, Field fab, blt up, cool/heat coils, fltrs, VAV, 75,000 CFM	120,000	39,500	159,500
1020	100,000 CFM	182,500	52,500	235,000
1030	150,000 CFM	302,500	83,500	386,000

D3040 Distribution Systems

Chilled Water Piping   Central Station Air Handling Unit   Hot Water Piping

System Components	QUANTITY	UNIT	COST EACH		
			MAT.	INST.	TOTAL
SYSTEM D3040 110 1010					
AHU, CENTRAL STATION, COOL/HEAT COILS, CONST. VOL., FLTRS., 2,000 CFM					
Central station air handling unit, chilled water, 2000 CFM	1.000	Ea.	10,900	1,100	12,000
Pipe, black steel, Sch 40, threaded, W/cplgs & hangers, 10' OC, 1" dia.	26.000	L.F.	269.75	404.63	674.38
Pipe, black steel, Sch 40, threaded, W/cplg & hangers, 10' OC, 1-1/4" dia.	20.000	L.F.	271.70	347.10	618.80
Elbow, 90°, black, straight, 1" dia.	4.000	Ea.	26.60	202	228.60
Elbow, 90°, black, straight, 1-1/4" dia.	4.000	Ea.	44	216	260
Tee, black, reducing, 1" dia.	8.000	Ea.	134	660	794
Tee, black, reducing, 1-1/4" dia.	8.000	Ea.	236	676	912
Reducer, concentric, black, 1" dia.	4.000	Ea.	48.40	176	224.40
Reducer, concentric, black, 1-1/4" dia.	4.000	Ea.	54.20	182	236.20
Union, black with brass seat, 1" dia.	4.000	Ea.	84	220	304
Union, black with brass seat, 1-1/4" dia.	2.000	Ea.	60	113	173
Pipe nipple, black, 1" dia	13.000	Ea.	53.95	80.93	134.88
Pipe nipple, black, 1-1/4" dia	12.000	Ea.	62.70	80.10	142.80
Valves, bronze, gate, N.R.S., threaded, class 150, 1" size	2.000	Ea.	190	69	259
Valves, bronze, gate, N.R.S., threaded, class 150, 1-1/4" size	2.000	Ea.	256	88	344
Strainer, Y type, bronze body, screwed, 150 lb., 1" pipe size	1.000	Ea.	42	39.50	81.50
Strainer, Y type, bronze body, screwed, 150 lb., 1-1/4" pipe size	1.000	Ea.	85	45	130
Valve, electric motor actuated, brass, 3 way, screwed, 3/4" pipe	1.000	Ea.	325	36	361
Valve, electric motor actuated, brass, 2 way, screwed, 1" pipe size	1.000	Ea.	605	34.50	639.50
Thermometers, stem type, 9" case, 8" stem, 3/4" NPT	4.000	Ea.	744	96	840
Pressure/temperature relief plug, 316 SS, 3/4"OD, 7-1/2" insertion	4.000	Ea.	376	84	460
Insulation, fiberglass pipe covering, 1" wall, 1" IPS	26.000	L.F.	29.64	129.48	159.12
Insulation, fiberglass pipe covering, 1" wall, 1-1/4" IPS	20.000	L.F.	24.80	104	128.80
Fan coil control system	1.000	Ea.	1,250	610	1,860
Re-heat coil balancing	2.000	Ea.		248	248
Multizone A/C balancing	1.000	Ea.		570	570
TOTAL			16,172.74	6,611.24	22,783.98

D3040 110	Central Station Air Handling Unit	COST EACH		
		MAT.	INST.	TOTAL
1010	AHU, Central station, cool/heat coils, constant vol, fltrs, 2,000 CFM	16,200	6,600	22,800
1020	5,000 CFM	22,700	8,525	31,225
1030	10,000 CFM	45,300	11,800	57,100
1040	15,000 CFM	64,000	16,000	80,000
1050	20,000 CFM	77,000	18,700	95,700

D30 HVAC

D3040 Distribution Systems

D3040 112	Central Station Air Handling Unit, VAV	COST EACH		
		MAT.	INST.	TOTAL
1010	AHU, Central station, cool/heat coils, VAV, fltrs, 5,000 CFM	26,500	8,875	35,375
1020	10,000 CFM	47,800	12,100	59,900
1030	15,000 CFM	67,000	15,700	82,700
1040	20,000 CFM	84,000	19,100	103,100
1050	30,000 CFM	110,500	22,000	132,500

Rooftop Air Handling Unit

System Components	QUANTITY	UNIT	COST EACH		
			MAT.	INST.	TOTAL
SYSTEM D3040 114 1010					
AHU, ROOFTOP, COOL/HEAT COILS, FLTRS., CONST. VOL., 2,000 CFM					
AHU, Built-up, cool/heat coils, filter, mix box, rooftop, constant volume	1.000	Ea.	11,100	1,875	12,975
Pipe, black steel, Sch 40, threaded, W/cplgs & hangers, 10' OC, 1" dia.	26.000	L.F.	269.75	404.63	674.38
Pipe, black steel, Sch 40, threaded, W/cplg & hangers, 10' OC, 1-1/4" dia.	20.000	L.F.	271.70	347.10	618.80
Elbow, 90°, black, straight, 1" dia.	4.000	Ea.	26.60	202	228.60
Elbow, 90°, black, straight, 1-1/4" dia.	4.000	Ea.	44	216	260
Tee, black, reducing, 1" dia.	8.000	Ea.	134	660	794
Tee, black, reducing, 1-1/4" dia.	8.000	Ea.	236	676	912
Reducer, black, concentric, 1" dia.	4.000	Ea.	48.40	176	224.40
Reducer, black, concentric, 1-1/4" dia.	4.000	Ea.	54.20	182	236.20
Union, black with brass seat, 1" dia.	4.000	Ea.	84	220	304
Union, black with brass seat, 1-1/4" dia.	2.000	Ea.	60	113	173
Pipe nipples, 1" dia	13.000	Ea.	53.95	80.93	134.88
Pipe nipples, 1-1/4" dia	12.000	Ea.	62.70	80.10	142.80
Valves, bronze, gate, N.R.S., threaded, class 150, 1" size	2.000	Ea.	190	69	259
Valves, bronze, gate, N.R.S., threaded, class 150, 1-1/4" size	2.000	Ea.	256	88	344
Strainer, Y type, bronze body, screwed, 150 lb., 1" pipe size	1.000	Ea.	42	39.50	81.50
Strainer, Y type, bronze body, screwed, 150 lb., 1-1/4" pipe size	1.000	Ea.	85	45	130
Valve, electric motor actuated, brass, 3 way, screwed, 3/4" pipe	1.000	Ea.	325	36	361
Valve, electric motor actuated, brass, 2 way, screwed, 1" pipe size	1.000	Ea.	605	34.50	639.50
Thermometers, stem type, 9" case, 8" stem, 3/4" NPT	4.000	Ea.	744	96	840
Pressure/temperature relief plug, 316 SS, 3/4"OD, 7-1/2" insertion	4.000	Ea.	376	84	460
Insulation, fiberglass pipe covering, 1" wall, 1" IPS	26.000	L.F.	29.64	129.48	159.12
Insulation, fiberglass pipe covering, 1" wall, 1-1/4" IPS	20.000	L.F.	24.80	104	128.80
Insulation pipe covering .016" aluminum jacket finish, add	45.000	S.F.	46.35	247.50	293.85
Fan coil control system	1.000	Ea.	1,250	610	1,860
Re-heat coil balancing	2.000	Ea.		248	248
Rooftop unit heat/cool balancing	1.000	Ea.		445	445
TOTAL			16,419.09	7,508.74	23,927.83

D3040 114	Rooftop Air Handling Unit	COST EACH		
		MAT.	INST.	TOTAL
1010	AHU, Rooftop, cool/heat coils, constant vol., fltrs, 2,000 CFM	16,400	7,500	23,900
1020	5,000 CFM	33,800	8,725	42,525
1030	10,000 CFM	66,500	12,100	78,600
1040	15,000 CFM	96,500	15,900	112,400

D3040 Distribution Systems

D3040 114	Rooftop Air Handling Unit	COST EACH		
		MAT.	INST.	TOTAL
1050	20,000 CFM	129,500	19,200	148,700

D3040 116	Rooftop Air Handling Unit, VAV	COST EACH		
		MAT.	INST.	TOTAL
1010	AHU, Rooftop, cool/heat coils, VAV, fltrs, 5,000 CFM	37,200	8,925	46,125
1020	10,000 CFM	73,500	12,200	85,700
1030	15,000 CFM	108,500	16,000	124,500
1040	20,000 CFM	136,000	19,500	155,500
1050	30,000 CFM	187,000	22,400	209,400

D3040   Distribution Systems

Galvanized Steel Duct

Fiberglass Duct Insulation

Flexible Fiberglass Duct

Horizontal Fan Coil Air Conditioning System

System Components	QUANTITY	UNIT	COST EACH		
			MAT.	INST.	TOTAL
SYSTEM D3040 124 1010					
FAN COIL A/C SYSTEM, HORIZONTAL, W/HOUSING, CONTROLS, 2 PIPE, 1/2 TON					
Fan coil A/C, horizontal housing, filters, chilled water, 1/2 ton cooling	1.000	Ea.	1,250	151	1,401
Pipe, black steel, Sch 40, threaded, W/cplgs & hangers, 10' OC, 3/4" dia.	20.000	L.F.	121.48	232.20	353.68
Elbow, 90°, black, straight, 3/4" dia.	6.000	Ea.	23.04	282	305.04
Tee, black, straight, 3/4" dia.	2.000	Ea.	12.20	146	158.20
Union, black with brass seat, 3/4" dia.	2.000	Ea.	32.30	101	133.30
Pipe nipples, 3/4" diam	3.000	Ea.	8.48	16.20	24.68
Valves, bronze, gate, N.R.S., threaded, class 150, 3/4" size	2.000	Ea.	150	66	216
Circuit setter, balance valve, bronze body, threaded, 3/4" pipe size	1.000	Ea.	83	33.50	116.50
Insulation, fiberglass pipe covering, 1" wall, 3/4" IPS	20.000	L.F.	21.40	95.40	116.80
Ductwork, 12" x 8" fabricated, galvanized steel, 12 LF	55.000	Lb.	42.35	418	460.35
Insulation, ductwork, blanket type, fiberglass, 1" thk, 1-1/2 LB density	40.000	S.F.	36	125.20	161.20
Diffusers, aluminum, OB damper, ceiling, perf, 24"x24" panel size, 6"x6"	2.000	Ea.	332	80	412
Ductwork, flexible, fiberglass fabric, insulated, 1"thk, PE jacket, 6" dia	16.000	L.F.	44	70.40	114.40
Round volume control damper 6" dia.	2.000	Ea.	53	58	111
Fan coil unit balancing	1.000	Ea.		82.50	82.50
Re-heat coil balancing	1.000	Ea.		124	124
Diffuser/register, high, balancing	2.000	Ea.		228	228
TOTAL			2,209.25	2,309.40	4,518.65

D3040 118	Fan Coil A/C Unit, Two Pipe	COST EACH		
		MAT.	INST.	TOTAL
1010	Fan coil A/C system, cabinet mounted, controls, 2 pipe, 1/2 Ton	1,225	1,250	2,475
1020	1 Ton	1,500	1,400	2,900
1030	1-1/2 Ton	1,625	1,400	3,025
1040	2 Ton	2,550	1,725	4,275
1050	3 Ton	3,175	1,800	4,975

D3040 120	Fan Coil A/C Unit, Two Pipe, Electric Heat	COST EACH		
		MAT.	INST.	TOTAL
1010	Fan coil A/C system, cabinet mntd, elect. ht, controls, 2 pipe, 1/2 Ton	1,800	1,250	3,050
1020	1 Ton	2,225	1,400	3,625
1030	1-1/2 Ton	2,575	1,400	3,975
1040	2 Ton	3,875	1,750	5,625
1050	3 Ton	6,450	1,800	8,250

D3040 Distribution Systems

D3040 122	Fan Coil A/C Unit, Four Pipe	COST EACH		
		MAT.	INST.	TOTAL
1010	Fan coil A/C system, cabinet mounted, controls, 4 pipe, 1/2 Ton	2,025	2,425	4,450
1020	1 Ton	2,325	2,575	4,900
1030	1-1/2 Ton	2,475	2,600	5,075
1040	2 Ton	3,075	2,675	5,750
1050	3 Ton	4,100	2,875	6,975

D3040 124	Fan Coil A/C, Horizontal, Duct Mount, 2 Pipe	COST EACH		
		MAT.	INST.	TOTAL
1010	Fan coil A/C system, horizontal w/housing, controls, 2 pipe, 1/2 Ton	2,200	2,300	4,500
1020	1 Ton	2,950	3,350	6,300
1030	1-1/2 Ton	3,625	4,350	7,975
1040	2 Ton	4,725	5,225	9,950
1050	3 Ton	5,750	6,900	12,650
1060	3-1/2 Ton	6,000	7,150	13,150
1070	4 Ton	6,150	8,100	14,250
1080	5 Ton	7,300	10,300	17,600
1090	6 Ton	7,400	11,100	18,500
1100	7 Ton	7,500	11,500	19,000
1110	8 Ton	7,500	11,700	19,200
1120	10 Ton	8,450	12,200	20,650

D3040 126	Fan Coil A/C, Horiz., Duct Mount, 2 Pipe, Elec. Ht.	COST EACH		
		MAT.	INST.	TOTAL
1010	Fan coil A/C system, horiz. hsng, elect. ht, ctrls, 2 pipe, 1/2 Ton	2,475	2,300	4,775
1020	1 Ton	3,275	3,350	6,625
1030	1-1/2 Ton	3,875	4,350	8,225
1040	2 Ton	5,150	5,225	10,375
1050	3 Ton	8,175	7,125	15,300
1060	3-1/2 Ton	9,150	7,150	16,300
1070	4 Ton	10,200	8,125	18,325
1080	5 Ton	12,200	10,300	22,500
1090	6 Ton	12,300	11,100	23,400
1100	7 Ton	12,500	11,700	24,200
1110	8 Ton	13,200	12,200	25,400
1120	10 Ton	14,000	11,500	25,500

D3040 128	Fan Coil A/C, Horizontal, Duct Mount, 4 Pipe	COST EACH		
		MAT.	INST.	TOTAL
1010	Fan coil A/C system, horiz. w/cabinet, controls, 4 pipe, 1/2 Ton	3,150	3,475	6,625
1020	1 Ton	4,000	4,650	8,650
1030	1-1/2 Ton	4,825	5,525	10,350
1040	2 Ton	5,625	6,200	11,825
1050	3 Ton	6,950	8,225	15,175
1060	3.5 Ton	7,975	10,100	18,075
1070	4 Ton	7,925	10,200	18,125
1080	5 Ton	9,525	14,000	23,525
1090	6 Ton	10,300	16,500	26,800
1100	7 Ton	11,900	18,500	30,400
1110	8 Ton	12,000	19,500	31,500
1120	10 Ton	15,000	24,000	39,000

D3040 Distribution Systems

VAV Terminal   Fan Powered VAV Terminal

System Components	QUANTITY	UNIT	COST EACH		
			MAT.	INST.	TOTAL
SYSTEM D3040 132 1010					
VAV TERMINAL, COOLING ONLY, WITH ACTUATOR/CONTROLS, 200 CFM					
Mixing box variable volume 300 to 600 CFM, cool only	1.000	Ea.	462	114.40	576.40
Ductwork, 12" x 8" fabricated, galvanized steel, 12 LF	55.000	Lb.	42.35	418	460.35
Insulation, ductwork, blanket type, fiberglass, 1" thk, 1-1/2 LB density	40.000	S.F.	36	125.20	161.20
Diffusers, aluminum, OB damper, ceiling, perf, 24"x24" panel size, 6"x6"	2.000	Ea.	332	80	412
Ductwork, flexible, fiberglass fabric, insulated, 1"thk, PE jacket, 6" dia	16.000	L.F.	44	70.40	114.40
Round volume control damper 6" dia.	2.000	Ea.	53	58	111
VAV box balancing	1.000	Ea.		76.50	76.50
Diffuser/register, high, balancing	2.000	Ea.		228	228
TOTAL			969.35	1,170.50	2,139.85

D3040 132	VAV Terminal, Cooling Only	COST EACH		
		MAT.	INST.	TOTAL
1010	VAV Terminal, cooling only, with actuator/controls, 200 CFM	970	1,175	2,145
1020	400 CFM	1,250	2,075	3,325
1030	600 CFM	1,675	3,075	4,750
1040	800 CFM	1,775	3,725	5,500
1050	1000 CFM	2,075	4,325	6,400
1060	1250 CFM	2,450	5,475	7,925
1070	1500 CFM	2,625	6,450	9,075
1080	2000 CFM	3,450	9,200	12,650

D3040 134	VAV Terminal, Hot Water Reheat	COST EACH		
		MAT.	INST.	TOTAL
1010	VAV Terminal, cooling, HW reheat, with actuator/controls, 200 CFM	2,350	2,200	4,550
1020	400 CFM	2,650	3,000	5,650
1030	600 CFM	3,050	4,075	7,125
1040	800 CFM	3,175	4,775	7,950
1050	1000 CFM	3,450	5,350	8,800
1060	1250 CFM	3,925	6,575	10,500
1070	1500 CFM	4,375	7,775	12,150
1080	2000 CFM	5,250	10,600	15,850

D3040 136	Fan Powered VAV Terminal, Cooling Only	COST EACH		
		MAT.	INST.	TOTAL
1010	VAV Terminal, cooling, fan powrd, with actuator/controls, 200 CFM	1,625	1,175	2,800
1020	400 CFM	1,975	1,925	3,900

D30 HVAC

D3040 Distribution Systems

D3040 136	Fan Powered VAV Terminal, Cooling Only	COST EACH		
		MAT.	INST.	TOTAL
1030	600 CFM	2,375	3,050	5,425
1040	800 CFM	2,550	3,650	6,200
1050	1000 CFM	2,825	4,225	7,050
1060	1250 CFM	3,300	5,550	8,850
1070	1500 CFM	3,450	6,500	9,950
1080	2000 CFM	4,400	9,475	13,875

D3040 138	Fan Powered VAV Terminal, Hot Water Reheat	COST EACH		
		MAT.	INST.	TOTAL
1010	VAV Terminal, cool, HW reht, fan powrd, with actuator/ctrls, 200 CFM	2,900	2,175	5,075
1020	400 CFM	3,225	3,000	6,225
1030	600 CFM	3,625	4,100	7,725
1040	800 CFM	3,800	4,700	8,500
1050	1000 CFM	4,100	5,275	9,375
1060	1250 CFM	4,675	6,600	11,275
1070	1500 CFM	5,150	7,850	13,000
1080	2000 CFM	6,075	10,900	16,975

D30 HVAC

D3040 Distribution Systems

Axial Flow Centrifugal Fan
Belt Drive

Belt Drive Utility Set

Centrifugal Roof Exhaust Fan
Direct Drive

System Components	QUANTITY	UNIT	COST EACH		
			MAT.	INST.	TOTAL
SYSTEM D3040 220 1010					
FAN SYSTEM, IN-LINE CENTRIFUGAL, 500 CFM					
Fans, in-line centrifugal, supply/exhaust, 500 CFM, 10" dia conn	1.000	Ea.	1,275	485	1,760
Louver, alum., W/screen, damper, mill fin, fxd blade, cont line, stormproof	4.050	S.F.	186.30	91.13	277.43
Motor for louver damper, electric or pneumatic	1.000	Ea.	530	45.50	575.50
Ductwork, 12" x 8" fabricated, galvanized steel, 60 LF	200.000	Lb.	197.60	1,885	2,082.60
Grilles, aluminum, air supply, single deflection, adjustable, 12" x 6"	1.000	Ea.	87	82.50	169.50
Fire damper, curtain type, vertical, 12" x 8"	1.000	Ea.	26.50	29	55.50
Duct access door, insulated, 10" x 10"	1.000	Ea.	20.50	58	78.50
Duct access door, insulated, 16" x 12"	1.000	Ea.	32.50	70.50	103
Pressure controller/switch, air flow controller	1.000	Ea.	180	56	236
Fan control switch and mounting base	1.000	Ea.	111	42	153
Fan balancing	1.000	Ea.		380	380
Diffuser/register balancing	3.000	Ea.		229.50	229.50
TOTAL			2,646.40	3,454.13	6,100.53

D3040 220	Centrifugal In Line Fan Systems	COST EACH		
		MAT.	INST.	TOTAL
1010	Fan system, in-line centrifugal, 500 CFM	2,650	3,450	6,100
1020	1300 CFM	3,200	6,000	9,200
1030	1500 CFM	3,600	6,925	10,525
1040	2500 CFM	5,725	21,000	26,725
1050	3500 CFM	7,200	28,400	35,600
1060	5000 CFM	9,550	42,200	51,750
1070	7500 CFM	11,200	43,200	54,400
1080	10,000 CFM	13,500	50,500	64,000

D3040 230	Utility Set Fan Systems	COST EACH		
		MAT.	INST.	TOTAL
1010	Utility fan set system, belt drive, 2000 CFM	2,700	11,200	13,900
1020	3500 CFM	4,600	19,700	24,300
1030	5000 CFM	5,850	27,400	33,250
1040	7500 CFM	8,100	31,800	39,900
1050	10,000 CFM	10,900	41,900	52,800
1060	15,000 CFM	11,500	42,700	54,200
1070	20,000 CFM	13,400	48,400	61,800

D30 HVAC

D3040 Distribution Systems

D3040 240	Roof Exhaust Fan Systems	COST EACH		
		MAT.	INST.	TOTAL
1010	Roof vent. system, centrifugal, alum., galv curb, BDD, 500 CFM	1,250	2,275	3,525
1020	800 CFM	1,550	4,375	5,925
1030	1500 CFM	2,300	6,500	8,800
1040	2750 CFM	3,400	14,600	18,000
1050	3500 CFM	4,200	18,800	23,000
1060	5000 CFM	5,950	31,100	37,050
1070	8500 CFM	7,900	40,000	47,900
1080	13,800 CFM	11,100	58,000	69,100

D3040 Controls & Instrumentation

Commercial/Industrial Dust Collection System

System Components	QUANTITY	UNIT	COST EACH		
			MAT.	INST.	TOTAL
SYSTEM D3040 250 1010					
COMMERCIAL/INDUSTRIAL VACUUM DUST COLLECTION SYSTEM, 500 CFM					
Dust collection central vac unit inc. stand, filter & shaker, 500 CFM 2 HP	1.000	Ea.	4,300	605	4,905
Galvanized tubing, 16 ga., 4" OD	80.000	L.F.	528	254.40	782.40
Galvanized tubing, 90° ell, 4" dia.	3.000	Ea.	112.50	69	181.50
Galvanized tubing, 45° ell, 4" dia.	4.000	Ea.	130	92	222
Galvanized tubing, TY slip fit, 4" dia.	4.000	Ea.	316	152	468
Flexible rubber hose, 4" dia.	32.000	L.F.	334.40	101.76	436.16
Galvanized air gate valve, 4" dia.	4.000	Ea.	1,320	200	1,520
Galvanized compression coupling, 4" dia.	36.000	Ea.	954	1,242	2,196
Pipe hangers, steel, 4" pipe size	16.000	Ea.	68.96	172.80	241.76
TOTAL			8,063.86	2,888.96	10,952.82

D3040 250	Commercial/Industrial Vacuum Dust Collection	COST EACH		
		MAT.	INST.	TOTAL
1010	Commercial/industrial, vacuum dust collection system, 500 CFM	8,075	2,900	10,975
1020	1000 CFM	10,700	3,300	14,000
1030	1500 CFM	13,500	3,650	17,150
1040	3000 CFM	29,300	5,100	34,400
1050	5000 CFM	37,100	7,675	44,775

D3040 Controls & Instrumentation

Commercial Kitchen Exhaust/Make-up Air Rooftop System

System Components	QUANTITY	UNIT	COST EACH		
			MAT.	INST.	TOTAL
SYSTEM D3040 260 1010					
COMMERCIAL KITCHEN EXHAUST/MAKE-UP AIR SYSTEM, ROOFTOP, GAS, 2000 CFM					
Make-up air rooftop unit, gas, 750 MBH	1.000	Ea.	3,480.80	143.13	3,623.93
Pipe, black steel, Sch 40, thrded, nipples, W/cplngs/hngrs, 10' OC, 1" dia.	20.000	L.F.	182.60	273.90	456.50
Elbow, 90°, black steel, straight, 3/4" dia.	2.000	Ea.	7.68	94	101.68
Elbow, 90°, black steel, straight, 1" dia.	3.000	Ea.	19.95	151.50	171.45
Tee, black steel, reducing, 1" dia.	1.000	Ea.	16.75	82.50	99.25
Union, black with brass seat, 1" dia.	1.000	Ea.	21	55	76
Pipe nipples, black, 3/4" dia	2.000	Ea.	11.30	21.60	32.90
Pipe cap, malleable iron, black, 1" dia.	1.000	Ea.	5.25	22	27.25
Gas cock, brass, 1" size	1.000	Ea.	34	34.50	68.50
Ductwork, 20" x 14" fabricated, galv. steel, 30 LF	220.000	Lb.	165	1,540	1,705
Ductwork, 18" x 10" fabricated, galv. steel, 12 LF	72.000	Lb.	54	504	558
Ductwork, 30" x 10" fabricated, galv. steel, 30 LF	260.000	Lb.	195	1,820	2,015
Ductwork, 16" x 10" fabricated, galv. steel, 12 LF	70.000	Lb.	52.50	490	542.50
Kitchen ventilation, island style, water wash, Stainless Steel	5.000	L.F.	12,250	1,255	13,505
Control system, Make-up Air Unit/Exhauster	1.000	Ea.	2,750	2,375	5,125
Rooftop unit heat/cool balancing	1.000	Ea.		445	445
Roof fan balancing	1.000	Ea.		254	254
TOTAL			19,245.83	9,561.13	28,806.96

D3040 260	Kitchen Exhaust/Make-Up Air	COST EACH		
		MAT.	INST.	TOTAL
1010	Commercial kitchen exhaust/make-up air system, rooftop, gas, 2000 CFM	19,200	9,550	28,750
1020	3000 CFM	28,600	13,200	41,800
1030	5000 CFM	31,500	15,700	47,200
1040	8000 CFM	47,500	23,200	70,700
1050	12,000 CFM	62,500	27,200	89,700
1060	16,000 CFM	77,500	41,600	119,100

D3040 Distribution Systems

Plate Heat Exchanger   Shell and Tube Heat Exchanger

System Components	QUANTITY	UNIT	COST EACH		
			MAT.	INST.	TOTAL
SYSTEM D3040 620 1010					
SHELL & TUBE HEAT EXCHANGER, 40 GPM					
Heat exchanger, 4 pass, 3/4" O.D. copper tubes, by steam at 10 psi, 40 GPM	1.000	Ea.	4,950	300	5,250
Pipe, black steel, Sch 40, threaded, W/couplings & hangers, 10' OC, 2" dia.	40.000	L.F.	828.20	936.78	1,764.98
Elbow, 90°, straight, 2" dia.	16.000	Ea.	400	1,056	1,456
Reducer, black steel, concentric, 2" dia.	2.000	Ea.	56	113	169
Valves, bronze, gate, rising stem, threaded, class 150, 2" size	6.000	Ea.	1,374	360	1,734
Valves, bronze, globe, class 150, rising stem, threaded, 2" size	2.000	Ea.	1,190	120	1,310
2" pipe size	2.000	Ea.	242	103	345
Valve, electric motor actuated, brass, 2 way, screwed, 1-1/2" pipe size	1.000	Ea.	660	51	711
Union, black with brass seat, 2" dia.	8.000	Ea.	352	560	912
Tee, black, straight, 2" dia.	9.000	Ea.	283.50	972	1,255.50
Tee, black, reducing run and outlet, 2" dia.	4.000	Ea.	230	432	662
Pipe nipple, black, 2" dia.	21.000	Ea.	8.20	9.28	17.48
Thermometers, stem type, 9" case, 8" stem, 3/4" NPT	2.000	Ea.	372	48	420
Gauges, pressure or vacuum, 3-1/2" diameter dial	2.000	Ea.	79	42	121
Insulation, fiberglass pipe covering, 1" wall, 2" IPS	40.000	L.F.	58	220	278
Heat exchanger control system	1.000	Ea.	2,675	2,125	4,800
Coil balancing	1.000	Ea.		124	124
TOTAL			13,757.90	7,572.06	21,329.96

D3040 610	Heat Exchanger, Plate Type	COST EACH		
		MAT.	INST.	TOTAL
1010	Plate heat exchanger, 400 GPM	52,000	15,200	67,200
1020	800 GPM	83,000	19,300	102,300
1030	1200 GPM	124,000	26,200	150,200
1040	1800 GPM	168,000	32,600	200,600

D3040 620	Heat Exchanger, Shell & Tube	COST EACH		
		MAT.	INST.	TOTAL
1010	Shell & tube heat exchanger, 40 GPM	13,800	7,575	21,375
1020	96 GPM	24,200	13,300	37,500
1030	240 GPM	43,900	18,100	62,000
1040	600 GPM	84,500	25,500	110,000

D30 HVAC

D3050 Terminal & Package Units

| Cabinet Unit Heater | Gas Unit Heater | Hydronic Unit Heater |

System Components	QUANTITY	UNIT	COST EACH		
			MAT.	INST.	TOTAL
SYSTEM D3050 120 1010					
SPACE HEATER, SUSPENDED, GAS FIRED, PROPELLER FAN, 20 MBH					
Space heater, propeller fan, 20 MBH output	1.000	Ea.	1,075	142	1,217
Pipe, black steel, Sch 40, threaded, W/coupling & hangers, 10' OC, 3/4" dia	20.000	L.F.	118.65	226.80	345.45
Elbow, 90°, black steel, straight, 1/2" dia.	3.000	Ea.	9.54	132	141.54
Elbow, 90°, black steel, straight, 3/4" dia.	3.000	Ea.	11.52	141	152.52
Tee, black steel, reducing, 3/4" dia.	1.000	Ea.	10.10	73	83.10
Union, black with brass seat, 3/4" dia.	1.000	Ea.	16.15	50.50	66.65
Pipe nipples, black, 1/2" dia	2.000	Ea.	9.64	20.90	30.54
Pipe nipples, black, 3/4" dia	2.000	Ea.	5.65	10.80	16.45
Pipe cap, black, 3/4" dia.	1.000	Ea.	4.36	20.50	24.86
Gas cock, brass, 3/4" size	1.000	Ea.	17.05	30	47.05
Thermostat, 1 set back, electric, timed	1.000	Ea.	38.50	84	122.50
Wiring, thermostat hook-up,25' of #18-3	1.000	Ea.	12.05	25.50	37.55
Vent chimney, prefab metal, U.L. listed, gas, double wall, galv. st, 4" dia	12.000	L.F.	84	202.20	286.20
Vent chimney, gas, double wall, galv. steel, elbow 90°, 4" dia.	2.000	Ea.	52	67	119
Vent chimney, gas, double wall, galv. steel, Tee, 4" dia.	1.000	Ea.	37	44	81
Vent chimney, gas, double wall, galv. steel, T cap, 4" dia.	1.000	Ea.	3.85	27.50	31.35
Vent chimney, gas, double wall, galv. steel, roof flashing, 4" dia.	1.000	Ea.	9.60	33.50	43.10
Vent chimney, gas, double wall, galv. steel, top, 4" dia.	1.000	Ea.	23.50	26	49.50
TOTAL			1,538.16	1,357.20	2,895.36

D3050 120	Unit Heaters, Gas	COST EACH		
		MAT.	INST.	TOTAL
1010	Space heater, suspended, gas fired, propeller fan, 20 MBH	1,550	1,350	2,900
1020	60 MBH	1,825	1,425	3,250
1030	100 MBH	2,050	1,500	3,550
1040	160 MBH	2,400	1,650	4,050
1050	200 MBH	2,850	1,825	4,675
1060	280 MBH	3,550	1,950	5,500
1070	320 MBH	4,500	2,200	6,700

D30 HVAC

D3050 Terminal & Package Units

D3050 130	Unit Heaters, Hydronic	COST EACH		
		MAT.	INST.	TOTAL
1010	Space heater, suspended, horiz. mount, HW, prop. fan, 20 MBH	1,975	1,450	3,425
1020	60 MBH	2,725	1,650	4,375
1030	100 MBH	3,275	1,800	5,075
1040	150 MBH	3,725	1,975	5,700
1050	200 MBH	4,175	2,225	6,400
1060	300 MBH	5,200	2,625	7,825

D3050 140	Cabinet Unit Heaters, Hydronic	COST EACH		
		MAT.	INST.	TOTAL
1010	Unit heater, cabinet type, horizontal blower, hot water, 20 MBH	2,300	1,425	3,725
1020	60 MBH	3,400	1,575	4,975
1030	100 MBH	3,800	1,725	5,525
1040	120 MBH	3,875	1,800	5,675

D30 HVAC

D3050 Terminal & Package Units

Roof • Roof Top Unit • Return Duct • Return Grille • Supply Diff. • Insulated Supply Duct • Finish Ceiling

System Description: Rooftop single zone units are electric cooling and gas heat. Duct systems are low velocity, galvanized steel supply and return. Price variations between sizes are due to several factors. Jumps in the cost of the rooftop unit occur when the manufacturer shifts from the largest capacity unit on a small frame to the smallest capacity on the next larger frame, or changes from one compressor to two. As the unit capacity increases for larger areas the duct distribution grows in proportion. For most applications there is a tradeoff point where it is less expensive and more efficient to utilize smaller units with short simple distribution systems. Larger units also require larger initial supply and return ducts which can create a space problem. Supplemental heat may be desired in colder locations. The table below is based on one unit supplying the area listed. The 10,000 S.F. unit for bars and taverns is not listed because a nominal 110 ton unit would be required and this is above the normal single zone rooftop capacity.

System Components	QUANTITY	UNIT	COST EACH MAT.	COST EACH INST.	COST EACH TOTAL
SYSTEM D3050 150 1280					
ROOFTOP, SINGLE ZONE, AIR CONDITIONER					
APARTMENT CORRIDORS, 500 S.F., .92 TON					
Rooftop air conditioner, 1 zone, electric cool, standard controls, curb	1.000	Ea.	1,817	793.50	2,610.50
Ductwork package for rooftop single zone units	1.000	System	262.20	1,104	1,366.20
TOTAL			2,079.20	1,897.50	3,976.70
COST PER S.F.			4.16	3.80	7.96
*Size would suggest multiple units.					

D3050 150	Rooftop Single Zone Unit Systems		COST PER S.F. MAT.	COST PER S.F. INST.	COST PER S.F. TOTAL
1260	Rooftop, single zone, air conditioner				
1280	Apartment corridors, 500 S.F., .92 ton		4.15	3.80	7.95
1320	1,000 S.F., 1.83 ton	R236000 -20	4.13	3.78	7.91
1360	1500 S.F., 2.75 ton		2.66	3.12	5.78
1400	3,000 S.F., 5.50 ton		2.53	2.99	5.52
1440	5,000 S.F., 9.17 ton		2.65	2.72	5.37
1480	10,000 S.F., 18.33 ton		2.73	2.55	5.28
1560	Banks or libraries, 500 S.F., 2.08 ton		9.40	8.60	18
1600	1,000 S.F., 4.17 ton		6.05	7.10	13.15
1640	1,500 S.F., 6.25 ton		5.75	6.80	12.55
1680	3,000 S.F., 12.50 ton		6	6.20	12.20
1720	5,000 S.F., 20.80 ton		6.20	5.80	12
1760	10,000 S.F., 41.67 ton		5	5.75	10.75
1840	Bars and taverns, 500 S.F. 5.54 ton		13.70	11.40	25.10
1880	1,000 S.F., 11.08 ton		14.45	9.80	24.25
1920	1,500 S.F., 16.62 ton		14.50	9.10	23.60
1960	3,000 S.F., 33.25 ton		11.95	8.65	20.60
2000	5,000 S.F., 55.42 ton		11.20	8.65	19.85
2040	10,000 S.F., 110.83 ton*				
2080	Bowling alleys, 500 S.F., 2.83 ton		8.25	9.60	17.85
2120	1,000 S.F., 5.67 ton		7.80	9.25	17.05
2160	1,500 S.F., 8.50 ton		8.20	8.40	16.60
2200	3,000 S.F., 17.00 ton		8.25	8.05	16.30
2240	5,000 S.F., 28.33 ton		6.90	7.85	14.75
2280	10,000 S.F., 56.67 ton		6.55	7.85	14.40
2360	Department stores, 500 S.F., 1.46 ton		6.60	6	12.60

D3050 Terminal & Package Units

D3050 150	Rooftop Single Zone Unit Systems	COST PER S.F.		
		MAT.	INST.	TOTAL
2400	1,000 S.F., 2.92 ton	4.24	4.96	9.20
2440	1,500 S.F., 4.37 ton	4.02	4.75	8.77
2480	3,000 S.F., 8.75 ton	4.21	4.32	8.53
2520	5,000 S.F., 14.58 ton	4.23	4.14	8.37
2560	10,000 S.F., 29.17 ton	3.56	4.03	7.59
2640	Drug stores, 500 S.F., 3.33 ton	9.70	11.30	21
2680	1,000 S.F., 6.67 ton	9.20	10.85	20.05
2720	1,500 S.F., 10.00 ton	9.65	9.90	19.55
2760	3,000 S.F., 20.00 ton	9.95	9.30	19.25
2800	5,000 S.F., 33.33 ton	8.15	9.20	17.35
2840	10,000 S.F., 66.67 ton	7.70	9.20	16.90
2920	Factories, 500 S.F., 1.67 ton	7.50	6.85	14.35
2960	1,000 S.F., 3.33 ton	4.84	5.65	10.49
3000	1,500 S.F., 5.00 ton	4.60	5.45	10.05
3040	3,000 S.F., 10.00 ton	4.82	4.94	9.76
3080	5,000 S.F., 16.67 ton	4.84	4.73	9.57
3120	10,000 S.F., 33.33 ton	4.07	4.61	8.68
3200	Food supermarkets, 500 S.F., 1.42 ton	6.40	5.85	12.25
3240	1,000 S.F., 2.83 ton	4.08	4.80	8.88
3280	1,500 S.F., 4.25 ton	3.91	4.62	8.53
3320	3,000 S.F., 8.50 ton	4.10	4.20	8.30
3360	5,000 S.F., 14.17 ton	4.11	4.02	8.13
3400	10,000 S.F., 28.33 ton	3.46	3.92	7.38
3480	Medical centers, 500 S.F., 1.17 ton	5.30	4.82	10.12
3520	1,000 S.F., 2.33 ton	5.25	4.81	10.06
3560	1,500 S.F., 3.50 ton	3.40	3.97	7.37
3600	3,000 S.F., 7.00 ton	3.23	3.80	7.03
3640	5,000 S.F., 11.67 ton	3.38	3.46	6.84
3680	10,000 S.F., 23.33 ton	3.47	3.25	6.72
3760	Offices, 500 S.F., 1.58 ton	7.15	6.50	13.65
3800	1,000 S.F., 3.17 ton	4.60	5.40	10
3840	1,500 S.F., 4.75 ton	4.37	5.15	9.52
3880	3,000 S.F., 9.50 ton	4.57	4.69	9.26
3920	5,000 S.F., 15.83 ton	4.60	4.50	9.10
3960	10,000 S.F., 31.67 ton	3.87	4.38	8.25
4000	Restaurants, 500 S.F., 2.50 ton	11.30	10.30	21.60
4040	1,000 S.F., 5.00 ton	6.90	8.15	15.05
4080	1,500 S.F., 7.50 ton	7.25	7.40	14.65
4120	3,000 S.F., 15.00 ton	7.25	7.10	14.35
4160	5,000 S.F., 25.00 ton	7.45	6.95	14.40
4200	10,000 S.F., 50.00 ton	5.80	6.90	12.70
4240	Schools and colleges, 500 S.F., 1.92 ton	8.65	7.90	16.55
4280	1,000 S.F., 3.83 ton	5.55	6.50	12.05
4320	1,500 S.F., 5.75 ton	5.30	6.25	11.55
4360	3,000 S.F., 11.50 ton	5.55	5.70	11.25
4400	5,000 S.F., 19.17 ton	5.70	5.35	11.05
4440	10,000 S.F., 38.33 ton	4.61	5.30	9.91
5000				
5100				
5200				
9000	Components of ductwork packages for above systems, per ton of cooling:			
9010	Ductwork; galvanized steel, 120 pounds			
9020	Insulation; fiberglass 2" thick, FRK faced, 52 S.F.			
9030	Diffusers; aluminum, 24" x 12", one			
9040	Registers; aluminum, return with dampers, one			

D3050 Terminal & Package Units

System Description: Rooftop units are multizone with up to 12 zones, and include electric cooling, gas heat, thermostats, filters, supply and return fans complete. Duct systems are low velocity, galvanized steel supply and return with insulated supplies.

Multizone units cost more per ton of cooling than single zone. However, they offer flexibility where load conditions are varied due to heat generating areas or exposure to radiational heating. For example, perimeter offices on the "sunny side" may require cooling at the same

time "shady side" or central offices may require heating. It is possible to accomplish similar results using duct heaters in branches of the single zone unit. However, heater location could be a problem and total system operating energy efficiency could be lower.

System Components				COST EACH		
	QUANTITY	UNIT		MAT.	INST.	TOTAL
SYSTEM D3050 155 1280						
ROOFTOP, MULTIZONE, AIR CONDITIONER						
APARTMENT CORRIDORS, 3,000 S.F., 5.50 TON						
Rooftop multizone unit, standard controls, curb	1.000	Ea.		28,820	1,848	30,668
Ductwork package for rooftop multizone units	1.000	System		2,145	12,650	14,795
TOTAL				30,965	14,498	45,463
COST PER S.F.				10.32	4.83	15.15

Note A: Small single zone unit recommended.
Note B: A combination of multizone units recommended.

D3050 155	Rooftop Multizone Unit Systems		COST PER S.F.		
			MAT.	INST.	TOTAL
1240	Rooftop, multizone, air conditioner				
1260	Apartment corridors, 1,500 S.F., 2.75 ton. See Note A.				
1280	3,000 S.F., 5.50 ton	R236000 -20	10.33	4.83	15.16
1320	10,000 S.F., 18.30 ton		7.15	4.65	11.80
1360	15,000 S.F., 27.50 ton		7.05	4.63	11.68
1400	20,000 S.F., 36.70 ton		7.35	4.64	11.99
1440	25,000 S.F., 45.80 ton		6.85	4.66	11.51
1520	Banks or libraries, 1,500 S.F., 6.25 ton		23.50	11	34.50
1560	3,000 S.F., 12.50 ton		19.80	10.75	30.55
1600	10,000 S.F., 41.67 ton		15.60	10.60	26.20
1640	15,000 S.F., 62.50 ton		11.55	10.55	22.10
1680	20,000 S.F., 83.33 ton		11.55	10.55	22.10
1720	25,000 S.F., 104.00 ton		10.35	10.50	20.85
1800	Bars and taverns, 1,500 S.F., 16.62 ton		50.50	15.85	66.35
1840	3,000 S.F., 33.24 ton		42	15.30	57.30
1880	10,000 S.F., 110.83 ton		25.50	15.20	40.70
1920	15,000 S.F., 165 ton, See Note B.				
1960	20,000 S.F., 220 ton, See Note B.				
2000	25,000 S.F., 275 ton, See Note B.				
2080	Bowling alleys, 1,500 S.F., 8.50 ton		32	14.95	46.95
2120	3,000 S.F., 17.00 ton		27	14.60	41.60
2160	10,000 S.F., 56.70 ton		21	14.45	35.45
2200	15,000 S.F., 85.00 ton		15.70	14.35	30.05
2240	20,000 S.F., 113.00 ton		14.05	14.25	28.30
2280	25,000 S.F., 140.00 ton see Note B.				
2360	Department stores, 1,500 S.F., 4.37 ton, See Note A.				

D3050 Terminal & Package Units

D3050 155	Rooftop Multizone Unit Systems	COST PER S.F.		
		MAT.	INST.	TOTAL
2400	3,000 S.F., 8.75 ton	16.40	7.70	24.10
2440	10,000 S.F., 29.17 ton	11.70	7.40	19.10
2480	15,000 S.F., 43.75 ton	10.90	7.45	18.35
2520	20,000 S.F., 58.33 ton	8.05	7.35	15.40
2560	25,000 S.F., 72.92 ton	8.10	7.40	15.50
2640	Drug stores, 1,500 S.F., 10.00 ton	37.50	17.55	55.05
2680	3,000 S.F., 20.00 ton	26	16.95	42.95
2720	10,000 S.F., 66.66 ton	18.45	16.85	35.30
2760	15,000 S.F., 100.00 ton	16.55	16.80	33.35
2800	20,000 S.F., 135 ton, See Note B.			
2840	25,000 S.F., 165 ton, See Note B.			
2920	Factories, 1,500 S.F., 5 ton, See Note A.			
2960	3,000 S.F., 10.00 ton	18.75	8.80	27.55
3000	10,000 S.F., 33.33 ton	13.35	8.45	21.80
3040	15,000 S.F., 50.00 ton	12.45	8.50	20.95
3080	20,000 S.F., 66.66 ton	9.25	8.45	17.70
3120	25,000 S.F., 83.33 ton	9.25	8.45	17.70
3200	Food supermarkets, 1,500 S.F., 4.25 ton, See Note A.			
3240	3,000 S.F., 8.50 ton	15.95	7.45	23.40
3280	10,000 S.F., 28.33 ton	10.85	7.15	18
3320	15,000 S.F., 42.50 ton	10.60	7.20	17.80
3360	20,000 S.F., 56.67 ton	7.85	7.15	15
3400	25,000 S.F., 70.83 ton	7.85	7.15	15
3480	Medical centers, 1,500 S.F., 3.5 ton, See Note A.			
3520	3,000 S.F., 7.00 ton	13.15	6.15	19.30
3560	10,000 S.F., 23.33 ton	8.80	5.90	14.70
3600	15,000 S.F., 35.00 ton	9.35	5.90	15.25
3640	20,000 S.F., 46.66 ton	8.75	5.95	14.70
3680	25,000 S.F., 58.33 ton	6.45	5.90	12.35
3760	Offices, 1,500 S.F., 4.75 ton, See Note A.			
3800	3,000 S.F., 9.50 ton	17.85	8.35	26.20
3840	10,000 S.F., 31.66 ton	12.70	8	20.70
3880	15,000 S.F., 47.50 ton	11.85	8.05	19.90
3920	20,000 S.F., 63.33 ton	8.75	8	16.75
3960	25,000 S.F., 79.16 ton	8.75	8	16.75
4000	Restaurants, 1,500 S.F., 7.50 ton	28	13.20	41.20
4040	3,000 S.F., 15.00 ton	24	12.90	36.90
4080	10,000 S.F., 50.00 ton	18.70	12.75	31.45
4120	15,000 S.F., 75.00 ton	13.85	12.65	26.50
4160	20,000 S.F., 100.00 ton	12.40	12.60	25
4200	25,000 S.F., 125 ton, See Note B.			
4240	Schools and colleges, 1,500 S.F., 5.75 ton	21.50	10.10	31.60
4280	3,000 S.F., 11.50 ton	18.20	9.90	28.10
4320	10,000 S.F., 38.33 ton	14.35	9.75	24.10
4360	15,000 S.F., 57.50 ton	10.60	9.70	20.30
4400	20,000 S.F.,76.66 ton	10.60	9.70	20.30
4440	25,000 S.F., 95.83 ton	10	9.70	19.70
4450				
9000	Components of ductwork packages for above systems, per ton of cooling:			
9010	Ductwork; galvanized steel, 240 pounds			
9020	Insulation; fiberglass, 2" thick, FRK faced, 104 S.F.			
9030	Diffusers; aluminum, 24" x 12", two			
9040	Registers; aluminum, return with dampers, one			

D3050 Terminal & Package Units

System Description: Self-contained, single package water cooled units include cooling tower, pump, piping allowance. Systems for 1000 S.F. and up include duct and diffusers to provide for even distribution of air. Smaller units distribute air through a supply air plenum, which is integral with the unit.

Returns are not ducted and supplies are not insulated.

Hot water or steam heating coils are included but piping to boiler and the boiler itself is not included.

Where local codes or conditions permit single pass cooling for the smaller units, deduct 10%.

System Components			COST EACH		
	QUANTITY	UNIT	MAT.	INST.	TOTAL
SYSTEM D3050 160 1300					
SELF-CONTAINED, WATER COOLED UNIT					
APARTMENT CORRIDORS, 500 S.F., .92 TON					
Self contained, water cooled, single package air conditioner unit	1.000	Ea.	1,285.20	630	1,915.20
Ductwork package for water or air cooled packaged units	1.000	System	75.44	837.20	912.64
Cooling tower, draw thru single flow, belt drive	1.000	Ea.	198.72	19.32	218.04
Cooling tower pumps & piping	1.000	System	99.36	45.54	144.90
TOTAL			1,658.72	1,532.06	3,190.78
COST PER S.F.			3.32	3.06	6.38

D3050 160	Self-contained, Water Cooled Unit Systems		COST PER S.F.		
			MAT.	INST.	TOTAL
1280	Self-contained, water cooled unit		3.32	3.06	6.38
1300	Apartment corridors, 500 S.F., .92 ton		3.30	3.05	6.35
1320	1,000 S.F., 1.83 ton	R236000	3.32	3.06	6.38
1360	3,000 S.F., 5.50 ton	-20	2.78	2.56	5.34
1400	5,000 S.F., 9.17 ton		2.65	2.38	5.03
1440	10,000 S.F., 18.33 ton		3.73	2.12	5.85
1520	Banks or libraries, 500 S.F., 2.08 ton		7.20	3.16	10.36
1560	1,000 S.F., 4.17 ton		6.30	5.80	12.10
1600	3,000 S.F., 12.50 ton		6	5.40	11.40
1640	5,000 S.F., 20.80 ton		8.45	4.82	13.27
1680	10,000 S.F., 41.66 ton		7.35	4.82	12.17
1760	Bars and taverns, 500 S.F., 5.54 ton		15.75	5.30	21.05
1800	1,000 S.F., 11.08 ton		15.40	9.25	24.65
1840	3,000 S.F., 33.25 ton		19.80	7.30	27.10
1880	5,000 S.F., 55.42 ton		18.65	7.60	26.25
1920	10,000 S.F., 110.00 ton		18.15	7.50	25.65
2000	Bowling alleys, 500 S.F., 2.83 ton		9.75	4.29	14.04
2040	1,000 S.F., 5.66 ton		8.55	7.90	16.45
2080	3,000 S.F., 17.00 ton		11.50	6.55	18.05
2120	5,000 S.F., 28.33 ton		10.40	6.30	16.70
2160	10,000 S.F., 56.66 ton		9.75	6.45	16.20
2200	Department stores, 500 S.F., 1.46 ton		5.05	2.21	7.26
2240	1,000 S.F., 2.92 ton		4.42	4.05	8.47
2280	3,000 S.F., 8.75 ton		4.21	3.76	7.97
2320	5,000 S.F., 14.58 ton		5.90	3.36	9.26
2360	10,000 S.F., 29.17 ton		5.35	3.24	8.59

D3050 Terminal & Package Units

D3050 160	Self-contained, Water Cooled Unit Systems	COST PER S.F.		
		MAT.	INST.	TOTAL
2440	Drug stores, 500 S.F., 3.33 ton	11.50	5.05	16.55
2480	1,000 S.F., 6.66 ton	10.10	9.30	19.40
2520	3,000 S.F., 20.00 ton	13.55	7.70	21.25
2560	5,000 S.F., 33.33 ton	14.15	7.60	21.75
2600	10,000 S.F., 66.66 ton	11.50	7.60	19.10
2680	Factories, 500 S.F., 1.66 ton	5.75	2.52	8.27
2720	1,000 S.F. 3.37 ton	5.10	4.70	9.80
2760	3,000 S.F., 10.00 ton	4.80	4.32	9.12
2800	5,000 S.F., 16.66 ton	6.75	3.85	10.60
2840	10,000 S.F., 33.33 ton	6.15	3.71	9.86
2920	Food supermarkets, 500 S.F., 1.42 ton	4.89	2.15	7.04
2960	1,000 S.F., 2.83 ton	5.10	4.73	9.83
3000	3,000 S.F., 8.50 ton	4.28	3.95	8.23
3040	5,000 S.F., 14.17 ton	4.08	3.67	7.75
3080	10,000 S.F., 28.33 ton	5.20	3.16	8.36
3160	Medical centers, 500 S.F., 1.17 ton	4.02	1.77	5.79
3200	1,000 S.F., 2.33 ton	4.21	3.89	8.10
3240	3,000 S.F., 7.00 ton	3.52	3.25	6.77
3280	5,000 S.F., 11.66 ton	3.35	3.02	6.37
3320	10,000 S.F., 23.33 ton	4.72	2.70	7.42
3400	Offices, 500 S.F., 1.58 ton	5.45	2.41	7.86
3440	1,000 S.F., 3.17 ton	5.70	5.30	11
3480	3,000 S.F., 9.50 ton	4.55	4.10	8.65
3520	5,000 S.F., 15.83 ton	6.40	3.67	10.07
3560	10,000 S.F., 31.67 ton	5.80	3.53	9.33
3640	Restaurants, 500 S.F., 2.50 ton	8.65	3.80	12.45
3680	1,000 S.F., 5.00 ton	7.55	6.95	14.50
3720	3,000 S.F., 15.00 ton	7.20	6.50	13.70
3760	5,000 S.F., 25.00 ton	10.15	5.80	15.95
3800	10,000 S.F., 50.00 ton	6.35	5.30	11.65
3880	Schools and colleges, 500 S.F., 1.92 ton	6.60	2.90	9.50
3920	1,000 S.F., 3.83 ton	5.80	5.35	11.15
3960	3,000 S.F., 11.50 ton	5.50	4.96	10.46
4000	5,000 S.F., 19.17 ton	7.75	4.43	12.18
4040	10,000 S.F., 38.33 ton	6.80	4.43	11.23
4050				
9000	Components of ductwork packages for above systems, per ton of cooling:			
9010	Ductwork; galvanized steel, 108 pounds			
9020	Diffusers, aluminum, 24" x 12", two			

D3050 Terminal & Package Units

System Description: Self-contained air cooled units with remote air cooled condenser and interconnecting tubing. Systems for 1000 S.F. and up include duct and diffusers. Smaller units distribute air directly.

Returns are not ducted and supplies are not insulated.

Potential savings may be realized by using a single zone rooftop system or through-the-wall unit, especially in the smaller capacities, if the application permits.

Hot water or steam heating coils are included but piping to boiler and the boiler itself is not included.

Condenserless models are available for 15% less where remote refrigerant source is available.

System Components			COST EACH		
	QUANTITY	UNIT	MAT.	INST.	TOTAL
SYSTEM D3050 165 1320					
SELF-CONTAINED, AIR COOLED UNIT					
APARTMENT CORRIDORS, 500 S.F., .92 TON					
Air cooled, package unit	1.000	Ea.	1,300.50	408	1,708.50
Ductwork package for water or air cooled packaged units	1.000	System	75.44	837.20	912.64
Refrigerant piping	1.000	System	547.40	556.60	1,104
Air cooled condenser, direct drive, propeller fan	1.000	Ea.	341	156.55	497.55
TOTAL			2,264.34	1,958.35	4,222.69
COST PER S.F.			4.53	3.92	8.45

D3050 165	Self-contained, Air Cooled Unit Systems	COST PER S.F.		
		MAT.	INST.	TOTAL
1300	Self-contained, air cooled unit			
1320	Apartment corridors, 500 S.F., .92 ton	4.55	3.90	8.45
1360	1,000 S.F., 1.83 ton	4.47	3.89	8.36
1400	3,000 S.F., 5.50 ton	3.83	3.64	7.47
1440	5,000 S.F., 9.17 ton	3.37	3.46	6.83
1480	10,000 S.F., 18.33 ton	3.42	3.17	6.59
1560	Banks or libraries, 500 S.F., 2.08 ton	9.80	5.05	14.85
1600	1,000 S.F., 4.17 ton	8.65	8.25	16.90
1640	3,000 S.F., 12.50 ton	7.65	7.85	15.50
1680	5,000 S.F., 20.80 ton	7.80	7.20	15
1720	10,000 S.F., 41.66 ton	8.20	7.05	15.25
1800	Bars and taverns, 500 S.F., 5.54 ton	20.50	10.95	31.45
1840	1,000 S.F., 11.08 ton	19.85	15.80	35.65
1880	3,000 S.F., 33.25 ton	21	13.70	34.70
1920	5,000 S.F., 55.42 ton	22	13.65	35.65
1960	10,000 S.F., 110.00 ton	22	13.60	35.60
2040	Bowling alleys, 500 S.F., 2.83 ton	13.40	6.85	20.25
2080	1,000 S.F., 5.66 ton	11.80	11.25	23.05
2120	3,000 S.F., 17.00 ton	10.60	9.80	20.40
2160	5,000 S.F., 28.33 ton	11.05	9.60	20.65
2200	10,000 S.F., 56.66 ton	11.45	9.55	21
2240	Department stores, 500 S.F., 1.46 ton	6.90	3.53	10.43
2280	1,000 S.F., 2.92 ton	6.10	5.75	11.85
2320	3,000 S.F., 8.75 ton	5.35	5.50	10.85

Note on row 1400: R236000 -20

D3050 Terminal & Package Units

D3050 165	Self-contained, Air Cooled Unit Systems	COST PER S.F.		
		MAT.	INST.	TOTAL
2360	5,000 S.F., 14.58 ton	5.35	5.50	10.85
2400	10,000 S.F., 29.17 ton	5.70	4.92	10.62
2480	Drug stores, 500 S.F., 3.33 ton	15.75	8.10	23.85
2520	1,000 S.F., 6.66 ton	13.90	13.20	27.10
2560	3,000 S.F., 20.00 ton	12.50	11.55	24.05
2600	5,000 S.F., 33.33 ton	13	11.25	24.25
2640	10,000 S.F., 66.66 ton	13.60	11.25	24.85
2720	Factories, 500 S.F., 1.66 ton	7.95	4.08	12.03
2760	1,000 S.F., 3.33 ton	7	6.65	13.65
2800	3,000 S.F., 10.00 ton	6.10	6.30	12.40
2840	5,000 S.F., 16.66 ton	6.20	5.75	11.95
2880	10,000 S.F., 33.33 ton	6.50	5.65	12.15
2960	Food supermarkets, 500 S.F., 1.42 ton	6.70	3.43	10.13
3000	1,000 S.F., 2.83 ton	6.90	6	12.90
3040	3,000 S.F., 8.50 ton	5.90	5.60	11.50
3080	5,000 S.F., 14.17 ton	5.20	5.35	10.55
3120	10,000 S.F., 28.33 ton	5.55	4.78	10.33
3200	Medical centers, 500 S.F., 1.17 ton	5.55	2.83	8.38
3240	1,000 S.F., 2.33 ton	5.75	4.95	10.70
3280	3,000 S.F., 7.00 ton	4.88	4.62	9.50
3320	5,000 S.F., 16.66 ton	4.30	4.39	8.69
3360	10,000 S.F., 23.33 ton	4.36	4.03	8.39
3440	Offices, 500 S.F., 1.58 ton	7.50	3.85	11.35
3480	1,000 S.F., 3.16 ton	7.80	6.75	14.55
3520	3,000 S.F., 9.50 ton	5.80	5.95	11.75
3560	5,000 S.F., 15.83 ton	5.95	5.50	11.45
3600	10,000 S.F., 31.66 ton	6.20	5.35	11.55
3680	Restaurants, 500 S.F., 2.50 ton	11.75	6.05	17.80
3720	1,000 S.F., 5.00 ton	10.45	9.90	20.35
3760	3,000 S.F., 15.00 ton	9.20	9.40	18.60
3800	5,000 S.F., 25.00 ton	9.75	8.45	18.20
3840	10,000 S.F., 50.00 ton	10.25	8.40	18.65
3920	Schools and colleges, 500 S.F., 1.92 ton	9.05	4.65	13.70
3960	1,000 S.F., 3.83 ton	8.05	7.60	15.65
4000	3,000 S.F., 11.50 ton	7.05	7.20	14.25
4040	5,000 S.F., 19.17 ton	7.15	6.65	13.80
4080	10,000 S.F., 38.33 ton	7.60	6.50	14.10
4090				
9000	Components of ductwork packages for above systems, per ton of cooling:			
9010	Ductwork; galvanized steel, 102 pounds			
9020	Diffusers; aluminum, 24" x 12", two			

D3050 Terminal & Package Units

Air Cooled Condensing Unit
Refrigerant Piping
Roof
Supply Duct
Fin. Ceiling
Return Grille
DX Air Handling Unit
Supply Diffuser

General: Split systems offer several important advantages which should be evaluated when a selection is to be made. They provide a greater degree of flexibility in component selection which permits an accurate match-up of the proper equipment size and type with the particular needs of the building. This allows for maximum use of modern energy saving concepts in heating and cooling. Outdoor installation of the air cooled condensing unit allows space savings in the building and also isolates the equipment operating sounds from building occupants.

Design Assumptions: The systems below are comprised of a direct expansion air handling unit and air cooled condensing unit with interconnecting copper tubing. Ducts and diffusers are also included for distribution of air. Systems are priced for cooling only. Heat can be added as desired either by putting hot water/steam coils into the air unit or into the duct supplying the particular area of need. Gas fired duct furnaces are also available. Refrigerant liquid line is insulated.

System Components	QUANTITY	UNIT	COST EACH		
			MAT.	INST.	TOTAL
SYSTEM D3050 170 1280					
SPLIT SYSTEM, AIR COOLED CONDENSING UNIT					
APARTMENT CORRIDORS, 1,000 S.F., 1.80 TON					
Fan coil AC unit, cabinet mntd & filters direct expansion air cool	1.000	Ea.	530.70	148.23	678.93
Ductwork package, for split system, remote condensing unit	1.000	System	70.46	791.48	861.94
Refrigeration piping	1.000	System	444.69	924.15	1,368.84
Condensing unit, air cooled, incls compressor & standard controls	1.000	Ea.	1,494.50	591.70	2,086.20
TOTAL			2,540.35	2,455.56	4,995.91
COST PER S.F.			2.54	2.46	5

*Cooling requirements would lead to choosing a water cooled unit.

D3050 170	Split Systems With Air Cooled Condensing Units	COST PER S.F.		
		MAT.	INST.	TOTAL
1260	Split system, air cooled condensing unit			
1280	Apartment corridors, 1,000 S.F., 1.83 ton	2.55	2.45	5
1320	2,000 S.F., 3.66 ton	1.98	2.48	4.46
1360	5,000 S.F., 9.17 ton	2.19	3.09	5.28
1400	10,000 S.F., 18.33 ton	2.51	3.38	5.89
1440	20,000 S.F., 36.66 ton	2.76	3.43	6.19
1520	Banks and libraries, 1,000 S.F., 4.17 ton	4.52	5.65	10.17
1560	2,000 S.F., 8.33 ton	4.96	7	11.96
1600	5,000 S.F., 20.80 ton	5.70	7.65	13.35
1640	10,000 S.F., 41.66 ton	6.25	7.80	14.05
1680	20,000 S.F., 83.32 ton	7.50	8.10	15.60
1760	Bars and taverns, 1,000 S.F., 11.08 ton	11.45	11.10	22.55
1800	2,000 S.F., 22.16 ton	15.25	13.25	28.50
1840	5,000 S.F., 55.42 ton	13.50	12.40	25.90
1880	10,000 S.F., 110.84 ton	16.35	12.95	29.30
1920	20,000 S.F., 220 ton*			
2000	Bowling alleys, 1,000 S.F., 5.66 ton	6.30	10.50	16.80
2040	2,000 S.F., 11.33 ton	6.75	9.55	16.30
2080	5,000 S.F., 28.33 ton	7.75	10.45	18.20
2120	10,000 S.F., 56.66 ton	8.50	10.60	19.10
2160	20,000 S.F., 113.32 ton	11.40	11.50	22.90
2320	Department stores, 1,000 S.F., 2.92 ton	3.20	3.87	7.07
2360	2,000 S.F., 5.83 ton	3.24	5.40	8.64
2400	5,000 S.F., 14.58 ton	3.47	4.91	8.38
2440	10,000 S.F., 29.17 ton	3.99	5.35	9.34
2480	20,000 S.F., 58.33 ton	4.39	5.45	9.84

R236000 -20

D30 HVAC

D3050 Terminal & Package Units

D3050 170	Split Systems With Air Cooled Condensing Units	COST PER S.F.		
		MAT.	INST.	TOTAL
2560	Drug stores, 1,000 S.F., 6.66 ton	7.40	12.35	19.75
2600	2,000 S.F., 13.32 ton	7.95	11.20	19.15
2640	5,000 S.F., 33.33 ton	10	12.45	22.45
2680	10,000 S.F., 66.66 ton	11	13.05	24.05
2720	20,000 S.F., 133.32 ton*			
2800	Factories, 1,000 S.F., 3.33 ton	3.66	4.42	8.08
2840	2,000 S.F., 6.66 ton	3.71	6.20	9.91
2880	5,000 S.F., 16.66 ton	4.56	6.15	10.71
2920	10,000 S.F., 33.33 ton	5	6.25	11.25
2960	20,000 S.F., 66.66 ton	5.50	6.50	12
3040	Food supermarkets, 1,000 S.F., 2.83 ton	3.11	3.76	6.87
3080	2,000 S.F., 5.66 ton	3.15	5.25	8.40
3120	5,000 S.F., 14.66 ton	3.38	4.78	8.16
3160	10,000 S.F., 28.33 ton	3.88	5.20	9.08
3200	20,000 S.F., 56.66 ton	4.27	5.30	9.57
3280	Medical centers, 1,000 S.F., 2.33 ton	2.76	3.04	5.80
3320	2,000 S.F., 4.66 ton	2.60	4.33	6.93
3360	5,000 S.F., 11.66 ton	2.78	3.94	6.72
3400	10,000 S.F., 23.33 ton	3.20	4.30	7.50
3440	20,000 S.F., 46.66 ton	3.52	4.36	7.88
3520	Offices, 1,000 S.F., 3.17 ton	3.47	4.21	7.68
3560	2,000 S.F., 6.33 ton	3.51	5.90	9.41
3600	5,000 S.F., 15.83 ton	3.78	5.35	9.13
3640	10,000 S.F., 31.66 ton	4.33	5.85	10.18
3680	20,000 S.F., 63.32 ton	5.20	6.20	11.40
3760	Restaurants, 1,000 S.F., 5.00 ton	5.55	9.30	14.85
3800	2,000 S.F., 10.00 ton	6	8.45	14.45
3840	5,000 S.F., 25.00 ton	6.85	9.20	16.05
3880	10,000 S.F., 50.00 ton	7.55	9.35	16.90
3920	20,000 S.F., 100.00 ton	10.05	10.15	20.20
4000	Schools and colleges, 1,000 S.F., 3.83 ton	4.15	5.20	9.35
4040	2,000 S.F., 7.66 ton	4.58	6.45	11.03
4080	5,000 S.F., 19.17 ton	5.25	7.05	12.30
4120	10,000 S.F., 38.33 ton	5.80	7.15	12.95
4160	20,000 S.F., 76.66 ton	6.35	7.50	13.85
5000				
5100				
5200				
9000	Components of ductwork packages for above systems, per ton of cooling:			
9010	Ductwork; galvanized steel, 102 pounds			
9020	Diffusers; aluminum, 24" x 12", two			

D3050 Terminal & Package Units

Gas Cock

Roof Curb

Gas Piping

Rooftop Air Conditioner Unit

System Components	QUANTITY	UNIT	COST EACH		
			MAT.	INST.	TOTAL
SYSTEM D3050 175 1010					
A/C, ROOFTOP, DX COOL, GAS HEAT, CURB, ECONOMIZER, FILTERS., 5 TON					
Roof top A/C, curb, economizer, sgl zone, elec cool, gas ht, 5 ton, 112 MBH	1.000	Ea.	5,475	2,150	7,625
Pipe, black steel, Sch 40, threaded, W/cplgs & hangers, 10' OC, 1" dia	20.000	L.F.	174.30	261.45	435.75
Elbow, 90°, black, straight, 3/4" dia.	3.000	Ea.	11.52	141	152.52
Elbow, 90°, black, straight, 1" dia.	3.000	Ea.	19.95	151.50	171.45
Tee, black, reducing, 1" dia.	1.000	Ea.	16.75	82.50	99.25
Union, black with brass seat, 1" dia.	1.000	Ea.	21	55	76
Pipe nipple, black, 3/4" dia	2.000	Ea.	11.30	21.60	32.90
Pipe nipple, black, 1" dia	2.000	Ea.	8.30	12.45	20.75
Cap, black, 1" dia.	1.000	Ea.	5.25	22	27.25
Gas cock, brass, 1" size	1.000	Ea.	34	34.50	68.50
Control system, pneumatic, Rooftop A/C unit	1.000	Ea.	2,750	2,375	5,125
Rooftop unit heat/cool balancing	1.000	Ea.		445	445
TOTAL			8,527.37	5,752	14,279.37

D3050 175	Rooftop Air Conditioner, Const. Volume	COST EACH		
		MAT.	INST.	TOTAL
1010	A/C, Rooftop, DX cool, gas heat, curb, economizer, fltrs, 5 Ton	8,525	5,750	14,275
1020	7-1/2 Ton	11,500	6,000	17,500
1030	12-1/2 Ton	17,900	6,575	24,475
1040	18 Ton	23,900	7,200	31,100
1050	25 Ton	30,700	8,200	38,900
1060	40 Ton	39,900	11,000	50,900

D3050 180	Rooftop Air Conditioner, Variable Air Volume	COST EACH		
		MAT.	INST.	TOTAL
1010	A/C, Rooftop, DX cool, gas heat, curb, ecmizr, fltrs, VAV, 12-1/2 Ton	19,900	7,025	26,925
1020	18 Ton	26,200	7,725	33,925
1030	25 Ton	33,500	8,900	42,400
1040	40 Ton	45,000	12,100	57,100
1050	60 Ton	65,000	16,400	81,400
1060	80 Ton	100,500	20,500	121,000

D3050 Terminal & Package Units

Computer rooms impose special requirements on air conditioning systems. A prime requirement is reliability, due to the potential monetary loss that could be incurred by a system failure. A second basic requirement is the tolerance of control with which temperature and humidity are regulated, and dust eliminated. As the air conditioning system reliability is so vital, the additional cost of reserve capacity and redundant components is often justified.

System Descriptions: Computer areas may be environmentally controlled by one of three methods as follows:

1. Self-contained Units
These are units built to higher standards of performance and reliability.

They usually contain alarms and controls to indicate component operation failure, filter change, etc. It should be remembered that these units in the room will occupy space that is relatively expensive to build and that all alterations and service of the equipment will also have to be accomplished within the computer area.

2. Decentralized Air Handling Units In operation these are similar to the self-contained units except that their cooling capability comes from remotely located refrigeration equipment as refrigerant or chilled water. As no compressors or refrigerating equipment are required in the air units, they are smaller and require less service than

self-contained units. An added plus for this type of system occurs if some of the computer components themselves also require chilled water for cooling.

3. Central System Supply Cooling is obtained from a central source which, since it is not located within the computer room, may have excess capacity and permit greater flexibility without interfering with the computer components. System performance criteria must still be met.

Note: The costs shown below do not include an allowance for ductwork or piping.

D3050 185	Computer Room Cooling Units	COST EACH		
		MAT.	INST.	TOTAL
0560	Computer room unit, air cooled, includes remote condenser			
0580	3 ton	19,600	2,425	22,025
0600	5 ton	21,000	2,700	23,700
0620	8 ton	39,200	4,475	43,675
0640	10 ton	40,900	4,850	45,750
0660	15 ton	45,000	5,500	50,500
0680	20 ton	54,500	7,850	62,350
0700	23 ton	67,000	8,950	75,950
0800	Chilled water, for connection to existing chiller system			
0820	5 ton	15,000	1,625	16,625
0840	8 ton	15,200	2,425	17,625
0860	10 ton	15,300	2,475	17,775
0880	15 ton	16,100	2,525	18,625
0900	20 ton	17,100	2,625	19,725
0920	23 ton	18,200	2,975	21,175
1000	Glycol system, complete except for interconnecting tubing			
1020	3 ton	24,600	3,025	27,625
1040	5 ton	26,900	3,175	30,075
1060	8 ton	43,300	5,250	48,550
1080	10 ton	46,000	5,750	51,750
1100	15 ton	57,000	7,225	64,225
1120	20 ton	62,500	7,850	70,350
1140	23 ton	66,000	8,175	74,175
1240	Water cooled, not including condenser water supply or cooling tower			
1260	3 ton	20,000	1,950	21,950
1280	5 ton	21,700	2,250	23,950
1300	8 ton	35,600	3,675	39,275
1320	15 ton	43,200	4,475	47,675
1340	20 ton	46,400	4,950	51,350
1360	23 ton	48,600	5,375	53,975

D3050 201	Packaged A/C, Elec. Ht., Const. Volume	COST EACH		
		MAT.	INST.	TOTAL
1010	A/C Packaged, DX, air cooled, electric heat, constant vol., 5 Ton	8,600	4,075	12,675
1020	10 Ton	13,800	5,600	19,400

D30 HVAC

D3050 Terminal & Package Units

D3050 201	Packaged A/C, Elec. Ht., Const. Volume	COST EACH		
		MAT.	INST.	TOTAL
1030	20 Ton	25,900	7,375	33,275
1040	30 Ton	40,300	8,175	48,475
1050	40 Ton	53,000	9,425	62,425
1060	50 Ton	70,000	10,600	80,600

D3050 202	Packaged Air Conditioner, Elect. Heat, VAV	COST EACH		
		MAT.	INST.	TOTAL
1010	A/C Packaged, DX, air cooled, electric heat, VAV, 10 Ton	15,500	7,000	22,500
1020	20 Ton	28,800	9,225	38,025
1030	30 Ton	44,700	10,100	54,800
1040	40 Ton	58,500	11,600	70,100
1050	50 Ton	76,500	12,900	89,400
1060	60 Ton	87,500	15,000	102,500

D3050 203	Packaged A/C, Hot Wtr. Heat, Const. Volume	COST EACH		
		MAT.	INST.	TOTAL
1010	A/C Packaged, DX, air cooled, H/W heat, constant vol., 5 Ton	7,300	6,025	13,325
1020	10 Ton	10,900	7,900	18,800
1030	20 Ton	22,600	10,600	33,200
1040	30 Ton	33,600	13,100	46,700
1050	40 Ton	46,800	14,700	61,500
1060	50 Ton	60,000	16,000	76,000

D3050 204	Packaged A/C, Hot Wtr. Heat, VAV	COST EACH		
		MAT.	INST.	TOTAL
1010	A/C Packaged, DX, air cooled, H/W heat, VAV, 10 Ton	12,600	9,150	21,750
1020	20 Ton	25,600	12,000	37,600
1030	30 Ton	38,100	14,800	52,900
1040	40 Ton	52,000	16,000	68,000
1050	50 Ton	66,500	18,600	85,100
1060	60 Ton	80,000	20,800	100,800

D30 HVAC

D3050   Terminal & Package Units

Condenser Supply Water Piping

Condenser Return Water Piping

Self—Contained Air Conditioner Unit, Water Cooled

System Components	QUANTITY	UNIT	COST EACH		
			MAT.	INST.	TOTAL
SYSTEM D3050 210 1010					
A/C, SELF CONTAINED, SINGLE PKG., WATER COOLED, ELECT. HEAT, 5 TON					
Self-contained, water cooled, elect. heat, not inc tower, 5 ton, const vol	1.000	Ea.	8,750	1,575	10,325
Pipe, black steel, Sch 40, threaded, W/cplg & hangers, 10' OC, 1-1/4" dia.	20.000	L.F.	224.68	287.03	511.71
Elbow, 90°, black, straight, 1-1/4" dia.	6.000	Ea.	66	324	390
Tee, black, straight, 1-1/4" dia.	2.000	Ea.	33.80	169	202.80
Tee, black, reducing, 1-1/4" dia.	2.000	Ea.	59	169	228
Thermometers, stem type, 9" case, 8" stem, 3/4" NPT	2.000	Ea.	372	48	420
Union, black with brass seat, 1-1/4" dia.	2.000	Ea.	60	113	173
Pipe nipple, black, 1-1/4" dia	3.000	Ea.	15.68	20.03	35.71
Valves, bronze, gate, N.R.S., threaded, class 150, 1-1/4" size	2.000	Ea.	256	88	344
Circuit setter, bal valve, bronze body, threaded, 1-1/4" pipe size	1.000	Ea.	157	45	202
Insulation, fiberglass pipe covering, 1" wall, 1-1/4" IPS	20.000	L.F.	24.80	104	128.80
Control system, pneumatic, A/C Unit with heat	1.000	Ea.	2,750	2,375	5,125
Re-heat coil balancing	1.000	Ea.		124	124
Rooftop unit heat/cool balancing	1.000	Ea.		445	445
TOTAL			12,768.96	5,886.06	18,655.02

D3050 210	AC Unit, Package, Elec. Ht., Water Cooled	COST EACH		
		MAT.	INST.	TOTAL
1010	A/C, Self contained, single pkg., water cooled, elect. heat, 5 Ton	12,800	5,875	18,675
1020	10 Ton	19,700	7,225	26,925
1030	20 Ton	28,800	9,125	37,925
1040	30 Ton	45,000	9,950	54,950
1050	40 Ton	58,000	11,000	69,000
1060	50 Ton	75,500	13,200	88,700

D3050 215	AC Unit, Package, Elec. Ht., Water Cooled, VAV	COST EACH		
		MAT.	INST.	TOTAL
1010	A/C, Self contained, single pkg., water cooled, elect. ht, VAV, 10 Ton	21,400	7,225	28,625
1020	20 Ton	31,600	9,125	40,725
1030	30 Ton	49,200	9,950	59,150
1040	40 Ton	63,000	11,000	74,000
1050	50 Ton	81,500	13,200	94,700
1060	60 Ton	93,500	16,000	109,500

D3050 Terminal & Package Units

D3050 220	AC Unit, Package, Hot Water Coil, Water Cooled	COST EACH		
		MAT.	INST.	TOTAL
1010	A/C, Self contn'd, single pkg., water cool, H/W ht, const. vol, 5 Ton	11,300	8,150	19,450
1020	10 Ton	16,500	9,725	26,225
1030	20 Ton	40,800	12,100	52,900
1040	30 Ton	53,000	15,200	68,200
1050	40 Ton	65,000	18,500	83,500
1060	50 Ton	80,000	22,800	102,800

D3050 225	AC Unit, Package, HW Coil, Water Cooled, VAV	COST EACH		
		MAT.	INST.	TOTAL
1010	A/C, Self contn'd, single pkg., water cool, H/W ht, VAV, 10 Ton	18,200	9,125	27,325
1020	20 Ton	28,300	11,800	40,100
1030	30 Ton	42,900	14,600	57,500
1040	40 Ton	57,000	15,900	72,900
1050	50 Ton	72,000	18,800	90,800
1060	60 Ton	85,500	20,300	105,800

D30 HVAC

D3050 Terminal & Package Units

Note: Water source units do not include an allowance for any type of water source or piping to it.

Heat Pump, Air/Air, Rooftop w/ Economizer

System Components	QUANTITY	UNIT	COST EACH MAT.	COST EACH INST.	COST EACH TOTAL
SYSTEM D3050 245 1010					
HEAT PUMP, ROOF TOP, AIR/AIR, CURB., ECONOMIZER., SUP. ELECT. HEAT, 10 TON					
Heat pump, air to air, rooftop, curb, economizer, elect ht, 10 ton cooling	1.000	Ea.	58,500	4,700	63,200
Ductwork, 32" x 12" fabricated, galvanized steel, 16 LF	176.000	Lb.	135.52	1,337.60	1,473.12
Insulation, ductwork, blanket type, fiberglass, 1" thk, 1-1/2 LB density	117.000	S.F.	105.30	366.21	471.51
Rooftop unit heat/cool balancing	1.000	Ea.		445	445
TOTAL			58,740.82	6,848.81	65,589.63

D3050 230	Heat Pump, Water Source, Central Station	COST EACH MAT.	COST EACH INST.	COST EACH TOTAL
1010	Heat pump, central station, water source, constant vol., 5 Ton	4,375	3,275	7,650
1020	10 Ton	11,300	4,575	15,875
1030	20 Ton	19,200	8,500	27,700
1040	30 Ton	27,700	12,400	40,100
1050	40 Ton	38,000	13,500	51,500
1060	50 Ton	43,200	18,200	61,400

D3050 235	Heat Pump, Water Source, Console	COST EACH MAT.	COST EACH INST.	COST EACH TOTAL
1020	Heat pump, console, water source, 1 Ton	2,475	1,800	4,275
1030	1-1/2 Ton	2,600	1,875	4,475
1040	2 Ton	3,350	2,200	5,550
1050	3 Ton	3,525	2,350	5,875
1060	3-1/2 Ton	3,825	2,425	6,250

D3050 240	Heat Pump, Horizontal, Duct Mounted	COST EACH MAT.	COST EACH INST.	COST EACH TOTAL
1020	Heat pump, horizontal, ducted, water source, 1 Ton	2,825	3,800	6,625
1030	1-1/2 Ton	3,125	4,775	7,900
1040	2 Ton	3,925	5,700	9,625
1050	3 Ton	4,425	7,475	11,900
1060	3-1/2 Ton	4,750	7,725	12,475

D30 HVAC

D3050 Terminal & Package Units

D3050 245	Heat Pump, Roof Top, Air/Air	COST EACH		
		MAT.	INST.	TOTAL
1010	Heat pump, roof top, air/air, curb, economizer, sup. elect heat, 10 Ton	58,500	6,850	65,350
1020	20 Ton	84,000	11,700	95,700
1030	30 Ton	113,500	16,400	129,900
1040	40 Ton	126,000	18,800	144,800
1050	50 Ton	146,500	21,200	167,700
1060	60 Ton	155,000	24,000	179,000

D3050 Terminal & Package Units

Thru—Wall Heat Pump   Thru—Wall Air Conditioner

System Components	QUANTITY	UNIT	COST EACH		
			MAT.	INST.	TOTAL
SYSTEM D3050 255 1010 A/C UNIT, THRU-THE-WALL, SUPPLEMENTAL ELECT. HEAT, CABINET, LOUVER, 1/2 TON					
A/C unit, thru-wall, electric heat., cabinet, louver, 1/2 ton	1.000	Ea.	790	202	992
TOTAL			790	202	992

D3050 255	Thru-Wall A/C Unit	COST EACH		
		MAT.	INST.	TOTAL
1010	A/C Unit, thru-the-wall, supplemental elect. heat, cabinet, louver, 1/2 Ton	790	202	992
1020	3/4 Ton	865	242	1,107
1030	1 Ton	935	300	1,235
1040	1-1/2 Ton	1,950	505	2,455
1050	2 Ton	1,975	635	2,610

D3050 260	Thru-Wall Heat Pump	COST EACH		
		MAT.	INST.	TOTAL
1010	Heat pump, thru-the-wall, cabinet, louver, 1/2 Ton	2,425	151	2,576
1020	3/4 Ton	2,650	202	2,852
1030	1 Ton	2,725	300	3,025
1040	Supplemental. elect. heat, 1-1/2 Ton	2,800	780	3,580
1050	2 Ton	3,025	805	3,830

D3090 Fume Exhaust Systems

Roof Exhaust Fan ←

10″ Dia. Fiberglass 90° Elbows →

← 10″ Dia. Fiberglass Reinforced Duct

Fume Hood →

Fume Hood Exhaust

System Components	QUANTITY	UNIT	COST EACH		
			MAT.	INST.	TOTAL
SYSTEM D3090 310 1010					
FUME HOOD EXHAUST SYSTEM, 3′ LONG, 1000 CFM					
Fume hood	3.000	L.F.	6,075	1,350	7,425
Ductwork, plastic, FM approved for acid fume & smoke, straight, 10″ dia	60.000	L.F.	1,410	807	2,217
Ductwork, plastic, FM approved for acid fume & smoke, elbow 90°, 10″ dia	3.000	Ea.	357	441	798
Fan, corrosive fume resistant plastic, 1630 CFM, 1/2 HP	1.000	Ea.	5,875	365	6,240
Fan control switch & mounting base	1.000	Ea.	111	42	153
Roof fan balancing	1.000	Ea.		254	254
TOTAL			13,828	3,259	17,087

D3090 310	Fume Hood Exhaust Systems	COST EACH		
		MAT.	INST.	TOTAL
1010	Fume hood exhaust system, 3′ long, 1000 CFM	13,800	3,250	17,050
1020	4′ long, 2000 CFM	16,400	4,125	20,525
1030	6′ long, 3500 CFM	22,400	6,150	28,550
1040	6′ long, 5000 CFM	31,300	7,225	38,525
1050	10′ long, 8000 CFM	41,900	9,900	51,800

D30 HVAC

D3090   Other HVAC Systems/Equip

Cast Iron Garage Exhaust System

Dual Exhaust System

System Components		QUANTITY	UNIT	COST EACH		
				MAT.	INST.	TOTAL
SYSTEM D3090 320 1040						
GARAGE, EXHAUST, SINGLE 3″ EXHAUST OUTLET, CARS & LIGHT TRUCKS						
A	Outlet top assy, for engine exhaust system with adapters and ftngs, 3″ diam	1.000	Ea.	330	40	370
F	Bullnose (guide) for engine exhaust system, 3″ diam	1.000	Ea.	38		38
G	Galvanized flexible tubing for engine exhaust system, 3″ diam	8.000	L.F.	128.40		128.40
H	Adapter for metal tubing end of engine exhaust system, 3″ tail pipe	1.000	Ea.	68.50		68.50
J	Pipe, sewer, cast iron, push-on joint, 8″ diam.	18.000	L.F.	909	729	1,638
	24″ deep	18.000	L.F.		31.32	31.32
	Backfill utility trench by hand, incl. compaction, 8″ wide 24″ deep	18.000	L.F.		43.74	43.74
	Stand for blower, concrete over polystyrene core, 6″ high	1.000	Ea.	5.05	19.90	24.95
	AC&V duct spiral reducer 10″x8″	1.000	Ea.	16.15	36	52.15
	AC&V duct spiral reducer 12″x10″	1.000	Ea.	18.50	47.50	66
	AC&V duct spiral preformed 45° elbow, 8″ diam	1.000	Ea.	8.90	41	49.90
	AC&V utility fan, belt drive, 3 phase, 2000 CFM, 1 HP	2.000	Ea.	2,450	630	3,080
	Safety switch, heavy duty fused, 240V, 3 pole, 30 amp	1.000	Ea.	211	193	404
	TOTAL			4,183.50	1,811.46	5,994.96

D3090 320	Garage Exhaust Systems	COST PER BAY		
		MAT.	INST.	TOTAL
1040	Garage, single 3″ exhaust outlet, cars & light trucks, one bay	4,175	1,800	5,975
1060	Additional bays up to seven bays	1,075	485	1,560
1500	4″ outlet, trucks, one bay	4,225	1,800	6,025
1520	Additional bays up to six bays	1,100	485	1,585
1600	5″ outlet, diesel trucks, one bay	4,625	1,800	6,425
1650	Additional single bays up to six	1,600	575	2,175
1700	Two adjoining bays	4,625	1,800	6,425
2000	Dual exhaust, 3″ outlets, pair of adjoining bays	5,250	2,275	7,525
2100	Additional pairs of adjoining bays	1,725	575	2,300

D3090   Other HVAC Systems/Equip

NOTES:
1) ALL HOUSEKEEPING PAD REINFORCING SHOULD TO ACI STANDARDS FOR MINIMUM AREA AND CONCRETE COVERAGE
2) HIGH CONCENTRATED LOADS OR POINT SUPPORTED EQUIPMENT REQUIRE SPECIAL TIE DOWN CONSIDERATIONS NOT COVERED BY THIS DETAIL
3) MINIMUM OF (4) HK PAD TO FLOOR ANCHOR BOLTS REQUIRED FOR EACH HOUSEKEEPING PAD.

System Components	QUANTITY	UNIT	COST EACH		
			MAT.	INST.	TOTAL
SYSTEM D3090 750 1000					
SEISMIC PAD FOR 20-38 SELF-CONTAINED UNIT					
Form equipment pad	28.000	L.F.	26.60	113.12	139.72
Reinforcing in hold down pad, #3 to #7	60.000	Lb.	32.40	36	68.40
Concrete 3000 PSI	.866	C.Y.	96.99		96.99
Place concrete pad	.866	C.Y.		30.31	30.31
Finish concrete equipment pad	47.000	S.F.		36.19	36.19
Drill for 3/8 inch slab anchors	10.000	Ea.	.50	86	86.50
Exisiting slab anchors 3/8 inch	10.000	Ea.	8.50	38.80	47.30
Equipment anchors 3/8 inch for plate/foot	8.000	Ea.	13.52	33.12	46.64
TOTAL			178.51	373.54	552.05

D3090 750	Seismic Concrete Equipment Pads	COST PER EACH		
		MAT.	INST.	TOTAL
0990	Seismic pad for self-contained AC units for plate/foot attachment			
1000	Seismic pad for 20-38 tons Self-contained AC unit without economizer .25g	179	375	554
1010	0.5 g seismic acceleration	179	375	554
1020	0.75 g seismic acceleration	179	375	554
1030	1.0 g seismic acceleration	179	375	554
1040	1.5 g seismic acceleration	182	425	607
1050	2.0 g seismic acceleration	196	580	776
1060	2.5 g seismic acceleration	207	730	937
1100	Seismic pad for 40-80 tons Self contained AC unit without economizer .25g	278	540	818
1110	0.5 g seismic acceleration	278	540	818
1120	0.75 g seismic acceleration	278	540	818
1130	1.0 g seismic acceleration	278	540	818
1140	1.5 g seismic acceleration	305	770	1,075
1150	2.0 g seismic acceleration	360	1,175	1,535

D3090   Other HVAC Systems/Equip

D3090 750	Seismic Concrete Equipment Pads	COST PER EACH		
		MAT.	INST.	TOTAL
1160	2.5 g seismic acceleration	420	1,700	2,120
1200	Seismic pad for 80-110 tons Self contained AC unit without economizer .25g	305	585	890
1210	0.5 g seismic acceleration	305	585	890
1220	0.75 g seismic acceleration	305	585	890
1230	1.0 g seismic acceleration	305	585	890
1240	1.5 g seismic acceleration	335	825	1,160
1250	2.0 g seismic acceleration	395	1,300	1,695
1260	2.5 g seismic acceleration	455	1,825	2,280
1990	Seismic pad for self-contained AC units for isolator/snubber bolts			
2000	Seismic pad for 20-38 tons Self contained AC unit without economizer .25g	192	405	597
2010	0.5 g seismic acceleration	192	405	597
2020	0.75 g seismic acceleration	192	405	597
2030	1.0 g seismic acceleration	192	405	597
2040	1.5 g seismic acceleration	196	455	651
2050	2.0 g seismic acceleration	213	620	833
2060	2.5 g seismic acceleration	224	770	994
2100	Seismic pad for 40-80 tons Self contained AC unit without economizer .25g	295	585	880
2110	0.5 g seismic acceleration	295	585	880
2120	0.75 g seismic acceleration	295	585	880
2130	1.0 g seismic acceleration	295	585	880
2140	1.5 g seismic acceleration	320	810	1,130
2150	2.0 g seismic acceleration	380	1,250	1,630
2160	2.5 g seismic acceleration	445	1,750	2,195
2200	Seismic pad for 80-110 tons Self contained AC unit without economizer .25g	325	625	950
2210	0.5 g seismic acceleration	325	625	950
2220	0.75 g seismic acceleration	325	625	950
2230	1.0 g seismic acceleration	325	625	950
2240	1.5 g seismic acceleration	350	870	1,220
2250	2.0 g seismic acceleration	415	1,350	1,765
2260	2.5 g seismic acceleration	485	1,900	2,385
2990	Seismic pad for self-contained AC economizer units for plate/foot attachment			
3000	Seismic pad for 20-38 tons Self contained AC unit economizer .25 g-2.0 g	119	218	337
3010	2.5 g seismic acceleration	127	289	416
3100	Seismic pad for 40-80 tons Self contained AC unit economizer .25-1.5 g	160	289	449
3110	2.0 g seismic acceleration	165	335	500
3120	2.5 g seismic acceleration	172	395	567
3190	Seismic pad for self-contained AC unit economizer for isolator/snubber bolts			
3200	Seismic pad for 20-38 tons Self contained AC unit economizer .25 g-2.0 g	125	231	356
3210	2.5 g seismic acceleration	136	310	446
3300	Seismic pad for 40-80 tons Self contained AC unit economizer .25-1.5 g	170	315	485
3310	2.0 g seismic acceleration	175	360	535
3320	2.5 g seismic acceleration	182	420	602

G1030 Site Earthwork

Trenching Systems are shown on a cost per linear foot basis. The systems include: excavation; backfill and removal of spoil; and compaction for various depths and trench bottom widths. The backfill has been reduced to accommodate a pipe of suitable diameter and bedding.

The slope for trench sides varies from none to 1:1.

The Expanded System Listing shows Trenching Systems that range from 2' to 12' in width. Depths range from 2' to 25'.

System Components			COST PER L.F.		
	QUANTITY	UNIT	EQUIP.	LABOR	TOTAL
SYSTEM G1030 805 1310					
TRENCHING COMMON EARTH, NO SLOPE, 2' WIDE, 2' DP, 3/8 C.Y. BUCKET					
Excavation, trench, hyd. backhoe, track mtd., 3/8 C.Y. bucket	.148	B.C.Y.	.36	.98	1.34
Backfill and load spoil, from stockpile	.153	L.C.Y.	.11	.30	.41
Compaction by vibrating plate, 6" lifts, 4 passes	.118	E.C.Y.	.03	.36	.39
Remove excess spoil, 8 C.Y. dump truck, 2 mile roundtrip	.040	L.C.Y.	.13	.14	.27
TOTAL			.63	1.78	2.41

G1030 805	Trenching Common Earth	COST PER L.F.		
		EQUIP.	LABOR	TOTAL
1310	Trenching, common earth, no slope, 2' wide, 2' deep, 3/8 C.Y. bucket	.63	1.78	2.41
1320	3' deep, 3/8 C.Y. bucket	.91	2.70	3.61
1330	4' deep, 3/8 C.Y. bucket	1.19	3.60	4.79
1340	6' deep, 3/8 C.Y. bucket	1.52	4.67	6.19
1350	8' deep, 1/2 C.Y. bucket	2.01	6.20	8.21
1360	10' deep, 1 C.Y. bucket	3.31	7.40	10.71
1400	4' wide, 2' deep, 3/8 C.Y. bucket	1.45	3.52	4.97
1410	3' deep, 3/8 C.Y. bucket	1.99	5.35	7.34
1420	4' deep, 1/2 C.Y. bucket	2.31	6	8.31
1430	6' deep, 1/2 C.Y. bucket	3.77	9.60	13.37
1440	8' deep, 1/2 C.Y. bucket	6.30	12.40	18.70
1450	10' deep, 1 C.Y. bucket	7.65	15.40	23.05
1460	12' deep, 1 C.Y. bucket	9.90	19.60	29.50
1470	15' deep, 1-1/2 C.Y. bucket	8.70	17.50	26.20
1480	18' deep, 2-1/2 C.Y. bucket	12	24.50	36.50
1520	6' wide, 6' deep, 5/8 C.Y. bucket w/trench box	8.35	14.20	22.55
1530	8' deep, 3/4 C.Y. bucket	11.10	18.70	29.80
1540	10' deep, 1 C.Y. bucket	10.85	19.40	30.25
1550	12' deep, 1-1/2 C.Y. bucket	11.70	21	32.70
1560	16' deep, 2-1/2 C.Y. bucket	16.75	26	42.75
1570	20' deep, 3-1/2 C.Y. bucket	20	31	51
1580	24' deep, 3-1/2 C.Y. bucket	24	37.50	61.50
1640	8' wide, 12' deep, 1-1/2 C.Y. bucket w/trench box	16.25	26.50	42.75
1650	15' deep, 1-1/2 C.Y. bucket	21	34.50	55.50
1660	18' deep, 2-1/2 C.Y. bucket	24	35	59
1680	24' deep, 3-1/2 C.Y. bucket	32.50	48.50	81
1730	10' wide, 20' deep, 3-1/2 C.Y. bucket w/trench box	26.50	46	72.50
1740	24' deep, 3-1/2 C.Y. bucket	39	55.50	94.50
1780	12' wide, 20' deep, 3-1/2 C.Y. bucket w/trench box	41.50	58	99.50
1790	25' deep, bucket	51.50	74	125.50
1800	1/2 to 1 slope, 2' wide, 2' deep, 3/8 C.Y. bucket	.91	2.70	3.61
1810	3' deep, 3/8 C.Y. bucket	1.52	4.75	6.27

G10 Site Preparation

G1030 Site Earthwork

G1030 805	Trenching Common Earth	COST PER L.F.		
		EQUIP.	LABOR	TOTAL
1820	4' deep, 3/8 C.Y. bucket	2.26	7.25	9.51
1840	6' deep, 3/8 C.Y. bucket	3.66	11.75	15.41
1860	8' deep, 1/2 C.Y. bucket	5.80	18.75	24.55
1880	10' deep, 1 C.Y. bucket	11.40	26	37.40
2300	4' wide, 2' deep, 3/8 C.Y. bucket	1.71	4.43	6.14
2310	3' deep, 3/8 C.Y. bucket	2.60	7.40	10
2320	4' deep, 1/2 C.Y. bucket	3.26	9.15	12.41
2340	6' deep, 1/2 C.Y. bucket	6.35	17.05	23.40
2360	8' deep, 1/2 C.Y. bucket	12.25	25	37.25
2380	10' deep, 1 C.Y. bucket	16.95	35.50	52.45
2400	12' deep, 1 C.Y. bucket	22.50	47.50	70
2430	15' deep, 1-1/2 C.Y. bucket	24.50	51	75.50
2460	18' deep, 2-1/2 C.Y. bucket	45.50	80	125.50
2840	6' wide, 6' deep, 5/8 C.Y. bucket w/trench box	12.35	21	33.35
2860	8' deep, 3/4 C.Y. bucket	17.95	31.50	49.45
2880	10' deep, 1 C.Y. bucket	17.55	32.50	50.05
2900	12' deep, 1-1/2 C.Y. bucket	22.50	42.50	65
2940	16' deep, 2-1/2 C.Y. bucket	38.50	62	100.50
2980	20' deep, 3-1/2 C.Y. bucket	50.50	83.50	134
3020	24' deep, 3-1/2 C.Y. bucket	71.50	115	186.50
3100	8' wide, 12' deep, 1-1/2 C.Y. bucket w/trench box	27.50	48	75.50
3120	15' deep, 1-1/2 C.Y. bucket	40	70	110
3140	18' deep, 2-1/2 C.Y. bucket	52.50	83	135.50
3180	24' deep, 3-1/2 C.Y. bucket	80	126	206
3270	10' wide, 20' deep, 3-1/2 C.Y. bucket w/trench box	51.50	96.50	148
3280	24' deep, 3-1/2 C.Y. bucket	88.50	137	225.50
3370	12' wide, 20' deep, 3-1/2 C.Y. bucket w/trench box	74.50	112	186.50
3380	25' deep, 3-1/2 C.Y. bucket	103	160	263
3500	1 to 1 slope, 2' wide, 2' deep, 3/8 C.Y. bucket	1.19	3.60	4.79
3520	3' deep, 3/8 C.Y. bucket	3.31	8.10	11.41
3540	4' deep, 3/8 C.Y. bucket	3.35	10.85	14.20
3560	6' deep, 3/8 C.Y. bucket	3.66	11.75	15.41
3580	8' deep, 1/2 C.Y. bucket	7.25	23.50	30.75
3600	10' deep, 1 C.Y. bucket	19.50	45	64.50
3800	4' wide, 2' deep, 3/8 C.Y. bucket	1.99	5.35	7.34
3820	3' deep, 3/8 C.Y. bucket	3.21	9.45	12.66
3840	4' deep, 1/2 C.Y. bucket	4.21	12.25	16.46
3860	6' deep, 1/2 C.Y. bucket	8.90	24.50	33.40
3880	8' deep, 1/2 C.Y. bucket	18.20	37.50	55.70
3900	10' deep, 1 C.Y. bucket	26.50	55	81.50
3920	12' deep, 1 C.Y. bucket	39	79.50	118.50
3940	15' deep, 1-1/2 C.Y. bucket	40.50	85	125.50
3960	18' deep, 2-1/2 C.Y. bucket	62.50	110	172.50
4030	6' wide, 6' deep, 5/8 C.Y. bucket w/trench box	16.25	28.50	44.75
4040	8' deep, 3/4 C.Y. bucket	23.50	39.50	63
4050	10' deep, 1 C.Y. bucket	25.50	47.50	73
4060	12' deep, 1-1/2 C.Y. bucket	34	64.50	98.50
4070	16' deep, 2-1/2 C.Y. bucket	60	98.50	158.50
4080	20' deep, 3-1/2 C.Y. bucket	82	137	219
4090	24' deep, 3-1/2 C.Y. bucket	119	192	311
4500	8' wide, 12' deep, 1-1/2 C.Y. bucket w/trench box	38.50	70	108.50
4550	15' deep, 1-1/2 C.Y. bucket	58.50	105	163.50
4600	18' deep, 2-1/2 C.Y. bucket	80	129	209
4650	24' deep, 3-1/2 C.Y. bucket	128	203	331
4800	10' wide, 20' deep, 3-1/2 C.Y. bucket w/trench box	76.50	147	223.50
4850	24' deep, 3-1/2 C.Y. bucket	136	214	350
4950	12' wide, 20' deep, 3-1/2 C.Y. bucket w/trench box	107	165	272
4980	25' deep, 3-1/2 C.Y. bucket	154	242	396

G1030 Site Earthwork

Trenching Systems are shown on a cost per linear foot basis. The systems include: excavation; backfill and removal of spoil; and compaction for various depths and trench bottom widths. The backfill has been reduced to accommodate a pipe of suitable diameter and bedding.

The slope for trench sides varies from none to 1:1.

The Expanded System Listing shows Trenching Systems that range from 2' to 12' in width. Depths range from 2' to 25'.

System Components	QUANTITY	UNIT	COST PER L.F.		
			EQUIP.	LABOR	TOTAL
SYSTEM G1030 806 1310					
TRENCHING LOAM & SANDY CLAY, NO SLOPE, 2' WIDE, 2' DP, 3/8 C.Y. BUCKET					
Excavation, trench, hyd. backhoe, track mtd., 3/8 C.Y. bucket	.148	B.C.Y.	.34	.91	1.25
Backfill and load spoil, from stockpile	.165	L.C.Y.	.12	.32	.44
Compaction by vibrating plate 18" wide, 6" lifts, 4 passes	.118	E.C.Y.	.03	.36	.39
Remove excess spoil, 8 C.Y. dump truck, 2 mile roundtrip	.042	L.C.Y.	.14	.15	.29
TOTAL			.63	1.78	2.41

G1030 806	Trenching Loam & Sandy Clay	COST PER L.F.		
		EQUIP.	LABOR	TOTAL
1310	Trenching, loam & sandy clay, no slope, 2' wide, 2' deep, 3/8 C.Y. bucket	.63	1.74	2.37
1320	3' deep, 3/8 C.Y. bucket	.99	2.88	3.87
1330	4' deep, 3/8 C.Y. bucket	1.16	3.51	4.67
1340	6' deep, 3/8 C.Y. bucket	1.65	4.19	5.85
1350	8' deep, 1/2 C.Y. bucket	2.17	5.55	7.70
1360	10' deep, 1 C.Y. bucket	2.46	5.95	8.40
1400	4' wide, 2' deep, 3/8 C.Y. bucket	1.44	3.45	4.89
1410	3' deep, 3/8 C.Y. bucket	1.96	5.20	7.15
1420	4' deep, 1/2 C.Y. bucket	2.29	5.90	8.20
1430	6' deep, 1/2 C.Y. bucket	4.04	8.60	12.65
1440	8' deep, 1/2 C.Y. bucket	6.15	12.20	18.35
1450	10' deep, 1 C.Y. bucket	5.95	12.50	18.45
1460	12' deep, 1 C.Y. bucket	7.45	15.55	23
1470	15' deep, 1-1/2 C.Y. bucket	9.05	18.10	27
1480	18' deep, 2-1/2 C.Y. bucket	11.20	19.85	31
1520	6' wide, 6' deep, 5/8 C.Y. bucket w/trench box	8.05	13.95	22
1530	8' deep, 3/4 C.Y. bucket	10.65	18.35	29
1540	10' deep, 1 C.Y. bucket	9.95	18.65	28.50
1550	12' deep, 1-1/2 C.Y. bucket	11.35	21	32.50
1560	16' deep, 2-1/2 C.Y. bucket	16.25	26.50	43
1570	20' deep, 3-1/2 C.Y. bucket	18.60	31	49.50
1580	24' deep, 3-1/2 C.Y. bucket	23.50	38	61.50
1640	8' wide, 12' deep, 1-1/4 C.Y. bucket w/trench box	16	26.50	42.50
1650	15' deep, 1-1/2 C.Y. bucket	19.55	33.50	53
1660	18' deep, 2-1/2 C.Y. bucket	24.50	38	62.50
1680	24' deep, 3-1/2 C.Y. bucket	31.50	49	80.50
1730	10' wide, 20' deep, 3-1/2 C.Y. bucket w/trench box	32	49.50	81.50
1740	24' deep, 3-1/2 C.Y. bucket	40	61	101
1780	12' wide, 20' deep, 3-1/2 C.Y. bucket w/trench box	38.50	58.50	97
1790	25' deep, bucket	50	75.50	126
1800	1/2:1 slope, 2' wide, 2' deep, 3/8 C.Y. bucket	.89	2.63	3.52
1810	3' deep, 3/8 C.Y. bucket	1.48	4.62	6.10
1820	4' deep, 3/8 C.Y. bucket	2.21	7.05	9.25
1840	6' deep, 3/8 C.Y. bucket	3.97	10.50	14.45

G1030 Site Earthwork

G1030 806	Trenching Loam & Sandy Clay	COST PER L.F.		
		EQUIP.	LABOR	TOTAL
1860	8' deep, 1/2 C.Y. bucket	6.30	16.75	23
1880	10' deep, 1 C.Y. bucket	8.35	21	29.50
2300	4' wide, 2' deep, 3/8 C.Y. bucket	1.69	4.34	6.05
2310	3' deep, 3/8 C.Y. bucket	2.55	7.20	9.75
2320	4' deep, 1/2 C.Y. bucket	3.21	8.95	12.15
2340	6' deep, 1/2 C.Y. bucket	6.80	15.30	22
2360	8' deep, 1/2 C.Y. bucket	11.90	24.50	36.50
2380	10' deep, 1 C.Y. bucket	13.05	28.50	41.50
2400	12' deep, 1 C.Y. bucket	22	47.50	69.50
2430	15' deep, 1-1/2 C.Y. bucket	25.50	53	78.50
2460	18' deep, 2-1/2 C.Y. bucket	44.50	81	126
2840	6' wide, 6' deep, 5/8 C.Y. bucket w/trench box	11.75	21	33
2860	8' deep, 3/4 C.Y. bucket	17.25	31	48.50
2880	10' deep, 1 C.Y. bucket	17.80	35	53
2900	12' deep, 1-1/2 C.Y. bucket	22	43	65
2940	16' deep, 2-1/2 C.Y. bucket	37	63	100
2980	20' deep, 3-1/2 C.Y. bucket	49	85	134
3020	24' deep, 3-1/2 C.Y. bucket	69	117	186
3100	8' wide, 12' deep, 1-1/2 C.Y. bucket w/trench box	27	48.50	75.50
3120	15' deep, 1-1/2 C.Y. bucket	36.50	68	105
3140	18' deep, 2-1/2 C.Y. bucket	51	84	135
3180	24' deep, 3-1/2 C.Y. bucket	77.50	128	206
3270	10' wide, 20' deep, 3-1/2 C.Y. bucket w/trench box	62.50	103	166
3280	24' deep, 3-1/2 C.Y. bucket	86	139	225
3320	12' wide, 20' deep, 3-1/2 C.Y. bucket w/trench box	69	112	181
3380	25' deep, 3-1/2 C.Y. bucket w/trench box	94	151	245
3500	1:1 slope, 2' wide, 2' deep, 3/8 C.Y. bucket	1.16	3.51	4.67
3520	3' deep, 3/8 C.Y. bucket	2.07	6.60	8.65
3540	4' deep, 3/8 C.Y. bucket	3.26	10.60	13.85
3560	6' deep, 3/8 C.Y. bucket	3.97	10.50	14.45
3580	8' deep, 1/2 C.Y. bucket	10.45	28	38.50
3600	10' deep, 1 C.Y. bucket	14.25	36	50.50
3800	4' wide, 2' deep, 3/8 C.Y. bucket	1.96	5.20	7.15
3820	3' deep, 3/8 C.Y. bucket	3.16	9.20	12.35
3840	4' deep, 1/2 C.Y. bucket	4.15	12.05	16.20
3860	6' deep, 1/2 C.Y. bucket	9.55	22	31.50
3880	8' deep, 1/2 C.Y. bucket	17.65	37	54.50
3900	10' deep, 1 C.Y. bucket	20	45	65
3920	12' deep, 1 C.Y. bucket	29	63.50	92.50
3940	15' deep, 1-1/2 C.Y. bucket	42	88	130
3960	18' deep, 2-1/2 C.Y. bucket	61	111	172
4030	6' wide, 6' deep, 5/8 C.Y. bucket w/trench box	15.45	28.50	44
4040	8' deep, 3/4 C.Y. bucket	24	44	68
4050	10' deep, 1 C.Y. bucket	25.50	51.50	77
4060	12' deep, 1-1/2 C.Y. bucket	33	65	98
4070	16' deep, 2-1/2 C.Y. bucket	58	99.50	158
4080	20' deep, 3-1/2 C.Y. bucket	79.50	139	219
4090	24' deep, 3-1/2 C.Y. bucket	115	195	310
4500	8' wide, 12' deep, 1-1/4 C.Y. bucket w/trench box	37.50	70.50	108
4550	15' deep, 1-1/2 C.Y. bucket	53.50	102	156
4600	18' deep, 2-1/2 C.Y. bucket	78	130	208
4650	24' deep, 3-1/2 C.Y. bucket	124	206	330
4800	10' wide, 20' deep, 3-1/2 C.Y. bucket w/trench box	93	157	250
4850	24' deep, 3-1/2 C.Y. bucket	132	218	350
4950	12' wide, 20' deep, 3-1/2 C.Y. bucket w/trench box	99.50	166	266
4980	25' deep, 3-1/2 C.Y. bucket	150	246	395

G1030 Site Earthwork

Trenching Systems are shown on a cost per linear foot basis. The systems include: excavation; backfill and removal of spoil; and compaction for various depths and trench bottom widths. The backfill has been reduced to accommodate a pipe of suitable diameter and bedding.

The slope for trench sides varies from none to 1:1.

The Expanded System Listing shows Trenching Systems that range from 2' to 12' in width. Depths range from 2' to 25'.

System Components		QUANTITY	UNIT	COST PER L.F.		
				EQUIP.	LABOR	TOTAL
SYSTEM G1030 807 1310						
TRENCHING SAND & GRAVEL, NO SLOPE, 2' WIDE, 2' DEEP, 3/8 C.Y. BUCKET						
Excavation, trench, hyd. backhoe, track mtd., 3/8 C.Y. bucket		.148	B.C.Y.	.33	.89	1.22
Backfill and load spoil, from stockpile		.140	L.C.Y.	.10	.27	.37
Compaction by vibrating plate 18" wide, 6" lifts, 4 passes		.118	E.C.Y.	.03	.36	.39
Remove excess spoil, 8 C.Y. dump truck, 2 mile roundtrip		.035	L.C.Y.	.12	.13	.25
	TOTAL			.58	1.65	2.23

G1030 807	Trenching Sand & Gravel	COST PER L.F.		
		EQUIP.	LABOR	TOTAL
1310	Trenching, sand & gravel, no slope, 2' wide, 2' deep, 3/8 C.Y. bucket	.58	1.65	2.23
1320	3' deep, 3/8 C.Y. bucket	.93	2.76	3.69
1330	4' deep, 3/8 C.Y. bucket	1.08	3.34	4.42
1340	6' deep, 3/8 C.Y. bucket	1.56	3.99	5.55
1350	8' deep, 1/2 C.Y. bucket	2.07	5.30	7.35
1360	10' deep, 1 C.Y. bucket	2.29	5.60	7.90
1400	4' wide, 2' deep, 3/8 C.Y. bucket	1.32	3.24	4.56
1410	3' deep, 3/8 C.Y. bucket	1.81	4.91	6.70
1420	4' deep, 1/2 C.Y. bucket	2.11	5.55	7.65
1430	6' deep, 1/2 C.Y. bucket	3.82	8.20	12
1440	8' deep, 1/2 C.Y. bucket	5.80	11.60	17.40
1450	10' deep, 1 C.Y. bucket	5.60	11.80	17.40
1460	12' deep, 1 C.Y. bucket	7.05	14.75	22
1470	15' deep, 1-1/2 C.Y. bucket	8.55	17.10	25.50
1480	18' deep, 2-1/2 C.Y. bucket	10.65	18.70	29.50
1520	6' wide, 6' deep, 5/8 C.Y. bucket w/trench box	7.65	13.20	21
1530	8' deep, 3/4 C.Y. bucket	10.10	17.45	27.50
1540	10' deep, 1 C.Y. bucket	9.40	17.60	27
1550	12' deep, 1-1/2 C.Y. bucket	10.75	19.75	30.50
1560	16' deep, 2 C.Y. bucket	15.60	25	40.50
1570	20' deep, 3-1/2 C.Y. bucket	17.65	29.50	47
1580	24' deep, 3-1/2 C.Y. bucket	22	35.50	57.50
1640	8' wide, 12' deep, 1-1/2 C.Y. bucket w/trench box	15.05	25	40
1650	15' deep, 1-1/2 C.Y. bucket	18.30	31.50	50
1660	18' deep, 2-1/2 C.Y. bucket	23.50	35.50	59
1680	24' deep, 3-1/2 C.Y. bucket	30	46	76
1730	10' wide, 20' deep, 3-1/2 C.Y. bucket w/trench box	30	46	76
1740	24' deep, 3-1/2 C.Y. bucket	37.50	57	94.50
1780	12' wide, 20' deep, 3-1/2 C.Y. bucket w/trench box	36	54.50	90.50
1790	25' deep, 3-1/2 C.Y. bucket	47	70.50	118
1800	1/2:1 slope, 2' wide, 2' deep, 3/8 C.Y. bucket	.84	2.49	3.33
1810	3' deep, 3/8 C.Y. bucket	1.39	4.39	5.80
1820	4' deep, 3/8 C.Y. bucket	2.07	6.70	8.75
1840	6' deep, 3/8 C.Y. bucket	3.78	10	13.80

G10 Site Preparation

G1030 Site Earthwork

G1030 807	Trenching Sand & Gravel	COST PER L.F.		
		EQUIP.	LABOR	TOTAL
1860	8' deep, 1/2 C.Y. bucket	6.05	16	22
1880	10' deep, 1 C.Y. bucket	7.85	19.80	27.50
2300	4' wide, 2' deep, 3/8 C.Y. bucket	1.56	4.08	5.65
2310	3' deep, 3/8 C.Y. bucket	2.36	6.80	9.15
2320	4' deep, 1/2 C.Y. bucket	2.97	8.50	11.45
2340	6' deep, 1/2 C.Y. bucket	6.50	14.65	21
2360	8' deep, 1/2 C.Y. bucket	11.30	23.50	35
2380	10' deep, 1 C.Y. bucket	12.35	27	39.50
2400	12' deep, 1 C.Y. bucket	20.50	45	65.50
2430	15' deep, 1-1/2 C.Y. bucket	24.50	50	74.50
2460	18' deep, 2-1/2 C.Y. bucket	42	76	118
2840	6' wide, 6' deep, 5/8 C.Y. bucket w/trench box	11.20	20	31
2860	8' deep, 3/4 C.Y. bucket	16.40	29.50	46
2880	10' deep, 1 C.Y. bucket	16.90	33	50
2900	12' deep, 1-1/2 C.Y. bucket	21	40.50	61.50
2940	16' deep, 2 C.Y. bucket	36	59.50	95.50
2980	20' deep, 3-1/2 C.Y. bucket	46.50	80	127
3020	24' deep, 3-1/2 C.Y. bucket	66	109	175
3100	8' wide, 12' deep, 1-1/4 C.Y. bucket w/trench box	25.50	45.50	71
3120	15' deep, 1-1/2 C.Y. bucket	34.50	64	98.50
3140	18' deep, 2-1/2 C.Y. bucket	49	79.50	129
3180	24' deep, 3-1/2 C.Y. bucket	73.50	120	194
3270	10' wide, 20' deep, 3-1/2 C.Y. bucket w/trench box	59	96.50	156
3280	24' deep, 3-1/2 C.Y. bucket	81.50	131	213
3370	12' wide, 20' deep, 3-1/2 C.Y. bucket w/trench box	66	107	173
3380	25' deep, 3-1/2 C.Y. bucket	94.50	151	246
3500	1:1 slope, 2' wide, 2' deep, 3/8 C.Y. bucket	1.81	4.07	5.90
3520	3' deep, 3/8 C.Y. bucket	1.95	6.30	8.25
3540	4' deep, 3/8 C.Y. bucket	3.06	10.10	13.15
3560	6' deep, 3/8 C.Y. bucket	3.79	10	13.80
3580	8' deep, 1/2 C.Y. bucket	9.95	26.50	36.50
3600	10' deep, 1 C.Y. bucket	13.35	34	47.50
3800	4' wide, 2' deep, 3/8 C.Y. bucket	1.81	4.92	6.75
3820	3' deep, 3/8 C.Y. bucket	2.93	8.70	11.65
3840	4' deep, 1/2 C.Y. bucket	3.85	11.45	15.30
3860	6' deep, 1/2 C.Y. bucket	9.15	21	30
3880	8' deep, 1/2 C.Y. bucket	16.80	35.50	52.50
3900	10' deep, 1 C.Y. bucket	19.10	42.50	61.50
3920	12' deep, 1 C.Y. bucket	27.50	60.50	88
3940	15' deep, 1-1/2 C.Y. bucket	40	83	123
3960	18' deep, 2-1/2 C.Y. bucket	58	105	163
4030	6' wide, 6' deep, 5/8 C.Y. bucket w/trench box	14.75	27	42
4040	8' deep, 3/4 C.Y. bucket	22.50	42	64.50
4050	10' deep, 1 C.Y. bucket	24.50	48.50	73
4060	12' deep, 1-1/2 C.Y. bucket	31.50	61	92.50
4070	16' deep, 2 C.Y. bucket	56	94	150
4080	20' deep, 3-1/2 C.Y. bucket	75.50	130	206
4090	24' deep, 3-1/2 C.Y. bucket	110	183	293
4500	8' wide, 12' deep, 1-1/2 C.Y. bucket w/trench box	36	66.50	103
4550	15' deep, 1-1/2 C.Y. bucket	50.50	96.50	147
4600	18' deep, 2-1/2 C.Y. bucket	74	123	197
4650	24' deep, 3-1/2 C.Y. bucket	118	193	310
4800	10' wide, 20' deep, 3-1/2 C.Y. bucket w/trench box	88	147	235
4850	24' deep, 3-1/2 C.Y. bucket	125	204	330
4950	12' wide, 20' deep, 3-1/2 C.Y. bucket w/trench box	94	156	250
4980	25' deep, 3-1/2 C.Y. bucket	142	231	375

G1030 Site Earthwork

The Pipe Bedding System is shown for various pipe diameters. Compacted bank sand is used for pipe bedding and to fill 12″ over the pipe. No backfill is included. Various side slopes are shown to accommodate different soil conditions. Pipe sizes vary from 6″ to 84″ diameter.

System Components	QUANTITY	UNIT	COST PER L.F.		
			MAT.	INST.	TOTAL
SYSTEM G1030 815 1440					
PIPE BEDDING, SIDE SLOPE 0 TO 1, 1′ WIDE, PIPE SIZE 6″ DIAMETER					
Borrow, bank sand, 2 mile haul, machine spread	.086	C.Y.	1.60	.61	2.21
Compaction, vibrating plate	.086	C.Y.		.20	.20
TOTAL			1.60	.81	2.41

G1030 815	Pipe Bedding	COST PER L.F.		
		MAT.	INST.	TOTAL
1440	Pipe bedding, side slope 0 to 1, 1′ wide, pipe size 6″ diameter	1.60	.81	2.41
1460	2′ wide, pipe size 8″ diameter	3.46	1.76	5.22
1480	Pipe size 10″ diameter	3.53	1.80	5.33
1500	Pipe size 12″ diameter	3.61	1.83	5.44
1520	3′ wide, pipe size 14″ diameter	5.85	2.97	8.82
1540	Pipe size 15″ diameter	5.90	3	8.90
1560	Pipe size 16″ diameter	5.95	3.03	8.98
1580	Pipe size 18″ diameter	6.10	3.09	9.19
1600	4′ wide, pipe size 20″ diameter	8.65	4.38	13.03
1620	Pipe size 21″ diameter	8.70	4.42	13.12
1640	Pipe size 24″ diameter	8.90	4.52	13.42
1660	Pipe size 30″ diameter	9.05	4.60	13.65
1680	6′ wide, pipe size 32″ diameter	15.50	7.90	23.40
1700	Pipe size 36″ diameter	15.90	8.05	23.95
1720	7′ wide, pipe size 48″ diameter	25.50	12.80	38.30
1740	8′ wide, pipe size 60″ diameter	30.50	15.60	46.10
1760	10′ wide, pipe size 72″ diameter	43	21.50	64.50
1780	12′ wide, pipe size 84″ diameter	56.50	28.50	85
2140	Side slope 1/2 to 1, 1′ wide, pipe size 6″ diameter	2.98	1.51	4.49
2160	2′ wide, pipe size 8″ diameter	5.05	2.58	7.63
2180	Pipe size 10″ diameter	5.45	2.76	8.21
2200	Pipe size 12″ diameter	5.75	2.93	8.68
2220	3′ wide, pipe size 14″ diameter	8.30	4.22	12.52
2240	Pipe size 15″ diameter	8.50	4.31	12.81
2260	Pipe size 16″ diameter	8.75	4.42	13.17
2280	Pipe size 18″ diameter	9.20	4.66	13.86
2300	4′ wide, pipe size 20″ diameter	12.10	6.15	18.25
2320	Pipe size 21″ diameter	12.40	6.30	18.70
2340	Pipe size 24″ diameter	13.15	6.70	19.85
2360	Pipe size 30″ diameter	14.60	7.40	22
2380	6′ wide, pipe size 32″ diameter	21.50	10.95	32.45
2400	Pipe size 36″ diameter	23	11.65	34.65
2420	7′ wide, pipe size 48″ diameter	36	18.15	54.15
2440	8′ wide, pipe size 60″ diameter	45.50	23	68.50
2460	10′ wide, pipe size 72″ diameter	62	31.50	93.50
2480	12′ wide, pipe size 84″ diameter	81.50	41.50	123
2620	Side slope 1 to 1, 1′ wide, pipe size 6″ diameter	4.37	2.21	6.58
2640	2′ wide, pipe size 8″ diameter	6.75	3.41	10.16

G10 Site Preparation

G1030 Site Earthwork

G1030 815	Pipe Bedding	COST PER L.F.		
		MAT.	INST.	TOTAL
2660	Pipe size 10" diameter	7.30	3.71	11.01
2680	Pipe size 12" diameter	7.95	4.04	11.99
2700	3' wide, pipe size 14" diameter	10.80	5.50	16.30
2720	Pipe size 15" diameter	11.15	5.65	16.80
2740	Pipe size 16" diameter	11.50	5.85	17.35
2760	Pipe size 18" diameter	12.30	6.25	18.55
2780	4' wide, pipe size 20" diameter	15.60	7.90	23.50
2800	Pipe size 21" diameter	16.05	8.15	24.20
2820	Pipe size 24" diameter	17.40	8.85	26.25
2840	Pipe size 30" diameter	20	10.20	30.20
2860	6' wide, pipe size 32" diameter	27.50	14	41.50
2880	Pipe size 36" diameter	30	15.15	45.15
2900	7' wide, pipe size 48" diameter	46	23.50	69.50
2920	8' wide, pipe size 60" diameter	60	30.50	90.50
2940	10' wide, pipe size 72" diameter	81.50	41.50	123
2960	12' wide, pipe size 84" diameter	107	54	161

G3010 Water Supply

G3010 110	Water Distribution Piping	COST PER L.F.		
		MAT.	INST.	TOTAL
2000	Piping, excav. & backfill excl., ductile iron class 250, mech. joint			
2130	4" diameter	13.85	15.70	29.55
2150	6" diameter	16.25	19.70	35.95
2160	8" diameter	23.50	23.50	47
2170	10" diameter	28.50	27.50	56
2180	12" diameter	34.50	29.50	64
2210	16" diameter	55.50	43.50	99
2220	18" diameter	59	45.50	104.50
3000	Tyton joint			
3130	4" diameter	12.55	7.90	20.45
3150	6" diameter	17.40	9.45	26.85
3160	8" diameter	24.50	15.70	40.20
3170	10" diameter	34.50	17.30	51.80
3180	12" diameter	36.50	19.70	56.20
3210	16" diameter	54.50	27.50	82
3220	18" diameter	60.50	31.50	92
3230	20" diameter	63	35.50	98.50
3250	24" diameter	79.50	41	120.50
4000	Copper tubing, type K			
4050	3/4" diameter	9.35	2.97	12.32
4060	1" diameter	12.45	3.71	16.16
4080	1-1/2" diameter	19.90	4.48	24.38
4090	2" diameter	30.50	5.15	35.65
4110	3" diameter	62.50	8.85	71.35
4130	4" diameter	104	12.50	116.50
4150	6" diameter	257	23	280
5000	Polyvinyl chloride class 160, S.D.R. 26			
5130	1-1/2" diameter	.36	1.11	1.47
5150	2" diameter	.50	1.21	1.71
5160	4" diameter	2.57	5.45	8.02
5170	6" diameter	6.30	6.55	12.85
5180	8" diameter	10.45	7.85	18.30
6000	Polyethylene 160 psi, S.D.R. 7			
6050	3/4" diameter	.61	1.58	2.19
6060	1" diameter	.88	1.71	2.59
6080	1-1/2" diameter	1.24	1.84	3.08
6090	2" diameter	1.78	2.27	4.05

G3020 Sanitary Sewer

G3020 110	Drainage & Sewage Piping	COST PER L.F.		
		MAT.	INST.	TOTAL
2000	Piping, excavation & backfill excluded, PVC, plain			
2130	4″ diameter	1.80	3.87	5.67
2150	6″ diameter	3.80	4.14	7.94
2160	8″ diameter	8.60	4.33	12.93
2900	Box culvert, precast, 8′ long			
3000	6′ x 3′	395	32	427
3020	6′ x 7′	595	36	631
3040	8′ x 3′	585	40	625
3060	8′ x 8′	750	45.50	795.50
3080	10′ x 3′	820	41	861
3100	10′ x 8′	1,050	57	1,107
3120	12′ x 3′	1,050	45.50	1,095.50
3140	12′ x 8′	1,250	67.50	1,317.50
4000	Concrete, nonreinforced			
4150	6″ diameter	7.05	11.70	18.75
4160	8″ diameter	7.75	13.80	21.55
4170	10″ diameter	8.60	14.30	22.90
4180	12″ diameter	10.50	15.50	26
4200	15″ diameter	14.35	17.20	31.55
4220	18″ diameter	16.95	21.50	38.45
4250	24″ diameter	28	31	59
4400	Reinforced, no gasket			
4580	12″ diameter	12.90	20.50	33.40
4600	15″ diameter	17.60	20.50	38.10
4620	18″ diameter	22	23.50	45.50
4650	24″ diameter	31	31	62
4670	30″ diameter	54	45.50	99.50
4680	36″ diameter	65	56	121
4690	42″ diameter	86	62.50	148.50
4700	48″ diameter	107	70	177
4720	60″ diameter	138	93	231
4730	72″ diameter	224	112	336
4740	84″ diameter	325	140	465
4800	With gasket			
4980	12″ diameter	14.20	11.20	25.40
5000	15″ diameter	19.35	11.75	31.10
5020	18″ diameter	24.50	12.40	36.90
5050	24″ diameter	38	13.85	51.85
5070	30″ diameter	61.50	45.50	107
5080	36″ diameter	74.50	56	130.50
5090	42″ diameter	96	56	152
5100	48″ diameter	120	70	190
5120	60″ diameter	179	89.50	268.50
5130	72″ diameter	244	112	356
5140	84″ diameter	385	187	572
5700	Corrugated metal, alum. or galv. bit. coated			
5760	8″ diameter	12.20	9.35	21.55
5770	10″ diameter	12.70	11.90	24.60
5780	12″ diameter	15.40	14.75	30.15
5800	15″ diameter	21.50	15.50	37
5820	18″ diameter	23	16.30	39.30
5850	24″ diameter	27.50	19.35	46.85
5870	30″ diameter	31	33.50	64.50
5880	36″ diameter	38.50	33.50	72
5900	48″ diameter	60.50	40	100.50
5920	60″ diameter	93.50	59.50	153
5930	72″ diameter	105	99.50	204.50
6000	Plain			

G3020 Sanitary Sewer

G3020 110	Drainage & Sewage Piping	COST PER L.F.		
		MAT.	INST.	TOTAL
6060	8" diameter	9.15	8.75	17.90
6070	10" diameter	9.70	11.05	20.75
6080	12" diameter	10.80	14.05	24.85
6100	15" diameter	14.20	14.05	28.25
6120	18" diameter	16.50	15.10	31.60
6140	24" diameter	21	17.65	38.65
6170	30" diameter	27	31	58
6180	36" diameter	34.50	31	65.50
6200	48" diameter	51	36.50	87.50
6220	60" diameter	76	57.50	133.50
6230	72" diameter	193	144	337
6300	Steel or alum. oval arch, coated & paved invert			
6400	15" equivalent diameter	18.70	15.50	34.20
6420	18" equivalent diameter	22.50	20.50	43
6450	24" equivalent diameter	31	25	56
6470	30" equivalent diameter	37.50	31	68.50
6480	36" equivalent diameter	43	40	83
6490	42" equivalent diameter	54	44.50	98.50
6500	48" equivalent diameter	64	54	118
6600	Plain			
6700	15" equivalent diameter	13.20	13.75	26.95
6720	18" equivalent diameter	16.80	17.65	34.45
6750	24" equivalent diameter	24.50	20.50	45
6770	30" equivalent diameter	30	37	67
6780	36" equivalent diameter	38	37	75
6790	42" equivalent diameter	48.50	44	92.50
6800	48" equivalent diameter	58.50	54	112.50
8000	Polyvinyl chloride SDR 35			
8130	4" diameter	1.80	3.87	5.67
8150	6" diameter	3.80	4.14	7.94
8160	8" diameter	8.60	4.33	12.93
8170	10" diameter	13.95	5.70	19.65
8180	12" diameter	16.15	5.90	22.05
8200	15" diameter	16.65	7.85	24.50

G3030 Storm Sewer

Manhole **Catch Basin**

The Manhole and Catch Basin System includes: excavation with a backhoe; a formed concrete footing; frame and cover; cast iron steps and compacted backfill.

The Expanded System Listing shows manholes that have a 4', 5' and 6' inside diameter riser. Depths range from 4' to 14'. Construction material shown is either concrete, concrete block, precast concrete, or brick.

System Components	QUANTITY	UNIT	COST PER EACH		
			MAT.	INST.	TOTAL
SYSTEM G3030 210 1920					
MANHOLE/CATCH BASIN, BRICK, 4' I.D. RISER, 4' DEEP					
Excavation, hydraulic backhoe, 3/8 C.Y. bucket	14.815	B.C.Y.		113.34	113.34
Trim sides and bottom of excavation	64.000	S.F.		58.24	58.24
Forms in place, manhole base, 4 uses	20.000	SFCA	13.60	99.60	113.20
Reinforcing in place footings, #4 to #7	.019	Ton	19.48	22.80	42.28
Concrete, 3000 psi	.925	C.Y.	103.60		103.60
Place and vibrate concrete, footing, direct chute	.925	C.Y.		46.35	46.35
Catch basin or MH, brick, 4' ID, 4' deep	1.000	Ea.	450	965	1,415
Catch basin or MH steps; heavy galvanized cast iron	1.000	Ea.	19.85	13.30	33.15
Catch basin or MH frame and cover	1.000	Ea.	275	227	502
Fill, granular	12.954	L.C.Y.	304.42		304.42
Backfill, spread with wheeled front end loader	12.954	L.C.Y.		30.83	30.83
Backfill compaction, 12" lifts, air tamp	12.954	E.C.Y.		109.59	109.59
TOTAL			1,185.95	1,686.05	2,872

G3030 210	Manholes & Catch Basins	COST PER EACH		
		MAT.	INST.	TOTAL
1920	Manhole/catch basin, brick, 4' I.D. riser, 4' deep	1,175	1,675	2,850
1940	6' deep	1,675	2,350	4,025
1960	8' deep	2,225	3,200	5,425
1980	10' deep	2,675	3,950	6,625
3000	12' deep	3,400	4,300	7,700
3020	14' deep	4,250	6,025	10,275
3200	Block, 4' I.D. riser, 4' deep	1,150	1,350	2,500
3220	6' deep	1,600	1,925	3,525
3240	8' deep	2,125	2,650	4,775
3260	10' deep	2,525	3,250	5,775
3280	12' deep	3,200	4,150	7,350
3300	14' deep	4,025	5,075	9,100
4620	Concrete, cast-in-place, 4' I.D. riser, 4' deep	1,225	2,350	3,575
4640	6' deep	1,750	3,125	4,875
4660	8' deep	2,450	4,500	6,950
4680	10' deep	2,925	5,575	8,500
4700	12' deep	3,700	6,925	10,625
4720	14' deep	4,575	8,300	12,875
5820	Concrete, precast, 4' I.D. riser, 4' deep	1,600	1,225	2,825
5840	6' deep	2,025	1,675	3,700

G30 Site Mechanical Utilities

G3030 Storm Sewer

G3030 210	Manholes & Catch Basins	COST PER EACH		
		MAT.	INST.	TOTAL
5860	8' deep	2,550	2,300	4,850
5880	10' deep	3,075	2,875	5,950
5900	12' deep	3,875	3,500	7,375
5920	14' deep	4,825	4,475	9,300
6000	5' I.D. riser, 4' deep	2,600	1,400	4,000
6020	6' deep	3,350	1,975	5,325
6040	8' deep	4,250	2,600	6,850
6060	10' deep	5,450	3,300	8,750
6080	12' deep	6,750	4,200	10,950
6100	14' deep	8,175	5,150	13,325
6200	6' I.D. riser, 4' deep	3,275	1,850	5,125
6220	6' deep	4,100	2,450	6,550
6240	8' deep	5,225	3,400	8,625
6260	10' deep	6,600	4,325	10,925
6280	12' deep	8,125	5,450	13,575
6300	14' deep	9,750	6,600	16,350

G30 Site Mechanical Utilities

G3060 Fuel Distribution

G3060 110	Gas Service Piping	COST PER L.F.		
		MAT.	INST.	TOTAL
2000	Piping, excavation & backfill excluded, polyethylene			
2070	1-1/4" diam, SDR 10	2.24	3.81	6.05
2090	2" diam, SDR 11	3.70	4.25	7.95
2110	3" diam, SDR 11.5	4.80	5.10	9.90
2130	4" diam, SDR 11	10.05	8.95	19
2150	6" diam, SDR 21	29	9.60	38.60
2160	8" diam, SDR 21	35.50	11.55	47.05
3000	Steel, schedule 40, plain end, tarred & wrapped			
3060	1" diameter	6.15	8.50	14.65
3090	2" diameter	9.65	9.10	18.75
3110	3" diameter	16	9.80	25.80
3130	4" diameter	21	15.45	36.45
3140	5" diameter	30	17.85	47.85
3150	6" diameter	37	22	59
3160	8" diameter	58.50	28.50	87

G3060 Fuel Distribution

Fiberglass Underground Fuel Storage Tank, Double Wall

System Components	QUANTITY	UNIT	COST EACH		
			MAT.	INST.	TOTAL
SYSTEM G3060 310 1010		Ea.			
STORAGE TANK, FUEL, UNDERGROUND, DOUBLE WALL FIBERGLASS, 600 GAL.					
Excavating trench, no sheeting or dewatering, 6'-10 ' D, 3/4 CY hyd backhoe	18.000	Ea.		137.70	137.70
Corrosion resistance wrap & coat, small diam pipe, 1" diam, add	120.000	Ea.	193.20		193.20
Fiberglass-reinforced elbows 90 & 45 degree, 2 inch	7.000	Ea.	315	549.50	864.50
Fiberglass-reinforced threaded adapters, 2 inch	2.000	Ea.	37.60	179	216.60
Remote tank gauging system, 30', 5" pointer travel	1.000	Ea.	5,725	335	6,060
Corrosion resistance wrap & coat, small diam pipe. 4 " diam, add	30.000	Ea.	73.80		73.80
Pea gravel	9.000	Ea.	711	423	1,134
Reinforcing in hold down pad, #3 to #7	120.000	Ea.	64.80	72	136.80
Tank leak detector system, 8 channel, external monitoring	1.000	Ea.	980		980
Tubbing copper, type L, 3/4" diam	120.000	Ea.	870	1,038	1,908
Elbow 90 degree ,wrought cu x cu 3/4 " diam	4.000	Ea.	28.20	138	166.20
Pipe, black steel welded, sch 40, 3" diam	30.000	Ea.	855	853.50	1,708.50
Elbow 90 degree, steel welded butt joint, 3 " diam	3.000	Ea.	96	524.40	620.40
Fiberglass-reinforced plastic pipe, 2 inch	156.000	Ea.	967.20	691.08	1,658.28
Fiberglass-reinforced plastic pipe, 3 inch	36.000	Ea.	268.20	180	448.20
Fiberglass-reinforced elbows 90 & 45 degree, 3 inch	3.000	Ea.	186	315	501
Tank leak detection system, probes, well monitoring, liquid phase detection	2.000	Ea.	1,010		1,010
Double wall fiberglass annular space	1.000	Ea.	345		345
Flange, weld neck, 150 lb, 3 " pipe size	1.000	Ea.	38.50	87.40	125.90
Vent protector/breather, 2" dia.	1.000	Ea.	31.50	21	52.50
Corrosion resistance wrap & coat, small diam pipe, 2" diam, add	36.000	Ea.	63.36		63.36
Concrete hold down pad, 6' x 5' x 8" thick	30.000	Ea.	89.10	43.20	132.30
600 gallon capacity	1.000	Ea.	8,650	500	9,150
Tank, for hold-downs 500-4000 gal., add	1.000	Ea.	445	160	605
Foot valve, single poppet, 3/4" dia	1.000	Ea.	78.50	37.50	116
Fuel fill box, locking inner cover, 3" dia.	1.000	Ea.	130	134	264
Fuel oil specialties, valve,ball chk, globe type fusible, 3/4" dia	2.000	Ea.	154	67	221
TOTAL			22,405.96	6,486.28	28,892.24

G3060 310	Fiberglass Fuel Tank, Double Wall	COST EACH		
		MAT.	INST.	TOTAL
1010	Storage tank, fuel, underground, double wall fiberglass, 600 Gal.	22,400	6,475	28,875
1020	2500 Gal.	34,000	8,950	42,950

G3060 Fuel Distribution

G3060 310	Fiberglass Fuel Tank, Double Wall	COST EACH		
		MAT.	INST.	TOTAL
1030	4000 Gal.	39,400	11,000	50,400
1040	6000 Gal.	46,300	12,500	58,800
1050	8000 Gal.	54,000	15,000	69,000
1060	10,000 Gal.	58,500	17,300	75,800
1070	15,000 Gal.	79,000	19,900	98,900
1080	20,000 Gal.	98,500	24,100	122,600
1090	25,000 Gal.	122,000	28,000	150,000
1100	30,000 Gal.	140,000	29,700	169,700

G3060 Fuel Distribution

Steel Underground Fuel Storage Tank, Double Wall

System Components	QUANTITY	UNIT	COST EACH MAT.	COST EACH INST.	COST EACH TOTAL
SYSTEM G3060 320 1010		Ea.			
STORAGE TANK, FUEL, UNDERGROUND, DOUBLE WALL STEEL, 550 GAL.					
Fiberglass-reinforced plastic pipe, 2 inch	156.000	Ea.	967.20	691.08	1,658.28
Fiberglass-reinforced plastic pipe, 3 inch	36.000	Ea.	268.20	180	448.20
Fiberglass-reinforced elbows 90 & 45 degree, 3 inch	3.000	Ea.	186	315	501
Tank leak detection system, probes, well monitoring, liquid phase detection	2.000	Ea.	1,010		1,010
Flange, weld neck, 150 lb, 3" pipe size	1.000	Ea.	38.50	87.40	125.90
Vent protector/breather, 2" dia.	1.000	Ea.	31.50	21	52.50
Concrete hold down pad, 6' x 5' x 8" thick	30.000	Ea.	89.10	43.20	132.30
Tanks, for hold-downs, 500-2000 gal, add	1.000	Ea.	183	160	343
Double wall steel tank annular space	1.000	Ea.	360		360
Foot valve, single poppet, 3/4" dia	1.000	Ea.	78.50	37.50	116
Fuel fill box, locking inner cover, 3" dia.	1.000	Ea.	130	134	264
Fuel oil specialties, valve, ball chk, globe type fusible, 3/4" dia	2.000	Ea.	154	67	221
Pea gravel	9.000	Ea.	711	423	1,134
Reinforcing in hold down pad, #3 to #7	120.000	Ea.	64.80	72	136.80
Tank, for manways, add	1.000	Ea.	1,800		1,800
Tank leak detector system, 8 channel, external monitoring	1.000	Ea.	980		980
Tubbing copper, type L, 3/4" diam	120.000	Ea.	870	1,038	1,908
Elbow 90 degree, wrought cu x cu 3/4" diam	8.000	Ea.	56.40	276	332.40
Pipe, black steel welded, sch 40, 3" diam	30.000	Ea.	855	853.50	1,708.50
Elbow 90 degree, steel welded butt joint, 3" diam	3.000	Ea.	96	524.40	620.40
Excavating trench, no sheeting or dewatering, 6'-10' D, 3/4 CY hyd backhoe	18.000	Ea.		137.70	137.70
Fiberglass-reinforced elbows 90 & 45 degree, 2 inch	7.000	Ea.	315	549.50	864.50
Fiberglass-reinforced threaded adapters, 2 inch	2.000	Ea.	37.60	179	216.60
500 gallon capacity	1.000	Ea.	4,725	505	5,230
Remote tank gauging system, 30', 5" pointer travel	1.000	Ea.	5,725	335	6,060
TOTAL			19,731.80	6,629.28	26,361.08

G3060 320	Steel Fuel Tank, Double Wall	COST EACH MAT.	COST EACH INST.	COST EACH TOTAL
1010	Storage tank, fuel, underground, double wall steel, 500 Gal.	19,700	6,625	26,325
1020	2000 Gal.	27,100	8,650	35,750
1030	4000 Gal.	37,200	11,200	48,400
1040	6000 Gal.	47,200	12,400	59,600
1050	8000 Gal.	53,000	15,300	68,300
1060	10,000 Gal.	58,000	17,500	75,500

G30 Site Mechanical Utilities

G3060 Fuel Distribution

G3060 320	Steel Fuel Tank, Double Wall	COST EACH		
		MAT.	INST.	TOTAL
1070	15,000 Gal.	65,000	20,400	85,400
1080	20,000 Gal.	78,500	24,400	102,900
1090	25,000 Gal.	117,500	27,900	145,400
1100	30,000 Gal.	135,000	29,900	164,900
1110	40,000 Gal.	169,000	37,500	206,500
1120	50,000 Gal.	202,500	44,900	247,400

G3060 325	Steel Tank, Above Ground, Single Wall	COST EACH		
		MAT.	INST.	TOTAL
1010	Storage tank, fuel, above ground, single wall steel, 550 Gal.	13,800	4,600	18,400
1020	2000 Gal.	20,100	4,700	24,800
1030	5000 Gal.	33,600	7,200	40,800
1040	10,000 Gal.	44,500	7,675	52,175
1050	15,000 Gal.	53,500	7,900	61,400
1060	20,000 Gal.	65,500	8,175	73,675
1070	25,000 Gal.	74,500	8,375	82,875
1080	30,000 Gal.	86,500	8,725	95,225

G3060 330	Steel Tank, Above Ground, Double Wall	COST EACH		
		MAT.	INST.	TOTAL
1010	Storage tank, fuel, above ground, double wall steel, 500 Gal.	14,400	4,650	19,050
1020	2000 Gal.	21,700	4,750	26,450
1030	4000 Gal.	29,900	4,850	34,750
1040	6000 Gal.	35,300	7,475	42,775
1050	8000 Gal.	41,700	7,675	49,375
1060	10,000 Gal.	44,900	7,825	52,725
1070	15,000 Gal.	60,500	8,100	68,600
1080	20,000 Gal.	67,000	8,375	75,375
1090	25,000 Gal.	78,000	8,625	86,625
1100	30,000 Gal.	84,000	8,950	92,950

Reference Section

All the reference information is in one section, making it easy to find what you need to know . . . and easy to use the book on a daily basis. This section is visually identified by a vertical gray bar on the page edges.

In this Reference Section, we've included Equipment Rental Costs, a listing of rental and operating costs; Crew Listings, a full listing of all crews and equipment, and their costs; Historical Cost Indexes for cost comparisons over time; City Cost Indexes and Location Factors for adjusting costs to the region you are in; Reference Tables, where you will find explanations, estimating information and procedures, or technical data; Change Orders, information on pricing changes to contract documents; Square Foot Costs that allow you to make a rough estimate for the overall cost of a project; and an explanation of all the Abbreviations in the book.

Table of Contents

Estimating Tips

- This section contains the average costs to rent and operate hundreds of pieces of construction equipment. This is useful information when estimating the time and material requirements of any particular operation in order to establish a unit or total cost. Equipment costs include not only rental, but also operating costs for equipment under normal use.

Rental Costs

- Equipment rental rates are obtained from industry sources throughout North America–contractors, suppliers, dealers, manufacturers, and distributors.
- Rental rates vary throughout the country, with larger cities generally having lower rates. Lease plans for new equipment are available for periods in excess of six months, with a percentage of payments applying toward purchase.
- Monthly rental rates vary from 2% to 5% of the purchase price of the equipment depending on the anticipated life of the equipment and its wearing parts.
- Weekly rental rates are about 1/3 the monthly rates, and daily rental rates are about 1/3 the weekly rate.
- Rental rates can also be treated as reimbursement costs for contractor-owned equipment. Owned equipment costs include depreciation, loan payments, interest, taxes, insurance, storage, and major repairs.

Operating Costs

- The operating costs include parts and labor for routine servicing, such as repair and replacement of pumps, filters and worn lines. Normal operating expendables, such as fuel, lubricants, tires and electricity (where applicable), are also included.
- Extraordinary operating expendables with highly variable wear patterns, such as diamond bits and blades, are excluded. These costs can be found as material costs in the Unit Price section.
- The hourly operating costs listed do not include the operator's wages.

Equipment Cost/Day

- Any power equipment required by a crew is shown in the Crew Listings with a daily cost.
- The daily cost of equipment needed by a crew is based on dividing the weekly rental rate by 5 (number of working days in the week), and then adding the hourly operating cost times 8 (the number of hours in a day). This "Equipment Cost/Day" is shown in the far right column of the Equipment Rental pages.
- If equipment is needed for only one or two days, it is best to develop your own cost by including components for daily rent and hourly operating cost. This is important when the listed Crew for a task does not contain the equipment needed, such as a crane for lifting mechanical heating/cooling equipment up onto a roof.

- If the quantity of work is less than the crew's Daily Output shown for a Unit Price line item that includes a bare unit equipment cost, it is recommended to estimate one day's rental cost and operating cost for equipment shown in the Crew Listing for that line item.

Mobilization/ Demobilization

- The cost to move construction equipment from an equipment yard or rental company to the jobsite and back again is not included in equipment rental costs listed in the Reference section, nor in the bare equipment cost of any Unit Price line item, nor in any equipment costs shown in the Crew listings.
- Mobilization (to the site) and demobilization (from the site) costs can be found in the Unit Price section.
- If a piece of equipment is already at the jobsite, it is not appropriate to utilize mobil./ demob. costs again in an estimate.

01 54 33 | Equipment Rental

			UNIT	HOURLY OPER. COST	RENT PER DAY	RENT PER WEEK	RENT PER MONTH	EQUIPMENT COST/DAY	
10	0010	**CONCRETE EQUIPMENT RENTAL** without operators							10
	0200	Bucket, concrete lightweight, 1/2 C.Y. [R015433-10]	Ea.	.75	22	66	198	19.20	
	0300	1 C.Y.		.80	26.50	80	240	22.40	
	0400	1-1/2 C.Y.		1.05	36.50	110	330	30.40	
	0500	2 C.Y.		1.15	43.50	130	390	35.20	
	0580	8 C.Y.		5.80	255	765	2,300	199.40	
	0600	Cart, concrete, self-propelled, operator walking, 10 C.F.		2.85	56.50	170	510	56.80	
	0700	Operator riding, 18 C.F.		4.80	93.50	280	840	94.40	
	0800	Conveyer for concrete, portable, gas, 16" wide, 26' long		11.00	122	365	1,100	161	
	0900	46' long		11.40	147	440	1,325	179.20	
	1000	56' long		11.50	157	470	1,400	186	
	1100	Core drill, electric, 2-1/2 H.P., 1" to 8" bit diameter		1.40	59.50	179	535	47	
	1150	11 H.P., 8" to 18" cores		5.40	112	335	1,000	110.20	
	1200	Finisher, concrete floor, gas, riding trowel, 96" wide		10.90	145	435	1,300	174.20	
	1300	Gas, walk-behind, 3 blade, 36" trowel		1.80	20	60	180	26.40	
	1400	4 blade, 48" trowel		3.55	27	81	243	44.60	
	1500	Float, hand-operated (Bull float) 48" wide		.08	13.65	41	123	8.85	
	1570	Curb builder, 14 H.P., gas, single screw		13.10	245	735	2,200	251.80	
	1590	Double screw		13.75	283	850	2,550	280	
	1600	Floor grinder, concrete and terrazzo, electric, 22" path		1.84	117	350	1,050	84.70	
	1700	Edger, concrete, electric, 7" path		.90	51.50	155	465	38.20	
	1750	Vacuum pick-up system for floor grinders, wet/dry		1.35	81.50	245	735	59.80	
	1800	Mixer, powered, mortar and concrete, gas, 6 C.F., 18 H.P.		7.60	117	350	1,050	130.80	
	1900	10 C.F., 25 H.P.		9.45	142	425	1,275	160.60	
	2000	16 C.F.		9.75	165	495	1,475	177	
	2100	Concrete, stationary, tilt drum, 2 C.Y.		6.55	230	690	2,075	190.40	
	2120	Pump, concrete, truck mounted 4" line 80' boom		23.95	875	2,620	7,850	715.60	
	2140	5" line, 110' boom		31.05	1,150	3,465	10,400	941.40	
	2160	Mud jack, 50 C.F. per hr.		6.55	125	375	1,125	127.40	
	2180	225 C.F. per hr.		8.70	142	425	1,275	154.60	
	2190	Shotcrete pump rig, 12 C.Y./hr.		13.75	220	660	1,975	242	
	2200	35 C.Y./hr.		15.85	237	710	2,125	268.80	
	2600	Saw, concrete, manual, gas, 18 H.P.		5.00	43.50	130	390	66	
	2650	Self-propelled, gas, 30 H.P.		11.00	100	300	900	148	
	2700	Vibrators, concrete, electric, 60 cycle, 2 H.P.		.30	8.65	26	78	7.60	
	2800	3 H.P.		.43	11.65	35	105	10.45	
	2900	Gas engine, 5 H.P.		1.70	16	48	144	23.20	
	3000	8 H.P.		2.30	15	45	135	27.40	
	3050	Vibrating screed, gas engine, 8 H.P.		2.81	71.50	215	645	65.50	
	3120	Concrete transit mixer, 6 x 4, 250 H.P., 8 C.Y., rear discharge		52.20	570	1,705	5,125	758.60	
	3200	Front discharge		61.30	695	2,090	6,275	908.40	
	3300	6 x 6, 285 H.P., 12 C.Y., rear discharge		60.40	655	1,970	5,900	877.20	
	3400	Front discharge	▼	63.10	705	2,115	6,350	927.80	
20	0010	**EARTHWORK EQUIPMENT RENTAL** without operators							20
	0040	Aggregate spreader, push type 8' to 12' wide [R015433-10]	Ea.	2.70	25.50	76	228	36.80	
	0045	Tailgate type, 8' wide		2.55	33	99	297	40.20	
	0055	Earth auger, truck-mounted, for fence & sign posts, utility poles		15.30	470	1,405	4,225	403.40	
	0060	For borings and monitoring wells		41.30	645	1,940	5,825	718.40	
	0070	Portable, trailer mounted		2.75	31.50	95	285	41	
	0075	Truck-mounted, for caissons, water wells		89.05	2,875	8,645	25,900	2,441	
	0080	Horizontal boring machine, 12" to 36" diameter, 45 H.P.		22.20	192	575	1,725	292.60	
	0090	12" to 48" diameter, 65 H.P.		30.95	335	1,000	3,000	447.60	
	0095	Auger, for fence posts, gas engine, hand held		.50	6	18	54	7.60	
	0100	Excavator, diesel hydraulic, crawler mounted, 1/2 C.Y. capacity		18.80	370	1,105	3,325	371.40	
	0120	5/8 C.Y. capacity		28.60	540	1,615	4,850	551.80	
	0140	3/4 C.Y. capacity		34.90	615	1,840	5,525	647.20	
	0150	1 C.Y. capacity	▼	42.70	680	2,035	6,100	748.60	

01 54 33 | Equipment Rental

		UNIT	HOURLY OPER. COST	RENT PER DAY	RENT PER WEEK	RENT PER MONTH	EQUIPMENT COST/DAY	
20	0200	1-1/2 C.Y. capacity	Ea.	51.80	910	2,730	8,200	960.40	20
	0300	2 C.Y. capacity		68.70	1,175	3,515	10,500	1,253	
	0320	2-1/2 C.Y. capacity		92.40	1,525	4,565	13,700	1,652	
	0325	3-1/2 C.Y. capacity		124.00	2,025	6,095	18,300	2,211	
	0330	4-1/2 C.Y. capacity		149.80	2,575	7,750	23,300	2,748	
	0335	6 C.Y. capacity		188.25	2,875	8,615	25,800	3,229	
	0340	7 C.Y. capacity		190.45	2,975	8,900	26,700	3,304	
	0342	Excavator attachments, bucket thumbs		3.05	240	720	2,150	168.40	
	0345	Grapples		2.75	208	625	1,875	147	
	0347	Hydraulic hammer for boom mounting, 5000 ft lb.		13.70	425	1,275	3,825	364.60	
	0349	11,000 ft lb.		22.35	755	2,260	6,775	630.80	
	0350	Gradall type, truck mounted, 3 ton @ 15' radius, 5/8 C.Y.		39.75	875	2,630	7,900	844	
	0370	1 C.Y. capacity		43.65	1,025	3,060	9,175	961.20	
	0400	Backhoe-loader, 40 to 45 H.P., 5/8 C.Y. capacity		12.90	240	720	2,150	247.20	
	0450	45 H.P. to 60 H.P., 3/4 C.Y. capacity		19.75	293	880	2,650	334	
	0460	80 H.P., 1-1/4 C.Y. capacity		21.60	320	955	2,875	363.80	
	0470	112 H.P., 1-1/2 C.Y. capacity		35.65	655	1,960	5,875	677.20	
	0482	Backhoe-loader attachment, compactor, 20,000 lb.		5.50	142	425	1,275	129	
	0485	Hydraulic hammer, 750 ft lb.		3.10	95	285	855	81.80	
	0486	Hydraulic hammer, 1200 ft lb.		6.05	217	650	1,950	178.40	
	0500	Brush chipper, gas engine, 6" cutter head, 35 H.P.		9.75	107	320	960	142	
	0550	Diesel engine, 12" cutter head, 130 H.P.		18.60	225	675	2,025	283.80	
	0600	15" cutter head, 165 H.P.		23.35	265	795	2,375	345.80	
	0750	Bucket, clamshell, general purpose, 3/8 C.Y.		1.20	38.50	115	345	32.60	
	0800	1/2 C.Y.		1.30	45	135	405	37.40	
	0850	3/4 C.Y.		1.45	53.50	160	480	43.60	
	0900	1 C.Y.		1.50	58.50	175	525	47	
	0950	1-1/2 C.Y.		2.45	80	240	720	67.60	
	1000	2 C.Y.		2.55	88.50	265	795	73.40	
	1010	Bucket, dragline, medium duty, 1/2 C.Y.		.70	23.50	70	210	19.60	
	1020	3/4 C.Y.		.70	24.50	74	222	20.40	
	1030	1 C.Y.		.75	26.50	80	240	22	
	1040	1-1/2 C.Y.		1.15	40	120	360	33.20	
	1050	2 C.Y.		1.25	45	135	405	37	
	1070	3 C.Y.		1.85	61.50	185	555	51.80	
	1200	Compactor, manually guided 2-drum vibratory smooth roller, 7.5 H.P.		6.70	197	590	1,775	171.60	
	1250	Rammer/tamper, gas, 8"		2.40	41.50	125	375	44.20	
	1260	15"		2.60	48.50	145	435	49.80	
	1300	Vibratory plate, gas, 18" plate, 3000 lb. blow		2.30	23	69	207	32.20	
	1350	21" plate, 5000 lb. blow		2.85	30	90	270	40.80	
	1370	Curb builder/extruder, 14 H.P., gas, single screw		13.10	245	735	2,200	251.80	
	1390	Double screw		13.75	283	850	2,550	280	
	1500	Disc harrow attachment, for tractor		.42	69.50	209	625	45.15	
	1810	Feller buncher, shearing & accumulating trees, 100 H.P.		31.15	545	1,640	4,925	577.20	
	1860	Grader, self-propelled, 25,000 lb.		27.85	525	1,580	4,750	538.80	
	1910	30,000 lb.		31.10	605	1,810	5,425	610.80	
	1920	40,000 lb.		48.75	1,025	3,105	9,325	1,011	
	1930	55,000 lb.		64.25	1,500	4,530	13,600	1,420	
	1950	Hammer, pavement breaker, self-propelled, diesel, 1000 to 1250 lb.		26.10	345	1,040	3,125	416.80	
	2000	1300 to 1500 lb.		39.15	695	2,080	6,250	729.20	
	2050	Pile driving hammer, steam or air, 4150 ft lb. @ 225 bpm		10.00	480	1,435	4,300	367	
	2100	8750 ft lb. @ 145 bpm		12.00	665	2,000	6,000	496	
	2150	15,000 ft lb. @ 60 bpm		13.55	805	2,415	7,250	591.40	
	2200	24,450 ft lb. @ 111 bpm		14.60	895	2,680	8,050	652.80	
	2250	Leads, 60' high for pile driving hammers up to 20,000 ft lb.		3.15	80.50	242	725	73.60	
	2300	90' high for hammers over 20,000 ft lb.		4.75	143	430	1,300	124	
	2350	Diesel type hammer, 22,400 ft lb.		27.60	620	1,860	5,575	592.80	
	2400	41,300 ft lb.		35.35	675	2,020	6,050	686.80	

			UNIT	HOURLY OPER. COST	RENT PER DAY	RENT PER WEEK	RENT PER MONTH	EQUIPMENT COST/DAY	
01 54 33 | Equipment Rental									
20	2450	141,000 ft lb.	Ea.	52.60	1,150	3,440	10,300	1,109	20
	2500	Vib. elec. hammer/extractor, 200 kW diesel generator, 34 H.P.		45.65	645	1,940	5,825	753.20	
	2550	80 H.P.		82.40	945	2,840	8,525	1,227	
	2600	150 H.P.		155.30	1,825	5,465	16,400	2,335	
	2800	Log chipper, up to 22" diameter, 600 H.P.		50.70	510	1,525	4,575	710.60	
	2850	Logger, for skidding & stacking logs, 150 H.P.		46.90	815	2,450	7,350	865.20	
	2860	Mulcher, diesel powered, trailer mounted		19.70	215	645	1,925	286.60	
	2900	Rake, spring tooth, with tractor		15.41	335	1,007	3,025	324.70	
	3000	Roller, vibratory, tandem, smooth drum, 20 H.P.		7.90	143	430	1,300	149.20	
	3050	35 H.P.		9.95	247	740	2,225	227.60	
	3100	Towed type vibratory compactor, smooth drum, 50 H.P.		23.60	335	1,000	3,000	388.80	
	3150	Sheepsfoot, 50 H.P.		24.90	370	1,105	3,325	420.20	
	3170	Landfill compactor, 220 H.P.		77.35	1,425	4,305	12,900	1,480	
	3200	Pneumatic tire roller, 80 H.P.		14.15	335	1,000	3,000	313.20	
	3250	120 H.P.		21.25	560	1,680	5,050	506	
	3300	Sheepsfoot vibratory roller, 240 H.P.		58.10	1,050	3,180	9,550	1,101	
	3320	340 H.P.		85.45	1,525	4,575	13,700	1,599	
	3350	Smooth drum vibratory roller, 75 H.P.		22.10	565	1,690	5,075	514.80	
	3400	125 H.P.		28.40	690	2,065	6,200	640.20	
	3410	Rotary mower, brush, 60", with tractor		19.80	310	925	2,775	343.40	
	3420	Rototiller, walk-behind, gas, 5 H.P.		2.23	67.50	203	610	58.45	
	3422	8 H.P.		3.47	103	310	930	89.75	
	3440	Scrapers, towed type, 7 C.Y. capacity		5.40	108	325	975	108.20	
	3450	10 C.Y. capacity		6.15	150	450	1,350	139.20	
	3500	15 C.Y. capacity		6.60	173	520	1,550	156.80	
	3525	Self-propelled, single engine, 14 C.Y. capacity		91.35	1,350	4,030	12,100	1,537	
	3550	Dual engine, 21 C.Y. capacity		131.60	1,525	4,605	13,800	1,974	
	3600	31 C.Y. capacity		181.80	2,350	7,070	21,200	2,868	
	3640	44 C.Y. capacity		230.40	3,200	9,625	28,900	3,768	
	3650	Elevating type, single engine, 11 C.Y. capacity		61.60	1,025	3,060	9,175	1,105	
	3700	22 C.Y. capacity		113.95	1,975	5,935	17,800	2,099	
	3710	Screening plant 110 H.P. w/5' x 10' screen		33.90	435	1,305	3,925	532.20	
	3720	5' x 16' screen		36.15	540	1,625	4,875	614.20	
	3850	Shovel, crawler-mounted, front-loading, 7 C.Y. capacity		200.60	2,750	8,270	24,800	3,259	
	3855	12 C.Y. capacity		268.10	3,500	10,520	31,600	4,249	
	3860	Shovel/backhoe bucket, 1/2 C.Y.		2.30	65	195	585	57.40	
	3870	3/4 C.Y.		2.40	71.50	215	645	62.20	
	3880	1 C.Y.		2.50	80	240	720	68	
	3890	1-1/2 C.Y.		2.60	93.50	280	840	76.80	
	3910	3 C.Y.		2.95	127	380	1,150	99.60	
	3950	Stump chipper, 18" deep, 30 H.P.		7.21	188	565	1,700	170.70	
	4110	Dozer, crawler, torque converter, diesel 80 H.P.		25.30	400	1,200	3,600	442.40	
	4150	105 H.P.		30.85	505	1,520	4,550	550.80	
	4200	140 H.P.		44.30	770	2,315	6,950	817.40	
	4260	200 H.P.		65.75	1,200	3,585	10,800	1,243	
	4310	300 H.P.		86.45	1,700	5,130	15,400	1,718	
	4360	410 H.P.		117.20	2,225	6,670	20,000	2,272	
	4370	500 H.P.		150.10	2,900	8,680	26,000	2,937	
	4380	700 H.P.		222.15	4,100	12,290	36,900	4,235	
	4400	Loader, crawler, torque conv., diesel, 1-1/2 C.Y., 80 H.P.		26.70	460	1,375	4,125	488.60	
	4450	1-1/2 to 1-3/4 C.Y., 95 H.P.		30.40	590	1,775	5,325	598.20	
	4510	1-3/4 to 2-1/4 C.Y., 130 H.P.		47.40	860	2,580	7,750	895.20	
	4530	2-1/2 to 3-1/4 C.Y., 190 H.P.		57.75	1,075	3,220	9,650	1,106	
	4560	3-1/2 to 5 C.Y., 275 H.P.		73.90	1,425	4,260	12,800	1,443	
	4610	Front end loader, 4WD, articulated frame, diesel, 1 to 1-1/4 C.Y., 70 H.P.		16.65	225	675	2,025	268.20	
	4620	1-1/2 to 1-3/4 C.Y., 95 H.P.		20.85	278	835	2,500	333.80	
	4650	1-3/4 to 2 C.Y., 130 H.P.		24.40	365	1,100	3,300	415.20	
	4710	2-1/2 to 3-1/2 C.Y., 145 H.P.		27.55	420	1,260	3,775	472.40	

01 54 33 | Equipment Rental

		UNIT	HOURLY OPER. COST	RENT PER DAY	RENT PER WEEK	RENT PER MONTH	EQUIPMENT COST/DAY	
20	4730	3 to 4-1/2 C.Y., 185 H.P.	Ea.	35.25	550	1,645	4,925	611	20
	4760	5-1/4 to 5-3/4 C.Y., 270 H.P.		56.50	845	2,540	7,625	960	
	4810	7 to 9 C.Y., 475 H.P.		98.35	1,775	5,345	16,000	1,856	
	4870	9 - 11 C.Y., 620 H.P.		132.15	2,500	7,495	22,500	2,556	
	4880	Skid steer loader, wheeled, 10 C.F., 30 H.P. gas		8.95	147	440	1,325	159.60	
	4890	1 C.Y., 78 H.P., diesel		16.90	243	730	2,200	281.20	
	4892	Skid-steer attachment, auger		.55	92	276	830	59.60	
	4893	Backhoe		.70	116	348	1,050	75.20	
	4894	Broom		.74	124	371	1,125	80.10	
	4895	Forks		.25	41	123	370	26.60	
	4896	Grapple		.57	94.50	283	850	61.15	
	4897	Concrete hammer		1.08	179	538	1,625	116.25	
	4898	Tree spade		.94	156	468	1,400	101.10	
	4899	Trencher		.76	126	378	1,125	81.70	
	4900	Trencher, chain, boom type, gas, operator walking, 12 H.P.		4.35	46.50	140	420	62.80	
	4910	Operator riding, 40 H.P.		17.10	293	880	2,650	312.80	
	5000	Wheel type, diesel, 4' deep, 12" wide		73.05	835	2,500	7,500	1,084	
	5100	6' deep, 20" wide		84.15	1,900	5,715	17,100	1,816	
	5150	Chain type, diesel, 5' deep, 8" wide		32.30	560	1,685	5,050	595.40	
	5200	Diesel, 8' deep, 16" wide		134.05	2,950	8,880	26,600	2,848	
	5202	Rock trencher, wheel type, 6" wide x 18" deep		19.05	320	960	2,875	344.40	
	5206	Chain type, 18" wide x 7' deep		103.05	2,825	8,465	25,400	2,517	
	5210	Tree spade, self-propelled		13.73	267	800	2,400	269.85	
	5250	Truck, dump, 2-axle, 12 ton, 8 C.Y. payload, 220 H.P.		27.80	225	675	2,025	357.40	
	5300	Three axle dump, 16 ton, 12 C.Y. payload, 400 H.P.		48.95	320	965	2,900	584.60	
	5310	Four axle dump, 25 ton, 18 C.Y. payload, 450 H.P.		58.00	470	1,405	4,225	745	
	5350	Dump trailer only, rear dump, 16-1/2 C.Y.		5.15	137	410	1,225	123.20	
	5400	20 C.Y.		5.60	155	465	1,400	137.80	
	5450	Flatbed, single axle, 1-1/2 ton rating		21.25	68.50	205	615	211	
	5500	3 ton rating		25.80	96.50	290	870	264.40	
	5550	Off highway rear dump, 25 ton capacity		67.70	1,225	3,645	10,900	1,271	
	5600	35 ton capacity		63.10	1,075	3,260	9,775	1,157	
	5610	50 ton capacity		85.40	1,475	4,425	13,300	1,568	
	5620	65 ton capacity		88.20	1,450	4,330	13,000	1,572	
	5630	100 ton capacity		113.50	1,950	5,815	17,400	2,071	
	6000	Vibratory plow, 25 H.P., walking		7.35	60	180	540	94.80	
40	0010	GENERAL EQUIPMENT RENTAL without operators	R015433-10						40
	0150	Aerial lift, scissor type, to 15' high, 1000 lb. capacity, electric	Ea.	3.00	53.50	160	480	56	
	0160	To 25' high, 2000 lb. capacity		3.40	68.50	205	615	68.20	
	0170	Telescoping boom to 40' high, 500 lb. capacity, gas		17.40	310	925	2,775	324.20	
	0180	To 45' high, 500 lb. capacity		18.50	355	1,070	3,200	362	
	0190	To 60' high, 600 lb. capacity		20.80	470	1,405	4,225	447.40	
	0195	Air compressor, portable, 6.5 CFM, electric		.31	12.65	38	114	10.10	
	0196	Gasoline		.77	19	57	171	17.55	
	0200	Towed type, gas engine, 60 CFM		11.55	46.50	140	420	120.40	
	0300	160 CFM		13.35	50	150	450	136.80	
	0400	Diesel engine, rotary screw, 250 CFM		14.00	108	325	975	177	
	0500	365 CFM		18.75	132	395	1,175	229	
	0550	450 CFM		23.70	165	495	1,475	288.60	
	0600	600 CFM		41.45	227	680	2,050	467.60	
	0700	750 CFM		41.60	237	710	2,125	474.80	
	0800	For silenced models, small sizes, add to rent		3%	5%	5%	5%		
	0900	Large sizes, add to rent		5%	7%	7%	7%		
	0930	Air tools, breaker, pavement, 60 lb.	Ea.	.50	9.65	29	87	9.80	
	0940	80 lb.		.50	10.35	31	93	10.20	
	0950	Drills, hand (jackhammer) 65 lb.		.60	16.65	50	150	14.80	
	0960	Track or wagon, swing boom, 4" drifter		55.90	815	2,450	7,350	937.20	
	0970	5" drifter		67.20	915	2,750	8,250	1,088	

01 54 33 | Equipment Rental

		UNIT	HOURLY OPER. COST	RENT PER DAY	RENT PER WEEK	RENT PER MONTH	EQUIPMENT COST/DAY	
40	0975	Track mounted quarry drill, 6" diameter drill	Ea.	102.85	1,350	4,060	12,200	1,635	40
	0980	Dust control per drill		.63	22	66	198	18.25	
	0990	Hammer, chipping, 12 lb.		.55	25.50	77	231	19.80	
	1000	Hose, air with couplings, 50' long, 3/4" diameter		.03	4.67	14	42	3.05	
	1100	1" diameter		.04	6.35	19	57	4.10	
	1200	1-1/2" diameter		.06	9.65	29	87	6.30	
	1300	2" diameter		.07	12	36	108	7.75	
	1400	2-1/2" diameter		.11	19	57	171	12.30	
	1410	3" diameter		.14	23	69	207	14.90	
	1450	Drill, steel, 7/8" x 2'		.05	8.65	26	78	5.60	
	1460	7/8" x 6'		.05	9	27	81	5.80	
	1520	Moil points		.02	4	12	36	2.55	
	1525	Pneumatic nailer w/accessories		.48	31.50	95	285	22.85	
	1530	Sheeting driver for 60 lb. breaker		.04	6	18	54	3.90	
	1540	For 90 lb. breaker		.12	8	24	72	5.75	
	1550	Spade, 25 lb.		.45	6.65	20	60	7.60	
	1560	Tamper, single, 35 lb.		.55	36.50	109	325	26.20	
	1570	Triple, 140 lb.		.82	54.50	164	490	39.35	
	1580	Wrenches, impact, air powered, up to 3/4" bolt		.40	11.35	34	102	10	
	1590	Up to 1-1/4" bolt		.50	23.50	70	210	18	
	1600	Barricades, barrels, reflectorized, 1 to 99 barrels		.03	4.60	13.80	41.50	3	
	1610	100 to 200 barrels		.02	3.53	10.60	32	2.30	
	1620	Barrels with flashers, 1 to 99 barrels		.03	5.25	15.80	47.50	3.40	
	1630	100 to 200 barrels		.03	4.20	12.60	38	2.75	
	1640	Barrels with steady burn type C lights		.04	7	21	63	4.50	
	1650	Illuminated board, trailer mounted, with generator		3.25	133	400	1,200	106	
	1670	Portable barricade, stock, with flashers, 1 to 6 units		.03	5.25	15.80	47.50	3.40	
	1680	25 to 50 units		.03	4.90	14.70	44	3.20	
	1685	Butt fusion machine, wheeled, 1.5 HP electric, 2" - 8" diameter pipe		2.56	167	500	1,500	120.50	
	1690	Tracked, 20 HP diesel, 4"-12" diameter pipe		10.43	490	1,465	4,400	376.45	
	1695	83 HP diesel, 8" - 24" diameter pipe		27.52	975	2,930	8,800	806.15	
	1700	Carts, brick, hand powered, 1000 lb. capacity		.44	72.50	218	655	47.10	
	1800	Gas engine, 1500 lb., 7-1/2' lift		4.04	115	345	1,025	101.30	
	1822	Dehumidifier, medium, 6 lb./hr., 150 CFM		.93	60	180	540	43.45	
	1824	Large, 18 lb./hr., 600 CFM		1.89	122	366	1,100	88.30	
	1830	Distributor, asphalt, trailer mounted, 2000 gal., 38 H.P. diesel		9.80	330	990	2,975	276.40	
	1840	3000 gal., 38 H.P. diesel		11.25	360	1,080	3,250	306	
	1850	Drill, rotary hammer, electric		.82	26.50	80	240	22.55	
	1860	Carbide bit, 1-1/2" diameter, add to electric rotary hammer		.02	4.97	14.90	44.50	3.15	
	1865	Rotary, crawler, 250 H.P.		131.70	2,050	6,175	18,500	2,289	
	1870	Emulsion sprayer, 65 gal., 5 H.P. gas engine		2.85	97	291	875	81	
	1880	200 gal., 5 H.P. engine		7.25	162	485	1,450	155	
	1900	Floor auto-scrubbing machine, walk-behind, 28" path		3.76	247	740	2,225	178.10	
	1930	Floodlight, mercury vapor, or quartz, on tripod, 1000 watt		.30	16	48	144	12	
	1940	2000 watt		.55	30.50	91	273	22.60	
	1950	Floodlights, trailer mounted with generator, 1 - 300 watt light		3.35	71.50	215	645	69.80	
	1960	2 - 1000 watt lights		4.35	96.50	290	870	92.80	
	2000	4 - 300 watt lights		4.10	91.50	275	825	87.80	
	2005	Foam spray rig, incl. box trailer, compressor, generator, proportioner		27.23	475	1,430	4,300	503.85	
	2020	Forklift, straight mast, 12' lift, 5000 lb., 2 wheel drive, gas		22.00	198	595	1,775	295	
	2040	21' lift, 5000 lb., 4 wheel drive, diesel		17.90	243	730	2,200	289.20	
	2050	For rough terrain, 42' lift, 35' reach, 9000 lb., 110 H.P.		25.10	470	1,405	4,225	481.80	
	2060	For plant, 4 ton capacity, 80 H.P., 2 wheel drive, gas		13.40	98.50	295	885	166.20	
	2080	10 ton capacity, 120 H.P., 2 wheel drive, diesel		19.95	172	515	1,550	262.60	
	2100	Generator, electric, gas engine, 1.5 kW to 3 kW		3.10	11.35	34	102	31.60	
	2200	5 kW		4.00	15	45	135	41	
	2300	10 kW		7.50	36.50	110	330	82	
	2400	25 kW		8.80	85	255	765	121.40	

01 54 33 | Equipment Rental

			UNIT	HOURLY OPER. COST	RENT PER DAY	RENT PER WEEK	RENT PER MONTH	EQUIPMENT COST/DAY	
40	2500	Diesel engine, 20 kW	Ea.	10.10	71.50	215	645	123.80	40
	2600	50 kW		18.15	98.50	295	885	204.20	
	2700	100 kW		35.05	138	415	1,250	363.40	
	2800	250 kW		69.05	243	730	2,200	698.40	
	2850	Hammer, hydraulic, for mounting on boom, to 500 ft lb.		2.40	75	225	675	64.20	
	2860	1000 ft lb.		4.15	125	375	1,125	108.20	
	2900	Heaters, space, oil or electric, 50 MBH		1.84	8	24	72	19.50	
	3000	100 MBH		3.32	11.35	34	102	33.35	
	3100	300 MBH		10.62	36.50	110	330	106.95	
	3150	500 MBH		21.42	48.50	145	435	200.35	
	3200	Hose, water, suction with coupling, 20' long, 2" diameter		.02	3	9	27	1.95	
	3210	3" diameter		.03	4.33	13	39	2.85	
	3220	4" diameter		.03	5	15	45	3.25	
	3230	6" diameter		.11	17.65	53	159	11.50	
	3240	8" diameter		.20	33.50	100	300	21.60	
	3250	Discharge hose with coupling, 50' long, 2" diameter		.02	2.67	8	24	1.75	
	3260	3" diameter		.03	4.67	14	42	3.05	
	3270	4" diameter		.04	7.35	22	66	4.70	
	3280	6" diameter		.11	18.65	56	168	12.10	
	3290	8" diameter		.20	33.50	100	300	21.60	
	3295	Insulation blower		.67	6	18	54	8.95	
	3300	Ladders, extension type, 16' to 36' long		.14	24	72	216	15.50	
	3400	40' to 60' long		.20	32.50	98	294	21.20	
	3405	Lance for cutting concrete		2.17	104	313	940	79.95	
	3407	Lawn mower, rotary, 22", 5 H.P.		2.14	63.50	190	570	55.10	
	3408	48" self propelled		2.88	75	225	675	68.05	
	3410	Level, electronic, automatic, with tripod and leveling rod		1.64	109	328	985	78.70	
	3430	Laser type, for pipe and sewer line and grade		.69	46	138	415	33.10	
	3440	Rotating beam for interior control		1.15	76.50	230	690	55.20	
	3460	Builder's optical transit, with tripod and rod		.09	15.35	46	138	9.90	
	3500	Light towers, towable, with diesel generator, 2000 watt		4.10	91.50	275	825	87.80	
	3600	4000 watt		4.35	96.50	290	870	92.80	
	3700	Mixer, powered, plaster and mortar, 6 C.F., 7 H.P.		2.30	19.65	59	177	30.20	
	3800	10 C.F., 9 H.P.		2.45	30.50	92	276	38	
	3850	Nailer, pneumatic		.49	32.50	98	294	23.50	
	3900	Paint sprayers complete, 8 CFM		.73	48.50	145	435	34.85	
	4000	17 CFM		1.35	89.50	269	805	64.60	
	4020	Pavers, bituminous, rubber tires, 8' wide, 50 H.P., diesel		29.45	490	1,465	4,400	528.60	
	4030	10' wide, 150 H.P.		96.65	1,800	5,395	16,200	1,852	
	4050	Crawler, 8' wide, 100 H.P., diesel		83.45	1,800	5,410	16,200	1,750	
	4060	10' wide, 150 H.P.		103.55	2,225	6,645	19,900	2,157	
	4070	Concrete paver, 12' to 24' wide, 250 H.P.		88.70	1,550	4,660	14,000	1,642	
	4080	Placer-spreader-trimmer, 24' wide, 300 H.P.		127.05	2,525	7,575	22,700	2,531	
	4100	Pump, centrifugal gas pump, 1-1/2" diameter, 65 GPM		3.70	48.50	145	435	58.60	
	4200	2" diameter, 130 GPM		4.85	53.50	160	480	70.80	
	4300	3" diameter, 250 GPM		5.10	55	165	495	73.80	
	4400	6" diameter, 1500 GPM		25.55	173	520	1,550	308.40	
	4500	Submersible electric pump, 1-1/4" diameter, 55 GPM		.31	16.35	49	147	12.30	
	4600	1-1/2" diameter, 83 GPM		.35	18.65	56	168	14	
	4700	2" diameter, 120 GPM		1.35	23.50	70	210	24.80	
	4800	3" diameter, 300 GPM		2.25	41.50	125	375	43	
	4900	4" diameter, 560 GPM		9.65	158	475	1,425	172.20	
	5000	6" diameter, 1590 GPM		14.15	213	640	1,925	241.20	
	5100	Diaphragm pump, gas, single, 1-1/2" diameter		1.15	49.50	148	445	38.80	
	5200	2" diameter		3.95	61.50	185	555	68.60	
	5300	3" diameter		3.95	61.50	185	555	68.60	
	5400	Double, 4" diameter		5.90	107	320	960	111.20	
	5450	Pressure washer 5 GPM, 3000 psi		4.25	48.50	145	435	63	

01 54 33 | Equipment Rental

		UNIT	HOURLY OPER. COST	RENT PER DAY	RENT PER WEEK	RENT PER MONTH	EQUIPMENT COST/DAY	
40	5500	Trash pump, self-priming, gas, 2" diameter	Ea.	4.05	21	63	189	45	40
	5600	Diesel, 4" diameter		7.75	73.50	220	660	106	
	5650	Diesel, 6" diameter		20.50	140	420	1,250	248	
	5655	Grout Pump		21.80	177	530	1,600	280.40	
	5700	Salamanders, L.P. gas fired, 100,000 Btu		3.33	12.65	38	114	34.25	
	5705	50,000 Btu		2.50	10.35	31	93	26.20	
	5720	Sandblaster, portable, open top, 3 C.F. capacity		.55	26.50	80	240	20.40	
	5730	6 C.F. capacity		.90	40	120	360	31.20	
	5740	Accessories for above		.12	20.50	62	186	13.35	
	5750	Sander, floor		.59	19.65	59	177	16.50	
	5760	Edger		.54	21.50	64	192	17.10	
	5800	Saw, chain, gas engine, 18" long		1.95	19.65	59	177	27.40	
	5900	Hydraulic powered, 36" long		.70	63.50	190	570	43.60	
	5950	60" long		.70	65	195	585	44.60	
	6000	Masonry, table mounted, 14" diameter, 5 H.P.		1.25	56.50	170	510	44	
	6050	Portable cut-off, 8 H.P.		2.10	32.50	98	294	36.40	
	6100	Circular, hand held, electric, 7-1/4" diameter		.14	4.67	14	42	3.90	
	6200	12" diameter		.21	7.65	23	69	6.30	
	6250	Wall saw, w/hydraulic power, 10 H.P.		7.00	60	180	540	92	
	6275	Shot blaster, walk-behind, 20" wide		4.65	290	870	2,600	211.20	
	6280	Sidewalk broom, walk-behind		2.09	60.50	182	545	53.10	
	6300	Steam cleaner, 100 gallons per hour		3.35	66.50	200	600	66.80	
	6310	200 gallons per hour		4.65	81.50	245	735	86.20	
	6340	Tar Kettle/Pot, 400 gallons		5.50	78.50	235	705	91	
	6350	Torch, cutting, acetylene-oxygen, 150' hose, excludes gases		.30	14	42	126	10.80	
	6360	Hourly operating cost includes tips and gas		10.80				86.40	
	6410	Toilet, portable chemical		.12	20	60	180	12.95	
	6420	Recycle flush type		.14	24	72	216	15.50	
	6430	Toilet, fresh water flush, garden hose,		.17	28.50	85	255	18.35	
	6440	Hoisted, non-flush, for high rise		.14	23.50	71	213	15.30	
	6465	Tractor, farm with attachment		18.25	275	825	2,475	311	
	6500	Trailers, platform, flush deck, 2 axle, 25 ton capacity		5.20	112	335	1,000	108.60	
	6600	40 ton capacity		6.75	155	465	1,400	147	
	6700	3 axle, 50 ton capacity		7.25	172	515	1,550	161	
	6800	75 ton capacity		9.05	225	675	2,025	207.40	
	6810	Trailer mounted cable reel for high voltage line work		5.14	245	734	2,200	187.90	
	6820	Trailer mounted cable tensioning rig		10.22	485	1,460	4,375	373.75	
	6830	Cable pulling rig		68.64	2,725	8,180	24,500	2,185	
	6900	Water tank trailer, engine driven discharge, 5000 gallons		6.75	145	435	1,300	141	
	6925	10,000 gallons		9.20	202	605	1,825	194.60	
	6950	Water truck, off highway, 6000 gallons		75.60	800	2,400	7,200	1,085	
	7010	Tram car for high voltage line work, powered, 2 conductor		4.44	133	399	1,200	115.30	
	7020	Transit (builder's level) with tripod		.09	15.35	46	138	9.90	
	7030	Trench box, 3000 lb., 6' x 8'		.56	93	279	835	60.30	
	7040	7200 lb., 6' x 20'		1.05	175	525	1,575	113.40	
	7050	8000 lb., 8' x 16'		1.05	175	525	1,575	113.40	
	7060	9500 lb., 8' x 20'		1.19	199	597	1,800	128.90	
	7065	11,000 lb., 8' x 24'		1.25	209	627	1,875	135.40	
	7070	12,000 lb., 10' x 20'		1.36	227	680	2,050	146.90	
	7100	Truck, pickup, 3/4 ton, 2 wheel drive		11.50	58.50	175	525	127	
	7200	4 wheel drive		11.75	75	225	675	139	
	7250	Crew carrier, 9 passenger		16.30	86.50	260	780	182.40	
	7290	Flat bed truck, 20,000 lb. GVW		17.60	125	375	1,125	215.80	
	7300	Tractor, 4 x 2, 220 H.P.		24.60	197	590	1,775	314.80	
	7410	330 H.P.		36.35	270	810	2,425	452.80	
	7500	6 x 4, 380 H.P.		41.65	315	945	2,825	522.20	
	7600	450 H.P.		50.75	380	1,145	3,425	635	
	7610	Tractor, with A frame, boom and winch, 225 H.P.		27.40	272	815	2,450	382.20	

01 54 33 | Equipment Rental

			UNIT	HOURLY OPER. COST	RENT PER DAY	RENT PER WEEK	RENT PER MONTH	EQUIPMENT COST/DAY	
40	7620	Vacuum truck, hazardous material, 2500 gallons	Ea.	11.55	298	895	2,675	271.40	40
	7625	5,000 gallons		13.40	415	1,250	3,750	357.20	
	7650	Vacuum, HEPA, 16 gallon, wet/dry		.74	18	54	162	16.70	
	7655	55 gallon, wet/dry		.59	27	81	243	20.90	
	7660	Water tank, portable		.16	27	80.70	242	17.40	
	7690	Sewer/catch basin vacuum, 14 C.Y., 1500 gallons		17.81	625	1,880	5,650	518.50	
	7700	Welder, electric, 200 amp		2.14	16.35	49	147	26.90	
	7800	300 amp		3.11	20	60	180	36.90	
	7900	Gas engine, 200 amp		11.70	23.50	70	210	107.60	
	8000	300 amp		13.35	24.50	74	222	121.60	
	8100	Wheelbarrow, any size		.08	12.65	38	114	8.25	
	8200	Wrecking ball, 4000 lb.		2.25	70	210	630	60	
50	0010	**HIGHWAY EQUIPMENT RENTAL** without operators							50
	0050	Asphalt batch plant, portable drum mixer, 100 ton/hr.	Ea.	70.30	1,425	4,310	12,900	1,424	
	0060	200 ton/hr.		78.75	1,525	4,570	13,700	1,544	
	0070	300 ton/hr.		91.25	1,800	5,375	16,100	1,805	
	0100	Backhoe attachment, long stick, up to 185 H.P., 10.5' long		.34	22.50	67	201	16.10	
	0140	Up to 250 H.P., 12' long		.36	24	72	216	17.30	
	0180	Over 250 H.P., 15' long		.50	33	99	297	23.80	
	0200	Special dipper arm, up to 100 H.P., 32' long		1.02	67.50	203	610	48.75	
	0240	Over 100 H.P., 33' long		1.27	84.50	253	760	60.75	
	0280	Catch basin/sewer cleaning truck, 3 ton, 9 C.Y., 1000 gal.		37.35	395	1,185	3,550	535.80	
	0300	Concrete batch plant, portable, electric, 200 C.Y./hr.		27.69	510	1,530	4,600	527.50	
	0520	Grader/dozer attachment, ripper/scarifier, rear mounted, up to 135 H.P.		3.35	65	195	585	65.80	
	0540	Up to 180 H.P.		3.95	83.50	250	750	81.60	
	0580	Up to 250 H.P.		4.35	95	285	855	91.80	
	0700	Pavement removal bucket, for hydraulic excavator, up to 90 H.P.		1.80	51.50	155	465	45.40	
	0740	Up to 200 H.P.		2.00	71.50	215	645	59	
	0780	Over 200 H.P.		2.15	85	255	765	68.20	
	0900	Aggregate spreader, self-propelled, 187 H.P.		46.10	690	2,065	6,200	781.80	
	1000	Chemical spreader, 3 C.Y.		3.00	43.50	130	390	50	
	1900	Hammermill, traveling, 250 H.P.		68.15	1,950	5,880	17,600	1,721	
	2000	Horizontal borer, 3" diameter, 13 H.P. gas driven		5.65	53.50	160	480	77.20	
	2150	Horizontal directional drill, 20,000 lb. thrust, 78 H.P. diesel		28.00	665	1,990	5,975	622	
	2160	30,000 lb. thrust, 115 H.P.		34.65	1,025	3,045	9,125	886.20	
	2170	50,000 lb. thrust, 170 H.P.		49.60	1,300	3,895	11,700	1,176	
	2190	Mud trailer for HDD, 1500 gallons, 175 H.P., gas		27.15	153	460	1,375	309.20	
	2200	Hydromulcher, diesel, 3000 gallon, for truck mounting		19.10	252	755	2,275	303.80	
	2300	Gas, 600 gallon		7.55	100	300	900	120.40	
	2400	Joint & crack cleaner, walk behind, 25 H.P.		3.40	50	150	450	57.20	
	2500	Filler, trailer mounted, 400 gallons, 20 H.P.		8.55	213	640	1,925	196.40	
	3000	Paint striper, self-propelled, 40 gallon, 22 H.P.		6.70	158	475	1,425	148.60	
	3100	120 gallon, 120 H.P.		20.45	410	1,225	3,675	408.60	
	3200	Post drivers, 6" I-Beam frame, for truck mounting		15.15	405	1,210	3,625	363.20	
	3400	Road sweeper, self-propelled, 8' wide, 90 H.P.		35.10	565	1,700	5,100	620.80	
	3450	Road sweeper, vacuum assisted, 4 C.Y., 220 gallons		63.20	620	1,855	5,575	876.60	
	4000	Road mixer, self-propelled, 130 H.P.		43.95	770	2,305	6,925	812.60	
	4100	310 H.P.		76.25	2,125	6,360	19,100	1,882	
	4220	Cold mix paver, incl. pug mill and bitumen tank, 165 H.P.		90.00	2,150	6,460	19,400	2,012	
	4240	Pavement brush, towed		3.10	95	285	855	81.80	
	4250	Paver, asphalt, wheel or crawler, 130 H.P., diesel		89.70	2,125	6,390	19,200	1,996	
	4300	Paver, road widener, gas 1' to 6', 67 H.P.		44.75	875	2,620	7,850	882	
	4400	Diesel, 2' to 14', 88 H.P.		56.90	1,050	3,155	9,475	1,086	
	4600	Slipform pavers, curb and gutter, 2 track, 75 H.P.		40.75	725	2,175	6,525	761	
	4700	4 track, 165 H.P.		36.65	735	2,200	6,600	733.20	
	4800	Median barrier, 215 H.P.		41.40	755	2,260	6,775	783.20	
	4901	Trailer, low bed, 75 ton capacity		9.75	225	675	2,025	213	
	5000	Road planer, walk behind, 10" cutting width, 10 H.P.		3.20	32.50	98	294	45.20	

R015433 -10

01 54 33 | Equipment Rental

		UNIT	HOURLY OPER. COST	RENT PER DAY	RENT PER WEEK	RENT PER MONTH	EQUIPMENT COST/DAY	
50	5100	Self-propelled, 12" cutting width, 64 H.P.	Ea.	8.90	112	335	1,000	138.20	**50**
	5120	Traffic line remover, metal ball blaster, truck mounted, 115 H.P.		44.60	740	2,220	6,650	800.80	
	5140	Grinder, truck mounted, 115 H.P.		50.10	805	2,410	7,225	882.80	
	5160	Walk-behind, 11 H.P.		3.65	53.50	160	480	61.20	
	5200	Pavement profiler, 4' to 6' wide, 450 H.P.		227.55	3,350	10,035	30,100	3,827	
	5300	8' to 10' wide, 750 H.P.		353.65	4,375	13,150	39,500	5,459	
	5400	Roadway plate, steel, 1" x 8' x 20'		.07	12.35	37	111	7.95	
	5600	Stabilizer, self-propelled, 150 H.P.		43.25	610	1,825	5,475	711	
	5700	310 H.P.		84.85	1,500	4,530	13,600	1,585	
	5800	Striper, thermal, truck mounted, 120 gallon paint, 460 H.P.		54.85	495	1,485	4,450	735.80	
	5900	Thermal paint heating kettle, 115 gallons		3.64	25.50	77	231	44.50	
	6000	Tar kettle, 330 gallon, trailer mounted		5.15	60	180	540	77.20	
	7000	Tunnel locomotive, diesel, 8 to 12 ton		29.20	570	1,710	5,125	575.60	
	7005	Electric, 10 ton		25.40	650	1,955	5,875	594.20	
	7010	Muck cars, 1/2 C.Y. capacity		2.00	23.50	71	213	30.20	
	7020	1 C.Y. capacity		2.20	31.50	95	285	36.60	
	7030	2 C.Y. capacity		2.30	36.50	110	330	40.40	
	7040	Side dump, 2 C.Y. capacity		2.50	43.50	130	390	46	
	7050	3 C.Y. capacity		3.40	50	150	450	57.20	
	7060	5 C.Y. capacity		4.85	63.50	190	570	76.80	
	7100	Ventilating blower for tunnel, 7-1/2 H.P.		1.75	50	150	450	44	
	7110	10 H.P.		1.88	51.50	155	465	46.05	
	7120	20 H.P.		2.68	67.50	202	605	61.85	
	7140	40 H.P.		4.17	95	285	855	90.35	
	7160	60 H.P.		6.38	147	440	1,325	139.05	
	7175	75 H.P.		8.35	196	587	1,750	184.20	
	7180	200 H.P.		15.40	293	880	2,650	299.20	
	7800	Windrow loader, elevating		51.85	1,325	3,960	11,900	1,207	
60	0010	**LIFTING AND HOISTING EQUIPMENT RENTAL** without operators R015433-10							**60**
	0120	Aerial lift truck, 2 person, to 80'	Ea.	26.70	705	2,120	6,350	637.60	
	0140	Boom work platform, 40' snorkel		15.80	270	810	2,425	288.40	
	0150	Crane, flatbed mounted, 3 ton capacity R015433-15		14.55	193	580	1,750	232.40	
	0200	Crane, climbing, 106' jib, 6000 lb. capacity, 410 fpm R312316-45		29.95	1,550	4,670	14,000	1,174	
	0300	101' jib, 10,250 lb. capacity, 270 fpm		36.20	1,975	5,920	17,800	1,474	
	0500	Tower, static, 130' high, 106' jib, 6200 lb. capacity at 400 fpm		33.60	1,800	5,400	16,200	1,349	
	0600	Crawler mounted, lattice boom, 1/2 C.Y., 15 tons at 12' radius		33.19	635	1,910	5,725	647.50	
	0700	3/4 C.Y., 20 tons at 12' radius		44.25	795	2,390	7,175	832	
	0800	1 C.Y., 25 tons at 12' radius		59.00	1,075	3,190	9,575	1,110	
	0900	1-1/2 C.Y., 40 tons at 12' radius		59.00	1,075	3,215	9,650	1,115	
	1000	2 C.Y., 50 tons at 12' radius		62.90	1,250	3,770	11,300	1,257	
	1100	3 C.Y., 75 tons at 12' radius		67.55	1,475	4,415	13,200	1,423	
	1200	100 ton capacity, 60' boom		76.50	1,700	5,080	15,200	1,628	
	1300	165 ton capacity, 60' boom		96.25	1,975	5,940	17,800	1,958	
	1400	200 ton capacity, 70' boom		118.45	2,475	7,440	22,300	2,436	
	1500	350 ton capacity, 80' boom		166.45	3,750	11,245	33,700	3,581	
	1600	Truck mounted, lattice boom, 6 x 4, 20 tons at 10' radius		35.08	1,125	3,350	10,100	950.65	
	1700	25 tons at 10' radius		37.95	1,225	3,650	11,000	1,034	
	1800	8 x 4, 30 tons at 10' radius		41.11	1,300	3,880	11,600	1,105	
	1900	40 tons at 12' radius		43.92	1,350	4,060	12,200	1,163	
	2000	60 tons at 15' radius		49.48	1,425	4,300	12,900	1,256	
	2050	82 tons at 15' radius		55.38	1,525	4,590	13,800	1,361	
	2100	90 tons at 15' radius		62.13	1,675	5,000	15,000	1,497	
	2200	115 tons at 15' radius		70.13	1,875	5,590	16,800	1,679	
	2300	150 tons at 18' radius		81.45	1,950	5,885	17,700	1,829	
	2350	165 tons at 18' radius		82.43	2,075	6,240	18,700	1,907	
	2400	Truck mounted, hydraulic, 12 ton capacity		36.75	530	1,590	4,775	612	
	2500	25 ton capacity		39.15	640	1,920	5,750	697.20	
	2550	33 ton capacity		39.70	655	1,970	5,900	711.60	

01 54 33 | Equipment Rental

		UNIT	HOURLY OPER. COST	RENT PER DAY	RENT PER WEEK	RENT PER MONTH	EQUIPMENT COST/DAY	
60	2560	40 ton capacity	Ea.	51.70	770	2,305	6,925	874.60	**60**
	2600	55 ton capacity		67.65	930	2,795	8,375	1,100	
	2700	80 ton capacity		88.65	1,400	4,225	12,700	1,554	
	2720	100 ton capacity		84.25	1,450	4,365	13,100	1,547	
	2740	120 ton capacity		96.15	1,575	4,690	14,100	1,707	
	2760	150 ton capacity		114.30	2,075	6,190	18,600	2,152	
	2800	Self-propelled, 4 x 4, with telescoping boom, 5 ton		15.70	232	695	2,075	264.60	
	2900	12-1/2 ton capacity		28.15	370	1,115	3,350	448.20	
	3000	15 ton capacity		28.85	390	1,175	3,525	465.80	
	3050	20 ton capacity		31.05	450	1,355	4,075	519.40	
	3100	25 ton capacity		32.65	505	1,520	4,550	565.20	
	3150	40 ton capacity		40.25	570	1,710	5,125	664	
	3200	Derricks, guy, 20 ton capacity, 60' boom, 75' mast		23.51	380	1,144	3,425	416.90	
	3300	100' boom, 115' mast		37.04	655	1,970	5,900	690.30	
	3400	Stiffleg, 20 ton capacity, 70' boom, 37' mast		25.93	495	1,490	4,475	505.45	
	3500	100' boom, 47' mast		39.91	795	2,380	7,150	795.30	
	3550	Helicopter, small, lift to 1250 lb. maximum, w/pilot		97.18	3,075	9,240	27,700	2,625	
	3600	Hoists, chain type, overhead, manual, 3/4 ton		.10	.33	1	3	1	
	3900	10 ton		.70	6	18	54	9.20	
	4000	Hoist and tower, 5000 lb. capacity, portable electric, 40' high		3.96	220	659	1,975	163.50	
	4100	For each added 10' section, add		.10	17.35	52	156	11.20	
	4200	Hoist and single tubular tower, 5000 lb. electric, 100' high		5.43	305	920	2,750	227.45	
	4300	For each added 6'-6" section, add		.18	29.50	89	267	19.25	
	4400	Hoist and double tubular tower, 5000 lb., 100' high		5.89	340	1,013	3,050	249.70	
	4500	For each added 6'-6" section, add		.20	33	99	297	21.40	
	4550	Hoist and tower, mast type, 6000 lb., 100' high		6.25	350	1,051	3,150	260.20	
	4570	For each added 10' section, add		.12	20.50	62	186	13.35	
	4600	Hoist and tower, personnel, electric, 2000 lb., 100' @ 125 fpm		14.61	930	2,790	8,375	674.90	
	4700	3000 lb., 100' @ 200 fpm		16.68	1,050	3,170	9,500	767.45	
	4800	3000 lb., 150' @ 300 fpm		18.58	1,175	3,550	10,700	858.65	
	4900	4000 lb., 100' @ 300 fpm		19.09	1,200	3,620	10,900	876.70	
	5000	6000 lb., 100' @ 275 fpm		20.27	1,275	3,790	11,400	920.15	
	5100	For added heights up to 500', add	L.F.	.01	1.67	5	15	1.10	
	5200	Jacks, hydraulic, 20 ton	Ea.	.05	2	6	18	1.60	
	5500	100 ton		.40	11.65	35	105	10.20	
	6100	Jacks, hydraulic, climbing w/50' jackrods, control console, 30 ton capacity		1.89	126	378	1,125	90.70	
	6150	For each added 10' jackrod section, add		.05	3.33	10	30	2.40	
	6300	50 ton capacity		3.05	203	609	1,825	146.20	
	6350	For each added 10' jackrod section, add		.06	4	12	36	2.90	
	6500	125 ton capacity		8.00	535	1,600	4,800	384	
	6550	For each added 10' jackrod section, add		.55	36.50	109	325	26.20	
	6600	Cable jack, 10 ton capacity with 200' cable		1.59	106	317	950	76.10	
	6650	For each added 50' of cable, add		.19	12.35	37	111	8.90	
70	0010	**WELLPOINT EQUIPMENT RENTAL** without operators							**70**
	0020	Based on 2 months rental							
	0100	Combination jetting & wellpoint pump, 60 H.P. diesel	Ea.	15.87	315	938	2,825	314.55	
	0200	High pressure gas jet pump, 200 H.P., 300 psi	"	36.61	267	802	2,400	453.30	
	0300	Discharge pipe, 8" diameter	L.F.	.01	.51	1.53	4.59	.40	
	0350	12" diameter		.01	.75	2.24	6.70	.55	
	0400	Header pipe, flows up to 150 GPM, 4" diameter		.01	.46	1.38	4.14	.35	
	0500	400 GPM, 6" diameter		.01	.54	1.63	4.89	.40	
	0600	800 GPM, 8" diameter		.01	.75	2.24	6.70	.55	
	0700	1500 GPM, 10" diameter		.01	.79	2.36	7.10	.55	
	0800	2500 GPM, 12" diameter		.02	1.49	4.47	13.40	1.05	
	0900	4500 GPM, 16" diameter		.03	1.91	5.72	17.15	1.40	
	0950	For quick coupling aluminum and plastic pipe, add		.03	1.97	5.92	17.75	1.40	
	1100	Wellpoint, 25' long, with fittings & riser pipe, 1-1/2" or 2" diameter	Ea.	.06	3.94	11.81	35.50	2.85	

R015433 -10

01 54 | Construction Aids

01 54 33 | Equipment Rental

			UNIT	HOURLY OPER. COST	RENT PER DAY	RENT PER WEEK	RENT PER MONTH	EQUIPMENT COST/DAY	
70	1200	Wellpoint pump, diesel powered, 4" suction, 20 H.P.	Ea.	6.89	180	541	1,625	163.30	70
	1300	6" suction, 30 H.P.		9.35	224	671	2,025	209	
	1400	8" suction, 40 H.P.		12.64	305	920	2,750	285.10	
	1500	10" suction, 75 H.P.		19.15	360	1,075	3,225	368.20	
	1600	12" suction, 100 H.P.		27.47	570	1,710	5,125	561.75	
	1700	12" suction, 175 H.P.		.36	630	1,890	5,675	700.90	
80	0010	**MARINE EQUIPMENT RENTAL** without operators R015433 -10	Ea.						80
	0200	Barge, 400 Ton, 30' wide x 90' long		16.65	1,075	3,230	9,700	779.20	
	0240	800 Ton, 45' wide x 90' long		20.15	1,300	3,915	11,700	944.20	
	2000	Tugboat, diesel, 100 H.P.		31.60	215	645	1,925	381.80	
	2040	250 H.P.		64.00	395	1,180	3,550	748	
	2080	380 H.P.		131.50	1,175	3,505	10,500	1,753	

Crew No.	Bare Costs		Incl. Subs O&P		Cost Per Labor-Hour	
Crew A-1	Hr.	Daily	Hr.	Daily	Bare Costs	Incl. O&P
1 Building Laborer	$35.10	$280.80	$54.00	$432.00	$35.10	$54.00
1 Concrete saw, gas manual		66.00		72.60	8.25	9.07
8 L.H., Daily Totals		$346.80		$504.60	$43.35	$63.08
Crew A-1A	Hr.	Daily	Hr.	Daily	Bare Costs	Incl. O&P
1 Skilled Worker	$45.40	$363.20	$70.20	$561.60	$45.40	$70.20
1 Shot Blaster, 20"		211.20		232.32	26.40	29.04
8 L.H., Daily Totals		$574.40		$793.92	$71.80	$99.24
Crew A-1B	Hr.	Daily	Hr.	Daily	Bare Costs	Incl. O&P
1 Building Laborer	$35.10	$280.80	$54.00	$432.00	$35.10	$54.00
1 Concrete Saw		148.00		162.80	18.50	20.35
8 L.H., Daily Totals		$428.80		$594.80	$53.60	$74.35
Crew A-1C	Hr.	Daily	Hr.	Daily	Bare Costs	Incl. O&P
1 Building Laborer	$35.10	$280.80	$54.00	$432.00	$35.10	$54.00
1 Chain Saw, gas, 18"		27.40		30.14	3.42	3.77
8 L.H., Daily Totals		$308.20		$462.14	$38.52	$57.77
Crew A-1D	Hr.	Daily	Hr.	Daily	Bare Costs	Incl. O&P
1 Building Laborer	$35.10	$280.80	$54.00	$432.00	$35.10	$54.00
1 Vibrating plate, gas, 18"		32.20		35.42	4.03	4.43
8 L.H., Daily Totals		$313.00		$467.42	$39.13	$58.43
Crew A-1E	Hr.	Daily	Hr.	Daily	Bare Costs	Incl. O&P
1 Building Laborer	$35.10	$280.80	$54.00	$432.00	$35.10	$54.00
1 Vibratory Plate, gas, 21"		40.80		44.88	5.10	5.61
8 L.H., Daily Totals		$321.60		$476.88	$40.20	$59.61
Crew A-1F	Hr.	Daily	Hr.	Daily	Bare Costs	Incl. O&P
1 Building Laborer	$35.10	$280.80	$54.00	$432.00	$35.10	$54.00
1 Rammer/tamper, gas, 8"		44.20		48.62	5.53	6.08
8 L.H., Daily Totals		$325.00		$480.62	$40.63	$60.08
Crew A-1G	Hr.	Daily	Hr.	Daily	Bare Costs	Incl. O&P
1 Building Laborer	$35.10	$280.80	$54.00	$432.00	$35.10	$54.00
1 Rammer/tamper, gas, 15"		49.80		54.78	6.22	6.85
8 L.H., Daily Totals		$330.60		$486.78	$41.33	$60.85
Crew A-1H	Hr.	Daily	Hr.	Daily	Bare Costs	Incl. O&P
1 Building Laborer	$35.10	$280.80	$54.00	$432.00	$35.10	$54.00
1 Exterior Steam Cleaner		66.80		73.48	8.35	9.19
8 L.H., Daily Totals		$347.60		$505.48	$43.45	$63.19
Crew A-1J	Hr.	Daily	Hr.	Daily	Bare Costs	Incl. O&P
1 Building Laborer	$35.10	$280.80	$54.00	$432.00	$35.10	$54.00
1 Cultivator, Walk-Behind, 5 H.P.		58.45		64.30	7.31	8.04
8 L.H., Daily Totals		$339.25		$496.30	$42.41	$62.04
Crew A-1K	Hr.	Daily	Hr.	Daily	Bare Costs	Incl. O&P
1 Building Laborer	$35.10	$280.80	$54.00	$432.00	$35.10	$54.00
1 Cultivator, Walk-Behind, 8 H.P.		89.75		98.72	11.22	12.34
8 L.H., Daily Totals		$370.55		$530.73	$46.32	$66.34
Crew A-1M	Hr.	Daily	Hr.	Daily	Bare Costs	Incl. O&P
1 Building Laborer	$35.10	$280.80	$54.00	$432.00	$35.10	$54.00
1 Snow Blower, Walk-Behind		53.10		58.41	6.64	7.30
8 L.H., Daily Totals		$333.90		$490.41	$41.74	$61.30

Crew No.	Bare Costs		Incl. Subs O&P		Cost Per Labor-Hour	
Crew A-2	Hr.	Daily	Hr.	Daily	Bare Costs	Incl. O&P
2 Laborers	$35.10	$561.60	$54.00	$864.00	$34.85	$53.37
1 Truck Driver (light)	34.35	274.80	52.10	416.80		
1 Flatbed Truck, Gas, 1.5 Ton		211.00		232.10	8.79	9.67
24 L.H., Daily Totals		$1047.40		$1512.90	$43.64	$63.04
Crew A-2A	Hr.	Daily	Hr.	Daily	Bare Costs	Incl. O&P
2 Laborers	$35.10	$561.60	$54.00	$864.00	$34.85	$53.37
1 Truck Driver (light)	34.35	274.80	52.10	416.80		
1 Flatbed Truck, Gas, 1.5 Ton		211.00		232.10		
1 Concrete Saw		148.00		162.80	14.96	16.45
24 L.H., Daily Totals		$1195.40		$1675.70	$49.81	$69.82
Crew A-2B	Hr.	Daily	Hr.	Daily	Bare Costs	Incl. O&P
1 Truck Driver (light)	$34.35	$274.80	$52.10	$416.80	$34.35	$52.10
1 Flatbed Truck, Gas, 1.5 Ton		211.00		232.10	26.38	29.01
8 L.H., Daily Totals		$485.80		$648.90	$60.73	$81.11
Crew A-3A	Hr.	Daily	Hr.	Daily	Bare Costs	Incl. O&P
1 Truck Driver (light)	$34.35	$274.80	$52.10	$416.80	$34.35	$52.10
1 Pickup truck, 4 x 4, 3/4 ton		139.00		152.90	17.38	19.11
8 L.H., Daily Totals		$413.80		$569.70	$51.73	$71.21
Crew A-3B	Hr.	Daily	Hr.	Daily	Bare Costs	Incl. O&P
1 Equip. Oper. (med.)	$46.55	$372.40	$70.25	$562.00	$40.92	$61.90
1 Truck Driver (heav.)	35.30	282.40	53.55	428.40		
1 Dump Truck, 12 C.Y., 400 H.P.		584.60		643.06		
1 F.E. Loader, W.M.,2.5 C.Y.		472.40		519.64	66.06	72.67
16 L.H., Daily Totals		$1711.80		$2153.10	$106.99	$134.57
Crew A-3C	Hr.	Daily	Hr.	Daily	Bare Costs	Incl. O&P
1 Equip. Oper. (light)	$44.75	$358.00	$67.55	$540.40	$44.75	$67.55
1 Loader, Skid Steer, 78 H.P.		281.20		309.32	35.15	38.66
8 L.H., Daily Totals		$639.20		$849.72	$79.90	$106.22
Crew A-3D	Hr.	Daily	Hr.	Daily	Bare Costs	Incl. O&P
1 Truck Driver, Light	$34.35	$274.80	$52.10	$416.80	$34.35	$52.10
1 Pickup truck, 4 x 4, 3/4 ton		139.00		152.90		
1 Flatbed Trailer, 25 Ton		108.60		119.46	30.95	34.05
8 L.H., Daily Totals		$522.40		$689.16	$65.30	$86.14
Crew A-3E	Hr.	Daily	Hr.	Daily	Bare Costs	Incl. O&P
1 Equip. Oper. (crane)	$47.80	$382.40	$72.15	$577.20	$41.55	$62.85
1 Truck Driver (heavy)	35.30	282.40	53.55	428.40		
1 Pickup truck, 4 x 4, 3/4 ton		139.00		152.90	8.69	9.56
16 L.H., Daily Totals		$803.80		$1158.50	$50.24	$72.41
Crew A-3F	Hr.	Daily	Hr.	Daily	Bare Costs	Incl. O&P
1 Equip. Oper. (crane)	$47.80	$382.40	$72.15	$577.20	$41.55	$62.85
1 Truck Driver (heavy)	35.30	282.40	53.55	428.40		
1 Pickup truck, 4 x 4, 3/4 ton		139.00		152.90		
1 Truck Tractor, 6x4, 380 H.P.		522.20		574.42		
1 Lowbed Trailer, 75 Ton		213.00		234.30	54.64	60.10
16 L.H., Daily Totals		$1539.00		$1967.22	$96.19	$122.95

Crews

Crew A-3G

Crew A-3G	Hr.	Daily	Hr.	Daily	Bare Costs	Incl. O&P
1 Equip. Oper. (crane)	$47.80	$382.40	$72.15	$577.20	$41.55	$62.85
1 Truck Driver (heavy)	35.30	282.40	53.55	428.40		
1 Pickup truck, 4 x 4, 3/4 ton		139.00		152.90		
1 Truck Tractor, 6x4, 450 H.P.		635.00		698.50		
1 Lowbed Trailer, 75 Ton		213.00		234.30	61.69	67.86
16 L.H., Daily Totals		$1651.80		$2091.30	$103.24	$130.71

Crew A-3H

Crew A-3H	Hr.	Daily	Hr.	Daily	Bare Costs	Incl. O&P
1 Equip. Oper. (crane)	$47.80	$382.40	$72.15	$577.20	$47.80	$72.15
1 Hyd. crane, 12 Ton (daily)		824.00		906.40	103.00	113.30
8 L.H., Daily Totals		$1206.40		$1483.60	$150.80	$185.45

Crew A-3I

Crew A-3I	Hr.	Daily	Hr.	Daily	Bare Costs	Incl. O&P
1 Equip. Oper. (crane)	$47.80	$382.40	$72.15	$577.20	$47.80	$72.15
1 Hyd. crane, 25 Ton (daily)		953.20		1048.52	119.15	131.07
8 L.H., Daily Totals		$1335.60		$1625.72	$166.95	$203.22

Crew A-3J

Crew A-3J	Hr.	Daily	Hr.	Daily	Bare Costs	Incl. O&P
1 Equip. Oper. (crane)	$47.80	$382.40	$72.15	$577.20	$47.80	$72.15
1 Hyd. crane, 40 Ton (daily)		1184.00		1302.40	148.00	162.80
8 L.H., Daily Totals		$1566.40		$1879.60	$195.80	$234.95

Crew A-3K

Crew A-3K	Hr.	Daily	Hr.	Daily	Bare Costs	Incl. O&P
1 Equip. Oper. (crane)	$47.80	$382.40	$72.15	$577.20	$44.52	$67.20
1 Equip. Oper. Oiler	41.25	330.00	62.25	498.00		
1 Hyd. crane, 55 Ton (daily)		1471.00		1618.10		
1 P/U Truck, 3/4 Ton (daily)		152.00		167.20	101.44	111.58
16 L.H., Daily Totals		$2335.40		$2860.50	$145.96	$178.78

Crew A-3L

Crew A-3L	Hr.	Daily	Hr.	Daily	Bare Costs	Incl. O&P
1 Equip. Oper. (crane)	$47.80	$382.40	$72.15	$577.20	$44.52	$67.20
1 Equip. Oper. Oiler	41.25	330.00	62.25	498.00		
1 Hyd. crane, 80 Ton (daily)		2119.00		2330.90		
1 P/U Truck, 3/4 Ton (daily)		152.00		167.20	141.94	156.13
16 L.H., Daily Totals		$2983.40		$3573.30	$186.46	$223.33

Crew A-3M

Crew A-3M	Hr.	Daily	Hr.	Daily	Bare Costs	Incl. O&P
1 Equip. Oper. (crane)	$47.80	$382.40	$72.15	$577.20	$44.52	$67.20
1 Equip. Oper. Oiler	41.25	330.00	62.25	498.00		
1 Hyd. crane, 100 Ton (daily)		2129.00		2341.90		
1 P/U Truck, 3/4 Ton (daily)		152.00		167.20	142.56	156.82
16 L.H., Daily Totals		$2993.40		$3584.30	$187.09	$224.02

Crew A-3N

Crew A-3N	Hr.	Daily	Hr.	Daily	Bare Costs	Incl. O&P
1 Equip. Oper. (crane)	$47.80	$382.40	$72.15	$577.20	$47.80	$72.15
1 Tower crane (monthly)		1005.00		1105.50	125.63	138.19
8 L.H., Daily Totals		$1387.40		$1682.70	$173.43	$210.34

Crew A-3P

Crew A-3P	Hr.	Daily	Hr.	Daily	Bare Costs	Incl. O&P
1 Equip. Oper., Light	$44.75	$358.00	$67.55	$540.40	$44.75	$67.55
1 A.T. Forklift, 42' lift		481.80		529.98	60.23	66.25
8 L.H., Daily Totals		$839.80		$1070.38	$104.97	$133.80

Crew A-4

Crew A-4	Hr.	Daily	Hr.	Daily	Bare Costs	Incl. O&P
2 Carpenters	$44.10	$705.60	$67.85	$1085.60	$42.15	$64.30
1 Painter, Ordinary	38.25	306.00	57.20	457.60		
24 L.H., Daily Totals		$1011.60		$1543.20	$42.15	$64.30

Crew A-5

Crew A-5	Hr.	Daily	Hr.	Daily	Bare Costs	Incl. O&P
2 Laborers	$35.10	$561.60	$54.00	$864.00	$35.02	$53.79
.25 Truck Driver (light)	34.35	68.70	52.10	104.20		
.25 Flatbed Truck, Gas, 1.5 Ton		52.75		58.02	2.93	3.22
18 L.H., Daily Totals		$683.05		$1026.22	$37.95	$57.01

Crew A-6

Crew A-6	Hr.	Daily	Hr.	Daily	Bare Costs	Incl. O&P
1 Instrument Man	$45.40	$363.20	$70.20	$561.60	$44.08	$67.47
1 Rodman/Chainman	42.75	342.00	64.75	518.00		
1 Level, electronic		78.70		86.57	4.92	5.41
16 L.H., Daily Totals		$783.90		$1166.17	$48.99	$72.89

Crew A-7

Crew A-7	Hr.	Daily	Hr.	Daily	Bare Costs	Incl. O&P
1 Chief Of Party	$56.40	$451.20	$87.15	$697.20	$48.18	$74.03
1 Instrument Man	45.40	363.20	70.20	561.60		
1 Rodman/Chainman	42.75	342.00	64.75	518.00		
1 Level, electronic		78.70		86.57	3.28	3.61
24 L.H., Daily Totals		$1235.10		$1863.37	$51.46	$77.64

Crew A-8

Crew A-8	Hr.	Daily	Hr.	Daily	Bare Costs	Incl. O&P
1 Chief of Party	$56.40	$451.20	$87.15	$697.20	$46.83	$71.71
1 Instrument Man	45.40	363.20	70.20	561.60		
2 Rodmen/Chainmen	42.75	684.00	64.75	1036.00		
1 Level, electronic		78.70		86.57	2.46	2.71
32 L.H., Daily Totals		$1577.10		$2381.37	$49.28	$74.42

Crew A-9

Crew A-9	Hr.	Daily	Hr.	Daily	Bare Costs	Incl. O&P
1 Asbestos Foreman	$49.35	$394.80	$76.90	$615.20	$48.91	$76.20
7 Asbestos Workers	48.85	2735.60	76.10	4261.60		
64 L.H., Daily Totals		$3130.40		$4876.80	$48.91	$76.20

Crew A-10A

Crew A-10A	Hr.	Daily	Hr.	Daily	Bare Costs	Incl. O&P
1 Asbestos Foreman	$49.35	$394.80	$76.90	$615.20	$49.02	$76.37
2 Asbestos Workers	48.85	781.60	76.10	1217.60		
24 L.H., Daily Totals		$1176.40		$1832.80	$49.02	$76.37

Crew A-10B

Crew A-10B	Hr.	Daily	Hr.	Daily	Bare Costs	Incl. O&P
1 Asbestos Foreman	$49.35	$394.80	$76.90	$615.20	$48.98	$76.30
3 Asbestos Workers	48.85	1172.40	76.10	1826.40		
32 L.H., Daily Totals		$1567.20		$2441.60	$48.98	$76.30

Crew A-10C

Crew A-10C	Hr.	Daily	Hr.	Daily	Bare Costs	Incl. O&P
3 Asbestos Workers	$48.85	$1172.40	$76.10	$1826.40	$48.85	$76.10
1 Flatbed Truck, Gas, 1.5 Ton		211.00		232.10	8.79	9.67
24 L.H., Daily Totals		$1383.40		$2058.50	$57.64	$85.77

Crew A-10D

Crew A-10D	Hr.	Daily	Hr.	Daily	Bare Costs	Incl. O&P
2 Asbestos Workers	$48.85	$781.60	$76.10	$1217.60	$46.69	$71.65
1 Equip. Oper. (crane)	47.80	382.40	72.15	577.20		
1 Equip. Oper. Oiler	41.25	330.00	62.25	498.00		
1 Hydraulic Crane, 33 Ton		711.60		782.76	22.24	24.46
32 L.H., Daily Totals		$2205.60		$3075.56	$68.92	$96.11

Crew A-11

Crew A-11	Hr.	Daily	Hr.	Daily	Bare Costs	Incl. O&P
1 Asbestos Foreman	$49.35	$394.80	$76.90	$615.20	$48.91	$76.20
7 Asbestos Workers	48.85	2735.60	76.10	4261.60		
2 Chip. Hammers, 12 Lb., Elec.		39.60		43.56	.62	.68
64 L.H., Daily Totals		$3170.00		$4920.36	$49.53	$76.88

Crew A-12

Crew A-12	Hr.	Daily	Hr.	Daily	Bare Costs	Incl. O&P
1 Asbestos Foreman	$49.35	$394.80	$76.90	$615.20	$48.91	$76.20
7 Asbestos Workers	48.85	2735.60	76.10	4261.60		
1 Trk-mtd vac, 14 CY, 1500 Gal.		518.50		570.35		
1 Flatbed Truck, 20,000 GVW		215.80		237.38	11.47	12.62
64 L.H., Daily Totals		$3864.70		$5684.53	$60.39	$88.82

Crew A-13

Crew A-13	Hr.	Daily	Hr.	Daily	Bare Costs	Incl. O&P
1 Equip. Oper. (light)	$44.75	$358.00	$67.55	$540.40	$44.75	$67.55
1 Trk-mtd vac, 14 CY, 1500 Gal.		518.50		570.35		
1 Flatbed Truck, 20,000 GVW		215.80		237.38	91.79	100.97
8 L.H., Daily Totals		$1092.30		$1348.13	$136.54	$168.52

Crew B-1

Crew B-1	Hr.	Daily	Hr.	Daily	Bare Costs	Incl. O&P
1 Labor Foreman (outside)	$37.10	$296.80	$57.10	$456.80	$35.77	$55.03
2 Laborers	35.10	561.60	54.00	864.00		
24 L.H., Daily Totals		$858.40		$1320.80	$35.77	$55.03

Crew B-1A

Crew B-1A	Hr.	Daily	Hr.	Daily	Bare Costs	Incl. O&P
1 Labor Foreman (outside)	$37.10	$296.80	$57.10	$456.80	$35.77	$55.03
2 Laborers	35.10	561.60	54.00	864.00		
2 Cutting Torches		21.60		23.76		
2 Sets of Gases		172.80		190.08	8.10	8.91
24 L.H., Daily Totals		$1052.80		$1534.64	$43.87	$63.94

Crew B-1B

Crew B-1B	Hr.	Daily	Hr.	Daily	Bare Costs	Incl. O&P
1 Labor Foreman (outside)	$37.10	$296.80	$57.10	$456.80	$38.77	$59.31
2 Laborers	35.10	561.60	54.00	864.00		
1 Equip. Oper. (crane)	47.80	382.40	72.15	577.20		
2 Cutting Torches		21.60		23.76		
2 Sets of Gases		172.80		190.08		
1 Hyd. Crane, 12 Ton		612.00		673.20	25.20	27.72
32 L.H., Daily Totals		$2047.20		$2785.04	$63.98	$87.03

Crew B-2

Crew B-2	Hr.	Daily	Hr.	Daily	Bare Costs	Incl. O&P
1 Labor Foreman (outside)	$37.10	$296.80	$57.10	$456.80	$35.50	$54.62
4 Laborers	35.10	1123.20	54.00	1728.00		
40 L.H., Daily Totals		$1420.00		$2184.80	$35.50	$54.62

Crew B-3

Crew B-3	Hr.	Daily	Hr.	Daily	Bare Costs	Incl. O&P
1 Labor Foreman (outside)	$37.10	$296.80	$57.10	$456.80	$37.41	$57.08
2 Laborers	35.10	561.60	54.00	864.00		
1 Equip. Oper. (med.)	46.55	372.40	70.25	562.00		
2 Truck Drivers (heavy)	35.30	564.80	53.55	856.80		
1 Crawler Loader, 3 C.Y.		1106.00		1216.60		
2 Dump Trucks, 12 C.Y., 400 H.P.		1169.20		1286.12	47.40	52.14
48 L.H., Daily Totals		$4070.80		$5242.32	$84.81	$109.22

Crew B-3A

Crew B-3A	Hr.	Daily	Hr.	Daily	Bare Costs	Incl. O&P
4 Laborers	$35.10	$1123.20	$54.00	$1728.00	$37.39	$57.25
1 Equip. Oper. (med.)	46.55	372.40	70.25	562.00		
1 Hyd. Excavator, 1.5 C.Y.		960.40		1056.44	24.01	26.41
40 L.H., Daily Totals		$2456.00		$3346.44	$61.40	$83.66

Crew B-3B

Crew B-3B	Hr.	Daily	Hr.	Daily	Bare Costs	Incl. O&P
2 Laborers	$35.10	$561.60	$54.00	$864.00	$38.01	$57.95
1 Equip. Oper. (med.)	46.55	372.40	70.25	562.00		
1 Truck Driver (heavy)	35.30	282.40	53.55	428.40		
1 Backhoe Loader, 80 H.P.		363.80		400.18		
1 Dump Truck, 12 C.Y., 400 H.P.		584.60		643.06	29.64	32.60
32 L.H., Daily Totals		$2164.80		$2897.64	$67.65	$90.55

Crew B-3C

Crew B-3C	Hr.	Daily	Hr.	Daily	Bare Costs	Incl. O&P
3 Laborers	$35.10	$842.40	$54.00	$1296.00	$37.96	$58.06
1 Equip. Oper. (med.)	46.55	372.40	70.25	562.00		
1 Crawler Loader, 4 C.Y.		1443.00		1587.30	45.09	49.60
32 L.H., Daily Totals		$2657.80		$3445.30	$83.06	$107.67

Crew B-4

Crew B-4	Hr.	Daily	Hr.	Daily	Bare Costs	Incl. O&P
1 Labor Foreman (outside)	$37.10	$296.80	$57.10	$456.80	$35.47	$54.44
4 Laborers	35.10	1123.20	54.00	1728.00		
1 Truck Driver (heavy)	35.30	282.40	53.55	428.40		
1 Truck Tractor, 220 H.P.		314.80		346.28		
1 Flatbed Trailer, 40 Ton		147.00		161.70	9.62	10.58
48 L.H., Daily Totals		$2164.20		$3121.18	$45.09	$65.02

Crew B-5

Crew B-5	Hr.	Daily	Hr.	Daily	Bare Costs	Incl. O&P
1 Labor Foreman (outside)	$37.10	$296.80	$57.10	$456.80	$38.66	$59.09
4 Laborers	35.10	1123.20	54.00	1728.00		
2 Equip. Oper. (med.)	46.55	744.80	70.25	1124.00		
1 Air Compressor, 250 cfm		177.00		194.70		
2 Breakers, Pavement, 60 lb.		19.60		21.56		
2 -50' Air Hoses, 1.5"		12.60		13.86		
1 Crawler Loader, 3 C.Y.		1106.00		1216.60	23.49	25.83
56 L.H., Daily Totals		$3480.00		$4755.52	$62.14	$84.92

Crew B-5A

Crew B-5A	Hr.	Daily	Hr.	Daily	Bare Costs	Incl. O&P
1 Labor Foreman (outside)	$37.10	$296.80	$57.10	$456.80	$38.01	$58.02
6 Laborers	35.10	1684.80	54.00	2592.00		
2 Equip. Oper. (med.)	46.55	744.80	70.25	1124.00		
1 Equip. Oper. (light)	44.75	358.00	67.55	540.40		
2 Truck Drivers (heavy)	35.30	564.80	53.55	856.80		
1 Air Compressor, 365 cfm		229.00		251.90		
2 Breakers, Pavement, 60 lb.		19.60		21.56		
8 -50' Air Hoses, 1"		32.80		36.08		
2 Dump Trucks, 8 C.Y., 220 H.P.		714.80		786.28	10.38	11.41
96 L.H., Daily Totals		$4645.40		$6665.82	$48.39	$69.44

Crew B-5B

Crew B-5B	Hr.	Daily	Hr.	Daily	Bare Costs	Incl. O&P
1 Powderman	$45.40	$363.20	$70.20	$561.60	$40.73	$61.89
2 Equip. Oper. (med.)	46.55	744.80	70.25	1124.00		
3 Truck Drivers (heavy)	35.30	847.20	53.55	1285.20		
1 F.E. Loader, W.M., 2.5 C.Y.		472.40		519.64		
3 Dump Trucks, 12 C.Y., 400 H.P.		1753.80		1929.18		
1 Air Compressor, 365 CFM		229.00		251.90	51.15	56.27
48 L.H., Daily Totals		$4410.40		$5671.52	$91.88	$118.16

Crew B-5C

Crew B-5C	Hr.	Daily	Hr.	Daily	Bare Costs	Incl. O&P
3 Laborers	$35.10	$842.40	$54.00	$1296.00	$38.94	$59.22
1 Equip. Oper. (med.)	46.55	372.40	70.25	562.00		
2 Truck Drivers (heav.)	35.30	564.80	53.55	856.80		
1 Equip. Oper. (crane)	47.80	382.40	72.15	577.20		
1 Equip. Oper. Oiler	41.25	330.00	62.25	498.00		
2 Dump Trucks, 12 C.Y., 400 H.P.		1169.20		1286.12		
1 Crawler Loader, 4 C.Y.		1443.00		1587.30		
1 S.P. Crane, 4x4, 25 Ton		565.20		621.72	49.65	54.61
64 L.H., Daily Totals		$5669.40		$7285.14	$88.58	$113.83

Crew No.	Bare Costs		Incl. Subs O&P		Cost Per Labor-Hour	

Crew B-5D

Crew B-5D	Hr.	Daily	Hr.	Daily	Bare Costs	Incl. O&P
1 Labor Foreman (outside)	$37.10	$296.80	$57.10	$456.80	$38.24	$58.39
4 Laborers	35.10	1123.20	54.00	1728.00		
2 Equip. Oper. (med.)	46.55	744.80	70.25	1124.00		
1 Truck Driver (heavy)	35.30	282.40	53.55	428.40		
1 Air Compressor, 250 cfm		177.00		194.70		
2 Breakers, Pavement, 60 lb.		19.60		21.56		
2 -50' Air Hoses, 1.5"		12.60		13.86		
1 Crawler Loader, 3 C.Y.		1106.00		1216.60		
1 Dump Truck, 12 C.Y., 400 H.P.		584.60		643.06	29.68	32.65
64 L.H., Daily Totals		$4347.00		$5826.98	$67.92	$91.05

Crew B-6	Hr.	Daily	Hr.	Daily	Bare Costs	Incl. O&P
2 Laborers	$35.10	$561.60	$54.00	$864.00	$38.32	$58.52
1 Equip. Oper. (light)	44.75	358.00	67.55	540.40		
1 Backhoe Loader, 48 H.P.		334.00		367.40	13.92	15.31
24 L.H., Daily Totals		$1253.60		$1771.80	$52.23	$73.83

Crew B-6A	Hr.	Daily	Hr.	Daily	Bare Costs	Incl. O&P
.5 Labor Foreman (outside)	$37.10	$148.40	$57.10	$228.40	$40.08	$61.12
1 Laborer	35.10	280.80	54.00	432.00		
1 Equip. Oper. (med.)	46.55	372.40	70.25	562.00		
1 Vacuum Trk.,5000 Gal.		357.20		392.92	17.86	19.65
20 L.H., Daily Totals		$1158.80		$1615.32	$57.94	$80.77

Crew B-6B	Hr.	Daily	Hr.	Daily	Bare Costs	Incl. O&P
2 Labor Foremen (outside)	$37.10	$593.60	$57.10	$913.60	$35.77	$55.03
4 Laborers	35.10	1123.20	54.00	1728.00		
1 S.P. Crane, 4x4, 5 Ton		264.60		291.06		
1 Flatbed Truck, Gas, 1.5 Ton		211.00		232.10		
1 Butt Fusion Mach., 4"-12" diam.		376.45		414.10	17.75	19.53
48 L.H., Daily Totals		$2568.85		$3578.86	$53.52	$74.56

Crew B-6C	Hr.	Daily	Hr.	Daily	Bare Costs	Incl. O&P
2 Labor Foremen (outside)	$37.10	$593.60	$57.10	$913.60	$35.77	$55.03
4 Laborers	35.10	1123.20	54.00	1728.00		
1 S.P. Crane, 4x4, 12 Ton		448.20		493.02		
1 Flatbed Truck, Gas, 3 Ton		264.40		290.84		
1 Butt Fusion Mach., 8"-24" diam.		806.15		886.76	31.64	34.80
48 L.H., Daily Totals		$3235.55		$4312.23	$67.41	$89.84

Crew B-7	Hr.	Daily	Hr.	Daily	Bare Costs	Incl. O&P
1 Labor Foreman (outside)	$37.10	$296.80	$57.10	$456.80	$37.34	$57.23
4 Laborers	35.10	1123.20	54.00	1728.00		
1 Equip. Oper. (med.)	46.55	372.40	70.25	562.00		
1 Brush Chipper, 12", 130 H.P.		283.80		312.18		
1 Crawler Loader, 3 C.Y.		1106.00		1216.60		
2 Chain Saws, gas, 36" Long		87.20		95.92	30.77	33.85
48 L.H., Daily Totals		$3269.40		$4371.50	$68.11	$91.07

Crew B-7A	Hr.	Daily	Hr.	Daily	Bare Costs	Incl. O&P
2 Laborers	$35.10	$561.60	$54.00	$864.00	$38.32	$58.52
1 Equip. Oper. (light)	44.75	358.00	67.55	540.40		
1 Rake w/Tractor		324.70		357.17		
2 Chain Saws, gas, 18"		54.80		60.28	15.81	17.39
24 L.H., Daily Totals		$1299.10		$1821.85	$54.13	$75.91

Crew B-7B	Hr.	Daily	Hr.	Daily	Bare Costs	Incl. O&P
1 Labor Foreman (outside)	$37.10	$296.80	$57.10	$456.80	$37.05	$56.70
4 Laborers	35.10	1123.20	54.00	1728.00		
1 Equip. Oper. (med.)	46.55	372.40	70.25	562.00		
1 Truck Driver (heavy)	35.30	282.40	53.55	428.40		
1 Brush Chipper, 12", 130 H.P.		283.80		312.18		
1 Crawler Loader, 3 C.Y.		1106.00		1216.60		
2 Chain Saws, gas, 36" Long		87.20		95.92		
1 Dump Truck, 8 C.Y., 220 H.P.		357.40		393.14	32.76	36.03
56 L.H., Daily Totals		$3909.20		$5193.04	$69.81	$92.73

Crew B-7C	Hr.	Daily	Hr.	Daily	Bare Costs	Incl. O&P
1 Labor Foreman (outside)	$37.10	$296.80	$57.10	$456.80	$37.05	$56.70
4 Laborers	35.10	1123.20	54.00	1728.00		
1 Equip. Oper. (med.)	46.55	372.40	70.25	562.00		
1 Truck Driver (heavy)	35.30	282.40	53.55	428.40		
1 Brush Chipper, 12", 130 H.P.		283.80		312.18		
1 Crawler Loader, 3 C.Y.		1106.00		1216.60		
2 Chain Saws, gas, 36" Long		87.20		95.92		
1 Dump Truck, 12 C.Y., 400 H.P.		584.60		643.06	36.81	40.50
56 L.H., Daily Totals		$4136.40		$5442.96	$73.86	$97.20

Crew B-8	Hr.	Daily	Hr.	Daily	Bare Costs	Incl. O&P
1 Labor Foreman (outside)	$37.10	$296.80	$57.10	$456.80	$39.03	$59.37
2 Laborers	35.10	561.60	54.00	864.00		
2 Equip. Oper. (med.)	46.55	744.80	70.25	1124.00		
1 Equip. Oper. Oiler	41.25	330.00	62.25	498.00		
2 Truck Drivers (heavy)	35.30	564.80	53.55	856.80		
1 Hyd. Crane, 25 Ton		697.20		766.92		
1 Crawler Loader, 3 C.Y.		1106.00		1216.60		
2 Dump Trucks, 12 C.Y., 400 H.P.		1169.20		1286.12	46.44	51.09
64 L.H., Daily Totals		$5470.40		$7069.24	$85.48	$110.46

Crew B-9	Hr.	Daily	Hr.	Daily	Bare Costs	Incl. O&P
1 Labor Foreman (outside)	$37.10	$296.80	$57.10	$456.80	$35.50	$54.62
4 Laborers	35.10	1123.20	54.00	1728.00		
1 Air Compressor, 250 cfm		177.00		194.70		
2 Breakers, Pavement, 60 lb.		19.60		21.56		
2 -50' Air Hoses, 1.5"		12.60		13.86	5.23	5.75
40 L.H., Daily Totals		$1629.20		$2414.92	$40.73	$60.37

Crew B-9A	Hr.	Daily	Hr.	Daily	Bare Costs	Incl. O&P
2 Laborers	$35.10	$561.60	$54.00	$864.00	$35.17	$53.85
1 Truck Driver (heavy)	35.30	282.40	53.55	428.40		
1 Water Tank Trailer, 5000 Gal.		141.00		155.10		
1 Truck Tractor, 220 H.P.		314.80		346.28		
2 -50' Discharge Hoses, 3"		6.10		6.71	19.25	21.17
24 L.H., Daily Totals		$1305.90		$1800.49	$54.41	$75.02

Crew B-9B	Hr.	Daily	Hr.	Daily	Bare Costs	Incl. O&P
2 Laborers	$35.10	$561.60	$54.00	$864.00	$35.17	$53.85
1 Truck Driver (heavy)	35.30	282.40	53.55	428.40		
2 -50' Discharge Hoses, 3"		6.10		6.71		
1 Water Tank Trailer, 5000 Gal.		141.00		155.10		
1 Truck Tractor, 220 H.P.		314.80		346.28		
1 Pressure Washer		63.00		69.30	21.87	24.06
24 L.H., Daily Totals		$1368.90		$1869.79	$57.04	$77.91

Crews

Crew B-9D

Crew B-9D	Bare Costs Hr.	Daily	Incl. Subs O&P Hr.	Daily	Cost Per Labor-Hour Bare Costs	Incl. O&P
1 Labor Foreman (Outside)	$37.10	$296.80	$57.10	$456.80	$35.50	$54.62
4 Common Laborers	35.10	1123.20	54.00	1728.00		
1 Air Compressor, 250 cfm		177.00		194.70		
2 -50' Air Hoses, 1.5"		12.60		13.86		
2 Air Powered Tampers		52.40		57.64	6.05	6.66
40 L.H., Daily Totals		$1662.00		$2451.00	$41.55	$61.27

Crew B-10

Crew B-10	Bare Costs Hr.	Daily	Incl. Subs O&P Hr.	Daily	Cost Per Labor-Hour Bare Costs	Incl. O&P
1 Equip. Oper. (med.)	$46.55	$372.40	$70.25	$562.00	$42.73	$64.83
.5 Laborer	35.10	140.40	54.00	216.00		
12 L.H., Daily Totals		$512.80		$778.00	$42.73	$64.83

Crew B-10A

Crew B-10A	Bare Costs Hr.	Daily	Incl. Subs O&P Hr.	Daily	Cost Per Labor-Hour Bare Costs	Incl. O&P
1 Equip. Oper. (med.)	$46.55	$372.40	$70.25	$562.00	$42.73	$64.83
.5 Laborer	35.10	140.40	54.00	216.00		
1 Roller, 2-Drum, W.B., 7.5 H.P.		171.60		188.76	14.30	15.73
12 L.H., Daily Totals		$684.40		$966.76	$57.03	$80.56

Crew B-10B

Crew B-10B	Bare Costs Hr.	Daily	Incl. Subs O&P Hr.	Daily	Cost Per Labor-Hour Bare Costs	Incl. O&P
1 Equip. Oper. (med.)	$46.55	$372.40	$70.25	$562.00	$42.73	$64.83
.5 Laborer	35.10	140.40	54.00	216.00		
1 Dozer, 200 H.P.		1243.00		1367.30	103.58	113.94
12 L.H., Daily Totals		$1755.80		$2145.30	$146.32	$178.78

Crew B-10C

Crew B-10C	Bare Costs Hr.	Daily	Incl. Subs O&P Hr.	Daily	Cost Per Labor-Hour Bare Costs	Incl. O&P
1 Equip. Oper. (med.)	$46.55	$372.40	$70.25	$562.00	$42.73	$64.83
.5 Laborer	35.10	140.40	54.00	216.00		
1 Dozer, 200 H.P.		1243.00		1367.30		
1 Vibratory Roller, Towed, 23 Ton		388.80		427.68	135.98	149.58
12 L.H., Daily Totals		$2144.60		$2572.98	$178.72	$214.41

Crew B-10D

Crew B-10D	Bare Costs Hr.	Daily	Incl. Subs O&P Hr.	Daily	Cost Per Labor-Hour Bare Costs	Incl. O&P
1 Equip. Oper. (med.)	$46.55	$372.40	$70.25	$562.00	$42.73	$64.83
.5 Laborer	35.10	140.40	54.00	216.00		
1 Dozer, 200 H.P.		1243.00		1367.30		
1 Sheepsft. Roller, Towed		420.20		462.22	138.60	152.46
12 L.H., Daily Totals		$2176.00		$2607.52	$181.33	$217.29

Crew B-10E

Crew B-10E	Bare Costs Hr.	Daily	Incl. Subs O&P Hr.	Daily	Cost Per Labor-Hour Bare Costs	Incl. O&P
1 Equip. Oper. (med.)	$46.55	$372.40	$70.25	$562.00	$42.73	$64.83
.5 Laborer	35.10	140.40	54.00	216.00		
1 Tandem Roller, 5 Ton		149.20		164.12	12.43	13.68
12 L.H., Daily Totals		$662.00		$942.12	$55.17	$78.51

Crew B-10F

Crew B-10F	Bare Costs Hr.	Daily	Incl. Subs O&P Hr.	Daily	Cost Per Labor-Hour Bare Costs	Incl. O&P
1 Equip. Oper. (med.)	$46.55	$372.40	$70.25	$562.00	$42.73	$64.83
.5 Laborer	35.10	140.40	54.00	216.00		
1 Tandem Roller, 10 Ton		227.60		250.36	18.97	20.86
12 L.H., Daily Totals		$740.40		$1028.36	$61.70	$85.70

Crew B-10G

Crew B-10G	Bare Costs Hr.	Daily	Incl. Subs O&P Hr.	Daily	Cost Per Labor-Hour Bare Costs	Incl. O&P
1 Equip. Oper. (med.)	$46.55	$372.40	$70.25	$562.00	$42.73	$64.83
.5 Laborer	35.10	140.40	54.00	216.00		
1 Sheepsft. Roll., 240 H.P.		1101.00		1211.10	91.75	100.93
12 L.H., Daily Totals		$1613.80		$1989.10	$134.48	$165.76

Crew B-10H

Crew B-10H	Bare Costs Hr.	Daily	Incl. Subs O&P Hr.	Daily	Cost Per Labor-Hour Bare Costs	Incl. O&P
1 Equip. Oper. (med.)	$46.55	$372.40	$70.25	$562.00	$42.73	$64.83
.5 Laborer	35.10	140.40	54.00	216.00		
1 Diaphragm Water Pump, 2"		68.60		75.46		
1 -20' Suction Hose, 2"		1.95		2.15		
2 -50' Discharge Hoses, 2"		3.50		3.85	6.17	6.79
12 L.H., Daily Totals		$586.85		$859.46	$48.90	$71.62

Crew B-10I

Crew B-10I	Bare Costs Hr.	Daily	Incl. Subs O&P Hr.	Daily	Cost Per Labor-Hour Bare Costs	Incl. O&P
1 Equip. Oper. (med.)	$46.55	$372.40	$70.25	$562.00	$42.73	$64.83
.5 Laborer	35.10	140.40	54.00	216.00		
1 Diaphragm Water Pump, 4"		111.20		122.32		
1 -20' Suction Hose, 4"		3.25		3.58		
2 -50' Discharge Hoses, 4"		9.40		10.34	10.32	11.35
12 L.H., Daily Totals		$636.65		$914.24	$53.05	$76.19

Crew B-10J

Crew B-10J	Bare Costs Hr.	Daily	Incl. Subs O&P Hr.	Daily	Cost Per Labor-Hour Bare Costs	Incl. O&P
1 Equip. Oper. (med.)	$46.55	$372.40	$70.25	$562.00	$42.73	$64.83
.5 Laborer	35.10	140.40	54.00	216.00		
1 Centrifugal Water Pump, 3"		73.80		81.18		
1 -20' Suction Hose, 3"		2.85		3.13		
2 -50' Discharge Hoses, 3"		6.10		6.71	6.90	7.59
12 L.H., Daily Totals		$595.55		$869.02	$49.63	$72.42

Crew B-10K

Crew B-10K	Bare Costs Hr.	Daily	Incl. Subs O&P Hr.	Daily	Cost Per Labor-Hour Bare Costs	Incl. O&P
1 Equip. Oper. (med.)	$46.55	$372.40	$70.25	$562.00	$42.73	$64.83
.5 Laborer	35.10	140.40	54.00	216.00		
1 Centr. Water Pump, 6"		308.40		339.24		
1 -20' Suction Hose, 6"		11.50		12.65		
2 -50' Discharge Hoses, 6"		24.20		26.62	28.68	31.54
12 L.H., Daily Totals		$856.90		$1156.51	$71.41	$96.38

Crew B-10L

Crew B-10L	Bare Costs Hr.	Daily	Incl. Subs O&P Hr.	Daily	Cost Per Labor-Hour Bare Costs	Incl. O&P
1 Equip. Oper. (med.)	$46.55	$372.40	$70.25	$562.00	$42.73	$64.83
.5 Laborer	35.10	140.40	54.00	216.00		
1 Dozer, 80 H.P.		442.40		486.64	36.87	40.55
12 L.H., Daily Totals		$955.20		$1264.64	$79.60	$105.39

Crew B-10M

Crew B-10M	Bare Costs Hr.	Daily	Incl. Subs O&P Hr.	Daily	Cost Per Labor-Hour Bare Costs	Incl. O&P
1 Equip. Oper. (med.)	$46.55	$372.40	$70.25	$562.00	$42.73	$64.83
.5 Laborer	35.10	140.40	54.00	216.00		
1 Dozer, 300 H.P.		1718.00		1889.80	143.17	157.48
12 L.H., Daily Totals		$2230.80		$2667.80	$185.90	$222.32

Crew B-10N

Crew B-10N	Bare Costs Hr.	Daily	Incl. Subs O&P Hr.	Daily	Cost Per Labor-Hour Bare Costs	Incl. O&P
1 Equip. Oper. (med.)	$46.55	$372.40	$70.25	$562.00	$42.73	$64.83
.5 Laborer	35.10	140.40	54.00	216.00		
1 F.E. Loader, T.M., 1.5 C.Y.		488.60		537.46	40.72	44.79
12 L.H., Daily Totals		$1001.40		$1315.46	$83.45	$109.62

Crew B-10O

Crew B-10O	Bare Costs Hr.	Daily	Incl. Subs O&P Hr.	Daily	Cost Per Labor-Hour Bare Costs	Incl. O&P
1 Equip. Oper. (med.)	$46.55	$372.40	$70.25	$562.00	$42.73	$64.83
.5 Laborer	35.10	140.40	54.00	216.00		
1 F.E. Loader, T.M., 2.25 C.Y.		895.20		984.72	74.60	82.06
12 L.H., Daily Totals		$1408.00		$1762.72	$117.33	$146.89

Crew B-10P

Crew B-10P	Bare Costs Hr.	Daily	Incl. Subs O&P Hr.	Daily	Cost Per Labor-Hour Bare Costs	Incl. O&P
1 Equip. Oper. (med.)	$46.55	$372.40	$70.25	$562.00	$42.73	$64.83
.5 Laborer	35.10	140.40	54.00	216.00		
1 Crawler Loader, 3 C.Y.		1106.00		1216.60	92.17	101.38
12 L.H., Daily Totals		$1618.80		$1994.60	$134.90	$166.22

Crews

Crew B-10Q

Crew No.	Bare Costs Hr.	Daily	Incl. Subs O&P Hr.	Daily	Cost Per Labor-Hour Bare Costs	Incl. O&P
1 Equip. Oper. (med.)	$46.55	$372.40	$70.25	$562.00	$42.73	$64.83
.5 Laborer	35.10	140.40	54.00	216.00		
1 Crawler Loader, 4 C.Y.		1443.00		1587.30	120.25	132.28
12 L.H., Daily Totals		$1955.80		$2365.30	$162.98	$197.11

Crew B-10R

Crew No.	Bare Costs Hr.	Daily	Incl. Subs O&P Hr.	Daily	Cost Per Labor-Hour Bare Costs	Incl. O&P
1 Equip. Oper. (med.)	$46.55	$372.40	$70.25	$562.00	$42.73	$64.83
.5 Laborer	35.10	140.40	54.00	216.00		
1 F.E. Loader, W.M., 1 C.Y.		268.20		295.02	22.35	24.59
12 L.H., Daily Totals		$781.00		$1073.02	$65.08	$89.42

Crew B-10S

Crew No.	Bare Costs Hr.	Daily	Incl. Subs O&P Hr.	Daily	Cost Per Labor-Hour Bare Costs	Incl. O&P
1 Equip. Oper. (med.)	$46.55	$372.40	$70.25	$562.00	$42.73	$64.83
.5 Laborer	35.10	140.40	54.00	216.00		
1 F.E. Loader, W.M., 1.5 C.Y.		333.80		367.18	27.82	30.60
12 L.H., Daily Totals		$846.60		$1145.18	$70.55	$95.43

Crew B-10T

Crew No.	Bare Costs Hr.	Daily	Incl. Subs O&P Hr.	Daily	Cost Per Labor-Hour Bare Costs	Incl. O&P
1 Equip. Oper. (med.)	$46.55	$372.40	$70.25	$562.00	$42.73	$64.83
.5 Laborer	35.10	140.40	54.00	216.00		
1 F.E. Loader, W.M.,2.5 C.Y.		472.40		519.64	39.37	43.30
12 L.H., Daily Totals		$985.20		$1297.64	$82.10	$108.14

Crew B-10U

Crew No.	Bare Costs Hr.	Daily	Incl. Subs O&P Hr.	Daily	Cost Per Labor-Hour Bare Costs	Incl. O&P
1 Equip. Oper. (med.)	$46.55	$372.40	$70.25	$562.00	$42.73	$64.83
.5 Laborer	35.10	140.40	54.00	216.00		
1 F.E. Loader, W.M., 5.5 C.Y.		960.00		1056.00	80.00	88.00
12 L.H., Daily Totals		$1472.80		$1834.00	$122.73	$152.83

Crew B-10V

Crew No.	Bare Costs Hr.	Daily	Incl. Subs O&P Hr.	Daily	Cost Per Labor-Hour Bare Costs	Incl. O&P
1 Equip. Oper. (med.)	$46.55	$372.40	$70.25	$562.00	$42.73	$64.83
.5 Laborer	35.10	140.40	54.00	216.00		
1 Dozer, 700 H.P.		4235.00		4658.50	352.92	388.21
12 L.H., Daily Totals		$4747.80		$5436.50	$395.65	$453.04

Crew B-10W

Crew No.	Bare Costs Hr.	Daily	Incl. Subs O&P Hr.	Daily	Cost Per Labor-Hour Bare Costs	Incl. O&P
1 Equip. Oper. (med.)	$46.55	$372.40	$70.25	$562.00	$42.73	$64.83
.5 Laborer	35.10	140.40	54.00	216.00		
1 Dozer, 105 H.P.		550.80		605.88	45.90	50.49
12 L.H., Daily Totals		$1063.60		$1383.88	$88.63	$115.32

Crew B-10X

Crew No.	Bare Costs Hr.	Daily	Incl. Subs O&P Hr.	Daily	Cost Per Labor-Hour Bare Costs	Incl. O&P
1 Equip. Oper. (med.)	$46.55	$372.40	$70.25	$562.00	$42.73	$64.83
.5 Laborer	35.10	140.40	54.00	216.00		
1 Dozer, 410 H.P.		2272.00		2499.20	189.33	208.27
12 L.H., Daily Totals		$2784.80		$3277.20	$232.07	$273.10

Crew B-10Y

Crew No.	Bare Costs Hr.	Daily	Incl. Subs O&P Hr.	Daily	Cost Per Labor-Hour Bare Costs	Incl. O&P
1 Equip. Oper. (med.)	$46.55	$372.40	$70.25	$562.00	$42.73	$64.83
.5 Laborer	35.10	140.40	54.00	216.00		
1 Vibr. Roller, Towed, 12 Ton		514.80		566.28	42.90	47.19
12 L.H., Daily Totals		$1027.60		$1344.28	$85.63	$112.02

Crew B-11A

Crew No.	Bare Costs Hr.	Daily	Incl. Subs O&P Hr.	Daily	Cost Per Labor-Hour Bare Costs	Incl. O&P
1 Equipment Oper. (med.)	$46.55	$372.40	$70.25	$562.00	$40.83	$62.13
1 Laborer	35.10	280.80	54.00	432.00		
1 Dozer, 200 H.P.		1243.00		1367.30	77.69	85.46
16 L.H., Daily Totals		$1896.20		$2361.30	$118.51	$147.58

Crew B-11B

Crew No.	Bare Costs Hr.	Daily	Incl. Subs O&P Hr.	Daily	Cost Per Labor-Hour Bare Costs	Incl. O&P
1 Equipment Oper. (light)	$44.75	$358.00	$67.55	$540.40	$39.92	$60.77
1 Laborer	35.10	280.80	54.00	432.00		
1 Air Powered Tamper		26.20		28.82		
1 Air Compressor, 365 cfm		229.00		251.90		
2 -50' Air Hoses, 1.5"		12.60		13.86	16.74	18.41
16 L.H., Daily Totals		$906.60		$1266.98	$56.66	$79.19

Crew B-11C

Crew No.	Bare Costs Hr.	Daily	Incl. Subs O&P Hr.	Daily	Cost Per Labor-Hour Bare Costs	Incl. O&P
1 Equipment Oper. (med.)	$46.55	$372.40	$70.25	$562.00	$40.83	$62.13
1 Laborer	35.10	280.80	54.00	432.00		
1 Backhoe Loader, 48 H.P.		334.00		367.40	20.88	22.96
16 L.H., Daily Totals		$987.20		$1361.40	$61.70	$85.09

Crew B-11J

Crew No.	Bare Costs Hr.	Daily	Incl. Subs O&P Hr.	Daily	Cost Per Labor-Hour Bare Costs	Incl. O&P
1 Equipment Oper. (med.)	$46.55	$372.40	$70.25	$562.00	$40.83	$62.13
1 Laborer	35.10	280.80	54.00	432.00		
1 Grader, 30,000 Lbs.		610.80		671.88		
1 Ripper, beam & 1 shank		81.60		89.76	43.27	47.60
16 L.H., Daily Totals		$1345.60		$1755.64	$84.10	$109.73

Crew B-11K

Crew No.	Bare Costs Hr.	Daily	Incl. Subs O&P Hr.	Daily	Cost Per Labor-Hour Bare Costs	Incl. O&P
1 Equipment Oper. (med.)	$46.55	$372.40	$70.25	$562.00	$40.83	$62.13
1 Laborer	35.10	280.80	54.00	432.00		
1 Trencher, Chain Type, 8' D		2848.00		3132.80	178.00	195.80
16 L.H., Daily Totals		$3501.20		$4126.80	$218.82	$257.93

Crew B-11L

Crew No.	Bare Costs Hr.	Daily	Incl. Subs O&P Hr.	Daily	Cost Per Labor-Hour Bare Costs	Incl. O&P
1 Equipment Oper. (med.)	$46.55	$372.40	$70.25	$562.00	$40.83	$62.13
1 Laborer	35.10	280.80	54.00	432.00		
1 Grader, 30,000 Lbs.		610.80		671.88	38.17	41.99
16 L.H., Daily Totals		$1264.00		$1665.88	$79.00	$104.12

Crew B-11M

Crew No.	Bare Costs Hr.	Daily	Incl. Subs O&P Hr.	Daily	Cost Per Labor-Hour Bare Costs	Incl. O&P
1 Equipment Oper. (med.)	$46.55	$372.40	$70.25	$562.00	$40.83	$62.13
1 Laborer	35.10	280.80	54.00	432.00		
1 Backhoe Loader, 80 H.P.		363.80		400.18	22.74	25.01
16 L.H., Daily Totals		$1017.00		$1394.18	$63.56	$87.14

Crew B-11N

Crew No.	Bare Costs Hr.	Daily	Incl. Subs O&P Hr.	Daily	Cost Per Labor-Hour Bare Costs	Incl. O&P
1 Labor Foreman (outside)	$37.10	$296.80	$57.10	$456.80	$38.00	$57.66
2 Equipment Operators (med.)	46.55	744.80	70.25	1124.00		
6 Truck Drivers (hvy.)	35.30	1694.40	53.55	2570.40		
1 F.E. Loader, W.M., 5.5 C.Y.		960.00		1056.00		
1 Dozer, 410 H.P.		2272.00		2499.20		
6 Dump Trucks, Off Hwy., 50 Ton		9408.00		10348.80	175.56	193.11
72 L.H., Daily Totals		$15376.00		$18055.20	$213.56	$250.77

Crew B-11Q

Crew No.	Bare Costs Hr.	Daily	Incl. Subs O&P Hr.	Daily	Cost Per Labor-Hour Bare Costs	Incl. O&P
1 Equipment Operator (med.)	$46.55	$372.40	$70.25	$562.00	$42.73	$64.83
.5 Laborer	35.10	140.40	54.00	216.00		
1 Dozer, 140 H.P.		817.40		899.14	68.12	74.93
12 L.H., Daily Totals		$1330.20		$1677.14	$110.85	$139.76

Crew B-11R

Crew No.	Bare Costs Hr.	Daily	Incl. Subs O&P Hr.	Daily	Cost Per Labor-Hour Bare Costs	Incl. O&P
1 Equipment Operator (med.)	$46.55	$372.40	$70.25	$562.00	$42.73	$64.83
.5 Laborer	35.10	140.40	54.00	216.00		
1 Dozer, 200 H.P.		1243.00		1367.30	103.58	113.94
12 L.H., Daily Totals		$1755.80		$2145.30	$146.32	$178.78

Crews

Crew B-11S

Crew B-11S	Hr.	Daily	Hr.	Daily	Bare Costs	Incl. O&P
1 Equipment Operator (med.)	$46.55	$372.40	$70.25	$562.00	$42.73	$64.83
.5 Laborer	35.10	140.40	54.00	216.00		
1 Dozer, 300 H.P.		1718.00		1889.80		
1 Ripper, beam & 1 shank		81.60		89.76	149.97	164.96
12 L.H., Daily Totals		$2312.40		$2757.56	$192.70	$229.80

Crew B-11T

Crew B-11T	Hr.	Daily	Hr.	Daily	Bare Costs	Incl. O&P
1 Equipment Operator (med.)	$46.55	$372.40	$70.25	$562.00	$42.73	$64.83
.5 Laborer	35.10	140.40	54.00	216.00		
1 Dozer, 410 H.P.		2272.00		2499.20		
1 Ripper, beam & 2 shanks		91.80		100.98	196.98	216.68
12 L.H., Daily Totals		$2876.60		$3378.18	$239.72	$281.51

Crew B-11U

Crew B-11U	Hr.	Daily	Hr.	Daily	Bare Costs	Incl. O&P
1 Equipment Operator (med.)	$46.55	$372.40	$70.25	$562.00	$42.73	$64.83
.5 Laborer	35.10	140.40	54.00	216.00		
1 Dozer, 520 H.P.		2937.00		3230.70	244.75	269.23
12 L.H., Daily Totals		$3449.80		$4008.70	$287.48	$334.06

Crew B-11V

Crew B-11V	Hr.	Daily	Hr.	Daily	Bare Costs	Incl. O&P
3 Laborers	$35.10	$842.40	$54.00	$1296.00	$35.10	$54.00
1 Roller, 2-Drum, W.B., 7.5 H.P.		171.60		188.76	7.15	7.87
24 L.H., Daily Totals		$1014.00		$1484.76	$42.25	$61.87

Crew B-11W

Crew B-11W	Hr.	Daily	Hr.	Daily	Bare Costs	Incl. O&P
1 Equipment Operator (med.)	$46.55	$372.40	$70.25	$562.00	$36.22	$54.98
1 Common Laborer	35.10	280.80	54.00	432.00		
10 Truck Drivers (hvy.)	35.30	2824.00	53.55	4284.00		
1 Dozer, 200 H.P.		1243.00		1367.30		
1 Vibratory Roller, Towed, 23 Ton		388.80		427.68		
10 Dump Trucks, 8 C.Y., 220 H.P.		3574.00		3931.40	54.23	59.65
96 L.H., Daily Totals		$8683.00		$11004.38	$90.45	$114.63

Crew B-11Y

Crew B-11Y	Hr.	Daily	Hr.	Daily	Bare Costs	Incl. O&P
1 Labor Foreman (Outside)	$37.10	$296.80	$57.10	$456.80	$39.14	$59.76
5 Common Laborers	35.10	1404.00	54.00	2160.00		
3 Equipment Operators (med.)	46.55	1117.20	70.25	1686.00		
1 Dozer, 80 H.P.		442.40		486.64		
2 Roller, 2-Drum, W.B., 7.5 H.P.		343.20		377.52		
4 Vibratory Plates, gas, 21"		163.20		179.52	13.18	14.50
72 L.H., Daily Totals		$3766.80		$5346.48	$52.32	$74.26

Crew B-12A

Crew B-12A	Hr.	Daily	Hr.	Daily	Bare Costs	Incl. O&P
1 Equip. Oper. (crane)	$47.80	$382.40	$72.15	$577.20	$41.45	$63.08
1 Laborer	35.10	280.80	54.00	432.00		
1 Hyd. Excavator, 1 C.Y.		748.60		823.46	46.79	51.47
16 L.H., Daily Totals		$1411.80		$1832.66	$88.24	$114.54

Crew B-12B

Crew B-12B	Hr.	Daily	Hr.	Daily	Bare Costs	Incl. O&P
1 Equip. Oper. (crane)	$47.80	$382.40	$72.15	$577.20	$41.45	$63.08
1 Laborer	35.10	280.80	54.00	432.00		
1 Hyd. Excavator, 1.5 C.Y.		960.40		1056.44	60.02	66.03
16 L.H., Daily Totals		$1623.60		$2065.64	$101.47	$129.10

Crew B-12C

Crew B-12C	Hr.	Daily	Hr.	Daily	Bare Costs	Incl. O&P
1 Equip. Oper. (crane)	$47.80	$382.40	$72.15	$577.20	$41.45	$63.08
1 Laborer	35.10	280.80	54.00	432.00		
1 Hyd. Excavator, 2 C.Y.		1253.00		1378.30	78.31	86.14
16 L.H., Daily Totals		$1916.20		$2387.50	$119.76	$149.22

Crew B-12D

Crew B-12D	Hr.	Daily	Hr.	Daily	Bare Costs	Incl. O&P
1 Equip. Oper. (crane)	$47.80	$382.40	$72.15	$577.20	$41.45	$63.08
1 Laborer	35.10	280.80	54.00	432.00		
1 Hyd. Excavator, 3.5 C.Y.		2211.00		2432.10	138.19	152.01
16 L.H., Daily Totals		$2874.20		$3441.30	$179.64	$215.08

Crew B-12E

Crew B-12E	Hr.	Daily	Hr.	Daily	Bare Costs	Incl. O&P
1 Equip. Oper. (crane)	$47.80	$382.40	$72.15	$577.20	$41.45	$63.08
1 Laborer	35.10	280.80	54.00	432.00		
1 Hyd. Excavator, .5 C.Y.		371.40		408.54	23.21	25.53
16 L.H., Daily Totals		$1034.60		$1417.74	$64.66	$88.61

Crew B-12F

Crew B-12F	Hr.	Daily	Hr.	Daily	Bare Costs	Incl. O&P
1 Equip. Oper. (crane)	$47.80	$382.40	$72.15	$577.20	$41.45	$63.08
1 Laborer	35.10	280.80	54.00	432.00		
1 Hyd. Excavator, .75 C.Y.		647.20		711.92	40.45	44.49
16 L.H., Daily Totals		$1310.40		$1721.12	$81.90	$107.57

Crew B-12G

Crew B-12G	Hr.	Daily	Hr.	Daily	Bare Costs	Incl. O&P
1 Equip. Oper. (crane)	$47.80	$382.40	$72.15	$577.20	$41.45	$63.08
1 Laborer	35.10	280.80	54.00	432.00		
1 Crawler Crane, 15 Ton		647.50		712.25		
1 Clamshell Bucket, .5 C.Y.		37.40		41.14	42.81	47.09
16 L.H., Daily Totals		$1348.10		$1762.59	$84.26	$110.16

Crew B-12H

Crew B-12H	Hr.	Daily	Hr.	Daily	Bare Costs	Incl. O&P
1 Equip. Oper. (crane)	$47.80	$382.40	$72.15	$577.20	$41.45	$63.08
1 Laborer	35.10	280.80	54.00	432.00		
1 Crawler Crane, 25 Ton		1110.00		1221.00		
1 Clamshell Bucket, 1 C.Y.		47.00		51.70	72.31	79.54
16 L.H., Daily Totals		$1820.20		$2281.90	$113.76	$142.62

Crew B-12I

Crew B-12I	Hr.	Daily	Hr.	Daily	Bare Costs	Incl. O&P
1 Equip. Oper. (crane)	$47.80	$382.40	$72.15	$577.20	$41.45	$63.08
1 Laborer	35.10	280.80	54.00	432.00		
1 Crawler Crane, 20 Ton		832.00		915.20		
1 Dragline Bucket, .75 C.Y.		20.40		22.44	53.27	58.60
16 L.H., Daily Totals		$1515.60		$1946.84	$94.72	$121.68

Crew B-12J

Crew B-12J	Hr.	Daily	Hr.	Daily	Bare Costs	Incl. O&P
1 Equip. Oper. (crane)	$47.80	$382.40	$72.15	$577.20	$41.45	$63.08
1 Laborer	35.10	280.80	54.00	432.00		
1 Gradall, 5/8 C.Y.		844.00		928.40	52.75	58.02
16 L.H., Daily Totals		$1507.20		$1937.60	$94.20	$121.10

Crew B-12K

Crew B-12K	Hr.	Daily	Hr.	Daily	Bare Costs	Incl. O&P
1 Equip. Oper. (crane)	$47.80	$382.40	$72.15	$577.20	$41.45	$63.08
1 Laborer	35.10	280.80	54.00	432.00		
1 Gradall, 3 Ton, 1 C.Y.		961.20		1057.32	60.08	66.08
16 L.H., Daily Totals		$1624.40		$2066.52	$101.53	$129.16

Crew B-12L

Crew B-12L	Hr.	Daily	Hr.	Daily	Bare Costs	Incl. O&P
1 Equip. Oper. (crane)	$47.80	$382.40	$72.15	$577.20	$41.45	$63.08
1 Laborer	35.10	280.80	54.00	432.00		
1 Crawler Crane, 15 Ton		647.50		712.25		
1 F.E. Attachment, .5 C.Y.		57.40		63.14	44.06	48.46
16 L.H., Daily Totals		$1368.10		$1784.59	$85.51	$111.54

Crew No.	Bare Costs		Incl. Subs O&P		Cost Per Labor-Hour	
Crew B-12M	Hr.	Daily	Hr.	Daily	Bare Costs	Incl. O&P
1 Equip. Oper. (crane)	$47.80	$382.40	$72.15	$577.20	$41.45	$63.08
1 Laborer	35.10	280.80	54.00	432.00		
1 Crawler Crane, 20 Ton		832.00		915.20		
1 F.E. Attachment, .75 C.Y.		62.20		68.42	55.89	61.48
16 L.H., Daily Totals		$1557.40		$1992.82	$97.34	$124.55
Crew B-12N	Hr.	Daily	Hr.	Daily	Bare Costs	Incl. O&P
1 Equip. Oper. (crane)	$47.80	$382.40	$72.15	$577.20	$41.45	$63.08
1 Laborer	35.10	280.80	54.00	432.00		
1 Crawler Crane, 25 Ton		1110.00		1221.00		
1 F.E. Attachment, 1 C.Y.		68.00		74.80	73.63	80.99
16 L.H., Daily Totals		$1841.20		$2305.00	$115.08	$144.06
Crew B-12O	Hr.	Daily	Hr.	Daily	Bare Costs	Incl. O&P
1 Equip. Oper. (crane)	$47.80	$382.40	$72.15	$577.20	$41.45	$63.08
1 Laborer	35.10	280.80	54.00	432.00		
1 Crawler Crane, 40 Ton		1115.00		1226.50		
1 F.E. Attachment, 1.5 C.Y.		76.80		84.48	74.49	81.94
16 L.H., Daily Totals		$1855.00		$2320.18	$115.94	$145.01
Crew B-12P	Hr.	Daily	Hr.	Daily	Bare Costs	Incl. O&P
1 Equip. Oper. (crane)	$47.80	$382.40	$72.15	$577.20	$41.45	$63.08
1 Laborer	35.10	280.80	54.00	432.00		
1 Crawler Crane, 40 Ton		1115.00		1226.50		
1 Dragline Bucket, 1.5 C.Y.		33.20		36.52	71.76	78.94
16 L.H., Daily Totals		$1811.40		$2272.22	$113.21	$142.01
Crew B-12Q	Hr.	Daily	Hr.	Daily	Bare Costs	Incl. O&P
1 Equip. Oper. (crane)	$47.80	$382.40	$72.15	$577.20	$41.45	$63.08
1 Laborer	35.10	280.80	54.00	432.00		
1 Hyd. Excavator, 5/8 C.Y.		551.80		606.98	34.49	37.94
16 L.H., Daily Totals		$1215.00		$1616.18	$75.94	$101.01
Crew B-12S	Hr.	Daily	Hr.	Daily	Bare Costs	Incl. O&P
1 Equip. Oper. (crane)	$47.80	$382.40	$72.15	$577.20	$41.45	$63.08
1 Laborer	35.10	280.80	54.00	432.00		
1 Hyd. Excavator, 2.5 C.Y.		1652.00		1817.20	103.25	113.58
16 L.H., Daily Totals		$2315.20		$2826.40	$144.70	$176.65
Crew B-12T	Hr.	Daily	Hr.	Daily	Bare Costs	Incl. O&P
1 Equip. Oper. (crane)	$47.80	$382.40	$72.15	$577.20	$41.45	$63.08
1 Laborer	35.10	280.80	54.00	432.00		
1 Crawler Crane, 75 Ton		1423.00		1565.30		
1 F.E. Attachment, 3 C.Y.		99.60		109.56	95.16	104.68
16 L.H., Daily Totals		$2185.80		$2684.06	$136.61	$167.75
Crew B-12V	Hr.	Daily	Hr.	Daily	Bare Costs	Incl. O&P
1 Equip. Oper. (crane)	$47.80	$382.40	$72.15	$577.20	$41.45	$63.08
1 Laborer	35.10	280.80	54.00	432.00		
1 Crawler Crane, 75 Ton		1423.00		1565.30		
1 Dragline Bucket, 3 C.Y.		51.80		56.98	92.17	101.39
16 L.H., Daily Totals		$2138.00		$2631.48	$133.63	$164.47
Crew B-12Y	Hr.	Daily	Hr.	Daily	Bare Costs	Incl. O&P
1 Equip. Oper. (crane)	$47.80	$382.40	$72.15	$577.20	$39.33	$60.05
2 Laborers	35.10	561.60	54.00	864.00		
1 Hyd. Excavator, 3.5 C.Y.		2211.00		2432.10	92.13	101.34
24 L.H., Daily Totals		$3155.00		$3873.30	$131.46	$161.39

Crew No.	Bare Costs		Incl. Subs O&P		Cost Per Labor-Hour	
Crew B-12Z	Hr.	Daily	Hr.	Daily	Bare Costs	Incl. O&P
1 Equip. Oper. (crane)	$47.80	$382.40	$72.15	$577.20	$39.33	$60.05
2 Laborers	35.10	561.60	54.00	864.00		
1 Hyd. Excavator, 2.5 C.Y.		1652.00		1817.20	68.83	75.72
24 L.H., Daily Totals		$2596.00		$3258.40	$108.17	$135.77
Crew B-13	Hr.	Daily	Hr.	Daily	Bare Costs	Incl. O&P
1 Labor Foreman (outside)	$37.10	$296.80	$57.10	$456.80	$38.08	$58.21
4 Laborers	35.10	1123.20	54.00	1728.00		
1 Equip. Oper. (crane)	47.80	382.40	72.15	577.20		
1 Equip. Oper. Oiler	41.25	330.00	62.25	498.00		
1 Hyd. Crane, 25 Ton		697.20		766.92	12.45	13.70
56 L.H., Daily Totals		$2829.60		$4026.92	$50.53	$71.91
Crew B-13A	Hr.	Daily	Hr.	Daily	Bare Costs	Incl. O&P
1 Labor Foreman (outside)	$37.10	$296.80	$57.10	$456.80	$38.71	$58.96
2 Laborers	35.10	561.60	54.00	864.00		
2 Equipment Operators (med.)	46.55	744.80	70.25	1124.00		
2 Truck Drivers (heavy)	35.30	564.80	53.55	856.80		
1 Crawler Crane, 75 Ton		1423.00		1565.30		
1 Crawler Loader, 4 C.Y.		1443.00		1587.30		
2 Dump Trucks, 8 C.Y., 220 H.P.		714.80		786.28	63.94	70.34
56 L.H., Daily Totals		$5748.80		$7240.48	$102.66	$129.29
Crew B-13B	Hr.	Daily	Hr.	Daily	Bare Costs	Incl. O&P
1 Labor Foreman (outside)	$37.10	$296.80	$57.10	$456.80	$38.08	$58.21
4 Laborers	35.10	1123.20	54.00	1728.00		
1 Equip. Oper. (crane)	47.80	382.40	72.15	577.20		
1 Equip. Oper. Oiler	41.25	330.00	62.25	498.00		
1 Hyd. Crane, 55 Ton		1100.00		1210.00	19.64	21.61
56 L.H., Daily Totals		$3232.40		$4470.00	$57.72	$79.82
Crew B-13C	Hr.	Daily	Hr.	Daily	Bare Costs	Incl. O&P
1 Labor Foreman (outside)	$37.10	$296.80	$57.10	$456.80	$38.08	$58.21
4 Laborers	35.10	1123.20	54.00	1728.00		
1 Equip. Oper. (crane)	47.80	382.40	72.15	577.20		
1 Equip. Oper. Oiler	41.25	330.00	62.25	498.00		
1 Crawler Crane, 100 Ton		1628.00		1790.80	29.07	31.98
56 L.H., Daily Totals		$3760.40		$5050.80	$67.15	$90.19
Crew B-13D	Hr.	Daily	Hr.	Daily	Bare Costs	Incl. O&P
1 Laborer	$35.10	$280.80	$54.00	$432.00	$41.45	$63.08
1 Equip. Oper. (crane)	47.80	382.40	72.15	577.20		
1 Hyd. Excavator, 1 C.Y.		748.60		823.46		
1 Trench Box		113.40		124.74	53.88	59.26
16 L.H., Daily Totals		$1525.20		$1957.40	$95.33	$122.34
Crew B-13E	Hr.	Daily	Hr.	Daily	Bare Costs	Incl. O&P
1 Laborer	$35.10	$280.80	$54.00	$432.00	$41.45	$63.08
1 Equip. Oper. (crane)	47.80	382.40	72.15	577.20		
1 Hyd. Excavator, 1.5 C.Y.		960.40		1056.44		
1 Trench Box		113.40		124.74	67.11	73.82
16 L.H., Daily Totals		$1737.00		$2190.38	$108.56	$136.90
Crew B-13F	Hr.	Daily	Hr.	Daily	Bare Costs	Incl. O&P
1 Laborer	$35.10	$280.80	$54.00	$432.00	$41.45	$63.08
1 Equip. Oper. (crane)	47.80	382.40	72.15	577.20		
1 Hyd. Excavator, 3.5 C.Y.		2211.00		2432.10		
1 Trench Box		113.40		124.74	145.28	159.80
16 L.H., Daily Totals		$2987.60		$3566.04	$186.72	$222.88

Crews

Crew No.	Bare Costs Hr.	Daily	Incl. Subs O&P Hr.	Daily	Cost Per Labor-Hour Bare Costs	Incl. O&P
Crew B-13G	Hr.	Daily	Hr.	Daily	Bare Costs	Incl. O&P
1 Laborer	$35.10	$280.80	$54.00	$432.00	$41.45	$63.08
1 Equip. Oper. (crane)	47.80	382.40	72.15	577.20		
1 Hyd. Excavator, .75 C.Y.		647.20		711.92		
1 Trench Box		113.40		124.74	47.54	52.29
16 L.H., Daily Totals		$1423.80		$1845.86	$88.99	$115.37
Crew B-13H	Hr.	Daily	Hr.	Daily	Bare Costs	Incl. O&P
1 Laborer	$35.10	$280.80	$54.00	$432.00	$41.45	$63.08
1 Equip. Oper. (crane)	47.80	382.40	72.15	577.20		
1 Gradall, 5/8 C.Y.		844.00		928.40		
1 Trench Box		113.40		124.74	59.84	65.82
16 L.H., Daily Totals		$1620.60		$2062.34	$101.29	$128.90
Crew B-13I	Hr.	Daily	Hr.	Daily	Bare Costs	Incl. O&P
1 Laborer	$35.10	$280.80	$54.00	$432.00	$41.45	$63.08
1 Equip. Oper. (crane)	47.80	382.40	72.15	577.20		
1 Gradall, 3 Ton, 1 C.Y.		961.20		1057.32		
1 Trench Box		113.40		124.74	67.16	73.88
16 L.H., Daily Totals		$1737.80		$2191.26	$108.61	$136.95
Crew B-13J	Hr.	Daily	Hr.	Daily	Bare Costs	Incl. O&P
1 Laborer	$35.10	$280.80	$54.00	$432.00	$41.45	$63.08
1 Equip. Oper. (crane)	47.80	382.40	72.15	577.20		
1 Hyd. Excavator, 2.5 C.Y.		1652.00		1817.20		
1 Trench Box		113.40		124.74	110.34	121.37
16 L.H., Daily Totals		$2428.60		$2951.14	$151.79	$184.45
Crew B-14	Hr.	Daily	Hr.	Daily	Bare Costs	Incl. O&P
1 Labor Foreman (outside)	$37.10	$296.80	$57.10	$456.80	$37.04	$56.77
4 Laborers	35.10	1123.20	54.00	1728.00		
1 Equip. Oper. (light)	44.75	358.00	67.55	540.40		
1 Backhoe Loader, 48 H.P.		334.00		367.40	6.96	7.65
48 L.H., Daily Totals		$2112.00		$3092.60	$44.00	$64.43
Crew B-14A	Hr.	Daily	Hr.	Daily	Bare Costs	Incl. O&P
1 Equip. Oper. (crane)	$47.80	$382.40	$72.15	$577.20	$43.57	$66.10
.5 Laborer	35.10	140.40	54.00	216.00		
1 Hyd. Excavator, 4.5 C.Y.		2748.00		3022.80	229.00	251.90
12 L.H., Daily Totals		$3270.80		$3816.00	$272.57	$318.00
Crew B-14B	Hr.	Daily	Hr.	Daily	Bare Costs	Incl. O&P
1 Equip. Oper. (crane)	$47.80	$382.40	$72.15	$577.20	$43.57	$66.10
.5 Laborer	35.10	140.40	54.00	216.00		
1 Hyd. Excavator, 6 C.Y.		3229.00		3551.90	269.08	295.99
12 L.H., Daily Totals		$3751.80		$4345.10	$312.65	$362.09
Crew B-14C	Hr.	Daily	Hr.	Daily	Bare Costs	Incl. O&P
1 Equip. Oper. (crane)	$47.80	$382.40	$72.15	$577.20	$43.57	$66.10
.5 Laborer	35.10	140.40	54.00	216.00		
1 Hyd. Excavator, 7 C.Y.		3304.00		3634.40	275.33	302.87
12 L.H., Daily Totals		$3826.80		$4427.60	$318.90	$368.97
Crew B-14F	Hr.	Daily	Hr.	Daily	Bare Costs	Incl. O&P
1 Equip. Oper. (crane)	$47.80	$382.40	$72.15	$577.20	$43.57	$66.10
.5 Laborer	35.10	140.40	54.00	216.00		
1 Hyd. Shovel, 7 C.Y.		3259.00		3584.90	271.58	298.74
12 L.H., Daily Totals		$3781.80		$4378.10	$315.15	$364.84
Crew B-14G	Hr.	Daily	Hr.	Daily	Bare Costs	Incl. O&P
1 Equip. Oper. (crane)	$47.80	$382.40	$72.15	$577.20	$43.57	$66.10
.5 Laborer	35.10	140.40	54.00	216.00		
1 Hyd. Shovel, 12 C.Y.		4249.00		4673.90	354.08	389.49
12 L.H., Daily Totals		$4771.80		$5467.10	$397.65	$455.59
Crew B-14J	Hr.	Daily	Hr.	Daily	Bare Costs	Incl. O&P
1 Equip. Oper. (med.)	$46.55	$372.40	$70.25	$562.00	$42.73	$64.83
.5 Laborer	35.10	140.40	54.00	216.00		
1 F.E. Loader, 8 C.Y.		1856.00		2041.60	154.67	170.13
12 L.H., Daily Totals		$2368.80		$2819.60	$197.40	$234.97
Crew B-14K	Hr.	Daily	Hr.	Daily	Bare Costs	Incl. O&P
1 Equip. Oper. (med.)	$46.55	$372.40	$70.25	$562.00	$42.73	$64.83
.5 Laborer	35.10	140.40	54.00	216.00		
1 F.E. Loader, 10 C.Y.		2556.00		2811.60	213.00	234.30
12 L.H., Daily Totals		$3068.80		$3589.60	$255.73	$299.13
Crew B-15	Hr.	Daily	Hr.	Daily	Bare Costs	Incl. O&P
1 Equipment Oper. (med.)	$46.55	$372.40	$70.25	$562.00	$38.49	$58.39
.5 Laborer	35.10	140.40	54.00	216.00		
2 Truck Drivers (heavy)	35.30	564.80	53.55	856.80		
2 Dump Trucks, 12 C.Y., 400 H.P.		1169.20		1286.12		
1 Dozer, 200 H.P.		1243.00		1367.30	86.15	94.77
28 L.H., Daily Totals		$3489.80		$4288.22	$124.64	$153.15
Crew B-16	Hr.	Daily	Hr.	Daily	Bare Costs	Incl. O&P
1 Labor Foreman (outside)	$37.10	$296.80	$57.10	$456.80	$35.65	$54.66
2 Laborers	35.10	561.60	54.00	864.00		
1 Truck Driver (heavy)	35.30	282.40	53.55	428.40		
1 Dump Truck, 12 C.Y., 400 H.P.		584.60		643.06	18.27	20.10
32 L.H., Daily Totals		$1725.40		$2392.26	$53.92	$74.76
Crew B-17	Hr.	Daily	Hr.	Daily	Bare Costs	Incl. O&P
2 Laborers	$35.10	$561.60	$54.00	$864.00	$37.56	$57.27
1 Equip. Oper. (light)	44.75	358.00	67.55	540.40		
1 Truck Driver (heavy)	35.30	282.40	53.55	428.40		
1 Backhoe Loader, 48 H.P.		334.00		367.40		
1 Dump Truck, 8 C.Y., 220 H.P.		357.40		393.14	21.61	23.77
32 L.H., Daily Totals		$1893.40		$2593.34	$59.17	$81.04
Crew B-17A	Hr.	Daily	Hr.	Daily	Bare Costs	Incl. O&P
2 Labor Foremen (outside)	$37.10	$593.60	$57.10	$913.60	$37.76	$58.17
6 Laborers	35.10	1684.80	54.00	2592.00		
1 Skilled Worker Foreman (out)	47.40	379.20	73.30	586.40		
1 Skilled Worker	45.40	363.20	70.20	561.60		
80 L.H., Daily Totals		$3020.80		$4653.60	$37.76	$58.17
Crew B-17B	Hr.	Daily	Hr.	Daily	Bare Costs	Incl. O&P
2 Laborers	$35.10	$561.60	$54.00	$864.00	$37.56	$57.27
1 Equip. Oper. (light)	44.75	358.00	67.55	540.40		
1 Truck Driver (heavy)	35.30	282.40	53.55	428.40		
1 Backhoe Loader, 48 H.P.		334.00		367.40		
1 Dump Truck, 12 C.Y., 400 H.P.		584.60		643.06	28.71	31.58
32 L.H., Daily Totals		$2120.60		$2843.26	$66.27	$88.85
Crew B-18	Hr.	Daily	Hr.	Daily	Bare Costs	Incl. O&P
1 Labor Foreman (outside)	$37.10	$296.80	$57.10	$456.80	$35.77	$55.03
2 Laborers	35.10	561.60	54.00	864.00		
1 Vibratory Plate, gas, 21"		40.80		44.88	1.70	1.87
24 L.H., Daily Totals		$899.20		$1365.68	$37.47	$56.90

621

Crew B-19

Crew B-19	Hr.	Daily	Hr.	Daily	Bare Costs	Incl. O&P
1 Pile Driver Foreman (outside)	$44.80	$358.40	$72.00	$576.00	$44.11	$69.22
4 Pile Drivers	42.80	1369.60	68.80	2201.60		
2 Equip. Oper. (crane)	47.80	764.80	72.15	1154.40		
1 Equip. Oper. Oiler	41.25	330.00	62.25	498.00		
1 Crawler Crane, 40 Ton		1115.00		1226.50		
1 Lead, 90' high		124.00		136.40		
1 Hammer, Diesel, 22k ft-lb		592.80		652.08	28.62	31.48
64 L.H., Daily Totals		$4654.60		$6444.98	$72.73	$100.70

Crew B-19A

Crew B-19A	Hr.	Daily	Hr.	Daily	Bare Costs	Incl. O&P
1 Pile Driver Foreman (outside)	$44.80	$358.40	$72.00	$576.00	$44.11	$69.22
4 Pile Drivers	42.80	1369.60	68.80	2201.60		
2 Equip. Oper. (crane)	47.80	764.80	72.15	1154.40		
1 Equip. Oper. Oiler	41.25	330.00	62.25	498.00		
1 Crawler Crane, 75 Ton		1423.00		1565.30		
1 Lead, 90' high		124.00		136.40		
1 Hammer, Diesel, 41k ft-lb		686.80		755.48	34.90	38.39
64 L.H., Daily Totals		$5056.60		$6887.18	$79.01	$107.61

Crew B-19B

Crew B-19B	Hr.	Daily	Hr.	Daily	Bare Costs	Incl. O&P
1 Pile Driver Foreman (outside)	$44.80	$358.40	$72.00	$576.00	$44.11	$69.22
4 Pile Drivers	42.80	1369.60	68.80	2201.60		
2 Equip. Oper. (crane)	47.80	764.80	72.15	1154.40		
1 Equip. Oper. Oiler	41.25	330.00	62.25	498.00		
1 Crawler Crane, 40 Ton		1115.00		1226.50		
1 Lead, 90' high		124.00		136.40		
1 Hammer, Diesel, 22k ft-lb		592.80		652.08		
1 Barge, 400 Ton		779.20		857.12	40.80	44.88
64 L.H., Daily Totals		$5433.80		$7302.10	$84.90	$114.10

Crew B-19C

Crew B-19C	Hr.	Daily	Hr.	Daily	Bare Costs	Incl. O&P
1 Pile Driver Foreman (outside)	$44.80	$358.40	$72.00	$576.00	$44.11	$69.22
4 Pile Drivers	42.80	1369.60	68.80	2201.60		
2 Equip. Oper. (crane)	47.80	764.80	72.15	1154.40		
1 Equip. Oper. Oiler	41.25	330.00	62.25	498.00		
1 Crawler Crane, 75 Ton		1423.00		1565.30		
1 Lead, 90' high		124.00		136.40		
1 Hammer, Diesel, 41k ft-lb		686.80		755.48		
1 Barge, 400 Ton		779.20		857.12	47.08	51.79
64 L.H., Daily Totals		$5835.80		$7744.30	$91.18	$121.00

Crew B-20

Crew B-20	Hr.	Daily	Hr.	Daily	Bare Costs	Incl. O&P
1 Labor Foreman (outside)	$37.10	$296.80	$57.10	$456.80	$39.20	$60.43
1 Skilled Worker	45.40	363.20	70.20	561.60		
1 Laborer	35.10	280.80	54.00	432.00		
24 L.H., Daily Totals		$940.80		$1450.40	$39.20	$60.43

Crew B-20A

Crew B-20A	Hr.	Daily	Hr.	Daily	Bare Costs	Incl. O&P
1 Labor Foreman (outside)	$37.10	$296.80	$57.10	$456.80	$42.63	$64.84
1 Laborer	35.10	280.80	54.00	432.00		
1 Plumber	54.60	436.80	82.35	658.80		
1 Plumber Apprentice	43.70	349.60	65.90	527.20		
32 L.H., Daily Totals		$1364.00		$2074.80	$42.63	$64.84

Crew B-21

Crew B-21	Hr.	Daily	Hr.	Daily	Bare Costs	Incl. O&P
1 Labor Foreman (outside)	$37.10	$296.80	$57.10	$456.80	$40.43	$62.11
1 Skilled Worker	45.40	363.20	70.20	561.60		
1 Laborer	35.10	280.80	54.00	432.00		
.5 Equip. Oper. (crane)	47.80	191.20	72.15	288.60		
.5 S.P. Crane, 4x4, 5 Ton		132.30		145.53	4.72	5.20
28 L.H., Daily Totals		$1264.30		$1884.53	$45.15	$67.30

Crew B-21A

Crew B-21A	Hr.	Daily	Hr.	Daily	Bare Costs	Incl. O&P
1 Labor Foreman (outside)	$37.10	$296.80	$57.10	$456.80	$43.66	$66.30
1 Laborer	35.10	280.80	54.00	432.00		
1 Plumber	54.60	436.80	82.35	658.80		
1 Plumber Apprentice	43.70	349.60	65.90	527.20		
1 Equip. Oper. (crane)	47.80	382.40	72.15	577.20		
1 S.P. Crane, 4x4, 12 Ton		448.20		493.02	11.21	12.33
40 L.H., Daily Totals		$2194.60		$3145.02	$54.87	$78.63

Crew B-21B

Crew B-21B	Hr.	Daily	Hr.	Daily	Bare Costs	Incl. O&P
1 Labor Foreman (outside)	$37.10	$296.80	$57.10	$456.80	$38.04	$58.25
3 Laborers	35.10	842.40	54.00	1296.00		
1 Equip. Oper. (crane)	47.80	382.40	72.15	577.20		
1 Hyd. Crane, 12 Ton		612.00		673.20	15.30	16.83
40 L.H., Daily Totals		$2133.60		$3003.20	$53.34	$75.08

Crew B-21C

Crew B-21C	Hr.	Daily	Hr.	Daily	Bare Costs	Incl. O&P
1 Labor Foreman (outside)	$37.10	$296.80	$57.10	$456.80	$38.08	$58.21
4 Laborers	35.10	1123.20	54.00	1728.00		
1 Equip. Oper. (crane)	47.80	382.40	72.15	577.20		
1 Equip. Oper. Oiler	41.25	330.00	62.25	498.00		
2 Cutting Torches		21.60		23.76		
2 Sets of Gases		172.80		190.08		
1 Lattice Boom Crane, 90 Ton		1497.00		1646.70	30.20	33.22
56 L.H., Daily Totals		$3823.80		$5120.54	$68.28	$91.44

Crew B-22

Crew B-22	Hr.	Daily	Hr.	Daily	Bare Costs	Incl. O&P
1 Labor Foreman (outside)	$37.10	$296.80	$57.10	$456.80	$40.92	$62.78
1 Skilled Worker	45.40	363.20	70.20	561.60		
1 Laborer	35.10	280.80	54.00	432.00		
.75 Equip. Oper. (crane)	47.80	286.80	72.15	432.90		
.75 S.P. Crane, 4x4, 5 Ton		198.45		218.29	6.62	7.28
30 L.H., Daily Totals		$1426.05		$2101.59	$47.53	$70.05

Crew B-22A

Crew B-22A	Hr.	Daily	Hr.	Daily	Bare Costs	Incl. O&P
1 Labor Foreman (outside)	$37.10	$296.80	$57.10	$456.80	$40.10	$61.49
1 Skilled Worker	45.40	363.20	70.20	561.60		
2 Laborers	35.10	561.60	54.00	864.00		
1 Equipment Oper. (crane)	47.80	382.40	72.15	577.20		
1 S.P. Crane, 4x4, 5 Ton		264.60		291.06		
1 Butt Fusion Mach., 4"-12" diam.		376.45		414.10	16.03	17.63
40 L.H., Daily Totals		$2245.05		$3164.76	$56.13	$79.12

Crew B-22B

Crew B-22B	Hr.	Daily	Hr.	Daily	Bare Costs	Incl. O&P
1 Labor Foreman (outside)	$37.10	$296.80	$57.10	$456.80	$40.10	$61.49
1 Skilled Worker	45.40	363.20	70.20	561.60		
2 Laborers	35.10	561.60	54.00	864.00		
1 Equip. Oper. (crane)	47.80	382.40	72.15	577.20		
1 S.P. Crane, 4x4, 5 Ton		264.60		291.06		
1 Butt Fusion Mach., 8"-24" diam.		806.15		886.76	26.77	29.45
40 L.H., Daily Totals		$2674.75		$3637.43	$66.87	$90.94

Crew B-22C

Crew B-22C	Hr.	Daily	Hr.	Daily	Bare Costs	Incl. O&P
1 Skilled Worker	$45.40	$363.20	$70.20	$561.60	$40.25	$62.10
1 Laborer	35.10	280.80	54.00	432.00		
1 Butt Fusion Mach., 2"-8" diam.		120.50		132.55	7.53	8.28
16 L.H., Daily Totals		$764.50		$1126.15	$47.78	$70.38

Crews

Crew B-23

Crew No.	Bare Costs Hr.	Bare Costs Daily	Incl. Subs O&P Hr.	Incl. Subs O&P Daily	Cost Per Labor-Hour Bare Costs	Cost Per Labor-Hour Incl. O&P
1 Labor Foreman (outside)	$37.10	$296.80	$57.10	$456.80	$35.50	$54.62
4 Laborers	35.10	1123.20	54.00	1728.00		
1 Drill Rig, Truck-Mounted		2441.00		2685.10		
1 Flatbed Truck, Gas, 3 Ton		264.40		290.84	67.64	74.40
40 L.H., Daily Totals		$4125.40		$5160.74	$103.14	$129.02

Crew B-23A

Crew No.	Bare Costs Hr.	Bare Costs Daily	Incl. Subs O&P Hr.	Incl. Subs O&P Daily	Bare Costs	Incl. O&P
1 Labor Foreman (outside)	$37.10	$296.80	$57.10	$456.80	$39.58	$60.45
1 Laborer	35.10	280.80	54.00	432.00		
1 Equip. Operator (med.)	46.55	372.40	70.25	562.00		
1 Drill Rig, Truck-Mounted		2441.00		2685.10		
1 Pickup Truck, 3/4 Ton		127.00		139.70	107.00	117.70
24 L.H., Daily Totals		$3518.00		$4275.60	$146.58	$178.15

Crew B-23B

Crew No.	Bare Costs Hr.	Bare Costs Daily	Incl. Subs O&P Hr.	Incl. Subs O&P Daily	Bare Costs	Incl. O&P
1 Labor Foreman (outside)	$37.10	$296.80	$57.10	$456.80	$39.58	$60.45
1 Laborer	35.10	280.80	54.00	432.00		
1 Equip. Operator (med.)	46.55	372.40	70.25	562.00		
1 Drill Rig, Truck-Mounted		2441.00		2685.10		
1 Pickup Truck, 3/4 Ton		127.00		139.70		
1 Centr. Water Pump, 6"		308.40		339.24	119.85	131.84
24 L.H., Daily Totals		$3826.40		$4614.84	$159.43	$192.29

Crew B-24

Crew No.	Bare Costs Hr.	Bare Costs Daily	Incl. Subs O&P Hr.	Incl. Subs O&P Daily	Bare Costs	Incl. O&P
1 Cement Finisher	$42.35	$338.80	$62.30	$498.40	$40.52	$61.38
1 Laborer	35.10	280.80	54.00	432.00		
1 Carpenter	44.10	352.80	67.85	542.80		
24 L.H., Daily Totals		$972.40		$1473.20	$40.52	$61.38

Crew B-25

Crew No.	Bare Costs Hr.	Bare Costs Daily	Incl. Subs O&P Hr.	Incl. Subs O&P Daily	Bare Costs	Incl. O&P
1 Labor Foreman (outside)	$37.10	$296.80	$57.10	$456.80	$38.40	$58.71
7 Laborers	35.10	1965.60	54.00	3024.00		
3 Equip. Oper. (med.)	46.55	1117.20	70.25	1686.00		
1 Asphalt Paver, 130 H.P.		1996.00		2195.60		
1 Tandem Roller, 10 Ton		227.60		250.36		
1 Roller, Pneum. Whl, 12 Ton		313.20		344.52	28.83	31.71
88 L.H., Daily Totals		$5916.40		$7957.28	$67.23	$90.42

Crew B-25B

Crew No.	Bare Costs Hr.	Bare Costs Daily	Incl. Subs O&P Hr.	Incl. Subs O&P Daily	Bare Costs	Incl. O&P
1 Labor Foreman (outside)	$37.10	$296.80	$57.10	$456.80	$39.08	$59.67
7 Laborers	35.10	1965.60	54.00	3024.00		
4 Equip. Oper. (med.)	46.55	1489.60	70.25	2248.00		
1 Asphalt Paver, 130 H.P.		1996.00		2195.60		
2 Tandem Rollers, 10 Ton		455.20		500.72		
1 Roller, Pneum. Whl, 12 Ton		313.20		344.52	28.80	31.68
96 L.H., Daily Totals		$6516.40		$8769.64	$67.88	$91.35

Crew B-25C

Crew No.	Bare Costs Hr.	Bare Costs Daily	Incl. Subs O&P Hr.	Incl. Subs O&P Daily	Bare Costs	Incl. O&P
1 Labor Foreman (outside)	$37.10	$296.80	$57.10	$456.80	$39.25	$59.93
3 Laborers	35.10	842.40	54.00	1296.00		
2 Equip. Oper. (med.)	46.55	744.80	70.25	1124.00		
1 Asphalt Paver, 130 H.P.		1996.00		2195.60		
1 Tandem Roller, 10 Ton		227.60		250.36	46.33	50.96
48 L.H., Daily Totals		$4107.60		$5322.76	$85.58	$110.89

Crew B-26

Crew No.	Bare Costs Hr.	Bare Costs Daily	Incl. Subs O&P Hr.	Incl. Subs O&P Daily	Bare Costs	Incl. O&P
1 Labor Foreman (outside)	$37.10	$296.80	$57.10	$456.80	$39.30	$60.21
6 Laborers	35.10	1684.80	54.00	2592.00		
2 Equip. Oper. (med.)	46.55	744.80	70.25	1124.00		
1 Rodman (reinf.)	49.10	392.80	78.40	627.20		
1 Cement Finisher	42.35	338.80	62.30	498.40		
1 Grader, 30,000 Lbs.		610.80		671.88		
1 Paving Mach. & Equip.		2531.00		2784.10	35.70	39.27
88 L.H., Daily Totals		$6599.80		$8754.38	$75.00	$99.48

Crew B-26A

Crew No.	Bare Costs Hr.	Bare Costs Daily	Incl. Subs O&P Hr.	Incl. Subs O&P Daily	Bare Costs	Incl. O&P
1 Labor Foreman (outside)	$37.10	$296.80	$57.10	$456.80	$39.30	$60.21
6 Laborers	35.10	1684.80	54.00	2592.00		
2 Equip. Oper. (med.)	46.55	744.80	70.25	1124.00		
1 Rodman (reinf.)	49.10	392.80	78.40	627.20		
1 Cement Finisher	42.35	338.80	62.30	498.40		
1 Grader, 30,000 Lbs.		610.80		671.88		
1 Paving Mach. & Equip.		2531.00		2784.10		
1 Concrete Saw		148.00		162.80	37.38	41.12
88 L.H., Daily Totals		$6747.80		$8917.18	$76.68	$101.33

Crew B-26B

Crew No.	Bare Costs Hr.	Bare Costs Daily	Incl. Subs O&P Hr.	Incl. Subs O&P Daily	Bare Costs	Incl. O&P
1 Labor Foreman (outside)	$37.10	$296.80	$57.10	$456.80	$39.90	$61.05
6 Laborers	35.10	1684.80	54.00	2592.00		
3 Equip. Oper. (med.)	46.55	1117.20	70.25	1686.00		
1 Rodman (reinf.)	49.10	392.80	78.40	627.20		
1 Cement Finisher	42.35	338.80	62.30	498.40		
1 Grader, 30,000 Lbs.		610.80		671.88		
1 Paving Mach. & Equip.		2531.00		2784.10		
1 Concrete Pump, 110' Boom		941.40		1035.54	42.53	46.79
96 L.H., Daily Totals		$7913.60		$10351.92	$82.43	$107.83

Crew B-27

Crew No.	Bare Costs Hr.	Bare Costs Daily	Incl. Subs O&P Hr.	Incl. Subs O&P Daily	Bare Costs	Incl. O&P
1 Labor Foreman (outside)	$37.10	$296.80	$57.10	$456.80	$35.60	$54.77
3 Laborers	35.10	842.40	54.00	1296.00		
1 Berm Machine		280.00		308.00	8.75	9.63
32 L.H., Daily Totals		$1419.20		$2060.80	$44.35	$64.40

Crew B-28

Crew No.	Bare Costs Hr.	Bare Costs Daily	Incl. Subs O&P Hr.	Incl. Subs O&P Daily	Bare Costs	Incl. O&P
2 Carpenters	$44.10	$705.60	$67.85	$1085.60	$41.10	$63.23
1 Laborer	35.10	280.80	54.00	432.00		
24 L.H., Daily Totals		$986.40		$1517.60	$41.10	$63.23

Crew B-29

Crew No.	Bare Costs Hr.	Bare Costs Daily	Incl. Subs O&P Hr.	Incl. Subs O&P Daily	Bare Costs	Incl. O&P
1 Labor Foreman (outside)	$37.10	$296.80	$57.10	$456.80	$38.08	$58.21
4 Laborers	35.10	1123.20	54.00	1728.00		
1 Equip. Oper. (crane)	47.80	382.40	72.15	577.20		
1 Equip. Oper. Oiler	41.25	330.00	62.25	498.00		
1 Gradall, 5/8 C.Y.		844.00		928.40	15.07	16.58
56 L.H., Daily Totals		$2976.40		$4188.40	$53.15	$74.79

Crew B-30

Crew No.	Bare Costs Hr.	Bare Costs Daily	Incl. Subs O&P Hr.	Incl. Subs O&P Daily	Bare Costs	Incl. O&P
1 Equip. Oper. (med.)	$46.55	$372.40	$70.25	$562.00	$39.05	$59.12
2 Truck Drivers (heavy)	35.30	564.80	53.55	856.80		
1 Hyd. Excavator, 1.5 C.Y.		960.40		1056.44		
2 Dump Trucks, 12 C.Y., 400 H.P.		1169.20		1286.12	88.73	97.61
24 L.H., Daily Totals		$3066.80		$3761.36	$127.78	$156.72

Crew B-31

Crew No.	Bare Costs Hr.	Bare Costs Daily	Incl. Subs O&P Hr.	Incl. Subs O&P Daily	Cost Per Labor-Hour Bare Costs	Cost Per Labor-Hour Incl. O&P
1 Labor Foreman (outside)	$37.10	$296.80	$57.10	$456.80	$37.30	$57.39
3 Laborers	35.10	842.40	54.00	1296.00		
1 Carpenter	44.10	352.80	67.85	542.80		
1 Air Compressor, 250 cfm		177.00		194.70		
1 Sheeting Driver		5.75		6.33		
2 -50' Air Hoses, 1.5"		12.60		13.86	4.88	5.37
40 L.H., Daily Totals		$1687.35		$2510.49	$42.18	$62.76

Crew B-32

Crew No.	Bare Costs Hr.	Bare Costs Daily	Incl. Subs O&P Hr.	Incl. Subs O&P Daily	Cost Per Labor-Hour Bare Costs	Cost Per Labor-Hour Incl. O&P
1 Laborer	$35.10	$280.80	$54.00	$432.00	$43.69	$66.19
3 Equip. Oper. (med.)	46.55	1117.20	70.25	1686.00		
1 Grader, 30,000 Lbs.		610.80		671.88		
1 Tandem Roller, 10 Ton		227.60		250.36		
1 Dozer, 200 H.P.		1243.00		1367.30	65.04	71.55
32 L.H., Daily Totals		$3479.40		$4407.54	$108.73	$137.74

Crew B-32A

Crew No.	Bare Costs Hr.	Bare Costs Daily	Incl. Subs O&P Hr.	Incl. Subs O&P Daily	Cost Per Labor-Hour Bare Costs	Cost Per Labor-Hour Incl. O&P
1 Laborer	$35.10	$280.80	$54.00	$432.00	$42.73	$64.83
2 Equip. Oper. (med.)	46.55	744.80	70.25	1124.00		
1 Grader, 30,000 Lbs.		610.80		671.88		
1 Roller, Vibratory, 25 Ton		640.20		704.22	52.13	57.34
24 L.H., Daily Totals		$2276.60		$2932.10	$94.86	$122.17

Crew B-32B

Crew No.	Bare Costs Hr.	Bare Costs Daily	Incl. Subs O&P Hr.	Incl. Subs O&P Daily	Cost Per Labor-Hour Bare Costs	Cost Per Labor-Hour Incl. O&P
1 Laborer	$35.10	$280.80	$54.00	$432.00	$42.73	$64.83
2 Equip. Oper. (med.)	46.55	744.80	70.25	1124.00		
1 Dozer, 200 H.P.		1243.00		1367.30		
1 Roller, Vibratory, 25 Ton		640.20		704.22	78.47	86.31
24 L.H., Daily Totals		$2908.80		$3627.52	$121.20	$151.15

Crew B-32C

Crew No.	Bare Costs Hr.	Bare Costs Daily	Incl. Subs O&P Hr.	Incl. Subs O&P Daily	Cost Per Labor-Hour Bare Costs	Cost Per Labor-Hour Incl. O&P
1 Labor Foreman (outside)	$37.10	$296.80	$57.10	$456.80	$41.16	$62.64
2 Laborers	35.10	561.60	54.00	864.00		
3 Equip. Oper. (med.)	46.55	1117.20	70.25	1686.00		
1 Grader, 30,000 Lbs.		610.80		671.88		
1 Tandem Roller, 10 Ton		227.60		250.36		
1 Dozer, 200 H.P.		1243.00		1367.30	43.36	47.70
48 L.H., Daily Totals		$4057.00		$5296.34	$84.52	$110.34

Crew B-33A

Crew No.	Bare Costs Hr.	Bare Costs Daily	Incl. Subs O&P Hr.	Incl. Subs O&P Daily	Cost Per Labor-Hour Bare Costs	Cost Per Labor-Hour Incl. O&P
1 Equip. Oper. (med.)	$46.55	$372.40	$70.25	$562.00	$43.28	$65.61
.5 Laborer	35.10	140.40	54.00	216.00		
.25 Equip. Oper. (med.)	46.55	93.10	70.25	140.50		
1 Scraper, Towed, 7 C.Y.		108.20		119.02		
1.25 Dozers, 300 H.P.		2147.50		2362.25	161.12	177.23
14 L.H., Daily Totals		$2861.60		$3399.77	$204.40	$242.84

Crew B-33B

Crew No.	Bare Costs Hr.	Bare Costs Daily	Incl. Subs O&P Hr.	Incl. Subs O&P Daily	Cost Per Labor-Hour Bare Costs	Cost Per Labor-Hour Incl. O&P
1 Equip. Oper. (med.)	$46.55	$372.40	$70.25	$562.00	$43.28	$65.61
.5 Laborer	35.10	140.40	54.00	216.00		
.25 Equip. Oper. (med.)	46.55	93.10	70.25	140.50		
1 Scraper, Towed, 10 C.Y.		139.20		153.12		
1.25 Dozers, 300 H.P.		2147.50		2362.25	163.34	179.67
14 L.H., Daily Totals		$2892.60		$3433.87	$206.61	$245.28

Crew B-33C

Crew No.	Bare Costs Hr.	Bare Costs Daily	Incl. Subs O&P Hr.	Incl. Subs O&P Daily	Cost Per Labor-Hour Bare Costs	Cost Per Labor-Hour Incl. O&P
1 Equip. Oper. (med.)	$46.55	$372.40	$70.25	$562.00	$43.28	$65.61
.5 Laborer	35.10	140.40	54.00	216.00		
.25 Equip. Oper. (med.)	46.55	93.10	70.25	140.50		
1 Scraper, Towed, 15 C.Y.		156.80		172.48		
1.25 Dozers, 300 H.P.		2147.50		2362.25	164.59	181.05
14 L.H., Daily Totals		$2910.20		$3453.23	$207.87	$246.66

Crew B-33D

Crew No.	Bare Costs Hr.	Bare Costs Daily	Incl. Subs O&P Hr.	Incl. Subs O&P Daily	Cost Per Labor-Hour Bare Costs	Cost Per Labor-Hour Incl. O&P
1 Equip. Oper. (med.)	$46.55	$372.40	$70.25	$562.00	$43.28	$65.61
.5 Laborer	35.10	140.40	54.00	216.00		
.25 Equip. Oper. (med.)	46.55	93.10	70.25	140.50		
1 S.P. Scraper, 14 C.Y.		1537.00		1690.70		
.25 Dozer, 300 H.P.		429.50		472.45	140.46	154.51
14 L.H., Daily Totals		$2572.40		$3081.65	$183.74	$220.12

Crew B-33E

Crew No.	Bare Costs Hr.	Bare Costs Daily	Incl. Subs O&P Hr.	Incl. Subs O&P Daily	Cost Per Labor-Hour Bare Costs	Cost Per Labor-Hour Incl. O&P
1 Equip. Oper. (med.)	$46.55	$372.40	$70.25	$562.00	$43.28	$65.61
.5 Laborer	35.10	140.40	54.00	216.00		
.25 Equip. Oper. (med.)	46.55	93.10	70.25	140.50		
1 S.P. Scraper, 21 C.Y.		1974.00		2171.40		
.25 Dozer, 300 H.P.		429.50		472.45	171.68	188.85
14 L.H., Daily Totals		$3009.40		$3562.35	$214.96	$254.45

Crew B-33F

Crew No.	Bare Costs Hr.	Bare Costs Daily	Incl. Subs O&P Hr.	Incl. Subs O&P Daily	Cost Per Labor-Hour Bare Costs	Cost Per Labor-Hour Incl. O&P
1 Equip. Oper. (med.)	$46.55	$372.40	$70.25	$562.00	$43.28	$65.61
.5 Laborer	35.10	140.40	54.00	216.00		
.25 Equip. Oper. (med.)	46.55	93.10	70.25	140.50		
1 Elev. Scraper, 11 C.Y.		1105.00		1215.50		
.25 Dozer, 300 H.P.		429.50		472.45	109.61	120.57
14 L.H., Daily Totals		$2140.40		$2606.45	$152.89	$186.18

Crew B-33G

Crew No.	Bare Costs Hr.	Bare Costs Daily	Incl. Subs O&P Hr.	Incl. Subs O&P Daily	Cost Per Labor-Hour Bare Costs	Cost Per Labor-Hour Incl. O&P
1 Equip. Oper. (med.)	$46.55	$372.40	$70.25	$562.00	$43.28	$65.61
.5 Laborer	35.10	140.40	54.00	216.00		
.25 Equip. Oper. (med.)	46.55	93.10	70.25	140.50		
1 Elev. Scraper, 22 C.Y.		2099.00		2308.90		
.25 Dozer, 300 H.P.		429.50		472.45	180.61	198.67
14 L.H., Daily Totals		$3134.40		$3699.85	$223.89	$264.27

Crew B-33H

Crew No.	Bare Costs Hr.	Bare Costs Daily	Incl. Subs O&P Hr.	Incl. Subs O&P Daily	Cost Per Labor-Hour Bare Costs	Cost Per Labor-Hour Incl. O&P
.5 Laborer	$35.10	$140.40	$54.00	$216.00	$43.28	$65.61
1 Equipment Operator (med.)	46.55	372.40	70.25	562.00		
.25 Equipment Operator (med.)	46.55	93.10	70.25	140.50		
1 S.P. Scraper, 44 C.Y.		3768.00		4144.80		
.25 Dozer, 410 H.P.		568.00		624.80	309.71	340.69
14 L.H., Daily Totals		$4941.90		$5688.10	$352.99	$406.29

Crew B-33J

Crew No.	Bare Costs Hr.	Bare Costs Daily	Incl. Subs O&P Hr.	Incl. Subs O&P Daily	Cost Per Labor-Hour Bare Costs	Cost Per Labor-Hour Incl. O&P
1 Equipment Operator (med.)	$46.55	$372.40	$70.25	$562.00	$46.55	$70.25
1 S.P. Scraper, 14 C.Y.		1537.00		1690.70	192.13	211.34
8 L.H., Daily Totals		$1909.40		$2252.70	$238.68	$281.59

Crew B-33K

Crew No.	Bare Costs Hr.	Bare Costs Daily	Incl. Subs O&P Hr.	Incl. Subs O&P Daily	Cost Per Labor-Hour Bare Costs	Cost Per Labor-Hour Incl. O&P
1 Equipment Operator (med.)	$46.55	$372.40	$70.25	$562.00	$43.28	$65.61
.25 Equipment Operator (med.)	46.55	93.10	70.25	140.50		
.5 Laborer	35.10	140.40	54.00	216.00		
1 S.P. Scraper, 31 C.Y.		2868.00		3154.80		
.25 Dozer, 410 H.P.		568.00		624.80	245.43	269.97
14 L.H., Daily Totals		$4041.90		$4698.10	$288.71	$335.58

Crews

Crew No.	Bare Costs Hr.	Daily	Incl. Subs O&P Hr.	Daily	Cost Per Labor-Hour Bare Costs	Incl. O&P
Crew B-34A						
1 Truck Driver (heavy)	$35.30	$282.40	$53.55	$428.40	$35.30	$53.55
1 Dump Truck, 8 C.Y., 220 H.P.		357.40		393.14	44.67	49.14
8 L.H., Daily Totals		$639.80		$821.54	$79.97	$102.69
Crew B-34B						
1 Truck Driver (heavy)	$35.30	$282.40	$53.55	$428.40	$35.30	$53.55
1 Dump Truck, 12 C.Y., 400 H.P.		584.60		643.06	73.08	80.38
8 L.H., Daily Totals		$867.00		$1071.46	$108.38	$133.93
Crew B-34C						
1 Truck Driver (heavy)	$35.30	$282.40	$53.55	$428.40	$35.30	$53.55
1 Truck Tractor, 6x4, 380 H.P.		522.20		574.42		
1 Dump Trailer, 16.5 C.Y.		123.20		135.52	80.67	88.74
8 L.H., Daily Totals		$927.80		$1138.34	$115.97	$142.29
Crew B-34D						
1 Truck Driver (heavy)	$35.30	$282.40	$53.55	$428.40	$35.30	$53.55
1 Truck Tractor, 6x4, 380 H.P.		522.20		574.42		
1 Dump Trailer, 20 C.Y.		137.80		151.58	82.50	90.75
8 L.H., Daily Totals		$942.40		$1154.40	$117.80	$144.30
Crew B-34E						
1 Truck Driver (heavy)	$35.30	$282.40	$53.55	$428.40	$35.30	$53.55
1 Dump Truck, Off Hwy., 25 Ton		1271.00		1398.10	158.88	174.76
8 L.H., Daily Totals		$1553.40		$1826.50	$194.18	$228.31
Crew B-34F						
1 Truck Driver (heavy)	$35.30	$282.40	$53.55	$428.40	$35.30	$53.55
1 Dump Truck, Off Hwy., 35 Ton		1157.00		1272.70	144.63	159.09
8 L.H., Daily Totals		$1439.40		$1701.10	$179.93	$212.64
Crew B-34G						
1 Truck Driver (heavy)	$35.30	$282.40	$53.55	$428.40	$35.30	$53.55
1 Dump Truck, Off Hwy., 50 Ton		1568.00		1724.80	196.00	215.60
8 L.H., Daily Totals		$1850.40		$2153.20	$231.30	$269.15
Crew B-34H						
1 Truck Driver (heavy)	$35.30	$282.40	$53.55	$428.40	$35.30	$53.55
1 Dump Truck, Off Hwy., 65 Ton		1572.00		1729.20	196.50	216.15
8 L.H., Daily Totals		$1854.40		$2157.60	$231.80	$269.70
Crew B-34I						
1 Truck Driver (heavy)	$35.30	$282.40	$53.55	$428.40	$35.30	$53.55
1 Dump Truck, 18 C.Y., 450 H.P.		745.00		819.50	93.13	102.44
8 L.H., Daily Totals		$1027.40		$1247.90	$128.43	$155.99
Crew B-34J						
1 Truck Driver (heavy)	$35.30	$282.40	$53.55	$428.40	$35.30	$53.55
1 Dump Truck, Off Hwy., 100 Ton		2071.00		2278.10	258.88	284.76
8 L.H., Daily Totals		$2353.40		$2706.50	$294.18	$338.31
Crew B-34K						
1 Truck Driver (heavy)	$35.30	$282.40	$53.55	$428.40	$35.30	$53.55
1 Truck Tractor, 6x4, 450 H.P.		635.00		698.50		
1 Lowbed Trailer, 75 Ton		213.00		234.30	106.00	116.60
8 L.H., Daily Totals		$1130.40		$1361.20	$141.30	$170.15
Crew B-34L						
1 Equip. Oper. (light)	$44.75	$358.00	$67.55	$540.40	$44.75	$67.55
1 Flatbed Truck, Gas, 1.5 Ton		211.00		232.10	26.38	29.01
8 L.H., Daily Totals		$569.00		$772.50	$71.13	$96.56
Crew B-34M						
1 Equip. Oper. (light)	$44.75	$358.00	$67.55	$540.40	$44.75	$67.55
1 Flatbed Truck, Gas, 3 Ton		264.40		290.84	33.05	36.35
8 L.H., Daily Totals		$622.40		$831.24	$77.80	$103.91
Crew B-34N						
1 Truck Driver (heavy)	$35.30	$282.40	$53.55	$428.40	$35.30	$53.55
1 Dump Truck, 8 C.Y., 220 H.P.		357.40		393.14		
1 Flatbed Trailer, 40 Ton		147.00		161.70	63.05	69.36
8 L.H., Daily Totals		$786.80		$983.24	$98.35	$122.91
Crew B-34P						
1 Pipe Fitter	$55.70	$445.60	$84.00	$672.00	$45.53	$68.78
1 Truck Driver (light)	34.35	274.80	52.10	416.80		
1 Equip. Oper. (med.)	46.55	372.40	70.25	562.00		
1 Flatbed Truck, Gas, 3 Ton		264.40		290.84		
1 Backhoe Loader, 48 H.P.		334.00		367.40	24.93	27.43
24 L.H., Daily Totals		$1691.20		$2309.04	$70.47	$96.21
Crew B-34Q						
1 Pipe Fitter	$55.70	$445.60	$84.00	$672.00	$45.95	$69.42
1 Truck Driver (light)	34.35	274.80	52.10	416.80		
1 Eqip. Oper. (crane)	47.80	382.40	72.15	577.20		
1 Flatbed Trailer, 25 Ton		108.60		119.46		
1 Dump Truck, 8 C.Y., 220 H.P.		357.40		393.14		
1 Hyd. Crane, 25 Ton		697.20		766.92	48.47	53.31
24 L.H., Daily Totals		$2266.00		$2945.52	$94.42	$122.73
Crew B-34R						
1 Pipe Fitter	$55.70	$445.60	$84.00	$672.00	$45.95	$69.42
1 Truck Driver (light)	34.35	274.80	52.10	416.80		
1 Eqip. Oper. (crane)	47.80	382.40	72.15	577.20		
1 Flatbed Trailer, 25 Ton		108.60		119.46		
1 Dump Truck, 8 C.Y., 220 H.P.		357.40		393.14		
1 Hyd. Crane, 25 Ton		697.20		766.92		
1 Hyd. Excavator, 1 C.Y.		748.60		823.46	79.66	87.62
24 L.H., Daily Totals		$3014.60		$3768.98	$125.61	$157.04
Crew B-34S						
2 Pipe Fitters	$55.70	$891.20	$84.00	$1344.00	$48.63	$73.42
1 Truck Driver (heavy)	35.30	282.40	53.55	428.40		
1 Eqip. Oper. (crane)	47.80	382.40	72.15	577.20		
1 Flatbed Trailer, 40 Ton		147.00		161.70		
1 Truck Tractor, 6x4, 380 H.P.		522.20		574.42		
1 Hyd. Crane, 80 Ton		1554.00		1709.40		
1 Hyd. Excavator, 2 C.Y.		1253.00		1378.30	108.63	119.49
32 L.H., Daily Totals		$5032.20		$6173.42	$157.26	$192.92
Crew B-34T						
2 Pipe Fitters	$55.70	$891.20	$84.00	$1344.00	$48.63	$73.42
1 Truck Driver (heavy)	35.30	282.40	53.55	428.40		
1 Eqip. Oper. (crane)	47.80	382.40	72.15	577.20		
1 Flatbed Trailer, 40 Ton		147.00		161.70		
1 Truck Tractor, 6x4, 380 H.P.		522.20		574.42		
1 Hyd. Crane, 80 Ton		1554.00		1709.40	69.47	76.42
32 L.H., Daily Totals		$3779.20		$4795.12	$118.10	$149.85

Crew No.	Bare Costs		Incl. Subs O&P		Cost Per Labor-Hour	

Crew B-35

	Hr.	Daily	Hr.	Daily	Bare Costs	Incl. O&P
1 Labor Foreman (outside)	$37.10	$296.80	$57.10	$456.80	$43.54	$66.34
1 Skilled Worker	45.40	363.20	70.20	561.60		
1 Welder (plumber)	54.60	436.80	82.35	658.80		
1 Laborer	35.10	280.80	54.00	432.00		
1 Equip. Oper. (crane)	47.80	382.40	72.15	577.20		
1 Equip. Oper. Oiler	41.25	330.00	62.25	498.00		
1 Welder, electric, 300 amp		36.90		40.59		
1 Hyd. Excavator, .75 C.Y.		647.20		711.92	14.25	15.68
48 L.H., Daily Totals		$2774.10		$3936.91	$57.79	$82.02

Crew B-35A

	Hr.	Daily	Hr.	Daily	Bare Costs	Incl. O&P
1 Labor Foreman (outside)	$37.10	$296.80	$57.10	$456.80	$42.34	$64.58
2 Laborers	35.10	561.60	54.00	864.00		
1 Skilled Worker	45.40	363.20	70.20	561.60		
1 Welder (plumber)	54.60	436.80	82.35	658.80		
1 Equip. Oper. (crane)	47.80	382.40	72.15	577.20		
1 Equip. Oper. Oiler	41.25	330.00	62.25	498.00		
1 Welder, gas engine, 300 amp		121.60		133.76		
1 Crawler Crane, 75 Ton		1423.00		1565.30	27.58	30.34
56 L.H., Daily Totals		$3915.40		$5315.46	$69.92	$94.92

Crew B-36

	Hr.	Daily	Hr.	Daily	Bare Costs	Incl. O&P
1 Labor Foreman (outside)	$37.10	$296.80	$57.10	$456.80	$40.08	$61.12
2 Laborers	35.10	561.60	54.00	864.00		
2 Equip. Oper. (med.)	46.55	744.80	70.25	1124.00		
1 Dozer, 200 H.P.		1243.00		1367.30		
1 Aggregate Spreader		36.80		40.48		
1 Tandem Roller, 10 Ton		227.60		250.36	37.69	41.45
40 L.H., Daily Totals		$3110.60		$4102.94	$77.77	$102.57

Crew B-36A

	Hr.	Daily	Hr.	Daily	Bare Costs	Incl. O&P
1 Labor Foreman (outside)	$37.10	$296.80	$57.10	$456.80	$41.93	$63.73
2 Laborers	35.10	561.60	54.00	864.00		
4 Equip. Oper. (med.)	46.55	1489.60	70.25	2248.00		
1 Dozer, 200 H.P.		1243.00		1367.30		
1 Aggregate Spreader		36.80		40.48		
1 Tandem Roller, 10 Ton		227.60		250.36		
1 Roller, Pneum. Whl, 12 Ton		313.20		344.52	32.51	35.76
56 L.H., Daily Totals		$4168.60		$5571.46	$74.44	$99.49

Crew B-36B

	Hr.	Daily	Hr.	Daily	Bare Costs	Incl. O&P
1 Labor Foreman (outside)	$37.10	$296.80	$57.10	$456.80	$41.10	$62.46
2 Laborers	35.10	561.60	54.00	864.00		
4 Equip. Oper. (med.)	46.55	1489.60	70.25	2248.00		
1 Truck Driver, Heavy	35.30	282.40	53.55	428.40		
1 Grader, 30,000 Lbs.		610.80		671.88		
1 F.E. Loader, crl, 1.5 C.Y.		598.20		658.02		
1 Dozer, 300 H.P.		1718.00		1889.80		
1 Roller, Vibratory, 25 Ton		640.20		704.22		
1 Truck Tractor, 6x4, 450 H.P.		635.00		698.50		
1 Water Tank Trailer, 5000 Gal.		141.00		155.10	67.86	74.65
64 L.H., Daily Totals		$6973.60		$8774.72	$108.96	$137.11

Crew B-36C

	Hr.	Daily	Hr.	Daily	Bare Costs	Incl. O&P
1 Labor Foreman (outside)	$37.10	$296.80	$57.10	$456.80	$42.41	$64.28
3 Equip. Oper. (med.)	46.55	1117.20	70.25	1686.00		
1 Truck Driver, Heavy	35.30	282.40	53.55	428.40		
1 Grader, 30,000 Lbs.		610.80		671.88		
1 Dozer, 300 H.P.		1718.00		1889.80		
1 Roller, Vibratory, 25 Ton		640.20		704.22		
1 Truck Tractor, 6x4, 450 H.P.		635.00		698.50		
1 Water Tank Trailer, 5000 Gal.		141.00		155.10	93.63	102.99
40 L.H., Daily Totals		$5441.40		$6690.70	$136.04	$167.27

Crew B-36D

	Hr.	Daily	Hr.	Daily	Bare Costs	Incl. O&P
1 Labor Foreman (outside)	$37.10	$296.80	$57.10	$456.80	$44.19	$66.96
3 Equip. Oper. (medium)	46.55	1117.20	70.25	1686.00		
1 Grader, 30,000 Lbs.		610.80		671.88		
1 Dozer, 300 H.P.		1718.00		1889.80		
1 Roller, Vibratory, 25 Ton		640.20		704.22	92.78	102.06
32 L.H., Daily Totals		$4383.00		$5408.70	$136.97	$169.02

Crew B-37

	Hr.	Daily	Hr.	Daily	Bare Costs	Incl. O&P
1 Labor Foreman (outside)	$37.10	$296.80	$57.10	$456.80	$37.04	$56.77
4 Laborers	35.10	1123.20	54.00	1728.00		
1 Equip. Oper. (light)	44.75	358.00	67.55	540.40		
1 Tandem Roller, 5 Ton		149.20		164.12	3.11	3.42
48 L.H., Daily Totals		$1927.20		$2889.32	$40.15	$60.19

Crew B-37A

	Hr.	Daily	Hr.	Daily	Bare Costs	Incl. O&P
2 Laborers	$35.10	$561.60	$54.00	$864.00	$34.85	$53.37
1 Truck Driver (light)	34.35	274.80	52.10	416.80		
1 Flatbed Truck, Gas, 1.5 Ton		211.00		232.10		
1 Tar Kettle, T.M.		77.20		84.92	12.01	13.21
24 L.H., Daily Totals		$1124.60		$1597.82	$46.86	$66.58

Crew B-37B

	Hr.	Daily	Hr.	Daily	Bare Costs	Incl. O&P
3 Laborers	$35.10	$842.40	$54.00	$1296.00	$34.91	$53.52
1 Truck Driver (light)	34.35	274.80	52.10	416.80		
1 Flatbed Truck, Gas, 1.5 Ton		211.00		232.10		
1 Tar Kettle, T.M.		77.20		84.92	9.01	9.91
32 L.H., Daily Totals		$1405.40		$2029.82	$43.92	$63.43

Crew B-37C

	Hr.	Daily	Hr.	Daily	Bare Costs	Incl. O&P
2 Laborers	$35.10	$561.60	$54.00	$864.00	$34.73	$53.05
2 Truck Drivers (light)	34.35	549.60	52.10	833.60		
2 Flatbed Trucks, Gas, 1.5 Ton		422.00		464.20		
1 Tar Kettle, T.M.		77.20		84.92	15.60	17.16
32 L.H., Daily Totals		$1610.40		$2246.72	$50.33	$70.21

Crew B-37D

	Hr.	Daily	Hr.	Daily	Bare Costs	Incl. O&P
1 Laborer	$35.10	$280.80	$54.00	$432.00	$34.73	$53.05
1 Truck Driver (light)	34.35	274.80	52.10	416.80		
1 Pickup Truck, 3/4 Ton		127.00		139.70	7.94	8.73
16 L.H., Daily Totals		$682.60		$988.50	$42.66	$61.78

Crews

| Crew No. | Bare Costs | | Incl. Subs O&P | | Cost Per Labor-Hour | |

Crew B-37E	Hr.	Daily	Hr.	Daily	Bare Costs	Incl. O&P
3 Laborers	$35.10	$842.40	$54.00	$1296.00	$37.90	$57.71
1 Equip. Oper. (light)	44.75	358.00	67.55	540.40		
1 Equip. Oper. (medium)	46.55	372.40	70.25	562.00		
2 Truck Drivers (light)	34.35	549.60	52.10	833.60		
4 Barrels w/ Flasher		13.60		14.96		
1 Concrete Saw		148.00		162.80		
1 Rotary Hammer Drill		22.55		24.81		
1 Hammer Drill Bit		3.15		3.46		
1 Loader, Skid Steer, 30 H.P., gas		159.60		175.56		
1 Conc. Hammer Attach.		116.25		127.88		
1 Vibrating plate, gas, 18"		32.20		35.42		
2 Flatbed Trucks, Gas, 1.5 Ton		422.00		464.20	16.38	18.02
56 L.H., Daily Totals		$3039.75		$4241.09	$54.28	$75.73

Crew B-37F	Hr.	Daily	Hr.	Daily	Bare Costs	Incl. O&P
3 Laborers	$35.10	$842.40	$54.00	$1296.00	$34.91	$53.52
1 Truck Driver (light)	34.35	274.80	52.10	416.80		
4 Barrels w/ Flasher		13.60		14.96		
1 Concrete Mixer, 10 C.F.		160.60		176.66		
1 Air Compressor, 60 cfm		120.40		132.44		
1 -50' Air Hose, 3/4"		3.05		3.36		
1 Spade (chipper)		7.60		8.36		
1 Flatbed Truck, Gas, 1.5 Ton		211.00		232.10	16.13	17.75
32 L.H., Daily Totals		$1633.45		$2280.68	$51.05	$71.27

Crew B-37G	Hr.	Daily	Hr.	Daily	Bare Costs	Incl. O&P
1 Labor Foreman (outside)	$37.10	$296.80	$57.10	$456.80	$37.04	$56.77
4 Laborers	35.10	1123.20	54.00	1728.00		
1 Equip. Oper. (light)	44.75	358.00	67.55	540.40		
1 Berm Machine		280.00		308.00		
1 Tandem Roller, 5 Ton		149.20		164.12	8.94	9.84
48 L.H., Daily Totals		$2207.20		$3197.32	$45.98	$66.61

Crew B-38	Hr.	Daily	Hr.	Daily	Bare Costs	Incl. O&P
1 Labor Foreman (outside)	$37.10	$296.80	$57.10	$456.80	$39.72	$60.58
2 Laborers	35.10	561.60	54.00	864.00		
1 Equip. Oper. (light)	44.75	358.00	67.55	540.40		
1 Equip. Oper. (med.)	46.55	372.40	70.25	562.00		
1 Backhoe Loader, 48 H.P.		334.00		367.40		
1 Hyd.Hammer, (1200 lb.)		178.40		196.24		
1 F.E. Loader, W.M., 4 C.Y.		611.00		672.10		
1 Pvmt. Rem. Bucket		59.00		64.90	29.56	32.52
40 L.H., Daily Totals		$2771.20		$3723.84	$69.28	$93.10

Crew B-39	Hr.	Daily	Hr.	Daily	Bare Costs	Incl. O&P
1 Labor Foreman (outside)	$37.10	$296.80	$57.10	$456.80	$37.04	$56.77
4 Laborers	35.10	1123.20	54.00	1728.00		
1 Equip. Oper. (light)	44.75	358.00	67.55	540.40		
1 Air Compressor, 250 cfm		177.00		194.70		
2 Breakers, Pavement, 60 lb.		19.60		21.56		
2 -50' Air Hoses, 1.5"		12.60		13.86	4.36	4.79
48 L.H., Daily Totals		$1987.20		$2955.32	$41.40	$61.57

Crew B-40	Hr.	Daily	Hr.	Daily	Bare Costs	Incl. O&P
1 Pile Driver Foreman (outside)	$44.80	$358.40	$72.00	$576.00	$44.11	$69.22
4 Pile Drivers	42.80	1369.60	68.80	2201.60		
2 Equip. Oper. (crane)	47.80	764.80	72.15	1154.40		
1 Equip. Oper. Oiler	41.25	330.00	62.25	498.00		
1 Crawler Crane, 40 Ton		1115.00		1226.50		
1 Vibratory Hammer & Gen.		2335.00		2568.50	53.91	59.30
64 L.H., Daily Totals		$6272.80		$8225.00	$98.01	$128.52

Crew B-40B	Hr.	Daily	Hr.	Daily	Bare Costs	Incl. O&P
1 Labor Foreman (outside)	$37.10	$296.80	$57.10	$456.80	$38.58	$58.92
3 Laborers	35.10	842.40	54.00	1296.00		
1 Equip. Oper. (crane)	47.80	382.40	72.15	577.20		
1 Equip. Oper. Oiler	41.25	330.00	62.25	498.00		
1 Lattice Boom Crane, 40 Ton		1163.00		1279.30	24.23	26.65
48 L.H., Daily Totals		$3014.60		$4107.30	$62.80	$85.57

Crew B-41	Hr.	Daily	Hr.	Daily	Bare Costs	Incl. O&P
1 Labor Foreman (outside)	$37.10	$296.80	$57.10	$456.80	$36.32	$55.76
4 Laborers	35.10	1123.20	54.00	1728.00		
.25 Equip. Oper. (crane)	47.80	95.60	72.15	144.30		
.25 Equip. Oper. Oiler	41.25	82.50	62.25	124.50		
.25 Crawler Crane, 40 Ton		278.75		306.63	6.34	6.97
44 L.H., Daily Totals		$1876.85		$2760.22	$42.66	$62.73

Crew B-42	Hr.	Daily	Hr.	Daily	Bare Costs	Incl. O&P
1 Labor Foreman (outside)	$37.10	$296.80	$57.10	$456.80	$39.49	$61.97
4 Laborers	35.10	1123.20	54.00	1728.00		
1 Equip. Oper. (crane)	47.80	382.40	72.15	577.20		
1 Equip. Oper. Oiler	41.25	330.00	62.25	498.00		
1 Welder	49.35	394.80	88.25	706.00		
1 Hyd. Crane, 25 Ton		697.20		766.92		
1 Welder, gas engine, 300 amp		121.60		133.76		
1 Horz. Boring Csg. Mch.		447.60		492.36	19.79	21.77
64 L.H., Daily Totals		$3793.60		$5359.04	$59.27	$83.74

Crew B-43	Hr.	Daily	Hr.	Daily	Bare Costs	Incl. O&P
1 Labor Foreman (outside)	$37.10	$296.80	$57.10	$456.80	$38.58	$58.92
3 Laborers	35.10	842.40	54.00	1296.00		
1 Equip. Oper. (crane)	47.80	382.40	72.15	577.20		
1 Equip. Oper. Oiler	41.25	330.00	62.25	498.00		
1 Drill Rig, Truck-Mounted		2441.00		2685.10	50.85	55.94
48 L.H., Daily Totals		$4292.60		$5513.10	$89.43	$114.86

Crew B-44	Hr.	Daily	Hr.	Daily	Bare Costs	Incl. O&P
1 Pile Driver Foreman (outside)	$44.80	$358.40	$72.00	$576.00	$43.34	$68.19
4 Pile Drivers	42.80	1369.60	68.80	2201.60		
2 Equip. Oper. (crane)	47.80	764.80	72.15	1154.40		
1 Laborer	35.10	280.80	54.00	432.00		
1 Crawler Crane, 40 Ton		1115.00		1226.50		
1 Lead, 60' high		73.60		80.96		
1 Hammer, diesel, 15K ft.-lbs.		591.40		650.54	27.81	30.59
64 L.H., Daily Totals		$4553.60		$6322.00	$71.15	$98.78

Crew B-45	Hr.	Daily	Hr.	Daily	Bare Costs	Incl. O&P
1 Equip. Oper. (med.)	$46.55	$372.40	$70.25	$562.00	$40.92	$61.90
1 Truck Driver (heavy)	35.30	282.40	53.55	428.40		
1 Dist. Tanker, 3000 Gallon		306.00		336.60		
1 Truck Tractor, 6x4, 380 H.P.		522.20		574.42	51.76	56.94
16 L.H., Daily Totals		$1483.00		$1901.42	$92.69	$118.84

Crew B-46	Hr.	Daily	Hr.	Daily	Bare Costs	Incl. O&P
1 Pile Driver Foreman (outside)	$44.80	$358.40	$72.00	$576.00	$39.28	$61.93
2 Pile Drivers	42.80	684.80	68.80	1100.80		
3 Laborers	35.10	842.40	54.00	1296.00		
1 Chain Saw, gas, 36" Long		43.60		47.96	.91	1.00
48 L.H., Daily Totals		$1929.20		$3020.76	$40.19	$62.93

Crews

Crew B-47	Hr.	Daily	Hr.	Daily	Bare Costs	Incl. O&P
1 Blast Foreman (outside)	$37.10	$296.80	$57.10	$456.80	$38.98	$59.55
1 Driller	35.10	280.80	54.00	432.00		
1 Equip. Oper. (light)	44.75	358.00	67.55	540.40		
1 Air Track Drill, 4"		937.20		1030.92		
1 Air Compressor, 600 cfm		467.60		514.36		
2 -50' Air Hoses, 3"		29.80		32.78	59.77	65.75
24 L.H., Daily Totals		$2370.20		$3007.26	$98.76	$125.30

Crew B-47A	Hr.	Daily	Hr.	Daily	Bare Costs	Incl. O&P
1 Drilling Foreman (outside)	$37.10	$296.80	$57.10	$456.80	$42.05	$63.83
1 Equip. Oper. (heavy)	47.80	382.40	72.15	577.20		
1 Oiler	41.25	330.00	62.25	498.00		
1 Air Track Drill, 5"		1088.00		1196.80	45.33	49.87
24 L.H., Daily Totals		$2097.20		$2728.80	$87.38	$113.70

Crew B-47C	Hr.	Daily	Hr.	Daily	Bare Costs	Incl. O&P
1 Laborer	$35.10	$280.80	$54.00	$432.00	$39.92	$60.77
1 Equip. Oper. (light)	44.75	358.00	67.55	540.40		
1 Air Compressor, 750 cfm		474.80		522.28		
2 -50' Air Hoses, 3"		29.80		32.78		
1 Air Track Drill, 4"		937.20		1030.92	90.11	99.12
16 L.H., Daily Totals		$2080.60		$2558.38	$130.04	$159.90

Crew B-47E	Hr.	Daily	Hr.	Daily	Bare Costs	Incl. O&P
1 Labor Foreman (outside)	$37.10	$296.80	$57.10	$456.80	$35.60	$54.77
3 Laborers	35.10	842.40	54.00	1296.00		
1 Flatbed Truck, Gas, 3 Ton		264.40		290.84	8.26	9.09
32 L.H., Daily Totals		$1403.60		$2043.64	$43.86	$63.86

Crew B-47G	Hr.	Daily	Hr.	Daily	Bare Costs	Incl. O&P
1 Labor Foreman (outside)	$37.10	$296.80	$57.10	$456.80	$38.01	$58.16
2 Laborers	35.10	561.60	54.00	864.00		
1 Equip. Oper. (light)	44.75	358.00	67.55	540.40		
1 Air Track Drill, 4"		937.20		1030.92		
1 Air Compressor, 600 cfm		467.60		514.36		
2 -50' Air Hoses, 3"		29.80		32.78		
1 Gunite Pump Rig		280.40		308.44	53.59	58.95
32 L.H., Daily Totals		$2931.40		$3747.70	$91.61	$117.12

Crew B-47H	Hr.	Daily	Hr.	Daily	Bare Costs	Incl. O&P
1 Skilled Worker Foreman (out)	$47.40	$379.20	$73.30	$586.40	$45.90	$70.97
3 Skilled Workers	45.40	1089.60	70.20	1684.80		
1 Flatbed Truck, Gas, 3 Ton		264.40		290.84	8.26	9.09
32 L.H., Daily Totals		$1733.20		$2562.04	$54.16	$80.06

Crew B-48	Hr.	Daily	Hr.	Daily	Bare Costs	Incl. O&P
1 Labor Foreman (outside)	$37.10	$296.80	$57.10	$456.80	$39.46	$60.15
3 Laborers	35.10	842.40	54.00	1296.00		
1 Equip. Oper. (crane)	47.80	382.40	72.15	577.20		
1 Equip. Oper. Oiler	41.25	330.00	62.25	498.00		
1 Equip. Oper. (light)	44.75	358.00	67.55	540.40		
1 Centr. Water Pump, 6"		308.40		339.24		
1 -20' Suction Hose, 6"		11.50		12.65		
1 -50' Discharge Hose, 6"		12.10		13.31		
1 Drill Rig, Truck-Mounted		2441.00		2685.10	49.52	54.47
56 L.H., Daily Totals		$4982.60		$6418.70	$88.97	$114.62

Crew B-49	Hr.	Daily	Hr.	Daily	Bare Costs	Incl. O&P
1 Labor Foreman (outside)	$37.10	$296.80	$57.10	$456.80	$40.99	$63.00
3 Laborers	35.10	842.40	54.00	1296.00		
2 Equip. Oper. (crane)	47.80	764.80	72.15	1154.40		
2 Equip. Oper. Oilers	41.25	660.00	62.25	996.00		
1 Equip. Oper. (light)	44.75	358.00	67.55	540.40		
2 Pile Drivers	42.80	684.80	68.80	1100.80		
1 Hyd. Crane, 25 Ton		697.20		766.92		
1 Centr. Water Pump, 6"		308.40		339.24		
1 -20' Suction Hose, 6"		11.50		12.65		
1 -50' Discharge Hose, 6"		12.10		13.31		
1 Drill Rig, Truck-Mounted		2441.00		2685.10	39.43	43.38
88 L.H., Daily Totals		$7077.00		$9361.62	$80.42	$106.38

Crew B-50	Hr.	Daily	Hr.	Daily	Bare Costs	Incl. O&P
2 Pile Driver Foremen (outside)	$44.80	$716.80	$72.00	$1152.00	$42.04	$66.10
6 Pile Drivers	42.80	2054.40	68.80	3302.40		
2 Equip. Oper. (crane)	47.80	764.80	72.15	1154.40		
1 Equip. Oper. Oiler	41.25	330.00	62.25	498.00		
3 Laborers	35.10	842.40	54.00	1296.00		
1 Crawler Crane, 40 Ton		1115.00		1226.50		
1 Lead, 60' high		73.60		80.96		
1 Hammer, diesel, 15K ft.-lbs.		591.40		650.54		
1 Air Compressor, 600 cfm		467.60		514.36		
2 -50' Air Hoses, 3"		29.80		32.78		
1 Chain Saw, gas, 36" Long		43.60		47.96	20.72	22.80
112 L.H., Daily Totals		$7029.40		$9955.90	$62.76	$88.89

Crew B-51	Hr.	Daily	Hr.	Daily	Bare Costs	Incl. O&P
1 Labor Foreman (outside)	$37.10	$296.80	$57.10	$456.80	$35.31	$54.20
4 Laborers	35.10	1123.20	54.00	1728.00		
1 Truck Driver (light)	34.35	274.80	52.10	416.80		
1 Flatbed Truck, Gas, 1.5 Ton		211.00		232.10	4.40	4.84
48 L.H., Daily Totals		$1905.80		$2833.70	$39.70	$59.04

Crew B-52	Hr.	Daily	Hr.	Daily	Bare Costs	Incl. O&P
1 Carpenter Foreman (outside)	$46.10	$368.80	$70.95	$567.60	$40.81	$62.49
1 Carpenter	44.10	352.80	67.85	542.80		
3 Laborers	35.10	842.40	54.00	1296.00		
1 Cement Finisher	42.35	338.80	62.30	498.40		
.5 Rodman (reinf.)	49.10	196.40	78.40	313.60		
.5 Equip. Oper. (med.)	46.55	186.20	70.25	281.00		
.5 Crawler Loader, 3 C.Y.		553.00		608.30	9.88	10.86
56 L.H., Daily Totals		$2838.40		$4107.70	$50.69	$73.35

Crew B-53	Hr.	Daily	Hr.	Daily	Bare Costs	Incl. O&P
1 Equip. Oper. (light)	$44.75	$358.00	$67.55	$540.40	$44.75	$67.55
1 Trencher, Chain, 12 H.P.		62.80		69.08	7.85	8.63
8 L.H., Daily Totals		$420.80		$609.48	$52.60	$76.19

Crew B-54	Hr.	Daily	Hr.	Daily	Bare Costs	Incl. O&P
1 Equip. Oper. (light)	$44.75	$358.00	$67.55	$540.40	$44.75	$67.55
1 Trencher, Chain, 40 H.P.		312.80		344.08	39.10	43.01
8 L.H., Daily Totals		$670.80		$884.48	$83.85	$110.56

Crew B-54A	Hr.	Daily	Hr.	Daily	Bare Costs	Incl. O&P
.17 Labor Foreman (outside)	$37.10	$50.46	$57.10	$77.66	$45.18	$68.34
1 Equipment Operator (med.)	46.55	372.40	70.25	562.00		
1 Wheel Trencher, 67 H.P.		1084.00		1192.40	115.81	127.39
9.36 L.H., Daily Totals		$1506.86		$1832.06	$160.99	$195.73

Crews

Crew No.	Bare Costs Hr.	Daily	Incl. Subs O&P Hr.	Daily	Cost Per Labor-Hour Bare Costs	Incl. O&P
Crew B-54B	Hr.	Daily	Hr.	Daily	Bare Costs	Incl. O&P
.25 Labor Foreman (outside)	$37.10	$74.20	$57.10	$114.20	$44.66	$67.62
1 Equipment Operator (med.)	46.55	372.40	70.25	562.00		
1 Wheel Trencher, 150 H.P.		1816.00		1997.60	181.60	199.76
10 L.H., Daily Totals		$2262.60		$2673.80	$226.26	$267.38

Crew No.	Bare Costs Hr.	Daily	Incl. Subs O&P Hr.	Daily	Cost Per Labor-Hour Bare Costs	Incl. O&P
Crew B-54C	Hr.	Daily	Hr.	Daily	Bare Costs	Incl. O&P
1 Laborer	$35.10	$280.80	$54.00	$432.00	$40.83	$62.13
1 Equipment Operator (med.)	46.55	372.40	70.25	562.00		
1 Wheel Trencher, 67 H.P.		1084.00		1192.40	67.75	74.53
16 L.H., Daily Totals		$1737.20		$2186.40	$108.58	$136.65

Crew No.	Bare Costs Hr.	Daily	Incl. Subs O&P Hr.	Daily	Cost Per Labor-Hour Bare Costs	Incl. O&P
Crew B-54D	Hr.	Daily	Hr.	Daily	Bare Costs	Incl. O&P
1 Laborer	$35.10	$280.80	$54.00	$432.00	$40.83	$62.13
1 Equipment Operator (med.)	46.55	372.40	70.25	562.00		
1 Rock trencher, 6" width		344.40		378.84	21.52	23.68
16 L.H., Daily Totals		$997.60		$1372.84	$62.35	$85.80

Crew No.	Bare Costs Hr.	Daily	Incl. Subs O&P Hr.	Daily	Cost Per Labor-Hour Bare Costs	Incl. O&P
Crew B-54E	Hr.	Daily	Hr.	Daily	Bare Costs	Incl. O&P
1 Laborer	$35.10	$280.80	$54.00	$432.00	$40.83	$62.13
1 Equipment Operator (med.)	46.55	372.40	70.25	562.00		
1 Rock trencher, 18" width		2517.00		2768.70	157.31	173.04
16 L.H., Daily Totals		$3170.20		$3762.70	$198.14	$235.17

Crew No.	Bare Costs Hr.	Daily	Incl. Subs O&P Hr.	Daily	Cost Per Labor-Hour Bare Costs	Incl. O&P
Crew B-55	Hr.	Daily	Hr.	Daily	Bare Costs	Incl. O&P
2 Laborers	$35.10	$561.60	$54.00	$864.00	$34.85	$53.37
1 Truck Driver (light)	34.35	274.80	52.10	416.80		
1 Truck-mounted earth auger		718.40		790.24		
1 Flatbed Truck, Gas, 3 Ton		264.40		290.84	40.95	45.05
24 L.H., Daily Totals		$1819.20		$2361.88	$75.80	$98.41

Crew No.	Bare Costs Hr.	Daily	Incl. Subs O&P Hr.	Daily	Cost Per Labor-Hour Bare Costs	Incl. O&P
Crew B-56	Hr.	Daily	Hr.	Daily	Bare Costs	Incl. O&P
1 Laborer	$35.10	$280.80	$54.00	$432.00	$39.92	$60.77
1 Equip. Oper. (light)	44.75	358.00	67.55	540.40		
1 Air Track Drill, 4"		937.20		1030.92		
1 Air Compressor, 600 cfm		467.60		514.36		
1 -50' Air Hose, 3"		14.90		16.39	88.73	97.60
16 L.H., Daily Totals		$2058.50		$2534.07	$128.66	$158.38

Crew No.	Bare Costs Hr.	Daily	Incl. Subs O&P Hr.	Daily	Cost Per Labor-Hour Bare Costs	Incl. O&P
Crew B-57	Hr.	Daily	Hr.	Daily	Bare Costs	Incl. O&P
1 Labor Foreman (outside)	$37.10	$296.80	$57.10	$456.80	$40.18	$61.17
2 Laborers	35.10	561.60	54.00	864.00		
1 Equip. Oper. (crane)	47.80	382.40	72.15	577.20		
1 Equip. Oper. (light)	44.75	358.00	67.55	540.40		
1 Equip. Oper. Oiler	41.25	330.00	62.25	498.00		
1 Crawler Crane, 25 Ton		1110.00		1221.00		
1 Clamshell Bucket, 1 C.Y.		47.00		51.70		
1 Centr. Water Pump, 6"		308.40		339.24		
1 -20' Suction Hose, 6"		11.50		12.65		
20 -50' Discharge Hoses, 6"		242.00		266.20	35.81	39.39
48 L.H., Daily Totals		$3647.70		$4827.19	$75.99	$100.57

Crew No.	Bare Costs Hr.	Daily	Incl. Subs O&P Hr.	Daily	Cost Per Labor-Hour Bare Costs	Incl. O&P
Crew B-58	Hr.	Daily	Hr.	Daily	Bare Costs	Incl. O&P
2 Laborers	$35.10	$561.60	$54.00	$864.00	$38.32	$58.52
1 Equip. Oper. (light)	44.75	358.00	67.55	540.40		
1 Backhoe Loader, 48 H.P.		334.00		367.40		
1 Small Helicopter, w/pilot		2625.00		2887.50	123.29	135.62
24 L.H., Daily Totals		$3878.60		$4659.30	$161.61	$194.14

Crew No.	Bare Costs Hr.	Daily	Incl. Subs O&P Hr.	Daily	Cost Per Labor-Hour Bare Costs	Incl. O&P
Crew B-59	Hr.	Daily	Hr.	Daily	Bare Costs	Incl. O&P
1 Truck Driver (heavy)	$35.30	$282.40	$53.55	$428.40	$35.30	$53.55
1 Truck Tractor, 220 H.P.		314.80		346.28		
1 Water Tank Trailer, 5000 Gal.		141.00		155.10	56.98	62.67
8 L.H., Daily Totals		$738.20		$929.78	$92.28	$116.22

Crew No.	Bare Costs Hr.	Daily	Incl. Subs O&P Hr.	Daily	Cost Per Labor-Hour Bare Costs	Incl. O&P
Crew B-59A	Hr.	Daily	Hr.	Daily	Bare Costs	Incl. O&P
2 Laborers	$35.10	$561.60	$54.00	$864.00	$35.17	$53.85
1 Truck Driver (heavy)	35.30	282.40	53.55	428.40		
1 Water Tank Trailer, 5000 Gal.		141.00		155.10		
1 Truck Tractor, 220 H.P.		314.80		346.28	18.99	20.89
24 L.H., Daily Totals		$1299.80		$1793.78	$54.16	$74.74

Crew No.	Bare Costs Hr.	Daily	Incl. Subs O&P Hr.	Daily	Cost Per Labor-Hour Bare Costs	Incl. O&P
Crew B-60	Hr.	Daily	Hr.	Daily	Bare Costs	Incl. O&P
1 Labor Foreman (outside)	$37.10	$296.80	$57.10	$456.80	$40.84	$62.09
2 Laborers	35.10	561.60	54.00	864.00		
1 Equip. Oper. (crane)	47.80	382.40	72.15	577.20		
2 Equip. Oper. (light)	44.75	716.00	67.55	1080.80		
1 Equip. Oper. Oiler	41.25	330.00	62.25	498.00		
1 Crawler Crane, 40 Ton		1115.00		1226.50		
1 Lead, 60' high		73.60		80.96		
1 Hammer, diesel, 15K ft.-lbs.		591.40		650.54		
1 Backhoe Loader, 48 H.P.		334.00		367.40	37.75	41.52
56 L.H., Daily Totals		$4400.80		$5802.20	$78.59	$103.61

Crew No.	Bare Costs Hr.	Daily	Incl. Subs O&P Hr.	Daily	Cost Per Labor-Hour Bare Costs	Incl. O&P
Crew B-61	Hr.	Daily	Hr.	Daily	Bare Costs	Incl. O&P
1 Labor Foreman (outside)	$37.10	$296.80	$57.10	$456.80	$37.43	$57.33
3 Laborers	35.10	842.40	54.00	1296.00		
1 Equip. Oper. (light)	44.75	358.00	67.55	540.00		
1 Cement Mixer, 2 C.Y.		190.40		209.44		
1 Air Compressor, 160 cfm		136.80		150.48	8.18	9.00
40 L.H., Daily Totals		$1824.40		$2653.12	$45.61	$66.33

Crew No.	Bare Costs Hr.	Daily	Incl. Subs O&P Hr.	Daily	Cost Per Labor-Hour Bare Costs	Incl. O&P
Crew B-62	Hr.	Daily	Hr.	Daily	Bare Costs	Incl. O&P
2 Laborers	$35.10	$561.60	$54.00	$864.00	$38.32	$58.52
1 Equip. Oper. (light)	44.75	358.00	67.55	540.40		
1 Loader, Skid Steer, 30 H.P.,gas		159.60		175.56	6.65	7.32
24 L.H., Daily Totals		$1079.20		$1579.96	$44.97	$65.83

Crew No.	Bare Costs Hr.	Daily	Incl. Subs O&P Hr.	Daily	Cost Per Labor-Hour Bare Costs	Incl. O&P
Crew B-63	Hr.	Daily	Hr.	Daily	Bare Costs	Incl. O&P
4 Laborers	$35.10	$1123.20	$54.00	$1728.00	$37.03	$56.71
1 Equip. Oper. (light)	44.75	358.00	67.55	540.40		
1 Loader, Skid Steer, 30 H.P.,gas		159.60		175.56	3.99	4.39
40 L.H., Daily Totals		$1640.80		$2443.96	$41.02	$61.10

Crew No.	Bare Costs Hr.	Daily	Incl. Subs O&P Hr.	Daily	Cost Per Labor-Hour Bare Costs	Incl. O&P
Crew B-64	Hr.	Daily	Hr.	Daily	Bare Costs	Incl. O&P
1 Laborer	$35.10	$280.80	$54.00	$432.00	$34.73	$53.05
1 Truck Driver (light)	34.35	274.80	52.10	416.80		
1 Power Mulcher (small)		142.00		156.20		
1 Flatbed Truck, Gas, 1.5 Ton		211.00		232.10	22.06	24.27
16 L.H., Daily Totals		$908.60		$1237.10	$56.79	$77.32

Crew No.	Bare Costs Hr.	Daily	Incl. Subs O&P Hr.	Daily	Cost Per Labor-Hour Bare Costs	Incl. O&P
Crew B-65	Hr.	Daily	Hr.	Daily	Bare Costs	Incl. O&P
1 Laborer	$35.10	$280.80	$54.00	$432.00	$34.73	$53.05
1 Truck Driver (light)	34.35	274.80	52.10	416.80		
1 Power Mulcher (large)		286.60		315.26		
1 Flatbed Truck, Gas, 1.5 Ton		211.00		232.10	31.10	34.21
16 L.H., Daily Totals		$1053.20		$1396.16	$65.83	$87.26

Crew No.	Bare Costs Hr.	Daily	Incl. Subs O&P Hr.	Daily	Cost Per Labor-Hour Bare Costs	Incl. O&P
Crew B-66	Hr.	Daily	Hr.	Daily	Bare Costs	Incl. O&P
1 Equip. Oper. (light)	$44.75	$358.00	$67.55	$540.40	$44.75	$67.55
1 Loader-Backhoe		247.20		271.92	30.90	33.99
8 L.H., Daily Totals		$605.20		$812.32	$75.65	$101.54
Crew B-67	Hr.	Daily	Hr.	Daily	Bare Costs	Incl. O&P
1 Millwright	$46.05	$368.40	$67.85	$542.80	$45.40	$67.70
1 Equip. Oper. (light)	44.75	358.00	67.55	540.40		
1 Forklift, R/T, 4,000 Lb.		289.20		318.12	18.07	19.88
16 L.H., Daily Totals		$1015.60		$1401.32	$63.48	$87.58
Crew B-68	Hr.	Daily	Hr.	Daily	Bare Costs	Incl. O&P
2 Millwrights	$46.05	$736.80	$67.85	$1085.60	$45.62	$67.75
1 Equip. Oper. (light)	44.75	358.00	67.55	540.40		
1 Forklift, R/T, 4,000 Lb.		289.20		318.12	12.05	13.26
24 L.H., Daily Totals		$1384.00		$1944.12	$57.67	$81.00
Crew B-69	Hr.	Daily	Hr.	Daily	Bare Costs	Incl. O&P
1 Labor Foreman (outside)	$37.10	$296.80	$57.10	$456.80	$38.58	$58.92
3 Laborers	35.10	842.40	54.00	1296.00		
1 Equip Oper. (crane)	47.80	382.40	72.15	577.20		
1 Equip Oper. Oiler	41.25	330.00	62.25	498.00		
1 Hyd. Crane, 80 Ton		1554.00		1709.40	32.38	35.61
48 L.H., Daily Totals		$3405.60		$4537.40	$70.95	$94.53
Crew B-69A	Hr.	Daily	Hr.	Daily	Bare Costs	Incl. O&P
1 Labor Foreman (outside)	$37.10	$296.80	$57.10	$456.80	$38.55	$58.61
3 Laborers	35.10	842.40	54.00	1296.00		
1 Equip. Oper. (med.)	46.55	372.40	70.25	562.00		
1 Concrete Finisher	42.35	338.80	62.30	498.40		
1 Curb/Gutter Paver, 2-Track		761.00		837.10	15.85	17.44
48 L.H., Daily Totals		$2611.40		$3650.30	$54.40	$76.05
Crew B-69B	Hr.	Daily	Hr.	Daily	Bare Costs	Incl. O&P
1 Labor Foreman (outside)	$37.10	$296.80	$57.10	$456.80	$38.55	$58.61
3 Laborers	35.10	842.40	54.00	1296.00		
1 Equip. Oper. (med.)	46.55	372.40	70.25	562.00		
1 Cement Finisher	42.35	338.80	62.30	498.40		
1 Curb/Gutter Paver, 4-Track		733.20		806.52	15.28	16.80
48 L.H., Daily Totals		$2583.60		$3619.72	$53.83	$75.41
Crew B-70	Hr.	Daily	Hr.	Daily	Bare Costs	Incl. O&P
1 Labor Foreman (outside)	$37.10	$296.80	$57.10	$456.80	$40.29	$61.41
3 Laborers	35.10	842.40	54.00	1296.00		
3 Equip. Oper. (med.)	46.55	1117.20	70.25	1686.00		
1 Grader, 30,000 Lbs.		610.80		671.88		
1 Ripper, beam & 1 shank		81.60		89.76		
1 Road Sweeper, S.P., 8' wide		620.80		682.88		
1 F.E. Loader, W.M., 1.5 C.Y.		333.80		367.18	29.41	32.35
56 L.H., Daily Totals		$3903.40		$5250.50	$69.70	$93.76
Crew B-70A	Hr.	Daily	Hr.	Daily	Bare Costs	Incl. O&P
1 Laborer	$35.10	$280.80	$54.00	$432.00	$44.26	$67.00
4 Equip. Oper. (med.)	46.55	1489.60	70.25	2248.00		
1 Grader, 40,000 Lbs.		1011.00		1112.10		
1 F.E. Loader, W.M.,2.5 C.Y.		472.40		519.64		
1 Dozer, 80 H.P.		442.40		486.64		
1 Roller, Pneum. Whl 12 Ton		313.20		344.52	55.98	61.57
40 L.H., Daily Totals		$4009.40		$5142.90	$100.24	$128.57

Crew No.	Bare Costs Hr.	Daily	Incl. Subs O&P Hr.	Daily	Cost Per Labor-Hour Bare Costs	Incl. O&P
Crew B-71	Hr.	Daily	Hr.	Daily	Bare Costs	Incl. O&P
1 Labor Foreman (outside)	$37.10	$296.80	$57.10	$456.80	$40.29	$61.41
3 Laborers	35.10	842.40	54.00	1296.00		
3 Equip. Oper. (med.)	46.55	1117.20	70.25	1686.00		
1 Pvmt. Profiler, 750 H.P.		5459.00		6004.90		
1 Road Sweeper, S.P., 8' wide		620.80		682.88		
1 F.E. Loader, W.M., 1.5 C.Y.		333.80		367.18	114.53	125.98
56 L.H., Daily Totals		$8670.00		$10493.76	$154.82	$187.39
Crew B-72	Hr.	Daily	Hr.	Daily	Bare Costs	Incl. O&P
1 Labor Foreman (outside)	$37.10	$296.80	$57.10	$456.80	$41.08	$62.51
3 Laborers	35.10	842.40	54.00	1296.00		
4 Equip. Oper. (med.)	46.55	1489.60	70.25	2248.00		
1 Pvmt. Profiler, 750 H.P.		5459.00		6004.90		
1 Hammermill, 250 H.P.		1721.00		1893.10		
1 Windrow Loader		1207.00		1327.70		
1 Mix Paver 165 H.P.		2012.00		2213.20		
1 Roller, Pneum. Whl, 12 Ton		313.20		344.52	167.38	184.12
64 L.H., Daily Totals		$13341.00		$15784.22	$208.45	$246.63
Crew B-73	Hr.	Daily	Hr.	Daily	Bare Costs	Incl. O&P
1 Labor Foreman (outside)	$37.10	$296.80	$57.10	$456.80	$42.51	$64.54
2 Laborers	35.10	561.60	54.00	864.00		
5 Equip. Oper. (med.)	46.55	1862.00	70.25	2810.00		
1 Road Mixer, 310 H.P.		1882.00		2070.20		
1 Tandem Roller, 10 Ton		227.60		250.36		
1 Hammermill, 250 H.P.		1721.00		1893.10		
1 Grader, 30,000 Lbs.		610.80		671.88		
.5 F.E. Loader, W.M., 1.5 C.Y.		166.90		183.59		
.5 Truck Tractor, 220 H.P.		157.40		173.14		
.5 Water Tank Trailer, 5000 Gal.		70.50		77.55	75.57	83.12
64 L.H., Daily Totals		$7556.60		$9450.62	$118.07	$147.67
Crew B-74	Hr.	Daily	Hr.	Daily	Bare Costs	Incl. O&P
1 Labor Foreman (outside)	$37.10	$296.80	$57.10	$456.80	$41.13	$62.40
1 Laborer	35.10	280.80	54.00	432.00		
4 Equip. Oper. (med.)	46.55	1489.60	70.25	2248.00		
2 Truck Drivers (heavy)	35.30	564.80	53.55	856.80		
1 Grader, 30,000 Lbs.		610.80		671.88		
1 Ripper, beam & 1 shank		81.60		89.76		
2 Stabilizers, 310 H.P.		3170.00		3487.00		
1 Flatbed Truck, Gas, 3 Ton		264.40		290.84		
1 Chem. Spreader, Towed		50.00		55.00		
1 Roller, Vibratory, 25 Ton		640.20		704.22		
1 Water Tank Trailer, 5000 Gal.		141.00		155.10		
1 Truck Tractor, 220 H.P.		314.80		346.28	82.39	90.63
64 L.H., Daily Totals		$7904.80		$9793.68	$123.51	$153.03
Crew B-75	Hr.	Daily	Hr.	Daily	Bare Costs	Incl. O&P
1 Labor Foreman (outside)	$37.10	$296.80	$57.10	$456.80	$41.96	$63.66
1 Laborer	35.10	280.80	54.00	432.00		
4 Equip. Oper. (med.)	46.55	1489.60	70.25	2248.00		
1 Truck Driver (heavy)	35.30	282.40	53.55	428.40		
1 Grader, 30,000 Lbs.		610.80		671.88		
1 Ripper, beam & 1 shank		81.60		89.76		
2 Stabilizers, 310 H.P.		3170.00		3487.00		
1 Dist. Tanker, 3000 Gallon		306.00		336.60		
1 Truck Tractor, 6x4, 380 H.P.		522.20		574.42		
1 Roller, Vibratory, 25 Ton		640.20		704.22	95.19	104.71
56 L.H., Daily Totals		$7680.40		$9429.08	$137.15	$168.38

Crew No.	Bare Costs		Incl. Subs O&P		Cost Per Labor-Hour	
Crew B-76	Hr.	Daily	Hr.	Daily	Bare Costs	Incl. O&P
1 Dock Builder Foreman (outside)	$44.80	$358.40	$72.00	$576.00	$43.96	$69.17
5 Dock Builders	42.80	1712.00	68.80	2752.00		
2 Equip. Oper. (crane)	47.80	764.80	72.15	1154.40		
1 Equip. Oper. Oiler	41.25	330.00	62.25	498.00		
1 Crawler Crane, 50 Ton		1257.00		1382.70		
1 Barge, 400 Ton		779.20		857.12		
1 Hammer, diesel, 15K ft.-lbs.		591.40		650.54		
1 Lead, 60' high		73.60		80.96		
1 Air Compressor, 600 cfm		467.60		514.36		
2 -50' Air Hoses, 3"		29.80		32.78	44.42	48.87
72 L.H., Daily Totals		$6363.80		$8498.86	$88.39	$118.04

Crew No.	Bare Costs		Incl. Subs O&P		Cost Per Labor-Hour	
Crew B-76A	Hr.	Daily	Hr.	Daily	Bare Costs	Incl. O&P
1 Labor Foreman (outside)	$37.10	$296.80	$57.10	$456.80	$37.71	$57.69
5 Laborers	35.10	1404.00	54.00	2160.00		
1 Equip. Oper. (crane)	47.80	382.40	72.15	577.20		
1 Equip. Oper. Oiler	41.25	330.00	62.25	498.00		
1 Crawler Crane, 50 Ton		1257.00		1382.70		
1 Barge, 400 Ton		779.20		857.12	31.82	35.00
64 L.H., Daily Totals		$4449.40		$5931.82	$69.52	$92.68

Crew No.	Bare Costs		Incl. Subs O&P		Cost Per Labor-Hour	
Crew B-77	Hr.	Daily	Hr.	Daily	Bare Costs	Incl. O&P
1 Labor Foreman (outside)	$37.10	$296.80	$57.10	$456.80	$35.35	$54.24
3 Laborers	35.10	842.40	54.00	1296.00		
1 Truck Driver (light)	34.35	274.80	52.10	416.80		
1 Crack Cleaner, 25 H.P.		57.20		62.92		
1 Crack Filler, Trailer Mtd.		196.40		216.04		
1 Flatbed Truck, Gas, 3 Ton		264.40		290.84	12.95	14.24
40 L.H., Daily Totals		$1932.00		$2739.40	$48.30	$68.48

Crew No.	Bare Costs		Incl. Subs O&P		Cost Per Labor-Hour	
Crew B-78	Hr.	Daily	Hr.	Daily	Bare Costs	Incl. O&P
1 Labor Foreman (outside)	$37.10	$296.80	$57.10	$456.80	$35.31	$54.20
4 Laborers	35.10	1123.20	54.00	1728.00		
1 Truck Driver (light)	34.35	274.80	52.10	416.80		
1 Paint Striper, S.P., 40 Gallon		148.60		163.46		
1 Flatbed Truck, Gas, 3 Ton		264.40		290.84		
1 Pickup Truck, 3/4 Ton		127.00		139.70	11.25	12.38
48 L.H., Daily Totals		$2234.80		$3195.60	$46.56	$66.58

Crew No.	Bare Costs		Incl. Subs O&P		Cost Per Labor-Hour	
Crew B-78A	Hr.	Daily	Hr.	Daily	Bare Costs	Incl. O&P
1 Equip. Oper. (light)	$44.75	$358.00	$67.55	$540.40	$44.75	$67.55
1 Line Rem. (metal balls) 115 H.P.		800.80		880.88	100.10	110.11
8 L.H., Daily Totals		$1158.80		$1421.28	$144.85	$177.66

Crew No.	Bare Costs		Incl. Subs O&P		Cost Per Labor-Hour	
Crew B-78B	Hr.	Daily	Hr.	Daily	Bare Costs	Incl. O&P
2 Laborers	$35.10	$561.60	$54.00	$864.00	$36.17	$55.51
.25 Equip. Oper. (light)	44.75	89.50	67.55	135.10		
1 Pickup Truck, 3/4 Ton		127.00		139.70		
1 Line Rem., 11 H.P.,walk behind		61.20		67.32		
.25 Road Sweeper, S.P., 8' wide		155.20		170.72	19.08	20.99
18 L.H., Daily Totals		$994.50		$1376.84	$55.25	$76.49

Crew No.	Bare Costs		Incl. Subs O&P		Cost Per Labor-Hour	
Crew B-78C	Hr.	Daily	Hr.	Daily	Bare Costs	Incl. O&P
1 Labor Foreman (outside)	$37.10	$296.80	$57.10	$456.80	$35.31	$54.20
4 Laborers	35.10	1123.20	54.00	1728.00		
1 Truck Driver (light)	34.35	274.80	52.10	416.80		
1 Paint Striper, T.M., 120 Gal.		735.80		809.38		
1 Flatbed Truck, Gas, 3 Ton		264.40		290.84		
1 Pickup Truck, 3/4 Ton		127.00		139.70	23.48	25.83
48 L.H., Daily Totals		$2822.00		$3841.52	$58.79	$80.03

Crew No.	Bare Costs		Incl. Subs O&P		Cost Per Labor-Hour	
Crew B-78D	Hr.	Daily	Hr.	Daily	Bare Costs	Incl. O&P
2 Labor Foremen (Outside)	$37.10	$593.60	$57.10	$913.60	$35.42	$54.43
7 Laborers	35.10	1965.60	54.00	3024.00		
1 Truck Driver (light)	34.35	274.80	52.10	416.80		
1 Paint Striper, T.M., 120 Gal.		735.80		809.38		
1 Flatbed Truck, Gas, 3 Ton		264.40		290.84		
3 Pickup Trucks, 3/4 Ton		381.00		419.10		
1 Air Compressor, 60 cfm		120.40		132.44		
1 -50' Air Hose, 3/4"		3.05		3.36		
1 Breakers, Pavement, 60 lb.		9.80		10.78	18.93	20.82
80 L.H., Daily Totals		$4348.45		$6020.30	$54.36	$75.25

Crew No.	Bare Costs		Incl. Subs O&P		Cost Per Labor-Hour	
Crew B-78E	Hr.	Daily	Hr.	Daily	Bare Costs	Incl. O&P
2 Labor Foremen (Outside)	$37.10	$593.60	$57.10	$913.60	$35.37	$54.36
9 Laborers	35.10	2527.20	54.00	3888.00		
1 Truck Driver (light)	34.35	274.80	52.10	416.80		
1 Paint Striper, T.M., 120 Gal.		735.80		809.38		
1 Flatbed Truck, Gas, 3 Ton		264.40		290.84		
4 Pickup Trucks, 3/4 Ton		508.00		558.80		
2 Air Compressor, 60 cfm		240.80		264.88		
2 -50' Air Hose, 3/4"		6.10		6.71		
2 Breakers, Pavement, 60 lb.		19.60		21.56	18.49	20.34
96 L.H., Daily Totals		$5170.30		$7170.57	$53.86	$74.69

Crew No.	Bare Costs		Incl. Subs O&P		Cost Per Labor-Hour	
Crew B-78F	Hr.	Daily	Hr.	Daily	Bare Costs	Incl. O&P
2 Labor Foremen (Outside)	$37.10	$593.60	$57.10	$913.60	$35.33	$54.31
11 Laborers	35.10	3088.80	54.00	4752.00		
1 Truck Driver (light)	34.35	274.80	52.10	416.80		
1 Paint Striper, T.M., 120 Gal.		735.80		809.38		
1 Flatbed Truck, Gas, 3 Ton		264.40		290.84		
7 Pickup Trucks, 3/4 Ton		889.00		977.90		
3 Air Compressor, 60 cfm		361.20		397.32		
3 -50' Air Hose, 3/4"		9.15		10.07		
3 Breakers, Pavement, 60 lb.		29.40		32.34	20.44	22.48
112 L.H., Daily Totals		$6246.15		$8600.25	$55.77	$76.79

Crew No.	Bare Costs		Incl. Subs O&P		Cost Per Labor-Hour	
Crew B-79	Hr.	Daily	Hr.	Daily	Bare Costs	Incl. O&P
1 Labor Foreman (outside)	$37.10	$296.80	$57.10	$456.80	$35.35	$54.24
3 Laborers	35.10	842.40	54.00	1296.00		
1 Truck Driver (light)	34.35	274.80	52.10	416.80		
1 Paint Striper, T.M., 120 Gal.		735.80		809.38		
1 Heating Kettle, 115 Gallon		44.50		48.95		
1 Flatbed Truck, Gas, 3 Ton		264.40		290.84		
2 Pickup Trucks, 3/4 Ton		254.00		279.40	32.47	35.71
40 L.H., Daily Totals		$2712.70		$3598.17	$67.82	$89.95

Crew No.	Bare Costs		Incl. Subs O&P		Cost Per Labor-Hour	
Crew B-79A	Hr.	Daily	Hr.	Daily	Bare Costs	Incl. O&P
1.5 Equip. Oper. (light)	$44.75	$537.00	$67.55	$810.60	$44.75	$67.55
.5 Line Remov. (grinder) 115 H.P.		441.40		485.54		
1 Line Rem. (metal balls) 115 H.P.		800.80		880.88	103.52	113.87
12 L.H., Daily Totals		$1779.20		$2177.02	$148.27	$181.42

Crew No.	Bare Costs		Incl. Subs O&P		Cost Per Labor-Hour	
Crew B-79B	Hr.	Daily	Hr.	Daily	Bare Costs	Incl. O&P
1 Laborer	$35.10	$280.80	$54.00	$432.00	$35.10	$54.00
1 Set of Gases		86.40		95.04	10.80	11.88
8 L.H., Daily Totals		$367.20		$527.04	$45.90	$65.88

Crew No.	Bare Costs		Incl. Subs O&P		Cost Per Labor-Hour	
Crew B-79C	Hr.	Daily	Hr.	Daily	Bare Costs	Incl. O&P
1 Labor Foreman (outside)	$37.10	$296.80	$57.10	$456.80	$35.28	$54.17
5 Laborers	35.10	1404.00	54.00	2160.00		
1 Truck Driver (light)	34.35	274.80	52.10	416.80		
1 Paint Striper, T.M., 120 Gal.		735.80		809.38		
1 Heating Kettle, 115 Gallon		44.50		48.95		
1 Flatbed Truck, Gas, 3 Ton		264.40		290.84		
3 Pickup Trucks, 3/4 Ton		381.00		419.10		
1 Air Compressor, 60 cfm		120.40		132.44		
1 -50' Air Hose, 3/4"		3.05		3.36		
1 Breakers, Pavement, 60 lb.		9.80		10.78	27.84	30.62
56 L.H., Daily Totals		$3534.55		$4748.44	$63.12	$84.79
Crew B-79D	Hr.	Daily	Hr.	Daily	Bare Costs	Incl. O&P
2 Labor Foremen (Outside)	$37.10	$593.60	$57.10	$913.60	$35.51	$54.54
5 Laborers	35.10	1404.00	54.00	2160.00		
1 Truck Driver (light)	34.35	274.80	52.10	416.80		
1 Paint Striper, T.M., 120 Gal.		735.80		809.38		
1 Heating Kettle, 115 Gallon		44.50		48.95		
1 Flatbed Truck, Gas, 3 Ton		264.40		290.84		
4 Pickup Trucks, 3/4 Ton		508.00		558.80		
1 Air Compressor, 60 cfm		120.40		132.44		
1 -50' Air Hose, 3/4"		3.05		3.36		
1 Breakers, Pavement, 60 lb.		9.80		10.78	26.34	28.98
64 L.H., Daily Totals		$3958.35		$5344.94	$61.85	$83.51
Crew B-79E	Hr.	Daily	Hr.	Daily	Bare Costs	Incl. O&P
2 Labor Foremen (Outside)	$37.10	$593.60	$57.10	$913.60	$35.42	$54.43
7 Laborers	35.10	1965.60	54.00	3024.00		
1 Truck Driver (light)	34.35	274.80	52.10	416.80		
1 Paint Striper, T.M., 120 Gal.		735.80		809.38		
1 Heating Kettle, 115 Gallon		44.50		48.95		
1 Flatbed Truck, Gas, 3 Ton		264.40		290.84		
5 Pickup Trucks, 3/4 Ton		635.00		698.50		
2 Air Compressors, 60 cfm		240.80		264.88		
2 -50' Air Hoses, 3/4"		6.10		6.71		
2 Breakers, Pavement, 60 lb.		19.60		21.56	24.33	26.76
80 L.H., Daily Totals		$4780.20		$6495.22	$59.75	$81.19
Crew B-80	Hr.	Daily	Hr.	Daily	Bare Costs	Incl. O&P
1 Labor Foreman (outside)	$37.10	$296.80	$57.10	$456.80	$37.83	$57.69
1 Laborer	35.10	280.80	54.00	432.00		
1 Truck Driver (light)	34.35	274.80	52.10	416.80		
1 Equip. Oper. (light)	44.75	358.00	67.55	540.40		
1 Flatbed Truck, Gas, 3 Ton		264.40		290.84		
1 Earth Auger, Truck-Mtd.		403.40		443.74	20.87	22.96
32 L.H., Daily Totals		$1878.20		$2580.58	$58.69	$80.64
Crew B-80A	Hr.	Daily	Hr.	Daily	Bare Costs	Incl. O&P
3 Laborers	$35.10	$842.40	$54.00	$1296.00	$35.10	$54.00
1 Flatbed Truck, Gas, 3 Ton		264.40		290.84	11.02	12.12
24 L.H., Daily Totals		$1106.80		$1586.84	$46.12	$66.12
Crew B-80B	Hr.	Daily	Hr.	Daily	Bare Costs	Incl. O&P
3 Laborers	$35.10	$842.40	$54.00	$1296.00	$37.51	$57.39
1 Equip. Oper. (light)	44.75	358.00	67.55	540.40		
1 Crane, Flatbed Mounted, 3 Ton		232.40		255.64	7.26	7.99
32 L.H., Daily Totals		$1432.80		$2092.04	$44.77	$65.38

Crew No.	Bare Costs		Incl. Subs O&P		Cost Per Labor-Hour	
Crew B-80C	Hr.	Daily	Hr.	Daily	Bare Costs	Incl. O&P
2 Laborers	$35.10	$561.60	$54.00	$864.00	$34.85	$53.37
1 Truck Driver (light)	34.35	274.80	52.10	416.80		
1 Flatbed Truck, Gas, 1.5 Ton		211.00		232.10		
1 Manual fence post auger, gas		7.60		8.36	9.11	10.02
24 L.H., Daily Totals		$1055.00		$1521.26	$43.96	$63.39
Crew B-81	Hr.	Daily	Hr.	Daily	Bare Costs	Incl. O&P
1 Laborer	$35.10	$280.80	$54.00	$432.00	$38.98	$59.27
1 Equip. Oper. (med.)	46.55	372.40	70.25	562.00		
1 Truck Driver (heavy)	35.30	282.40	53.55	428.40		
1 Hydromulcher, T.M., 3000 Gal.		303.80		334.18		
1 Truck Tractor, 220 H.P.		314.80		346.28	25.77	28.35
24 L.H., Daily Totals		$1554.20		$2102.86	$64.76	$87.62
Crew B-81A	Hr.	Daily	Hr.	Daily	Bare Costs	Incl. O&P
1 Laborer	$35.10	$280.80	$54.00	$432.00	$34.73	$53.05
1 Truck Driver (light)	34.35	274.80	52.10	416.80		
1 Hydromulcher, T.M., 600 Gal.		120.40		132.44		
1 Flatbed Truck, Gas, 3 Ton		264.40		290.84	24.05	26.45
16 L.H., Daily Totals		$940.40		$1272.08	$58.77	$79.50
Crew B-82	Hr.	Daily	Hr.	Daily	Bare Costs	Incl. O&P
1 Laborer	$35.10	$280.80	$54.00	$432.00	$39.92	$60.77
1 Equip. Oper. (light)	44.75	358.00	67.55	540.40		
1 Horiz. Borer, 6 H.P.		77.20		84.92	4.83	5.31
16 L.H., Daily Totals		$716.00		$1057.32	$44.75	$66.08
Crew B-82A	Hr.	Daily	Hr.	Daily	Bare Costs	Incl. O&P
1 Laborer	$35.10	$280.80	$54.00	$432.00	$39.92	$60.77
1 Equip. Oper. (light)	44.75	358.00	67.55	540.40		
1 Flatbed Truck, Gas, 3 Ton		264.40		290.84		
1 Flatbed Trailer, 25 Ton		108.60		119.46		
1 Horiz. Dir. Drill, 20k lb. thrust		622.00		684.20	62.19	68.41
16 L.H., Daily Totals		$1633.80		$2066.90	$102.11	$129.18
Crew B-82B	Hr.	Daily	Hr.	Daily	Bare Costs	Incl. O&P
2 Laborers	$35.10	$561.60	$54.00	$864.00	$38.32	$58.52
1 Equip. Oper. (light)	44.75	358.00	67.55	540.40		
1 Flatbed Truck, Gas, 3 Ton		264.40		290.84		
1 Flatbed Trailer, 25 Ton		108.60		119.46		
1 Horiz. Dir. Drill, 30k lb. thrust		886.20		974.82	52.47	57.71
24 L.H., Daily Totals		$2178.80		$2789.52	$90.78	$116.23
Crew B-82C	Hr.	Daily	Hr.	Daily	Bare Costs	Incl. O&P
2 Laborers	$35.10	$561.60	$54.00	$864.00	$38.32	$58.52
1 Equip. Oper. (light)	44.75	358.00	67.55	540.40		
1 Flatbed Truck, Gas, 3 Ton		264.40		290.84		
1 Flatbed Trailer, 25 Ton		108.60		119.46		
1 Horiz. Dir. Drill, 50k lb. thrust		1176.00		1293.60	64.54	71.00
24 L.H., Daily Totals		$2468.60		$3108.30	$102.86	$129.51
Crew B-82D	Hr.	Daily	Hr.	Daily	Bare Costs	Incl. O&P
1 Equip. Oper. (light)	$44.75	$358.00	$67.55	$540.40	$44.75	$67.55
1 Mud Trailer for HDD, 1500 gallon		309.20		340.12	38.65	42.52
8 L.H., Daily Totals		$667.20		$880.52	$83.40	$110.07

Crew B-83

Crew No.	Bare Costs Hr.	Bare Costs Daily	Incl. Subs O&P Hr.	Incl. Subs O&P Daily	Cost Per Labor-Hour Bare Costs	Cost Per Labor-Hour Incl. O&P
1 Tugboat Captain	$46.55	$372.40	$70.25	$562.00	$40.83	$62.13
1 Tugboat Hand	35.10	280.80	54.00	432.00		
1 Tugboat, 250 H.P.		748.00		822.80	46.75	51.42
16 L.H., Daily Totals		$1401.20		$1816.80	$87.58	$113.55

Crew B-84

Crew No.	Hr.	Daily	Hr.	Daily	Bare Costs	Incl. O&P
1 Equip. Oper. (med.)	$46.55	$372.40	$70.25	$562.00	$46.55	$70.25
1 Rotary Mower/Tractor		343.40		377.74	42.92	47.22
8 L.H., Daily Totals		$715.80		$939.74	$89.47	$117.47

Crew B-85

Crew No.	Hr.	Daily	Hr.	Daily	Bare Costs	Incl. O&P
3 Laborers	$35.10	$842.40	$54.00	$1296.00	$37.43	$57.16
1 Equip. Oper. (med.)	46.55	372.40	70.25	562.00		
1 Truck Driver (heavy)	35.30	282.40	53.55	428.40		
1 Aerial Lift Truck, 80'		637.60		701.36		
1 Brush Chipper, 12", 130 H.P.		283.80		312.18		
1 Pruning Saw, Rotary		6.30		6.93	23.19	25.51
40 L.H., Daily Totals		$2424.90		$3306.87	$60.62	$82.67

Crew B-86

Crew No.	Hr.	Daily	Hr.	Daily	Bare Costs	Incl. O&P
1 Equip. Oper. (med.)	$46.55	$372.40	$70.25	$562.00	$46.55	$70.25
1 Stump Chipper, S.P.		170.70		187.77	21.34	23.47
8 L.H., Daily Totals		$543.10		$749.77	$67.89	$93.72

Crew B-86A

Crew No.	Hr.	Daily	Hr.	Daily	Bare Costs	Incl. O&P
1 Equip. Oper. (med.)	$46.55	$372.40	$70.25	$562.00	$46.55	$70.25
1 Grader, 30,000 Lbs.		610.80		671.88	76.35	83.98
8 L.H., Daily Totals		$983.20		$1233.88	$122.90	$154.24

Crew B-86B

Crew No.	Hr.	Daily	Hr.	Daily	Bare Costs	Incl. O&P
1 Equip. Oper. (med.)	$46.55	$372.40	$70.25	$562.00	$46.55	$70.25
1 Dozer, 200 H.P.		1243.00		1367.30	155.38	170.91
8 L.H., Daily Totals		$1615.40		$1929.30	$201.93	$241.16

Crew B-87

Crew No.	Hr.	Daily	Hr.	Daily	Bare Costs	Incl. O&P
1 Laborer	$35.10	$280.80	$54.00	$432.00	$44.26	$67.00
4 Equip. Oper. (med.)	46.55	1489.60	70.25	2248.00		
2 Feller Bunchers, 100 H.P.		1154.40		1269.84		
1 Log Chipper, 22" Tree		710.60		781.66		
1 Dozer, 105 H.P.		550.80		605.88		
1 Chain Saw, gas, 36" Long		43.60		47.96	61.48	67.63
40 L.H., Daily Totals		$4229.80		$5385.34	$105.75	$134.63

Crew B-88

Crew No.	Hr.	Daily	Hr.	Daily	Bare Costs	Incl. O&P
1 Laborer	$35.10	$280.80	$54.00	$432.00	$44.91	$67.93
6 Equip. Oper. (med.)	46.55	2234.40	70.25	3372.00		
2 Feller Bunchers, 100 H.P.		1154.40		1269.84		
1 Log Chipper, 22" Tree		710.60		781.66		
2 Log Skidders, 50 H.P.		1730.40		1903.44		
1 Dozer, 105 H.P.		550.80		605.88		
1 Chain Saw, gas, 36" Long		43.60		47.96	74.82	82.30
56 L.H., Daily Totals		$6705.00		$8412.78	$119.73	$150.23

Crew B-89

Crew No.	Hr.	Daily	Hr.	Daily	Bare Costs	Incl. O&P
1 Equip. Oper. (light)	$44.75	$358.00	$67.55	$540.40	$39.55	$59.83
1 Truck Driver (light)	34.35	274.80	52.10	416.80		
1 Flatbed Truck, Gas, 3 Ton		264.40		290.84		
1 Concrete Saw		148.00		162.80		
1 Water Tank, 65 Gal.		17.40		19.14	26.86	29.55
16 L.H., Daily Totals		$1062.60		$1429.98	$66.41	$89.37

Crew B-89A

Crew No.	Hr.	Daily	Hr.	Daily	Bare Costs	Incl. O&P
1 Skilled Worker	$45.40	$363.20	$70.20	$561.60	$40.25	$62.10
1 Laborer	35.10	280.80	54.00	432.00		
1 Core Drill (large)		110.20		121.22	6.89	7.58
16 L.H., Daily Totals		$754.20		$1114.82	$47.14	$69.68

Crew B-89B

Crew No.	Hr.	Daily	Hr.	Daily	Bare Costs	Incl. O&P
1 Equip. Oper. (light)	$44.75	$358.00	$67.55	$540.40	$39.55	$59.83
1 Truck Driver, Light	34.35	274.80	52.10	416.80		
1 Wall Saw, Hydraulic, 10 H.P.		92.00		101.20		
1 Generator, Diesel, 100 kW		363.40		399.74		
1 Water Tank, 65 Gal.		17.40		19.14		
1 Flatbed Truck, Gas, 3 Ton		264.40		290.84	46.08	50.68
16 L.H., Daily Totals		$1370.00		$1768.12	$85.63	$110.51

Crew B-90

Crew No.	Hr.	Daily	Hr.	Daily	Bare Costs	Incl. O&P
1 Labor Foreman (outside)	$37.10	$296.80	$57.10	$456.80	$37.81	$57.66
3 Laborers	35.10	842.40	54.00	1296.00		
2 Equip. Oper. (light)	44.75	716.00	67.55	1080.80		
2 Truck Drivers (heavy)	35.30	564.80	53.55	856.80		
1 Road Mixer, 310 H.P.		1882.00		2070.20		
1 Dist. Truck, 2000 Gal.		276.40		304.04	33.73	37.10
64 L.H., Daily Totals		$4578.40		$6064.64	$71.54	$94.76

Crew B-90A

Crew No.	Hr.	Daily	Hr.	Daily	Bare Costs	Incl. O&P
1 Labor Foreman (outside)	$37.10	$296.80	$57.10	$456.80	$41.93	$63.73
2 Laborers	35.10	561.60	54.00	864.00		
4 Equip. Oper. (med.)	46.55	1489.60	70.25	2248.00		
2 Graders, 30,000 Lbs.		1221.60		1343.76		
1 Tandem Roller, 10 Ton		227.60		250.36		
1 Roller, Pneum. Whl, 12 Ton		313.20		344.52	31.47	34.62
56 L.H., Daily Totals		$4110.40		$5507.44	$73.40	$98.35

Crew B-90B

Crew No.	Hr.	Daily	Hr.	Daily	Bare Costs	Incl. O&P
1 Labor Foreman (outside)	$37.10	$296.80	$57.10	$456.80	$41.16	$62.64
2 Laborers	35.10	561.60	54.00	864.00		
3 Equip. Oper. (med.)	46.55	1117.20	70.25	1686.00		
1 Roller, Pneum. Whl, 12 Ton		313.20		344.52		
1 Road Mixer, 310 H.P.		1882.00		2070.20	45.73	50.31
48 L.H., Daily Totals		$4170.80		$5421.52	$86.89	$112.95

Crew B-90C

Crew No.	Hr.	Daily	Hr.	Daily	Bare Costs	Incl. O&P
1 Labor Foreman (outside)	$37.10	$296.80	$57.10	$456.80	$38.46	$58.59
4 Laborers	35.10	1123.20	54.00	1728.00		
3 Equip. Oper. (med.)	46.55	1117.20	70.25	1686.00		
3 Truck Drivers (heavy)	35.30	847.20	53.55	1285.20		
3 Road Mixers, 310 H.P.		5646.00		6210.60	64.16	70.58
88 L.H., Daily Totals		$9030.40		$11366.60	$102.62	$129.17

Crew B-90D

Crew No.	Hr.	Daily	Hr.	Daily	Bare Costs	Incl. O&P
1 Labor Foreman (outside)	$37.10	$296.80	$57.10	$456.80	$37.94	$57.88
6 Laborers	35.10	1684.80	54.00	2592.00		
3 Equip. Oper. (med.)	46.55	1117.20	70.25	1686.00		
3 Truck Drivers (heavy)	35.30	847.20	53.55	1285.20		
3 Road Mixers, 310 H.P.		5646.00		6210.60	54.29	59.72
104 L.H., Daily Totals		$9592.00		$12230.60	$92.23	$117.60

Crews

Crew No.	Bare Costs Hr.	Daily	Incl. Subs O&P Hr.	Daily	Cost Per Labor-Hour Bare Costs	Incl. O&P
Crew B-91	Hr.	Daily	Hr.	Daily	Bare Costs	Incl. O&P
1 Labor Foreman (outside)	$37.10	$296.80	$57.10	$456.80	$41.10	$62.46
2 Laborers	35.10	561.60	54.00	864.00		
4 Equip. Oper. (med.)	46.55	1489.60	70.25	2248.00		
1 Truck Driver (heavy)	35.30	282.40	53.55	428.40		
1 Dist. Tanker, 3000 Gallon		306.00		336.60		
1 Truck Tractor, 6x4, 380 H.P.		522.20		574.42		
1 Aggreg. Spreader, S.P.		781.80		859.98		
1 Roller, Pneum. Whl, 12 Ton		313.20		344.52		
1 Tandem Roller, 10 Ton		227.60		250.36	33.61	36.97
64 L.H., Daily Totals		$4781.20		$6363.08	$74.71	$99.42
Crew B-91B	Hr.	Daily	Hr.	Daily	Bare Costs	Incl. O&P
1 Laborer	$35.10	$280.80	$54.00	$432.00	$40.83	$62.13
1 Equipment Oper. (med.)	46.55	372.40	70.25	562.00		
1 Road Sweeper, Vac. Assist.		876.60		964.26	54.79	60.27
16 L.H., Daily Totals		$1529.80		$1958.26	$95.61	$122.39
Crew B-91C	Hr.	Daily	Hr.	Daily	Bare Costs	Incl. O&P
1 Laborer	$35.10	$280.80	$54.00	$432.00	$34.73	$53.05
1 Truck Driver (light)	34.35	274.80	52.10	416.80		
1 Catch Basin Cleaning Truck		535.80		589.38	33.49	36.84
16 L.H., Daily Totals		$1091.40		$1438.18	$68.21	$89.89
Crew B-91D	Hr.	Daily	Hr.	Daily	Bare Costs	Incl. O&P
1 Labor Foreman (outside)	$37.10	$296.80	$57.10	$456.80	$39.69	$60.42
5 Laborers	35.10	1404.00	54.00	2160.00		
5 Equip. Oper. (med.)	46.55	1862.00	70.25	2810.00		
2 Truck Drivers (heavy)	35.30	564.80	53.55	856.80		
1 Aggreg. Spreader, S.P.		781.80		859.98		
2 Truck Tractor, 6x4, 380 H.P.		1044.40		1148.84		
2 Dist. Tanker, 3000 Gallon		612.00		673.20		
2 Pavement brush, towed		163.60		179.96		
2 Roller, Pneum. Whl, 12 Ton		626.40		689.04	31.04	34.14
104 L.H., Daily Totals		$7355.80		$9834.62	$70.73	$94.56
Crew B-92	Hr.	Daily	Hr.	Daily	Bare Costs	Incl. O&P
1 Labor Foreman (outside)	$37.10	$296.80	$57.10	$456.80	$35.60	$54.77
3 Laborers	35.10	842.40	54.00	1296.00		
1 Crack Cleaner, 25 H.P.		57.20		62.92		
1 Air Compressor, 60 cfm		120.40		132.44		
1 Tar Kettle, T.M.		77.20		84.92		
1 Flatbed Truck, Gas, 3 Ton		264.40		290.84	16.23	17.85
32 L.H., Daily Totals		$1658.40		$2323.92	$51.83	$72.62
Crew B-93	Hr.	Daily	Hr.	Daily	Bare Costs	Incl. O&P
1 Equip. Oper. (med.)	$46.55	$372.40	$70.25	$562.00	$46.55	$70.25
1 Feller Buncher, 100 H.P.		577.20		634.92	72.15	79.36
8 L.H., Daily Totals		$949.60		$1196.92	$118.70	$149.62
Crew B-94A	Hr.	Daily	Hr.	Daily	Bare Costs	Incl. O&P
1 Laborer	$35.10	$280.80	$54.00	$432.00	$35.10	$54.00
1 Diaphragm Water Pump, 2"		68.60		75.46		
1 -20' Suction Hose, 2"		1.95		2.15		
2 -50' Discharge Hoses, 2"		3.50		3.85	9.26	10.18
8 L.H., Daily Totals		$354.85		$513.46	$44.36	$64.18

Crew No.	Bare Costs Hr.	Daily	Incl. Subs O&P Hr.	Daily	Cost Per Labor-Hour Bare Costs	Incl. O&P
Crew B-94B	Hr.	Daily	Hr.	Daily	Bare Costs	Incl. O&P
1 Laborer	$35.10	$280.80	$54.00	$432.00	$35.10	$54.00
1 Diaphragm Water Pump, 4"		111.20		122.32		
1 -20' Suction Hose, 4"		3.25		3.58		
2 -50' Discharge Hoses, 4"		9.40		10.34	15.48	17.03
8 L.H., Daily Totals		$404.65		$568.24	$50.58	$71.03
Crew B-94C	Hr.	Daily	Hr.	Daily	Bare Costs	Incl. O&P
1 Laborer	$35.10	$280.80	$54.00	$432.00	$35.10	$54.00
1 Centrifugal Water Pump, 3"		73.80		81.18		
1 -20' Suction Hose, 3"		2.85		3.13		
2 -50' Discharge Hoses, 3"		6.10		6.71	10.34	11.38
8 L.H., Daily Totals		$363.55		$523.02	$45.44	$65.38
Crew B-94D	Hr.	Daily	Hr.	Daily	Bare Costs	Incl. O&P
1 Laborer	$35.10	$280.80	$54.00	$432.00	$35.10	$54.00
1 Centr. Water Pump, 6"		308.40		339.24		
1 -20' Suction Hose, 6"		11.50		12.65		
2 -50' Discharge Hoses, 6"		24.20		26.62	43.01	47.31
8 L.H., Daily Totals		$624.90		$810.51	$78.11	$101.31
Crew C-1	Hr.	Daily	Hr.	Daily	Bare Costs	Incl. O&P
3 Carpenters	$44.10	$1058.40	$67.85	$1628.40	$41.85	$64.39
1 Laborer	35.10	280.80	54.00	432.00		
32 L.H., Daily Totals		$1339.20		$2060.40	$41.85	$64.39
Crew C-2	Hr.	Daily	Hr.	Daily	Bare Costs	Incl. O&P
1 Carpenter Foreman (outside)	$46.10	$368.80	$70.95	$567.60	$42.93	$66.06
4 Carpenters	44.10	1411.20	67.85	2171.20		
1 Laborer	35.10	280.80	54.00	432.00		
48 L.H., Daily Totals		$2060.80		$3170.80	$42.93	$66.06
Crew C-2A	Hr.	Daily	Hr.	Daily	Bare Costs	Incl. O&P
1 Carpenter Foreman (outside)	$46.10	$368.80	$70.95	$567.60	$42.64	$65.13
3 Carpenters	44.10	1058.40	67.85	1628.40		
1 Cement Finisher	42.35	338.80	62.30	498.40		
1 Laborer	35.10	280.80	54.00	432.00		
48 L.H., Daily Totals		$2046.80		$3126.40	$42.64	$65.13
Crew C-3	Hr.	Daily	Hr.	Daily	Bare Costs	Incl. O&P
1 Rodman Foreman (outside)	$51.10	$408.80	$81.60	$652.80	$45.31	$71.34
4 Rodmen (reinf.)	49.10	1571.20	78.40	2508.80		
1 Equip. Oper. (light)	44.75	358.00	67.55	540.40		
2 Laborers	35.10	561.60	54.00	864.00		
3 Stressing Equipment		30.60		33.66		
.5 Grouting Equipment		77.30		85.03	1.69	1.85
64 L.H., Daily Totals		$3007.50		$4684.69	$46.99	$73.20
Crew C-4	Hr.	Daily	Hr.	Daily	Bare Costs	Incl. O&P
1 Rodman Foreman (outside)	$51.10	$408.80	$81.60	$652.80	$49.60	$79.20
3 Rodmen (reinf.)	49.10	1178.40	78.40	1881.60		
3 Stressing Equipment		30.60		33.66	.96	1.05
32 L.H., Daily Totals		$1617.80		$2568.06	$50.56	$80.25
Crew C-4A	Hr.	Daily	Hr.	Daily	Bare Costs	Incl. O&P
2 Rodmen (reinf.)	$49.10	$785.60	$78.40	$1254.40	$49.10	$78.40
4 Stressing Equipment		40.80		44.88	2.55	2.81
16 L.H., Daily Totals		$826.40		$1299.28	$51.65	$81.20

Crew No.	Bare Costs		Incl. Subs O&P		Cost Per Labor-Hour	
Crew C-5	**Hr.**	**Daily**	**Hr.**	**Daily**	**Bare Costs**	**Incl. O&P**
1 Rodman Foreman (outside)	$51.10	$408.80	$81.60	$652.80	$48.08	$75.66
4 Rodmen (reinf.)	49.10	1571.20	78.40	2508.80		
1 Equip. Oper. (crane)	47.80	382.40	72.15	577.20		
1 Equip. Oper. Oiler	41.25	330.00	62.25	498.00		
1 Hyd. Crane, 25 Ton		697.20		766.92	12.45	13.70
56 L.H., Daily Totals		$3389.60		$5003.72	$60.53	$89.35
Crew C-6	**Hr.**	**Daily**	**Hr.**	**Daily**	**Bare Costs**	**Incl. O&P**
1 Labor Foreman (outside)	$37.10	$296.80	$57.10	$456.80	$36.64	$55.90
4 Laborers	35.10	1123.20	54.00	1728.00		
1 Cement Finisher	42.35	338.80	62.30	498.40		
2 Gas Engine Vibrators		54.80		60.28	1.14	1.26
48 L.H., Daily Totals		$1813.60		$2743.48	$37.78	$57.16
Crew C-7	**Hr.**	**Daily**	**Hr.**	**Daily**	**Bare Costs**	**Incl. O&P**
1 Labor Foreman (outside)	$37.10	$296.80	$57.10	$456.80	$38.08	$57.99
5 Laborers	35.10	1404.00	54.00	2160.00		
1 Cement Finisher	42.35	338.80	62.30	498.40		
1 Equip. Oper. (med.)	46.55	372.40	70.25	562.00		
1 Equip. Oper. (oiler)	41.25	330.00	62.25	498.00		
2 Gas Engine Vibrators		54.80		60.28		
1 Concrete Bucket, 1 C.Y.		22.40		24.64		
1 Hyd. Crane, 55 Ton		1100.00		1210.00	16.35	17.98
72 L.H., Daily Totals		$3919.20		$5470.12	$54.43	$75.97
Crew C-7A	**Hr.**	**Daily**	**Hr.**	**Daily**	**Bare Costs**	**Incl. O&P**
1 Labor Foreman (outside)	$37.10	$296.80	$57.10	$456.80	$35.40	$54.27
5 Laborers	35.10	1404.00	54.00	2160.00		
2 Truck Drivers (Heavy)	35.30	564.80	53.55	856.80		
2 Conc. Transit Mixers		1855.60		2041.16	28.99	31.89
64 L.H., Daily Totals		$4121.20		$5514.76	$64.39	$86.17
Crew C-7B	**Hr.**	**Daily**	**Hr.**	**Daily**	**Bare Costs**	**Incl. O&P**
1 Labor Foreman (outside)	$37.10	$296.80	$57.10	$456.80	$37.71	$57.69
5 Laborers	35.10	1404.00	54.00	2160.00		
1 Equipment Oper. (crane)	47.80	382.40	72.15	577.20		
1 Equipment Oiler	41.25	330.00	62.25	498.00		
1 Conc. Bucket, 2 C.Y.		35.20		38.72		
1 Lattice Boom Crane, 165 Ton		1907.00		2097.70	30.35	33.38
64 L.H., Daily Totals		$4355.40		$5828.42	$68.05	$91.07
Crew C-7C	**Hr.**	**Daily**	**Hr.**	**Daily**	**Bare Costs**	**Incl. O&P**
1 Labor Foreman (outside)	$37.10	$296.80	$57.10	$456.80	$38.21	$58.45
5 Laborers	35.10	1404.00	54.00	2160.00		
2 Equipment Operators (med.)	46.55	744.80	70.25	1124.00		
2 F.E. Loaders, W.M., 4 C.Y.		1222.00		1344.20	19.09	21.00
64 L.H., Daily Totals		$3667.60		$5085.00	$57.31	$79.45
Crew C-7D	**Hr.**	**Daily**	**Hr.**	**Daily**	**Bare Costs**	**Incl. O&P**
1 Labor Foreman (outside)	$37.10	$296.80	$57.10	$456.80	$37.02	$56.76
5 Laborers	35.10	1404.00	54.00	2160.00		
1 Equip. Oper. (med.)	46.55	372.40	70.25	562.00		
1 Concrete Conveyer		186.00		204.60	3.32	3.65
56 L.H., Daily Totals		$2259.20		$3383.40	$40.34	$60.42

Crew No.	Bare Costs		Incl. Subs O&P		Cost Per Labor-Hour	
Crew C-8	**Hr.**	**Daily**	**Hr.**	**Daily**	**Bare Costs**	**Incl. O&P**
1 Labor Foreman (outside)	$37.10	$296.80	$57.10	$456.80	$39.09	$59.14
3 Laborers	35.10	842.40	54.00	1296.00		
2 Cement Finishers	42.35	677.60	62.30	996.80		
1 Equip. Oper. (med.)	46.55	372.40	70.25	562.00		
1 Concrete Pump (small)		715.60		787.16	12.78	14.06
56 L.H., Daily Totals		$2904.80		$4098.76	$51.87	$73.19
Crew C-8A	**Hr.**	**Daily**	**Hr.**	**Daily**	**Bare Costs**	**Incl. O&P**
1 Labor Foreman (outside)	$37.10	$296.80	$57.10	$456.80	$37.85	$57.28
3 Laborers	35.10	842.40	54.00	1296.00		
2 Cement Finishers	42.35	677.60	62.30	996.80		
48 L.H., Daily Totals		$1816.80		$2749.60	$37.85	$57.28
Crew C-8B	**Hr.**	**Daily**	**Hr.**	**Daily**	**Bare Costs**	**Incl. O&P**
1 Labor Foreman (outside)	$37.10	$296.80	$57.10	$456.80	$37.79	$57.87
3 Laborers	35.10	842.40	54.00	1296.00		
1 Equip. Oper. (med.)	46.55	372.40	70.25	562.00		
1 Vibrating Power Screed		65.50		72.05		
1 Roller, Vibratory, 25 Ton		640.20		704.22		
1 Dozer, 200 H.P.		1243.00		1367.30	48.72	53.59
40 L.H., Daily Totals		$3460.30		$4458.37	$86.51	$111.46
Crew C-8C	**Hr.**	**Daily**	**Hr.**	**Daily**	**Bare Costs**	**Incl. O&P**
1 Labor Foreman (outside)	$37.10	$296.80	$57.10	$456.80	$38.55	$58.61
3 Laborers	35.10	842.40	54.00	1296.00		
1 Cement Finisher	42.35	338.80	62.30	498.40		
1 Equip. Oper. (med.)	46.55	372.40	70.25	562.00		
1 Shotcrete Rig, 12 C.Y./hr		242.00		266.20		
1 Air Compressor, 160 cfm		136.80		150.48		
4 -50' Air Hoses, 1"		16.40		18.04		
4 -50' Air Hoses, 2"		31.00		34.10	8.88	9.77
48 L.H., Daily Totals		$2276.60		$3282.02	$47.43	$68.38
Crew C-8D	**Hr.**	**Daily**	**Hr.**	**Daily**	**Bare Costs**	**Incl. O&P**
1 Labor Foreman (outside)	$37.10	$296.80	$57.10	$456.80	$39.83	$60.24
1 Laborer	35.10	280.80	54.00	432.00		
1 Cement Finisher	42.35	338.80	62.30	498.40		
1 Equipment Oper. (light)	44.75	358.00	67.55	540.40		
1 Air Compressor, 250 cfm		177.00		194.70		
2 -50' Air Hoses, 1"		8.20		9.02	5.79	6.37
32 L.H., Daily Totals		$1459.60		$2131.32	$45.61	$66.60
Crew C-8E	**Hr.**	**Daily**	**Hr.**	**Daily**	**Bare Costs**	**Incl. O&P**
1 Labor Foreman (outside)	$37.10	$296.80	$57.10	$456.80	$38.25	$58.16
3 Laborers	35.10	842.40	54.00	1296.00		
1 Cement Finisher	42.35	338.80	62.30	498.40		
1 Equipment Oper. (light)	44.75	358.00	67.55	540.40		
1 Shotcrete Rig, 35 C.Y./hr		268.80		295.68		
1 Air Compressor, 250 cfm		177.00		194.70		
4 -50' Air Hoses, 1"		16.40		18.04		
4 -50' Air Hoses, 2"		31.00		34.10	10.28	11.30
48 L.H., Daily Totals		$2329.20		$3334.12	$48.52	$69.46
Crew C-10	**Hr.**	**Daily**	**Hr.**	**Daily**	**Bare Costs**	**Incl. O&P**
1 Laborer	$35.10	$280.80	$54.00	$432.00	$39.93	$59.53
2 Cement Finishers	42.35	677.60	62.30	996.80		
24 L.H., Daily Totals		$958.40		$1428.80	$39.93	$59.53

Crews

Crew No.	Bare Costs Hr.	Bare Costs Daily	Incl. Subs O&P Hr.	Incl. Subs O&P Daily	Cost Per Labor-Hour Bare Costs	Cost Per Labor-Hour Incl. O&P
Crew C-10B						
3 Laborers	$35.10	$842.40	$54.00	$1296.00	$38.00	$57.32
2 Cement Finishers	42.35	677.60	62.30	996.80		
1 Concrete Mixer, 10 C.F.		160.60		176.66		
2 Trowels, 48" Walk-Behind		89.20		98.12	6.25	6.87
40 L.H., Daily Totals		$1769.80		$2567.58	$44.24	$64.19
Crew C-10C						
1 Laborer	$35.10	$280.80	$54.00	$432.00	$39.93	$59.53
2 Cement Finishers	42.35	677.60	62.30	996.80		
1 Trowel, 48" Walk-Behind		44.60		49.06	1.86	2.04
24 L.H., Daily Totals		$1003.00		$1477.86	$41.79	$61.58
Crew C-10D						
1 Laborer	$35.10	$280.80	$54.00	$432.00	$39.93	$59.53
2 Cement Finishers	42.35	677.60	62.30	996.80		
1 Vibrating Power Screed		65.50		72.05		
1 Trowel, 48" Walk-Behind		44.60		49.06	4.59	5.05
24 L.H., Daily Totals		$1068.50		$1549.91	$44.52	$64.58
Crew C-10E						
1 Laborer	$35.10	$280.80	$54.00	$432.00	$39.93	$59.53
2 Cement Finishers	42.35	677.60	62.30	996.80		
1 Vibrating Power Screed		65.50		72.05		
1 Cement Trowel, 96" Ride-On		174.20		191.62	9.99	10.99
24 L.H., Daily Totals		$1198.10		$1692.47	$49.92	$70.52
Crew C-11						
1 Struc. Steel Foreman (outside)	$51.35	$410.80	$91.80	$734.40	$48.50	$83.97
6 Struc. Steel Workers	49.35	2368.80	88.25	4236.00		
1 Equip. Oper. (crane)	47.80	382.40	72.15	577.20		
1 Equip. Oper. Oiler	41.25	330.00	62.25	498.00		
1 Lattice Boom Crane, 150 Ton		1829.00		2011.90	25.40	27.94
72 L.H., Daily Totals		$5321.00		$8057.50	$73.90	$111.91
Crew C-12						
1 Carpenter Foreman (outside)	$46.10	$368.80	$70.95	$567.60	$43.55	$66.78
3 Carpenters	44.10	1058.40	67.85	1628.40		
1 Laborer	35.10	280.80	54.00	432.00		
1 Equip. Oper. (crane)	47.80	382.40	72.15	577.20		
1 Hyd. Crane, 12 Ton		612.00		673.20	12.75	14.03
48 L.H., Daily Totals		$2702.40		$3878.40	$56.30	$80.80
Crew C-13						
1 Struc. Steel Worker	$49.35	$394.80	$88.25	$706.00	$47.60	$81.45
1 Welder	49.35	394.80	88.25	706.00		
1 Carpenter	44.10	352.80	67.85	542.80		
1 Welder, gas engine, 300 amp		121.60		133.76	5.07	5.57
24 L.H., Daily Totals		$1264.00		$2088.56	$52.67	$87.02
Crew C-14						
1 Carpenter Foreman (outside)	$46.10	$368.80	$70.95	$567.60	$43.17	$66.60
5 Carpenters	44.10	1764.00	67.85	2714.00		
4 Laborers	35.10	1123.20	54.00	1728.00		
4 Rodmen (reinf.)	49.10	1571.20	78.40	2508.80		
2 Cement Finishers	42.35	677.60	62.30	996.80		
1 Equip. Oper. (crane)	47.80	382.40	72.15	577.20		
1 Equip. Oper. Oiler	41.25	330.00	62.25	498.00		
1 Hyd. Crane, 80 Ton		1554.00		1709.40	10.79	11.87
144 L.H., Daily Totals		$7771.20		$11299.80	$53.97	$78.47

Crew No.	Bare Costs Hr.	Bare Costs Daily	Incl. Subs O&P Hr.	Incl. Subs O&P Daily	Cost Per Labor-Hour Bare Costs	Cost Per Labor-Hour Incl. O&P
Crew C-14A						
1 Carpenter Foreman (outside)	$46.10	$368.80	$70.95	$567.60	$44.29	$68.43
16 Carpenters	44.10	5644.80	67.85	8684.80		
4 Rodmen (reinf.)	49.10	1571.20	78.40	2508.80		
2 Laborers	35.10	561.60	54.00	864.00		
1 Cement Finisher	42.35	338.80	62.30	498.40		
1 Equip. Oper. (med.)	46.55	372.40	70.25	562.00		
1 Gas Engine Vibrator		27.40		30.14		
1 Concrete Pump (small)		715.60		787.16	3.71	4.09
200 L.H., Daily Totals		$9600.60		$14502.90	$48.00	$72.51
Crew C-14B						
1 Carpenter Foreman (outside)	$46.10	$368.80	$70.95	$567.60	$44.21	$68.19
16 Carpenters	44.10	5644.80	67.85	8684.80		
4 Rodmen (reinf.)	49.10	1571.20	78.40	2508.80		
2 Laborers	35.10	561.60	54.00	864.00		
2 Cement Finishers	42.35	677.60	62.30	996.80		
1 Equip. Oper. (med.)	46.55	372.40	70.25	562.00		
1 Gas Engine Vibrator		27.40		30.14		
1 Concrete Pump (small)		715.60		787.16	3.57	3.93
208 L.H., Daily Totals		$9939.40		$15001.30	$47.79	$72.12
Crew C-14C						
1 Carpenter Foreman (outside)	$46.10	$368.80	$70.95	$567.60	$42.26	$65.22
6 Carpenters	44.10	2116.80	67.85	3256.80		
2 Rodmen (reinf.)	49.10	785.60	78.40	1254.40		
4 Laborers	35.10	1123.20	54.00	1728.00		
1 Cement Finisher	42.35	338.80	62.30	498.40		
1 Gas Engine Vibrator		27.40		30.14	.24	.27
112 L.H., Daily Totals		$4760.60		$7335.34	$42.51	$65.49
Crew C-14D						
1 Carpenter Foreman (outside)	$46.10	$368.80	$70.95	$567.60	$43.89	$67.58
18 Carpenters	44.10	6350.40	67.85	9770.40		
2 Rodmen (reinf.)	49.10	785.60	78.40	1254.40		
2 Laborers	35.10	561.60	54.00	864.00		
1 Cement Finisher	42.35	338.80	62.30	498.40		
1 Equip. Oper. (med.)	46.55	372.40	70.25	562.00		
1 Gas Engine Vibrator		27.40		30.14		
1 Concrete Pump (small)		715.60		787.16	3.71	4.09
200 L.H., Daily Totals		$9520.60		$14334.10	$47.60	$71.67
Crew C-14E						
1 Carpenter Foreman (outside)	$46.10	$368.80	$70.95	$567.60	$43.49	$67.69
2 Carpenters	44.10	705.60	67.85	1085.60		
4 Rodmen (reinf.)	49.10	1571.20	78.40	2508.80		
3 Laborers	35.10	842.40	54.00	1296.00		
1 Cement Finisher	42.35	338.80	62.30	498.40		
1 Gas Engine Vibrator		27.40		30.14	.31	.34
88 L.H., Daily Totals		$3854.20		$5986.54	$43.80	$68.03
Crew C-14F						
1 Labor Foreman (outside)	$37.10	$296.80	$57.10	$456.80	$40.16	$59.88
2 Laborers	35.10	561.60	54.00	864.00		
6 Cement Finishers	42.35	2032.80	62.30	2990.40		
1 Gas Engine Vibrator		27.40		30.14	.38	.42
72 L.H., Daily Totals		$2918.60		$4341.34	$40.54	$60.30

Crews

Crew C-14G

Crew C-14G	Hr.	Daily	Hr.	Daily	Bare Costs	Incl. O&P
1 Labor Foreman (outside)	$37.10	$296.80	$57.10	$456.80	$39.53	$59.19
2 Laborers	35.10	561.60	54.00	864.00		
4 Cement Finishers	42.35	1355.20	62.30	1993.60		
1 Gas Engine Vibrator		27.40		30.14	.49	.54
56 L.H., Daily Totals		$2241.00		$3344.54	$40.02	$59.72

Crew C-14H

Crew C-14H	Hr.	Daily	Hr.	Daily	Bare Costs	Incl. O&P
1 Carpenter Foreman (outside)	$46.10	$368.80	$70.95	$567.60	$43.48	$66.89
2 Carpenters	44.10	705.60	67.85	1085.60		
1 Rodman (reinf.)	49.10	392.80	78.40	627.20		
1 Laborer	35.10	280.80	54.00	432.00		
1 Cement Finisher	42.35	338.80	62.30	498.40		
1 Gas Engine Vibrator		27.40		30.14	.57	.63
48 L.H., Daily Totals		$2114.20		$3240.94	$44.05	$67.52

Crew C-14L

Crew C-14L	Hr.	Daily	Hr.	Daily	Bare Costs	Incl. O&P
1 Carpenter Foreman (outside)	$46.10	$368.80	$70.95	$567.60	$41.12	$63.03
6 Carpenters	44.10	2116.80	67.85	3256.80		
4 Laborers	35.10	1123.20	54.00	1728.00		
1 Cement Finisher	42.35	338.80	62.30	498.40		
1 Gas Engine Vibrator		27.40		30.14	.29	.31
96 L.H., Daily Totals		$3975.00		$6080.94	$41.41	$63.34

Crew C-15

Crew C-15	Hr.	Daily	Hr.	Daily	Bare Costs	Incl. O&P
1 Carpenter Foreman (outside)	$46.10	$368.80	$70.95	$567.60	$41.49	$63.52
2 Carpenters	44.10	705.60	67.85	1085.60		
3 Laborers	35.10	842.40	54.00	1296.00		
2 Cement Finishers	42.35	677.60	62.30	996.80		
1 Rodman (reinf.)	49.10	392.80	78.40	627.20		
72 L.H., Daily Totals		$2987.20		$4573.20	$41.49	$63.52

Crew C-16

Crew C-16	Hr.	Daily	Hr.	Daily	Bare Costs	Incl. O&P
1 Labor Foreman (outside)	$37.10	$296.80	$57.10	$456.80	$39.09	$59.14
3 Laborers	35.10	842.40	54.00	1296.00		
2 Cement Finishers	42.35	677.60	62.30	996.80		
1 Equip. Oper. (med.)	46.55	372.40	70.25	562.00		
1 Gunite Pump Rig		280.40		308.44		
2 -50' Air Hoses, 3/4"		6.10		6.71		
2 -50' Air Hoses, 2"		15.50		17.05	5.39	5.93
56 L.H., Daily Totals		$2491.20		$3643.80	$44.49	$65.07

Crew C-17

Crew C-17	Hr.	Daily	Hr.	Daily	Bare Costs	Incl. O&P
2 Skilled Worker Foremen (out)	$47.40	$758.40	$73.30	$1172.80	$45.80	$70.82
8 Skilled Workers	45.40	2905.60	70.20	4492.80		
80 L.H., Daily Totals		$3664.00		$5665.60	$45.80	$70.82

Crew C-17A

Crew C-17A	Hr.	Daily	Hr.	Daily	Bare Costs	Incl. O&P
2 Skilled Worker Foremen (out)	$47.40	$758.40	$73.30	$1172.80	$45.82	$70.84
8 Skilled Workers	45.40	2905.60	70.20	4492.80		
.125 Equip. Oper. (crane)	47.80	47.80	72.15	72.15		
.125 Hyd. Crane, 80 Ton		194.25		213.68	2.40	2.64
81 L.H., Daily Totals		$3906.05		$5951.43	$48.22	$73.47

Crew C-17B

Crew C-17B	Hr.	Daily	Hr.	Daily	Bare Costs	Incl. O&P
2 Skilled Worker Foremen (out)	$47.40	$758.40	$73.30	$1172.80	$45.85	$70.85
8 Skilled Workers	45.40	2905.60	70.20	4492.80		
.25 Equip. Oper. (crane)	47.80	95.60	72.15	144.30		
.25 Hyd. Crane, 80 Ton		388.50		427.35		
.25 Trowel, 48" Walk-Behind		11.15		12.27	4.87	5.36
82 L.H., Daily Totals		$4159.25		$6249.52	$50.72	$76.21

Crew C-17C

Crew C-17C	Hr.	Daily	Hr.	Daily	Bare Costs	Incl. O&P
2 Skilled Worker Foremen (out)	$47.40	$758.40	$73.30	$1172.80	$45.87	$70.87
8 Skilled Workers	45.40	2905.60	70.20	4492.80		
.375 Equip. Oper. (crane)	47.80	143.40	72.15	216.45		
.375 Hyd. Crane, 80 Ton		582.75		641.02	7.02	7.72
83 L.H., Daily Totals		$4390.15		$6523.07	$52.89	$78.59

Crew C-17D

Crew C-17D	Hr.	Daily	Hr.	Daily	Bare Costs	Incl. O&P
2 Skilled Worker Foremen (out)	$47.40	$758.40	$73.30	$1172.80	$45.90	$70.88
8 Skilled Workers	45.40	2905.60	70.20	4492.80		
.5 Equip. Oper. (crane)	47.80	191.20	72.15	288.60		
.5 Hyd. Crane, 80 Ton		777.00		854.70	9.25	10.18
84 L.H., Daily Totals		$4632.20		$6808.90	$55.15	$81.06

Crew C-17E

Crew C-17E	Hr.	Daily	Hr.	Daily	Bare Costs	Incl. O&P
2 Skilled Worker Foremen (out)	$47.40	$758.40	$73.30	$1172.80	$45.80	$70.82
8 Skilled Workers	45.40	2905.60	70.20	4492.80		
1 Hyd. Jack with Rods		90.70		99.77	1.13	1.25
80 L.H., Daily Totals		$3754.70		$5765.37	$46.93	$72.07

Crew C-18

Crew C-18	Hr.	Daily	Hr.	Daily	Bare Costs	Incl. O&P
.125 Labor Foreman (outside)	$37.10	$37.10	$57.10	$57.10	$35.32	$54.34
1 Laborer	35.10	280.80	54.00	432.00		
1 Concrete Cart, 10 C.F.		56.80		62.48	6.31	6.94
9 L.H., Daily Totals		$374.70		$551.58	$41.63	$61.29

Crew C-19

Crew C-19	Hr.	Daily	Hr.	Daily	Bare Costs	Incl. O&P
.125 Labor Foreman (outside)	$37.10	$37.10	$57.10	$57.10	$35.32	$54.34
1 Laborer	35.10	280.80	54.00	432.00		
1 Concrete Cart, 18 C.F.		94.40		103.84	10.49	11.54
9 L.H., Daily Totals		$412.30		$592.94	$45.81	$65.88

Crew C-20

Crew C-20	Hr.	Daily	Hr.	Daily	Bare Costs	Incl. O&P
1 Labor Foreman (outside)	$37.10	$296.80	$57.10	$456.80	$37.69	$57.46
5 Laborers	35.10	1404.00	54.00	2160.00		
1 Cement Finisher	42.35	338.80	62.30	498.40		
1 Equip. Oper. (med.)	46.55	372.40	70.25	562.00		
2 Gas Engine Vibrators		54.80		60.28		
1 Concrete Pump (small)		715.60		787.16	12.04	13.24
64 L.H., Daily Totals		$3182.40		$4524.64	$49.73	$70.70

Crew C-21

Crew C-21	Hr.	Daily	Hr.	Daily	Bare Costs	Incl. O&P
1 Labor Foreman (outside)	$37.10	$296.80	$57.10	$456.80	$37.69	$57.46
5 Laborers	35.10	1404.00	54.00	2160.00		
1 Cement Finisher	42.35	338.80	62.30	498.40		
1 Equip. Oper. (med.)	46.55	372.40	70.25	562.00		
2 Gas Engine Vibrators		54.80		60.28		
1 Concrete Conveyer		186.00		204.60	3.76	4.14
64 L.H., Daily Totals		$2652.80		$3942.08	$41.45	$61.60

Crew C-22

Crew C-22	Hr.	Daily	Hr.	Daily	Bare Costs	Incl. O&P
1 Rodman Foreman (outside)	$51.10	$408.80	$81.60	$652.80	$49.26	$78.48
4 Rodmen (reinf.)	49.10	1571.20	78.40	2508.80		
.125 Equip. Oper. (crane)	47.80	47.80	72.15	72.15		
.125 Equip. Oper. Oiler	41.25	41.25	62.25	62.25		
.125 Hyd. Crane, 25 Ton		87.15		95.86	2.08	2.28
42 L.H., Daily Totals		$2156.20		$3391.86	$51.34	$80.76

Crews

Crew No.	Bare Costs		Incl. Subs O&P		Cost Per Labor-Hour	
Crew C-23	Hr.	Daily	Hr.	Daily	**Bare Costs**	**Incl. O&P**
2 Skilled Worker Foremen (out)	$47.40	$758.40	$73.30	$1172.80	$45.63	$70.22
6 Skilled Workers	45.40	2179.20	70.20	3369.60		
1 Equip. Oper. (crane)	47.80	382.40	72.15	577.20		
1 Equip. Oper. Oiler	41.25	330.00	62.25	498.00		
1 Lattice Boom Crane, 90 Ton		1497.00		1646.70	18.71	20.58
80 L.H., Daily Totals		$5147.00		$7264.30	$64.34	$90.80
Crew C-23A	Hr.	Daily	Hr.	Daily	**Bare Costs**	**Incl. O&P**
1 Labor Foreman (outside)	$37.10	$296.80	$57.10	$456.80	$39.27	$59.90
2 Laborers	35.10	561.60	54.00	864.00		
1 Equip. Oper. (crane)	47.80	382.40	72.15	577.20		
1 Equip. Oper. Oiler	41.25	330.00	62.25	498.00		
1 Crawler Crane, 100 Ton		1628.00		1790.80		
3 Conc. Buckets, 8 C.Y.		598.20		658.02	55.66	61.22
40 L.H., Daily Totals		$3797.00		$4844.82	$94.92	$121.12
Crew C-24	Hr.	Daily	Hr.	Daily	**Bare Costs**	**Incl. O&P**
2 Skilled Worker Foremen (out)	$47.40	$758.40	$73.30	$1172.80	$45.63	$70.22
6 Skilled Workers	45.40	2179.20	70.20	3369.60		
1 Equip. Oper. (crane)	47.80	382.40	72.15	577.20		
1 Equip. Oper. Oiler	41.25	330.00	62.25	498.00		
1 Lattice Boom Crane, 150 Ton		1829.00		2011.90	22.86	25.15
80 L.H., Daily Totals		$5479.00		$7629.50	$68.49	$95.37
Crew C-25	Hr.	Daily	Hr.	Daily	**Bare Costs**	**Incl. O&P**
2 Rodmen (reinf.)	$49.10	$785.60	$78.40	$1254.40	$38.48	$62.55
2 Rodmen Helpers	27.85	445.60	46.70	747.20		
32 L.H., Daily Totals		$1231.20		$2001.60	$38.48	$62.55
Crew C-27	Hr.	Daily	Hr.	Daily	**Bare Costs**	**Incl. O&P**
2 Cement Finishers	$42.35	$677.60	$62.30	$996.80	$42.35	$62.30
1 Concrete Saw		148.00		162.80	9.25	10.18
16 L.H., Daily Totals		$825.60		$1159.60	$51.60	$72.47
Crew C-28	Hr.	Daily	Hr.	Daily	**Bare Costs**	**Incl. O&P**
1 Cement Finisher	$42.35	$338.80	$62.30	$498.40	$42.35	$62.30
1 Portable Air Compressor, Gas		17.55		19.31	2.19	2.41
8 L.H., Daily Totals		$356.35		$517.71	$44.54	$64.71
Crew C-29	Hr.	Daily	Hr.	Daily	**Bare Costs**	**Incl. O&P**
1 Laborer	$35.10	$280.80	$54.00	$432.00	$35.10	$54.00
1 Pressure Washer		63.00		69.30	7.88	8.66
8 L.H., Daily Totals		$343.80		$501.30	$42.98	$62.66
Crew C-30	Hr.	Daily	Hr.	Daily	**Bare Costs**	**Incl. O&P**
1 Laborer	$35.10	$280.80	$54.00	$432.00	$35.10	$54.00
1 Concrete Mixer, 10 C.F.		160.60		176.66	20.07	22.08
8 L.H., Daily Totals		$441.40		$608.66	$55.17	$76.08
Crew D-1	Hr.	Daily	Hr.	Daily	**Bare Costs**	**Incl. O&P**
1 Bricklayer	$44.10	$352.80	$66.60	$532.80	$39.85	$60.17
1 Bricklayer Helper	35.60	284.80	53.75	430.00		
16 L.H., Daily Totals		$637.60		$962.80	$39.85	$60.17
Crew D-2	Hr.	Daily	Hr.	Daily	**Bare Costs**	**Incl. O&P**
3 Bricklayers	$44.10	$1058.40	$66.60	$1598.40	$41.01	$62.04
2 Bricklayer Helpers	35.60	569.60	53.75	860.00		
.5 Carpenter	44.10	176.40	67.85	271.40		
44 L.H., Daily Totals		$1804.40		$2729.80	$41.01	$62.04
Crew D-3	Hr.	Daily	Hr.	Daily	**Bare Costs**	**Incl. O&P**
3 Bricklayers	$44.10	$1058.40	$66.60	$1598.40	$40.86	$61.76
2 Bricklayer Helpers	35.60	569.60	53.75	860.00		
.25 Carpenter	44.10	88.20	67.85	135.70		
42 L.H., Daily Totals		$1716.20		$2594.10	$40.86	$61.76
Crew D-4	Hr.	Daily	Hr.	Daily	**Bare Costs**	**Incl. O&P**
1 Bricklayer	$44.10	$352.80	$66.60	$532.80	$40.01	$60.41
2 Bricklayer Helpers	35.60	569.60	53.75	860.00		
1 Equip. Oper. (light)	44.75	358.00	67.55	540.40		
1 Grout Pump, 50 C.F./hr.		127.40		140.14	3.98	4.38
32 L.H., Daily Totals		$1407.80		$2073.34	$43.99	$64.79
Crew D-5	Hr.	Daily	Hr.	Daily	**Bare Costs**	**Incl. O&P**
1 Bricklayer	$44.10	$352.80	$66.60	$532.80	$44.10	$66.60
8 L.H., Daily Totals		$352.80		$532.80	$44.10	$66.60
Crew D-6	Hr.	Daily	Hr.	Daily	**Bare Costs**	**Incl. O&P**
3 Bricklayers	$44.10	$1058.40	$66.60	$1598.40	$40.02	$60.48
3 Bricklayer Helpers	35.60	854.40	53.75	1290.00		
.25 Carpenter	44.10	88.20	67.85	135.70		
50 L.H., Daily Totals		$2001.00		$3024.10	$40.02	$60.48
Crew D-7	Hr.	Daily	Hr.	Daily	**Bare Costs**	**Incl. O&P**
1 Tile Layer	$40.75	$326.00	$59.85	$478.80	$36.42	$53.50
1 Tile Layer Helper	32.10	256.80	47.15	377.20		
16 L.H., Daily Totals		$582.80		$856.00	$36.42	$53.50
Crew D-8	Hr.	Daily	Hr.	Daily	**Bare Costs**	**Incl. O&P**
3 Bricklayers	$44.10	$1058.40	$66.60	$1598.40	$40.70	$61.46
2 Bricklayer Helpers	35.60	569.60	53.75	860.00		
40 L.H., Daily Totals		$1628.00		$2458.40	$40.70	$61.46
Crew D-9	Hr.	Daily	Hr.	Daily	**Bare Costs**	**Incl. O&P**
3 Bricklayers	$44.10	$1058.40	$66.60	$1598.40	$39.85	$60.17
3 Bricklayer Helpers	35.60	854.40	53.75	1290.00		
48 L.H., Daily Totals		$1912.80		$2888.40	$39.85	$60.17
Crew D-10	Hr.	Daily	Hr.	Daily	**Bare Costs**	**Incl. O&P**
1 Bricklayer Foreman (outside)	$46.10	$368.80	$69.60	$556.80	$43.40	$65.53
1 Bricklayer	44.10	352.80	66.60	532.80		
1 Bricklayer Helper	35.60	284.80	53.75	430.00		
1 Equip. Oper. (crane)	47.80	382.40	72.15	577.20		
1 S.P. Crane, 4x4, 12 Ton		448.20		493.02	14.01	15.41
32 L.H., Daily Totals		$1837.00		$2589.82	$57.41	$80.93
Crew D-11	Hr.	Daily	Hr.	Daily	**Bare Costs**	**Incl. O&P**
1 Bricklayer Foreman (outside)	$46.10	$368.80	$69.60	$556.80	$41.93	$63.32
1 Bricklayer	44.10	352.80	66.60	532.80		
1 Bricklayer Helper	35.60	284.80	53.75	430.00		
24 L.H., Daily Totals		$1006.40		$1519.60	$41.93	$63.32
Crew D-12	Hr.	Daily	Hr.	Daily	**Bare Costs**	**Incl. O&P**
1 Bricklayer Foreman (outside)	$46.10	$368.80	$69.60	$556.80	$40.35	$60.92
1 Bricklayer	44.10	352.80	66.60	532.80		
2 Bricklayer Helpers	35.60	569.60	53.75	860.00		
32 L.H., Daily Totals		$1291.20		$1949.60	$40.35	$60.92

Crew D-13

Crew D-13	Hr.	Daily	Hr.	Daily	Bare Costs	Incl. O&P
1 Bricklayer Foreman (outside)	$46.10	$368.80	$69.60	$556.80	$42.22	$63.95
1 Bricklayer	44.10	352.80	66.60	532.80		
2 Bricklayer Helpers	35.60	569.60	53.75	860.00		
1 Carpenter	44.10	352.80	67.85	542.80		
1 Equip. Oper. (crane)	47.80	382.40	72.15	577.20		
1 S.P. Crane, 4x4, 12 Ton		448.20		493.02	9.34	10.27
48 L.H., Daily Totals		$2474.60		$3562.62	$51.55	$74.22

Crew E-1

Crew E-1	Hr.	Daily	Hr.	Daily	Bare Costs	Incl. O&P
1 Welder Foreman (outside)	$51.35	$410.80	$91.80	$734.40	$48.48	$82.53
1 Welder	49.35	394.80	88.25	706.00		
1 Equip. Oper. (light)	44.75	358.00	67.55	540.40		
1 Welder, gas engine, 300 amp		121.60		133.76	5.07	5.57
24 L.H., Daily Totals		$1285.20		$2114.56	$53.55	$88.11

Crew E-2

Crew E-2	Hr.	Daily	Hr.	Daily	Bare Costs	Incl. O&P
1 Struc. Steel Foreman (outside)	$51.35	$410.80	$91.80	$734.40	$48.26	$82.74
4 Struc. Steel Workers	49.35	1579.20	88.25	2824.00		
1 Equip. Oper. (crane)	47.80	382.40	72.15	577.20		
1 Equip. Oper. Oiler	41.25	330.00	62.25	498.00		
1 Lattice Boom Crane, 90 Ton		1497.00		1646.70	26.73	29.41
56 L.H., Daily Totals		$4199.40		$6280.30	$74.99	$112.15

Crew E-3

Crew E-3	Hr.	Daily	Hr.	Daily	Bare Costs	Incl. O&P
1 Struc. Steel Foreman (outside)	$51.35	$410.80	$91.80	$734.40	$50.02	$89.43
1 Struc. Steel Worker	49.35	394.80	88.25	706.00		
1 Welder	49.35	394.80	88.25	706.00		
1 Welder, gas engine, 300 amp		121.60		133.76	5.07	5.57
24 L.H., Daily Totals		$1322.00		$2280.16	$55.08	$95.01

Crew E-4

Crew E-4	Hr.	Daily	Hr.	Daily	Bare Costs	Incl. O&P
1 Struc. Steel Foreman (outside)	$51.35	$410.80	$91.80	$734.40	$49.85	$89.14
3 Struc. Steel Workers	49.35	1184.40	88.25	2118.00		
1 Welder, gas engine, 300 amp		121.60		133.76	3.80	4.18
32 L.H., Daily Totals		$1716.80		$2986.16	$53.65	$93.32

Crew E-5

Crew E-5	Hr.	Daily	Hr.	Daily	Bare Costs	Incl. O&P
2 Struc. Steel Foremen (outside)	$51.35	$821.60	$91.80	$1468.80	$48.78	$84.75
5 Struc. Steel Workers	49.35	1974.00	88.25	3530.00		
1 Equip. Oper. (crane)	47.80	382.40	72.15	577.20		
1 Welder	49.35	394.80	88.25	706.00		
1 Equip. Oper. Oiler	41.25	330.00	62.25	498.00		
1 Lattice Boom Crane, 90 Ton		1497.00		1646.70		
1 Welder, gas engine, 300 amp		121.60		133.76	20.23	22.26
80 L.H., Daily Totals		$5521.40		$8560.46	$69.02	$107.01

Crew E-6

Crew E-6	Hr.	Daily	Hr.	Daily	Bare Costs	Incl. O&P
3 Struc. Steel Foremen (outside)	$51.35	$1232.40	$91.80	$2203.20	$48.83	$84.99
9 Struc. Steel Workers	49.35	3553.20	88.25	6354.00		
1 Equip. Oper. (crane)	47.80	382.40	72.15	577.20		
1 Welder	49.35	394.80	88.25	706.00		
1 Equip. Oper. Oiler	41.25	330.00	62.25	498.00		
1 Equip. Oper. (light)	44.75	358.00	67.55	540.40		
1 Lattice Boom Crane, 90 Ton		1497.00		1646.70		
1 Welder, gas engine, 300 amp		121.60		133.76		
1 Air Compressor, 160 cfm		136.80		150.48		
2 Impact Wrenches		36.00		39.60	14.00	15.39
128 L.H., Daily Totals		$8042.20		$12849.34	$62.83	$100.39

Crew E-7

Crew E-7	Hr.	Daily	Hr.	Daily	Bare Costs	Incl. O&P
1 Struc. Steel Foreman (outside)	$51.35	$410.80	$91.80	$734.40	$48.78	$84.75
4 Struc. Steel Workers	49.35	1579.20	88.25	2824.00		
1 Equip. Oper. (crane)	47.80	382.40	72.15	577.20		
1 Equip. Oper. Oiler	41.25	330.00	62.25	498.00		
1 Welder Foreman (outside)	51.35	410.80	91.80	734.40		
2 Welders	49.35	789.60	88.25	1412.00		
1 Lattice Boom Crane, 90 Ton		1497.00		1646.70		
2 Welders, gas engine, 300 amp		243.20		267.52	21.75	23.93
80 L.H., Daily Totals		$5643.00		$8694.22	$70.54	$108.68

Crew E-8

Crew E-8	Hr.	Daily	Hr.	Daily	Bare Costs	Incl. O&P
1 Struc. Steel Foreman (outside)	$51.35	$410.80	$91.80	$734.40	$48.56	$83.97
4 Struc. Steel Workers	49.35	1579.20	88.25	2824.00		
1 Welder Foreman (outside)	51.35	410.80	91.80	734.40		
4 Welders	49.35	1579.20	88.25	2824.00		
1 Equip. Oper. (crane)	47.80	382.40	72.15	577.20		
1 Equip. Oper. Oiler	41.25	330.00	62.25	498.00		
1 Equip. Oper. (light)	44.75	358.00	67.55	540.40		
1 Lattice Boom Crane, 90 Ton		1497.00		1646.70		
4 Welders, gas engine, 300 amp		486.40		535.04	19.07	20.98
104 L.H., Daily Totals		$7033.80		$10914.14	$67.63	$104.94

Crew E-9

Crew E-9	Hr.	Daily	Hr.	Daily	Bare Costs	Incl. O&P
2 Struc. Steel Foremen (outside)	$51.35	$821.60	$91.80	$1468.80	$48.83	$84.99
5 Struc. Steel Workers	49.35	1974.00	88.25	3530.00		
1 Welder Foreman (outside)	51.35	410.80	91.80	734.40		
5 Welders	49.35	1974.00	88.25	3530.00		
1 Equip. Oper. (crane)	47.80	382.40	72.15	577.20		
1 Equip. Oper. Oiler	41.25	330.00	62.25	498.00		
1 Equip. Oper. (light)	44.75	358.00	67.55	540.40		
1 Lattice Boom Crane, 90 Ton		1497.00		1646.70		
5 Welders, gas engine, 300 amp		608.00		668.80	16.45	18.09
128 L.H., Daily Totals		$8355.80		$13194.30	$65.28	$103.08

Crew E-10

Crew E-10	Hr.	Daily	Hr.	Daily	Bare Costs	Incl. O&P
1 Welder Foreman (outside)	$51.35	$410.80	$91.80	$734.40	$50.35	$90.03
1 Welder	49.35	394.80	88.25	706.00		
1 Welder, gas engine, 300 amp		121.60		133.76		
1 Flatbed Truck, Gas, 3 Ton		264.40		290.84	24.13	26.54
16 L.H., Daily Totals		$1191.60		$1865.00	$74.47	$116.56

Crew E-11

Crew E-11	Hr.	Daily	Hr.	Daily	Bare Costs	Incl. O&P
2 Painters, Struc. Steel	$39.30	$628.80	$71.15	$1138.40	$39.61	$65.96
1 Building Laborer	35.10	280.80	54.00	432.00		
1 Equip. Oper. (light)	44.75	358.00	67.55	540.40		
1 Air Compressor, 250 cfm		177.00		194.70		
1 Sandblaster, portable, 3 C.F.		20.40		22.44		
1 Set Sand Blasting Accessories		13.35		14.69	6.59	7.24
32 L.H., Daily Totals		$1478.35		$2342.63	$46.20	$73.21

Crew E-12

Crew E-12	Hr.	Daily	Hr.	Daily	Bare Costs	Incl. O&P
1 Welder Foreman (outside)	$51.35	$410.80	$91.80	$734.40	$48.05	$79.67
1 Equip. Oper. (light)	44.75	358.00	67.55	540.40		
1 Welder, gas engine, 300 amp		121.60		133.76	7.60	8.36
16 L.H., Daily Totals		$890.40		$1408.56	$55.65	$88.03

Crew E-13

Crew E-13	Hr.	Daily	Hr.	Daily	Bare Costs	Incl. O&P
1 Welder Foreman (outside)	$51.35	$410.80	$91.80	$734.40	$49.15	$83.72
.5 Equip. Oper. (light)	44.75	179.00	67.55	270.20		
1 Welder, gas engine, 300 amp		121.60		133.76	10.13	11.15
12 L.H., Daily Totals		$711.40		$1138.36	$59.28	$94.86

Crews

Crew E-14	Hr.	Daily	Hr.	Daily	Bare Costs	Incl. O&P
1 Welder Foreman (outside)	$51.35	$410.80	$91.80	$734.40	$51.35	$91.80
1 Welder, gas engine, 300 amp		121.60		133.76	15.20	16.72
8 L.H., Daily Totals		$532.40		$868.16	$66.55	$108.52

Crew E-16	Hr.	Daily	Hr.	Daily	Bare Costs	Incl. O&P
1 Welder Foreman (outside)	$51.35	$410.80	$91.80	$734.40	$50.35	$90.03
1 Welder	49.35	394.80	88.25	706.00		
1 Welder, gas engine, 300 amp		121.60		133.76	7.60	8.36
16 L.H., Daily Totals		$927.20		$1574.16	$57.95	$98.39

Crew E-17	Hr.	Daily	Hr.	Daily	Bare Costs	Incl. O&P
1 Struc. Steel Foreman (outside)	$51.35	$410.80	$91.80	$734.40	$50.35	$90.03
1 Structural Steel Worker	49.35	394.80	88.25	706.00		
16 L.H., Daily Totals		$805.60		$1440.40	$50.35	$90.03

Crew E-18	Hr.	Daily	Hr.	Daily	Bare Costs	Incl. O&P
1 Struc. Steel Foreman (outside)	$51.35	$410.80	$91.80	$734.40	$49.19	$85.36
3 Structural Steel Workers	49.35	1184.40	88.25	2118.00		
1 Equipment Operator (med.)	46.55	372.40	70.25	562.00		
1 Lattice Boom Crane, 20 Ton		950.65		1045.71	23.77	26.14
40 L.H., Daily Totals		$2918.25		$4460.11	$72.96	$111.50

Crew E-19	Hr.	Daily	Hr.	Daily	Bare Costs	Incl. O&P
1 Structural Steel Worker	$49.35	$394.80	$88.25	$706.00	$48.48	$82.53
1 Struc. Steel Foreman (outside)	51.35	410.80	91.80	734.40		
1 Equip. Oper. (light)	44.75	358.00	67.55	540.40		
1 Lattice Boom Crane, 20 Ton		950.65		1045.71	39.61	43.57
24 L.H., Daily Totals		$2114.25		$3026.51	$88.09	$126.10

Crew E-20	Hr.	Daily	Hr.	Daily	Bare Costs	Incl. O&P
1 Struc. Steel Foreman (outside)	$51.35	$410.80	$91.80	$734.40	$48.39	$83.43
5 Structural Steel Workers	49.35	1974.00	88.25	3530.00		
1 Equip. Oper. (crane)	47.80	382.40	72.15	577.20		
1 Oiler	41.25	330.00	62.25	498.00		
1 Lattice Boom Crane, 40 Ton		1163.00		1279.30	18.17	19.99
64 L.H., Daily Totals		$4260.20		$6618.90	$66.57	$103.42

Crew E-22	Hr.	Daily	Hr.	Daily	Bare Costs	Incl. O&P
1 Skilled Worker Foreman (out)	$47.40	$379.20	$73.30	$586.40	$46.07	$71.23
2 Skilled Workers	45.40	726.40	70.20	1123.20		
24 L.H., Daily Totals		$1105.60		$1709.60	$46.07	$71.23

Crew E-24	Hr.	Daily	Hr.	Daily	Bare Costs	Incl. O&P
3 Structural Steel Workers	$49.35	$1184.40	$88.25	$2118.00	$48.65	$83.75
1 Equipment Operator (med.)	46.55	372.40	70.25	562.00		
1 Hyd. Crane, 25 Ton		697.20		766.92	21.79	23.97
32 L.H., Daily Totals		$2254.00		$3446.92	$70.44	$107.72

Crew E-25	Hr.	Daily	Hr.	Daily	Bare Costs	Incl. O&P
1 Welder Foreman (outside)	$51.35	$410.80	$91.80	$734.40	$51.35	$91.80
1 Cutting Torch		10.80		11.88		
1 Set of Gases		86.40		95.04	12.15	13.37
8 L.H., Daily Totals		$508.00		$841.32	$63.50	$105.17

Crew F-3	Hr.	Daily	Hr.	Daily	Bare Costs	Incl. O&P
4 Carpenters	$44.10	$1411.20	$67.85	$2171.20	$44.84	$68.71
1 Equip. Oper. (crane)	47.80	382.40	72.15	577.20		
1 Hyd. Crane, 12 Ton		612.00		673.20	15.30	16.83
40 L.H., Daily Totals		$2405.60		$3421.60	$60.14	$85.54

Crew F-4	Hr.	Daily	Hr.	Daily	Bare Costs	Incl. O&P
4 Carpenters	$44.10	$1411.20	$67.85	$2171.20	$44.24	$67.63
1 Equip. Oper. (crane)	47.80	382.40	72.15	577.20		
1 Equip. Oper. Oiler	41.25	330.00	62.25	498.00		
1 Hyd. Crane, 55 Ton		1100.00		1210.00	22.92	25.21
48 L.H., Daily Totals		$3223.60		$4456.40	$67.16	$92.84

Crew F-5	Hr.	Daily	Hr.	Daily	Bare Costs	Incl. O&P
1 Carpenter Foreman (outside)	$46.10	$368.80	$70.95	$567.60	$44.60	$68.63
3 Carpenters	44.10	1058.40	67.85	1628.40		
32 L.H., Daily Totals		$1427.20		$2196.00	$44.60	$68.63

Crew F-6	Hr.	Daily	Hr.	Daily	Bare Costs	Incl. O&P
2 Carpenters	$44.10	$705.60	$67.85	$1085.60	$41.24	$63.17
2 Building Laborers	35.10	561.60	54.00	864.00		
1 Equip. Oper. (crane)	47.80	382.40	72.15	577.20		
1 Hyd. Crane, 12 Ton		612.00		673.20	15.30	16.83
40 L.H., Daily Totals		$2261.60		$3200.00	$56.54	$80.00

Crew F-7	Hr.	Daily	Hr.	Daily	Bare Costs	Incl. O&P
2 Carpenters	$44.10	$705.60	$67.85	$1085.60	$39.60	$60.92
2 Building Laborers	35.10	561.60	54.00	864.00		
32 L.H., Daily Totals		$1267.20		$1949.60	$39.60	$60.92

Crew G-1	Hr.	Daily	Hr.	Daily	Bare Costs	Incl. O&P
1 Roofer Foreman (outside)	$39.40	$315.20	$66.05	$528.40	$34.96	$58.61
4 Roofers, Composition	37.40	1196.80	62.70	2006.40		
2 Roofer Helpers	27.85	445.60	46.70	747.20		
1 Application Equipment		179.20		197.12		
1 Tar Kettle/Pot		91.00		100.10		
1 Crew Truck		182.40		200.64	8.08	8.89
56 L.H., Daily Totals		$2410.20		$3779.86	$43.04	$67.50

Crew G-2	Hr.	Daily	Hr.	Daily	Bare Costs	Incl. O&P
1 Plasterer	$40.35	$322.80	$60.40	$483.20	$37.07	$55.97
1 Plasterer Helper	35.75	286.00	53.50	428.00		
1 Building Laborer	35.10	280.80	54.00	432.00		
1 Grout Pump, 50 C.F./hr.		127.40		140.14	5.31	5.84
24 L.H., Daily Totals		$1017.00		$1483.34	$42.38	$61.81

Crew G-2A	Hr.	Daily	Hr.	Daily	Bare Costs	Incl. O&P
1 Roofer, composition	$37.40	$299.20	$62.70	$501.60	$33.45	$54.47
1 Roofer Helper	27.85	222.80	46.70	373.60		
1 Building Laborer	35.10	280.80	54.00	432.00		
1 Foam spray rig, trailer-mtd.		503.85		554.24		
1 Pickup Truck, 3/4 Ton		127.00		139.70	26.29	28.91
24 L.H., Daily Totals		$1433.65		$2001.14	$59.74	$83.38

Crew G-3	Hr.	Daily	Hr.	Daily	Bare Costs	Incl. O&P
2 Sheet Metal Workers	$52.15	$834.40	$79.50	$1272.00	$43.63	$66.75
2 Building Laborers	35.10	561.60	54.00	864.00		
32 L.H., Daily Totals		$1396.00		$2136.00	$43.63	$66.75

Crew G-4	Hr.	Daily	Hr.	Daily	Bare Costs	Incl. O&P
1 Labor Foreman (outside)	$37.10	$296.80	$57.10	$456.80	$35.77	$55.03
2 Building Laborers	35.10	561.60	54.00	864.00		
1 Flatbed Truck, Gas, 1.5 Ton		211.00		232.10		
1 Air Compressor, 160 cfm		136.80		150.48	14.49	15.94
24 L.H., Daily Totals		$1206.20		$1703.38	$50.26	$70.97

Crew No.	Bare Costs		Incl. Subs O&P		Cost Per Labor-Hour	

Crew G-5	Hr.	Daily	Hr.	Daily	Bare Costs	Incl. O&P
1 Roofer Foreman (outside)	$39.40	$315.20	$66.05	$528.40	$33.98	$56.97
2 Roofers, Composition	37.40	598.40	62.70	1003.20		
2 Roofer Helpers	27.85	445.60	46.70	747.20		
1 Application Equipment		179.20		197.12	4.48	4.93
40 L.H., Daily Totals		$1538.40		$2475.92	$38.46	$61.90

Crew G-6A	Hr.	Daily	Hr.	Daily	Bare Costs	Incl. O&P
2 Roofers Composition	$37.40	$598.40	$62.70	$1003.20	$37.40	$62.70
1 Small Compressor, Electric		10.10		11.11		
2 Pneumatic Nailers		45.70		50.27	3.49	3.84
16 L.H., Daily Totals		$654.20		$1064.58	$40.89	$66.54

Crew G-7	Hr.	Daily	Hr.	Daily	Bare Costs	Incl. O&P
1 Carpenter	$44.10	$352.80	$67.85	$542.80	$44.10	$67.85
1 Small Compressor, Electric		10.10		11.11		
1 Pneumatic Nailer		22.85		25.14	4.12	4.53
8 L.H., Daily Totals		$385.75		$579.04	$48.22	$72.38

Crew H-1	Hr.	Daily	Hr.	Daily	Bare Costs	Incl. O&P
2 Glaziers	$42.75	$684.00	$64.75	$1036.00	$46.05	$76.50
2 Struc. Steel Workers	49.35	789.60	88.25	1412.00		
32 L.H., Daily Totals		$1473.60		$2448.00	$46.05	$76.50

Crew H-2	Hr.	Daily	Hr.	Daily	Bare Costs	Incl. O&P
2 Glaziers	$42.75	$684.00	$64.75	$1036.00	$40.20	$61.17
1 Building Laborer	35.10	280.80	54.00	432.00		
24 L.H., Daily Totals		$964.80		$1468.00	$40.20	$61.17

Crew H-3	Hr.	Daily	Hr.	Daily	Bare Costs	Incl. O&P
1 Glazier	$42.75	$342.00	$64.75	$518.00	$38.02	$57.98
1 Helper	33.30	266.40	51.20	409.60		
16 L.H., Daily Totals		$608.40		$927.60	$38.02	$57.98

Crew H-4	Hr.	Daily	Hr.	Daily	Bare Costs	Incl. O&P
1 Carpenter	$44.10	$352.80	$67.85	$542.80	$41.27	$63.03
1 Carpenter Helper	33.30	266.40	51.20	409.60		
.5 Electrician	51.55	206.20	77.05	308.20		
20 L.H., Daily Totals		$825.40		$1260.60	$41.27	$63.03

Crew J-1	Hr.	Daily	Hr.	Daily	Bare Costs	Incl. O&P
3 Plasterers	$40.35	$968.40	$60.40	$1449.60	$38.51	$57.64
2 Plasterer Helpers	35.75	572.00	53.50	856.00		
1 Mixing Machine, 6 C.F.		130.80		143.88	3.27	3.60
40 L.H., Daily Totals		$1671.20		$2449.48	$41.78	$61.24

Crew J-2	Hr.	Daily	Hr.	Daily	Bare Costs	Incl. O&P
3 Plasterers	$40.35	$968.40	$60.40	$1449.60	$38.63	$57.63
2 Plasterer Helpers	35.75	572.00	53.50	856.00		
1 Lather	39.25	314.00	57.60	460.80		
1 Mixing Machine, 6 C.F.		130.80		143.88	2.73	3.00
48 L.H., Daily Totals		$1985.20		$2910.28	$41.36	$60.63

Crew J-3	Hr.	Daily	Hr.	Daily	Bare Costs	Incl. O&P
1 Terrazzo Worker	$40.40	$323.20	$59.35	$474.80	$37.08	$54.48
1 Terrazzo Helper	33.75	270.00	49.60	396.80		
1 Floor Grinder, 22" path		84.70		93.17		
1 Terrazzo Mixer		177.00		194.70	16.36	17.99
16 L.H., Daily Totals		$854.90		$1159.47	$53.43	$72.47

Crew J-4	Hr.	Daily	Hr.	Daily	Bare Costs	Incl. O&P
2 Cement Finishers	$42.35	$677.60	$62.30	$996.80	$39.93	$59.53
1 Laborer	35.10	280.80	54.00	432.00		
1 Floor Grinder, 22" path		84.70		93.17		
1 Floor Edger, 7" path		38.20		42.02		
1 Vacuum Pick-Up System		59.80		65.78	7.61	8.37
24 L.H., Daily Totals		$1141.10		$1629.77	$47.55	$67.91

Crew J-4A	Hr.	Daily	Hr.	Daily	Bare Costs	Incl. O&P
2 Cement Finishers	$42.35	$677.60	$62.30	$996.80	$38.73	$58.15
2 Laborers	35.10	561.60	54.00	864.00		
1 Floor Grinder, 22" path		84.70		93.17		
1 Floor Edger, 7" path		38.20		42.02		
1 Vacuum Pick-Up System		59.80		65.78		
1 Floor Auto Scrubber		178.10		195.91	11.28	12.40
32 L.H., Daily Totals		$1600.00		$2257.68	$50.00	$70.55

Crew J-4B	Hr.	Daily	Hr.	Daily	Bare Costs	Incl. O&P
1 Laborer	$35.10	$280.80	$54.00	$432.00	$35.10	$54.00
1 Floor Auto Scrubber		178.10		195.91	22.26	24.49
8 L.H., Daily Totals		$458.90		$627.91	$57.36	$78.49

Crew J-6	Hr.	Daily	Hr.	Daily	Bare Costs	Incl. O&P
2 Painters	$38.25	$612.00	$57.20	$915.20	$39.09	$58.99
1 Building Laborer	35.10	280.80	54.00	432.00		
1 Equip. Oper. (light)	44.75	358.00	67.55	540.40		
1 Air Compressor, 250 cfm		177.00		194.70		
1 Sandblaster, portable, 3 C.F.		20.40		22.44		
1 Set Sand Blasting Accessories		13.35		14.69	6.59	7.24
32 L.H., Daily Totals		$1461.55		$2119.43	$45.67	$66.23

Crew K-1	Hr.	Daily	Hr.	Daily	Bare Costs	Incl. O&P
1 Carpenter	$44.10	$352.80	$67.85	$542.80	$39.23	$59.98
1 Truck Driver (light)	34.35	274.80	52.10	416.80		
1 Flatbed Truck, Gas, 3 Ton		264.40		290.84	16.52	18.18
16 L.H., Daily Totals		$892.00		$1250.44	$55.75	$78.15

Crew K-2	Hr.	Daily	Hr.	Daily	Bare Costs	Incl. O&P
1 Struc. Steel Foreman (outside)	$51.35	$410.80	$91.80	$734.40	$45.02	$77.38
1 Struc. Steel Worker	49.35	394.80	88.25	706.00		
1 Truck Driver (light)	34.35	274.80	52.10	416.80		
1 Flatbed Truck, Gas, 3 Ton		264.40		290.84	11.02	12.12
24 L.H., Daily Totals		$1344.80		$2148.04	$56.03	$89.50

Crew L-1	Hr.	Daily	Hr.	Daily	Bare Costs	Incl. O&P
1 Electrician	$51.55	$412.40	$77.05	$616.40	$53.08	$79.70
1 Plumber	54.60	436.80	82.35	658.80		
16 L.H., Daily Totals		$849.20		$1275.20	$53.08	$79.70

Crew L-2	Hr.	Daily	Hr.	Daily	Bare Costs	Incl. O&P
1 Carpenter	$44.10	$352.80	$67.85	$542.80	$38.70	$59.52
1 Carpenter Helper	33.30	266.40	51.20	409.60		
16 L.H., Daily Totals		$619.20		$952.40	$38.70	$59.52

Crew L-3	Hr.	Daily	Hr.	Daily	Bare Costs	Incl. O&P
1 Carpenter	$44.10	$352.80	$67.85	$542.80	$47.98	$73.06
.5 Electrician	51.55	206.20	77.05	308.20		
.5 Sheet Metal Worker	52.15	208.60	79.50	318.00		
16 L.H., Daily Totals		$767.60		$1169.00	$47.98	$73.06

Crew No.	Bare Costs		Incl. Subs O&P		Cost Per Labor-Hour	

Crew L-3A

	Hr.	Daily	Hr.	Daily	Bare Costs	Incl. O&P
1 Carpenter Foreman (outside)	$46.10	$368.80	$70.95	$567.60	$48.12	$73.80
.5 Sheet Metal Worker	52.15	208.60	79.50	318.00		
12 L.H., Daily Totals		$577.40		$885.60	$48.12	$73.80

Crew L-4

	Hr.	Daily	Hr.	Daily	Bare Costs	Incl. O&P
2 Skilled Workers	$45.40	$726.40	$70.20	$1123.20	$41.37	$63.87
1 Helper	33.30	266.40	51.20	409.60		
24 L.H., Daily Totals		$992.80		$1532.80	$41.37	$63.87

Crew L-5

	Hr.	Daily	Hr.	Daily	Bare Costs	Incl. O&P
1 Struc. Steel Foreman (outside)	$51.35	$410.80	$91.80	$734.40	$49.41	$86.46
5 Struc. Steel Workers	49.35	1974.00	88.25	3530.00		
1 Equip. Oper. (crane)	47.80	382.40	72.15	577.20		
1 Hyd. Crane, 25 Ton		697.20		766.92	12.45	13.70
56 L.H., Daily Totals		$3464.40		$5608.52	$61.86	$100.15

Crew L-5A

	Hr.	Daily	Hr.	Daily	Bare Costs	Incl. O&P
1 Struc. Steel Foreman (outside)	$51.35	$410.80	$91.80	$734.40	$49.46	$85.11
2 Structural Steel Workers	49.35	789.60	88.25	1412.00		
1 Equip. Oper. (crane)	47.80	382.40	72.15	577.20		
1 S.P. Crane, 4x4, 25 Ton		565.20		621.72	17.66	19.43
32 L.H., Daily Totals		$2148.00		$3345.32	$67.13	$104.54

Crew L-5B

	Hr.	Daily	Hr.	Daily	Bare Costs	Incl. O&P
1 Struc. Steel Foreman (outside)	$51.35	$410.80	$91.80	$734.40	$50.40	$80.53
2 Structural Steel Workers	49.35	789.60	88.25	1412.00		
2 Electricians	51.55	824.80	77.05	1232.80		
2 Steamfitters/Pipefitters	55.70	891.20	84.00	1344.00		
1 Equip. Oper. (crane)	47.80	382.40	72.15	577.20		
1 Equip. Oper. Oiler	41.25	330.00	62.25	498.00		
1 Hyd. Crane, 80 Ton		1554.00		1709.40	21.58	23.74
72 L.H., Daily Totals		$5182.80		$7507.80	$71.98	$104.28

Crew L-6

	Hr.	Daily	Hr.	Daily	Bare Costs	Incl. O&P
1 Plumber	$54.60	$436.80	$82.35	$658.80	$53.58	$80.58
.5 Electrician	51.55	206.20	77.05	308.20		
12 L.H., Daily Totals		$643.00		$967.00	$53.58	$80.58

Crew L-7

	Hr.	Daily	Hr.	Daily	Bare Costs	Incl. O&P
2 Carpenters	$44.10	$705.60	$67.85	$1085.60	$42.59	$65.21
1 Building Laborer	35.10	280.80	54.00	432.00		
.5 Electrician	51.55	206.20	77.05	308.20		
28 L.H., Daily Totals		$1192.60		$1825.80	$42.59	$65.21

Crew L-8

	Hr.	Daily	Hr.	Daily	Bare Costs	Incl. O&P
2 Carpenters	$44.10	$705.60	$67.85	$1085.60	$46.20	$70.75
.5 Plumber	54.60	218.40	82.35	329.40		
20 L.H., Daily Totals		$924.00		$1415.00	$46.20	$70.75

Crew L-9

	Hr.	Daily	Hr.	Daily	Bare Costs	Incl. O&P
1 Labor Foreman (inside)	$35.60	$284.80	$54.80	$438.40	$40.21	$64.35
2 Building Laborers	35.10	561.60	54.00	864.00		
1 Struc. Steel Worker	49.35	394.80	88.25	706.00		
.5 Electrician	51.55	206.20	77.05	308.20		
36 L.H., Daily Totals		$1447.40		$2316.60	$40.21	$64.35

Crew L-10

	Hr.	Daily	Hr.	Daily	Bare Costs	Incl. O&P
1 Struc. Steel Foreman (outside)	$51.35	$410.80	$91.80	$734.40	$49.50	$84.07
1 Structural Steel Worker	49.35	394.80	88.25	706.00		
1 Equip. Oper. (crane)	47.80	382.40	72.15	577.20		
1 Hyd. Crane, 12 Ton		612.00		673.20	25.50	28.05
24 L.H., Daily Totals		$1800.00		$2690.80	$75.00	$112.12

Crew L-11

	Hr.	Daily	Hr.	Daily	Bare Costs	Incl. O&P
2 Wreckers	$35.10	$561.60	$59.40	$950.40	$40.69	$64.63
1 Equip. Oper. (crane)	47.80	382.40	72.15	577.20		
1 Equip. Oper. (light)	44.75	358.00	67.55	540.40		
1 Hyd. Excavator, 2.5 C.Y.		1652.00		1817.20		
1 Loader, Skid Steer, 78 H.P.		281.20		309.32	60.41	66.45
32 L.H., Daily Totals		$3235.20		$4194.52	$101.10	$131.08

Crew M-1

	Hr.	Daily	Hr.	Daily	Bare Costs	Incl. O&P
3 Elevator Constructors	$70.85	$1700.40	$106.15	$2547.60	$67.31	$100.85
1 Elevator Apprentice	56.70	453.60	84.95	679.60		
5 Hand Tools		46.00		50.60	1.44	1.58
32 L.H., Daily Totals		$2200.00		$3277.80	$68.75	$102.43

Crew M-3

	Hr.	Daily	Hr.	Daily	Bare Costs	Incl. O&P
1 Electrician Foreman (outside)	$53.55	$428.40	$80.05	$640.40	$53.61	$80.64
1 Common Laborer	35.10	280.80	54.00	432.00		
.25 Equipment Operator, Med.	46.55	93.10	70.25	140.50		
1 Elevator Constructor	70.85	566.80	106.15	849.20		
1 Elevator Apprentice	56.70	453.60	84.95	679.60		
.25 S.P. Crane, 4x4, 20 Ton		129.85		142.84	3.82	4.20
34 L.H., Daily Totals		$1952.55		$2884.53	$57.43	$84.84

Crew M-4

	Hr.	Daily	Hr.	Daily	Bare Costs	Incl. O&P
1 Electrician Foreman (outside)	$53.55	$428.40	$80.05	$640.40	$52.99	$79.72
1 Common Laborer	35.10	280.80	54.00	432.00		
.25 Equipment Operator, Crane	47.80	95.60	72.15	144.30		
.25 Equipment Operator, Oiler	41.25	82.50	62.25	124.50		
1 Elevator Constructor	70.85	566.80	106.15	849.20		
1 Elevator Apprentice	56.70	453.60	84.95	679.60		
.25 S.P. Crane, 4x4, 40 Ton		166.00		182.60	4.61	5.07
36 L.H., Daily Totals		$2073.70		$3052.60	$57.60	$84.79

Crew Q-1

	Hr.	Daily	Hr.	Daily	Bare Costs	Incl. O&P
1 Plumber	$54.60	$436.80	$82.35	$658.80	$49.15	$74.13
1 Plumber Apprentice	43.70	349.60	65.90	527.20		
16 L.H., Daily Totals		$786.40		$1186.00	$49.15	$74.13

Crew Q-1A

	Hr.	Daily	Hr.	Daily	Bare Costs	Incl. O&P
.25 Plumber Foreman (outside)	$56.60	$113.20	$85.35	$170.70	$55.00	$82.95
1 Plumber	54.60	436.80	82.35	658.80		
10 L.H., Daily Totals		$550.00		$829.50	$55.00	$82.95

Crew Q-1C

	Hr.	Daily	Hr.	Daily	Bare Costs	Incl. O&P
1 Plumber	$54.60	$436.80	$82.35	$658.80	$48.28	$72.83
1 Plumber Apprentice	43.70	349.60	65.90	527.20		
1 Equip. Oper. (medium)	46.55	372.40	70.25	562.00		
1 Trencher, Chain Type, 8' D		2848.00		3132.80	118.67	130.53
24 L.H., Daily Totals		$4006.80		$4880.80	$166.95	$203.37

Crew Q-2

	Hr.	Daily	Hr.	Daily	Bare Costs	Incl. O&P
2 Plumbers	$54.60	$873.60	$82.35	$1317.60	$50.97	$76.87
1 Plumber Apprentice	43.70	349.60	65.90	527.20		
24 L.H., Daily Totals		$1223.20		$1844.80	$50.97	$76.87

Crews

Crew Q-3

Crew Q-3	Hr.	Daily	Hr.	Daily	Bare Costs	Incl. O&P
1 Plumber Foreman (inside)	$55.10	$440.80	$83.10	$664.80	$52.00	$78.42
2 Plumbers	54.60	873.60	82.35	1317.60		
1 Plumber Apprentice	43.70	349.60	65.90	527.20		
32 L.H., Daily Totals		$1664.00		$2509.60	$52.00	$78.42

Crew Q-4

Crew Q-4	Hr.	Daily	Hr.	Daily	Bare Costs	Incl. O&P
1 Plumber Foreman (inside)	$55.10	$440.80	$83.10	$664.80	$52.00	$78.42
1 Plumber	54.60	436.80	82.35	658.80		
1 Welder (plumber)	54.60	436.80	82.35	658.80		
1 Plumber Apprentice	43.70	349.60	65.90	527.20		
1 Welder, electric, 300 amp		36.90		40.59	1.15	1.27
32 L.H., Daily Totals		$1700.90		$2550.19	$53.15	$79.69

Crew Q-5

Crew Q-5	Hr.	Daily	Hr.	Daily	Bare Costs	Incl. O&P
1 Steamfitter	$55.70	$445.60	$84.00	$672.00	$50.13	$75.60
1 Steamfitter Apprentice	44.55	356.40	67.20	537.60		
16 L.H., Daily Totals		$802.00		$1209.60	$50.13	$75.60

Crew Q-6

Crew Q-6	Hr.	Daily	Hr.	Daily	Bare Costs	Incl. O&P
2 Steamfitters	$55.70	$891.20	$84.00	$1344.00	$51.98	$78.40
1 Steamfitter Apprentice	44.55	356.40	67.20	537.60		
24 L.H., Daily Totals		$1247.60		$1881.60	$51.98	$78.40

Crew Q-7

Crew Q-7	Hr.	Daily	Hr.	Daily	Bare Costs	Incl. O&P
1 Steamfitter Foreman (inside)	$56.20	$449.60	$84.75	$678.00	$53.04	$79.99
2 Steamfitters	55.70	891.20	84.00	1344.00		
1 Steamfitter Apprentice	44.55	356.40	67.20	537.60		
32 L.H., Daily Totals		$1697.20		$2559.60	$53.04	$79.99

Crew Q-8

Crew Q-8	Hr.	Daily	Hr.	Daily	Bare Costs	Incl. O&P
1 Steamfitter Foreman (inside)	$56.20	$449.60	$84.75	$678.00	$53.04	$79.99
1 Steamfitter	55.70	445.60	84.00	672.00		
1 Welder (steamfitter)	55.70	445.60	84.00	672.00		
1 Steamfitter Apprentice	44.55	356.40	67.20	537.60		
1 Welder, electric, 300 amp		36.90		40.59	1.15	1.27
32 L.H., Daily Totals		$1734.10		$2600.19	$54.19	$81.26

Crew Q-9

Crew Q-9	Hr.	Daily	Hr.	Daily	Bare Costs	Incl. O&P
1 Sheet Metal Worker	$52.15	$417.20	$79.50	$636.00	$46.92	$71.53
1 Sheet Metal Apprentice	41.70	333.60	63.55	508.40		
16 L.H., Daily Totals		$750.80		$1144.40	$46.92	$71.53

Crew Q-10

Crew Q-10	Hr.	Daily	Hr.	Daily	Bare Costs	Incl. O&P
2 Sheet Metal Workers	$52.15	$834.40	$79.50	$1272.00	$48.67	$74.18
1 Sheet Metal Apprentice	41.70	333.60	63.55	508.40		
24 L.H., Daily Totals		$1168.00		$1780.40	$48.67	$74.18

Crew Q-11

Crew Q-11	Hr.	Daily	Hr.	Daily	Bare Costs	Incl. O&P
1 Sheet Metal Foreman (inside)	$52.65	$421.20	$80.25	$642.00	$49.66	$75.70
2 Sheet Metal Workers	52.15	834.40	79.50	1272.00		
1 Sheet Metal Apprentice	41.70	333.60	63.55	508.40		
32 L.H., Daily Totals		$1589.20		$2422.40	$49.66	$75.70

Crew Q-12

Crew Q-12	Hr.	Daily	Hr.	Daily	Bare Costs	Incl. O&P
1 Sprinkler Installer	$54.05	$432.40	$81.55	$652.40	$48.65	$73.40
1 Sprinkler Apprentice	43.25	346.00	65.25	522.00		
16 L.H., Daily Totals		$778.40		$1174.40	$48.65	$73.40

Crew Q-13

Crew Q-13	Hr.	Daily	Hr.	Daily	Bare Costs	Incl. O&P
1 Sprinkler Foreman (inside)	$54.55	$436.40	$82.30	$658.40	$51.48	$77.66
2 Sprinkler Installers	54.05	864.80	81.55	1304.80		
1 Sprinkler Apprentice	43.25	346.00	65.25	522.00		
32 L.H., Daily Totals		$1647.20		$2485.20	$51.48	$77.66

Crew Q-14

Crew Q-14	Hr.	Daily	Hr.	Daily	Bare Costs	Incl. O&P
1 Asbestos Worker	$48.85	$390.80	$76.10	$608.80	$43.98	$68.50
1 Asbestos Apprentice	39.10	312.80	60.90	487.20		
16 L.H., Daily Totals		$703.60		$1096.00	$43.98	$68.50

Crew Q-15

Crew Q-15	Hr.	Daily	Hr.	Daily	Bare Costs	Incl. O&P
1 Plumber	$54.60	$436.80	$82.35	$658.80	$49.15	$74.13
1 Plumber Apprentice	43.70	349.60	65.90	527.20		
1 Welder, electric, 300 amp		36.90		40.59	2.31	2.54
16 L.H., Daily Totals		$823.30		$1226.59	$51.46	$76.66

Crew Q-16

Crew Q-16	Hr.	Daily	Hr.	Daily	Bare Costs	Incl. O&P
2 Plumbers	$54.60	$873.60	$82.35	$1317.60	$50.97	$76.87
1 Plumber Apprentice	43.70	349.60	65.90	527.20		
1 Welder, electric, 300 amp		36.90		40.59	1.54	1.69
24 L.H., Daily Totals		$1260.10		$1885.39	$52.50	$78.56

Crew Q-17

Crew Q-17	Hr.	Daily	Hr.	Daily	Bare Costs	Incl. O&P
1 Steamfitter	$55.70	$445.60	$84.00	$672.00	$50.13	$75.60
1 Steamfitter Apprentice	44.55	356.40	67.20	537.60		
1 Welder, electric, 300 amp		36.90		40.59	2.31	2.54
16 L.H., Daily Totals		$838.90		$1250.19	$52.43	$78.14

Crew Q-17A

Crew Q-17A	Hr.	Daily	Hr.	Daily	Bare Costs	Incl. O&P
1 Steamfitter	$55.70	$445.60	$84.00	$672.00	$49.35	$74.45
1 Steamfitter Apprentice	44.55	356.40	67.20	537.60		
1 Equip. Oper. (crane)	47.80	382.40	72.15	577.20		
1 Hyd. Crane, 12 Ton		612.00		673.20		
1 Welder, electric, 300 amp		36.90		40.59	27.04	29.74
24 L.H., Daily Totals		$1833.30		$2500.59	$76.39	$104.19

Crew Q-18

Crew Q-18	Hr.	Daily	Hr.	Daily	Bare Costs	Incl. O&P
2 Steamfitters	$55.70	$891.20	$84.00	$1344.00	$51.98	$78.40
1 Steamfitter Apprentice	44.55	356.40	67.20	537.60		
1 Welder, electric, 300 amp		36.90		40.59	1.54	1.69
24 L.H., Daily Totals		$1284.50		$1922.19	$53.52	$80.09

Crew Q-19

Crew Q-19	Hr.	Daily	Hr.	Daily	Bare Costs	Incl. O&P
1 Steamfitter	$55.70	$445.60	$84.00	$672.00	$50.60	$76.08
1 Steamfitter Apprentice	44.55	356.40	67.20	537.60		
1 Electrician	51.55	412.40	77.05	616.40		
24 L.H., Daily Totals		$1214.40		$1826.00	$50.60	$76.08

Crew Q-20

Crew Q-20	Hr.	Daily	Hr.	Daily	Bare Costs	Incl. O&P
1 Sheet Metal Worker	$52.15	$417.20	$79.50	$636.00	$47.85	$72.63
1 Sheet Metal Apprentice	41.70	333.60	63.55	508.40		
.5 Electrician	51.55	206.20	77.05	308.20		
20 L.H., Daily Totals		$957.00		$1452.60	$47.85	$72.63

Crew Q-21

Crew Q-21	Hr.	Daily	Hr.	Daily	Bare Costs	Incl. O&P
2 Steamfitters	$55.70	$891.20	$84.00	$1344.00	$51.88	$78.06
1 Steamfitter Apprentice	44.55	356.40	67.20	537.60		
1 Electrician	51.55	412.40	77.05	616.40		
32 L.H., Daily Totals		$1660.00		$2498.00	$51.88	$78.06

Crew Q-22

Crew No.	Bare Costs Hr.	Daily	Incl. Subs O&P Hr.	Daily	Cost Per Labor-Hour Bare Costs	Incl. O&P
1 Plumber	$54.60	$436.80	$82.35	$658.80	$49.15	$74.13
1 Plumber Apprentice	43.70	349.60	65.90	527.20		
1 Hyd. Crane, 12 Ton		612.00		673.20	38.25	42.08
16 L.H., Daily Totals		$1398.40		$1859.20	$87.40	$116.20

Crew Q-22A

Crew No.	Bare Costs Hr.	Daily	Incl. Subs O&P Hr.	Daily	Cost Per Labor-Hour Bare Costs	Incl. O&P
1 Plumber	$54.60	$436.80	$82.35	$658.80	$45.30	$68.60
1 Plumber Apprentice	43.70	349.60	65.90	527.20		
1 Laborer	35.10	280.80	54.00	432.00		
1 Equip. Oper. (crane)	47.80	382.40	72.15	577.20		
1 Hyd. Crane, 12 Ton		612.00		673.20	19.13	21.04
32 L.H., Daily Totals		$2061.60		$2868.40	$64.42	$89.64

Crew Q-23

Crew No.	Bare Costs Hr.	Daily	Incl. Subs O&P Hr.	Daily	Cost Per Labor-Hour Bare Costs	Incl. O&P
1 Plumber Foreman (outside)	$56.60	$452.80	$85.35	$682.80	$52.58	$79.32
1 Plumber	54.60	436.80	82.35	658.80		
1 Equip. Oper. (med.)	46.55	372.40	70.25	562.00		
1 Lattice Boom Crane, 20 Ton		950.65		1045.71	39.61	43.57
24 L.H., Daily Totals		$2212.65		$2949.32	$92.19	$122.89

Crew R-1

Crew No.	Bare Costs Hr.	Daily	Incl. Subs O&P Hr.	Daily	Cost Per Labor-Hour Bare Costs	Incl. O&P
1 Electrician Foreman	$52.05	$416.40	$77.80	$622.40	$45.55	$68.56
3 Electricians	51.55	1237.20	77.05	1849.20		
2 Helpers	33.30	532.80	51.20	819.20		
48 L.H., Daily Totals		$2186.40		$3290.80	$45.55	$68.56

Crew R-1A

Crew No.	Bare Costs Hr.	Daily	Incl. Subs O&P Hr.	Daily	Cost Per Labor-Hour Bare Costs	Incl. O&P
1 Electrician	$51.55	$412.40	$77.05	$616.40	$42.42	$64.13
1 Helper	33.30	266.40	51.20	409.60		
16 L.H., Daily Totals		$678.80		$1026.00	$42.42	$64.13

Crew R-2

Crew No.	Bare Costs Hr.	Daily	Incl. Subs O&P Hr.	Daily	Cost Per Labor-Hour Bare Costs	Incl. O&P
1 Electrician Foreman	$52.05	$416.40	$77.80	$622.40	$45.87	$69.07
3 Electricians	51.55	1237.20	77.05	1849.20		
2 Helpers	33.30	532.80	51.20	819.20		
1 Equip. Oper. (crane)	47.80	382.40	72.15	577.20		
1 S.P. Crane, 4x4, 5 Ton		264.60		291.06	4.72	5.20
56 L.H., Daily Totals		$2833.40		$4159.06	$50.60	$74.27

Crew R-3

Crew No.	Bare Costs Hr.	Daily	Incl. Subs O&P Hr.	Daily	Cost Per Labor-Hour Bare Costs	Incl. O&P
1 Electrician Foreman	$52.05	$416.40	$77.80	$622.40	$51.00	$76.37
1 Electrician	51.55	412.40	77.05	616.40		
.5 Equip. Oper. (crane)	47.80	191.20	72.15	288.60		
.5 S.P. Crane, 4x4, 5 Ton		132.30		145.53	6.62	7.28
20 L.H., Daily Totals		$1152.30		$1672.93	$57.62	$83.65

Crew R-4

Crew No.	Bare Costs Hr.	Daily	Incl. Subs O&P Hr.	Daily	Cost Per Labor-Hour Bare Costs	Incl. O&P
1 Struc. Steel Foreman (outside)	$51.35	$410.80	$91.80	$734.40	$50.19	$86.72
3 Struc. Steel Workers	49.35	1184.40	88.25	2118.00		
1 Electrician	51.55	412.40	77.05	616.40		
1 Welder, gas engine, 300 amp		121.60		133.76	3.04	3.34
40 L.H., Daily Totals		$2129.20		$3602.56	$53.23	$90.06

Crew R-5

Crew No.	Bare Costs Hr.	Daily	Incl. Subs O&P Hr.	Daily	Cost Per Labor-Hour Bare Costs	Incl. O&P
1 Electrician Foreman	$52.05	$416.40	$77.80	$622.40	$44.96	$67.72
4 Electrician Linemen	51.55	1649.60	77.05	2465.60		
2 Electrician Operators	51.55	824.80	77.05	1232.80		
4 Electrician Groundmen	33.30	1065.60	51.20	1638.40		
1 Crew Truck		182.40		200.64		
1 Flatbed Truck, 20,000 GVW		215.80		237.38		
1 Pickup Truck, 3/4 Ton		127.00		139.70		
.2 Hyd. Crane, 55 Ton		220.00		242.00		
.2 Hyd. Crane, 12 Ton		122.40		134.64		
.2 Earth Auger, Truck-Mtd.		80.68		88.75		
1 Tractor w/Winch		382.20		420.42	15.12	16.63
88 L.H., Daily Totals		$5286.88		$7422.73	$60.08	$84.35

Crew R-6

Crew No.	Bare Costs Hr.	Daily	Incl. Subs O&P Hr.	Daily	Cost Per Labor-Hour Bare Costs	Incl. O&P
1 Electrician Foreman	$52.05	$416.40	$77.80	$622.40	$44.96	$67.72
4 Electrician Linemen	51.55	1649.60	77.05	2465.60		
2 Electrician Operators	51.55	824.80	77.05	1232.80		
4 Electrician Groundmen	33.30	1065.60	51.20	1638.40		
1 Crew Truck		182.40		200.64		
1 Flatbed Truck, 20,000 GVW		215.80		237.38		
1 Pickup Truck, 3/4 Ton		127.00		139.70		
.2 Hyd. Crane, 55 Ton		220.00		242.00		
.2 Hyd. Crane, 12 Ton		122.40		134.64		
.2 Earth Auger, Truck-Mtd.		80.68		88.75		
1 Tractor w/Winch		382.20		420.42		
3 Cable Trailers		563.70		620.07		
.5 Tensioning Rig		186.88		205.56		
.5 Cable Pulling Rig		1092.50		1201.75	36.06	39.67
88 L.H., Daily Totals		$7129.95		$9450.11	$81.02	$107.39

Crew R-7

Crew No.	Bare Costs Hr.	Daily	Incl. Subs O&P Hr.	Daily	Cost Per Labor-Hour Bare Costs	Incl. O&P
1 Electrician Foreman	$52.05	$416.40	$77.80	$622.40	$36.42	$55.63
5 Electrician Groundmen	33.30	1332.00	51.20	2048.00		
1 Crew Truck		182.40		200.64	3.80	4.18
48 L.H., Daily Totals		$1930.80		$2871.04	$40.23	$59.81

Crew R-8

Crew No.	Bare Costs Hr.	Daily	Incl. Subs O&P Hr.	Daily	Cost Per Labor-Hour Bare Costs	Incl. O&P
1 Electrician Foreman	$52.05	$416.40	$77.80	$622.40	$45.55	$68.56
3 Electrician Linemen	51.55	1237.20	77.05	1849.20		
2 Electrician Groundmen	33.30	532.80	51.20	819.20		
1 Pickup Truck, 3/4 Ton		127.00		139.70		
1 Crew Truck		182.40		200.64	6.45	7.09
48 L.H., Daily Totals		$2495.80		$3631.14	$52.00	$75.65

Crew R-9

Crew No.	Bare Costs Hr.	Daily	Incl. Subs O&P Hr.	Daily	Cost Per Labor-Hour Bare Costs	Incl. O&P
1 Electrician Foreman	$52.05	$416.40	$77.80	$622.40	$42.49	$64.22
1 Electrician Lineman	51.55	412.40	77.05	616.40		
2 Electrician Operators	51.55	824.80	77.05	1232.80		
4 Electrician Groundmen	33.30	1065.60	51.20	1638.40		
1 Pickup Truck, 3/4 Ton		127.00		139.70		
1 Crew Truck		182.40		200.64	4.83	5.32
64 L.H., Daily Totals		$3028.60		$4450.34	$47.32	$69.54

Crew R-10

Crew No.	Bare Costs Hr.	Daily	Incl. Subs O&P Hr.	Daily	Cost Per Labor-Hour Bare Costs	Incl. O&P
1 Electrician Foreman	$52.05	$416.40	$77.80	$622.40	$48.59	$72.87
4 Electrician Linemen	51.55	1649.60	77.05	2465.60		
1 Electrician Groundman	33.30	266.40	51.20	409.60		
1 Crew Truck		182.40		200.64		
3 Tram Cars		345.90		380.49	11.01	12.11
48 L.H., Daily Totals		$2860.70		$4078.73	$59.60	$84.97

Crew No.	Bare Costs		Incl. Subs O&P		Cost Per Labor-Hour	
Crew R-11	Hr.	Daily	Hr.	Daily	Bare Costs	Incl. O&P
1 Electrician Foreman	$52.05	$416.40	$77.80	$622.40	$48.74	$73.16
4 Electricians	51.55	1649.60	77.05	2465.60		
1 Equip. Oper. (crane)	47.80	382.40	72.15	577.20		
1 Common Laborer	35.10	280.80	54.00	432.00		
1 Crew Truck		182.40		200.64		
1 Hyd. Crane, 12 Ton		612.00		673.20	14.19	15.60
56 L.H., Daily Totals		$3523.60		$4971.04	$62.92	$88.77
Crew R-12	Hr.	Daily	Hr.	Daily	Bare Costs	Incl. O&P
1 Carpenter Foreman (inside)	$44.60	$356.80	$68.65	$549.20	$41.57	$64.96
4 Carpenters	44.10	1411.20	67.85	2171.20		
4 Common Laborers	35.10	1123.20	54.00	1728.00		
1 Equip. Oper. (med.)	46.55	372.40	70.25	562.00		
1 Steel Worker	49.35	394.80	88.25	706.00		
1 Dozer, 200 H.P.		1243.00		1367.30		
1 Pickup Truck, 3/4 Ton		127.00		139.70	15.57	17.13
88 L.H., Daily Totals		$5028.40		$7223.40	$57.14	$82.08
Crew R-13	Hr.	Daily	Hr.	Daily	Bare Costs	Incl. O&P
1 Electrician Foreman	$52.05	$416.40	$77.80	$622.40	$49.50	$74.14
3 Electricians	51.55	1237.20	77.05	1849.20		
.25 Equip. Oper. (crane)	47.80	95.60	72.15	144.30		
1 Equipment Oiler	41.25	330.00	62.25	498.00		
.25 Hydraulic Crane, 33 Ton		177.90		195.69	4.24	4.66
42 L.H., Daily Totals		$2257.10		$3309.59	$53.74	$78.80
Crew R-15	Hr.	Daily	Hr.	Daily	Bare Costs	Incl. O&P
1 Electrician Foreman	$52.05	$416.40	$77.80	$622.40	$50.50	$75.59
4 Electricians	51.55	1649.60	77.05	2465.60		
1 Equipment Oper. (light)	44.75	358.00	67.55	540.40		
1 Aerial Lift Truck		324.20		356.62	6.75	7.43
48 L.H., Daily Totals		$2748.20		$3985.02	$57.25	$83.02
Crew R-18	Hr.	Daily	Hr.	Daily	Bare Costs	Incl. O&P
.25 Electrician Foreman	$52.05	$104.10	$77.80	$155.60	$40.36	$61.20
1 Electrician	51.55	412.40	77.05	616.40		
2 Helpers	33.30	532.80	51.20	819.20		
26 L.H., Daily Totals		$1049.30		$1591.20	$40.36	$61.20
Crew R-19	Hr.	Daily	Hr.	Daily	Bare Costs	Incl. O&P
.5 Electrician Foreman	$52.05	$208.20	$77.80	$311.20	$51.65	$77.20
2 Electricians	51.55	824.80	77.05	1232.80		
20 L.H., Daily Totals		$1033.00		$1544.00	$51.65	$77.20
Crew R-21	Hr.	Daily	Hr.	Daily	Bare Costs	Incl. O&P
1 Electrician Foreman	$52.05	$416.40	$77.80	$622.40	$51.55	$77.07
3 Electricians	51.55	1237.20	77.05	1849.20		
.1 Equip. Oper. (med.)	46.55	37.24	70.25	56.20		
.1 S.P. Crane, 4x4, 25 Ton		56.52		62.17	1.72	1.90
32.8 L.H., Daily Totals		$1747.36		$2589.97	$53.27	$78.96
Crew R-22	Hr.	Daily	Hr.	Daily	Bare Costs	Incl. O&P
.66 Electrician Foreman	$52.05	$274.82	$77.80	$410.78	$43.79	$66.06
2 Helpers	33.30	532.80	51.20	819.20		
2 Electricians	51.55	824.80	77.05	1232.80		
37.28 L.H., Daily Totals		$1632.42		$2462.78	$43.79	$66.06

Crew No.	Bare Costs		Incl. Subs O&P		Cost Per Labor-Hour	
Crew R-30	Hr.	Daily	Hr.	Daily	Bare Costs	Incl. O&P
.25 Electrician Foreman (outside)	$53.55	$107.10	$80.05	$160.10	$41.58	$63.10
1 Electrician	51.55	412.40	77.05	616.40		
2 Laborers, (Semi-Skilled)	35.10	561.60	54.00	864.00		
26 L.H., Daily Totals		$1081.10		$1640.50	$41.58	$63.10
Crew R-31	Hr.	Daily	Hr.	Daily	Bare Costs	Incl. O&P
1 Electrician	$51.55	$412.40	$77.05	$616.40	$51.55	$77.05
1 Core Drill, Electric, 2.5 H.P.		47.00		51.70	5.88	6.46
8 L.H., Daily Totals		$459.40		$668.10	$57.42	$83.51
Crew W-41E	Hr.	Daily	Hr.	Daily	Bare Costs	Incl. O&P
.5 Plumber Foreman (outside)	$56.60	$226.40	$85.35	$341.40	$47.20	$71.61
1 Plumber	54.60	436.80	82.35	658.80		
1 Laborer	35.10	280.80	54.00	432.00		
20 L.H., Daily Totals		$944.00		$1432.20	$47.20	$71.61

Historical Cost Indexes

The table below lists both the RSMeans Historical Cost Index based on Jan. 1, 1993 = 100 as well as the computed value of an index based on Jan. 1, 2012 costs. Since the Jan. 1, 2012 figure is estimated, space is left to write in the actual index figures as they become available through either the quarterly *Means Construction Cost Indexes* or as printed in the *Engineering News-Record*. To compute the actual index based on Jan. 1, 2012 = 100, divide the Historical Cost Index for a particular year by the actual Jan. 1, 2012 Construction Cost Index. Space has been left to advance the index figures as the year progresses.

Year	Historical Cost Index Jan. 1, 1993 = 100		Current Index Based on Jan. 1, 2012 = 100		Year	Historical Cost Index Jan. 1, 1993 = 100	Current Index Based on Jan. 1, 2012 = 100		Year	Historical Cost Index Jan. 1, 1993 = 100	Current Index Based on Jan. 1, 2012 = 100	
	Est.	Actual	Est.	Actual		Actual	Est.	Actual		Actual	Est.	Actual
Oct 2012*					July 1997	112.8	58.5		July 1979	57.8	30.0	
July 2012*					1996	110.2	57.2		1978	53.5	27.7	
April 2012*					1995	107.6	55.8		1977	49.5	25.7	
Jan 2012*	192.8		100.0	100.0	1994	104.4	54.1		1976	46.9	24.3	
July 2011		185.7	96.3		1993	101.7	52.7		1975	44.8	23.2	
2010		183.5	95.2		1992	99.4	51.6		1974	41.4	21.5	
2009		180.1	93.4		1991	96.8	50.2		1973	37.7	19.6	
2008		180.4	93.6		1990	94.3	48.9		1972	34.8	18.0	
2007		169.4	87.9		1989	92.1	47.8		1971	32.1	16.6	
2006		162.0	84.0		1988	89.9	46.6		1970	28.7	14.9	
2005		151.6	78.6		1987	87.7	45.5		1969	26.9	14.0	
2004		143.7	74.5		1986	84.2	43.7		1968	24.9	12.9	
2003		132.0	68.5		1985	82.6	42.8		1967	23.5	12.2	
2002		128.7	66.8		1984	82.0	42.5		1966	22.7	11.8	
2001		125.1	64.9		1983	80.2	41.6		1965	21.7	11.3	
2000		120.9	62.7		1982	76.1	39.5		1964	21.2	11.0	
1999		117.6	61.0		1981	70.0	36.3		1963	20.7	10.7	
1998		115.1	59.7		1980	62.9	32.6		1962	20.2	10.5	

Adjustments to Costs

The Historical Cost Index can be used to convert National Average building costs at a particular time to the approximate building costs for some other time.

Example:

Estimate and compare construction costs for different years in the same city.

To estimate the National Average construction cost of a building in 1970, knowing that it cost $900,000 in 2012:

INDEX in 1970 = 28.7

INDEX in 2012 = 192.8

Time Adjustment using the Historical Cost Indexes:

$$\frac{\text{Index for Year A}}{\text{Index for Year B}} \times \text{Cost in Year B} = \text{Cost in Year A}$$

$$\frac{\text{INDEX 1970}}{\text{INDEX 2012}} \times \text{Cost 2012} = \text{Cost 1970}$$

$$\frac{28.7}{192.8} \times \$900,000 = .149 \times \$900,000 = \$134,100$$

The construction cost of the building in 1970 is $134,100.

Note: The City Cost Indexes for Canada can be used to convert U.S. National averages to local costs in Canadian dollars.

*Historical Cost Index updates and other resources are provided on the following website.
http://www.reedconstructiondata.com/rsmeans/chgnotice/176028

How to Use the City Cost Indexes

What you should know before you begin

RSMeans City Cost Indexes (CCI) are an extremely useful tool to use when you want to compare costs from city to city and region to region.

This publication contains average construction cost indexes for 731 U.S. and Canadian cities covering over 930 three-digit zip code locations, as listed directly under each city.

Keep in mind that a City Cost Index number is a percentage ratio of a specific city's cost to the national average cost of the same item at a stated time period.

In other words, these index figures represent relative construction factors (or, if you prefer, multipliers) for Material and Installation costs, as well as the weighted average for Total In Place costs for each CSI MasterFormat division. Installation costs include both labor and equipment rental costs. When estimating equipment rental rates only, for a specific location, use 015433 CONTRACTOR EQUIPMENT index.

The 30 City Average Index is the average of 30 major U.S. cities and serves as a National Average.

Index figures for both material and installation are based on the 30 major city average of 100 and represent the cost relationship as of July 1, 2011. The index for each division is computed from representative material and labor quantities for that division. The weighted average for each city is a weighted total of the components listed above it, but does not include relative productivity between trades or cities.

As changes occur in local material prices, labor rates, and equipment rental rates, (including fuel costs) the impact of these changes should be accurately measured by the change in the City Cost Index for each particular city (as compared to the 30 City Average).

Therefore, if you know (or have estimated) building costs in one city today, you can easily convert those costs to expected building costs in another city.

In addition, by using the Historical Cost Index, you can easily convert National Average building costs at a particular time to the approximate building costs for some other time. The City Cost Indexes can then be applied to calculate the costs for a particular city.

Quick Calculations

Location Adjustment Using the City Cost Indexes:

$$\frac{\text{Index for City A}}{\text{Index for City B}} \times \text{Cost in City B} = \text{Cost in City A}$$

Time Adjustment for the National Average Using the Historical Cost Index:

$$\frac{\text{Index for Year A}}{\text{Index for Year B}} \times \text{Cost in Year B} = \text{Cost in Year A}$$

Adjustment from the National Average:

$$\frac{\text{Index for City A}}{100} \times \text{National Average Cost} = \text{Cost in City A}$$

Since each of the other RSMeans publications contains many different items, any *one* item multiplied by the particular city index may give incorrect results. However, the larger the number of items compiled, the closer the results should be to actual costs for that particular city.

The City Cost Indexes for Canadian cities are calculated using Canadian material and equipment prices and labor rates, in Canadian dollars. Therefore, indexes for Canadian cities can be used to convert U.S. National Average prices to local costs in Canadian dollars.

How to use this section

1. Compare costs from city to city.

In using the RSMeans Indexes, remember that an index number is not a fixed number but a ratio: It's a percentage ratio of a building component's cost at any stated time to the National Average cost of that same component at the same time period. Put in the form of an equation:

$$\frac{\text{Specific City Cost}}{\text{National Average Cost}} \times 100 = \text{City Index Number}$$

Therefore, when making cost comparisons between cities, do not subtract one city's index number from the index number of another city and read the result as a percentage difference. Instead, divide one city's index number by that of the other city. The resulting number may then be used as a multiplier to calculate cost differences from city to city.

The formula used to find cost differences between cities for the purpose of comparison is as follows:

$$\frac{\text{City A Index}}{\text{City B Index}} \times \text{City B Cost (Known)} = \text{City A Cost (Unknown)}$$

In addition, you can use RSMeans CCI to calculate and compare costs division by division between cities using the same basic formula. (Just be sure that you're comparing similar divisions.)

2. Compare a specific city's construction costs with the National Average.

When you're studying construction location feasibility, it's advisable to compare a prospective project's cost index with an index of the National Average cost.

For example, divide the weighted average index of construction costs of a specific city by that of the 30 City Average, which = 100.

$$\frac{\text{City Index}}{100} = \% \text{ of National Average}$$

As a result, you get a ratio that indicates the relative cost of construction in that city in comparison with the National Average.

3. Convert U.S. National Average to actual costs in Canadian City.

$$\frac{\text{Index for Canadian City}}{100} \times \text{National Average Cost} = \text{Cost in Canadian City in \$ CAN}$$

4. Adjust construction cost data based on a National Average.

When you use a source of construction cost data which is based on a National Average (such as RSMeans cost data publications), it is necessary to adjust those costs to a specific location.

$$\frac{\text{City Index}}{100} \times \frac{\text{"Book" Cost Based on}}{\text{National Average Costs}} = \frac{\text{City Cost}}{\text{(Unknown)}}$$

5. When applying the City Cost Indexes to demolition projects, use the appropriate division installation index. For example, for removal of existing doors and windows, use Division 8 (Openings) index.

What you might like to know about how we developed the Indexes

The information presented in the CCI is organized according to the Construction Specifications Institute (CSI) MasterFormat 2010.

To create a reliable index, RSMeans researched the building type most often constructed in the United States and Canada. Because it was concluded that no one type of building completely represented the building construction industry, nine different types of buildings were combined to create a composite model.

The exact material, labor, and equipment quantities are based on detailed analyses of these nine building types, then each quantity is weighted in proportion to expected usage. These various material items, labor hours, and equipment rental rates are thus combined to form a composite building representing as closely as possible the actual usage of materials, labor and equipment used in the North American Building Construction Industry.

The following structures were chosen to make up that composite model:

1. Factory, 1 story
2. Office, 2–4 story
3. Store, Retail
4. Town Hall, 2–3 story
5. High School, 2–3 story
6. Hospital, 4–8 story
7. Garage, Parking
8. Apartment, 1–3 story
9. Hotel/Motel, 2–3 story

For the purposes of ensuring the timeliness of the data, the components of the index for the composite model have been streamlined. They currently consist of:

- specific quantities of 66 commonly used construction materials;
- specific labor-hours for 21 building construction trades; and
- specific days of equipment rental for 6 types of construction equipment (normally used to install the 66 material items by the 21 trades.) Fuel costs and routine maintenance costs are included in the equipment cost.

A sophisticated computer program handles the updating of all costs for each city on a quarterly basis. Material and equipment price quotations are gathered quarterly from 731 cities in the United States and Canada. These prices and the latest negotiated labor wage rates for 21 different building trades are used to compile the quarterly update of the City Cost Index.

The 30 major U.S. cities used to calculate the National Average are:

Atlanta, GA	Memphis, TN
Baltimore, MD	Milwaukee, WI
Boston, MA	Minneapolis, MN
Buffalo, NY	Nashville, TN
Chicago, IL	New Orleans, LA
Cincinnati, OH	New York, NY
Cleveland, OH	Philadelphia, PA
Columbus, OH	Phoenix, AZ
Dallas, TX	Pittsburgh, PA
Denver, CO	St. Louis, MO
Detroit, MI	San Antonio, TX
Houston, TX	San Diego, CA
Indianapolis, IN	San Francisco, CA
Kansas City, MO	Seattle, WA
Los Angeles, CA	Washington, DC

What the CCI does not indicate

The weighted average for each city is a total of the divisional components weighted to reflect typical usage, but it does not include the productivity variations between trades or cities.

In addition, the CCI does not take into consideration factors such as the following:

- managerial efficiency
- competitive conditions
- automation
- restrictive union practices
- unique local requirements
- regional variations due to specific building codes

City Cost Indexes

Table 1

DIVISION		UNITED STATES 30 CITY AVERAGE			ALABAMA ANNISTON 362			BIRMINGHAM 350 - 352			BUTLER 369			DECATUR 356			DOTHAN 363		
		MAT.	INST.	TOTAL	MAT.	INST.	TOTAL	MAT.	INST.	TOTAL	MAT.	INST.	TOTAL	MAT.	INST.	TOTAL	MAT.	INST.	TOTAL
015433	CONTRACTOR EQUIPMENT		100.0	100.0		100.7	100.7		100.8	100.8		98.0	98.0		100.7	100.7		98.0	98.0
0241, 31 - 34	SITE & INFRASTRUCTURE, DEMOLITION	100.0	100.0	100.0	87.6	93.4	91.6	85.6	94.0	91.4	103.5	87.5	92.4	80.6	92.0	88.5	100.8	87.5	91.6
0310	Concrete Forming & Accessories	100.0	100.0	100.0	91.9	49.9	55.4	92.3	72.4	75.0	88.6	45.2	50.8	96.0	48.1	54.3	96.8	44.6	51.4
0320	Concrete Reinforcing	100.0	100.0	100.0	93.3	83.3	88.3	93.3	83.7	88.5	98.6	48.8	73.5	93.3	78.1	85.7	98.6	48.2	73.2
0330	Cast-in-Place Concrete	100.0	100.0	100.0	92.5	51.8	76.5	98.7	66.6	86.0	90.2	57.3	77.2	91.9	64.9	81.3	90.2	48.2	73.7
03	CONCRETE	100.0	100.0	100.0	95.3	58.4	77.3	94.3	73.5	84.2	96.1	51.9	74.6	91.1	61.2	76.5	95.5	48.4	72.6
04	MASONRY	100.0	100.0	100.0	92.0	70.5	78.9	94.8	79.1	85.2	96.9	51.3	69.1	93.0	54.2	69.3	98.1	42.0	63.8
05	METALS	100.0	100.0	100.0	93.6	91.3	92.9	94.5	93.1	94.0	92.6	78.9	88.1	95.8	87.9	93.2	92.7	77.7	87.7
06	WOOD, PLASTICS & COMPOSITES	100.0	100.0	100.0	94.1	45.4	66.0	96.0	71.0	81.5	89.3	45.0	63.7	99.0	45.6	68.1	100.4	45.0	68.4
07	THERMAL & MOISTURE PROTECTION	100.0	100.0	100.0	93.1	55.8	78.0	95.1	82.0	89.8	93.2	59.5	79.5	92.9	61.3	80.1	93.1	51.8	76.3
08	OPENINGS	100.0	100.0	100.0	93.8	51.1	83.1	97.6	73.3	91.4	93.9	46.8	82.0	97.9	52.6	86.4	93.9	46.8	82.1
0920	Plaster & Gypsum Board	100.0	100.0	100.0	88.2	44.1	56.7	97.1	70.5	78.1	86.0	43.7	55.8	93.2	44.4	58.3	96.0	43.7	58.7
0950, 0980	Ceilings & Acoustic Treatment	100.0	100.0	100.0	89.3	44.1	59.4	94.9	70.5	78.8	89.3	43.7	59.2	93.8	44.4	61.2	89.3	43.7	59.2
0960	Flooring	100.0	100.0	100.0	101.8	42.1	84.3	104.5	63.1	92.4	107.6	58.6	93.2	104.5	53.0	89.4	114.6	28.8	89.4
0970, 0990	Wall Finishes & Painting/Coating	100.0	100.0	100.0	96.6	33.2	57.5	96.6	58.6	73.1	96.6	56.2	71.7	96.6	59.8	73.9	96.6	56.2	71.7
09	FINISHES	100.0	100.0	100.0	95.4	45.5	67.6	98.5	68.8	81.9	99.4	48.4	70.9	97.1	49.4	70.5	102.3	42.4	68.9
COVERS	DIVS. 10 - 14, 25, 28, 41, 43, 44, 46	100.0	100.0	100.0	100.0	73.9	94.8	100.0	88.7	97.8	100.0	44.7	89.0	100.0	46.7	89.4	100.0	44.8	89.0
21, 22, 23	FIRE SUPPRESSION, PLUMBING & HVAC	100.0	100.0	100.0	99.2	59.4	83.0	99.9	65.9	86.1	96.7	35.7	72.0	99.9	43.7	77.2	96.7	35.6	72.0
26, 27, 3370	ELECTRICAL, COMMUNICATIONS & UTIL.	100.0	100.0	100.0	96.6	60.9	78.2	103.0	62.5	82.1	98.5	42.7	69.7	98.2	65.6	81.4	97.3	61.0	78.6
MF2010	WEIGHTED AVERAGE	100.0	100.0	100.0	96.0	64.5	82.1	97.6	74.6	87.4	96.5	52.0	76.9	96.5	60.1	80.5	96.6	52.0	76.9

Table 2

DIVISION		ALABAMA EVERGREEN 364			GADSDEN 359			HUNTSVILLE 357 - 358			JASPER 355			MOBILE 365 - 366			MONTGOMERY 360 - 361		
		MAT.	INST.	TOTAL	MAT.	INST.	TOTAL	MAT.	INST.	TOTAL	MAT.	INST.	TOTAL	MAT.	INST.	TOTAL	MAT.	INST.	TOTAL
015433	CONTRACTOR EQUIPMENT		98.0	98.0		100.7	100.7		100.7	100.7		100.7	100.7		98.0	98.0		98.0	98.0
0241, 31 - 34	SITE & INFRASTRUCTURE, DEMOLITION	104.0	87.8	92.8	86.3	92.9	90.9	80.4	93.1	89.1	85.7	92.7	90.6	95.1	88.5	90.5	93.6	88.4	90.0
0310	Concrete Forming & Accessories	85.4	46.9	51.9	88.7	43.9	49.7	96.0	64.3	68.4	93.6	36.4	43.9	96.1	56.9	62.0	94.0	45.9	52.2
0320	Concrete Reinforcing	98.7	48.8	73.5	98.9	82.5	90.6	93.3	78.6	85.9	93.3	82.4	87.8	96.3	81.7	89.0	96.3	82.3	89.3
0330	Cast-in-Place Concrete	90.2	59.9	78.3	92.0	51.0	75.8	89.6	63.3	79.2	101.9	45.9	79.8	94.5	69.3	84.6	94.8	48.6	77.6
03	CONCRETE	96.3	53.6	75.5	95.1	55.3	75.7	89.9	67.9	79.2	98.6	50.3	75.0	92.9	67.3	80.4	93.7	55.4	75.1
04	MASONRY	96.9	56.2	72.0	91.4	45.4	63.3	94.5	60.3	73.6	88.0	43.6	60.9	95.2	55.7	71.1	93.3	41.6	61.7
05	METALS	92.7	78.9	88.1	93.7	90.5	92.6	95.8	89.5	93.7	93.6	89.8	92.4	94.6	91.6	93.6	94.5	90.1	93.0
06	WOOD, PLASTICS & COMPOSITES	85.9	45.0	62.3	89.9	41.1	61.7	99.0	65.2	79.4	96.0	33.5	59.9	99.1	56.1	74.3	95.6	45.0	66.4
07	THERMAL & MOISTURE PROTECTION	93.1	60.1	79.7	93.0	66.1	82.1	92.8	74.7	85.4	93.0	47.8	74.7	92.8	73.3	84.9	92.4	64.8	81.2
08	OPENINGS	93.9	46.8	82.0	93.8	49.9	82.8	97.9	63.2	89.1	93.8	48.8	82.5	97.9	60.7	88.5	97.9	54.3	86.9
0920	Plaster & Gypsum Board	85.1	43.7	55.5	85.5	39.7	52.8	93.2	64.5	72.7	88.7	31.9	48.1	93.2	55.2	66.1	97.1	43.7	59.0
0950, 0980	Ceilings & Acoustic Treatment	89.3	43.7	59.2	89.3	39.7	56.6	95.8	64.5	75.2	89.3	31.9	54.4	95.8	55.2	69.0	94.9	43.7	61.1
0960	Flooring	105.0	58.6	91.4	100.0	47.1	84.5	104.5	56.6	90.4	102.6	42.1	84.9	113.6	58.6	97.5	112.0	31.0	88.4
0970, 0990	Wall Finishes & Painting/Coating	96.6	56.2	71.7	96.6	64.0	76.5	96.6	61.6	75.0	96.6	40.7	62.1	100.1	57.2	73.6	96.6	56.2	71.7
09	FINISHES	98.6	49.6	71.2	94.4	44.9	66.8	97.6	62.2	77.8	95.4	36.5	62.5	102.6	56.1	76.7	101.8	42.8	68.9
COVERS	DIVS. 10 - 14, 25, 28, 41, 43, 44, 46	100.0	46.4	89.3	100.0	80.4	96.1	100.0	85.1	97.0	100.0	42.9	88.6	100.0	81.6	96.3	100.0	80.3	96.1
21, 22, 23	FIRE SUPPRESSION, PLUMBING & HVAC	96.7	38.2	73.0	101.8	38.6	76.2	99.9	55.5	81.9	101.8	56.4	83.4	99.9	64.6	85.6	100.0	36.4	74.2
26, 27, 3370	ELECTRICAL, COMMUNICATIONS & UTIL.	95.9	42.7	68.5	98.3	62.5	79.9	99.4	65.6	82.0	97.7	62.5	79.6	99.4	60.7	79.5	98.5	64.7	81.0
MF2010	WEIGHTED AVERAGE	96.2	53.4	77.3	96.6	57.6	79.4	96.6	68.1	84.1	96.8	57.6	79.5	97.7	67.5	84.4	97.4	56.6	79.4

Table 3

DIVISION		ALABAMA PHENIX CITY 368			SELMA 367			TUSCALOOSA 354			ALASKA ANCHORAGE 995 - 996			FAIRBANKS 997			JUNEAU 998		
		MAT.	INST.	TOTAL	MAT.	INST.	TOTAL	MAT.	INST.	TOTAL	MAT.	INST.	TOTAL	MAT.	INST.	TOTAL	MAT.	INST.	TOTAL
015433	CONTRACTOR EQUIPMENT		98.0	98.0		98.0	98.0		100.7	100.7		114.5	114.5		114.5	114.5		114.5	114.5
0241, 31 - 34	SITE & INFRASTRUCTURE, DEMOLITION	108.1	88.4	94.5	100.6	88.3	92.2	80.8	93.1	89.3	125.9	129.7	128.5	118.0	129.7	126.1	125.5	129.7	128.4
0310	Concrete Forming & Accessories	91.9	40.7	47.4	89.8	45.1	50.9	95.9	49.5	55.6	139.3	117.2	120.1	142.3	117.3	120.6	138.5	117.2	119.9
0320	Concrete Reinforcing	98.6	65.1	81.7	98.6	82.1	90.3	93.3	82.4	87.9	148.6	108.8	128.5	143.5	108.9	126.0	111.7	108.8	110.3
0330	Cast-in-Place Concrete	90.2	49.2	74.0	90.2	48.4	73.7	93.3	51.0	76.6	144.5	116.5	133.5	136.6	116.9	128.8	144.4	116.5	133.4
03	CONCRETE	98.7	50.1	75.1	95.0	54.9	75.5	91.7	57.9	75.2	131.5	114.7	123.3	119.6	114.9	117.3	122.1	114.7	118.5
04	MASONRY	96.9	43.4	64.2	100.2	40.8	64.0	93.3	48.5	66.0	193.3	121.7	149.6	195.8	121.7	150.6	178.8	121.7	144.0
05	METALS	92.6	83.8	89.7	92.6	89.0	91.4	94.9	90.5	93.4	120.1	101.7	114.0	117.1	101.8	112.1	117.1	101.6	112.0
06	WOOD, PLASTICS & COMPOSITES	93.8	37.6	61.4	90.9	45.0	64.4	99.0	47.2	69.0	116.7	116.0	116.3	121.5	116.0	118.4	116.7	116.0	116.3
07	THERMAL & MOISTURE PROTECTION	93.5	64.7	81.8	93.0	54.7	77.4	92.9	68.2	82.9	191.0	116.3	160.6	179.7	117.6	154.4	181.2	116.3	154.8
08	OPENINGS	93.8	46.1	81.8	93.8	54.3	83.9	97.9	60.4	88.4	119.9	112.9	118.1	116.4	113.0	115.5	115.7	112.9	115.0
0920	Plaster & Gypsum Board	89.6	36.1	51.4	87.3	43.7	56.2	93.2	46.0	59.5	143.4	116.3	124.1	150.2	116.3	126.0	130.9	116.3	120.5
0950, 0980	Ceilings & Acoustic Treatment	89.3	36.1	54.2	89.3	43.7	59.2	95.8	46.0	62.9	136.0	116.3	123.0	122.5	116.3	118.4	116.2	116.3	116.3
0960	Flooring	110.1	31.0	86.9	108.3	29.8	85.3	104.5	39.3	85.4	160.1	128.4	150.8	150.4	128.4	143.9	150.6	128.4	144.1
0970, 0990	Wall Finishes & Painting/Coating	96.6	56.2	71.7	96.6	56.2	71.7	96.6	48.4	66.9	150.9	116.9	129.9	150.4	125.8	135.2	150.9	116.9	129.9
09	FINISHES	101.1	38.7	66.3	99.4	42.6	67.7	97.5	46.3	69.0	150.9	119.6	133.4	143.6	120.5	130.8	140.5	119.6	128.8
COVERS	DIVS. 10 - 14, 25, 28, 41, 43, 44, 46	100.0	79.9	96.0	100.0	44.7	89.0	100.0	82.3	96.5	100.0	108.7	101.7	100.0	108.7	101.7	100.0	108.7	101.7
21, 22, 23	FIRE SUPPRESSION, PLUMBING & HVAC	96.7	36.8	72.4	96.7	35.9	72.1	99.9	36.2	74.1	100.3	104.5	102.0	100.3	108.2	103.5	100.3	104.0	101.8
26, 27, 3370	ELECTRICAL, COMMUNICATIONS & UTIL.	98.0	73.9	85.5	97.0	42.7	69.0	98.9	62.5	80.1	133.3	116.7	124.7	143.5	116.7	129.6	129.3	116.7	122.8
MF2010	WEIGHTED AVERAGE	97.1	55.9	78.9	96.3	51.9	76.7	96.6	58.6	79.9	124.5	114.0	119.9	122.4	115.0	119.1	120.3	113.9	117.5

City Cost Indexes

DIVISION		ALASKA KETCHIKAN 999 MAT.	INST.	TOTAL	ARIZONA CHAMBERS 865 MAT.	INST.	TOTAL	FLAGSTAFF 860 MAT.	INST.	TOTAL	GLOBE 855 MAT.	INST.	TOTAL	KINGMAN 864 MAT.	INST.	TOTAL	MESA/TEMPE 852 MAT.	INST.	TOTAL
015433	CONTRACTOR EQUIPMENT		114.5	114.5		94.0	94.0		94.0	94.0		95.9	95.9		94.0	94.0		95.9	95.9
0241, 31 - 34	SITE & INFRASTRUCTURE, DEMOLITION	176.4	129.7	144.2	64.0	96.6	86.5	82.4	98.5	93.5	96.6	98.8	98.1	64.0	98.6	87.9	86.8	100.4	96.2
0310	Concrete Forming & Accessories	134.3	117.2	119.4	96.5	45.5	52.2	101.3	68.1	72.4	99.2	45.4	52.4	94.8	67.3	70.9	101.8	67.2	71.7
0320	Concrete Reinforcing	112.2	108.8	110.5	98.0	78.0	87.9	97.8	85.2	91.5	102.6	77.9	90.2	98.1	85.2	91.6	103.3	85.2	94.1
0330	Cast-in-Place Concrete	276.4	116.5	213.4	89.3	54.1	75.4	89.4	75.5	83.9	86.2	54.2	73.6	89.0	71.9	82.3	86.9	71.9	81.0
03	CONCRETE	203.0	114.7	159.9	94.8	55.0	75.4	112.9	73.8	93.9	105.5	55.0	80.9	94.4	72.3	83.6	97.5	72.3	85.2
04	MASONRY	204.8	121.7	154.1	92.9	41.2	61.3	93.0	62.8	74.6	107.4	41.1	66.9	92.9	61.3	73.6	107.5	61.3	79.3
05	METALS	117.3	101.6	112.1	94.0	68.6	85.6	94.5	76.8	88.7	90.6	68.8	83.4	94.7	76.6	88.7	90.9	76.8	86.3
06	WOOD, PLASTICS & COMPOSITES	112.9	116.0	114.7	94.6	43.4	65.0	99.9	68.3	81.6	88.8	43.5	62.6	90.6	68.3	77.7	92.0	68.4	78.3
07	THERMAL & MOISTURE PROTECTION	182.8	116.3	155.8	96.4	50.8	77.9	98.2	66.3	85.2	102.6	48.4	80.6	96.4	62.1	82.5	101.8	62.8	86.0
08	OPENINGS	118.6	112.9	117.2	104.8	50.8	91.2	105.0	73.2	97.0	97.7	50.9	85.9	105.0	72.0	96.7	97.8	72.0	91.3
0920	Plaster & Gypsum Board	137.9	116.3	122.5	91.3	41.7	55.9	94.8	67.3	75.2	97.8	41.7	57.7	85.2	67.3	72.4	100.6	67.3	76.8
0950, 0980	Ceilings & Acoustic Treatment	117.4	116.3	116.7	112.4	41.7	65.7	113.3	67.3	82.9	98.9	41.7	61.1	113.3	67.3	82.9	98.9	67.3	78.0
0960	Flooring	150.4	128.4	143.9	92.7	41.4	77.7	95.1	41.6	79.4	98.1	41.4	81.4	91.6	56.2	81.2	99.5	51.9	85.5
0970, 0990	Wall Finishes & Painting/Coating	150.4	116.9	129.7	93.2	38.9	59.7	93.2	57.7	71.3	97.8	38.9	61.5	93.2	57.7	71.3	97.8	57.7	73.1
09	FINISHES	146.4	119.6	131.4	97.4	42.8	67.0	100.7	61.4	78.8	98.1	42.9	67.3	96.5	63.5	78.1	97.7	62.7	78.2
COVERS	DIVS. 10 - 14, 25, 28, 41, 43, 44, 46	100.0	108.7	101.7	100.0	77.7	95.6	100.0	82.9	96.6	100.0	77.9	95.6	100.0	82.3	96.5	100.0	82.6	96.5
21, 22, 23	FIRE SUPPRESSION, PLUMBING & HVAC	98.6	104.0	100.8	96.4	74.0	87.3	100.2	83.0	93.2	94.3	73.7	86.0	96.4	82.0	90.6	100.2	76.9	90.8
26, 27, 3370	ELECTRICAL, COMMUNICATIONS & UTIL.	143.4	116.7	129.6	101.4	68.5	84.4	100.4	62.3	80.7	96.6	63.7	79.7	101.4	62.3	81.2	93.6	62.3	77.4
MF2010	WEIGHTED AVERAGE	134.1	113.9	125.2	96.5	63.0	81.7	100.3	73.9	88.7	97.4	62.5	82.0	96.4	73.4	86.3	97.4	72.4	86.3

DIVISION		ARIZONA PHOENIX 850,853 MAT.	INST.	TOTAL	PRESCOTT 863 MAT.	INST.	TOTAL	SHOW LOW 859 MAT.	INST.	TOTAL	TUCSON 856 - 857 MAT.	INST.	TOTAL	ARKANSAS BATESVILLE 725 MAT.	INST.	TOTAL	CAMDEN 717 MAT.	INST.	TOTAL
015433	CONTRACTOR EQUIPMENT		96.4	96.4		94.0	94.0		95.9	95.9		95.9	95.9		88.3	88.3		88.3	88.3
0241, 31 - 34	SITE & INFRASTRUCTURE, DEMOLITION	87.3	100.9	96.7	70.3	96.6	88.4	98.8	98.8	98.8	82.3	100.7	95.0	71.0	84.4	80.2	71.7	83.9	80.1
0310	Concrete Forming & Accessories	102.7	70.4	74.6	97.8	45.3	52.1	105.3	45.7	53.4	102.0	70.0	74.2	83.5	47.6	52.3	83.3	32.4	39.0
0320	Concrete Reinforcing	101.5	85.4	93.4	97.8	78.2	87.9	103.3	78.1	90.6	85.5	85.2	85.3	95.4	64.5	79.8	96.7	64.3	80.4
0330	Cast-in-Place Concrete	87.0	75.7	82.5	89.3	54.0	75.4	86.2	54.3	73.6	89.4	75.5	84.0	80.2	47.4	67.3	82.2	40.0	65.6
03	CONCRETE	97.1	75.1	86.3	99.7	54.9	77.9	107.6	55.2	82.0	95.8	74.7	85.5	85.2	51.5	68.8	86.9	42.2	65.1
04	MASONRY	94.3	65.9	77.0	93.0	46.4	64.5	107.4	42.7	67.9	92.4	62.8	74.3	105.5	43.1	67.4	113.6	33.2	64.5
05	METALS	92.5	78.2	87.7	94.6	68.7	86.0	90.4	69.2	83.4	91.7	77.0	86.8	96.9	66.9	87.0	97.0	66.4	86.9
06	WOOD, PLASTICS & COMPOSITES	92.9	71.2	80.3	95.8	43.4	65.5	96.2	43.5	65.8	92.3	71.2	80.1	86.9	48.3	64.6	86.7	31.5	54.8
07	THERMAL & MOISTURE PROTECTION	101.5	67.0	87.4	96.9	50.2	77.9	102.8	50.8	81.7	102.9	62.7	86.6	96.2	46.4	76.0	96.0	37.7	72.3
08	OPENINGS	98.9	74.8	92.9	105.0	50.8	91.3	96.7	50.9	85.2	94.0	74.8	89.2	95.1	46.9	83.0	91.3	41.3	78.7
0920	Plaster & Gypsum Board	103.2	70.2	79.6	91.5	41.7	55.9	103.3	41.7	59.3	107.3	70.2	80.8	76.7	47.2	55.6	76.7	29.9	43.3
0950, 0980	Ceilings & Acoustic Treatment	106.1	70.2	82.4	111.5	41.7	65.4	98.9	41.7	61.1	99.8	70.2	80.2	88.4	47.2	61.2	88.4	29.9	49.7
0960	Flooring	99.8	54.2	86.4	93.6	41.4	78.3	101.3	47.2	85.4	90.5	41.6	76.1	102.7	61.9	90.7	102.6	41.5	84.6
0970, 0990	Wall Finishes & Painting/Coating	97.8	64.0	76.9	93.2	38.9	59.7	97.8	38.9	61.5	98.4	57.7	73.3	96.2	43.4	63.6	96.2	49.9	67.6
09	FINISHES	99.7	66.1	81.0	98.0	42.8	67.2	99.9	43.9	68.7	95.9	63.2	77.6	89.7	49.5	67.3	89.8	35.1	59.3
COVERS	DIVS. 10 - 14, 25, 28, 41, 43, 44, 46	100.0	83.5	96.7	100.0	77.7	95.6	100.0	77.9	95.6	100.0	83.4	96.7	100.0	42.7	88.6	100.0	38.4	87.7
21, 22, 23	FIRE SUPPRESSION, PLUMBING & HVAC	100.2	83.1	93.2	100.2	71.2	88.4	94.3	74.1	86.1	100.2	73.5	89.4	94.3	53.6	77.8	94.3	50.9	76.7
26, 27, 3370	ELECTRICAL, COMMUNICATIONS & UTIL.	100.7	70.9	85.3	100.1	62.2	80.5	93.9	63.6	78.3	95.6	59.9	77.2	98.4	63.4	80.3	94.9	60.4	77.1
MF2010	WEIGHTED AVERAGE	97.9	76.6	88.5	98.2	62.1	82.2	97.5	62.9	82.2	96.1	72.1	85.5	94.2	56.1	77.4	94.1	50.1	74.7

DIVISION		ARKANSAS FAYETTEVILLE 727 MAT.	INST.	TOTAL	FORT SMITH 729 MAT.	INST.	TOTAL	HARRISON 726 MAT.	INST.	TOTAL	HOT SPRINGS 719 MAT.	INST.	TOTAL	JONESBORO 724 MAT.	INST.	TOTAL	LITTLE ROCK 720 - 722 MAT.	INST.	TOTAL
015433	CONTRACTOR EQUIPMENT		88.3	88.3		88.3	88.3		88.3	88.3		88.3	88.3		106.3	106.3		88.3	88.3
0241, 31 - 34	SITE & INFRASTRUCTURE, DEMOLITION	70.4	85.9	81.1	75.1	85.8	82.5	75.5	84.4	81.6	74.9	85.3	82.1	94.8	99.4	97.9	82.1	85.8	84.6
0310	Concrete Forming & Accessories	79.5	40.9	45.9	96.7	58.2	63.2	87.6	47.6	52.8	81.0	37.7	43.4	86.9	51.1	55.7	89.3	62.6	66.1
0320	Concrete Reinforcing	95.4	69.4	82.3	96.6	70.1	83.2	95.0	64.4	79.6	94.9	64.5	79.6	92.3	66.8	79.4	96.7	65.2	80.9
0330	Cast-in-Place Concrete	80.2	51.7	69.0	91.7	66.6	81.8	89.0	45.4	71.8	84.1	40.5	66.9	87.4	57.5	75.6	92.1	66.6	82.1
03	CONCRETE	85.0	50.9	68.4	93.1	63.8	78.8	92.5	50.7	72.1	90.4	44.7	68.2	89.8	57.6	74.1	92.9	64.9	79.2
04	MASONRY	95.0	43.7	63.7	100.3	52.0	70.8	105.9	41.3	66.4	85.2	35.4	54.8	96.4	44.3	64.6	97.1	52.0	69.6
05	METALS	96.9	69.0	87.7	99.3	70.7	89.8	98.1	66.6	87.7	96.9	66.9	87.0	93.8	80.0	89.2	95.4	69.1	86.7
06	WOOD, PLASTICS & COMPOSITES	82.9	37.7	56.8	102.5	60.6	78.3	92.0	48.3	66.8	84.0	37.9	57.4	90.3	51.3	67.8	97.2	66.4	79.4
07	THERMAL & MOISTURE PROTECTION	97.1	47.9	77.1	97.4	56.0	80.6	96.5	45.1	75.6	96.2	40.0	73.4	100.9	51.9	81.0	96.5	56.6	80.3
08	OPENINGS	95.1	46.4	82.8	96.0	57.0	86.2	96.0	47.6	83.8	91.3	43.2	79.1	98.2	55.4	87.4	96.0	60.2	87.0
0920	Plaster & Gypsum Board	74.5	36.3	47.2	82.8	59.9	66.5	81.4	47.2	57.0	75.4	36.5	47.6	90.7	50.0	61.6	88.4	65.9	72.3
0950, 0980	Ceilings & Acoustic Treatment	88.4	36.3	54.0	92.0	59.9	70.8	92.0	47.2	62.4	88.4	36.5	54.1	92.5	50.0	64.4	93.8	65.9	75.4
0960	Flooring	99.6	61.9	88.5	110.3	63.7	96.6	105.4	61.9	92.6	101.3	61.9	89.7	73.6	55.9	68.4	111.7	63.7	97.6
0970, 0990	Wall Finishes & Painting/Coating	96.2	31.0	55.9	96.2	56.7	71.8	96.2	43.4	63.6	96.2	49.9	67.6	86.3	51.0	64.5	96.2	58.2	72.8
09	FINISHES	88.6	42.4	62.8	93.7	59.3	74.5	92.2	49.5	68.4	89.6	42.5	63.3	86.8	51.4	67.0	95.4	62.9	77.3
COVERS	DIVS. 10 - 14, 25, 28, 41, 43, 44, 46	100.0	52.6	90.6	100.0	77.1	95.4	100.0	53.1	90.7	100.0	39.4	87.9	100.0	48.7	89.8	100.0	77.7	95.6
21, 22, 23	FIRE SUPPRESSION, PLUMBING & HVAC	94.3	52.2	77.2	100.3	51.6	80.5	94.3	51.3	76.9	94.3	50.4	76.5	100.5	54.5	81.9	100.2	59.3	83.6
26, 27, 3370	ELECTRICAL, COMMUNICATIONS & UTIL.	92.3	54.4	72.7	95.7	68.6	81.7	97.0	39.4	67.3	97.1	67.2	81.6	103.4	63.4	82.8	100.5	69.7	84.6
MF2010	WEIGHTED AVERAGE	92.9	54.1	75.8	97.1	62.5	81.8	95.5	52.3	76.5	93.4	52.9	75.5	96.8	60.7	80.9	97.0	65.0	82.9

		ARKANSAS												CALIFORNIA					
		PINE BLUFF			RUSSELLVILLE			TEXARKANA			WEST MEMPHIS			ALHAMBRA			ANAHEIM		
	DIVISION	716			728			718			723			917 - 918			928		
		MAT.	INST.	TOTAL	MAT.	INST.	TOTAL	MAT.	INST.	TOTAL	MAT.	INST.	TOTAL	MAT.	INST.	TOTAL	MAT.	INST.	TOTAL
015433	CONTRACTOR EQUIPMENT		88.3	88.3		88.3	88.3		88.9	88.9		106.3	106.3		99.3	99.3		100.8	100.8
0241, 31 - 34	SITE & INFRASTRUCTURE, DEMOLITION	76.8	85.8	83.0	72.2	84.3	80.5	89.7	86.3	87.4	101.5	99.4	100.0	97.9	109.3	105.8	96.8	108.4	104.8
0310	Concrete Forming & Accessories	80.7	62.5	64.9	84.1	56.5	60.1	86.5	42.6	48.3	91.7	51.3	56.5	121.6	119.9	120.1	107.0	121.9	119.9
0320	Concrete Reinforcing	96.6	65.2	80.8	96.1	64.3	80.1	96.2	64.5	80.2	92.3	66.8	79.4	109.7	118.2	114.0	95.9	118.1	107.1
0330	Cast-in-Place Concrete	84.1	66.6	77.2	84.1	47.3	69.6	91.7	45.3	73.4	91.6	57.5	78.2	89.2	118.3	100.7	92.9	120.8	103.9
03	CONCRETE	91.2	64.8	78.3	88.4	55.4	72.3	89.6	48.5	69.6	96.9	57.8	77.8	100.0	118.0	108.8	99.7	119.8	109.5
04	MASONRY	122.3	52.0	79.4	99.5	39.5	62.9	100.3	35.0	60.5	81.7	44.3	58.9	116.0	118.2	117.4	80.3	116.4	102.4
05	METALS	97.8	69.0	88.3	96.9	66.5	86.9	90.9	67.0	83.0	92.8	80.2	88.6	83.5	101.6	89.5	100.7	101.8	101.1
06	WOOD, PLASTICS & COMPOSITES	83.5	66.4	73.6	88.1	60.6	72.2	91.5	44.6	64.4	96.0	51.3	70.2	96.8	117.7	108.9	97.0	120.3	110.5
07	THERMAL & MOISTURE PROTECTION	96.3	56.6	80.2	97.3	46.1	76.5	97.1	46.7	76.6	101.4	51.9	81.2	101.2	117.4	107.8	101.6	121.3	109.6
08	OPENINGS	91.3	60.2	83.4	95.1	56.2	85.3	96.5	47.6	84.2	98.2	55.4	87.4	91.5	119.7	98.8	103.4	121.3	107.9
0920	Plaster & Gypsum Board	74.9	65.9	68.5	76.7	59.9	64.7	79.7	43.4	53.8	93.4	50.0	62.4	98.5	118.3	112.7	103.2	120.9	115.8
0950, 0980	Ceilings & Acoustic Treatment	88.4	65.9	73.5	88.4	59.9	69.6	93.8	43.4	60.5	90.5	50.0	63.7	92.8	118.3	109.7	107.5	120.9	116.3
0960	Flooring	101.0	63.7	90.0	102.3	61.9	90.4	103.4	53.4	88.7	76.2	55.9	70.2	97.2	105.0	99.4	108.9	111.4	109.6
0970, 0990	Wall Finishes & Painting/Coating	96.2	58.2	72.8	96.2	36.9	59.6	96.2	32.0	56.6	86.3	51.0	64.5	108.1	108.5	108.4	102.8	106.7	105.2
09	FINISHES	89.5	62.9	74.7	89.9	56.0	71.0	92.6	42.7	64.8	88.2	51.4	67.7	97.3	115.9	107.7	104.4	118.3	112.2
COVERS	DIVS. 10 - 14, 25, 28, 41, 43, 44, 46	100.0	77.7	95.6	100.0	44.0	88.9	100.0	35.2	87.1	100.0	48.7	89.8	100.0	109.9	102.0	100.0	110.5	102.1
21, 22, 23	FIRE SUPPRESSION, PLUMBING & HVAC	100.3	54.0	81.5	94.3	53.4	77.8	100.3	57.3	82.9	94.5	66.3	83.1	94.1	111.1	101.0	100.1	112.0	104.9
26, 27, 3370	ELECTRICAL, COMMUNICATIONS & UTIL.	95.0	69.7	82.0	95.7	47.5	70.8	97.0	38.2	66.7	105.0	60.3	81.9	112.7	115.8	114.3	92.2	105.4	99.0
MF2010	WEIGHTED AVERAGE	96.7	63.8	82.2	94.1	55.4	77.0	95.9	51.3	76.2	95.8	62.8	81.2	97.1	113.5	104.3	98.9	112.8	105.1

		CALIFORNIA																	
		BAKERSFIELD			BERKELEY			EUREKA			FRESNO			INGLEWOOD			LONG BEACH		
	DIVISION	932 - 933			947			955			936 - 938			903 - 905			906 - 908		
		MAT.	INST.	TOTAL	MAT.	INST.	TOTAL	MAT.	INST.	TOTAL	MAT.	INST.	TOTAL	MAT.	INST.	TOTAL	MAT.	INST.	TOTAL
015433	CONTRACTOR EQUIPMENT		98.7	98.7		98.5	98.5		98.4	98.4		98.7	98.7		96.5	96.5		96.5	96.5
0241, 31 - 34	SITE & INFRASTRUCTURE, DEMOLITION	99.1	106.0	103.9	120.8	105.3	110.1	110.3	102.8	105.2	102.0	105.5	104.4	91.4	103.8	100.0	98.8	103.8	102.3
0310	Concrete Forming & Accessories	105.5	121.4	119.3	119.6	148.1	144.4	117.0	132.1	130.1	103.0	133.1	129.2	111.2	119.8	118.7	106.4	119.8	118.1
0320	Concrete Reinforcing	108.0	118.0	113.0	95.0	119.4	107.3	104.7	118.8	111.8	91.5	118.7	105.2	107.6	118.1	112.9	106.6	118.1	112.4
0330	Cast-in-Place Concrete	94.6	119.4	104.5	128.5	121.8	125.9	100.7	116.2	106.8	97.9	117.0	105.4	88.4	118.7	100.3	100.7	118.7	107.8
03	CONCRETE	100.2	119.1	109.4	114.5	131.6	122.8	110.2	122.7	116.3	101.3	123.4	112.1	97.2	118.2	107.4	107.0	118.2	107.4
04	MASONRY	99.4	115.9	109.4	130.4	132.7	131.8	103.8	127.3	118.1	102.6	122.1	114.5	76.5	118.3	102.0	85.4	118.3	105.5
05	METALS	96.1	100.9	97.7	105.9	101.0	104.3	100.6	100.0	100.4	100.7	101.6	101.0	91.1	102.0	94.7	90.9	102.0	94.6
06	WOOD, PLASTICS & COMPOSITES	92.1	120.4	108.4	118.6	153.8	138.9	110.4	137.2	125.9	103.5	137.2	123.0	99.9	117.6	110.1	93.6	117.6	107.5
07	THERMAL & MOISTURE PROTECTION	100.5	111.9	105.1	114.4	135.6	123.0	105.7	115.6	109.7	95.3	115.0	103.3	99.4	118.7	107.2	99.6	119.0	107.5
08	OPENINGS	100.9	116.8	104.9	101.4	141.2	111.4	102.2	114.6	105.3	102.7	126.0	108.6	93.5	119.6	100.1	93.5	119.6	100.1
0920	Plaster & Gypsum Board	94.5	120.9	113.3	110.4	154.9	142.2	108.4	138.2	129.7	97.4	138.2	126.6	103.7	118.3	114.2	99.2	118.3	112.9
0950, 0980	Ceilings & Acoustic Treatment	108.0	120.9	116.5	109.4	154.9	139.4	112.9	138.2	129.6	110.5	138.2	128.8	100.7	118.3	112.3	100.7	118.3	112.3
0960	Flooring	109.1	97.4	105.7	115.8	126.8	119.1	113.5	122.0	116.0	115.5	139.8	122.6	100.0	105.0	101.5	97.3	105.0	99.6
0970, 0990	Wall Finishes & Painting/Coating	104.9	93.8	98.0	103.9	141.5	127.1	104.2	48.7	70.0	120.2	111.0	114.5	99.7	108.5	105.2	99.7	108.5	105.2
09	FINISHES	105.4	114.7	110.6	111.0	145.5	130.2	110.9	123.9	118.1	109.8	133.8	123.2	102.5	115.8	109.9	101.8	115.8	109.6
COVERS	DIVS. 10 - 14, 25, 28, 41, 43, 44, 46	100.0	107.6	101.5	100.0	124.0	104.8	100.0	120.3	104.0	100.0	120.3	104.0	100.0	109.6	101.9	100.0	109.6	101.9
21, 22, 23	FIRE SUPPRESSION, PLUMBING & HVAC	100.1	105.5	102.3	94.3	147.5	115.9	94.1	103.5	97.9	100.2	113.2	105.5	93.7	111.0	100.7	93.7	111.0	100.7
26, 27, 3370	ELECTRICAL, COMMUNICATIONS & UTIL.	101.6	101.2	101.4	106.6	138.5	123.1	99.8	116.8	108.6	91.7	100.4	96.2	103.4	115.9	109.8	103.1	115.9	109.7
MF2010	WEIGHTED AVERAGE	100.0	109.5	104.2	105.5	133.2	117.7	101.6	114.2	107.2	100.5	115.7	107.2	95.3	113.1	103.2	96.9	113.2	104.1

		CALIFORNIA																	
		LOS ANGELES			MARYSVILLE			MODESTO			MOJAVE			OAKLAND			OXNARD		
	DIVISION	900 - 902			959			953			935			946			930		
		MAT.	INST.	TOTAL	MAT.	INST.	TOTAL	MAT.	INST.	TOTAL	MAT.	INST.	TOTAL	MAT.	INST.	TOTAL	MAT.	INST.	TOTAL
015433	CONTRACTOR EQUIPMENT		100.1	100.1		98.4	98.4		98.4	98.4		98.7	98.7		98.5	98.5		97.6	97.6
0241, 31 - 34	SITE & INFRASTRUCTURE, DEMOLITION	98.8	107.5	104.8	106.2	105.0	105.4	100.5	105.0	103.6	95.5	106.0	102.7	127.4	105.3	112.2	102.3	104.1	103.5
0310	Concrete Forming & Accessories	108.2	121.9	120.1	107.6	133.0	129.7	104.2	133.2	129.5	116.2	116.2	116.2	109.1	148.1	143.0	108.1	121.9	120.1
0320	Concrete Reinforcing	108.4	118.3	113.4	104.7	118.5	111.7	108.5	118.7	113.7	110.0	117.9	114.0	97.1	119.4	108.4	108.0	118.0	113.0
0330	Cast-in-Place Concrete	95.5	119.4	104.9	112.6	117.0	114.3	100.8	117.1	107.2	84.7	119.6	98.5	121.8	121.8	121.8	98.6	120.0	107.0
03	CONCRETE	102.8	119.4	110.9	112.2	123.4	117.7	103.3	123.6	113.2	93.8	116.8	105.0	113.9	131.7	122.6	102.3	119.4	110.7
04	MASONRY	90.2	120.1	108.5	104.8	119.1	113.5	103.8	123.0	115.5	100.7	115.1	109.5	138.3	132.7	134.9	104.1	114.5	110.5
05	METALS	98.1	103.5	99.9	100.1	101.6	100.6	97.3	102.1	98.9	97.7	100.7	98.7	99.9	101.0	100.3	95.9	101.3	97.7
06	WOOD, PLASTICS & COMPOSITES	99.6	120.2	111.5	98.2	137.2	119.1	94.4	137.2	119.1	102.8	113.6	109.0	106.6	153.8	133.9	98.1	120.4	111.0
07	THERMAL & MOISTURE PROTECTION	98.8	121.0	107.8	105.2	118.0	110.4	101.8	117.7	110.0	101.2	110.4	105.0	112.1	135.6	121.6	104.7	116.9	109.7
08	OPENINGS	100.6	121.3	105.8	101.4	125.9	107.6	100.2	126.6	106.8	96.7	113.1	100.9	101.4	141.2	111.4	99.8	121.4	105.2
0920	Plaster & Gypsum Board	103.7	120.9	115.9	100.4	138.2	127.4	103.6	138.2	128.3	109.9	113.9	112.7	103.8	154.9	140.3	103.2	120.9	115.8
0950, 0980	Ceilings & Acoustic Treatment	110.8	120.9	117.4	112.0	138.2	129.3	107.5	138.2	127.8	112.0	113.9	113.2	112.3	154.9	140.4	112.5	120.9	118.0
0960	Flooring	97.7	111.4	101.7	108.6	110.5	109.2	109.1	116.7	111.3	115.9	97.4	110.5	110.2	126.8	115.1	107.5	111.4	108.7
0970, 0990	Wall Finishes & Painting/Coating	98.8	108.5	104.8	104.2	115.2	111.0	104.2	118.4	112.9	104.2	93.8	97.7	103.9	141.5	127.1	104.2	99.7	101.4
09	FINISHES	104.2	118.4	112.1	107.7	129.4	119.8	106.6	130.8	120.1	110.0	110.6	110.3	109.9	145.5	129.7	107.2	117.6	113.0
COVERS	DIVS. 10 - 14, 25, 28, 41, 43, 44, 46	100.0	110.2	102.0	100.0	120.3	104.0	100.0	120.3	104.0	100.0	106.8	101.3	100.0	124.0	104.8	100.0	110.7	102.1
21, 22, 23	FIRE SUPPRESSION, PLUMBING & HVAC	100.2	111.9	104.9	94.1	108.9	100.1	100.1	113.2	105.4	94.1	100.9	96.9	100.2	147.5	119.4	100.1	112.0	104.9
26, 27, 3370	ELECTRICAL, COMMUNICATIONS & UTIL.	101.7	122.2	112.3	96.4	103.8	100.2	98.9	110.5	104.9	90.3	98.2	94.4	105.8	143.6	125.3	96.2	107.5	102.0
MF2010	WEIGHTED AVERAGE	100.1	115.5	106.9	100.9	114.4	106.8	100.7	116.9	107.9	97.0	106.9	101.3	106.3	133.9	118.5	100.2	112.3	105.5

CALIFORNIA

DIVISION		PALM SPRINGS 922			PALO ALTO 943			PASADENA 910 - 912			REDDING 960			RICHMOND 948			RIVERSIDE 925		
		MAT.	INST.	TOTAL	MAT.	INST.	TOTAL	MAT.	INST.	TOTAL	MAT.	INST.	TOTAL	MAT.	INST.	TOTAL	MAT.	INST.	TOTAL
015433	CONTRACTOR EQUIPMENT		99.6	99.6		98.5	98.5		99.3	99.3		98.4	98.4		98.5	98.5		99.6	99.6
0241, 31 - 34	SITE & INFRASTRUCTURE, DEMOLITION	88.3	106.5	100.8	116.5	105.3	108.8	94.7	109.3	104.8	106.2	105.0	105.4	126.8	105.3	112.0	95.1	106.5	102.9
0310	Concrete Forming & Accessories	103.5	119.9	117.7	107.3	140.1	135.9	111.8	119.9	118.9	107.4	133.0	129.7	122.0	147.7	144.4	107.1	121.9	119.9
0320	Concrete Reinforcing	110.2	118.0	114.1	95.0	119.2	107.2	110.6	118.2	114.4	104.7	118.5	111.7	95.0	119.2	107.2	107.0	118.0	112.6
0330	Cast-in-Place Concrete	88.5	120.7	101.2	108.7	121.6	113.8	84.7	118.3	97.9	111.6	117.0	113.7	125.0	121.6	123.7	96.3	120.8	105.9
03	CONCRETE	95.0	118.8	106.6	102.8	128.0	115.1	95.7	118.1	106.6	111.2	123.4	117.1	116.0	131.4	123.5	101.0	119.7	110.1
04	MASONRY	78.1	115.4	100.8	109.6	128.8	121.3	100.8	118.2	111.4	104.8	119.1	113.5	130.1	128.8	129.3	79.1	115.4	101.2
05	METALS	101.3	101.5	101.4	97.4	100.3	98.3	83.6	101.6	89.5	100.4	101.6	100.8	97.4	100.4	98.4	100.9	101.7	101.2
06	WOOD, PLASTICS & COMPOSITES	91.9	117.8	106.9	104.0	143.6	126.9	84.4	117.7	103.7	97.9	137.2	120.6	122.2	153.8	140.4	97.0	120.3	110.5
07	THERMAL & MOISTURE PROTECTION	101.3	119.3	108.6	111.6	128.7	118.6	100.9	117.9	107.8	105.2	117.5	110.2	122.2	133.9	121.0	101.8	120.7	109.5
08	OPENINGS	98.8	118.2	103.7	101.4	134.7	109.8	91.5	119.7	98.6	102.4	125.9	108.3	101.4	140.2	111.2	101.9	121.3	106.8
0920	Plaster & Gypsum Board	97.3	118.3	112.3	101.5	144.3	132.1	91.2	118.3	110.6	100.7	138.2	127.5	112.4	154.9	142.8	102.3	120.9	115.6
0950, 0980	Ceilings & Acoustic Treatment	104.8	118.3	113.7	110.3	144.3	132.8	92.8	118.3	109.7	118.0	138.2	131.3	110.3	154.9	139.7	109.8	120.9	117.1
0960	Flooring	111.1	105.0	109.3	109.3	120.8	112.7	91.7	105.0	95.6	108.6	110.5	109.1	117.7	120.8	118.6	112.9	111.4	112.5
0970, 0990	Wall Finishes & Painting/Coating	100.9	117.3	111.0	103.9	139.2	125.6	108.1	108.5	108.4	104.2	115.2	111.0	103.9	139.2	125.6	100.9	106.7	104.5
09	FINISHES	102.9	116.9	110.7	108.0	138.2	124.8	94.6	115.9	106.5	108.9	129.4	120.3	112.6	144.2	130.2	105.6	118.3	112.7
COVERS	DIVS. 10 - 14, 25, 28, 41, 43, 44, 46	100.0	110.2	102.0	100.0	122.9	104.5	100.0	109.9	102.0	100.0	120.3	104.0	100.0	124.0	104.8	100.0	110.5	102.1
21, 22, 23	FIRE SUPPRESSION, PLUMBING & HVAC	94.1	107.3	99.5	94.3	141.2	113.3	94.1	111.1	101.0	100.1	108.9	103.6	94.3	136.5	111.4	100.1	112.0	104.9
26, 27, 3370	ELECTRICAL, COMMUNICATIONS & UTIL.	95.9	104.4	100.3	105.7	142.0	124.4	109.7	115.8	112.9	99.3	103.8	101.6	106.2	135.0	121.1	92.4	104.4	98.6
MF2010	WEIGHTED AVERAGE	96.4	110.9	102.8	101.3	129.9	113.9	95.2	113.6	103.3	102.8	114.4	107.9	104.7	129.7	115.7	98.9	112.4	104.9

CALIFORNIA

DIVISION		SACRAMENTO 942,956 - 958			SALINAS 939			SAN BERNARDINO 923 - 924			SAN DIEGO 919 - 921			SAN FRANCISCO 940 - 941			SAN JOSE 951		
		MAT.	INST.	TOTAL	MAT.	INST.	TOTAL	MAT.	INST.	TOTAL	MAT.	INST.	TOTAL	MAT.	INST.	TOTAL	MAT.	INST.	TOTAL
015433	CONTRACTOR EQUIPMENT		98.0	98.0		98.7	98.7		99.6	99.6		99.3	99.3		109.1	109.1		99.1	99.1
0241, 31 - 34	SITE & INFRASTRUCTURE, DEMOLITION	100.9	110.7	107.6	116.7	105.7	109.1	74.3	106.5	96.5	100.8	103.0	102.3	129.7	111.0	116.8	135.8	100.2	111.2
0310	Concrete Forming & Accessories	107.4	136.1	132.3	110.7	136.4	133.0	110.5	119.8	118.6	108.2	110.6	110.3	108.7	148.9	143.7	110.0	147.9	142.9
0320	Concrete Reinforcing	89.7	118.8	104.4	108.5	119.1	113.9	107.0	118.0	112.5	107.2	118.0	112.6	110.6	119.7	115.2	95.5	119.4	107.6
0330	Cast-in-Place Concrete	103.0	118.1	109.0	97.4	117.4	105.3	66.5	120.7	87.8	92.8	106.6	98.2	124.9	123.1	124.2	117.1	121.0	118.6
03	CONCRETE	103.2	124.7	113.7	111.5	125.2	118.1	75.6	118.8	96.7	100.5	110.0	105.1	117.5	133.1	125.1	109.8	131.7	120.5
04	MASONRY	111.6	123.0	118.5	100.4	128.2	117.4	85.8	115.4	103.8	92.0	113.7	105.2	138.8	135.9	137.0	132.7	132.8	132.7
05	METALS	95.6	96.0	95.7	100.3	103.2	101.2	100.9	101.4	101.0	98.7	102.7	100.0	106.5	110.8	107.9	95.7	107.7	99.6
06	WOOD, PLASTICS & COMPOSITES	99.3	140.7	123.2	102.3	140.4	124.3	100.6	117.8	110.6	97.9	107.2	103.3	106.6	153.9	134.0	106.5	153.5	133.6
07	THERMAL & MOISTURE PROTECTION	118.7	122.1	120.1	102.0	125.8	111.7	100.4	119.3	108.1	106.5	105.1	106.0	114.2	137.1	123.5	101.2	136.7	115.6
08	OPENINGS	114.1	128.5	117.7	101.2	133.9	109.4	98.9	118.2	103.7	99.5	111.9	102.6	105.9	141.3	114.8	93.1	141.0	105.1
0920	Plaster & Gypsum Board	97.8	141.5	129.0	104.5	141.5	130.9	104.1	118.3	114.3	98.8	107.2	104.8	106.8	154.9	141.1	97.5	154.9	138.5
0950, 0980	Ceilings & Acoustic Treatment	110.3	141.5	130.9	112.0	141.5	131.5	107.5	118.3	114.6	100.7	107.2	104.8	120.2	154.9	143.1	102.6	154.9	137.1
0960	Flooring	109.4	116.7	111.5	110.9	126.8	114.9	115.1	105.0	112.1	100.1	111.4	103.4	110.2	126.8	115.1	101.4	126.8	108.9
0970, 0990	Wall Finishes & Painting/Coating	101.1	118.4	111.8	105.3	141.5	127.7	100.9	104.9	103.4	104.5	109.4	107.5	103.9	151.4	133.2	104.7	141.5	127.4
09	FINISHES	106.3	132.9	121.1	110.0	137.0	125.0	104.1	115.6	110.5	100.3	110.2	105.9	112.1	146.7	131.4	104.7	145.3	127.3
COVERS	DIVS. 10 - 14, 25, 28, 41, 43, 44, 46	100.0	121.3	104.2	100.0	120.7	104.1	100.0	107.1	101.4	100.0	108.4	101.7	100.0	124.5	104.9	100.0	123.4	104.7
21, 22, 23	FIRE SUPPRESSION, PLUMBING & HVAC	100.1	116.8	106.9	94.1	120.0	104.6	94.1	107.3	99.5	100.1	110.4	104.3	100.2	169.6	128.3	100.1	146.7	118.9
26, 27, 3370	ELECTRICAL, COMMUNICATIONS & UTIL.	101.1	113.3	107.4	91.7	125.8	109.3	95.9	103.6	99.9	96.0	101.0	98.6	105.9	155.0	131.2	102.1	152.2	128.0
MF2010	WEIGHTED AVERAGE	102.9	118.6	109.9	100.5	122.7	110.3	94.3	110.5	101.4	99.3	107.8	103.0	108.5	142.3	123.4	103.2	135.1	117.3

CALIFORNIA

DIVISION		SAN LUIS OBISPO 934			SAN MATEO 944			SAN RAFAEL 949			SANTA ANA 926 - 927			SANTA BARBARA 931			SANTA CRUZ 950		
		MAT.	INST.	TOTAL	MAT.	INST.	TOTAL	MAT.	INST.	TOTAL	MAT.	INST.	TOTAL	MAT.	INST.	TOTAL	MAT.	INST.	TOTAL
015433	CONTRACTOR EQUIPMENT		98.7	98.7		98.5	98.5		98.5	98.5		99.6	99.6		98.7	98.7		99.1	99.1
0241, 31 - 34	SITE & INFRASTRUCTURE, DEMOLITION	108.1	106.0	106.7	124.1	105.3	111.1	114.7	110.7	112.0	86.7	106.5	100.3	102.3	106.0	104.9	135.1	100.0	110.9
0310	Concrete Forming & Accessories	117.8	119.6	119.4	112.9	147.8	143.2	115.2	147.5	143.3	110.8	119.8	118.6	109.1	121.8	120.1	110.1	136.5	133.1
0320	Concrete Reinforcing	110.0	117.9	114.0	95.0	119.4	107.3	95.5	119.3	107.5	110.7	118.0	114.4	108.0	118.0	113.0	118.3	119.2	118.7
0330	Cast-in-Place Concrete	104.7	119.7	110.6	121.0	121.7	121.3	140.9	120.6	132.9	85.0	120.7	99.0	98.2	119.8	106.7	116.3	119.3	117.5
03	CONCRETE	110.0	118.3	114.1	112.3	131.4	121.6	134.4	130.8	132.6	92.6	118.8	105.4	102.2	119.4	110.6	112.9	126.1	119.4
04	MASONRY	102.3	115.1	110.1	129.8	132.2	131.3	106.7	132.2	122.2	75.1	115.7	99.9	100.9	115.1	109.6	136.8	128.4	131.7
05	METALS	98.3	100.9	99.2	97.2	100.6	98.4	98.8	97.7	98.4	101.0	101.4	101.1	96.3	101.3	97.9	102.6	106.6	103.9
06	WOOD, PLASTICS & COMPOSITES	105.0	117.9	112.5	111.6	153.8	135.9	106.4	153.5	133.6	102.2	117.8	111.2	98.1	120.4	111.0	106.5	140.5	126.1
07	THERMAL & MOISTURE PROTECTION	102.1	115.9	107.7	112.0	134.8	121.3	116.6	131.7	122.7	101.6	119.3	108.8	101.4	116.2	107.4	101.1	128.6	112.3
08	OPENINGS	99.0	115.5	103.2	101.4	140.2	111.2	111.3	140.1	118.5	98.1	118.2	103.1	100.9	121.4	106.1	94.3	134.0	104.3
0920	Plaster & Gypsum Board	111.8	118.3	116.5	107.4	154.9	141.3	109.6	154.9	141.9	105.0	118.3	114.5	103.2	120.9	115.8	104.0	141.5	130.8
0950, 0980	Ceilings & Acoustic Treatment	112.0	118.3	116.2	110.3	154.9	139.7	118.4	154.9	142.5	107.5	118.3	114.6	112.5	120.9	118.0	109.3	141.5	130.6
0960	Flooring	116.9	97.4	111.1	112.3	120.8	114.8	123.2	120.8	122.5	115.7	105.0	112.5	109.1	97.4	105.7	105.9	126.8	112.0
0970, 0990	Wall Finishes & Painting/Coating	104.2	99.7	101.4	103.9	139.2	125.6	99.9	139.2	124.1	100.9	104.9	103.4	104.2	99.7	101.4	104.9	141.5	127.5
09	FINISHES	111.7	112.9	112.4	110.2	143.9	129.0	112.8	144.0	130.2	105.7	115.6	111.2	107.9	115.3	112.0	108.3	137.0	124.3
COVERS	DIVS. 10 - 14, 25, 28, 41, 43, 44, 46	100.0	117.5	103.5	100.0	124.0	104.8	100.0	123.3	104.6	100.0	112.0	102.0	100.0	110.7	102.1	100.0	121.0	104.2
21, 22, 23	FIRE SUPPRESSION, PLUMBING & HVAC	94.1	107.3	99.5	94.3	138.4	112.2	94.2	146.1	115.3	94.1	107.4	99.5	100.1	112.0	104.9	100.1	120.0	108.2
26, 27, 3370	ELECTRICAL, COMMUNICATIONS & UTIL.	90.3	98.1	94.3	105.7	141.1	124.0	102.3	116.2	109.5	95.9	105.0	100.6	89.3	108.2	99.0	101.0	125.8	113.8
MF2010	WEIGHTED AVERAGE	99.7	109.4	104.0	103.8	131.3	115.9	106.0	129.5	116.4	96.1	110.8	102.6	99.5	112.3	105.1	105.0	122.8	112.9

City Cost Indexes

CALIFORNIA / COLORADO

DIVISION		SANTA ROSA 954 MAT.	INST.	TOTAL	STOCKTON 952 MAT.	INST.	TOTAL	SUSANVILLE 961 MAT.	INST.	TOTAL	VALLEJO 945 MAT.	INST.	TOTAL	VAN NUYS 913-916 MAT.	INST.	TOTAL	ALAMOSA 811 MAT.	INST.	TOTAL
015433	CONTRACTOR EQUIPMENT		99.0	99.0		98.4	98.4		98.4	98.4		98.5	98.5		99.3	99.3		95.2	95.2
0241, 31 - 34	SITE & INFRASTRUCTURE, DEMOLITION	100.9	105.1	103.8	100.2	105.0	103.5	113.2	105.0	107.5	100.3	110.6	107.4	112.4	109.3	110.3	131.0	91.6	103.8
0310	Concrete Forming & Accessories	104.5	146.9	141.4	107.9	133.3	130.0	108.7	133.0	129.8	106.1	146.6	141.4	117.6	119.9	119.6	105.9	71.5	76.0
0320	Concrete Reinforcing	105.7	119.6	112.7	108.5	118.8	113.7	104.7	118.5	111.7	96.7	119.5	108.2	110.6	118.2	114.4	105.8	80.7	93.2
0330	Cast-in-Place Concrete	110.6	118.7	113.8	98.2	117.1	105.6	101.6	117.0	107.6	112.2	119.3	115.0	89.3	118.3	100.7	99.6	82.0	92.7
03	CONCRETE	111.7	130.4	120.8	102.2	123.6	112.6	112.1	123.4	117.6	108.8	130.0	119.1	108.8	118.0	113.3	113.2	77.2	95.6
04	MASONRY	102.8	133.5	121.5	103.8	123.0	115.5	103.2	119.1	112.9	80.2	133.5	112.7	116.0	118.2	117.4	126.0	75.6	95.2
05	METALS	101.3	104.9	102.5	97.5	102.2	99.0	99.5	101.6	100.2	98.8	98.0	98.5	82.6	101.6	88.9	96.0	82.7	91.6
06	WOOD, PLASTICS & COMPOSITES	93.2	153.3	127.9	99.7	137.2	121.4	99.8	137.2	121.4	96.0	153.5	129.2	92.1	117.7	106.9	93.2	71.8	80.8
07	THERMAL & MOISTURE PROTECTION	102.1	133.9	115.0	104.9	119.8	111.0	105.8	117.5	110.5	114.2	133.6	122.1	101.8	117.4	108.2	106.1	80.8	95.8
08	OPENINGS	99.8	140.9	110.2	100.2	126.6	106.8	102.3	125.9	108.3	113.7	141.0	120.6	91.3	119.7	98.5	95.6	78.0	91.2
0920	Plaster & Gypsum Board	99.1	154.9	138.9	103.6	138.2	128.3	101.8	138.2	127.8	103.7	154.9	140.3	96.1	118.3	112.0	81.6	70.7	73.8
0950, 0980	Ceilings & Acoustic Treatment	107.5	154.9	138.8	112.5	138.2	129.5	112.0	138.2	129.3	120.4	154.9	143.2	91.0	118.3	109.0	108.8	70.7	83.6
0960	Flooring	111.7	120.4	114.3	109.1	116.7	111.3	109.1	110.5	109.5	118.0	126.8	120.6	94.9	105.0	97.8	111.5	57.4	95.6
0970, 0990	Wall Finishes & Painting/Coating	100.9	141.5	126.0	104.2	118.4	112.9	104.2	115.2	111.0	100.8	141.5	125.9	108.1	108.5	108.4	107.9	24.9	56.7
09	FINISHES	105.0	143.5	126.5	107.7	130.8	120.6	108.9	129.4	120.3	109.3	144.7	129.0	97.2	115.9	107.6	106.9	63.5	82.7
COVERS	DIVS. 10 - 14, 25, 28, 41, 43, 44, 46	100.0	122.0	104.4	100.0	120.3	104.0	100.0	120.3	104.0	100.0	122.6	104.5	100.0	109.9	102.0	100.0	90.2	98.0
21, 22, 23	FIRE SUPPRESSION, PLUMBING & HVAC	94.1	168.2	124.1	100.1	113.2	105.4	94.1	108.9	100.1	100.2	130.4	112.4	94.1	111.1	101.0	94.1	74.6	86.2
26, 27, 3370	ELECTRICAL, COMMUNICATIONS & UTIL.	96.2	120.9	108.9	98.9	112.2	105.8	99.7	103.8	101.8	98.1	129.6	114.4	109.7	115.8	112.9	95.7	75.1	85.1
MF2010	WEIGHTED AVERAGE	100.3	135.0	115.6	100.7	117.2	108.0	101.5	114.4	107.2	102.2	128.2	113.7	98.1	113.5	104.9	101.5	76.7	90.6

COLORADO

DIVISION		BOULDER 803 MAT.	INST.	TOTAL	COLORADO SPRINGS 808-809 MAT.	INST.	TOTAL	DENVER 800-802 MAT.	INST.	TOTAL	DURANGO 813 MAT.	INST.	TOTAL	FORT COLLINS 805 MAT.	INST.	TOTAL	FORT MORGAN 807 MAT.	INST.	TOTAL
015433	CONTRACTOR EQUIPMENT		96.2	96.2		94.7	94.7		99.1	99.1		95.2	95.2		96.2	96.2		96.2	96.2
0241, 31 - 34	SITE & INFRASTRUCTURE, DEMOLITION	91.9	97.2	95.6	93.3	95.4	94.7	92.4	103.6	100.1	123.9	91.6	101.6	103.6	96.8	98.9	94.1	96.8	96.0
0310	Concrete Forming & Accessories	104.0	80.0	83.1	95.1	80.4	82.3	100.4	80.7	83.2	111.3	71.8	77.0	101.4	79.1	82.0	104.3	79.5	82.7
0320	Concrete Reinforcing	98.9	80.8	89.8	98.1	85.2	91.6	98.1	85.2	91.6	105.8	80.7	93.2	99.0	79.6	89.2	99.1	80.7	89.8
0330	Cast-in-Place Concrete	103.2	82.4	95.0	106.0	85.8	98.0	100.3	85.5	94.5	114.5	82.1	101.8	116.5	81.2	102.6	101.3	81.3	93.4
03	CONCRETE	102.3	81.3	92.0	105.5	83.4	94.8	100.0	83.5	91.9	116.2	77.4	97.3	112.8	80.1	96.9	100.9	80.5	90.9
04	MASONRY	92.8	76.1	82.6	93.5	76.1	82.9	95.5	76.1	83.7	113.4	75.6	90.3	110.8	55.2	76.9	107.6	75.8	88.2
05	METALS	99.5	86.0	95.0	102.6	88.5	98.0	105.2	88.7	99.7	96.0	83.0	91.7	100.7	81.1	94.2	99.2	82.9	93.8
06	WOOD, PLASTICS & COMPOSITES	97.6	82.1	88.7	88.7	82.2	85.0	95.6	82.2	87.8	101.0	71.8	84.1	95.4	82.1	87.7	97.8	82.1	88.7
07	THERMAL & MOISTURE PROTECTION	105.0	78.8	94.4	105.9	83.1	96.6	104.2	77.0	93.2	106.0	80.8	95.7	105.4	67.9	90.2	105.0	82.4	95.8
08	OPENINGS	101.5	83.6	96.9	106.1	84.9	100.8	106.3	84.8	100.9	103.4	78.0	97.0	101.4	83.6	96.9	101.4	83.6	96.9
0920	Plaster & Gypsum Board	108.6	81.8	89.4	89.1	81.8	83.9	104.6	81.8	88.3	93.4	70.7	77.2	102.7	81.8	87.8	109.1	81.8	89.6
0950, 0980	Ceilings & Acoustic Treatment	99.5	81.8	87.8	106.8	81.8	90.3	105.9	81.8	90.0	108.8	70.7	83.6	99.5	81.8	87.8	99.5	81.8	87.8
0960	Flooring	109.4	87.8	103.1	100.7	71.5	92.1	105.8	88.8	100.8	116.4	57.4	99.1	105.7	57.4	91.5	109.9	57.4	94.5
0970, 0990	Wall Finishes & Painting/Coating	103.0	70.2	82.8	102.7	42.7	65.7	103.0	79.8	88.7	107.9	24.9	56.7	103.0	42.4	65.6	103.0	56.4	74.3
09	FINISHES	104.2	80.5	91.0	101.0	74.7	86.3	103.9	81.9	91.6	108.8	63.5	83.5	103.0	71.4	85.4	104.3	73.0	86.8
COVERS	DIVS. 10 - 14, 25, 28, 41, 43, 44, 46	100.0	90.4	98.1	100.0	90.8	98.2	100.0	90.4	98.1	100.0	90.1	98.0	100.0	90.4	98.1	100.0	90.4	98.1
21, 22, 23	FIRE SUPPRESSION, PLUMBING & HVAC	94.1	80.2	88.4	100.2	74.8	89.9	99.9	80.5	92.1	94.1	89.1	92.1	100.0	80.1	91.9	94.1	80.1	88.4
26, 27, 3370	ELECTRICAL, COMMUNICATIONS & UTIL.	98.9	84.0	91.2	102.4	84.7	93.3	104.1	87.0	95.3	95.1	73.7	84.1	98.9	86.8	92.6	99.3	86.8	92.8
MF2010	WEIGHTED AVERAGE	98.6	82.9	91.7	101.6	81.7	92.8	101.7	84.7	94.2	101.9	79.6	92.1	102.6	79.1	92.2	99.3	82.0	91.7

COLORADO

DIVISION		GLENWOOD SPRINGS 816 MAT.	INST.	TOTAL	GOLDEN 804 MAT.	INST.	TOTAL	GRAND JUNCTION 815 MAT.	INST.	TOTAL	GREELEY 806 MAT.	INST.	TOTAL	MONTROSE 814 MAT.	INST.	TOTAL	PUEBLO 810 MAT.	INST.	TOTAL
015433	CONTRACTOR EQUIPMENT		97.9	97.9		96.2	96.2		97.9	97.9		96.2	96.2		96.5	96.5		95.2	95.2
0241, 31 - 34	SITE & INFRASTRUCTURE, DEMOLITION	140.5	98.5	111.5	105.6	97.1	99.7	123.1	98.2	105.9	90.5	96.2	94.5	133.7	94.7	106.8	114.8	94.1	100.5
0310	Concrete Forming & Accessories	103.3	79.6	82.7	97.4	79.5	81.8	110.1	79.2	83.2	99.6	83.0	85.2	102.9	79.4	82.4	107.8	80.7	84.2
0320	Concrete Reinforcing	104.7	80.7	92.6	99.1	80.7	89.8	105.0	80.7	92.7	98.9	79.3	89.0	104.6	80.7	92.5	101.2	85.2	93.1
0330	Cast-in-Place Concrete	99.5	81.5	92.4	101.3	81.4	93.5	110.2	80.8	98.6	97.4	60.3	82.8	99.6	81.4	92.4	98.8	86.6	94.0
03	CONCRETE	117.9	80.7	99.8	110.1	80.5	95.7	112.6	80.1	96.8	97.6	74.6	86.4	109.6	80.4	95.4	102.7	83.9	93.5
04	MASONRY	100.2	75.8	85.3	110.4	75.8	89.3	133.2	75.6	98.0	104.7	51.6	72.3	106.6	75.6	87.7	96.7	76.1	84.1
05	METALS	95.7	83.5	91.7	99.4	83.0	94.0	97.3	82.2	92.3	100.7	80.0	93.8	94.9	82.5	90.8	98.9	89.3	95.7
06	WOOD, PLASTICS & COMPOSITES	88.7	82.2	85.0	90.7	82.1	85.7	98.8	82.2	89.2	92.9	88.2	90.2	89.9	82.4	85.6	95.5	82.5	88.0
07	THERMAL & MOISTURE PROTECTION	105.9	81.9	96.2	105.9	76.4	93.9	104.9	70.8	91.0	104.8	63.3	87.9	106.1	81.9	96.3	104.4	82.6	95.6
08	OPENINGS	102.5	83.6	97.8	101.4	83.6	96.9	103.4	83.6	98.4	101.4	86.9	97.8	103.6	83.7	98.6	97.5	85.0	94.4
0920	Plaster & Gypsum Board	113.3	81.8	90.8	100.0	81.8	87.0	125.1	81.8	94.2	100.9	88.1	91.8	80.7	81.8	81.5	86.6	81.8	83.1
0950, 0980	Ceilings & Acoustic Treatment	107.9	81.8	90.6	99.5	81.8	87.8	107.9	81.8	90.6	99.5	88.1	92.0	108.8	81.8	90.9	117.8	81.8	94.0
0960	Flooring	110.6	52.8	93.6	103.3	57.4	89.8	115.8	57.4	98.7	104.5	57.4	90.7	113.9	47.5	94.4	112.6	88.8	105.6
0970, 0990	Wall Finishes & Painting/Coating	107.9	56.4	76.2	103.0	70.2	82.8	107.9	70.2	84.6	103.0	26.4	55.8	107.9	24.9	56.7	107.9	39.6	65.8
09	FINISHES	110.7	72.3	89.3	102.9	75.3	87.5	111.4	74.6	90.9	101.5	73.3	85.8	107.5	67.7	85.3	107.7	77.7	91.0
COVERS	DIVS. 10 - 14, 25, 28, 41, 43, 44, 46	100.0	90.6	98.1	100.0	90.4	98.1	100.0	90.5	98.1	100.0	91.1	98.2	100.0	90.9	98.1	100.0	91.4	98.3
21, 22, 23	FIRE SUPPRESSION, PLUMBING & HVAC	94.1	88.9	92.0	94.1	79.7	88.3	100.0	88.6	95.4	100.0	80.0	91.9	94.1	88.9	92.0	100.0	74.8	89.8
26, 27, 3370	ELECTRICAL, COMMUNICATIONS & UTIL.	92.7	73.8	82.9	99.3	83.9	91.4	94.8	57.2	75.4	98.9	86.8	92.6	94.8	59.9	76.8	95.7	75.1	85.1
MF2010	WEIGHTED AVERAGE	101.6	82.2	93.1	100.7	81.7	92.3	104.2	79.6	93.4	100.0	78.2	90.4	100.8	79.3	91.3	100.4	80.8	91.8

653

DIVISION		COLORADO SALIDA 812			CONNECTICUT BRIDGEPORT 066			BRISTOL 060			HARTFORD 061			MERIDEN 064			NEW BRITAIN 060		
		MAT.	INST.	TOTAL	MAT.	INST.	TOTAL	MAT.	INST.	TOTAL	MAT.	INST.	TOTAL	MAT.	INST.	TOTAL	MAT.	INST.	TOTAL
015433	CONTRACTOR EQUIPMENT		96.5	96.5		100.4	100.4		100.4	100.4		100.4	100.4		100.9	100.9		100.4	100.4
0241, 31 - 34	SITE & INFRASTRUCTURE, DEMOLITION	123.6	95.0	103.9	111.8	103.3	105.9	111.0	103.3	105.7	103.6	103.3	103.4	109.2	104.0	105.6	111.2	103.3	105.7
0310	Concrete Forming & Accessories	110.1	79.2	83.3	99.3	121.7	118.8	99.3	121.6	118.7	97.3	121.6	118.4	99.0	121.6	118.6	99.6	121.6	118.7
0320	Concrete Reinforcing	104.3	80.7	92.4	103.6	128.8	116.3	103.6	128.8	116.3	103.6	128.8	116.3	103.6	128.8	116.3	103.6	128.8	116.3
0330	Cast-in-Place Concrete	114.1	81.4	101.2	107.8	125.0	114.6	101.0	125.0	110.4	107.0	125.0	114.1	97.1	125.0	108.1	102.6	125.0	111.1
03	CONCRETE	111.5	80.4	96.3	110.6	124.0	117.1	107.1	123.9	115.3	110.0	123.9	116.8	105.2	123.9	114.3	108.0	123.9	115.7
04	MASONRY	134.8	75.6	98.7	104.1	129.8	119.8	96.7	129.8	116.9	97.2	129.8	117.1	96.3	129.8	116.7	98.0	129.8	117.4
05	METALS	94.6	82.4	90.6	99.1	125.2	107.7	99.1	125.0	107.7	103.9	125.0	110.9	96.5	125.0	105.9	95.7	125.0	105.4
06	WOOD, PLASTICS & COMPOSITES	96.5	82.4	88.3	98.6	120.3	111.1	98.6	120.3	111.1	97.1	120.3	110.5	98.6	120.3	111.1	98.6	120.3	111.1
07	THERMAL & MOISTURE PROTECTION	105.0	81.9	95.6	101.2	126.6	111.6	101.3	123.7	110.4	102.6	123.7	111.2	101.3	123.7	110.4	101.3	123.7	110.4
08	OPENINGS	95.7	83.7	92.7	102.4	130.1	109.4	102.4	130.1	109.4	103.1	130.1	109.9	105.1	130.1	111.4	102.4	130.1	109.4
0920	Plaster & Gypsum Board	81.2	81.8	81.6	97.8	120.3	113.8	97.8	120.3	113.8	95.9	120.3	113.3	99.6	120.3	114.4	97.8	120.3	113.8
0950, 0980	Ceilings & Acoustic Treatment	108.8	81.8	90.9	102.0	120.3	114.1	102.0	120.3	114.1	100.2	120.3	113.5	106.3	120.3	115.5	102.0	120.3	114.1
0960	Flooring	119.1	47.5	98.1	94.5	134.4	106.2	94.5	134.4	106.2	94.5	134.4	106.2	94.5	134.4	106.2	94.5	134.4	106.2
0970, 0990	Wall Finishes & Painting/Coating	107.9	24.9	56.7	90.1	117.5	107.0	90.1	117.5	107.0	90.1	117.5	107.0	90.1	117.5	107.0	90.1	117.5	107.0
09	FINISHES	107.9	67.7	85.5	101.7	123.2	113.7	101.8	123.2	113.7	99.9	123.2	112.9	102.9	123.2	114.2	101.8	123.2	113.7
COVERS	DIVS. 10 - 14, 25, 28, 41, 43, 44, 46	100.0	91.0	98.2	100.0	108.6	101.7	100.0	108.6	101.7	100.0	108.6	101.7	100.0	108.6	101.7	100.0	108.6	101.7
21, 22, 23	FIRE SUPPRESSION, PLUMBING & HVAC	94.1	74.6	86.2	100.0	114.7	106.0	100.0	114.7	106.0	100.1	114.7	106.0	94.1	114.7	102.4	100.0	114.7	106.0
26, 27, 3370	ELECTRICAL, COMMUNICATIONS & UTIL.	95.1	75.1	84.8	102.2	109.9	106.2	102.2	109.6	106.0	99.2	110.5	105.1	102.1	109.6	106.0	102.3	109.6	106.1
MF2010	WEIGHTED AVERAGE	101.3	78.3	91.2	102.2	118.7	109.5	101.5	118.6	109.0	102.0	118.7	109.4	99.7	118.6	108.0	101.1	118.6	108.8

DIVISION		CONNECTICUT NEW HAVEN 065			NEW LONDON 063			NORWALK 068			STAMFORD 069			WATERBURY 067			WILLIMANTIC 062		
		MAT.	INST.	TOTAL	MAT.	INST.	TOTAL	MAT.	INST.	TOTAL	MAT.	INST.	TOTAL	MAT.	INST.	TOTAL	MAT.	INST.	TOTAL
015433	CONTRACTOR EQUIPMENT		100.9	100.9		100.9	100.9		100.4	100.4		100.4	100.4		100.4	100.4		100.4	100.4
0241, 31 - 34	SITE & INFRASTRUCTURE, DEMOLITION	111.1	104.0	106.2	102.8	104.0	103.6	111.6	103.3	105.9	112.3	103.3	106.1	111.4	103.3	105.8	111.9	103.3	105.9
0310	Concrete Forming & Accessories	99.0	121.6	118.6	99.0	121.6	118.6	99.3	122.1	119.1	99.3	122.1	119.1	99.3	121.6	118.7	99.3	121.5	118.6
0320	Concrete Reinforcing	103.6	128.8	116.3	81.2	128.8	105.2	103.6	129.0	116.4	103.6	129.0	116.4	103.6	128.8	116.3	103.6	128.8	116.3
0330	Cast-in-Place Concrete	104.4	125.0	112.5	88.9	125.0	103.1	106.0	126.5	114.1	107.8	126.5	115.2	107.8	125.0	114.6	100.7	124.9	110.2
03	CONCRETE	123.2	123.9	123.5	94.7	123.9	108.9	109.7	124.7	117.0	110.6	124.7	117.4	110.6	123.9	117.0	107.0	123.8	115.2
04	MASONRY	96.9	129.8	117.0	95.3	129.8	116.3	96.4	131.3	117.7	97.2	131.3	118.0	97.2	129.8	117.1	96.5	129.8	116.8
05	METALS	95.9	125.0	105.5	95.6	125.0	105.3	99.1	125.7	107.9	99.1	125.7	107.9	99.1	125.0	107.7	98.9	124.9	107.5
06	WOOD, PLASTICS & COMPOSITES	98.6	120.3	111.1	98.6	120.3	111.1	98.6	120.3	111.1	98.6	120.3	111.1	98.6	120.3	111.1	98.6	120.3	111.1
07	THERMAL & MOISTURE PROTECTION	101.4	123.6	110.4	101.3	123.7	110.4	101.4	127.3	111.9	101.3	127.3	111.9	101.3	123.6	110.4	101.5	123.3	110.4
08	OPENINGS	102.4	130.1	109.4	105.6	130.1	111.8	102.4	130.1	109.4	102.4	130.1	109.4	102.4	130.1	109.4	105.6	130.1	111.8
0920	Plaster & Gypsum Board	97.8	120.3	113.8	97.8	120.3	113.8	97.8	120.3	113.8	97.8	120.3	113.8	97.8	120.3	113.8	97.8	120.3	113.8
0950, 0980	Ceilings & Acoustic Treatment	102.0	120.3	114.1	100.0	120.3	113.4	102.0	120.3	114.1	102.0	120.3	114.1	102.0	120.3	114.1	100.0	120.3	113.4
0960	Flooring	94.5	134.4	106.2	94.5	134.4	106.2	94.5	134.4	106.2	94.5	134.4	106.2	94.5	134.4	106.2	94.5	119.7	101.9
0970, 0990	Wall Finishes & Painting/Coating	90.1	117.5	107.0	90.1	117.5	107.0	90.1	117.5	107.0	90.1	117.5	107.0	90.1	117.5	107.0	90.1	117.5	107.0
09	FINISHES	101.8	123.2	113.7	100.6	123.2	113.2	101.8	123.2	113.7	101.9	123.2	113.7	101.6	123.2	113.6	101.5	120.7	112.2
COVERS	DIVS. 10 - 14, 25, 28, 41, 43, 44, 46	100.0	108.6	101.7	100.0	108.6	101.7	100.0	108.8	101.7	100.0	108.8	101.7	100.0	108.6	101.7	100.0	108.6	101.7
21, 22, 23	FIRE SUPPRESSION, PLUMBING & HVAC	100.0	114.7	106.0	94.1	114.7	102.4	100.0	114.8	106.0	100.0	114.8	106.0	100.0	114.7	106.0	100.0	114.7	106.0
26, 27, 3370	ELECTRICAL, COMMUNICATIONS & UTIL.	102.1	109.6	106.0	98.7	109.6	104.3	102.2	162.3	133.2	102.2	162.3	133.2	101.6	109.9	105.9	102.2	110.5	106.5
MF2010	WEIGHTED AVERAGE	102.8	118.6	109.8	97.6	118.6	106.9	101.8	126.3	112.6	101.9	126.3	112.7	101.8	118.6	109.2	101.7	118.4	109.1

DIVISION		D.C. WASHINGTON 200 - 205			DELAWARE DOVER 199			NEWARK 197			WILMINGTON 198			FLORIDA DAYTONA BEACH 321			FORT LAUDERDALE 333		
		MAT.	INST.	TOTAL	MAT.	INST.	TOTAL	MAT.	INST.	TOTAL	MAT.	INST.	TOTAL	MAT.	INST.	TOTAL	MAT.	INST.	TOTAL
015433	CONTRACTOR EQUIPMENT		103.2	103.2		116.9	116.9		116.9	116.9		117.0	117.0		98.0	98.0		90.9	90.9
0241, 31 - 34	SITE & INFRASTRUCTURE, DEMOLITION	109.6	92.6	97.9	98.2	111.9	107.6	98.6	111.9	107.8	88.8	112.2	104.9	116.5	89.6	97.9	99.7	77.9	84.6
0310	Concrete Forming & Accessories	97.4	81.1	83.2	98.3	102.7	102.1	100.4	102.7	102.4	101.4	102.7	102.5	96.7	72.1	75.3	95.3	72.8	75.7
0320	Concrete Reinforcing	98.5	89.7	94.1	96.0	102.1	99.1	96.8	102.1	99.5	96.8	102.1	99.5	96.3	77.0	86.6	96.3	76.7	86.4
0330	Cast-in-Place Concrete	129.8	90.0	114.1	95.5	101.9	98.0	85.8	101.9	92.2	92.6	101.9	96.3	91.8	73.9	84.7	96.2	81.0	90.2
03	CONCRETE	115.7	87.0	101.7	97.3	103.2	100.2	92.7	103.2	97.8	96.2	103.2	99.6	91.6	74.8	83.4	93.8	77.5	85.8
04	MASONRY	101.4	81.4	89.2	103.8	96.8	99.5	102.1	96.8	98.9	108.2	96.8	101.2	93.6	69.4	78.8	93.9	72.2	80.6
05	METALS	96.5	106.6	99.8	103.9	116.9	108.2	103.9	116.9	108.2	100.8	116.9	106.1	96.1	92.2	94.8	96.0	93.1	95.1
06	WOOD, PLASTICS & COMPOSITES	101.9	79.9	89.2	97.2	102.6	100.3	100.1	102.6	101.6	102.5	102.6	102.5	100.0	73.6	84.7	95.9	71.4	81.8
07	THERMAL & MOISTURE PROTECTION	100.2	84.9	94.0	97.9	112.4	103.8	97.9	112.4	103.8	98.4	112.4	104.1	95.1	77.8	88.1	95.1	85.4	91.2
08	OPENINGS	103.0	88.8	99.4	95.6	110.4	99.3	95.6	110.4	99.3	95.3	110.4	99.1	100.2	70.5	92.7	97.9	69.5	90.7
0920	Plaster & Gypsum Board	108.6	79.3	87.7	105.9	102.5	103.5	107.3	102.5	103.9	107.8	102.5	104.0	93.2	73.2	78.9	92.3	71.0	77.1
0950, 0980	Ceilings & Acoustic Treatment	105.8	79.3	88.3	104.2	102.5	103.1	104.2	102.5	103.1	99.5	102.5	101.5	95.8	73.2	80.9	95.8	71.0	79.4
0960	Flooring	115.0	97.2	109.8	97.1	107.6	100.1	97.3	107.6	100.3	96.9	107.6	100.0	117.7	77.1	105.8	117.7	72.6	104.5
0970, 0990	Wall Finishes & Painting/Coating	121.0	86.6	99.8	98.1	102.8	101.0	98.1	102.8	101.0	98.1	102.8	101.0	111.2	78.1	90.8	105.7	74.0	86.2
09	FINISHES	107.0	83.9	94.1	100.1	103.1	101.8	100.6	103.1	102.0	99.4	103.1	101.5	107.1	73.4	88.3	103.9	72.1	86.2
COVERS	DIVS. 10 - 14, 25, 28, 41, 43, 44, 46	100.0	99.4	99.9	100.0	93.7	98.7	100.0	93.7	98.7	100.0	93.7	98.7	100.0	78.3	95.7	100.0	84.8	97.0
21, 22, 23	FIRE SUPPRESSION, PLUMBING & HVAC	100.2	94.2	97.7	99.9	113.4	105.4	100.0	113.4	105.5	100.1	113.4	105.5	99.9	77.0	90.6	99.9	70.6	88.1
26, 27, 3370	ELECTRICAL, COMMUNICATIONS & UTIL.	98.8	106.0	102.5	96.4	110.1	103.5	100.3	110.1	105.3	98.6	110.1	104.5	98.0	58.4	77.6	98.0	74.3	85.8
MF2010	WEIGHTED AVERAGE	102.4	92.8	98.2	99.5	107.9	103.2	99.4	107.9	103.2	99.1	108.0	103.0	98.8	75.2	88.4	98.1	75.9	88.3

City Cost Indexes

FLORIDA

DIVISION		FORT MYERS 339,341			GAINESVILLE 326,344			JACKSONVILLE 320,322			LAKELAND 338			MELBOURNE 329			MIAMI 330 - 332,340		
		MAT.	INST.	TOTAL	MAT.	INST.	TOTAL	MAT.	INST.	TOTAL	MAT.	INST.	TOTAL	MAT.	INST.	TOTAL	MAT.	INST.	TOTAL
015433	CONTRACTOR EQUIPMENT		98.0	98.0		98.0	98.0		98.0	98.0		98.0	98.0		98.0	98.0		90.9	90.9
0241, 31 - 34	SITE & INFRASTRUCTURE, DEMOLITION	113.5	88.9	96.5	127.3	88.6	100.6	116.5	88.9	97.5	115.7	89.1	97.3	124.9	88.8	100.0	101.6	77.6	85.1
0310	Concrete Forming & Accessories	91.1	79.5	81.1	92.0	57.5	62.0	96.5	57.9	62.9	87.6	80.1	81.1	93.1	73.8	76.3	99.7	73.2	76.6
0320	Concrete Reinforcing	97.4	98.6	98.0	102.3	67.6	84.8	96.3	67.7	81.9	99.9	99.5	99.7	97.4	77.0	87.1	96.3	76.7	86.5
0330	Cast-in-Place Concrete	100.4	71.6	89.1	105.3	65.3	89.6	92.7	71.4	84.3	102.7	72.9	90.9	110.6	76.4	97.1	98.1	82.0	91.8
03	CONCRETE	94.7	81.3	88.2	102.6	63.6	83.6	92.0	65.9	79.3	96.6	82.1	89.6	103.3	76.4	90.2	95.0	78.0	86.7
04	MASONRY	87.5	65.4	74.0	109.0	64.6	81.9	93.6	64.7	76.0	105.5	80.1	90.0	92.7	73.7	81.1	94.4	76.0	83.2
05	METALS	98.2	100.5	99.0	95.1	87.1	92.4	94.7	87.5	92.3	98.1	101.2	99.1	104.2	92.3	100.3	100.9	91.9	97.9
06	WOOD, PLASTICS & COMPOSITES	92.8	82.3	86.7	94.0	55.0	71.5	100.0	55.0	74.0	88.6	82.3	85.0	95.6	73.6	82.9	101.6	71.4	84.2
07	THERMAL & MOISTURE PROTECTION	94.9	84.5	90.7	95.4	64.7	82.9	95.3	65.3	83.1	94.9	89.3	92.6	95.5	80.3	89.3	103.6	79.5	93.8
08	OPENINGS	98.8	79.0	93.8	98.2	55.6	87.4	100.2	58.9	89.8	98.7	79.7	93.9	99.3	73.9	92.9	97.9	69.5	90.7
0920	Plaster & Gypsum Board	87.3	82.2	83.7	88.2	54.1	63.8	93.2	54.1	65.3	85.1	82.2	83.0	88.2	73.2	77.5	90.6	71.0	76.6
0950, 0980	Ceilings & Acoustic Treatment	89.3	82.2	84.6	89.3	54.1	66.0	95.8	54.1	68.2	89.3	82.2	84.6	91.3	73.2	79.3	93.1	71.0	78.5
0960	Flooring	114.1	57.7	97.5	114.6	45.2	94.2	117.7	67.6	103.0	111.4	59.2	96.1	114.8	77.1	103.7	125.3	76.4	111.0
0970, 0990	Wall Finishes & Painting/Coating	111.2	64.1	82.1	111.2	64.1	82.1	111.2	65.3	82.9	111.2	64.1	82.1	111.2	96.9	102.4	105.7	74.0	86.2
09	FINISHES	103.7	74.1	87.2	105.5	54.8	77.2	107.1	59.4	80.5	102.8	74.4	86.9	105.5	76.6	89.4	105.5	73.3	87.6
COVERS	DIVS. 10 - 14, 25, 28, 41, 43, 44, 46	100.0	78.6	95.7	100.0	76.6	95.3	100.0	74.6	95.0	100.0	78.6	95.7	100.0	79.8	96.0	100.0	85.4	97.1
21, 22, 23	FIRE SUPPRESSION, PLUMBING & HVAC	96.7	66.2	84.4	98.8	68.6	86.6	99.9	68.6	87.3	96.7	86.7	92.7	99.9	79.2	91.5	99.9	71.3	88.3
26, 27, 3370	ELECTRICAL, COMMUNICATIONS & UTIL.	100.3	65.5	82.3	98.3	76.3	87.0	97.7	66.1	81.4	98.3	65.4	81.3	99.4	68.0	83.2	99.9	76.9	88.0
MF2010	WEIGHTED AVERAGE	98.1	75.8	88.3	100.4	69.7	86.9	98.7	69.4	85.7	99.0	82.0	91.5	101.5	78.2	91.2	99.6	76.7	89.6

FLORIDA

DIVISION		ORLANDO 327 - 328,347			PANAMA CITY 324			PENSACOLA 325			SARASOTA 342			ST. PETERSBURG 337			TALLAHASSEE 323		
		MAT.	INST.	TOTAL	MAT.	INST.	TOTAL	MAT.	INST.	TOTAL	MAT.	INST.	TOTAL	MAT.	INST.	TOTAL	MAT.	INST.	TOTAL
015433	CONTRACTOR EQUIPMENT		98.0	98.0		98.0	98.0		98.0	98.0		98.0	98.0		98.0	98.0		98.0	98.0
0241, 31 - 34	SITE & INFRASTRUCTURE, DEMOLITION	116.7	88.7	97.4	131.7	87.8	101.4	130.9	88.3	101.5	117.9	88.8	97.8	117.3	88.4	97.4	112.6	88.0	95.6
0310	Concrete Forming & Accessories	96.3	76.4	79.0	95.8	46.6	53.0	93.8	55.0	60.0	96.7	79.6	81.9	94.8	54.1	59.4	98.6	46.8	53.5
0320	Concrete Reinforcing	96.3	76.3	86.2	100.6	77.1	88.7	103.2	77.6	90.3	96.3	99.4	97.9	99.9	86.2	93.0	96.3	67.5	81.8
0330	Cast-in-Place Concrete	115.0	73.8	98.7	97.4	59.3	82.4	120.3	68.9	100.0	104.9	72.7	92.2	103.8	67.2	89.4	100.2	58.8	83.9
03	CONCRETE	104.5	76.5	90.8	100.2	58.4	79.8	111.1	65.6	88.9	98.2	81.8	90.2	98.1	66.2	82.6	95.9	56.6	76.8
04	MASONRY	99.2	69.4	81.0	98.6	49.9	68.9	116.3	57.5	80.4	94.5	80.1	85.7	148.1	51.7	89.3	96.8	56.8	72.4
05	METALS	101.6	91.5	98.3	95.9	89.3	93.7	97.0	90.8	95.0	98.8	100.7	99.4	99.0	93.7	97.3	89.8	86.8	88.8
06	WOOD, PLASTICS & COMPOSITES	99.5	79.9	88.2	98.8	44.4	67.3	96.9	54.8	72.6	100.0	82.3	89.8	97.3	53.2	71.9	97.3	43.9	66.5
07	THERMAL & MOISTURE PROTECTION	96.3	78.4	89.0	95.6	59.7	81.0	95.5	65.8	83.4	95.1	89.3	92.8	95.1	61.0	81.2	101.0	75.5	90.6
08	OPENINGS	100.2	72.9	93.3	97.7	49.3	85.5	97.7	60.4	88.3	100.2	78.7	94.8	98.7	63.3	89.8	100.7	49.9	87.9
0920	Plaster & Gypsum Board	104.6	79.8	86.9	91.0	43.1	56.8	91.5	53.8	64.6	93.2	82.2	85.4	90.1	52.2	63.0	107.2	42.6	61.0
0950, 0980	Ceilings & Acoustic Treatment	98.5	79.8	86.1	91.3	43.1	59.4	91.3	53.8	66.5	93.8	82.2	86.1	91.3	52.2	65.5	98.5	42.6	61.6
0960	Flooring	117.9	77.1	105.9	117.2	45.0	96.0	112.0	65.9	98.5	117.7	60.6	100.9	116.3	57.8	99.2	117.7	64.9	102.2
0970, 0990	Wall Finishes & Painting/Coating	111.2	74.0	88.3	111.2	66.3	83.5	111.2	66.3	83.5	111.2	64.1	82.1	111.2	64.1	82.1	111.2	66.3	83.5
09	FINISHES	108.8	76.8	90.9	107.5	47.2	73.9	105.6	57.5	78.8	106.7	74.6	88.8	105.4	54.8	77.2	108.7	50.8	76.4
COVERS	DIVS. 10 - 14, 25, 28, 41, 43, 44, 46	100.0	79.0	95.8	100.0	49.9	90.0	100.0	50.0	90.1	100.0	78.6	95.7	100.0	60.3	92.1	100.0	71.2	94.3
21, 22, 23	FIRE SUPPRESSION, PLUMBING & HVAC	99.9	60.6	84.0	99.9	55.8	82.1	99.9	56.2	82.2	99.8	64.8	85.6	99.9	60.1	83.8	99.9	41.8	76.4
26, 27, 3370	ELECTRICAL, COMMUNICATIONS & UTIL.	100.1	62.8	80.8	96.7	60.1	77.8	100.7	57.2	78.3	98.0	65.4	81.2	98.3	65.4	81.3	103.8	60.1	81.3
MF2010	WEIGHTED AVERAGE	101.8	73.0	89.1	100.1	60.5	82.7	102.6	64.1	85.6	100.0	77.3	90.0	102.5	65.8	86.3	99.4	59.3	81.7

FLORIDA / GEORGIA

DIVISION		TAMPA 335 - 336,346			WEST PALM BEACH 334,349			ALBANY 317,398			ATHENS 306			ATLANTA 300 - 303,399			AUGUSTA 308 - 309		
		MAT.	INST.	TOTAL	MAT.	INST.	TOTAL	MAT.	INST.	TOTAL	MAT.	INST.	TOTAL	MAT.	INST.	TOTAL	MAT.	INST.	TOTAL
015433	CONTRACTOR EQUIPMENT		98.0	98.0		90.9	90.9		91.8	91.8		93.2	93.2		93.7	93.7		93.2	93.2
0241, 31 - 34	SITE & INFRASTRUCTURE, DEMOLITION	117.6	89.0	97.9	96.4	77.9	83.6	99.9	79.2	85.6	103.6	92.3	95.8	99.4	94.1	95.7	95.8	92.0	93.2
0310	Concrete Forming & Accessories	97.6	80.2	82.4	98.6	72.4	75.8	96.0	45.8	52.3	93.6	43.5	50.0	96.9	75.3	78.1	94.5	67.0	70.6
0320	Concrete Reinforcing	96.3	99.5	97.9	99.1	76.4	87.6	96.0	83.5	89.7	102.7	82.7	92.6	102.0	84.9	93.4	103.0	75.5	89.1
0330	Cast-in-Place Concrete	101.4	72.9	90.2	91.5	78.0	86.2	98.0	47.8	78.2	111.6	53.1	88.5	111.6	71.7	95.9	105.4	50.0	83.6
03	CONCRETE	96.5	82.2	89.5	90.7	76.2	83.7	94.5	55.1	75.3	103.1	55.0	79.7	101.1	75.9	88.8	96.6	63.0	80.2
04	MASONRY	94.9	80.1	85.9	93.4	70.4	79.4	96.0	44.6	64.7	82.4	56.9	66.8	96.8	67.7	79.1	97.1	41.4	63.1
05	METALS	98.1	101.2	99.1	95.2	92.6	94.3	95.4	86.9	92.6	91.2	75.4	86.0	92.1	79.5	87.9	90.9	72.9	84.9
06	WOOD, PLASTICS & COMPOSITES	101.2	82.3	90.3	100.6	71.4	83.7	99.0	40.3	65.1	93.8	37.3	61.2	97.7	78.0	86.3	95.1	72.7	82.1
07	THERMAL & MOISTURE PROTECTION	95.3	89.3	92.9	94.9	74.1	86.4	92.8	61.4	80.0	94.5	54.7	78.3	94.4	74.2	86.2	94.1	58.5	79.6
08	OPENINGS	100.2	82.1	95.6	97.0	69.5	90.0	97.9	46.6	84.9	91.2	45.2	79.6	97.0	73.7	91.1	91.3	64.4	84.5
0920	Plaster & Gypsum Board	93.2	82.2	85.4	96.0	71.0	78.1	93.0	38.9	54.4	96.5	35.7	53.1	98.7	77.7	83.7	97.4	72.2	79.4
0950, 0980	Ceilings & Acoustic Treatment	95.8	82.2	86.8	89.3	71.0	77.2	94.9	38.9	57.9	95.8	35.7	56.1	95.8	77.7	83.8	96.8	72.2	80.6
0960	Flooring	117.7	59.2	100.5	120.1	69.6	105.3	117.7	37.5	94.2	89.2	56.4	79.5	90.6	68.3	84.1	89.6	41.1	75.4
0970, 0990	Wall Finishes & Painting/Coating	111.2	64.1	82.1	105.7	74.0	86.2	105.7	55.0	74.4	96.6	36.9	59.8	96.6	84.6	89.2	96.6	38.5	60.8
09	FINISHES	107.2	74.4	88.9	103.2	71.5	85.6	103.7	43.2	70.0	94.6	43.5	66.1	94.8	75.0	83.8	94.2	59.9	75.1
COVERS	DIVS. 10 - 14, 25, 28, 41, 43, 44, 46	100.0	79.1	95.9	100.0	84.8	97.0	100.0	80.6	96.1	100.0	42.2	88.5	100.0	85.3	97.1	100.0	53.6	90.8
21, 22, 23	FIRE SUPPRESSION, PLUMBING & HVAC	99.9	86.7	94.6	96.7	67.3	84.8	99.9	68.2	87.1	94.0	72.9	85.4	99.9	73.4	89.2	100.0	65.7	86.1
26, 27, 3370	ELECTRICAL, COMMUNICATIONS & UTIL.	98.0	65.4	81.2	99.4	74.3	86.5	93.5	60.1	76.3	102.3	73.9	87.7	101.7	75.5	88.2	103.0	65.6	83.7
MF2010	WEIGHTED AVERAGE	99.8	82.1	92.0	96.7	74.4	86.9	97.6	61.5	81.7	95.5	64.2	81.7	98.0	76.5	88.5	96.7	64.5	82.5

GEORGIA

DIVISION		COLUMBUS 318-319 MAT.	INST.	TOTAL	DALTON 307 MAT.	INST.	TOTAL	GAINESVILLE 305 MAT.	INST.	TOTAL	MACON 310-312 MAT.	INST.	TOTAL	SAVANNAH 313-314 MAT.	INST.	TOTAL	STATESBORO 304 MAT.	INST.	TOTAL
015433	CONTRACTOR EQUIPMENT		91.8	91.8		104.7	104.7		93.2	93.2		101.9	101.9		92.7	92.7		92.6	92.6
0241, 31 - 34	SITE & INFRASTRUCTURE, DEMOLITION	99.8	79.3	85.7	104.0	96.3	98.7	103.0	92.3	95.6	101.1	94.0	96.2	100.8	80.0	86.5	104.5	77.0	85.6
0310	Concrete Forming & Accessories	95.9	57.1	62.2	87.3	49.0	54.0	96.6	45.3	52.0	95.2	54.3	59.6	96.0	50.7	56.6	82.3	42.5	47.6
0320	Concrete Reinforcing	96.3	84.2	90.2	102.2	78.3	90.1	102.5	82.7	92.5	97.6	83.5	90.5	97.2	75.7	86.4	101.8	44.0	72.6
0330	Cast-in-Place Concrete	97.6	56.3	81.3	108.4	47.0	84.2	117.3	52.9	91.9	96.3	50.2	78.1	107.4	49.2	84.5	111.4	61.7	91.8
03	CONCRETE	94.4	63.2	79.2	102.0	55.4	79.3	105.3	55.8	81.2	93.9	59.8	77.3	99.4	56.3	78.4	102.6	51.2	77.5
04	MASONRY	96.0	58.4	73.1	84.2	33.9	53.5	91.4	57.3	70.6	108.2	39.4	66.3	95.1	51.5	68.5	85.6	41.6	58.8
05	METALS	94.9	88.6	92.8	91.9	85.0	89.6	90.4	75.1	85.3	91.1	87.7	90.0	91.4	84.2	89.1	95.4	72.4	87.8
06	WOOD, PLASTICS & COMPOSITES	99.0	55.4	73.8	76.7	50.4	61.5	97.5	40.2	64.4	108.9	54.4	77.4	115.1	47.5	76.1	70.7	41.8	54.0
07	THERMAL & MOISTURE PROTECTION	92.7	65.7	81.7	96.3	52.7	78.6	94.4	57.6	79.4	91.3	63.1	79.9	95.0	58.2	80.1	95.0	51.0	77.1
08	OPENINGS	97.9	56.7	87.5	92.9	47.1	81.3	91.2	42.4	78.9	96.2	55.2	85.9	99.1	48.5	86.4	93.6	33.4	78.4
0920	Plaster & Gypsum Board	93.0	54.5	65.4	80.3	49.2	58.1	98.7	38.7	55.9	101.8	53.4	67.2	92.2	46.4	59.5	82.2	40.4	52.3
0950, 0980	Ceilings & Acoustic Treatment	94.9	54.5	68.2	107.8	49.2	69.1	95.8	38.7	58.1	89.7	53.4	65.7	98.5	46.4	64.1	104.0	40.4	62.0
0960	Flooring	117.7	52.8	98.6	90.0	37.5	74.6	90.6	37.5	75.0	91.6	38.0	75.9	118.3	48.6	97.8	106.1	47.0	88.8
0970, 0990	Wall Finishes & Painting/Coating	105.7	68.2	82.5	87.3	56.3	68.2	96.6	36.9	59.8	108.1	55.0	75.3	107.1	57.2	76.3	94.6	34.6	57.6
09	FINISHES	103.6	56.4	77.3	103.6	47.0	72.0	95.0	40.9	64.8	91.3	50.2	68.4	104.7	50.1	74.2	106.4	41.6	70.3
COVERS	DIVS. 10 - 14, 25, 28, 41, 43, 44, 46	100.0	82.3	96.5	100.0	24.2	84.9	100.0	42.5	88.6	100.0	80.3	96.1	100.0	52.6	90.6	100.0	39.2	87.9
21, 22, 23	FIRE SUPPRESSION, PLUMBING & HVAC	99.9	49.9	79.7	94.1	59.2	79.9	94.0	72.8	85.4	99.9	66.3	86.3	99.9	61.6	84.4	94.5	56.7	79.2
26, 27, 3370	ELECTRICAL, COMMUNICATIONS & UTIL.	93.5	74.0	83.4	113.8	72.0	92.2	102.3	73.9	87.7	92.5	62.1	76.8	95.0	57.4	75.6	102.6	57.4	79.3
MF2010	WEIGHTED AVERAGE	97.5	64.6	83.0	97.6	60.1	81.1	96.1	64.0	82.0	96.4	64.2	82.2	98.1	60.5	81.5	97.4	54.0	78.3

GEORGIA / HAWAII / IDAHO

DIVISION		VALDOSTA 316 MAT.	INST.	TOTAL	WAYCROSS 315 MAT.	INST.	TOTAL	HILO 967 MAT.	INST.	TOTAL	HONOLULU 968 MAT.	INST.	TOTAL	STATES & POSS., GUAM 969 MAT.	INST.	TOTAL	BOISE 836-837 MAT.	INST.	TOTAL
015433	CONTRACTOR EQUIPMENT		91.8	91.8		91.8	91.8		99.4	99.4		99.4	99.4		162.1	162.1		99.3	99.3
0241, 31 - 34	SITE & INFRASTRUCTURE, DEMOLITION	110.3	79.2	88.9	106.8	78.0	86.9	124.4	107.4	112.6	127.4	107.4	113.6	166.7	104.8	124.0	77.8	98.3	91.9
0310	Concrete Forming & Accessories	86.0	44.9	50.2	87.8	68.6	71.1	110.2	135.0	131.8	117.2	135.0	132.7	112.4	67.0	72.9	100.7	73.9	77.4
0320	Concrete Reinforcing	98.3	71.4	84.8	98.3	77.2	87.7	109.0	122.1	115.6	108.0	122.1	115.1	192.4	32.0	111.5	99.8	74.9	87.2
0330	Cast-in-Place Concrete	95.9	51.7	78.5	108.3	50.4	85.5	187.8	125.4	163.2	158.4	125.4	145.4	162.8	108.9	141.6	90.1	74.5	84.0
03	CONCRETE	98.4	53.9	76.7	102.6	64.7	84.1	147.4	128.1	138.0	132.9	128.1	130.5	148.0	75.4	112.6	98.8	74.4	86.9
04	MASONRY	102.1	51.1	71.0	103.0	41.5	65.5	121.3	127.0	124.8	114.1	127.0	122.0	173.3	46.0	95.6	122.1	62.5	85.8
05	METALS	94.6	83.1	90.8	93.6	79.9	89.1	107.4	108.1	107.6	128.1	108.1	121.5	138.5	77.6	118.4	99.9	74.8	91.6
06	WOOD, PLASTICS & COMPOSITES	87.0	39.3	59.5	88.8	77.0	82.0	101.4	137.6	122.4	111.7	137.6	126.7	112.0	70.9	88.3	87.9	76.2	81.2
07	THERMAL & MOISTURE PROTECTION	92.9	64.4	81.3	92.7	53.1	76.6	104.7	124.7	112.8	114.5	124.7	118.6	120.8	69.9	100.1	96.0	66.6	84.1
08	OPENINGS	93.2	42.7	80.4	93.2	60.7	85.0	99.7	131.3	107.7	105.0	131.3	111.6	104.5	57.0	92.5	96.3	70.8	89.9
0920	Plaster & Gypsum Board	85.1	37.9	51.4	85.5	76.7	79.2	103.7	138.6	128.6	134.7	138.6	137.5	202.8	59.2	100.2	86.8	75.4	78.7
0950, 0980	Ceilings & Acoustic Treatment	91.3	37.9	56.0	89.3	76.7	81.0	109.3	138.6	128.7	114.4	138.6	130.4	220.9	59.2	114.0	111.7	75.4	87.7
0960	Flooring	110.4	48.7	92.3	111.8	31.3	88.2	133.3	133.6	133.4	157.0	133.6	150.1	156.7	48.6	125.0	96.5	66.5	87.7
0970, 0990	Wall Finishes & Painting/Coating	105.7	55.0	74.4	105.7	42.0	66.4	98.7	144.2	126.8	103.1	144.2	128.5	104.2	37.9	63.3	98.8	41.6	63.5
09	FINISHES	100.9	45.0	69.7	100.4	60.1	77.9	115.8	136.8	127.5	128.5	136.8	133.1	190.9	61.9	118.9	99.3	70.1	83.0
COVERS	DIVS. 10 - 14, 25, 28, 41, 43, 44, 46	100.0	51.7	90.4	100.0	43.0	88.7	100.0	115.6	103.1	100.0	115.6	103.1	100.0	79.7	96.0	100.0	62.2	92.5
21, 22, 23	FIRE SUPPRESSION, PLUMBING & HVAC	99.9	68.1	87.0	96.1	58.1	80.7	100.1	109.7	104.0	100.1	109.7	104.0	102.1	40.0	76.9	100.0	67.6	86.9
26, 27, 3370	ELECTRICAL, COMMUNICATIONS & UTIL.	91.6	59.8	75.2	95.8	60.5	77.6	107.0	127.2	117.4	105.9	127.2	116.9	154.1	43.8	97.2	96.4	73.0	84.3
MF2010	WEIGHTED AVERAGE	97.6	60.8	81.4	97.3	61.4	81.5	110.3	121.2	115.1	113.3	121.2	116.8	131.1	60.8	100.1	99.3	72.4	87.4

IDAHO / ILLINOIS

DIVISION		COEUR D'ALENE 838 MAT.	INST.	TOTAL	IDAHO FALLS 834 MAT.	INST.	TOTAL	LEWISTON 835 MAT.	INST.	TOTAL	POCATELLO 832 MAT.	INST.	TOTAL	TWIN FALLS 833 MAT.	INST.	TOTAL	BLOOMINGTON 617 MAT.	INST.	TOTAL
015433	CONTRACTOR EQUIPMENT		93.8	93.8		99.3	99.3		93.8	93.8		99.3	99.3		99.3	99.3		100.8	100.8
0241, 31 - 34	SITE & INFRASTRUCTURE, DEMOLITION	76.2	93.9	88.4	76.3	97.4	90.8	82.2	94.4	90.6	79.6	98.2	92.3	86.4	96.6	93.4	97.8	96.9	97.1
0310	Concrete Forming & Accessories	117.9	57.8	65.6	95.4	41.4	48.4	122.5	59.1	67.4	100.9	73.6	77.2	101.6	29.6	39.0	86.0	120.1	115.6
0320	Concrete Reinforcing	107.4	93.5	100.4	101.8	77.7	89.6	107.4	93.6	100.5	100.2	74.9	87.5	102.1	77.9	89.9	98.6	107.6	103.1
0330	Cast-in-Place Concrete	97.4	86.9	93.3	85.8	52.0	72.5	101.3	87.8	96.0	92.7	74.3	85.4	95.1	39.8	73.3	97.9	114.2	104.3
03	CONCRETE	105.9	75.0	90.9	91.4	52.8	72.6	109.5	76.0	93.1	98.3	74.2	86.6	105.5	43.4	75.2	96.3	115.6	105.7
04	MASONRY	123.7	82.4	98.5	117.2	34.6	66.8	124.1	83.3	99.2	119.8	64.4	86.0	122.3	32.6	67.6	113.8	119.2	117.1
05	METALS	94.2	84.0	90.8	107.5	73.7	96.4	93.6	85.0	90.8	107.6	74.7	96.7	107.6	73.1	96.2	96.8	111.3	101.6
06	WOOD, PLASTICS & COMPOSITES	93.4	50.5	68.6	82.6	39.8	57.9	98.0	50.5	70.6	88.0	76.2	81.2	88.7	28.3	53.8	85.6	119.8	105.4
07	THERMAL & MOISTURE PROTECTION	147.8	73.7	117.7	95.6	44.6	74.9	148.0	73.7	117.8	96.1	61.3	81.9	96.9	38.7	73.2	97.9	113.9	104.4
08	OPENINGS	115.3	56.0	100.4	100.5	46.8	87.0	115.3	58.7	101.0	97.1	65.5	89.1	100.5	38.4	84.9	89.4	107.0	93.8
0920	Plaster & Gypsum Board	154.5	49.0	79.1	81.0	37.8	50.1	155.4	49.0	79.4	83.8	75.4	77.8	84.5	25.9	42.6	97.2	120.3	113.7
0950, 0980	Ceilings & Acoustic Treatment	147.1	49.0	82.3	109.7	37.8	62.2	147.1	49.0	82.3	117.8	75.4	89.8	112.4	25.9	55.3	94.9	120.3	111.7
0960	Flooring	135.3	48.0	109.7	96.2	45.1	81.2	138.5	89.5	124.1	99.7	66.5	90.0	100.9	45.1	84.6	97.4	112.2	101.8
0970, 0990	Wall Finishes & Painting/Coating	116.6	61.9	82.8	98.8	34.2	59.0	116.6	61.9	82.8	98.7	43.3	64.5	98.8	25.5	53.6	96.0	124.2	113.4
09	FINISHES	167.7	54.8	104.7	97.5	40.6	65.8	168.9	63.3	110.0	101.2	70.3	84.0	101.2	30.9	62.0	97.5	119.8	109.9
COVERS	DIVS. 10 - 14, 25, 28, 41, 43, 44, 46	100.0	52.4	90.5	100.0	39.5	88.0	100.0	65.0	93.0	100.0	62.2	92.5	100.0	35.5	87.2	100.0	105.0	101.0
21, 22, 23	FIRE SUPPRESSION, PLUMBING & HVAC	99.6	83.2	93.0	100.9	61.5	84.9	100.8	90.2	96.5	100.0	67.5	86.8	100.0	55.6	82.0	94.0	106.7	99.1
26, 27, 3370	ELECTRICAL, COMMUNICATIONS & UTIL.	87.4	80.3	83.7	87.6	73.0	80.1	85.5	80.8	83.1	93.9	73.0	83.1	88.9	62.9	75.5	94.3	96.7	95.6
MF2010	WEIGHTED AVERAGE	107.2	76.3	93.6	98.9	58.7	81.2	107.9	79.7	95.5	100.3	72.2	87.9	101.3	52.5	79.8	96.3	109.3	102.0

ILLINOIS

DIVISION		CARBONDALE 629 MAT.	INST.	TOTAL	CENTRALIA 628 MAT.	INST.	TOTAL	CHAMPAIGN 618-619 MAT.	INST.	TOTAL	CHICAGO 606-608 MAT.	INST.	TOTAL	DECATUR 625 MAT.	INST.	TOTAL	EAST ST. LOUIS 620-622 MAT.	INST.	TOTAL
015433	CONTRACTOR EQUIPMENT		107.0	107.0		107.0	107.0		101.6	101.6		92.7	92.7		101.6	101.6		107.0	107.0
0241, 31 - 34	SITE & INFRASTRUCTURE, DEMOLITION	104.8	97.4	99.7	105.2	98.7	100.7	107.5	97.7	100.7	111.8	93.7	99.3	91.6	97.7	95.8	107.2	98.6	101.3
0310	Concrete Forming & Accessories	94.0	104.1	102.8	95.9	112.4	110.2	91.7	118.5	115.0	98.0	156.1	148.5	95.8	118.0	115.1	91.7	112.7	110.0
0320	Concrete Reinforcing	97.6	94.6	96.1	97.6	104.5	101.1	98.6	102.5	100.6	99.0	161.1	130.3	95.6	102.9	99.3	97.5	108.5	103.1
0330	Cast-in-Place Concrete	91.6	99.1	94.6	92.1	116.1	101.5	113.5	109.9	112.1	107.8	147.0	123.2	100.0	112.9	105.1	93.6	116.2	102.5
03	CONCRETE	87.4	101.4	94.2	87.9	112.8	100.0	108.7	112.4	110.5	101.0	152.5	126.1	97.5	113.3	105.2	88.8	113.7	101.0
04	MASONRY	75.5	102.6	92.0	75.6	116.7	100.6	137.4	116.3	124.5	98.4	153.1	131.8	72.3	115.4	98.6	75.8	116.6	100.7
05	METALS	96.0	111.1	101.0	96.0	117.9	103.3	96.8	107.3	100.3	95.3	133.9	108.1	99.5	107.8	102.3	97.2	119.8	104.6
06	WOOD, PLASTICS & COMPOSITES	99.2	103.4	101.6	101.6	109.8	106.4	92.0	118.1	107.1	101.5	155.5	132.7	98.8	118.1	110.0	96.8	109.8	104.3
07	THERMAL & MOISTURE PROTECTION	93.1	98.9	95.5	93.2	112.9	101.2	98.6	113.3	104.5	99.7	143.6	117.6	98.7	108.0	102.5	93.2	112.4	101.0
08	OPENINGS	85.7	108.5	91.4	85.7	113.9	92.8	90.1	113.0	95.9	97.5	158.0	112.7	96.0	113.1	100.3	85.7	115.7	93.3
0920	Plaster & Gypsum Board	100.8	103.4	102.7	102.2	110.1	107.8	99.9	118.6	113.3	101.0	157.2	141.1	104.1	118.6	114.5	99.9	110.1	107.2
0950, 0980	Ceilings & Acoustic Treatment	94.9	103.4	100.5	94.9	110.1	104.9	94.9	118.6	110.6	109.9	157.2	141.1	101.2	118.6	112.7	94.9	110.1	104.9
0960	Flooring	116.3	125.8	119.1	117.4	118.6	117.8	100.5	125.8	107.9	97.0	148.5	112.1	104.0	117.6	108.0	115.1	118.6	116.2
0970, 0990	Wall Finishes & Painting/Coating	104.0	101.0	102.1	104.0	108.3	106.6	96.0	112.3	106.1	95.1	161.0	135.8	96.0	110.6	105.0	104.0	108.3	106.6
09	FINISHES	100.9	107.0	104.3	101.4	113.0	107.9	99.6	119.8	110.9	101.2	156.2	131.9	101.7	118.2	110.9	100.5	113.2	107.6
COVERS	DIVS. 10 - 14, 25, 28, 41, 43, 44, 46	100.0	100.5	100.1	100.0	103.9	100.8	100.0	104.7	100.9	100.0	125.2	105.0	100.0	104.4	100.9	100.0	103.9	100.8
21, 22, 23	FIRE SUPPRESSION, PLUMBING & HVAC	93.9	96.7	95.1	93.9	92.8	93.5	94.0	105.5	98.6	100.0	133.9	113.7	99.9	101.5	100.6	99.9	97.1	98.8
26, 27, 3370	ELECTRICAL, COMMUNICATIONS & UTIL.	93.0	101.5	97.4	94.4	105.4	100.1	97.6	95.8	96.7	95.4	133.4	115.0	97.1	90.3	93.6	94.0	105.4	99.8
MF2010	WEIGHTED AVERAGE	93.1	102.0	97.1	93.4	107.0	99.4	99.8	108.1	103.5	99.1	138.9	116.6	97.4	106.3	101.3	95.1	108.3	100.9

ILLINOIS

DIVISION		EFFINGHAM 624 MAT.	INST.	TOTAL	GALESBURG 614 MAT.	INST.	TOTAL	JOLIET 604 MAT.	INST.	TOTAL	KANKAKEE 609 MAT.	INST.	TOTAL	LA SALLE 613 MAT.	INST.	TOTAL	NORTH SUBURBAN 600-603 MAT.	INST.	TOTAL
015433	CONTRACTOR EQUIPMENT		101.6	101.6		100.8	100.8		90.9	90.9		90.9	90.9		100.8	100.8		90.9	90.9
0241, 31 - 34	SITE & INFRASTRUCTURE, DEMOLITION	99.0	97.2	97.7	100.3	96.7	97.8	111.7	92.6	98.5	104.8	92.0	96.0	99.7	97.6	98.2	110.7	91.8	97.7
0310	Concrete Forming & Accessories	100.1	111.5	110.0	91.6	115.7	112.6	100.1	154.6	147.5	94.2	135.5	130.1	104.0	121.0	118.8	99.5	148.9	142.4
0320	Concrete Reinforcing	98.6	99.9	99.3	98.1	107.2	102.7	99.0	146.2	122.8	99.8	140.4	120.3	98.3	133.4	116.0	99.0	155.2	127.3
0330	Cast-in-Place Concrete	99.7	105.3	101.9	100.8	105.2	102.5	107.7	142.3	121.3	100.4	127.1	110.9	100.6	114.4	106.1	107.8	139.8	120.4
03	CONCRETE	98.3	107.2	102.7	99.0	110.5	104.6	101.1	147.4	123.7	95.3	132.6	113.5	99.8	121.1	110.2	101.1	145.7	122.8
04	MASONRY	79.3	104.4	94.6	113.9	113.7	113.8	101.0	146.3	128.6	97.8	132.5	119.0	113.9	117.0	115.8	98.3	142.4	125.2
05	METALS	96.7	111.6	101.9	96.8	110.1	101.2	93.2	125.8	104.0	93.2	121.4	102.5	96.9	125.6	106.4	94.4	128.7	105.7
06	WOOD, PLASTICS & COMPOSITES	101.2	113.3	108.2	91.8	115.0	105.2	103.2	156.1	133.8	96.5	134.4	118.4	105.5	120.3	114.1	101.5	150.6	129.9
07	THERMAL & MOISTURE PROTECTION	98.2	106.0	101.4	98.1	106.6	101.5	99.6	140.1	116.0	98.8	131.9	112.2	98.2	114.9	105.0	100.0	138.5	115.7
08	OPENINGS	89.9	109.7	94.9	89.4	108.8	94.3	95.8	154.3	110.5	87.5	139.4	100.5	89.4	122.7	97.8	95.8	152.1	110.0
0920	Plaster & Gypsum Board	104.0	113.6	110.9	99.9	115.4	111.0	97.8	157.8	140.7	95.5	135.5	124.1	106.3	120.9	116.7	101.0	152.2	137.6
0950, 0980	Ceilings & Acoustic Treatment	94.9	113.6	107.3	94.9	115.4	108.4	109.9	157.8	141.6	109.9	135.5	126.8	94.9	120.9	112.1	109.9	152.2	137.8
0960	Flooring	105.3	125.8	111.3	100.4	112.2	103.9	96.6	138.1	108.8	93.7	138.1	106.7	107.4	116.3	110.0	97.0	138.1	109.1
0970, 0990	Wall Finishes & Painting/Coating	96.0	105.9	102.1	96.0	93.9	94.7	93.2	151.2	129.0	93.2	124.2	112.4	96.0	124.2	113.4	95.1	151.2	129.7
09	FINISHES	100.7	114.7	108.5	98.9	113.6	107.1	100.7	152.6	129.6	99.0	133.0	118.0	101.7	119.6	111.7	101.2	148.4	127.5
COVERS	DIVS. 10 - 14, 25, 28, 41, 43, 44, 46	100.0	72.5	94.5	100.0	100.9	100.2	100.0	123.8	104.7	100.0	114.8	102.9	100.0	101.0	100.2	100.0	117.0	103.4
21, 22, 23	FIRE SUPPRESSION, PLUMBING & HVAC	94.0	101.1	96.9	94.0	102.7	97.5	100.1	133.2	113.5	94.1	127.3	107.5	94.0	124.7	106.4	100.0	123.2	109.4
26, 27, 3370	ELECTRICAL, COMMUNICATIONS & UTIL.	95.0	101.5	98.4	95.3	87.7	91.4	94.7	137.9	117.0	89.5	137.1	114.0	92.4	134.8	114.2	94.5	133.3	114.6
MF2010	WEIGHTED AVERAGE	95.3	103.9	99.1	96.9	104.8	100.4	98.6	136.4	115.3	94.6	127.4	109.1	97.0	120.8	107.5	98.7	132.4	113.5

ILLINOIS

DIVISION		PEORIA 615-616 MAT.	INST.	TOTAL	QUINCY 623 MAT.	INST.	TOTAL	ROCK ISLAND 612 MAT.	INST.	TOTAL	ROCKFORD 610-611 MAT.	INST.	TOTAL	SOUTH SUBURBAN 605 MAT.	INST.	TOTAL	SPRINGFIELD 626-627 MAT.	INST.	TOTAL
015433	CONTRACTOR EQUIPMENT		100.8	100.8		101.6	101.6		100.8	100.8		100.8	100.8		90.9	90.9		101.6	101.6
0241, 31 - 34	SITE & INFRASTRUCTURE, DEMOLITION	100.5	96.8	97.9	97.8	97.3	97.4	98.4	96.1	96.8	99.6	98.0	98.5	110.7	91.8	97.7	99.2	97.8	98.2
0310	Concrete Forming & Accessories	94.2	116.9	113.9	98.0	114.6	112.4	93.1	100.0	99.1	98.2	132.3	127.9	99.5	148.9	142.5	96.5	118.5	115.6
0320	Concrete Reinforcing	95.6	107.3	101.5	98.3	99.8	99.0	98.1	99.8	99.0	90.4	140.0	115.4	99.0	155.2	127.3	95.6	102.9	99.3
0330	Cast-in-Place Concrete	97.7	115.2	104.6	99.8	97.6	99.0	98.6	96.0	97.6	100.1	125.9	110.2	107.8	139.8	120.4	89.9	108.1	97.1
03	CONCRETE	96.3	114.5	105.2	98.0	106.0	101.9	97.1	99.0	98.0	96.9	131.2	113.6	101.1	145.7	122.8	92.5	111.9	101.9
04	MASONRY	114.0	114.4	114.3	99.5	101.1	100.5	113.8	95.6	102.7	88.9	137.3	118.4	98.3	142.4	125.2	77.2	116.5	101.2
05	METALS	99.5	111.0	103.3	96.7	105.3	99.6	96.8	106.1	99.9	99.5	128.8	109.2	94.4	128.7	105.7	102.0	107.9	103.9
06	WOOD, PLASTICS & COMPOSITES	98.8	115.0	108.2	98.7	118.1	109.9	93.3	99.3	96.7	98.8	131.0	117.4	101.5	150.6	129.9	100.1	118.1	110.5
07	THERMAL & MOISTURE PROTECTION	98.8	112.1	104.2	98.2	103.5	100.4	98.1	97.2	97.7	101.3	129.6	112.8	100.0	138.7	115.8	98.4	112.1	104.0
08	OPENINGS	96.1	112.8	100.3	90.8	112.4	96.2	89.4	98.4	91.7	96.1	132.0	105.1	95.8	152.1	110.0	97.1	113.1	101.1
0920	Plaster & Gypsum Board	104.1	115.4	112.2	102.2	118.6	113.9	99.9	99.1	99.4	104.1	131.9	124.0	101.0	152.2	137.6	105.9	118.6	115.0
0950, 0980	Ceilings & Acoustic Treatment	101.2	115.4	110.6	94.9	118.6	110.6	94.9	99.1	97.7	101.2	131.9	121.5	109.9	152.2	137.8	100.3	118.6	112.4
0960	Flooring	104.0	112.2	106.4	104.0	104.0	104.0	101.6	94.7	99.6	104.0	116.3	107.6	97.0	138.1	109.1	104.0	109.0	105.5
0970, 0990	Wall Finishes & Painting/Coating	96.0	124.2	113.4	96.0	108.2	103.5	96.0	97.0	96.6	96.0	131.3	117.8	95.1	151.2	129.7	96.0	108.2	103.5
09	FINISHES	101.8	117.1	110.4	100.1	113.5	107.6	99.1	98.6	98.9	101.8	129.7	117.4	101.2	148.4	127.5	101.5	116.5	109.9
COVERS	DIVS. 10 - 14, 25, 28, 41, 43, 44, 46	100.0	104.7	100.9	100.0	75.5	95.1	100.0	98.1	99.6	100.0	94.4	98.9	100.0	117.0	103.4	100.0	104.7	100.9
21, 22, 23	FIRE SUPPRESSION, PLUMBING & HVAC	99.9	105.7	102.3	94.0	98.3	95.7	94.0	99.4	96.2	100.0	115.6	106.3	100.0	123.2	109.4	99.8	104.8	101.8
26, 27, 3370	ELECTRICAL, COMMUNICATIONS & UTIL.	96.2	97.2	96.7	92.5	81.6	86.9	87.4	98.4	93.1	96.6	131.8	114.8	94.5	133.3	114.6	97.5	92.4	94.9
MF2010	WEIGHTED AVERAGE	99.5	108.3	103.4	96.0	100.1	97.8	95.9	98.9	97.2	98.4	124.3	109.8	98.7	132.4	113.5	97.8	107.1	101.9

INDIANA

DIVISION		ANDERSON 460			BLOOMINGTON 474			COLUMBUS 472			EVANSVILLE 476 - 477			FORT WAYNE 467 - 468			GARY 463 - 464		
		MAT.	INST.	TOTAL	MAT.	INST.	TOTAL	MAT.	INST.	TOTAL	MAT.	INST.	TOTAL	MAT.	INST.	TOTAL	MAT.	INST.	TOTAL
015433	CONTRACTOR EQUIPMENT		96.6	96.6		88.1	88.1		88.1	88.1		116.9	116.9		96.6	96.6		96.6	96.6
0241, 31 - 34	SITE & INFRASTRUCTURE, DEMOLITION	94.9	94.9	94.9	79.4	95.4	90.4	76.4	95.1	89.3	84.4	124.7	112.2	95.4	94.6	94.8	95.4	98.2	97.3
0310	Concrete Forming & Accessories	95.0	81.5	83.3	100.5	82.4	84.8	95.0	79.3	81.4	94.6	80.5	82.3	93.4	74.7	77.1	95.1	110.3	108.3
0320	Concrete Reinforcing	97.9	82.7	90.3	89.6	82.5	86.0	90.0	82.5	86.2	98.1	76.6	87.3	97.9	77.8	87.8	97.9	103.3	100.6
0330	Cast-in-Place Concrete	98.2	79.7	90.9	98.2	80.8	91.3	97.8	74.5	88.6	93.8	87.5	91.3	104.4	75.3	93.0	102.7	107.9	104.7
03	CONCRETE	94.7	81.6	88.3	100.8	81.6	91.4	100.2	78.1	89.4	101.0	82.4	91.9	99.7	76.2	87.2	96.9	108.0	102.3
04	MASONRY	87.4	81.7	83.9	88.8	79.1	82.9	88.6	77.9	82.1	84.5	83.0	83.6	91.2	79.2	83.9	88.7	113.2	103.7
05	METALS	94.2	89.5	92.7	94.6	78.8	89.4	94.7	78.1	89.2	88.3	84.7	87.1	94.2	86.9	91.8	94.2	104.8	97.7
06	WOOD, PLASTICS & COMPOSITES	107.1	81.7	92.4	119.4	82.1	97.9	114.6	78.8	93.9	98.2	79.1	87.1	106.8	74.0	87.8	104.7	108.2	106.8
07	THERMAL & MOISTURE PROTECTION	98.2	80.2	90.9	93.9	82.8	89.3	93.5	82.0	88.8	97.6	84.4	92.2	98.0	82.6	91.7	97.1	109.5	102.1
08	OPENINGS	98.3	82.0	94.2	106.5	82.3	100.4	101.5	80.4	96.2	98.2	78.9	93.3	98.3	74.2	92.2	98.3	111.6	101.7
0920	Plaster & Gypsum Board	99.8	81.6	86.8	97.7	82.2	86.6	94.5	78.8	83.3	93.0	77.8	82.1	98.8	73.6	80.8	92.9	108.9	104.4
0950, 0980	Ceilings & Acoustic Treatment	91.1	81.6	84.8	83.4	82.2	82.6	83.4	78.8	80.3	88.4	77.8	81.4	91.1	73.6	79.5	91.1	108.9	102.9
0960	Flooring	98.3	81.3	93.3	105.9	78.5	97.9	100.9	78.5	94.3	99.1	84.5	94.8	98.3	78.5	92.4	98.3	121.4	105.1
0970, 0990	Wall Finishes & Painting/Coating	98.8	70.0	81.0	91.4	83.3	86.4	91.4	83.3	86.4	96.0	85.8	89.7	98.8	75.2	84.2	98.8	122.6	113.5
09	FINISHES	96.5	80.3	87.5	96.7	81.8	88.4	94.9	79.5	86.3	95.2	81.6	87.6	96.2	75.5	84.7	95.6	113.6	105.7
COVERS	DIVS. 10 - 14, 25, 28, 41, 43, 44, 46	100.0	92.5	98.5	100.0	87.8	97.6	100.0	87.0	97.4	100.0	92.0	98.4	100.0	87.5	97.5	100.0	103.4	100.7
21, 22, 23	FIRE SUPPRESSION, PLUMBING & HVAC	100.0	77.4	90.8	99.8	80.8	92.1	93.8	78.7	87.7	99.9	81.1	92.3	100.0	74.5	89.7	100.0	105.7	102.3
26, 27, 3370	ELECTRICAL, COMMUNICATIONS & UTIL.	88.2	86.3	87.2	99.7	85.7	92.5	98.9	86.3	92.4	95.8	85.6	90.6	89.0	74.1	81.3	100.4	114.3	107.6
MF2010	WEIGHTED AVERAGE	96.1	83.4	90.5	98.4	82.9	91.6	96.0	81.5	89.6	96.0	86.5	91.8	96.7	78.7	88.8	97.6	108.5	102.4

INDIANA

DIVISION		INDIANAPOLIS 461 - 462			KOKOMO 469			LAFAYETTE 479			LAWRENCEBURG 470			MUNCIE 473			NEW ALBANY 471		
		MAT.	INST.	TOTAL	MAT.	INST.	TOTAL	MAT.	INST.	TOTAL	MAT.	INST.	TOTAL	MAT.	INST.	TOTAL	MAT.	INST.	TOTAL
015433	CONTRACTOR EQUIPMENT		92.4	92.4		96.6	96.6		88.1	88.1		105.8	105.8		96.4	96.4		96.0	96.0
0241, 31 - 34	SITE & INFRASTRUCTURE, DEMOLITION	95.1	97.9	97.0	91.5	94.8	93.8	77.3	95.2	89.6	74.4	111.8	100.2	79.2	95.5	90.5	71.8	98.1	90.0
0310	Concrete Forming & Accessories	95.7	85.2	86.6	98.2	77.1	79.9	92.9	82.0	83.5	91.6	75.9	78.0	93.2	81.3	82.9	88.8	73.7	75.7
0320	Concrete Reinforcing	97.3	82.8	90.0	88.6	82.6	85.6	89.6	82.7	86.1	88.9	78.8	83.8	99.1	82.7	90.8	90.2	76.5	83.3
0330	Cast-in-Place Concrete	94.5	86.4	91.3	97.3	84.0	92.0	98.3	83.1	92.3	91.9	73.6	84.7	103.2	79.9	94.0	94.9	72.5	86.1
03	CONCRETE	96.5	84.9	90.8	91.6	81.1	86.5	100.3	82.3	91.6	93.6	76.3	85.1	100.1	81.6	91.1	98.6	74.3	86.8
04	MASONRY	94.6	82.9	87.4	87.1	79.6	82.5	93.5	81.5	86.2	73.6	77.8	76.2	90.7	81.6	85.2	80.7	71.0	74.8
05	METALS	96.3	80.9	91.2	90.8	89.2	90.3	93.1	78.9	88.4	90.0	86.5	88.8	96.5	89.8	94.3	91.8	81.8	88.5
06	WOOD, PLASTICS & COMPOSITES	103.8	85.5	93.2	110.1	75.5	90.1	111.9	81.9	94.5	97.0	75.2	84.4	114.3	81.6	95.4	98.7	74.2	84.6
07	THERMAL & MOISTURE PROTECTION	96.2	84.6	91.5	97.8	79.9	90.5	93.5	83.3	89.3	96.8	79.3	89.6	96.4	80.5	90.0	85.6	70.4	79.4
08	OPENINGS	106.5	84.1	100.8	92.4	78.7	89.0	99.8	82.1	95.4	99.9	76.5	94.0	101.3	81.9	96.4	97.7	76.1	92.3
0920	Plaster & Gypsum Board	97.7	85.3	88.8	105.2	75.2	83.8	91.4	81.9	84.6	72.1	74.9	74.1	93.0	81.6	84.9	91.2	73.7	78.7
0950, 0980	Ceilings & Acoustic Treatment	95.6	85.3	88.8	91.1	75.2	80.6	78.9	81.9	80.9	93.8	74.9	81.3	84.3	81.6	82.5	88.4	73.7	78.7
0960	Flooring	98.1	87.5	94.9	102.4	88.8	98.4	99.7	89.1	96.6	73.7	87.5	77.7	99.4	81.3	94.1	97.3	65.8	88.1
0970, 0990	Wall Finishes & Painting/Coating	98.8	83.3	89.3	98.8	75.6	84.5	91.4	98.1	95.6	92.5	74.4	81.3	91.4	70.0	78.2	96.0	87.2	90.6
09	FINISHES	97.5	85.6	90.9	98.1	78.8	87.3	93.2	85.1	88.7	86.4	78.2	81.8	94.1	80.2	86.3	94.7	74.0	83.1
COVERS	DIVS. 10 - 14, 25, 28, 41, 43, 44, 46	100.0	93.8	98.8	100.0	87.1	97.4	100.0	92.2	98.4	100.0	46.4	89.3	100.0	92.0	98.4	100.0	45.8	89.2
21, 22, 23	FIRE SUPPRESSION, PLUMBING & HVAC	99.9	83.3	93.2	94.0	80.7	88.6	93.8	79.6	88.1	94.5	75.6	86.8	99.8	77.3	90.7	94.0	77.0	87.1
26, 27, 3370	ELECTRICAL, COMMUNICATIONS & UTIL.	102.4	86.3	94.1	92.7	79.2	85.7	98.4	83.4	90.7	93.7	75.6	84.4	91.5	80.3	85.7	94.3	76.4	85.0
MF2010	WEIGHTED AVERAGE	99.2	85.6	93.2	93.7	82.2	88.6	95.7	83.2	90.2	92.5	79.6	86.8	97.1	82.6	90.7	93.6	76.6	86.1

DIVISION		INDIANA									IOWA								
		SOUTH BEND 465 - 466			TERRE HAUTE 478			WASHINGTON 475			BURLINGTON 526			CARROLL 514			CEDAR RAPIDS 522 - 524		
		MAT.	INST.	TOTAL	MAT.	INST.	TOTAL	MAT.	INST.	TOTAL	MAT.	INST.	TOTAL	MAT.	INST.	TOTAL	MAT.	INST.	TOTAL
015433	CONTRACTOR EQUIPMENT		104.8	104.8		116.9	116.9		116.9	116.9		99.8	99.8		99.8	99.8		96.5	96.5
0241, 31 - 34	SITE & INFRASTRUCTURE, DEMOLITION	97.8	95.1	95.9	86.1	125.0	113.0	86.3	122.8	111.5	100.9	96.9	98.2	88.6	97.1	94.4	103.1	96.4	98.5
0310	Concrete Forming & Accessories	98.2	78.8	81.3	95.5	80.5	82.4	96.2	79.3	81.5	99.1	77.1	79.9	88.1	52.7	57.3	104.3	81.6	84.6
0320	Concrete Reinforcing	97.9	77.9	87.8	98.1	82.9	90.5	90.7	51.8	71.1	100.6	82.3	91.4	101.5	81.8	91.5	101.4	84.8	93.1
0330	Cast-in-Place Concrete	95.6	79.5	89.3	90.8	88.9	90.1	98.8	88.2	94.7	111.3	56.9	89.8	111.3	61.8	91.8	111.6	80.4	99.3
03	CONCRETE	89.6	80.2	85.0	103.4	84.1	94.0	108.9	77.3	93.5	104.3	71.9	88.5	103.3	62.7	83.5	104.4	82.4	93.7
04	MASONRY	87.2	80.0	82.8	91.9	82.2	86.0	84.6	83.2	83.7	100.0	68.3	80.7	102.2	74.9	85.6	106.1	80.3	90.3
05	METALS	94.2	99.3	95.9	89.0	88.1	88.7	83.7	70.8	79.5	89.2	91.4	90.0	89.3	91.1	89.9	91.6	93.4	92.2
06	WOOD, PLASTICS & COMPOSITES	104.4	78.5	89.5	100.1	79.4	88.1	100.5	78.9	88.0	97.1	77.9	86.0	85.2	47.7	63.5	102.9	80.6	90.1
07	THERMAL & MOISTURE PROTECTION	92.8	83.8	89.2	97.6	82.7	91.6	97.8	84.5	92.4	106.8	76.9	94.6	107.1	71.5	92.7	107.7	80.3	96.6
08	OPENINGS	91.4	78.1	88.1	98.8	80.8	94.3	95.2	69.1	88.6	91.9	71.2	86.7	97.0	56.1	86.7	98.0	81.7	93.9
0920	Plaster & Gypsum Board	90.8	78.3	81.9	93.0	78.1	82.4	92.5	77.7	81.9	104.2	77.2	84.9	100.1	46.1	61.5	108.9	80.3	88.5
0950, 0980	Ceilings & Acoustic Treatment	85.6	78.3	80.8	88.4	78.1	81.6	82.0	77.7	79.1	109.7	77.2	88.2	109.7	46.1	67.7	113.3	80.3	91.5
0960	Flooring	96.5	83.4	92.7	99.1	87.5	95.7	100.2	80.0	94.3	113.3	39.6	91.7	106.4	34.8	85.4	131.2	82.0	116.8
0970, 0990	Wall Finishes & Painting/Coating	98.3	87.2	91.4	96.0	85.2	89.3	96.0	85.8	89.7	99.0	82.8	89.0	99.0	78.3	86.2	101.0	72.4	83.3
09	FINISHES	93.7	80.5	86.4	95.2	82.1	87.9	94.3	80.7	86.8	107.8	70.8	87.2	103.3	50.3	73.7	114.3	80.6	95.5
COVERS	DIVS. 10 - 14, 25, 28, 41, 43, 44, 46	100.0	71.1	94.2	100.0	94.6	98.9	100.0	92.0	98.4	100.0	87.3	97.5	100.0	69.8	94.0	100.0	88.3	97.7
21, 22, 23	FIRE SUPPRESSION, PLUMBING & HVAC	99.9	77.4	90.8	99.9	79.9	91.8	94.0	80.3	88.4	94.3	77.9	87.7	94.3	71.1	84.9	100.3	81.9	92.8
26, 27, 3370	ELECTRICAL, COMMUNICATIONS & UTIL.	99.7	84.2	91.7	94.0	85.7	89.7	94.5	85.6	89.9	100.8	71.9	85.9	101.5	82.4	91.7	98.4	81.0	89.4
MF2010	WEIGHTED AVERAGE	95.7	82.9	90.1	96.7	86.9	92.4	94.4	83.7	89.7	97.6	77.3	88.6	97.4	72.4	86.4	100.7	84.0	93.3

IOWA

DIVISION		COUNCIL BLUFFS 515			CRESTON 508			DAVENPORT 527 - 528			DECORAH 521			DES MOINES 500 - 503,509			DUBUQUE 520		
		MAT.	INST.	TOTAL	MAT.	INST.	TOTAL	MAT.	INST.	TOTAL	MAT.	INST.	TOTAL	MAT.	INST.	TOTAL	MAT.	INST.	TOTAL
015433	CONTRACTOR EQUIPMENT		96.0	96.0		99.8	99.8		99.8	99.8		99.8	99.8		101.4	101.4		95.3	95.3
0241, 31 - 34	SITE & INFRASTRUCTURE, DEMOLITION	111.3	92.7	98.5	88.5	96.6	94.1	100.8	99.4	99.8	99.4	96.5	97.4	89.8	100.2	96.9	100.9	93.6	95.9
0310	Concrete Forming & Accessories	87.6	72.0	74.0	88.6	68.7	71.3	103.7	88.0	90.1	96.8	46.5	53.0	105.2	78.3	81.8	88.8	70.9	73.2
0320	Concrete Reinforcing	103.5	77.8	90.5	100.7	81.8	91.2	101.4	95.8	98.6	100.6	81.3	90.9	101.4	82.0	91.7	100.0	84.7	92.3
0330	Cast-in-Place Concrete	116.0	76.6	100.5	113.0	65.8	93.2	107.4	86.9	99.3	108.3	58.5	88.7	93.5	90.5	92.3	109.2	87.7	100.8
03	CONCRETE	107.0	75.5	91.7	103.0	71.1	87.5	102.3	89.7	96.2	102.2	58.6	81.0	94.4	84.0	89.3	101.3	80.2	91.0
04	MASONRY	107.6	75.8	88.2	102.2	82.0	89.8	102.7	85.8	92.4	121.3	71.1	90.7	96.6	83.1	88.3	107.0	76.6	88.5
05	METALS	96.9	89.9	94.6	89.2	91.4	89.9	91.6	101.5	94.9	89.4	89.3	89.3	91.7	93.6	92.4	90.3	92.9	91.1
06	WOOD, PLASTICS & COMPOSITES	84.2	71.4	76.8	85.7	65.5	74.0	102.9	87.0	93.8	94.3	39.3	62.6	102.7	76.1	87.4	85.7	67.2	75.0
07	THERMAL & MOISTURE PROTECTION	107.2	69.8	92.0	107.9	78.9	96.1	107.2	85.9	98.6	107.0	54.9	85.8	108.6	80.1	97.0	107.5	72.1	93.1
08	OPENINGS	97.0	76.6	91.9	109.5	66.2	98.6	98.0	89.0	95.7	95.3	51.6	84.3	98.0	82.1	94.0	97.0	76.1	91.7
0920	Plaster & Gypsum Board	100.1	70.8	79.2	100.1	64.5	74.7	108.9	86.7	93.0	102.8	37.5	56.2	97.7	75.4	81.8	100.1	66.4	76.1
0950, 0980	Ceilings & Acoustic Treatment	109.7	70.8	84.0	109.7	64.5	79.8	113.3	86.7	95.7	109.7	37.5	62.0	110.6	75.4	87.4	109.7	66.4	81.1
0960	Flooring	105.4	84.5	99.3	106.6	34.8	85.5	116.0	86.9	107.5	112.8	49.4	94.2	115.6	84.5	106.5	120.5	79.7	108.5
0970, 0990	Wall Finishes & Painting/Coating	96.0	67.5	78.4	99.0	78.3	86.2	99.0	88.6	92.6	99.0	34.7	59.3	99.0	82.5	88.8	100.0	67.2	79.8
09	FINISHES	104.6	73.5	87.3	103.3	62.6	80.6	109.8	87.7	97.5	107.4	44.0	72.0	106.3	79.5	91.3	109.1	71.2	88.0
COVERS	DIVS. 10 - 14, 25, 28, 41, 43, 44, 46	100.0	81.7	96.4	100.0	74.2	94.9	100.0	90.2	98.1	100.0	81.9	96.4	100.0	88.2	97.7	100.0	86.3	97.3
21, 22, 23	FIRE SUPPRESSION, PLUMBING & HVAC	100.3	74.6	89.9	94.3	80.7	88.8	100.3	89.6	96.0	94.3	73.3	85.8	100.2	81.3	92.5	100.3	76.4	90.6
26, 27, 3370	ELECTRICAL, COMMUNICATIONS & UTIL.	103.6	82.0	92.5	96.3	82.4	89.1	95.3	86.7	90.8	98.4	47.1	71.9	107.5	82.5	94.6	102.2	79.1	90.3
MF2010	WEIGHTED AVERAGE	101.7	78.8	91.6	98.1	78.8	89.6	99.6	90.4	95.5	98.5	65.7	84.0	99.1	84.7	92.7	99.9	79.7	91.0

IOWA

DIVISION		FORT DODGE 505			MASON CITY 504			OTTUMWA 525			SHENANDOAH 516			SIBLEY 512			SIOUX CITY 510 - 511		
		MAT.	INST.	TOTAL	MAT.	INST.	TOTAL	MAT.	INST.	TOTAL	MAT.	INST.	TOTAL	MAT.	INST.	TOTAL	MAT.	INST.	TOTAL
015433	CONTRACTOR EQUIPMENT		99.8	99.8		99.8	99.8		95.3	95.3		96.0	96.0		99.8	99.8		99.8	99.8
0241, 31 - 34	SITE & INFRASTRUCTURE, DEMOLITION	96.4	95.4	95.7	96.4	96.5	96.5	101.7	91.7	94.8	109.3	91.8	97.2	112.0	95.3	100.4	113.2	96.1	101.4
0310	Concrete Forming & Accessories	89.2	47.5	52.9	93.5	47.2	53.2	95.0	59.3	64.0	89.1	59.4	63.2	89.4	39.7	46.1	104.3	65.8	70.8
0320	Concrete Reinforcing	100.7	64.4	82.4	100.6	81.3	90.9	100.6	82.6	91.5	103.5	68.7	85.9	103.5	64.3	83.7	101.4	64.7	82.9
0330	Cast-in-Place Concrete	104.1	46.1	81.2	104.1	59.1	86.4	112.0	56.3	90.1	112.2	62.1	92.4	109.9	46.5	84.9	110.6	57.3	89.6
03	CONCRETE	98.4	51.7	75.6	98.6	59.2	79.4	104.0	63.9	84.4	104.3	63.2	84.3	103.2	48.3	76.5	103.8	63.7	84.2
04	MASONRY	100.7	40.0	63.7	114.1	69.9	87.1	103.5	59.4	76.6	107.1	75.8	88.0	126.0	40.3	73.7	99.9	56.3	73.3
05	METALS	89.3	81.0	86.6	89.3	89.6	89.3	89.2	91.1	89.8	95.9	84.7	92.2	89.5	79.8	86.3	91.6	82.5	88.5
06	WOOD, PLASTICS & COMPOSITES	86.1	48.0	64.1	90.1	39.3	60.8	92.0	60.8	74.0	85.7	56.1	68.6	86.4	38.0	58.5	102.9	65.9	81.5
07	THERMAL & MOISTURE PROTECTION	107.3	59.7	87.9	106.8	65.1	89.8	107.6	64.5	90.1	106.5	68.1	90.9	106.8	50.6	84.0	107.2	65.2	90.2
08	OPENINGS	102.2	50.4	89.2	92.8	51.5	82.4	97.0	66.2	89.2	86.8	56.9	79.3	93.1	45.1	81.0	98.0	62.0	88.9
0920	Plaster & Gypsum Board	100.1	46.4	61.7	100.1	37.5	55.4	101.0	59.9	71.6	100.1	55.0	67.9	100.1	36.2	54.4	108.9	64.9	77.4
0950, 0980	Ceilings & Acoustic Treatment	109.7	46.4	67.9	109.7	37.5	62.0	109.7	59.9	76.8	109.7	55.0	73.6	109.7	36.2	61.1	113.3	64.9	81.3
0960	Flooring	108.5	49.4	91.1	111.1	49.4	93.0	124.0	52.5	103.1	106.3	35.9	85.7	107.4	35.6	86.3	116.3	56.2	98.7
0970, 0990	Wall Finishes & Painting/Coating	99.0	62.0	76.2	99.0	31.7	57.5	100.0	81.2	88.4	96.0	67.5	78.4	99.0	62.0	76.2	99.5	62.0	76.4
09	FINISHES	105.5	48.4	73.7	106.3	43.9	71.5	110.4	59.5	82.0	104.7	54.8	76.9	107.4	39.9	69.8	111.9	63.5	84.9
COVERS	DIVS. 10 - 14, 25, 28, 41, 43, 44, 46	100.0	77.8	95.6	100.0	82.3	96.5	100.0	80.1	96.0	100.0	71.0	94.2	100.0	76.8	95.4	100.0	84.2	96.9
21, 22, 23	FIRE SUPPRESSION, PLUMBING & HVAC	94.3	66.8	83.2	94.3	74.4	86.2	94.3	72.6	85.5	94.3	72.1	85.3	94.3	62.7	81.5	100.3	69.3	87.7
26, 27, 3370	ELECTRICAL, COMMUNICATIONS & UTIL.	103.2	44.5	72.9	102.2	59.1	80.0	100.6	67.9	83.7	98.4	82.0	89.9	98.4	44.0	70.3	98.4	74.4	86.0
MF2010	WEIGHTED AVERAGE	97.9	59.7	81.0	97.6	67.8	84.5	98.4	70.7	86.2	98.2	72.3	86.8	98.9	56.5	80.2	100.5	70.7	87.3

DIVISION		IOWA						KANSAS											
		SPENCER 513			WATERLOO 506 - 507			BELLEVILLE 669			COLBY 677			DODGE CITY 678			EMPORIA 668		
		MAT.	INST.	TOTAL	MAT.	INST.	TOTAL	MAT.	INST.	TOTAL	MAT.	INST.	TOTAL	MAT.	INST.	TOTAL	MAT.	INST.	TOTAL
015433	CONTRACTOR EQUIPMENT		99.8	99.8		99.8	99.8		102.5	102.5		102.5	102.5		102.5	102.5		100.8	100.8
0241, 31 - 34	SITE & INFRASTRUCTURE, DEMOLITION	112.0	95.3	98.0	101.2	96.5	98.0	115.8	93.8	100.6	113.1	93.8	99.8	115.5	93.4	100.3	106.5	91.6	96.2
0310	Concrete Forming & Accessories	94.9	39.7	46.9	104.6	49.7	56.8	94.1	56.6	61.5	100.0	61.1	66.2	93.6	61.0	65.3	86.5	68.5	70.8
0320	Concrete Reinforcing	103.5	64.3	83.7	101.4	84.5	92.9	103.5	55.5	79.3	106.1	55.5	80.6	103.5	55.6	79.4	102.0	56.1	78.9
0330	Cast-in-Place Concrete	109.9	46.5	84.9	111.6	56.5	89.9	118.6	57.9	94.7	114.0	57.9	91.9	116.0	57.6	93.0	114.6	48.5	88.6
03	CONCRETE	103.6	48.3	76.6	104.5	60.0	82.8	116.2	58.2	88.0	113.4	60.2	87.5	114.6	60.0	88.0	109.0	60.4	85.3
04	MASONRY	126.0	40.3	73.7	101.4	75.9	85.8	97.3	58.4	73.6	98.4	58.4	74.0	106.5	60.9	78.7	102.8	68.7	82.0
05	METALS	89.4	79.8	86.3	91.6	92.4	91.9	95.0	78.6	89.5	95.3	78.5	89.8	96.8	77.5	90.4	94.7	79.8	89.8
06	WOOD, PLASTICS & COMPOSITES	91.9	38.0	60.8	103.5	39.3	66.4	93.4	55.4	71.4	100.1	61.5	77.8	92.7	61.5	74.7	85.8	70.8	77.2
07	THERMAL & MOISTURE PROTECTION	107.7	50.6	84.5	107.0	72.1	92.8	99.5	59.3	83.1	99.4	59.9	83.4	99.4	60.9	83.8	98.0	74.3	88.4
08	OPENINGS	106.2	45.1	90.8	93.8	54.1	83.8	95.9	50.6	84.5	95.9	53.9	85.3	95.9	53.9	85.3	93.4	59.0	84.8
0920	Plaster & Gypsum Board	101.0	36.2	54.7	108.9	37.5	57.9	101.7	53.9	67.6	106.3	60.2	73.4	100.8	60.2	71.8	98.5	69.8	78.0
0950, 0980	Ceilings & Acoustic Treatment	109.7	36.2	61.1	113.3	37.5	63.2	94.9	53.9	67.8	94.9	60.2	72.0	94.9	60.2	72.0	94.9	69.8	78.4
0960	Flooring	110.6	35.6	88.6	117.7	79.0	106.4	103.6	41.0	85.2	107.3	41.0	87.8	103.4	41.0	85.1	98.6	38.1	80.8
0970, 0990	Wall Finishes & Painting/Coating	99.0	62.0	76.2	99.5	82.0	88.7	96.0	41.0	62.1	96.0	41.0	62.1	96.0	41.0	62.1	96.0	41.0	62.1
09	FINISHES	108.5	39.9	70.2	110.4	56.3	80.2	101.5	51.9	73.8	102.9	55.5	76.5	101.3	55.5	75.7	98.5	60.4	77.3
COVERS	DIVS. 10 - 14, 25, 28, 41, 43, 44, 46	100.0	76.8	95.4	100.0	83.6	96.7	100.0	43.6	88.8	100.0	44.2	88.9	100.0	44.3	88.9	100.0	43.3	88.7
21, 22, 23	FIRE SUPPRESSION, PLUMBING & HVAC	94.3	62.7	81.5	100.3	81.2	92.6	94.0	70.8	84.6	94.0	67.4	83.2	99.9	67.4	86.8	94.0	71.0	84.7
26, 27, 3370	ELECTRICAL, COMMUNICATIONS & UTIL.	100.1	44.0	71.2	98.4	59.1	78.1	99.9	67.3	83.1	99.9	67.3	83.1	96.7	73.7	84.8	97.1	73.6	84.9
MF2010	WEIGHTED AVERAGE	100.6	56.5	81.2	99.7	72.2	87.6	99.6	65.5	84.6	99.5	65.8	84.6	101.2	66.8	86.0	97.9	69.7	85.4

KANSAS

DIVISION		FORT SCOTT 667 MAT.	INST.	TOTAL	HAYS 676 MAT.	INST.	TOTAL	HUTCHINSON 675 MAT.	INST.	TOTAL	INDEPENDENCE 673 MAT.	INST.	TOTAL	KANSAS CITY 660-662 MAT.	INST.	TOTAL	LIBERAL 679 MAT.	INST.	TOTAL
015433	CONTRACTOR EQUIPMENT		101.7	101.7		102.5	102.5		102.5	102.5		102.5	102.5		99.2	99.2		102.5	102.5
0241, 31-34	SITE & INFRASTRUCTURE, DEMOLITION	102.8	92.0	95.4	119.6	93.8	101.8	95.2	93.9	94.3	116.8	94.0	101.0	95.0	91.8	92.8	119.8	93.9	102.0
0310	Concrete Forming & Accessories	100.7	80.7	83.3	97.7	61.1	65.9	88.8	61.0	64.6	107.8	69.5	74.5	97.6	97.1	97.2	94.1	61.0	65.3
0320	Concrete Reinforcing	101.4	89.1	95.2	103.5	55.5	79.3	103.5	55.6	79.3	102.9	60.5	81.5	98.3	94.4	96.3	105.0	55.6	80.1
0330	Cast-in-Place Concrete	106.3	56.7	86.7	89.9	57.9	77.3	83.3	47.9	69.4	116.5	48.2	89.6	91.1	96.1	93.0	89.9	47.9	73.4
03	CONCRETE	103.9	74.6	89.7	104.1	60.2	82.7	87.8	56.7	72.6	115.8	61.4	89.3	91.6	96.5	96.0	106.1	56.7	82.0
04	MASONRY	104.0	59.4	76.8	106.7	58.4	77.3	97.7	60.6	75.1	95.7	63.2	75.9	106.0	97.5	100.8	104.3	60.4	77.6
05	METALS	94.6	91.1	93.5	94.9	78.5	89.5	94.7	77.4	89.0	94.6	79.9	89.8	102.1	98.7	101.0	95.2	77.4	89.3
06	WOOD, PLASTICS & COMPOSITES	102.0	88.8	94.4	97.5	61.5	76.7	88.1	61.5	72.7	109.2	72.3	87.9	98.3	97.7	97.9	93.4	61.5	75.0
07	THERMAL & MOISTURE PROTECTION	98.8	71.0	87.5	99.7	59.9	83.6	98.4	60.8	83.1	99.5	72.9	88.7	98.2	97.3	97.8	99.9	60.8	84.0
08	OPENINGS	93.4	80.6	90.2	95.8	53.9	85.3	95.8	53.9	85.3	93.4	61.0	85.3	94.8	90.8	93.8	95.9	53.9	85.3
0920	Plaster & Gypsum Board	104.5	88.4	93.0	104.5	60.2	72.9	99.9	60.2	71.6	112.2	71.4	83.0	96.2	97.5	97.1	101.7	60.2	72.1
0950, 0980	Ceilings & Acoustic Treatment	94.9	88.4	90.6	94.9	60.2	72.0	94.9	60.2	72.0	94.9	71.4	79.4	94.9	97.5	96.6	94.9	60.2	72.0
0960	Flooring	115.0	41.3	93.4	106.1	41.0	87.0	100.4	41.0	83.2	112.0	41.0	91.2	91.6	98.3	93.6	103.6	41.0	85.2
0970, 0990	Wall Finishes & Painting/Coating	98.0	41.0	62.8	96.0	41.0	62.1	96.0	41.0	62.1	96.0	41.0	62.1	104.0	71.4	83.9	96.0	41.0	62.1
09	FINISHES	104.2	70.7	85.5	103.0	55.5	76.5	98.4	55.5	74.5	105.2	61.9	81.0	98.4	93.7	95.8	102.3	55.5	76.2
COVERS	DIVS. 10-14, 25, 28, 41, 43, 44, 46	100.0	49.7	90.0	100.0	44.2	88.9	100.0	44.3	88.9	100.0	45.5	89.2	100.0	66.4	93.3	100.0	44.3	88.9
21, 22, 23	FIRE SUPPRESSION, PLUMBING & HVAC	94.0	69.1	83.9	94.0	67.4	83.2	94.0	67.4	83.2	94.0	69.4	84.0	99.9	99.0	99.5	94.0	67.4	83.2
26, 27, 3370	ELECTRICAL, COMMUNICATIONS & UTIL.	96.3	73.6	84.6	98.8	67.3	82.5	93.7	67.3	80.1	95.9	73.6	84.4	102.3	95.9	99.0	96.7	69.6	82.7
MF2010	WEIGHTED AVERAGE	97.7	73.9	87.2	98.8	65.8	84.3	94.8	65.4	81.8	99.2	69.5	86.1	99.5	95.4	97.7	98.7	65.8	84.2

KANSAS / KENTUCKY

DIVISION		SALINA 674 MAT.	INST.	TOTAL	TOPEKA 664-666 MAT.	INST.	TOTAL	WICHITA 670-672 MAT.	INST.	TOTAL	ASHLAND 411-412 MAT.	INST.	TOTAL	BOWLING GREEN 421-422 MAT.	INST.	TOTAL	CAMPTON 413-414 MAT.	INST.	TOTAL
015433	CONTRACTOR EQUIPMENT		102.5	102.5		100.8	100.8		102.5	102.5		98.5	98.5		96.0	96.0		102.2	102.2
0241, 31-34	SITE & INFRASTRUCTURE, DEMOLITION	105.0	93.8	97.3	97.0	90.7	92.6	96.9	92.6	93.9	106.0	87.7	93.4	71.9	98.8	90.5	80.4	100.0	93.9
0310	Concrete Forming & Accessories	90.7	57.0	61.4	97.4	42.8	49.9	96.6	46.4	53.0	89.5	100.8	99.4	85.3	80.1	80.8	90.0	87.7	88.0
0320	Concrete Reinforcing	102.9	64.3	83.5	95.6	96.6	96.1	95.6	75.8	85.6	91.7	106.6	99.2	88.9	89.0	88.9	89.8	105.6	97.8
0330	Cast-in-Place Concrete	100.7	51.5	81.3	90.6	47.7	73.7	88.6	50.6	73.6	86.4	101.2	92.2	85.7	99.8	91.2	95.6	63.7	83.0
03	CONCRETE	101.7	57.8	80.3	92.9	56.2	75.0	91.8	54.8	73.8	94.5	102.6	98.4	92.7	88.7	90.8	96.8	82.8	90.0
04	MASONRY	121.5	58.4	83.0	100.2	56.8	73.7	93.8	53.1	69.0	90.6	104.8	99.3	92.4	73.6	80.9	90.3	73.0	79.7
05	METALS	96.6	82.2	91.8	102.0	96.1	100.0	102.0	84.1	96.1	90.9	110.1	97.3	92.5	86.6	90.6	91.8	94.2	92.6
06	WOOD, PLASTICS & COMPOSITES	89.5	55.4	69.8	94.5	39.6	62.8	96.0	45.2	66.6	80.0	99.3	91.2	93.9	78.7	85.1	92.6	94.7	93.8
07	THERMAL & MOISTURE PROTECTION	99.0	59.3	82.8	100.0	63.3	85.0	98.3	54.6	80.6	89.9	98.9	93.6	85.5	81.3	83.8	97.9	72.3	87.5
08	OPENINGS	95.8	51.5	84.6	96.1	56.5	86.1	96.1	53.0	85.2	96.9	96.7	96.9	97.8	77.0	92.5	99.5	92.4	97.7
0920	Plaster & Gypsum Board	99.9	53.9	67.1	98.6	37.6	55.0	98.3	43.3	59.0	59.3	99.3	87.9	87.1	78.4	80.8	87.1	93.9	91.9
0950, 0980	Ceilings & Acoustic Treatment	94.9	53.9	67.8	95.8	37.6	57.4	94.9	43.3	60.9	83.3	99.3	93.9	88.4	78.4	81.7	88.4	93.9	92.0
0960	Flooring	101.7	64.9	90.9	105.0	77.2	96.8	103.8	66.0	92.7	78.5	104.9	86.3	95.1	90.1	93.6	96.5	43.2	80.9
0970, 0990	Wall Finishes & Painting/Coating	96.0	41.0	62.1	96.0	55.4	70.9	96.0	50.6	67.9	98.3	95.6	96.6	96.0	69.9	79.9	96.0	69.0	79.3
09	FINISHES	99.8	56.5	75.6	100.0	48.6	71.4	99.6	49.9	71.9	82.5	101.1	92.9	93.4	80.8	86.4	94.1	78.4	85.4
COVERS	DIVS. 10-14, 25, 28, 41, 43, 44, 46	100.0	54.1	90.9	100.0	51.0	90.2	100.0	50.3	90.1	100.0	99.4	99.9	100.0	61.4	92.3	100.0	60.3	92.1
21, 22, 23	FIRE SUPPRESSION, PLUMBING & HVAC	99.9	67.5	86.8	99.9	57.4	82.7	99.7	63.6	85.1	93.9	91.3	92.9	99.9	83.9	93.5	94.1	80.9	88.7
26, 27, 3370	ELECTRICAL, COMMUNICATIONS & UTIL.	96.4	73.7	84.7	102.0	73.6	87.4	99.9	73.7	86.4	92.2	97.3	94.8	94.8	83.7	89.1	92.2	70.3	80.9
MF2010	WEIGHTED AVERAGE	100.0	66.9	85.4	99.2	64.5	83.9	98.4	64.1	83.3	93.3	98.5	95.6	95.0	83.5	90.0	94.5	81.2	88.6

KENTUCKY

DIVISION		CORBIN 407-409 MAT.	INST.	TOTAL	COVINGTON 410 MAT.	INST.	TOTAL	ELIZABETHTOWN 427 MAT.	INST.	TOTAL	FRANKFORT 406 MAT.	INST.	TOTAL	HAZARD 417-418 MAT.	INST.	TOTAL	HENDERSON 424 MAT.	INST.	TOTAL
015433	CONTRACTOR EQUIPMENT		102.2	102.2		105.8	105.8		96.0	96.0		102.2	102.2		102.2	102.2		116.9	116.9
0241, 31-34	SITE & INFRASTRUCTURE, DEMOLITION	77.8	99.7	92.9	75.9	113.8	102.1	67.0	98.7	88.8	82.9	100.7	95.2	78.3	101.4	94.2	75.4	125.3	109.8
0310	Concrete Forming & Accessories	87.3	69.2	71.5	86.1	96.4	95.1	81.0	79.1	79.3	97.1	75.2	78.1	87.3	88.4	88.3	92.9	83.1	84.4
0320	Concrete Reinforcing	89.4	68.8	79.0	88.4	95.8	92.2	89.4	92.5	91.0	90.7	92.5	91.6	90.2	105.6	98.0	89.1	90.0	89.5
0330	Cast-in-Place Concrete	90.5	61.2	78.9	91.5	94.0	92.5	77.5	76.0	76.9	87.5	71.7	81.3	91.9	87.2	90.1	75.7	89.4	81.1
03	CONCRETE	92.1	66.9	79.8	95.1	95.5	95.3	85.2	80.8	83.0	91.4	77.6	84.7	93.7	91.2	92.5	89.7	86.7	88.2
04	MASONRY	90.5	65.5	75.2	103.6	107.4	105.9	77.0	79.6	78.6	87.4	81.8	84.0	87.7	75.7	80.4	96.3	92.5	93.9
05	METALS	91.7	78.8	87.4	89.9	93.5	91.1	91.7	88.5	90.6	98.7	89.4	95.6	91.8	94.4	92.7	83.5	89.6	85.5
06	WOOD, PLASTICS & COMPOSITES	89.8	73.1	80.1	90.8	89.5	90.1	89.5	78.7	83.3	101.2	73.1	84.9	89.8	94.7	92.6	96.2	80.6	87.2
07	THERMAL & MOISTURE PROTECTION	97.7	67.5	85.4	97.0	97.7	97.3	85.2	78.2	82.4	97.6	76.9	89.2	97.8	71.0	86.9	97.3	93.0	95.5
08	OPENINGS	98.7	64.1	90.0	101.0	88.3	97.8	97.8	82.7	94.0	97.9	79.5	93.3	99.9	82.6	95.5	95.7	83.0	92.5
0920	Plaster & Gypsum Board	86.2	71.6	75.8	69.3	89.6	83.8	86.2	78.4	80.6	97.9	71.6	79.1	86.2	93.9	91.7	89.3	79.4	82.2
0950, 0980	Ceilings & Acoustic Treatment	88.4	71.6	77.3	92.0	89.6	90.4	88.4	78.4	81.7	91.1	71.6	78.2	88.4	93.9	92.0	82.0	79.4	80.3
0960	Flooring	94.9	43.2	79.7	71.3	88.1	76.2	92.5	90.1	91.8	99.5	57.0	87.0	94.9	44.0	79.9	98.3	90.1	95.9
0970, 0990	Wall Finishes & Painting/Coating	96.0	52.1	68.9	92.5	85.5	88.2	96.0	78.3	85.1	96.0	84.1	88.7	96.0	69.0	79.3	96.0	93.8	94.6
09	FINISHES	93.2	62.8	76.3	85.2	93.5	89.9	92.2	80.3	85.6	96.9	72.3	83.2	93.3	79.3	85.5	92.6	85.4	88.6
COVERS	DIVS. 10-14, 25, 28, 41, 43, 44, 46	100.0	51.5	90.3	100.0	104.5	100.9	100.0	90.4	98.1	100.0	70.1	94.1	100.0	61.2	92.3	100.0	69.6	93.9
21, 22, 23	FIRE SUPPRESSION, PLUMBING & HVAC	94.0	69.6	84.1	94.5	93.1	93.9	94.4	82.4	89.5	100.0	83.6	93.4	94.1	81.8	89.1	94.4	78.2	87.8
26, 27, 3370	ELECTRICAL, COMMUNICATIONS & UTIL.	92.4	83.7	87.9	96.0	80.3	87.9	92.0	83.7	87.7	100.0	92.6	96.2	92.1	62.0	76.6	94.2	83.9	88.9
MF2010	WEIGHTED AVERAGE	93.7	72.5	84.4	94.4	95.2	94.8	91.4	83.9	88.1	97.2	83.5	91.2	93.9	81.5	88.4	92.4	87.9	90.4

KENTUCKY

DIVISION		LEXINGTON 403 - 405			LOUISVILLE 400 - 402			OWENSBORO 423			PADUCAH 420			PIKEVILLE 415 - 416			SOMERSET 425 - 426		
		MAT.	INST.	TOTAL	MAT.	INST.	TOTAL	MAT.	INST.	TOTAL	MAT.	INST.	TOTAL	MAT.	INST.	TOTAL	MAT.	INST.	TOTAL
015433	CONTRACTOR EQUIPMENT		102.2	102.2		96.0	96.0		116.9	116.9		116.9	116.9		98.5	98.5		102.2	102.2
0241, 31 - 34	SITE & INFRASTRUCTURE, DEMOLITION	79.5	101.7	94.8	69.8	98.7	89.7	84.6	125.2	112.6	78.1	124.8	110.3	116.7	87.0	96.2	71.7	100.3	91.4
0310	Concrete Forming & Accessories	98.1	76.1	79.0	93.5	79.1	80.9	91.5	82.6	83.8	89.6	79.3	80.6	97.3	94.3	94.7	87.9	73.9	75.7
0320	Concrete Reinforcing	98.1	92.0	95.0	98.1	92.5	95.3	89.1	89.7	89.4	89.6	86.1	87.8	92.2	106.5	99.4	89.4	91.8	90.6
0330	Cast-in-Place Concrete	92.5	86.7	90.3	94.5	75.9	87.2	88.3	98.0	92.1	80.7	87.5	83.4	94.9	98.7	96.4	75.7	102.8	86.4
03	CONCRETE	95.2	83.1	89.3	95.9	80.7	88.5	101.3	89.4	95.5	94.0	83.6	89.0	107.4	98.7	103.2	80.6	87.5	84.0
04	MASONRY	88.7	70.1	77.4	89.9	79.4	83.5	88.8	83.7	85.7	91.8	91.6	91.7	88.1	101.0	96.0	83.0	66.6	73.0
05	METALS	94.1	89.2	92.5	100.9	88.6	96.9	85.0	89.3	86.4	82.0	87.6	83.8	90.9	108.9	96.8	91.7	88.0	90.5
06	WOOD, PLASTICS & COMPOSITES	103.7	73.1	86.0	101.2	78.7	88.2	94.4	80.6	86.4	92.1	77.7	83.8	88.4	94.0	91.6	90.3	73.1	80.3
07	THERMAL & MOISTURE PROTECTION	97.9	86.3	93.2	92.0	78.2	86.4	97.6	88.8	94.0	97.3	81.8	91.0	90.5	84.0	87.9	97.3	67.5	85.2
08	OPENINGS	98.8	77.0	93.3	98.8	82.7	94.8	95.7	83.8	92.7	94.8	77.4	90.4	97.8	90.6	96.0	98.7	77.3	93.3
0920	Plaster & Gypsum Board	95.9	71.6	78.5	89.0	78.4	81.4	87.9	79.4	81.8	86.5	76.4	79.3	62.0	93.9	84.8	86.2	71.6	75.8
0950, 0980	Ceilings & Acoustic Treatment	93.8	71.6	79.1	91.1	78.4	82.7	82.0	79.4	80.3	82.0	76.4	78.3	83.3	93.9	90.3	88.4	71.6	77.3
0960	Flooring	99.9	73.6	92.2	98.3	90.1	95.9	97.7	90.1	95.4	96.3	62.2	86.3	82.9	104.9	89.3	95.1	43.2	79.9
0970, 0990	Wall Finishes & Painting/Coating	96.0	84.1	88.7	96.0	78.3	85.1	96.0	97.0	96.6	96.0	81.0	86.7	98.3	85.6	90.5	96.0	78.3	85.1
09	FINISHES	97.1	75.7	85.2	94.7	80.9	87.0	92.9	85.2	88.6	91.9	76.0	83.1	85.0	95.9	91.1	92.6	68.3	79.1
COVERS	DIVS. 10 - 14, 25, 28, 41, 43, 44, 46	100.0	92.6	98.5	100.0	90.3	98.1	100.0	98.7	99.7	100.0	65.5	93.1	100.0	61.0	92.2	100.0	61.8	92.4
21, 22, 23	FIRE SUPPRESSION, PLUMBING & HVAC	99.9	76.7	90.5	100.0	82.3	92.8	99.9	77.2	90.7	94.4	82.5	89.6	93.9	88.8	91.8	94.4	75.1	86.6
26, 27, 3370	ELECTRICAL, COMMUNICATIONS & UTIL.	95.3	83.7	89.3	102.7	80.8	91.4	94.3	83.9	88.9	96.6	80.5	88.3	95.2	78.0	86.3	92.6	83.7	88.0
MF2010	WEIGHTED AVERAGE	96.5	81.8	90.0	97.8	83.5	91.5	95.2	87.9	92.0	92.6	85.7	89.6	95.6	91.7	93.9	91.9	79.1	86.2

LOUISIANA

DIVISION		ALEXANDRIA 713 - 714			BATON ROUGE 707 - 708			HAMMOND 704			LAFAYETTE 705			LAKE CHARLES 706			MONROE 712		
		MAT.	INST.	TOTAL	MAT.	INST.	TOTAL	MAT.	INST.	TOTAL	MAT.	INST.	TOTAL	MAT.	INST.	TOTAL	MAT.	INST.	TOTAL
015433	CONTRACTOR EQUIPMENT		88.9	88.9		88.7	88.7		89.4	89.4		89.4	89.4		88.7	88.7		88.9	88.9
0241, 31 - 34	SITE & INFRASTRUCTURE, DEMOLITION	96.1	85.7	88.9	104.0	85.2	91.1	105.3	86.5	92.3	106.0	86.4	92.5	106.7	85.0	91.8	96.1	85.0	88.5
0310	Concrete Forming & Accessories	82.5	36.4	42.4	93.8	62.0	66.1	79.3	48.7	52.7	95.1	53.7	59.1	96.6	57.3	62.4	82.1	36.7	42.6
0320	Concrete Reinforcing	98.0	57.5	77.6	99.0	59.3	79.0	97.6	61.1	79.2	99.0	59.3	79.0	99.0	58.2	78.5	96.9	57.3	76.9
0330	Cast-in-Place Concrete	95.8	39.4	73.6	94.8	57.7	80.2	97.6	45.1	76.9	97.1	45.7	76.9	102.2	66.5	88.2	95.8	55.8	80.1
03	CONCRETE	95.1	42.8	69.6	95.1	60.5	78.2	95.4	50.7	73.6	96.3	52.8	75.1	99.0	61.3	80.6	94.9	48.4	72.3
04	MASONRY	118.1	49.3	76.2	106.1	51.1	72.5	105.6	52.8	73.4	105.6	50.3	71.8	104.6	56.7	75.4	113.4	45.8	72.1
05	METALS	89.5	71.8	83.7	101.3	70.2	91.1	97.0	70.9	88.4	96.1	70.4	87.6	96.1	70.1	87.5	89.5	69.5	82.9
06	WOOD, PLASTICS & COMPOSITES	86.7	35.1	56.9	100.8	67.8	81.8	86.7	49.9	65.5	107.0	57.0	78.1	105.2	61.1	79.7	86.0	35.5	56.8
07	THERMAL & MOISTURE PROTECTION	97.5	50.9	78.6	95.5	57.9	80.2	97.2	58.8	81.6	97.7	56.4	80.9	96.9	58.9	81.5	97.5	50.1	78.2
08	OPENINGS	98.2	41.5	83.9	101.1	59.6	90.7	96.8	54.3	86.1	101.1	53.8	89.2	101.1	56.8	90.0	98.2	45.4	84.9
0920	Plaster & Gypsum Board	76.2	33.6	45.8	95.1	67.2	75.2	89.4	48.7	60.3	98.8	56.0	68.3	98.8	60.2	71.3	75.7	34.0	45.9
0950, 0980	Ceilings & Acoustic Treatment	91.1	33.6	53.1	102.2	67.2	79.1	99.3	48.7	65.9	97.5	56.0	70.1	98.5	60.2	73.2	91.1	34.0	53.3
0960	Flooring	101.3	66.9	91.2	102.1	66.9	91.8	93.4	66.9	85.6	102.3	66.9	91.9	102.3	76.4	94.7	100.8	59.8	88.8
0970, 0990	Wall Finishes & Painting/Coating	96.2	33.6	57.6	99.9	38.5	62.0	99.9	50.9	69.7	99.9	38.5	62.0	99.9	35.4	60.1	96.2	40.1	61.6
09	FINISHES	91.6	40.7	63.2	100.4	61.1	78.5	96.5	52.3	71.8	99.8	54.5	74.5	100.0	58.7	77.0	91.4	40.3	62.9
COVERS	DIVS. 10 - 14, 25, 28, 41, 43, 44, 46	100.0	51.0	90.2	100.0	79.6	95.9	100.0	49.0	89.8	100.0	78.1	95.6	100.0	78.9	95.8	100.0	46.8	89.4
21, 22, 23	FIRE SUPPRESSION, PLUMBING & HVAC	100.3	51.2	80.4	100.1	59.1	83.5	94.2	45.9	74.6	100.2	59.4	83.6	100.2	59.8	83.8	100.3	50.1	80.0
26, 27, 3370	ELECTRICAL, COMMUNICATIONS & UTIL.	93.9	56.5	74.6	110.9	61.3	85.3	102.0	56.6	78.6	103.3	67.0	84.5	102.7	67.0	84.3	95.8	57.7	76.1
MF2010	WEIGHTED AVERAGE	97.1	53.5	77.9	101.2	63.0	84.4	97.5	56.1	79.3	99.9	61.5	83.0	100.1	64.1	84.2	97.0	53.6	77.9

LOUISIANA / MAINE

DIVISION		NEW ORLEANS 700 - 701			SHREVEPORT 710 - 711			THIBODAUX 703			AUGUSTA 043			BANGOR 044			BATH 045		
		MAT.	INST.	TOTAL	MAT.	INST.	TOTAL	MAT.	INST.	TOTAL	MAT.	INST.	TOTAL	MAT.	INST.	TOTAL	MAT.	INST.	TOTAL
015433	CONTRACTOR EQUIPMENT		89.6	89.6		88.9	88.9		89.4	89.4		100.4	100.4		100.4	100.4		100.4	100.4
0241, 31 - 34	SITE & INFRASTRUCTURE, DEMOLITION	109.6	88.0	94.7	98.6	84.9	89.1	107.9	86.4	93.1	87.9	100.2	96.4	90.9	97.9	95.7	89.1	100.2	96.7
0310	Concrete Forming & Accessories	98.5	68.9	72.7	96.1	38.8	46.2	91.7	61.6	65.5	98.1	100.3	100.0	93.7	91.0	91.3	90.1	100.3	98.9
0320	Concrete Reinforcing	99.0	61.8	80.3	96.6	57.7	77.0	97.6	61.0	79.1	84.6	101.0	92.9	84.3	101.1	92.8	83.4	100.9	92.2
0330	Cast-in-Place Concrete	101.2	69.9	88.9	95.3	44.9	75.5	104.9	48.0	82.5	95.3	61.9	82.2	83.5	104.4	91.8	83.5	61.9	75.0
03	CONCRETE	98.6	68.4	83.9	94.9	45.7	70.9	100.8	57.4	79.6	105.7	86.6	96.4	99.1	96.8	98.0	99.1	86.5	93.0
04	MASONRY	105.9	62.0	79.1	103.4	47.4	69.2	133.9	48.5	81.8	95.4	60.0	73.8	109.0	59.7	78.9	115.5	56.9	79.7
05	METALS	109.1	74.3	97.6	86.3	69.6	80.7	97.0	70.6	88.3	86.7	85.0	86.1	86.3	80.8	84.5	84.7	84.7	84.7
06	WOOD, PLASTICS & COMPOSITES	101.7	70.5	83.7	101.8	38.5	65.2	94.6	67.0	78.7	97.2	112.0	105.8	92.2	98.8	96.0	87.9	112.0	101.8
07	THERMAL & MOISTURE PROTECTION	97.4	70.4	86.5	96.6	49.1	77.3	97.5	54.5	80.0	100.9	66.1	86.8	101.5	65.7	86.9	101.5	65.3	86.8
08	OPENINGS	101.9	68.4	93.5	96.0	43.5	82.8	102.1	63.6	92.4	99.3	90.9	97.2	99.2	83.5	95.3	99.2	90.7	97.1
0920	Plaster & Gypsum Board	97.0	70.0	77.7	82.8	37.1	50.1	92.6	66.4	73.9	95.2	111.7	107.0	92.4	98.1	96.5	90.2	111.7	105.6
0950, 0980	Ceilings & Acoustic Treatment	97.5	70.0	79.3	92.0	37.1	55.7	99.3	66.4	77.6	94.8	111.7	106.0	94.8	98.1	97.0	92.7	111.7	105.3
0960	Flooring	102.7	66.9	92.2	109.5	64.2	96.2	99.6	46.2	83.9	94.5	57.9	83.7	92.3	64.4	84.1	90.5	57.9	80.9
0970, 0990	Wall Finishes & Painting/Coating	101.3	67.6	80.5	96.2	33.6	57.6	101.3	50.9	70.2	90.1	36.4	57.0	90.1	37.8	57.8	90.1	36.4	57.0
09	FINISHES	100.3	68.6	82.6	95.1	42.1	65.6	99.0	58.3	76.3	97.4	87.6	91.9	96.9	81.6	88.4	95.6	87.6	91.1
COVERS	DIVS. 10 - 14, 25, 28, 41, 43, 44, 46	100.0	83.6	96.7	100.0	64.9	93.0	100.0	80.1	96.0	100.0	93.7	98.7	100.0	106.1	101.2	100.0	93.7	98.7
21, 22, 23	FIRE SUPPRESSION, PLUMBING & HVAC	100.1	65.8	86.2	100.2	55.1	81.9	94.2	59.6	80.2	99.9	65.4	85.9	100.0	61.4	84.4	94.1	65.4	82.4
26, 27, 3370	ELECTRICAL, COMMUNICATIONS & UTIL.	103.4	71.7	87.0	100.2	66.6	82.8	100.4	69.3	84.4	98.5	80.1	89.0	100.1	80.1	89.8	98.0	80.1	88.8
MF2010	WEIGHTED AVERAGE	102.3	70.5	88.3	96.7	56.3	78.9	100.2	63.4	84.0	97.6	79.8	89.8	97.7	78.9	89.4	96.0	79.5	88.7

City Cost Indexes

MAINE

DIVISION		HOULTON 047 MAT.	INST.	TOTAL	KITTERY 039 MAT.	INST.	TOTAL	LEWISTON 042 MAT.	INST.	TOTAL	MACHIAS 046 MAT.	INST.	TOTAL	PORTLAND 040-041 MAT.	INST.	TOTAL	ROCKLAND 048 MAT.	INST.	TOTAL
015433	CONTRACTOR EQUIPMENT		100.4	100.4		100.4	100.4		100.4	100.4		100.4	100.4		100.4	100.4		100.4	100.4
0241, 31 - 34	SITE & INFRASTRUCTURE, DEMOLITION	90.8	100.0	97.2	84.7	100.2	95.4	87.5	97.9	94.7	90.1	100.0	97.0	85.0	97.9	93.9	86.0	100.1	95.7
0310	Concrete Forming & Accessories	96.7	99.4	99.0	90.7	100.7	99.4	98.3	91.0	91.9	94.3	99.5	98.8	97.2	91.0	91.8	95.2	99.7	99.1
0320	Concrete Reinforcing	84.3	101.0	92.7	82.9	101.0	92.0	103.6	101.1	102.3	84.3	101.0	92.7	103.6	101.1	102.3	84.3	101.1	92.8
0330	Cast-in-Place Concrete	83.5	60.1	74.3	83.5	62.8	75.4	85.2	104.4	92.8	83.5	60.2	74.4	105.7	104.4	105.2	85.3	61.3	75.8
03	CONCRETE	100.0	85.5	93.0	94.6	87.0	90.9	99.2	96.8	98.0	99.5	85.6	92.7	109.4	96.8	103.2	96.7	86.1	91.5
04	MASONRY	93.4	58.0	71.8	106.2	59.5	77.7	94.0	59.7	73.1	93.4	58.3	72.0	94.3	59.7	73.2	88.0	59.7	70.8
05	METALS	84.9	84.9	84.9	84.7	84.8	84.7	89.3	80.8	86.5	85.0	84.9	84.9	90.6	80.8	87.4	84.8	84.9	84.9
06	WOOD, PLASTICS & COMPOSITES	96.0	112.0	105.3	88.3	112.0	102.0	97.9	98.8	98.4	93.1	112.0	104.0	97.1	98.8	98.1	93.9	112.0	104.4
07	THERMAL & MOISTURE PROTECTION	101.6	63.6	86.1	101.1	66.3	86.9	101.3	65.7	86.8	101.5	63.6	86.1	104.6	65.7	88.8	101.3	64.5	86.3
08	OPENINGS	99.3	89.0	96.7	99.2	90.2	96.9	102.4	83.5	97.7	99.3	89.0	96.7	102.4	83.5	97.7	99.2	89.0	96.7
0920	Plaster & Gypsum Board	95.2	111.7	107.0	90.2	111.7	105.6	98.7	98.1	98.3	93.3	111.7	106.5	99.5	98.1	98.5	93.3	111.7	106.5
0950, 0980	Ceilings & Acoustic Treatment	92.7	111.7	105.3	92.7	111.7	105.3	102.0	98.1	99.4	92.7	111.7	105.3	99.3	98.1	98.5	92.7	111.7	105.3
0960	Flooring	93.5	54.2	82.0	90.6	60.4	81.7	95.1	64.4	86.1	92.6	54.2	81.3	94.5	64.4	85.6	92.9	54.2	81.5
0970, 0990	Wall Finishes & Painting/Coating	90.1	37.8	57.8	90.1	36.4	57.0	90.1	37.8	57.8	90.1	37.8	57.8	90.1	37.8	57.8	90.1	37.8	57.8
09	FINISHES	97.2	86.6	91.3	95.2	88.3	91.3	99.6	81.6	89.6	96.6	86.6	91.0	98.3	81.6	89.0	96.3	86.8	91.0
COVERS	DIVS. 10 - 14, 25, 28, 41, 43, 44, 46	100.0	92.9	98.6	100.0	95.2	99.1	100.0	106.1	101.2	100.0	93.0	98.6	100.0	106.1	101.2	100.0	93.2	98.7
21, 22, 23	FIRE SUPPRESSION, PLUMBING & HVAC	94.1	64.3	82.0	94.1	66.0	82.7	100.0	61.4	84.4	94.1	64.4	82.0	99.9	61.4	84.3	94.1	64.7	82.2
26, 27, 3370	ELECTRICAL, COMMUNICATIONS & UTIL.	102.3	80.1	90.9	98.0	80.1	88.8	102.3	80.1	90.9	102.3	80.1	90.9	103.9	80.1	91.6	102.2	80.1	90.8
MF2010	WEIGHTED AVERAGE	95.7	78.9	88.3	94.8	80.1	88.3	98.1	78.9	89.7	95.5	79.0	88.2	99.5	78.9	90.4	94.7	79.4	88.0

MAINE / MARYLAND

DIVISION		WATERVILLE (MAINE) 049 MAT.	INST.	TOTAL	ANNAPOLIS 214 MAT.	INST.	TOTAL	BALTIMORE 210-212 MAT.	INST.	TOTAL	COLLEGE PARK 207-208 MAT.	INST.	TOTAL	CUMBERLAND 215 MAT.	INST.	TOTAL	EASTON 216 MAT.	INST.	TOTAL
015433	CONTRACTOR EQUIPMENT		100.4	100.4		98.6	98.6		102.0	102.0		103.1	103.1		98.6	98.6		98.6	98.6
0241, 31 - 34	SITE & INFRASTRUCTURE, DEMOLITION	91.0	100.2	97.3	99.7	90.5	93.4	100.2	94.4	96.2	106.9	92.8	97.2	91.2	90.2	90.5	98.2	87.6	90.9
0310	Concrete Forming & Accessories	89.7	100.3	98.9	94.1	71.0	74.0	96.9	75.3	78.1	85.5	71.8	73.6	88.5	77.8	79.2	86.7	72.4	74.3
0320	Concrete Reinforcing	84.3	101.0	92.7	99.8	82.5	91.1	99.8	82.5	91.1	98.5	80.9	89.6	88.2	74.7	81.4	87.4	80.7	84.0
0330	Cast-in-Place Concrete	83.5	61.9	75.0	140.3	79.5	116.4	124.9	80.3	107.3	131.0	80.5	111.1	111.5	84.1	100.7	123.8	50.6	95.0
03	CONCRETE	100.8	86.6	93.8	120.9	77.2	99.6	113.4	79.4	96.8	115.7	77.8	97.2	101.2	80.3	91.0	110.1	67.4	89.3
04	MASONRY	103.1	60.0	76.8	101.1	75.8	85.7	102.2	75.8	86.1	115.1	70.5	87.9	100.2	78.5	86.9	114.3	45.4	72.3
05	METALS	84.9	85.0	84.9	94.9	94.7	94.9	96.1	95.3	95.8	83.9	96.9	88.2	92.5	91.3	92.1	92.8	88.8	91.4
06	WOOD, PLASTICS & COMPOSITES	87.3	112.0	101.6	90.0	70.8	78.9	92.8	76.5	83.4	87.6	71.1	78.1	83.3	76.3	79.2	81.3	79.5	80.2
07	THERMAL & MOISTURE PROTECTION	101.6	66.1	87.1	97.1	79.7	90.0	97.4	80.5	90.6	100.5	77.8	91.3	96.8	77.3	88.9	96.9	61.6	82.5
08	OPENINGS	99.3	90.9	97.2	93.9	78.5	90.0	96.1	81.6	92.4	97.2	75.0	91.6	95.1	77.5	90.7	93.1	73.4	88.2
0920	Plaster & Gypsum Board	90.2	111.7	105.6	98.3	70.3	78.3	99.9	76.0	82.9	99.7	70.3	78.7	94.5	75.9	81.2	94.0	79.2	83.4
0950, 0980	Ceilings & Acoustic Treatment	92.7	111.7	105.3	98.9	70.3	80.0	99.8	76.0	84.1	95.8	70.3	78.9	99.8	75.9	84.0	99.8	79.2	86.2
0960	Flooring	90.2	57.9	80.7	93.8	80.9	90.0	93.8	80.9	90.0	107.1	80.9	99.4	89.8	82.2	87.6	89.1	54.1	78.8
0970, 0990	Wall Finishes & Painting/Coating	90.1	36.4	57.0	96.8	83.5	88.6	96.8	83.5	88.6	121.0	78.7	94.9	96.8	77.3	84.8	96.8	78.7	85.6
09	FINISHES	95.8	87.6	91.2	96.0	73.2	83.3	96.6	76.6	85.4	101.4	73.5	85.8	94.1	78.3	85.3	94.3	71.3	81.4
COVERS	DIVS. 10 - 14, 25, 28, 41, 43, 44, 46	100.0	93.7	98.7	100.0	86.1	97.2	100.0	87.1	97.4	100.0	82.2	96.5	100.0	89.8	98.0	100.0	81.1	96.2
21, 22, 23	FIRE SUPPRESSION, PLUMBING & HVAC	94.1	65.4	82.4	99.9	83.7	93.3	99.9	83.8	93.4	94.3	86.1	91.0	93.9	72.0	85.0	93.9	69.5	84.0
26, 27, 3370	ELECTRICAL, COMMUNICATIONS & UTIL.	102.3	80.1	90.9	96.2	93.2	94.7	99.4	93.8	96.5	98.3	98.9	98.6	97.1	82.0	89.3	96.6	66.1	80.9
MF2010	WEIGHTED AVERAGE	96.1	79.8	88.9	100.2	83.2	92.7	100.2	84.7	93.3	98.5	84.2	92.2	95.8	80.2	89.0	97.5	70.3	85.5

MARYLAND / MASSACHUSETTS

DIVISION		ELKTON 219 MAT.	INST.	TOTAL	HAGERSTOWN 217 MAT.	INST.	TOTAL	SALISBURY 218 MAT.	INST.	TOTAL	SILVER SPRING 209 MAT.	INST.	TOTAL	WALDORF 206 MAT.	INST.	TOTAL	BOSTON (MASS.) 020-022, 024 MAT.	INST.	TOTAL
015433	CONTRACTOR EQUIPMENT		98.6	98.6		98.6	98.6		98.6	98.6		96.1	96.1		96.1	96.1		106.0	106.0
0241, 31 - 34	SITE & INFRASTRUCTURE, DEMOLITION	85.3	88.3	87.4	89.2	91.1	90.5	98.2	87.7	90.9	94.3	86.0	88.6	101.6	86.0	90.9	95.2	107.4	103.6
0310	Concrete Forming & Accessories	92.1	85.8	86.6	87.8	78.1	79.3	99.2	54.9	60.7	93.9	70.1	73.2	100.6	70.2	74.1	101.8	142.2	136.9
0320	Concrete Reinforcing	87.4	104.7	96.1	88.2	74.7	81.4	87.4	67.5	77.4	97.4	76.0	86.6	98.0	76.0	86.9	102.5	149.5	126.2
0330	Cast-in-Place Concrete	100.2	78.9	91.8	106.2	84.2	97.5	123.8	49.2	94.5	134.1	79.4	112.5	150.3	79.4	122.4	107.8	149.9	124.4
03	CONCRETE	92.9	87.6	90.3	97.1	80.5	89.0	110.9	56.8	84.5	114.3	75.6	95.5	126.1	75.7	101.5	113.4	145.1	128.9
04	MASONRY	100.1	62.3	77.0	106.0	78.5	89.2	114.1	50.0	75.0	114.2	68.7	86.4	97.9	68.7	80.1	112.0	162.5	142.8
05	METALS	92.8	101.2	95.6	92.7	91.5	92.3	92.8	83.9	89.9	87.9	93.3	89.7	87.9	93.4	89.7	101.2	129.1	110.4
06	WOOD, PLASTICS & COMPOSITES	87.5	92.3	90.3	82.4	76.4	78.9	96.6	58.5	74.6	93.8	70.4	80.3	101.0	70.4	83.3	101.1	141.6	124.5
07	THERMAL & MOISTURE PROTECTION	96.5	75.1	87.8	96.5	76.1	88.2	97.1	66.4	84.6	103.1	81.4	94.3	103.6	81.4	94.6	101.6	150.1	121.3
08	OPENINGS	93.1	84.4	90.9	93.1	76.3	88.9	93.4	64.7	86.2	90.3	74.6	86.4	91.1	74.6	87.0	98.5	143.3	109.8
0920	Plaster & Gypsum Board	96.7	92.4	93.7	94.0	76.0	81.2	102.7	57.5	70.4	105.4	70.3	80.3	109.0	70.3	81.4	101.7	142.2	130.7
0950, 0980	Ceilings & Acoustic Treatment	99.8	92.4	94.9	100.8	76.0	84.4	99.8	57.5	71.9	105.8	70.3	82.3	105.8	70.3	82.3	101.0	142.2	128.2
0960	Flooring	91.6	61.2	82.7	89.5	82.2	87.4	95.3	67.8	87.2	113.9	80.9	104.2	118.0	80.9	107.1	95.0	178.2	119.4
0970, 0990	Wall Finishes & Painting/Coating	96.8	78.7	85.6	96.8	78.7	85.6	96.8	78.7	85.6	128.5	78.7	97.8	128.5	78.7	97.8	92.8	153.8	130.4
09	FINISHES	94.5	81.1	87.0	94.0	78.5	85.3	97.1	59.2	76.0	101.6	71.7	84.9	103.6	72.3	86.1	99.4	150.6	128.0
COVERS	DIVS. 10 - 14, 25, 28, 41, 43, 44, 46	100.0	64.7	93.0	100.0	89.8	98.0	100.0	41.7	88.4	100.0	79.7	96.0	100.0	79.7	96.0	100.0	120.2	104.0
21, 22, 23	FIRE SUPPRESSION, PLUMBING & HVAC	93.9	83.3	89.6	99.9	84.4	93.6	93.9	64.3	81.9	94.3	84.8	90.4	94.3	84.8	90.4	100.1	128.6	111.6
26, 27, 3370	ELECTRICAL, COMMUNICATIONS & UTIL.	98.4	93.2	95.7	96.9	82.0	89.2	95.4	71.4	83.0	95.4	98.9	97.2	93.0	98.9	96.0	101.5	132.0	117.2
MF2010	WEIGHTED AVERAGE	94.7	84.3	90.1	96.8	82.9	90.7	97.9	65.3	83.5	97.7	82.3	90.9	98.5	82.4	91.4	102.2	136.8	117.5

City Cost Indexes

MASSACHUSETTS

DIVISION		BROCKTON 023 MAT.	INST.	TOTAL	BUZZARDS BAY 025 MAT.	INST.	TOTAL	FALL RIVER 027 MAT.	INST.	TOTAL	FITCHBURG 014 MAT.	INST.	TOTAL	FRAMINGHAM 017 MAT.	INST.	TOTAL	GREENFIELD 013 MAT.	INST.	TOTAL
015433	CONTRACTOR EQUIPMENT		102.2	102.2		102.2	102.2		103.1	103.1		100.4	100.4		101.6	101.6		100.4	100.4
0241, 31 - 34	SITE & INFRASTRUCTURE, DEMOLITION	92.5	104.0	100.4	82.7	103.9	97.3	91.6	104.0	100.2	84.5	103.9	97.9	81.0	103.6	96.6	88.4	102.4	98.1
0310	Concrete Forming & Accessories	102.4	127.9	124.6	100.1	127.2	123.7	102.4	127.5	124.2	94.8	127.1	122.9	101.1	127.7	124.3	93.3	108.3	106.3
0320	Concrete Reinforcing	103.6	149.4	126.7	83.0	121.5	102.4	103.6	121.5	112.6	83.0	142.0	112.7	83.0	149.0	116.3	86.5	125.7	106.2
0330	Cast-in-Place Concrete	102.6	152.3	122.2	85.3	152.0	111.6	99.3	152.6	120.3	89.4	145.9	111.6	89.4	139.7	109.2	91.9	124.2	104.6
03	CONCRETE	110.5	139.5	124.7	93.3	133.9	113.1	108.9	134.2	121.2	91.7	135.4	113.0	94.6	135.0	114.3	95.7	116.5	105.8
04	MASONRY	107.9	158.8	139.0	99.3	158.8	135.6	108.4	158.8	139.1	95.5	151.9	129.9	101.7	152.0	132.4	99.8	125.9	115.7
05	METALS	98.0	126.9	107.6	93.0	115.2	100.3	98.0	115.6	103.8	92.9	120.7	102.1	93.0	126.1	103.9	95.1	109.4	99.8
06	WOOD, PLASTICS & COMPOSITES	100.0	124.7	114.3	97.2	124.7	113.1	100.0	125.0	114.4	93.7	124.5	111.5	99.7	124.5	114.0	92.0	106.0	100.1
07	THERMAL & MOISTURE PROTECTION	101.6	145.9	119.6	101.0	141.2	117.3	101.6	140.4	117.4	101.0	137.8	116.0	101.1	142.8	118.1	101.1	118.2	108.0
08	OPENINGS	96.6	133.8	105.9	92.1	120.5	99.3	96.6	120.6	102.6	101.1	131.7	108.8	92.6	133.6	102.9	101.2	111.9	103.9
0920	Plaster & Gypsum Board	95.7	124.8	116.5	91.3	124.8	115.2	95.7	124.8	116.5	92.4	124.6	115.4	95.6	124.8	116.5	93.7	105.5	102.1
0950, 0980	Ceilings & Acoustic Treatment	103.0	124.8	117.4	93.7	124.8	114.3	103.0	124.8	117.4	92.7	124.6	113.8	92.7	124.8	113.9	100.0	105.5	103.6
0960	Flooring	95.5	178.2	119.7	94.2	178.2	118.8	95.3	178.2	119.6	92.3	178.2	117.5	93.9	178.2	118.7	91.6	140.6	106.0
0970, 0990	Wall Finishes & Painting/Coating	92.3	139.1	121.2	92.3	139.1	121.2	92.3	139.1	121.2	90.1	139.1	120.4	91.2	139.1	120.8	90.1	109.4	102.0
09	FINISHES	99.4	138.1	121.0	95.6	138.1	119.3	99.3	138.3	121.1	95.0	138.0	119.0	95.6	137.9	119.2	96.9	114.2	106.5
COVERS	DIVS. 10 - 14, 25, 28, 41, 43, 44, 46	100.0	117.1	103.4	100.0	117.1	103.4	100.0	117.7	103.5	100.0	107.0	101.4	100.0	116.6	103.3	100.0	105.3	101.1
21, 22, 23	FIRE SUPPRESSION, PLUMBING & HVAC	100.0	111.9	104.8	94.1	111.6	101.2	100.0	111.7	104.7	95.0	115.0	103.1	95.0	124.6	107.0	95.0	102.0	97.8
26, 27, 3370	ELECTRICAL, COMMUNICATIONS & UTIL.	100.6	98.8	99.7	97.6	98.8	98.3	100.5	98.8	99.7	102.8	101.8	102.3	99.1	128.4	114.2	102.8	93.0	97.7
MF2010	WEIGHTED AVERAGE	100.8	124.7	111.4	94.9	122.1	106.9	100.6	122.2	110.1	96.1	123.3	108.1	95.5	129.9	110.7	97.3	108.4	102.2

MASSACHUSETTS

DIVISION		HYANNIS 026 MAT.	INST.	TOTAL	LAWRENCE 019 MAT.	INST.	TOTAL	LOWELL 018 MAT.	INST.	TOTAL	NEW BEDFORD 027 MAT.	INST.	TOTAL	PITTSFIELD 012 MAT.	INST.	TOTAL	SPRINGFIELD 010 - 011 MAT.	INST.	TOTAL
015433	CONTRACTOR EQUIPMENT		102.2	102.2		102.2	102.2		100.4	100.4		103.1	103.1		100.4	100.4		100.4	100.4
0241, 31 - 34	SITE & INFRASTRUCTURE, DEMOLITION	88.8	103.9	99.2	93.1	104.0	100.6	92.4	103.9	100.3	90.0	104.0	99.7	93.4	102.2	99.4	92.8	102.4	99.5
0310	Concrete Forming & Accessories	95.0	127.2	123.1	102.1	128.0	124.6	99.4	128.0	124.3	102.4	127.5	124.2	99.3	106.5	105.5	99.6	108.4	107.2
0320	Concrete Reinforcing	83.0	121.5	102.4	102.7	135.5	119.2	103.6	135.2	119.5	103.6	121.5	112.6	85.8	108.6	97.3	103.6	125.7	114.7
0330	Cast-in-Place Concrete	93.6	152.0	116.6	103.5	146.8	120.5	94.1	146.8	114.8	87.4	152.6	113.1	102.6	121.8	110.2	97.9	124.3	108.3
03	CONCRETE	100.4	133.9	116.7	110.8	135.0	122.6	101.4	134.8	117.7	102.9	134.2	118.2	102.9	111.7	107.2	103.3	116.6	109.8
04	MASONRY	106.9	158.8	138.6	107.1	158.8	138.7	94.7	151.9	129.6	106.8	158.8	138.5	95.4	121.6	111.4	95.0	126.1	114.0
05	METALS	94.5	115.2	101.3	95.5	121.4	104.0	95.4	118.6	103.1	98.0	115.6	103.8	95.3	102.4	97.6	98.0	109.4	101.7
06	WOOD, PLASTICS & COMPOSITES	91.2	124.7	110.6	100.0	124.7	114.3	99.5	124.7	114.1	100.0	125.0	114.4	99.5	106.0	103.3	99.5	106.0	103.3
07	THERMAL & MOISTURE PROTECTION	101.2	141.2	117.5	101.5	145.1	119.2	101.4	143.2	118.4	101.5	140.4	117.3	101.4	116.3	107.5	101.4	118.3	108.2
08	OPENINGS	92.8	120.5	99.8	96.6	130.0	105.0	102.4	130.0	109.4	96.6	120.6	102.6	102.4	107.3	103.6	102.4	111.9	104.8
0920	Plaster & Gypsum Board	87.6	124.8	114.2	98.7	124.8	117.4	98.7	124.8	117.4	95.7	124.8	116.5	98.7	105.5	103.6	98.7	105.5	103.6
0950, 0980	Ceilings & Acoustic Treatment	95.8	124.8	115.0	102.0	124.8	117.1	102.0	124.8	117.1	103.0	124.8	117.4	102.0	105.5	104.3	102.0	105.5	104.3
0960	Flooring	92.0	178.2	117.3	94.5	178.2	119.0	94.5	178.2	119.0	95.3	178.2	119.6	94.7	140.6	108.1	94.3	140.6	107.9
0970, 0990	Wall Finishes & Painting/Coating	92.3	139.1	121.2	90.2	139.1	120.4	90.1	139.1	120.4	92.3	139.1	121.2	90.1	109.4	102.0	91.7	109.4	102.6
09	FINISHES	95.5	138.1	119.3	99.0	138.1	120.8	99.0	138.1	120.8	99.2	138.3	121.0	99.1	113.1	106.9	99.1	114.2	107.5
COVERS	DIVS. 10 - 14, 25, 28, 41, 43, 44, 46	100.0	117.1	103.4	100.0	117.2	103.4	100.0	117.2	103.4	100.0	117.7	103.5	100.0	103.8	100.8	100.0	105.4	101.1
21, 22, 23	FIRE SUPPRESSION, PLUMBING & HVAC	100.0	111.6	104.7	100.0	119.0	107.7	100.0	124.5	109.9	100.0	111.7	104.7	100.0	97.6	99.1	100.0	102.1	100.9
26, 27, 3370	ELECTRICAL, COMMUNICATIONS & UTIL.	98.1	98.8	98.5	101.8	128.4	115.5	102.3	124.2	113.6	101.4	98.8	100.1	102.3	93.0	97.5	102.3	94.9	98.5
MF2010	WEIGHTED AVERAGE	98.0	122.1	108.6	100.5	129.0	113.1	99.4	128.5	112.3	99.9	122.2	109.7	99.6	105.3	102.1	100.0	108.7	103.9

DIVISION		MASSACHUSETTS WORCESTER 015 - 016 MAT.	INST.	TOTAL	MICHIGAN ANN ARBOR 481 MAT.	INST.	TOTAL	BATTLE CREEK 490 MAT.	INST.	TOTAL	BAY CITY 487 MAT.	INST.	TOTAL	DEARBORN 481 MAT.	INST.	TOTAL	DETROIT 482 MAT.	INST.	TOTAL
015433	CONTRACTOR EQUIPMENT		100.4	100.4		110.6	110.6		103.2	103.2		110.6	110.6		110.6	110.6		98.9	98.9
0241, 31 - 34	SITE & INFRASTRUCTURE, DEMOLITION	92.8	103.9	100.4	74.7	96.5	89.8	84.8	88.5	87.4	66.5	95.7	86.6	74.5	96.6	89.7	89.3	98.2	95.4
0310	Concrete Forming & Accessories	99.8	127.1	123.6	100.7	110.6	109.3	98.6	89.8	90.9	100.8	89.2	90.7	100.5	114.6	112.8	101.3	114.6	112.9
0320	Concrete Reinforcing	103.6	144.3	124.1	99.7	123.6	111.8	98.1	91.1	94.6	99.7	122.8	111.4	99.7	123.8	111.9	99.0	123.8	111.5
0330	Cast-in-Place Concrete	97.3	145.9	116.5	81.9	112.4	93.9	92.4	102.5	96.4	78.4	93.3	84.2	80.1	111.5	92.5	87.9	111.6	97.2
03	CONCRETE	103.0	135.8	119.0	90.3	113.9	101.8	95.2	93.8	94.5	88.5	97.6	92.9	89.3	115.4	102.0	93.2	114.3	103.5
04	MASONRY	94.5	151.9	129.5	97.9	108.5	104.4	96.0	86.8	90.3	97.5	88.5	92.0	97.8	111.9	106.4	96.9	111.9	106.1
05	METALS	98.0	121.6	105.8	93.8	119.0	102.1	93.0	87.3	91.1	94.5	115.9	101.5	93.9	119.4	102.3	97.9	102.2	99.3
06	WOOD, PLASTICS & COMPOSITES	99.9	124.5	114.1	97.8	111.1	105.5	100.1	89.6	94.1	97.8	88.4	92.4	97.8	115.7	108.1	98.2	115.7	108.3
07	THERMAL & MOISTURE PROTECTION	101.4	137.8	116.2	101.3	110.0	104.8	93.7	87.4	91.2	99.1	96.0	97.8	99.9	114.7	105.9	98.3	114.8	105.0
08	OPENINGS	102.4	132.4	110.0	95.1	109.8	98.8	92.7	83.8	90.5	95.1	95.6	95.2	95.1	112.3	99.4	96.6	112.3	100.6
0920	Plaster & Gypsum Board	98.7	124.6	117.2	104.7	110.4	108.8	94.6	85.4	88.0	104.7	87.0	92.1	104.7	115.1	112.2	104.7	115.1	112.2
0950, 0980	Ceilings & Acoustic Treatment	102.0	124.6	116.9	93.7	110.4	104.7	93.8	85.4	88.2	94.7	87.0	89.6	93.7	115.1	107.9	94.7	115.1	108.2
0960	Flooring	94.5	170.9	116.9	94.2	117.1	100.9	98.7	96.2	98.0	94.0	80.5	90.0	93.8	117.8	100.8	93.9	117.8	100.9
0970, 0990	Wall Finishes & Painting/Coating	90.1	139.1	120.4	92.8	102.0	98.5	96.0	82.6	87.7	92.8	83.3	87.0	92.8	102.1	98.5	94.3	102.1	99.1
09	FINISHES	99.0	136.5	119.9	94.8	111.1	103.9	96.5	90.1	92.9	94.5	86.2	89.9	94.7	114.3	105.6	96.2	114.3	106.3
COVERS	DIVS. 10 - 14, 25, 28, 41, 43, 44, 46	100.0	110.4	102.1	100.0	106.8	101.4	100.0	103.0	100.6	100.0	97.1	99.4	100.0	107.6	101.5	100.0	107.6	101.5
21, 22, 23	FIRE SUPPRESSION, PLUMBING & HVAC	100.0	115.1	106.1	100.0	100.2	100.1	99.9	90.9	96.3	100.0	87.9	95.1	100.0	110.5	104.3	100.1	111.8	104.8
26, 27, 3370	ELECTRICAL, COMMUNICATIONS & UTIL.	102.3	102.6	102.4	95.6	110.4	103.2	94.8	83.4	88.9	94.4	91.3	92.8	95.6	109.2	102.6	96.7	109.1	103.1
MF2010	WEIGHTED AVERAGE	100.0	123.5	110.4	95.8	108.1	101.2	96.0	89.2	93.0	95.2	93.6	94.5	95.7	111.4	102.6	97.4	110.1	103.0

MICHIGAN

DIVISION		FLINT 484 - 485			GAYLORD 497			GRAND RAPIDS 493,495			IRON MOUNTAIN 498 - 499			JACKSON 492			KALAMAZOO 491		
		MAT.	INST.	TOTAL	MAT.	INST.	TOTAL	MAT.	INST.	TOTAL	MAT.	INST.	TOTAL	MAT.	INST.	TOTAL	MAT.	INST.	TOTAL
015433	CONTRACTOR EQUIPMENT		110.6	110.6		105.6	105.6		103.2	103.2		94.9	94.9		105.6	105.6		103.2	103.2
0241, 31 - 34	SITE & INFRASTRUCTURE, DEMOLITION	64.3	95.9	86.1	79.0	86.7	84.3	86.3	88.4	87.7	87.5	94.9	92.6	101.3	88.4	92.4	85.1	88.5	87.4
0310	Concrete Forming & Accessories	103.5	91.4	93.0	95.9	56.1	61.2	98.9	81.0	83.4	88.0	86.1	86.4	93.4	88.0	88.7	98.6	89.5	90.7
0320	Concrete Reinforcing	99.7	123.1	111.5	91.5	92.7	92.1	98.1	90.8	94.4	91.3	94.4	92.8	88.9	122.9	106.0	98.1	91.0	94.6
0330	Cast-in-Place Concrete	82.5	95.4	87.6	92.2	71.4	84.0	98.4	95.5	97.3	109.2	89.4	101.4	92.1	94.5	93.0	94.3	102.4	97.5
03	CONCRETE	90.7	99.4	95.0	91.6	69.8	81.0	98.2	87.5	93.0	101.2	88.9	95.2	86.8	97.4	91.9	98.4	93.6	96.1
04	MASONRY	98.0	96.2	96.9	106.1	82.9	91.9	91.8	81.9	85.8	92.5	88.8	90.3	86.7	93.2	90.7	94.6	86.8	89.8
05	METALS	93.9	116.5	101.4	94.1	100.6	96.3	94.2	86.3	91.6	93.5	90.7	92.6	94.3	113.8	100.8	93.0	87.0	91.0
06	WOOD, PLASTICS & COMPOSITES	100.9	89.7	94.5	92.5	48.8	67.3	97.2	79.1	86.8	87.3	86.1	86.6	91.3	86.3	88.4	100.1	89.6	94.1
07	THERMAL & MOISTURE PROTECTION	99.1	99.3	99.2	92.2	70.8	83.5	95.5	77.1	88.0	95.4	84.1	90.8	91.6	96.6	93.6	93.7	87.4	91.2
08	OPENINGS	95.1	96.3	95.4	95.0	53.9	84.7	96.6	82.2	92.9	100.6	73.4	93.7	94.0	87.2	92.3	92.7	83.8	90.5
0920	Plaster & Gypsum Board	106.5	88.4	93.5	94.0	46.0	59.7	95.5	74.6	80.6	58.1	86.1	78.1	92.5	84.6	86.8	94.6	85.4	88.0
0950, 0980	Ceilings & Acoustic Treatment	93.7	88.4	90.2	92.0	46.0	61.6	92.9	74.6	80.8	91.8	86.1	88.0	92.9	84.6	87.4	93.8	85.4	88.2
0960	Flooring	94.0	83.2	90.8	91.8	50.4	79.7	98.9	70.5	90.5	112.8	96.8	108.1	90.5	69.4	84.3	98.7	75.8	92.0
0970, 0990	Wall Finishes & Painting/Coating	92.8	90.0	91.1	92.5	45.6	63.5	96.0	81.3	86.9	111.5	58.8	79.0	92.5	75.7	82.1	96.0	82.6	87.7
09	FINISHES	94.0	89.0	91.2	96.7	51.8	71.7	96.6	78.4	86.5	99.3	85.3	91.5	98.0	82.4	89.3	96.5	86.2	90.7
COVERS	DIVS. 10 - 14, 25, 28, 41, 43, 44, 46	100.0	98.2	99.6	100.0	91.8	98.4	100.0	101.6	100.3	100.0	93.7	98.7	100.0	98.0	99.6	100.0	103.0	100.6
21, 22, 23	FIRE SUPPRESSION, PLUMBING & HVAC	100.0	94.1	97.6	94.4	82.8	89.7	99.9	83.2	93.1	94.3	86.8	91.3	94.4	92.0	93.4	99.9	83.0	93.1
26, 27, 3370	ELECTRICAL, COMMUNICATIONS & UTIL.	95.6	95.0	95.3	92.9	49.0	70.3	99.1	75.1	86.7	99.2	87.6	93.2	96.8	110.3	103.8	94.7	86.9	90.7
MF2010	WEIGHTED AVERAGE	95.5	97.1	96.2	94.7	72.8	85.1	97.2	83.0	90.9	96.7	87.8	92.8	94.3	95.9	95.0	96.3	87.4	92.4

DIVISION		LANSING 488 - 489			MUSKEGON 494			ROYAL OAK 480,483			SAGINAW 486			TRAVERSE CITY 496			MINNESOTA BEMIDJI 566		
		MAT.	INST.	TOTAL	MAT.	INST.	TOTAL	MAT.	INST.	TOTAL	MAT.	INST.	TOTAL	MAT.	INST.	TOTAL	MAT.	INST.	TOTAL
015433	CONTRACTOR EQUIPMENT		110.6	110.6		103.2	103.2		96.4	96.4		110.6	110.6		94.9	94.9		98.7	98.7
0241, 31 - 34	SITE & INFRASTRUCTURE, DEMOLITION	83.2	95.8	91.9	82.9	88.4	86.7	79.0	96.0	90.7	67.4	95.7	86.9	74.3	94.6	88.3	98.4	98.6	98.6
0310	Concrete Forming & Accessories	104.2	88.4	90.5	99.1	88.1	89.5	97.1	111.7	109.8	100.7	89.0	90.5	88.0	71.1	73.3	90.8	94.2	93.7
0320	Concrete Reinforcing	99.7	122.9	111.4	98.8	90.5	94.6	90.4	122.0	105.6	99.7	122.8	111.3	92.7	90.2	91.4	103.5	109.4	106.5
0330	Cast-in-Place Concrete	87.0	93.7	89.6	92.1	96.5	93.8	71.7	110.4	87.0	80.9	93.2	85.8	85.2	63.7	76.7	105.6	106.6	106.0
03	CONCRETE	93.1	97.5	95.2	93.6	90.9	92.3	78.0	111.9	94.5	89.8	97.5	93.6	83.4	72.7	78.2	99.5	102.4	100.9
04	MASONRY	91.7	93.8	92.9	93.1	76.2	82.8	93.0	111.9	104.5	99.5	88.5	92.8	90.7	82.8	85.8	100.3	107.1	104.4
05	METALS	92.5	115.9	100.2	90.7	85.9	89.1	97.0	99.9	98.0	93.9	115.7	101.1	93.5	88.8	91.9	92.6	122.5	102.5
06	WOOD, PLASTICS & COMPOSITES	100.3	86.5	92.3	96.1	88.5	91.7	93.2	112.2	104.2	93.6	88.4	90.6	87.3	69.5	77.0	72.8	90.9	83.3
07	THERMAL & MOISTURE PROTECTION	100.2	92.0	96.9	92.9	78.2	86.9	97.7	114.0	104.4	99.8	96.0	98.3	94.5	71.4	85.1	108.5	99.7	104.9
08	OPENINGS	95.1	94.5	94.9	92.0	87.7	90.9	95.3	110.1	99.0	92.9	95.6	93.6	100.6	64.9	91.6	97.7	111.9	101.3
0920	Plaster & Gypsum Board	97.4	85.0	88.6	75.1	84.2	81.6	101.5	111.5	108.6	104.7	87.0	92.1	58.1	69.0	65.9	105.6	91.0	95.1
0950, 0980	Ceilings & Acoustic Treatment	93.7	85.0	88.0	94.7	84.2	87.8	92.9	111.5	105.2	93.7	87.0	89.3	91.8	69.0	76.7	137.6	91.0	106.8
0960	Flooring	104.0	83.2	97.9	97.9	65.3	88.3	91.8	116.4	99.0	94.2	80.5	90.2	112.8	50.4	94.5	108.9	126.5	114.7
0970, 0990	Wall Finishes & Painting/Coating	103.9	84.1	91.7	95.3	81.3	86.7	94.3	102.0	99.0	92.8	83.3	87.0	111.5	45.6	70.8	96.0	101.0	99.1
09	FINISHES	98.5	86.3	91.7	93.4	83.0	87.6	93.8	111.9	103.9	94.4	86.2	89.9	98.2	63.8	79.0	112.4	100.2	105.6
COVERS	DIVS. 10 - 14, 25, 28, 41, 43, 44, 46	100.0	97.6	99.5	100.0	102.8	100.6	100.0	102.7	100.5	100.0	97.1	99.4	100.0	90.3	98.1	100.0	95.7	99.1
21, 22, 23	FIRE SUPPRESSION, PLUMBING & HVAC	99.9	92.2	96.8	99.8	85.2	93.9	94.5	109.6	100.6	100.0	87.5	95.0	94.3	82.4	89.5	94.5	88.1	91.9
26, 27, 3370	ELECTRICAL, COMMUNICATIONS & UTIL.	98.7	93.0	95.8	95.2	80.1	87.4	97.6	94.0	95.8	92.7	91.3	92.0	94.6	76.7	85.3	104.5	104.0	104.2
MF2010	WEIGHTED AVERAGE	96.4	95.1	95.9	94.9	84.9	90.5	93.4	106.2	99.1	95.0	93.5	94.4	93.6	78.7	87.0	98.7	101.3	99.9

MINNESOTA

DIVISION		BRAINERD 564			DETROIT LAKES 565			DULUTH 556 - 558			MANKATO 560			MINNEAPOLIS 553 - 555			ROCHESTER 559		
		MAT.	INST.	TOTAL	MAT.	INST.	TOTAL	MAT.	INST.	TOTAL	MAT.	INST.	TOTAL	MAT.	INST.	TOTAL	MAT.	INST.	TOTAL
015433	CONTRACTOR EQUIPMENT		101.4	101.4		98.7	98.7		101.2	101.2		101.4	101.4		104.7	104.7		101.2	101.2
0241, 31 - 34	SITE & INFRASTRUCTURE, DEMOLITION	96.6	103.5	101.3	96.4	99.1	98.2	98.8	102.3	101.2	92.9	104.1	100.6	101.3	107.6	105.7	100.3	102.1	101.6
0310	Concrete Forming & Accessories	94.0	97.0	96.6	88.1	96.9	95.7	101.1	116.4	114.4	101.0	104.7	104.2	103.2	129.6	126.1	103.8	110.6	109.7
0320	Concrete Reinforcing	102.3	109.6	106.0	103.5	109.4	106.5	98.8	109.9	104.4	102.1	119.8	111.0	99.0	120.2	109.7	98.8	119.9	109.4
0330	Cast-in-Place Concrete	114.8	111.6	113.6	102.6	110.8	105.8	107.4	109.8	108.4	105.8	110.7	107.7	120.3	119.0	119.8	117.9	103.0	112.0
03	CONCRETE	103.9	105.4	104.6	97.0	105.0	100.9	102.3	113.5	107.7	99.0	110.4	104.6	110.5	124.5	117.3	107.7	110.5	109.1
04	MASONRY	123.6	117.6	119.9	123.6	114.8	118.2	108.6	121.3	116.3	111.9	114.4	113.4	108.1	129.1	120.9	107.3	117.0	113.2
05	METALS	93.8	122.5	103.3	92.6	122.3	102.4	99.6	125.1	108.0	93.6	128.2	105.1	102.4	131.9	112.1	99.5	130.1	109.6
06	WOOD, PLASTICS & COMPOSITES	93.7	90.7	92.0	70.2	90.9	82.2	110.4	116.3	113.8	101.9	102.6	102.3	113.6	127.8	121.8	113.6	109.4	111.2
07	THERMAL & MOISTURE PROTECTION	107.6	112.3	109.5	108.3	112.5	110.0	109.0	119.9	113.5	108.0	103.2	106.0	108.8	132.6	118.5	109.1	104.6	107.3
08	OPENINGS	85.7	111.8	92.2	97.6	111.9	101.2	93.9	121.1	100.7	90.4	121.3	98.2	97.2	135.7	106.9	93.9	125.7	101.9
0920	Plaster & Gypsum Board	86.5	91.0	89.7	104.7	91.0	94.9	94.3	117.2	110.7	90.6	103.2	99.6	102.2	129.0	121.3	101.7	110.1	107.7
0950, 0980	Ceilings & Acoustic Treatment	67.9	91.0	83.1	137.6	91.0	106.8	92.0	117.2	108.7	67.9	103.2	91.2	93.8	129.0	117.1	92.0	110.1	103.9
0960	Flooring	108.6	126.5	113.9	108.4	126.5	113.7	105.9	127.8	112.4	110.7	126.5	115.4	103.7	126.5	110.4	106.1	126.5	112.1
0970, 0990	Wall Finishes & Painting/Coating	90.2	101.0	96.9	96.0	101.0	99.1	88.5	111.6	102.7	101.7	105.1	103.8	97.6	132.1	118.9	92.0	105.1	100.1
09	FINISHES	94.1	101.9	98.5	111.7	102.1	106.4	97.0	118.4	108.9	95.7	108.6	102.9	98.4	129.7	115.8	98.2	113.1	106.5
COVERS	DIVS. 10 - 14, 25, 28, 41, 43, 44, 46	100.0	97.9	99.6	100.0	98.2	99.6	100.0	105.4	101.1	100.0	98.1	99.6	100.0	110.2	102.0	100.0	104.1	100.8
21, 22, 23	FIRE SUPPRESSION, PLUMBING & HVAC	93.7	92.0	93.0	94.5	91.7	93.3	100.1	101.0	100.5	93.7	91.7	92.9	100.0	121.6	108.8	100.0	99.4	99.8
26, 27, 3370	ELECTRICAL, COMMUNICATIONS & UTIL.	102.1	108.9	105.6	104.1	70.5	86.8	99.5	108.9	104.3	108.7	89.0	98.5	101.6	113.1	107.6	100.6	89.1	94.7
MF2010	WEIGHTED AVERAGE	97.6	105.3	101.0	99.4	99.3	99.4	100.1	112.0	105.4	97.7	104.6	100.7	102.1	123.0	111.3	100.9	107.6	103.8

City Cost Indexes

MINNESOTA / MISSISSIPPI

DIVISION		SAINT PAUL 550-551 MAT.	INST.	TOTAL	ST. CLOUD 563 MAT.	INST.	TOTAL	THIEF RIVER FALLS 567 MAT.	INST.	TOTAL	WILLMAR 562 MAT.	INST.	TOTAL	WINDOM 561 MAT.	INST.	TOTAL	BILOXI 395 MAT.	INST.	TOTAL
015433	CONTRACTOR EQUIPMENT		101.2	101.2		101.4	101.4		98.7	98.7		101.4	101.4		101.4	101.4		98.5	98.5
0241, 31 - 34	SITE & INFRASTRUCTURE, DEMOLITION	101.0	102.9	102.3	91.1	105.4	101.0	97.1	98.6	98.1	90.8	103.2	99.4	84.1	101.9	96.4	101.8	88.9	92.9
0310	Concrete Forming & Accessories	97.8	129.3	125.2	91.3	124.9	120.5	91.4	93.4	93.2	91.2	96.2	95.5	95.2	87.9	88.9	94.7	56.1	61.2
0320	Concrete Reinforcing	95.4	120.1	107.8	102.3	120.0	111.2	103.9	109.3	106.7	101.9	119.6	110.8	101.9	118.7	110.4	96.3	60.1	78.1
0330	Cast-in-Place Concrete	120.3	118.4	119.5	101.3	117.9	107.8	104.7	91.3	99.4	102.9	89.3	97.5	89.0	67.0	80.4	106.6	55.2	86.4
03	CONCRETE	112.0	124.1	117.9	94.9	121.9	108.0	98.2	96.8	97.5	95.0	99.3	97.1	85.6	87.8	86.6	98.8	58.2	79.0
04	MASONRY	117.2	129.1	124.4	108.6	126.5	119.5	100.2	107.1	104.4	113.0	117.6	115.8	123.1	90.1	102.9	95.6	45.7	65.1
05	METALS	99.0	131.6	109.8	94.5	129.5	106.0	92.8	121.8	102.3	93.6	127.0	104.6	93.5	124.6	103.8	92.5	83.7	89.6
06	WOOD, PLASTICS & COMPOSITES	106.6	127.6	118.7	91.3	122.2	109.2	73.6	90.4	83.6	91.1	91.0	91.0	94.9	88.1	91.0	99.3	59.6	76.4
07	THERMAL & MOISTURE PROTECTION	110.3	132.4	119.3	107.8	122.8	113.9	109.4	101.5	106.2	107.6	109.6	108.4	107.6	86.6	99.0	92.8	57.0	78.3
08	OPENINGS	91.7	135.6	102.7	90.4	132.7	101.1	97.7	111.9	101.3	88.0	96.2	90.0	92.1	94.6	92.8	97.9	60.7	88.5
0920	Plaster & Gypsum Board	91.2	128.9	118.1	86.5	123.4	112.9	105.2	91.0	95.0	86.5	91.2	89.9	86.5	88.2	87.8	97.3	58.8	69.8
0950, 0980	Ceilings & Acoustic Treatment	89.3	128.9	115.4	67.9	123.4	104.6	137.6	91.0	106.8	67.9	91.2	83.3	67.9	88.2	81.3	95.8	58.8	71.4
0960	Flooring	100.0	126.5	107.8	104.6	126.5	111.1	109.4	126.5	114.4	106.5	126.5	112.4	109.2	126.5	114.3	117.7	55.3	99.4
0970, 0990	Wall Finishes & Painting/Coating	97.6	127.6	116.1	101.7	132.1	120.5	96.0	101.0	99.1	96.0	101.0	99.1	96.0	105.1	101.6	105.7	45.8	68.7
09	FINISHES	95.0	129.0	114.0	93.2	126.2	111.6	112.2	100.2	105.5	93.4	99.6	96.8	93.5	95.0	94.3	104.4	55.1	76.9
COVERS	DIVS. 10 - 14, 25, 28, 41, 43, 44, 46	100.0	109.9	102.0	100.0	104.5	100.9	100.0	95.6	99.1	100.0	97.8	99.6	100.0	92.9	98.6	100.0	59.9	92.0
21, 22, 23	FIRE SUPPRESSION, PLUMBING & HVAC	100.0	117.1	106.9	99.7	121.3	108.4	94.5	87.7	91.7	93.7	110.0	100.3	93.7	86.1	90.6	99.9	50.4	79.9
26, 27, 3370	ELECTRICAL, COMMUNICATIONS & UTIL.	98.7	113.1	106.1	102.1	113.1	107.8	101.7	70.5	85.6	102.1	90.5	96.1	108.7	89.0	98.5	98.8	59.0	78.3
MF2010	WEIGHTED AVERAGE	101.1	121.5	110.1	97.6	120.8	107.9	98.3	95.8	97.2	96.0	105.1	100.0	96.4	93.8	95.2	98.3	60.2	81.5

MISSISSIPPI

DIVISION		CLARKSDALE 386 MAT.	INST.	TOTAL	COLUMBUS 397 MAT.	INST.	TOTAL	GREENVILLE 387 MAT.	INST.	TOTAL	GREENWOOD 389 MAT.	INST.	TOTAL	JACKSON 390-392 MAT.	INST.	TOTAL	LAUREL 394 MAT.	INST.	TOTAL
015433	CONTRACTOR EQUIPMENT		98.5	98.5		98.5	98.5		98.5	98.5		98.5	98.5		98.5	98.5		98.5	98.5
0241, 31 - 34	SITE & INFRASTRUCTURE, DEMOLITION	99.2	88.7	91.9	100.5	89.0	92.6	105.7	88.9	94.1	102.4	88.4	92.8	97.3	88.9	91.5	107.1	88.8	94.5
0310	Concrete Forming & Accessories	86.1	52.4	56.8	84.3	54.5	58.4	83.0	67.7	69.7	94.6	52.3	57.8	94.0	61.1	65.4	84.4	56.3	59.9
0320	Concrete Reinforcing	103.8	44.2	73.8	103.2	45.2	74.0	104.4	64.0	84.0	103.8	55.5	79.6	96.3	59.1	77.6	103.8	41.5	72.4
0330	Cast-in-Place Concrete	103.9	56.1	85.1	108.7	61.4	90.1	107.0	58.3	87.8	111.8	55.7	89.7	90.7	59.1	78.2	106.3	57.8	87.2
03	CONCRETE	97.0	53.8	76.6	100.6	56.8	79.2	102.0	65.1	84.0	103.3	55.7	80.1	90.8	61.5	76.5	102.6	55.7	79.8
04	MASONRY	95.4	47.6	66.2	122.5	54.6	81.1	141.8	51.1	86.4	96.0	47.4	66.4	96.6	51.1	68.8	118.2	50.9	77.1
05	METALS	89.6	76.2	85.2	89.5	77.1	85.4	90.7	85.6	89.0	89.6	77.7	85.7	92.4	83.5	89.5	89.6	76.1	85.1
06	WOOD, PLASTICS & COMPOSITES	87.3	54.4	68.3	85.4	55.5	68.1	84.1	72.4	77.4	99.3	54.4	73.4	98.0	63.3	78.0	86.4	58.0	70.0
07	THERMAL & MOISTURE PROTECTION	92.7	49.8	75.2	92.8	54.3	77.1	93.0	63.0	80.8	93.0	49.7	75.4	94.6	62.0	81.4	92.9	56.1	77.9
08	OPENINGS	97.1	52.4	85.9	97.1	52.5	85.9	97.1	65.1	89.1	97.1	53.8	86.2	98.3	58.8	88.3	93.7	53.3	83.5
0920	Plaster & Gypsum Board	85.5	53.5	62.6	85.1	54.5	63.3	85.1	72.0	75.7	96.0	53.5	65.6	91.2	62.7	70.8	85.1	57.2	65.2
0950, 0980	Ceilings & Acoustic Treatment	89.3	53.5	65.6	89.3	54.5	66.3	91.3	72.0	78.6	89.3	53.5	65.6	93.1	62.7	73.0	89.3	57.2	68.1
0960	Flooring	111.4	55.3	95.0	110.2	62.1	96.1	109.4	55.3	93.5	117.7	55.3	99.4	118.1	55.3	99.7	108.4	55.3	92.8
0970, 0990	Wall Finishes & Painting/Coating	105.7	48.6	70.5	105.7	55.8	74.9	105.7	69.4	83.3	105.7	48.6	70.5	105.7	69.4	83.3	105.7	64.2	80.1
09	FINISHES	99.5	52.8	73.5	99.4	56.4	75.4	100.0	66.6	81.4	103.0	52.8	75.0	103.4	61.3	79.9	99.5	57.5	76.1
COVERS	DIVS. 10 - 14, 25, 28, 41, 43, 44, 46	100.0	60.3	92.1	100.0	61.5	92.3	100.0	63.2	92.7	100.0	60.2	92.1	100.0	62.2	92.5	100.0	40.4	88.1
21, 22, 23	FIRE SUPPRESSION, PLUMBING & HVAC	97.4	44.3	75.9	96.7	40.3	73.8	99.9	51.1	80.1	97.4	42.2	75.0	99.9	56.5	82.3	96.7	49.2	77.5
26, 27, 3370	ELECTRICAL, COMMUNICATIONS & UTIL.	98.1	49.3	72.9	96.3	52.2	73.5	98.1	66.6	81.9	98.1	46.2	71.3	99.5	66.6	82.5	97.8	59.5	78.1
MF2010	WEIGHTED AVERAGE	96.4	55.5	78.4	97.8	56.9	79.8	100.3	65.1	84.7	97.6	55.1	78.8	97.4	64.4	82.9	97.9	58.8	80.6

MISSISSIPPI / MISSOURI

DIVISION		MCCOMB 396 MAT.	INST.	TOTAL	MERIDIAN 393 MAT.	INST.	TOTAL	TUPELO 388 MAT.	INST.	TOTAL	BOWLING GREEN 633 MAT.	INST.	TOTAL	CAPE GIRARDEAU 637 MAT.	INST.	TOTAL	CHILLICOTHE 646 MAT.	INST.	TOTAL
015433	CONTRACTOR EQUIPMENT		98.5	98.5		98.5	98.5		98.5	98.5		106.1	106.1		106.1	106.1		102.2	102.2
0241, 31 - 34	SITE & INFRASTRUCTURE, DEMOLITION	92.8	88.6	89.9	97.0	89.2	91.6	96.8	88.6	91.1	91.4	93.6	92.9	92.7	93.5	93.3	100.3	90.9	93.8
0310	Concrete Forming & Accessories	84.3	54.2	58.1	81.9	67.2	69.1	83.5	54.5	58.3	91.8	87.1	87.7	85.7	75.0	76.4	90.3	90.0	90.0
0320	Concrete Reinforcing	104.4	43.6	73.8	103.2	59.1	81.0	101.6	55.8	78.5	100.9	96.9	98.9	102.1	83.3	92.7	97.5	100.1	98.8
0330	Cast-in-Place Concrete	94.4	55.6	79.1	101.0	61.6	85.4	103.9	57.6	85.7	94.6	75.6	87.1	93.7	82.5	89.2	93.0	65.8	82.3
03	CONCRETE	90.5	54.2	72.8	94.8	65.1	80.3	96.5	57.3	77.4	96.3	86.1	91.4	95.5	80.6	88.3	99.8	83.9	92.1
04	MASONRY	123.9	46.9	76.9	95.3	55.3	70.9	131.6	50.6	82.2	124.4	95.9	107.0	121.5	77.3	94.5	98.6	90.8	93.8
05	METALS	89.7	74.3	84.6	90.6	83.7	88.3	89.5	77.9	85.7	97.9	110.8	102.1	98.9	104.4	100.8	95.5	96.5	95.8
06	WOOD, PLASTICS & COMPOSITES	85.4	54.2	68.9	83.0	69.3	75.1	84.7	55.5	67.8	88.9	87.4	88.0	82.6	72.3	76.6	91.9	96.0	94.3
07	THERMAL & MOISTURE PROTECTION	92.4	48.9	74.7	92.6	64.5	81.1	92.6	55.8	77.7	101.0	98.4	99.9	100.9	81.1	92.8	97.6	84.9	92.4
08	OPENINGS	97.2	54.1	86.3	97.1	67.9	89.8	97.1	53.7	86.2	99.0	83.1	95.0	99.0	74.3	92.7	90.8	84.5	89.2
0920	Plaster & Gypsum Board	85.1	56.5	64.7	85.1	68.8	73.4	85.1	54.5	63.3	97.3	87.0	89.9	95.5	71.3	78.2	103.1	95.7	97.8
0950, 0980	Ceilings & Acoustic Treatment	89.3	56.5	67.6	91.3	68.8	76.4	89.3	54.5	66.3	90.1	87.0	88.0	90.1	71.3	77.7	89.5	95.7	93.6
0960	Flooring	110.2	55.3	94.1	108.4	55.3	92.8	109.7	55.3	93.7	101.2	95.8	99.6	97.5	88.0	94.7	93.5	45.0	79.3
0970, 0990	Wall Finishes & Painting/Coating	105.7	44.6	68.0	105.7	80.3	90.0	105.7	61.9	78.7	102.0	103.4	102.8	102.0	72.7	83.9	94.3	47.3	65.3
09	FINISHES	98.6	54.0	73.7	98.9	67.0	81.1	98.9	55.7	74.8	98.5	89.4	93.4	97.1	75.3	84.9	96.4	79.5	87.0
COVERS	DIVS. 10 - 14, 25, 28, 41, 43, 44, 46	100.0	63.3	92.8	100.0	64.3	92.9	100.0	61.5	92.3	100.0	89.5	97.9	100.0	90.4	98.1	100.0	55.7	91.2
21, 22, 23	FIRE SUPPRESSION, PLUMBING & HVAC	96.7	37.1	72.6	99.9	58.7	83.2	97.7	46.4	76.9	93.9	86.7	91.0	99.9	94.9	97.8	94.2	44.0	73.9
26, 27, 3370	ELECTRICAL, COMMUNICATIONS & UTIL.	94.8	52.5	73.0	97.8	59.2	77.9	97.8	52.3	74.4	99.7	82.9	91.0	99.7	107.9	103.70	95.9	34.9	64.5
MF2010	WEIGHTED AVERAGE	96.3	54.6	77.9	96.7	66.1	83.2	98.0	57.9	80.4	98.4	90.5	94.9	99.7	89.6	95.3	96.1	70.0	84.6

MISSOURI

DIVISION		COLUMBIA 652			FLAT RIVER 636			HANNIBAL 634			HARRISONVILLE 647			JEFFERSON CITY 650 - 651			JOPLIN 648		
		MAT.	INST.	TOTAL	MAT.	INST.	TOTAL	MAT.	INST.	TOTAL	MAT.	INST.	TOTAL	MAT.	INST.	TOTAL	MAT.	INST.	TOTAL
015433	CONTRACTOR EQUIPMENT		107.0	107.0		106.1	106.1		106.1	106.1		102.2	102.2		107.0	107.0		105.7	105.7
0241, 31 - 34	SITE & INFRASTRUCTURE, DEMOLITION	105.3	95.9	98.8	94.1	93.6	93.8	89.0	93.4	92.0	91.7	95.8	94.5	101.7	95.8	97.6	100.4	98.5	99.1
0310	Concrete Forming & Accessories	87.3	79.5	80.5	97.1	87.1	88.4	90.2	77.3	79.0	87.6	104.1	101.9	96.7	79.3	81.6	101.1	73.5	77.1
0320	Concrete Reinforcing	99.3	115.6	107.5	102.1	105.8	104.0	100.3	96.8	98.5	97.1	111.9	104.5	98.1	106.7	102.4	100.6	72.3	86.3
0330	Cast-in-Place Concrete	89.5	82.6	86.8	97.7	94.2	96.3	89.6	75.1	83.9	95.3	106.7	99.8	90.0	82.5	87.1	100.7	66.1	87.1
03	CONCRETE	86.1	88.8	87.4	99.3	94.2	96.8	92.5	81.6	87.2	96.4	106.7	101.4	87.5	87.0	87.2	99.6	71.6	86.0
04	MASONRY	133.3	85.6	104.2	122.0	78.8	95.6	115.2	95.9	103.4	93.1	107.9	102.1	96.0	85.6	89.7	92.4	84.8	87.7
05	METALS	94.5	119.5	102.7	97.8	113.8	103.1	97.9	109.6	101.7	95.9	112.3	101.4	93.9	115.8	101.1	98.6	88.4	95.2
06	WOOD, PLASTICS & COMPOSITES	92.4	77.1	83.6	95.6	87.4	90.9	87.1	75.1	80.2	88.6	103.7	97.3	102.4	77.1	87.8	102.8	74.5	86.4
07	THERMAL & MOISTURE PROTECTION	93.3	86.0	90.3	101.2	93.8	98.2	100.8	92.3	97.4	96.9	107.7	101.3	93.4	86.0	90.4	97.4	72.2	87.1
08	OPENINGS	90.6	94.5	91.6	99.0	85.7	95.8	99.0	76.4	93.3	91.2	106.0	94.9	87.8	92.1	88.9	92.0	72.4	87.1
0920	Plaster & Gypsum Board	99.9	76.3	83.1	102.7	87.0	91.5	95.9	74.3	80.5	97.1	103.6	101.8	104.2	76.3	84.3	110.2	73.5	84.0
0950, 0980	Ceilings & Acoustic Treatment	94.9	76.3	82.6	90.1	87.0	88.0	90.1	74.3	79.7	89.5	103.6	98.8	94.0	76.3	82.3	90.4	73.5	79.2
0960	Flooring	112.4	95.9	107.5	104.5	88.0	99.6	100.3	95.8	99.0	89.0	107.3	94.4	120.0	95.9	112.9	118.8	42.2	96.3
0970, 0990	Wall Finishes & Painting/Coating	104.0	79.4	88.8	102.0	62.6	77.7	102.0	103.4	102.8	99.2	107.0	104.0	104.0	79.4	88.8	93.8	37.0	58.7
09	FINISHES	99.5	81.1	89.2	100.2	83.4	90.9	97.8	82.1	89.1	93.9	104.8	100.0	102.4	81.1	90.5	103.0	64.4	81.5
COVERS	DIVS. 10 - 14, 25, 28, 41, 43, 44, 46	100.0	95.3	99.1	100.0	92.6	98.5	100.0	54.7	91.0	100.0	97.6	99.5	100.0	95.3	99.1	100.0	62.0	92.4
21, 22, 23	FIRE SUPPRESSION, PLUMBING & HVAC	99.9	95.2	98.0	93.9	86.7	91.0	93.9	86.6	91.0	94.1	103.3	97.8	99.9	89.5	95.7	100.2	48.0	79.0
26, 27, 3370	ELECTRICAL, COMMUNICATIONS & UTIL.	95.6	88.0	91.7	104.2	107.9	106.1	98.4	82.9	90.4	102.6	101.7	102.1	99.3	88.0	93.4	93.7	69.0	81.0
MF2010	WEIGHTED AVERAGE	97.7	92.4	95.4	99.4	92.9	96.5	97.3	87.1	92.8	95.7	104.5	99.6	96.2	90.5	93.7	98.2	70.4	85.9

MISSOURI

DIVISION		KANSAS CITY 640 - 641			KIRKSVILLE 635			POPLAR BLUFF 639			ROLLA 654 - 655			SEDALIA 653			SIKESTON 638		
		MAT.	INST.	TOTAL	MAT.	INST.	TOTAL	MAT.	INST.	TOTAL	MAT.	INST.	TOTAL	MAT.	INST.	TOTAL	MAT.	INST.	TOTAL
015433	CONTRACTOR EQUIPMENT		103.4	103.4		98.5	98.5		100.9	100.9		107.0	107.0		99.2	99.2		100.9	100.9
0241, 31 - 34	SITE & INFRASTRUCTURE, DEMOLITION	93.2	98.2	96.7	90.3	89.5	89.8	77.2	92.9	88.1	104.8	94.0	97.3	96.7	91.8	93.3	80.7	93.2	89.3
0310	Concrete Forming & Accessories	100.1	107.9	106.9	83.5	77.9	78.6	83.7	72.6	74.0	93.9	90.4	90.8	91.3	79.8	81.3	84.7	73.6	75.0
0320	Concrete Reinforcing	95.6	116.5	106.1	101.2	86.0	93.5	104.2	83.3	93.7	99.8	67.8	83.7	98.3	104.7	101.5	103.6	83.2	93.3
0330	Cast-in-Place Concrete	93.7	108.0	99.3	110.1	75.1	96.2	85.1	79.7	77.0	91.6	85.5	89.2	95.7	83.2	90.8	80.3	82.0	81.0
03	CONCRETE	95.6	109.7	102.5	110.1	79.3	95.1	85.7	78.1	82.0	87.8	85.8	86.8	99.2	86.5	93.0	89.4	79.3	84.5
04	MASONRY	95.1	109.7	104.0	128.1	87.4	103.2	119.9	71.6	90.4	109.8	78.8	90.8	115.7	86.0	97.5	119.6	76.2	93.1
05	METALS	106.5	114.9	109.3	97.4	96.4	97.1	98.0	96.5	97.5	93.8	102.3	96.6	92.4	106.7	97.1	98.3	95.7	97.5
06	WOOD, PLASTICS & COMPOSITES	102.0	107.6	105.2	75.9	77.1	76.6	75.1	72.3	73.5	99.1	93.2	95.7	92.0	77.1	83.4	76.5	72.3	74.1
07	THERMAL & MOISTURE PROTECTION	97.0	109.6	102.1	107.3	85.8	98.6	105.9	80.9	95.7	93.4	91.0	92.4	98.8	93.0	96.4	106.1	79.4	95.2
08	OPENINGS	98.2	109.8	101.2	103.3	74.9	96.2	104.3	73.6	96.6	90.6	87.3	89.8	93.9	87.1	92.2	104.3	67.1	94.9
0920	Plaster & Gypsum Board	106.1	107.6	107.2	90.4	76.3	80.3	90.9	71.3	76.9	100.8	92.9	95.1	93.9	76.3	81.4	92.7	71.3	77.5
0950, 0980	Ceilings & Acoustic Treatment	96.7	107.6	103.9	88.3	76.3	80.4	90.1	71.3	77.7	94.9	92.9	93.6	94.9	76.3	82.6	90.1	71.3	77.7
0960	Flooring	94.3	109.0	98.6	77.5	95.9	82.9	92.2	81.4	89.1	116.3	95.9	110.3	88.4	97.1	90.9	92.7	81.4	89.4
0970, 0990	Wall Finishes & Painting/Coating	99.2	114.7	108.7	97.2	79.4	86.2	96.7	72.1	81.5	104.0	86.4	93.1	104.0	105.7	105.0	96.7	57.6	72.6
09	FINISHES	98.1	108.6	104.0	96.7	80.2	87.5	97.0	72.7	83.4	100.9	90.4	95.0	97.4	84.5	90.2	97.7	71.6	83.1
COVERS	DIVS. 10 - 14, 25, 28, 41, 43, 44, 46	100.0	101.5	100.3	100.0	53.1	90.7	100.0	88.4	97.7	100.0	57.1	91.5	100.0	89.7	97.9	100.0	90.0	98.0
21, 22, 23	FIRE SUPPRESSION, PLUMBING & HVAC	100.0	110.9	104.4	93.9	86.1	90.7	93.9	91.3	92.9	93.9	86.9	91.1	93.9	96.0	94.7	93.9	84.4	90.1
26, 27, 3370	ELECTRICAL, COMMUNICATIONS & UTIL.	104.3	102.0	103.1	98.6	82.8	90.5	98.9	107.8	103.5	94.1	87.9	90.9	95.7	101.6	98.8	97.9	107.8	103.0
MF2010	WEIGHTED AVERAGE	100.1	108.0	103.6	100.4	83.8	93.1	97.0	86.8	92.5	95.2	87.9	92.0	96.6	92.8	94.9	97.5	85.5	92.2

MISSOURI / MONTANA

DIVISION		SPRINGFIELD 656 - 658			ST. JOSEPH 644 - 645			ST. LOUIS 630 - 631			BILLINGS 590 - 591			BUTTE 597			GREAT FALLS 594		
		MAT.	INST.	TOTAL	MAT.	INST.	TOTAL	MAT.	INST.	TOTAL	MAT.	INST.	TOTAL	MAT.	INST.	TOTAL	MAT.	INST.	TOTAL
015433	CONTRACTOR EQUIPMENT		101.7	101.7		102.2	102.2		107.1	107.1		98.9	98.9		98.7	98.7		98.7	98.7
0241, 31 - 34	SITE & INFRASTRUCTURE, DEMOLITION	99.2	93.6	95.4	94.7	94.0	94.2	92.6	97.5	96.0	98.6	97.0	97.5	109.4	96.3	100.4	113.3	97.1	102.1
0310	Concrete Forming & Accessories	98.8	74.1	77.4	99.9	87.6	89.2	97.1	103.4	102.6	101.9	65.9	70.6	90.3	64.0	67.5	101.7	67.4	71.8
0320	Concrete Reinforcing	95.6	115.1	105.4	94.4	111.1	102.8	93.4	107.6	100.5	101.4	80.2	90.7	110.0	80.3	95.0	101.4	80.2	90.7
0330	Cast-in-Place Concrete	97.2	72.4	87.5	93.6	104.1	97.7	93.7	106.3	98.7	115.2	66.3	95.9	126.8	67.9	103.6	134.0	64.4	106.5
03	CONCRETE	96.3	82.1	89.4	95.4	98.4	96.9	94.9	106.0	100.3	106.3	69.7	88.5	110.4	69.5	90.5	115.5	69.7	93.2
04	MASONRY	89.5	84.5	86.4	94.9	93.9	94.3	101.5	109.4	106.3	125.4	69.9	91.5	120.7	71.7	90.8	125.3	73.9	93.9
05	METALS	98.4	106.2	101.0	102.5	110.5	105.1	103.8	118.1	108.5	110.2	89.8	103.5	103.0	89.9	98.7	106.8	89.8	101.2
06	WOOD, PLASTICS & COMPOSITES	99.0	73.3	84.2	102.8	85.1	92.5	95.5	101.7	99.1	97.8	66.2	79.6	86.9	63.6	73.4	98.9	66.2	80.0
07	THERMAL & MOISTURE PROTECTION	97.5	80.1	90.5	97.5	95.5	96.7	100.9	106.7	103.3	107.4	69.0	91.8	107.3	69.5	91.9	107.8	68.4	91.8
08	OPENINGS	96.1	81.5	92.4	96.8	96.4	96.7	98.2	108.6	100.9	96.6	66.3	89.0	94.6	66.1	87.4	98.0	65.6	89.8
0920	Plaster & Gypsum Board	102.2	72.3	80.9	111.8	84.4	92.2	103.9	101.7	102.3	96.9	65.5	74.4	100.6	62.7	73.6	108.9	65.5	77.9
0950, 0980	Ceilings & Acoustic Treatment	94.9	72.3	80.0	95.8	84.4	88.3	95.5	101.7	99.6	106.2	65.5	79.3	111.5	62.7	79.3	113.3	65.5	81.7
0960	Flooring	113.8	42.2	92.8	97.5	97.1	97.4	104.2	99.3	102.8	109.2	73.6	98.7	106.4	77.7	98.0	114.8	77.7	103.9
0970, 0990	Wall Finishes & Painting/Coating	98.0	52.9	70.2	94.3	88.8	90.9	102.0	106.7	104.9	97.5	54.5	71.0	96.0	54.0	70.1	96.0	51.3	68.4
09	FINISHES	103.2	65.4	82.1	99.2	88.7	93.4	101.4	102.4	101.9	104.5	66.3	82.8	105.0	65.0	82.7	109.2	67.0	85.7
COVERS	DIVS. 10 - 14, 25, 28, 41, 43, 44, 46	100.0	93.4	98.7	100.0	96.8	99.4	100.0	102.3	100.5	100.0	74.9	95.0	100.0	74.7	95.0	100.0	76.3	95.3
21, 22, 23	FIRE SUPPRESSION, PLUMBING & HVAC	99.9	70.0	88.1	100.2	87.3	94.9	99.9	101.7	100.6	100.2	71.4	88.5	100.3	68.4	87.4	100.3	73.5	89.4
26, 27, 3370	ELECTRICAL, COMMUNICATIONS & UTIL.	99.8	72.4	85.7	102.7	76.5	89.2	102.2	108.3	105.3	97.3	76.7	86.7	104.9	72.6	88.2	97.5	73.5	85.1
MF2010	WEIGHTED AVERAGE	98.5	79.9	90.3	99.3	91.8	96.0	100.0	105.7	102.5	103.5	74.7	90.8	103.5	73.5	90.3	105.0	75.3	91.9

MONTANA

DIVISION		HAVRE 595 MAT.	INST.	TOTAL	HELENA 596 MAT.	INST.	TOTAL	KALISPELL 599 MAT.	INST.	TOTAL	MILES CITY 593 MAT.	INST.	TOTAL	MISSOULA 598 MAT.	INST.	TOTAL	WOLF POINT 592 MAT.	INST.	TOTAL
015433	CONTRACTOR EQUIPMENT		98.7	98.7		98.7	98.7		98.7	98.7		98.7	98.7		98.7	98.7		98.7	98.7
0241, 31 - 34	SITE & INFRASTRUCTURE, DEMOLITION	118.8	96.7	103.6	101.9	96.2	98.0	98.2	96.0	96.7	105.9	96.4	99.3	89.2	96.2	94.0	127.4	96.5	106.1
0310	Concrete Forming & Accessories	84.2	57.2	60.7	101.9	66.6	71.2	93.2	55.2	60.1	100.4	55.7	61.5	93.2	62.3	66.4	93.7	50.7	56.3
0320	Concrete Reinforcing	110.8	64.3	87.4	104.9	64.0	84.3	112.9	80.0	96.3	110.4	64.3	87.2	111.8	80.2	95.9	112.0	64.3	88.0
0330	Cast-in-Place Concrete	136.5	62.9	107.5	104.0	63.3	88.0	110.1	60.6	90.6	120.5	62.6	97.7	93.4	62.6	81.3	135.0	63.0	106.6
03	CONCRETE	118.9	61.7	91.0	101.0	65.9	83.9	99.8	62.9	81.8	107.2	60.9	84.6	87.9	66.8	77.7	122.5	58.8	91.5
04	MASONRY	121.6	72.0	91.3	116.6	68.5	87.2	119.6	66.9	87.4	127.2	67.2	90.6	145.2	70.2	99.4	128.3	67.9	91.5
05	METALS	99.4	82.0	93.7	106.0	81.3	97.8	99.3	88.2	95.6	98.6	81.9	93.1	99.8	89.0	96.3	98.7	81.8	93.1
06	WOOD, PLASTICS & COMPOSITES	79.6	54.1	64.9	98.9	66.2	80.0	89.8	52.4	68.2	96.4	54.5	72.2	89.8	62.4	74.0	88.9	47.5	65.0
07	THERMAL & MOISTURE PROTECTION	107.6	65.6	90.5	107.6	70.4	92.5	106.9	66.5	90.5	107.2	63.8	89.5	106.5	68.9	91.2	108.0	62.8	89.6
08	OPENINGS	94.7	54.5	84.6	97.4	60.0	88.0	94.7	58.1	85.5	94.2	54.7	84.2	94.7	63.3	86.8	94.2	50.7	83.2
0920	Plaster & Gypsum Board	96.1	52.9	65.3	97.7	65.5	74.7	100.6	51.2	65.3	107.8	53.4	68.9	100.6	61.5	72.7	102.3	46.2	62.2
0950, 0980	Ceilings & Acoustic Treatment	111.5	52.9	72.8	110.6	65.5	80.8	111.5	51.2	71.7	109.7	53.4	72.5	111.5	61.5	78.5	109.7	46.2	67.7
0960	Flooring	103.1	77.7	95.6	114.8	61.9	99.3	108.5	77.7	99.4	114.6	73.6	102.5	108.5	77.7	99.4	110.2	73.6	99.4
0970, 0990	Wall Finishes & Painting/Coating	96.0	51.3	68.4	96.0	45.6	64.9	96.0	39.4	61.1	96.0	47.3	66.0	96.0	50.2	67.7	96.0	51.3	68.4
09	FINISHES	104.3	59.4	79.2	106.6	63.7	82.7	104.9	56.7	78.0	107.6	57.3	79.6	104.2	63.5	81.5	107.4	53.7	77.4
COVERS	DIVS. 10 - 14, 25, 28, 41, 43, 44, 46	100.0	74.3	94.9	100.0	76.3	95.3	100.0	73.4	94.7	100.0	72.7	94.6	100.0	74.1	94.9	100.0	72.1	94.5
21, 22, 23	FIRE SUPPRESSION, PLUMBING & HVAC	94.3	72.1	85.3	100.2	69.9	87.9	94.3	68.1	83.7	94.3	69.6	84.3	100.3	67.6	87.0	94.3	70.0	84.5
26, 27, 3370	ELECTRICAL, COMMUNICATIONS & UTIL.	97.5	66.0	81.2	101.9	73.5	87.3	101.7	71.9	86.3	97.5	68.8	82.7	102.7	71.9	86.8	97.5	64.0	80.2
MF2010	WEIGHTED AVERAGE	102.0	70.2	88.0	102.6	72.0	89.1	99.6	70.1	86.6	100.7	69.1	86.8	100.8	72.2	88.2	103.1	67.5	87.4

NEBRASKA

DIVISION		ALLIANCE 693 MAT.	INST.	TOTAL	COLUMBUS 686 MAT.	INST.	TOTAL	GRAND ISLAND 688 MAT.	INST.	TOTAL	HASTINGS 689 MAT.	INST.	TOTAL	LINCOLN 683 - 685 MAT.	INST.	TOTAL	MCCOOK 690 MAT.	INST.	TOTAL
015433	CONTRACTOR EQUIPMENT		97.0	97.0		100.8	100.8		100.8	100.8		100.8	100.8		100.8	100.8		100.8	100.8
0241, 31 - 34	SITE & INFRASTRUCTURE, DEMOLITION	99.4	97.5	98.1	98.7	90.9	93.3	103.4	92.1	95.6	102.3	91.3	94.7	91.0	92.1	91.7	103.2	91.1	94.9
0310	Concrete Forming & Accessories	88.2	56.3	60.5	96.3	59.1	64.0	95.9	76.0	78.6	98.8	74.3	77.4	100.2	60.3	65.5	93.7	56.6	61.5
0320	Concrete Reinforcing	113.6	47.6	80.3	104.7	46.4	75.3	104.1	75.5	89.7	104.1	47.1	75.4	95.6	74.9	85.2	106.1	75.0	90.4
0330	Cast-in-Place Concrete	108.2	58.5	88.6	110.2	55.4	88.6	116.7	69.8	98.2	116.7	64.1	96.0	87.2	72.3	81.3	116.7	58.2	93.7
03	CONCRETE	117.8	56.1	87.7	104.1	56.6	81.0	108.7	74.4	92.0	108.8	66.4	88.2	91.3	68.3	80.1	108.8	61.8	85.9
04	MASONRY	110.1	66.8	83.7	115.3	71.6	88.7	108.6	79.0	90.6	117.7	88.6	99.9	96.8	69.7	80.2	105.1	66.9	81.8
05	METALS	100.6	65.3	88.9	92.7	74.6	86.8	94.5	86.3	91.8	95.2	76.2	88.9	99.6	85.3	94.9	95.5	84.2	91.7
06	WOOD, PLASTICS & COMPOSITES	85.2	55.5	68.0	96.4	60.3	75.6	95.8	76.8	84.8	99.3	76.8	86.3	98.5	55.8	73.8	93.9	55.5	71.7
07	THERMAL & MOISTURE PROTECTION	104.5	67.8	89.6	98.3	64.8	84.7	98.4	75.3	89.0	98.5	86.7	93.7	97.9	70.6	86.8	98.4	65.0	84.8
08	OPENINGS	89.9	51.7	80.3	89.8	56.2	81.4	89.8	72.7	85.5	89.8	65.2	83.6	95.3	57.3	85.7	89.9	58.7	82.0
0920	Plaster & Gypsum Board	91.3	54.1	64.7	100.4	59.0	70.8	99.9	76.0	82.8	101.7	76.0	83.4	101.6	54.4	67.9	99.9	54.1	67.2
0950, 0980	Ceilings & Acoustic Treatment	99.2	54.1	69.4	94.9	59.0	71.2	94.9	76.0	82.4	94.9	76.0	82.4	97.6	54.4	69.0	94.9	54.1	67.9
0960	Flooring	103.9	86.0	98.6	102.6	105.1	103.3	102.4	112.3	105.3	103.8	105.1	104.2	104.0	87.5	99.2	101.5	86.0	96.9
0970, 0990	Wall Finishes & Painting/Coating	173.8	57.7	102.2	96.0	67.2	78.2	96.0	71.3	80.7	96.0	67.2	78.2	96.0	82.1	87.4	96.0	50.3	67.8
09	FINISHES	103.3	61.1	79.7	100.1	67.4	81.8	100.3	81.4	89.8	100.9	78.6	88.5	100.9	66.7	81.9	100.0	60.2	77.8
COVERS	DIVS. 10 - 14, 25, 28, 41, 43, 44, 46	100.0	68.0	93.6	100.0	77.2	95.5	100.0	82.6	96.5	100.0	81.2	96.3	100.0	80.2	96.1	100.0	67.3	93.5
21, 22, 23	FIRE SUPPRESSION, PLUMBING & HVAC	94.2	59.4	80.1	94.0	72.3	85.2	99.9	78.2	91.1	94.0	75.4	86.5	99.8	78.2	91.1	94.0	72.8	85.4
26, 27, 3370	ELECTRICAL, COMMUNICATIONS & UTIL.	92.7	73.7	82.9	92.3	81.9	86.9	91.0	67.3	78.8	90.4	88.8	89.6	99.8	67.3	83.0	94.8	73.7	83.9
MF2010	WEIGHTED AVERAGE	99.7	65.8	84.8	96.8	71.7	85.7	98.7	78.4	89.8	97.8	79.3	89.6	98.0	73.6	87.2	97.6	70.7	85.7

NEBRASKA / NEVADA

DIVISION		NORFOLK 687 MAT.	INST.	TOTAL	NORTH PLATTE 691 MAT.	INST.	TOTAL	OMAHA 680 - 681 MAT.	INST.	TOTAL	VALENTINE 692 MAT.	INST.	TOTAL	CARSON CITY 897 MAT.	INST.	TOTAL	ELKO 898 MAT.	INST.	TOTAL
015433	CONTRACTOR EQUIPMENT		92.2	92.2		100.8	100.8		92.2	92.2		95.1	95.1		99.3	99.3		99.3	99.3
0241, 31 - 34	SITE & INFRASTRUCTURE, DEMOLITION	81.1	90.5	87.6	104.3	91.3	95.3	81.5	91.1	88.1	86.2	95.0	92.3	69.7	101.3	91.5	56.0	101.0	87.0
0310	Concrete Forming & Accessories	83.1	73.4	74.7	95.8	74.1	76.9	91.5	73.1	75.5	84.3	55.9	59.6	101.5	97.6	98.1	108.0	84.0	87.1
0320	Concrete Reinforcing	104.8	49.1	76.7	105.5	76.1	90.7	100.1	75.5	87.7	106.1	46.1	75.9	105.0	117.5	111.3	106.7	91.8	99.2
0330	Cast-in-Place Concrete	111.4	63.3	92.4	116.7	65.5	96.5	93.6	78.7	87.7	103.2	55.9	84.6	94.6	87.8	91.9	95.4	83.5	90.7
03	CONCRETE	103.0	65.7	84.9	108.9	72.2	91.0	93.9	75.7	85.0	105.5	54.9	80.8	100.1	97.9	99.0	97.9	85.5	91.9
04	MASONRY	122.3	69.5	90.1	92.9	88.6	90.3	102.3	79.9	88.6	105.4	67.0	81.9	116.9	76.6	92.3	119.2	69.9	89.1
05	METALS	96.0	68.0	86.8	94.7	86.2	91.9	98.9	78.6	92.2	106.5	66.3	93.3	94.1	103.2	97.1	93.2	90.7	92.4
06	WOOD, PLASTICS & COMPOSITES	80.0	76.3	77.9	95.7	76.8	84.8	89.6	72.5	79.8	79.7	55.0	65.5	87.7	100.4	95.1	96.7	84.4	89.6
07	THERMAL & MOISTURE PROTECTION	97.9	73.7	88.1	98.4	80.6	91.2	94.1	80.5	88.6	98.8	67.6	86.1	99.6	87.0	94.5	100.9	75.9	90.7
08	OPENINGS	91.3	65.7	84.9	89.1	72.0	84.8	98.0	72.4	91.6	91.4	52.9	81.7	97.0	112.6	100.9	99.8	82.2	95.4
0920	Plaster & Gypsum Board	100.7	76.0	83.1	99.9	76.0	82.8	104.9	72.1	81.5	102.6	54.1	67.9	90.4	100.3	97.5	94.5	83.8	86.9
0950, 0980	Ceilings & Acoustic Treatment	109.8	76.0	87.5	94.9	76.0	82.4	111.6	72.1	85.5	113.1	54.1	74.1	109.7	100.3	103.5	112.4	83.8	93.5
0960	Flooring	130.7	105.1	123.2	102.4	105.1	103.2	135.4	85.8	120.8	133.2	83.6	118.6	101.1	82.0	95.5	106.6	53.5	91.0
0970, 0990	Wall Finishes & Painting/Coating	172.0	67.2	107.3	96.0	67.2	78.2	172.0	68.9	108.4	172.0	69.6	108.8	99.8	83.3	89.6	98.8	83.3	89.2
09	FINISHES	121.5	78.6	97.6	100.3	78.6	88.2	123.9	74.7	96.5	123.8	61.5	89.0	100.8	93.4	96.7	101.9	78.3	88.7
COVERS	DIVS. 10 - 14, 25, 28, 41, 43, 44, 46	100.0	80.0	96.0	100.0	70.8	94.2	100.0	81.0	96.2	100.0	65.2	93.1	100.0	97.1	99.4	100.0	67.8	93.6
21, 22, 23	FIRE SUPPRESSION, PLUMBING & HVAC	93.8	75.3	86.3	99.9	73.7	89.3	99.7	78.0	90.9	93.7	57.5	79.0	99.9	84.2	93.5	97.2	83.8	91.8
26, 27, 3370	ELECTRICAL, COMMUNICATIONS & UTIL.	91.2	82.5	86.7	93.0	81.9	87.3	99.2	82.8	90.8	89.9	92.0	91.0	91.1	98.5	94.9	93.9	98.4	96.3
MF2010	WEIGHTED AVERAGE	98.5	75.1	88.2	98.1	79.4	89.9	100.0	79.2	90.8	99.7	67.6	85.6	97.8	93.5	95.9	97.2	85.3	92.0

NEVADA / NEW HAMPSHIRE

DIVISION		ELY 893 MAT.	INST.	TOTAL	LAS VEGAS 889-891 MAT.	INST.	TOTAL	RENO 894-895 MAT.	INST.	TOTAL	CHARLESTON 036 MAT.	INST.	TOTAL	CLAREMONT 037 MAT.	INST.	TOTAL	CONCORD 032-033 MAT.	INST.	TOTAL
015433	CONTRACTOR EQUIPMENT		99.3	99.3		99.3	99.3		99.3	99.3		100.4	100.4		100.4	100.4		100.4	100.4
0241, 31-34	SITE & INFRASTRUCTURE, DEMOLITION	60.8	101.2	88.6	63.1	103.8	91.1	60.7	101.3	88.7	85.6	96.0	92.8	79.1	96.0	90.7	91.9	98.0	96.1
0310	Concrete Forming & Accessories	101.8	104.9	104.5	103.6	114.8	113.3	98.9	97.6	97.7	88.6	43.4	49.3	93.8	43.4	50.0	95.5	87.1	88.2
0320	Concrete Reinforcing	105.5	85.0	95.1	97.2	125.4	111.4	99.7	124.1	112.0	82.9	46.7	64.6	82.9	46.7	64.6	82.9	91.9	87.4
0330	Cast-in-Place Concrete	102.5	103.1	102.7	99.2	110.8	103.8	108.4	87.8	100.3	100.0	50.2	80.4	91.9	50.2	75.5	108.8	86.5	100.0
03	CONCRETE	106.0	100.3	103.3	101.3	114.9	107.9	106.0	99.0	102.6	104.8	47.3	76.8	96.2	47.3	72.4	107.6	87.7	97.9
04	MASONRY	124.0	79.1	96.6	111.6	106.7	108.6	118.3	76.6	92.8	90.1	37.8	58.2	90.1	37.8	58.2	93.0	80.2	85.2
05	METALS	93.1	90.2	92.2	100.3	110.4	103.6	94.6	105.8	98.3	92.3	62.2	82.3	92.3	62.2	82.3	93.0	88.7	91.6
06	WOOD, PLASTICS & COMPOSITES	88.6	106.8	99.1	87.8	114.8	103.4	84.3	100.4	93.6	86.7	45.0	62.6	92.5	45.0	65.0	96.2	91.2	93.3
07	THERMAL & MOISTURE PROTECTION	101.5	87.3	95.7	115.1	101.8	109.7	101.0	87.1	95.3	100.6	41.5	76.7	100.6	41.5	76.6	99.4	84.9	93.5
08	OPENINGS	99.7	92.5	97.9	98.6	122.2	104.6	97.4	108.0	100.1	99.1	40.7	84.4	100.3	40.7	85.3	100.3	81.9	95.7
0920	Plaster & Gypsum Board	90.9	106.9	102.3	90.9	115.2	108.3	83.8	100.3	95.6	90.2	42.5	56.1	91.5	42.5	56.5	94.2	90.3	91.4
0950, 0980	Ceilings & Acoustic Treatment	112.4	106.9	108.8	121.4	115.2	117.3	117.8	100.3	106.3	92.7	42.5	59.6	92.7	42.5	59.6	91.8	90.3	90.8
0960	Flooring	104.0	59.9	91.0	94.9	103.4	97.4	100.7	82.0	95.2	89.2	33.6	72.9	91.6	33.6	74.6	89.2	93.7	90.5
0970, 0990	Wall Finishes & Painting/Coating	98.8	118.3	110.8	101.6	122.1	114.2	98.8	83.3	89.2	90.1	48.2	64.3	90.1	48.2	64.3	90.1	100.6	96.6
09	FINISHES	101.3	98.9	100.0	100.7	113.8	108.0	100.5	93.4	96.5	93.7	42.6	65.2	93.9	42.6	65.3	94.9	90.6	92.5
COVERS	DIVS. 10-14, 25, 28, 41, 43, 44, 46	100.0	66.9	93.4	100.0	93.2	98.7	100.0	97.1	99.4	100.0	38.6	87.8	100.0	38.6	87.8	100.0	62.1	92.5
21, 22, 23	FIRE SUPPRESSION, PLUMBING & HVAC	97.2	104.8	100.3	100.1	108.5	103.5	100.0	84.2	93.6	94.1	39.3	71.9	94.1	39.4	71.9	99.9	83.5	93.2
26, 27, 3370	ELECTRICAL, COMMUNICATIONS & UTIL.	94.2	112.0	103.4	98.5	116.6	107.8	94.5	98.5	96.5	99.5	34.1	65.8	99.5	34.1	65.8	98.3	59.4	78.2
MF2010	WEIGHTED AVERAGE	98.5	98.1	98.3	99.8	110.7	104.6	98.7	93.7	96.5	96.3	47.1	74.6	95.3	47.1	74.1	98.6	82.4	91.5

NEW HAMPSHIRE / NEW JERSEY

DIVISION		KEENE 034 MAT.	INST.	TOTAL	LITTLETON 035 MAT.	INST.	TOTAL	MANCHESTER 031 MAT.	INST.	TOTAL	NASHUA 030 MAT.	INST.	TOTAL	PORTSMOUTH 038 MAT.	INST.	TOTAL	ATLANTIC CITY 082,084 MAT.	INST.	TOTAL
015433	CONTRACTOR EQUIPMENT		100.4	100.4		100.4	100.4		100.4	100.4		100.4	100.4		100.4	100.4		98.7	98.7
0241, 31-34	SITE & INFRASTRUCTURE, DEMOLITION	94.3	96.2	95.6	79.0	95.7	90.5	89.6	98.1	95.4	94.9	98.1	97.1	88.6	99.5	96.1	98.9	103.0	101.7
0310	Concrete Forming & Accessories	92.6	41.5	48.1	102.2	46.3	53.6	97.6	87.7	89.0	99.6	87.7	89.3	89.7	92.6	92.3	107.0	124.2	121.9
0320	Concrete Reinforcing	82.9	55.6	69.1	83.6	33.8	58.5	103.6	92.0	97.7	103.6	92.0	97.7	82.9	92.1	87.5	79.0	114.8	97.0
0330	Cast-in-Place Concrete	100.4	51.7	81.2	90.1	52.4	75.3	112.0	108.4	110.5	95.1	108.4	102.3	90.2	115.8	100.3	85.3	130.0	102.9
03	CONCRETE	104.5	48.6	77.3	95.4	46.9	71.8	112.5	95.5	104.2	104.2	95.5	100.0	95.5	100.4	97.9	97.1	123.4	109.9
04	MASONRY	93.9	40.0	61.0	101.2	43.4	65.9	95.6	80.2	86.2	94.7	80.2	85.9	90.6	92.3	91.6	97.3	127.6	115.8
05	METALS	93.0	66.3	84.1	93.0	57.0	81.1	98.0	89.3	95.1	98.0	89.3	95.1	94.5	92.1	93.7	92.7	104.6	96.6
06	WOOD, PLASTICS & COMPOSITES	90.9	40.1	61.6	100.8	45.9	69.1	96.2	91.2	93.3	99.5	91.2	94.7	87.9	91.2	89.8	109.4	123.9	117.8
07	THERMAL & MOISTURE PROTECTION	101.2	43.5	77.7	100.7	47.3	79.0	100.7	88.2	95.6	101.5	88.2	96.1	101.2	112.4	105.7	101.2	124.8	110.8
08	OPENINGS	97.6	45.4	84.5	101.4	38.5	85.6	102.4	81.9	97.2	102.4	81.9	97.2	103.1	77.2	96.6	100.0	121.6	105.4
0920	Plaster & Gypsum Board	90.6	37.6	52.7	103.3	43.5	60.6	102.2	90.3	93.7	98.7	90.3	92.7	90.2	90.3	90.2	102.9	124.0	118.0
0950, 0980	Ceilings & Acoustic Treatment	92.7	37.6	56.3	92.7	43.5	60.2	98.4	90.3	94.2	102.0	90.3	94.2	94.8	90.3	91.8	92.7	124.0	113.4
0960	Flooring	91.1	55.1	80.6	100.4	33.6	80.8	95.4	93.7	94.9	94.5	93.7	94.2	89.6	93.7	91.8	98.1	133.1	108.4
0970, 0990	Wall Finishes & Painting/Coating	90.1	48.2	64.3	90.1	63.2	73.5	90.1	100.6	96.6	90.1	100.6	96.6	90.1	100.6	96.6	90.1	121.1	109.2
09	FINISHES	95.8	44.4	67.1	97.8	46.0	68.9	98.5	90.6	94.1	99.7	90.6	94.6	95.1	93.5	94.2	100.0	125.9	114.4
COVERS	DIVS. 10-14, 25, 28, 41, 43, 44, 46	100.0	52.8	90.6	100.0	40.4	88.1	100.0	62.2	92.5	100.0	62.2	92.5	100.0	66.2	93.3	100.0	110.4	102.1
21, 22, 23	FIRE SUPPRESSION, PLUMBING & HVAC	94.1	42.6	73.2	94.1	65.6	82.5	99.9	83.5	93.2	100.0	83.5	93.3	100.0	89.6	95.8	99.6	123.3	109.2
26, 27, 3370	ELECTRICAL, COMMUNICATIONS & UTIL.	99.5	34.1	65.8	100.7	59.3	79.3	100.3	81.4	90.6	102.1	81.4	91.5	100.0	81.5	90.5	97.2	136.9	117.7
MF2010	WEIGHTED AVERAGE	96.9	49.4	76.0	96.5	56.6	78.9	100.7	86.7	94.5	100.2	86.7	94.3	97.8	91.2	94.9	98.1	122.1	108.7

NEW JERSEY

DIVISION		CAMDEN 081 MAT.	INST.	TOTAL	DOVER 078 MAT.	INST.	TOTAL	ELIZABETH 072 MAT.	INST.	TOTAL	HACKENSACK 076 MAT.	INST.	TOTAL	JERSEY CITY 073 MAT.	INST.	TOTAL	LONG BRANCH 077 MAT.	INST.	TOTAL
015433	CONTRACTOR EQUIPMENT		98.7	98.7		100.4	100.4		100.4	100.4		100.4	100.4		98.7	98.7		98.3	98.3
0241, 31-34	SITE & INFRASTRUCTURE, DEMOLITION	99.4	103.5	102.3	111.1	104.1	106.3	115.9	104.1	107.8	111.3	104.6	106.7	99.4	104.5	102.9	105.2	104.4	104.7
0310	Concrete Forming & Accessories	99.6	124.3	121.1	96.2	125.0	121.2	106.6	125.0	122.6	96.2	125.0	121.2	99.6	125.0	121.7	100.1	124.7	121.5
0320	Concrete Reinforcing	103.6	116.4	110.1	79.8	123.6	101.9	79.8	123.6	101.9	79.8	123.6	101.9	103.6	123.6	113.7	79.8	123.6	101.9
0330	Cast-in-Place Concrete	82.7	131.7	102.0	106.0	130.9	115.8	91.0	130.9	106.8	103.6	131.0	114.4	82.7	131.0	101.7	91.9	129.9	106.9
03	CONCRETE	98.0	124.3	110.8	105.8	125.9	115.6	100.6	125.9	112.9	103.8	125.9	114.6	98.0	125.8	111.5	102.8	125.3	113.7
04	MASONRY	89.2	127.6	112.6	93.0	128.1	114.4	108.0	128.1	120.2	96.7	128.1	115.8	86.5	128.1	111.9	100.9	127.6	117.1
05	METALS	97.8	104.7	100.1	92.7	111.9	99.1	94.2	111.9	100.1	92.8	111.9	99.1	97.9	109.6	101.8	92.8	109.4	98.3
06	WOOD, PLASTICS & COMPOSITES	99.5	123.9	113.6	98.9	123.9	113.4	112.4	123.9	119.1	98.9	123.9	113.4	99.5	123.9	113.6	100.5	123.9	114.0
07	THERMAL & MOISTURE PROTECTION	101.1	124.5	110.6	101.6	126.4	111.6	101.7	126.4	111.7	101.3	123.9	110.5	101.1	126.4	111.4	101.2	125.0	110.9
08	OPENINGS	102.4	121.6	107.2	105.4	123.6	110.0	103.4	123.6	108.5	102.6	123.6	107.9	102.4	123.6	107.8	98.4	123.6	104.8
0920	Plaster & Gypsum Board	98.7	124.0	116.8	95.2	124.0	115.8	102.9	124.0	118.0	95.2	124.0	115.8	98.7	124.0	116.8	97.4	124.0	116.4
0950, 0980	Ceilings & Acoustic Treatment	102.0	124.0	116.5	92.7	124.0	113.4	94.8	124.0	114.1	92.7	124.0	113.4	102.0	124.0	116.5	92.7	124.0	113.4
0960	Flooring	94.5	133.1	105.8	93.4	164.3	114.2	98.7	164.3	117.9	93.4	164.3	114.2	94.5	164.3	114.9	94.7	164.3	115.1
0970, 0990	Wall Finishes & Painting/Coating	90.1	121.1	109.2	90.0	123.1	110.4	90.0	123.1	110.4	90.0	123.1	110.4	90.1	123.1	110.5	90.1	121.1	109.2
09	FINISHES	100.2	125.9	114.6	97.8	131.5	116.6	101.4	131.5	118.2	97.6	131.5	116.5	100.2	131.5	117.7	98.8	131.1	116.9
COVERS	DIVS. 10-14, 25, 28, 41, 43, 44, 46	100.0	110.5	102.1	100.0	110.3	102.1	100.0	110.3	102.1	100.0	110.3	102.1	100.0	110.4	102.1	100.0	110.4	102.1
21, 22, 23	FIRE SUPPRESSION, PLUMBING & HVAC	100.0	124.9	110.1	99.6	125.7	110.2	100.0	125.6	110.4	99.6	125.7	110.2	100.0	125.7	110.4	99.6	124.7	109.8
26, 27, 3370	ELECTRICAL, COMMUNICATIONS & UTIL.	102.6	136.9	120.3	98.6	137.0	118.4	99.3	137.0	118.8	98.6	136.9	118.4	103.8	136.9	120.9	98.3	132.7	116.0
MF2010	WEIGHTED AVERAGE	99.4	122.6	109.6	99.7	124.6	110.7	100.6	124.5	111.2	99.4	124.5	110.5	99.4	124.4	110.4	99.0	123.3	109.7

NEW JERSEY

DIVISION		NEW BRUNSWICK 088 - 089			NEWARK 070 - 071			PATERSON 074 - 075			POINT PLEASANT 087			SUMMIT 079			TRENTON 085 - 086		
		MAT.	INST.	TOTAL	MAT.	INST.	TOTAL	MAT.	INST.	TOTAL	MAT.	INST.	TOTAL	MAT.	INST.	TOTAL	MAT.	INST.	TOTAL
015433	CONTRACTOR EQUIPMENT		98.3	98.3		100.4	100.4		100.4	100.4		98.3	98.3		100.4	100.4		98.3	98.3
0241, 31 - 34	SITE & INFRASTRUCTURE, DEMOLITION	114.2	104.4	107.5	115.2	104.1	107.5	113.0	104.6	107.2	115.7	104.4	107.9	113.1	104.1	106.9	96.1	104.4	101.8
0310	Concrete Forming & Accessories	102.1	124.9	121.9	96.0	125.0	121.2	98.1	125.0	121.5	97.5	124.4	120.9	98.8	125.0	121.6	96.7	124.6	121.0
0320	Concrete Reinforcing	79.8	123.6	101.9	103.6	123.6	113.7	103.6	123.6	113.7	79.8	123.5	101.8	79.8	123.6	101.9	103.6	119.0	111.3
0330	Cast-in-Place Concrete	105.3	130.2	115.1	109.9	131.0	118.2	105.4	131.0	115.5	105.3	129.8	115.0	88.0	131.0	104.9	101.5	129.9	112.7
03	CONCRETE	115.3	125.5	120.3	111.4	125.9	118.5	109.3	125.9	117.4	115.0	125.1	119.9	97.4	125.9	111.3	107.3	124.4	115.6
04	MASONRY	95.5	128.0	115.3	98.2	128.1	116.4	93.5	128.1	114.6	86.9	127.6	111.7	95.2	128.1	115.3	85.8	127.6	111.3
05	METALS	92.8	109.5	98.3	97.9	111.9	102.5	93.0	111.9	99.3	92.8	109.2	98.2	92.7	111.9	99.1	93.0	107.2	97.7
06	WOOD, PLASTICS & COMPOSITES	103.6	123.9	115.3	98.2	123.9	113.1	101.3	123.9	114.4	97.2	123.9	112.6	102.4	123.9	114.8	96.6	123.9	112.4
07	THERMAL & MOISTURE PROTECTION	101.4	125.2	111.1	101.3	126.4	111.5	101.6	123.9	110.7	101.4	125.0	111.0	102.0	126.4	111.9	97.2	124.6	108.3
08	OPENINGS	94.5	123.6	101.8	108.3	123.6	112.1	108.3	123.6	112.1	96.5	124.5	103.6	110.6	123.6	113.9	103.0	122.1	107.8
0920	Plaster & Gypsum Board	99.7	124.0	117.1	96.2	124.0	116.1	98.7	124.0	116.8	95.2	124.0	115.8	97.4	124.0	116.4	96.5	124.0	116.1
0950, 0980	Ceilings & Acoustic Treatment	92.7	124.0	113.4	98.4	124.0	115.3	102.0	124.0	116.5	92.7	124.0	113.4	92.7	124.0	113.4	99.3	124.0	115.6
0960	Flooring	95.9	164.3	116.0	94.7	164.3	115.1	94.5	164.3	114.9	93.4	133.1	105.1	94.8	164.3	115.2	94.8	164.3	115.2
0970, 0990	Wall Finishes & Painting/Coating	90.1	123.1	110.5	90.0	123.1	110.4	90.0	123.1	110.4	90.1	121.1	109.2	90.0	123.1	110.4	90.1	121.1	109.2
09	FINISHES	100.5	131.5	117.8	99.0	131.5	117.2	100.4	131.5	117.8	99.3	125.9	114.1	98.9	131.5	117.1	98.8	131.1	116.9
COVERS	DIVS. 10 - 14, 25, 28, 41, 43, 44, 46	100.0	110.2	102.0	100.0	110.3	102.1	100.0	110.4	102.1	100.0	107.1	101.4	100.0	110.3	102.1	100.0	110.3	102.1
21, 22, 23	FIRE SUPPRESSION, PLUMBING & HVAC	99.6	125.0	109.9	100.1	126.1	110.6	100.0	125.7	110.4	99.6	124.5	109.7	99.6	126.1	110.3	100.2	124.7	110.1
26, 27, 3370	ELECTRICAL, COMMUNICATIONS & UTIL.	98.0	138.0	118.7	105.5	136.9	121.7	103.8	137.0	120.9	97.2	132.7	115.5	99.3	137.0	118.8	105.1	137.6	121.9
MF2010	WEIGHTED AVERAGE	100.1	124.3	110.8	102.7	124.6	112.4	101.4	124.5	111.6	99.7	122.5	109.7	99.6	124.7	110.7	99.6	123.6	110.2

DIVISION		NEW JERSEY VINELAND 080,083			NEW MEXICO ALBUQUERQUE 870 - 872			CARRIZOZO 883			CLOVIS 881			FARMINGTON 874			GALLUP 873		
		MAT.	INST.	TOTAL	MAT.	INST.	TOTAL	MAT.	INST.	TOTAL	MAT.	INST.	TOTAL	MAT.	INST.	TOTAL	MAT.	INST.	TOTAL
015433	CONTRACTOR EQUIPMENT		98.7	98.7		111.1	111.1		111.1	111.1		111.1	111.1		111.1	111.1		111.1	111.1
0241, 31 - 34	SITE & INFRASTRUCTURE, DEMOLITION	104.1	103.5	103.7	78.9	106.9	98.2	100.5	106.9	104.9	87.9	106.9	101.0	85.1	106.9	100.1	93.6	106.9	102.8
0310	Concrete Forming & Accessories	95.3	124.3	120.5	99.4	65.8	70.2	99.4	65.8	70.2	99.4	65.6	70.0	99.4	65.8	70.2	99.4	65.8	70.2
0320	Concrete Reinforcing	79.0	124.8	97.0	100.4	71.1	85.6	107.7	71.1	89.2	108.9	71.0	89.8	109.7	71.1	90.2	105.0	71.1	87.9
0330	Cast-in-Place Concrete	91.9	130.0	106.9	101.4	73.4	90.4	94.3	73.4	86.1	94.3	73.4	86.0	102.3	73.4	90.9	96.3	73.4	87.3
03	CONCRETE	102.3	123.5	112.6	102.6	70.5	87.0	116.2	70.5	93.9	105.5	70.4	88.4	106.2	70.5	88.8	111.7	70.5	91.6
04	MASONRY	85.9	127.6	111.3	107.7	62.9	80.4	104.4	62.9	79.1	104.5	62.9	79.1	114.7	62.9	83.1	104.5	62.9	79.2
05	METALS	92.7	104.7	96.6	100.4	88.2	96.4	97.3	88.2	94.3	96.9	88.1	94.0	98.2	88.2	94.9	97.3	88.2	94.3
06	WOOD, PLASTICS & COMPOSITES	94.4	123.9	111.5	87.9	66.1	75.3	88.0	66.1	75.4	88.0	66.1	75.4	88.0	66.1	75.4	88.0	66.1	75.4
07	THERMAL & MOISTURE PROTECTION	101.0	124.8	110.7	100.6	73.4	89.5	102.2	73.4	90.5	101.0	73.4	89.8	100.9	73.4	89.7	101.9	73.4	90.3
08	OPENINGS	96.0	121.6	102.5	97.1	68.8	90.0	95.8	68.8	89.0	96.0	68.8	89.2	100.1	68.8	92.2	100.1	68.8	92.2
0920	Plaster & Gypsum Board	93.3	124.0	115.2	89.3	64.7	71.7	81.2	64.7	69.4	81.2	64.7	69.4	81.2	64.7	69.4	81.2	64.7	69.4
0950, 0980	Ceilings & Acoustic Treatment	92.7	124.0	113.4	112.0	64.7	80.7	108.8	64.7	79.7	108.8	64.7	79.7	108.8	64.7	79.7	108.8	64.7	79.7
0960	Flooring	92.6	133.1	104.4	98.4	69.1	89.8	100.7	69.1	91.4	100.7	69.1	91.4	100.7	69.1	91.4	100.7	69.1	91.4
0970, 0990	Wall Finishes & Painting/Coating	90.1	121.1	109.2	103.7	51.7	71.6	98.8	51.7	69.8	98.8	51.7	69.8	98.8	51.7	69.8	98.8	51.7	69.8
09	FINISHES	97.7	125.9	113.5	100.3	64.6	80.4	101.2	64.6	80.8	99.7	64.6	80.2	99.3	64.6	80.0	100.6	64.6	80.5
COVERS	DIVS. 10 - 14, 25, 28, 41, 43, 44, 46	100.0	110.5	102.1	100.0	80.2	96.1	100.0	80.2	96.1	100.0	80.2	96.1	100.0	80.2	96.1	100.0	80.2	96.1
21, 22, 23	FIRE SUPPRESSION, PLUMBING & HVAC	99.6	124.8	109.8	100.1	68.2	87.2	96.6	68.2	85.1	96.6	67.8	84.9	100.0	68.2	87.1	96.4	68.2	85.0
26, 27, 3370	ELECTRICAL, COMMUNICATIONS & UTIL.	97.2	136.9	117.7	89.5	71.1	80.0	89.5	71.1	80.0	87.2	71.1	78.9	87.8	71.1	79.2	87.1	71.1	78.8
MF2010	WEIGHTED AVERAGE	97.6	122.4	108.6	98.7	73.6	87.7	99.4	73.6	88.1	97.4	73.5	86.9	99.4	73.6	88.0	98.8	73.6	87.7

NEW MEXICO

DIVISION		LAS CRUCES 880			LAS VEGAS 877			ROSWELL 882			SANTA FE 875			SOCORRO 878			TRUTH/CONSEQUENCES 879		
		MAT.	INST.	TOTAL	MAT.	INST.	TOTAL	MAT.	INST.	TOTAL	MAT.	INST.	TOTAL	MAT.	INST.	TOTAL	MAT.	INST.	TOTAL
015433	CONTRACTOR EQUIPMENT		87.3	87.3		111.1	111.1		111.1	111.1		111.1	111.1		111.1	111.1		87.3	87.3
0241, 31 - 34	SITE & INFRASTRUCTURE, DEMOLITION	90.5	86.0	87.4	84.4	106.9	99.9	90.0	106.9	101.7	83.4	106.9	99.6	81.0	106.9	98.9	101.7	86.0	90.9
0310	Concrete Forming & Accessories	96.3	64.6	68.7	99.4	65.8	70.2	99.4	65.8	70.2	98.6	65.8	70.1	99.4	65.8	70.2	96.3	64.6	68.7
0320	Concrete Reinforcing	103.6	70.9	87.1	106.7	71.1	88.8	108.9	71.1	89.8	107.7	71.1	89.2	108.9	71.1	89.8	102.4	70.9	86.5
0330	Cast-in-Place Concrete	89.0	65.8	79.9	99.5	73.4	89.2	94.3	73.4	86.1	103.6	73.4	91.7	97.5	73.4	88.0	106.9	65.8	90.7
03	CONCRETE	85.1	67.0	76.3	103.5	70.5	87.4	106.2	70.5	88.8	104.8	70.5	88.1	102.3	70.5	86.8	96.9	67.0	82.4
04	MASONRY	100.5	62.6	77.4	104.8	62.9	79.3	115.3	62.9	83.3	108.8	62.9	80.8	104.7	62.9	79.2	102.1	62.6	77.9
05	METALS	98.1	81.7	92.7	97.0	88.2	94.1	98.2	88.2	94.9	98.2	88.2	94.9	97.3	88.2	94.3	96.9	81.7	91.9
06	WOOD, PLASTICS & COMPOSITES	79.3	65.0	71.0	88.0	66.1	75.4	88.0	66.1	75.4	87.5	66.1	75.2	88.0	66.1	75.4	79.3	65.0	71.0
07	THERMAL & MOISTURE PROTECTION	87.1	68.7	79.6	100.5	73.4	89.5	101.1	73.4	89.8	100.2	73.4	89.3	100.4	73.4	89.4	87.6	68.7	79.9
08	OPENINGS	90.1	68.2	84.6	96.0	68.8	89.2	95.8	68.8	89.0	96.0	68.8	89.1	95.8	68.8	89.0	90.0	68.2	84.5
0920	Plaster & Gypsum Board	83.3	64.7	70.0	81.2	64.7	69.4	81.2	64.7	69.4	89.2	64.7	71.7	81.2	64.7	69.4	83.3	64.7	70.0
0950, 0980	Ceilings & Acoustic Treatment	97.8	64.7	75.9	108.8	64.7	79.7	108.8	64.7	79.7	109.7	64.7	80.0	108.8	64.7	79.7	97.8	64.7	75.9
0960	Flooring	133.3	69.1	114.4	100.7	69.1	91.4	100.7	69.1	91.4	100.7	69.1	91.4	100.7	69.1	91.4	133.3	69.1	114.4
0970, 0990	Wall Finishes & Painting/Coating	90.0	51.7	66.4	98.8	51.7	69.8	98.8	51.7	69.8	98.8	51.7	69.8	98.8	51.7	69.8	90.0	51.7	66.4
09	FINISHES	112.8	63.8	85.5	99.1	64.6	79.9	99.8	64.6	80.2	100.6	64.6	80.5	99.0	64.6	79.9	113.6	63.8	85.8
COVERS	DIVS. 10 - 14, 25, 28, 41, 43, 44, 46	100.0	77.4	95.5	100.0	80.2	96.1	100.0	80.2	96.1	100.0	80.2	96.1	100.0	80.2	96.1	100.0	77.4	95.5
21, 22, 23	FIRE SUPPRESSION, PLUMBING & HVAC	100.3	67.9	87.2	96.4	68.2	85.0	100.0	68.2	87.1	99.9	68.2	87.1	96.4	68.2	85.0	96.3	67.9	84.8
26, 27, 3370	ELECTRICAL, COMMUNICATIONS & UTIL.	88.4	66.3	77.0	89.5	71.1	80.0	88.6	71.1	79.6	96.6	71.1	83.4	87.6	71.1	79.1	91.2	71.1	80.8
MF2010	WEIGHTED AVERAGE	96.1	69.6	84.4	97.3	73.6	86.8	99.3	73.6	88.0	99.4	73.6	88.0	96.8	73.6	86.6	97.0	70.3	85.3

NEW MEXICO / NEW YORK

DIVISION		TUCUMCARI 884			ALBANY 120-122			BINGHAMTON 137-139			BRONX 104			BROOKLYN 112			BUFFALO 140-142		
		MAT.	INST.	TOTAL	MAT.	INST.	TOTAL	MAT.	INST.	TOTAL	MAT.	INST.	TOTAL	MAT.	INST.	TOTAL	MAT.	INST.	TOTAL
015433	CONTRACTOR EQUIPMENT		111.1	111.1		113.6	113.6		114.2	114.2		113.9	113.9		114.5	114.5		96.5	96.5
0241, 31 - 34	SITE & INFRASTRUCTURE, DEMOLITION	87.6	106.9	100.9	70.5	106.9	95.6	93.4	92.7	92.9	114.2	124.5	121.3	119.7	128.0	125.4	97.5	97.3	97.3
0310	Concrete Forming & Accessories	99.4	65.6	70.0	97.8	95.5	95.8	102.1	82.7	85.2	101.7	176.5	166.8	108.5	176.2	167.4	102.0	115.7	113.9
0320	Concrete Reinforcing	106.7	71.0	88.7	98.3	91.8	95.0	97.3	95.1	96.2	95.9	179.8	138.2	98.8	187.6	143.5	102.5	101.8	102.1
0330	Cast-in-Place Concrete	94.3	73.4	86.0	76.6	102.0	86.6	98.4	94.5	96.8	89.2	164.2	118.8	100.4	162.5	124.9	103.1	117.8	108.9
03	CONCRETE	104.7	70.4	88.0	93.9	97.8	95.8	96.7	90.8	93.8	96.2	171.0	132.6	108.5	171.5	139.2	106.4	113.0	109.6
04	MASONRY	116.0	62.9	83.6	92.4	100.8	97.6	107.9	89.5	96.7	93.8	175.1	143.4	117.3	175.0	152.5	106.8	116.8	112.9
05	METALS	96.9	88.1	94.1	100.3	104.0	101.5	96.9	114.2	102.6	104.9	142.9	117.5	105.2	141.8	117.3	101.5	94.7	99.2
06	WOOD, PLASTICS & COMPOSITES	88.0	66.1	75.4	96.1	94.3	95.1	106.3	81.2	91.8	103.1	178.3	146.6	107.9	177.9	148.3	99.6	116.5	109.3
07	THERMAL & MOISTURE PROTECTION	101.0	73.4	89.7	88.6	93.7	90.7	103.4	83.3	95.2	104.1	164.3	128.6	105.8	163.1	129.1	100.9	108.4	104.0
08	OPENINGS	95.8	68.8	89.0	94.3	87.7	92.6	89.3	80.3	87.0	85.0	172.8	107.1	88.7	172.1	109.7	90.7	103.7	94.0
0920	Plaster & Gypsum Board	81.2	64.7	69.4	101.2	93.9	96.0	112.3	80.2	89.3	103.6	180.4	158.4	109.8	180.4	160.2	109.2	116.7	114.6
0950, 0980	Ceilings & Acoustic Treatment	108.8	64.7	79.7	94.4	93.9	94.1	97.1	80.2	85.9	83.5	180.4	147.5	93.6	180.4	150.9	105.9	116.7	113.1
0960	Flooring	100.7	69.1	91.4	91.7	103.9	95.3	103.7	89.6	99.6	99.0	177.0	121.9	110.9	177.0	130.3	102.3	116.7	106.5
0970, 0990	Wall Finishes & Painting/Coating	98.8	51.7	69.8	89.3	78.4	82.6	90.8	81.8	85.2	106.1	152.7	134.8	121.2	152.7	140.6	98.1	112.6	107.1
09	FINISHES	99.7	64.6	80.1	95.0	95.3	95.2	97.4	83.5	89.7	101.2	175.0	142.3	113.7	174.7	147.7	102.0	116.7	110.2
COVERS	DIVS. 10 - 14, 25, 28, 41, 43, 44, 46	100.0	80.2	96.1	100.0	93.6	98.9	100.0	94.3	98.9	100.0	134.3	106.8	100.0	133.5	106.7	100.0	106.5	101.3
21, 22, 23	FIRE SUPPRESSION, PLUMBING & HVAC	96.6	67.8	84.9	100.0	92.1	96.8	100.4	80.7	92.4	100.1	166.8	127.1	99.7	166.7	126.9	99.9	92.8	97.0
26, 27, 3370	ELECTRICAL, COMMUNICATIONS & UTIL.	89.5	71.1	80.0	99.2	91.6	95.3	100.7	90.2	95.3	96.9	173.3	136.3	100.9	173.3	138.3	98.6	99.7	99.2
MF2010	WEIGHTED AVERAGE	98.1	73.5	87.3	96.7	96.4	96.5	98.4	89.2	94.4	98.9	163.6	127.4	103.4	163.8	130.0	100.3	104.0	101.9

NEW YORK

DIVISION		ELMIRA 148-149			FAR ROCKAWAY 116			FLUSHING 113			GLENS FALLS 128			HICKSVILLE 115,117,118			JAMAICA 114		
		MAT.	INST.	TOTAL	MAT.	INST.	TOTAL	MAT.	INST.	TOTAL	MAT.	INST.	TOTAL	MAT.	INST.	TOTAL	MAT.	INST.	TOTAL
015433	CONTRACTOR EQUIPMENT		115.2	115.2		114.5	114.5		114.5	114.5		113.6	113.6		114.5	114.5		114.5	114.5
0241, 31 - 34	SITE & INFRASTRUCTURE, DEMOLITION	93.1	93.6	93.4	123.6	128.0	126.7	123.6	128.0	126.7	62.4	106.2	92.6	112.3	126.6	122.2	117.5	128.0	124.8
0310	Concrete Forming & Accessories	87.4	85.3	85.6	95.4	176.2	165.7	99.1	176.2	166.2	86.7	88.8	88.5	92.1	146.0	139.0	99.1	176.2	166.2
0320	Concrete Reinforcing	103.7	85.9	94.8	98.8	187.6	143.5	100.5	187.6	144.4	97.9	88.6	93.2	98.8	179.5	139.5	98.8	187.6	143.5
0330	Cast-in-Place Concrete	96.4	94.5	95.6	108.5	162.5	129.8	108.5	162.5	129.8	74.8	99.7	84.6	92.2	153.5	116.4	100.4	162.5	124.9
03	CONCRETE	100.2	90.4	95.4	114.7	171.5	142.4	115.2	171.5	142.6	86.9	93.4	90.0	100.4	153.5	126.3	107.9	171.5	138.9
04	MASONRY	103.2	91.0	95.7	121.4	175.0	154.1	115.4	175.0	151.8	93.8	96.8	95.6	111.9	160.6	141.6	119.3	175.0	153.3
05	METALS	96.8	113.1	102.2	105.2	141.8	117.3	105.2	141.8	117.3	96.4	102.7	98.5	106.7	136.5	116.5	105.2	141.8	117.3
06	WOOD, PLASTICS & COMPOSITES	83.9	84.4	84.2	92.0	177.9	141.7	96.6	177.9	143.6	83.6	87.5	85.9	88.6	145.9	121.7	96.6	177.9	143.6
07	THERMAL & MOISTURE PROTECTION	101.8	84.8	94.9	105.8	163.1	129.1	105.8	163.1	129.1	88.0	90.6	89.0	105.4	149.6	123.3	105.6	163.1	129.0
08	OPENINGS	91.6	79.9	88.7	87.1	172.1	108.5	87.1	172.1	108.5	88.0	83.3	86.8	87.1	152.9	103.7	87.1	172.1	108.5
0920	Plaster & Gypsum Board	103.6	83.7	89.4	98.4	180.4	156.9	101.1	180.4	157.7	95.8	86.9	89.5	97.9	147.3	133.2	101.1	180.4	157.7
0950, 0980	Ceilings & Acoustic Treatment	101.4	83.7	89.7	82.7	180.4	147.2	82.7	180.4	147.2	91.8	86.9	88.6	81.7	147.3	125.0	82.7	180.4	147.2
0960	Flooring	91.5	89.6	90.9	105.5	177.0	126.5	107.0	177.0	127.5	83.3	103.9	89.4	104.4	149.4	117.6	107.0	177.0	127.5
0970, 0990	Wall Finishes & Painting/Coating	96.6	77.9	85.0	121.2	152.7	140.6	121.2	152.7	140.6	89.3	81.9	84.7	121.2	152.7	140.6	121.2	152.7	140.6
09	FINISHES	96.8	85.1	90.3	108.9	174.7	145.6	109.6	174.7	145.9	90.6	90.7	90.7	107.2	146.7	129.2	109.1	174.7	145.7
COVERS	DIVS. 10 - 14, 25, 28, 41, 43, 44, 46	100.0	87.8	97.6	100.0	133.5	106.7	100.0	133.5	106.7	100.0	91.5	98.3	100.0	123.0	104.6	100.0	133.5	106.7
21, 22, 23	FIRE SUPPRESSION, PLUMBING & HVAC	94.2	86.3	91.0	93.8	166.7	123.3	93.8	166.7	123.3	94.3	84.6	90.4	99.7	148.7	119.6	93.8	166.7	123.3
26, 27, 3370	ELECTRICAL, COMMUNICATIONS & UTIL.	97.3	93.5	95.3	108.1	173.3	141.7	108.1	173.3	141.7	96.2	91.6	93.9	100.1	141.0	121.2	99.0	173.3	137.4
MF2010	WEIGHTED AVERAGE	96.7	91.0	94.2	103.1	163.8	129.8	102.9	163.8	129.7	92.3	92.6	92.5	101.3	145.6	120.8	101.1	163.8	128.7

NEW YORK

DIVISION		JAMESTOWN 147			KINGSTON 124			LONG ISLAND CITY 111			MONTICELLO 127			MOUNT VERNON 105			NEW ROCHELLE 108		
		MAT.	INST.	TOTAL	MAT.	INST.	TOTAL	MAT.	INST.	TOTAL	MAT.	INST.	TOTAL	MAT.	INST.	TOTAL	MAT.	INST.	TOTAL
015433	CONTRACTOR EQUIPMENT		93.5	93.5		114.5	114.5		114.5	114.5		114.5	114.5		113.9	113.9		113.9	113.9
0241, 31 - 34	SITE & INFRASTRUCTURE, DEMOLITION	94.3	92.9	93.3	119.2	124.7	123.0	121.0	128.0	125.9	114.5	124.7	121.5	122.3	119.2	120.2	121.1	119.2	119.8
0310	Concrete Forming & Accessories	87.5	81.0	81.8	88.4	108.3	105.7	103.2	176.2	166.7	95.0	108.4	106.6	92.6	129.3	124.5	106.7	129.3	126.4
0320	Concrete Reinforcing	103.9	97.6	100.7	98.2	134.7	116.6	98.8	187.6	143.5	97.5	134.7	116.2	94.6	178.4	136.9	94.7	178.4	136.9
0330	Cast-in-Place Concrete	100.0	93.5	97.5	101.1	130.7	112.8	103.5	162.5	126.8	94.7	130.7	108.9	99.7	129.7	111.5	99.7	129.7	111.5
03	CONCRETE	103.4	88.4	96.1	108.8	120.6	114.6	111.0	171.5	140.5	103.6	120.7	111.9	105.7	137.6	121.3	105.1	137.6	121.0
04	MASONRY	111.8	90.0	99.0	109.1	135.1	124.9	110.4	175.0	151.2	102.1	135.1	122.2	99.7	127.3	116.5	99.7	127.3	116.5
05	METALS	94.1	89.2	92.5	105.2	115.1	108.4	105.2	141.8	117.3	105.1	115.2	108.4	104.7	132.6	113.9	105.0	132.6	114.1
06	WOOD, PLASTICS & COMPOSITES	82.5	78.0	79.9	84.9	102.6	95.1	102.0	177.9	145.9	92.5	102.6	98.3	93.2	132.4	115.9	110.3	132.4	123.1
07	THERMAL & MOISTURE PROTECTION	101.2	85.8	95.0	107.5	136.0	119.1	105.7	163.1	129.1	107.1	136.0	118.9	105.0	137.9	118.3	105.1	137.9	118.4
08	OPENINGS	91.5	81.4	88.9	92.3	119.6	99.2	87.1	172.1	108.5	87.2	119.6	95.3	85.0	145.6	100.2	85.0	145.6	100.3
0920	Plaster & Gypsum Board	98.0	77.1	83.0	94.2	102.6	100.2	104.8	180.4	158.8	96.5	102.6	100.9	98.5	133.0	123.2	111.2	133.0	126.8
0950, 0980	Ceilings & Acoustic Treatment	98.6	77.1	84.4	76.4	102.6	93.7	82.7	180.4	147.2	76.4	102.6	93.7	81.7	133.0	115.6	81.7	133.0	115.6
0960	Flooring	94.5	92.3	93.9	97.7	75.9	91.3	108.8	177.0	128.8	100.4	75.9	93.2	91.1	172.3	114.9	97.9	172.3	119.8
0970, 0990	Wall Finishes & Painting/Coating	98.1	78.2	85.9	118.7	106.3	111.0	121.2	152.7	140.6	118.7	108.8	112.6	104.1	152.7	134.1	104.1	152.7	134.1
09	FINISHES	96.7	82.1	88.5	104.2	99.9	101.8	110.3	174.7	146.2	104.8	100.2	102.2	98.7	139.1	121.2	102.0	139.1	122.7
COVERS	DIVS. 10 - 14, 25, 28, 41, 43, 44, 46	100.0	93.3	98.7	100.0	108.4	101.7	100.0	133.5	106.7	100.0	108.4	101.7	100.0	117.2	103.4	100.0	117.2	103.4
21, 22, 23	FIRE SUPPRESSION, PLUMBING & HVAC	94.1	82.2	89.3	94.2	115.7	102.9	99.7	166.7	126.9	94.2	118.1	103.9	94.3	117.9	103.8	94.3	117.9	103.8
26, 27, 3370	ELECTRICAL, COMMUNICATIONS & UTIL.	96.0	86.4	91.1	98.0	115.7	107.1	99.6	173.3	137.6	98.0	115.7	107.1	95.2	157.5	127.4	95.2	157.5	127.4
MF2010	WEIGHTED AVERAGE	96.9	86.4	92.3	100.9	117.4	108.2	103.0	163.8	129.8	99.4	118.0	107.6	98.6	133.0	113.8	99.0	133.0	114.0

NEW YORK

DIVISION		NEW YORK 100-102 MAT.	INST.	TOTAL	NIAGARA FALLS 143 MAT.	INST.	TOTAL	PLATTSBURGH 129 MAT.	INST.	TOTAL	POUGHKEEPSIE 125-126 MAT.	INST.	TOTAL	QUEENS 110 MAT.	INST.	TOTAL	RIVERHEAD 119 MAT.	INST.	TOTAL
015433	CONTRACTOR EQUIPMENT		114.3	114.3		93.5	93.5		99.5	99.5		114.5	114.5		114.5	114.5		114.5	114.5
0241, 31-34	SITE & INFRASTRUCTURE, DEMOLITION	123.0	125.1	124.5	96.5	94.7	95.3	85.4	102.9	97.5	115.3	124.3	121.5	115.7	128.0	124.2	113.2	126.8	122.6
0310	Concrete Forming & Accessories	106.0	184.9	174.6	87.4	117.3	113.5	91.0	86.4	87.0	88.8	153.4	144.9	92.3	176.2	165.3	96.5	146.8	140.3
0320	Concrete Reinforcing	101.5	179.8	141.0	102.5	102.3	102.4	102.6	88.2	95.4	98.2	134.9	116.7	100.5	187.6	144.4	100.6	176.6	138.9
0330	Cast-in-Place Concrete	100.4	180.1	131.8	103.4	122.6	111.0	91.6	95.4	93.1	97.9	128.2	109.9	95.4	162.5	121.8	93.7	154.7	117.8
03	CONCRETE	106.4	180.1	142.3	105.7	115.4	110.4	100.5	89.5	95.2	105.9	139.8	122.4	103.6	171.5	136.7	101.1	153.7	126.7
04	MASONRY	103.9	178.2	149.2	119.6	123.4	121.9	89.5	90.7	90.2	102.2	129.4	118.8	108.3	175.0	149.0	117.2	162.8	145.1
05	METALS	119.0	141.2	126.9	96.9	93.5	95.8	101.0	83.5	95.2	105.2	116.8	109.0	105.2	141.8	117.3	107.1	135.4	116.5
06	WOOD, PLASTICS & COMPOSITES	107.5	187.8	153.9	82.4	115.3	101.4	90.5	85.1	87.4	84.9	164.5	130.9	88.7	177.9	140.3	93.7	145.9	123.8
07	THERMAL & MOISTURE PROTECTION	104.1	166.8	129.6	101.3	110.7	105.1	101.1	88.2	95.9	107.4	140.3	120.8	105.4	163.1	128.9	106.0	150.5	124.1
08	OPENINGS	90.2	178.0	112.3	91.5	103.2	94.4	96.7	81.2	92.8	92.3	151.4	107.2	87.1	172.1	108.5	87.1	152.2	103.5
0920	Plaster & Gypsum Board	112.0	190.1	167.8	98.0	115.5	110.5	117.0	83.9	93.4	94.2	166.5	145.9	97.9	180.4	156.8	99.6	147.3	133.6
0950, 0980	Ceilings & Acoustic Treatment	102.5	190.1	160.4	98.6	115.5	109.8	104.9	83.9	91.0	76.4	166.5	135.9	82.7	180.4	147.2	82.6	147.3	125.3
0960	Flooring	100.3	177.0	122.8	94.4	117.0	101.0	107.8	103.9	106.7	97.7	145.8	111.8	104.4	177.0	125.7	105.5	149.4	118.4
0970, 0990	Wall Finishes & Painting/Coating	106.1	155.0	136.2	98.1	113.1	107.4	116.5	78.8	93.2	118.7	106.3	111.0	121.2	152.7	140.6	121.2	152.7	140.6
09	FINISHES	107.5	181.6	148.8	96.8	117.8	108.5	101.2	88.9	94.3	103.9	149.2	129.2	107.6	174.7	145.0	107.8	147.2	129.8
COVERS	DIVS. 10-14, 25, 28, 41, 43, 44, 46	100.0	137.9	107.5	100.0	104.2	100.8	100.0	51.4	90.3	100.0	113.5	102.7	100.0	133.5	106.7	100.0	123.8	104.7
21, 22, 23	FIRE SUPPRESSION, PLUMBING & HVAC	100.0	168.4	127.7	94.1	99.4	96.2	94.2	84.6	90.3	94.2	117.2	103.5	99.7	166.7	126.9	99.9	149.8	120.1
26, 27, 3370	ELECTRICAL, COMMUNICATIONS & UTIL.	105.0	173.3	140.3	94.7	98.8	96.8	93.9	85.7	89.7	98.0	115.7	107.1	100.1	173.3	137.9	101.7	141.0	122.0
MF2010	WEIGHTED AVERAGE	104.8	166.9	132.2	97.9	106.1	101.5	96.9	87.0	92.6	100.1	128.4	112.6	101.4	163.8	128.9	102.1	146.1	121.5

NEW YORK

DIVISION		ROCHESTER 144-146 MAT.	INST.	TOTAL	SCHENECTADY 123 MAT.	INST.	TOTAL	STATEN ISLAND 103 MAT.	INST.	TOTAL	SUFFERN 109 MAT.	INST.	TOTAL	SYRACUSE 130-132 MAT.	INST.	TOTAL	UTICA 133-135 MAT.	INST.	TOTAL
015433	CONTRACTOR EQUIPMENT		115.6	115.6		113.6	113.6		113.9	113.9		113.9	113.9		113.6	113.6		113.6	113.6
0241, 31-34	SITE & INFRASTRUCTURE, DEMOLITION	74.5	107.6	97.3	71.9	106.9	96.0	127.1	124.5	125.3	117.7	120.3	119.5	92.4	106.6	102.2	70.2	104.2	93.7
0310	Concrete Forming & Accessories	103.5	91.7	93.3	102.0	95.1	96.0	92.1	176.5	165.6	100.6	126.4	123.1	101.0	88.0	89.7	102.5	80.6	83.5
0320	Concrete Reinforcing	103.4	89.2	96.2	96.9	91.8	94.3	95.9	179.8	138.2	94.7	135.0	115.0	98.3	95.5	96.9	98.3	87.1	92.6
0330	Cast-in-Place Concrete	96.8	96.6	96.7	90.4	101.4	94.7	99.7	164.2	125.1	96.7	126.8	108.5	91.3	95.8	93.1	83.6	87.5	85.1
03	CONCRETE	112.7	93.9	103.5	100.8	97.4	99.2	107.4	171.0	138.4	102.1	127.4	114.4	99.7	93.0	96.5	97.7	85.3	91.7
04	MASONRY	103.3	96.3	99.0	91.9	99.8	96.7	106.6	175.1	148.4	99.0	123.0	113.6	98.9	101.8	100.6	90.6	88.2	89.1
05	METALS	98.0	104.2	100.1	100.4	104.0	101.6	102.8	142.9	116.0	102.8	118.0	107.8	100.3	105.0	101.8	98.3	101.6	99.4
06	WOOD, PLASTICS & COMPOSITES	96.6	91.7	93.8	102.5	94.3	97.8	91.7	178.3	141.7	102.8	132.6	120.0	102.5	85.6	92.7	102.5	82.4	90.9
07	THERMAL & MOISTURE PROTECTION	96.7	93.9	95.5	89.1	93.2	90.8	104.4	164.3	128.8	104.9	134.4	116.9	99.5	96.2	98.2	88.9	90.0	89.4
08	OPENINGS	94.2	86.1	92.2	94.3	87.7	92.6	85.0	172.8	107.1	85.0	136.9	98.1	92.3	79.9	89.2	94.3	78.6	90.4
0920	Plaster & Gypsum Board	114.8	91.4	98.1	106.3	93.9	97.5	98.6	180.4	157.0	102.6	133.3	124.5	106.3	84.8	91.0	106.3	81.6	88.7
0950, 0980	Ceilings & Acoustic Treatment	106.9	91.4	96.7	97.1	93.9	95.0	83.5	180.4	147.5	81.7	133.3	115.7	97.1	84.8	89.0	97.1	81.6	86.9
0960	Flooring	90.3	103.0	94.1	91.0	103.9	94.8	95.2	177.0	119.2	94.3	149.4	110.4	93.1	95.0	93.7	91.0	90.4	90.8
0970, 0990	Wall Finishes & Painting/Coating	97.9	95.5	96.4	89.3	78.4	82.6	106.1	152.7	134.8	104.1	114.4	110.5	96.6	98.5	97.8	89.3	98.5	95.0
09	FINISHES	102.9	94.4	98.2	96.0	95.1	95.5	100.8	175.0	142.2	99.6	126.9	114.9	97.9	90.0	93.5	96.0	84.2	89.4
COVERS	DIVS. 10-14, 25, 28, 41, 43, 44, 46	100.0	94.1	98.8	100.0	93.3	98.7	100.0	134.3	106.8	100.0	115.6	103.1	100.0	95.7	99.2	100.0	87.2	97.4
21, 22, 23	FIRE SUPPRESSION, PLUMBING & HVAC	100.0	87.1	94.8	100.2	91.5	96.7	100.1	166.8	127.1	94.3	112.0	101.4	100.2	88.3	95.3	100.2	78.4	91.3
26, 27, 3370	ELECTRICAL, COMMUNICATIONS & UTIL.	99.2	89.6	94.2	100.9	91.6	96.1	96.9	173.3	136.3	103.2	123.8	113.8	100.9	94.3	97.5	99.0	94.3	96.6
MF2010	WEIGHTED AVERAGE	100.0	94.0	97.3	97.8	96.1	97.0	100.8	163.6	128.5	98.7	122.0	109.0	98.9	94.5	97.0	96.8	88.2	93.0

NEW YORK / NORTH CAROLINA

DIVISION		WATERTOWN 136 MAT.	INST.	TOTAL	WHITE PLAINS 106 MAT.	INST.	TOTAL	YONKERS 107 MAT.	INST.	TOTAL	ASHEVILLE 287-288 MAT.	INST.	TOTAL	CHARLOTTE 281-282 MAT.	INST.	TOTAL	DURHAM 277 MAT.	INST.	TOTAL
015433	CONTRACTOR EQUIPMENT		113.6	113.6		113.9	113.9		113.9	113.9		94.7	94.7		94.7	94.7		99.9	99.9
0241, 31-34	SITE & INFRASTRUCTURE, DEMOLITION	78.2	106.5	97.7	113.8	119.2	117.5	122.5	119.1	120.1	108.4	75.5	85.7	109.7	75.6	86.2	108.6	84.0	91.6
0310	Concrete Forming & Accessories	88.2	90.3	90.1	105.3	129.3	126.2	105.7	129.3	126.2	92.5	37.4	44.6	96.6	39.2	46.7	94.8	38.0	45.4
0320	Concrete Reinforcing	98.9	95.6	97.2	94.7	178.4	136.9	98.5	178.4	138.8	93.6	41.0	67.1	94.0	38.3	65.9	95.2	47.9	71.4
0330	Cast-in-Place Concrete	97.3	94.7	96.3	88.5	129.7	104.8	99.0	129.8	111.1	118.0	45.0	89.3	124.5	47.0	93.9	119.9	45.3	90.5
03	CONCRETE	110.4	93.6	102.2	95.6	137.6	116.1	105.3	137.6	121.1	109.0	42.7	76.7	111.9	43.6	78.6	109.7	44.3	77.8
04	MASONRY	91.6	101.4	97.6	98.5	127.3	116.1	103.4	127.3	118.0	87.1	38.2	57.3	93.2	41.8	61.8	92.4	34.4	57.0
05	METALS	98.3	105.0	100.5	104.3	132.6	113.7	114.4	132.6	120.4	87.2	72.4	82.3	91.2	71.6	84.7	100.4	75.5	92.2
06	WOOD, PLASTICS & COMPOSITES	85.2	89.4	87.6	108.6	132.4	122.4	108.4	132.4	122.3	94.5	36.9	61.3	99.7	39.0	64.6	96.9	38.3	63.1
07	THERMAL & MOISTURE PROTECTION	89.2	96.3	92.1	104.8	137.9	118.2	105.1	137.9	118.4	99.9	41.2	76.1	97.3	42.7	75.1	100.7	43.2	77.3
08	OPENINGS	94.3	85.7	92.1	85.1	145.6	100.3	88.2	145.6	102.7	93.2	36.7	79.0	97.3	38.1	82.4	97.3	40.5	83.0
0920	Plaster & Gypsum Board	97.7	88.8	91.3	106.2	133.0	125.4	111.4	133.0	126.9	104.3	34.8	54.7	100.7	36.9	55.1	108.3	36.2	56.8
0950, 0980	Ceilings & Acoustic Treatment	97.1	88.8	91.6	81.7	133.0	115.6	100.7	133.0	122.1	93.7	34.8	54.8	96.4	36.9	57.1	97.3	36.2	57.0
0960	Flooring	83.8	91.2	85.9	96.3	172.3	118.6	95.9	172.3	118.3	103.7	43.6	86.1	106.7	43.8	88.2	107.3	43.6	88.6
0970, 0990	Wall Finishes & Painting/Coating	89.3	88.9	89.1	104.1	152.7	134.1	104.1	152.7	134.1	114.8	33.7	64.8	114.8	38.5	67.7	114.8	35.4	65.8
09	FINISHES	93.7	90.1	91.7	100.1	139.1	121.8	105.6	139.1	124.3	100.8	37.9	65.7	101.5	39.8	67.1	103.2	38.4	67.0
COVERS	DIVS. 10-14, 25, 28, 41, 43, 44, 46	100.0	95.7	99.2	100.0	117.2	103.4	100.0	120.4	104.1	100.0	64.5	92.9	100.0	65.0	93.0	100.0	72.4	94.5
21, 22, 23	FIRE SUPPRESSION, PLUMBING & HVAC	100.2	83.8	93.5	100.3	117.9	107.4	100.3	117.9	107.4	100.2	36.9	74.6	99.9	37.1	74.5	100.3	35.8	74.2
26, 27, 3370	ELECTRICAL, COMMUNICATIONS & UTIL.	100.9	91.7	96.2	95.2	157.5	127.4	103.3	157.5	131.3	96.6	36.6	65.7	97.2	47.6	71.6	97.5	46.3	71.1
MF2010	WEIGHTED AVERAGE	98.5	93.5	96.3	98.8	133.0	113.9	103.5	133.1	116.5	97.8	45.5	74.7	99.4	47.8	76.7	100.8	47.9	77.5

NORTH CAROLINA

DIVISION		ELIZABETH CITY 279 MAT.	INST.	TOTAL	FAYETTEVILLE 283 MAT.	INST.	TOTAL	GASTONIA 280 MAT.	INST.	TOTAL	GREENSBORO 270,272-274 MAT.	INST.	TOTAL	HICKORY 286 MAT.	INST.	TOTAL	KINSTON 285 MAT.	INST.	TOTAL
015433	CONTRACTOR EQUIPMENT		103.9	103.9		99.9	99.9		94.7	94.7		99.9	99.9		99.9	99.9		99.9	99.9
0241, 31-34	SITE & INFRASTRUCTURE, DEMOLITION	114.3	85.0	94.1	107.4	84.1	91.3	108.0	75.5	85.6	108.5	84.1	91.7	107.6	84.0	91.4	106.2	84.1	90.9
0310	Concrete Forming & Accessories	82.0	33.0	39.4	92.1	38.8	45.7	98.4	38.3	46.1	94.5	38.6	45.9	88.9	36.6	43.4	85.5	38.8	44.8
0320	Concrete Reinforcing	93.1	39.9	66.3	97.3	48.1	72.5	94.0	40.9	67.3	94.0	56.2	75.0	93.6	18.6	55.8	93.1	18.1	55.3
0330	Cast-in-Place Concrete	120.1	36.9	87.4	123.7	48.2	94.0	115.3	52.1	90.4	119.0	46.5	90.5	117.9	46.1	89.6	113.8	39.3	84.5
03	CONCRETE	109.9	37.7	74.7	111.4	45.7	79.4	107.4	45.5	77.2	109.0	46.6	78.6	108.7	38.6	74.6	105.4	37.2	72.2
04	MASONRY	105.0	25.7	56.6	90.6	39.1	59.2	91.7	36.1	57.8	90.5	35.0	56.6	76.8	39.3	53.9	82.8	31.5	51.5
05	METALS	89.2	71.9	83.5	104.3	75.6	94.9	88.1	72.4	82.9	94.5	78.6	89.2	87.3	66.1	80.3	86.3	65.2	79.3
06	WOOD, PLASTICS & COMPOSITES	81.9	34.2	54.3	93.5	38.3	61.6	102.4	38.3	65.3	96.6	38.3	62.9	89.3	36.7	58.9	86.3	39.6	59.3
07	THERMAL & MOISTURE PROTECTION	100.0	32.5	72.6	99.8	41.7	76.2	100.2	41.5	76.3	100.5	40.8	76.2	100.3	40.2	75.8	100.1	33.8	73.2
08	OPENINGS	94.2	32.1	78.5	93.3	40.5	80.0	97.3	38.2	82.4	97.3	42.8	83.6	93.3	29.8	77.3	93.4	31.4	77.7
0920	Plaster & Gypsum Board	101.8	31.3	51.4	109.0	36.2	57.0	110.4	36.2	57.4	110.4	36.2	57.4	104.3	34.6	54.5	104.5	37.6	56.7
0950, 0980	Ceilings & Acoustic Treatment	97.3	31.3	53.7	94.6	36.2	56.0	97.3	36.2	56.9	97.3	36.2	56.9	93.7	34.6	54.6	97.3	37.6	57.9
0960	Flooring	98.0	23.7	76.2	103.8	43.6	86.2	107.3	43.6	88.6	107.3	40.3	87.6	103.5	33.6	83.0	100.7	19.2	76.8
0970, 0990	Wall Finishes & Painting/Coating	114.8	43.6	70.9	114.8	33.7	64.8	114.8	38.7	67.9	114.8	32.8	64.2	114.8	32.8	64.2	114.8	29.9	62.4
09	FINISHES	100.1	32.2	62.2	101.5	38.7	66.5	103.3	39.1	67.5	103.4	38.1	67.0	101.0	35.3	64.3	100.7	34.6	63.8
COVERS	DIVS. 10-14, 25, 28, 41, 43, 44, 46	100.0	72.8	94.6	100.0	73.1	94.7	100.0	64.5	92.9	100.0	64.7	93.0	100.0	64.5	92.9	100.0	73.6	94.7
21, 22, 23	FIRE SUPPRESSION, PLUMBING & HVAC	94.3	29.0	67.8	100.2	36.9	74.5	100.2	36.6	74.4	100.2	37.0	74.6	94.3	30.4	68.4	94.3	31.0	68.6
26, 27, 3370	ELECTRICAL, COMMUNICATIONS & UTIL.	97.1	29.0	62.0	95.6	50.5	72.3	96.1	34.0	64.1	96.4	36.8	65.7	94.2	30.8	61.5	94.0	47.9	70.2
MF2010	WEIGHTED AVERAGE	97.8	40.6	72.6	100.7	49.4	78.1	98.6	45.4	75.1	99.7	47.3	76.6	95.5	42.3	72.1	95.2	43.8	72.6

NORTH CAROLINA / NORTH DAKOTA

DIVISION		MURPHY 289 MAT.	INST.	TOTAL	RALEIGH 275-276 MAT.	INST.	TOTAL	ROCKY MOUNT 278 MAT.	INST.	TOTAL	WILMINGTON 284 MAT.	INST.	TOTAL	WINSTON-SALEM 271 MAT.	INST.	TOTAL	BISMARCK 585 MAT.	INST.	TOTAL
015433	CONTRACTOR EQUIPMENT		94.7	94.7		99.9	99.9		99.9	99.9		94.7	94.7		99.9	99.9		98.7	98.7
0241, 31-34	SITE & INFRASTRUCTURE, DEMOLITION	110.1	75.3	86.1	109.1	84.1	91.9	112.0	84.2	92.8	109.5	75.7	86.2	108.8	84.0	91.7	100.1	97.4	98.2
0310	Concrete Forming & Accessories	99.0	23.9	33.7	94.9	39.5	46.7	87.7	31.6	38.9	93.7	44.1	50.5	95.8	37.7	45.2	99.8	42.5	49.9
0320	Concrete Reinforcing	93.2	17.9	55.2	94.0	48.1	70.9	93.1	26.3	59.5	94.3	46.4	70.2	94.0	38.0	65.8	110.0	85.6	97.7
0330	Cast-in-Place Concrete	122.0	35.2	87.8	127.6	51.5	97.6	117.5	38.5	86.4	117.5	48.0	90.1	122.0	44.0	91.3	101.1	49.3	80.7
03	CONCRETE	112.2	29.2	71.8	113.3	47.1	81.1	110.4	35.1	73.7	108.8	47.7	79.0	110.6	41.9	77.1	100.3	54.3	77.9
04	MASONRY	79.4	25.4	46.4	91.7	40.0	60.2	83.2	33.1	52.6	77.1	40.0	54.5	90.7	36.0	57.3	104.3	59.6	77.0
05	METALS	85.3	64.5	78.4	92.2	75.5	86.7	88.4	65.4	80.8	87.0	74.9	83.0	92.2	71.1	85.2	96.5	86.1	93.0
06	WOOD, PLASTICS & COMPOSITES	103.1	22.1	56.3	96.9	38.9	63.4	88.6	28.9	54.1	96.2	44.1	66.1	96.6	37.6	62.5	82.3	36.9	56.0
07	THERMAL & MOISTURE PROTECTION	100.1	30.6	71.9	99.5	42.0	76.1	100.5	31.8	72.6	99.9	46.1	78.0	100.5	40.5	76.1	107.4	52.6	85.1
08	OPENINGS	93.2	24.5	75.9	94.1	40.6	80.6	93.4	25.6	76.3	93.4	43.9	80.9	97.3	37.5	82.2	98.0	48.4	85.5
0920	Plaster & Gypsum Board	109.3	19.5	45.1	100.7	36.9	55.1	103.7	26.5	48.6	106.0	42.2	60.4	110.4	35.5	56.9	98.3	35.2	53.2
0950, 0980	Ceilings & Acoustic Treatment	93.7	19.5	44.7	96.4	36.9	57.1	94.6	26.5	49.6	94.6	42.2	60.0	97.3	35.5	56.5	144.8	35.2	72.4
0960	Flooring	107.6	24.6	83.3	107.3	43.6	88.6	102.0	22.3	78.6	104.5	45.5	87.2	107.3	43.6	88.6	115.3	75.5	103.6
0970, 0990	Wall Finishes & Painting/Coating	114.8	18.1	55.1	114.8	37.2	66.9	114.8	40.0	68.6	114.8	40.2	68.8	114.8	34.4	65.2	96.0	31.0	55.9
09	FINISHES	102.8	22.7	58.1	101.8	39.7	67.2	101.1	30.3	61.6	101.4	43.9	69.3	103.4	38.2	67.1	114.9	45.3	76.1
COVERS	DIVS. 10-14, 25, 28, 41, 43, 44, 46	100.0	61.8	92.4	100.0	73.5	94.7	100.0	72.9	94.6	100.0	74.7	95.0	100.0	64.4	92.9	100.0	81.2	96.3
21, 22, 23	FIRE SUPPRESSION, PLUMBING & HVAC	94.3	18.5	63.6	100.0	35.3	73.8	94.3	35.7	70.6	100.2	38.3	75.1	100.2	35.7	74.1	100.3	60.7	84.3
26, 27, 3370	ELECTRICAL, COMMUNICATIONS & UTIL.	97.5	25.7	60.5	100.6	36.5	67.5	99.1	38.8	68.0	96.8	36.9	65.9	96.4	40.1	67.4	98.1	71.7	84.5
MF2010	WEIGHTED AVERAGE	96.4	33.2	68.5	99.8	47.6	76.8	96.8	42.5	72.9	97.4	48.5	75.8	99.5	46.0	75.9	100.7	64.4	84.7

NORTH DAKOTA

DIVISION		DEVILS LAKE 583 MAT.	INST.	TOTAL	DICKINSON 586 MAT.	INST.	TOTAL	FARGO 580-581 MAT.	INST.	TOTAL	GRAND FORKS 582 MAT.	INST.	TOTAL	JAMESTOWN 584 MAT.	INST.	TOTAL	MINOT 587 MAT.	INST.	TOTAL
015433	CONTRACTOR EQUIPMENT		98.7	98.7		98.7	98.7		98.7	98.7		98.7	98.7		98.7	98.7		98.7	98.7
0241, 31-34	SITE & INFRASTRUCTURE, DEMOLITION	109.6	95.4	99.8	119.7	94.1	102.1	100.7	97.4	98.4	114.2	94.1	100.4	108.5	94.1	98.6	111.2	97.4	101.7
0310	Concrete Forming & Accessories	103.3	36.9	45.6	93.3	36.1	43.6	101.0	43.2	50.7	96.9	36.1	44.0	94.6	35.8	43.4	93.0	60.8	65.0
0320	Concrete Reinforcing	110.0	85.9	97.9	111.0	42.0	76.2	101.4	85.7	93.5	108.3	85.8	96.9	110.6	49.8	80.0	112.0	85.9	98.9
0330	Cast-in-Place Concrete	122.8	47.9	93.3	111.1	46.3	85.6	100.2	51.2	80.9	111.1	46.3	85.6	121.3	46.2	91.7	111.1	48.3	86.4
03	CONCRETE	114.0	51.4	83.5	113.0	42.2	78.5	107.8	55.3	82.2	110.1	50.2	80.9	112.6	43.4	78.9	108.8	62.1	86.1
04	MASONRY	112.8	65.2	83.8	114.8	59.0	80.8	106.0	59.6	77.7	107.3	64.8	81.3	125.1	34.7	69.9	106.5	64.2	80.7
05	METALS	96.5	85.1	92.8	96.4	64.8	86.0	98.8	86.4	94.7	96.5	80.5	91.2	96.5	65.9	86.4	96.8	86.7	93.4
06	WOOD, PLASTICS & COMPOSITES	85.5	34.0	55.7	75.2	34.0	51.4	82.1	37.4	56.3	78.9	34.0	53.0	76.9	34.0	52.1	74.9	61.3	67.1
07	THERMAL & MOISTURE PROTECTION	108.2	50.8	84.9	108.8	48.4	84.2	105.7	53.7	84.6	108.5	50.8	85.0	108.1	43.0	81.6	108.2	56.4	87.2
08	OPENINGS	98.0	42.3	84.0	97.9	31.9	81.3	97.9	48.7	85.5	98.0	42.3	83.9	98.0	34.1	81.9	98.1	61.7	88.9
0920	Plaster & Gypsum Board	118.9	32.2	57.0	109.9	32.2	54.4	98.3	35.7	53.6	111.7	32.2	54.9	111.2	32.2	54.8	109.9	60.4	74.5
0950, 0980	Ceilings & Acoustic Treatment	145.7	32.2	70.7	145.7	32.2	70.7	144.8	35.7	72.8	145.7	32.2	70.7	145.7	32.2	70.7	145.7	60.4	89.4
0960	Flooring	119.5	37.6	95.4	111.2	37.6	89.6	114.9	75.5	103.3	113.6	37.6	91.3	112.2	37.6	90.3	111.0	84.2	103.1
0970, 0990	Wall Finishes & Painting/Coating	96.0	23.7	51.4	96.0	23.7	51.4	96.0	73.8	82.3	96.0	23.7	51.4	96.0	23.7	51.4	96.0	26.0	52.8
09	FINISHES	119.5	34.1	71.9	117.1	34.1	70.8	114.9	50.4	78.9	117.4	34.1	70.9	116.4	34.1	70.5	116.1	60.9	85.3
COVERS	DIVS. 10-14, 25, 28, 41, 43, 44, 46	100.0	34.9	87.1	100.0	35.1	87.1	100.0	81.3	96.3	100.0	35.0	87.1	100.0	79.1	95.8	100.0	84.0	96.8
21, 22, 23	FIRE SUPPRESSION, PLUMBING & HVAC	94.5	63.0	81.7	94.5	70.5	84.7	100.3	66.0	86.4	100.4	35.6	74.2	94.5	37.5	71.4	100.4	60.7	84.3
26, 27, 3370	ELECTRICAL, COMMUNICATIONS & UTIL.	96.3	38.0	66.3	105.1	71.7	87.8	99.7	66.9	82.8	99.9	56.9	77.7	96.3	38.0	66.2	103.1	80.4	91.4
MF2010	WEIGHTED AVERAGE	101.7	57.0	82.0	102.7	58.8	83.3	102.1	65.7	86.0	102.8	53.1	80.9	101.9	46.4	77.4	102.7	70.2	88.4

DIVISION		NORTH DAKOTA WILLISTON 588			OHIO AKRON 442 - 443			ATHENS 457			CANTON 446 - 447			CHILLICOTHE 456			CINCINNATI 451 - 452		
		MAT.	INST.	TOTAL	MAT.	INST.	TOTAL	MAT.	INST.	TOTAL	MAT.	INST.	TOTAL	MAT.	INST.	TOTAL	MAT.	INST.	TOTAL
015433	CONTRACTOR EQUIPMENT		98.7	98.7		97.0	97.0		91.7	91.7		97.0	97.0		101.6	101.6		101.4	101.4
0241, 31 - 34	SITE & INFRASTRUCTURE, DEMOLITION	112.2	94.1	99.7	91.7	104.6	100.6	103.8	94.8	97.6	91.8	104.1	100.3	89.0	106.6	101.2	86.1	106.1	99.9
0310	Concrete Forming & Accessories	98.4	36.1	44.2	100.3	92.6	93.6	91.7	89.0	89.4	100.3	82.7	85.0	93.3	95.4	95.1	95.0	82.2	83.8
0320	Concrete Reinforcing	113.2	42.0	77.3	93.4	92.0	92.7	93.4	87.6	90.4	93.4	77.3	85.3	90.6	81.0	85.8	96.0	83.2	89.6
0330	Cast-in-Place Concrete	111.1	46.3	85.6	95.5	98.4	96.6	108.5	95.2	103.3	96.4	96.0	96.2	98.5	94.3	96.8	90.7	86.6	89.1
03	CONCRETE	110.2	42.2	77.1	95.1	93.8	94.5	102.6	90.3	96.6	95.6	85.9	90.9	96.9	92.1	94.6	91.6	84.0	87.9
04	MASONRY	101.2	59.0	75.5	90.4	95.6	93.6	76.1	91.1	85.2	91.1	86.5	88.3	82.9	100.4	93.6	82.5	87.3	85.4
05	METALS	96.6	64.8	86.1	92.7	82.5	89.3	100.5	79.3	93.5	92.7	76.2	87.2	92.8	85.1	90.3	95.2	84.7	91.7
06	WOOD, PLASTICS & COMPOSITES	80.2	34.0	53.5	102.2	91.4	96.0	83.8	90.3	87.5	102.7	80.9	90.1	96.2	94.1	95.0	98.5	80.0	87.8
07	THERMAL & MOISTURE PROTECTION	108.4	48.4	84.0	107.2	96.9	103.0	99.8	93.0	97.0	108.2	92.7	101.9	100.9	96.4	99.1	99.3	91.1	95.9
08	OPENINGS	98.0	31.9	81.4	112.2	91.5	107.0	101.0	86.3	97.3	105.9	78.0	98.9	92.9	86.1	91.2	101.7	79.7	96.1
0920	Plaster & Gypsum Board	111.7	32.2	54.9	91.0	90.8	90.8	91.1	89.6	90.1	92.3	80.0	83.5	91.7	94.2	93.5	93.8	79.6	83.7
0950, 0980	Ceilings & Acoustic Treatment	145.7	32.2	70.7	94.7	90.8	92.1	103.6	89.6	94.4	94.7	80.0	85.0	97.7	94.2	95.4	98.6	79.6	86.1
0960	Flooring	114.7	37.6	92.1	100.4	92.1	98.0	127.7	100.1	119.6	100.6	82.1	95.2	103.9	103.6	103.8	104.8	90.6	100.7
0970, 0990	Wall Finishes & Painting/Coating	96.0	23.7	51.4	100.8	102.3	101.7	103.1	96.1	98.8	100.8	83.3	90.0	100.1	92.5	95.4	100.1	86.1	91.5
09	FINISHES	117.6	34.1	71.0	98.1	93.3	95.4	103.0	92.7	97.3	98.3	82.1	89.3	99.6	97.1	98.2	100.1	83.7	90.9
COVERS	DIVS. 10 - 14, 25, 28, 41, 43, 44, 46	100.0	35.1	87.1	100.0	94.0	98.8	100.0	56.1	91.3	100.0	91.5	98.3	100.0	92.0	98.4	100.0	92.4	98.5
21, 22, 23	FIRE SUPPRESSION, PLUMBING & HVAC	94.5	70.5	84.7	100.0	97.0	98.8	94.0	55.0	78.2	100.0	83.9	93.5	94.4	93.4	94.0	99.9	83.0	93.1
26, 27, 3370	ELECTRICAL, COMMUNICATIONS & UTIL.	100.2	71.7	85.5	97.9	94.5	96.1	99.3	102.6	101.0	97.2	90.9	93.9	98.9	85.2	91.8	97.7	80.4	88.8
MF2010	WEIGHTED AVERAGE	101.1	58.8	82.4	98.7	94.5	96.9	98.0	83.1	91.4	98.2	86.3	93.0	95.2	93.4	94.4	96.9	85.8	92.0

DIVISION		OHIO CLEVELAND 441			COLUMBUS 430 - 432			DAYTON 453 - 454			HAMILTON 450			LIMA 458			LORAIN 440		
		MAT.	INST.	TOTAL	MAT.	INST.	TOTAL	MAT.	INST.	TOTAL	MAT.	INST.	TOTAL	MAT.	INST.	TOTAL	MAT.	INST.	TOTAL
015433	CONTRACTOR EQUIPMENT		97.3	97.3		95.9	95.9		96.7	96.7		101.6	101.6		94.2	94.2		97.0	97.0
0241, 31 - 34	SITE & INFRASTRUCTURE, DEMOLITION	91.7	104.9	100.8	93.2	100.9	98.5	84.9	106.0	99.4	84.8	106.2	99.5	97.6	94.5	95.5	91.1	103.4	99.6
0310	Concrete Forming & Accessories	100.4	97.9	98.2	100.6	87.4	89.1	95.0	81.6	83.4	95.0	81.7	83.4	91.6	85.9	86.6	100.4	87.9	89.5
0320	Concrete Reinforcing	93.8	92.3	93.0	103.7	83.0	93.3	96.0	81.2	88.6	96.0	83.2	89.6	93.4	81.4	87.4	93.4	92.1	92.8
0330	Cast-in-Place Concrete	93.6	106.4	98.7	88.9	94.0	90.9	84.4	87.6	85.6	90.4	86.0	88.7	99.7	97.4	98.8	90.9	104.2	96.1
03	CONCRETE	94.3	99.0	96.6	93.5	88.5	91.1	88.4	83.4	85.9	91.5	83.6	87.6	95.8	88.7	92.4	92.8	93.8	93.3
04	MASONRY	95.0	103.4	100.1	91.4	95.0	93.6	82.0	83.7	83.1	82.4	86.0	84.6	104.8	84.9	92.6	87.1	97.6	93.5
05	METALS	94.3	84.9	91.2	94.3	81.2	90.0	94.4	77.9	88.9	94.5	84.7	91.2	100.5	81.1	94.1	93.3	83.0	89.9
06	WOOD, PLASTICS & COMPOSITES	101.2	94.9	97.6	98.6	84.9	90.7	99.9	80.3	88.6	98.5	80.0	87.8	83.7	85.2	84.6	102.2	85.3	92.5
07	THERMAL & MOISTURE PROTECTION	105.9	107.7	106.6	100.7	95.1	98.5	104.2	89.0	98.0	101.0	90.7	96.8	99.3	95.8	97.9	108.1	101.0	105.3
08	OPENINGS	101.7	93.4	99.6	103.4	81.6	97.9	101.8	79.9	96.3	99.1	79.7	94.2	101.0	80.0	95.7	105.9	88.2	101.4
0920	Plaster & Gypsum Board	90.0	94.4	93.1	96.1	84.5	87.8	93.8	80.0	83.9	93.8	79.6	83.7	91.1	84.5	86.4	91.0	84.5	86.3
0950, 0980	Ceilings & Acoustic Treatment	92.9	94.4	93.9	95.5	84.5	88.2	99.7	80.0	86.7	98.6	79.6	86.1	102.6	84.5	90.6	94.7	84.5	88.0
0960	Flooring	100.2	105.0	101.6	95.2	90.0	93.7	107.7	83.0	100.5	104.8	90.6	100.7	126.8	90.8	116.3	100.6	105.0	101.9
0970, 0990	Wall Finishes & Painting/Coating	100.8	106.5	104.3	99.0	92.5	95.0	100.1	85.9	91.4	100.1	86.1	91.5	103.2	84.9	91.9	100.8	106.5	104.3
09	FINISHES	97.6	99.7	98.8	97.3	88.0	92.1	101.1	82.0	90.4	100.0	83.4	90.7	102.1	86.4	93.3	98.1	92.6	95.1
COVERS	DIVS. 10 - 14, 25, 28, 41, 43, 44, 46	100.0	98.3	99.7	100.0	94.7	98.9	100.0	91.9	98.4	100.0	92.0	98.4	100.0	92.9	98.6	100.0	95.2	99.0
21, 22, 23	FIRE SUPPRESSION, PLUMBING & HVAC	99.9	98.8	99.5	99.9	93.9	97.5	100.6	84.8	94.2	100.4	82.4	93.1	94.0	86.2	90.9	100.0	84.7	93.8
26, 27, 3370	ELECTRICAL, COMMUNICATIONS & UTIL.	97.5	107.4	102.6	98.7	88.1	93.2	96.3	83.8	89.9	96.7	81.9	89.1	99.7	80.8	89.9	97.4	89.9	93.5
MF2010	WEIGHTED AVERAGE	97.9	99.8	98.7	97.8	90.6	94.6	96.7	85.2	91.6	96.6	85.6	91.7	98.4	86.1	93.0	97.7	91.3	94.9

DIVISION		OHIO MANSFIELD 448 - 449			MARION 433			SPRINGFIELD 455			STEUBENVILLE 439			TOLEDO 434 - 436			YOUNGSTOWN 444 - 445		
		MAT.	INST.	TOTAL	MAT.	INST.	TOTAL	MAT.	INST.	TOTAL	MAT.	INST.	TOTAL	MAT.	INST.	TOTAL	MAT.	INST.	TOTAL
015433	CONTRACTOR EQUIPMENT		97.0	97.0		95.6	95.6		96.7	96.7		100.3	100.3		98.3	98.3		97.0	97.0
0241, 31 - 34	SITE & INFRASTRUCTURE, DEMOLITION	87.9	104.4	99.3	89.2	99.8	96.5	85.2	104.6	98.6	134.7	109.2	117.1	92.4	101.8	98.9	91.6	105.0	100.8
0310	Concrete Forming & Accessories	91.1	86.6	87.2	97.5	84.4	86.1	95.0	84.7	86.1	100.5	86.7	88.5	100.5	95.9	96.5	100.3	86.0	87.9
0320	Concrete Reinforcing	85.0	77.9	81.4	95.6	83.0	89.3	96.0	81.2	88.6	93.1	85.4	89.2	103.7	89.8	96.7	93.4	86.9	90.1
0330	Cast-in-Place Concrete	88.4	93.0	90.2	81.2	91.1	85.1	86.6	87.7	87.1	88.2	93.1	90.1	88.9	103.4	94.6	94.6	98.5	96.1
03	CONCRETE	87.8	86.7	87.2	85.8	86.1	86.0	89.6	84.7	87.2	89.7	88.1	88.9	93.5	97.0	95.2	94.7	90.0	92.4
04	MASONRY	89.6	97.4	94.3	92.9	96.1	94.8	82.2	84.0	83.3	79.8	91.2	86.7	99.5	100.1	99.8	90.7	92.7	91.9
05	METALS	93.5	77.1	88.1	93.4	79.2	88.7	94.3	77.6	88.8	90.1	79.6	86.6	94.1	87.6	91.9	92.7	80.3	88.6
06	WOOD, PLASTICS & COMPOSITES	91.2	85.3	87.8	94.9	84.9	89.2	101.5	84.7	91.8	90.9	85.1	87.6	98.6	95.1	96.6	102.2	83.8	91.6
07	THERMAL & MOISTURE PROTECTION	107.6	95.8	102.8	100.3	84.8	94.0	104.0	89.6	98.1	112.3	94.3	105.0	102.5	103.6	102.9	108.3	94.9	102.9
08	OPENINGS	105.1	79.6	98.7	97.3	80.2	93.0	99.5	80.4	94.7	98.3	82.9	94.4	101.2	91.4	98.7	105.9	84.7	100.6
0920	Plaster & Gypsum Board	84.9	84.5	84.6	93.8	84.5	87.1	93.8	84.5	87.1	94.4	84.1	87.1	96.1	94.9	95.2	91.0	83.0	85.3
0950, 0980	Ceilings & Acoustic Treatment	95.6	84.5	88.3	95.5	84.5	88.2	99.7	84.5	89.6	92.3	84.1	86.9	95.5	94.9	95.1	94.7	83.0	87.0
0960	Flooring	95.7	104.5	98.3	93.8	73.0	87.7	107.7	83.0	100.5	122.3	95.1	114.3	94.5	101.8	96.6	100.6	93.7	98.6
0970, 0990	Wall Finishes & Painting/Coating	100.8	91.2	94.9	99.0	50.1	68.8	100.1	85.9	91.4	113.1	95.5	102.2	99.0	102.9	101.4	100.8	93.5	96.3
09	FINISHES	95.9	90.3	92.8	96.1	78.9	86.5	101.1	84.6	91.9	114.7	88.6	100.2	97.0	97.5	97.3	98.2	87.6	92.3
COVERS	DIVS. 10 - 14, 25, 28, 41, 43, 44, 46	100.0	92.4	98.5	100.0	57.9	91.6	100.0	92.5	98.5	100.0	96.3	99.3	100.0	98.5	99.7	100.0	92.3	98.5
21, 22, 23	FIRE SUPPRESSION, PLUMBING & HVAC	94.0	83.4	89.7	94.0	89.0	92.0	100.6	85.0	94.3	94.3	91.2	93.0	100.0	99.2	99.7	100.0	92.1	96.8
26, 27, 3370	ELECTRICAL, COMMUNICATIONS & UTIL.	95.0	80.6	87.6	92.6	80.6	86.4	96.3	84.0	89.9	87.8	111.5	100.0	98.7	104.1	101.5	97.4	86.1	91.5
MF2010	WEIGHTED AVERAGE	95.2	87.4	91.7	93.9	85.4	90.2	96.6	85.8	91.8	96.1	93.5	95.0	97.9	98.3	98.1	98.1	90.1	94.6

City Cost Indexes

OHIO / OKLAHOMA

DIVISION		ZANESVILLE 437-438 MAT.	INST.	TOTAL	ARDMORE 734 MAT.	INST.	TOTAL	CLINTON 736 MAT.	INST.	TOTAL	DURANT 747 MAT.	INST.	TOTAL	ENID 737 MAT.	INST.	TOTAL	GUYMON 739 MAT.	INST.	TOTAL
015433	CONTRACTOR EQUIPMENT		95.6	95.6		81.8	81.8		81.0	81.0		81.0	81.0		81.0	81.0		81.0	81.0
0241, 31 - 34	SITE & INFRASTRUCTURE, DEMOLITION	92.0	101.1	98.2	98.9	90.4	93.0	100.5	89.0	92.5	93.8	88.8	90.3	101.9	89.0	93.0	105.1	87.6	93.0
0310	Concrete Forming & Accessories	94.8	84.5	85.9	91.3	39.6	46.3	90.2	34.3	41.5	83.8	39.5	45.3	93.4	33.6	41.4	96.7	21.9	31.6
0320	Concrete Reinforcing	95.0	84.9	89.9	96.4	77.7	87.0	96.9	77.7	87.2	97.3	61.6	79.3	96.3	77.7	86.9	96.9	27.3	61.8
0330	Cast-in-Place Concrete	85.6	90.1	87.3	97.9	43.1	76.3	94.6	43.1	74.3	91.5	43.0	72.4	94.6	45.4	75.2	94.6	31.2	69.6
03	CONCRETE	89.2	86.2	87.7	96.9	48.5	73.3	96.3	46.1	71.8	91.5	45.4	69.1	96.7	46.7	72.3	99.5	27.0	64.1
04	MASONRY	90.3	82.2	85.4	97.2	55.8	72.0	125.5	55.8	83.0	95.8	63.6	76.2	106.1	55.8	75.4	100.3	22.2	52.6
05	METALS	94.8	80.4	90.0	91.0	69.6	84.0	91.1	69.6	84.0	91.1	63.2	81.8	92.5	69.6	85.0	91.6	40.7	74.8
06	WOOD, PLASTICS & COMPOSITES	91.3	84.9	87.6	97.2	38.2	63.1	96.2	31.0	58.6	88.4	38.2	59.4	99.9	30.2	59.6	103.5	20.0	55.3
07	THERMAL & MOISTURE PROTECTION	100.5	89.1	95.8	97.5	59.2	81.9	97.6	58.5	81.7	97.2	57.0	80.9	97.6	58.4	81.7	97.9	28.2	69.6
08	OPENINGS	97.3	82.1	93.5	94.3	48.7	82.8	94.4	44.8	81.9	94.4	44.6	81.8	94.3	44.1	81.7	94.5	21.4	76.1
0920	Plaster & Gypsum Board	91.1	84.5	86.4	79.5	36.9	49.1	79.0	29.5	43.7	74.9	36.9	47.8	80.4	28.6	43.4	81.2	18.2	36.2
0950, 0980	Ceilings & Acoustic Treatment	95.5	84.5	88.2	83.8	36.9	52.9	83.8	29.5	48.0	83.8	36.9	52.9	83.8	28.6	47.4	86.5	18.2	41.4
0960	Flooring	92.0	87.4	90.7	107.2	45.2	89.0	105.8	43.1	87.4	102.0	64.8	91.1	108.0	43.1	88.9	110.0	25.5	85.2
0970, 0990	Wall Finishes & Painting/Coating	99.0	78.4	86.3	96.2	54.1	70.2	96.2	54.1	70.2	96.2	54.1	70.2	96.2	54.1	70.2	96.2	19.3	48.7
09	FINISHES	95.6	84.2	89.2	92.7	40.3	63.5	92.5	35.7	60.8	90.3	44.4	64.7	93.4	35.2	60.9	95.1	21.9	54.3
COVERS	DIVS. 10 - 14, 25, 28, 41, 43, 44, 46	100.0	88.0	97.6	100.0	72.6	94.5	100.0	71.8	94.4	100.0	72.7	94.6	100.0	71.7	94.4	100.0	69.8	94.0
21, 22, 23	FIRE SUPPRESSION, PLUMBING & HVAC	94.0	88.9	92.0	94.3	61.3	80.9	94.3	61.3	80.9	94.3	61.4	81.0	100.3	61.3	84.5	94.3	23.1	65.5
26, 27, 3370	ELECTRICAL, COMMUNICATIONS & UTIL.	93.1	81.1	86.9	94.4	68.6	81.1	95.5	68.6	81.6	97.1	51.7	73.7	95.5	68.6	81.6	97.1	16.4	55.5
MF2010	WEIGHTED AVERAGE	94.5	86.1	90.8	95.0	60.1	79.6	96.5	58.8	79.8	94.1	57.7	78.1	97.3	58.7	80.3	96.2	31.0	67.5

OKLAHOMA

DIVISION		LAWTON 735 MAT.	INST.	TOTAL	MCALESTER 745 MAT.	INST.	TOTAL	MIAMI 743 MAT.	INST.	TOTAL	MUSKOGEE 744 MAT.	INST.	TOTAL	OKLAHOMA CITY 730-731 MAT.	INST.	TOTAL	PONCA CITY 746 MAT.	INST.	TOTAL
015433	CONTRACTOR EQUIPMENT		81.8	81.8		81.0	81.0		88.9	88.9		88.9	88.9		82.1	82.1		81.0	81.0
0241, 31 - 34	SITE & INFRASTRUCTURE, DEMOLITION	97.6	90.4	92.6	86.9	89.1	88.4	88.4	86.3	87.0	88.6	85.0	86.1	96.1	90.9	92.5	94.4	89.0	90.6
0310	Concrete Forming & Accessories	96.5	45.2	51.9	82.0	40.9	46.2	93.6	69.2	72.4	97.6	30.1	38.9	95.7	39.3	46.6	89.6	39.9	46.4
0320	Concrete Reinforcing	96.6	77.7	87.1	96.9	40.9	68.7	95.4	77.8	86.5	96.3	31.1	63.5	96.6	77.7	87.1	96.3	77.7	86.9
0330	Cast-in-Place Concrete	91.5	45.5	73.3	80.2	45.5	66.5	84.0	44.9	68.6	85.0	35.9	65.7	92.4	48.1	75.0	93.9	38.4	72.0
03	CONCRETE	93.0	51.8	72.9	82.3	43.0	63.2	86.7	63.0	75.1	88.4	33.7	61.7	93.5	50.1	72.3	93.5	47.0	70.9
04	MASONRY	100.2	55.8	73.1	114.9	56.4	79.2	98.6	57.0	73.2	117.7	45.3	73.5	99.8	57.5	74.0	91.1	56.4	69.9
05	METALS	96.1	69.7	87.4	91.0	53.9	78.8	91.0	81.7	87.9	92.5	56.2	80.5	98.0	69.6	88.6	91.0	69.3	83.8
06	WOOD, PLASTICS & COMPOSITES	102.5	45.8	69.8	86.0	41.4	60.3	99.8	77.5	86.9	103.8	29.9	61.1	101.8	36.9	64.3	95.6	38.8	62.8
07	THERMAL & MOISTURE PROTECTION	97.4	60.0	82.2	96.9	55.9	80.2	97.2	60.5	82.3	97.3	41.5	74.6	94.2	59.8	80.2	97.4	58.4	81.5
08	OPENINGS	96.0	52.6	85.1	94.3	40.2	80.7	94.3	70.5	88.3	94.3	29.0	77.9	96.0	47.8	83.9	94.3	49.0	82.9
0920	Plaster & Gypsum Board	82.8	44.8	55.6	73.6	40.2	49.8	80.4	77.3	78.2	82.8	28.2	43.8	84.9	35.6	49.7	79.0	37.5	49.4
0950, 0980	Ceilings & Acoustic Treatment	92.0	44.8	60.8	83.8	40.2	55.0	83.8	77.3	79.5	92.0	28.2	49.8	92.0	35.6	54.7	83.8	37.5	53.2
0960	Flooring	110.3	43.1	90.6	100.8	43.1	83.9	108.8	64.8	95.9	111.4	41.7	90.9	110.3	43.1	90.6	105.4	43.1	87.1
0970, 0990	Wall Finishes & Painting/Coating	96.2	54.1	70.2	96.2	39.8	61.4	96.2	81.7	87.2	96.2	28.9	54.7	96.2	54.1	70.2	96.2	54.1	70.2
09	FINISHES	95.5	44.4	67.0	89.1	40.4	61.9	92.1	70.8	80.2	95.1	32.0	59.9	95.5	39.6	64.3	91.9	40.4	63.2
COVERS	DIVS. 10 - 14, 25, 28, 41, 43, 44, 46	100.0	73.5	94.7	100.0	73.1	94.7	100.0	77.8	95.6	100.0	71.3	94.3	100.0	73.0	94.6	100.0	72.8	94.6
21, 22, 23	FIRE SUPPRESSION, PLUMBING & HVAC	100.3	61.3	84.5	94.3	30.2	68.3	94.3	60.2	80.5	100.3	23.4	69.1	100.2	62.1	84.7	94.3	59.9	80.4
26, 27, 3370	ELECTRICAL, COMMUNICATIONS & UTIL.	97.1	68.6	82.4	95.5	66.4	80.5	97.0	66.5	81.2	95.1	28.0	60.5	98.7	68.6	83.2	95.1	62.6	78.3
MF2010	WEIGHTED AVERAGE	97.5	61.4	81.6	93.6	50.6	74.6	93.8	67.9	82.3	96.7	39.3	71.4	97.8	60.6	81.4	94.1	58.7	78.5

OKLAHOMA / OREGON

DIVISION		POTEAU 749 MAT.	INST.	TOTAL	SHAWNEE 748 MAT.	INST.	TOTAL	TULSA 740-741 MAT.	INST.	TOTAL	WOODWARD 738 MAT.	INST.	TOTAL	BEND 977 MAT.	INST.	TOTAL	EUGENE 974 MAT.	INST.	TOTAL
015433	CONTRACTOR EQUIPMENT		88.3	88.3		81.0	81.0		88.9	88.9		81.0	81.0		98.7	98.7		98.7	98.7
0241, 31 - 34	SITE & INFRASTRUCTURE, DEMOLITION	73.2	85.1	81.4	97.5	88.9	91.6	94.7	86.4	89.0	100.9	89.0	92.7	113.0	103.8	106.6	101.4	103.8	103.0
0310	Concrete Forming & Accessories	87.7	42.1	48.1	83.7	38.6	44.5	97.5	39.1	46.7	90.3	34.2	41.5	111.3	94.4	96.6	108.0	94.3	96.1
0320	Concrete Reinforcing	97.4	77.7	87.5	96.3	45.0	70.4	96.6	77.6	87.0	96.3	77.7	86.9	100.8	104.5	102.7	105.2	104.5	104.8
0330	Cast-in-Place Concrete	84.1	44.4	68.4	97.0	42.6	75.5	92.7	44.4	73.7	94.6	43.1	74.3	99.4	104.7	101.5	96.2	104.7	99.6
03	CONCRETE	88.8	50.8	70.3	95.4	41.8	69.2	93.6	49.5	72.1	96.5	46.1	72.0	109.1	99.7	104.5	100.7	99.6	100.2
04	MASONRY	99.5	56.4	73.2	116.2	55.2	79.0	99.4	57.6	73.9	93.9	55.8	70.7	106.4	108.5	107.8	103.9	108.5	106.7
05	METALS	91.0	81.3	87.8	90.9	55.7	79.3	95.7	80.4	90.6	91.2	69.6	84.0	86.8	98.1	90.5	87.5	98.0	90.9
06	WOOD, PLASTICS & COMPOSITES	92.7	41.5	63.1	88.3	38.0	59.2	103.1	38.0	65.5	96.4	30.9	58.6	102.0	91.3	95.8	98.0	91.3	94.1
07	THERMAL & MOISTURE PROTECTION	97.3	56.3	80.6	97.4	59.0	81.8	97.3	54.8	80.0	97.6	58.4	81.7	105.3	95.4	101.2	104.5	92.4	99.6
08	OPENINGS	94.3	51.0	83.4	94.3	37.4	80.0	96.0	48.0	83.9	94.4	44.7	81.9	97.8	99.5	98.2	98.1	99.5	98.5
0920	Plaster & Gypsum Board	77.7	40.2	50.9	74.9	36.7	47.6	82.8	36.6	49.8	79.8	29.4	43.8	102.2	90.9	94.1	99.9	90.9	93.5
0950, 0980	Ceilings & Acoustic Treatment	83.8	40.2	55.0	83.8	36.7	52.7	92.0	36.6	55.4	86.5	29.4	48.8	96.6	90.9	92.8	97.6	90.9	93.2
0960	Flooring	104.7	64.8	93.0	102.0	34.3	82.1	110.1	44.8	91.0	105.9	45.2	88.1	109.2	108.2	108.9	107.4	108.2	107.6
0970, 0990	Wall Finishes & Painting/Coating	96.2	54.1	70.2	96.2	36.0	59.0	96.2	42.7	63.2	96.2	54.1	70.2	108.7	69.0	84.2	108.7	69.0	84.2
09	FINISHES	89.7	46.4	65.5	90.6	36.1	60.2	94.9	39.3	63.9	93.3	36.0	61.4	105.7	93.4	98.8	103.8	93.4	98.0
COVERS	DIVS. 10 - 14, 25, 28, 41, 43, 44, 46	100.0	73.4	94.7	100.0	72.4	94.5	100.0	73.4	94.7	100.0	71.8	94.4	100.0	102.9	100.6	100.0	102.9	100.6
21, 22, 23	FIRE SUPPRESSION, PLUMBING & HVAC	94.3	59.9	80.4	94.3	60.6	80.6	100.3	47.3	78.8	94.3	61.3	80.9	94.1	97.6	95.5	100.1	97.6	99.1
26, 27, 3370	ELECTRICAL, COMMUNICATIONS & UTIL.	95.2	66.5	80.4	97.2	68.6	82.4	97.1	36.5	65.9	97.0	68.6	82.3	100.5	93.9	97.1	99.1	93.9	96.4
MF2010	WEIGHTED AVERAGE	93.2	61.4	79.2	95.7	56.5	78.4	97.4	53.5	78.0	95.1	58.8	79.1	98.8	98.6	98.7	98.6	98.5	98.6

City Cost Indexes

OREGON

DIVISION		KLAMATH FALLS 976 MAT.	INST.	TOTAL	MEDFORD 975 MAT.	INST.	TOTAL	PENDLETON 978 MAT.	INST.	TOTAL	PORTLAND 970-972 MAT.	INST.	TOTAL	SALEM 973 MAT.	INST.	TOTAL	VALE 979 MAT.	INST.	TOTAL
015433	CONTRACTOR EQUIPMENT		98.7	98.7		98.7	98.7		96.2	96.2		98.7	98.7		98.7	98.7		96.2	96.2
0241, 31-34	SITE & INFRASTRUCTURE, DEMOLITION	117.6	103.8	108.1	110.0	103.8	105.7	107.8	97.3	100.6	104.0	103.8	103.9	96.6	103.8	101.5	94.7	97.3	96.5
0310	Concrete Forming & Accessories	104.9	94.3	95.6	104.1	94.3	95.5	104.4	94.5	95.8	109.1	94.6	96.5	106.9	94.4	96.1	110.3	93.7	95.8
0320	Concrete Reinforcing	100.8	104.5	102.7	102.6	104.5	103.5	100.0	104.5	102.3	106.0	104.5	105.2	106.2	104.5	105.3	97.5	104.4	101.0
0330	Cast-in-Place Concrete	99.4	104.7	101.5	99.3	104.7	101.4	100.1	106.1	102.5	98.9	104.8	101.2	88.2	104.7	94.7	78.9	105.7	89.4
03	CONCRETE	111.9	99.6	105.9	106.7	99.6	103.2	93.1	100.2	96.6	102.2	99.8	101.0	96.8	99.7	98.2	78.2	99.7	88.6
04	MASONRY	120.1	108.5	113.0	100.9	108.5	105.5	110.4	108.6	109.3	104.5	108.5	107.0	108.7	108.5	108.6	108.7	108.6	108.6
05	METALS	86.8	97.9	90.5	87.1	97.9	90.6	92.6	98.5	94.5	88.3	98.2	91.6	87.8	98.1	91.2	92.5	97.6	94.2
06	WOOD, PLASTICS & COMPOSITES	93.4	91.3	92.2	92.3	91.3	91.7	94.8	91.4	92.9	98.9	91.3	94.5	95.2	91.3	93.0	102.9	91.4	96.3
07	THERMAL & MOISTURE PROTECTION	105.5	93.9	100.8	105.1	93.9	100.6	97.3	94.2	96.0	104.5	98.0	101.8	102.5	95.4	99.6	96.7	91.9	94.7
08	OPENINGS	97.8	99.5	98.2	100.7	99.5	100.4	93.2	99.6	94.8	95.7	99.5	96.7	97.6	99.5	98.1	93.1	92.3	92.9
0920	Plaster & Gypsum Board	97.3	90.9	92.7	96.4	90.9	92.5	80.4	90.9	87.9	100.2	90.9	93.5	94.4	90.9	91.9	87.2	90.9	89.8
0950, 0980	Ceilings & Acoustic Treatment	104.8	90.9	95.6	109.8	90.9	97.3	67.6	90.9	83.0	99.7	90.9	93.9	99.9	90.9	93.9	67.6	90.9	83.0
0960	Flooring	105.9	108.2	106.6	105.2	108.2	106.1	74.1	108.2	84.1	104.9	108.2	105.9	107.6	108.2	107.8	76.1	108.2	85.5
0970, 0990	Wall Finishes & Painting/Coating	108.7	61.3	79.4	108.7	61.3	79.4	98.3	69.0	80.2	108.3	69.0	84.0	108.7	69.0	84.2	98.3	69.0	80.2
09	FINISHES	105.6	92.6	98.7	106.3	92.6	98.7	72.6	93.5	84.3	103.6	93.4	97.9	103.2	93.4	97.7	72.8	93.5	84.3
COVERS	DIVS. 10-14, 25, 28, 41, 43, 44, 46	100.0	102.9	100.6	100.0	102.9	100.6	100.0	95.8	99.2	100.0	103.0	100.6	100.0	102.9	100.6	100.0	103.2	100.6
21, 22, 23	FIRE SUPPRESSION, PLUMBING & HVAC	94.1	97.6	95.5	100.1	97.6	99.1	95.8	106.9	100.3	100.1	100.9	100.4	100.1	97.6	99.1	95.8	74.9	87.3
26, 27, 3370	ELECTRICAL, COMMUNICATIONS & UTIL.	99.2	83.4	91.1	102.6	83.4	92.7	91.4	94.3	92.9	99.4	100.2	99.8	103.5	93.9	98.6	91.4	76.7	83.8
MF2010	WEIGHTED AVERAGE	99.8	97.0	98.6	100.1	97.0	98.7	94.1	100.0	96.7	98.8	100.3	99.5	98.6	98.6	98.6	91.9	90.5	91.3

PENNSYLVANIA

DIVISION		ALLENTOWN 181 MAT.	INST.	TOTAL	ALTOONA 166 MAT.	INST.	TOTAL	BEDFORD 155 MAT.	INST.	TOTAL	BRADFORD 167 MAT.	INST.	TOTAL	BUTLER 160 MAT.	INST.	TOTAL	CHAMBERSBURG 172 MAT.	INST.	TOTAL
015433	CONTRACTOR EQUIPMENT		113.6	113.6		113.6	113.6		110.9	110.9		113.6	113.6		113.6	113.6		112.9	112.9
0241, 31-34	SITE & INFRASTRUCTURE, DEMOLITION	91.4	105.4	101.1	95.6	105.6	102.5	109.6	102.5	104.7	90.6	105.0	100.5	86.7	107.1	100.8	84.9	103.1	97.4
0310	Concrete Forming & Accessories	100.4	113.5	111.8	86.4	79.5	80.4	85.6	82.0	82.4	88.4	80.2	81.2	87.8	93.7	92.9	86.1	81.1	81.8
0320	Concrete Reinforcing	98.3	111.7	105.0	95.3	90.1	92.7	96.3	81.9	89.1	97.3	90.3	93.8	96.0	110.0	103.0	95.7	102.2	99.0
0330	Cast-in-Place Concrete	82.8	104.8	91.5	92.2	84.8	89.3	107.1	72.8	93.6	88.1	89.2	88.6	81.5	96.8	87.5	89.5	72.5	82.8
03	CONCRETE	94.4	110.9	102.4	90.1	84.8	87.5	101.7	80.1	91.2	96.3	86.7	91.6	82.1	99.0	90.4	102.0	83.6	93.0
04	MASONRY	95.7	104.8	101.3	97.8	68.1	79.7	107.4	85.2	93.9	95.0	83.6	88.1	100.0	96.2	97.7	96.0	90.3	92.5
05	METALS	100.6	123.5	108.2	94.4	110.6	99.7	96.9	105.0	99.6	98.5	110.2	102.4	94.1	121.9	103.3	98.5	114.9	103.9
06	WOOD, PLASTICS & COMPOSITES	101.9	115.4	109.7	81.3	81.7	81.5	82.7	81.7	82.1	87.6	78.4	82.3	82.6	91.5	87.7	91.0	81.7	85.6
07	THERMAL & MOISTURE PROTECTION	99.5	117.2	106.7	98.9	90.5	95.4	104.8	88.5	98.2	99.5	91.2	96.1	98.5	100.1	99.2	98.7	75.5	89.3
08	OPENINGS	92.3	114.6	97.9	86.8	85.4	86.4	94.6	83.2	91.8	92.7	87.3	91.3	86.8	103.0	90.9	89.1	83.4	87.7
0920	Plaster & Gypsum Board	103.9	115.6	112.3	96.6	80.9	85.4	95.4	80.9	85.0	97.2	77.5	83.1	96.6	91.0	92.6	100.8	80.9	86.6
0950, 0980	Ceilings & Acoustic Treatment	88.9	115.6	106.6	93.5	80.9	85.2	89.7	80.9	83.9	91.8	77.5	82.4	94.5	91.0	92.2	91.8	80.9	84.6
0960	Flooring	93.1	98.0	94.6	86.9	92.2	88.4	88.4	92.3	89.5	87.0	100.1	90.8	87.7	84.8	86.9	90.8	48.3	78.3
0970, 0990	Wall Finishes & Painting/Coating	96.6	74.4	82.9	92.6	106.9	101.4	97.3	86.0	90.3	96.6	92.3	93.9	92.6	106.9	101.4	96.6	86.0	90.1
09	FINISHES	95.8	106.8	101.9	94.6	84.0	88.7	94.2	82.9	87.9	93.9	83.3	88.0	94.4	92.2	93.2	94.4	75.3	83.7
COVERS	DIVS. 10-14, 25, 28, 41, 43, 44, 46	100.0	106.2	101.2	100.0	95.9	99.2	100.0	99.0	99.8	100.0	98.9	99.8	100.0	102.9	100.6	100.0	96.2	99.2
21, 22, 23	FIRE SUPPRESSION, PLUMBING & HVAC	100.2	112.2	105.0	99.7	83.7	93.2	94.1	88.4	91.7	94.3	90.3	92.7	93.8	95.0	94.3	94.3	89.9	92.5
26, 27, 3370	ELECTRICAL, COMMUNICATIONS & UTIL.	99.9	97.7	98.7	89.8	107.8	99.1	92.6	107.8	100.5	93.5	107.8	100.9	90.4	102.0	96.4	92.1	85.8	88.8
MF2010	WEIGHTED AVERAGE	97.9	109.2	102.9	94.8	90.6	93.0	97.2	91.7	94.8	95.5	93.8	94.7	92.3	100.5	95.9	95.5	89.5	92.9

PENNSYLVANIA

DIVISION		DOYLESTOWN 189 MAT.	INST.	TOTAL	DUBOIS 158 MAT.	INST.	TOTAL	ERIE 164-165 MAT.	INST.	TOTAL	GREENSBURG 156 MAT.	INST.	TOTAL	HARRISBURG 170-171 MAT.	INST.	TOTAL	HAZLETON 182 MAT.	INST.	TOTAL
015433	CONTRACTOR EQUIPMENT		94.9	94.9		110.9	110.9		113.6	113.6		110.9	110.9		112.9	112.9		113.6	113.6
0241, 31-34	SITE & INFRASTRUCTURE, DEMOLITION	104.8	91.7	95.8	115.4	102.6	106.6	92.2	106.2	101.8	105.1	104.7	104.8	81.2	104.7	97.4	84.5	106.0	99.3
0310	Concrete Forming & Accessories	85.3	128.2	122.6	85.0	83.0	83.2	100.0	87.4	89.0	91.4	93.7	93.4	93.7	90.7	91.1	83.2	88.3	87.6
0320	Concrete Reinforcing	95.1	138.9	117.2	95.7	90.5	93.1	97.3	92.0	94.6	95.7	110.0	102.9	98.3	102.6	100.5	95.4	106.5	101.0
0330	Cast-in-Place Concrete	78.3	89.1	82.5	103.2	91.4	98.6	90.7	84.2	88.1	99.4	96.4	98.2	87.2	96.3	90.8	78.2	91.6	83.5
03	CONCRETE	90.2	116.4	103.0	102.6	88.6	95.8	89.0	88.4	88.7	96.6	98.8	97.7	94.5	96.1	95.3	87.3	94.2	90.6
04	MASONRY	99.0	128.9	117.3	107.4	86.0	94.4	87.8	90.1	89.2	118.0	96.2	104.7	95.5	93.5	94.3	108.2	96.8	101.2
05	METALS	98.1	127.7	107.9	96.9	109.8	101.1	94.6	110.9	100.0	96.8	120.7	104.7	102.7	118.6	107.9	100.3	120.3	106.9
06	WOOD, PLASTICS & COMPOSITES	83.3	130.2	110.4	81.6	81.7	81.6	97.9	85.9	91.0	89.0	91.4	90.4	95.9	90.0	92.5	82.0	86.8	84.8
07	THERMAL & MOISTURE PROTECTION	97.8	132.0	111.7	105.1	94.8	100.9	99.2	93.5	96.9	104.7	99.8	102.7	105.2	108.9	106.7	99.1	105.7	101.8
08	OPENINGS	94.1	139.9	105.6	94.6	89.0	93.2	87.0	88.0	87.2	94.6	102.9	96.7	92.3	94.4	92.8	93.0	92.9	93.0
0920	Plaster & Gypsum Board	94.8	130.9	120.6	94.0	80.9	84.6	103.9	85.2	90.5	96.5	91.0	92.5	100.9	89.4	92.7	95.3	86.1	88.7
0950, 0980	Ceilings & Acoustic Treatment	88.1	130.9	116.4	89.7	80.9	83.9	88.9	85.2	86.5	88.8	91.0	90.2	93.5	89.4	90.8	90.0	86.1	87.4
0960	Flooring	76.9	133.3	93.4	88.1	100.1	91.7	92.3	96.1	93.4	91.8	71.2	85.7	93.7	133.3	93.7	84.3	96.7	87.9
0970, 0990	Wall Finishes & Painting/Coating	96.1	72.7	81.7	97.3	106.9	103.2	100.7	90.2	94.2	97.3	106.9	103.2	96.6	89.0	91.9	96.6	100.5	99.0
09	FINISHES	86.8	122.4	106.6	94.6	87.9	90.8	96.4	88.9	92.2	94.7	90.5	92.4	95.1	90.8	92.7	92.0	89.1	90.4
COVERS	DIVS. 10-14, 25, 28, 41, 43, 44, 46	100.0	74.2	94.9	100.0	99.0	99.8	100.0	101.1	100.2	100.0	102.8	100.6	100.0	98.2	99.6	100.0	96.5	99.3
21, 22, 23	FIRE SUPPRESSION, PLUMBING & HVAC	93.8	126.9	107.2	94.1	88.6	91.8	99.7	93.0	97.0	94.1	92.8	93.6	100.0	92.2	96.9	94.3	98.3	95.9
26, 27, 3370	ELECTRICAL, COMMUNICATIONS & UTIL.	92.7	117.9	105.7	93.2	107.8	100.8	91.7	87.4	89.5	93.2	107.8	100.8	96.7	85.8	91.1	94.3	85.8	89.9
MF2010	WEIGHTED AVERAGE	94.7	120.1	105.9	97.6	94.5	96.2	94.6	93.6	94.1	97.2	100.3	98.5	97.7	96.1	97.0	95.1	97.2	96.0

PENNSYLVANIA

DIVISION		INDIANA 157			JOHNSTOWN 159			KITTANNING 162			LANCASTER 175 - 176			LEHIGH VALLEY 180			MONTROSE 188		
		MAT.	INST.	TOTAL	MAT.	INST.	TOTAL	MAT.	INST.	TOTAL	MAT.	INST.	TOTAL	MAT.	INST.	TOTAL	MAT.	INST.	TOTAL
015433	CONTRACTOR EQUIPMENT		110.9	110.9		110.9	110.9		113.6	113.6		112.9	112.9		113.6	113.6		113.6	113.6
0241, 31 - 34	SITE & INFRASTRUCTURE, DEMOLITION	103.1	103.6	103.4	110.2	103.7	105.8	89.4	107.1	101.6	77.0	104.6	96.1	88.6	105.6	100.3	87.5	103.9	98.8
0310	Concrete Forming & Accessories	86.1	86.2	86.2	85.0	83.3	83.5	87.8	93.8	93.0	87.9	89.8	89.6	94.3	112.4	110.1	84.0	87.6	87.2
0320	Concrete Reinforcing	94.9	110.0	102.6	96.3	109.8	103.1	96.0	110.1	103.1	95.4	102.5	99.0	95.4	111.7	103.6	100.0	106.3	103.1
0330	Cast-in-Place Concrete	97.4	96.3	97.0	108.0	89.9	100.9	84.7	96.8	89.5	76.2	95.5	83.8	84.7	103.5	92.1	83.0	90.6	86.0
03	CONCRETE	94.3	95.5	94.9	102.5	91.9	97.3	84.6	99.1	91.7	89.6	95.5	92.5	93.5	109.9	101.5	92.2	93.3	92.7
04	MASONRY	103.3	97.9	100.0	104.1	85.6	92.8	103.7	97.9	100.2	101.3	92.4	95.9	95.7	102.7	100.0	95.7	97.8	97.0
05	METALS	96.9	120.5	104.7	96.9	118.7	104.1	94.2	122.2	103.4	98.5	118.1	105.0	100.3	122.7	107.7	98.6	115.0	104.0
06	WOOD, PLASTICS & COMPOSITES	83.4	81.7	82.4	81.6	81.7	81.6	82.6	91.5	87.7	93.5	90.0	91.5	94.2	115.4	106.5	82.7	86.9	85.1
07	THERMAL & MOISTURE PROTECTION	104.6	97.8	101.8	104.8	93.3	100.2	98.6	100.6	99.4	98.3	97.3	97.9	99.4	105.2	101.7	99.1	94.3	97.1
08	OPENINGS	94.6	94.9	94.7	94.6	91.2	93.8	86.8	100.2	90.2	89.1	98.1	91.4	93.0	114.6	98.5	89.3	92.9	90.2
0920	Plaster & Gypsum Board	95.8	80.9	85.2	93.7	80.9	84.6	96.6	91.0	92.6	103.1	89.4	93.3	98.5	115.6	110.7	95.8	86.2	88.9
0950, 0980	Ceilings & Acoustic Treatment	89.7	80.9	83.9	88.8	80.9	83.6	94.5	91.0	92.2	91.8	89.4	90.2	90.0	115.6	106.9	91.8	86.2	88.1
0960	Flooring	88.9	100.1	92.2	88.1	92.3	89.4	87.7	102.4	92.0	91.8	93.7	92.3	89.8	98.0	92.2	84.9	60.6	77.8
0970, 0990	Wall Finishes & Painting/Coating	97.3	106.9	103.2	97.3	106.9	103.2	92.6	106.9	101.4	96.6	60.2	74.2	96.6	70.0	80.2	96.6	100.5	99.0
09	FINISHES	93.8	89.1	91.2	93.8	86.4	89.7	94.6	95.3	95.0	94.3	87.3	90.4	94.3	104.8	100.1	92.9	83.7	87.8
COVERS	DIVS. 10 - 14, 25, 28, 41, 43, 44, 46	100.0	101.7	100.3	100.0	99.2	99.8	100.0	102.9	100.6	100.0	97.6	99.5	100.0	102.1	100.4	100.0	97.1	99.4
21, 22, 23	FIRE SUPPRESSION, PLUMBING & HVAC	94.1	92.8	93.5	94.1	89.0	92.0	93.8	97.7	95.4	94.3	91.6	93.2	94.3	111.1	101.1	94.3	99.6	96.4
26, 27, 3370	ELECTRICAL, COMMUNICATIONS & UTIL.	93.2	107.8	100.8	93.2	107.8	100.8	89.8	107.9	99.1	93.5	46.8	69.4	94.3	138.5	117.1	93.5	94.4	93.9
MF2010	WEIGHTED AVERAGE	96.0	99.1	97.4	97.2	95.8	96.6	92.8	102.4	97.0	94.3	89.7	92.3	95.6	113.5	103.5	94.5	97.0	95.6

PENNSYLVANIA

DIVISION		NEW CASTLE 161			NORRISTOWN 194			OIL CITY 163			PHILADELPHIA 190 - 191			PITTSBURGH 150 - 152			POTTSVILLE 179		
		MAT.	INST.	TOTAL	MAT.	INST.	TOTAL	MAT.	INST.	TOTAL	MAT.	INST.	TOTAL	MAT.	INST.	TOTAL	MAT.	INST.	TOTAL
015433	CONTRACTOR EQUIPMENT		113.6	113.6		98.2	98.2		113.6	113.6		97.6	97.6		112.1	112.1		112.9	112.9
0241, 31 - 34	SITE & INFRASTRUCTURE, DEMOLITION	87.2	107.0	100.9	91.9	99.2	96.9	85.6	105.2	99.1	98.6	98.3	98.4	108.7	106.8	107.4	79.9	104.8	97.1
0310	Concrete Forming & Accessories	87.8	96.2	95.1	87.0	132.2	126.3	87.8	81.4	82.3	102.8	134.7	130.6	98.5	97.4	97.5	80.2	88.4	87.3
0320	Concrete Reinforcing	94.7	93.7	94.2	95.5	146.3	121.1	96.0	93.5	94.7	98.5	146.3	122.6	96.8	110.5	103.7	94.6	102.0	98.3
0330	Cast-in-Place Concrete	82.3	95.9	87.6	81.1	128.6	99.8	79.9	93.7	85.4	99.4	128.6	110.9	103.2	96.6	100.6	81.1	78.3	80.0
03	CONCRETE	82.5	96.8	89.4	87.6	133.2	109.8	80.9	89.4	85.0	100.0	134.3	116.7	99.9	100.6	100.3	93.4	88.8	91.2
04	MASONRY	99.3	96.2	97.4	109.3	129.0	121.3	99.8	89.9	93.8	96.2	129.1	116.3	97.1	103.6	101.0	95.4	94.4	94.8
05	METALS	94.2	114.0	100.7	99.7	133.0	110.7	94.2	111.8	100.0	103.5	133.2	113.3	98.3	121.7	106.0	98.7	118.1	105.1
06	WOOD, PLASTICS & COMPOSITES	82.6	95.8	90.3	84.3	132.2	112.0	82.6	78.4	80.2	102.7	135.5	121.7	98.2	95.8	96.8	84.3	86.8	85.7
07	THERMAL & MOISTURE PROTECTION	98.6	97.7	98.2	97.5	132.5	111.7	98.5	93.8	96.6	98.4	132.9	112.4	104.9	102.2	103.8	98.3	105.9	101.4
08	OPENINGS	86.8	97.5	89.5	89.6	143.1	103.1	86.8	80.3	85.2	98.1	145.0	109.9	97.6	106.0	99.7	89.2	91.5	89.8
0920	Plaster & Gypsum Board	96.6	95.4	95.8	90.8	133.0	121.0	96.6	77.5	83.0	98.6	136.5	125.7	103.1	95.4	97.6	97.6	86.1	89.4
0950, 0980	Ceilings & Acoustic Treatment	94.5	95.4	95.1	99.7	133.0	121.7	94.5	77.5	83.3	99.7	136.5	124.0	89.7	95.4	93.5	91.8	86.1	88.0
0960	Flooring	87.7	60.2	79.6	91.9	139.3	105.8	87.7	100.1	91.4	99.8	141.2	112.0	95.3	107.4	98.9	87.8	93.7	89.6
0970, 0990	Wall Finishes & Painting/Coating	92.6	106.9	101.4	99.6	146.7	128.7	92.6	106.9	101.4	99.6	146.7	128.7	97.3	114.0	107.6	96.6	100.5	99.0
09	FINISHES	94.5	90.3	92.1	95.6	134.9	117.5	94.3	85.7	89.5	99.2	137.2	120.4	96.9	100.3	98.8	92.8	90.4	91.4
COVERS	DIVS. 10 - 14, 25, 28, 41, 43, 44, 46	100.0	103.3	100.7	100.0	115.0	103.0	100.0	100.0	100.0	100.0	119.0	103.8	100.0	103.3	100.7	100.0	94.5	98.9
21, 22, 23	FIRE SUPPRESSION, PLUMBING & HVAC	93.8	94.7	94.2	93.9	128.3	107.9	93.8	92.3	93.2	99.9	128.4	111.5	100.0	100.3	100.1	94.3	99.5	96.4
26, 27, 3370	ELECTRICAL, COMMUNICATIONS & UTIL.	90.4	91.4	90.9	94.7	142.8	119.5	92.4	102.0	97.4	99.1	142.8	121.7	95.5	107.9	101.9	91.7	90.2	90.9
MF2010	WEIGHTED AVERAGE	92.4	97.5	94.6	95.2	130.2	110.6	92.4	94.7	93.4	99.9	130.9	113.6	99.1	104.6	101.5	94.2	96.8	95.4

PENNSYLVANIA

DIVISION		READING 195 - 196			SCRANTON 184 - 185			STATE COLLEGE 168			STROUDSBURG 183			SUNBURY 178			UNIONTOWN 154		
		MAT.	INST.	TOTAL	MAT.	INST.	TOTAL	MAT.	INST.	TOTAL	MAT.	INST.	TOTAL	MAT.	INST.	TOTAL	MAT.	INST.	TOTAL
015433	CONTRACTOR EQUIPMENT		116.9	116.9		113.6	113.6		112.9	112.9		113.6	113.6		113.6	113.6		110.9	110.9
0241, 31 - 34	SITE & INFRASTRUCTURE, DEMOLITION	96.3	110.9	106.4	91.8	106.1	101.7	82.1	104.4	97.4	86.3	104.0	98.5	90.3	105.8	101.0	103.6	104.7	104.4
0310	Concrete Forming & Accessories	102.3	86.0	88.1	100.6	89.2	90.7	85.2	79.4	80.2	89.1	88.8	88.8	92.3	87.5	88.1	79.8	93.7	91.9
0320	Concrete Reinforcing	96.8	102.1	99.5	98.3	106.5	102.4	96.5	90.8	93.6	98.6	118.6	108.7	97.3	102.6	100.0	95.7	110.0	102.9
0330	Cast-in-Place Concrete	72.7	96.7	82.1	86.5	92.6	88.9	83.4	68.3	77.4	81.5	75.1	79.0	88.7	95.3	91.3	97.4	96.4	97.0
03	CONCRETE	86.3	94.2	90.1	96.2	95.0	95.6	96.3	79.2	88.0	91.0	90.8	90.9	96.9	94.4	95.7	94.0	98.8	96.4
04	MASONRY	97.8	95.5	96.4	96.1	98.3	97.4	101.4	81.5	89.3	92.5	102.3	98.5	95.0	92.0	93.1	120.8	96.2	105.8
05	METALS	99.9	118.9	106.2	102.7	120.6	108.6	98.3	111.5	102.7	100.4	120.2	106.9	98.4	118.4	105.0	96.6	120.7	104.6
06	WOOD, PLASTICS & COMPOSITES	102.8	82.8	91.3	101.9	86.9	93.2	89.7	81.7	85.1	88.5	86.9	87.6	91.8	86.8	88.9	75.5	91.4	84.7
07	THERMAL & MOISTURE PROTECTION	97.9	108.9	102.4	99.4	98.0	98.9	98.5	91.5	95.7	99.3	87.1	94.3	99.4	104.9	101.6	104.5	99.8	102.6
08	OPENINGS	95.3	94.0	95.0	92.3	92.9	92.5	89.1	85.4	88.2	93.0	89.7	92.2	89.3	91.7	89.9	94.6	102.9	96.7
0920	Plaster & Gypsum Board	103.0	82.1	88.0	106.3	86.2	92.0	98.7	80.9	86.0	96.6	86.2	89.2	97.3	86.1	89.3	91.0	91.0	91.0
0950, 0980	Ceilings & Acoustic Treatment	88.7	82.1	84.3	97.1	86.2	89.9	89.0	80.9	83.7	88.1	86.2	86.9	89.0	86.1	87.1	88.8	91.0	90.2
0960	Flooring	97.3	93.7	96.2	93.1	110.2	98.1	90.3	102.1	93.8	87.5	53.8	77.6	88.7	91.8	89.6	85.4	100.1	89.7
0970, 0990	Wall Finishes & Painting/Coating	98.1	100.9	99.8	96.6	100.5	99.0	96.6	106.9	103.0	96.6	68.1	79.0	96.6	100.9	99.2	97.3	106.9	103.2
09	FINISHES	96.5	87.6	91.5	97.9	93.6	95.5	93.1	86.0	89.1	92.8	79.9	85.6	93.9	89.5	91.4	92.0	94.6	93.5
COVERS	DIVS. 10 - 14, 25, 28, 41, 43, 44, 46	100.0	99.6	99.9	100.0	97.1	99.4	100.0	93.1	98.6	100.0	65.9	93.2	100.0	93.6	98.7	100.0	102.8	100.6
21, 22, 23	FIRE SUPPRESSION, PLUMBING & HVAC	100.0	107.9	103.2	100.2	100.5	100.3	94.3	85.7	90.8	94.3	102.2	97.5	94.3	91.3	93.1	94.1	92.8	93.6
26, 27, 3370	ELECTRICAL, COMMUNICATIONS & UTIL.	101.3	90.2	95.6	99.9	94.5	97.1	92.6	107.8	100.5	94.3	142.6	119.2	92.0	86.7	89.3	90.2	107.8	99.3
MF2010	WEIGHTED AVERAGE	97.6	100.0	98.6	98.6	99.5	99.0	95.0	91.8	93.6	94.9	103.0	98.5	95.1	95.1	95.1	96.4	100.8	98.3

City Cost Indexes

		PENNSYLVANIA																
DIVISION		WASHINGTON			WELLSBORO			WESTCHESTER			WILKES-BARRE			WILLIAMSPORT			YORK		
		153			169			193			186 - 187			177			173 - 174		
		MAT.	INST.	TOTAL	MAT.	INST.	TOTAL	MAT.	INST.	TOTAL	MAT.	INST.	TOTAL	MAT.	INST.	TOTAL	MAT.	INST.	TOTAL
015433	CONTRACTOR EQUIPMENT		110.9	110.9		113.6	113.6		98.2	98.2		113.6	113.6		113.6	113.6		112.9	112.9
0241, 31 - 34	SITE & INFRASTRUCTURE, DEMOLITION	103.7	104.7	104.4	94.7	103.8	101.0	98.0	96.9	97.2	84.3	106.1	99.3	81.6	104.4	97.3	80.5	104.7	97.2
0310	Concrete Forming & Accessories	86.2	93.8	92.9	87.8	85.9	86.1	93.5	129.2	124.6	91.5	89.2	89.5	89.1	61.9	65.4	83.3	87.9	87.3
0320	Concrete Reinforcing	95.7	110.1	103.0	96.5	106.1	101.4	94.6	112.9	103.8	97.3	106.5	102.0	96.5	68.5	82.4	97.3	102.6	100.0
0330	Cast-in-Place Concrete	97.4	96.5	97.1	87.4	88.5	87.8	89.7	128.0	104.8	78.2	92.6	83.9	75.0	74.0	74.6	81.5	95.7	87.1
03	CONCRETE	94.4	99.0	96.6	98.7	91.8	95.3	95.0	125.4	109.8	88.1	95.0	91.4	84.9	69.3	77.3	94.6	94.7	94.7
04	MASONRY	103.1	97.9	99.9	101.1	92.0	95.6	103.4	129.0	119.0	108.8	98.3	102.4	86.9	92.3	90.2	96.1	92.4	93.9
05	METALS	96.6	121.0	104.6	98.4	115.2	104.0	99.7	117.0	105.4	98.6	120.7	105.9	98.5	101.5	99.5	100.1	118.6	106.2
06	WOOD, PLASTICS & COMPOSITES	83.5	91.4	88.1	87.1	86.8	86.9	91.6	130.1	113.8	90.9	86.7	88.5	88.5	54.2	68.7	87.8	86.8	87.2
07	THERMAL & MOISTURE PROTECTION	104.6	100.2	102.8	99.7	92.0	96.6	97.8	131.9	111.7	99.0	106.3	102.0	98.9	101.4	99.9	98.4	108.1	102.4
08	OPENINGS	94.5	102.9	96.7	92.6	92.9	92.7	89.6	126.7	99.0	89.3	97.5	91.4	89.3	56.8	81.1	89.1	92.6	90.0
0920	Plaster & Gypsum Board	95.6	91.0	92.3	96.4	86.1	89.1	92.7	130.9	120.0	97.6	86.0	89.4	97.6	52.5	65.4	99.0	86.1	89.8
0950, 0980	Ceilings & Acoustic Treatment	88.8	91.0	90.2	89.0	86.1	87.1	99.7	130.9	120.3	91.8	86.0	88.0	91.8	52.5	65.9	90.8	86.1	87.7
0960	Flooring	88.9	100.1	92.2	86.7	53.2	76.9	95.4	141.2	108.9	88.4	96.7	90.9	87.5	52.1	77.1	89.2	93.7	90.5
0970, 0990	Wall Finishes & Painting/Coating	97.3	106.9	103.2	96.6	100.5	99.0	99.6	146.7	128.7	96.6	103.2	100.7	96.6	103.2	100.7	96.6	89.0	91.9
09	FINISHES	93.6	95.0	94.4	93.6	81.2	86.7	97.4	131.9	116.6	93.8	91.1	92.3	93.4	63.5	76.7	93.1	88.7	90.6
COVERS	DIVS. 10 - 14, 25, 28, 41, 43, 44, 46	100.0	102.8	100.6	100.0	93.6	98.7	100.0	114.7	102.9	100.0	97.1	99.4	100.0	93.3	98.7	100.0	97.5	99.5
21, 22, 23	FIRE SUPPRESSION, PLUMBING & HVAC	94.1	97.9	95.6	94.3	90.6	92.8	93.9	125.8	106.8	94.3	99.2	96.3	94.3	90.7	92.8	100.2	91.7	96.7
26, 27, 3370	ELECTRICAL, COMMUNICATIONS & UTIL.	92.6	107.8	100.5	93.5	84.0	88.6	94.6	120.8	108.1	94.3	85.8	89.9	92.5	49.5	70.3	93.5	85.8	89.5
MF2010	WEIGHTED AVERAGE	95.9	102.1	98.6	96.1	92.4	94.5	96.1	122.8	107.9	94.8	98.2	96.3	93.0	79.6	87.1	96.3	95.2	95.8

		PUERTO RICO			RHODE ISLAND						SOUTH CAROLINA								
DIVISION		SAN JUAN			NEWPORT			PROVIDENCE			AIKEN			BEAUFORT			CHARLESTON		
		009			028			029			298			299			294		
		MAT.	INST.	TOTAL	MAT.	INST.	TOTAL	MAT.	INST.	TOTAL	MAT.	INST.	TOTAL	MAT.	INST.	TOTAL	MAT.	INST.	TOTAL
015433	CONTRACTOR EQUIPMENT		90.2	90.2		101.9	101.9		101.9	101.9		99.5	99.5		99.5	99.5		99.5	99.5
0241, 31 - 34	SITE & INFRASTRUCTURE, DEMOLITION	131.5	90.1	103.0	87.5	102.9	98.1	88.6	102.9	98.5	128.4	86.4	99.4	122.8	84.5	96.4	103.7	84.1	90.2
0310	Concrete Forming & Accessories	95.4	17.4	27.6	102.3	117.2	115.2	101.0	117.2	115.0	96.3	71.7	74.9	95.2	39.4	46.6	94.3	41.1	48.1
0320	Concrete Reinforcing	186.3	12.2	98.6	103.6	112.7	108.2	103.6	112.7	108.2	95.1	69.3	82.1	94.2	27.3	60.5	94.0	58.9	76.3
0330	Cast-in-Place Concrete	107.8	31.0	77.6	83.5	117.3	96.8	102.6	117.3	108.4	93.1	73.1	85.2	93.1	48.6	75.6	109.2	49.3	85.6
03	CONCRETE	115.0	22.2	69.8	100.9	115.9	108.2	110.4	115.9	113.1	110.3	72.8	92.0	107.6	42.4	75.8	104.1	49.0	77.2
04	MASONRY	84.4	16.3	42.8	101.1	122.3	114.0	104.6	122.3	115.4	81.2	65.0	71.3	97.2	34.8	59.1	98.6	38.8	62.1
05	METALS	111.9	35.1	86.5	98.0	108.9	101.6	98.0	108.9	101.6	86.1	86.6	86.2	86.1	69.5	80.6	87.9	77.0	84.3
06	WOOD, PLASTICS & COMPOSITES	93.4	17.2	49.4	99.9	117.8	110.2	99.1	117.8	109.9	99.8	72.9	84.2	97.8	40.1	64.5	96.6	40.1	64.0
07	THERMAL & MOISTURE PROTECTION	129.6	21.4	85.6	101.5	114.5	106.8	99.1	114.5	105.3	101.3	70.2	88.7	101.0	37.8	75.3	100.1	42.3	76.6
08	OPENINGS	146.8	14.6	113.5	96.5	115.7	101.4	97.2	115.7	101.9	93.2	68.7	87.1	93.3	38.8	79.6	97.3	43.8	83.8
0920	Plaster & Gypsum Board	115.3	14.4	43.3	95.1	117.7	111.2	93.0	117.7	110.6	108.4	71.9	82.3	111.3	38.1	59.0	113.4	38.1	59.6
0950, 0980	Ceilings & Acoustic Treatment	243.9	14.4	92.3	99.2	117.7	111.4	98.5	117.7	111.2	93.7	71.9	79.3	97.3	38.1	58.2	97.3	38.1	58.2
0960	Flooring	197.1	13.7	143.3	95.3	134.8	106.9	94.9	134.8	106.6	106.2	71.6	96.0	107.8	53.6	91.9	107.3	61.0	93.7
0970, 0990	Wall Finishes & Painting/Coating	193.0	12.6	81.7	92.3	120.8	109.9	92.3	120.8	109.9	114.8	74.1	89.7	114.8	36.6	66.5	114.8	41.3	69.4
09	FINISHES	207.2	16.4	100.8	98.5	121.4	111.2	97.7	121.4	110.9	105.4	72.0	86.7	106.5	42.0	70.5	104.2	44.3	70.8
COVERS	DIVS. 10 - 14, 25, 28, 41, 43, 44, 46	100.0	17.0	83.5	100.0	103.1	100.6	100.0	103.1	100.6	100.0	77.6	95.5	100.0	46.7	89.4	100.0	70.3	94.1
21, 22, 23	FIRE SUPPRESSION, PLUMBING & HVAC	102.8	13.3	66.5	100.0	108.3	103.4	99.9	108.3	103.3	94.3	67.7	83.5	94.3	25.4	66.4	100.2	39.9	75.8
26, 27, 3370	ELECTRICAL, COMMUNICATIONS & UTIL.	130.6	12.6	69.7	101.4	99.0	100.2	99.7	99.0	99.3	94.3	70.0	81.8	97.7	32.2	63.9	96.2	94.3	95.2
MF2010	WEIGHTED AVERAGE	121.3	24.1	78.4	99.2	111.1	104.5	100.2	111.1	105.0	96.8	72.8	86.2	97.5	42.5	73.3	98.4	57.4	80.3

		SOUTH CAROLINA															SOUTH DAKOTA		
DIVISION		COLUMBIA			FLORENCE			GREENVILLE			ROCK HILL			SPARTANBURG			ABERDEEN		
		290 - 292			295			296			297			293			574		
		MAT.	INST.	TOTAL	MAT.	INST.	TOTAL	MAT.	INST.	TOTAL	MAT.	INST.	TOTAL	MAT.	INST.	TOTAL	MAT.	INST.	TOTAL
015433	CONTRACTOR EQUIPMENT		99.5	99.5		99.5	99.5		99.5	99.5		99.5	99.5		99.5	99.5		98.7	98.7
0241, 31 - 34	SITE & INFRASTRUCTURE, DEMOLITION	101.5	84.0	89.5	115.4	84.1	93.8	109.7	83.7	91.8	107.1	83.6	90.9	109.5	83.7	91.7	98.8	94.9	96.1
0310	Concrete Forming & Accessories	96.0	40.2	47.5	83.0	40.3	45.9	93.9	40.2	47.2	92.5	37.9	45.0	96.8	40.2	47.6	100.2	38.9	46.9
0320	Concrete Reinforcing	94.0	58.7	76.2	93.7	58.8	76.1	93.6	46.9	70.1	94.4	46.7	70.4	93.6	46.9	70.1	108.5	40.4	74.1
0330	Cast-in-Place Concrete	112.1	49.9	87.6	93.0	49.1	75.7	93.0	49.0	75.7	93.0	44.1	73.7	93.0	49.0	75.7	105.9	45.7	82.2
03	CONCRETE	105.6	48.7	77.9	102.2	48.5	76.1	100.8	46.3	74.2	98.9	43.5	71.9	101.0	46.3	74.3	103.1	43.0	73.8
04	MASONRY	92.9	36.8	58.6	81.3	38.8	55.4	79.1	38.8	54.5	105.1	34.1	61.8	81.3	38.8	55.4	108.2	56.7	76.8
05	METALS	87.9	76.3	84.1	86.9	76.6	83.5	86.9	72.3	82.1	86.1	71.8	81.4	86.9	72.3	82.1	102.9	66.1	90.8
06	WOOD, PLASTICS & COMPOSITES	99.0	39.7	64.7	83.1	39.7	58.0	96.6	39.7	63.7	94.9	37.7	61.8	100.4	39.7	65.3	96.9	38.2	63.0
07	THERMAL & MOISTURE PROTECTION	98.8	41.0	75.3	100.4	42.2	76.8	100.3	42.2	76.7	100.2	39.9	75.7	100.4	42.2	76.7	107.2	50.3	84.0
08	OPENINGS	97.3	43.5	83.7	93.3	43.5	80.8	93.2	40.7	80.0	93.3	39.8	79.8	93.3	40.7	80.0	93.8	39.0	80.0
0920	Plaster & Gypsum Board	100.7	37.6	55.6	101.0	37.6	55.7	106.6	37.6	57.3	105.7	35.6	55.6	108.9	37.6	58.0	111.3	36.6	57.9
0950, 0980	Ceilings & Acoustic Treatment	96.4	37.6	57.6	94.6	37.6	57.0	93.7	37.6	56.6	93.7	35.6	55.3	93.7	37.6	56.6	112.9	36.6	62.5
0960	Flooring	104.0	45.7	86.8	98.5	45.7	83.0	104.9	59.9	91.7	104.0	46.5	87.1	106.4	59.9	92.7	115.7	52.7	97.2
0970, 0990	Wall Finishes & Painting/Coating	112.2	41.3	69.4	114.8	41.3	69.4	114.8	41.3	69.4	114.8	41.3	69.4	114.8	41.3	69.4	96.0	39.1	60.9
09	FINISHES	100.8	41.0	67.5	101.0	41.5	67.8	102.9	43.9	70.0	102.2	39.5	67.2	103.6	43.9	70.3	109.1	41.1	71.1
COVERS	DIVS. 10 - 14, 25, 28, 41, 43, 44, 46	100.0	70.1	94.0	100.0	70.1	94.0	100.0	70.1	94.0	100.0	69.3	93.9	100.0	70.1	94.0	100.0	43.8	88.8
21, 22, 23	FIRE SUPPRESSION, PLUMBING & HVAC	99.9	35.3	73.7	100.2	35.3	73.9	100.2	33.9	73.3	94.3	32.9	69.4	100.2	33.9	73.3	100.2	42.7	76.9
26, 27, 3370	ELECTRICAL, COMMUNICATIONS & UTIL.	95.2	48.2	71.0	94.2	45.9	69.3	96.2	49.6	72.2	96.2	49.6	72.2	96.2	49.6	72.2	100.3	54.4	76.6
MF2010	WEIGHTED AVERAGE	97.8	49.3	76.4	96.6	49.3	75.8	96.6	49.0	75.6	96.0	47.2	74.5	96.8	49.0	75.7	101.6	52.2	79.8

677

SOUTH DAKOTA

DIVISION		MITCHELL 573 MAT.	INST.	TOTAL	MOBRIDGE 576 MAT.	INST.	TOTAL	PIERRE 575 MAT.	INST.	TOTAL	RAPID CITY 577 MAT.	INST.	TOTAL	SIOUX FALLS 570 - 571 MAT.	INST.	TOTAL	WATERTOWN 572 MAT.	INST.	TOTAL
015433	CONTRACTOR EQUIPMENT		98.7	98.7		98.7	98.7		98.7	98.7		98.7	98.7		99.6	99.6		98.7	98.7
0241, 31 - 34	SITE & INFRASTRUCTURE, DEMOLITION	95.7	94.9	95.1	95.6	94.9	95.1	94.0	94.9	94.7	96.9	95.0	95.6	94.6	96.6	96.0	95.5	94.9	95.1
0310	Concrete Forming & Accessories	99.5	39.3	47.1	91.1	39.1	45.8	98.9	40.0	47.7	106.9	38.1	47.0	99.6	42.6	50.0	88.1	38.9	45.3
0320	Concrete Reinforcing	107.8	49.2	78.2	110.6	40.4	75.2	108.0	59.1	83.3	101.4	59.2	80.1	101.4	59.3	80.2	104.9	40.5	72.4
0330	Cast-in-Place Concrete	102.9	44.4	79.9	102.9	45.7	80.4	88.8	44.0	71.2	102.1	44.6	79.5	94.5	45.0	75.0	102.9	45.7	80.4
03	CONCRETE	100.8	44.2	73.2	100.7	43.1	72.6	93.7	46.5	70.7	99.9	45.8	73.5	94.5	48.0	71.8	99.6	43.0	72.0
04	MASONRY	96.8	54.5	71.0	105.7	56.7	75.8	103.8	54.8	73.9	105.7	55.9	75.3	101.3	56.6	74.0	131.0	58.9	87.0
05	METALS	101.9	66.3	90.2	102.0	66.1	90.1	102.9	74.6	93.6	104.7	75.1	94.9	104.9	75.4	95.1	101.9	66.6	90.3
06	WOOD, PLASTICS & COMPOSITES	96.0	38.8	62.9	86.3	38.5	58.7	94.8	39.0	62.6	100.2	35.4	62.7	95.6	41.7	64.5	83.3	38.2	57.2
07	THERMAL & MOISTURE PROTECTION	107.0	48.0	83.0	107.1	50.3	84.0	106.9	48.3	83.1	107.5	49.8	84.1	109.4	51.2	85.7	106.8	50.9	84.1
08	OPENINGS	92.3	39.5	79.0	95.2	38.5	80.9	96.9	44.9	83.8	98.0	43.0	84.1	98.2	46.4	85.2	92.3	38.7	78.8
0920	Plaster & Gypsum Board	109.3	37.1	57.8	103.1	36.8	55.8	98.3	37.4	54.8	110.5	33.7	55.6	108.3	40.2	59.6	101.1	36.6	55.0
0950, 0980	Ceilings & Acoustic Treatment	109.2	37.1	61.6	112.9	36.8	62.6	108.3	37.4	61.5	114.7	33.7	61.2	112.0	40.2	64.6	109.2	36.6	61.2
0960	Flooring	115.1	52.7	96.8	109.6	52.7	92.9	114.8	37.5	92.1	114.8	75.4	103.2	114.8	78.2	104.1	108.1	52.7	91.8
0970, 0990	Wall Finishes & Painting/Coating	96.0	42.8	63.2	96.0	43.9	63.9	96.0	47.0	65.8	96.0	47.0	65.8	96.0	47.0	65.8	96.0	39.1	60.9
09	FINISHES	107.7	41.8	70.9	106.2	41.8	70.2	105.9	39.5	68.9	109.0	45.0	73.3	108.0	49.1	75.2	104.6	41.1	69.2
COVERS	DIVS. 10 - 14, 25, 28, 41, 43, 44, 46	100.0	46.0	88.2	100.0	43.8	88.8	100.0	74.2	94.8	100.0	74.0	94.8	100.0	74.5	94.9	100.0	43.7	88.8
21, 22, 23	FIRE SUPPRESSION, PLUMBING & HVAC	94.2	42.3	73.2	94.2	42.8	73.4	100.1	42.4	76.7	100.2	42.9	77.0	100.2	41.2	76.3	94.2	42.8	73.4
26, 27, 3370	ELECTRICAL, COMMUNICATIONS & UTIL.	98.7	46.7	71.9	100.3	47.6	73.2	100.1	52.1	75.3	97.0	52.1	73.8	99.2	63.1	80.6	97.9	47.6	72.0
MF2010	WEIGHTED AVERAGE	98.6	51.0	77.6	99.3	51.4	78.2	100.1	53.8	79.7	101.4	54.6	80.7	100.7	57.1	81.5	99.8	51.6	78.5

TENNESSEE

DIVISION		CHATTANOOGA 373 - 374 MAT.	INST.	TOTAL	COLUMBIA 384 MAT.	INST.	TOTAL	COOKEVILLE 385 MAT.	INST.	TOTAL	JACKSON 383 MAT.	INST.	TOTAL	JOHNSON CITY 376 MAT.	INST.	TOTAL	KNOXVILLE 377 - 379 MAT.	INST.	TOTAL
015433	CONTRACTOR EQUIPMENT		103.8	103.8		98.0	98.0		98.0	98.0		104.0	104.0		97.8	97.8		97.8	97.8
0241, 31 - 34	SITE & INFRASTRUCTURE, DEMOLITION	102.1	98.6	99.7	89.3	87.3	87.9	95.5	86.7	89.4	98.8	97.1	97.6	110.0	87.5	94.5	87.2	88.0	87.7
0310	Concrete Forming & Accessories	96.6	57.1	62.3	83.4	61.3	64.1	83.5	37.4	43.4	89.7	47.5	53.0	84.5	40.7	46.4	95.3	43.8	50.5
0320	Concrete Reinforcing	88.5	62.6	75.5	90.9	62.6	76.7	90.9	62.6	76.6	90.9	62.9	76.8	89.1	61.0	75.0	88.5	61.1	74.7
0330	Cast-in-Place Concrete	97.3	62.1	83.4	92.7	53.3	77.2	105.0	45.2	81.5	102.6	51.5	82.4	78.3	62.7	72.1	91.4	50.1	75.1
03	CONCRETE	93.3	61.6	77.9	93.9	60.4	77.6	103.7	47.0	76.1	95.7	53.7	75.3	98.9	54.2	77.1	90.6	51.3	71.4
04	MASONRY	103.9	51.6	72.0	121.4	56.6	81.8	115.6	46.2	73.3	121.6	49.9	77.8	118.8	47.3	75.2	81.4	55.0	65.3
05	METALS	96.2	87.4	93.3	90.6	88.0	89.7	90.7	86.9	89.4	92.9	87.6	91.1	93.5	86.1	91.0	96.8	86.3	93.3
06	WOOD, PLASTICS & COMPOSITES	106.2	58.8	78.8	74.0	62.8	67.6	74.2	35.7	52.0	90.5	48.2	66.0	79.2	39.2	56.1	92.4	39.2	61.7
07	THERMAL & MOISTURE PROTECTION	95.6	59.6	81.0	90.4	61.1	78.5	90.8	48.2	73.5	92.6	51.5	75.8	91.1	55.5	76.6	89.2	59.3	77.0
08	OPENINGS	102.1	57.3	90.8	92.0	57.6	83.4	92.0	44.0	79.9	101.5	53.9	89.5	97.5	46.9	84.8	94.3	47.0	82.4
0920	Plaster & Gypsum Board	76.1	58.0	63.2	82.3	62.1	67.9	82.3	34.2	47.9	83.9	47.0	57.6	98.3	37.8	55.1	105.8	37.8	57.3
0950, 0980	Ceilings & Acoustic Treatment	99.7	58.0	72.2	82.9	62.1	69.2	82.9	34.2	50.7	91.8	47.0	62.2	95.8	37.8	57.5	96.7	37.8	57.8
0960	Flooring	98.1	59.3	86.7	92.8	21.5	71.9	92.9	61.4	83.7	91.7	42.7	77.3	94.7	42.6	79.4	99.5	58.4	87.4
0970, 0990	Wall Finishes & Painting/Coating	104.4	55.7	74.3	94.6	35.2	57.9	94.6	38.4	59.9	96.0	52.3	69.0	101.6	44.4	66.3	101.6	51.2	70.5
09	FINISHES	96.1	57.4	74.5	94.7	51.5	70.6	95.3	40.7	64.8	95.0	46.3	67.8	100.1	40.3	66.8	92.6	46.1	66.7
COVERS	DIVS. 10 - 14, 25, 28, 41, 43, 44, 46	100.0	44.4	88.9	100.0	50.7	90.2	100.0	44.2	88.9	100.0	46.5	89.3	100.0	46.6	89.4	100.0	49.3	89.9
21, 22, 23	FIRE SUPPRESSION, PLUMBING & HVAC	100.2	63.3	85.2	96.9	77.4	89.0	96.9	72.1	86.9	100.0	71.6	88.5	99.9	56.3	82.2	99.9	66.7	86.5
26, 27, 3370	ELECTRICAL, COMMUNICATIONS & UTIL.	102.4	69.3	85.3	95.1	61.0	77.5	96.8	61.9	78.8	102.5	62.1	81.7	92.3	49.2	70.1	97.9	58.1	77.3
MF2010	WEIGHTED AVERAGE	99.0	66.2	84.6	95.7	67.1	83.1	97.0	60.2	80.8	99.2	63.8	83.6	98.7	56.7	80.2	95.4	61.4	80.4

TENNESSEE / TEXAS

DIVISION		MCKENZIE 382 MAT.	INST.	TOTAL	MEMPHIS 375,380 - 381 MAT.	INST.	TOTAL	NASHVILLE 370 - 372 MAT.	INST.	TOTAL	ABILENE 795 - 796 MAT.	INST.	TOTAL	AMARILLO 790 - 791 MAT.	INST.	TOTAL	AUSTIN 786 - 787 MAT.	INST.	TOTAL
015433	CONTRACTOR EQUIPMENT		98.0	98.0		102.2	102.2		104.1	104.1		88.9	88.9		88.9	88.9		88.6	88.6
0241, 31 - 34	SITE & INFRASTRUCTURE, DEMOLITION	95.0	87.0	89.5	90.5	93.3	92.5	96.6	99.5	98.6	95.1	86.0	88.8	95.3	87.1	89.6	97.0	86.8	90.0
0310	Concrete Forming & Accessories	90.8	40.3	46.9	95.4	60.4	64.9	97.0	64.0	68.3	95.1	40.2	47.4	95.6	54.1	59.5	90.2	53.4	58.2
0320	Concrete Reinforcing	91.1	62.9	76.9	97.3	63.5	80.3	92.6	63.0	77.7	93.8	51.8	72.6	93.8	50.0	71.7	88.8	48.8	68.7
0330	Cast-in-Place Concrete	102.8	60.0	85.9	90.8	62.7	79.8	86.1	66.3	78.3	96.1	48.7	77.4	95.3	55.4	79.6	92.4	49.3	75.4
03	CONCRETE	102.3	53.5	78.5	91.9	63.4	78.0	88.9	66.1	77.8	94.8	46.5	71.3	94.4	54.7	75.0	87.5	51.9	70.2
04	MASONRY	119.9	48.8	76.5	96.6	63.7	76.6	86.2	59.2	69.7	103.1	57.5	75.3	103.1	58.3	75.8	99.7	47.6	67.9
05	METALS	90.7	87.9	89.8	97.8	89.5	95.0	97.8	88.7	94.8	99.3	68.9	89.2	99.3	68.6	89.2	95.5	64.8	85.4
06	WOOD, PLASTICS & COMPOSITES	82.6	38.5	57.1	100.8	61.2	78.0	99.9	65.0	79.8	99.6	38.7	64.4	98.1	56.5	74.1	94.3	56.6	72.5
07	THERMAL & MOISTURE PROTECTION	90.8	49.4	74.0	90.2	64.8	79.9	93.9	61.9	80.9	97.4	51.0	78.5	97.4	54.2	79.8	86.7	51.1	72.2
08	OPENINGS	92.0	45.8	80.4	101.4	61.7	91.4	99.6	64.1	90.6	92.6	42.1	79.9	92.6	53.7	82.8	98.2	54.2	87.1
0920	Plaster & Gypsum Board	85.5	37.0	50.9	91.7	60.4	69.3	92.1	64.3	72.3	82.8	37.3	50.3	84.4	55.7	63.9	81.5	55.8	63.1
0950, 0980	Ceilings & Acoustic Treatment	82.9	37.0	52.6	99.8	60.4	73.7	94.7	64.3	74.6	92.0	37.3	55.9	92.0	55.7	68.0	93.7	55.8	68.6
0960	Flooring	96.1	41.2	80.0	94.8	37.8	78.0	99.8	67.3	90.2	110.3	77.2	100.6	110.1	77.2	100.5	95.9	41.4	79.9
0970, 0990	Wall Finishes & Painting/Coating	94.6	52.3	68.5	99.3	55.3	72.2	102.2	68.9	81.7	94.7	51.8	68.2	94.7	51.1	67.8	92.2	42.1	61.3
09	FINISHES	96.5	40.5	65.2	96.3	55.1	73.3	98.3	64.9	79.7	94.9	47.5	68.5	95.2	58.1	74.5	90.4	49.9	67.8
COVERS	DIVS. 10 - 14, 25, 28, 41, 43, 44, 46	100.0	29.5	86.0	100.0	81.1	96.2	100.0	81.8	96.4	100.0	76.2	95.3	100.0	71.3	94.3	100.0	78.0	95.6
21, 22, 23	FIRE SUPPRESSION, PLUMBING & HVAC	96.9	71.8	86.8	100.0	70.2	87.9	100.0	77.3	90.8	100.3	45.2	78.0	100.2	51.2	80.3	100.1	55.3	82.0
26, 27, 3370	ELECTRICAL, COMMUNICATIONS & UTIL.	96.5	66.8	81.2	103.7	65.9	84.2	95.6	61.9	78.2	97.3	50.5	73.1	99.5	67.1	82.8	96.4	64.5	79.9
MF2010	WEIGHTED AVERAGE	97.1	61.8	81.6	98.2	69.6	85.6	96.8	72.2	86.0	97.9	54.2	78.6	98.1	61.0	81.7	96.1	58.8	79.6

City Cost Indexes

TEXAS

DIVISION		BEAUMONT 776 - 777			BROWNWOOD 768			BRYAN 778			CHILDRESS 792			CORPUS CHRISTI 783 - 784			DALLAS 752 - 753		
		MAT.	INST.	TOTAL	MAT.	INST.	TOTAL	MAT.	INST.	TOTAL	MAT.	INST.	TOTAL	MAT.	INST.	TOTAL	MAT.	INST.	TOTAL
015433	CONTRACTOR EQUIPMENT		89.8	89.8		88.9	88.9		89.8	89.8		88.9	88.9		95.7	95.7		98.0	98.0
0241, 31 - 34	SITE & INFRASTRUCTURE, DEMOLITION	86.6	86.3	86.4	101.1	85.5	90.3	78.2	87.9	84.9	106.1	85.9	92.1	137.0	82.6	99.5	109.8	87.3	94.2
0310	Concrete Forming & Accessories	101.5	50.1	56.8	93.6	34.1	41.8	81.2	41.6	46.8	93.7	61.5	65.7	96.4	38.1	45.7	93.9	64.3	68.1
0320	Concrete Reinforcing	91.2	42.7	66.7	94.1	49.1	71.4	93.7	48.9	71.1	93.9	49.3	71.4	88.2	47.3	67.6	101.0	52.3	76.5
0330	Cast-in-Place Concrete	86.3	53.1	73.2	103.7	43.8	80.1	69.1	66.0	67.9	98.6	50.1	79.5	102.5	46.2	80.3	96.5	56.2	80.6
03	CONCRETE	93.0	50.7	72.4	102.2	41.5	72.6	78.1	52.6	65.7	103.2	55.9	80.2	95.3	44.5	70.5	97.3	60.6	79.4
04	MASONRY	104.5	58.5	76.5	132.2	50.2	82.2	143.7	57.2	90.9	107.8	51.5	73.4	88.8	49.3	64.7	102.6	58.4	75.6
05	METALS	97.0	65.3	86.5	96.9	62.5	85.6	96.5	68.2	87.1	96.7	64.4	86.0	95.1	75.2	88.5	100.4	79.9	93.6
06	WOOD, PLASTICS & COMPOSITES	111.8	50.2	76.2	98.3	30.2	59.0	78.2	34.9	53.2	99.0	66.6	80.3	113.9	37.3	69.7	98.2	67.2	80.3
07	THERMAL & MOISTURE PROTECTION	103.6	56.8	84.6	97.5	45.7	76.4	96.1	56.9	80.1	98.0	50.3	78.6	95.4	46.1	75.4	92.6	64.0	81.0
08	OPENINGS	95.9	46.8	83.5	88.6	37.5	75.7	97.6	43.0	83.9	89.6	55.9	81.1	105.0	38.6	88.3	100.7	58.4	90.1
0920	Plaster & Gypsum Board	95.1	49.3	62.4	81.7	28.6	43.8	83.6	33.4	47.8	81.7	66.1	70.5	86.3	35.8	50.2	88.7	66.6	72.9
0950, 0980	Ceilings & Acoustic Treatment	99.7	49.3	66.4	88.4	28.6	48.9	93.0	33.4	53.7	88.4	66.1	73.6	93.7	35.8	55.4	94.6	66.6	76.1
0960	Flooring	109.1	74.6	99.0	109.2	46.8	90.9	82.1	55.2	74.2	108.2	42.8	89.0	109.0	66.0	96.4	99.3	50.0	84.8
0970, 0990	Wall Finishes & Painting/Coating	91.8	50.2	66.1	94.7	30.2	54.9	89.0	62.4	72.6	94.7	39.9	60.9	104.7	59.6	76.8	103.0	53.2	72.3
09	FINISHES	91.2	54.3	70.6	94.3	35.2	61.3	79.8	44.5	60.1	94.8	56.8	73.6	98.7	44.9	68.7	97.7	60.8	77.1
COVERS	DIVS. 10 - 14, 25, 28, 41, 43, 44, 46	100.0	79.6	95.9	100.0	39.2	87.9	100.0	78.8	95.8	100.0	73.4	94.7	100.0	77.0	95.4	100.0	82.1	96.4
21, 22, 23	FIRE SUPPRESSION, PLUMBING & HVAC	100.1	59.3	83.6	94.3	48.4	75.7	94.1	66.4	82.9	94.3	52.7	77.5	100.1	40.1	75.8	100.0	63.7	85.3
26, 27, 3370	ELECTRICAL, COMMUNICATIONS & UTIL.	94.8	72.6	83.4	93.3	45.4	68.6	92.9	67.4	79.8	97.3	45.1	70.3	92.7	54.7	73.1	95.5	67.6	81.1
MF2010	WEIGHTED AVERAGE	97.2	62.0	81.7	97.7	49.0	76.2	94.3	61.7	79.9	97.3	57.2	79.6	98.9	52.3	78.4	99.4	66.8	85.0

TEXAS

DIVISION		DEL RIO 788			DENTON 762			EASTLAND 764			EL PASO 798 - 799,885			FORT WORTH 760 - 761			GALVESTON 775		
		MAT.	INST.	TOTAL	MAT.	INST.	TOTAL	MAT.	INST.	TOTAL	MAT.	INST.	TOTAL	MAT.	INST.	TOTAL	MAT.	INST.	TOTAL
015433	CONTRACTOR EQUIPMENT		88.6	88.6		94.7	94.7		88.9	88.9		88.9	88.9		88.9	88.9		98.5	98.5
0241, 31 - 34	SITE & INFRASTRUCTURE, DEMOLITION	117.8	85.1	95.2	101.7	78.7	85.9	104.0	85.4	91.2	92.4	85.4	87.6	97.1	86.4	89.7	107.8	85.7	92.6
0310	Concrete Forming & Accessories	91.2	37.7	44.7	99.0	33.5	42.0	94.2	37.1	44.5	94.4	45.0	51.4	91.3	63.7	67.3	89.8	61.9	65.5
0320	Concrete Reinforcing	88.8	44.3	66.4	95.5	50.3	72.7	94.3	49.0	71.5	93.8	47.2	70.3	93.8	52.2	72.8	93.1	64.0	78.4
0330	Cast-in-Place Concrete	110.4	43.7	84.1	80.2	42.9	66.6	109.6	44.5	83.9	89.8	41.8	70.9	99.0	52.1	80.5	91.7	67.1	82.0
03	CONCRETE	112.3	42.1	78.1	80.7	42.9	62.3	106.9	43.0	75.8	91.6	45.3	69.0	96.0	58.2	77.6	94.4	65.6	80.4
04	MASONRY	103.6	51.9	72.0	140.8	48.6	84.6	101.6	50.1	70.2	100.8	47.9	68.5	97.3	58.3	73.5	99.9	57.2	73.9
05	METALS	94.0	59.6	82.6	96.5	75.6	89.6	96.7	62.9	85.6	99.0	63.4	87.3	96.3	68.7	87.2	98.0	87.1	94.4
06	WOOD, PLASTICS & COMPOSITES	93.7	35.9	60.3	107.9	33.1	64.7	105.3	34.0	64.1	99.2	47.5	69.3	100.9	67.1	81.4	95.3	61.8	76.0
07	THERMAL & MOISTURE PROTECTION	92.3	45.2	73.2	96.0	45.6	75.5	97.9	44.9	76.3	93.6	53.8	77.4	98.3	54.2	80.3	95.3	65.2	83.1
08	OPENINGS	99.0	34.2	82.6	102.7	38.2	86.4	76.9	39.5	67.5	92.6	43.6	80.3	86.7	58.3	79.5	102.3	61.6	92.0
0920	Plaster & Gypsum Board	80.9	34.4	47.7	85.3	31.4	46.8	81.7	32.4	46.5	87.4	46.4	58.1	85.4	66.6	72.0	89.9	61.1	69.3
0950, 0980	Ceilings & Acoustic Treatment	89.2	34.4	53.0	92.9	31.4	52.3	88.4	32.4	51.4	92.0	46.4	61.9	93.8	66.6	75.8	95.7	61.1	72.8
0960	Flooring	92.8	35.7	76.0	101.7	44.8	85.0	143.0	46.8	114.7	110.3	65.3	97.1	144.3	42.6	114.5	95.7	55.2	83.8
0970, 0990	Wall Finishes & Painting/Coating	92.2	26.5	51.7	104.7	30.5	59.0	96.2	31.5	56.3	94.7	36.0	58.5	96.2	52.7	69.3	99.2	48.5	67.9
09	FINISHES	90.6	35.8	60.0	90.7	34.6	59.4	104.7	37.5	67.2	95.1	47.9	68.8	106.0	59.2	79.9	89.3	58.8	72.3
COVERS	DIVS. 10 - 14, 25, 28, 41, 43, 44, 46	100.0	39.0	87.9	100.0	37.8	87.6	100.0	40.3	88.1	100.0	77.9	95.6	100.0	81.8	96.4	100.0	83.6	96.7
21, 22, 23	FIRE SUPPRESSION, PLUMBING & HVAC	94.1	46.3	74.7	94.3	39.8	72.2	94.3	48.7	75.8	100.2	35.4	73.9	100.2	59.1	83.5	94.1	65.9	82.7
26, 27, 3370	ELECTRICAL, COMMUNICATIONS & UTIL.	94.1	31.2	61.7	95.8	45.5	69.9	93.2	45.4	68.5	93.9	53.3	72.9	93.4	62.4	77.4	94.5	67.3	80.4
MF2010	WEIGHTED AVERAGE	98.0	46.5	75.3	97.1	47.8	75.4	96.5	49.7	75.9	96.8	51.2	76.7	97.2	63.2	82.2	96.5	68.2	84.0

TEXAS

DIVISION		GIDDINGS 789			GREENVILLE 754			HOUSTON 770 - 772			HUNTSVILLE 773			LAREDO 780			LONGVIEW 756		
		MAT.	INST.	TOTAL	MAT.	INST.	TOTAL	MAT.	INST.	TOTAL	MAT.	INST.	TOTAL	MAT.	INST.	TOTAL	MAT.	INST.	TOTAL
015433	CONTRACTOR EQUIPMENT		88.6	88.6		95.6	95.6		98.4	98.4		89.8	89.8		88.6	88.6		90.5	90.5
0241, 31 - 34	SITE & INFRASTRUCTURE, DEMOLITION	103.3	85.4	90.9	102.5	82.2	88.5	106.0	85.5	91.9	94.1	86.0	88.5	96.9	86.6	89.8	97.8	89.3	91.9
0310	Concrete Forming & Accessories	89.4	57.6	61.7	86.6	28.2	35.8	91.7	62.0	65.9	87.7	57.1	61.1	91.2	38.3	45.2	83.7	29.0	36.2
0320	Concrete Reinforcing	89.4	46.2	67.6	101.6	25.6	63.3	92.9	64.5	78.6	94.0	48.3	70.9	88.8	47.2	67.9	100.4	23.4	61.6
0330	Cast-in-Place Concrete	93.5	44.1	74.1	87.9	38.2	68.3	88.9	67.1	80.3	95.0	48.5	76.7	78.9	59.2	71.2	102.2	35.8	76.0
03	CONCRETE	91.2	51.4	71.8	90.1	33.2	62.4	92.1	65.8	79.3	100.4	53.3	77.4	85.8	48.3	67.5	105.5	31.7	69.5
04	MASONRY	111.6	52.0	75.2	160.5	47.4	91.5	99.7	67.2	79.9	142.0	43.8	82.1	97.3	47.4	66.9	156.1	43.7	87.5
05	METALS	93.4	61.9	83.0	97.7	63.6	86.4	101.0	88.0	96.7	96.4	63.8	85.6	96.5	63.8	85.7	91.2	51.2	78.0
06	WOOD, PLASTICS & COMPOSITES	92.7	61.8	74.8	89.6	27.3	53.6	97.5	61.8	76.9	86.1	60.4	71.2	93.7	37.2	61.1	83.9	29.5	52.5
07	THERMAL & MOISTURE PROTECTION	92.9	49.4	75.2	92.7	40.8	71.6	94.9	67.5	83.8	97.0	47.4	76.9	91.3	49.4	74.3	93.9	36.2	70.5
08	OPENINGS	98.2	50.2	86.1	99.5	26.9	81.2	104.5	61.6	93.7	97.6	49.3	85.5	98.8	39.2	83.8	90.5	26.9	74.5
0920	Plaster & Gypsum Board	79.5	61.1	66.4	82.8	25.5	41.8	92.8	61.1	70.2	87.2	59.7	67.6	82.2	35.8	49.1	80.6	27.9	42.9
0950, 0980	Ceilings & Acoustic Treatment	89.2	61.1	70.6	90.1	25.5	47.4	101.1	61.1	74.7	93.0	59.7	71.0	93.7	35.8	55.4	87.3	27.9	48.1
0960	Flooring	92.8	35.7	76.0	95.0	49.1	81.5	97.0	55.2	84.7	85.6	35.7	70.9	92.7	66.0	84.9	100.6	36.1	81.6
0970, 0990	Wall Finishes & Painting/Coating	92.2	31.5	54.8	103.0	25.9	55.5	99.2	62.4	76.5	89.0	32.3	54.0	92.2	56.1	69.9	94.6	30.3	54.9
09	FINISHES	89.2	52.0	68.4	94.1	31.4	59.2	97.1	60.4	76.6	82.3	51.7	65.2	89.9	44.4	64.5	99.7	30.4	61.0
COVERS	DIVS. 10 - 14, 25, 28, 41, 43, 44, 46	100.0	45.2	89.1	100.0	36.1	87.3	100.0	83.6	96.7	100.0	45.4	89.1	100.0	74.9	95.0	100.0	22.9	84.7
21, 22, 23	FIRE SUPPRESSION, PLUMBING & HVAC	94.1	60.1	80.3	94.1	45.7	74.5	100.0	66.6	86.5	94.1	61.0	80.7	100.0	38.8	75.2	94.1	28.9	67.6
26, 27, 3370	ELECTRICAL, COMMUNICATIONS & UTIL.	91.1	45.1	67.3	92.2	28.1	59.1	96.5	67.5	81.5	92.9	45.1	68.2	94.3	62.2	77.7	92.4	45.6	68.3
MF2010	WEIGHTED AVERAGE	95.1	56.2	77.9	98.6	43.3	74.2	99.1	69.8	86.2	97.5	55.9	79.2	95.8	52.7	76.8	98.6	40.4	72.9

TEXAS

DIVISION		LUBBOCK 793-794 MAT.	INST.	TOTAL	LUFKIN 759 MAT.	INST.	TOTAL	MCALLEN 785 MAT.	INST.	TOTAL	MCKINNEY 750 MAT.	INST.	TOTAL	MIDLAND 797 MAT.	INST.	TOTAL	ODESSA 797 MAT.	INST.	TOTAL
015433	CONTRACTOR EQUIPMENT		97.2	97.2		90.5	90.5		95.7	95.7		95.6	95.6		97.2	97.2		88.9	88.9
0241, 31 - 34	SITE & INFRASTRUCTURE, DEMOLITION	120.9	84.3	95.7	92.5	90.3	91.0	142.0	82.5	101.0	98.5	82.8	87.6	124.3	84.3	96.7	95.2	86.3	89.1
0310	Concrete Forming & Accessories	93.2	52.6	57.9	86.6	58.7	62.3	95.8	35.7	43.5	85.7	37.6	43.9	96.6	39.6	47.0	95.0	39.5	46.7
0320	Concrete Reinforcing	95.0	51.8	73.2	102.1	60.8	81.3	88.3	47.2	67.6	101.6	50.3	75.7	96.1	51.1	73.4	93.8	51.0	72.2
0330	Cast-in-Place Concrete	96.3	49.0	77.6	91.4	45.2	73.2	111.4	44.5	85.1	82.4	46.4	68.2	102.3	46.3	80.3	96.1	45.3	76.1
03	CONCRETE	93.6	52.9	73.7	97.9	55.0	77.0	101.2	42.9	72.8	85.6	44.9	65.8	98.1	46.1	72.8	94.8	44.9	70.5
04	MASONRY	102.4	55.9	74.0	119.7	43.8	73.4	103.4	49.3	70.4	172.7	49.9	97.8	120.6	43.6	73.7	103.1	43.6	66.8
05	METALS	102.6	80.4	95.3	97.8	67.5	87.8	93.9	74.8	87.6	97.6	74.6	90.0	100.8	79.2	93.7	98.6	67.4	88.3
06	WOOD, PLASTICS & COMPOSITES	98.7	56.7	74.4	92.0	61.7	74.5	112.6	34.8	67.7	88.3	37.7	59.1	103.0	39.3	66.2	99.6	39.1	64.7
07	THERMAL & MOISTURE PROTECTION	88.0	53.3	73.9	93.7	47.1	74.8	95.4	44.9	74.9	92.6	47.5	74.2	88.2	44.9	70.6	97.4	44.0	75.7
08	OPENINGS	102.2	50.7	89.2	73.0	54.6	68.4	103.3	37.7	86.8	99.5	40.6	84.7	101.1	40.9	85.9	92.6	40.8	79.6
0920	Plaster & Gypsum Board	83.3	55.7	63.6	79.8	61.1	66.5	86.3	33.2	48.4	81.4	36.3	49.2	84.8	37.7	51.2	82.8	37.7	50.6
0950, 0980	Ceilings & Acoustic Treatment	93.8	55.7	68.6	80.1	61.1	67.5	93.7	33.2	53.7	90.1	36.3	54.5	91.1	37.7	55.9	92.0	37.7	56.2
0960	Flooring	102.8	40.5	84.5	135.1	39.2	107.0	108.5	66.0	96.0	94.6	36.6	77.6	104.3	50.0	88.3	110.3	50.0	92.6
0970, 0990	Wall Finishes & Painting/Coating	105.2	51.1	71.8	94.6	39.0	60.3	104.7	29.8	58.5	103.0	42.5	65.7	105.2	51.1	71.8	94.7	51.1	67.8
09	FINISHES	97.7	50.3	71.2	107.8	53.8	77.7	99.1	40.1	66.2	93.5	37.9	62.5	98.1	42.0	66.8	94.9	41.9	65.3
COVERS	DIVS. 10 - 14, 25, 28, 41, 43, 44, 46	100.0	77.9	95.6	100.0	74.6	94.9	100.0	74.8	95.0	100.0	41.7	88.4	100.0	77.6	95.5	100.0	77.3	95.5
21, 22, 23	FIRE SUPPRESSION, PLUMBING & HVAC	99.9	44.3	77.3	94.1	61.0	80.7	94.1	30.4	68.3	94.1	43.4	73.6	93.9	44.5	73.9	100.3	44.4	77.6
26, 27, 3370	ELECTRICAL, COMMUNICATIONS & UTIL.	95.9	51.5	73.0	93.7	45.1	68.6	91.9	35.5	62.8	92.3	46.9	68.9	95.9	41.9	68.0	97.4	41.8	68.8
MF2010	WEIGHTED AVERAGE	99.6	56.8	80.7	95.8	58.3	79.3	98.6	46.6	75.7	98.5	50.2	77.2	99.4	51.4	78.2	97.8	50.2	76.8

TEXAS

DIVISION		PALESTINE 758 MAT.	INST.	TOTAL	SAN ANGELO 769 MAT.	INST.	TOTAL	SAN ANTONIO 781-782 MAT.	INST.	TOTAL	TEMPLE 765 MAT.	INST.	TOTAL	TEXARKANA 755 MAT.	INST.	TOTAL	TYLER 757 MAT.	INST.	TOTAL
015433	CONTRACTOR EQUIPMENT		90.5	90.5		88.9	88.9		91.0	91.0		88.9	88.9		90.5	90.5		90.5	90.5
0241, 31 - 34	SITE & INFRASTRUCTURE, DEMOLITION	99.6	90.1	93.1	97.3	86.8	90.1	96.6	91.3	92.9	85.6	85.2	85.3	86.6	90.1	89.0	97.2	90.1	92.3
0310	Concrete Forming & Accessories	79.0	57.8	60.6	93.9	37.4	44.7	91.2	56.8	61.3	96.8	35.2	43.2	92.5	35.2	42.6	88.0	34.1	41.1
0320	Concrete Reinforcing	99.6	49.1	74.2	94.0	51.0	72.3	95.1	48.1	71.4	94.1	48.8	71.3	99.5	52.0	75.6	100.4	52.2	76.1
0330	Cast-in-Place Concrete	83.5	43.8	67.9	97.8	43.5	76.4	77.4	67.5	73.5	80.2	48.9	67.8	84.2	44.6	68.6	100.4	43.5	78.0
03	CONCRETE	99.0	51.9	76.1	97.6	43.2	71.1	86.0	59.7	73.2	83.4	43.7	64.1	90.9	42.9	67.5	105.0	42.1	74.3
04	MASONRY	115.0	50.4	75.6	128.8	43.0	76.4	97.2	59.3	74.1	140.2	48.8	84.4	177.1	46.4	97.3	166.5	49.3	94.9
05	METALS	97.5	62.4	86.0	97.1	64.6	86.4	97.2	68.3	87.7	96.8	63.5	85.8	91.1	67.2	83.2	97.4	67.7	87.6
06	WOOD, PLASTICS & COMPOSITES	83.1	61.7	70.8	98.5	37.4	63.2	93.7	54.9	71.3	107.6	34.0	65.1	94.2	33.5	59.1	93.5	31.6	57.7
07	THERMAL & MOISTURE PROTECTION	94.2	48.2	75.5	97.3	43.7	75.5	91.0	63.9	80.0	96.9	45.3	75.9	93.5	48.8	75.4	94.0	53.2	77.4
08	OPENINGS	72.9	51.6	67.6	88.6	39.8	76.3	100.7	53.0	88.7	74.8	36.2	65.1	90.5	38.7	77.4	72.9	37.7	64.0
0920	Plaster & Gypsum Board	75.3	61.1	65.2	81.7	36.0	49.1	82.2	53.9	62.0	81.7	32.4	46.5	84.7	32.0	47.1	79.8	30.0	44.3
0950, 0980	Ceilings & Acoustic Treatment	80.1	61.1	67.5	88.4	36.0	53.8	93.7	53.9	67.4	88.4	32.4	51.4	87.3	32.0	50.8	80.1	30.0	47.0
0960	Flooring	126.5	60.6	107.1	109.3	35.7	87.7	92.7	66.2	84.9	145.6	42.9	115.5	108.5	61.0	94.6	137.0	38.1	108.0
0970, 0990	Wall Finishes & Painting/Coating	94.6	31.5	55.7	94.7	51.1	67.8	92.2	56.1	69.9	96.2	34.7	58.3	94.6	40.6	61.3	94.6	40.6	61.3
09	FINISHES	105.5	56.4	78.1	94.0	37.7	62.6	89.9	57.4	71.8	104.0	36.0	66.1	101.8	39.5	67.0	108.7	33.8	66.9
COVERS	DIVS. 10 - 14, 25, 28, 41, 43, 44, 46	100.0	42.8	88.6	100.0	74.8	95.0	100.0	81.0	96.2	100.0	37.3	87.5	100.0	74.9	95.0	100.0	74.6	94.9
21, 22, 23	FIRE SUPPRESSION, PLUMBING & HVAC	94.1	57.7	79.3	94.3	43.7	73.8	99.9	66.1	86.2	94.3	34.9	70.3	94.1	34.4	69.9	94.1	59.2	79.9
26, 27, 3370	ELECTRICAL, COMMUNICATIONS & UTIL.	89.9	45.1	66.8	97.3	47.5	71.6	94.7	62.3	78.0	94.4	67.4	80.5	93.6	63.5	78.1	92.4	54.0	72.6
MF2010	WEIGHTED AVERAGE	95.2	56.6	78.2	97.3	49.6	76.3	96.2	65.0	82.4	95.1	49.4	75.0	98.0	51.0	77.2	99.0	54.4	79.4

TEXAS / UTAH

DIVISION		VICTORIA 779 MAT.	INST.	TOTAL	WACO 766-767 MAT.	INST.	TOTAL	WAXAHACHIE 751 MAT.	INST.	TOTAL	WHARTON 774 MAT.	INST.	TOTAL	WICHITA FALLS 763 MAT.	INST.	TOTAL	LOGAN 843 MAT.	INST.	TOTAL
015433	CONTRACTOR EQUIPMENT		97.4	97.4		88.9	88.9		95.6	95.6		98.5	98.5		88.9	88.9		98.6	98.6
0241, 31 - 34	SITE & INFRASTRUCTURE, DEMOLITION	112.8	81.1	90.9	94.0	86.4	88.7	100.6	83.3	88.7	118.9	83.9	94.8	94.7	86.0	88.7	90.7	98.4	96.0
0310	Concrete Forming & Accessories	90.1	36.4	43.4	95.5	40.5	47.7	85.7	59.2	62.6	85.1	37.9	44.0	95.4	38.4	45.8	105.4	60.2	66.1
0320	Concrete Reinforcing	89.4	31.2	60.1	93.8	48.8	71.1	101.6	50.4	75.8	93.0	53.1	72.9	93.8	51.0	72.2	100.2	75.9	87.9
0330	Cast-in-Place Concrete	103.0	42.0	79.0	86.7	53.2	73.5	87.0	42.4	69.4	105.8	52.1	84.7	92.7	45.8	74.2	86.0	72.1	80.5
03	CONCRETE	101.7	39.6	71.4	90.1	47.7	69.4	89.2	53.1	71.7	105.7	47.7	77.4	93.1	44.6	69.5	105.3	67.8	87.0
04	MASONRY	116.7	35.4	67.1	99.9	55.8	73.0	161.1	50.0	93.3	101.0	46.2	67.5	100.3	57.5	74.2	106.8	62.0	79.4
05	METALS	96.6	70.9	88.1	99.2	66.7	88.5	97.7	76.6	90.7	98.0	78.0	91.4	99.1	68.9	89.1	99.9	76.8	92.3
06	WOOD, PLASTICS & COMPOSITES	99.2	37.2	63.4	106.1	36.4	65.8	88.3	66.5	75.8	89.5	33.8	57.3	106.1	36.3	65.8	79.9	58.4	67.5
07	THERMAL & MOISTURE PROTECTION	98.9	40.9	75.3	97.9	48.7	77.9	92.7	47.5	74.3	95.6	50.7	77.4	97.9	52.0	79.2	99.6	63.7	85.0
08	OPENINGS	102.1	36.4	85.6	86.7	37.5	74.3	99.5	56.3	88.7	102.3	38.3	86.2	86.7	41.3	75.3	91.7	57.6	83.1
0920	Plaster & Gypsum Board	87.8	35.7	50.6	82.8	34.9	48.6	82.0	66.1	70.6	85.8	32.1	47.5	82.8	34.8	48.5	81.4	57.0	64.0
0950, 0980	Ceilings & Acoustic Treatment	96.6	35.7	56.4	92.0	34.9	54.3	91.9	66.1	74.8	95.7	32.1	53.7	92.0	34.8	54.2	109.7	57.0	74.9
0960	Flooring	95.1	39.2	78.7	144.3	46.4	115.6	94.6	39.2	78.3	93.2	46.8	79.6	145.2	77.2	125.3	100.7	50.0	85.8
0970, 0990	Wall Finishes & Painting/Coating	99.4	39.0	62.1	96.2	34.7	58.3	103.0	39.0	63.5	99.2	32.3	57.9	98.7	51.1	69.3	98.8	62.0	76.1
09	FINISHES	87.5	37.3	59.5	105.1	39.8	68.7	94.2	54.7	72.2	89.0	38.0	60.5	105.5	46.0	72.3	100.6	57.8	76.8
COVERS	DIVS. 10 - 14, 25, 28, 41, 43, 44, 46	100.0	38.4	87.7	100.0	78.3	95.7	100.0	42.2	88.5	100.0	40.6	88.2	100.0	68.7	93.8	100.0	57.0	91.5
21, 22, 23	FIRE SUPPRESSION, PLUMBING & HVAC	94.1	32.8	69.3	100.3	51.3	80.4	94.1	42.5	73.2	94.1	61.0	80.7	100.3	46.6	78.5	100.0	71.3	88.4
26, 27, 3370	ELECTRICAL, COMMUNICATIONS & UTIL.	99.4	41.2	69.4	97.5	67.6	82.0	92.3	67.6	79.5	98.1	45.5	71.0	99.2	57.9	77.9	94.5	73.7	83.8
MF2010	WEIGHTED AVERAGE	98.6	44.0	74.5	97.4	56.4	79.4	98.5	57.3	80.3	98.5	54.0	78.9	98.0	54.8	79.0	99.2	70.0	86.3

City Cost Indexes

UTAH / VERMONT

DIVISION		OGDEN 842,844 MAT.	INST.	TOTAL	PRICE 845 MAT.	INST.	TOTAL	PROVO 846-847 MAT.	INST.	TOTAL	SALT LAKE CITY 840-841 MAT.	INST.	TOTAL	BELLOWS FALLS 051 MAT.	INST.	TOTAL	BENNINGTON 052 MAT.	INST.	TOTAL
015433	CONTRACTOR EQUIPMENT		98.6	98.6		97.6	97.6		97.6	97.6		98.6	98.6		100.4	100.4		100.4	100.4
0241, 31 - 34	SITE & INFRASTRUCTURE, DEMOLITION	78.7	98.4	92.3	88.4	96.7	94.1	87.1	96.7	93.7	78.3	98.3	92.1	81.9	97.8	92.8	81.3	97.5	92.5
0310	Concrete Forming & Accessories	105.5	60.2	66.1	107.4	51.0	58.4	106.6	60.1	66.1	107.9	60.1	66.3	99.3	48.8	55.4	97.2	53.0	58.8
0320	Concrete Reinforcing	99.9	75.9	87.8	107.5	75.7	91.5	108.4	75.8	92.0	102.1	75.8	88.9	82.9	63.7	73.2	82.9	63.6	73.2
0330	Cast-in-Place Concrete	87.3	72.1	81.3	86.0	61.7	76.4	86.0	72.0	80.5	95.4	72.0	86.2	96.9	71.2	86.8	96.9	67.9	85.5
03	CONCRETE	95.8	67.8	82.2	106.6	60.1	84.0	105.2	67.7	86.9	114.2	67.7	91.5	100.9	60.0	81.0	100.7	60.7	81.2
04	MASONRY	100.3	62.0	76.9	112.2	62.0	81.6	112.3	62.0	81.6	114.0	62.0	82.3	93.6	60.6	73.5	102.3	60.5	76.8
05	METALS	100.4	76.8	92.6	97.1	76.1	90.2	98.1	76.7	91.1	105.0	76.7	95.6	92.5	69.6	85.0	92.5	68.7	84.7
06	WOOD, PLASTICS & COMPOSITES	79.9	58.4	67.5	82.5	47.1	62.1	81.2	58.4	68.0	81.5	58.4	68.2	99.5	38.4	64.2	96.7	44.9	66.8
07	THERMAL & MOISTURE PROTECTION	98.5	63.7	84.4	101.4	59.4	84.4	101.4	63.7	86.1	105.1	63.7	88.3	100.7	59.6	84.0	100.7	54.7	82.0
08	OPENINGS	91.7	57.6	83.1	96.2	50.3	84.6	96.2	57.6	86.5	93.7	57.6	84.6	99.2	41.1	84.5	99.2	43.4	85.1
0920	Plaster & Gypsum Board	81.4	57.0	64.0	83.7	45.3	56.3	81.9	57.0	64.1	84.4	57.0	64.8	96.5	35.8	53.1	94.2	42.5	57.3
0950, 0980	Ceilings & Acoustic Treatment	109.7	57.0	74.9	109.7	45.3	67.2	109.7	57.0	74.9	103.6	57.0	72.8	92.7	35.8	55.1	92.7	42.5	59.5
0960	Flooring	98.5	50.0	84.2	101.8	37.1	82.8	101.4	50.0	86.3	102.1	50.0	86.8	94.5	31.9	76.1	93.4	31.9	75.3
0970, 0990	Wall Finishes & Painting/Coating	98.8	62.0	76.1	98.8	39.6	62.3	98.8	50.6	69.1	101.9	50.6	70.2	90.1	28.1	51.9	90.1	28.1	51.9
09	FINISHES	98.9	57.8	75.9	101.8	46.1	70.7	101.3	56.6	76.4	99.4	56.6	75.5	95.6	42.0	65.7	95.0	45.9	67.6
COVERS	DIVS. 10 - 14, 25, 28, 41, 43, 44, 46	100.0	57.0	91.5	100.0	49.5	90.0	100.0	57.0	91.4	100.0	57.0	91.4	100.0	45.9	89.2	100.0	46.5	89.4
21, 22, 23	FIRE SUPPRESSION, PLUMBING & HVAC	100.0	71.3	88.4	97.0	68.8	85.6	100.0	71.3	88.4	100.1	71.3	88.4	94.1	95.7	94.7	94.1	89.5	92.2
26, 27, 3370	ELECTRICAL, COMMUNICATIONS & UTIL.	94.8	73.7	83.9	100.0	73.7	86.4	95.4	63.5	78.9	97.8	63.5	80.1	102.0	94.8	98.3	102.0	64.9	82.8
MF2010	WEIGHTED AVERAGE	97.3	70.0	85.3	99.5	65.9	84.7	99.7	68.3	85.8	101.6	68.4	86.9	96.5	72.7	86.0	96.8	67.8	84.0

VERMONT

DIVISION		BRATTLEBORO 053 MAT.	INST.	TOTAL	BURLINGTON 054 MAT.	INST.	TOTAL	GUILDHALL 059 MAT.	INST.	TOTAL	MONTPELIER 056 MAT.	INST.	TOTAL	RUTLAND 057 MAT.	INST.	TOTAL	ST. JOHNSBURY 058 MAT.	INST.	TOTAL
015433	CONTRACTOR EQUIPMENT		100.4	100.4		100.4	100.4		100.4	100.4		100.4	100.4		100.4	100.4		100.4	100.4
0241, 31 - 34	SITE & INFRASTRUCTURE, DEMOLITION	82.9	97.8	93.1	83.8	96.5	92.5	80.9	95.8	91.1	84.8	96.5	92.9	84.8	96.5	92.8	80.9	96.0	91.3
0310	Concrete Forming & Accessories	99.6	48.7	55.3	96.8	51.3	57.3	97.6	43.8	50.8	101.5	51.4	57.9	99.8	51.4	57.7	96.5	43.9	50.7
0320	Concrete Reinforcing	82.0	63.7	72.8	103.6	82.7	93.1	83.6	37.7	60.4	82.5	82.7	82.6	103.6	82.7	93.1	82.0	42.9	62.3
0330	Cast-in-Place Concrete	100.0	68.3	87.5	105.7	98.9	103.0	94.0	54.9	78.6	111.9	98.9	106.8	95.0	98.9	96.5	94.0	55.2	78.7
03	CONCRETE	103.3	59.0	81.7	109.4	74.2	92.2	98.3	47.4	73.5	109.5	74.2	92.3	104.1	74.2	89.6	98.0	48.4	73.8
04	MASONRY	101.3	60.6	76.4	104.9	49.1	70.8	101.5	39.0	63.4	89.6	49.1	64.9	85.0	49.1	63.1	126.1	39.1	73.0
05	METALS	92.5	69.5	84.9	99.7	78.9	92.8	92.5	58.5	81.3	92.5	78.9	88.0	98.0	78.9	91.7	92.5	59.0	81.5
06	WOOD, PLASTICS & COMPOSITES	99.8	38.4	64.3	94.7	50.7	69.3	96.2	44.9	66.6	98.8	50.7	71.0	99.9	50.7	71.5	92.3	44.9	64.9
07	THERMAL & MOISTURE PROTECTION	100.8	53.6	81.6	100.7	59.7	84.0	100.6	41.4	76.5	100.1	60.1	83.9	100.9	60.1	84.3	100.5	41.4	76.5
08	OPENINGS	99.2	41.1	84.5	102.4	52.5	89.9	99.2	38.2	83.8	99.2	52.5	87.4	102.4	52.5	89.9	99.2	38.2	83.8
0920	Plaster & Gypsum Board	96.5	35.8	53.1	98.1	48.5	62.7	102.4	42.5	59.6	105.6	48.5	64.8	97.3	48.5	62.5	105.2	42.5	60.4
0950, 0980	Ceilings & Acoustic Treatment	92.7	35.8	55.1	94.8	48.5	64.2	92.7	42.5	59.5	91.8	48.5	63.2	97.5	48.5	65.1	92.7	42.5	59.5
0960	Flooring	94.6	31.9	76.2	94.7	57.7	83.8	97.7	31.9	78.4	101.3	57.7	88.5	94.5	57.7	83.7	101.3	31.9	80.9
0970, 0990	Wall Finishes & Painting/Coating	90.1	28.1	51.9	90.1	32.7	54.7	90.1	21.8	48.0	90.1	32.7	54.7	90.1	32.7	54.7	90.1	22.9	48.7
09	FINISHES	95.7	42.0	65.8	96.4	49.3	70.1	97.1	39.4	64.9	98.5	49.3	71.1	96.8	49.3	70.3	98.5	39.6	65.6
COVERS	DIVS. 10 - 14, 25, 28, 41, 43, 44, 46	100.0	45.9	89.2	100.0	70.6	94.1	100.0	38.6	87.8	100.0	70.6	94.1	100.0	70.6	94.1	100.0	38.6	87.8
21, 22, 23	FIRE SUPPRESSION, PLUMBING & HVAC	94.1	97.8	95.6	99.9	62.1	84.5	94.1	60.4	80.4	93.9	62.1	81.0	100.0	62.1	84.6	94.1	60.4	80.4
26, 27, 3370	ELECTRICAL, COMMUNICATIONS & UTIL.	102.0	94.8	98.3	99.4	64.9	81.6	102.0	64.9	82.8	100.7	64.9	82.2	102.0	64.9	82.9	102.0	64.9	82.8
MF2010	WEIGHTED AVERAGE	97.2	72.9	86.5	100.6	65.4	85.1	96.6	55.0	78.3	97.4	65.4	83.3	99.2	65.4	84.3	97.9	55.2	79.1

VERMONT / VIRGINIA

DIVISION		WHITE RIVER JCT. 050 MAT.	INST.	TOTAL	ALEXANDRIA 223 MAT.	INST.	TOTAL	ARLINGTON 222 MAT.	INST.	TOTAL	BRISTOL 242 MAT.	INST.	TOTAL	CHARLOTTESVILLE 229 MAT.	INST.	TOTAL	CULPEPER 227 MAT.	INST.	TOTAL
015433	CONTRACTOR EQUIPMENT		100.4	100.4		101.1	101.1		99.9	99.9		99.9	99.9		104.0	104.0		99.9	99.9
0241, 31 - 34	SITE & INFRASTRUCTURE, DEMOLITION	85.4	95.9	92.7	118.6	88.3	97.7	130.3	85.1	99.2	113.8	84.7	93.7	119.2	86.7	96.8	116.8	85.5	95.2
0310	Concrete Forming & Accessories	94.8	42.1	49.0	89.8	75.3	77.2	89.3	71.8	74.1	85.7	44.1	49.5	84.2	50.2	54.6	81.7	70.4	71.9
0320	Concrete Reinforcing	82.9	37.6	60.1	83.6	79.9	81.7	94.4	71.6	82.9	94.3	68.5	81.3	93.7	69.4	81.5	94.4	65.7	79.9
0330	Cast-in-Place Concrete	100.0	54.7	82.1	122.1	83.8	107.0	118.8	79.2	103.2	118.3	48.9	91.0	123.1	57.0	97.0	121.6	66.3	99.8
03	CONCRETE	105.2	46.6	76.6	111.6	80.1	96.2	115.8	75.0	95.9	112.2	52.2	83.0	113.3	57.9	86.3	110.3	69.0	90.2
04	MASONRY	113.5	37.8	67.3	93.7	72.5	80.7	107.7	66.1	82.3	95.8	41.5	62.7	121.9	48.0	76.8	109.7	61.8	80.5
05	METALS	92.5	58.7	81.4	95.8	94.2	95.3	94.5	81.8	90.3	93.3	85.4	90.7	93.6	88.0	91.8	93.7	80.6	89.4
06	WOOD, PLASTICS & COMPOSITES	93.7	43.2	64.5	95.7	74.4	83.4	92.9	74.4	82.2	85.9	42.4	60.8	84.5	48.3	63.6	83.2	74.4	78.1
07	THERMAL & MOISTURE PROTECTION	100.9	36.6	74.7	99.0	80.9	91.6	101.0	68.6	87.8	100.5	48.1	79.2	100.1	53.5	81.2	100.3	62.0	84.7
08	OPENINGS	99.2	39.5	84.1	97.3	75.4	91.8	95.2	69.4	88.7	98.6	48.4	86.0	96.6	53.3	85.7	96.9	65.0	88.9
0920	Plaster & Gypsum Board	92.4	40.7	55.5	110.4	73.5	84.0	107.8	73.5	83.3	103.4	40.5	58.4	103.4	45.9	62.3	103.7	73.5	82.1
0950, 0980	Ceilings & Acoustic Treatment	92.7	40.7	58.4	97.3	73.5	81.6	94.6	73.5	80.6	93.7	40.5	58.5	93.7	45.9	62.1	94.6	73.5	80.6
0960	Flooring	92.3	31.9	74.6	107.3	86.1	101.1	105.6	63.4	93.2	101.8	39.2	83.4	100.3	46.2	84.4	100.3	63.4	89.5
0970, 0990	Wall Finishes & Painting/Coating	90.1	19.1	46.3	130.0	81.1	99.8	130.0	81.1	99.8	114.8	43.8	71.0	114.8	62.0	82.2	130.0	55.1	83.8
09	FINISHES	94.8	37.9	63.1	104.4	77.4	89.3	104.5	71.9	86.3	100.8	42.4	68.2	100.4	49.9	72.2	101.1	68.8	83.1
COVERS	DIVS. 10 - 14, 25, 28, 41, 43, 44, 46	100.0	38.2	87.7	100.0	89.3	97.9	100.0	70.2	94.1	100.0	73.2	94.7	100.0	73.1	94.6	100.0	59.7	92.0
21, 22, 23	FIRE SUPPRESSION, PLUMBING & HVAC	94.1	60.0	80.2	100.2	88.8	95.6	100.2	84.6	93.9	94.3	53.8	77.9	94.3	56.9	79.1	94.3	62.8	81.5
26, 27, 3370	ELECTRICAL, COMMUNICATIONS & UTIL.	102.0	64.9	82.8	96.3	102.5	99.5	94.0	98.3	96.2	96.0	37.6	65.9	95.9	71.0	83.1	98.4	55.4	76.2
MF2010	WEIGHTED AVERAGE	98.0	54.4	78.8	100.6	86.0	94.2	101.6	79.9	92.0	98.6	54.3	79.1	100.0	62.8	83.6	99.3	67.0	85.1

681

City Cost Indexes

VIRGINIA

DIVISION		FAIRFAX 220-221 MAT.	INST.	TOTAL	FARMVILLE 239 MAT.	INST.	TOTAL	FREDERICKSBURG 224-225 MAT.	INST.	TOTAL	GRUNDY 246 MAT.	INST.	TOTAL	HARRISONBURG 228 MAT.	INST.	TOTAL	LYNCHBURG 245 MAT.	INST.	TOTAL
015433	CONTRACTOR EQUIPMENT		99.9	99.9		104.0	104.0		99.9	99.9		99.9	99.9		99.9	99.9		99.9	99.9
0241,31-34	SITE & INFRASTRUCTURE, DEMOLITION	129.2	85.9	99.4	114.8	86.0	94.9	116.2	85.8	95.3	111.3	83.6	92.2	125.8	84.8	97.5	112.2	84.9	93.3
0310	Concrete Forming & Accessories	84.3	72.3	73.9	95.1	45.7	52.1	84.3	50.0	54.5	88.6	38.1	44.7	80.7	44.2	49.0	85.7	63.1	66.1
0320	Concrete Reinforcing	94.4	79.8	87.0	94.3	52.9	73.5	95.1	78.8	86.9	93.0	53.5	73.1	94.4	48.1	71.1	93.7	69.1	81.3
0330	Cast-in-Place Concrete	118.8	80.1	103.5	123.0	54.9	96.2	120.6	53.8	94.3	118.3	49.3	91.1	118.7	60.0	95.6	118.3	59.8	95.3
03	CONCRETE	115.5	77.6	97.0	112.4	51.9	82.9	109.9	58.4	84.8	111.0	46.4	79.5	113.3	52.5	83.7	110.9	64.5	88.3
04	MASONRY	107.6	66.4	82.4	104.7	47.3	69.7	108.8	46.0	70.5	99.2	50.0	69.2	105.8	52.1	73.0	114.0	54.2	77.5
05	METALS	93.7	95.1	94.2	93.6	77.5	88.3	93.7	91.6	93.0	93.3	71.5	86.1	93.6	83.7	90.4	93.5	86.7	91.3
06	WOOD, PLASTICS & COMPOSITES	85.9	74.4	79.2	97.7	46.7	68.2	85.9	47.7	63.8	88.6	37.2	58.9	82.3	41.4	58.6	85.9	66.5	74.7
07	THERMAL & MOISTURE PROTECTION	100.9	68.9	87.9	100.1	48.5	79.1	100.3	51.6	80.5	100.4	47.8	79.0	100.7	61.4	84.7	100.3	55.7	82.2
08	OPENINGS	95.2	76.6	90.5	96.9	45.6	84.0	96.6	55.2	86.2	98.6	36.5	83.0	96.9	51.9	85.6	96.9	61.5	88.0
0920	Plaster & Gypsum Board	103.7	73.5	82.1	109.3	44.2	62.8	103.7	45.9	62.4	103.4	35.1	54.6	103.4	39.4	57.7	103.4	65.3	76.2
0950,0980	Ceilings & Acoustic Treatment	94.6	73.5	80.6	93.7	44.2	61.0	94.6	45.9	62.4	93.7	35.1	55.0	93.7	39.4	57.8	93.7	65.3	74.9
0960	Flooring	102.1	66.2	91.6	107.3	63.1	94.3	102.1	77.5	94.9	103.3	35.3	83.3	100.0	77.5	93.4	101.8	43.7	84.7
0970,0990	Wall Finishes & Painting/Coating	130.0	81.1	99.8	114.8	40.8	69.2	130.0	67.7	91.6	114.8	37.0	66.8	130.0	53.5	82.8	114.8	43.8	71.0
09	FINISHES	102.9	72.4	85.9	102.8	48.7	72.6	101.6	55.7	76.0	101.0	37.1	65.4	101.7	50.2	73.0	100.6	57.9	76.8
COVERS	DIVS. 10-14, 25, 28, 41, 43, 44, 46	100.0	70.2	94.1	100.0	49.1	89.9	100.0	74.0	94.8	100.0	47.1	89.5	100.0	72.9	94.6	100.0	76.6	95.3
21,22,23	FIRE SUPPRESSION, PLUMBING & HVAC	94.3	84.9	90.5	94.3	36.7	70.9	94.3	82.3	89.4	94.3	41.1	72.7	94.3	53.7	77.8	94.3	56.4	78.9
26,27,3370	ELECTRICAL, COMMUNICATIONS & UTIL.	97.1	98.3	97.7	93.3	49.9	70.9	94.2	91.3	92.7	96.0	47.4	70.9	96.2	83.0	89.4	97.0	55.9	75.8
MF2010	WEIGHTED AVERAGE	100.1	82.0	92.1	98.9	52.3	78.4	98.8	71.8	86.9	98.6	49.7	77.0	99.6	63.0	83.4	99.3	63.6	83.5

VIRGINIA

DIVISION		NEWPORT NEWS 236 MAT.	INST.	TOTAL	NORFOLK 233-235 MAT.	INST.	TOTAL	PETERSBURG 238 MAT.	INST.	TOTAL	PORTSMOUTH 237 MAT.	INST.	TOTAL	PULASKI 243 MAT.	INST.	TOTAL	RICHMOND 230-232 MAT.	INST.	TOTAL
015433	CONTRACTOR EQUIPMENT		104.0	104.0		104.6	104.6		104.0	104.0		103.9	103.9		99.9	99.9		104.0	104.0
0241,31-34	SITE & INFRASTRUCTURE, DEMOLITION	113.0	87.4	95.3	111.3	88.3	95.4	117.7	87.7	97.0	111.5	86.7	94.4	110.7	83.6	92.0	110.4	87.7	94.7
0310	Concrete Forming & Accessories	94.5	66.1	69.8	95.9	66.2	70.1	88.5	59.6	63.3	84.9	54.3	58.3	88.6	38.3	44.8	94.0	59.6	64.1
0320	Concrete Reinforcing	94.0	72.3	83.1	94.0	72.3	83.1	93.7	70.1	81.8	93.7	69.8	81.6	93.0	53.5	73.1	94.0	70.1	82.0
0330	Cast-in-Place Concrete	119.6	60.2	96.2	130.7	60.3	102.9	127.0	55.2	98.7	118.4	59.7	95.3	118.3	49.3	91.1	115.2	55.2	91.6
03	CONCRETE	109.3	66.5	88.4	114.9	66.6	91.4	115.2	61.5	89.1	108.0	60.6	84.9	111.0	46.5	79.6	107.1	61.5	84.9
04	MASONRY	99.5	54.1	71.8	105.6	54.1	74.2	113.2	55.6	78.1	105.0	53.9	73.8	92.5	50.0	66.6	97.3	55.6	71.9
05	METALS	95.8	89.9	93.9	94.8	90.0	93.2	93.7	89.5	92.3	94.8	87.2	92.3	93.4	71.6	86.2	98.0	89.5	95.2
06	WOOD, PLASTICS & COMPOSITES	96.6	70.3	81.4	98.6	70.3	82.2	89.0	62.1	73.5	85.7	54.5	67.7	88.6	37.2	58.9	95.7	62.1	76.3
07	THERMAL & MOISTURE PROTECTION	100.1	56.1	82.2	97.5	56.1	80.6	100.1	56.3	82.3	100.1	53.8	81.3	100.4	47.8	79.0	98.7	56.3	81.5
08	OPENINGS	97.3	64.9	89.1	97.3	64.9	89.1	96.6	60.8	87.6	97.4	55.7	86.9	98.6	36.5	83.0	97.3	60.8	88.1
0920	Plaster & Gypsum Board	110.4	68.5	80.5	101.0	68.5	77.8	103.7	60.1	72.6	104.1	52.3	67.1	103.4	35.1	54.6	114.0	60.1	75.5
0950,0980	Ceilings & Acoustic Treatment	97.3	68.5	78.3	97.3	68.5	78.3	94.6	60.1	71.8	97.3	52.3	67.6	93.7	35.1	55.0	100.9	60.1	74.0
0960	Flooring	107.3	52.9	91.3	106.7	52.9	90.9	102.8	74.6	94.5	99.5	66.9	90.0	103.3	35.3	83.3	106.7	74.6	97.3
0970,0990	Wall Finishes & Painting/Coating	114.8	44.3	71.3	114.8	67.8	85.8	114.8	62.0	82.2	114.8	67.8	85.8	114.8	37.0	66.8	114.8	62.0	82.2
09	FINISHES	103.5	61.7	80.2	101.8	64.4	80.9	101.3	62.7	79.8	100.5	57.4	76.5	101.0	37.1	65.4	104.0	62.7	81.0
COVERS	DIVS. 10-14, 25, 28, 41, 43, 44, 46	100.0	78.3	95.7	100.0	78.3	95.7	100.0	73.3	94.7	100.0	76.6	95.3	100.0	47.1	89.5	100.0	73.3	94.7
21,22,23	FIRE SUPPRESSION, PLUMBING & HVAC	100.2	63.9	85.5	100.0	63.7	85.3	94.3	55.0	78.4	100.2	62.1	84.8	94.3	41.4	72.9	100.0	55.0	81.8
26,27,3370	ELECTRICAL, COMMUNICATIONS & UTIL.	96.0	60.4	77.6	101.2	59.9	79.9	96.2	71.0	83.2	94.3	59.8	76.5	96.0	51.2	72.9	99.3	71.0	84.7
MF2010	WEIGHTED AVERAGE	100.4	67.3	85.8	101.4	67.6	86.5	99.9	66.0	85.0	99.9	64.4	84.3	98.3	50.3	77.1	100.6	66.0	85.3

VIRGINIA / WASHINGTON

DIVISION		ROANOKE 240-241 MAT.	INST.	TOTAL	STAUNTON 244 MAT.	INST.	TOTAL	WINCHESTER 226 MAT.	INST.	TOTAL	CLARKSTON 994 MAT.	INST.	TOTAL	EVERETT 982 MAT.	INST.	TOTAL	OLYMPIA 985 MAT.	INST.	TOTAL
015433	CONTRACTOR EQUIPMENT		99.9	99.9		104.0	104.0		99.9	99.9		91.0	91.0		104.1	104.1		104.1	104.1
0241,31-34	SITE & INFRASTRUCTURE, DEMOLITION	110.3	84.8	92.7	115.4	86.5	95.5	124.3	84.9	97.1	96.4	90.4	92.2	92.9	112.9	106.7	94.4	112.9	107.1
0310	Concrete Forming & Accessories	94.3	62.9	67.0	88.1	52.4	57.0	82.9	49.2	53.6	124.9	70.5	77.6	113.7	99.4	101.2	103.5	99.5	100.0
0320	Concrete Reinforcing	94.0	69.2	81.5	93.7	51.9	72.6	93.7	83.8	88.7	106.6	84.5	95.5	116.6	103.0	109.7	117.2	103.0	110.1
0330	Cast-in-Place Concrete	134.4	59.7	105.0	123.0	53.2	95.5	118.7	56.3	94.1	102.5	82.4	94.6	101.0	105.8	102.9	91.9	106.0	97.5
03	CONCRETE	116.7	64.3	91.2	112.6	54.3	84.2	112.7	59.7	86.9	99.5	77.4	88.7	98.4	101.8	100.0	94.4	101.9	98.0
04	MASONRY	100.6	55.8	73.3	110.2	54.3	76.1	103.4	49.9	70.8	104.1	79.6	89.2	122.3	99.2	108.2	112.2	99.3	104.3
05	METALS	95.6	86.6	92.6	93.6	82.3	89.9	93.7	90.2	92.6	87.3	80.3	84.9	100.8	92.9	98.2	95.8	93.0	94.9
06	WOOD, PLASTICS & COMPOSITES	96.6	66.5	79.2	88.6	52.9	68.0	84.5	47.7	63.2	101.0	67.8	81.8	106.4	99.0	102.1	93.4	99.0	96.6
07	THERMAL & MOISTURE PROTECTION	100.0	54.7	81.6	100.1	52.3	80.6	100.8	58.7	83.7	151.2	76.5	120.8	102.4	99.0	101.1	102.1	96.8	99.9
08	OPENINGS	97.3	61.5	88.3	96.9	51.0	85.4	98.7	56.5	88.1	106.4	71.0	97.5	101.2	100.2	101.0	101.0	100.2	100.8
0920	Plaster & Gypsum Board	110.4	65.3	78.2	103.4	50.6	65.7	103.7	45.9	62.4	130.2	66.6	84.8	115.5	98.9	103.6	105.1	98.9	100.7
0950,0980	Ceilings & Acoustic Treatment	97.3	65.3	76.2	93.7	50.6	65.2	94.6	45.9	62.4	99.3	66.6	77.7	107.8	98.9	101.9	101.2	98.9	99.7
0960	Flooring	107.3	47.1	89.6	102.7	41.3	84.7	101.4	77.5	94.4	103.2	49.4	87.4	116.5	95.9	110.5	109.2	96.1	105.3
0970,0990	Wall Finishes & Painting/Coating	114.8	43.8	71.0	114.8	30.6	62.8	130.0	47.1	78.8	110.1	61.7	80.2	105.5	74.8	86.6	105.5	84.1	92.3
09	FINISHES	103.3	58.7	78.4	100.8	48.6	71.7	102.2	53.4	75.0	116.9	64.5	87.7	108.7	96.0	101.6	100.4	97.1	100.1
COVERS	DIVS. 10-14, 25, 28, 41, 43, 44, 46	100.0	76.5	95.3	100.0	76.3	95.3	100.0	55.1	91.1	100.0	81.0	96.2	100.0	96.6	99.3	100.0	101.0	100.2
21,22,23	FIRE SUPPRESSION, PLUMBING & HVAC	100.2	47.5	78.9	94.3	55.4	78.5	94.3	67.4	83.4	94.4	87.9	91.8	100.0	90.9	96.3	99.9	90.9	96.2
26,27,3370	ELECTRICAL, COMMUNICATIONS & UTIL.	96.0	40.4	67.3	94.9	43.9	68.6	94.6	45.6	69.3	99.9	92.2	96.0	103.8	82.3	92.7	98.1	97.0	97.6
MF2010	WEIGHTED AVERAGE	101.2	59.8	82.9	99.2	58.2	81.1	99.4	62.2	83.0	100.4	81.3	92.0	102.2	95.6	99.3	99.4	97.9	98.7

City Cost Indexes

		RICHLAND 993			SEATTLE 980 - 981,987			SPOKANE 990 - 992			TACOMA 983 - 984			VANCOUVER 986			WENATCHEE 988		
DIVISION		MAT.	INST.	TOTAL	MAT.	INST.	TOTAL	MAT.	INST.	TOTAL	MAT.	INST.	TOTAL	MAT.	INST.	TOTAL	MAT.	INST.	TOTAL
015433	CONTRACTOR EQUIPMENT		91.0	91.0		103.9	103.9		91.0	91.0		104.1	104.1		98.8	98.8		104.1	104.1
0241, 31 - 34	SITE & INFRASTRUCTURE, DEMOLITION	98.0	91.3	93.4	97.0	111.1	106.7	97.4	91.3	93.1	96.1	112.9	107.7	107.4	100.2	102.5	107.0	111.5	110.1
0310	Concrete Forming & Accessories	125.0	79.9	85.7	105.2	100.3	100.9	129.2	79.7	86.1	105.2	99.5	100.2	106.3	86.6	89.2	106.6	78.0	81.7
0320	Concrete Reinforcing	102.3	84.6	93.4	115.1	103.1	109.1	103.0	84.6	93.7	115.1	103.0	109.0	116.1	102.7	109.4	116.1	91.2	103.6
0330	Cast-in-Place Concrete	102.7	84.5	95.5	106.0	106.3	106.1	106.7	84.4	97.9	103.9	106.0	104.7	116.0	100.3	109.8	106.0	79.4	95.5
03	CONCRETE	99.0	82.4	90.9	101.2	102.5	101.8	101.4	82.2	92.1	100.1	101.9	101.0	110.1	94.3	102.4	107.3	81.1	94.5
04	MASONRY	105.0	81.9	90.9	116.4	99.3	106.0	105.6	81.9	91.2	116.2	99.3	105.9	117.3	95.8	104.1	119.0	81.3	96.0
05	METALS	87.6	82.9	86.1	102.5	95.1	100.1	89.9	82.7	87.6	102.5	93.0	99.4	100.0	93.5	97.8	100.0	86.7	95.6
06	WOOD, PLASTICS & COMPOSITES	101.2	78.7	88.2	97.9	99.0	98.5	109.7	78.7	91.8	96.5	99.0	98.0	88.4	83.7	85.7	97.6	76.5	85.4
07	THERMAL & MOISTURE PROTECTION	152.4	78.6	122.4	102.3	99.1	101.0	148.9	79.5	120.6	102.2	96.8	100.0	102.7	91.2	98.0	102.8	79.8	93.5
08	OPENINGS	109.0	72.5	99.8	103.4	100.2	102.6	109.6	72.9	100.3	101.8	100.2	101.4	99.5	90.0	97.1	101.3	72.9	94.1
0920	Plaster & Gypsum Board	130.2	77.9	92.8	109.6	98.9	101.9	130.6	77.9	92.9	112.5	98.9	102.8	110.2	83.4	91.0	114.1	75.7	86.7
0950, 0980	Ceilings & Acoustic Treatment	104.4	77.9	86.9	110.3	98.9	102.7	101.4	77.9	85.8	110.5	98.9	102.8	105.2	83.4	90.8	103.0	75.7	85.0
0960	Flooring	103.4	83.9	97.7	109.1	103.9	107.6	103.5	89.3	99.4	109.6	96.1	105.6	115.2	107.0	112.8	112.7	65.6	98.9
0970, 0990	Wall Finishes & Painting/Coating	110.1	61.7	80.2	105.5	84.1	92.3	110.1	61.7	80.3	105.5	84.1	92.3	108.9	65.2	82.0	105.5	61.7	78.5
09	FINISHES	118.3	78.3	96.0	106.6	98.7	102.2	117.9	79.4	96.4	107.0	97.1	101.5	104.9	87.7	95.3	107.6	73.2	88.4
COVERS	DIVS. 10 - 14, 25, 28, 41, 43, 44, 46	100.0	66.9	93.4	100.0	101.0	100.2	100.0	66.8	93.4	100.0	101.0	100.2	100.0	64.1	92.9	100.0	82.3	96.5
21, 22, 23	FIRE SUPPRESSION, PLUMBING & HVAC	100.4	100.1	100.3	100.0	122.1	109.0	100.3	89.0	95.7	100.1	90.9	96.4	100.2	93.0	97.3	94.1	85.4	90.6
26, 27, 3370	ELECTRICAL, COMMUNICATIONS & UTIL.	97.1	93.1	95.1	103.6	107.9	105.8	95.1	79.1	86.8	103.6	97.0	100.2	108.5	98.0	103.1	104.4	80.2	91.9
MF2010	WEIGHTED AVERAGE	102.1	86.8	95.4	102.5	106.3	104.2	102.5	82.7	93.7	102.2	97.9	100.3	103.5	93.0	98.8	101.8	83.6	93.8

		WASHINGTON YAKIMA 989			WEST VIRGINIA														
					BECKLEY 258 - 259			BLUEFIELD 247 - 248			BUCKHANNON 262			CHARLESTON 250 - 253			CLARKSBURG 263 - 264		
DIVISION		MAT.	INST.	TOTAL	MAT.	INST.	TOTAL	MAT.	INST.	TOTAL	MAT.	INST.	TOTAL	MAT.	INST.	TOTAL	MAT.	INST.	TOTAL
015433	CONTRACTOR EQUIPMENT		104.1	104.1		99.9	99.9		99.9	99.9		99.9	99.9		99.9	99.9		99.9	99.9
0241, 31 - 34	SITE & INFRASTRUCTURE, DEMOLITION	98.9	112.3	108.2	104.9	86.9	92.5	104.7	86.9	92.4	111.5	86.7	94.4	102.7	88.4	92.9	112.1	86.7	94.6
0310	Concrete Forming & Accessories	105.5	95.1	96.5	84.6	86.5	86.3	85.8	86.2	86.1	85.2	84.5	84.6	99.5	88.5	89.9	82.9	84.4	84.2
0320	Concrete Reinforcing	115.7	91.3	103.4	92.7	84.2	88.4	92.7	66.3	79.4	93.3	83.1	88.2	94.0	84.4	89.2	93.3	83.7	88.4
0330	Cast-in-Place Concrete	111.0	84.2	100.4	115.7	102.7	110.6	115.7	102.6	110.5	115.4	100.0	109.3	107.0	100.9	104.6	126.4	100.0	116.0
03	CONCRETE	104.9	90.3	97.8	106.5	92.3	99.6	106.6	88.8	97.9	109.5	90.3	100.2	103.3	92.6	98.1	114.6	90.4	102.8
04	MASONRY	109.5	81.3	92.3	99.4	89.6	93.5	94.2	89.6	91.4	105.6	86.9	94.2	96.2	91.5	93.3	108.1	86.9	95.2
05	METALS	100.7	87.0	96.2	93.6	95.2	94.1	93.6	88.7	91.9	93.7	95.7	94.4	95.8	96.4	96.0	93.7	95.8	94.4
06	WOOD, PLASTICS & COMPOSITES	97.0	99.0	98.2	86.0	87.8	87.1	87.7	87.8	87.8	87.0	83.3	84.9	102.6	87.8	94.1	83.9	83.3	83.6
07	THERMAL & MOISTURE PROTECTION	102.3	81.4	93.8	100.2	87.2	94.9	100.2	87.2	94.9	100.5	86.7	94.9	97.3	87.7	93.4	100.4	86.7	94.8
08	OPENINGS	101.3	81.7	96.4	98.0	81.2	93.7	98.8	77.1	93.4	98.9	78.5	93.8	98.5	81.2	94.2	98.9	80.5	94.2
0920	Plaster & Gypsum Board	112.3	98.9	102.7	101.5	87.3	91.4	102.4	87.3	91.6	103.0	82.7	88.5	100.5	87.3	91.1	100.7	82.7	87.8
0950, 0980	Ceilings & Acoustic Treatment	105.0	98.9	101.0	91.9	87.3	88.9	91.9	87.3	88.9	93.7	82.7	86.4	95.5	87.3	90.1	93.7	82.7	86.4
0960	Flooring	110.8	60.7	96.1	98.9	110.4	102.3	99.5	110.4	102.7	99.2	104.1	100.6	107.3	110.4	108.2	98.0	104.1	99.8
0970, 0990	Wall Finishes & Painting/Coating	105.5	61.7	78.5	114.8	36.9	66.7	114.8	36.9	66.7	114.8	89.3	99.0	114.8	89.5	99.2	114.8	89.3	99.0
09	FINISHES	106.4	85.5	94.8	98.6	86.4	91.8	98.9	86.4	91.9	99.9	88.4	93.5	101.2	92.7	96.5	99.2	88.4	93.2
COVERS	DIVS. 10 - 14, 25, 28, 41, 43, 44, 46	100.0	98.2	99.6	100.0	57.3	91.5	100.0	57.2	91.5	100.0	94.6	98.9	100.0	95.6	99.1	100.0	94.6	98.9
21, 22, 23	FIRE SUPPRESSION, PLUMBING & HVAC	100.1	100.2	100.1	94.3	80.1	88.6	94.3	79.7	88.4	94.3	88.0	91.7	100.0	82.2	92.8	94.3	87.7	91.6
26, 27, 3370	ELECTRICAL, COMMUNICATIONS & UTIL.	106.6	93.1	99.6	92.4	90.9	91.6	95.0	71.5	82.9	96.3	91.5	93.8	97.2	90.9	93.9	96.3	91.5	93.8
MF2010	WEIGHTED AVERAGE	102.5	92.6	98.1	97.3	86.6	92.6	97.4	82.6	90.9	98.8	89.0	94.5	99.2	89.5	94.9	99.4	89.1	94.9

		WEST VIRGINIA																	
		GASSAWAY 266			HUNTINGTON 255 - 257			LEWISBURG 249			MARTINSBURG 254			MORGANTOWN 265			PARKERSBURG 261		
DIVISION		MAT.	INST.	TOTAL	MAT.	INST.	TOTAL	MAT.	INST.	TOTAL	MAT.	INST.	TOTAL	MAT.	INST.	TOTAL	MAT.	INST.	TOTAL
015433	CONTRACTOR EQUIPMENT		99.9	99.9		99.9	99.9		99.9	99.9		99.9	99.9		99.9	99.9		99.9	99.9
0241, 31 - 34	SITE & INFRASTRUCTURE, DEMOLITION	108.5	87.2	93.8	109.3	89.4	95.5	122.2	86.9	97.9	108.8	84.9	92.3	105.6	87.0	92.8	114.4	88.4	96.5
0310	Concrete Forming & Accessories	84.7	84.6	84.6	95.4	91.3	91.8	83.2	86.2	85.8	84.6	76.9	77.9	83.2	84.1	84.0	86.9	86.0	86.1
0320	Concrete Reinforcing	93.3	84.4	88.8	94.0	90.6	92.3	93.3	66.3	79.7	92.7	74.1	83.3	93.3	83.7	88.4	92.7	83.0	87.8
0330	Cast-in-Place Concrete	120.8	100.1	112.6	126.2	105.1	117.9	115.8	102.6	110.6	121.2	89.7	108.8	115.3	99.9	109.2	117.9	91.5	107.5
03	CONCRETE	110.4	90.6	100.8	112.7	96.4	104.7	115.9	88.8	102.7	110.5	81.5	96.4	106.3	90.2	98.5	111.7	88.0	100.1
04	MASONRY	109.2	90.1	97.6	99.9	91.8	95.0	98.6	89.6	93.1	101.2	79.5	87.9	128.6	86.9	103.2	84.3	84.7	84.5
05	METALS	93.7	96.4	94.6	95.9	98.6	96.8	93.7	88.7	92.0	93.9	85.3	91.1	93.8	95.5	94.4	94.4	95.5	94.8
06	WOOD, PLASTICS & COMPOSITES	86.2	83.3	84.5	96.6	89.9	92.7	84.2	87.8	86.3	86.0	78.1	81.5	84.2	83.3	83.7	87.1	84.9	85.8
07	THERMAL & MOISTURE PROTECTION	100.2	87.5	95.1	100.3	88.4	95.5	101.1	87.2	95.5	100.4	72.7	89.2	100.3	86.7	94.8	100.1	86.0	94.4
08	OPENINGS	96.8	78.8	92.2	97.3	83.8	93.9	98.9	77.1	93.4	100.2	66.9	91.8	100.3	80.5	95.3	97.9	79.4	93.2
0920	Plaster & Gypsum Board	102.1	82.7	88.2	109.3	89.5	95.2	100.7	87.3	91.1	102.1	77.3	84.4	100.7	82.7	87.8	103.4	84.3	89.7
0950, 0980	Ceilings & Acoustic Treatment	93.7	82.7	86.4	93.7	89.5	90.9	93.7	87.3	89.5	93.7	77.3	82.9	93.7	82.7	86.4	93.7	84.3	87.5
0960	Flooring	99.0	110.4	102.3	107.1	105.1	106.5	98.1	110.4	101.7	98.9	56.2	86.4	98.1	104.1	99.9	102.3	96.6	100.6
0970, 0990	Wall Finishes & Painting/Coating	114.8	89.5	99.2	114.8	83.2	95.3	114.8	36.9	66.7	114.8	43.6	70.9	114.8	89.3	99.0	114.8	88.4	98.5
09	FINISHES	99.4	89.7	94.0	102.3	92.9	97.1	100.5	86.4	92.6	99.4	70.1	83.0	98.7	88.4	93.0	100.9	88.0	93.7
COVERS	DIVS. 10 - 14, 25, 28, 41, 43, 44, 46	100.0	94.6	98.9	100.0	96.9	99.4	100.0	57.2	91.5	100.0	55.4	91.1	100.0	66.6	93.4	100.0	95.1	99.0
21, 22, 23	FIRE SUPPRESSION, PLUMBING & HVAC	94.3	88.8	92.1	100.2	84.4	93.8	94.3	80.0	88.5	94.3	82.6	89.6	94.3	87.6	91.6	100.2	87.8	95.1
26, 27, 3370	ELECTRICAL, COMMUNICATIONS & UTIL.	96.3	90.9	93.5	96.0	93.9	94.9	92.4	71.5	81.6	98.0	81.6	89.6	96.5	91.5	93.9	96.4	90.3	93.3
MF2010	WEIGHTED AVERAGE	98.7	89.8	94.8	100.6	91.4	96.6	99.1	82.7	91.9	98.9	79.1	90.2	99.5	88.2	94.5	99.6	88.4	94.7

683

WEST VIRGINIA / WISCONSIN

DIVISION		PETERSBURG 268 MAT.	INST.	TOTAL	ROMNEY 267 MAT.	INST.	TOTAL	WHEELING 260 MAT.	INST.	TOTAL	BELOIT 535 MAT.	INST.	TOTAL	EAU CLAIRE 547 MAT.	INST.	TOTAL	GREEN BAY 541 - 543 MAT.	INST.	TOTAL
015433	CONTRACTOR EQUIPMENT		99.9	99.9		99.9	99.9		99.9	99.9		100.9	100.9		100.8	100.8		98.7	98.7
0241, 31 - 34	SITE & INFRASTRUCTURE, DEMOLITION	104.9	87.3	92.8	108.0	87.3	93.7	115.1	87.6	96.1	97.8	106.2	103.6	98.6	103.4	101.9	102.8	99.5	100.5
0310	Concrete Forming & Accessories	86.0	79.7	80.5	82.6	79.8	80.1	88.6	84.5	85.1	103.3	94.6	95.7	101.9	96.3	97.0	107.3	95.6	97.1
0320	Concrete Reinforcing	92.7	74.6	83.6	93.3	71.8	82.5	92.1	83.7	87.9	102.0	118.4	110.3	100.1	101.7	100.9	98.1	88.4	93.2
0330	Cast-in-Place Concrete	115.3	94.0	106.9	120.8	94.0	110.2	117.9	100.1	110.9	103.5	92.8	99.3	103.6	93.5	99.6	107.2	98.0	103.6
03	CONCRETE	106.4	84.5	95.7	110.3	84.1	97.5	111.7	90.5	101.3	99.7	98.6	99.2	101.1	96.6	98.9	104.0	95.4	99.8
04	MASONRY	101.2	86.9	92.5	99.0	83.7	89.7	108.9	86.9	95.5	104.6	93.9	98.1	92.6	97.9	95.8	124.4	97.2	107.8
05	METALS	93.8	91.8	93.2	93.9	90.8	92.9	94.6	95.9	95.0	95.9	108.3	100.0	95.7	102.8	98.1	97.9	96.9	97.6
06	WOOD, PLASTICS & COMPOSITES	88.0	78.1	82.3	83.3	78.1	80.3	88.6	83.3	85.5	101.5	97.0	98.9	108.3	97.1	101.8	109.3	97.1	102.2
07	THERMAL & MOISTURE PROTECTION	100.3	75.1	90.1	100.4	74.2	89.8	100.5	87.3	95.2	105.8	91.4	99.9	106.3	84.9	97.6	107.8	85.2	98.6
08	OPENINGS	100.3	73.8	93.6	100.2	73.1	93.4	98.8	80.5	94.2	102.1	105.3	102.9	99.6	95.9	98.7	97.8	94.6	97.0
0920	Plaster & Gypsum Board	103.0	77.3	84.6	100.3	77.3	83.8	103.4	82.7	88.6	100.3	97.3	98.1	105.2	97.3	99.5	96.6	97.3	97.1
0950, 0980	Ceilings & Acoustic Treatment	93.7	77.3	82.9	93.7	77.3	82.9	93.7	82.7	86.4	87.5	97.3	93.9	101.5	97.3	98.7	93.4	97.3	96.0
0960	Flooring	100.0	104.1	101.2	97.9	97.8	97.9	103.3	104.1	103.5	104.5	117.5	108.3	96.3	113.3	101.3	115.9	113.3	115.1
0970, 0990	Wall Finishes & Painting/Coating	114.8	89.3	99.0	114.8	89.3	99.0	114.8	89.3	99.0	91.9	97.4	95.3	88.4	91.1	90.1	98.0	80.3	87.1
09	FINISHES	99.5	85.4	91.6	98.9	84.1	90.6	101.2	88.4	94.1	100.3	99.3	99.7	99.7	99.3	99.5	104.0	97.9	100.6
COVERS	DIVS. 10 - 14, 25, 28, 41, 43, 44, 46	100.0	66.0	93.2	100.0	94.0	98.8	100.0	96.2	99.2	100.0	89.4	97.9	100.0	91.8	98.4	100.0	91.5	98.3
21, 22, 23	FIRE SUPPRESSION, PLUMBING & HVAC	94.3	88.7	92.0	94.3	88.6	92.0	100.2	87.7	95.2	99.9	89.1	95.5	100.2	84.8	93.9	100.4	82.9	93.3
26, 27, 3370	ELECTRICAL, COMMUNICATIONS & UTIL.	99.6	81.7	90.4	98.8	81.7	90.0	93.7	91.5	92.6	101.1	87.5	94.1	103.7	90.2	96.7	98.4	82.8	90.3
MF2010	WEIGHTED AVERAGE	98.5	84.9	92.5	98.7	85.1	92.7	100.7	89.2	95.7	100.0	96.0	98.3	99.7	94.3	97.3	101.8	91.6	97.3

WISCONSIN

DIVISION		KENOSHA 531 MAT.	INST.	TOTAL	LA CROSSE 546 MAT.	INST.	TOTAL	LANCASTER 538 MAT.	INST.	TOTAL	MADISON 537 MAT.	INST.	TOTAL	MILWAUKEE 530,532 MAT.	INST.	TOTAL	NEW RICHMOND 540 MAT.	INST.	TOTAL
015433	CONTRACTOR EQUIPMENT		98.8	98.8		100.8	100.8		100.9	100.9		100.9	100.9		89.3	89.3		101.4	101.4
0241, 31 - 34	SITE & INFRASTRUCTURE, DEMOLITION	104.7	103.6	103.9	91.8	103.5	99.9	97.2	106.6	103.7	93.3	106.7	102.5	98.6	97.2	97.6	93.7	103.7	100.6
0310	Concrete Forming & Accessories	107.0	103.3	103.7	90.2	96.4	95.6	102.7	95.4	96.4	102.8	97.2	97.9	105.4	120.2	118.3	98.0	103.1	102.4
0320	Concrete Reinforcing	101.8	101.1	101.5	99.7	90.6	95.1	103.4	90.4	96.9	102.0	90.8	96.4	102.0	101.7	101.8	97.1	101.6	99.3
0330	Cast-in-Place Concrete	112.7	97.4	106.7	93.2	91.0	92.3	102.9	96.5	100.4	94.6	97.2	95.6	101.1	113.3	105.9	107.9	81.0	97.3
03	CONCRETE	104.5	100.9	102.7	92.3	93.7	93.0	99.5	95.0	97.3	95.2	96.1	95.6	98.8	113.4	105.9	99.3	95.3	97.4
04	MASONRY	101.9	107.0	105.0	91.7	99.8	96.7	104.7	99.6	101.6	102.0	102.1	102.1	104.5	122.3	115.4	119.1	94.3	104.0
05	METALS	96.6	102.4	98.5	95.6	97.6	96.3	93.4	94.5	93.8	98.5	96.5	97.8	99.2	96.4	98.3	95.8	101.9	97.8
06	WOOD, PLASTICS & COMPOSITES	102.0	102.5	102.3	95.1	97.1	96.2	100.9	97.0	98.6	98.8	97.0	97.7	103.3	120.5	113.2	97.7	109.0	104.2
07	THERMAL & MOISTURE PROTECTION	105.4	96.3	101.7	105.9	84.5	97.2	105.6	79.8	95.1	102.4	90.8	97.7	103.7	115.0	108.3	107.8	92.1	101.4
08	OPENINGS	97.5	105.6	99.5	99.6	83.8	95.6	97.2	84.6	94.0	102.1	97.5	100.9	104.3	115.3	107.1	87.7	102.4	91.4
0920	Plaster & Gypsum Board	88.1	103.0	98.8	100.1	97.3	98.1	99.0	97.3	97.8	102.7	97.3	98.8	101.7	121.4	115.7	87.2	109.8	103.3
0950, 0980	Ceilings & Acoustic Treatment	87.5	103.0	97.7	99.7	97.3	98.1	82.9	97.3	92.4	92.2	97.3	95.5	92.0	121.4	111.4	67.0	109.8	95.3
0960	Flooring	123.0	112.2	119.8	89.2	113.3	96.2	103.7	106.2	104.5	98.6	106.2	100.8	107.5	119.4	111.0	108.5	113.3	109.9
0970, 0990	Wall Finishes & Painting/Coating	100.5	103.6	102.4	88.4	72.5	78.6	91.9	70.0	78.4	91.9	97.4	95.3	83.9	117.5	108.5	101.7	91.1	95.2
09	FINISHES	105.2	105.4	105.3	96.1	97.7	97.0	98.9	94.4	96.4	99.4	99.2	99.3	102.5	120.6	112.6	94.5	103.7	99.6
COVERS	DIVS. 10 - 14, 25, 28, 41, 43, 44, 46	100.0	99.3	99.9	100.0	92.4	98.5	100.0	51.0	90.3	100.0	92.2	98.5	100.0	104.2	100.8	100.0	89.5	97.9
21, 22, 23	FIRE SUPPRESSION, PLUMBING & HVAC	100.1	94.8	97.9	100.2	85.5	94.3	93.9	85.3	90.4	99.8	94.6	97.7	99.9	103.7	101.4	93.7	82.2	89.1
26, 27, 3370	ELECTRICAL, COMMUNICATIONS & UTIL.	101.7	99.4	100.5	104.0	90.4	97.0	100.9	90.4	95.5	99.4	94.1	96.7	102.6	100.1	101.3	102.0	90.4	96.0
MF2010	WEIGHTED AVERAGE	100.8	101.0	100.9	98.1	93.2	95.9	97.6	91.5	94.9	99.3	97.2	98.4	100.9	108.3	104.2	97.3	94.4	96.0

WISCONSIN

DIVISION		OSHKOSH 549 MAT.	INST.	TOTAL	PORTAGE 539 MAT.	INST.	TOTAL	RACINE 534 MAT.	INST.	TOTAL	RHINELANDER 545 MAT.	INST.	TOTAL	SUPERIOR 548 MAT.	INST.	TOTAL	WAUSAU 544 MAT.	INST.	TOTAL
015433	CONTRACTOR EQUIPMENT		98.7	98.7		100.9	100.9		100.9	100.9		98.7	98.7		101.4	101.4		98.7	98.7
0241, 31 - 34	SITE & INFRASTRUCTURE, DEMOLITION	93.9	98.5	97.0	87.1	106.6	100.6	97.6	107.3	104.3	107.9	99.6	102.2	90.2	104.1	99.7	89.3	99.5	96.3
0310	Concrete Forming & Accessories	92.2	84.6	85.6	96.3	96.3	96.3	103.6	103.3	103.3	89.9	95.5	94.8	96.5	92.7	93.2	91.6	95.6	95.1
0320	Concrete Reinforcing	98.2	77.7	87.9	103.5	90.5	97.0	102.0	101.1	101.6	98.4	92.7	95.5	97.1	93.7	95.4	98.4	90.6	94.4
0330	Cast-in-Place Concrete	99.4	88.3	95.0	88.3	98.7	92.4	101.5	97.2	99.8	112.7	98.7	107.2	101.6	96.9	99.8	92.6	98.0	94.7
03	CONCRETE	94.0	85.1	89.7	87.6	96.2	91.8	98.7	100.8	99.7	106.2	96.3	101.4	93.8	94.7	94.2	89.0	95.8	92.3
04	MASONRY	105.6	87.9	94.8	103.6	99.5	101.1	104.6	107.0	106.0	122.5	99.1	108.2	118.4	104.0	109.6	105.1	97.2	100.3
05	METALS	96.0	89.8	94.0	94.1	95.4	94.5	97.5	102.4	99.1	95.9	97.9	96.5	96.7	99.7	97.7	95.8	97.8	96.4
06	WOOD, PLASTICS & COMPOSITES	91.8	86.2	88.5	93.0	97.0	95.3	101.7	102.5	102.2	89.6	97.1	93.9	96.2	91.2	93.3	91.3	97.1	94.6
07	THERMAL & MOISTURE PROTECTION	106.9	78.3	95.3	105.1	89.3	98.7	105.8	95.9	101.8	107.7	83.5	97.9	107.5	95.1	102.5	106.8	84.2	97.6
08	OPENINGS	93.2	83.2	90.7	97.4	91.6	95.9	102.1	105.6	103.0	93.2	86.8	91.6	87.5	92.3	88.7	93.4	95.2	93.9
0920	Plaster & Gypsum Board	85.7	86.0	85.9	93.6	97.3	96.2	100.3	103.0	102.2	85.7	97.3	94.0	87.0	91.5	90.2	85.7	97.3	94.0
0950, 0980	Ceilings & Acoustic Treatment	93.4	86.0	88.5	84.7	97.3	93.0	87.5	103.0	97.7	93.4	97.3	96.0	67.9	91.5	83.5	93.4	97.3	96.0
0960	Flooring	106.5	99.7	104.5	99.6	112.7	103.5	104.5	112.2	106.7	105.6	113.3	107.9	110.0	122.5	113.6	106.3	113.3	108.4
0970, 0990	Wall Finishes & Painting/Coating	96.0	68.3	78.9	91.9	70.0	78.4	91.9	108.7	102.2	96.0	63.6	76.0	90.2	100.4	96.5	96.0	80.3	86.3
09	FINISHES	99.1	85.2	91.4	96.7	96.4	96.5	100.3	105.9	103.4	100.1	95.5	97.5	94.0	98.9	96.7	98.7	97.9	98.3
COVERS	DIVS. 10 - 14, 25, 28, 41, 43, 44, 46	100.0	64.1	92.8	100.0	65.9	93.2	100.0	99.3	99.9	100.0	56.9	91.4	100.0	89.2	97.8	100.0	91.5	98.3
21, 22, 23	FIRE SUPPRESSION, PLUMBING & HVAC	94.5	74.6	86.4	93.9	90.2	92.4	99.9	94.8	97.8	94.5	84.8	90.5	93.7	92.3	93.1	94.5	83.6	90.0
26, 27, 3370	ELECTRICAL, COMMUNICATIONS & UTIL.	102.6	76.2	89.0	104.8	93.7	99.0	100.9	97.3	99.1	101.9	81.4	91.3	107.0	96.9	101.8	103.7	81.4	92.2
MF2010	WEIGHTED AVERAGE	97.2	82.6	90.8	96.1	94.5	95.4	100.1	101.0	100.5	99.8	90.5	95.7	97.1	96.9	97.0	96.5	91.7	94.4

WYOMING

DIVISION		CASPER 826 MAT.	INST.	TOTAL	CHEYENNE 820 MAT.	INST.	TOTAL	NEWCASTLE 827 MAT.	INST.	TOTAL	RAWLINS 823 MAT.	INST.	TOTAL	RIVERTON 825 MAT.	INST.	TOTAL	ROCK SPRINGS 829-831 MAT.	INST.	TOTAL
015433	CONTRACTOR EQUIPMENT		99.3	99.3		99.3	99.3		99.3	99.3		99.3	99.3		99.3	99.3		99.3	99.3
0241, 31 - 34	SITE & INFRASTRUCTURE, DEMOLITION	96.2	97.4	97.0	88.5	97.4	94.7	79.6	96.4	91.2	94.4	96.4	95.8	87.6	96.4	93.6	82.9	96.4	92.2
0310	Concrete Forming & Accessories	103.0	41.3	49.3	104.6	56.0	62.3	96.0	43.8	50.6	99.8	43.8	51.1	95.0	43.8	50.5	101.4	43.8	51.3
0320	Concrete Reinforcing	106.8	64.1	85.3	100.8	64.9	82.7	108.3	64.7	86.3	107.9	64.7	86.1	108.9	64.7	86.6	108.9	66.3	87.4
0330	Cast-in-Place Concrete	92.9	74.7	85.7	91.3	74.9	84.8	92.2	51.9	76.3	92.3	51.9	76.4	92.3	51.9	76.4	92.2	51.9	76.3
03	CONCRETE	99.6	58.0	79.3	98.3	64.7	81.9	99.0	51.3	75.8	111.4	51.3	82.2	106.5	51.3	79.6	99.5	51.6	76.2
04	MASONRY	101.3	35.8	61.4	98.1	49.4	68.4	94.8	44.3	64.0	94.8	44.3	64.0	94.8	44.3	64.0	152.6	44.3	86.5
05	METALS	97.6	68.4	87.9	98.8	69.8	89.2	93.9	67.7	85.2	93.9	67.7	85.2	94.0	67.7	85.3	94.7	68.3	86.0
06	WOOD, PLASTICS & COMPOSITES	91.8	38.4	64.4	93.5	57.8	72.9	84.3	44.8	61.5	87.9	44.8	63.0	83.3	44.8	61.0	91.2	44.8	64.4
07	THERMAL & MOISTURE PROTECTION	97.8	47.5	77.3	99.5	53.1	80.6	100.8	46.6	78.8	102.5	46.6	79.8	101.9	46.6	79.4	100.9	46.6	78.8
08	OPENINGS	96.3	43.2	83.0	98.6	53.8	87.3	102.8	46.7	88.7	102.5	46.7	88.4	102.7	46.7	88.6	103.2	47.1	89.1
0920	Plaster & Gypsum Board	100.7	36.4	54.8	89.0	56.4	65.7	83.7	42.9	54.6	84.1	42.9	54.7	83.7	42.9	54.6	92.8	42.9	57.2
0950, 0980	Ceilings & Acoustic Treatment	114.2	36.4	62.8	106.7	56.4	73.5	108.8	42.9	65.3	108.8	42.9	65.3	108.8	42.9	65.3	108.8	42.9	65.3
0960	Flooring	99.6	34.6	80.5	104.1	55.5	89.8	97.6	48.8	83.3	100.6	48.8	85.4	97.0	48.8	82.8	102.9	48.8	87.1
0970, 0990	Wall Finishes & Painting/Coating	98.8	45.4	65.9	102.3	45.4	67.2	98.1	29.1	55.5	98.1	29.1	55.5	98.1	29.1	55.5	98.1	29.1	55.5
09	FINISHES	105.1	39.1	68.3	104.1	54.8	76.6	98.5	42.4	67.2	101.2	42.4	68.4	99.4	42.4	67.6	101.1	42.4	68.4
COVERS	DIVS. 10 - 14, 25, 28, 41, 43, 44, 46	100.0	74.3	94.9	100.0	76.5	95.3	100.0	57.2	91.5	100.0	57.2	91.5	100.0	57.2	91.5	100.0	57.2	91.5
21, 22, 23	FIRE SUPPRESSION, PLUMBING & HVAC	100.0	55.0	81.8	100.0	55.0	81.8	97.0	52.6	79.0	97.0	52.6	79.0	97.0	52.6	79.0	100.0	52.7	80.8
26, 27, 3370	ELECTRICAL, COMMUNICATIONS & UTIL.	94.9	66.9	80.5	97.6	72.9	84.9	95.1	66.8	80.5	95.1	66.8	80.5	95.1	66.9	80.5	93.4	66.9	79.7
MF2010	WEIGHTED AVERAGE	98.9	57.7	80.7	99.1	63.8	83.5	96.9	57.0	79.3	99.0	57.0	80.5	98.1	57.0	80.0	101.0	57.2	81.7

WYOMING / CANADA

DIVISION		SHERIDAN 828 MAT.	INST.	TOTAL	WHEATLAND 822 MAT.	INST.	TOTAL	WORLAND 824 MAT.	INST.	TOTAL	YELLOWSTONE NAT'L PA 821 MAT.	INST.	TOTAL	BARRIE, ONTARIO MAT.	INST.	TOTAL	BATHURST, NEW BRUNSWICK MAT.	INST.	TOTAL
015433	CONTRACTOR EQUIPMENT		99.3	99.3		99.3	99.3		99.3	99.3		99.3	99.3		101.7	101.7		102.0	102.0
0241, 31 - 34	SITE & INFRASTRUCTURE, DEMOLITION	88.1	97.4	94.5	83.8	96.4	92.5	81.2	96.4	91.7	81.3	96.7	91.9	114.9	101.4	105.6	94.6	97.7	96.7
0310	Concrete Forming & Accessories	102.6	46.2	53.5	97.9	44.2	51.2	97.9	43.8	50.9	97.9	46.1	52.9	123.2	93.6	97.5	103.1	66.6	71.4
0320	Concrete Reinforcing	108.9	64.8	86.7	108.3	64.7	86.3	108.9	64.7	86.6	110.8	69.6	90.0	180.2	87.6	133.5	148.8	59.1	103.6
0330	Cast-in-Place Concrete	95.4	74.8	87.3	96.2	52.4	79.0	92.2	51.9	76.3	92.2	55.2	77.6	167.6	92.3	137.9	138.2	64.1	109.0
03	CONCRETE	106.6	60.3	84.1	103.7	51.7	78.3	99.2	51.3	75.9	99.5	54.4	77.5	153.4	92.1	123.5	135.8	65.0	101.3
04	MASONRY	95.1	48.8	66.9	95.1	45.2	64.7	94.8	44.3	64.0	94.9	50.3	67.7	167.0	102.0	127.3	158.0	67.6	102.8
05	METALS	97.5	69.6	88.3	93.8	67.7	85.2	94.0	67.7	85.3	94.6	69.5	86.3	107.3	92.6	102.5	104.7	73.5	94.4
06	WOOD, PLASTICS & COMPOSITES	94.7	44.8	66.2	85.9	44.8	62.2	86.0	44.8	62.2	86.0	44.8	62.2	117.4	92.2	102.8	94.7	66.9	78.6
07	THERMAL & MOISTURE PROTECTION	101.9	51.5	81.4	101.1	47.5	79.3	100.9	46.6	78.8	100.4	49.7	79.8	111.6	93.1	104.0	105.0	65.1	88.8
08	OPENINGS	103.5	47.6	89.4	101.4	46.7	87.6	103.0	46.7	88.9	95.9	47.9	83.8	92.4	90.3	91.8	87.4	58.3	80.1
0920	Plaster & Gypsum Board	111.2	42.9	62.5	83.7	42.9	54.6	83.7	42.9	54.6	84.0	42.9	54.7	155.0	91.9	109.9	162.1	65.7	93.3
0950, 0980	Ceilings & Acoustic Treatment	111.8	42.9	66.3	108.8	42.9	65.3	108.8	42.9	65.3	109.7	42.9	65.6	95.8	91.9	93.2	96.7	65.7	76.2
0960	Flooring	100.8	48.8	85.5	99.2	48.8	84.4	99.2	48.8	84.4	99.2	48.8	84.4	132.5	101.8	123.5	115.8	48.6	96.1
0970, 0990	Wall Finishes & Painting/Coating	100.4	45.4	66.5	98.1	29.1	55.5	98.1	29.1	55.5	98.1	29.1	55.5	112.8	93.1	100.7	112.0	53.5	75.9
09	FINISHES	106.5	45.4	72.4	99.4	42.6	67.7	99.0	42.4	67.4	99.2	43.9	68.3	118.4	95.4	105.5	112.6	62.1	84.5
COVERS	DIVS. 10 - 14, 25, 28, 41, 43, 44, 46	100.0	75.0	95.0	100.0	57.5	91.5	100.0	57.2	91.5	100.0	59.2	91.9	140.0	79.2	127.9	140.5	69.5	126.4
21, 22, 23	FIRE SUPPRESSION, PLUMBING & HVAC	97.0	55.0	80.8	97.0	53.1	79.2	97.0	52.6	79.0	97.0	55.7	80.3	103.0	104.9	103.8	103.2	73.7	91.3
26, 27, 3370	ELECTRICAL, COMMUNICATIONS & UTIL.	97.8	66.9	81.9	95.1	72.8	83.6	95.1	66.9	80.5	94.1	66.9	80.1	119.3	94.5	106.5	119.9	64.6	91.4
MF2010	WEIGHTED AVERAGE	99.7	60.6	82.4	97.5	58.2	80.2	97.1	57.0	79.4	96.4	59.3	80.1	118.6	96.9	109.1	114.1	70.1	94.7

CANADA

DIVISION		BRANDON, MANITOBA MAT.	INST.	TOTAL	BRANTFORD, ONTARIO MAT.	INST.	TOTAL	BRIDGEWATER, NOVA SCOTIA MAT.	INST.	TOTAL	CALGARY, ALBERTA MAT.	INST.	TOTAL	CAP-DE-LA-MADELEINE, QUEBEC MAT.	INST.	TOTAL	CHARLESBOURG, QUEBEC MAT.	INST.	TOTAL
015433	CONTRACTOR EQUIPMENT		103.9	103.9		101.7	101.7		101.7	101.7		106.4	106.4		102.6	102.6		102.6	102.6
0241, 31 - 34	SITE & INFRASTRUCTURE, DEMOLITION	110.7	100.3	103.5	112.7	101.7	105.1	97.0	99.3	98.5	125.9	105.2	111.6	92.7	100.9	98.4	92.7	100.9	98.4
0310	Concrete Forming & Accessories	122.5	75.8	81.9	123.0	101.4	104.2	97.4	75.0	77.9	127.5	96.2	100.3	128.1	92.1	96.8	128.1	92.1	96.8
0320	Concrete Reinforcing	161.8	55.6	108.3	175.1	86.3	130.3	148.8	48.8	98.4	143.8	72.5	107.9	148.8	82.4	115.3	148.8	82.4	115.3
0330	Cast-in-Place Concrete	151.1	79.4	122.8	163.5	114.5	144.2	168.1	74.8	131.3	201.8	106.1	164.1	131.9	101.5	119.9	131.9	101.5	119.9
03	CONCRETE	135.9	73.9	105.7	150.5	103.0	127.4	148.4	70.7	110.5	167.2	95.3	132.2	130.9	93.6	112.7	130.9	93.6	112.7
04	MASONRY	161.7	70.4	106.0	163.3	106.7	128.8	158.8	74.8	107.6	212.7	90.7	138.3	159.0	90.6	117.3	159.0	90.6	117.3
05	METALS	107.5	78.8	98.0	106.7	93.4	102.3	105.0	76.3	96.1	143.7	89.0	125.6	105.0	90.0	100.1	105.0	90.0	100.1
06	WOOD, PLASTICS & COMPOSITES	112.9	76.8	92.0	115.2	100.1	106.5	87.4	74.3	79.8	113.5	96.0	103.4	126.1	92.0	106.4	126.1	92.0	106.4
07	THERMAL & MOISTURE PROTECTION	105.2	75.0	92.0	111.5	98.9	106.3	106.5	73.1	92.9	123.7	94.0	111.6	105.4	93.9	100.7	105.4	93.9	100.7
08	OPENINGS	93.4	67.6	86.9	92.2	96.7	93.4	83.9	67.7	79.9	93.4	85.7	91.4	93.4	84.6	91.2	93.4	84.6	91.2
0920	Plaster & Gypsum Board	130.0	75.6	91.2	155.0	100.1	115.8	155.9	73.4	96.9	171.9	95.4	117.2	185.9	91.5	118.5	185.9	91.5	118.5
0950, 0980	Ceilings & Acoustic Treatment	95.8	75.6	82.5	95.8	100.1	98.6	95.8	73.4	81.0	151.3	95.4	114.4	95.8	91.5	93.0	95.8	91.5	93.0
0960	Flooring	132.5	72.3	114.8	132.5	101.8	123.5	112.1	69.3	99.5	134.6	95.4	123.1	132.5	102.5	123.7	132.5	102.5	123.7
0970, 0990	Wall Finishes & Painting/Coating	112.0	60.8	80.5	112.0	102.2	106.0	112.0	66.5	83.9	111.9	109.7	110.5	112.0	95.0	101.5	112.0	95.0	101.5
09	FINISHES	114.5	74.0	91.9	117.1	102.0	108.7	110.3	73.2	89.6	133.8	98.0	113.8	119.7	94.6	105.7	119.7	94.6	105.7
COVERS	DIVS. 10 - 14, 25, 28, 41, 43, 44, 46	140.5	71.8	126.9	140.5	81.5	128.8	140.5	70.8	126.7	140.5	101.4	132.8	140.5	90.7	130.6	140.5	90.7	130.6
21, 22, 23	FIRE SUPPRESSION, PLUMBING & HVAC	103.2	88.8	97.3	103.2	100.8	105.2	103.2	89.2	97.5	100.5	92.6	97.3	103.8	96.1	100.7	103.8	96.1	100.7
26, 27, 3370	ELECTRICAL, COMMUNICATIONS & UTIL.	122.0	72.8	96.6	117.2	94.0	105.2	123.2	67.3	94.4	123.5	84.2	103.2	116.9	75.9	95.8	116.9	75.9	95.8
MF2010	WEIGHTED AVERAGE	116.2	79.0	99.8	117.7	101.0	110.4	115.6	77.8	98.9	129.8	93.1	113.6	114.8	91.3	104.4	114.8	91.3	104.4

City Cost Indexes

CANADA

		CHARLOTTETOWN, PRINCE EDWARD ISLAND			CHICOUTIMI, QUEBEC			CORNER BROOK, NEWFOUNDLAND			CORNWALL, ONTARIO			DALHOUSIE, NEW BRUNSWICK			DARTMOUTH, NOVA SCOTIA		
DIVISION		MAT.	INST.	TOTAL	MAT.	INST.	TOTAL	MAT.	INST.	TOTAL	MAT.	INST.	TOTAL	MAT.	INST.	TOTAL	MAT.	INST.	TOTAL
015433	CONTRACTOR EQUIPMENT		101.6	101.6		102.6	102.6		103.3	103.3		101.7	101.7		102.0	102.0		101.7	101.7
0241, 31 - 34	SITE & INFRASTRUCTURE, DEMOLITION	108.2	96.8	100.3	92.2	99.7	97.4	112.8	98.3	102.8	110.8	101.2	104.2	94.5	97.7	96.7	104.7	99.3	100.9
0310	Concrete Forming & Accessories	97.8	60.9	65.7	128.1	89.7	94.7	104.5	64.5	69.7	121.0	93.8	97.3	103.1	66.9	71.6	97.5	75.0	77.9
0320	Concrete Reinforcing	155.0	48.9	101.5	112.2	92.1	102.1	148.8	50.8	99.4	175.1	86.0	130.2	148.8	59.1	103.6	155.2	48.8	101.6
0330	Cast-in-Place Concrete	160.5	63.3	122.2	130.1	96.8	117.0	172.3	73.2	133.2	147.0	104.4	130.2	138.2	64.2	109.1	169.8	74.8	132.4
03	CONCRETE	153.8	60.3	108.3	124.3	92.7	108.9	162.3	65.9	115.3	142.1	96.0	119.7	135.8	65.1	101.4	150.3	70.7	111.5
04	MASONRY	164.1	65.2	103.7	159.5	90.6	117.5	159.2	66.7	102.8	162.0	97.8	122.8	155.8	67.6	101.9	170.6	74.8	112.2
05	METALS	111.6	69.4	97.7	104.5	91.1	100.1	107.9	75.0	97.1	106.7	92.0	101.8	104.7	73.8	94.5	108.0	76.3	97.5
06	WOOD, PLASTICS & COMPOSITES	87.7	60.4	71.9	126.1	89.8	105.1	95.7	63.5	77.1	114.1	93.1	102.0	94.7	66.9	78.6	87.4	74.3	79.8
07	THERMAL & MOISTURE PROTECTION	106.6	62.5	88.6	105.4	93.0	100.3	108.6	64.7	90.7	111.3	93.2	103.9	108.9	65.1	91.1	106.5	73.1	92.9
08	OPENINGS	95.7	52.1	84.7	92.9	77.9	89.1	99.7	59.6	89.6	93.4	90.0	92.5	87.4	58.3	80.1	83.9	67.7	79.9
0920	Plaster & Gypsum Board	157.7	59.1	87.2	185.9	89.3	116.9	162.1	62.2	90.7	224.8	92.8	130.5	162.1	65.7	93.3	158.9	73.4	97.8
0950, 0980	Ceilings & Acoustic Treatment	110.3	59.1	76.5	95.8	89.3	91.5	96.7	62.2	73.9	98.5	92.8	94.8	96.7	65.7	76.2	105.8	73.4	84.4
0960	Flooring	112.2	64.8	98.2	132.5	102.5	123.7	116.5	59.0	99.6	132.5	100.3	123.1	115.8	74.3	103.6	112.1	69.3	99.5
0970, 0990	Wall Finishes & Painting/Coating	112.0	44.5	70.4	112.0	101.1	105.3	112.0	64.0	82.4	112.0	95.3	101.7	112.0	53.5	75.9	112.0	66.5	83.9
09	FINISHES	115.2	60.2	84.5	119.7	93.7	105.2	114.0	63.5	85.8	125.8	95.4	108.8	112.6	67.2	87.3	112.9	73.2	90.7
COVERS	DIVS. 10 - 14, 25, 28, 41, 43, 44, 46	140.5	68.9	126.3	140.5	90.1	130.5	140.5	69.8	126.5	140.5	78.8	128.2	140.5	69.4	126.4	140.5	70.8	126.7
21, 22, 23	FIRE SUPPRESSION, PLUMBING & HVAC	103.3	67.4	88.8	103.2	95.6	100.1	103.2	75.9	92.1	103.8	105.6	104.6	103.2	73.7	91.3	103.2	89.2	97.5
26, 27, 3370	ELECTRICAL, COMMUNICATIONS & UTIL.	113.6	54.7	83.2	116.5	83.0	99.2	119.1	60.9	89.1	118.3	95.0	106.3	120.0	61.1	89.6	123.7	67.3	94.6
MF2010	WEIGHTED AVERAGE	118.2	65.4	95.0	113.7	91.6	104.0	119.5	70.5	97.9	117.7	97.2	108.7	114.1	70.3	94.8	117.2	77.8	99.8

CANADA

		EDMONTON, ALBERTA			FORT MCMURRAY, ALBERTA			FREDERICTON, NEW BRUNSWICK			GATINEAU, QUEBEC			GRANBY, QUEBEC			HALIFAX, NOVA SCOTIA		
DIVISION		MAT.	INST.	TOTAL	MAT.	INST.	TOTAL	MAT.	INST.	TOTAL	MAT.	INST.	TOTAL	MAT.	INST.	TOTAL	MAT.	INST.	TOTAL
015433	CONTRACTOR EQUIPMENT		106.4	106.4		103.7	103.7		102.0	102.0		102.6	102.6		102.6	102.6		101.7	101.7
0241, 31 - 34	SITE & INFRASTRUCTURE, DEMOLITION	151.7	105.2	119.6	118.6	102.2	107.3	96.4	97.7	97.3	92.5	100.9	98.3	93.0	100.9	98.5	99.9	99.0	99.3
0310	Concrete Forming & Accessories	129.7	96.2	100.6	121.2	96.4	99.6	120.7	67.2	74.1	128.1	92.0	96.7	128.1	91.9	96.6	97.8	77.3	80.0
0320	Concrete Reinforcing	143.8	72.5	107.9	161.8	72.5	116.8	145.2	59.3	101.9	157.4	82.4	119.6	157.4	82.4	119.6	153.0	61.2	106.7
0330	Cast-in-Place Concrete	210.4	106.1	169.3	217.2	105.3	173.1	132.5	64.3	105.6	130.1	101.4	118.8	134.5	101.4	121.4	172.4	80.6	136.2
03	CONCRETE	171.7	95.3	134.5	175.3	95.1	136.2	133.6	65.3	100.4	131.3	93.5	112.9	133.5	93.5	114.0	151.2	76.1	114.6
04	MASONRY	200.5	90.7	133.5	202.4	90.7	134.2	175.9	69.2	110.8	158.9	90.6	117.2	159.2	90.6	117.3	171.4	82.4	117.1
05	METALS	144.2	89.0	126.0	132.2	89.1	118.0	110.3	74.3	98.4	105.0	89.9	100.0	105.0	89.8	100.0	126.5	81.6	111.7
06	WOOD, PLASTICS & COMPOSITES	110.0	96.0	101.9	109.8	96.0	101.8	115.9	66.9	87.6	126.1	92.0	106.4	126.1	92.0	106.4	87.5	76.2	81.0
07	THERMAL & MOISTURE PROTECTION	125.1	94.0	112.5	118.9	93.5	108.5	109.8	66.1	92.0	105.4	93.9	100.7	105.4	92.3	100.0	107.3	77.1	95.0
08	OPENINGS	93.4	85.7	91.4	93.4	85.7	91.4	87.3	57.1	79.7	93.4	79.7	89.9	93.4	79.7	89.9	83.9	71.4	80.8
0920	Plaster & Gypsum Board	166.3	95.4	115.6	154.6	95.5	112.4	177.8	65.7	97.7	147.1	91.5	107.4	150.1	91.5	108.3	158.0	75.4	99.0
0950, 0980	Ceilings & Acoustic Treatment	158.0	95.4	116.6	105.8	95.5	99.0	107.6	65.7	79.9	95.8	91.5	93.0	95.8	91.5	93.0	111.2	75.4	87.5
0960	Flooring	135.8	95.4	123.9	132.5	95.4	121.6	128.0	77.5	113.2	132.5	102.5	123.7	132.5	102.5	123.7	112.1	91.0	105.9
0970, 0990	Wall Finishes & Painting/Coating	112.0	109.7	110.6	112.0	99.0	104.0	112.0	68.2	84.9	112.0	95.0	101.5	112.0	95.0	101.5	112.0	79.8	92.1
09	FINISHES	137.0	98.0	115.2	120.8	96.8	107.4	120.8	69.4	92.2	115.2	94.6	103.7	115.5	94.6	103.9	114.2	80.4	95.4
COVERS	DIVS. 10 - 14, 25, 28, 41, 43, 44, 46	140.5	101.4	132.8	140.5	101.3	132.7	140.5	69.5	126.4	140.5	90.7	130.6	140.5	90.7	130.6	140.5	71.5	126.8
21, 22, 23	FIRE SUPPRESSION, PLUMBING & HVAC	100.6	92.6	97.4	103.5	104.4	103.9	103.3	83.8	95.4	103.8	96.1	100.7	103.2	96.1	100.4	99.8	78.0	91.0
26, 27, 3370	ELECTRICAL, COMMUNICATIONS & UTIL.	115.6	84.2	99.4	111.0	89.3	99.8	124.5	80.5	101.8	116.9	75.9	95.8	117.6	75.9	96.1	120.9	79.8	99.7
MF2010	WEIGHTED AVERAGE	130.0	93.1	113.7	126.5	95.8	113.0	117.0	75.6	98.8	114.4	91.1	104.2	114.7	91.0	104.3	119.0	80.3	101.9

CANADA

		HAMILTON, ONTARIO			HULL, QUEBEC			JOLIETTE, QUEBEC			KAMLOOPS, BRITISH COLUMBIA			KINGSTON, ONTARIO			KITCHENER, ONTARIO		
DIVISION		MAT.	INST.	TOTAL	MAT.	INST.	TOTAL	MAT.	INST.	TOTAL	MAT.	INST.	TOTAL	MAT.	INST.	TOTAL	MAT.	INST.	TOTAL
015433	CONTRACTOR EQUIPMENT		108.4	108.4		102.6	102.6		102.6	102.6		105.7	105.7		104.0	104.0		103.9	103.9
0241, 31 - 34	SITE & INFRASTRUCTURE, DEMOLITION	116.3	112.8	113.9	92.5	100.9	98.3	93.2	100.9	98.5	117.7	104.3	108.5	110.8	104.9	106.7	100.3	105.1	103.6
0310	Concrete Forming & Accessories	130.8	94.3	99.0	128.1	92.0	96.7	128.1	92.1	96.8	123.5	95.0	98.7	121.2	93.8	97.4	117.6	85.6	89.8
0320	Concrete Reinforcing	162.7	85.9	124.0	157.4	82.4	119.6	148.8	82.4	115.3	116.8	80.3	98.4	175.1	86.0	130.2	110.5	85.8	98.1
0330	Cast-in-Place Concrete	153.0	95.8	130.4	130.1	101.4	118.8	135.6	101.5	122.1	117.3	105.3	112.5	147.0	104.4	130.2	140.8	86.9	119.5
03	CONCRETE	143.8	93.3	119.2	131.3	93.5	112.9	132.7	93.6	113.7	137.7	95.8	117.3	142.1	96.1	119.7	122.6	86.4	105.0
04	MASONRY	179.1	100.4	131.1	158.9	90.6	117.2	159.3	90.6	117.4	165.6	98.8	124.8	168.6	97.9	125.4	159.8	92.6	118.8
05	METALS	125.5	92.3	114.6	105.0	89.9	100.0	105.0	90.0	100.1	107.3	89.9	101.6	108.4	91.9	102.9	115.4	92.1	107.7
06	WOOD, PLASTICS & COMPOSITES	114.5	93.4	102.3	126.1	92.0	106.4	126.1	92.0	106.4	98.3	93.4	95.5	114.1	93.2	102.0	108.7	84.9	94.9
07	THERMAL & MOISTURE PROTECTION	122.5	95.7	111.6	105.4	93.9	100.7	105.4	93.9	100.7	120.7	90.7	108.5	111.3	94.4	104.4	110.8	90.8	102.7
08	OPENINGS	93.4	91.9	93.0	93.4	79.7	89.9	93.4	84.6	91.2	89.1	89.4	89.2	93.4	89.6	92.4	84.5	85.5	84.7
0920	Plaster & Gypsum Board	191.9	93.2	121.4	147.1	91.5	107.4	185.9	91.5	118.5	136.1	92.7	105.1	229.1	93.0	131.9	153.0	84.4	104.0
0950, 0980	Ceilings & Acoustic Treatment	130.9	93.2	106.0	95.8	91.5	93.0	95.8	91.5	93.0	95.8	92.7	93.8	113.0	93.0	99.8	105.8	84.4	91.6
0960	Flooring	134.6	105.3	126.0	132.5	102.5	123.7	132.5	102.5	123.7	130.3	57.3	108.8	132.5	100.3	123.1	128.5	105.3	121.7
0970, 0990	Wall Finishes & Painting/Coating	112.0	100.9	105.2	112.0	95.0	101.5	112.0	95.0	101.5	112.0	87.0	96.6	112.0	88.0	97.2	112.0	91.1	99.1
09	FINISHES	130.9	97.2	112.1	115.2	94.6	103.7	119.7	94.6	105.7	116.6	87.7	100.5	129.5	94.7	110.1	116.9	89.5	101.6
COVERS	DIVS. 10 - 14, 25, 28, 41, 43, 44, 46	140.5	104.0	133.3	140.5	90.7	130.6	140.5	90.7	130.6	140.5	101.7	132.8	140.5	78.8	128.2	140.5	100.9	132.7
21, 22, 23	FIRE SUPPRESSION, PLUMBING & HVAC	100.7	84.0	93.9	103.2	96.1	100.4	103.2	96.1	100.4	103.2	99.7	101.8	103.8	105.9	104.7	99.8	89.1	95.4
26, 27, 3370	ELECTRICAL, COMMUNICATIONS & UTIL.	119.7	87.5	103.1	119.0	75.9	96.7	117.6	75.9	96.1	121.3	85.6	102.9	118.3	93.6	105.6	117.6	85.1	100.8
MF2010	WEIGHTED AVERAGE	121.9	93.7	109.4	114.5	91.1	104.2	114.9	91.3	104.5	116.9	94.4	107.0	118.6	97.3	109.2	113.7	90.4	103.4

City Cost Indexes

CANADA

DIVISION		LAVAL, QUEBEC			LETHBRIDGE, ALBERTA			LLOYDMINSTER, ALBERTA			LONDON, ONTARIO			MEDICINE HAT, ALBERTA			MONCTON, NEW BRUNSWICK		
		MAT.	INST.	TOTAL	MAT.	INST.	TOTAL	MAT.	INST.	TOTAL	MAT.	INST.	TOTAL	MAT.	INST.	TOTAL	MAT.	INST.	TOTAL
015433	CONTRACTOR EQUIPMENT		102.6	102.6		103.7	103.7		103.7	103.7		104.0	104.0		103.7	103.7		102.0	102.0
0241, 31 - 34	SITE & INFRASTRUCTURE, DEMOLITION	93.0	100.9	98.5	110.9	102.8	105.3	110.9	102.2	104.9	115.1	105.3	108.4	109.5	102.3	104.5	94.0	97.8	96.7
0310	Concrete Forming & Accessories	128.2	92.0	96.7	122.4	96.5	99.9	120.7	86.2	90.7	130.9	88.2	93.8	122.3	86.2	90.9	103.1	67.1	71.8
0320	Concrete Reinforcing	157.4	82.4	119.6	161.8	72.5	116.8	161.8	72.5	116.8	142.3	84.7	113.2	161.8	72.5	116.8	148.8	62.3	105.2
0330	Cast-in-Place Concrete	134.5	101.4	121.4	162.9	105.3	140.2	151.1	101.5	131.5	164.1	93.7	136.3	151.1	101.5	131.5	133.1	64.5	106.1
03	CONCRETE	133.5	93.5	114.0	148.1	95.2	122.3	142.1	89.3	116.4	146.2	89.7	118.6	142.2	89.3	116.4	133.2	66.1	100.5
04	MASONRY	159.2	90.6	117.3	176.5	90.7	124.1	158.7	83.8	113.0	183.3	97.7	131.1	158.7	83.8	113.0	157.6	67.6	102.7
05	METALS	105.1	89.9	100.1	125.8	89.1	113.7	107.5	89.0	101.4	124.2	91.6	113.5	107.5	88.9	101.4	104.7	79.4	96.4
06	WOOD, PLASTICS & COMPOSITES	126.3	92.0	106.5	113.0	96.0	103.2	109.8	85.7	95.9	114.5	86.5	98.3	113.0	85.7	97.2	94.7	66.9	78.6
07	THERMAL & MOISTURE PROTECTION	105.9	93.9	101.0	116.4	93.5	107.1	113.6	88.8	103.5	123.3	93.4	111.1	119.6	88.8	107.1	108.9	66.6	91.7
08	OPENINGS	93.4	79.7	89.9	93.4	85.7	91.4	93.4	80.1	90.0	94.4	87.0	92.5	93.4	80.1	90.0	87.4	61.6	80.9
0920	Plaster & Gypsum Board	150.5	91.5	108.4	139.1	95.5	107.9	133.7	84.9	98.8	193.7	86.0	116.8	136.4	84.9	99.6	162.1	65.7	93.3
0950, 0980	Ceilings & Acoustic Treatment	95.8	91.5	93.0	104.9	95.5	98.7	95.8	84.9	88.6	137.2	86.0	103.4	95.8	84.9	88.6	96.7	65.7	76.2
0960	Flooring	132.5	102.5	123.7	132.5	95.4	121.6	132.5	95.4	121.6	134.8	105.3	126.2	132.5	95.4	121.6	115.8	74.3	103.6
0970, 0990	Wall Finishes & Painting/Coating	112.0	95.0	101.5	111.9	108.0	109.5	112.0	84.2	94.8	112.0	97.7	103.2	111.9	84.2	94.8	112.0	53.5	75.9
09	FINISHES	115.6	94.6	103.9	117.8	97.8	106.6	115.3	87.4	99.7	123.1	92.3	109.9	115.4	87.4	99.8	112.6	67.2	87.3
COVERS	DIVS. 10 - 14, 25, 28, 41, 43, 44, 46	140.5	90.7	130.6	140.5	101.3	132.7	140.5	97.8	132.0	140.5	102.6	133.0	140.5	97.8	132.0	140.5	69.5	126.3
21, 22, 23	FIRE SUPPRESSION, PLUMBING & HVAC	99.8	96.1	98.3	103.4	100.8	102.4	103.8	100.9	102.6	100.7	81.2	92.8	103.2	97.3	100.8	103.2	73.8	91.3
26, 27, 3370	ELECTRICAL, COMMUNICATIONS & UTIL.	118.9	75.9	96.7	112.5	89.3	100.5	109.9	89.3	99.3	112.9	85.1	98.6	109.9	89.3	99.3	124.6	64.6	93.7
MF2010	WEIGHTED AVERAGE	114.0	91.1	103.9	120.8	95.3	109.5	116.0	91.8	105.4	121.6	90.2	107.8	116.1	91.1	105.1	114.3	71.7	95.5

CANADA

DIVISION		MONTREAL, QUEBEC			MOOSE JAW, SASKATCHEWAN			NEW GLASGOW, NOVA SCOTIA			NEWCASTLE, NEW BRUNSWICK			NORTH BAY, ONTARIO			OSHAWA, ONTARIO		
		MAT.	INST.	TOTAL	MAT.	INST.	TOTAL	MAT.	INST.	TOTAL	MAT.	INST.	TOTAL	MAT.	INST.	TOTAL	MAT.	INST.	TOTAL
015433	CONTRACTOR EQUIPMENT		104.2	104.2		100.2	100.2		101.7	101.7		102.0	102.0		101.7	101.7		103.9	103.9
0241, 31 - 34	SITE & INFRASTRUCTURE, DEMOLITION	102.6	100.0	100.8	110.6	96.8	101.1	97.2	99.3	98.6	94.6	97.7	96.7	112.7	100.8	104.5	112.6	104.9	107.3
0310	Concrete Forming & Accessories	135.8	90.0	96.0	106.7	63.3	69.0	97.4	75.0	77.9	103.1	66.9	71.6	123.0	91.1	95.2	123.2	93.2	97.1
0320	Concrete Reinforcing	150.6	92.1	121.1	114.2	64.7	89.2	148.8	48.8	98.4	148.8	59.1	103.6	175.1	85.5	129.9	175.1	88.2	131.3
0330	Cast-in-Place Concrete	182.2	98.1	149.1	146.6	73.7	117.9	169.8	74.8	132.4	138.2	64.2	109.1	163.5	90.3	134.7	162.8	91.2	134.6
03	CONCRETE	156.9	93.2	125.9	125.4	67.8	97.4	149.3	70.7	111.0	135.8	65.2	101.4	150.5	89.9	121.0	150.2	91.7	121.7
04	MASONRY	166.1	90.6	120.1	157.3	67.0	102.2	159.0	74.8	107.6	158.0	67.6	102.8	163.3	93.5	120.7	162.9	98.2	123.4
05	METALS	124.2	91.6	113.4	103.9	75.9	94.7	105.8	76.3	96.1	104.7	73.8	94.5	106.7	91.6	101.7	106.8	93.8	102.5
06	WOOD, PLASTICS & COMPOSITES	126.3	90.0	105.3	96.2	61.8	76.3	87.4	74.3	79.8	94.7	66.9	78.6	115.2	91.6	101.6	115.4	92.2	102.0
07	THERMAL & MOISTURE PROTECTION	119.4	93.5	108.9	104.8	67.1	89.5	106.5	73.1	92.9	108.9	65.1	91.1	111.5	89.4	102.5	111.8	91.2	103.4
08	OPENINGS	93.4	79.8	89.9	88.2	59.2	80.9	83.9	67.7	79.9	87.4	58.3	80.1	92.2	87.4	91.0	92.2	91.7	92.1
0920	Plaster & Gypsum Board	171.6	89.3	112.8	131.9	60.5	80.9	155.9	73.4	96.9	162.1	65.7	93.3	155.0	91.3	109.5	156.8	91.9	110.4
0950, 0980	Ceilings & Acoustic Treatment	115.6	89.3	98.2	95.8	60.5	72.5	95.8	73.4	81.0	96.7	65.7	76.2	95.8	91.3	92.8	100.3	91.9	94.8
0960	Flooring	134.1	102.5	124.8	121.1	65.2	104.7	112.1	69.3	99.5	115.8	74.3	103.6	132.5	100.3	123.1	132.5	108.0	125.3
0970, 0990	Wall Finishes & Painting/Coating	112.0	101.1	105.3	112.0	69.2	85.6	112.0	66.5	83.9	112.0	53.5	75.9	112.0	94.5	101.2	112.0	104.9	107.6
09	FINISHES	123.5	93.9	107.0	111.5	64.0	85.0	110.3	73.2	89.6	112.6	67.2	87.3	117.1	93.6	104.0	118.2	97.2	106.5
COVERS	DIVS. 10 - 14, 25, 28, 41, 43, 44, 46	140.5	90.6	130.6	140.5	68.6	126.2	140.5	70.8	126.7	140.5	69.5	126.4	140.5	77.4	128.0	140.5	103.5	133.2
21, 22, 23	FIRE SUPPRESSION, PLUMBING & HVAC	100.7	95.6	98.6	103.8	80.4	94.3	103.2	89.2	97.5	103.2	73.7	91.3	103.2	103.6	103.4	99.8	106.3	102.4
26, 27, 3370	ELECTRICAL, COMMUNICATIONS & UTIL.	123.4	83.0	102.5	120.0	65.6	91.9	119.4	67.3	92.5	119.2	64.6	91.0	119.4	94.9	106.8	118.7	94.5	106.2
MF2010	WEIGHTED AVERAGE	121.9	91.9	108.7	113.4	72.4	95.3	115.3	77.8	98.8	114.1	70.8	95.0	118.0	94.9	107.8	117.1	98.2	108.7

CANADA

DIVISION		OTTAWA, ONTARIO			OWEN SOUND, ONTARIO			PETERBOROUGH, ONTARIO			PORTAGE LA PRAIRIE, MANITOBA			PRINCE ALBERT, SASKATCHEWAN			PRINCE GEORGE, BRITISH COLUMBIA		
		MAT.	INST.	TOTAL	MAT.	INST.	TOTAL	MAT.	INST.	TOTAL	MAT.	INST.	TOTAL	MAT.	INST.	TOTAL	MAT.	INST.	TOTAL
015433	CONTRACTOR EQUIPMENT		103.9	103.9		101.7	101.7		101.7	101.7		103.9	103.9		100.2	100.2		105.7	105.7
0241, 31 - 34	SITE & INFRASTRUCTURE, DEMOLITION	112.3	105.1	107.3	114.9	101.2	105.5	112.7	101.1	104.7	111.2	100.2	103.6	105.5	97.0	99.7	121.2	104.3	109.6
0310	Concrete Forming & Accessories	131.7	90.8	96.1	123.2	89.5	93.9	123.0	92.2	96.2	122.5	75.3	81.5	106.7	63.1	68.8	111.9	89.5	92.4
0320	Concrete Reinforcing	155.4	84.6	119.7	180.2	87.6	133.5	175.1	86.0	130.2	161.8	55.6	108.3	119.4	64.4	91.8	116.8	80.3	98.4
0330	Cast-in-Place Concrete	168.5	92.9	138.7	167.6	86.2	135.5	163.5	92.0	135.4	151.1	78.7	122.6	132.8	73.6	109.5	147.1	105.3	130.6
03	CONCRETE	150.5	90.5	121.3	153.4	88.2	121.6	150.5	91.1	121.6	135.9	73.5	105.5	119.4	67.7	94.2	151.9	93.4	123.4
04	MASONRY	180.1	97.6	129.8	167.0	99.5	125.8	163.3	100.6	125.0	161.7	69.3	105.3	156.3	67.0	101.8	167.9	98.8	125.8
05	METALS	129.3	91.5	116.8	107.3	92.4	102.4	106.7	92.1	101.9	107.5	78.7	98.0	104.0	75.7	94.6	107.3	89.9	101.6
06	WOOD, PLASTICS & COMPOSITES	114.4	90.0	100.3	117.4	88.1	100.5	115.2	90.2	100.8	112.9	76.8	92.0	96.2	61.8	76.3	98.3	85.8	91.1
07	THERMAL & MOISTURE PROTECTION	125.1	92.9	112.0	111.6	90.3	102.9	111.5	95.2	104.9	105.2	74.5	92.8	104.7	65.9	88.9	114.9	89.9	104.8
08	OPENINGS	93.4	88.9	92.2	92.4	86.7	90.9	92.2	89.2	91.5	93.4	67.6	86.9	86.7	59.2	79.8	89.1	85.3	88.2
0920	Plaster & Gypsum Board	230.4	89.7	129.9	155.0	87.7	107.0	155.0	89.9	108.5	130.0	75.6	91.2	131.9	60.5	80.9	136.1	84.9	99.5
0950, 0980	Ceilings & Acoustic Treatment	140.8	89.7	107.0	95.8	87.7	90.5	95.8	89.9	91.9	95.8	75.6	82.5	95.8	60.5	72.5	95.8	84.9	88.6
0960	Flooring	134.6	100.3	124.6	132.5	101.8	123.5	132.5	100.3	123.1	132.5	72.3	114.8	121.1	65.2	104.7	127.3	78.5	113.0
0970, 0990	Wall Finishes & Painting/Coating	112.0	92.6	100.0	112.8	93.1	100.7	112.0	96.9	102.7	112.0	60.8	80.5	112.0	59.0	79.3	112.0	87.0	96.6
09	FINISHES	136.5	92.9	112.2	118.4	92.3	103.8	117.1	94.3	104.4	114.6	73.7	91.8	111.5	62.9	84.4	115.7	86.8	99.6
COVERS	DIVS. 10 - 14, 25, 28, 41, 43, 44, 46	140.5	100.6	132.6	140.0	77.9	127.7	140.5	79.0	128.3	140.5	71.4	126.8	140.5	68.7	126.2	140.5	100.8	132.6
21, 22, 23	FIRE SUPPRESSION, PLUMBING & HVAC	100.7	81.7	93.0	103.0	103.5	103.2	103.2	107.4	104.9	103.2	88.2	97.2	103.8	72.4	91.1	103.2	99.7	101.8
26, 27, 3370	ELECTRICAL, COMMUNICATIONS & UTIL.	112.3	85.9	98.7	120.9	93.6	106.8	117.2	94.5	105.5	119.7	62.8	90.3	120.0	65.6	91.9	117.4	85.6	101.0
MF2010	WEIGHTED AVERAGE	122.9	90.7	108.7	118.8	95.0	108.3	117.7	97.0	108.6	116.0	77.2	98.9	112.3	70.5	93.9	118.1	93.7	107.3

CANADA

DIVISION		QUEBEC, QUEBEC			RED DEER, ALBERTA			REGINA, SASKATCHEWAN			RIMOUSKI, QUEBEC			ROUYN-NORANDA, QUEBEC			SAINT HYACINTHE, QUEBEC		
		MAT.	INST.	TOTAL	MAT.	INST.	TOTAL	MAT.	INST.	TOTAL	MAT.	INST.	TOTAL	MAT.	INST.	TOTAL	MAT.	INST.	TOTAL
015433	CONTRACTOR EQUIPMENT		104.5	104.5		103.7	103.7		100.2	100.2		102.6	102.6		102.6	102.6		102.6	102.6
0241, 31 - 34	SITE & INFRASTRUCTURE, DEMOLITION	100.7	100.1	100.3	109.5	102.3	104.5	115.5	98.5	103.8	93.0	99.7	97.7	92.5	100.9	98.3	93.0	100.9	98.5
0310	Concrete Forming & Accessories	137.2	90.3	96.4	139.2	86.2	93.1	107.0	88.1	90.6	128.1	89.7	94.7	128.1	92.0	96.7	128.1	92.0	96.7
0320	Concrete Reinforcing	141.0	92.2	116.4	161.8	72.5	116.8	128.8	77.8	103.1	112.2	92.1	102.1	157.4	82.4	119.6	157.4	82.4	119.6
0330	Cast-in-Place Concrete	149.3	98.5	129.3	151.1	101.5	131.5	170.8	93.2	140.2	136.9	96.8	121.1	130.1	101.4	118.8	134.5	101.4	121.4
03	CONCRETE	139.0	93.5	116.8	143.2	89.3	116.9	139.9	88.0	114.6	127.7	92.7	110.6	131.3	93.5	112.9	133.5	93.5	114.0
04	MASONRY	173.5	90.7	122.9	158.7	83.8	113.0	167.7	91.1	121.0	158.7	90.6	117.1	158.9	90.6	117.2	159.1	90.6	117.3
05	METALS	124.2	91.8	113.5	107.5	88.9	101.4	110.6	83.7	101.7	104.5	91.1	100.1	105.0	89.9	100.0	105.0	89.9	100.0
06	WOOD, PLASTICS & COMPOSITES	126.9	90.1	105.6	113.0	85.7	97.2	96.3	88.8	92.0	126.1	89.8	105.1	126.1	92.0	106.4	126.1	92.0	106.4
07	THERMAL & MOISTURE PROTECTION	121.4	93.7	110.1	129.1	88.8	112.8	106.7	84.3	97.6	105.4	93.0	100.3	105.4	93.9	100.7	105.6	93.9	100.9
08	OPENINGS	93.4	87.8	92.0	93.4	80.1	90.0	88.2	77.7	85.5	92.9	77.9	89.1	93.4	79.7	89.9	93.4	79.7	89.9
0920	Plaster & Gypsum Board	191.4	89.3	118.4	136.4	84.9	99.6	168.2	88.5	111.2	185.7	89.3	116.8	146.8	91.5	107.3	149.8	91.5	108.2
0950, 0980	Ceilings & Acoustic Treatment	120.7	89.3	99.9	95.8	84.9	88.6	125.7	88.5	101.1	94.9	89.3	91.2	94.9	91.5	92.7	94.9	91.5	92.7
0960	Flooring	134.6	102.5	125.2	134.6	95.4	123.1	121.1	67.4	105.4	132.5	102.5	123.7	132.5	102.5	123.7	132.5	102.5	123.7
0970, 0990	Wall Finishes & Painting/Coating	112.5	101.1	105.4	111.9	84.2	94.8	112.0	87.3	96.8	112.0	101.1	105.3	112.0	95.0	101.5	112.0	95.0	101.5
09	FINISHES	127.5	93.9	108.8	116.0	87.4	100.0	123.0	84.8	101.7	119.5	93.7	105.1	114.9	94.6	103.6	115.3	94.6	103.8
COVERS	DIVS. 10 - 14, 25, 28, 41, 43, 44, 46	140.5	90.7	130.6	140.5	97.8	132.0	140.5	75.1	127.5	140.5	90.1	130.5	140.5	90.7	130.6	140.5	90.7	130.6
21, 22, 23	FIRE SUPPRESSION, PLUMBING & HVAC	100.6	95.7	98.6	103.2	97.3	100.8	99.9	82.3	92.8	103.2	95.6	100.1	103.2	96.1	100.4	98.6	96.1	97.6
26, 27, 3370	ELECTRICAL, COMMUNICATIONS & UTIL.	116.5	83.0	99.2	109.9	89.3	99.3	119.9	87.3	103.1	117.6	83.0	99.7	117.6	75.9	96.1	118.5	75.9	96.5
MF2010	WEIGHTED AVERAGE	119.8	92.3	107.7	116.6	91.1	105.3	116.7	86.2	103.2	114.2	91.6	104.2	114.4	91.1	104.1	113.6	91.1	103.7

CANADA

DIVISION		SAINT JOHN, NEW BRUNSWICK			SARNIA, ONTARIO			SASKATOON, SASKATCHEWAN			SAULT STE MARIE, ONTARIO			SHERBROOKE, QUEBEC			SOREL, QUEBEC		
		MAT.	INST.	TOTAL	MAT.	INST.	TOTAL	MAT.	INST.	TOTAL	MAT.	INST.	TOTAL	MAT.	INST.	TOTAL	MAT.	INST.	TOTAL
015433	CONTRACTOR EQUIPMENT		102.0	102.0		101.7	101.7		100.2	100.2		101.7	101.7		102.6	102.6		102.6	102.6
0241, 31 - 34	SITE & INFRASTRUCTURE, DEMOLITION	94.8	98.6	97.4	111.2	101.2	104.3	106.6	98.5	101.0	101.2	100.8	100.9	93.0	100.9	98.5	93.2	100.9	98.5
0310	Concrete Forming & Accessories	120.5	63.9	71.3	121.9	99.7	102.6	106.9	88.1	90.5	112.0	88.0	91.1	128.1	92.0	96.7	128.1	92.1	96.8
0320	Concrete Reinforcing	148.8	62.5	105.3	124.0	87.4	105.6	119.4	77.8	98.4	112.4	85.6	98.9	157.4	82.4	119.6	148.8	82.4	115.3
0330	Cast-in-Place Concrete	136.2	64.3	107.8	150.9	106.0	133.2	142.0	93.2	122.8	135.5	90.4	117.8	134.5	101.4	121.4	135.6	101.5	122.1
03	CONCRETE	136.0	64.7	101.3	136.1	99.5	118.3	124.0	88.0	106.4	120.0	88.6	104.7	133.5	93.5	114.0	132.7	93.6	113.7
04	MASONRY	176.3	69.8	111.3	174.1	103.5	131.0	164.2	91.1	119.6	159.7	95.1	120.3	159.2	90.6	117.3	159.3	90.6	117.4
05	METALS	104.6	79.9	96.5	106.6	92.5	102.0	104.9	83.7	97.9	105.9	90.8	100.9	105.0	89.9	100.0	105.0	90.0	100.1
06	WOOD, PLASTICS & COMPOSITES	115.9	62.4	85.0	114.3	99.0	105.5	94.6	88.8	91.3	102.6	87.0	93.6	126.1	92.0	106.4	126.1	92.0	106.4
07	THERMAL & MOISTURE PROTECTION	109.2	65.5	91.4	111.5	98.9	106.4	105.4	84.3	97.6	110.3	91.0	102.4	105.4	93.9	100.7	105.4	93.9	100.7
08	OPENINGS	87.3	58.0	79.9	94.4	93.3	94.1	87.2	77.7	84.8	84.9	85.4	85.0	93.4	79.7	89.9	93.4	84.6	91.2
0920	Plaster & Gypsum Board	179.4	61.1	94.9	178.2	98.9	121.6	144.8	88.5	104.6	143.4	86.6	102.8	149.8	91.5	108.2	185.7	91.5	118.4
0950, 0980	Ceilings & Acoustic Treatment	103.1	61.1	75.3	100.3	98.9	99.4	117.5	88.5	98.3	95.8	86.6	89.7	94.9	91.5	92.7	94.9	91.5	92.7
0960	Flooring	128.0	74.3	112.2	132.5	109.7	125.8	121.1	67.4	105.4	124.3	103.8	118.3	132.5	102.5	123.7	132.5	102.5	123.7
0970, 0990	Wall Finishes & Painting/Coating	112.0	71.6	87.1	112.0	109.5	110.5	112.0	87.3	96.8	112.0	101.5	105.5	112.0	95.0	101.5	112.0	95.0	101.5
09	FINISHES	119.7	66.4	90.0	120.8	103.1	110.9	117.8	84.8	99.4	112.4	92.2	101.2	115.3	94.6	103.8	119.5	94.6	105.6
COVERS	DIVS. 10 - 14, 25, 28, 41, 43, 44, 46	140.5	68.9	126.3	140.5	80.5	128.6	140.5	75.1	127.5	140.5	102.1	132.9	140.5	90.7	130.6	140.5	90.7	130.6
21, 22, 23	FIRE SUPPRESSION, PLUMBING & HVAC	103.2	78.9	93.4	103.2	113.8	107.5	99.8	82.3	92.7	103.2	100.0	101.9	103.8	96.1	100.7	103.2	96.1	100.4
26, 27, 3370	ELECTRICAL, COMMUNICATIONS & UTIL.	127.7	84.5	105.4	120.2	96.9	108.2	121.9	87.3	104.1	118.9	94.9	106.5	117.6	75.9	96.1	117.6	75.9	96.1
MF2010	WEIGHTED AVERAGE	116.6	75.3	98.4	117.4	101.6	110.5	113.2	86.2	101.3	112.6	94.5	104.6	114.8	91.1	104.4	114.9	91.3	104.5

CANADA

DIVISION		ST CATHARINES, ONTARIO			ST JEROME, QUEBEC			ST JOHNS, NEWFOUNDLAND			SUDBURY, ONTARIO			SUMMERSIDE, PRINCE EDWARD ISLAND			SYDNEY, NOVA SCOTIA		
		MAT.	INST.	TOTAL	MAT.	INST.	TOTAL	MAT.	INST.	TOTAL	MAT.	INST.	TOTAL	MAT.	INST.	TOTAL	MAT.	INST.	TOTAL
015433	CONTRACTOR EQUIPMENT		101.7	101.7		102.6	102.6		103.3	103.3		101.7	101.7		101.6	101.6		101.7	101.7
0241, 31 - 34	SITE & INFRASTRUCTURE, DEMOLITION	101.1	101.9	101.7	92.5	100.9	98.3	113.3	99.7	103.9	101.2	101.4	101.3	105.2	96.8	99.4	92.7	99.3	97.2
0310	Concrete Forming & Accessories	115.6	94.0	96.8	128.1	92.0	96.7	104.7	72.5	76.7	112.0	88.0	91.1	97.7	61.0	65.8	97.4	75.0	77.9
0320	Concrete Reinforcing	111.5	85.8	98.6	157.4	82.4	119.6	160.7	64.0	112.0	112.4	84.3	98.2	146.6	48.9	97.4	148.8	48.8	98.4
0330	Cast-in-Place Concrete	134.4	95.6	119.1	130.1	101.4	118.8	173.5	85.2	138.7	135.5	92.0	118.4	161.2	63.4	122.6	130.9	74.8	108.8
03	CONCRETE	119.5	93.1	106.6	131.3	93.5	112.9	164.8	75.9	121.5	120.0	89.0	104.9	152.9	60.4	107.8	129.7	70.7	101.0
04	MASONRY	159.3	100.4	123.4	158.9	90.6	117.2	164.8	77.3	111.4	159.4	95.6	120.4	158.1	65.2	101.4	155.9	74.8	106.5
05	METALS	105.9	92.0	101.3	105.0	89.9	100.0	113.8	79.9	102.6	105.9	91.6	101.1	105.8	69.5	93.8	105.8	76.3	96.1
06	WOOD, PLASTICS & COMPOSITES	106.4	93.4	98.9	126.1	92.0	106.4	95.8	71.2	81.6	102.6	87.0	93.6	87.7	60.4	71.9	87.4	74.3	79.8
07	THERMAL & MOISTURE PROTECTION	110.8	96.4	105.0	105.4	93.9	100.7	110.3	75.5	96.2	110.3	90.9	102.4	106.0	63.9	88.9	106.5	73.1	92.9
08	OPENINGS	84.0	90.5	85.6	93.4	79.7	89.9	99.7	66.2	91.2	84.9	85.4	85.0	95.7	52.1	84.7	83.9	67.7	79.9
0920	Plaster & Gypsum Board	137.6	93.2	105.9	146.8	91.5	107.3	172.6	70.1	99.4	143.4	86.6	102.8	156.4	59.1	86.9	155.9	73.4	96.9
0950, 0980	Ceilings & Acoustic Treatment	100.3	93.2	95.6	94.9	91.5	92.7	110.3	70.1	83.8	95.8	86.6	89.7	95.8	59.1	71.5	95.8	73.4	81.0
0960	Flooring	126.9	101.8	119.5	132.5	102.5	123.7	116.5	61.0	100.2	124.3	103.8	118.3	112.2	64.8	98.2	112.1	69.3	99.5
0970, 0990	Wall Finishes & Painting/Coating	112.0	100.9	105.2	112.0	95.0	101.5	112.0	74.7	89.0	112.0	92.1	99.7	112.0	44.5	70.4	112.0	66.5	83.9
09	FINISHES	113.5	96.6	104.1	114.9	94.6	103.6	118.2	70.6	91.6	112.4	91.3	100.6	111.4	60.2	82.9	110.3	73.2	89.6
COVERS	DIVS. 10 - 14, 25, 28, 41, 43, 44, 46	140.5	78.9	128.3	140.5	90.7	130.6	140.5	72.2	126.9	140.5	102.2	132.9	140.5	68.9	126.3	140.5	70.8	126.7
21, 22, 23	FIRE SUPPRESSION, PLUMBING & HVAC	99.8	82.9	92.9	103.2	96.1	100.4	100.1	71.3	88.4	103.2	85.9	96.2	103.2	67.4	88.7	103.2	89.2	97.5
26, 27, 3370	ELECTRICAL, COMMUNICATIONS & UTIL.	119.2	86.0	102.1	118.3	75.9	96.4	116.0	72.3	93.4	116.2	86.0	100.6	118.4	54.7	85.5	119.4	67.3	92.5
MF2010	WEIGHTED AVERAGE	111.7	91.3	102.8	114.4	91.1	104.1	120.3	75.7	100.6	112.3	90.4	102.7	117.0	65.5	94.3	112.8	77.8	97.4

City Cost Indexes

		CANADA																
DIVISION		THUNDER BAY, ONTARIO			TIMMINS, ONTARIO			TORONTO, ONTARIO			TROIS RIVIERES, QUEBEC			TRURO, NOVA SCOTIA			VANCOUVER, BRITISH COLUMBIA		
		MAT.	INST.	TOTAL	MAT.	INST.	TOTAL	MAT.	INST.	TOTAL	MAT.	INST.	TOTAL	MAT.	INST.	TOTAL	MAT.	INST.	TOTAL
015433	CONTRACTOR EQUIPMENT		101.7	101.7		101.7	101.7		104.0	104.0		102.6	102.6		101.7	101.7		112.1	112.1
0241, 31 - 34	SITE & INFRASTRUCTURE, DEMOLITION	106.5	101.9	103.3	112.7	100.8	104.5	139.0	105.9	116.2	93.2	100.9	98.5	97.2	99.3	98.6	121.1	108.5	112.4
0310	Concrete Forming & Accessories	123.1	91.6	95.7	123.0	91.1	95.2	132.2	99.5	103.7	128.1	92.1	96.8	97.4	75.0	77.9	126.6	87.0	92.2
0320	Concrete Reinforcing	99.7	85.3	92.4	175.1	85.5	129.9	162.1	86.5	124.0	148.8	82.4	115.3	148.8	48.8	98.4	152.8	79.7	116.0
0330	Cast-in-Place Concrete	148.0	94.0	126.7	163.5	90.3	134.7	154.3	114.8	138.8	135.6	101.5	122.1	169.8	74.8	132.4	164.0	101.0	139.2
03	CONCRETE	128.2	91.4	110.3	150.5	89.9	121.0	144.5	102.2	123.9	132.7	93.6	113.7	149.3	70.7	111.0	153.3	90.8	122.9
04	MASONRY	160.1	99.7	123.2	163.3	93.5	120.7	193.0	105.0	139.3	159.3	90.6	117.4	159.0	74.8	107.6	157.9	91.2	126.6
05	METALS	105.7	90.9	100.8	106.7	91.6	101.7	127.1	92.9	115.8	105.0	90.0	100.1	105.8	76.3	96.1	157.9	91.2	135.9
06	WOOD, PLASTICS & COMPOSITES	115.4	90.3	100.9	115.2	91.6	101.6	115.4	98.1	105.4	126.1	92.0	106.4	87.4	74.3	79.8	114.9	85.2	97.7
07	THERMAL & MOISTURE PROTECTION	111.0	93.1	103.8	111.5	89.4	102.5	123.5	100.4	114.1	105.4	93.9	100.7	106.5	73.1	92.9	133.7	89.0	115.5
08	OPENINGS	82.9	88.1	84.2	92.2	87.4	91.0	92.2	96.5	93.3	93.4	84.6	91.2	83.9	67.7	79.9	95.1	84.3	92.4
0920	Plaster & Gypsum Board	170.4	89.9	112.9	155.0	91.3	109.5	176.3	98.0	120.3	185.7	91.5	118.4	155.9	73.4	96.9	162.8	84.1	106.6
0950, 0980	Ceilings & Acoustic Treatment	95.8	89.9	91.9	95.8	91.3	92.8	132.8	98.0	109.8	94.9	91.5	92.7	95.8	73.4	81.0	157.5	84.1	109.0
0960	Flooring	132.5	109.0	125.6	132.5	100.3	123.1	135.8	111.6	128.7	132.5	102.5	123.7	112.1	69.3	99.5	135.0	98.8	124.4
0970, 0990	Wall Finishes & Painting/Coating	112.0	89.5	98.1	112.0	94.5	101.2	114.0	104.9	108.4	112.0	95.0	101.5	112.0	66.5	83.9	111.9	81.4	93.1
09	FINISHES	118.4	94.8	105.3	117.1	93.6	104.0	131.6	102.4	115.4	119.5	94.6	105.6	110.3	73.2	89.6	133.9	88.2	108.4
COVERS	DIVS. 10 - 14, 25, 28, 41, 43, 44, 46	140.5	78.7	128.2	140.5	77.4	128.0	140.5	105.7	133.6	140.5	90.7	130.6	140.5	70.8	126.7	140.5	99.5	132.4
21, 22, 23	FIRE SUPPRESSION, PLUMBING & HVAC	99.8	82.7	92.8	103.2	103.6	103.4	100.6	97.7	99.4	103.2	96.1	100.4	103.2	89.2	97.5	100.6	84.7	94.2
26, 27, 3370	ELECTRICAL, COMMUNICATIONS & UTIL.	117.5	84.5	100.5	118.9	94.9	106.5	114.0	88.1	100.7	119.8	75.9	97.1	117.3	67.3	91.5	115.1	77.7	95.8
MF2010	WEIGHTED AVERAGE	113.1	90.2	103.0	117.9	94.9	107.8	123.0	98.8	112.3	115.1	91.3	104.6	115.1	77.8	98.6	128.1	89.1	110.9

		CANADA																	
DIVISION		VICTORIA, BRITISH COLUMBIA			WHITEHORSE, YUKON			WINDSOR, ONTARIO			WINNIPEG, MANITOBA			YARMOUTH, NOVA SCOTIA			YELLOWKNIFE, NWT		
		MAT.	INST.	TOTAL	MAT.	INST.	TOTAL	MAT.	INST.	TOTAL	MAT.	INST.	TOTAL	MAT.	INST.	TOTAL	MAT.	INST.	TOTAL
015433	CONTRACTOR EQUIPMENT		108.8	108.8		101.8	101.8		101.7	101.7		105.9	105.9		101.7	101.7		101.7	101.7
0241, 31 - 34	SITE & INFRASTRUCTURE, DEMOLITION	121.1	108.0	112.1	108.8	97.7	101.2	96.3	101.8	100.1	121.5	101.6	107.8	97.0	99.3	98.5	128.6	102.3	110.5
0310	Concrete Forming & Accessories	111.9	86.4	89.7	107.0	62.3	68.1	123.1	89.9	94.3	131.6	69.8	77.8	97.4	75.0	77.9	106.9	85.3	88.2
0320	Concrete Reinforcing	116.8	79.6	98.0	115.8	62.7	89.0	109.3	84.6	96.9	143.8	58.2	100.7	148.8	48.8	98.4	118.4	66.6	92.3
0330	Cast-in-Place Concrete	147.1	100.3	128.6	162.2	72.9	127.0	137.7	94.9	120.8	192.3	75.4	146.2	168.1	74.8	131.3	245.0	92.6	185.0
03	CONCRETE	151.9	90.1	121.8	133.5	66.8	101.0	121.3	90.8	106.4	162.7	70.1	117.6	148.4	70.7	110.5	175.5	84.6	131.2
04	MASONRY	167.0	93.9	122.4	170.1	65.3	106.2	159.5	98.5	122.3	188.0	70.9	116.5	158.8	74.8	107.6	177.2	79.2	117.4
05	METALS	107.3	87.2	100.7	110.9	75.6	99.2	105.7	91.4	101.0	154.6	75.5	128.5	105.8	76.3	96.1	109.7	81.6	100.4
06	WOOD, PLASTICS & COMPOSITES	98.3	85.1	90.7	96.2	60.9	75.8	115.4	88.8	100.0	113.4	70.6	88.7	87.4	74.3	79.8	96.2	87.0	90.9
07	THERMAL & MOISTURE PROTECTION	114.9	88.8	104.3	105.3	64.9	88.9	110.8	92.2	103.3	116.3	72.4	98.5	106.5	73.1	92.9	108.2	83.1	98.0
08	OPENINGS	89.1	80.4	86.9	86.7	57.9	79.5	82.6	87.8	84.0	93.4	62.8	85.7	83.9	67.7	79.9	86.7	73.1	83.3
0920	Plaster & Gypsum Board	136.1	84.1	99.0	124.3	59.5	78.0	158.4	88.4	108.4	161.4	69.1	95.5	155.9	73.4	96.9	175.0	86.5	111.8
0950, 0980	Ceilings & Acoustic Treatment	95.8	84.1	88.1	100.3	59.5	73.4	95.8	88.4	90.9	142.8	69.1	94.1	95.8	73.4	81.0	130.2	86.5	101.3
0960	Flooring	127.3	78.5	113.0	121.1	63.2	104.1	132.5	106.1	124.8	133.7	74.8	116.4	112.1	69.3	99.5	121.1	96.9	114.0
0970, 0990	Wall Finishes & Painting/Coating	112.0	84.3	93.1	112.0	58.1	78.7	112.0	93.9	100.8	112.0	56.2	77.6	112.0	66.5	83.9	112.0	84.6	95.1
09	FINISHES	115.7	84.7	98.4	111.7	61.7	83.9	116.6	93.6	103.8	129.7	69.6	96.2	110.3	73.2	89.6	124.3	86.8	103.4
COVERS	DIVS. 10 - 14, 25, 28, 41, 43, 44, 46	140.5	74.5	127.4	140.5	67.9	126.1	140.5	78.1	128.1	140.5	70.5	126.6	140.5	70.8	126.7	140.5	72.5	127.0
21, 22, 23	FIRE SUPPRESSION, PLUMBING & HVAC	103.2	84.6	95.7	103.3	79.0	93.5	99.8	82.3	92.7	100.5	67.9	87.3	103.2	89.2	97.5	103.6	100.9	102.5
26, 27, 3370	ELECTRICAL, COMMUNICATIONS & UTIL.	118.3	77.7	97.4	127.6	65.0	95.3	122.0	86.0	103.4	117.9	68.3	92.3	119.4	67.3	92.5	131.3	90.6	110.3
MF2010	WEIGHTED AVERAGE	118.1	87.2	104.5	116.5	71.3	96.6	112.2	90.0	102.4	128.4	72.4	103.7	115.2	77.8	98.7	123.5	88.9	108.3

Location Factors

Costs shown in RSMeans cost data publications are based on national averages for materials and installation. To adjust these costs to a specific location, simply multiply the base cost by the factor and divide by 100 for that city. The data is arranged alphabetically by state and postal zip code numbers. For a city not listed, use the factor for a nearby city with similar economic characteristics.

STATE/ZIP	CITY	MAT.	INST.	TOTAL
ALABAMA				
350-352	Birmingham	97.6	74.6	87.4
354	Tuscaloosa	96.6	58.6	79.9
355	Jasper	96.8	57.6	79.5
356	Decatur	96.5	60.1	80.5
357-358	Huntsville	96.6	68.1	84.1
359	Gadsden	96.6	57.6	79.4
360-361	Montgomery	97.4	56.6	79.4
362	Anniston	96.0	64.5	82.1
363	Dothan	96.6	52.0	76.9
364	Evergreen	96.2	53.4	77.3
365-366	Mobile	97.7	67.5	84.4
367	Selma	96.3	51.9	76.7
368	Phenix City	97.1	55.9	78.9
369	Butler	96.5	52.0	76.9
ALASKA				
995-996	Anchorage	124.5	114.0	119.9
997	Fairbanks	122.4	115.0	119.1
998	Juneau	120.3	113.9	117.5
999	Ketchikan	134.1	113.9	125.2
ARIZONA				
850,853	Phoenix	97.9	76.6	88.5
851,852	Mesa/Tempe	97.4	72.4	86.3
855	Globe	97.4	62.5	82.0
856-857	Tucson	96.1	72.1	85.5
859	Show Low	97.5	62.9	82.2
860	Flagstaff	100.3	73.9	88.7
863	Prescott	98.2	62.1	82.2
864	Kingman	96.4	73.4	86.3
865	Chambers	96.5	63.0	81.7
ARKANSAS				
716	Pine Bluff	96.7	63.8	82.2
717	Camden	94.1	50.1	74.7
718	Texarkana	95.9	51.3	76.2
719	Hot Springs	93.4	52.9	75.5
720-722	Little Rock	97.0	65.0	82.9
723	West Memphis	95.8	62.8	81.2
724	Jonesboro	96.8	60.7	80.9
725	Batesville	94.2	56.1	77.4
726	Harrison	95.5	52.3	76.5
727	Fayetteville	92.9	54.1	75.8
728	Russellville	94.1	55.4	77.0
729	Fort Smith	97.1	62.5	81.8
CALIFORNIA				
900-902	Los Angeles	100.1	115.5	106.9
903-905	Inglewood	95.3	113.1	103.2
906-908	Long Beach	96.9	113.2	104.1
910-912	Pasadena	95.2	113.6	103.3
913-916	Van Nuys	98.1	113.5	104.9
917-918	Alhambra	97.1	113.5	104.3
919-921	San Diego	99.3	107.8	103.0
922	Palm Springs	96.4	110.9	102.8
923-924	San Bernardino	94.3	110.5	101.4
925	Riverside	98.9	112.4	104.9
926-927	Santa Ana	96.1	110.8	102.6
928	Anaheim	98.9	112.8	105.1
930	Oxnard	100.2	112.3	105.5
931	Santa Barbara	99.5	112.3	105.1
932-933	Bakersfield	100.0	109.5	104.2
934	San Luis Obispo	99.7	109.4	104.0
935	Mojave	97.0	106.9	101.3
936-938	Fresno	100.5	115.7	107.2
939	Salinas	100.5	122.7	110.3
940-941	San Francisco	108.5	142.3	123.4
942,956-958	Sacramento	102.9	118.6	109.9
943	Palo Alto	101.3	129.9	113.9
944	San Mateo	103.8	131.3	115.9
945	Vallejo	102.2	128.2	113.7
946	Oakland	106.3	133.9	118.5
947	Berkeley	105.5	133.2	117.7
948	Richmond	104.7	129.7	115.7
949	San Rafael	106.0	129.5	116.4
950	Santa Cruz	105.0	122.8	112.9

STATE/ZIP	CITY	MAT.	INST.	TOTAL
CALIFORNIA (CONT'D)				
951	San Jose	103.2	135.1	117.3
952	Stockton	100.7	117.2	108.0
953	Modesto	100.7	116.9	107.9
954	Santa Rosa	100.3	135.0	115.6
955	Eureka	101.6	114.2	107.2
959	Marysville	100.9	114.4	106.8
960	Redding	102.8	114.4	107.9
961	Susanville	101.5	114.4	107.2
COLORADO				
800-802	Denver	101.7	84.7	94.2
803	Boulder	98.6	82.9	91.7
804	Golden	100.7	81.7	92.3
805	Fort Collins	102.6	79.1	92.2
806	Greeley	100.0	78.2	90.4
807	Fort Morgan	99.3	82.0	91.7
808-809	Colorado Springs	101.6	81.7	92.8
810	Pueblo	100.4	80.8	91.8
811	Alamosa	101.5	76.7	90.6
812	Salida	101.3	78.3	91.2
813	Durango	101.9	79.6	92.1
814	Montrose	100.8	79.3	91.3
815	Grand Junction	104.2	79.6	93.4
816	Glenwood Springs	101.6	82.2	93.1
CONNECTICUT				
060	New Britain	101.1	118.6	108.8
061	Hartford	102.0	118.7	109.4
062	Willimantic	101.7	118.4	109.1
063	New London	97.6	118.6	106.9
064	Meriden	99.7	118.6	108.0
065	New Haven	102.8	118.6	109.8
066	Bridgeport	102.2	118.7	109.5
067	Waterbury	101.8	118.6	109.2
068	Norwalk	101.8	126.3	112.6
069	Stamford	101.9	126.3	112.7
D.C.				
200-205	Washington	102.4	92.8	98.2
DELAWARE				
197	Newark	99.4	107.9	103.2
198	Wilmington	99.1	108.0	103.0
199	Dover	99.5	107.9	103.2
FLORIDA				
320,322	Jacksonville	98.7	69.4	85.7
321	Daytona Beach	98.8	75.2	88.4
323	Tallahassee	99.4	59.3	81.7
324	Panama City	100.1	60.5	82.7
325	Pensacola	102.6	64.1	85.6
326,344	Gainesville	100.4	69.7	86.9
327-328,347	Orlando	101.8	73.0	89.1
329	Melbourne	101.5	78.2	91.2
330-332,340	Miami	99.6	76.7	89.6
333	Fort Lauderdale	98.1	75.9	88.3
334,349	West Palm Beach	96.7	74.4	86.9
335-336,346	Tampa	99.8	82.1	92.0
337	St. Petersburg	102.5	65.8	86.3
338	Lakeland	99.0	82.0	91.5
339,341	Fort Myers	98.1	75.8	88.3
342	Sarasota	100.0	77.3	90.0
GEORGIA				
300-303,399	Atlanta	98.0	76.5	88.5
304	Statesboro	97.4	54.0	78.3
305	Gainesville	96.1	64.0	82.0
306	Athens	95.5	64.2	81.7
307	Dalton	97.6	60.1	81.1
308-309	Augusta	96.7	64.5	82.5
310-312	Macon	96.4	64.2	82.2
313-314	Savannah	98.1	60.5	81.5
315	Waycross	97.3	61.4	81.5
316	Valdosta	97.6	60.8	81.4
317,398	Albany	97.6	61.5	81.7
318-319	Columbus	97.5	64.6	83.0

Location Factors

STATE/ZIP	CITY	MAT.	INST.	TOTAL
HAWAII				
967	Hilo	110.3	121.2	115.1
968	Honolulu	113.3	121.2	116.8
STATES & POSS.				
969	Guam	131.1	60.8	100.1
IDAHO				
832	Pocatello	100.3	72.2	87.9
833	Twin Falls	101.3	52.5	79.8
834	Idaho Falls	98.9	58.7	81.2
835	Lewiston	107.9	79.7	95.5
836-837	Boise	99.3	72.4	87.4
838	Coeur d'Alene	107.2	76.3	93.6
ILLINOIS				
600-603	North Suburban	98.7	132.4	113.5
604	Joliet	98.6	136.4	115.3
605	South Suburban	98.7	132.4	113.5
606-608	Chicago	99.1	138.9	116.6
609	Kankakee	94.6	127.4	109.1
610-611	Rockford	98.4	124.3	109.8
612	Rock Island	95.9	98.9	97.2
613	La Salle	97.0	120.8	107.5
614	Galesburg	96.9	104.8	100.4
615-616	Peoria	99.5	108.3	103.4
617	Bloomington	96.3	109.3	102.0
618-619	Champaign	99.8	108.1	103.5
620-622	East St. Louis	95.1	108.3	100.9
623	Quincy	96.0	100.1	97.8
624	Effingham	95.3	103.9	99.1
625	Decatur	97.4	106.3	101.3
626-627	Springfield	97.8	107.1	101.9
628	Centralia	93.4	107.0	99.4
629	Carbondale	93.1	102.0	97.1
INDIANA				
460	Anderson	96.1	83.4	90.5
461-462	Indianapolis	99.2	85.6	93.2
463-464	Gary	97.6	108.5	102.4
465-466	South Bend	95.7	82.9	90.1
467-468	Fort Wayne	96.7	78.7	88.8
469	Kokomo	93.7	82.2	88.6
470	Lawrenceburg	92.5	79.6	86.8
471	New Albany	93.6	76.6	86.1
472	Columbus	96.0	81.5	89.6
473	Muncie	97.1	82.6	90.7
474	Bloomington	98.4	82.9	91.6
475	Washington	94.4	83.7	89.7
476-477	Evansville	96.0	86.5	91.8
478	Terre Haute	96.7	86.9	92.4
479	Lafayette	95.7	83.2	90.2
IOWA				
500-503,509	Des Moines	99.1	84.7	92.7
504	Mason City	97.6	67.8	84.5
505	Fort Dodge	97.9	59.7	81.0
506-507	Waterloo	99.7	72.2	87.6
508	Creston	98.1	78.8	89.6
510-511	Sioux City	100.5	70.7	87.3
512	Sibley	98.9	56.5	80.2
513	Spencer	100.6	56.5	81.2
514	Carroll	97.4	72.4	86.4
515	Council Bluffs	101.7	78.8	91.6
516	Shenandoah	98.2	72.3	86.8
520	Dubuque	99.9	79.7	91.0
521	Decorah	98.5	65.7	84.0
522-524	Cedar Rapids	100.7	84.0	93.3
525	Ottumwa	98.4	70.7	86.2
526	Burlington	97.6	77.3	88.6
527-528	Davenport	99.6	90.4	95.5
KANSAS				
660-662	Kansas City	99.5	95.4	97.7
664-666	Topeka	99.2	64.5	83.9
667	Fort Scott	97.7	73.9	87.2
668	Emporia	97.9	69.7	85.4
669	Belleville	99.6	65.5	84.6
670-672	Wichita	98.4	64.1	83.3
673	Independence	99.2	69.5	86.1
674	Salina	100.0	66.9	85.4
675	Hutchinson	94.8	65.4	81.8
676	Hays	98.8	65.8	84.3
677	Colby	99.5	65.8	84.6

STATE/ZIP	CITY	MAT.	INST.	TOTAL
KANSAS (CONT'D)				
678	Dodge City	101.2	66.8	86.0
679	Liberal	98.7	65.8	84.2
KENTUCKY				
400-402	Louisville	97.8	83.5	91.5
403-405	Lexington	96.5	81.8	90.0
406	Frankfort	97.2	83.5	91.2
407-409	Corbin	93.7	72.5	84.4
410	Covington	94.4	95.2	94.8
411-412	Ashland	93.3	98.5	95.6
413-414	Campton	94.5	81.2	88.6
415-416	Pikeville	95.6	91.7	93.9
417-418	Hazard	93.9	81.5	88.4
420	Paducah	92.6	85.7	89.6
421-422	Bowling Green	95.0	83.5	90.0
423	Owensboro	95.2	87.9	92.0
424	Henderson	92.4	87.9	90.4
425-426	Somerset	91.9	79.1	86.2
427	Elizabethtown	91.4	83.9	88.1
LOUISIANA				
700-701	New Orleans	102.3	70.5	88.3
703	Thibodaux	100.2	63.4	84.0
704	Hammond	97.5	56.1	79.3
705	Lafayette	99.9	61.5	83.0
706	Lake Charles	100.1	64.1	84.2
707-708	Baton Rouge	101.2	63.0	84.4
710-711	Shreveport	96.7	56.3	78.9
712	Monroe	97.0	53.6	77.9
713-714	Alexandria	97.1	53.5	77.9
MAINE				
039	Kittery	94.8	80.1	88.3
040-041	Portland	99.5	78.9	90.4
042	Lewiston	98.1	78.9	89.7
043	Augusta	97.6	79.8	89.8
044	Bangor	97.7	78.9	89.4
045	Bath	96.0	79.5	88.7
046	Machias	95.5	79.0	88.2
047	Houlton	95.7	78.9	88.3
048	Rockland	94.7	79.4	88.0
049	Waterville	96.1	79.8	88.9
MARYLAND				
206	Waldorf	98.5	82.4	91.4
207-208	College Park	98.5	84.2	92.2
209	Silver Spring	97.7	82.3	90.9
210-212	Baltimore	100.2	84.7	93.3
214	Annapolis	100.2	83.2	92.7
215	Cumberland	95.8	80.2	89.0
216	Easton	97.5	70.3	85.5
217	Hagerstown	96.8	82.9	90.7
218	Salisbury	97.9	65.3	83.5
219	Elkton	94.7	84.3	90.1
MASSACHUSETTS				
010-011	Springfield	100.0	108.7	103.9
012	Pittsfield	99.6	105.3	102.1
013	Greenfield	97.3	108.4	102.2
014	Fitchburg	96.1	123.3	108.1
015-016	Worcester	100.0	123.5	110.4
017	Framingham	95.5	129.9	110.7
018	Lowell	99.4	128.5	112.3
019	Lawrence	100.5	129.0	113.1
020-022, 024	Boston	102.2	136.8	117.5
023	Brockton	100.8	124.7	111.4
025	Buzzards Bay	94.9	122.1	106.9
026	Hyannis	98.0	122.1	108.6
027	New Bedford	99.9	122.2	109.7
MICHIGAN				
480,483	Royal Oak	93.4	106.2	99.1
481	Ann Arbor	95.8	108.1	101.2
482	Detroit	97.4	110.1	103.0
484-485	Flint	95.5	97.1	96.2
486	Saginaw	95.0	93.5	94.4
487	Bay City	95.2	93.6	94.5
488-489	Lansing	96.4	95.1	95.9
490	Battle Creek	96.0	89.2	93.0
491	Kalamazoo	96.3	87.4	92.4
492	Jackson	94.3	95.9	95.0
493,495	Grand Rapids	97.2	83.0	90.9
494	Muskegon	94.9	84.9	90.5

Location Factors

STATE/ZIP	CITY	MAT.	INST.	TOTAL	STATE/ZIP	CITY	MAT.	INST.	TOTAL
MICHIGAN (CONT'D)					**NEW HAMPSHIRE (CONT'D)**				
496	Traverse City	93.6	78.7	87.0	032-033	Concord	98.6	82.4	91.5
497	Gaylord	94.7	72.8	85.1	034	Keene	96.9	49.4	76.0
498-499	Iron mountain	96.7	87.8	92.8	035	Littleton	96.5	56.6	78.9
					036	Charleston	96.3	47.1	74.6
MINNESOTA					037	Claremont	95.3	47.1	74.1
550-551	Saint Paul	101.1	121.5	110.1	038	Portsmouth	97.8	91.2	94.9
553-555	Minneapolis	102.1	123.0	111.3					
556-558	Duluth	100.1	112.0	105.4	**NEW JERSEY**				
559	Rochester	100.9	107.6	103.8	070-071	Newark	102.7	124.6	112.4
560	Mankato	97.7	104.6	100.7	072	Elizabeth	100.6	124.5	111.2
561	Windom	96.4	93.8	95.2	073	Jersey City	99.4	124.4	110.4
562	Willmar	96.0	105.1	100.0	074-075	Paterson	101.4	124.5	111.6
563	St. Cloud	97.6	120.8	107.9	076	Hackensack	99.4	124.5	110.5
564	Brainerd	97.6	105.3	101.0	077	Long Branch	99.0	123.3	109.7
565	Detroit Lakes	99.4	99.3	99.4	078	Dover	99.7	124.6	110.7
566	Bemidji	98.7	101.3	99.9	079	Summit	99.6	124.7	110.7
567	Thief River Falls	98.3	95.8	97.2	080,083	Vineland	97.6	122.4	108.6
					081	Camden	99.4	122.6	109.6
MISSISSIPPI					082,084	Atlantic City	98.1	122.1	108.7
386	Clarksdale	96.4	55.5	78.4	085-086	Trenton	99.6	123.6	110.2
387	Greenville	100.3	65.1	84.7	087	Point Pleasant	99.7	122.5	109.7
388	Tupelo	98.0	57.9	80.4	088-089	New Brunswick	100.1	124.3	110.8
389	Greenwood	97.6	55.1	78.8					
390-392	Jackson	97.4	64.4	82.9	**NEW MEXICO**				
393	Meridian	96.7	66.1	83.2	870-872	Albuquerque	98.7	73.6	87.7
394	Laurel	97.9	58.8	80.6	873	Gallup	98.8	73.6	87.7
395	Biloxi	98.3	60.2	81.5	874	Farmington	99.4	73.6	88.0
396	Mccomb	96.3	54.6	77.9	875	Santa Fe	99.4	73.6	88.0
397	Columbus	97.8	56.9	79.8	877	Las Vegas	97.3	73.6	86.8
					878	Socorro	96.8	73.6	86.6
MISSOURI					879	Truth/Consequences	97.0	70.3	85.3
630-631	St. Louis	100.0	105.7	102.5	880	Las Cruces	96.1	69.6	84.4
633	Bowling Green	98.4	90.5	94.9	881	Clovis	97.4	73.5	86.9
634	Hannibal	97.3	87.1	92.8	882	Roswell	99.3	73.6	88.0
635	Kirksville	100.4	83.8	93.1	883	Carrizozo	99.4	73.6	88.1
636	Flat River	99.4	92.9	96.5	884	Tucumcari	98.1	73.5	87.3
637	Cape Girardeau	99.7	89.6	95.3					
638	Sikeston	97.5	85.5	92.2	**NEW YORK**				
639	Poplar Bluff	97.0	86.8	92.5	100-102	New York	104.8	166.9	132.2
640-641	Kansas City	100.1	108.0	103.6	103	Staten Island	100.8	163.6	128.5
644-645	St. Joseph	99.3	91.8	96.0	104	Bronx	98.9	163.6	127.4
646	Chillicothe	96.1	70.0	84.6	105	Mount Vernon	98.6	133.0	113.8
647	Harrisonville	95.7	104.5	99.6	106	White Plains	98.8	133.0	113.9
648	Joplin	98.2	70.4	85.9	107	Yonkers	103.5	133.1	116.5
650-651	Jefferson City	96.2	90.5	93.7	108	New Rochelle	99.0	133.0	114.0
652	Columbia	97.7	92.4	95.4	109	Suffern	98.7	122.0	109.0
653	Sedalia	96.6	92.8	94.9	110	Queens	101.4	163.8	128.9
654-655	Rolla	95.2	87.9	92.0	111	Long Island City	103.0	163.8	129.8
656-658	Springfield	98.5	79.9	90.3	112	Brooklyn	103.4	163.8	130.0
					113	Flushing	102.9	163.8	129.7
MONTANA					114	Jamaica	101.1	163.8	128.7
590-591	Billings	103.5	74.7	90.8	115,117,118	Hicksville	101.3	145.6	120.8
592	Wolf Point	103.1	67.5	87.4	116	Far Rockaway	103.1	163.8	129.8
593	Miles City	100.7	69.1	86.8	119	Riverhead	102.1	146.1	121.5
594	Great Falls	105.0	75.3	91.9	120-122	Albany	96.7	96.4	96.5
595	Havre	102.0	70.2	88.0	123	Schenectady	97.8	96.1	97.0
596	Helena	102.6	72.0	89.1	124	Kingston	100.9	117.4	108.2
597	Butte	103.5	73.5	90.3	125-126	Poughkeepsie	100.1	128.4	112.6
598	Missoula	100.8	72.2	88.2	127	Monticello	99.4	118.0	107.6
599	Kalispell	99.6	70.1	86.6	128	Glens Falls	92.3	92.6	92.5
					129	Plattsburgh	96.9	87.0	92.6
NEBRASKA					130-132	Syracuse	98.9	94.5	97.0
680-681	Omaha	100.0	79.2	90.8	133-135	Utica	96.8	88.2	93.0
683-685	Lincoln	98.0	73.6	87.2	136	Watertown	98.5	93.5	96.3
686	Columbus	96.8	71.7	85.7	137-139	Binghamton	98.4	89.2	94.4
687	Norfolk	98.5	75.1	88.2	140-142	Buffalo	100.3	104.0	101.9
688	Grand Island	98.7	78.4	89.8	143	Niagara Falls	97.9	106.1	101.5
689	Hastings	97.8	79.3	89.6	144-146	Rochester	100.0	94.0	97.3
690	Mccook	97.6	70.7	85.7	147	Jamestown	96.9	86.4	92.3
691	North Platte	98.1	79.4	89.9	148-149	Elmira	96.7	91.0	94.2
692	Valentine	99.7	67.6	85.6					
693	Alliance	99.7	65.8	84.8	**NORTH CAROLINA**				
					270,272-274	Greensboro	99.7	47.3	76.6
NEVADA					271	Winston-Salem	99.5	46.0	75.9
889-891	Las Vegas	99.8	110.7	104.6	275-276	Raleigh	99.8	47.6	76.8
893	Ely	98.5	98.1	98.3	277	Durham	100.8	47.9	77.5
894-895	Reno	98.7	93.7	96.5	278	Rocky Mount	96.8	42.5	72.9
897	Carson City	97.8	93.5	95.9	279	Elizabeth City	97.8	40.6	72.6
898	Elko	97.2	85.3	92.0	280	Gastonia	98.6	45.4	75.1
					281-282	Charlotte	99.4	47.8	76.7
NEW HAMPSHIRE					283	Fayetteville	100.7	49.4	78.1
030	Nashua	100.2	86.7	94.3	284	Wilmington	97.4	48.5	75.8
031	Manchester	100.7	86.7	94.5	285	Kinston	95.2	43.8	72.6

Location Factors

STATE/ZIP	CITY	MAT.	INST.	TOTAL
NORTH CAROLINA (CONT'D)				
286	Hickory	95.5	42.3	72.1
287-288	Asheville	97.8	45.5	74.7
289	Murphy	96.4	33.2	68.5
NORTH DAKOTA				
580-581	Fargo	102.1	65.7	86.0
582	Grand Forks	102.8	53.1	80.9
583	Devils Lake	101.7	57.0	82.0
584	Jamestown	101.9	46.4	77.4
585	Bismarck	100.7	64.4	84.7
586	Dickinson	102.7	58.8	83.3
587	Minot	102.7	70.2	88.4
588	Williston	101.1	58.8	82.4
OHIO				
430-432	Columbus	97.8	90.6	94.6
433	Marion	93.9	85.4	90.2
434-436	Toledo	97.9	98.3	98.1
437-438	Zanesville	94.5	86.1	90.8
439	Steubenville	96.1	93.5	95.0
440	Lorain	97.7	91.3	94.9
441	Cleveland	97.9	99.8	98.7
442-443	Akron	98.7	94.5	96.9
444-445	Youngstown	98.1	90.1	94.6
446-447	Canton	98.2	86.3	93.0
448-449	Mansfield	95.2	87.4	91.7
450	Hamilton	96.6	85.6	91.7
451-452	Cincinnati	96.9	85.8	92.0
453-454	Dayton	96.7	85.2	91.6
455	Springfield	96.6	85.8	91.8
456	Chillicothe	95.2	93.4	94.4
457	Athens	98.0	83.1	91.4
458	Lima	98.4	86.1	93.0
OKLAHOMA				
730-731	Oklahoma City	97.8	60.6	81.4
734	Ardmore	95.0	60.1	79.6
735	Lawton	97.5	61.4	81.6
736	Clinton	96.5	58.8	79.8
737	Enid	97.3	58.7	80.3
738	Woodward	95.1	58.8	79.1
739	Guymon	96.2	31.0	67.5
740-741	Tulsa	97.4	53.5	78.0
743	Miami	93.8	67.9	82.3
744	Muskogee	96.7	39.3	71.4
745	Mcalester	93.6	50.6	74.6
746	Ponca City	94.1	58.7	78.5
747	Durant	94.1	57.7	78.1
748	Shawnee	95.7	56.5	78.4
749	Poteau	93.2	61.4	79.2
OREGON				
970-972	Portland	98.8	100.3	99.5
973	Salem	98.6	98.6	98.6
974	Eugene	98.6	98.5	98.6
975	Medford	100.1	97.0	98.7
976	Klamath Falls	99.8	97.0	98.6
977	Bend	98.8	98.6	98.7
978	Pendleton	94.1	100.0	96.7
979	Vale	91.9	90.5	91.3
PENNSYLVANIA				
150-152	Pittsburgh	99.1	104.6	101.5
153	Washington	95.9	102.1	98.6
154	Uniontown	96.4	100.8	98.3
155	Bedford	97.2	91.7	94.8
156	Greensburg	97.2	100.3	98.5
157	Indiana	96.0	99.1	97.4
158	Dubois	97.6	94.5	96.2
159	Johnstown	97.2	95.8	96.6
160	Butler	92.3	100.5	95.9
161	New Castle	92.4	97.5	94.6
162	Kittanning	92.8	102.4	97.0
163	Oil City	92.4	94.7	93.4
164-165	Erie	94.6	93.6	94.1
166	Altoona	94.8	90.6	93.0
167	Bradford	95.5	93.8	94.7
168	State College	95.0	91.8	93.6
169	Wellsboro	96.1	92.4	94.5
170-171	Harrisburg	97.7	96.1	97.0
172	Chambersburg	95.5	89.5	92.9
173-174	York	96.3	95.2	95.8
175-176	Lancaster	94.3	89.7	92.3

STATE/ZIP	CITY	MAT.	INST.	TOTAL
PENNSYLVANIA (CONT'D)				
177	Williamsport	93.0	79.6	87.1
178	Sunbury	95.1	95.1	95.1
179	Pottsville	94.2	96.8	95.4
180	Lehigh Valley	95.6	113.5	103.5
181	Allentown	97.9	109.2	102.9
182	Hazleton	95.1	97.2	96.0
183	Stroudsburg	94.9	103.0	98.5
184-185	Scranton	98.6	99.5	99.0
186-187	Wilkes-Barre	94.8	98.2	96.3
188	Montrose	94.5	97.0	95.6
189	Doylestown	94.7	120.1	105.9
190-191	Philadelphia	99.9	130.9	113.6
193	Westchester	96.1	122.8	107.9
194	Norristown	95.2	130.2	110.6
195-196	Reading	97.6	100.0	98.6
PUERTO RICO				
009	San Juan	121.3	24.1	78.4
RHODE ISLAND				
028	Newport	99.2	111.1	104.5
029	Providence	100.2	111.1	105.0
SOUTH CAROLINA				
290-292	Columbia	97.8	49.3	76.4
293	Spartanburg	96.8	49.0	75.7
294	Charleston	98.4	57.4	80.3
295	Florence	96.6	49.3	75.8
296	Greenville	96.6	49.0	75.6
297	Rock Hill	96.0	47.2	74.5
298	Aiken	96.8	72.8	86.2
299	Beaufort	97.5	42.5	73.3
SOUTH DAKOTA				
570-571	Sioux Falls	100.7	57.1	81.5
572	Watertown	99.8	51.6	78.5
573	Mitchell	98.6	51.0	77.6
574	Aberdeen	101.6	52.2	79.8
575	Pierre	100.1	53.8	79.7
576	Mobridge	99.3	51.4	78.2
577	Rapid City	101.4	54.6	80.7
TENNESSEE				
370-372	Nashville	96.8	72.2	86.0
373-374	Chattanooga	99.0	66.2	84.6
375,380-381	Memphis	98.2	69.6	85.6
376	Johnson City	98.7	56.7	80.2
377-379	Knoxville	95.4	61.4	80.4
382	Mckenzie	97.1	61.8	81.6
383	Jackson	99.2	63.8	83.6
384	Columbia	95.7	67.1	83.1
385	Cookeville	97.0	60.2	80.8
TEXAS				
750	Mckinney	98.5	50.2	77.2
751	Waxahachie	98.5	57.3	80.3
752-753	Dallas	99.4	66.8	85.0
754	Greenville	98.6	43.3	74.2
755	Texarkana	98.0	51.0	77.2
756	Longview	98.6	40.4	72.9
757	Tyler	99.0	54.4	79.4
758	Palestine	95.2	56.6	78.2
759	Lufkin	95.8	58.3	79.3
760-761	Fort Worth	97.2	63.2	82.2
762	Denton	97.1	47.8	75.4
763	Wichita Falls	98.0	54.8	79.0
764	Eastland	96.5	49.7	75.9
765	Temple	95.1	49.4	75.0
766-767	Waco	97.4	56.4	79.4
768	Brownwood	97.7	49.0	76.2
769	San Angelo	97.3	49.6	76.3
770-772	Houston	99.1	69.8	86.2
773	Huntsville	97.5	55.9	79.2
774	Wharton	98.5	54.0	78.9
775	Galveston	96.5	68.2	84.0
776-777	Beaumont	97.2	62.0	81.7
778	Bryan	94.3	61.7	79.9
779	Victoria	98.6	44.0	74.5
780	Laredo	95.8	52.7	76.8
781-782	San Antonio	96.2	65.0	82.4
783-784	Corpus Christi	98.9	52.3	78.4
785	Mc Allen	98.6	46.6	75.7
786-787	Austin	96.1	58.8	79.6

Location Factors

STATE/ZIP	CITY	MAT.	INST.	TOTAL	STATE/ZIP	CITY	MAT.	INST.	TOTAL
TEXAS (CONT'D)					**WISCONSIN (CONT'D)**				
788	Del Rio	98.0	46.5	75.3	538	Lancaster	97.6	91.5	94.9
789	Giddings	95.1	56.2	77.9	539	Portage	96.1	94.5	95.4
790-791	Amarillo	98.1	61.0	81.7	540	New Richmond	97.3	94.4	96.0
792	Childress	97.3	57.2	79.6	541-543	Green Bay	101.8	91.6	97.3
793-794	Lubbock	99.6	56.8	80.7	544	Wausau	96.5	91.7	94.4
795-796	Abilene	97.9	54.2	78.6	545	Rhinelander	99.8	90.5	95.7
797	Midland	99.4	51.4	78.2	546	La Crosse	98.1	93.2	95.9
798-799,885	El Paso	96.8	51.2	76.7	547	Eau Claire	99.7	94.3	97.3
					548	Superior	97.1	96.9	97.0
UTAH					549	Oshkosh	97.2	82.6	90.8
840-841	Salt Lake City	101.6	68.4	86.9					
842,844	Ogden	97.3	70.0	85.3	**WYOMING**				
843	Logan	99.2	70.0	86.3	820	Cheyenne	99.1	63.8	83.5
845	Price	99.5	65.9	84.7	821	Yellowstone Nat'l Park	96.4	59.3	80.1
846-847	Provo	99.7	68.3	85.8	822	Wheatland	97.5	58.2	80.2
					823	Rawlins	99.0	57.0	80.5
VERMONT					824	Worland	97.1	57.0	79.4
050	White River Jct.	98.0	54.4	78.8	825	Riverton	98.1	57.0	80.0
051	Bellows Falls	96.5	72.7	86.0	826	Casper	98.9	57.7	80.7
052	Bennington	96.8	67.8	84.0	827	Newcastle	96.9	57.0	79.3
053	Brattleboro	97.2	72.9	86.5	828	Sheridan	99.7	60.6	82.4
054	Burlington	100.6	65.4	85.1	829-831	Rock Springs	101.0	57.2	81.7
056	Montpelier	97.4	65.4	83.3					
057	Rutland	99.2	65.4	84.3	**CANADIAN FACTORS (reflect Canadian currency)**				
058	St. Johnsbury	97.9	55.2	79.1	**ALBERTA**				
059	Guildhall	96.6	55.0	78.3		Calgary	129.8	93.1	113.6
						Edmonton	130.0	93.1	113.7
VIRGINIA						Fort McMurray	126.5	95.8	113.0
220-221	Fairfax	100.1	82.0	92.1		Lethbridge	120.8	95.3	109.5
222	Arlington	101.6	79.9	92.0		Lloydminster	116.0	91.8	105.4
223	Alexandria	100.6	86.0	94.2		Medicine Hat	116.1	91.1	105.1
224-225	Fredericksburg	98.8	71.8	86.9		Red Deer	116.6	91.1	105.3
226	Winchester	99.4	62.2	83.0					
227	Culpeper	99.3	67.0	85.1	**BRITISH COLUMBIA**				
228	Harrisonburg	99.6	63.0	83.4		Kamloops	116.9	94.4	107.0
229	Charlottesville	100.0	62.8	83.6		Prince George	118.1	93.7	107.3
230-232	Richmond	100.6	66.0	85.3		Vancouver	128.1	89.1	110.9
233-235	Norfolk	101.4	67.6	86.5		Victoria	118.1	87.2	104.5
236	Newport News	100.4	67.3	85.8					
237	Portsmouth	99.9	64.4	84.3	**MANITOBA**				
238	Petersburg	99.9	66.0	85.0		Brandon	116.2	79.0	99.8
239	Farmville	98.9	52.3	78.4		Portage la Prairie	116.0	77.2	98.9
240-241	Roanoke	101.2	59.8	82.9		Winnipeg	128.4	72.4	103.7
242	Bristol	98.6	54.3	79.1					
243	Pulaski	98.3	50.3	77.1	**NEW BRUNSWICK**				
244	Staunton	99.2	58.2	81.1		Bathurst	114.1	70.1	94.7
245	Lynchburg	99.3	63.6	83.5		Dalhousie	114.1	70.3	94.8
246	Grundy	98.6	49.7	77.0		Fredericton	117.0	75.6	98.8
						Moncton	114.3	71.7	95.5
WASHINGTON						Newcastle	114.1	70.8	95.0
980-981,987	Seattle	102.5	106.3	104.2		St. John	116.6	75.3	98.4
982	Everett	102.2	95.6	99.3					
983-984	Tacoma	102.2	97.9	100.3	**NEWFOUNDLAND**				
985	Olympia	99.4	97.9	98.7		Corner Brook	119.5	70.5	97.9
986	Vancouver	103.5	93.0	98.8		St Johns	120.3	75.7	100.6
988	Wenatchee	101.8	83.6	93.8					
989	Yakima	102.5	92.6	98.1	**NORTHWEST TERRITORIES**				
990-992	Spokane	102.5	82.7	93.7		Yellowknife	123.5	88.9	108.3
993	Richland	102.1	86.8	95.4					
994	Clarkston	100.4	81.3	92.0	**NOVA SCOTIA**				
						Bridgewater	115.6	77.8	98.9
WEST VIRGINIA						Dartmouth	117.2	77.8	99.8
247-248	Bluefield	97.4	82.6	90.9		Halifax	119.0	80.3	101.9
249	Lewisburg	99.1	82.7	91.9		New Glasgow	115.3	77.8	98.8
250-253	Charleston	99.2	89.5	94.9		Sydney	112.8	77.8	97.4
254	Martinsburg	98.9	79.1	90.2		Truro	115.1	77.8	98.6
255-257	Huntington	100.6	91.4	96.6		Yarmouth	115.2	77.8	98.7
258-259	Beckley	97.3	86.6	92.6					
260	Wheeling	100.7	89.2	95.7	**ONTARIO**				
261	Parkersburg	99.6	88.4	94.7		Barrie	118.6	96.9	109.1
262	Buckhannon	98.8	89.0	94.5		Brantford	117.7	101.0	110.4
263-264	Clarksburg	99.4	89.1	94.9		Cornwall	117.7	97.2	108.7
265	Morgantown	99.5	88.2	94.5		Hamilton	121.9	93.7	109.4
266	Gassaway	98.7	89.8	94.8		Kingston	118.6	97.3	109.2
267	Romney	98.7	85.1	92.7		Kitchener	113.7	90.4	103.4
268	Petersburg	98.5	84.9	92.5		London	121.6	90.2	107.8
						North Bay	118.0	94.9	107.8
WISCONSIN						Oshawa	117.1	98.2	108.7
530,532	Milwaukee	100.9	108.3	104.2		Ottawa	122.9	90.7	108.7
531	Kenosha	100.8	101.0	100.9		Owen Sound	118.8	95.0	108.3
534	Racine	100.1	101.0	100.5		Peterborough	117.7	97.0	108.6
535	Beloit	100.0	96.0	98.3		Sarnia	117.4	101.6	110.5
537	Madison	99.3	97.2	98.4					

Location Factors

STATE/ZIP	CITY	MAT.	INST.	TOTAL
ONTARIO (CONT'D)	Sault Ste Marie	112.6	94.5	104.6
	St. Catharines	111.7	91.3	102.8
	Sudbury	112.3	90.4	102.7
	Thunder Bay	113.1	90.2	103.0
	Timmins	117.9	94.9	107.8
	Toronto	123.0	98.8	112.3
	Windsor	112.2	90.0	102.4
PRINCE EDWARD ISLAND				
	Charlottetown	118.2	65.4	95.0
	Summerside	117.0	65.5	94.3
QUEBEC				
	Cap-de-la-Madeleine	114.8	91.3	104.4
	Charlesbourg	114.8	91.3	104.4
	Chicoutimi	113.7	91.6	104.0
	Gatineau	114.4	91.1	104.2
	Granby	114.7	91.0	104.3
	Hull	114.5	91.1	104.2
	Joliette	114.9	91.3	104.5
	Laval	114.0	91.1	103.9
	Montreal	121.9	91.9	108.7
	Quebec	119.8	92.3	107.7
	Rimouski	114.2	91.6	104.2
	Rouyn-Noranda	114.4	91.1	104.1
	Saint Hyacinthe	113.6	91.1	103.7
	Sherbrooke	114.8	91.1	104.4
	Sorel	114.9	91.3	104.5
	St Jerome	114.4	91.1	104.1
	Trois Rivieres	115.1	91.3	104.6
SASKATCHEWAN				
	Moose Jaw	113.4	72.4	95.3
	Prince Albert	112.3	70.5	93.9
	Regina	116.7	86.2	103.2
	Saskatoon	113.2	86.2	101.3
YUKON				
	Whitehorse	116.5	71.3	96.6

R011105-05   Tips for Accurate Estimating

1. Use pre-printed or columnar forms for orderly sequence of dimensions and locations and for recording telephone quotations.

2. Use only the front side of each paper or form except for certain pre-printed summary forms.

3. Be consistent in listing dimensions: For example, length x width x height. This helps in rechecking to ensure that, the total length of partitions is appropriate for the building area.

4. Use printed (rather than measured) dimensions where given.

5. Add up multiple printed dimensions for a single entry where possible.

6. Measure all other dimensions carefully.

7. Use each set of dimensions to calculate multiple related quantities.

8. Convert foot and inch measurements to decimal feet when listing. Memorize decimal equivalents to .01 parts of a foot (1/8" equals approximately .01').

9. Do not "round off" quantities until the final summary.

10. Mark drawings with different colors as items are taken off.

11. Keep similar items together, different items separate.

12. Identify location and drawing numbers to aid in future checking for completeness.

13. Measure or list everything on the drawings or mentioned in the specifications.

14. It may be necessary to list items not called for to make the job complete.

15. Be alert for: Notes on plans such as N.T.S. (not to scale); changes in scale throughout the drawings; reduced size drawings; discrepancies between the specifications and the drawings.

16. Develop a consistent pattern of performing an estimate. For example:
    a. Start the quantity takeoff at the lower floor and move to the next higher floor.
    b. Proceed from the main section of the building to the wings.
    c. Proceed from south to north or vice versa, clockwise or counterclockwise.
    d. Take off floor plan quantities first, elevations next, then detail drawings.

17. List all gross dimensions that can be either used again for different quantities, or used as a rough check of other quantities for verification (exterior perimeter, gross floor area, individual floor areas, etc.).

18. Utilize design symmetry or repetition (repetitive floors, repetitive wings, symmetrical design around a center line, similar room layouts, etc.). Note: Extreme caution is needed here so as not to omit or duplicate an area.

19. Do not convert units until the final total is obtained. For instance, when estimating concrete work, keep all units to the nearest cubic foot, then summarize and convert to cubic yards.

20. When figuring alternatives, it is best to total all items involved in the basic system, then total all items involved in the alternates. Therefore you work with positive numbers in all cases. When adds and deducts are used, it is often confusing whether to add or subtract a portion of an item; especially on a complicated or involved alternate.

R011105-10   Unit Gross Area Requirements

The figures in the table below indicate typical ranges in square feet as a function of the "occupant" unit. This table is best used in the preliminary design stages to help determine the probable size requirement for the total project.

Building Type	Unit	Gross Area in S.F.		
		1/4	Median	3/4
Apartments	Unit	660	860	1,100
Auditorium & Play Theaters	Seat	18	25	38
Bowling Alleys	Lane		940	
Churches & Synagogues	Seat	20	28	39
Dormitories	Bed	200	230	275
Fraternity & Sorority Houses	Bed	220	315	370
Garages, Parking	Car	325	355	385
Hospitals	Bed	685	850	1,075
Hotels	Rental Unit	475	600	710
Housing for the elderly	Unit	515	635	755
Housing, Public	Unit	700	875	1,030
Ice Skating Rinks	Total	27,000	30,000	36,000
Motels	Rental Unit	360	465	620
Nursing Homes	Bed	290	350	450
Restaurants	Seat	23	29	39
Schools, Elementary	Pupil	65	77	90
Junior High & Middle		85	110	129
Senior High		102	130	145
Vocational		110	135	195
Shooting Ranges	Point		450	
Theaters & Movies	Seat		15	

R011105-20 Floor Area Ratios

Table below lists commonly used gross to net area and net to gross area ratios expressed in % for various building types.

Building Type	Gross to Net Ratio	Net to Gross Ratio	Building Type	Gross to Net Ratio	Net to Gross Ratio
Apartment	156	64	School Buildings (campus type)		
Bank	140	72	Administrative	150	67
Church	142	70	Auditorium	142	70
Courthouse	162	61	Biology	161	62
Department Store	123	81	Chemistry	170	59
Garage	118	85	Classroom	152	66
Hospital	183	55	Dining Hall	138	72
Hotel	158	63	Dormitory	154	65
Laboratory	171	58	Engineering	164	61
Library	132	76	Fraternity	160	63
Office	135	75	Gymnasium	142	70
Restaurant	141	70	Science	167	60
Warehouse	108	93	Service	120	83
			Student Union	172	59

The gross area of a building is the total floor area based on outside dimensions.

The net area of a building is the usable floor area for the function intended and excludes such items as stairways, corridors and mechanical rooms. In the case of a commercial building, it might be considered as the "leasable area."

R011105-30 Occupancy Determinations

Description		S.F. Required per Person		
		BOCA	SBC	UBC
Assembly Areas	Fixed Seats	**	6	7
	Movable Seats		15	15
	Concentrated	7		
	Unconcentrated	15		
	Standing Space	3		
Educational	Unclassified			
	Classrooms	20	40	20
	Shop Areas	50	100	50
Institutional	Unclassified		125	
	In-Patient Areas	240		
	Sleeping Areas	120		
Mercantile	Basement	30	30	20
	Ground Floor	30	30	30
	Upper Floors	60	60	50
Office		100	100	100

BOCA=Building Officials & Code Administrators
SBC=Southern Building Code
UBC=Uniform Building Code

** The occupancy load for assembly area with fixed seats shall be determined by the number of fixed seats installed.

R011110-10 Architectural Fees

Tabulated below are typical percentage fees by project size, for good professional architectural service. Fees may vary from those listed depending upon degree of design difficulty and economic conditions in any particular area.

Rates can be interpolated horizontally and vertically. Various portions of the same project requiring different rates should be adjusted proportionally. For alterations, add 50% to the fee for the first $500,000 of project cost and add 25% to the fee for project cost over $500,000.

Architectural fees tabulated below include Structural, Mechanical and Electrical Engineering Fees. They do not include the fees for special consultants such as kitchen planning, security, acoustical, interior design, etc.

Civil Engineering fees are included in the Architectural fee for project sites requiring minimal design such as city sites. However, separate Civil Engineering fees must be added when utility connections require design, drainage calculations are needed, stepped foundations are required, or provisions are required to protect adjacent wetlands.

Building Types	Total Project Size in Thousands of Dollars						
	100	250	500	1,000	5,000	10,000	50,000
Factories, garages, warehouses, repetitive housing	9.0%	8.0%	7.0%	6.2%	5.3%	4.9%	4.5%
Apartments, banks, schools, libraries, offices, municipal buildings	12.2	12.3	9.2	8.0	7.0	6.6	6.2
Churches, hospitals, homes, laboratories, museums, research	15.0	13.6	12.7	11.9	9.5	8.8	8.0
Memorials, monumental work, decorative furnishings	—	16.0	14.5	13.1	10.0	9.0	8.3

R011110-30 Engineering Fees

Typical **Structural Engineering Fees** based on type of construction and total project size. These fees are included in Architectural Fees.

Type of Construction	Total Project Size (in thousands of dollars)			
	$500	$500-$1,000	$1,000-$5,000	Over $5000
Industrial buildings, factories & warehouses	Technical payroll times 2.0 to 2.5	1.60%	1.25%	1.00%
Hotels, apartments, offices, dormitories, hospitals, public buildings, food stores		2.00%	1.70%	1.20%
Museums, banks, churches and cathedrals		2.00%	1.75%	1.25%
Thin shells, prestressed concrete, earthquake resistive		2.00%	1.75%	1.50%
Parking ramps, auditoriums, stadiums, convention halls, hangars & boiler houses		2.50%	2.00%	1.75%
Special buildings, major alterations, underpinning & future expansion		Add to above 0.5%	Add to above 0.5%	Add to above 0.5%

For complex reinforced concrete or unusually complicated structures, add 20% to 50%.

Typical **Mechanical and Electrical Engineering Fees** are based on the size of the subcontract. The fee structure for both are shown below. These fees are included in Architectural Fees.

Type of Construction	Subcontract Size							
	$25,000	$50,000	$100,000	$225,000	$350,000	$500,000	$750,000	$1,000,000
Simple structures	6.4%	5.7%	4.8%	4.5%	4.4%	4.3%	4.2%	4.1%
Intermediate structures	8.0	7.3	6.5	5.6	5.1	5.0	4.9	4.8
Complex structures	10.1	9.0	9.0	8.0	7.5	7.5	7.0	7.0

For renovations, add 15% to 25% to applicable fee.

R012153-10   Repair and Remodeling

Cost figures are based on new construction utilizing the most cost-effective combination of labor, equipment and material with the work scheduled in proper sequence to allow the various trades to accomplish their work in an efficient manner.

The costs for repair and remodeling work must be modified due to the following factors that may be present in any given repair and remodeling project.

1. Equipment usage curtailment due to the physical limitations of the project, with only hand-operated equipment being used.

2. Increased requirement for shoring and bracing to hold up the building while structural changes are being made and to allow for temporary storage of construction materials on above-grade floors.

3. Material handling becomes more costly due to having to move within the confines of an enclosed building. For multi-story construction, low capacity elevators and stairwells may be the only access to the upper floors.

4. Large amount of cutting and patching and attempting to match the existing construction is required. It is often more economical to remove entire walls rather than create many new door and window openings. This sort of trade-off has to be carefully analyzed.

5. Cost of protection of completed work is increased since the usual sequence of construction usually cannot be accomplished.

6. Economies of scale usually associated with new construction may not be present. If small quantities of components must be custom fabricated due to job requirements, unit costs will naturally increase. Also, if only small work areas are available at a given time, job scheduling between trades becomes difficult and subcontractor quotations may reflect the excessive start-up and shut-down phases of the job.

7. Work may have to be done on other than normal shifts and may have to be done around an existing production facility which has to stay in production during the course of the repair and remodeling.

8. Dust and noise protection of adjoining non-construction areas can involve substantial special protection and alter usual construction methods.

9. Job may be delayed due to unexpected conditions discovered during demolition or removal. These delays ultimately increase construction costs.

10. Piping and ductwork runs may not be as simple as for new construction. Wiring may have to be snaked through walls and floors.

11. Matching "existing construction" may be impossible because materials may no longer be manufactured. Substitutions may be expensive.

12. Weather protection of existing structure requires additional temporary structures to protect building at openings.

13. On small projects, because of local conditions, it may be necessary to pay a tradesman for a minimum of four hours for a task that is completed in one hour.

All of the above areas can contribute to increased costs for a repair and remodeling project. Each of the above factors should be considered in the planning, bidding and construction stage in order to minimize the increased costs associated with repair and remodeling jobs.

R012909-80   Sales Tax by State

State sales tax on materials is tabulated below (5 states have no sales tax). Many states allow local jurisdictions, such as a county or city, to levy additional sales tax.

Some projects may be sales tax exempt, particularly those constructed with public funds.

State	Tax (%)	State	Tax (%)	State	Tax (%)	State	Tax (%)
Alabama	4	Illinois	6.25	Montana	0	Rhode Island	7
Alaska	0	Indiana	7	Nebraska	5.5	South Carolina	6
Arizona	6.6	Iowa	6	Nevada	6.85	South Dakota	4
Arkansas	6	Kansas	5.3	New Hampshire	0	Tennessee	7
California	9.25	Kentucky	6	New Jersey	7	Texas	6.25
Colorado	2.9	Louisiana	4	New Mexico	5.13	Utah	4.75
Connecticut	6	Maine	5	New York	4	Vermont	6
Delaware	0	Maryland	6	North Carolina	5.75	Virginia	4
District of Columbia	6	Massachusetts	6.25	North Dakota	5	Washington	6.5
Florida	6	Michigan	6	Ohio	5.5	West Virginia	6
Georgia	4	Minnesota	6.875	Oklahoma	4.5	Wisconsin	5
Hawaii	4	Mississippi	7	Oregon	0	Wyoming	4
Idaho	6	Missouri	4.225	Pennsylvania	6	Average	5.07 %

Sales Tax by Province (Canada)

GST - a value-added tax, which the government imposes on most goods and services provided in or imported into Canada. PST - a retail sales tax, which three of the provinces impose on the price of most goods and some

services. QST - a value-added tax, similar to the federal GST, which Quebec imposes. HST - Five provinces have combined their retail sales tax with the federal GST into one harmonized tax.

Province	PST (%)	QST (%)	GST(%)	HST(%)
Alberta	0	0	5	0
British Columbia	0	0	0	12
Manitoba	7	0	5	0
New Brunswick	0	0	0	13
Newfoundland	0	0	0	13
Northwest Territories	0	0	5	0
Nova Scotia	0	0	0	15
Ontario	0	0	0	13
Prince Edward Island	10	0	5	0
Quebec	0	8.5	5	0
Saskatchewan	5	0	5	0
Yukon	0	0	5	0

R012909-85   Unemployment Taxes and Social Security Taxes

State Unemployment Tax rates vary not only from state to state, but also with the experience rating of the contractor. The Federal Unemployment Tax rate is 6.2% of the first $7,000 of wages. This is reduced by a credit of up to 5.4% for timely payment to the state. The minimum Federal Unemployment Tax is 0.8% after all credits.

Social Security (FICA) for 2012 is estimated at time of publication to be 7.65% of wages up to $110,100.

R012909-90   Overtime

One way to improve the completion date of a project or eliminate negative float from a schedule is to compress activity duration times. This can be achieved by increasing the crew size or working overtime with the proposed crew.

To determine the costs of working overtime to compress activity duration times, consider the following examples. Below is an overtime efficiency and

cost chart based on a five, six, or seven day week with an eight through twelve hour day. Payroll percentage increases for time and one half and double time are shown for the various working days.

Days per Week	Hours per Day	Production Efficiency					Payroll Cost Factors	
		1st Week	2nd Week	3rd Week	4th Week	Average 4 Weeks	@ 1-1/2 Times	@ 2 Times
5	8	100%	100%	100%	100%	100 %	100 %	100 %
	9	100	100	95	90	96.25	105.6	111.1
	10	100	95	90	85	91.25	110.0	120.0
	11	95	90	75	65	81.25	113.6	127.3
	12	90	85	70	60	76.25	116.7	133.3
6	8	100	100	95	90	96.25	108.3	116.7
	9	100	95	90	85	92.50	113.0	125.9
	10	95	90	85	80	87.50	116.7	133.3
	11	95	85	70	65	78.75	119.7	139.4
	12	90	80	65	60	73.75	122.2	144.4
7	8	100	95	85	75	88.75	114.3	128.6
	9	95	90	80	70	83.75	118.3	136.5
	10	90	85	75	65	78.75	121.4	142.9
	11	85	80	65	60	72.50	124.0	148.1
	12	85	75	60	55	68.75	126.2	152.4

R013113-40 Builder's Risk Insurance

Builder's Risk Insurance is insurance on a building during construction. Premiums are paid by the owner or the contractor. Blasting, collapse and underground insurance would raise total insurance costs above those listed. Floater policy for materials delivered to the job runs $.75 to $1.25 per $100 value. Contractor equipment insurance runs $.50 to $1.50 per $100 value. Insurance for miscellaneous tools to $1,500 value runs from $3.00 to $7.50 per $100 value.

Tabulated below are New England Builder's Risk insurance rates in dollars per $100 value for $1,000 deductible. For $25,000 deductible, rates can be reduced 13% to 34%. On contracts over $1,000,000, rates may be lower than those tabulated. Policies are written annually for the total completed value in place. For "all risk" insurance (excluding flood, earthquake and certain other perils) add $.025 to total rates below.

Coverage	Frame Construction (Class 1)		Brick Construction (Class 4)		Fire Resistive (Class 6)	
	Range	Average	Range	Average	Range	Average
Fire Insurance	$.350 to $ .850	$.600	$.158 to $.189	$.174	$.052 to $.080	$.070
Extended Coverage	.115 to .200	.158	.080 to .105	.101	.081 to .105	.100
Vandalism	.012 to .016	.014	.008 to .011	.011	.008 to .011	.010
Total Annual Rate	$.477 to $1.066	$.772	$.246 to $.305	$.286	$.141 to $.196	$.180

R013113-50 General Contractor's Overhead

There are two distinct types of overhead on a construction project: Project Overhead and Main Office Overhead. Project Overhead includes those costs at a construction site not directly associated with the installation of construction materials. Examples of Project Overhead costs include the following:

1. Superintendent
2. Construction office and storage trailers
3. Temporary sanitary facilities
4. Temporary utilities
5. Security fencing
6. Photographs
7. Clean up
8. Performance and payment bonds

The above Project Overhead items are also referred to as General Requirements and therefore are estimated in Division 1. Division 1 is the first division listed in the CSI MasterFormat but it is usually the last division estimated. The sum of the costs in Divisions 1 through 49 is referred to as the sum of the direct costs.

All construction projects also include indirect costs. The primary components of indirect costs are the contractor's Main Office Overhead and profit. The amount of the Main Office Overhead expense varies depending on the following:

1. Owner's compensation
2. Project managers and estimator's wages
3. Clerical support wages
4. Office rent and utilities
5. Corporate legal and accounting costs
6. Advertising
7. Automobile expenses
8. Association dues
9. Travel and entertainment expenses

These costs are usually calculated as a percentage of annual sales volume. This percentage can range from 35% for a small contractor doing less than $500,000 to 5% for a large contractor with sales in excess of $100 million.

R013113-60   Workers' Compensation Insurance Rates by Trade

The table below tabulates the national averages for Workers' Compensation insurance rates by trade and type of building. The average "Insurance Rate" is multiplied by the "% of Building Cost" for each trade. This produces the "Workers' Compensation Cost" by % of total labor cost, to be added for each trade by building type to determine the weighted average Workers' Compensation rate for the building types analyzed.

Trade	Insurance Rate (% Labor Cost)		% of Building Cost			Workers' Compensation		
	Range	Average	Office Bldgs.	Schools & Apts.	Mfg.	Office Bldgs.	Schools & Apts.	Mfg.
Excavation, Grading, etc.	3.9 % to 18.1%	9.0%	4.8%	4.9%	4.5%	0.43%	0.44%	0.41%
Piles & Foundations	5.1 to 59.5	16.8	7.1	5.2	8.7	1.19	0.87	1.46
Concrete	4.9 to 29.7	12.7	5.0	14.8	3.7	0.64	1.88	0.47
Masonry	4.4 to 28.7	12.1	6.9	7.5	1.9	0.83	0.91	0.23
Structural Steel	5.1 to 124.1	36.9	10.7	3.9	17.6	3.95	1.44	6.49
Miscellaneous & Ornamental Metals	4.2 to 22.6	10.1	2.8	4.0	3.6	0.28	0.40	0.36
Carpentry & Millwork	5.1 to 37	15.0	3.7	4.0	0.5	0.56	0.60	0.08
Metal or Composition Siding	4.9 to 43.3	14.9	2.3	0.3	4.3	0.34	0.04	0.64
Roofing	5.1 to 75.2	28.8	2.3	2.6	3.1	0.66	0.75	0.89
Doors & Hardware	2.8 to 37	10.5	0.9	1.4	0.4	0.09	0.15	0.04
Sash & Glazing	4.9 to 33.1	12.6	3.5	4.0	1.0	0.44	0.50	0.13
Lath & Plaster	2.5 to 30.5	10.8	3.3	6.9	0.8	0.36	0.75	0.09
Tile, Marble & Floors	2.3 to 18.9	8.0	2.6	3.0	0.5	0.21	0.24	0.04
Acoustical Ceilings	3.2 to 30.3	7.8	2.4	0.2	0.3	0.19	0.02	0.02
Painting	4.3 to 28.9	10.7	1.5	1.6	1.6	0.16	0.17	0.17
Interior Partitions	5.1 to 37	15.0	3.9	4.3	4.4	0.59	0.65	0.66
Miscellaneous Items	2.5 to 90.6	14.6	5.2	3.7	9.7	0.76	0.54	1.42
Elevators	1.8 to 12.8	5.9	2.1	1.1	2.2	0.12	0.06	0.13
Sprinklers	1.9 to 17.2	7.0	0.5	—	2.0	0.04	—	0.14
Plumbing	2.7 to 17.1	6.9	4.9	7.2	5.2	0.34	0.50	0.36
Heat., Vent., Air Conditioning	3.8 to 19.3	8.5	13.5	11.0	12.9	1.15	0.94	1.10
Electrical	2.6 to 13.2	5.6	10.1	8.4	11.1	0.57	0.47	0.62
Total	1.8 % to 124.1%	—	100.0%	100.0%	100.0%	13.90%	12.32%	15.95%
	Overall Weighted Average 14.06%							

Workers' Compensation Insurance Rates by States

The table below lists the weighted average Workers' Compensation base rate for each state with a factor comparing this with the national average of 13.7%.

State	Weighted Average	Factor	State	Weighted Average	Factor	State	Weighted Average	Factor
Alabama	19.6%	143	Kentucky	17.0%	124	North Dakota	10.8%	79
Alaska	16.3	119	Louisiana	15.6	114	Ohio	8.7	64
Arizona	9.0	66	Maine	14.0	102	Oklahoma	14.7	107
Arkansas	10.2	74	Maryland	15.6	114	Oregon	12.0	88
California	27.9	204	Massachusetts	12.4	91	Pennsylvania	16.3	119
Colorado	7.1	52	Michigan	20.6	150	Rhode Island	11.9	87
Connecticut	23.1	169	Minnesota	24.1	176	South Carolina	20.1	147
Delaware	9.3	68	Mississippi	13.1	96	South Dakota	16.0	117
District of Columbia	11.2	82	Missouri	17.4	127	Tennessee	13.2	96
Florida	10.8	79	Montana	14.2	104	Texas	10.6	77
Georgia	27.8	203	Nebraska	18.1	132	Utah	7.8	57
Hawaii	9.0	66	Nevada	10.4	76	Vermont	14.6	107
Idaho	10.8	79	New Hampshire	21.1	154	Virginia	8.7	64
Illinois	22.6	165	New Jersey	13.4	98	Washington	11.1	81
Indiana	5.5	40	New Mexico	17.8	130	West Virginia	12.6	92
Iowa	10.8	79	New York	5.9	43	Wisconsin	14.9	109
Kansas	8.0	58	North Carolina	17.6	128	Wyoming	5.7	42
	Weighted Average for U.S. is 14.1% of payroll = 100%							

Rates in the following table are the base or manual costs per $100 of payroll for Workers' Compensation in each state. Rates are usually applied to straight time wages only and not to premium time wages and bonuses.

The weighted average skilled worker rate for 35 trades is 13.7%. For bidding purposes, apply the full value of Workers' Compensation directly to total labor costs, or if labor is 38%, materials 42% and overhead and profit 20% of total cost, carry 38/80 x 13.7% =6.5% of cost (before overhead and profit) into overhead. Rates vary not only from state to state but also with the experience rating of the contractor.

Rates are the most current available at the time of publication.

R013113-60 Workers' Compensation Insurance Rates by Trade and State (cont.)

State	Carpentry — 3 stories or less 5651	Carpentry — interior cab. work 5437	Carpentry — general 5403	Concrete Work — NOC 5213	Concrete Work — flat (flr., sdwk.) 5221	Electrical Wiring — inside 5190	Excavation — earth NOC 6217	Excavation — rock 6217	Glaziers 5462	Insulation Work 5479	Lathing 5443	Masonry 5022	Painting & Decorating 5474	Pile Driving 6003	Plastering 5480	Plumbing 5183	Roofing 5551	Sheet Metal Work (HVAC) 5538	Steel Erection — door & sash 5102	Steel Erection — inter, ornam. 5102	Steel Erection — structure 5040	Steel Erection — NOC 5057	Tile Work — (interior ceramic) 5348	Waterproofing 9014	Wrecking 5701
AL	29.28	13.11	25.00	12.94	9.22	8.58	11.91	11.91	20.78	14.99	8.43	22.04	16.81	18.81	14.91	8.97	48.49	9.00	10.13	10.13	46.10	24.11	14.15	8.68	46.10
AK	12.44	9.33	13.86	11.33	10.80	6.86	9.06	9.06	32.79	17.54	8.30	16.08	11.68	33.22	13.00	7.53	25.29	7.47	7.41	7.41	25.75	41.66	5.15	5.48	25.75
AZ	11.78	5.44	15.76	6.99	4.24	4.37	4.81	4.81	6.09	10.18	3.64	7.06	7.21	8.53	5.15	4.56	18.34	6.49	9.20	9.20	21.81	10.32	2.89	3.58	21.81
AR	11.58	5.85	10.93	6.39	5.50	4.31	6.73	6.73	7.95	8.55	4.39	7.75	8.88	10.93	12.95	4.70	17.06	5.13	6.99	6.99	28.58	21.04	6.21	2.97	28.58
CA	36.98	36.98	36.98	19.36	19.34	13.20	18.05	18.05	27.35	17.74	16.02	27.71	21.08	23.37	30.46	17.05	64.15	19.29	22.60	22.60	41.64	23.39	2.30	21.08	23.39
CO	7.62	4.14	5.79	6.03	4.35	2.67	4.88	4.88	4.93	7.66	3.52	7.28	5.10	7.13	5.24	3.62	13.42	3.77	5.01	5.01	24.23	9.35	3.77	2.76	21.38
CT	19.80	17.42	27.18	22.71	13.56	7.85	14.62	14.62	19.83	24.28	12.69	27.26	21.51	23.20	18.28	10.85	48.23	13.52	15.52	15.52	64.75	22.28	13.05	6.77	65.75
DE	9.15	9.15	7.05	7.35	6.12	3.18	5.54	5.54	7.90	7.05	7.90	8.28	9.53	11.07	7.90	4.76	17.93	6.13	8.83	8.83	17.30	8.83	5.60	8.28	17.30
DC	8.25	8.16	7.71	12.10	7.65	4.34	9.06	9.06	13.00	6.41	6.70	10.21	5.60	15.02	8.73	7.96	16.80	7.20	15.77	15.77	19.23	10.98	9.00	4.18	19.23
FL	9.33	7.33	10.95	11.45	5.16	5.13	5.96	5.96	8.48	8.55	4.12	8.77	7.91	38.24	11.10	4.82	17.10	6.49	8.06	8.06	19.04	10.13	4.43	4.41	19.04
GA	43.26	19.77	27.19	20.25	15.13	10.28	16.31	16.31	18.41	19.10	12.62	28.72	28.86	23.32	21.44	12.2	75.23	17.15	19.64	19.64	73.28	34.09	12.76	10.18	73.28
HI	7.84	6.87	14.67	7.64	4.33	4.13	5.18	5.18	8.07	5.61	6.55	7.82	6.96	9.14	8.22	4.26	13.77	4.11	6.51	6.51	28.23	9.49	5.22	5.37	20.79
ID	12.77	6.43	10.55	11.76	5.76	3.47	7.06	7.06	9.63	7.67	6.29	7.80	8.43	9.30	13.57	4.27	22.62	7.21	8.55	8.55	32.97	8.02	6.84	4.80	27.50
IL	23.60	15.01	21.72	29.69	12.06	8.24	11.22	11.22	18.09	20.32	12.88	20.85	13.07	21.77	22.24	10.77	36.73	12.98	19.24	19.24	79.82	21.35	16.91	5.78	29.82
IN	8.38	4.15	6.38	4.95	3.41	2.68	4.15	4.15	5.28	6.02	3.24	4.43	4.34	5.34	3.28	2.65	10.05	4.13	4.21	4.21	11.63	5.11	2.89	2.59	11.63
IA	10.34	8.42	12.90	12.72	8.24	4.47	6.88	6.88	9.20	5.82	4.64	8.40	6.76	8.73	10.98	6.40	19.92	4.80	5.70	5.70	36.26	14.65	6.70	4.60	24.10
KS	12.27	5.30	8.09	6.46	5.62	3.67	4.59	4.59	8.35	8.35	3.41	6.73	6.60	7.80	5.04	4.43	13.94	4.61	4.75	4.75	18.81	13.14	5.31	3.99	13.14
KY	12.63	12.30	24.88	12.96	7.51	5.36	11.65	11.65	16.68	13.04	8.83	7.70	11.00	21.98	12.55	5.87	34.41	11.42	10.07	10.07	60.00	17.23	18.88	4.22	60.00
LA	18.20	12.54	20.92	11.92	9.35	6.46	12.02	12.02	14.16	10.50	6.61	13.71	15.78	15.66	10.45	6.08	32.48	12.91	12.19	12.19	44.77	9.67	7.08	6.58	44.77
ME	14.80	10.05	21.30	15.69	9.73	5.57	10.34	10.34	14.40	14.60	5.58	10.56	14.17	12.31	10.83	7.41	24.74	8.22	7.40	7.40	38.54	15.25	5.97	5.13	38.54
MD	17.56	13.32	14.28	19.37	5.51	7.07	7.60	7.60	12.50	14.18	5.58	10.00	7.28	21.24	10.47	7.02	30.67	7.73	10.49	10.49	59.74	22.48	6.69	5.43	22.48
MA	8.68	5.23	9.61	18.85	6.24	2.84	4.35	4.35	9.58	7.78	5.27	10.55	5.09	12.92	4.68	3.50	30.99	5.72	6.89	6.89	54.08	33.00	5.81	2.48	23.75
MI	21.01	11.98	21.01	17.15	10.48	6.35	14.00	14.00	15.12	13.11	13.59	18.32	13.30	59.47	10.34	7.71	42.64	12.58	12.03	12.03	59.47	16.23	11.70	6.95	59.47
MN	19.68	20.00	29.85	10.35	13.68	5.50	10.18	10.18	33.05	22.80	10.63	15.00	14.53	30.90	10.63	8.08	62.73	17.35	9.73	9.73	124.08	8.93	11.70	7.20	8.93
MS	17.32	9.93	13.14	9.84	5.57	4.62	9.84	9.84	11.42	9.11	4.97	12.50	9.60	17.78	10.10	8.54	33.19	6.45	13.01	13.01	30.00	8.32	7.92	4.45	30.00
MO	18.26	12.25	13.57	17.90	11.00	7.12	11.34	11.34	10.74	13.27	9.16	15.43	11.27	18.34	14.38	10.70	36.70	9.28	11.58	11.58	38.70	38.11	13.39	6.50	38.70
MT	13.20	10.71	20.41	12.22	10.37	5.23	12.92	12.92	10.67	19.74	7.41	9.78	8.66	15.08	10.75	7.27	39.34	8.38	9.64	9.64	24.14	9.36	8.36	7.78	9.36
NE	20.53	15.68	20.38	19.08	12.10	7.83	15.30	15.30	12.18	19.13	8.00	18.20	11.23	15.73	13.68	9.48	34.05	11.63	13.15	13.15	44.88	22.70	8.23	6.70	63.83
NV	10.76	7.25	11.35	10.52	7.16	4.80	8.48	8.48	6.75	8.06	3.45	6.62	6.07	8.88	6.41	6.22	17.81	8.84	7.73	7.73	25.26	15.85	13.93	5.16	15.85
NH	20.77	11.63	18.79	25.37	13.01	5.70	13.22	13.22	12.59	13.98	7.47	19.78	24.64	15.55	10.58	10.41	35.43	8.15	11.93	11.93	99.47	28.64	12.59	6.79	99.47
NJ	15.50	9.86	15.50	14.21	9.79	4.45	8.75	8.75	7.99	10.68	12.42	14.48	10.11	14.56	12.42	6.24	38.07	6.71	10.85	10.85	16.29	15.14	7.82	5.82	15.93
NM	19.58	8.17	18.99	13.33	10.11	8.08	8.28	8.28	18.17	11.75	6.68	15.36	11.43	18.20	14.39	8.14	37.47	9.92	12.79	12.79	54.49	40.63	7.66	6.66	54.49
NY	4.93	2.81	6.01	7.46	5.60	2.64	3.94	3.94	6.56	3.28	4.63	6.16	4.85	6.74	2.51	3.31	12.36	4.57	5.46	5.46	10.44	6.29	3.12	3.09	4.57
NC	15.50	11.55	18.63	17.12	8.14	9.96	13.11	13.11	11.87	12.57	9.34	11.05	11.85	16.82	13.63	8.92	33.88	11.87	11.97	11.97	70.40	20.61	8.12	5.41	70.40
ND	10.78	10.78	10.78	4.92	4.92	3.79	4.18	4.18	10.78	10.78	8.88	6.00	6.57	12.68	8.88	6.21	19.53	6.21	12.68	12.68	12.68	12.68	10.78	19.53	8.53
OH	6.82	4.77	6.03	4.98	4.96	3.17	4.83	4.83	9.26	9.83	30.29	7.62	7.64	7.67	7.20	3.94	15.01	4.87	6.17	6.17	12.91	6	6.11	4.90	6.00
OK	13.42	9.17	11.76	11.76	6.34	5.73	10.83	10.83	16.07	19.47	8.45	10.02	8.47	20.25	12.19	7.09	21.13	9.05	13.76	13.76	39.72	23.97	6.50	5.71	39.72
OR	19.79	8.26	13.53	10.34	8.96	5.18	9.03	9.03	10.65	10.89	6.79	11.80	10.85	12.18	9.08	5.38	26.12	6.49	6.82	6.82	20.28	15.61	6.68	5.72	20.28
PA	16.83	16.83	13.22	16.61	11.93	6.69	9.79	9.79	12.75	13.22	12.75	14.24	14.78	17.14	12.75	8.62	33.19	8.74	16.63	16.63	25.25	16.63	9.61	14.24	25.25
RI	9.69	10.13	12.42	13.18	10.51	4.12	8.56	8.56	10.26	13.56	4.93	8.95	9.48	20.95	8.02	5.77	19.37	6.38	6.06	6.06	28.84	20.64	4.60	4.61	28.84
SC	21.43	18.13	22.49	16.89	9.59	11.45	11.78	11.78	16.99	18.58	11.06	13.93	15.50	20.61	15.75	12.36	50.08	13.06	13.91	13.91	41.22	32.53	10.50	6.33	41.22
SD	18.86	13.19	18.65	20.78	8.58	4.84	9.13	9.13	14.61	14.35	6.47	11.88	10.04	15.98	10.23	9.60	31.05	9.72	11.92	11.92	45.18	23.68	6.07	6.02	45.18
TN	16.91	10.01	10.79	11.98	5.04	5.70	11.30	11.30	11.59	8.82	7.16	12.26	9.19	21.55	10.85	5.70	30.21	7.60	8.74	8.74	22.74	23.16	7.39	4.11	22.74
TX	9.68	7.76	9.68	8.61	6.25	5.65	7.33	7.33	7.82	10.32	4.91	8.32	8.04	12.94	8.04	5.47	17.96	13.94	7.16	7.16	29.32	11.95	5.11	5.97	8.11
UT	9.81	5.76	7.93	7.13	5.38	3.09	6.77	6.77	7.13	5.43	4.01	6.86	5.93	7.69	4.67	3.28	21.47	5.41	4.91	4.91	17.18	8.18	3.74	4.02	18.30
VT	13.01	12.79	15.72	11.55	8.77	4.46	10.51	10.51	13.83	14.05	6.01	13.93	9.03	12.33	8.89	8.77	26.46	7.73	10.42	10.42	45.01	23.47	7.90	7.15	45.01
VA	8.91	6.79	7.37	8.34	4.22	3.84	6.23	6.23	6.35	5.77	6.19	6.15	7.43	7.98	6.26	4.34	21.14	5.67	6.19	6.19	25.35	11.51	4.06	2.65	25.35
WA	8.93	8.93	8.93	8.93	8.93	3.27	5.79	5.79	13.83	8.00	8.93	11.74	14.05	20.72	10.68	4.12	19.61	4.58	8.62	8.62	8.62	8.62	7.66	19.61	8.62
WV	13.52	9.63	10.91	11.26	6.25	6.07	9.18	9.18	11.22	9.76	7.21	10.37	10.25	15.47	9.74	6.22	25.10	7.93	8.31	8.31	34.41	16.71	7.86	3.96	32.85
WI	13.04	10.81	16.27	12.16	8.90	5.66	7.72	7.72	12.52	12.83	4.69	15.44	12.07	26.59	10.07	5.82	31.84	8.36	11.02	11.02	21.68	30.03	16.47	5.33	21.68
WY	5.07	5.07	5.07	5.07	5.07	5.07	5.07	5.07	5.07	5.07	5.07	5.07	5.07	5.07	5.07	5.07	5.07	5.07	5.07	5.07	5.07	5.07	5.07	5.07	5.07
AVG.	14.90	10.53	14.96	12.70	8.24	5.58	9.01	9.01	12.57	11.85	7.82	12.10	10.70	16.76	10.78	6.91	28.83	8.47	10.07	10.07	36.86	17.78	8.01	6.41	30.43

R013113-60 Workers' Compensation (cont.) (Canada in Canadian dollars)

Province		Alberta	British Columbia	Manitoba	Ontario	New Brunswick	Newfndld. & Labrador	Northwest Territories	Nova Scotia	Prince Edward Island	Quebec	Saskat-chewan	Yukon
Carpentry—3 stories or less	Rate	6.07	3.93	3.96	4.44	4.62	9.44	3.92	5.70	6.62	12.61	3.74	8.55
	Code	42143	721028	40102	723	238130	4226	4-41	4226	403	80110	B1226	202
Carpentry—interior cab. work	Rate	2.16	2.68	3.96	4.44	4.37	4.24	3.92	4.83	3.69	12.61	2.24	8.55
	Code	42133	721021	40102	723	238350	4279	4-41	4274	402	80110	B1127	202
CARPENTRY—general	Rate	6.07	3.93	3.93	4.44	4.62	4.24	3.92	5.70	6.62	12.61	3.74	8.55
	Code	42143	721028	40102	723	238130	4299	4-41	4226	403	80110	B1202	202
CONCRETE WORK—NOC	Rate	3.86	3.28	6.27	17.86	4.62	9.44	3.92	5.03	3.69	12.86	4.28	8.55
	Code	42104	721010	40110	748	238110	4224	4-41	4224	402	80100	B1314	203
CONCRETE WORK—flat (flr. sidewalk)	Rate	3.86	3.28	6.27	17.86	4.62	9.44	3.92	5.03	3.69	12.86	4.28	8.55
	Code	42104	721010	40110	748	238110	4224	4-41	4224	402	80100	B1314	203
ELECTRICAL Wiring—inside	Rate	1.72	1.71	1.74	3.60	2.09	2.57	2.67	2.68	3.69	4.55	2.24	4.96
	Code	42124	721019	40203	704	238210	4261	4-46	4261	402	80170	B1105	206
EXCAVATION—earth NOC	Rate	2.18	3.62	4.52	5.16	4.62	3.59	3.90	3.16	3.69	8.33	2.21	4.96
	Code	40604	721031	4	711	238190	4214	4-43	4214	402	80030	R1106	207
EXCAVATION—rock	Rate	2.18	3.62	4.19	5.16	4.62	3.59	3.90	3.16	3.69	8.33	2.21	4.96
	Code	40604	721031	40706	711	238190	4214	4-43	4214	402	80030	R1106	207
GLAZIERS	Rate	2.34	3.05	3.96	10.00	4.62	5.25	3.92	5.70	3.69	14.52	4.28	4.96
	Code	42121	715020	40109	751	238150	4233	4-41	4233	402	80150	B1304	212
INSULATION WORK	Rate	1.74	6.88	3.96	10.00	4.37	5.25	3.92	5.70	3.69	12.61	3.74	8.55
	Code	42184	721029	40102	751	238310	4234	4-41	4234	402	80110	B1207	202
LATHING	Rate	3.78	7.08	3.96	4.44	4.37	4.24	3.92	4.83	3.69	12.61	4.28	8.55
	Code	42135	721042	40102	723	238390	4279	4-41	4271	402	80110	B1316	202
MASONRY	Rate	3.84	3.02	3.96	12.39	4.62	5.25	3.92	5.70	3.69	12.86	4.28	8.55
	Code	42102	721037	40102	741	238140	4231	4-41	4231	402	80100	B1318	202
PAINTING & DECORATING	Rate	2.90	3.12	3.44	7.33	4.37	4.24	3.92	4.83	3.69	12.61	3.74	8.55
	Code	42111	721041	40105	719	238320	4275	4-41	4275	402	80110	B1201	202
PILE DRIVING	Rate	3.77	3.92	4.19	6.86	4.62	3.59	3.90	5.03	6.62	8.33	4.28	8.55
	Code	42159	722004	40706	732	238190	4129	4-43	4221	403	80030	B1310	202
PLASTERING	Rate	3.78	7.08	4.48	7.33	4.37	4.24	3.92	4.83	3.69	12.61	3.74	8.55
	Code	42135	721042	40108	719	238390	4271	4-41	4271	402	80110	B1221	202
PLUMBING	Rate	1.72	2.26	2.93	4.06	2.09	2.68	2.67	3.14	2.21	6.44	2.24	4.96
	Code	42122	721043	40204	707	238220	4241	4-46	4241	401	80160	B1101	214
ROOFING	Rate	5.85	6.52	6.74	14.44	4.62	9.44	3.92	7.76	3.69	19.78	4.28	8.55
	Code	42118	721036	40403	728	238160	4236	4-41	4236	402	80130	B1320	202
SHEET METAL WORK (HVAC)	Rate	1.72	2.26	6.74	4.06	2.09	2.68	2.67	3.14	2.21	6.44	2.24	4.96
	Code	42117	721043	40402	707	238220	4244	4-46	4244	401	80160	B1107	208
STEEL ERECTION—door & sash	Rate	1.74	12.03	8.24	17.86	4.62	9.44	3.92	5.70	3.69	20.90	4.28	8.55
	Code	42106	722005	40502	748	238120	4227	4-41	4227	402	80080	B1322	202
STEEL ERECTION—inter., ornam.	Rate	1.74	12.03	8.24	17.86	4.62	9.44	3.92	5.70	3.69	20.90	4.28	8.55
	Code	42106	722005	40502	748	238120	4227	4-41	4227	402	80080	B1322	202
STEEL ERECTION—structure	Rate	1.74	12.03	8.24	17.86	4.62	9.44	3.92	5.70	3.69	20.90	4.28	8.55
	Code	42106	722005	40502	748	238120	4227	4-41	4227	402	80080	B1322	202
STEEL ERECTION—NOC	Rate	1.74	12.03	8.24	17.86	4.62	9.44	3.92	5.70	3.69	20.90	4.28	8.55
	Code	42106	722005	40502	748	238120	4227	4-41	4227	402	80080	B1322	202
TILE WORK—inter. (ceramic)	Rate	2.80	3.34	1.90	7.33	4.37	4.24	3.92	4.83	3.69	12.61	4.28	8.55
	Code	42113	721054	40103	719	238340	4276	4-41	4276	402	80110	B1301	202
WATERPROOFING	Rate	2.90	3.10	3.96	4.44	4.62	4.24	3.92	5.70	3.69	17.81	3.74	8.55
	Code	42139	721016	40102	723	238190	4299	4-41	4239	402	80130	B1217	202
WRECKING	Rate	2.18	4.81	7.34	17.86	4.62	3.59	3.90	3.16	5.61	12.61	2.21	8.55
	Code	40604	721005	40106	748	238190	4211	4-43	4211	402	80110	R1125	202

R013113-80   Performance Bond

This table shows the cost of a Performance Bond for a construction job scheduled to be completed in 12 months. Add 1% of the premium cost per month for jobs requiring more than 12 months to complete. The rates are "standard" rates offered to contractors that the bonding company considers financially sound and capable of doing the work. Preferred rates are offered by some bonding companies based upon financial strength of the contractor. Actual rates vary from contractor to contractor and from bonding company to bonding company. Contractors should prequalify through a bonding agency before submitting a bid on a contract that requires a bond.

Contract Amount	Building Construction Class B Projects		Highways & Bridges					
			Class A New Construction			Class A-1 Highway Resurfacing		
First $ 100,000 bid	$25.00 per M		$15.00 per M			$9.40 per M		
Next 400,000 bid	$ 2,500	plus $15.00 per M	$ 1,500	plus $10.00	per M	$ 940	plus $7.20	per M
Next 2,000,000 bid	8,500	plus 10.00 per M	5,500	plus 7.00	per M	3,820	plus 5.00	per M
Next 2,500,000 bid	28,500	plus 7.50 per M	19,500	plus 5.50	per M	15,820	plus 4.50	per M
Next 2,500,000 bid	47,250	plus 7.00 per M	33,250	plus 5.00	per M	28,320	plus 4.50	per M
Over 7,500,000 bid	64,750	plus 6.00 per M	45,750	plus 4.50	per M	39,570	plus 4.00	per M

R015423-10   Steel Tubular Scaffolding

On new construction, tubular scaffolding is efficient up to 60' high or five stories. Above this it is usually better to use a hung scaffolding if construction permits. Swing scaffolding operations may interfere with tenants. In this case, the tubular is more practical at all heights.

In repairing or cleaning the front of an existing building the cost of tubular scaffolding per S.F. of building front increases as the height increases above the first tier. The first tier cost is relatively high due to leveling and alignment.

The minimum efficient crew for erecting and dismantling is three workers. They can set up and remove 18 frame sections per day up to 5 stories high. For 6 to 12 stories high, a crew of four is most efficient. Use two or more on top and two on the bottom for handing up or hoisting. They can also set up and remove 18 frame sections per day. At 7' horizontal spacing, this will run about 800 S.F. per day of erecting and dismantling. Time for placing and removing planks must be added to the above. A crew of three can place and remove 72 planks per day up to 5 stories. For over 5 stories, a crew of four can place and remove 80 planks per day.

The table below shows the number of pieces required to erect tubular steel scaffolding for 1000 S.F. of building frontage. This area is made up of a scaffolding system that is 12 frames (11 bays) long by 2 frames high.

For jobs under twenty-five frames, add 50% to rental cost. Rental rates will be lower for jobs over three months duration. Large quantities for long periods can reduce rental rates by 20%.

Description of Component	Number of Pieces for 1000 S.F. of Building Front	Unit
5' Wide Standard Frame, 6'-4" High	24	Ea.
Leveling Jack & Plate	24	
Cross Brace	44	
Side Arm Bracket, 21"	12	
Guardrail Post	12	
Guardrail, 7' section	22	
Stairway Section	2	
Stairway Starter Bar	1	
Stairway Inside Handrail	2	
Stairway Outside Handrail	2	
Walk-Thru Frame Guardrail	2	

Scaffolding is often used as falsework over 15' high during construction of cast-in-place concrete beams and slabs. Two foot wide scaffolding is generally used for heavy beam construction. The span between frames depends upon the load to be carried with a maximum span of 5'.

Heavy duty shoring frames with a capacity of 10,000#/leg can be spaced up to 10' O.C. depending upon form support design and loading.

Scaffolding used as horizontal shoring requires less than half the material required with conventional shoring.

On new construction, erection is done by carpenters.

Rolling towers supporting horizontal shores can reduce labor and speed the job. For maintenance work, catwalks with spans up to 70' can be supported by the rolling towers.

R015433-10 Contractor Equipment

Rental Rates shown elsewhere in the book pertain to late model high quality machines in excellent working condition, rented from equipment dealers. Rental rates from contractors may be substantially lower than the rental rates from equipment dealers depending upon economic conditions; for older, less productive machines, reduce rates by a maximum of 15%. Any overtime must be added to the base rates. For shift work, rates are lower. Usual rule of thumb is 150% of one shift rate for two shifts; 200% for three shifts.

For periods of less than one week, operated equipment is usually more economical to rent than renting bare equipment and hiring an operator.

Costs to move equipment to a job site (mobilization) or from a job site (demobilization) are not included in rental rates, nor in any Equipment costs on any Unit Price line items or crew listings. These costs can be found elsewhere. If a piece of equipment is already at a job site, it is not appropriate to utilize mob/demob costs in an estimate again.

Rental rates vary throughout the country with larger cities generally having lower rates. Lease plans for new equipment are available for periods in excess of six months with a percentage of payments applying toward purchase.

Rental rates can also be treated as reimbursement costs for contractor-owned equipment. Owned equipment costs include depreciation, loan payments, interest, taxes, insurance, storage, and major repairs.

Monthly rental rates vary from 2% to 5% of the cost of the equipment depending on the anticipated life of the equipment and its wearing parts. Weekly rates are about 1/3 the monthly rates and daily rental rates about 1/3 the weekly rate.

The hourly operating costs for each piece of equipment include costs to the user such as fuel, oil, lubrication, normal expendables for the equipment, and a percentage of mechanic's wages chargeable to maintenance. The hourly operating costs listed do not include the operator's wages.

The daily cost for equipment used in the standard crews is figured by dividing the weekly rate by five, then adding eight times the hourly operating cost to give the total daily equipment cost, not including the operator. This figure is in the right hand column of the Equipment listings under Equipment Cost/Day.

Pile Driving rates shown for pile hammer and extractor do not include leads, crane, boiler or compressor. Vibratory pile driving requires an added field specialist during set-up and pile driving operation for the electric model. The hydraulic model requires a field specialist for set-up only. Up to 125 reuses of sheet piling are possible using vibratory drivers. For normal conditions, crane capacity for hammer type and size are as follows.

Crane Capacity	Hammer Type and Size		
	Air or Steam	Diesel	Vibratory
25 ton	to 8,750 ft.-lb.		70 H.P.
40 ton	15,000 ft.-lb.	to 32,000 ft.-lb.	170 H.P.
60 ton	25,000 ft.-lb.		300 H.P.
100 ton		112,000 ft.-lb.	

Cranes should be specified for the job by size, building and site characteristics, availability, performance characteristics, and duration of time required.

Backhoes & Shovels rent for about the same as equivalent size cranes but maintenance and operating expense is higher. Crane operators rate must be adjusted for high boom heights. Average adjustments: for 150' boom add 2% per hour; over 185', add 4% per hour; over 210', add 6% per hour; over 250', add 8% per hour and over 295', add 12% per hour.

Tower Cranes of the climbing or static type have jibs from 50' to 200' and capacities at maximum reach range from 4,000 to 14,000 pounds. Lifting capacities increase up to maximum load as the hook radius decreases.

Typical rental rates, based on purchase price are about 2% to 3% per month.

Erection and dismantling runs between 500 and 2000 labor hours. Climbing operation takes 10 labor hours per 20' climb. Crane dead time is about 5 hours per 40' climb. If crane is bolted to side of the building add cost of ties and extra mast sections. Climbing cranes have from 80' to 180' of mast while static cranes have 80' to 800' of mast.

Truck Cranes can be converted to tower cranes by using tower attachments. Mast heights over 400' have been used.

A single 100' high material **Hoist and Tower** can be erected and dismantled in about 400 labor hours; a double 100' high hoist and tower in about 600 labor hours. Erection times for additional heights are 3 and 4 labor hours

per vertical foot respectively up to 150', and 4 to 5 labor hours per vertical foot over 150' high. A 40' high portable Buck hoist takes about 160 labor hours to erect and dismantle. Additional heights take 2 labor hours per vertical foot to 80' and 3 labor hours per vertical foot for the next 100'. Most material hoists do not meet local code requirements for carrying personnel.

A 150' high **Personnel Hoist** requires about 500 to 800 labor hours to erect and dismantle. Budget erection time at 5 labor hours per vertical foot for all trades. Local code requirements or labor scarcity requiring overtime can add up to 50% to any of the above erection costs.

Earthmoving Equipment: The selection of earthmoving equipment depends upon the type and quantity of material, moisture content, haul distance, haul road, time available, and equipment available. Short haul cut and fill operations may require dozers only, while another operation may require excavators, a fleet of trucks, and spreading and compaction equipment. Stockpiled material and granular material are easily excavated with front end loaders. Scrapers are most economically used with hauls between 300' and 1-1/2 miles if adequate haul roads can be maintained. Shovels are often used for blasted rock and any material where a vertical face of 8' or more can be excavated. Special conditions may dictate the use of draglines, clamshells, or backhoes. Spreading and compaction equipment must be matched to the soil characteristics, the compaction required and the rate the fill is being supplied.

Existing Conditions | R0241 Demolition

R024119-10   Demolition Defined

Whole Building Demolition - Demolition of the whole building with no concern for any particular building element, component, or material type being demolished. This type of demolition is accomplished with large pieces of construction equipment that break up the structure, load it into trucks and haul it to a disposal site, but disposal or dump fees are not included. Demolition of below-grade foundation elements, such as footings, foundation walls, grade beams, slabs on grade, etc., is not included. Certain mechanical equipment containing flammable liquids or ozone-depleting refrigerants, electric lighting elements, communication equipment components, and other building elements may contain hazardous waste, and must be removed, either selectively or carefully, as hazardous waste before the building can be demolished.

Foundation Demolition - Demolition of below-grade foundation footings, foundation walls, grade beams, and slabs on grade. This type of demolition is accomplished by hand or pneumatic hand tools, and does not include saw cutting, or handling, loading, hauling, or disposal of the debris.

Gutting - Removal of building interior finishes and electrical/mechanical systems down to the load-bearing and sub-floor elements of the rough building frame, with no concern for any particular building element, component, or material type being demolished. This type of demolition is accomplished by hand or pneumatic hand tools, and includes loading into trucks, but not hauling, disposal or dump fees, scaffolding, or shoring. Certain mechanical equipment containing flammable liquids or ozone-depleting refrigerants, electric lighting elements, communication equipment components, and other building elements may contain hazardous waste, and must be removed, either selectively or carefully, as hazardous waste, before the building is gutted.

Selective Demolition - Demolition of a selected building element, component, or finish, with some concern for surrounding or adjacent elements, components, or finishes (see the first Subdivision (s) at the beginning of appropriate Divisions). This type of demolition is accomplished by hand or pneumatic hand tools, and does not include handling, loading, storing, hauling, or disposal of the debris, scaffolding, or shoring. "Gutting" methods may be used in order to save time, but damage that is caused to surrounding or adjacent elements, components, or finishes may have to be repaired at a later time.

Careful Removal - Removal of a piece of service equipment, building element or component, or material type, with great concern for both the removed item and surrounding or adjacent elements, components or finishes. The purpose of careful removal may be to protect the removed item for later re-use, preserve a higher salvage value of the removed item, or replace an item while taking care to protect surrounding or adjacent elements, components, connections, or finishes from cosmetic and/or structural damage. An approximation of the time required to perform this type of removal is 1/3 to 1/2 the time it would take to install a new item of like kind (see Reference Number R220105-10). This type of removal is accomplished by hand or pneumatic hand tools, and does not include loading, hauling, or storing the removed item, scaffolding, shoring, or lifting equipment.

Cutout Demolition - Demolition of a small quantity of floor, wall, roof, or other assembly, with concern for the appearance and structural integrity of the surrounding materials. This type of demolition is accomplished by hand or pneumatic hand tools, and does not include saw cutting, handling, loading, hauling, or disposal of debris, scaffolding, or shoring.

Rubbish Handling - Work activities that involve handling, loading or hauling of debris. Generally, the cost of rubbish handling must be added to the cost of all types of demolition, with the exception of whole building demolition.

Minor Site Demolition - Demolition of site elements outside the footprint of a building. This type of demolition is accomplished by hand or pneumatic hand tools, or with larger pieces of construction equipment, and may include loading a removed item onto a truck (check the Crew for equipment used). It does not include saw cutting, hauling or disposal of debris, and, sometimes, handling or loading.

R024119-20   Dumpsters

Dumpster rental costs on construction sites are presented in two ways.

The cost per week rental includes the delivery of the dumpster; its pulling or emptying once per week, and its final removal. The assumption is made that the dumpster contractor could choose to empty a dumpster by simply bringing in an empty unit and removing the full one. These costs also include the disposal of the materials in the dumpster.

The Alternate Pricing can be used when actual planned conditions are not approximated by the weekly numbers. For example, these lines can be used when a dumpster is needed for 4 weeks and will need to be emptied 2 or 3 times per week. Conversely the Alternate Pricing lines can be used when a dumpster will be rented for several weeks or months but needs to be emptied only a few times over this period.

Existing Conditions | R0265 Underground Storage Tank Removal

R026510-20   Underground Storage Tank Removal

Underground Storage Tank Removal can be divided into two categories: Non-Leaking and Leaking. Prior to removing an underground storage tank, tests should be made, with the proper authorities present, to determine whether a tank has been leaking or the surrounding soil has been contaminated.

To safely remove Liquid Underground Storage Tanks:
1. Excavate to the top of the tank.
2. Disconnect all piping.
3. Open all tank vents and access ports.
4. Remove all liquids and/or sludge.
5. Purge the tank with an inert gas.
6. Provide access to the inside of the tank and clean out the interior using proper personal protective equipment (PPE).
7. Excavate soil surrounding the tank using proper PPE for on-site personnel.
8. Pull and properly dispose of the tank.
9. Clean up the site of all contaminated material.
10. Install new tanks or close the excavation.

Existing Conditions — R0282 Asbestos Remediation

R028213-20   Asbestos Removal Process

Asbestos removal is accomplished by a specialty contractor who understands the federal and state regulations regarding the handling and disposal of the material. The process of asbestos removal is divided into many individual steps. An accurate estimate can be calculated only after all the steps have been priced.

The steps are generally as follows:
1. Obtain an asbestos abatement plan from an industrial hygienist.
2. Monitor the air quality in and around the removal area and along the path of travel between the removal area and transport area. This establishes the background contamination.
3. Construct a two part decontamination chamber at entrance to removal area.
4. Install a HEPA filter to create a negative pressure in the removal area.
5. Install wall, floor and ceiling protection as required by the plan, usually 2 layers of fireproof 6 mil polyethylene.

6. Industrial hygienist visually inspects work area to verify compliance with plan.
7. Provide temporary supports for conduit and piping affected by the removal process.
8. Proceed with asbestos removal and bagging process. Monitor air quality as described in Step #2. Discontinue operations when contaminate levels exceed applicable standards.
9. Document the legal disposal of materials in accordance with EPA standards.
10. Thoroughly clean removal area including all ledges, crevices and surfaces.
11. Post abatement inspection by industrial hygienist to verify plan compliance.
12. Provide a certificate from a licensed industrial hygienist attesting that contaminate levels are within acceptable standards before returning area to regular use.

Thermal & Moist. Protec. — R0784 Firestopping

R078413-30   Firestopping

Firestopping is the sealing of structural, mechanical, electrical and other penetrations through fire-rated assemblies. The basic components of firestop systems are safing insulation and firestop sealant on both sides of wall penetrations and the top side of floor penetrations.

Pipe penetrations are assumed to be through concrete, grout, or joint compound and can be sleeved or unsleeved. Costs for the penetrations and sleeves are not included. An annular space of 1″ is assumed. Escutcheons are not included.

Metallic pipe is assumed to be copper, aluminum, cast iron or similar metallic material. Insulated metallic pipe is assumed to be covered with a thermal insulating jacket of varying thickness and materials.

Non-metallic pipe is assumed to be PVC, CPVC, FR Polypropylene or similar plastic piping material. Intumescent firestop sealant or wrap strips are included. Collars on both sides of wall penetrations and a sheet metal plate on the underside of floor penetrations are included.

Ductwork is assumed to be sheet metal, stainless steel or similar metallic material. Duct penetrations are assumed to be through concrete, grout or joint compound. Costs for penetrations and sleeves are not included. An annular space of 1/2″ is assumed.

Multi-trade openings include costs for sheet metal forms, firestop mortar, wrap strips, collars and sealants as necessary.

Structural penetrations joints are assumed to be 1/2″ or less. CMU walls are assumed to be within 1-1/2″ of metal deck. Drywall walls are assumed to be tight to the underside of metal decking.

Metal panel, glass or curtain wall systems include a spandrel area of 5′ filled with mineral wool foil-faced insulation. Fasteners and stiffeners are included.

Finishes — R0991 Painting

R099100-10   Painting Estimating Techniques

Proper estimating methodology is needed to obtain an accurate painting estimate. There is no known reliable shortcut or square foot method. The following steps should be followed:

- List all surfaces to be painted, with an accurate quantity (area) of each. Items having similar surface condition, finish, application method and accessibility may be grouped together.
- List all the tasks required for each surface to be painted, including surface preparation, masking, and protection of adjacent surfaces. Surface preparation may include minor repairs, washing, sanding and puttying.
- Select the proper Means line for each task. Review and consider all adjustments to labor and materials for type of paint and location of work. Apply the height adjustment carefully. For instance, when applying the adjustment for work over 8' high to a wall that is 12' high, apply the adjustment only to the area between 8' and 12' high, and not to the entire wall.

When applying more than one percent (%) adjustment, apply each to the base cost of the data, rather than applying one percentage adjustment on top of the other.

When estimating the cost of painting walls and ceilings remember to add the brushwork for all cut-ins at inside corners and around windows and doors as a LF measure. One linear foot of cut-in with brush equals one square foot of painting.

All items for spray painting include the labor for roll-back.

Deduct for openings greater than 100 SF, or openings that extend from floor to ceiling and are greater than 5' wide. Do not deduct small openings.

The cost of brushes, rollers, ladders and spray equipment are considered to be part of a painting contractor's overhead, and should not be added to the estimate. The cost of rented equipment such as scaffolding and swing staging should be added to the estimate.

R220102-20 Labor Adjustment Factors

Labor Adjustment Factors are provided for Divisions 21, 22, and 23 to assist the mechanical estimator account for the various complexities and special conditions of any particular project. While a single percentage has been entered on each line of Division 22 01 02.20, it should be understood that these are just suggested midpoints of ranges of values commonly used by mechanical estimators. They may be increased or decreased depending on the severity of the special conditions.

The group for "existing occupied buildings", has been the subject of requests for explanation. Actually there are two stages to this group: buildings that are existing and "finished" but unoccupied, and those that also are occupied. Buildings that are "finished" may result in higher labor costs due to the

workers having to be more careful not to damage finished walls, ceilings, floors, etc. and may necessitate special protective coverings and barriers. Also corridor bends and doorways may not accommodate long pieces of pipe or larger pieces of equipment. Work above an already hung ceiling can be very time consuming. The addition of occupants may force the work to be done on premium time (nights and/or weekends), eliminate the possible use of some preferred tools such as pneumatic drivers, powder charged drivers etc. The estimator should evaluate the access to the work area and just how the work is going to be accomplished to arrive at an increase in labor costs over "normal" new construction productivity.

R220105-10   Demolition (Selective vs. Removal for Replacement)

Demolition can be divided into two basic categories.

One type of demolition involves the removal of material with no concern for its replacement. The labor-hours to estimate this work are found under "Selective Demolition" in the Fire Protection, Plumbing and HVAC Divisions. It is selective in that individual items or all the material installed as a system or trade grouping such as plumbing or heating systems are removed. This may be accomplished by the easiest way possible, such as sawing, torch cutting, or sledge hammer as well as simple unbolting.

The second type of demolition is the removal of some item for repair or replacement. This removal may involve careful draining, opening of unions, disconnecting and tagging of electrical connections, capping of pipes/ducts to prevent entry of debris or leakage of the material contained as well as transport of the item away from its in-place location to a truck/dumpster. An approximation of the time required to accomplish this type of demolition is to use half of the time indicated as necessary to install a new unit. For example; installation of a new pump might be listed as requiring 6 labor-hours so if we had to estimate the removal of the old pump we would allow an additional 3 hours for a total of 9 hours. That is, the complete replacement of a defective pump with a new pump would be estimated to take 9 labor-hours.

R220523-80   Valve Materials

VALVE MATERIALS

Bronze:
Bronze is one of the oldest materials used to make valves. It is most commonly used in hot and cold water systems and other non-corrosive services. It is often used as a seating surface in larger iron body valves to ensure tight closure.

Carbon Steel:
Carbon steel is a high strength material. Therefore, valves made from this metal are used in higher pressure services, such as steam lines up to 600 psi at 850° F. Many steel valves are available with butt-weld ends for economy and are generally used in high pressure steam service as well as other higher pressure non-corrosive services.

Forged Steel:
Valves from tough carbon steel are used in service up to 2000 psi and temperatures up to 1000° F in Gate, Globe and Check valves.

Iron:
Valves are normally used in medium to large pipe lines to control non-corrosive fluid and gases, where pressures do not exceed 250 psi at 450° F or 500 psi cold water, oil or gas.

Stainless Steel:
Developed steel alloys can be used in over 90% corrosive services.

Plastic PVC:
This is used in a great variety of valves generally in high corrosive service with lower temperatures and pressures.

VALVE SERVICE PRESSURES

Pressure ratings on valves provide an indication of the safe operating pressure for a valve at some elevated temperature. This temperature is dependent upon the materials used and the fabrication of the valve. When specific data is not available, a good "rule-of-thumb" to follow is the temperature of saturated steam on the primary rating indicated on the valve body. Example: The valve has the number 150S printed on the side indicating 150 psi and hence, a maximum operating temperature of 367° F (temperature of saturated steam and 150 psi).

DEFINITIONS

1. "WOG" – Water, oil, gas (cold working pressures).
2. "SWP" – Steam working pressure.
3. 100% area (full port) – means the area through the valve is equal to or greater than the area of standard pipe.
4. "Standard Opening" – means that the area through the valve is less than the area of standard pipe and therefore these valves should be used only where restriction of flow is unimportant.
5. "Round Port" – means the valve has a full round opening through the plug and body, of the same size and area as standard pipe.
6. "Rectangular Port" – valves have rectangular shaped ports through the plug body. The area of the port is either equal to 100% of the area of standard pipe, or restricted (standard opening). In either case it is clearly marked.
7. "ANSI" – American National Standards Institute.

R220523-90   Valve Selection Considerations

INTRODUCTION: In any piping application, valve performance is critical. Valves should be selected to give the best performance at the lowest cost.

The following is a list of performance characteristics generally expected of valves.

1. Stopping flow or starting it.
2. Throttling flow (Modulation).
3. Flow direction changing.
4. Checking backflow (Permitting flow in only one direction).
5. Relieving or regulating pressure.

In order to properly select the right valve, some facts must be determined.

A. What liquid or gas will flow through the valve?
B. Does the fluid contain suspended particles?
C. Does the fluid remain in liquid form at all times?
D. Which metals does fluid corrode?
E. What are the pressure and temperature limits? (As temperature and pressure rise, so will the price of the valve.)
F. Is there constant line pressure?
G. Is the valve merely an on-off valve?
H. Will checking of backflow be required?
I. Will the valve operate frequently or infrequently?

Valves are classified by design type into such classifications as Gate, Globe, Angle, Check, Ball, Butterfly and Plug. They are also classified by end connection, stem, pressure restrictions and material such as bronze, cast iron, etc. Each valve has a specific use. A quality valve used correctly will provide a lifetime of trouble-free service, but a high quality valve installed in the wrong service may require frequent attention.

STEM TYPES
(OS & Y)—Rising Stem-Outside Screw and Yoke

Offers a visual indication of whether the valve is open or closed. Recommended where high temperatures, corrosives, and solids in the line might cause damage to inside-valve stem threads. The stem threads are engaged by the yoke bushing so the stem rises through the hand wheel as it is turned.

(R.S.)—Rising Stem-Inside Screw

Adequate clearance for operation must be provided because both the hand wheel and the stem rise.
The valve wedge position is indicated by the position of the stem and hand wheel.

(N.R.S.)—Non-Rising Stem-Inside Screw

A minimum clearance is required for operating this type of valve. Excessive wear or damage to stem threads inside the valve may be caused by heat, corrosion, and solids. Because the hand wheel and stem do not rise, wedge position cannot be visually determined.

VALVE TYPES
Gate Valves

Provide full flow, minute pressure drop, minimum turbulence and minimum fluid trapped in the line.
They are normally used where operation is infrequent.

Globe Valves

Globe valves are designed for throttling and/or frequent operation with positive shut-off. Particular attention must be paid to the several types of seating materials available to avoid unnecessary wear. The seats must be compatible with the fluid in service and may be composition or metal. The configuration of the Globe valve opening causes turbulence which results in increased resistance. Most bronze Globe valves are rising stem-inside screw, but they are also available on O.S. & Y.

Angle Valves

The fundamental difference between the Angle valve and the Globe valve is the fluid flow through the Angle valve. It makes a 90° turn and offers less resistance to flow than the Globe valve while replacing an elbow. An Angle valve thus reduces the number of joints and installation time.

Check Valves

Check valves are designed to prevent backflow by automatically seating when the direction of fluid is reversed.
Swing Check valves are generally installed with Gate-valves, as they provide comparable full flow. Usually recommended for lines where flow velocities are low and should not be used on lines with pulsating flow. Recommended for horizontal installation, or in vertical lines only where flow is upward.

Lift Check Valves

These are commonly used with Globe and Angle valves since they have similar diaphragm seating arrangements and are recommended for preventing backflow of steam, air, gas and water, and on vapor lines with high flow velocities. For horizontal lines, horizontal lift checks should be used and vertical lift checks for vertical lines.

Ball Valves

Ball valves are light and easily installed, yet because of modern elastomeric seats, provide tight closure. Flow is controlled by rotating up to 90° a drilled ball which fits tightly against resilient seals. This ball seats with flow in either direction, and valve handle indicates the degree of opening. Recommended for frequent operation readily adaptable to automation, ideal for installation where space is limited.

Butterfly Valves

Butterfly valves provide bubble-tight closure with excellent throttling characteristics. They can be used for full-open, closed and for throttling applications.

The Butterfly valve consists of a disc within the valve body which is controlled by a shaft. In its closed position, the valve disc seals against a resilient seat. The disc position throughout the full 90° rotation is visually indicated by the position of the operator.

A Butterfly valve is only a fraction of the weight of a Gate valve and requires no gaskets between flanges in most cases. Recommended for frequent operation and adaptable to automation where space is limited.

Wafer and Lug type bodies when installed between two pipe flanges, can be easily removed from the line. The pressure of the bolted flanges holds the valve in place.
Locating lugs makes installation easier.

Plug Valves

Lubricated plug valves, because of the wide range of service to which they are adapted, may be classified as all purpose valves. They can be safely used at all pressure and vacuums, and at all temperatures up to the limits of available lubricants. They are the most satisfactory valves for the handling of gritty suspensions and many other destructive, erosive, corrosive and chemical solutions.

R221113-50   Pipe Material Considerations

1. Malleable fittings should be used for gas service.
2. Malleable fittings are used where there are stresses/strains due to expansion and vibration.
3. Cast fittings may be broken as an aid to disassembling of heating lines frozen by long use, temperature and minerals.
4. Cast iron pipe is extensively used for underground and submerged service.
5. Type M (light wall) copper tubing is available in hard temper only and is used for nonpressure and less severe applications than K and L.

6. Type L (medium wall) copper tubing, available hard or soft for interior service.
7. Type K (heavy wall) copper tubing, available in hard or soft temper for use where conditions are severe. For underground and interior service.
8. Hard drawn tubing requires fewer hangers or supports but should not be bent. Silver brazed fittings are recommended, however soft solder is normally used.
9. Type DMV (very light wall) copper tubing designed for drainage, waste and vent plus other non-critical pressure services.

Domestic/Imported Pipe and Fittings Cost

The prices shown in this publication for steel/cast iron pipe and steel, cast iron, malleable iron fittings are based on domestic production sold at the normal trade discounts. The above listed items of foreign manufacture may be available at prices of 1/3 to 1/2 those shown. Some imported items after minor machining or finishing operations are being sold as domestic to further complicate the system.

Caution: Most pipe prices in this book also include a coupling and pipe hangers which for the larger sizes can add significantly to the per foot cost and should be taken into account when comparing "book cost" with quoted supplier's cost.

R221113-70   Piping to 10' High

When taking off pipe, it is important to identify the different material types and joining procedures, as well as distances between supports and components required for proper support.

During the takeoff, measure through all fittings. Do not subtract the lengths of the fittings, valves, or strainers, etc. This added length plus the final rounding of the totals will compensate for nipples and waste.

When rounding off totals always increase the actual amount to correspond with manufacturer's shipping lengths.

A. Both red brass and yellow brass pipe are normally furnished in 12' lengths, plain end. The Unit Price section includes in the linear foot costs two field threads and one coupling per 10' length. A carbon steel clevis type hanger assembly every 10' is also prorated into the linear foot costs, including both material and labor.

B. Cast iron soil pipe is furnished in either 5' or 10' lengths. For pricing purposes, the Unit Price section features 10' lengths with a joint and a carbon steel clevis hanger assembly every 5' prorated into the per foot costs of both material and labor.

   Three methods of joining are considered: lead and oakum poured joints or push-on gasket type joints for the bell and spigot pipe and a joint clamp for the no-hub soil pipe. The labor and material costs for each of these individual joining procedures are also prorated into the linear costs per foot.

C. Copper tubing covers types K, L, M, and DWV which are furnished in 20' lengths. Means pricing data is based on a tubing cut each length and a coupling and two soft soldered joints every 10'. A carbon steel, clevis type hanger assembly every 10' is also prorated into the per foot costs. The prices for refrigeration tubing are for materials only. Labor for full lengths may be based on the type L labor but short cut measures in tight areas can increase the installation labor-hours from 20 to 40%.

D. Corrosion-resistant piping does not lend itself to one particular standard of hanging or support assembly due to its diversity of application and placement. The several varieties of corrosion-resistant piping do not include any material or labor costs for hanger assemblies (See the Unit Price section for appropriate selection).

E. Glass pipe is furnished in standard lengths either 5' or 10' long, beaded on one end. Special orders for diverse lengths beaded on both ends are also available. For pricing purposes, R.S. Means features 10' lengths with a coupling and a carbon steel band hanger assembly every 10' prorated into the per foot linear costs.

   Glass pipe is also available with conical ends and standard lengths ranging from 6" through 3' in 6" increments, then up to 10' in 12" increments. Special lengths can be customized for particular installation requirements.

   For pricing purposes, Means has based the labor and material pricing on 10' lengths. Included in these costs per linear foot are the prorated costs for a flanged assembly every 10' consisting of two flanges, a gasket, two insertable seals, and the required number of bolts and nuts. A carbon steel band hanger assembly based on 10' center lines has also been prorated into the costs per foot for labor and materials.

F. Plastic pipe of several compositions and joining methods are considered. Fiberglass reinforced pipe (FRP) is priced, based on 10' lengths (20' lengths are also available), with coupling and epoxy joints every 10'. FRP is furnished in both "General Service" and "High Strength." A carbon steel clevis hanger assembly, 3 for every 10', is built into the prorated labor and material costs on a per foot basis.

   The PVC and CPVC pipe schedules 40, 80 and 120, plus SDR ratings are all based on 20' lengths with a coupling installed every 10', as well as a carbon steel clevis hanger assembly every 3'. The PVC and

ABS type DWV piping is based on 10' lengths with solvent weld couplings every 10', and with carbon steel clevis hanger assemblies, 3 for every 10'. The rest of the plastic piping in this section is based on flexible 100' coils and does not include any coupling or supports.

   This section ends with PVC drain and sewer piping based on 10' lengths with bell and spigot ends and 0-ring type, push-on joints.

G. Stainless steel piping includes both weld end and threaded piping, both in the type 304 and 316 specification and in the following schedules, 5, 10, 40, 80, and 160. Although this piping is usually furnished in 20' lengths, this cost grouping has a joint (either heli-arc butt-welded or threads and coupling) every 10'. A carbon steel clevis type hanger assembly is also included at 10' intervals and prorated into the linear foot costs.

H. Carbon steel pipe includes both black and galvanized. This section encompasses schedules 40 (standard) and 80 (extra heavy).

   Several common methods of joining steel pipe — such as thread and coupled, butt welded, and flanged (150 lb. weld neck flanges) are also included.

   For estimating purposes, it is assumed that the piping is purchased in 20' lengths and that a compatible joint is made up every 10'. These joints are prorated into the labor and material costs per linear foot. The following hanger and support assemblies every 10' are also included: carbon steel clevis for the T & C pipe, and single rod roll type for both the welded and flanged piping. All of these hangers are oversized to accommodate pipe insulation 3/4" thick through 5" pipe size and 1-1/2" thick from 6" through 12" pipe size.

I. Grooved joint steel pipe is priced both black and galvanized, in schedules 10, 40, and 80, furnished in 20' lengths. This section describes two joining methods: cut groove and roll groove. The schedule 10 piping is roll-grooved, while the heavier schedules are cut-grooved. The labor and material costs are prorated into per linear foot prices, including a coupled joint every 10', as well as a carbon steel clevis hanger assembly.

Notes:

The pipe hanger assemblies mentioned in the preceding paragraphs include the described hanger; appropriately sized steel, box-type insert and nut; plus 18" of threaded hanger rod.

C clamps are used when the pipe is to be supported from steel shapes rather than anchored in the slab. C clamps are slightly less costly than inserts. However, to save time in estimating, it is advisable to use the given line number cost, rather than substituting a C clamp for the insert.

Add to piping labor for elevated installation:

10' to 14.5' high	10%	30' to 34.5' high	40%
15' to 19.5' high	20%	35' to 39.5' high	50%
20' to 24.5' high	25%	Over 40' and higher	55%
25' to 29.5' high	35%		

When using the percentage adds for elevated piping installations as shown above, bear in mind that the given heights are for the pipe supports, even though the insert, anchor, or clamp may be several feet higher than the pipe itself.

An allowance has been included in the piping installation time for testing and minor tightening of leaking joints, fittings, stuffing boxes, packing glands, etc. For extraordinary test requirements such as x-rays, prolonged pressure or demonstration tests, a percentage of the piping labor, based on the estimator's experience, must be added to the labor total. A testing service specializing in weld x-rays should be consulted for pricing if it is an estimate requirement. Equipment installation time includes start-up with associated adjustments.

R230500-10   Subcontractors

On the unit cost pages of the R.S. Means Cost Data books, the last column is entitled "Total Incl. O&P". This is normally the cost of the installing contractor. In the HVAC Division, this is the cost of the mechanical contractor. If the particular work being estimated is to be performed by a sub to the mechanical contractor, the mechanical's profit and handling charge (usually 10%) is added to the total of the last column.

R233100-10   Loudness Levels for Moving Air thru Fans, Diffusers, Register, Etc. (Measured in Sones)

Area	Very Quiet	Quiet	Noisy	Area	Very Quiet	Quiet	Noisy	Area	Very Quiet	Quiet	Noisy
Auditoriums				**Hotels**				**Offices**			
Auditorium lobbies	3	4	6	Banquet Rooms	1.5	3	6	Conference rooms	1	1.7	3
Concert and opera halls	0.8	1	1.5	Individual rooms, suites	1	2	4	Drafting	2	4	8
Courtrooms	2	3	4	Kitchens and laundries	4	7	10	General open offices	2	4	8
Lecture halls	1.5	2	3	Lobbies	2	4	8	Halls and corridors	2.5	5	10
Movie theaters	1.5	2	3	**Indoor Sports**				Professional offices	1.5	3	6
Churches and Schools				Bowling alleys	3	4	6	Reception room	1.5	3	6
Kitchens	4	6	8	Gymnasiums	2	4	6	Tabulation & computation	3	6	12
Laboratories	2	4	6	Swimming pools	4	7	10	**Public Buildings**			
Libraries	1.5	2	3	**Manufacturing Areas**				Banks	2	4	6
Recreation halls	2	4	8	Assembly lines	5	12	30	Court houses	2.5	4	6
Sanctuaries	1	1.7	3	Foreman's office	3	5	8	Museums	2	3	4
Schools and classrooms	1.5	2.5	4	Foundries	10	20	40	Planetariums	1.5	2	3
Hospital and Clinics				General storage	5	10	20	Post offices	2.5	4	6
Laboratories	2	4	6	Heavy machinery	10	25	60	Public libraries	1.5	2	4
Lobbies, waiting rooms	2	4	6	Light machinery	5	12	30	Waiting rooms	3	5	8
Halls and corridors	2	4	6	Tool maintenance	4	7	10	**Restaurants**			
Operating rooms	1.5	2.5	4	**Stores**				Cafeterias	3	6	10
Private rooms	1	1.7	3	Department stores	3	6	8	Night clubs	2.5	4	6
Wards	1.5	2.5	4	Supermarkets	4	7	10	Restaurants	2	4	8

(Table header: Recommended Loudness Levels (Sones))

R233100-20   Ductwork

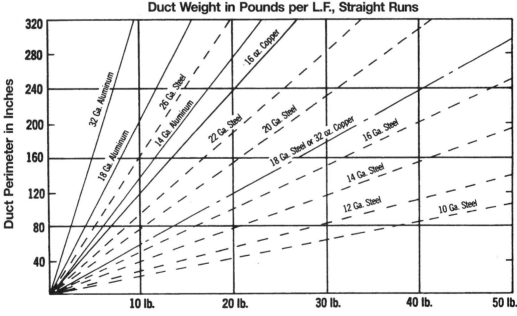

Duct Weight in Pounds per L.F., Straight Runs

Add to the above for fittings; 90° elbow is 3 L.F.; 45° elbow is 2.5 L.F.; offset is 4 L.F.; transition offset is 6 L.F.; square-to-round transition is 4 L.F.; 90° reducing elbow is 5 L.F. For bracing and waste, add 20% to aluminum and copper, 15% to steel.

R233100-30   Duct Fabrication/Installation

The labor cost for fabricated sheet metal duct includes both the cost of fabrication and installation of the duct. The split is approximately 40% for fabrication, 60% for installation. It is for this reason that the percentage add for elevated installation of fabricated duct is less than the percentage add for prefabricated/preformed duct.

Example: assume a piece of duct cost $100 installed (labor only)

Sheet Metal Fabrication = 40% = $40

Installation = 60% = $60

The add for elevated installation is:

$$\frac{\text{Based on total labor}}{\text{(fabrication \& installation)}} = \$100 \text{ x } 6\% = \$6.00$$

$$\frac{\text{Based on installation cost only}}{\text{(Material purchased prefabricated)}} = \$60 \text{ x } 10\% = \$6.00$$

The $6.00 markup (10′ to 15′ high) is the same.

R233100-40 Steel Sheet Metal Calculator (Weight in Lb./Ft. of Length)

Gauge	26	24	22	20	18	16	Gauge	26	24	22	20	18	16
Wt.-Lb./S.F.	.906	1.156	1.406	1.656	2.156	2.656	Wt.-Lb./S.F.	.906	1.156	1.406	1.656	2.156	2.656
SMACNA Max. Dimension – Long Side		30″	54″	84″	85″ Up		SMACNA Max. Dimension – Long Side		30″	54″	84″	85″ Up	
Sum-2 sides							Sum-2 Sides						
2	.3	.40	.50	.60	.80	.90	56	9.3	12.0	14.0	16.2	21.3	25.2
3	.5	.65	.80	.90	1.1	1.4	57	9.5	12.3	14.3	16.5	21.7	25.7
4	.7	.85	1.0	1.2	1.5	1.8	58	9.7	12.5	14.5	16.8	22.0	26.1
5	.8	1.1	1.3	1.5	1.9	2.3	59	9.8	12.7	14.8	17.1	22.4	26.6
6	1.0	1.3	1.5	1.7	2.3	2.7	60	10.0	12.9	15.0	17.4	22.8	27.0
7	1.2	1.5	1.8	2.0	2.7	3.2	61	10.2	13.1	15.3	17.7	23.2	27.5
8	1.3	1.7	2.0	2.3	3.0	3.6	62	10.3	13.3	15.5	18.0	23.6	27.9
9	1.5	1.9	2.3	2.6	3.4	4.1	63	10.5	13.5	15.8	18.3	24.0	28.4
10	1.7	2.2	2.5	2.9	3.8	4.5	64	10.7	13.7	16.0	18.6	24.3	28.8
11	1.8	2.4	2.8	3.2	4.2	5.0	65	10.8	13.9	16.3	18.9	24.7	29.3
12	2.0	2.6	3.0	3.5	4.6	5.4	66	11.0	14.1	16.5	19.1	25.1	29.7
13	2.2	2.8	3.3	3.8	4.9	5.9	67	11.2	14.3	16.8	19.4	25.5	30.2
14	2.3	3.0	3.5	4.1	5.3	6.3	68	11.3	14.6	17.0	19.7	25.8	30.6
15	2.5	3.2	3.8	4.4	5.7	6.8	69	11.5	14.8	17.3	20.0	26.2	31.1
16	2.7	3.4	4.0	4.6	6.1	7.2	70	11.7	15.0	17.5	20.3	26.6	31.5
17	2.8	3.7	4.3	4.9	6.5	7.7	71	11.8	15.2	17.8	20.6	27.0	32.0
18	3.0	3.9	4.5	5.2	6.8	8.1	72	12.0	15.4	18.0	20.9	27.4	32.4
19	3.2	4.1	4.8	5.5	7.2	8.6	73	12.2	15.6	18.3	21.2	27.7	32.9
20	3.3	4.3	5.0	5.8	7.6	9.0	74	12.3	15.8	18.5	21.5	28.1	33.3
21	3.5	4.5	5.3	6.1	8.0	9.5	75	12.5	16.1	18.8	21.8	28.5	33.8
22	3.7	4.7	5.5	6.4	8.4	9.9	76	12.7	16.3	19.0	22.0	28.9	34.2
23	3.8	5.0	5.8	6.7	8.7	10.4	77	12.8	16.5	19.3	22.3	29.3	34.7
24	4.0	5.2	6.0	7.0	9.1	10.8	78	13.0	16.7	19.5	22.6	29.6	35.1
25	4.2	5.4	6.3	7.3	9.5	11.3	79	13.2	16.9	19.8	22.9	30.0	35.6
26	4.3	5.6	6.5	7.5	9.9	11.7	80	13.3	17.1	20.0	23.2	30.4	36.0
27	4.5	5.8	6.8	7.8	10.3	12.2	81	13.5	17.3	20.3	23.5	30.8	36.5
28	4.7	6.0	7.0	8.1	10.6	12.6	82	13.7	17.5	20.5	23.8	31.2	36.9
29	4.8	6.2	7.3	8.4	11.0	13.1	83	13.8	17.8	20.8	24.1	31.5	37.4
30	5.0	6.5	7.5	8.7	11.4	13.5	84	14.0	18.0	21.0	24.4	31.9	37.8
31	5.2	6.7	7.8	9.0	11.8	14.0	85	14.2	18.2	21.3	24.7	32.3	38.3
32	5.3	6.9	8.0	9.3	12.2	14.4	86	14.3	18.4	21.5	24.9	32.7	38.7
33	5.5	7.1	8.3	9.6	12.5	14.9	87	14.5	18.6	21.8	25.2	33.1	39.2
34	5.7	7.3	8.5	9.9	12.9	15.3	88	14.7	18.8	22.0	25.5	33.4	39.6
35	5.8	7.5	8.8	10.2	13.3	15.8	89	14.8	19.0	22.3	25.8	33.8	40.1
36	6.0	7.8	9.0	10.4	13.7	16.2	90	15.0	19.3	22.5	26.1	34.2	40.5
37	6.2	8.0	9.3	10.7	14.1	16.7	91	15.2	19.5	22.8	26.4	34.6	41.0
38	6.3	8.2	9.5	11.0	14.4	17.1	92	15.3	19.7	23.0	26.7	35.0	41.4
39	6.5	8.4	9.8	11.3	14.8	17.6	93	15.5	19.9	23.3	27.0	35.3	41.9
40	6.7	8.6	10.0	11.6	15.2	18.0	94	15.7	20.1	23.5	27.3	35.7	42.3
41	6.8	8.8	10.3	11.9	15.6	18.5	95	15.8	20.3	23.8	27.6	36.1	42.8
42	7.0	9.0	10.5	12.2	16.0	18.9	96	16.0	20.5	24.0	27.8	36.5	43.2
43	7.2	9.2	10.8	12.5	16.3	19.4	97	16.2	20.8	24.3	28.1	36.9	43.7
44	7.3	9.5	11.0	12.8	16.7	19.8	98	16.3	21.0	24.5	28.4	37.2	44.1
45	7.5	9.7	11.3	13.1	17.1	20.3	99	16.5	21.2	24.8	28.7	37.6	44.6
46	7.7	9.9	11.5	13.3	17.5	20.7	100	16.7	21.4	25.0	29.0	38.0	45.0
47	7.8	10.1	11.8	13.6	17.9	21.2	101	16.8	21.6	25.3	29.3	38.4	45.5
48	8.0	10.3	12.0	13.9	18.2	21.6	102	17.0	21.8	25.5	29.6	38.8	45.9
49	8.2	10.5	12.3	14.2	18.6	22.1	103	17.2	22.0	25.8	29.9	39.1	46.4
50	8.3	10.7	12.5	14.5	19.0	22.5	104	17.3	22.3	26.0	30.2	39.5	46.8
51	8.5	11.0	12.8	14.8	19.4	23.0	105	17.5	22.5	26.3	30.5	39.9	47.3
52	8.7	11.2	13.0	15.1	19.8	23.4	106	17.7	22.7	26.5	30.7	40.3	47.7
53	8.8	11.4	13.3	15.4	20.1	23.9	107	17.8	22.9	26.8	31.0	40.7	48.2
54	9.0	11.6	13.5	15.7	20.5	24.3	108	18.0	23.1	27.0	31.3	41.0	48.6
55	9.2	11.8	13.8	16.0	20.9	24.8	109	18.2	23.3	27.3	31.6	41.4	49.1
							110	18.3	23.5	27.5	31.9	41.8	49.5

Example: If duct is 34″ x 20″ x 15′ long, 34″ is greater than 30″ maximum, for 24 ga. so must be 22 ga. 34″ + 20″ = 54″ going across from 54″ find 13.5 lb. per foot. 13.5 x 15′ = 202.5 lbs. For S.F. of surface area

202.5 ÷ 1.406 = 144 S.F.

Note: Figures include an allowance for scrap.

R233100-50 Ductwork Packages (per Ton of Cooling)

System	Sheet Metal	Insulation	Diffusers	Return Register
Roof Top Unit Single Zone	120 Lbs.	52 S.F.	1	1
Roof Top Unit Multizone	240 Lbs.	104 S.F.	2	1
Self-contained Air or Water Cooled	108 Lbs.	—	2	—
Split System Air Cooled	102 Lbs.	—	2	—

Systems reflect most common usage.
Refer to system graphics for duct layout.

Heating, Ventilating & A.C. R2334 HVAC Fans

R233400-10 Recommended Ventilation Air Changes

Table below lists range of time in minutes per change for various types of facilities.

Assembly Halls	2-10	Dance Halls	2-10	Laundries	1-3
Auditoriums	2-10	Dining Rooms	3-10	Markets	2-10
Bakeries	2-3	Dry Cleaners	1-5	Offices	2-10
Banks	3-10	Factories	2-5	Pool Rooms	2-5
Bars	2-5	Garages	2-10	Recreation Rooms	2-10
Beauty Parlors	2-5	Generator Rooms	2-5	Sales Rooms	2-10
Boiler Rooms	1-5	Gymnasiums	2-10	Theaters	2-8
Bowling Alleys	2-10	Kitchens-Hospitals	2-5	Toilets	2-5
Churches	5-10	Kitchens-Restaurant	1-3	Transformer Rooms	1-5

CFM air required for changes = Volume of room in cubic feet ÷ Minutes per change.

Heating, Ventilating & A.C. R2337 Air Outlets & Inlets

R233700-60 Diffuser Evaluation

CFM = V × An × K where V = Outlet velocity in feet per minute. An = Neck area in square feet and K = Diffuser delivery factor. An undersized diffuser for a desired CFM will produce a high velocity and noise level. When air moves past people at a velocity in excess of 25 FPM, an annoying draft is felt. An oversized diffuser will result in low velocity with poor mixing. Consideration must be given to avoid vertical stratification or horizontal areas of stagnation.

R235000-10 Heating Systems

Heating Systems

The basic function of a heating system is to bring an enclosed volume up to a desired temperature and then maintain that temperature within a reasonable range. To accomplish this, the selected system must have sufficient capacity to offset transmission losses resulting from the temperature difference on the interior and exterior of the enclosing walls in addition to losses due to cold air infiltration through cracks, crevices and around doors and windows. The amount of heat to be furnished is dependent upon the building size, construction, temperature difference, air leakage, use, shape, orientation and exposure. Air circulation is also an important consideration. Circulation will prevent stratification which could result in heat losses through uneven temperatures at various levels. For example, the most

efficient use of unit heaters can usually be achieved by circulating the space volume through the total number of units once every 20 minutes or 3 times an hour. This general rule must, of course, be adapted for special cases such as large buildings with low ratios of heat transmitting surface to cubical volume. The type of occupancy of a building will have considerable bearing on the number of heat transmitting units and the location selected. It is axiomatic, however, that the basis of any successful heating system is to provide the maximum amount of heat at the points of maximum heat loss such as exposed walls, windows, and doors. Large roof areas, wind direction, and wide doorways create problems of excessive heat loss and require special consideration and treatment.

Heat Transmission

Heat transfer is an important parameter to be considered during selection of the exterior wall style, material and window area. A high rate of transfer will permit greater heat loss during the wintertime with the resultant increase in heating energy costs and a greater rate of heat gain in the summer with proportionally greater cooling cost. Several terms are used to describe various aspects of heat transfer. However, for general estimating purposes this book lists U values for systems of construction materials. U is the "overall heat transfer coefficient." It is defined as the heat flow per hour through one square foot when the temperature difference in the air on either side of the structure wall, roof, ceiling or floor is one degree Fahrenheit. The structural segment may be a single homogeneous material or a composite.

Total heat transfer is found using the following equation:

$Q = AU(T_2 - T_1)$ where
- Q = Heat flow, BTU per hour
- A = Area, square feet
- U = Overall heat transfer coefficient
- $(T_2 - T_1)$ = Difference in temperature of air on each side of the construction component. (Also abbreviated TD)

Note that heat can flow through all surfaces of any building and this flow is in addition to heat gain or loss due to ventilation, infiltration and generation (appliances, machinery, people).

R235000-20 Heating Approximations for Quick Estimating

Oil Piping & Boiler Room Piping

Small System . . . . 20 to 30% of Boiler

Complex System
with Pumps, Headers, Etc. . . . . 80 to 110% of Boiler

Breeching With Insulation:

Small . . . . 10 to 15% of Boiler

Large . . . . 15 to 25% of Boiler

Coils: . . . . 15 to 30% of Containing Unit

Balancing (Independent) . . . . 1/2% of H.V.A.C. Estimate

Quality/Complexity Adjustment: For all heating installations add these adjustments to the estimate to more closely allow for the equipment and conditions of the particular job under consideration.

Economy installation, add . . . . 0 to 5% of System

Good quality, medium complexity, add . . . . 5 to 15% of System

Above average quality and complexity, add . . . . 15 to 25% of System

R235000-30   The Basics of a Heating System

The function of a heating system is to achieve and maintain a desired temperature in a room or building by replacing the amount of heat being dissipated. There are four kinds of heating systems: hot-water, steam, warm-air and electric resistance. Each has certain essential and similar elements with the exception of electric resistance heating.

The basic elements of a heating system are:

A. A **combustion chamber** in which fuel is burned and heat transferred to a conveying medium.

B. The **"fluid"** used for conveying the heat (water, steam or air).

C. **Conductors** or pipes for transporting the fluid to specific desired locations.

D. A means of disseminating the heat, sometimes called **terminal units.**

A. The **combustion chamber** in a furnace heats air which is then distributed. This is called a warm-air system.

The combustion chamber in a boiler heats water which is either distributed as hot water or steam and this is termed a hydronic system.

The maximum allowable working pressures are limited by ASME "Code for Heating Boilers" to 15 PSI for steam and 160 PSI for hot water heating boilers, with a maximum temperature limitation of 250° F. Hot water boilers are generally rated for a working pressure of 30 PSI. High pressure boilers are governed by the ASME "Code for Power Boilers" which is used almost universally for boilers operating over 15 PSIG. High pressure boilers used for a combination of heating/process loads are usually designed for 150 PSIG.

Boiler ratings are usually indicated as either Gross or Net Output. The Gross Load is equal to the Net Load plus a piping and pickup allowance. When this allowance cannot be determined, divide the gross output rating by 1.25 for a value equal to or greater than the net heat loss requirement of the building.

B. Of the three **fluids** used, steam carries the greatest amount of heat per unit volume. This is due to the fact that it gives up its latent heat of vaporization at a temperature considerably above room temperature. Another advantage is that the pressure to produce a positive circulation is readily available. Piping conducts the steam to terminal units and returns condensate to the boiler.

The **steam system** is well adapted to large buildings because of its positive circulation, its comparatively economical installation and its ability to deliver large quantities of heat. Nearly all large office buildings, stores, hotels, and industrial buildings are so heated, in addition to many residences.

Hot water, when used as the heat carrying fluid, gives up a portion of its sensible heat and then returns to the boiler or heating apparatus for reheating. As the heat conveyed by each pound of water is about one-fiftieth of the heat conveyed by a pound of steam, it is necessary to circulate about fifty times as much water as steam by weight (although only one-thirtieth as much by volume). The hot water system is usually, although not necessarily, designed to operate at temperatures below that of the ordinary steam system and so the amount of heat transfer surface must be correspondingly greater. A temperature of 190° F to 200° F is normally the maximum. Circulation in small buildings may depend on the difference in density between hot water and the cool water returning to the boiler; circulating pumps are normally used to maintain a desired rate of flow. Pumps permit a greater degree of flexibility and better control.

In **warm-air** furnace systems, cool air is taken from one or more points in the building, passed over the combustion chamber and flue gas passages and then distributed through a duct system. A disadvantage of this system is that the ducts take up much more building volume than steam or hot water pipes. Advantages of this system are the relative ease with which humidification can be accomplished by the evaporation of water as the air circulates through the heater, and the lack of need for expensive disseminating units as the warm air simply becomes part of the interior atmosphere of the building.

C. **Conductors** (pipes and ducts) have been lightly treated in the discussion of conveying fluids. For more detailed information such as sizing and distribution methods, the reader is referred to technical publications such as the American Society of Heating, Refrigerating and Air-Conditioning Engineers "Handbook of Fundamentals."

D. **Terminal units** come in an almost infinite variety of sizes and styles, but the basic principles of operation are very limited. As previously mentioned, warm-air systems require only a simple register or diffuser to mix heated air with that present in the room. Special application items such as radiant coils and infrared heaters are available to meet particular conditions but are not usually considered for general heating needs. Most heating is accomplished by having air flow over coils or pipes containing the heat transporting medium (steam, hot-water, electricity). These units, while varied, may be separated into two general types, (1) radiator/convectors and (2) unit heaters.

Radiator/convectors may be cast, fin-tube or pipe assemblies. They may be direct, indirect, exposed, concealed or mounted within a cabinet enclosure, upright or baseboard style. These units are often collectively referred to as "radiatiors" or "radiation" although none gives off heat either entirely by radiation or by convection but rather a combination of both. The air flows over the units as a gravity "current." It is necessary to have one or more heat-emitting units in each room. The most efficient placement is low along an outside wall or under a window to counteract the cold coming into the room and achieve an even distribution.

In contrast to radiator/convectors which operate most effectively against the walls of smaller rooms, **unit heaters** utilize a fan to move air over heating coils and are very effective in locations of relatively large volume. Unit heaters, while usually suspended overhead, may be floor mounted. They also may take in fresh outside air for ventilation. The heat distributed by unit heaters may be from a remote source and conveyed by a fluid or it may be from the combustion of fuel in each individual heater. In the latter case the only piping required would be for fuel, however, a vent for the products of combustion would be necessary.

The following list gives may of the advantages of unit heaters for applications other than office or residential:

a. Large capacity so smaller number of units are required, **b.** Piping system simplified, **c.** Space saved where they are located overhead out of the way, **d.** Rapid heating directed where needed with effective wide distribution, **e.** Difference between floor and ceiling temperature reduced, **f.** Circulation of air obtained, and ventilation with introduction of fresh air possible, **g.** Heat output flexible and easily controlled.

R235000-50   Factor for Determining Heat Loss for Various Types of Buildings

General: While the most accurate estimates of heating requirements would naturally be based on detailed information about the building being considered, it is possible to arrive at a reasonable approximation using the following procedure:

1. Calculate the cubic volume of the room or building.
2. Select the appropriate factor from Table 1 below. Note that the factors apply only to inside temperatures listed in the first column and to 0° F outside temperature.

3. If the building has bad north and west exposures, multiply the heat loss factor by 1.1.
4. If the outside design temperature is other than 0° F, multiply the factor from Table 1 by the factor from Table 2.
5. Multiply the cubic volume by the factor selected from Table 1. This will give the estimated BTUH heat loss which must be made up to maintain inside temperature.

Table 1 — Building Type	Conditions	Qualifications	Loss Factor*
Factories & Industrial Plants General Office Areas at 70° F	One Story	Skylight in Roof	6.2
		No Skylight in Roof	5.7
	Multiple Story	Two Story	4.6
		Three Story	4.3
		Four Story	4.1
		Five Story	3.9
		Six Story	3.6
	All Walls Exposed	Flat Roof	6.9
		Heated Space Above	5.2
	One Long Warm Common Wall	Flat Roof	6.3
		Heated Space Above	4.7
	Warm Common Walls on Both Long Sides	Flat Roof	5.8
		Heated Space Above	4.1
Warehouses at 60° F	All Walls Exposed	Skylights in Roof	5.5
		No Skylight in Roof	5.1
		Heated Space Above	4.0
	One Long Warm Common Wall	Skylight in Roof	5.0
		No Skylight in Roof	4.9
		Heated Space Above	3.4
	Warm Common Walls on Both Long Sides	Skylight in Roof	4.7
		No Skylight in Roof	4.4
		Heated Space Above	3.0

*Note: This table tends to be conservative particularly for new buildings designed for minimum energy consumption.

Table 2 — Outside Design Temperature Correction Factor (for Degrees Fahrenheit)									
Outside Design Temperature	50	40	30	20	10	0	-10	-20	-30
Correction Factor	.29	.43	.57	.72	.86	1.00	1.14	1.28	1.43

R235000-70 Transmission of Heat

R235000-70 and R235000-80 provide a way to calculate heat transmission of various construction materials from their U values and the TD (Temperature Difference).

1. From the Exterior Enclosure Division or elsewhere, determine U values for the construction desired.
2. Determine the coldest design temperature. The difference between this temperature and the desired interior temperature is the TD (temperature difference).

3. Enter R235000-70 or R235000-80 at correct U Value. Cross horizontally to the intersection with appropriate TD. Read transmission per square foot from bottom of figure.
4. Multiply this value of BTU per hour transmission per square foot of area by the total surface area of that type of construction.

R235000-80 Transmission of Heat (Low Rate)

Heating, Ventilating & A.C. R2356 Solar Energy Heating Equipment

R235616-60 Solar Heating (Space and Hot Water)

Collectors should face as close to due South as possible, however, variations of up to 20 degrees on either side of true South are acceptable. Local climate and collector type may influence the choice between east or west deviations. Obviously they should be located so they are not shaded from the sun's rays. Incline collectors at a slope of latitude minus 5 degrees for domestic hot water and latitude plus 15 degrees for space heating.

Flat plate collectors consist of a number of components as follows: Insulation to reduce heat loss through the bottom and sides of the collector. The enclosure which contains all the components in this assembly is usually weatherproof and prevents dust, wind and water from coming in contact with the absorber plate. The cover plate usually consists of one or more layers of a variety of glass or plastic and reduces the reradiation by creating an air space which traps the heat between the cover and the absorber plates.

The absorber plate must have a good thermal bond with the fluid passages. The absorber plate is usually metallic and treated with a surface coating which improves absorptivity. Black or dark paints or selective coatings are used for this purpose, and the design of this passage and plate combination helps determine a solar system's effectiveness.

Heat transfer fluid passage tubes are attached above and below or integral with an absorber plate for the purpose of transferring thermal energy from the absorber plate to a heat transfer medium. The heat exchanger is a device for transferring thermal energy from one fluid to another.

Piping and storage tanks should be well insulated to minimize heat losses.

Size domestic water heating storage tanks to hold 20 gallons of water per user, minimum, plus 10 gallons per dishwasher or washing machine. For domestic water heating an optimum collector size is approximately 3/4 square foot of area per gallon of water storage. For space heating of residences and small commercial applications the collector is commonly sized between 30% and 50% of the internal floor area. For space heating of large commercial applications, collector areas less than 30% of the internal floor area can still provide significant heat reductions.

A supplementary heat source is recommended for Northern states for December through February.

The solar energy transmission per square foot of collector surface varies greatly with the material used. Initial cost, heat transmittance and useful life are obviously interrelated.

Heating, Ventilating & A.C. R2360 Central Cooling Equipment

R236000-10 Air Conditioning

General: The purpose of air conditioning is to control the environment of a space so that comfort is provided for the occupants and/or conditions are suitable for the processes or equipment contained therein. The several items which should be evaluated to define system objectives are:

Temperature Control
Humidity Control
Cleanliness
Odor, smoke and fumes
Ventilation

Efforts to control the above parameters must also include consideration of the degree or tolerance of variation, the noise level introduced, the velocity of air motion and the energy requirements to accomplish the desired results.

The variation in **temperature** and **humidity** is a function of the sensor and the controller. The controller reacts to a signal from the sensor and produces the appropriate suitable response in either the terminal unit, the conductor of the transporting medium (air, steam, chilled water, etc.), or the source (boiler, evaporating coils, etc.).

The **noise level** is a by-product of the energy supplied to moving components of the system. Those items which usually contribute the most noise are pumps, blowers, fans, compressors and diffusers. The level of noise can be partially controlled through use of vibration pads, isolators, proper sizing, shields, baffles and sound absorbing liners.

Some **air motion** is necessary to prevent stagnation and stratification. The maximum acceptable velocity varies with the degree of heating or cooling

which is taking place. Most people feel air moving past them at velocities in excess of 25 FPM as an annoying draft. However, velocities up to 45 FPM may be acceptable in certain cases. Ventilation, expressed as air changes per hour and percentage of fresh air, is usually an item regulated by local codes.

Selection of the system to be used for a particular application is usually a trade-off. In some cases the building size, style, or room available for mechanical use limits the range of possibilities. Prime factors influencing the decision are first cost and total life (operating, maintenance and replacement costs). The accuracy with which each parameter is determined will be an important measure of the reliability of the decision and subsequent satisfactory operation of the installed system.

Heat delivery may be desired from an air conditioning system. Heating capability usually is added as follows: A gas fired burner or hot water/steam/electric coils may be added to the air handling unit directly and heat all air equally. For limited or localized heat requirements the water/steam/electric coils may be inserted into the duct branch supplying the cold areas. Gas fired duct furnaces are also available.

Note: When water or steam coils are used the cost of the piping and boiler must also be added. For a rough estimate use the cost per square foot of the appropriate sized hydronic system with unit heaters. This will provide a cost for the boiler and piping, and the unit heaters of the system would equate to the approximate cost of the heating coils.

R236000-20   Air Conditioning Requirements

BTUs per hour per S.F. of floor area and S.F. per ton of air conditioning.

Type of Building	BTU/Hr per S.F.	S.F. per Ton	Type of Building	BTU/Hr per S.F.	S.F. per Ton	Type of Building	BTU/Hr per S.F.	S.F. per Ton
Apartments, Individual	26	450	Dormitory, Rooms	40	300	Libraries	50	240
Corridors	22	550	Corridors	30	400	Low Rise Office, Exterior	38	320
Auditoriums & Theaters	40	300/18*	Dress Shops	43	280	Interior	33	360
Banks	50	240	Drug Stores	80	150	Medical Centers	28	425
Barber Shops	48	250	Factories	40	300	Motels	28	425
Bars & Taverns	133	90	High Rise Office—Ext. Rms.	46	263	Office (small suite)	43	280
Beauty Parlors	66	180	Interior Rooms	37	325	Post Office, Individual Office	42	285
Bowling Alleys	68	175	Hospitals, Core	43	280	Central Area	46	260
Churches	36	330/20*	Perimeter	46	260	Residences	20	600
Cocktail Lounges	68	175	Hotel, Guest Rooms	44	275	Restaurants	60	200
Computer Rooms	141	85	Corridors	30	400	Schools & Colleges	46	260
Dental Offices	52	230	Public Spaces	55	220	Shoe Stores	55	220
Dept. Stores, Basement	34	350	Industrial Plants, Offices	38	320	Shop'g. Ctrs., Supermarkets	34	350
Main Floor	40	300	General Offices	34	350	Retail Stores	48	250
Upper Floor	30	400	Plant Areas	40	300	Specialty	60	200

*Persons per ton
12,000 BTU = 1 ton of air conditioning

R236000-30   Psychrometric Table

Dewpoint or Saturation Temperature (F)

Relative humidity (%)

100	32	35	40	45	50	55	60	65	70	75	80	85	90	95	100
90	30	33	37	42	47	52	57	62	67	72	77	82	87	92	97
80	27	30	34	39	44	49	54	58	64	68	73	78	83	88	93
70	24	27	31	36	40	45	50	55	60	64	69	74	79	84	88
60	20	24	28	32	36	41	46	51	55	60	65	69	74	79	83
50	16	20	24	28	33	36	41	46	50	55	60	64	69	73	78
40	12	15	18	23	27	31	35	40	45	49	53	58	62	67	71
30	8	10	14	18	21	25	29	33	37	42	46	50	54	59	62
20	6	7	8	9	13	16	20	24	28	31	35	40	43	48	52
10	4	4	5	5	6	8	9	10	13	17	20	24	27	30	34
	32	35	40	45	50	55	60	65	70	75	80	85	90	95	100

Dry bulb temperature (F)

This table shows the relationship between RELATIVE HUMIDITY, DRY BULB TEMPERATURE AND DEWPOINT.

As an example, assume that the thermometer in a room reads 75° F, and we know that the relative humidity is 50%. The chart shows the dewpoint temperature to be 55° F. That is, any surface colder than 55° F will "sweat" or collect condensing moisture. This surface could be the outside of an uninsulated chilled water pipe in the summertime, or the inside surface of a wall or deck in the wintertime. After determining the extreme ambient parameters, the table at the left is useful in determining which surfaces need insulation or vapor barrier protection.

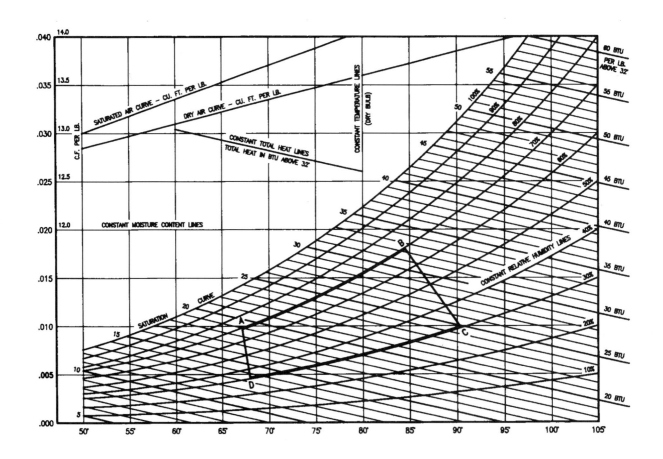

TEMPERATURE DEGREES FAHRENHEIT
TOTAL PRESSURE = 14.696 LB. PER SQ. IN. ABS.

Psychrometric chart showing different variables based on one pound of dry air. Space marked A B C D is temperature-humidity range which is most comfortable for majority of people.

R236000-90 Quality/Complexity Adjustment for Air Conditioning Systems

Economy installation, add . . . . 0 to 5%
Good quality, medium complexity, add . . . . 5 to 15%
Above average quality and complexity, add . . . . 15 to 25%

Add the above adjustments to the estimate to more closely allow for the equipment and conditions of the particular job under consideration.

Fig. R238313-11

R238313-10   Heat Trace Systems

Before you can determine the cost of a HEAT TRACE installation, the method of attachment must be established. There are (4) common methods:

1. Cable is simply attached to the pipe with polyester tape every 12'.
2. Cable is attached with a continuous cover of 2" wide aluminum tape.
3. Cable is attached with factory extruded heat transfer cement and covered with metallic raceway with clips every 10'.
4. Cable is attached between layers of pipe insulation using either clips or polyester tape.

Example: Components for method 3 must include:

A. Heat trace cable by voltage and watts per linear foot.
B. Heat transfer cement, 1 gallon per 60 linear feet of cover.
C. Metallic raceway by size and type.
D. Raceway clips by size of pipe.

When taking off linear foot lengths of cable add the following for each valve in the system. (E)

In all of the above methods each component of the system must be priced individually.

SCREWED OR WELDED VALVE:			FLANGED VALVE:			BUTTERFLY VALVES:		
1/2"	=	6"	1/2"	=	1' -0"	1/2"	=	0'
3/4"	=	9"	3/4"	=	1' -6"	3/4"	=	0'
1"	=	1' -0"	1"	=	2' -0"	1"	=	1' -0"
1-1/2"	=	1' -6"	1-1/2"	=	2' -6"	1-1/2"	=	1' -6"
2"	=	2'	2"	=	2' -6"	2"	=	2' -0"
2-1/2"	=	2' -6"	2-1/2"	=	3' -0"	2-1/2"	=	2' -6"
3"	=	2' -6"	3"	=	3' -6"	3"	=	2' -6"
4"	=	4' -0"	4"	=	4' -0"	4"	=	3' -0"
6"	=	7' -0"	6"	=	8' -0"	6"	=	3' -6"
8"	=	9' -6"	8"	=	11' -0"	8"	=	4' -0"
10"	=	12' -6"	10"	=	14' -0"	10"	=	4' -0"
12"	=	15' -0"	12"	=	16' -6"	12"	=	5' -0"
14"	=	18' -0"	14"	=	19' -6"	14"	=	5' -6"
16"	=	21' -6"	16"	=	23' -0"	16"	=	6' -0"
18"	=	25' -6"	18"	=	27' -0"	18"	=	6' -6"
20"	=	28' -6"	20"	=	30' -0"	20"	=	7' -0"
24"	=	34' -0"	24"	=	36' -0"	24"	=	8' -0"
30"	=	40' -0"	30"	=	42' -0"	30"	=	10' -0"

R238313-10 Heat Trace Systems (cont.)

Add the following quantities of heat transfer cement to linear foot totals for each valve:

Nominal Valve Size	Gallons of Cement per Valve
1/2"	0.14
3/4"	0.21
1"	0.29
1-1/2"	0.36
2"	0.43
2-1/2"	0.70
3"	0.71
4"	1.00
6"	1.43
8"	1.48
10"	1.50
12"	1.60
14"	1.75
16"	2.00
18"	2.25
20"	2.50
24"	3.00
30"	3.75

The following must be added to the list of components to accurately price HEAT TRACE systems:

1. Expediter fitting and clamp fasteners (F)
2. Junction box and nipple connected to expediter fitting (G)
3. Field installed terminal blocks within junction box
4. Ground lugs
5. Piping from power source to expediter fitting
6. Controls
7. Thermostats
8. Branch wiring
9. Cable splices
10. End of cable terminations
11. Branch piping fittings and boxes

Deduct the following percentages from labor if cable lengths in the same area exceed:

150' to 250'	10%	351' to 500'	20%
251' to 350'	15%	Over 500'	25%

Add the following percentages to labor for elevated installations:

15' to 20' high	10%	31' to 35' high	40%
21' to 25' high	20%	36' to 40' high	50%
26' to 30' high	30%	Over 40' high	60%

R238313-20 Spiral-Wrapped Heat Trace Cable (Pitch Table)

In order to increase the amount of heat, occasionally heat trace cable is wrapped in a spiral fashion around a pipe; increasing the number of feet of heater cable per linear foot of pipe.

Engineers first determine the heat loss per foot of pipe (based on the insulating material, its thickness, and the temperature differential across it). A ratio is then calculated by the formula:

$$\text{Feet of Heat Trace per Foot of Pipe} = \frac{\text{Watts/Foot of Heat Loss}}{\text{Watts/Foot of the Cable}}$$

The linear distance between wraps (pitch) is then taken from a chart or table. Generally, the pitch is listed on a drawing leaving the estimator to calculate the total length of heat tape required. An approximation may be taken from this table.

Feet of Heat Trace Per Foot of Pipe																
	Nominal Pipe Size in Inches															
Pitch In Inches	1	1¼	1½	2	2½	3	4	6	8	10	12	14	16	18	20	24
3.5	1.80															
4	1.65															
5	1.46	1.60	1.80													
6	1.34	1.45	1.55	1.75												
7	1.25	1.35	1.43	1.57	1.75											
8	1.20	1.28	1.34	1.45	1.60	1.80										
9	1.16	1.23	1.28	1.37	1.51	1.68										
10	1.13	1.19	1.24	1.32	1.44	1.57	1.82									
15	1.06	1.08	1.10	1.15	1.21	1.29	1.42	1.78								
20	1.04	1.05	1.06	1.08	1.13	1.17	1.25	1.49	1.73							
25		1.04	1.04	1.06	1.08	1.11	1.17	1.33	1.51	1.72						
30				1.04	1.05	1.07	1.12	1.24	1.37	1.54	1.70	1.80				
35					1.06	1.06	1.09	1.17	1.28	1.42	1.54	1.64	1.78			
40						1.05	1.07	1.14	1.22	1.33	1.44	1.52	1.64	1.75		
50							1.05	1.09	1.15	1.22	1.29	1.35	1.44	1.53	1.64	1.83
60								1.06	1.11	1.16	1.21	1.25	1.31	1.39	1.46	1.62
70								1.05	1.08	1.12	1.17	1.19	1.24	1.30	1.35	1.47
80									1.06	1.09	1.13	1.15	1.19	1.24	1.28	1.38
90									1.04	1.06	1.10	1.13	1.16	1.19	1.23	1.32
100										1.05	1.08	1.10	1.13	1.15	1.19	1.23

Note: Common practice would normally limit the lower end of the table to 5% of additional heat and above 80% an engineer would likely opt for two (2) parallel cables.

R312319-90   Wellpoints

A single stage wellpoint system is usually limited to dewatering an average 15′ depth below normal ground water level. Multi-stage systems are employed for greater depth with the pumping equipment installed only at the lowest header level. Ejectors with unlimited lift capacity can be economical when two or more stages of wellpoints can be replaced or when horizontal clearance is restricted, such as in deep trenches or tunneling projects, and where low water flows are expected. Wellpoints are usually spaced on 2-1/2′ to 10′ centers along a header pipe. Wellpoint spacing, header size, and pump size are all determined by the expected flow as dictated by soil conditions.

In almost all soils encountered in wellpoint dewatering, the wellpoints may be jetted into place. Cemented soils and stiff clays may require sand wicks about 12″ in diameter around each wellpoint to increase efficiency and eliminate weeping into the excavation. These sand wicks require 1/2 to 3 C.Y. of washed filter sand and are installed by using a 12″ diameter steel casing and hole puncher jetted into the ground 2′ deeper than the wellpoint. Rock may require predrilled holes.

Labor required for the complete installation and removal of a single stage wellpoint system is in the range of 3/4 to 2 labor-hours per linear foot of header, depending upon jetting conditions, wellpoint spacing, etc.

Continuous pumping is necessary except in some free draining soil where temporary flooding is permissible (as in trenches which are backfilled after each day's work). Good practice requires provision of a stand-by pump during the continuous pumping operation.

Systems for continuous trenching below the water table should be installed three to four times the length of expected daily progress to ensure uninterrupted digging, and header pipe size should not be changed during the job.

For pervious free draining soils, deep wells in place of wellpoints may be economical because of lower installation and maintenance costs. Daily production ranges between two to three wells per day, for 25′ to 40′ depths, to one well per day for depths over 50′.

Detailed analysis and estimating for any dewatering problem is available at no cost from wellpoint manufacturers. Major firms will quote "sufficient equipment" quotes or their affiliates offer lump sum proposals to cover complete dewatering responsibility.

Description for 200′ System with 8″ Header		Quantities
Equipment & Material	Wellpoints 25′ long, 2″ diameter @ 5′ O.C.	40 Each
	Header pipe, 8″ diameter	200 L.F.
	Discharge pipe, 8″ diameter	100 L.F.
	8″ valves	3 Each
	Combination jetting & wellpoint pump (standby)	1 Each
	Wellpoint pump, 8″ diameter	1 Each
	Transportation to and from site	1 Day
	Fuel for 30 days x 60 gal./day	1800 Gallons
	Lubricants for 30 days x 16 lbs./day	480 Lbs.
	Sand for points	40 C.Y.
Labor	Technician to supervise installation	1 Week
	Labor for installation and removal of system	300 Labor-hours
	4 Operators straight time 40 hrs./wk. for 4.33 wks.	693 Hrs.
	4 Operators overtime 2 hrs./wk. for 4.33 wks.	35 Hrs.

R314116-40   Wood Sheet Piling

Wood sheet piling may be used for depths to 20' where there is no ground water. If moderate ground water is encountered Tongue & Groove sheeting will help to keep it out. When considerable ground water is present, steel sheeting must be used.

For estimating purposes on trench excavation, sizes are as follows:

Depth	Sheeting	Wales	Braces	B.F. per S.F.
To 8'	3 x 12's	6 x 8's, 2 line	6 x 8's, @ 10'	4.0 @ 8'
8' x 12'	3 x 12's	10 x 10's, 2 line	10 x 10's, @ 9'	5.0 average
12' to 20'	3 x 12's	12 x 12's, 3 line	12 x 12's, @ 8'	7.0 average

Sheeting to be toed in at least 2' depending upon soil conditions. A five person crew with an air compressor and sheeting driver can drive and brace 440 SF/day at 8' deep, 360 SF/day at 12' deep, and 320 SF/day at 16' deep.

For normal soils, piling can be pulled in 1/3 the time to install. Pulling difficulty increases with the time in the ground. Production can be increased by high pressure jetting.

R314116-45   Steel Sheet Piling

Limiting weights are 22 to 38#/S.F. of wall surface with 27#/S.F. average for usual types and sizes. (Weights of piles themselves are from 30.7#/L.F. to 57#/L.F. but they are 15" to 21" wide.) Lightweight sections 12" to 28" wide from 3 ga. to 12 ga. thick are also available for shallow excavations. Piles may be driven two at a time with an impact or vibratory hammer (use vibratory to pull) hung from a crane without leads. A reasonable estimate of the life of steel sheet piling is 10 uses with up to 125 uses possible if a vibratory hammer is used. Used piling costs from 50% to 80% of new piling depending on location and market conditions. Sheet piling and H piles

can be rented for about 30% of the delivered mill price for the first month and 5% per month thereafter. Allow 1 labor-hour per pile for cleaning and trimming after driving. These costs increase with depth and hydrostatic head. Vibratory drivers are faster in wet granular soils and are excellent for pile extraction. Pulling difficulty increases with the time in the ground and may cost more than driving. It is often economical to abandon the sheet piling, especially if it can be used as the outer wall form. Allow about 1/3 additional length or more for toeing into ground. Add bracing, waler and strut costs. Waler costs can equal the cost per ton of sheeting.

Utilities | R3311 Water Utility Distribution Piping

R331113-80   Piping Designations

There are several systems currently in use to describe pipe and fittings. The following paragraphs will help to identify and clarify classifications of piping systems used for water distribution.

Piping may be classified by schedule. Piping schedules include 5S, 10S, 10, 20, 30, Standard, 40, 60, Extra Strong, 80, 100, 120, 140, 160 and Double Extra Strong. These schedules are dependent upon the pipe wall thickness. The wall thickness of a particular schedule may vary with pipe size.

Ductile iron pipe for water distribution is classified by Pressure Classes such as Class 150, 200, 250, 300 and 350. These classes are actually the rated water working pressure of the pipe in pounds per square inch (psi). The pipe in these pressure classes is designed to withstand the rated water working pressure plus a surge allowance of 100 psi.

The American Water Works Association (AWWA) provides standards for various types of **plastic pipe**. C-900 is the specification for polyvinyl chloride (PVC) piping used for water distribution in sizes ranging from 4" through 12". C-901 is the specification for polyethylene (PE) pressure pipe, tubing and fittings used for water distribution in sizes ranging from 1/2" through 3". C-905 is the specification for PVC piping sizes 14" and greater.

PVC pressure-rated pipe is identified using the standard dimensional ratio (SDR) method. This method is defined by the American Society for Testing and Materials (ASTM) Standard D 2241. This pipe is available in SDR numbers 64, 41, 32.5, 26, 21, 17, and 13.5. Pipe with an SDR of 64 will have the thinnest wall while pipe with an SDR of 13.5 will have the thickest wall. When the pressure rating (PR) of a pipe is given in psi, it is based on a line supplying water at 73 degrees F.

The National Sanitation Foundation (NSF) seal of approval is applied to products that can be used with potable water. These products have been tested to ANSI/NSF Standard 14.

Valves and strainers are classified by American National Standards Institute (ANSI) Classes. These Classes are 125, 150, 200, 250, 300, 400, 600, 900, 1500 and 2500. Within each class there is an operating pressure range dependent upon temperature. Design parameters should be compared to the appropriate material dependent, pressure-temperature rating chart for accurate valve selection.

Change Orders

Change Order Considerations

A change order is a written document, usually prepared by the design professional, and signed by the owner, the architect/engineer, and the contractor. A change order states the agreement of the parties to: an addition, deletion, or revision in the work; an adjustment in the contract sum, if any; or an adjustment in the contract time, if any. Change orders, or "extras" in the construction process occur after execution of the construction contract and impact architects/engineers, contractors, and owners.

Change orders that are properly recognized and managed can ensure orderly, professional, and profitable progress for all who are involved in the project. There are many causes for change orders and change order requests. In all cases, change orders or change order requests should be addressed promptly and in a precise and prescribed manner. The following paragraphs include information regarding change order pricing and procedures.

The Causes of Change Orders

Reasons for issuing change orders include:

- Unforeseen field conditions that require a change in the work
- Correction of design discrepancies, errors, or omissions in the contract documents
- Owner-requested changes, either by design criteria, scope of work, or project objectives
- Completion date changes for reasons unrelated to the construction process
- Changes in building code interpretations, or other public authority requirements that require a change in the work
- Changes in availability of existing or new materials and products

Procedures

Properly written contract documents must include the correct change order procedures for all parties—owners, design professionals and contractors—to follow in order to avoid costly delays and litigation.

Being "in the right" is not always a sufficient or acceptable defense. The contract provisions requiring notification and documentation must be adhered to within a defined or reasonable time frame.

The appropriate method of handling change orders is by a written proposal and acceptance by all parties involved. Prior to starting work on a project, all parties should identify their authorized agents who may sign and accept change orders, as well as any limits placed on their authority.

Time may be a critical factor when the need for a change arises. For such cases, the contractor might be directed to proceed on a "time and materials" basis, rather than wait for all paperwork to be processed—a delay that could impede progress. In this situation, the contractor must still follow the prescribed change order procedures including, but not limited to, notification and documentation.

All forms used for change orders should be dated and signed by the proper authority. Lack of documentation can be very costly, especially if legal judgments are to be made, and if certain field personnel are no longer available. For time and material change orders, the contractor should keep accurate daily records of all labor and material allocated to the change.

Owners or awarding authorities who do considerable and continual building construction (such as the federal government) realize the inevitability of change orders for numerous reasons, both predictable and unpredictable. As a result, the federal government, the American Institute of Architects (AIA), the Engineers Joint Contract Documents Committee (EJCDC) and other contractor, legal, and technical organizations have developed standards and procedures to be followed by all parties to achieve contract continuance and timely completion, while being financially fair to all concerned.

In addition to the change order standards put forth by industry associations, there are also many books available on the subject.

Pricing Change Orders

When pricing change orders, regardless of their cause, the most significant factor is when the change occurs. The need for a change may be perceived in the field or requested by the architect/engineer *before* any of the actual installation has begun, or may evolve or appear *during* construction when the item of work in question is partially installed. In the latter cases, the original sequence of construction is disrupted, along with all contiguous and supporting systems. Change orders cause the greatest impact when they occur *after* the installation has been completed and must be uncovered, or even replaced. Post-completion changes may be caused by necessary design changes, product failure, or changes in the owner's requirements that are not discovered until the building or the systems begin to function.

Specified procedures of notification and record keeping must be adhered to and enforced regardless of the stage of construction: *before, during,* or *after* installation. Some bidding documents anticipate change orders by requiring that unit prices including overhead and profit percentages—for additional as well as deductible changes—be listed. Generally these unit prices do not fully take into account the ripple effect, or impact on other trades, and should be used for general guidance only.

When pricing change orders, it is important to classify the time frame in which the change occurs. There are two basic time frames for change orders: *pre-installation change orders,* which occur before the start of construction, and *post-installation change orders,* which involve reworking after the original installation. Change orders that occur between these stages may be priced according to the extent of work completed using a combination of techniques developed for pricing *pre-* and *post-installation* changes.

The following factors are the basis for a check list to use when preparing a change order estimate.

Factors To Consider When Pricing Change Orders

As an estimator begins to prepare a change order, the following questions should be reviewed to determine their impact on the final price.

General

- *Is the change order work* pre-installation *or* post-installation?

Change order work costs vary according to how much of the installation has been completed. Once workers have the project scoped in their minds, even though they have not started, it can be difficult to refocus.

Consequently they may spend more than the normal amount of time understanding the change. Also, modifications to work in place, such as trimming or refitting, usually take more time than was initially estimated. The greater the amount of work in place, the more reluctant workers are to change it. Psychologically they may resent the change and as a result the rework takes longer than normal. Post-installation change order estimates must include demolition of existing work as required to accomplish the change. If the work is performed at a later time, additional obstacles, such as building finishes, may be present which must be protected. Regardless of whether the change

occurs pre-installation or post-installation, attempt to isolate the identifiable factors and price them separately. For example, add shipping costs that may be required pre-installation or any demolition required post-installation. Then analyze the potential impact on productivity of psychological and/or learning curve factors and adjust the output rates accordingly. One approach is to break down the typical workday into segments and quantify the impact on each segment. The following chart may be useful as a guide:

	Activities (Productivity) Expressed as Percentages of a Workday		
Task	**Means Mechanical Cost Data (for New Construction)**	**Pre-Installation Change Orders**	**Post-Installation Change Orders**
1. Study plans	3%	6%	6%
2. Material procurement	3%	3%	3%
3. Receiving and storing	3%	3%	3%
4. Mobilization	5%	5%	5%
5. Site movement	5%	5%	8%
6. Layout and marking	8%	10%	12%
7. Actual installation	64%	59%	54%
8. Clean-up	3%	3%	3%
9. Breaks—non-productive	6%	6%	6%
Total	100%	100%	100%

Change Order Installation Efficiency

The labor-hours expressed (for new construction) are based on average installation time, using an efficiency level of approximately 60%–65%. For change order situations, adjustments to this efficiency level should reflect the daily labor-hour allocation for that particular occurrence.

If any of the specific percentages expressed in the above chart do not apply to a particular project situation, then those percentage points should be reallocated to the appropriate task(s). Example: Using data for new construction, assume there is no new material being utilized. The percentages for Tasks 2 and 3 would therefore be reallocated to other tasks. If the time required for Tasks 2 and 3 can now be applied to installation, we can add the time allocated for *Material Procurement* and *Receiving and Storing* to the *Actual Installation* time for new construction, thereby increasing the Actual Installation percentage.

This chart shows that, due to reduced productivity, labor costs will be higher than those for new construction by 5%–15% for pre-installation change orders and by 15%–25% for post-installation change orders. Each job and change order is unique and must be examined individually. Many factors, covered elsewhere in this section, can each have a significant impact on productivity and change order costs. All such factors should be considered in every case.

- *Will the change substantially delay the original completion date?*

  A significant change in the project may cause the original completion date to be extended. The extended schedule may subject the contractor to new wage rates dictated by relevant labor contracts. Project supervision and other project overhead must also be extended beyond the original completion date. The schedule extension may also put installation into a new weather season. For example, underground piping scheduled for October installation was delayed until January. As a result, frost penetrated the trench area, thereby changing the degree of difficulty of the task. Changes and delays may have a ripple effect throughout the project. This effect must be analyzed and negotiated with the owner.

- *What is the net effect of a deduct change order?*

  In most cases, change orders resulting in a deduction or credit reflect only bare costs. The contractor may retain the overhead and profit based on the original bid.

Materials

- *Will you have to pay more or less for the new material, required by the change order, than you paid for the original purchase?*

  The same material prices or discounts will usually apply to materials purchased for change orders as new construction. In some instances, however, the contractor may forfeit the advantages of competitive pricing for change orders. Consider the following example:

  A contractor purchased over $20,000 worth of fan coil units for an installation, and obtained the maximum discount. Some time later it was determined the project required an additional matching unit. The contractor has to purchase this unit from the original supplier to ensure a match. The supplier at this time may not discount the unit because of the small quantity, and the fact that he is no longer in a competitive situation. The impact of quantity on purchase can add between 0% and 25% to material prices and/or subcontractor quotes.

- *If materials have been ordered or delivered to the job site, will they be subject to a cancellation charge or restocking fee?*

  Check with the supplier to determine if ordered materials are subject to a cancellation charge. Delivered materials not used as result of a change order may be subject to a restocking fee if returned to the supplier. Common restocking charges run between 20% and 40%. Also, delivery charges to return the goods to the supplier must be added.

Labor

- *How efficient is the existing crew at the actual installation?*

  Is the same crew that performed the initial work going to do the change order? Possibly the change consists of the installation of a unit identical to one already installed; therefore, the change should take less time. Be sure to consider this potential productivity increase and modify the productivity rates accordingly.

- *If the crew size is increased, what impact will that have on supervision requirements?*

  Under most bargaining agreements or management practices, there is a point at which a working foreman is replaced by a nonworking foreman. This replacement increases project overhead by adding a nonproductive worker. If additional workers are added to accelerate the project or to perform changes while maintaining the schedule, be sure to add additional supervision time if warranted. Calculate the hours involved and the additional cost directly if possible.

- *What are the other impacts of increased crew size?*

  The larger the crew, the greater the potential for productivity to decrease. Some of the factors that cause this productivity loss are: overcrowding (producing restrictive conditions in the working space), and possibly a shortage of any special tools and equipment required. Such factors affect not only the crew working on the elements directly involved in the change order, but other crews whose movement may also be hampered.

As the crew increases, check its basic composition for changes by the addition or deletion of apprentices or nonworking foreman, and quantify the potential effects of equipment shortages or other logistical factors.

- *As new crews, unfamiliar with the project, are brought onto the site, how long will it take them to become oriented to the project requirements?*

  The orientation time for a new crew to become 100% effective varies with the site and type of project. Orientation is easiest at a new construction site, and most difficult at existing, very restrictive renovation sites. The type of work also affects orientation time. When all elements of the work are exposed, such as concrete or masonry work, orientation is decreased. When the work is concealed or less visible, such as existing electrical systems, orientation takes longer. Usually orientation can be accomplished in one day or less. Costs for added orientation should be itemized and added to the total estimated cost.

- *How much actual production can be gained by working overtime?*

  Short term overtime can be used effectively to accomplish more work in a day. However, as overtime is scheduled to run beyond several weeks, studies have shown marked decreases in output. The following chart shows the effect of long term overtime on worker efficiency. If the anticipated change requires extended overtime to keep the job on schedule, these factors can be used as a guide to predict the impact on time and cost. Add project overhead, particularly supervision, that may also be incurred.

Days per Week	Hours per Day	Production Efficiency					Payroll Cost Factors	
		1 Week	2 Weeks	3 Weeks	4 Weeks	Average 4 Weeks	@ 1-1/2 Times	@ 2 Times
5	8	100%	100%	100%	100%	100%	100%	100%
	9	100	100	95	90	96.25	105.6	111.1
	10	100	95	90	85	91.25	110.0	120.0
	11	95	90	75	65	81.25	113.6	127.3
	12	90	85	70	60	76.25	116.7	133.3
6	8	100	100	95	90	96.25	108.3	116.7
	9	100	95	90	85	92.50	113.0	125.9
	10	95	90	85	80	87.50	116.7	133.3
	11	95	85	70	65	78.75	119.7	139.4
	12	90	80	65	60	73.75	122.2	144.4
7	8	100	95	85	75	88.75	114.3	128.6
	9	95	90	80	70	83.75	118.3	136.5
	10	90	85	75	65	78.75	121.4	142.9
	11	85	80	65	60	72.50	124.0	148.1
	12	85	75	60	55	68.75	126.2	152.4

Effects of Overtime

Caution: Under many labor agreements, Sundays and holidays are paid at a higher premium than the normal overtime rate.

The use of long-term overtime is counterproductive on almost any construction job; that is, the longer the period of overtime, the lower the actual production rate. Numerous studies have been conducted, and while they have resulted in slightly different numbers, all reach the same conclusion. The figure above tabulates the effects of overtime work on efficiency.

As illustrated, there can be a difference between the *actual* payroll cost per hour and the *effective* cost per hour for overtime work. This is due to the reduced production efficiency with the increase in weekly hours beyond 40. This difference between actual and effective cost results from overtime work over a prolonged period. Short-term overtime work does not result in as great a reduction in efficiency and, in such cases, effective cost may not vary significantly from the actual payroll cost. As the total hours per week are increased on a regular basis, more time is lost due to fatigue, lowered morale, and an increased accident rate.

As an example, assume a project where workers are working 6 days a week, 10 hours per day. From the figure above (based on productivity studies), the average effective productive hours over a 4-week period are:

$$0.875 \times 60 = 52.5$$

Depending upon the locale and day of week, overtime hours may be paid at time and a half or double time. For time and a half, the overall (average) *actual* payroll cost (including regular and overtime hours) is determined as follows:

$$\frac{40 \text{ reg. hrs.} + (20 \text{ overtime hrs.} \times 1.5)}{60 \text{ hrs.}} = 1.167$$

Based on 60 hours, the payroll cost per hour will be 116.7% of the normal rate at 40 hours per week. However, because the effective production (efficiency) for 60 hours is reduced to the equivalent of 52.5 hours, the effective cost of overtime is calculated as follows:

For time and a half:

$$\frac{40 \text{ reg. hrs.} + (20 \text{ overtime hrs.} \times 1.5)}{52.5 \text{ hrs.}} = 1.33$$

Installed cost will be 133% of the normal rate (for labor).

Thus, when figuring overtime, the actual cost per unit of work will be higher than the apparent overtime payroll dollar increase, due to the reduced productivity of the longer workweek. These efficiency calculations are true only for those cost factors determined by hours worked. Costs that are applied weekly or monthly, such as equipment rentals, will not be similarly affected.

Equipment

- *What equipment is required to complete the change order?*

Change orders may require extending the rental period of equipment already on the job site, or the addition of special equipment brought in to accomplish the change work. In either case, the additional rental charges and operator labor charges must be added.

Summary

The preceding considerations and others you deem appropriate should be analyzed and applied to a change order estimate. The impact of each should be quantified and listed on the estimate to form an audit trail.

Change orders that are properly identified, documented, and managed help to ensure the orderly, professional and profitable progress of the work. They also minimize potential claims or disputes at the end of the project.

Estimating Tips

- The cost figures in this Square Foot Cost section were derived from approximately 11,200 projects contained in the RSMeans database of completed construction projects. They include the contractor's overhead and profit, but do not generally include architectural fees or land costs. The figures have been adjusted to January of the current year. New projects are added to our files each year, and outdated projects are discarded. For this reason, certain costs may not show a uniform annual progression. In no case are all subdivisions of a project listed.

- These projects were located throughout the U.S. and reflect a tremendous variation in square foot (S.F.) and cubic foot (C.F.) costs. This is due to differences, not only in labor and material costs, but also in individual owners' requirements. For instance, a bank in a large city would have different features than one in a rural area. This is true of all the different types of buildings analyzed. Therefore, caution should be exercised when using these Square Foot costs. For example, for court houses, costs in the database are local court house costs and will not apply to the larger, more elaborate federal court houses. As a general rule, the projects in the 1/4 column do not include any site work or equipment, while the projects in the 3/4 column may include both equipment and site work. The median figures do not generally include site work.

- None of the figures "go with" any others. All individual cost items were computed and tabulated separately. Thus, the sum of the median figures for Plumbing, HVAC and Electrical will not normally total up to the total Mechanical and Electrical costs arrived at by separate analysis and tabulation of the projects.

- Each building was analyzed as to total and component costs and percentages. The figures were arranged in ascending order with the results tabulated as shown. The 1/4 column shows that 25% of the projects had lower costs and 75% had higher. The 3/4 column shows that 75% of the projects had lower costs and 25% had higher. The median column shows that 50% of the projects had lower costs and 50% had higher.

- There are two times when square foot costs are useful. The first is in the conceptual stage when no details are available. Then square foot costs make a useful starting point. The second is after the bids are in and the costs can be worked back into their appropriate units for information purposes. As soon as details become available in the project design, the square foot approach should be discontinued and the project priced as to its particular components. When more precision is required, or for estimating the replacement cost of specific buildings, the current edition of *RSMeans Square Foot Costs* should be used.

- In using the figures in this section, it is recommended that the median column be used for preliminary figures if no additional information is available. The median figures, when multiplied by the total city construction cost index figures (see City Cost Indexes) and then multiplied by the project size modifier at the end of this section, should present a fairly accurate base figure, which would then have to be adjusted in view of the estimator's experience, local economic conditions, code requirements, and the owner's particular requirements. There is no need to factor the percentage figures, as these should remain constant from city to city. All tabulations mentioning air conditioning had at least partial air conditioning.

- The editors of this book would greatly appreciate receiving cost figures on one or more of your recent projects, which would then be included in the averages for next year. All cost figures received will be kept confidential, except that they will be averaged with other similar projects to arrive at Square Foot cost figures for next year's book. See the last page of the book for details and the discount available for submitting one or more of your projects.

50 17 00 | S.F. Costs

			UNIT	UNIT COSTS			% OF TOTAL			
				1/4	MEDIAN	3/4	1/4	MEDIAN	3/4	
01	0010	**APARTMENTS Low Rise (1 to 3 story)**	S.F.	69.50	87	116				01
	0020	Total project cost	C.F.	6.25	8.25	10.20				
	0100	Site work	S.F.	5.95	8.10	14.30	6.05%	10.55%	14.05%	
	0500	Masonry		1.37	3.18	5.50	1.54%	3.67%	6.35%	
	1500	Finishes		7.35	10	12.50	9.05%	10.75%	12.85%	
	1800	Equipment		2.27	3.45	5.10	2.73%	4.03%	5.95%	
	2720	Plumbing		5.40	6.95	8.85	6.65%	8.95%	10.05%	
	2770	Heating, ventilating, air conditioning		3.45	4.25	6.25	4.20%	5.60%	7.60%	
	2900	Electrical		4.02	5.35	7.20	5.20%	6.65%	8.40%	
	3100	Total: Mechanical & Electrical	▼	13.95	17.75	22	15.90%	18.05%	23%	
	9000	Per apartment unit, total cost	Apt.	65,000	99,000	146,000				
	9500	Total: Mechanical & Electrical	"	12,300	19,300	25,200				
02	0010	**APARTMENTS Mid Rise (4 to 7 story)**	S.F.	92.50	111	138				02
	0020	Total project costs	C.F.	7.20	9.95	13.60				
	0100	Site work	S.F.	3.69	7.30	13.15	5.25%	6.70%	9.15%	
	0500	Masonry		6.15	8.45	11.55	5.10%	7.25%	10.50%	
	1500	Finishes		11.60	15.15	19.10	10.55%	13.45%	17.70%	
	1800	Equipment		2.68	4.01	5.25	2.54%	3.48%	4.31%	
	2500	Conveying equipment		1.99	2.53	3.07	1.94%	2.27%	2.69%	
	2720	Plumbing		5.40	8.65	9.15	5.70%	7.20%	8.95%	
	2900	Electrical		6.10	8.25	10.05	6.65%	7.20%	8.95%	
	3100	Total: Mechanical & Electrical	▼	19.45	24.50	29.50	18.50%	21%	23%	
	9000	Per apartment unit, total cost	Apt.	104,500	123,000	204,000				
	9500	Total: Mechanical & Electrical	"	19,700	22,800	28,800				
03	0010	**APARTMENTS High Rise (8 to 24 story)**	S.F.	105	120	145				03
	0020	Total project costs	C.F.	10.15	11.80	15.10				
	0100	Site work	S.F.	3.79	6.15	8.60	2.58%	4.84%	6.15%	
	0500	Masonry		6.05	11	13.70	4.74%	9.65%	11.05%	
	1500	Finishes		11.60	14.50	17.15	9.75%	11.80%	13.70%	
	1800	Equipment		3.36	4.14	5.50	2.78%	3.49%	4.35%	
	2500	Conveying equipment		2.38	3.61	4.91	2.23%	2.78%	3.37%	
	2720	Plumbing		7.70	9.10	12.65	6.80%	7.20%	10.45%	
	2900	Electrical		7.20	9.10	12.25	6.45%	7.65%	8.80%	
	3100	Total: Mechanical & Electrical	▼	21.50	27.50	33	17.95%	22.50%	24.50%	
	9000	Per apartment unit, total cost	Apt.	108,500	119,500	166,000				
	9500	Total: Mechanical & Electrical	"	23,500	26,800	28,400				
04	0010	**AUDITORIUMS**	S.F.	109	148	212				04
	0020	Total project costs	C.F.	6.80	9.45	13.60				
	2720	Plumbing	S.F.	6.45	9.50	11.40	5.85%	7.20%	8.70%	
	2900	Electrical		8.40	12.25	20	6.80%	9.05%	11.35%	
	3100	Total: Mechanical & Electrical	▼	52.50	68.50	94	24.50%	29%	31.50%	
05	0010	**AUTOMOTIVE SALES**	S.F.	80.50	109	135				05
	0020	Total project costs	C.F.	5.30	6.35	8.25				
	2720	Plumbing	S.F.	3.67	6.35	6.95	2.89%	6.05%	6.50%	
	2770	Heating, ventilating, air conditioning		5.65	8.65	9.35	4.61%	10%	10.35%	
	2900	Electrical		6.35	9.95	13.80	7.25%	8.80%	12.15%	
	3100	Total: Mechanical & Electrical	▼	20.50	29	35	18.90%	20.50%	22%	
06	0010	**BANKS**	S.F.	158	197	250				06
	0020	Total project costs	C.F.	11.25	15.30	20				
	0100	Site work	S.F.	18.05	27.50	40	7.85%	12.95%	16.95%	
	0500	Masonry		8.20	15.70	28.50	3.36%	6.95%	10.05%	
	1500	Finishes		14.60	21.50	26.50	5.85%	8.60%	11.55%	
	1800	Equipment		5.95	13.05	26.50	1%	5.55%	10.50%	
	2720	Plumbing		4.94	7.05	10.30	2.82%	3.90%	4.93%	
	2770	Heating, ventilating, air conditioning		9.40	12.55	16.70	4.86%	7.15%	8.50%	
	2900	Electrical		15	20	26	8.20%	10.20%	12.20%	
	3100	Total: Mechanical & Electrical	▼	36	48.50	58	16.25%	19.45%	23%	
	3500	See also division 11020 & 11030 (MF2004 11 16 00 & 11 17 00)									

		**50 17 00	S.F. Costs**	UNIT	UNIT COSTS			% OF TOTAL			
				1/4	MEDIAN	3/4	1/4	MEDIAN	3/4	
13	0010	**CHURCHES**	S.F.	106	135	175				13
	0020	Total project costs	C.F.	6.60	8.30	10.95				
	1800	Equipment	S.F.	1.27	3.04	6.45	.95%	2.11%	4.31%	
	2720	Plumbing		4.13	5.80	8.50	3.51%	4.96%	6.25%	
	2770	Heating, ventilating, air conditioning		9.65	12.60	17.85	7.50%	10%	12%	
	2900	Electrical		8.95	12.30	16.60	7.30%	8.80%	10.95%	
	3100	Total: Mechanical & Electrical	↓	27.50	37	49	18.30%	22%	25%	
	3500	See also division 11040 (MF2004 11 91 00)								
15	0010	**CLUBS, COUNTRY**	S.F.	114	137	173				15
	0020	Total project costs	C.F.	9.20	11.20	15.45				
	2720	Plumbing	S.F.	6.90	10.20	23.50	5.60%	7.90%	10%	
	2900	Electrical		8.95	12.25	16	7%	8.95%	11%	
	3100	Total: Mechanical & Electrical	↓	47.50	59.50	63	19%	26.50%	29.50%	
17	0010	**CLUBS, SOCIAL Fraternal**	S.F.	96	131	175				17
	0020	Total project costs	C.F.	5.70	8.60	10.30				
	2720	Plumbing	S.F.	5.70	7.10	10.75	5.60%	6.90%	8.55%	
	2770	Heating, ventilating, air conditioning		8.25	9.95	12.80	8.20%	9.25%	14.40%	
	2900	Electrical		6.85	11.25	12.90	5.95%	9.30%	10.55%	
	3100	Total: Mechanical & Electrical	↓	35.50	38.50	48.50	21%	23%	23.50%	
18	0010	**CLUBS, Y.M.C.A.**	S.F.	119	154	194				18
	0020	Total project costs	C.F.	5.25	8.80	13.10				
	2720	Plumbing	S.F.	7.20	14.35	16.10	5.65%	7.60%	10.85%	
	2900	Electrical		9.35	11.40	17.05	6.25%	7.95%	9.20%	
	3100	Total: Mechanical & Electrical	↓	35	42	71	20.50%	21.50%	28.50%	
19	0010	**COLLEGES Classrooms & Administration**	S.F.	115	156	207				19
	0020	Total project costs	C.F.	8.25	12.25	18.90				
	0500	Masonry	S.F.	8.45	16	19.55	5.65%	8.05%	10.50%	
	2720	Plumbing		5.85	12	22.50	5.10%	6.60%	8.95%	
	2900	Electrical		9.40	14.55	20	7.70%	9.75%	12%	
	3100	Total: Mechanical & Electrical	↓	39.50	54	72	23.50%	28%	32%	
21	0010	**COLLEGES Science, Engineering, Laboratories**	S.F.	214	251	291				21
	0020	Total project costs	C.F.	12.30	17.95	20.50				
	1800	Equipment	S.F.	11.95	27	29.50	2%	6.45%	12.65%	
	2900	Electrical		17.70	25.50	38.50	7.10%	9.40%	12.10%	
	3100	Total: Mechanical & Electrical	↓	65.50	78	121	28.50%	31.50%	41%	
	3500	See also division 11600 (MF2004 11 53 00)								
23	0010	**COLLEGES Student Unions**	S.F.	137	185	225				23
	0020	Total project costs	C.F.	7.65	10	12.35				
	3100	Total: Mechanical & Electrical	S.F.	51.50	55.50	66	23.50%	26%	29%	
25	0010	**COMMUNITY CENTERS**	S.F.	113	139	189				25
	0020	Total project costs	C.F.	7.35	10.55	13.65				
	1800	Equipment	S.F.	2.73	4.51	7.35	1.48%	3.01%	5.30%	
	2720	Plumbing		5.35	9.35	12.75	4.85%	7%	8.95%	
	2770	Heating, ventilating, air conditioning		8.55	12.45	17.85	6.80%	10.35%	12.90%	
	2900	Electrical		9.25	12.50	17.95	7.15%	8.95%	10.45%	
	3100	Total: Mechanical & Electrical	↓	31.50	40	57	19.05%	24%	31%	
28	0010	**COURT HOUSES**	S.F.	163	192	265				28
	0020	Total project costs	C.F.	12.50	14.95	18.85				
	2720	Plumbing	S.F.	7.75	10.80	12.25	5.95%	7.45%	8.20%	
	2900	Electrical		17.30	19.25	28	8.90%	10.45%	11.85%	
	3100	Total: Mechanical & Electrical	↓	48.50	63.50	69.50	22.50%	27.50%	30%	
30	0010	**DEPARTMENT STORES**	S.F.	60	81.50	103				30
	0020	Total project costs	C.F.	3.23	4.18	5.70				
	2720	Plumbing	S.F.	1.87	2.37	3.59	1.82%	4.21%	5.90%	
	2770	Heating, ventilating, air conditioning		5.45	8.45	12.70	8.20%	9.10%	14.80%	

50 17 00 | S.F. Costs

			UNIT	UNIT COSTS			% OF TOTAL			
				1/4	MEDIAN	3/4	1/4	MEDIAN	3/4	
30	2900	Electrical	S.F.	6.90	9.50	11.20	9.05%	12.15%	14.95%	30
	3100	Total: Mechanical & Electrical	↓	12.15	15.55	27	13.20%	21.50%	50%	
31	0010	**DORMITORIES Low Rise (1 to 3 story)**	S.F.	114	158	198				31
	0020	Total project costs	C.F.	6.45	10.45	15.65				
	2720	Plumbing	S.F.	6.85	9.20	11.60	8.05%	9%	9.65%	
	2770	Heating, ventilating, air conditioning		7.25	8.70	11.60	4.61%	8.05%	10%	
	2900	Electrical		7.55	11.50	15.75	6.40%	8.65%	9.50%	
	3100	Total: Mechanical & Electrical	↓	39.50	42	65.50	22%	25%	27%	
	9000	Per bed, total cost	Bed	48,400	53,500	115,500				
32	0010	**DORMITORIES Mid Rise (4 to 8 story)**	S.F.	140	183	226				32
	0020	Total project costs	C.F.	15.45	16.95	20.50				
	2900	Electrical	S.F.	14.90	16.90	23	8.20%	10.20%	11.95%	
	3100	Total: Mechanical & Electrical	"	41.50	83	84.50	25.50%	34.50%	37.50%	
	9000	Per bed, total cost	Bed	20,000	45,600	263,500				
34	0010	**FACTORIES**	S.F.	53	79	122				34
	0020	Total project costs	C.F.	3.40	5.10	8.40				
	0100	Site work	S.F.	6.05	11.05	17.50	6.95%	11.45%	17.95%	
	2720	Plumbing		2.86	5.30	8.80	3.73%	6.05%	8.10%	
	2770	Heating, ventilating, air conditioning		5.55	8	10.80	5.25%	8.45%	11.35%	
	2900	Electrical		6.60	10.45	15.90	8.10%	10.50%	14.20%	
	3100	Total: Mechanical & Electrical	↓	18.85	29	38	21%	28.50%	35.50%	
36	0010	**FIRE STATIONS**	S.F.	106	145	197				36
	0020	Total project costs	C.F.	6.15	8.45	11.25				
	0500	Masonry	S.F.	15.45	28	36.50	8.35%	11.30%	15.70%	
	1140	Roofing		3.43	9.30	10.55	1.90%	4.94%	5.05%	
	1580	Painting		2.66	3.98	4.07	1.37%	1.57%	2.07%	
	1800	Equipment		1.31	2.51	4.63	.62%	1.63%	3.42%	
	2720	Plumbing		5.90	9.40	13.30	5.85%	7.35%	9.45%	
	2770	Heating, ventilating, air conditioning		5.85	9.45	14.60	5.15%	7.40%	9.40%	
	2900	Electrical		7.60	13.20	18	6.85%	8.60%	10.60%	
	3100	Total: Mechanical & Electrical	↓	38.50	49.50	56	18.40%	23%	27%	
37	0010	**FRATERNITY HOUSES & Sorority Houses**	S.F.	105	136	186				37
	0020	Total project costs	C.F.	10.50	10.95	13.15				
	2720	Plumbing	S.F.	7.95	9.10	16.65	6.80%	8%	10.85%	
	2900	Electrical		6.95	15	18.40	6.60%	9.90%	10.65%	
	3100	Total: Mechanical & Electrical	↓	8.55	26.50	32		15.10%	15.90%	
38	0010	**FUNERAL HOMES**	S.F.	111	151	275				38
	0020	Total project costs	C.F.	11.35	12.60	24				
	2900	Electrical	S.F.	4.91	9	9.85	3.58%	4.44%	5.95%	
	3100	Total: Mechanical & Electrical	↓	17.45	25.50	35.50	12.90%	12.90%	12.90%	
39	0010	**GARAGES, COMMERCIAL (Service)**	S.F.	63	97	134				39
	0020	Total project costs	C.F.	4.14	6.10	8.90				
	1800	Equipment	S.F.	3.55	7.95	12.40	2.21%	4.62%	6.80%	
	2720	Plumbing		4.36	6.70	12.25	5.45%	7.85%	10.65%	
	2730	Heating & ventilating		5.70	7.45	9.45	5.25%	6.85%	8.20%	
	2900	Electrical		5.95	9.10	13.15	7.15%	9.25%	10.85%	
	3100	Total: Mechanical & Electrical	↓	13.20	25.50	37.50	12.35%	17.40%	26%	
40	0010	**GARAGES, MUNICIPAL (Repair)**	S.F.	97.50	123	173				40
	0020	Total project costs	C.F.	5.75	7.30	12.60				
	0500	Masonry	S.F.	8.65	16.95	26.50	4.03%	9.15%	12.50%	
	2720	Plumbing		4.14	7.95	15	3.59%	6.70%	7.95%	
	2730	Heating & ventilating		7.10	10.25	19.80	6.15%	7.45%	13.50%	
	2900	Electrical		6.80	10.75	15.60	6.65%	8.15%	11.15%	
	3100	Total: Mechanical & Electrical	↓	31.50	44	63.50	21.50%	23%	28.50%	

		**50 17 00	S.F. Costs**		UNIT COSTS			% OF TOTAL		
			UNIT	1/4	MEDIAN	3/4	1/4	MEDIAN	3/4
41	0010	**GARAGES, PARKING**	S.F.	35.50	52.50	90				**41**
	0020	Total project costs	C.F.	3.38	4.59	6.70			
	2720	Plumbing	S.F.	1.02	1.58	2.44	1.72%	2.70%	3.85%
	2900	Electrical		1.97	2.42	3.80	4.33%	5.20%	6.30%
	3100	Total: Mechanical & Electrical	↓	4.04	5.60	7	7%	8.90%	11.05%
	3200								
	9000	Per car, total cost	Car	15,200	19,100	24,300			
43	0010	**GYMNASIUMS**	S.F.	100	133	176				**43**
	0020	Total project costs	C.F.	4.99	6.75	8.30			
	1800	Equipment	S.F.	2.38	4.46	8.55	1.98%	3.30%	6.70%
	2720	Plumbing		6.35	7.40	9.70	4.65%	6.40%	7.75%
	2770	Heating, ventilating, air conditioning		6.80	10.35	21	5.15%	9.05%	11.10%
	2900	Electrical		7.70	10.25	13.80	6.60%	8.30%	10.30%
	3100	Total: Mechanical & Electrical	↓	28	37	44	19.60%	23.50%	28%
	3500	See also division 11480 (MF2004 11 67 00)							
46	0010	**HOSPITALS**	S.F.	192	240	325				**46**
	0020	Total project costs	C.F.	14.55	18.10	26			
	1800	Equipment	S.F.	4.87	9.35	16.15	.80%	2.53%	4.80%
	2720	Plumbing		16.55	23.50	30	7.60%	9.10%	10.85%
	2770	Heating, ventilating, air conditioning		24.50	31	43.50	7.80%	12.95%	16.65%
	2900	Electrical		21	28.50	40.50	9.90%	11.75%	14.10%
	3100	Total: Mechanical & Electrical	↓	62	86	128	28%	33.50%	37%
	9000	Per bed or person, total cost	Bed	222,500	306,500	353,000			
	9900	See also division 11700 (MF2004 11 71 00)							
48	0010	**HOUSING For the Elderly**	S.F.	94.50	120	147				**48**
	0020	Total project costs	C.F.	6.75	9.35	11.95			
	0100	Site work	S.F.	6.60	10.20	14.95	5.05%	7.90%	12.10%
	0500	Masonry		2.88	10.75	15.70	1.30%	6.05%	11%
	1800	Equipment		2.28	3.14	5	1.88%	3.23%	4.43%
	2510	Conveying systems		2.30	3.09	4.18	1.78%	2.20%	2.81%
	2720	Plumbing		7	8.95	11.25	8.15%	9.55%	10.50%
	2730	Heating, ventilating, air conditioning		3.60	5.10	7.60	3.30%	5.60%	7.25%
	2900	Electrical		7.05	9.55	12.25	7.30%	8.50%	10.25%
	3100	Total: Mechanical & Electrical	↓	26	30	38.50	18.10%	22.50%	29%
	9000	Per rental unit, total cost	Unit	88,000	102,500	114,500			
	9500	Total: Mechanical & Electrical	"	19,600	22,500	26,300			
50	0010	**HOUSING Public (Low Rise)**	S.F.	79.50	110	143				**50**
	0020	Total project costs	C.F.	7.05	8.80	10.95			
	0100	Site work	S.F.	10.10	14.55	23.50	8.35%	11.75%	16.50%
	1800	Equipment		2.16	3.52	5.35	2.26%	3.03%	4.24%
	2720	Plumbing		5.70	7.55	9.55	7.15%	9.05%	11.60%
	2730	Heating, ventilating, air conditioning		2.88	5.60	6.10	4.26%	6.05%	6.45%
	2900	Electrical		4.80	7.15	9.90	5.10%	6.55%	8.25%
	3100	Total: Mechanical & Electrical	↓	23	29.50	33	14.50%	17.55%	26.50%
	9000	Per apartment, total cost	Apt.	87,000	99,000	124,500			
	9500	Total: Mechanical & Electrical	"	18,600	22,900	25,400			
51	0010	**ICE SKATING RINKS**	S.F.	68	159	174				**51**
	0020	Total project costs	C.F.	4.99	5.10	5.90			
	2720	Plumbing	S.F.	2.53	4.75	4.86	3.12%	3.23%	5.65%
	2900	Electrical		7.25	11.15	11.80	6.30%	10.15%	15.05%
	3100	Total: Mechanical & Electrical	↓	12	17	21	18.95%	18.95%	18.95%
52	0010	**JAILS**	S.F.	206	267	345				**52**
	0020	Total project costs	C.F.	18.60	26	30.50			
	1800	Equipment	S.F.	8.05	24	40.50	2.80%	6.05%	10.35%
	2720	Plumbing		19.90	26.50	35	7%	8.90%	13.35%
	2770	Heating, ventilating, air conditioning		18.65	25	48	7.50%	9.45%	17.75%
	2900	Electrical		21.50	29.50	36.50	8.80%	11.65%	14.95%

		50 17 00 | S.F. Costs		UNIT COSTS			% OF TOTAL			
			UNIT	**1/4**	**MEDIAN**	**3/4**	**1/4**	**MEDIAN**	**3/4**	
52	3100	Total: Mechanical & Electrical	S.F.	56	103	122	27.50%	30%	34%	52
53	0010	**LIBRARIES**	S.F.	132	168	218				53
	0020	Total project costs	C.F.	8.95	11.20	14.30				
	0500	Masonry	S.F.	10.45	18.05	30.50	5.80%	7.60%	11.60%	
	1800	Equipment		1.78	4.80	7.25	.34%	1.50%	4.07%	
	2720	Plumbing		4.82	6.85	9.50	3.38%	4.60%	5.70%	
	2770	Heating, ventilating, air conditioning		10.65	18.05	22	7.80%	10.95%	12.80%	
	2900	Electrical		13.40	17.35	22.50	8.35%	10.30%	11.95%	
	3100	Total: Mechanical & Electrical		39.50	51.50	62	20.50%	23%	26.50%	
54	0010	**LIVING, ASSISTED**	S.F.	121	142	168				54
	0020	Total project costs	C.F.	10.15	11.85	13.50				
	0500	Masonry	S.F.	3.50	4.23	5.20	2.36%	3.16%	3.90%	
	1800	Equipment		2.68	3.13	4.09	2.06%	2.45%	2.87%	
	2720	Plumbing		10.10	13.55	14.05	6.05%	8.15%	10.60%	
	2770	Heating, ventilating, air conditioning		12	12.55	13.75	7.95%	9.35%	9.70%	
	2900	Electrical		11.80	13.05	15	8.95%	9.95%	10.65%	
	3100	Total: Mechanical & Electrical		33	38.50	44.50	25%	28.50%	31.50%	
55	0010	**MEDICAL CLINICS**	S.F.	123	151	192				55
	0020	Total project costs	C.F.	9	11.65	15.50				
	1800	Equipment	S.F.	3.32	7	10.85	1.05%	2.94%	6.35%	
	2720	Plumbing		8.15	11.50	15.40	6.15%	8.40%	10.10%	
	2770	Heating, ventilating, air conditioning		9.75	12.75	18.75	6.65%	8.85%	11.35%	
	2900	Electrical		10.55	15	19.60	8.10%	10%	12.25%	
	3100	Total: Mechanical & Electrical		33.50	46	63	22.50%	27%	33.50%	
	3500	See also division 11700 (MF2004 11 71 00)								
57	0010	**MEDICAL OFFICES**	S.F.	115	143	175				57
	0020	Total project costs	C.F.	8.60	11.70	15.80				
	1800	Equipment	S.F.	3.81	7.55	10.70	.68%	4.97%	7.05%	
	2720	Plumbing		6.40	9.85	13.25	5.60%	6.80%	8.50%	
	2770	Heating, ventilating, air conditioning		7.70	11.15	14.70	6.10%	8%	9.70%	
	2900	Electrical		9.25	13.45	18.80	7.60%	9.80%	11.40%	
	3100	Total: Mechanical & Electrical		25	36	52	19.35%	23%	28.50%	
59	0010	**MOTELS**	S.F.	73	106	138				59
	0020	Total project costs	C.F.	6.50	8.70	14.20				
	2720	Plumbing	S.F.	7.40	9.40	11.25	9.45%	10.60%	12.55%	
	2770	Heating, ventilating, air conditioning		4.50	6.70	12.05	5.60%	5.60%	10%	
	2900	Electrical		6.90	8.70	10.85	7.45%	9.05%	10.45%	
	3100	Total: Mechanical & Electrical		22	29.50	50.50	18.50%	24%	25.50%	
	5000										
	9000	Per rental unit, total cost	Unit	37,100	70,500	76,500				
	9500	Total: Mechanical & Electrical	"	7,225	10,900	12,700				
60	0010	**NURSING HOMES**	S.F.	114	147	181				60
	0020	Total project costs	C.F.	9	11.25	15.35				
	1800	Equipment	S.F.	3.60	4.77	7.95	2.02%	3.62%	4.99%	
	2720	Plumbing		9.80	14.85	17.90	8.75%	10.10%	12.70%	
	2770	Heating, ventilating, air conditioning		10.30	15.65	21	9.70%	11.45%	11.80%	
	2900	Electrical		11.35	14.15	19.25	9.40%	10.55%	12.45%	
	3100	Total: Mechanical & Electrical		27	38	63.50	26%	29.50%	30.50%	
	9000	Per bed or person, total cost	Bed	50,500	63,500	82,000				
61	0010	**OFFICES Low Rise (1 to 4 story)**	S.F.	96.50	125	163				61
	0020	Total project costs	C.F.	6.85	9.50	12.50				
	0100	Site work	S.F.	7.75	13.70	20	6.20%	9.70%	13.55%	
	0500	Masonry		3.84	7.65	13.80	2.62%	5.45%	8.50%	
	1800	Equipment		1.02	2.01	5.45	.60%	1.50%	3.50%	
	2720	Plumbing		3.44	5.30	7.80	3.66%	4.50%	6.10%	
	2770	Heating, ventilating, air conditioning		7.60	10.60	15.55	7.20%	10.30%	11.70%	
	2900	Electrical		7.90	11.25	16.05	7.45%	9.65%	11.40%	

			UNIT	UNIT COSTS			% OF TOTAL			
				1/4	MEDIAN	3/4	1/4	MEDIAN	3/4	
		**50 17 00	S.F. Costs**								
61	3100	Total: Mechanical & Electrical	S.F.	21.50	30	45	18.20%	22%	27%	61
62	0010	**OFFICES Mid Rise (5 to 10 story)**	S.F.	102	124	168				62
	0020	Total project costs	C.F.	7.20	9.20	13.10				
	2720	Plumbing	S.F.	3.08	4.78	6.85	2.83%	3.74%	4.50%	
	2770	Heating, ventilating, air conditioning		7.75	11.05	17.65	7.65%	9.40%	11%	
	2900	Electrical		7.55	9.70	14.65	6.35%	7.80%	10%	
	3100	Total: Mechanical & Electrical		19.60	25.50	48	18.95%	21%	27.50%	
63	0010	**OFFICES High Rise (11 to 20 story)**	S.F.	125	158	194				63
	0020	Total project costs	C.F.	8.75	10.95	15.70				
	2900	Electrical	S.F.	7.60	9.30	13.80	5.80%	7.85%	10.50%	
	3100	Total: Mechanical & Electrical		24.50	33	55.50	16.90%	23.50%	34%	
64	0010	**POLICE STATIONS**	S.F.	151	197	249				64
	0020	Total project costs	C.F.	11.95	14.65	20				
	0500	Masonry	S.F.	14.10	25	31.50	6.70%	9.10%	11.35%	
	1800	Equipment		2.39	10.50	16.65	.98%	3.35%	6.70%	
	2720	Plumbing		8.40	16.75	21	5.65%	6.90%	10.75%	
	2770	Heating, ventilating, air conditioning		13.15	17.45	24.50	5.85%	10.55%	11.70%	
	2900	Electrical		16.45	23.50	31	9.80%	11.85%	14.80%	
	3100	Total: Mechanical & Electrical		54	64.50	87.50	25%	31.50%	32.50%	
65	0010	**POST OFFICES**	S.F.	119	146	187				65
	0020	Total project costs	C.F.	7.15	9	10.30				
	2720	Plumbing	S.F.	5.35	6.60	8.35	4.24%	5.30%	5.60%	
	2770	Heating, ventilating, air conditioning		8.35	10.30	11.45	6.65%	7.15%	9.35%	
	2900	Electrical		9.80	13.75	16.35	7.25%	9%	11%	
	3100	Total: Mechanical & Electrical		28.50	37	42	16.25%	18.80%	22%	
66	0010	**POWER PLANTS**	S.F.	825	1,075	2,000				66
	0020	Total project costs	C.F.	22.50	49.50	106				
	2900	Electrical	S.F.	58	123	184	9.30%	12.75%	21.50%	
	8100	Total: Mechanical & Electrical		145	470	1,050	32.50%	32.50%	52.50%	
67	0010	**RELIGIOUS EDUCATION**	S.F.	95.50	125	154				67
	0020	Total project costs	C.F.	5.30	7.60	9.50				
	2720	Plumbing	S.F.	3.99	5.65	7.95	4.40%	5.30%	7.10%	
	2770	Heating, ventilating, air conditioning		10.10	11.45	16.15	10.05%	11.45%	12.35%	
	2900	Electrical		7.60	10.70	14.15	7.60%	9.05%	10.35%	
	3100	Total: Mechanical & Electrical		31	40.50	49.50	22%	23%	27%	
69	0010	**RESEARCH Laboratories & Facilities**	S.F.	146	207	300				69
	0020	Total project costs	C.F.	10.65	21	25				
	1800	Equipment	S.F.	6.35	12.50	30.50	.94%	4.58%	9.10%	
	2720	Plumbing		14.35	18.35	29.50	6.15%	8.30%	10.80%	
	2770	Heating, ventilating, air conditioning		12.85	43	51	7.25%	16.50%	17.50%	
	2900	Electrical		17.20	27.50	45	9.55%	11.50%	15.40%	
	3100	Total: Mechanical & Electrical		55	95.50	137	29.50%	37%	41%	
70	0010	**RESTAURANTS**	S.F.	139	179	233				70
	0020	Total project costs	C.F.	11.65	15.30	20				
	1800	Equipment	S.F.	8.95	22	33.50	6.10%	13%	15.65%	
	2720	Plumbing		11	13.30	17.50	6.10%	8.15%	9%	
	2770	Heating, ventilating, air conditioning		13.95	19.30	23.50	9.20%	12%	12.40%	
	2900	Electrical		14.65	18.10	23.50	8.35%	10.55%	11.55%	
	3100	Total: Mechanical & Electrical		45.50	48.50	63	21%	25%	29.50%	
	9000	Per seat unit, total cost	Seat	5,100	6,775	8,025				
	9500	Total: Mechanical & Electrical	"	1,275	1,700	2,000				
72	0010	**RETAIL STORES**	S.F.	65	87	115				72
	0020	Total project costs	C.F.	4.39	6.25	8.70				
	2720	Plumbing	S.F.	2.35	3.92	6.70	3.26%	4.60%	6.80%	
	2770	Heating, ventilating, air conditioning		5.05	6.95	10.45	6.75%	8.75%	10.15%	
	2900	Electrical		5.85	7.95	11.50	7.25%	9.90%	11.60%	
	3100	Total: Mechanical & Electrical		15.50	19.85	27.50	17.05%	21%	23.50%	

			UNIT COSTS			% OF TOTAL			
50 17 00 | S.F. Costs		UNIT	1/4	MEDIAN	3/4	1/4	MEDIAN	3/4	
74	0010	**SCHOOLS Elementary**	S.F.	106	132	161				74
	0020	Total project costs	C.F.	6.90	8.85	11.45				
	0500	Masonry	S.F.	9.20	16.15	24	5.25%	10.65%	14.05%	
	1800	Equipment		2.89	4.88	9	1.83%	3.13%	4.61%	
	2720	Plumbing		6.10	8.60	11.50	5.70%	7.15%	9.35%	
	2730	Heating, ventilating, air conditioning		9.10	14.50	20.50	8.15%	10.80%	14.90%	
	2900	Electrical		10	13.25	16.90	8.45%	10.05%	11.80%	
	3100	Total: Mechanical & Electrical	↓	36.50	44.50	55	25%	27.50%	30%	
	9000	Per pupil, total cost	Ea.	12,100	18,000	40,400				
	9500	Total: Mechanical & Electrical	"	3,425	4,325	10,900				
76	0010	**SCHOOLS Junior High & Middle**	S.F.	109	134	163				76
	0020	Total project costs	C.F.	6.90	8.95	10.05				
	0500	Masonry	S.F.	13.60	17.80	21.50	8%	11.60%	14.35%	
	1800	Equipment		3.48	5.60	8.25	1.80%	3.09%	4.86%	
	2720	Plumbing		6.35	7.80	9.70	5.30%	6.80%	7.25%	
	2770	Heating, ventilating, air conditioning		12.70	15.45	27	8.90%	11.55%	14.20%	
	2900	Electrical		10.70	12.90	16.60	7.90%	9.35%	10.60%	
	3100	Total: Mechanical & Electrical	↓	35	44.50	55.50	23.50%	26.50%	29.50%	
	9000	Per pupil, total cost	Ea.	13,800	18,100	24,400				
78	0010	**SCHOOLS Senior High**	S.F.	113	139	174				78
	0020	Total project costs	C.F.	6.85	9.85	16.25				
	1800	Equipment	S.F.	2.98	7	9.75	1.88%	2.91%	4.56%	
	2720	Plumbing		6.35	9.55	17.45	5.60%	6.90%	8.30%	
	2770	Heating, ventilating, air conditioning		13	14.85	22.50	8.95%	11.60%	15%	
	2900	Electrical		11.45	14.85	22.50	8.65%	10.20%	12.25%	
	3100	Total: Mechanical & Electrical	↓	37.50	44	74	23.50%	26.50%	28.50%	
	9000	Per pupil, total cost	Ea.	10,700	21,700	27,200				
80	0010	**SCHOOLS Vocational**	S.F.	92	133	165				80
	0020	Total project costs	C.F.	5.70	8.20	11.35				
	0500	Masonry	S.F.	5.40	13.30	20.50	3.20%	4.61%	10.95%	
	1800	Equipment		2.87	7.15	9.85	1.24%	3.10%	4.26%	
	2720	Plumbing		5.85	8.75	12.85	5.40%	6.90%	8.55%	
	2770	Heating, ventilating, air conditioning		8.20	15.30	25.50	8.60%	11.90%	14.65%	
	2900	Electrical		9.55	13.05	17.85	8.45%	11%	13.20%	
	3100	Total: Mechanical & Electrical	↓	36	36.50	63	27.50%	29.50%	31%	
	9000	Per pupil, total cost	Ea.	12,800	34,200	51,000				
83	0010	**SPORTS ARENAS**	S.F.	80	107	165				83
	0020	Total project costs	C.F.	4.35	7.80	10.05				
	2720	Plumbing	S.F.	4.65	7.05	14.90	4.35%	6.35%	9.40%	
	2770	Heating, ventilating, air conditioning		10	11.85	16.45	8.80%	10.20%	13.55%	
	2900	Electrical		8.35	11.35	14.65	8.60%	9.90%	12.25%	
	3100	Total: Mechanical & Electrical	↓	21	37	49.50	21.50%	25%	27.50%	
85	0010	**SUPERMARKETS**	S.F.	74	85.50	101				85
	0020	Total project costs	C.F.	4.13	4.99	7.55				
	2720	Plumbing	S.F.	4.14	5.20	6.05	5.40%	6%	7.45%	
	2770	Heating, ventilating, air conditioning		6.10	8.10	9.85	8.60%	8.65%	9.60%	
	2900	Electrical		9.30	10.60	12.60	10.40%	12.45%	13.60%	
	3100	Total: Mechanical & Electrical	↓	23.50	25.50	34	23.50%	27.50%	28.50%	
86	0010	**SWIMMING POOLS**	S.F.	120	201	430				86
	0020	Total project costs	C.F.	9.60	12	13.10				
	2720	Plumbing	S.F.	11.10	12.70	17	4.80%	9.70%	20.50%	
	2900	Electrical		9	14.60	21.50	5.75%	6.95%	7.60%	
	3100	Total: Mechanical & Electrical	↓	22	56	76.50	11.15%	14.10%	23.50%	
87	0010	**TELEPHONE EXCHANGES**	S.F.	159	227	296				87
	0020	Total project costs	C.F.	9.90	15.90	22				
	2720	Plumbing	S.F.	6.70	10.40	15.20	4.52%	5.80%	6.90%	
	2770	Heating, ventilating, air conditioning		15.60	31.50	39	11.80%	16.05%	18.40%	

		50 17 00 | S.F. Costs	UNIT	UNIT COSTS			% OF TOTAL			
				1/4	MEDIAN	3/4	1/4	MEDIAN	3/4	
87	2900	Electrical	S.F.	16.20	25.50	45.50	10.90%	14%	17.85%	87
	3100	Total: Mechanical & Electrical	↓	48	91	128	29.50%	33.50%	44.50%	
91	0010	**THEATERS**	S.F.	100	129	189				91
	0020	Total project costs	C.F.	4.63	6.85	10.05				
	2720	Plumbing	S.F.	3.34	3.62	14.80	2.92%	4.70%	6.80%	
	2770	Heating, ventilating, air conditioning		9.75	11.80	14.60	8%	12.25%	13.40%	
	2900	Electrical		8.75	11.80	24	8.05%	9.35%	12.25%	
	3100	Total: Mechanical & Electrical	↓	22.50	30.50	36	21.50%	25.50%	27.50%	
94	0010	**TOWN HALLS City Halls & Municipal Buildings**	S.F.	112	142	185				94
	0020	Total project costs	C.F.	10.20	11.95	17.20				
	2720	Plumbing	S.F.	4.67	8.75	15.55	4.31%	5.95%	7.95%	
	2770	Heating, ventilating, air conditioning		8.45	16.75	24.50	7.05%	9.05%	13.45%	
	2900	Electrical		10.60	14.75	19.95	8.05%	9.45%	11.65%	
	3100	Total: Mechanical & Electrical	↓	37	46.50	71.50	22%	26.50%	31%	
97	0010	**WAREHOUSES & Storage Buildings**	S.F.	41.50	60.50	88.50				97
	0020	Total project costs	C.F.	2.19	3.42	5.65				
	0100	Site work	S.F.	4.31	8.55	12.95	6.05%	12.95%	19.85%	
	0500	Masonry		2.47	5.95	12.80	3.73%	7.40%	12.30%	
	1800	Equipment		.67	1.45	8.10	.72%	1.69%	5.55%	
	2720	Plumbing		1.39	2.50	4.67	2.90%	4.80%	6.55%	
	2730	Heating, ventilating, air conditioning		1.59	4.48	6	2.41%	5%	8.90%	
	2900	Electrical		2.47	4.65	7.70	5.15%	7.20%	10.10%	
	3100	Total: Mechanical & Electrical	↓	6.90	10.55	21	13.30%	19.10%	26%	
99	0010	**WAREHOUSE & OFFICES Combination**	S.F.	51.50	68.50	93.50				99
	0020	Total project costs	C.F.	2.63	3.81	5.65				
	1800	Equipment	S.F.	.89	1.72	2.56	.52%	1.20%	2.40%	
	2720	Plumbing		1.98	3.45	5.15	3.74%	4.76%	6.30%	
	2770	Heating, ventilating, air conditioning		3.13	4.89	6.85	5%	5.65%	10.05%	
	2900	Electrical		3.44	5.10	8.10	5.75%	8%	10%	
	3100	Total: Mechanical & Electrical	↓	9.55	14.80	23.50	14.40%	19.95%	24.50%	

Square Foot Project Size Modifier

One factor that affects the S.F. cost of a particular building is the size. In general, for buildings built to the same specifications in the same locality, the larger building will have the lower S.F. cost. This is due mainly to the decreasing contribution of the exterior walls plus the economy of scale usually achievable in larger buildings. The Area Conversion Scale shown below will give a factor to convert costs for the typical size building to an adjusted cost for the particular project.

The Square Foot Base Size lists the median costs, most typical project size in our accumulated data, and the range in size of the projects.

The Size Factor for your project is determined by dividing your project area in S.F. by the typical project size for the particular Building Type. With this factor, enter the Area Conversion Scale at the appropriate Size Factor and determine the appropriate cost multiplier for your building size.

Example: Determine the cost per S.F. for a 100,000 S.F. Mid-rise apartment building.

$$\frac{\text{Proposed building area} = 100,000 \text{ S.F.}}{\text{Typical size from below} = 50,000 \text{ S.F.}} = 2.00$$

Enter Area Conversion scale at 2.0, intersect curve, read horizontally the appropriate cost multiplier of .94. Size adjusted cost becomes .94 x $111.00 = $104.00 based on national average costs.

Note: For Size Factors less than .50, the Cost Multiplier is 1.1
For Size Factors greater than 3.5, the Cost Multiplier is .90

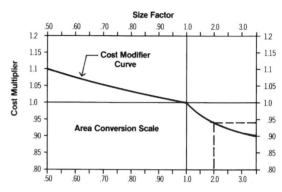

Square Foot Base Size

Building Type	Median Cost per S.F.	Typical Size Gross S.F.	Typical Range Gross S.F.	Building Type	Median Cost per S.F.	Typical Size Gross S.F.	Typical Range Gross S.F.
Apartments, Low Rise	$ 87.00	21,000	9,700 - 37,200	Jails	$ 267.00	40,000	5,500 - 145,000
Apartments, Mid Rise	111.00	50,000	32,000 - 100,000	Libraries	168.00	12,000	7,000 - 31,000
Apartments, High Rise	120.00	145,000	95,000 - 600,000	Living, Assisted	142.00	32,300	23,500 - 50,300
Auditoriums	148.00	25,000	7,600 - 39,000	Medical Clinics	151.00	7,200	4,200 - 15,700
Auto Sales	109.00	20,000	10,800 - 28,600	Medical Offices	143.00	6,000	4,000 - 15,000
Banks	197.00	4,200	2,500 - 7,500	Motels	106.00	40,000	15,800 - 120,000
Churches	135.00	17,000	2,000 - 42,000	Nursing Homes	147.00	23,000	15,000 - 37,000
Clubs, Country	137.00	6,500	4,500 - 15,000	Offices, Low Rise	125.00	20,000	5,000 - 80,000
Clubs, Social	131.00	10,000	6,000 - 13,500	Offices, Mid Rise	124.00	120,000	20,000 - 300,000
Clubs, YMCA	154.00	28,300	12,800 - 39,400	Offices, High Rise	158.00	260,000	120,000 - 800,000
Colleges (Class)	156.00	50,000	15,000 - 150,000	Police Stations	197.00	10,500	4,000 - 19,000
Colleges (Science Lab)	251.00	45,600	16,600 - 80,000	Post Offices	146.00	12,400	6,800 - 30,000
College (Student Union)	185.00	33,400	16,000 - 85,000	Power Plants	1075.00	7,500	1,000 - 20,000
Community Center	139.00	9,400	5,300 - 16,700	Religious Education	125.00	9,000	6,000 - 12,000
Court Houses	192.00	32,400	17,800 - 106,000	Research	207.00	19,000	6,300 - 45,000
Dept. Stores	81.50	90,000	44,000 - 122,000	Restaurants	179.00	4,400	2,800 - 6,000
Dormitories, Low Rise	158.00	25,000	10,000 - 95,000	Retail Stores	87.00	7,200	4,000 - 17,600
Dormitories, Mid Rise	183.00	85,000	20,000 - 200,000	Schools, Elementary	132.00	41,000	24,500 - 55,000
Factories	79.00	26,400	12,900 - 50,000	Schools, Jr. High	134.00	92,000	52,000 - 119,000
Fire Stations	145.00	5,800	4,000 - 8,700	Schools, Sr. High	139.00	101,000	50,500 - 175,000
Fraternity Houses	136.00	12,500	8,200 - 14,800	Schools, Vocational	133.00	37,000	20,500 - 82,000
Funeral Homes	151.00	10,000	4,000 - 20,000	Sports Arenas	107.00	15,000	5,000 - 40,000
Garages, Commercial	97.00	9,300	5,000 - 13,600	Supermarkets	85.50	44,000	12,000 - 60,000
Garages, Municipal	123.00	8,300	4,500 - 12,600	Swimming Pools	201.00	20,000	10,000 - 32,000
Garages, Parking	52.50	163,000	76,400 - 225,300	Telephone Exchange	227.00	4,500	1,200 - 10,600
Gymnasiums	133.00	19,200	11,600 - 41,000	Theaters	129.00	10,500	8,800 - 17,500
Hospitals	240.00	55,000	27,200 - 125,000	Town Halls	142.00	10,800	4,800 - 23,400
House (Elderly)	120.00	37,000	21,000 - 66,000	Warehouses	60.50	25,000	8,000 - 72,000
Housing (Public)	110.00	36,000	14,400 - 74,400	Warehouse & Office	68.50	25,000	8,000 - 72,000
Ice Rinks	159.00	29,000	27,200 - 33,600				

Abbreviations

A	Area Square Feet; Ampere	BTUH	BTU per Hour	Cwt.	100 Pounds
ABS	Acrylonitrile Butadiene Stryrene; Asbestos Bonded Steel	B.U.R.	Built-up Roofing	C.W.X.	Cool White Deluxe
A.C.	Alternating Current;	BX	Interlocked Armored Cable	C.Y.	Cubic Yard (27 cubic feet)
	Air-Conditioning;	°C	degree centegrade	C.Y./Hr.	Cubic Yard per Hour
	Asbestos Cement;	c	Conductivity, Copper Sweat	Cyl.	Cylinder
	Plywood Grade A & C	C	Hundred; Centigrade	d	Penny (nail size)
A.C.I.	American Concrete Institute	C/C	Center to Center, Cedar on Cedar	D	Deep; Depth; Discharge
AD	Plywood, Grade A & D	C-C	Center to Center	Dis., Disch.	Discharge
Addit.	Additional	Cab.	Cabinet	Db.	Decibel
Adj.	Adjustable	Cair.	Air Tool Laborer	Dbl.	Double
af	Audio-frequency	Calc	Calculated	DC	Direct Current
A.G.A.	American Gas Association	Cap.	Capacity	DDC	Direct Digital Control
Agg.	Aggregate	Carp.	Carpenter	Demob.	Demobilization
A.H.	Ampere Hours	C.B.	Circuit Breaker	d.f.u.	Drainage Fixture Units
A hr.	Ampere-hour	C.C.A.	Chromate Copper Arsenate	D.H.	Double Hung
A.H.U.	Air Handling Unit	C.C.F.	Hundred Cubic Feet	DHW	Domestic Hot Water
A.I.A.	American Institute of Architects	cd	Candela	DI	Ductile Iron
AIC	Ampere Interrupting Capacity	cd/sf	Candela per Square Foot	Diag.	Diagonal
Allow.	Allowance	CD	Grade of Plywood Face & Back	Diam., Dia	Diameter
alt.	Altitude	CDX	Plywood, Grade C & D, exterior glue	Distrib.	Distribution
Alum.	Aluminum			Div.	Division
a.m.	Ante Meridiem	Cefi.	Cement Finisher	Dk.	Deck
Amp.	Ampere	Cem.	Cement	D.L.	Dead Load; Diesel
Anod.	Anodized	CF	Hundred Feet	DLH	Deep Long Span Bar Joist
Approx.	Approximate	C.F.	Cubic Feet	Do.	Ditto
Apt.	Apartment	CFM	Cubic Feet per Minute	Dp.	Depth
Asb.	Asbestos	c.g.	Center of Gravity	D.P.S.T.	Double Pole, Single Throw
A.S.B.C.	American Standard Building Code	CHW	Chilled Water; Commercial Hot Water	Dr.	Drive
Asbe.	Asbestos Worker			Drink.	Drinking
ASCE.	American Society of Civil Engineers	C.I.	Cast Iron	D.S.	Double Strength
A.S.H.R.A.E.	American Society of Heating, Refrig. & AC Engineers	C.I.P.	Cast in Place	D.S.A.	Double Strength A Grade
		Circ.	Circuit	D.S.B.	Double Strength B Grade
A.S.M.E.	American Society of Mechanical Engineers	C.L.	Carload Lot	Dty.	Duty
		Clab.	Common Laborer	DWV	Drain Waste Vent
A.S.T.M.	American Society for Testing and Materials	Clam	Common maintenance laborer	DX	Deluxe White, Direct Expansion
		C.L.F.	Hundred Linear Feet	dyn	Dyne
Attchmt.	Attachment	CLF	Current Limiting Fuse	e	Eccentricity
Avg., Ave.	Average	CLP	Cross Linked Polyethylene	E	Equipment Only; East
A.W.G.	American Wire Gauge	cm	Centimeter	Ea.	Each
AWWA	American Water Works Assoc.	CMP	Corr. Metal Pipe	E.B.	Encased Burial
Bbl.	Barrel	C.M.U.	Concrete Masonry Unit	Econ.	Economy
B&B	Grade B and Better; Balled & Burlapped	CN	Change Notice	E.C.Y	Embankment Cubic Yards
		Col.	Column	EDP	Electronic Data Processing
B.&S.	Bell and Spigot	CO₂	Carbon Dioxide	EIFS	Exterior Insulation Finish System
B.&W.	Black and White	Comb.	Combination	E.D.R.	Equiv. Direct Radiation
b.c.c.	Body-centered Cubic	Compr.	Compressor	Eq.	Equation
B.C.Y.	Bank Cubic Yards	Conc.	Concrete	EL	elevation
BE	Bevel End	Cont.	Continuous; Continued, Container	Elec.	Electrician; Electrical
B.F.	Board Feet	Corr.	Corrugated	Elev.	Elevator; Elevating
Bg. cem.	Bag of Cement	Cos	Cosine	EMT	Electrical Metallic Conduit; Thin Wall Conduit
BHP	Boiler Horsepower; Brake Horsepower	Cot	Cotangent		
		Cov.	Cover	Eng.	Engine, Engineered
B.I.	Black Iron	C/P	Cedar on Paneling	EPDM	Ethylene Propylene Diene Monomer
Bit., Bitum.	Bituminous	CPA	Control Point Adjustment		
Bit., Conc.	Bituminous Concrete	Cplg.	Coupling	EPS	Expanded Polystyrene
Bk.	Backed	C.P.M.	Critical Path Method	Eqhv.	Equip. Oper., Heavy
Bkrs.	Breakers	CPVC	Chlorinated Polyvinyl Chloride	Eqlt.	Equip. Oper., Light
Bldg.	Building	C.Pr.	Hundred Pair	Eqmd.	Equip. Oper., Medium
Blk.	Block	CRC	Cold Rolled Channel	Eqmm.	Equip. Oper., Master Mechanic
Bm.	Beam	Creos.	Creosote	Eqol.	Equip. Oper., Oilers
Boil.	Boilermaker	Crpt.	Carpet & Linoleum Layer	Equip.	Equipment
B.P.M.	Blows per Minute	CRT	Cathode-ray Tube	ERW	Electric Resistance Welded
BR	Bedroom	CS	Carbon Steel, Constant Shear Bar Joist	E.S.	Energy Saver
Brg.	Bearing			Est.	Estimated
Brhe.	Bricklayer Helper	Csc	Cosecant	esu	Electrostatic Units
Bric.	Bricklayer	C.S.F.	Hundred Square Feet	E.W.	Each Way
Brk.	Brick	CSI	Construction Specifications Institute	EWT	Entering Water Temperature
Brng.	Bearing			Excav.	Excavation
Brs.	Brass	C.T.	Current Transformer	Exp.	Expansion, Exposure
Brz.	Bronze	CTS	Copper Tube Size	Ext.	Exterior
Bsn.	Basin	Cu	Copper, Cubic	Extru.	Extrusion
Btr.	Better	Cu. Ft.	Cubic Foot	f.	Fiber stress
Btu	British Thermal Unit	cw	Continuous Wave	F	Fahrenheit; Female; Fill
		C.W.	Cool White; Cold Water	Fab.	Fabricated

747

FBGS	Fiberglass	H.P.	Horsepower; High Pressure	LE	Lead Equivalent
F.C.	Footcandles	H.P.F.	High Power Factor	LED	Light Emitting Diode
f.c.c.	Face-centered Cubic	Hr.	Hour	L.F.	Linear Foot
f'c.	Compressive Stress in Concrete;	Hrs./Day	Hours per Day	L.F. Nose	Linear Foot of Stair Nosing
	Extreme Compressive Stress	HSC	High Short Circuit	L.F. Rsr	Linear Foot of Stair Riser
F.E.	Front End	Ht.	Height	Lg.	Long; Length; Large
FEP	Fluorinated Ethylene Propylene	Htg.	Heating	L & H	Light and Heat
	(Teflon)	Htrs.	Heaters	LH	Long Span Bar Joist
F.G.	Flat Grain	HVAC	Heating, Ventilation & Air-	L.H.	Labor Hours
F.H.A.	Federal Housing Administration		Conditioning	L.L.	Live Load
Fig.	Figure	Hvy.	Heavy	L.L.D.	Lamp Lumen Depreciation
Fin.	Finished	HW	Hot Water	lm	Lumen
Fixt.	Fixture	Hyd.;Hydr.	Hydraulic	lm/sf	Lumen per Square Foot
Fl. Oz.	Fluid Ounces	Hz.	Hertz (cycles)	lm/W	Lumen per Watt
Flr.	Floor	I.	Moment of Inertia	L.O.A.	Length Over All
F.M.	Frequency Modulation;	IBC	International Building Code	log	Logarithm
	Factory Mutual	I.C.	Interrupting Capacity	L-O-L	Lateralolet
Fmg.	Framing	ID	Inside Diameter	long.	longitude
Fdn.	Foundation	I.D.	Inside Dimension; Identification	L.P.	Liquefied Petroleum; Low Pressure
Fori.	Foreman, Inside	I.F.	Inside Frosted	L.P.F.	Low Power Factor
Foro.	Foreman, Outside	I.M.C.	Intermediate Metal Conduit	LR	Long Radius
Fount.	Fountain	In.	Inch	L.S.	Lump Sum
fpm	Feet per Minute	Incan.	Incandescent	Lt.	Light
FPT	Female Pipe Thread	Incl.	Included; Including	Lt. Ga.	Light Gauge
Fr.	Frame	Int.	Interior	L.T.L.	Less than Truckload Lot
F.R.	Fire Rating	Inst.	Installation	Lt. Wt.	Lightweight
FRK	Foil Reinforced Kraft	Insul.	Insulation/Insulated	L.V.	Low Voltage
FRP	Fiberglass Reinforced Plastic	I.P.	Iron Pipe	M	Thousand; Material; Male;
FS	Forged Steel	I.P.S.	Iron Pipe Size		Light Wall Copper Tubing
FSC	Cast Body; Cast Switch Box	I.P.T.	Iron Pipe Threaded	M²CA	Meters Squared Contact Area
Ft.	Foot; Feet	I.W.	Indirect Waste	m/hr.; M.H.	Man-hour
Ftng.	Fitting	J	Joule	mA	Milliampere
Ftg.	Footing	J.I.C.	Joint Industrial Council	Mach.	Machine
Ft lb.	Foot Pound	K	Thousand; Thousand Pounds;	Mag. Str.	Magnetic Starter
Furn.	Furniture		Heavy Wall Copper Tubing, Kelvin	Maint.	Maintenance
FVNR	Full Voltage Non-Reversing	K.A.H.	Thousand Amp. Hours	Marb.	Marble Setter
FXM	Female by Male	KCMIL	Thousand Circular Mils	Mat; Mat'l.	Material
Fy.	Minimum Yield Stress of Steel	KD	Knock Down	Max.	Maximum
g	Gram	K.D.A.T.	Kiln Dried After Treatment	MBF	Thousand Board Feet
G	Gauss	kg	Kilogram	MBH	Thousand BTU's per hr.
Ga.	Gauge	kG	Kilogauss	MC	Metal Clad Cable
Gal., gal.	Gallon	kgf	Kilogram Force	M.C.F.	Thousand Cubic Feet
gpm, GPM	Gallon per Minute	kHz	Kilohertz	M.C.F.M.	Thousand Cubic Feet per Minute
Galv.	Galvanized	Kip.	1000 Pounds	M.C.M.	Thousand Circular Mils
Gen.	General	KJ	Kiljoule	M.C.P.	Motor Circuit Protector
G.F.I.	Ground Fault Interrupter	K.L.	Effective Length Factor	MD	Medium Duty
Glaz.	Glazier	K.L.F.	Kips per Linear Foot	M.D.O.	Medium Density Overlaid
GPD	Gallons per Day	Km	Kilometer	Med.	Medium
GPH	Gallons per Hour	K.S.F.	Kips per Square Foot	MF	Thousand Feet
GPM	Gallons per Minute	K.S.I.	Kips per Square Inch	M.F.B.M.	Thousand Feet Board Measure
GR	Grade	kV	Kilovolt	Mfg.	Manufacturing
Gran.	Granular	kVA	Kilovolt Ampere	Mfrs.	Manufacturers
Grnd.	Ground	K.V.A.R.	Kilovar (Reactance)	mg	Milligram
H	High Henry	KW	Kilowatt	MGD	Million Gallons per Day
H.C.	High Capacity	KWh	Kilowatt-hour	MGPH	Thousand Gallons per Hour
H.D.	Heavy Duty; High Density	L	Labor Only; Length; Long;	MH, M.H.	Manhole; Metal Halide; Man-Hour
H.D.O.	High Density Overlaid		Medium Wall Copper Tubing	MHz	Megahertz
H.D.P.E.	high density polyethelene	Lab.	Labor	Mi.	Mile
Hdr.	Header	lat	Latitude	MI	Malleable Iron; Mineral Insulated
Hdwe.	Hardware	Lath.	Lather	mm	Millimeter
Help.	Helper Average	Lav.	Lavatory	Mill.	Millwright
HEPA	High Efficiency Particulate Air	lb.; #	Pound	Min., min.	Minimum, minute
	Filter	L.B.	Load Bearing; L Conduit Body	Misc.	Miscellaneous
Hg	Mercury	L. & E.	Labor & Equipment	ml	Milliliter, Mainline
HIC	High Interrupting Capacity	lb./hr.	Pounds per Hour	M.L.F.	Thousand Linear Feet
HM	Hollow Metal	lb./L.F.	Pounds per Linear Foot	Mo.	Month
HMWPE	high molecular weight	lbf/sq.in.	Pound-force per Square Inch	Mobil.	Mobilization
	polyethylene	L.C.L.	Less than Carload Lot	Mog.	Mogul Base
H.O.	High Output	L.C.Y.	Loose Cubic Yard	MPH	Miles per Hour
Horiz.	Horizontal	Ld.	Load	MPT	Male Pipe Thread

MRT	Mile Round Trip	Pl.	Plate	S.F.C.A.	Square Foot Contact Area
ms	Millisecond	Plah.	Plasterer Helper	S.F. Flr.	Square Foot of Floor
M.S.F.	Thousand Square Feet	Plas.	Plasterer	S.F.G.	Square Foot of Ground
Mstz.	Mosaic & Terrazzo Worker	Pluh.	Plumbers Helper	S.F. Hor.	Square Foot Horizontal
M.S.Y.	Thousand Square Yards	Plum.	Plumber	S.F.R.	Square Feet of Radiation
Mtd., mtd.	Mounted	Ply.	Plywood	S.F. Shlf.	Square Foot of Shelf
Mthe.	Mosaic & Terrazzo Helper	p.m.	Post Meridiem	S4S	Surface 4 Sides
Mtng.	Mounting	Pntd.	Painted	Shee.	Sheet Metal Worker
Mult.	Multi; Multiply	Pord.	Painter, Ordinary	Sin.	Sine
M.V.A.	Million Volt Amperes	pp	Pages	Skwk.	Skilled Worker
M.V.A.R.	Million Volt Amperes Reactance	PP, PPL	Polypropylene	SL	Saran Lined
MV	Megavolt	P.P.M.	Parts per Million	S.L.	Slimline
MW	Megawatt	Pr.	Pair	Sldr.	Solder
MXM	Male by Male	P.E.S.B.	Pre-engineered Steel Building	SLH	Super Long Span Bar Joist
MYD	Thousand Yards	Prefab.	Prefabricated	S.N.	Solid Neutral
N	Natural; North	Prefin.	Prefinished	S-O-L	Socketolet
nA	Nanoampere	Prop.	Propelled	sp	Standpipe
NA	Not Available; Not Applicable	PSF, psf	Pounds per Square Foot	S.P.	Static Pressure; Single Pole; Self-Propelled
N.B.C.	National Building Code	PSI, psi	Pounds per Square Inch		
NC	Normally Closed	PSIG	Pounds per Square Inch Gauge	Spri.	Sprinkler Installer
N.E.M.A.	National Electrical Manufacturers Assoc.	PSP	Plastic Sewer Pipe	spwg	Static Pressure Water Gauge
		Pspr.	Painter, Spray	S.P.D.T.	Single Pole, Double Throw
NEHB	Bolted Circuit Breaker to 600V.	Psst.	Painter, Structural Steel	SPF	Spruce Pine Fir
N.L.B.	Non-Load-Bearing	P.T.	Potential Transformer	S.P.S.T.	Single Pole, Single Throw
NM	Non-Metallic Cable	P. & T.	Pressure & Temperature	SPT	Standard Pipe Thread
nm	Nanometer	Ptd.	Painted	Sq.	Square; 100 Square Feet
No.	Number	Ptns.	Partitions	Sq. Hd.	Square Head
NO	Normally Open	Pu	Ultimate Load	Sq. In.	Square Inch
N.O.C.	Not Otherwise Classified	PVC	Polyvinyl Chloride	S.S.	Single Strength; Stainless Steel
Nose.	Nosing	Pvmt.	Pavement	S.S.B.	Single Strength B Grade
N.P.T.	National Pipe Thread	Pwr.	Power	sst, ss	Stainless Steel
NQOD	Combination Plug-on/Bolt on Circuit Breaker to 240V.	Q	Quantity Heat Flow	Sswk.	Structural Steel Worker
		Qt.	Quart	Sswl.	Structural Steel Welder
N.R.C.	Noise Reduction Coefficient/ Nuclear Regulator Commission	Quan., Qty.	Quantity	St.;Stl.	Steel
		Q.C.	Quick Coupling	S.T.C.	Sound Transmission Coefficient
N.R.S.	Non Rising Stem	r	Radius of Gyration	Std.	Standard
ns	Nanosecond	R	Resistance	Stg.	Staging
nW	Nanowatt	R.C.P.	Reinforced Concrete Pipe	STK	Select Tight Knot
OB	Opposing Blade	Rect.	Rectangle	STP	Standard Temperature & Pressure
OC	On Center	Reg.	Regular	Stpi.	Steamfitter, Pipefitter
OD	Outside Diameter	Reinf.	Reinforced	Str.	Strength; Starter; Straight
O.D.	Outside Dimension	Req'd.	Required	Strd.	Stranded
ODS	Overhead Distribution System	Res.	Resistant	Struct.	Structural
O.G.	Ogee	Resi.	Residential	Sty.	Story
O.H.	Overhead	Rgh.	Rough	Subj.	Subject
O&P	Overhead and Profit	RGS	Rigid Galvanized Steel	Subs.	Subcontractors
Oper.	Operator	R.H.W.	Rubber, Heat & Water Resistant; Residential Hot Water	Surf.	Surface
Opng.	Opening			Sw.	Switch
Orna.	Ornamental	rms	Root Mean Square	Swbd.	Switchboard
OSB	Oriented Strand Board	Rnd.	Round	S.Y.	Square Yard
O.S.&Y.	Outside Screw and Yoke	Rodm.	Rodman	Syn.	Synthetic
Ovhd.	Overhead	Rofc.	Roofer, Composition	S.Y.P.	Southern Yellow Pine
OWG	Oil, Water or Gas	Rofp.	Roofer, Precast	Sys.	System
Oz.	Ounce	Rohe.	Roofer Helpers (Composition)	t.	Thickness
P.	Pole; Applied Load; Projection	Rots.	Roofer, Tile & Slate	T	Temperature; Ton
p.	Page	R.O.W.	Right of Way	Tan	Tangent
Pape.	Paperhanger	RPM	Revolutions per Minute	T.C.	Terra Cotta
P.A.P.R.	Powered Air Purifying Respirator	R.S.	Rapid Start	T & C	Threaded and Coupled
PAR	Parabolic Reflector	Rsr	Riser	T.D.	Temperature Difference
Pc., Pcs.	Piece, Pieces	RT	Round Trip	Tdd	Telecommunications Device for the Deaf
P.C.	Portland Cement; Power Connector	S.	Suction; Single Entrance; South		
P.C.F.	Pounds per Cubic Foot	SC	Screw Cover	T.E.M.	Transmission Electron Microscopy
P.C.M.	Phase Contrast Microscopy	SCFM	Standard Cubic Feet per Minute	TFE	Tetrafluoroethylene (Teflon)
P.E.	Professional Engineer; Porcelain Enamel; Polyethylene; Plain End	Scaf.	Scaffold	T. & G.	Tongue & Groove; Tar & Gravel
		Sch., Sched.	Schedule		
		S.C.R.	Modular Brick	Th., Thk.	Thick
Perf.	Perforated	S.D.	Sound Deadening	Thn.	Thin
PEX	Cross linked polyethylene	S.D.R.	Standard Dimension Ratio	Thrded	Threaded
Ph.	Phase	S.E.	Surfaced Edge	Tilf.	Tile Layer, Floor
P.I.	Pressure Injected	Sel.	Select	Tilh.	Tile Layer, Helper
Pile.	Pile Driver	S.E.R., S.E.U.	Service Entrance Cable	THHN	Nylon Jacketed Wire
Pkg.	Package	S.F.	Square Foot	THW.	Insulated Strand Wire

Abbreviations

THWN	Nylon Jacketed Wire	USP	United States Primed	Wrck.	Wrecker		
T.L.	Truckload	UTP	Unshielded Twisted Pair	W.S.P.	Water, Steam, Petroleum		
T.M.	Track Mounted	V	Volt	WT., Wt.	Weight		
Tot.	Total	V.A.	Volt Amperes	WWF	Welded Wire Fabric		
T-O-L	Threadolet	V.C.T.	Vinyl Composition Tile	XFER	Transfer		
T.S.	Trigger Start	VAV	Variable Air Volume	XFMR	Transformer		
Tr.	Trade	VC	Veneer Core	XHD	Extra Heavy Duty		
Transf.	Transformer	Vent.	Ventilation	XHHW,	Cross-Linked Polyethylene Wire		
Trhv.	Truck Driver, Heavy	Vert.	Vertical	XLPE	Insulation		
Trlr	Trailer	V.F.	Vinyl Faced	XLP	Cross-linked Polyethylene		
Trlt.	Truck Driver, Light	V.G.	Vertical Grain	Y	Wye		
TTY	Teletypewriter	V.H.F.	Very High Frequency	yd	Yard		
TV	Television	VHO	Very High Output	yr	Year		
T.W.	Thermoplastic Water Resistant	Vib.	Vibrating	Δ	Delta		
	Wire	V.L.F.	Vertical Linear Foot	%	Percent		
UCI	Uniform Construction Index	Vol.	Volume	~	Approximately		
UF	Underground Feeder	VRP	Vinyl Reinforced Polyester	Ø	Phase; diameter		
UGND	Underground Feeder	W	Wire; Watt; Wide; West	@	At		
U.H.F.	Ultra High Frequency	w/	With	#	Pound; Number		
U.I.	United Inch	W.C.	Water Column; Water Closet	<	Less Than		
U.L.	Underwriters Laboratory	W.F.	Wide Flange	>	Greater Than		
Uld.	unloading	W.G.	Water Gauge	Z	zone		
Unfin.	Unfinished	Wldg.	Welding				
URD	Underground Residential	W. Mile	Wire Mile				
	Distribution	W-O-L	Weldolet				
US	United States	W.R.	Water Resistant				

Index

Index

Index

Index

Index

Division Notes

	CREW	DAILY OUTPUT	LABOR-HOURS	UNIT	2012 BARE COSTS				TOTAL INCL O&P
					MAT.	LABOR	EQUIP.	TOTAL	

Division Notes

		CREW	DAILY OUTPUT	LABOR-HOURS	UNIT	2012 BARE COSTS				TOTAL INCL O&P
						MAT.	LABOR	EQUIP.	TOTAL	

Division Notes

	CREW	DAILY OUTPUT	LABOR-HOURS	UNIT	2012 BARE COSTS				TOTAL INCL O&P
					MAT.	LABOR	EQUIP.	TOTAL	

Division Notes

	CREW	DAILY OUTPUT	LABOR-HOURS	UNIT	2012 BARE COSTS				TOTAL INCL O&P
					MAT.	LABOR	EQUIP.	TOTAL	

Division Notes

	CREW	DAILY OUTPUT	LABOR-HOURS	UNIT	2012 BARE COSTS				TOTAL INCL O&P
					MAT.	LABOR	EQUIP.	TOTAL	

Reed Construction Data/RSMeans— a tradition of excellence in construction cost information and services since 1942

For more information visit the RSMeans website at **www.rsmeans.com**

Unit prices according to the latest MasterFormat!

Book Selection Guide The following table provides definitive information on the content of each cost data publication. The number of lines of data provided in each unit price or assemblies division, as well as the number of reference tables and crews, is listed for each book. The presence of other elements such as equipment rental costs, historical cost indexes, city cost indexes, square foot models, or cross-referenced indexes is also indicated. You can use the table to help select the RSMeans book that has the quantity and type of information you most need in your work.

Unit Cost Divisions	Building Construction	Mechanical	Electrical	Commercial Renovation	Square Foot	Site Work Landsc.	Green Building	Interior	Concrete Masonry	Open Shop	Heavy Construction	Light Commercial	Facilities Construction	Plumbing	Residential
1	571	392	407	495		515	124	319	461	570	505	231	1001	408	174
2	745	264	83	684		965	180	363	219	742	704	439	1174	288	240
3	1539	222	212	906		1342	874	313	1847	1539	1481	386	1567	189	366
4	902	24	0	698		701	183	573	1137	878	593	490	1149	0	405
5	1912	263	168	1022		871	1799	1021	834	1903	1118	893	1905	339	724
6	1986	67	69	1573		401	534	1294	300	1965	380	1667	1602	22	2179
7	1456	208	125	1484		555	778	543	505	1453	26	1161	1516	217	915
8	2081	61	10	2277		296	1155	1765	658	2036	0	1661	2495	0	1412
9	1875	72	26	1670		306	444	1966	386	1817	15	1589	2111	54	1400
10	988	17	10	612		215	27	808	159	988	29	494	1074	231	221
11	1029	208	166	493		126	54	885	28	1014	0	235	1049	169	110
12	562	0	2	318		248	150	1707	12	551	19	364	1757	23	317
13	732	117	111	247		347	128	249	69	731	261	80	760	72	79
14	280	36	0	229		28	0	259	0	279	0	12	299	21	6
21	78	0	16	30		0	0	249	0	78	0	60	430	436	224
22	1144	7289	155	1108		1536	1100	609	20	1106	1660	834	7150	9008	662
23	1201	7048	605	784		157	900	691	38	1121	110	688	5126	1870	411
26	1249	496	9967	1010		763	572	1085	55	1237	539	1095	9903	441	559
27	67	0	261	34		9	0	59	0	67	35	48	263	0	4
28	96	58	124	71		0	21	78	0	99	0	40	139	44	25
31	1477	735	608	798		3186	290	7	1208	1421	3257	600	1540	660	606
32	767	54	0	838		4324	343	359	274	738	1797	380	1645	166	428
33	506	1008	465	205		1964	41	0	228	505	1887	117	1549	1197	115
34	109	0	20	4		144	0	0	31	64	122	0	129	0	0
35	18	0	0	0		166	0	0	0	18	281	0	83	0	0
41	52	0	0	24		7	0	22	0	52	30	0	59	14	0
44	75	83	0	0		0	0	0	0	0	0	0	75	75	0
46	23	16	0	0		162	149	0	0	23	152	0	33	33	0
48	0	0	0	0		0	19	0	0	0	0	0	0	0	0
Totals	23520	18738	13610	17614		19334	9865	15224	8469	22995	15001	13564	47583	15977	11582

Assem Div	Building Construction	Mechanical	Electrical	Commercial Renovation	Square Foot	Site Work Landscape	Assemblies	Green Building	Interior	Concrete Masonry	Heavy Construction	Light Commercial	Facilities Construction	Plumbing	Asm Div	Residential
A		15	0	188	150	577	598	0	0	536	571	154	24	0	1	368
B		0	0	825	2472	0	5572	56	330	1914	368	2032	143	0	2	211
C		0	0	647	864	0	1233	0	1558	146	0	763	245	0	3	588
D		1067	812	712	1798	72	2425	281	769	0	0	1272	1027	1083	4	859
E		0	0	86	259	0	297	0	5	0	0	256	5	0	5	392
F		0	0	0	122	0	122	0	0	0	0	122	3	0	6	357
G		527	294	317	202	3006	668	0	0	535	1372	200	293	685	7	300
															8	760
															9	80
															10	0
															11	0
															12	0
Totals		1609	1106	2775	5867	3655	10915	337	2662	3131	2311	4799	1740	1768		3915

Reference Section	Building Construction Costs	Mechanical	Electrical	Commercial Renovation	Square Foot	Site Work Landscape	Assem.	Green Building	Interior	Concrete Masonry	Open Shop	Heavy Construction	Light Commercial	Facilities Construction	Plumbing	Resi.
Reference Tables	yes	yes	yes	yes	no	yes	yes	yes	yes	yes	yes	yes	yes	yes	yes	yes
Models					107								46			28
Crews	527	527	527	505		527		527	527	527	503	527	503	505	527	503
Equipment Rental Costs	yes	yes	yes	yes		yes		yes	yes	yes	yes	yes	yes	yes	yes	yes
Historical Cost Indexes	yes	yes	yes	yes	yes	yes	yes	yes	yes	yes	yes	yes	yes	yes	yes	no
City Cost Indexes	yes	yes	yes	yes	yes	yes	yes	yes	yes	yes	yes	yes	yes	yes	yes	yes

RSMeans Building Construction Cost Data 2012

Offers you unchallenged unit price reliability in an easy-to-use format. Whether used for verifying complete, finished estimates or for periodic checks, it supplies more cost facts better and faster than any comparable source. Over 23,000 unit prices have been updated for 2012. The City Cost Indexes and Location Factors cover over 930 areas, for indexing to any project location in North America. Order and get *RSMeans Quarterly Update Service* FREE. You'll have year-long access to the RSMeans Estimating **HOTLINE** FREE with your subscription. Expert assistance when using RSMeans data is just a phone call away.

$177.95 per copy | Available Sept. 2011 | Catalog no. 60012

RSMeans Green Building Cost Data 2012

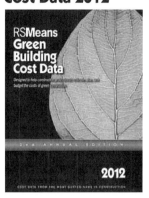

Estimate, plan, and budget the costs of green building for both new commercial construction and renovation work with this first edition of RSMeans Green Building Cost Data. More than 9,000 unit costs for a wide array of green building products plus assemblies costs. Easily identified cross references to LEED and Green Globes building rating systems criteria.

$147.95 per copy | Available Nov. 2011 | Catalog no. 60552

RSMeans Mechanical Cost Data 2012

Total unit and systems price guidance for mechanical construction. . . materials, parts, fittings, and complete labor cost information. Includes prices for piping, heating, air conditioning, ventilation, and all related construction.

Plus new 2012 unit costs for:

- Thousands of installed HVAC/ controls assemblies components
- "On-site" Location Factors for over 930 cities and towns in the U.S. and Canada
- Crews, labor, and equipment

$174.95 per copy | Available Oct. 2011 | Catalog no. 60022

RSMeans Facilities Construction Cost Data 2012

For the maintenance and construction of commercial, industrial, municipal, and institutional properties. Costs are shown for new and remodeling construction and are broken down into materials, labor, equipment, and overhead and profit. Special emphasis is given to sections on mechanical, electrical, furnishings, site work, building maintenance, finish work, and demolition.

More than 47,000 unit costs, plus assemblies costs and a comprehensive Reference Section are included.

$453.95 per copy | Available Nov. 2011 | Catalog no. 60202

RSMeans Square Foot Costs 2012

Accurate and Easy To Use

- **Updated price information** based on nationwide figures from suppliers, estimators, labor experts, and contractors
- "How-to-Use" sections, with **clear examples** of commercial, residential, industrial, and institutional structures
- Realistic graphics, offering true-to-life illustrations of building projects
- Extensive information on using square foot cost data, including sample estimates and alternate pricing methods

$187.95 per copy | Available Oct. 2011 | Catalog no. 60052

RSMeans Commercial Renovation Cost Data 2012

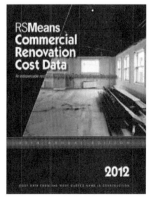

Commercial/Multifamily Residential

Use this valuable tool to estimate commercial and multifamily residential renovation and remodeling.

Includes: New costs for hundreds of unique methods, materials, and conditions that only come up in repair and remodeling, PLUS:

- Unit costs for more than 17,000 construction components
- Installed costs for more than 2,000 assemblies
- More than 930 "on-site" localization factors for the U.S. and Canada

$144.95 per copy | Available Oct. 2011 | Catalog no. 60042

RSMeans Electrical Cost Data 2012

Pricing information for every part of electrical cost planning. More than 13,000 unit and systems costs with design tables; clear specifications and drawings; engineering guides; illustrated estimating procedures; complete labor-hour and materials costs for better scheduling and procurement; and the latest electrical products and construction methods.

- A variety of special electrical systems including cathodic protection
- Costs for maintenance, demolition, HVAC/mechanical, specialties, equipment, and more

$179.95 per copy | Available Oct. 2011 | Catalog no. 60032

RSMeans Assemblies Cost Data 2012

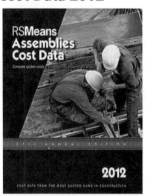

RSMeans Assemblies Cost Data takes the guesswork out of preliminary or conceptual estimates. Now you don't have to try to calculate the assembled cost by working up individual component costs. We've done all the work for you.

Presents detailed illustrations, descriptions, specifications, and costs for every conceivable building assembly—over 350 types in all—arranged in the easy-to-use UNIFORMAT II system. Each illustrated "assembled" cost includes a complete grouping of materials and associated installation costs, including the installing contractor's overhead and profit.

$290.95 per copy | Available Sept. 2011 | Catalog no. 60062

RSMeans Residential Cost Data 2012

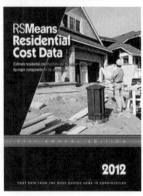

Contains square foot costs for 28 basic home models with the look of today, plus hundreds of custom additions and modifications you can quote right off the page. Includes costs for more than 700 residential systems. Complete with blank estimating forms, sample estimates, and step-by-step instructions.

Now contains line items for cultured stone and brick, PVC trim lumber, and TPO roofing.

$127.95 per copy | Available Oct. 2011 | Catalog no. 60172

RSMeans Electrical Change Order Cost Data 2012

RSMeans Electrical Change Order Cost Data provides you with electrical unit prices exclusively for pricing change orders—based on the recent, direct experience of contractors and suppliers. Analyze and check your own change order estimates against the experience others have had doing the same work. It also covers productivity analysis and change order cost justifications. With useful information for calculating the effects of change orders and dealing with their administration.

$174.95 per copy | Available Dec. 2011 | Catalog no. 60232

RSMeans Open Shop Building Construction Cost Data 2012

The latest costs for accurate budgeting and estimating of new commercial and residential construction. . . renovation work. . . change orders. . . cost engineering.

RSMeans Open Shop "BCCD" will assist you to:

- Develop benchmark prices for change orders
- Plug gaps in preliminary estimates and budgets
- Estimate complex projects
- Substantiate invoices on contracts
- Price ADA-related renovations

$152.95 per copy | Available Dec. 2011 | Catalog no. 60152

RSMeans Site Work & Landscape Cost Data 2012

Includes unit and assemblies costs for earthwork, sewerage, piped utilities, site improvements, drainage, paving, trees and shrubs, street openings/repairs, underground tanks, and more. Contains 78 types of assemblies costs for accurate conceptual estimates.

Includes:

- Estimating for infrastructure improvements
- Environmentally-oriented construction
- ADA-mandated handicapped access
- Hazardous waste line items

$172.95 per copy | Available Dec. 2011 | Catalog no. 60282

RSMeans Facilities Maintenance & Repair Cost Data 2012

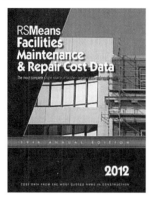

RSMeans Facilities Maintenance & Repair Cost Data gives you a complete system to manage and plan your facility repair and maintenance costs and budget efficiently. Guidelines for auditing a facility and developing an annual maintenance plan. Budgeting is included, along with reference tables on cost and management, and information on frequency and productivity of maintenance operations.

The only nationally recognized source of maintenance and repair costs. Developed in cooperation with the Civil Engineering Research Laboratory (CERL) of the Army Corps of Engineers.

$399.95 per copy | Available Nov. 2011 | Catalog no. 60302

RSMeans Concrete & Masonry Cost Data 2012

Provides you with cost facts for virtually all concrete/masonry estimating needs, from complicated formwork to various sizes and face finishes of brick and block—all in great detail. The comprehensive Unit Price Section contains more than 8,000 selected entries. Also contains an Assemblies [Cost] Section, and a detailed Reference Section that supplements the cost data.

$162.95 per copy | Available Dec. 2011 | Catalog no. 60112

RSMeans Construction Cost Indexes 2012

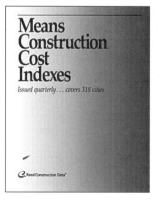

What materials and labor costs will change unexpectedly this year? By how much?

• Breakdowns for 318 major cities
• National averages for 30 key cities
• Expanded five major city indexes
• Historical construction cost indexes

$362.00 per year (subscription) | Catalog no. 50142
$90.50 individual quarters | Catalog no. 60142 A,B,C,D

RSMeans Light Commercial Cost Data 2012

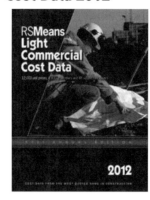

Specifically addresses the light commercial market, which is a specialized niche in the construction industry. Aids you, the owner/designer/contractor, in preparing all types of estimates—from budgets to detailed bids. Includes new advances in methods and materials.

Assemblies Section allows you to evaluate alternatives in the early stages of design/planning.

Over 13,000 unit costs ensure that you have the prices you need. . . when you need them.

$132.95 per copy | Available Nov. 2011 | Catalog no. 60182

RSMeans Labor Rates for the Construction Industry 2012

Complete information for estimating labor costs, making comparisons, and negotiating wage rates by trade for more than 300 U.S. and Canadian cities. With 46 construction trades listed by local union number in each city, and historical wage rates included for comparison. Each city chart lists the county and is alphabetically arranged with handy visual flip tabs for quick reference.

$395.95 per copy | Available Dec. 2011 | Catalog no. 60122

RSMeans Interior Cost Data 2012

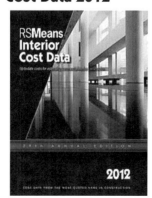

Provides you with prices and guidance needed to make accurate interior work estimates. Contains costs on materials, equipment, hardware, custom installations, furnishings, and labor costs. . . for new and remodel commercial and industrial interior construction, including updated information on office furnishings, and reference information.

$182.95 per copy | Available Nov. 2011 | Catalog no. 60092

Annual Cost Guides

For more information visit the RSMeans website at **www.rsmeans.com**

Unit prices according to the latest MasterFormat!

RSMeans Heavy Construction Cost Data 2012

A comprehensive guide to heavy construction costs. Includes costs for highly specialized projects such as tunnels, dams, highways, airports, and waterways. Information on labor rates, equipment, and materials costs is included. Features unit price costs, systems costs, and numerous reference tables for costs and design.

$177.95 per copy | Available Dec. 2011 | Catalog no. 60162

RSMeans Plumbing Cost Data 2012

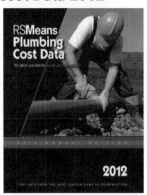

Comprehensive unit prices and assemblies for plumbing, irrigation systems, commercial and residential fire protection, point-of-use water heaters, and the latest approved materials. This publication and its companion, *RSMeans Mechanical Cost Data*, provide full-range cost estimating coverage for all the mechanical trades.

Now contains updated costs for potable water and radiant heat systems and high efficiency fixtures.

$179.95 per copy | Available Oct. 2011 | Catalog no. 60212

2012 RSMeans Seminar Schedule

Note: call for exact dates and details.

Location	Dates	Location	Dates
Las Vegas, NV	March	Las Vegas, NV	October
Washington, DC	April	Orlando, FL	November
San Francisco, CA	June	San Diego, CA	December
Washington, DC	September		
Dallas, TX	September		

1-800-334-3509, ext. 925115

2012 Regional Seminar Schedule

Note: call for exact dates and details.

Location	Dates	Location	Dates
Seattle, WA	January and August	Columbus, GA	June
Dallas/Ft. Worth, TX	January	El Segundo, CA	August
Austin, TX	February	Jacksonville FL	September
Oklahoma City, OK	February	Birmingham, AL	October
Anchorage, AK	March and September	St. Louis, MO	October
Phoenix, AZ	March	Houston, TX	October
San Bernardino, CA	April	Portland, OR	November
Aiea, HI	April	Baltimore, MD	November
Kansas City, MO	April	San Antonio, TX	December
Toronto	May	Raleigh, NC	December
Denver, CO	May		
Bethesda, MD	June		

1-800-334-3509, ext. 925115

Professional Development

Registration Information

Register early... Save up to $100! Register 30 days before the start date of a seminar and save $100 off your total fee. *Note: This discount can be applied only once per order. It cannot be applied to team discount registrations or any other special offer.*

How to register Register by phone today! The RSMeans toll-free number for making reservations is **1-800-334-3509, ext. 925115.**

Individual seminar registration fee - $935. *Means CostWorks®* training registration fee - $375. To register by mail, complete the registration form and return, with your full fee, to: RSMeans Seminars, 700 Longwater Drive, Norwell, MA 02061.

Government pricing All federal government employees save off the regular seminar price. Other promotional discounts cannot be combined with the government discount.

Team discount program for two to four seminar registrations. Call for pricing: 1-800-334-3509, ext. 925115

Multiple course discounts When signing up for two or more courses, call for pricing.

Refund policy Cancellations will be accepted up to ten business days prior to the seminar start. There are no refunds for cancellations received later than ten working days prior to the first day of the seminar. A $150 processing fee will be applied for all cancellations. Written notice of cancellation is required. Substitutions can be made at any time before the session starts. **No-shows are subject to the full seminar fee.**

AACE approved courses Many seminars described and offered here have been approved for 14 hours (1.4 recertification credits) of credit by the AACE International Certification Board toward meeting the continuing education requirements for recertification as a Certified Cost Engineer/Certified Cost Consultant.

AIA Continuing Education We are registered with the AIA Continuing Education System (AIA/CES) and are committed to developing quality learning activities in accordance with the CES criteria. Many seminars meet the AIA/CES criteria for Quality Level 2. AIA members may receive (14) learning units (LUs) for each two-day RSMeans course.

Daily course schedule The first day of each seminar session begins at 8:30 a.m. and ends at 4:30 p.m. The second day begins at 8:00 a.m. and ends at 4:00 p.m. Participants are urged to bring a hand-held calculator, since many actual problems will be worked out in each session.

Continental breakfast Your registration includes the cost of a continental breakfast, and a morning and afternoon refreshment break. These informal segments allow you to discuss topics of mutual interest with other seminar attendees. (You are free to make your own lunch and dinner arrangements.)

Hotel/transportation arrangements RSMeans arranges to hold a block of rooms at most host hotels. To take advantage of special group rates when making your reservation, be sure to mention that you are attending the RSMeans seminar. You are, of course, free to stay at the lodging place of your choice. **(Hotel reservations and transportation arrangements should be made directly by seminar attendees.)**

Important Class sizes are limited, so please register as soon as possible.

Note: *Pricing subject to change.*

Registration Form

ADDS-1000

Call 1-800-334-3509, ext. 925115 to register or FAX this form 1-800-632-6732. Visit our website: www.rsmeans.com

Please register the following people for the RSMeans construction seminars as shown here. We understand that we must make our own hotel reservations if overnight stays are necessary.

☐ Full payment of $_____enclosed.

☐ Bill me.

Please print name of registrant(s).

(To appear on certificate of completion)

_____

_____

_____

_____

P.O. #: _____
GOVERNMENT AGENCIES MUST SUPPLY PURCHASE ORDER NUMBER OR TRAINING FORM.

Firm name_____

Address_____

City/State/Zip_____

Telephone no._____ Fax no._____

E-mail address_____

Charge registration(s) to: ☐ MasterCard ☐ VISA ☐ American Express

Account no._____ Exp. date_____

Cardholder's signature_____

Seminar name_____

Seminar City _____

Please mail check to: RSMeans Seminars, 700 Longwater Drive, Norwell, MA 02061 USA

Professional Development

Means CostWorks.com Training

Construction estimating is vital to the decision-making process at each state of every project. Means CostWorks.com works the way you do. It's systematic, flexible and intuitive. In this one day class you will see how you can estimate any phase of any project faster and better.

Some of what you'll learn:
- Customizing Means CostWorks.com
- Making the most of RSMeans "Circle Reference" numbers
- How to integrate your cost data
- Generate reports, exporting estimates to MS Excel, sharing, collaborating and more

Who should attend: architects & engineers, facility managers, contractors, construction estimators, and anyone using this powerful web-based tool.

Facilities Construction Estimating

In this *two-day* course, professionals working in facilities management can get help with their daily challenges to establish budgets for all phases of a project.

Some of what you'll learn:
- Determining the full scope of a project
- Identifying the scope of risks and opportunities
- Creative solutions to estimating issues
- Organizing estimates for presentation and discussion
- Special techniques for repair/remodel and maintenance projects
- Negotiating project change orders

Who should attend: facility managers, engineers, contractors, facility tradespeople, planners, and project managers.

Scheduling with Microsoft Project

Two days of hands-on training gives you a look at the basics to putting it all together with MS Project to create a complete project schedule. Learn to work better and faster, manage changes and updates, enhance tracking, generate actionable reports, and boost control of your time and budget.

Some of what you'll learn:
- Defining task/activity relationships: link tasks, establish predecessor/successor relationships and create logs
- Baseline scheduling: the essential what/when
- Using MS Project to determine the critical path
- Integrate RSMeans data with MS Project
- The dollar-loaded schedule: enhance the reliability of this "must-know" technique for scheduling public projects.

Who should attend: Contractors' project-management teams, architects and engineers, project owners and their representatives, and those interested in improving their project planning and scheduling and management skills.

Site Work & Heavy Construction Estimating

This *two-day* course teaches attendees how to estimate earthwork, site utilities, foundations, and site improvements, using the assemblies and the unit price methods.

Some of what you'll learn:
- Basic site work and heavy construction estimating skills
- Estimating foundations, utilities, earthwork, and site improvements
- Correct equipment usage, quality control, and site investigation for estimating purposes

Who should attend: project managers, design engineers, estimators, and contractors doing site work and heavy construction.

Practical Project Management for Construction Professionals

In this *two-day* course, acquire the essential knowledge and develop the skills to effectively and efficiently execute the day-to-day responsibilities of the construction project manager.

Covers:
- General conditions of the construction contract
- Contract modifications: change orders and construction change directives
- Negotiations with subcontractors and vendors
- Effective writing: notification and communications
- Dispute resolution: claims and liens

Who should attend: architects, engineers, owner's representatives, project managers.

Mechanical & Electrical Estimating

This *two-day* course teaches attendees how to prepare more accurate and complete mechanical/electrical estimates, avoiding the pitfalls of omission and double-counting, while understanding the composition and rationale within the RSMeans mechanical/electrical database.

Some of what you'll learn:
- The unique way mechanical and electrical systems are interrelated
- M&E estimates—conceptual, planning, budgeting, and bidding stages
- Order of magnitude, square foot, assemblies, and unit price estimating
- Comparative cost analysis of equipment and design alternatives

Who should attend: architects, engineers, facilities managers, mechanical and electrical contractors, and others who need a highly reliable method for developing, understanding, and evaluating mechanical and electrical contracts.

Professional Development

Unit Price Estimating

This interactive *two-day* seminar teaches attendees how to interpret project information and process it into final, detailed estimates with the greatest accuracy level.

The most important credential an estimator can take to the job is the ability to visualize construction and estimate accurately.

Some of what you'll learn:
- Interpreting the design in terms of cost
- The most detailed, time-tested methodology for accurate pricing
- Key cost drivers—material, labor, equipment, staging, and subcontracts
- Understanding direct and indirect costs for accurate job cost accounting and change order management

Who should attend: Corporate and government estimators and purchasers, architects, engineers, and others who need to produce accurate project estimates.

RSMeans CostWorks® CD Training

This one-day course helps users become more familiar with the functionality of *RSMeans CostWorks* program. Each menu, icon, screen, and function found in the program is explained in depth. Time is devoted to hands-on estimating exercises.

Some of what you'll learn:
- Searching the database using all navigation methods
- Exporting RSMeans data to your preferred spreadsheet format
- Viewing crews, assembly components, and much more
- Automatically regionalizing the database

You are required to bring your own laptop computer for this course.

When you register for this course you will receive an outline for your laptop requirements.

Also offering web training for CostWorks CD!

Facilities Maintenance & Repair Estimating

This *two-day* course teaches attendees how to plan, budget, and estimate the cost of ongoing and preventive maintenance and repair for existing buildings and grounds.

Some of what you'll learn:
- The most financially favorable maintenance, repair, and replacement scheduling and estimating
- Auditing and value engineering facilities
- Preventive planning and facilities upgrading
- Determining both in-house and contract-out service costs
- Annual, asset-protecting M&R plan

Who should attend: Facility managers, maintenance supervisors, buildings and grounds superintendents, plant managers, planners, estimators, and others involved in facilities planning and budgeting.

Square Foot Estimating using Means CostWorks

This *two day* class uses the leading industry data and a powerful software package to develop highly accurate conceptual estimates for your construction projects. All attendees must bring a laptop computer loaded with the current year *Square Foot Model Costs* and the *Assemblies Cost Data* CostWorks titles.

Some of what you'll learn:
- Introduction to conceptual estimating
- Types of conceptual estimates
- Helpful hints
- Order of magnitude estimating
- Square foot estimating
- Assemblies estimating

Who should attend: architects, engineers, contractors, construction estimators, owner's representatives, and anyone looking for an electronic method for performing square foot estimating.

Assessing Scope of Work for Facility Construction Estimating

This *two-day* practical training program addresses the vital importance of understanding the SCOPE of projects in order to produce accurate cost estimates for facility repair and remodeling.

Some of what you'll learn:
- Discussions of site visits, plans/specs, record drawings of facilities, and site-specific lists
- Review of CSI divisions, including means, methods, materials, and the challenges of scoping each topic
- Exercises in SCOPE identification and SCOPE writing for accurate estimating of projects
- Hands-on exercises that require SCOPE, take-off, and pricing

Who should attend: corporate and government estimators, planners, facility managers, and others who need to produce accurate project estimates.

Reference Books

For more information visit the RSMeans website at **www.rsmeans.com**

Value Engineering: Practical Applications

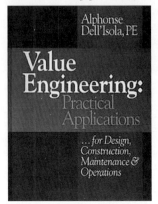

For Design, Construction, Maintenance & Operations
by Alphonse Dell'Isola, PE

A tool for immediate application—for engineers, architects, facility managers, owners, and contractors. Includes making the case for VE—the management briefing; integrating VE into planning, budgeting, and design; conducting life cycle costing; using VE methodology in design review and consultant selection; case studies; VE workbook; and a life cycle costing program on disk.

$79.95 per copy | Over 450 pages, illustrated, softcover | Catalog no. 67319A

The Building Professional's Guide to Contract Documents

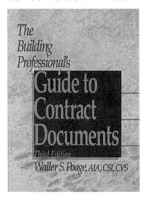

3rd Edition
by Waller S. Poage, AIA, CSI, CVS

A comprehensive reference for owners, design professionals, contractors, and students

- Structure your documents for maximum efficiency.
- Effectively communicate construction requirements.
- Understand the roles and responsibilities of construction professionals.
- Improve methods of project delivery.

$64.95 per copy | 400 pages Diagrams and construction forms, hardcover
Catalog no. 67261A

Cost Planning & Estimating for Facilities Maintenance

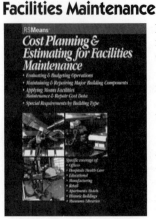

In this unique book, a team of facilities management authorities shares their expertise on:

- Evaluating and budgeting maintenance operations
- Maintaining and repairing key building components
- Applying *RSMeans Facilities Maintenance & Repair Cost Data* to your estimating

Covers special maintenance requirements of the ten major building types

$89.95 per copy | Over 475 pages, hardcover | Catalog no. 67314

Facilities Operations & Engineering Reference

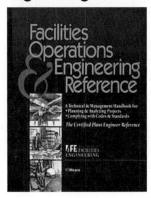

by the Association for Facilities Engineering and RSMeans

An all-in-one technical reference for planning and managing facility projects and solving day-to-day operations problems. Selected as the official certified plant engineer reference, this handbook covers financial analysis, maintenance, HVAC and energy efficiency, and more.

$109.95 per copy | Over 700 pages, illustrated, hardcover | Catalog no. 67318

Complete Book of Framing

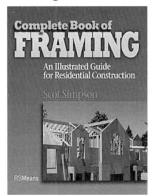

by Scot Simpson

This straightforward, easy-to-learn method will help framers, carpenters, and handy homeowners build their skills in rough carpentry and framing. Shows how to frame all the parts of a house: floors, walls, roofs, door & window openings, and stairs—with hundreds of color photographs and drawings that show every detail.

The book gives beginners all the basics they need to go from zero framing knowledge to a journeyman level.

$29.95 per copy | 336 pages, softcover | Catalog no. 67353

Life Cycle Costing for Facilities

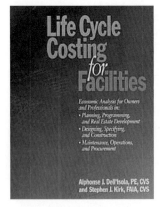

by Alphonse Dell'Isola and Dr. Steven Kirk

Guidance for achieving higher quality design and construction projects at lower costs! Cost-cutting efforts often sacrifice quality to yield the cheapest product. Life cycle costing enables building designers and owners to achieve both. The authors of this book show how LCC can work for a variety of projects — from roads to HVAC upgrades to different types of buildings.

$99.95 per copy | 396 pages, hardcover | Catalog no. 67341

Reference Books

For more information visit the RSMeans website at **www.rsmeans.com**

Interior Home Improvement Costs

9th Edition

Updated estimates for the most popular remodeling and repair projects—from small, do-it-yourself jobs to major renovations and new construction. Includes: kitchens & baths; new living space from your attic, basement, or garage; new floors, paint, and wallpaper; tearing out or building new walls; closets, stairs, and fireplaces; new energy-saving improvements, home theaters, and more!

$24.95 per copy | 250 pages, illustrated, softcover | Catalog no. 67308E

Exterior Home Improvement Costs

9th Edition

Updated estimates for the most popular remodeling and repair projects—from small, do-it-yourself jobs, to major renovations and new construction. Includes: curb appeal projects—landscaping, patios, porches, driveways, and walkways; new windows and doors; decks, greenhouses, and sunrooms; room additions and garages; roofing, siding, and painting; "green" improvements to save energy & water.

$24.95 per copy | Over 275 pages, illustrated, softcover | Catalog no. 67309E

Builder's Essentials: Plan Reading & Material Takeoff

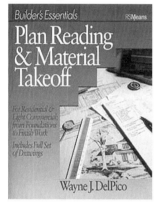

For Residential and Light Commercial Construction
by Wayne J. DelPico

A valuable tool for understanding plans and specs, and accurately calculating material quantities. Step-by-step instructions and takeoff procedures based on a full set of working drawings.

$35.95 per copy | Over 420 pages, softcover | Catalog no. 67307

Means Unit Price Estimating Methods

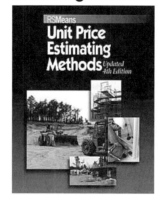

New 4th Edition

This new edition includes up-to-date cost data and estimating examples, updated to reflect changes to the CSI numbering system and new features of RSMeans cost data. It describes the most productive, universally accepted ways to estimate, and uses checklists and forms to illustrate shortcuts and timesavers. A model estimate demonstrates procedures. A new chapter explores computer estimating alternatives.

$59.95 per copy | Over 350 pages, illustrated, softcover | Catalog no. 67303B

Concrete Repair and Maintenance Illustrated

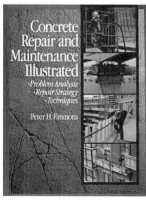

by Peter Emmons

Hundreds of illustrations show users how to analyze, repair, clean, and maintain concrete structures for optimal performance and cost effectiveness. From parking garages to roads and bridges to structural concrete, this comprehensive book describes the causes, effects, and remedies for concrete wear and failure. Invaluable for planning jobs, selecting materials, and training employees, this book is a must-have for concrete specialists, general contractors, facility managers, civil and structural engineers, and architects.

$69.95 per copy | 300 pages, illustrated, softcover | Catalog no. 67146

Total Productive Facilities Management

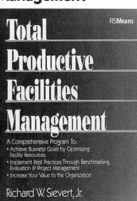

by Richard W. Sievert, Jr.

Today, facilities are viewed as strategic resources. . . elevating the facility manager to the role of asset manager supporting the organization's overall business goals. Now, Richard Sievert Jr., in this well-articulated guidebook, sets forth a new operational standard for the facility manager's emerging role. . . a comprehensive program for managing facilities as a true profit center.

$79.95 per copy | 275 pages, softcover | Catalog no. 67321

Reference Books

For more information visit the RSMeans website at **www.rsmeans.com**

Means Illustrated Construction Dictionary

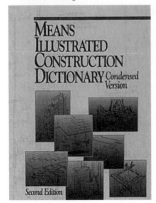

Condensed, 2nd Edition

The best portable dictionary for office or field use—an essential tool for contractors, architects, insurance and real estate personnel, facility managers, homeowners, and anyone who needs quick, clear definitions for construction terms. The second edition has been further enhanced with updates and hundreds of new terms and illustrations . . . in keeping with the most recent developments in the construction industry.

Now with a quick-reference Spanish section. Includes tools and equipment, materials, tasks, and more!

$59.95 per copy | Over 500 pages, softcover | Catalog no. 67282A

Facilities Planning & Relocation

by David D. Owen

A complete system for planning space needs and managing relocations. Includes step-by-step manual, over 50 forms, and extensive reference section on materials and furnishings.

New lower price and user-friendly format.

$89.95 per copy | Over 450 pages, softcover | Catalog no. 67301

Electrical Estimating Methods

3rd Edition

Expanded edition includes sample estimates and cost information in keeping with the latest version of the CSI MasterFormat and UNIFORMAT II. Complete coverage of fiber optic and uninterruptible power supply electrical systems, broken down by components, and explained in detail. Includes a new chapter on computerized estimating methods. A practical companion to *RSMeans Electrical Cost Data.*

$64.95 per copy | Over 325 pages, hardcover | Catalog no. 67230B

Square Foot & UNIFORMAT Assemblies Estimating Methods

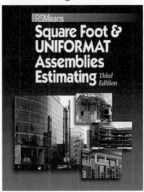

3rd Edition

Develop realistic square foot and assemblies costs for budgeting and construction funding. The new edition features updated guidance on square foot and assemblies estimating using UNIFORMAT II. An essential reference for anyone who performs conceptual estimates.

$69.95 per copy | Over 300 pages, illustrated, softcover | Catalog no. 67145B

Mechanical Estimating Methods

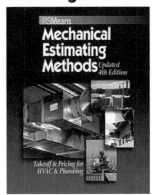

4th Edition

Completely updated, this guide assists you in making a review of plans, specs, and bid packages, with suggestions for takeoff procedures, listings, substitutions, and pre-bid scheduling for all components of HVAC. Includes suggestions for budgeting labor and equipment usage. Compares materials and construction methods to allow you to select the best option.

$64.95 per copy | Over 350 pages, illustrated, softcover | Catalog no. 67294B

Residential & Light Commercial Construction Standards

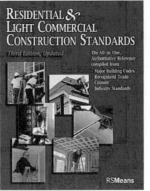

3rd Edition, Updated by RSMeans and contributing authors

This book provides authoritative requirements and recommendations compiled from leading professional associations, industry publications, and building code organizations. This all-in-one reference helps establish a standard for workmanship, quickly resolve disputes, and avoid defect claims. Updated third edition includes new coverage of green building, seismic, hurricane, and mold-resistant construction.

$59.95 | Over 550 pages, illustrated, softcover | Catalog no. 67322B

Reference Books

For more information visit the RSMeans website at **www.rsmeans.com**

Construction Business Management

by Nick Ganaway

Only 43% of construction firms stay in business after four years. Make sure your company thrives with valuable guidance from a pro with 25 years of success as a commercial contractor. Find out what it takes to build all aspects of a business that is profitable, enjoyable, and enduring. With a bonus chapter on retail construction.

$49.95 per copy | 200 pages, softcover | Catalog no. 67352

The Practice of Cost Segregation Analysis

by Bruce A. Desrosiers and Wayne J. DelPico

This expert guide walks you through the practice of cost segregation analysis, which enables property owners to defer taxes and benefit from "accelerated cost recovery" through depreciation deductions on assets that are properly identified and classified.

With a glossary of terms, sample cost segregation estimates for various building types, key information resources, and updates via a dedicated website, this book is a critical resource for anyone involved in cost segregation analysis.

$99.95 per copy | Over 225 pages | Catalog no. 67345

How to Estimate with Means Data & CostWorks

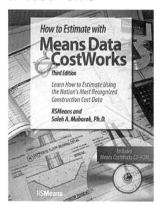

New 3rd Edition
by RSMeans and Saleh A. Mubarak, Ph.D.

New 3rd Edition—fully updated with new chapters, plus new CD with updated *CostWorks* cost data and MasterFormat organization. Includes all major construction items—with more than 300 exercises and two sets of plans that show how to estimate for a broad range of construction items and systems—including general conditions and equipment costs.

$59.95 per copy | 272 pages, softcover | Includes CostWorks CD
Catalog no. 67324B

Project Scheduling & Management for Construction

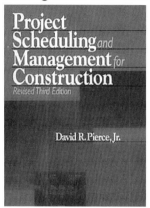

3rd Edition
by David R. Pierce, Jr.

A comprehensive yet easy-to-follow guide to construction project scheduling and control—from vital project management principles through the latest scheduling, tracking, and controlling techniques. The author is a leading authority on scheduling, with years of field and teaching experience at leading academic institutions. Spend a few hours with this book and come away with a solid understanding of this essential management topic.

$64.95 per copy | Over 300 pages, illustrated, hardcover | Catalog no. 67247B

Preventive Maintenance for Multi-Family Housing

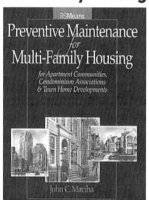

by John C. Maciha

Prepared by one of the nation's leading experts on multi-family housing.

This complete PM system for apartment and condominium communities features expert guidance, checklists for buildings and grounds maintenance tasks and their frequencies, a reusable wall chart to track maintenance, and a dedicated website featuring customizable electronic forms. A must-have for anyone involved with multi-family housing maintenance and upkeep.

$89.95 per copy | 225 pages | Catalog no. 67346

Job Order Contracting Expediting Construction Project Delivery

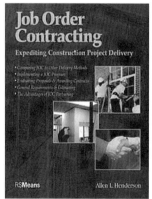

by Allen Henderson

Expert guidance to help you implement JOC—fast becoming the preferred project delivery method for repair and renovation, minor new construction, and maintenance projects in the public sector and in many states and municipalities. The author, a leading JOC expert and practitioner, shows how to:

- Establish a JOC program
- Evaluate proposals and award contracts
- Handle general requirements and estimating
- Partner for maximum benefits

$89.95 per copy | 192 pages, illustrated, hardcover | Catalog no. 67348

Reference Books

For more information visit the RSMeans website at **www.rsmeans.com**

Estimating Building Costs

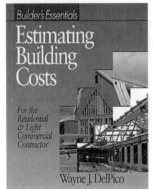

For the Residential & Light Commercial Contractor
by Wayne J. DelPico

Step-by-step estimating methods for residential and light commercial contractors. Includes a detailed look at every construction specialty—explaining all the components, takeoff units, and labor needed for well-organized, complete estimates. Covers correctly interpreting plans and specifications, and developing accurate and complete labor and material costs.

$29.95 per copy | Over 400 pages, illustrated, softcover | Catalog no. 67343

The Homeowner's Guide to Mold

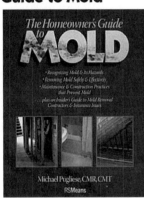

By Michael Pugliese

Expert guidance to protect your health and your home.

Mold, whether caused by leaks, humidity or flooding, is a real health and financial issue—for homeowners and contractors.

This full-color book explains:

- Construction and maintenance practices to prevent mold
- How to inspect for and remove mold
- Mold remediation procedures and costs
- What to do after a flood
- How to deal with insurance companies

$21.95 per copy | 144 pages, softcover | Catalog no. 67344

Landscape Estimating Methods

5th Edition

Answers questions about preparing competitive landscape construction estimates, with up-to-date cost estimates and the new MasterFormat classification system. Expanded and revised to address the latest materials and methods, including new coverage on approaches to green building. Includes:

- Step-by-step explanation of the estimating process
- Sample forms and worksheets that save time and prevent errors

$64.95 per copy | Over 350 pages, softcover | Catalog no. 67295C

Building & Renovating Schools

This all-inclusive guide covers every step of the school construction process—from initial planning, needs assessment, and design, right through moving into the new facility. A must-have resource for anyone concerned with new school construction or renovation. With square foot cost models for elementary, middle, and high school facilities, and real-life case studies of recently completed school projects.

The contributors to this book—architects, construction project managers, contractors, and estimators who specialize in school construction—provide start-to-finish, expert guidance on the process.

$99.95 per copy | Over 425 pages, hardcover | Catalog no. 67342

Universal Design Ideas for Style, Comfort & Safety

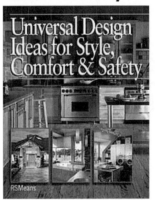

by RSMeans and Lexicon Consulting, Inc.

Incorporating universal design when building or remodeling helps people of any age and physical ability more fully and safely enjoy their living spaces. This book shows how universal design can be artfully blended into the most attractive homes. It discusses specialized products like adjustable countertops and chair lifts, as well as simple ways to enhance a home's safety and comfort. With color photos and expert guidance, every area of the home is covered. Includes budget estimates that give an idea how much projects will cost.

$21.95 | 160 pages, illustrated, softcover | Catalog no. 67354

Plumbing Estimating Methods

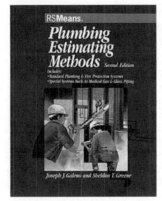

3rd Edition
by Joseph Galeno and Sheldon Greene

Updated and revised! This practical guide walks you through a plumbing estimate, from basic materials and installation methods through change order analysis. *Plumbing Estimating Methods* covers residential, commercial, industrial, and medical systems, and features sample takeoff and estimate forms and detailed illustrations of systems and components.

$59.95 per copy | 330+ pages, softcover | Catalog no. 67283B

Understanding & Negotiating Construction Contracts

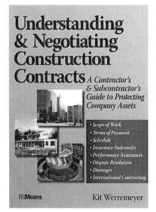

by Kit Werremeyer

Take advantage of the author's 30 years' experience in small-to-large (including international) construction projects. Learn how to identify, understand, and evaluate high risk terms and conditions typically found in all construction contracts—then negotiate to lower or eliminate the risk, improve terms of payment, and reduce exposure to claims and disputes. The author avoids "legalese" and gives real-life examples from actual projects.

$69.95 per copy | 300 pages, softcover | Catalog no. 67350

How Your House Works

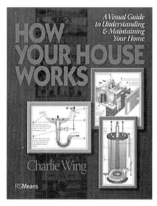

by Charlie Wing

A must-have reference for every homeowner, handyman, and contractor—for repair, remodeling, and new construction. This book uncovers the mysteries behind just about every major appliance and building element in your house—from electrical, heating and AC, to plumbing, framing, foundations and appliances. Clear, "exploded" drawings show exactly how things should be put together and how they function—what to check if they don't work, and what you can do that might save you having to call in a professional.

$21.95 per copy | 160 pages, softcover | Catalog no. 67351

RSMeans Estimating Handbook

3rd Edition

Widely used in the industry for tasks ranging from routine estimates to special cost analysis projects, this handbook has been completely updated and reorganized with new and expanded technical information.

RSMeans Estimating Handbook will help construction professionals:

- Evaluate architectural plans and specifications
- Prepare accurate quantity takeoffs
- Compare design alternatives and costs
- Perform value engineering
- Double-check estimates and quotes
- Estimate change orders

$99.95 per copy | Over 900 pages, hardcover | Catalog No. 67276B

Spanish/English Construction Dictionary

2nd Edition
by RSMeans and the International Code Council

This expanded edition features thousands of the most common words and useful phrases in the construction industry with easy-to-follow pronunciations in both Spanish and English. Over 800 new terms, phrases, and illustrations have been added. It also features a new stand-alone "Safety & Emergencies" section, with colored pages for quick access.

Unique to this dictionary are the systems illustrations showing the relationship of components in the most common building systems for all major trades.

$23.95 per copy | Over 400 pages | Catalog no. 67327A

The Gypsum Construction Handbook

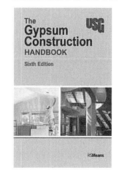

by USG

An invaluable reference of construction procedures for gypsum drywall, cement board, veneer plaster, and conventional plaster. This new edition includes the newest product developments, installation methods, fire- and sound-rated construction information, illustrated framing-to-finish application instructions, estimating and planning information, and more. Great for architects and engineers; contractors, builders, and dealers; apprentices and training programs; building inspectors and code officials; and anyone interested in gypsum construction. Features information on tools and safety practices, a glossary of construction terms, and a list of important agencies and associations. Also available in Spanish.

$29.95 | Over 575 pages, illustrated, softcover | Catalog no. 67357A

Means Illustrated Construction Dictionary

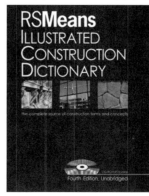

Unabridged 4th Edition, with CD-ROM

Long regarded as the industry's finest, *Means Illustrated Construction Dictionary* is now even better. With nearly 20,000 terms and more than 1,400 illustrations and photos, it is the clear choice for the most comprehensive and current information. The companion CD-ROM that comes with this new edition adds extra features such as: larger graphics and expanded definitions.

$99.95 per copy | Over 790 pages, illust., hardcover | Catalog no. 67292B

Reference Books

For more information visit the RSMeans website at **www.rsmeans.com**

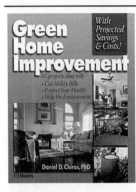

Green
Home Improvement
by Daniel D. Chiras, PhD

With energy costs rising and environmental awareness increasing, people are looking to make their homes greener. This book, with 65 projects and actual costs and projected savings help homeowners prioritize their green improvements.

Projects range from simple water savers that cost only a few dollars, to bigger-ticket items such as HVAC systems. With color photos and cost estimates, each project compares options and describes the work involved, the benefits, and the savings.

$24.95 | 320 pages, illustrated, softcover | Catalog no. 67355

New Titles

Construction Supervision

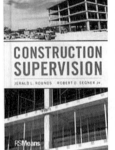

This brand new title inspires supervisory excellence with proven tactics and techniques applied by thousands of construction supervisors over the past decade. Recognizing the unique and critical role the supervisor plays in project success, the book's leadership guidelines carve out a practical blueprint for motivating work performance and increasing productivity through effective communication.

Features:

• A unique focus on field supervision and crew management

• Coverage of supervision from the foreman to the superintendent level

• An overview of technical skills whose mastery will build confidence and success for the supervisor

• A detailed view of "soft" management and communication skills

$90.00 per copy | Over 450 pages, softcover | Catalog no. 67358

Risk Management for Design and Construction

This book introduces risk as a central pillar of project management and shows how a project manager can be prepared for dealing with uncertainty. Written by experts in the field, *Risk Management for Design and Construction* uses clear, straightforward terminology to demystify the concepts of project uncertainty and risk.

Highlights include:

• Integrated cost and schedule risk analysis

• An introduction to a ready-to-use system of analyzing a project's risks and tools to proactively manage risks

• A methodology that was developed and used by the Washington State Department of Transportation

• Case studies and examples on the proper application of principles

• Information about combining value analysis with risk analysis

$125.00 per copy | Over 250 pages, softcover | Catalog no. 67359

Green Building: Project Planning & Cost Estimating

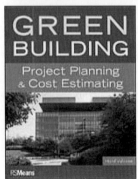

3rd Edition

Since the widely read first edition of this book, green building has gone from a growing trend to a major force in design and construction.

This new edition has been updated with the latest in green building technologies, design concepts, standards, and costs. Full-color with all new case studies—plus a new chapter on commercial real estate.

$99.95 per copy | Over 450 pages, softcover | Catalog no. 67338B

2012 Order Form

For more information visit the RSMeans website at **www.rsmeans.com**

Qty.	Book no.	COST ESTIMATING BOOKS	Unit Price	Total
	60062	Assemblies Cost Data 2012	$290.95	
	60012	Building Construction Cost Data 2012	177.95	
	60112	Concrete & Masonry Cost Data 2012	162.95	
	50142	Construction Cost Indexes 2012 (subscription)	362.00	
	60142A	Construction Cost Index–January 2012	90.50	
	60142B	Construction Cost Index–April 2012	90.50	
	60142C	Construction Cost Index–July 2012	90.50	
	60142D	Construction Cost Index–October 2012	90.50	
	60342	Contr. Pricing Guide: Resid. R & R Costs 2012	39.95	
	60232	Electrical Change Order Cost Data 2012	174.95	
	60032	Electrical Cost Data 2012	179.95	
	60202	Facilities Construction Cost Data 2012	453.95	
	60302	Facilities Maintenance & Repair Cost Data 2012	399.95	
	60552	Green Building Cost Data 2012	147.95	
	60162	Heavy Construction Cost Data 2012	177.95	
	60092	Interior Cost Data 2012	182.95	
	60122	Labor Rates for the Const. Industry 2012	395.95	
	60182	Light Commercial Cost Data 2012	132.95	
	60022	Mechanical Cost Data 2012	174.95	
	60152	Open Shop Building Const. Cost Data 2012	152.95	
	60212	Plumbing Cost Data 2012	179.95	
	60042	Commercial Renovation Cost Data 2012	144.95	
	60172	Residential Cost Data 2012	127.95	
	60282	Site Work & Landscape Cost Data 2012	172.95	
	60052	Square Foot Costs 2012	187.95	
	62011	Yardsticks for Costing (2011)	174.95	
	62012	Yardsticks for Costing (2012)	176.95	
		REFERENCE BOOKS		
	67329	Bldrs Essentials: Best Bus. Practices for Bldrs	29.95	
	67298A	Bldrs Essentials: Framing/Carpentry 2nd Ed.	24.95	
	67298AS	Bldrs Essentials: Framing/Carpentry Spanish	24.95	
	67307	Bldrs Essentials: Plan Reading & Takeoff	35.95	
	67342	Building & Renovating Schools	99.95	
	67339	Building Security: Strategies & Costs	89.95	
	67353	Complete Book of Framing	29.95	
	67146	Concrete Repair & Maintenance Illustrated	69.95	
	67352	Construction Business Management	49.95	
	67358	Construction Supervision	90.00	
	67314	Cost Planning & Est. for Facil. Maint.	89.95	
	67328A	Designing & Building with the IBC, 2nd Ed.	99.95	
	67230B	Electrical Estimating Methods, 3rd Ed.	64.95	
	67343	Estimating Bldg. Costs for Resi. & Lt. Comm.	29.95	
	67276B	Estimating Handbook, 3rd Ed.	99.95	
	67318	Facilities Operations & Engineering Reference	109.95	
	67301	Facilities Planning & Relocation	89.95	
	67338B	Green Building: Proj. Planning & Cost Est., 3rd Ed.	99.95	
	67355	Green Home Improvement	24.95	
	67357A	The Gypsum Construction Handbook	29.95	
	67357S	The Gypsum Construction Handbook (Spanish)	29.95	
	67148	Heavy Construction Handbook	99.95	
	67323	Historic Preservation: Proj. Planning & Est.	99.95	

Qty.	Book no.	REFERENCE BOOKS (Cont.)	Unit Price	Total
	67308E	Home Improvement Costs–Int. Projects, 9th Ed.	24.95	
	67309E	Home Improvement Costs–Ext. Projects, 9th Ed.	24.95	
	67344	Homeowner's Guide to Mold	21.95	
	67324B	How to Est.w/Means Data & CostWorks, 3rd Ed.	59.95	
	67351	How Your House Works	21.95	
	67282A	Illustrated Const. Dictionary, Condensed, 2nd Ed.	59.95	
	67292B	Illustrated Const. Dictionary, w/CD-ROM, 4th Ed.	99.95	
	67348	Job Order Contracting	89.95	
	67295C	Landscape Estimating Methods, 5th Ed.	64.95	
	67341	Life Cycle Costing for Facilities	99.95	
	67294B	Mechanical Estimating Methods, 4th Ed.	64.95	
	67283B	Plumbing Estimating Methods, 3rd Ed.	59.95	
	67345	Practice of Cost Segregation Analysis	99.95	
	67346	Preventive Maint. for Multi-Family Housing	89.95	
	67326	Preventive Maint. Guidelines for School Facil.	149.95	
	67247B	Project Scheduling & Manag. for Constr. 3rd Ed.	64.95	
	67322B	Resi. & Light Commercial Const. Stds., 3rd Ed.	59.95	
	67359	Risk Management for Design & Construction	125.00	
	67327A	Spanish/English Construction Dictionary, 2nd Ed.	23.95	
	67145B	Sq. Ft. & Assem. Estimating Methods, 3rd Ed.	69.95	
	67321	Total Productive Facilities Management	79.95	
	67350	Understanding and Negotiating Const. Contracts	69.95	
	67303B	Unit Price Estimating Methods, 4th Ed.	59.95	
	67354	Universal Design	21.95	
	67319A	Value Engineering: Practical Applications	79.95	

MA residents add 6.25% state sales tax

Shipping & Handling**

Total (U.S. Funds)*

Prices are subject to change and are for U.S. delivery only. *Canadian customers may call for current prices. **Shipping & handling charges: Add 7% of total order for check and credit card payments. Add 9% of total order for invoiced orders.

Send order to: ADDV-1000

Name (please print) _____

Company _____

☐ Company

☐ Home Address _____

_____

City/State/Zip _____

Phone # _____ P.O. # _____

(Must accompany all orders being billed)

Mail to: RSMeans, 700 Longwater Drive, Norwell, MA 02061

RSMeans Project Cost Report

By filling out this report, your project data will contribute to the database that supports the RSMeans Project Cost Square Foot Data. When you fill out this form, RSMeans will provide a $30 discount off one of the RSMeans products advertised in the preceding pages. Please complete the form including all items where you have cost data, and all the items marked (☑).

$30.00 Discount per product for each report you submit

Project Description (no remodeling projects, please)

☑ Building Use (Office School...)_____

☑ Address (City, State)_____

_____

☑ Total Building Area (SF) _____

☑ Ground Floor (SF) _____

☑ Frame (Wood, Steel...) _____

☑ Exterior Wall (Brick, Tilt-up...) _____

☑ Basement: (checkone)   ☐ Full   ☐ Partial   ☐ None

☑ Number of Stories _____

☑ Floor-to-Floor Height_____

☑ Volume (C.F.)_____

% Air Conditioned _____ Tons_____

Total Project Cost _____ $ _____

Owner _____

Architect_____

General Contractor _____

☑ Bid Date _____

☑ Typical Bay Size _____

☑ Capacity _____

☑ Labor Force: _____ % Union _____ % Non-Union

☑ Project Description (Circle one number in each line.)

1. Economy 2. Average 3. Custom 4. Luxury

1. Square 2. Rectangular 3. Irregular 4. Very Irregular

Comments _____

_____

A	☑	General Conditions	$	
B	☑	Site Work	$	
C	☑	Concrete	$	
D	☑	Masonry	$	
E	☑	Metals	$	
F	☑	Wood & Plastics	$	
G	☑	Thermal &Moisture Protection	$	
GR		Roofing & Flashing	$	
H	☑	Doors and Windows	$	
J	☑	Finishes	$	
JP		Painting & Wall Covering	$	

K	☑	Specialties	$	
L	☑	Equipment	$	
M	☑	Furnishings	$	
N	☑	SpecialConstruction	$	
P	☑	ConveyingSystems	$	
Q	☑	Mechanical	$	
QP		Plumbing	$	
QB		HVAC	$	
R	☑	Electrical	$	
S	☑	Mech./Elec. Combined	$	

Please specify the RSMeans product you wish to receive. Complete the address information.

Product Name _____

Product Number _____

Your Name _____

Title _____

Company_____
  ☐ Company
  ☐ Home   Street Address_____

City, State, Zip _____

Return by mail or fax 888-492-6770.

Method of Payment:

Credit Card # _____

Expiration Date _____

Check_____

Purchase Order _____

Phone Number _____
(for those not comfortable mailing in credit card information)

RSMeans
a division of Reed Construction Data
Square Foot Costs Department
700 Longwater Drive
Norwell, MA 02061

DISCARD